RAND McNALLY

D1781191

Chicago & Cook County
street guide

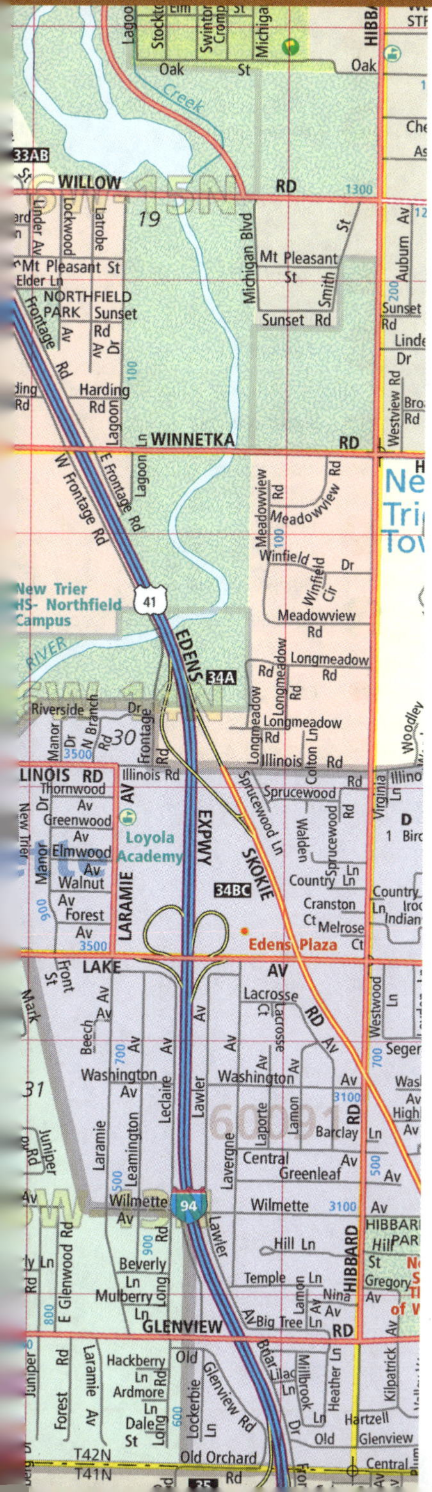

TELL US WHAT YOU THINK
comment card on last page

Contents

Introduction

Maps

Lists and Indexes

RAND McNALLY
Rand McNally Consumer Affairs
P.O. Box 7600
Chicago, IL 60680-9915
randmcnally.com
For comments or suggestions, please call
(800) 777-MAPS (-6277)
or email us at:
consumeraffairs@randmcnally.com

NAVTEQ ON BOARD™

Legend

- Interstate highway
- Interstate (Business) highway
- U.S. highway
- State/provincial highway
- Secondary state/provincial highway/county highway
- Trans-Canada Highway
- Canadian autoroute
- Mexican highway
- Other highway designation
- 456 Exit number
- Free limited-access highway (with tunnel)
- Toll highway, toll plaza
- Interchange
- Ramp
- Highway
- Primary road
- Secondary road
- Minor road, unpaved road
- Walkway or trail
- One-way road

- Ferry, waterway
- Levee
- Trolley
- Railroad, station, mass transit line
- Bus station
- Park and ride
- Parking lot/ parking garage
- Rest area, service area
- Airport
- 1200 Block number
- International boundary, state boundary
- County boundary
- Township/range boundary, section corner
- 12345 ZIP code boundary, ZIP code
- 4W-2N Chicago Grid Boundary, Chicago Grid
- 45°33'30" 90°33'30" Latitude, longitude
- Hospital
- School
- University or college

- Information/visitor center/ welcome center
- Police/sheriff, etc.
- Fire station
- City/town/village hall and other government buildings
- Courthouse
- Post office
- Library
- Museum
- Border crossing/ Port of entry
- Theater/ performing arts center
- Golf course
- Other point of interest

Chicago Block Numbers

This page explains the block-numbering system used in the city of Chicago. This system should not be confused with the grid system that Rand McNally uses throughout the Chicago 7-County Street Guide — see page A for details

For the most part, streets in Chicago lie in a grid pattern, and the intersection of State and Madison streets is designated as the city center. Madison Street, running east and west, and State Street, running north and south, represent the base lines, or axis, from which all block and house numbers are determined.

Generally, block numbers in Chicago ascend in all directions by multiples of 100. Chicago street names and block numbers extend into some but not all neighboring suburbs. Here is a list of the major streets in Chicago along with their distance from the base line in both miles and block numbers.

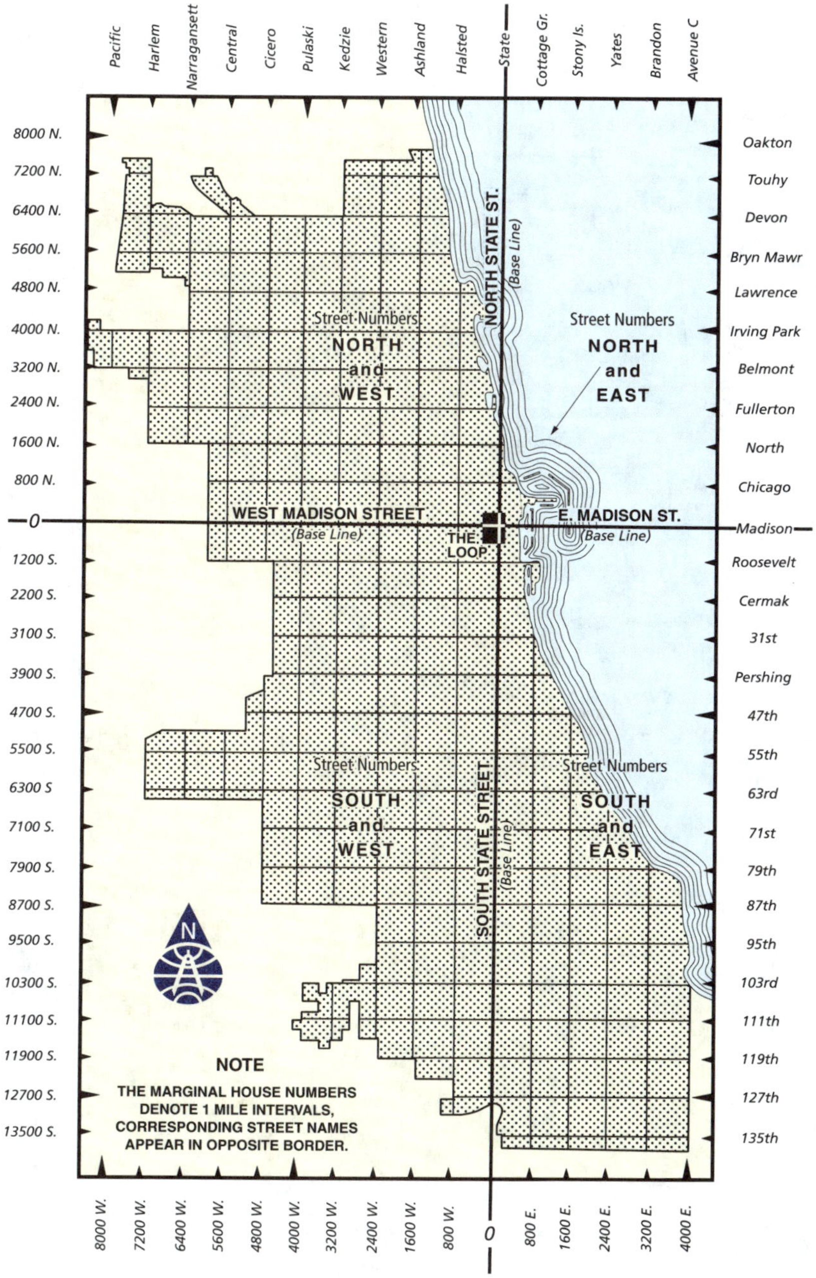

North of Madison Street		Block No.
Chicago Av	1 Mile	800
North Av	2 Miles	1600
Fullerton Av	3 Miles	2400
Belmont Av	4 Miles	3200
Irving Park Rd	5 Miles	4000
Lawrence Av	6 Miles	4800
Bryn Mawr Av	7 Miles	5600
Devon Av	8 Miles	6400
Touhy Av	9 Miles	7200
Oakton St	10 Miles	8000

South of Madison Street		Block No.
Roosevelt Rd	1 Mile	1200
Cermak Rd	2 Miles	2200
Thirty-First St	3 Miles	3100
Pershing Rd	4 Miles	3900
Forty-Seventh St	5 Miles	4700
Fifty-Fifth St	6 Miles	5500
Sixty-Third St	7 Miles	6300
Seventy-First St	8 Miles	7100
Seventy-Ninth St	9 Miles	7900
Eighty-Seventh St	10 Miles	8700
Ninety-Fifth St	11 Miles	9500

West of State Street		Block No.
Halsted St	1 Mile	800
Ashland Av	2 Miles	1600
Western Av	3 Miles	2400
Kedzie Av	4 Miles	3200
Pulaski Rd	5 Miles	4000
Cicero Av	6 Miles	4800
Central Av	7 Miles	5600
Narragansett Av	8 Miles	6400
Harlem Av	9 Miles	7200

East of State Street		Block No.
South Park Av	1/2 Mile	400
Cottage Grove Av	1 Miles	800
Woodlawn Av	1 1/2 Miles	1200
Stony Island Av	2 Miles	1600
Jeffrey Av	2 1/2 Miles	2000
Yates Av	3 Miles	2400
Brandon Av	4 Miles	3200

Downtown Chicago

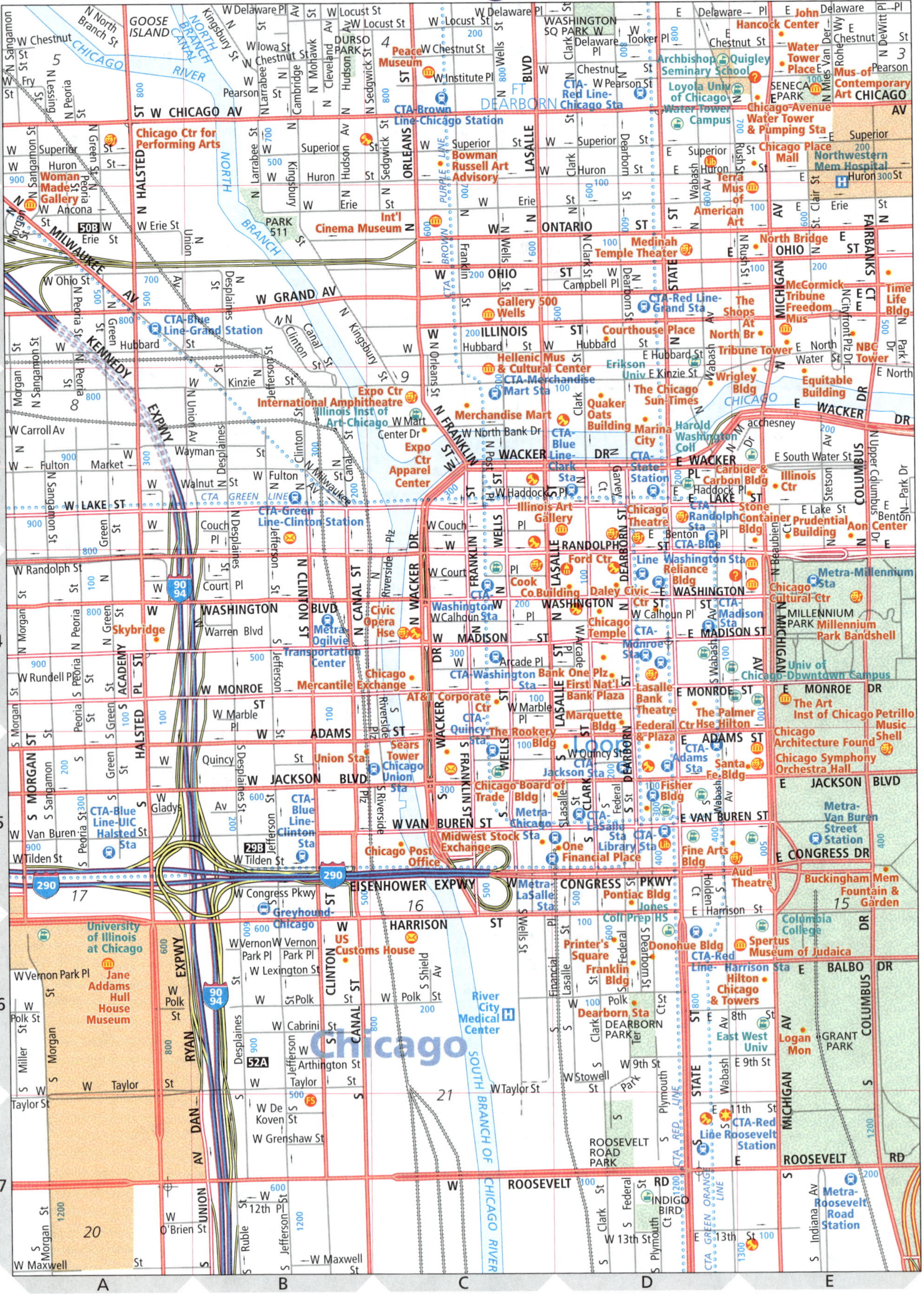

Note: This grid references this map only

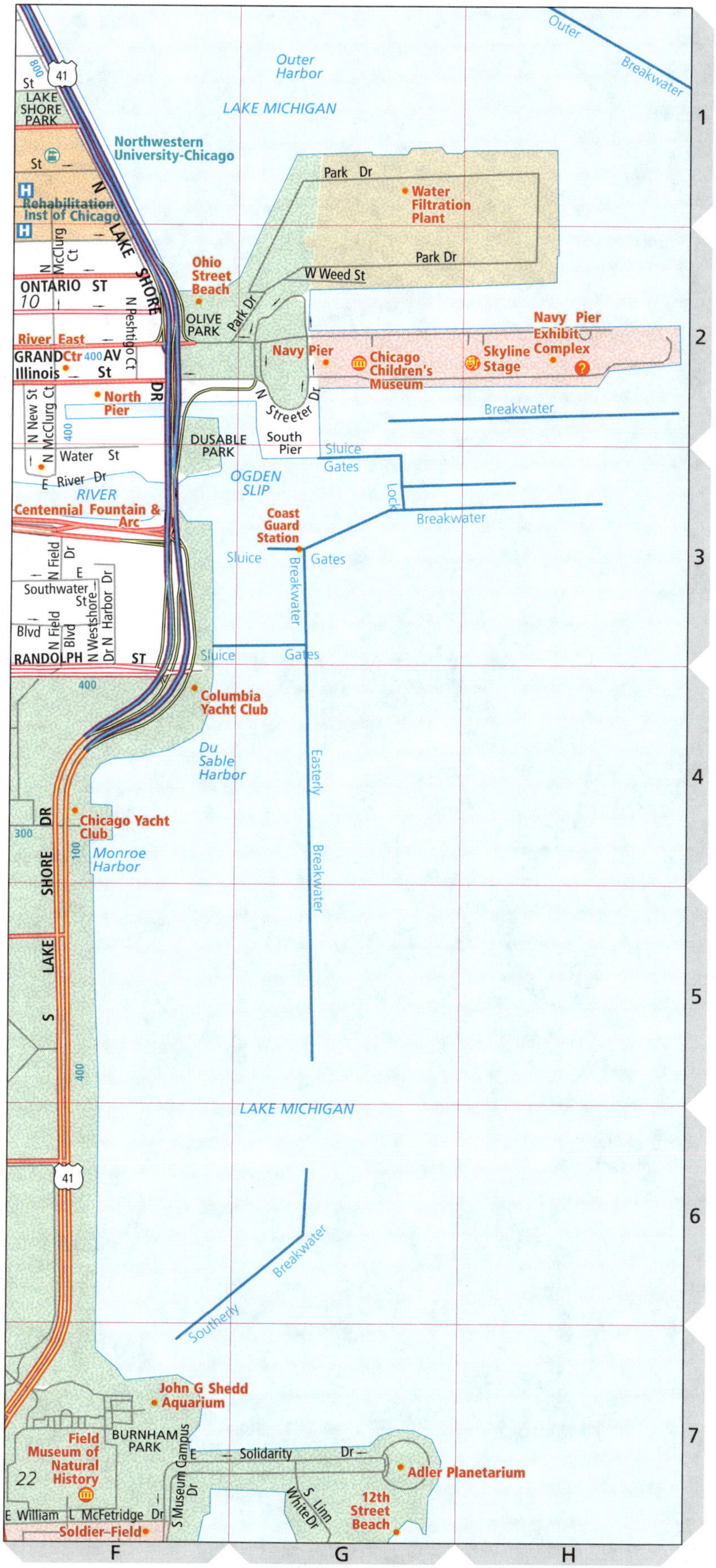
Outer Harbor
LAKE MICHIGAN
Outer Breakwater
Northwestern University-Chicago
LAKE SHORE PARK
Rehabilitation Inst of Chicago
Park Dr
Water Filtration Plant
W Weed St
Ohio Street Beach
ONTARIO ST
OLIVE PARK
Navy Pier
Navy Pier Exhibit Complex
Chicago Children's Museum
Skyline Stage
River East
GRAND AV
Illinois St
North Pier
Streeter Dr
South Pier
DUSABLE PARK
Water St
E River Dr
RIVER
OGDEN SLIP
Centennial Fountain & Arc
Coast Guard Station
Sluice Gates
Breakwater
Lock
RANDOLPH ST
Columbia Yacht Club
Du Sable Harbor
Easterly Breakwater
Chicago Yacht Club
Monroe Harbor
S LAKE SHORE DR
Southerly Breakwater
John G Shedd Aquarium
Field Museum of Natural History
BURNHAM PARK
E Solidarity Dr
Adler Planetarium
12th Street Beach
S Linn White Dr
S Museum Campus Dr
E William L McFetridge Dr
Soldier Field
F
G
H
1
2
3
4
5
6
7

Points of Interest

Adler Planetarium	G7
Aon Center	E3
AT&T Corporate Center	C4
Buckingham Memorial Fountain & Garden	E5
Burnham Park	F7
Carbide-Carbon Building	E3
Chicago Avenue Water Tower & Pumping Station	E1
Chicago Center for Performing Arts	A1
Chicago Children's Museum	G2
Chicago City Hall	D4
Chicago Mercantile Exchange	C4
Chicago Symphony Orchestra Hall	E5
Chicago Theatre	D3
Chicago Union Station	C5
Civic Opera House	C4
Coast Guard Station	G3
Columbia College	E6
Cook County Building	C4
Cook County Circuit Court	D3
Cook County Circuit Court	D4
Cook County Circuit Court	D7
Cook County Circuit Court	E7
Daley Civic Center	D4
Dearborn Station	D6
Equitable Building	E3
Field Museum of Natural History	F7
Fine Arts Building	D5
First National Bank Plaza	D4
Grant Park	E6
Greyhound-Chicago	B5
Harold Washington College	D3
Harold Washington Library Center	D5
Hilton Chicago & Towers	D6
Illinois Center	E3
Illinois Supreme Court	C3
John G Shedd Aquarium	F7
John Hancock Center	E1
John Marshall Law School	D5
Marina City	D3
Merchandise Mart	C3
Metra-Chicago Station	D5
Metra-LaSalle Station	D5
Metra-Millennium Station	E4
Metra-Ogilvie Transportation Center	B4
Metra-Roosevelt Road Station	E7
Metra-Van Buren Street Station	E5
Midwest Stock Exchange	C5
Navy Pier	G2
Navy Pier Exhibit Complex	H2
NBC Tower	E2
North Pier	G2
Northwestern Memorial Hospital	E1
Northwestern University-Chicago	F1
One Financial Place	D5
Petrillo Music Shell	E4
Prudential Building	E3
Roosevelt University	E5
Sears Tower	C5
Soldier Field	F7
Stone Container Building	E3
The Art Institute of Chicago	E4
The Chicago Sun-Times	D3
The Palmer House Hilton	D4
Tribune Tower	D2
United States Courthouse	D5
University of Illinois at Chicago	A6
Washington Square Park	D1
Water Tower Place	E1
Wrigley Building	D3

1 in. = 1400 ft.

0 — 0.25 — 0.5 miles

1:24,000
1 in. = 2000 ft.
0 0.25 0.5
miles

SEE B MAP

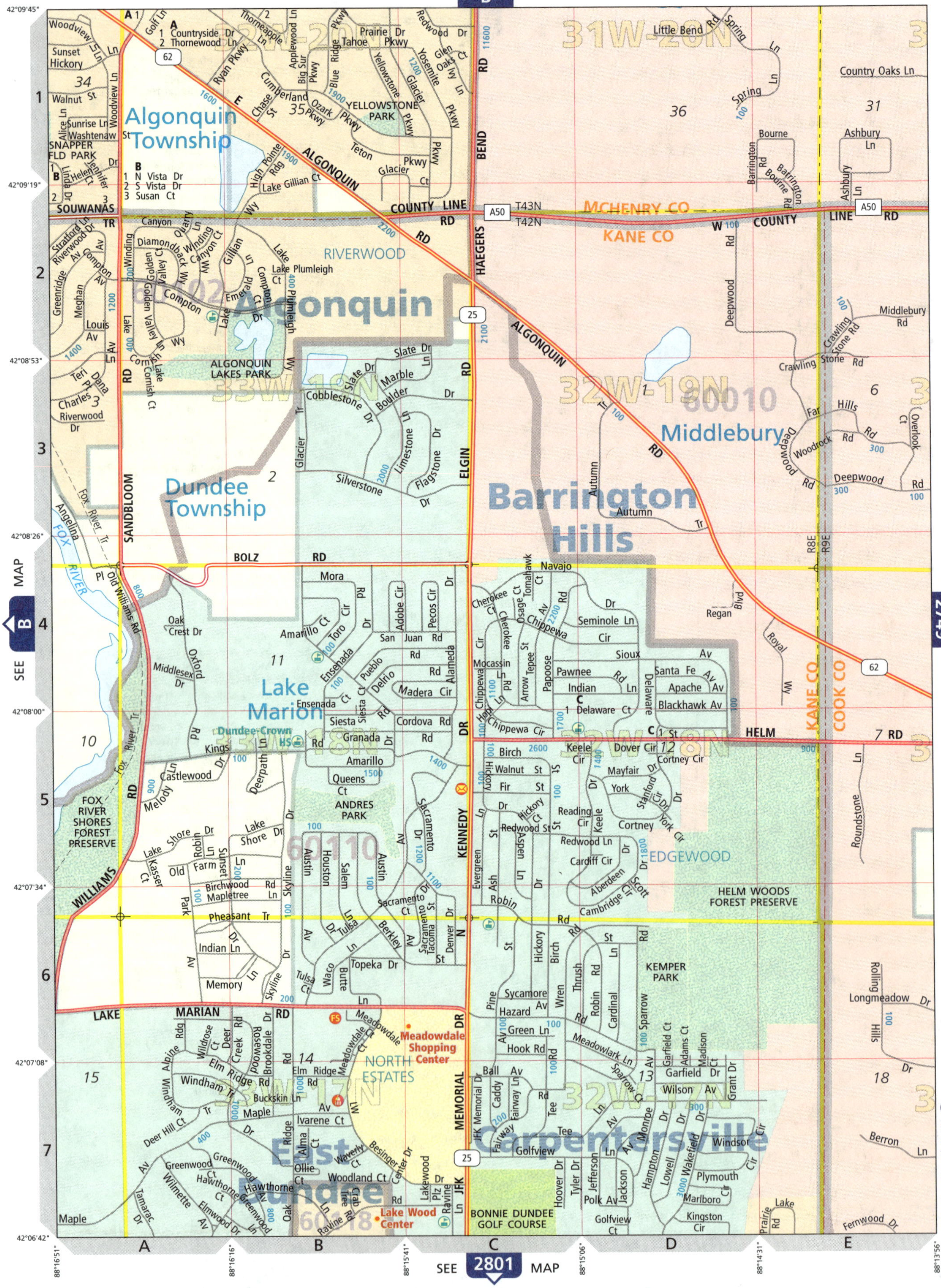
Algonquin Township
Algonquin
Dundee Township
Barrington Hills
Middlebury
Lake Marion
Carpentersville
East Dundee
McHENRY CO
KANE CO
COOK CO
RIVERWOOD
ALGONQUIN LAKES PARK
YELLOWSTONE PARK
SNAPPER FLD PARK
ANDRES PARK
EDGEWOOD
HELM WOODS FOREST PRESERVE
KEMPER PARK
FOX RIVER SHORES FOREST PRESERVE
NORTH ESTATES
Meadowdale Shopping Center
Lake Wood Center
BONNIE DUNDEE GOLF COURSE
Dundee-Crown HS
FOX RIVER
ALGONQUIN RD
COUNTY LINE RD
HAEGERS BEND RD
ELGIN RD
KENNEDY DR
MEMORIAL DR
SANDBLOOM RD
BOLZ RD
HELM RD
LAKE MARIAN RD
WILLIAMS RD
31W-20N
32W-19N
33W-18N
32W-18N
32W-17N
33W-17N
60102
60010
60110
60118
T43N
T42N
R8E
R9E
42°09'45"
42°09'19"
42°08'53"
42°08'26"
42°08'00"
42°07'34"
42°07'08"
42°06'42"
88°16'51"
88°16'16"
88°15'41"
88°15'06"
88°14'31"
88°13'56"

SEE 2749 MAP

SEE B MAP

SEE 2801 MAP

1:24,000
1 in. = 2000 ft.
0 0.25 0.5
miles

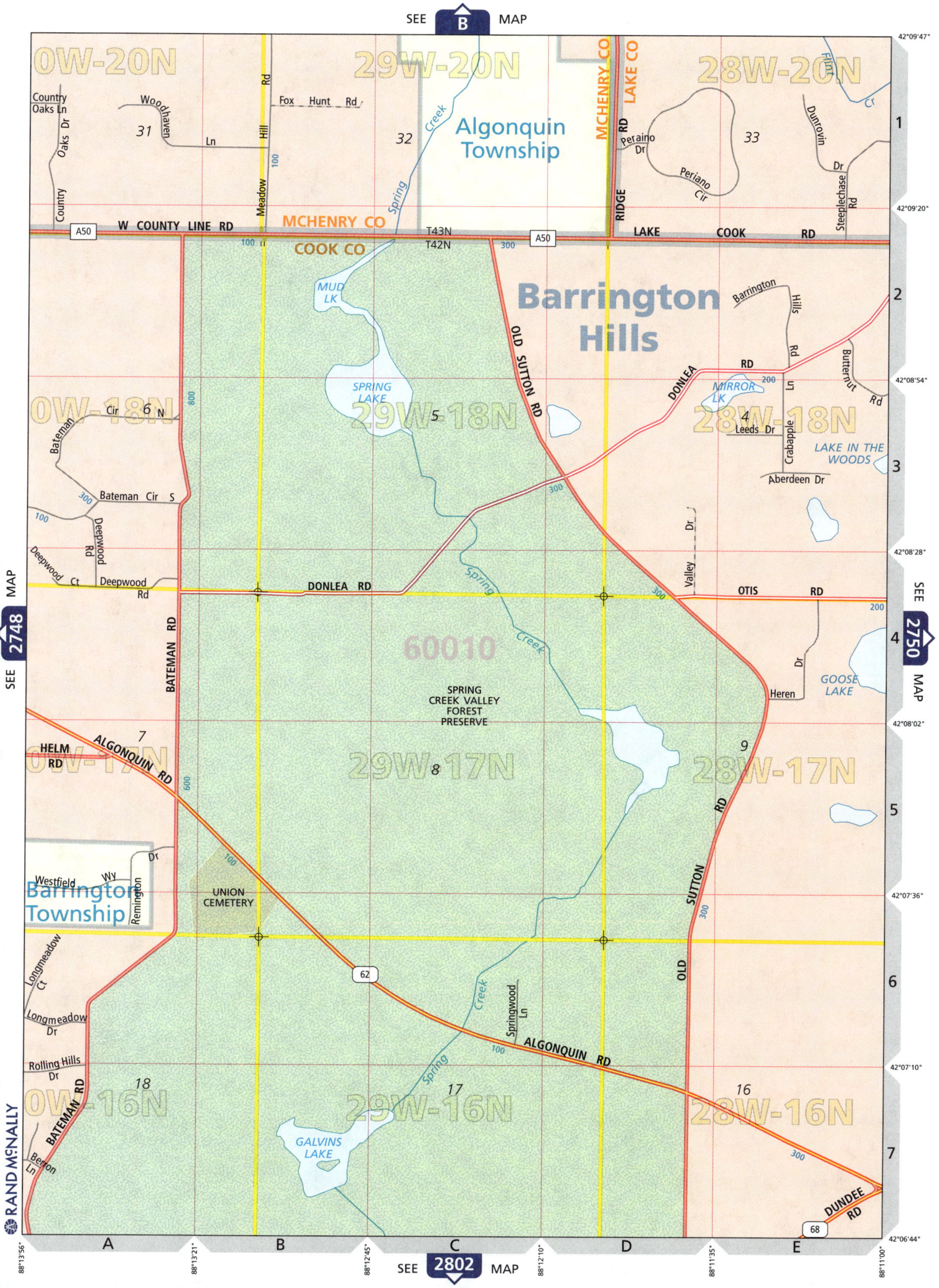
SEE B MAP
SEE 2802 MAP
SEE 2748 MAP
SEE 2750 MAP
0W-20N
29W-20N
28W-20N
Algonquin
Township
Country
Oaks Ln
Oaks Dr
Country
Woodhaven
Ln
31
32
33
Fox Hunt Rd
Meadow
Hill
Rd
Spring
Creek
MCHENRY CO
LAKE CO
RD
Peraino
Dr
Periano
Cir
Dunrovin
Dr
Steeplechase
Rd
Flint
Cr
RIDGE
W COUNTY LINE RD
A50
MCHENRY CO
COOK CO
T43N
T42N
LAKE COOK RD
MUD
LK
Barrington
Hills
Barrington
Hills
Rd
OLD SUTTON RD
DONLEA
RD
MIRROR
LK
Butternut
Rd
SPRING
LAKE
0W-18N
6
Cir
N
Bateman
29W-18N
5
28W-18N
4
Leeds Dr
Crabapple
Ln
LAKE IN THE
WOODS
Aberdeen Dr
Bateman Cir S
Deepwood
Rd
Deepwood
Ct
Deepwood
Rd
Valley
Dr
DONLEA RD
OTIS RD
Spring
Creek
60010
SPRING
CREEK VALLEY
FOREST
PRESERVE
BATEMAN RD
Heren
Dr
GOOSE
LAKE
7
HELM
RD
ALGONQUIN RD
0W-17N
29W-17N
8
28W-17N
9
SUTTON
RD
Westfield
Wy
Dr
Remington
Barrington
Township
UNION
CEMETERY
Longmeadow
Ct
Longmeadow
Dr
62
OLD
Creek
Springwood
Ln
ALGONQUIN RD
Rolling Hills
Dr
18
0W-16N
BATEMAN RD
Benton
Ln
Spring
17
29W-16N
GALVINS
LAKE
16
28W-16N
DUNDEE
RD
68
A B C D E
1 2 3 4 5 6 7
100 200 300 600 800
42°09'47"
42°09'20"
42°08'54"
42°08'28"
42°08'02"
42°07'36"
42°07'10"
42°06'44"
88°13'56"
88°13'21"
88°12'45"
88°12'10"
88°11'35"
88°11'00"
RAND McNALLY

1:24,000
1 in. = 2000 ft.
0 0.25 0.5
miles

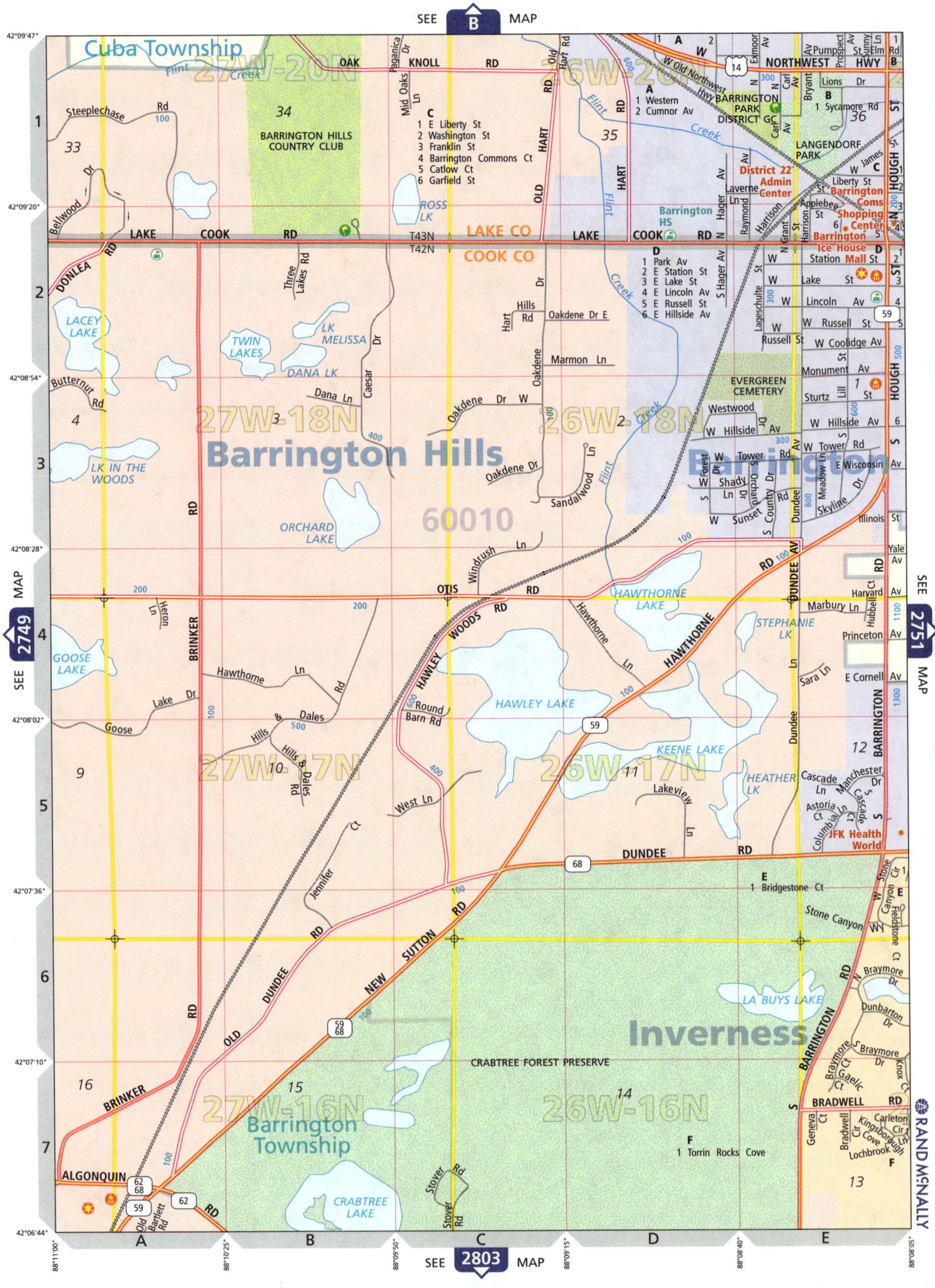
SEE B MAP
Cuba Township
27W-20N
26W-20N
OAK KNOLL RD
BARRINGTON HILLS COUNTRY CLUB
34
33
35
36
C
1 E Liberty St
2 Washington St
3 Franklin St
4 Barrington Commons Ct
5 Catlow Ct
6 Garfield St
A
1 Western
2 Cumnor Av
B
1 Sycamore Rd
BARRINGTON PARK DISTRICT GC
LANGENDORF PARK
District 22 Admin Center
Barrington HS
Barrington Coms Shopping Center
Barrington Ice House Mall
ROSS LK
LAKE CO
COOK CO
T43N
T42N
LAKE COOK RD
NORTHWEST HWY
D
1 Park Av
2 E Station St
3 E Lake St
4 E Lincoln Av
5 E Russell St
6 E Hillside Av
LACEY LAKE
TWIN LAKES
LK MELISSA
DANA LK
EVERGREEN CEMETERY
27W-18N
26W-18N
Barrington Hills
Barrington
LK IN THE WOODS
ORCHARD LAKE
60010
OTIS RD
HAWTHORNE LAKE
STEPHANIE LK
GOOSE LAKE
HAWLEY LAKE
KEENE LAKE
HEATHER LK
27W-17N
26W-17N
9
10
11
12
JFK Health World
DUNDEE RD
E
1 Bridgestone Ct
LA BUYS LAKE
Inverness
CRABTREE FOREST PRESERVE
27W-16N
26W-16N
Barrington Township
16
15
14
13
F
1 Torrin Rocks Cove
BRADWELL RD
ALGONQUIN RD
CRABTREE LAKE
SEE 2749 MAP
SEE 2751 MAP
SEE 2803 MAP
A B C D E
1 2 3 4 5 6 7
RAND McNALLY

1:24,000
1 in. = 2000 ft.
0 0.25 0.5
miles

SEE B MAP

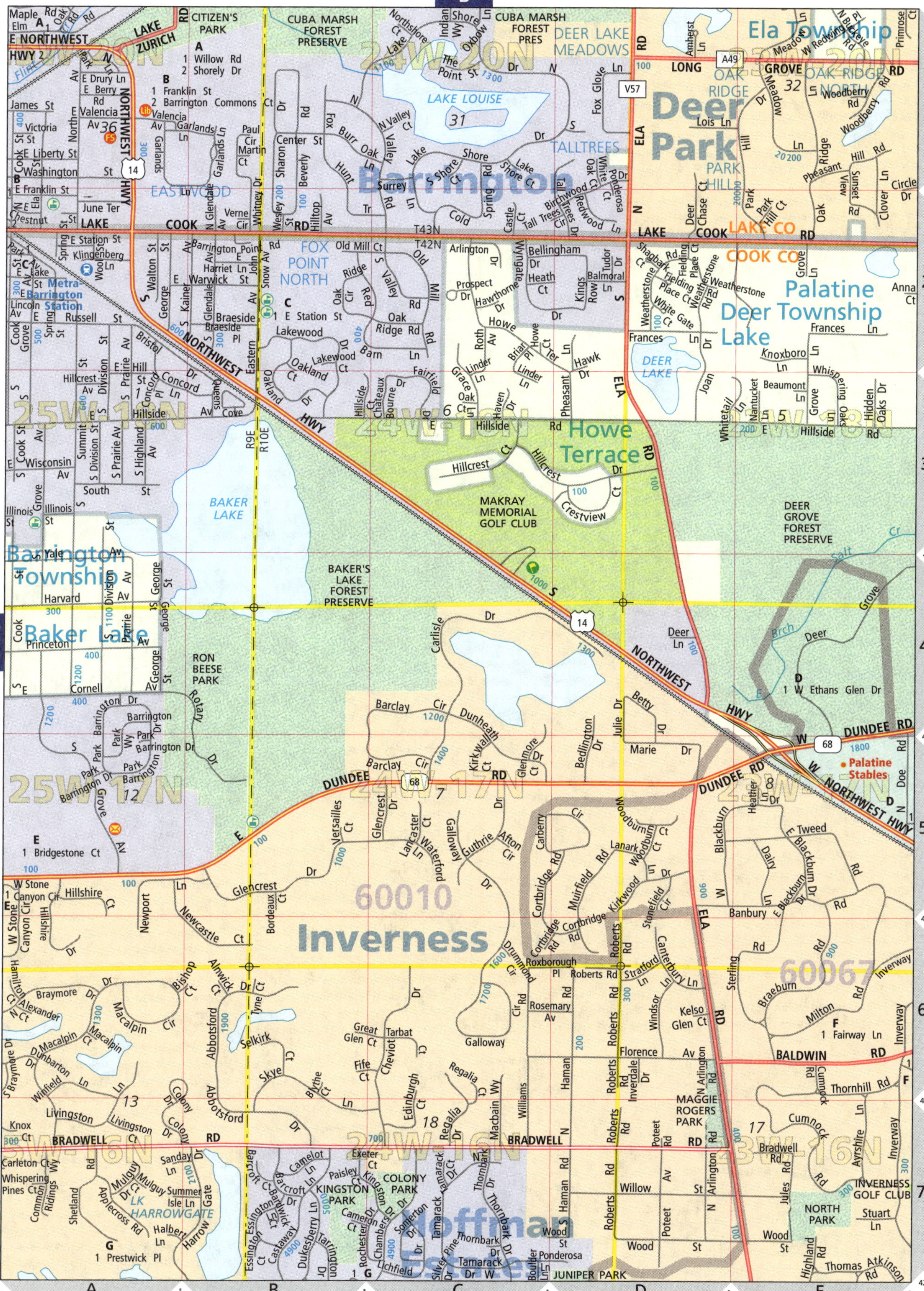

SEE 2750 MAP

SEE 2752 MAP

SEE 2804 MAP

RAND McNALLY

1:24,000
1 in. = 2000 ft.
0 0.25 0.5
miles

SEE B MAP
SEE 2751 MAP
SEE 2753 MAP
SEE 2805 MAP
LONG GROVE RD
W LONG GROVE RD
The Shops of Kildeer
PRESTONFIELD
Deer Park Town Center
Ela Township
Kildeer
Deer Park
60074
60010
60047
60067
RUE VALLEE
MICHAEL D' ANGELO PARK
DOVER PND PARK
DOVER POND
FERNDALE WOODS
HARTZ FARM
LAKE COOK RD
LAKE CO
COOK CO
T43N
T42N
Barrington Woods
Brentwood
Palatine Township
DEER GRV LK
DEER GROVE FOREST PRESERVE
East Branch Salt Creek
QUENTIN RD
W DUNDEE RD
E DUNDEE RD
EAGLE PARK
Pepper Tree
Kenilwicke
HUMMINGBIRD PARK
Morgan's Gate
PALATINE HILLS GOLF COURSE
THOMAS T HAMILTON PARK
Heatherlea
CHERRYWOOD PARK
THOMAS HAMILTON RES
Lake Park Estates
PALATINE HILLS PARK
Quentin Corners
North Quentin Ctr
NORTHWEST HWY
BALDWIN RD
ROSELLE RD
SMITH ST
ASHWOOD PARK
Century Plaza
Village Oasis
Eurofresh Plaza
MULBERRY PARK
Palatine
Palatine Plaza
Inverness
INVERNESS GOLF CLUB
COLFAX ST
RIEMER RESERVOIR PARK
Cutting Hall
PLUM GROVE RD
22W-20N
21W-20N
22W-18N
21W-18N
22W-17N
21W-17N
22W-16N
21W-16N
A
1 N Long Meadow Ct
B
1 N Broadmoor Ct
2 N Dartmoor Av
3 W Denton Av
4 W Broadmoor Ct
5 W Dresden Av
6 N Denton Av
7 Cherrywood Av
8 N Tanglewood Av
9 N Chelsea Av
10 N Wellington Ct
C
1 Old Wick Ln
2 Crichton Ln
3 Strome Ln
4 Burleigh Ln
5 Borthwick Ln
6 Duntrune Ln
7 Tantallon Ln
8 Knockderry Ln
9 Dirleton Ln
10 Ravenscraig Ln
11 Brodick Ln
D
1 N Crabtree Dr
2 N Edgewater Ct
E
1 W Chesterfield Ct
2 N Aurelia Ct
RAND McNALLY

1:24,000
1 in. = 2000 ft.
0 0.25 0.5
miles

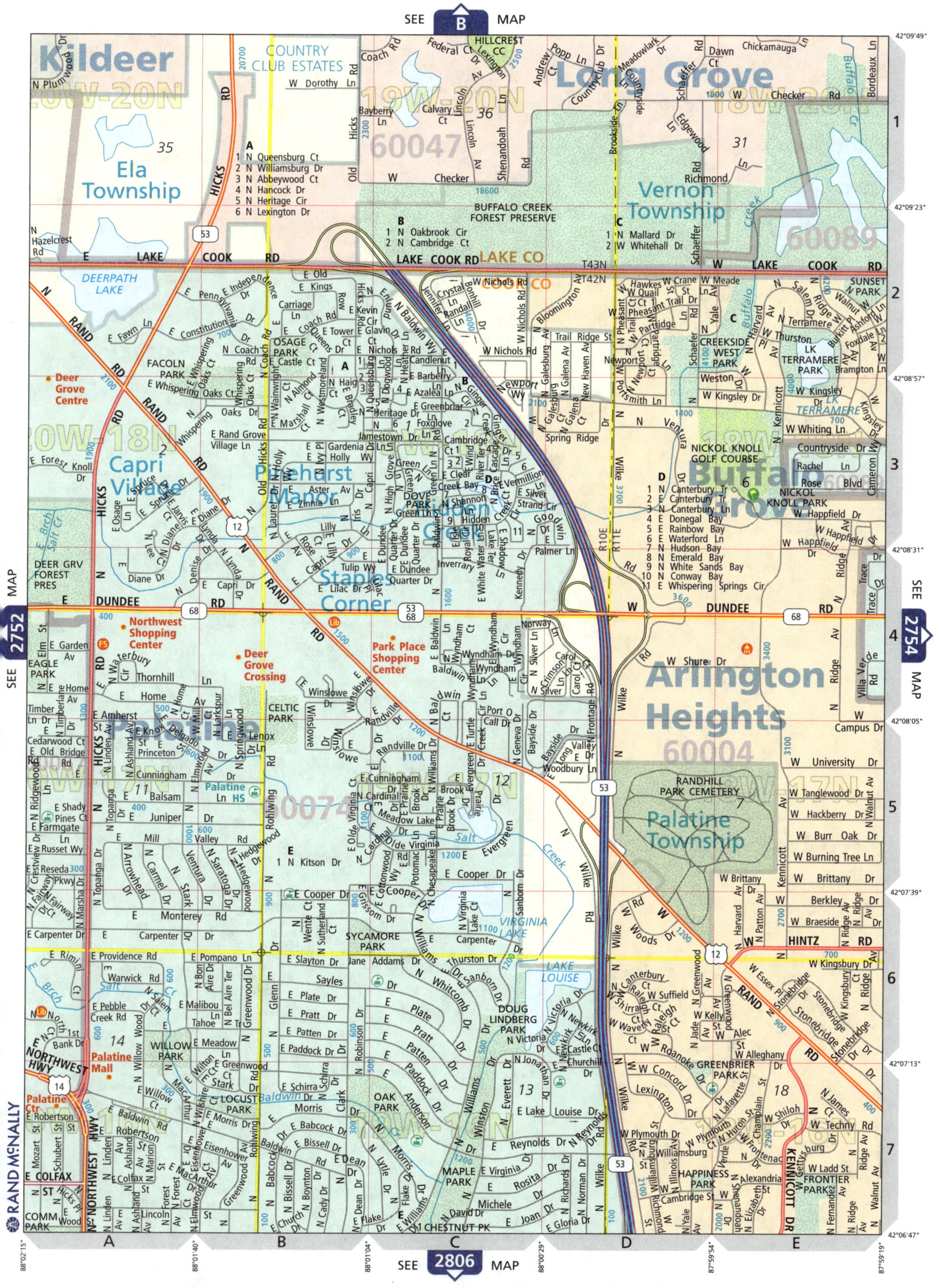
SEE B MAP
SEE 2752 MAP
SEE 2754 MAP
SEE 2806 MAP
Kildeer
COUNTRY CLUB ESTATES
Long Grove
Ela Township
Vernon Township
60047
60089
BUFFALO CREEK FOREST PRESERVE
HILLCREST CC
LAKE CO
COOK CO
LAKE COOK RD
DEERPATH LAKE
Deer Grove Centre
FACOLN PARK
OSAGE PARK
Capri Village
Pinehurst Manor
Hidden Creek
Staples Corner
DOVE PARK
TERRAMERE PARK
CREEKSIDE WEST PARK
NICKOL KNOLL GOLF COURSE
NICKOL KNOLL PARK
Buffalo Grove
DEER GRV FOREST PRES
DUNDEE RD
Northwest Shopping Center
Deer Grove Crossing
Park Place Shopping Center
EAGLE PARK
CELTIC PARK
Palatine
Palatine HS
60074
Arlington Heights
60004
RANDHILL PARK CEMETERY
Palatine Township
SYCAMORE PARK
VIRGINIA LAKE
LAKE LOUISE
DOUG LINDBERG PARK
WILLOW PARK
Palatine Mall
LOCUST PARK
OAK PARK
MAPLE PARK
GREENBRIER PARK
HAPPINESS PARK
FRONTIER PARK
Palatine Ctr
NORTHWEST HWY
HICKS RD
RAND RD
HINTZ RD
KENNICOTT DR
COMM PARK
A
1 N Queensburg Ct
2 N Williamsburg Dr
3 N Abbeywood Ct
4 N Hancock Dr
5 N Heritage Cir
6 N Lexington Dr
B
1 N Oakbrook Cir
2 N Cambridge Ct
C
1 N Mallard Dr
2 W Whitehall Dr
D
1 N Canterbury Tr
2 E Canterbury Tr
3 N Canterbury Ln
4 E Donegal Bay
5 E Rainbow Bay
6 E Waterford Ln
7 N Hudson Bay
8 N Emerald Bay
9 N White Sands Bay
10 N Conway Bay
11 E Whispering Springs Cir
RAND McNALLY

1:24,000
1 in. = 2000 ft.
0 0.25 0.5
miles

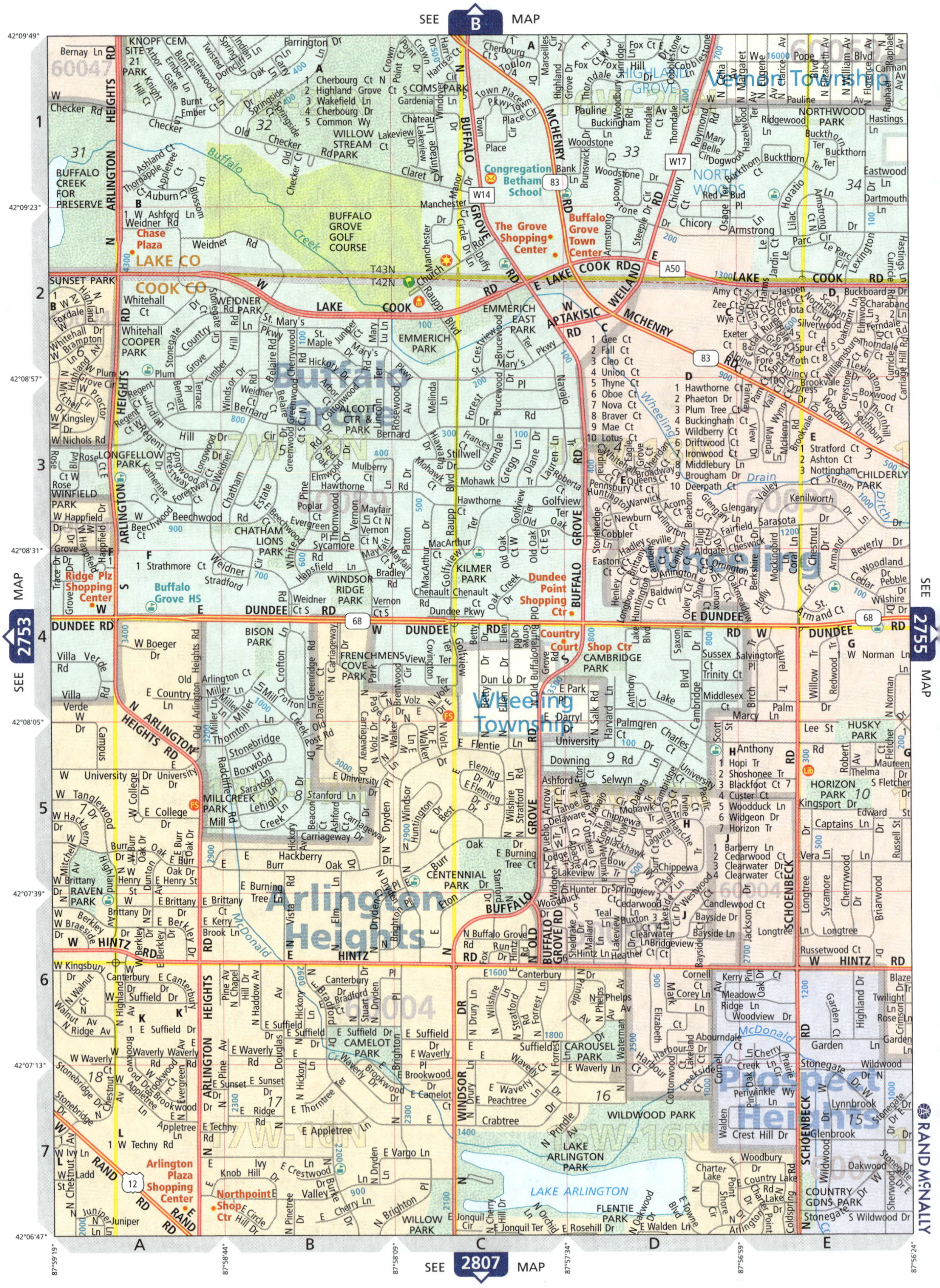
SEE B MAP
SEE 2753 MAP
SEE 2755 MAP
SEE 2807 MAP
Buffalo Grove
Wheeling
Wheeling Township
Arlington Heights
Prospect Heights
Vernon Township
BUFFALO GROVE GOLF COURSE
BUFFALO CREEK FOREST PRESERVE
LAKE CO
COOK CO
LAKE ARLINGTON
LAKE ARLINGTON PARK
Chase Plaza
The Grove Shopping Center
Buffalo Grove Town Center
Congregation Betham School
Buffalo Grove HS
Ridge Plz Shopping Center
Dundee Point Shopping Ctr
Country Court Shop Ctr
Arlington Plaza Shopping Center
Northpoint Shop Ctr
LAKE COOK RD
DUNDEE RD
HINTZ RD
ARLINGTON HEIGHTS RD
BUFFALO GROVE RD
MCHENRY RD
WEILAND RD
SCHOENBECK RD
WINDSOR DR
RAND RD
APTAKISIC RD
EMMERICH PARK
EMMERICH EAST PARK
KILMER PARK
WINDSOR RIDGE PARK
CHATHAM LIONS PARK
CAMBRIDGE PARK
CENTENNIAL PARK
CAROUSEL PARK
WILDWOOD PARK
HORIZON PARK
HUSKY PARK
NORTHWOOD PARK
CHILDERLY PARK
COUNTRY GDNS PARK
FLENTIE PARK
WILLOW PARK
RAVEN PARK
CAMELOT PARK
MILLCREEK PARK
FRENCHMENS COVE PARK
BISON PARK
WINFIELD PARK
LONGFELLOW PARK
COOPER PARK
WEIDNER PARK
SUNSET PARK
ALCOTT CTR & PARK
WILLOW STREAM PARK
KNOPF CEM
RAND McNALLY

1:24,000
1 in. = 2000 ft.
0 0.25 0.5
miles

SEE B MAP

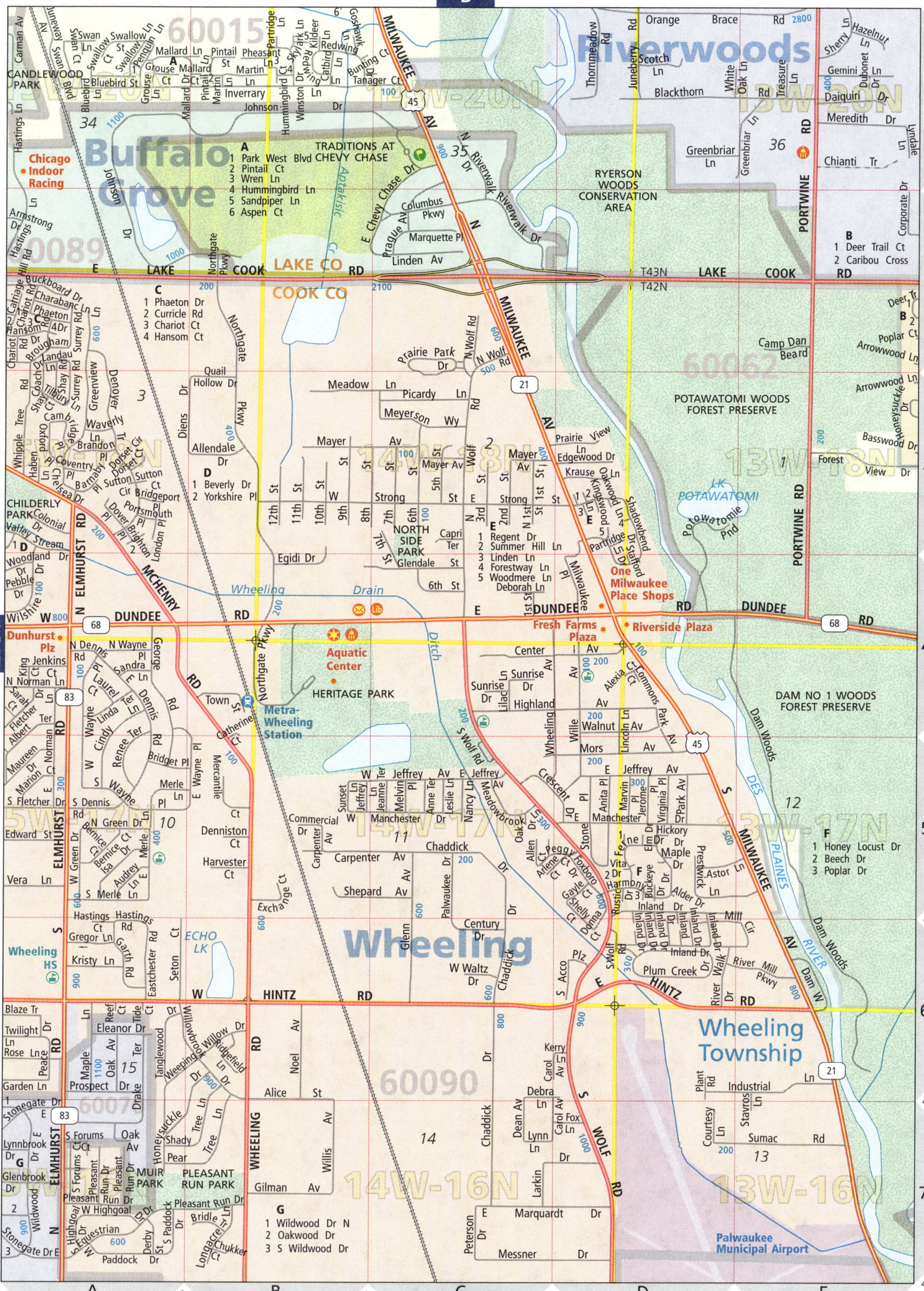

SEE 2754 MAP
SEE 2756 MAP
SEE 2808 MAP

1:24,000
1 in. = 2000 ft.
0 0.25 0.5
miles

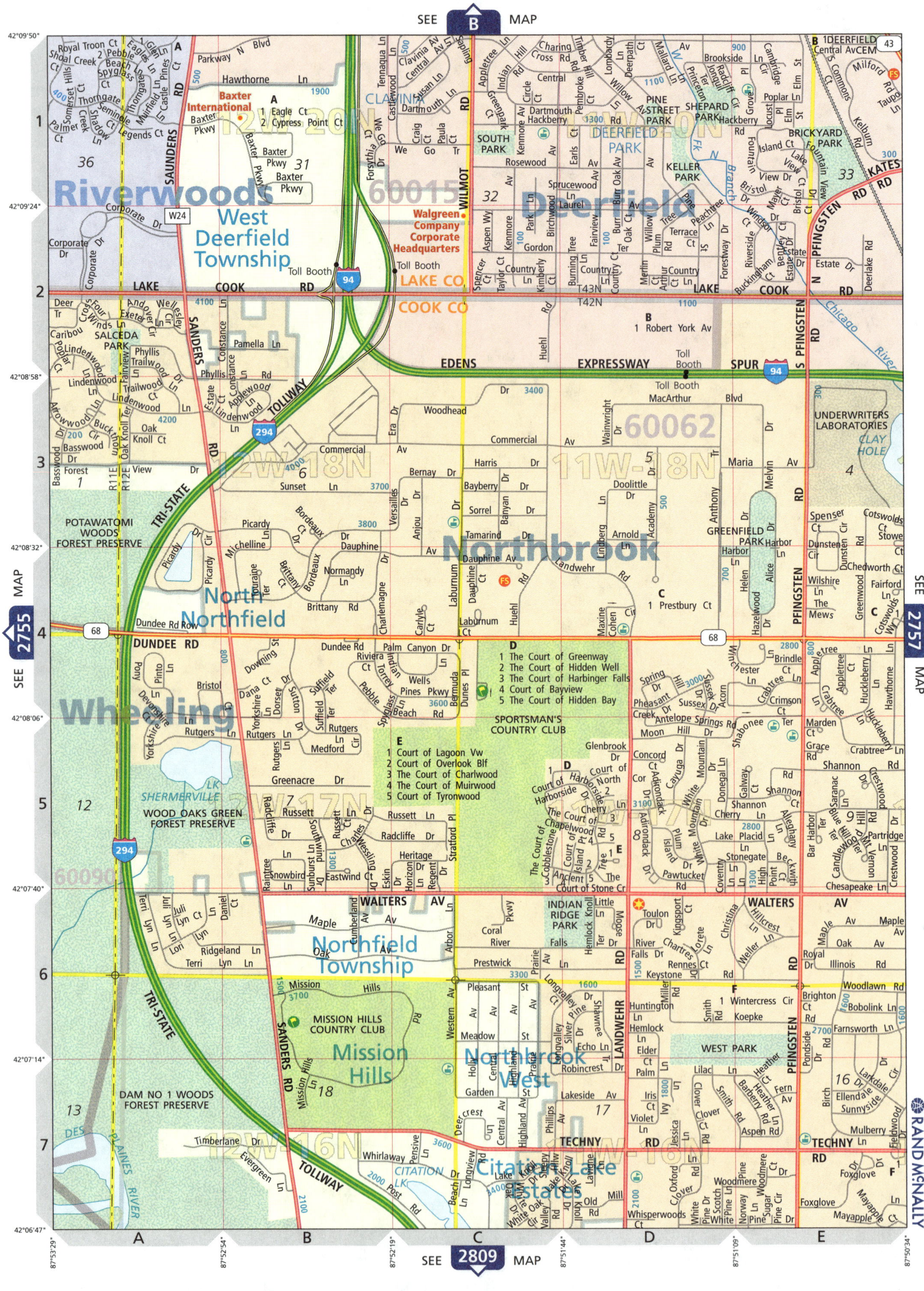

1:24,000
1 in. = 2000 ft.
0 0.25 0.5
miles

SEE B MAP

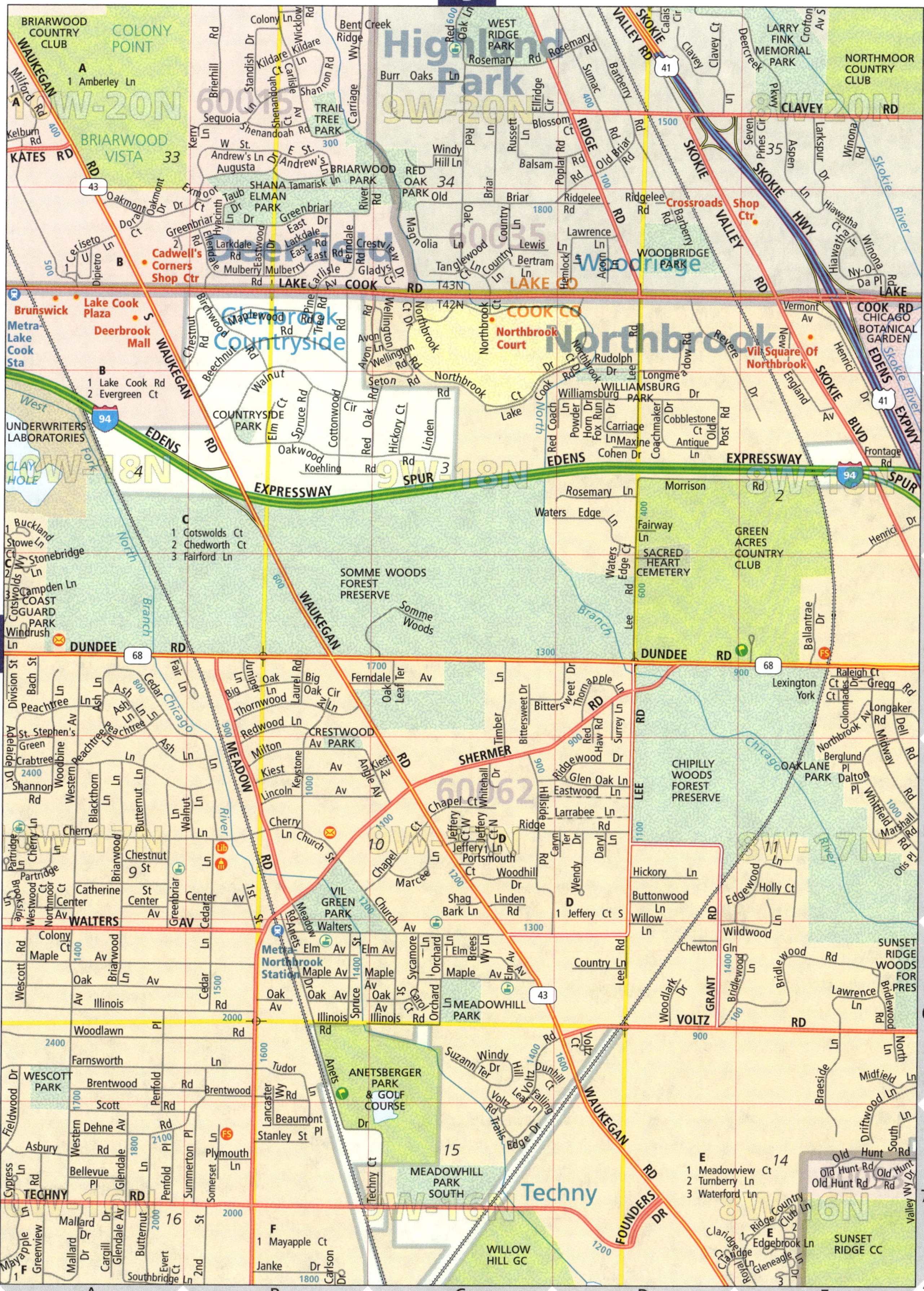
Highland Park
Northbrook
Glenbrook Countryside
Woodridge
Techny
Oakfield
BRIARWOOD COUNTRY CLUB
COLONY POINT
BRIARWOOD VISTA
WEST RIDGE PARK
TRAIL TREE PARK
BRIARWOOD PARK
RED OAK PARK
SHANA ELMAN PARK
WOODBRIDGE PARK
LARRY FINK MEMORIAL PARK
NORTHMOOR COUNTRY CLUB
Crossroads Shop Ctr
Cadwell's Corners Shop Ctr
Lake Cook Plaza
Deerbrook Mall
Brunswick
Metra-Lake Cook Sta
Northbrook Court
CHICAGO BOTANICAL GARDEN
Vil Square Of Northbrook
COUNTRYSIDE PARK
WILLIAMSBURG PARK
UNDERWRITERS LABORATORIES
CLAY HOLE
SOMME WOODS FOREST PRESERVE
SACRED HEART CEMETERY
GREEN ACRES COUNTRY CLUB
COAST GUARD PARK
CRESTWOOD PARK
CHIPILLY WOODS FOREST PRESERVE
OAKLANE PARK
VIL GREEN PARK
Metra-Northbrook Station
MEADOWHILL PARK
SUNSET RIDGE WOODS FOR PRES
WESCOTT PARK
ANETSBERGER PARK & GOLF COURSE
MEADOWHILL PARK SOUTH
WILLOW HILL GC
SUNSET RIDGE CC
LAKE CO
COOK CO
EDENS EXPRESSWAY
SPUR
SKOKIE VALLEY RD
SKOKIE HWY
SKOKIE BLVD
EDENS EXPWY
WAUKEGAN RD
DUNDEE RD
LAKE COOK RD
CLAVEY RD
KATES RD
SHERMER RD
WALTERS AV
VOLTZ RD
TECHNY RD
FOUNDERS DR
MEADOW RD
LEE RD
GRANT RD
RIDGE RD
60015
60035
60062
9W-20N
8W-20N
9W-18N
8W-18N
10W-18N
9W-17N
8W-17N
10W-17N
9W-16N
8W-16N
10W-16N
A 1 Amberley Ln
B 1 Lake Cook Rd 2 Evergreen Ct
C 1 Cotswolds Ct 2 Chedworth Ct 3 Fairford Ln
D 1 Jeffery Ct S
E 1 Meadowview Ct 2 Turnberry Ln 3 Waterford Ln
F 1 Mayapple Ct
42°09'51"
42°09'25"
42°08'59"
42°08'32"
42°08'06"
42°07'40"
42°07'14"
42°06'48"
87°50'34"
87°49'59"
87°49'23"
87°48'48"
87°48'13"
87°47'38"
A B C D E
1 2 3 4 5 6 7

SEE 2756 MAP

SEE 2758 MAP

SEE 2810 MAP

1:24,000
1 in. = 2000 ft.
0 0.25 0.5
miles

SEE B MAP

Highland Park
LAKE MICHIGAN
Braeside
LAKE CO
COOK CO
New Trier Township
Chicago Botanical Garden
Ravinia Festival Music Center
Metra Braeside Station
GLENCOE PIONEER CEM
NORTHMOOR COUNTRY CLUB
KENNEDY PARK
LAKE SHORE COUNTRY CLUB
TURNBULL WOODS FOREST PRESERVE
GLENCOE GOLF CLUB
Glencoe Comm Center
Glencoe Historical Society Museum
Metra Glencoe Sta
VET MEM PARK
HENRY J KALK PARK
LAKEFRONT PARK
Public Beach
Glencoe
SKOKIE LAGOONS
SKOKIE COUNTRY CLUB
WILLIAM N ERICKSON FOREST PRESERVE
SHELTON PARK
WATTS PARK
LINDEN PARK
SUNSET RIDGE WOODS FOR PRESERVE
Greyhound-Northbrook
Northbrook
Northfield
Northfield Township
NICK CORWIN PARK
WINNETKA GOLF CLUB
Winnetka
SUNSET RIDGE CC
EDENS EXPRESSWAY SPUR
EDENS EXPWY
SKOKIE BLVD
GREEN BAY RD
SHERIDAN RD
LAKE COOK RD
COUNTY LINE RD
DUNDEE RD
TOWER RD
FORESTWAY DR
HOHLFELDER RD
FRONTAGE RD
VOLTZ RD
SUNSET RIDGE RD
HIBBARD RD
7W-20N
6W-20N
5W-20N
7W-18N
6W-18N
7W-17N
6W-17N
7W-16N
6W-16N
60035
60062
60022
60093
RAND McNALLY

SEE 2757 MAP
SEE 2759 MAP
SEE 2811 MAP

1:24,000
1 in. = 2000 ft.
0 0.25 0.5
miles

SEE B MAP
LAKE MICHIGAN
SEE 2758 MAP
SEE B MAP
SEE 2812 MAP
42°09'51"
42°09'25"
42°08'59"
42°08'33"
42°08'07"
42°07'41"
42°07'14"
42°06'48"
87°44'43"
87°44'08"
87°43'33"
87°42'58"
87°42'23"
87°41'48"
A
B
C
D
E
1
2
3
4
5
6
7
18N
Glencoe
A
1 Keystone Ct
Lakeside Ter
South Ct
Sunrise Cir
Surfside Pl
Shoreline
Harbor St
Wentworth Av
Mary St
B
1 Whitebridge Ln
Whitebridge Hill Dr
Whitebridge Hill Rd
Old
Woodlawn Av
Taylorsport Ln
Green
Glen Wood Av
Crescent Ln
SHERIDAN RD
C
1 Merrill St
Scott Av
Bay
Fisher
17
Sheridan Rd
Glen Oak Dr
D
1 Rosewood Av
Granite Gallery
Metra- Hubbard Woods Sta
Hubbard Pl
Ravine Rd
Hubbard Woods
Private Rd
Gage St
Hubbard St
Tower Manor Dr
Lamson Dr
TOWER ROAD PARK
16
4W-16N
GREEN BAY RD
TOWER RD
Chatfield Rd
Lincoln Av
Foxdale Av
Eldorado St
Prospect Av
Bryant Av
Lloyd Pl
Winnetka
LLOYD PARK
Laurel Av

1:24,000
1 in. = 2000 ft.
0 0.25 0.5
miles

SEE 2748 MAP
SEE 2855 MAP
SEE B MAP
SEE 2802 MAP
Carpentersville
Barrington Hills
East Dundee
West Dundee
Hoffman Estates
Elgin
Dundee Township
Hanover Township
60110
60010
60118
60123
60192
60120
33W-16N
32W-16N
33W-15N
32W-15N
32W-14N
32W-12N
31W-1
KANE CO
COOK CO
R8E
R9E
T42N
T41N
BONNIE DUNDEE GOLF COURSE
GOLFVIEW PARK
Comm Unit School District 300 Board of Education
MAX FREEMAN MEM PARK
Dolphin Cove Water Park
LIONS PARK
CARMEN GARCIA MEM ARBORETUM PARK
Clearwater Theater
Haegar Pottery Factory
Summit School
River Valley Square
DUNDEE TOWNSHIP CEMETERY EAST
Santa's Village Amusement Park
WILLIAM ALDIS SR PARK
SOUTH END PARK
THE RESERVE
MAX MCGRAW WILDLIFE FOUNDATION
RIVER VALLEY MEM GDNS CEM
FOX RIVER BUSINESS PARK
VOYAGEUR LNDG FOREST PRES
SPRING CREEK VALLEY FOR PRES
SPRING CREEK VALLEY FOREST PRESERVE
TROUT PARK
COBBLERS CROSSING
NORTHWEST TOLLWAY
Toll Booth
FOX RIVER
Jelkes Cr
Sleepy Cr
MEMORIAL DR
JFK
DUNDEE AV
BARRINGTON AV
PENNY AV
PENNY RD
DUNDEE RD
MAIN ST
HIGGINS RD
W HIGGINS RD
ELGIN AV
DUNCAN AV
VAN BUREN ST
WATER ST
W MAIN ST
WILLIAMS PL
Airport Rd
Brandt Dr
Massey Rd
Sunset Dr
Sunset Park Dr
Elmwood
Richardson Rd
Piemonte Dr
McGraw Ln
Maple Av
Knollwood Av
Cleveland Av
Edwards Av
Springwood Dr
Geneva St
Huron Dr
Deep Woods Ct
Elma Av
Stewart Av
Parkway Av
Glenwood Av
Oakhill Rd
Trout Park Blvd
A
1 Springwood Cir
D
1 Geneva St
B
1 Entrance Rd
2 Cheryl Ln
3 Willow Lake Rd
4 Big Peninsula Rd
5 Little Peninsula Rd
68
40
72
25
90
42°06'42"
42°06'16"
42°05'50"
42°05'24"
42°04'58"
42°04'32"
42°04'05"
42°03'39"
88°16'49"
88°16'14"
88°15'39"
88°15'04"
88°14'29"
88°13'54"
A B C D E
1 2 3 4 5 6 7
RAND McNALLY

1:24,000
1 in. = 2000 ft.
0 0.25 0.5
miles

SEE 2749 MAP

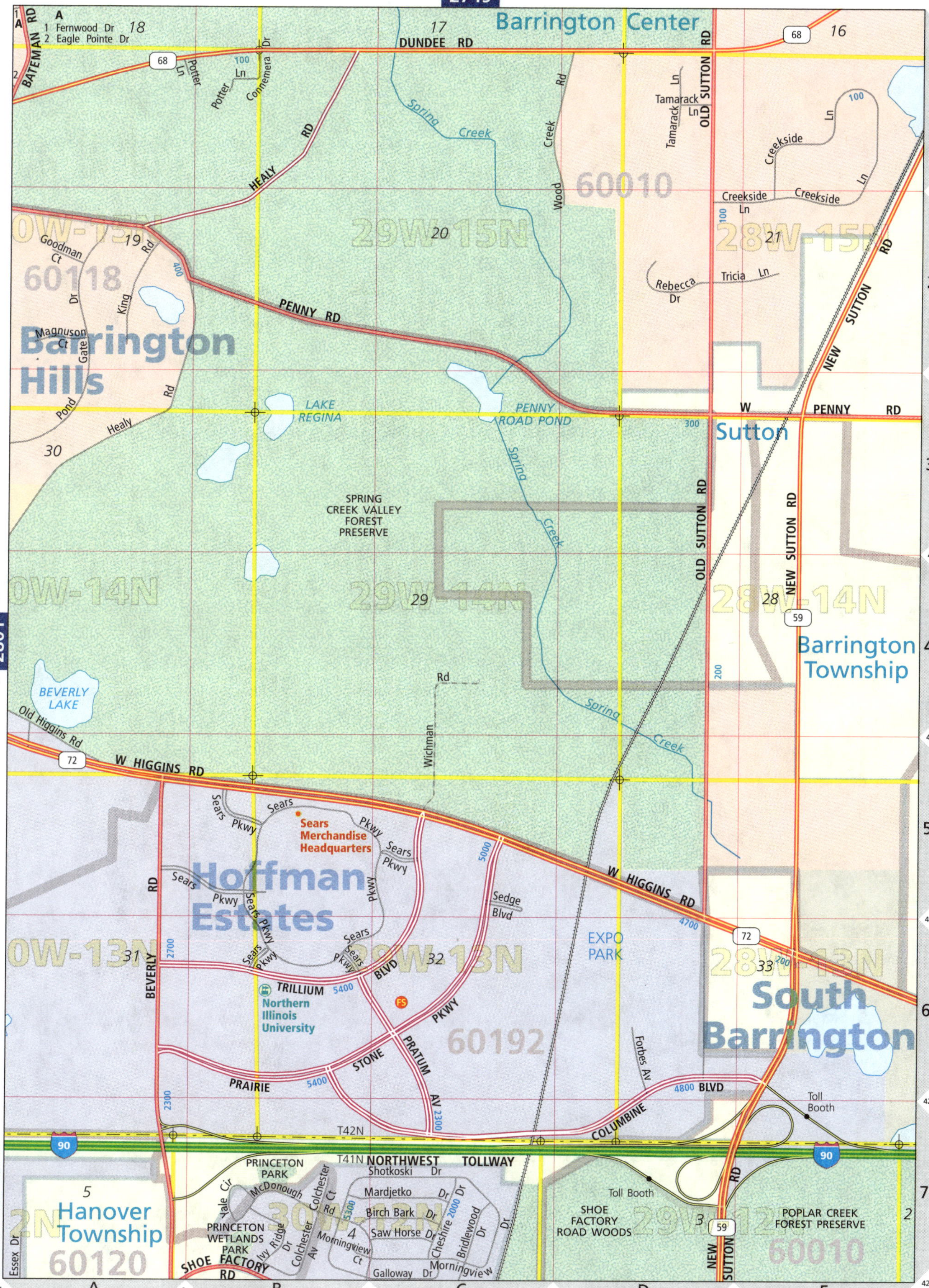

SEE 2801 MAP

SEE 2803 MAP

SEE 2856 MAP

1:24,000
1 in. = 2000 ft.
0 0.25 0.5
miles

SEE 2750 MAP

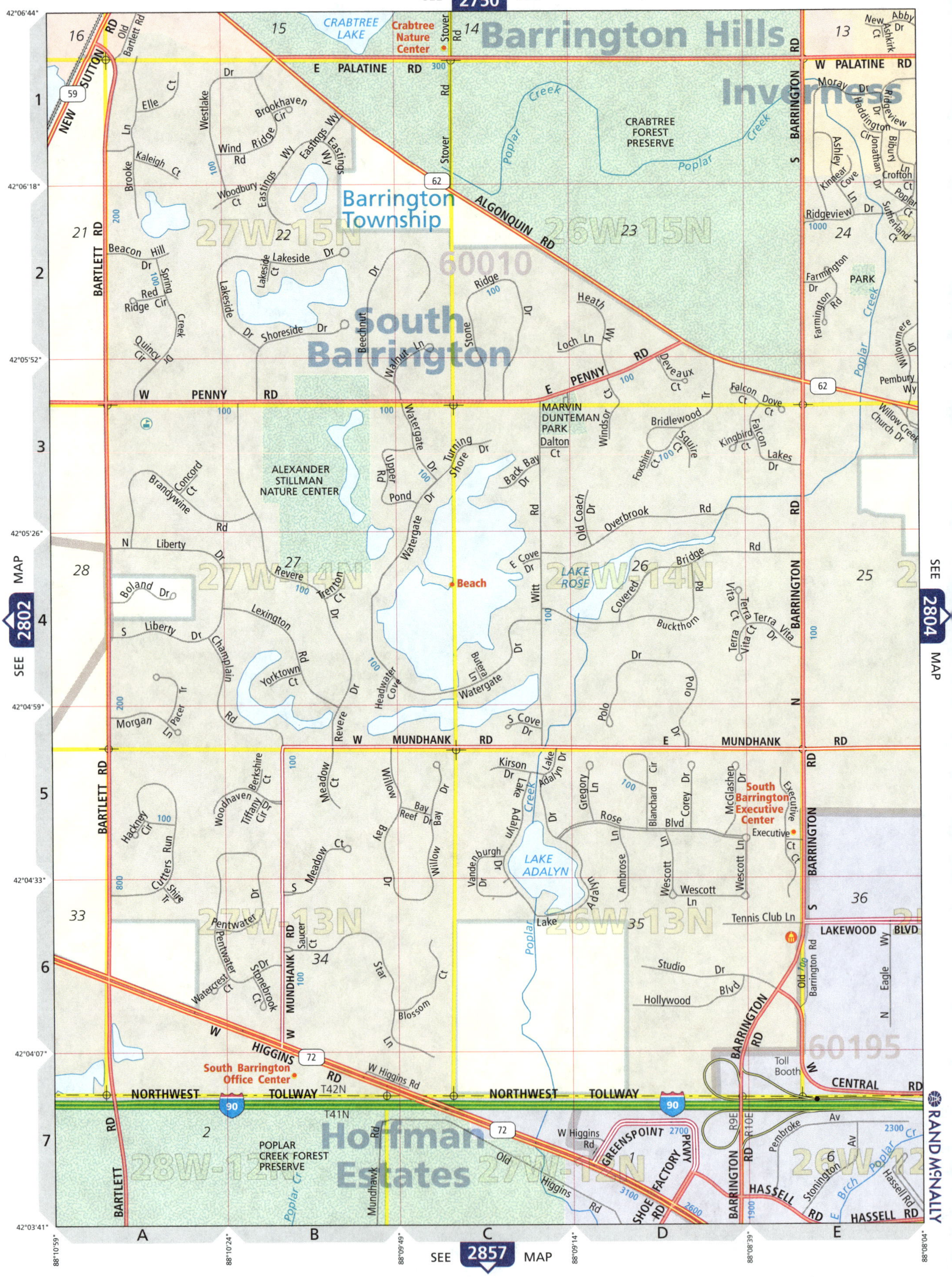
Barrington Hills
Inverness
Barrington Township
South Barrington
Hoffman Estates
CRABTREE LAKE
Crabtree Nature Center
CRABTREE FOREST PRESERVE
ALEXANDER STILLMAN NATURE CENTER
MARVIN DUNTEMAN PARK
LAKE ROSE
LAKE ADALYN
Beach
South Barrington Executive Center
South Barrington Office Center
POPLAR CREEK FOREST PRESERVE
PARK
Toll Booth
60010
60195
27W-15N
26W-15N
27W-14N
26W-14N
27W-13N
26W-13N
28W-12N
27W-12N
26W-12N
T42N
T41N
R9E
R10E
E PALATINE RD
W PALATINE RD
ALGONQUIN RD
W PENNY RD
E PENNY RD
W MUNDHANK RD
E MUNDHANK RD
BARTLETT RD
S BARRINGTON RD
N BARRINGTON RD
W MUNDHANK RD
W HIGGINS RD
NORTHWEST TOLLWAY
NEW SUTTON RD
W CENTRAL RD
LAKEWOOD BLVD
GREENSPOINT PKWY
SHOE FACTORY RD
HASSELL RD
E HASSELL RD
Poplar Creek
59
62
72
90
42°06'44"
42°06'18"
42°05'52"
42°05'26"
42°04'59"
42°04'33"
42°04'07"
42°03'41"
88°10'59"
88°10'24"
88°09'49"
88°09'14"
88°08'39"
88°08'04"
A
B
C
D
E
1
2
3
4
5
6
7

SEE 2802 MAP

SEE 2804 MAP

SEE 2857 MAP

RAND McNALLY

1:24,000
1 in. = 2000 ft.
0 0.25 0.5
miles

SEE 2751 MAP

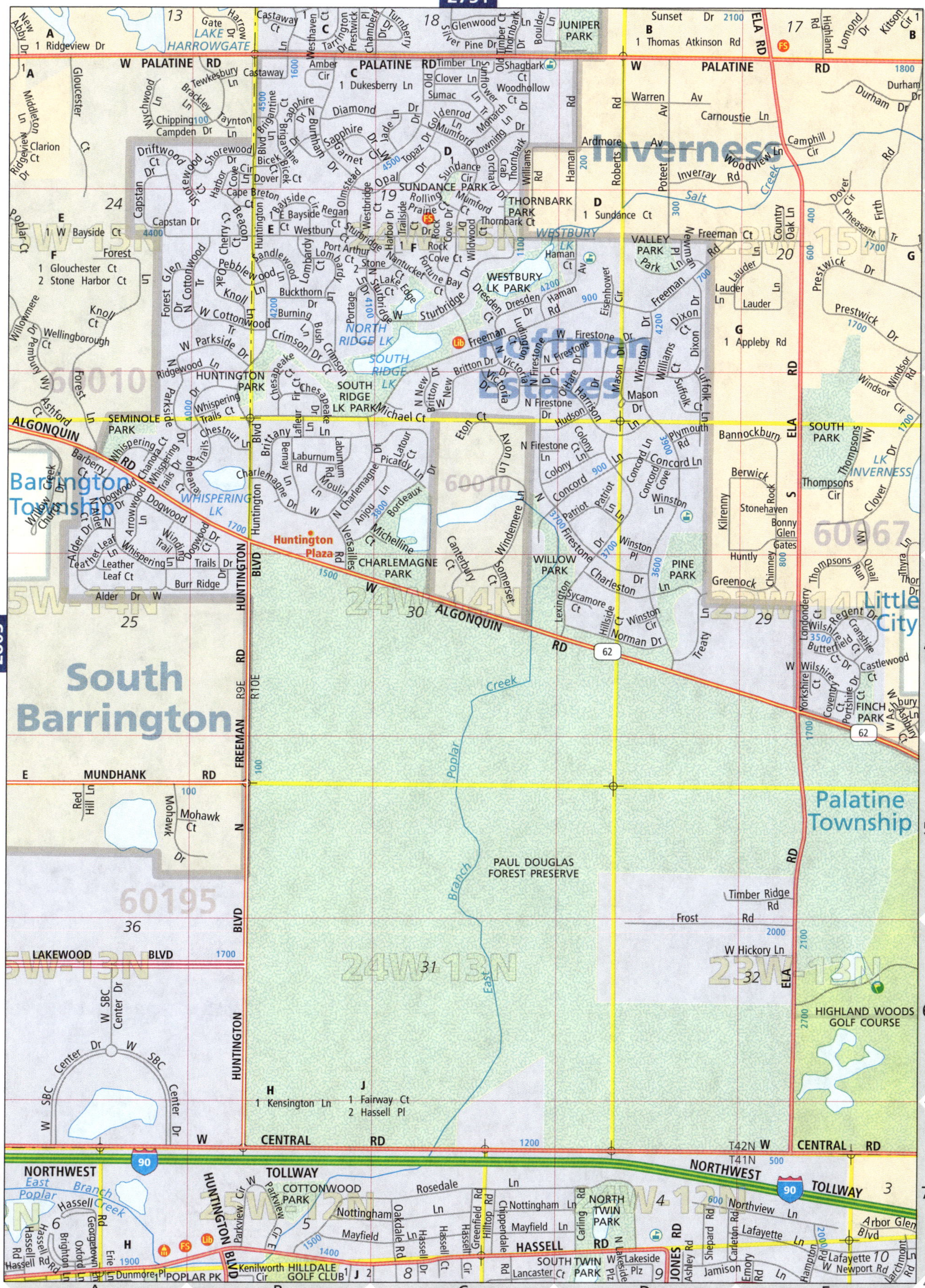

SEE 2803 MAP
SEE 2805 MAP
SEE 2858 MAP

1:24,000
1 in. = 2000 ft.
0 0.25 0.5
miles

SEE 2752 MAP

Inverness
Palatine Township
Palatine
Rolling Meadows
Schaumburg
Hoffman Estates
Schaumburg Township
Forest Estates
INVERNESS GOLF CLUB
RIEMER RES
RIEMER RES PARK
WALLY DEGNER PARK
ROBIN PARK
CEDAR PARK
HAWTHORNE PARK
HERON PARK
SPARROW PARK
MALLARD PARK
PARTRIDGE PARK
WHIPPOORWILL PARK
PEREGRINE PARK
PEREGRINE LAKE
CARDINAL PARK
BIRCHWOOD PARK
BIRCHWOOD SOUTH PARK
COUNTRYSIDE PARK
LK INVERNESS
William Fremd HS
Regency Plaza
Harper College
PLUM GROVE RESERVOIR PARK
PLUM GRV RES
PAUL DOUGLAS FOREST PRESERVE
HIGHLAND WOODS GOLF COURSE
ST. MICHAEL THE ARCHANGEL CEMETERY
COTTONWOOD
The Grove
George Clayson Hse
Palatine Sta
Metra
Motorola Museum of Electronics
Motorola Corporate Headquarters
Motorola Corporate Office Tower
60067
60195
60173
PALATINE
ROSELLE
QUENTIN
PLUM GROVE
EUCLID
ILLINOIS
ALGONQUIN
CENTRAL
MEACHAM
NORTHWEST TOLLWAY
KIRCHOFF
MOTOROLA
Toll Booth
Salt Creek
T42N
T41N
J
1 St. Albans on Oxford
2 Scarborough on Oxford
3 Stuart on Oxford
4 Eton on Oxford
5 Exeter on Oxford
6 Falmouth on Oxford
7 Grimsby on Oxford
8 Kendall on Oxford
9 Kensington on Oxford
10 Pembroke on Duxbury
11 Ealing on Duxbury
12 Kettering on Oxford
13 Windermere on Duxbury
14 Cheviot on Duxbury
15 Croydon on Duxbury
16 Hastings on Oxford
17 Harrogate on Oxford
18 Carlisle on Duxbury
19 Coventry on Duxbury
20 Barrow on Duxbury
21 Belford Ln
22 St. George Dr
23 Prestwick Ln
K
1 California Ct
L
1 Post Oak Pl
G
1 Plum Tree Ln
2 Jonquil Ct
3 New Castle Ct
4 Butterfield Ct
H
1 Still Water Ct
42°06'45"
42°06'19"
42°05'53"
42°05'27"
42°05'01"
42°04'35"
42°04'09"
42°03'43"
88°05'09"
88°04'34"
88°03'59"
88°03'24"
88°02'48"
88°02'13"

SEE 2804 MAP
SEE 2806 MAP
SEE 2859 MAP

1:24,000
1 in. = 2000 ft.
0 0.25 0.5
miles

SEE 2753 MAP

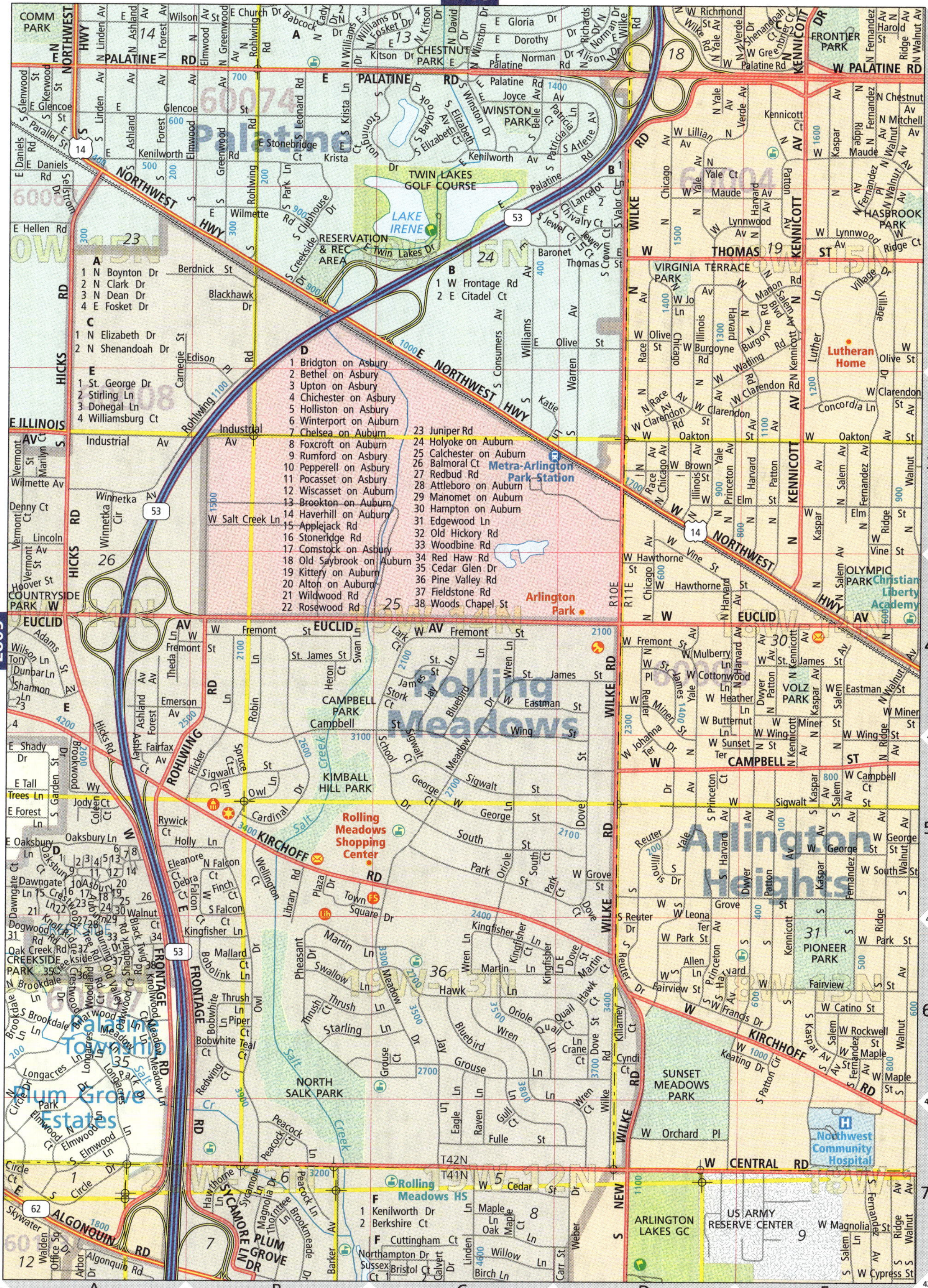
Palatine
60074
Rolling Meadows
Arlington Heights
60004
60005
60067
60008
TWIN LAKES GOLF COURSE
LAKE IRENE
RESERVATION & REC AREA
WINSTON PARK
CHESTNUT PARK
COMM PARK
FRONTIER PARK
HASBROOK PARK
VIRGINIA TERRACE PARK
Lutheran Home
Metra-Arlington Park Station
Arlington Park
OLYMPIC PARK
Christian Liberty Academy
VOLZ PARK
CAMPBELL PARK
KIMBALL HILL PARK
Rolling Meadows Shopping Center
Town Square Dr
COUNTRYSIDE PARK
CREEKSIDE PARK
Palatine Township
Plum Grove Estates
NORTH SALK PARK
SUNSET MEADOWS PARK
PIONEER PARK
Northwest Community Hospital
Rolling Meadows HS
ARLINGTON LAKES GC
US ARMY RESERVE CENTER
PLUM GROVE
ALGONQUIN RD
CENTRAL RD
KIRCHHOFF RD
EUCLID AV
NORTHWEST HWY
W PALATINE RD
THOMAS ST
WILKE RD
KENNICOTT AV
HICKS RD
ROHLWING RD
FRONTAGE RD
SYCAMORE LN
NEW WILKE RD
CAMPBELL ST
A
1 N Boynton Dr
2 N Clark Dr
3 N Dean Dr
4 E Fosket Dr
B
1 W Frontage Rd
2 E Citadel Ct
C
1 N Elizabeth Dr
2 N Shenandoah Dr
E
1 St. George Dr
2 Stirling Ln
3 Donegal Ln
4 Williamsburg Ct
D
1 Bridgton on Asbury
2 Bethel on Asbury
3 Upton on Asbury
4 Chichester on Asbury
5 Holliston on Asbury
6 Winterport on Auburn
7 Chelsea on Auburn
8 Foxcroft on Auburn
9 Rumford on Asbury
10 Pepperell on Asbury
11 Pocasset on Auburn
12 Wiscasset on Auburn
13 Brookton on Asbury
14 Haverhill on Auburn
15 Applejack Rd
16 Stoneridge Rd
17 Comstock on Asbury
18 Old Saybrook on Auburn
19 Kittery on Auburn
20 Alton on Auburn
21 Wildwood Rd
22 Rosewood Rd
23 Juniper Rd
24 Holyoke on Auburn
25 Calchester on Auburn
26 Balmoral Ct
27 Redbud Rd
28 Attleboro on Auburn
29 Manomet on Auburn
30 Hampton on Auburn
31 Edgewood Ln
32 Old Hickory Rd
33 Woodbine Rd
34 Red Haw Rd
35 Cedar Glen Dr
36 Pine Valley Rd
37 Fieldstone Rd
38 Woods Chapel St
F
1 Kenilworth Dr
2 Berkshire Ct
42°06'47"
42°06'20"
42°05'54"
42°05'28"
42°05'02"
42°04'36"
42°04'10"
42°03'44"
88°02'13"
88°01'38"
88°01'03"
88°00'28"
87°59'53"
87°59'18"

SEE 2805 MAP

SEE 2807 MAP

SEE 2860 MAP

1:24,000
1 in. = 2000 ft.
0 0.25 0.5
miles

SEE 2754 MAP

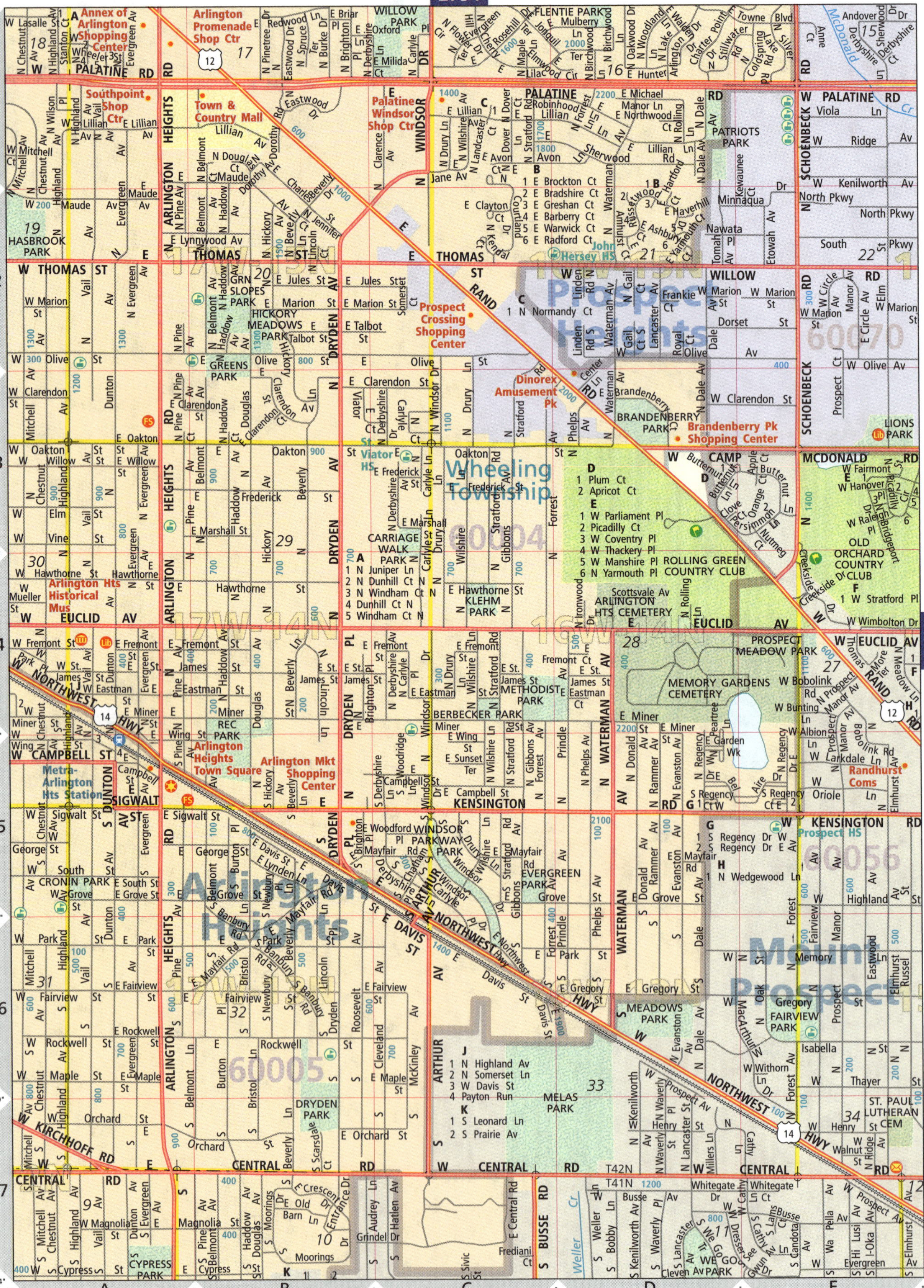
Arlington Heights
Prospect Heights
Mount Prospect
Wheeling Township
60004
60005
60056
60070
17W-13N
17W-14N
16W-13N
16W-14N
W PALATINE RD
E THOMAS ST
W OAKTON ST
E EUCLID AV
W CAMPBELL ST
E SIGWALT ST
E KENSINGTON RD
W CENTRAL RD
NORTHWEST HWY
N ARLINGTON HEIGHTS RD
DRYDEN AV
N WINDSOR DR
N WATERMAN AV
SCHOENBECK RD
BUSSE RD
RAND RD
W MCDONALD RD
W KIRCHHOFF RD
Annex of Arlington Shopping Center
Arlington Promenade Shop Ctr
Southpoint Shop Ctr
Town & Country Mall
Palatine Windsor Shop Ctr
Prospect Crossing Shopping Center
Dinorex Amusement Pk
Brandenberry Pk Shopping Center
Arlington Hts Historical Mus
Arlington Heights Town Square
Arlington Mkt Shopping Center
Metra-Arlington Hts Station
Randhurst Coms
John Hersey HS
Prospect HS
St Viator HS
HASBROOK PARK
PATRIOTS PARK
GRN SLOPES PARK
HICKORY MEADOWS PARK
GREENS PARK
BRANDENBERRY PARK
LIONS PARK
ROLLING GREEN COUNTRY CLUB
OLD ORCHARD COUNTRY CLUB
ARLINGTON HTS CEMETERY
KLEHM PARK
CARRIAGE WALK PARK
REC PARK
BERBECKER PARK
METHODIST PARK
MEMORY GARDENS CEMETERY
PROSPECT MEADOW PARK
WINDSOR PARKWAY PARK
EVERGREEN PARK
CRONIN PARK
MEADOWS PARK
FAIRVIEW PARK
DRYDEN PARK
MELAS PARK
ST. PAUL LUTHERAN CEM
CYPRESS PARK
WE GO PARK
FLENTIE PARK
WILLOW PARK
Weller Cr
McDonald Cr
T42N
T41N
42°06'47"
42°06'20"
42°05'54"
42°05'28"
42°05'02"
42°04'36"
42°04'10"
42°03'44"
87°59'18"
87°58'43"
87°58'08"
87°57'33"
87°56'58"
87°56'23"
A B C D E
1 2 3 4 5 6 7

SEE 2806 MAP
SEE 2808 MAP
SEE 2861 MAP

1:24,000
1 in. = 2000 ft.
0 0.25 0.5
miles

SEE 2755 MAP

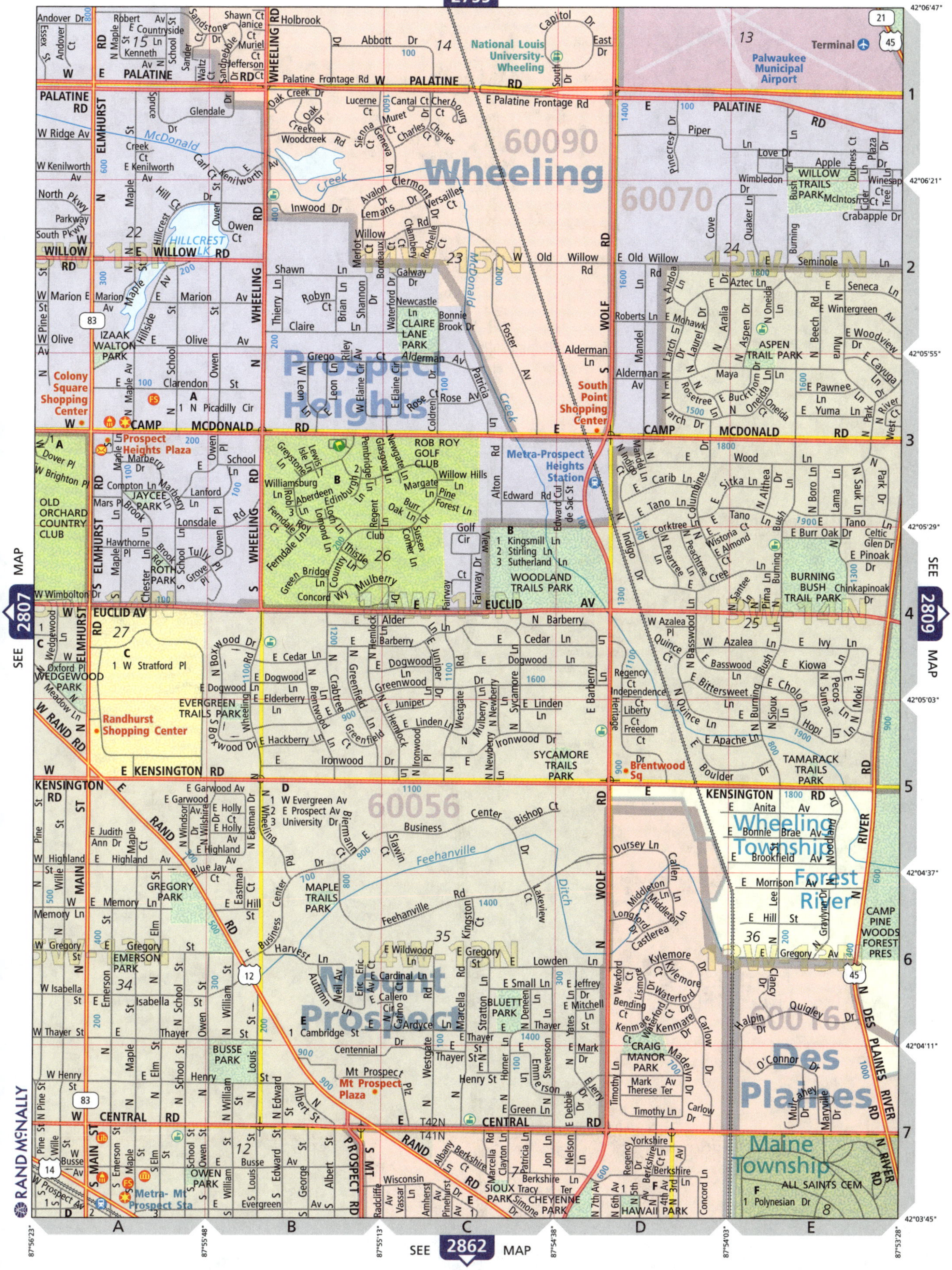

SEE 2807 MAP
SEE 2809 MAP
SEE 2862 MAP

1:24,000
1 in. = 2000 ft.
0 0.25 0.5
miles

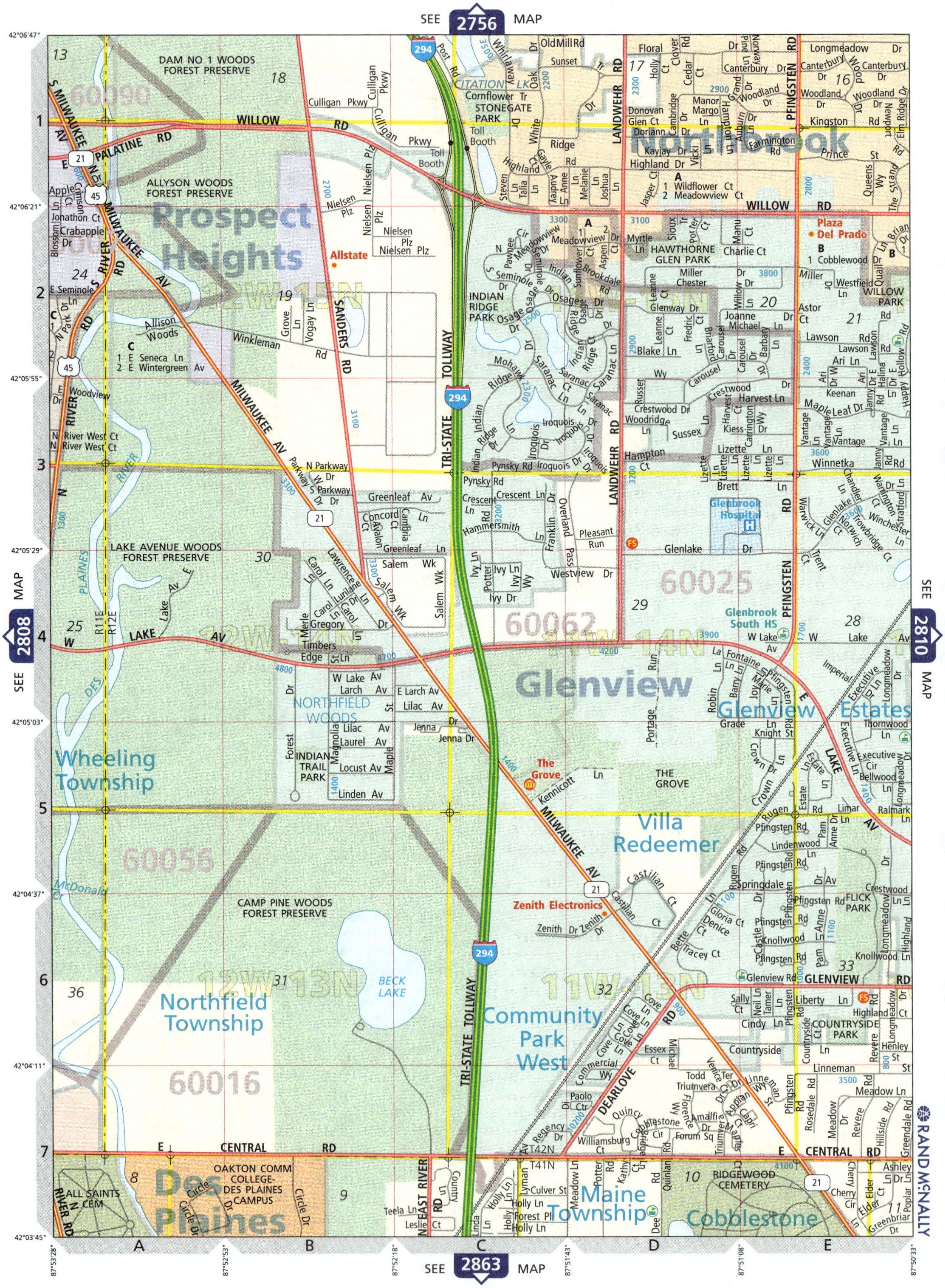
SEE 2756 MAP
SEE 2863 MAP
SEE 2808 MAP
SEE 2810 MAP
DAM NO 1 WOODS FOREST PRESERVE
ALLYSON WOODS FOREST PRESERVE
LAKE AVENUE WOODS FOREST PRESERVE
CAMP PINE WOODS FOREST PRESERVE
Prospect Heights
Northbrook
Glenview
Glenview Estates
Wheeling Township
Northfield Township
Maine Township
Des Plaines
Cobblestone
Villa Redeemer
Community Park West
NORTHFIELD WOODS
INDIAN TRAIL PARK
INDIAN RIDGE PARK
STONEGATE PARK
HAWTHORNE GLEN PARK
WILLOW PARK
FLICK PARK
COUNTRYSIDE PARK
THE GROVE
The Grove
BECK LAKE
OAKTON COMM COLLEGE-DES PLAINES CAMPUS
ALL SAINTS CEM
RIDGEWOOD CEMETERY
Glenbrook Hospital
Glenbrook South HS
Allstate
Zenith Electronics
Plaza Del Prado
WILLOW RD
LAKE AV
CENTRAL RD
GLENVIEW RD
MILWAUKEE AV
SANDERS RD
TRI-STATE TOLLWAY
LANDWEHR RD
PFINGSTEN RD
DEARLOVE RD
RIVER RD
60090
60062
60025
60056
60016
12W-15N
12W-14N
12W-13N
11W-14N
11W-13N
RAND McNALLY

1:24,000
1 in. = 2000 ft.
0 0.25 0.5
miles

SEE 2757 MAP

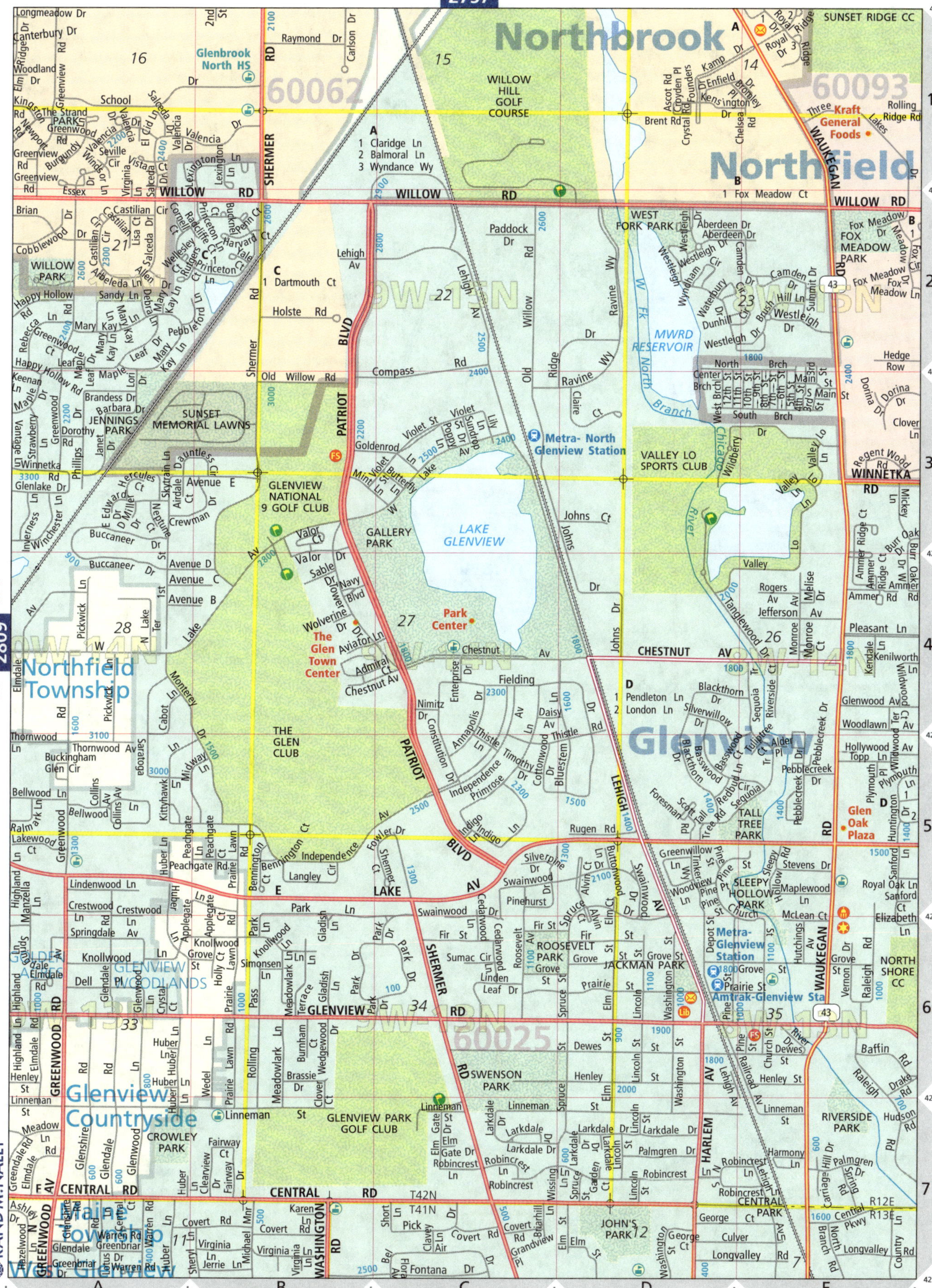
Northbrook
Northfield
Glenview
Northfield Township
Glenview Countryside
Glenview Woodlands
Maine Township
West Glenview
60062
60093
60025
9W-15N
9W-14N
9W-13N
Glenbrook North HS
WILLOW HILL GOLF COURSE
SUNSET RIDGE CC
Kraft General Foods
FOX MEADOW PARK
WEST FORK PARK
MWRD RESERVOIR
WILLOW PARK
JENNINGS PARK
SUNSET MEMORIAL LAWNS
GLENVIEW NATIONAL 9 GOLF CLUB
GALLERY PARK
LAKE GLENVIEW
Park Center
The Glen Town Center
THE GLEN CLUB
Metra- North Glenview Station
VALLEY LO SPORTS CLUB
TALL TREE PARK
SLEEPY HOLLOW PARK
Glen Oak Plaza
NORTH SHORE CC
ROOSEVELT PARK
JACKMAN PARK
Metra- Glenview Station
Amtrak-Glenview Sta
SWENSON PARK
GLENVIEW PARK GOLF CLUB
CROWLEY PARK
RIVERSIDE PARK
JOHN'S PARK
CENTRAL PARK
WILLOW RD
SHERMER RD
PATRIOT BLVD
CHESTNUT AV
LAKE AV
GLENVIEW RD
CENTRAL RD
GREENWOOD RD
WAUKEGAN RD
WINNETKA RD
LEHIGH
HARLEM AV
WASHINGTON RD
Chicago River
W Fk North Branch
T42N
T41N
R12E
R13E
RAND McNALLY

SEE 2809 MAP

SEE 2811 MAP

SEE 2864 MAP

1:24,000
1 in. = 2000 ft.
0 0.25 0.5
miles

SEE 2758 MAP

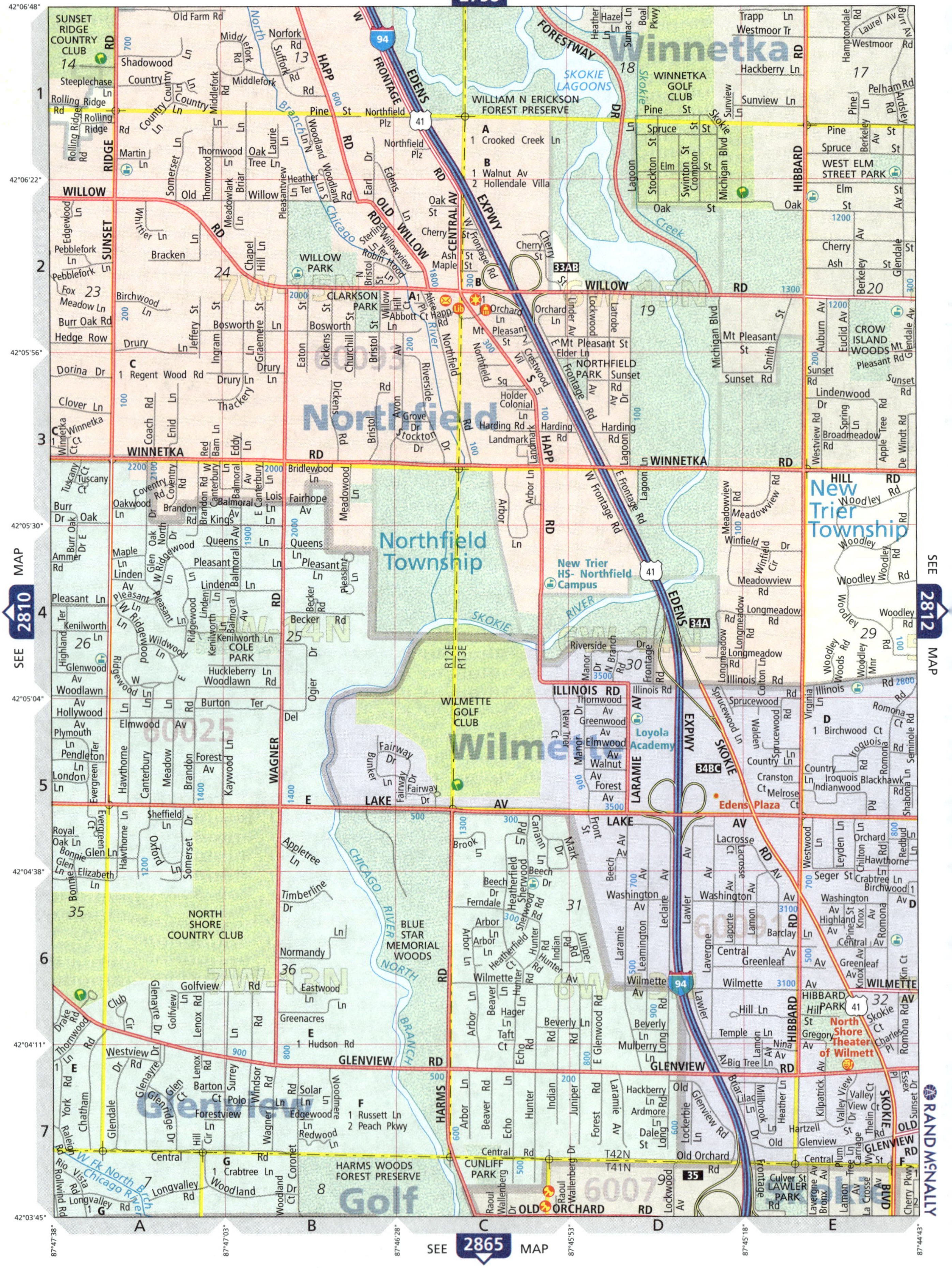

SEE 2810 MAP

SEE 2812 MAP

SEE 2865 MAP

1:24,000
1 in. = 2000 ft.
0 0.25 0.5
miles

SEE 2759 MAP

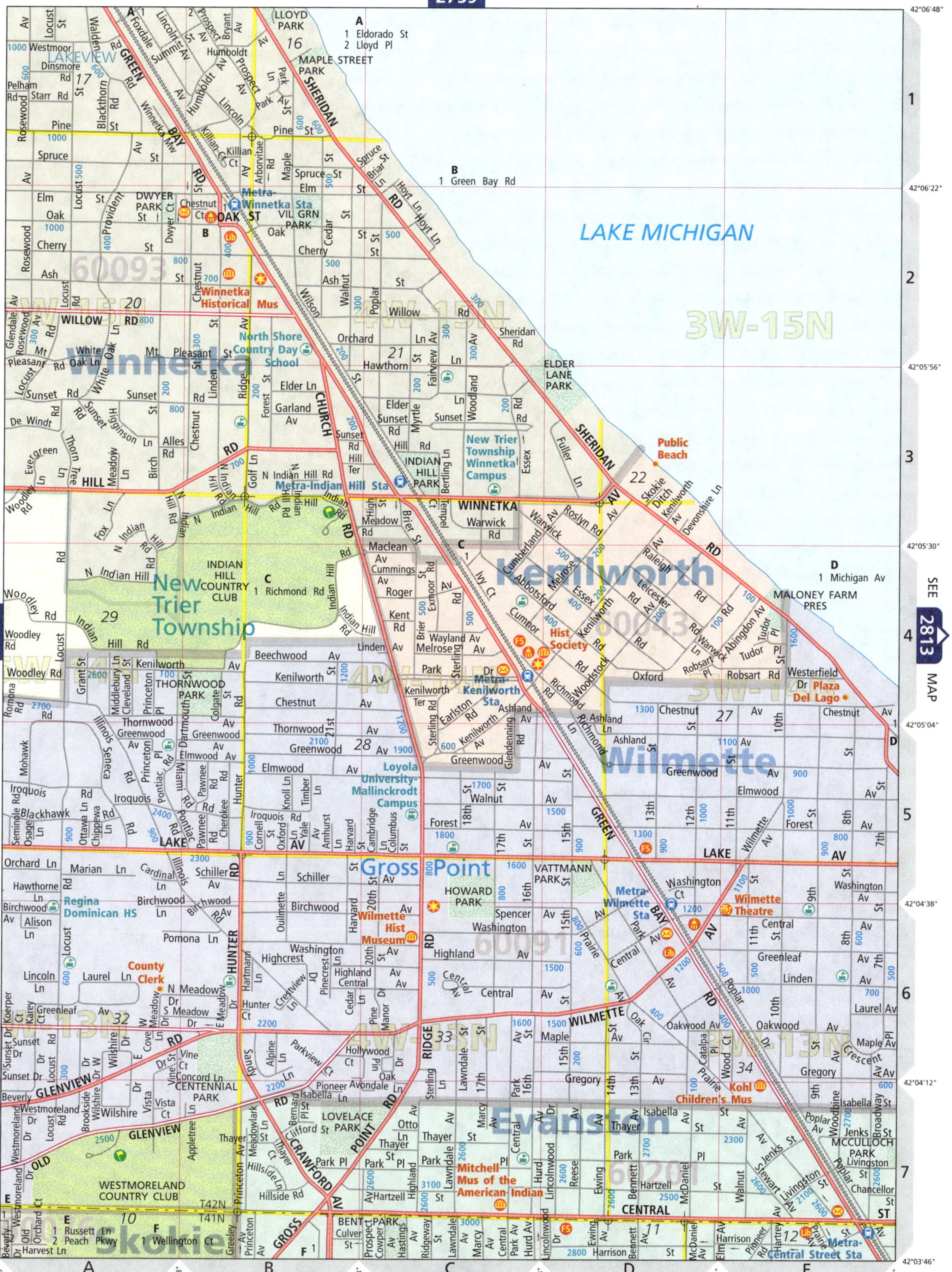
LAKE MICHIGAN
Winnetka
Kenilworth
Wilmette
Evanston
Skokie
New Trier Township
Gross Point
3W-15N
4W-15N
3W-14N
4W-14N
3W-13N
4W-13N
60093
60043
60091
60201
SHERIDAN RD
GREEN BAY RD
HILL RD
WILLOW RD
LAKE AV
WILMETTE AV
CENTRAL ST
GLENVIEW RD
RIDGE AV
HUNTER RD
CRAWFORD AV
CHURCH RD
INDIAN HILL COUNTRY CLUB
WESTMORELAND COUNTRY CLUB
LLOYD PARK
MAPLE STREET PARK
ELDER LANE PARK
DWYER PARK
VIL GRN PARK
INDIAN HILL PARK
THORNWOOD PARK
HOWARD PARK
VATTMANN PARK
CENTENNIAL PARK
LOVELACE PARK
MCCULLOCH PARK
MALONEY FARM PRES
Metra-Winnetka Sta
Metra-Indian Hill Sta
Metra-Kenilworth Sta
Metra-Wilmette Sta
Metra-Central Street Sta
Winnetka Historical Mus
North Shore Country Day School
New Trier Township Winnetka Campus
Hist Society
Loyola University-Mallinckrodt Campus
Regina Dominican HS
County Clerk
Wilmette Hist Museum
Wilmette Theatre
Kohl Children's Mus
Mitchell Mus of the American Indian
Public Beach
Plaza Del Lago
A 1 Eldorado St 2 Lloyd Pl
B 1 Green Bay Rd
C 1 Richmond Rd
D 1 Michigan Av
E 1 Russett Ln 2 Peach Pkwy
F 1 Wellington Ct
42°06'48"
42°06'22"
42°05'56"
42°05'30"
42°05'04"
42°04'38"
42°04'12"
42°03'46"
87°44'43"
87°44'08"
87°43'33"
87°42'58"
87°42'23"
87°41'48"

SEE 2811 MAP
SEE 2813 MAP
SEE 2866 MAP

1:24,000
1 in. = 2000 ft.
0
0.25
0.5
miles
N
SEE B MAP
SEE 2812 MAP
SEE B MAP
SEE 2867 MAP
42°06'48"
42°06'22"
42°05'56"
42°05'30"
42°05'04"
42°04'38"
42°04'12"
42°03'46"
87°41'48"
87°41'13"
87°40'38"
87°40'03"
87°39'28"
87°38'53"
1
2
3
4
5
6
7
A
B
C
D
E
LAKE MICHIGAN
2W-14N
2W-13N
Wilmette
Evanston
Michigan
27
Elmwood Av
Elmwood Av
Forest Av
Forest Av
26
GILLSON PARK
Overlook Dr
Upper Dr
Middle Dr
Harbor Dr
Wilmette Hbr
SHERIDAN RD
LAKE AV
Washington Av
Washington
Central Av
Greenleaf
35
US Coast Guard Station
Baha'i Place of Worship
NORTH SHORE CHANNEL
Linden
Laurel Av
CTA-Purple Line-Linden Station
MAPLE PARK
34
Maple Av
Gregory
Isabella St
Golf Ter
Driftwood Ln
Girard Av
Garrison Av
Linden Av
Canterbury Ct
Roslyn Ter
Sheridan Pl
Lakeside Ct
Nat'l Louis University-Evanston
SHERIDAN RD
PETER N JANS COMM GOLF COURSE
Jenks St
MCCULLOCH PARK
Livingston St
Welsh-Ryan Arena
Chancellor St
Northwestern University-Ryan Fld
Evanston Northwestern Health Care
CTA-Purple Line Sta
Euclid Park Pl
Ingleside Pl
INGLESIDE PARK
Ingleside Pk
NORTHEAST PARK
Monticello Pl
Clinton Pl
Orrington Av
DEERING ESTATE PARK
Evanston Art Ctr
CENTRAL ST
RIDGE AV
Milburn St
Milburn Pk
NORTHWESTERN UNIVERSITY-EVANSTON CAMPUS
T41N
T42N
12
7
Harrison St
Ashland Av
Jackson Av
Rosalie St
Asbury Av
CHANDLER PARK
Sherman Av
Hampton Pkwy
Dupee Pl
Bryant Av
Eastwood Av
RAND McNALLY

1:24,000
1 in. = 2000 ft.
0 0.25 0.5
miles

SEE 2801 MAP

Elgin
Hoffman Estates
Hanover Township
Elgin Township
KANE CO
COOK CO
60120
60123
60103
Summit Square Shopping Center
Cobblers Crossing Shopping Center
LORDS PARK
Elgin Public Museum
Elgin Academy
Elgin Area Mus
Elgin Armory
Grand Victoria Casino
Clock Tower Shop Ctr
Elgin U-46 Planetarium
Fire Barn Mus & Park
Memorial Aud
Elgin HS
CAMPUS PARK
WRIGHT PARK
MT HOPE CEMETERY
BLUFF CITY CEMETERY
DRAKE FLD
CONTINENTAL PARK
MARIE GROLICH PK
ROLLING KNOLLS COUNTRY CLUB
CANTERBURY PARK PLACE
CANTERBURY FIELDS PARK
BLACKHAWK
NEWSOME PARK
ST. FRANCIS PARK
GIFFORD PARK
CITY PARK
OBSERVATORY PKS
FOX RIVER
Poplar Creek
SUMMIT ST
GOLF RD
BODE RD
CHICAGO ST
IRVING PARK RD
VILLA ST
LAKE ST
BLUFF CITY BLVD
SHALES PKWY
LIBERTY ST
DUNDEE AV
CONGDON AV
SHOE FACTORY RD
DWIGHT ST
NATIONAL ST
RAYMOND ST
GRACE ST
CHARLES ST
ILLINOIS AV
LAVOIE AV
GIFFORD RD
33W-12N
32W-12N
33W-11N
32W-11N
33W-10N
32W-10N
A B C D E
1 2 3 4 5 6 7
RAND McNALLY

SEE 2856 MAP

SEE B MAP

SEE 2909 MAP

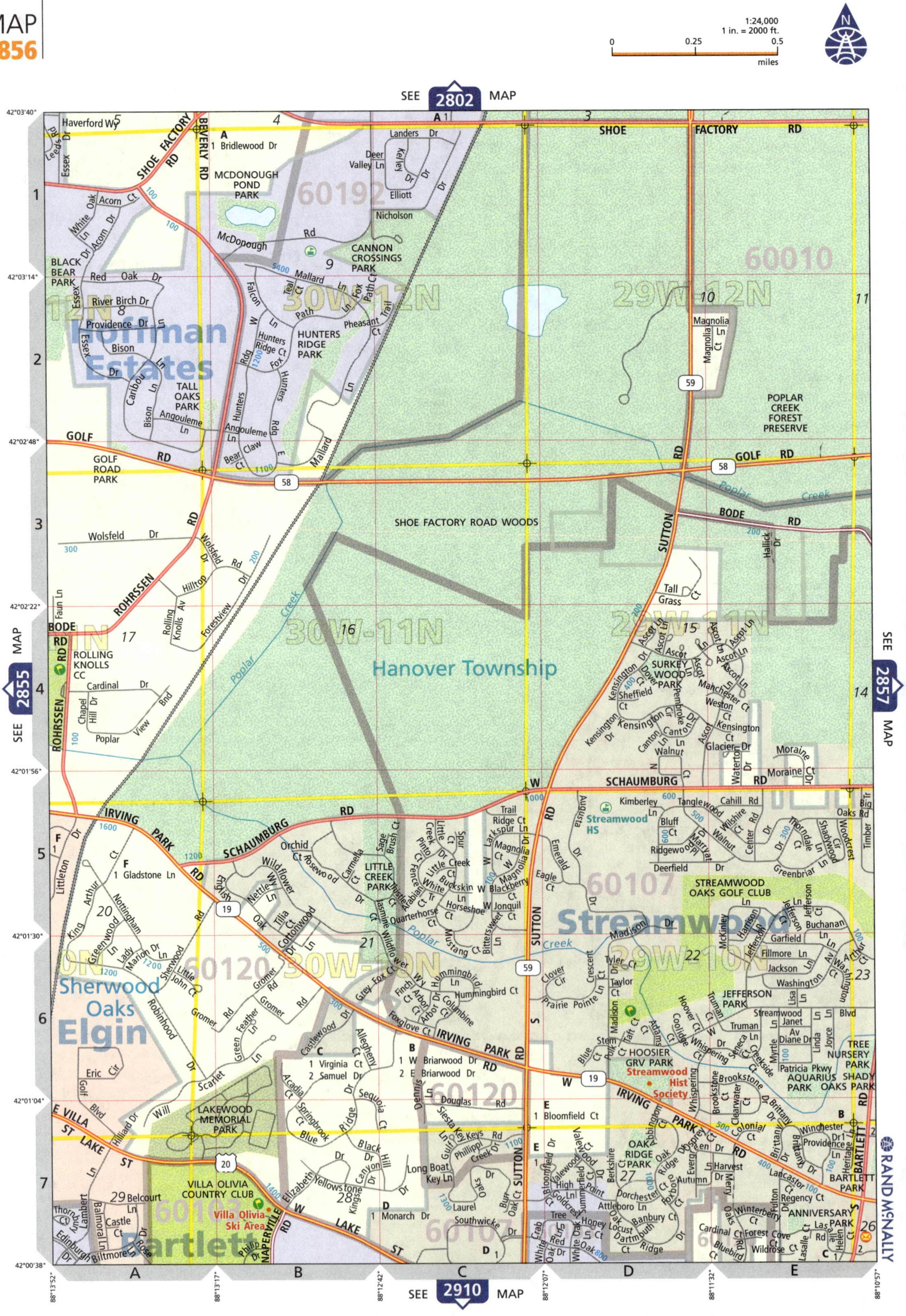
1:24,000
1 in. = 2000 ft.
0 0.25 0.5
miles
N
SEE 2802 MAP
SEE 2855 MAP
SEE 2857 MAP
SEE 2910 MAP
SHOE FACTORY RD
BEVERLY RD
MCDONOUGH POND PARK
60192
CANNON CROSSINGS PARK
BLACK BEAR PARK
Hoffman Estates
HUNTERS RIDGE PARK
TALL OAKS PARK
30W-12N
29W-12N
60010
POPLAR CREEK FOREST PRESERVE
GOLF RD
GOLF ROAD PARK
SHOE FACTORY ROAD WOODS
BODE RD
SUTTON RD
ROHRSSEN RD
ROLLING KNOLLS CC
30W-11N
29W-11N
Hanover Township
SURREY WOOD PARK
Poplar Creek
SCHAUMBURG RD
IRVING PARK RD
LITTLE CREEK PARK
Streamwood HS
STREAMWOOD OAKS GOLF CLUB
60107
Streamwood
60120
30W-10N
29W-10N
Sherwood Oaks
Elgin
JEFFERSON PARK
HOOSIER GRV PARK
Streamwood Hist Society
TREE NURSERY PARK
AQUARIUS PARK
SHADY OAKS PARK
LAKEWOOD MEMORIAL PARK
VILLA OLIVIA COUNTRY CLUB
Villa Olivia Ski Area
OAK RIDGE PARK
BARTLETT PARK
ANNIVERSARY PARK
LAKE ST
NAPERVILLE RD
BARTLETT RD
Bartlett
RAND McNALLY
A B C D E
1 2 3 4 5 6 7

1:24,000
1 in. = 2000 ft.
0 0.25 0.5
miles

SEE 2803 MAP

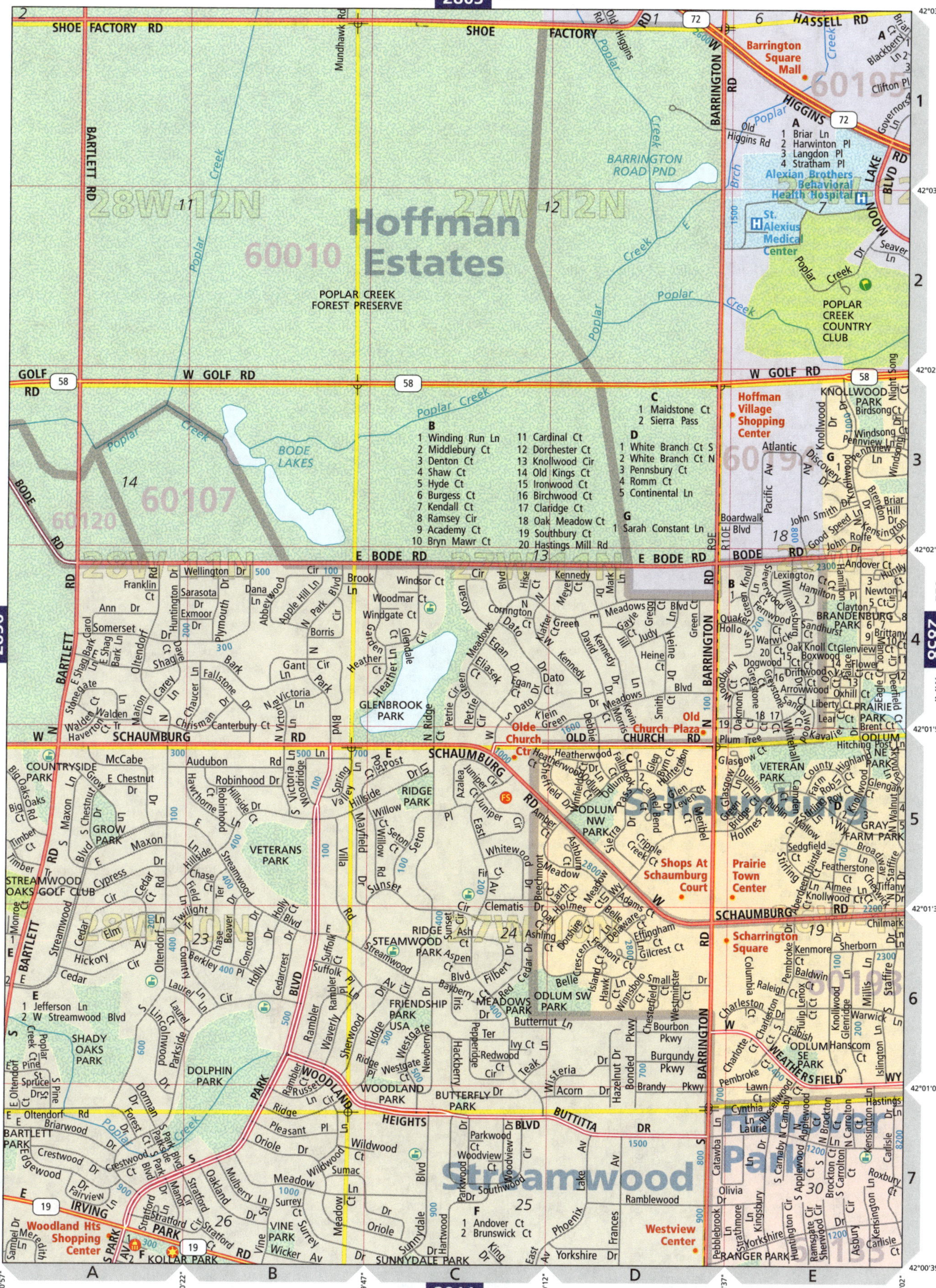
SHOE FACTORY RD
HASSELL RD
Barrington Square Mall
60195
HIGGINS RD
BARRINGTON RD
BARRINGTON ROAD PND
Alexian Brothers Behavioral Health Hospital
St. Alexius Medical Center
POPLAR CREEK COUNTRY CLUB
28W-12N
27W-12N
Hoffman Estates
60010
POPLAR CREEK FOREST PRESERVE
W GOLF RD
BODE LAKES
60107
60120
Hoffman Village Shopping Center
B
1 Winding Run Ln
2 Middlebury Ct
3 Denton Ct
4 Shaw Ct
5 Hyde Ct
6 Burgess Ct
7 Kendall Ct
8 Ramsey Cir
9 Academy Ct
10 Bryn Mawr Ct
11 Cardinal Ct
12 Dorchester Ct
13 Knollwood Cir
14 Old Kings Ct
15 Ironwood Ct
16 Birchwood Ct
17 Claridge Ct
18 Oak Meadow Ct
19 Southbury Ct
20 Hastings Mill Rd
C
1 Maidstone Ct
2 Sierra Pass
D
1 White Branch Ct S
2 White Branch Ct N
3 Pennsbury Ct
4 Romm Ct
5 Continental Ln
G
1 Sarah Constant Ln
E BODE RD
GLENBROOK PARK
W SCHAUMBURG RD
Olde Church Ctr
Old Church Plaza
OLD CHURCH RD
VETERANS PARK
COUNTRYSIDE PARK
GROW PARK
STREAMWOOD OAKS GOLF CLUB
RIDGE PARK
ODLUM NW PARK
Schaumburg
Shops At Schaumburg Court
Prairie Town Center
VETERAN PARK
GRAY FARM PARK
BRANDENBURG PARK
Scharrington Square
28W-10N
27W-10N
RIDGE STEAMWOOD PARK
FRIENDSHIP PARK USA
MEADOWS PARK
ODLUM SW PARK
ODLUM SE PARK
WEATHERSFIELD WY
E
1 Jefferson Ln
2 W Streamwood Blvd
SHADY OAKS PARK
DOLPHIN PARK
WOODLAND PARK
BUTTERFLY PARK
WOODLAND HEIGHTS BLVD
BUTTITTA DR
BARTLETT PARK
Streamwood
Hanover Park
60133
Westview Center
Woodland Hts Shopping Center
F
1 Andover Ct
2 Brunswick Ct
IRVING PARK RD
VINE PARK
KOLLAR PARK
SUNNYDALE PARK
RANGER PARK
A B C D E
1 2 3 4 5 6 7

SEE 2856 MAP
SEE 2858 MAP
SEE 2911 MAP

1:24,000
1 in. = 2000 ft.
0 0.25 0.5
miles

SEE 2804 MAP

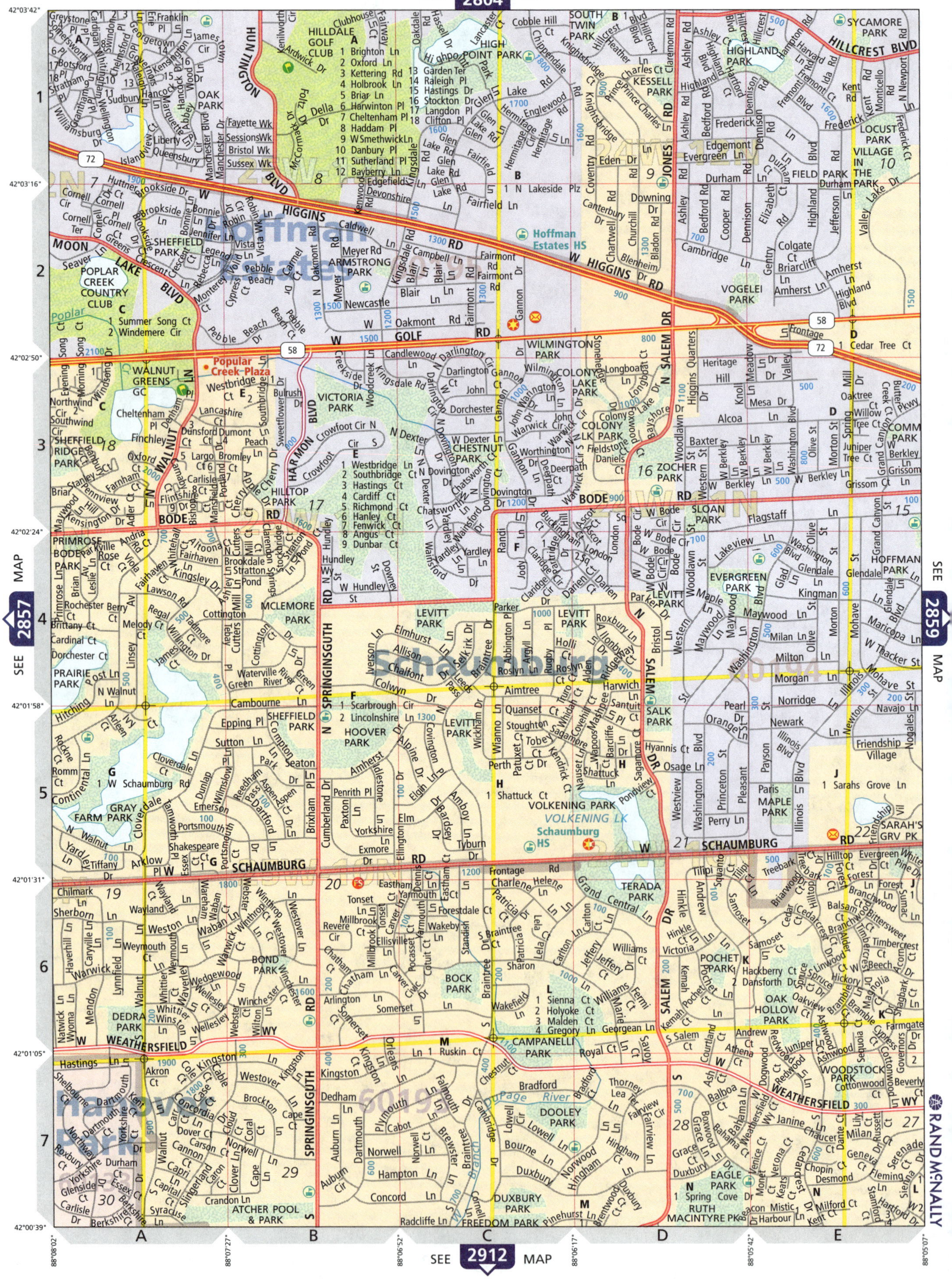
Hoffman Estates
Schaumburg
Hanover Park
HIGGINS RD
GOLF RD
SCHAUMBURG RD
WEATHERSFIELD WY
BODE RD
HILLCREST BLVD
N SALEM DR
N SPRINGINSGUTH RD
HUNTINGTON BLVD
WALNUT LN
MOON LAKE BLVD
JONES RD
HARMON BLVD
HILLDALE GOLF CLUB
HIGH POINT PARK
SOUTH TWIN PARK
KESSELL PARK
HIGHLAND PARK
SYCAMORE PARK
LOCUST PARK
VILLAGE IN THE PARK
OAK PARK
POPLAR CREEK COUNTRY CLUB
SHEFFIELD PARK
ARMSTRONG PARK
VOGELEI PARK
Hoffman Estates HS
Popular Creek Plaza
WALNUT GREENS GC
VICTORIA PARK
WILMINGTON PARK
COLONY LAKE PARK
COLONY PARK
CHESTNUT PARK
ZOCHER PARK
SHEFFIELD RIDGE PARK
HILLTOP PARK
PRIMROSE BODE PARK
SLOAN PARK
EVERGREEN PARK
HOFFMAN PARK
LEVITT PARK
MCLEMORE PARK
PRAIRIE PARK
SHEFFIELD PARK
HOOVER PARK
SALK PARK
Friendship Village
GRAY FARM PARK
VOLKENING PARK
VOLKENING LK
Schaumburg HS
MAPLE PARK
SARAH'S GRV PK
TERADA PARK
BOND PARK
BOCK PARK
DEDRA PARK
POCHET PARK
OAK HOLLOW PARK
CAMPANELLI PARK
WOODSTOCK PARK
DOOLEY PARK
EAGLE PARK
RUTH MACINTYRE PK
DUXBURY PARK
ATCHER POOL & PARK
FREEDOM PARK
Page River
42°03'42"
42°03'16"
42°02'50"
42°02'24"
42°01'58"
42°01'31"
42°01'05"
42°00'39"
88°08'02"
88°07'27"
88°06'52"
88°06'17"
88°05'42"
88°05'07"
A B C D E
1 2 3 4 5 6 7

SEE 2857 MAP

SEE 2859 MAP

SEE 2912 MAP

1:24,000
1 in. = 2000 ft.
0 0.25 0.5
miles

SEE 2805 MAP

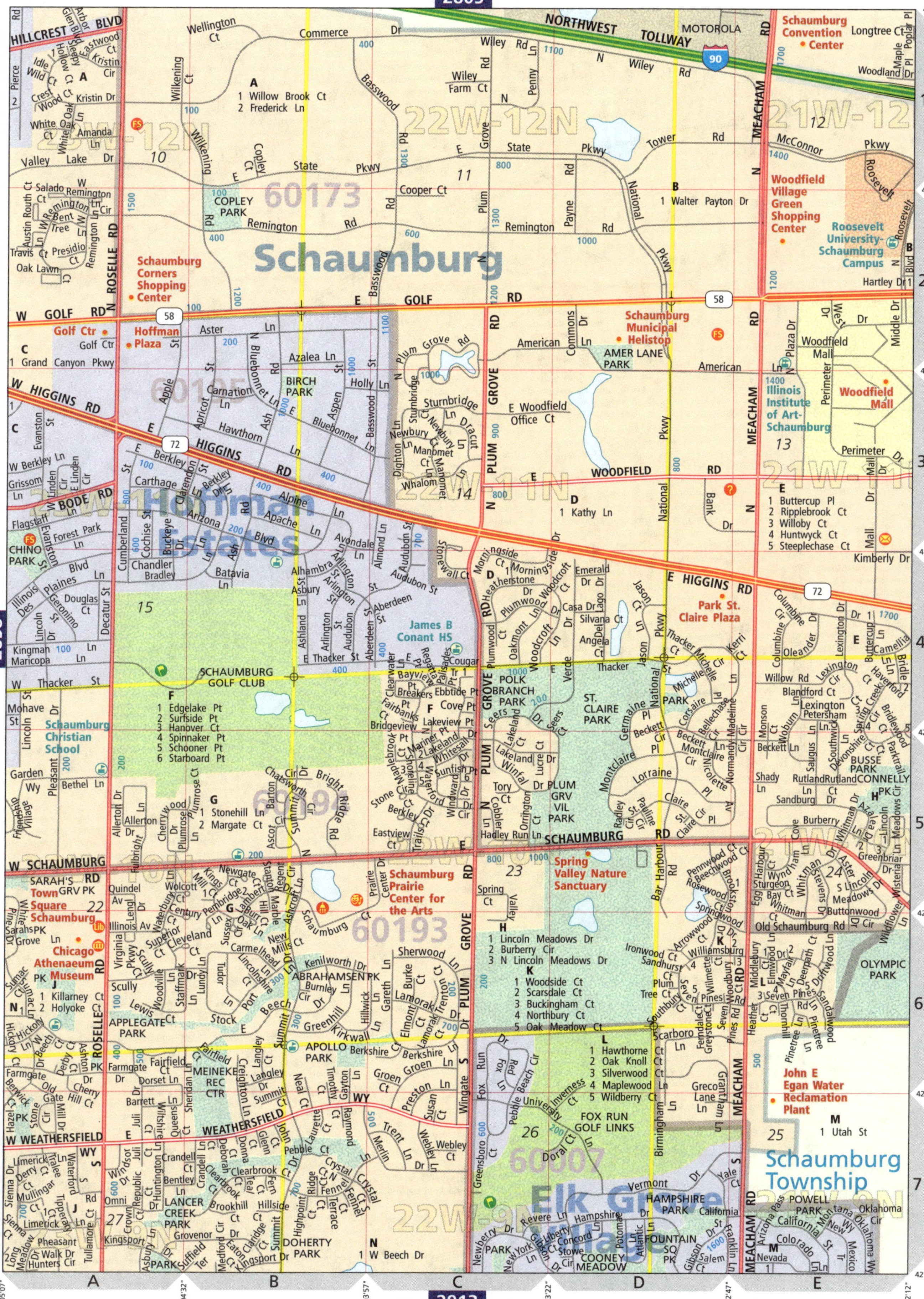
Schaumburg
Hoffman Estates
Elk Grove Village
Schaumburg Township
60173
60195
60194
60193
60007
22W-12N
21W-12
22W-11N
21W-11
22W-10N
21W-10N
22W-9N
21W-9N
NORTHWEST TOLLWAY
90
MOTOROLA
Schaumburg Convention Center
Longtree Ct
Woodland Dr
Commerce Dr
Wellington Ct
Wiley Rd
Wiley Farm Ct
1 Willow Brook Ct
2 Frederick Ln
State Pkwy
Tower Rd
McConnor Pkwy
Roosevelt
Woodfield Village Green Shopping Center
Roosevelt University-Schaumburg Campus
Hartley Dr
1 Walter Payton Dr
Remington Rd
Cooper Ct
COPLEY PARK
National Pkwy
Schaumburg Corners Shopping Center
W GOLF RD
GOLF RD
58
Golf Ctr
Hoffman Plaza
1 Grand Canyon Pkwy
Aster Ln
Azalea Ln
BIRCH PARK
Holly Ln
Schaumburg Municipal Helistop
AMER LANE PARK
American Ln
American
Woodfield Mall
Illinois Institute of Art-Schaumburg
Perimeter Dr
E Woodfield Office Ct
W HIGGINS RD
E HIGGINS RD
72
WOODFIELD RD
1 Kathy Ln
1 Buttercup Pl
2 Ripplebrook Ct
3 Willoby Ct
4 Huntwyck Ct
5 Steeplechase Ct
Kimberly Dr
PLUM GROVE RD
MEACHAM RD
ROSELLE RD
Park St. Claire Plaza
James B Conant HS
CHINO PARK
BODE RD
Schaumburg Golf Club
Thacker St
1 Edgelake Pt
2 Surfside Pt
3 Hanover Ct
4 Spinnaker Pt
5 Schooner Pt
6 Starboard Pt
1 Stonehill Ln
2 Margate Ct
POLK BRANCH PARK
ST. CLAIRE PARK
PLUM GRV VIL PARK
BUSSE PARK
CONNELLY PK
Schaumburg Christian School
W SCHAUMBURG RD
SCHAUMBURG RD
SARAH'S GRV PK
Town Square Schaumburg
Chicago Athenaeum Museum
1 Killarney Ct
2 Holyoke Ct
Schaumburg Prairie Center for the Arts
Spring Valley Nature Sanctuary
1 Lincoln Meadows Dr
2 Burberry Cir
3 N Lincoln Meadows Dr
1 Woodside Ct
2 Scarsdale Ct
3 Buckingham Ct
4 Northbury Ct
5 Oak Meadow Ct
1 Hawthorne Ct
2 Oak Knoll Ct
3 Silverwood Ct
4 Maplewood Ct
5 Wildberry Ct
Old Schaumburg Rd
OLYMPIC PARK
ABRAHAMSEN PK
APPLEGATE PARK
APOLLO PARK
MEINEKE REC CTR
John E Egan Water Reclamation Plant
1 Utah St
W WEATHERSFIELD
WEATHERSFIELD WY
FOX RUN GOLF LINKS
LANCER CREEK PARK
DOHERTY PARK
1 W Beech Dr
HAMPSHIRE PARK
FOUNTAIN SQ PK
COONEY MEADOW
POWELL PARK
Oklahoma Cir
A B C D E
1 2 3 4 5 6 7
42°03'43"
42°03'17"
42°02'51"
42°02'25"
42°01'59"
42°01'33"
42°01'07"
42°00'41"
88°05'07"
88°04'32"
88°03'57"
88°03'22"
88°02'47"
88°02'12"
RAND McNALLY

SEE 2858 MAP

SEE 2860 MAP

SEE 2913 MAP

1:24,000
1 in. = 2000 ft.
0 0.25 0.5
miles

SEE 2806 MAP

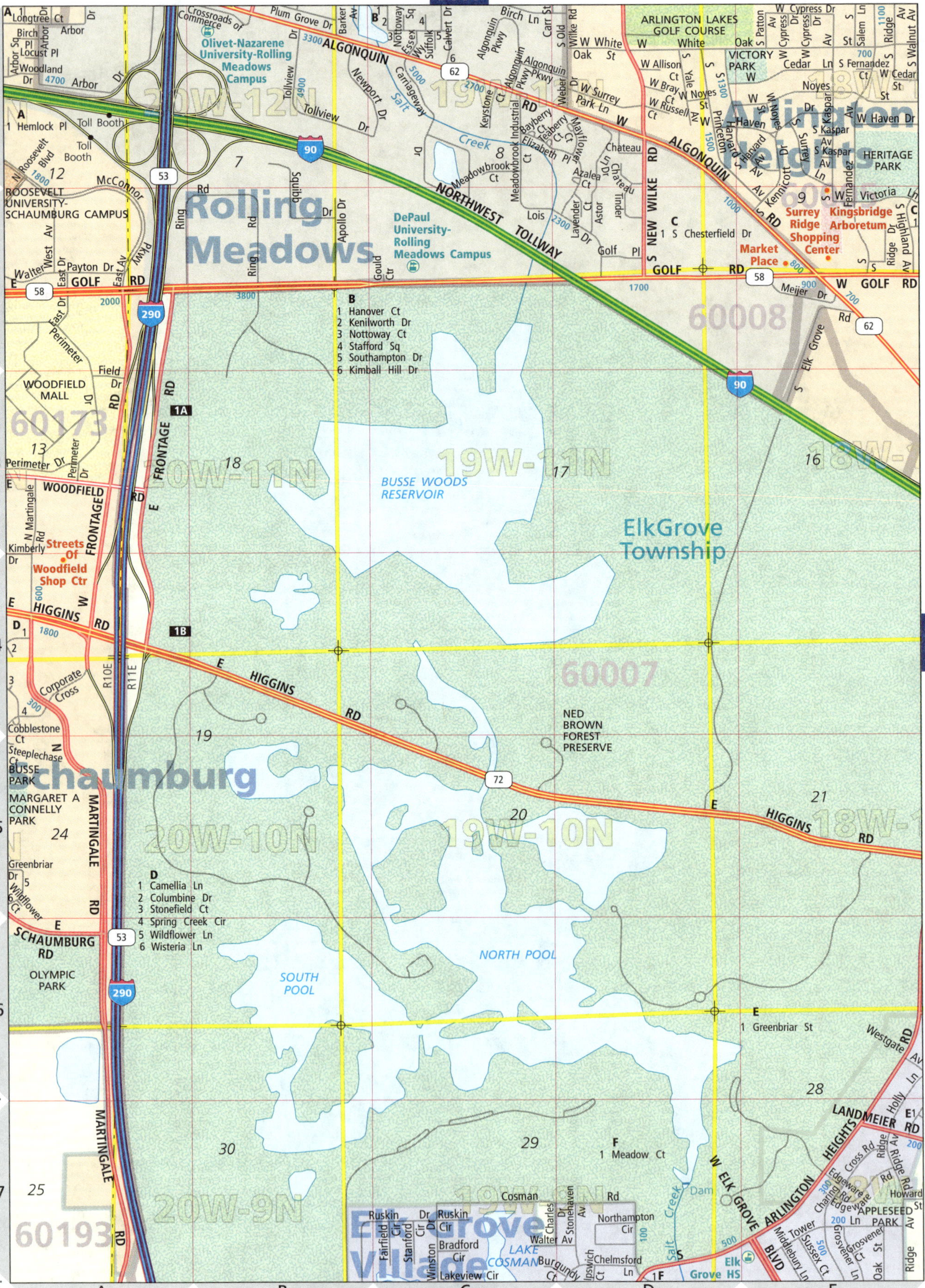

SEE 2859 MAP

SEE 2861 MAP

SEE 2914 MAP

1:24,000
1 in. = 2000 ft.
0 0.25 0.5
miles

SEE 2807 MAP

Arlington Heights
Mount Prospect
Elk Grove Village
Elk Grove Township
Des Plaines
Branigar Estates
60005
60056
60007
60018
MT PROSPECT GOLF COURSE
ROBERT T JACKSON CLEARWATER PARK
HERITAGE PARK
CAREFREE PARK
PRAIRIE PARK
FALCON PARK
WELLERS CREEK PARK
SUNSET PARK
KOPP PARK
REDWOOD PARK
BEAU DRIVE PARK
NED BROWN FOR PRESERVE
ELK GRV CEM
LAKE BRIARWOOD
BRIARWOOD LK
OSBORN PARK
ANDREWS PARK
UDALL PARK
Int'l Plaza Shopping Center
Arlington Towne Sq
Golf Plz
Golf Plaza II
Countryside Court Shop Ctr
United Plaza
Crystal Court Shop Ctr
United Airlines
Higgins Industrial Park
Metro Prep School
W GOLF RD
GOLF
ALGONQUIN RD
DEMPSTER
HIGGINS
OAKTON ST
NORTHWEST TOLLWAY
ARLINGTON HEIGHTS RD
BUSSE RD
ELMHURST RD
LANDMEIER RD
TONNE RD
Toll Booth
58
62
72
83
90
16W-12N
17W-12N
17W-11N
16W-11N
17W-10N
16W-10N
17W-9N
16W-9N
A
B
C
D
E
1
2
3
4
5
6
7
42°03'44"
42°03'18"
42°02'52"
42°02'26"
42°02'00"
42°01'34"
42°01'08"
42°00'42"
87°59'17"
87°58'42"
87°58'07"
87°57'32"
87°56'57"
87°56'22"
RAND McNALLY

SEE 2860 MAP
SEE 2862 MAP
SEE 2915 MAP

1:24,000
1 in. = 2000 ft.
0 0.25 0.5
miles

SEE 2808 MAP

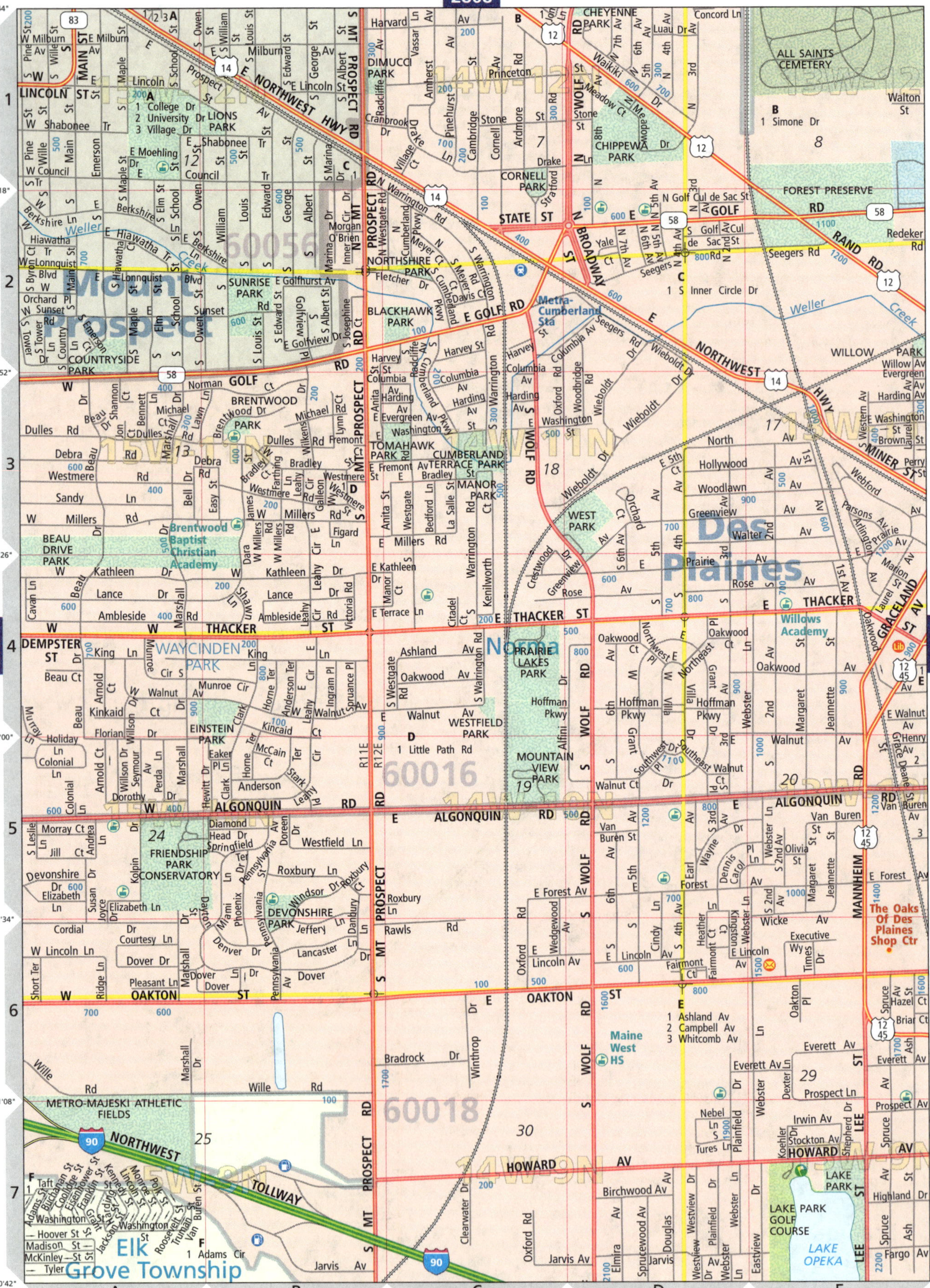
Mount Prospect
Des Plaines
Norma
Elk Grove Township
60056
60016
60018
ALL SAINTS CEMETERY
FOREST PRESERVE
LIONS PARK
DIMUCCI PARK
CHIPPEWA PARK
CORNELL PARK
SUNRISE PARK
BLACKHAWK PARK
NORTHSHIRE PARK
COUNTRYSIDE PARK
Metra-Cumberland Sta
BRENTWOOD PARK
TOMAHAWK PARK
CUMBERLAND TERRACE PARK
MANOR PARK
WEST PARK
BEAU DRIVE PARK
Brentwood Baptist Christian Academy
WAYCINDEN PARK
EINSTEIN PARK
PRAIRIE LAKES PARK
WESTFIELD PARK
MOUNTAIN VIEW PARK
Willows Academy
FRIENDSHIP PARK CONSERVATORY
DEVONSHIRE PARK
The Oaks Of Des Plaines Shop Ctr
Maine West HS
METRO-MAJESKI ATHLETIC FIELDS
LAKE PARK
LAKE PARK GOLF COURSE
LAKE OPEKA
WILLOW PARK
NORTHWEST HWY
GOLF RD
THACKER ST
DEMPSTER ST
ALGONQUIN RD
OAKTON ST
HOWARD AV
MT PROSPECT RD
WOLF RD
MANNHEIM RD
LEE ST
GRACELAND AV
RAND RD
MINER ST
NORTHWEST TOLLWAY
BROADWAY
Weller Creek
15W-12N
14W-12N
13W-12N
15W-11N
14W-11N
13W-11N
14W-10N
13W-10N
15W-9N
14W-9N
13W-9N
RAND McNALLY

SEE 2861 MAP
SEE 2863 MAP
SEE 2916 MAP

1:24,000
1 in. = 2000 ft.
0 0.25 0.5
miles

SEE 2809 MAP

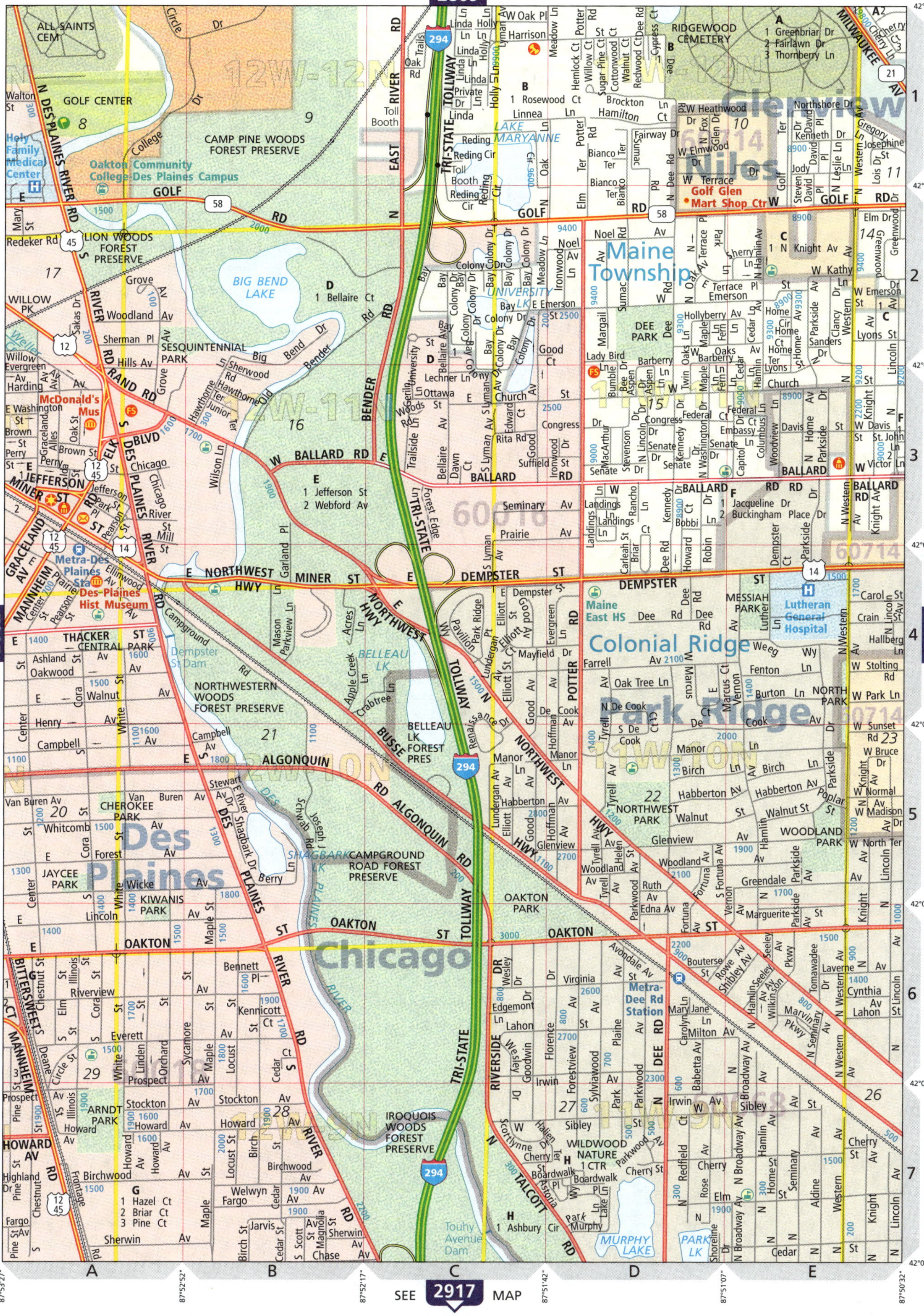

SEE 2862 MAP
SEE 2864 MAP
SEE 2917 MAP

1:24,000
1 in. = 2000 ft.
0 0.25 0.5
miles

SEE 2810 MAP

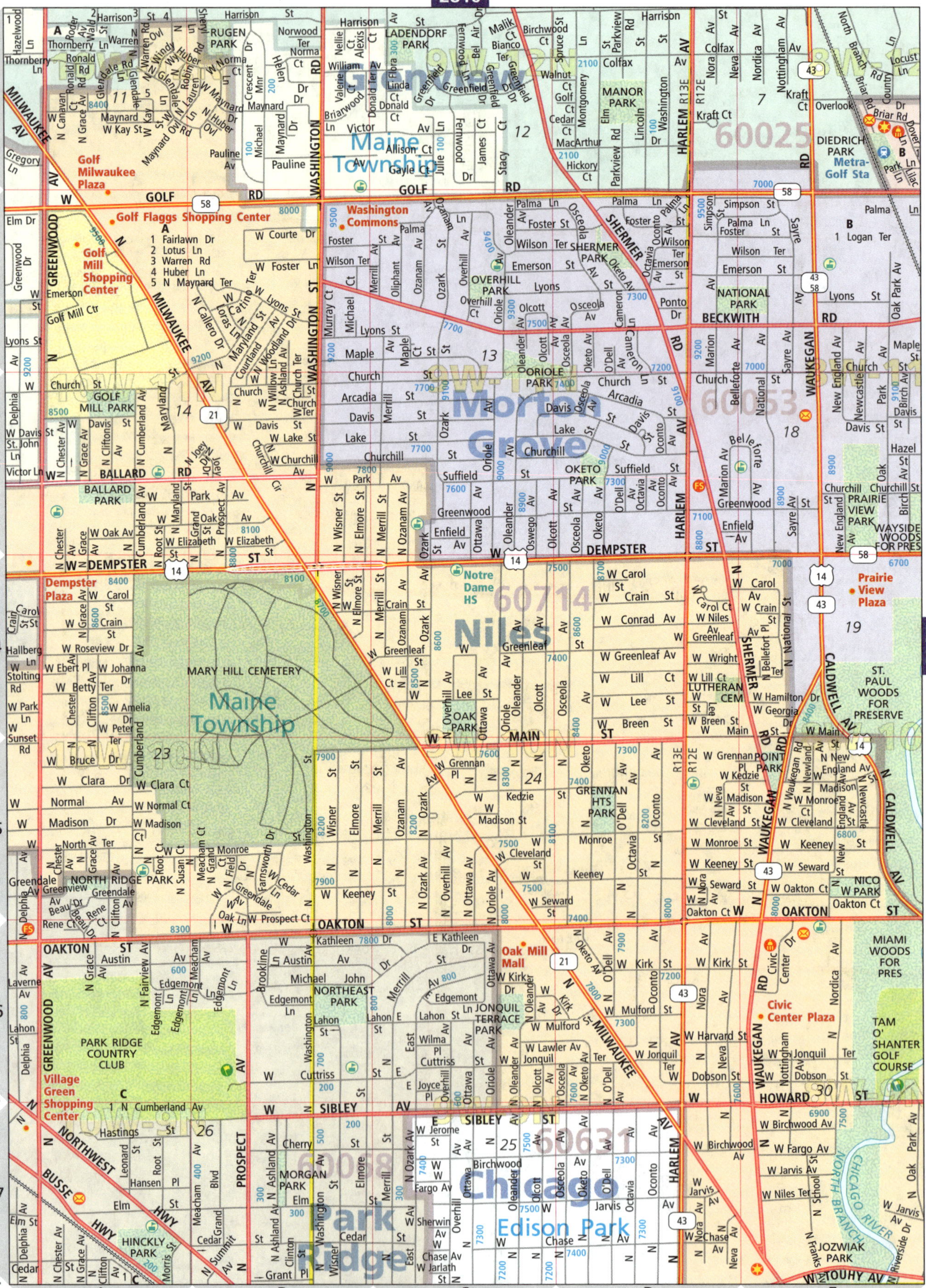
Glenview
Maine Township
Morton Grove
Niles
Park Ridge
Chicago
Edison Park
60025
60053
60714
60631
60068
Golf Milwaukee Plaza
Golf Flaggs Shopping Center
Golf Mill Shopping Center
GOLF MILL PARK
Washington Commons
LADENDORF PARK
RUGEN PARK
MANOR PARK
DIEDRICH PARK
Metra-Golf Sta
OVERHILL PARK
SHERMER PARK
NATIONAL PARK
BECKWITH
ORIOLE PARK
OKETO PARK
BALLARD PARK
Dempster Plaza
Notre Dame HS
MARY HILL CEMETERY
OAK PARK
GRENNAN HTS PARK
LUTHERAN CEM
POINT PARK
ST. PAUL WOODS FOR PRESERVE
PRAIRIE VIEW PARK
WAYSIDE WOODS FOR PRES
Prairie View Plaza
NICO W PARK
NORTH RIDGE PARK
PARK RIDGE COUNTRY CLUB
Village Green Shopping Center
NORTHEAST PARK
JONQUIL TERRACE PARK
Oak Mill Mall
Civic Center Plaza
MIAMI WOODS FOR PRES
TAM O' SHANTER GOLF COURSE
MORGAN PARK
HINCKLY PARK
JOZWIAK PARK
NORTH BRANCH CHICAGO RIVER
MILWAUKEE AV
GOLF RD
DEMPSTER ST
OAKTON ST
MAIN ST
HOWARD ST
SIBLEY AV
TOUHY AV
BALLARD RD
BECKWITH RD
GREENWOOD AV
WASHINGTON
HARLEM AV
SHERMER RD
WAUKEGAN RD
CALDWELL AV
NORTHWEST HWY
BUSSE HWY
PROSPECT
A
1 Fairlawn Dr
2 Lotus Ln
3 Warren Rd
4 Huber Ln
5 N Maynard Ter
B
1 Logan Ter
C
1 N Cumberland Av
58
14
21
43

42°03'45" 42°03'19" 42°02'53" 42°02'27" 42°02'01" 42°01'35" 42°01'09" 42°00'42"

1 2 3 4 5 6 7

A B C D E

87°50'32" 87°49'57" 87°49'22" 87°48'47" 87°48'12" 87°47'38"

SEE 2863 MAP

SEE 2865 MAP

SEE 2918 MAP

1:24,000
1 in. = 2000 ft.
0 0.25 0.5
miles

SEE 2811 MAP

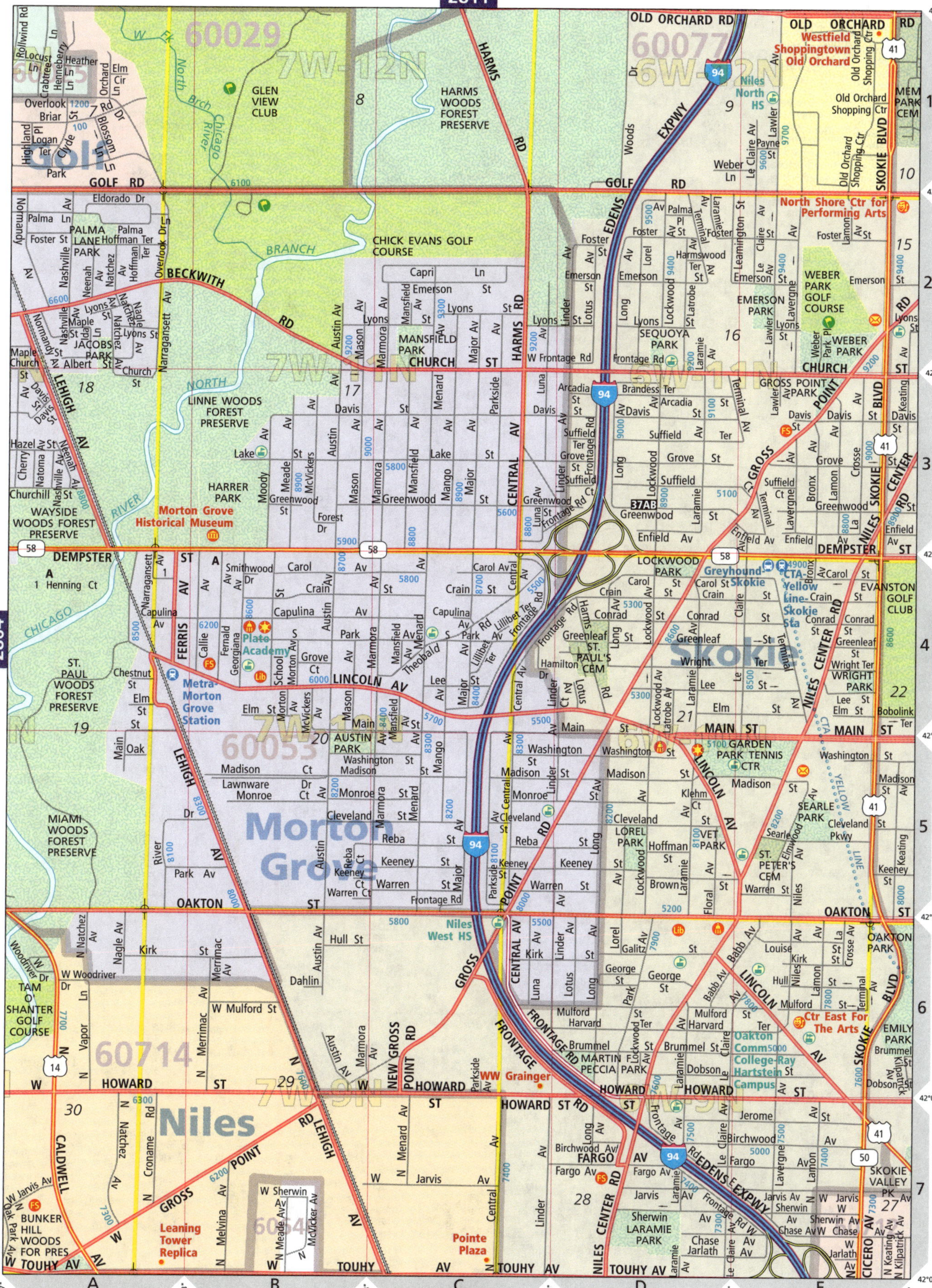

SEE 2864 MAP

SEE 2866 MAP

SEE 2919 MAP

1:24,000
1 in. = 2000 ft.
0 0.25 0.5
miles

SEE 2812 MAP

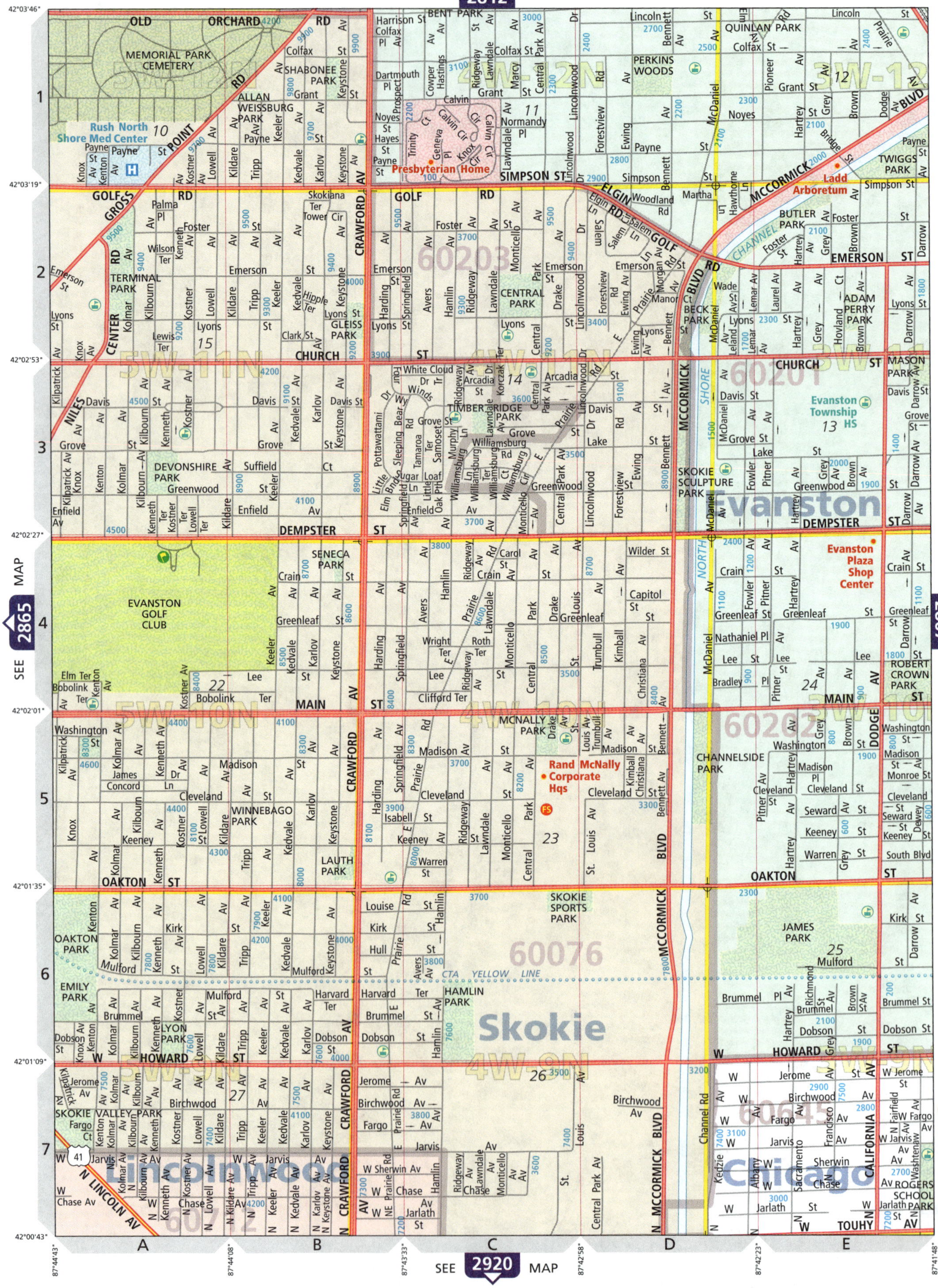

SEE 2865 MAP
SEE 2867 MAP
SEE 2920 MAP

1:24,000
1 in. = 2000 ft.
0 0.25 0.5
miles

SEE 2813 MAP

SEE 2866 MAP
SEE B MAP
SEE 2921 MAP

RAND McNALLY

1:24,000
1 in. = 2000 ft.
0 0.25 0.5
miles

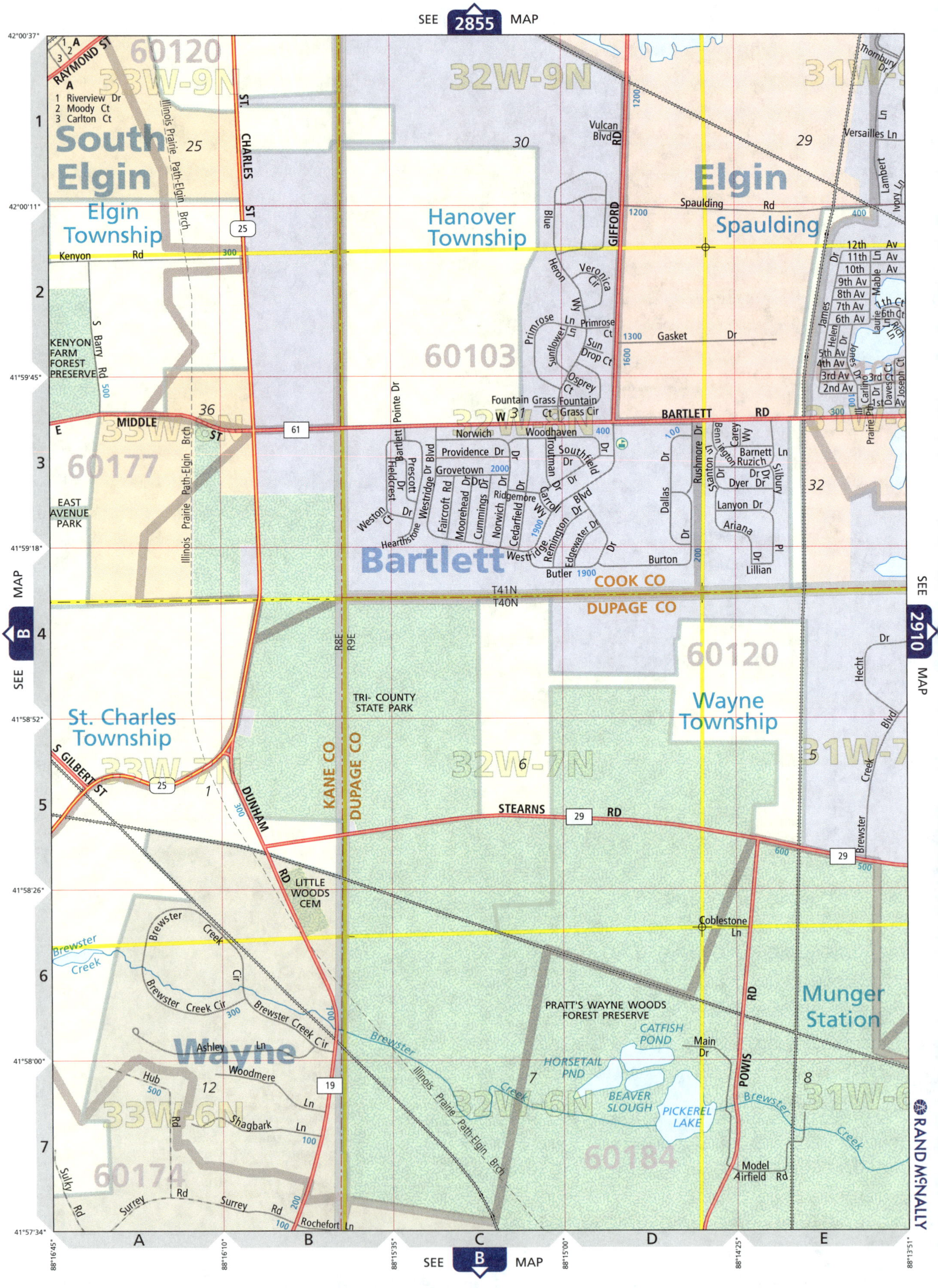

1:24,000
1 in. = 2000 ft.
0 0.25 0.5
miles

SEE 2856 MAP

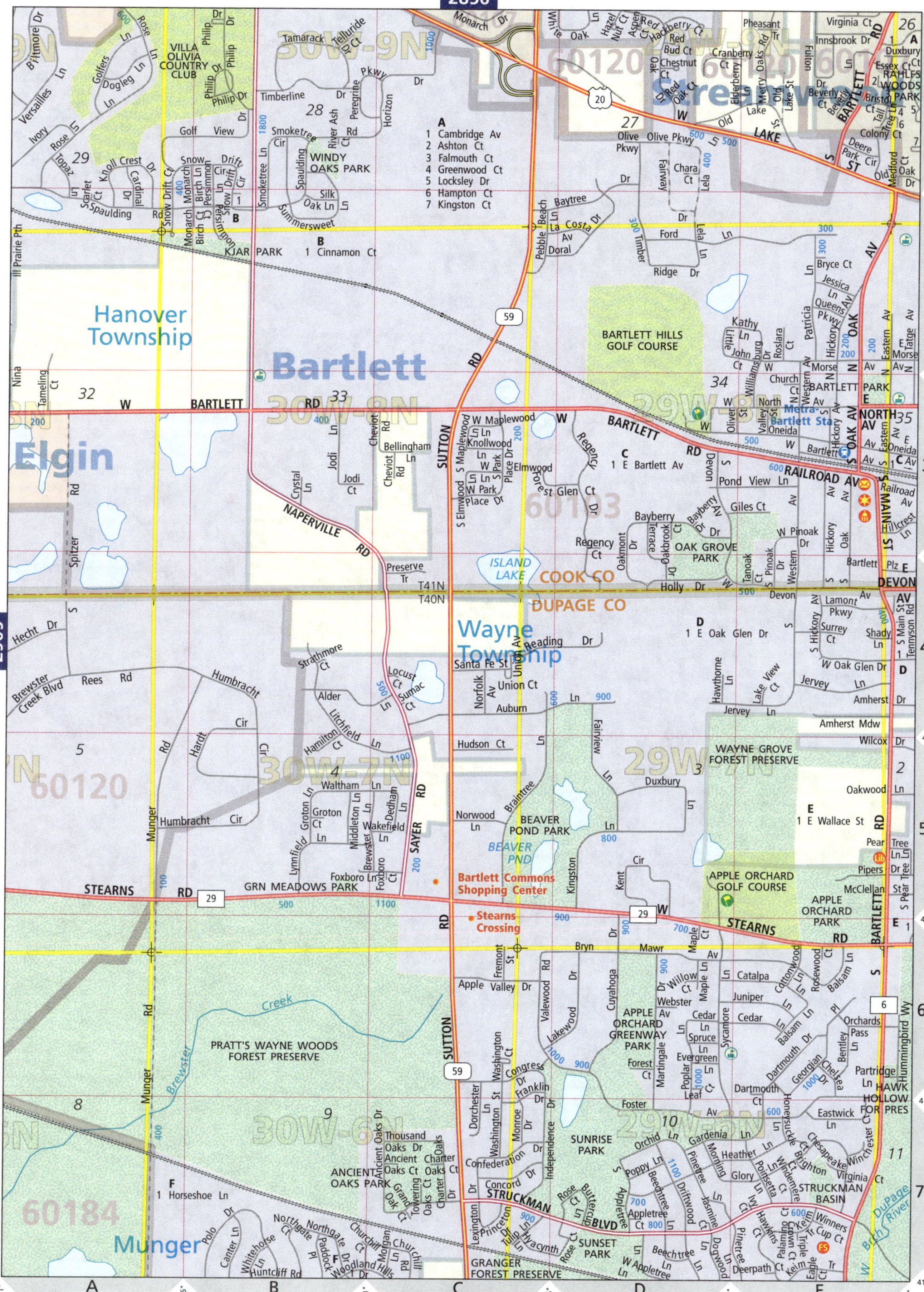
Bartlett
Streamwood
Elgin
Hanover Township
Wayne Township
Munger
VILLA OLIVIA COUNTRY CLUB
WINDY OAKS PARK
KJAR PARK
BARTLETT HILLS GOLF COURSE
BARTLETT PARK
Metra-Bartlett Sta
OAK GROVE PARK
ISLAND LAKE
COOK CO
DUPAGE CO
T41N
T40N
WAYNE GROVE FOREST PRESERVE
BEAVER POND PARK
BEAVER PND
Bartlett Commons Shopping Center
Stearns Crossing
APPLE ORCHARD GOLF COURSE
APPLE ORCHARD PARK
GRN MEADOWS PARK
PRATT'S WAYNE WOODS FOREST PRESERVE
APPLE ORCHARD GREENWAY PARK
SUNRISE PARK
ANCIENT OAKS PARK
SUNSET PARK
GRANGER FOREST PRESERVE
STRUCKMAN BASIN
HAWK HOLLOW FOR PRES
RAHLFS WOODS PARK
30W-9N
30W-8N
30W-7N
30W-6N
29W-8N
29W-7N
29W-6N
60120
60103
60184
A
1 Cambridge Av
2 Ashton Ct
3 Falmouth Ct
4 Greenwood Ct
5 Locksley Dr
6 Hampton Ct
7 Kingston Ct
B
1 Cinnamon Ct
C
1 E Bartlett Av
D
1 E Oak Glen Dr
E
1 E Wallace St
F
1 Horseshoe Ln
W BARTLETT RD
SUTTON RD
NAPERVILLE RD
SAYER RD
STEARNS RD
STRUCKMAN BLVD
W LAKE ST
RAILROAD AV
S MAIN ST
S OAK AV
N OAK AV
BARTLETT RD
DEVON AV
Munger Rd
Union Av
Bryn Mawr Av
59
20
29
6
RAND MCNALLY
A B C D E
1 2 3 4 5 6 7
42°00'39"
42°00'12"
41°59'46"
41°59'20"
41°58'54"
41°58'28"
41°58'02"
41°57'36"
88°13'51"
88°13'16"
88°12'41"
88°12'06"
88°11'31"
88°10'56"

SEE 2909 MAP

SEE 2911 MAP

SEE B MAP

1:24,000
1 in. = 2000 ft.
0 0.25 0.5
miles

SEE 2857 MAP

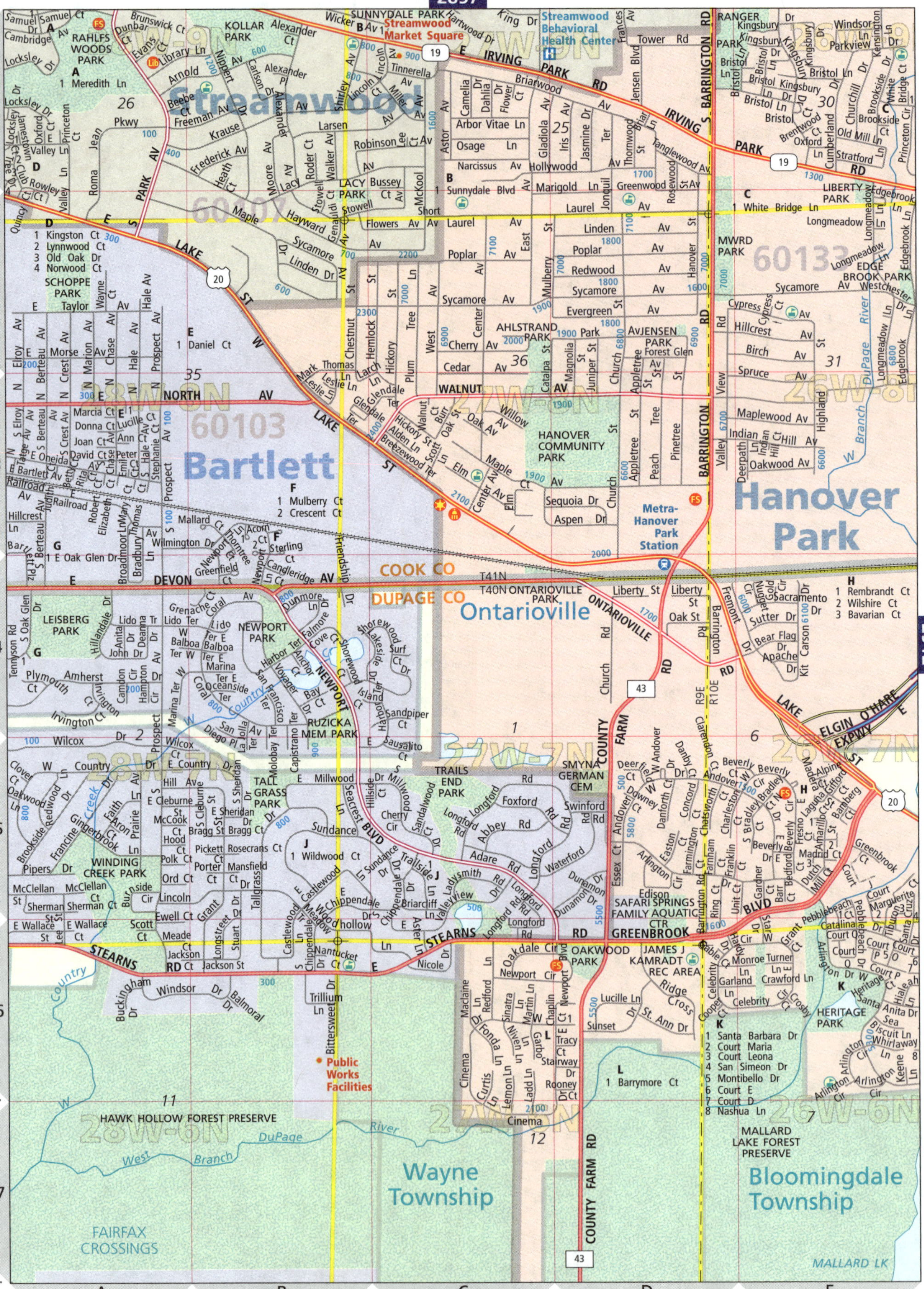
Streamwood
Bartlett
Hanover Park
Ontarioville
Streamwood Market Square
Streamwood Behavioral Health Center
KOLLAR PARK
RAHLFS WOODS PARK
LACY PARK
SCHOPPE PARK
AHLSTRAND PARK
AVJENSEN PARK
HANOVER COMMUNITY PARK
MWRD PARK
EDGE BROOK PARK
LIBERTY PARK
RANGER PARK
Metra-Hanover Park Station
COOK CO
DUPAGE CO
T41N
T40N
ONTARIOVILLE PARK
LEISBERG PARK
NEWPORT PARK
RUZICKA MEM PARK
TALL GRASS PARK
TRAILS END PARK
SMYNA GERMAN CEM
WINDING CREEK PARK
SAFARI SPRINGS FAMILY AQUATIC CTR
OAKWOOD PARK
JAMES J KAMRADT REC AREA
HERITAGE PARK
Public Works Facilities
HAWK HOLLOW FOREST PRESERVE
FAIRFAX CROSSINGS
MALLARD LAKE FOREST PRESERVE
Wayne Township
Bloomingdale Township
MALLARD LK
60107
60103
60133
IRVING PARK RD
LAKE ST
NORTH AV
DEVON AV
STEARNS RD
GREENBROOK BLVD
COUNTY FARM RD
S BARRINGTON RD
ELGIN O'HARE EXPWY
West Branch DuPage River
Country Creek
1 Kingston Ct
2 Lynnwood Ct
3 Old Oak Dr
4 Norwood Ct
1 Rembrandt Ct
2 Wilshire Ct
3 Bavarian Ct
1 Mulberry Ct
2 Crescent Ct
1 Santa Barbara Dr
2 Court Maria
3 Court Leona
4 San Simeon Dr
5 Montibello Dr
6 Court E
7 Court D
8 Nashua Ln
1 Barrymore Ct
RAND McNALLY

SEE 2910 MAP

SEE 2912 MAP

SEE B MAP

1:24,000
1 in. = 2000 ft.
0 0.25 0.5
miles

SEE 2858 MAP

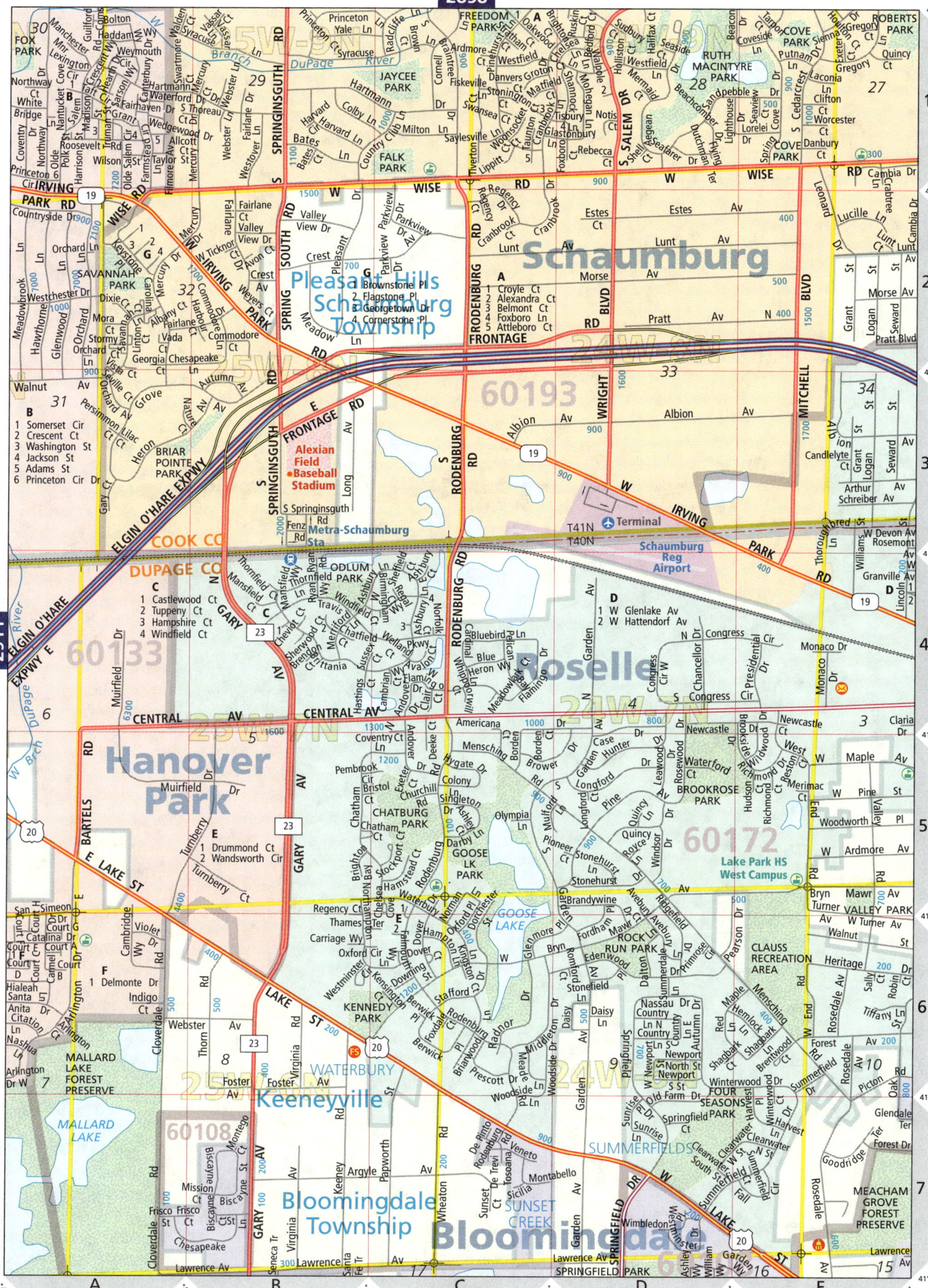

SEE 2911 MAP

SEE 2913 MAP

SEE B MAP

1:24,000
1 in. = 2000 ft.
0 0.25 0.5
miles

SEE 2859 MAP

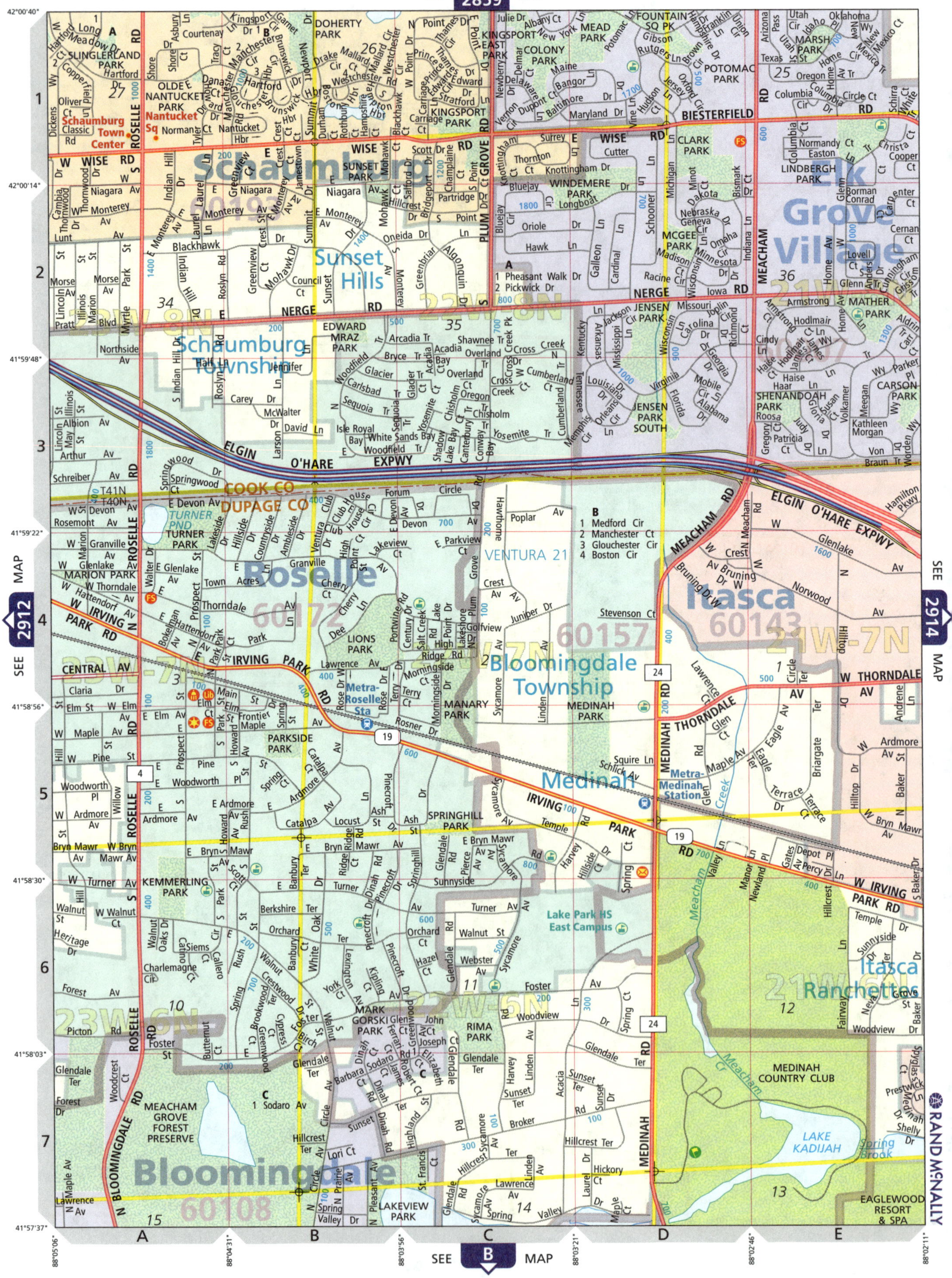

SEE 2912 MAP

SEE 2914 MAP

SEE B MAP

1:24,000
1 in. = 2000 ft.
0 0.25 0.5
miles

SEE 2860 MAP

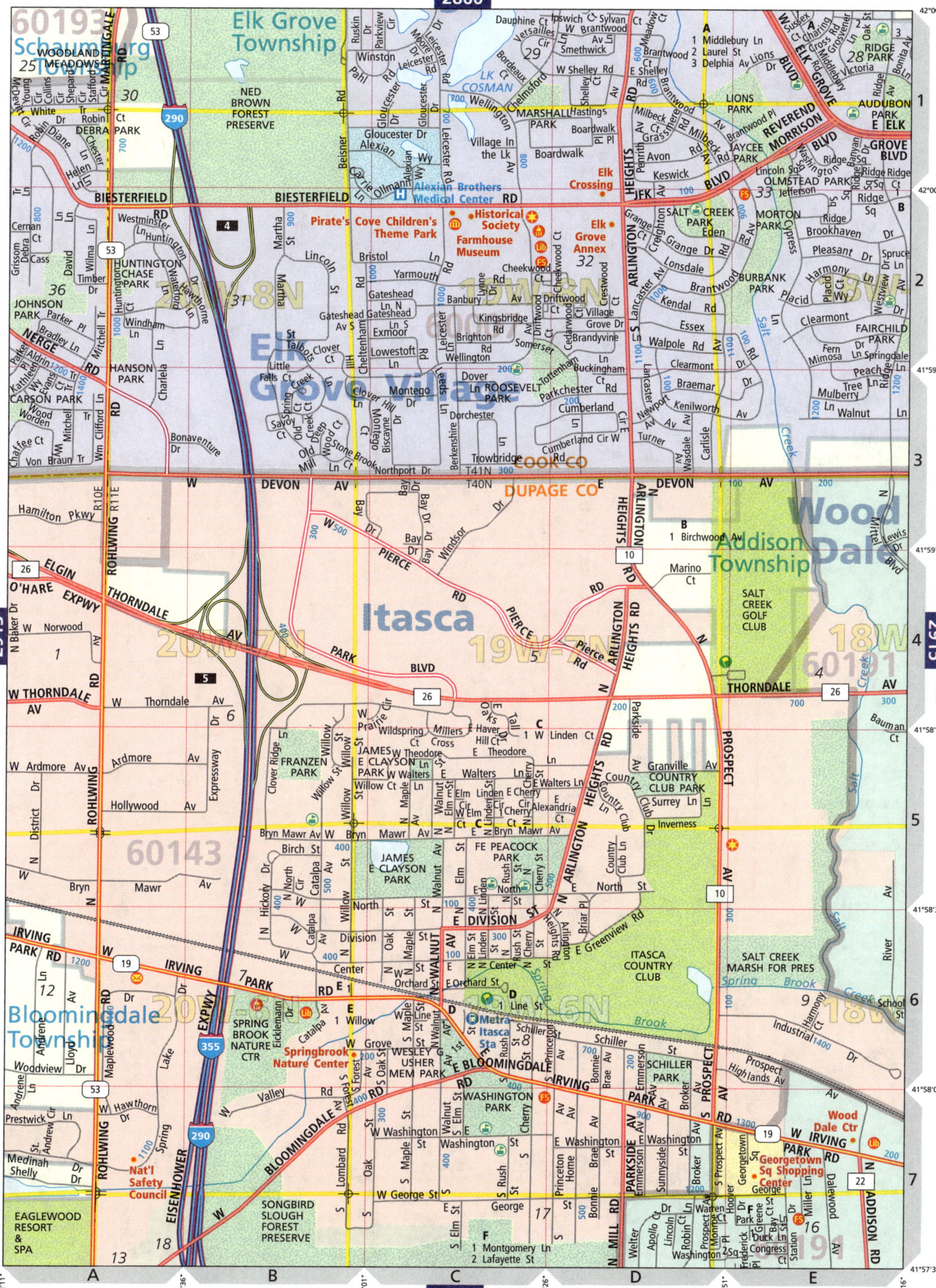

SEE 2913 MAP
SEE 2915 MAP
SEE B MAP

1:24,000
1 in. = 2000 ft.
0 0.25 0.5
miles

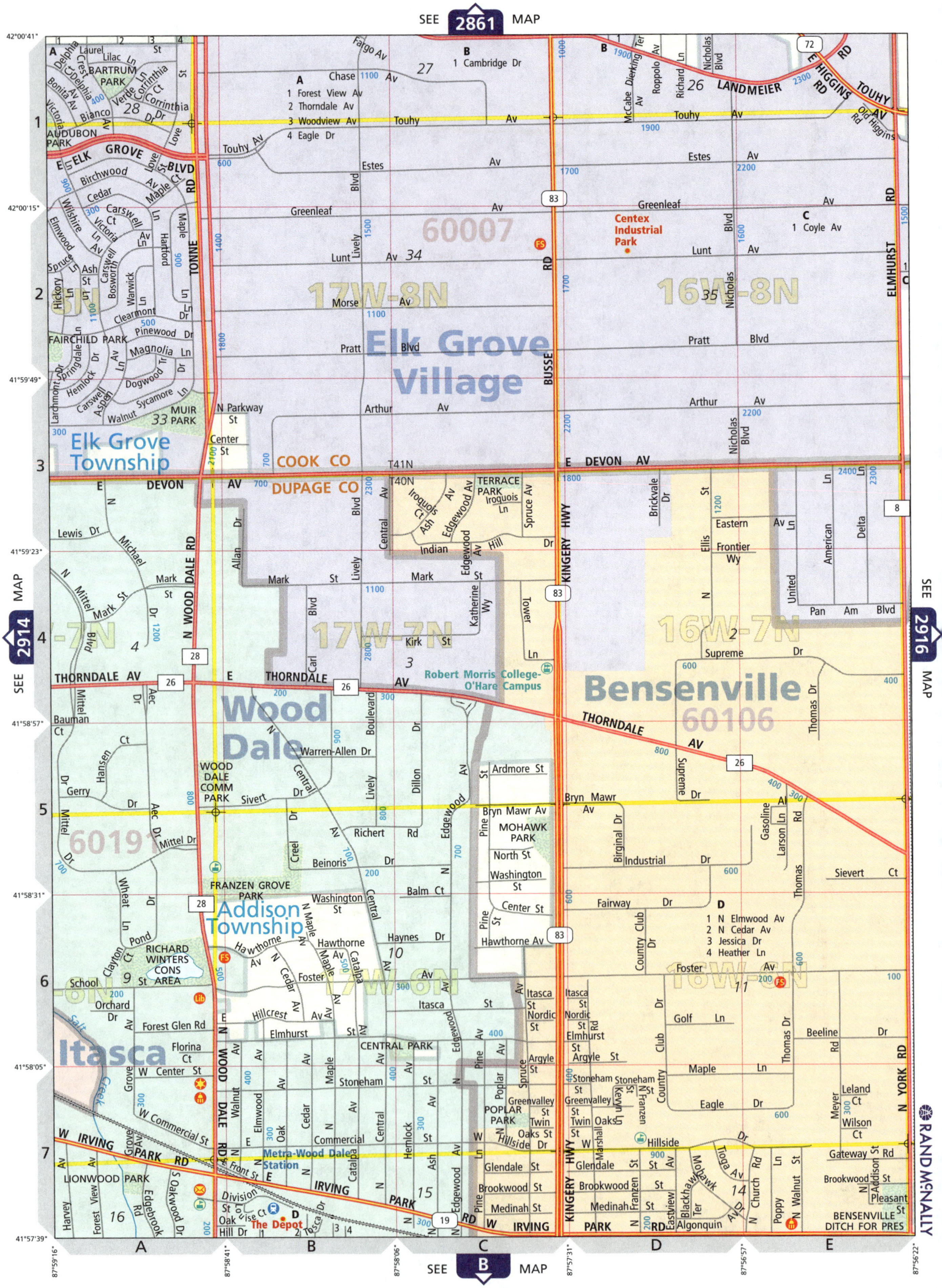
SEE 2861 MAP
SEE 2914 MAP
SEE 2916 MAP
SEE B MAP
Elk Grove Village
60007
17W-8N
16W-8N
Elk Grove Township
COOK CO
DUPAGE CO
T41N
T40N
17W-7N
16W-7N
Bensenville
60106
Wood Dale
60191
Addison Township
17W-6N
16W-6N
Itasca
Centex Industrial Park
Robert Morris College-O'Hare Campus
BARTRUM PARK
AUDUBON PARK
FAIRCHILD PARK
MUIR PARK
TERRACE PARK
WOOD DALE COMM PARK
FRANZEN GROVE PARK
MOHAWK PARK
RICHARD WINTERS CONS AREA
CENTRAL PARK
POPLAR PARK
LIONWOOD PARK
BENSENVILLE DITCH FOR PRES
Metra-Wood Dale Station
The Depot
ELK GROVE BLVD
TOUHY AV
DEVON AV
THORNDALE AV
IRVING PARK RD
BUSSE RD
KINGERY HWY
TONNE RD
N WOOD DALE RD
ELMHURST RD
N YORK RD
LANDMEIER RD
E HIGGINS RD
A 1 Forest View Av 2 Thorndale Av 3 Woodview Av 4 Eagle Dr
B 1 Cambridge Dr
C 1 Coyle Av
D 1 N Elmwood Av 2 N Cedar Av 3 Jessica Dr 4 Heather Ln
A B C D E
1 2 3 4 5 6 7
RAND McNALLY

1:24,000
1 in. = 2000 ft.
0 0.25 0.5
miles

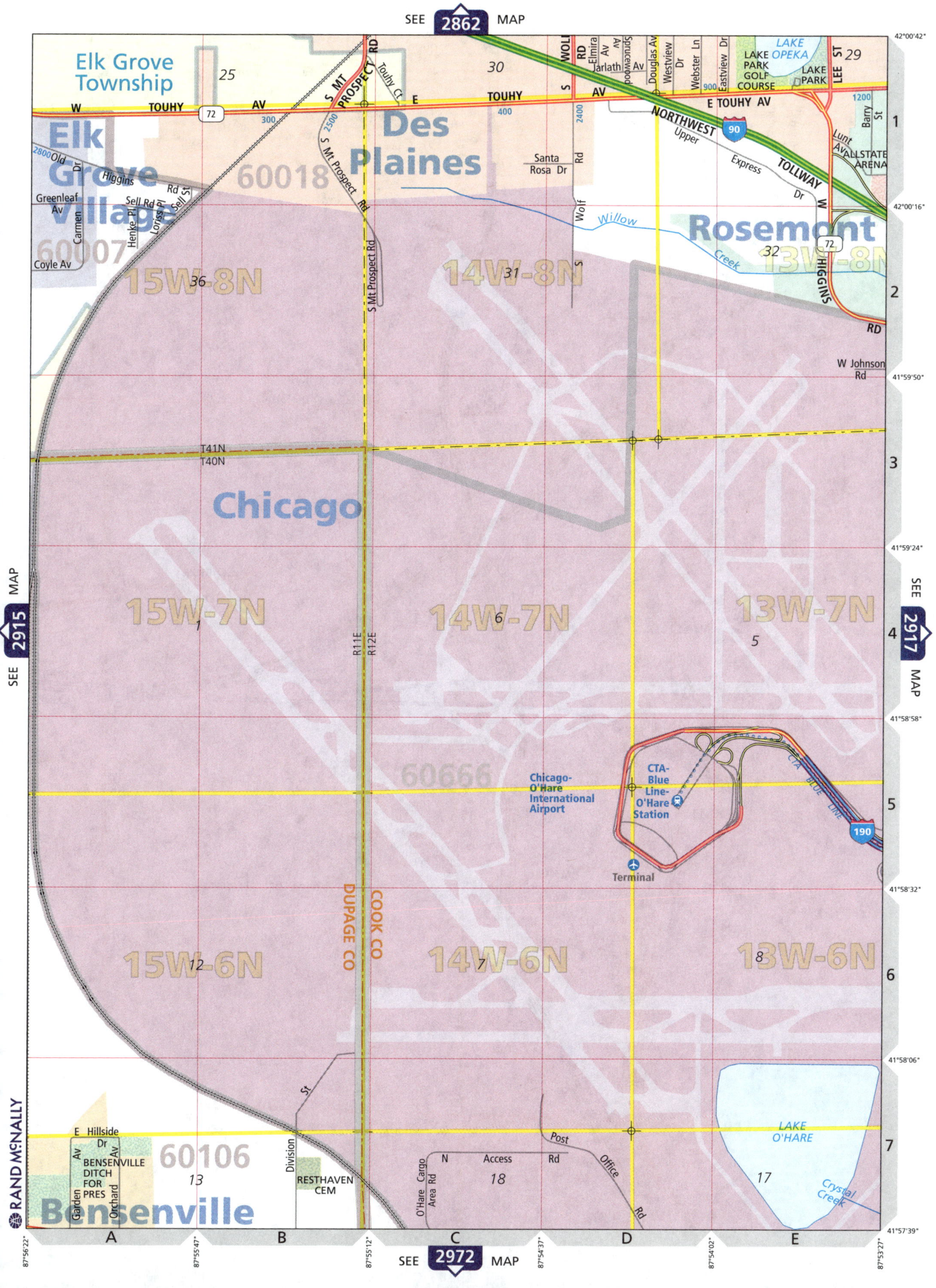

1:24,000
1 in. = 2000 ft.
0 0.25 0.5
miles

SEE 2863 MAP

Des Plaines
Park Ridge
Rosemont
Chicago
Schiller Park
Norridge
Allstate Arena
O'Hare Air Force Base & Air National Guard
Chicago-O'Hare International Airport
Metra-O'Hare Transfer Station
Rosemont Station
Rosemont Theatre
Donald E Stephens Convention Center
DePaul University-O'Hare Campus
Maine South HS
IROQUOIS WOODS FOREST PRESERVE
CHIPPEWA WOODS FOREST PRES
AXEHEAD LAKE
PETERSON LK
EATON FLD PARK
SEMINOLE PARK
CENTENNIAL PARK
SOUTHWEST PARK
MAINE CEM
DAM NO 4 FOREST PRESERVE
ALL SAINTS CEMETERY
ST. NICHOLAS CEM
CATHERINE CHEVALIER FOREST PRESERVE
SCHILLER WOODS FOREST PRESERVE
DES PLAINES RIVER
NORTHWEST TOLLWAY
TRI-STATE TOLLWAY
KENNEDY EXPWY
MANNHEIM RD
RIVER RD
EAST RIVER RD
HIGGINS RD
DEVON AV
TOUHY AV
TALCOTT RD
BALMORAL AV
LAWRENCE AV
FOSTER AV
BRYN MAWR AV
CTA BLUE LINE
12W-8N
11W-8N
12W-7N
11W-7N
12W-6N
11W-6N
60018
60068
60631
60656
60666
60706
60176
A
B
C
D
E
1
2
3
4
5
6
7
A
1 N Broadway Av
2 N Seminary Av
3 N Western Av
4 N Lincoln Av
B
1 1st Park Av
2 3rd Park Av
3 2nd Park Av
4 4th Park Av
5 5th Park AV
6 Van Selow Dr

SEE 2916 MAP

SEE 2918 MAP

SEE 2973 MAP

1:24,000
1 in. = 2000 ft.
0 0.25 0.5
miles
SEE 2864 MAP
SEE 2917 MAP
SEE 2919 MAP
SEE 2974 MAP
Park Ridge
Niles
Norwood Park
Chicago
Maine Township
Norwood Park Township
Leyden Township
Harwood Heights
Norridge
TOUHY AV
DEVON AV
TALCOTT RD
HIGGINS RD
KENNEDY EXPWY
FOSTER AV
LAWRENCE AV
BRYN MAWR AV
NORTHWEST HWY
MILWAUKEE AV
HARLEM AV
CUMBERLAND AV
CANFIELD RD
OZANAM AV
ORIOLE AV
NEWARK AV
PIONEER PARK
BROOKS PARK
EDISON PARK
OLYMPIA PARK
SOUTH PARK
JAYCEE PARK
ORIOLE PARK
NORRIDGE PARK
NORWOOD CIRCLE PARK
NORWOOD PARK
CENTENNIAL PARK
MYRTLE GRV PARK
NORWOOD PLGND PARK
ST. ADALBERT CEMETERY
UNION RIDGE CEM
RIDGEMOOR CC
MIAMI WOODS FOR PRES
BUNKER HILL WOODS FOR PRES
Metra-Park Ridge Sta
Metra-Edison Pk Station
Metra-Norwood Park Station
CTA-Blue Line-Cumberland
CTA-Blue Line-Harlem Sta
Greyhound-Chicago
Resurrection HS
Resurrection Medical Center
Harlem-Foster Shopping Center
Harwood Commons
Holiday Plaza Shopping Center
60068
60631
60656
60706
RAND McNALLY

1:24,000
1 in. = 2000 ft.
0 0.25 0.5
miles

SEE 2865 MAP

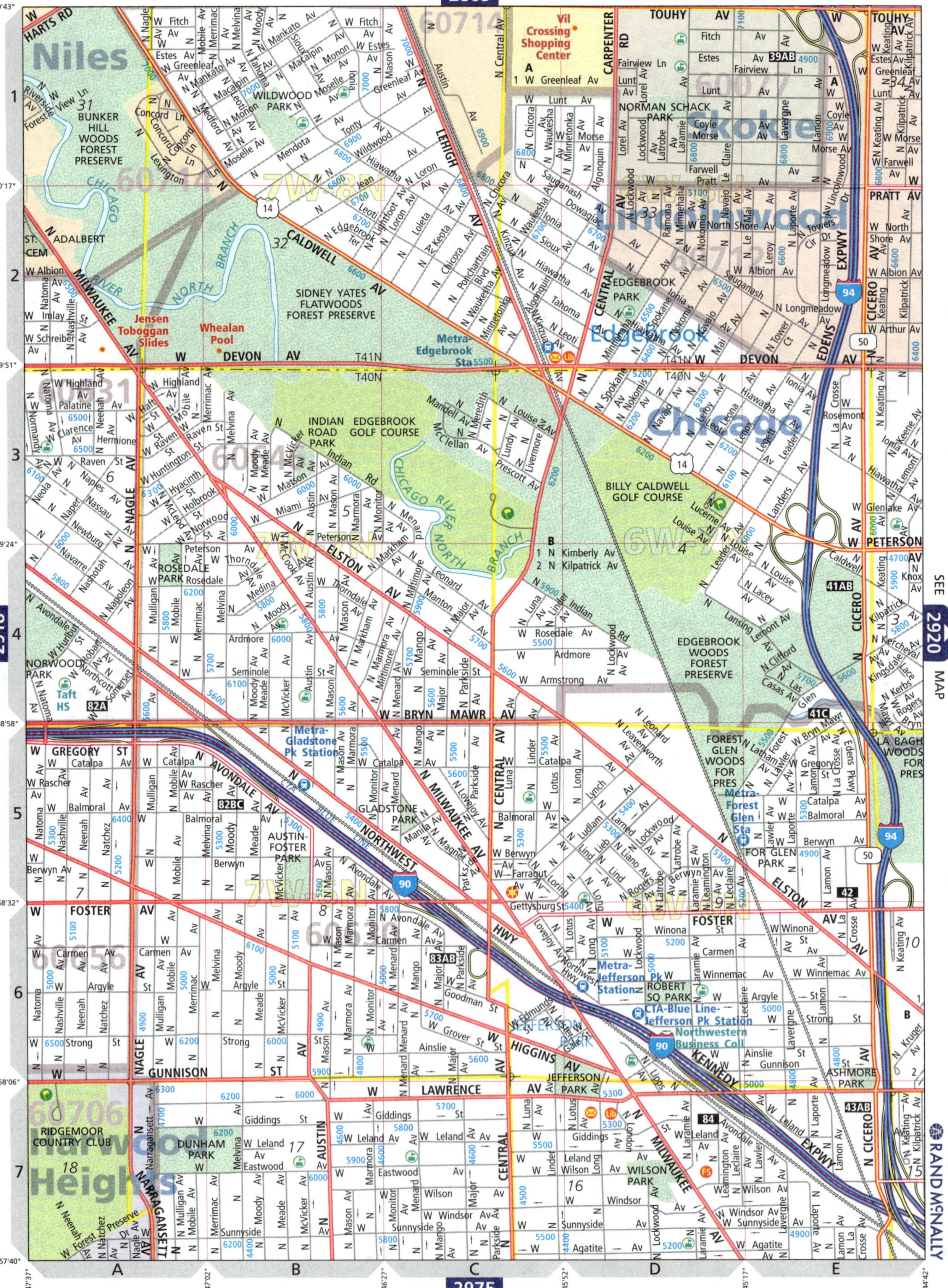
Niles
Skokie
Lincolnwood
Chicago
Edgebrook
Harwood Heights
BUNKER HILL WOODS FOREST PRESERVE
SIDNEY YATES FLATWOODS FOREST PRESERVE
INDIAN ROAD PARK
EDGEBROOK GOLF COURSE
BILLY CALDWELL GOLF COURSE
EDGEBROOK WOODS FOREST PRESERVE
FOREST GLEN WOODS FOR PRES
NORMAN SCHACK PARK
EDGEBROOK PARK
WILDWOOD PARK
ROSEDALE PARK
NORWOOD PARK
GLADSTONE PARK
AUSTIN-FOSTER PARK
ROBERT SQ PARK
JEFFERSON PARK
DUNHAM PARK
WILSON PARK
ASHMORE PARK
FOR GLEN PARK
RIDGEMOOR COUNTRY CLUB
Vil Crossing Shopping Center
Jensen Toboggan Slides
Whealan Pool
Metra-Edgebrook Sta
Metra-Gladstone Pk Station
Metra-Forest Glen Sta
Metra-Jefferson Pk Station
CTA-Blue Line-Jefferson Pk Station
Northwestern Business Coll
Taft HS
TOUHY AV
DEVON AV
PETERSON AV
BRYN MAWR AV
FOSTER AV
LAWRENCE AV
GUNNISON ST
HIGGINS AV
MILWAUKEE AV
CALDWELL AV
ELSTON AV
NORTHWEST HWY
KENNEDY EXPWY
EDENS EXPWY
NAGLE AV
AUSTIN AV
CENTRAL AV
CICERO AV
NARRAGANSETT AV
LEHIGH AV
CARPENTER RD
CHICAGO RIVER NORTH BRANCH
60714
60077
60712
60631
60646
60656
60630
60706
7W-8N
6W-8N
7W-7N
6W-7N
7W-6N
6W-6N
T41N
T40N
RAND McNALLY

SEE 2918 MAP

SEE 2920 MAP

SEE 2975 MAP

1:24,000
1 in. = 2000 ft.
0 0.25 0.5
miles

SEE 2866 MAP

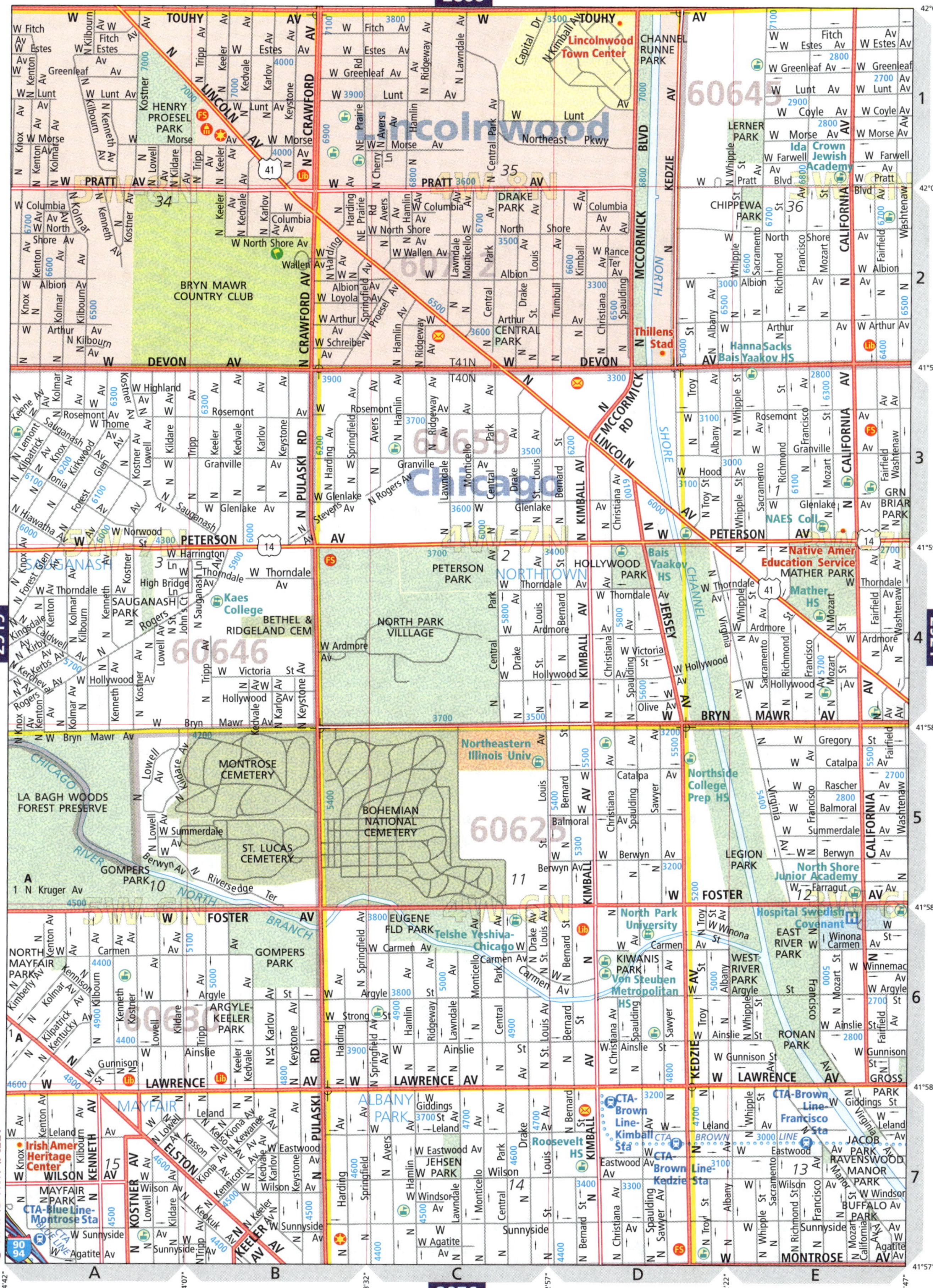

SEE 2919 MAP
SEE 2921 MAP
SEE 2976 MAP

1:24,000
1 in. = 2000 ft.
0 0.25 0.5
miles

SEE 2867 MAP

LAKE MICHIGAN
Chicago
ROGERS PARK
WEST RIDGE
EDGEWATER
UPTOWN
RAVENSWOOD
SUMMERDALE
ROSEHILL CEMETERY
ST. BONIFACE CEM
ROBERT A BLACK GOLF COURSE
WARREN PARK
INDIAN BOUNDARY PARK
EUGENE MATANKY PARK
PASCHEN PARK
EMMERSON PARK
SCHREIBER PARK
LOYOLA PARK
PRATT BOULEVARD BCH & PARK
COLUMBIA AVENUE BCH & PARK
NORTH SHORE AVENUE BCH & PARK
HARTIGAN PARK & BCH
BERGER BCH & PARK
LANE BCH & PARK
LINCOLN PARK
WINNEMAC PARK
GROSS PARK
SUNKEN GDNS PARK
WELLES PARK
CHASE PARK
CLARENDON PARK
SENN PARK
GRN BRIAR PARK
Loyola Beach
Loyola Avenue Beach
Ardmore Hollywood Beach
Loyola Univ of Chicago-Lakeshore Campus
Loyola Mundelein Coll
Kindred Hosp Chicago-Lakeshore
Kindred Hosp Chicago-North Campus
Methodist Hosp of Chicago
Louis A Weiss Mem Hospital
Swedish Amer Museum Ctr
Vietnam War Mus
Uptown Theatre
Aragon Ballroom
Riviera Theatre
Hse Theatre of Chicago
Appetite Theatre
Raven Theatre
Lifeline Theatre
Theo Ubique Theatre
Sullivan HS
Nicholas Senn HS
Amundsen HS
St. Gregory HS
St. Augustine College
Harry S Truman Coll
Eagles Wings Urban Academy
Ravenswood Baptist Christian School
Armory
Metra-Rogers Park Station
Metra-Ravenswood Sta
CTA-Red Line-Morse Sta
CTA-Red Line-Loyola Sta
CTA-Red Line-Granville Sta
CTA-Red Line-Thorndale Sta
CTA-Red Line-Bryn Mawr Sta
CTA-Red Line-Berwyn Station
CTA-Red Line-Argyle Station
CTA-Red Line-Lawrence Sta
CTA-Red Line-Wilson Sta
CTA-Brown Line-Damen Sta
CTA-Brown Line-Montrose Sta
CTA-Brown Line-Rockwell Sta
CTA-Brown Line-Western Sta
WESTERN AV
RIDGE BLVD
RAVENSWOOD AV
CLARK ST
ASHLAND AV
BROADWAY
SHERIDAN RD
LAKE SHORE DR
LINCOLN AV
DAMEN AV
DEVON AV
PRATT BLVD
PETERSON AV
MAWR AV
BRYN
FOSTER AV
LAWRENCE AV
MONTROSE
HOLLYWOOD AV
GLENWOOD AV
CLARENDON AV
60645
60626
60659
60660
60640
60625
A B C D E
1 2 3 4 5 6 7
42°00'43"
42°00'17"
41°59'51"
41°59'25"
41°58'59"
41°58'33"
41°58'06"
41°57'40"
87°41'47"
87°41'12"
87°40'37"
87°40'03"
87°39'28"
87°38'53"

SEE 2920 MAP

SEE 2922 MAP

SEE 2977 MAP

1:24,000
1 in. = 2000 ft.
0 0.25 0.5
miles

SEE B MAP

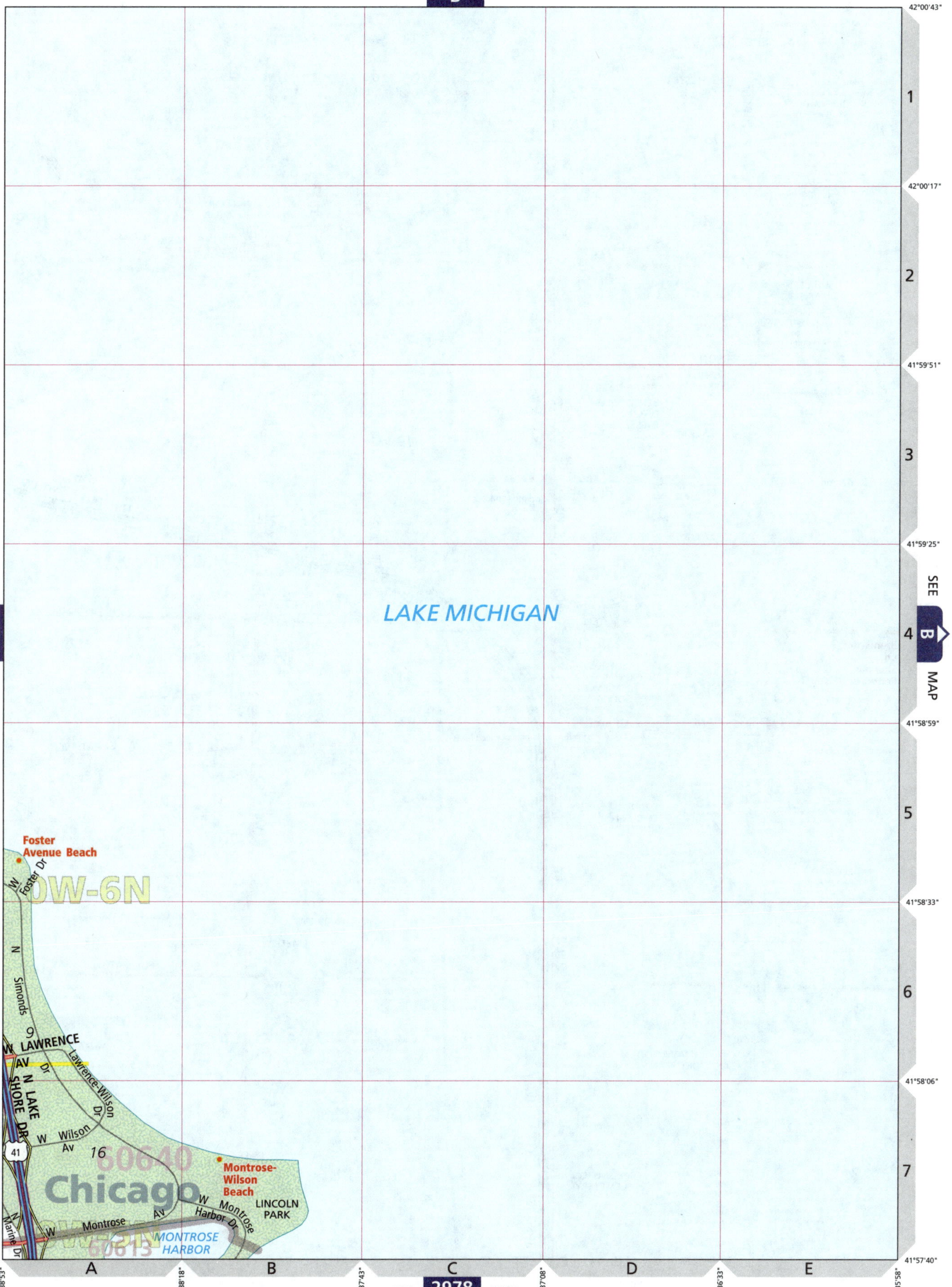

SEE 2921 MAP

SEE B MAP

SEE 2978 MAP

1:24,000
1 in. = 2000 ft.
0 0.25 0.5
miles

SEE 2916 MAP

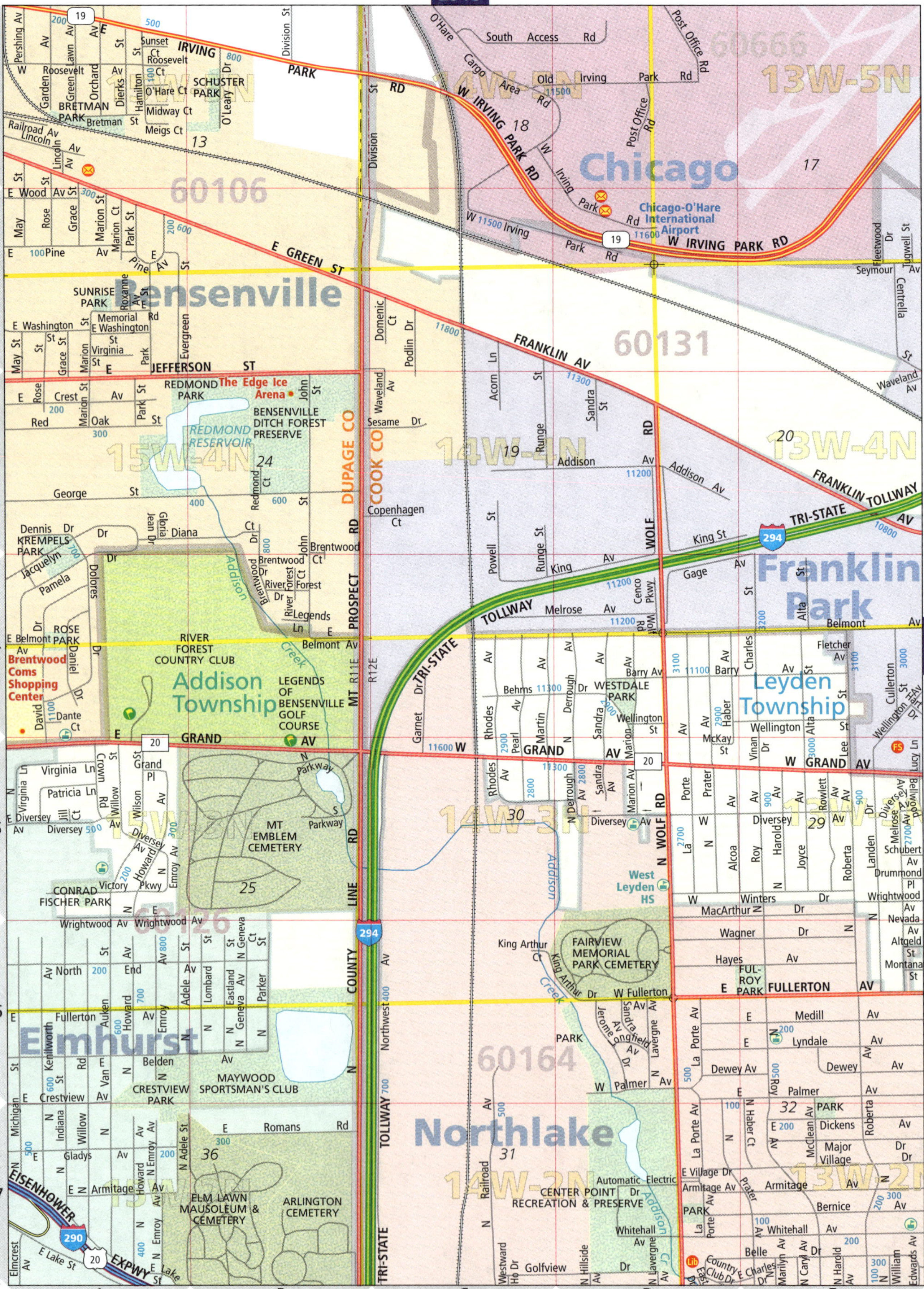
Bensenville
Chicago
Franklin Park
Elmhurst
Northlake
Addison Township
Leyden Township
60106
60666
60131
60126
60164
15W-4N
14W-5N
13W-5N
14W-4N
13W-4N
15W-3N
14W-3N
13W-3N
15W-2N
14W-2N
13W-2N
Chicago-O'Hare International Airport
IRVING PARK RD
W IRVING PARK RD
E GREEN ST
FRANKLIN AV
JEFFERSON ST
TRI-STATE TOLLWAY
FRANKLIN TOLLWAY
E GRAND AV
W GRAND AV
FULLERTON AV
EISENHOWER EXPWY
COUNTY LINE RD
MT PROSPECT RD
N WOLF RD
DUPAGE CO
COOK CO
SCHUSTER PARK
BRETMAN PARK
SUNRISE PARK
REDMOND PARK
The Edge Ice Arena
REDMOND RESERVOIR
BENSENVILLE DITCH FOREST PRESERVE
KREMPELS PARK
ROSE PARK
RIVER FOREST COUNTRY CLUB
LEGENDS OF BENSENVILLE GOLF COURSE
Brentwood Coms Shopping Center
MT EMBLEM CEMETERY
CONRAD FISCHER PARK
WESTDALE PARK
West Leyden HS
FAIRVIEW MEMORIAL PARK CEMETERY
FULLROY PARK
CRESTVIEW PARK
MAYWOOD SPORTSMAN'S CLUB
ELM LAWN MAUSOLEUM & CEMETERY
ARLINGTON CEMETERY
CENTER POINT RECREATION & PRESERVE
R11E
R12E
A
B
C
D
E
1
2
3
4
5
6
7

SEE B MAP
SEE 2973 MAP
SEE 3028 MAP

1:24,000
1 in. = 2000 ft.
0 0.25 0.5
miles

SEE 2917 MAP

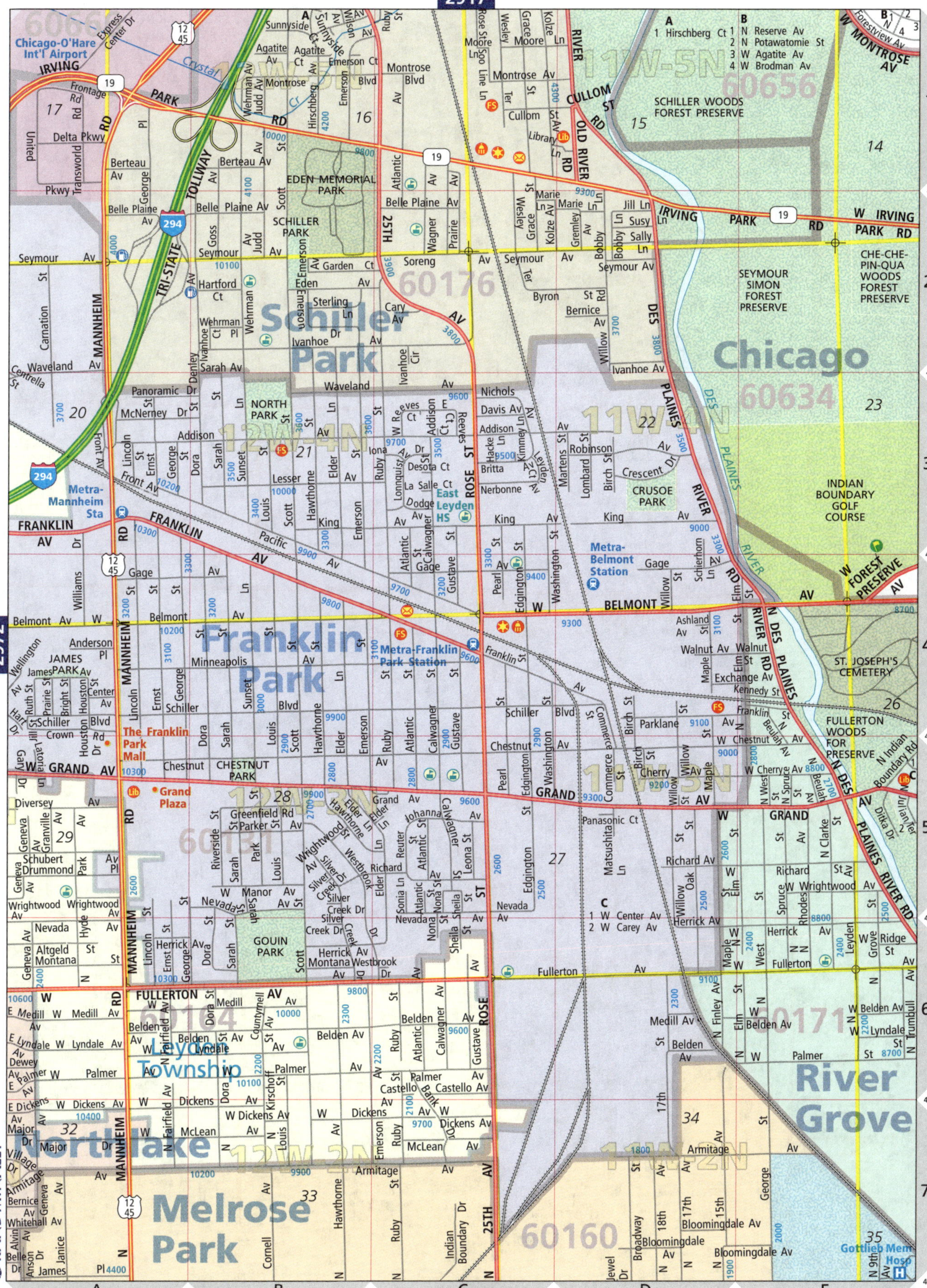

Chicago-O'Hare Int'l Airport
Schiller Park
60176
Franklin Park
60131
Chicago
60634
60656
Schiller Woods Forest Preserve
Seymour Simon Forest Preserve
Che-Che-Pin-Qua Woods Forest Preserve
Indian Boundary Golf Course
St. Joseph's Cemetery
Fullerton Woods For Preserve
Eden Memorial Park
Schiller Park
North Park
Crusoe Park
Chestnut Park
Gouin Park
Metra-Mannheim Sta
Metra-Belmont Station
Metra-Franklin Park Station
East Leyden HS
The Franklin Park Mall
Grand Plaza
Leyden Township
Northlake
60164
Melrose Park
60160
River Grove
60171
Gottlieb Mem Hosp
Mannheim Rd
Irving Park Rd
Tri-State Tollway
Franklin Av
Belmont Av
Grand Av
Fullerton Av
Des Plaines River Rd
25th Av
Rose St
11W-5N
12W-4N
11W-4N
12W-3N
11W-3N
12W-2N
11W-2N
RAND McNALLY

SEE 2972 MAP
SEE 2974 MAP
SEE 3029 MAP

1:24,000
1 in. = 2000 ft.
0 0.25 0.5
miles

SEE 2918 MAP

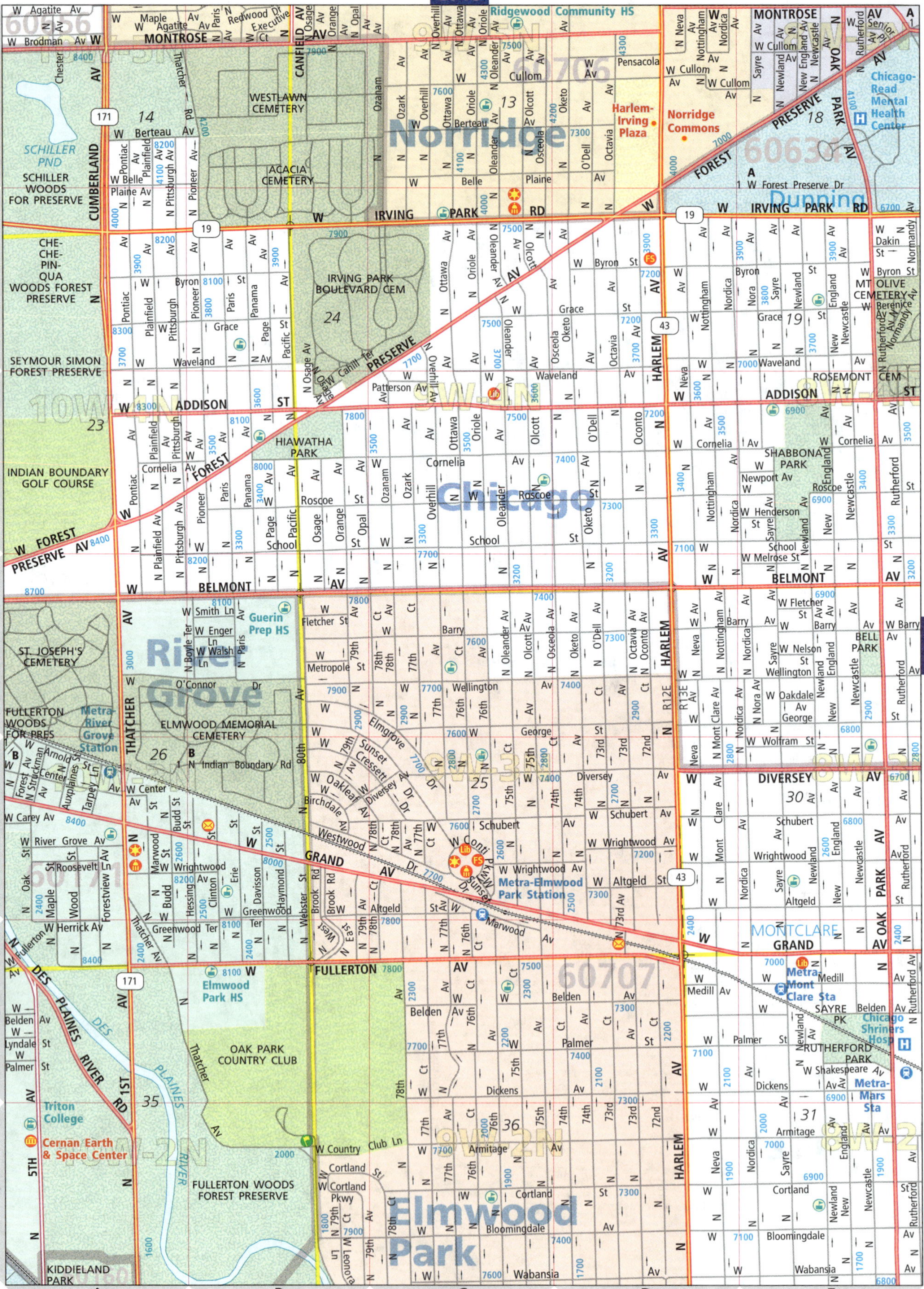
MONTROSE
IRVING PARK RD
ADDISON ST
BELMONT AV
DIVERSEY AV
GRAND AV
FULLERTON AV
CUMBERLAND AV
THATCHER AV
HARLEM AV
OAK PARK AV
CANFIELD AV
FOREST PRESERVE AV
DES PLAINES RIVER RD
Norridge
Chicago
River Grove
Elmwood Park
Dunning
MONTCLARE
SCHILLER POND
SCHILLER WOODS FOR PRESERVE
CHE-CHE-PIN-QUA WOODS FOREST PRESERVE
SEYMOUR SIMON FOREST PRESERVE
INDIAN BOUNDARY GOLF COURSE
WESTLAWN CEMETERY
ACACIA CEMETERY
IRVING PARK BOULEVARD CEM
HIAWATHA PARK
ST. JOSEPH'S CEMETERY
FULLERTON WOODS FOR PRES
ELMWOOD MEMORIAL CEMETERY
OAK PARK COUNTRY CLUB
FULLERTON WOODS FOREST PRESERVE
KIDDIELAND PARK
Triton College
Cernan Earth & Space Center
Guerin Prep HS
Elmwood Park HS
Ridgewood Community HS
Harlem-Irving Plaza
Norridge Commons
Chicago-Read Mental Health Center
MT OLIVE CEMETERY
ROSEMONT CEM
SHABBONA PARK
BELL PARK
RUTHERFORD SAYRE PK
Chicago Shriners Hosp
Metra-River Grove Station
Metra-Elmwood Park Station
Metra-Mont Clare Sta
Metra-Mars Sta
60656
60706
60634
60171
60707
1
2
3
4
5
6
7
A
B
C
D
E
41°57'40"
41°57'14"
41°56'48"
41°56'21"
41°55'55"
41°55'29"
41°55'03"
41°54'37"
87°50'31"
87°49'56"
87°49'21"
87°48'47"
87°48'12"
87°47'37"
RAND McNALLY

SEE 2973 MAP
SEE 2975 MAP
SEE 3030 MAP

1:24,000
1 in. = 2000 ft.
0 0.25 0.5
miles

SEE 2919 MAP

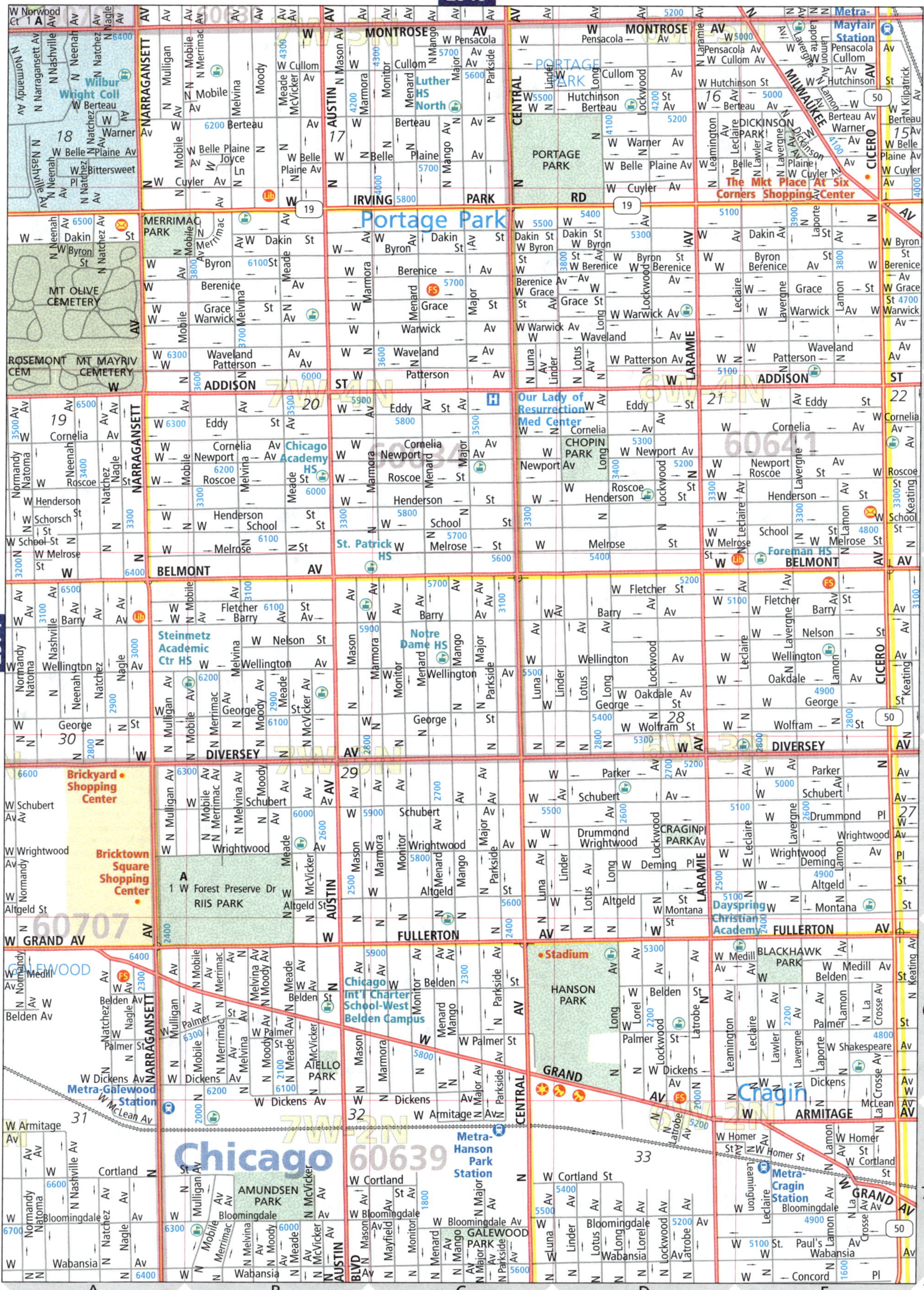

SEE 2974 MAP

SEE 2976 MAP

SEE 3031 MAP

RAND McNALLY

1:24,000
1 in. = 2000 ft.
0 0.25 0.5
miles

SEE 2920 MAP

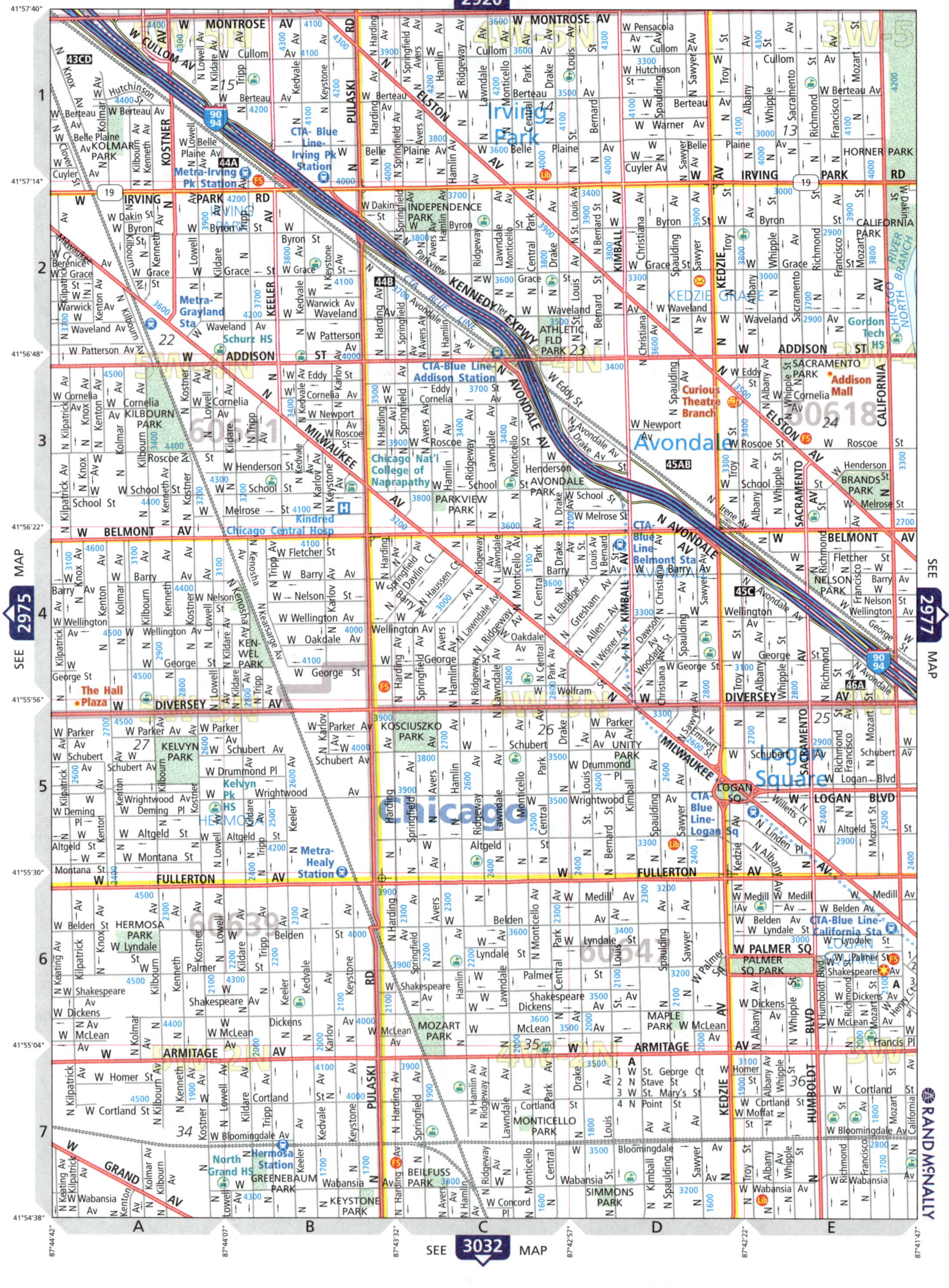

SEE 2975 MAP

SEE 2977 MAP

SEE 3032 MAP

1:24,000
1 in. = 2000 ft.
0 0.25 0.5
miles

SEE 2921 MAP

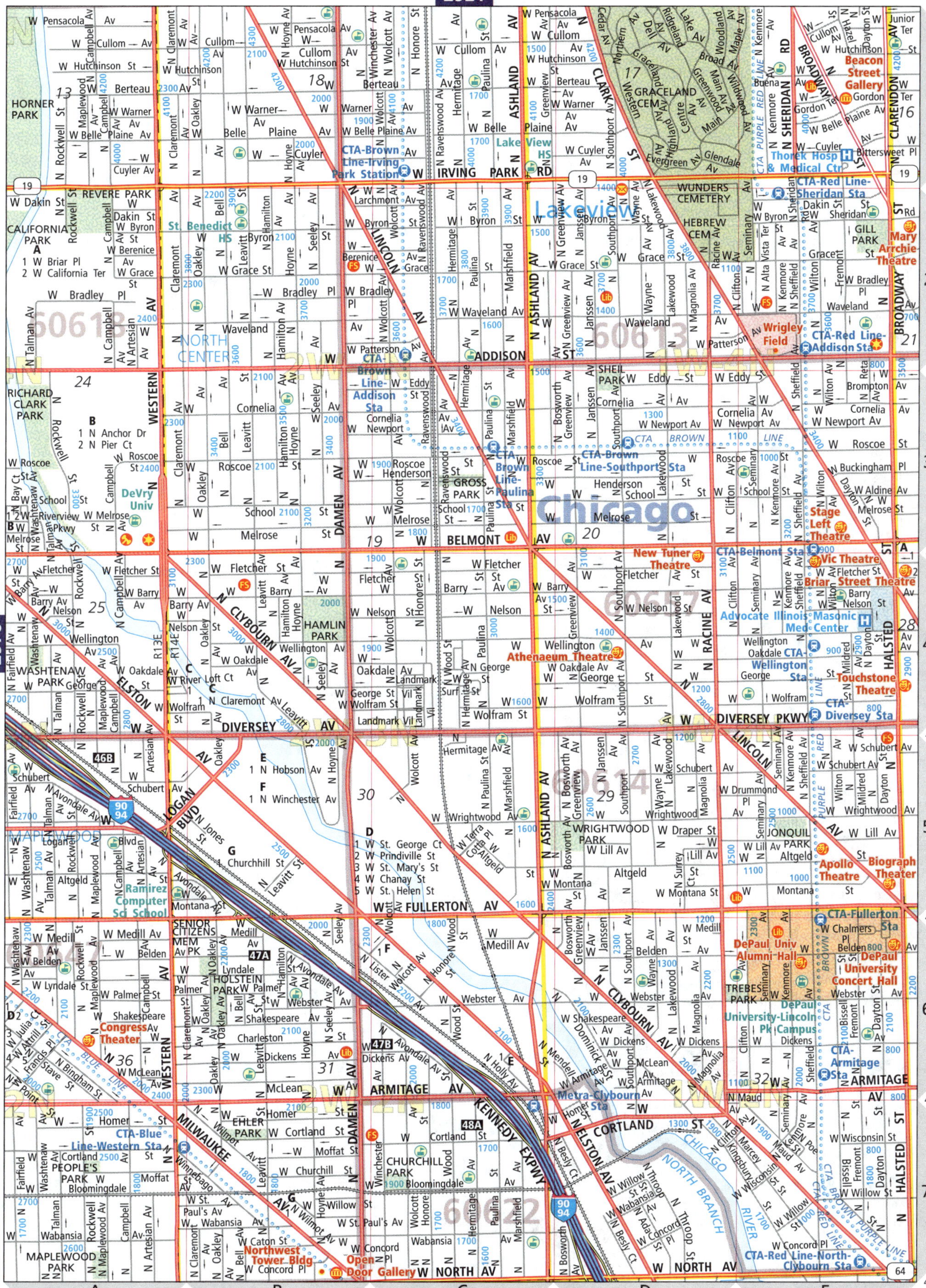

SEE 2976 MAP
SEE 2978 MAP
SEE 3033 MAP

1:24,000
1 in. = 2000 ft.
0 0.25 0.5
miles

1:24,000
1 in. = 2000 ft.
0 0.25 0.5
miles

SEE 2972 MAP

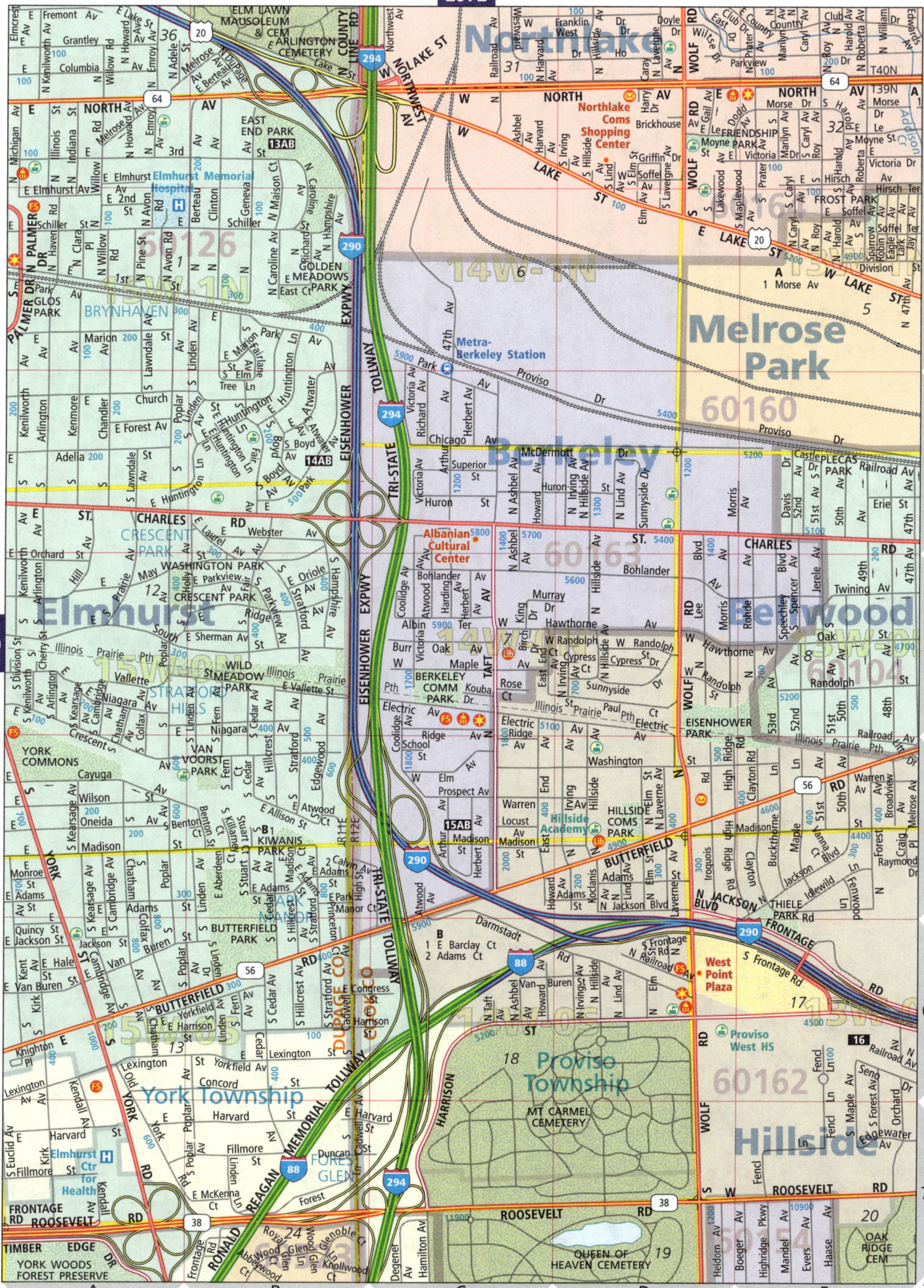
Northlake
Melrose Park
60160
Berkeley
60163
Bellwood
60104
Elmhurst
60126
Hillside
60162
York Township
Proviso Township
ELM LAWN MAUSOLEUM & CEM
ARLINGTON CEMETERY
Elmhurst Memorial Hospital
Northlake Coms Shopping Center
Metra-Berkeley Station
Albanian Cultural Center
BERKELEY COMM PARK
EISENHOWER PARK
Hillside Academy
HILLSIDE COMS PARK
West Point Plaza
Proviso West HS
MT CARMEL CEMETERY
QUEEN OF HEAVEN CEMETERY
OAK RIDGE CEM
YORK WOODS FOREST PRESERVE
Elmhurst Ctr for Health
YORK COMMONS
FOREST GLEN
BRYNHAVEN
GOLDEN MEADOWS PARK
EAST END PARK
CRESCENT PARK
WASHINGTON PARK
WILD MEADOW PARK
STRATFORD HILLS
VAN VOORST PARK
KIWANIS PARK
BUTTERFIELD PARK
FRIENDSHIP PARK
FROST PARK
PLECAS PARK
THIELE PARK
EISENHOWER EXPWY
TRI-STATE TOLLWAY
REAGAN MEMORIAL TOLLWAY
NORTH AV
LAKE ST
ROOSEVELT RD
BUTTERFIELD RD
CHARLES ST
WOLF RD
YORK RD
HARRISON
COUNTY LINE RD
14W-1N
15W-1N
14W-0N
15W-0N
14W-0S
15W-0S
41°54'37"
41°54'11"
41°53'45"
41°53'18"
41°52'52"
41°52'26"
41°52'00"
41°51'34"
87°56'20"
87°55'45"
87°55'10"
87°54'35"
87°54'00"
87°53'25"
A
B
C
D
E
1
2
3
4
5
6
7

SEE B MAP

SEE 3029 MAP

SEE 3086 MAP

1:24,000
1 in. = 2000 ft.
0 0.25 0.5
miles

SEE 2973 MAP

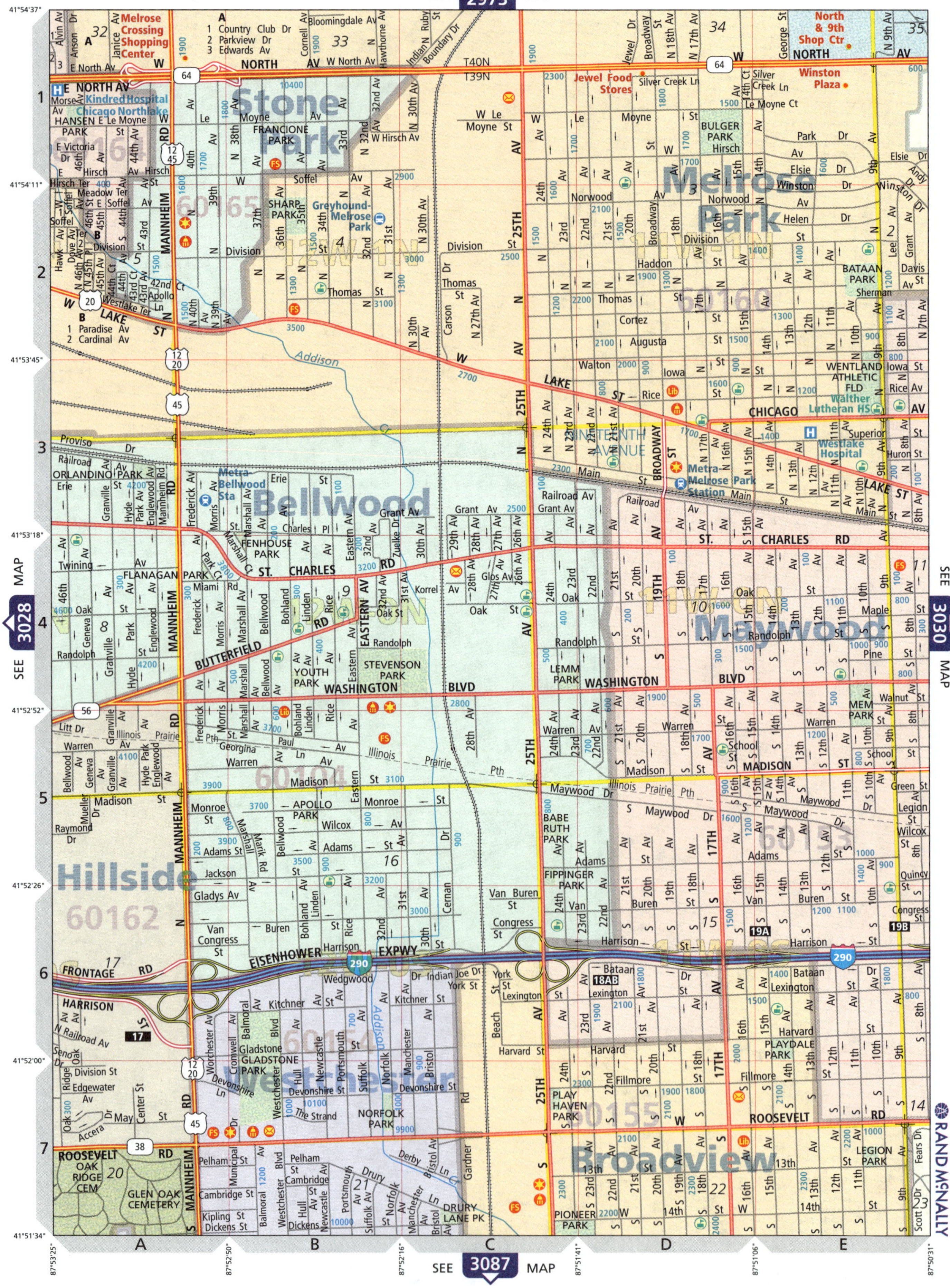

SEE 3028 MAP
SEE 3030 MAP
SEE 3087 MAP

1:24,000
1 in. = 2000 ft.
0 0.25 0.5
miles

SEE 2974 MAP

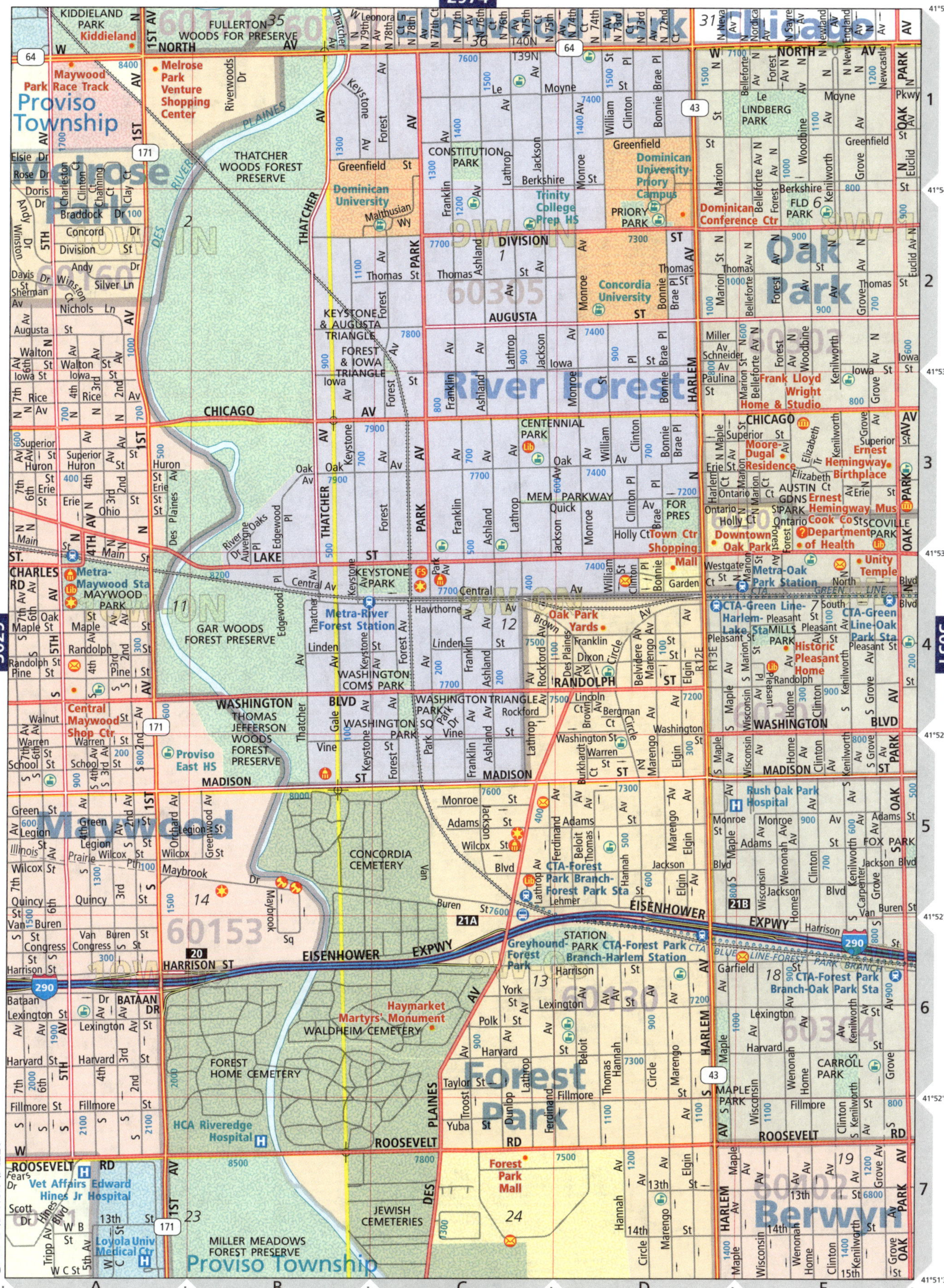

SEE 3029 MAP

SEE 3031 MAP

SEE 3088 MAP

1:24,000
1 in. = 2000 ft.
0 0.25 0.5
miles

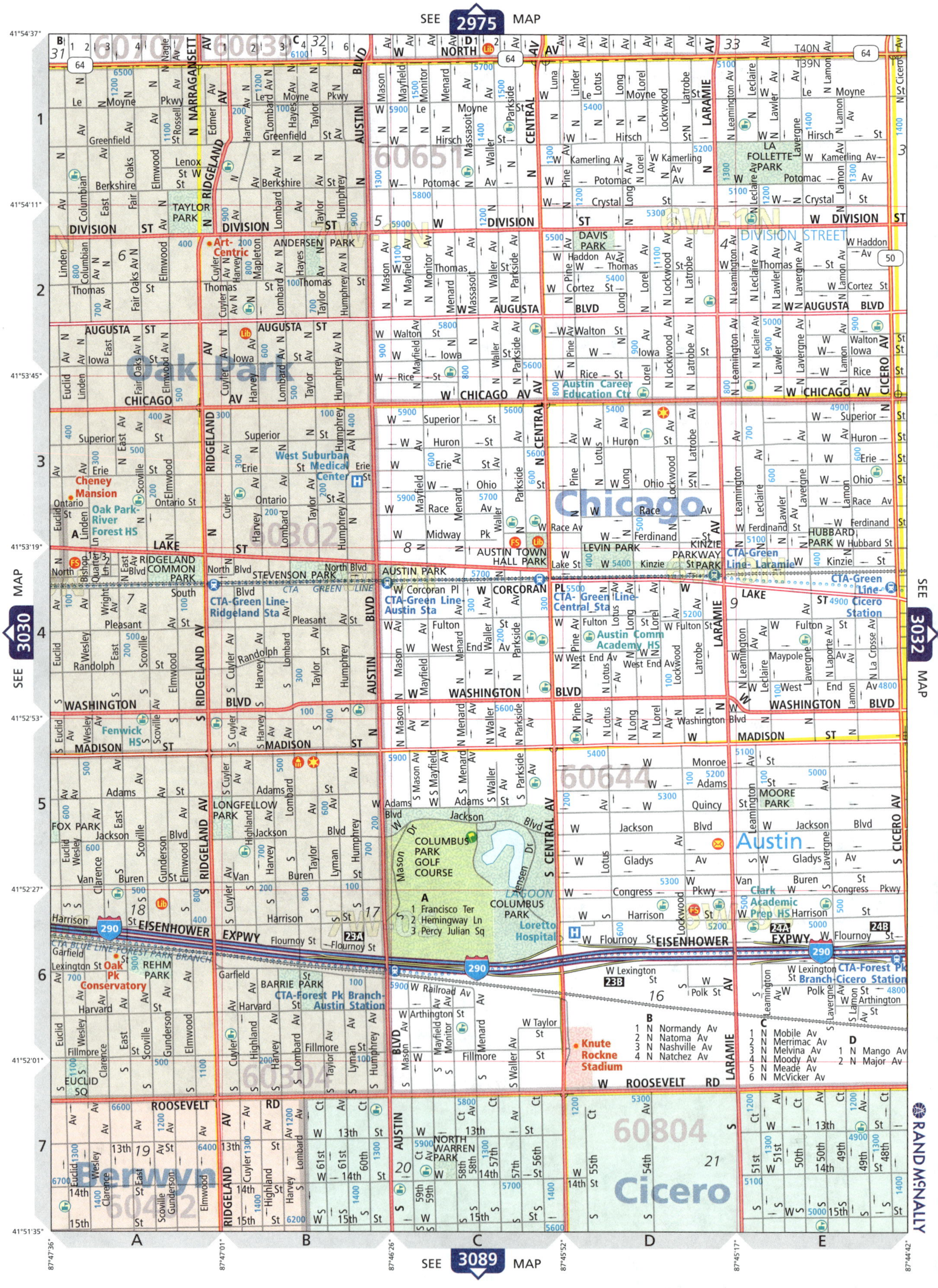
SEE 2975 MAP
SEE 3030 MAP
SEE 3032 MAP
SEE 3089 MAP
Oak Park
Chicago
Austin
Berwyn
Cicero
60707
60639
60651
60302
60644
60304
60804
60402
N NARRAGANSETT AV
N RIDGELAND AV
AUSTIN BLVD
N CENTRAL AV
LARAMIE AV
CICERO AV
NORTH AV
DIVISION ST
AUGUSTA BLVD
CHICAGO AV
LAKE ST
WASHINGTON BLVD
MADISON ST
EISENHOWER EXPWY
ROOSEVELT RD
TAYLOR PARK
ANDERSEN PARK
DAVIS PARK
LA FOLLETTE PARK
DIVISION STREET
Art-Centric
West Suburban Medical Center
Cheney Mansion
Oak Park-River Forest HS
RIDGELAND COMMON PARK
STEVENSON PARK
AUSTIN PARK
AUSTIN TOWN HALL PARK
LEVIN PARK
PARKWAY PARK
HUBBARD PARK
KINZIE
CTA-Green Line-Ridgeland Sta
CTA-Green Line-Austin Sta
CTA-Green Line-Central Sta
CTA-Green Line-Laramie
CTA-Green Line-Cicero Station
Austin Career Education Ctr
Austin Comm Academy HS
Fenwick HS
FOX PARK
LONGFELLOW PARK
COLUMBUS PARK GOLF COURSE
COLUMBUS PARK
LAGOON
Loretto Hospital
MOORE PARK
Clark Academic Prep HS
REHM PARK
Oak Pk Conservatory
BARRIE PARK
CTA-Forest Pk Branch-Austin Station
CTA-Forest Pk Branch-Cicero Station
CTA BLUE LINE-FOREST PARK BRANCH
Knute Rockne Stadium
NORTH WARREN PARK
EUCLID SQ
A
1 Francisco Ter
2 Hemingway Ln
3 Percy Julian Sq
B
1 N Normandy Av
2 N Natoma Av
3 N Nashville Av
4 N Natchez Av
C
1 N Mobile Av
2 N Merrimac Av
3 N Melvina Av
4 N Moody Av
5 N Meade Av
6 N McVicker Av
D
1 N Mango Av
2 N Major Av
6W-1N
7W-0
T40N
T39N
41°54'37"
41°54'11"
41°53'45"
41°53'19"
41°52'53"
41°52'27"
41°52'01"
41°51'35"
87°47'36"
87°47'01"
87°46'26"
87°45'52"
87°45'17"
87°44'42"
A B C D E
1 2 3 4 5 6 7

1:24,000
1 in. = 2000 ft.
0 0.25 0.5
miles

SEE 2976 MAP

Chicago
Cicero
NORTH AV
DIVISION ST
AUGUSTA BLVD
CHICAGO AV
FRANKLIN BLVD
LAKE ST
WASHINGTON BLVD
WARREN BLVD
MADISON ST
JACKSON BLVD
VAN BUREN ST
CONGRESS PKWY
EISENHOWER EXPWY
ROOSEVELT RD
DOUGLAS BLVD
W OGDEN AV
GRAND AV
PULASKI RD
HAMLIN BLVD
INDEPENDENCE BLVD
CENTRAL PARK AV
CONSERVATORY DR
KEDZIE AV
SACRAMENTO BLVD
HUMBOLDT DR
KOSTNER AV
KILBOURN AV
CICERO AV
HUMBOLDT PARK
GARFIELD PARK
DOUGLAS PARK
LAGOON
Northwest Armory
Norwegian Amer Hospital
Orr HS
Hartgrove Hosp
Sacred Heart Hospital
Garfield Park Conservatory
CTA- Green Line-Conservatory
Westinghouse Achievement Ctr
Carroll Metra-Kedzie Station
CTA- Green Line-LAKE Pulaski Sta
CTA-Green Line-Kedzie Sta
CTA- Green Line-California Sta
Garfield Hosp
ACT Charter HS
Academy of Scholastic Achievement
Providence St. Mel School
Marshall Metro HS
CTA-For Pk Branch-Kedzie-Homan Station
Advocate Bethany Hosp
CTA-Forest Park Branch-Pulaski Station
Crossroads Adult Transition Ctr
Manley Career Academy HS
North Lawndale Adult Transition Ctr
Collins HS
60651
60624
60612
60644
60623
60804
290
64
50
41°54'38"
41°54'12"
41°53'45"
41°53'19"
41°52'53"
41°52'27"
41°52'01"
41°51'35"
87°44'42"
87°44'07"
87°43'32"
87°42'57"
87°42'22"
87°41'47"
RAND McNALLY

SEE 3031 MAP
SEE 3033 MAP
SEE 3090 MAP

1:24,000
1 in. = 2000 ft.
0 0.25 0.5
miles

SEE 2977 MAP

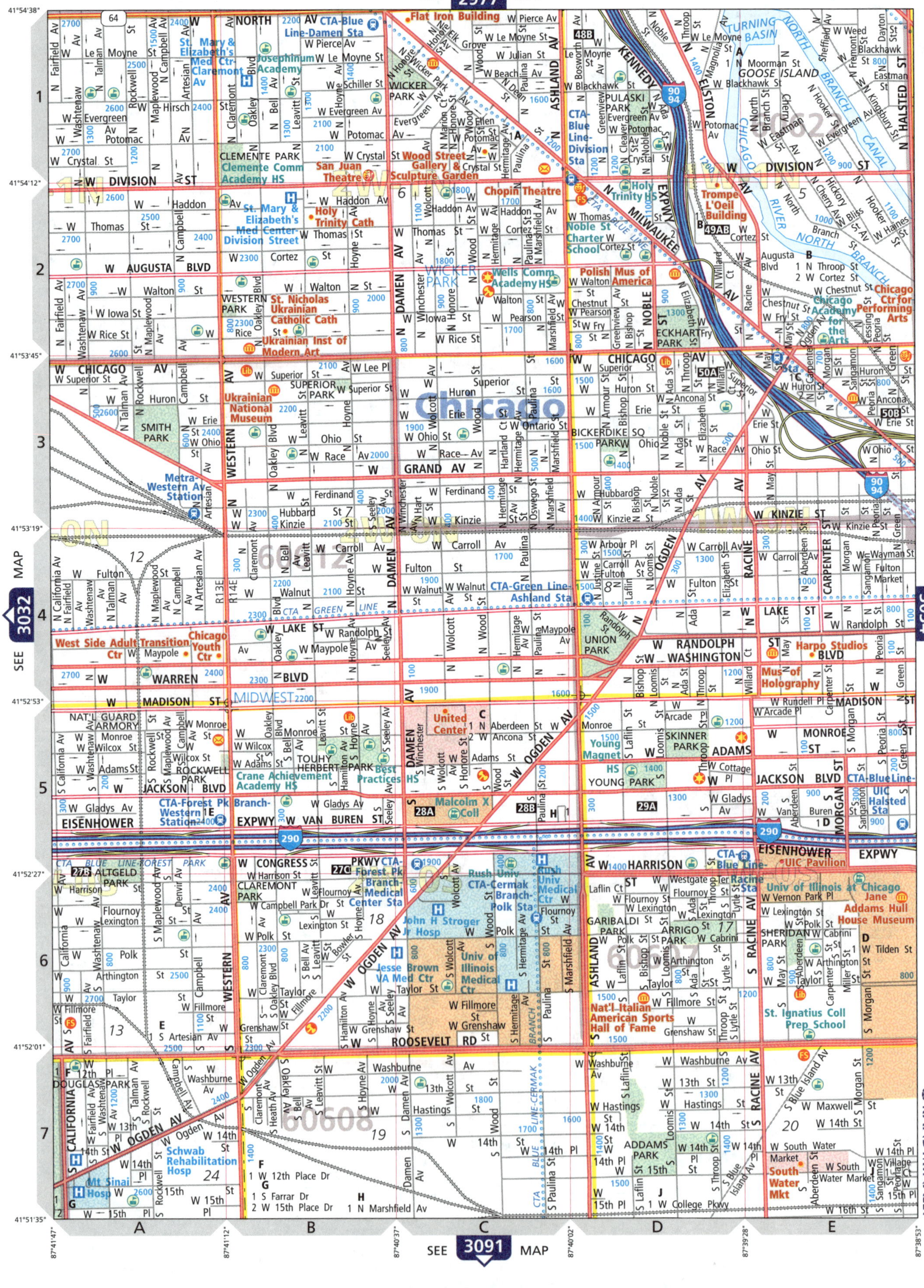
Chicago
W NORTH AV
W DIVISION ST
W AUGUSTA BLVD
W CHICAGO AV
W GRAND AV
W KINZIE ST
W LAKE ST
W RANDOLPH ST
W WARREN BLVD
W MADISON ST
JACKSON BLVD
EISENHOWER EXPWY
CONGRESS PKWY
W HARRISON ST
ROOSEVELT RD
KENNEDY EXPWY
MILWAUKEE AV
OGDEN AV
N WESTERN AV
N DAMEN AV
N ASHLAND AV
RACINE
N HALSTED ST
S CALIFORNIA AV
GOOSE ISLAND
NORTH BRANCH CHICAGO RIVER
Flat Iron Building
Wood Street Gallery & Sculpture Garden
San Juan Theatre
Chopin Theatre
Holy Trinity Cath
St. Mary & Elizabeth's Med Center Division Street
St. Nicholas Ukrainian Catholic Cath
Ukrainian Inst of Modern Art
Ukrainian National Museum
Polish Mus of America
Trompe L'Oeil Building
Chicago Ctr for Performing Arts
Harpo Studios
Mus of Holography
United Center
Malcolm X Coll
Rush Univ Medical Ctr
John H Stroger Jr Hosp
Jesse Brown VA Med Ctr
Univ of Illinois Medical Ctr
Univ of Illinois at Chicago
Jane Addams Hull House Museum
UIC Pavilion
Nat'l Italian American Sports Hall of Fame
St. Ignatius Coll Prep School
Schwab Rehabilitation Hosp
Mt Sinai Hosp
South Water Mkt
West Side Adult Transition Ctr
Chicago Youth Ctr
Crane Achievement Academy HS
Wells Comm Academy HS
Noble St Charter School
Clemente Comm Academy HS
Chicago Academy for the Arts
Young Magnet HS
Best Practices HS
CTA-Blue Line-Damen Sta
CTA-Blue Line-Division Sta
CTA-Green Line-Ashland Sta
CTA-Forest Pk Branch-Western Station
CTA-Cermak Branch-Polk Sta
CTA-Blue Line-Halsted Sta
Metra-Western Av Station
SMITH PARK
WICKER PARK
ECKHART PARK
UNION PARK
SKINNER PARK
ALTGELD PARK
ARRIGO PARK
ADAMS PARK
DOUGLAS PARK
60622
60612
60607
60608

SEE 3032 MAP
SEE 3034 MAP
SEE 3091 MAP

RAND McNALLY

1:24,000
1 in. = 2000 ft.
0 0.25 0.5
miles

SEE 2978 MAP

SEE 3033 MAP
SEE B MAP
SEE 3092 MAP

1:24,000
1 in. = 2000 ft.
0 0.25 0.5
miles

SEE 3028 MAP

SEE MAP B 4
SEE 3087 MAP
SEE 3146 MAP

1:24,000
1 in. = 2000 ft.
0 0.25 0.5
miles

SEE 3029 MAP

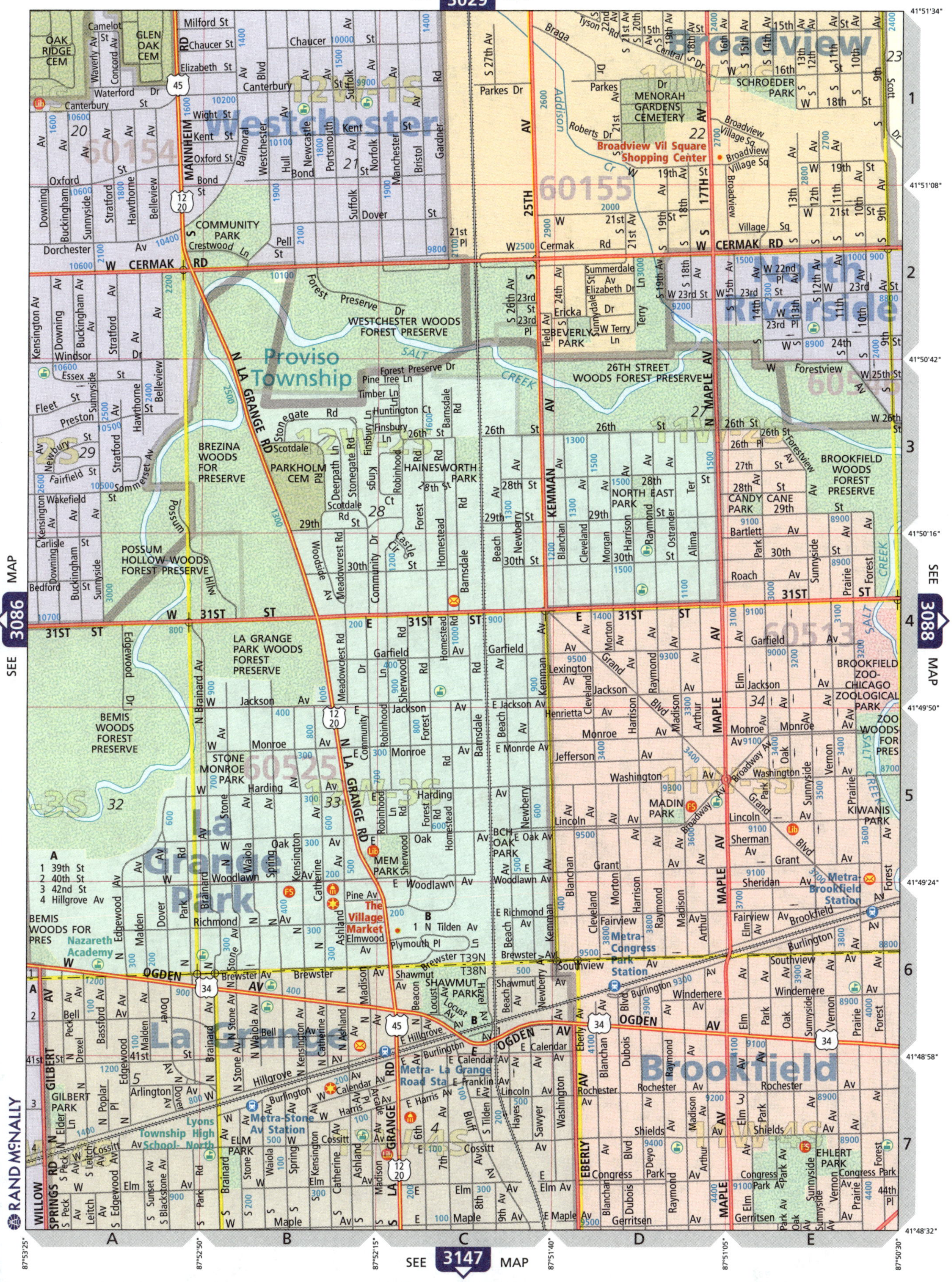
Westchester
Broadview
North Riverside
La Grange Park
La Grange
Brookfield
Proviso Township
60154
60155
60525
60513
12W-1S
11W-1S
12W-2S
11W-2S
12W-3S
11W-3S
12W-4S
11W-4S
OAK RIDGE CEM
GLEN OAK CEM
MENORAH GARDENS CEMETERY
SCHROEDER PARK
Broadview Vil Square Shopping Center
COMMUNITY PARK
WESTCHESTER WOODS FOREST PRESERVE
26TH STREET WOODS FOREST PRESERVE
BEVERLY PARK
BREZINA WOODS FOR PRESERVE
PARKHOLM CEM
HAINESWORTH PARK
NORTH EAST PARK
CANDY CANE PARK
BROOKFIELD WOODS FOREST PRESERVE
POSSUM HOLLOW WOODS FOREST PRESERVE
LA GRANGE PARK WOODS FOREST PRESERVE
BEMIS WOODS FOREST PRESERVE
BEMIS WOODS FOR PRES
STONE MONROE PARK
MEM PARK
BCH OAK PARK
MADIN PARK
KIWANIS PARK
BROOKFIELD ZOO-CHICAGO ZOOLOGICAL PARK
ZOO WOODS FOR PRES
SHAWMUT PARK
GILBERT PARK
ELM PARK
EHLERT PARK
The Village Market
Nazareth Academy
Lyons Township High School- North
Metra- La Grange Road Sta
Metra- Stone Av Station
Metra- Congress Park Station
Metra- Brookfield Station
SALT CREEK
Addison Cr
W CERMAK RD
W 31ST ST
OGDEN AV
MANNHEIM RD
N LA GRANGE RD
25TH AV
17TH AV
KEMMAN AV
N MAPLE AV
GILBERT AV
WILLOW SPRINGS RD
EBERLY AV
A
1 39th St
2 40th St
3 42nd St
4 Hillgrove Av
1 N Tilden Av
SEE 3086 MAP
SEE 3088 MAP
SEE 3147 MAP
A B C D E
1 2 3 4 5 6 7
41°51'34"
41°51'08"
41°50'42"
41°50'16"
41°49'50"
41°49'24"
41°48'58"
41°48'32"
87°53'25"
87°52'50"
87°52'15"
87°51'40"
87°51'05"
87°50'30"
RAND McNALLY

SEE 3147 MAP

1:24,000
1 in. = 2000 ft.
0 0.25 0.5
miles

SEE 3030 MAP

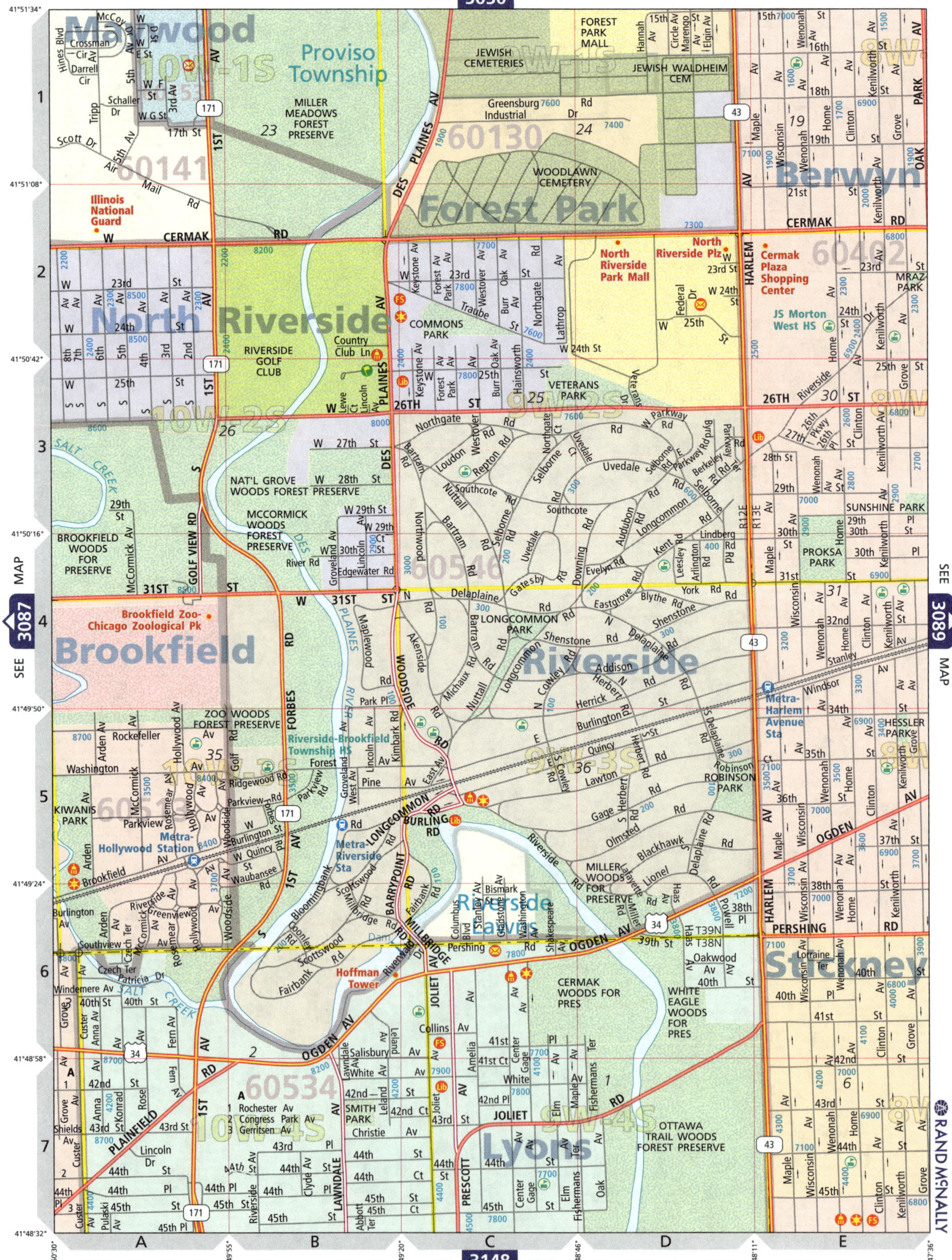
Maywood
Proviso Township
MILLER MEADOWS FOREST PRESERVE
JEWISH CEMETERIES
FOREST PARK MALL
JEWISH WALDHEIM CEM
Greensburg Industrial Dr
WOODLAWN CEMETERY
Forest Park
60130
60141
Berwyn
Illinois National Guard
CERMAK RD
North Riverside
North Riverside Park Mall
North Riverside Plz
Cermak Plaza Shopping Center
60402
MRAZ PARK
JS Morton West HS
COMMONS PARK
RIVERSIDE GOLF CLUB
Country Club Ln
VETERANS PARK
26TH ST
NAT'L GROVE WOODS FOREST PRESERVE
MCCORMICK WOODS FOREST PRESERVE
BROOKFIELD WOODS FOR PRESERVE
SALT CREEK
DES PLAINES RIVER
SUNSHINE PARK
PROKSA PARK
60546
31ST ST
Brookfield Zoo-Chicago Zoological Pk
Brookfield
LONGCOMMON PARK
Riverside
ZOO WOODS FOREST PRESERVE
Riverside-Brookfield Township HS
Metra-Harlem Avenue Sta
HESSLER PARK
ROBINSON PARK
KIWANIS PARK
60513
Metra-Hollywood Station
Metra-Riverside Sta
Riverside Lawns
MILLER WOODS FOR PRESERVE
OGDEN AV
PERSHING RD
Stickney
Hoffman Tower
CERMAK WOODS FOR PRES
WHITE EAGLE WOODS FOR PRES
60534
SMITH PARK
1 Rochester Av
2 Congress Park Av
3 Gerritsen Av
Lyons
OTTAWA TRAIL WOODS FOREST PRESERVE
JOLIET RD
HARLEM AV
DES PLAINES AV
1ST AV
FORBES RD
PLAINFIELD RD
RAND McNALLY

SEE 3087 MAP

SEE 3089 MAP

SEE 3148 MAP

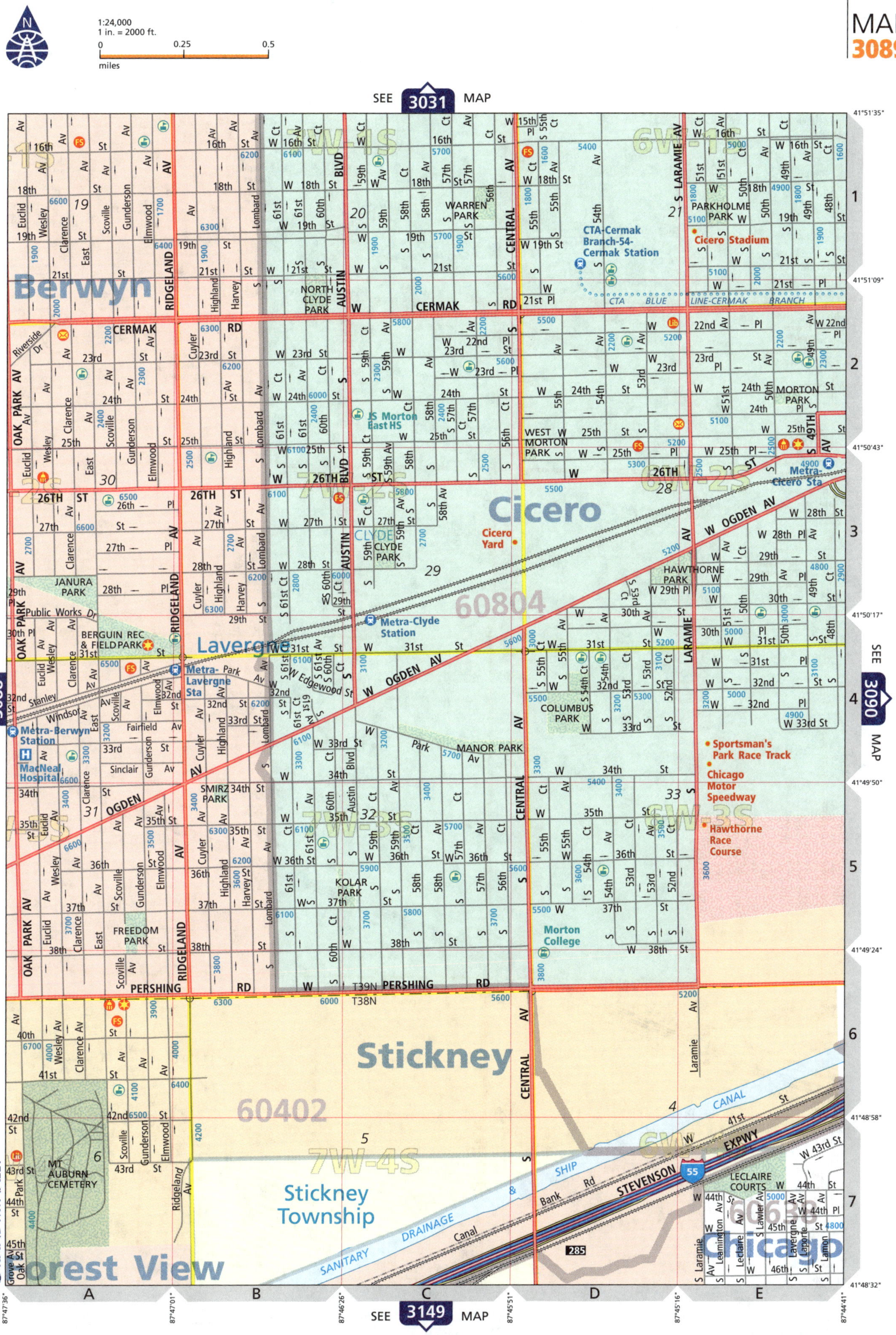
1:24,000
1 in. = 2000 ft.
0 0.25 0.5
miles
SEE 3031 MAP
SEE 3149 MAP
SEE MAP 3088
SEE MAP 3090
Berwyn
Cicero
Lavergne
Stickney
Stickney Township
Forest View
Chicago
60804
60402
60638
CERMAK RD
26TH ST
PERSHING RD
W OGDEN AV
OGDEN
OAK PARK AV
RIDGELAND AV
AUSTIN BLVD
CENTRAL AV
S LARAMIE AV
49TH AV
STEVENSON EXPWY
55
SANITARY & SHIP CANAL
DRAINAGE
Canal Bank Rd
CTA BLUE LINE-CERMAK BRANCH
CTA-Cermak Branch-54-Cermak Station
Metra-Cicero Sta
Metra-Clyde Station
Metra-Park Lavergne Sta
Metra-Berwyn Station
MacNeal Hospital
Cicero Stadium
Cicero Yard
JS Morton East HS
Morton College
Sportsman's Park Race Track
Chicago Motor Speedway
Hawthorne Race Course
MT AUBURN CEMETERY
WARREN PARK
PARKHOLME PARK
NORTH CLYDE PARK
CLYDE PARK
WEST MORTON PARK
MORTON PARK
HAWTHORNE PARK
JANURA PARK
BERGUIN REC & FIELD PARK
COLUMBUS PARK
MANOR PARK
SMIRZ PARK
KOLAR PARK
FREEDOM PARK
LECLAIRE COURTS
Public Works Dr
Riverside Dr
T39N
T38N
7W-1S
6W-1S
7W-2S
6W-2S
7W-3S
6W-3S
7W-4S
1 2 3 4 5 6 7
A B C D E
41°51'35"
41°51'09"
41°50'43"
41°50'17"
41°49'50"
41°49'24"
41°48'58"
41°48'32"
87°47'36"
87°47'01"
87°46'26"
87°45'51"
87°45'16"
87°44'41"
RAND McNALLY

1:24,000
1 in. = 2000 ft.
0 0.25 0.5
miles

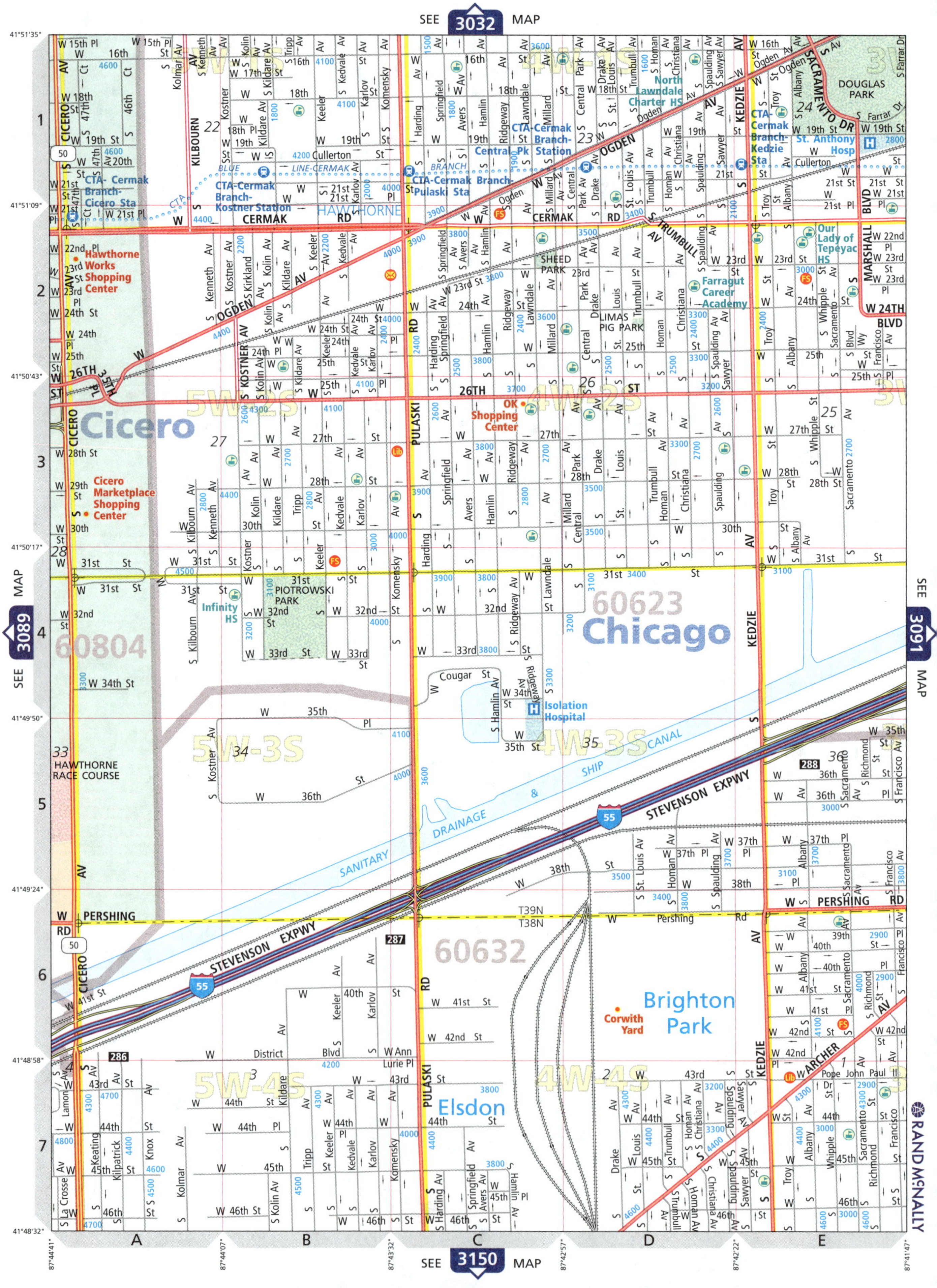
SEE 3032 MAP
SEE 3089 MAP
SEE 3091 MAP
SEE 3150 MAP
Cicero
Chicago
60804
60623
60632
HAWTHORNE
Hawthorne Works Shopping Center
Cicero Marketplace Shopping Center
CTA-Cermak Branch-Cicero Sta
CTA-Cermak Branch-Kostner Station
CTA-Cermak Branch-Pulaski Sta
CTA-Cermak Branch-Central Pk Station
CTA-Cermak Branch-Kedzie Sta
BLUE LINE-CERMAK BRANCH
North Lawndale Charter HS
St. Anthony Hosp
DOUGLAS PARK
Our Lady of Tepeyac HS
Farragut Career Academy
SHEED PARK
LIMAS PIG PARK
OK Shopping Center
PIOTROWSKI PARK
Infinity HS
Isolation Hospital
HAWTHORNE RACE COURSE
SANITARY & SHIP CANAL
DRAINAGE
STEVENSON EXPWY
Corwith Yard
Brighton Park
Elsdon
CICERO AV
KILBOURN AV
KOSTNER AV
PULASKI RD
KEDZIE AV
SACRAMENTO DR
MARSHALL BLVD
W 24TH BLVD
CERMAK RD
OGDEN AV
26TH ST
W 26TH
35TH PL
W 31st St
W PERSHING RD
ARCHER AV
TRUMBULL AV
T39N
T38N
5W-1S
4W-1S
5W-2S
4W-2S
5W-3S
4W-3S
5W-4S
4W-4S
A
B
C
D
E
1
2
3
4
5
6
7
41°51'35"
41°51'09"
41°50'43"
41°50'17"
41°49'50"
41°49'24"
41°48'58"
41°48'32"
87°44'41"
87°44'07"
87°43'32"
87°42'57"
87°42'22"
87°41'47"

RAND McNALLY

1:24,000
1 in. = 2000 ft.
0 0.25 0.5
miles

SEE 3033 MAP

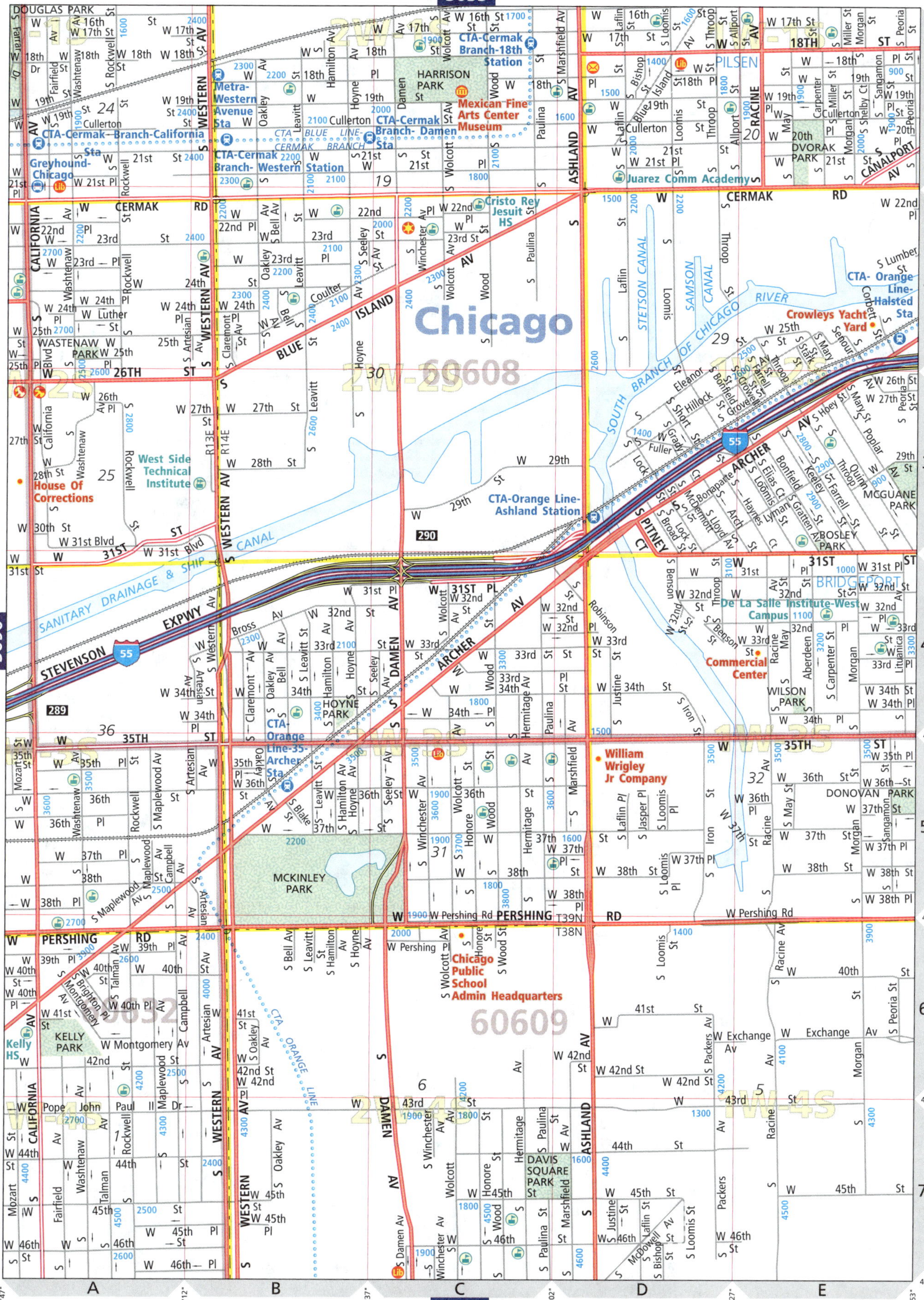

SEE 3090 MAP

SEE 3092 MAP

SEE 3151 MAP

1:24,000
1 in. = 2000 ft.
0 0.25 0.5
miles

SEE 3034 MAP

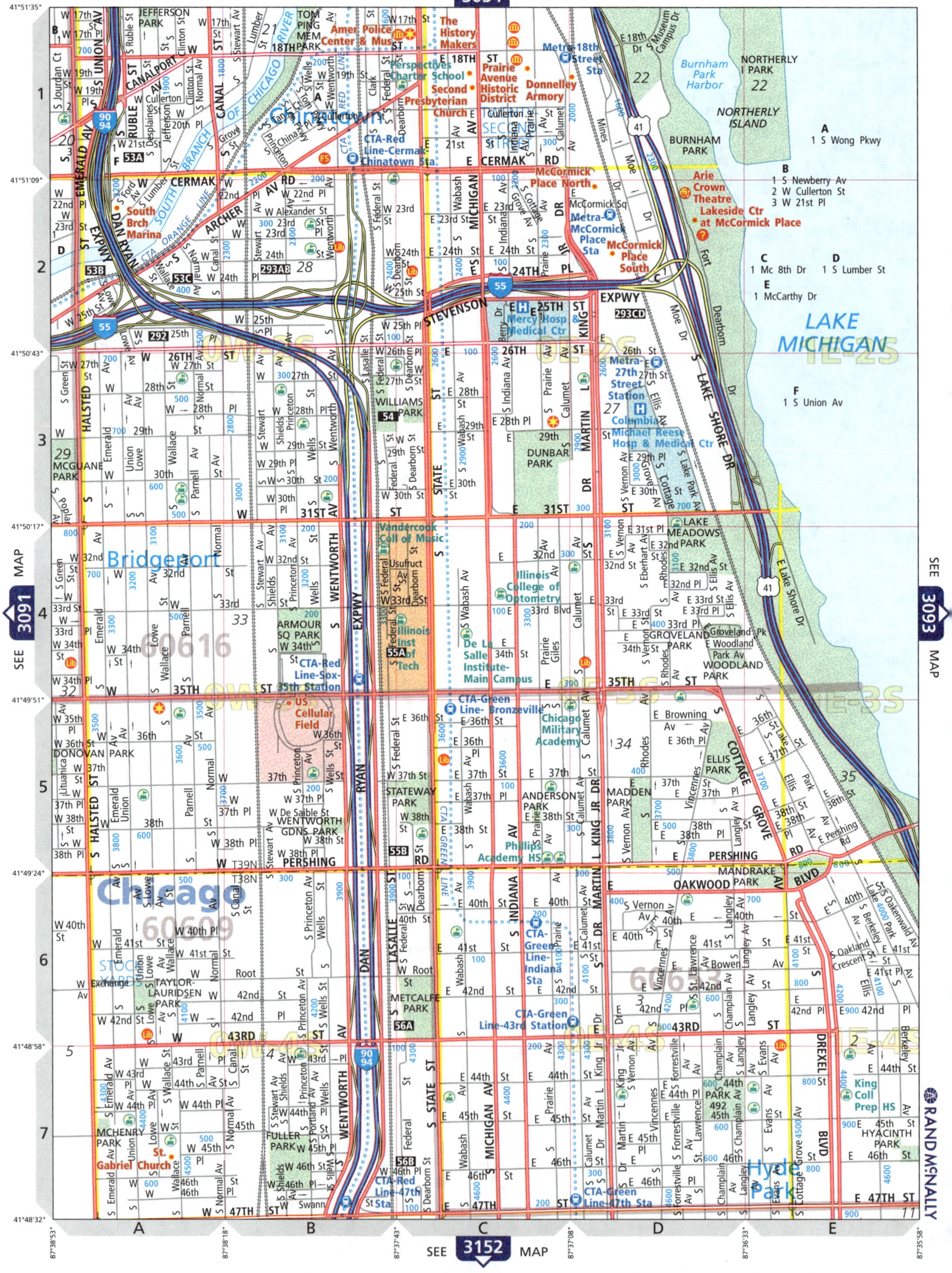
Chinatown
Bridgeport
Chicago
60616
60609
60653
Hyde Park
LAKE MICHIGAN
Burnham Park Harbor
NORTHERLY ISLAND
NORTHERLY I PARK
BURNHAM PARK
DAN RYAN EXPWY
STEVENSON EXPWY
S LAKE SHORE DR
CERMAK RD
ARCHER AV
31ST ST
35TH ST
PERSHING RD
43RD ST
47TH ST
HALSTED ST
WENTWORTH AV
STATE ST
MICHIGAN AV
INDIANA AV
MARTIN L KING JR DR
COTTAGE GROVE AV
DREXEL BLVD
OAKWOOD BLVD
The History Makers
Amer Police Center & Mus
Perspectives Charter School
Second Presbyterian Church
Prairie Avenue Historic District
Donnelley Armory
Metra-18th Street Sta
CTA-Red Line-Cermak-Chinatown Sta
McCormick Place North
Metra-McCormick Place Sta
McCormick Place South
Arie Crown Theatre
Lakeside Ctr at McCormick Place
Mercy Hosp & Medical Ctr
Metra-27th Street Station
Columbia Michael Reese Hosp & Medical Ctr
South Brch Marina
WILLIAMS PARK
MCGUANE PARK
DUNBAR PARK
LAKE MEADOWS PARK
Vandercook Coll of Music
Illinois College of Optometry
Illinois Inst of Tech
ARMOUR SQ PARK
CTA-Red Line-Sox-35th Station
US Cellular Field
De La Salle Institute-Main Campus
CTA-Green Line-Bronzeville
Chicago Military Academy
DONOVAN PARK
GROVELAND PARK
WOODLAND PARK
ELLIS PARK
STATEWAY PARK
ANDERSON PARK
MADDEN PARK
WENTWORTH GDNS PARK
Phillips Academy HS
MANDRAKE PARK
STOCK YARDS
TAYLOR-LAURIDSEN PARK
METCALFE PARK
CTA-Green Line-Indiana Sta
CTA-Green Line-43rd Station
MCHENRY PARK
St. Gabriel Church
FULLER PARK
CTA-Red Line-47th St Sta
CTA-Green Line-47th Sta
PARK 492
King Coll Prep HS
HYACINTH PARK
A 1 S Wong Pkwy
B 1 S Newberry Av
2 W Cullerton St
3 W 21st Pl
C 1 Mc 8th Dr
D 1 S Lumber St
E 1 McCarthy Dr
F 1 S Union Av
41°51'35"
41°51'09"
41°50'43"
41°50'17"
41°49'51"
41°49'24"
41°48'58"
41°48'32"
87°38'53"
87°38'18"
87°37'43"
87°37'08"
87°36'33"
87°35'58"

SEE 3091 MAP

SEE 3093 MAP

SEE 3152 MAP

1:24,000
1 in. = 2000 ft.
0 0.25 0.5
miles

SEE B MAP

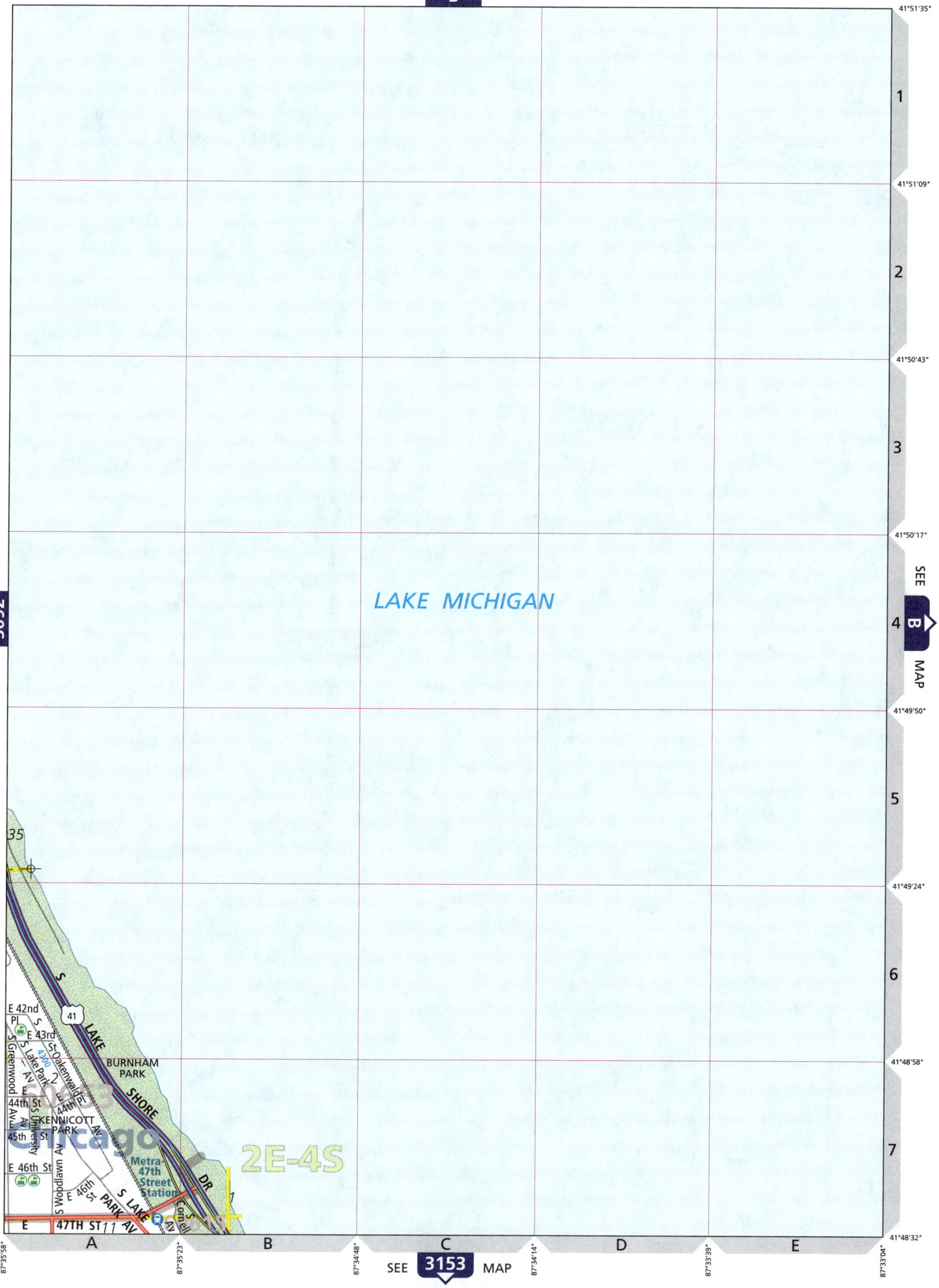

SEE 3092 MAP

SEE B MAP

SEE 3153 MAP

1:24,000
1 in. = 2000 ft.
0 0.25 0.5
miles

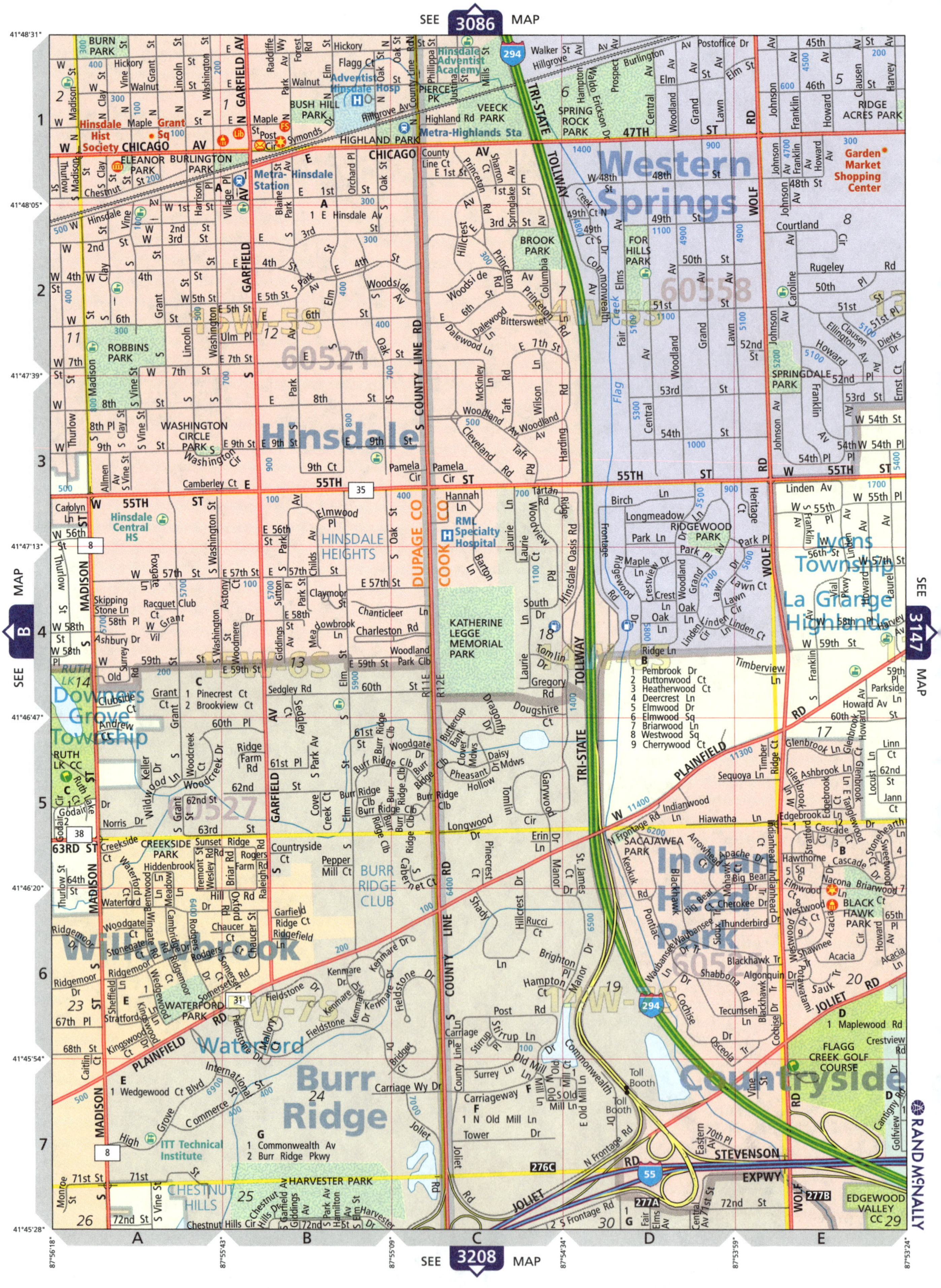
SEE 3086 MAP
SEE 3208 MAP
SEE B MAP
SEE 3147 MAP
Western Springs
60558
Hinsdale
60521
60527
Downers Grove Township
Willowbrook
Waterford
Burr Ridge
Indian Head Park
60525
Countryside
Lyons Township
La Grange Highlands
TRI-STATE TOLLWAY
294
55
STEVENSON EXPWY
JOLIET RD
PLAINFIELD RD
55TH ST
47TH ST
W CHICAGO AV
GARFIELD AV
MADISON ST
COUNTY LINE RD
WOLF RD
63RD ST
71st St
DUPAGE CO
COOK CO
Hinsdale Adventist Academy
Adventist Hinsdale Hosp
Metra-Highlands Sta
Metra-Hinsdale Station
Hinsdale Hist Society
Hinsdale Central HS
RML Specialty Hospital
KATHERINE LEGGE MEMORIAL PARK
BURR RIDGE CLUB
ITT Technical Institute
Garden Market Shopping Center
FLAGG CREEK GOLF COURSE
EDGEWOOD VALLEY CC
RUTH LK CC
HARVESTER PARK
CHESTNUT HILLS
ROBBINS PARK
WASHINGTON CIRCLE PARK
BROOK PARK
SPRING ROCK PARK
VEECK PARK
BUSH HILL PARK
HIGHLAND PARK
BURN PARK
ELEANOR PARK
BURLINGTON PARK
FOR HILLS PARK
RIDGE ACRES PARK
SPRINGDALE PARK
RIDGEWOOD PARK
CREEKSIDE PARK
WATERFORD PARK
SACAJAWEA PARK
BLACK HAWK PARK
HINSDALE HEIGHTS
1 Pembrook Dr
2 Buttonwood Ct
3 Heatherwood Ct
4 Deercrest Ln
5 Elmwood Dr
6 Elmwood Sq
7 Briarwood Ln
8 Westwood Sq
9 Cherrywood Ct
1 Pinecrest Ct
2 Brookview Ct
1 Wedgewood Ct
1 Commonwealth Av
2 Burr Ridge Pkwy
1 N Old Mill Ln
1 Maplewood Rd
RAND McNALLY

1:24,000
1 in. = 2000 ft.
0 0.25 0.5
miles

SEE 3087 MAP

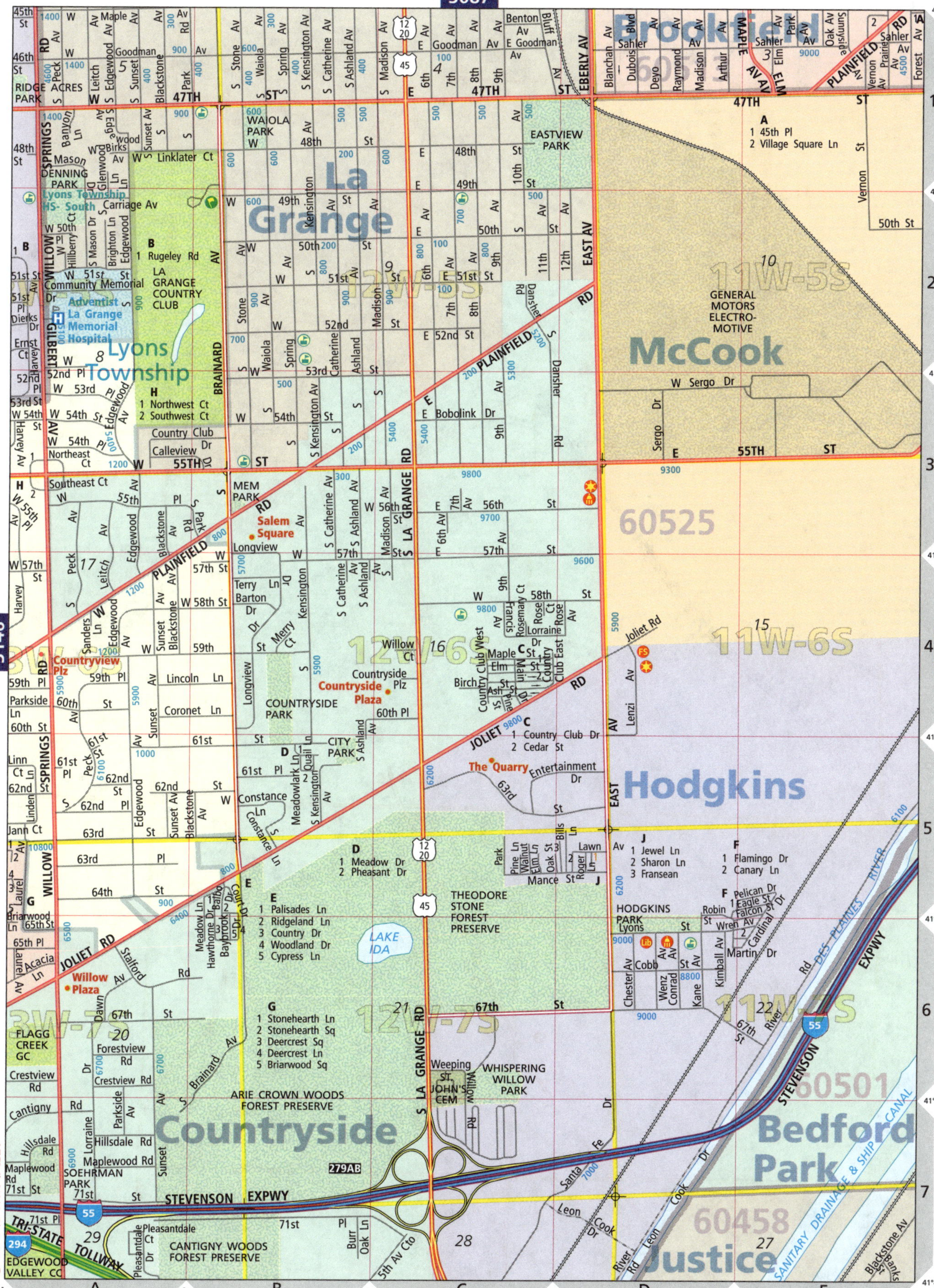

Brookfield
60513
La Grange
Lyons Township
McCook
GENERAL MOTORS ELECTRO-MOTIVE
60525
Hodgkins
Countryside
Bedford Park
Justice
60501
60458
12W-5S
11W-5S
12W-6S
11W-6S
12W-7S
11W-7S
LA GRANGE COUNTRY CLUB
Adventist La Grange Memorial Hospital
Lyons Township HS- South
EASTVIEW PARK
WAIOLA PARK
DENNING PARK
MEM PARK
Salem Square
Countryview Plz
Countryside Plaza
COUNTRYSIDE PARK
CITY PARK
The Quarry
THEODORE STONE FOREST PRESERVE
LAKE IDA
ARIE CROWN WOODS FOREST PRESERVE
WHISPERING WILLOW PARK
ST JOHN'S CEM
Willow Plaza
FLAGG CREEK GC
SOEHRMAN PARK
CANTIGNY WOODS FOREST PRESERVE
EDGEWOOD VALLEY CC
HODGKINS PARK
RIDGE ACRES PARK
47TH ST
55TH ST
67th St
PLAINFIELD RD
JOLIET RD
S LA GRANGE RD
EAST AV
WILLOW SPRINGS RD
BRAINARD AV
STEVENSON EXPWY
TRI-STATE TOLLWAY
DES PLAINES RIVER
SANITARY DRAINAGE & SHIP CANAL
279AB

SEE 3146 MAP
SEE 3148 MAP
SEE 3209 MAP

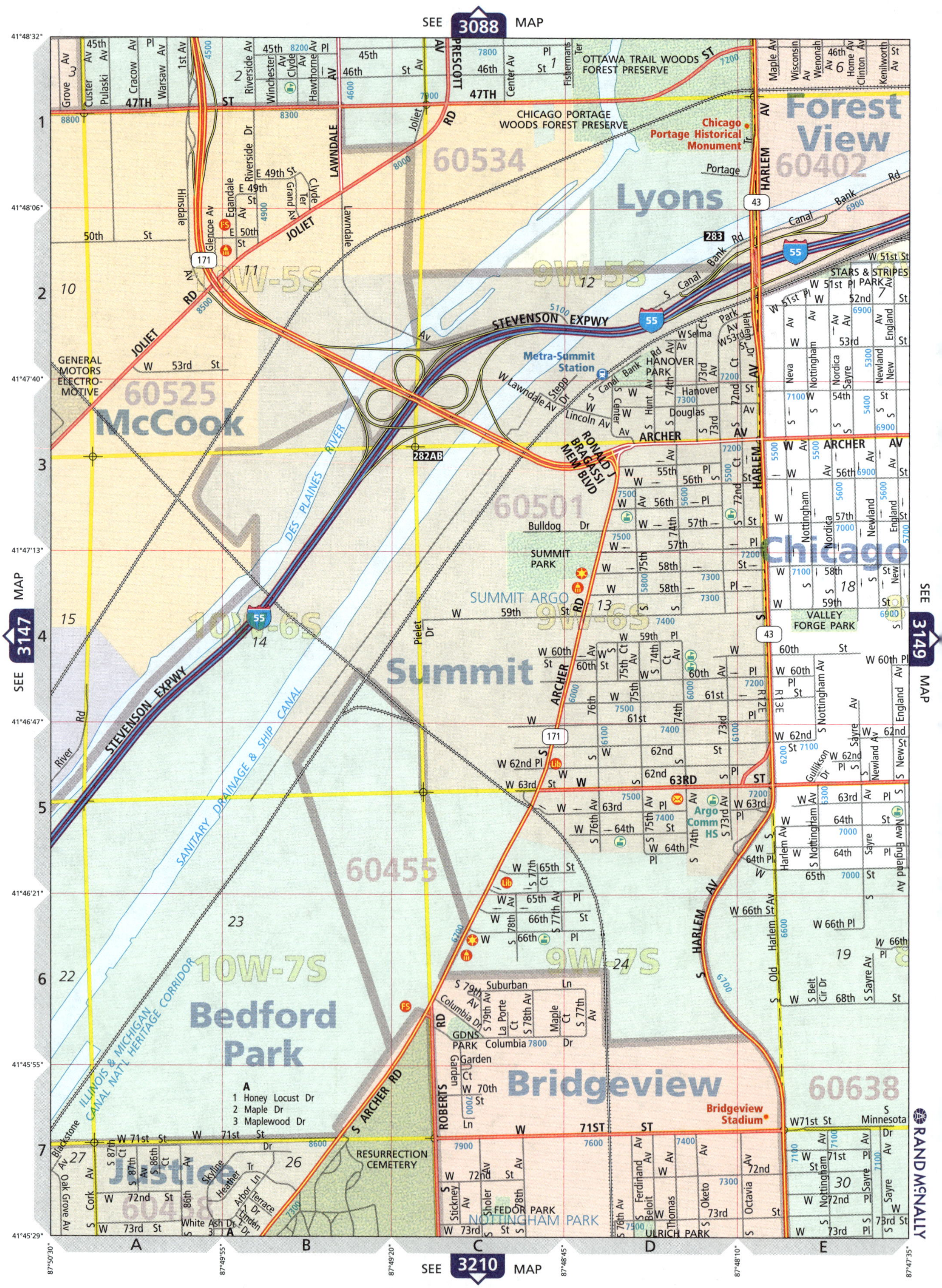
1:24,000
1 in. = 2000 ft.
0
0.25
0.5
miles
SEE 3088 MAP
SEE 3147 MAP
SEE 3149 MAP
SEE 3210 MAP
Forest View
60402
Lyons
60534
60525
McCook
60501
Summit
SUMMIT ARGO
60455
Bedford Park
Bridgeview
60638
Chicago
Justice
60458
OTTAWA TRAIL WOODS FOREST PRESERVE
CHICAGO PORTAGE WOODS FOREST PRESERVE
Chicago Portage Historical Monument
GENERAL MOTORS ELECTRO-MOTIVE
Metra-Summit Station
SUMMIT PARK
STARS & STRIPES PARK
VALLEY FORGE PARK
Argo Comm HS
RESURRECTION CEMETERY
Bridgeview Stadium
FEDOR PARK
NOTTINGHAM PARK
ULRICH PARK
HANOVER PARK
GDNS PARK
STEVENSON EXPWY
DES PLAINES RIVER
SANITARY DRAINAGE & SHIP CANAL
ILLINOIS & MICHIGAN CANAL NAT'L HERITAGE CORRIDOR
RONALD J BRAGASSI MEM BLVD
JOLIET RD
ARCHER RD
HARLEM AV
47TH ST
63RD ST
71ST ST
ROBERTS RD
S ARCHER RD
10W-5S
9W-5S
10W-6S
9W-6S
10W-7S
9W-7S
A
1 Honey Locust Dr
2 Maple Dr
3 Maplewood Dr
RAND McNALLY

1:24,000
1 in. = 2000 ft.
0 0.25 0.5
miles

SEE 3089 MAP

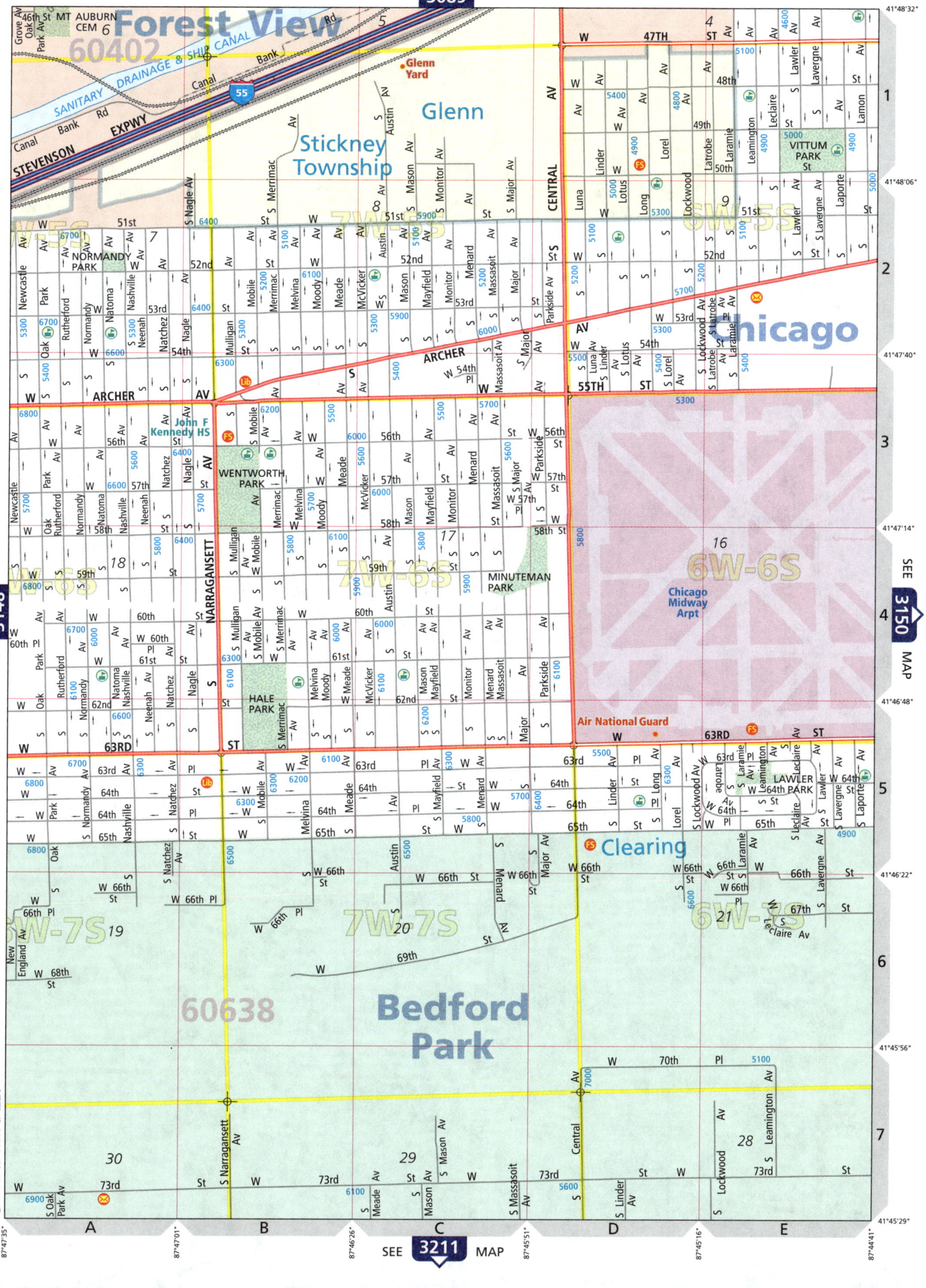
Forest View
60402
MT AUBURN CEM
SANITARY DRAINAGE & SHIP CANAL
STEVENSON EXPWY
55
Canal Bank Rd
Glenn Yard
Glenn
Stickney Township
W 47TH ST
CENTRAL AV
W 51st St
NORMANDY PARK
ARCHER AV
W 55TH ST
Chicago
John F Kennedy HS
WENTWORTH PARK
NARRAGANSETT AV
MINUTEMAN PARK
Chicago Midway Arpt
HALE PARK
Air National Guard
W 63RD ST
LAWLER PARK
VITTUM PARK
Clearing
60638
Bedford Park
W 73rd St
7W-5S
6W-5S
7W-6S
6W-6S
7W-7S
6W-7S
1
2
3
4
5
6
7
A
B
C
D
E
41°48'32"
41°48'06"
41°47'40"
41°47'14"
41°46'48"
41°46'22"
41°45'56"
41°45'29"
87°47'35"
87°47'01"
87°46'26"
87°45'51"
87°45'16"
87°44'41"

SEE MAP 3148

SEE MAP 3150

SEE 3211 MAP

1:24,000
1 in. = 2000 ft.
0 0.25 0.5
miles

SEE 3090 MAP

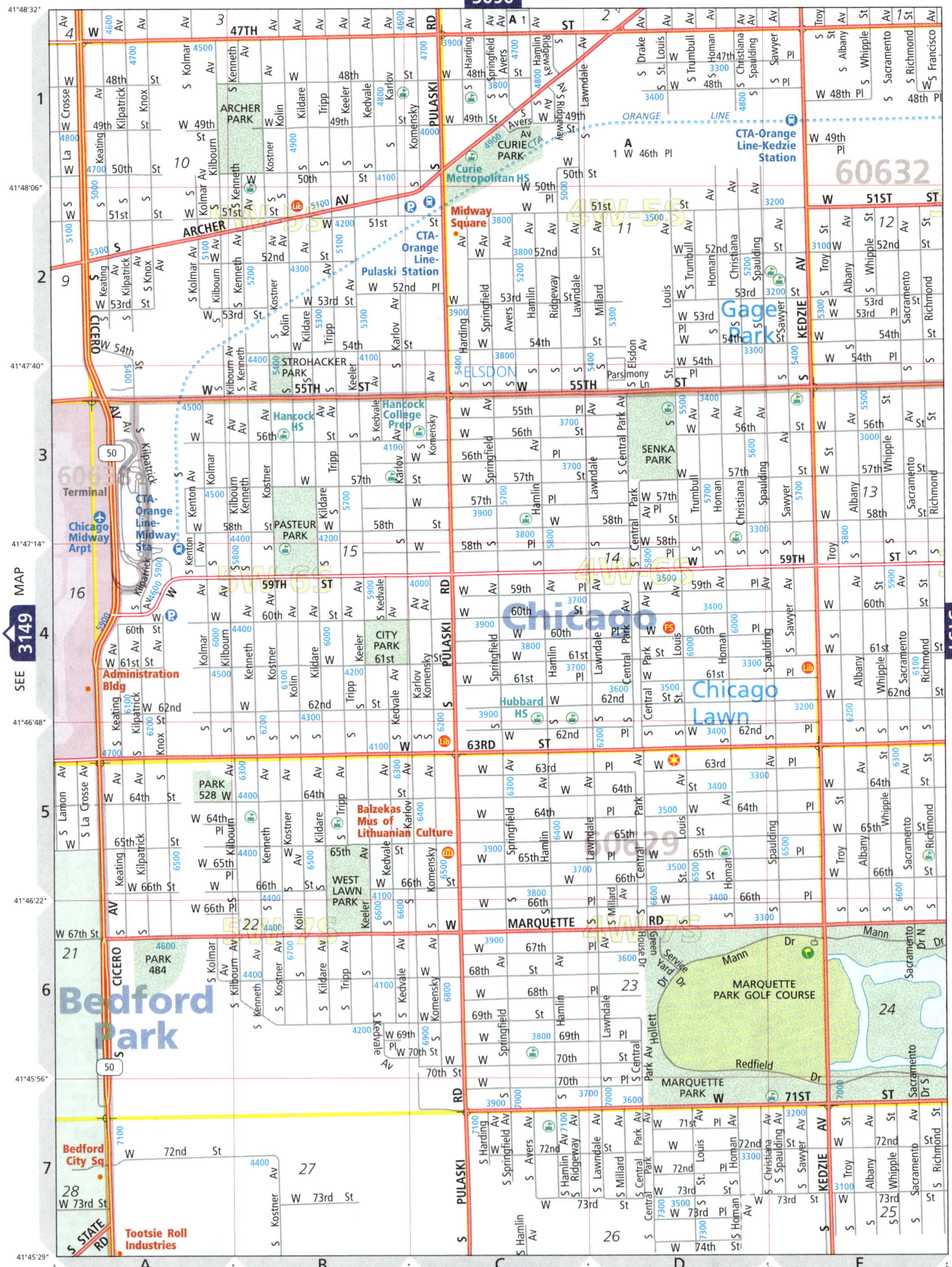
ARCHER PARK
CURIE PARK
Curie Metropolitan HS
Midway Square
CTA-Orange Line-Pulaski Station
CTA-Orange Line-Kedzie Station
60632
Gage Park
ELSDON
STROHACKER PARK
Hancock College Prep
Hancock HS
SENKA PARK
PASTEUR PARK
Chicago Midway Arpt
Terminal
CTA-Orange Line-Midway Sta
Administration Bldg
CITY PARK
Chicago
Chicago Lawn
Hubbard HS
PARK 528
Balzekas Mus of Lithuanian Culture
WEST LAWN PARK
60629
PARK 484
Bedford Park
MARQUETTE PARK GOLF COURSE
MARQUETTE PARK
Bedford City Sq
Tootsie Roll Industries
47TH
ARCHER AV
55TH ST
59TH ST
63RD ST
MARQUETTE RD
71ST
CICERO AV
PULASKI RD
KEDZIE AV
ORANGE LINE

SEE 3149 MAP
SEE 3151 MAP
SEE 3212 MAP

RAND McNALLY

1:24,000
1 in. = 2000 ft.
0 0.25 0.5
miles

SEE 3091 MAP

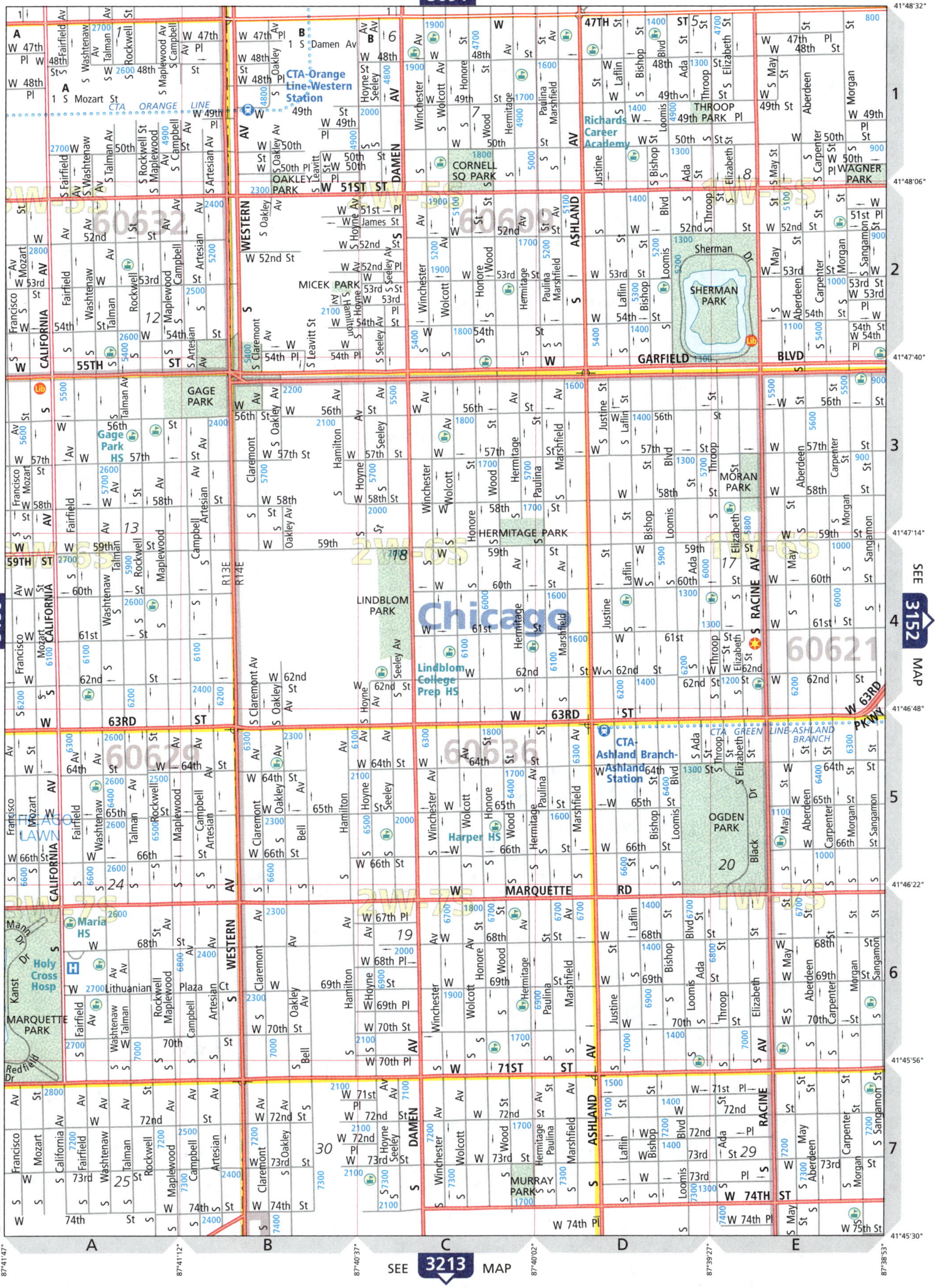

W 47th St
47TH ST
W 51ST ST
W 55TH ST
GARFIELD BLVD
W 63RD ST
W 63RD PKWY
W MARQUETTE RD
W 71ST ST
W 74TH ST
CALIFORNIA AV
WESTERN AV
DAMEN AV
ASHLAND AV
S RACINE AV
CTA-Orange Line-Western Station
CTA ORANGE LINE
CTA GREEN LINE-ASHLAND BRANCH
CTA-Ashland Branch-Ashland Station
OAKLEY PARK
CORNELL SQ PARK
THROOP PARK
WAGNER PARK
Richards Career Academy
MICEK PARK
SHERMAN PARK
Sherman Dr
GAGE PARK
Gage Park HS
HERMITAGE PARK
MORAN PARK
LINDBLOM PARK
Lindblom College Prep HS
Chicago
CHICAGO LAWN
Harper HS
OGDEN PARK
Maria HS
Holy Cross Hosp
MARQUETTE PARK
Mann Dr
Redfield Dr
MURRAY PARK
Lithuanian Plaza Ct
60632
60609
60629
60636
60621
2W-5S
1W-5S
2W-6S
1W-6S
2W-7S
1W-7S
R13E
R14E
41°48'32"
41°48'06"
41°47'40"
41°47'14"
41°46'48"
41°46'22"
41°45'56"
41°45'30"
87°41'47"
87°41'12"
87°40'37"
87°40'02"
87°39'27"
87°38'53"
A
B
C
D
E
1
2
3
4
5
6
7
SEE 3150 MAP
SEE 3152 MAP
RAND McNALLY

SEE 3213 MAP

1:24,000
1 in. = 2000 ft.
0 0.25 0.5
miles

SEE 3092 MAP

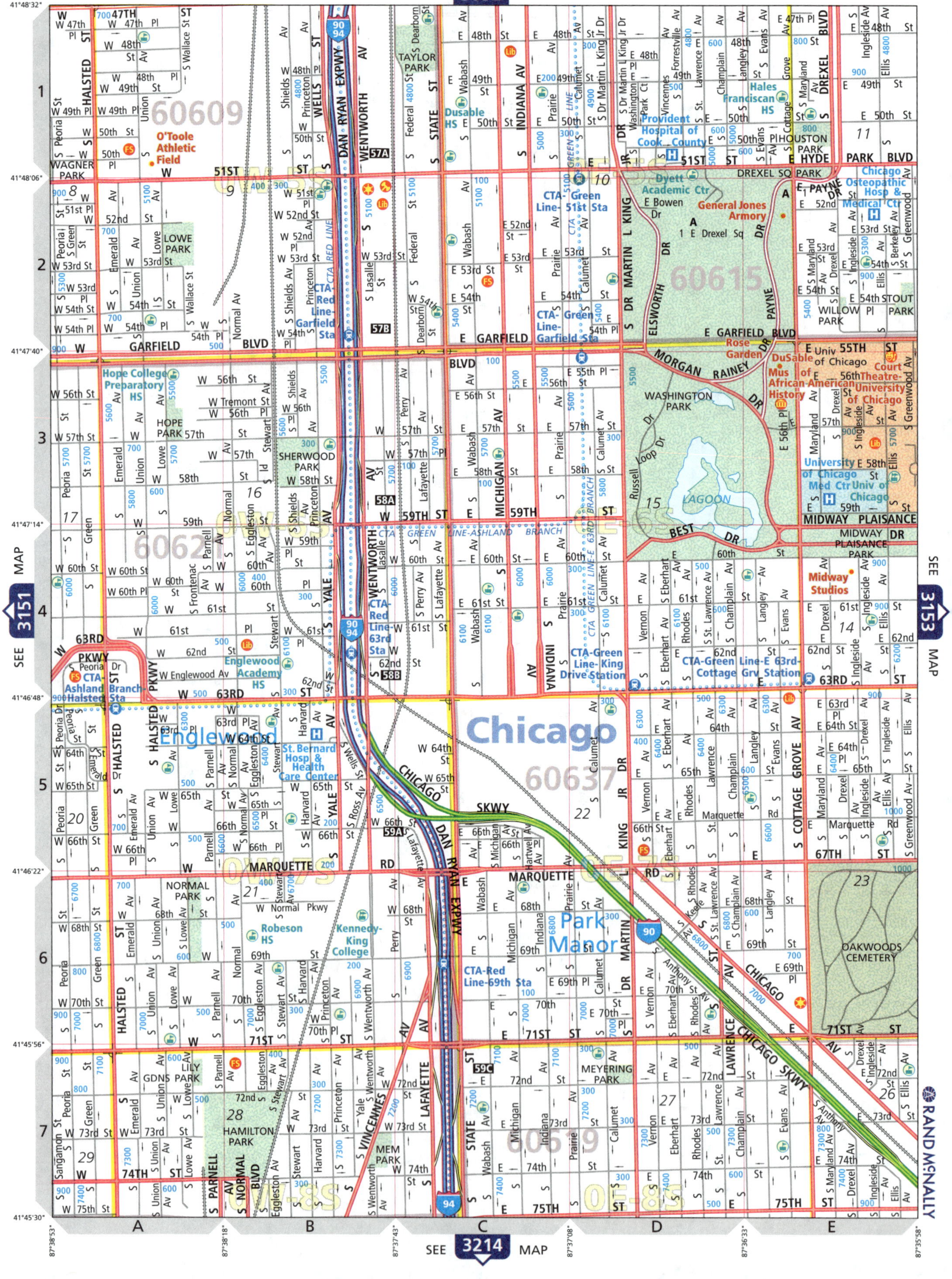
Chicago
60609
60615
60621
60637
60619
O'Toole Athletic Field
WAGNER PARK
LOWE PARK
HOPE PARK
SHERWOOD PARK
TAYLOR PARK
Dusable HS
Provident Hospital of Cook County
Hales Franciscan HS
Dyett Academic Ctr
General Jones Armory
CTA-Green Line-51st Sta
CTA-Green Line-Garfield Sta
CTA-Red Line-Garfield Sta
CTA-Red Line-63rd Sta
CTA-Green Line-King Drive Station
CTA-Green Line-E 63rd-Cottage Grv Station
CTA-Ashland Branch-Halsted Sta
CTA-Red Line-69th Sta
WASHINGTON PARK
LAGOON
Rose Garden
DuSable Mus of African-American History
Univ of Chicago
Court Theatre-University of Chicago
University of Chicago Med Ctr
Chicago Osteopathic Hosp & Medical Ctr
MIDWAY PLAISANCE PARK
Midway Studios
Hope College Preparatory HS
Englewood
Englewood Academy HS
St. Bernard Hosp & Health Care Center
NORMAL PARK
Robeson HS
Kennedy-King College
Park Manor
OAKWOODS CEMETERY
LILY GDNS PARK
HAMILTON PARK
MEM PARK
MEYERING PARK
WILLOW PARK
STOUT PARK
DREXEL SQ PARK
HOUSTON PARK
DAN RYAN EXPWY
CHICAGO SKWY
GARFIELD BLVD
MARQUETTE RD
MIDWAY PLAISANCE
S DR MARTIN L KING JR DR
S COTTAGE GROVE AV
S HALSTED ST
WENTWORTH AV
STATE ST
INDIANA AV
DREXEL BLVD
51ST ST
55TH ST
59TH ST
63RD ST
67TH ST
71ST ST
75TH ST
MORGAN DR
RAINEY DR
BEST DR
ELSWORTH DR
PAYNE DR
VINCENNES AV
LAFAYETTE AV
YALE AV
NORMAL BLVD
PARNELL AV
SEE 3151 MAP
SEE 3153 MAP
RAND McNALLY

SEE 3214 MAP

1:24,000
1 in. = 2000 ft.
0 0.25 0.5
miles

SEE 3093 MAP

LAKE MICHIGAN
KENWOOD
60615
HYDE PARK
60637
60649
60619
Chicago
Brookdale
South Shore
SOUTH SHORE
KENWOOD COMM ST PARK
MADISON PARK
SPRUCE PARK
NICHOLS PARK
CORNELL PARK
BURNHAM PARK
BIXLER PARK
MIDWAY PLAISANCE PARK
MIDWAY PLAISANCE DR
JACKSON PARK
WOODED ISLAND
EAST LAGOON
WEST LAGOON
SOUTH LAGOON
COLUMBIA BASIN
YACHT HARBOR
JACKSON PARK GOLF COURSE
HARPER PLGND PARK
OAKWOODS CEM
HASAN PARK
SOUTH SHORE COUNTRY CLUB
WOODHULL PARK
HOARD PARK
RAINBOW PARK & BEACH
UNIV OF CHICAGO
Mus of Science & Industry
Coast Guard Station
La Rabida Childrens Hospital & Research Center
Morton B Weiss Mus of Judaica
Kenwood Academy HS
Heller Hse
McCormick Theol Seminary
Hyde Pk Hist Society
Meadville Lombard Theol School
Frederick C Robie Hse
Mandel Hall
Oriental Inst Museum
International Hse
Catholic Theol Union Chicago
Hyde Park Academy HS
Mt Carmel HS
Metra-53rd St Sta
Metra-55th-56th-57th Street Sta
Metra-59th Street Sta
Metra-63rd Street Station
Metra-Stony I Station
Metra-Bryn Mawr Station
Metra-South Shore Station
Metra-75th Street Sta
Metra-Windsor Pk Station
S LAKE SHORE DR
S LAKE PARK AV
HYDE PARK BLVD
S WOODLAWN AV
E 55TH ST
S CORNELL AV
HAYES DR
S RICHARDS DR
S COAST GUARD DR
MARQUETTE DR
E 63RD ST
E 67TH ST
E 71ST ST
S STONY ISLAND AV
S JEFFERY BLVD
S SOUTH SHORE DR
S YATES BLVD
S EXCHANGE AV
E 75TH ST
S CHICAGO AV
E SOUTH SHORE DR
1E-7S
2E-6S
2E-7S
3E-7S
A
B
C
D
E
1
2
3
4
5
6
7
41
90
A 1 S Saginaw Av

SEE 3152 MAP
SEE B MAP
SEE 3215 MAP

1:24,000
1 in. = 2000 ft.
0 0.25 0.5
miles

SEE 3146 MAP

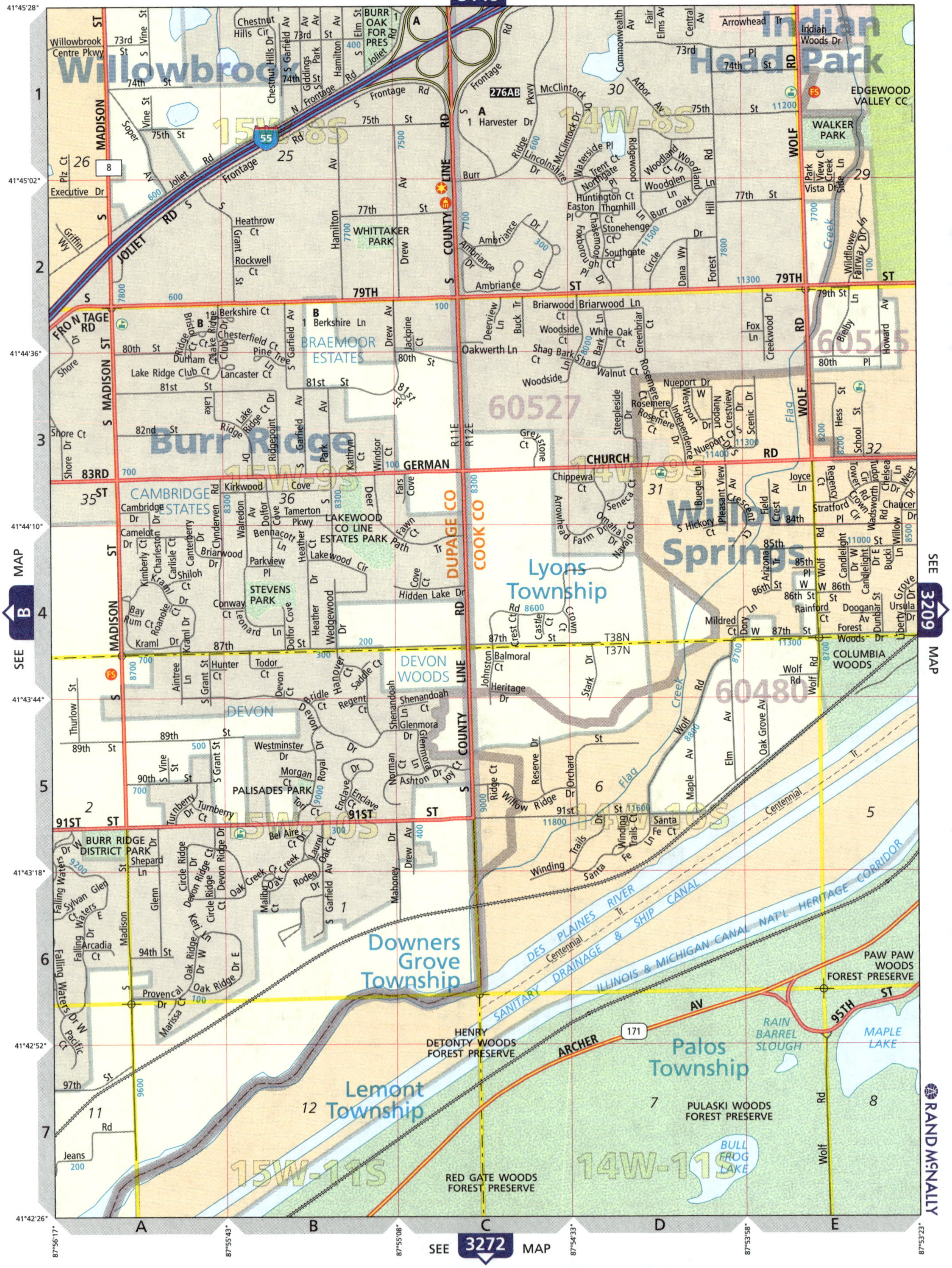
Willowbrook
Burr Ridge
Indian Head Park
Willow Springs
Lyons Township
Downers Grove Township
Lemont Township
Palos Township
BRAEMOOR ESTATES
CAMBRIDGE ESTATES
DEVON WOODS
DEVON
LAKEWOOD CO LINE ESTATES PARK
STEVENS PARK
WHITTAKER PARK
WALKER PARK
PALISADES PARK
BURR RIDGE DISTRICT PARK
BURR OAK FOR PRES
EDGEWOOD VALLEY CC
COLUMBIA WOODS
PAW PAW WOODS FOREST PRESERVE
HENRY DETONTY WOODS FOREST PRESERVE
RED GATE WOODS FOREST PRESERVE
PULASKI WOODS FOREST PRESERVE
RAIN BARREL SLOUGH
MAPLE LAKE
BULL FROG LAKE
DES PLAINES RIVER
SANITARY DRAINAGE & SHIP CANAL
ILLINOIS & MICHIGAN CANAL NAT'L HERITAGE CORRIDOR
DUPAGE CO
COOK CO
60527
60525
60480
15W-8S
14W-8S
15W-9S
14W-9S
15W-10S
14W-10S
15W-11S
14W-11S
T38N
T37N
R11E
R12E
79TH ST
83RD ST
91ST ST
95TH ST
GERMAN
CHURCH RD
ARCHER AV
171
55
JOLIET RD
S MADISON ST
COUNTY LINE RD
WOLF RD
S FRONTAGE RD
SEE B MAP
SEE 3209 MAP
41°45'28"
41°45'02"
41°44'36"
41°44'10"
41°43'44"
41°43'18"
41°42'52"
41°42'26"
87°56'17"
87°55'43"
87°55'08"
87°54'33"
87°53'58"
87°53'23"

SEE 3272 MAP

1:24,000
1 in. = 2000 ft.
0 0.25 0.5
miles

SEE 3147 MAP

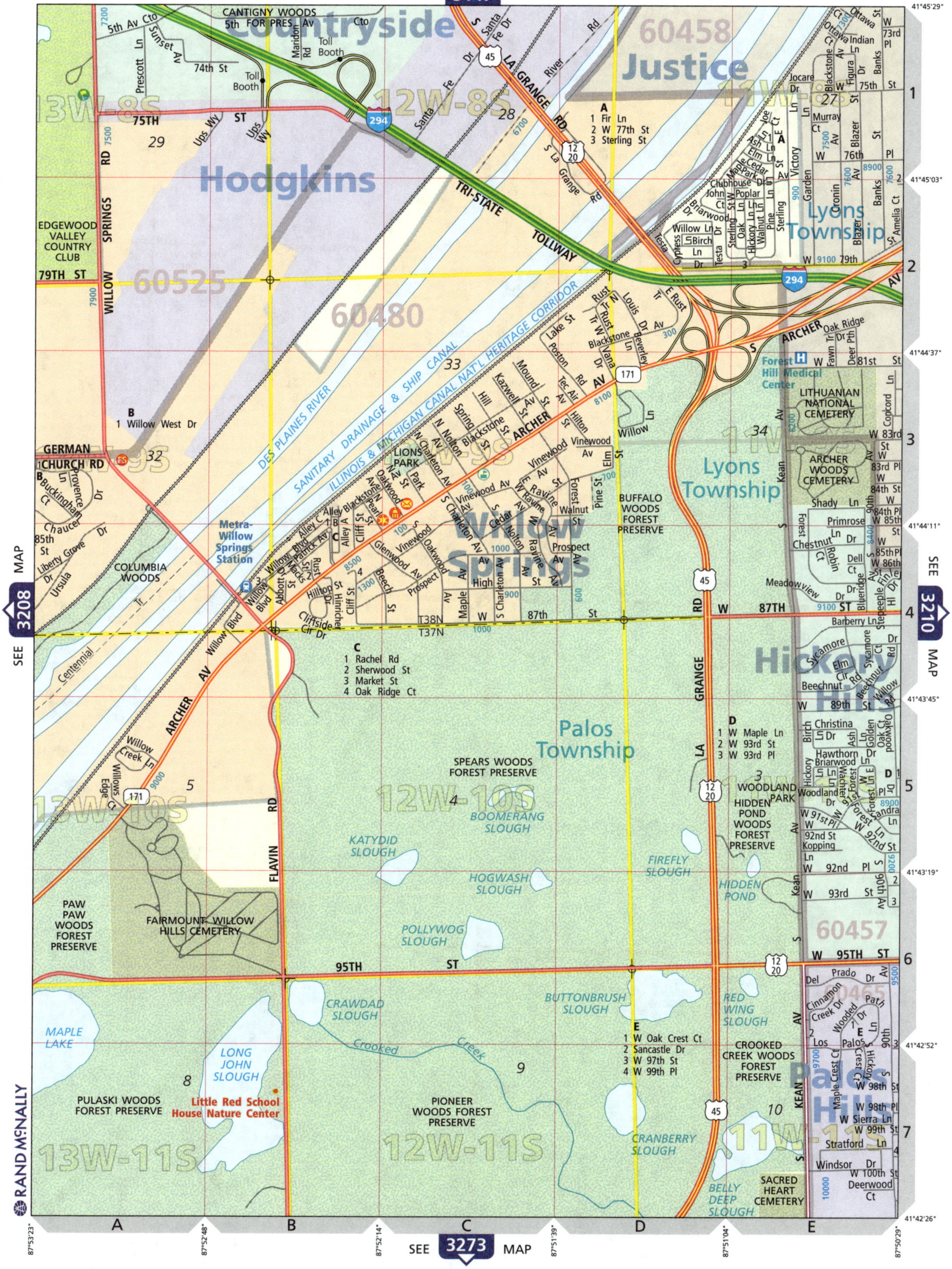

SEE 3273 MAP

1:24,000
1 in. = 2000 ft.
0 0.25 0.5
miles

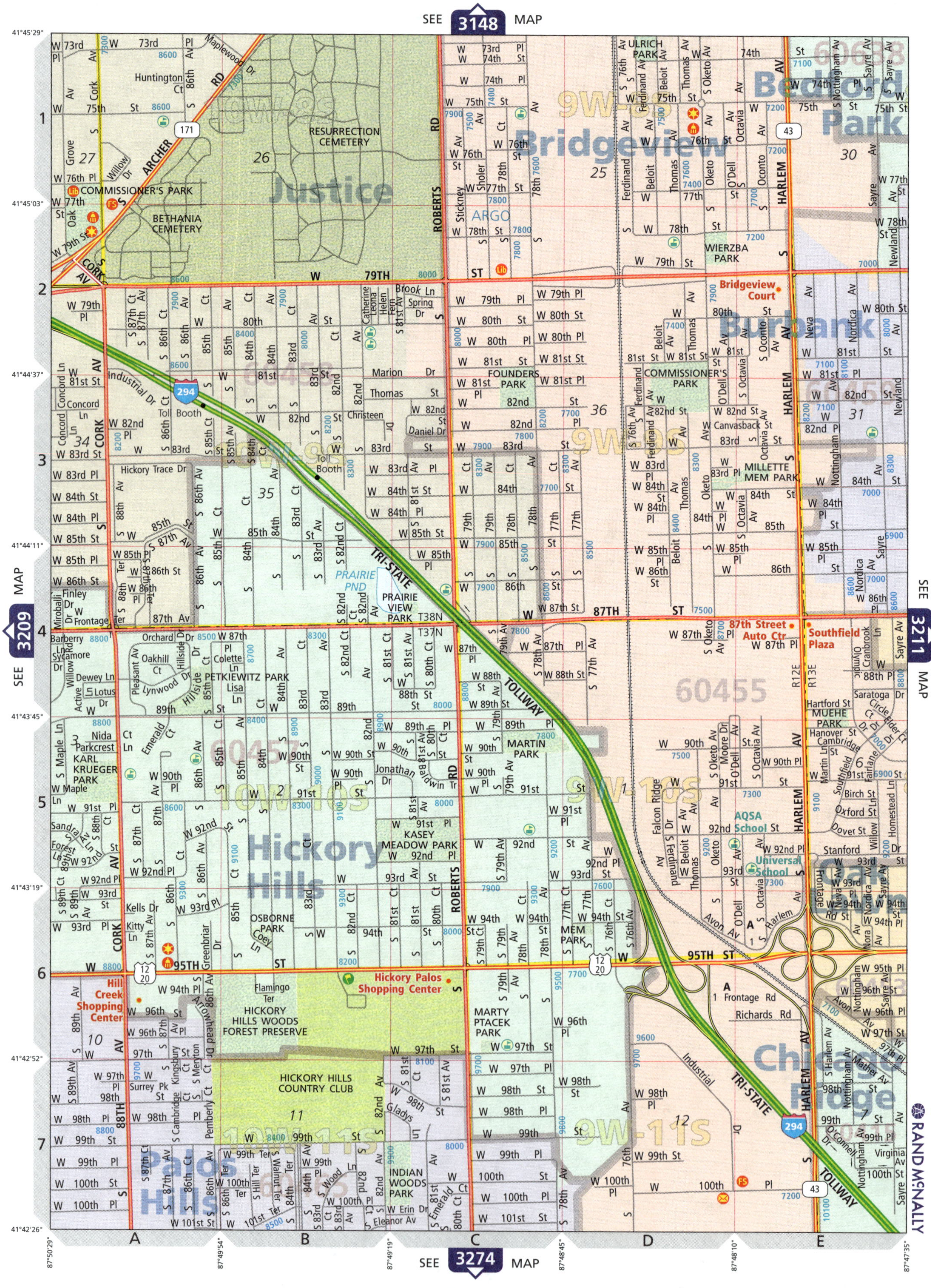
SEE 3148 MAP
SEE 3209 MAP
SEE 3211 MAP
SEE 3274 MAP
Justice
Bridgeview
Bedford Park
Burbank
Hickory Hills
Palos Hills
Chicago Ridge
RESURRECTION CEMETERY
BETHANIA CEMETERY
COMMISSIONER'S PARK
ARGO
WIERZBA PARK
FOUNDERS PARK
MILLETTE MEM PARK
ULRICH PARK
Bridgeview Court
87th Street Auto Ctr
Southfield Plaza
PRAIRIE VIEW PARK
PRAIRIE PND
PETKIEWITZ PARK
KARL KRUEGER PARK
KASEY MEADOW PARK
MARTIN PARK
MUEHE PARK
OSBORNE PARK
MEM PARK
AQSA School
Universal School
Hickory Palos Shopping Center
Hill Creek Shopping Center
HICKORY HILLS WOODS FOREST PRESERVE
HICKORY HILLS COUNTRY CLUB
MARTY PTACEK PARK
INDIAN WOODS PARK
TRI-STATE
TOLLWAY
Toll Booth
ARCHER
ROBERTS RD
HARLEM AV
CORK AV
88TH AV
W 79TH ST
87TH ST
95TH ST
60455
60457
60458
60465
60638
10W-9S
9W-9S
10W-10S
9W-10S
10W-11S
9W-11S
T38N
T37N
R12E
R13E
RAND McNALLY

1:24,000
1 in. = 2000 ft.
0 0.25 0.5
miles

SEE 3149 MAP

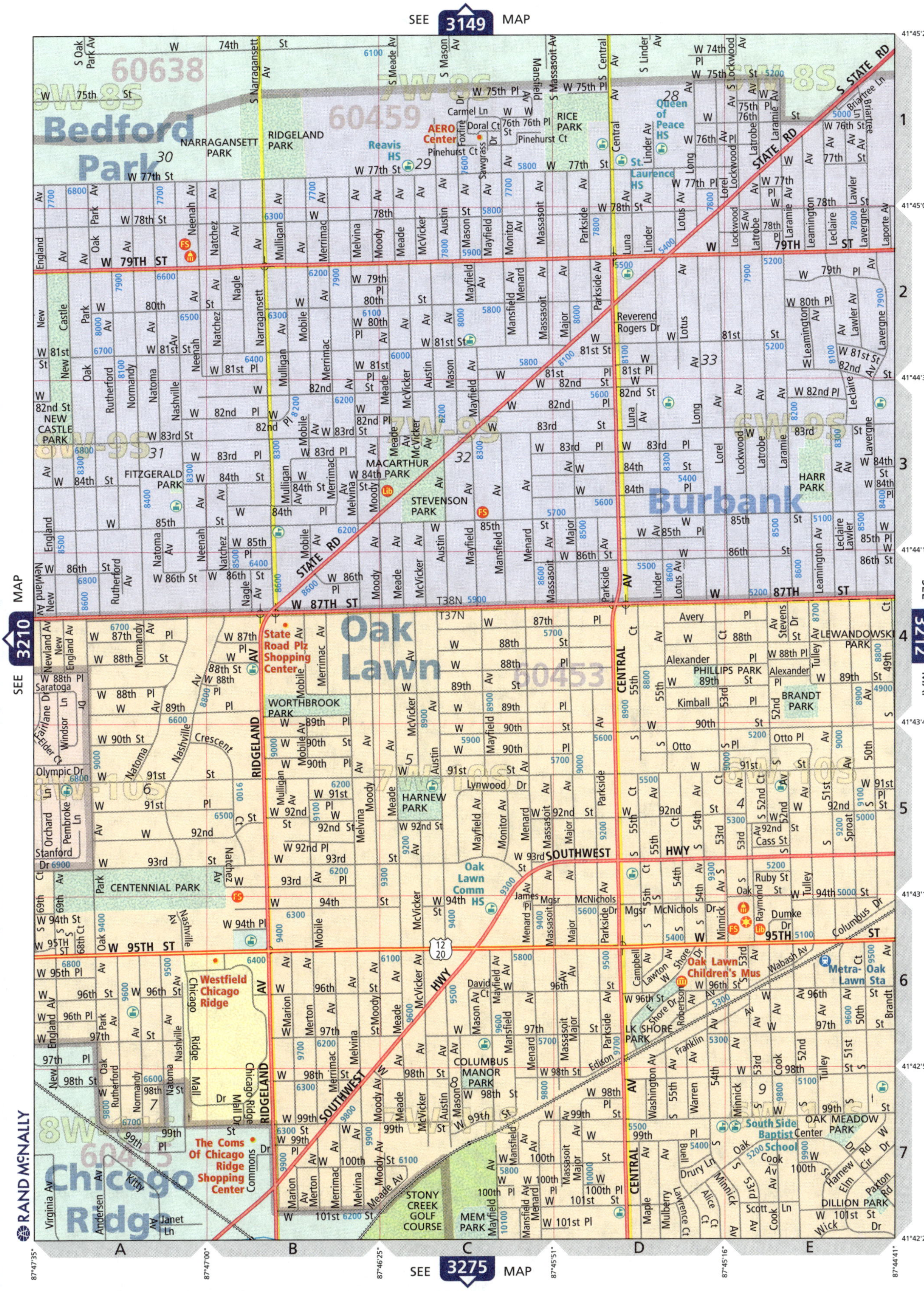

SEE 3210 MAP
SEE 3212 MAP
SEE 3275 MAP

1:24,000
1 in. = 2000 ft.
0 0.25 0.5
miles

SEE 3150 MAP

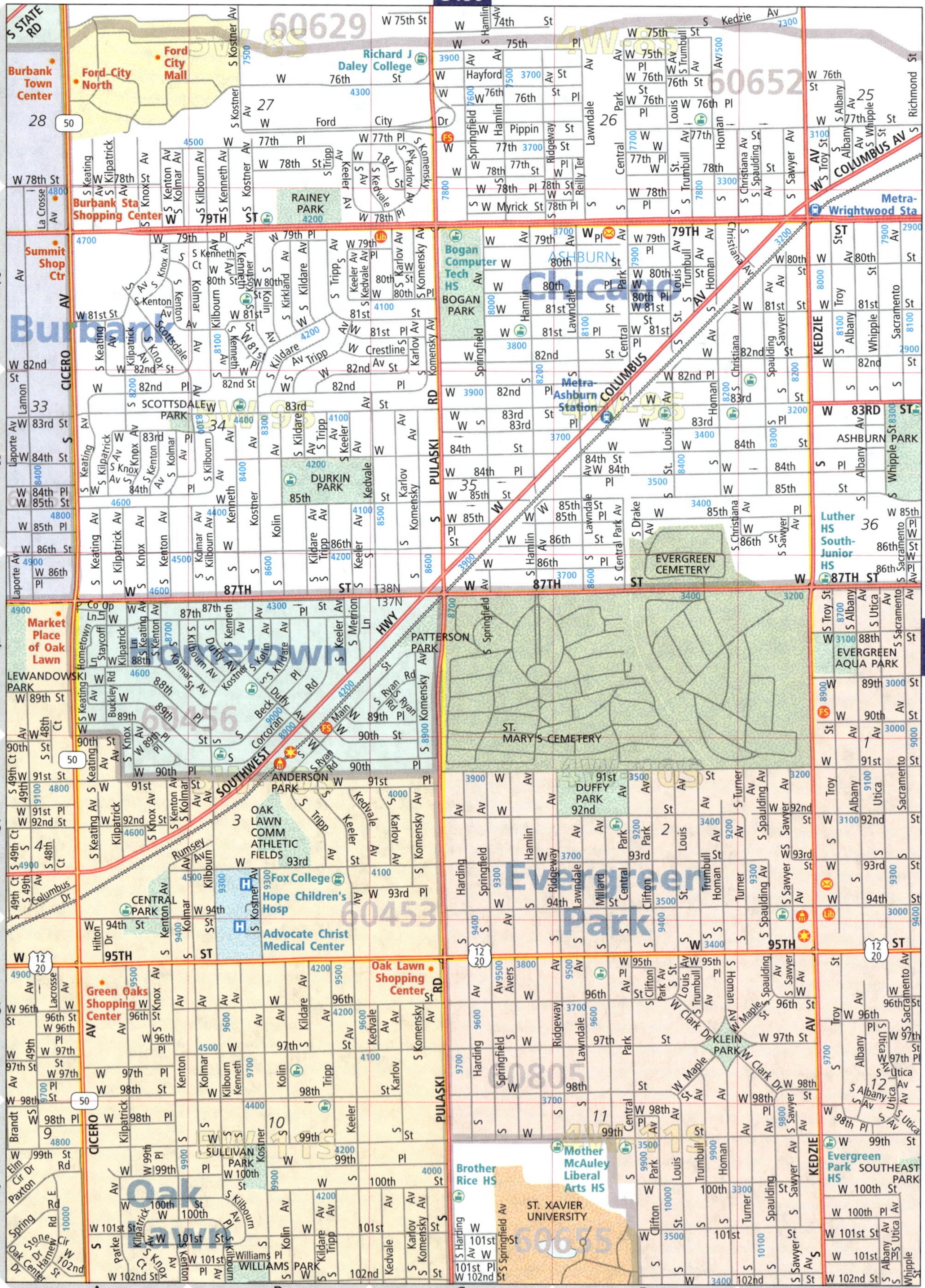
Burbank
Chicago
Hometown
Evergreen Park
Oak Lawn
Burbank Town Center
Ford City North
Ford City Mall
Richard J Daley College
Burbank Sta Shopping Center
RAINEY PARK
Summit Shop Ctr
Bogan Computer Tech HS
BOGAN PARK
ASHBURN
Metra-Wrightwood Sta
Metra-Ashburn Station
SCOTTSDALE PARK
DURKIN PARK
ASHBURN PARK
Luther HS South-Junior HS
EVERGREEN CEMETERY
Market Place of Oak Lawn
LEWANDOWSKI PARK
PATTERSON PARK
ST. MARY'S CEMETERY
EVERGREEN AQUA PARK
ANDERSON PARK
OAK LAWN COMM ATHLETIC FIELDS
DUFFY PARK
Fox College
Hope Children's Hosp
Advocate Christ Medical Center
CENTRAL PARK
Green Oaks Shopping Center
Oak Lawn Shopping Center
KLEIN PARK
SULLIVAN PARK
WILLIAMS PARK
Brother Rice HS
Mother McAuley Liberal Arts HS
ST. XAVIER UNIVERSITY
Evergreen Park HS
SOUTHEAST PARK
CICERO AV
PULASKI RD
KEDZIE AV
COLUMBUS AV
SOUTHWEST HWY
79TH ST
87TH ST
95TH ST
60629
60652
60456
60453
60805
60655

SEE 3211 MAP
SEE 3213 MAP
SEE 3276 MAP

1:24,000
1 in. = 2000 ft.
0 0.25 0.5
miles

SEE 3151 MAP

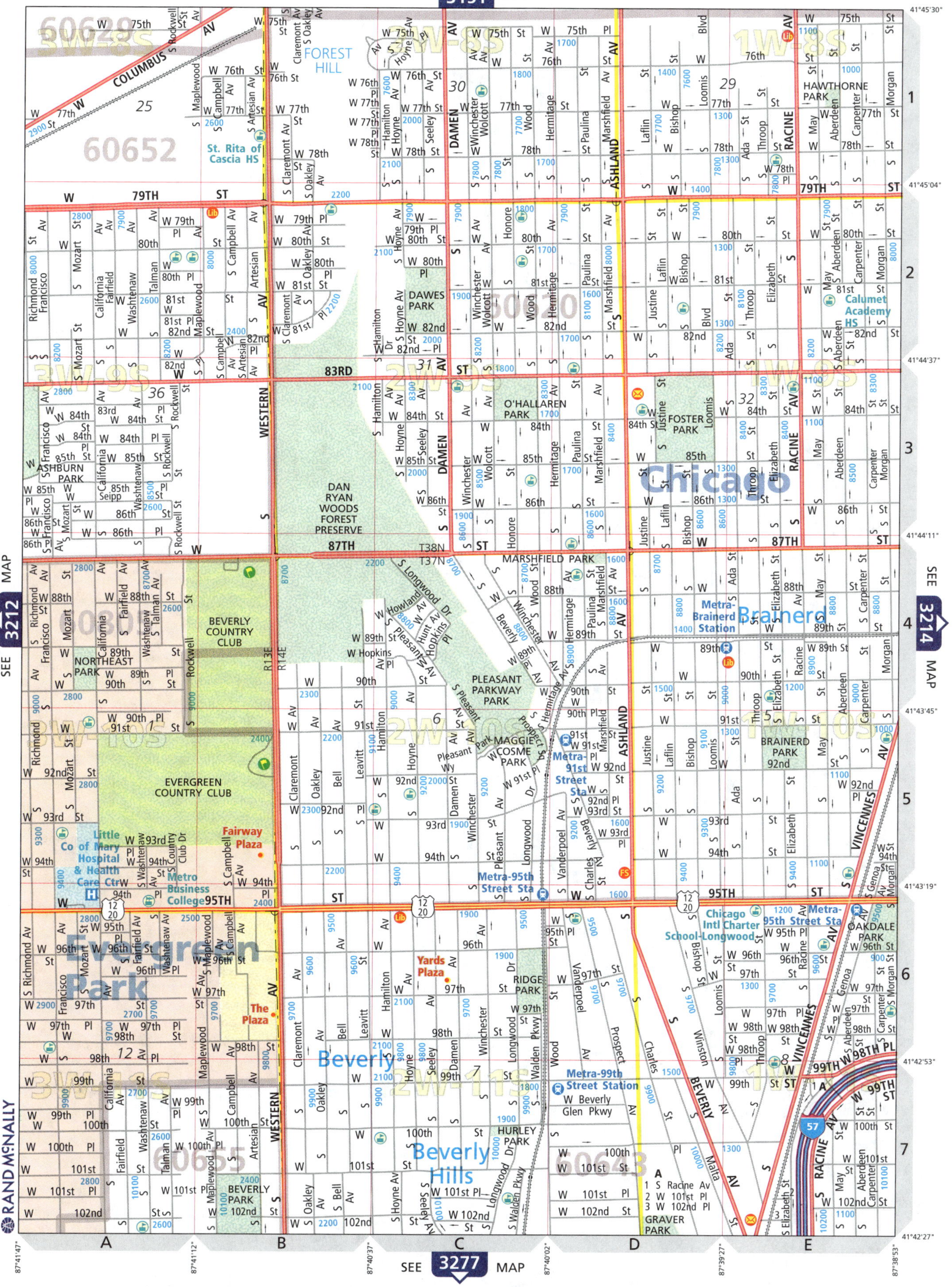
Chicago
Beverly
Beverly Hills
Evergreen Park
Brainerd
FOREST HILL
HAWTHORNE PARK
DAWES PARK
O'HALLAREN PARK
FOSTER PARK
ASHBURN PARK
DAN RYAN WOODS FOREST PRESERVE
BEVERLY COUNTRY CLUB
EVERGREEN COUNTRY CLUB
NORTHEAST PARK
MARSHFIELD PARK
PLEASANT PARKWAY PARK
MAGGIE COSME PARK
BRAINERD PARK
OAKDALE PARK
RIDGE PARK
HURLEY PARK
BEVERLY PARK
GRAVER PARK
St. Rita of Cascia HS
Calumet Academy HS
Little Co of Mary Hospital & Health Care Ctr
Metro Business College
Chicago Intl Charter School-Longwood
Fairway Plaza
Yards Plaza
The Plaza
Metra-Brainerd Station
Metra-91st Street Sta
Metra-95th Street Sta
Metra-99th Street Station
Metra-95th Street Sta
COLUMBUS AV
W 79TH ST
83RD ST
87TH ST
95TH ST
99TH ST
WESTERN AV
DAMEN AV
ASHLAND AV
RACINE AV
VINCENNES AV
BEVERLY AV
W Beverly Glen Pkwy
60628
60652
60620
60805
60655
60643
3W-8S
2W-8S
1W-8S
3W-9S
2W-9S
1W-9S
3W-10S
2W-10S
1W-10S
3W-11S
2W-11S
1W-11S
T38N
T37N
R13E
R14E
A 1 S Racine Av 2 W 101st Pl 3 W 102nd Pl
1 2 3 4 5 6 7
A B C D E
41°45'30"
41°45'04"
41°44'37"
41°44'11"
41°43'45"
41°43'19"
41°42'53"
41°42'27"
87°41'47"
87°41'12"
87°40'37"
87°40'02"
87°39'27"
87°38'53"

SEE 3212 MAP

SEE 3214 MAP

SEE 3277 MAP

1:24,000
1 in. = 2000 ft.
0 0.25 0.5
miles

SEE 3152 MAP

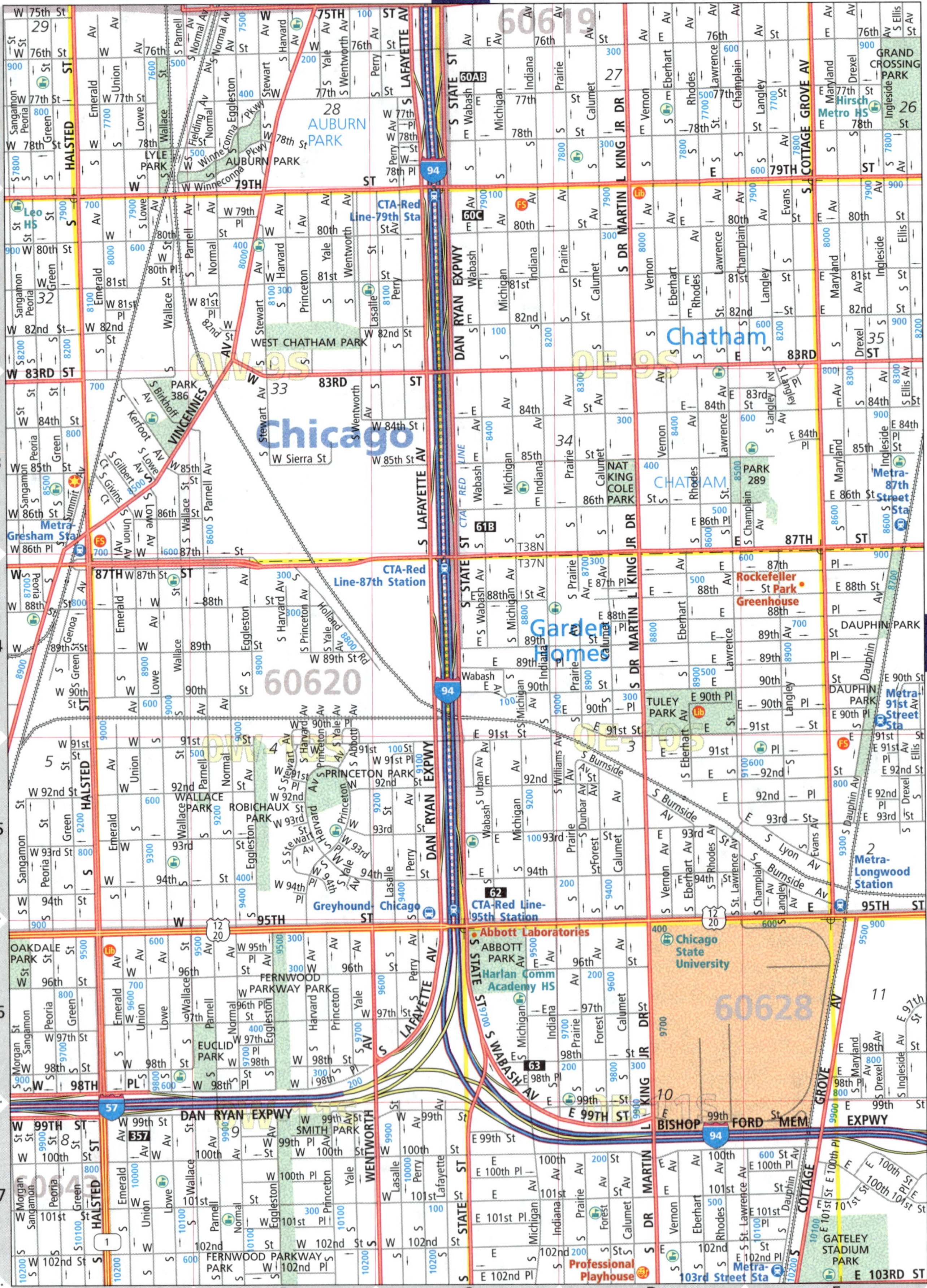
Chicago
Chatham
Garden Homes
60619
60620
60628
AUBURN PARK
AUBURN PARK
LYLE PARK
WEST CHATHAM PARK
PARK 386
NAT KING COLE PARK
PARK 289
GRAND CROSSING PARK
Hirsch Metro HS
Leo HS
CTA-Red Line-79th Sta
CTA-Red Line-87th Station
CTA-Red Line-95th Station
Metra-Gresham Sta
Metra-87th Street Sta
Metra-91st Street Sta
Metra-Longwood Station
Metra-103rd Street Sta
Rockefeller Park Greenhouse
DAUPHIN PARK
TULEY PARK
PRINCETON PARK
WALLACE PARK
ROBICHAUX PARK
Greyhound-Chicago
Abbott Laboratories
ABBOTT PARK
Harlan Comm Academy HS
Chicago State University
OAKDALE PARK
FERNWOOD PARKWAY PARK
EUCLID PARK
SMITH PARK
GATELEY STADIUM PARK
Professional Playhouse
DAN RYAN EXPWY
BISHOP FORD MEM EXPWY
S STATE ST
S LAFAYETTE AV
HALSTED ST
VINCENNES AV
S DR MARTIN L KING JR DR
S COTTAGE GROVE AV
W 75th St
79TH ST
W 83RD ST
87TH ST
95TH ST
98TH PL
99TH ST
E 103RD ST
94
57
12 20
1

SEE 3213 MAP
SEE 3215 MAP
SEE 3278 MAP

RAND McNALLY

1:24,000
1 in. = 2000 ft.
0 0.25 0.5
miles

SEE 3153 MAP

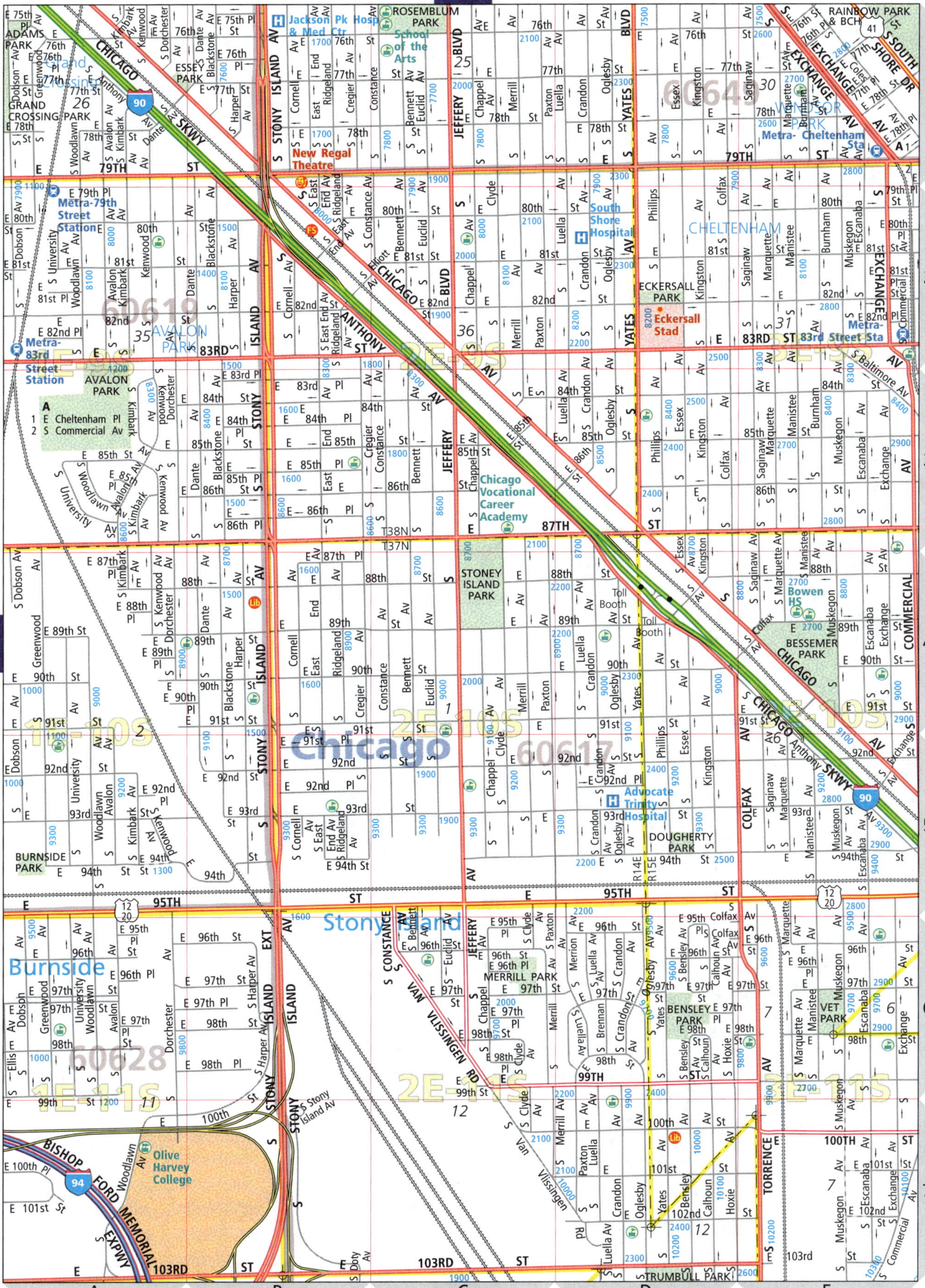
Chicago
Burnside
Stony Island
CHELTENHAM
60619
60617
60628
60649
CHICAGO SKWY
90
94
BISHOP FORD MEMORIAL EXPWY
S STONY ISLAND AV
JEFFERY BLVD
YATES BLVD
COLFAX AV
TORRENCE AV
S SOUTH SHORE DR
EXCHANGE AV
COMMERCIAL AV
ANTHONY AV
VAN VLISSINGEN RD
79TH ST
83RD ST
87TH ST
95TH ST
99TH ST
100TH ST
103RD ST
ADAMS PARK
GRAND CROSSING PARK
ESSEX PARK
ROSEMBLUM PARK
RAINBOW PARK & BCH
WINDSOR PARK
AVALON PARK
ECKERSALL PARK
Eckersall Stad
STONEY ISLAND PARK
BESSEMER PARK
DOUGHERTY PARK
MERRILL PARK
BENSLEY PARK
VET PARK
BURNSIDE PARK
TRUMBULL PARK
Jackson Pk Hosp & Med Ctr
School of the Arts
New Regal Theatre
Metra-79th Street Station
Metra-83rd Street Station
Metra-Cheltenham Sta
Metra-83rd Street Sta
South Shore Hospital
Chicago Vocational Career Academy
Bowen HS
Advocate Trinity Hospital
Olive Harvey College
Toll Booth
A
1 E Cheltenham Pl
2 S Commercial Av
2E-9S
2E-10S
2E-11S
1E-10S
1E-11S
3E-9S
3E-10S
3E-11S
T38N
T37N
R14E
R15E
1
2
3
4
5
6
7
A
B
C
D
E
41°45'29"
41°45'03"
41°44'37"
41°44'11"
41°43'45"
41°43'19"
41°42'53"
41°42'27"
87°35'58"
87°35'24"
87°34'49"
87°34'14"
87°33'39"
87°33'04"
RAND McNALLY

SEE 3214 MAP

SEE 3216 MAP

SEE 3279 MAP

1:24,000
1 in. = 2000 ft.
0
0.25
0.5
miles
N
SEE B MAP
SEE 3215 MAP
SEE B MAP
SEE 3280 MAP
LAKE MICHIGAN
Chicago
South Chicago
60617
60649
4E-8S
4E-9S
4E-10S
Water Filtration Plant
RAINBOW PARK & BEACH
RUSSELL PARK
Metra-87th Street Station
Metra-South Chicago Station
PARK 523
PARK 503
CALUMET
Calumet Harbor
NORTH SLIP
SOUTH SLIP
CALUMET RIVER
TURNING BASIN
HOWARD SLIP
SLIP NO 1
SLIP NO 2
SLIP NO 3
CALUMET PARK
US Coast Guard
St. Francis de Sales HS
East Side
Hammond
46320
COOK CO
LAKE CO
ILLINOIS
INDIANA
T38N
T37N
E 79TH ST
E 83RD ST
E 87TH ST
95TH ST
E 100TH ST
S SOUTH SHORE DR
S BAKER AV
S BURLEY AV
S MACKINAW AV
S COMMERCIAL AV
S CHICAGO AV
CHICAGO SKWY
S EWING AV
INDIANAPOLIS AV
S Kreiter Av
S Harbor Av
Avenue G
Foreman
Crilly
Walton
Barron
A
B
C
D
E
1
2
3
4
5
6
7
41°45'29"
41°45'03"
41°44'37"
41°44'11"
41°43'45"
41°43'19"
41°42'53"
41°42'27"
87°33'04"
87°32'30"
87°31'55"
87°31'20"
87°30'45"
87°30'10"
RAND McNALLY

1:24,000
1 in. = 2000 ft.
0 0.25 0.5
miles

SEE B MAP

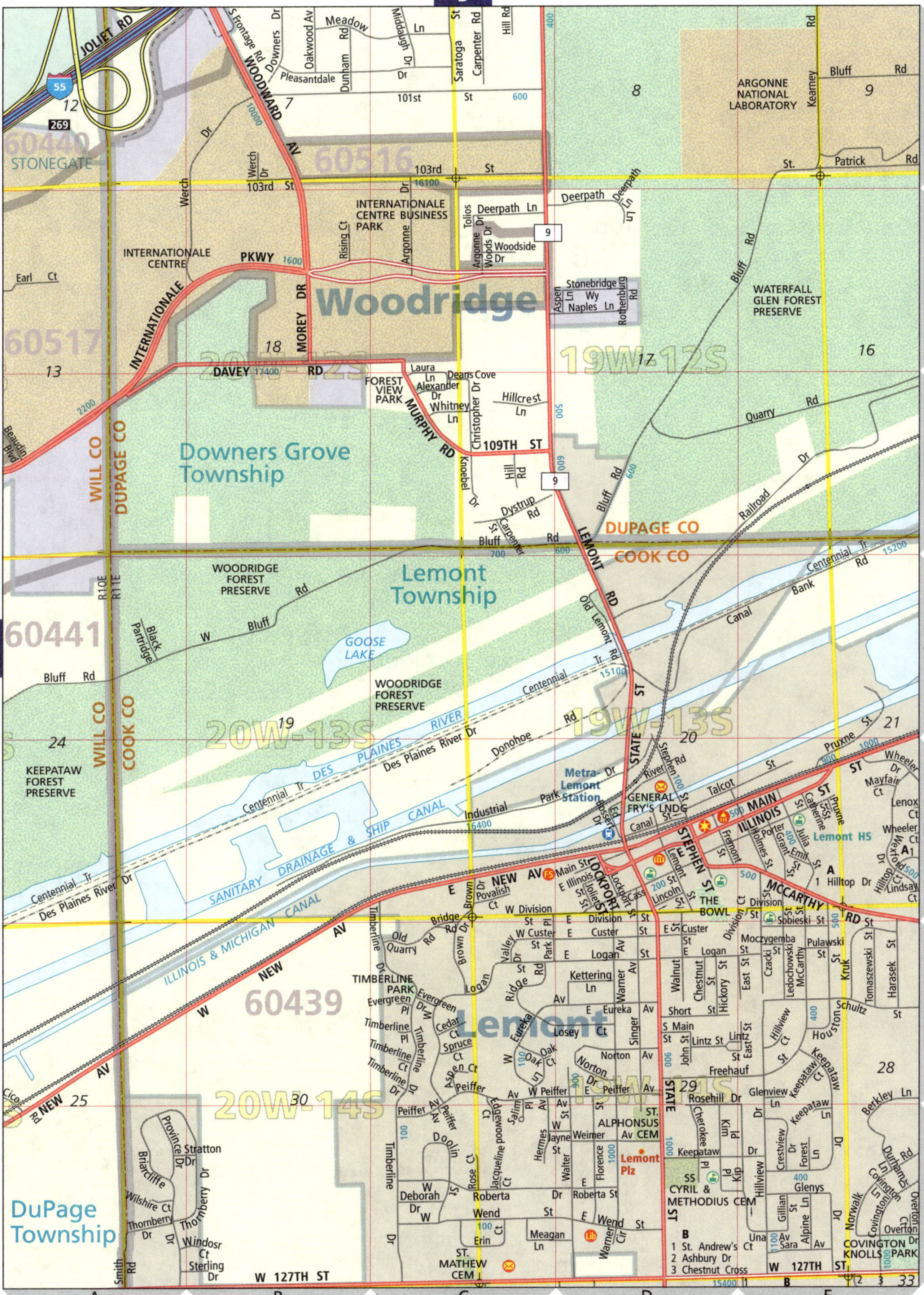
JOLIET RD
55
269
60440
STONEGATE
12
S Frontage Rd
WOODWARD AV
Downers Dr
Oakwood Av
Meadow
Dunham Rd
Middaugh Dr
Ln
Saratoga St
Carpenter Rd
Hill Rd
Pleasantdale Dr
101st St
600
400
7
8
9
ARGONNE NATIONAL LABORATORY
Kearney Rd
Bluff Rd
Patrick Rd
60516
103rd St
103rd St
Werch Dr
Werch
16100
INTERNATIONALE CENTRE BUSINESS PARK
Rising Ct
Argonne Dr
Tolios Dr
Deerpath Ln
Deerpath
Woods Dr
Woodside Dr
9
INTERNATIONALE CENTRE
PKWY
1600
Earl Ct
INTERNATIONALE
MOREY DR
Woodridge
Stonebridge Wy
Aspen Ln
Naples Ln
Rothenburg Rd
WATERFALL GLEN FOREST PRESERVE
60517
18
13
17
16
19W-12S
20W-12S
DAVEY 17400 RD
Laura Ln
Alexander Dr
Deans Cove
Whitney Ln
FOREST VIEW PARK
MURPHY RD
Christopher Dr
Hillcrest Ln
500
2200
Beaudin Blvd
109TH ST
Quarry Rd
Downers Grove Township
WILL CO
DUPAGE CO
Hill Rd
Knoebel Dr
9
Dystrup Rd
Bluff Rd
600
Railroad Dr
Bluff Rd
Carpenter St
700
600
DUPAGE CO
COOK CO
LEMONT RD
Centennial Tr
Rd
15200
WOODRIDGE FOREST PRESERVE
Lemont Township
Bank
Canal
60441
R10E
R11E
Black Partridge
W Bluff Rd
Old Lemont Rd
GOOSE LAKE
Bluff Rd
WOODRIDGE FOREST PRESERVE
Tr
15100
Centennial
STATE ST
21
Pruxne St
20W-13S
19
24
19W-13S
20
KEEPATAW FOREST PRESERVE
WILL CO
COOK CO
DES PLAINES RIVER
Des Plaines River Dr
Donohoe Rd
Stephen Rd
Rd
1000
900
Wheeler Dr
Mayfair Ct
Centennial Tr
Metra-Lemont Station
Park Dr
River
GENERAL FRY'S LNDG
Talcot St
ST
Lenox Ct
SANITARY DRAINAGE & SHIP CANAL
Industrial
16400
Canal St
MAIN ST
ILLINOIS
Porter St
Grant St
Catherine St
Pruxne St
Wheeler Ct
Lemont HS
Wexford Dr
Centennial Tr
Des Plaines River Dr
E NEW AV
Main St
E Illinois St
LOCKPORT ST
STEPHEN ST
Fremont St
Holmes St
Julia St
Emily St
Hilltop Dr
Lindsay Ct
1500
ILLINOIS & MICHIGAN CANAL
Povalish Ct
W Division St
Division St
200 St
Lincoln St
THE BOWL
McCARTHY RD
Division Ct
Division St
Sobieski St
A
1 Hilltop Dr
Timberline Dr
Brown Dr
Bridge Rd
Old Quarry Rd
W Custer St
Custer St
Custer St
Logan St
Logan St
Moczygemba St
Pulawski St
Kettering Ln
Walnut St
Chestnut St
Hickory St
East St
Czacki St
Ledochowski St
McCarthy St
Kruk St
Tomaszewski St
Harasek St
TIMBERLINE PARK
Evergreen Pl
Evergreen Dr
60439
W NEW AV
Valley Dr
Ridge Rd
Logan
Eureka Av
Short St
S Main St
Lintz St
Lintz St
East St
Schultz St
Timberline Pl
Timberline Ct
Cedar Ct
Spruce Ct
Lemont
Losey Ct
Oak Ct
Oak Ln
Norton Dr
Norton Av
Singer Av
John St
Freehauf St
Hillview Ct
Houston St
Keepataw Ct
Keepataw Dr
28
Aspen Ct
Peiffer Av
W Peiffer Av
E Peiffer Av
Rosehill Dr
Glenview Ln
Keepataw Ln
Berkley Ln
NEW RD
Cicero
25
30
20W-14S
29
Peiffer Av
Edgewood Ct
Salim St
ST. ALPHONSUS CEM
Cherokee Pl
Kim Pl
Province Dr
Stratton Dr
Briarcliffe
Doolin St
Hermes St
Jayne St
Weimer Av
Walter St
Florence Dr
Lemont Plz
Keepataw Dr
Hillview Dr
Crestview Dr
Forest Ln
Durham Rd
Covington Ln
Wilshire Ct
Thornberry Dr
Rose Ct
Jacqueline Ct
Roberta Dr
Roberta St
SS CYRIL & METHODIUS CEM
Glenys
Gillian St
Alpine Ln
Norwalk Dr
Overton Ct
Overton Dr
Timberline Dr
W Deborah Dr
W Wend St
E Wend St
Warner Cir
B
1 St. Andrew's Ct
2 Ashbury Dr
3 Chestnut Cross
Una Av
Sara Av
COVINGTON KNOLLS PARK
Windsor Ct
Sterling Dr
Erin Ct
Meagan Ln
ST. MATHEW CEM
Smith Rd
W 127TH ST
15400
W 127TH ST
33
DuPage Township

SEE B MAP
SEE 3271 MAP
SEE 3342 MAP

RAND McNALLY

1:24,000
1 in. = 2000 ft.
0 0.25 0.5
miles

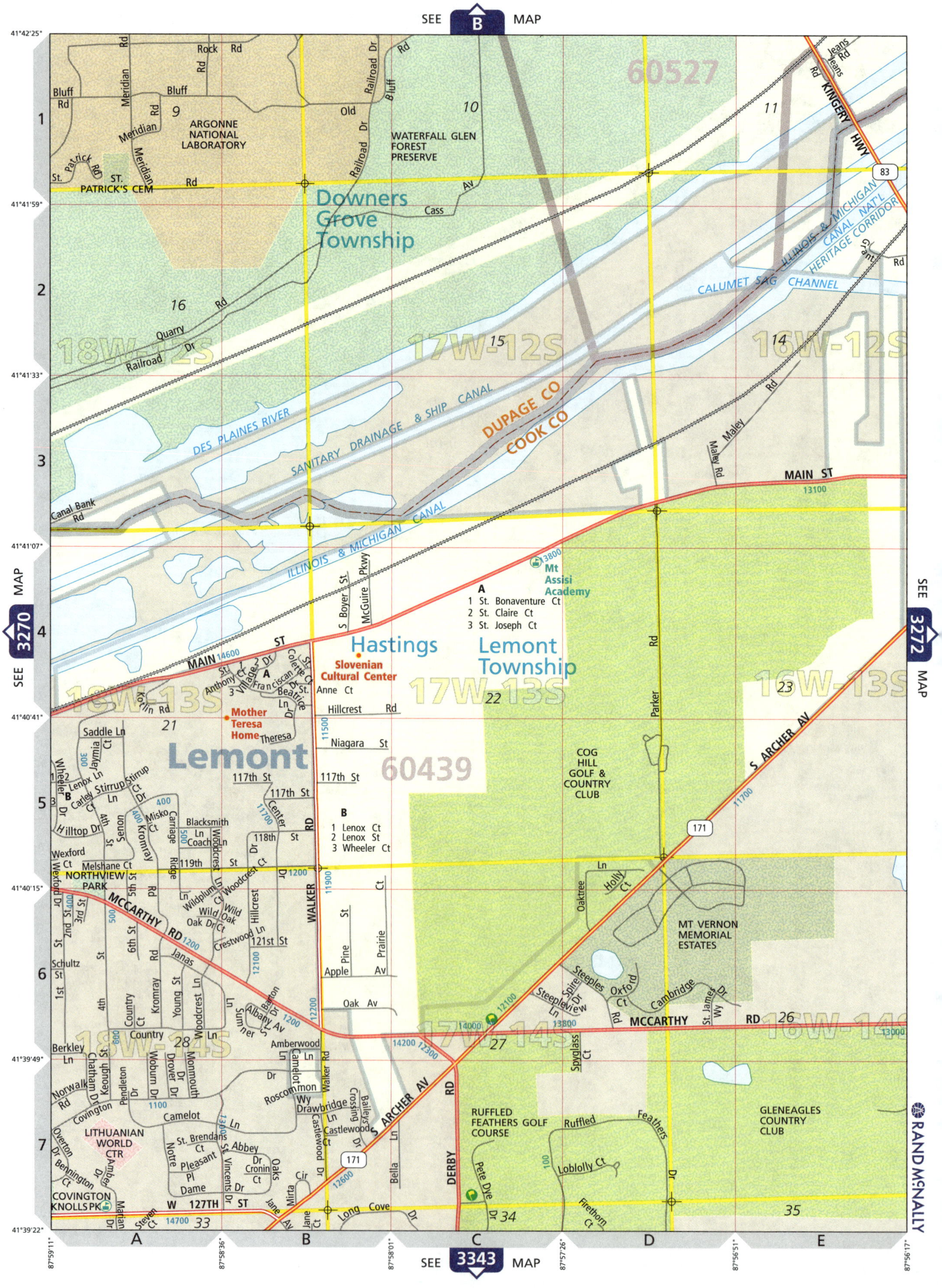
SEE B MAP
SEE 3270 MAP
SEE 3272 MAP
SEE 3343 MAP
41°42'25"
41°41'59"
41°41'33"
41°41'07"
41°40'41"
41°40'15"
41°39'49"
41°39'22"
87°59'11"
87°58'36"
87°58'01"
87°57'26"
87°56'51"
87°56'17"
A
B
C
D
E
1
2
3
4
5
6
7
60527
60439
ARGONNE NATIONAL LABORATORY
WATERFALL GLEN FOREST PRESERVE
Downers Grove Township
Lemont Township
Lemont
Hastings
ST. PATRICK'S CEM
DES PLAINES RIVER
SANITARY DRAINAGE & SHIP CANAL
ILLINOIS & MICHIGAN CANAL
CALUMET SAG CHANNEL
ILLINOIS & MICHIGAN CANAL NAT'L HERITAGE CORRIDOR
DUPAGE CO
COOK CO
18W-12S
17W-12S
16W-12S
18W-13S
17W-13S
16W-13S
18W-14S
17W-14S
16W-14S
9
10
11
14
15
16
21
22
23
26
27
28
33
34
35
Mt Assisi Academy
Slovenian Cultural Center
Mother Teresa Home
COG HILL GOLF & COUNTRY CLUB
MT VERNON MEMORIAL ESTATES
RUFFLED FEATHERS GOLF COURSE
GLENEAGLES COUNTRY CLUB
LITHUANIAN WORLD CTR
NORTHVIEW PARK
COVINGTON KNOLLS PK
A
1 St. Bonaventure Ct
2 St. Claire Ct
3 St. Joseph Ct
B
1 Lenox Ct
2 Lenox St
3 Wheeler Ct
MAIN ST
MCCARTHY RD
WALKER RD
S ARCHER AV
KINGERY HWY
DERBY RD
Parker Rd
W 127TH ST
Bluff Rd
Rock Rd
Meridian Rd
Railroad Dr
Old Railroad Dr
Cass Av
Quarry Rd
Canal Bank Rd
Maley Rd
Jeans Rd
Grant Rd
83
171
13100
14600
11500
11700
11900
12100
12200
12300
12600
13000
13800
14000
14200
14700
1100
1200
3800
100
300
400
500
600
St. Patrick Rd
Saddle Ln
Jaymia Ct
Wheeler Dr
Lenox Ln
Carley Ct
Stirrup Ln
Stirrup Ct
Hilltop Dr
Wexford Ct
Wexford Dr
Melshane Ct
Senon
4th St
Misko Ct
Kromray Rd
Carriage Ridge
Blacksmith Ln
Coach Ln
Woodcrest Ln
119th St
117th St
118th St
Center St
Hillcrest Rd
Niagara St
Theresa
Anne Ct
Korlin Rd
Franciscan
Village Dr
Anthony
Colette Ct
Beatrice Ln
Wildplum Ln
Wild Oak Dr
Wild Oak Ct
Woodcrest Ct
Crestwood Ln
121st St
Hillcrest
S Boyer St
McGuire Pkwy
Pine St
Prairie Ct
Apple Av
Oak Av
2nd St
3rd St
5th St
6th St
Schultz St
1st St
Janas
Country Ct
Country Ln
Kromray
Young St
Woodcrest Ln
Barton Dr
Albany Av
Sumner St
Amberwood Ln
Camelot Ln
Roscommon Wy
Drawbridge Ln
Crossing Ct
Baileys Dr
Castlewood Ct
Castlewood Dr
Berkley Ln
Norwalk Rd
Chatham Dr
Keough St
Pendleton Dr
Woburn Dr
Drover Dr
Monmouth Dr
Covington Ct
Camelot
Overton Dr
Bennington Ct
Amber Dr
St. Brendans Ct
Notre Dame
Pleasant Pl
Abbey Dr
Vincents Dr
Cronin Ct
Oaks
Mirta Cir
Jane Ct
Jane Av
Steven Ct
Marian Dr
Long Cove Dr
Bella Ln
Oaktree
Holly Ct
Steeples Dr
Spire Dr
Steepleview Ln
Oxford Ct
Cambridge
St. James Wy
Spyglass Ct
Ruffled Feathers Dr
Pete Dye Dr
Loblolly Ct
Firethorn Ct
RAND McNALLY

1:24,000
1 in. = 2000 ft.
0 0.25 0.5
miles

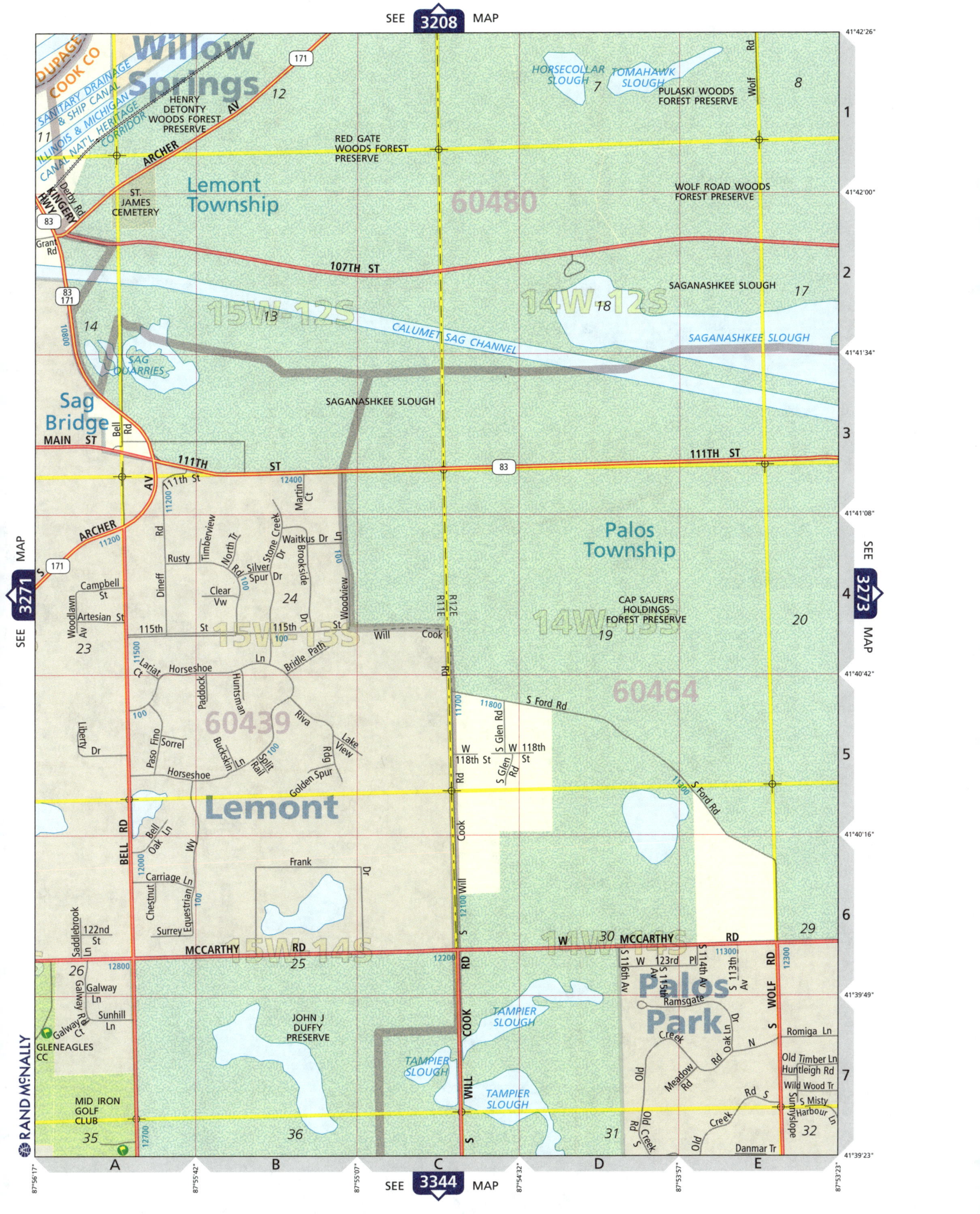

1:24,000
1 in. = 2000 ft.
0 0.25 0.5
miles

SEE 3209 MAP

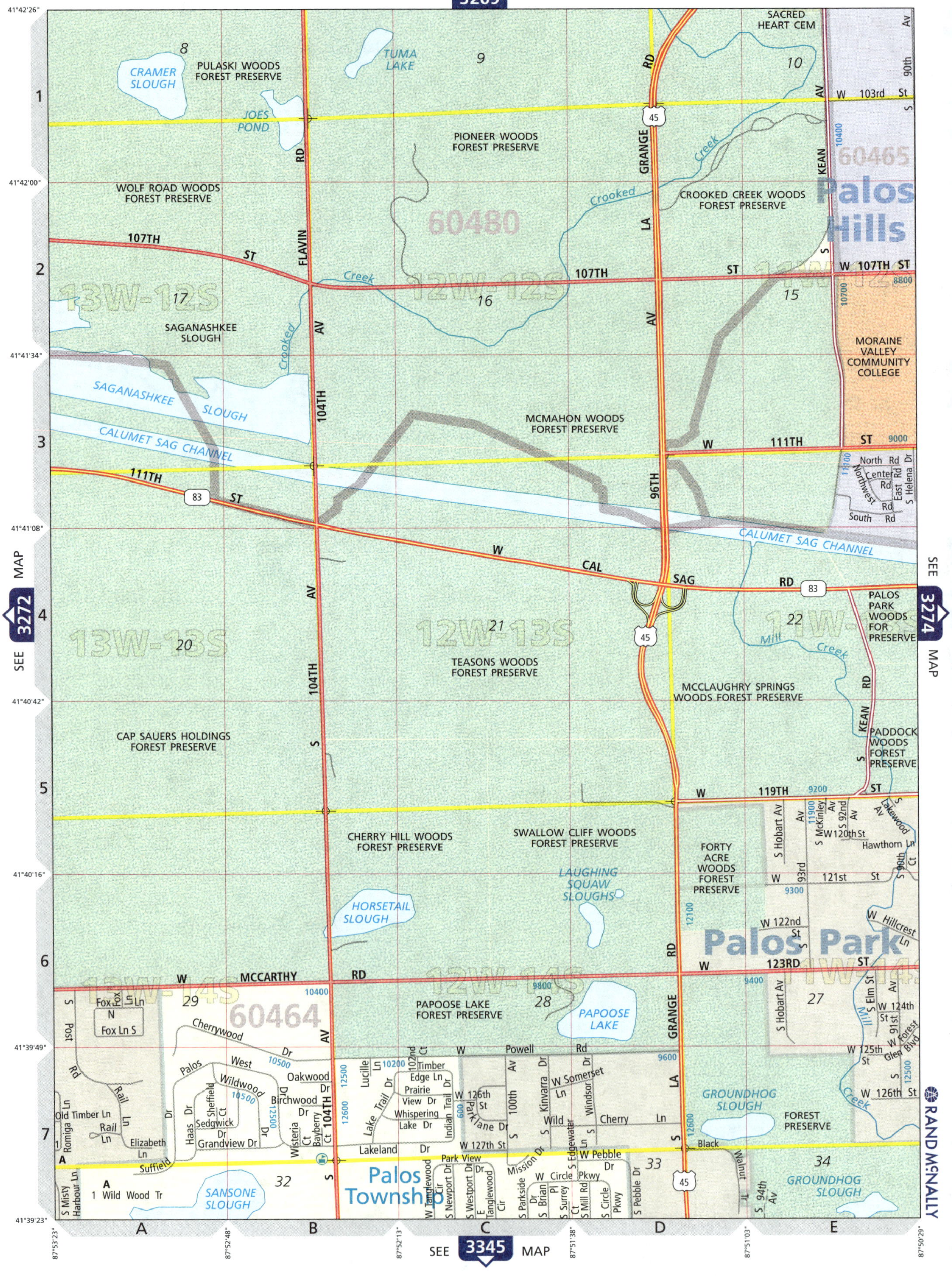

SEE 3272 MAP

SEE 3274 MAP

SEE 3345 MAP

1:24,000
1 in. = 2000 ft.
0 0.25 0.5
miles

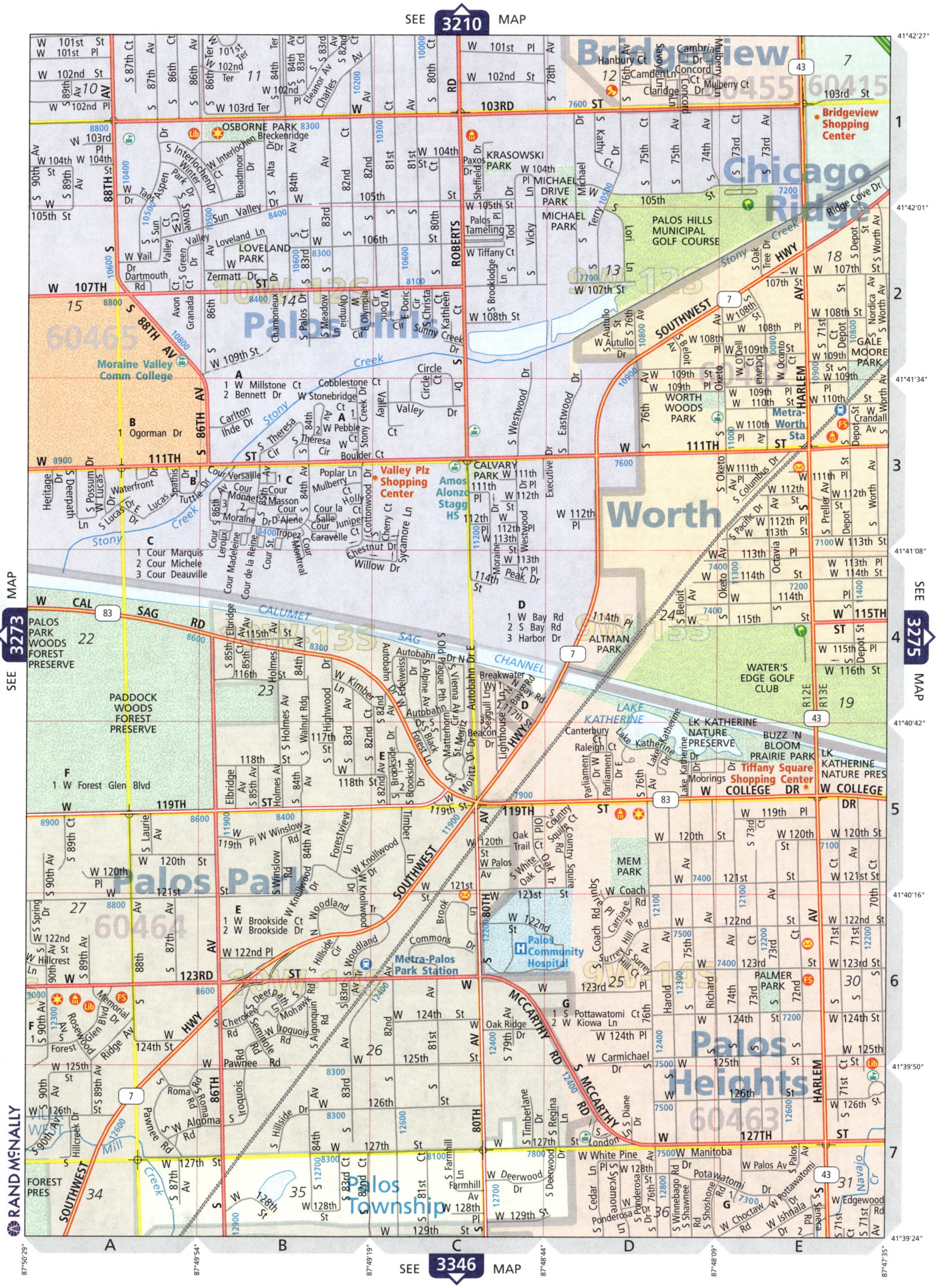

1:24,000
1 in. = 2000 ft.
0 0.25 0.5
miles

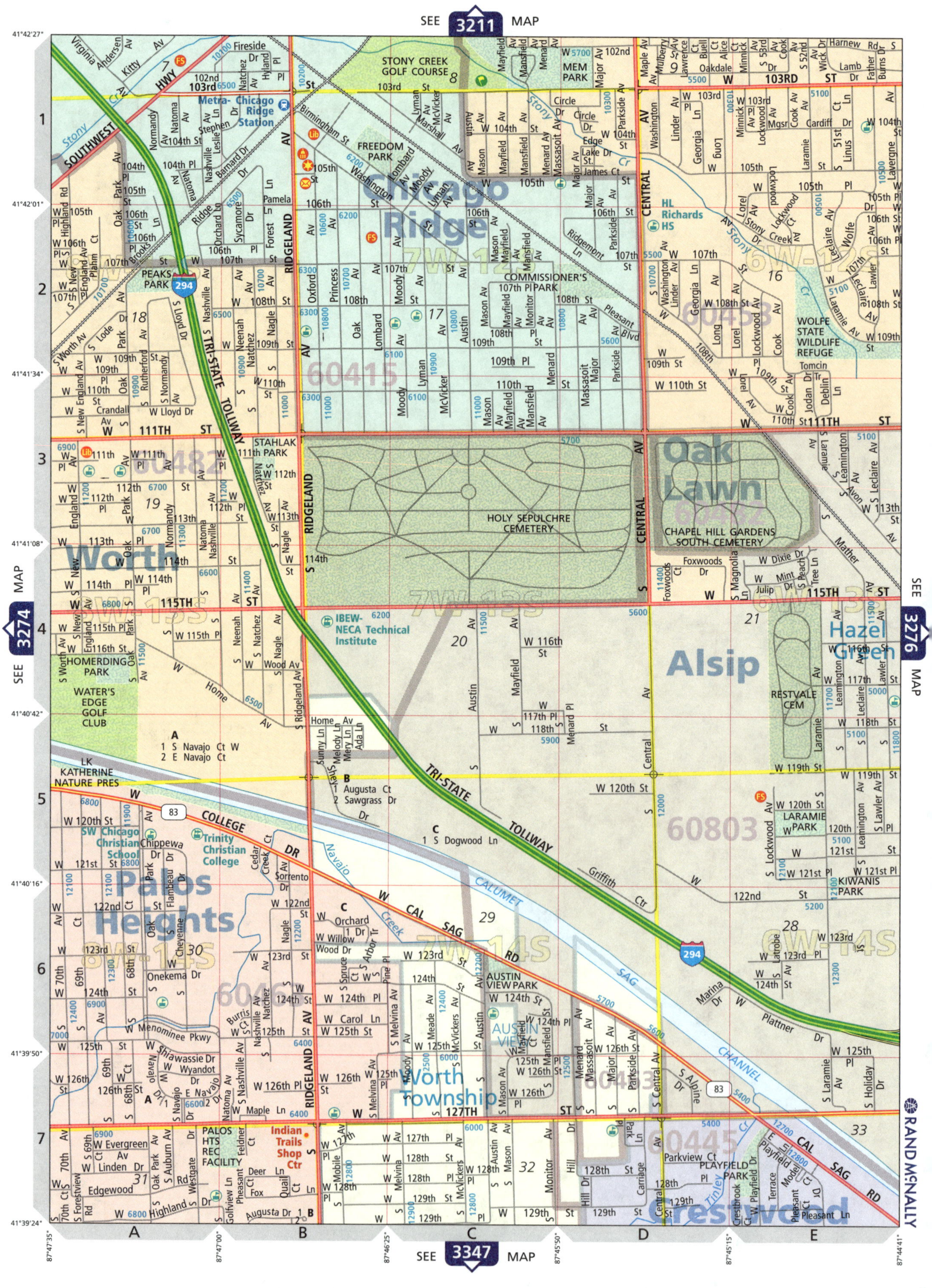
SEE 3211 MAP
SEE 3274 MAP
SEE 3276 MAP
SEE 3347 MAP
Chicago Ridge
Worth
Oak Lawn
Alsip
Hazel Green
Palos Heights
Worth Township
Crestwood
60415
60482
60453
60803
60463
60445
STONY CREEK GOLF COURSE
MEM PARK
Metra- Chicago Ridge Station
FREEDOM PARK
PEAKS PARK
COMMISSIONER'S PARK
HL Richards HS
WOLFE STATE WILDLIFE REFUGE
STAHLAK PARK
HOLY SEPULCHRE CEMETERY
CHAPEL HILL GARDENS SOUTH CEMETERY
IBEW-NECA Technical Institute
HOMERDING PARK
WATER'S EDGE GOLF CLUB
RESTVALE CEM
LK KATHERINE NATURE PRES
SW Chicago Christian School
Trinity Christian College
LARAMIE PARK
KIWANIS PARK
AUSTIN VIEW PARK
PALOS HTS REC FACILITY
Indian Trails Shop Ctr
PLAYFIELD PARK
TRI-STATE TOLLWAY
SOUTHWEST HWY
COLLEGE DR
CAL SAG RD
CALUMET SAG CHANNEL
RIDGELAND AV
CENTRAL AV
103RD ST
111TH ST
115TH ST
127TH ST
Navajo Creek
Stony Cr
Tinley Cr
294
83
7W-13S
6W-13S
7W-12S
6W-12S
5W-13S
7W-14S
6W-14S
8W-14S
A
B
C
D
E
1
2
3
4
5
6
7
41°42'27"
41°42'01"
41°41'34"
41°41'08"
41°40'42"
41°40'16"
41°39'50"
41°39'24"
87°47'35"
87°47'00"
87°46'25"
87°45'50"
87°45'15"
87°44'41"
RAND McNALLY

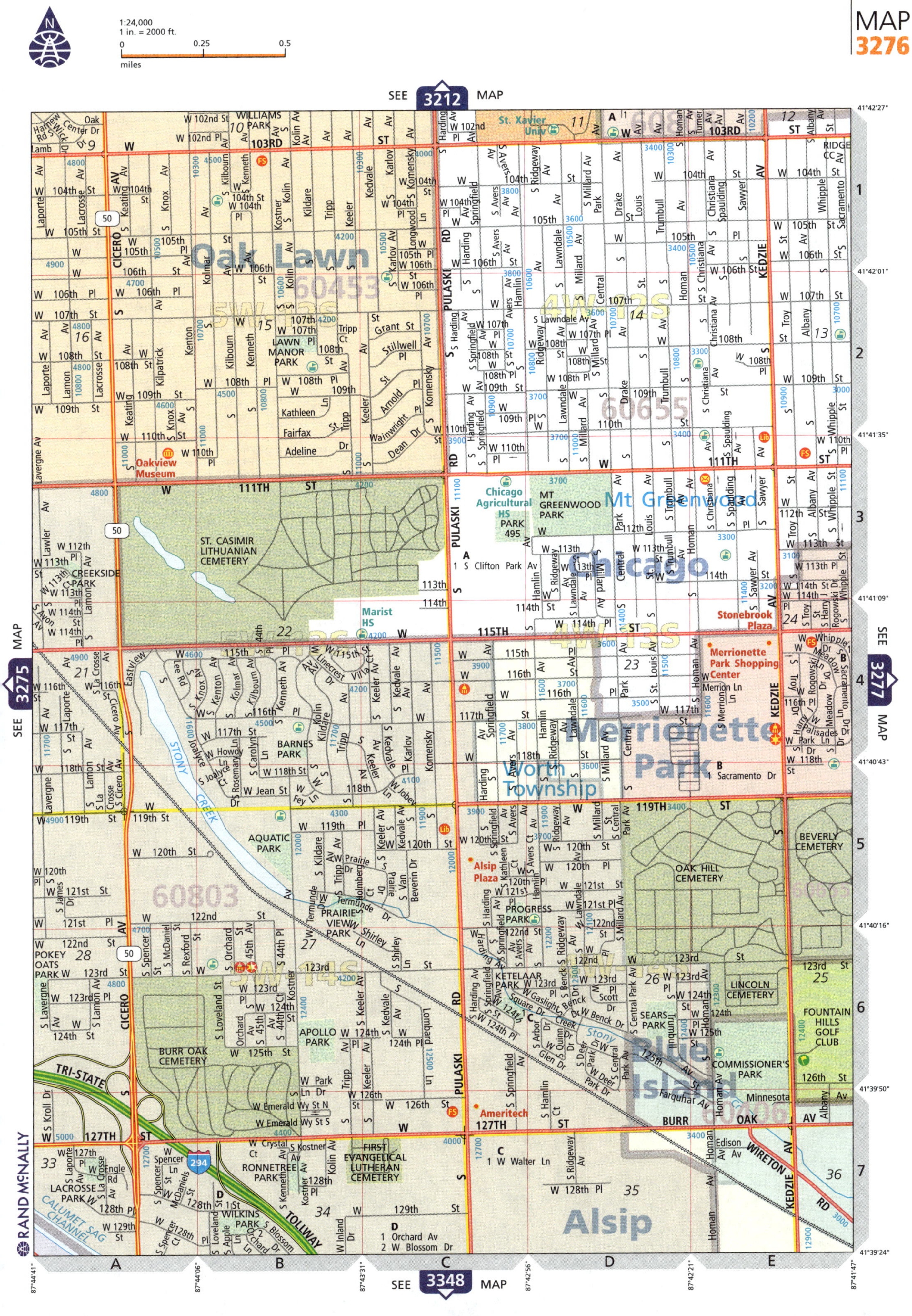
1:24,000
1 in. = 2000 ft.
0 0.25 0.5
miles
SEE 3212 MAP
SEE 3348 MAP
SEE 3275 MAP
SEE 3277 MAP
Oak Lawn
60453
60655
60803
60406
Chicago
Mt Greenwood
Merrionette Park
Worth Township
Blue Island
Alsip
5W-13S
4W-13S
5W-14S
4W-14S
St. Xavier Univ
Oakview Museum
ST. CASIMIR LITHUANIAN CEMETERY
CREEKSIDE PARK
LAWN MANOR PARK
Chicago Agricultural HS
PARK 495
MT GREENWOOD PARK
Marist HS
Stonebrook Plaza
Merrionette Park Shopping Center
BARNES PARK
AQUATIC PARK
STONY CREEK
PRAIRIE VIEW PARK
Alsip Plaza
PROGRESS PARK
KETELAAR PARK
OAK HILL CEMETERY
BEVERLY CEMETERY
LINCOLN CEMETERY
SEARS PARK
FOUNTAIN HILLS GOLF CLUB
COMMISSIONER'S PARK
POKEY OATS PARK
BURR OAK CEMETERY
APOLLO PARK
Ameritech
FIRST EVANGELICAL LUTHERAN CEMETERY
RONNETREE PARK
LACROSSE PARK
WILKINS PARK
CALUMET SAG CHANNEL
TRI-STATE TOLLWAY
294
50
CICERO AV
PULASKI RD
KEDZIE AV
103RD ST
111TH ST
115TH ST
119TH ST
127TH ST
BURR OAK AV
WIRETON RD
RIDGE CC
RAND McNALLY

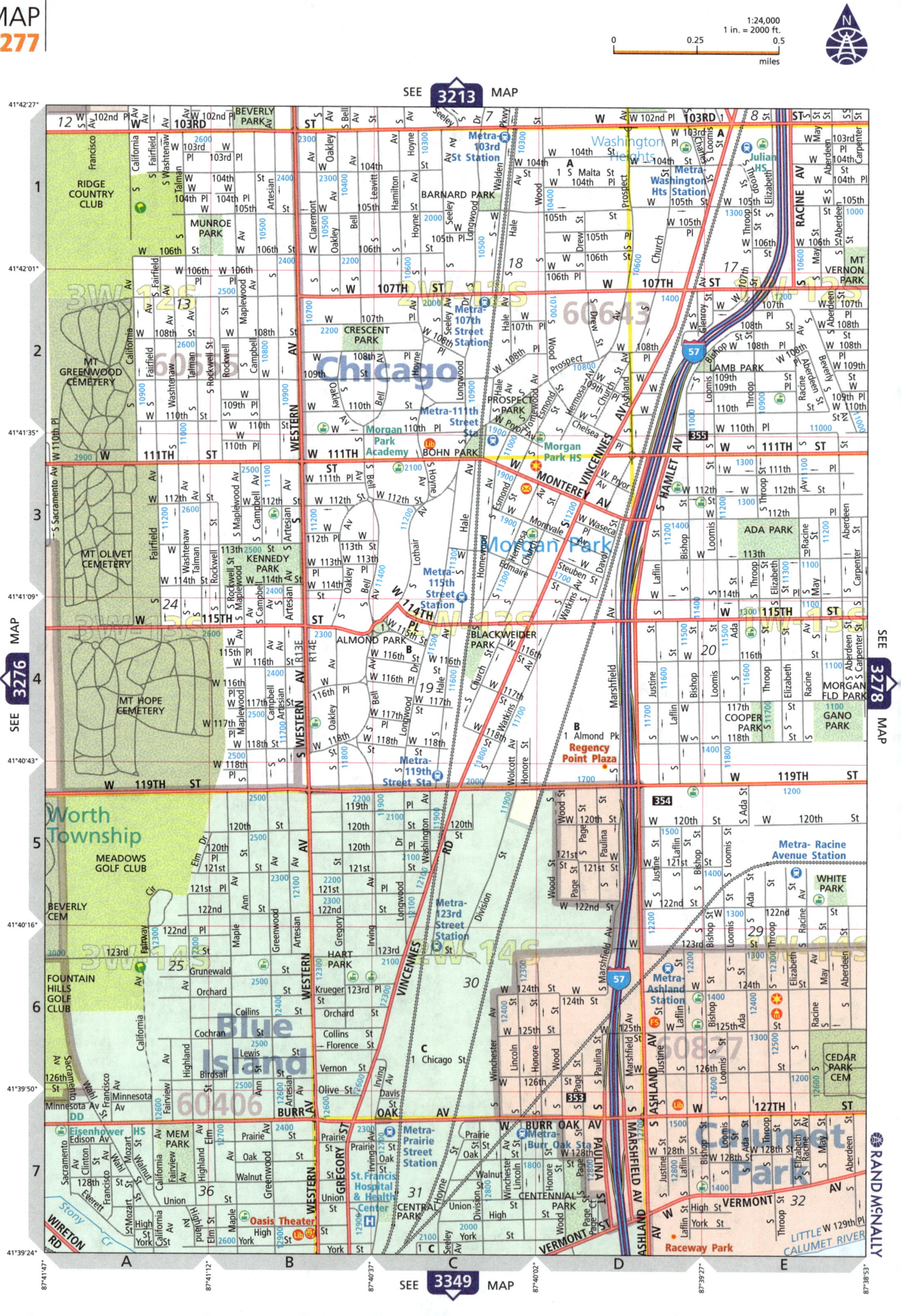
1:24,000
1 in. = 2000 ft.
0 0.25 0.5
miles
N
SEE 3213 MAP
SEE 3276 MAP
SEE 3278 MAP
SEE 3349 MAP
Chicago
Blue Island
Calumet Park
Morgan Park
Washington Heights
Worth Township
60655
60643
60406
60827
RIDGE COUNTRY CLUB
MUNROE PARK
MT GREENWOOD CEMETERY
MT OLIVET CEMETERY
MT HOPE CEMETERY
MEADOWS GOLF CLUB
BEVERLY CEM
FOUNTAIN HILLS GOLF CLUB
CRESCENT PARK
KENNEDY PARK
BARNARD PARK
PROSPECT PARK
BOHN PARK
ALMOND PARK
BLACKWEIDER PARK
LAMB PARK
ADA PARK
MT VERNON PARK
MORGAN FLD PARK
COOPER PARK
GANO PARK
WHITE PARK
HART PARK
MEM PARK
CENTENNIAL PARK
CENTRAL PARK
CEDAR PARK CEM
Metra-103rd St Station
Metra-107th Street Station
Metra-111th Street Sta
Metra-115th Street Station
Metra-119th Street Sta
Metra-123rd Street Station
Metra-Washington Hts Station
Metra-Racine Avenue Station
Metra-Ashland Station
Metra-Prairie Street Station
Metra-Burr Oak Sta
Morgan Park Academy
Morgan Park HS
Julian HS
Eisenhower HS
Regency Point Plaza
Oasis Theater
St. Francis Hospital & Health Center
Raceway Park
W 103RD ST
W 107TH ST
W 111TH ST
115TH ST
119TH ST
127TH ST
BURR OAK AV
VERMONT ST
WESTERN AV
VINCENNES AV
VINCENNES RD
ASHLAND AV
MARSHFIELD AV
RACINE AV
S HAMLET AV
W MONTEREY AV
W 114TH PL
GREGORY ST
WIRETON RD
PAULINA ST
LITTLE CALUMET RIVER
Stony Cr
57
RAND McNALLY

1:24,000
1 in. = 2000 ft.
0 0.25 0.5
miles

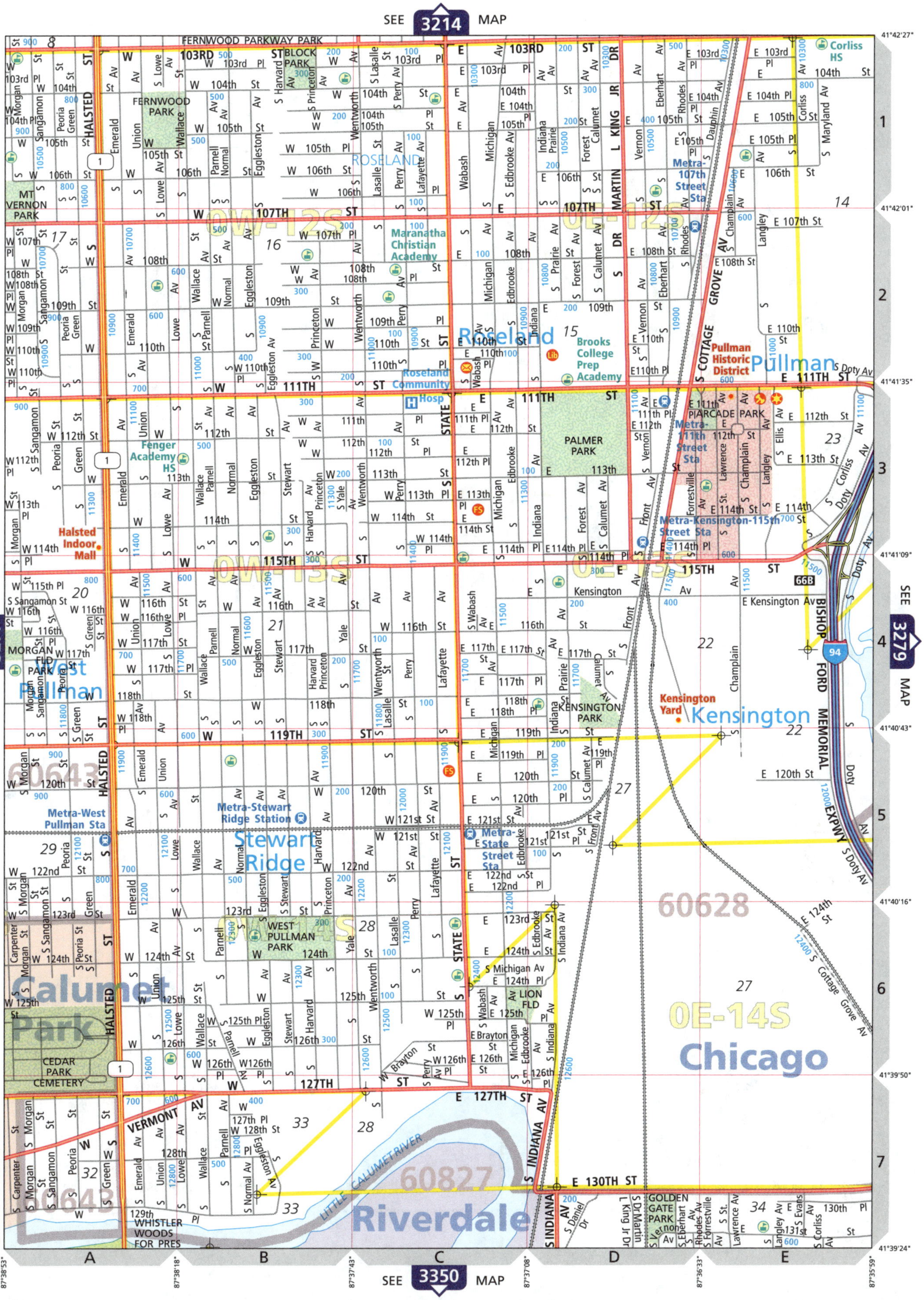
SEE 3214 MAP
SEE 3350 MAP
SEE 3277 MAP
SEE 3279 MAP
Roseland
Pullman
Kensington
West Pullman
Stewart Ridge
Calumet Park
Riverdale
Chicago
0W-12S
0E-12S
0W-13S
0E-13S
0W-14S
0E-14S
60643
60628
60827
FERNWOOD PARKWAY PARK
FERNWOOD PARK
BLOCK PARK
MT VERNON PARK
Maranatha Christian Academy
Roseland Community Hosp
Brooks College Prep Academy
Pullman Historic District
PALMER PARK
ARCADE PARK
Metra-107th Street Sta
Metra-111th Street Sta
Metra-Kensington-115th Street Sta
Metra-West Pullman Sta
Metra-Stewart Ridge Station
Metra-State Street Sta
Fenger Academy HS
Halsted Indoor Mall
MORGAN FLD PARK
KENSINGTON PARK
Kensington Yard
WEST PULLMAN PARK
LION FLD
CEDAR PARK CEMETERY
WHISTLER WOODS FOR PRES
GOLDEN GATE PARK
Corliss HS
LITTLE CALUMET RIVER
HALSTED
STATE
103RD
107TH ST
111TH ST
115TH ST
119TH ST
127TH ST
E 130TH ST
COTTAGE GROVE AV
MARTIN L KING JR DR
BISHOP FORD MEMORIAL EXPWY
VERMONT AV
INDIANA AV
94
66B
1
A B C D E
1 2 3 4 5 6 7
41°42'27"
41°42'01"
41°41'35"
41°41'09"
41°40'43"
41°40'16"
41°39'50"
41°39'24"
87°38'53"
87°38'18"
87°37'43"
87°37'08"
87°36'33"
87°35'59"

1:24,000
1 in. = 2000 ft.
0 0.25 0.5
miles

SEE 3215 MAP

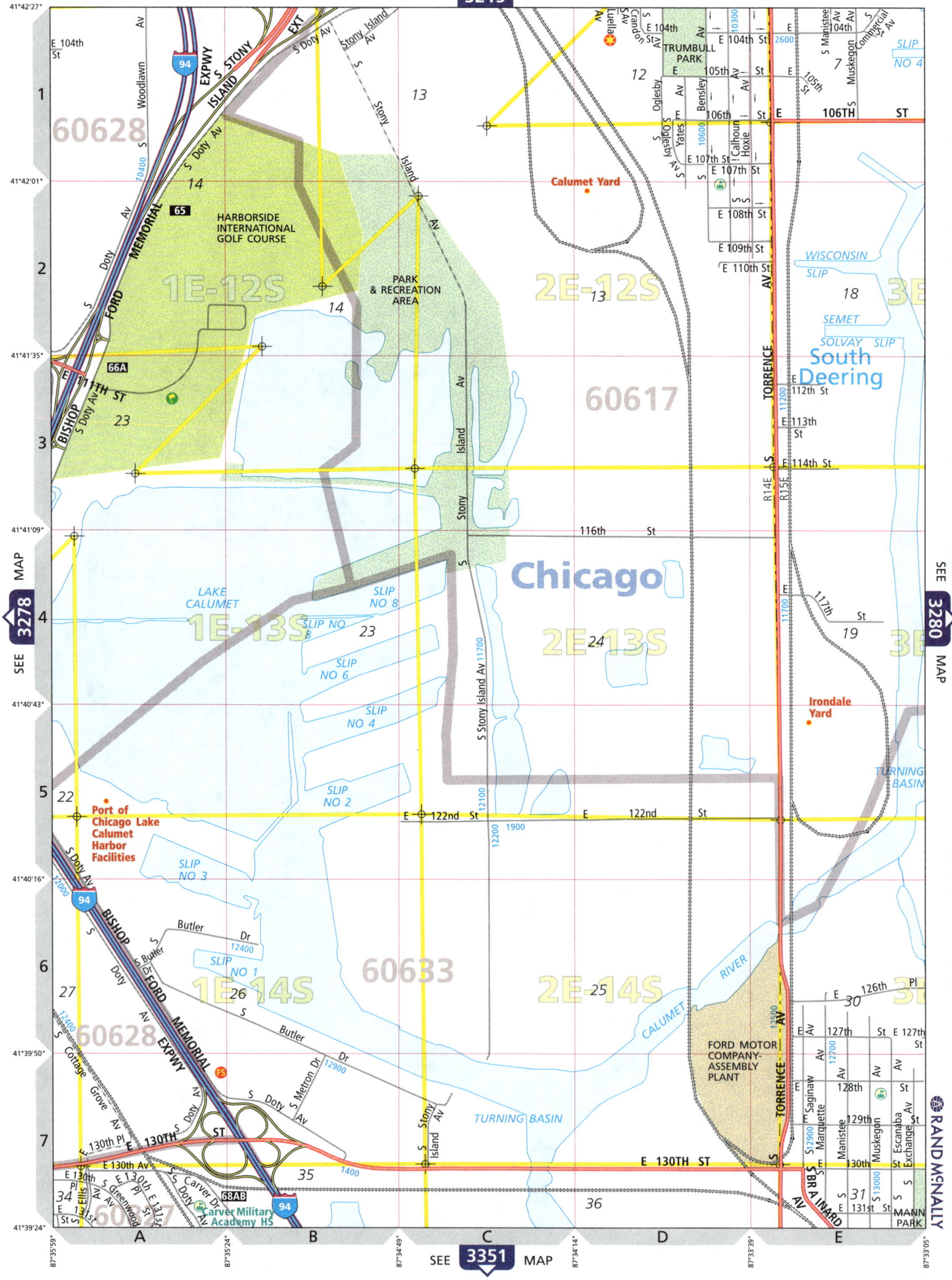

SEE 3278 MAP
SEE 3280 MAP
SEE 3351 MAP

1:24,000
1 in. = 2000 ft.
0 0.25 0.5
miles

SEE 3216 MAP

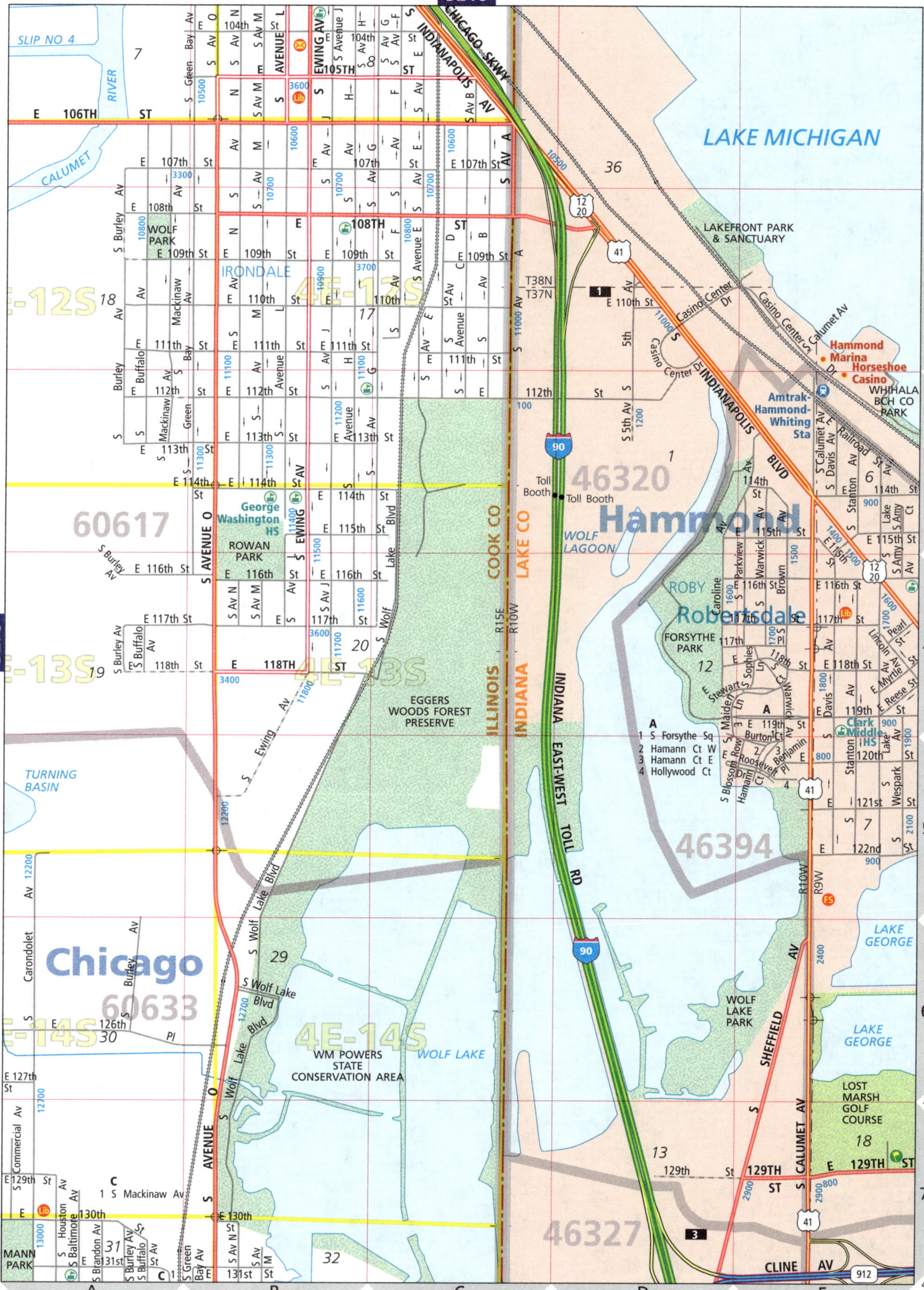
LAKE MICHIGAN
SLIP NO 4
CALUMET RIVER
TURNING BASIN
E 106TH ST
CHICAGO SKWY
INDIANAPOLIS AV
INDIANAPOLIS BLVD
IRONDALE
WOLF PARK
ROWAN PARK
George Washington HS
60617
60633
Chicago
4E-12S
4E-13S
4E-14S
EGGERS WOODS FOREST PRESERVE
WM POWERS STATE CONSERVATION AREA
WOLF LAKE
COOK CO
LAKE CO
ILLINOIS
INDIANA
INDIANA EAST-WEST TOLL RD
Toll Booth
WOLF LAGOON
LAKEFRONT PARK & SANCTUARY
Hammond Marina
Horseshoe Casino
WHIHALA BCH CO PARK
Amtrak-Hammond-Whiting Sta
Casino Center Dr
46320
Hammond
ROBY
Robertsdale
FORSYTHE PARK
Clark Middle HS
46394
46327
LAKE GEORGE
WOLF LAKE PARK
LOST MARSH GOLF COURSE
SHEFFIELD AV
CALUMET AV
CLINE AV
E 129TH ST
E 130th
MANN PARK
S AVENUE O
S EWING AV
T38N
T37N
R15E
R10W
R9W
A
1 S Forsythe Sq
2 Hamann Ct W
3 Hamann Ct E
4 Hollywood Ct
C
1 S Mackinaw Av

SEE 3279 MAP

SEE B MAP

SEE 3352 MAP

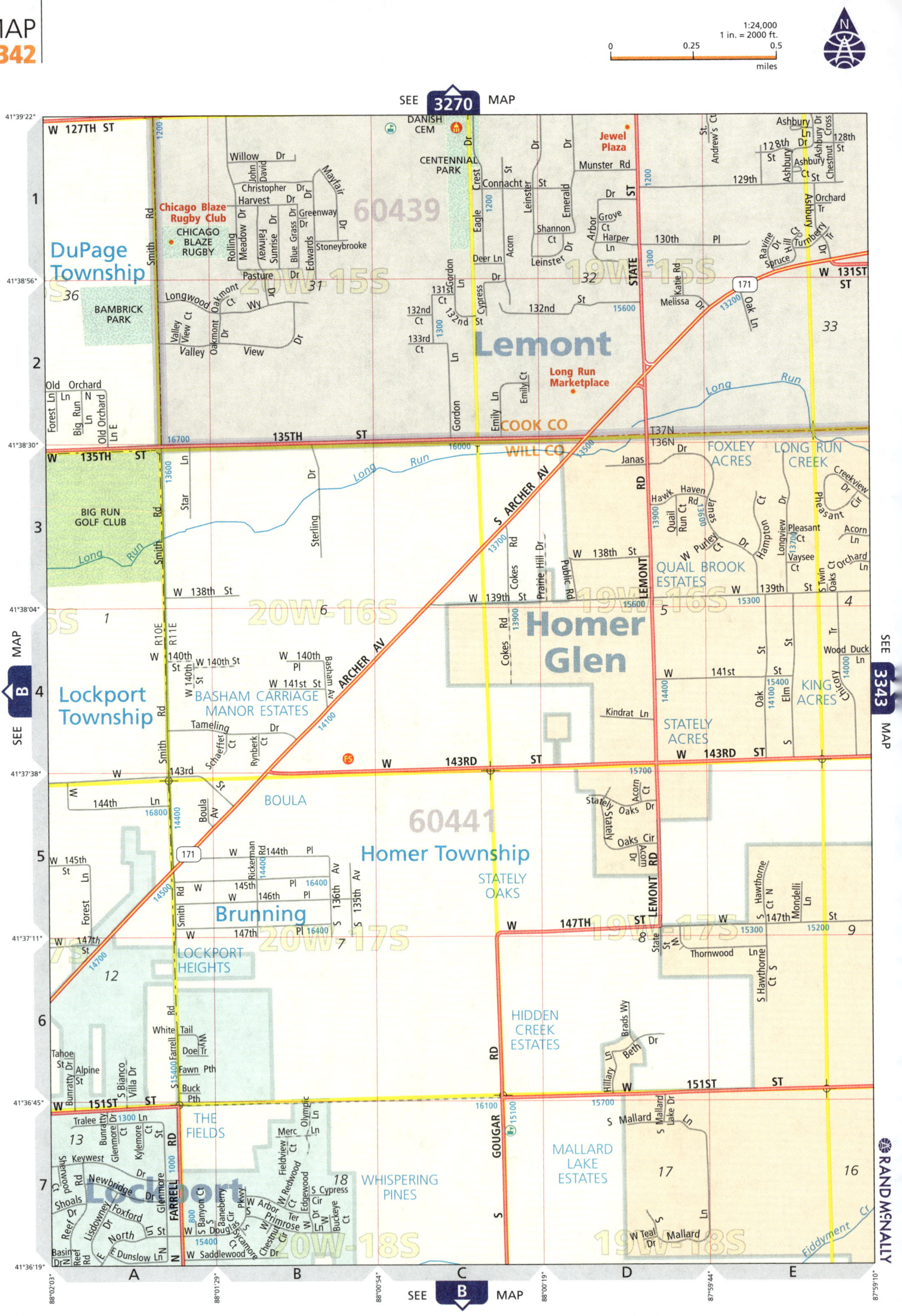
1:24,000
1 in. = 2000 ft.
0 0.25 0.5
miles
N
SEE 3270 MAP
SEE B MAP
SEE 3343 MAP
SEE B MAP
DuPage Township
Lockport Township
Homer Township
Lemont
Homer Glen
Lockport
Brunning
COOK CO
WILL CO
T37N
T36N
R10E
R11E
60439
60441
20W-15S
19W-15S
20W-16S
19W-16S
20W-17S
19W-17S
20W-18S
19W-18S
W 127TH ST
W 131ST ST
135TH ST
W 135TH ST
W 143RD ST
W 147TH ST
W 151ST ST
W 138th St
W 139th St
W 141st St
W 144th Ln
W 145th St
S ARCHER AV
ARCHER AV
STATE RD
LEMONT RD
GOUGAR RD
FARRELL RD
Smith Rd
DANISH CEM
CENTENNIAL PARK
Jewel Plaza
Chicago Blaze Rugby Club
CHICAGO BLAZE RUGBY
BAMBRICK PARK
Long Run Marketplace
BIG RUN GOLF CLUB
Long Run
FOXLEY ACRES
LONG RUN CREEK
QUAIL BROOK ESTATES
BASHAM CARRIAGE MANOR ESTATES
STATELY ACRES
KING ACRES
BOULA
STATELY OAKS
LOCKPORT HEIGHTS
HIDDEN CREEK ESTATES
THE FIELDS
WHISPERING PINES
MALLARD LAKE ESTATES
Stately Oaks Dr
Oaks Cir
Kindrat Ln
Thornwood Ln
S Mallard Ln
W Teal Dr
Mallard
Fiddyment Ct
Brads Wy
Beth Dr
Hillary Ln
171
31 32 33 36 1 5 4 6 12 7 8 9 13 18 17 16
A B C D E
1 2 3 4 5 6 7
41°39'22"
41°38'56"
41°38'30"
41°38'04"
41°37'38"
41°37'11"
41°36'45"
41°36'19"
88°02'03"
88°01'29"
88°00'54"
88°00'19"
87°59'44"
87°59'10"
RAND McNALLY

1:24,000
1 in. = 2000 ft.
0 0.25 0.5
miles

SEE 3271 MAP

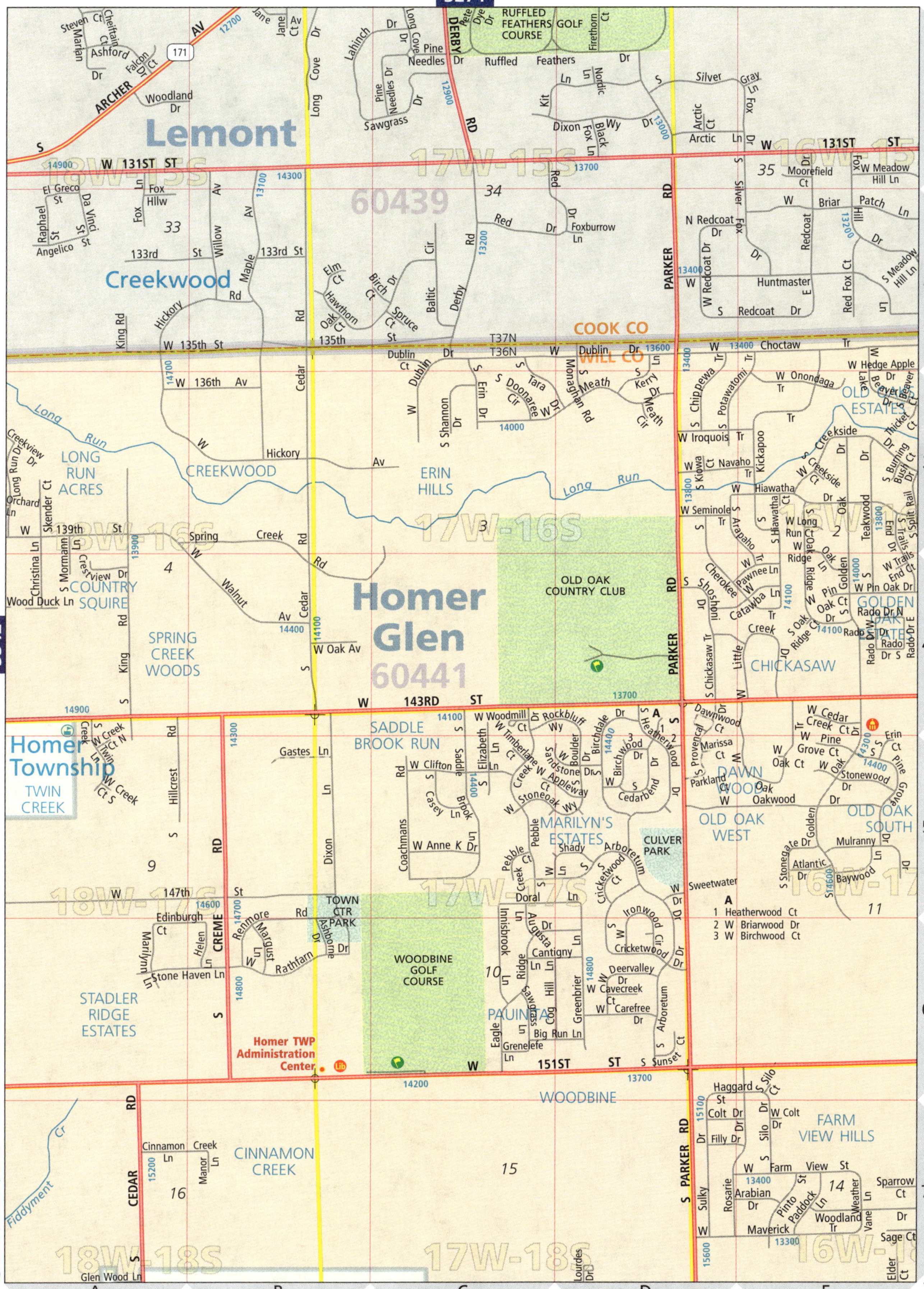

A B C D E
1 2 3 4 5 6 7

SEE 3342 MAP
SEE 3344 MAP
SEE B MAP

RAND McNALLY

1:24,000
1 in. = 2000 ft.
0 0.25 0.5
miles

SEE 3272 MAP

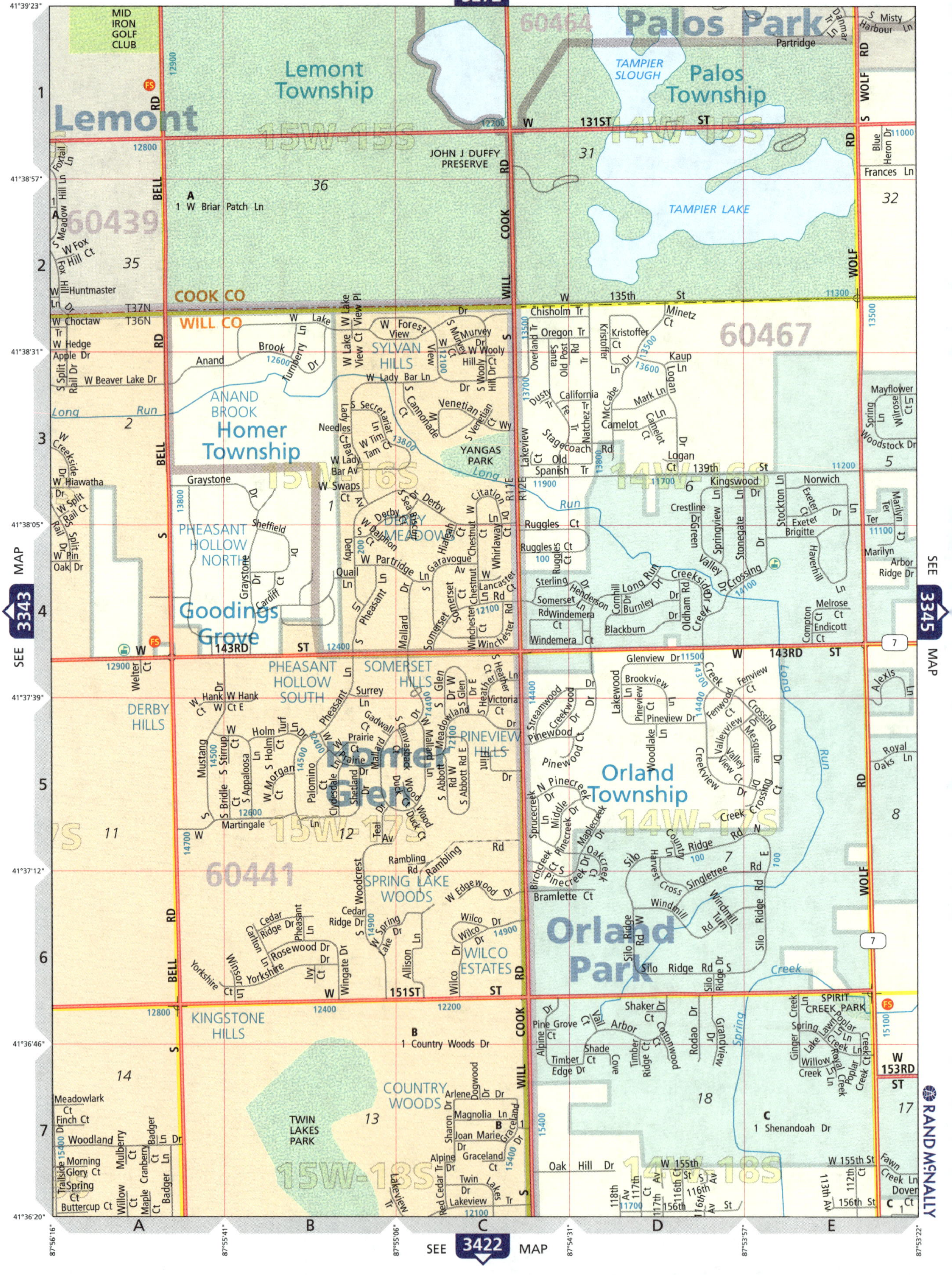
MID IRON GOLF CLUB
Lemont
Lemont Township
Palos Park
Palos Township
TAMPIER SLOUGH
TAMPIER LAKE
JOHN J DUFFY PRESERVE
W 131ST ST
W 135th St
COOK CO
WILL CO
T37N
T36N
60439
60464
60467
60441
15W-15S
14W-15S
15W-16S
14W-16S
15W-17S
14W-17S
15W-18S
14W-18S
1 W Briar Patch Ln
SYLVAN HILLS
ANAND BROOK
Homer Township
YANGAS PARK
DERBY MEADOWS
PHEASANT HOLLOW NORTH
Goodings Grove
W 143RD ST
PHEASANT HOLLOW SOUTH
SOMERSET HILLS
DERBY HILLS
Homer Glen
PINEVIEW HILLS
Orland Township
SPRING LAKE WOODS
WILCO ESTATES
Orland Park
W 151ST ST
KINGSTONE HILLS
1 Country Woods Dr
COUNTRY WOODS
TWIN LAKES PARK
SPIRIT CREEK PARK
W 153RD ST
1 Shenandoah Dr
W 155th St
BELL RD
S BELL RD
COOK RD
S WILL COOK RD
WOLF RD
S WOLF RD
Long Run
Spring Creek
RAND McNALLY

SEE 3343 MAP
SEE 3345 MAP
SEE 3422 MAP

1:24,000
1 in. = 2000 ft.
0 0.25 0.5
miles

SEE 3273 MAP

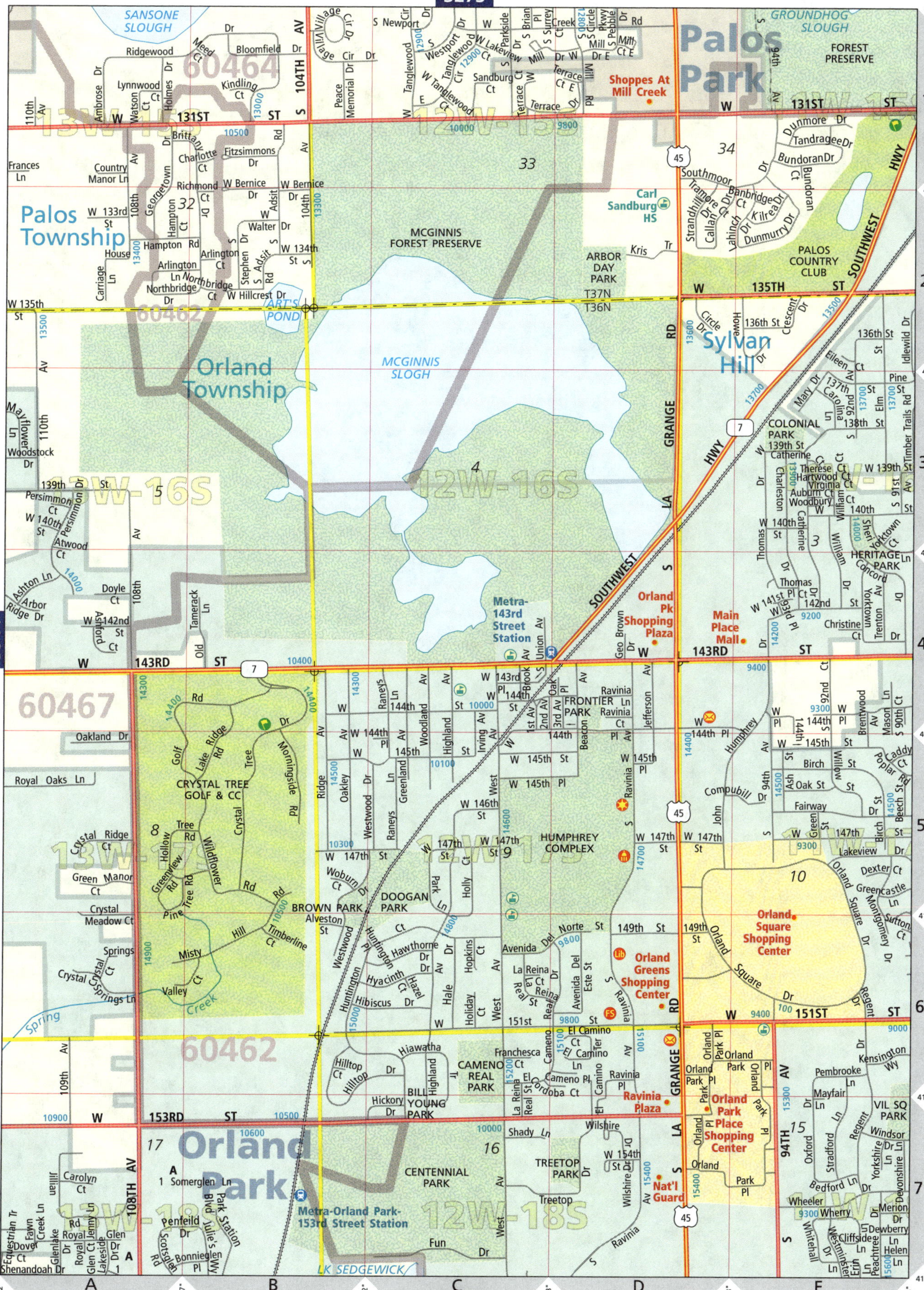
SANSONE SLOUGH
GROUNDHOG SLOUGH
FOREST PRESERVE
Palos Park
Shoppes At Mill Creek
Palos Township
Orland Township
MCGINNIS FOREST PRESERVE
MCGINNIS SLOGH
ART'S POND
Carl Sandburg HS
ARBOR DAY PARK
PALOS COUNTRY CLUB
Sylvan Hill
COLONIAL PARK
HERITAGE PARK
Metra-143rd Street Station
Orland Pk Shopping Plaza
Main Place Mall
FRONTIER PARK
CRYSTAL TREE GOLF & CC
BROWN PARK
DOOGAN PARK
HUMPHREY COMPLEX
Orland Greens Shopping Center
Orland Square Shopping Center
CAMENO REAL PARK
BILL YOUNG PARK
Ravinia Plaza
Orland Park Place Shopping Center
VIL SQ PARK
Orland Park
Metra-Orland Park-153rd Street Station
CENTENNIAL PARK
TREETOP PARK
Nat'l Guard
LK SEDGEWICK
60464
60462
60467
W 131ST ST
W 135TH ST
W 143RD ST
W 151ST ST
W 153RD ST
104TH AV
108TH AV
94TH AV
S LA GRANGE RD
SOUTHWEST HWY
T37N
T36N
13W-15S
12W-15S
13W-16S
12W-16S
13W-17S
12W-17S
12W-18S
13W-18S
33
34
32
4
5
3
8
9
10
16
17
15
A
B
C
D
E
1
2
3
4
5
6
7
41°39'24"
41°38'58"
41°38'31"
41°38'05"
41°37'39"
41°37'13"
41°36'47"
41°36'21"
87°53'22"
87°52'47"
87°52'12"
87°51'38"
87°51'03"
87°50'28"

SEE 3344 MAP

SEE 3346 MAP

SEE 3423 MAP

1:24,000
1 in. = 2000 ft.
0 0.25 0.5
miles

SEE 3274 MAP

SEE 3345 MAP

SEE 3347 MAP

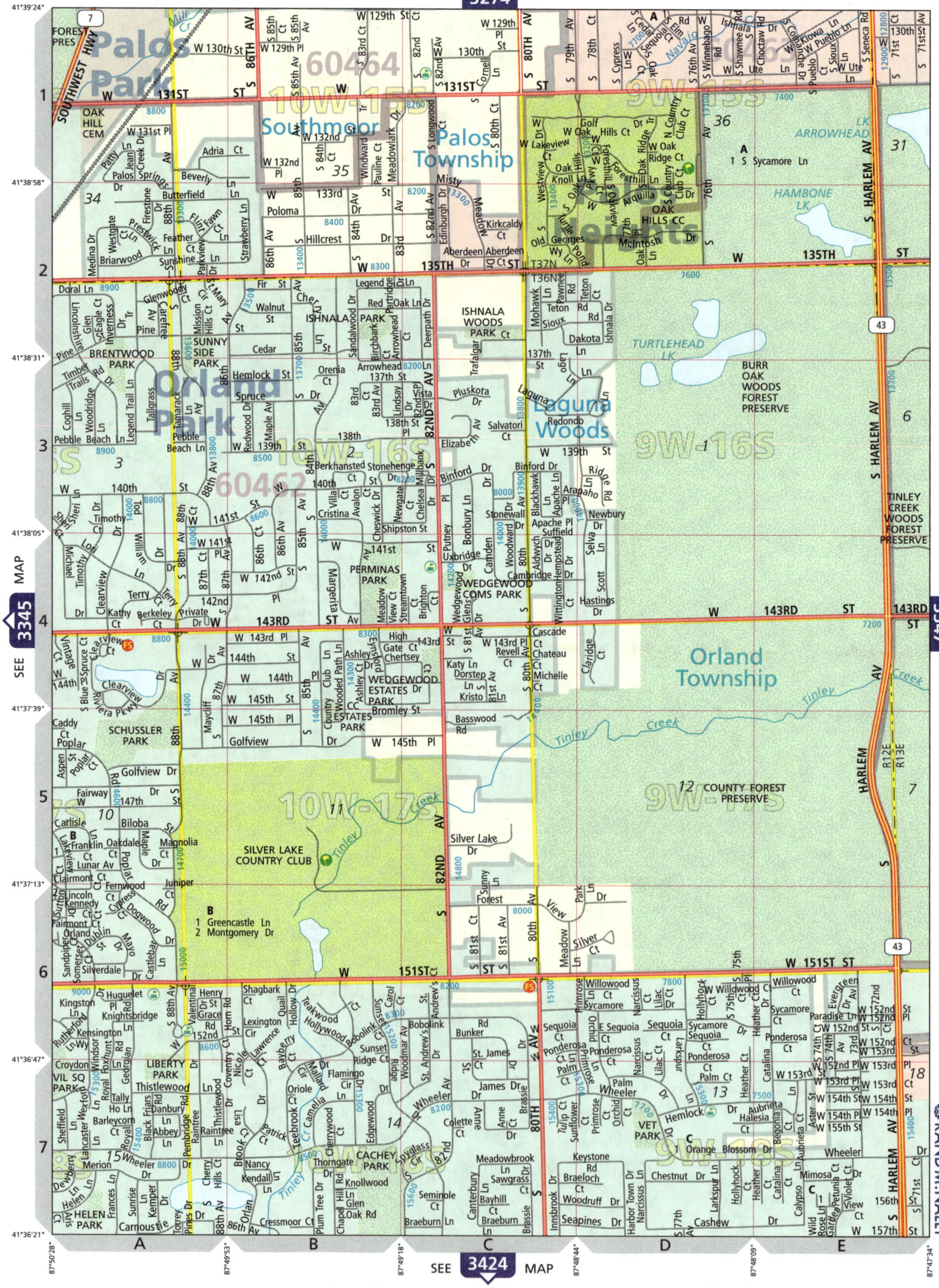
Palos Park
Southmoor
Palos Township
Palos Heights
Orland Park
Laguna Woods
Orland Township
60464
60462
10W-15S
9W-15S
10W-16S
9W-16S
10W-17S
9W-17S
10W-18S
9W-18S
SOUTHWEST HWY
W 131ST ST
W 135TH ST
W 143RD ST
W 151ST ST
S HARLEM AV
S 82ND AV
S 80TH AV
86TH AV
88TH AV
OAK HILL CEM
OAK HILLS CC
ARROWHEAD LK
HAMBONE LK
TURTLEHEAD LK
BURR OAK WOODS FOREST PRESERVE
TINLEY CREEK WOODS FOREST PRESERVE
COUNTY FOREST PRESERVE
ISHNALA WOODS PARK
ISHNALA PARK
SUNNY SIDE PARK
BRENTWOOD PARK
PERMINAS PARK
WEDGEWOOD COMS PARK
WEDGEWOOD ESTATES PARK
SCHUSSLER PARK
SILVER LAKE COUNTRY CLUB
LIBERTY PARK
VIL SQ PARK
HELEN PARK
CACHEY PARK
VET PARK
Tinley Creek
FOREST PRES
A 1 S Sycamore Ln
B 1 Greencastle Ln 2 Montgomery Dr
C 1 Orange Blossom Dr
41°39'24"
41°38'58"
41°38'31"
41°38'05"
41°37'39"
41°37'13"
41°36'47"
41°36'21"
87°50'28"
87°49'53"
87°49'18"
87°48'44"
87°48'09"
87°47'34"

SEE 3424 MAP

1:24,000
1 in. = 2000 ft.
0 0.25 0.5
miles

SEE 3275 MAP

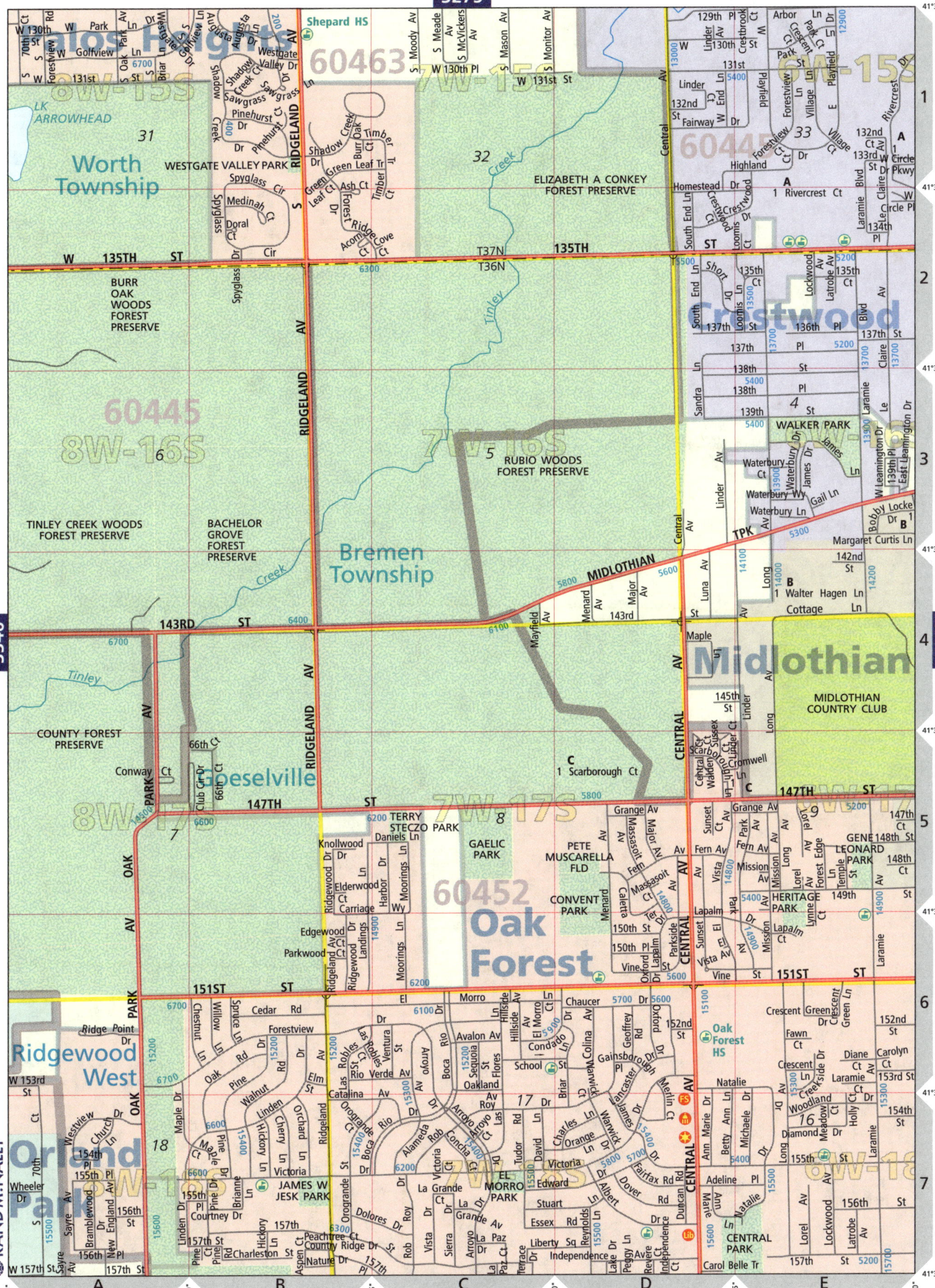
Palos Heights
Worth Township
WESTGATE VALLEY PARK
LK ARROWHEAD
Shepard HS
60463
8W-15S
7W-15S
6W-15S
ELIZABETH A CONKEY FOREST PRESERVE
60445
Crestwood
BURR OAK WOODS FOREST PRESERVE
8W-16S
7W-16S
RUBIO WOODS FOREST PRESERVE
WALKER PARK
TINLEY CREEK WOODS FOREST PRESERVE
BACHELOR GROVE FOREST PRESERVE
Bremen Township
MIDLOTHIAN TPK
Midlothian
MIDLOTHIAN COUNTRY CLUB
COUNTY FOREST PRESERVE
Goeselville
8W-17S
7W-17S
TERRY STECZO PARK
GAELIC PARK
PETE MUSCARELLA FLD
CONVENT PARK
60452
Oak Forest
GENE LEONARD PARK
HERITAGE PARK
Ridgewood West
Orland Park
8W-18S
7W-18S
JAMES W JESK PARK
EL MORRO PARK
Oak Forest HS
CENTRAL PARK
W 135TH ST
143RD ST
147TH ST
151ST ST
RIDGELAND AV
CENTRAL AV
OAK PARK AV
T37N
T36N
Tinley Creek
41°39'24"
41°38'58"
41°38'32"
41°38'06"
41°37'40"
41°37'14"
41°36'48"
41°36'21"
87°47'34"
87°46'59"
87°46'25"
87°45'50"
87°45'15"
87°44'40"
A
B
C
D
E
1
2
3
4
5
6
7

SEE 3346 MAP

SEE 3348 MAP

SEE 3425 MAP

1:24,000
1 in. = 2000 ft.
0 0.25 0.5
miles

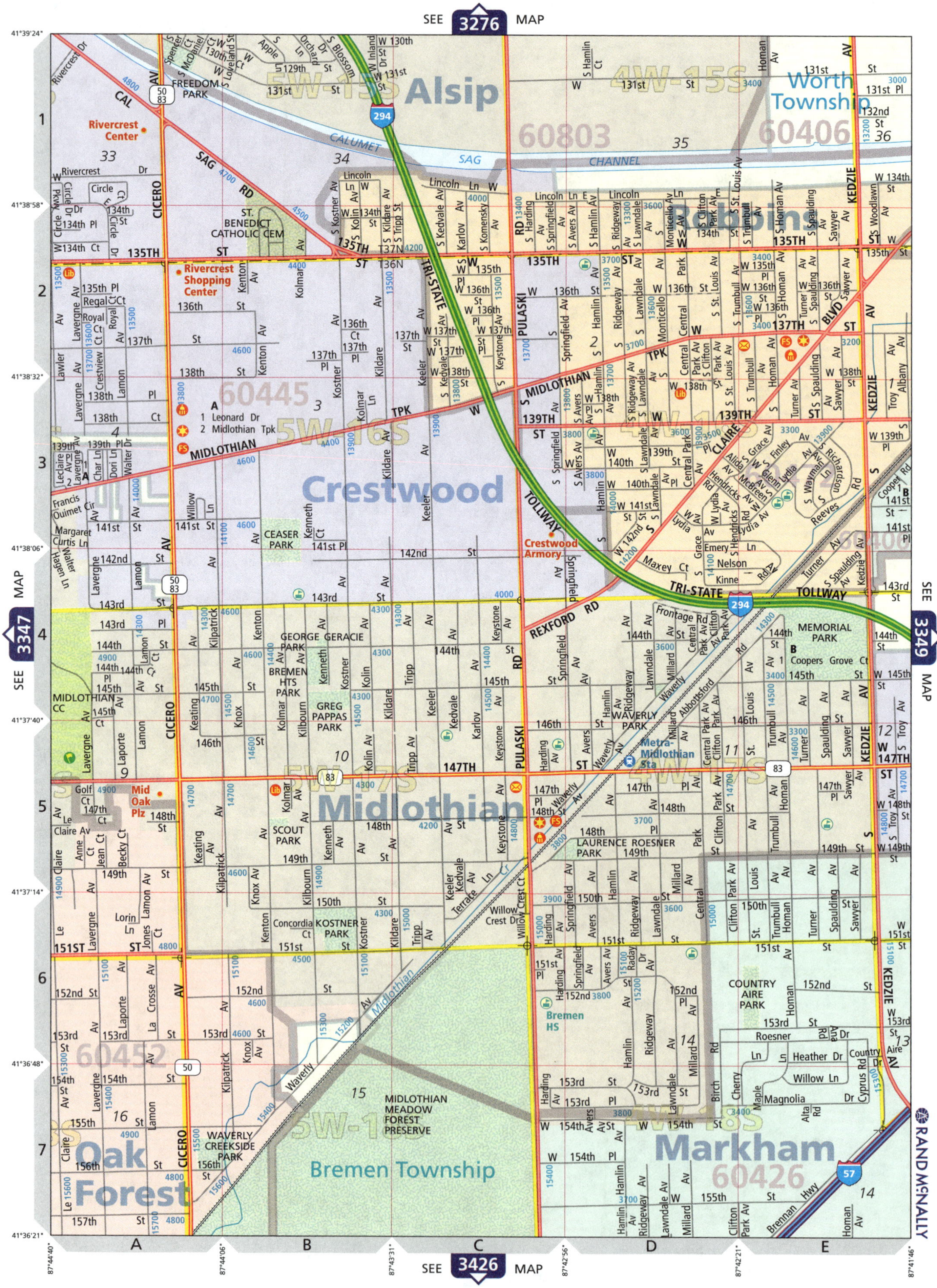
SEE 3276 MAP
SEE 3347 MAP
SEE 3349 MAP
SEE 3426 MAP
Alsip
Worth Township
Robbins
Crestwood
Midlothian
Oak Forest
Markham
Bremen Township
60803
60406
60445
60452
60426
5W-15S
4W-15S
5W-16S
5W-17S
4W-17S
5W-18S
4W-18S
CALUMET SAG CHANNEL
FREEDOM PARK
Rivercrest Center
ST. BENEDICT CATHOLIC CEM
Rivercrest Shopping Center
CEASER PARK
Crestwood Armory
GEORGE GERACIE PARK
BREMEN HTS PARK
GREG PAPPAS PARK
MIDLOTHIAN CC
Mid Oak Plz
SCOUT PARK
KOSTNER PARK
Metra-Midlothian Sta
LAURENCE ROESNER PARK
WAVERLY PARK
MEMORIAL PARK
COUNTRY AIRE PARK
Bremen HS
MIDLOTHIAN MEADOW FOREST PRESERVE
WAVERLY CREEKSIDE PARK
CICERO AV
PULASKI RD
KEDZIE AV
135TH ST
147TH ST
151ST ST
MIDLOTHIAN TPK
TRI-STATE TOLLWAY
REXFORD RD
A
1 Leonard Dr
2 Midlothian Tpk
B
Coopers Grove Ct
A B C D E
1 2 3 4 5 6 7
RAND McNALLY

1:24,000
1 in. = 2000 ft.
0 0.25 0.5
miles

SEE 3277 MAP

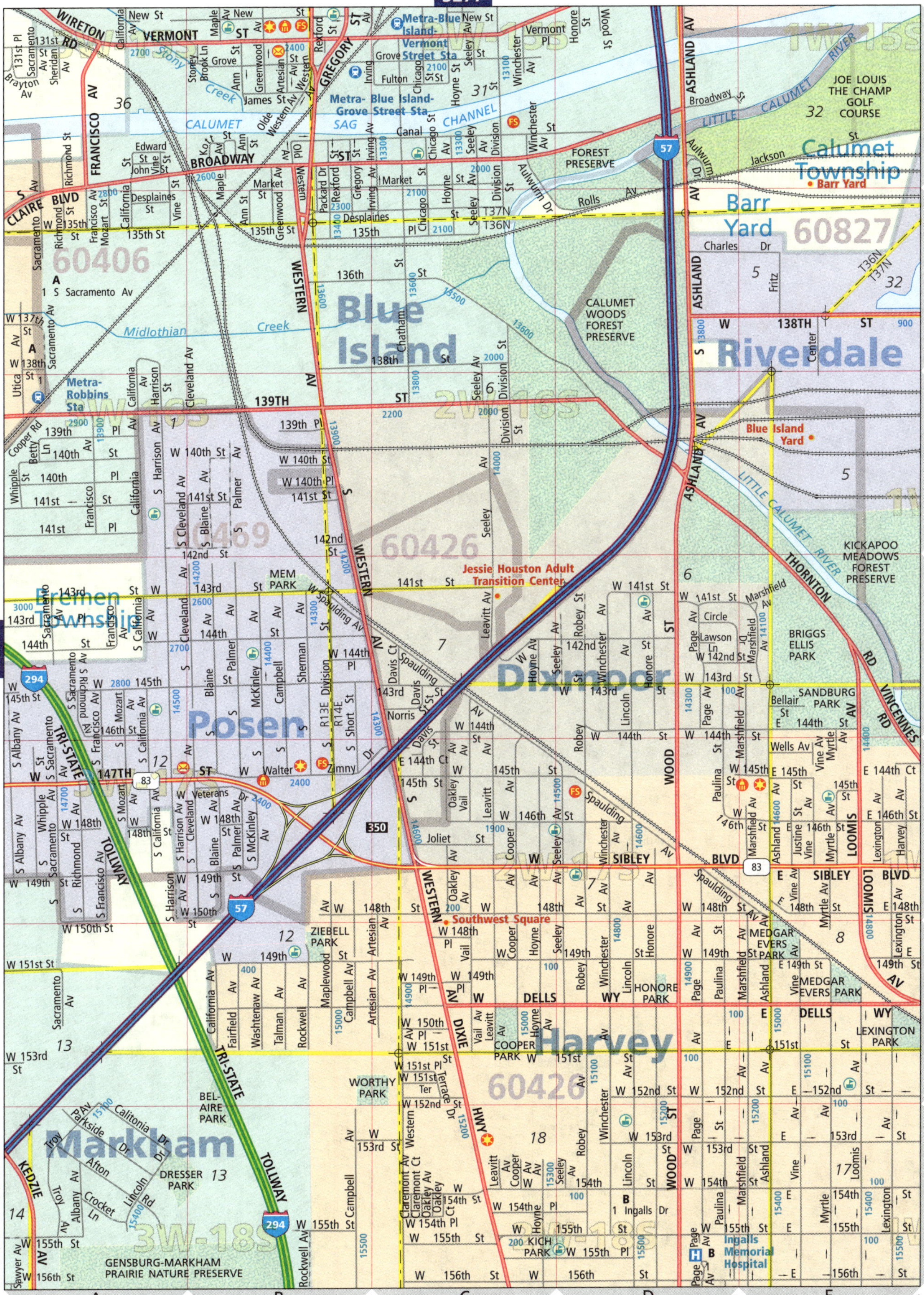

SEE 3348 MAP

SEE 3350 MAP

SEE 3427 MAP

1:24,000
1 in. = 2000 ft.
0 0.25 0.5
miles

SEE 3278 MAP

Riverdale
Calumet Township
JOE LOUIS THE CHAMP GOLF COURSE
Triplex Marina
WHISTLER WOODS FOREST PRESERVE
Chicago
Altgeld Gardens
CARVER PARK
LITTLE CALUMET RIVER
MOHAWK PARK
Metra-Riverdale Station
RIVERDALE PARK
60827
60419
SUNSHINE PARK
LAKE COTTAGE GROVE
KICKAPOO MEADOWS FOREST PRESERVE
IVANHOE PARK
Metra-Ivanhoe Sta
CONTAINER PARK
FRANSON PARK
STREAMSIDE PARK
CALUMET PARK
Harvey
North Harvey
Dolton
TOWN & COUNTRY PARK
DOLTON PARK
LAKE VICTORY
Metra-147th St Station
Yard Center
60426
HARMON PARK
South Holland
RIVERSIDE PARK
CALUMET RIVER
Thornton Township HS
New Covenant Christian Academy
PHOENIX PARK DISTRICT
TOMAHAWK PARK
Phoenix
60473
Metra-Harvey Station
South Suburban College
TEE PEE PARK
WIGWAM PARK
YOUNGS GRV PARK
VAN OOSTENBRUGGE PARK
VET MEMORIAL PARK
PHOENIX PARK DISTRICT
S HALSTED ST
INDIANA AV
SIBLEY BLVD
W 138TH ST
W 144TH ST
E 154TH ST
155TH ST
VINCENNES RD
LINCOLN AV
SOUTH PARK AV
CHICAGO RD
STATE ST

SEE 3349 MAP
SEE 3351 MAP
SEE 3428 MAP

RAND McNALLY

1:24,000
1 in. = 2000 ft.
0 0.25 0.5
miles

SEE 3279 MAP

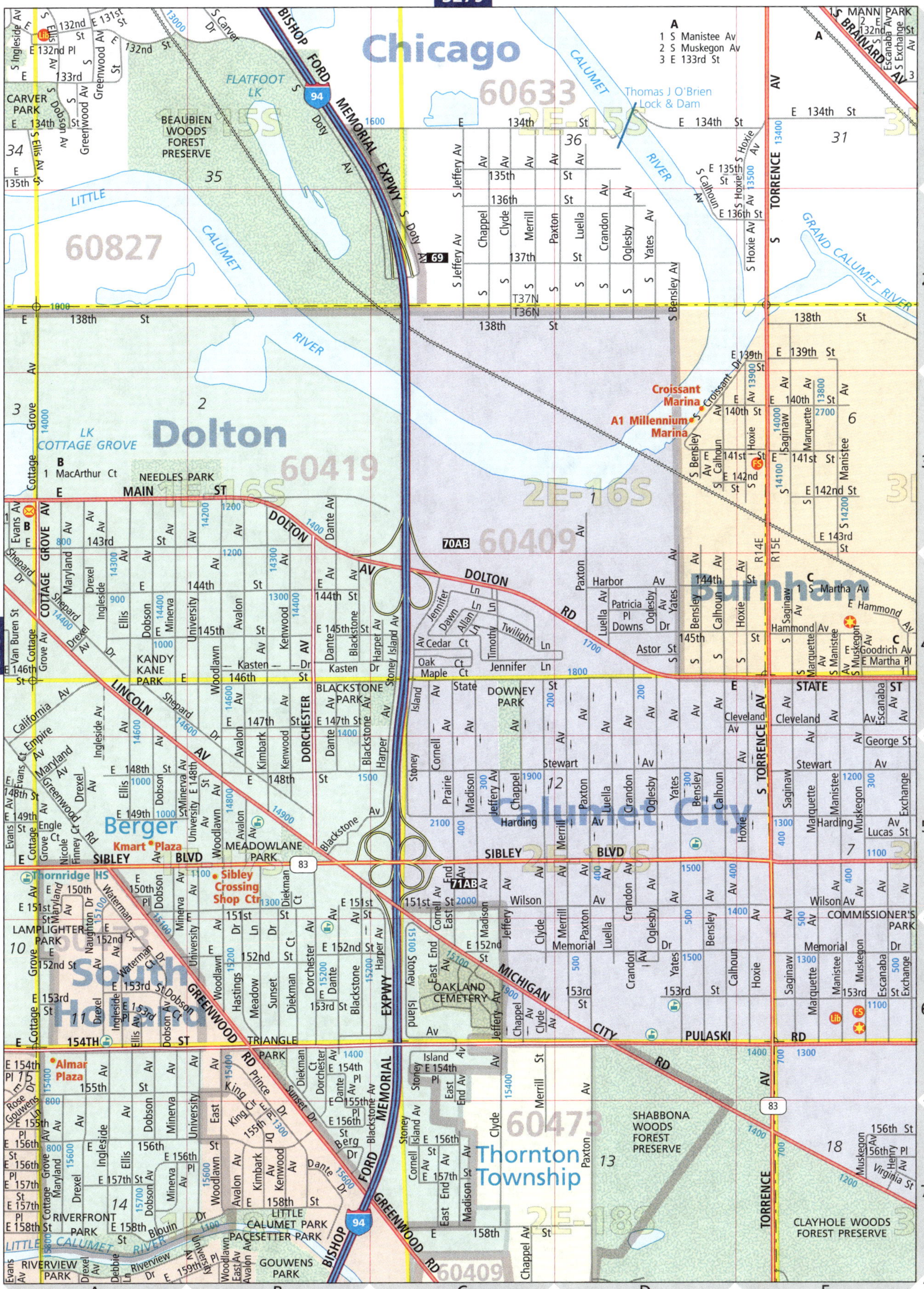
Chicago
60633
60827
Dolton
60419
60409
Burnham
Calumet City
Berger
South Holland
Thornton Township
60473
BEAUBIEN WOODS FOREST PRESERVE
FLATFOOT LK
LITTLE CALUMET RIVER
CALUMET RIVER
GRAND CALUMET RIVER
Thomas J O'Brien Lock & Dam
LK COTTAGE GROVE
CARVER PARK
NEEDLES PARK
KANDY KANE PARK
BLACKSTONE PARK
DOWNEY PARK
MEADOWLANE PARK
LAMPLIGHTER PARK
OAKLAND CEMETERY
TRIANGLE PARK
RIVERFRONT PARK
RIVERVIEW PARK
LITTLE CALUMET PARK
PACESETTER PARK
GOUWENS PARK
COMMISSIONER'S PARK
SHABBONA WOODS FOREST PRESERVE
CLAYHOLE WOODS FOREST PRESERVE
Croissant Marina
A1 Millennium Marina
Kmart Plaza
Sibley Crossing Shop Ctr
Almar Plaza
Thornridge HS
BISHOP FORD MEMORIAL EXPWY
94
83
70AB
71AB
69
TORRENCE AV
COTTAGE GROVE AV
MAIN ST
DOLTON AV
DOLTON RD
LINCOLN AV
SIBLEY BLVD
STATE ST
MICHIGAN CITY RD
PULASKI RD
154TH ST
GREENWOOD RD
E 134th St
138th St
T37N
T36N
R14E
R15E
1E-15S
2E-15S
1E-16S
2E-16S
2E-17S
2E-18S
A
1 S Manistee Av
2 S Muskegon Av
3 E 133rd St
B
1 MacArthur Ct
C
1 S Martha Av

41°39'24"
41°38'58"
41°38'32"
41°38'06"
41°37'40"
41°37'14"
41°36'48"
41°36'21"
87°35'59"
87°35'24"
87°34'49"
87°34'14"
87°33'40"
87°33'05"

SEE 3350 MAP

SEE 3352 MAP

SEE 3429 MAP

RAND McNALLY

1:24,000
1 in. = 2000 ft.
0 0.25 0.5
miles

SEE 3280 MAP

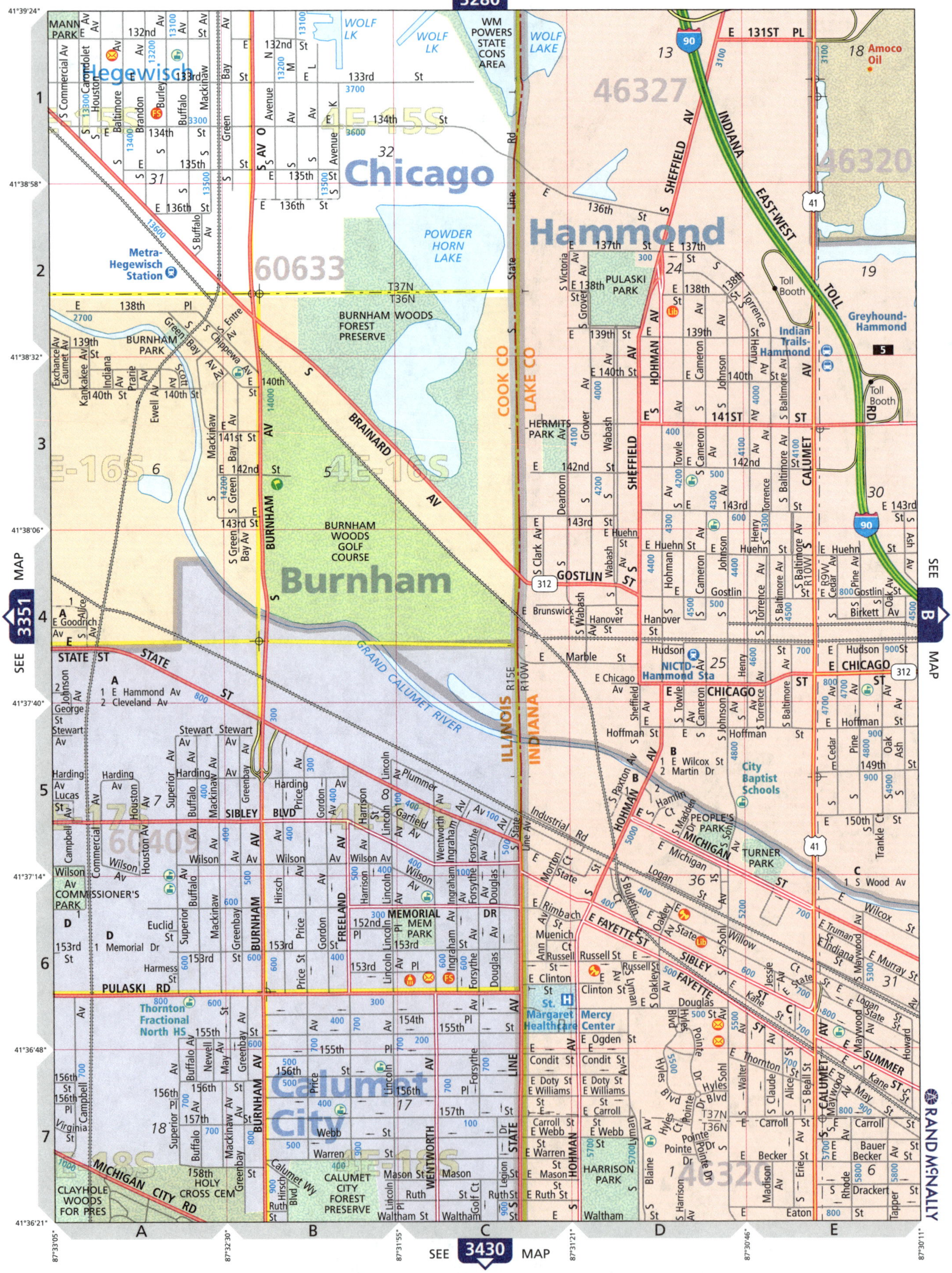
Hegewisch
Chicago
60633
Hammond
46327
46320
Burnham
60409
Calumet City
WOLF LK
WOLF LAKE
WM POWERS STATE CONS AREA
POWDER HORN LAKE
BURNHAM WOODS FOREST PRESERVE
BURNHAM WOODS GOLF COURSE
BURNHAM PARK
Metra-Hegewisch Station
GRAND CALUMET RIVER
ILLINOIS
INDIANA
COOK CO
LAKE CO
INDIANA EAST-WEST TOLL RD
Amoco Oil
Greyhound-Hammond
Indian Trails-Hammond
Toll Booth
PULASKI PARK
HERMITS PARK
NICTD-Hammond Sta
City Baptist Schools
PEOPLE'S PARK
TURNER PARK
COMMISSIONER'S PARK
MEMORIAL MEM PARK
Thornton Fractional North HS
St. Margaret Mercy Healthcare Center
HARRISON PARK
CALUMET CITY FOREST PRESERVE
CLAYHOLE WOODS FOR PRES
HOLY CROSS CEM
BRAINARD AV
BURNHAM AV
SHEFFIELD AV
HOHMAN AV
CALUMET AV
STATE LINE RD
STATE ST
SIBLEY BLVD
PULASKI RD
MICHIGAN CITY RD
GOSTLIN ST
CHICAGO ST
FAYETTE ST
SUMMER ST
141ST ST
E 131ST PL
T37N
T36N
R15E
R10W

SEE 3351 MAP
SEE B MAP
SEE 3430 MAP

RAND McNALLY

1:24,000
1 in. = 2000 ft.
0 0.25 0.5
miles

SEE 3344 MAP

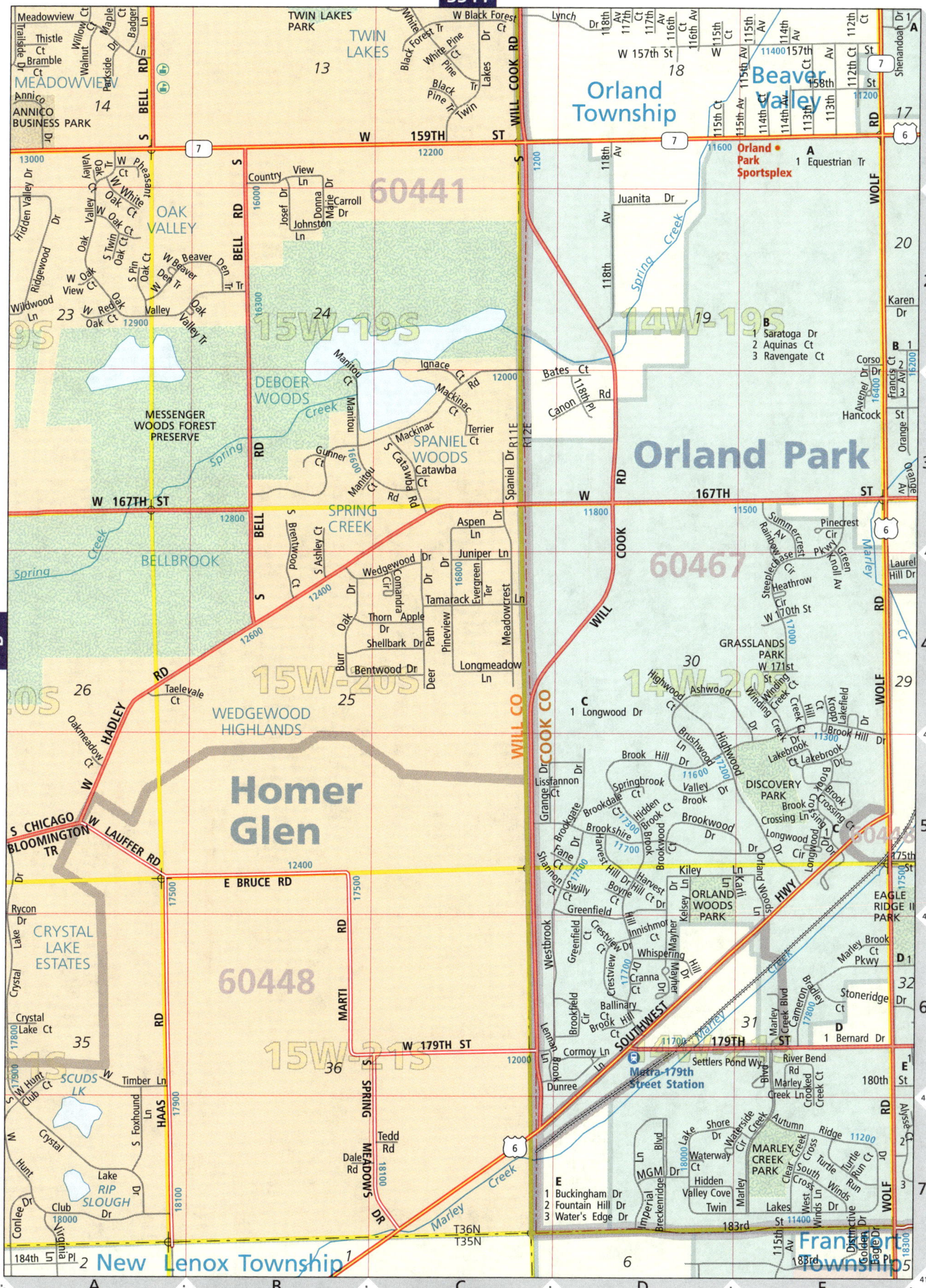

TWIN LAKES PARK
TWIN LAKES
MEADOWVIEW
ANNICO BUSINESS PARK
OAK VALLEY
DEBOER WOODS
MESSENGER WOODS FOREST PRESERVE
SPANIEL WOODS
SPRING CREEK
BELLBROOK
WEDGEWOOD HIGHLANDS
Homer Glen
CRYSTAL LAKE ESTATES
SCUDS LK
RIP SLOUGH
New Lenox Township
Orland Township
Beaver Valley
Orland Park Sportsplex
Orland Park
GRASSLANDS PARK
DISCOVERY PARK
ORLAND WOODS PARK
EAGLE RIDGE II PARK
Metra-179th Street Station
MARLEY CREEK PARK
Frankfort Township
60441
60467
60448
15W-19S
14W-19S
15W-20S
14W-20S
15W-21S
W 159TH ST
W 167TH ST
W 179TH ST
E BRUCE RD
S BELL RD
WILL COOK RD
WOLF RD
W HADLEY RD
S CHICAGO BLOOMINGTON TR
W LAUFFER RD
HAAS RD
MARTI RD
S SPRING MEADOWS DR
SOUTHWEST HWY
WILL CO
COOK CO
R11E
R12E
T36N
T35N
A
1 Equestrian Tr
B
1 Saratoga Dr
2 Aquinas Ct
3 Ravengate Ct
C
1 Longwood Dr
D
1 Bernard Dr
E
1 Buckingham Dr
2 Fountain Hill Dr
3 Water's Edge Dr

SEE 3423 MAP
SEE B MAP
SEE B MAP

1:24,000
1 in. = 2000 ft.
0 0.25 0.5
miles

SEE 3345 MAP

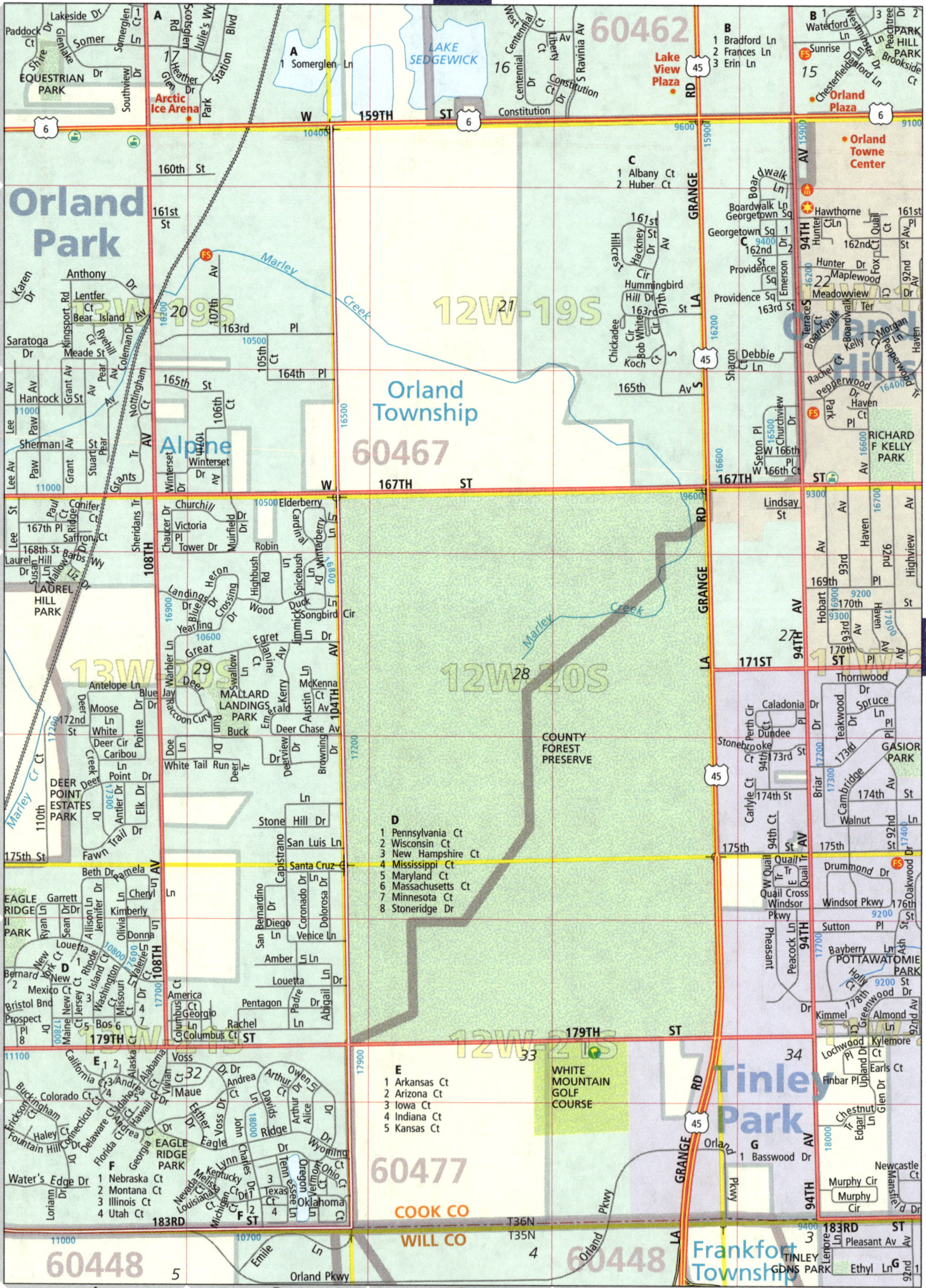
Orland Park
Orland Township
Alpine
Orland Hills
Tinley Park
Frankfort Township
60462
60467
60477
60448
13W-19S
12W-19S
13W-20S
12W-20S
12W-21S
COOK CO
WILL CO
T36N
T35N
W 159TH ST
160th St
161st St
163rd Pl
164th Pl
165th St
W 167TH ST
179TH ST
183RD ST
108TH AV
104TH AV
LA GRANGE RD
94TH AV
171ST ST
175th St
Marley Creek
LAKE SEDGEWICK
EQUESTRIAN PARK
Arctic Ice Arena
Lake View Plaza
Orland Plaza
Orland Towne Center
LAUREL HILL PARK
DEER POINT ESTATES PARK
MALLARD LANDINGS PARK
EAGLE RIDGE II PARK
EAGLE RIDGE PARK
COUNTY FOREST PRESERVE
WHITE MOUNTAIN GOLF COURSE
RICHARD F KELLY PARK
GASIOR PARK
POTTAWATOMIE PARK
TINLEY GDNS PARK
Orland Pkwy
A
1 Somerglen Ln
B
1 Bradford Ln
2 Frances Ln
3 Erin Ln
C
1 Albany Ct
2 Huber Ct
D
1 Pennsylvania Ct
2 Wisconsin Ct
3 New Hampshire Ct
4 Mississippi Ct
5 Maryland Ct
6 Massachusetts Ct
7 Minnesota Ct
8 Stoneridge Dr
E
1 Arkansas Ct
2 Arizona Ct
3 Iowa Ct
4 Indiana Ct
5 Kansas Ct
F
1 Nebraska Ct
2 Montana Ct
3 Illinois Ct
4 Utah Ct
G
1 Basswood Dr
41°36'21"
41°35'55"
41°35'28"
41°35'02"
41°34'36"
41°34'10"
41°33'44"
41°33'18"
87°53'21"
87°52'46"
87°52'12"
87°51'37"
87°51'02"
87°50'27"
A B C D E
1 2 3 4 5 6 7

SEE 3422 MAP

SEE 3424 MAP

SEE B MAP

1:24,000
1 in. = 2000 ft.
0 0.25 0.5
miles

SEE 3346 MAP

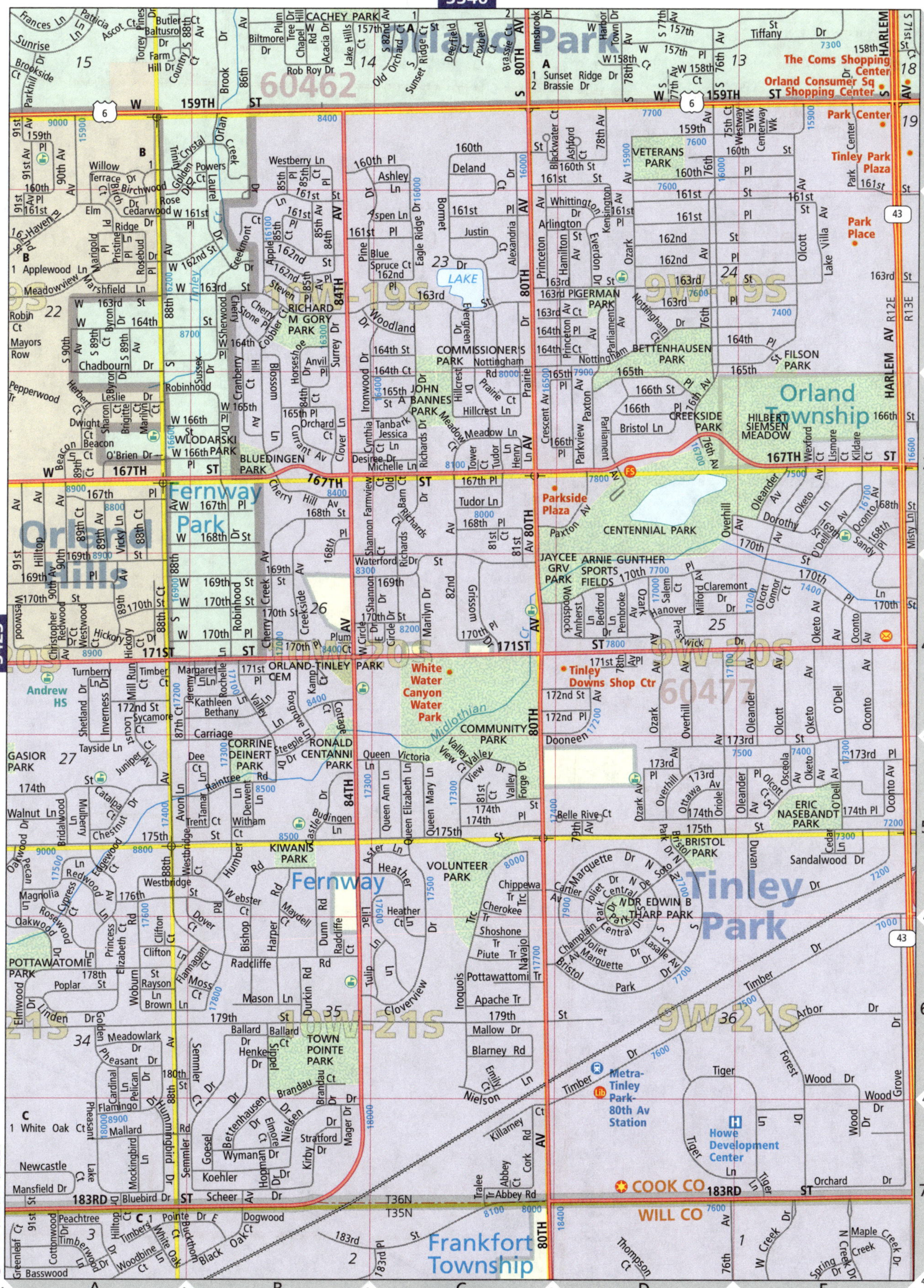
Orland Park
60462
159TH ST
W 159TH ST
The Coms Shopping Center
Orland Consumer Sq Shopping Center
Park Center
Tinley Park Plaza
Park Place
HARLEM AV
80TH AV
84TH AV
88th Av
167TH ST
171ST
175th St
179th St
183RD ST
Orland Hills
Fernway Park
Fernway
Orland Township
Tinley Park
60477
Centennial Park
Parkside Plaza
Veterans Park
Bettenhausen Park
Commissioner's Park
John A Bannes Park
Creekside Park
Hilbert Siemsen Meadow
Filson Park
Pigerman Park
Richard M Gory Park
Wlodarski Park
Bluedingen Park
Jaycee Grv Park
Arnie Gunther Sports Fields
Orland-Tinley Cem
Tinley Downs Shop Ctr
White Water Canyon Water Park
Community Park
Corrine Deinert Park
Ronald Centanni Park
Gasior Park
Andrew HS
Kiwanis Park
Volunteer Park
Eric Nasebandt Park
Bristol Park
Dr Edwin B Tharp Park
Pottawatomie Park
Town Pointe Park
Metra-Tinley Park-80th Av Station
Howe Development Center
Cook Co
Will Co
Frankfort Township
Midlothian Cr
Lake
10W-19S
9W-19S
10W-20S
9W-20S
10W-21S
9W-21S
T36N
T35N
R12E
R13E

SEE 3423 MAP

SEE 3425 MAP

SEE 3504 MAP

1:24,000
1 in. = 2000 ft.
0 0.25 0.5
miles

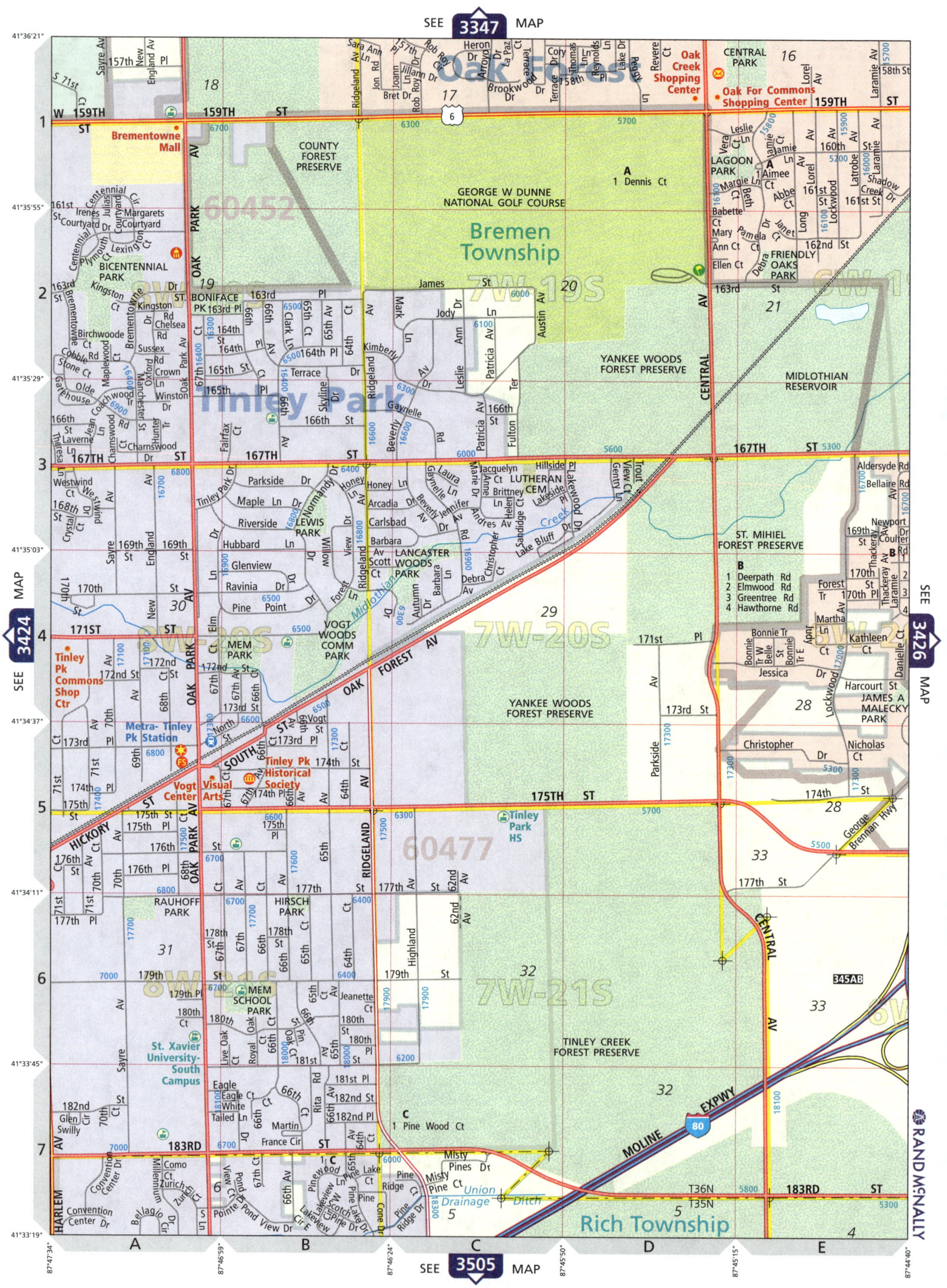
SEE 3347 MAP
SEE 3505 MAP
SEE 3424 MAP
SEE 3426 MAP
Oak Forest
Tinley Park
Bremen Township
Rich Township
60452
60477
7W-19S
7W-20S
7W-21S
8W-19S
8W-20S
8W-21S
159TH ST
167TH ST
171ST ST
175TH ST
183RD ST
OAK PARK AV
RIDGELAND AV
CENTRAL AV
HARLEM AV
OAK FOREST AV
SOUTH ST
HICKORY ST
MOLINE EXPWY
80
6
George Brennan Hwy
Brementowne Mall
COUNTY FOREST PRESERVE
GEORGE W DUNNE NATIONAL GOLF COURSE
YANKEE WOODS FOREST PRESERVE
MIDLOTHIAN RESERVOIR
ST. MIHIEL FOREST PRESERVE
TINLEY CREEK FOREST PRESERVE
BICENTENNIAL PARK
ST. BONIFACE PK
LEWIS PARK
LANCASTER WOODS PARK
VOGT WOODS COMM PARK
MEM PARK
LUTHERAN CEM
CENTRAL PARK
LAGOON PARK
FRIENDLY OAKS PARK
JAMES A MALECKY PARK
RAUHOFF PARK
HIRSCH PARK
MEM SCHOOL PARK
Tinley Pk Commons Shop Ctr
Metra- Tinley Pk Station
Vogt Center
Visual Arts
Tinley Pk Historical Society
Tinley Park HS
St. Xavier University- South Campus
Oak Creek Shopping Center
Oak For Commons Shopping Center
Midlothian Creek
Union Drainage Ditch
A 1 Dennis Ct
B 1 Deerpath Rd 2 Elmwood Rd 3 Greentree Rd 4 Hawthorne Rd
C 1 Pine Wood Ct
T36N
T35N
345AB
41°36'21"
41°35'55"
41°35'29"
41°35'03"
41°34'37"
41°34'11"
41°33'45"
41°33'19"
87°47'34"
87°46'59"
87°46'24"
87°45'50"
87°45'15"
87°44'40"
A B C D E
1 2 3 4 5 6 7
RAND McNALLY

1:24,000
1 in. = 2000 ft.
0 0.25 0.5
miles

SEE 3348 MAP

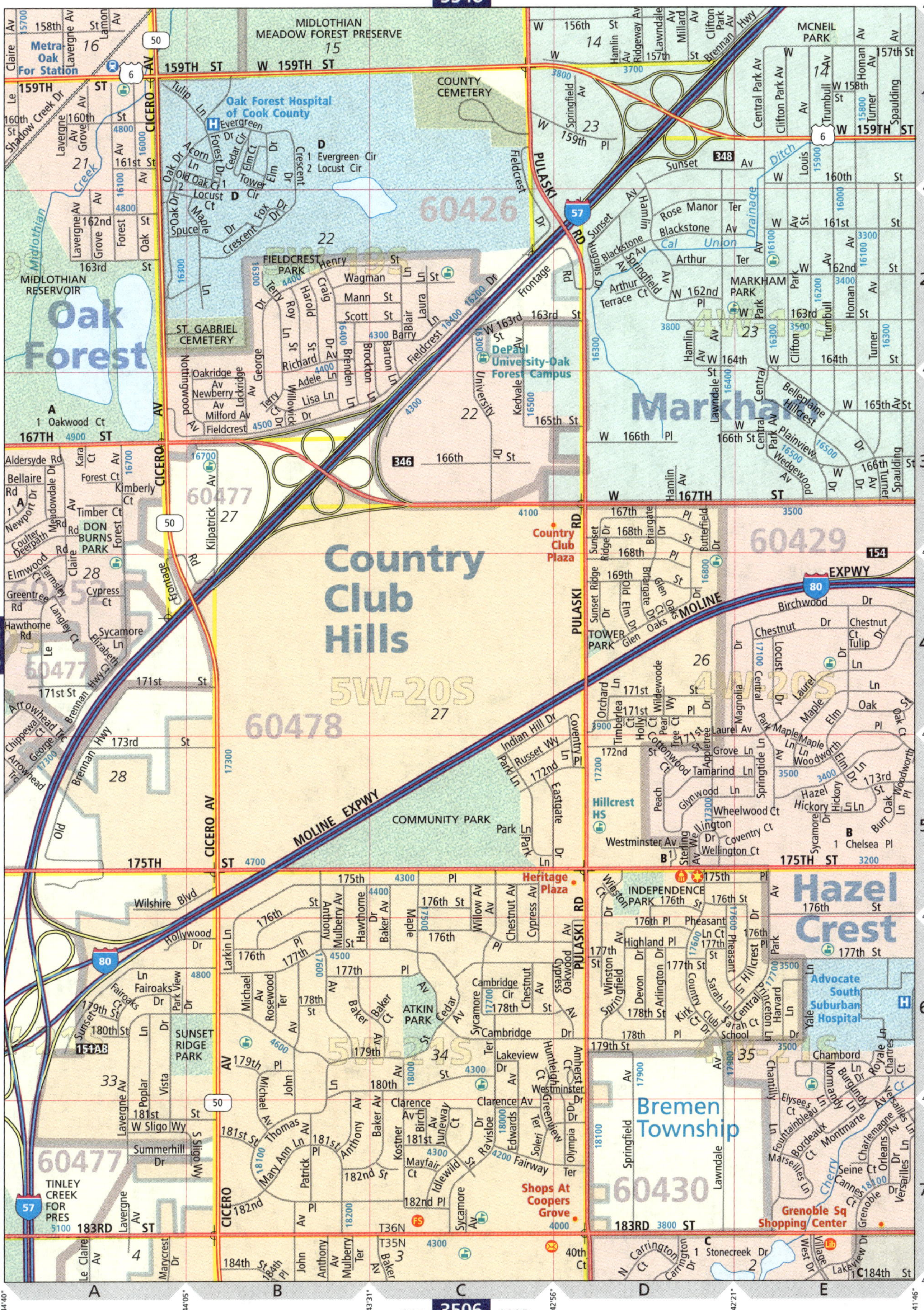
Oak Forest
Country Club Hills
Markham
Hazel Crest
Bremen Township
MIDLOTHIAN MEADOW FOREST PRESERVE
Oak Forest Hospital of Cook County
COUNTY CEMETERY
ST. GABRIEL CEMETERY
MIDLOTHIAN RESERVOIR
Metra-Oak Forest Station
FIELDCREST PARK
DePaul University-Oak Forest Campus
MCNEIL PARK
MARKHAM PARK
DON BURNS PARK
Country Club Plaza
TOWER PARK
COMMUNITY PARK
Hillcrest HS
Heritage Plaza
INDEPENDENCE PARK
Advocate South Suburban Hospital
ATKIN PARK
SUNSET RIDGE PARK
TINLEY CREEK FOR PRES
Shops At Coopers Grove
Grenoble Sq Shopping Center
60426
60477
60478
60429
60430
5W-19S
4W-19S
5W-20S
4W-20S
5W-21S
4W-21S
159TH ST
167TH ST
175TH ST
183RD ST
CICERO AV
PULASKI RD
MOLINE EXPWY
Cal Union Drainage Ditch
Midlothian Creek
D 1 Evergreen Cir 2 Locust Cir
A 1 Oakwood Ct
B 1 Chelsea Pl
C 1 Stonecreek Dr
RAND McNALLY

SEE 3425 MAP
SEE 3427 MAP
SEE 3506 MAP

1:24,000
1 in. = 2000 ft.
0 0.25 0.5
miles

SEE 3349 MAP

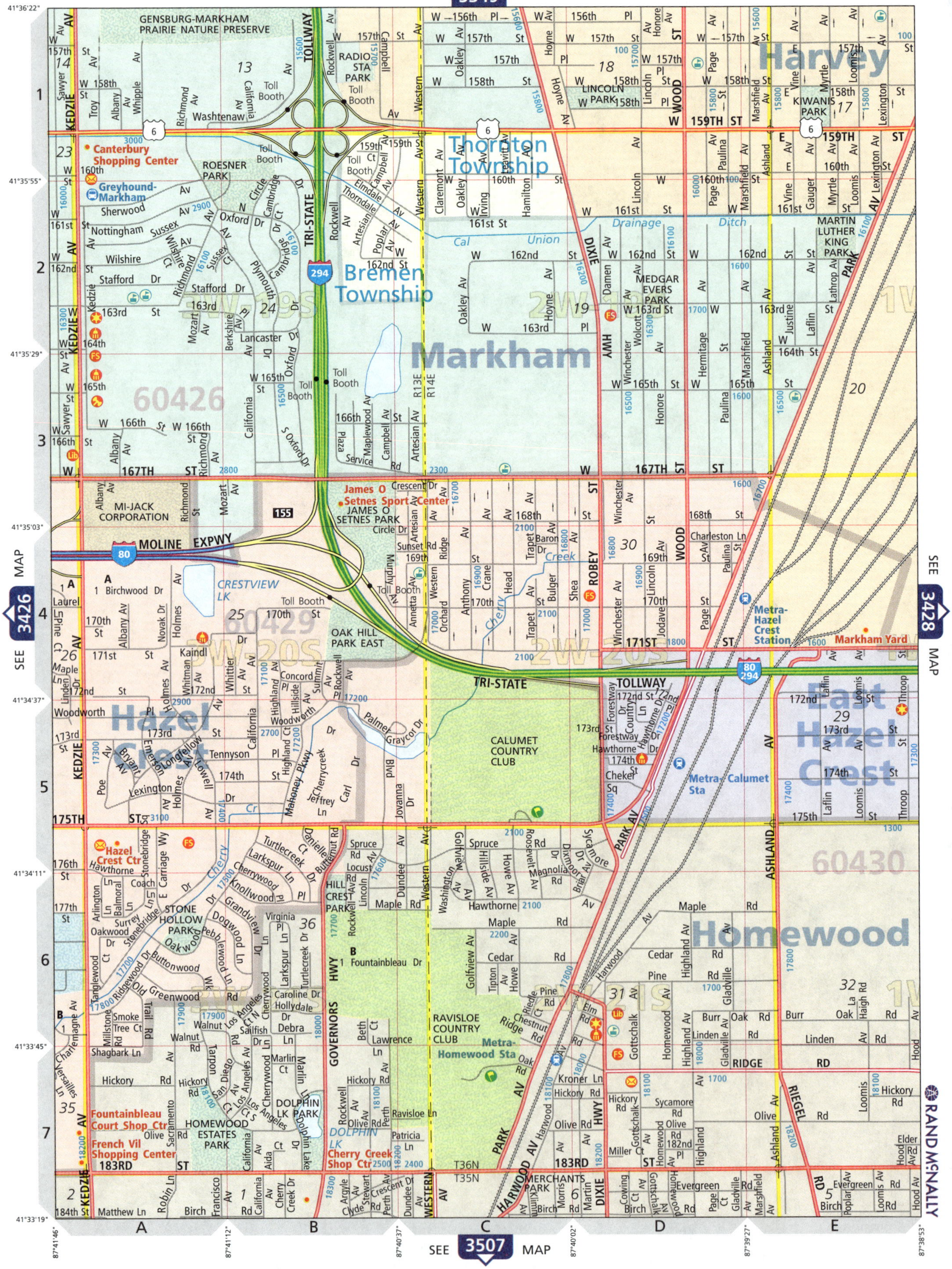
GENSBURG-MARKHAM PRAIRIE NATURE PRESERVE
RADIO STA PARK
Harvey
KIWANIS PARK
LINCOLN PARK
Canterbury Shopping Center
Greyhound-Markham
ROESNER PARK
Thornton Township
Bremen Township
Cal Union Drainage Ditch
MARTIN LUTHER KING PARK
MEDGAR EVERS PARK
Markham
60426
TRI-STATE TOLLWAY
MI-JACK CORPORATION
James O Setnes Sport Center
JAMES O SETNES PARK
MOLINE EXPWY
CRESTVIEW LK
60429
OAK HILL PARK EAST
Metra-Hazel Crest Station
Markham Yard
Hazel Crest
CALUMET COUNTRY CLUB
East Hazel Crest
Metra-Calumet Sta
60430
Hazel Crest Ctr
STONE HOLLOW PARK
HILL CREST PARK
Homewood
RAVISLOE COUNTRY CLUB
Metra-Homewood Sta
Fountainbleau Court Shop Ctr
French Vil Shopping Center
HOMEWOOD ESTATES PARK
DOLPHIN LK PARK
Cherry Creek Shop Ctr
MERCHANTS PARK
KEDZIE AV
159TH ST
167TH ST
171ST ST
175TH ST
183RD ST
WESTERN AV
DIXIE HWY
ASHLAND AV
GOVERNORS HWY
HARWOOD AV
PARK AV
RIDGE RD
RIEGEL RD
ROBEY
WOOD ST
RAND McNALLY

SEE 3426 MAP
SEE 3428 MAP
SEE 3507 MAP

1:24,000
1 in. = 2000 ft.
0 0.25 0.5
miles

SEE 3350 MAP

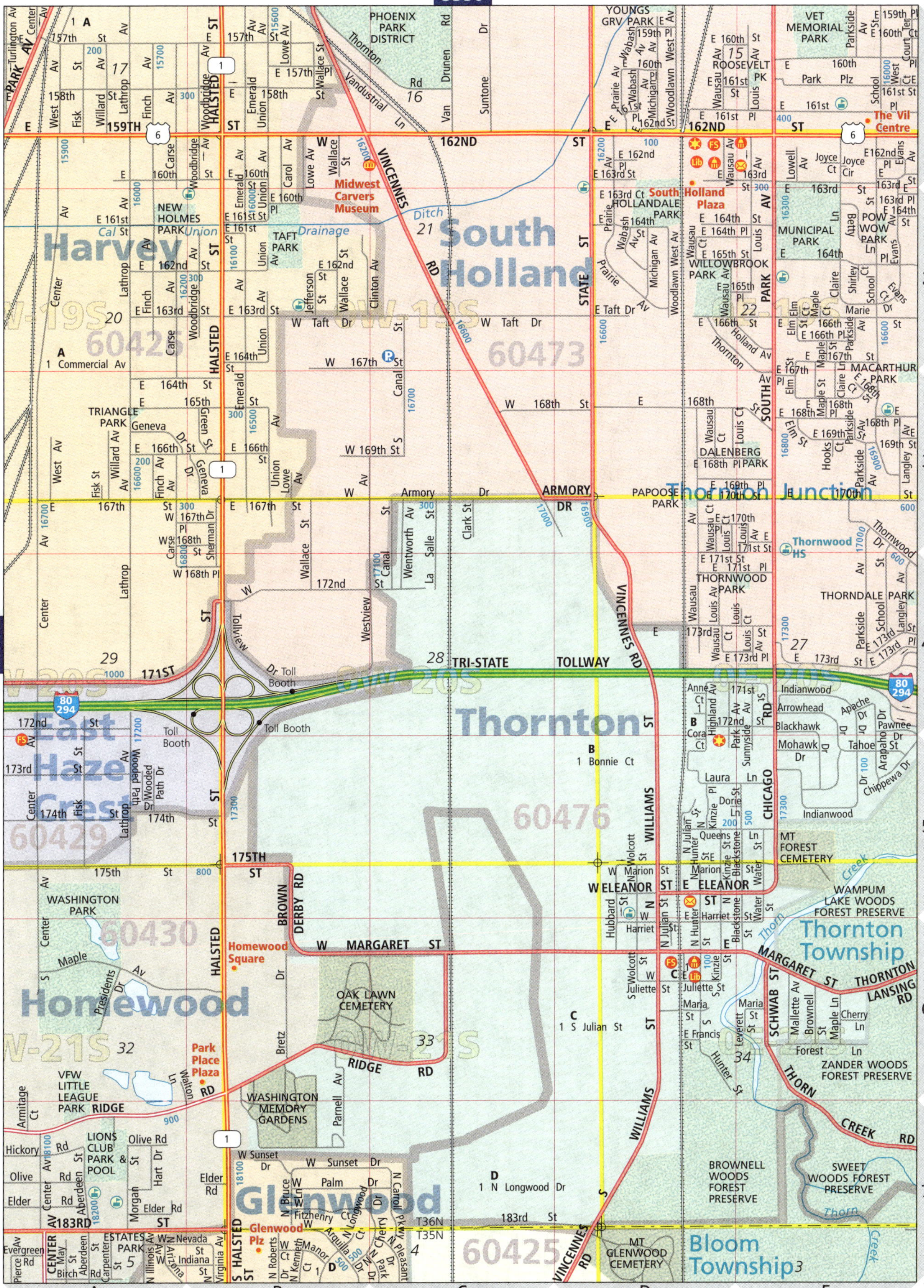

SEE 3427 MAP
SEE 3429 MAP
SEE 3508 MAP

1:24,000
1 in. = 2000 ft.
0 0.25 0.5
miles

SEE 3351 MAP

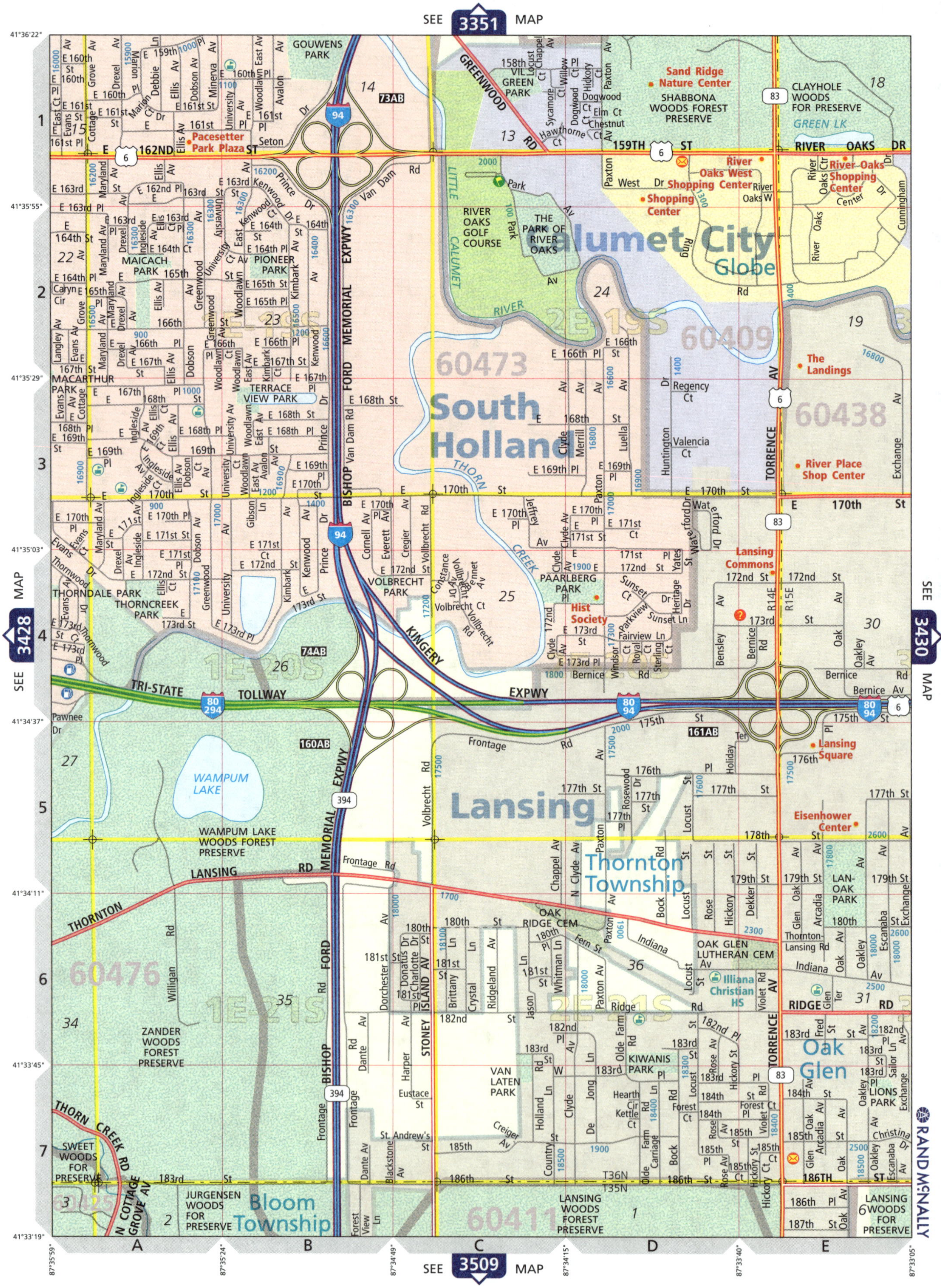
South Holland
Lansing
Calumet City
Globe
Thornton Township
Bloom Township
Oak Glen
60473
60409
60438
60476
60411
60425
2E-19S
1E-20S
1E-21S
2E-21S
TRI-STATE TOLLWAY
KINGERY EXPWY
BISHOP FORD MEMORIAL EXPWY
TORRENCE AV
LANSING RD
THORNTON
159TH ST
RIVER OAKS DR
E 162ND ST
170th St
186TH ST
RIDGE RD
STONEY ISLAND AV
GREENWOOD RD
THORN CREEK RD
N COTTAGE GROVE AV
Pacesetter Park Plaza
Sand Ridge Nature Center
SHABBONA WOODS FOREST PRESERVE
CLAYHOLE WOODS FOR PRESERVE
GREEN LK
River Oaks West Shopping Center
River Oaks Shopping Center
Shopping Center
RIVER OAKS GOLF COURSE
THE PARK OF RIVER OAKS
LITTLE CALUMET RIVER
THORN CREEK
The Landings
River Place Shop Center
Lansing Commons
Lansing Square
Eisenhower Center
Hist Society
PAARLBERG PARK
VOLBRECHT PARK
GOUWENS PARK
VIL GREEN PARK
MAICACH PARK
PIONEER PARK
TERRACE VIEW PARK
MACARTHUR PARK
THORNDALE PARK
THORNCREEK PARK
WAMPUM LAKE
WAMPUM LAKE WOODS FOREST PRESERVE
ZANDER WOODS FOREST PRESERVE
SWEET WOODS FOR PRESERVE
JURGENSEN WOODS FOR PRESERVE
LANSING WOODS FOREST PRESERVE
LANSING WOODS FOR PRESERVE
OAK RIDGE CEM
OAK GLEN LUTHERAN CEM
Illiana Christian HS
KIWANIS PARK
VAN LATEN PARK
LAN-OAK PARK
LIONS PARK
73AB
74AB
160AB
161AB
T36N
T35N
R14E
R15E
A
B
C
D
E
1
2
3
4
5
6
7
41°36'22"
41°35'55"
41°35'29"
41°35'03"
41°34'37"
41°34'11"
41°33'45"
41°33'19"
87°35'59"
87°35'24"
87°34'49"
87°34'15"
87°33'40"
87°33'05"

SEE 3428 MAP

SEE 3430 MAP

SEE 3509 MAP

1:24,000
1 in. = 2000 ft.
0 0.25 0.5
miles

SEE 3352 MAP

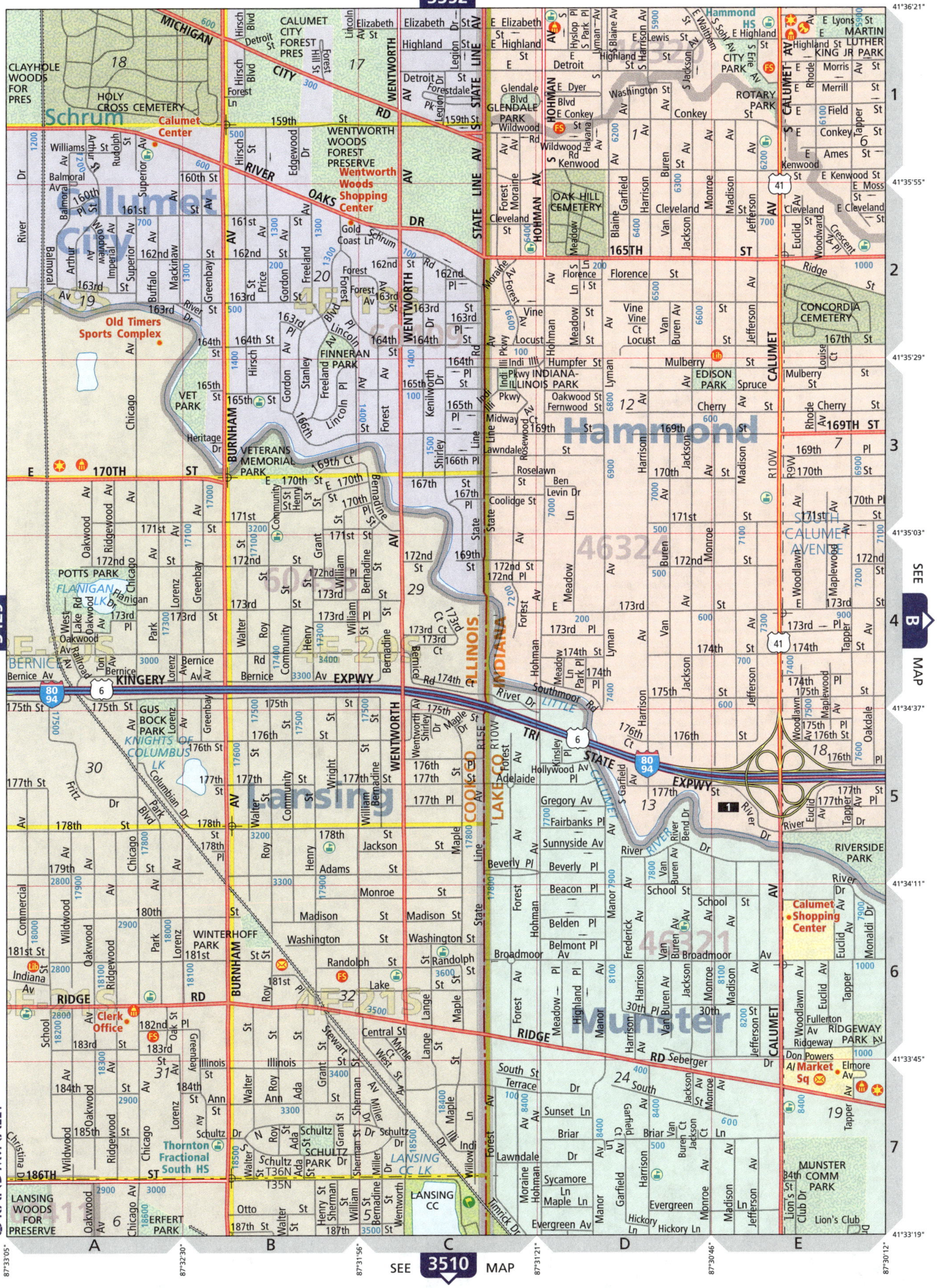

SEE 3429 MAP

SEE B MAP

SEE 3510 MAP

1:24,000
1 in. = 2000 ft.
0 0.25 0.5
miles

SEE 3424 MAP

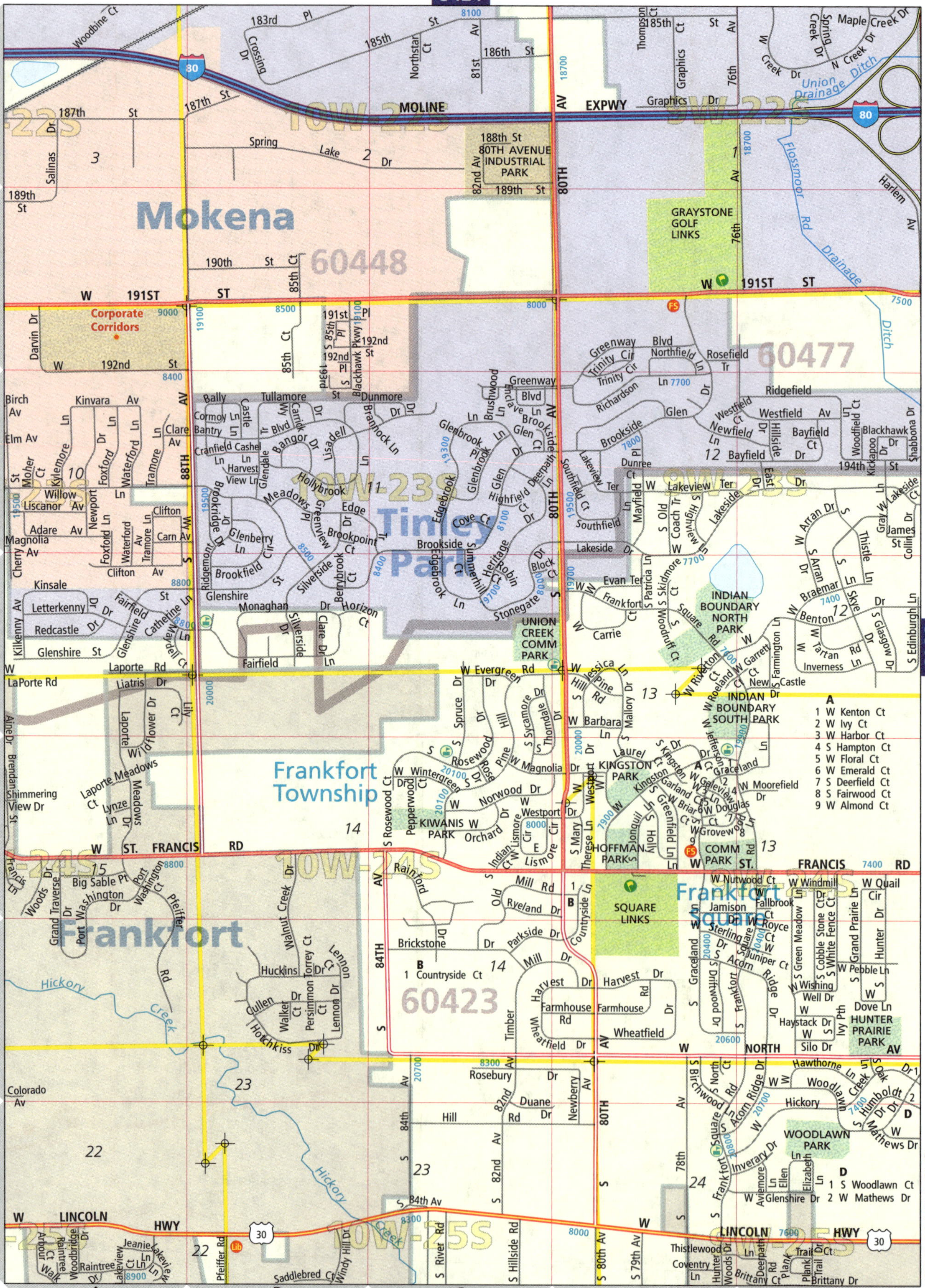
Mokena
60448
Tinley Park
Frankfort Township
Frankfort
Frankfort Square
60477
60423
MOLINE EXPWY
W 191ST ST
W ST. FRANCIS RD
W LINCOLN HWY
88TH AV
80TH AV
84TH AV
80TH AVENUE INDUSTRIAL PARK
Corporate Corridors
GRAYSTONE GOLF LINKS
UNION CREEK COMM PARK
INDIAN BOUNDARY NORTH PARK
INDIAN BOUNDARY SOUTH PARK
KINGSTON PARK
KIWANIS PARK
HOFFMAN PARK
COMM PARK
SQUARE LINKS
HUNTER PRAIRIE PARK
WOODLAWN PARK
Hickory Creek
Union Drainage Ditch
Flossmoor Rd Drainage Ditch
10W-22S
9W-22S
10W-23S
9W-23S
10W-24S
10W-25S
9W-25S
A
1 W Kenton Ct
2 W Ivy Ct
3 W Harbor Ct
4 S Hampton Ct
5 W Floral Ct
6 W Emerald Ct
7 S Deerfield Ct
8 S Fairwood Ct
9 W Almond Ct
B
1 Countryside Ct
D
1 S Woodlawn Ct
2 W Mathews Dr
A
B
C
D
E
1
2
3
4
5
6
7
41°33'18"
41°32'52"
41°32'26"
41°32'00"
41°31'34"
41°31'08"
41°30'42"
41°30'16"
87°50'27"
87°49'52"
87°49'18"
87°48'43"
87°48'08"
87°47'33"

SEE B MAP

SEE 3505 MAP

SEE B MAP

1:24,000
1 in. = 2000 ft.
0 0.25 0.5
miles

SEE 3425 MAP

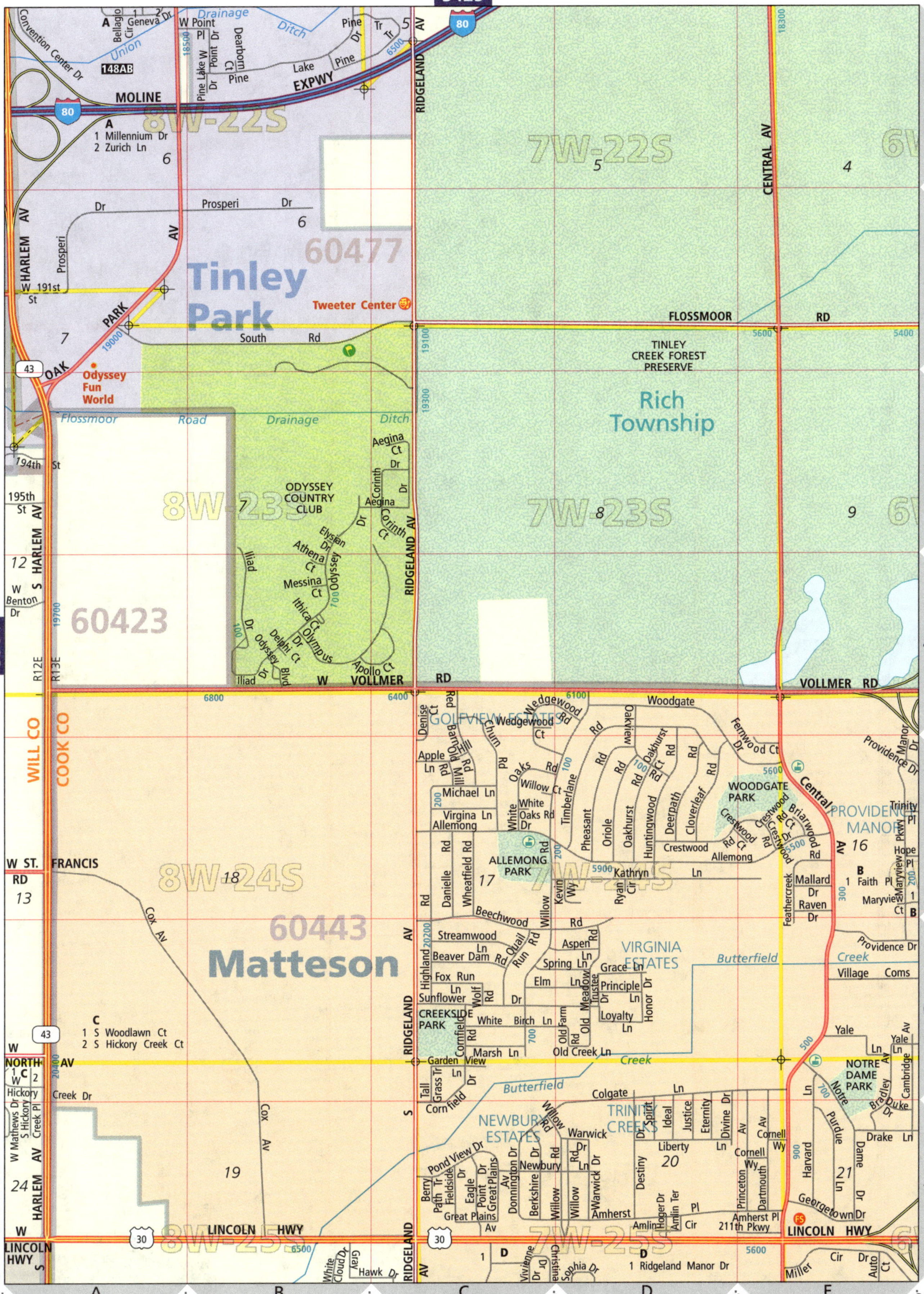
Tinley Park
Matteson
Rich Township
60477
60423
60443
8W-22S
7W-22S
8W-23S
7W-23S
8W-24S
7W-24S
8W-25S
7W-25S
Tweeter Center
Odyssey Fun World
ODYSSEY COUNTRY CLUB
TINLEY CREEK FOREST PRESERVE
GOLFVIEW ESTATES
ALLEMONG PARK
WOODGATE PARK
PROVIDENCE MANOR
VIRGINIA ESTATES
CREEKSIDE PARK
NEWBURY ESTATES
TRINITY CREEK
NOTRE DAME PARK
WILL CO
COOK CO
MOLINE EXPWY
FLOSSMOOR RD
W VOLLMER RD
VOLLMER RD
RIDGELAND AV
CENTRAL AV
HARLEM AV
OAK PARK AV
W ST. FRANCIS RD
W NORTH AV
LINCOLN HWY
Prosperi Dr
South Rd
Woodgate
Butterfield Creek
Flossmoor Road Drainage Ditch
Union Drainage Ditch
Cox Av
A
1 Millennium Dr
2 Zurich Ln
B
1 Faith Pl
C
1 S Woodlawn Ct
2 S Hickory Creek Ct
D
1 Ridgeland Manor Dr
41°33'19"
41°32'53"
41°32'27"
41°32'00"
41°31'34"
41°31'08"
41°30'42"
41°30'16"
87°47'33"
87°46'59"
87°46'24"
87°45'49"
87°45'15"
87°44'40"

SEE 3504 MAP

SEE 3506 MAP

SEE 3593 MAP

1:24,000
1 in. = 2000 ft.
0 0.25 0.5
miles

SEE 3426 MAP

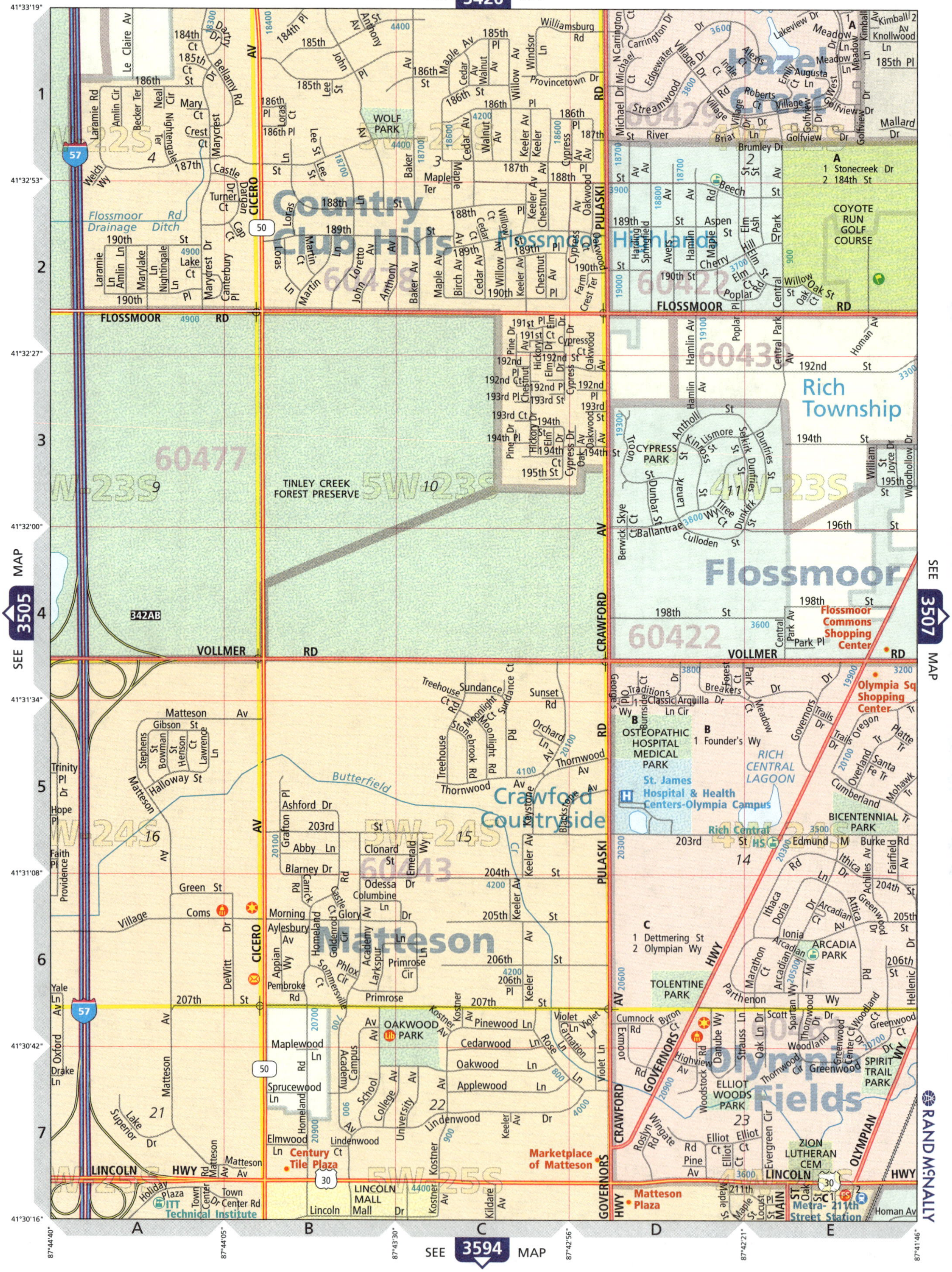
Country Club Hills
60478
Flossmoor Highland
60422
Hazel Crest
60429
WOLF PARK
COYOTE RUN GOLF COURSE
A
1 Stonecreek Dr
2 184th St
FLOSSMOOR RD
60477
TINLEY CREEK FOREST PRESERVE
Rich Township
60430
CYPRESS PARK
Flossmoor
Flossmoor Commons Shopping Center
342AB
VOLLMER RD
CICERO AV
PULASKI RD
CRAWFORD AV
Olympia Sq Shopping Center
B
1 Founder's Wy
OSTEOPATHIC HOSPITAL MEDICAL PARK
St. James Hospital & Health Centers-Olympia Campus
RICH CENTRAL LAGOON
Rich Central HS
BICENTENNIAL PARK
Crawford Countryside
Butterfield
Matteson
60443
C
1 Dettmering St
2 Olympian Wy
ARCADIA PARK
TOLENTINE PARK
OAKWOOD PARK
ELLIOT WOODS PARK
SPIRIT TRAIL PARK
Olympia Fields
ZION LUTHERAN CEM
Century Tile Plaza
Marketplace of Matteson
Matteson Plaza
LINCOLN MALL
ITT Technical Institute
LINCOLN HWY
GOVERNORS HWY
Metra-211th Street Station
SEE 3505 MAP
SEE 3507 MAP
A B C D E
1 2 3 4 5 6 7

SEE 3594 MAP

RAND McNALLY

1:24,000
1 in. = 2000 ft.
0 0.25 0.5
miles

SEE 3427 MAP

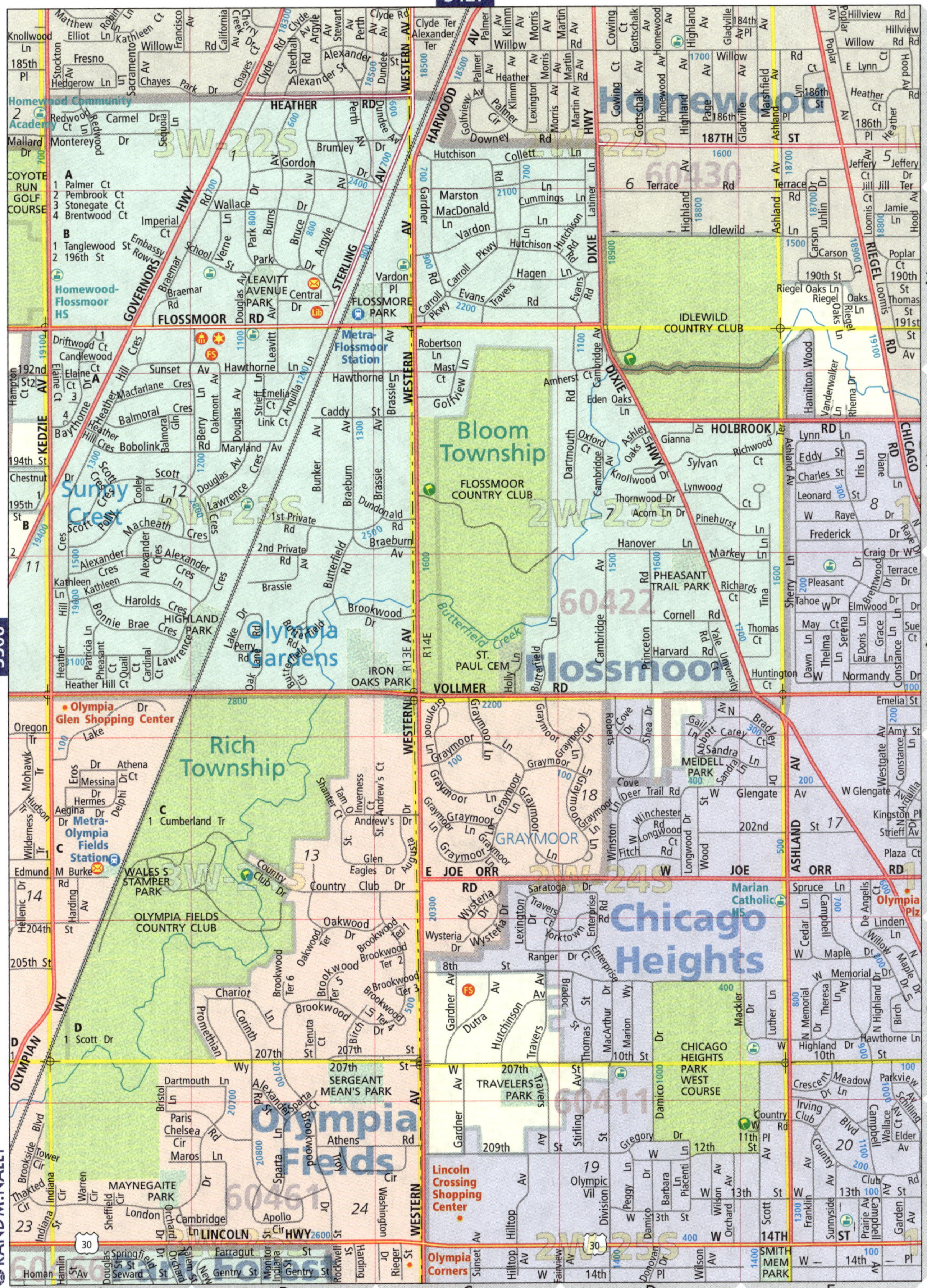

SEE 3506 MAP

SEE 3508 MAP

SEE 3595 MAP

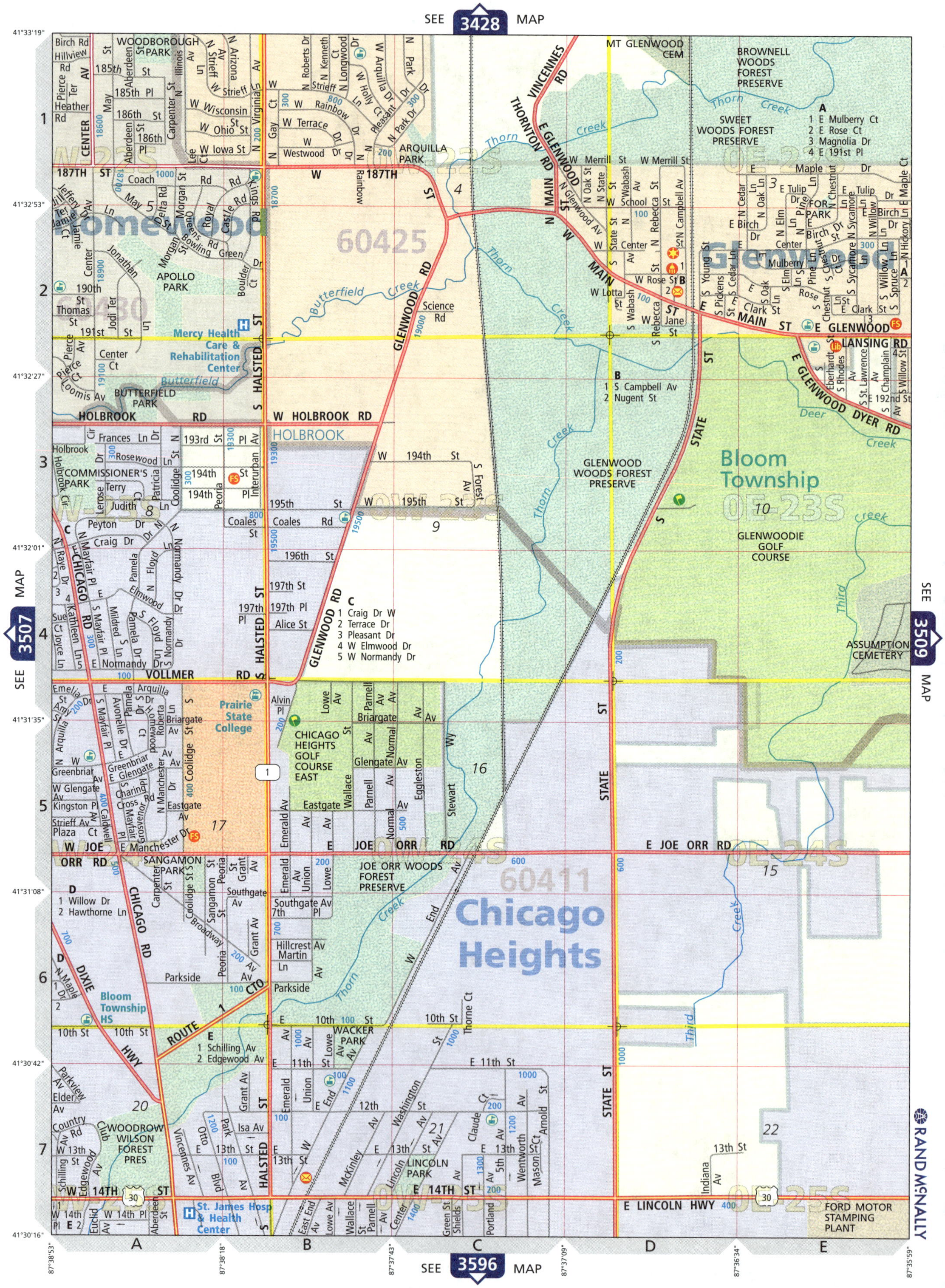
1:24,000
1 in. = 2000 ft.
0 0.25 0.5 miles
SEE 3428 MAP
SEE 3596 MAP
SEE 3507 MAP
SEE 3509 MAP
Homewood
Glenwood
Chicago Heights
Bloom Township
60425
60411
60430
WOODBOROUGH PARK
APOLLO PARK
Mercy Health Care & Rehabilitation Center
BUTTERFIELD PARK
HOLBROOK
COMMISSIONER'S PARK
Prairie State College
CHICAGO HEIGHTS GOLF COURSE EAST
SANGAMON PARK
JOE ORR WOODS FOREST PRESERVE
Bloom Township HS
WACKER PARK
WOODROW WILSON FOREST PRES
LINCOLN PARK
St. James Hosp & Health Center
MT GLENWOOD CEM
BROWNELL WOODS FOREST PRESERVE
SWEET WOODS FOREST PRESERVE
ARQUILLA PARK
FOR PARK
GLENWOOD WOODS FOREST PRESERVE
GLENWOODIE GOLF COURSE
ASSUMPTION CEMETERY
FORD MOTOR STAMPING PLANT
187TH ST
HOLBROOK RD
VOLLMER RD
W JOE ORR RD
E JOE ORR RD
E LINCOLN HWY
W 14TH ST
E 14TH ST
GLENWOOD RD
HALSTED ST
CHICAGO RD
STATE ST
DIXIE HWY
ROUTE 1
VINCENNES RD
THORNTON RD
E GLENWOOD DYER RD
LANSING RD
MAIN ST
Thorn Creek
Butterfield Creek
Deer Creek
Third Creek
A
1 E Mulberry Ct
2 E Rose Ct
3 Magnolia Dr
4 E 191st Pl
B
1 S Campbell Av
2 Nugent St
C
1 Craig Dr W
2 Terrace Dr
3 Pleasant Dr
4 W Elmwood Dr
5 W Normandy Dr
D
1 Willow Dr
2 Hawthorne Ln
E
1 Schilling Av
2 Edgewood Av
RAND McNALLY

1:24,000
1 in. = 2000 ft.
0 0.25 0.5
miles

SEE 3429 MAP

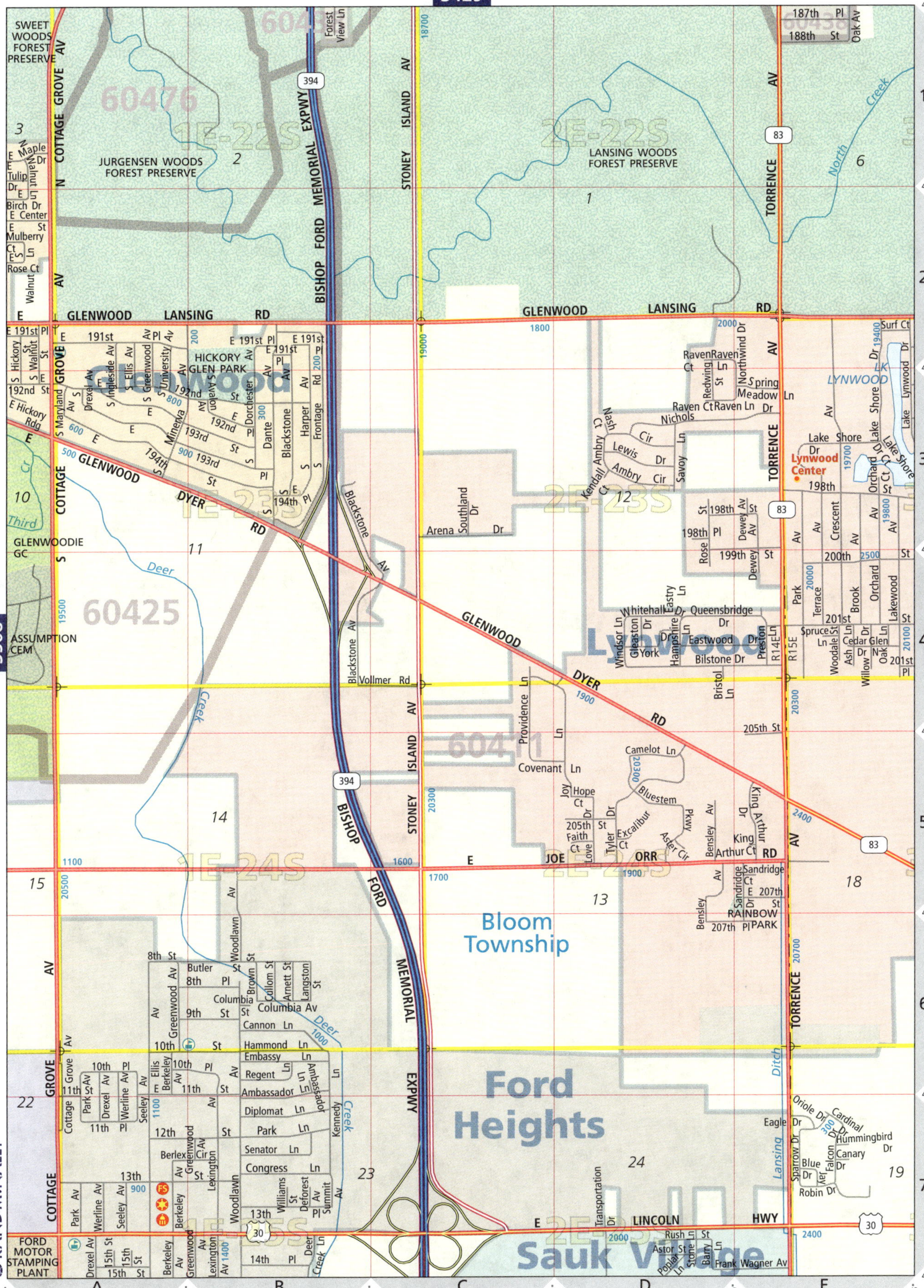

SEE 3508 MAP
SEE 3510 MAP
SEE 3597 MAP

1:24,000
1 in. = 2000 ft.
0 0.25 0.5
miles

SEE 3430 MAP

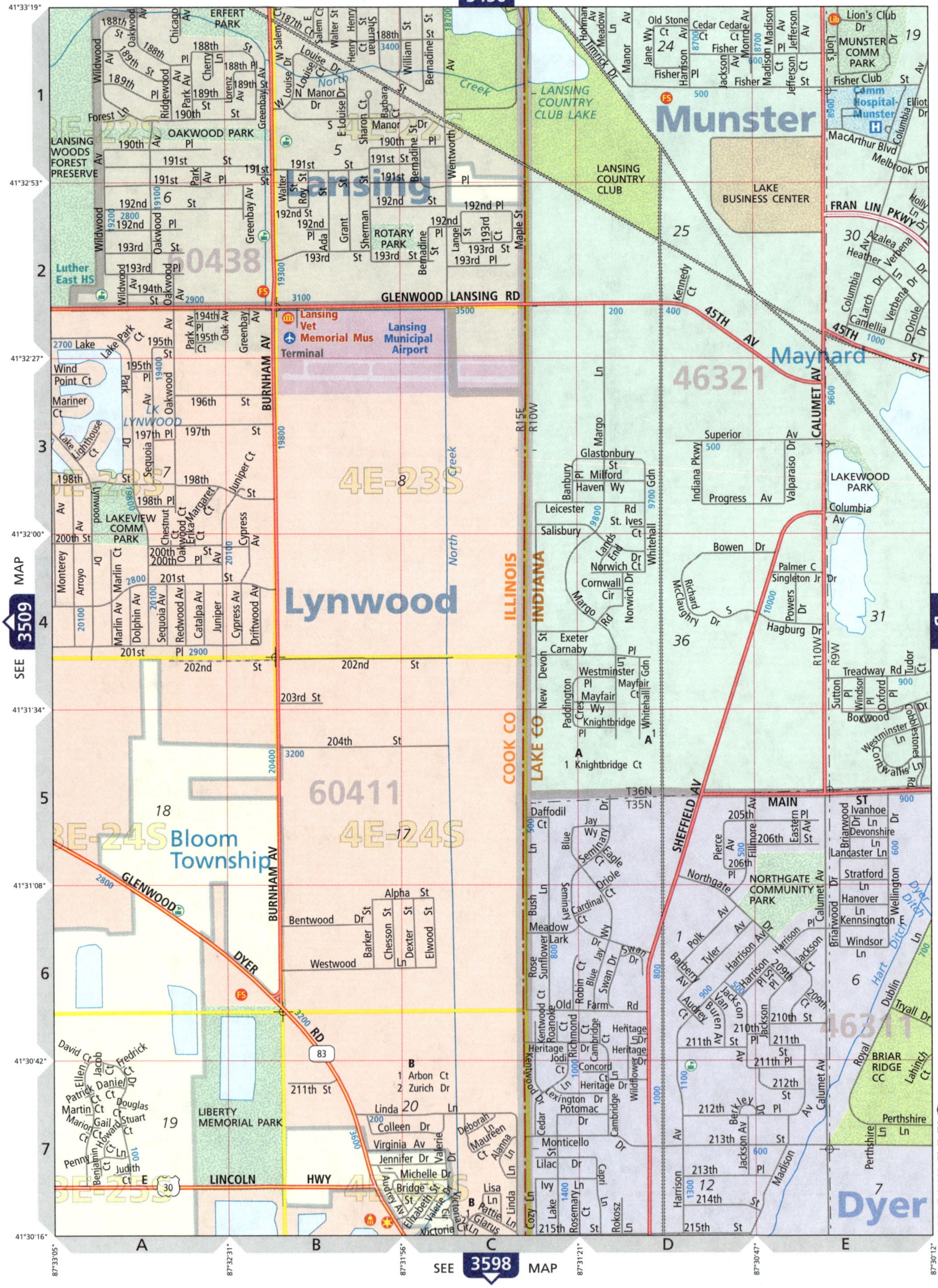
Munster
Lansing
Lynwood
Maynard
Dyer
Bloom Township
60438
60411
46321
46311
4E-22S
4E-23S
4E-24S
3E-22S
3E-23S
3E-24S
3E-25S
ILLINOIS
INDIANA
COOK CO
LAKE CO
R15E
R10W
R9W
T36N
T35N
GLENWOOD LANSING RD
45TH AV
BURNHAM AV
CALUMET AV
SHEFFIELD AV
GLENWOOD DYER RD
LINCOLN HWY
30
83
ERFERT PARK
OAKWOOD PARK
LANSING WOODS FOREST PRESERVE
Luther East HS
ROTARY PARK
LANSING COUNTRY CLUB LAKE
LANSING COUNTRY CLUB
LAKE BUSINESS CENTER
Lion's Club
MUNSTER COMM PARK
Comm Hospital-Munster
FRAN LIN PKWY
Lansing Vet Memorial Mus
Lansing Municipal Airport
Terminal
LK LYNWOOD
LAKEVIEW COMM PARK
LAKEWOOD PARK
NORTHGATE COMMUNITY PARK
BRIAR RIDGE CC
LIBERTY MEMORIAL PARK
North Creek
Hart Ditch
Dyer Ditch
A
1 Knightbridge Ct
B
1 Arbon Ct
2 Zurich Dr
41°33'19"
41°32'53"
41°32'27"
41°32'00"
41°31'34"
41°31'08"
41°30'42"
41°30'16"
87°33'05"
87°32'31"
87°31'56"
87°31'21"
87°30'47"
87°30'12"
A
B
C
D
E
1
2
3
4
5
6
7

SEE 3509 MAP

SEE B MAP

SEE 3598 MAP

1:24,000
1 in. = 2000 ft.
0 0.25 0.5
miles

SEE 3505 MAP

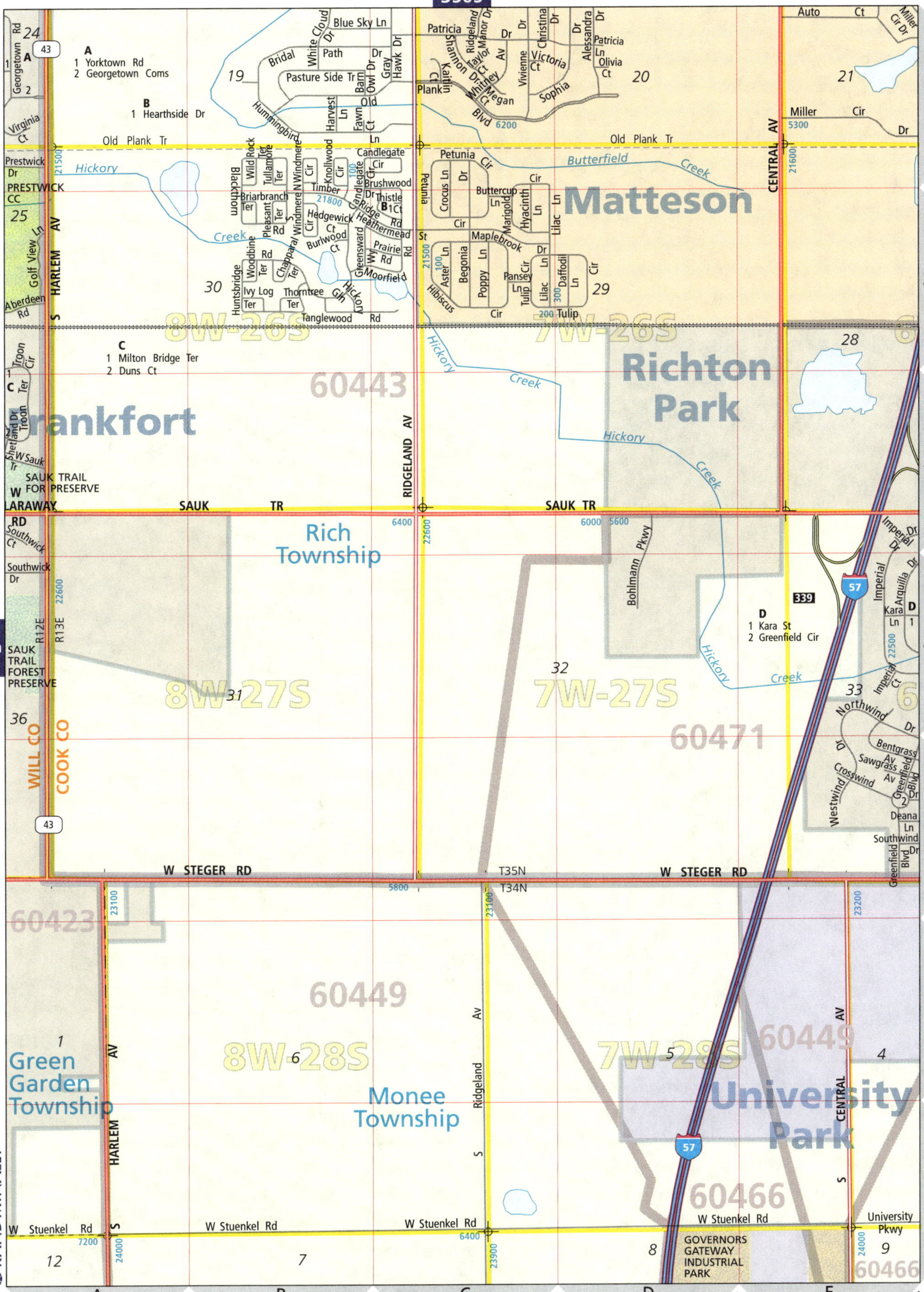

SEE 3682 MAP
SEE MAP B
SEE 3594 MAP

1:24,000
1 in. = 2000 ft.
0 0.25 0.5
miles

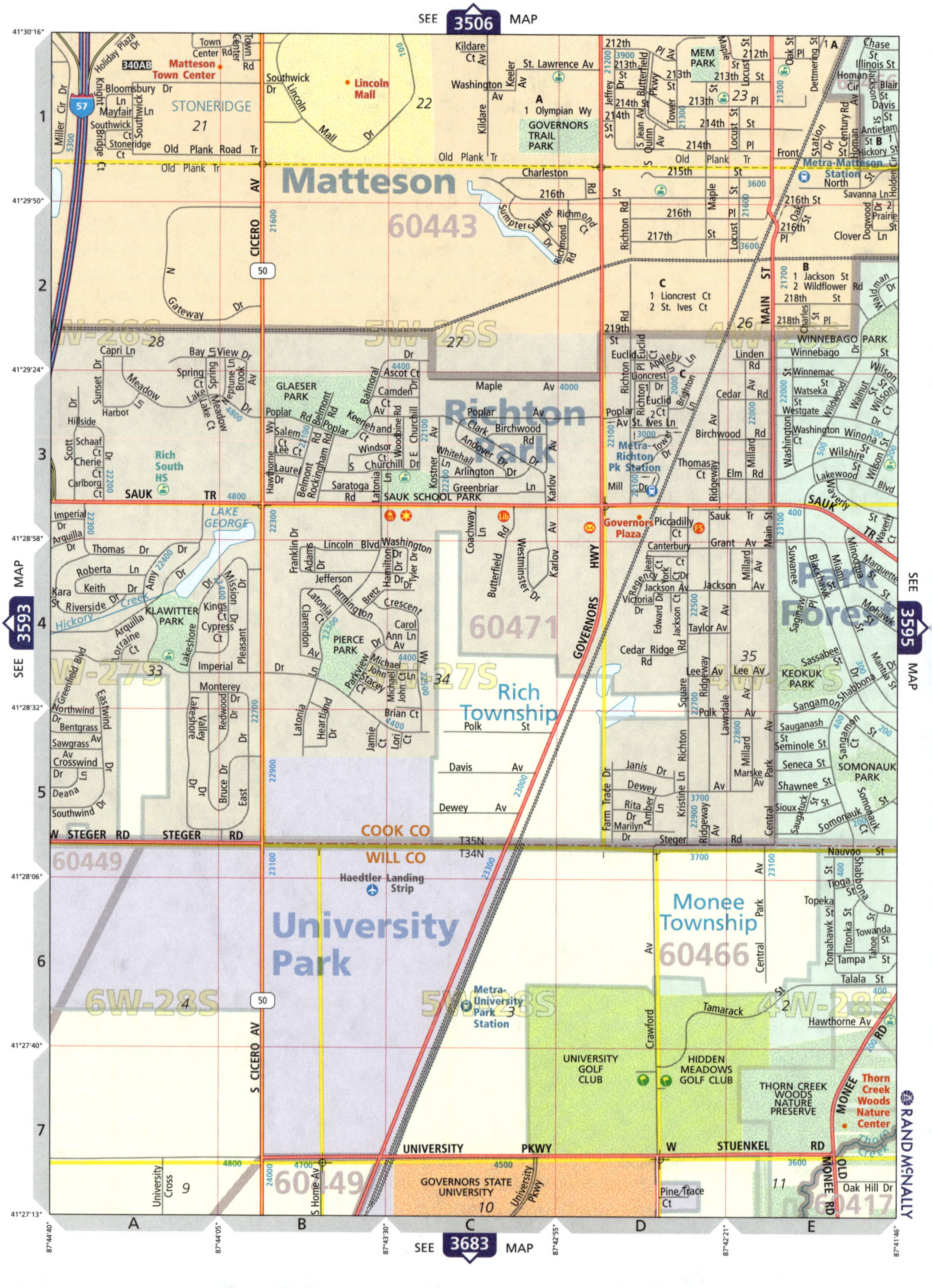
SEE 3506 MAP
SEE 3593 MAP
SEE 3595 MAP
SEE 3683 MAP
Matteson
60443
Richton Park
60471
University Park
60449
Monee Township
60466
Rich Township
60417
STONERIDGE
Matteson Town Center
Lincoln Mall
GOVERNORS TRAIL PARK
MEM PARK
Metra-Matteson Station
GLAESER PARK
Rich South HS
SAUK SCHOOL PARK
Metra-Richton Pk Station
Governors Plaza
LAKE GEORGE
KLAWITTER PARK
PIERCE PARK
WINNEBAGO PARK
KEOKUK PARK
SOMONAUK PARK
Park Forest
COOK CO
WILL CO
T35N
T34N
Haedtler Landing Strip
Metra-University Park Station
UNIVERSITY GOLF CLUB
HIDDEN MEADOWS GOLF CLUB
THORN CREEK WOODS NATURE PRESERVE
Thorn Creek Woods Nature Center
GOVERNORS STATE UNIVERSITY
UNIVERSITY PKWY
W STUENKEL RD
STEGER RD
SAUK TR
CICERO AV
S CICERO AV
GOVERNORS HWY
MAIN ST
MONEE RD
OLD MONEE RD
Old Plank Road Tr
N Gateway Dr
4W-26S
5W-26S
6W-27S
5W-27S
4W-27S
6W-28S
5W-28S
4W-28S
21 22 23 26 27 28 33 34 35 2 3 4 9 10 11
A B C D E
1 2 3 4 5 6 7
41°30'16"
41°29'50"
41°29'24"
41°28'58"
41°28'32"
41°28'06"
41°27'40"
41°27'13"
87°44'40"
87°44'05"
87°43'30"
87°42'55"
87°42'21"
87°41'46"
RAND McNALLY

1:24,000
1 in. = 2000 ft.
0 0.25 0.5
miles

SEE 3507 MAP

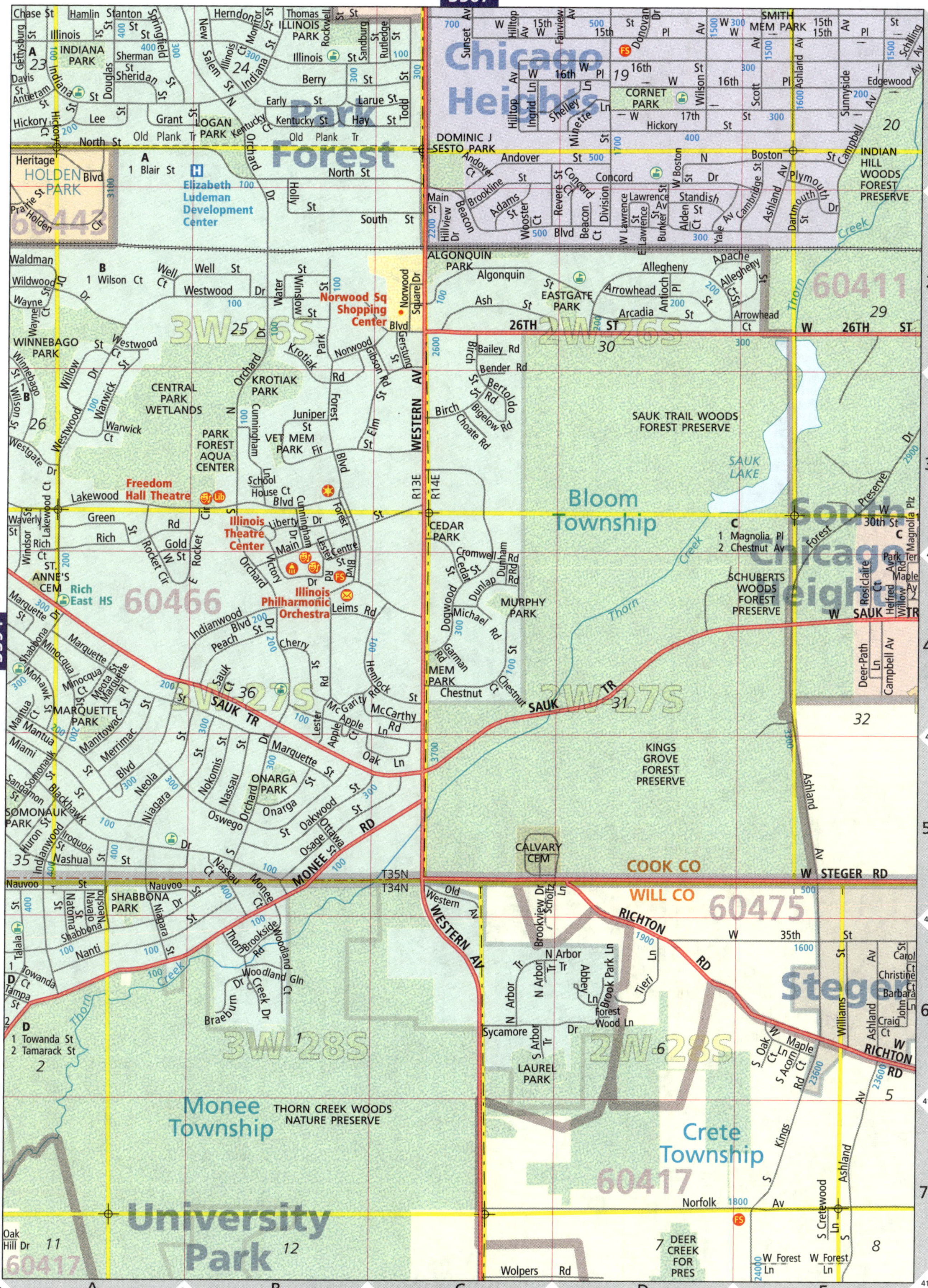

SEE 3594 MAP

SEE 3596 MAP

SEE 3684 MAP

RAND McNALLY

1:24,000
1 in. = 2000 ft.
0 0.25 0.5
miles

SEE 3508 MAP

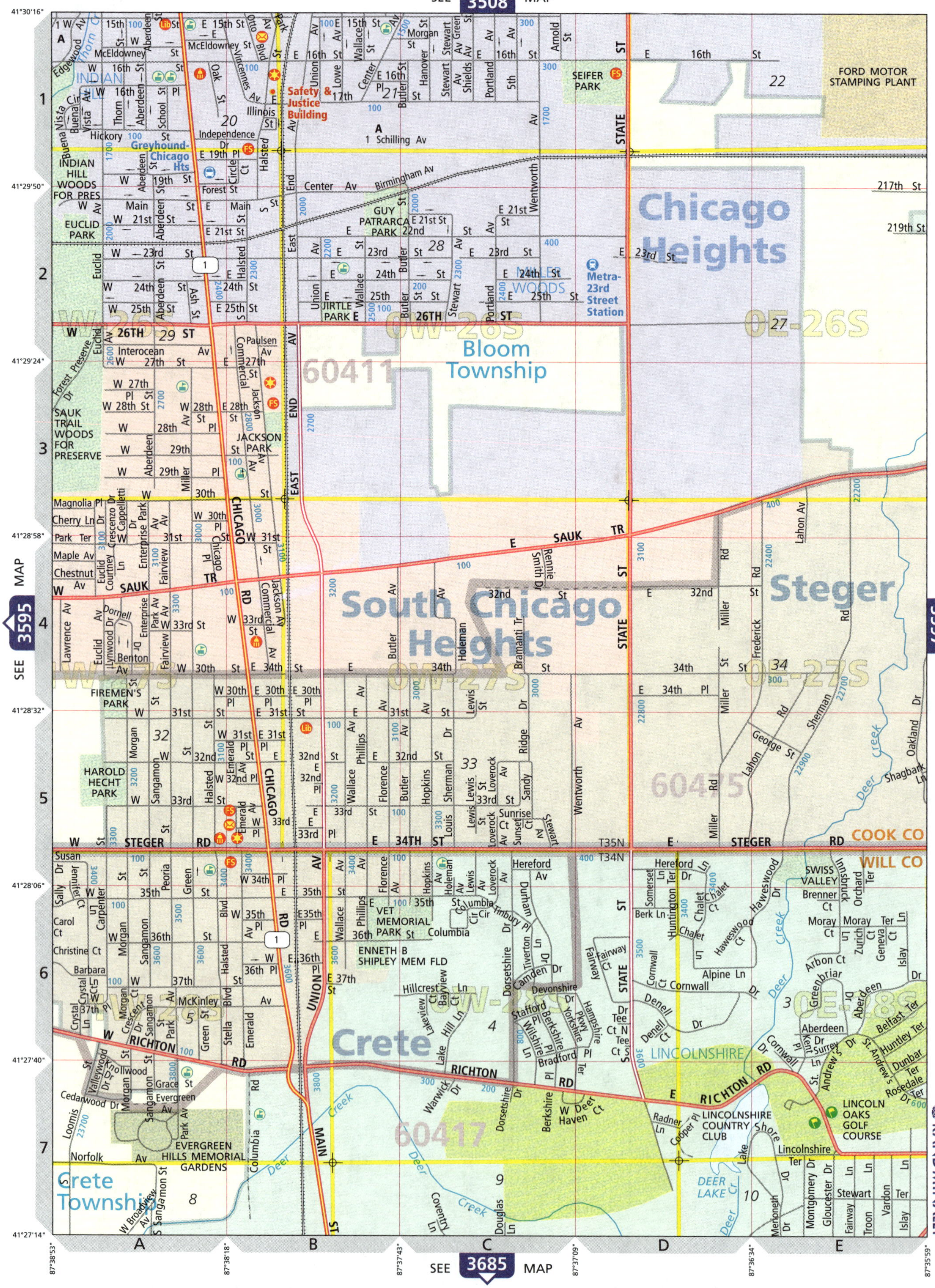
Chicago Heights
Bloom Township
South Chicago Heights
Steger
Crete
Crete Township
FORD MOTOR STAMPING PLANT
SEIFER PARK
Safety & Justice Building
Greyhound-Chicago Hts
INDIAN HILL WOODS FOR PRES
EUCLID PARK
GUY PATRARCA PARK
MILLER WOODS
Metra-23rd Street Station
JIRTLE PARK
JACKSON PARK
SAUK TRAIL WOODS FOR PRESERVE
FIREMEN'S PARK
HAROLD HECHT PARK
VET MEMORIAL PARK
ENNETH B SHIPLEY MEM FLD
EVERGREEN HILLS MEMORIAL GARDENS
LINCOLNSHIRE
LINCOLNSHIRE COUNTRY CLUB
LINCOLN OAKS GOLF COURSE
SWISS VALLEY
DEER LAKE
COOK CO
WILL CO
60411
60475
60417
0W-26S
0E-26S
0W-27S
0E-27S
0E-28S
T35N
T34N
STATE ST
CHICAGO RD
EAST END AV
UNION AV
MAIN ST
E SAUK TR
W SAUK TR
W STEGER RD
E STEGER RD
E 34TH ST
W 26TH ST
E 26TH ST
W RICHTON RD
E RICHTON RD
Deer Creek
Thorn Cr

SEE 3595 MAP

SEE 3597 MAP

SEE 3685 MAP

1:24,000
1 in. = 2000 ft.
0 0.25 0.5
miles

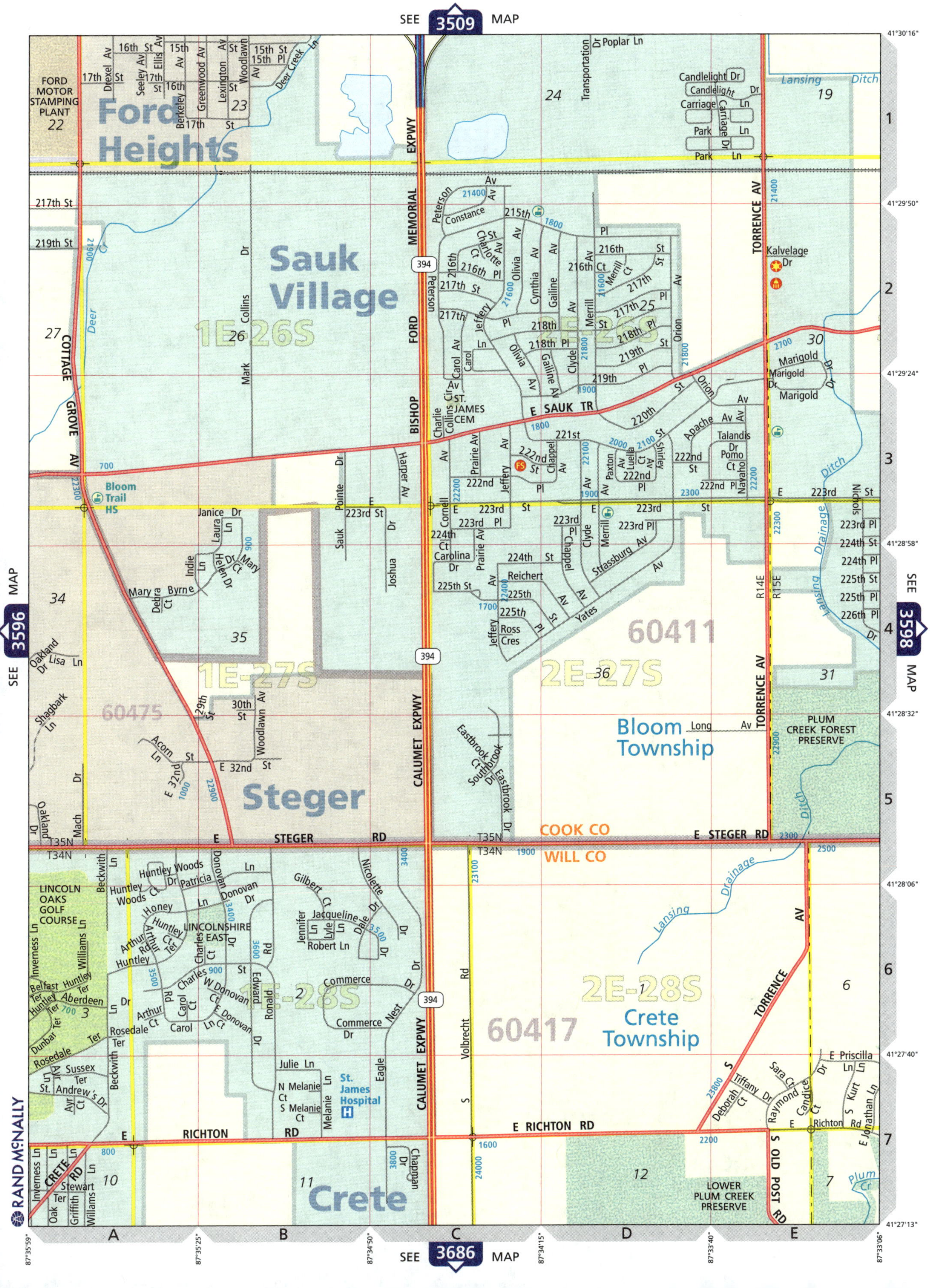

1:24,000
1 in. = 2000 ft.
0 0.25 0.5
miles

SEE 3510 MAP

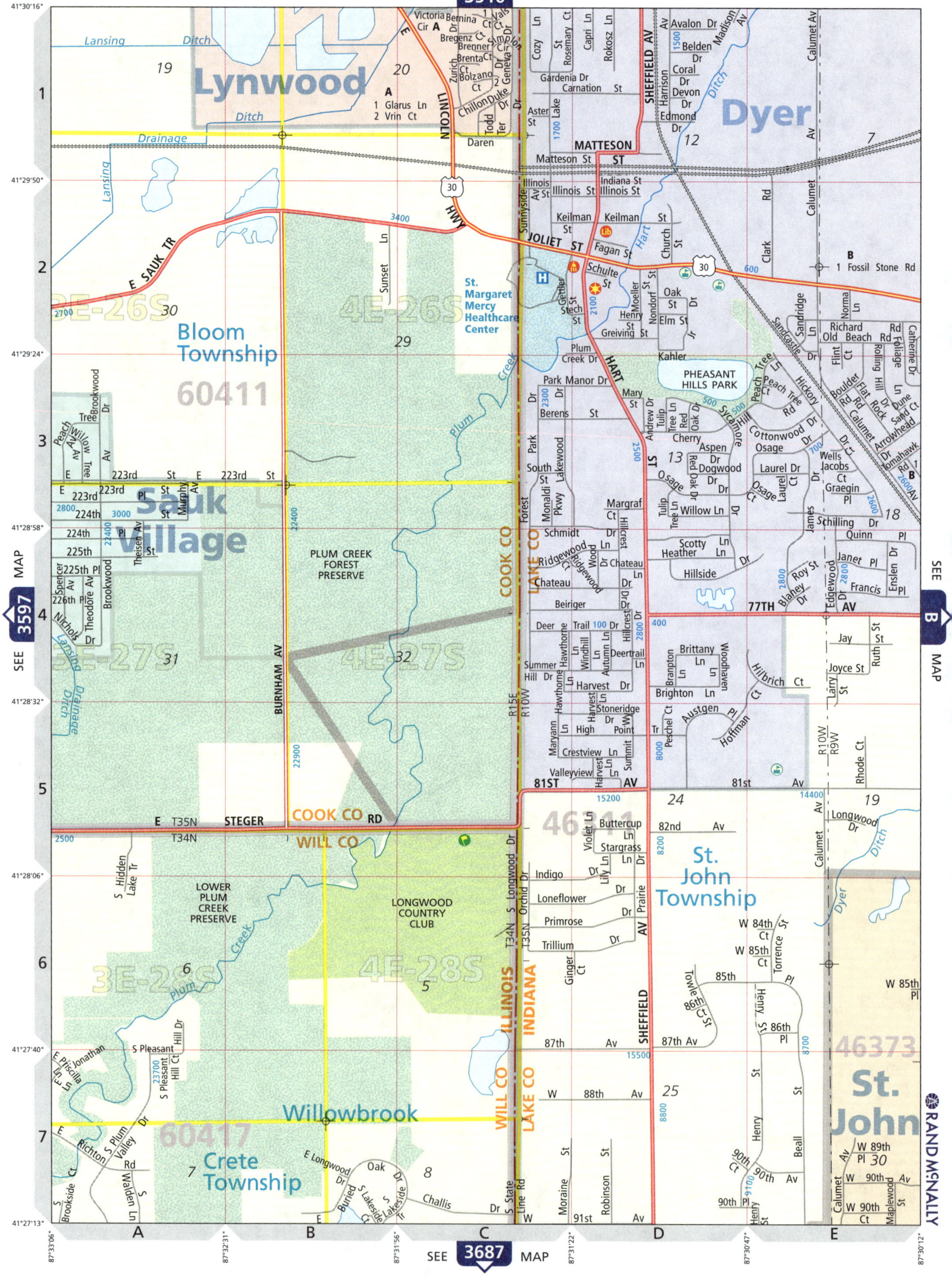
Lynwood
Dyer
Bloom Township
Sauk Village
St. John Township
St. John
Crete Township
Willowbrook
60411
60417
46311
46373
St. Margaret Mercy Healthcare Center
PLUM CREEK FOREST PRESERVE
LOWER PLUM CREEK PRESERVE
LONGWOOD COUNTRY CLUB
PHEASANT HILLS PARK
E SAUK TR
JOLIET ST
MATTESON ST
SHEFFIELD AV
LINCOLN HWY
BURNHAM AV
HART ST
77TH AV
81ST AV
E STEGER RD
COOK CO
WILL CO
LAKE CO
ILLINOIS
INDIANA
Lansing Ditch
Drainage Ditch
Plum Creek
Dyer Ditch
Hart Ditch
3E-26S
4E-26S
3E-27S
4E-27S
3E-28S
4E-28S
T35N
T34N
R15E
R10W
R9W
A
1 Glarus Ln
2 Vrin Ct
B
1 Fossil Stone Rd
E 223rd St
225th St
Theodore Av
Brookwood Dr
Sunset Ln
Calumet Av
Clark Rd
Longwood Dr
Challis Dr
87th Av
88th Av
90th Av
S State Line Rd
Moraine St
Robinson St
Henry St
Torrence St
Beall St

SEE 3597 MAP
SEE B MAP
SEE 3687 MAP

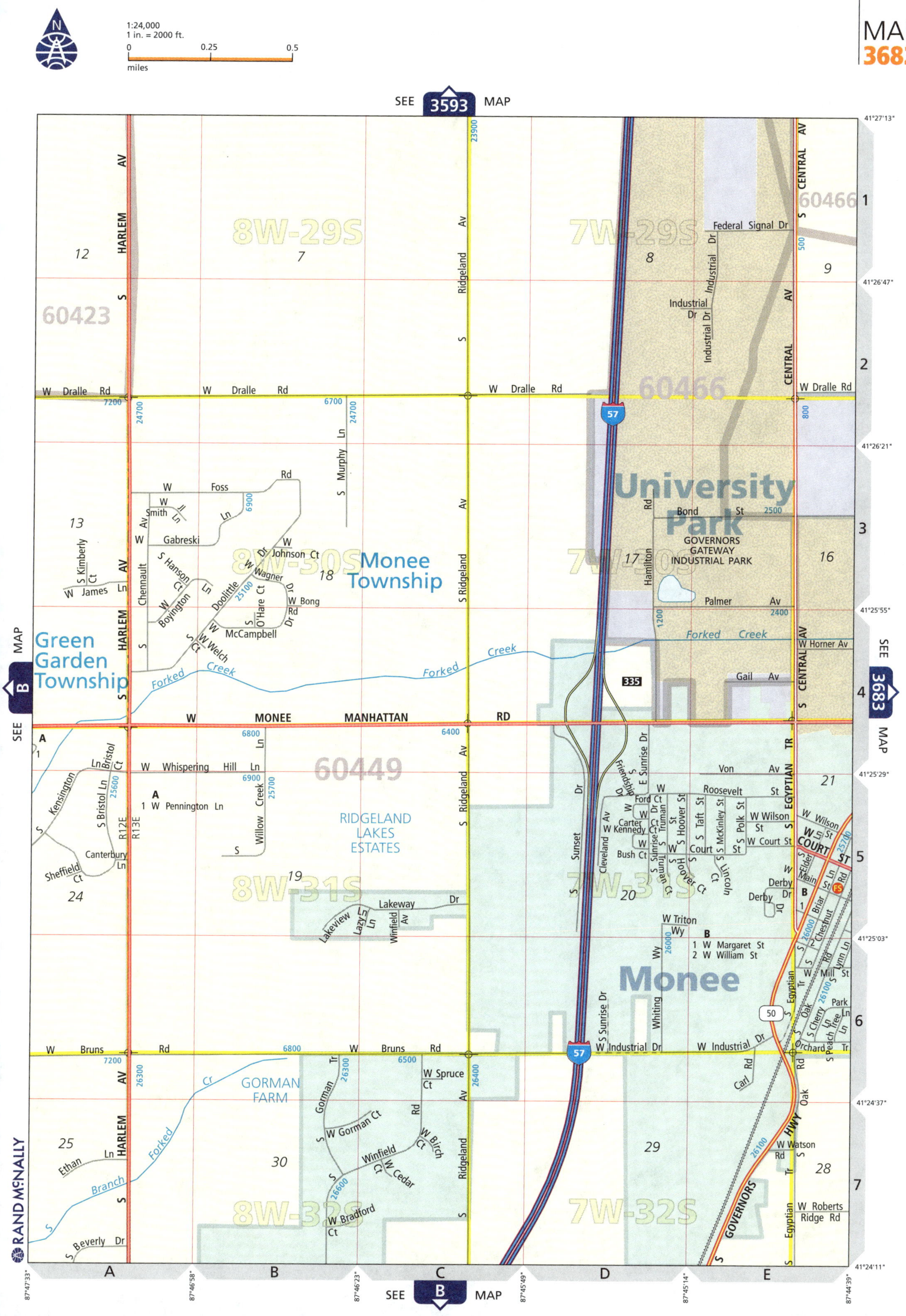
1:24,000
1 in. = 2000 ft.
0
0.25
0.5
miles
SEE 3593 MAP
SEE B MAP
SEE B MAP
SEE 3683 MAP
University Park
GOVERNORS GATEWAY INDUSTRIAL PARK
Monee Township
Green Garden Township
Monee
RIDGELAND LAKES ESTATES
GORMAN FARM
8W-29S
7W-29S
8W-30S
7W-30S
8W-31S
7W-31S
8W-32S
7W-32S
60423
60466
60449
S HARLEM AV
S Ridgeland Av
S CENTRAL AV
W Dralle Rd
W MONEE MANHATTAN RD
W Bruns Rd
Federal Signal Dr
Industrial Dr
W Foss Rd
Gabreski
W James Ln
S Kimberly Ct
Chennault
W Johnson Ct
W Wagner Dr
W Bong Rd
McCampbell
S O'Hare Ct
Doolittle Ln
W Boyington Ln
S Hanson Ct
W Smith Ln
S Murphy Ln
Forked Creek
Bond St
Palmer Av
W Horner Av
Gail Av
Hamilton Rd
W Whispering Hill Ln
1 W Pennington Ln
S Willow Creek Ln
Kensington
S Bristol Ln
Bristol Ct
Canterbury Ln
Sheffield Ct
Lakeway Dr
Lakeview
Lazy Ln
Winfield Av
S Sunset Dr
S Sunrise Dr
E Sunrise Dr
Friendship Dr
Von Av
W Roosevelt St
W Wilson St
W Court St
S EGYPTIAN TR
W COURT ST
W Triton Wy
1 W Margaret St
2 W William St
W Industrial Dr
Whiting Wy
Cleveland Av
W Kennedy Ct
Carter
Truman Ct
Hoover Ct
Taft St
McKinley St
Polk St
Lincoln Ct
Bush Ct
Ford Ct
Derby Dr
W Mill St
Park Ln
Oak
Cherry Tree Ln
Peach Tree Ln
Orchard Tr
S GOVERNORS HWY
W Watson Rd
W Roberts Ridge Rd
Carl Rd
W Spruce Ct
W Gorman Ct
Gorman Tr
W Birch Ct
Winfield Ct
W Cedar Ct
W Bradford Ct
Ethan Ln
Forked Branch
S Beverly Dr
57
335
50
RAND McNALLY

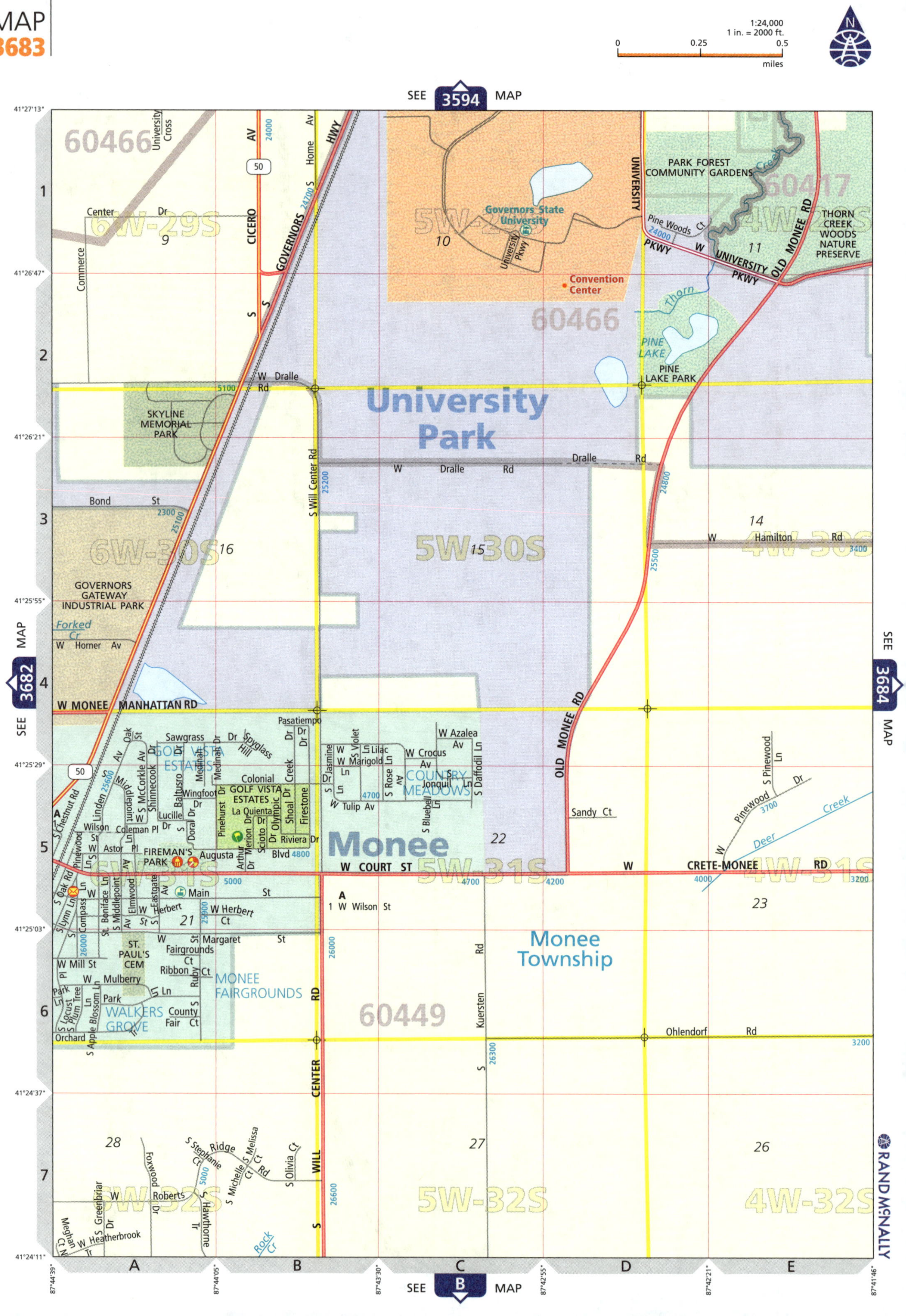
1:24,000
1 in. = 2000 ft.
0
0.25
0.5
miles
N
SEE 3594 MAP
SEE 3682 MAP
SEE 3684 MAP
SEE B MAP
University Park
Monee
Monee Township
60466
60417
60449
6W-29S
5W-29S
4W-29S
6W-30S
5W-30S
4W-30S
6W-31S
5W-31S
4W-31S
6W-32S
5W-32S
4W-32S
Governors State University
Convention Center
PARK FOREST COMMUNITY GARDENS
THORN CREEK WOODS NATURE PRESERVE
PINE LAKE PARK
PINE LAKE
Thorn
Creek
SKYLINE MEMORIAL PARK
GOVERNORS GATEWAY INDUSTRIAL PARK
Forked Cr
GOLF VISTA ESTATES
COUNTRY MEADOWS
FIREMAN'S PARK
ST. PAUL'S CEM
MONEE FAIRGROUNDS
WALKERS GROVE
Deer Creek
Rock Cr
S CICERO AV
S GOVERNORS HWY
UNIVERSITY PKWY
W UNIVERSITY PKWY
OLD MONEE RD
W Dralle Rd
Dralle Rd
S Will Center Rd
S WILL CENTER RD
W Hamilton Rd
W MONEE MANHATTAN RD
W COURT ST
W CRETE-MONEE RD
Ohlendorf Rd
S Kuersten Rd
Bond St
W Horner Av
Center Dr
Commerce
University Cross
Pine Woods Ct
University Pkwy
S Home Av
Sandy Ct
S Pinewood Ln
W Pinewood Dr
Main St
W Herbert Ct
W Margaret St
Fairgrounds Ct
Ribbon Ct
Ruby Ct
W Mill St
W Mulberry
Park Ln
County Fair Ct
Orchard
W Roberts Dr
W Heatherbrook Tr
S Greenbriar Dr
Foxwood Dr
S Hawthorne Tr
Ridge Rd
S Stephanie Ct
S Melissa Ct
S Michelle Ct
S Olivia Ct
Meghan Ct N
1 W Wilson St
50
24000
24700
5100
25100
2300
25200
24800
25500
3400
25600
4700
4800
5000
4700
4200
4000
3700
3200
25900
26000
26000
26300
3200
26600
5000
9
10
11
14
15
16
21
22
23
26
27
28
1
2
3
4
5
6
7
A
B
C
D
E
41°27'13"
41°26'47"
41°26'21"
41°25'55"
41°25'29"
41°25'03"
41°24'37"
41°24'11"
87°44'39"
87°44'05"
87°43'30"
87°42'55"
87°42'21"
87°41'46"
RAND McNALLY

1:24,000
1 in. = 2000 ft.
0 0.25 0.5
miles

SEE 3595 MAP

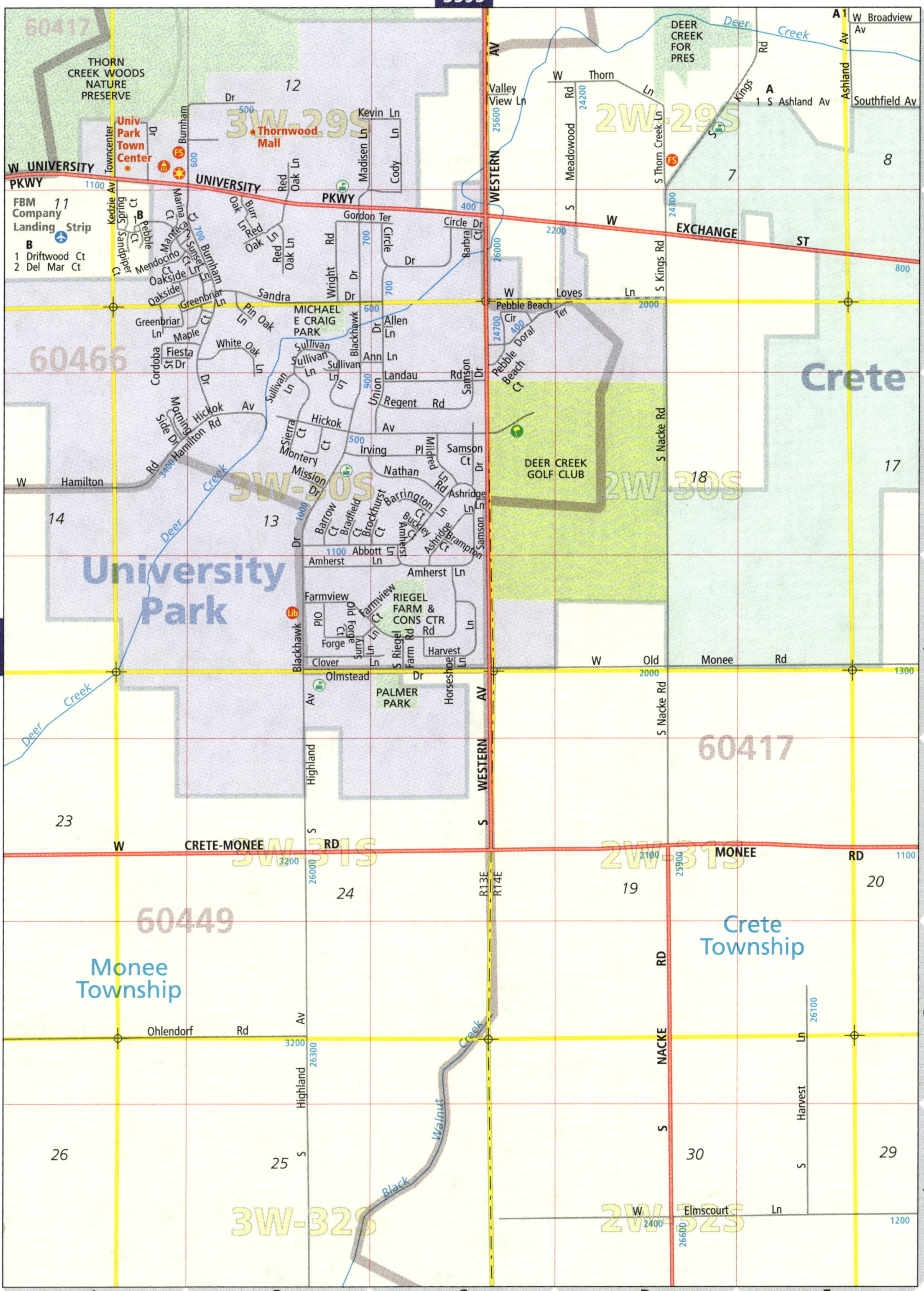

SEE 3683 MAP
SEE 3685 MAP
SEE B MAP

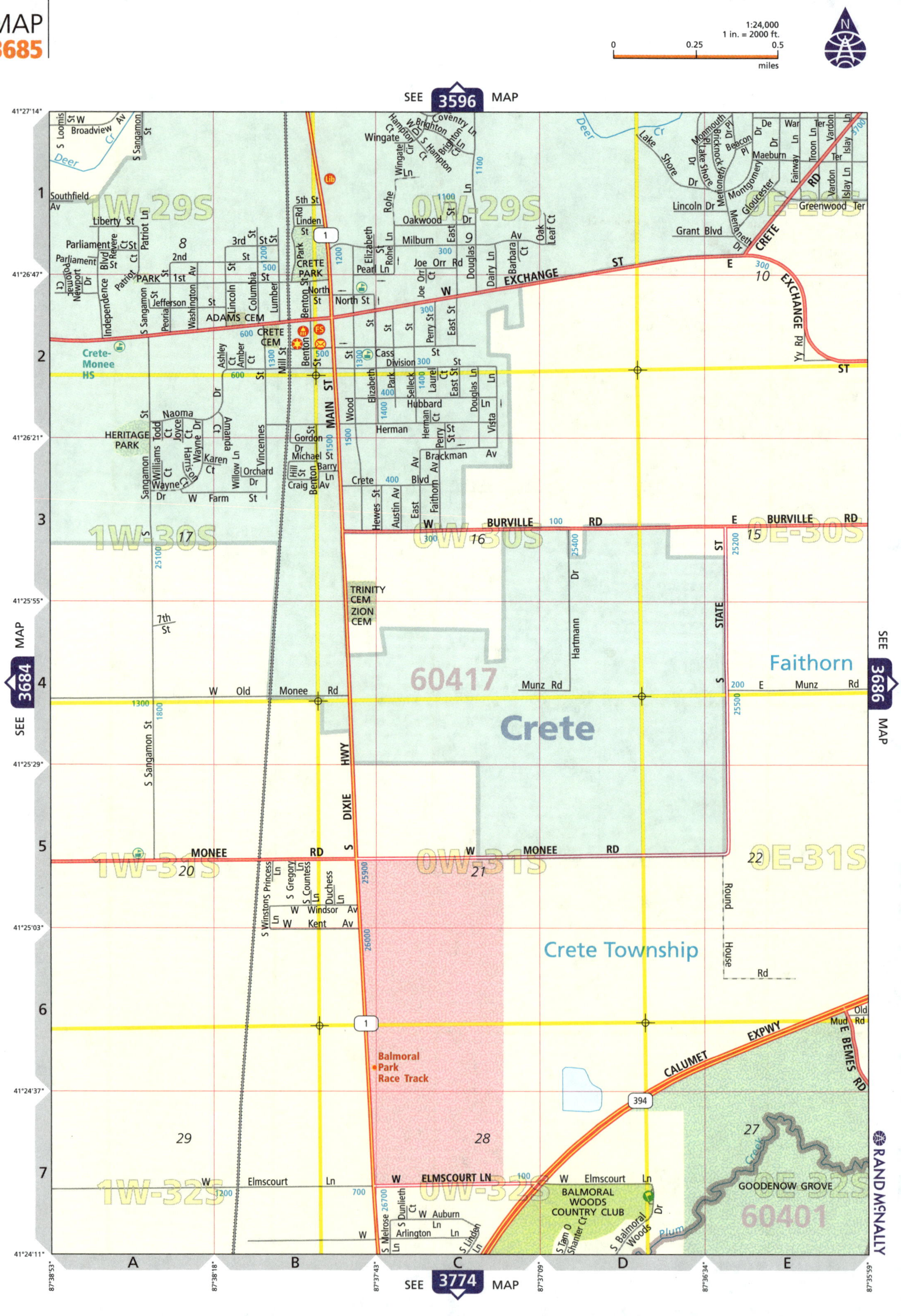
1:24,000
1 in. = 2000 ft.
0 0.25 0.5
miles
N
SEE 3596 MAP
SEE 3684 MAP
SEE 3686 MAP
SEE 3774 MAP
1W-29S
0W-29S
0E-29S
1W-30S
0W-30S
0E-30S
1W-31S
0W-31S
0E-31S
1W-32S
0W-32S
0E-32S
60417
60401
Crete
Faithorn
Crete Township
Crete-Monee HS
HERITAGE PARK
CRETE PARK
ADAMS CEM
CRETE CEM
TRINITY CEM
ZION CEM
Balmoral Park Race Track
BALMORAL WOODS COUNTRY CLUB
GOODENOW GROVE
Lib
FS
W EXCHANGE ST
E EXCHANGE ST
CRETE RD
W BURVILLE RD
E BURVILLE RD
W Old Monee Rd
Munz Rd
E Munz Rd
MONEE RD
W MONEE RD
W ELMSCOURT LN
W Elmscourt Ln
MAIN ST
S DIXIE HWY
S STATE ST
CALUMET EXPWY
E BEMES RD
Old Mud Rd
Round House Rd
S Sangamon St
Hartmann Dr
Deer Cr
Plum Creek
RAND McNALLY

1:24,000
1 in. = 2000 ft.
0 0.25 0.5
miles

SEE 3597 MAP

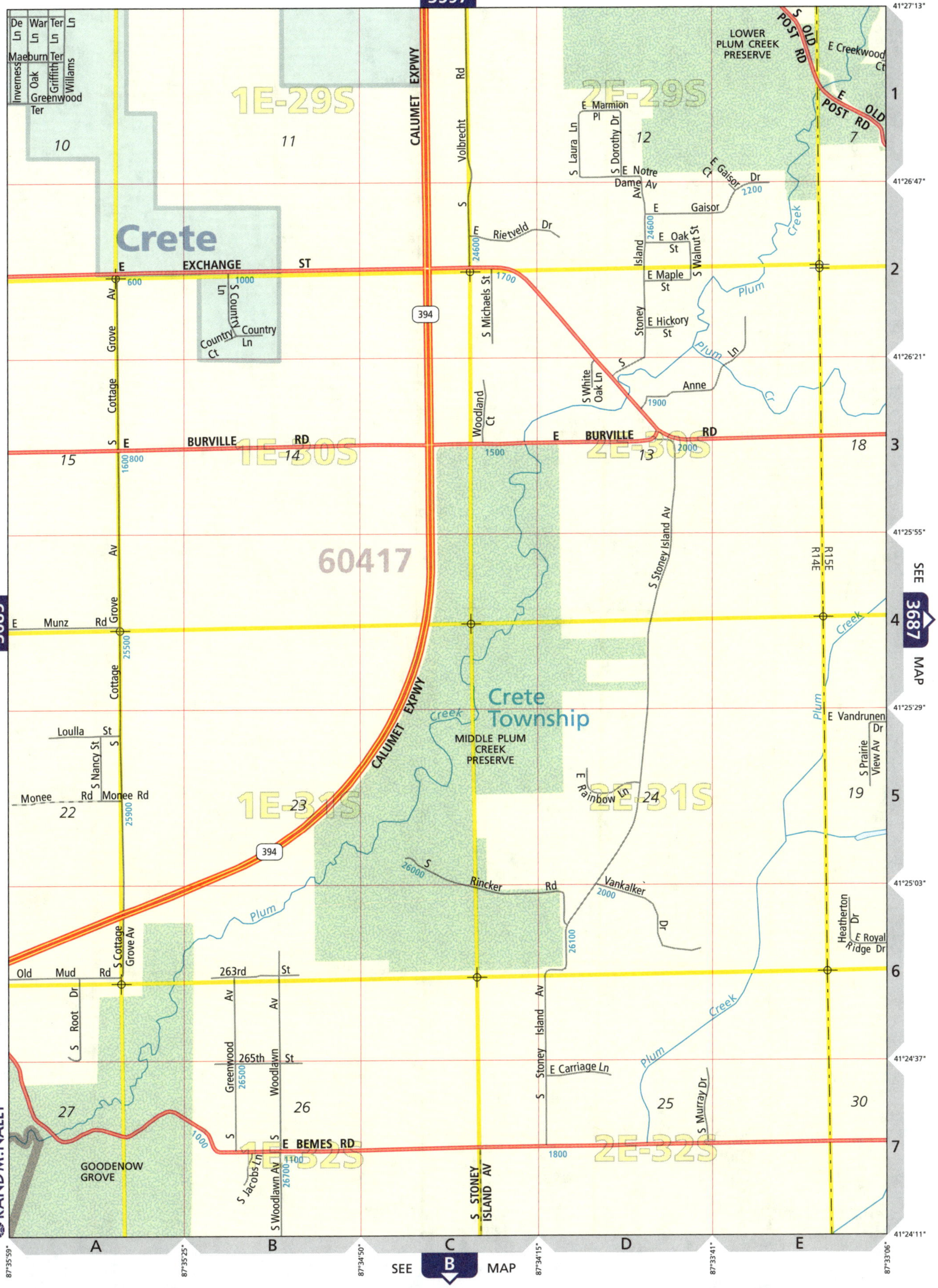
Crete
Crete Township
60417
1E-29S
2E-29S
1E-30S
2E-30S
1E-31S
2E-31S
1E-32S
2E-32S
LOWER PLUM CREEK PRESERVE
MIDDLE PLUM CREEK PRESERVE
GOODENOW GROVE
CALUMET EXPWY
394
E EXCHANGE ST
E BURVILLE RD
E Munz Rd
Old Mud Rd
E BEMES RD
S STONEY ISLAND AV
S OLD POST RD
E OLD POST RD
S Cottage Grove Av
S Volbrecht Rd
S Stoney Island Av
E Rietveld Dr
S Michaels St
Woodland Ct
S Country Ln
Country Ln
Country Ct
De Ln
War Ln
Ter Ln
Maeburn Ter
Inverness
Oak
Griffith
Willams
Greenwood Ter
E Marmion Pl
S Laura Ln
S Dorothy Dr
E Notre Dame Av
E Gaisor Ct
E Gaisor Dr
E Oak St
S Walnut St
E Maple St
E Hickory St
S White Oak Ln
Plum Ln
Anne
E Creekwood Ct
Plum Creek
Loulla St
S Nancy St
Monee Rd
S Rincker Rd
Vankalker Dr
E Rainbow Ln
E Vandrunen Dr
S Prairie View Av
Heatherton Dr
E Royal Ridge Dr
263rd St
265th St
S Greenwood Av
S Woodlawn Av
S Root Dr
E Carriage Ln
S Murray Dr
S Jacobs Ln
R15E
R14E
10
11
12
7
15
14
13
18
22
23
24
19
27
26
25
30
600
1000
1700
24600
1900
2000
2200
1600
800
1500
25500
25900
26000
26100
26500
26700
1000
1100
1800
A
B
C
D
E
1
2
3
4
5
6
7
41°27'13"
41°26'47"
41°26'21"
41°25'55"
41°25'29"
41°25'03"
41°24'37"
41°24'11"
87°35'59"
87°35'25"
87°34'50"
87°34'15"
87°33'41"
87°33'06"

SEE 3685 MAP

SEE 3687 MAP

SEE B MAP

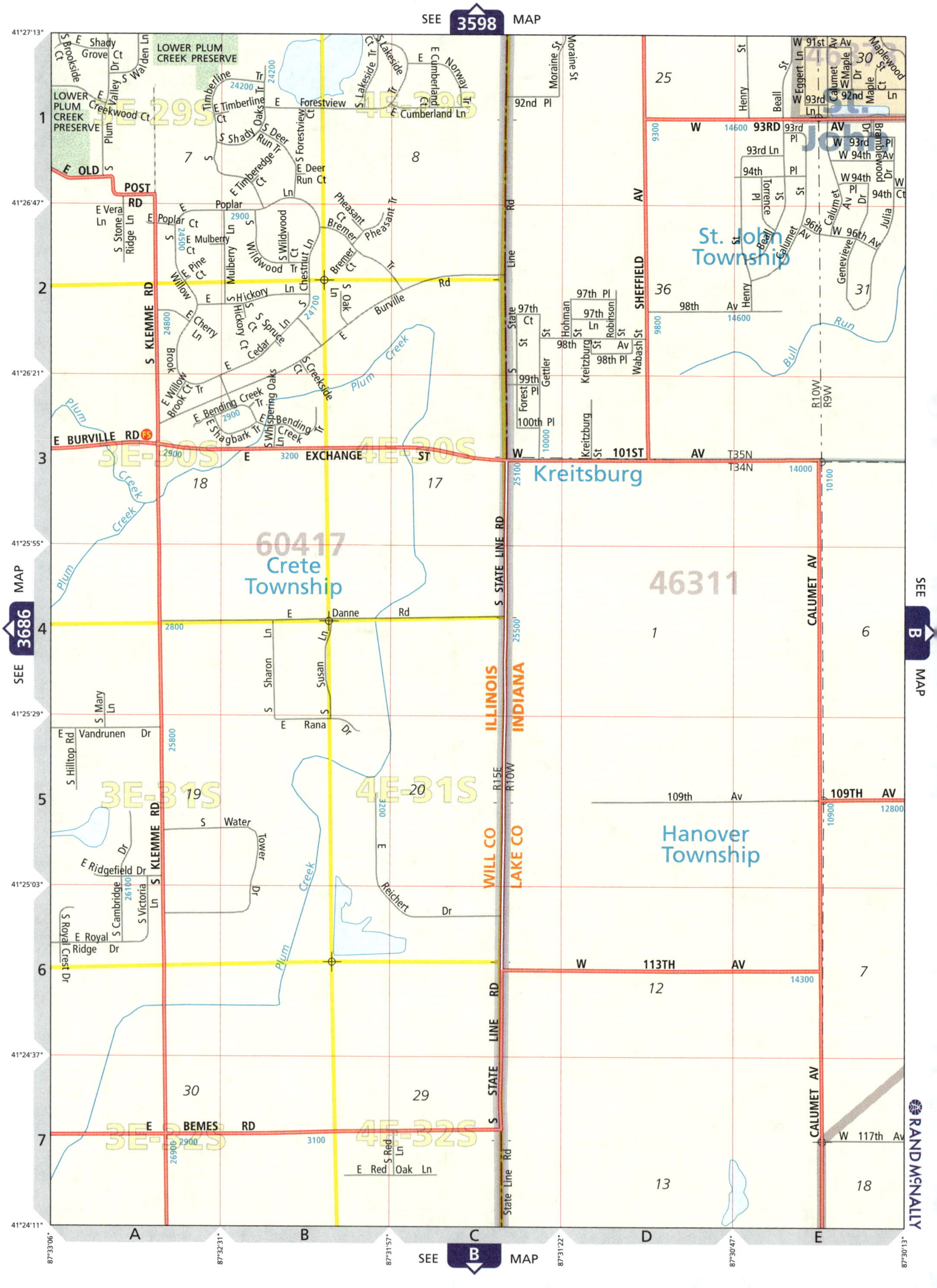
1:24,000
1 in. = 2000 ft.
0
0.25
0.5
miles
N
SEE 3598 MAP
SEE 3686 MAP
SEE B MAP
SEE B MAP
LOWER PLUM CREEK PRESERVE
LOWER PLUM CREEK PRESERVE
E Shady Grove Ct
S Brookside Ct
S Walden Ln
Valley Dr
E Creekwood Ct
Plum
E OLD POST RD
E Timberline Tr
E Timberline Ct
24200
Forestview
S Forestview Ct
S Shady Oaks Tr
S Deer Run Tr
E Timberedge Ct
E Deer Run Ct
S Lakeside Ct
S Lakeside Tr
E Cumberland Ct
E Cumberland Ln
Norway Tr
3E-29S
4E-29S
7
8
E Vera Ln
S Stone Ridge Ln
E Poplar Ct
Poplar
2900
E Mulberry Ct
S Mulberry Ln
S Wildwood Ct
Wildwood Tr
Chestnut Ln
Pheasant Ct
Pheasant Tr
Bremer Ct
E Pine Ct
Willow
E Hickory Ln
S Hickory Ct
S Spruce Ln
Cedar Ct
24700
S Oak Ln
Burville Rd
E Cherry Ln
Brook
24800
S KLEMME RD
E Willow Brook Ct
E Bending Creek Tr
S Whispering Oaks Ln
E Bending Creek Tr
S Creekside Ct
S Creekside
S Shagbark Tr
Plum Creek
Plum
E BURVILLE RD
FS
2900
3200
E EXCHANGE ST
3E-30S
4E-30S
18
17
Creek
Creek
60417
Crete Township
Plum
E Danne Rd
2800
S Sharon Ln
S Susan Ln
E Rana Dr
S Mary Ln
E Vandrunen Dr
S Hilltop Rd
25800
3E-31S
19
4E-31S
20
3200
S Water Tower Dr
S KLEMME RD
E Ridgefield Dr
S Cambridge
26100
S Victoria Ln
E Reichert Dr
Creek
Plum
S Royal Crest Dr
E Royal Ridge Dr
30
29
E BEMES RD
3E-32S
4E-32S
2900
26900
3100
S Red Ln
E Red Oak Ln
S STATE LINE RD
State Line Rd
S State Line Rd
State Line Rd
ILLINOIS
INDIANA
WILL CO
LAKE CO
R15E
R10W
25100
25500
Moraine St
Moraine St
92nd Pl
97th Ct
99th Pl
Forest Pl
100th Pl
Gettler St
Hohman St
97th Pl
97th Ln
98th
Robinson St
Kreitzburg St
98th Pl
Av
Wabash St
Kreitzburg St
10000
W 101ST AV
SHEFFIELD AV
25
36
9300
9800
W 93RD AV
14600
93rd Ln
94th Pl
Torrence St
Henry St
Beall St
St. John Township
98th Av
14600
Henry
Calumet
W 91st Av
Eggert Ln
W 93rd Ln
Calumet Av
W Maple Dr
92nd
Maple Ct
Maplewood
30
St. John
93rd Pl
W 93rd Pl
W 94th Av
Bramblewood Dr
W 94th Pl
Calumet Av
Calumet Dr
94th Ct
96th Av
W 96th Av
Genevieve
Julia
31
Bull Run
R10W
R9W
T35N
T34N
14000
10100
Kreitsburg
46311
CALUMET AV
1
6
109th Av
109TH AV
12800
10900
Hanover Township
W 113TH AV
14300
12
7
CALUMET AV
W 117th Av
13
18
A
B
C
D
E
1
2
3
4
5
6
7
41°27'13"
41°26'47"
41°26'21"
41°25'55"
41°25'29"
41°25'03"
41°24'37"
41°24'11"
87°33'06"
87°32'31"
87°31'57"
87°31'22"
87°30'47"
87°30'13"
RAND McNALLY

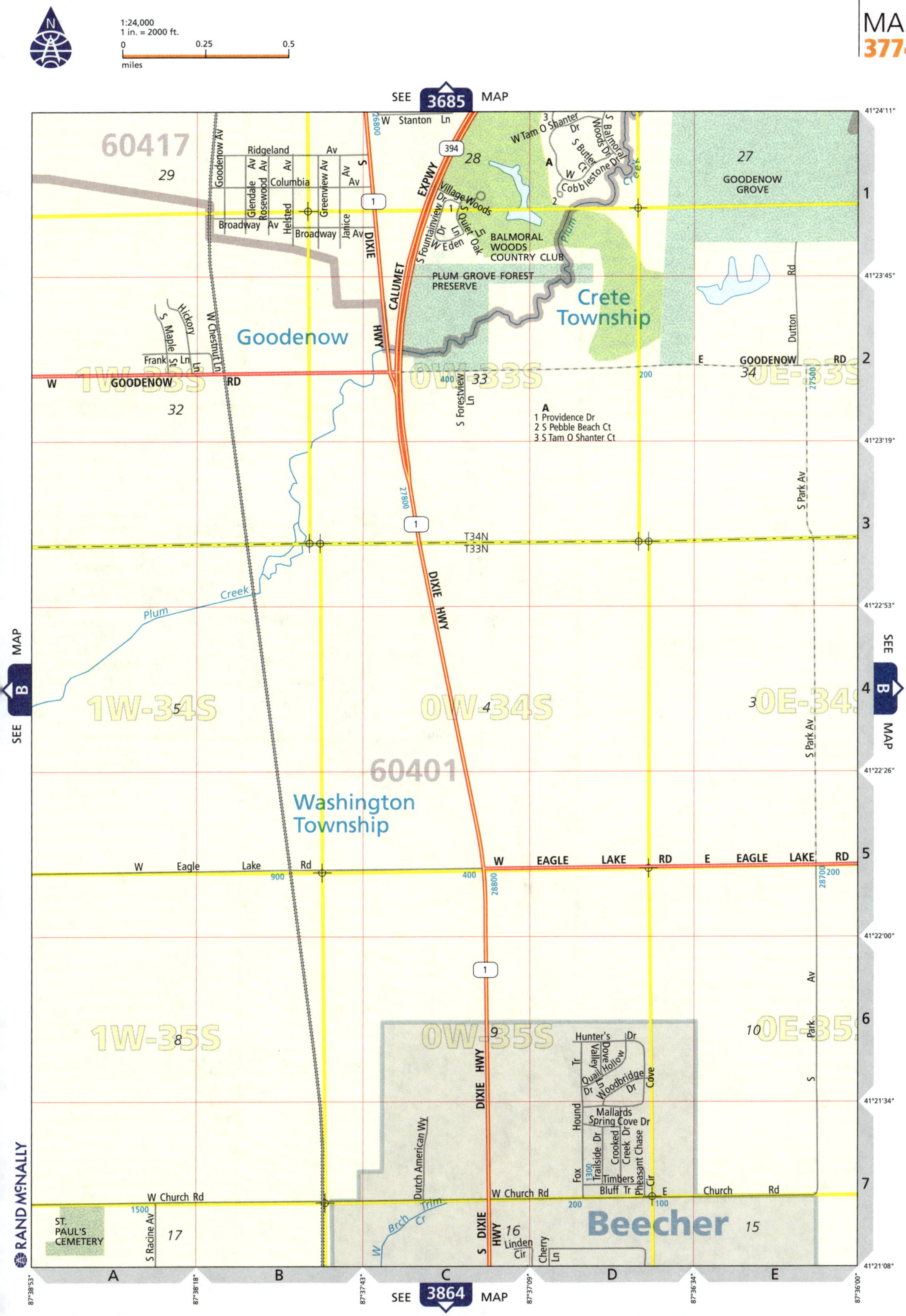
1:24,000
1 in. = 2000 ft.
0
0.25
0.5
miles
SEE 3685 MAP
SEE B MAP
SEE 3864 MAP
60417
60401
Goodenow
Crete Township
Washington Township
Beecher
GOODENOW GROVE
BALMORAL WOODS COUNTRY CLUB
PLUM GROVE FOREST PRESERVE
ST. PAUL'S CEMETERY
W GOODENOW RD
E GOODENOW RD
W Eagle Lake Rd
W EAGLE LAKE RD
E EAGLE LAKE RD
W Church Rd
E Church Rd
CALUMET EXPWY
DIXIE HWY
S DIXIE HWY
W Stanton Ln
Ridgeland Av
Columbia
Broadway Av
Goodenow Av
Glendale Av
Rosewood Av
Helsted Av
Greenview Av
Janice Av
S Av
W Chestnut Ln
Hickory
S Maple St
Frank Ln
Ln
S Forestview Ln
S Fountainview Dr
Village Woods Dr
S Quiet Oak Ln
W Eden Ln
W Tam O Shanter Dr
S Butler Ct
S Balmoral Woods Dr
W Cobblestone Dr
Plum Creek
Dutton Rd
S Park Av
S Racine Av
Dutch American Wy
Hunter's Dr
Valley Tr
Dove Ln
Quail Hollow Dr
Woodbridge Dr
Cove
Mallards
Spring Cove Dr
Hound
Trailside Dr
Crooked Creek Dr
Pheasant Chase Cir
Fox
Timbers
Bluff Tr
W Brch Cr
Trim
Linden Cir
Cherry Ln
A
1 Providence Dr
2 S Pebble Beach Ct
3 S Tam O Shanter Ct
T34N
T33N
1W-33S
0W-33S
0E-33S
1W-34S
0W-34S
0E-34S
1W-35S
0W-35S
0E-35S
27
28
29
32
33
34
3
4
5
8
9
10
15
16
17
1
394
26800
27800
27500
28800
28700
400
200
900
1500
1300
100
1
2
3
4
5
6
7
A
B
C
D
E
41°24'11"
41°23'45"
41°23'19"
41°22'53"
41°22'26"
41°22'00"
41°21'34"
41°21'08"
87°38'53"
87°38'18"
87°37'43"
87°37'09"
87°36'34"
87°36'00"
RAND McNALLY

1:24,000
1 in. = 2000 ft.
0 0.25 0.5
miles

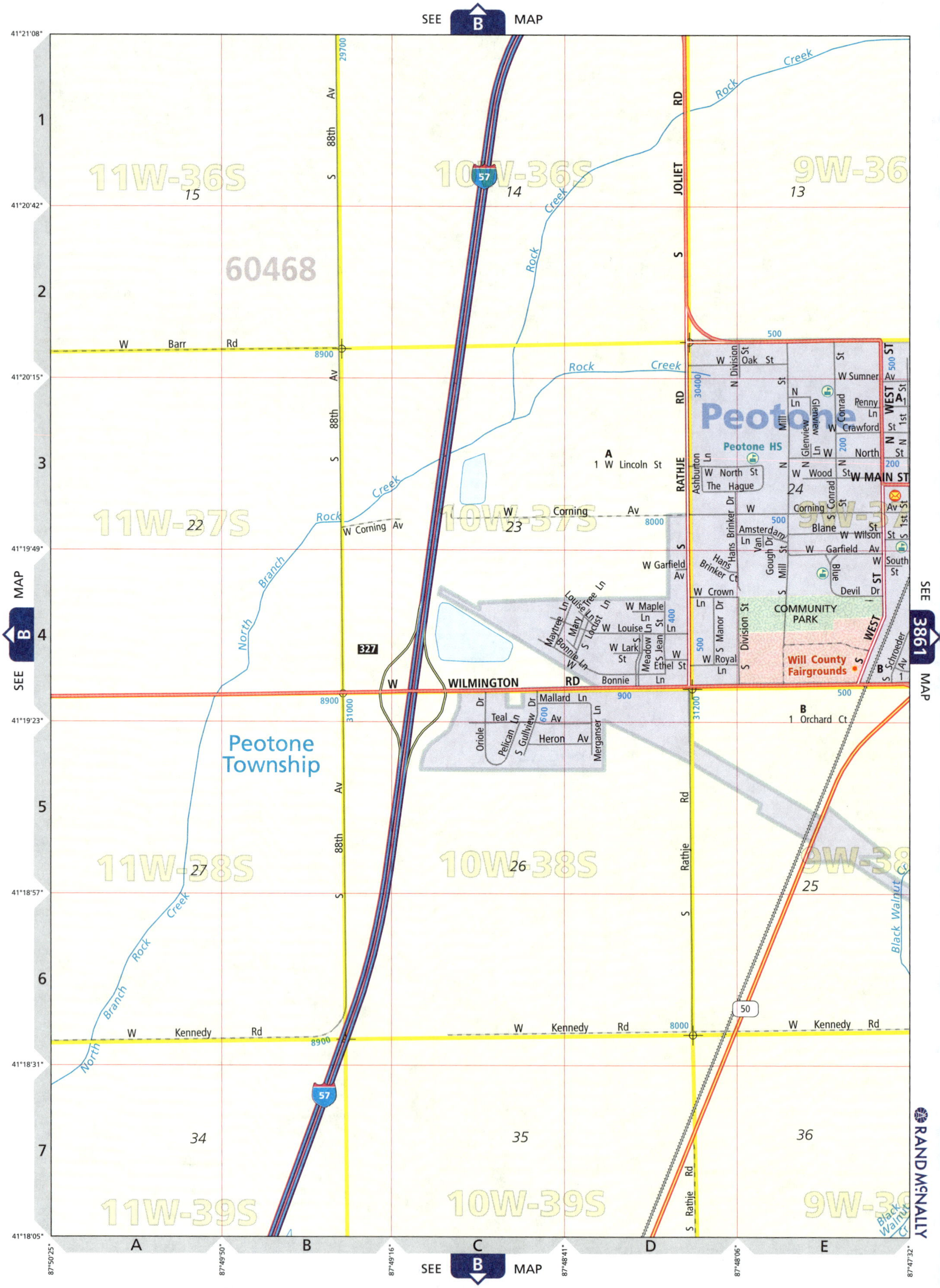

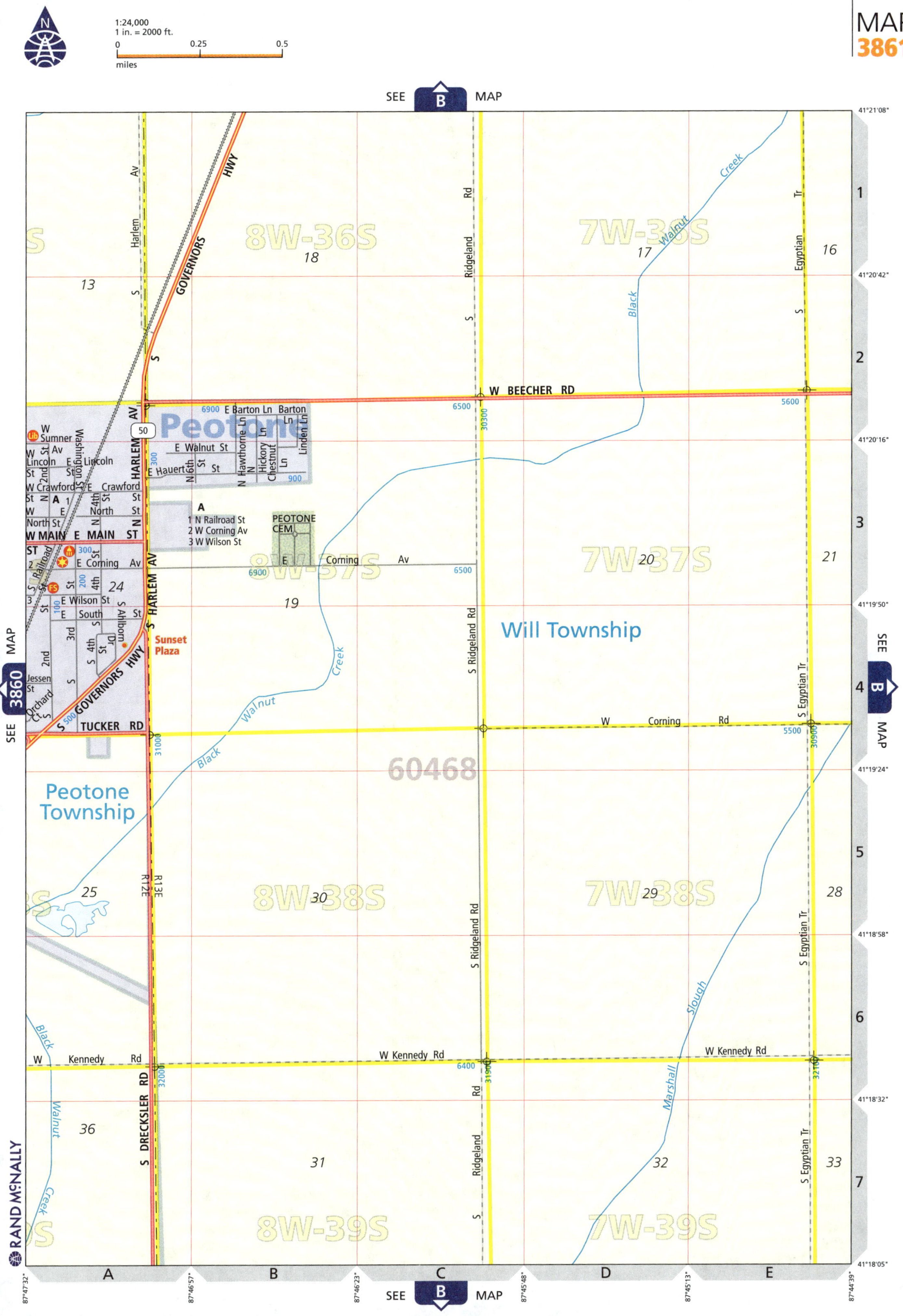
1:24,000
1 in. = 2000 ft.
0
0.25
0.5
miles
SEE B MAP
SEE 3860 MAP
SEE B MAP
SEE B MAP
Peotone
Will Township
Peotone Township
Sunset Plaza
PEOTONE CEM
60468
8W-36S
7W-36S
8W-37S
7W-37S
8W-38S
7W-38S
8W-39S
7W-39S
W BEECHER RD
W Corning Rd
W Kennedy Rd
W Kennedy Rd
W Kennedy Rd
TUCKER RD
GOVERNORS HWY
GOVERNORS HWY
S HARLEM AV
S Harlem Av
HARLEM AV
S DRECKSLER RD
S Ridgeland Rd
S Egyptian Tr
E Corning Av
E Barton Ln
Barton Ln
Linden Ln
E Walnut St
E Hauert St
N 6th St
N Hawthorne Ln
N Hickory Ln
Chestnut Ln
W Sumner Av
W Lincoln St
E Lincoln St
Washington St
W Crawford St
E Crawford St
W North St
E North St
W MAIN ST
E MAIN ST
Railroad St
E Wilson St
E South St
S Allhorn Dr
Jessen St
Orchard Ct
3rd
2nd
4th
A
1 N Railroad St
2 W Corning Av
3 W Wilson St
Black Walnut Creek
Black Walnut Creek
Marshall Slough
R12E
R13E
50
6900
6500
5600
5500
6400
30300
31000
30900
32000
31900
32100
300
200
100
500
900
13
16
17
18
19
20
21
24
25
28
29
30
31
32
33
36
1
2
3
4
5
6
7
A
B
C
D
E
41°21'08"
41°20'42"
41°20'16"
41°19'50"
41°19'24"
41°18'58"
41°18'32"
41°18'05"
87°47'32"
87°46'57"
87°46'23"
87°45'48"
87°45'13"
87°44'39"
RAND McNALLY

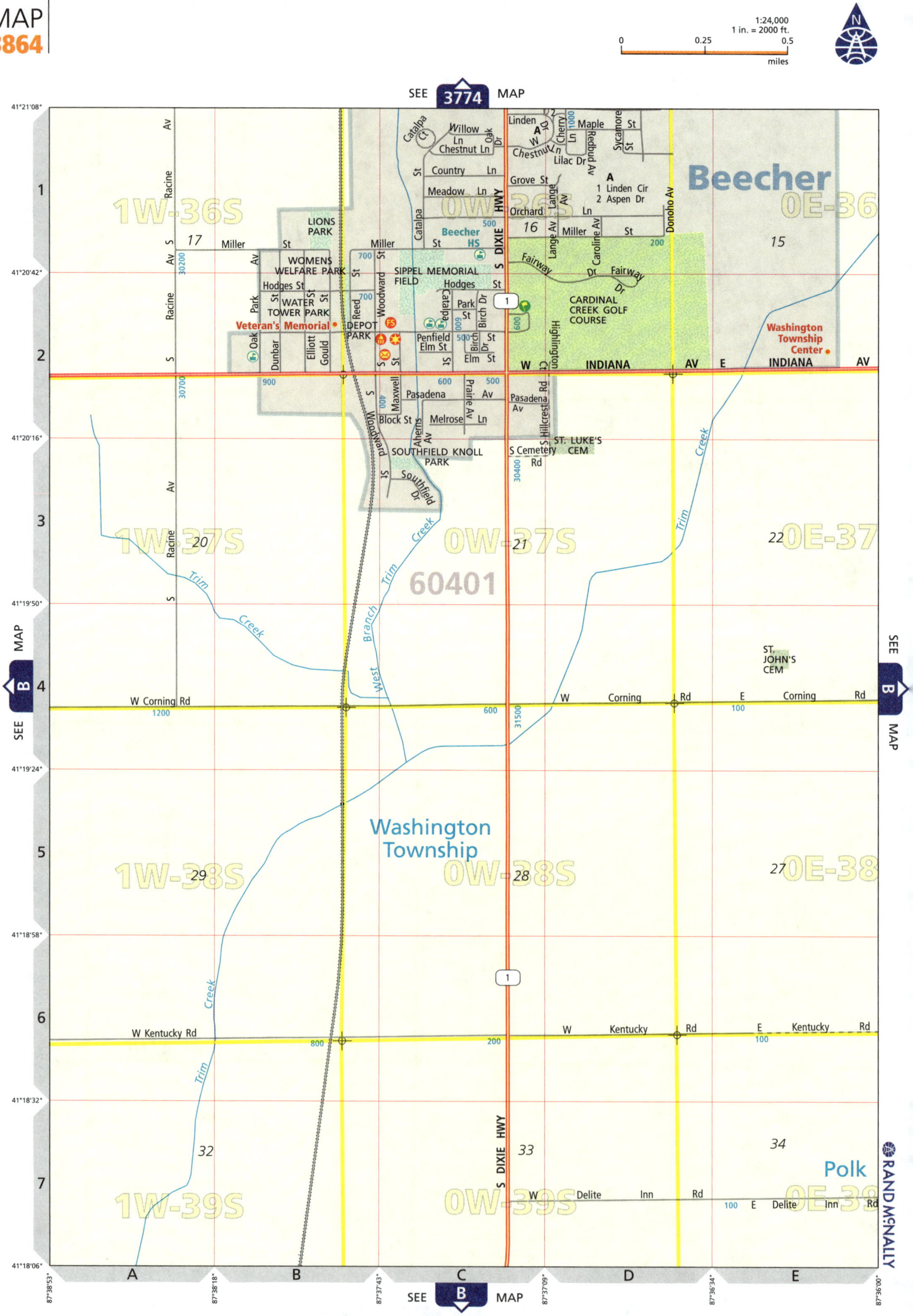
1:24,000
1 in. = 2000 ft.
0 0.25 0.5
miles
N
SEE 3774 MAP
SEE B MAP
Beecher
Washington Township
60401
Washington Township Center
Polk
1W-36S
0W-36S
0E-36
1W-37S
0W-37S
0E-37
1W-38S
0W-38S
0E-38
1W-39S
0W-39S
0E-39
LIONS PARK
WOMENS WELFARE PARK
WATER TOWER PARK
Veteran's Memorial
DEPOT PARK
SIPPEL MEMORIAL FIELD
Beecher HS
CARDINAL CREEK GOLF COURSE
SOUTHFIELD KNOLL PARK
ST. LUKE'S CEM
ST. JOHN'S CEM
S DIXIE HWY
W INDIANA AV
E INDIANA AV
W Corning Rd
E Corning Rd
W Kentucky Rd
E Kentucky Rd
W Delite Inn Rd
E Delite Inn Rd
S Racine Av
Miller St
Trim Creek
West Branch Trim Creek
Donoho Av
Highlington Ct
S Hillcrest Rd
S Cemetery Rd
Pasadena Av
Maxwell
Block St
Melrose Ln
Prairie Av
Aherns Av
S Woodward St
Southfield Dr
Penfield St
Elm St
Birch Dr
Park St
Catalpa
Hodges St
Reed St
Oak
Dunbar
Elliott
Gould
Park St
Country Ln
Meadow Ln
Willow Ln
Chestnut Ln
Catalpa Ct
Oak Dr
Linden Dr
W Chestnut Ln
Cherry Ln
Maple St
Redbud Av
Sycamore St
Lilac Dr
Grove St
Orchard Ln
Lange Av
Caroline Av
Fairway Dr
1 Linden Cir
2 Aspen Dr
15
16
17
20
21
22
27
28
29
32
33
34
1
2
3
4
5
6
7
A
B
C
D
E
41°21'08"
41°20'42"
41°20'16"
41°19'50"
41°19'24"
41°18'58"
41°18'32"
41°18'06"
87°38'53"
87°38'18"
87°37'43"
87°37'09"
87°36'34"
87°36'00"
RAND McNALLY

Cities and Communities

Community Name	Abbr.	County	ZIP Code	Map Page
*Addison	ADSN	DuPage	60143	2914
Addison Township	AddT	DuPage	60126	2972
*Algonquin	ALGN	McHenry	60102	2748
*Algonquin	ALGN	Kane	60102	2748
Algonquin Township	AlqT	McHenry	60010	2749
Alpine		Cook	60467	3423
*Alsip	ALSP	Cook	60803	3276
Altgeld Gardens		Cook	60827	3350
*Arlington Heights	ANHT	Cook	60004	2753
Austin		Cook	60644	3031
Avondale		Cook	60618	2976
Baker Lake		Cook	60010	2751
*Barrington	BRTN	Cook	60010	2750
*Barrington	BRTN	Lake	60010	2751
Barrington Center		Cook	60010	2802
*Barrington Hills	BNHL	McHenry	60010	2748
*Barrington Hills	BNHL	Kane	60010	2748
*Barrington Hills	BNHL	Lake	60010	2750
*Barrington Hills	BNHL	Cook	60010	2750
Barrington Township	BrnT	Cook	60010	2750
Barrington Woods		Cook	60074	2752
Barr Yard		Cook	60827	3349
*Bartlett	BRLT	DuPage	60103	2910
*Bartlett	BRLT	Cook	60103	2910
*Bartlett	BRLT	Kane	60103	2909
Beaver Valley		Cook	60467	3422
*Bedford Park	BDPK	Cook	60501	3148
*Beecher	BCHR	Will	60401	3864
*Bellwood	BLWD	Cook	60104	3029
*Bensenville	BNVL	DuPage	60106	2915
*Bensenville	BNVL	Cook	60131	2972
Berger		Cook	60419	3351
*Berkeley	BKLY	Cook	60163	3028
*Berwyn	BRWN	Cook	60402	3089
Beverly		Cook	60643	3213
Beverly Hills		Cook	60643	3213
*Bloomingdale	BMDL	DuPage	60108	2913
Bloomingdale Township	BmdT	DuPage	60108	2912
Bloom Township	BlmT	Cook	60466	3595
*Blue Island	BLID	Cook	60406	3349
*Bolingbrook	BGBK	Will	60440	3270
Braeside		Lake	60035	2758
Brainerd		Cook	60620	3213
Branigar Estates		Cook	60007	2861
Bremen Township	BmnT	Cook	60426	3426
Brentwood		Cook	60074	2752
Bridgeport		Cook	60616	3092
*Bridgeview	BGVW	Cook	60455	3210
Brighton Park		Cook	60632	3090
*Broadview	BDVW	Cook	60155	3029
Brookdale		Cook	60637	3153
*Brookfield	BKFD	Cook	60513	3088
Brunning		Will	60441	3342
*Buffalo Grove	BFGV	Cook	60089	2754
*Buffalo Grove	BFGV	Lake	60089	2754
*Burbank	BRBK	Cook	60459	3211
*Burnham	BNHM	Cook	60633	3352
Burnside		Cook	60628	3215
*Burr Ridge	BRRG	Cook	60527	3208
*Burr Ridge	BRRG	DuPage	60527	3208
*Calumet City	CTCY	Cook	60409	3352
*Calumet Park	CTPK	Cook	60827	3277
Calumet Township	ClmT	Cook	60827	3349
Capri Village		Cook	60074	2753
*Carpentersville	CPVL	Kane	60110	2748
Chatham		Cook	60619	3214
*Chicago	CHCG	DuPage	60666	2916
*Chicago	CHCG	Cook	60602	3034
*Chicago Heights	CHHT	Cook	60411	3596
Chicago Lawn		Cook	60629	3150
*Chicago Ridge	CHRG	Cook	60415	3275
Chinatown		Cook	60616	3092
*Cicero	CCRO	Cook	60804	3089
Citation Lake Estates		Cook	60062	2756
Clearing		Cook	60638	3149
Cobblestone		Cook	60016	2809
Colonial Ridge		Cook	60016	2863
Community Park West		Cook	60025	2809
--Cook County	CokC			
*Country Club Hills	CCHL	Cook	60478	3426
*Countryside	CTSD	Cook	60525	3147
Cragin		Cook	60639	2975
Crawford Countryside		Cook	60443	3506
Creekwood		Cook	60439	3343
*Crestwood	CTWD	Cook	60445	3348
*Crete	CRTE	Will	60417	3685
Crete Township	CteT	Will	60417	3686
Cuba Township	CbaT	Lake	60010	2750
*Deerfield	DRFD	Cook	60015	2756
*Deerfield	DRFD	Lake	60015	2756
Deer Lake		Cook	60010	2751
*Deer Park	DRPK	Lake	60010	2752
*Des Plaines	DSPN	Cook	60016	2863
*Dixmoor	DXMR	Cook	60406	3349
*Dolton	DLTN	Cook	60419	3350
Downers Grove Township	DGvT	DuPage	60439	3270
Dundee Township	DndT	Kane	60118	2801
Dunning		Cook	60634	2974
--DuPage County	DPgC			
DuPage Township	DPgT	Will	60441	3270
*Dyer	DYR	Lake	46311	3598
*East Dundee	EDND	Cook	60118	2801
*East Dundee	EDND	Kane	60118	2801
*East Hazel Crest	EHZC	Cook	60429	3427
East Side		Cook	60617	3216
Edgebrook		Cook	60646	2919
Edison Park		Cook	60631	2864
Ela Township	ElaT	Lake	60074	2752
*Elgin	ELGN	Cook	60120	2855
*Elgin	ELGN	Kane	60120	2855
Elgin Township	ElgT	Cook	60103	2909
Elgin Township	ElgT	Kane	60120	2855
Elk Grove Township	EGvT	Cook	60018	2916
*Elk Grove Village	EGVV	Cook	60007	2914
*Elk Grove Village	EGVV	DuPage	60007	2915
*Elmhurst	EMHT	Cook	60126	3028
*Elmhurst	EMHT	DuPage	60126	3028
*Elmwood Park	EDPK	Cook	60707	2974
Elsdon		Cook	60632	3090
Englewood		Cook	60621	3152
*Evanston	EVTN	Cook	60201	2867
*Evergreen Park	ENGN	Cook	60805	3212
Faithorn		Will	60417	3685
Fernway		Cook	60477	3424
Fernway Park		Cook	60462	3424
*Flossmoor	FSMR	Cook	60422	3507
Flossmoor Highlands		Cook	60422	3506
*Ford Heights	FDHT	Cook	60411	3509
Forest Estates		Cook	60067	2805
*Forest Park	FTPK	Cook	60130	3030
Forest River		Cook	60056	2808
*Forest View	FTVW	Cook	60402	3088
*Frankfort	FKFT	Will	60423	3593
Frankfort Square		Will	60423	3504
Frankfort Township	FftT	Will	60423	3505
*Franklin Park	FNPK	Cook	60131	2973
Gage Park		Cook	60632	3150
Garden Homes		Cook	60619	3214
Glenbrook Countryside		Cook	60062	2757
*Glencoe	GLNC	Cook	60022	2758
Glenn		Cook	60638	3149
*Glenview	GNVW	Cook	60025	2810
Glenview Countryside		Cook	60025	2810
Glenview Estates		Cook	60025	2809
*Glenwood	GNWD	Cook	60425	3508
Globe		Cook	60409	3429
Goeselville		Cook	60452	3347
*Golf	GLF	Cook	60029	2864
Goodenow		Will	60401	3774
Goodings Grove		Will	60441	3344
Green Garden Township	GGnT	Will	60449	3682
Gross Point		Cook	60091	2812
*Hammond	HMND	Lake	46320	3430
*Hanover Park	HRPK	Cook	60133	2911
*Hanover Park	HRPK	DuPage	60133	2911
Hanover Township	HnrT	Cook	60103	2909
*Harvey	HRVY	Cook	60426	3350
*Harwood Heights	HDHT	Cook	60706	2918
Hastings		Cook	60439	3271
*Hazel Crest	HLCT	Cook	60429	3427
Hazel Green		Cook	60803	3275
Heatherlea		Cook	60067	2752
Hegewisch		Cook	60633	3352
*Hickory Hills	HYHL	Cook	60457	3210
Hidden Creek		Cook	60074	2753
*Highland Park	HDPK	Lake	60035	2758
*Hillside	HLSD	Cook	60162	3028
*Hinsdale	HNDL	Cook	60521	3146
*Hinsdale	HNDL	DuPage	60521	3146
*Hodgkins	HGKN	Cook	60525	3147
*Hoffman Estates	HFET	Cook	60195	2804
*Homer Glen	HMGN	Will	60441	3343
Homer Township	HmrT	Will	60467	3344
*Hometown	HMTN	Cook	60456	3212
*Homewood	HMWD	Cook	60430	3427
Howe Terrace		Cook	60010	2751
Hubbard Woods		Cook	60093	2759
Hyde Park		Cook	60653	3092
*Indian Head Park	IHPK	Cook	60525	3146
*Inverness	IVNS	Cook	60067	2752
Irving Park		Cook	60618	2976
*Itasca	ITSC	DuPage	60143	2914
Itasca Ranchettes		DuPage	60143	2913
*Justice	JSTC	Cook	60458	3210
--Kane County	KneC			
Keeneyville		DuPage	60172	2912
Kenilwicke		Cook	60067	2752
*Kenilworth	KLWH	Cook	60043	2812
Kensington		Cook	60628	3278
*Kildeer	KLDR	Lake	60074	2752
Kreitsburg		Lake	46311	3687
*La Grange	LGNG	Cook	60525	3087
La Grange Highlands		Cook	60525	3146
*La Grange Park	LGPK	Cook	60525	3087
Laguna Woods		Cook	60462	3346

*Indicates incorporated city

Cities and Communities

Community Name	Abbr.	County	ZIP Code	Map Page
--Lake County	LkeC			
Lake Marion		Kane	60110	2748
Lake Park Estates		Cook	60067	2752
Lakeview		Cook	60613	2977
*Lansing	LNSG	Cook	60438	3430
Lavergne		Cook	60402	3089
*Lemont	LMNT	Cook	60439	3342
*Lemont	LMNT	DuPage	60439	3271
Lemont Township	LmnT	Cook	60480	3272
Leyden Township	LydT	Cook	60164	2973
*Lincolnwood	LNWD	Cook	60712	2920
Little City		Cook	60067	2804
*Lockport	LKPT	Will	60441	3342
Lockport Township	LktT	Will	60441	3342
Logan Square		Cook	60647	2976
*Long Grove	LGGV	Lake	60047	2753
Loop		Cook	60604	3034
*Lynwood	LYWD	Cook	60411	3510
*Lyons	LYNS	Cook	60534	3088
Lyons Township	LynT	Cook	60480	3209
Maine Township	MaiT	Cook	60068	2863
*Markham	MKHM	Cook	60426	3427
*Matteson	MTSN	Cook	60443	3506
Maynard		Lake	46321	3510
*Maywood	MYWD	Cook	60153	3030
*McCook	MCCK	Cook	60525	3148
--McHenry County	McHC			
Medinah		DuPage	60157	2913
*Melrose Park	MLPK	Cook	60160	3029
*Merrionette Park	MTPK	Cook	60803	3276
Middlebury		Kane	60010	2748
*Midlothian	MDLN	Cook	60445	3348
Mission Hills		Cook	60062	2756
*Mokena	MKNA	Will	60448	3504
*Monee	MONE	Will	60449	3683
Monee Township	MonT	Will	60449	3684
Morgan Park		Cook	60643	3277
Morgan's Gate		Cook	60067	2752
*Morton Grove	MNGV	Cook	60053	2865
Mt Greenwood		Cook	60655	3276
*Mt Prospect	MPPT	Cook	60056	2808
Munger		DuPage	60103	2910
Munger Station		DuPage	60184	2909
*Munster	MNSR	Lake	46321	3430
Near North Side		Cook	60610	3034
New Lenox Township	NlxT	Will	60448	3422
New Trier Township	NtrT	Cook	60093	2812
*Niles	NLES	Cook	60714	2864
Norma		Cook	60016	2862
*Norridge	NRDG	Cook	60706	2974
*Northbrook	NHBK	Cook	60062	2757
Northbrook West		Cook	60062	2756
*Northfield	NHFD	Cook	60093	2811
Northfield Township	NfdT	Cook	60056	2809
North Harvey		Cook	60426	3350
*Northlake	NHLK	Cook	60164	3028
North Northfield		Cook	60062	2756
*North Riverside	NRIV	Cook	60546	3088
Norwood Park		Cook	60631	2918
Norwood Park Township	NpkT	Cook	60656	2918
*Oak Brook	OKBK	DuPage	60523	3086
*Oak Brook	OKBK	Cook	60523	3086
*Oak Forest	OKFT	Cook	60452	3347
Oak Glen		Cook	60438	3429
*Oak Lawn	OKLN	Cook	60453	3211
*Oak Park	OKPK	Cook	60304	3031
Oakton		Cook	60202	2867
*Olympia Fields	OMFD	Cook	60461	3506
Olympia Gardens		Cook	60422	3507
Ontarioville		DuPage	60133	2911
*Orland Hills	ODHL	Cook	60477	3423
*Orland Park	ODPK	Will	60448	3423
*Orland Park	ODPK	Cook	60462	3345
Orland Township	OrlT	Cook	60464	3345
*Palatine	PLTN	Cook	60067	2752
Palatine Township	PltT	Cook	60074	2752
Palisades		DuPage	60527	3208
*Palos Heights	PSHT	Cook	60463	3274
*Palos Hills	PSHL	Cook	60465	3274
*Palos Park	PSPK	Cook	60464	3274
Palos Township	PlsT	Cook	60464	3273
*Park Forest	PKFT	Cook	60466	3595
*Park Forest	PKFT	Will	60466	3683
Park Manor		Cook	60637	3152
*Park Ridge	PKRG	Cook	60068	2918
*Peotone	PTON	Will	60468	3861
Peotone Township	PtnT	Will	60468	3861
Pepper Tree		Cook	60067	2752
*Phoenix	PHNX	Cook	60426	3350
Pinehurst Manor		Cook	60074	2753
Pleasant Hills		Cook	60193	2912
Plum Grove Estates		Cook	60067	2806
Polk		Will	60401	3864
Portage Park		Cook	60634	2975
*Posen	POSN	Cook	60469	3349
*Prospect Heights	PTHT	Cook	60070	2808
Proviso Township	PvsT	Cook	60558	3086
Pullman		Cook	60628	3278
*Richton Park	RNPK	Cook	60471	3594
Rich Township	RchT	Cook	60443	3593
Ridgewood West		Cook	60452	3347
*Riverdale	RVDL	Cook	60827	3350
*River Forest	RVFT	Cook	60305	3030
*River Grove	RVGV	Cook	60171	2974
*Riverside	RVSD	Cook	60546	3088
Riverside Lawns		Cook	60546	3088
Riverside Township	RvsT	Cook	60546	3088
*Riverwoods	RVWD	Lake	60015	2755
*Robbins	RBBN	Cook	60472	3348
Robertsdale		Lake	46394	3280
Rogers Park		Cook	60660	2921
*Rolling Meadows	RGMW	Cook	60008	2806
Roseland		Cook	60628	3278
*Roselle	ROSL	Cook	60172	2913
*Roselle	ROSL	DuPage	60172	2913
*Rosemont	RSMT	Cook	60018	2917
Sag Bridge		Cook	60439	3272
St. Charles Township	SchT	Kane	60177	2909
*St. John	SJHN	Lake	46373	3598
St. John Township	SjnT	Lake	46311	3687
*Sauk Village	SLVL	Cook	60411	3597
*Schaumburg	SMBG	Cook	60193	2859
*Schaumburg	SMBG	DuPage	60172	2912
Schaumburg Township	SmbT	Cook	60193	2913
*Schiller Park	SRPK	Cook	60176	2973
Schrum		Cook	60409	3430
Sherwood Oaks		Cook	60120	2856
*Skokie	SKOK	Cook	60077	2865
*South Barrington	SBTN	Cook	60010	2803
South Chicago		Cook	60617	3216
*South Chicago Heights	SCHT	Cook	60411	3596
South Deering		Cook	60617	3279
*South Elgin	SEGN	Kane	60177	2909
*South Holland	SHLD	Cook	60473	3428
Southmoor		Cook	60464	3346
South Shore		Cook	60649	3153
Spaulding		Cook	60120	2909
Staples Corner		Cook	60074	2753
*Steger	STGR	Cook	60475	3596
*Steger	STGR	Will	60475	3596
Stewart Ridge		Cook	60628	3278
*Stickney	SKNY	Cook	60402	3089
Stickney Township	StkT	Cook	60402	3089
*Stone Park	SNPK	Cook	60165	3029
Stony Island		Cook	60617	3215
*Streamwood	SMWD	Cook	60107	2857
*Summit	SMMT	Cook	60501	3148
Sunny Crest		Cook	60422	3507
Sunset Hills		Cook	60193	2913
Sutton		Cook	60010	2802
Sylvan Hill		Cook	60462	3345
Techny		Cook	60062	2757
*Thornton	TNTN	Cook	60476	3428
Thornton Junction		Cook	60473	3428
Thornton Township	ThtT	Cook	60476	3429
*Tinley Park	TYPK	Cook	60477	3425
*Tinley Park	TYPK	Will	60477	3504
*University Park	UYPK	Cook	60471	3594
*University Park	UYPK	Will	60466	3684
Uptown		Cook	60640	2921
Vernon Township	VrnT	Lake	60062	2755
Villa Redeemer		Cook	60025	2809
Washington Township	WshT	Will	60401	3864
Waterford		DuPage	60527	3146
*Wayne	WYNE	DuPage	60184	2909
*Wayne	WYNE	Kane	60120	2909
Wayne Township	WynT	DuPage	60120	2909
*Westchester	WSTR	Cook	60154	3029
West Deerfield Township	WdfT	Lake	60015	2756
*West Dundee	WDND	Kane	60118	2801
*Western Springs	WNSP	Cook	60558	3086
West Glenview		Cook	60025	2810
West Pullman		Cook	60628	3278
*Wheeling	WLNG	Cook	60090	2755
*Wheeling	WLNG	Lake	60089	2754
Wheeling Township	WhlT	Cook	60056	2808
--Will County	WilC			
*Willowbrook	WLBK	DuPage	60527	3146
Willowbrook		Will	60417	3598
*Willow Springs	WLSP	Cook	60480	3209
Will Township	WllT	Will	60468	3861
*Wilmette	WLMT	Cook	60091	2812
*Winnetka	WNKA	Cook	60093	2812
*Wood Dale	WDDL	DuPage	60191	2915
Woodridge		Lake	60035	2757
*Woodridge	WDRG	Will	60517	3270
*Woodridge	WDRG	DuPage	60517	3270
*Worth	WRTH	Cook	60482	3274
Worth Township	WthT	Cook	60463	3347
York Township	YkTp	DuPage	60126	3028

*Indicates incorporated city

List of Abbreviations

Admin	Administration
Agri	Agricultural
Ag	Agriculture
AFB	Air Force Base
Arpt	Airport
Al	Alley
Amer	American
Anx	Annex
Arc	Arcade
Arch	Archaeological
Aud	Auditorium
Avd	Avenida
Av	Avenue
Bfld	Battlefield
Bch	Beach
Bnd	Bend
Bio	Biological
Blf	Bluff
Blvd	Boulevard
Brch	Branch
Br	Bridge
Brk	Brook
Bldg	Building
Bur	Bureau
Byp	Bypass
Bywy	Byway
Cl	Calle
Cljn	Callejon
Cmto	Caminito
Cm	Camino
Cap	Capitol
Cath	Cathedral
Cswy	Causeway
Cem	Cemetery
Ctr	Center
Ctr	Centre
Cir	Circle
Crlo	Circulo
CH	City Hall
Clf	Cliff
Clfs	Cliffs
Clb	Club
Cltr	Cluster
Col	Coliseum
Coll	College
Com	Common
Coms	Commons
Comm	Community
Co.	Company
Cons	Conservation
Conv & Vis Bur	Convention and Visitors Bureau
Cor	Corner
Cors	Corners
Corp	Corporation
Corr	Corridor
Cte	Corte
CC	Country Club
Co	County
Ct	Court
Ct Hse	Court House
Cts	Courts
Cr	Creek
Cres	Crescent
Cross	Crossing
Curv	Curve
Cto	Cut Off
Dept	Department
Dev	Development
Diag	Diagonal
Div	Division
Dr	Drive
Drwy	Driveway
E	East
El	Elevation
Env	Environmental
Est	Estate
Ests	Estates
Exh	Exhibition
Expm	Experimental
Expo	Exposition
Expwy	Expressway
Ext	Extension
Frgds	Fairgrounds
ft	Feet
Fy	Ferry
Fld	Field
Flds	Fields
Flt	Flat
Flts	Flats
For	Forest
Fk	Fork
Ft	Fort
Found	Foundation
Frwy	Freeway
Gdn	Garden
Gdns	Gardens
Gen Hosp	General Hospital
Gln	Glen
GC	Golf Course
Grn	Green
Grds	Grounds
Grv	Grove
Hbr	Harbor/Harbour
Hvn	Haven
HQs	Headquarters
Ht	Height
Hts	Heights
HS	High School
Hwy	Highway
Hl	Hill
Hls	Hills
Hist	Historical
Hllw	Hollow
Hosp	Hospital
Hse	House
Ind Res	Indian Reservation
Info	Information
Inst	Institute
Int'l	International
I	Island
Is	Islands
Isl	Isle
Jct	Junction
Knl	Knoll
Knls	Knolls
Lk	Lake
Lndg	Landing
Ln	Lane
Lib	Library
Ldg	Lodge
Lp	Loop
Mnr	Manor
Mkt	Market
Mdw	Meadow
Mdws	Meadows
Med	Medical
Mem	Memorial
Metro	Metropolitan
Mw	Mews
Mil	Military
Ml	Mill
Mls	Mills
Mon	Monument
Mtwy	Motorway
Mnd	Mound
Mnds	Mounds
Mt	Mount
Mtn	Mountain
Mtns	Mountains
Mun	Municipal
Mus	Museum
Nat'l	National
Nat'l For	National Forest
Nat'l Hist Pk	National Historic Park
Nat'l Hist Site	National Historic Site
Nat'l Mon	National Monument
Nat'l Park	National Park
Nat'l Rec Area	National Recreation Area
Nat'l Wld Ref	National Wildlife Refuge
Nat	Natural
NAS	Naval Air Station
Nk	Nook
N	North
Orch	Orchard
Ohwy	Outer Highway
Ovl	Oval
Ovlk	Overlook
Ovps	Overpass
Pk	Park
Pkwy	Parkway
Pas	Paseo
Psg	Passage
Pass	Passenger
Pth	Path
Pn	Pine
Pns	Pines
Pl	Place
Pln	Plain
Plns	Plains
Plgnd	Playground
Plz	Plaza
Pt	Point
Pnd	Pond
PO	Post Office
Pres	Preserve
Prov	Provincial
Rwy	Railway
Rec	Recreation
Reg	Regional
Res	Reservoir
Rst	Rest
Rdg	Ridge
Rd	Road
Rds	Roads
St.	Saint
Ste.	Sainte
Sci	Science
Sci	Sciences
Sci	Scientific
Shop Ctr	Shopping Center
Shr	Shore
Shrs	Shores
Skwy	Skyway
S	South
Spr	Spring
Sprs	Springs
Sq	Square
Stad	Stadium
St For	State Forest
St Hist Site	State Historic Site
St Nat Area	State Natural Area
St Pk	State Park
St Rec Area	State Recreation Area
Sta	Station
St	Street
Smt	Summit
Sys	Systems
Tech	Technical
Tech	Technological
Tech	Technology
Ter	Terrace
Terr	Territory
Theol	Theological
Thwy	Throughway
Toll Fy	Toll Ferry
TIC	Tourist Information Center
Trc	Trace
Trfwy	Trafficway
Tr	Trail
Tun	Tunnel
Tpk	Turnpike
Unps	Underpass
Univ	University
Vly	Valley
Vet	Veterans
Vw	View
Vil	Village
Wk	Walk
Wall	Wall
Wy	Way
W	West
WMA	Wildlife Management Area

Chicago & Cook County Street Index

HIGHWAYS

- **ALT** - Alternate Route
- **BUS** - Business Route
- **CO** - County Highway/Road
- **FM** - Farm To Market Road
- **HIST** - Historic Highway
- **I** - Interstate Highway
- **LP** - State Loop
- **P** - Provincial Highway
- **PK** - Park & Recreation Road
- **RTE** - Other Route
- **SPR** - State Spur
- **SR** - State Route/Highway
- **US** - United States Highway

STREET Block	City	ZIP	Map#	CGS	Grid
CO-4					
10	ROSL	60172	2913		A5
100	BMDL	60108	2913		A7
300	BMDL	60172	2913		A6
CO-4 N Bloomingdale Rd					
100	BMDL	60108	2913		A7
CO-4 Roselle Rd					
300	BMDL	60108	2913		A6
300	BMDL	60172	2913		A6
300	ROSL	60172	2913		A6
CO-4 N Roselle Rd					
300	ROSL	60172	2913		A3
CO-4 S Roselle Rd					
10	ROSL	60172	2913		A5
700	BMDL	60108	2913		A6
CO-6					
200	BRLT	60103	2910		E6
200	WynT	60103	2910		E5
CO-6 S Bartlett Rd					
200	WynT	60103	2910		E5
400	BRLT	60103	2910		E6
CO-8					
200	BNVL	60106	2915		E7
300	CHCG	60106	2915		E7
800	EGVV	60106	2915		E4
2300	EGvT	60007	2915		E3
2300	EGVV	60007	2915		E3
2700	OKBK	60523	3086		B5
3600	HNDL	60521	3086		B6
3700	OKBK	60521	3086		B6
5400	DGvT	60521	3146		A7
5400	HNDL	60521	3146		A7
5800	DGvT	60527	3146		A4
5900	BRRG	60527	3146		A5
6300	WLBK	60527	3146		A5
7200	DGvT	60527	3208		A1
7200	WLBK	60527	3208		A1
7600	BRRG	60527	3208		A2
CO-8 Elmhurst Rd					
2300	EGvT	60007	2915		E3
2300	EGVV	60007	2915		E3
CO-8 S Madison St					
5400	DGvT	60521	3146		A7
5400	HNDL	60521	3146		A7
5800	DGvT	60527	3146		A4
5900	BRRG	60527	3146		A5
6300	WLBK	60527	3146		A5
7200	DGvT	60527	3208		A1
7200	WLBK	60527	3208		A1
7600	BRRG	60527	3208		A2
CO-8 York Rd					
2700	OKBK	60523	3086		B5
3600	HNDL	60521	3086		B6
3700	OKBK	60521	3086		B6
CO-8 N York Rd					
200	BNVL	60106	2915		E7
300	CHCG	60106	2915		E7
800	EGVV	60007	2915		E4
800	EGVV	60106	2915		E4
CO-9					
10	DGvT	60439	3270		C1
10	WDRG	60439	3270		C3
10	WDRG	60516	3270		C1
200	DGvT	60517	3270		D3
200	WDRG	60517	3270		C3
500	LMNT	60439	3270		C3
600	DGvT	60516	3270		C1
CO-9 Lemont Rd					
10	DGvT	60439	3270		C1
10	WDRG	60439	3270		C3
10	WDRG	60516	3270		C1
200	DGvT	60517	3270		C3
200	WDRG	60517	3270		C3
500	LMNT	60439	3270		C3
600	DGvT	60516	3270		C1
CO-10					
10	ITSC	60143	2914		D5
200	WDDL	60143	2914		D7
200	WDDL	60191	2914		D7
300	AddT	60143	2914		D4
1200	EGVV	60007	2914		D4
CO-10 N Arlington Heights Rd					
1200	AddT	60143	2914		D4
1200	EGVV	60007	2914		D4
1200	ITSC	60143	2914		D4
CO-10 N Prospect Av					
10	ITSC	60143	2914		D5
300	AddT	60143	2914		D5
CO-10 S Prospect Av					
100	ITSC	60143	2914		D6
200	WDDL	60143	2914		D7
200	WDDL	60191	2914		D7
CO-19					
-	SchT	60177	2909		B5
10	WYNE	60120	2909		B7
200	BRLT	60120	2909		B7
200	SchT	60120	2909		B5
200	WYNE	60174	2909		B7
CO-19 Dunham Rd					
-	SchT	60177	2909		B5
10	WYNE	60120	2909		B7
200	BRLT	60120	2909		B5
200	SchT	60120	2909		B5
200	WYNE	60174	2909		B7
CO-20					
10	BNVL	60106	2972		D5
10	EMHT	60106	2972		A5
10	EMHT	60126	2972		A5
100	AddT	60106	2972		D5
100	AddT	60126	2972		D5
100	BNVL	60126	2972		A5
100	FNPK	60131	2972		B5
100	LydT	60131	2972		B5
CO-20 E Grand Av					
10	BNVL	60106	2972		D5
10	EMHT	60106	2972		A5
10	EMHT	60126	2972		A5
100	AddT	60106	2972		D5
CO-20 E Grand Av					
100	AddT	60126	2972		D5
100	BNVL	60126	2972		A5
100	FNPK	60131	2972		B5
100	LydT	60131	2972		B5
CO-22					
200	WDDL	60191	2914		E7
CO-22 N Addison Rd					
200	WDDL	60191	2914		E7
CO-23					
-	HRPK	60133	2912		B4
10	BMDL	60108	2912		B7
10	BMDL	60172	2912		B7
10	BmdT	60172	2912		B7
200	BmdT	60108	2912		B7
200	ROSL	60172	2912		B6
200	SMBG	60193	2912		B6
CO-23 Gary Av					
-	HRPK	60133	2912		B5
10	BMDL	60108	2912		B7
10	BMDL	60172	2912		B7
10	BmdT	60172	2912		B7
200	BmdT	60108	2912		B7
500	ROSL	60172	2912		B6
CO-23 N Gary Av					
-	HRPK	60133	2912		B4
200	ROSL	60172	2912		B6
200	SMBG	60193	2912		B6
CO-24					
10	BMDL	60157	2913		D7
10	BmdT	60143	2913		D5
10	BmdT	60157	2913		D7
300	ITSC	60143	2913		D6
300	ITSC	60157	2913		D4
300	ROSL	60157	2913		D4
400	ROSL	60143	2913		D6
700	BMDL	60101	2913		D7
CO-24 Meacham Rd					
-	ITSC	60143	2913		D3
CO-24 Medinah Rd					
10	BMDL	60157	2913		D7
10	BmdT	60143	2913		D5
10	BmdT	60157	2913		D7
300	ITSC	60143	2913		D6
300	ITSC	60157	2913		D4
300	ROSL	60157	2913		D4
400	ROSL	60143	2913		D6
700	BMDL	60101	2913		D7
CO-25					
500	PtnT	60468	3861	9W-37S	A4
500	PTON	60468	3861	9W-37S	A4
500	WllT	60468	3861	9W-37S	A4
CO-25 Tucker Rd					
500	PtnT	60468	3861	9W-37S	A4
500	PTON	60468	3861	9W-37S	A4
500	WllT	60468	3861	9W-37S	A4
CO-26					
10	BNVL	60106	2915		E5
10	CHCG	60106	2915		E5
10	WDDL	60191	2915		B4
100	AddT	60143	2914		A4
100	EGVV	60007	2915		B4
100	EGVV	60191	2915		B4
100	WDDL	60007	2915		B4
300	ITSC	60143	2914		C4
300	ITSC	60191	2914		E4
300	WDDL	60191	2914		E4
500	WDDL	60106	2915		C4
700	AddT	60191	2914		E4
CO-26 Thorndale Av					
-	WDDL	60106	2915		C4
10	BNVL	60106	2915		E5
10	CHCG	60106	2915		E5
10	WDDL	60191	2915		A4
100	AddT	60143	2914		A4
300	ITSC	60143	2914		C4
300	ITSC	60191	2914		E4
300	WDDL	60191	2914		E4
700	AddT	60191	2914		E4
CO-26 E Thorndale Av					
10	WDDL	60191	2915		B4
100	EGVV	60007	2915		B4
100	EGVV	60191	2915		B4
100	WDDL	60007	2915		B4
500	BNVL	60106	2915		C4
500	WDDL	60106	2915		C4
CO-28					
-	EGvT	60007	2915		A4
-	EGVV	60007	2915		A4
-	WDDL	60007	2915		A4
200	WDDL	60191	2915		A4
400	AddT	60191	2915		A6
1300	EGVV	60191	2915		A3
CO-28 N Wood Dale Rd					
-	EGvT	60007	2915		A4
-	EGVV	60007	2915		A4
-	WDDL	60007	2915		A4
200	WDDL	60191	2915		A4
400	AddT	60191	2915		A6
1300	EGVV	60191	2915		A3
CO-29					
10	BRLT	60103	2910		B5
10	BRLT	60120	2909		D5
10	BRLT	60120	2910		A5
10	BRLT	60133	2911		D6
10	BRLT	60184	2909		E5
10	SchT	60120	2909		D5
10	WynT	60120	2909		D5
10	WynT	60184	2909		E5
100	BRLT	60103	2911		B6
200	WynT	60103	2911		B6
1300	BmdT	60133	2911		E5
1300	HRPK	60133	2911		E5
CO-29 Greenbrook Blvd					
10	BRLT	60133	2911		D6
1300	BmdT	60133	2911		E5
1300	HRPK	60133	2911		E5
1600	BRLT	60103	2911		D6
CO-29 Stearns Rd					
10	BRLT	60103	2910		A5
10	BRLT	60120	2909		D5
10	BRLT	60120	2910		A5
10	BRLT	60184	2909		E5
10	SchT	60120	2909		D5
10	WynT	60120	2909		D5
10	WynT	60184	2909		E5
100	BRLT	60103	2911		B6
500	WynT	60103	2911		A6
CO-29 E Stearns Rd					
-	BRLT	60133	2911		D6
-	HRPK	60133	2911		C6
200	BRLT	60103	2911		B6
200	WynT	60103	2911		B6
CO-29 W Stearns Rd					
100	BRLT	60103	2910		B5
CO-29 W Stearns Rd					
500	BRLT	60120	2910		A5
CO-31					
100	BRRG	60527	3146		B6
100	WLBK	60527	3146		B6
CO-31 Plainfield Rd					
100	BRRG	60527	3146		B6
100	WLBK	60527	3146		B6
CO-34					
100	OKBK	60523	3086		B4
100	PvsT	60523	3086		C4
CO-34 Oak Brook Rd					
100	OKBK	60523	3086		B4
100	PvsT	60523	3086		C4
CO-35					
300	DGvT	60521	3146		A3
400	HNDL	60521	3146		B3
CO-35 E 55th St					
400	HNDL	60521	3146		B3
CO-35 W 55th St					
10	HNDL	60521	3146		A3
300	WLBK	60521	3146		A3
CO-38					
10	DGvT	60527	3146		A5
CO-38 63rd St					
10	DGvT	60527	3146		A5
CO-40					
10	BNHL	60118	2801		E2
10	CPVL	60110	2801		E2
10	EDND	60110	2801		E2
10	EDND	60118	2801		E2
CO-40 Penny Rd					
10	BNHL	60118	2801		E2
10	CPVL	60110	2801		E2
10	EDND	60110	2801		E2
10	EDND	60118	2801		E2
CO-43					
10	HRPK	60133	2911		D7
10	WynT	60133	2911		D7
500	BRLT	60103	2911		D5
5500	BRLT	60133	2911		D6
5500	HRPK	60103	2911		D5
CO-43 County Farm Rd					
10	HRPK	60133	2911		D7
10	WynT	60133	2911		D7
500	BRLT	60103	2911		D5
5500	BRLT	60133	2911		D6
5500	HRPK	60103	2911		D5
CO-61					
2100	BRLT	60103	2909		B3
2100	BRLT	60120	2909		B3
2100	HnrT	60103	2909		B3
2100	SEGN	60103	2909		B3
2100	SEGN	60120	2909		B3
2100	SEGN	60177	2909		B3
CO-61 W Bartlett Rd					
2100	BRLT	60103	2909		B3
2100	BRLT	60120	2909		B3
2100	HnrT	60103	2909		B3
2100	SEGN	60103	2909		B3
2100	SEGN	60120	2909		B3
2100	SEGN	60177	2909		B3
CO-A49					
10	DRPK	60010	2752	22W-20N	B1
100	BRTN	60010	2751	23W-20N	D1
100	DRPK	60010	2751	23W-20N	D1
100	ElaT	60010	2751	23W-20N	E1
100	ElaT	60010	2752	23W-20N	A1
500	DRPK	60074	2752	22W-20N	C1
21600	ElaT	60074	2752	21W-20N	D1
CO-A49 Long Grove Rd					
10	DRPK	60010	2752	22W-20N	B1
100	BRTN	60010	2751	23W-20N	D1
100	DRPK	60010	2751	23W-20N	D1
100	ElaT	60010	2751	23W-20N	E1
100	ElaT	60010	2752	23W-20N	A1
500	DRPK	60074	2752	22W-20N	C1
CO-A49 W Long Grove Rd					
21600	DRPK	60074	2752	21W-20N	D1
21600	ElaT	60074	2752	21W-20N	D1
21700	DRPK	60010	2752	21W-20N	C1
CO-A50					
10	BNHL	60010	2749	29W-18N	C2
100	ALGN	60010	2748		E2
100	ALGN	60102	2748		E2
100	BFGV	60089	2754	16W-20N	D2
100	BNHL	60010	2748		E2
100	WLNG	60089	2754	16W-20N	D2
300	AlqT	60010	2749	29W-20N	D2
1300	WLNG	60090	2754	16W-20N	D2
2000	AlqT	60102	2748		B2
CO-A50 County Line Rd					
2000	ALGN	60102	2748		B2
2000	AlqT	60102	2748		B2
2200	ALGN	60010	2748		C2
2200	BNHL	60010	2748		C2
CO-A50 W County Line Rd					
10	BNHL	60010	2749	29W-18N	C2
100	ALGN	60010	2748		E2
100	ALGN	60102	2748		E2
100	BNHL	60010	2748		E2
300	AlqT	60010	2749	29W-20N	D2
CO-A50 E Lake Cook Rd					
100	BFGV	60089	2754	16W-20N	D2
100	WLNG	60089	2754	16W-20N	D2
1300	WLNG	60090	2754	16W-20N	D2
CO-V57					
10	BRTN	60010	2751	24W-20N	D1
10	DRPK	60010	2751	24W-20N	D1
10	ElaT	60010	2751	24W-20N	E1
10	PltT	60010	2751	24W-20N	D1
CO-V57 N Ela Rd					
10	BRTN	60010	2751	24W-20N	D1
10	DRPK	60010	2751	24W-20N	D1
10	ElaT	60010	2751	24W-20N	D1
10	PltT	60010	2751	24W-20N	D1
CO-V62					
20000	DRPK	60010	2752	22W-20N	C2
20000	DRPK	60074	2752	22W-20N	C2
20000	PltT	60074	2752	21W-20N	C2
20600	KLDR	60010	2752	22W-20N	C2
CO-V62 N Quentin Rd					
20000	DRPK	60010	2752	22W-20N	C2
20000	DRPK	60074	2752	22W-20N	C2
20000	PltT	60074	2752	21W-20N	C2
20600	KLDR	60010	2752	22W-20N	C2
CO-W14					
10	BFGV	60089	2754	16W-20N	C1
CO-W14 N Buffalo Grove Rd					
10	BFGV	60089	2754	16W-20N	C1
CO-W17					
100	BFGV	60089	2754	16W-20N	D1
100	WLNG	60089	2754	16W-20N	D2
300	BFGV	60069	2754	16W-20N	D1
300	VrnT	60069	2754	16W-20N	D1
CO-W17 Weiland Rd					
100	BFGV	60089	2754	16W-20N	D1
100	WLNG	60089	2754	16W-20N	D2
300	BFGV	60069	2754	16W-20N	D1
300	VrnT	60069	2754	16W-20N	D1
CO-W24					
10	NHBK	60062	2756	12W-20N	A2
10	RVWD	60015	2756	12W-20N	A2
10	RVWD	60062	2756	12W-20N	A2
10	WdfT	60015	2756	12W-20N	A2
10	WdfT	60062	2756	12W-20N	A2
400	DRFD	60015	2756	12W-20N	A1
CO-W24 Saunders Rd					
10	NHBK	60062	2756	12W-20N	A2
10	RVWD	60015	2756	12W-20N	A2
10	RVWD	60062	2756	12W-20N	A2
10	WdfT	60015	2756	12W-20N	A2
10	WdfT	60062	2756	12W-20N	A2
400	DRFD	60015	2756	12W-20N	A1
I-55					
-	BDPK	-	3147	13W-8S	A7
-	BDPK	-	3148	10W-6S	B4
-	BGBK	-	3270		A1
-	BRRG	-	3146		D7
-	BRRG	-	3208		B1
-	CHCG	-	3089	6W-4S	E6
-	CHCG	-	3090	4W-3S	D5
-	CHCG	-	3091	1W-2S	D3
-	CHCG	-	3092	0W-2S	A2
-	CTSD	-	3146		D7
-	CTSD	-	3147	12W-7S	C7
-	DGvT	-	3270		A1
-	DPgT	-	3270		A1
-	FTVW	-	3089	6W-4S	E7
-	FTVW	-	3148	10W-6S	B4
-	FTVW	-	3149	7W-5S	B1
-	HGKN	-	3147	13W-8S	A7
-	IHPK	-	3146		D7
-	SKNY	-	3089	6W-4S	E6
-	SMMT	-	3148	9W-5S	D2
-	StkT	-	3089	6W-4S	E7
-	WDRG	-	3270		A1
-	WLBK	-	3208		B1
I-55 Joliet Rd					
-	BGBK	-	3270		A1
-	BRRG	-	3146		D7
-	BRRG	-	3208		B1
-	DGvT	-	3270		A1
-	DPgT	-	3270		A1
-	IHPK	-	3146		D7
-	WDRG	-	3270		A1
-	WLBK	-	3208		B1
I-55 Stevenson Expwy					
-	BDPK	-	3147	11W-7S	E6
-	BDPK	-	3148	10W-6S	B4
-	CHCG	-	3089	6W-4S	E6
-	CHCG	-	3090	5W-4S	A6
-	CHCG	-	3091	1W-2S	D3
-	CHCG	-	3092	0E-2S	C2
-	CTSD	-	3146		D7
-	CTSD	-	3147	13W-7S	A7
-	FTVW	-	3089	6W-4S	E7
-	FTVW	-	3148	10W-6S	B4
-	FTVW	-	3149	7W-5S	B1
-	HGKN	-	3147	11W-7S	E6
-	IHPK	-	3146		D7
-	SKNY	-	3089	6W-4S	E6
-	SMMT	-	3148	10W-6S	B4
-	StkT	-	3089	6W-4S	E7
I-57					
-	BLID	-	3277	2W-15S	D7
-	BLID	-	3349	2W-15S	D1
-	BmnT	-	3349	3W-17S	A6
-	BmnT	-	3425	6W-21S	E6
-	BmnT	-	3426	5W-20S	B4
-	CCHL	-	3426	6W-20S	B4
-	CCHL	-	3506	6W-22S	A1
-	CHCG	-	3213	1W-11S	E7
-	CHCG	-	3214	0W-11S	A7
-	CHCG	-	3277	1W-12S	D2
-	ClmT	-	3349	2W-15S	D1
-	CTPK	-	3277	2W-15S	D7
-	DXMR	-	3349	3W-17S	B5
-	MKHM	-	3348	4W-18S	E7
-	MKHM	-	3349	3W-18S	A6
-	MKHM	-	3426	5W-19S	D2
-	MONE	-	3682	7W-30S	D2
-	MonT	-	3593	7W-28S	D7
-	MonT	-	3682	7W-32S	D6
-	MTSN	-	3506	6W-23S	A4
-	MTSN	-	3594	6W-25S	A1
-	OKFT	-	3426	5W-19S	C2
-	POSN	-	3349	2W-17S	C5
-	PtnT	-	3860	11W-39S	B7
-	RchT	-	3426	6W-22S	A7
-	RchT	-	3506	6W-22S	A1
-	RchT	-	3593	7W-28S	D7
-	RNPK	-	3593	6W-26S	E3
-	RNPK	-	3594	6W-26S	A2
-	RVDL	-	3349	2W-15S	D1
-	UYPK	-	3593	7W-28S	D6
-	UYPK	-	3682	7W-29S	D1
I-57 Dan Ryan Expwy					
-	CHCG	-	3214	0W-11S	A7
I-80					
-	BmnT	-	3425	7W-21S	D7
-	BmnT	-	3426	6W-21S	A6
-	CCHL	-	3426	6W-21S	A6
-	EHZC	-	3427	2W-20S	E4
-	EHZC	-	3428	1W-20S	A4
-	FftT	-	3504	10W-22S	A1
-	HLCT	-	3426	4W-20S	E4
-	HLCT	-	3427	3W-20S	B4
-	HMND	-	3430		D5
-	LNSG	-	3429	2E-20S	C4
-	LNSG	-	3430	3E-20S	A4
-	MKHM	-	3427	3W-20S	A4
-	MKNA	-	3504	10W-22S	A1
-	MNSR	-	3430		D5
-	RchT	-	3425	7W-21S	D7
-	RchT	-	3505	7W-22S	C1
-	SHLD	-	3428	0E-20S	E4
-	SHLD	-	3429	1E-20S	A4
-	ThtT	-	3429	1E-20S	A4
-	TNTN	-	3428	0W-20S	C4
-	TYPK	-	3504	9W-22S	E1
-	TYPK	-	3505	7W-22S	C1
I-80 Kingery Expwy					
-	LNSG	-	3429	2E-20S	D4
-	LNSG	-	3430		D5
-	MNSR	-	3430	4E-20S	C4
-	ThtT	-	3429	2E-20S	C4
I-80 Moline Expwy					
-	BmnT	-	3425	7W-21S	D7
-	BmnT	-	3426	6W-21S	A6
I-80 Moline Expwy					
-	CCHL	-	3426	6W-21S	A6
-	FftT	-	3504	10W-22S	A1
-	HLCT	-	3426	4W-20S	E4
-	HLCT	-	3427	3W-20S	B4
-	MKHM	-	3427	3W-20S	A4
-	MKNA	-	3504	10W-22S	A1
-	RchT	-	3425	7W-21S	D7
-	RchT	-	3505	7W-22S	C1
-	TYPK	-	3504	9W-22S	E1
-	TYPK	-	3505	7W-22S	C1
I-80 Tri State Expwy					
-	HMND	-	3430		D5
-	LNSG	-	3430	4E-20S	C4
-	MNSR	-	3430		D5
I-80 Tri-State Tollway					
-	EHZC	-	3427	2W-20S	D4
-	EHZC	-	3428	0W-20S	C4
-	HLCT	-	3427	3W-20S	C4
-	LNSG	-	3429	1E-20S	C4
-	SHLD	-	3428	0E-20S	E4
-	SHLD	-	3429	1E-20S	A4
-	ThtT	-	3429	1E-20S	A4
-	TNTN	-	3428	0W-20S	C4
I-88					
-	EMHT	-	3028		C6
-	HLSD	-	3028		C6
-	OKBK	-	3028		B7
-	OKBK	-	3086		A1
-	PvsT	-	3028		C6
-	YkTp	-	3028		B7
-	YkTp	-	3086		B1
I-88 Ronald Reagan Mem Tollway					
-	EMHT	-	3028		C6
-	HLSD	-	3028		C6
-	OKBK	-	3028		B7
-	OKBK	-	3086		A1
-	PvsT	-	3028		C6
-	YkTp	-	3028		B7
-	YkTp	-	3086		B1
I-90					
-	ANHT	-	2860	18W-11N	E3
-	ANHT	-	2861	17W-11N	B4
-	CHCG	-	2916		E1
-	CHCG	-	2917	11W-7N	D4
-	CHCG	-	2918	10W-7N	A4
-	CHCG	-	2919	6W-6N	D6
-	CHCG	-	2920	5W-5N	A7
-	CHCG	-	2976	4W-4N	C3
-	CHCG	-	2977	1W-2N	D7
-	CHCG	-	3033	1W-1N	D1
-	CHCG	-	3034	0W-1S	A7
-	CHCG	-	3092	0W-3S	B5
-	CHCG	-	3152	0W-6S	B4
-	CHCG	-	3153	1E-8S	A7
-	CHCG	-	3215	2E-10S	D4
-	CHCG	-	3216	3E-10S	A6
-	CHCG	-	3280		C1
-	DSPN	-	2861	16W-9N	E6
-	DSPN	-	2862	14W-9N	C7
-	DSPN	-	2916		E1
-	DSPN	-	2917	12W-8N	B2
-	EGvT	-	2860	18W-11N	D3
-	EGvT	-	2861	16W-9N	E6
-	EGvT	-	2862	15W-9N	A7
-	EGVV	-	2861	17W-11N	B4
-	ELGN	-	2801		C7
-	ElgT	-	2801		A7
-	HFET	-	2802	29W-12N	D7
-	HFET	-	2803	27W-12N	D7
-	HFET	-	2804	24W-12N	E7
-	HMND	-	3280		D7
-	HMND	-	3352		E4
-	HnrT	-	2801		C7
-	HnrT	-	2802	30W-12N	C7
-	MPPT	-	2861	16W-10N	C6
-	RGMW	-	2859	21W-12N	E1
-	RGMW	-	2860	20W-12N	B1
-	RSMT	-	2916		E1
-	RSMT	-	2917	11W-7N	D4
-	SMBG	-	2804	24W-12N	E7
-	SMBG	-	2805	23W-12N	A7
-	SMBG	-	2859	21W-12N	D1
-	SmbT	-	2805	23W-12N	B7
-	SmbT	-	2859	21W-12N	D1
I-90 Chicago Skwy					
-	CHCG	-	3152	0E-7S	E6
-	CHCG	-	3153	1E-8S	A7
-	CHCG	-	3215	3E-10S	E5
-	CHCG	-	3216	3E-10S	A6
-	CHCG	-	3280	4E-11S	C1
-	HMND	-	3280	4E-11S	C1
I-90 Chicago Skwy W					
-	CHCG	-	3152	0E-7S	D6
-	CHCG	-	3215	3E-10S	D4
I-90 Dan Ryan Expwy					
-	CHCG	-	3034	0W-1S	A7
-	CHCG	-	3092	0W-3S	B5
-	CHCG	-	3152	0W-6S	B3
I-90 Indiana East-West Toll Rd					
-	CHCG	-	3280		C1
-	HMND	-	3280		D7
-	HMND	-	3352		E4
I-90 Indiana East-W Toll Road					
-	HMND	-	3280		C4
I-90 Kennedy Expwy					
-	CHCG	-	2917	10W-7N	E4
-	CHCG	-	2918	10W-7N	A4
-	CHCG	-	2919	6W-6N	D6
-	CHCG	-	2920	5W-5N	A7
-	CHCG	-	2976	3W-3N	E4
-	CHCG	-	2977	1W-2N	D7
-	CHCG	-	3033	1W-1N	D1
-	CHCG	-	3034	0W-0S	A5
I-90 Kennedy Expwy E					
-	CHCG	-	2919	7W-6N	C6
-	CHCG	-	3034	0W-0S	A5
I-90 Kennedy Expwy W					
-	CHCG	-	3034	0W-0N	A4
I-90 Northwest Tollway					
-	ANHT	-	2860	18W-11N	D3
-	ANHT	-	2861	17W-11N	B4
-	CHCG	-	2916		E1
-	CHCG	-	2917	11W-7N	E4
-	DSPN	-	2861	16W-9N	E6
-	DSPN	-	2862	14W-9N	C7
-	DSPN	-	2916		E1
-	DSPN	-	2917	12W-8N	B2
-	EGvT	-	2860	18W-11N	D3
-	EGvT	-	2861	16W-9N	E6
-	EGvT	-	2862	15W-9N	A7
-	EGVV	-	2861	17W-11N	B4

Chicago & Cook County Street Index

STREET Block	City	ZIP	Map#	CGS	Grid
I-90 Northwest Tollway					
-	ELGN	-	2801		A7
-	ElgT	-	2801		A7
-	HFET	-	2802	29W-12N	D7
-	HFET	-	2803	27W-12N	C7
-	HFET	-	2804	24W-12N	E7
-	HnrT	-	2801		C7
-	HnrT	-	2802	29W-12N	D7
-	MPPT	-	2861	16W-10N	C6
-	RGMW	-	2859	21W-12N	E1
-	RGMW	-	2860	18W-11N	D3
-	RSMT	-	2916		E1
-	RSMT	-	2917	11W-7N	D4
-	SMBG	-	2804	24W-12N	E7
-	SMBG	-	2805	23W-12N	B7
-	SMBG	-	2859	21W-12N	D1
-	SmbT	-	2805	23W-12N	B7
-	SmbT	-	2859	21W-12N	D1
I-94					
-	CHCG	-	2919	6W-7N	E4
-	CHCG	-	2920	5W-5N	A7
-	CHCG	-	2976	5W-4N	B2
-	CHCG	-	2977	3W-3N	A5
-	CHCG	-	3033	1W-1N	D1
-	CHCG	-	3034	0W-0N	A4
-	CHCG	-	3092	0W-4S	B7
-	CHCG	-	3152	0W-7S	C6
-	CHCG	-	3214	0W-8S	C1
-	CHCG	-	3215	1E-11S	A7
-	CHCG	-	3278	0E-13S	E4
-	CHCG	-	3279	1E-14S	B7
-	CHCG	-	3351	1E-15S	B1
-	CTCY	-	3351	2E-16S	C2
-	DLTN	-	3351	1E-17S	C5
-	DRFD	-	2756	11W-18N	E3
-	DRFD	-	2757	10W-18N	A3
-	GLNC	-	2758	7W-17N	B6
-	GNVW	-	2811	6W-13N	D6
-	HMND	-	3430		D5
-	LNSG	-	3429	2E-20S	D4
-	LNSG	-	3430		D5
-	LNWD	-	2919	6W-8N	E2
-	MNGV	-	2865	6W-10N	D4
-	MNSR	-	3430		D5
-	NfdT	-	2756	12W-20N	B2
-	NfdT	-	2757	8W-18N	E3
-	NfdT	-	2758	7W-17N	B6
-	NfdT	-	2811	7W-16N	C1
-	NHBK	-	2756	11W-18N	E3
-	NHBK	-	2757	8W-18N	E3
-	NHBK	-	2758	7W-17N	B6
-	NHFD	-	2758	7W-16N	B7
-	NHFD	-	2811	6W-14N	D4
-	NtrT	-	2758	7W-18N	A4
-	NtrT	-	2811	6W-14N	D4
-	SHLD	-	3351	1E-18S	B7
-	SHLD	-	3429	1E-20S	B3
-	SKOK	-	2811	6W-13N	E7
-	SKOK	-	2865	6W-9N	D7
-	SKOK	-	2919	6W-9N	E1
-	ThtT	-	3429	2E-20S	C4
-	WdfT	-	2756	12W-20N	B2
-	WLMT	-	2811	6W-13N	D7
I-94 Bishop Ford Mem Expwy					
-	CHCG	-	3214	0W-11S	C6
-	CHCG	-	3215	1E-11S	A7
-	CHCG	-	3278	0E-14S	E5
-	CHCG	-	3279	1E-14S	B7
-	CHCG	-	3351	1E-15S	B1
-	CTCY	-	3351	2E-16S	C2
-	DLTN	-	3351	1E-17S	C5
-	SHLD	-	3351	1E-18S	B7
-	SHLD	-	3429	1E-20S	B3
I-94 Dan Ryan Expwy					
-	CHCG	-	3034	0W-1S	A7
-	CHCG	-	3092	0W-4S	B7
-	CHCG	-	3152	0W-8S	C7
-	CHCG	-	3214	0E-9S	C3
I-94 Edens Expwy					
-	CHCG	-	2919	6W-6N	E5
-	CHCG	-	2920	5W-5N	A7
-	GLNC	-	2758	7W-16N	B7
-	GNVW	-	2811	6W-13N	D6
-	LNWD	-	2919	6W-8N	E2
-	MNGV	-	2865	6W-10N	D4
-	NfdT	-	2811	7W-16N	C1
-	NHBK	-	2758	8W-18N	A4
-	NHFD	-	2758	7W-16N	B7
-	NHFD	-	2811	7W-16N	B1
-	NtrT	-	2758	7W-18N	A4
-	NtrT	-	2811	6W-14N	D4
-	SKOK	-	2811	6W-13N	E7
-	SKOK	-	2865	6W-10N	D4
-	SKOK	-	2919	6W-8N	E1
-	WLMT	-	2811	6W-13N	D6
I-94 Edens Expressway Spur					
-	DRFD	-	2756	11W-18N	E3
-	DRFD	-	2757	10W-18N	A3
-	NfdT	-	2756	12W-18N	B2
-	NfdT	-	2757	10W-18N	A3
-	NfdT	-	2758	7W-17N	B6
-	NHBK	-	2756	11W-18N	E3
-	NHBK	-	2757	8W-18N	E3
-	NHBK	-	2758	7W-17N	B6
-	WdfT	-	2756	12W-20N	B2
I-94 Edens Expressway Spur E					
-	NfdT	-	2756	12W-20N	B2
-	NfdT	-	2757	10W-18N	A3
-	NHBK	-	2757	8W-18N	E3
-	WdfT	-	2756	12W-20N	B2
I-94 Edens Expressway Spur W					
-	DRFD	-	2756	12W-20N	B1
-	NfdT	-	2757	10W-18N	A3
-	WdfT	-	2756	12W-20N	B1
I-94 Kennedy Expwy					
-	CHCG	-	2920	5W-5N	A7
-	CHCG	-	2976	3W-3N	E4
-	CHCG	-	2977	3W-3N	A5
-	CHCG	-	3033	1W-1N	D1
-	CHCG	-	3034	0W-0N	A4
I-94 Kennedy Expwy E					
-	CHCG	-	3034	0W-0S	A5
I-94 Kennedy Expwy W					
-	CHCG	-	3034	0W-0N	A4
I-94 Kingery Expwy					
-	LNSG	-	3429	2E-20S	C4
-	LNSG	-	3430	3E-20S	A4
-	MNSR	-	3430	4E-20S	C4
-	SHLD	-	3429	1E-18S	B1
-	ThtT	-	3429	1E-20S	C4
I-94 Tri State Expwy					
-	HMND	-	3430		D5
-	LNSG	-	3430	4E-20S	C5
-	MNSR	-	3430		C5

STREET Block	City	ZIP	Map#	CGS	Grid
I-94 Tri-State Tollway					
-	DRFD	-	2756	12W-20N	B1
-	WdfT	-	2756	12W-20N	B2
I-190					
-	CHCG	-	2916		E5
-	CHCG	-	2917	12W-7N	B5
-	RSMT	-	2917	11W-7N	E4
I-290					
-	ADSN	-	2914		B7
-	BDVW	-	3029	11W-0S	C6
-	BKLY	-	3028		C5
-	BLWD	-	3029	11W-0S	C6
-	CHCG	-	3031	6W-0S	E6
-	CHCG	-	3032	5W-0S	A6
-	CHCG	-	3033	1W-0S	D5
-	CHCG	-	3034	0W-0S	A5
-	EGvT	-	2860	21W-11N	A3
-	EGvT	-	2914		A1
-	EGVV	-	2914		A1
-	EMHT	-	2972		A7
-	EMHT	-	3028		B2
-	FTPK	-	3030	10W-0S	B6
-	HLSD	-	3028		E6
-	HLSD	-	3029	13W-0S	A6
-	ITSC	-	2914		B5
-	MYWD	-	3029	11W-0S	D6
-	MYWD	-	3030	10W-0S	B6
-	NHLK	-	3028		B2
-	OKPK	-	3030	8W-0S	E6
-	OKPK	-	3031	8W-0S	A6
-	PvsT	-	3028		C6
-	RGMW	-	2860	20W-12N	A1
-	SMBG	-	2860	20W-11N	A3
-	WSTR	-	3029	12W-0S	C6
I-290 Eisenhower Expwy					
-	ADSN	-	2914		B7
-	BDVW	-	3029	12W-0S	C6
-	BKLY	-	3028		C5
-	BLWD	-	3029	12W-0S	A6
-	CHCG	-	3031	7W-0S	C6
-	CHCG	-	3032	3W-0S	E5
-	CHCG	-	3033	1W-0S	D5
-	CHCG	-	3034	0W-0S	A5
-	EMHT	-	2972		A7
-	EMHT	-	3028		B2
-	FTPK	-	3030	10W-0S	A6
-	HLSD	-	3028		E6
-	HLSD	-	3029	13W-0S	A6
-	ITSC	-	2914		B7
-	MYWD	-	3029	11W-0S	D6
-	MYWD	-	3030	10W-0S	B6
-	NHLK	-	3028		B2
-	OKPK	-	3030	10W-0S	A6
-	OKPK	-	3031	8W-0S	A6
-	PvsT	-	3028		C6
-	WSTR	-	3029	12W-0S	B6
I-294					
-	ALSP	-	3275	7W-13S	C5
-	ALSP	-	3276	5W-15S	A7
-	ALSP	-	3348	5W-15S	B1
-	BGVW	-	3210	9W-10S	C4
-	BKLY	-	3028		C3
-	BmnT	-	3348	3W-17S	E4
-	BmnT	-	3349	3W-18S	B7
-	BRRG	-	3146		D4
-	CHCG	-	2863	12W-9N	C7
-	CHCG	-	2917	12W-6N	B6
-	CHRG	-	3210	9W-11S	E7
-	CHRG	-	3274	8W-11S	E1
-	CHRG	-	3275	8W-12S	A2
-	CTSD	-	3146		E7
-	CTSD	-	3147	13W-8S	A7
-	CTSD	-	3209	13W-8S	A1
-	CTWD	-	3348	4W-17S	D4
-	DRFD	-	2756	12W-20N	B2
-	DSPN	-	2863	12W-10N	C4
-	DSPN	-	2917	12W-8N	C2
-	EHZC	-	3427	2W-20S	C4
-	EHZC	-	3428	1W-20S	A4
-	EMHT	-	3028		C6
-	FNPK	-	2972		B6
-	FNPK	-	2973	12W-4N	A3
-	GNVW	-	2809	11W-13N	C6
-	HGKN	-	3209	12W-8S	B1
-	HLCT	-	3427	2W-20S	C4
-	HLSD	-	3028		C6
-	HNDL	-	3086		C6
-	HNDL	-	3146		D6
-	HYHL	-	3210	9W-10S	C4
-	IHPK	-	3146		D5
-	JSTC	-	3209	11W-9S	E2
-	JSTC	-	3210	10W-9S	B3
-	LNSG	-	3429	1E-20S	C4
-	LydT	-	2972		E3
-	LydT	-	2973	13W-4N	A3
-	LynT	-	3086		C6
-	LynT	-	3146		D4
-	LynT	-	3147	13W-8S	A7
-	LynT	-	3209	12W-8S	D2
-	MaiT	-	2809	11W-13N	C7
-	MaiT	-	2863	12W-12N	C1
-	MDLN	-	3348	4W-16S	D4
-	MKHM	-	3349	3W-18S	B7
-	MKHM	-	3427	3W-19S	B2
-	NfdT	-	2756	12W-17N	A5
-	NfdT	-	2809	11W-13N	C7
-	NHBK	-	2756	12W-18N	B3
-	NHBK	-	2809	12W-16N	C1
-	NHLK	-	2972		C4
-	NHLK	-	3028		B2
-	OKBK	-	3086		B2
-	PKRG	-	2863	12W-10N	C5
-	POSN	-	3349	3W-18S	B7
-	PvsT	-	3028		C7
-	PvsT	-	3086		C6
-	RBBN	-	3348	4W-16S	D4
-	RSMT	-	2917	12W-8N	C3
-	SHLD	-	3428	0E-20S	E4
-	SHLD	-	3429	1E-20S	A4
-	SRPK	-	2917	12W-6N	C6
-	SRPK	-	2973	12W-4N	A3
-	ThtT	-	3429	1E-20S	A4
-	TNTN	-	3428	0W-20S	C4
-	WdfT	-	2756	13W-17N	A5
-	WhlT	-	2756	12W-18N	A4
-	WLNG	-	2756	12W-18N	A4
-	WLSP	-	3209	12W-8S	C1
-	WNSP	-	3086		C7
-	WNSP	-	3146		D6
-	WRTH	-	3275	8W-12S	A2
-	WthT	-	3275	7W-13S	B5
I-294 Tri-State Tollway					
-	ALSP	-	3275	7W-13S	C5
-	ALSP	-	3276	5W-15S	A7
-	ALSP	-	3348	5W-15S	B1

STREET Block	City	ZIP	Map#	CGS	Grid
I-294 Tri-State Tollway					
-	BGVW	-	3210	9W-11S	D6
-	BKLY	-	3028		C6
-	BmnT	-	3348	3W-17S	E4
-	BmnT	-	3349	3W-18S	B7
-	BRRG	-	3146		D5
-	CHCG	-	2863	12W-9N	C7
-	CHCG	-	2917	12W-6N	B6
-	CHRG	-	3210	9W-11S	E7
-	CHRG	-	3274	8W-11S	E1
-	CHRG	-	3275	8W-12S	A2
-	CTSD	-	3146		E7
-	CTSD	-	3147	13W-8S	A7
-	CTSD	-	3209	12W-8S	B1
-	CTWD	-	3348	4W-17S	D4
-	DRFD	-	2756	12W-18N	B2
-	DSPN	-	2863	12W-10N	C4
-	DSPN	-	2917	12W-8N	C2
-	EHZC	-	3427	2W-20S	D4
-	EHZC	-	3428	1W-20S	A4
-	EMHT	-	3028		C6
-	FNPK	-	2972		B6
-	FNPK	-	2973	12W-4N	A3
-	GNVW	-	2809	11W-13N	C6
-	HGKN	-	3209	12W-8S	C1
-	HLCT	-	3427	3W-19S	B3
-	HLSD	-	3028		C6
-	HNDL	-	3086		C6
-	HNDL	-	3146		D6
-	HYHL	-	3210	9W-10S	C4
-	IHPK	-	3146		E7
-	JSTC	-	3209	11W-9S	E2
-	JSTC	-	3210	10W-9S	B3
-	LNSG	-	3429	1E-20S	C4
-	LydT	-	2972		B5
-	LydT	-	2973	13W-4N	A3
-	LynT	-	3086		C6
-	LynT	-	3146		D4
-	LynT	-	3147	13W-8S	A7
-	LynT	-	3209	12W-8S	D2
-	MaiT	-	2809	11W-13N	C7
-	MaiT	-	2863	12W-12N	C1
-	MDLN	-	3348	4W-16S	D4
-	MKHM	-	3349	3W-18S	B7
-	MKHM	-	3427	3W-19S	B2
-	NfdT	-	2756	13W-17N	A5
-	NfdT	-	2809	11W-13N	C6
-	NHBK	-	2756	12W-18N	B3
-	NHBK	-	2809	12W-16N	C1
-	NHLK	-	2972		C4
-	NHLK	-	3028		B1
-	OKBK	-	3086		B2
-	PKRG	-	2863	12W-10N	C4
-	POSN	-	3349	3W-18S	B7
-	PvsT	-	3028		C7
-	PvsT	-	3086		C1
-	RBBN	-	3348	4W-16S	D4
-	RSMT	-	2917	12W-8N	C3
-	SHLD	-	3428	0E-20S	E4
-	SHLD	-	3429	1E-20S	A4
-	SRPK	-	2917	12W-6N	C6
-	SRPK	-	2973	12W-4N	A3
-	ThtT	-	3429	1E-20S	B4
-	TNTN	-	3428	0W-20S	C4
-	WdfT	-	2756	13W-17N	A5
-	WhlT	-	2756	12W-18N	A4
-	WLNG	-	2756	12W-18N	A4
-	WLSP	-	3209	12W-8S	C1
-	WNSP	-	3086		C7
-	WNSP	-	3146		D6
-	WRTH	-	3275	8W-12S	A2
-	WthT	-	3275	7W-13S	B5
I-355					
-	ADSN	-	2914		B7
-	ITSC	-	2914		B6
SR-1					
-	EHZC	60426	3428	0W-20S	B4
-	EHZC	60473	3428	0W-20S	B4
-	PHNX	60426	3350	1W-18S	B7
-	RVDL	60628	3278	0W-15S	A7
-	RVDL	60643	3278	0W-15S	A7
-	RVDL	60827	3278	0W-15S	A7
100	CHHT	60411	3508	0W-23S	B4
300	BCHR	60401	3864	0W-36S	C2
300	WshT	60401	3864	0W-37S	C2
800	CRTE	60417	3596	1W-29S	B7
800	CRTE	60417	3685	0W-32S	B6
1100	BCHR	60401	3774	0W-35S	C6
1500	CHHT	60411	3596	1W-28S	B6
1500	CteT	60417	3685	0W-30S	B3
2500	SCHT	60411	3596	1W-26S	A2
3000	STGR	60475	3596	1W-27S	B4
9900	CHCG	60628	3214	0W-11S	A7
9900	CHCG	60643	3214	1W-11S	A7
10300	CHCG	60628	3278	0W-13S	A3
10300	CHCG	60643	3278	1W-13S	A3
12200	CTPK	60827	3278	1W-14S	A6
12500	CTPK	60628	3278	1W-14S	A6
12600	CHCG	60827	3278	1W-14S	A7
13100	RVDL	60827	3350	1W-17S	A6
14300	HRVY	60426	3350	0W-18S	B7
15600	HRVY	60426	3428	0W-21S	B7
16900	SHLD	60473	3428	0W-20S	B4
17200	EHZC	60429	3428	0W-20S	B5
17300	HMWD	60430	3428	0W-20S	B5
18000	GNWD	60425	3428	0W-21S	B7
18000	GNWD	60430	3428	0W-21S	B7
18300	GNWD	60425	3508	0W-24S	B5
18500	HMWD	60430	3508	1W-24S	B5
19000	HMWD	60425	3508	0W-23S	B2
19100	BlmT	60411	3508	0W-23S	B3
19300	GNWD	60411	3508	0W-23S	B3
26800	CteT	60417	3774	0W-32S	C1
27000	CteT	60401	3774	0W-33S	C3
27800	WshT	60401	3774	0W-35S	C6
SR-1 Chicago Rd					
1100	CHHT	60411	3508	1W-25S	A7
1500	CHHT	60411	3596	1W-28S	B6
2500	SCHT	60411	3596	1W-26S	A2
3000	STGR	60475	3596	1W-27S	B4
3700	CRTE	60417	3596	1W-28S	B7
SR-1 Dixie Hwy					
27000	CteT	60401	3774	0W-33S	C3
27800	WshT	60401	3774	0W-35S	C6
28800	BCHR	60401	3774	0W-35S	C6
SR-1 S Dixie Hwy					
300	BCHR	60401	3864	0W-36S	C2
300	WshT	60401	3864	0W-37S	C2
1100	BCHR	60401	3774	0W-36S	C7
1800	CRTE	60417	3685	0W-31S	B4
1800	CteT	60417	3685	0W-31S	B5
26800	CteT	60401	3774	0W-33S	C2
26800	CteT	60417	3774	0W-32S	C1
SR-1 Halsted St					
-	EHZC	60426	3428	0W-20S	B4

STREET Block	City	ZIP	Map#	CGS	Grid
SR-1 Halsted St					
-	EHZC	60473	3428	0W-20S	B4
-	PHNX	60426	3350	0W-18S	B7
14300	HRVY	60426	3350	1W-17S	A4
14300	RVDL	60827	3350	1W-16S	A4
15600	HRVY	60426	3428	0W-21S	B7
16900	SHLD	60473	3428	0W-20S	B4
17200	EHZC	60429	3428	0W-20S	B5
17300	HMWD	60430	3428	0W-20S	B5
18000	GNWD	60425	3428	0W-21S	B7
18000	GNWD	60430	3428	0W-21S	B7
SR-1 S Halsted St					
-	RVDL	60628	3278	0W-15S	A7
-	RVDL	60643	3278	0W-15S	A7
-	RVDL	60827	3278	0W-15S	A7
100	CHHT	60411	3508	0W-23S	B4
9900	CHCG	60628	3214	1W-11S	A7
9900	CHCG	60643	3214	1W-11S	A7
10300	CHCG	60628	3278	1W-13S	A3
10300	CHCG	60643	3278	1W-13S	A3
12200	CTPK	60827	3278	1W-14S	A6
12500	CTPK	60628	3278	1W-14S	A6
12600	CTPK	60827	3278	1W-14S	A7
13100	RVDL	60827	3350	1W-17S	A6
14500	HRVY	60426	3350	1W-16S	A4
18300	GNWD	60425	3428	0W-22S	B7
18300	GNWD	60425	3508	1W-24S	B5
18300	GNWD	60430	3428	0W-21S	B7
18300	HMWD	60430	3428	0W-21S	B7
18500	HMWD	60430	3508	1W-24S	B5
19000	HMWD	60425	3508	0W-23S	B2
19100	BlmT	60411	3508	0W-23S	B3
19300	GNWD	60411	3508	0W-23S	B3
SR-1 Main St					
800	CRTE	60417	3596	1W-29S	B7
800	CRTE	60417	3685	0W-32S	B6
1500	CteT	60417	3685	0W-30S	B3
SR-1 Route 1 Cto					
-	CHHT	60411	3508	1W-24S	B6
SR-1 Vincennes Rd					
-	PHNX	60426	3350	1W-18S	B7
14900	HRVY	60426	3350	1W-18S	B7
SR-7					
9800	ODPK	60462	3345	11W-16S	E3
10600	CHRG	60482	3274	9W-12S	E2
10600	OrlT	60462	3345	11W-16S	E3
10600	WRTH	60482	3274	9W-12S	E2
10700	ODPK	60467	3345	13W-16S	A4
10700	OrlT	60467	3345	13W-16S	A4
10800	PSHL	60465	3274	9W-13S	D4
10900	ODPK	60467	3344	13W-17S	E6
10900	OrlT	60467	3344	13W-17S	E6
11100	WRTH	60465	3274	9W-13S	D3
11200	ODPK	60467	3422	15W-19S	B1
11200	OrlT	60467	3422	15W-19S	B1
11200	PSHT	60465	3274	9W-13S	D4
11400	PSHT	60463	3274	9W-13S	D4
11800	HMGN	60441	3422	14W-18S	C1
11800	PSPK	60464	3274	11W-14S	A7
12600	PlsT	60464	3346	11W-15S	A1
12600	PSPK	60464	3346	11W-15S	A1
13000	ODPK	60462	3346	11W-15S	A1
13000	PlsT	60462	3346	11W-15S	A1
13100	PlsT	60462	3345	11W-16S	E3
SR-7 W 143rd St					
9800	ODPK	60462	3345	12W-16S	C4
10600	OrlT	60462	3345	13W-16S	B4
10700	ODPK	60467	3345	13W-16S	A4
10700	OrlT	60467	3345	13W-16S	A4
10900	ODPK	60467	3344	13W-17S	E6
10900	OrlT	60467	3344	13W-17S	E6
SR-7 W 159th St					
11200	ODPK	60467	3422	14W-18S	E1
11200	OrlT	60467	3422	13W-18S	E1
11800	HMGN	60441	3422	14W-18S	C1
SR-7 Southwest Hwy					
10600	CHRG	60482	3274	9W-12S	E2
10600	WRTH	60482	3274	9W-12S	E2
10800	PSHL	60465	3274	9W-13S	D4
11100	WRTH	60465	3274	9W-13S	D3
11200	PSHT	60465	3274	9W-13S	D4
11400	PSHT	60463	3274	9W-13S	D4
11800	PSPK	60464	3274	11W-14S	A7
12600	PlsT	60464	3346	11W-15S	A1
12600	PSPK	60464	3346	11W-15S	A1
13000	ODPK	60462	3346	11W-15S	A1
13000	PlsT	60462	3346	11W-15S	A1
13100	ODPK	60462	3345	11W-16S	E3
13100	OrlT	60462	3345	11W-16S	E3
13100	PlsT	60462	3345	11W-16S	E3
SR-7 Wolf Rd					
14300	ODPK	60467	3344	13W-17S	E4
14300	OrlT	60467	3344	13W-17S	E4
15600	ODPK	60467	3422	15W-19S	B1
15600	OrlT	60467	3422	15W-19S	B1
SR-19					
-	CHCG	60131	2972		D2
-	CHCG	60176	2973	11W-5N	E2
-	CHCG	60634	2973	11W-5N	E2
-	CHCG	60666	2973	12W-5N	A1
-	FNPK	60131	2972		E1
-	FNPK	60666	2972		D2
-	FNPK	60666	2973	13W-5N	A1
-	SRPK	60666	2973	13W-5N	A1
10	BmdT	60143	2913		D5
10	BmdT	60143	2914		E7
10	BmdT	60157	2913		D5
10	BNVL	60106	2915		E7
10	BNVL	60106	2972		A1
10	HnrT	60120	2856	30W-10N	B5
10	ITSC	60143	2914		E7
10	ROSL	60172	2913		D5
10	SMWD	60107	2856	29W-10N	D6
10	SMWD	60107	2857	28W-9N	A7
100	HnrT	60107	2856	29W-10N	D6
100	ROSL	60172	2912		E4
100	SMWD	60120	2856	30W-10N	B5
100	WDDL	60191	2915		C7
200	WDDL	60191	2914		E7
300	BmdT	60172	2913		C5
300	ELGN	60120	2855		B4
400	ITSC	60143	2913		E6
400	ITSC	60191	2914		E7
400	SMBG	60172	2912		D3
400	SMBG	60193	2912		D3
600	CHCG	60613	2978	0W-4N	A1
700	CHCG	60613	2977	3W-4N	A2
700	SmbT	60193	2912		B2
800	HRPK	60133	2912		C3
800	SMBG	60133	2912		A2
800	SMWD	60107	2911		C1
900	HRPK	60107	2911		C1
1000	HRPK	60133	2911		C1
1000	SMWD	60133	2911		C1
1100	BNVL	60131	2972		C1

STREET Block	City	ZIP	Map#	CGS	Grid
SR-19					
1100	CHCG	60106	2972		C1
1100	WDDL	60143	2914		D7
1400	HnrT	60120	2855		E5
1600	ELGN	60120	2856	31W-10N	A5
1900	CHCG	60618	2977	2W-5N	B1
2700	CHCG	60618	2976	3W-4N	E2
3900	CHCG	60641	2976	5W-4N	A2
4600	CHCG	60641	2975	7W-4N	B2
5500	CHCG	60634	2975	6W-5N	C2
6600	CHCG	60634	2974	8W-4N	D2
7100	NRDG	60634	2974	8W-5N	D2
7100	NRDG	60706	2974	8W-5N	D2
7500	CHCG	60706	2974	9W-5N	C2
9200	SRPK	60176	2973	13W-5N	A1
11500	CHCG	60666	2972		D2
SR-19 E Chicago St					
300	ELGN	60120	2855		B4
1400	HnrT	60120	2855		E5
SR-19 Irving Park Rd					
-	CHCG	60176	2973	11W-5N	E2
-	CHCG	60634	2973	11W-5N	E2
-	CHCG	60666	2973	13W-5N	A1
-	ELGN	60120	2855		E5
-	FNPK	60666	2973	13W-5N	A1
-	HnrT	60120	2855		E5
-	ROSL	60172	2913		C5
-	SRPK	60666	2973	13W-5N	A1
10	BmdT	60143	2913		D5
10	BmdT	60143	2914		E7
10	BmdT	60157	2913		D5
10	HnrT	60120	2856	30W-10N	B5
10	ITSC	60143	2914		E7
100	HnrT	60107	2856	30W-10N	C6
100	SMWD	60107	2856	30W-10N	C6
100	SMWD	60120	2856	30W-10N	B5
300	BmdT	60172	2913		C5
400	ITSC	60143	2913		E6
800	HRPK	60133	2912		C3
800	SMBG	60133	2912		A2
1200	HRPK	60133	2911		C1
1600	ELGN	60120	2856	31W-10N	A5
1700	SMWD	60107	2911		D1
1700	SMWD	60133	2911		D1
9200	SRPK	60176	2973	13W-5N	A1
SR-19 E Irving Park Rd					
10	BNVL	60106	2972		A1
10	ROSL	60172	2913		A4
10	SMWD	60107	2857	28W-9N	A7
100	ITSC	60143	2914		C6
100	WDDL	60191	2915		B7
400	BmdT	60172	2913		C5
400	BNVL	60106	2915		C7
800	SMWD	60107	2911		C1
900	CHCG	60131	2972		B1
900	HRPK	60107	2911		C1
1000	HRPK	60133	2911		C1
1000	SMWD	60133	2911		C1
1100	BNVL	60131	2972		C1
1100	CHCG	60106	2972		C1
1100	WDDL	60143	2914		D7
1200	WDDL	60191	2914		D7
1300	ITSC	60191	2914		E7
11500	CHCG	60666	2972		C1
SR-19 W Irving Park Rd					
-	BmdT	60143	2914		A6
-	BNVL	60131	2972		C1
-	CHCG	60131	2972		C1
-	CHCG	60176	2973	11W-5N	E2
-	CHCG	60634	2973	10W-5N	E2
-	CHCG	60666	2972		D2
-	FNPK	60131	2972		E1
-	FNPK	60666	2972		D2
-	HnrT	60107	2856	29W-10N	D6
-	HnrT	60120	2856	29W-10N	C6
-	SMWD	60120	2856	29W-10N	C6
10	BNVL	60106	2915		E7
10	ROSL	60172	2913		D5
10	SMWD	60107	2856	29W-10N	D6
100	ROSL	60172	2912		E4
100	WDDL	60191	2915		C7
200	ITSC	60143	2914		C6
200	WDDL	60191	2914		E7
400	ITSC	60191	2914		E7
400	SMBG	60172	2912		D3
400	SMBG	60193	2912		D3
600	CHCG	60613	2978	0W-5N	A1
700	CHCG	60613	2977	3W-4N	A2
700	SmbT	60193	2912		B2
1400	BmdT	60143	2913		E6
1400	ITSC	60143	2913		E6
1800	SMBG	60133	2912		A2
1900	CHCG	60618	2977	2W-5N	B1
1900	HRPK	60133	2912		A2
2700	CHCG	60618	2976	3W-4N	E2
3900	CHCG	60641	2976	5W-4N	A2
4600	CHCG	60641	2975	7W-4N	B2
5500	CHCG	60634	2975	6W-5N	C2
6600	CHCG	60634	2974	8W-4N	D2
7100	NRDG	60634	2974	8W-5N	D2
7100	NRDG	60706	2974	8W-5N	D2
7500	CHCG	60706	2974	9W-5N	C2
SR-19 N Recreation Dr					
-	CHCG	60613	2978	0W-4N	A1
SR-21					
500	MaiT	60016	2809	10W-13N	E7
500	MaiT	60025	2809	10W-13N	E7
500	NfdT	60016	2809	10W-13N	E7
500	NfdT	60025	2809	11W-13N	E7
500	PTHT	60062	2809	13W-15N	A1
500	PTHT	60070	2809	13W-15N	A1
500	PTHT	60090	2809	13W-15N	A1
500	WhlT	60062	2809	13W-15N	A1
500	WhlT	60090	2809	13W-15N	A1
500	WLNG	60090	2755	14W-18N	C3
600	WhlT	60090	2755	13W-17N	E5
700	GNVW	60025	2809	11W-13N	D6
800	BFGV	60090	2755	14W-20N	C2
900	BFGV	60089	2755	14W-20N	C1
900	VrnT	60015	2755	14W-20N	C1
900	VrnT	60062	2755	14W-20N	C1
900	VrnT	60089	2755	14W-20N	C1
1000	RVWD	60015	2755	14W-20N	C1
1100	PTHT	60070	2755	13W-16N	E7
1100	PTHT	60070	2808	13W-16N	E1
1100	WhlT	60090	2808	13W-16N	E1
1600	GNVW	60062	2809	12W-14N	C4
1800	NfdT	60062	2809	12W-14N	C4
7500	CHCG	60631	2864	9W-9N	D7
7500	CHCG	60714	2864	9W-9N	D7
7500	NLES	60631	2864	9W-9N	D7
7500	NLES	60714	2864	9W-9N	D6
8300	NLES	60714	2864	9W-10N	C5
9600	GNVW	60025	2864	10W-12N	A1
9600	MaiT	60016	2864	10W-12N	A1

Block	City	ZIP	Map#	CGS	Grid
SR-21					
9700	GNVW	60025	2863	10W-12N	E1
9700	MaiT	60025	2863	10W-12N	E1
9800	MaiT	60016	2863	10W-12N	E1
SR-21 Milwaukee Av					
500	MaiT	60016	2809	10W-13N	E7
500	MaiT	60025	2809	10W-13N	E7
500	NfdT	60016	2809	10W-13N	E7
500	NfdT	60025	2809	11W-13N	E7
700	GNVW	60025	2809	11W-13N	D6
900	BFGV	60089	2755	14W-20N	C1
900	VrnT	60015	2755	14W-20N	C1
900	VrnT	60062	2755	14W-20N	C1
900	VrnT	60089	2755	14W-20N	C1
1000	RVWD	60015	2755	14W-20N	C1
1600	GNVW	60062	2809	12W-14N	C4
1800	NfdT	60062	2809	12W-14N	C4
2800	PTHT	60062	2809	12W-15N	A2
2800	PTHT	60070	2809	12W-15N	A2
9700	GNVW	60025	2863	10W-12N	E1
9700	GNVW	60025	2864	10W-12N	A1
9700	MaiT	60016	2864	10W-12N	A1
9700	MaiT	60025	2863	10W-12N	E1
9700	MaiT	60714	2864	10W-12N	A1
9700	NLES	60714	2864	10W-12N	A1
9800	MaiT	60016	2863	10W-12N	E1
20400	BFGV	60090	2755	14W-20N	C1
SR-21 N Milwaukee Av					
-	NfdT	60062	2809	12W-15N	A2
500	PTHT	60062	2809	13W-15N	A1
500	PTHT	60070	2809	13W-15N	A1
500	PTHT	60090	2809	13W-15N	A1
500	WhlT	60062	2809	13W-15N	A1
500	WhlT	60090	2809	13W-15N	A1
500	WLNG	60090	2755	14W-18N	C3
800	BFGV	60090	2755	14W-20N	C2
900	BFGV	60089	2755	14W-20N	C1
900	VrnT	60062	2755	14W-20N	C1
900	VrnT	60089	2755	14W-20N	C1
7500	CHCG	60631	2864	9W-9N	D7
7500	CHCG	60714	2864	9W-9N	D7
7500	NLES	60631	2864	9W-9N	D7
7500	NLES	60714	2864	9W-9N	D6
8300	MaiT	60714	2864	9W-10N	C5
9600	GNVW	60025	2864	10W-12N	A1
9600	MaiT	60016	2864	10W-12N	A1
SR-21 S Milwaukee Av					
10	WLNG	60090	2755	14W-18N	D4
600	WhlT	60090	2755	13W-17N	E5
1100	PTHT	60070	2755	13W-16N	E7
1100	PTHT	60070	2808	13W-16N	E1
1100	PTHT	60070	2809	13W-16N	A1
1100	PTHT	60090	2809	13W-16N	A1
1100	WhlT	60090	2808	13W-16N	E1
1100	WhlT	60090	2809	13W-16N	A1
SR-25					
-	BRLT	60103	2909		B3
-	BRLT	60120	2909		B4
-	BRLT	60177	2909		B4
-	ElgT	60177	2909		B2
-	SchT	60120	2909		A5
-	SchT	60177	2909		A5
-	SEGN	60103	2909		B3
-	SEGN	60120	2909		B3
-	SEGN	60177	2909		B3
10	CPVL	60110	2748		C2
10	CPVL	60118	2801		C2
10	EDND	60118	2801		C2
10	ELGN	60120	2855		B2
100	BNHL	60110	2748		C2
200	EDND	60110	2748		C7
600	DndT	60118	2801		C4
800	CPVL	60110	2801		C1
800	EDND	60110	2801		C1
900	ElgT	60120	2855		B7
1100	ElgT	60120	2909		B1
1300	ELGN	60120	2801		B7
1500	DndT	60120	2801		B6
1500	ELGN	60118	2801		B7
1900	DndT	60110	2748		C2
2100	ALGN	60102	2748		C2
2100	ALGN	60110	2748		C2
2100	BNHL	60010	2748		C2
2100	BNHL	60102	2748		C2
SR-25 Bluff City Blvd					
500	ELGN	60120	2855		B6
SR-25 Dundee Av					
10	CPVL	60118	2801		C2
10	EDND	60118	2801		C2
600	DndT	60118	2801		C4
1100	ELGN	60120	2855		B1
1300	ELGN	60120	2801		B7
1500	DndT	60120	2801		B6
1500	ELGN	60118	2801		B7
SR-25 Elgin Rd					
1600	BNHL	60110	2748		C2
1600	CPVL	60110	2748		C2
1900	DndT	60110	2748		C2
2100	ALGN	60102	2748		C2
2100	ALGN	60110	2748		C2
2100	BNHL	60010	2748		C2
2100	BNHL	60102	2748		C2
SR-25 JFK Memorial Dr					
-	CPVL	60118	2801		C1
-	EDND	60118	2801		C1
10	CPVL	60110	2748		C6
200	EDND	60110	2748		C7
800	CPVL	60110	2801		C1
800	EDND	60110	2801		C1
SR-25 N Kennedy Dr					
10	CPVL	60110	2748		C6
100	BNHL	60110	2748		C4
SR-25 N Liberty St					
10	ELGN	60120	2855		B2
SR-25 S Liberty St					
10	ELGN	60120	2855		B4
SR-25 St. Charles St					
800	ELGN	60120	2855		B6
900	ElgT	60120	2855		B7
1100	ElgT	60120	2909		B1
SR-38					
-	EMHT	60126	3028		B7
-	EMHT	60523	3028		B7
-	OKBK	60126	3028		B7
-	OKBK	60523	3028		A7
-	PvsT	60126	3028		B7
-	PvsT	60523	3028		B7
-	YkTp	60126	3028		B7
-	YkTp	60523	3028		B7
4000	HLSD	60162	3029	13W-1S	A7
4000	PvsT	60162	3029	13W-1S	A7
4000	WSTR	60154	3029	13W-0S	A7
4300	HLSD	60162	3028		D7
4300	PvsT	60162	3028		D7
4400	HLSD	60154	3028		E7
4400	WSTR	60154	3028		E7
SR-38					
11900	PvsT	60126	3028		B7
SR-38 Roosevelt Rd					
-	EMHT	60126	3028		B7
-	EMHT	60523	3028		B7
-	OKBK	60126	3028		B7
-	OKBK	60523	3028		A7
-	PvsT	60523	3028		B7
-	WSTR	60154	3028		D7
-	YkTp	60126	3028		B7
-	YkTp	60523	3028		B7
4000	HLSD	60162	3029	13W-1S	A7
4000	PvsT	60162	3029	13W-1S	A7
4000	WSTR	60154	3029	13W-0S	A7
4300	HLSD	60162	3028		D7
4300	PvsT	60162	3028		D7
4400	HLSD	60154	3028		E7
11900	PvsT	60126	3028		B7
SR-38 W Roosevelt Rd					
10900	HLSD	60154	3028		E7
10900	HLSD	60162	3028		E7
10900	WSTR	60154	3028		E7
SR-43					
-	BGVW	60453	3210	9W-10S	E5
-	FTPK	60305	3030	8W-0N	D4
-	LYNS	60402	3148	8W-5S	E1
-	OKLN	60453	3210	9W-10S	E5
-	OKLN	60455	3210	9W-10S	E5
-	OrlT	60452	3346	9W-17S	E5
-	PlsT	60462	3346	8W-16S	E2
-	PSHT	60462	3346	9W-17S	E6
-	PSHT	60463	3346	9W-17S	E6
-	SMMT	60534	3148	9W-5S	E2
-	TYPK	60423	3505	8W-23S	A3
10	DRFD	60015	2757	10W-20N	A2
10	DRFD	60062	2757	10W-20N	A2
10	FTPK	60130	3030	8W-0N	D4
10	FTPK	60304	3030	9W-0S	D5
10	GNVW	60025	2864	8W-12N	E1
10	MNGV	60053	2864	8W-10N	E4
10	NfdT	60062	2757	10W-18N	A2
10	OKPK	60302	3030	8W-0S	D6
10	OKPK	60304	3030	9W-0N	D5
100	GNVW	60025	2810	8W-13N	E6
100	GNVW	60093	2810	8W-15N	E3
100	NHFD	60025	2810	8W-15N	E3
100	NHFD	60093	2810	8W-15N	E2
300	NHBK	60062	2810	8W-15N	E2
300	OKPK	60130	3030	9W-0S	D5
400	OKPK	60301	3030	8W-0N	D4
400	OKPK	60305	3030	9W-0S	D6
400	RVFT	60301	3030	8W-0N	D4
400	RVFT	60305	3030	9W-0S	D6
600	DRFD	60015	2756	10W-20N	E1
600	NHBK	60062	2757	9W-18N	B4
1100	BRWN	60402	3030	8W-0S	D7
1500	BRWN	60402	3088	8W-1S	D1
1500	CHCG	60707	3030	8W-2N	D1
1500	EDPK	60707	3030	8W-2N	D1
1500	FTPK	60130	3088	8W-1S	D1
1500	NRIV	60130	3088	9W-1S	D1
1700	CHCG	60707	2974	8W-2N	D7
1700	EDPK	60707	2974	8W-2N	D7
1700	NRIV	60402	3088	8W-1S	D1
2100	NHFD	60062	2810	8W-16N	E1
2100	NRIV	60546	3088	8W-1S	D2
2500	RVSD	60546	3088	8W-2S	D3
2700	CHCG	60634	2974	8W-3N	D5
3200	RVSD	60402	3088	9W-3S	E4
3600	LYNS	60402	3088	8W-3S	E5
3600	LYNS	60534	3088	8W-3S	E5
3800	SKNY	60402	3088	8W-3S	E6
3900	NRDG	60634	2974	8W-3N	D5
3900	NRDG	60706	2974	8W-3N	D5
4400	FTVW	60402	3088	8W-4S	E7
4400	HDHT	60706	2918	8W-5N	D7
4400	NRDG	60706	2918	8W-5N	D7
4600	FTVW	60402	3148	9W-5S	E1
4600	LYNS	60534	3148	8W-4S	E1
4700	CHCG	60656	2918	8W-5N	D7
5100	CHCG	60501	3148	8W-5S	E1
5100	CHCG	60638	3148	9W-5S	E1
5100	CHCG	60706	2918	8W-6N	D6
5100	SMMT	60501	3148	9W-5S	E1
5400	SMMT	60638	3148	8W-5S	E3
5600	CHCG	60631	2918	8W-6N	D6
6300	BDPK	60638	3148	8W-7S	E5
6500	BDPK	60501	3148	9W-7S	D5
6500	CHCG	60714	2918	8W-8N	D2
6500	NLES	60631	2918	8W-8N	D2
6500	NLES	60714	2918	9W-6N	D6
6700	BGVW	60455	3148	9W-7S	E6
7000	NLES	60714	2864	8W-10N	E5
7100	BGVW	60638	3148	8W-8S	E7
7200	CHCG	60631	2864	8W-9N	D7
7300	BDPK	60638	3210	8W-8S	E1
7300	BGVW	60455	3210	8W-8S	E1
7400	BGVW	60638	3210	8W-8S	E1
7500	CHCG	60714	2864	8W-9N	D7
7500	NLES	60631	2864	8W-9N	D7
7700	BGVW	60459	3210	9W-8S	E2
7700	BRBK	60455	3210	9W-8S	E2
7700	BRBK	60459	3210	9W-8S	E2
8300	MNGV	60714	2864	8W-10N	E5
9800	CHRG	60415	3210	9W-11S	E7
9800	CHRG	60455	3210	9W-11S	E7
10100	BGVW	60455	3274	9W-11S	E1
10100	CHRG	60415	3274	9W-11S	E1
10100	PSHL	60455	3274	9W-11S	E1
10100	PSHL	60465	3274	9W-11S	E1
10400	CHRG	60482	3274	9W-15S	E7
10400	WRTH	60465	3274	9W-15S	E7
10500	WRTH	60482	3274	9W-15S	E7
11600	PSHT	60463	3274	8W-13S	E5
11600	WRTH	60463	3274	8W-13S	E5
13500	BmnT	60445	3346	8W-17S	E6
13500	BmnT	60462	3346	9W-17S	E6
13500	OrlT	60462	3346	8W-16S	E2
13500	WthT	60445	3346	9W-17S	E6
13500	WthT	60462	3346	9W-17S	E6
13500	WthT	60463	3346	9W-17S	E6
14100	BmnT	60452	3346	8W-16S	E4
15100	ODPK	60462	3346	9W-18S	E6
15200	OKFT	60462	3346	9W-18S	E6
15700	ODPK	60462	3424	9W-18S	E1
15800	ODPK	60477	3424	9W-18S	E1
15800	TYPK	60477	3424	9W-21S	E6
16300	OrlT	60477	3424	8W-19S	E2
18200	TYPK	60477	3425	8W-21S	A7
19300	FftT	60423	3505	8W-23S	A3
19300	FftT	60477	3505	8W-23S	A3
19300	RchT	60423	3505	9W-24S	A6
19300	RchT	60477	3505	8W-23S	A3
19300	TYPK	60477	3505	8W-23S	A3
19700	MTSN	60443	3505	9W-24S	A6
SR-43					
19700	RchT	60443	3505	9W-24S	A6
19800	MTSN	60423	3505	9W-24S	A6
20600	FKFT	60423	3505	9W-25S	A7
21500	RchT	60443	3593	9W-25S	A1
22400	FKFT	60423	3593	9W-27S	A5
22400	FKFT	60443	3593	9W-27S	A5
22400	RchT	60423	3593	9W-27S	A3
SR-43 Harlem Av					
-	CHCG	60638	3148	8W-5S	E2
-	FftT	60477	3505	8W-23S	A2
-	LYNS	60402	3148	9W-5S	E1
-	SMMT	60501	3148	9W-5S	E2
-	SMMT	60534	3148	8W-5S	E2
-	TYPK	60477	3505	8W-23S	A3
1100	BRWN	60402	3030	8W-0S	D7
1100	FTPK	60130	3030	8W-0S	D7
1100	OKPK	60304	3030	8W-0S	D7
1500	BRWN	60402	3088	9W-1S	D1
1500	FTPK	60130	3088	9W-1S	D1
1500	NRIV	60130	3088	9W-1S	D1
1700	NRIV	60402	3088	9W-1S	D1
2100	NRIV	60546	3088	8W-1S	D2
2500	RVSD	60546	3088	8W-2S	D3
3200	RVSD	60402	3088	9W-3S	E4
3600	LYNS	60402	3088	9W-3S	E5
3600	LYNS	60534	3088	8W-3S	E5
3800	SKNY	60402	3088	8W-3S	E6
4400	FTVW	60402	3148	8W-4S	E7
4600	FTVW	60402	3148	8W-4S	E1
4600	LYNS	60534	3148	8W-4S	E1
15900	ODPK	60462	3424	9W-18S	E1
15900	ODPK	60477	3424	9W-18S	E1
15900	TYPK	60477	3424	9W-21S	E6
16300	OrlT	60477	3424	9W-19S	E2
18200	TYPK	60477	3425	8W-21S	A7
19300	TYPK	60423	3505	8W-23S	A3
SR-43 N Harlem Av					
-	FTPK	60305	3030	8W-0N	D4
10	FTPK	60130	3030	8W-0N	D4
10	OKPK	60302	3030	9W-0S	D6
10	OKPK	60304	3030	9W-0S	D5
400	OKPK	60301	3030	8W-0N	D4
400	OKPK	60305	3030	9W-0S	D6
400	RVFT	60301	3030	8W-0N	D4
400	RVFT	60305	3030	9W-0S	D6
1500	CHCG	60707	3030	9W-2N	D1
1500	EDPK	60707	3030	8W-2N	D1
1700	CHCG	60707	2974	8W-2N	D7
1700	EDPK	60707	2974	8W-2N	D7
2700	CHCG	60634	2974	9W-3N	D5
3900	NRDG	60634	2974	9W-3N	D5
3900	NRDG	60706	2974	9W-3N	D5
4400	HDHT	60706	2918	8W-5N	D7
4400	NRDG	60706	2918	8W-5N	D7
4700	CHCG	60656	2918	8W-5N	D7
5100	CHCG	60706	2918	8W-6N	D6
5600	CHCG	60631	2918	9W-6N	D6
6500	CHCG	60714	2918	8W-8N	D2
6500	NLES	60631	2918	8W-8N	D2
6500	NLES	60714	2918	9W-6N	D6
7200	CHCG	60631	2864	8W-9N	D7
7200	NLES	60714	2864	8W-9N	D7
7500	CHCG	60714	2864	8W-9N	D7
7500	NLES	60631	2864	8W-9N	D7
SR-43 S Harlem Av					
-	BGVW	60453	3210	9W-10S	E5
-	FKFT	60423	3505	9W-25S	A7
-	OKLN	60453	3210	9W-10S	E5
-	OKLN	60455	3210	9W-10S	E5
-	OrlT	60452	3346	9W-17S	E5
-	PlsT	60462	3346	8W-16S	E2
-	PSHT	60462	3346	9W-17S	E6
-	PSHT	60463	3346	9W-17S	E6
-	SMMT	60534	3148	9W-5S	E2
-	TYPK	60423	3505	8W-23S	A3
10	FTPK	60130	3030	9W-0S	D5
10	FTPK	60304	3030	9W-0S	D5
10	OKPK	60302	3030	9W-0S	D5
10	OKPK	60304	3030	9W-0S	D5
300	OKPK	60130	3030	9W-0S	D5
5100	CHCG	60501	3148	9W-5S	E1
5100	CHCG	60638	3148	9W-5S	E1
5100	FTVW	60402	3148	9W-5S	E1
5300	SMMT	60501	3148	9W-6S	E4
5400	SMMT	60638	3148	8W-5S	E3
6300	BDPK	60638	3148	8W-7S	E5
6500	BDPK	60501	3148	9W-7S	D5
6700	BGVW	60455	3148	9W-7S	E6
7100	BGVW	60638	3148	8W-8S	E7
7300	BDPK	60638	3210	8W-8S	E1
7300	BGVW	60455	3210	9W-8S	E1
7400	BGVW	60638	3210	9W-8S	E1
7700	BGVW	60459	3210	9W-8S	E2
7700	BRBK	60455	3210	9W-8S	E2
7700	BRBK	60459	3210	9W-8S	E2
9800	CHRG	60415	3210	9W-11S	E7
9800	CHRG	60455	3210	9W-11S	E7
10100	BGVW	60455	3274	9W-11S	E1
10100	CHRG	60415	3274	9W-11S	E1
10100	PSHL	60455	3274	9W-11S	E1
10100	PSHL	60465	3274	9W-11S	E1
10400	CHRG	60482	3274	9W-15S	E7
10400	WRTH	60465	3274	9W-15S	E7
10500	WRTH	60482	3274	9W-15S	E7
11600	PSHT	60463	3274	8W-13S	E5
11600	WRTH	60463	3274	8W-13S	E5
13500	BmnT	60445	3346	9W-17S	E6
13500	BmnT	60462	3346	9W-17S	E6
13500	OrlT	60462	3346	8W-16S	E2
13500	WthT	60445	3346	9W-17S	E6
13500	WthT	60462	3346	9W-17S	E6
13500	WthT	60463	3346	9W-17S	E6
14100	BmnT	60452	3346	8W-16S	E4
15100	ODPK	60462	3346	9W-18S	E6
15200	OKFT	60462	3346	9W-18S	E6
15700	ODPK	60462	3424	9W-18S	E1
15800	ODPK	60477	3424	9W-18S	E1
15800	TYPK	60477	3424	9W-18S	E1
19300	FftT	60423	3505	8W-23S	A3
19300	FftT	60477	3505	8W-23S	A3
19300	RchT	60423	3505	9W-24S	A6
19300	RchT	60477	3505	8W-23S	A3
19300	TYPK	60477	3505	8W-23S	A3
19700	MTSN	60443	3505	9W-24S	A6
19700	RchT	60443	3505	9W-24S	A6
19800	MTSN	60423	3505	9W-24S	A6
21500	FKFT	60423	3593	9W-25S	A1
21500	RchT	60443	3593	9W-25S	A1
22400	FKFT	60443	3593	9W-27S	A5
22400	RchT	60423	3593	9W-27S	A3
SR-43 W Oakton St					
7000	NLES	60714	2864	8W-10N	E5
SR-43 Waukegan Rd					
10	DRFD	60015	2757	10W-20N	A2
SR-43 Waukegan Rd					
10	DRFD	60062	2757	10W-20N	A2
10	GNVW	60025	2864	8W-12N	E1
10	MNGV	60053	2864	8W-10N	E4
100	GNVW	60025	2810	8W-13N	E6
100	GNVW	60093	2810	8W-15N	E3
100	NHFD	60025	2810	8W-15N	E3
100	NHFD	60093	2810	8W-15N	E2
300	NHBK	60062	2810	8W-15N	E2
400	NfdT	60062	2757	10W-18N	B3
600	DRFD	60015	2756	10W-20N	E1
600	NHBK	60062	2757	9W-18N	B4
2100	NHFD	60062	2810	8W-16N	E1
8400	MNGV	60714	2864	8W-10N	E4
8400	NLES	60714	2864	8W-10N	E4
SR-43 N Waukegan Rd					
8000	NLES	60714	2864	8W-10N	E5
8300	MNGV	60053	2864	8W-10N	E5
8300	MNGV	60714	2864	8W-10N	E5
SR-43 S Waukegan Rd					
10	DRFD	60015	2757	10W-18N	A2
10	DRFD	60062	2757	10W-18N	A2
10	NfdT	60062	2757	10W-18N	A2
SR-50					
-	CTWD	60803	3348	5W-15S	A1
-	MonT	60466	3683	6W-29S	B2
-	PtnT	60468	3860	9W-38S	E6
-	PTON	60468	3860	9W-38S	E6
-	UYPK	60466	3683	6W-29S	B2
10	CHCG	60644	3031	6W-0N	E5
100	PTON	60468	3861	9W-37S	A3
100	WIIT	60468	3861	9W-37S	A2
300	PtnT	60468	3861	9W-37S	A2
700	CHCG	60651	3031	6W-1N	E2
800	CHCG	60644	3032	6W-0S	A6
1000	CCRO	60804	3032	6W-0S	A7
1500	CCRO	60804	3090	6W-1S	A1
1500	CHCG	60639	3031	6W-2N	E1
1600	CHCG	60639	2975	6W-2N	E7
2700	CHCG	60641	2975	6W-5N	E1
3400	SKNY	60804	3090	6W-3S	A5
3700	CHCG	60804	3090	6W-3S	A6
4200	CHCG	60632	3090	6W-4S	A7
4200	CHCG	60638	3090	6W-4S	A7
4300	CHCG	60630	2975	6W-5N	E1
4400	CHCG	60630	2919	6W-5N	E7
4600	CHCG	60632	3150	5W-6S	A3
4600	CHCG	60638	3150	5W-6S	A3
5600	CHCG	60646	2919	6W-7N	E4
6100	CHCG	60629	3150	6W-7S	A6
6300	LNWD	60712	2919	6W-6N	E5
6400	BDPK	60638	3150	5W-7S	A6
6700	BDPK	60629	3150	5W-7S	A7
7200	LNWD	60712	2865	5W-9N	E7
7300	BDPK	60638	3212	5W-8S	A1
7300	CHCG	60629	3212	5W-8S	A1
7300	CHCG	60638	3212	5W-8S	A1
7300	SKOK	60077	2865	6W-9N	E7
7400	BRBK	60459	3212	5W-8S	A1
7400	CHCG	60652	3212	6W-8S	A1
7500	SKOK	60076	2865	5W-9N	E7
8500	CHCG	60459	3212	5W-9S	A4
8600	BRBK	60453	3212	6W-9S	A4
8600	CHCG	60456	3212	6W-9S	A4
8600	HMTN	60456	3212	6W-9S	A4
8600	OKLN	60453	3212	6W-9S	A4
8700	OKLN	60456	3212	6W-10S	A4
10200	OKLN	60453	3276	5W-13S	A3
11000	ALSP	60803	3276	5W-12S	A3
11000	CHCG	60655	3276	5W-12S	A3
13100	ALSP	60803	3348	5W-15S	A1
13100	CTWD	60445	3348	5W-15S	A1
13900	BmnT	60445	3348	5W-16S	A3
14300	MDLN	60445	3348	5W-18S	A7
14700	MDLN	60452	3348	5W-18S	A7
14800	OKFT	60452	3348	5W-17S	A5
14900	OKFT	60445	3348	5W-17S	A6
15700	BmnT	60426	3426	5W-21S	B7
15700	OKFT	60452	3426	6W-21S	B7
16200	OKFT	60426	3426	6W-21S	B7
16700	BmnT	60477	3426	5W-20S	A3
16700	OKFT	60477	3426	5W-20S	A3
16800	BmnT	60452	3426	5W-20S	A4
17000	BmnT	60478	3426	6W-20S	B4
17000	CCHL	60477	3426	6W-20S	B4
17000	CCHL	60478	3426	6W-20S	B4
18400	CCHL	60478	3506	5W-25S	B7
18800	CCHL	60477	3506	5W-22S	B2
18800	RchT	60477	3506	5W-22S	B2
19900	MTSN	60443	3506	5W-24S	B5
19900	MTSN	60477	3506	5W-24S	B4
19900	RchT	60443	3506	5W-24S	B4
21100	MTSN	60443	3594	6W-26S	B2
21900	RNPK	60471	3594	6W-26S	B2
22900	UYPK	60466	3594	6W-27S	B5
22900	UYPK	60471	3594	6W-27S	B5
23100	MonT	60449	3594	6W-28S	B7
23100	MonT	60466	3594	6W-28S	B7
24000	MonT	60449	3683	6W-31S	A5
25100	UYPK	60449	3683	6W-30S	A5
25500	MONE	60449	3682	7W-31S	E6
25500	MONE	60449	3683	6W-31S	A6
26100	MonT	60449	3682	7W-32S	E7
SR-50 Cicero Av					
-	ALSP	60803	3348	5W-15S	A1
-	CTWD	60803	3348	5W-15S	A1
13100	CTWD	60445	3348	6W-15S	A1
13900	BmnT	60445	3348	5W-16S	A3
14300	MDLN	60445	3348	5W-18S	A7
14700	MDLN	60452	3348	5W-18S	A7
14800	OKFT	60452	3348	5W-17S	A5
14900	OKFT	60445	3348	5W-17S	A6
15700	BmnT	60426	3426	6W-21S	B7
15700	OKFT	60452	3426	6W-21S	B7
16200	OKFT	60426	3426	6W-21S	B7
16700	BmnT	60477	3426	5W-20S	A3
16700	OKFT	60477	3426	5W-20S	A3
16800	BmnT	60452	3426	5W-20S	A3
17000	BmnT	60478	3426	6W-20S	B4
17000	CCHL	60477	3426	6W-20S	B4
17000	CCHL	60478	3426	6W-20S	B4
18400	CCHL	60478	3506	6W-25S	B7
18800	CCHL	60477	3506	5W-22S	B2
18800	RchT	60477	3506	5W-22S	B2
19900	MTSN	60443	3506	5W-24S	B5
19900	MTSN	60477	3506	5W-24S	B4
19900	RchT	60443	3506	5W-24S	B4
21100	MTSN	60443	3594	6W-26S	B2
21900	RNPK	60471	3594	6W-26S	B2
22700	UYPK	60471	3594	6W-27S	B5
22900	UYPK	60466	3594	6W-27S	B5
SR-50 N Cicero Av					
10	CHCG	60644	3031	6W-0N	E5
700	CHCG	60651	3031	6W-1N	E2
1500	CHCG	60639	3031	6W-2N	E1
SR-50 N Cicero Av					
1600	CHCG	60639	2975	6W-2N	E7
2700	CHCG	60641	2975	6W-5N	E1
4300	CHCG	60630	2975	6W-5N	E1
4400	CHCG	60630	2919	6W-5N	E7
5600	CHCG	60646	2919	6W-7N	E4
6300	LNWD	60712	2919	6W-6N	E5
7200	LNWD	60712	2865	5W-9N	E7
7300	SKOK	60077	2865	5W-9N	E7
SR-50 S Cicero Av					
-	CTWD	60445	3348	5W-15S	A1
-	CTWD	60803	3348	5W-15S	A1
-	MonT	60466	3683	6W-29S	B2
-	UYPK	60466	3683	6W-29S	B2
10	CHCG	60644	3031	6W-0S	E5
800	CHCG	60644	3032	6W-0S	A6
1000	CCRO	60804	3032	6W-0S	A7
1500	CCRO	60804	3090	6W-1S	A1
3400	SKNY	60804	3090	6W-3S	A5
3700	CHCG	60804	3090	6W-3S	A6
4200	CHCG	60632	3090	6W-4S	A7
4200	CHCG	60638	3090	6W-4S	A7
4600	CHCG	60632	3150	5W-6S	A3
4600	CHCG	60638	3150	5W-6S	A3
6100	CHCG	60629	3150	6W-7S	A6
6400	BDPK	60638	3150	6W-7S	A6
6700	BDPK	60629	3150	5W-7S	A7
7300	BDPK	60638	3212	5W-8S	A1
7300	CHCG	60629	3212	5W-8S	A1
7300	CHCG	60638	3212	5W-8S	A1
7400	BRBK	60459	3212	6W-8S	A1
7400	CHCG	60652	3212	6W-8S	A1
8500	CHCG	60459	3212	5W-9S	A4
8600	BRBK	60453	3212	6W-9S	A4
8600	CHCG	60456	3212	6W-9S	A4
8600	HMTN	60456	3212	6W-9S	A4
8600	OKLN	60453	3212	6W-9S	A4
8700	OKLN	60456	3212	6W-10S	A4
10200	OKLN	60453	3276	6W-13S	A3
11000	CHCG	60655	3276	5W-12S	A3
12800	ALSP	60803	3276	5W-15S	A7
13100	ALSP	60803	3348	5W-15S	A1
23100	MonT	60449	3594	6W-28S	B7
23100	MonT	60466	3594	6W-28S	B7
23100	RNPK	60471	3594	6W-27S	B5
23100	UYPK	60466	3594	6W-28S	B6
23100	UYPK	60471	3594	6W-27S	B5
24000	MonT	60449	3683	6W-31S	A5
SR-50 S Governors Hwy					
-	MonT	60466	3683	6W-29S	B2
-	UYPK	60466	3683	6W-29S	B2
400	PTON	60468	3861	9W-37S	A4
25100	MonT	60449	3683	6W-30S	A3
25100	UYPK	60449	3683	6W-30S	A3
25500	MONE	60449	3682	7W-31S	E6
25500	MONE	60449	3683	6W-31S	A4
26100	MonT	60449	3682	7W-32S	E7
29800	PtnT	60468	3861	9W-36S	A2
29800	WIIT	60468	3861	9W-37S	A2
SR-50 N Harlem Av					
100	PTON	60468	3861	9W-37S	A3
200	WIIT	60468	3861	9W-37S	A3
300	PtnT	60468	3861	9W-37S	A2
SR-50 S Harlem Av					
100	PTON	60468	3861	9W-37S	A3
100	WIIT	60468	3861	9W-37S	A3
SR-50 Skokie Blvd					
7400	LNWD	60712	2865	5W-9N	E7
7400	SKOK	60077	2865	6W-9N	E7
7500	SKOK	60076	2865	6W-9N	E7
SR-53					
-	ANHT	-	2753	19W-17N	D5
-	ANHT	-	2806	19W-15N	C2
-	EGvT	-	2860	21W-11N	A3
-	EGvT	-	2914		A1
-	PLTN	-	2753	18W-16N	D7
-	PLTN	-	2806	20W-14N	A3
-	PltT	-	2753	18W-16N	D7
-	PltT	-	2806	20W-13N	A6
-	RGMW	-	2806	19W-15N	B2
-	RGMW	-	2860	20W-12N	A1
-	SMBG	-	2806	20W-13N	A6
-	SMBG	-	2860	20W-9N	A7
10	BmdT	60143	2914		A7
10	ITSC	60143	2914		A7
800	EGVV	60007	2914		A7
1000	ITSC	60007	2914		A3
1100	AddT	60143	2914		A4
2300	ElaT	60047	2753	20W-20N	A2
2300	LGGV	60047	2753	20W-20N	A2
2300	PLTN	60047	2753	20W-20N	A2
SR-53 EXT					
-	ANHT	-	2753	19W-18N	D4
-	ElaT	-	2753	19W-20N	C2
-	PLTN	-	2753	19W-18N	C3
-	PltT	-	2753	19W-18N	D4
SR-53 Biesterfield Rd					
1000	EGVV	60007	2914		A7
SR-53 E Dundee Rd					
-	PltT	60004	2753	19W-18N	D4
900	PLTN	60074	2753	19W-18N	C4
1500	PltT	60074	2753	19W-18N	C4
SR-53 W Dundee Rd					
-	ANHT	60004	2753	19W-18N	D4
-	PltT	60004	2753	19W-18N	D4
-	PltT	60074	2753	19W-18N	D4
SR-53 Hicks Rd					
2700	LGGV	60047	2753	20W-20N	B1
2700	PLTN	60047	2753	20W-20N	A2
2700	PLTN	60074	2753	20W-20N	A2
20700	ElaT	60047	2753	20W-20N	B1
SR-53 N Hicks Rd					
2100	PLTN	60074	2753	20W-20N	B2
2300	ElaT	60047	2753	20W-20N	A2
2300	LGGV	60047	2753	20W-20N	A2
2300	PLTN	60047	2753	20W-20N	A2
SR-53 Rand Rd					
2000	PLTN	60074	2753	20W-18N	A3
SR-53 N Rand Rd					
1600	PLTN	60074	2753	19W-18N	B4
SR-53 Rohlwing Rd					
10	BmdT	60143	2914		A7
800	EGVV	60007	2914		A2
1000	ITSC	60007	2914		A3
1000	ITSC	60143	2914		A3
1100	AddT	60143	2914		A4
SR-53 N Rohlwing Rd					
200	BmdT	60143	2914		A6
200	ITSC	60143	2914		A6
SR-56					
500	BKLY	60162	3028		B6
500	BKLY	60163	3028		B6
500	EMHT	60126	3028		B6
500	EMHT	60162	3028		B6
4000	BLWD	60104	3029	13W-0N	A5

Block	City	ZIP	Map#	CGS	Grid
SR-56					
4000	BLWD	60162	3029	12W-0N	A4
4000	HLSD	60162	3029	13W-0N	A5
4300	BLWD	60104	3028		E5
4300	HLSD	60162	3028		E5
5200	HLSD	60163	3028		C5
SR-56 Butterfield Rd					
4000	BLWD	60104	3029	13W-0N	A5
4000	BLWD	60162	3029	13W-0N	A4
4000	HLSD	60162	3029	13W-0N	A5
4300	BLWD	60104	3028		E5
4300	HLSD	60162	3028		E5
5200	BKLY	60162	3028		C5
5200	BKLY	60163	3028		C5
5200	HLSD	60163	3028		C5
5900	EMHT	60162	3028		C6
6000	EMHT	60126	3028		B6
SR-56 E Butterfield Rd					
500	BKLY	60162	3028		B6
500	BKLY	60163	3028		B6
500	EMHT	60126	3028		B6
500	EMHT	60162	3028		B6
SR-56 Washington Blvd					
4000	BLWD	60104	3029	12W-0N	A4
4000	BLWD	60162	3029	12W-0N	A4
4000	HLSD	60162	3029	13W-0N	A4
SR-58					
-	HFET	60010	2856	29W-11N	E3
-	HFET	60010	2857	27W-12N	C3
-	HFET	60107	2856	29W-11N	D3
-	RGMW	60007	2860	20W-12N	A2
10	ANHT	60005	2861	17W-11N	B2
10	DSPN	60056	2862	15W-11N	A3
10	HFET	60195	2859	23W-12N	A2
10	MPPT	60016	2862	15W-11N	A3
10	MPPT	60056	2862	15W-11N	A3
10	SMBG	60195	2859	23W-12N	A2
100	HFET	60173	2859	23W-12N	B2
100	SMBG	60195	2858	25W-11N	B2
300	DSPN	60016	2861	16W-11N	E3
300	HFET	60195	2858	23W-12N	E2
300	MPPT	60056	2861	16W-11N	D3
500	ANHT	60005	2860	18W-11N	E2
500	DSPN	60016	2862	13W-12N	E2
500	HFET	60120	2856	30W-11N	B3
500	HFET	60192	2856	30W-11N	B3
500	HnrT	60120	2856	30W-11N	B3
500	HnrT	60192	2856	30W-11N	B3
600	ELGN	60120	2855		C3
700	RGMW	60005	2860	18W-11N	E2
700	RGMW	60008	2860	21W-11N	A2
800	ANHT	60056	2861	17W-11N	B2
900	MPPT	60005	2861	17W-11N	B2
1200	HFET	60194	2858	25W-11N	C2
1300	DSPN	60016	2863	11W-11N	D2
1300	HnrT	60120	2855		C3
1400	SMBG	60173	2859	23W-11N	A2
1600	SMBG	60194	2858	25W-12N	B2
1700	GNVW	60025	2864	10W-11N	B2
1700	GNVW	60053	2864	10W-11N	B2
1700	MaiT	60016	2863	11W-11N	D2
1700	MNGV	60053	2864	8W-10N	E4
1800	SMBG	60173	2860	21W-11N	A2
2000	RGMW	60173	2860	20W-12N	A2
2100	EGvT	60007	2860	21W-11N	A2
2100	HFET	60194	2857	27W-11N	C3
2100	SMBG	60194	2857	27W-11N	C3
2400	MaiT	60025	2864	9W-12N	C2
2500	MaiT	60714	2864	9W-12N	B2
3100	EGvT	60008	2860	20W-12N	B2
4800	SKOK	60076	2865	5W-11N	E4
4800	SKOK	60077	2865	6W-11N	E4
5600	MNGV	60053	2865	7W-10N	C4
8000	NLES	60025	2864	10W-12N	B2
8000	NLES	60714	2864	10W-12N	B2
8500	MaiT	60016	2864	10W-12N	A2
8700	MaiT	60714	2863	11W-12N	E2
8700	NLES	60714	2863	11W-12N	E2
8800	NLES	60016	2863	11W-12N	E2
SR-58 Dempster St					
4800	SKOK	60076	2865	5W-11N	E4
4800	SKOK	60077	2865	6W-11N	E4
5600	MNGV	60053	2865	7W-10N	B4
6700	MNGV	60053	2864	8W-10N	E4
SR-58 Golf Rd					
-	ELGN	60120	2855		E3
-	HFET	60010	2856	29W-11N	E3
-	HFET	60010	2857	28W-12N	A3
-	HFET	60107	2856	29W-11N	D3
-	HnrT	60120	2855		E3
-	RGMW	60007	2860	20W-12N	A2
-	RGMW	60173	2860	20W-12N	A2
-	SMBG	60173	2860	20W-12N	A2
500	HFET	60120	2856	30W-11N	B3
500	HFET	60192	2856	30W-11N	B3
500	HnrT	60120	2856	30W-11N	B3
500	HnrT	60192	2856	30W-11N	B3
900	ANHT	60005	2860	18W-11N	E2
900	RGMW	60005	2860	18W-11N	E2
900	RGMW	60008	2860	21W-11N	A2
1700	GNVW	60025	2864	10W-11N	B2
1700	GNVW	60053	2864	10W-11N	B2
1700	MNGV	60053	2864	10W-11N	B2
2100	EGvT	60007	2860	21W-11N	A2
2400	MaiT	60025	2864	9W-12N	C2
2500	MaiT	60714	2864	9W-12N	B2
3100	EGvT	60008	2860	20W-12N	B2
9200	MaiT	60016	2863	11W-12N	D2
9200	NLES	60714	2863	11W-12N	D2
9500	DSPN	60016	2863	11W-12N	C2
SR-58 E Golf Rd					
10	ANHT	60005	2861	17W-11N	B2
10	HFET	60195	2859	23W-12N	A2
10	SMBG	60195	2859	23W-12N	A2
100	HFET	60173	2859	23W-12N	B2
500	DSPN	60016	2862	13W-12N	E2
600	MPPT	60056	2861	17W-11N	B2
800	ANHT	60056	2861	17W-11N	B2
900	MPPT	60005	2861	17W-11N	B2
1300	DSPN	60016	2863	11W-11N	D2
1400	SMBG	60173	2859	23W-11N	A2
1700	MaiT	60016	2863	11W-11N	D2
2000	EGvT	60007	2860	20W-11N	A2
2000	RGMW	60008	2860	20W-12N	A2
2000	RGMW	60173	2860	20W-12N	A2
2000	SMBG	60173	2860	20W-12N	A2
SR-58 W Golf Rd					
-	HFET	60010	2857	27W-12N	C3
10	ANHT	60005	2861	18W-11N	A2
10	DSPN	60016	2862	15W-11N	A2
10	DSPN	60056	2862	15W-11N	A3
10	HFET	60195	2859	23W-12N	A2
10	MPPT	60016	2862	15W-11N	A3
10	MPPT	60056	2862	15W-11N	A3
10	SMBG	60173	2859	23W-12N	A2

Block	City	ZIP	Map#	CGS	Grid
SR-58 W Golf Rd					
10	SMBG	60195	2859	23W-12N	A2
100	SMBG	60195	2858	25W-11N	B2
300	DSPN	60016	2861	16W-11N	E3
300	HFET	60195	2858	23W-12N	E2
300	MPPT	60056	2861	16W-11N	D3
500	ANHT	60005	2860	18W-11N	E2
600	HFET	60194	2858	24W-12N	D2
700	RGMW	60005	2860	18W-11N	E2
700	RGMW	60008	2860	18W-11N	E2
1600	SMBG	60194	2858	25W-12N	B2
2000	ANHT	60056	2861	17W-11N	B2
2000	MPPT	60005	2861	17W-11N	B2
2100	HFET	60194	2857	27W-11N	C3
2100	SMBG	60194	2857	27W-11N	C3
8000	MaiT	60025	2864	10W-12N	B2
8000	MaiT	60714	2864	10W-12N	B2
8000	MNGV	60053	2864	9W-12N	B2
8000	NLES	60025	2864	10W-12N	B2
8000	NLES	60714	2864	10W-12N	B2
8500	MaiT	60016	2864	10W-12N	A2
8700	MaiT	60016	2863	10W-12N	E2
8700	MaiT	60714	2863	11W-12N	E2
8700	NLES	60714	2863	11W-12N	E2
8800	NLES	60016	2863	11W-12N	E2
SR-58 Summit St					
600	ELGN	60120	2855		C3
1300	HnrT	60120	2855		C3
SR-58 Waukegan Rd					
8800	MNGV	60053	2864	8W-11N	E3
9500	GNVW	60025	2864	8W-11N	E2
SR-59					
-	BNHL	60010	2803	28W-15N	A1
-	BRLT	60103	2856	29W-9N	C7
-	BRLT	60107	2856	30W-9N	C7
-	BRLT	60120	2910		C6
-	BrnT	60010	2802	28W-13N	E6
-	BrnT	60010	2803	28W-15N	A1
-	BrnT	60192	2802	28W-13N	E6
-	HFET	60010	2802	29W-12N	D7
-	HFET	60010	2856	29W-12N	D1
-	HFET	60120	2856	29W-11N	D3
-	HFET	60192	2802	28W-13N	E6
-	HnrT	60010	2802	29W-12N	D7
-	SBTN	60010	2802	28W-13N	E6
-	SBTN	60118	2802	28W-13N	E6
-	SMWD	60107	2910		C1
-	SMWD	60120	2910		C1
10	BNHL	60010	2750	27W-16N	A7
10	BRLT	60103	2910		C6
10	BRTN	60010	2750	25W-18N	E2
10	HnrT	60107	2856	29W-10N	C6
10	SMWD	60107	2856	30W-10N	C6
10	WynT	60103	2910		C4
100	BrnT	60010	2750	27W-16N	B6
100	HnrT	60120	2856	29W-10N	C6
100	SMWD	60120	2856	29W-10N	C6
200	HFET	60107	2856	29W-11N	D3
700	BNHL	60118	2802	28W-14N	E4
700	BrnT	60118	2802	28W-14N	E4
SR-59 Hawthorne Rd					
10	BNHL	60010	2750	25W-18N	E3
10	BRTN	60010	2750	25W-18N	E3
SR-59 N Hough St					
100	BRTN	60010	2750	25W-20N	E2
SR-59 S Hough St					
100	BRTN	60010	2750	25W-18N	E2
SR-59 New Sutton Rd					
-	BNHL	60010	2803	28W-15N	A1
-	BrnT	60010	2802	28W-13N	E6
-	BrnT	60010	2803	28W-15N	A1
-	BrnT	60192	2802	28W-13N	E6
-	HFET	60010	2802	29W-12N	D7
-	HFET	60192	2802	28W-13N	E6
-	HnrT	60010	2802	29W-12N	D7
-	SBTN	60010	2802	28W-13N	E6
-	SBTN	60118	2802	28W-13N	E6
100	BNHL	60010	2750	27W-16N	A7
100	BrnT	60010	2750	27W-16N	B6
700	BNHL	60118	2802	28W-14N	E4
700	BrnT	60118	2802	28W-14N	E4
SR-59 Sutton Rd					
-	BRLT	60103	2856	29W-9N	C7
-	BRLT	60107	2856	30W-9N	C7
-	BRLT	60120	2910		C6
-	HFET	60010	2856	29W-12N	D1
-	HFET	60120	2856	29W-11N	D3
-	SMWD	60107	2910		C1
-	SMWD	60120	2910		C1
10	BRLT	60103	2910		C6
10	WynT	60103	2910		C4
100	HnrT	60120	2856	29W-10N	C6
100	SMWD	60120	2856	29W-10N	C6
200	HFET	60107	2856	29W-11N	D3
200	HnrT	60107	2856	30W-10N	C6
200	SMWD	60107	2856	30W-10N	C6
SR-59 S Sutton Rd					
10	HnrT	60107	2856	29W-11N	D5
10	SMWD	60107	2856	29W-10N	D5
SR-62					
-	RGMW	60067	2806	20W-12N	A7
10	ANHT	60005	2861	16W-10N	D5
10	BNHL	60010	2750	27W-16N	A7
10	BNHL	60010	2803	27W-15N	C1
10	BrnT	60010	2750	27W-16N	A7
10	BrnT	60010	2803	27W-15N	C1
10	SBTN	60010	2803	27W-15N	C1
100	ALGN	60102	2748		C2
100	ALGN	60110	2748		C2
100	BNHL	60010	2748		A1
100	BNHL	60010	2749	29W-16N	B6
100	BNHL	60102	2748		C2
100	BNHL	60110	2748		C2
200	PLTN	60067	2805	22W-13N	B6
200	PltT	60173	2805	22W-13N	B6
200	SMBG	60173	2805	22W-13N	B6
300	DSPN	60016	2861	16W-10N	E5
300	DSPN	60018	2861	16W-10N	E5
300	MPPT	60056	2861	16W-10N	E5
400	ANHT	60005	2860	18W-11N	E2
400	RGMW	60005	2860	18W-11N	E2
500	EGvT	60005	2861	16W-10N	E5
700	HFET	60067	2804	23W-14N	E4
700	HFET	60195	2804	23W-14N	E4
700	PltT	60195	2804	23W-14N	E4
700	RGMW	60008	2860	18W-11N	E2
800	AlqT	60102	2748		A1
1000	EGvT	60056	2861	16W-10N	D5
1300	HFET	60010	2804	24W-14N	C4
1300	SBTN	60010	2804	23W-14N	E4
1400	PltT	60067	2805	21W-13N	E7
1400	PltT	60195	2805	21W-13N	E7
1500	MPPT	60005	2861	16W-10N	E5
1600	IVNS	60067	2804	23W-14N	E5
1600	IVNS	60067	2805	21W-13N	E7

Block	City	ZIP	Map#	CGS	Grid
SR-62					
1600	IVNS	60195	2804	23W-14N	E5
1600	PltT	60067	2804	23W-14N	E5
1600	SMBG	60067	2805	21W-12N	E7
1700	SMBG	60067	2806	21W-12N	A7
1700	SMBG	60173	2806	21W-12N	A7
2000	RGMW	60008	2806	21W-12N	A7
2000	RGMW	60173	2806	21W-12N	A7
2000	SMBG	60008	2806	21W-12N	A7
SR-62 Algonquin Rd					
-	HFET	60195	2804	23W-14N	E4
-	RGMW	60005	2806	20W-12N	A7
-	SBTN	60010	2804	23W-14N	E4
10	BNHL	60010	2750	27W-16N	A7
10	BNHL	60010	2803	27W-15N	C1
10	BrnT	60010	2750	27W-16N	A7
10	BrnT	60010	2803	27W-15N	C1
10	SBTN	60010	2803	27W-15N	C1
100	ALGN	60102	2748		C2
100	ALGN	60110	2748		C2
100	BNHL	60010	2748		A1
100	BNHL	60010	2749	29W-16N	B6
100	BNHL	60102	2748		C2
100	BNHL	60110	2748		C2
2200	ANHT	60005	2860	19W-12N	D1
2200	RGMW	60005	2860	19W-12N	D1
2200	RGMW	60008	2860	19W-12N	C1
SR-62 E Algonquin Rd					
-	RGMW	60067	2806	20W-12N	A7
10	ANHT	60005	2861	18W-11N	A3
200	PLTN	60067	2805	22W-13N	B6
200	PltT	60173	2805	22W-13N	B6
200	SMBG	60173	2805	22W-13N	B6
800	AlqT	60102	2748		A1
1000	EGvT	60005	2861	16W-10N	D5
1000	EGvT	60056	2861	16W-10N	D5
1500	MPPT	60005	2861	16W-10N	E5
1500	PltT	60067	2805	20W-13N	E7
1600	MPPT	60056	2861	16W-10N	E5
1600	SMBG	60067	2805	21W-12N	E7
1700	SMBG	60067	2806	21W-12N	A7
1700	SMBG	60173	2806	21W-12N	A7
1900	ALGN	60102	2748		B2
2000	RGMW	60008	2806	21W-12N	A7
2000	RGMW	60173	2806	21W-12N	A7
2000	SMBG	60008	2806	21W-12N	A7
2200	ALGN	60110	2748		C2
2200	BNHL	60010	2748		C2
2200	BNHL	60102	2748		C2
2200	BNHL	60110	2748		C2
SR-62 W Algonquin Rd					
10	ANHT	60005	2861	16W-10N	D5
300	DSPN	60016	2861	16W-10N	E5
300	DSPN	60018	2861	16W-10N	E5
400	ANHT	60005	2860	18W-11N	E2
400	RGMW	60005	2860	18W-11N	E2
700	HFET	60067	2804	23W-14N	E4
700	HFET	60195	2804	23W-14N	D4
700	PltT	60195	2804	23W-14N	E4
700	RGMW	60008	2860	18W-11N	E2
1100	PLTN	60067	2805	22W-13N	B6
1100	PltT	60173	2805	22W-13N	B6
1100	SMBG	60173	2805	22W-13N	B6
1300	HFET	60010	2804	24W-14N	C4
1300	SBTN	60010	2804	24W-14N	C4
1400	PltT	60067	2805	21W-13N	E7
1400	PltT	60195	2805	21W-13N	E7
1500	EGvT	60005	2861	16W-10N	D4
1500	EGvT	60056	2861	16W-10N	D4
1500	MPPT	60056	2861	16W-10N	D4
1600	IVNS	60067	2804	23W-14N	E5
1600	IVNS	60067	2805	21W-13N	E7
1600	IVNS	60195	2804	23W-14N	E5
1600	PltT	60067	2804	23W-14N	E5
1700	MPPT	60005	2861	17W-11N	C4
SR-64					
-	CHCG	60614	2978	0W-1N	A7
-	EMHT	60126	3028		B1
-	MLPK	60164	3029	13W-2N	A1
-	NHLK	60164	3029	13W-2N	A1
-	SNPK	60164	3029	13W-2N	A1
10	NHLK	60164	3028		A1
100	CHCG	60610	2978	0W-2N	B7
500	MLPK	60160	3030	10W-2N	A1
500	PvsT	60160	3030	10W-1N	A1
600	MLPK	60160	3029	12W-2N	A1
700	CHCG	60610	2977	1W-1N	E7
700	CHCG	60614	2977	1W-1N	E7
700	CHCG	60622	2977	1W-1N	E7
1900	CHCG	60622	3033	3W-1N	A1
1900	CHCG	60647	3033	3W-1N	A1
2500	MLPK	60165	3029	12W-2N	A1
2500	SNPK	60165	3029	12W-2N	A1
2800	CHCG	60622	3032	3W-1N	E1
2800	CHCG	60647	3032	3W-1N	E1
3100	CHCG	60651	3032	4W-2N	D1
3900	CHCG	60639	3032	5W-2N	B1
4700	CHCG	60639	3031	8W-1N	A1
4700	CHCG	60651	3031	8W-1N	A1
5900	CHCG	60302	3031	7W-2N	B1
5900	OKPK	60302	3031	7W-2N	B1
6300	CHCG	60707	3031	7W-2N	A1
6700	CHCG	60302	3030	10W-1N	A1
6700	CHCG	60707	3030	10W-2N	A1
6700	OKPK	60302	3030	10W-2N	A1
6700	OKPK	60707	3030	8W-2N	E1
7100	EDPK	60707	3030	8W-2N	D1
7100	RVFT	60305	3030	8W-2N	D1
7200	RVFT	60707	3030	9W-2N	D1
7300	EDPK	60305	3030	9W-2N	D1
8300	MLPK	60171	3030	10W-2N	B1
8300	RVFT	60160	3030	10W-1N	B1
8300	RVGV	60171	3030	10W-2N	B1
8300	RVGV	60305	3030	10W-1N	B1
8300	RVGV	60707	3030	10W-1N	B1
10400	SNPK	60160	3029	12W-2N	A1
SR-64 W Eugenie St					
100	CHCG	60614	2978	0W-2N	B7
SR-64 N Lasalle Dr					
1600	CHCG	60610	2978	0W-2N	B7
1600	CHCG	60614	2978	0W-2N	B7
SR-64 W La Salle Dr					
-	CHCG	60614	2978	0W-1N	A7
SR-64 E North Av					
-	MLPK	60160	3029	13W-2N	A1
-	MLPK	60164	3029	13W-2N	A1
-	MLPK	60165	3029	13W-2N	A1
-	NHLK	60164	3029	13W-2N	A1
-	SNPK	60164	3029	13W-2N	A1
-	SNPK	60165	3029	13W-2N	A1
10	NHLK	60164	3028		D1
100	EMHT	60126	3028		A1
SR-64 W North Av					
-	EMHT	60126	3028		B1
10	NHLK	60164	3028		E1

Block	City	ZIP	Map#	CGS	Grid
SR-64 W North Av					
100	CHCG	60610	2978	0W-2N	B7
100	CHCG	60614	2978	0W-2N	B7
500	MLPK	60160	3030	10W-2N	A1
500	PvsT	60160	3030	10W-1N	A1
600	MLPK	60160	3029	12W-2N	A1
700	CHCG	60610	2977	1W-1N	E7
700	CHCG	60614	2977	1W-1N	E7
700	CHCG	60622	2977	1W-1N	E7
1900	CHCG	60622	3033	3W-1N	A1
1900	CHCG	60647	3033	3W-1N	A1
2500	MLPK	60165	3029	12W-2N	A1
2500	SNPK	60165	3029	12W-2N	A1
2800	CHCG	60622	3032	3W-1N	E1
2800	CHCG	60647	3032	3W-1N	E1
3100	CHCG	60651	3032	4W-2N	D1
3900	CHCG	60639	3032	5W-2N	B1
4700	CHCG	60639	3031	8W-1N	A1
4700	CHCG	60651	3031	8W-1N	A1
5900	CHCG	60302	3031	7W-2N	B1
5900	OKPK	60302	3031	7W-2N	B1
6300	CHCG	60707	3031	7W-2N	A1
6700	CHCG	60302	3030	10W-2N	A1
6700	CHCG	60707	3030	10W-2N	A1
6700	OKPK	60302	3030	10W-2N	A1
6700	OKPK	60707	3030	8W-2N	E1
7100	EDPK	60707	3030	8W-2N	D1
7100	RVFT	60305	3030	8W-2N	D1
7200	RVFT	60707	3030	9W-2N	D1
7300	EDPK	60305	3030	9W-2N	D1
8300	MLPK	60171	3030	10W-2N	B1
8300	RVFT	60160	3030	10W-1N	B1
8300	RVGV	60171	3030	10W-2N	B1
8300	RVGV	60305	3030	10W-1N	B1
8300	RVGV	60707	3030	10W-1N	B1
10400	SNPK	60160	3029	12W-2N	A1
SR-68					
-	BNHL	60010	2801		E1
-	BNHL	60110	2801		E1
-	BNHL	60118	2801		E1
-	CPVL	60110	2801		D1
-	EDND	60110	2801		D1
-	GLNC	60062	2758	8W-17N	A4
-	NtrT	60062	2758	8W-17N	A4
-	PltT	60004	2753	19W-18N	D4
-	WhlT	60062	2755	15W-18N	A4
-	WhlT	60062	2756	13W-18N	A4
-	WLNG	60090	2756	13W-18N	A4
10	BFGV	60089	2754	17W-17N	B4
10	BFGV	60090	2754	16W-18N	D4
10	BNHL	60010	2750	27W-16N	A7
10	BRTN	60010	2750	26W-17N	D5
10	BRTN	60010	2751	25W-17N	A5
10	IVNS	60010	2750	26W-17N	D5
10	IVNS	60010	2751	25W-17N	A5
10	PLTN	60067	2752	21W-18N	E4
10	PLTN	60067	2753	20W-17N	A4
10	PltT	60067	2753	20W-17N	A4
10	PltT	60074	2752	21W-18N	E4
10	PltT	60074	2753	20W-17N	A4
10	WLNG	60089	2754	16W-18N	D4
10	WLNG	60090	2754	16W-18N	D4
10	WLNG	60090	2755	15W-18N	A4
100	BNHL	60010	2802	30W-15N	A1
100	BrnT	60010	2750	27W-16N	A7
100	EDND	60118	2801		D1
100	IVNS	60067	2751	23W-17N	D5
100	PLTN	60074	2753	19W-17N	C4
200	BNHL	60010	2749	28W-16N	E7
200	DndT	60118	2801		D1
400	ANHT	60004	2754	17W-17N	B4
400	NHBK	60062	2758	8W-17N	A4
500	CPVL	60118	2801		C2
500	NHBK	60062	2757	8W-17N	E4
500	PLTN	60074	2752	21W-17N	C4
700	ANHT	60004	2753	18W-17N	E4
700	BFGV	60089	2753	18W-17N	E4
700	PltT	60067	2752	21W-17N	C4
1000	ANHT	60089	2754	17W-17N	B4
1000	BFGV	60004	2754	17W-17N	B4
1200	PltT	60010	2752	22W-17N	A4
1500	PLTN	60010	2752	23W-17N	A4
1700	PLTN	60010	2751	24W-17N	C5
1700	PLTN	60067	2751	24W-17N	C5
1700	PltT	60010	2751	24W-17N	C5
1800	PltT	60067	2751	23W-17N	E5
2500	NHBK	60062	2756	10W-18N	E4
4100	NfdT	60062	2756	13W-18N	A4
SR-68 Algonquin Rd					
100	BNHL	60010	2750	27W-16N	A7
100	BrnT	60010	2750	27W-16N	A7
SR-68 Barrington Av					
500	CPVL	60118	2801		C2
500	DndT	60118	2801		B2
500	EDND	60118	2801		B2
SR-68 Dundee Rd					
-	BNHL	60010	2801		E1
-	BNHL	60110	2801		E1
-	BNHL	60118	2801		E1
-	BRTN	60010	2750	25W-17N	E5
-	CPVL	60110	2801		D1
-	EDND	60110	2801		E1
-	EDND	60118	2801		E1
-	GLNC	60062	2758	8W-17N	A4
-	IVNS	60010	2750	25W-17N	E5
-	NtrT	60062	2758	8W-17N	A4
-	PLTN	60067	2751	23W-17N	E5
-	PltT	60067	2751	23W-17N	E5
-	WhlT	60062	2755	13W-18N	E4
-	WhlT	60062	2756	13W-18N	A4
-	WLNG	60090	2755	13W-18N	E4
-	WLNG	60090	2756	13W-18N	A4
10	BNHL	60010	2750	26W-17N	D5
100	BNHL	60010	2802	30W-15N	A1
200	BNHL	60010	2749	28W-16N	E7
400	NHBK	60062	2758	8W-17N	A4
500	NHBK	60062	2757	8W-17N	E4
2000	IVNS	60010	2751	23W-17N	D5
2000	IVNS	60067	2751	23W-17N	D5
2000	PltT	60010	2751	23W-17N	E5
2500	NHBK	60062	2756	10W-18N	E4
4100	NfdT	60062	2756	13W-18N	A4
SR-68 E Dundee Rd					
-	ANHT	60089	2754	17W-17N	B4
-	BFGV	60004	2754	17W-17N	B4
-	PltT	60004	2753	19W-18N	D4
-	WhlT	60062	2755	15W-18N	A4
10	BRTN	60010	2750	26W-17N	D5
10	BRTN	60010	2751	25W-17N	A5
10	IVNS	60010	2750	26W-17N	D5
10	IVNS	60010	2751	25W-17N	A5
10	PLTN	60067	2752	20W-18N	E4
10	PLTN	60067	2753	20W-17N	A4
10	PltT	60067	2753	20W-17N	A4
10	PltT	60074	2752	20W-18N	E4

Block	City	ZIP	Map#	CGS	Grid
SR-68 E Dundee Rd					
10	PltT	60074	2753	20W-17N	A4
10	WLNG	60090	2755	15W-18N	A4
100	IVNS	60067	2751	23W-17N	D5
100	PLTN	60074	2753	19W-17N	C4
300	BFGV	60090	2754	16W-18N	D4
600	ANHT	60004	2754	17W-17N	B4
600	BFGV	60089	2754	17W-17N	B4
SR-68 W Dundee Rd					
-	PltT	60004	2753	19W-18N	D4
-	PltT	60074	2753	19W-18N	D4
10	BFGV	60089	2754	16W-18N	C4
10	BFGV	60090	2754	16W-18N	D4
10	WLNG	60089	2754	16W-18N	D4
10	WLNG	60090	2755	14W-18N	C4
100	PLTN	60067	2752	21W-18N	E4
100	PltT	60074	2752	21W-18N	E4
500	PLTN	60074	2752	21W-17N	C4
700	ANHT	60004	2753	18W-17N	E4
700	BFGV	60089	2753	18W-17N	E4
700	PltT	60067	2752	21W-17N	C4
800	WLNG	60090	2754	15W-18N	E4
1200	ANHT	60004	2754	18W-18N	A4
1200	ANHT	60089	2754	18W-18N	A4
1200	PltT	60010	2752	22W-17N	A4
1500	PLTN	60010	2752	23W-17N	A4
1700	PLTN	60010	2751	24W-17N	C5
1700	PLTN	60067	2751	24W-17N	C5
1700	PltT	60010	2751	24W-17N	C5
1800	PltT	60067	2751	23W-17N	E5
SR-68 New Sutton Rd					
100	BNHL	60010	2750	27W-16N	B6
100	BrnT	60010	2750	27W-16N	B6
SR-68 Penny Av					
100	EDND	60118	2801		D1
200	DndT	60118	2801		D1
SR-72					
-	CHCG	60018	2916		E1
-	EGvT	60007	2860	20W-11N	A4
-	HFET	60118	2801		E4
-	HFET	60192	2802	28W-13N	E6
10	BrnT	60010	2803	27W-13N	A6
10	DSPN	60018	2916		B1
10	EDND	60118	2801		E4
10	EGvT	60007	2861	17W-10N	B5
10	EGvT	60018	2916		B1
10	HFET	60194	2859	21W-11N	E4
10	HFET	60195	2859	23W-11N	A3
10	MaiT	60018	2916		C1
10	SBTN	60010	2803	27W-13N	B7
10	WDND	60118	2801		A2
100	SMBG	60194	2859	23W-11N	A3
100	SMBG	60195	2859	23W-11N	A3
200	BrnT	60010	2802	28W-13N	E6
200	HFET	60010	2802	28W-13N	D6
200	HFET	60118	2802	28W-13N	E6
200	HFET	60194	2858	24W-11N	E2
200	SBTN	60010	2802	28W-13N	E6
200	SMBG	60194	2858	23W-11N	E3
200	SMBG	60195	2858	23W-11N	E3
300	CHCG	60007	2916		A1
400	DndT	60118	2801		E4
400	EGVV	60007	2861	16W-9N	C6
400	SBTN	60118	2802	28W-13N	E6
600	HFET	60195	2858	26W-12N	A1
600	SMBG	60173	2859	22W-11N	C3
700	CHCG	60068	2918	10W-7N	B4
700	CHCG	60631	2918	9W-7N	D5
700	PKRG	60068	2918	10W-7N	B4
1500	CHCG	60018	2917	11W-7N	E4
1500	CHCG	60068	2917	11W-7N	E4
1500	CHCG	60631	2917	11W-7N	E4
1500	PKRG	60068	2917	11W-7N	E4
1700	SMBG	60173	2860	19W-10N	C5
1900	HFET	60194	2857	26W-12N	E1
2200	HFET	60195	2857	27W-12N	D1
2400	EGVV	60007	2915		E1
2500	EGvT	60007	2915		E1
2500	EGvT	60018	2915		E1
2600	HFET	60010	2803	27W-12N	D7
2600	HFET	60010	2857	26W-12N	E1
2600	HFET	60195	2803	27W-12N	D7
2800	EGVV	60007	2916		A1
2800	EGVV	60018	2916		A1
7200	CHCG	60656	2918	9W-7N	D5
7700	PKRG	60631	2918	9W-7N	B4
9300	RSMT	60018	2917	12W-7N	C3
10000	DSPN	60018	2917	12W-8N	B3
10200	CHCG	60666	2917	13W-8N	A2
10200	RSMT	60666	2917	13W-8N	A2
10700	CHCG	60666	2916		E2
10700	RSMT	60018	2916		E2
SR-72 W Higgins Av					
7200	CHCG	60631	2918	9W-7N	D5
7200	CHCG	60656	2918	9W-7N	D5
SR-72 Higgins Rd					
-	DndT	60118	2801		D4
-	EDND	60118	2801		E4
-	EGvT	60007	2860	20W-11N	A4
-	HFET	60118	2801		E4
-	SMBG	60173	2860	20W-11N	A4
700	CHCG	60068	2918	10W-7N	A4
700	CHCG	60631	2918	10W-7N	A4
700	PKRG	60068	2918	10W-7N	A4
1500	CHCG	60018	2917	11W-7N	E4
1500	CHCG	60068	2917	11W-7N	E4
1500	CHCG	60631	2917	11W-7N	E4
1500	PKRG	60068	2917	11W-7N	E4
SR-72 E Higgins Rd					
-	EGvT	60007	2860	20W-10N	B4
10	EGvT	60007	2861	17W-10N	B5
10	HFET	60195	2859	23W-11N	A3
200	HFET	60194	2859	23W-11N	A3
600	SMBG	60173	2859	22W-11N	C3
600	SMBG	60194	2859	22W-11N	C3
1700	SMBG	60173	2860	19W-10N	C5
1900	EGVV	60007	2861	16W-9N	E7
2400	EGVV	60007	2915		E1
2600	EGvT	60007	2915		E1
SR-72 W Higgins Rd					
-	CHCG	60018	2916		E1
-	DSPN	60018	2916		E1
-	EDND	60118	2801		E4
-	HFET	60118	2801		E4
-	HFET	60192	2802	28W-13N	E6
-	PKRG	60068	2917	11W-7N	D4
10	BrnT	60010	2803	27W-13N	A6
10	HFET	60194	2859	21W-11N	E4
10	HFET	60195	2859	23W-11N	A3
10	SBTN	60010	2803	27W-12N	C7
100	SMBG	60194	2859	23W-11N	A3
100	SMBG	60195	2859	23W-11N	A3
200	BrnT	60010	2802	28W-13N	E6
200	HFET	60010	2802	28W-13N	D6
200	HFET	60118	2802	28W-13N	E6

STREET Block	City	ZIP	Map#	CGS	Grid
SR-72 W Higgins Rd					
200	HFET	60194	2858	24W-11N	E2
200	SBTN	60010	2802	28W-13N	E6
200	SMBG	60194	2858	23W-11N	E3
200	SMBG	60195	2858	23W-11N	E3
400	SBTN	60118	2802	28W-13N	E6
600	HFET	60195	2858	26W-12N	A1
1900	HFET	60194	2857	26W-12N	E1
2200	HFET	60195	2857	27W-12N	D1
2600	HFET	60010	2857	26W-12N	E1
2600	HFET	60195	2803	27W-12N	D7
2900	HFET	60010	2803	27W-12N	D7
7700	PKRG	60631	2918	9W-7N	B4
8300	CHCG	60631	2918	10W-7N	B4
8300	PKRG	60068	2918	10W-7N	B4
8400	CHCG	60068	2918	10W-7N	B4
8400	CHCG	60631	2917	10W-7N	E4
9300	CHCG	60018	2917	11W-7N	D4
9300	CHCG	60068	2917	11W-7N	D4
9300	RSMT	60018	2917	12W-7N	C3
10000	DSPN	60018	2917	12W-8N	B3
10200	CHCG	60666	2917	13W-8N	A2
10200	RSMT	60666	2917	13W-8N	A2
10700	CHCG	60666	2916		E2
10700	RSMT	60018	2916		E2
SR-72 E Main St					
10	EDND	60118	2801		E4
400	DndT	60118	2801		E4
SR-72 W Main St					
10	EDND	60118	2801		A2
10	WDND	60118	2801		A2
SR-72 Oakton St					
1500	EGVV	60007	2861	16W-9N	C6
1800	EGvT	60007	2861	16W-9N	C6
SR-72 N Oriole Av					
-	CHCG	60631	2918	9W-7N	C4
SR-72 Touhy Av					
2500	EGvT	60007	2915		E1
2500	EGvT	60018	2915		E1
2500	EGVV	60007	2915		E1
SR-72 E Touhy Av					
200	CHCG	60018	2916		C1
200	DSPN	60018	2916		B1
200	MaiT	60018	2916		C1
SR-72 W Touhy Av					
10	DSPN	60018	2916		B1
10	EGvT	60018	2916		B1
10	MaiT	60018	2916		C1
300	CHCG	60007	2916		A1
300	CHCG	60018	2916		A1
2800	EGvT	60007	2915		E1
2800	EGvT	60018	2915		E1
2800	EGVV	60007	2915		E1
2800	EGVV	60007	2916		A1
2800	EGVV	60018	2916		A1
SR-83					
-	CTWD	60803	3348	5W-15S	A1
-	DGvT	60439	3271		E1
-	DGvT	60527	3271		E1
-	DLTN	60409	3351	1E-17S	C5
-	LmnT	60439	3271		E1
-	PlsT	60464	3272	14W-12S	D3
-	PlsT	60480	3273	13W-13S	A3
10	BFGV	60089	2754	16W-20N	C1
10	DLTN	60419	3350	0E-17S	E5
10	HRVY	60426	3349	2W-17S	E5
10	MPPT	60056	2808	15W-14N	A3
10	MPPT	60070	2808	15W-14N	A3
10	PTHT	60056	2808	15W-15N	A3
10	PTHT	60070	2808	15W-13N	A7
10	SHLD	60419	3350	0W-17S	D5
10	SHLD	60473	3350	0E-17S	E5
10	WLNG	60090	2755	15W-17N	A4
100	DLTN	60473	3350	0E-17S	D5
100	DXMR	60426	3349	2W-17S	D5
100	HRVY	60426	3350	1W-17S	A5
200	EGVV	60007	2861	17W-9N	C7
200	MPPT	60056	2862	15W-12N	A1
400	BNVL	60106	2915		C6
400	CTCY	60409	3351	2E-18S	E7
400	HRVY	60419	3350	0W-17S	B5
400	MPPT	60056	2861	16W-9N	E6
500	DLTN	60426	3350	0W-17S	B5
500	WLNG	60090	2754	15W-18N	E3
600	DSPN	60016	2861	16W-11N	E3
600	EGvT	60007	2861	16W-9N	C6
700	DLTN	60419	3351	0E-17S	A5
700	DLTN	60473	3351	1E-17S	A5
800	DSPN	60056	2861	16W-10N	E4
800	SHLD	60473	3351	1E-17S	A5
900	CTCY	60409	3429	2E-21S	E7
900	DSPN	60018	2861	16W-9N	E6
900	EGvT	60005	2861	16W-9N	E6
900	EGvT	60056	2861	16W-9N	E6
900	EGVV	60007	2915		C1
900	MPPT	60018	2861	16W-9N	E6
900	PTHT	60070	2755	15W-16N	A7
900	PTHT	60090	2755	15W-17N	A6
900	WLNG	60089	2754	16W-18N	D2
1000	EGVV	60106	2915		C6
1400	LNSG	60438	3429	2E-19S	E3
1900	EGVV	60005	2861	16W-9N	D6
2200	POSN	60469	3349	3W-17S	A5
2300	MPPT	60005	2861	16W-9N	D6
2400	BlmT	60411	3510	4E-25S	B6
2400	LYWD	60411	3509	2E-23S	E3
2400	LYWD	60411	3510	4E-25S	B6
3100	MDLN	60445	3348	3W-17S	E5
3100	POSN	60469	3348	5W-17S	B5
4800	ALSP	60803	3276	5W-14S	A7
5100	ALSP	60803	3275	8W-14S	A5
5200	CTWD	60445	3275	6W-14S	E7
5200	CTWD	60803	3275	6W-14S	E7
5500	WthT	60463	3275	6W-14S	D6
5500	WthT	60803	3275	8W-14S	A5
6300	PSHT	60463	3275	8W-14S	B5
7000	PSHT	60463	3274	9W-14S	D5
7900	PSHT	60464	3274	9W-13S	C5
7900	PSPK	60463	3274	9W-13S	C5
7900	PSPK	60464	3274	9W-13S	C5
8500	PlsT	60464	3274	11W-13S	A4
8600	PlsT	60464	3273	11W-13S	E4
10800	LMNT	60439	3272	14W-13S	C3
10800	LmnT	60480	3272	16W-12S	A3
12200	LMNT	60464	3272	15W-12S	B3
13100	ALSP	60803	3348	5W-15S	A1
13100	CTWD	60445	3348	5W-15S	A1
13900	BmnT	60445	3348	5W-16S	A3
18500	BlmT	60438	3429	2E-22S	E7
19000	BlmT	60411	3509	2E-23S	E3
19000	BlmT	60438	3509	2E-22S	E1
19000	LNSG	60411	3509	2E-22S	E1
19000	LNSG	60438	3509	2E-22S	E1
SR-83 111th St					
-	PlsT	60464	3272	14W-12S	D3

STREET Block	City	ZIP	Map#	CGS	Grid
SR-83 111th St					
-	PlsT	60464	3273	13W-13S	A3
-	PlsT	60480	3273	13W-13S	A3
12200	LMNT	60439	3272	14W-13S	C3
12200	LmnT	60464	3272	15W-12S	B3
SR-83 119th St					
7500	PSHT	60463	3274	9W-14S	D5
7900	PSHT	60464	3274	9W-13S	C5
7900	PSPK	60463	3274	9W-13S	C5
7900	PSPK	60464	3274	9W-13S	C5
SR-83 W 127th St					
4800	ALSP	60803	3276	5W-14S	A7
5100	ALSP	60803	3275	6W-14S	E7
5200	CTWD	60445	3275	6W-14S	E7
5200	CTWD	60803	3275	6W-14S	E7
SR-83 147th St					
3200	MDLN	60445	3348	4W-17S	E5
3200	POSN	60469	3348	3W-17S	E5
SR-83 W 147th St					
2300	DXMR	60426	3349	2W-17S	C5
2300	HRVY	60426	3349	2W-17S	C5
2300	POSN	60469	3349	3W-17S	A5
3100	MDLN	60445	3348	3W-17S	E5
3100	POSN	60469	3348	5W-17S	B5
SR-83 S Archer Av					
10800	LmnT	60439	3272	16W-12S	A2
10800	LmnT	60480	3272	16W-12S	A3
SR-83 Busse Rd					
200	EGVV	60007	2861	17W-9N	C7
600	EGvT	60007	2861	16W-9N	C7
900	EGVV	60007	2915		C1
1000	BNVL	60106	2915		C4
1000	EGVV	60106	2915		C4
SR-83 W Cal Sag Rd					
-	PlsT	60480	3273	12W-13S	B3
-	PSHT	60463	3275	7W-14S	B5
5400	ALSP	60803	3275	8W-14S	A5
5400	CTWD	60445	3275	6W-14S	E7
5500	WthT	60463	3275	6W-14S	D6
5500	WthT	60803	3275	8W-14S	A5
8000	PSHT	60463	3274	10W-13S	C5
8000	PSPK	60464	3274	10W-13S	C5
8500	PlsT	60464	3274	11W-13S	A4
8600	PlsT	60464	3273	11W-13S	E4
SR-83 Cicero Av					
-	ALSP	60803	3348	5W-15S	A1
-	CTWD	60803	3348	5W-15S	A1
13100	CTWD	60445	3348	6W-15S	A1
13900	BmnT	60445	3348	5W-16S	A3
14300	MDLN	60445	3348	5W-17S	A4
SR-83 S Cicero Av					
-	CTWD	60445	3348	5W-15S	A1
-	CTWD	60803	3348	5W-15S	A1
12700	ALSP	60803	3276	6W-15S	A7
13100	ALSP	60803	3348	5W-15S	A1
SR-83 W College Dr					
6300	PSHT	60463	3275	8W-14S	B5
6300	WthT	60463	3275	8W-14S	B5
7000	PSHT	60463	3274	8W-14S	E5
SR-83 Elmhurst Rd					
600	DSPN	60016	2861	16W-11N	E3
900	DSPN	60056	2861	16W-10N	E4
900	MPPT	60056	2861	16W-10N	E4
SR-83 N Elmhurst Rd					
10	MPPT	60070	2808	15W-14N	A3
10	PTHT	60056	2808	15W-15N	A3
10	PTHT	60070	2808	15W-13N	A7
900	MPPT	60056	2808	15W-14N	A5
900	PTHT	60070	2755	15W-16N	A7
900	WLNG	60090	2755	15W-16N	A7
1000	PTHT	60090	2755	15W-16N	A7
SR-83 S Elmhurst Rd					
10	MPPT	60056	2808	15W-14N	A3
10	MPPT	60070	2808	15W-14N	A3
10	PTHT	60056	2808	15W-14N	A3
10	PTHT	60070	2808	15W-14N	A3
10	WLNG	60090	2755	15W-18N	A4
400	MPPT	60056	2861	16W-9N	E6
800	DSPN	60056	2861	16W-10N	E4
900	DSPN	60016	2861	16W-11N	E3
900	PTHT	60090	2755	15W-17N	A6
1400	DSPN	60018	2861	16W-10N	E6
1400	MPPT	60018	2861	16W-10N	E6
SR-83 Glenwood Dyer Rd					
2400	BlmT	60411	3510	4E-25S	B6
2400	LYWD	60411	3509	3E-24S	E5
2400	LYWD	60411	3510	4E-25S	B6
SR-83 Kingery Hwy					
-	DGvT	60439	3271		E1
-	DGvT	60527	3271		E1
-	EGVV	60106	2915		C6
-	LmnT	60439	3271		E1
-	LmnT	60439	3272	16W-12S	A2
400	BNVL	60106	2915		C6
SR-83 W Lincoln St					
-	MPPT	60056	2861	15W-12N	E1
-	MPPT	60056	2862	15W-12N	A1
SR-83 N Main St					
10	MPPT	60056	2808	15W-13N	A7
SR-83 S Main St					
10	MPPT	60056	2808	15W-12N	A7
200	MPPT	60056	2862	15W-12N	A1
SR-83 McHenry Rd					
10	BFGV	60089	2754	16W-20N	C1
400	WLNG	60090	2755	15W-17N	A4
500	WLNG	60090	2754	15W-18N	E3
900	WLNG	60089	2754	16W-18N	D2
SR-83 Oakton St					
1800	EGvT	60007	2861	16W-9N	C6
1800	EGVV	60007	2861	16W-9N	C6
1900	EGvT	60005	2861	16W-9N	D6
1900	EGVV	60005	2861	16W-9N	D6
SR-83 E Oakton St					
2200	EGvT	60005	2861	16W-9N	D6
2200	EGvT	60007	2861	16W-9N	D6
2200	EGVV	60005	2861	16W-9N	D6
2200	EGVV	60007	2861	16W-9N	D6
2300	MPPT	60005	2861	16W-9N	D6
2400	EGvT	60056	2861	16W-9N	E6
2500	MPPT	60056	2861	16W-9N	E6
2600	DSPN	60018	2861	16W-9N	E6
2600	DSPN	60056	2861	16W-9N	E6
SR-83 W Oakton St					
900	DSPN	60018	2861	16W-9N	E6
900	DSPN	60056	2861	16W-9N	E6
900	EGvT	60005	2861	16W-9N	E6
900	EGvT	60056	2861	16W-9N	E6
900	MPPT	60018	2861	16W-9N	E6
900	MPPT	60056	2861	16W-9N	E6
SR-83 Sibley Blvd					
-	DLTN	60409	3351	1E-17S	C5
-	DLTN	60419	3351	1E-17S	C5
1400	CTCY	60409	3351	2E-18S	E7
SR-83 E Sibley Blvd					
-	DLTN	60409	3351	1E-17S	C5

STREET Block	City	ZIP	Map#	CGS	Grid
SR-83 E Sibley Blvd					
10	DLTN	60419	3350	0E-17S	D5
10	HRVY	60426	3349	1W-17S	E5
10	SHLD	60419	3350	0E-17S	D5
10	SHLD	60473	3350	0E-17S	D5
100	DLTN	60473	3350	0E-17S	D5
100	HRVY	60426	3350	1W-17S	A5
400	HRVY	60419	3350	0W-17S	B5
500	DLTN	60426	3350	0W-17S	B5
700	DLTN	60419	3351	0E-17S	A5
700	DLTN	60473	3351	1E-17S	A5
800	SHLD	60473	3351	1E-17S	A5
SR-83 W Sibley Blvd					
10	DLTN	60419	3350	0E-17S	E5
10	HRVY	60426	3349	2W-17S	E5
10	SHLD	60419	3350	0W-17S	D5
10	SHLD	60473	3350	0E-17S	E5
100	DXMR	60426	3349	2W-17S	D5
200	HRVY	60426	3350	0W-17S	C5
2200	POSN	60469	3349	2W-17S	C5
SR-83 Torrence Av					
400	CTCY	60409	3351	3E-17S	E5
900	CTCY	60409	3429	2E-21S	E7
1400	LNSG	60438	3429	2E-19S	E3
18500	BlmT	60438	3429	2E-22S	E7
19000	BlmT	60411	3509	2E-23S	E3
19000	BlmT	60438	3509	2E-22S	E1
19000	LNSG	60411	3509	2E-22S	E1
19000	LNSG	60438	3509	2E-22S	E1
19300	LYWD	60411	3509	2E-23S	E3
SR-171					
-	JSTC	60458	3209	11W-9S	D3
-	JSTC	60480	3209	11W-9S	E2
-	LmnT	60480	3208		C7
-	LYNS	60534	3148	10W-4S	A1
-	MCCK	60525	3148	10W-5S	A2
-	MYWD	60153	3088	10W-3S	B5
-	PKRG	60068	2918	10W-6N	A5
-	PlsT	60480	3208		D6
-	PvsT	60130	3088	10W-3S	B5
-	SMMT	60525	3148	10W-5S	B2
-	WLSP	60480	3209	11W-9S	E2
10	MYWD	60153	3030	10W-0N	A4
100	RVFT	60305	3030	10W-0N	A4
700	MLPK	60153	3030	10W-1N	A2
700	MLPK	60160	3030	10W-1N	A1
1600	MLPK	60160	2974	10W-2N	A7
1600	MLPK	60171	3030	10W-2N	A1
1600	PvsT	60160	3030	10W-1N	A1
1600	RVGV	60171	2974	10W-2N	A7
1600	RVGV	60171	3030	10W-2N	A1
1700	FTPK	60130	3030	10W-0S	A6
1700	FTPK	60153	3030	10W-0S	A6
2100	PvsT	60130	3030	10W-1S	A7
2200	NRIV	60546	3088	10W-2S	A2
2200	PvsT	60141	3088	10W-3S	B5
2500	BKFD	60546	3088	10W-2S	A3
3000	RVGV	60634	2974	10W-3N	A4
3500	RVSD	60546	3088	10W-3S	B5
3700	CHCG	60634	2974	10W-2N	A6
3900	BKFD	60513	3088	10W-3S	B6
3900	LYNS	60534	3088	10W-4S	A7
3900	RVSD	60513	3088	10W-3S	B6
4200	CHCG	60656	2974	10W-2N	A6
4200	NRDG	60634	2974	10W-2N	A6
4200	NRDG	60706	2974	10W-2N	A6
4600	CHCG	60656	2918	10W-5N	A7
4600	NRDG	60706	2918	10W-5N	A7
4900	CHCG	60706	2918	10W-5N	A7
5200	NRDG	60656	2918	10W-6N	A6
5500	CHCG	60631	2918	10W-6N	A5
5500	SMMT	60501	3148	9W-6S	C5
6300	BDPK	60501	3148	9W-7S	C5
6600	BDPK	60455	3148	9W-7S	C6
6700	BGVW	60455	3148	9W-7S	C6
7000	BGVW	60458	3148	10W-7S	B7
7000	BGVW	60501	3148	10W-7S	B7
7000	JSTC	60458	3148	10W-7S	B7
7000	JSTC	60501	3148	10W-7S	B7
7300	JSTC	60458	3210	10W-8S	A1
9000	PlsT	60480	3209	13W-10S	A5
10800	LMNT	60439	3272	16W-13S	A4
10800	LmnT	60480	3272	15W-11S	B1
11300	LMNT	60439	3271		B7
12700	LMNT	60439	3343	18W-15S	A1
12900	LMNT	60439	3342	18W-15S	E1
13400	HMGN	60441	3342	19W-15S	D2
13500	HmrT	60441	3342	20W-17S	A5
14400	LktT	60441	3342	20W-17S	A5
14500	LKPT	60441	3342	21W-17S	A5
SR-171 1st Av					
-	FTPK	60130	3030	10W-0S	A7
-	MYWD	60153	3088	10W-3S	B5
-	NRIV	60546	3088	10W-1S	A2
-	PvsT	60130	3088	10W-3S	B5
-	PvsT	60141	3088	10W-3S	B5
1900	MLPK	60160	3030	10W-2N	A1
1900	MLPK	60171	3030	10W-2N	A1
1900	PvsT	60160	3030	10W-1N	A1
1900	RVGV	60171	3030	10W-2N	A1
2100	MYWD	60153	3030	10W-1S	A7
2100	PvsT	60130	3030	10W-1S	A7
3900	BKFD	60513	3088	10W-3S	B6
3900	LYNS	60534	3088	10W-4S	A6
3900	RVSD	60513	3088	10W-3S	B6
3900	RVSD	60546	3088	10W-3S	B6
SR-171 N 1st Av					
10	MYWD	60153	3030	10W-0N	A4
700	MLPK	60153	3030	10W-1N	A2
700	MLPK	60160	3030	10W-1N	A1
700	RVFT	60305	3030	10W-1N	A3
1600	MLPK	60160	2974	10W-2N	A7
1600	MLPK	60171	3030	10W-2N	A1
1600	PvsT	60160	3030	10W-1N	A1
1600	RVGV	60171	2974	10W-2N	A7
1600	RVGV	60171	3030	10W-2N	A1
SR-171 S 1st Av					
-	BKFD	60513	3088	10W-3S	B6
-	LYNS	60534	3088	10W-3S	B6
-	PvsT	60130	3030	10W-0S	A7
-	RVSD	60513	3088	10W-3S	B6
100	MYWD	60153	3030	10W-0N	A4
100	RVFT	60305	3030	10W-0N	A4
1700	FTPK	60130	3030	10W-0S	A6
1700	FTPK	60153	3030	10W-0S	A6
2200	NRIV	60546	3088	10W-2S	A2
2200	PvsT	60141	3088	10W-1S	A2
2500	BKFD	60546	3088	10W-2S	A3
3500	RVSD	60546	3088	10W-3S	B5
SR-171 Archer Av					
-	JSTC	60458	3209	11W-9S	E2
-	JSTC	60480	3209	11W-9S	E2
-	LmnT	60439	3272	15W-11S	B1
-	LmnT	60480	3208		C7
-	LmnT	60480	3272	15W-11S	B1

STREET Block	City	ZIP	Map#	CGS	Grid
SR-171 Archer Av					
-	PlsT	60480	3208		D6
-	WLSP	60480	3209	11W-9S	E2
9000	PlsT	60480	3209	13W-10S	A5
13900	HmrT	60441	3342	20W-17S	A5
14400	LktT	60441	3342	20W-17S	A5
14500	LKPT	60441	3342	21W-17S	A5
SR-171 S Archer Av					
-	JSTC	60458	3209	11W-9S	D3
-	JSTC	60458	3210	11W-8S	A2
-	JSTC	60480	3209	11W-9S	E2
-	WLSP	60480	3209	11W-9S	E2
10800	LMNT	60439	3272	16W-13S	A4
10800	LmnT	60480	3272	16W-12S	A3
11300	LMNT	60439	3271		B7
12700	LMNT	60439	3343	18W-15S	A1
12900	LMNT	60439	3342	18W-15S	E1
13400	HMGN	60441	3342	19W-15S	D2
13500	HmrT	60441	3342	19W-16S	D3
SR-171 S Archer Rd					
5500	SMMT	60501	3148	9W-6S	C5
6300	BDPK	60501	3148	9W-7S	C5
6600	BDPK	60455	3148	9W-7S	C6
6700	BGVW	60455	3148	9W-7S	C6
7000	BGVW	60458	3148	10W-7S	B7
7000	BGVW	60501	3148	10W-7S	B7
7000	JSTC	60458	3148	10W-7S	B7
7000	JSTC	60501	3148	10W-7S	B7
7300	JSTC	60458	3210	10W-8S	A1
SR-171 N Cumberland Av					
-	PKRG	60068	2918	10W-6N	A5
3200	RVGV	60171	2974	10W-4N	A4
3200	RVGV	60634	2974	10W-4N	A4
3700	CHCG	60634	2974	10W-2N	A6
4200	CHCG	60656	2974	10W-2N	A6
4200	NRDG	60634	2974	10W-2N	A6
4200	NRDG	60706	2974	10W-2N	A6
4600	CHCG	60656	2918	10W-5N	A7
4600	NRDG	60706	2918	10W-5N	A7
4900	CHCG	60706	2918	10W-5N	A7
5200	NRDG	60656	2918	10W-6N	A6
5500	CHCG	60631	2918	10W-6N	A5
SR-171 Forbes Rd					
-	NRIV	60546	3088	10W-3S	B4
-	RVSD	60546	3088	10W-3S	B4
SR-171 RJ Bragassi Mem Blvd					
-	SMMT	60501	3148	9W-6S	D3
SR-171 N Thatcher Av					
2500	RVGV	60171	2974	10W-3N	A5
3000	CHCG	60634	2974	10W-3N	A4
3000	RVGV	60634	2974	10W-3N	A4
SR-312					
10	BNHM	60633	3352		C4
800	HMND	46327	3352		E4
SR-312 E Chicago St					
800	HMND	46327	3352		E4
SR-312 Gostlin St					
10	BNHM	60633	3352		C4
10	HMND	46327	3352		C4
SR-394					
-	BlmT	-	3429	1E-21S	B7
-	BlmT	-	3509	1E-22S	B1
-	BlmT	-	3597	1E-26S	C2
-	CRTE	60417	3597	1E-28S	C6
-	CRTE	60417	3686	1E-30S	C2
-	CteT	60401	3774	0W-33S	C2
-	CteT	60417	3597	1E-28S	C6
-	CteT	60417	3685	0W-32S	D7
-	CteT	60417	3686	1E-31S	B5
-	CteT	60417	3774	0W-32S	C1
-	FDHT	-	3509	1E-24S	C6
-	GNWD	-	3509	1E-23S	B3
-	LYWD	-	3509	1E-23S	B4
-	SHLD	-	3429	1E-21S	B7
-	SLVL	60411	3597	1E-26S	C2
-	STGR	60411	3597	1E-27S	C4
-	STGR	60475	3597	1E-27S	C4
-	ThtT	-	3429	1E-20S	B4
SR-394 Bishop Ford Mem Expwy					
-	BlmT	-	3429	1E-21S	B7
-	BlmT	-	3509	1E-24S	B5
-	BlmT	-	3597	1E-26S	C2
-	FDHT	-	3509	1E-24S	C6
-	GNWD	-	3509	1E-23S	B3
-	LYWD	-	3509	1E-23S	B4
-	SHLD	-	3429	1E-21S	B7
-	SLVL	60411	3597	1E-26S	C2
-	ThtT	-	3429	1E-20S	B5
SR-394 Calumet Expwy					
-	CRTE	60417	3597	1E-28S	C6
-	CRTE	60417	3686	1E-30S	C2
-	CteT	60401	3774	0W-33S	C2
-	CteT	60417	3597	1E-28S	C6
-	CteT	60417	3685	0W-32S	D7
-	CteT	60417	3686	1E-31S	B5
-	CteT	60417	3774	0W-32S	C1
-	SLVL	60411	3597	1E-28S	C6
-	STGR	60411	3597	1E-28S	C6
-	STGR	60475	3597	1E-27S	C4
SR-394 Kingery Expwy					
-	SHLD	-	3429	1E-20S	B3
SR-912					
-	HMND	-	3280		E7
SR-912 Cline Av					
-	HMND	-	3280		E7
US-6					
-	HMND	-	3430		D5
-	LNSG	-	3429	3E-20S	E4
-	LNSG	-	3430	3E-20S	A4
-	MNSR	-	3430		D5
-	NlxT	60448	3422	15W-21S	C7
10	HRVY	60426	3427	1W-18S	E1
10	SHLD	60473	3428	0E-19S	E1
100	HRVY	60426	3428	1W-18S	A1
200	MKHM	60426	3427	2W-19S	C1
200	ThtT	60426	3427	2W-18S	C1
300	HRVY	60473	3428	0W-18S	B1
300	SHLD	60426	3428	0W-18S	B1
700	SHLD	60473	3429	0E-19S	A1
1100	CTCY	60409	3429	2E-19S	D1
2300	BmnT	60426	3427	2W-19S	C1
3300	MKHM	60426	3426	4W-19S	E1
3800	BmnT	60426	3426	4W-19S	E1
4700	OKFT	60452	3426	5W-18S	B1
5100	OKFT	60452	3425	7W-19S	C1
5400	BmnT	60477	3425	6W-18S	D1
5400	OKFT	60477	3425	6W-18S	D1
6400	TYPK	60452	3425	8W-18S	B1
6500	BmnT	60452	3425	8W-18S	B1
6700	TYPK	60477	3425	8W-18S	A1
6900	ODPK	60477	3425	8W-18S	A1
7000	ODPK	60462	3425	8W-18S	A1
7100	ODPK	60462	3424	11W-18S	A1
7100	TYPK	60477	3424	11W-18S	A1
7200	ODPK	60477	3424	9W-18S	E1

STREET Block	City	ZIP	Map#	CGS	Grid
US-6					
7400	TYPK	60462	3424	9W-18S	E1
8700	ODHL	60462	3424	10W-18S	A1
8700	ODHL	60477	3424	10W-18S	A1
9100	ODHL	60477	3423	11W-18S	E1
9100	ODPK	60462	3423	11W-18S	E1
9100	ODPK	60477	3423	11W-18S	E1
9300	ODPK	60467	3423	11W-18S	E1
9900	OrlT	60467	3423	12W-18S	C1
10800	ODPK	60467	3422	13W-19S	E1
10800	OrlT	60467	3422	13W-19S	E1
16800	OrlT	60448	3422	13W-20S	E4
17200	ODPK	60448	3422	13W-20S	E5
17900	HMGN	60448	3422	14W-21S	C7
US-6 159th St					
-	SHLD	60473	3429	1E-19S	C1
1400	CTCY	60409	3429	2E-19S	E1
4700	BmnT	60426	3426	5W-18S	B1
4700	OKFT	60452	3426	5W-18S	B1
5100	OKFT	60452	3425	7W-19S	C1
5400	BmnT	60477	3425	6W-18S	D1
5400	OKFT	60477	3425	6W-18S	D1
6400	TYPK	60452	3425	8W-18S	B1
6500	BmnT	60452	3425	8W-18S	B1
6700	TYPK	60477	3425	8W-18S	A1
6900	ODPK	60477	3425	8W-18S	A1
US-6 E 159th St					
10	HRVY	60426	3427	1W-18S	E1
100	HRVY	60426	3428	1W-18S	A1
300	HRVY	60473	3428	0W-18S	B1
300	SHLD	60426	3428	0W-18S	B1
300	SHLD	60473	3428	0W-18S	B1
US-6 W 159th St					
-	OKFT	60452	3426	5W-18S	B1
10	HRVY	60426	3427	2W-18S	E1
200	MKHM	60426	3427	2W-19S	C1
200	ThtT	60426	3427	2W-18S	C1
2300	BmnT	60426	3427	2W-19S	C1
3300	MKHM	60426	3426	4W-19S	E1
3800	BmnT	60426	3426	4W-19S	E1
7000	ODPK	60462	3425	8W-18S	A1
7000	ODPK	60477	3425	8W-18S	A1
7000	TYPK	60477	3425	8W-18S	A1
7100	ODPK	60462	3424	11W-18S	A1
7100	TYPK	60477	3424	11W-18S	A1
7200	ODPK	60477	3424	9W-18S	E1
7400	TYPK	60462	3424	9W-18S	E1
8700	ODHL	60462	3424	10W-18S	A1
8700	ODHL	60477	3424	10W-18S	A1
9100	ODHL	60477	3423	11W-18S	E1
9100	ODPK	60462	3423	11W-18S	E1
9100	ODPK	60477	3423	11W-18S	E1
9300	ODPK	60467	3423	11W-18S	E1
9900	OrlT	60467	3423	12W-18S	C1
10800	ODPK	60467	3422	13W-18S	E1
10800	OrlT	60467	3422	13W-18S	E1
US-6 E 162nd St					
10	SHLD	60473	3428	0E-19S	D1
700	SHLD	60473	3429	0E-19S	A1
US-6 W 162nd St					
10	SHLD	60473	3428	0E-19S	E1
500	HRVY	60426	3428	0W-18S	B1
500	HRVY	60473	3428	0W-18S	B1
500	SHLD	60426	3428	0W-18S	B1
US-6 Kingery Expwy					
-	LNSG	-	3429	3E-20S	E4
-	LNSG	-	3430	3E-20S	A4
-	MNSR	-	3430	3E-20S	A4
US-6 Southwest Hwy					
-	NlxT	60448	3422	15W-21S	C7
-	OrlT	60467	3422	14W-21S	D6
11300	ODPK	60467	3422	14W-21S	E5
17700	ODPK	60448	3422	14W-21S	D6
17700	OrlT	60448	3422	14W-21S	D6
17900	HMGN	60448	3422	14W-21S	C7
US-6 Torrence Av					
1100	CTCY	60409	3429	2E-19S	D1
1400	LNSG	60438	3429	2E-19S	E3
US-6 Tri State Expwy					
-	HMND	-	3430		D5
-	LNSG	-	3430	4E-20S	C5
-	MNSR	-	3430		C5
US-6 Wolf Rd					
15900	ODPK	60467	3422	13W-19S	E1
15900	OrlT	60467	3422	13W-19S	E1
16800	OrlT	60448	3422	13W-20S	E4
17200	ODPK	60448	3422	13W-20S	E5
US-12					
-	ANHT	60074	2753	19W-17N	D5
-	BGVW	60455	3210	8W-10S	E6
-	BGVW	60457	3210	9W-11S	D6
-	CHCG	60176	2917	12W-6N	B6
-	CHCG	60666	2973	12W-5N	A1
-	CTSD	60525	3147	12W-8S	C7
-	HGKN	60525	3209	12W-8S	C1
-	HLSD	60104	3029	12W-0S	A6
-	HLSD	60154	3029	12W-0S	A6
-	HYHL	60455	3210	9W-11S	D6
-	LynT	60458	3209	12W-8S	D1
-	LynT	60480	3209	12W-8S	D1
-	OKLN	60453	3210	9W-11S	D6
-	SRPK	60176	2917	12W-6N	B6
-	SRPK	60176	2973	12W-5N	A1
-	WLSP	60458	3209	12W-8S	D1
-	WLSP	60480	3209	11W-10S	D5
-	WLSP	60525	3209	12W-8S	C1
10	ANHT	60004	2754	17W-16N	A7
10	BLWD	60104	3029	12W-0N	A3
10	BLWD	60160	3029	12W-1N	A3
10	BLWD	60162	3029	12W-0S	A6
10	CHCG	60619	3214	0E-10S	D5
10	CHCG	60620	3214	0W-10S	B6
10	CHCG	60628	3214	0W-10S	B6
10	DSPN	60016	2808	14W-12N	C7
10	HLSD	60162	3029	12W-0S	A7
10	LGNG	60525	3087	12W-4S	C6
10	MLPK	60160	3029	12W-1N	A2
10	MPPT	60016	2808	14W-12N	C7
10	MPPT	60056	2808	15W-13N	B6
10	WSTR	60154	3029	13W-0S	A7
100	LGPK	60525	3087	12W-3S	C6
200	ANHT	60004	2807	15W-14N	E4
300	DSPN	60016	2863	13W-11N	A3
300	LGNG	60525	3147	12W-7S	C5
300	MPPT	60056	2807	15W-14N	E4
300	PvsT	60162	3029	12W-0S	A7
400	ANHT	60004	2753	18W-17N	E6
600	ANHT	60056	2807	15W-14N	E4
600	DRPK	60074	2752	21W-20N	D1
600	ElaT	60074	2752	21W-20N	D1
700	CHCG	60643	3214	0W-10S	A6
700	MPPT	60004	2807	16W-14N	E4
900	CHCG	60619	3215	1E-10S	A5
900	CHCG	60628	3215	1E-10S	A5
900	DSPN	60016	2862	13W-10N	E4

Chicago & Cook County Street Index

STREET Block	City	ZIP	Map#	CGS	Grid
US-12					
1000	DSPN	60018	2862	13W-10N	E5
1000	HMND	46320	3280		D2
1000	HMND	46394	3280		E4
1000	PvsT	60525	3087	12W-2S	B4
1200	PLTN	60074	2753	20W-18N	B3
1200	PltT	60004	2753	18W-17N	D6
1200	PltT	60074	2753	19W-17N	D5
1200	PTHT	60004	2807	17W-15N	C2
1300	PvsT	60154	3029	12W-1S	A7
1400	PvsT	60154	3087	12W-1S	A1
1400	PvsT	60162	3087	12W-1S	A1
1400	WSTR	60154	3087	12W-3S	B5
1500	CHCG	60617	3215	3E-10S	E5
1500	MLPK	60165	3029	13W-1N	A2
1500	SNPK	60165	3029	13W-1N	A2
1700	DSPN	60018	2863	13W-9N	A7
2000	DSPN	60018	2917	12W-8N	A2
2000	LydT	60164	2973	12W-2N	A7
2000	MLPK	60160	2973	12W-2N	A7
2000	NHLK	60164	2973	12W-2N	A7
2000	RSMT	60018	2917	13W-8N	A2
2200	PltT	60074	2752	20W-18N	E2
2300	LydT	60131	2973	13W-2N	A6
2400	CHCG	60620	3213	3W-10S	A6
2400	CHCG	60643	3213	3W-10S	A6
2400	ENGN	60805	3213	3W-10S	A6
2400	FNPK	60131	2973	13W-3N	A6
2400	FNPK	60164	2973	13W-3N	A6
2400	WhlT	60004	2807	16W-14N	D3
2900	CHCG	60666	2917	12W-7N	B4
2900	ENGN	60805	3212	3W-10S	E6
2900	RSMT	60666	2917	12W-8N	A2
3000	CHCG	60617	3216	4E-11S	B6
3900	OKLN	60453	3212	4W-10S	C6
4000	FNPK	60176	2973	12W-2N	A7
4900	OKLN	60453	3211	7W-10S	C6
6000	HGKN	60525	3147	12W-6S	C5
6300	CHRG	60453	3211	7W-10S	B6
7600	HYHL	60457	3210	9W-11S	D6
8700	HYHL	60465	3210	10W-10S	A6
8700	PSHL	60465	3210	10W-10S	A6
8900	HYHL	60457	3209	11W-10S	E6
8900	PSHL	60465	3209	11W-10S	E6
9000	HYHL	60465	3209	11W-10S	E6
9000	PlsT	60465	3209	11W-10S	E6
9000	PlsT	60480	3209	11W-10S	E6
10300	CHCG	60617	3280	4E-11S	C1
10500	CHCG	46320	3280	4E-12S	C1
20200	KLDR	60074	2752	21W-20N	E1
20400	KLDR	60047	2752	21W-20N	D1
US-12 95th St					
-	HYHL	60457	3209	11W-10S	E6
-	HYHL	60465	3209	11W-10S	E6
-	PlsT	60465	3209	11W-10S	E6
-	PlsT	60480	3209	11W-10S	E6
-	PSHL	60465	3209	11W-10S	E6
US-12 E 95th St					
10	CHCG	60619	3214	0E-10S	D5
10	CHCG	60620	3214	0E-10S	C6
10	CHCG	60628	3214	0E-10S	D5
900	CHCG	60619	3215	1E-10S	A5
900	CHCG	60628	3215	1E-10S	A5
1500	CHCG	60617	3215	3E-10S	E5
3000	CHCG	60617	3216	3E-10S	A5
US-12 W 95th St					
-	BGVW	60455	3210	8W-10S	E6
-	BGVW	60457	3210	9W-11S	D6
-	CHCG	60619	3214	0E-10S	C6
-	HYHL	60455	3210	9W-11S	D6
-	OKLN	60453	3210	9W-11S	D6
10	CHCG	60620	3214	0W-10S	B6
10	CHCG	60628	3214	0W-10S	B6
700	CHCG	60643	3214	0W-10S	A6
900	CHCG	60620	3213	1W-10S	D6
2400	CHCG	60643	3213	3W-10S	A6
2400	ENGN	60805	3213	3W-10S	A6
2900	ENGN	60805	3212	3W-10S	E6
3900	OKLN	60453	3212	4W-10S	C6
4900	OKLN	60453	3211	7W-10S	C6
6300	CHRG	60453	3211	7W-10S	B6
7600	HYHL	60457	3210	9W-11S	D6
8700	HYHL	60465	3210	10W-10S	A6
8700	PSHL	60465	3210	10W-10S	A6
8900	HYHL	60457	3209	11W-10S	E6
8900	PSHL	60465	3209	11W-10S	E6
9000	HYHL	60465	3209	11W-10S	E6
9000	PlsT	60465	3209	11W-10S	E6
9000	PlsT	60480	3209	11W-10S	E6
US-12 S Ewing Av					
9500	CHCG	60617	3216	4E-11S	B6
US-12 Graceland Av					
800	DSPN	60016	2862	13W-10N	E4
US-12 S Indianapolis Av					
-	CHCG	46320	3280	4E-11S	C1
10000	CHCG	60617	3216	4E-11S	B7
10300	CHCG	60617	3280	4E-11S	C1
10600	HMND	46320	3280	4E-12S	C1
US-12 S Indianapolis Blvd					
1000	HMND	46320	3280		D2
1000	HMND	46394	3280		E4
10500	CHCG	46320	3280		C1
10500	CHCG	60617	3280		C1
US-12 La Grange Rd					
-	LynT	60458	3209	12W-8S	D1
-	LynT	60480	3209	12W-8S	D1
-	PlsT	60480	3209	11W-9S	D4
-	WLSP	60458	3209	12W-8S	D1
-	WLSP	60480	3209	11W-10S	D5
-	WLSP	60525	3209	12W-8S	D1
US-12 N La Grange Rd					
-	WSTR	60154	3087	12W-2S	A2
10	LGNG	60525	3087	12W-4S	C6
100	LGPK	60525	3087	12W-3S	C6
1000	PvsT	60525	3087	12W-2S	B4
2500	PvsT	60154	3087	12W-2S	B2
US-12 S La Grange Rd					
-	HGKN	60525	3209	12W-8S	C1
-	WLSP	60525	3209	12W-8S	C1
10	LGNG	60525	3087	12W-4S	C7
300	LGNG	60525	3147	12W-7S	C5
5200	CTSD	60525	3147	12W-5S	C3
6000	HGKN	60525	3147	12W-6S	C5
US-12 Mannheim Rd					
-	CHCG	60176	2917	12W-6N	B6
-	CHCG	60666	2973	12W-5N	A1
-	SRPK	60176	2917	12W-6N	B6
-	SRPK	60176	2973	12W-5N	A1
10	BLWD	60104	3029	12W-0N	A3
10	BLWD	60160	3029	12W-1N	A3
10	MLPK	60160	3029	12W-1N	A3
500	BLWD	60162	3029	12W-0N	A4
500	HLSD	60162	3029	12W-0N	A4
600	DSPN	60016	2863	13W-11N	A3
900	DSPN	60016	2862	13W-10N	E4

STREET Block	City	ZIP	Map#	CGS	Grid
US-12 Mannheim Rd					
1000	DSPN	60018	2862	13W-10N	E5
1700	DSPN	60018	2863	13W-9N	A7
2000	DSPN	60018	2917	13W-8N	A2
2000	RSMT	60018	2917	13W-8N	A2
2400	FNPK	60131	2973	13W-3N	A6
2400	FNPK	60164	2973	13W-3N	A6
2400	LydT	60131	2973	13W-3N	A6
2400	LydT	60164	2973	13W-3N	A6
2900	CHCG	60666	2917	12W-7N	B4
2900	RSMT	60666	2917	12W-8N	A2
4000	FNPK	60176	2973	13W-2N	A7
US-12 N Mannheim Rd					
-	BLWD	60104	3029	12W-1N	A3
-	BLWD	60160	3029	12W-1N	A3
-	HLSD	60104	3029	12W-0S	A6
-	HLSD	60154	3029	12W-0S	A6
-	WSTR	60154	3029	12W-0S	A6
10	BLWD	60162	3029	12W-0S	A6
10	HLSD	60162	3029	12W-0S	A6
1500	MLPK	60160	3029	13W-1N	A2
1500	MLPK	60165	3029	13W-1N	A2
1500	SNPK	60165	3029	13W-1N	A2
2000	LydT	60164	2973	12W-2N	A7
2000	MLPK	60160	2973	12W-2N	A7
2000	NHLK	60164	2973	12W-2N	A7
2300	LydT	60131	2973	13W-2N	A6
US-12 S Mannheim Rd					
-	BLWD	60104	3029	12W-0S	A6
-	HLSD	60154	3029	12W-0S	A6
10	HLSD	60162	3029	13W-0S	A7
10	WSTR	60154	3029	13W-0S	A7
300	PvsT	60162	3029	12W-0S	A7
1300	PvsT	60154	3029	12W-1S	A7
1400	PvsT	60154	3087	12W-1S	A1
1400	PvsT	60162	3087	12W-1S	A1
1400	WSTR	60154	3087	12W-3S	B5
US-12 Rand Rd					
10	DSPN	60016	2808	14W-12N	C7
10	MPPT	60016	2808	14W-12N	C7
10	MPPT	60056	2808	14W-12N	B7
300	DSPN	60016	2862	13W-11N	E2
600	DRPK	60074	2752	21W-20N	D1
600	ElaT	60074	2752	21W-20N	D1
1200	DSPN	60016	2863	13W-11N	A2
2000	PLTN	60074	2753	20W-18N	A3
US-12 E Rand Rd					
10	ANHT	60004	2754	17W-16N	A7
10	MPPT	60056	2808	15W-13N	A5
200	ANHT	60004	2807	15W-14N	E4
900	DSPN	60016	2808	14W-13N	B7
900	MPPT	60016	2808	14W-13N	B7
1200	PTHT	60004	2807	17W-15N	C2
2400	MPPT	60004	2807	16W-14N	D3
2400	MPPT	60056	2807	16W-14N	D3
2400	WhlT	60004	2807	16W-14N	D3
2500	ANHT	60056	2807	16W-14N	E4
US-12 N Rand Rd					
-	ANHT	60004	2753	19W-17N	D5
-	ANHT	60074	2753	19W-17N	D5
-	PltT	60004	2753	19W-17N	D5
1200	PLTN	60074	2753	20W-18N	B3
2100	PltT	60074	2753	20W-18N	A2
2200	DRPK	60074	2752	20W-20N	E2
2200	ElaT	60074	2752	20W-20N	E2
2200	PltT	60074	2752	20W-18N	E2
20200	KLDR	60074	2752	21W-20N	E1
20400	KLDR	60047	2752	21W-20N	D1
US-12 W Rand Rd					
-	ANHT	60074	2753	19W-17N	D5
10	ANHT	60004	2754	17W-16N	A7
10	MPPT	60056	2808	15W-13N	B6
300	MPPT	60056	2807	15W-14N	E4
400	ANHT	60004	2753	18W-17N	D6
600	ANHT	60056	2807	15W-14N	E4
700	ANHT	60004	2807	16W-14N	E4
700	MPPT	60004	2807	16W-14N	E4
1200	PltT	60004	2753	18W-17N	D6
US-12 S River Rd					
-	DSPN	60016	2863	13W-11N	A3
US-14					
-	NLES	60053	2865	8W-9N	A6
-	PltT	60067	2751	23W-17N	E5
10	ANHT	60004	2807	17W-14N	A4
10	ANHT	60005	2807	17W-14N	A4
10	DSPN	60016	2862	14W-12N	C1
10	MPPT	60056	2808	15W-12N	A7
10	MPPT	60056	2862	13W-11N	E3
10	PLTN	60067	2752	22W-17N	A5
10	PLTN	60067	2806	18W-14N	D3
10	PLTN	60074	2806	18W-14N	D3
100	BRTN	60010	2751	24W-17N	D4
100	PLTN	60074	2753	20W-16N	A7
200	MPPT	60056	2807	15W-12N	E7
200	PLTN	60067	2753	20W-16N	A7
500	ANHT	60004	2806	18W-14N	E4
500	ANHT	60005	2806	18W-14N	E4
500	BRTN	60010	2750	26W-20N	E1
500	PltT	60067	2752	21W-17N	C6
1100	PltT	60010	2751	23W-17N	D4
1200	NLES	60714	2863	10W-10N	E4
1200	NLES	60714	2864	8W-10N	E4
1200	PKRG	60068	2863	10W-10N	E4
1200	PKRG	60068	2864	10W-10N	A4
1200	PKRG	60714	2863	10W-10N	E4
1300	DSPN	60016	2863	11W-10N	E4
1500	PLTN	60067	2751	23W-17N	E5
1700	CHCG	60660	2921	2W-7N	B3
1800	ANHT	60074	2806	19W-14N	D3
1900	CHCG	60659	2921	2W-7N	B3
2000	MaiT	60016	2863	11W-11N	D4
2400	PKRG	60016	2863	11W-10N	D4
2500	MaiT	60068	2863	11W-10N	D4
2700	CHCG	60659	2920	3W-7N	E3
3800	CHCG	60646	2920	4W-7N	B4
4700	CHCG	60646	2919	6W-7N	D3
5200	CHCG	60640	2921	1W-6N	D5
6800	CHCG	60714	2919	7W-8N	B1
6800	NLES	60646	2919	7W-8N	B1
6800	NLES	60714	2919	7W-8N	B1
6900	MNGV	60053	2864	8W-10N	E4
7000	NLES	60053	2864	8W-11N	E4
7100	MNGV	60714	2864	8W-11N	D4
7200	CHCG	60646	2865	8W-9N	A7
7200	NLES	60714	2865	8W-9N	A6
7900	MNGV	60053	2865	8W-9N	A6
7900	MNGV	60714	2865	8W-9N	A6
US-14 N Broadway St					
5200	CHCG	60640	2921	1W-6N	D5
5500	CHCG	60660	2921	1W-6N	D4
US-14 Caldwell Av					
7900	MNGV	60053	2864	8W-10N	E4
7900	NLES	60714	2864	8W-10N	E4
US-14 N Caldwell Av					
-	NLES	60053	2865	8W-9N	A6

STREET Block	City	ZIP	Map#	CGS	Grid
US-14 N Caldwell Av					
6000	CHCG	60646	2919	6W-7N	D3
6800	CHCG	60714	2919	7W-8N	B1
6800	NLES	60646	2919	7W-8N	B1
6800	NLES	60714	2919	7W-8N	B1
7200	CHCG	60646	2865	8W-9N	A7
7200	NLES	60714	2865	8W-9N	A6
7900	MNGV	60053	2865	8W-9N	A6
7900	MNGV	60714	2865	8W-9N	A6
8000	MNGV	60053	2864	8W-10N	E5
8000	MNGV	60714	2864	8W-10N	E5
8000	NLES	60714	2864	8W-10N	E5
US-14 Dempster St					
1200	NLES	60714	2863	10W-10N	E4
1200	PKRG	60068	2863	10W-10N	E4
1200	PKRG	60068	2864	10W-10N	A4
1200	PKRG	60714	2863	10W-10N	E4
2000	MaiT	60016	2863	11W-11N	D4
2600	DSPN	60016	2863	11W-10N	D4
2600	MaiT	60068	2863	11W-10N	D4
2600	PKRG	60016	2863	11W-10N	D4
6900	MNGV	60053	2864	8W-10N	E4
7000	NLES	60714	2864	8W-10N	E4
US-14 E Dempster St					
2300	DSPN	60016	2863	12W-10N	C4
2300	PKRG	60068	2863	12W-10N	C4
2400	PKRG	60016	2863	11W-10N	D4
2500	MaiT	60016	2863	11W-10N	D4
2500	MaiT	60068	2863	11W-10N	D4
US-14 W Dempster St					
7000	MNGV	60053	2864	8W-11N	E4
7000	NLES	60053	2864	8W-11N	E4
7000	NLES	60714	2864	8W-11N	E4
7100	MNGV	60714	2864	8W-11N	D4
8500	PKRG	60068	2864	10W-10N	A4
US-14 Miner St					
1200	DSPN	60016	2862	13W-11N	E3
1300	DSPN	60016	2863	11W-10N	E4
US-14 E Northwest Hwy					
10	ANHT	60004	2807	17W-14N	A4
10	ANHT	60005	2807	17W-14N	A4
10	DSPN	60016	2862	14W-12N	C1
10	MPPT	60056	2808	15W-12N	A7
10	MPPT	60056	2862	13W-11N	E3
10	PLTN	60067	2752	20W-16N	E6
100	BRTN	60010	2751	25W-20N	A1
200	PLTN	60067	2753	20W-16N	A7
200	PLTN	60074	2753	20W-16N	A7
400	PLTN	60067	2806	20W-15N	A1
400	PLTN	60074	2806	20W-15N	A1
1700	DSPN	60016	2863	12W-11N	A4
2100	MPPT	60056	2807	16W-13N	D6
US-14 N Northwest Hwy					
10	PLTN	60067	2806	20W-16N	A1
10	PLTN	60074	2806	20W-16N	A1
100	BRTN	60010	2751	25W-20N	A2
300	PLTN	60067	2753	20W-16N	A7
300	PLTN	60074	2753	20W-16N	A7
US-14 S Northwest Hwy					
-	PLTN	60067	2751	23W-17N	E5
-	PltT	60067	2751	23W-17N	E5
10	PLTN	60067	2806	18W-14N	D3
10	PLTN	60074	2806	18W-14N	D3
100	BRTN	60010	2751	24W-17N	D4
1100	PltT	60010	2751	23W-17N	D4
US-14 W Northwest Hwy					
-	PltT	60010	2751	23W-17N	E5
-	PltT	60067	2751	23W-17N	E5
10	ANHT	60004	2807	17W-14N	A4
10	ANHT	60005	2807	17W-14N	A4
10	MPPT	60056	2808	15W-12N	A7
10	PLTN	60067	2752	22W-17N	A5
200	MPPT	60056	2807	15W-12N	E7
500	ANHT	60004	2806	18W-14N	E4
500	ANHT	60005	2806	18W-14N	E4
500	BRTN	60010	2750	26W-20N	D1
500	PltT	60067	2752	21W-17N	C6
1500	PLTN	60067	2751	23W-17N	E5
1800	ANHT	60074	2806	19W-14N	D3
1800	PLTN	60074	2806	19W-14N	D3
US-14 W Peterson Av					
1700	CHCG	60660	2921	2W-7N	B3
1900	CHCG	60659	2921	2W-7N	B3
2700	CHCG	60659	2920	3W-7N	E3
3800	CHCG	60646	2920	4W-7N	B4
4700	CHCG	60646	2919	5W-7N	E4
US-14 N Ridge Av					
5600	CHCG	60640	2921	1W-7N	D4
5600	CHCG	60660	2921	1W-7N	D4
US-14 Waukegan Rd					
8500	MNGV	60053	2864	8W-10N	E4
US-20					
-	BGVW	60455	3210	8W-10S	E6
-	BGVW	60457	3210	9W-11S	D6
-	ELGN	-	2855		A6
-	ELGN	60103	2856	31W-9N	A7
-	EMHT	-	2972		A7
-	EMHT	-	3028		B1
-	HGKN	60525	3147	12W-8S	C7
-	HGKN	60525	3209	12W-8S	C1
-	HLSD	60104	3029	12W-0S	A6
-	HLSD	60154	3029	12W-0S	A6
-	HnrT	60103	2910		C1
-	HYHL	60455	3210	9W-11S	D6
-	LynT	60458	3209	12W-8S	D1
-	LynT	60480	3209	12W-8S	D1
-	OKLN	60453	3210	9W-11S	D6
-	PlsT	60480	3209	11W-9S	D4
-	SMWD	60120	2910		C1
-	WLSP	60458	3209	12W-8S	D1
-	WLSP	60480	3209	11W-10S	D5
-	WLSP	60525	3209	12W-8S	C1
10	BLWD	60104	3029	12W-0N	A3
10	BLWD	60160	3029	12W-1N	A3
10	BLWD	60162	3029	12W-0S	A6
10	BmdT	60172	2912		C6
10	CHCG	60619	3214	0E-11S	D6
10	CHCG	60620	3214	0W-11S	B6
10	CHCG	60628	3214	0W-11S	B6
10	HLSD	60162	3029	12W-0S	A7
10	LGNG	60525	3087	12W-4S	C6
10	MLPK	60160	3028		E2
10	MLPK	60160	3029	12W-1N	A3
10	NHLK	60164	3028		E2
10	ROSL	60172	2912		E7
10	WSTR	60154	3029	13W-0S	A7
100	BRLT	60103	2910		D1
100	BRLT	60103	2911		B2
100	BRLT	60107	2910		D1
100	BRLT	60107	2911		B2
100	LGPK	60525	3087	12W-3S	C6
100	SMWD	60103	2910		D1
100	SMWD	60107	2910		D1
100	SMWD	60107	2911		B2
200	BMDL	60108	2912		E7

STREET Block	City	ZIP	Map#	CGS	Grid
US-20					
200	BMDL	60172	2912		E7
200	BmdT	60108	2912		E7
200	BmdT	60133	2911		E5
200	HRPK	60133	2911		E5
200	ROSL	60108	2912		E7
300	HRPK	60133	2912		A5
300	LGNG	60525	3147	12W-7S	C5
300	PvsT	60162	3029	12W-0S	A7
400	HRPK	60172	2912		B6
500	BRLT	60120	2910		D1
500	HnrT	60120	2910		D1
500	SMWD	60103	2911		A2
600	BmdT	60133	2912		A5
600	HRPK	60103	2911		B2
700	CHCG	60643	3214	0W-10S	A6
900	CHCG	60619	3215	1E-10S	A5
900	CHCG	60620	3213	2W-11S	C6
900	CHCG	60628	3215	1E-10S	A5
1000	HMND	46320	3280		D2
1000	HMND	46394	3280		E4
1000	PvsT	60525	3087	12W-2S	B4
1100	BRLT	60103	2856	30W-9N	B7
1100	BRLT	60107	2856	30W-9N	B7
1100	BRLT	60120	2856	30W-9N	B7
1100	HnrT	60103	2856	30W-9N	B7
1100	HnrT	60107	2856	30W-9N	B7
1100	HnrT	60120	2856	30W-9N	B7
1100	SMWD	60107	2856	30W-9N	C7
1300	PvsT	60154	3029	12W-1S	A7
1400	PvsT	60154	3087	12W-1S	A1
1400	PvsT	60162	3087	12W-1S	A1
1400	WSTR	60154	3087	12W-3S	B5
1500	CHCG	60617	3215	3E-11S	E5
1500	ELGN	60120	2855		B6
1500	ELGN	60120	2856	30W-9N	B7
2200	BRLT	60133	2911		C3
2400	CHCG	60643	3213	3W-11S	A6
2400	ENGN	60805	3213	3W-11S	A6
2900	ENGN	60805	3212	3W-11S	E6
3000	CHCG	60617	3216	4E-11S	B6
3900	OKLN	60453	3212	4W-10S	C6
4100	MLPK	60165	3029	13W-1N	A3
4100	SNPK	60165	3029	13W-1N	A3
4900	OKLN	60453	3211	7W-11S	C6
5200	CTSD	60525	3147	12W-5S	C3
6300	CHRG	60453	3211	7W-10S	B6
7600	HYHL	60457	3210	9W-11S	D6
8700	HYHL	60465	3210	10W-10S	A6
8700	PSHL	60465	3210	10W-10S	A6
8900	HYHL	60457	3209	11W-11S	E6
8900	PSHL	60465	3209	11W-11S	E6
9000	HYHL	60465	3209	11W-10S	E6
9000	PlsT	60465	3209	11W-10S	E6
10500	CHCG	46320	3280		C1
10500	CHCG	60617	3280		C1
US-20 BUS					
-	ELGN	60120	2855		D6
US-20 95th St					
-	HYHL	60457	3209	11W-10S	E6
-	HYHL	60465	3209	11W-10S	E6
-	PlsT	60465	3209	11W-10S	E6
-	PlsT	60480	3209	11W-10S	E6
-	PSHL	60465	3209	11W-10S	E6
US-20 E 95th St					
10	CHCG	60619	3214	0E-11S	D6
10	CHCG	60620	3214	0E-10S	C6
10	CHCG	60628	3214	0E-11S	D6
900	CHCG	60619	3215	1E-10S	A5
900	CHCG	60628	3215	1E-10S	A5
1500	CHCG	60617	3215	3E-11S	E5
3000	CHCG	60617	3216	3E-10S	A5
US-20 W 95th St					
-	BGVW	60455	3210	8W-10S	E6
-	BGVW	60457	3210	9W-11S	D6
-	CHCG	60619	3214	0E-10S	C6
-	HYHL	60455	3210	9W-11S	D6
-	OKLN	60453	3210	9W-11S	D6
10	CHCG	60620	3214	0W-11S	B6
10	CHCG	60628	3214	0W-11S	B6
700	CHCG	60643	3214	0W-10S	A6
2400	CHCG	60620	3213	3W-11S	A6
2400	CHCG	60643	3213	3W-11S	A6
2400	ENGN	60805	3213	3W-11S	A6
2900	ENGN	60805	3212	3W-11S	E6
3900	OKLN	60453	3212	4W-10S	C6
4900	OKLN	60453	3211	7W-11S	C6
6300	CHRG	60453	3211	7W-10S	B6
7600	HYHL	60457	3210	9W-11S	D6
8700	HYHL	60465	3210	10W-10S	A6
8700	PSHL	60465	3210	10W-10S	A6
8900	HYHL	60457	3209	11W-11S	E6
8900	PSHL	60465	3209	11W-11S	E6
9000	HYHL	60465	3209	11W-10S	E6
9000	PlsT	60465	3209	11W-10S	E6
9000	PlsT	60480	3209	11W-10S	E6
US-20 Eisenhower Expwy					
-	EMHT	-	2972		A7
-	EMHT	-	3028		B1
US-20 S Ewing Av					
9500	CHCG	60617	3216	4E-11S	B6
US-20 S Indianapolis Av					
-	CHCG	46320	3280	4E-11S	C1
-	HMND	46320	3280	4E-11S	C1
10000	CHCG	60617	3216	4E-11S	B7
10300	CHCG	60617	3280	4E-11S	C1
US-20 S Indianapolis Blvd					
1000	HMND	46320	3280		D2
1000	HMND	46394	3280		E4
10500	CHCG	46320	3280		C1
10500	CHCG	60617	3280		C1
US-20 La Grange Rd					
-	LynT	60458	3209	12W-8S	D1
-	LynT	60480	3209	12W-8S	D1
-	PlsT	60480	3209	11W-9S	D4
-	WLSP	60458	3209	12W-8S	D1
-	WLSP	60480	3209	11W-10S	D5
-	WLSP	60525	3209	12W-8S	D1
US-20 N La Grange Rd					
-	WSTR	60154	3087	12W-2S	A2
10	LGNG	60525	3087	12W-4S	C6
100	LGPK	60525	3087	12W-3S	C6
1000	PvsT	60525	3087	12W-2S	B4
2500	PvsT	60154	3087	12W-2S	B2
US-20 S La Grange Rd					
-	CTSD	60525	3147	12W-8S	C7
-	HGKN	60525	3209	12W-8S	C1
-	WLSP	60525	3209	12W-8S	C1
10	LGNG	60525	3087	12W-4S	C7
300	LGNG	60525	3147	12W-7S	C5
6000	HGKN	60525	3147	12W-6S	C5
US-20 Lake St					
-	BRLT	60103	2856	31W-9N	A7
-	ELGN	-	2855		D6
-	ELGN	60103	2856	31W-9N	A7

STREET Block	City	ZIP	Map#	CGS	Grid
US-20 Lake St					
-	ELGN	60120	2856	31W-10N	A7
-	HnrT	60120	2856	31W-9N	A7
10	BmdT	60172	2912		C6
10	ROSL	60172	2912		C6
200	BmdT	60133	2911		E5
200	HRPK	60133	2911		E5
300	BMDL	60108	2912		D7
300	BMDL	60172	2912		D7
300	BmdT	60108	2912		D7
300	HRPK	60133	2912		B6
400	HRPK	60172	2912		B6
600	BmdT	60133	2912		A5
US-20 E Lake St					
10	MLPK	60160	3028		E2
10	NHLK	60164	3028		D2
100	BRLT	60103	2910		E2
100	BRLT	60103	2911		B2
100	BRLT	60107	2910		E2
100	BRLT	60107	2911		B2
100	SMWD	60103	2910		E1
100	SMWD	60107	2910		E2
100	SMWD	60107	2911		B2
500	SMWD	60103	2911		A2
1000	BmdT	60133	2911		E5
1000	BmdT	60133	2912		A5
1000	HRPK	60133	2911		E5
1000	HRPK	60133	2912		A5
US-20 W Lake St					
-	HnrT	60103	2910		C1
-	SMWD	60120	2910		C1
10	NHLK	60164	3028		E2
200	BMDL	60108	2912		E7
200	BMDL	60172	2912		E7
200	BmdT	60108	2912		E7
200	BmdT	60172	2912		E7
200	ROSL	60108	2912		E7
200	ROSL	60172	2912		E7
500	BRLT	60103	2910		D1
500	BRLT	60107	2910		D1
500	BRLT	60120	2910		D1
500	HnrT	60120	2910		D1
500	SMWD	60103	2910		D1
500	SMWD	60107	2910		D1
600	BRLT	60103	2911		B2
600	HRPK	60103	2911		B2
600	HRPK	60133	2911		B2
600	SMWD	60107	2911		B2
1100	BRLT	60103	2856	30W-9N	B7
1100	BRLT	60107	2856	30W-9N	B7
1100	BRLT	60120	2856	30W-9N	B7
1100	HnrT	60103	2856	30W-9N	B7
1100	HnrT	60107	2856	30W-9N	B7
1100	HnrT	60120	2856	30W-9N	B7
1100	SMWD	60107	2856	30W-9N	C7
2200	BRLT	60133	2911		C3
4100	MLPK	60160	3029	13W-1N	A2
4100	MLPK	60165	3029	12W-1N	A2
4100	SNPK	60165	3029	13W-1N	A2
4700	MLPK	60160	3028		E2
US-20 Mannheim Rd					
10	BLWD	60104	3029	12W-0N	A3
10	BLWD	60160	3029	12W-1N	A3
10	MLPK	60160	3029	12W-1N	A3
500	BLWD	60162	3029	12W-0N	A4
500	HLSD	60162	3029	12W-0N	A4
US-20 N Mannheim Rd					
-	BLWD	60104	3029	12W-1N	A3
-	BLWD	60160	3029	12W-1N	A3
-	HLSD	60104	3029	12W-0S	A6
-	HLSD	60154	3029	12W-0S	A6
-	MLPK	60160	3029	13W-1N	A3
-	MLPK	60165	3029	13W-1N	A3
-	SNPK	60165	3029	13W-1N	A3
-	WSTR	60154	3029	12W-0S	A6
10	BLWD	60162	3029	12W-0S	A6
10	HLSD	60162	3029	12W-0S	A6
US-20 S Mannheim Rd					
-	BLWD	60104	3029	12W-0S	A6
-	HLSD	60154	3029	12W-0S	A6
10	HLSD	60162	3029	13W-0S	A7
10	WSTR	60154	3029	13W-0S	A7
300	PvsT	60162	3029	12W-0S	A7
1300	PvsT	60154	3029	12W-1S	A7
1400	PvsT	60154	3087	12W-1S	A1
1400	PvsT	60162	3087	12W-1S	A1
1400	WSTR	60154	3087	12W-3S	B5
US-20 Villa St					
-	ELGN	-	2855		E6
US-20 BUS Villa St					
-	ELGN	60120	2855		D6
US-20 E Villa St					
1500	ELGN	60120	2855		E7
1500	ELGN	60120	2856	30W-9N	B7
US-30					
10	BlmT	60411	3598		D2
10	CHHT	60411	3508	0E-25S	E7
10	DYR	46311	3598		C2
10	DYR	60411	3598	4E-26S	C2
100	CHHT	60411	3507	1W-25S	E7
300	BlmT	60411	3508	0E-25S	E7
700	OMFD	60461	3507	3W-25S	A7
800	CHHT	60411	3509	1E-25S	A7
800	FDHT	60411	3509	1E-25S	A7
1400	BlmT	60411	3509	3E-25S	E7
1600	SLVL	60411	3509	3E-25S	E7
2400	BlmT	60411	3510	3E-25S	A7
2500	PKFT	60466	3507	3W-25S	A7
2600	PKFT	60461	3507	3W-25S	A7
2800	LYWD	60411	3510	3E-25S	A7
3200	MTSN	60443	3506	4W-25S	E7
3200	OMFD	60461	3506	4W-25S	E7
3200	OMFD	60466	3506	4W-25S	E7
3200	PKFT	60466	3506	4W-25S	E7
3600	OMFD	60443	3506	4W-25S	E7
5300	MTSN	60443	3505	7W-25S	C7
6200	RchT	60443	3505	8W-25S	A7
6500	FftT	60423	3505	8W-25S	A7
6500	FKFT	60423	3505	8W-25S	A7
6500	RchT	60423	3505	8W-25S	A7
7200	FftT	60423	3504	9W-25S	E7
7200	FKFT	60423	3504	9W-25S	E7
21400	LYWD	60411	3598		D2
US-30 E 14th St					
10	CHHT	60411	3508	1W-25S	A7
300	BlmT	60411	3508	0W-25S	D7
US-30 W 14th St					
10	CHHT	60411	3508	1W-25S	A7
100	CHHT	60411	3507	1W-25S	E7
700	OMFD	60461	3507	2W-25S	C7
US-30 Joliet St					
10	BlmT	60411	3598	4E-26S	C2
10	DYR	46311	3598		C2
10	DYR	60411	3598	4E-26S	C2

STREET Block	City	ZIP	Map#	CGS	Grid
US-30 Lincoln Hwy					
-	CHHT	60411	3507	2W-25S	C7
2400	OMFD	60461	3507	3W-25S	A7
2500	PKFT	60466	3507	3W-25S	A7
2600	PKFT	60461	3507	3W-25S	A7
3200	MTSN	60443	3506	4W-25S	E7
3200	OMFD	60461	3506	4W-25S	E7
3200	OMFD	60466	3506	4W-25S	E7
3200	PKFT	60466	3506	4W-25S	E7
3600	OMFD	60443	3506	4W-25S	E7
5300	MTSN	60443	3505	7W-25S	C7
6200	RchT	60443	3505	7W-25S	C7
6500	FftT	60423	3505	9W-25S	A7
6500	FKFT	60423	3505	9W-25S	A7
6500	RchT	60423	3505	9W-25S	A7
US-30 E Lincoln Hwy					
400	BlmT	60411	3508	0E-25S	E7
400	CHHT	60411	3508	0E-25S	E7
800	CHHT	60411	3509	1E-25S	A7
800	FDHT	60411	3509	1E-25S	A7
1400	BlmT	60411	3509	3E-25S	E7
1600	SLVL	60411	3509	3E-25S	E7
2400	BlmT	60411	3510	3E-25S	A7
2800	LYWD	60411	3510	3E-25S	A7
21400	BlmT	60411	3598		D2
21400	LYWD	60411	3598		D2
US-30 W Lincoln Hwy					
7200	FftT	60423	3504	9W-25S	E7
7200	FftT	60423	3505	8W-25S	A7
7200	FKFT	60423	3504	9W-25S	E7
7200	FKFT	60423	3505	8W-25S	A7
7200	RchT	60423	3505	8W-25S	A7
7200	RchT	60443	3505	8W-25S	A7
US-30 E Sauk Tr					
3600	BlmT	60411	3598	4E-26S	C2
3600	DYR	46311	3598	4E-26S	C2
3600	DYR	60411	3598	4E-26S	C2
US-34					
-	PvsT	60521	3086		C6
10	LGNG	60525	3087	12W-4S	C6
10	LGPK	60525	3087	13W-4S	B6
10	PvsT	60558	3087	13W-4S	B6
10	WNSP	60558	3087	13W-4S	B6
100	PvsT	60558	3086		A7
100	WNSP	60558	3086		A7
400	HNDL	60521	3086		C6
400	LynT	60521	3086		C6
500	LynT	60558	3086		C6
7200	BRWN	60402	3088	9W-3S	D6
7200	LYNS	60402	3088	9W-3S	D6
7200	LYNS	60534	3088	9W-3S	D6
7200	RVSD	60402	3088	9W-3S	D6
7200	RVSD	60546	3088	9W-3S	D6
7300	LYNS	60546	3088	9W-3S	D6
8700	BKFD	60513	3088	10W-4S	A6
8800	BKFD	60513	3087	11W-4S	E6
US-34 Ogden Av					
-	HNDL	60521	3086		C6
-	LynT	60521	3086		C6
-	LynT	60558	3086		C6
-	PvsT	60521	3086		C6
10	LGPK	60525	3087	13W-4S	B6
10	PvsT	60558	3087	13W-4S	B6
10	WNSP	60558	3087	13W-4S	B6
100	PvsT	60558	3086		A7
100	WNSP	60558	3086		A7
7200	BRWN	60402	3088	9W-3S	D6
7200	LYNS	60402	3088	9W-3S	D6
7200	LYNS	60534	3088	9W-3S	D6
7200	RVSD	60402	3088	9W-3S	D6
7200	RVSD	60546	3088	9W-3S	D6
7300	LYNS	60546	3088	9W-3S	D6
8700	BKFD	60513	3088	10W-4S	A6
8800	BKFD	60513	3087	11W-4S	E6
9500	LGNG	60525	3087	12W-4S	D6
US-34 E Ogden Av					
10	LGNG	60525	3087	12W-4S	C6
400	HNDL	60521	3086		C6
400	LynT	60521	3086		C6
500	LynT	60558	3086		C6
9600	BKFD	60513	3087	12W-4S	D6
US-34 W Ogden Av					
10	HNDL	60521	3086		A7
10	LGNG	60525	3087	12W-4S	C6
1200	LGPK	60525	3087	13W-3S	A6
1500	WNSP	60558	3087	13W-3S	A6
1600	PvsT	60558	3087	13W-3S	A6
US-41					
-	CHCG	-	2921	0W-6N	E6
-	CHCG	-	2922	0W-5N	A7
-	CHCG	-	2978	0W-5N	A1
-	CHCG	-	3034	0E-1N	C1
-	CHCG	-	3092	1E-3S	E5
-	CHCG	-	3093	1E-4S	A6
-	CokC	-	3034	0E-0N	D4
-	CokC	60637	3153	2E-6S	C3
-	GLNC	-	2758	7W-17N	B6
-	HDPK	-	2757	8W-20N	D1
-	NfdT	-	2757	8W-18N	E3
-	NfdT	-	2811	7W-16N	C1
-	NHBK	-	2757	8W-18N	E3
-	NHBK	-	2758	7W-17N	A4
-	NHFD	-	2758	7W-16N	B7
-	NHFD	-	2811	7W-15N	C1
-	NtrT	-	2758	7W-18N	A4
-	NtrT	-	2811	6W-14N	D4
-	WLMT	60093	2811	5W-13N	E6
10	CHCG	60601	3034	0E-1S	D7
10	CHCG	60603	3034	0E-1S	D7
100	CHCG	60605	3034	0E-0S	D5
1000	HMND	46320	3280		D2
1000	HMND	46394	3280		E7
1500	CHCG	60616	3034	0E-1S	D7
1900	CHCG	60625	2921	2W-6N	B5
2000	CHCG	60637	3153	2E-7S	D5
2000	CHCG	60649	3153	2E-7S	C5
3000	HMND	46320	3352		E5
3000	HMND	46327	3280		E7
3000	HMND	46327	3352		E5
3200	CHCG	60617	3216	4E-10S	B6
5300	CHCG	60615	3153	2E-7S	D5
5500	CHCG	60659	2921	1W-6N	E5
5600	CHCG	60659	2920	3W-7N	E4
5900	HMND	46320	3430		E2
6100	HMND	46324	3430		E2
6300	CHCG	60712	2920	4W-7N	C3
6300	LNWD	60712	2920	3W-7N	E4
7200	LNWD	60712	2866	5W-9N	A7
7200	SKOK	60076	2866	5W-9N	A7
7500	SKOK	60076	2865	5W-12N	E1
7500	SKOK	60077	2865	6W-12N	E1
7700	CHCG	60649	3215	3E-8S	E1
7800	CHCG	60649	3216	3E-8S	A1
10000	SKOK	60076	2811	5W-12N	E7
10000	SKOK	60077	2811	5W-12N	E7

STREET Block	City	ZIP	Map#	CGS	Grid
US-41					
10000	WLMT	60076	2811	5W-12N	E7
10000	WLMT	60077	2811	5W-12N	E7
10000	WLMT	60091	2811	5W-13N	E6
10300	CHCG	60617	3280	4E-11S	C1
10500	CHCG	46320	3280	4E-12S	C1
US-41 E 85th St					
3200	CHCG	60617	3216	4E-9S	A3
US-41 E 87th St					
3200	CHCG	60617	3216	4E-9S	A3
US-41 S Baker Av					
8400	CHCG	60617	3216	3E-9S	A3
US-41 S Burley Av					
8500	CHCG	60617	3216	4E-9S	A3
US-41 Calumet Av					
-	HMND	46320	3430		E1
6200	HMND	46324	3430		E1
US-41 S Calumet Av					
1400	HMND	46394	3280		E7
2100	HMND	46320	3280		E5
3000	HMND	46320	3352		E5
3000	HMND	46327	3280		E7
3000	HMND	46327	3352		E5
5900	HMND	46320	3430		E2
6100	HMND	46324	3430		E2
US-41 S Coast Guard Dr					
6400	CHCG	60637	3153	2E-7S	C5
6400	CHCG	60649	3153	2E-7S	C5
US-41 Edens Expwy					
-	GLNC	-	2758	7W-16N	B7
-	HDPK	-	2757	8W-20N	E2
-	NfdT	-	2757	8W-18N	E2
-	NfdT	-	2811	7W-16N	C1
-	NHBK	-	2757	8W-18N	E2
-	NHBK	-	2758	7W-17N	A4
-	NHFD	-	2758	7W-16N	B7
-	NHFD	-	2811	6W-14N	D4
-	NtrT	-	2758	7W-18N	A4
-	NtrT	-	2811	6W-14N	D4
US-41 S Ewing Av					
9200	CHCG	60617	3216	4E-10S	A5
US-41 W Foster Av					
900	CHCG	60640	2921	1W-6N	E5
1900	CHCG	60625	2921	2W-6N	B5
US-41 S Indianapolis Av					
-	CHCG	60617	3280	4E-11S	C1
10000	CHCG	60617	3216	4E-11S	B7
10600	CHCG	46320	3280	4E-11S	C1
10600	HMND	46320	3280	4E-12S	C1
US-41 S Indianapolis Blvd					
1000	HMND	46320	3280		D2
1000	HMND	46394	3280		D3
10500	CHCG	46320	3280	4E-12S	C1
10500	CHCG	60617	3280		C1
US-41 N Lake Shore Dr					
-	CHCG	-	2921	0W-6N	E6
-	CHCG	-	2922	0W-5N	A7
-	CHCG	-	2978	0W-4N	A3
-	CHCG	-	3034	0E-1N	C1
-	CokC	-	3034	0E-0N	D4
US-41 S Lake Shore Dr					
-	CHCG	-	3092	0E-1S	D1
-	CHCG	-	3093	1E-4S	A6
-	CHCG	-	3153	2E-5S	B1
-	CokC	60637	3153	2E-6S	C3
10	CHCG	60601	3034	0E-1S	D7
10	CHCG	60603	3034	0E-1S	D7
100	CHCG	60605	3034	0E-0S	D5
1400	CHCG	60616	3034	0E-1S	D7
5300	CHCG	60637	3153	2E-7S	D5
US-41 Lincoln Av					
7400	LNWD	60712	2866	5W-9N	A7
7400	SKOK	60076	2866	5W-9N	A7
7500	SKOK	60076	2865	5W-9N	E7
7500	SKOK	60077	2865	5W-9N	E7
US-41 N Lincoln Av					
5200	CHCG	60625	2921	3W-6N	A5
5500	CHCG	60659	2921	1W-6N	D5
5600	CHCG	60659	2920	3W-7N	E4
6300	CHCG	60712	2920	4W-7N	C3
6300	LNWD	60712	2920	3W-7N	E4
7200	LNWD	60712	2866	5W-9N	A7
7200	SKOK	60076	2866	5W-9N	A7
US-41 S Mackinaw Av					
8700	CHCG	60617	3216	4E-10S	B6
US-41 E Marquette Dr					
2000	CHCG	60637	3153	2E-7S	C5
2000	CHCG	60649	3153	2E-7S	C5
US-41 Skokie Blvd					
7500	SKOK	60076	2865	6W-12N	E1
7500	SKOK	60077	2865	6W-12N	E1
10000	SKOK	60076	2811	5W-12N	E7
10000	SKOK	60077	2811	5W-12N	E7
10000	WLMT	60076	2811	5W-12N	E7
10000	WLMT	60077	2811	5W-12N	E7
10000	WLMT	60091	2811	5W-12N	E7
US-41 Skokie Hwy					
-	HDPK	-	2757	8W-18N	E3
-	NfdT	-	2757	8W-18N	E3
-	NHBK	-	2757	8W-18N	E3
US-41 Skokie Rd					
-	NHFD	60093	2811	5W-13N	E6
-	SKOK	60077	2811	5W-13N	E7
-	WLMT	60077	2811	5W-13N	E7
-	WLMT	60091	2811	5W-13N	E6
-	WLMT	60093	2811	5W-13N	E6
US-41 Skokie Valley Rd					
-	HDPK	60035	2757	9W-20N	D1
US-41 E South Shore Dr					
2400	CHCG	60649	3153	3E-7S	D6
US-41 S South Shore Dr					
6700	CHCG	60649	3153	2E-7S	D5
7700	CHCG	60649	3215	3E-8S	E1
7800	CHCG	60617	3216	3E-8S	A1
7800	CHCG	60649	3216	3E-8S	A1
US-41 Tri State Expwy					
-	HMND	-	3430		E5
US-45					
-	CHCG	60176	2917	12W-6N	B6
-	CHCG	60666	2973	12W-5N	A1
-	HGKN	60525	3209	12W-8S	C1
-	HLSD	60104	3029	12W-0S	A6
-	HLSD	60154	3029	12W-0S	A6
-	LynT	60458	3209	12W-8S	C1
-	LynT	60480	3209	12W-8S	C1
-	MKNA	60448	3423	12W-22S	D7
-	PlsT	60465	3273	12W-13S	D4
-	PlsT	60480	3209	11W-11S	D7
-	PlsT	60480	3273	12W-13S	D4
-	SRPK	60176	2917	12W-6N	B6
-	WLSP	60458	3209	12W-8S	C1
-	WLSP	60480	3209	11W-9S	D4
-	WLSP	60525	3209	12W-8S	C1
10	BLWD	60104	3029	12W-1N	A3
10	BLWD	60160	3029	13W-1N	A3

STREET Block	City	ZIP	Map#	CGS	Grid
US-45					
10	BLWD	60162	3029	12W-0S	A6
10	DSPN	60016	2863	13W-11N	A3
10	HLSD	60162	3029	12W-0S	A7
10	LGNG	60525	3087	12W-4S	C6
10	MLPK	60160	3029	13W-1N	A3
10	WSTR	60154	3029	13W-0S	A7
100	LGPK	60525	3087	12W-3S	C6
100	MaiT	60016	2863	13W-12N	A1
300	LGNG	60525	3147	12W-7S	C5
300	PvsT	60162	3029	12W-0S	A7
400	WhlT	60056	2808	13W-13N	E6
500	PTHT	60062	2809	13W-15N	A1
500	PTHT	60070	2809	13W-15N	A1
500	PTHT	60090	2809	13W-15N	A1
500	WhlT	60062	2809	13W-15N	A1
500	WhlT	60090	2809	13W-15N	A1
500	WLNG	60090	2755	13W-17N	D5
600	MPPT	60056	2808	13W-13N	E6
600	WhlT	60025	2808	13W-13N	E6
600	WhlT	60090	2755	13W-17N	E5
700	DSPN	60016	2808	13W-12N	E7
700	DSPN	60016	2809	13W-12N	A7
700	MaiT	60016	2808	13W-12N	E7
700	MaiT	60016	2809	13W-12N	A7
800	BFGV	60090	2755	14W-20N	C2
900	BFGV	60089	2755	14W-20N	C1
900	DSPN	60016	2862	13W-10N	E4
900	VrnT	60015	2755	14W-20N	C1
900	VrnT	60062	2755	14W-20N	C1
900	VrnT	60089	2755	14W-20N	C1
900	WhlT	60016	2808	13W-13N	E7
1000	DSPN	60018	2862	13W-10N	E5
1000	PvsT	60525	3087	12W-2S	B4
1000	RVWD	60015	2755	14W-20N	C1
1100	PTHT	60070	2755	13W-16N	E7
1100	PTHT	60070	2808	13W-16N	E1
1100	WhlT	60090	2808	13W-16N	E1
1200	MPPT	60056	2809	13W-15N	A2
1300	PvsT	60154	3029	12W-1S	A7
1300	WhlT	60025	2809	13W-14N	A3
1400	PvsT	60154	3087	12W-1S	A1
1400	PvsT	60162	3087	12W-1S	A1
1400	WSTR	60154	3087	12W-4S	C6
1500	MLPK	60165	3029	12W-1N	A2
1500	SNPK	60165	3029	12W-1N	A1
1700	DSPN	60018	2863	13W-9N	A7
2000	DSPN	60018	2917	12W-8N	A2
2000	LydT	60164	2973	12W-2N	A7
2000	MLPK	60160	2973	12W-2N	A7
2000	NHLK	60164	2973	12W-2N	A7
2000	RSMT	60018	2917	13W-8N	A2
2300	LydT	60131	2973	13W-2N	A6
2400	FNPK	60131	2973	13W-3N	A6
2400	FNPK	60164	2973	13W-3N	A6
2900	CHCG	60666	2917	12W-6N	B7
2900	RSMT	60666	2917	12W-8N	A2
3700	SRPK	60176	2973	13W-4N	A4
4000	FNPK	60176	2973	13W-4N	A4
5200	CTSD	60525	3147	12W-5S	C3
6000	HGKN	60525	3147	12W-6S	C5
11800	PlsT	60464	3273	12W-15S	D7
11800	PSPK	60464	3273	12W-15S	D7
12700	PSPK	60464	3345	11W-15S	D1
13000	PlsT	60462	3345	11W-15S	D1
13000	PSPK	60462	3345	11W-15S	D1
13400	OrlT	60462	3345	11W-15S	D2
13500	ODPK	60462	3345	12W-16S	D2
15700	ODPK	60462	3423	11W-18S	D1
15800	ODPK	60467	3423	11W-20S	D5
16600	ODHL	60477	3423	11W-19S	D3
16600	OrlT	60467	3423	11W-19S	D3
16900	TYPK	60477	3423	11W-20S	D4
17500	OrlT	60477	3423	11W-21S	D6
18200	FftT	60448	3423	12W-21S	D7
18200	ODPK	60448	3423	12W-21S	D7
18200	ODPK	60477	3423	12W-21S	D7
US-45 96th Av					
-	PlsT	60464	3273	11W-13S	D4
-	PlsT	60465	3273	12W-13S	D4
-	PlsT	60480	3273	12W-13S	D4
US-45 N Des Plaines River Rd					
10	DSPN	60016	2863	13W-12N	A2
100	MaiT	60016	2863	13W-12N	A1
900	DSPN	60016	2808	13W-13N	E7
900	MaiT	60016	2808	13W-13N	E7
900	WhlT	60016	2808	13W-13N	E7
1000	WhlT	60056	2808	13W-13N	E6
US-45 Graceland Av					
800	DSPN	60016	2862	13W-10N	E4
US-45 La Grange Rd					
-	LynT	60458	3209	12W-8S	C1
-	LynT	60480	3209	12W-8S	C1
-	MKNA	60448	3423	12W-22S	D7
-	PlsT	60480	3209	11W-11S	D7
-	PlsT	60480	3273	11W-12S	D1
-	WLSP	60458	3209	12W-8S	C1
-	WLSP	60480	3209	11W-9S	D4
-	WLSP	60525	3209	12W-8S	D1
16700	ODHL	60477	3423	11W-20S	D3
16700	ODPK	60467	3423	11W-19S	D3
16700	OrlT	60467	3423	11W-20S	D3
16700	OrlT	60477	3423	11W-20S	D3
16900	TYPK	60477	3423	11W-20S	D4
18200	FftT	60448	3423	12W-21S	D7
18200	ODPK	60448	3423	12W-21S	D7
18200	ODPK	60477	3423	12W-21S	D7
US-45 N La Grange Rd					
-	WSTR	60154	3087	12W-2S	A2
10	LGNG	60525	3087	12W-4S	C6
100	LGPK	60525	3087	12W-3S	C6
1000	PvsT	60525	3087	12W-2S	B4
2500	PvsT	60154	3087	12W-2S	B2
US-45 S La Grange Rd					
-	HGKN	60525	3147	12W-8S	C7
-	HGKN	60525	3209	12W-8S	C1
-	PlsT	60480	3273	12W-13S	D4
-	WLSP	60525	3209	12W-8S	C1
10	LGNG	60525	3087	12W-4S	C7
300	LGNG	60525	3147	12W-7S	C5
5200	CTSD	60525	3147	12W-5S	C3
11800	PlsT	60464	3273	12W-15S	D7
11800	PSPK	60464	3273	12W-15S	D7
12700	PSPK	60464	3345	12W-15S	D1
13000	PlsT	60462	3345	11W-15S	D1
13000	PSPK	60462	3345	11W-15S	D1
13400	OrlT	60462	3345	11W-15S	D2
13500	ODPK	60462	3345	12W-16S	D2
15700	ODPK	60462	3423	11W-18S	D1
15800	ODPK	60467	3423	12W-20S	D5
16600	ODHL	60477	3423	11W-19S	D3
16600	OrlT	60467	3423	11W-19S	D3
US-45 Mannheim Rd					
-	CHCG	60176	2917	12W-6N	B6
-	CHCG	60666	2973	12W-5N	A1

STREET Block	City	ZIP	Map#	CGS	Grid
US-45 Mannheim Rd					
-	SRPK	60176	2917	12W-6N	B6
-	SRPK	60176	2973	12W-5N	A1
10	BLWD	60104	3029	12W-0N	A3
10	BLWD	60160	3029	12W-1N	A3
10	MLPK	60160	3029	12W-1N	A3
500	BLWD	60162	3029	12W-0N	A4
500	HLSD	60162	3029	12W-0N	A4
600	DSPN	60016	2863	13W-11N	A4
900	DSPN	60016	2862	13W-10N	E4
1000	DSPN	60018	2862	13W-10N	E5
1700	DSPN	60018	2863	13W-9N	A7
2000	DSPN	60018	2917	13W-8N	A2
2000	RSMT	60018	2917	13W-8N	A2
2400	FNPK	60131	2973	13W-3N	A6
2400	FNPK	60164	2973	13W-3N	A6
2400	LydT	60131	2973	13W-3N	A6
2400	LydT	60164	2973	13W-3N	A6
2900	CHCG	60666	2917	12W-6N	B7
2900	RSMT	60666	2917	12W-8N	A2
4000	FNPK	60176	2973	13W-4N	A4
US-45 N Mannheim Rd					
-	BLWD	60104	3029	13W-1N	A3
-	BLWD	60160	3029	13W-1N	A3
-	HLSD	60104	3029	12W-0S	A6
-	HLSD	60154	3029	12W-0S	A6
-	WSTR	60154	3029	12W-0S	A6
10	BLWD	60162	3029	12W-0S	A6
10	HLSD	60162	3029	12W-0S	A6
1500	MLPK	60160	3029	13W-1N	A3
1500	MLPK	60165	3029	12W-1N	A2
1500	SNPK	60165	3029	13W-1N	A1
2000	LydT	60164	2973	12W-2N	A7
2000	MLPK	60160	2973	12W-2N	A7
2000	NHLK	60164	2973	12W-2N	A7
2300	LydT	60131	2973	13W-2N	A6
US-45 S Mannheim Rd					
-	BLWD	60104	3029	12W-0S	A6
-	HLSD	60154	3029	12W-0S	A6
10	HLSD	60162	3029	13W-0S	A7
10	WSTR	60154	3029	13W-0S	A7
300	PvsT	60162	3029	12W-0S	A7
1300	PvsT	60154	3029	12W-1S	A7
1400	PvsT	60154	3087	12W-1S	A1
1400	PvsT	60162	3087	12W-1S	A1
1400	WSTR	60154	3087	12W-4S	C6
US-45 Milwaukee Av					
900	BFGV	60089	2755	14W-20N	C1
900	VrnT	60015	2755	14W-20N	C1
900	VrnT	60062	2755	14W-20N	C1
900	VrnT	60089	2755	14W-20N	C1
1000	RVWD	60015	2755	14W-20N	C1
20400	BFGV	60090	2755	14W-20N	C1
US-45 N Milwaukee Av					
500	PTHT	60062	2809	13W-15N	A1
500	PTHT	60070	2809	13W-15N	A1
500	PTHT	60090	2809	13W-15N	A1
500	WhlT	60062	2809	13W-15N	A1
500	WhlT	60090	2809	13W-15N	A1
500	WLNG	60090	2755	13W-17N	D5
800	BFGV	60090	2755	14W-20N	C2
900	BFGV	60089	2755	14W-20N	C1
900	VrnT	60062	2755	14W-20N	C1
900	VrnT	60089	2755	14W-20N	C1
US-45 S Milwaukee Av					
10	WLNG	60090	2755	14W-18N	D4
600	WhlT	60090	2755	13W-17N	E5
1100	PTHT	60070	2755	13W-16N	E7
1100	PTHT	60070	2808	13W-16N	E1
1100	PTHT	60070	2809	13W-16N	A1
1100	PTHT	60090	2809	13W-16N	A1
1100	WhlT	60090	2808	13W-16N	E1
1100	WhlT	60090	2809	13W-16N	A1
US-45 N River Rd					
400	WhlT	60056	2808	13W-13N	E6
600	MPPT	60056	2808	13W-13N	E6
600	WhlT	60025	2808	13W-13N	E6
700	DSPN	60016	2808	13W-12N	E7
700	DSPN	60016	2809	13W-12N	A7
700	MaiT	60016	2808	13W-12N	E7
700	MaiT	60016	2809	13W-12N	A7
1300	MPPT	60056	2809	13W-14N	A3
1300	WhlT	60025	2809	13W-14N	A3
1300	WhlT	60062	2809	13W-14N	A3
1500	PTHT	60070	2809	13W-15N	A2
US-45 S River Rd					
10	DSPN	60016	2863	13W-11N	A3
1200	MPPT	60056	2809	13W-15N	A2
1200	PTHT	60070	2809	12W-15N	A2
1200	WhlT	60062	2809	13W-15N	A2

A

STREET Block	City	ZIP	Map#	CGS	Grid
Abbe Ct					
5400	OKFT	60452	3425	6W-19S	E1
Abbey Ct					
-	TYPK	60477	3424	10W-21S	C7
Abbey Ln					
10	PKFT	60466	3595	2W-28S	D6
8800	ODPK	60462	3346	11W-18S	A7
Abbey Rd					
-	TYPK	60477	3424	10W-21S	C7
500	BRLT	60103	2911		C5
S Abbey Hill Ln					
400	PLTN	60067	2805	22W-15N	C2
Abbey Oaks Dr					
1200	LMNT	60439	3271		B7
Abbeywood Cir					
100	SMWD	60107	2857	28W-11N	B4
Abbeywood Ct					
500	OKBK	60523	3028		B7
1000	ELGN	60120	2855		D2
N Abbeywood Ct					
2100	PLTN	60074	2753	20W-20N	B1
Abbey Wood Ln					
-	HFET	60195	2858	25W-12N	A1
Abbington Ct					
10	SMWD	60107	2856	29W-9N	D7
Abbington Pl					
400	SMBG	60194	2858	24W-11N	C4
Abbotsford Dr					
1900	IVNS	60010	2751	25W-16N	B6
2000	HFET	60010	2751	24W-16N	B7
Abbotsford Rd					
10	KLWH	60043	2812	4W-14N	C3
10	WNKA	60043	2812	4W-14N	C3
10	WNKA	60093	2812	4W-14N	C4
Abbott Av					
200	CHHT	60411	3507	2W-24S	D5
200	CHHT	60422	3507	2W-24S	D5
200	FSMR	60422	3507	2W-24S	D5
S Abbott Av					
9000	CHCG	60620	3214	0W-10S	B5
Abbott Ct					
1800	NHFD	60093	2811	7W-15N	B2
Abbott Dr					
100	WLNG	60090	2808	14W-16N	B1
Abbott Ln					
1000	UYPK	60466	3684	3W-30S	B3
S Abbott Rd E					
14400	HMGN	60441	3344	15W-17S	C5
S Abbott Rd W					
14500	HMGN	60441	3344	15W-17S	C5
Abbott St					
100	WLSP	60480	3209	12W-9S	B4
Abbott Ter					
4500	LYNS	60534	3088	10W-4S	B7
Abbottsford Rd					
14300	MDLN	60445	3348	4W-17S	D4
Abby Ln					
4600	MTSN	60443	3506	5W-24S	B5
Aberdeen Ct					
10	SMBG	60194	2857	26W-10N	E6
8000	PSHT	60464	3346	10W-15S	C2
E Aberdeen Ct					
300	EMHT	60126	3028		B5
Aberdeen Dr					
100	EDND	60118	2801		C2
200	BNHL	60010	2749	28W-18N	E3
400	CRTE	60417	3596	0E-28S	E6
600	CRTE	60417	3597	0E-28S	A6
1800	GNVW	60025	2810	8W-15N	D2
2100	CPVL	60110	2748		D6
8100	PSHT	60464	3346	10W-15S	C2
Aberdeen Ln					
500	PTHT	60070	2808	14W-14N	B3
1000	IVNS	60067	2752	22W-16N	B7
Aberdeen Rd					
500	FKFT	60423	3593	9W-26S	A2
500	IVNS	60067	2752	22W-16N	B6
500	RchT	60443	3593	9W-26S	A2
Aberdeen St					
500	HFET	60194	2859	22W-11N	C4
1400	CHHT	60411	3508	1W-25S	A7
1400	CHHT	60411	3596	1W-25S	A1
2500	SCHT	60411	3596	1W-26S	A3
18100	HMWD	60430	3428	1W-22S	A7
18400	HMWD	60430	3508	1W-22S	A1
N Aberdeen St					
10	CHCG	60607	3033	1W-0N	E4
300	CHCG	60622	3033	1W-0N	E4
S Aberdeen St					
10	CHCG	60607	3033	1W-0S	E5
1400	CHCG	60608	3033	1W-1S	E7
3100	CHCG	60608	3091	1W-3S	E4
3400	CHCG	60609	3091	1W-3S	E5
4700	CHCG	60609	3151	1W-6S	E3
5500	CHCG	60621	3151	1W-7S	E6
7500	CHCG	60620	3213	1W-9S	E2
9900	CHCG	60643	3213	1W-11S	E7
10300	CHCG	60643	3277	1W-12S	E1
12700	CTPK	60827	3277	1W-15S	E7
Aberdour Ln					
100	IVNS	60067	2752	22W-16N	B7
Abigail Ln					
17700	ODPK	60467	3423	13W-21S	B6
Abingdon Av					
100	KLWH	60043	2812	3W-14N	E4
Abourndale Ct					
1400	PTHT	60070	2754	16W-16N	D6
1400	WLNG	60090	2754	16W-16N	D6
Acacia Cir					
100	IHPK	60525	3146		E6
Acacia Dr					
100	IHPK	60525	3146		E6
15700	ODPK	60462	3424	10W-18S	B1
Acacia Ln					
10	BmdT	60143	2913		C7
10	BmdT	60157	2913		C7
10	ROSL	60143	2913		C7
10	ROSL	60157	2913		C7
1600	CTSD	60525	3147	13W-7S	A6
1600	IHPK	60525	3147	13W-7S	A6
1700	IHPK	60525	3146		E6
Academy Av					
500	MTSN	60443	3506	5W-25S	B7
Academy Ct					
600	SMBG	60194	2857	27W-11N	C3
Academy Dr					
400	NHBK	60062	2756	11W-18N	D3
Academy Pl					
200	ELGN	60120	2855		A3
S Academy Pl					
10	CHCG	60607	3034	0W-0S	A5
Acadia Ct					
-	HnrT	60107	2856	30W-10N	B6
-	HnrT	60120	2856	30W-10N	B6
600	ROSL	60172	2913		C3
Acadia Bay					
600	ROSL	60172	2913		C2
Accera Dr					
10	HLSD	60162	3029	13W-0S	A7
N Access Rd					
-	CHCG	60666	2916		C7
S Acco Plz					
700	WLNG	60090	2755	14W-17N	D6
Achilles Av					
20300	OMFD	60461	3506	4W-24S	E6
W Acme Dr					
100	RVDL	60827	3350	0W-15S	C1
Acorn Ct					
200	SMBG	60193	2858	23W-10N	E6
700	BRLT	60103	2911		B3
1500	WLNG	60090	2754	16W-18N	D3
5700	HFET	60120	2856	31W-12N	A1
13300	PSHT	60463	3347	7W-15S	B2
14300	HMGN	60441	3342	19W-17S	D5
S Acorn Ct					
23500	CteT	60417	3595	2W-28S	E6
Acorn Dr					
200	SMWD	60107	2857	27W-10N	D7
1600	HFET	60120	2856	31W-12N	A1
14500	HMGN	60441	3342	19W-17S	D5
Acorn Ln					
-	BmnT	60426	3426	5W-19S	B1
10	HDPK	60035	2757	9W-20N	D2
10	STGR	60475	3597	1E-27S	A5
2800	NHBK	60062	2756	11W-17N	D4
3600	FNPK	60131	2972		C3
3600	LydT	60131	2972		C3
15000	HMGN	60441	3342	18W-16S	E3
Acorn St					
1200	LMNT	60439	3342	19W-15S	C1
Acorn Hill Ln					
500	OKBK	60523	3086		A6
Acorn Ln Dr					
1800	FSMR	60422	3507	2W-23S	D3
S Acorn Ridge Dr					
20400	FftT	60423	3504	9W-25S	E7

Chicago & Cook County Street Index

STREET Block	City	ZIP	Map#	CGS	Grid
Alley C					
-	WLSP	60480	3209	12W-9S	B4
Allison Ct					
2500	MaiT	60025	2864	9W-12N	C1
W Allison Ct					
1400	ANHT	60005	2860	19W-12N	D1
Allison Ln					
1200	SMBG	60194	2858	25W-11N	B4
14900	HMGN	60441	3344	15W-17S	C6
17500	ODPK	60467	3423	13W-21S	A6
E Allison St					
300	EMHT	60126	3028		B5
Allison Woods					
10000	NfdT	60062	2809	12W-15N	A2
10000	PTHT	60062	2809	12W-15N	A2
Allmen Av					
900	HNDL	60521	3146		A3
Allonby Dr					
400	SMBG	60194	2858	24W-11N	D4
S Allport St					
1600	CHCG	60608	3091	1W-1S	D1
Alma Ct					
700	CPVL	60110	2748		B7
E Almond Ct					
1800	MPPT	60056	2808	13W-14N	D4
N Almond Ct					
2000	PLTN	60074	2753	19W-18N	B3
W Almond Ct					
7700	FftT	60423	3504	9W-24S	E5
Almond Ln					
600	HFET	60194	2859	22W-11N	C4
9200	TYPK	60477	3423	11W-21S	E6
Almond Pk					
-	CHCG	60643	3277	2W-13S	D4
Alnwick Ct					
600	IVNS	60010	2751	25W-17N	B6
Aloha Ln					
10	PvsT	60558	3086		D4
10	WSTR	60523	3086		D4
Alpha St					
-	LYWD	60411	3510	4E-24S	B6
S Alpine Av					
11500	PSPK	60464	3274	10W-13S	C4
Alpine Ct					
1300	HRPK	60133	2911		E5
1300	WLNG	60090	2754	16W-18N	D2
Alpine Dr					
100	SMBG	60194	2858	25W-10N	C5
12100	HMGN	60441	3344	15W-18S	C7
15100	ODPK	60467	3344	14W-18S	C7
S Alpine Dr					
12500	ALSP	60445	3275	6W-14S	D7
12500	ALSP	60463	3275	6W-14S	D7
12500	ALSP	60803	3275	6W-14S	D7
12500	CTWD	60445	3275	6W-14S	D7
12500	CTWD	60803	3275	6W-14S	D7
12500	WthT	60463	3275	6W-14S	D7
Alpine Ln					
-	DSPN	60018	2917	12W-8N	B2
10	CRTE	60417	3596	0E-28S	D6
300	HFET	60194	2859	23W-11N	B3
400	WLMT	60091	2812	4W-13N	B6
1100	LMNT	60439	3270		E7
Alpine Rdg					
-	CPVL	60110	2748		A7
Alpine St					
-	LKPT	60441	3342	21W-17S	A6
S Alta Dr					
10300	PSHL	60465	3274	10W-12S	B1
Alta Rd					
15400	MKHM	60426	3348	4W-18S	E7
Alta St					
2900	LydT	60164	2972		E4
3200	FNPK	60131	2972		E4
N Alta Vista Ter					
3800	CHCG	60613	2977	1W-4N	E2
Altgeld St					
10500	LydT	60164	2973	13W-3N	A6
10600	LydT	60164	2972		E6
10600	NHLK	60164	2972		E6
W Altgeld St					
800	CHCG	60614	2977	1W-3N	D5
2400	CHCG	60647	2977	3W-3N	A5
3200	CHCG	60647	2976	4W-3N	C5
4400	CHCG	60639	2976	5W-3N	A5
4800	CHCG	60639	2975	7W-3N	B5
6700	CHCG	60707	2974	8W-3N	E5
6700	CHCG	60707	2975	8W-3N	A5
7600	EDPK	60707	2974	9W-3N	C5
N Althea Dr					
1400	MPPT	60056	2808	13W-14N	E3
Alton Rd					
10	PTHT	60070	2808	14W-14N	C3
100	MPPT	60056	2808	14W-14N	C3
Alton on Auburn					
10	RGMW	60008	2806	19W-14N	B4
Altoona Ct					
1800	SMBG	60194	2858	25W-11N	A4
W Alva St					
800	PLTN	60067	2752	22W-16N	C6
Alveston St					
10300	ODPK	60462	3345	13W-17S	B6
Alvin Av					
100	MLPK	60160	2973	13W-2N	A7
100	MLPK	60164	2973	13W-2N	A7
100	NHLK	60164	2973	13W-2N	A7
100	NHLK	60164	3029	13W-2N	A1
Alvin Ct					
1200	GNVW	60025	2810	9W-13N	D5
Alvin Pl					
-	CHHT	60411	3508	0W-24S	B4
Alysse Ct					
-	ODPK	60467	3422	13W-21S	E7
Amaarja Ct					
4800	RGMW	60067	2805	21W-13N	E5
Amalfi Dr					
4000	NfdT	60025	2809	11W-13N	D7
Amanda Ct					
10	CRTE	60417	3685	1W-30S	B2
5500	RGMW	60008	2805	21W-13N	C5
Amanda Ln					
-	SMBG	60173	2859	23W-12N	A1
-	SMBG	60195	2859	23W-12N	A1
Amarillo Ct					
400	CPVL	60110	2748		B4
Amarillo Dr					
10	CPVL	60110	2748		B5
Amarillo St					
-	HRPK	60133	2911		E5
Ambassador Ln					
1500	FDHT	60411	3509	1E-25S	B6
Amber Cir					
4700	HFET	60195	2804	24W-15N	B1
Amber Ct					
10	CRTE	60417	3685	1W-29S	B2
Amber Ct					
10	SMBG	60193	2857	27W-10N	C5
Amber Dr					
1000	LMNT	60439	3271		A7
Amber Ln					
10400	ODPK	60467	3423	13W-21S	B6
23000	RNPK	60471	3594	4W-27S	D5
Amberley Ln					
400	DRFD	60015	2757	10W-20N	A1
Amberwood Ln					
1400	LmnT	60439	3271		B6
Ambleside Dr					
300	ROSL	60172	2913		B4
Ambleside Rd					
200	DSPN	60016	2862	15W-11N	A4
Amboy Ln					
10	SMBG	60194	2858	25W-10N	C5
Ambriance Dr					
-	BRRG	60527	3208		C2
Ambrose Dr					
-	PlsT	60464	3345	13W-15S	A1
-	PlsT	60467	3345	13W-15S	A1
Ambrose Ln					
10	SBTN	60010	2803	26W-13N	D6
Ambry Cir					
-	LYWD	60411	3509	2E-23S	D3
Amelia Av					
3900	LYNS	60534	3088	9W-4S	C7
Amelia Ct					
7800	JSTC	60458	3209	11W-8S	E2
W Amelia Dr					
8400	MaiT	60714	2864	10W-10N	A4
8400	NLES	60714	2864	10W-10N	A4
America Ct					
17800	ODPK	60467	3423	13W-21S	A6
American Ln					
800	SMBG	60173	2859	21W-11N	D2
2300	EGVV	60007	2915		E4
American Wy					
10	ELGN	60120	2855		C3
900	EDND	60118	2801		B3
Americana Ct					
10	ROSL	60172	2912		C4
E Ames St					
800	HMND	46320	3430		E1
Amherst Av					
100	DSPN	60016	2862	14W-12N	C1
500	DSPN	60016	2808	14W-12N	C7
Amherst Ct					
2000	FSMR	60422	3507	2W-23S	C3
17900	CCHL	60478	3426	5W-21S	D6
Amherst Dr					
100	BRLT	60103	2910		E4
100	BRLT	60103	2911		A4
1300	SMBG	60194	2858	25W-10N	B5
Amherst Ln					
400	SMBG	60195	2858	24W-12N	E2
500	HFET	60195	2858	24W-12N	E2
1000	UYPK	60449	3684	3W-30S	B4
1000	UYPK	60466	3684	3W-30S	C4
17000	TYPK	60477	3424	9W-20S	D4
20500	DRPK	60010	2751	23W-20N	D1
Amherst Mdw					
100	BRLT	60103	2910		E4
100	WynT	60103	2910		E4
Amherst Pl					
5600	MTSN	60443	3505	7W-25S	D7
E Amherst St					
300	PLTN	60067	2753	20W-17N	A5
300	PLTN	60074	2753	20W-17N	A5
E Amhurst Ct					
2200	ANHT	60004	2807	16W-15N	D2
Amhurst Ln					
900	WLMT	60091	2812	4W-14N	B5
Amlin Cir					
-	MTSN	60443	3505	7W-25S	D7
18600	CCHL	60478	3506	6W-22S	A1
Amlin Ln					
19000	CCHL	60478	3506	6W-22S	A2
Amlin Ter					
-	MTSN	60443	3505	7W-25S	D7
Ammer Rd					
1400	GNVW	60025	2810	8W-14N	E4
1400	GNVW	60025	2811	8W-14N	A4
Ammer Ridge Ct					
1900	GNVW	60025	2810	8W-14N	E4
Amsterdam Ln					
500	PTON	60468	3860	9W-37S	E3
S Amy Av					
1500	HMND	46394	3280		E4
Amy Ct					
1300	WLNG	60090	2754	16W-18N	D2
S Amy Ct					
1400	HMND	46394	3280		E3
Amy Dr					
22400	RNPK	60471	3594	6W-27S	A4
Amy St					
100	CHHT	60411	3507	1W-24S	E5
100	CHHT	60411	3508	1W-24S	A4
Ana Rd					
-	MKHM	60426	3348	4W-18S	E6
Anand Brook Dr					
12400	HmrT	60467	3344	15W-16S	A3
12600	HMGN	60441	3344	15W-16S	A3
12600	HmrT	60441	3344	15W-16S	A3
Anchor Ct					
800	BRLT	60103	2911		B4
N Anchor Dr					
3200	CHCG	60618	2977	3W-4N	A3
Ancient Oaks Ct					
1100	BRLT	60103	2910		C7
Ancient Oaks Dr					
1100	BRLT	60103	2910		C7
Ancient Tree Rd					
-	NHBK	60062	2756	11W-17N	C5
W Ancona St					
-	CHCG	60622	3033	2W-0S	C5
Anders Dr					
-	EGVV	60007	2913		E2
Andersen Av					
9900	CHRG	60415	3211	8W-11S	A7
9900	CHRG	60415	3275	8W-11S	A1
E Anderson Dr					
800	PLTN	60074	2753	19W-16N	C7
1500	ANHT	60004	2753	18W-16N	D7
Anderson Pl					
10400	FNPK	60131	2973	13W-3N	A4
Anderson Ter					
200	DSPN	60016	2862	15W-10N	B5
Anderson Ter E					
800	DSPN	60016	2862	15W-10N	B4
N Andoa Ln					
1800	MPPT	60056	2808	13W-15N	D2
1800	PTHT	60070	2808	13W-15N	D2
Andover Cir					
10	NHBK	60062	2756	12W-18N	A2
Andover Ct					
300	SMWD	60107	2857	27W-9N	C7
800	PTHT	60070	2808	15W-16N	A1
1800	CHHT	60411	3595	2W-26S	C1
2200	SMBG	60194	2857	26W-11N	E4
W Andover Ct					
900	PLTN	60067	2752	22W-16N	B6
Andover Dr					
10	PTHT	60070	2808	15W-16N	A1
10	ROSL	60172	2912		C4
100	PTHT	60070	2807	15W-16N	E1
4200	RNPK	60471	3594	5W-26S	C3
N Andover Dr					
10	ROSL	60172	2912		C4
W Andover Dr					
5900	HRPK	60133	2911		D5
Andover Dr E					
1500	HRPK	60133	2911		D5
Andover Dr W					
5800	HRPK	60133	2911		D5
Andover St					
500	CHHT	60411	3595	2W-26S	C1
Andrea Ct					
10600	ODPK	60467	3423	13W-21S	B6
Andrea Dr					
10600	ODPK	60467	3423	13W-21S	A6
Andrea Ln					
1200	DSPN	60016	2862	15W-10N	A5
1200	DSPN	60018	2862	15W-10N	A5
Andrene Ln					
10	BmdT	60143	2914		A6
200	BmdT	60143	2913		E5
200	ITSC	60143	2913		E5
Andres Av					
6000	TYPK	60477	3425	7W-20S	C3
Andrew Ct					
10	DGvT	60527	3146		A5
600	SMBG	60193	2858	24W-9N	D6
1700	LGGV	60047	2753	19W-20N	C1
Andrew Dr					
2400	DYR	46311	3598		D3
Andrew Ln					
10	HFET	60193	2858	24W-10N	D6
10	HFET	60194	2858	24W-10N	D6
10	SMBG	60193	2858	24W-10N	D6
Andria Ct					
2000	SMBG	60194	2858	26W-11N	A4
Andy Dr					
100	MLPK	60160	3030	10W-1N	A2
600	MLPK	60160	3029	10W-1N	E1
Andy Ln					
1800	DSPN	60018	2917	12W-8N	B2
Anets Dr					
100	NfdT	60062	2757	9W-16N	B6
100	NHBK	60062	2757	9W-16N	B6
Angela Ct					
1000	SMBG	60173	2859	22W-11N	D4
Angelico St					
14900	LMNT	60439	3343	18W-15S	A2
Angelina Pl					
10	ALGN	60102	2748		A3
10	DndT	60102	2748		A3
Angeline Ct					
4600	PltT	60067	2805	20W-14N	E4
4600	RGMW	60067	2805	20W-14N	E4
Angle Av					
1000	NHBK	60062	2757	9W-17N	B5
Angouleme Ln					
5600	HFET	60120	2856	30W-12N	B2
5600	HFET	60192	2856	30W-12N	B2
Angus Ct					
1800	SMBG	60194	2858	25W-11N	B4
E Anita Av					
100	WhlT	60056	2808	13W-13N	E5
Anita Dr					
400	BRLT	60103	2911		A4
Anita Pl					
300	WLNG	60090	2755	14W-17N	D5
Anita St					
200	DSPN	60016	2862	14W-11N	B3
Anjou Dr					
300	NHBK	60062	2756	12W-18N	C3
Anjou Ln					
3700	HFET	60195	2804	24W-14N	B3
Ann Av					
5200	HMND	46320	3352		C6
Ann Ct					
100	BRLT	60103	2911		A3
Ann Ln					
600	UYPK	60466	3684	3W-30S	B2
Ann St					
200	ELGN	60120	2855		A3
500	DLTN	60419	3350	0E-16S	E4
3100	LNSG	60438	3430	3E-21S	B7
11900	BLID	60406	3277	3W-14S	B5
11900	CHCG	60655	3277	3W-14S	B5
13400	BLID	60406	3349	3W-15S	B2
Anna Av					
4000	LYNS	60534	3088	10W-4S	A7
Anna Ct					
-	PltT	60010	2751	23W-18N	E2
-	PltT	60010	2752	23W-18N	A2
S Anna Marie Dr					
1800	MPPT	60056	2861	17W-10N	C5
Annapolis Dr					
1500	GNVW	60025	2810	9W-14N	C5
Anne Ct					
100	TNTN	60476	3428	0E-20S	D4
300	ANHT	60004	2807	15W-16N	E1
300	PTHT	60004	2807	15W-16N	E1
300	PTHT	60070	2807	15W-16N	E1
8000	ODPK	60462	3346	10W-18S	C7
10400	RSMT	60018	2917	13W-8N	A1
14800	OKFT	60452	3348	6W-17S	A5
Anne Dr					
8000	ODPK	60462	3346	10W-18S	C7
Anne Ln					
1900	CteT	60417	3686	2E-30S	D3
2500	NHBK	60062	2809	11W-15N	D1
Anne Ter					
300	WLNG	60090	2755	14W-17N	C5
W Anne K Dr					
14000	HMGN	60441	3343	17W-17S	C5
Anne Marie Dr					
16700	TYPK	60477	3425	7W-20S	C3
Annetta Av					
16900	HLCT	60429	3427	3W-20S	C4
Annico Dr					
15700	HMGN	60441	3422	16W-18S	A1
W Ann Lurie Pl					
4000	CHCG	60632	3090	5W-4S	C6
Ann Marie Dr					
15300	OKFT	60452	3347	6W-18S	D7
Ann Marie Ln					
5500	OKFT	60452	3347	6W-18S	D7
Anson Dr					
1900	MLPK	60160	3029	13W-2N	A1
1900	MLPK	60164	3029	13W-2N	A1
1900	NHLK	60164	3029	13W-2N	A1
2000	MLPK	60160	2973	13W-2N	A7
2000	MLPK	60164	2973	13W-2N	A7
2000	NHLK	60164	2973	13W-2N	A7
Antelope Ln					
10800	ODPK	60467	3423	13W-20S	A4
Antelope Springs Rd					
3000	NHBK	60062	2756	11W-17N	D5
Antholl St					
3700	FSMR	60422	3506	4W-23S	D3
N Anthon Av					
4500	CHCG	60656	2918	10W-5N	A7
4700	NRDG	60656	2918	10W-5N	A7
4700	NRDG	60706	2918	10W-5N	A7
Anthony Av					
16700	HLCT	60429	3427	2W-20S	C4
16700	MKHM	60426	3427	2W-20S	C4
18300	CCHL	60478	3426	5W-22S	B7
18900	CCHL	60478	3506	5W-22S	B2
18900	RchT	60477	3506	5W-22S	B2
S Anthony Av					
-	CHCG	60619	3152	1E-8S	E7
6800	CHCG	60637	3152	0E-7S	D6
7700	CHCG	60619	3215	1E-8S	A1
8000	CHCG	60617	3215	3E-10S	E5
Anthony Ct					
200	BFGV	60089	2754	16W-17N	D4
Anthony Dr					
10800	ODPK	60467	3423	13W-19S	A2
Anthony Rd					
200	BFGV	60089	2754	16W-17N	E5
400	WLNG	60089	2754	16W-17N	D5
400	WLNG	60090	2754	16W-17N	D5
Anthony Tr					
200	NHBK	60062	2756	11W-18N	D3
Antietam St					
500	MTSN	60443	3594	4W-25S	E1
500	MTSN	60466	3594	4W-25S	E1
500	PKFT	60466	3594	4W-25S	E1
500	PKFT	60466	3595	4W-25S	A1
Antioch Pl					
10	PKFT	60466	3595	2W-26S	D2
Antique Ln					
1000	NHBK	60062	2757	8W-18N	D3
Antler Dr					
17300	ODPK	60467	3423	13W-20S	A5
Anvil Pl					
8400	TYPK	60477	3424	10W-19S	B2
Apache Av					
500	CPVL	60110	2748		D4
2400	SLVL	60411	3597	2E-26S	D3
Apache Dr					
10	TNTN	60476	3428	0E-20S	E4
1400	HRPK	60133	2911		E4
6400	IHPK	60525	3146		D5
Apache Ln					
300	HFET	60194	2859	23W-11N	B3
13900	ODPK	60462	3346	9W-16S	C3
E Apache Ln					
1800	MPPT	60056	2808	13W-14N	D5
Apache Pl					
7900	ODPK	60462	3346	9W-16S	C3
Apache St					
10	PKFT	60466	3595	2W-26S	D2
Apache Tr					
500	WLNG	60090	2754	16W-17N	D5
8000	TYPK	60477	3424	10W-21S	C6
Apollo Cir					
2600	OMFD	60461	3507	3W-25S	B7
Apollo Ct					
-	TYPK	60477	3505	8W-23S	B4
200	WDDL	60191	2914		D7
Apollo Dr					
5600	EGvT	60007	2860	19W-12N	B2
5600	RGMW	60008	2860	19W-12N	B2
Apollo Ln					
4200	SNPK	60165	3029	13W-1N	A2
S Appaloosa Ln					
14400	HMGN	60441	3344	15W-17S	B5
Appian Wy					
500	MTSN	60443	3506	5W-24S	B6
3800	NfdT	60025	2809	11W-13N	D7
Apple Av					
100	LmnT	60439	3271		B6
Apple Ct					
10	PKFT	60466	3595	3W-27S	B5
1400	MPPT	60056	2807	16W-14N	E3
Apple Dr					
800	PTHT	60070	2808	13W-15N	E1
800	SMBG	60194	2858	25W-11N	B3
900	PTHT	60062	2809	13W-15N	A1
900	PTHT	60070	2809	13W-15N	A1
900	PTHT	60090	2809	13W-15N	A1
900	WhlT	60062	2809	13W-15N	A1
900	WhlT	60090	2809	13W-15N	A1
Apple Ln					
10	BlmT	60466	3595	3W-27S	C5
10	PKFT	60466	3595	3W-27S	B4
1200	ELGN	60120	2855		D4
16100	TYPK	60477	3424	10W-19S	B2
S Apple Ln					
12800	ALSP	60803	3276	5W-15S	B7
12800	ALSP	60803	3348	5W-15S	B1
Apple St					
900	HFET	60195	2859	23W-11N	A3
1100	SMBG	60173	2859	23W-12N	A2
Applebee St					
100	BRTN	60010	2750	25W-20N	E2
S Apple Blossom Ln					
26100	MONE	60449	3683	6W-32S	A6
Appleby Ln					
4000	RNPK	60471	3594	4W-26S	D2
Appleby Rd					
100	IVNS	60067	2805	22W-15N	A1
1400	PLTN	60067	2805	22W-15N	A1
1700	IVNS	60067	2804	23W-15N	D2
Apple Creek Ln					
900	DSPN	60016	2863	12W-10N	B4
Applecross Rd					
2100	IVNS	60010	2751	25W-16N	A7
Applegate Ct					
2900	NfdT	60025	2810	10W-13N	B6
Applegate Ln					
2900	NfdT	60025	2810	10W-13N	A6
Apple Hill Ct					
1100	ELGN	60120	2855		D1
Apple Hill Ln					
10	MTSN	60443	3505	7W-24S	C5
200	SMWD	60107	2857	28W-11N	B4
Applejack Rd					
10	RGMW	60008	2806	19W-14N	B3
Appletree Ct					
200	BFGV	60089	2754	17W-20N	A1
800	BRLT	60103	2910		D7
800	NHBK	60062	2756	10W-17N	E4
N Apple Tree Ct					
900	PLTN	60067	2752	20W-17N	E5
Appletree Dr					
17100	CCHL	60478	3426	4W-20S	D5
17100	HLCT	60429	3426	4W-20S	D5
Apple Tree Ln					
600	GLNC	60022	2758	7W-17N	B4
Appletree Ln					
200	WLMT	60091	2812	5W-13N	B7
500	DRFD	60015	2756	11W-20N	C1
800	GNVW	60025	2811	7W-13N	B5
2600	NHBK	60062	2756	10W-17N	E4
E Appletree Ln					
10	ANHT	60004	2754	17W-16N	A7
S Appletree Ln					
1100	BRLT	60103	2910		D7
W Appletree Ln					
10	ANHT	60004	2754	17W-16N	A7
800	BRLT	60103	2910		D7
Apple Tree Rd					
100	NtrT	60093	2811	5W-15N	E3
100	WNKA	60093	2811	5W-15N	E3
Appletree St					
6600	HRPK	60133	2911		D3
Apple Valley Dr					
900	BRLT	60103	2910		C6
W Appleway Ct					
13800	HMGN	60441	3343	17W-17S	C5
N Applewood Ct					
8100	HRPK	60133	2857	26W-9N	E7
S Applewood Ct					
8000	HRPK	60133	2857	26W-9N	E7
Applewood Ln					
900	ALGN	60102	2748		B1
4000	NHBK	60062	2756	12W-18N	B3
4100	MTSN	60443	3506	5W-25S	C7
16000	ODHL	60462	3424	10W-19S	A1
16000	ODHL	60477	3424	11W-19S	A2
16000	ODPK	60462	3424	10W-19S	A1
16000	ODPK	60477	3424	10W-19S	A1
Apricot Ct					
1400	MPPT	60056	2807	16W-14N	D3
Apricot St					
900	HFET	60195	2859	23W-11N	B3
W Aptakisic Rd					
700	BFGV	60089	2754	16W-18N	C2
700	WLNG	60089	2754	16W-18N	C2
Aquinas Ct					
11100	ODPK	60467	3422	14W-19S	E2
Arabian Ct					
10	SMWD	60107	2856	30W-10N	C5
Arabian Dr					
13400	HMGN	60441	3343	16W-18S	E7
N Aralia Dr					
1700	MPPT	60056	2808	13W-15N	D2
1800	PTHT	60070	2808	13W-15N	D2
Arapaho Dr					
10	TNTN	60476	3428	0E-20S	E5
Arapaho Pl					
7900	ODPK	60462	3346	9W-16S	C3
7900	OrlT	60462	3346	9W-16S	C3
S Arapaho Tr					
13800	HMGN	60441	3343	16W-16S	D3
Arbeleda Ln					
2200	NHBK	60062	2810	10W-15N	A2
Arbon Ct					
100	LYWD	60411	3510	4E-25S	C7
200	CRTE	60417	3596	0E-28S	E6
Arbor Av					
7400	BRRG	60527	3208		D1
Arbor Ct					
10	BFGV	60089	2754	17W-18N	B3
10	SMWD	60107	2856	30W-10N	C6
1000	ANHT	60005	2861	17W-11N	B2
1000	MPPT	60005	2861	17W-11N	B2
1000	MPPT	60056	2861	17W-11N	B2
W Arbor Ct					
1600	PLTN	60067	2752	23W-17N	A5
Arbor Dr					
-	RGMW	60173	2806	21W-12N	A7
-	SMBG	60067	2806	21W-12N	A7
-	SMBG	60173	2805	22W-12N	C7
-	SMBG	60173	2806	21W-12N	A7
10	SMWD	60107	2856	30W-10N	C6
1200	LMNT	60439	3342	19W-15S	D1
4700	RGMW	60008	2806	21W-12N	A7
4700	RGMW	60008	2860	21W-12N	A1
4700	RGMW	60173	2860	21W-12N	A1
4700	SMBG	60008	2806	21W-12N	A7
4700	SMBG	60008	2860	21W-12N	A1
4700	SMBG	60173	2860	21W-12N	A1
7200	TYPK	60477	3424	9W-21S	E6
11700	ODPK	60467	3344	14W-18S	D6
S Arbor Dr					
12500	ALSP	60803	3276	4W-14S	D6
Arbor Ln					
1000	GNVW	60025	2811	6W-13N	C6
1400	NfdT	60062	2756	12W-17N	C6
1400	NHBK	60062	2756	12W-17N	C6
2000	NHFD	60093	2811	6W-14N	C3
5200	CTWD	60445	3347	6W-15S	E1
7200	JSTC	60458	3148	10W-8S	B7
N Arbor Ln					
1100	PLTN	60067	2752	23W-17N	A5
1300	PLTN	60010	2752	23W-17N	A5
1300	PltT	60010	2752	23W-17N	A5
Arbor Sq					
-	SMBG	60173	2860	21W-12N	A1
W Arbor Ter					
16500	LKPT	60441	3342	20W-18S	B7
N Arbor Tr					
100	PKFT	60466	3595	2W-28S	C6
S Arbor Tr					
10	PKFT	60466	3595	2W-28S	C6
12200	PSHT	60463	3275	7W-14S	B6
12200	WthT	60463	3275	7W-14S	B6
Arbor Cove					
800	PLTN	60067	2752	22W-17N	B6
S Arboretum Dr					
14600	HMGN	60441	3343	17W-17S	D6
Arbor Gate Ln					
300	BFGV	60089	2754	17W-20N	A1
Arbor Glen Blvd					
-	HFET	60195	2805	23W-12N	A7
-	HFET	60195	2859	23W-12N	A1
-	SMBG	60195	2804	23W-12N	E7
-	SMBG	60195	2805	23W-12N	A7
-	SMBG	60195	2859	23W-12N	A1

STREET Block	City	ZIP	Map#	CGS	Grid
Arbor Ridge Dr					
11000	ODPK	60467	3344	13W-16S	E4
11000	ODPK	60467	3345	13W-16S	A4
11000	OrlT	60467	3344	13W-16S	E4
Arbor Vitae Ln					
2000	HRPK	60133	2911		C1
Arborvitae Rd					
500	WNKA	60093	2812	4W-15N	B1
W Arbour Pl					
-	CHCG	60607	3033	1W-0N	D4
-	CHCG	60612	3033	1W-0N	D4
Arbour Walk Dr					
8900	FKFT	60423	3504	11W-25S	A7
Arcade Pl					
10	LGNG	60525	3087	12W-4S	B7
W Arcade Pl					
-	CHCG	60602	3034		D5
100	CHCG	60603	3034		D5
100	CHCG	60606	3034	0W-0S	B5
1000	CHCG	60607	3033	1W-0S	E5
Arcadia Av					
17700	LNSG	60438	3429	3E-21S	E6
Arcadia Ct					
10	BRRG	60527	3208		A6
Arcadia Dr					
6200	TYPK	60477	3425	7W-20S	B3
Arcadia St					
200	PKFT	60466	3595	2W-26S	D2
3400	SKOK	60203	2866	4W-11N	C3
3700	SKOK	60076	2866	4W-11N	C3
5100	SKOK	60077	2865	6W-11N	D3
5400	MNGV	60053	2865	6W-11N	D3
7200	MNGV	60053	2864	9W-11N	D3
7800	MNGV	60714	2864	9W-11N	B3
7800	NLES	60714	2864	9W-11N	B3
Arcadia Tr					
500	ROSL	60172	2913		B2
Arcadian Ct					
20400	OMFD	60461	3506	4W-24S	E6
Arcadian Dr					
20300	OMFD	60461	3506	4W-24S	E6
Arcadian Wy					
20500	OMFD	60461	3506	4W-24S	E6
S Arch St					
2900	CHCG	60608	3091	1W-2S	D3
Archbury Ln					
2300	PKRG	60068	2917	11W-8N	D1
Archer Av					
-	JSTC	60458	3209	11W-9S	E2
-	JSTC	60480	3209	11W-9S	E2
-	LmnT	60439	3272	15W-12S	A1
-	LmnT	60480	3208		C7
-	LmnT	60480	3272	15W-12S	A1
-	PlsT	60480	3208		C7
-	SMMT	60501	3148	9W-6S	D3
7200	CHCG	60638	3148	8W-5S	E3
7200	SMMT	60638	3148	8W-5S	E3
8000	WLSP	60480	3209	12W-9S	C3
9000	PlsT	60480	3209	13W-10S	A5
13900	HmrT	60441	3342	20W-16S	B4
14400	LktT	60441	3342	20W-17S	A5
14500	LKPT	60441	3342	21W-17S	A5
Archer Av SR-171					
-	JSTC	60458	3209	11W-9S	E2
-	JSTC	60480	3209	11W-9S	E2
-	LmnT	60439	3272	15W-12S	A1
-	LmnT	60480	3208		C7
-	LmnT	60480	3272	15W-12S	A1
-	PlsT	60480	3208		C7
8000	WLSP	60480	3209	12W-9S	C3
9000	PlsT	60480	3209	13W-10S	A5
13900	HmrT	60441	3342	20W-16S	B4
14400	LktT	60441	3342	20W-17S	A5
14500	LKPT	60441	3342	21W-17S	A5
S Archer Av					
-	JSTC	60458	3209	11W-9S	E2
-	JSTC	60458	3210	11W-8S	A2
-	JSTC	60480	3209	11W-9S	E2
-	WLSP	60480	3209	11W-9S	E2
1900	CHCG	60616	3092	0W-2S	A2
2400	CHCG	60608	3092	1W-2S	A2
2500	CHCG	60608	3091	2W-3S	C4
3400	CHCG	60609	3091	2W-3S	B5
3700	CHCG	60632	3091	3W-3S	B5
4000	CHCG	60632	3090	3W-4S	E7
4600	CHCG	60632	3150	5W-5S	A2
5300	CHCG	60638	3150	5W-5S	A2
5400	CHCG	60638	3149	7W-5S	C3
10800	LMNT	60439	3272	16W-13S	A4
10800	LmnT	60480	3272	16W-12S	A3
11300	LMNT	60439	3271		E5
12700	LMNT	60439	3343	18W-15S	A1
12900	LMNT	60439	3342	19W-16S	C3
13400	HMGN	60441	3342	19W-15S	D2
13500	HmrT	60441	3342	19W-16S	D3
S Archer Av SR-83					
10800	LMNT	60439	3272	16W-12S	A3
10800	LmnT	60480	3272	16W-12S	A3
S Archer Av SR-171					
-	JSTC	60458	3209	11W-9S	E2
-	JSTC	60458	3210	11W-8S	A2
-	JSTC	60480	3209	11W-9S	E2
-	WLSP	60480	3209	11W-9S	E2
10800	LMNT	60439	3272	16W-13S	A4
10800	LmnT	60480	3272	16W-12S	A3
11300	LMNT	60439	3271		E5
12700	LMNT	60439	3343	18W-15S	A1
12900	LMNT	60439	3342	19W-16S	C3
13400	HMGN	60441	3342	19W-15S	D2
13500	HmrT	60441	3342	19W-16S	D3
W Archer Av					
6400	CHCG	60638	3149	8W-5S	A3
6800	CHCG	60638	3148	9W-5S	D3
7100	SMMT	60501	3148	8W-5S	E3
7100	SMMT	60638	3148	8W-5S	E3
S Archer Rd					
5500	SMMT	60501	3148	10W-7S	B7
6300	BDPK	60501	3148	9W-7S	C5
6600	BDPK	60455	3148	9W-7S	C6
6700	BGVW	60455	3148	9W-7S	C6
7000	BGVW	60458	3148	10W-7S	B7
7000	BGVW	60501	3148	10W-7S	B7
7000	JSTC	60458	3148	10W-7S	B7
7000	JSTC	60501	3148	10W-7S	B7
7300	JSTC	60458	3210	10W-8S	A1
S Archer Rd SR-171					
5500	SMMT	60501	3148	10W-7S	B7
6300	BDPK	60501	3148	9W-7S	C5
6600	BDPK	60455	3148	9W-7S	C6
6700	BGVW	60455	3148	9W-7S	C6
7000	BGVW	60458	3148	10W-7S	B7
7000	BGVW	60501	3148	10W-7S	B7
7000	JSTC	60458	3148	10W-7S	B7
7000	JSTC	60501	3148	10W-7S	B7
7300	JSTC	60458	3210	10W-8S	A1

STREET Block	City	ZIP	Map#	CGS	Grid
Arctic Ct					
13000	LMNT	60439	3343	16W-15S	D1
Arctic Ln					
13400	LMNT	60439	3343	16W-15S	D1
Arden Av					
3500	BKFD	60513	3088	10W-3S	A5
3800	LYNS	60513	3088	10W-3S	A6
Ardmore Av					
900	ITSC	60143	2914		A5
2200	IVNS	60067	2804	24W-15N	D1
2400	HFET	60067	2804	24W-15N	D1
2400	HFET	60195	2804	24W-15N	D1
E Ardmore Av					
300	ROSL	60172	2913		B5
W Ardmore Av					
-	CHCG	60646	2920	4W-7N	B4
-	CHCG	60659	2920	4W-7N	B4
300	BmdT	60172	2912		E5
300	ROSL	60172	2912		E5
400	BmdT	60172	2913		A5
1200	CHCG	60660	2921	1W-7N	D4
1200	ITSC	60143	2914		A5
1300	ITSC	60143	2913		E5
2400	CHCG	60659	2921	3W-7N	A4
5200	CHCG	60646	2919	6W-7N	C4
6300	CHCG	60631	2919	8W-7N	A4
7700	CHCG	60068	2918	9W-7N	C4
7700	CHCG	60631	2918	9W-7N	C4
7700	PKRG	60068	2918	9W-7N	C4
Ardmore Ct					
1100	SMBG	60193	2912		C1
Ardmore Ln					
10	GNVW	60025	2811	6W-13N	D7
Ardmore Rd					
100	DSPN	60016	2862	14W-12N	C1
Ardmore St					
10	AddT	60106	2915		C5
Ardsley Rd					
600	WNKA	60093	2811	5W-16N	E1
Ardwick Dr					
1600	HFET	60195	2858	25W-12N	B1
E Ardyce Ln					
900	MPPT	60056	2808	14W-13N	C6
Arena Dr					
-	BlmT	60411	3509	2E-23S	C3
-	LYWD	60411	3509	2E-23S	C3
Argonne Dr					
10300	WDRG	60516	3270		C2
10300	WDRG	60517	3270		C2
Argonne Woods Dr					
10300	DGvT	60517	3270		C2
10300	WDRG	60517	3270		C2
Argyle Av					
10	BmdT	60172	2912		B7
300	BMDL	60108	2912		B7
300	BMDL	60172	2912		B7
600	FSMR	60422	3507	3W-22S	B2
600	HMWD	60430	3507	3W-22S	B1
18300	HMWD	60430	3427	3W-22S	B7
Argyle St					
1000	BNVL	60106	2915		D6
W Argyle St					
1800	CHCG	60640	2921	2W-6N	B6
1900	CHCG	60625	2921	2W-6N	B6
2700	CHCG	60625	2920	3W-6N	E6
3900	CHCG	60630	2920	5W-6N	B6
6000	CHCG	60630	2919	7W-6N	B6
6300	CHCG	60656	2919	8W-6N	A6
7200	CHCG	60656	2918	9W-6N	C6
7600	CHCG	60706	2918	9W-6N	C6
7600	HDHT	60656	2918	9W-6N	C6
7600	HDHT	60706	2918	9W-6N	C6
7800	NRDG	60706	2918	9W-6N	B6
8600	NRDG	60706	2917	10W-6N	E6
8700	CHCG	60706	2917	10W-6N	E6
Argyll Ln					
400	SMBG	60194	2858	24W-11N	C4
Ari Dr E					
3500	GNVW	60025	2809	10W-15N	E3
Ari Dr W					
3700	GNVW	60025	2809	10W-15N	E3
Ari Ln					
3600	GNVW	60025	2809	10W-15N	E2
Ariana Dr					
-	BRLT	60120	2909		D3
Aris Ct					
15600	ODPK	60462	3346	11W-18S	A7
N Arizona Av					
300	GNWD	60425	3428	1W-22S	A7
300	GNWD	60425	3508	1W-22S	B1
Arizona Blvd					
10	HFET	60194	2859	23W-11N	B3
Arizona Ct					
17900	ODPK	60467	3423	12W-21S	C6
Arizona Tr					
8500	WLSP	60480	3208		E4
Arizona Pass					
600	EGVV	60007	2859	21W-9N	E7
700	EGVV	60007	2913		E1
Arkansas Ct					
17900	ODPK	60467	3423	12W-21S	C6
Arkansas Dr					
900	EGVV	60007	2913		D2
Arklow Pl					
1900	SMBG	60194	2858	26W-10N	A5
Arleen Ct					
2000	SMBG	60194	2858	26W-10N	A5
S Arlene Av					
10	PLTN	60074	2806	19W-15N	D1
Arlene Ct					
100	WLNG	60090	2755	14W-17N	C5
Arlene Dr					
12000	HMGN	60441	3344	15W-18S	C7
Arlingdale Ct					
2500	RGMW	60067	2805	22W-14N	C5
Arlingdale Dr					
2400	RGMW	60067	2805	22W-14N	B4
5700	RGMW	60008	2805	21W-14N	C5
Arlington Av					
400	ELGN	60120	2855		B5
500	DSPN	60016	2862	13W-11N	E3
800	LGNG	60525	3087	13W-4S	A7
S Arlington Av					
100	EMHT	60126	3028		A3
Arlington Cir					
5200	HRPK	60133	2911		E6
Arlington Ct					
1100	HRPK	60133	2912		A6
10600	PlsT	60462	3345	13W-15S	B2
Arlington Dr					
-	BRLT	60103	2911		D5
-	CPVL	60110	2801		A1
-	EDND	60118	2801		A1
-	HRPK	60103	2911		D5
-	WLNG	60089	2754	16W-18N	D3

STREET Block	City	ZIP	Map#	CGS	Grid
Arlington Dr					
100	PltT	60010	2751	24W-18N	C2
200	HRPK	60133	2911		D5
1600	WLNG	60090	2754	16W-18N	D3
4100	RNPK	60471	3594	5W-26S	C3
17600	CCHL	60478	3426	4W-21S	D6
Arlington Dr E					
5200	HRPK	60133	2912		A6
5500	BmdT	60133	2912		A6
Arlington Dr W					
1200	HRPK	60133	2911		E6
1200	HRPK	60133	2912		A6
Arlington Ln					
1400	SMBG	60193	2858	25W-10N	B6
10600	PlsT	60462	3345	13W-15S	A2
10600	PlsT	60467	3345	13W-15S	A2
17600	HLCT	60429	3427	3W-21S	A6
W Arlington Ln					
400	CteT	60417	3685	0W-32S	C7
W Arlington Pl					
500	CHCG	60614	2978	0W-3N	A5
Arlington Rd					
700	RVSD	60546	3088	9W-2S	D4
N Arlington Rd					
100	IVNS	60010	2751	23W-16N	D6
Arlington St					
500	HFET	60194	2859	22W-11N	B4
7800	TYPK	60477	3424	9W-19S	C2
Arlington Heights Rd					
100	ANHT	60004	2754	18W-18N	A2
100	BFGV	60004	2754	18W-18N	A2
100	BFGV	60089	2754	18W-18N	A2
N Arlington Heights Rd					
-	ANHT	60007	2861	18W-11N	A4
10	ANHT	60004	2807	17W-15N	A2
10	ANHT	60005	2807	17W-14N	A5
10	VrnT	60089	2754	18W-20N	A2
100	EGvT	60007	2861	18W-10N	A5
100	EGVV	60007	2861	18W-10N	A5
100	VrnT	60004	2754	17W-20N	A2
300	BFGV	60047	2754	18W-20N	A1
300	ITSC	60143	2914		D4
300	LGGV	60047	2754	18W-20N	A1
300	VrnT	60047	2754	18W-20N	A1
1200	AddT	60143	2914		D3
1200	EGVV	60007	2914		D3
2000	ANHT	60004	2754	17W-17N	A5
2900	BFGV	60004	2754	17W-17N	A4
2900	BFGV	60089	2754	17W-16N	A7
3300	ANHT	60089	2754	17W-16N	A7
N Arlington Heights Rd CO-10					
1200	AddT	60143	2914		D3
1200	EGVV	60007	2914		D3
1200	ITSC	60143	2914		D3
S Arlington Heights Rd					
-	ANHT	60004	2807	17W-13N	A6
10	ANHT	60005	2807	17W-13N	A6
10	EGvT	60007	2860	18W-9N	E7
10	EGvT	60007	2861	18W-10N	A6
10	EGVV	60007	2860	18W-9N	E7
10	EGVV	60007	2861	18W-10N	A6
100	VrnT	60004	2754	17W-18N	A2
100	VrnT	60089	2754	17W-18N	A2
400	ANHT	60004	2754	17W-18N	A3
400	BFGV	60004	2754	17W-18N	A3
400	BFGV	60089	2754	17W-18N	A3
500	ANHT	60089	2754	18W-18N	A3
600	EGVV	60007	2914		D2
1200	ANHT	60005	2861	18W-11N	A3
1400	ITSC	60143	2914		D3
2400	ANHT	60007	2861	18W-11N	A3
2400	EGVV	60005	2861	18W-11N	A3
Armitage Av					
-	NHLK	60164	2972		D7
300	NHLK	60164	2973	13W-2N	A7
400	LydT	60164	2973	13W-2N	A7
1300	MLPK	60160	2973	11W-2N	D7
1300	RVGV	60171	2973	11W-2N	E7
1700	FNPK	60131	2973	11W-2N	D7
1700	FNPK	60160	2973	11W-2N	D7
2500	MLPK	60131	2973	12W-2N	B7
9600	MLPK	60164	2973	12W-2N	C7
E Armitage Av					
200	EMHT	60126	2972		A7
W Armitage Av					
300	CHCG	60614	2978	0W-2N	A6
1600	CHCG	60614	2977	2W-2N	C6
1600	CHCG	60622	2977	2W-2N	B6
1900	CHCG	60647	2977	2W-2N	B6
2700	CHCG	60647	2976	4W-2N	D7
3900	CHCG	60639	2976	5W-2N	B7
4800	CHCG	60639	2975	6W-2N	D7
6600	CHCG	60707	2975	8W-2N	A7
6700	CHCG	60707	2974	9W-2N	C7
7100	EDPK	60707	2974	9W-2N	C7
Armitage Ct					
18000	HMWD	60430	3428	1W-21S	A7
Armory Dr					
-	SHLD	60473	3428	0W-19S	C3
-	SHLD	60476	3428	0W-19S	C3
-	TNTN	60473	3428	0W-19S	C3
-	TNTN	60476	3428	0W-19S	C3
W Armory Dr					
100	SHLD	60473	3428	0W-19S	C3
100	TNTN	60473	3428	0W-19S	C3
100	TNTN	60476	3428	0W-19S	C3
500	HRVY	60473	3428	0W-19S	B3
N Armour St					
400	CHCG	60622	3033	1W-0N	D3
W Armstrong Av					
5200	CHCG	60630	2919	6W-7N	C4
5200	CHCG	60646	2919	6W-7N	C4
Armstrong Ct					
1400	EGVV	60007	2913		E2
Armstrong Ct N					
600	BFGV	60089	2754	15W-20N	E1
Armstrong Dr					
100	BFGV	60089	2754	16W-20N	D2
200	WLNG	60089	2754	16W-20N	D2
700	BFGV	60089	2755	15W-20N	A2
Armstrong Ln					
1400	EGVV	60007	2913		E2
Arnett St					
-	FDHT	60411	3509	1E-24S	B6
Arnold Av					
400	SMWD	60107	2911		A1
Arnold Ct					
800	DSPN	60016	2862	15W-10N	A4
Arnold Ln					
3100	NHBK	60062	2756	11W-18N	D3
Arnold Pl					
-	EVTN	60202	2867	1W-9N	C6
4000	OKLN	60453	3276	5W-12S	C2
Arnold St					
1000	CHHT	60411	3508	0W-25S	C7

STREET Block	City	ZIP	Map#	CGS	Grid
Arnold St					
1400	CHHT	60411	3596	0W-25S	C1
W Arnold St					
8400	RVGV	60171	2974	10W-3N	A5
Aron Ct					
200	BRLT	60103	2911		A5
Arquilla Cir					
-	OMFD	60461	3506	4W-24S	D5
Arquilla Dr					
4900	RNPK	60471	3594	6W-27S	A4
5300	RNPK	60471	3593	6W-27S	E4
E Arquilla Dr					
10	CHHT	60411	3508	1W-24S	A4
N Arquilla Dr					
200	CHHT	60411	3508	1W-24S	A4
300	CHHT	60411	3507	1W-24S	E5
W Arquilla Dr					
300	GNWD	60425	3508	0W-22S	B1
500	GNWD	60425	3428	0W-22S	B7
7600	PSHT	60463	3346	9W-15S	D2
Arquilla Ln					
1200	FSMR	60422	3507	3W-23S	B3
S Arran Dr					
19600	FftT	60423	3504	9W-23S	E4
W Arran Dr					
7400	FftT	60423	3504	9W-23S	E3
Arrow St					
2300	CPVL	60110	2748		C4
Arrow Tr					
400	WLNG	60090	2754	16W-17N	C5
Arrowhead Ct					
10	PKFT	60466	3595	2W-26S	D2
6300	IHPK	60525	3146		D5
13600	ODPK	60462	3346	10W-16S	B2
Arrowhead Dr					
10	TNTN	60476	3428	0E-20S	E4
600	ELGN	60120	2855		B2
900	DYR	46311	3598		E3
9500	HYHL	60465	3210	10W-11S	A6
9500	PSHL	60465	3210	10W-11S	A6
N Arrowhead Dr					
900	PLTN	60074	2753	20W-17N	A5
Arrowhead Ln					
8200	ODPK	60462	3346	10W-16S	B3
8200	OrlT	60462	3346	10W-16S	B3
Arrowhead St					
200	PKFT	60466	3595	2W-26S	D2
Arrowhead Tr					
11200	IHPK	60527	3208		D1
Arrowhead Trc					
5000	BmnT	60477	3426	6W-20S	A5
17200	BmnT	60478	3426	6W-20S	A5
17200	OKFT	60452	3425	6W-20S	E5
17200	OKFT	60452	3426	6W-20S	A5
17200	OKFT	60478	3426	6W-20S	A5
Arrowhead Farm Dr					
8300	BRRG	60527	3208		C3
Arrowwood Ct					
10	SMWD	60107	2857	26W-11N	E4
200	SMBG	60193	2859	21W-10N	D6
Arrowwood Ln					
100	NHBK	60062	2755	13W-18N	E2
200	NHBK	60062	2756	13W-18N	A3
2600	RGMW	60008	2805	21W-14N	C5
3700	HFET	60195	2804	25W-14N	A3
Arroyo Av					
19800	LYWD	60411	3510	3E-23S	A4
Arroyo Ct					
15400	OKFT	60452	3347	7W-18S	C7
Arroyo Dr					
15200	OKFT	60452	3347	7W-18S	C7
15700	OKFT	60452	3425	7W-18S	C1
15800	BmnT	60477	3425	7W-18S	C1
Artesian Av					
-	MKHM	60426	3427	3W-19S	C3
11900	BLID	60406	3277	3W-14S	B6
11900	CHCG	60655	3277	3W-14S	B6
13100	BLID	60406	3349	3W-15S	B1
14900	HRVY	60426	3349	3W-17S	C6
15900	BmnT	60426	3427	3W-19S	B2
16700	HLCT	60429	3427	3W-20S	C4
N Artesian Av					
400	CHCG	60612	3033	3W-0N	A3
1200	CHCG	60622	3033	3W-1N	A1
1500	CHCG	60647	3033	3W-1N	A1
2400	CHCG	60647	2977	3W-3N	A5
2700	CHCG	60618	2977	3W-3N	A5
4400	CHCG	60618	2921	3W-5N	A7
5400	CHCG	60625	2921	3W-6N	A5
5500	CHCG	60659	2921	3W-6N	A5
6300	CHCG	60645	2921	3W-7N	A3
7400	CHCG	60645	2867	3W-9N	A7
S Artesian Av					
300	CHCG	60612	3033	3W-0S	A6
2500	CHCG	60608	3091	3W-2S	B2
3500	CHCG	60632	3091	3W-3S	B5
5400	CHCG	60632	3151	3W-5S	B3
5600	CHCG	60629	3151	3W-6S	B7
7600	CHCG	60652	3213	3W-8S	B1
9800	CHCG	60655	3213	3W-11S	B7
9800	ENGN	60655	3213	3W-11S	B7
9800	ENGN	60805	3213	3W-11S	B7
10200	CHCG	60655	3277	3W-12S	B1
11800	BLID	60406	3277	3W-13S	B5
Artesian St					
12800	LMNT	60439	3272	16W-13S	A4
W Arthington St					
-	CHCG	60607	3034		D6
1000	CHCG	60607	3033	1W-0S	E6
2400	CHCG	60612	3033	3W-0S	A6
2800	CHCG	60612	3032	3W-0S	E6
3100	CHCG	60624	3032	4W-0S	D6
4600	CHCG	60644	3032	5W-0S	A6
4800	CHCG	60644	3031	6W-0S	E6
5900	OKPK	60304	3031	7W-0S	B6
Arthur Av					
10	ROSL	60172	2913		A3
200	ROSL	60172	2912		E3
700	EGVV	60007	2915		B3
1000	BKLY	60163	3028		C3
2200	EGvT	60007	2915		D3
3100	BKFD	60513	3087	11W-3S	D5
3100	LGPK	60525	3087	11W-3S	D5
4500	BKFD	60513	3147	11W-4S	D1
4600	MCCK	60513	3147	11W-4S	D1
4600	MCCK	60525	3147	11W-4S	D1
S Arthur Av					
-	ANHT	60004	2807	17W-13N	C5
-	ANHT	60005	2807	17W-13N	C5
400	MPPT	60056	2807	16W-13N	C6
W Arthur Av					
1200	CHCG	60626	2921	1W-8N	D2
2000	CHCG	60645	2921	3W-8N	A2
2600	CHCG	60645	2920	3W-8N	E2
3100	LNWD	60645	2920	3W-8N	D2

STREET Block	City	ZIP	Map#	CGS	Grid
W Arthur Av					
3800	LNWD	60712	2920	4W-8N	B2
4700	LNWD	60712	2919	5W-8N	E2
7100	CHCG	60631	2918	8W-8N	D2
Arthur Ct					
10	CRTE	60417	3597	1E-28S	A6
10	DRFD	60015	2756	11W-20N	D2
10	SMWD	60107	2856	29W-10N	E6
14400	DLTN	60419	3350	0E-16S	D4
17900	ODPK	60467	3423	13W-21S	B6
Arthur Dr					
-	MONE	60449	3683	6W-31S	B5
800	ELGN	60120	2855		C2
17900	ODPK	60467	3423	13W-21S	B7
Arthur Rd					
3400	CRTE	60417	3597	0E-28S	A6
Arthur St					
10	CHCG	60631	2918	10W-8N	B2
10	PKRG	60068	2918	10W-8N	B2
1200	CTCY	60409	3430	3E-19S	A1
2000	PKRG	60068	2917	11W-8N	D2
Arthur Ter					
3600	MKHM	60426	3426	4W-19S	D2
Arthur Terrace Ct					
3900	MKHM	60426	3426	4W-19S	D2
Arts Cir Dr					
-	EVTN	60201	2867	2W-11N	C2
Asbury					
-	RGMW	60008	2806	20W-13N	A5
Asbury Av					
100	CHCG	60645	2867	2W-9N	A6
100	EVTN	60202	2867	3W-9N	A6
1100	WNKA	60093	2758	6W-16N	D7
1200	EVTN	60201	2867	3W-11N	A3
2500	EVTN	60201	2813	3W-12N	A7
2700	WLMT	60091	2813	2W-13N	A7
Asbury Cir					
7700	HRPK	60133	2857	26W-9N	E7
Asbury Ct					
900	WNKA	60093	2758	6W-16N	D7
1200	ELGN	60120	2801		D7
Asbury Ln					
400	HFET	60194	2859	22W-11N	B4
400	SMBG	60194	2859	23W-11N	B4
800	SMBG	60193	2859	23W-9N	A7
800	SMBG	60193	2913		A1
Asbury Rd					
2200	NHBK	60062	2757	10W-16N	A7
Ascot Cir					
10	SMBG	60194	2859	23W-10N	B5
Ascot Ct					
700	HFET	60194	2858	24W-11N	D3
4400	RNPK	60471	3594	5W-26S	C3
8800	ODPK	60462	3424	11W-18S	A1
Ascot Dr					
-	PKRG	60068	2917	11W-8N	D1
Ascot Ln					
300	SMWD	60107	2856	29W-11N	D4
600	HnrT	60107	2856	29W-11N	D4
Ascot Rd					
2300	NHBK	60062	2810	8W-16N	D1
Ash Av					
1200	BNVL	60106	2915		C3
1200	EGVV	60007	2915		C3
N Ash Av					
200	WDDL	60191	2915		C7
400	AddT	60191	2915		C7
S Ash Av					
4300	HMND	46327	3352		E4
Ash Ct					
10	SMWD	60107	2857	27W-10N	C6
500	SMBG	60193	2858	24W-9N	D7
13300	PSHT	60463	3347	7W-15S	B2
Ash Dr					
1000	ELGN	60120	2855		D4
W Ash Dr					
1100	MPPT	60056	2861	16W-11N	D3
Ash Ln					
10	LynT	60458	3209	11W-8S	E1
600	WLNG	60090	2754	16W-17N	D5
800	NHBK	60062	2757	10W-17N	A4
8900	HYHL	60457	3209	11W-10S	E5
20100	LYWD	60411	3509	3E-23S	E4
Ash Rd					
600	HFET	60194	2859	23W-11N	B4
600	SMBG	60194	2859	23W-11N	B4
900	HFET	60195	2859	23W-11N	B3
1100	HFET	60173	2859	23W-12N	B2
1100	SMBG	60173	2859	23W-12N	B2
Ash St					
-	ROSL	60172	2913		B5
10	BlmT	60466	3595	2W-26S	C2
10	CPVL	60110	2748		C6
10	CTSD	60525	3147	12W-6S	C4
10	HGKN	60525	3147	12W-6S	C4
10	PKFT	60466	3595	2W-26S	C2
300	EGVV	60007	2915		A2
700	FSMR	60422	3506	4W-22S	E2
700	FSMR	60429	3506	4W-22S	E2
700	HLCT	60429	3506	4W-22S	E2
700	WNKA	60093	2812	5W-15N	A2
1100	WNKA	60093	2811	5W-15N	E2
1600	DSPN	60018	2862	13W-9N	E7
1700	NHFD	60093	2811	7W-15N	C2
2400	CHHT	60411	3596	1W-26S	A2
2400	SCHT	60411	3596	1W-26S	A2
14500	ODPK	60462	3345	11W-17S	E5
14500	OrlT	60462	3345	11W-17S	E5
17600	TYPK	60477	3423	11W-21S	E6
S Ash St					
10	PLTN	60067	2805	21W-15N	C1
100	PltT	60067	2805	21W-15N	C1
Ashbel Av					
10	NHLK	60164	3028		C1
N Ashbel Av					
10	HLSD	60162	3028		C6
10	PvsT	60162	3028		C6
1200	BKLY	60163	3028		C4
Ashborne Dr					
14700	HMGN	60441	3343	17W-17S	B6
Ashbrook Ln					
11000	IHPK	60525	3146		E5
Ashburn Ct					
10	SMBG	60193	2857	27W-10N	D5
Ashburton Ln					
100	PTON	60468	3860	9W-37S	D3
Ashbury Cir					
100	PKRG	60068	2863	11W-9N	C7
Ashbury Ct					
200	ROSL	60172	2912		C4
400	LMNT	60439	3342	19W-15S	E1
E Ashbury Ct					
2200	ANHT	60004	2807	16W-15N	D2
W Ashbury Ct					
1800	IVNS	60067	2804	23W-14N	E4

STREET Block	City	ZIP	Map#	CGS	Grid
W Ashbury Ct					
1800	IVNS	60067	2805	23W-14N	A4
Ashbury Dr					
400	DGvT	60521	3146		A4
400	HNDL	60521	3146		A4
1200	LMNT	60439	3270		D7
1200	LMNT	60439	3342	18W-15S	E1
Ashbury Ln					
10	BNHL	60010	2748		E1
400	LMNT	60439	3342	19W-15S	E1
W Ashbury Ln					
1800	IVNS	60067	2804	23W-14N	E4
1800	IVNS	60195	2804	23W-14N	E5
1800	PltT	60067	2804	23W-14N	E5
1800	PltT	60195	2804	23W-14N	E5
1900	IVNS	60067	2805	23W-14N	A4
Ashbury Ln E					
100	ROSL	60172	2912		C4
Ashbury Ln W					
200	ROSL	60172	2912		B4
Ashcroft Ln					
10	SMBG	60193	2859	22W-10N	B6
Ashford Cir					
1700	ANHT	60004	2754	16W-17N	C5
1700	WLNG	60090	2754	16W-17N	C5
Ashford Ct					
10	BFGV	60089	2754	17W-17N	B5
10	SBTN	60010	2804	25W-15N	A3
14200	ODPK	60467	3345	13W-16S	A4
15900	TYPK	60477	3424	9W-19S	D1
Ashford Dr					
4600	MTSN	60443	3506	5W-24S	B5
14700	LMNT	60439	3343	18W-15S	A1
W Ashford Ln					
500	ANHT	60004	2753	18W-18N	E2
500	ANHT	60004	2754	17W-20N	A2
Ashkirk Ct					
10	IVNS	60010	2803	25W-16N	E1
Ashland Av					
-	CHHT	60411	3507	1W-23S	E3
-	CRTE	60417	3684	1W-29S	E1
-	CteT	60417	3684	1W-29S	E1
-	DXMR	60426	3349	2W-16S	D3
-	FSMR	60422	3507	1W-23S	E3
-	RVDL	60827	3349	2W-16S	D3
10	DSPN	60016	2862	14W-10N	C4
10	FTPK	60130	3030	9W-0N	C5
100	CHCG	60645	2867	3W-9N	A6
500	EDND	60118	2801		B1
800	RVFT	60305	3030	9W-1N	C3
1100	EVTN	60202	2867	3W-10N	A4
1300	DSPN	60016	2863	13W-10N	A4
1500	EDPK	60707	3030	9W-1N	C1
1600	KLWH	60043	2812	4W-14N	C4
1600	WLMT	60091	2812	4W-14N	C4
1900	CHHT	60411	3595	2W-26S	E2
2000	EVTN	60201	2867	3W-12N	A1
2200	RGWW	60008	2806	20W-14N	A4
2400	EVTN	60201	2813	3W-12N	A7
2600	WLMT	60091	2813	3W-13N	A7
2600	WLMT	60201	2813	3W-13N	A7
3300	BlmT	60466	3595	1W-27S	E5
3300	BlmT	60475	3595	1W-27S	E5
3300	CteT	60466	3595	1W-27S	E5
3300	CteT	60475	3595	1W-27S	E5
3500	CteT	60417	3595	1W-28S	E6
3500	STGR	60475	3595	1W-28S	E6
9100	FNPK	60131	2973	11W-3N	D4
12900	BLID	60406	3277	2W-15S	D7
12900	CTPK	60406	3277	1W-15S	D7
12900	CTPK	60406	3349	2W-15S	D1
12900	CTPK	60827	3277	1W-15S	D7
12900	CTPK	60827	3349	2W-15S	D1
13200	BLID	60406	3349	1W-15S	D1
13200	ClmT	60827	3349	1W-15S	D1
14300	HRVY	60426	3349	2W-17S	E6
14300	ThtT	60426	3349	2W-17S	E6
15600	HRVY	60426	3427	1W-19S	E1
16100	MKHM	60426	3427	1W-19S	E3
16500	HLCT	60426	3427	1W-19S	E3
17100	EHZC	60429	3427	1W-21S	E6
17100	HRVY	60429	3427	1W-20S	E4
17400	EHZC	60430	3427	1W-20S	E5
18100	HMWD	60430	3427	1W-21S	E7
18500	HMWD	60430	3507	1W-22S	E2
18800	BlmT	60430	3507	1W-22S	E2
20200	BlmT	60411	3595	1W-27S	E5
20200	SCHT	60411	3595	1W-27S	E5
20200	SCHT	60466	3595	1W-27S	E5
N Ashland Av					
10	CHCG	60607	3033	2W-0N	D4
10	CHCG	60612	3033	2W-0N	D4
10	LGNG	60525	3087	12W-4S	B6
10	PLTN	60074	2806	20W-16N	A1
200	LGPK	60525	3087	12W-3S	B6
200	PKRG	60068	2864	10W-9N	B7
300	CHCG	60622	3033	2W-1N	C1
1200	PLTN	60074	2753	20W-17N	A5
1600	CHCG	60622	2977	2W-2N	C7
1900	CHCG	60614	2977	2W-2N	C6
2600	CHCG	60657	2977	2W-3N	C4
3500	CHCG	60613	2977	1W-3N	C5
4400	CHCG	60613	2921	2W-5N	C7
4400	CHCG	60640	2921	1W-6N	C6
6400	CHCG	60626	2921	1W-8N	C2
6400	CHCG	60660	2921	2W-8N	C2
7600	CHCG	60626	2867	2W-9N	C6
9200	NLES	60714	2864	10W-11N	B3
S Ashland Av					
-	BLID	60406	3349	1W-15S	D1
-	CTPK	60827	3349	1W-15S	D1
-	CTSD	60525	3147	12W-6S	B5
10	CHCG	60607	3033	1W-0S	D6
10	CHCG	60612	3033	1W-0S	D6
10	LGNG	60525	3087	12W-4S	B7
10	PLTN	60074	2806	20W-15N	A1
300	LGNG	60525	3147	12W-4S	B1
1000	CHCG	60608	3033	2W-0S	D7
1600	CHCG	60608	3091	2W-1S	D1
1600	PKRG	60068	2918	10W-7N	B4
1900	CHCG	60631	2918	10W-7N	B4
1900	PKRG	60631	2918	10W-7N	B4
3400	CHCG	60609	3091	2W-4S	D7
4700	CHCG	60609	3151	2W-5S	D2
5500	CHCG	60636	3151	1W-6S	D3
7500	CHCG	60620	3213	1W-8S	D1
9400	CHCG	60643	3213	2W-10S	D6
10900	CHCG	60643	3277	2W-12S	D2
11800	CHCG	60827	3277	1W-13S	D5
11800	CTPK	60643	3277	1W-13S	D5
11800	CTPK	60827	3277	1W-14S	D7
12800	BLID	60406	3277	1W-15S	D7
12800	CTPK	60406	3277	1W-15S	D7
13300	ClmT	60827	3349	1W-16S	D2
13300	RVDL	60827	3349	1W-16S	D2
S Ashland Av					
13300	ThtT	60827	3349	1W-16S	D2
13800	DXMR	60426	3349	1W-16S	D3
23600	CteT	60417	3595	1W-28S	E7
23600	STGR	60475	3595	1W-28S	E7
24000	CteT	60417	3684	2W-29S	E1
N Ashland Blvd					
6800	CHCG	60626	2921	1W-8N	C1
7200	CHCG	60626	2867	1W-9N	C7
Ashland Ct					
200	BFGV	60089	2754	17W-20N	A1
Ashland Ln					
1300	WLMT	60091	2812	4W-14N	D4
Ashland Pl					
400	HDPK	60035	2758	7W-20N	B1
Ashland St					
300	HFET	60194	2859	22W-11N	B4
600	EDND	60118	2801		B1
Ashley Ct					
10	CRTE	60417	3685	1W-29S	B2
200	ROSL	60172	2912		C5
700	HFET	60195	2858	24W-12N	D1
3800	RGMW	60008	2806	20W-14N	A5
14400	ODPK	60462	3346	10W-17S	B4
S Ashley Ct					
16700	HMGN	60441	3422	15W-20S	B4
Ashley Dr					
3300	MaiT	60025	2810	10W-12N	A7
3400	MaiT	60025	2809	10W-12N	E7
8300	ODPK	60462	3346	10W-17S	B4
Ashley Ln					
-	IVNS	60010	2803	25W-15N	E1
-	SBTN	60010	2803	25W-15N	E1
200	WYNE	60120	2909		A6
600	SMBG	60194	2858	25W-11N	B4
8200	TYPK	60477	3424	10W-19S	C1
Ashley Rd					
1600	HFET	60195	2858	24W-12N	D1
1900	HFET	60195	2804	24W-12N	D7
Ashley Wy					
-	BMDL	60108	2912		D7
Ashley Oaks Ln					
10	FSMR	60422	3507	2W-23S	D3
Ashley Woods Dr					
-	PvsT	60154	3086		D3
-	PvsT	60523	3086		D3
-	WSTR	60523	3086		D3
2600	WSTR	60154	3086		D3
Ashling Ct					
2800	SMBG	60193	2857	27W-10N	C6
Ashridge Ln					
-	UYPK	60417	3684	3W-30S	C3
-	UYPK	60466	3684	3W-30S	C3
Ashton Ct					
400	SMBG	60193	2859	23W-10N	A6
1000	SMWD	60107	2910		C1
1400	WLNG	60090	2754	15W-18N	E3
2800	WSTR	60154	3086		E4
Ashton Dr					
-	WLSP	60527	3208		C5
10	BRRG	60527	3208		C5
Ashton Ln					
10900	ODPK	60467	3345	13W-16S	A4
Ashwood Ct					
400	SMBG	60193	2858	24W-10N	E6
Ashwood Dr					
200	SMBG	60193	2858	24W-9N	E7
17100	ODPK	60467	3422	14W-20S	D4
Aspen Ct					
10	LMNT	60439	3270		C6
10	SMWD	60107	2857	27W-10N	C6
100	SMBG	60194	2858	25W-10N	B5
600	BRLT	60103	2910		D1
1300	ELGN	60120	2855		E4
2700	NHBK	60062	2809	11W-15N	D2
15800	OKFT	60452	3347	8W-18S	B7
20700	VrnT	60015	2755	15W-20N	B2
W Aspen Ct					
900	PltT	60067	2752	22W-17N	C4
900	PltT	60074	2752	22W-17N	C4
Aspen Dr					
-	BCHR	60401	3864	0W-36S	D1
10	SMBG	60194	2858	25W-10N	B5
400	DYR	46311	3598		D3
1800	HRPK	60133	2911		D3
9200	MaiT	60016	2863	11W-11N	D3
N Aspen Dr					
1700	MPPT	60056	2808	13W-15N	E2
S Aspen Dr					
10300	PSHL	60465	3274	10W-12S	A1
Aspen Ln					
10	CPVL	60110	2748		C5
10	GLNC	60022	2758	6W-18N	D3
100	HDPK	60035	2757	8W-20N	E1
1200	EGVV	60007	2915		A3
6000	MTSN	60443	3505	7W-24S	D6
8200	TYPK	60477	3424	10W-19S	B2
9200	MaiT	60016	2863	11W-11N	D3
10500	DGvT	60439	3270		D2
10500	WDRG	60439	3270		D2
12000	HMGN	60441	3422	15W-20S	C3
Aspen Rd					
2800	NHBK	60062	2756	11W-16N	E7
Aspen St					
900	HFET	60195	2859	22W-11N	B3
3700	FSMR	60422	3506	4W-22S	D2
14500	ODPK	60462	3346	11W-17S	A5
Aspen Wy					
100	DRFD	60015	2756	11W-20N	C2
E Aster Av					
800	PLTN	60074	2753	19W-18N	B3
Aster Cir					
2100	LYWD	60411	3509	2E-24S	D5
Aster Dr					
10	SMBG	60173	2859	21W-10N	E5
100	SMBG	60193	2859	21W-10N	E6
Aster Ln					
100	HFET	60195	2859	23W-11N	B2
100	MTSN	60443	3593	7W-26S	C2
400	BRLT	60103	2911		C6
8200	TYPK	60477	3424	10W-21S	B5
Aster St					
10	DYR	46311	3598		C1
15300	ODPK	60462	3346	9W-18S	E7
15300	OrlT	60462	3346	9W-18S	E7
Astony Ct					
5700	HNDL	60521	3146		B4
Astor Av					
7000	HRPK	60133	2911		C1
Astor Ct					
2500	GNVW	60025	2809	10W-15N	E2
Astor Ln					
600	WLNG	60090	2755	13W-17N	D5
5400	ANHT	60005	2860	19W-12N	D2
5400	RGMW	60005	2860	19W-12N	D2
Astor Ln					
5400	RGMW	60008	2860	19W-12N	D2
Astor Pl					
-	GLNC	60022	2758	7W-18N	B4
200	NHBK	60062	2758	7W-16N	B7
200	NHFD	60062	2758	7W-16N	B7
200	NHFD	60093	2758	7W-16N	B7
W Astor Pl					
5200	MONE	60449	3683	6W-31S	A5
Astor St					
1600	BNHM	60633	3351	2E-16S	D4
1600	CTCY	60409	3351	2E-16S	D4
2200	SLVL	60411	3509	2E-25S	D7
N Astor St					
1200	CHCG	60611	3034	0E-1N	C1
1400	CHCG	60610	3034	0E-1N	C1
1500	CHCG	60610	2978		D7
Astoria Ct					
200	BRTN	60010	2750	25W-17N	E5
Astoria Wy					
10	PKRG	60068	2863	11W-9N	C7
Athena Ct					
-	OMFD	60461	3507	3W-24S	A5
10	TYPK	60477	3505	8W-23S	B3
600	SMBG	60193	2858	24W-9N	D6
Athens Rd					
2400	BlmT	60411	3507	2W-25S	C7
2400	OMFD	60461	3507	3W-25S	B7
Atlantic Av					
-	HFET	60107	2857	26W-11N	E4
-	SMWD	60107	2857	26W-11N	E4
800	HFET	60194	2857	26W-11N	E3
2200	LydT	60164	2973	12W-2N	C6
2300	FNPK	60131	2973	12W-2N	C6
2300	FNPK	60164	2973	12W-2N	C6
4100	SRPK	60176	2973	12W-5N	C1
14600	DLTN	60419	3350	0W-17S	B5
14600	RVDL	60827	3350	0W-17S	B5
S Atlantic Av					
14000	RVDL	60827	3350	0W-16S	C3
14500	DLTN	60419	3350	0W-17S	C4
Atlantic Dr					
13300	HMGN	60441	3343	16W-17S	E5
Atlantic Ln					
400	EGVV	60007	2859	22W-9N	D7
Atlantic St					
3300	FNPK	60131	2973	12W-4N	C4
S Atlantic St					
13600	RVDL	60827	3350	0W-16S	C2
Attica Rd					
3400	OMFD	60461	3506	4W-24S	E6
Attleboro Ct					
1100	SMBG	60193	2912		C2
Attleboro Ln					
-	BRLT	60107	2856	29W-9N	D7
-	SMWD	60107	2856	29W-9N	D7
Attleboro on Auburn					
10	RGMW	60008	2806	19W-14N	C3
W Attrill St					
2600	CHCG	60647	2977	3W-2N	A6
E Atwater Av					
400	EMHT	60126	3028		B3
Atwood Av					
1400	BKLY	60163	3028		C4
2000	HLSD	60162	3028		C5
Atwood Ct					
10900	ODPK	60467	3345	13W-16S	A3
E Atwood Ct					
400	EMHT	60126	3028		B5
Aubrieta Ct					
15400	ODPK	60462	3346	9W-18S	E7
15400	OrlT	60462	3346	9W-18S	E7
Aubrieta Ln					
15300	ODPK	60462	3346	9W-18S	E7
Auburn					
10	RGMW	60008	2806	20W-13N	A5
Auburn Av					
200	WNKA	60093	2811	5W-15N	E2
S Auburn Av					
12700	PSHT	60463	3275	8W-15S	A7
Auburn Cir					
600	SMBG	60193	2858	25W-9N	B7
Auburn Ct					
9200	ODPK	60462	3345	11W-16S	E3
Auburn Ln					
500	SMBG	60193	2858	25W-9N	B7
900	BRLT	60103	2910		C4
1000	BFGV	60089	2754	17W-20N	A1
1100	VrnT	60089	2754	17W-20N	A1
2300	NHBK	60062	2809	11W-15N	E1
W Auburn Ln					
400	CteT	60417	3685	0W-32S	C7
Auburn Rd					
800	WNKA	60093	2758	5W-16N	E7
W Auburn Woods Ct					
400	PLTN	60067	2752	21W-17N	D6
N Auburn Woods Dr					
1000	PLTN	60067	2752	21W-17N	D5
Audrey Av					
800	BlmT	60411	3510	4E-25S	B7
Audrey Ct					
400	DYR	46311	3510		D6
S Audrey Ct					
200	MPPT	60056	2861	17W-12N	B1
Audrey Ln					
500	WLNG	60090	2755	15W-17N	A5
2500	NHBK	60062	2809	11W-15N	C1
S Audrey Ln					
10	ANHT	60005	2807	17W-12N	C7
10	MPPT	60056	2807	17W-12N	C7
100	MPPT	60056	2861	17W-12N	B1
Audubon Rd					
300	RVSD	60546	3088	9W-2S	D4
300	SMWD	60107	2857	28W-10N	B5
Audubon St					
-	SMBG	60173	2859	22W-11N	C3
600	HFET	60194	2859	22W-11N	C4
700	SMBG	60194	2859	22W-11N	C3
Augusta Av					
900	ELGN	60120	2855		A1
Augusta Blvd					
4800	MONE	60449	3683	6W-31S	A5
W Augusta Blvd					
1200	CHCG	60622	3033	1W-1N	E2
2800	CHCG	60622	3032	4W-1N	C2
3000	CHCG	60651	3032	4W-1N	D2
4700	CHCG	60651	3031	7W-1N	C2
5900	CHCG	60302	3031	7W-1N	B2
5900	OKPK	60302	3031	7W-1N	B2
Augusta Ct					
100	PSHT	60463	3275	7W-14S	B5
Augusta Dr					
10	DRFD	60015	2757	10W-20N	B1
10	SMWD	60107	2856	29W-10N	D5
100	PSHT	60463	3275	8W-15S	B7
Augusta Dr					
100	PSHT	60463	3347	8W-15S	B1
20100	OMFD	60461	3507	3W-24S	C5
Augusta Ln					
100	PSHT	60463	3347	8W-15S	B1
14700	HMGN	60441	3343	17W-17S	C6
18600	HLCT	60429	3506	4W-22S	E1
Augusta St					
10	CHCG	60302	3031	7W-1N	B2
10	CHCG	60651	3031	7W-1N	B2
10	OKPK	60302	3031	8W-1N	A2
200	MYWD	60153	3030	10W-1N	A2
600	MYWD	60153	3029	11W-1N	D2
700	OKPK	60302	3030	8W-1N	E2
800	MLPK	60160	3029	10W-1N	E2
1100	RVFT	60305	3030	9W-1N	C2
Aulwurm Dr					
-	ClmT	60827	3349	1W-15S	D1
13300	BLID	60406	3349	2W-15S	C1
13300	ClmT	60406	3349	2W-15S	C1
N Aurelia Ct					
600	PLTN	60067	2752	21W-16N	D7
Austgen Pl					
500	DYR	46311	3598		D5
3100	SjnT	46311	3598		D5
Austin Av					
10	CPVL	60110	2748		B5
500	PKRG	60068	2864	10W-9N	A6
1500	CRTE	60417	3685	0W-30S	C3
1500	CteT	60417	3685	0W-30S	C3
7600	BRBK	60459	3211	7W-8S	C2
7600	SKOK	60077	2865	7W-9N	B6
7800	MNGV	60053	2865	7W-9N	B6
8500	OKLN	60459	3211	7W-9S	C4
8700	OKLN	60453	3211	7W-10S	C5
10300	CHRG	60415	3275	7W-12S	C1
10300	CHRG	60453	3275	7W-12S	C1
10300	OKLN	60453	3275	7W-12S	C1
10400	OKLN	60415	3275	7W-12S	C1
11000	ALSP	60482	3275	7W-12S	C3
11000	CHRG	60482	3275	7W-12S	C3
16300	BmnT	60477	3425	7W-19S	C2
N Austin Av					
1700	CHCG	60639	2975	7W-2N	B7
2700	CHCG	60634	2975	7W-3N	B5
4300	CHCG	60630	2975	7W-5N	B1
4400	CHCG	60630	2919	7W-5N	B7
5400	CHCG	60646	2919	7W-7N	B4
6900	NLES	60714	2919	7W-8N	C1
S Austin Av					
4700	StkT	60638	3149	7W-5S	C1
4900	CHCG	60638	3149	7W-7S	C5
6400	BDPK	60638	3149	7W-7S	C5
11500	ALSP	60482	3275	7W-13S	C4
12200	ALSP	60803	3275	7W-14S	C6
12200	WthT	60803	3275	7W-14S	C6
12700	WthT	60463	3275	7W-15S	C7
N Austin Blvd					
10	CHCG	60644	3031	7W-0N	B5
10	OKPK	60302	3031	7W-1N	B1
10	OKPK	60304	3031	7W-0N	B5
700	CHCG	60651	3031	7W-1N	B1
800	CHCG	60302	3031	7W-1N	B2
1500	CHCG	60639	3031	7W-2N	B1
1600	CHCG	60639	2975	7W-2N	B7
S Austin Blvd					
10	CHCG	60644	3031	7W-1S	C7
10	OKPK	60302	3031	7W-0S	B5
10	OKPK	60304	3031	7W-1S	C7
1000	CCRO	60804	3031	7W-0S	B7
1000	CHCG	60804	3031	7W-0S	B7
1000	OKPK	60804	3031	7W-0S	B7
1500	CCRO	60804	3089	7W-3S	C5
3800	CCRO	60402	3089	7W-3S	C6
3800	SKNY	60402	3089	7W-3S	C6
Austin Ln					
200	SMBG	60195	2859	23W-12N	A2
17000	ODPK	60467	3423	13W-20S	B4
W Austin Ln					
1000	PLTN	60067	2805	22W-15N	B2
Austin St					
1000	EVTN	60202	2867	2W-9N	A6
Auto Ct					
-	MTSN	60443	3505	6W-25S	E7
5500	MTSN	60443	3593	6W-25S	E1
Autobahn Dr E					
11500	PSPK	60464	3274	9W-13S	C4
Autobahn Dr N					
8000	PSPK	60464	3274	10W-13S	C4
Autobahn Dr S					
8000	PSPK	60464	3274	10W-13S	C4
Autobahn Dr W					
11500	PSPK	60464	3274	10W-13S	C4
Automatic Electric Dr					
-	NHLK	60164	2972		D7
W Autullo Dr					
7600	WRTH	60482	3274	9W-12S	D2
S Autullo St					
10800	WRTH	60482	3274	9W-12S	D2
Autumn Av					
1600	SMBG	60193	2912		B3
Autumn Dr					
600	ROSL	60172	2912		D6
16900	TYPK	60477	3425	7W-20S	C4
Autumn Ln					
10	SMWD	60107	2856	29W-9N	D7
200	MPPT	60056	2808	14W-13N	B6
2900	DYR	46311	3598		D4
W Autumn Rd					
1400	PLTN	60067	2752	22W-17N	A5
1400	PltT	60067	2752	22W-17N	A5
Autumn Tr					
10	BNHL	60010	2748		D3
Autumn Ridge Dr					
11200	ODPK	60467	3422	14W-21S	E7
Auvergne Pl					
500	RVFT	60305	3030	10W-0N	B4
N Auxplaines St					
2700	RVGV	60171	2974	10W-3N	A5
Avalon Av					
6000	OKFT	60452	3347	7W-18S	C6
14200	DLTN	60419	3351	1E-16S	B4
15600	SHLD	60473	3351	1E-18S	B7
15900	SHLD	60473	3429	1E-18S	B1
S Avalon Av					
300	GNWD	60425	3509	1E-23S	B3
7600	CHCG	60619	3215	1E-9S	A2
9500	CHCG	60628	3215	1E-11S	A6
Avalon Ct					
100	ROSL	60172	2912		C4
2000	GNVW	60062	2809	12W-14N	B3
14000	ODPK	60462	3346	10W-16S	B3
Avalon Dr					
500	DYR	46311	3598		D1
1800	WLNG	60090	2808	14W-15N	B1
Avebury Ct					
400	ROSL	60172	2912		D5
Avebury Ln					
400	ROSL	60172	2912		D6
Avenel Dr					
16400	ODPK	60467	3422	14W-19S	E3
Avenida Del Este St					
9800	ODPK	60462	3345	12W-17S	D6
Avenida Del Norte St					
9800	ODPK	60462	3345	12W-17S	C6
Avenue E					
2800	GNVW	60025	2810	10W-14N	A3
S Avenue A					
10600	CHCG	46320	3280	4E-12S	C1
10600	CHCG	60617	3280	4E-12S	C1
10600	HMND	46320	3280	4E-12S	C1
Avenue B					
2900	GNVW	60025	2810	10W-14N	A4
S Avenue B					
10600	CHCG	60617	3280	4E-12S	C1
Avenue C					
2900	GNVW	60025	2810	10W-14N	A4
S Avenue C					
10600	CHCG	60617	3280	4E-12S	C2
Avenue D					
2900	GNVW	60025	2810	10W-14N	A4
S Avenue D					
10600	CHCG	60617	3280	4E-12S	C1
S Avenue E					
10800	CHCG	60617	3280	4E-12S	C2
S Avenue F					
10300	CHCG	60617	3216	4E-11S	C7
10300	CHCG	60617	3280	4E-11S	C1
S Avenue G					
9700	CHCG	60617	3216	4E-11S	C6
10300	CHCG	60617	3280	4E-11S	C1
Avenue G Dr					
-	CHCG	60617	3216	4E-11S	C7
-	HMND	46320	3216	4E-11S	C7
S Avenue H					
9700	CHCG	60617	3216	4E-10S	B6
10300	CHCG	60617	3280	4E-12S	B3
S Avenue J					
10100	CHCG	60617	3216	4E-11S	B7
10300	CHCG	60617	3280	4E-11S	B1
S Avenue K					
13300	CHCG	60633	3352	4E-15S	B1
S Avenue L					
9500	CHCG	60617	3216	4E-10S	B5
10300	CHCG	60617	3280	4E-11S	B1
13200	CHCG	60633	3352	4E-15S	B1
S Avenue M					
9500	CHCG	60617	3216	4E-10S	B5
10300	CHCG	60617	3280	4E-11S	B1
13000	CHCG	60633	3280	4E-15S	B7
13100	CHCG	60633	3352	4E-15S	B1
S Avenue N					
9500	CHCG	60617	3216	4E-10S	B5
11600	CHCG	60617	3280	4E-13S	B4
13000	CHCG	60633	3280	4E-15S	B7
13100	CHCG	60633	3352	4E-15S	B1
S Avenue O					
10200	CHCG	60617	3216	4E-11S	B7
10300	CHCG	60617	3280	3E-14S	B7
11800	CHCG	60633	3280	4E-13S	B5
13100	CHCG	60633	3352	4E-15S	B1
13600	BNHM	60633	3352	3E-16S	B2
Avers Av					
8400	SKOK	60076	2866	4W-10N	C4
9200	SKOK	60203	2866	4W-11N	C2
9500	EVTN	60201	2866	4W-11N	C2
15500	MDLN	60426	3348	4W-18S	D7
15500	MDLN	60445	3348	4W-18S	D7
18700	FSMR	60422	3506	4W-22S	D2
19000	RchT	60430	3506	4W-22S	D2
19000	RchT	60478	3506	4W-22S	D2
N Avers Av					
300	CHCG	60624	3032	4W-0N	C4
700	CHCG	60651	3032	4W-0N	C3
1500	CHCG	60647	3032	4W-2N	C1
2000	CHCG	60647	2976	4W-3N	C5
3800	CHCG	60618	2976	4W-4N	C2
4300	CHCG	60625	2976	4W-5N	C1
4400	CHCG	60625	2920	4W-5N	C7
6100	CHCG	60659	2920	4W-7N	C3
6900	LNWD	60712	2920	4W-8N	C1
S Avers Av					
1200	CHCG	60623	3032	4W-1S	C7
1200	CHCG	60624	3032	4W-1S	C7
1600	CHCG	60623	3090	4W-1S	C1
4500	CHCG	60632	3090	4W-4S	C7
5100	CHCG	60632	3150	4W-5S	C2
7100	CHCG	60629	3150	4W-8S	C7
9100	CHCG	60805	3212	4W-11S	C6
9100	ENGN	60805	3212	4W-11S	C6
9800	CHCG	60655	3212	4W-11S	C7
10500	CHCG	60655	3276	4W-12S	C1
11700	WthT	60803	3276	4W-13S	C5
12200	ALSP	60803	3276	4W-14S	C6
13400	CTWD	60472	3348	4W-15S	D2
13400	RBBN	60472	3348	4W-15S	D2
S Avers Ct					
12000	ALSP	60803	3276	4W-14S	D5
N Avery Ct					
10	PLTN	60067	2805	22W-16N	C1
10	PltT	60067	2805	22W-16N	C1
Avery Pl					
5200	OKLN	60453	3211	6W-10S	D4
Aviator Ln					
2600	GNVW	60025	2810	9W-14N	B4
Aviemore Ln					
20900	FftT	60423	3504	9W-25S	E7
Avon Av					
-	BGVW	60455	3210	9W-10S	D6
100	NfdT	60093	2811	7W-15N	B3
100	NHFD	60093	2811	7W-15N	C3
7000	CHRG	60415	3210	8W-11S	E6
7000	OKLN	60415	3210	8W-11S	E6
7000	OKLN	60453	3210	8W-11S	E6
S Avon Av					
11100	ALSP	60803	3275	6W-13S	E3
11300	ALSP	60803	3276	6W-13S	A4
Avon Ct					
1300	SMBG	60193	2912		B2
10600	PSHL	60465	3274	10W-12S	A2
E Avon Ct					
1600	ANHT	60004	2807	16W-15N	C1
Avon Dr					
1800	HFET	60120	2855		E1
Avon Ln					
-	NHBK	60062	2757	9W-18N	B2
10	SBTN	60010	2804	24W-14N	C3
17300	TYPK	60477	3424	10W-20S	A5
E Avon Ln					
1700	ANHT	60004	2807	16W-15N	C1

Chicago & Cook County Street Index

STREET Block	City	ZIP	Map#	CGS	Grid
Avon Rd					
10	DRFD	60015	2757	9W-18N	B2
10	EGVV	60007	2914		D1
10	NHBK	60062	2757	9W-18N	B2
100	NfdT	60062	2757	9W-18N	B2
N Avon Rd					
100	EMHT	60126	3028		A2
Avondale Av					
-	PKRG	60068	2918	9W-8N	B1
2300	PKRG	60068	2863	11W-9N	D6
N Avondale Av					
-	CHCG	60614	2977	2W-2N	C6
2600	CHCG	60647	2977	3W-3N	A5
2800	CHCG	60618	2976	3W-3N	E4
3800	CHCG	60641	2976	4W-4N	C2
5100	CHCG	60630	2919	7W-6N	C6
5600	CHCG	60631	2919	8W-7N	A4
5600	CHCG	60646	2919	7W-7N	A4
6700	CHCG	60631	2918	9W-8N	C2
6700	PKRG	60068	2918	9W-8N	C2
W Avondale Dr					
200	PLTN	60067	2752	21W-17N	D4
Avondale Ln					
500	HFET	60194	2859	22W-11N	B3
2000	WLMT	60091	2812	4W-13N	B7
Avonelle Dr					
200	CHHT	60411	3508	1W-24S	A4
Aylesbury Av					
4700	MTSN	60443	3506	5W-24S	B6
Ayr Ct					
-	CRTE	60417	3597	0E-28S	A7
Ayr Ln					
3600	CRTE	60417	3597	0E-28S	A7
E Ayres St					
10	HNDL	60521	3086		B7
W Ayres St					
10	HNDL	60521	3086		A7
Ayrshire Ln					
300	IVNS	60067	2751	23W-16N	E7
W Azalea Av					
4500	MONE	60449	3683	5W-31S	C4
Azalea Cir					
100	SMWD	60107	2857	27W-10N	C5
Azalea Ct					
5500	RGMW	60008	2860	19W-12N	D1
Azalea Dr					
10	SMBG	60173	2859	21W-10N	E5
1000	MNSR	46321	3510		E2
Azalea Ln					
400	HFET	60195	2859	23W-11N	B2
E Azalea Ln					
1100	PLTN	60074	2753	19W-18N	C3
W Azalea Ln					
1800	MPPT	60056	2808	13W-14N	E4
W Azalea Pl					
1700	MPPT	60056	2808	13W-14N	D4
E Aztec Ln					
1700	MPPT	60056	2808	13W-15N	E2

B

STREET Block	City	ZIP	Map#	CGS	Grid
W B St					
-	MYWD	60153	3030	10W-1S	A7
-	PvsT	60141	3030	10W-1S	A7
Babb Av					
7800	SKOK	60077	2865	6W-9N	D6
E Babcock Dr					
800	PLTN	60074	2753	19W-16N	B7
N Babcock Dr					
100	PLTN	60074	2753	19W-16N	B7
100	PLTN	60074	2806	19W-16N	B1
Babetta Av					
600	PKRG	60068	2863	11W-9N	D7
Babette Ct					
5500	BmnT	60452	3425	6W-19S	D2
5500	BmnT	60477	3425	6W-19S	D2
5500	OKFT	60452	3425	6W-19S	D2
Bach St					
800	NHBK	60062	2757	10W-17N	A4
Back Bay Dr					
10	SBTN	60010	2803	26W-14N	C3
Badger Ln					
-	HMGN	60441	3344	16W-18S	A7
15400	HMGN	60441	3422	16W-18S	A1
Badger Rd					
3400	EGvT	60005	2861	16W-10N	D6
3400	MPPT	60005	2861	16W-10N	D6
Baffin Rd					
1400	GNVW	60025	2810	8W-13N	E6
Bahama Ct					
600	SMBG	60193	2858	24W-9N	D7
Bahama Ln					
500	SMBG	60193	2858	24W-9N	D7
Bailey Rd					
10	PKFT	60466	3595	2W-26S	C2
Baileys Crossing Dr					
1200	LMNT	60439	3271		B7
Baker Av					
800	DndT	60118	2801		C5
17500	CCHL	60478	3426	5W-21S	C6
18500	CCHL	60478	3506	5W-22S	C1
18900	RchT	60477	3506	5W-22S	C2
18900	RchT	60478	3506	5W-22S	C2
S Baker Av					
8300	CHCG	60617	3216	3E-9S	A3
S Baker Av US-41					
8400	CHCG	60617	3216	3E-9S	A3
Baker Ct					
17800	CCHL	60478	3426	5W-21S	C6
Baker Dr					
300	BmdT	60143	2913		E6
500	ITSC	60143	2913		E6
N Baker Dr					
1000	ITSC	60143	2913		E4
1000	ITSC	60143	2914		A4
S Baker Dr					
400	BmdT	60143	2913		E6
400	ITSC	60143	2913		E6
N Baker St					
600	ITSC	60143	2913		E5
Balbo Dr					
-	LynT	60525	3147	13W-7S	B5
10	CTSD	60525	3147	13W-7S	B5
E Balbo Dr					
10	CHCG	60605	3034	0E-0S	C6
Balboa Ct					
600	SMBG	60193	2858	24W-9N	D7
Balboa Ter E					
700	BRLT	60103	2911		B4
Balboa Ter W					
700	BRLT	60103	2911		A4
S Baldwin Av					
7400	CHCG	60649	3153	2E-8S	C7
Baldwin Ct					
1500	WLNG	60090	2754	16W-18N	D4

STREET Block	City	ZIP	Map#	CGS	Grid
Baldwin Ct					
2400	SMBG	60193	2857	26W-10N	E6
N Baldwin Ct					
1300	PLTN	60074	2753	19W-17N	C4
E Baldwin Ln					
1200	PLTN	60074	2753	19W-17N	C4
N Baldwin Ln					
-	PLTN	60074	2753	19W-17N	C4
Baldwin Rd					
1300	IVNS	60067	2752	22W-16N	A6
1300	PLTN	60067	2752	22W-16N	A6
1600	IVNS	60067	2751	23W-16N	E6
2100	IVNS	60010	2751	23W-16N	D6
E Baldwin Rd					
400	PLTN	60074	2753	19W-16N	B7
N Baldwin Rd					
1600	PLTN	60074	2753	19W-18N	C3
Baldwin Tr					
8000	HYHL	60457	3210	10W-10S	C5
N Baldwin Wy					
2200	PLTN	60074	2753	19W-18N	C2
2200	PltT	60074	2753	19W-18N	C2
Ball Av					
10	CPVL	60110	2748		C7
Ballantrae Dr					
600	NHBK	60062	2757	8W-18N	E4
Ballantrae Wy					
3700	FSMR	60422	3506	4W-23S	D4
3900	FSMR	60443	3506	4W-23S	D3
3900	RchT	60443	3506	4W-23S	D3
Ballard Ct					
-	TYPK	60477	3424	10W-21S	B6
Ballard Dr					
-	TYPK	60477	3424	10W-21S	B6
Ballard Rd					
1600	MaiT	60068	2863	11W-11N	E3
1600	PKRG	60068	2863	11W-11N	E3
1700	MaiT	60016	2863	11W-11N	E3
1700	PKRG	60016	2863	11W-11N	E3
E Ballard Rd					
2200	DSPN	60016	2863	12W-11N	C3
2500	MaiT	60016	2863	12W-11N	C3
W Ballard Rd					
8100	NLES	60714	2864	10W-11N	A3
8500	MaiT	60016	2864	10W-11N	A3
8500	MaiT	60714	2864	10W-11N	A3
8700	MaiT	60068	2863	10W-11N	E3
8700	NLES	60714	2863	10W-11N	E3
9000	MaiT	60016	2863	11W-11N	D3
9000	PKRG	60016	2863	11W-11N	D3
9000	PKRG	60068	2863	11W-11N	D3
9700	DSPN	60016	2863	12W-11N	B3
Ballinary Ct					
11700	ODPK	60467	3422	14W-21S	D6
Bally Castle Ln					
8600	TYPK	60477	3504	10W-23S	B3
Balm Ct					
300	WDDL	60191	2915		C6
Balmoral Av					
-	CHCG	60018	2917	12W-6N	B5
-	CHCG	60666	2917	12W-6N	B5
-	RSMT	60018	2917	12W-6N	C5
10	NHFD	60093	2811	7W-14N	B3
600	WSTR	60154	3029	12W-0S	B6
1200	CTCY	60409	3430	3E-19S	A1
1400	WSTR	60154	3087	12W-1S	B1
2000	GNVW	60025	2811	7W-14N	A3
W Balmoral Av					
1000	CHCG	60640	2921	2W-6N	B5
2400	CHCG	60625	2921	3W-6N	A5
2600	CHCG	60625	2920	3W-6N	E5
5400	CHCG	60630	2919	6W-6N	C5
6300	CHCG	60656	2919	8W-6N	A5
7900	CHCG	60656	2918	10W-6N	B5
7900	LydT	60656	2918	10W-6N	B5
7900	NpkT	60656	2918	10W-6N	B5
Balmoral Cir					
1600	IVNS	60067	2805	22W-14N	A3
Balmoral Cres					
2800	FSMR	60422	3507	3W-23S	A3
Balmoral Ct					
800	EDND	60118	2801		C2
4900	RGMW	60008	2806	19W-14N	C3
8700	LynT	60527	3208		C3
Balmoral Dr					
300	BRLT	60103	2911		B6
800	EDND	60118	2801		C2
1500	IVNS	60067	2805	22W-14N	A3
1500	PLTN	60067	2805	22W-14N	A3
4400	RNPK	60443	3594	5W-26S	B3
4400	RNPK	60471	3594	5W-26S	B3
Balmoral Gln					
1300	FSMR	60422	3507	3W-23S	A3
Balmoral Ln					
200	BRTN	60010	2751	24W-18N	D2
200	PltT	60010	2751	24W-18N	D2
500	IVNS	60067	2805	22W-14N	A3
800	NHBK	60062	2810	9W-15N	B1
1000	ELGN	60120	2856	31W-9N	A7
17600	HLCT	60429	3427	3W-21S	A6
S Balmoral Woods Dr					
26700	CteT	60417	3685	0W-32S	D7
26800	CteT	60417	3774	0W-32S	D1
Balsam Ct					
300	SMBG	60193	2858	24W-10N	E6
Balsam Ln					
-	DSPN	60018	2917	12W-8N	B2
900	BRLT	60103	2910		E6
E Balsam Ln					
400	PLTN	60074	2753	20W-17N	A5
Balsam Rd					
1700	HDPK	60035	2757	9W-20N	C1
Baltic Cir					
13200	LMNT	60439	3343	17W-15S	C2
S Baltimore Av					
4600	HMND	46327	3352		E5
8300	CHCG	60617	3215	3E-9S	E2
8700	CHCG	60617	3216	3E-10S	A4
12900	CHCG	60633	3280	3E-15S	A7
13100	CHCG	60633	3352	3E-15S	A1
Baltimore Dr					
1700	EGVV	60007	2913		C1
Baltusro Dr					
-	MONE	60449	3683	6W-31S	A5
Baltusrol Dr					
8800	ODPK	60462	3424	11W-18S	A1
Bamberg Ct					
1200	HRPK	60133	2911		E5
Banbridge Ct					
9400	PlsT	60462	3345	11W-15S	D2
Banbury Av					
200	EGVV	60007	2914		C2
Banbury Ct					
10	SMWD	60107	2856	29W-9N	D7
600	ROSL	60172	2913		B6

STREET Block	City	ZIP	Map#	CGS	Grid
Banbury Ct					
900	SMBG	60194	2858	26W-11N	A3
Banbury Pl					
9700	MNSR	46321	3510		C3
Banbury Rd					
1400	IVNS	60067	2751	23W-17N	E5
1400	IVNS	60067	2752	23W-17N	A6
S Banbury Rd					
600	ANHT	60005	2807	17W-13N	B6
Banbury Ter					
400	ROSL	60172	2913		B6
S Baneberry Cir					
15300	LKPT	60441	3342	20W-18S	B7
Bangor Dr					
8500	TYPK	60477	3504	10W-23S	B3
Bangor Ln					
1800	EGVV	60007	2913		C1
Bank Dr					
-	LydT	60164	2973	12W-2N	C6
-	MLPK	60160	2973	12W-2N	C6
1200	SMBG	60173	2859	21W-11N	D3
Bank Ln					
10	BFGV	60089	2754	16W-20N	C1
Banks St					
7200	JSTC	60458	3147	11W-8S	E7
7200	JSTC	60458	3209	11W-8S	E1
E Banks St					
10	CHCG	60610	3034	0E-1N	C1
Bannock Ct					
100	EDND	60118	2801		C2
Bannock Rd					
800	EDND	60118	2801		C2
Bannockburn					
2100	IVNS	60067	2804	23W-14N	D3
Bantry Blvd					
-	MKNA	60448	3504	10W-23S	B3
8600	TYPK	60477	3504	10W-23S	B3
Banyan Dr					
400	NHBK	60062	2756	11W-18N	C3
800	EGVV	60007	2914		E1
S Banyon Ct					
15300	LKPT	60441	3342	20W-18S	A7
Banyon Ln					
500	LGNG	60525	3147	13W-5S	A1
Barbara Av					
6200	TYPK	60477	3425	7W-20S	B3
Barbara Ct					
600	BMDL	60157	2913		B7
1200	CRTE	60417	3685	0W-29S	C1
18900	LNSG	60438	3510	4E-22S	B1
Barbara Dr					
3100	GNVW	60025	2810	10W-15N	A3
Barbara Ln					
100	STGR	60475	3596	1W-28S	A6
200	STGR	60475	3595	1W-28S	E6
1200	CHHT	60411	3507	2W-25S	D7
16900	TYPK	60477	3425	7W-20S	C4
W Barbara Ln					
7800	FftT	60423	3504	9W-24S	D4
Barbary Ln					
2400	GNVW	60025	2809	11W-15N	E2
2400	GNVW	60062	2809	11W-15N	E2
W Barber St					
-	CHCG	60607	3034	0W-1S	A7
-	CHCG	60608	3034	1W-1S	A7
Barberry Av					
400	DYR	46311	3510		D6
Barberry Ct					
1000	ELGN	60120	2855		D2
3800	HFET	60195	2804	25W-14N	A3
E Barberry Ct					
2300	ANHT	60004	2807	16W-15N	C2
Barberry Ln					
600	WLNG	60090	2754	16W-17N	D5
8900	HYHL	60457	3209	11W-10S	E4
8900	HYHL	60457	3210	11W-10S	A4
9000	MaiT	60016	2863	11W-11N	D2
9100	PlsT	60480	3209	11W-10S	E4
E Barberry Ln					
1100	PLTN	60074	2753	19W-18N	C3
1600	MPPT	60056	2808	14W-14N	D4
N Barberry Ln					
1600	MPPT	60056	2808	14W-14N	C4
Barberry Rd					
100	HDPK	60035	2757	8W-20N	D2
1800	NHBK	60062	2756	11W-16N	E7
Barbra Ct					
500	UYPK	60466	3684	3W-29S	C2
Barbs Wy					
10900	ODPK	60467	3423	13W-20S	A4
Barclay Cir					
1200	IVNS	60010	2751	24W-17N	C4
E Barclay Ct					
400	EMHT	60126	3028		C6
Barclay Ln					
3000	WLMT	60091	2811	6W-13N	E6
Barcliffe Ln					
100	SMBG	60194	2858	24W-10N	D5
Barcroft Ct					
5100	HFET	60010	2751	24W-16N	B7
Barcroft Dr					
5100	HFET	60010	2751	24W-16N	B7
5100	IVNS	60010	2751	24W-16N	B7
Bardsey Dr					
10	SMBG	60194	2858	25W-10N	C5
Bardwick Ct					
5000	HFET	60010	2751	24W-16N	B7
Bar Harbor Ter					
1200	NHBK	60062	2756	10W-17N	E5
Bar Harbour Rd					
10	SMBG	60173	2859	21W-10N	D5
10	SMBG	60193	2859	21W-10N	D5
Barker Av					
4700	RGMW	60008	2806	19W-12N	B7
4700	RGMW	60008	2860	19W-12N	B1
Barker St					
-	LYWD	60411	3510	4E-24S	B6
Bark Wood Rd					
2500	SMBG	60173	2805	21W-13N	D6
Barleycorn Ct					
8900	ODPK	60462	3346	11W-18S	A7
Barnaby Pl					
700	WLNG	60090	2755	15W-18N	A3
Barnard Dr					
10300	CHRG	60415	3275	8W-12S	B1
Barnard Ln					
10	HDPK	60035	2758	7W-20N	A2
10	NtrT	60035	2758	7W-20N	A2
Barnett Ln					
-	BRLT	60120	2909		E3
Barn Owl Dr					
-	RchT	60443	3593	8W-25S	B1
Barnsdale Rd					
500	LGPK	60525	3087	12W-3S	C5

STREET Block	City	ZIP	Map#	CGS	Grid
Barnsley Pl					
400	NHBK	60062	2758	8W-17N	A5
Baron Dr					
2100	HLCT	60429	3427	2W-20S	C4
E Baronet Ln					
-	ANHT	60004	2806	19W-15N	C2
1300	PLTN	60074	2806	19W-15N	C2
Barr Ct					
5700	HRPK	60133	2911		E5
W Barr Rd					
8900	PtnT	60468	3860	11W-36S	A2
Barra Ln					
100	IVNS	60067	2752	22W-16N	B7
Barrett Ln					
100	SMBG	60193	2859	23W-9N	A7
Barrett St					
400	ELGN	60120	2855		A4
Barrington Av					
10	EDND	60118	2801		A2
500	CPVL	60110	2801		B2
500	DndT	60118	2801		B2
500	EDND	60110	2801		A2
600	CPVL	60118	2801		B2
Barrington Av SR-68					
500	CPVL	60118	2801		B2
500	DndT	60118	2801		B2
500	EDND	60118	2801		B2
Barrington Ct					
500	UYPK	60466	3684	3W-30S	C3
Barrington Rd					
700	HFET	60194	2857	27W-12N	D1
700	SMWD	60107	2857	27W-11N	D4
700	SMWD	60194	2857	27W-11N	D4
1800	HFET	60195	2857	27W-12N	D1
1900	HFET	60195	2803	27W-12N	D7
6100	HRPK	60133	2911		D3
7600	SMWD	60107	2911		D1
N Barrington Rd					
10	BrnT	60010	2803	25W-15N	E3
10	SBTN	60010	2803	26W-14N	E4
10	SMBG	60194	2857	27W-11N	D5
10	SMWD	60107	2857	27W-11N	D4
200	HFET	60107	2857	27W-11N	D4
200	HFET	60194	2857	27W-11N	D4
200	SMWD	60194	2857	27W-11N	D4
S Barrington Rd					
-	SBTN	60195	2803	25W-13N	E5
10	HFET	60195	2803	25W-13N	E5
10	SBTN	60010	2803	25W-13N	E5
10	SMBG	60193	2857	27W-10N	D6
10	SMBG	60194	2857	27W-10N	D6
100	BNHL	60010	2750	25W-16N	E7
100	BRTN	60010	2750	25W-16N	E7
100	IVNS	60010	2750	25W-17N	E5
300	BNHL	60010	2803	26W-15N	E1
300	BrnT	60010	2803	26W-15N	E1
300	HRPK	60107	2857	26W-10N	D7
300	HRPK	60133	2857	26W-10N	D7
300	IVNS	60010	2803	26W-15N	E1
300	SMBG	60133	2857	26W-10N	D7
300	SMWD	60107	2857	26W-10N	D6
900	BrnT	60010	2750	25W-16N	E7
1000	HRPK	60133	2911		D1
1000	SMWD	60107	2911		D1
Barrington Bourne Rd					
10	BNHL	60010	2748		E1
Barrington Commons Ct					
100	BRTN	60010	2750	27W-20N	C1
100	BRTN	60010	2751	25W-20N	A1
Barrington Hills Rd					
10	BNHL	60010	2749	28W-18N	E2
Barrington Point Rd					
800	BRTN	60010	2751	25W-18N	B2
N Barrington Woods Rd					
2200	PLTN	60074	2752	21W-18N	D2
2300	DRPK	60074	2752	21W-18N	D2
2300	PltT	60074	2752	21W-18N	D2
Barron Dr					
1800	CHCG	60617	3216	4E-10S	C5
Barrow Ct					
1000	UYPK	60466	3684	3W-30S	B3
Barrow on Duxbury					
10	RGMW	60008	2805	22W-13N	B7
Barry Av					
10800	FNPK	60131	2972		D4
10800	LydT	60164	2972		D4
W Barry Av					
600	CHCG	60657	2978	0W-3N	A4
800	CHCG	60657	2977	2W-3N	B4
1900	CHCG	60618	2977	2W-3N	A4
2700	CHCG	60618	2976	3W-3N	E4
3900	CHCG	60641	2976	5W-3N	B4
4700	CHCG	60641	2975	7W-3N	C4
5500	CHCG	60634	2975	8W-3N	A4
7000	CHCG	60634	2974	9W-3N	C4
7100	CHCG	60707	2974	9W-3N	C4
7500	EDPK	60707	2974	9W-3N	C4
7900	RVGV	60171	2974	9W-3N	B4
Barry Ln					
500	CRTE	60417	3685	0W-30S	B3
1100	SLVL	60411	3509	2E-25S	D7
1600	GNVW	60025	2809	11W-14N	D4
4100	OKFT	60452	3426	5W-19S	C2
S Barry Rd					
500	ElgT	60177	2909		A2
500	SEGN	60177	2909		A2
Barry St					
7000	RSMT	60018	2916		E1
7100	DSPN	60018	2916		E1
Barrymore Ct					
2000	HRPK	60133	2911		D6
Barrypoint Rd					
100	RVSD	60546	3088	10W-3S	B6
Bartels Rd					
5500	BmdT	60133	2912		A5
5500	HRPK	60133	2912		A5
Bartlett Av					
9000	BKFD	60513	3087	11W-2S	E4
9100	LGPK	60525	3087	11W-2S	D4
E Bartlett Av					
-	BRLT	60103	2910		D3
-	BRLT	60103	2911		A3
W Bartlett Av					
100	BRLT	60103	2910		E3
Bartlett Pl					
200	ELGN	60120	2855		A5
Bartlett Plz					
10	BRLT	60103	2910		E4
10	BRLT	60103	2911		A3
Bartlett Rd					
-	BNHL	60010	2803	28W-16N	A1
-	HFET	60010	2803	28W-12N	A7
-	HFET	60010	2857	28W-12N	A1
-	HFET	60120	2857	28W-12N	A1
-	SMWD	60107	2857	28W-11N	A4

STREET Block	City	ZIP	Map#	CGS	Grid
Bartlett Rd					
10	BrnT	60010	2803	28W-15N	A2
10	BrnT	60118	2803	28W-15N	A2
10	SBTN	60010	2803	28W-13N	A5
N Bartlett Rd					
-	HFET	60120	2857	28W-11N	A4
10	SMWD	60107	2857	28W-11N	A4
S Bartlett Rd					
-	BRLT	60120	2910		E1
10	SMWD	60107	2857	28W-10N	A6
200	BRLT	60103	2910		E6
200	WynT	60103	2910		E5
500	SMWD	60107	2856	28W-9N	E7
1100	SMWD	60107	2910		E1
2000	BRLT	60107	2910		E1
S Bartlett Rd CO-6					
200	WynT	60103	2910		E5
400	BRLT	60103	2910		E6
W Bartlett Rd					
10	BRLT	60103	2909		D3
10	BRLT	60103	2910		D3
10	BRLT	60120	2909		D3
10	ELGN	60103	2910		A3
10	ELGN	60120	2909		E3
10	HnrT	60103	2909		D3
10	HnrT	60103	2910		B3
10	HnrT	60120	2909		E3
200	ELGN	60103	2909		E3
2100	SEGN	60103	2909		B3
2100	SEGN	60120	2909		B3
2100	SEGN	60177	2909		B3
W Bartlett Rd CO-61					
2100	BRLT	60103	2909		B3
2100	BRLT	60120	2909		B3
2100	HnrT	60103	2909		B3
2100	SEGN	60103	2909		B3
2100	SEGN	60120	2909		B3
2100	SEGN	60177	2909		B3
Bartlett Pointe Dr					
-	BRLT	60103	2909		C3
-	HnrT	60103	2909		C3
Barton Av					
100	CHCG	60202	2867	2W-9N	A6
100	CHCG	60645	2867	2W-9N	A6
100	EVTN	60202	2867	2W-9N	A6
Barton Cir					
100	SMBG	60194	2859	23W-10N	B5
Barton Ct					
1000	GNVW	60025	2811	7W-13N	A7
Barton Dr					
-	LMNT	60439	3271		B6
700	CTSD	60525	3147	12W-6S	B4
700	LynT	60525	3147	12W-6S	B4
Barton Ln					
-	HNDL	60521	3146		C4
900	PTON	60468	3861	8W-37S	B2
1000	WllT	60468	3861	8W-37S	B2
16400	OKFT	60452	3426	5W-19S	C2
E Barton Ln					
700	PTON	60468	3861	8W-37S	B2
Bartram Rd					
300	RVSD	60546	3088	9W-2S	C3
400	NRIV	60546	3088	9W-2S	C3
Basham Av					
14000	HmrT	60441	3342	20W-16S	B4
Basin Dr					
1200	LKPT	60441	3342	21W-18S	A7
Bassford Av					
10	LGNG	60525	3087	13W-4S	A6
10	LGPK	60525	3087	13W-4S	A6
Basswood Cir					
1400	GNVW	60025	2810	8W-14N	D5
Basswood Ct					
100	EGVV	60007	2861	17W-9N	A6
1200	ELGN	60120	2855		D4
1500	GNVW	60025	2810	8W-14N	D5
Basswood Dr					
100	EGVV	60007	2861	17W-9N	A7
300	NHBK	60062	2755	13W-18N	E3
300	NHBK	60062	2756	13W-18N	A3
300	WhlT	60062	2756	13W-18N	A3
8900	TYPK	60477	3424	11W-22S	A7
9100	TYPK	60477	3423	11W-21S	E7
E Basswood Ln					
1800	MPPT	60056	2808	13W-14N	D4
N Basswood Ln					
1200	MPPT	60056	2808	13W-14N	D4
Basswood Rd					
1200	HFET	60173	2859	22W-12N	C2
1200	HFET	60195	2859	22W-12N	C2
1200	SMBG	60173	2859	22W-12N	C2
8100	ODPK	60462	3346	10W-17S	C5
8100	OrlT	60462	3346	10W-17S	C5
Basswood St					
800	HFET	60194	2859	22W-11N	B3
800	HFET	60195	2859	22W-11N	C3
1100	HFET	60173	2859	22W-11N	C2
1100	SMBG	60173	2859	22W-11N	C2
Bataan Dr					
-	FTPK	60130	3030	10W-0S	A6
-	MYWD	60153	3030	10W-0S	A6
-	MYWD	60155	3029	11W-0S	D6
1300	BDVW	60155	3029	11W-0S	E6
1300	MYWD	60153	3029	11W-0S	D6
Batavia Ln					
200	HFET	60194	2859	23W-11N	B4
Bateman Cir N					
300	BNHL	60010	2749	30W-18N	A3
Bateman Cir S					
300	BNHL	60010	2749	30W-18N	A3
Bateman Rd					
-	BNHL	60010	2801		E2
-	BNHL	60010	2802	30W-15N	A1
-	BNHL	60118	2801		E2
800	BNHL	60010	2749	30W-17N	A4
Bates Ct					
-	OrlT	60467	3422	14W-19S	C3
1500	SMBG	60193	2912		B1
Bates Ln					
1400	SMBG	60193	2912		B1
Bath & Tennis Dr					
-	OKBK	60523	3086		A4
E Bauer St					
800	HMND	46320	3352		E7
Bauman Ct					
300	WDDL	60191	2914		E4
300	WDDL	60191	2915		A4
Bavarian Ct					
5700	HRPK	60133	2911		E4
Baxter Ln					
500	HFET	60194	2858	24W-11N	D3
Baxter Pkwy					
10	RVWD	60015	2756	12W-20N	A1
10	WdfT	60015	2756	12W-20N	B1

STREET Block	City	ZIP	Map#	CGS	Grid
Bay Ct					
800	BRLT	60103	2911		B4
N Bay Ct					
3200	CHCG	60618	2977	3W-4N	A3
Bay Dr					
-	EGVV	60007	2914		C3
-	EGVV	60143	2914		C3
200	ITSC	60143	2914		B3
N Bay Rd					
10	PSHT	60463	3274	9W-13S	C4
10	PSHT	60465	3274	9W-13S	C4
S Bay Rd					
10	PSHT	60463	3274	9W-13S	C4
10	PSHT	60465	3274	9W-13S	C4
W Bay Rd					
10	PSHT	60463	3274	9W-13S	C4
10	PSHT	60465	3274	9W-13S	C4
Bay St					
200	WDDL	60191	2914		E7
Bayberry Ct					
10	SMWD	60107	2857	27W-10N	C6
5300	RGMW	60008	2860	19W-12N	C1
12600	PlsT	60464	3273	13W-14S	B7
15200	ODPK	60462	3346	10W-18S	B7
Bayberry Dr					
700	BRLT	60103	2910		D3
3400	NHBK	60062	2756	11W-18N	C3
Bayberry Ln					
2000	HFET	60195	2858	25W-12N	B1
2300	ElaT	60047	2753	19W-20N	B1
2300	LGGV	60047	2753	19W-20N	B1
9200	TYPK	60477	3423	11W-21S	E6
Baybrook Dr					
10	CTSD	60525	3147	13W-7S	B6
S Baybrook Dr					
10	PLTN	60074	2806	19W-15N	C1
Bay Colony Dr					
-	DSPN	60016	2863	12W-11N	C2
-	MaiT	60016	2863	12W-11N	C2
W Bayer Dr					
600	PLTN	60067	2752	21W-17N	C5
600	PltT	60067	2752	21W-17N	C5
Bayfield Ct					
-	TYPK	60477	3504	9W-23S	E3
Bayfield Dr					
-	TYPK	60477	3504	9W-23S	D3
Bayhill Ct					
8100	ODPK	60462	3346	10W-18S	C7
Bay Reef Dr					
10	SBTN	60010	2803	27W-13N	C5
Bay Rum Ct					
10	BRRG	60527	3208		A4
Bayshore Dr					
900	SMBG	60194	2858	24W-11N	D3
Bayside Cir					
4400	HFET	60195	2804	24W-15N	B2
Bayside Ct					
700	WLNG	60090	2754	16W-17N	D6
E Bayside Ct					
1500	HFET	60195	2804	24W-15N	B2
W Bayside Ct					
1600	HFET	60195	2804	25W-15N	A2
Bayside Dr					
200	PLTN	60074	2753	19W-17N	D5
200	PltT	60074	2753	19W-17N	C5
1400	WLNG	60004	2754	16W-17N	D6
1400	WLNG	60090	2754	16W-17N	D6
Bayside Ln					
1400	WLNG	60090	2754	16W-17N	D6
Baythorne Dr					
1100	FSMR	60422	3507	3W-23S	A3
3100	RchT	60422	3507	3W-23S	A3
Baytree Dr					
800	BRLT	60103	2910		D2
Bayview Ct					
100	CRTE	60475	3596	0W-28S	C6
Bay View Dr					
4800	RNPK	60471	3594	6W-26S	A2
Bayview Pt					
300	SMBG	60194	2859	22W-10N	C4
Bayview Rd					
100	ELGN	60123	2801		A7
100	ELGN	60123	2855		A1
Baywood Ln					
13100	HMGN	60441	3343	16W-17S	E5
Beach Av					
10	LGNG	60525	3087	12W-4S	C6
300	LGPK	60525	3087	12W-3S	C5
W Beach Av					
1600	CHCG	60622	3033	2W-1N	C1
3200	CHCG	60622	3032	4W-1N	D1
3200	CHCG	60651	3032	4W-1N	D1
Beach Ln					
3500	NfdT	60062	2756	12W-16N	C7
Beach Rd					
10	GLNC	60022	2758	6W-18N	D4
Beach St					
1800	BDVW	60155	3029	12W-0S	C6
Beachcomber Dr					
1100	SMBG	60193	2912		D1
Beachview Ter					
14600	DLTN	60419	3350	0E-17S	E5
14900	DLTN	60473	3350	0E-17S	E6
14900	SHLD	60419	3350	0E-17S	E6
14900	SHLD	60473	3350	0E-17S	E6
Beacon Av					
14300	ODPK	60462	3345	12W-17S	D5
N Beacon Av					
10	LGNG	60525	3087	12W-4S	C6
Beacon Blvd					
200	CHHT	60411	3595	2W-26S	C2
1900	PKFT	60411	3595	2W-26S	C1
1900	PKFT	60466	3595	2W-26S	C1
Beacon Ct					
10	BFGV	60089	2754	17W-17N	B5
1900	CHHT	60411	3595	2W-26S	D2
4400	HFET	60195	2804	25W-15N	B2
8900	ODHL	60477	3424	11W-19S	A3
Beacon Dr					
800	SMBG	60193	2858	24W-9N	D7
800	SMBG	60193	2912		D1
7900	PSHT	60463	3274	10W-13S	C5
Beacon Ln					
8900	ODHL	60477	3424	11W-19S	A3
Beacon Pl					
-	CRTE	60417	3685	0E-29S	E1
200	MNSR	46321	3430		D6
N Beacon St					
4400	CHCG	60613	2921	1W-5N	D7
4400	CHCG	60640	2921	1W-5N	D7
Beacon Hill Dr					
10	BrnT	60010	2803	28W-15N	A2
10	SBTN	60010	2803	27W-15N	A2
Beall St					
8400	SjnT	46311	3598		E7

STREET Block	City	ZIP	Map#	CGS	Grid
Beall St					
9000	SjnT	46311	3687		E2
S Beall St					
5500	HMND	46320	3352		E7
Bear Claw Ct					
5500	HFET	60192	2856	30W-12N	B3
Bear Flag Dr					
1400	HRPK	60133	2911		E4
Bear Island Av					
10800	ODPK	60467	3423	13W-19S	A2
Beatrice Ln					
1100	LMNT	60439	3271		B4
Beau Ct					
600	DSPN	60016	2862	15W-10N	A4
Beau Dr					
200	DSPN	60016	2862	15W-11N	A3
200	DSPN	60056	2862	15W-11N	A3
200	MPPT	60056	2862	15W-11N	A3
1200	PKRG	60068	2864	10W-10N	A5
N Beaubien Ct					
100	CHCG	60601	3034	0E-0N	C4
100	CHCG	60602	3034	0E-0N	C4
Beaudin Blvd					
-	WDRG	60440	3270		A3
-	WDRG	60517	3270		A3
Beaumont Ln					
200	PltT	60010	2751	23W-18N	E3
Beaumont Pl					
-	NHBK	60062	2757	9W-16N	B7
S Beaver Ct					
13600	HMGN	60441	3343	16W-16S	E3
Beaver Dr					
400	SMWD	60107	2857	28W-10N	B6
Beaver Ln					
900	GNVW	60025	2811	6W-13N	C6
Beaver Rd					
600	GNVW	60025	2811	6W-13N	C7
Beaver Dam Rd					
6200	MTSN	60443	3505	7W-24S	C6
W Beaver Den Tr					
-	HMGN	60441	3422	15W-19S	A2
W Beaver Lake Dr					
12800	HMGN	60441	3344	16W-16S	A3
12800	HmrT	60441	3344	16W-16S	A3
12800	HmrT	60467	3344	16W-16S	A3
13000	HMGN	60441	3343	16W-16S	E3
Beaver Pond Rd					
1600	IVNS	60067	2805	23W-15N	A1
S Beck Pl					
8700	HMTN	60456	3212	5W-10S	B4
Becker Rd					
800	GNVW	60025	2811	7W-14N	B4
E Becker St					
600	HMND	46320	3352		E7
Becker Ter					
18600	CCHL	60478	3506	6W-22S	A1
Becket Av					
2900	WSTR	60154	3086		E4
3000	PvsT	60558	3086		E4
Beckett Cir					
1300	SMBG	60173	2859	22W-10N	D5
Beckett Ln					
1300	SMBG	60173	2859	21W-10N	E5
Beckwith Ct					
2800	NHBK	60062	2756	11W-17N	E5
Beckwith Ln					
3400	CRTE	60417	3597	0E-28S	A6
3400	CRTE	60475	3597	0E-28S	A6
3400	STGR	60417	3597	0E-28S	A6
3400	STGR	60475	3597	0E-28S	A6
Beckwith Rd					
6400	MNGV	60053	2865	7W-11N	A2
6700	MNGV	60053	2864	8W-11N	D2
7900	MNGV	60714	2864	8W-11N	D2
7900	NLES	60714	2864	8W-11N	D2
Becky Ct					
14800	OKFT	60452	3348	6W-17S	A5
Bedford Ct					
800	SMBG	60193	2912		D1
1000	ELGN	60120	2855		C2
5700	HRPK	60133	2911		E5
W Bedford Dr					
1100	PLTN	60067	2805	22W-15N	B2
Bedford Ln					
500	DSPN	60016	2862	14W-11N	C3
9200	ODPK	60462	3345	11W-18S	E7
17000	TYPK	60477	3424	9W-20S	D4
Bedford Rd					
1600	HFET	60195	2858	24W-12N	D1
Bedford St					
-	WSTR	60154	3086		E4
-	WSTR	60154	3087	13W-2S	A4
Bedlington Dr					
1500	IVNS	60010	2751	24W-17N	D5
Beebe Ct					
400	SMWD	60107	2911		A1
Beech Av					
-	WLMT	60091	2811	6W-13N	D6
W Beech Ct					
300	SMBG	60193	2859	23W-10N	A6
Beech Dr					
300	WLNG	60090	2755	13W-17N	E5
400	GNVW	60025	2811	6W-13N	C6
E Beech Dr					
10	SMBG	60193	2859	23W-10N	B6
W Beech Dr					
10	SMBG	60193	2859	22W-9N	C7
200	SMBG	60193	2858	23W-10N	E6
N Beech Rd					
1700	MPPT	60056	2808	13W-15N	E2
Beech St					
200	WLSP	60480	3209	12W-9S	B4
300	PlsT	60480	3209	12W-9S	C4
3600	FSMR	60422	3506	4W-22S	D2
14500	ODPK	60462	3345	11W-17S	E5
W Beecher Rd					
4900	WlIT	60468	3861	7W-36S	C2
6500	PTON	60468	3861	7W-36S	C2
6900	PtnT	60468	3861	8W-36S	A2
Beechmont Ct					
10	SMBG	60193	2857	27W-10N	C5
Beechnut Dr					
10	SBTN	60010	2803	27W-15N	B2
Beechnut Rd					
1800	NfdT	60062	2757	10W-18N	B3
2000	DRFD	60062	2757	10W-18N	B3
8700	HYHL	60457	3209	11W-10S	E4
9000	PlsT	60480	3209	11W-10S	E4
Beechtree Ln					
800	BRLT	60103	2910		D7
Beechwood Av					
1900	KLWH	60043	2812	4W-14N	C4
1900	WLMT	60091	2812	4W-14N	B4
Beechwood Ct					
1200	SMBG	60193	2859	21W-10N	D5

STREET Block	City	ZIP	Map#	CGS	Grid
E Beechwood Ct					
10	BFGV	60089	2754	17W-18N	B3
W Beechwood Ct					
10	BFGV	60089	2754	17W-18N	A3
S Beechwood Dr					
1000	MPPT	60056	2861	16W-11N	D3
Beechwood Rd					
500	BFGV	60089	2754	17W-18N	A3
1000	ANHT	60004	2754	18W-18N	A3
1000	BFGV	60004	2754	18W-18N	A3
5900	MTSN	60443	3505	7W-24S	C5
Beeline Dr					
100	BNVL	60106	2915		E6
100	CHCG	60106	2915		E6
Begonia Ct					
15400	ODPK	60462	3346	9W-18S	E7
Begonia Dr					
10	MTSN	60443	3593	7W-26S	C2
Behrns Dr					
2900	LydT	60164	2972		C4
Beinlich Ct					
-	GLNC	60022	2758	7W-18N	B4
Beinoris Dr					
100	WDDL	60191	2915		B5
Beiriger Dr					
10	DYR	46311	3598		C4
Beisner Rd					
800	EGvT	60007	2914		B1
800	EGVV	60007	2914		B1
Bel Air Dr					
300	GNVW	60025	2864	9W-12N	C1
400	GNVW	60025	2810	9W-12N	C7
Bel Aire Ct					
10	BRRG	60527	3208		B5
Belaire Ct					
10	BFGV	60089	2754	17W-18N	B3
E Bel Aire Dr					
2600	ANHT	60004	2807	16W-14N	D5
W Bel Aire Ln					
600	MPPT	60056	2861	16W-11N	E3
Belaire Rd					
100	BFGV	60089	2754	17W-18N	B3
N Bel Aire Ter					
500	PLTN	60074	2753	20W-16N	B6
Belcourt Ln					
-	BRLT	60103	2856	31W-9N	A7
-	ELGN	60103	2856	31W-9N	A7
-	ELGN	60120	2856	31W-9N	A7
Belden Av					
9100	FNPK	60131	2973	11W-2N	D6
9600	LydT	60164	2973	12W-2N	C6
E Belden Av					
100	EMHT	60126	2972		A6
300	AddT	60126	2972		A6
W Belden Av					
300	CHCG	60614	2978	0W-2N	A6
800	CHCG	60614	2977	1W-2N	D6
2400	CHCG	60647	2977	3W-2N	A6
2800	CHCG	60647	2976	3W-2N	E6
3900	CHCG	60639	2976	5W-2N	B6
6400	CHCG	60639	2975	8W-2N	A6
6400	CHCG	60707	2975	8W-2N	A6
7000	CHCG	60707	2974	8W-2N	E6
7600	EDPK	60707	2974	9W-2N	C6
8600	RVGV	60171	2973	10W-2N	E6
8600	RVGV	60171	2974	10W-2N	A6
Belden Dr					
500	DYR	46311	3598		D1
Belden Pl					
200	MNSR	46321	3430		D6
W Belden St					
4000	CHCG	60639	2976	5W-2N	B6
4000	CHCG	60647	2976	5W-2N	B6
4700	CHCG	60639	2975	6W-2N	D6
Belfast Ter					
500	CRTE	60417	3596	0E-28S	E6
500	CRTE	60417	3597	0E-28S	A6
Belford Ln					
10	RGMW	60008	2805	23W-12N	B7
Belinder Ln					
-	RGMW	60173	2805	21W-13N	C6
600	SMBG	60173	2805	21W-13N	C5
Bell Av					
800	LGNG	60525	3087	13W-4S	A6
1400	WNSP	60558	3087	13W-4S	A6
N Bell Av					
300	CHCG	60612	3033	2W-0N	B4
1300	CHCG	60622	3033	2W-1N	B1
1500	CHCG	60647	3033	2W-1N	B1
2100	CHCG	60647	2977	2W-2N	B6
3300	CHCG	60618	2977	2W-4N	B3
5300	CHCG	60625	2921	2W-6N	B5
6200	CHCG	60659	2921	2W-7N	B3
6800	CHCG	60645	2921	2W-8N	B1
7500	CHCG	60645	2867	2W-9N	B7
7500	EVTN	60202	2867	2W-9N	B7
S Bell Av					
100	CHCG	60612	3033	2W-0S	B5
1300	CHCG	60608	3033	2W-1S	B7
2200	CHCG	60608	3091	2W-2S	B2
4000	CHCG	60609	3091	2W-4S	B6
6300	CHCG	60636	3151	2W-7S	B6
8900	CHCG	60620	3213	2W-11S	B6
9500	CHCG	60643	3213	2W-11S	B6
10300	CHCG	60643	3277	2W-12S	B1
11800	BLID	60406	3277	2W-13S	C5
11800	CHCG	60406	3277	2W-13S	C5
Bell Dr					
400	DSPN	60016	2862	15W-11N	A3
Bell Ln					
800	WNKA	60093	2758	6W-16N	E7
Bell Rd					
-	LMNT	60439	3272	16W-12S	A3
-	LmnT	60480	3272	15W-12S	A2
12700	LMNT	60439	3344	16W-15S	A2
13100	HMGN	60441	3344	16W-15S	A2
13100	HmrT	60441	3344	16W-15S	A2
13100	HmrT	60467	3344	16W-15S	A2
S Bell Rd					
13500	HMGN	60441	3344	16W-16S	A3
13500	HmrT	60441	3344	16W-16S	A3
13500	HmrT	60467	3344	16W-16S	A2
13500	LmnT	60439	3344	16W-15S	A2
16300	HMGN	60441	3422	15W-20S	B3
Bell Rd S					
16000	HMGN	60441	3422	15W-19S	B2
Bella Ln					
12500	LMNT	60439	3271		C7
Bellagio Cir					
18400	TYPK	60477	3425	8W-22S	A7
18400	TYPK	60477	3505	8W-22S	A1
Bellair St					
10	DXMR	60426	3349	1W-17S	E4
10	HRVY	60426	3349	1W-17S	E4

STREET Block	City	ZIP	Map#	CGS	Grid
Bellaire Av					
300	DSPN	60016	2863	12W-11N	C3
300	MaiT	60016	2863	12W-11N	C3
Bellaire Ct					
2300	DSPN	60016	2863	12W-11N	B2
Bellaire Rd					
5100	OKFT	60452	3425	6W-20S	E3
5100	OKFT	60452	3426	6W-20S	A3
Bellamy Rd					
-	CCHL	60478	3506	6W-22S	A1
S Belle Av					
10	PLTN	60074	2806	19W-15N	C1
Belle Ct					
500	HRVY	60426	3350	0W-18S	B7
600	PHNX	60426	3350	0W-18S	B7
Belle Dr					
10	NHLK	60164	2972		E7
300	MLPK	60160	2973	13W-2N	A7
300	MLPK	60164	2973	13W-2N	A7
300	NHLK	60164	2973	13W-2N	A7
Belle Ln					
2800	SMBG	60193	2857	27W-10N	D6
Belle St					
17000	OKFT	60452	3425	6W-20S	E4
Bellechase Cir					
10	SMBG	60173	2859	21W-10N	D4
N Bellefort Pl					
8500	NLES	60714	2864	8W-10N	E4
Belleforte Av					
8800	NLES	60053	2864	8W-11N	E3
8800	NLES	60714	2864	8W-11N	E3
9100	MNGV	60053	2864	8W-11N	E3
Belleforte Av N					
700	OKPK	60302	3030	8W-1N	E2
1200	CHCG	60707	3030	8W-2N	E1
Belle Plaine Av					
-	CHCG	60631	2918	10W-8N	A2
-	SRPK	60176	2973	12W-5N	C2
10	PKRG	60068	2918	10W-8N	A2
1400	PKRG	60068	2917	11W-8N	E2
10200	FNPK	60176	2973	12W-5N	A2
W Belle Plaine Av					
1300	CHCG	60613	2977	2W-5N	C1
2000	CHCG	60618	2977	3W-5N	A1
2800	CHCG	60618	2976	4W-5N	C1
4600	CHCG	60641	2976	5W-5N	A1
5600	CHCG	60641	2975	7W-5N	C1
6200	CHCG	60634	2975	7W-5N	B1
7300	NRDG	60706	2974	9W-5N	C1
7700	NRDG	60634	2974	9W-5N	C1
8200	CHCG	60634	2974	10W-5N	A1
Belleplaine Dr					
16400	MKHM	60426	3426	4W-19S	E3
Belle Rive Ct					
7800	TYPK	60477	3424	9W-20S	D5
Belleview Av					
1600	WSTR	60154	3087	13W-1S	A2
Bellevue Av					
700	ELGN	60120	2855		A1
Bellevue Pl					
2200	NHBK	60062	2757	10W-16N	A7
E Bellevue Pl					
10	CHCG	60610	3034	0E-1N	C2
10	CHCG	60611	3034	0E-1N	C2
Bellingham Dr					
200	BRTN	60010	2751	24W-18N	C2
Bellingham Ln					
200	BRLT	60103	2910		C3
200	HnrT	60103	2910		C3
Bell Oak Ln					
10	LMNT	60439	3272	15W-14S	A5
Bellwood Av					
-	WSTR	60104	3029	12W-0S	B6
-	WSTR	60154	3029	12W-0S	B6
10	BLWD	60104	3029	12W-0S	B5
400	HLSD	60162	3029	13W-0N	A5
2700	LydT	60164	2972		E5
2800	FNPK	60131	2972		E5
Bellwood Dr					
10	BNHL	60010	2750	28W-20N	A2
Bellwood Ln					
3300	GNVW	60025	2810	10W-14N	A5
3400	GNVW	60025	2809	10W-14N	E5
Belmont Av					
10500	FNPK	60131	2972		E4
10500	FNPK	60131	2973	13W-4N	A4
10700	FNPK	60164	2972		E4
10800	LydT	60164	2972		E4
E Belmont Av					
800	AddT	60106	2972		B4
800	AddT	60126	2972		B4
800	BNVL	60106	2972		B4
800	FNPK	60131	2972		B4
N Belmont Av					
1300	ANHT	60004	2807	17W-15N	B2
S Belmont Av					
10	ANHT	60004	2807	17W-14N	B5
100	ANHT	60005	2807	17W-13N	B5
1400	ANHT	60005	2861	17W-12N	B1
W Belmont Av					
-	CHCG	60171	2973	11W-3N	E4
-	RVGV	60634	2973	10W-3N	E4
300	CHCG	60657	2978	0W-4N	A3
700	CHCG	60657	2977	2W-4N	C3
1900	CHCG	60618	2977	2W-4N	B3
2700	CHCG	60618	2976	5W-4N	A4
3900	CHCG	60641	2976	5W-4N	B4
4700	CHCG	60641	2975	6W-4N	E4
5500	CHCG	60634	2975	6W-4N	C4
6700	CHCG	60634	2974	10W-4N	B4
7100	CHCG	60707	2974	10W-4N	B4
7500	EDPK	60707	2974	9W-4N	C4
7900	RVGV	60171	2974	9W-4N	B4
7900	RVGV	60707	2974	9W-4N	B4
8000	CHCG	60171	2974	10W-4N	B4
8300	RVGV	60634	2974	10W-4N	A4
8700	CHCG	60634	2974	11W-4N	D4
8700	RVGV	60171	2973	11W-4N	D4
9900	FNPK	60131	2973	12W-4N	A4
Belmont Ct					
1000	SMBG	60193	2912		C2
N Belmont Ct					
1600	ANHT	60004	2807	17W-15N	B1
S Belmont Ln					
700	ANHT	60005	2807	17W-13N	A7
Belmont Pl					
200	MNSR	46321	3430		D6
Belmont Rd					
22000	RNPK	60471	3594	5W-26S	B3
Belmont Harbor Dr					
-	CHCG	60613	2978		A2
Beloit Av					
400	FTPK	60130	3030	9W-0S	D5
7100	BGVW	60455	3148	9W-8S	D7
9100	BGVW	60455	3210	9W-10S	D5

STREET Block	City	ZIP	Map#	CGS	Grid
S Beloit Av					
10800	WRTH	60482	3274	9W-12S	D2
S Belt Cir Dr					
6700	BDPK	60638	3148	8W-7S	E6
Belvidere Av					
100	FTPK	60130	3030	9W-0N	D4
E Bemes Rd					
400	CteT	60417	3685	0E-32S	E6
400	CteT	60417	3686	1E-32S	B7
2100	CteT	60417	3687	3E-32S	A7
3300	CteT	46311	3687	3E-32S	A7
3300	HnrT	46311	3687	3E-32S	A7
S Benck Dr					
12300	ALSP	60803	3276	4W-14S	D6
W Benck Dr					
3600	ALSP	60803	3276	4W-14S	D6
Bender Rd					
-	DSPN	60016	2863	12W-11N	C3
10	PKFT	60466	3595	2W-26S	C3
Bending Ct					
600	DSPN	60016	2808	13W-13N	D6
E Bending Creek Tr					
2800	CteT	60417	3687	3E-30S	A3
Benjamin Ct					
10	BlmT	60411	3510	3E-25S	A7
Benjamin Pl					
2000	HMND	46394	3280		E5
Ben Levin Dr					
200	HMND	46324	3430		D3
Bennacott Ln					
400	BRRG	60527	3208		B4
Bennet Av					
17200	SHLD	60473	3429	2E-20S	C4
Bennett Av					
2400	EVTN	60201	2866	4W-12N	D1
2500	EVTN	60201	2812	4W-12N	D7
2700	EVTN	60091	2812	3W-13N	D7
2700	WLMT	60091	2812	3W-13N	D7
8300	SKOK	60076	2866	4W-10N	D5
8800	SKOK	60203	2866	4W-11N	D3
S Bennett Av					
400	PLTN	60067	2805	21W-15N	D3
6700	CHCG	60649	3153	2E-7S	C6
7600	CHCG	60649	3215	2E-9S	C2
8300	CHCG	60617	3215	2E-10S	C4
Bennett Dr					
-	PSHL	60465	3274	10W-12S	B3
600	ELGN	60120	2855		C2
Bennett Ln					
200	DSPN	60016	2862	15W-11N	A3
Bennett Pl					
1800	DSPN	60018	2863	12W-9N	B6
Bennett Rd					
300	EGvT	60007	2861	18W-10N	A5
300	EGVV	60007	2861	18W-10N	A5
Bennington Ct					
10	LMNT	60439	3271		A7
1300	GNVW	60025	2810	9W-13N	B5
Bennington Ln					
-	BRLT	60120	2909		D3
-	ELGN	60120	2909		D3
Bensley Av					
-	LNSG	60438	3429	2E-20S	D4
200	BNHM	60409	3351	2E-17S	D5
200	BNHM	60633	3351	2E-17S	D5
200	CTCY	60409	3351	2E-17S	D5
20200	LYWD	60411	3509	2E-24S	D5
S Bensley Av					
-	CHCG	60633	3351	2E-16S	D2
9500	CHCG	60617	3215	3E-11S	D6
10300	CHCG	60617	3279	2E-11S	D1
14300	BNHM	60633	3351	2E-16S	D4
14500	BNHM	60409	3351	2E-16S	D4
14500	CTCY	60409	3351	2E-16S	D4
Benson Av					
1600	EVTN	60201	2867	2W-11N	B3
S Benson St					
3100	CHCG	60608	3091	1W-3S	D4
Bent St					
600	ELGN	60120	2855		B5
Bent Creek Ct					
100	RGMW	60067	2805	21W-13N	D5
200	SMBG	60173	2805	21W-13N	D5
Bent Creek Rdg					
10	DRFD	60015	2757	9W-20N	B1
Bentgrass Av					
-	RNPK	60471	3593	6W-27S	E5
-	RNPK	60471	3594	6W-27S	A5
Bentley Ct					
10	DRFD	60015	2756	11W-20N	E2
Bentley Ln					
100	SMBG	60193	2859	23W-9N	A7
1000	BRLT	60103	2910		E6
Benton Av					
100	SCHT	60411	3596	1W-27S	A4
400	LGNG	60525	3147	12W-4S	C1
E Benton Blvd					
-	CHCG	60601	3034	0E-0N	D4
S Benton Ct					
700	EMHT	60126	3028		A5
W Benton Dr					
7200	FftT	60423	3505	9W-23S	A4
7200	RchT	60423	3505	9W-23S	A4
7300	FftT	60423	3504	9W-23S	E4
E Benton Pl					
10	CHCG	60601	3034	0E-0N	C4
Benton St					
700	EMHT	60126	3028		B5
1500	CRTE	60417	3685	0W-30S	B3
2400	PltT	60067	2805	20W-13N	E5
2400	RGMW	60008	2805	20W-13N	E5
2400	RGMW	60067	2805	20W-13N	E5
N Benton St					
10	PLTN	60067	2805	20W-16N	E1
100	PLTN	60067	2752	20W-16N	E7
S Benton St					
600	PLTN	60067	2805	20W-15N	E3
Bent Ridge Ln					
600	ELGN	60120	2855		D2
Bent Tree Ct					
1000	ELGN	60120	2855		C1
Bent Tree Ln					
100	SMBG	60195	2859	23W-12N	A2
Bentwood Dr					
-	BlmT	60411	3510	4E-24S	B6
-	LYWD	60411	3510	4E-24S	B6
12200	HMGN	60441	3422	15W-20S	B4
Bentwood Ln					
6300	WLBK	60527	3146		A6
Berdnick St					
3600	RGMW	60008	2806	20W-15N	A2
W Berenice Av					
1800	CHCG	60613	2977	2W-4N	B2
2400	CHCG	60618	2977	3W-4N	A2
4700	CHCG	60641	2975	6W-4N	D2

Chicago & Cook County Street Index

STREET Block	City	ZIP	Map#	CGS	Grid
W Berenice Av					
4700	CHCG	60641	2976	5W-4N	A2
5500	CHCG	60634	2975	7W-4N	B2
6700	CHCG	60634	2974	8W-4N	E2
Berens St					
10	DYR	46311	3598		C3
Berg Dr					
1400	DLTN	60419	3351	1E-18S	B7
1400	SHLD	60419	3351	1E-18S	B7
1400	SHLD	60473	3351	1E-18S	B7
Berglund Pl					
600	NHBK	60062	2757	8W-17N	E5
Bergman Ct					
10	FTPK	60130	3030	9W-0N	D4
Berk Ln					
10	CRTE	60417	3596	0W-28S	D6
Berkeley Av					
600	WNKA	60093	2811	5W-15N	E1
900	FDHT	60411	3509	1E-25S	A6
1400	FDHT	60411	3597	1E-25S	A1
S Berkeley Av					
4100	CHCG	60653	3092	1E-4S	E6
5200	CHCG	60615	3152	1E-5S	E2
Berkeley Ct					
8800	ODPK	60462	3346	11W-16S	A4
Berkeley Rd					
500	BRWN	60402	3088	9W-2S	D3
500	RVSD	60546	3088	9W-2S	D3
Berkenshire Ln					
1100	EGVV	60007	2914		C3
1300	ITSC	60143	2914		C3
Berkhansted Ct					
8300	ODPK	60462	3346	10W-16S	B3
Berkley Ct					
600	SMBG	60194	2859	22W-10N	C5
Berkley Dr					
-	HFET	60194	2859	23W-11N	B3
500	DYR	46311	3510		D7
E Berkley Dr					
10	ANHT	60004	2754	17W-17N	A6
W Berkley Dr					
10	ANHT	60004	2754	18W-17N	A6
400	ANHT	60004	2753	18W-17N	E6
Berkley Ln					
1000	LMNT	60439	3270		E7
1000	LMNT	60439	3271		A6
E Berkley Ln					
10	HFET	60194	2859	23W-11N	A3
W Berkley Ln					
100	HFET	60194	2858	23W-11N	E3
100	HFET	60194	2859	23W-11N	A3
Berkley Pl					
300	SMWD	60107	2857	28W-10N	B6
Berkley St					
900	CPVL	60110	2748		B6
Berkshire Av					
-	MKHM	60426	3427	3W-19S	B2
Berkshire Cir					
2000	CPVL	60110	2801		D1
Berkshire Ct					
-	RGMW	60008	2806	19W-12N	C7
10	BRRG	60527	3208		B2
10	SBTN	60010	2803	27W-13N	B5
10	SMWD	60107	2856	29W-9N	D7
300	DSPN	60016	2808	14W-12N	C7
500	SMBG	60193	2859	22W-9N	B6
1000	ELGN	60120	2855		D5
4000	CPVL	60110	2801		D1
7800	HRPK	60133	2858	26W-9N	A7
Berkshire Dr					
10	WLNG	60090	2754	16W-18N	E4
900	MTSN	60443	3505	7W-25S	C7
7700	HRPK	60133	2858	26W-9N	A7
Berkshire Ln					
10	BRRG	60527	3208		B2
300	DSPN	60016	2808	14W-12N	D7
600	SMBG	60193	2859	22W-9N	C6
E Berkshire Ln					
400	MPPT	60056	2862	15W-12N	A2
W Berkshire Ln					
100	MPPT	60056	2862	15W-12N	A2
Berkshire Pl					
800	CRTE	60417	3596	0W-28S	C6
Berkshire St					
-	CHCG	60651	3031	7W-1N	B1
400	OKPK	60302	3031	8W-1N	A1
800	OKPK	60302	3030	8W-1N	E2
1100	OKPK	60305	3030	8W-1N	D1
7400	RVFT	60305	3030	9W-1N	C1
10800	WSTR	60154	3086		E2
Berkshire Ter					
300	ROSL	60172	2913		B6
Berlex Cir					
-	FDHT	60411	3509	1E-25S	A7
Bermuda Dunes Pl					
800	NHBK	60062	2756	12W-17N	C4
Bernadine St					
17400	LNSG	60438	3430	4E-20S	C4
19200	LNSG	60438	3510	4E-22S	C2
Bernard Ct					
10	BFGV	60089	2754	17W-18N	A3
Bernard Dr					
-	ODPK	60467	3422	13W-21S	E6
10	BFGV	60089	2754	17W-18N	B3
10	WLNG	60090	2754	16W-18N	D3
1000	BFGV	60004	2754	18W-18N	A3
17700	ODPK	60467	3423	13W-21S	A6
Bernard Pl					
2700	EVTN	60201	2812	4W-13N	B7
2700	WLMT	60091	2812	4W-13N	B7
N Bernard St					
2400	CHCG	60647	2976	4W-3N	D5
3600	CHCG	60618	2976	4W-4N	D2
4300	CHCG	60625	2976	4W-5N	D1
5000	CHCG	60625	2920	4W-6N	D5
5500	CHCG	60659	2920	4W-6N	D5
Bernay Dr					
3600	NHBK	60062	2756	12W-18N	C3
Bernay Ln					
-	BFGV	60089	2754	17W-20N	A1
1600	BFGV	60047	2754	18W-20N	A1
1600	LGGV	60047	2754	18W-20N	A1
3800	HFET	60195	2804	24W-14N	B3
Berner Dr					
100	ELGN	60120	2855		E2
100	HnrT	60120	2855		E2
400	HFET	60120	2855		E2
Bernice Av					
10	NHLK	60164	2972		E7
300	MLPK	60160	2973	13W-2N	A7
300	NHLK	60164	2973	13W-2N	A7
2500	LNSG	60438	3429	3E-20S	E4
2800	LNSG	60438	3430	4E-20S	B4
9300	SRPK	60176	2973	11W-4N	D2
Bernice Ct					
400	WLNG	60090	2755	15W-17N	A5
W Bernice Dr					
10500	PlsT	60464	3345	13W-15S	B1
Bernice Rd					
-	MNSR	46321	3430	4E-20S	C4
1800	SHLD	60473	3429	2E-20S	D4
2400	LNSG	60438	3429	3E-20S	E4
2600	LNSG	60438	3430	4E-20S	C4
Bernina Ct					
10	LYWD	60411	3598	4E-25S	C1
Berron Ln					
-	BNHL	60010	2748		E7
-	BNHL	60010	2749	30W-16N	A7
Berry Ct					
2100	SMBG	60194	2858	26W-11N	A4
Berry Dr					
-	CHCG	60616	3092	0E-2S	C2
Berry Ln					
1100	FSMR	60422	3507	3W-23S	B3
1800	DSPN	60018	2863	12W-10N	B5
Berry Pkwy					
10	PKRG	60068	2918	9W-8N	B1
E Berry Rd					
400	BRTN	60010	2751	25W-20N	A1
Berry St					
100	PKFT	60466	3595	3W-25S	B1
Berrybrook Ct					
19600	TYPK	60477	3504	10W-23S	B4
Berry Path Tr					
900	MTSN	60443	3505	7W-25S	C7
Berteau Av					
10000	SRPK	60176	2973	12W-5N	B1
E Berteau Av					
400	EMHT	60126	3028		B1
N Berteau Av					
100	BRLT	60103	2911		A3
100	EMHT	60126	3028		B2
S Berteau Av					
100	BRLT	60103	2911		A3
W Berteau Av					
1400	CHCG	60613	2977	2W-5N	B1
1900	CHCG	60618	2977	3W-5N	A1
2800	CHCG	60618	2976	3W-5N	E1
3900	CHCG	60641	2976	5W-5N	B1
4800	CHCG	60641	2975	7W-5N	C1
5500	CHCG	60634	2975	7W-5N	B1
7300	NRDG	60706	2974	9W-5N	C1
8200	CHCG	60634	2974	10W-5N	A1
Bertling Ln					
100	WNKA	60093	2812	4W-15N	C3
Bertoldo Rd					
10	PKFT	60466	3595	2W-26S	C3
Bertram Ln					
1900	HDPK	60035	2757	9W-20N	C2
Berwick					
2100	IVNS	60067	2804	23W-14N	D3
Berwick Ct					
400	SMBG	60193	2859	23W-9N	A6
1600	FSMR	60422	3506	4W-23S	D4
Berwick Pl					
600	ROSL	60172	2912		C6
W Berwyn Av					
1800	CHCG	60640	2921	2W-6N	B5
1900	CHCG	60625	2921	3W-6N	A5
2600	CHCG	60625	2920	3W-6N	E5
4300	CHCG	60630	2920	5W-6N	A5
4800	CHCG	60630	2919	6W-6N	E5
6600	CHCG	60656	2918	8W-6N	E5
6600	CHCG	60656	2919	8W-6N	A5
7800	NpkT	60656	2918	9W-6N	B5
8400	NRDG	60656	2918	10W-6N	A6
8400	NRDG	60706	2918	10W-6N	A6
8600	CHCG	60656	2917	10W-6N	E6
Berwyn St					
9700	RSMT	60018	2917	12W-6N	B6
N Besly Ct					
1600	CHCG	60622	2977	1W-2N	D7
Bessie Coleman Dr					
500	CHCG	60666	2917	13W-6N	A5
Best Dr					
-	CHCG	60637	3152	0E-6S	D4
E Best Dr					
1300	ANHT	60004	2754	17W-17N	C5
Beth Ct					
16000	OKFT	60452	3425	6W-19S	E1
17900	HMWD	60430	3427	3W-21S	B6
Beth Dr					
10800	ODPK	60467	3423	13W-21S	A5
15600	HMGN	60441	3342	19W-17S	D6
15600	HmrT	60441	3342	19W-17S	D6
Bethany Ln					
8500	TYPK	60477	3424	10W-20S	B4
Bethel Ln					
10	SMBG	60194	2859	23W-10N	A5
Bethel on Asbury					
10	RGMW	60008	2806	19W-15N	B3
Bette Ln					
1000	GNVW	60025	2809	11W-13N	D6
Bettenhausen Dr					
18000	TYPK	60477	3424	10W-21S	B7
Betty Ct					
100	BRLT	60103	2911		A3
10400	RSMT	60018	2917	13W-8N	A1
Betty Dr					
100	IVNS	60010	2751	23W-17N	D4
900	BFGV	60089	2754	16W-17N	C4
900	WhlT	60004	2754	16W-17N	C4
N Betty Dr					
3100	ANHT	60004	2754	16W-17N	C5
3100	WhlT	60004	2754	16W-17N	C4
3200	BFGV	60089	2754	16W-17N	C4
Betty Ln					
500	SHLD	60473	3428	0E-19S	E2
13900	BLID	60406	3349	3W-16S	A3
W Betty Ter					
8400	MaiT	60714	2864	10W-10N	A4
8500	NLES	60714	2864	10W-10N	A4
Betty Ann Ln					
15300	OKFT	60452	3347	6W-18S	D7
N Beulah Av					
2700	RVGV	60171	2973	11W-3N	E5
Beulah Ln					
800	ELGN	60120	2855		C5
Beverley Ln					
100	WLSP	60480	3209	11W-9S	D2
Beverly Av					
16700	TYPK	60477	3425	7W-20S	C3
S Beverly Av					
8700	CHCG	60620	3213	2W-10S	C4
9500	CHCG	60643	3213	1W-11S	D7
10700	CHCG	60643	3277	1W-12S	E2
W Beverly Cir					
1500	HRPK	60133	2911		E5
Beverly Cir E					
5800	HRPK	60133	2911		E5
Beverly Ct					
100	SMWD	60107	2910		E1
200	SMBG	60193	2858	23W-9N	E7
1600	HRPK	60133	2911		D5
Beverly Dr					
300	WLMT	60091	2812	5W-13N	A7
900	WLNG	60090	2754	15W-18N	E4
900	WLNG	60090	2755	15W-18N	B3
1700	ANHT	60004	2807	17W-15N	B2
10000	SKOK	60076	2812	5W-12N	A7
10000	WLMT	60076	2812	5W-12N	A7
S Beverly Dr					
26700	GGnT	60449	3682	9W-32S	A7
26700	MonT	60449	3682	9W-32S	A7
Beverly Dr E					
-	HRPK	60133	2911		E5
Beverly Ln					
200	GNVW	60025	2811	6W-13N	C6
1300	SMWD	60107	2910		E1
8600	ODPK	60462	3346	10W-15S	A1
8700	PlsT	60462	3346	10W-15S	A1
N Beverly Ln					
1500	ANHT	60004	2807	17W-15N	B2
S Beverly Ln					
10	ANHT	60004	2807	17W-14N	B5
300	ANHT	60005	2807	17W-13N	B7
300	MPPT	60056	2861	17W-12N	C1
Beverly Pl					
10	LNSG	60438	3430		C5
10	MNSR	46321	3430		D5
10	MNSR	60438	3430	4E-21S	C5
Beverly Rd					
100	BRTN	60010	2751	24W-20N	B1
100	HnrT	60120	2802	30W-13N	A6
100	HnrT	60120	2856	30W-12N	A1
100	HFET	60192	2802	30W-13N	A6
200	HFET	60192	2802	30W-13N	A6
2900	HFET	60118	2802	30W-13N	A5
Beverly Tr					
-	ELGN	60120	2855		C5
W Beverly Glen Pkwy					
1600	CHCG	60643	3213	2W-11S	D7
Bianco Dr					
300	EGVV	60007	2915		A1
Bianco Ter					
2300	GNVW	60025	2864	9W-12N	C1
9700	MaiT	60016	2863	11W-12N	D2
S Bianco Villa Dr					
1300	LKPT	60441	3342	21W-17S	A6
Bibury Ln					
1200	IVNS	60010	2803	25W-15N	E1
Bicek Ct					
4400	HFET	60195	2804	24W-15N	B1
Bicek Dr					
1500	HFET	60195	2804	24W-15N	B1
Bielby Ln					
7900	LynT	60525	3208		E2
7900	WLSP	60525	3208		E2
Biermann Ct					
600	MPPT	60056	2808	14W-13N	B5
Biesterfield Rd					
10	EGVV	60007	2914		A2
1300	EGVV	60007	2913		D1
Biesterfield Rd SR-53					
1000	EGVV	60007	2914		A2
Big Bear Ct					
6400	IHPK	60525	3146		D6
Big Bear Dr					
6400	IHPK	60525	3146		E5
Big Bend Dr					
1800	DSPN	60016	2863	12W-11N	B2
Bigelow Rd					
10	PKFT	60466	3595	2W-26S	C3
Big Oak Cir					
1800	NHBK	60062	2757	9W-17N	B4
Big Oak Ln					
1900	NHBK	60062	2757	10W-17N	B4
Big Oaks Ct					
10	SMWD	60107	2857	28W-10N	A5
Big Oaks Rd					
10	SMWD	60107	2856	28W-10N	E5
10	SMWD	60107	2857	28W-10N	A5
2300	DRPK	60074	2752	21W-18N	D2
2300	PLTN	60074	2752	21W-18N	D2
2300	PltT	60074	2752	21W-18N	D2
Big Peninsula Rd					
100	ELGN	60123	2801		B6
Big Run Ln					
13300	DPgT	60441	3342	21W-15S	A2
13800	HMGN	60441	3343	17W-17S	C6
Big Sable Pt					
8800	FKFT	60423	3504	11W-24S	A5
Big Sur Pkwy					
1200	ALGN	60102	2748		B1
Big Tree Ln					
3100	WLMT	60091	2811	6W-13N	D7
Bills Ln					
-	HGKN	60525	3147	12W-7S	D5
Biloba St					
8800	ODPK	60462	3346	11W-17S	A5
Bilstone Dr					
-	LYWD	60411	3509	2E-23S	D4
Biltmore Dr					
600	BRLT	60103	2856	31W-9N	A7
600	BRLT	60103	2910		A1
600	ELGN	60120	2856	31W-9N	A7
8500	ODPK	60462	3424	10W-18S	B1
Binford Dr					
7900	ODPK	60462	3346	10W-16S	C3
N Bingham St					
2000	CHCG	60647	2977	3W-2N	A6
Birch Av					
1400	HRPK	60133	2911		E2
9000	MNGV	60053	2864	8W-11N	E3
9200	MKNA	60448	3504	11W-23S	A3
18000	CCHL	60478	3426	5W-21S	C7
18900	CCHL	60478	3506	5W-22S	C2
Birch Ct					
300	ROSL	60172	2913		B6
13600	LMNT	60439	3343	17W-15S	B2
16000	ODHL	60477	3424	11W-19S	A1
W Birch Ct					
6400	MONE	60449	3682	8W-32S	C7
Birch Dr					
600	BCHR	60401	3864	0W-36S	C2
1100	ELGN	60120	2855		D4
1600	BKLY	60163	3028		C4
1600	HLSD	60163	3028		C4
E Birch Dr					
400	GNWD	60425	3508	0E-22S	E2
500	GNWD	60425	3509	0E-22S	A2
S Birch Dr					
1100	MPPT	60056	2861	16W-11N	D3
Birch Ln					
600	OMFD	60461	3507	3W-24S	B6
800	CHHT	60411	3507	1W-24S	E6
1100	LynT	60458	3209	11W-8S	D2
1100	WNSP	60558	3146		D3
1500	PKRG	60068	2863	11W-10N	E5
2200	ANHT	60005	2860	19W-12N	D1
2200	RGMW	60008	2806	19W-12N	C7
2200	RGMW	60008	2860	19W-12N	C1
8900	HYHL	60457	3209	11W-10S	E5
Birch Pl					
1700	RGMW	60008	2860	21W-12N	A1
1700	RGMW	60173	2860	21W-12N	A1
1700	SMBG	60173	2860	21W-12N	A1
Birch Rd					
600	GLNC	60022	2758	7W-17N	C5
1000	HMWD	60430	3428	1W-22S	A7
1200	HMWD	60430	3508	1W-22S	A1
1300	HMWD	60430	3427	1W-22S	E7
1600	NHBK	60062	2756	10W-16N	E7
15300	MKHM	60426	3348	4W-18S	D7
Birch St					
10	CPVL	60110	2748		C5
10	CTSD	60525	3147	12W-6S	C4
10	HGKN	60525	3147	12W-6S	C4
10	PKFT	60466	3595	2W-26S	C3
100	WNKA	60093	2812	5W-15N	A3
500	ITSC	60143	2914		B5
1700	DSPN	60018	2863	12W-9N	B7
2100	DSPN	60018	2917	12W-9N	B1
3400	FNPK	60131	2973	11W-4N	D3
7000	BGVW	60455	3210	8W-10S	E5
9100	ODPK	60462	3345	11W-17S	E5
Birch Tr					
10	WLNG	60090	2754	16W-17N	E4
Birchbark Ct					
13600	ODPK	60462	3346	10W-16S	B2
Birch Bark Dr					
5200	HFET	60192	2802	30W-12N	C7
Birchcreek Ct					
11900	OrlT	60467	3344	14W-17S	C6
W Birchdale Av					
7900	EDPK	60707	2974	9W-3N	B5
7900	RVGV	60171	2974	10W-3N	B5
S Birchdale Dr					
14400	HMGN	60441	3343	17W-17S	D5
Birchwood Av					
10	DRFD	60015	2756	11W-20N	C2
300	EGVV	60007	2914		D3
300	EGVV	60007	2915		A1
600	DSPN	60018	2862	14W-9N	D7
1900	DSPN	60018	2863	12W-9N	B7
2300	WLMT	60091	2812	5W-13N	B6
2700	WLMT	60091	2811	5W-13N	E6
3200	SKOK	60076	2866	4W-9N	D7
5300	SKOK	60077	2865	6W-9N	D7
E Birchwood Av					
10	HNDL	60521	3086		A6
W Birchwood Av					
10	HNDL	60521	3086		A6
300	PLTN	60067	2752	21W-17N	D4
1300	CHCG	60626	2867	1W-9N	C7
1300	CokC	60626	2867	1W-9N	D7
2400	CHCG	60645	2867	3W-9N	A7
2700	CHCG	60645	2866	3W-9N	E7
3100	SKOK	60076	2866	3W-9N	D7
3100	SKOK	60645	2866	3W-9N	D7
6800	NLES	60714	2864	8W-9N	E7
7200	CHCG	60631	2864	9W-9N	C7
Birchwood Ct					
10	SMWD	60107	2857	27W-11N	C3
2200	GNVW	60025	2864	9W-12N	C1
2800	WLMT	60091	2811	5W-14N	E5
W Birchwood Ct					
14300	HMGN	60441	3343	16W-17S	E6
Birchwood Dr					
10	PlsT	60464	3273	13W-14S	B7
100	BRTN	60010	2751	24W-20N	C2
200	DRPK	60010	2751	24W-20N	C2
3200	HLCT	60429	3427	3W-20S	A4
3300	HLCT	60429	3426	4W-20S	E4
8800	ODHL	60477	3424	11W-19S	A2
W Birchwood Dr					
13600	HMGN	60441	3343	17W-17S	D5
Birchwood Ln					
2200	NHFD	60093	2811	7W-15N	A2
2400	WLMT	60091	2812	5W-13N	A6
N Birchwood Ln					
2000	ANHT	60004	2807	16W-16N	D1
S Birchwood Ln					
20700	FftT	60423	3504	9W-25S	D6
Birchwood Rd					
10	DRFD	60015	2757	10W-18N	B2
10	NfdT	60062	2757	10W-18N	B2
100	DndT	60110	2748		A6
200	HNDL	60521	3086		A6
3600	PKFT	60466	3594	4W-26S	D3
3600	RNPK	60471	3594	4W-26S	D3
Birchwoode Ct					
7000	TYPK	60477	3425	8W-19S	A2
Birdsall St					
2400	BLID	60406	3277	3W-14S	A6
Birdsong Ct					
2300	SMBG	60194	2857	26W-11N	E3
Birginal Dr					
700	BNVL	60106	2915		D5
Birkett Av					
800	HMND	46327	3352		E4
S Birkhoff Av					
8300	CHCG	60620	3214	0W-9S	A3
W Birks Av					
1200	LGNG	60525	3147	13W-5S	A1
1200	LynT	60525	3147	13W-5S	A1
Birmingham Av					
100	CHHT	60411	3596	0W-26S	B2
Birmingham Ct					
100	ROSL	60172	2912		C4
Birmingham Ln					
-	SMBG	60193	2859	21W-9N	D7
Birmingham St					
6000	CHRG	60415	3275	7W-12S	B1
Biscayne Ct					
200	BMDL	60108	2912		B7
Biscayne Dr					
1200	EGVV	60007	2914		C3
Biscayne St					
200	BMDL	60108	2912		B7
200	BMDL	60172	2912		B7
200	BmdT	60172	2912		B7
Bishop Ct					
300	IVNS	60010	2751	25W-16N	A6
800	SMBG	60194	2858	25W-11N	A3
1500	MPPT	60056	2808	14W-13N	C5
W Bishop Ct					
1000	PLTN	60067	2805	22W-15N	B3
Bishop Rd					
-	TYPK	60477	3424	10W-21S	B6
N Bishop St					
10	CHCG	60607	3033	1W-0N	D4
800	CHCG	60622	3033	1W-1N	D2
S Bishop St					
800	CHCG	60607	3033	1W-0S	D6
1800	CHCG	60608	3091	1W-1S	D1
4600	CHCG	60609	3091	1W-4S	D7
5000	CHCG	60609	3151	1W-5S	D2
5500	CHCG	60636	3151	1W-7S	D6
7500	CHCG	60620	3213	1W-8S	D1
9400	CHCG	60643	3213	1W-11S	D6
12000	CHCG	60643	3277	1W-14S	D5
12200	CTPK	60827	3277	1W-14S	E6
Bishop Ford Memorial Expwy					
-	BlmT	-	3429	1E-21S	B7
-	BlmT	-	3509	1E-24S	B5
-	BlmT	-	3597	1E-26S	C3
-	CHCG	-	3214	0E-11S	D7
-	CHCG	-	3215	1E-11S	A7
-	CHCG	-	3278	1E-13S	E4
-	CHCG	-	3279	1E-14S	B7
-	CHCG	-	3351	1E-15S	B1
-	CTCY	-	3351	2E-16S	C2
-	DLTN	-	3351	1E-17S	C5
-	FDHT	-	3509	2E-25S	C7
-	GNWD	-	3509	1E-23S	B3
-	LYWD	-	3509	1E-23S	B4
-	SHLD	-	3351	1E-18S	B7
-	SHLD	-	3429	1E-21S	B7
-	SLVL	60411	3597	1E-26S	C3
-	ThtT	-	3429	1E-20S	B5
Bishop Ford Mem Expwy I-94					
-	CHCG	-	3214	0E-11S	D7
-	CHCG	-	3215	1E-11S	A7
-	CHCG	-	3278	1E-13S	E4
-	CHCG	-	3279	1E-13S	A3
-	CHCG	-	3351	1E-15S	B1
-	CTCY	-	3351	2E-16S	C2
-	DLTN	-	3351	1E-18S	B7
-	SHLD	-	3351	1E-18S	B7
-	SHLD	-	3429	1E-20S	B3
Bishop Ford Mem Expwy SR-394					
-	BlmT	-	3429	1E-21S	B7
-	BlmT	-	3509	1E-22S	B2
-	BlmT	-	3597	1E-26S	C3
-	FDHT	-	3509	1E-24S	C6
-	GNWD	-	3509	1E-23S	B3
-	LYWD	-	3509	1E-23S	B4
-	SHLD	-	3429	1E-21S	B7
-	SLVL	60411	3597	1E-26S	C3
-	ThtT	-	3429	1E-20S	B5
Bishop Quarter Ln					
100	OKPK	60302	3031	8W-0N	A4
Bismark Ct					
700	EGVV	60007	2913		D2
Bismark St					
7700	RvsT	60546	3088	9W-3S	C6
Bison Ln					
1200	HFET	60120	2856	31W-12N	A2
E Bissell Dr					
800	PLTN	60074	2753	19W-16N	B7
N Bissell Dr					
100	PLTN	60074	2753	19W-16N	B7
N Bissell St					
1600	CHCG	60614	2977	1W-2N	E7
Bittersweet Ct					
-	DSPN	60018	2863	13W-9N	A6
300	SMBG	60193	2858	23W-10N	E6
Bittersweet Dr					
800	NHBK	60062	2757	9W-17N	C4
1000	BRLT	60103	2911		B6
1000	WynT	60103	2911		B6
Bittersweet Ln					
100	SMWD	60107	2856	30W-10N	C6
700	HNDL	60521	3146		C2
E Bittersweet Ln					
1800	MPPT	60056	2808	13W-14N	D4
W Bittersweet Pl					
600	CHCG	60613	2977	1W-5N	E1
600	CHCG	60613	2978		A1
6500	CHCG	60634	2975	8W-5N	A1
Black Dr					
-	CHCG	60636	3151	1W-7S	E5
W Blackberry Ct					
10	SMWD	60107	2856	30W-10N	C5
Blackberry Ln					
1900	HFET	60195	2857	26W-12N	E1
Blackburn Dr					
11600	ODPK	60467	3344	14W-16S	D4
E Blackburn Dr					
900	IVNS	60067	2751	23W-17N	E5
W Blackburn Dr					
900	IVNS	60067	2751	23W-17N	D5
Blackfoot Ct					
500	WLNG	60090	2754	16W-17N	D5
W Black Forest Ct					
12000	HMGN	60441	3422	15W-18S	C1
S Black Forest Ln					
11600	PSPK	60464	3274	10W-13S	C5
Black Forest Tr					
12100	HMGN	60441	3422	15W-18S	C1
Black Fox Ln					
13000	LMNT	60439	3343	17W-15S	D1
Black Friars Rd					
15300	ODPK	60462	3346	11W-18S	A7
Blackhawk Av					
400	CPVL	60110	2748		D5
Blackhawk Ct					
1100	SMBG	60193	2913		C1
Blackhawk Dr					
10	MonT	60466	3595	3W-28S	B5
10	PKFT	60466	3595	4W-27S	A5
10	SmbT	60193	2913		A2
10	TNTN	60476	3428	0E-20S	E4
200	PKFT	60466	3594	4W-27S	E4
700	UYPK	60466	3684	3W-31S	B4
800	ELGN	60120	2855		C1
800	ROSL	60172	2913		B2
800	SmbT	60172	2913		B2
1000	UYPK	60449	3684	3W-30S	B4
1200	ELGN	60120	2801		C7
1400	MPPT	60056	2861	16W-12N	C2
3600	RGMW	60008	2806	20W-15N	B2
7200	TYPK	60477	3504	9W-23S	E3
Blackhawk Ln					
13900	ODPK	60462	3346	9W-16S	C3
S Blackhawk Pkwy					
19100	MKNA	60448	3504	10W-23S	B3
Blackhawk Rd					
10	GLNC	60022	2758	7W-20N	C2
10	HDPK	60022	2758	7W-20N	C2
10	HDPK	60035	2758	7W-20N	B2
200	RVSD	60546	3088	9W-3S	D5

Chicago & Cook County Street Index

STREET Block	City	ZIP	Map#	CGS	Grid
Blackhawk Rd					
300	BRWN	60402	3088	9W-3S	D5
300	RVSD	60402	3088	9W-3S	D5
2500	WLMT	60091	2812	5W-14N	A5
2800	WLMT	60091	2811	5W-14N	E5
W Blackhawk St					
400	CHCG	60610	3034	0W-1N	A1
800	CHCG	60610	3033	1W-1N	E1
800	CHCG	60622	3033	1W-1N	E1
Blackhawk Ter					
200	BNVL	60106	2915		D7
Blackhawk Tr					
1500	WLNG	60090	2754	16W-17N	D5
6500	IHPK	60525	3146		E6
Black Hill Dr					
100	HnrT	60107	2856	30W-9N	B7
Black Oak Av					
18300	TYPK	60477	3424	10W-22S	B7
Black Partridge					
-	LmnT	60439	3270		A4
Black Pine Tr					
12100	HMGN	60441	3422	15W-18S	C1
Blacksmith Ln					
1000	LMNT	60439	3271		A5
Blackstone Av					
-	LNSG	60438	3429	1E-21S	B7
-	ThtT	60438	3429	1E-22S	B7
300	WLSP	60480	3209	12W-9S	D2
3600	MKHM	60426	3426	4W-19S	D2
6200	CTSD	60525	3147	13W-6S	B5
6200	LynT	60525	3147	13W-6S	B5
7100	JSTC	60458	3147	11W-8S	E7
7100	JSTC	60458	3148	11W-8S	A7
7200	JSTC	60458	3209	11W-8S	E1
14200	DLTN	60419	3351	1E-16S	B4
19900	BlmT	60411	3509	1E-23S	B3
19900	LYWD	60411	3509	1E-23S	B3
20200	MTSN	60443	3506	5W-24S	C5
20200	OMFD	60461	3506	5W-24S	C5
S Blackstone Av					
100	LGNG	60525	3087	13W-4S	A7
200	GNWD	60425	3509	1E-23S	B3
200	LGNG	60525	3147	13W-4S	A1
500	LynT	60525	3147	13W-5S	A1
4900	CHCG	60615	3153	1E-5S	A2
5500	CHCG	60637	3153	1E-6S	A3
7100	CHCG	60619	3153	1E-8S	B7
8300	CHCG	60619	3215	1E-9S	B3
Blackstone Pl					
500	HDPK	60035	2758	7W-20N	B1
Blackstone St					
100	TNTN	60476	3428	0E-21S	E5
Blackthorn Dr					
1400	GNVW	60025	2810	8W-14N	D4
Blackthorn Ln					
1000	NHBK	60062	2757	10W-17N	A5
Blackthorn Rd					
200	RchT	60443	3593	8W-26S	B1
600	WNKA	60093	2812	5W-16N	A1
1000	RVWD	60015	2755	13W-20N	D1
Black Twig Rd					
10	RGMW	60008	2806	20W-13N	A6
Black Walnut Tr					
10	PlsT	60464	3273	11W-14S	D7
10	PSPK	60464	3273	11W-14S	D7
Blackwater Ct					
15900	TYPK	60477	3424	9W-19S	C1
Bladon Rd					
1300	SMBG	60195	2858	24W-12N	D2
Blaine Av					
6200	HMND	46320	3430		D2
6200	HMND	46324	3430		D2
S Blaine Av					
5800	HMND	46320	3352		D7
5800	HMND	46320	3430		D1
14200	POSN	60469	3349	3W-17S	B4
14800	POSN	60426	3349	3W-17S	B5
Blaine Ct					
700	SMBG	60173	2805	21W-13N	C6
Blaine St					
10	HNDL	60521	3146		B2
Blair Ln					
100	IVNS	60067	2752	22W-16N	A7
1200	HFET	60194	2858	25W-12N	C2
16400	OKFT	60452	3426	5W-19S	C2
Blair St					
500	PKFT	60466	3594	4W-25S	E1
500	PKFT	60466	3595	3W-26S	A1
Blake Ln					
4000	GNVW	60062	2809	11W-15N	D2
4100	GNVW	60025	2809	11W-15N	D2
S Blake St					
3600	CHCG	60609	3091	2W-3S	B5
Blanchan Av					
1100	LGPK	60525	3087	11W-2S	D4
1500	PvsT	60525	3087	11W-2S	D4
3500	BKFD	60513	3087	11W-3S	D6
4500	BKFD	60513	3147	11W-4S	D1
4600	MCCK	60513	3147	11W-4S	D1
4600	MCCK	60525	3147	11W-4S	D1
Blanchard Cir					
10	SBTN	60010	2803	26W-13N	D5
Blandford Ct					
1500	SMBG	60173	2859	21W-10N	E4
Blane St					
200	PTON	60468	3860	9W-37S	E3
Blaney Dr					
700	DYR	46311	3598		E4
2800	SjnT	46311	3598		E4
Blarney Dr					
4600	MTSN	60443	3506	5W-24S	B5
Blarney Rd					
8000	TYPK	60477	3424	10W-21S	C6
Blaze Tr					
900	WLNG	60090	2754	15W-16N	E6
900	WLNG	60090	2755	15W-16N	A6
Blazer Av					
7600	JSTC	60458	3209	11W-8S	E2
Blazer St					
7500	JSTC	60458	3209	11W-8S	E1
Blenheim Dr					
800	SMBG	60195	2858	24W-12N	D2
Bliss Dr					
100	OKBK	60523	3086		B2
W Bliss St					
800	CHCG	60622	3033	1W-1N	E2
Block Ct					
8000	TYPK	60477	3504	10W-23S	C4
Block St					
700	BCHR	60401	3864	0W-37S	C2
Bloomfield Ct					
1100	SMWD	60107	2856	29W-10N	D7
W Bloomfield Ct					
700	PLTN	60067	2805	21W-14N	C4

STREET Block	City	ZIP	Map#	CGS	Grid
Bloomfield Dr					
1100	BRLT	60107	2856	29W-9N	D7
1100	SMWD	60107	2856	29W-9N	D7
10400	PlsT	60464	3345	13W-15S	B1
Bloomingbank Rd					
10	RVSD	60546	3088	10W-3S	B6
Bloomingdale Av					
1600	MLPK	60160	2973	11W-2N	D7
3300	MLPK	60160	3029	12W-2N	B1
W Bloomingdale Av					
1500	CHCG	60622	2977	2W-2N	C7
2300	CHCG	60647	2977	3W-2N	A7
2800	CHCG	60647	2976	3W-2N	E7
4200	CHCG	60639	2976	5W-2N	B7
4800	CHCG	60639	2975	6W-2N	D7
6300	CHCG	60707	2975	8W-2N	A7
6700	CHCG	60707	2974	9W-2N	C7
7100	EDPK	60707	2974	9W-2N	C7
7900	RVGV	60171	2974	9W-2N	B7
7900	RVGV	60707	2974	9W-2N	B7
E Bloomingdale Rd					
100	ITSC	60143	2914		C6
N Bloomingdale Rd					
100	BMDL	60108	2913		A7
N Bloomingdale Rd CO-4					
100	BMDL	60108	2913		A7
W Bloomingdale Rd					
100	ITSC	60143	2914		B7
600	ADSN	60143	2914		B7
N Bloomington Av					
3900	ANHT	60004	2753	19W-18N	C2
3900	PltT	60004	2753	19W-18N	C2
4000	ElaT	60047	2753	19W-18N	C2
Bloomsbury Ln					
-	MTSN	60443	3594	6W-25S	A1
Blossom Ct					
10	SBTN	60010	2803	27W-13N	C6
200	BFGV	60089	2754	17W-20N	A1
1700	HDPK	60035	2757	9W-20N	C1
S Blossom Dr					
12800	ALSP	60803	3276	5W-15S	B7
12800	ALSP	60803	3348	5W-15S	B1
W Blossom Dr					
4400	ALSP	60803	3276	5W-15S	C7
Blossom Ln					
10	GLF	60029	2865	8W-12N	A1
800	PTHT	60070	2809	13W-15N	A2
8500	TYPK	60477	3424	10W-19S	B2
S Blossom Row					
1900	HMND	46394	3280		D5
Blouin Dr					
1000	DLTN	60419	3351	1E-18S	A7
1100	SHLD	60419	3351	1E-18S	A7
1100	SHLD	60473	3351	1E-18S	A7
S Bluebell Ln					
-	MONE	60449	3683	5W-31S	C5
Bluebird Ct					
10	SMWD	60120	2856	29W-9N	E7
Bluebird Dr					
8800	TYPK	60477	3424	11W-21S	A7
Bluebird Ln					
400	VrnT	60015	2755	15W-20N	A1
1000	ROSL	60172	2912		C4
2100	RGMW	60008	2806	19W-14N	C4
Bluebird St					
800	VrnT	60015	2755	15W-20N	A1
E Bluebonnet Ln					
300	HFET	60195	2859	22W-11N	B3
500	HFET	60173	2859	22W-11N	C3
500	SMBG	60173	2859	22W-11N	C3
N Bluebonnet Ln					
1000	HFET	60195	2859	23W-11N	B2
Blue Devil Dr					
10	PTON	60468	3860	9W-37S	E4
Blue Grass Dr					
12900	LMNT	60439	3342	20W-15S	B1
Blue Heron Dr					
10600	ODPK	60467	3423	13W-20S	B4
13100	PlsT	60467	3344	13W-15S	E1
Blue Heron Wy					
-	BRLT	60103	2909		C2
1100	ROSL	60172	2912		C4
Blue Hill Ter					
1200	NHBK	60062	2756	10W-17N	E5
S Blue Island Av					
1200	CHCG	60607	3033	1W-1S	E7
1200	CHCG	60608	3033	1W-1S	D7
1600	CHCG	60608	3091	1W-1S	D1
Blue Island-Riverdale Rd					
-	RVDL	60827	3350	1W-15S	B2
Bluejay Cir					
700	EGVV	60007	2913		C2
Blue Jay Ct					
400	MPPT	60056	2808	15W-13N	A6
Blue Jay Dr					
-	ODPK	60467	3423	13W-20S	A4
100	BlmT	60411	3509	3E-25S	E7
Blue Jay Wy					
10	DYR	46311	3510		C5
Blueridge Av					
8400	HYHL	60457	3209	11W-9S	E4
Blue Ridge Dr					
700	HnrT	60107	2856	30W-9N	B7
700	SMWD	60107	2856	30W-10N	C6
700	SMWD	60120	2856	30W-10N	C6
Blue Ridge Pkwy					
1000	ALGN	60102	2748		B1
Blue Sky Ln					
-	RchT	60443	3593	8W-25S	B1
Blue Spruce Ct					
8200	TYPK	60477	3424	10W-19S	C2
S Blue Spruce Ct					
14300	ODPK	60462	3346	11W-17S	A4
Blue Stem Ct					
10	SMWD	60107	2856	29W-10N	D6
Bluestem Ln					
1500	GNVW	60025	2810	9W-14N	D5
Bluestem Pkwy					
2000	LYWD	60411	3509	2E-24S	D5
Bluff Av					
10	LGNG	60525	3087	12W-4S	C7
300	LGNG	60525	3147	12W-4S	C1
Bluff Ct					
600	SMWD	60107	2856	29W-10N	D5
Bluff Rd					
-	DGvT	60439	3270		E1
-	DGvT	60439	3271		A1
600	LMNT	60439	3270		C3
900	GLNC	60022	2758	6W-18N	C4
16900	DPgT	60441	3270		A4
W Bluff Rd					
10	DGvT	60439	3270		B4
10	DPgT	60441	3270		B4
10	LmnT	60439	3270		B4

STREET Block	City	ZIP	Map#	CGS	Grid
Bluff St					
300	WNKA	60093	2758	6W-16N	D7
600	GLNC	60022	2758	6W-17N	C4
Bluff City Blvd					
700	ELGN	60120	2855		D6
Bluff City Blvd SR-25					
500	ELGN	60120	2855		A6
Blythe Ct					
2000	IVNS	60010	2751	24W-16N	B6
Blythe Rd					
300	RVSD	60546	3088	9W-3S	D4
Boal Pkwy					
700	WNKA	60093	2758	6W-16N	D7
700	WNKA	60093	2811	6W-16N	D1
Boardwalk					
-	ODHL	60477	3423	11W-19S	E2
Boardwalk Blvd					
2500	HFET	60194	2857	26W-11N	D3
S Boardwalk Ct					
800	PLTN	60067	2805	21W-14N	D3
W Boardwalk Dr					
100	PLTN	60067	2805	21W-14N	D3
Boardwalk Ln					
-	ODHL	60477	3423	11W-19S	E1
-	ODPK	60462	3423	11W-19S	E1
9400	ODPK	60467	3423	11W-19S	D2
Boardwalk Pl					
10	PKRG	60068	2863	11W-9N	D7
100	EGVV	60007	2914		D1
Boardwalk Ter					
9100	ODHL	60477	3423	11W-19S	E2
Bobbi Ln					
-	MaiT	60016	2863	11W-11N	D3
-	PKRG	60016	2863	11W-11N	D3
-	PKRG	60068	2863	11W-11N	D3
Bobby Ln					
-	SRPK	60176	2973	11W-4N	D2
S Bobby Ln					
100	MPPT	60056	2807	16W-12N	D7
100	MPPT	60056	2861	16W-12N	D1
Bobby Locke Dr					
5100	MDLN	60445	3347	6W-16S	E3
Bobolink Ct					
8300	ODPK	60462	3346	10W-18S	B6
Bobolink Dr					
500	HNDL	60521	3086		C6
E Bobolink Dr					
10	CTSD	60525	3147	12W-5S	C3
Bobolink Ln					
2600	NHBK	60062	2756	10W-16N	E6
3300	RGMW	60008	2806	20W-13N	B6
Bobolink Rd					
2800	FSMR	60422	3507	3W-23S	A3
8000	ODPK	60462	3346	10W-18S	C6
N Bobolink Rd					
400	MPPT	60056	2807	15W-14N	E4
W Bobolink Rd					
400	MPPT	60056	2807	16W-14N	E4
600	ANHT	60004	2807	16W-14N	E4
600	ANHT	60056	2807	16W-14N	E4
Bobolink Ter					
4200	SKOK	60076	2866	5W-10N	A4
4700	SKOK	60076	2865	5W-10N	E4
4700	SKOK	60077	2865	5W-10N	E4
Bob White Cir					
16300	ODPK	60467	3423	12W-19S	D2
Bobwhite Ct					
3700	PltT	60067	2806	20W-13N	B6
3700	RGMW	60008	2806	20W-13N	B6
Bobwhite Ln					
3600	RGMW	60008	2806	20W-13N	B6
Boca Rio Dr					
6100	OKFT	60452	3347	7W-18S	C6
15100	BmnT	60452	3347	7W-18S	C6
Bock Rd					
17700	LNSG	60438	3429	2E-21S	D6
17700	ThtT	60438	3429	2E-21S	D6
18500	BlmT	60411	3429	2E-21S	D7
W Bode Cir					
600	HFET	60194	2858	24W-11N	D4
700	SMBG	60194	2858	24W-11N	D4
Bode Rd					
-	HnrT	60120	2856	31W-11N	A4
10	HFET	60107	2856	29W-11N	E3
10	HFET	60107	2857	28W-11N	A3
10	HFET	60120	2856	29W-11N	E3
10	HFET	60120	2857	28W-11N	A3
10	HFET	60194	2859	23W-11N	A3
10	SMWD	60107	2856	29W-11N	E3
10	SMWD	60107	2857	28W-11N	A3
10	SMWD	60120	2856	29W-11N	E3
100	HFET	60194	2858	25W-11N	A3
300	ELGN	60120	2855		E4
300	HnrT	60120	2855		C4
800	SMBG	60194	2858	24W-11N	D3
2300	HFET	60194	2857	26W-11N	E4
2300	SMBG	60194	2857	26W-11N	E4
2500	SMWD	60194	2857	26W-11N	E4
E Bode Rd					
-	HFET	60194	2857	27W-11N	D4
-	SMWD	60194	2857	27W-11N	D4
10	HFET	60107	2857	28W-11N	A4
10	HFET	60120	2857	28W-11N	A4
10	SMWD	60107	2857	27W-11N	D4
500	HFET	60010	2857	27W-11N	D4
500	SMWD	60010	2857	27W-11N	D4
Boeger Av					
1200	HLSD	60162	3028		E7
1200	WSTR	60154	3028		E7
1400	WSTR	60154	3086		E3
Boeger Ct					
11000	WSTR	60154	3086		E2
W Boeger Dr					
100	ANHT	60004	2754	17W-17N	A4
100	ANHT	60089	2754	17W-17N	A4
100	BFGV	60089	2754	17W-17N	A4
W Bogey Ln					
1000	PLTN	60067	2805	22W-14N	B4
Bohland Av					
10	BLWD	60104	3029	12W-0N	B5
Bohlander Av					
-	BLWD	60104	3028		E4
5400	BKLY	60163	3028		D4
Bohlmann Pkwy					
22500	RNPK	60443	3593	7W-27S	D4
22500	RNPK	60471	3593	7W-27S	D4
Bokelman Av					
100	ROSL	60172	2913		A4
Boland Dr					
10	BrnT	60010	2803	27W-14N	A4
10	BrnT	60118	2803	27W-14N	A4
Bolleana Ct					
1800	HFET	60195	2804	25W-14N	A3
Bolton Wy					
700	HRPK	60133	2912		A1

STREET Block	City	ZIP	Map#	CGS	Grid
Bolz Rd					
10	BNHL	60110	2748		B4
10	CPVL	60110	2748		B4
200	DndT	60110	2748		B4
700	CPVL	60102	2748		A4
700	DndT	60102	2748		A4
Bolzano Ct					
10	LYWD	60411	3598	4E-25S	C1
W Bombay Wy					
900	PLTN	60067	2752	22W-16N	B7
900	PltT	60067	2752	22W-16N	B7
N Bon Aire Dr					
700	PLTN	60074	2753	20W-16N	B6
S Bonaparte St					
2900	CHCG	60608	3091	1W-2S	D3
Bonaventure Dr					
1000	EGVV	60007	2914		A3
Bonbury Ln					
14000	ODPK	60462	3346	10W-16S	C4
S Bond Av					
8400	CHCG	60617	3216	3E-9S	A3
Bond St					
-	BDVW	60155	3087	12W-1S	B1
-	WSTR	60154	3087	12W-1S	B1
10	EGvT	60007	2861	17W-10N	B5
10	EGVV	60007	2861	17W-10N	B5
2300	MonT	60449	3682	7W-30S	D3
2300	MonT	60449	3683	6W-30S	A3
2300	UYPK	60449	3682	7W-30S	D3
2300	UYPK	60449	3683	6W-30S	A3
2300	UYPK	60466	3682	7W-30S	D3
Bonded Pkwy					
600	SMBG	60107	2857	27W-10N	D6
600	SMBG	60193	2857	27W-10N	D7
600	SMWD	60107	2857	27W-10N	D7
S Bonfield St					
2700	CHCG	60608	3091	1W-2S	D3
W Bong Rd					
6800	MonT	60449	3682	8W-30S	B3
Bonhill Dr					
3900	PltT	60004	2753	19W-18N	C2
Bonita Av					
700	EGVV	60007	2914		E1
700	EGVV	60007	2915		A1
W Bonita Av					
1400	MPPT	60056	2861	16W-12N	C1
Bonita Dr					
1000	PKRG	60068	2918	10W-7N	A3
1200	PKRG	60068	2917	10W-7N	E3
Bonnie Av					
1000	PKRG	60068	2918	10W-7N	A3
Bonnie Ct					
100	TNTN	60476	3428	0W-20S	D5
Bonnie Ln					
-	PTON	60468	3860	10W-37S	C4
300	EGvT	60007	2861	17W-9N	B7
300	EGVV	60007	2861	17W-9N	B7
500	IVNS	60067	2752	22W-16N	B7
1800	HFET	60194	2858	25W-12N	A2
W Bonnie Ln					
800	PTON	60468	3860	10W-37S	D4
Bonnie Tr					
5400	OKFT	60452	3425	6W-20S	E4
Bonnie Tr E					
17000	OKFT	60452	3425	6W-20S	E4
Bonnie Tr W					
17000	OKFT	60452	3425	6W-20S	E4
Bonnie Brae Av					
200	ITSC	60143	2914		D7
E Bonnie Brae Av					
100	WhlT	60056	2808	13W-13N	E5
Bonnie Brae Cres					
2900	FSMR	60422	3507	3W-23S	A4
Bonnie Brae Pl					
700	RVFT	60305	3030	9W-0N	D3
1500	EDPK	60707	3030	9W-1N	D1
1500	RVFT	60707	3030	9W-1N	D1
Bonnie Brae Rd					
10	HNDL	60521	3086		A7
Bonnie Brook Dr					
800	PTHT	60070	2808	14W-15N	C2
Bonnie Dundee Rd					
400	CPVL	60110	2801		B1
400	CPVL	60118	2801		B1
400	EDND	60118	2801		B1
500	EDND	60110	2801		B1
Bonnie Glen Ln					
1300	GNVW	60025	2811	8W-13N	A5
Bonnieglen Pl					
-	ODPK	60467	3345	13W-18S	A7
Bonny Glen Gates					
-	IVNS	60067	2804	23W-14N	E3
Booth Ct					
300	ELGN	60120	2855		A5
Bordeaux Ct					
700	EGVV	60007	2914		C1
700	IVNS	60010	2751	24W-17N	B6
1900	WLNG	60090	2808	14W-15N	C2
3500	HLCT	60429	3426	4W-21S	E7
3900	NHBK	60062	2756	12W-18N	B3
Bordeaux Dr					
600	NHBK	60062	2756	12W-18N	B4
3700	HFET	60195	2804	24W-14N	C3
Bordeaux Ln					
1600	LGGV	60047	2753	18W-20N	E1
1600	LGGV	60089	2753	18W-20N	E1
1600	VrnT	60089	2753	18W-20N	E1
Borden Cir					
1300	ELGN	60120	2855		E3
Borden Ct					
10	ROSL	60172	2912		C5
1200	ELGN	60120	2855		D3
Borden Dr					
900	ROSL	60172	2912		C5
1300	ELGN	60120	2855		E3
W Borders Dr					
1200	PLTN	60067	2805	22W-15N	A2
1300	IVNS	60067	2805	22W-15N	B2
Borman Ct					
900	EGVV	60007	2913		E2
Bormet Dr					
8100	TYPK	60477	3424	10W-19S	C2
N Boro Ln					
1400	MPPT	60056	2808	13W-14N	E3
Borris Cir					
100	SMWD	60107	2857	28W-11N	B4
Borthwick Ln					
100	IVNS	60067	2752	22W-18N	B4
Bos Dr					
17800	ODPK	60467	3423	13W-21S	A6
Boston Cir					
1000	SMBG	60193	2913		D4
Boston Hbr					
1000	SMBG	60193	2913		B1

STREET Block	City	ZIP	Map#	CGS	Grid
N Boston St					
200	CHHT	60411	3595	2W-26S	E1
W Boston St					
1800	CHHT	60411	3595	2W-26S	D1
N Bosworth Av					
1400	CHCG	60622	3033	1W-1N	D1
1600	CHCG	60622	2977	1W-2N	D7
2500	CHCG	60614	2977	1W-3N	D5
2600	CHCG	60657	2977	1W-3N	D5
3500	CHCG	60613	2977	1W-4N	D3
6400	CHCG	60626	2921	1W-8N	C2
6400	CHCG	60660	2921	1W-8N	C2
7600	CHCG	60626	2867	1W-9N	C6
Bosworth Ln					
900	EGVV	60007	2915		A2
1800	NHFD	60093	2811	7W-15N	B2
N Bothwell St					
10	PLTN	60067	2805	22W-14N	B4
100	PLTN	60067	2752	21W-16N	E7
S Bothwell St					
10	PLTN	60067	2805	21W-15N	E1
Botsford Pl					
2100	HFET	60195	2858	26W-12N	A1
Boula Av					
10	HmrT	60441	3342	20W-17S	A5
Boulder Ct					
18900	HMWD	60430	3508	1W-22S	B2
W Boulder Ct					
10	PSHL	60465	3274	10W-12S	B3
Boulder Dr					
-	BNHL	60110	2748		B3
-	CPVL	60110	2748		B3
E Boulder Dr					
1800	MPPT	60056	2808	13W-14N	D5
S Boulder Dr					
14300	HMGN	60441	3343	17W-17S	D5
Boulder Ln					
4800	HFET	60010	2751	24W-16N	C7
4800	HFET	60010	2804	24W-16N	C1
4800	HFET	60195	2804	24W-16N	C1
Boulder Rd					
2300	DYR	46311	3598		E3
S Boulevard Wy					
2400	CHCG	60623	3090	3W-2S	E2
Bourbon Pkwy					
1500	SMBG	60193	2857	27W-10N	D6
1500	SMWD	60107	2857	27W-10N	D6
Bourne Ln					
1000	SMBG	60193	2858	24W-9N	C7
Bouterse St					
2100	PKRG	60068	2863	11W-9N	D6
Bow Tr					
1500	WLNG	60090	2754	16W-17N	D5
E Bowen Av					
400	CHCG	60653	3092	0E-4S	D6
Bowen Ct					
400	ELGN	60120	2855		B5
Bowen Dr					
400	MNSR	46321	3510		D4
E Bowen Dr					
-	CHCG	60615	3152	0E-5S	D2
W Bowler St					
2100	CHCG	60612	3033	2W-0S	B6
Bowling Green Dr					
800	GNWD	60425	3508	1W-22S	A2
800	HMWD	60430	3508	1W-22S	A2
Bowman St					
-	MTSN	60443	3506	6W-24S	A5
N Bowmanville Av					
5300	CHCG	60625	2921	2W-6N	B5
5400	CHCG	60640	2921	2W-6N	B5
Boxwood Ct					
10	SMWD	60107	2857	26W-11N	E4
1000	WLNG	60090	2754	15W-18N	E3
Boxwood Dr					
500	SMBG	60193	2858	24W-9N	D7
800	MNSR	46321	3510		E5
N Boxwood Dr					
1100	MPPT	60056	2808	15W-14N	B4
S Boxwood Dr					
900	MPPT	60056	2808	15W-14N	B5
Boxwood Ln					
700	BFGV	60089	2754	17W-17N	B5
S Boyd Av					
200	EMHT	60126	3028		B3
S Boyer St					
11200	LmnT	60439	3271		B4
W Boyington Ln					
7000	MonT	60449	3682	8W-30S	A4
N Boyle Ter					
3000	RVGV	60171	2974	10W-3N	B4
3100	CHCG	60171	2974	10W-3N	B4
3100	CHCG	60634	2974	10W-3N	B4
Boyne Ct					
11800	ODPK	60467	3422	14W-21S	D5
N Boynton Dr					
100	PLTN	60074	2753	19W-16N	B7
100	PLTN	60074	2806	20W-15N	A2
Bracken Ln					
400	NHFD	60093	2811	7W-15N	A2
Brackley Ln					
10	SBTN	60010	2804	25W-15N	A1
Brackman Av					
200	CRTE	60417	3685	0W-30S	C3
Bradbury Ln					
300	BRLT	60103	2911		A4
Braddock Dr					
100	MLPK	60160	3030	10W-1N	A2
Bradfield Ct					
1000	UYPK	60466	3684	3W-30S	B3
Bradford Cir					
400	EGVV	60007	2860	19W-9N	C7
Bradford Ct					
900	SMBG	60193	2858	24W-9N	D7
1000	ELGN	60120	2855		D1
E Bradford Ct					
700	ANHT	60004	2754	17W-16N	B6
W Bradford Ct					
6600	MONE	60449	3682	8W-32S	B7
N Bradford Dr					
2600	ANHT	60004	2754	17W-16N	B6
Bradford Ln					
10	OKBK	60523	3086		B3
900	SMBG	60193	2858	24W-9N	C7
9300	ODPK	60462	3423	11W-18S	D1
Bradford Pl					
10	CRTE	60417	3596	0W-28S	C7
Bradley Av					
600	MTSN	60443	3505	6W-25S	E7
Bradley Cir					
1200	ELGN	60120	2801		D7
Bradley Ct					
200	DSPN	60016	2862	15W-11N	B3
11200	ODPK	60467	3422	14W-21S	E6
11200	OrlT	60467	3422	14W-21S	E6

Chicago & Cook County Street Index

STREET Block	City	ZIP	Map#	CGS	Grid
E Bradley Ct					
900	PLTN	60074	2753	19W-18N	B3
S Bradley Ct					
5700	HRPK	60133	2911		E5
Bradley Ct N					
5900	HRPK	60133	2911		E5
N Bradley Dr					
200	CHHT	60411	3507	2W-24S	E4
Bradley Ln					
10	HFET	60194	2859	23W-11N	A4
1200	EGVV	60007	2914		A2
Bradley Pl					
2300	EVTN	60202	2866	3W-10N	D4
W Bradley Pl					
1900	CHCG	60613	2977	2W-4N	B2
1900	CHCG	60618	2977	2W-4N	B2
Bradley Rd					
400	BFGV	60089	2754	17W-18N	B4
E Bradley St					
10	DSPN	60016	2862	14W-11N	C3
W Bradley St					
10	DSPN	60016	2862	15W-11N	B3
Bradoc St					
800	CHHT	60411	3507	2W-24S	D6
Bradrock Dr					
10	DSPN	60018	2862	14W-9N	C6
Brads Wy					
14800	HMGN	60441	3342	19W-17S	D6
14800	HmrT	60441	3342	19W-17S	D6
E Bradshire Ct					
2300	ANHT	60004	2807	16W-15N	C2
Bradwell Cir					
2000	IVNS	60010	2750	25W-16N	E7
Bradwell Rd					
100	HFET	60010	2751	24W-16N	C7
100	IVNS	60010	2750	25W-16N	E7
100	IVNS	60010	2751	25W-16N	A7
2000	IVNS	60067	2751	23W-16N	E7
Braeborn Ct					
1400	WLNG	60090	2754	16W-18N	D3
Braeburn Av					
1100	FSMR	60422	3507	3W-23S	C3
Braeburn Dr					
10	PKFT	60466	3595	3W-28S	B6
Braeburn Ln					
100	HDPK	60035	2758	7W-20N	C1
8000	ODPK	60462	3346	10W-18S	C7
Braeburn Rd					
600	EDND	60118	2801		B2
600	IVNS	60067	2751	23W-16N	E6
Braeloch Ct					
7800	ODPK	60462	3346	9W-18S	C7
Braemar Dr					
10	EGVV	60007	2914		D3
W Braemar Ln					
7400	FftT	60423	3504	9W-23S	E4
Braemar Rd					
700	FSMR	60422	3507	3W-22S	A2
Braeside					
-	BRTN	60010	2751	25W-18N	B2
W Braeside Dr					
300	ANHT	60004	2753	18W-17N	E6
300	ANHT	60004	2754	18W-17N	A6
Braeside Ln					
1600	NHBK	60062	2757	8W-16N	E6
Braeside Pl					
700	BRTN	60010	2751	25W-18N	B2
Braeside Rd					
300	HDPK	60035	2758	7W-20N	C2
Braga Dr					
2400	BDVW	60155	3087	11W-1S	C1
Bragg Ct					
300	BRLT	60103	2911		B5
Bragg St					
200	BRLT	60103	2911		B5
N Brainard Av					
10	LGNG	60525	3087	13W-4S	B7
200	LGPK	60525	3087	12W-3S	B6
900	WSTR	60525	3087	12W-3S	B6
S Brainard Av					
10	LGNG	60525	3087	12W-4S	B7
300	LGNG	60525	3147	13W-5S	B3
500	LynT	60525	3147	13W-5S	B1
5400	CTSD	60525	3147	13W-7S	B6
13000	CHCG	60633	3279	3E-15S	E7
13100	CHCG	60633	3351	3E-15S	E1
13300	CHCG	60633	3352	3E-15S	A1
13700	BNHM	60633	3352	4E-16S	B3
13800	HMND	46327	3352		C4
S Braintree Ct					
100	SMBG	60193	2858	25W-10N	C6
N Braintree Dr					
10	SMBG	60193	2858	25W-10N	C5
10	SMBG	60194	2858	25W-11N	C4
500	HFET	60194	2858	25W-11N	C4
S Braintree Dr					
10	SMBG	60193	2858	25W-9N	C7
10	SMBG	60194	2858	25W-10N	C6
800	SMBG	60193	2912		C1
Braintree Ln					
600	BRLT	60103	2910		C5
Brair Cove					
800	PLTN	60067	2752	22W-17N	B5
Bramanti Tr					
3200	SCHT	60475	3596	0W-27S	C4
3200	STGR	60475	3596	0W-27S	C4
Bramble Ct					
300	SMBG	60193	2858	23W-10N	E6
13000	HMGN	60441	3422	16W-18S	A1
Bramble Ln					
300	SMBG	60193	2858	24W-10N	E6
Bramblewood Dr					
-	SJHN	46373	3687		E1
-	SjnT	46311	3687		E1
15500	OKFT	60452	3347	8W-18S	A7
Bramlette Ct					
11800	HMGN	60441	3344	14W-17S	C6
11800	ODPK	60441	3344	14W-17S	C6
11800	ODPK	60467	3344	14W-17S	C6
11800	OrlT	60467	3344	14W-17S	C6
Brampton Ct					
1000	UYPK	60466	3684	3W-30S	C3
W Brampton Ln					
300	ANHT	60004	2754	18W-18N	A2
500	ANHT	60004	2753	18W-18N	E2
N Branch Rd					
1200	WLMT	60091	2811	6W-14N	D4
Branchwood Ct					
300	SMBG	60193	2858	23W-10N	E6
Branchwood Dr					
10	SMBG	60193	2858	24W-10N	E6
10	SMBG	60194	2858	24W-10N	E6
Brandau Ct					
8400	TYPK	60477	3424	10W-21S	B6
Brandau Dr					
18000	TYPK	60477	3424	10W-21S	B7
E Brandenberry Ct					
2400	ANHT	60004	2807	16W-15N	D3
2400	PTHT	60004	2807	16W-15N	D3
2400	WhlT	60004	2807	16W-15N	D3
Brandess Dr					
3100	GNVW	60025	2810	10W-15N	A3
Brandess Ter					
5300	SKOK	60077	2865	6W-11N	D3
S Brandon Av					
-	CHCG	60617	3216	3E-10S	A4
7900	CHCG	60649	3216	3E-9S	A2
13000	CHCG	60633	3280	3E-15S	A7
13100	CHCG	60633	3352	3E-15S	A1
W Brandon Ct					
100	PLTN	60067	2752	21W-17N	E6
Brandon Pl					
700	WLNG	60090	2755	15W-18N	A3
Brandon Rd					
10	NHFD	60093	2811	7W-14N	A3
2000	GNVW	60025	2811	7W-14N	A3
2000	GNVW	60093	2811	7W-14N	A3
Brandt Av					
9500	OKLN	60453	3211	6W-11S	E6
9700	OKLN	60453	3212	6W-11S	A7
Brandt Dr					
900	DndT	60118	2801		C6
900	DndT	60120	2801		C6
900	ELGN	60118	2801		C6
900	ELGN	60120	2801		C6
Brandy Pkwy					
1500	SMBG	60193	2857	27W-10N	D7
1500	SMWD	60107	2857	27W-10N	D7
Brandyvine Ln					
100	EGVV	60007	2914		D2
Brandywine Dr					
700	ROSL	60172	2912		D5
Brandywine Rd					
10	SBTN	60010	2803	27W-14N	A3
Brannock Ln					
-	TYPK	60477	3504	10W-23S	B3
Brampton Ln					
3000	DYR	46311	3598		D4
Brantwood Av					
10	EGVV	60007	2914		D1
W Brantwood Av					
10	EGVV	60007	2914		D1
Brantwood Ct					
600	EGVV	60007	2914		D1
Brantwood Pl					
800	EGVV	60007	2914		E1
Brassie Av					
1000	FSMR	60422	3507	3W-23S	B4
Brassie Ct					
15700	ODPK	60462	3424	10W-18S	C1
Brassie Dr					
2700	GNVW	60025	2810	9W-13N	B6
15200	ODPK	60462	3346	10W-18S	C7
15600	ODPK	60462	3424	9W-18S	C1
Braver Ct					
1300	WLNG	60090	2754	16W-18N	D3
W Bray Ct					
1400	ANHT	60005	2860	19W-12N	D1
Braymore Ct					
100	IVNS	60010	2750	25W-16N	E7
N Braymore Dr					
1800	IVNS	60010	2750	25W-16N	E6
1800	IVNS	60010	2751	25W-16N	A6
S Braymore Dr					
1600	IVNS	60010	2750	25W-16N	E6
1600	IVNS	60010	2751	25W-16N	A6
Brayton Av					
13100	WthT	60406	3349	3W-15S	A1
E Brayton St					
10	CHCG	60628	3278	0W-14S	C6
W Brayton St					
10	CHCG	60628	3278	0W-14S	C6
Breakers Dr					
3600	FSMR	60422	3506	4W-24S	D4
3600	OMFD	60461	3506	4W-24S	D4
Breakers Pt					
600	SMBG	60194	2859	22W-10N	C4
Breakwater Wy					
7900	PSHT	60463	3274	9W-13S	C4
Breckenridge Blvd					
18200	FftT	60448	3422	14W-21S	D7
18200	ODPK	60467	3422	14W-22S	D7
Breckenridge Dr					
8400	PSHL	60465	3274	10W-12S	B1
W Breen St					
7100	NLES	60714	2864	9W-10N	D4
Brees Wy Ln					
1400	NHBK	60062	2757	9W-17N	C6
Breezewood Ter					
2200	HRPK	60133	2911		C3
Bregenz Ct					
100	LYWD	60411	3598	4E-25S	C1
Brementowne Dr					
6800	BmnT	60452	3425	8W-19S	A2
6800	BmnT	60477	3425	8W-19S	A2
6800	TYPK	60477	3425	8W-19S	A2
Brementowne Rd					
6800	TYPK	60477	3425	8W-19S	A2
Bremer Ct					
-	CteT	60417	3687	4E-29S	B2
Bremer Tr					
-	CteT	60417	3687	4E-29S	B2
Brendan St					
20100	FKFT	60423	3504	11W-24S	A5
Brenden Ln					
16400	OKFT	60452	3426	5W-19S	B2
Brendon Ct					
10	ROSL	60172	2912		B4
Brendon Dr					
800	SMBG	60194	2857	26W-11N	E3
S Brennan Av					
9500	CHCG	60617	3215	2E-11S	D6
Brennan Hwy					
15300	MKHM	60426	3348	4W-18S	E7
15400	MKHM	60426	3426	4W-18S	D1
Brenner Ct					
10	LYWD	60411	3598	4E-25S	C1
200	CRTE	60417	3596	0E-28S	E6
Brent Ct					
2200	SMBG	60194	2857	26W-11N	E5
Brent Rd					
1100	NHBK	60062	2810	8W-15N	D1
Brenta Ct					
100	LYWD	60411	3598	4E-25S	C1
Brentwood Av					
14400	ODPK	60462	3345	11W-17S	E4
Brentwood Cir					
1000	BFGV	60089	2754	17W-17N	C4
Brentwood Ct					
-	BNVL	60106	2972		B3
400	ROSL	60172	2912		E6
800	SMBG	60193	2858	24W-9N	D7
1100	HRPK	60133	2911		E1
1200	FSMR	60422	3507	3W-22S	A2
S Brentwood Ct					
16700	HMGN	60441	3422	15W-20S	B3
Brentwood Dr					
10	GLNC	60022	2758	6W-18N	D3
200	CHHT	60411	3507	1W-23S	E4
300	DSPN	60016	2862	15W-11N	B3
700	BNVL	60106	2972		B4
W Brentwood Dr					
100	PltT	60074	2752	21W-18N	D2
N Brentwood Ln					
800	MPPT	60056	2808	14W-14N	B4
Brentwood Rd					
2100	NHBK	60062	2757	10W-16N	A6
Brentwood Tr					
10	ELGN	60120	2855		E4
Bret Dr					
6200	OKFT	60452	3425	7W-18S	B1
Bretman St					
-	BNVL	60106	2972		A1
E Brett Ct					
200	ANHT	60005	2861	17W-12N	A1
Brett Ln					
3800	GNVW	60025	2809	11W-14N	D3
Bretz Dr					
4400	RNPK	60471	3594	5W-27S	B4
17700	HMWD	60430	3428	0W-21S	B6
17700	TNTN	60430	3428	0W-21S	B6
Brewster Av					
-	BKFD	60513	3087	12W-3S	C6
-	LGNG	60513	3087	12W-3S	C6
10	LGPK	60525	3087	12W-4S	B6
500	LGNG	60525	3087	12W-4S	B6
Brewster Ln					
10	LGNG	60525	3087	12W-3S	C6
100	LGPK	60525	3087	12W-4S	C6
500	SMBG	60193	2858	25W-9N	C7
800	BRLT	60103	2910		C5
Brewster Creek Blvd					
-	BRLT	60120	2909		E5
-	BRLT	60120	2910		A4
-	WynT	60184	2909		E5
Brewster Creek Cir					
10	WYNE	60120	2909		A6
Brian Av					
600	SMBG	60194	2858	26W-11N	A4
Brian Ct					
22500	RNPK	60471	3594	5W-27S	C5
Brian Dr					
2300	NHBK	60062	2810	10W-15N	A2
2400	NHBK	60062	2809	10W-15N	E2
Brian Ln					
200	PTHT	60070	2808	14W-15N	B2
S Brian Pl					
12800	PlsT	60464	3273	12W-15S	C7
12800	PlsT	60464	3345	12W-15S	C1
Brianne Ln					
15500	OKFT	60452	3347	8W-18S	B7
Briar Av					
17600	HMWD	60430	3427	2W-21S	D6
Briar Ct					
1300	DSPN	60018	2862	13W-9N	E6
1300	DSPN	60018	2863	12W-9N	A7
2200	HFET	60195	2857	26W-12N	E1
8800	MaiT	60016	2863	11W-11N	D4
8800	MaiT	60068	2863	11W-11N	D4
8800	PKRG	60068	2863	11W-11N	D4
W Briar Ct					
7700	FftT	60423	3504	9W-24S	D5
Briar Dr					
-	SKOK	60077	2811	6W-13N	E7
-	SKOK	60091	2811	6W-13N	E7
200	WLMT	60091	2811	6W-13N	D7
17100	TYPK	60477	3423	11W-20S	E5
Briar Ln					
-	HFET	60195	2857	26W-12N	E1
-	HFET	60195	2858	25W-12N	B1
10	GLNC	60022	2758	6W-17N	D6
200	HDPK	60035	2757	9W-20N	C2
400	MNSR	46321	3430		D7
500	NHFD	60093	2811	7W-15N	B2
500	WNKA	60093	2812	4W-15N	C1
3600	HLCT	60429	3506	4W-22S	D1
7400	HRPK	60133	2911		D1
15100	OKFT	60452	3347	7W-18S	D7
S Briar Ln					
13000	PSHT	60463	3347	8W-15S	A1
13000	WthT	60463	3347	8W-15S	A1
25900	MONE	60449	3682	6W-31S	E5
Briar Pl					
100	PltT	60010	2751	24W-18N	C2
300	ITSC	60143	2914		D6
E Briar Pl					
900	ANHT	60004	2807	17W-16N	B1
W Briar Pl					
300	CHCG	60657	2978	0W-3N	A4
700	CHCG	60657	2977	3W-4N	A2
Briar Rd					
-	GNVW	60025	2864	8W-12N	E1
10	GLF	60029	2864	8W-12N	E1
10	GLF	60029	2865	8W-12N	A1
6300	WLBK	60527	3146		B5
Briar Tr					
2500	SMBG	60173	2805	21W-13N	D6
Briarbranch Ter					
200	RchT	60443	3593	8W-26S	B2
Briarcliff Ln					
400	BRLT	60103	2911		C5
500	HFET	60195	2858	24W-12N	E2
Briarcliffe Dr					
12300	LMNT	60439	3270		A7
Briarford Ln					
2400	GNVW	60062	2809	11W-15N	D2
Briargate Av					
-	BLMT	60411	3508	0W-24S	E7
-	CHHT	60411	3508	1W-24S	A5
Briargate Dr					
16700	CCHL	60478	3426	4W-20S	D3
16700	MKHM	60426	3426	4W-20S	D3
Briargate Ln					
300	DRPK	60010	2752	22W-20N	B1
Briargate Ter					
10	BmdT	60157	2913		E5
300	HNDL	60521	3086		A6
Briar Hill Dr					
2000	SMBG	60194	2858	26W-11N	A3
2100	SMBG	60194	2857	26W-11N	E3
Briarhill Ln					
400	GNVW	60025	2810	9W-12N	C7
W Briar Patch Ln					
13100	LMNT	60439	3343	16W-15S	E2
13100	LMNT	60439	3344	15W-15S	A2
Briartree Ln					
5000	BDPK	60638	3211	6W-8S	E1
5000	BRBK	60459	3211	6W-8S	E1
5000	BRBK	60638	3211	6W-8S	E1
Briarwood Av					
-	HRPK	60107	2911		C1
-	SMWD	60107	2911		C1
100	CPVL	60110	2801		A1
1700	HRPK	60133	2911		C1
Briarwood Ct					
10	IHPK	60525	3146		E5
10	SMBG	60193	2858	24W-10N	E6
100	ELGN	60120	2855		D3
100	MTSN	60443	3505	6W-24S	E5
11700	BRRG	60527	3208		C2
Briarwood Dr					
400	WLNG	60090	2754	15W-17N	E6
500	BRRG	60527	3208		A4
500	DYR	46311	3510		E5
700	LynT	60458	3209	11W-8S	D2
E Briarwood Dr					
10	SMWD	60107	2856	30W-10N	C6
10	SMWD	60107	2857	28W-9N	A7
S Briarwood Dr E					
2800	MPPT	60005	2861	17W-10N	C5
S Briarwood Dr W					
2700	ANHT	60005	2861	17W-10N	B5
2700	MPPT	60005	2861	17W-10N	B4
2700	MPPT	60056	2861	17W-10N	B4
W Briarwood Dr					
10	SMWD	60107	2856	30W-10N	C6
13600	HMGN	60441	3343	16W-17S	E6
Briarwood Ln					
10	IHPK	60525	3146		D5
10	IHPK	60525	3147	13W-7S	A6
10	PltT	60067	2805	20W-13N	E6
10	PltT	60173	2805	20W-13N	E6
10	SMBG	60173	2805	20W-13N	E6
200	PltT	60067	2805	21W-13N	A6
500	EGVV	60007	2861	18W-10N	A6
600	ROSL	60172	2912		C6
1000	NHBK	60062	2757	10W-17N	A6
2600	MaiT	60025	2864	9W-12N	B1
8800	ODPK	60462	3346	11W-15S	A2
9100	HYHL	60457	3209	11W-10S	E5
11500	BRRG	60527	3208		D2
Briarwood Pl					
400	HDPK	60035	2758	7W-20N	B1
Briarwood Sq					
10	IHPK	60525	3147	12W-7S	B6
Briarwood St					
100	ELGN	60120	2855		D3
N Brice Ct					
1900	PLTN	60074	2753	19W-18N	C3
Brickhouse Av					
-	NHLK	60164	3028		D1
Bricknock Pl					
-	CRTE	60417	3685	0E-29S	E1
Brickstone Dr					
8100	FftT	60423	3504	10W-24S	C6
Brickton Pl					
100	CHCG	60068	2918	9W-7N	B4
100	CHCG	60631	2918	9W-7N	B4
100	PKRG	60068	2918	9W-7N	B4
100	PKRG	60631	2918	9W-7N	B4
Brickton Reau					
400	PKRG	60068	2917	11W-8N	D2
Brickvale Dr					
2300	EGVV	60007	2915		D3
2300	EGVV	60106	2915		D3
Bridal Path Dr					
-	RchT	60443	3593	8W-25S	B1
Bridalwood Ln					
17400	TYPK	60477	3424	11W-20S	A5
Bridge Rd					
-	LMNT	60439	3270		C6
Bridge St					
-	EVTN	60201	2866	3W-12N	E1
-	LYWD	60411	3510	4E-25S	B7
800	BlmT	60411	3510	4E-25S	B7
Bridgeport Dr					
-	SmbT	60193	2913		C2
1200	SMBG	60193	2913		C2
N Bridgeport Dr					
1400	MPPT	60056	2807	15W-14N	E3
Bridgeport Pl					
600	WLNG	60090	2755	15W-18N	A3
Bridgestone Ct					
500	IVNS	60010	2750	26W-17N	E6
500	IVNS	60010	2751	25W-17N	A5
Bridget Ct					
6000	BRRG	60527	3146		C7
Bridget Pl					
500	WLNG	60090	2755	15W-17N	A5
Bridgeview Ct					
700	WLNG	60090	2754	16W-17N	D6
W Bridgeview Ct					
500	PLTN	60067	2805	21W-16N	C1
Bridgeview Pt					
600	SMBG	60194	2859	22W-10N	C4
N Bridgeview St					
10	PLTN	60067	2805	21W-16N	C1
Bridgton on Asbury					
10	RGMW	60008	2806	19W-15N	B2
Bridle Ct					
10	BRRG	60527	3208		B5
S Bridle Ct					
14600	HMGN	60441	3344	15W-17S	B5
Bridle Ln					
200	SMBG	60173	2859	21W-10N	E4
Bridle Tr					
400	WLNG	60090	2755	15W-16N	B7
Bridlegate Ln					
800	NHFD	60093	2758	7W-16N	B7
Bridle Path					
-	LMNT	60439	3272	15W-13S	B4
Bridlewood Ct					
200	SMBG	60173	2859	21W-10N	E4
Bridlewood Dr					
1900	HFET	60192	2802	30W-12N	C7
1900	HFET	60192	2856	30W-12N	B1
Bridlewood Ln					
10	NHBK	60062	2757	8W-17N	D6
10	NHFD	60093	2811	7W-14N	B3
Bridlewood Rd					
10	NHBK	60062	2757	8W-17N	E6
Bridlewood Tr					
10	BrnT	60010	2803	26W-14N	D3
10	SBTN	60010	2803	26W-14N	D3
Brier St					
10	KLWH	60043	2812	4W-14N	C3
10	KLWH	60093	2812	4W-14N	C3
Brier St					
10	WNKA	60093	2812	4W-14N	C4
600	WNKA	60043	2812	4W-14N	C4
Brierhill Rd					
400	DRFD	60015	2757	10W-20N	B1
Brigantine Ct					
4600	HFET	60195	2804	24W-15N	B1
Brigantine Ln					
4500	HFET	60195	2804	24W-15N	B1
4600	SBTN	60010	2804	24W-15N	B1
Bright St					
3000	FNPK	60131	2973	13W-3N	A4
Brighton Ct					
300	CRTE	60417	3685	0W-29S	C1
600	BRLT	60103	2910		E7
1000	SMBG	60193	2912		C1
1600	NHBK	60062	2756	10W-16N	E6
2800	WSTR	60154	3086		E4
8200	ODPK	60462	3346	10W-16S	C4
S Brighton Ct					
400	PLTN	60067	2805	22W-15N	B2
Brighton Ln					
10	OKBK	60523	3086		B3
300	CRTE	60417	3685	0W-29S	C1
400	DYR	46311	3598		D4
700	LGNG	60525	3147	13W-5S	A2
1900	HFET	60195	2804	26W-12N	A7
1900	HFET	60195	2858	25W-12N	B1
5000	RNPK	60471	3594	4W-26S	D3
S Brighton Ln					
500	PLTN	60067	2805	22W-15N	B2
Brighton Pl					
10	BRRG	60527	3146		C6
600	WLNG	60090	2755	15W-18N	A3
N Brighton Pl					
200	ANHT	60004	2807	17W-14N	C4
2700	ANHT	60004	2754	17W-17N	C6
S Brighton Pl					
100	ANHT	60004	2807	17W-13N	B5
3900	CHCG	60632	3091	3W-4S	A6
W Brighton Pl					
100	MPPT	60056	2807	15W-14N	E3
100	MPPT	60056	2808	15W-14N	A3
Brighton Rd					
200	EGVV	60007	2914		C2
Brighton Bay					
200	ROSL	60172	2912		B5
Bright Ridge Rd					
10	SMBG	60193	2859	22W-10N	B5
10	SMBG	60194	2859	22W-10N	B5
Brigitte Ct					
16500	ODHL	60477	3424	11W-19S	A3
Brigitte Ter					
11100	ODPK	60467	3344	14W-16S	E4
Brindle Ct					
2800	NHBK	60062	2756	11W-17N	E4
Brinker Rd					
10	BNHL	60010	2750	28W-16N	A7
Bristol Av					
600	WSTR	60154	3029	12W-1S	C7
1400	WSTR	60154	3087	12W-1S	C1
Bristol Bnd					
11100	ODPK	60467	3423	13W-21S	A6
Bristol Cir					
1900	CPVL	60110	2801		D1
Bristol Ct					
-	RGMW	60008	2806	19W-12N	C7
10	BRRG	60527	3208		A2
200	DRFD	60015	2756	11W-20N	E2
1000	SMWD	60107	2910		E1
1200	HRPK	60133	2911		E1
1300	ROSL	60172	2912		B5
4100	NHBK	60062	2756	12W-17N	A4
5000	CPVL	60110	2801		D1
7200	GGnT	60449	3682	9W-31S	A4
S Bristol Ct					
400	PLTN	60067	2805	22W-15N	B2
Bristol Dr					
600	BRTN	60010	2751	25W-18N	A2
800	DRFD	60015	2756	11W-20N	E1
Bristol Ln					
-	LYWD	60411	3509	2E-24S	D4
400	SMBG	60194	2858	24W-11N	D4
500	EGVV	60007	2914		B2
1900	CPVL	60110	2801		D1
7500	HRPK	60133	2911		D1
7700	TYPK	60477	3424	9W-19S	D3
20700	OMFD	60461	3507	3W-25S	A7
S Bristol Ln					
700	ANHT	60005	2807	17W-13N	B7
25600	GGnT	60449	3682	9W-31S	A5
Bristol Rd					
10	NHFD	60093	2811	7W-15N	B3
Bristol St					
200	NHFD	60093	2811	7W-15N	B3
N Bristol St					
200	NHFD	60093	2811	7W-15N	B2
Bristol Wk					
1700	HFET	60195	2858	25W-12N	B1
Bristol Park Dr N					
7800	TYPK	60477	3424	9W-20S	D5
Bristol Park Dr S					
7700	TYPK	60477	3424	9W-21S	D6
Britta Av					
3500	FNPK	60131	2973	11W-4N	C3
Brittania Wy					
1400	ROSL	60172	2912		B4
Brittany Ct					
1600	WLNG	60090	2754	16W-18N	D4
2200	SMBG	60194	2857	26W-11N	E4
2200	SMBG	60194	2858	26W-11N	A4
4000	NHBK	60062	2756	12W-18N	B4
7600	FKFT	60423	3504	9W-25S	E7
E Brittany Ct					
200	ANHT	60004	2754	17W-17N	A6
Brittany Dr					
100	SMWD	60107	2856	29W-9N	E7
10600	PlsT	60462	3345	13W-15S	A1
21200	FKFT	60423	3504	9W-25S	E7
E Brittany Dr					
10	ANHT	60004	2754	17W-17N	A6
W Brittany Dr					
10	ANHT	60004	2754	18W-17N	A6
400	ANHT	60004	2753	18W-17N	E5
Brittany Ln					
400	DYR	46311	3598		D4
1400	HFET	60195	2804	24W-14N	B3
18000	LNSG	60438	3429	2E-21S	C6
18100	ThtT	60438	3429	2E-21S	C6
Brittany Rd					
3800	NHBK	60062	2756	12W-18N	B4
Brittany Tr					
-	HnrT	60120	2855		E4
100	ELGN	60120	2855		E3

STREET Block	City	ZIP	Map#	CGS	Grid
Brittney Ln					
6000	TYPK	60477	3425	7W-20S	C3
Brixham Pl					
10	SMBG	60194	2858	25W-10N	B5
Broad Av					
-	CHCG	60613	2977	1W-5N	D1
S Broad St					
2900	CHCG	60608	3091	1W-2S	D3
Broadmeadow Rd					
1100	WNKA	60093	2811	5W-15N	E3
Broadmoor Av					
10	LNSG	60438	3430		C6
10	MNSR	46321	3430		C6
N Broadmoor Ct					
1500	PLTN	60067	2752	21W-18N	D3
W Broadmoor Ct					
200	PLTN	60067	2752	21W-18N	D3
Broadmoor Dr					
8400	PSHL	60465	3274	10W-12S	B1
Broadmoor Ln					
200	BRLT	60103	2911		A4
Broadview Av					
-	BLWD	60104	3028		E5
400	HDPK	60035	2758	7W-20N	A1
400	HLSD	60162	3028		E5
W Broadview Av					
1200	CteT	60417	3596	1W-29S	A7
1200	CteT	60417	3685	1W-29S	A1
1400	CteT	60417	3684	1W-29S	E1
Broadview Village Sq					
-	NRIV	60155	3087	11W-1S	E2
-	NRIV	60546	3087	11W-1S	E2
700	BDVW	60155	3087	11W-1S	E1
Broadway Av					
-	CteT	60417	3774	1W-33S	B1
10	CHHT	60411	3508	1W-24S	A6
100	EVTN	60091	2812	3W-13N	E7
100	EVTN	60201	2812	3W-13N	E7
100	WLMT	60091	2812	3W-13N	E7
9100	BKFD	60513	3087	11W-3S	E5
14700	HRVY	60426	3350	1W-17S	A6
N Broadway Av					
10	PKRG	60068	2917	11W-8N	D2
500	PKRG	60068	2863	11W-9N	E7
S Broadway Av					
900	PKRG	60068	2917	11W-8N	E2
Broadway Ct					
1500	WLNG	60090	2754	16W-18N	D3
Broadway Ln					
2200	SMBG	60194	2857	26W-10N	E5
Broadway St					
10	MLPK	60160	3029	11W-2N	D1
10	MYWD	60153	3029	11W-0N	D3
1300	BLID	60406	3349	3W-15S	B1
1900	MLPK	60160	2973	11W-2N	D7
2000	FNPK	60131	2973	11W-2N	D7
2800	RBBN	60406	3349	3W-15S	A1
N Broadway St					
10	DSPN	60016	2862	14W-12N	D2
2800	CHCG	60614	2978	0W-3N	A4
2800	CHCG	60657	2978	0W-3N	A4
3500	CHCG	60613	2978	0W-4N	A3
3700	CHCG	60613	2977	1W-5N	E1
4400	CHCG	60613	2921	1W-5N	E7
4400	CHCG	60640	2921	1W-5N	D7
5500	CHCG	60660	2921	1W-7N	D3
6300	CHCG	60626	2921	1W-7N	D3
N Broadway St US-14					
5200	CHCG	60640	2921	1W-6N	D5
5500	CHCG	60660	2921	1W-6N	D4
Brockhurst Ct					
1000	UYPK	60466	3684	3W-30S	B3
E Brockton Ct					
2400	ANHT	60004	2807	16W-15N	C1
N Brockton Ct					
8100	HRPK	60133	2857	26W-9N	E7
S Brockton Ct					
8000	HRPK	60133	2857	26W-9N	E7
Brockton Ln					
500	SMBG	60193	2858	25W-9N	B7
9200	MaiT	60016	2863	11W-12N	D1
16400	OKFT	60452	3426	5W-19S	B2
Brockway St					
2100	PLTN	60067	2805	21W-14N	E4
2700	RGMW	60008	2805	21W-13N	E5
2700	RGMW	60067	2805	21W-13N	E5
N Brockway St					
10	PLTN	60067	2805	21W-16N	E1
100	PLTN	60067	2752	21W-16N	E7
S Brockway St					
10	PLTN	60067	2805	21W-15N	E1
1100	RGMW	60067	2805	21W-14N	E4
Brodick Ln					
10	IVNS	60067	2752	22W-17N	B4
W Brodman Av					
8400	CHCG	60656	2974	10W-5N	A1
8400	NRDG	60706	2974	10W-5N	A1
8500	CHCG	60656	2973	11W-5N	E1
Broker Av					
200	ITSC	60143	2914		D7
200	WDDL	60143	2914		D7
400	WDDL	60191	2914		D7
Broker Rd					
10	BmdT	60157	2913		C7
200	BMDL	60108	2913		B7
400	BmdT	60108	2913		C7
500	BMDL	60157	2913		B7
Bromley Ct					
1800	SMBG	60194	2858	25W-11N	A3
Bromley Pl					
800	NHBK	60062	2810	8W-16N	D1
Bromley St					
8200	ODPK	60462	3346	10W-17S	B5
W Brompton Av					
700	CHCG	60657	2977	1W-4N	E3
700	CHCG	60657	2978	0W-4N	A3
Bronx Av					
8700	SKOK	60077	2865	6W-10N	E4
10000	SKOK	60077	2811	6W-12N	E7
10000	WLMT	60091	2811	6W-12N	E7
Brook Av					
14300	ODPK	60462	3345	12W-17S	C4
19800	LYWD	60411	3509	3E-23S	E4
22000	RNPK	60471	3594	6W-26S	B3
E Brook Dr					
500	ANHT	60005	2861	17W-11N	B4
Brook Ln					
-	BGVW	60455	3210	10W-9S	C2
-	BGVW	60458	3210	10W-9S	C2
-	JSTC	60455	3210	10W-9S	C2
-	JSTC	60458	3210	10W-9S	C2
10	PSHT	60463	3274	10W-14S	C6
10	PSPK	60464	3274	10W-14S	C6
100	PTHT	60070	2808	15W-14N	A3
400	GNVW	60025	2811	6W-13N	C5
Brook Ln					
700	SMWD	60107	2857	28W-11N	B4
Brook Pl					
-	HNDL	60521	3086		A6
Brook Rd					
100	PTHT	60070	2808	15W-14N	A4
Brook Crossing Ct					
11200	ODPK	60467	3422	14W-20S	E5
Brook Crossing Dr					
11300	ODPK	60467	3422	14W-20S	E5
Brook Crossing Ln					
17300	ODPK	60467	3422	14W-20S	E5
Brookdale Ct					
2000	PltT	60067	2805	20W-13N	E6
11800	ODPK	60467	3422	14W-20S	D5
Brookdale Dr					
1000	CPVL	60110	2748		B7
1100	DndT	60110	2748		B7
N Brookdale Dr					
600	SMBG	60194	2858	25W-11N	B4
Brookdale Ln					
10	SMBG	60067	2805	20W-13N	E6
10	SMBG	60173	2805	20W-13N	E6
100	PltT	60067	2805	20W-13N	E6
200	PltT	60067	2806	20W-13N	A6
N Brookdale Ln					
200	PltT	60067	2806	20W-13N	A6
S Brookdale Ln					
200	PltT	60067	2806	20W-13N	A6
Brookdale Rd					
2700	GNVW	60025	2809	11W-15N	D2
2700	GNVW	60062	2809	11W-15N	D2
2700	NHBK	60025	2809	11W-15N	D2
2700	NHBK	60062	2809	11W-15N	D2
Brooke Ln					
-	SBTN	60010	2803	27W-15N	A1
Brookfield Av					
8400	BKFD	60513	3088	10W-3S	A6
8400	RVSD	60513	3088	10W-3S	A6
8400	RVSD	60546	3088	10W-3S	A6
8700	BKFD	60513	3087	11W-3S	E6
E Brookfield Av					
100	WhlT	60056	2808	13W-13N	E5
Brookfield Cir					
17700	ODPK	60467	3422	14W-21S	D6
19500	TYPK	60477	3504	10W-23S	B4
Brookgate Dr					
17200	ODPK	60467	3422	14W-20S	D5
Brookhaven Cir					
10	SBTN	60010	2803	27W-15N	B1
Brookhaven Dr					
200	EGVV	60007	2914		E2
Brook Hill Ct					
11800	ODPK	60467	3422	14W-21S	D6
Brookhill Ct					
200	SMBG	60193	2859	23W-9N	B7
Brook Hill Dr					
-	ODPK	60448	3422	14W-21S	D6
11200	ODPK	60467	3422	14W-20S	E4
11200	OrlT	60448	3422	13W-20S	E4
Brookhill Dr					
10	NHFD	60093	2758	7W-16N	B7
W Brookline Ct					
400	PLTN	60067	2805	21W-14N	D4
Brookline Ln					
800	PKRG	60068	2864	10W-9N	B6
Brookline St					
500	CHHT	60411	3595	2W-26S	C2
S Brooklodge Ln					
10600	PSHL	60465	3274	9W-12S	C2
Brookmeade Dr					
3200	RGMW	60008	2806	20W-12N	B7
Brook Park Ln					
10	PKFT	60466	3595	2W-28S	D6
Brookpoint Ct					
8400	TYPK	60477	3504	10W-23S	B3
Brookridge Dr					
19500	TYPK	60477	3504	10W-23S	B3
Brooks Ln					
10400	CHRG	60415	3275	8W-12S	A2
10400	CHRG	60482	3275	8W-12S	A2
10400	WRTH	60482	3275	8W-12S	A2
Brookshire Dr					
11500	ODPK	60467	3422	14W-20S	D5
11900	HMGN	60448	3422	14W-20S	D5
11900	HMGN	60467	3422	14W-20S	D5
Brookside Blvd					
20800	OMFD	60461	3507	4W-25S	A7
Brookside Ct					
1000	HRPK	60133	2911		E1
9100	ODPK	60462	3423	11W-18S	E1
9100	ODPK	60462	3424	11W-18S	A1
S Brookside Ct					
24000	CteT	60417	3598	3E-29S	A7
24000	CteT	60417	3687	3E-29S	A1
W Brookside Ct					
8100	PSPK	60464	3274	10W-14S	B6
Brookside Dr					
10	LMNT	60439	3272	15W-13S	B4
10	ROSL	60172	2912		E4
300	WLMT	60091	2812	5W-13N	A7
800	BRLT	60103	2911		A5
1400	HFET	60194	2858	26W-12N	A2
7400	HRPK	60133	2911		E1
S Brookside Dr					
11700	PSPK	60464	3274	10W-13S	C5
W Brookside Dr					
8100	PSPK	60464	3274	10W-14S	B6
Brookside Ln					
300	GLNC	60022	2758	6W-16N	D7
800	DRFD	60015	2756	11W-20N	D1
1300	NHBK	60062	2757	10W-17N	A5
1700	ElaT	60047	2753	18W-20N	D1
1700	LGGV	60047	2753	18W-20N	D1
1800	HFET	60194	2858	25W-12N	A2
2600	SMBG	60173	2805	21W-13N	C6
Brookside Rd					
10	PKFT	60466	3595	3W-28S	B6
W Brookside St					
800	PLTN	60067	2805	22W-15N	C1
800	PltT	60067	2805	22W-15N	C1
Brookside Glen Ct					
19300	TYPK	60477	3504	10W-23S	C3
Brookside Glen Dr					
7600	TYPK	60477	3504	10W-23S	C3
8700	FftT	60448	3504	10W-23S	C3
8700	MKNA	60448	3504	10W-23S	C3
Brookston Dr					
10	SMBG	60193	2859	21W-10N	D5
200	SMBG	60173	2859	21W-10N	D5
Brookstone Ct					
10	SMWD	60107	2856	29W-10N	E7
Brookstone Dr					
10	SMWD	60107	2856	29W-10N	E6
Brookton on Auburn					
10	RGMW	60008	2806	19W-14N	B3
Brookvale Dr					
700	WLNG	60090	2754	16W-18N	E3
Brookvale Ter					
700	GLNC	60022	2758	6W-16N	C7
Brookview Ct					
10	DGvT	60527	3146		A4
Brookview Dr					
23100	BlmT	60466	3595	2W-28S	C6
23100	CteT	60475	3595	2W-28S	C6
Brookview Ln					
11600	OrlT	60467	3344	14W-17S	D4
S Brookview Ln					
1700	RGMW	60067	2805	21W-13N	D5
Brookwood Av					
22300	SLVL	60411	3598	3E-27S	A4
Brookwood Ct					
10	ANHT	60004	2754	17W-16N	A7
17400	ODPK	60467	3422	14W-20S	D5
Brookwood Dr					
300	OMFD	60461	3507	3W-25S	B7
1700	FSMR	60422	3507	3W-23S	B4
6000	OKFT	60452	3425	7W-18S	C1
11500	ODPK	60467	3422	14W-20S	D5
20900	PKFT	60466	3507	3W-25S	B7
22100	BlmT	60411	3598	3E-26S	A3
22100	SLVL	60411	3598	3E-26S	A3
E Brookwood Dr					
1200	ANHT	60004	2754	17W-16N	C7
W Brookwood Dr					
10	ANHT	60004	2754	17W-16N	A6
Brookwood St					
10	BNVL	60106	2915		E7
Brookwood Ter					
300	ROSL	60172	2913		B6
Brookwood Ter 1					
300	OMFD	60461	3507	3W-24S	B6
Brookwood Ter 2					
400	OMFD	60461	3507	3W-24S	B6
Brookwood Ter 3					
500	OMFD	60461	3507	3W-24S	C6
Brookwood Ter 4					
500	OMFD	60461	3507	3W-24S	B6
Brookwood Ter 5					
600	OMFD	60461	3507	3W-24S	B6
Brookwood Ter 6					
700	OMFD	60461	3507	3W-24S	B6
Brookwood Wy Dr					
2600	RGMW	60008	2806	20W-14N	A5
Brophy Av					
1200	PKRG	60068	2918	10W-7N	A3
1800	CHCG	60631	2918	10W-7N	A4
W Bross Av					
2200	CHCG	60608	3091	2W-3S	B4
Brougham Dr					
10	WLNG	60090	2754	16W-18N	D3
10	WLNG	60090	2755	15W-18N	A2
Brower Dr					
900	ROSL	60172	2912		C5
Brown Av					
200	FTPK	60130	3030	9W-0N	D4
700	EVTN	60202	2866	3W-10N	E5
2100	EVTN	60201	2866	3W-12N	E1
7500	RVFT	60305	3030	9W-0N	C4
S Brown Av					
1300	HMND	46394	3280		E4
Brown Cir					
500	EGVV	60007	2913		D1
Brown Ct					
800	SMBG	60193	2912		C1
Brown Dr					
11800	LMNT	60439	3270		C6
Brown Ln					
8700	TYPK	60477	3424	11W-21S	A6
Brown St					
-	FDHT	60411	3509	1E-24S	B6
1200	DSPN	60016	2862	13W-11N	E3
1300	DSPN	60016	2863	13W-11N	A3
5100	SKOK	60077	2865	6W-10N	D5
W Brown St					
1400	ANHT	60004	2806	18W-14N	D3
Brown Derby Rd					
-	HMWD	60430	3428	0W-21S	B5
-	TNTN	60430	3428	0W-21S	B6
-	TNTN	60476	3428	0W-21S	B6
Brownell St					
200	ThtT	60476	3428	0E-21S	E6
200	TNTN	60476	3428	0E-21S	E6
Browning Av					
10	WDND	60118	2801		A3
E Browning Av					
500	CHCG	60653	3092	0E-3S	D5
Browning Dr					
17200	ODPK	60467	3423	13W-20S	B5
S Brownstone Av					
1400	ANHT	60005	2861	17W-11N	C4
1400	MPPT	60005	2861	17W-11N	C4
1400	MPPT	60056	2861	17W-11N	C4
Brownstone Pl					
-	SMBG	60193	2912		B2
Brownville Rd					
200	HDPK	60035	2758	7W-20N	C2
Bruce Av					
600	FSMR	60422	3507	3W-22S	B2
600	HMWD	60430	3507	3W-22S	B1
Bruce Dr					
900	ELGN	60120	2855		C4
4800	RNPK	60471	3594	6W-27S	B5
4800	UYPK	60471	3594	6W-27S	B5
W Bruce Dr					
8400	MaiT	60714	2864	10W-10N	A5
8400	NLES	60714	2864	10W-10N	A5
8700	NLES	60714	2863	10W-10N	E5
N Bruce Ln					
700	GNWD	60425	3428	0W-21S	B7
E Bruce Rd					
12400	HMGN	60448	3422	15W-21S	B5
Brucewood Ct					
10	BFGV	60089	2754	16W-18N	C2
Brucewood Dr					
200	BFGV	60089	2754	16W-18N	C3
Brumley Dr					
2400	FSMR	60422	3507	3W-22S	B1
3600	FSMR	60422	3506	4W-22S	D1
3600	FSMR	60429	3506	4W-22S	D1
3600	HLCT	60429	3506	4W-22S	D1
Brummel Dr					
1200	EGVV	60007	2861	17W-9N	C7
1800	EGvT	60007	2861	16W-9N	D7
Brummel Pl					
2200	EVTN	60202	2866	3W-9N	D6
Brummel St					
900	EVTN	60202	2867	2W-9N	A6
1900	EVTN	60202	2866	3W-9N	E6
Brummel St					
3800	SKOK	60076	2866	4W-9N	B6
4600	SKOK	60076	2865	5W-9N	E6
4900	SKOK	60077	2865	6W-9N	D6
Bruning Dr W					
-	ITSC	60143	2913		D4
W Bruns Rd					
5700	MONE	60449	3682	8W-31S	C6
5700	MonT	60449	3682	8W-31S	C6
6800	GGnT	60449	3682	8W-32S	A6
Brunswick Cir					
900	SMBG	60193	2913		B1
Brunswick Ct					
300	SMWD	60107	2857	28W-9N	A7
300	SMWD	60107	2911		A1
1300	ELGN	60120	2801		D7
Brunswick Dr					
200	BFGV	60089	2754	16W-20N	D1
Brunswick Hbr					
1000	SMBG	60193	2913		B1
E Brunswick St					
10	HMND	46327	3352		C4
Brush Rd					
2500	SMBG	60173	2805	21W-13N	D6
Brush Hill Ln					
1700	GNVW	60025	2810	8W-15N	E2
Brushwood Dr					
10	RchT	60443	3593	8W-26S	B1
Brushwood Ln					
8100	TYPK	60477	3504	10W-23S	C3
17100	ODPK	60467	3422	14W-20S	D5
Bryant Av					
-	PLTN	60067	2805	21W-14N	D4
600	BRTN	60010	2750	25W-20N	E1
700	WNKA	60093	2759	5W-16N	B7
700	WNKA	60093	2812	5W-16N	B1
2300	EVTN	60201	2867	2W-12N	A1
2600	EVTN	60201	2813	2W-13N	A7
17300	HLCT	60429	3427	3W-20S	A5
W Bryant Av					
10	PLTN	60067	2805	21W-14N	D4
10	RGMW	60008	2805	21W-14N	E4
Bryce Ct					
300	BRLT	60103	2910		E2
Bryce Tr					
500	ROSL	60172	2913		B3
Brynhaven Ct					
500	EGVV	60007	2861	18W-10N	A6
Brynhaven St					
500	EGVV	60007	2861	18W-10N	A6
Bryn Mawr Av					
-	CHCG	60018	2917	12W-6N	B6
-	CHCG	60666	2917	12W-6N	B6
-	ITSC	60143	2914		B5
-	RSMT	60018	2917	12W-6N	B6
-	SRPK	60176	2917	12W-6N	B6
-	SRPK	60666	2917	12W-6N	B6
-	WDDL	60191	2915		C5
10	AddT	60106	2915		C5
10	BNVL	60106	2915		D5
400	BmdT	60172	2913		A5
400	ROSL	60172	2913		A5
500	BmdT	60172	2912		E5
600	BRLT	60103	2910		D6
600	ROSL	60172	2912		E5
E Bryn Mawr Av					
100	ITSC	60143	2914		C5
800	ROSL	60172	2913		C5
W Bryn Mawr Av					
10	BmdT	60172	2913		A5
10	ROSL	60172	2913		A5
100	ITSC	60143	2914		B5
500	BmdT	60172	2912		D6
500	ROSL	60172	2912		C6
900	CHCG	60640	2921	1W-7N	D4
900	CHCG	60660	2921	1W-7N	E4
1500	ITSC	60143	2913		E5
2400	CHCG	60625	2921	3W-7N	A4
2400	CHCG	60659	2921	3W-7N	A4
2700	CHCG	60625	2920	5W-7N	B5
2700	CHCG	60659	2920	5W-7N	A5
3900	CHCG	60630	2920	5W-7N	A5
3900	CHCG	60646	2920	5W-6N	A5
5400	CHCG	60630	2919	7W-7N	C4
5400	CHCG	60646	2919	7W-7N	C4
6300	CHCG	60631	2919	7W-7N	A4
6300	CHCG	60656	2919	7W-7N	A4
6600	CHCG	60656	2918	8W-7N	D4
7800	NpkT	60631	2918	9W-7N	B5
7900	LydT	60656	2918	9W-6N	B5
7900	NpkT	60656	2918	9W-6N	B5
8000	LydT	60631	2918	10W-6N	A5
8000	MaiT	60631	2918	10W-6N	A5
8000	MaiT	60656	2918	10W-6N	B5
8200	CHCG	60631	2918	10W-7N	A5
8600	CHCG	60631	2917	10W-7N	E5
8600	CHCG	60656	2917	10W-7N	E5
Bryn Mawr Ct					
600	SMBG	60194	2857	27W-11N	C3
Buccaneer Dr					
900	GNVW	60025	2810	10W-14N	A3
900	SMBG	60173	2805	21W-13N	C5
Buchanan Ln					
10	SMWD	60107	2856	29W-10N	E5
Buchanan St					
10	EGvT	60018	2862	15W-9N	A7
Buck Dr					
10400	ODPK	60467	3423	13W-20S	B4
Buck Pth					
16700	LKPT	60441	3342	20W-17S	A6
16700	LktT	60441	3342	20W-17S	A6
Buck Tr					
7900	BRRG	60527	3208		C2
Buckboard Dr					
10	WLNG	60090	2755	15W-18N	A2
400	WLNG	60090	2754	15W-18N	E2
W Buckeye Ct					
15300	LKPT	60441	3342	20W-18S	B7
Buckeye Dr					
400	WLNG	60090	2755	13W-17N	D5
600	HFET	60194	2859	23W-11N	A4
N Buckeye Rd					
20500	DRPK	60010	2751	23W-20N	E1
20500	ElaT	60010	2751	23W-20N	E1
Bucki Ln					
8500	WLSP	60480	3208		E4
Buckingham Av					
1600	WSTR	60154	3087	13W-1S	A2
3000	LGPK	60525	3087	13W-2S	A4
Buckingham Cir					
300	ELGN	60120	2855		C4
Buckingham Ct					
10	DRFD	60015	2756	11W-20N	E2
100	EGVV	60007	2914		D3
200	SMBG	60193	2859	22W-10N	C6
Buckingham Ct					
700	HFET	60194	2858	24W-11N	C3
1100	WLNG	60090	2754	16W-18N	D3
8400	WLSP	60480	3209	13W-9S	A3
Buckingham Dr					
-	ODPK	60467	3422	14W-21S	D7
-	ODPK	60467	3423	13W-21S	A6
200	BRLT	60103	2911		A6
Buckingham Ln					
10	BFGV	60089	2754	16W-20N	D1
W Buckingham Pl					
600	CHCG	60657	2977	1W-4N	E3
600	CHCG	60657	2978	0W-4N	A3
Buckingham Glen Cir					
1500	NfdT	60025	2810	10W-14N	A5
Buckingham Place Dr					
9000	MaiT	60016	2863	11W-11N	E3
9000	NLES	60714	2863	10W-11N	E3
Buckland Ln					
2500	NHBK	60062	2757	10W-18N	A3
Buckley Ct					
500	UYPK	60466	3684	3W-30S	C3
Buckley Rd					
8800	HMTN	60456	3212	5W-10S	A4
Bucknel Ct					
100	GNVW	60025	2810	10W-15N	B2
Buckskin					
10	LMNT	60439	3272	15W-13S	B5
Buckskin Ln					
10	HnrT	60107	2856	30W-10N	C5
10	SMWD	60107	2856	30W-10N	C5
600	CPVL	60110	2748		B7
Buckthorn Cir					
300	NHBK	60062	2756	13W-18N	A3
Buckthorn Ct					
400	BFGV	60089	2754	16W-20N	D1
18300	TYPK	60477	3424	10W-22S	A7
Buckthorn Dr					
1500	HFET	60195	2804	24W-15N	B2
E Buckthorn Dr					
1800	MPPT	60056	2808	13W-15N	E3
Buckthorn Ln					
300	ELGN	60120	2855		E3
Buckthorn Rd					
10	SBTN	60010	2803	26W-14N	D4
Buckthorn Ter					
600	BFGV	60089	2754	15W-20N	E1
Buckthorne Ln					
200	HLSD	60162	3028		E5
N Budd St					
2400	RVGV	60171	2974	10W-3N	A5
Budingen Ln					
8400	TYPK	60477	3424	10W-20S	B5
Buege Ln					
-	WLSP	60480	3208		D3
Buell Ct					
9900	OKLN	60453	3211	6W-11S	D7
10100	OKLN	60453	3275	6W-11S	D1
W Buena Av					
600	CHCG	60613	2977	1W-5N	E1
600	CHCG	60613	2978	0W-5N	A1
Buena Vista Av					
1600	CHHT	60411	3596	1W-25S	A1
Buena Vista Cir					
1600	CHHT	60411	3596	1W-26S	A1
Buffalo Av					
700	CTCY	60409	3352	3E-18S	A7
1300	CTCY	60409	3430	3E-19S	A2
S Buffalo Av					
8700	CHCG	60617	3216	4E-10S	A4
10600	CHCG	60617	3280	3E-12S	A3
13000	CHCG	60633	3280	3E-15S	A7
13100	CHCG	60633	3352	3E-15S	A1
Buffalo Tr					
400	WLNG	60090	2754	16W-17N	D5
N Buffalo Grove Rd					
-	ANHT	60090	2754	16W-17N	C6
-	WLNG	60090	2754	16W-17N	C5
10	BFGV	60089	2754	16W-20N	C1
2700	ANHT	60004	2754	16W-17N	C6
3300	WhlT	60004	2754	16W-17N	C6
3500	WhlT	60089	2754	16W-17N	C6
N Buffalo Grove Rd CO-W14					
10	BFGV	60089	2754	17W-20N	C1
S Buffalo Grove Rd					
-	WhlT	60004	2754	16W-17N	C4
10	BFGV	60089	2754	16W-18N	D4
10	WLNG	60089	2754	16W-18N	C2
100	WLNG	60090	2754	16W-18N	D3
800	WhlT	60089	2754	16W-17N	C4
Bulger Av					
16700	HLCT	60429	3427	2W-20S	C4
16700	MKHM	60426	3427	2W-20S	C4
Bulldog Dr					
7600	SMMT	60501	3148	9W-6S	C3
S Bulletin Ct					
5100	HMND	46320	3352		D6
Bulrush Dr					
1600	HFET	60194	2858	25W-11N	B3
Bumble Bee Dr					
9200	MaiT	60016	2863	11W-11N	D3
Bundoran Ct					
13200	PlsT	60462	3345	11W-15S	E1
Bundoran Dr					
9200	PlsT	60462	3345	11W-15S	E1
Bunker Av					
1300	FSMR	60422	3507	3W-23S	B3
Bunker Dr					
8000	ODPK	60462	3346	10W-18S	C6
Bunker Ln					
1300	CPVL	60110	2801		C1
4000	WLMT	60091	2811	7W-14N	B5
Bunker St					
1900	CHHT	60411	3595	2W-26S	D2
Bunratty Dr					
1000	LKPT	60441	3342	21W-18S	A7
Bunting Ct					
200	VrnT	60015	2755	14W-20N	B1
W Bunting Ln					
600	ANHT	60004	2807	16W-14N	E4
600	MPPT	60004	2807	16W-14N	E4
600	MPPT	60056	2807	16W-14N	E4
Burberry Cir					
10	SMBG	60173	2859	22W-10N	C6
Burberry Ln					
1400	SMBG	60173	2859	21W-10N	E5
Burgess Ct					
600	SMBG	60194	2857	27W-11N	C3
N Burgoyne Rd					
1000	ANHT	60004	2806	18W-15N	E2
W Burgoyne Rd					
1200	ANHT	60004	2806	18W-15N	D2
Burgundy Ct					
600	EGVV	60007	2860	19W-9N	C7

STREET Block	City	ZIP	Map#	CGS	Grid
Burgundy Ln					
2400	NHBK	60062	2810	10W-15N	A1
18000	HLCT	60429	3426	4W-21S	E6
Burgundy Pkwy					
1500	SMBG	60193	2857	27W-10N	D6
1500	SMWD	60107	2857	27W-10N	D6
E Buried Oak Dr					
3100	CteT	60417	3598	4E-29S	B7
Burke Ct					
200	SMBG	60193	2859	22W-10N	C6
N Burke Dr					
1900	ANHT	60004	2807	17W-16N	B1
2000	ANHT	60004	2754	17W-16N	B7
Burkhardt Ct					
300	FTPK	60130	3030	9W-0N	D5
W Burkhardt Dr					
2800	CHCG	60623	3032	3W-1S	E7
W Burkitt Pl					
700	ANHT	60004	2753	18W-18N	E2
Burleigh Ln					
100	IVNS	60067	2752	22W-18N	B4
S Burley Av					
-	CHCG	60617	3280	3E-12S	A3
8700	CHCG	60617	3216	4E-10S	A4
12300	CHCG	60633	3280	3E-14S	A6
13100	CHCG	60633	3352	3E-15S	A1
S Burley Av US-41					
8500	CHCG	60617	3216	4E-9S	A3
Burling Rd					
10	RVSD	60546	3088	9W-3S	C5
N Burling St					
1300	CHCG	60610	3034	0W-1N	A1
2400	CHCG	60614	2978	0W-3N	A5
2800	CHCG	60657	2978	0W-3N	A4
Burlington Av					
10	LGNG	60525	3087	13W-4S	A7
10	WNSP	60558	3086		E7
10	WNSP	60558	3087	13W-4S	A7
1000	WNSP	60558	3146		D1
8800	BKFD	60513	3088	11W-3S	A6
8900	BKFD	60513	3087	11W-4S	D6
E Burlington Av					
10	LGNG	60525	3087	12W-4S	C7
W Burlington Av					
10	LGNG	60525	3087	12W-4S	B7
E Burlington St					
10	RVSD	60546	3088	9W-3S	D5
300	BRWN	60402	3088	9W-3S	D5
300	RVSD	60402	3088	9W-3S	D5
W Burlington St					
100	BKFD	60513	3088	10W-3S	B5
100	RVSD	60513	3088	10W-3S	B5
100	RVSD	60546	3088	10W-3S	B5
Burlwood Ct					
400	RchT	60443	3593	8W-26S	B2
Burnham Av					
100	BNHM	60409	3352	3E-18S	B7
100	BNHM	60633	3352	3E-18S	B7
100	CTCY	60409	3352	3E-17S	B6
900	CTCY	60409	3430	4E-19S	B3
1500	LNSG	60438	3430	3E-19S	B3
18700	LNSG	60438	3510	3E-24S	B6
19300	LNSG	60411	3510	3E-22S	B2
19400	LYWD	60411	3510	3E-23S	B2
20300	BlmT	60411	3510	4E-24S	B5
21100	BlmT	60411	3598	3E-27S	B5
22300	SLVL	60411	3598	3E-27S	B5
22400	BlmT	46311	3598	3E-27S	B4
22900	CteT	60417	3598	3E-27S	B5
S Burnham Av					
-	BNHM	60409	3352	4E-16S	B4
-	CTCY	60409	3352	4E-16S	B4
7600	CHCG	60649	3215	3E-8S	E1
7800	CHCG	60617	3215	3E-8S	E1
13800	BNHM	60633	3352	4E-16S	B4
13800	CHCG	60633	3352	3E-16S	B2
Burnham Ct					
900	GNVW	60025	2810	9W-13N	B6
Burnham Dr					
-	HFET	60010	2804	24W-15N	B1
500	UYPK	60466	3684	3W-29S	B2
4500	HFET	60195	2804	24W-15N	B1
Burnham Pl					
100	EVTN	60202	2867	2W-10N	C4
S Burning Bush Ct					
13800	HMGN	60441	3343	16W-16S	E3
Burning Bush Ln					
-	MPPT	60056	2808	13W-15N	E2
-	PTHT	60056	2808	13W-15N	E2
-	PTHT	60070	2808	13W-15N	E2
1500	HFET	60195	2804	24W-15N	B2
N Burning Bush Ln					
800	MPPT	60056	2808	13W-14N	E5
800	WhlT	60056	2808	13W-13N	E5
1800	PTHT	60056	2808	13W-15N	E2
1800	PTHT	60070	2808	13W-15N	E2
E Burning Tree Ct					
1600	ANHT	60004	2754	16W-17N	C5
1600	WLNG	60090	2754	16W-17N	C5
Burning Tree Ln					
10	DRFD	60015	2756	11W-20N	D2
E Burning Tree Ln					
400	ANHT	60004	2754	17W-17N	B5
W Burning Tree Ln					
400	ANHT	60004	2753	18W-17N	E5
Burning Tree Rd					
10	RGMW	60008	2806	20W-13N	A6
Burnley Cir					
400	SMBG	60193	2859	22W-10N	B6
Burnley Dr					
11600	ODPK	60467	3344	14W-16S	D4
S Burno Dr					
400	PLTN	60067	2805	21W-15N	D2
Burns Av					
600	FSMR	60422	3507	3W-22S	B2
600	FSMR	60430	3507	3W-22S	B2
600	HMWD	60430	3507	3W-22S	B2
1600	WSTR	60154	3086		E1
Burns Dr					
1300	ELGN	60120	2855		D6
S Burnside Av					
9100	CHCG	60619	3214	0E-10S	D5
Burnside Cir					
200	BRLT	60103	2911		A5
Burnside Ct					
-	OMFD	60461	3506	4W-24S	D5
Burnt Ember Ct					
10	BFGV	60089	2754	17W-20N	A1
Burnt Ember Ln					
300	BFGV	60089	2754	17W-20N	A1
Burr Av					
700	WNKA	60093	2811	5W-16N	E1
700	WNKA	60093	2812	5W-16N	A1
800	WNKA	60093	2759	5W-16N	A7

STREET Block	City	ZIP	Map#	CGS	Grid
Burris Ct					
10	PSHT	60463	3275	8W-14S	B6
Burr Oak Av					
200	DRFD	60015	2756	11W-20N	D1
2000	BLID	60406	3277	3W-14S	B7
2000	BLID	60827	3277	3W-14S	B7
2000	CTPK	60827	3277	3W-14S	B7
2200	FTPK	60406	3088	9W-2S	C2
2200	FTPK	60546	3088	9W-2S	C2
2200	NRIV	60546	3088	9W-2S	C2
2500	RVSD	60546	3088	9W-2S	C3
3000	ALSP	60406	3276	4W-14S	D7
3000	BLID	60406	3276	4W-14S	D7
3300	WthT	60406	3276	4W-14S	E7
3400	WthT	60803	3276	4W-14S	D7
3500	ALSP	60803	3276	4W-14S	D7
5800	BKLY	60163	3028		C4
W Burr Oak Av					
-	BLID	60827	3277	2W-15S	C7
1600	CTPK	60827	3277	2W-15S	C7
1700	BLID	60406	3277	2W-14S	D7
Burr Oak Av E					
-	ELGN	60120	2855		C7
Burr Oak Av S					
-	ELGN	60120	2855		C7
Burr Oak Ct					
-	PSHT	60463	3347	7W-15S	B1
-	SMWD	60107	2856	30W-9N	C7
100	DRFD	60015	2756	11W-20N	D2
900	OKBK	60523	3086		B1
1400	HNDL	60521	3086		B5
Burr Oak Dr					
1300	GNVW	60025	2811	8W-14N	A3
1400	GNVW	60025	2810	8W-14N	E3
16800	HMGN	60441	3422	15W-20S	B4
E Burr Oak Dr					
100	ANHT	60004	2754	17W-17N	B5
1300	MPPT	60056	2808	13W-14N	E4
1700	WLNG	60090	2754	17W-17N	C5
W Burr Oak Dr					
10	ANHT	60004	2754	17W-17N	A5
500	ANHT	60004	2753	18W-17N	E5
Burr Oak Dr E					
1900	GNVW	60025	2811	8W-14N	A4
Burr Oak Dr W					
1900	GNVW	60025	2810	8W-14N	E3
Burr Oak Ln					
10	SMBG	60193	2859	23W-10N	B6
700	PTHT	60070	2808	14W-14N	C3
700	UYPK	60466	3684	3W-29S	B2
1200	BRTN	60010	2751	24W-20N	B1
7100	CTSD	60525	3147	12W-8S	B7
11400	BRRG	60527	3208		D2
17300	HLCT	60429	3426	4W-20S	E5
Burr Oak Pl					
500	HNDL	60521	3086		B5
Burr Oak Rd					
1400	HNDL	60521	3086		B5
1600	HMWD	60430	3427	2W-21S	D6
2300	NHFD	60093	2811	8W-15N	A2
Burr Oak St					
2100	HRPK	60133	2911		C3
Burr Oaks Ln					
1900	HDPK	60035	2757	9W-20N	C1
Burr Ridge Clb					
200	BRRG	60527	3146		C5
Burr Ridge Dr					
1700	HFET	60195	2804	25W-14N	A4
Burr Ridge Pkwy					
10	BRRG	60527	3208		C1
1000	BRRG	60527	3146		B7
Burton Av					
400	HDPK	60035	2758	7W-20N	B1
Burton Ct					
11500	WSTR	60154	3086		C3
E Burton Ct					
600	HMND	46394	3280		E5
Burton Dr					
200	BRLT	60103	2909		D4
2600	WSTR	60154	3086		D3
Burton Ln					
1800	PKRG	60068	2863	11W-10N	E4
E Burton Pl					
10	CHCG	60610	3034	0E-1N	C1
S Burton Pl					
100	ANHT	60005	2807	17W-13N	B5
W Burton Pl					
10	CHCG	60610	3034	0W-1N	B1
Burton Ter					
900	GNVW	60025	2811	7W-14N	A5
E Burville Rd					
10	CteT	60417	3685	0E-30S	E3
10	CteT	60417	3686	1E-30S	B3
2900	CteT	60417	3687	4E-30S	B2
3200	CteT	46311	3687	4E-30S	B2
3200	SjnT	46311	3687	4E-30S	B2
W Burville Rd					
10	CRTE	60417	3685	0W-30S	C3
10	CteT	60417	3685	0W-30S	C3
W Bush Ct					
6000	MONE	60449	3682	7W-31S	D5
E Business Center Dr					
400	MPPT	60056	2808	14W-13N	C5
E Busse Av					
-	DSPN	60016	2808	15W-12N	B7
10	MPPT	60056	2808	15W-12N	B7
N Busse Av					
5000	CHCG	60656	2918	8W-6N	E6
W Busse Av					
10	MPPT	60056	2808	15W-12N	A7
1100	MPPT	60056	2807	16W-12N	D7
Busse Hwy					
10	PKRG	60068	2918	10W-9N	A1
200	PKRG	60068	2864	10W-9N	A7
500	PKRG	60068	2863	10W-9N	E7
1700	DSPN	60016	2863	12W-10N	C5
Busse Rd					
10	EGVV	60007	2861	16W-9N	C7
10	MPPT	60005	2861	17W-10N	C6
10	MPPT	60056	2861	17W-10N	C6
600	EGvT	60007	2861	16W-9N	C7
900	EGVV	60007	2915		C3
1000	BNVL	60106	2915		C4
1000	EGVV	60106	2915		C4
Busse Rd SR-83					
200	EGVV	60007	2861	16W-9N	C7
600	EGvT	60007	2861	16W-9N	C7
900	EGVV	60007	2915		C3
1000	BNVL	60106	2915		C4
1000	EGVV	60106	2915		C4
S Busse Rd					
10	ANHT	60056	2807	16W-12N	C7
10	MPPT	60056	2807	16W-12N	C7
200	MPPT	60056	2861	16W-10N	C5
1700	EGvT	60056	2861	16W-10N	C5

STREET Block	City	ZIP	Map#	CGS	Grid
S Busse Rd					
2100	MPPT	60005	2861	16W-10N	C5
2200	EGVV	60007	2861	17W-10N	C6
Bussey Ct					
800	SMWD	60107	2911		C1
Butera Ln					
10	SBTN	60010	2803	26W-14N	C4
Butler Av					
3200	CHHT	60411	3596	0W-27S	B4
3200	SCHT	60411	3596	0W-27S	B4
3200	STGR	60475	3596	0W-27S	B4
Butler Ct					
8800	ODPK	60462	3424	10W-18S	A1
S Butler Ct					
26900	CteT	60417	3774	0W-32S	D1
Butler Dr					
200	BRLT	60103	2909		C4
S Butler Dr					
-	CHCG	60628	3279	1E-14S	A6
12400	CHCG	60633	3279	1E-14S	A6
Butler Pl					
500	PKRG	60068	2918	10W-8N	B1
Butler St					
-	BlmT	60411	3509	1E-24S	B6
-	FDHT	60411	3509	1E-24S	B6
2500	BlmT	60411	3596	0W-26S	C2
2500	CHHT	60411	3596	0W-26S	C2
Butler Bay Ct					
1000	ELGN	60120	2855		D1
Butte Ln					
200	CPVL	60110	2748		B6
Butter Creek Ct					
-	HFET	60194	2858	23W-11N	E3
Buttercup Ct					
13000	HMGN	60441	3344	16W-18S	A7
Buttercup Ln					
100	MTSN	60443	3593	7W-26S	C2
100	SjnT	46311	3598		D5
400	SMBG	60173	2859	21W-10N	E4
1100	BRLT	60103	2910		D7
Buttercup Pl					
500	SMBG	60173	2859	21W-11N	E3
Buttercup Bank					
100	BRRG	60527	3146		C5
Butterfield Cir					
1800	FSMR	60422	3507	3W-23S	B4
1800	FSMR	60461	3507	3W-23S	B4
1800	RchT	60461	3507	3W-23S	B4
Butterfield Ct					
100	RGMW	60008	2805	22W-13N	B5
400	HFET	60067	2804	23W-14N	E4
Butterfield Dr					
16700	CCHL	60478	3426	4W-20S	D3
16700	MKHM	60426	3426	4W-20S	D3
Butterfield Ln					
1700	FSMR	60422	3507	2W-23S	C4
1700	OMFD	60422	3507	2W-23S	C4
1700	OMFD	60461	3507	2W-23S	C4
8600	ODPK	60462	3346	11W-15S	A2
Butterfield Pkwy					
21200	MTSN	60443	3594	4W-25S	D1
Butterfield Rd					
1500	FSMR	60422	3507	3W-23S	B4
3300	BLWD	60104	3029	12W-0N	A4
3900	BLWD	60162	3029	12W-0N	A4
3900	HLSD	60162	3029	12W-0N	A4
4000	BLWD	60104	3028		D5
4300	HLSD	60162	3028		D5
5200	BKLY	60162	3028		C5
5200	BKLY	60163	3028		C5
5200	HLSD	60163	3028		C5
5900	EMHT	60162	3028		C6
6000	EMHT	60126	3028		B6
22300	RNPK	60471	3594	5W-27S	C4
Butterfield Rd SR-56					
4000	BLWD	60104	3029	13W-0N	A4
4000	BLWD	60162	3029	13W-0N	A4
4000	HLSD	60162	3029	13W-0N	A4
4300	BLWD	60104	3028		D5
4300	HLSD	60162	3028		D5
5200	BKLY	60162	3028		C5
5200	HLSD	60162	3028		C5
5200	HLSD	60163	3028		C5
5900	EMHT	60162	3028		C6
6000	EMHT	60126	3028		B6
E Butterfield Rd					
500	BKLY	60162	3028		A6
500	BKLY	60163	3028		A6
500	EMHT	60126	3028		A6
500	EMHT	60162	3028		A6
E Butterfield Rd SR-56					
100	EMHT	60126	3028		A6
500	BKLY	60162	3028		A6
500	BKLY	60163	3028		A6
500	EMHT	60162	3028		A6
Butterfly Ln					
2200	GNVW	60025	2810	9W-15N	C3
Butternut Ct					
800	ROSL	60172	2913		A7
Butternut Ln					
200	SMWD	60107	2857	27W-10N	C6
900	NHBK	60062	2757	10W-17N	A5
1000	MPPT	60056	2807	16W-14N	D3
1000	WhlT	60004	2807	16W-14N	D3
W Butternut Ln					
1300	ANHT	60005	2806	18W-14N	D4
Butternut Rd					
200	BNHL	60010	2749	28W-18N	E2
200	BNHL	60010	2750	28W-18N	A3
17500	HLCT	60429	3427	3W-21S	B5
Buttitta Dr					
1500	HRPK	60107	2857	27W-9N	D7
1500	HRPK	60133	2857	27W-9N	D7
1500	SMWD	60107	2857	27W-9N	D7
Buttonwood Cir					
1600	SMBG	60173	2859	21W-10N	E6
Buttonwood Ct					
10	IHPK	60525	3146		D4
Buttonwood Ln					
1100	NHBK	60062	2757	8W-17N	D5
1300	GNVW	60025	2810	9W-13N	D5
Buttonwood Wk					
2900	HLCT	60429	3427	3W-21S	A6
Buxton Ct					
1500	WLNG	60090	2754	16W-17N	D6
Byrd Rd					
500	RVSD	60546	3088	9W-2S	D3
Byron Ct					
700	OMFD	60461	3506	4W-25S	D6
S Byron Ct					
700	MPPT	60056	2862	15W-11N	A2
Byron Dr					
16300	ODHL	60462	3424	11W-19S	A2
16300	ODHL	60477	3424	11W-19S	A2
16300	ODPK	60462	3424	11W-19S	A2

STREET Block	City	ZIP	Map#	CGS	Grid
Byron St					
6000	RSMT	60018	2917	12W-7N	B4
9300	SRPK	60176	2973	11W-4N	C2
W Byron St					
1000	CHCG	60613	2977	1W-4N	E2
1900	CHCG	60618	2977	3W-4N	A2
2800	CHCG	60618	2976	4W-4N	D2
4100	CHCG	60641	2976	5W-4N	A2
5500	CHCG	60641	2975	7W-4N	C2
6400	CHCG	60634	2975	8W-4N	A2
6800	CHCG	60634	2974	9W-4N	D2
C					
W C St					
-	MYWD	60153	3030	10W-1S	A7
-	PvsT	60141	3030	10W-1S	A7
S Cabernet Ct					
10	BRRG	60527	3146		C5
Cable Ct					
400	SMBG	60193	2858	25W-9N	A7
Cabot Ln					
1300	SMBG	60193	2858	25W-9N	B7
1600	GNVW	60025	2810	10W-14N	A4
W Cabrini St					
600	CHCG	60607	3034	0W-0S	A6
1200	CHCG	60607	3033	1W-0S	D6
Caddy Av					
100	CPVL	60110	2748		C7
Caddy Ct					
9000	ODPK	60462	3345	11W-17S	E5
9000	ODPK	60462	3346	11W-17S	A5
Caddy St					
2400	FSMR	60422	3507	3W-23S	B3
S Cadwell Av					
400	EMHT	60126	3028		B6
800	BKLY	60162	3028		B6
800	BKLY	60163	3028		B6
800	EMHT	60162	3028		B6
1000	PvsT	60126	3028		B7
1000	YkTp	60126	3028		B7
N Cady Dr					
100	PLTN	60074	2753	19W-16N	B7
100	PLTN	60074	2806	19W-16N	B1
Caesar Dr					
400	BNHL	60010	2750	27W-18N	B3
Cahill Rd					
400	SMWD	60107	2856	29W-10N	E5
W Cahill Ter					
7800	CHCG	60634	2974	9W-4N	B3
Caitlin Ct					
6800	WLBK	60527	3146		A7
Caladonia Dr					
9400	TYPK	60477	3423	11W-20S	E4
Calais Cir					
600	HDPK	60035	2757	8W-20N	D1
Calchester on Auburn					
10	RGMW	60008	2806	19W-14N	C3
Caldwell Av					
300	CHHT	60411	3508	1W-24S	A5
7900	MNGV	60053	2864	8W-10N	E4
7900	NLES	60714	2864	8W-10N	E4
Caldwell Av US-14					
7900	MNGV	60053	2864	8W-10N	E4
7900	NLES	60714	2864	8W-10N	E4
N Caldwell Av					
-	NLES	60053	2865	8W-9N	A7
5700	CHCG	60646	2920	5W-7N	A4
6000	CHCG	60646	2919	7W-8N	B2
6800	CHCG	60714	2919	7W-8N	B2
6800	NLES	60646	2919	7W-8N	B2
6800	NLES	60714	2919	7W-8N	B2
7200	CHCG	60646	2865	8W-9N	A7
7200	NLES	60714	2865	8W-9N	A7
7900	MNGV	60053	2865	8W-9N	A7
7900	MNGV	60714	2865	8W-9N	A7
8000	MNGV	60053	2864	8W-10N	E5
8000	MNGV	60714	2864	8W-10N	E5
8000	NLES	60714	2864	8W-10N	E5
N Caldwell Av US-14					
-	NLES	60053	2865	8W-9N	A7
6000	CHCG	60646	2919	7W-8N	B2
6800	CHCG	60714	2919	7W-8N	B2
6800	NLES	60646	2919	7W-8N	B2
6800	NLES	60714	2919	7W-8N	B2
7200	CHCG	60646	2865	8W-9N	A7
7200	NLES	60714	2865	8W-9N	A7
7900	MNGV	60053	2865	8W-9N	A7
7900	MNGV	60714	2865	8W-9N	A7
8000	MNGV	60053	2864	8W-10N	E5
8000	MNGV	60714	2864	8W-10N	E5
8000	NLES	60714	2864	8W-10N	E5
Caldwell Ln					
1400	HFET	60194	2858	25W-12N	B2
E Calendar Av					
400	LGNG	60525	3087	12W-4S	C6
700	BKFD	60513	3087	12W-4S	C6
700	LGNG	60513	3087	12W-4S	C6
W Calendar Av					
10	LGNG	60525	3087	12W-4S	B7
Caletta Ter					
5700	OKFT	60452	3347	7W-17S	D5
Calhoun Av					
200	BNHM	60409	3351	2E-17S	E6
200	BNHM	60633	3351	2E-17S	E6
200	CTCY	60409	3351	2E-17S	E6
S Calhoun Av					
9500	CHCG	60617	3215	3E-11S	D6
10300	CHCG	60617	3279	2E-12S	D1
13400	CHCG	60633	3351	2E-15S	D1
14300	BNHM	60633	3351	2E-16S	D4
14500	BNHM	60409	3351	2E-16S	D4
14500	CTCY	60409	3351	2E-16S	D4
W Calhoun Pl					
10	CHCG	60602	3034		D5
100	CHCG	60606	3034		D5
California Av					
-	BLID	60469	3349	3W-16S	A3
-	HLCT	60426	3427	3W-19S	B3
-	POSN	60406	3349	3W-16S	A3
600	PLTN	60008	2805	20W-14N	E3
600	PLTN	60067	2805	20W-14N	E3
600	RGMW	60008	2805	20W-14N	E3
700	DLTN	60419	3351	0E-17S	A4
3000	PltT	60067	2805	20W-13N	E6
3000	RGMW	60067	2805	20W-13N	E5
12300	BLID	60406	3277	3W-15S	A7
13000	WthT	60406	3349	3W-15S	A1
13700	BLID	60406	3349	3W-16S	A3
13700	POSN	60469	3349	3W-16S	A3
14800	BmnT	60426	3349	3W-17S	B6
14800	HRVY	60426	3349	3W-17S	B6
14800	POSN	60426	3349	3W-17S	B6
15000	MKHM	60426	3349	3W-17S	B6
15700	MKHM	60426	3427	3W-18S	B1

STREET Block	City	ZIP	Map#	CGS	Grid
California Av					
17000	HLCT	60429	3427	3W-20S	B5
18200	HMWD	60430	3427	3W-21S	B7
18400	HMWD	60430	3507	3W-22S	B1
N California Av					
10	CHCG	60612	3033	3W-0N	A4
700	CHCG	60612	3032	3W-0N	E3
700	CHCG	60622	3032	3W-1N	E2
1500	CHCG	60647	3032	3W-2N	E1
1600	CHCG	60647	2976	3W-2N	E7
2700	CHCG	60618	2976	3W-4N	E3
4400	CHCG	60618	2920	3W-5N	E7
4400	CHCG	60625	2920	3W-5N	E7
5500	CHCG	60659	2920	3W-6N	E5
6300	CHCG	60645	2920	3W-8N	E2
7200	CHCG	60645	2866	3W-9N	E7
7500	EVTN	60202	2866	3W-9N	E7
S California Av					
10	CHCG	60612	3033	3W-1S	A7
1100	CHCG	60608	3033	3W-1S	A7
1100	CHCG	60623	3033	3W-1S	A7
1500	PltT	60067	2805	20W-13N	E5
1500	RGMW	60008	2805	20W-13N	E5
1600	CHCG	60608	3091	3W-2S	A2
1600	CHCG	60623	3091	3W-2S	A2
3300	CHCG	60632	3091	3W-4S	A7
4700	CHCG	60632	3151	3W-7S	A6
5400	CHCG	60629	3151	3W-8S	A7
8700	CHCG	60652	3213	3W-10S	A4
8700	ENGN	60805	3213	3W-11S	A7
9800	CHCG	60655	3213	3W-11S	A7
9800	ENGN	60655	3213	3W-11S	A7
9900	CHCG	60805	3213	3W-11S	A7
10200	ENGN	60655	3277	3W-11S	A1
10500	CHCG	60655	3277	3W-12S	A2
14400	BmnT	60469	3349	3W-17S	A4
14500	POSN	60469	3349	3W-17S	A5
14800	BmnT	60426	3349	3W-17S	A5
S California Blvd					
2400	CHCG	60608	3091	3W-2S	A3
2400	CHCG	60623	3091	3W-2S	A2
California Ct					
3100	RGMW	60008	2805	22W-13N	B6
10900	ODPK	60467	3423	13W-21S	A6
California St					
1500	EGVV	60007	2859	21W-9N	E7
13300	BLID	60406	3349	3W-15S	A2
W California Ter					
700	CHCG	60657	2977	3W-4N	A2
California Tr					
11800	OrlT	60467	3344	14W-16S	C3
Calitonia Dr					
15200	MKHM	60426	3349	3W-18S	A7
Callan Av					
100	CHCG	60626	2867	2W-9N	B6
100	EVTN	60202	2867	2W-9N	B6
Callan Dr					
9500	PlsT	60462	3345	11W-15S	D2
Callen Ln					
1200	DSPN	60016	2808	13W-13N	D5
E Callero Cir					
1000	MPPT	60056	2808	14W-13N	C6
Callero Ct					
600	ROSL	60172	2913		A6
N Callero Dr					
9200	NLES	60714	2864	10W-11N	B2
Calleview Dr					
10	CTSD	60525	3147	13W-5S	A3
10	LGNG	60525	3147	13W-5S	A3
Callie Av					
8500	MNGV	60053	2865	7W-10N	B4
Cal Sag Rd					
-	ALSP	60803	3275	6W-14S	E7
-	RBBN	60445	3348	5W-15S	B2
-	RBBN	60472	3348	5W-15S	B2
4400	CTWD	60445	3348	6W-15S	A1
5100	CTWD	60445	3275	6W-15S	E7
W Cal Sag Rd					
-	PlsT	60480	3273	12W-13S	D4
-	PSHT	60463	3275	7W-14S	B5
5400	ALSP	60803	3275	7W-14S	C6
5400	CTWD	60445	3275	6W-14S	E7
5500	WthT	60463	3275	6W-14S	D6
5500	WthT	60803	3275	7W-14S	C6
8000	PSHT	60463	3274	10W-13S	C5
8000	PSPK	60464	3274	10W-13S	C5
8500	PlsT	60464	3274	11W-13S	A4
8600	PlsT	60464	3273	12W-13S	D4
W Cal Sag Rd SR-83					
-	PlsT	60480	3273	12W-13S	D4
-	PSHT	60463	3275	7W-14S	B5
5400	ALSP	60803	3275	7W-14S	C6
5400	CTWD	60445	3275	6W-14S	E7
5500	WthT	60463	3275	6W-14S	D6
5500	WthT	60803	3275	7W-14S	C6
8000	PSHT	60463	3274	10W-13S	C5
8000	PSPK	60464	3274	10W-13S	C5
8500	PlsT	60464	3274	11W-13S	A4
8600	PlsT	60464	3273	12W-13S	D4
Calumet Av					
-	HMND	46320	3430		E3
1300	DYR	46311	3510		E7
1300	DYR	46311	3598		E2
6200	HMND	46324	3430		E6
7800	MNSR	46321	3430		E5
8100	SjnT	46311	3598		E5
8200	SjnT	46373	3598		E5
8600	MNSR	46321	3510		E7
8900	SJHN	46373	3598		E7
9000	SJHN	46373	3687		E1
9300	SjnT	46373	3687		E2
10100	HnrT	46311	3687		E4
14100	DLTN	60419	3350	0E-16S	D3
15400	SHLD	60473	3350	0E-18S	D7
Calumet Av US-41					
-	HMND	46320	3430		E3
6200	HMND	46324	3430		E3
S Calumet Av					
1000	HMND	46320	3280		E2
1100	HMND	46394	3280		E7
3000	HMND	46320	3352		E1
3000	HMND	46327	3280		E7
3000	HMND	46327	3352		E3
3500	CHCG	60616	3092	0E-3S	D5
3500	CHCG	60653	3092	0E-3S	D5
4600	CHCG	60615	3092	0E-4S	D7
4700	CHCG	60615	3152	0E-5S	D1
5900	HMND	46320	3430		E1
6100	HMND	46324	3430		E1
6700	CHCG	60637	3152	0E-8S	D7
7000	CHCG	60619	3152	0E-8S	D7
9200	CHCG	60619	3214	0E-11S	D5
9400	CHCG	60628	3214	0E-11S	D6
11300	CHCG	60628	3278	0E-13S	D3
13300	CHCG	60827	3350	0E-15S	D1

Chicago & Cook County Street Index

STREET Block	City	ZIP	Map#	CGS	Grid
S Calumet Av US-41					
1400	HMND	46394	3280		E7
2100	HMND	46320	3280		E5
3000	HMND	46320	3352		E1
3000	HMND	46327	3280		E7
3000	HMND	46327	3352		E3
5900	HMND	46320	3430		E1
6100	HMND	46324	3430		E1
Calumet Blvd					
100	HRVY	60426	3350	1W-17S	A4
Calumet Expwy					
-	CRTE	60417	3597	2E-27S	C5
-	CRTE	60417	3686	1E-29S	C1
-	CteT	60401	3774	0W-33S	C2
-	CteT	60417	3597	1E-28S	C7
-	CteT	60417	3685	0E-32S	D6
-	CteT	60417	3686	1E-31S	C5
-	CteT	60417	3774	0W-33S	C2
-	SLVL	60411	3597	1E-27S	C5
-	STGR	60411	3597	1E-27S	C4
-	STGR	60475	3597	1E-27S	C4
Calumet Expwy SR-394					
-	CRTE	60417	3597	1E-27S	C5
-	CRTE	60417	3686	1E-29S	C1
-	CteT	60401	3774	0W-33S	C2
-	CteT	60417	3597	1E-28S	C7
-	CteT	60417	3685	0E-32S	D6
-	CteT	60417	3686	1E-31S	C5
-	CteT	60417	3774	0W-33S	C2
-	SLVL	60411	3597	1E-27S	C5
-	STGR	60411	3597	1E-27S	C4
-	STGR	60475	3597	1E-27S	C4
Calumet St					
9300	SjnT	46311	3687		E2
Calumet Wy					
500	CTCY	60409	3352	4E-18S	B7
Calvary Ct					
2500	LGGV	60047	2753	19W-20N	C1
Calvert Dr					
4600	RGMW	60008	2806	19W-12N	C7
4700	RGMW	60008	2860	19W-12N	C1
Calvin Av					
-	EMHT	60126	3028		B5
2000	BKLY	60162	3028		C6
2000	BKLY	60163	3028		B5
2000	EMHT	60162	3028		C6
Calvin Cir					
-	EVTN	60201	2866	4W-12N	C1
Calwagner Av					
2200	LydT	60164	2973	12W-2N	C6
2400	FNPK	60131	2973	12W-3N	C6
2400	FNPK	60164	2973	12W-3N	C6
2400	LydT	60131	2973	12W-3N	C6
Calwagner St					
2600	FNPK	60131	2973	12W-3N	C5
Calypso Ln					
15500	ODPK	60462	3346	9W-18S	E7
Camberley Ct					
10	HNDL	60521	3146		A3
Cambia Dr					
300	SMBG	60193	2912		E1
1300	SMBG	60193	2913		A2
Cambourne Ln					
1600	SMBG	60194	2858	25W-10N	B5
Cambria Ct					
2000	GNVW	60062	2809	12W-14N	C3
Cambria Dr					
-	BGVW	60455	3274	9W-11S	D1
Cambrian Ct					
100	ROSL	60172	2912		C4
Cambridge Av					
10	SMWD	60107	2910		C1
10	SMWD	60107	2911		A1
600	MTSN	60443	3505	6W-25S	E6
1100	BlmT	60430	3507	2W-23S	D3
1100	FSMR	60422	3507	2W-23S	D3
1500	CHHT	60422	3507	2W-23S	D4
1500	OMFD	60422	3507	2W-23S	D4
1500	OMFD	60461	3507	2W-23S	D4
N Cambridge Av					
800	CHCG	60610	3034	0W-1N	A2
2300	CHCG	60614	2978	0W-2N	A6
2800	CHCG	60657	2978	0W-3N	A4
S Cambridge Av					
700	EMHT	60126	3028		A5
Cambridge Cir					
500	DRFD	60015	2756	11W-20N	E1
4100	CCHL	60478	3426	5W-21S	C6
Cambridge Ct					
10	BFGV	60089	2754	16W-17N	D5
1000	DYR	46311	3510		D6
1900	PLTN	60074	2753	19W-18N	C3
16000	MKHM	60426	3427	3W-19S	B2
N Cambridge Ct					
1900	PLTN	60074	2753	19W-20N	C2
S Cambridge Ct					
9700	PSHL	60465	3210	10W-11S	A7
Cambridge Dr					
500	SMBG	60193	2858	25W-9N	C7
700	BRRG	60527	3208		A3
800	BFGV	60089	2754	16W-17N	D5
800	BFGV	60090	2754	16W-17N	D5
800	WLNG	60090	2754	16W-17N	D5
900	EGVV	60007	2861	16W-9N	D7
900	EGVV	60007	2915		C1
1800	CPVL	60110	2748		D6
2300	NHBK	60062	2809	11W-15N	D1
4000	CCHL	60478	3426	5W-21S	C6
7900	ODPK	60462	3346	10W-16S	C4
13400	LMNT	60439	3271		D6
16100	MKHM	60426	3427	3W-19S	B2
N Cambridge Dr					
400	PLTN	60067	2752	22W-16N	C7
S Cambridge Dr					
25900	CteT	60417	3687	3E-31S	A6
Cambridge Ln					
600	HFET	60195	2858	24W-12N	D2
700	SMBG	60195	2858	24W-12N	D2
900	WLMT	60091	2812	4W-14N	C5
1000	DYR	46311	3510		D7
2800	OMFD	60461	3507	3W-25S	A7
Cambridge Pl					
800	WLNG	60090	2755	15W-18N	A3
17100	ODHL	60477	3423	11W-20S	E5
17100	TYPK	60477	3423	11W-20S	E5
Cambridge Rd					
6400	WLBK	60527	3146		A6
Cambridge St					
100	DSPN	60016	2862	14W-12N	C1
500	DSPN	60016	2808	14W-13N	B6
1900	CHHT	60411	3595	2W-26S	E2
7100	BGVW	60455	3210	8W-10S	E5
10100	WSTR	60154	3029	12W-1S	B7
10200	PvsT	60162	3029	12W-1S	A7
W Cambridge St					
1300	ANHT	60004	2753	18W-16N	D7
Cambridge Wy					
-	BmdT	60172	2912		A6
-	HRPK	60133	2912		A6
Camden Ct					
100	SMBG	60194	2857	26W-10N	E5
1500	WLNG	60090	2754	16W-18N	D4
4400	RNPK	60471	3594	5W-26S	B3
Camden Dr					
200	CRTE	60417	3596	0W-28S	C6
200	CRTE	60475	3596	0W-28S	C6
1700	GNVW	60025	2810	8W-15N	E2
13900	ODPK	60462	3346	10W-16S	C4
Camden Ln					
-	BGVW	60455	3274	9W-11S	D1
800	NHFD	60093	2758	7W-16N	B7
Camdon Cir					
500	BRLT	60103	2911		A4
Camel Bend Ct					
200	SMBG	60194	2857	27W-10N	D5
Camelia Dr					
7300	HRPK	60133	2911		C1
Camelia Ln					
8400	ODPK	60462	3346	10W-18S	B7
Camellia Dr					
900	MNSR	46321	3510		E2
Camellia Ln					
1600	SMBG	60173	2859	21W-11N	E4
1700	SMBG	60173	2860	20W-10N	A5
Camelot Ct					
13800	OrlT	60467	3344	14W-16S	D3
E Camelot Ct					
1300	ANHT	60004	2754	17W-16N	C7
Camelot Dr					
600	BRRG	60527	3208		A4
Camelot Ln					
1100	LMNT	60439	3271		A7
1500	HFET	60010	2751	24W-16N	B7
2000	LYWD	60411	3509	2E-24S	D5
11600	OrlT	60467	3344	14W-16S	D3
Camelot St					
10500	PvsT	60154	3087	13W-1S	A1
10500	PvsT	60162	3087	13W-1S	A1
10500	WSTR	60154	3087	13W-1S	A1
10500	WSTR	60162	3087	13W-1S	A1
Cameno Pl					
9800	ODPK	60462	3345	12W-18S	D6
S Cameron Av					
4600	HMND	46327	3352		D5
Cameron Ct					
1400	HFET	60010	2751	24W-16N	B7
Cameron Ln					
9300	MNGV	60053	2864	9W-11N	D2
Cameron Pkwy					
11200	ODPK	60467	3422	14W-21S	E6
Cameron Wy					
400	ANHT	60004	2753	18W-18N	E3
400	BFGV	60004	2753	18W-18N	E3
400	BFGV	60089	2753	18W-18N	E3
Camp Alphonse					
4000	PltT	60010	2752	22W-17N	A4
4000	PltT	60067	2752	22W-17N	A4
4000	PltT	60074	2752	22W-17N	A4
Campbell Av					
-	CTCY	60409	3352	3E-17S	A5
-	MKHM	60426	3427	3W-19S	B3
700	CHHT	60411	3507	1W-25S	E7
1100	DSPN	60016	2862	13W-9N	D6
1100	DSPN	60016	2863	13W-10N	A5
1400	CHHT	60411	3595	1W-26S	E1
3200	SCHT	60411	3595	1W-27S	E4
9500	OKLN	60453	3211	6W-11S	D6
14900	HRVY	60426	3349	3W-17S	B6
15500	HRVY	60426	3427	3W-18S	B1
15900	BmnT	60426	3427	3W-19S	B2
N Campbell Av					
10	GNWD	60425	3508	0E-22S	D2
400	CHCG	60612	3033	3W-0N	A3
700	CHCG	60622	3033	3W-0N	A3
1500	CHCG	60647	3033	3W-1N	A1
2400	CHCG	60647	2977	3W-3N	A5
3800	CHCG	60618	2977	3W-4N	A2
4400	CHCG	60618	2921	3W-5N	A7
5300	CHCG	60625	2921	3W-6N	A5
5500	CHCG	60659	2921	3W-6N	A5
6300	CHCG	60645	2921	3W-7N	A3
7200	CHCG	60645	2867	3W-9N	A7
S Campbell Av					
10	GNWD	60425	3508	0E-23S	D3
1200	CHCG	60608	3033	3W-1S	A7
1200	CHCG	60612	3033	3W-0S	A7
3700	CHCG	60632	3091	3W-4S	B6
4700	CHCG	60632	3151	3W-5S	A1
5600	CHCG	60629	3151	3W-7S	B6
7900	CHCG	60652	3213	3W-9S	B2
9800	CHCG	60655	3213	3W-11S	B7
9800	ENGN	60655	3213	3W-11S	B7
9800	ENGN	60805	3213	3W-11S	B7
10300	CHCG	60655	3277	3W-13S	B3
11800	BLID	60406	3277	3W-13S	B5
14300	POSN	60469	3349	3W-17S	B4
W Campbell Ct					
600	ANHT	60005	2806	18W-14N	E5
Campbell Ln					
1200	HFET	60194	2858	25W-12N	C2
W Campbell Pl					
-	CHCG	60610	3034		D2
Campbell St					
2000	ANHT	60005	2806	19W-14N	D5
2000	RGMW	60005	2806	19W-14N	D5
2000	RGMW	60008	2806	19W-14N	B4
12800	LMNT	60439	3272	16W-13S	A4
E Campbell St					
10	ANHT	60005	2807	17W-14N	A5
1100	ANHT	60004	2807	17W-14N	C5
W Campbell St					
10	ANHT	60005	2807	18W-14N	A5
400	ANHT	60005	2806	18W-14N	D5
1500	RGMW	60005	2806	19W-14N	D5
1500	RGMW	60008	2806	19W-14N	D5
W Campbell Park Dr					
2200	CHCG	60612	3033	2W-0S	B6
Camp Dan Beard					
5300	WhlT	60062	2755	13W-18N	E2
Campden Ln					
2500	NHBK	60062	2757	10W-18N	A4
Camp Flint Dr					
200	DndT	60118	2801		A4
Campground Rd					
1100	DSPN	60016	2863	12W-10N	A4
Camphill Cir					
1900	IVNS	60067	2804	23W-15N	E1
E Camp McDonald Rd					
10	MPPT	60056	2808	13W-15N	D3
10	MPPT	60070	2808	13W-15N	D3
10	PTHT	60056	2808	13W-15N	D3
10	PTHT	60070	2808	13W-15N	D3
900	PTHT	60090	2808	14W-14N	C3
900	WLNG	60070	2808	14W-14N	D3
900	WLNG	60090	2808	14W-14N	C3
W Camp McDonald Rd					
10	MPPT	60056	2808	15W-15N	A3
10	MPPT	60070	2808	15W-14N	A3
10	PTHT	60056	2808	15W-15N	A3
10	PTHT	60070	2808	15W-15N	A3
100	MPPT	60056	2807	16W-14N	D3
100	PTHT	60056	2807	15W-14N	E3
100	PTHT	60070	2807	16W-14N	D3
400	ANHT	60004	2807	16W-14N	D3
400	WhlT	60004	2807	16W-14N	D3
Campus Av					
-	RchT	60443	3506	5W-25S	B7
700	MTSN	60443	3506	5W-25S	B7
Campus Dr					
300	ELGN	60120	2855		D5
N Campus Dr					
2200	EVTN	60201	2867	2W-12N	C1
S Campus Dr					
1800	EVTN	60201	2867	2W-11N	C2
W Campus Dr					
200	ANHT	60004	2753	18W-17N	E5
200	ANHT	60004	2754	18W-17N	A5
S Campus Pkwy					
1400	CHCG	60608	3034		E7
Canal St					
200	LMNT	60439	3270		D5
1800	BLID	60406	3349	2W-15S	C1
16700	SHLD	60473	3428	0W-20S	C4
16700	SHLD	60476	3428	0W-20S	C4
16700	TNTN	60473	3428	0W-20S	C4
16700	TNTN	60476	3428	0W-20S	C4
N Canal St					
10	CHCG	60606	3034	0W-0N	A4
10	CHCG	60661	3034	0W-0N	A4
300	CHCG	60610	3034	0W-0N	A4
S Canal St					
-	CHCG	60609	3092	0W-4S	B7
-	CHCG	60661	3034	0W-0S	A5
10	CHCG	60606	3034	0W-0S	A5
300	CHCG	60607	3034	0W-0S	A6
1500	CHCG	60616	3034	0W-1S	A7
1600	CHCG	60616	3092	0W-2S	A2
16600	SHLD	60473	3428	0W-19S	C3
Canal Bank Rd					
-	FTVW	60402	3089	7W-4S	C7
-	SKNY	60804	3089	7W-4S	C7
6600	FTVW	60402	3148	8W-5S	E2
6600	FTVW	60402	3149	8W-5S	A1
7100	SMMT	60534	3148	8W-5S	E2
7300	LYNS	60534	3148	9W-5S	E2
7300	SMMT	60501	3148	9W-5S	D2
15100	DGvT	60439	3270		D4
15100	LMNT	60439	3270		D4
15100	LMNT	60439	3271		A3
S Canal Bank Rd					
-	SMMT	60534	3148	9W-5S	D2
7400	SMMT	60501	3148	9W-5S	D2
S Canalport Av					
1700	CHCG	60616	3092	0W-1S	A1
2000	CHCG	60608	3091	1W-1S	E1
2000	CHCG	60608	3092	1W-1S	A1
Canary Dr					
-	BlmT	60411	3509	3E-25S	E7
Canary Ln					
6400	HGKN	60525	3147	11W-7S	E5
N Canavan Ct					
9800	NLES	60714	2864	10W-12N	A1
Canbury Ct					
1500	WLNG	60090	2754	16W-18N	D4
Candice Ct					
23800	CteT	60417	3597	2E-28S	E7
Candida Rd					
1000	ELGN	60123	2801		A7
Candlegate Cir					
100	RchT	60443	3593	8W-26S	B1
Candlelight Dr					
10	SLVL	60411	3597	2E-25S	D1
Candlelight Dr E					
8500	WLSP	60480	3208		E4
Candlelight Dr W					
8500	WLSP	60480	3208		E4
Candlelyte Ct					
300	ROSL	60172	2912		E3
E Candlenut Ln					
1100	PLTN	60074	2753	19W-18N	C2
Candleridge Ct					
700	BRLT	60103	2911		B4
Candlewood Ct					
1400	WLNG	60004	2754	16W-17N	D6
1400	WLNG	60090	2754	16W-17N	D6
3000	FSMR	60422	3507	3W-23S	A2
Candlewood Ln					
1300	HFET	60194	2858	25W-11N	B2
Candlewood Rd					
1000	ELGN	60123	2801		A7
Candlewood Hill Rd					
1200	NHBK	60062	2756	10W-17N	E5
S Candota Av					
100	MPPT	60056	2807	16W-12N	E7
200	MPPT	60056	2861	16W-12N	E1
N Canfield Av					
2100	CHCG	60068	2918	9W-7N	B4
2100	CHCG	60631	2918	9W-7N	B4
2100	PKRG	60068	2918	9W-7N	B4
2100	PKRG	60631	2918	9W-7N	B4
4400	CHCG	60634	2974	9W-5N	B1
4400	CHCG	60706	2974	9W-5N	B1
4400	NRDG	60634	2974	9W-5N	B1
4400	NRDG	60706	2918	10W-5N	B7
4400	NRDG	60706	2974	9W-5N	B1
5100	CHCG	60656	2918	10W-5N	B7
5100	CHCG	60706	2918	9W-6N	B6
5100	NRDG	60656	2918	10W-5N	B7
5200	NpkT	60656	2918	9W-6N	B5
5500	NpkT	60631	2918	9W-7N	B5
S Canford Cliffs Dr					
1400	MPPT	60056	2861	17W-11N	C4
Cannes Ct					
3400	HLCT	60429	3426	4W-21S	E7
Cannon Ct					
1800	SMBG	60193	2858	25W-9N	A7
Cannon Dr					
-	CHCG	60614	2978	0W-2N	B7
N Cannon Dr					
-	CHCG	60657	2978	0W-3N	A4
1800	CHCG	60614	2978	0W-2N	B6
S Cannon Dr					
2300	EGvT	60005	2861	16W-10N	E6
2300	EGvT	60056	2861	16W-10N	E6
2300	MPPT	60056	2861	16W-10N	E6
Cannon Ln					
-	FDHT	60411	3509	1E-24S	B6
S Cannonade Ct					
13700	HMGN	60467	3344	15W-16S	C3
Canon Rd					
11800	ODPK	60467	3422	14W-19S	D3
11800	OrlT	60467	3422	14W-19S	C3
Cantal Ct					
10	WLNG	60090	2808	14W-15N	C1
Canter Ln					
1400	BRLT	60103	2910		B7
Canterberry Dr					
8400	BRRG	60527	3208		A4
Canterberry Ln					
10	OKBK	60523	3086		B5
Canterbury Ct					
10	PSHT	60463	3274	9W-13S	D5
10	SMWD	60107	2857	28W-11N	B5
10	WLMT	60091	2813	2W-13N	B6
300	HNDL	60521	3086		A7
1100	ELGN	60120	2855		D5
2700	SBTN	60010	2804	24W-14N	C3
3800	RNPK	60471	3594	4W-27S	D4
W Canterbury Ct					
1500	ANHT	60004	2753	18W-16N	D6
Canterbury Dr					
600	HRPK	60133	2912		A1
900	SMBG	60195	2858	24W-12N	D2
2500	NHBK	60062	2810	10W-16N	A1
2700	NHBK	60062	2809	11W-16N	D1
E Canterbury Dr					
1400	ANHT	60004	2754	16W-16N	C6
W Canterbury Dr					
10	ANHT	60004	2754	18W-16N	A6
Canterbury Ln					
300	IVNS	60010	2751	23W-17N	D6
300	IVNS	60067	2751	23W-16N	D6
1200	GNVW	60025	2811	7W-14N	A5
6000	HFET	60120	2855		E1
6100	ELGN	60120	2855		E1
7200	GGnT	60449	3682	9W-31S	A5
7200	MonT	60449	3682	9W-31S	A5
15500	ODPK	60462	3346	10W-18S	C7
E Canterbury Ln					
10	NHFD	60093	2811	7W-14N	B3
N Canterbury Ln					
1700	PLTN	60074	2753	18W-18N	D3
W Canterbury Ln					
10	NHFD	60093	2811	7W-14N	A3
Canterbury Pl					
-	CCHL	60478	3506	6W-22S	A2
Canterbury St					
-	HLSD	60154	3086		D1
9800	BDVW	60155	3087	12W-1S	B1
9800	WSTR	60154	3087	13W-1S	A1
10700	PvsT	60154	3086		E1
10700	PvsT	60162	3086		E1
10700	WSTR	60154	3086		E1
Canterbury Tr					
400	ROSL	60172	2913		C3
E Canterbury Tr					
1200	PLTN	60074	2753	18W-18N	D3
N Canterbury Tr					
1700	PLTN	60074	2753	18W-18N	D3
Cantigny Ln					
13800	HMGN	60441	3343	17W-17S	C6
Cantigny Rd					
10700	CTSD	60525	3147	13W-7S	A7
10800	CTSD	60525	3146		E7
Canton Ln					
100	SMWD	60107	2856	29W-11N	D4
S Canvasback Ct					
14400	HMGN	60441	3344	15W-17S	C5
W Canvasback St					
10	BGVW	60455	3210	9W-9S	D3
Cap Ct					
-	CCHL	60478	3506	6W-22S	B2
Cape Ct					
-	SMBG	60193	2858	25W-9N	B7
Cape Ln					
600	SMBG	60193	2858	25W-9N	B7
Cape Breton Ct					
1600	HFET	60195	2804	25W-15N	B2
Capistrano Ln					
10400	ODPK	60467	3423	13W-21S	B5
10400	OrlT	60467	3423	13W-21S	B5
Capistrano Ter					
900	BRLT	60103	2911		B5
Capital Ct					
1800	SMBG	60193	2858	25W-9N	A7
Capital Dr					
-	LNWD	60712	2920	4W-8N	C1
-	SKOK	60076	2920	4W-8N	C1
Capitol Dr					
1000	WLNG	60090	2808	14W-16N	C1
9000	MaiT	60016	2863	11W-11N	E3
9000	PKRG	60016	2863	11W-11N	E3
Capitol St					
3300	SKOK	60076	2866	4W-10N	D4
Cappelletti Dr					
3000	SCHT	60411	3596	1W-27S	A3
Capri Ct					
3700	NfdT	60025	2809	11W-13N	E7
E Capri Dr					
800	PLTN	60074	2753	19W-18N	B4
N Capri Dr					
1800	PLTN	60074	2753	19W-18N	C3
Capri Ln					
1300	DYR	46311	3510		D7
1600	DYR	46311	3598		D1
1900	SMBG	60193	2858	25W-9N	A7
5000	RNPK	60471	3594	6W-26S	A2
5600	MNGV	60053	2865	7W-11N	C2
Capri Ter					
100	WLNG	60090	2755	14W-18N	C3
Capstan Dr					
4400	HFET	60195	2804	25W-15N	A2
Captains Ln					
1000	WLNG	60090	2754	15W-17N	E5
Capulina Av					
5800	MNGV	60053	2865	8W-10N	A4
Carberry Cir					
1100	IVNS	60067	2751	24W-17N	C5
Carboy Rd					
1600	EGvT	60005	2861	16W-10N	E5
1600	MPPT	60005	2861	16W-10N	E5
1600	MPPT	60056	2861	16W-10N	E5
W Carboy Rd					
500	EGvT	60005	2861	16W-10N	E5
500	MPPT	60056	2861	16W-10N	E5
Cardiff Cir					
1900	CPVL	60110	2748		C5
Cardiff Ct					
-	HmrT	60441	3344	15W-16S	B4
900	SMBG	60194	2858	25W-11N	B3
Cardigan Pl					
-	HFET	60195	2804	26W-12N	A7
1900	HFET	60195	2858	26W-12N	A1
Cardinal Av					
1400	MLPK	60160	3029	13W-1N	A2
Cardinal Ct					
10	SMWD	60120	2856	29W-9N	D7
100	DYR	46311	3510		C6
1700	WLNG	60090	2754	16W-18N	D3
1800	FSMR	60422	3507	3W-23S	A4
2200	SMBG	60194	2857	26W-11N	E4
2200	SMBG	60194	2858	26W-11N	A4
N Cardinal Ct					
1100	PLTN	60074	2753	19W-17N	B5
Cardinal Dr					
-	BlmT	60411	3509	3E-25S	E7
400	BRLT	60103	2910		A1
2100	RGMW	60008	2806	19W-13N	B5
2600	HnrT	60120	2856	31W-11N	A4
6400	HGKN	60525	3147	11W-7S	E6
16700	ODPK	60467	3423	13W-20S	B3
N Cardinal Dr					
1000	PLTN	60074	2753	19W-17N	C5
Cardinal Ln					
10	CPVL	60110	2748		D6
10	ROSL	60172	2912		C4
700	EGVV	60007	2913		D2
2400	WLMT	60091	2812	5W-13N	A5
18000	TYPK	60477	3424	11W-21S	A7
E Cardinal Ln					
1000	MPPT	60056	2808	14W-13N	C6
Carefree Av					
8800	ODPK	60462	3346	11W-16S	A2
W Carefree Dr					
13600	HMGN	60441	3343	17W-17S	D6
W Carey Av					
8600	RVGV	60171	2973	11W-3N	D6
8600	RVGV	60171	2974	10W-3N	A5
Carey Ct					
300	CHHT	60411	3507	2W-24S	D5
Carey Dr					
-	ROSL	60172	2913		B3
-	SmbT	60172	2913		B3
Carey Ln					
10	SMWD	60107	2857	28W-11N	A4
Carey Wy					
-	BRLT	60120	2909		E3
Cargill Dr					
2000	NHBK	60062	2757	10W-16N	A7
Cariann Ln					
1300	GNVW	60025	2811	6W-13N	C5
1300	WLMT	60091	2811	6W-13N	C5
E Carib Ln					
1700	MPPT	60056	2808	13W-14N	D3
Caribou Cross					
-	NHBK	60015	2756	13W-18N	A2
-	RVWD	60015	2756	13W-18N	A2
10	NHBK	60062	2755	13W-20N	E2
10	NHBK	60062	2756	13W-18N	A2
Caribou Ln					
1200	HFET	60120	2856	31W-12N	A2
10800	ODPK	60467	3423	13W-20S	A5
Carl Av					
-	BRTN	60010	2750	26W-20N	E1
800	ELGN	60120	2855		C3
N Carl Av					
500	BRTN	60010	2750	26W-20N	E1
Carl Blvd					
2600	EGVV	60007	2915		B4
2600	EGVV	60191	2915		B4
2600	WDDL	60191	2915		B4
Carl Ct					
500	PTHT	60070	2808	15W-15N	A1
Carl Rd					
-	MONE	60449	3682	7W-32S	E6
Carlborg Ct					
22200	RNPK	60471	3594	6W-26S	A3
Carleah St					
8800	MaiT	60016	2863	11W-11N	D4
8800	MaiT	60068	2863	11W-11N	D4
8800	PKRG	60068	2863	11W-11N	D4
Carleton Cir					
10	IVNS	60010	2750	25W-16N	E7
Carleton Ct					
10	IVNS	60010	2751	25W-16N	A7
Carleton Rd					
2000	HFET	60195	2804	24W-12N	E7
Carley Ct					
10	LMNT	60439	3271		A5
Carling Rd					
2000	HFET	60195	2804	24W-12N	D7
Carlino Dr					
100	BRLT	60103	2909		E3
Carlisle Av					
10	DRFD	60015	2757	9W-20N	B2
10	NfdT	60062	2757	9W-20N	B2
1100	EGVV	60007	2914		D3
1300	ITSC	60143	2914		D3
Carlisle Ct					
1800	SMBG	60194	2858	25W-11N	A3
8200	HRPK	60133	2857	26W-9N	E7
8400	BRRG	60527	3208		A4
Carlisle Dr					
-	HRPK	60193	2857	26W-9N	E7
-	SMBG	60193	2857	26W-9N	E7
1300	BRTN	60010	2751	24W-17N	C4
1300	IVNS	60010	2751	24W-17N	C4
7800	HRPK	60133	2858	26W-9N	A7
8000	HRPK	60133	2857	26W-9N	E7
Carlisle Ln					
9000	ODPK	60462	3346	11W-17S	A5
Carlisle St					
-	WSTR	60154	3086		E4
-	WSTR	60154	3087	13W-2S	A4
Carlisle on Duxbury					
10	RGMW	60008	2805	22W-13N	B7
Carlow Dr					
800	DSPN	60016	2808	13W-13N	D7
Carl P Cassata Sr Ln					
6800	HDHT	60706	2918	8W-5N	E7
6900	NRDG	60706	2918	8W-5N	E7
Carlsbad Dr					
6100	TYPK	60477	3425	7W-20S	B3
Carlsbad Tr					
400	ROSL	60172	2913		B3
Carlson Dr					
1300	SMWD	60107	2911		B1
2000	NHBK	60062	2757	9W-16N	B7
2000	NHBK	60062	2810	9W-16N	B1
Carlton Ct					
100	SMBG	60193	2858	24W-10N	D6
300	SEGN	60177	2909		A1

Chicago & Cook County Street Index

STREET Block	City	ZIP	Map#	CGS	Grid
Carlton Ct					
3000	WSTR	60154	3086		E4
Carlton Dr					
600	ELGN	60120	2855		C2
Carlton Ln					
900	SMBG	60193	2858	24W-10N	C6
14900	HMGN	60441	3344	15W-17S	B6
Carlton Ihde Dr					
-	PSHL	60465	3274	10W-12S	B3
Carlyle Ct					
100	ELGN	60120	2855		E3
700	NHBK	60062	2756	12W-18N	C4
17300	TYPK	60477	3423	11W-20S	E5
N Carlyle Ct					
1100	ANHT	60004	2807	17W-15N	C3
N Carlyle Ln					
900	ANHT	60004	2807	17W-14N	C3
N Carlyle Pl					
300	ANHT	60004	2807	17W-14N	C4
S Carlyle Pl					
300	ANHT	60004	2807	16W-13N	C5
Carman Av					
-	BFGV	60089	2754	15W-20N	E1
-	VrnT	60069	2754	15W-20N	E1
-	VrnT	60089	2754	15W-20N	E1
400	BFGV	60089	2755	15W-20N	A1
Carmel Ct					
1600	HFET	60194	2858	25W-12N	B2
Carmel Dr					
2900	FSMR	60422	3507	3W-22S	A1
5500	HRPK	60133	2912		A6
N Carmel Dr					
900	PLTN	60074	2753	20W-17N	A5
Carmel Ln					
10	BRBK	60459	3211	7W-8S	C1
Carmelhead Ln					
200	SMBG	60193	2859	23W-10N	B6
Carmella Ct					
-	SMWD	60120	2856	30W-10N	B5
Carmella Ln					
800	ELGN	60120	2855		C5
W Carmen Av					
1200	CHCG	60640	2921	1W-6N	D6
2400	CHCG	60625	2921	3W-6N	A6
3400	CHCG	60625	2920	4W-6N	C6
4100	CHCG	60630	2920	5W-6N	A6
5600	CHCG	60630	2919	7W-6N	B6
6300	CHCG	60656	2919	7W-6N	A6
6600	CHCG	60656	2918	8W-6N	E6
7200	HDHT	60706	2918	9W-6N	C6
7500	HDHT	60656	2918	9W-6N	C6
7700	NRDG	60706	2918	9W-6N	C6
8600	NRDG	60706	2917	10W-6N	E6
8700	CHCG	60706	2917	10W-6N	E6
Carmen Dr					
1500	EGVV	60007	2916		A2
W Carmichael Dr					
7600	PSHT	60463	3274	9W-14S	D6
Carn Av					
-	MKNA	60448	3504	11W-23S	A3
-	TYPK	60477	3504	11W-23S	A3
N Carnaby					
8100	HRPK	60133	2857	26W-9N	E7
S Carnaby					
8000	HRPK	60133	2857	26W-9N	E7
Carnaby Ct					
800	SMBG	60194	2858	25W-11N	A3
Carnaby Pl					
-	MNSR	46321	3510		C4
Carnation Ln					
200	HFET	60195	2859	23W-11N	B3
700	MTSN	60443	3506	5W-25S	C6
Carnation St					
10	DYR	46311	3598		C1
3400	FNPK	60131	2973	13W-4N	A2
Carnegie St					
900	RGMW	60008	2806	20W-15N	A3
Carnoustie Dr					
8800	ODPK	60462	3346	11W-18S	A7
Carnoustie Ln					
10	IVNS	60067	2804	23W-15N	D1
Carol Av					
1000	WLNG	60090	2755	14W-16N	C6
5600	MNGV	60053	2865	7W-10N	C4
15900	HRVY	60426	3428	0W-19S	B1
15900	SHLD	60426	3428	0W-19S	B1
21700	SLVL	60411	3597	2E-26S	C2
W Carol Av					
6900	NLES	60714	2864	8W-10N	E4
Carol Ct					
10	CRTE	60417	3597	1E-28S	A6
200	STGR	60475	3595	1W-28S	E6
200	STGR	60475	3596	1W-28S	A6
300	HDPK	60035	2758	7W-20N	C2
1400	PLTN	60074	2753	19W-17N	D4
1400	PltT	60074	2753	19W-17N	D4
1500	NHBK	60062	2757	9W-17N	C6
10400	RSMT	60018	2917	13W-8N	A1
15100	ODPK	60462	3346	10W-18S	B6
W Carol Ct					
7100	NLES	60714	2864	8W-10N	D4
Carol Ln					
800	CRTE	60417	3597	1E-28S	A6
1100	GLNC	60022	2758	6W-18N	C3
1300	DSPN	60018	2862	13W-10N	D5
1600	SLVL	60411	3597	2E-26S	C2
3400	GNVW	60062	2809	12W-14N	B4
S Carol Ln					
400	MPPT	60056	2861	17W-12N	C1
W Carol Ln					
6200	PSHT	60463	3275	7W-14S	B6
Carol St					
1200	NLES	60714	2864	10W-10N	A4
1200	PKRG	60068	2864	10W-10N	A4
1300	PKRG	60068	2863	10W-10N	E4
3600	SKOK	60076	2866	4W-10N	C4
4800	SKOK	60076	2865	5W-10N	E4
5000	SKOK	60077	2865	6W-10N	D4
W Carol St					
7300	NLES	60714	2864	9W-10N	D4
8500	PKRG	60068	2864	10W-10N	A4
Carol Ann Dr					
10	SMWD	60107	2857	28W-11N	A4
Carol Ann Ln					
4500	RNPK	60471	3594	5W-27S	C4
Carol Belle Tr					
5500	OKFT	60452	3347	6W-18S	D7
Carolina Ct					
1400	SMBG	60193	2912		A2
Carolina Dr					
1600	EGVV	60007	2913		D2
1600	SLVL	60411	3597	2E-27S	C4
Carolina Ln					
9200	ODPK	60462	3345	11W-16S	E3

STREET Block	City	ZIP	Map#	CGS	Grid
Caroline Av					
-	BCHR	60401	3864	0W-36S	D1
1400	HMND	46394	3280		D4
4900	WNSP	60558	3146		E2
N Caroline Av					
200	EMHT	60126	3028		B1
Caroline Dr					
2700	HMWD	60430	3427	3W-21S	B6
Carolyn Ct					
5100	OKFT	60452	3347	6W-18S	E6
10800	ODPK	60467	3345	13W-18S	A7
W Carolyn Dr					
900	PLTN	60067	2805	22W-15N	B2
Carolyn Ln					
800	PKRG	60068	2863	11W-9N	D6
5500	DGvT	60521	3146		A3
5500	HNDL	60521	3146		A3
S Carolyn Ln					
11700	ALSP	60803	3276	5W-13S	B4
Caron Ct					
600	SMBG	60193	2858	25W-9N	A7
S Carondolet Av					
12200	CHCG	60633	3280	3E-14S	A6
13100	CHCG	60633	3352	3E-15S	A1
Carousel Dr					
4000	GNVW	60062	2809	11W-15N	D3
Carpenter Av					
-	WLNG	60090	2755	14W-17N	B5
500	OKPK	60302	3030	8W-0S	E5
500	OKPK	60304	3030	8W-0S	E5
Carpenter Ct					
1000	EGVV	60007	2913		E2
E Carpenter Dr					
200	PLTN	60067	2752	20W-17N	E6
200	PLTN	60067	2753	20W-17N	A6
300	PLTN	60074	2753	20W-17N	A6
1300	PltT	60074	2753	19W-17N	C6
Carpenter Rd					
-	SKOK	60646	2919	6W-8N	D1
400	DGvT	60439	3270		C1
7000	SKOK	60077	2919	6W-8N	D1
Carpenter St					
10	DGvT	60439	3270		C3
10	LmnT	60439	3270		C3
600	CHHT	60411	3508	1W-24S	A6
3300	BlmT	60475	3596	1W-28S	A6
3300	STGR	60475	3596	1W-28S	A6
18300	HMWD	60430	3428	1W-22S	A7
18500	HMWD	60430	3508	1W-22S	A1
N Carpenter St					
10	CHCG	60607	3033	1W-0S	E5
600	CHCG	60622	3033	1W-0N	E3
S Carpenter St					
700	CHCG	60607	3033	1W-0S	E6
1800	CHCG	60608	3091	1W-1S	E1
5000	CHCG	60609	3151	1W-5S	E2
5500	CHCG	60621	3151	1W-7S	E6
8900	CHCG	60620	3213	1W-10S	E5
9600	CHCG	60643	3213	1W-11S	E6
11200	CHCG	60643	3277	1W-13S	E4
12200	CHCG	60643	3278	1W-14S	A6
12200	CTPK	60643	3278	1W-14S	A6
12200	CTPK	60827	3278	1W-14S	A6
Carr Ct					
500	SMBG	60193	2858	25W-9N	A7
1400	EGVV	60007	2913		E2
Carr St					
4500	RGMW	60008	2806	19W-12N	D7
4600	RGMW	60008	2860	19W-12N	C1
Carriage Av					
1200	LGNG	60525	3147	13W-5S	A2
Carriage Ct					
600	SMBG	60193	2913		C1
Carriage Dr					
10	SLVL	60411	3597	2E-25S	E1
Carriage Ln					
10	LMNT	60439	3272	15W-14S	A6
10	SLVL	60411	3597	2E-25S	D1
1100	SMBG	60193	2913		C1
1200	NHBK	60062	2757	9W-18N	D3
8400	TYPK	60477	3424	10W-20S	B5
12700	CTWD	60445	3275	7W-15S	D7
12700	WthT	60463	3275	7W-15S	D7
18300	LNSG	60438	3429	2E-21S	D7
18500	BlmT	60411	3429	2E-21S	D7
E Carriage Ln					
800	PLTN	60074	2753	19W-18N	B2
1700	CteT	60417	3686	2E-32S	D7
Carriage Pl					
10	BRRG	60527	3146		C6
Carriage Tr					
10	PSHT	60463	3274	9W-14S	D6
Carriage Wy					
100	WLMT	60091	2811	5W-13N	E7
300	DRFD	60015	2757	9W-20N	B1
800	ELGN	60120	2855		C1
1300	ROSL	60172	2912		B6
6200	OKFT	60452	3347	7W-17S	B5
E Carriage Wy					
10	HLCT	60429	3427	3W-21S	A6
Carriage Hill Dr					
600	GNVW	60025	2810	8W-13N	E7
Carriage Hill Rd					
10	WLNG	60090	2755	15W-18N	A2
100	WLNG	60090	2754	15W-18N	E3
Carriage House Ln					
10	PlsT	60467	3345	13W-15S	A2
Carriage Ridge Ln					
400	LMNT	60439	3271		A5
W Carriageway Cir					
700	PLTN	60067	2805	21W-14N	C3
S Carriageway Ct					
700	PLTN	60067	2805	21W-15N	D2
Carriageway Dr					
100	BRRG	60527	3146		C7
500	BFGV	60089	2754	17W-17N	B5
5000	RGMW	60008	2860	19W-12N	C1
N Carriageway Dr					
-	BFGV	60004	2754	17W-17N	B5
3400	ANHT	60004	2754	17W-17N	B4
3400	BFGV	60089	2754	17W-18N	B4
S Carriageway Ln					
800	PLTN	60067	2805	21W-14N	C3
Carriage Wy Dr					
-	BRRG	60527	3146		B7
Carrick Rd					
400	MTSN	60443	3506	5W-24S	B6
Carrick Wy					
-	TYPK	60477	3504	10W-23S	B3
W Carrie Ct					
7800	FftT	60423	3504	9W-23S	D4
Carrie Ollmann Ln					
800	EGVV	60007	2914		B1
N Carrington Ct					
3900	HLCT	60429	3426	4W-22S	D7

STREET Block	City	ZIP	Map#	CGS	Grid
N Carrington Ct					
18400	HLCT	60429	3506	4W-22S	D1
Carrington Dr					
3800	HLCT	60429	3426	4W-22S	D7
3800	HLCT	60429	3506	4W-22S	D1
3900	CCHL	60429	3506	4W-22S	D1
3900	CCHL	60478	3506	4W-22S	D1
18300	BmnT	60430	3426	4W-22S	D7
Carrington Wy					
2300	GNVW	60025	2809	11W-15N	E3
2300	GNVW	60062	2809	11W-15N	E3
W Carroll Av					
1600	CHCG	60607	3033	2W-0N	C4
1600	CHCG	60612	3033	2W-0N	B4
2900	CHCG	60612	3032	4W-0N	D4
4000	CHCG	60624	3032	5W-0N	B4
4700	CHCG	60644	3032	5W-0N	A4
Carroll Dr					
-	HMGN	60441	3422	15W-19S	B2
Carroll Pkwy					
2200	FSMR	60422	3507	2W-22S	C2
N Carroll Pkwy					
500	GNWD	60425	3428	0W-21S	C7
Carroll Sq					
600	EGvT	60007	2861	18W-10N	A6
600	EGVV	60007	2861	18W-10N	A6
E Carroll St					
10	CTCY	60409	3352		C7
600	HMND	46320	3352		E7
Carroll Wy					
200	BRLT	60103	2909		C3
N Carrolton Ct					
8100	HRPK	60133	2857	26W-9N	E7
S Carrolton Ct					
8000	HRPK	60133	2857	26W-9N	E7
Carry Ln					
-	BFGV	60089	2754	17W-20N	B1
Carse Av					
15700	HRVY	60426	3428	1W-19S	A1
Carson Ct					
1400	HMWD	60430	3507	1W-22S	E2
1800	SMBG	60193	2858	25W-9N	A7
Carson Dr					
1000	MLPK	60160	3029	12W-1N	C2
1400	HMWD	60430	3507	1W-22S	E2
18900	BlmT	60430	3507	1W-22S	E2
Carswell Av					
900	EGVV	60007	2915		A3
Carswell Ct					
900	EGVV	60007	2915		A2
Carter Ct					
200	NHBK	60062	2758	7W-16N	A6
W Carter Ct					
6000	MONE	60449	3682	7W-31S	D5
N Carter St					
400	PLTN	60067	2752	21W-16N	D7
Carthage Ln					
10	HFET	60194	2859	23W-11N	A3
Cartier Av					
-	TYPK	60477	3424	9W-21S	D5
S Carver Dr					
-	CHCG	60827	3279	1E-15S	A7
-	CHCG	60827	3351	1E-15S	B1
Carver Ln					
100	SMBG	60193	2858	25W-10N	B6
100	SMBG	60194	2858	25W-10N	B6
Cary Av					
9600	SRPK	60176	2973	12W-4N	C2
N Caryl Av					
100	NHLK	60164	2972		E7
100	NHLK	60164	3028		E1
1500	MLPK	60160	3028		E2
S Caryl Av					
100	NHLK	60164	3028		E1
200	MLPK	60160	3028		E2
Caryn Cir					
700	SHLD	60473	3429	0E-19S	A2
Caryn Ter					
1100	NHBK	60062	2757	9W-17N	D5
Caryville Ln					
100	SMBG	60193	2858	26W-10N	A6
Casa Dr					
1000	SMBG	60173	2859	22W-11N	D4
Cascade Ct					
7900	ODPK	60462	3346	9W-17S	C4
S Cascade Ct					
1400	BRTN	60010	2750	25W-17N	E5
Cascade Dr					
10	IHPK	60525	3146		E5
Cascade Ln					
1300	PLTN	60074	2753	19W-18N	C3
1400	BRTN	60010	2750	25W-17N	E5
Case Ct					
400	SMBG	60193	2858	25W-9N	A7
Case Dr					
700	ROSL	60172	2912		D5
Case Ln					
1100	ELGN	60120	2855		D3
Case Pl					
600	EVTN	60202	2867	2W-9N	B6
Case St					
700	EVTN	60202	2867	2W-9N	B6
Casey Ct					
900	SMBG	60173	2805	21W-13N	C6
S Casey Ln					
14400	HMGN	60441	3343	17W-17S	C5
Cashel Ln					
8700	TYPK	60477	3504	10W-23S	B3
Cashew Dr					
7400	ODPK	60462	3346	9W-18S	D7
Casino Center Dr					
700	HMND	46320	3280		E2
900	LkeC	46320	3280		E3
Cass Av					
-	DGvT	60439	3271		C2
Cass Ln					
800	EGVV	60007	2914		A2
Cass St					
10	LMNT	60439	3270		D5
300	CRTE	60417	3685	0W-29S	C2
5200	OKLN	60453	3211	6W-10S	E5
Castaway Ct					
1600	HFET	60010	2804	24W-16N	B1
Castaway Ln					
1600	HFET	60010	2804	25W-15N	B1
1600	HFET	60195	2804	25W-15N	B1
1600	SBTN	60010	2804	25W-15N	B1
4800	HFET	60010	2751	24W-16N	B7
5100	IVNS	60010	2751	24W-16N	B7
Castello Av					
9600	FNPK	60131	2973	12W-2N	C6
9600	LydT	60164	2973	12W-2N	C6
Castilian Cir					
2200	NHBK	60062	2810	10W-15N	A2

STREET Block	City	ZIP	Map#	CGS	Grid
Castilian Ct					
1000	GNVW	60025	2809	11W-13N	D6
1000	NfdT	60025	2809	11W-13N	D6
Castle Av					
10	DndT	60118	2801		C5
Castle Cir					
300	LGPK	60525	3087	12W-2S	C4
Castle Ct					
100	BRTN	60010	2751	24W-20N	C2
100	PltT	60010	2751	24W-20N	C2
400	MTSN	60443	3506	5W-24S	B6
1700	ELGN	60120	2856	31W-9N	A7
8600	LynT	60527	3208		C4
E Castle Ct					
800	PLTN	60074	2753	19W-18N	B2
Castle Dr					
1000	GNVW	60025	2809	11W-13N	E6
1200	PKRG	60068	2917	10W-7N	E3
1200	PKRG	60068	2918	10W-7N	A3
5100	BLWD	60104	3028		E3
8400	TYPK	60477	3424	10W-20S	B5
Castle Rd					
18700	HMWD	60430	3508	1W-22S	B2
Castlebar Ln					
15000	ODPK	60462	3346	11W-17S	A6
Castle Dargan Dr					
-	CCHL	60478	3506	6W-22S	A1
W Castle Island Av					
8400	CHCG	60656	2918	10W-5N	A7
Castle Pines Ct					
-	RVWD	60015	2756	12W-20N	A1
Castlerea Ln					
600	DSPN	60016	2808	13W-13N	D6
Castlewood Ct					
100	ROSL	60172	2912		A4
300	HFET	60067	2804	23W-14N	E4
1300	LMNT	60439	3271		B7
Castlewood Dr					
10	CPVL	60110	2748		A5
10	DndT	60110	2748		A5
600	HnrT	60107	2856	30W-10N	B6
600	HnrT	60120	2856	30W-10N	B6
600	SMWD	60107	2856	30W-10N	B6
600	SMWD	60120	2856	30W-10N	B6
1300	LMNT	60439	3271		B7
Castlewood Ln					
300	BFGV	60089	2754	17W-20N	A1
300	BRLT	60103	2911		B6
300	DRFD	60015	2756	12W-20N	C1
E Castlewood Ln					
800	BRLT	60103	2911		B5
W Castlewood Ter					
700	CHCG	60640	2921	1W-6N	E6
Catalina Av					
6200	OKFT	60452	3347	7W-18S	B7
Catalina Ct					
15500	ODPK	60462	3346	9W-18S	E7
Catalina Dr					
1100	HRPK	60133	2912		A6
1300	HRPK	60133	2911		E6
15100	ODPK	60462	3346	9W-18S	E7
15100	OrlT	60462	3346	9W-18S	E7
Catalpa Av					
200	WDDL	60191	2915		B7
300	ROSL	60172	2913		B5
400	AddT	60191	2915		B5
400	ITSC	60143	2914		B5
20100	LYWD	60411	3510	3E-23S	A4
W Catalpa Av					
1000	CHCG	60640	2921	2W-6N	C5
2400	CHCG	60625	2921	3W-6N	A5
3200	CHCG	60625	2920	4W-6N	D5
5800	CHCG	60630	2919	7W-6N	B5
6300	CHCG	60656	2919	8W-6N	A5
7200	CHCG	60656	2918	9W-6N	D5
7800	NpkT	60656	2918	9W-6N	B5
8600	CHCG	60656	2917	10W-6N	E5
Catalpa Ct					
-	BCHR	60401	3864	0W-36S	C1
200	ROSL	60172	2913		B5
8900	TYPK	60477	3424	11W-20S	A5
Catalpa Ln					
400	DLTN	60419	3350	0E-16S	E3
600	BRLT	60103	2910		E6
W Catalpa Ln					
1700	MPPT	60056	2861	17W-11N	C3
Catalpa Pl					
200	WLMT	60091	2812	3W-13N	D6
Catalpa St					
800	BCHR	60401	3864	0W-36S	C1
6800	HRPK	60133	2911		C3
Catawba Ct					
12100	HMGN	60441	3422	15W-19S	C3
Catawba Ln					
8000	HRPK	60133	2857	26W-9N	D7
W Catawba Ln					
13400	HMGN	60441	3343	16W-16S	E4
S Catawba Rd					
16500	HMGN	60441	3422	15W-19S	C3
Catbird Ln					
300	VrnT	60015	2755	14W-20N	B1
Catherine					
-	JSTC	60458	3210	10W-9S	B2
N Catherine Av					
10	LGNG	60525	3087	12W-4S	B6
200	LGPK	60525	3087	12W-3S	B6
S Catherine Av					
10	LGNG	60525	3087	12W-4S	B7
300	LGNG	60525	3147	12W-4S	B1
5500	CTSD	60525	3147	12W-6S	B3
W Catherine Av					
7900	LydT	60656	2918	10W-6N	A5
7900	NpkT	60656	2918	10W-6N	A5
8400	CHCG	60656	2918	10W-6N	A5
8600	CHCG	60656	2917	10W-6N	E5
Catherine Ct					
-	WLNG	60090	2755	15W-17N	B5
13900	ODPK	60462	3345	11W-16S	E3
Catherine Dr					
900	DYR	46311	3598		E2
13900	ODPK	60462	3345	11W-16S	E3
Catherine Ln					
19700	TYPK	60448	3504	11W-23S	A4
Catherine St					
300	LMNT	60439	3270		E5
2200	NHBK	60062	2757	10W-17N	A5
N Cathy Ln					
100	MPPT	60056	2807	16W-13N	E7
S Cathy Ln					
700	MPPT	60056	2807	16W-12N	E7
W Cathy Ln					
800	MPPT	60056	2807	16W-12N	E7
Catino Ct					
600	ROSL	60172	2913		A6

STREET Block	City	ZIP	Map#	CGS	Grid
N Catino Ct					
200	MPPT	60056	2808	14W-13N	C6
W Catino St					
600	ANHT	60005	2806	18W-13N	E6
W Catino Ter					
8100	NLES	60714	2864	10W-11N	B2
Catlow Ct					
-	BRTN	60010	2750	27W-20N	C1
W Caton St					
2100	CHCG	60647	2977	2W-2N	B7
Caumet Av					
-	BNHM	60633	3352	3E-16S	A3
Cavan Ln					
600	DSPN	60016	2862	15W-11N	A4
W Cavecreek Ct					
13700	HMGN	60441	3343	17W-17S	D6
Cawdor Ln					
100	IVNS	60067	2752	22W-16N	B7
E Cayuga Av					
100	EMHT	60126	3028		A5
Cayuga Dr					
1000	NHBK	60062	2756	11W-17N	D5
E Cayuga Ln					
2000	MPPT	60056	2808	13W-15N	E3
Cedar Av					
-	CHCG	60613	2977	1W-5N	D1
400	EMHT	60126	3028		B6
400	YkTp	60126	3028		B6
700	ELGN	60120	2855		A2
2000	HRPK	60133	2911		C2
17700	CCHL	60478	3426	5W-21S	C6
18600	CCHL	60478	3506	5W-22S	C1
N Cedar Av					
300	WDDL	60191	2915		B7
500	AddT	60191	2915		B6
S Cedar Av					
500	EMHT	60126	3028		B4
900	YkTp	60126	3028		B6
4400	HMND	46327	3352		E4
Cedar Cir					
-	BmnT	60426	3426	5W-19S	B1
100	SMWD	60107	2857	28W-10N	A6
Cedar Ct					
10	CTCY	60409	3351	2E-16S	C4
10	LMNT	60439	3270		C6
100	SMBG	60193	2858	24W-10N	E6
300	SMWD	60107	2857	28W-10N	A5
500	MNSR	46321	3510		D1
1800	DSPN	60018	2863	12W-9N	B6
2100	GNVW	60025	2864	9W-12N	D1
2200	NHBK	60062	2809	11W-16N	D1
18800	CCHL	60478	3506	5W-22S	C2
W Cedar Ct					
6500	MONE	60449	3682	8W-32S	C7
Cedar Dr					
10	WLNG	60090	2754	15W-18N	E4
Cedar Ln					
10	LynT	60458	3209	11W-8S	E1
200	GLNC	60022	2758	6W-17N	D5
300	EGVV	60007	2915		A1
400	WLMT	60091	2812	4W-13N	B6
700	BRLT	60103	2910		D6
700	CHHT	60411	3507	1W-24S	E6
800	NHBK	60062	2757	10W-17N	A4
1000	DYR	46311	3510		C7
9200	PKRG	60016	2863	11W-11N	E3
9300	MaiT	60016	2863	11W-11N	E2
17500	TYPK	60477	3424	9W-21S	E5
E Cedar Ln					
1300	MPPT	60056	2808	14W-14N	C4
2900	CteT	60417	3687	3E-30S	B2
N Cedar Ln					
10	GNWD	60425	3508	0E-22S	E1
S Cedar Ln					
10	GNWD	60425	3508	0E-22S	D2
12700	PSHT	60463	3274	9W-15S	D7
12700	PSHT	60463	3346	9W-15S	D1
W Cedar Ln					
900	ANHT	60005	2860	18W-12N	E1
8000	NLES	60714	2864	10W-10N	B5
Cedar Rd					
-	HMGN	60441	3343	18W-16S	B3
-	LMNT	60439	3343	18W-16S	B3
1600	HMWD	60430	3427	2W-21S	D6
3600	PKFT	60466	3594	4W-26S	D3
3600	PKFT	60471	3594	4W-26S	D3
3600	RNPK	60471	3594	4W-26S	D3
6400	OKFT	60452	3347	8W-18S	B6
S Cedar Rd					
13800	HMGN	60441	3343	18W-16S	B4
15400	HmrT	60441	3343	18W-18S	A7
Cedar St					
10	CTSD	60525	3147	12W-6S	C5
10	PKFT	60466	3595	2W-27S	C4
100	PKRG	60068	2864	10W-9N	B7
300	WNKA	60093	2812	4W-15N	B2
700	WLSP	60480	3209	12W-9S	C4
1400	PKRG	60068	2863	11W-9N	E7
2000	DSPN	60018	2863	12W-9N	B7
2200	DSPN	60018	2917	12W-9N	B1
8300	ODPK	60462	3346	10W-16S	B2
E Cedar St					
10	ANHT	60005	2861	18W-12N	A1
10	CHCG	60610	3034	0E-1N	C2
10	CHCG	60611	3034	0E-1N	C2
N Cedar St					
10	PLTN	60067	2805	21W-16N	D1
100	PLTN	60067	2752	21W-16N	D7
S Cedar St					
10	PLTN	60067	2805	21W-14N	D3
100	PltT	60067	2805	21W-15N	D2
W Cedar St					
200	ANHT	60005	2861	18W-12N	A1
400	ANHT	60005	2860	18W-12N	E1
2200	ANHT	60008	2806	19W-12N	C7
2200	RGMW	60008	2806	19W-12N	C7
S Cedarbend Dr					
13600	HMGN	60441	3343	17W-17S	D5
Cedar Creek Ct					
10	PSHT	60463	3275	8W-14S	B5
W Cedar Creek Ct					
13200	HMGN	60441	3343	16W-17S	E4
Cedarcrest Dr					
400	SMWD	60107	2857	28W-10N	B6
S Cedarcrest Dr					
10	SMBG	60193	2858	24W-9N	E7
800	SMBG	60193	2912		E1
Cedarfield Dr					
100	BRLT	60103	2909		C3
Cedar Glen Dr					
10	PltT	60067	2806	19W-14N	C4
10	RGMW	60008	2806	19W-14N	C4
S Cedar Glen Dr					
2300	ANHT	60005	2861	17W-11N	B4
2300	ANHT	60056	2861	17W-11N	B4

STREET Block	City	ZIP	Map#	CGS	Grid
S Cedar Glen Dr					
2300	MPPT	60056	2861	17W-11N	B4
2600	MPPT	60005	2861	17W-10N	B4
Cedar Glen Dr N					
2500	LYWD	60411	3509	3E-23S	E4
Cedar Ridge Dr					
12400	HMGN	60441	3344	15W-17S	B6
Cedar Ridge Rd					
100	RNPK	60471	3594	4W-27S	D4
Cedar Run Dr					
600	WLNG	60090	2754	16W-18N	E2
Cedar Tree Ct					
300	HFET	60194	2858	23W-11N	E2
Cedarwood Ct					
600	WLNG	60090	2754	16W-17N	D5
1000	EGVV	60007	2914		D2
E Cedarwood Ct					
100	PLTN	60067	2753	20W-17N	A5
200	PLTN	60074	2753	20W-17N	A5
Cedarwood Dr					
100	CteT	60417	3596	1W-28S	A7
100	CteT	60475	3596	1W-28S	A7
100	STGR	60475	3596	1W-28S	A7
8800	ODHL	60462	3424	11W-19S	A2
8800	ODHL	60477	3424	11W-19S	A2
8800	ODPK	60462	3424	11W-19S	A2
Cedarwood Ln					
1200	GNVW	60025	2810	9W-13N	C5
1500	WLNG	60090	2754	16W-17N	D6
4100	MTSN	60443	3506	5W-25S	C6
Celebrity Cir E					
1500	HRPK	60133	2911		E6
Celebrity Cir W					
1500	HRPK	60133	2911		D6
N Celia Av					
20500	BFGV	60069	2754	16W-20N	D1
20500	BFGV	60089	2754	16W-20N	D1
20500	VrnT	60069	2754	16W-20N	D1
20500	VrnT	60089	2754	16W-20N	D1
Celtic Glen Dr					
2000	MPPT	60056	2808	13W-14N	E4
2000	WhlT	60025	2808	13W-14N	E4
S Cemetery Rd					
30300	WshT	60401	3864	0W-37S	C3
Cenco Pkwy					
3300	FNPK	60131	2972		D4
Centennial Cir					
16000	TYPK	60477	3425	8W-19S	A1
Centennial Ct					
15600	ODPK	60462	3423	12W-18S	C1
Centennial Dr					
900	MPPT	60056	2808	14W-13N	B7
6800	BmnT	60452	3425	8W-19S	A2
6800	TYPK	60477	3425	8W-19S	A2
15700	ODPK	60462	3423	12W-18S	C1
Center					
-	RVDL	60827	3349	1W-16S	E2
Center Av					
-	CHCG	60827	3350	0E-16S	E2
10	WLNG	60090	2755	14W-17N	C4
1200	CHHT	60411	3508	0W-25S	C7
1400	CHHT	60411	3596	0W-25S	B1
2000	NHBK	60062	2757	10W-17N	B5
3900	LYNS	60534	3088	9W-4S	C7
4500	LYNS	60534	3148	9W-4S	C1
4600	MCCK	60534	3148	9W-4S	C1
6600	HRPK	60133	2911		C2
10400	FNPK	60131	2973	13W-3N	A4
13900	DLTN	60419	3350	0E-16S	E3
14400	HRVY	60426	3350	1W-18S	A7
15600	HRVY	60426	3428	1W-18S	A1
16700	EHZC	60429	3428	1W-20S	A5
18100	HMWD	60430	3428	1W-21S	A7
18300	HMWD	60430	3508	1W-22S	A1
S Center Av					
5400	SMMT	60501	3148	9W-5S	D3
17500	EHZC	60429	3428	1W-21S	A6
17500	HMWD	60430	3428	1W-21S	A6
W Center Av					
8300	RVGV	60171	2974	10W-3N	A5
8600	RVGV	60171	2973	11W-3N	D6
Center Brch					
10	GNVW	60093	2810	8W-15N	D3
Center Ct					
1100	HMWD	60430	3508	1W-23S	A2
W Center Ct					
100	HFET	60195	2805	23W-12N	A7
100	PltT	60195	2805	23W-12N	A7
100	SMBG	60195	2805	23W-12N	A7
Center Dr					
-	CPVL	60110	2748		B7
-	EDND	60118	2748		B7
-	SMBG	60173	2805	22W-12N	D7
1800	CPVL	60110	2801		B1
1800	CPVL	60118	2801		B1
1800	EDND	60110	2801		B1
1800	EDND	60118	2801		B1
11600	LMNT	60439	3271		B5
Center Ln					
1200	ANHT	60004	2807	16W-15N	D3
1200	PTHT	60004	2807	16W-15N	D3
Center Rd					
-	HnrT	60107	2856	29W-10N	E5
10	SMWD	60107	2856	29W-10N	E5
11100	PSHL	60465	3273	11W-13S	E3
W Center Rd					
300	PLTN	60074	2752	21W-18N	C2
300	PltT	60074	2752	21W-18N	C2
Center St					
-	BRTN	60010	2751	24W-20N	B1
10	AddT	60106	2915		C6
10	BNVL	60106	2915		C6
10	HNDL	60521	3086		A7
300	HLSD	60162	3029	13W-0S	A7
300	PvsT	60162	3029	13W-0S	A7
600	EGvT	60007	2915		A3
700	DSPN	60016	2863	13W-10N	A6
1100	DSPN	60018	2863	13W-10N	A6
E Center St					
10	GNWD	60425	3508	0E-22S	E2
100	ITSC	60143	2914		C6
500	GNWD	60425	3509	0E-22S	A2
W Center St					
100	GNWD	60425	3508	0E-22S	D2
100	ITSC	60143	2914		B6
100	WDDL	60191	2915		A7
Centerway Wk					
15900	TYPK	60477	3424	9W-19S	E1
Central Av					
-	ELGN	60120	2855		C7
-	RchT	60471	3593	7W-26S	E3
-	RVFT	60305	3030	10W-0N	B4
10	MTSN	60443	3505	6W-24S	E5
10	RchT	60443	3505	7W-23S	E4
10	RchT	60477	3505	7W-22S	E2
Central Av					
10	ROSL	60172	2913		A4
100	ROSL	60172	2912		B4
200	WLMT	60091	2813	3W-13N	A6
300	NHFD	60093	2811	7W-15N	C2
400	AddT	60191	2915		B6
400	WDDL	60191	2915		B5
500	MonT	60449	3682	7W-29S	E2
500	MonT	60466	3682	7W-29S	E2
500	UYPK	60449	3682	7W-29S	E2
500	UYPK	60466	3682	7W-29S	E2
600	HRPK	60133	2912		A4
600	ROSL	60133	2912		A4
700	WLMT	60091	2812	3W-13N	D6
800	DRFD	60015	2756	12W-20N	C1
1100	BNVL	60007	2915		B4
1100	BNVL	60106	2915		B3
1200	EGVV	60007	2915		B3
1600	NfdT	60062	2756	11W-16N	C7
1600	NHBK	60062	2756	11W-16N	C7
1700	DSPN	60018	2917	12W-8N	A2
3000	WLMT	60091	2811	6W-13N	D6
3800	PvsT	60558	3086		D7
3800	WNSP	60558	3086		D7
4700	WNSP	60558	3146		D3
7100	BRRG	60527	3146		D7
7100	BRRG	60527	3208		D1
7100	IHPK	60525	3146		D7
7200	OKPK	60301	3030	9W-0N	C4
7200	OKPK	60302	3030	9W-0N	C4
7300	FTPK	60130	3030	9W-0N	D4
7300	FTPK	60305	3030	9W-0N	D4
7500	BDPK	60459	3211	6W-8S	D1
7500	BDPK	60638	3211	6W-8S	D1
7500	BRBK	60459	3211	6W-10S	D4
7800	SKOK	60053	2865	6W-9N	C6
7800	SKOK	60077	2865	6W-9N	C6
8600	OKLN	60453	3211	6W-11S	D7
8700	MNGV	60053	2865	7W-10N	C4
10200	OKLN	60453	3275	7W-12S	D2
10400	CHRG	60415	3275	7W-12S	D2
11000	CHRG	60453	3275	6W-12S	D3
11000	OKLN	60803	3275	6W-12S	D3
12700	ALSP	60463	3275	7W-15S	D7
12700	ALSP	60803	3275	7W-15S	D7
12700	CTWD	60445	3275	7W-15S	D7
12700	CTWD	60463	3275	7W-15S	D7
12700	CTWD	60803	3275	7W-15S	D7
12900	CTWD	60445	3347	7W-15S	D1
13000	WthT	60445	3347	6W-15S	D1
13000	WthT	60463	3347	6W-15S	D1
13300	BmnT	60463	3347	6W-15S	D2
13900	BmnT	60445	3347	7W-17S	D5
14100	MDLN	60445	3347	7W-17S	D5
14500	OKFT	60445	3347	6W-17S	D4
14500	OKFT	60452	3347	6W-17S	D4
14600	BmnT	60452	3347	6W-17S	D5
15700	OKFT	60452	3425	6W-18S	D1
15800	BmnT	60477	3425	6W-21S	E6
15800	OKFT	60477	3425	6W-18S	D1
16100	BmnT	60452	3425	6W-19S	D1
18100	RchT	60477	3425	7W-21S	E7
21100	MTSN	60443	3593	7W-26S	E1
21600	MTSN	60471	3593	7W-26S	E2
21600	RNPK	60443	3593	7W-26S	E2
21600	RNPK	60471	3593	7W-26S	E2
N Central Av					
10	CHCG	60644	3031	7W-0N	C3
200	WDDL	60191	2915		B7
400	AddT	60191	2915		B7
700	CHCG	60651	3031	7W-0N	C3
1500	CHCG	60639	3031	7W-2N	C1
1700	CHCG	60639	2975	7W-2N	C7
2700	CHCG	60634	2975	7W-2N	C7
2700	CHCG	60641	2975	7W-2N	C7
4300	CHCG	60630	2975	7W-5N	C1
4400	CHCG	60630	2919	7W-5N	C7
5500	CHCG	60646	2919	6W-6N	C5
6600	CHCG	60712	2919	6W-8N	D2
6600	LNWD	60712	2919	6W-8N	D2
7000	NLES	60714	2919	6W-8N	C1
7000	SKOK	60077	2919	6W-8N	C1
7000	SKOK	60646	2919	6W-8N	C1
7000	SKOK	60714	2919	6W-8N	C1
7200	NLES	60077	2865	7W-9N	C7
7200	NLES	60714	2865	7W-9N	C7
7200	SKOK	60077	2865	7W-9N	C7
S Central Av					
-	MONE	60449	3682	6W-30S	E4
-	StkT	60402	3089	7W-4S	D7
10	CHCG	60644	3031	7W-0S	C5
1100	CCRO	60804	3031	6W-0S	D7
1500	CCRO	60804	3089	7W-1S	D1
3800	SKNY	60402	3089	7W-3S	D6
3800	SKNY	60804	3089	7W-3S	D6
4600	FTVW	60402	3089	7W-4S	D7
4600	FTVW	60638	3089	6W-4S	D7
4600	FTVW	60638	3149	6W-4S	D1
4600	StkT	60638	3089	6W-4S	D7
4600	StkT	60638	3149	6W-4S	D1
5000	CHCG	60638	3149	7W-5S	D2
7000	BDPK	60638	3149	7W-8S	D7
7300	BDPK	60459	3211	6W-8S	D1
7300	BDPK	60638	3211	6W-8S	D1
7300	BRBK	60459	3211	6W-8S	D1
11100	ALSP	60803	3275	7W-13S	D5
11100	CHRG	60415	3275	7W-13S	D3
11100	CHRG	60453	3275	7W-13S	D3
11100	OKLN	60453	3275	7W-13S	D3
11100	OKLN	60803	3275	7W-13S	D5
12500	ALSP	60463	3275	6W-14S	D7
12500	WthT	60463	3275	6W-14S	D7
12500	WthT	60803	3275	6W-14S	D7
12600	CTWD	60445	3275	6W-14S	D7
12600	CTWD	60463	3275	6W-14S	D7
12600	CTWD	60803	3275	6W-14S	D7
23200	MonT	60449	3593	7W-28S	E7
23200	MonT	60466	3593	7W-28S	E7
23200	RchT	60449	3593	6W-27S	E5
23200	RchT	60471	3593	6W-27S	E5
23200	UYPK	60449	3593	7W-28S	E7
24000	MonT	60466	3682	6W-29S	E1
24000	UYPK	60466	3682	6W-29S	E1
25300	MonT	60449	3682	6W-30S	E4
25300	UYPK	60449	3682	6W-30S	E4
Central Ct					
3100	GNVW	60025	2810	10W-12N	A7
3100	NfdT	60025	2810	10W-12N	A7
14500	OKFT	60452	3347	6W-17S	D5
Central Dr					
2500	BDVW	60155	3087	11W-1S	D1
2500	FSMR	60422	3507	3W-22S	B2
Central Pkwy					
1400	GNVW	60025	2810	8W-12N	E7
Central Rd					
800	GLF	60025	2811	7W-13N	B7
800	GNVW	60025	2811	8W-12N	A7
1700	GNVW	60025	2810	9W-13N	B7
E Central Rd					
-	ANHT	60056	2807	17W-12N	C7
-	MaiT	60025	2810	10W-13N	A7
-	MPPT	60005	2807	17W-12N	C7
10	ANHT	60005	2807	17W-13N	B7
200	MPPT	60056	2808	14W-13N	C7
400	DSPN	60016	2808	14W-13N	C7
400	MPPT	60016	2808	14W-13N	C7
800	DSPN	60056	2808	13W-13N	D7
800	MaiT	60016	2808	13W-13N	D7
800	WhlT	60016	2808	13W-13N	D7
800	WhlT	60056	2808	13W-13N	D7
1500	DSPN	60016	2809	12W-13N	B7
1500	MPPT	60056	2807	17W-12N	C7
1500	NfdT	60016	2809	12W-13N	A7
3100	GNVW	60025	2810	10W-13N	A7
3100	NfdT	60025	2810	10W-13N	A7
3500	MaiT	60025	2809	10W-13N	E7
3500	NfdT	60025	2809	10W-13N	E7
3600	MaiT	60016	2809	12W-13N	A7
9500	GNVW	60016	2809	11W-13N	C7
9500	GNVW	60025	2809	11W-13N	C7
W Central Rd					
10	HFET	60195	2803	25W-13N	E7
10	MPPT	60056	2808	15W-13N	A7
10	PltT	60195	2805	22W-13N	A7
10	SBTN	60010	2803	25W-13N	E7
10	SMBG	60195	2805	22W-13N	A7
100	ANHT	60005	2807	18W-12N	A7
100	HFET	60195	2805	22W-13N	A7
200	HFET	60195	2804	24W-13N	B7
200	MPPT	60056	2807	16W-13N	C7
200	SMBG	60195	2804	23W-13N	E7
500	ANHT	60005	2806	18W-12N	E7
1500	ANHT	60056	2807	16W-13N	C7
1600	RGMW	60008	2806	18W-13N	E7
1700	ANHT	60008	2806	19W-13N	D7
1700	MPPT	60005	2807	16W-13N	C7
Central St					
-	SKOK	60076	2812	5W-13N	B7
-	SKOK	60077	2811	5W-13N	E7
-	SKOK	60201	2812	4W-13N	B7
-	WLMT	60077	2811	5W-13N	E7
-	WLMT	60091	2811	5W-13N	E7
-	WLMT	60091	2812	5W-13N	B7
-	WLMT	60201	2812	4W-13N	B7
600	EVTN	60201	2813	2W-13N	B7
1700	EVTN	60201	2812	3W-13N	D7
3500	LNSG	60438	3430	4E-21S	C6
Central Park Av					
-	PKFT	60466	3594	4W-27S	E5
-	RNPK	60466	3594	4W-27S	E5
-	RNPK	60471	3594	4W-27S	E5
100	EVTN	60201	2812	4W-12N	C7
100	WLMT	60091	2812	4W-13N	C7
100	WLMT	60201	2812	4W-13N	C7
700	FSMR	60422	3506	4W-23S	E3
700	FSMR	60429	3506	4W-22S	E2
700	HLCT	60429	3506	4W-22S	E2
1000	RchT	60430	3506	4W-23S	E3
1700	RchT	60422	3506	4W-23S	E4
2100	EVTN	60201	2866	4W-11N	C2
2100	SKOK	60203	2866	4W-11N	C3
7200	SKOK	60076	2866	4W-9N	D7
13300	RBBN	60472	3348	4W-16S	D3
14300	MDLN	60445	3348	4W-17S	D4
14800	MDLN	60426	3348	4W-17S	D5
14800	MKHM	60426	3348	4W-17S	D5
14800	MKHM	60445	3348	4W-17S	D5
15700	MKHM	60426	3426	4W-18S	E1
16900	HLCT	60429	3426	4W-20S	E4
17500	CCHL	60429	3426	4W-21S	E6
17500	CCHL	60478	3426	4W-21S	E6
19800	OMFD	60461	3506	4W-23S	E4
23100	MonT	60466	3594	4W-28S	E6
N Central Park Av					
400	CHCG	60624	3032	4W-0N	C3
700	CHCG	60651	3032	4W-0N	C3
1500	CHCG	60647	3032	4W-1N	C1
1600	CHCG	60647	2976	4W-2N	C7
3600	CHCG	60618	2976	4W-4N	C2
4300	CHCG	60625	2976	4W-5N	C1
4400	CHCG	60625	2920	4W-5N	C7
5600	CHCG	60659	2920	4W-7N	C4
6300	CHCG	60712	2920	4W-7N	C3
6800	LNWD	60712	2920	4W-8N	C1
S Central Park Av					
-	CHCG	60629	3150	4W-6S	D3
-	CHCG	60632	3150	4W-6S	D3
10	CHCG	60624	3032	4W-1S	D7
1100	CHCG	60623	3032	4W-1S	D7
1600	CHCG	60623	3090	4W-2S	D3
7500	CHCG	60652	3212	4W-9S	D2
9100	CHCG	60805	3212	4W-10S	D5
9100	ENGN	60805	3212	4W-11S	D7
10100	CHCG	60655	3212	4W-11S	D7
10200	CHCG	60655	3276	4W-13S	D4
10200	CHCG	60805	3276	4W-11S	D1
10200	ENGN	60805	3276	4W-11S	D1
11600	MTPK	60655	3276	4W-13S	D4
11900	MTPK	60803	3276	4W-14S	D5
11900	WthT	60803	3276	4W-14S	D5
12500	ALSP	60803	3276	4W-14S	D6
Centre Av					
-	CHCG	60613	2977	1W-5N	D1
Centre St					
10	PKFT	60466	3595	3W-27S	B4
Centrella St					
3700	FNPK	60131	2972		E2
3700	FNPK	60131	2973	13W-4N	A3
3700	LydT	60131	2972		E2
Century Ct					
100	SMBG	60193	2859	23W-10N	A6
Century Dr					
10	ROSL	60172	2913		C4
10	WLNG	60090	2755	14W-17N	C6
Century Rd					
21400	MTSN	60443	3594	4W-25S	E1
Ceriseto U					
-	DRFD	60015	2757	10W-20N	A2
Cermak Rd					
-	OKBK	60523	3086		B2
6200	BRWN	60402	3089	8W-2S	A2
6200	CCRO	60804	3089	7W-1S	B2
6800	BRWN	60402	3088	8W-1S	E2
7100	NRIV	60130	3088	8W-1S	D2
7100	NRIV	60546	3088	8W-1S	D2
11300	HLSD	60154	3086		C2
11300	PvsT	60162	3086		C2
11300	PvsT	60523	3086		C2
11300	WSTR	60154	3086		C2
Cermak Rd					
11300	WSTR	60523	3086		C2
E Cermak Rd					
10	CHCG	60616	3092	0E-1S	C1
W Cermak Rd					
-	PvsT	60155	3087	12W-1S	C2
10	CHCG	60616	3092	0W-2S	A2
700	CHCG	60608	3092	1W-1S	A1
800	CHCG	60608	3091	3W-2S	A2
900	BDVW	60155	3087	11W-1S	C2
900	NRIV	60546	3087	13W-1S	A2
900	PvsT	60546	3087	13W-1S	A2
1100	NRIV	60155	3087	11W-1S	E2
1700	BDVW	60546	3087	11W-1S	D2
2700	CHCG	60623	3091	3W-1S	A2
3400	CHCG	60623	3090	5W-1S	B2
4500	CCRO	60804	3090	5W-1S	A2
4700	HLSD	60154	3086		D2
4700	HLSD	60162	3086		D2
4700	PvsT	60162	3086		D2
4800	CCRO	60804	3089	7W-1S	C2
6100	BRWN	60402	3089	7W-1S	B2
7200	BRWN	60402	3088	10W-1S	A2
7200	NRIV	60130	3088	10W-1S	A2
7200	NRIV	60546	3088	10W-1S	A2
7300	FTPK	60130	3088	9W-1S	D2
7300	FTPK	60546	3088	9W-1S	D2
7900	PvsT	60546	3088	9W-1S	B2
8000	PvsT	60141	3088	10W-1S	B2
8600	NRIV	60141	3088	10W-1S	A2
8700	PvsT	60141	3087	13W-1S	A2
9800	BDVW	60154	3087	12W-1S	C2
9800	PvsT	60154	3087	12W-2S	C2
9800	WSTR	60154	3087	12W-1S	C2
10100	PvsT	60525	3087	12W-1S	B2
10700	WSTR	60154	3086		E2
11200	PvsT	60523	3086		D2
11200	WSTR	60523	3086		D2
Cernan Ct					
1000	EGVV	60007	2914		A2
1100	EGVV	60007	2913		E2
Cernan Dr					
800	BLWD	60104	3029	12W-0S	C6
Chadbourn Dr					
8800	ODPK	60462	3424	11W-19S	A2
8900	ODHL	60462	3424	11W-19S	A3
8900	ODHL	60477	3424	11W-19S	A3
Chaddick Dr					
100	WLNG	60090	2755	14W-17N	C6
Chaffee Ct					
1400	EGVV	60007	2914		A3
N Chalary Ct					
300	PLTN	60067	2752	22W-16N	C7
Chalet Ct					
100	CRTE	60417	3596	0E-28S	D6
Chalet Ln					
10	CRTE	60417	3596	0E-28S	D6
Chalfont Dr					
1300	SMBG	60194	2858	25W-11N	B4
Challis Dr					
3300	CteT	60417	3598	4E-29S	C7
3300	SjnT	46311	3598	4E-29S	C7
W Chalmers Pl					
800	CHCG	60614	2977	1W-2N	E6
Chambers Dr					
-	HFET	60195	2804	24W-16N	B1
4900	HFET	60010	2751	24W-16N	C7
4900	HFET	60010	2804	24W-16N	B1
5000	IVNS	60010	2751	24W-16N	C7
Chambery Ct					
1900	WLNG	60090	2808	14W-15N	C2
Chambord Ln					
3300	HLCT	60429	3426	4W-21S	E6
Chamonieux Dr					
10600	PSHL	60465	3274	10W-12S	B2
Champlain Av					
7900	TYPK	60477	3424	9W-21S	D6
14800	DLTN	60419	3350	0E-17S	E6
S Champlain Av					
200	BlmT	60425	3508	0E-23S	E3
200	GNWD	60425	3508	0E-23S	E3
4200	CHCG	60653	3092	0E-4S	D7
4600	CHCG	60615	3092	0E-4S	D7
4700	CHCG	60615	3152	0E-5S	D1
7100	CHCG	60619	3152	0E-8S	D7
7100	CHCG	60637	3152	0E-8S	D7
7500	CHCG	60619	3214	0E-9S	E2
9400	CHCG	60628	3214	0E-10S	E5
10500	CHCG	60628	3278	0E-12S	E2
Champlain Rd					
10	SBTN	60010	2803	27W-14N	A4
Champlain St					
15400	DLTN	60419	3350	0E-18S	E6
15400	SHLD	60473	3350	0E-18S	E7
N Champlain St					
2200	ANHT	60004	2753	18W-16N	E7
Champlaine Ct					
1200	SMBG	60193	2913		C2
W Chanay St					
2700	CHCG	60647	2977	2W-3N	C5
Chancellor Dr					
10	ROSL	60172	2912		D4
Chancellor St					
1300	EVTN	60201	2813	2W-13N	A7
1700	EVTN	60201	2812	3W-13N	E7
S Chandler Av					
100	EMHT	60126	3028		A3
Chandler Ln					
10	HFET	60194	2859	23W-11N	A4
2100	GNVW	60025	2809	10W-15N	E3
Channel Rd					
7200	CHCG	60645	2866	3W-9N	D7
7200	SKOK	60076	2866	3W-9N	D7
7200	SKOK	60645	2866	3W-9N	D7
Channing Ct					
200	ELGN	60120	2855		A3
1600	MLPK	60160	3030	10W-1N	A2
N Channing St					
10	ELGN	60120	2855		A4
S Channing St					
10	ELGN	60120	2855		A4
Chanora Ct					
-	HFET	60195	2804	25W-14N	A3
Chanticleer Ln					
100	HNDL	60521	3146		B4
Chantilly Ln					
18000	HLCT	60429	3426	4W-21S	E6
Chaparral Cir					
200	ELGN	60120	2855		E4
Chaparral Ct					
300	ELGN	60120	2855		E4
Chapel Ct					
1500	NHBK	60062	2757	9W-17N	C5
N Chapel St					
10	ELGN	60120	2855		A4
S Chapel St					
10	ELGN	60120	2855		A4
Chapel Hill Dr					
2600	HnrT	60120	2856	31W-11N	A4
N Chapel Hill Dr					
2600	ANHT	60004	2754	17W-16N	B6
Chapel Hill Ln					
400	NHFD	60093	2811	7W-15N	B2
Chapel Hill Rd					
15500	ODPK	60462	3346	10W-18S	B7
15600	ODPK	60462	3424	10W-18S	B1
Chaplin Ct					
2000	HRPK	60133	2911		D6
Chapman Ct					
2400	RGMW	60008	2805	20W-14N	E5
Chapman Dr					
-	CRTE	60417	3597	1E-29S	C7
Chapparal Ter					
700	RchT	60443	3593	8W-26S	B2
Chappel Av					
200	CTCY	60409	3351	2E-17S	C5
500	ThtT	60473	3351	2E-17S	C6
15800	ThtT	60473	3429	2E-18S	C1
17800	LNSG	60438	3429	2E-21S	C5
22100	SLVL	60411	3597	2E-26S	D3
S Chappel Av					
-	CHCG	60633	3351	2E-15S	C2
-	CTCY	60409	3351	2E-16S	C2
6700	CHCG	60649	3153	2E-7S	C6
7500	CHCG	60649	3215	2E-9S	C2
9500	CHCG	60617	3215	2E-11S	C6
Char Ln					
13900	BmnT	60445	3348	6W-16S	A3
13900	CTWD	60445	3348	6W-16S	A3
Chara Ct					
400	BRLT	60103	2910		D1
Charabanc Ln					
10	WLNG	60090	2754	15W-18N	E2
100	WLNG	60090	2755	15W-18N	A2
Charal Ln					
300	HDPK	60035	2758	7W-20N	A1
Charing Cross Rd					
10	CHHT	60411	3508	1W-24S	A5
300	EGVV	60007	2860	18W-9N	E7
500	EGVV	60007	2914		E1
1300	DRFD	60015	2756	11W-20N	C1
Chariot Ct					
100	WLNG	60090	2755	15W-18N	A2
W Chariot Ct					
1700	EGvT	60056	2861	17W-10N	C5
1700	MPPT	60056	2861	17W-10N	C5
Chariot Ln					
2700	OMFD	60461	3507	3W-24S	B6
Chariot Rd					
100	WLNG	60090	2755	15W-18N	A2
Charlela Ln					
900	EGVV	60007	2914		A3
Charlemagne Av					
3200	HLCT	60429	3426	4W-21S	E7
3200	HLCT	60429	3427	4W-21S	A7
Charlemagne Cir					
10	ROSL	60172	2913		A6
Charlemagne Dr					
500	NHBK	60062	2756	12W-18N	B4
N Charlemagne Dr					
3800	HFET	60195	2804	24W-14N	B3
Charlemagne Dr W					
1500	HFET	60195	2804	25W-14N	B3
Charlene Ln					
1000	SMBG	60193	2858	24W-10N	C6
Charles Av					
1200	ALGN	60102	2748		A3
10100	PSHL	60465	3274	10W-11S	B1
Charles Ct					
10	BFGV	60089	2754	16W-17N	D5
10	CRTE	60417	3597	1E-28S	B6
1600	WLNG	60090	2808	14W-15N	C1
Charles Dr					
-	RVDL	60827	3349	1W-16S	D2
400	EGvT	60007	2860	19W-9N	C7
400	EGVV	60007	2860	19W-9N	C7
1600	WLNG	60090	2808	14W-15N	C1
3700	NHBK	60062	2756	12W-17N	B5
E Charles Dr					
10	NHLK	60164	2972		E7
Charles Ln					
5800	OKFT	60452	3347	7W-18S	D7
Charles Pl					
200	WLMT	60091	2811	5W-13N	E7
Charles St					
200	CHHT	60411	3507	1W-23S	E3
800	CRTE	60417	3597	1E-28S	A6
3000	LydT	60164	2972		E4
3100	FNPK	60131	2972		E4
4700	HLSD	60154	3086		D1
4700	HLSD	60162	3086		D1
4700	PvsT	60162	3086		D1
4700	WSTR	60154	3086		D1
21800	MTSN	60443	3594	4W-26S	E2
E Charles St					
600	ANHT	60004	2807	17W-15N	B1
S Charles St					
9400	CHCG	60620	3213	2W-10S	D6
9400	CHCG	60643	3213	2W-10S	D6
10300	CHCG	60643	3277	1W-12S	D1
Charleston Ct					
200	SMBG	60193	2857	26W-10N	E6
1600	MLPK	60160	3030	10W-1N	A2
5800	HRPK	60133	2911		D5
Charleston Dr					
2400	SMBG	60193	2857	26W-10N	E6
8400	BRRG	60527	3208		A4
13900	ODPK	60462	3345	11W-16S	E3
Charleston Ln					
700	HFET	60195	2804	24W-14N	D4
700	IVNS	60067	2804	24W-14N	D4
1600	HLCT	60429	3427	2W-20S	D4
Charleston Rd					
10	HNDL	60521	3146		B4
4000	MTSN	60443	3594	5W-26S	C1
Charleston St					
6400	OKFT	60452	3347	8W-18S	B7
W Charleston St					
2000	CHCG	60614	2977	2W-2N	B6
2000	CHCG	60647	2977	2W-2N	B6
N Charleton Av					
100	WLSP	60480	3209	12W-9S	C3
S Charleton Av					
100	WLSP	60480	3209	12W-9S	C3
600	PlsT	60480	3209	12W-9S	C4
Charlie Ct					
2700	GNVW	60025	2809	11W-15N	D2
2700	GNVW	60062	2809	11W-15N	D2
2700	NHBK	60062	2809	11W-15N	D2

STREET Block	City	ZIP	Map#	CGS	Grid
E Chicago St					
1400	HnrT	60120	2855		E5
E Chicago St SR-19					
300	ELGN	60120	2855		D5
1400	HnrT	60120	2855		E5
E Chicago St SR-312					
800	HMND	46327	3352		E4
S Chicago Beach Dr					
4800	CHCG	60615	3153	2E-5S	B1
S Chicago Bloomington Tr					
12900	HMGN	60441	3422	16W-20S	A5
12900	HMGN	60448	3422	16W-20S	A5
Chicago Ridge Mall Dr					
-	CHRG	60415	3211	8W-11S	B6
-	CHRG	60453	3211	8W-11S	B6
-	OKLN	60453	3211	8W-11S	B7
Chichester on Asbury					
10	RGMW	60008	2806	19W-15N	B3
Chickadee Cir					
16300	ODPK	60467	3423	12W-19S	D2
Chickamauga Ln					
1500	LGGV	60047	2753	18W-20N	E1
S Chickasaw Tr					
14000	HMGN	60441	3343	16W-16S	D4
N Chicora Av					
6700	NLES	60646	2919	7W-8N	C2
6700	SKOK	60646	2919	7W-8N	C2
6900	CHCG	60646	2919	6W-8N	C1
Chicory Ct					
100	RGMW	60008	2805	21W-14N	D5
200	BFGV	60089	2754	16W-20N	D1
Chicory Ln					
200	BFGV	60089	2754	16W-20N	D2
Chicory Tr					
13900	HMGN	60441	3342	18W-16S	E4
14100	HmrT	60441	3342	18W-16S	E4
N Childrens Plz					
2300	CHCG	60614	2978		C5
Childs Av					
5500	HNDL	60521	3146		B4
Chillon Dr					
10	LYWD	60411	3598	4E-25S	C1
Chilmark Ln					
2100	SMBG	60193	2857	26W-10N	E6
2100	SMBG	60193	2858	26W-10N	A6
Chilton Ln					
700	WLMT	60091	2811	5W-13N	E5
Chimney Rock					
800	IVNS	60067	2804	23W-14N	E4
S China Pl					
2100	CHCG	60616	3092	0W-1S	B1
Chinkapinoak Dr					
2000	MPPT	60056	2808	13W-14N	E4
2000	WhlT	60025	2808	13W-14N	E4
Chipili Dr					
200	NHBK	60062	2758	7W-17N	A6
E Chippendale Dr					
300	BRLT	60103	2911		B5
S Chippendale Dr					
900	BRLT	60103	2911		C6
Chippendale Rd					
1700	HFET	60195	2858	24W-12N	C1
1900	HFET	60195	2804	24W-12N	C7
S Chippewa Av					
13800	BNHM	60633	3352	3E-16S	A2
Chippewa Cir					
900	CPVL	60110	2748		C5
Chippewa Ct					
10	BRRG	60527	3208		C3
5100	OKFT	60452	3426	6W-20S	A5
Chippewa Dr					
10	TNTN	60476	3428	0E-20S	E5
600	ELGN	60120	2855		C2
6700	PSHT	60463	3275	8W-14S	A5
Chippewa Ln					
900	WLMT	60091	2812	5W-14N	A5
Chippewa Tr					
1300	WLNG	60090	2754	16W-17N	D5
8000	TYPK	60477	3424	10W-21S	C5
S Chippewa Tr					
13500	HMGN	60441	3343	16W-16S	D3
Chipping Campden Dr					
10	IVNS	60010	2804	25W-15N	A1
10	SBTN	60010	2804	25W-15N	A1
Chisholm Ct					
500	ROSL	60172	2913		C3
Chisholm Tr					
700	ROSL	60172	2913		C3
11800	OrlT	60467	3344	14W-16S	C2
E Chivalry Ct					
1500	PLTN	60074	2806	19W-15N	D2
Choate Rd					
10	PKFT	60466	3595	2W-26S	C3
S Choctaw Rd					
12900	PSHT	60463	3346	9W-15S	E1
W Choctaw Rd					
7300	PSHT	60463	3274	9W-15S	E7
W Choctaw Tr					
13000	HMGN	60441	3343	16W-16S	E2
13000	HMGN	60441	3344	16W-16S	A2
E Cholo Ln					
1900	MPPT	60056	2808	13W-14N	E4
Chopin Ct					
400	SMBG	60193	2858	24W-9N	E7
S Chris Ln					
700	MPPT	60056	2861	17W-12N	B2
Chrisman Dr					
200	SMWD	60107	2857	28W-11N	A5
Christa Ct					
900	EGVV	60007	2913		E1
S Christa Ct					
10700	PSHL	60465	3274	10W-12S	C2
Christeen Dr					
8100	JSTC	60458	3210	10W-9S	B3
Christiana Av					
8200	SKOK	60076	2866	4W-10N	D5
N Christiana Av					
800	CHCG	60624	3032	4W-1N	D2
800	CHCG	60651	3032	4W-1N	D2
2800	CHCG	60647	2976	4W-3N	D5
3000	CHCG	60618	2976	4W-3N	D4
5100	CHCG	60625	2920	4W-6N	D5
5500	CHCG	60659	2920	4W-6N	D5
6400	LNWD	60712	2920	4W-8N	D2
S Christiana Av					
1200	CHCG	60624	3032	4W-1S	D7
1400	CHCG	60623	3032	4W-1S	D7
1500	CHCG	60623	3090	4W-1S	D1
4300	CHCG	60632	3090	4W-4S	D7
4700	CHCG	60632	3150	4W-5S	D1
7100	CHCG	60629	3150	4W-8S	E7
7700	CHCG	60652	3212	4W-8S	E2
10300	ENGN	60805	3276	4W-11S	E1
10800	CHCG	60655	3276	4W-12S	E2

STREET Block	City	ZIP	Map#	CGS	Grid
Christie Av					
8000	LYNS	60534	3088	10W-4S	B7
Christina Dr					
-	MTSN	60443	3505	7W-25S	C7
-	MTSN	60443	3593	7W-25S	C1
2600	LNSG	60438	3429	3E-21S	E7
2600	LNSG	60438	3430	3E-21S	A7
9000	HYHL	60457	3209	11W-10S	E5
9100	PlsT	60480	3209	11W-10S	E5
18500	BlmT	60411	3430	3E-22S	A7
18500	LNSG	60411	3430	3E-21S	A7
Christina Ln					
1300	NHBK	60062	2756	11W-17N	D6
13800	HMGN	60441	3343	18W-16S	A4
Christine Ct					
200	STGR	60475	3595	1W-28S	E6
200	STGR	60475	3596	1W-28S	A6
9100	ODPK	60462	3345	11W-16S	E4
Christopher Av					
17000	ODHL	60477	3424	11W-20S	A4
17000	TYPK	60477	3424	11W-20S	A4
Christopher Ct					
1200	ELGN	60120	2855		D2
16900	TYPK	60477	3425	7W-20S	C4
Christopher Dr					
-	LMNT	60439	3342	20W-15S	B1
400	DGvT	60439	3270		C3
5300	BmnT	60477	3425	6W-20S	E5
5300	OKFT	60452	3425	6W-20S	E5
5300	OKFT	60477	3425	6W-20S	E5
Chukker Ct					
400	WLNG	60090	2755	15W-16N	B7
Church Ct					
400	BRLT	60103	2910		E3
Church Dr					
15600	SHLD	60473	3350	0E-18S	E7
E Church Dr					
800	PLTN	60074	2753	19W-16N	B7
800	PLTN	60074	2806	20W-16N	B1
Church Ln					
15400	OKFT	60452	3347	8W-18S	A7
Church Rd					
-	KLWH	60043	2812	4W-14N	B3
-	NtrT	60043	2812	4W-14N	B3
-	WNKA	60043	2812	4W-14N	B3
10	NtrT	60093	2812	4W-14N	B3
10	WNKA	60093	2812	4W-15N	B3
200	BFGV	60089	2754	17W-18N	C2
6200	HRPK	60133	2911		D4
E Church Rd					
10	BCHR	60401	3774	0E-35S	E7
10	WshT	60401	3774	0E-35S	E7
N Church Rd					
200	BNVL	60106	2915		E7
S Church Rd					
1000	MPPT	60056	2861	16W-11N	D3
W Church Rd					
10	BCHR	60401	3774	0W-35S	C7
600	WshT	60401	3774	0W-35S	B7
Church St					
300	EVTN	60201	2867	2W-11N	B3
1000	GNVW	60025	2810	8W-13N	E6
1100	NHBK	60062	2757	9W-17N	C5
1600	EVTN	60201	2866	3W-11N	E3
1900	DYR	46311	3598		D2
2500	SKOK	60201	2866	4W-11N	D2
2500	SKOK	60203	2866	4W-11N	D2
3700	SKOK	60076	2866	5W-11N	B3
4700	SKOK	60076	2865	6W-11N	E2
4700	SKOK	60077	2865	5W-11N	E3
5500	MNGV	60053	2865	7W-11N	C2
6600	HRPK	60133	2911		D3
6700	MNGV	60053	2864	9W-11N	D3
7800	MNGV	60714	2864	9W-11N	D3
7800	NLES	60714	2864	9W-11N	B3
E Church St					
100	EMHT	60126	3028		A3
2300	DSPN	60016	2863	11W-11N	C3
2300	MaiT	60016	2863	11W-11N	C3
S Church St					
10300	CHCG	60643	3277	1W-12S	D1
W Church St					
8000	MNGV	60053	2864	10W-11N	B3
8000	MNGV	60714	2864	10W-11N	B3
8000	NLES	60714	2864	10W-11N	B3
8500	MaiT	60016	2864	10W-11N	A3
8500	NLES	60016	2864	10W-11N	A3
8600	MaiT	60016	2863	11W-11N	E3
8700	PKRG	60016	2863	10W-11N	E3
8700	PKRG	60068	2863	10W-11N	E3
9300	DSPN	60016	2863	11W-11N	D3
W Church Ter					
8000	NLES	60714	2864	10W-11N	B3
Churchhill St					
-	CHCG	60647	2977	2W-3N	B5
W Churchill Av					
8000	MNGV	60053	2864	10W-11N	B3
8000	NLES	60053	2864	10W-11N	B3
8000	NLES	60714	2864	10W-11N	B3
N Churchill Cir					
9000	NLES	60714	2864	10W-11N	B3
Churchill Ct					
1200	BRLT	60103	2910		B7
Churchill Dr					
7400	HRPK	60133	2911		E1
10600	ODPK	60467	3423	13W-20S	A3
E Churchill Dr					
1500	PLTN	60074	2753	19W-16N	D7
21900	RNPK	60471	3594	5W-26S	C3
S Churchill Dr					
4400	RNPK	60471	3594	5W-26S	B3
Churchill Rd					
-	SMBG	60194	2858	24W-12N	D2
1200	BRLT	60103	2910		C7
1200	ROSL	60172	2912		C5
1300	SMBG	60195	2858	24W-12N	D2
Churchill St					
-	MNGV	60053	2865	8W-11N	A3
200	NHFD	60093	2811	7W-15N	B3
7400	MNGV	60053	2864	9W-11N	C3
7700	NLES	60053	2864	9W-11N	C3
7700	NLES	60714	2864	9W-11N	C3
W Churchill St					
2000	CHCG	60622	2977	2W-2N	B7
2000	CHCG	60647	2977	2W-2N	B7
Churchview Dr					
16500	ODPK	60467	3423	11W-19S	E3
Churn Rd					
10	MTSN	60443	3505	7W-24S	C4
Cicero Av					
-	ALSP	60803	3348	5W-15S	A1
-	CTWD	60803	3348	5W-15S	A1
13100	CTWD	60445	3348	6W-15S	A2
13900	BmnT	60445	3348	5W-16S	A3
14300	MDLN	60445	3348	5W-17S	A4

STREET Block	City	ZIP	Map#	CGS	Grid
Cicero Av					
14700	MDLN	60452	3348	5W-17S	A5
14800	OKFT	60452	3348	5W-17S	A5
14900	OKFT	60445	3348	5W-17S	A6
15700	BmnT	60426	3426	5W-20S	A3
15700	OKFT	60452	3426	5W-20S	A3
16200	OKFT	60426	3426	5W-20S	A3
16700	BmnT	60477	3426	5W-20S	A3
16700	OKFT	60477	3426	5W-20S	A3
16800	BmnT	60452	3426	5W-20S	A4
17000	BmnT	60478	3426	6W-20S	B4
17000	CCHL	60477	3426	5W-21S	B7
17000	CCHL	60478	3426	6W-20S	B4
18400	CCHL	60478	3506	5W-24S	B6
18800	CCHL	60477	3506	5W-22S	B2
18800	RchT	60477	3506	5W-22S	B2
19900	MTSN	60443	3506	5W-24S	B5
19900	MTSN	60477	3506	5W-24S	B4
19900	RchT	60443	3506	5W-24S	B4
21100	MTSN	60443	3594	6W-26S	B2
21900	RNPK	60471	3594	6W-26S	B2
22700	UYPK	60471	3594	6W-27S	B5
22900	UYPK	60466	3594	6W-27S	B5
Cicero Av SR-50					
-	ALSP	60803	3348	5W-15S	A1
-	CTWD	60803	3348	5W-15S	A1
13100	CTWD	60445	3348	6W-15S	A2
13900	BmnT	60445	3348	5W-16S	A3
14300	MDLN	60445	3348	5W-17S	A4
14700	MDLN	60452	3348	5W-17S	A5
14800	OKFT	60452	3348	5W-17S	A5
14900	OKFT	60445	3348	5W-17S	A6
15700	BmnT	60426	3426	5W-20S	A3
15700	OKFT	60452	3426	5W-20S	A3
16200	OKFT	60426	3426	5W-20S	A3
16700	BmnT	60477	3426	5W-20S	A3
16700	OKFT	60477	3426	5W-20S	A3
16800	BmnT	60452	3426	5W-20S	A4
16800	BmnT	60478	3426	6W-20S	B4
17000	BmnT	60478	3426	6W-20S	B4
17000	CCHL	60477	3426	5W-21S	B7
17000	CCHL	60478	3426	6W-20S	B4
18400	CCHL	60478	3506	5W-24S	B6
18800	CCHL	60477	3506	5W-22S	B2
18800	RchT	60477	3506	5W-22S	B2
19900	MTSN	60443	3506	5W-24S	B5
19900	MTSN	60477	3506	5W-24S	B4
19900	RchT	60443	3506	5W-24S	B4
21100	MTSN	60443	3594	6W-26S	B2
21900	RNPK	60471	3594	6W-26S	B2
22900	UYPK	60466	3594	6W-27S	B5
22900	UYPK	60471	3594	6W-27S	B5
Cicero Av SR-83					
-	ALSP	60803	3348	5W-15S	A1
-	CTWD	60803	3348	5W-15S	A1
13100	CTWD	60445	3348	6W-15S	A2
13900	BmnT	60445	3348	5W-16S	A3
14300	MDLN	60445	3348	5W-17S	A4
N Cicero Av					
10	CHCG	60644	3031	6W-0N	E5
1600	CHCG	60639	2975	6W-2N	E7
1600	CHCG	60639	3031	5W-1N	E1
1600	CHCG	60651	3031	5W-1N	E1
2700	CHCG	60641	2975	6W-5N	E1
4300	CHCG	60630	2975	6W-5N	E1
4400	CHCG	60630	2919	6W-5N	E7
5600	CHCG	60646	2919	6W-7N	E4
6300	LNWD	60712	2919	5W-8N	E2
7200	LNWD	60712	2865	5W-9N	E7
7300	SKOK	60077	2865	5W-9N	E7
N Cicero Av SR-50					
10	CHCG	60644	3031	6W-0N	E5
700	CHCG	60651	3031	6W-1N	E3
1500	CHCG	60639	3031	6W-2N	E1
1600	CHCG	60639	2975	6W-2N	E7
2700	CHCG	60641	2975	6W-5N	E1
4300	CHCG	60630	2975	6W-5N	E1
4400	CHCG	60630	2919	6W-5N	E7
5600	CHCG	60646	2919	6W-7N	E4
6300	LNWD	60712	2919	5W-8N	E2
7200	LNWD	60712	2865	5W-9N	E7
7300	SKOK	60077	2865	5W-9N	E7
S Cicero Av					
-	CTWD	60445	3348	5W-15S	A1
-	CTWD	60803	3348	5W-15S	A1
-	MonT	60466	3683	6W-29S	B2
-	UYPK	60466	3683	6W-29S	B2
10	CHCG	60644	3031	6W-0S	E5
800	CHCG	60644	3032	6W-0S	A6
1000	CCRO	60804	3032	6W-0S	A7
1500	CCRO	60804	3090	5W-4S	A6
3400	SKNY	60804	3090	6W-3S	A5
3700	CHCG	60804	3090	6W-3S	A6
3900	CHCG	60632	3090	6W-4S	A6
4200	CHCG	60638	3090	6W-4S	A7
4600	CHCG	60632	3150	5W-5S	A2
4600	CHCG	60638	3150	5W-7S	A6
5600	CHCG	60629	3150	5W-7S	A6
6400	BDPK	60638	3150	5W-7S	A6
6700	BDPK	60629	3150	5W-7S	A7
7300	BDPK	60638	3212	5W-8S	A1
7300	CHCG	60629	3212	5W-8S	A1
7300	CHCG	60638	3212	5W-8S	A1
7400	BRBK	60459	3212	6W-9S	A3
7400	CHCG	60652	3212	6W-9S	A3
8500	CHCG	60459	3212	5W-9S	A4
8600	BRBK	60453	3212	6W-9S	A4
8600	CHCG	60456	3212	6W-9S	A4
8600	HMTN	60456	3212	6W-9S	A4
8600	OKLN	60453	3212	6W-9S	A4
8700	OKLN	60456	3212	6W-10S	A4
10200	OKLN	60453	3276	5W-12S	A1
11000	CHCG	60655	3276	5W-12S	A3
11600	ALSP	60803	3276	6W-13S	A4
13100	ALSP	60803	3348	5W-15S	A1
23100	MonT	60449	3594	6W-28S	B7
23100	MonT	60466	3594	6W-28S	B7
23100	RNPK	60471	3594	6W-28S	B7
23100	UYPK	60466	3594	6W-28S	B7
23100	UYPK	60471	3594	6W-28S	B7
24000	MonT	60449	3683	6W-29S	B1
S Cicero Av SR-50					
-	CTWD	60445	3348	5W-15S	A1
-	CTWD	60803	3348	5W-15S	A1
-	MonT	60466	3683	6W-29S	B2
-	UYPK	60466	3683	6W-29S	B2
10	CHCG	60644	3031	6W-0S	E5
800	CHCG	60644	3032	6W-0S	A6
1000	CCRO	60804	3032	6W-0S	A7
1500	CCRO	60804	3090	5W-4S	A6
3400	SKNY	60804	3090	6W-3S	A5
3700	CHCG	60804	3090	6W-3S	A6
3900	CHCG	60632	3090	6W-4S	A6
4200	CHCG	60638	3090	6W-4S	A7
4600	CHCG	60632	3150	5W-5S	A2
4600	CHCG	60638	3150	5W-7S	A6

STREET Block	City	ZIP	Map#	CGS	Grid
S Cicero Av SR-50					
5600	CHCG	60629	3150	5W-7S	A6
6400	BDPK	60638	3150	5W-7S	A6
7100	BDPK	60629	3150	5W-8S	A7
7300	BDPK	60638	3212	5W-8S	A1
7300	CHCG	60629	3212	5W-8S	A1
7300	CHCG	60638	3212	5W-8S	A1
7400	BRBK	60459	3212	6W-9S	A3
7400	CHCG	60652	3212	6W-9S	A3
8500	CHCG	60459	3212	5W-9S	A4
8600	BRBK	60453	3212	6W-9S	A4
8600	CHCG	60456	3212	6W-9S	A4
8600	HMTN	60456	3212	6W-9S	A4
8600	OKLN	60453	3212	6W-9S	A4
8700	OKLN	60456	3212	6W-10S	A4
10200	OKLN	60453	3276	5W-12S	A1
11000	CHCG	60655	3276	5W-12S	A3
12800	ALSP	60803	3276	5W-15S	A7
13100	ALSP	60803	3348	5W-15S	A1
23100	MonT	60449	3594	6W-28S	B7
23100	MonT	60466	3594	6W-28S	B7
23100	RNPK	60471	3594	6W-28S	B7
23100	UYPK	60466	3594	6W-28S	B7
23100	UYPK	60471	3594	6W-28S	B7
24000	MonT	60449	3683	6W-29S	B1
S Cicero Av SR-83					
-	CTWD	60445	3348	5W-15S	A1
-	CTWD	60803	3348	5W-15S	A1
12700	ALSP	60803	3276	6W-15S	A7
13100	ALSP	60803	3348	5W-15S	A1
Cico Rd					
-	DPgT	60441	3270		A6
Cider Ln					
800	PTHT	60070	2808	13W-15N	E2
Cimarron Ct					
1300	ELGN	60120	2855		E4
Cindy Ln					
-	EGVV	60007	2913		E2
100	WLNG	60090	2755	15W-17N	A5
1400	DSPN	60018	2862	14W-10N	D6
3700	GNVW	60025	2809	11W-13N	E6
3800	NfdT	60025	2809	11W-13N	E6
Cinema Dr E					
2100	HRPK	60133	2911		C7
Cinema Dr W					
2000	HRPK	60133	2911		C6
Cinnamon Ct					
400	BRLT	60103	2910		B2
Cinnamon Creek Dr					
-	PlsT	60480	3209	11W-11S	E6
10	PSHL	60465	3209	11W-11S	E6
Cinnamon Creek Ln					
14600	HMGN	60441	3343	18W-18S	A7
Circle Av					
100	BMDL	60108	2913		B7
100	BMDL	60157	2913		B7
100	BmdT	60108	2913		B7
100	BmdT	60157	2913		B7
100	FTPK	60130	3030	9W-1S	D7
300	ROSL	60108	2913		B7
300	ROSL	60157	2913		B7
300	ROSL	60172	2913		B7
1400	FTPK	60130	3088	9W-1S	D1
1500	NRIV	60130	3088	9W-1S	D1
7200	OKPK	60302	3030	9W-0N	D4
E Circle Av					
200	PTHT	60070	2807	15W-15N	E2
N Circle Av					
100	BMDL	60108	2913		B7
W Circle Av					
200	PTHT	60070	2807	15W-15N	E2
Circle Ct					
200	SMBG	60067	2806	21W-12N	A7
400	DRFD	60015	2756	11W-20N	C1
1400	EGVV	60007	2913		E1
1900	CHHT	60411	3596	1W-26S	B1
4900	CTWD	60445	3348	6W-15S	A1
7000	BGVW	60455	3210	8W-10S	E4
10900	PSHL	60465	3274	10W-12S	C3
Circle Dr					
-	DSPN	60016	2809	12W-12N	A7
-	DSPN	60016	2863	12W-12N	A1
-	NfdT	60016	2809	12W-12N	A7
10	BFGV	60089	2754	17W-20N	C2
10	DRPK	60010	2751	23W-20N	E1
10	DRPK	60010	2752	23W-20N	A1
10	DXMR	60426	3349	2W-16S	D4
500	CteT	60417	3684	3W-29S	C2
500	UYPK	60466	3684	3W-29S	C2
600	ROSL	60172	2913		C3
1400	HnrT	60120	2855		E4
2400	HLCT	60429	3427	3W-20S	B4
2700	MKHM	60426	3427	3W-19S	B2
5600	OKLN	60453	3275	7W-12S	C1
7800	BRRG	60527	3208		D2
8000	PSHL	60465	3274	10W-12S	C2
13500	OrlT	60462	3345	11W-16S	D2
13500	PlsT	60462	3345	11W-16S	D2
E Circle Dr					
1900	NHFD	60093	2758	8W-16N	A7
4900	CTWD	60445	3348	6W-15S	A2
8300	TYPK	60477	3424	10W-20S	C4
N Circle Dr					
2200	PltT	60067	2806	20W-13N	A7
S Circle Dr					
200	EGvT	60067	2806	20W-13N	A7
200	PltT	60067	2806	21W-12N	A7
200	SMBG	60067	2806	21W-12N	A7
1000	MPPT	60056	2861	16W-11N	D3
W Circle Dr					
4900	CTWD	60445	3348	6W-15S	A2
8300	TYPK	60477	3424	10W-20S	B4
S Circle Ln					
1500	PltT	60067	2805	20W-14N	E5
S Circle Pkwy					
12700	PlsT	60464	3273	12W-15S	D7
12700	PlsT	60464	3345	12W-15S	D1
W Circle Pkwy					
9700	PlsT	60464	3273	12W-15S	C7
W Circle Pl					
5000	CTWD	60445	3347	6W-15S	E2
Circle St					
1800	DSPN	60018	2863	13W-9N	A6
Circle Ter					
300	BmdT	60157	2913		E4
W Circle Dr Pkwy					
13200	CTWD	60445	3347	6W-15S	E1
13200	CTWD	60445	3348	6W-15S	A1
E Circle Hill Dr					
300	ANHT	60004	2754	17W-16N	B7
Circle Ridge Ct					
10	BRRG	60527	3208		A6
Circle Ridge Dr					
100	BRRG	60527	3208		A6

STREET Block	City	ZIP	Map#	CGS	Grid
Citadel Ct					
700	DSPN	60016	2862	14W-11N	C4
E Citadel Ct					
1500	PLTN	60074	2806	19W-15N	C2
W Citation Dr					
12000	HMGN	60467	3344	15W-16S	C3
Citation Ln					
1200	HRPK	60133	2912		A6
N Cityfront Plaza Dr					
400	CHCG	60611	3034		E4
Civic Dr					
200	SMBG	60193	2858	25W-10N	C6
Civic Center Dr					
700	NLES	60714	2864	8W-9N	E6
Clair Ct					
10	ROSL	60172	2912		C4
S Claire Blvd					
-	CTWD	60445	3348	4W-16S	D4
-	RBBN	60445	3348	4W-16S	D4
2900	BLID	60406	3349	3W-15S	A2
2900	RBBN	60406	3349	3W-15S	A2
2900	RBBN	60472	3349	3W-15S	A2
13500	RBBN	60406	3348	3W-16S	E2
13500	RBBN	60472	3348	4W-16S	D3
14200	CTWD	60472	3348	4W-16S	D4
Claire Ct					
2000	GNVW	60025	2810	9W-15N	D3
Claire Ln					
400	PTHT	60070	2808	14W-15N	B2
16200	SHLD	60473	3428	0E-19S	E2
Clairmont Ct					
9100	ODPK	60462	3346	11W-17S	A5
Clancy Dr					
-	DSPN	60016	2808	13W-13N	E6
9200	MaiT	60016	2863	11W-11N	E2
9200	NLES	60714	2863	11W-11N	E2
W Clara Ct					
8300	NLES	60714	2864	10W-10N	A5
W Clara Dr					
8400	MaiT	60714	2864	10W-10N	A5
8400	NLES	60714	2864	10W-10N	A5
N Clara Pl					
100	EMHT	60126	3028		A2
Clare Av					
8800	MKNA	60448	3504	11W-23S	A3
8800	TYPK	60477	3504	11W-23S	A3
E Clare Ct					
10	PLTN	60067	2805	20W-14N	E3
Clare Dr					
19800	FftT	60423	3504	10W-23S	B4
19800	FftT	60477	3504	10W-23S	B4
19800	TYPK	60477	3504	10W-23S	B4
Claremont Av					
15400	HRVY	60426	3349	2W-18S	C7
15900	MKHM	60426	3427	2W-19S	C2
15900	ThtT	60426	3427	2W-19S	C2
N Claremont Av					
300	CHCG	60612	3033	2W-0N	B4
1200	CHCG	60622	3033	2W-1N	B1
1500	CHCG	60647	3033	2W-1N	B1
2100	CHCG	60647	2977	2W-2N	B6
4100	CHCG	60618	2977	2W-5N	A1
5000	CHCG	60625	2921	2W-6N	A6
6000	CHCG	60659	2921	2W-7N	A3
6300	CHCG	60645	2921	2W-7N	A3
7500	CHCG	60202	2867	2W-9N	A7
7500	CHCG	60645	2867	2W-9N	A7
7500	EVTN	60202	2867	2W-9N	A7
S Claremont Av					
700	CHCG	60612	3033	2W-0S	B6
1300	CHCG	60608	3033	2W-1S	B7
2500	CHCG	60608	3091	2W-2S	B2
3400	CHCG	60609	3091	2W-3S	B5
5400	CHCG	60609	3151	2W-5S	B2
5600	CHCG	60636	3151	2W-6S	B3
7400	CHCG	60636	3213	2W-8S	B1
7500	CHCG	60620	3213	2W-8S	B1
9500	CHCG	60643	3213	2W-11S	B7
10300	CHCG	60643	3277	2W-12S	B1
Claremont Ct					
15400	HRVY	60426	3349	2W-18S	C7
Claremont Dr					
7500	TYPK	60477	3424	9W-20S	D4
Claremont Rd					
1800	HFET	60195	2858	24W-12N	D1
Clarence Av					
-	CCHL	60478	3426	5W-21S	C7
500	OKPK	60302	3031	8W-0S	A5
500	OKPK	60304	3031	8W-0S	A6
1100	BRWN	60402	3031	8W-1S	A7
3900	BRWN	60402	3089	8W-4S	A6
3900	SKNY	60402	3089	8W-4S	A6
N Clarence Av					
1600	ANHT	60004	2807	17W-15N	C1
W Clarence Av					
6500	CHCG	60631	2919	8W-7N	A3
7200	CHCG	60631	2918	9W-7N	D3
Clarendon Av					
4600	RNPK	60471	3594	5W-27S	B4
N Clarendon Av					
3900	CHCG	60613	2977	0W-5N	E1
4400	CHCG	60613	2921	1W-5N	E7
4400	CHCG	60640	2921	1W-5N	E7
Clarendon Ct					
5900	HRPK	60133	2911		D4
E Clarendon Ct					
600	ANHT	60004	2807	17W-15N	B3
W Clarendon Rd					
1000	ANHT	60004	2806	18W-15N	E3
Clarendon St					
800	HFET	60194	2859	23W-11N	A3
E Clarendon St					
10	PTHT	60070	2808	15W-15N	A3
1000	ANHT	60004	2807	17W-15N	B3
W Clarendon St					
200	ANHT	60004	2807	18W-15N	A3
400	PTHT	60070	2807	16W-15N	D3
500	ANHT	60004	2806	18W-15N	E3
Clarendon Springs Ct					
700	SMBG	60194	2858	25W-11N	B3
Claret Dr					
400	BFGV	60089	2754	17W-20N	C1
Claria Dr					
10	ROSL	60172	2913		A4
100	ROSL	60172	2912		E4
N Clarice Av					
20500	BFGV	60069	2754	16W-20N	E1
20500	BFGV	60089	2754	16W-20N	E1
20500	VrnT	60069	2754	16W-20N	E1
Claridge Cir					
600	HFET	60194	2858	24W-11N	C4
Claridge Ct					
10	SMWD	60107	2857	27W-11N	C3
800	SMBG	60193	2859	23W-9N	B7
2000	NHBK	60062	2757	8W-16N	D7

STREET Block	City	ZIP	Map#	CGS	Grid
Claridge Ct					
14300	ODPK	60462	3346	9W-17S	D4
W Claridge Ct					
1200	PLTN	60067	2752	22W-17N	B5
Claridge Dr					
-	BGVW	60455	3274	9W-11S	D1
Claridge Ln					
2100	NHBK	60062	2757	8W-16N	D7
2100	NHBK	60062	2810	9W-15N	B1
Claridge St					
10800	WSTR	60154	3086		E2
Clarion Ct					
900	IVNS	60010	2804	25W-15N	A1
S Clark Av					
4300	HMND	46327	3352		C4
Clark Dr					
4100	RNPK	60471	3594	5W-26S	C3
N Clark Dr					
100	PLTN	60074	2806	20W-15N	A2
200	PLTN	60074	2753	19W-16N	B7
W Clark Dr					
3400	ENGN	60805	3212	4W-11S	D6
Clark Ln					
800	DSPN	60016	2862	15W-10N	B5
1100	DSPN	60018	2862	15W-10N	B5
16300	TYPK	60477	3425	8W-19S	B2
Clark Rd					
1900	DYR	46311	3598		E2
Clark St					
-	SHLD	60473	3428	0W-20S	C3
-	SKOK	60076	2866	5W-11N	B2
-	TNTN	60473	3428	0W-20S	C3
-	TNTN	60476	3428	0W-20S	C3
400	EVTN	60201	2867	2W-11N	B2
14600	DLTN	60419	3350	0W-17S	C5
14600	RVDL	60827	3350	0W-17S	C5
14900	HRVY	60426	3350	0W-17S	C5
15200	SHLD	60473	3350	0W-17S	C6
E Clark St					
10	GNWD	60425	3508	0E-22S	E2
N Clark St					
10	CHCG	60602	3034	0W-0N	B4
10	CHCG	60603	3034	0W-0N	B4
100	CHCG	60601	3034	0W-0N	B4
300	CHCG	60610	3034	0W-0N	B3
1600	CHCG	60610	2978	0W-2N	B7
1600	CHCG	60614	2978	0W-2N	B7
2700	CHCG	60657	2978	0W-3N	A4
3000	CHCG	60657	2977	0W-3N	E4
3500	CHCG	60613	2977	1W-5N	D1
4400	CHCG	60613	2921	1W-5N	D7
4400	CHCG	60640	2921	1W-5N	D7
5700	CHCG	60660	2921	2W-7N	C3
6300	CHCG	60626	2921	2W-7N	C3
7200	CHCG	60626	2867	2W-9N	C7
7500	EVTN	60202	2867	2W-9N	C6
S Clark St					
10	CHCG	60602	3034	0W-0S	B5
10	CHCG	60603	3034	0W-0S	B5
100	CHCG	60604	3034	0W-0S	B5
300	CHCG	60605	3034	0W-1S	B7
1400	CHCG	60616	3034	0W-1S	B7
1600	CHCG	60616	3092	0W-1S	B1
13900	RVDL	60827	3350	0W-16S	C3
14500	DLTN	60419	3350	0W-16S	C4
N Clarke St					
2400	RVGV	60171	2973	11W-3N	E5
Classic Ln					
-	OMFD	60461	3506	4W-24S	D5
Classic Rd					
100	SMBG	60193	2913		A1
S Claude Av					
5500	HMND	46320	3352		E7
Claude Ct					
1100	CHHT	60411	3508	0W-25S	C7
Clausen Av					
3800	PvsT	60558	3086		E7
3800	WNSP	60558	3086		E7
5100	WNSP	60558	3146		E2
Claussen Ct					
13900	DLTN	60419	3350	0E-16S	E2
Clavey Ct					
400	HDPK	60035	2757	8W-20N	D1
Clavey Ln					
-	GNVW	60025	2810	9W-12N	C7
400	HDPK	60035	2757	8W-20N	D1
Clavey Rd					
700	HDPK	60035	2758	8W-20N	A1
1000	HDPK	60035	2757	8W-20N	E1
Clavinia Av					
1600	DRFD	60015	2756	12W-20N	C1
Clay Ct					
1600	MLPK	60160	3030	10W-1N	A2
N Clay St					
100	HNDL	60521	3146		A1
400	HNDL	60521	3086		A7
S Clay St					
10	HNDL	60521	3146		A1
Claymoor St					
300	HNDL	60521	3146		B4
Clayton Cir					
700	SMBG	60194	2857	26W-11N	E4
Clayton Ct					
500	WDDL	60191	2915		A6
E Clayton Ct					
1600	ANHT	60004	2807	16W-15N	C2
Clayton Ln					
500	DSPN	60016	2808	14W-12N	C7
500	MPPT	60016	2808	14W-12N	C7
500	MPPT	60056	2808	14W-12N	C7
Clayton Rd					
200	HLSD	60162	3028		E5
Clear Vw					
10	LMNT	60439	3272	15W-13S	B4
Clearbrook Ct					
200	SMBG	60193	2859	23W-9N	B7
S Clearbrook Dr					
2500	ANHT	60005	2861	17W-11N	B4
Clear Creek Cross					
18100	ODPK	60467	3422	14W-21S	E7
E Clear Creek Bay					
1700	PLTN	60074	2753	19W-18N	C3
Clearmont Dr					
200	EGVV	60007	2914		E2
300	EGVV	60007	2915		A2
Clearview Ct					
14300	ODPK	60462	3346	11W-17S	A4
Clearview Dr					
600	GNVW	60025	2810	10W-13N	B7
8800	ODPK	60462	3346	11W-17S	A4
Clearwater Ct					
10	SMWD	60107	2856	29W-10N	E7
700	WLNG	60090	2754	16W-17N	D5
N Clearwater Ct					
1100	PLTN	60067	2752	22W-17N	A5
Clearwater Dr					
1500	WLNG	60090	2754	16W-17N	D5
2000	DSPN	60018	2862	14W-9N	C7
2000	OKBK	60523	3086		A2
Clearwater Ln					
300	SMBG	60194	2859	22W-10N	C4
1500	WLNG	60090	2754	16W-17N	D6
Clearwater N St					
400	ROSL	60172	2912		E7
Clearwater South St					
500	ROSL	60172	2912		D7
Clearwater W St					
900	ROSL	60172	2912		D7
N Cleaver St					
1100	CHCG	60622	3033	1W-1N	D1
E Cleburne St					
200	BRLT	60103	2911		A5
S Cleburne St					
800	BRLT	60103	2911		B5
Clematis Dr					
1200	SMBG	60193	2857	27W-10N	C6
1200	SMWD	60107	2857	27W-10N	C6
Cleo Ct					
600	WLNG	60090	2754	16W-18N	D2
Clermont Dr					
1800	WLNG	60090	2808	14W-15N	C2
Cleveland Av					
100	CPVL	60110	2801		A1
100	CPVL	60118	2801		A1
100	EDND	60118	2801		A1
400	ELGN	60120	2855		B5
900	PKRG	60068	2918	9W-8N	C3
1000	CTCY	60409	3352	3E-17S	A5
1100	BKFD	60513	3087	11W-3S	D5
1100	LGPK	60525	3087	11W-3S	D5
1400	CTCY	60409	3351	2E-17S	D4
1500	PvsT	60525	3087	11W-2S	D4
13800	BLID	60406	3349	3W-16S	B3
13800	BLID	60469	3349	3W-16S	B3
13800	POSN	60406	3349	3W-16S	B3
13800	POSN	60469	3349	3W-16S	B3
25700	MONE	60449	3682	7W-31S	D5
N Cleveland Av					
-	CHCG	60610	2978	0W-2N	A7
1000	CHCG	60610	3034	0W-1N	A2
1700	CHCG	60614	2978	0W-2N	A7
S Cleveland Av					
400	ANHT	60005	2807	17W-13N	C6
900	MPPT	60056	2807	17W-13N	C7
14500	POSN	60469	3349	3W-17S	B5
14900	BmnT	60426	3349	3W-17S	B5
Cleveland Ct					
100	SMBG	60193	2859	23W-10N	A6
Cleveland Rd					
700	HNDL	60521	3146		C3
Cleveland St					
10	CTCY	60409	3430		C2
300	HMND	46324	3430		E2
1000	EVTN	60202	2867	3W-10N	A5
1200	WLMT	60091	2812	5W-14N	A4
1300	NtrT	60093	2812	5W-14N	A4
1900	EVTN	60202	2866	3W-10N	E5
3300	SKOK	60076	2866	4W-10N	D5
4700	SKOK	60076	2865	6W-10N	E5
5200	SKOK	60077	2865	6W-10N	D5
5700	MNGV	60053	2865	7W-10N	B5
E Cleveland St					
1000	HMND	46320	3430		E2
W Cleveland St					
6800	MNGV	60053	2864	8W-10N	E5
6800	NLES	60714	2864	8W-10N	E5
Cleven Av					
1100	MPPT	60056	2807	16W-12N	D7
1100	MPPT	60056	2861	16W-12N	D1
Cliff St					
100	WLSP	60480	3209	12W-9S	B4
N Clifford Av					
5700	CHCG	60646	2919	6W-7N	E4
Clifford St					
3400	EVTN	60201	2812	4W-13N	B7
Clifford Ter					
3700	SKOK	60076	2866	4W-10N	C4
Cliffside Ln					
9200	ODPK	60462	3345	11W-18S	E7
Cliffside Cir Dr					
10	WLSP	60480	3209	12W-9S	B4
Clifton Av					
-	MKNA	60448	3504	11W-23S	A4
N Clifton Av					
10	PKRG	60068	2864	10W-9N	A7
10	PKRG	60068	2918	8W-8N	D1
1800	CHCG	60614	2977	1W-2N	D7
3000	CHCG	60657	2977	1W-3N	D4
3700	CHCG	60613	2977	1W-4N	E2
4400	CHCG	60613	2921	1W-5N	D7
4700	CHCG	60640	2921	1W-6N	D6
4800	CHCG	60656	2918	10W-6N	A6
4800	NRDG	60706	2918	10W-6N	A6
4900	CHCG	60706	2918	10W-6N	A6
8400	NLES	60714	2864	10W-10N	A4
S Clifton Av					
10	PKRG	60068	2918	10W-8N	A2
Clifton Ct					
400	SMBG	60193	2912		E1
17700	TYPK	60477	3424	11W-21S	A6
Clifton Ln					
8800	TYPK	60477	3424	11W-21S	A6
W Clifton Ln					
13900	HMGN	60441	3343	17W-17S	C5
Clifton Pl					
2200	HFET	60195	2857	26W-12N	E1
2200	HFET	60195	2858	25W-12N	C1
Clifton Wy					
-	MKNA	60448	3504	11W-23S	A3
Clifton Park Av					
-	MKHM	60426	3348	4W-17S	D6
-	MKHM	60445	3348	4W-17S	D5
14300	MDLN	60445	3348	4W-17S	D4
15900	MKHM	60426	3426	4W-19S	E2
S Clifton Park Av					
9100	ENGN	60805	3212	4W-10S	D5
10200	ENGN	60805	3276	4W-13S	C3
13700	RBBN	60472	3348	4W-16S	D2
Cline Av					
-	HMND	-	3280		E7
Cline Av SR-912					
-	HMND	-	3280		E7
Clinton Av					
-	HRVY	60426	3350	1W-17S	B6
-	OKPK	60301	3030	8W-0N	E4
100	OKPK	60302	3030	8W-0N	E5
900	OKPK	60304	3030	8W-0S	E7
1200	BRWN	60402	3030	8W-1S	E7
1500	BRWN	60402	3088	8W-2S	E3
3900	SKNY	60402	3088	8W-4S	E6
4400	FTVW	60402	3088	8W-4S	E7
4500	FTVW	60402	3148	8W-4S	E1
16100	HRVY	60426	3428	0W-19S	C2
16100	SHLD	60426	3428	0W-19S	C2
16100	SHLD	60473	3428	0W-19S	C2
N Clinton Av					
100	EMHT	60126	3028		B2
Clinton Ct					
1600	MLPK	60160	3030	10W-1N	A2
W Clinton Ct					
1200	PLTN	60067	2805	22W-15N	B2
Clinton Pl					
400	FTPK	60130	3030	9W-0N	D4
500	RVFT	60305	3030	9W-0N	D3
600	EVTN	60201	2813	2W-13N	B7
1500	EDPK	60707	3030	9W-1N	D1
Clinton St					
100	PKRG	60068	2864	10W-9N	B7
12700	BLID	60406	3277	3W-15S	A7
14500	HRVY	60426	3350	1W-17S	B5
E Clinton St					
10	CTCY	60409	3352		C6
10	HMND	46320	3352		C6
N Clinton St					
10	CHCG	60661	3034	0W-0N	A4
400	CHCG	60610	3034	0W-0N	A3
2400	RVGV	60171	2974	10W-3N	B5
S Clinton St					
10	CHCG	60661	3034	0W-0S	A6
300	CHCG	60607	3034	0W-0S	A5
1600	CHCG	60616	3092	0W-1S	A1
Clipper Dr					
-	RGMW	60008	2805	21W-13N	C6
-	RGMW	60173	2805	21W-13N	C6
-	SMBG	60173	2805	21W-13N	C6
Clipper Cove					
2600	SMBG	60173	2805	21W-13N	C6
Clonard St					
-	MTSN	60443	3506	5W-24S	B5
Cloud Ct					
500	SMBG	60193	2858	25W-9N	B7
Clove Ct					
1400	MPPT	60056	2807	16W-14N	D3
Clover Cir					
10	SMWD	60107	2856	29W-10N	D6
Clover Ct					
100	BRLT	60103	2911		A5
800	GNVW	60025	2810	9W-13N	B7
1900	NHBK	60062	2756	11W-16N	D7
Clover Dr					
1500	IVNS	60067	2805	23W-15N	A3
1600	IVNS	60067	2804	23W-14N	E3
Clover Ln					
10	DRPK	60010	2751	23W-20N	E2
600	SMBG	60193	2858	25W-9N	B7
600	UYPK	60449	3684	3W-30S	B2
600	UYPK	60466	3684	3W-30S	B2
700	GLNC	60022	2758	7W-17N	B5
1200	HFET	60195	2804	24W-15N	C1
2300	NHFD	60093	2810	8W-15N	E3
2300	NHFD	60093	2811	8W-15N	A3
3300	MTSN	60443	3594	4W-26S	E2
16500	TYPK	60477	3424	10W-19S	B3
Clover Mdws					
100	BRRG	60527	3146		C5
Clover Rd					
1800	NHBK	60062	2756	11W-16N	D7
2100	NHBK	60062	2809	11W-16N	D1
N Clover St					
4000	CHCG	60641	2976	5W-5N	A1
Cloverdale Ct					
1900	SMBG	60194	2858	25W-10N	A5
Cloverdale Ln					
10	SMBG	60194	2858	26W-10N	A5
Cloverdale Rd					
10	BMDL	60108	2912		A7
10	BMDL	60172	2912		A7
10	BmdT	60108	2912		A7
10	BmdT	60172	2912		A7
100	HRPK	60133	2912		A7
500	HRPK	60172	2912		A7
Clover Hill Ct					
700	EGVV	60007	2914		B2
1000	ELGN	60120	2855		D1
Clover Hill Ln					
600	EGVV	60007	2914		B3
1000	ELGN	60120	2855		D1
Cloverleaf Rd					
10	MTSN	60443	3505	7W-24S	D5
Clover Ridge Ln					
-	ITSC	60143	2914		B5
Cloverview Dr					
8300	TYPK	60477	3424	10W-21S	C6
Club Cir					
900	GNVW	60025	2811	7W-13N	A6
Club Cir Dr					
14500	BmnT	60445	3347	8W-17S	B5
14500	OKFT	60452	3347	8W-17S	B5
Club House Cir					
500	ROSL	60172	2913		B3
Clubhouse Dr					
100	LynT	60458	3209	11W-8S	D2
S Clubhouse Dr					
200	PLTN	60074	2806	19W-15N	B2
Clubhouse Ln					
-	HFET	60195	2858	25W-12N	B1
Clubside Ct					
10	DGvT	60527	3146		A4
Club Tree Dr					
-	BRLT	60103	2911		A2
-	BRLT	60107	2911		A2
3000	SMWD	60107	2911		A1
N Clybourn Av					
1200	CHCG	60610	3034	0W-1N	A1
1600	CHCG	60614	2977	1W-2N	E7
1600	CHCG	60622	2977	1W-2N	E7
2700	CHCG	60618	2977	2W-3N	B4
2700	CHCG	60647	2977	2W-3N	B4
2700	CHCG	60657	2977	2W-3N	B5
Clyde Av					
100	CHCG	60626	2867	2W-9N	B6
100	EVTN	60202	2867	2W-9N	B6
200	CTCY	60409	3351	2E-17S	C6
4300	LYNS	60534	3088	10W-4S	B7
4500	LYNS	60534	3148	10W-4S	B1
4600	MCCK	60525	3148	10W-4S	B1
15400	DLTN	60419	3351	2E-18S	C7
15400	DLTN	60473	3351	2E-18S	C7
15400	ThtT	60409	3351	2E-18S	C7
15400	ThtT	60419	3351	2E-18S	C7
15400	ThtT	60473	3351	2E-18S	C7
16600	SHLD	60473	3429	2E-19S	D3
17900	ThtT	60438	3429	2E-21S	D7
18000	LNSG	60438	3429	2E-21S	D7
18400	HMWD	60430	3507	3W-22S	B1
18500	BlmT	60411	3429	2E-21S	D7
22100	SLVL	60411	3597	2E-27S	D3
N Clyde Av					
10	PltT	60067	2805	22W-16N	B1
100	PltT	60067	2752	22W-16N	B7
200	PLTN	60067	2752	22W-16N	B7
300	IVNS	60067	2752	22W-16N	B7
17700	LNSG	60438	3429	2E-21S	D5
17700	ThtT	60438	3429	2E-21S	D5
S Clyde Av					
-	CHCG	60633	3351	2E-15S	C2
-	CTCY	60409	3351	2E-16S	C2
10	PltT	60067	2805	22W-15N	B1
6700	CHCG	60649	3153	2E-7S	C6
7500	CHCG	60649	3215	2E-9S	C2
9800	CHCG	60617	3215	2E-11S	C6
Clyde Rd					
2400	HMWD	60430	3507	3W-22S	C1
2500	HMWD	60430	3427	3W-22S	B7
18400	FSMR	60422	3507	3W-22S	B1
18400	FSMR	60430	3507	3W-22S	B1
Clyde St					
10	GLF	60029	2865	8W-12N	A1
100	GLF	60025	2865	8W-12N	A1
100	GNVW	60025	2865	8W-12N	A1
Clyde Ter					
2300	HMWD	60430	3507	2W-22S	C1
4800	MCCK	60525	3148	10W-5S	B1
Clydesdale Ln					
14500	HMGN	60441	3344	15W-17S	B5
Clynderven Rd					
8300	BRRG	60527	3208		A4
CO-4 N Bloomingdale Rd					
100	BMDL	60108	2913		A7
CO-4 Roselle Rd					
300	BMDL	60108	2913		A6
300	BMDL	60172	2913		A6
300	ROSL	60172	2913		A6
CO-4 N Roselle Rd					
300	ROSL	60172	2913		A3
CO-4 S Roselle Rd					
10	ROSL	60172	2913		A5
700	BMDL	60108	2913		A6
CO-6 S Bartlett Rd					
200	WynT	60103	2910		E5
400	BRLT	60103	2910		E6
CO-8 Elmhurst Rd					
2300	EGvT	60007	2915		E3
2300	EGVV	60007	2915		E3
CO-8 S Madison St					
5400	DGvT	60521	3146		A7
5400	HNDL	60521	3146		A7
5800	DGvT	60527	3146		A4
5900	BRRG	60527	3146		A5
6300	WLBK	60527	3146		A5
7200	DGvT	60527	3208		A1
7200	WLBK	60527	3208		A1
7600	BRRG	60527	3208		A2
CO-8 York Rd					
2700	OKBK	60523	3086		B5
3600	HNDL	60521	3086		B6
3700	OKBK	60521	3086		B6
CO-8 N York Rd					
200	BNVL	60106	2915		E7
300	CHCG	60106	2915		E7
800	EGVV	60007	2915		E4
800	EGVV	60106	2915		E4
CO-9 Lemont Rd					
10	DGvT	60439	3270		C1
10	WDRG	60439	3270		C3
10	WDRG	60516	3270		C1
200	DGvT	60517	3270		C3
200	WDRG	60517	3270		C3
500	LMNT	60439	3270		C3
600	DGvT	60516	3270		C1
CO-10 N Arlington Heights Rd					
1200	AddT	60143	2914		D4
1200	EGVV	60007	2914		D4
1200	ITSC	60143	2914		D4
CO-10 N Prospect Av					
10	ITSC	60143	2914		D5
300	AddT	60143	2914		D5
CO-10 S Prospect Av					
100	ITSC	60143	2914		D6
200	WDDL	60143	2914		D7
200	WDDL	60191	2914		D7
CO-19 Dunham Rd					
-	SchT	60177	2909		B5
10	WYNE	60120	2909		B7
200	BRLT	60120	2909		B5
200	SchT	60120	2909		B5
200	WYNE	60174	2909		B7
CO-20 E Grand Av					
10	BNVL	60106	2972		D5
10	EMHT	60106	2972		A5
10	EMHT	60126	2972		A5
100	AddT	60106	2972		D5
100	AddT	60126	2972		D5
100	BNVL	60126	2972		A5
100	FNPK	60131	2972		B5
100	LydT	60131	2972		B5
CO-22 N Addison Rd					
200	WDDL	60191	2914		E7
CO-23 Gary Av					
-	HRPK	60133	2912		B5
10	BMDL	60108	2912		B7
10	BMDL	60172	2912		B7
10	BmdT	60172	2912		B7
200	BmdT	60108	2912		B7
500	ROSL	60172	2912		B6
CO-23 N Gary Av					
-	HRPK	60133	2912		B4
200	ROSL	60172	2912		B6
200	SMBG	60193	2912		B6
CO-24 Meacham Rd					
-	ITSC	60143	2913		D3
CO-24 Medinah Rd					
10	BMDL	60157	2913		D7
10	BmdT	60143	2913		D5
10	BmdT	60157	2913		D7
300	ITSC	60143	2913		D6
300	ITSC	60157	2913		D6
300	ROSL	60157	2913		D7
400	ROSL	60143	2913		D6
700	BMDL	60101	2913		D7
CO-25 Tucker Rd					
500	PtnT	60468	3861	9W-37S	A4
500	PTON	60468	3861	9W-37S	A4
500	WlIT	60468	3861	9W-37S	A4
CO-26 Thorndale Av					
-	WDDL	60106	2915		C4
10	BNVL	60106	2915		E5
10	CHCG	60106	2915		E5
10	WDDL	60191	2915		A4
100	AddT	60143	2914		A4
300	ITSC	60143	2914		C4
300	ITSC	60191	2914		E4
300	WDDL	60191	2914		E4
700	AddT	60191	2914		E4
CO-26 E Thorndale Av					
10	WDDL	60191	2915		B4
100	EGVV	60007	2915		B4
100	EGVV	60191	2915		B4
100	WDDL	60007	2915		B4
500	BNVL	60106	2915		C4
500	WDDL	60106	2915		C4
CO-28 N Wood Dale Rd					
-	EGvT	60007	2915		A4
-	EGVV	60007	2915		A4
-	WDDL	60007	2915		A4
200	WDDL	60191	2915		A4
400	AddT	60191	2915		A6
1300	EGVV	60191	2915		A3
CO-29 Greenbrook Blvd					
10	BRLT	60133	2911		D6
1300	BmdT	60133	2911		E5
1300	HRPK	60133	2911		E5
1600	BRLT	60103	2911		D6
CO-29 Stearns Rd					
10	BRLT	60103	2910		A5
10	BRLT	60120	2909		D5
10	BRLT	60133	2910		A5
10	BRLT	60184	2909		E5
10	SchT	60120	2909		D5
10	WynT	60120	2909		D5
10	WynT	60184	2909		E5
100	BRLT	60103	2911		B6
500	WynT	60103	2911		A6
CO-29 E Stearns Rd					
-	BRLT	60133	2911		D6
-	HRPK	60133	2911		C6
200	BRLT	60103	2911		B6
200	WynT	60103	2911		B6
CO-29 W Stearns Rd					
100	BRLT	60103	2910		B5
500	BRLT	60120	2910		A5
CO-31 Plainfield Rd					
100	BRRG	60527	3146		B6
100	WLBK	60527	3146		B6
CO-34 Oak Brook Rd					
100	OKBK	60523	3086		B4
100	PvsT	60523	3086		C4
CO-35 E 55th St					
400	HNDL	60521	3146		B3
CO-35 W 55th St					
10	HNDL	60521	3146		A3
300	DGvT	60521	3146		A3
CO-38 63rd St					
10	DGvT	60527	3146		A5
CO-40 Penny Rd					
10	BNHL	60118	2801		E2
10	CPVL	60110	2801		E2
10	EDND	60110	2801		E2
10	EDND	60118	2801		E2
CO-43 County Farm Rd					
10	HRPK	60133	2911		D7
10	WynT	60133	2911		D7
500	BRLT	60133	2911		D5
5500	BRLT	60133	2911		D6
5500	HRPK	60103	2911		D5
CO-61 W Bartlett Rd					
2100	BRLT	60103	2909		B3
2100	BRLT	60120	2909		B3
2100	HnrT	60103	2909		B3
2100	SEGN	60103	2909		B3
2100	SEGN	60120	2909		B3
2100	SEGN	60177	2909		B3
CO-A49 Long Grove Rd					
10	DRPK	60010	2752	22W-20N	B1
100	BRTN	60010	2751	23W-20N	D1
100	DRPK	60010	2751	23W-20N	D1
100	ElaT	60010	2751	23W-20N	E1
100	ElaT	60010	2752	23W-20N	A1
500	DRPK	60074	2752	22W-20N	C1
CO-A49 W Long Grove Rd					
21600	DRPK	60074	2752	21W-20N	D1
21600	ElaT	60074	2752	21W-20N	D1
21700	DRPK	60010	2752	21W-20N	C1
CO-A50 County Line Rd					
2000	ALGN	60102	2748		B2
2000	AlqT	60102	2748		B2
2200	ALGN	60010	2748		C2
2200	BNHL	60010	2748		C2
CO-A50 W County Line Rd					
10	BNHL	60010	2749	29W-18N	C2
100	ALGN	60010	2748		E2
100	ALGN	60102	2748		E2
100	BNHL	60010	2748		E2
300	AlqT	60010	2749	29W-20N	D2
CO-A50 E Lake Cook Rd					
100	BFGV	60089	2754	16W-20N	D2
100	WLNG	60089	2754	16W-20N	D2
1300	WLNG	60090	2754	16W-20N	D2
Coach Dr					
-	DSPN	60018	2917	12W-8N	B2
Coach Ln					
-	HLCT	60429	3427	3W-21S	A6
1000	LMNT	60439	3271		A5
Coach Rd					
10	WLNG	60090	2755	15W-18N	A3
100	NHFD	60093	2811	7W-15N	A3
800	HMWD	60430	3508	1W-22S	A1
2300	ElaT	60047	2753	19W-20N	B1
2300	LGGV	60047	2753	19W-20N	B1
E Coach Rd					
800	PLTN	60074	2753	19W-18N	B2
N Coach Rd					
2100	PLTN	60074	2753	19W-18N	B2
S Coach Rd					
12100	PSHT	60463	3274	9W-14S	D6
W Coach Rd					
7600	PSHT	60463	3274	9W-14S	D6
Coachmaker Dr					
200	NHBK	60062	2757	8W-18N	D3
Coachmans Rd					
14000	HMGN	60441	3343	17W-17S	C5
Coachway Ln					
22400	RNPK	60471	3594	5W-27S	C4
Coachwood Tr					
6900	TYPK	60477	3425	8W-19S	A3
Coales Rd					
700	BlmT	60411	3508	0W-23S	B3
700	CHHT	60411	3508	0W-23S	B3
Coales St					
800	CHHT	60411	3508	1W-23S	B3
S Coast Guard Dr					
6400	CHCG	60637	3153	2E-7S	C5

Chicago & Cook County Street Index

STREET Block	City	ZIP	Map#	CGS	Grid
Coolidge Av					
1500	BKLY	60163	3028		C4
N Coolidge Av					
600	PLTN	60067	2752	22W-16N	B6
W Coolidge Av					
100	BRTN	60010	2750	25W-18N	E2
Coolidge Ct					
10	SMWD	60107	2856	29W-10N	D6
Coolidge St					
10	CTCY	60409	3430		C3
10	EGvT	60018	2862	15W-9N	A7
10	HMND	46324	3430		C3
3000	OKBK	60523	3086		A4
Coolidge St N					
300	BlmT	60411	3508	1W-23S	A3
300	CHHT	60411	3508	1W-23S	A3
300	CHHT	60425	3508	1W-23S	A3
300	HMWD	60425	3508	1W-23S	A3
Coolidge St S					
200	CHHT	60411	3508	1W-24S	A6
Coonley Rd					
300	RVSD	60546	3088	10W-3S	B6
Co Op Ln					
4700	HMTN	60456	3212	5W-10S	A4
4700	OKLN	60453	3212	5W-10S	A4
4700	OKLN	60456	3212	5W-10S	A4
Cooper Av					
600	ELGN	60120	2855		B1
14400	DXMR	60426	3349	2W-17S	C6
15300	HRVY	60426	3349	2W-18S	C7
Cooper Ct					
600	SMBG	60173	2859	22W-12N	C2
900	EGVV	60007	2913		E1
1600	HRPK	60133	2911		D6
E Cooper Dr					
1200	PLTN	60074	2753	19W-17N	C5
Cooper Pl					
3700	CRTE	60417	3596	0W-28S	D7
Cooper Rd					
1300	HFET	60195	2858	24W-12N	D2
13900	BLID	60406	3348	3W-16S	E3
13900	BLID	60406	3349	3W-16S	A3
13900	RBBN	60406	3348	3W-16S	E3
13900	RBBN	60406	3349	3W-16S	A3
Coopers Grove Ct					
3000	BLID	60406	3348	4W-17S	E4
3000	RBBN	60406	3348	4W-17S	E4
Copenhagen Ct					
11600	BNVL	60106	2972		C3
11600	FNPK	60131	2972		B3
Copley Ct					
-	SMBG	60173	2859	23W-12N	B1
Copperfield Ln					
1000	SMBG	60193	2913		A1
Cora Ct					
100	TNTN	60476	3428	0E-20S	D5
S Cora St					
900	DSPN	60016	2863	13W-10N	A5
1100	DSPN	60018	2863	13W-10N	A5
Coral Av					
600	BRLT	60103	2911		B4
Coral Ct					
500	SMBG	60193	2858	25W-9N	B7
Coral Dr					
500	DYR	46311	3598		D1
W Coral Dr					
8300	CHCG	60656	2918	10W-5N	A7
8300	NRDG	60706	2918	10W-5N	A7
Coral Ln					
100	WLNG	60090	2754	16W-18N	E4
Coral Pkwy					
1400	NHBK	60062	2756	11W-17N	C6
S Corbett St					
2500	CHCG	60608	3091	1W-2S	E2
W Corcoran Pl					
5500	CHCG	60644	3031	7W-0N	C4
5900	OKPK	60302	3031	7W-0N	B4
S Corcoran Rd					
8700	HMTN	60456	3212	5W-10S	B5
Cordial Dr					
400	DSPN	60018	2862	15W-10N	A6
600	DSPN	60018	2861	16W-10N	E5
600	MPPT	60018	2861	16W-10N	D5
600	MPPT	60056	2861	16W-10N	D5
Cordoba Ct					
9800	ODPK	60462	3345	12W-18S	C6
Cordoba St					
900	UYPK	60466	3684	3W-30S	A3
Cordova Rd					
100	CPVL	60110	2748		B5
Corey Dr					
10	SBTN	60010	2803	26W-13N	D5
Corey Ln					
800	PTHT	60070	2754	16W-16N	D6
800	WLNG	60090	2754	16W-16N	D6
Corinth Ct					
10	TYPK	60477	3505	8W-23S	C3
Corinth Dr					
10	TYPK	60477	3505	8W-23S	C3
Corinth Rd					
2600	OMFD	60461	3507	3W-24S	B6
Cork Av					
8700	HYHL	60457	3210	11W-10S	A6
8700	HYHL	60458	3210	11W-10S	A4
8700	JSTC	60458	3210	11W-10S	A4
9400	HYHL	60465	3210	10W-10S	A6
9400	PSHL	60465	3210	10W-10S	A6
S Cork Av					
7100	JSTC	60458	3148	11W-8S	A7
7300	JSTC	60458	3210	11W-8S	A1
8500	HYHL	60457	3210	10W-9S	A4
8600	HYHL	60458	3210	10W-9S	A4
8600	JSTC	60457	3210	10W-9S	A4
Cork Rd					
-	TYPK	60477	3424	10W-21S	C7
E Corktree Ln					
1700	MPPT	60056	2808	13W-14N	D4
Corley Ct					
1300	ELGN	60120	2855		D3
Corley Dr					
1300	ELGN	60120	2855		E3
S Corliss Av					
10300	CHCG	60628	3278	1E-12S	E1
13100	CHCG	60827	3278	0E-15S	E7
13100	CHCG	60827	3350	0E-15S	E1
Cormoy Ln					
11800	ODPK	60467	3422	14W-21S	D6
19300	TYPK	60477	3504	10W-23S	B3
W Cornelia Av					
500	CHCG	60657	2978	0W-4N	A3
1000	CHCG	60657	2977	2W-4N	B3
1900	CHCG	60618	2977	2W-4N	B3
3600	CHCG	60618	2976	4W-4N	C3
4300	CHCG	60641	2976	5W-4N	A3
4700	CHCG	60641	2975	5W-4N	E3
W Cornelia Av					
5500	CHCG	60634	2975	8W-4N	A3
6700	CHCG	60634	2974	8W-4N	E3
Cornell Av					
-	SNPK	60160	3029	12W-2N	B1
-	SNPK	60165	3029	12W-2N	B1
100	DSPN	60016	2862	14W-12N	C1
200	CTCY	60409	3351	2E-17S	C5
1000	ANHT	60004	2754	16W-16N	D7
1000	PTHT	60004	2754	16W-16N	D7
1000	PTHT	60070	2754	16W-16N	D7
1000	WLNG	60004	2754	16W-16N	D7
1000	WLNG	60090	2754	16W-16N	D7
1900	MLPK	60160	3029	12W-2N	B1
2000	LydT	60164	2973	12W-2N	B7
2000	MLPK	60160	2973	12W-2N	B7
15100	DLTN	60419	3351	2E-17S	C6
17000	SHLD	60473	3429	1E-20S	B4
22100	SLVL	60411	3597	2E-27S	C3
E Cornell Av					
-	BrnT	60010	2750	25W-17N	E4
-	BRTN	60010	2750	25W-17N	E4
400	BrnT	60010	2751	25W-17N	A4
400	BRTN	60010	2751	25W-17N	A4
S Cornell Av					
-	CHCG	60615	3093	1E-4S	A7
-	CHCG	60637	3153	2E-6S	B3
-	CHCG	60649	3153	2E-7S	B6
-	CHCG	60653	3093	1E-4S	A7
4800	CHCG	60615	3153	1E-5S	B1
7500	CHCG	60649	3215	2E-8S	B1
8100	CHCG	60617	3215	2E-9S	B2
W Cornell Av					
900	IVNS	60067	2752	22W-16N	C7
1100	PLTN	60067	2752	22W-16N	B7
1100	PltT	60067	2752	22W-16N	B7
Cornell Cir					
1600	HFET	60194	2858	26W-12N	A2
Cornell Ct					
100	GNVW	60025	2810	10W-15N	A2
1400	HFET	60194	2858	26W-12N	A2
1400	PTHT	60070	2754	16W-16N	D6
1400	WLNG	60090	2754	16W-16N	D6
Cornell Dr					
-	CHCG	60607	3033	1W-0S	D5
1400	HFET	60194	2858	26W-12N	A2
S Cornell Dr					
-	CHCG	60637	3153	2E-6S	B4
-	CHCG	60649	3153	2E-7S	B5
Cornell Ln					
800	SMBG	60193	2858	25W-9N	C7
800	SMBG	60193	2912		C1
S Cornell Ln					
13000	PlsT	60464	3346	10W-15S	C1
Cornell Pl					
1500	HFET	60194	2858	26W-12N	A2
Cornell Rd					
1700	FSMR	60422	3507	2W-23S	D4
Cornell St					
900	WLMT	60091	2812	4W-14N	B5
Cornell Ter					
1400	HFET	60194	2858	26W-12N	A2
Cornell Wy					
5600	MTSN	60443	3505	7W-25S	E7
Cornerstone Pl					
-	SMBG	60193	2912		B2
Cornfield Dr					
800	MTSN	60443	3505	7W-25S	C7
Cornfield Rd					
700	MTSN	60443	3505	7W-24S	C6
Cornflower Tr					
3400	NHBK	60062	2809	11W-16N	C1
Cornhill Dr					
-	ODPK	60467	3344	14W-16S	D4
E Corning Av					
200	PTON	60468	3861	9W-37S	A3
400	WIIT	60468	3861	9W-37S	A3
W Corning Av					
100	PTON	60468	3861	8W-37S	B3
200	PTON	60468	3860	10W-37S	C3
8700	PtnT	60468	3860	10W-37S	B3
E Corning Rd					
100	WshT	60401	3864	0E-37S	E4
W Corning Rd					
10	WshT	60401	3864	1W-37S	A4
4900	WIIT	60468	3861	7W-37S	D4
Cornwall Cir					
-	MNSR	46321	3510		D4
Cornwall Ct					
10	CRTE	60417	3596	0W-28S	D6
Cornwall Dr					
10	CRTE	60417	3596	0W-28S	D6
Cornwallis Ln					
900	MNSR	46321	3510		E5
N Corona Dr					
5700	RGMW	60008	2805	22W-13N	C5
5700	RGMW	60067	2805	22W-13N	C5
S Corona Dr					
5700	RGMW	60008	2805	22W-13N	C5
5700	RGMW	60067	2805	22W-13N	C5
Coronado Dr					
17500	ODPK	60467	3423	13W-21S	B6
Coronet Ln					
800	CTSD	60525	3147	13W-6S	A4
800	LynT	60525	3147	13W-6S	A4
Coronet Rd					
500	GLF	60025	2811	7W-12N	B7
500	GNVW	60025	2811	7W-12N	B7
Corporate Cross					
-	SMBG	60173	2860	21W-10N	A4
Corporate Dr					
-	NHBK	60015	2756	13W-20N	A2
-	NHBK	60062	2756	13W-20N	A2
-	RVWD	60015	2755	13W-20N	E2
-	RVWD	60015	2756	13W-20N	A2
-	WdfT	60015	2756	13W-20N	A2
100	ELGN	60123	2801		A6
Corrington Ct					
200	SMWD	60107	2857	27W-11N	C4
Corrinthia Ct					
500	EGVV	60007	2915		A1
Corrinthia Dr					
400	EGVV	60007	2915		A1
Corsaire Ln					
10	SMBG	60173	2859	21W-10N	D4
Corso Dr					
-	ODPK	60467	3422	14W-19S	E2
Cortbridge Rd					
800	IVNS	60067	2751	24W-17N	D6
W Cortez Dr					
3100	CHCG	60622	3032	3W-1N	E2
3100	CHCG	60651	3032	3W-1N	E2
Cortez St					
1200	MLPK	60160	3029	11W-1N	D2
W Cortez St					
1300	CHCG	60622	3033	1W-1N	E2
W Cortez St					
2800	CHCG	60622	3032	3W-1N	E2
3200	CHCG	60651	3032	4W-1N	D2
4800	CHCG	60651	3031	6W-1N	E2
W Cortland Pkwy					
7900	EDPK	60707	2974	9W-2N	B7
W Cortland St					
1200	CHCG	60614	2977	1W-2N	D7
1400	CHCG	60622	2977	2W-2N	C7
2000	CHCG	60647	2977	2W-2N	B7
2800	CHCG	60647	2976	5W-2N	B7
3900	CHCG	60639	2976	5W-2N	B7
5800	CHCG	60639	2975	7W-2N	B7
6300	CHCG	60707	2975	8W-2N	A7
6700	CHCG	60707	2974	8W-2N	E7
7800	EDPK	60707	2974	9W-2N	B7
Cortney Cir					
900	CPVL	60110	2748		D5
Cortney Dr					
900	CPVL	60110	2748		D5
Cory Ln					
5800	OKFT	60452	3425	7W-18S	C1
Cosman Rd					
10	EGvT	60007	2860	19W-9N	C7
10	EGVV	60007	2860	19W-9N	C7
E Cossitt Av					
10	LGNG	60525	3087	12W-4S	C7
700	BKFD	60513	3087	12W-4S	C7
700	BKFD	60525	3087	12W-4S	C7
W Cossitt Av					
10	LGNG	60525	3087	12W-4S	B7
1400	WNSP	60558	3087	13W-4S	A7
Cotswolds Ct					
2500	NHBK	60062	2756	10W-18N	E3
2500	NHBK	60062	2757	10W-18N	B3
Cotswolds Wy					
700	NHBK	60062	2756	10W-18N	E4
700	NHBK	60062	2757	10W-18N	A4
Cottage Ct					
17200	TYPK	60477	3424	10W-20S	B4
Cottage Ln					
10	MDLN	60445	3347	6W-16S	E4
W Cottage Pl					
-	CHCG	60607	3033	1W-0S	D5
Cottage Grove Av					
-	BlmT	60425	3509	0E-25S	A7
1000	CHHT	60411	3509	0E-25S	A7
1000	FDHT	60411	3509	1E-25S	A7
1400	CHHT	60411	3597	1E-25S	A1
1400	FDHT	60411	3597	1E-25S	A1
13800	CHCG	60827	3351	0E-16S	A3
13800	DLTN	60419	3351	0E-16S	A3
14900	DLTN	60473	3351	1E-17S	A6
15300	SHLD	60419	3351	1E-17S	A6
15600	SHLD	60473	3351	1E-18S	A7
15900	SHLD	60473	3429	1E-18S	A1
20400	BlmT	60411	3509	0E-25S	A7
21500	BlmT	60411	3597	0E-26S	A2
21500	SLVL	60411	3597	0E-26S	A2
21900	STGR	60411	3597	0E-26S	A2
21900	STGR	60475	3597	0E-26S	A2
22500	BlmT	60475	3597	1E-27S	A4
22500	SLVL	60475	3597	1E-27S	A4
22900	CRTE	60417	3597	1E-27S	B5
22900	CRTE	60475	3597	1E-27S	B5
N Cottage Grove Av					
-	BlmT	60425	3429	1E-22S	A7
-	ThtT	60425	3429	1E-22S	A7
-	ThtT	60476	3429	1E-22S	A7
10	GNWD	60425	3509	0E-22S	A1
100	BlmT	60425	3509	0E-22S	A1
100	BlmT	60476	3509	0E-22S	A1
S Cottage Grove Av					
10	BlmT	60425	3509	1E-23S	A3
10	GNWD	60425	3509	0E-22S	A2
1400	CRTE	60417	3686	0E-30S	A3
1400	CteT	60417	3686	1E-31S	A6
3300	CHCG	60616	3092	0E-3S	D5
3400	CHCG	60653	3092	1E-4S	E7
4600	CHCG	60615	3092	1E-4S	E7
4700	CHCG	60615	3152	0E-7S	E5
5400	CHCG	60637	3152	1E-5S	E2
7000	CHCG	60619	3152	1E-7S	E6
9500	CHCG	60619	3214	0E-11S	E7
9500	CHCG	60628	3214	0E-11S	E7
10300	CHCG	60628	3278	0E-12S	E2
12400	CHCG	60628	3279	0E-14S	A7
20000	BlmT	60411	3509	0E-24S	A5
20000	CHHT	60411	3509	0E-24S	A5
Cottington Ct					
500	SMBG	60194	2858	25W-11N	B4
Cottington Dr					
1600	SMBG	60194	2858	25W-11N	A4
Cottonwood Ct					
300	SMBG	60193	2858	24W-9N	E7
1000	WLNG	60090	2754	16W-16N	D7
3700	HLCT	60429	3426	4W-20S	D5
9400	MaiT	60016	2863	11W-12N	D1
15200	ODPK	60467	3344	14W-18S	D6
Cottonwood Dr					
-	HnrT	60120	2856	30W-10N	B6
-	SMWD	60120	2856	30W-10N	B6
200	EGVV	60007	2861	17W-9N	B7
600	DYR	46311	3598		E3
1500	GNVW	60025	2810	9W-14N	C5
11100	PSHL	60465	3274	10W-13S	B3
18300	TYPK	60477	3424	11W-22S	A7
Cottonwood Ln					
400	SMBG	60193	2858	23W-9N	E7
900	BRLT	60103	2910		E6
W Cottonwood Ln					
900	MPPT	60056	2861	16W-11N	D4
1300	ANHT	60005	2806	18W-14N	D4
Cottonwood Rd					
10	DRFD	60015	2757	9W-18N	B3
10	NfdT	60062	2757	9W-18N	B3
100	BFGV	60089	2754	17W-18N	B3
N Cottonwood Tr					
4200	HFET	60195	2804	25W-15N	A2
W Cottonwood Tr					
1700	HFET	60195	2804	25W-15N	B2
E Cottonwood Wy					
1000	PLTN	60074	2753	19W-17N	C6
Cotuit Ct					
100	SMBG	60193	2858	25W-10N	C6
W Couch Pl					
-	CHCG	60601	3034		E4
200	CHCG	60606	3034	0W-0N	B4
600	CHCG	60661	3034	0W-0N	A4
700	CHCG	60607	3034	0W-0N	A4
W Cougar St					
10	CHCG	60623	3090	4W-3S	C4
10	CHCG	60632	3090	4W-3S	C4
E Cougar Tr					
700	HFET	60194	2859	22W-11N	C4
E Cougar Tr					
700	SMBG	60173	2859	22W-11N	C4
700	SMBG	60194	2859	22W-11N	C4
Coulter Rd					
5100	OKFT	60452	3425	6W-20S	E3
5100	OKFT	60452	3426	6W-20S	A3
W Coulter St					
2000	CHCG	60608	3091	2W-2S	B2
Council Ct					
300	SmbT	60193	2913		B2
E Council Tr					
100	ANHT	60005	2861	17W-12N	A2
100	MPPT	60056	2862	15W-12N	A1
1000	MPPT	60016	2862	15W-12N	B1
W Council Tr					
10	MPPT	60056	2862	15W-12N	A1
300	MPPT	60056	2861	16W-12N	E2
Council Hill Rd					
600	EDND	60110	2801		B1
600	EDND	60118	2801		B1
S Countess Ln					
25900	CteT	60417	3685	1W-31S	B5
Country Ct					
10	DRFD	60015	2756	11W-20N	D2
10	LMNT	60439	3271		A6
1000	CRTE	60417	3686	1E-30S	B2
15800	ODPK	60462	3424	10W-18S	A1
Country Dr					
10	CTSD	60525	3147	12W-7S	B6
E Country Dr					
200	BRLT	60103	2911		A5
S Country Dr					
700	BRTN	60010	2750	26W-18N	E3
800	BNHL	60010	2750	26W-18N	E3
W Country Dr					
200	BRLT	60103	2911		A5
Country Ln					
10	DRPK	60010	2752	22W-20N	A1
10	HDPK	60035	2757	9W-20N	C2
10	NfdT	60093	2811	7W-16N	A1
10	NHFD	60093	2811	7W-16N	A1
10	ODPK	60467	3344	14W-17S	D5
100	MaiT	60016	2809	12W-12N	C7
200	GLF	60029	2864	8W-12N	E1
200	GNVW	60025	2864	8W-12N	E1
200	GNVW	60029	2864	8W-12N	E1
300	GNVW	60025	2810	8W-12N	E7
400	SMWD	60107	2857	28W-10N	A6
500	BCHR	60401	3864	0W-36S	C1
600	GLNC	60022	2758	6W-16N	C6
800	BFGV	60089	2754	17W-18N	A2
1000	CRTE	60417	3686	1E-30S	B2
1100	DRFD	60015	2756	11W-20N	D2
1100	LMNT	60439	3271		A6
1200	NHBK	60062	2757	9W-17N	D6
3100	WLMT	60091	2811	6W-14N	E5
17200	EHZC	60429	3427	2W-20S	D5
18300	LNSG	60438	3429	2E-21S	C7
18500	BlmT	60411	3429	2E-21S	C7
E Country Ln					
10	ANHT	60004	2754	17W-17N	A4
10	BFGV	60089	2754	17W-17N	A4
S Country Ln					
900	DSPN	60016	2862	15W-11N	A3
900	MPPT	60056	2862	15W-11N	A2
24700	CRTE	60417	3686	1E-30S	B2
Country Ln E					
600	ROSL	60172	2912		D6
Country Ln N					
600	ROSL	60172	2912		D6
Country Ln S					
700	ROSL	60172	2912		D6
Country Aire Dr					
-	MKHM	60426	3348	4W-18S	E6
E Country Club Ct					
10	PLTN	60067	2752	20W-17N	E4
N Country Club Ct					
13100	PSHT	60463	3346	9W-15S	D1
S Country Club Ct					
13200	PSHT	60463	3346	9W-15S	D2
Country Club Dr					
-	MPPT	60056	2808	14W-14N	B4
10	CTSD	60525	3147	12W-6S	C5
10	NHLK	60164	2972		D7
10	PTHT	60070	2808	14W-14N	B4
100	NHLK	60164	3028		E1
400	NHLK	60164	3029	12W-2N	A1
500	ITSC	60143	2914		D5
600	BNVL	60106	2915		D6
800	LGNG	60525	3147	13W-5S	A3
2400	OMFD	60461	3507	3W-24S	B5
2600	RchT	60461	3507	3W-24S	B5
17500	CCHL	60429	3426	4W-21S	D6
17500	CCHL	60478	3426	4W-21S	D6
17500	HLCT	60429	3426	4W-21S	D6
17800	BmnT	60430	3426	4W-21S	D6
Countryclub Dr					
1700	LGGV	60047	2753	19W-20N	D1
E Country Club Dr					
10	NHLK	60164	2972		D7
10	NHLK	60164	3028		E1
S Country Club Dr					
9300	ENGN	60805	3213	3W-10S	A5
Country Club Ln					
600	ITSC	60143	2914		D5
800	NHBK	60062	2757	8W-16N	E7
1000	SMBG	60193	2912		B1
1100	SmbT	60193	2912		B1
8000	NRIV	60546	3088	10W-2S	B2
8400	ODPK	60462	3346	10W-17S	B5
W Country Club Ln					
7900	EDPK	60707	2974	9W-2N	B7
7900	RVGV	60171	2974	9W-2N	B7
Country Club Rd					
100	CHHT	60411	3507	1W-25S	E7
100	CHHT	60411	3508	1W-25S	A7
1000	ELGN	60123	2801		A7
Country Club East					
-	CTSD	60525	3147	12W-6S	C4
Country Club West					
-	CTSD	60525	3147	12W-6S	C4
Countryfield Ln					
700	ELGN	60120	2855		E2
E Country Lake Rd					
2700	ANHT	60004	2754	16W-16N	E7
Country Manor Ln					
10	PlsT	60467	3345	13W-15S	A1
Country Oak Ln					
300	IVNS	60067	2804	23W-15N	E2
Country Oaks Dr					
10	BNHL	60010	2749	30W-20N	A2
Country Oaks Ln					
10	BNHL	60010	2748		E1
10	BNHL	60010	2749	30W-20N	A1
Country Ridge Dr					
6400	OKFT	60452	3347	8W-18S	B7
Countryside Ct					
10	BRRG	60527	3146		B5
10	WLBK	60527	3146		B5
900	GNVW	60025	2809	10W-13N	E6
900	NfdT	60025	2809	10W-13N	E6
20200	FftT	60423	3504	10W-24S	C6
Countryside Dr					
100	ALGN	60102	2748		A1
100	AlqT	60102	2748		A1
300	ROSL	60172	2913		B4
900	HRPK	60133	2912		A2
1400	BFGV	60089	2753	18W-18N	E3
W Countryside Dr					
900	PLTN	60067	2752	22W-17N	B6
Countryside Ln					
1400	LGGV	60047	2753	18W-20N	D1
3500	GNVW	60025	2809	11W-13N	D6
3500	NfdT	60025	2809	11W-13N	D6
20300	FftT	60423	3504	10W-24S	D6
E Countryside Ln					
10	PTHT	60070	2808	15W-16N	A1
Countryside Plz					
10	CTSD	60525	3147	12W-6S	B4
Country Squire Ct					
10	PSHT	60463	3274	9W-14S	D5
S Country Squire Rd					
10	PSHT	60463	3274	9W-14S	D5
Country View Ln					
12400	HMGN	60441	3422	15W-19S	B1
Country Woods Dr					
12000	HMGN	60441	3344	15W-18S	C7
12000	OrlT	60467	3344	15W-18S	C7
County Fair Ct					
5100	MONE	60449	3683	6W-31S	A6
County Farm Ln					
2300	SMBG	60194	2857	26W-10N	E5
County Farm Rd					
10	HRPK	60133	2911		D7
10	WynT	60133	2911		D7
500	BRLT	60103	2911		D5
5500	BRLT	60133	2911		D6
5500	HRPK	60103	2911		D5
County Farm Rd CO-43					
10	HRPK	60133	2911		D7
10	WynT	60133	2911		D7
500	BRLT	60103	2911		D5
5500	BRLT	60133	2911		D6
5500	HRPK	60103	2911		D5
County Line Ct					
500	HNDL	60521	3146		C1
County Line Ln					
6700	BRRG	60527	3146		C7
County Line Rd					
300	GLNC	60022	2758	6W-18N	C2
300	HDPK	60022	2758	6W-18N	C2
300	HDPK	60035	2758	7W-18N	B2
700	NtrT	60062	2758	7W-18N	B2
900	NtrT	60035	2758	7W-18N	B2
2000	ALGN	60102	2748		B2
2000	AlqT	60102	2748		B2
2200	ALGN	60010	2748		B2
2200	BNHL	60010	2748		B2
County Line Rd CO-A50					
2000	ALGN	60102	2748		B2
2000	AlqT	60102	2748		B2
2200	ALGN	60010	2748		B2
2200	BNHL	60010	2748		B2
N County Line Rd					
100	HNDL	60521	3146		C1
300	HNDL	60521	3086		C7
600	AddT	60126	2972		B6
600	EMHT	60126	2972		B6
600	EMHT	60126	3028		B1
600	EMHT	60164	3028		B1
600	NHLK	60126	2972		B7
600	NHLK	60126	3028		B1
600	NHLK	60164	2972		B7
600	NHLK	60164	3028		B1
700	LydT	60126	2972		B6
700	LydT	60164	2972		B6
800	LynT	60521	3086		C7
900	FNPK	60131	2972		B6
900	LydT	60131	2972		B6
S County Line Rd					
10	HNDL	60521	3146		C6
400	DGvT	60527	3208		C5
400	WLSP	60480	3208		C6
400	WLSP	60527	3208		C5
5800	BRRG	60521	3146		C4
5800	HNDL	60527	3146		C4
6000	BRRG	60067	3146		C4
7400	BRRG	60527	3208		C2
8000	LynT	60527	3208		C2
8800	BRRG	60480	3208		C4
8800	DGvT	60480	3208		C5
8800	LynT	60480	3208		C5
W County Line Rd					
10	BNHL	60010	2749	30W-20N	A2
100	ALGN	60010	2748		E2
100	ALGN	60102	2748		E2
100	BNHL	60010	2748		E2
300	AlqT	60010	2749	29W-20N	D2
W County Line Rd CO-A50					
10	BNHL	60010	2749	30W-20N	A2
100	ALGN	60010	2748		E2
100	ALGN	60102	2748		E2
100	BNHL	60010	2748		E2
300	AlqT	60010	2749	29W-20N	D2
Countrynell Av					
10	LydT	60164	2973	12W-2N	B6
Cour Caravelle					
10	PSHL	60465	3274	10W-13S	B3
Cour D'Alene					
10	PSHL	60465	3274	10W-13S	B3
Cour Deauville					
10	PSHL	60465	3274	10W-13S	A4
Cour de la Reine					
10	PSHL	60465	3274	10W-13S	B4
Cour la Salle					
10	PSHL	60465	3274	10W-13S	B3
Cour Leroux					
10	PSHL	60465	3274	10W-13S	B3
Cour Madeleine					
10	PSHL	60465	3274	10W-13S	B4
Cour Marquis					
10	PSHL	60465	3274	10W-13S	A4
Cour Masson					
10	PSHL	60465	3274	10W-13S	B3
Cour Michele					
10	PSHL	60465	3274	10W-13S	A4
Cour Monnet					
10	PSHL	60465	3274	10W-13S	B3

STREET Block	City	ZIP	Map#	CGS	Grid
Cour Montreal					
10	PSHL	60465	3274	10W-13S	B3
Cour St. Tropez					
10	PSHL	60465	3274	10W-13S	B4
Court Dr					
10	CTSD	60525	3147	13W-7S	B5
W Court Pl					
-	CHCG	60606	3034	0W-0N	B4
10	CHCG	60602	3034	0W-0N	B4
600	CHCG	60661	3034	0W-0N	A4
700	CHCG	60607	3034	0W-0N	A4
W Court St					
4700	MONE	60449	3683	5W-31S	B5
4700	MonT	60449	3683	5W-31S	B5
4700	UYPK	60449	3683	5W-31S	C5
5500	MONE	60449	3682	6W-31S	E5
Court Ter					
-	SHLD	60473	3428	0E-18S	E1
Court A					
1100	HRPK	60133	2912		A6
Court B					
1100	HRPK	60133	2912		A6
Court C					
1200	HRPK	60133	2912		A6
Court D					
1200	HRPK	60133	2911		D7
1200	HRPK	60133	2912		A6
Court E					
1200	HRPK	60133	2911		D6
1200	HRPK	60133	2912		A6
W Courte Dr					
8000	MaiT	60714	2864	10W-11N	B2
8000	MNGV	60053	2864	10W-11N	B2
8000	NLES	60714	2864	10W-11N	B2
Courtenay Ln					
100	SMBG	60193	2913		A1
Courtesy Ln					
400	DSPN	60018	2862	15W-10N	A6
1000	WLNG	60090	2755	13W-16N	D7
Court F					
5500	HRPK	60133	2912		A6
Court G					
1100	HRPK	60133	2912		A6
Court H					
1200	HRPK	60133	2912		A6
Court J					
1300	HRPK	60133	2911		E5
Court la Grov					
200	DRPK	60010	2752	22W-20N	C1
Courtland Av					
10	PKRG	60068	2918	10W-7N	B3
2000	CHCG	60631	2918	10W-7N	B4
N Courtland Av					
-	NRDG	60706	2918	10W-6N	B6
5300	CHCG	60656	2918	10W-6N	B6
5300	CHCG	60706	2918	10W-6N	B6
5300	LydT	60656	2918	10W-6N	B6
5600	CHCG	60631	2918	10W-7N	B5
5600	LydT	60631	2918	10W-6N	B5
5600	MaiT	60631	2918	10W-6N	B5
9200	NLES	60714	2864	10W-11N	B3
W Courtland Av					
7900	NRDG	60706	2918	10W-5N	B7
Courtland Cir					
600	WNSP	60558	3146		E2
Courtland Ct					
400	SMBG	60193	2858	24W-9N	D7
N Courtland Dr					
1500	ANHT	60004	2807	16W-15N	C2
Court Leona					
1300	HRPK	60133	2911		D6
Court Marguerite					
1300	HRPK	60133	2911		E5
Court Maria					
1300	HRPK	60133	2911		D6
Courtney Dr					
6500	OKFT	60452	3347	8W-18S	B7
Courtney Ln					
3100	SCHT	60411	3596	1W-27S	A4
Court O					
1300	HRPK	60133	2911		E6
Court of Bayview					
10	NHBK	60062	2756	11W-17N	C4
Court of Harborside					
10	NHBK	60062	2756	11W-17N	C5
Court of Island Pt					
10	NHBK	60062	2756	11W-17N	D5
Court of Lagoon Vw					
10	NHBK	60062	2756	12W-17N	C5
Court of North Cor					
10	NHBK	60062	2756	11W-17N	D5
Court of Overlook Blf					
10	NHBK	60062	2756	12W-17N	C5
Court of Tyronwood					
10	NHBK	60062	2756	12W-17N	C5
Court P					
1300	HRPK	60133	2911		E6
Court Q					
1300	HRPK	60133	2911		E6
Court Touraine					
500	DRPK	60010	2752	22W-20N	C2
Cour Versaille					
10	PSHL	60465	3274	10W-13S	B3
CO-V57 N Ela Rd					
10	BRTN	60010	2751	24W-20N	D1
10	DRPK	60010	2751	24W-20N	D1
10	ElaT	60010	2751	24W-20N	D1
10	PltT	60010	2751	24W-20N	D1
CO-V62 N Quentin Rd					
20000	DRPK	60010	2752	22W-20N	C2
20000	DRPK	60074	2752	22W-20N	C2
20000	PltT	60074	2752	21W-20N	C2
20600	KLDR	60010	2752	22W-20N	C2
Cove Ct					
10	BRRG	60527	3208		C4
700	BRLT	60103	2911		B4
8100	TYPK	60477	3504	10W-23S	C3
13400	PSHT	60463	3347	7W-15S	C2
Cove Dr					
200	CHHT	60422	3507	2W-24S	D4
1000	PTHT	60070	2808	13W-15N	D2
1100	MPPT	60056	2808	13W-15N	D2
E Cove Dr					
10	SBTN	60010	2803	26W-14N	C4
N Cove Dr					
800	PLTN	60067	2752	22W-17N	B6
S Cove Dr					
10	SBTN	60010	2803	26W-14N	C5
Cove Ln					
-	NfdT	60025	2809	11W-13N	D6
400	WLMT	60091	2812	5W-13N	A6
4100	GNVW	60025	2809	11W-13N	D6
4400	HFET	60195	2804	25W-15N	B1
Cove Pt					
700	SMBG	60194	2859	22W-10N	C4
Cove Creek Ct					
6200	BRRG	60527	3146		B5
Covehill Ct					
200	SMBG	60194	2858	24W-10N	D5
Covenant Ln					
-	LYWD	60411	3509	2E-24S	C5
Coventry Ct					
1200	ROSL	60172	2912		B5
3300	HFET	60067	2804	23W-14N	E4
3600	HLCT	60429	3426	4W-20S	D5
15200	ODPK	60462	3346	10W-18S	B7
Coventry Dr					
7200	HRPK	60133	2912		A1
Coventry Ln					
300	CRTE	60417	3596	0W-29S	C7
300	CRTE	60417	3685	0W-29S	C1
1300	NHBK	60062	2756	11W-17N	D6
7700	FftT	60423	3504	9W-25S	D7
7700	FKFT	60423	3504	9W-25S	D7
17100	CCHL	60478	3426	5W-20S	D4
Coventry Pl					
700	WLNG	60090	2755	15W-18N	A3
W Coventry Pl					
200	MPPT	60056	2807	16W-14N	D3
Coventry Rd					
10	NHFD	60093	2811	7W-14N	A3
1400	SMBG	60195	2858	24W-12N	D2
Coventry on Duxbury					
10	RGMW	60008	2805	22W-13N	B7
Covered Bridge Rd					
10	SBTN	60010	2803	26W-14N	D4
Covert Rd					
2300	GNVW	60025	2810	9W-12N	C7
Coveside Ln					
500	SMBG	60193	2912		E1
Covey St					
800	DndT	60118	2801		A5
Covington Dr					
1000	LMNT	60439	3270		E7
1100	LMNT	60439	3271		A7
22500	DRPK	60010	2752	22W-20N	B1
Covington Ln					
1300	LMNT	60439	3270		E7
Covington Pl					
200	SMBG	60194	2858	25W-10N	C5
Covington Ter					
300	BFGV	60089	2754	17W-17N	C4
300	WhlT	60004	2754	17W-17N	C4
300	WhlT	60089	2754	17W-17N	C4
CO-W14 N Buffalo Grove Rd					
10	BFGV	60089	2754	16W-20N	C1
CO-W17 Weiland Rd					
100	BFGV	60089	2754	16W-20N	D1
100	WLNG	60089	2754	16W-20N	D2
300	BFGV	60069	2754	16W-20N	D1
300	VrnT	60069	2754	16W-20N	D1
CO-W24 Saunders Rd					
10	NHBK	60062	2756	12W-20N	A2
10	RVWD	60015	2756	12W-20N	A2
10	RVWD	60062	2756	12W-20N	A2
10	WdfT	60015	2756	12W-20N	A2
10	WdfT	60062	2756	12W-20N	A2
400	DRFD	60015	2756	12W-20N	A1
Cowing Ct					
18300	HMWD	60430	3427	2W-22S	D7
18400	HMWD	60430	3507	2W-22S	D1
N Cowley Rd					
10	RVSD	60546	3088	9W-3S	C4
S Cowley Rd					
10	RVSD	60546	3088	9W-3S	C5
Cowper Av					
2300	EVTN	60201	2866	4W-12N	C1
2500	EVTN	60201	2812	4W-12N	C7
Cox Av					
-	FftT	60423	3505	8W-25S	B7
-	MTSN	60423	3505	8W-25S	B7
-	MTSN	60443	3505	8W-25S	B7
-	RchT	60423	3505	8W-25S	B7
-	RchT	60443	3505	8W-25S	B7
Coyle Av					
2600	EGVV	60007	2915		E2
2600	EGVV	60007	2916		A2
4900	LNWD	60712	2919	6W-8N	D1
4900	SKOK	60077	2919	6W-8N	D1
4900	SKOK	60712	2919	6W-8N	D1
W Coyle Av					
2400	CHCG	60645	2921	3W-8N	A1
2600	CHCG	60645	2920	3W-8N	E1
4800	LNWD	60712	2919	6W-8N	E1
4800	SKOK	60077	2919	6W-8N	E1
4800	SKOK	60712	2919	6W-8N	E1
7200	CHCG	60631	2918	9W-8N	D1
7200	NLES	60631	2918	9W-8N	D1
7200	NLES	60714	2918	9W-8N	D1
Cozy Ln					
1300	DYR	46311	3510		C7
1400	DYR	46311	3598		C1
Crabapple Dr					
-	PTHT	60070	2808	13W-15N	E2
900	PTHT	60070	2809	13W-15N	A2
Crabapple Ln					
10	BNHL	60010	2749	28W-18N	E3
Crab Orchard Dr					
4400	HFET	60195	2804	24W-15N	C1
E Crabtree Dr					
700	ANHT	60004	2754	16W-16N	C7
N Crabtree Dr					
1300	PLTN	60010	2752	23W-17N	A4
1300	PLTN	60067	2752	23W-17N	A4
1300	PltT	60010	2752	23W-17N	A4
1300	PltT	60067	2752	23W-17N	A4
Crab Tree Ln					
700	BRLT	60103	2856	29W-9N	C7
Crabtree Ln					
200	GLF	60029	2865	8W-12N	A1
200	GNVW	60025	2865	8W-12N	A1
300	GNVW	60025	2811	7W-12N	B7
900	DSPN	60016	2863	12W-10N	B4
900	PKRG	60068	2863	12W-10N	B4
1200	SMBG	60193	2912		E1
2100	NHBK	60062	2757	10W-17N	A5
2700	NHBK	60062	2756	11W-17N	E4
2900	WLMT	60091	2811	5W-13N	E6
N Crabtree Ln					
1100	MPPT	60056	2808	14W-14N	B4
1200	PTHT	60070	2808	14W-14N	B4
Crab Tree Rd					
100	EDND	60118	2748		B7
Cracow Av					
4500	LYNS	60525	3148	10W-4S	A1
4500	LYNS	60534	3148	10W-4S	A1
4500	MCCK	60525	3148	10W-4S	A1
Craig Av					
500	CRTE	60417	3685	1W-30S	B3
Craig Ct					
300	DRFD	60015	2756	12W-20N	C1
300	STGR	60475	3595	1W-28S	E6
400	MPPT	60005	2861	17W-12N	B1
400	MPPT	60056	2861	17W-12N	B1
Craig Dr					
16400	OKFT	60452	3426	5W-19S	B2
E Craig Dr					
10	CHHT	60411	3508	1W-23S	A3
2000	DSPN	60018	2917	12W-8N	B2
S Craig Dr					
2600	DSPN	60018	2917	12W-8N	C2
Craig Dr W					
10	CHHT	60411	3508	0W-23S	B4
100	CHHT	60411	3507	1W-23S	E4
Craig Pl					
300	HLSD	60162	3028		E5
Craigie Ln					
100	IVNS	60067	2752	22W-16N	B7
Crain St					
800	EVTN	60202	2867	2W-10N	B4
1200	PKRG	60068	2863	10W-10N	E4
1200	PKRG	60068	2864	10W-10N	A4
1700	EVTN	60202	2866	3W-10N	E4
3300	SKOK	60076	2866	5W-10N	B4
4700	SKOK	60076	2865	6W-10N	E4
5000	SKOK	60077	2865	6W-10N	D4
5400	SKOK	60053	2865	6W-10N	D4
5600	MNGV	60053	2865	7W-10N	C4
W Crain St					
7000	NLES	60714	2864	8W-10N	E4
7900	MaiT	60714	2864	9W-10N	B4
8500	PKRG	60068	2864	10W-10N	A4
Cranberry Ct					
10	HnrT	60120	2910		D1
8600	TYPK	60477	3424	10W-19S	B3
15400	HMGN	60441	3344	16W-18S	A7
Cranbrook Ct					
1300	SMBG	60193	2912		C2
Cranbrook Dr					
10	DSPN	60016	2862	14W-12N	B1
10	MPPT	60016	2862	14W-12N	B1
10	MPPT	60056	2862	14W-12N	B1
900	SMBG	60193	2912		C2
Cranbrook Ln					
8700	BGVW	60455	3210	8W-10S	E4
8700	BRBK	60459	3210	8W-10S	E4
8700	OKLN	60453	3210	8W-10S	E4
8700	OKLN	60455	3210	8W-10S	E4
W Crandall Av					
6800	WRTH	60482	3275	8W-12S	A3
7000	WRTH	60482	3274	8W-12S	E3
Crandell Ct					
100	SMBG	60193	2859	23W-9N	A7
Crandell Ln					
600	SMBG	60193	2859	23W-9N	B7
Crandon Av					
500	CTCY	60409	3351	2E-17S	D6
S Crandon Av					
-	CHCG	60633	3351	2E-15S	D2
-	CTCY	60409	3351	2E-15S	D2
6700	CHCG	60649	3153	2E-7S	D6
7500	CHCG	60649	3215	2E-9S	D2
7800	CHCG	60617	3215	2E-9S	D3
10300	CHCG	60617	3279	2E-11S	D1
Crandon Ln					
1700	SMBG	60193	2858	25W-9N	A7
Crane Av					
16700	HLCT	60429	3427	2W-20S	C4
16700	MKHM	60426	3427	2W-20S	C4
Crane Ct					
2100	RGMW	60008	2806	19W-13N	D6
W Crane St					
1400	ANHT	60004	2753	18W-18N	D2
Cranfield Ln					
19400	TYPK	60477	3504	10W-23S	B3
Cranna Ct					
11700	ODPK	60467	3422	14W-21S	D6
Cranshire Ct					
3500	HFET	60067	2804	23W-14N	E4
Cranston Ct					
3100	WLMT	60091	2811	6W-14N	E5
Crawford Av					
2100	EVTN	60201	2866	4W-12N	B1
2100	SKOK	60203	2866	4W-12N	B2
2300	SKOK	60201	2866	4W-12N	B1
2500	EVTN	60201	2812	4W-13N	B7
2700	WLMT	60091	2812	4W-13N	B7
2700	WLMT	60201	2812	4W-13N	B7
7400	LNWD	60712	2866	4W-9N	B7
7400	SKOK	60076	2866	5W-11N	B2
19600	CCHL	60443	3506	4W-23S	D4
19600	CCHL	60478	3506	4W-23S	D4
19600	FSMR	60422	3506	4W-23S	D4
19600	FSMR	60443	3506	4W-23S	D4
19600	RchT	60443	3506	4W-23S	D4
21000	MTSN	60443	3506	4W-25S	D7
21000	OMFD	60461	3506	4W-25S	D7
23100	MonT	60466	3594	5W-28S	D6
23100	MonT	60471	3594	5W-28S	D7
23100	PKFT	60466	3594	5W-28S	D7
23100	RNPK	60466	3594	5W-28S	D7
23100	RNPK	60471	3594	5W-28S	D7
23500	UYPK	60466	3594	5W-28S	D7
N Crawford Av					
6400	CHCG	60646	2920	5W-8N	B3
6400	CHCG	60659	2920	5W-8N	B3
6700	LNWD	60712	2920	5W-8N	B2
7200	LNWD	60712	2866	5W-9N	B7
7300	SKOK	60076	2866	5W-9N	B7
Crawford Ln					
1500	HRPK	60133	2911		E6
E Crawford St					
100	PTON	60468	3861	9W-37S	A3
400	WIIT	60468	3861	9W-37S	A3
W Crawford St					
100	PTON	60468	3860	9W-37S	E3
100	PTON	60468	3861	9W-37S	A3
Crawling Stone Rd					
10	BNHL	60010	2748		E2
E Cree Ln					
1700	MPPT	60056	2808	13W-14N	D4
Creek Ct					
100	PTHT	60070	2808	15W-15N	A1
W Creek Ct N					
14800	HMGN	60441	3343	18W-17S	A5
W Creek Ct S					
14800	HMGN	60441	3343	18W-17S	A5
Creek Dr					
-	ALSP	60803	3276	4W-14S	D6
4800	WNSP	60558	3146		D1
N Creek Dr					
18300	TYPK	60477	3424	9W-22S	E7
18500	TYPK	60477	3504	9W-22S	E1
W Creek Dr					
18300	TYPK	60477	3424	9W-22S	E7
18300	TYPK	60477	3504	9W-22S	E1
W Creek Rd					
9600	PlsT	60464	3345	12W-15S	D1
9600	PSPK	60464	3345	12W-15S	C1
Creek Bend Rd					
2400	SMBG	60173	2805	21W-13N	D6
Creek Crossing Ct					
14600	OrlT	60467	3344	14W-17S	D5
Creek Crossing Dr					
13900	ODPK	60467	3344	14W-17S	D4
13900	OrlT	60467	3344	14W-17S	D4
Creekmont Ct					
16100	TYPK	60477	3424	10W-19S	B2
Creekside Av					
16800	TYPK	60477	3424	10W-20S	B4
Creekside Ct					
10	SMWD	60107	2856	29W-10N	E6
400	DGvT	60527	3146		A5
400	WLBK	60527	3146		A5
1000	PTHT	60070	2754	16W-16N	D7
1000	WLNG	60090	2754	16W-16N	D7
S Creekside Ct					
13800	HMGN	60441	3343	16W-16S	E3
24900	CteT	60417	3687	3E-30S	B2
Creekside Dr					
-	ANHT	60056	2807	15W-14N	E4
-	MPPT	60056	2807	15W-14N	E4
-	RGMW	60008	2806	20W-13N	A6
1400	HFET	60194	2858	25W-11N	B2
5300	OKFT	60452	3347	6W-18S	E7
11600	ODPK	60467	3344	14W-16S	D4
S Creekside Dr					
300	PLTN	60074	2806	19W-15N	B2
W Creekside Dr					
13000	HMGN	60441	3343	16W-16S	E3
13000	HMGN	60441	3344	16W-16S	A3
Creek Side Ln					
-	WLSP	60527	3208		E1
Creekside Ln					
10	BNHL	60010	2802	28W-15N	E2
Creekview Dr					
14400	OrlT	60467	3344	14W-17S	D5
14900	HMGN	60441	3342	18W-16S	E3
14900	HMGN	60441	3343	18W-16S	A3
E Creekwood Ct					
2500	CteT	60417	3686	3E-29S	E1
2500	CteT	60417	3687	3E-29S	A1
Creekwood Dr					
7900	BRRG	60527	3208		E3
14300	OrlT	60467	3344	14W-17S	C5
W Creekwood Dr					
300	PLTN	60074	2752	21W-18N	D2
Creel Dr					
600	WDDL	60191	2915		B5
Cregier Av					
17000	SHLD	60473	3429	1E-20S	C4
S Cregier Av					
6700	CHCG	60649	3153	2E-7S	B6
7500	CHCG	60649	3215	2E-8S	B1
8300	CHCG	60617	3215	2E-10S	B4
Creiger Av					
18000	LNSG	60438	3429	2E-21S	C7
Creighton Av					
900	EGVV	60007	2914		D2
Creighton Ln					
400	SMBG	60193	2859	23W-9N	B6
S Creme Rd					
14300	HMGN	60441	3343	18W-17S	B6
Crescent Av					
-	BlmT	60411	3509	3E-22S	E2
16500	TYPK	60477	3424	9W-19S	C3
19600	LYWD	60411	3509	3E-23S	E3
E Crescent Av					
100	EMHT	60126	3028		A5
N Crescent Av					
10	PLTN	60067	2805	22W-16N	C1
10	PltT	60067	2805	22W-16N	C1
100	PLTN	60067	2752	22W-16N	C7
4800	NRDG	60706	2918	10W-6N	B7
5600	CHCG	60631	2918	10W-7N	B5
5600	LydT	60631	2918	10W-7N	B5
5600	MaiT	60631	2918	10W-7N	B5
S Crescent Av					
200	PLTN	60067	2805	22W-15N	C2
200	PltT	60067	2805	22W-15N	C2
1500	PKRG	60068	2918	10W-7N	B4
1900	CHCG	60631	2918	10W-7N	B4
W Crescent Av					
800	PLTN	60067	2752	22W-16N	C7
900	PKRG	60068	2918	10W-8N	A1
1300	PKRG	60068	2917	10W-8N	E1
Crescent Ct					
10	SMWD	60107	2856	29W-10N	D6
700	BRLT	60103	2911		B3
700	HRPK	60133	2912		A3
1900	HFET	60194	2858	25W-12N	A2
6500	OKLN	60453	3211	8W-10S	A5
8400	WLSP	60480	3208		D3
12900	CTWD	60445	3347	6W-15S	E1
W Crescent Ct					
900	PLTN	60067	2752	22W-16N	B7
Crescent Dr					
-	BmnT	60426	3426	5W-19S	B1
10	GLNC	60022	2758	6W-18N	D4
10	MaiT	60025	2864	10W-12N	B1
200	CHHT	60411	3507	1W-25S	E6
300	WLNG	60090	2755	14W-17N	C5
2400	HLCT	60429	3427	3W-20S	C3
2400	HMWD	60430	3427	3W-22S	B7
3700	STGR	60475	3596	1W-28S	A6
9100	FNPK	60131	2973	11W-4N	D3
13500	OrlT	60462	3345	11W-16S	E2
13500	PlsT	60462	3345	11W-16S	E2
E Crescent Dr					
600	ANHT	60005	2807	17W-12N	B7
Crescent Ln					
100	SMBG	60193	2857	27W-10N	D6
1000	GLNC	60093	2759	5W-16N	A6
1000	WNKA	60093	2759	5W-16N	A6
1800	HFET	60194	2858	26W-12N	A2
3400	GNVW	60062	2809	11W-14N	C3
5300	OKFT	60452	3347	6W-18S	E6
Crescent Pl					
10	WLMT	60091	2812	3W-13N	E6
6400	HMND	46324	3430		E2
Crescent Wy					
700	HRPK	60133	2912		A1
22500	RNPK	60471	3594	5W-27S	C4
Crescent Green Dr					
5200	OKFT	60452	3347	6W-18S	E6
Crescent Green Ln					
15100	OKFT	60452	3347	6W-18S	E6
Crescenzo Dr					
3000	SCHT	60411	3596	1W-27S	A4
W Cressett Dr					
7700	EDPK	60707	2974	9W-3N	B5
7900	RVGV	60171	2974	9W-3N	B5
Cressmoor Ct					
8500	ODPK	60462	3346	10W-18S	B7
Crest Av					
-	SMBG	60193	2912		B2
100	EGVV	60007	2861	18W-9N	A7
200	EGvT	60007	2861	18W-9N	A7
300	BmdT	60157	2913		C4
300	ROSL	60157	2913		C4
300	ROSL	60172	2913		C4
400	EGvT	60007	2915		A1
400	EGVV	60007	2915		A1
700	SmbT	60193	2912		B2
E Crest Av					
100	BNVL	60106	2972		A3
N Crest Av					
100	BRLT	60103	2911		A3
S Crest Av					
100	BRLT	60103	2911		A3
W Crest Av					
300	ITSC	60143	2913		D4
Crest Ct					
1100	SMBG	60193	2913		B1
4900	CCHL	60478	3506	6W-22S	A1
8600	LynT	60527	3208		C4
Crest Ln					
1100	WNSP	60558	3146		D4
Crest St					
1300	SMBG	60193	2913		B2
1300	SmbT	60193	2913		B2
Crestbrook Ct					
12800	CTWD	60445	3275	6W-15S	E7
12800	CTWD	60445	3347	6W-15S	E1
Crest Hill Dr					
400	PTHT	60070	2754	16W-16N	D7
W Crestline Av					
4100	CHCG	60652	3212	5W-9S	B2
Crestline Dr					
-	ODPK	60467	3344	14W-16S	D3
E Crestview Av					
100	EMHT	60126	2972		A6
Crestview Ct					
100	BRTN	60010	2751	24W-18N	D3
100	PltT	60010	2751	24W-18N	D3
13600	CTWD	60445	3348	6W-16S	A3
17600	ODPK	60467	3422	14W-21S	D6
Crestview Dr					
10	DRFD	60015	2757	9W-20N	B2
1000	LMNT	60439	3270		E7
5700	WNSP	60558	3146		D4
8100	WLSP	60480	3208		D3
13900	HMGN	60441	3343	18W-16S	A4
17600	ODPK	60467	3422	14W-21S	D6
N Crestview Dr					
-	PLTN	60067	2752	20W-17N	E5
800	PLTN	60067	2753	20W-17N	A5
Crestview Ln					
100	DYR	46311	3598		C5
2200	WLMT	60091	2812	4W-13N	B6
Crestview Rd					
10800	CTSD	60525	3146		E6
10800	CTSD	60525	3147	13W-7S	A6
Crestview Ter					
10	BFGV	60089	2754	16W-18N	C2
Crest Wood Ct					
100	HFET	60195	2859	23W-12N	A1
100	SMBG	60195	2859	23W-12N	A1
Crestwood Ct					
900	SMWD	60107	2857	28W-9N	A7
1000	EGVV	60007	2914		D2
5600	MTSN	60443	3505	7W-24S	D5
13400	CTWD	60445	3347	6W-15S	D2
Crestwood Dr					
10	SMWD	60107	2857	28W-9N	A7
100	EDND	60118	2801		B2
300	ROSL	60172	2913		B6
400	DSPN	60016	2862	14W-11N	C4
1100	NHBK	60062	2756	10W-17N	E5
2000	PltT	60067	2806	20W-13N	A6
2000	RGMW	60008	2806	20W-13N	A6
3700	GNVW	60025	2809	11W-15N	D3
3700	GNVW	60062	2809	11W-15N	D3
4100	NfdT	60062	2809	11W-15N	D3
5400	CTWD	60445	3347	6W-15S	D2
E Crestwood Dr					
600	ANHT	60004	2754	17W-16N	B7
Crestwood Ln					
-	GNVW	60025	2809	10W-13N	E5
-	LMNT	60439	3271		A6
-	PltT	60067	2806	20W-13N	A6
-	RGMW	60008	2806	20W-13N	A5
3100	GNVW	60025	2810	10W-13N	A5
10200	PvsT	60154	3087	12W-1S	A2
10200	WSTR	60154	3087	12W-1S	A2
S Crestwood Ln					
400	MPPT	60056	2861	17W-12N	C2
Crestwood Rd					
5600	MTSN	60443	3505	7W-24S	D5
Crestwood Vil					
200	NHFD	60093	2811	6W-15N	C3
Crete Blvd					
300	CRTE	60417	3685	0W-30S	B3
Crete Rd					
3700	CRTE	60417	3597	0E-29S	A7
3700	CRTE	60417	3685	0E-29S	E1
3700	CteT	60417	3685	0E-29S	E1
W Crete-Monee Rd					
-	CteT	60417	3684	3W-31S	C5
-	MonT	60417	3684	3W-31S	C5
3200	MonT	60449	3683	4W-31S	D5
3200	MonT	60449	3684	3W-31S	B5
4000	UYPK	60449	3683	5W-31S	D5
4200	MONE	60449	3683	5W-31S	C5
S Cretewood Ln					
23900	CteT	60417	3595	2W-29S	E7
Crewman Dr					
100	GNVW	60025	2810	10W-14N	A3
Crichton Ln					
100	IVNS	60067	2752	22W-18N	B3
S Cricketwood Ct					
14600	HMGN	60441	3343	17W-17S	D5
S Cricketwood Dr					
14600	HMGN	60441	3343	17W-17S	D6
N Crilly Ct					
1700	CHCG	60614	2978		C7
S Crilly Dr					
-	CHCG	60617	3216	4E-10S	C6
Crimson Ct					
800	PTHT	60070	2809	13W-15N	A1
2800	NHBK	60062	2756	11W-17N	E4
4100	HFET	60195	2804	24W-15N	B2

STREET Block	City	ZIP	Map#	CGS	Grid
Crimson Dr					
1000	WLNG	60090	2754	15W-16N	E6
4100	HFET	60195	2804	24W-15N	B2
Crimson Ln					
1500	PLTN	60074	2753	19W-17N	D4
1500	PltT	60074	2753	19W-17N	D4
Cripple Creek Ct					
100	SMBG	60194	2857	27W-10N	D5
Criss Cir					
300	EGVV	60007	2861	17W-10N	B5
Cristina Av					
8300	ODPK	60462	3346	10W-16S	B3
Crocket Ln					
15400	MKHM	60426	3349	3W-18S	A7
W Crocus Av					
4600	MONE	60449	3683	5W-31S	C4
Crocus Ln					
10	MTSN	60443	3593	7W-26S	C2
Croft Ln					
1200	EVTN	60202	2867	2W-10N	A4
Crofton Av S					
600	HDPK	60035	2757	8W-20N	E1
Crofton Ct					
700	SBTN	60010	2803	25W-15N	E1
Crofton Ln					
900	BFGV	60089	2754	17W-17N	B4
Croftwood Ct					
100	RGMW	60008	2805	21W-13N	D5
S Croissant Dr					
13800	BNHM	60633	3351	2E-16S	D3
Crompton St					
-	WNKA	60093	2811	6W-15N	D2
Cromwell Av					
700	WSTR	60154	3029	12W-0S	B7
Cromwell Ln					
5500	OKFT	60452	3347	6W-17S	D5
Cromwell Rd					
10	PKFT	60466	3595	2W-27S	C4
N Croname Rd					
7300	NLES	60714	2865	7W-9N	A7
Cronin Av					
7500	JSTC	60458	3209	11W-8S	E2
Cronin Ct					
1200	LMNT	60439	3271		B7
Crooked Creek Ct					
17900	ODPK	60467	3422	14W-21S	E7
Crooked Creek Dr					
1300	BCHR	60401	3774	0W-35S	D7
Crooked Creek Ln					
300	NHFD	60093	2811	6W-15N	C1
Crooked Creek Rd					
2500	SMBG	60173	2805	21W-13N	D6
Crooked Creek Tr					
10	DRPK	60010	2752	22W-18N	A2
10	PltT	60010	2752	22W-18N	A2
W Crooked Willow Ln					
1200	PLTN	60067	2805	22W-14N	B3
Crosby Ct					
1500	HRPK	60133	2911		E6
N Crosby St					
900	CHCG	60610	3034	0W-1N	A2
Cross Creek Ct					
800	ROSL	60172	2913		C3
Cross Creek Dr N					
800	ROSL	60172	2913		C2
Cross Creek Pk W					
600	ROSL	60172	2913		C3
Crossen Av					
10	EGVV	60007	2861	17W-9N	C7
Crossing Ct					
500	RGMW	60008	2805	21W-13N	C5
Crossing Dr					
18300	TYPK	60477	3504	10W-22S	B1
Crossman Cir					
-	PvsT	60141	3088	10W-1S	A1
Crossroads of Commerce					
10	RGMW	60008	2806	20W-12N	B7
10	RGMW	60008	2860	20W-12N	B1
Crosswind Dr					
-	RNPK	60471	3593	6W-27S	E5
-	RNPK	60471	3594	6W-27S	A5
Crow Ln					
400	WLNG	60090	2754	16W-17N	D5
S Crowell St					
2700	CHCG	60608	3091	1W-2S	E3
Crowfoot Cir N					
1400	HFET	60194	2858	25W-11N	B3
Crowfoot Cir S					
1400	HFET	60194	2858	25W-11N	B3
Crown Cir					
8400	WLSP	60480	3208		E3
Crown Ct					
700	SMBG	60193	2859	23W-9N	A7
8600	LynT	60527	3208		C4
S Crown Ct					
300	PLTN	60074	2806	19W-15N	D2
Crown Dr					
1500	GNVW	60025	2809	11W-14N	E5
Crown Hl					
-	ELGN	60120	2855		C7
Crown Ln					
1400	GNVW	60025	2809	11W-14N	E5
6800	TYPK	60477	3425	8W-19S	A2
W Crown Ln					
600	PTON	60468	3860	9W-37S	D4
Crown Rd					
400	AddT	60126	2972		A5
500	AddT	60106	2972		A5
500	BNVL	60106	2972		A5
10400	FNPK	60131	2973	13W-3N	A5
Crown Point Ct					
500	BFGV	60089	2754	17W-20N	C1
Crown Point Dr					
500	BFGV	60089	2754	17W-20N	C1
Croyden Pl					
2300	NHBK	60062	2810	8W-16N	D1
Croydon Ln					
10	OKBK	60523	3086		B2
8900	ODPK	60462	3346	11W-18S	A7
Croydon on Duxbury					
10	RGMW	60008	2805	22W-13N	B6
Croyle Ct					
1100	SMBG	60193	2912		C2
Crystal Ct					
100	STGR	60475	3596	1W-28S	A6
1000	GNVW	60025	2810	10W-13N	A6
1000	NfdT	60025	2810	10W-13N	A6
16800	TYPK	60477	3425	8W-20S	A3
W Crystal Ct					
4400	ALSP	60803	3276	5W-15S	B7
Crystal Ct N					
600	SMBG	60193	2859	22W-9N	B7
Crystal Ct S					
600	SMBG	60193	2859	22W-9N	B7
Crystal Ln					
100	BRLT	60103	2910		B3
100	HnrT	60103	2910		B3
200	CteT	60417	3596	1W-28S	A6
200	CteT	60475	3596	1W-28S	A6
200	STGR	60475	3596	1W-28S	A6
2400	PltT	60004	2753	19W-18N	C2
18000	LNSG	60438	3429	2E-21S	C6
18100	ThtT	60438	3429	2E-21S	C6
W Crystal Ln					
-	EGvT	60056	2861	17W-10N	C4
-	MPPT	60056	2861	17W-10N	C4
Crystal Rd					
2300	NHBK	60062	2810	8W-15N	D1
W Crystal St					
2600	CHCG	60622	3033	3W-1N	A1
2700	CHCG	60622	3032	3W-1N	E1
3200	CHCG	60651	3032	4W-1N	D1
4800	CHCG	60651	3031	6W-1N	D2
Crystal Creek Dr					
8700	ODHL	60462	3424	10W-19S	A1
8700	ODHL	60477	3424	10W-19S	A1
8700	ODPK	60477	3424	10W-19S	A1
16000	ODPK	60462	3424	10W-19S	A1
16000	TYPK	60462	3424	10W-19S	A1
16000	TYPK	60477	3424	10W-19S	A1
Crystal Lake Ct					
13000	HMGN	60441	3422	16W-21S	A6
Crystal Lake Dr					
17400	HMGN	60441	3422	16W-21S	A6
17800	HMGN	60448	3422	16W-21S	A6
S Crystal Lake Dr					
17900	HMGN	60441	3422	16W-21S	A7
17900	HMGN	60448	3422	16W-21S	A7
Crystal Meadow Ct					
10800	ODPK	60462	3345	13W-17S	A6
10800	ODPK	60467	3345	13W-17S	A6
Crystal Ridge Ct					
10800	ODPK	60462	3345	13W-17S	A5
10800	ODPK	60467	3345	13W-17S	A5
Crystal Springs Ct					
14900	ODPK	60467	3345	13W-17S	A6
Crystal Springs Ln					
10800	ODPK	60462	3345	13W-17S	A6
10800	ODPK	60467	3345	13W-17S	A6
Crystal Tree Dr					
14400	ODPK	60462	3345	13W-17S	B5
Cullen Dr					
8500	FKFT	60423	3504	10W-24S	B6
Cullerton St					
3000	FNPK	60131	2972		E4
3000	LydT	60164	2972		E5
E Cullerton St					
10	CHCG	60616	3092	0E-1S	C1
W Cullerton St					
500	CHCG	60616	3092	0W-1S	A1
800	CHCG	60608	3092		E2
1300	CHCG	60608	3091	2W-1S	B1
3000	CHCG	60623	3090	3W-1S	E1
Culligan Pkwy					
10	NfdT	60062	2809	12W-16N	B1
Culloden St					
3700	FSMR	60422	3506	4W-23S	D4
W Cullom Av					
900	CHCG	60613	2977	1W-5N	E1
1900	CHCG	60618	2977	3W-5N	A1
2800	CHCG	60618	2976	4W-5N	C1
4000	CHCG	60641	2976	5W-5N	B1
4800	CHCG	60641	2975	7W-5N	C1
5500	CHCG	60634	2975	7W-5N	B1
6800	HDHT	60706	2974	8W-5N	E1
7100	NRDG	60706	2974	9W-5N	C1
7700	CHCG	60634	2974	9W-5N	C1
7700	NRDG	60634	2974	9W-5N	C1
Cullom St					
-	FDHT	60411	3509	1E-24S	B6
-	SRPK	60176	2973	11W-5N	C1
Culver Ln					
1700	GNVW	60025	2810	8W-12N	D7
Culver St					
3300	EVTN	60201	2812	4W-12N	B7
5000	SKOK	60077	2811	6W-12N	E7
9500	MaiT	60016	2809	11W-12N	C7
Culzean Ln					
10	IVNS	60067	2805	22W-16N	A1
Cumberland Av					
200	KLWH	60043	2812	4W-14N	C4
1400	NfdT	60062	2756	12W-17N	B6
1400	NHBK	60062	2756	12W-17N	B6
N Cumberland Av					
10	PKRG	60068	2864	10W-9N	A7
10	PKRG	60068	2918	8W-8N	D1
1000	NLES	60714	2864	10W-10N	A5
3200	RVGV	60171	2974	10W-4N	A4
3200	RVGV	60634	2974	10W-4N	A4
3700	CHCG	60634	2974	10W-5N	A2
4200	CHCG	60656	2974	10W-5N	A2
4200	NRDG	60634	2974	10W-5N	A2
4200	NRDG	60706	2974	10W-5N	A2
4600	CHCG	60656	2918	10W-6N	A5
4600	NRDG	60706	2918	10W-6N	A6
4900	CHCG	60706	2918	10W-6N	A6
5200	NRDG	60656	2918	10W-6N	A6
5500	CHCG	60631	2918	10W-6N	A5
8400	MaiT	60016	2864	10W-10N	A5
N Cumberland Av SR-171					
-	PKRG	60068	2918	10W-7N	A4
3200	RVGV	60171	2974	10W-4N	A4
3200	RVGV	60634	2974	10W-4N	A4
3700	CHCG	60634	2974	10W-5N	A2
4200	CHCG	60656	2974	10W-5N	A2
4200	NRDG	60634	2974	10W-5N	A2
4200	NRDG	60706	2974	10W-5N	A2
4600	CHCG	60656	2918	10W-6N	A6
4600	NRDG	60706	2918	10W-6N	A6
4900	CHCG	60706	2918	10W-6N	A6
5200	NRDG	60656	2918	10W-6N	A6
5500	CHCG	60631	2918	10W-6N	A5
S Cumberland Av					
10	PKRG	60068	2918	10W-8N	A2
1800	CHCG	60631	2918	10W-7N	A4
Cumberland Cir E					
1300	EGVV	60007	2914		D3
Cumberland Cir W					
1300	EGVV	60007	2914		C3
Cumberland Ct					
900	ROSL	60172	2913		C3
E Cumberland Ct					
24200	CteT	60417	3687	4E-29S	C1
Cumberland Dr					
10	SMBG	60194	2858	25W-10N	B5
7300	HRPK	60133	2911		E1
E Cumberland Ln					
3300	CteT	60417	3687	4E-29S	C1
Cumberland Pkwy					
1400	ALGN	60102	2748		B1
N Cumberland Pkwy					
10	DSPN	60016	2862	14W-12N	C2
S Cumberland Pkwy					
10	DSPN	60016	2862	14W-11N	C2
Cumberland St					
600	HFET	60194	2859	23W-11N	A4
Cumberland Tr					
500	ROSL	60172	2913		C3
3200	OMFD	60461	3506	4W-24S	E5
3200	OMFD	60461	3507	3W-24S	A5
Cummings Av					
700	KLWH	60043	2812	4W-14N	C4
700	NtrT	60093	2812	4W-14N	C4
Cummings Dr					
100	BRLT	60103	2909		C3
Cummings Ln					
2000	FSMR	60422	3507	2W-22S	C2
Cumnock Rd					
300	IVNS	60067	2751	23W-16N	E7
700	MTSN	60443	3506	4W-25S	D6
700	MTSN	60461	3506	4W-25S	D6
700	OMFD	60461	3506	4W-25S	D6
Cumnor Av					
600	BRTN	60010	2750	26W-20N	D1
Cumnor Rd					
200	KLWH	60043	2812	4W-14N	C4
200	WLMT	60043	2812	3W-14N	D4
200	WLMT	60091	2812	3W-14N	D4
Cunningham Cir					
1100	EGVV	60007	2913		E2
Cunningham Dr					
200	PKFT	60466	3595	3W-26S	B3
1200	CTCY	60409	3429	3E-19S	E2
E Cunningham Dr					
10	PLTN	60067	2752	20W-17N	E5
100	PLTN	60067	2753	20W-17N	A5
200	PLTN	60074	2753	20W-17N	A5
W Cunningham Dr					
10	PLTN	60067	2752	21W-17N	D5
Cunningham Ln					
10	PKFT	60466	3595	3W-26S	B3
Currant Av					
8400	TYPK	60477	3424	10W-19S	B3
Curricle Rd					
10	WLNG	60090	2754	15W-20N	E2
10	WLNG	60090	2755	15W-18N	A2
Curtis Ln					
5200	HRPK	60133	2911		C6
Curtis St					
2800	DSPN	60018	2917	12W-8N	B2
Custer Av					
100	CHCG	60626	2867	2W-9N	B6
100	CHCG	60645	2867	2W-9N	B6
1000	EVTN	60202	2867	2W-10N	B4
3900	BKFD	60513	3088	11W-4S	A7
3900	LYNS	60534	3088	11W-4S	A7
4100	LYNS	60513	3088	11W-4S	A7
4500	BKFD	60513	3148	10W-4S	A1
4500	LYNS	60534	3148	10W-4S	A1
4500	MCCK	60513	3148	11W-4S	A1
4500	MCCK	60525	3148	11W-4S	A1
Custer Ct					
500	WLNG	60090	2754	16W-17N	D5
E Custer St					
10	LMNT	60439	3270		D6
W Custer St					
10	LMNT	60439	3270		C6
N Cutcheon Ter					
-	CHCG	60640	2921	1W-6N	E6
Cutter Ln					
600	EGVV	60007	2913		D1
600	EGVV	60193	2913		D1
Cutters Run					
10	BrnT	60010	2803	27W-13N	A6
10	SBTN	60010	2803	27W-13N	A6
Cutters Mill Ct					
700	SMBG	60194	2858	25W-11N	B4
Cutters Mill Ln					
400	SMBG	60194	2858	25W-11N	B4
Cuttingham Ct					
2600	RGMW	60008	2806	19W-12N	C7
E Cuttriss St					
10	PKRG	60068	2864	9W-9N	C6
200	NLES	60714	2864	9W-9N	C6
W Cuttriss St					
200	PKRG	60068	2864	10W-9N	B6
Cuyahoga Dr					
900	BRLT	60103	2910		D6
Cuyler Av					
-	NHBK	60062	2758	7W-17N	A6
1200	BRWN	60304	3031	7W-1S	B7
1200	BRWN	60402	3031	7W-1S	B7
1200	OKPK	60304	3031	7W-1S	B7
1500	BRWN	60402	3089	7W-2S	B3
3800	SKNY	60402	3089	7W-3S	B6
N Cuyler Av					
100	OKPK	60302	3031	7W-0N	B3
S Cuyler Av					
500	OKPK	60302	3031	7W-0S	B5
500	OKPK	60304	3031	7W-0S	B5
1100	BRWN	60304	3031	7W-0S	B7
1100	BRWN	60402	3031	7W-0S	B7
W Cuyler Av					
900	CHCG	60613	2977	1W-5N	E1
2000	CHCG	60618	2977	2W-5N	B1
3300	CHCG	60618	2976	4W-5N	D1
4600	CHCG	60641	2976	5W-5N	A1
4900	CHCG	60641	2975	6W-5N	E1
6200	CHCG	60634	2975	7W-5N	A1
Cuyler Av N					
800	OKPK	60302	3031	7W-1N	A2
Cyndi Ct					
1900	RGMW	60008	2806	18W-13N	D6
Cynthia Av					
1400	PKRG	60068	2863	10W-9N	E7
21500	SLVL	60411	3597	2E-26S	C2
Cynthia Ct					
16600	TYPK	60477	3424	10W-19S	B3
Cynthia Ln					
1400	HRPK	60133	2857	26W-9N	E7
Cypress Av					
1400	HRPK	60133	2911		D2
17500	CCHL	60478	3426	5W-21S	C6
18800	CCHL	60478	3506	5W-22S	D2
20100	LYWD	60411	3510	3E-23S	B4
S Cypress Cir					
16400	LKPT	60441	3342	20W-18S	B7
Cypress Ct					
10	PLTN	60067	2752	20W-17N	E4
400	SMBG	60193	2858	23W-9N	E6
800	ROSL	60172	2913		B6
1500	HFET	60194	2858	25W-12N	B2
1500	HRPK	60133	2911		E2
Cypress Ct					
4000	CCHL	60478	3506	5W-23S	C2
4800	RNPK	60471	3594	6W-27S	A4
4900	BmnT	60477	3426	6W-20S	A4
4900	OKFT	60452	3426	6W-20S	A4
5000	HLSD	60162	3028		D4
8900	ODPK	60462	3346	11W-17S	A6
9000	TYPK	60477	3424	11W-21S	A5
9300	MaiT	60016	2863	11W-12N	D1
Cypress Dr					
-	LMNT	60439	3342	19W-15S	C2
100	SMWD	60107	2857	28W-10N	A5
1200	WLNG	60090	2754	16W-18N	E3
4800	HLSD	60162	3028		D4
19100	CCHL	60478	3506	5W-23S	D3
S Cypress Dr					
1000	MPPT	60056	2861	16W-11N	D3
W Cypress Dr					
900	ANHT	60005	2860	18W-12N	E1
Cypress Ln					
10	CTSD	60525	3147	12W-7S	B6
1000	EGVV	60007	2914		E2
1100	LynT	60458	3209	11W-8S	D2
1900	NHBK	60062	2757	10W-16N	A7
S Cypress Ln					
12900	PSHT	60463	3346	9W-15S	D1
E Cypress St					
10	ANHT	60005	2807	17W-12N	B7
W Cypress St					
10	ANHT	60005	2807	18W-12N	A7
400	ANHT	60005	2806	18W-12N	E7
Cypress Point Ct					
500	RVWD	60015	2756	12W-20N	B1
Cyprus Rd					
15300	MKHM	60426	3348	4W-18S	E7
S Cyril Ct					
7100	CHCG	60649	3153	2E-8S	C7
Czacki St					
500	LMNT	60439	3270		E6
Czech Ter					
3900	BKFD	60513	3088	10W-4S	A6
3900	LYNS	60513	3088	10W-4S	A6
D					
W D St					
-	MYWD	60153	3088	10W-1S	A1
-	PvsT	60141	3088	10W-1S	A1
-	PvsT	60153	3088	10W-1S	A1
Daffodil Ct					
-	DYR	46311	3510		C5
-	LYWD	60411	3510		C5
Daffodil Ln					
300	MTSN	60443	3593	7W-26S	D2
S Daffodil Ln					
25600	MONE	60449	3683	5W-31S	C5
Dahlia Ct					
100	RGMW	60008	2805	21W-13N	D5
Dahlia Dr					
7300	HRPK	60133	2911		C1
Dahlin					
-	SKOK	60077	2865	7W-9N	B6
Daiquiri Dr					
2600	RVWD	60015	2755	13W-20N	E1
Dairy Ln					
900	IVNS	60067	2751	23W-17N	E5
1200	CRTE	60417	3685	0W-29S	C2
Daisy Av					
2200	GNVW	60025	2810	9W-14N	C4
Daisy Ln					
600	BmdT	60172	2912		D6
600	ROSL	60172	2912		D6
Daisy Mdws					
100	BRRG	60527	3146		C5
W Dakin St					
800	CHCG	60613	2977	1W-4N	E2
2500	CHCG	60618	2976	3W-4N	E2
2500	CHCG	60618	2977	3W-4N	A2
3900	CHCG	60641	2976	4W-4N	B2
5500	CHCG	60634	2975	7W-4N	B2
5500	CHCG	60641	2975	7W-4N	C2
6600	CHCG	60634	2974	8W-4N	E2
Dakota Dr					
1200	ELGN	60120	2801		C7
1600	EGVV	60007	2913		D2
Dakota Ln					
7800	ODPK	60462	3346	9W-16S	C2
Dakota Tr					
400	WLNG	60090	2754	16W-17N	D5
Dale Av					
200	ANHT	60004	2807	16W-15N	D2
200	PTHT	60004	2807	16W-15N	D2
200	PTHT	60070	2807	16W-15N	D2
N Dale Av					
200	MPPT	60056	2807	16W-13N	D6
300	ANHT	60056	2807	16W-13N	D6
1100	PTHT	60004	2807	16W-15N	D3
1100	PTHT	60056	2807	16W-15N	D3
1100	PTHT	60070	2807	16W-15N	D3
1100	WhlT	60004	2807	16W-15N	D3
1800	ANHT	60004	2807	16W-15N	D1
S Dale Av					
300	ANHT	60004	2807	16W-13N	D6
300	ANHT	60056	2807	16W-13N	D6
300	MPPT	60004	2807	16W-13N	D6
300	MPPT	60056	2807	16W-13N	D6
Dale Dr					
1300	HnrT	60120	2855		E2
3400	CRTE	60417	3597	1E-28S	B6
Dale Rd					
-	HMGN	60448	3422	15W-21S	B7
Dale St					
10	GNVW	60025	2811	6W-13N	D7
2400	DSPN	60018	2917	12W-8N	A1
Dalewood Av					
200	WDDL	60191	2914		E7
Dalewood Ln					
500	HNDL	60521	3146		C2
Dallas Dr					
100	BRLT	60103	2909		D3
W Dalphon Ct					
12300	HMGN	60467	3344	15W-16S	B4
Dalton Ct					
10	SBTN	60010	2803	26W-14N	C3
Dalton Ln					
400	ROSL	60172	2912		D6
Dalton Pl					
600	NHBK	60062	2757	8W-17N	E5
Dam W					
10000	WhlT	60090	2755	13W-17N	E6
Damen Av					
1200	CHCG	60608	3033	2W-1S	C7
16100	MKHM	60426	3427	2W-19S	D2
N Damen Av					
10	CHCG	60612	3033	2W-0N	C4
N Damen Av					
300	CHCG	60622	3033	2W-1N	C2
1500	CHCG	60647	3033	2W-1N	B1
1600	CHCG	60622	2977	2W-2N	B7
1600	CHCG	60647	2977	2W-2N	B7
1900	CHCG	60614	2977	2W-2N	B7
2600	CHCG	60618	2977	2W-2N	B7
2600	CHCG	60657	2977	2W-3N	B5
3500	CHCG	60613	2977	2W-2N	B7
4400	CHCG	60613	2921	2W-5N	B7
4400	CHCG	60618	2921	2W-5N	B7
4400	CHCG	60625	2921	2W-6N	B6
4400	CHCG	60640	2921	2W-6N	B6
6000	CHCG	60659	2921	2W-7N	B3
6000	CHCG	60660	2921	2W-7N	B3
7000	CHCG	60626	2921	2W-8N	B1
7000	CHCG	60645	2921	2W-8N	B1
7200	CHCG	60626	2867	2W-9N	B7
7200	CHCG	60645	2867	2W-9N	B7
7500	EVTN	60202	2867	2W-9N	B7
S Damen Av					
10	CHCG	60612	3033	2W-1S	C7
1100	CHCG	60608	3033	2W-1S	C7
1600	CHCG	60608	3091	2W-4S	C7
4300	CHCG	60609	3091	2W-4S	C7
4700	CHCG	60609	3151	2W-5S	C1
5500	CHCG	60636	3151	2W-6S	C3
7500	CHCG	60620	3213	2W-8S	C1
9500	CHCG	60643	3213	2W-11S	C7
Damico Dr					
800	CHHT	60411	3507	2W-25S	D7
Dam Woods					
10000	WhlT	60062	2755	13W-17N	E6
10000	WhlT	60090	2755	13W-17N	E5
10000	WLNG	60090	2755	13W-17N	E5
Dana Ct					
100	SMBG	60193	2913		A1
4000	NHBK	60062	2756	12W-17N	B4
Dana Ln					
400	BNHL	60010	2750	27W-18N	B3
500	SMWD	60107	2857	28W-11N	B4
Dana Pt					
1700	ALGN	60102	2748		A3
Dana Wy					
7800	BRRG	60527	3208		D2
Danbury Ct					
400	SMBG	60193	2912		E1
Danbury Ln					
1300	DSPN	60018	2862	15W-10N	B6
8800	ODPK	60462	3346	11W-18S	A7
Danbury Pl					
2000	HFET	60195	2858	25W-12N	B1
Danby Ct					
5900	HRPK	60133	2911		D5
Dancing Bear Ln					
1300	ELGN	60120	2855		E3
Dandridge Ct					
800	ELGN	60120	2855		D2
Danford Ln					
15700	ODPK	60462	3423	11W-18S	E1
Danforth Ct					
5800	HRPK	60133	2911		D5
Daniel Ct					
10	BlmT	60411	3510	3E-25S	A7
100	BRLT	60103	2911		B2
1400	NHBK	60062	2756	12W-17N	B6
Daniel Dr					
100	BNVL	60106	2972		A4
8000	BGVW	60455	3210	10W-9S	C3
8000	JSTC	60455	3210	10W-9S	C3
8000	JSTC	60458	3210	10W-9S	C3
S Daniel Dr					
13000	CHCG	60628	3278	0E-15S	D7
13000	CHCG	60827	3278	0E-15S	D7
13000	CHCG	60827	3350	0W-15S	C1
Danielle Ct					
-	HLCT	60429	3427	3W-21S	B5
17000	OKFT	60452	3425	6W-20S	E4
17000	OKFT	60477	3425	6W-20S	E4
Danielle Rd					
300	MTSN	60443	3505	7W-24S	C5
Daniels Ct					
900	SMBG	60194	2858	24W-11N	D3
N Daniels Ct					
3000	ANHT	60004	2754	17W-17N	B4
Daniels Ln					
6200	OKFT	60452	3347	7W-17S	C5
E Daniels Rd					
10	PLTN	60067	2805	20W-15N	E1
200	PLTN	60067	2806	20W-15N	A1
W Daniels Rd					
400	PLTN	60067	2805	21W-15N	C1
400	PltT	60067	2805	21W-15N	C1
Danmar Tr					
10	PSPK	60464	3272	14W-15S	E7
10	PSPK	60464	3344	14W-15S	E1
E Danne Rd					
2800	CteT	60417	3687	4E-30S	B4
3200	HnrT	46311	3687	4E-30S	B4
Dan Ryan Expwy					
-	CHCG	-	3034	0W-1S	A7
-	CHCG	-	3092	0W-3S	B5
-	CHCG	-	3152	0W-6S	B4
-	CHCG	-	3214	0W-8S	C1
Dan Ryan Expwy I-57					
-	CHCG	-	3214	0W-11S	A7
Dan Ryan Expwy I-90					
-	CHCG	-	3034	0W-1S	A7
-	CHCG	-	3092	0W-4S	B6
-	CHCG	-	3152	0W-7S	C5
Dan Ryan Expwy I-94					
-	CHCG	-	3034	0W-1S	A7
-	CHCG	-	3092	0W-2S	A2
-	CHCG	-	3152	0W-7S	C5
-	CHCG	-	3214	0W-8S	C1
Dansforth Dr					
200	SMBG	60193	2858	24W-10N	D6
Dansher Rd					
5100	CTSD	60525	3147	12W-5S	C2
S Dansher Rd					
5200	CTSD	60525	3147	12W-5S	C2
Dante Av					
15400	DLTN	60419	3351	1E-18S	B6
18200	ThtT	60438	3429	1E-21S	B7
18500	LNSG	60438	3429	1E-21S	B7
S Dante Av					
-	BlmT	60411	3509	1E-23S	B3
200	GNWD	60425	3509	1E-23S	B3
500	BlmT	60425	3509	1E-23S	B3
6800	CHCG	60637	3153	1E-7S	B6
7300	CHCG	60619	3153	1E-8S	B7
8700	CHCG	60619	3215	1E-10S	B4
Dante Ct					
-	BNVL	60106	2972		A4
700	SMBG	60193	2858	23W-9N	E7

STREET Block	City	ZIP	Map#	CGS	Grid
Dante Dr					
15600	SHLD	60473	3351	1E-18S	B7
Danube Wy					
10	OMFD	60461	3506	4W-25S	D7
Danvers Ct					
1100	SMBG	60193	2912		C1
Dara James St					
400	DSPN	60016	2862	15W-11N	B4
Darby Ln					
1100	ROSL	60172	2912		C5
Daren Dr					
200	BlmT	60411	3598	4E-26S	C1
200	LYWD	60411	3598	4E-26S	C1
Darien Ct					
600	HFET	60194	2858	24W-11N	D4
N Darlington Cir					
1200	HFET	60194	2858	25W-11N	C3
W Darlington Cir					
1300	HFET	60194	2858	25W-11N	C3
Darlington Ct					
1200	HFET	60194	2858	25W-11N	C3
Darmstadt Rd					
-	BKLY	60163	3028		C6
-	HLSD	60162	3028		C6
Darrell Cir					
-	PvsT	60141	3088	10W-1S	A1
Darrow Av					
1000	EVTN	60202	2866	3W-10N	E4
1400	EVTN	60201	2866	3W-11N	E3
E Darryl Dr					
1800	WhlT	60004	2754	16W-17N	C5
Dartford Ln					
10	SMBG	60194	2858	25W-10N	B5
N Dartmoor Av					
1500	PLTN	60067	2752	21W-18N	D3
W Dartmoor Av					
200	PLTN	60067	2752	21W-17N	D4
Dartmouth Av					
800	MTSN	60443	3505	7W-25S	E7
Dartmouth Ct					
10	SMWD	60107	2856	29W-9N	D7
100	GNVW	60025	2810	9W-15N	B2
800	BRLT	60103	2910		E6
800	HRPK	60133	2858	26W-9N	A7
Dartmouth Dr					
1000	BRLT	60103	2910		E6
Dartmouth Ln					
400	SMBG	60193	2858	25W-9N	B7
700	BFGV	60089	2754	15W-20N	E1
1100	DRFD	60015	2756	11W-20N	C1
2800	OMFD	60461	3507	3W-25S	A6
8000	HRPK	60133	2858	26W-9N	A7
Dartmouth Pl					
600	EVTN	60201	2867	2W-12N	B1
3300	EVTN	60201	2866	4W-12N	B1
3300	SKOK	60076	2866	4W-12N	B1
Dartmouth Rd					
1100	FSMR	60422	3507	2W-23S	D3
8700	PSHL	60465	3274	10W-12S	A2
Dartmouth St					
1100	WLMT	60091	2812	5W-14N	B5
1900	CHHT	60411	3595	1W-26S	E2
Dartry Dr					
-	CCHL	60478	3506	6W-22S	A1
Darvin Dr					
19100	MKNA	60448	3504	11W-23S	A2
Daryl Ln					
1100	NHBK	60062	2757	9W-17N	D5
Dato Ct					
100	SMWD	60107	2857	27W-11N	C4
Dato Dr					
10	SMWD	60107	2857	27W-11N	C4
Dauntless Cir					
300	GNVW	60025	2810	10W-15N	A3
S Dauphin Av					
8700	CHCG	60619	3214	1E-10S	E4
10000	CHCG	60628	3214	0E-11S	E7
10300	CHCG	60628	3278	0E-12S	E1
Dauphine Av					
600	NHBK	60062	2756	12W-18N	B4
Dauphine Ct					
600	EGVV	60007	2914		C1
600	NHBK	60062	2756	11W-18N	C4
Dave Ct					
100	SMWD	60107	2857	28W-11N	A4
Daves Ct					
100	BRLT	60103	2909		E3
Davey Rd					
16900	DGvT	60439	3270		B3
16900	WDRG	60517	3270		B3
17400	DGvT	60517	3270		C2
17400	WDRG	60439	3270		B3
David Ct					
10	BlmT	60411	3510	3E-25S	A6
300	BRLT	60103	2911		A3
5900	OKLN	60453	3211	7W-11S	C6
David Dr					
100	BNVL	60106	2972		A4
100	SMWD	60107	2857	27W-11N	D4
300	ELGN	60120	2855		C5
1100	EMHT	60106	2972		A5
1100	EMHT	60126	2972		A5
2000	DSPN	60018	2917	12W-8N	B1
N David Dr					
10	PLTN	60074	2753	19W-16N	C7
10	PLTN	60074	2806	19W-16N	C1
David Ln					
300	SmbT	60172	2913		B3
900	EGVV	60007	2914		A2
15400	OKFT	60452	3347	7W-18S	C7
David Pl					
8800	NLES	60016	2863	11W-12N	E2
8800	NLES	60714	2863	11W-12N	E2
8900	MaiT	60016	2863	11W-12N	E1
Davids Ln					
17900	ODPK	60467	3423	13W-21S	B6
Da Vinci St					
13100	LMNT	60439	3343	18W-15S	A2
Davis Av					
4000	RchT	60471	3594	5W-27S	C5
9500	FNPK	60131	2973	11W-4N	C3
S Davis Av					
1200	HMND	46394	3280		E3
Davis Ct					
200	DSPN	60016	2862	14W-11N	C2
2100	RGMW	60008	2805	20W-14N	E4
14200	DXMR	60406	3349	2W-17S	C4
Davis Dr					
10	BKLY	60163	3028		E3
10	BLWD	60104	3028		E3
10	BLWD	60163	3028		E3
Davis St					
200	EVTN	60201	2867	2W-11N	B3
500	PKFT	60466	3594	4W-25S	E1
500	PKFT	60466	3595	4W-25S	A1

STREET Block	City	ZIP	Map#	CGS	Grid
Davis St					
600	MLPK	60160	3029	10W-1N	E2
600	MLPK	60160	3030	10W-1N	A2
1500	MaiT	60016	2863	11W-11N	E3
1500	PKRG	60016	2863	11W-11N	E3
1500	PKRG	60068	2863	11W-11N	E3
1800	EVTN	60201	2866	3W-11N	E3
2200	BLID	60406	3277	2W-14S	C7
2200	DXMR	60406	3349	2W-17S	C4
3300	SKOK	60203	2866	4W-11N	D3
4000	SKOK	60076	2866	5W-11N	B3
4700	SKOK	60076	2865	5W-11N	E3
4700	SKOK	60077	2865	6W-11N	E3
6600	MNGV	60053	2865	8W-11N	A3
6700	MNGV	60053	2864	8W-11N	E3
7800	NLES	60714	2864	9W-11N	B3
E Davis St					
-	ANHT	60004	2807	16W-13N	C6
1900	ANHT	60005	2807	16W-13N	C6
W Davis St					
10	ANHT	60005	2807	16W-13N	C6
8000	MNGV	60053	2864	10W-11N	B3
8000	MNGV	60714	2864	10W-11N	B3
8400	NLES	60714	2864	10W-11N	A3
8500	NLES	60016	2864	10W-11N	A3
8600	MaiT	60016	2863	10W-11N	E3
8600	MaiT	60016	2864	10W-11N	A3
8600	MaiT	60714	2864	10W-11N	A3
8700	PKRG	60016	2863	10W-11N	E3
8700	PKRG	60068	2863	10W-11N	E3
N Davisson St					
2400	RVGV	60171	2974	10W-3N	B5
N Davlin Ct					
3000	CHCG	60618	2976	4W-3N	C4
S Davol St					
11200	CHCG	60643	3277	2W-13S	D3
Dawn Av					
6600	CTSD	60525	3147	13W-7S	A6
Dawn Ct					
500	DSPN	60016	2863	12W-11N	C3
1500	LGGV	60047	2753	18W-20N	D1
Dawn Ln					
10	CTCY	60409	3351	2E-16S	C4
100	CHHT	60411	3507	1W-23S	E4
Dawngate Ct					
4400	RGMW	60008	2806	20W-13N	A5
Dawngate Ln					
4400	RGMW	60008	2805	20W-13N	E5
4400	RGMW	60008	2806	20W-13N	A5
4400	RGMW	60067	2805	20W-13N	E5
Dawnwood Ct					
14300	HMGN	60441	3343	16W-17S	D4
N Dawson Av					
2800	CHCG	60618	2976	4W-3N	D4
N Days Ter					
7100	NLES	60714	2918	8W-8N	E1
Dayton St					
1400	DSPN	60018	2862	15W-10N	A5
N Dayton St					
1400	CHCG	60622	3033	1W-1N	E1
1600	CHCG	60614	2977	1W-2N	E7
2700	CHCG	60657	2977	1W-3N	E5
4300	CHCG	60613	2921	1W-5N	E7
4300	CHCG	60613	2977	1W-5N	E1
4300	CHCG	60640	2921	1W-5N	E7
Dean Av					
1000	WLNG	60090	2755	14W-16N	C7
Dean Dr					
4000	OKLN	60453	3276	5W-12S	C3
E Dean Dr					
100	PLTN	60074	2753	19W-16N	B7
N Dean Dr					
100	PLTN	60074	2753	19W-16N	B7
100	PLTN	60074	2806	20W-15N	A2
N Dean St					
1300	CHCG	60622	3033	2W-1N	C1
Deana Ln					
-	RNPK	60471	3593	6W-27S	E5
-	RNPK	60471	3594	6W-27S	A5
Deane St					
-	DSPN	60016	2862	13W-10N	E5
1200	DSPN	60018	2862	13W-10N	E5
1900	DSPN	60018	2863	13W-9N	A6
De Angelis Ct					
600	CHHT	60411	3507	1W-24S	E6
Deanna Dr					
400	BRLT	60103	2911		A4
Deans Cove					
-	DGvT	60439	3270		C3
S Dearborn Av					
4100	HMND	46327	3352		C3
Dearborn Ct					
18500	TYPK	60477	3505	8W-22S	B1
N Dearborn Pkwy					
1200	CHCG	60610	3034	0W-1N	B1
1500	CHCG	60610	2978		D7
1500	CHCG	60614	2978		D7
Dearborn St					
10	SHLD	60473	3350	0W-17S	D6
14600	DLTN	60419	3350	0W-17S	C5
14600	RVDL	60827	3350	0W-17S	C5
N Dearborn St					
10	CHCG	60602	3034	0W-0N	B4
10	CHCG	60603	3034	0W-0N	B4
100	CHCG	60601	3034	0W-0N	B4
300	CHCG	60610	3034	0W-0N	B3
S Dearborn St					
10	CHCG	60602	3034	0W-0S	B5
10	CHCG	60603	3034	0W-0S	B5
100	CHCG	60604	3034	0W-0S	B5
300	CHCG	60605	3034	0W-0S	B6
1500	CHCG	60616	3034	0W-1S	C7
1900	CHCG	60616	3092	0W-1S	C1
3800	CHCG	60609	3092	0W-4S	C6
5400	CHCG	60609	3152	0W-5S	C2
13800	RVDL	60827	3350	0W-16S	C3
14500	DLTN	60419	3350	0W-16S	C4
Dearlove Rd					
10200	GNVW	60016	2809	11W-13N	C7
10200	GNVW	60025	2809	11W-13N	D7
10200	MaiT	60016	2809	11W-13N	C7
10200	NfdT	60025	2809	11W-13N	C7
E Debbie Dr					
10	MPPT	60056	2808	14W-13N	D7
Debbie Ln					
-	ODHL	60477	3423	11W-19S	E2
-	ODPK	60477	3423	11W-19S	E2
10	SMBG	60107	2857	27W-11N	D4
10	SMBG	60194	2857	27W-11N	D4
10	SMWD	60107	2857	27W-11N	D4
10	SMWD	60194	2857	27W-11N	D4
9400	ODPK	60467	3423	11W-19S	E2
15900	SHLD	60473	3351	1E-18S	A7
15900	SHLD	60473	3429	1E-18S	A1

STREET Block	City	ZIP	Map#	CGS	Grid
Deblin Ln					
5100	OKLN	60453	3275	6W-12S	E3
Deborah Ct					
600	SMBG	60193	2859	23W-9N	B7
23800	CteT	60417	3597	2E-28S	E7
Deborah Dr					
10	LMNT	60439	3270		C7
Deborah Ln					
100	WLNG	60090	2755	14W-18N	C4
500	LYWD	60411	3510	4E-25S	C7
S Deborah Ln					
400	MPPT	60056	2861	17W-12N	C1
Debra Av					
6100	TYPK	60477	3425	7W-20S	C4
Debra Ct					
10	SLVL	60411	3597	1E-27S	A4
3700	RGMW	60008	2806	20W-13N	A5
Debra Dr					
15800	OKFT	60452	3425	6W-19S	E2
16100	BmnT	60477	3425	6W-19S	E2
Debra Ln					
10	WLNG	60090	2755	14W-16N	C6
800	EGVV	60007	2914		A2
2500	GNVW	60025	2810	10W-15N	A2
2500	NHBK	60025	2810	10W-15N	A2
2500	NHBK	60062	2810	10W-15N	A2
2700	HMWD	60430	3427	3W-21S	B6
Debra Rd					
400	DSPN	60016	2862	15W-11N	A3
600	DSPN	60016	2861	16W-11N	E3
Decatur St					
500	HFET	60194	2859	23W-11N	A4
De Cook Av					
2700	PKRG	60068	2863	11W-10N	C4
N De Cook Ct					
2300	PKRG	60068	2863	11W-10N	D4
S De Cook Ct					
2300	PKRG	60068	2863	11W-10N	D5
Dedham Ln					
800	BRLT	60103	2910		C5
1500	SMBG	60193	2858	25W-9N	B7
Dee Ct					
8700	TYPK	60477	3424	10W-20S	B5
Dee Ln					
400	ROSL	60172	2913		B4
Dee Rd					
-	NLES	60016	2863	11W-12N	D1
100	DRPK	60074	2752	21W-18N	E2
100	PltT	60074	2752	21W-18N	E2
8800	MaiT	60016	2863	11W-11N	D4
8800	MaiT	60068	2863	11W-11N	D4
8800	PKRG	60068	2863	11W-11N	D4
9500	NLES	60714	2863	11W-11N	D2
10000	MaiT	60016	2809	11W-12N	D7
10000	NfdT	60016	2809	11W-12N	D7
10000	NfdT	60025	2809	11W-12N	D7
N Dee Rd					
10	PKRG	60068	2917	11W-9N	D1
100	PKRG	60068	2863	11W-9N	D6
9600	MaiT	60016	2863	11W-12N	D1
9600	NLES	60714	2863	11W-12N	D2
S Dee Rd					
-	CHCG	60631	2917	10W-7N	E4
10	PKRG	60068	2917	11W-8N	D1
Deeke Ct					
10	ROSL	60172	2912		C5
Deep Wood Ct					
700	EGVV	60007	2914		B3
Deepwood Ct					
100	BNHL	60010	2749	30W-18N	A4
Deep Wood Ln					
4800	RGMW	60008	2805	21W-13N	E5
4800	RGMW	60067	2805	21W-13N	D5
Deepwood Rd					
10	BNHL	60010	2749	30W-18N	A3
100	BNHL	60010	2748		D2
Deep Woods Ct					
1100	ELGN	60120	2801		C7
Deep Woods Dr					
1100	ELGN	60120	2801		C7
Deer Av					
-	PLTN	60067	2752	22W-17N	A5
-	PltT	60067	2752	22W-17N	A5
-	PltT	60074	2752	22W-17N	A5
N Deer Av					
900	PLTN	60067	2752	22W-17N	A5
1100	PltT	60067	2752	22W-17N	A5
W Deer Ct					
1300	PLTN	60067	2752	22W-17N	A5
Deer Ln					
10	LMNT	60439	3342	19W-15S	C1
100	BRTN	60010	2751	23W-17N	D4
100	PltT	60010	2751	23W-17N	D4
6400	PSHT	60463	3275	8W-15S	B7
Deer Pth					
8000	JSTC	60458	3209	11W-9S	E3
Deer Run					
100	PltT	60010	2752	22W-18N	A2
Deer Tr					
4500	NHBK	60062	2755	13W-18N	E2
4500	NHBK	60062	2756	13W-18N	A2
17200	ODPK	60467	3423	13W-20S	B5
Deer Chase Av					
10400	ODPK	60467	3423	13W-20S	B4
10400	OrlT	60467	3423	13W-20S	B4
Deer Chase Ct					
20000	DRPK	60010	2751	23W-20N	D2
20000	PltT	60010	2751	23W-20N	D2
Deer Creek Dr					
17100	ODPK	60467	3423	13W-20S	A4
Deer Creek Ln					
1400	BlmT	60411	3509	1E-25S	B7
1400	FDHT	60411	3509	1E-25S	B7
1400	FDHT	60411	3597	1E-25S	B1
1400	SLVL	60411	3509	1E-25S	B7
1400	SLVL	60411	3597	1E-25S	B1
Deercreek Pkwy					
700	HDPK	60035	2757	8W-20N	D1
Deer Creek Rd					
1000	CPVL	60110	2748		A6
1000	DndT	60110	2748		A6
Deercrest Ln					
10	IHPK	60525	3146		D4
10	IHPK	60525	3147	12W-7S	B6
1900	NfdT	60062	2756	11W-16N	C7
Deercrest Sq					
10	IHPK	60525	3147	12W-7S	B6
Deere Park Cir					
500	BRLT	60103	2910		E1
Deere Park Ct					
100	HDPK	60035	2758	6W-20N	C2
N Deere Park Dr E					
200	HDPK	60035	2758	6W-20N	C1
N Deere Park Dr W					
200	HDPK	60035	2758	6W-20N	C1

STREET Block	City	ZIP	Map#	CGS	Grid
S Deere Park Dr					
10	HDPK	60035	2758	6W-20N	D2
100	GLNC	60022	2758	6W-20N	D2
100	HDPK	60022	2758	6W-20N	D2
Deerfield Ct					
500	SMBG	60194	2857	26W-11N	E4
1800	HRPK	60133	2911		D5
15700	ODPK	60462	3424	10W-18S	C1
S Deerfield Ct					
20100	FftT	60423	3504	9W-24S	E5
Deerfield Dr					
500	SMWD	60107	2856	29W-10N	D5
Deerfield Ln					
2600	RGMW	60008	2805	21W-13N	D5
Deer Grove					
16700	PltT	60010	2751	23W-17N	E4
16700	PltT	60010	2752	22W-18N	A3
16700	PltT	60067	2751	23W-17N	E4
16700	PltT	60074	2752	22W-18N	A3
Deer Grove Ln					
100	PltT	60010	2752	22W-18N	A3
W Deer Haven Ct					
10	CRTE	60417	3596	0W-28S	D7
Deer Hill Ct					
600	CPVL	60110	2748		A7
Deerlake Rd					
10	DRFD	60015	2756	10W-20N	E2
10	DRFD	60062	2756	10W-20N	E2
N Deer Park Blvd					
-	DRPK	60074	2752	21W-20N	D1
-	KLDR	60047	2752	21W-20N	D1
-	KLDR	60074	2752	21W-20N	D1
20300	PltT	60074	2752	21W-20N	D2
S Deer Park Dr					
12500	ALSP	60803	3276	4W-14S	D6
W Deer Park Dr					
3600	ALSP	60803	3276	4W-14S	D6
Deerpath Ct					
200	SMBG	60193	2859	21W-10N	E6
500	DRFD	60015	2756	11W-20N	D1
800	HFET	60194	2858	24W-11N	C3
1000	WLNG	60090	2754	16W-18N	D3
1200	BRLT	60103	2910		E7
Deer Path Dr					
16700	HMGN	60441	3422	15W-20S	C4
Deerpath Dr					
13500	ODPK	60462	3346	10W-16S	C2
Deer-Path Ln					
3200	SCHT	60411	3595	1W-27S	E4
Deerpath Ln					
-	DSPN	60018	2917	12W-8N	B2
10	LGPK	60525	3087	12W-2S	B3
10	PSPK	60464	3274	10W-14S	B6
200	CPVL	60110	2748		B5
200	DndT	60110	2748		B5
500	DGvT	60439	3270		C2
800	HFET	60194	2858	24W-11N	C3
6600	HRPK	60133	2911		E3
8000	TYPK	60477	3504	10W-23S	C3
S Deerpath Ln					
11100	PSHL	60465	3274	11W-13S	A3
Deerpath Rd					
10	MTSN	60443	3505	7W-24S	D5
10	PltT	60010	2752	22W-20N	A2
600	EDND	60118	2801		B2
5100	OKFT	60452	3425	6W-20S	E4
5100	OKFT	60452	3426	6W-20S	A4
20500	DRPK	60010	2752	22W-20N	A1
21100	FKFT	60423	3504	9W-25S	E7
S Deerpath Rd					
100	DRPK	60010	2752	22W-18N	A2
100	PltT	60010	2752	22W-18N	A2
Deer Path Tr					
10	BRRG	60527	3208		B3
10	LynT	60527	3208		C4
Deer Point Dr					
10800	ODPK	60467	3423	13W-20S	A5
E Deer Run Ct					
1200	CteT	60417	3687	3E-29S	B1
Deer Run Dr					
10700	ODPK	60467	3423	13W-20S	B4
N Deer Run Dr					
500	PLTN	60067	2752	21W-16N	C6
Deer Run Ln					
-	HnrT	60120	2855		E4
S Deer Run Tr					
24300	CteT	60417	3687	3E-29S	B1
Deer Trail Ct					
4500	NHBK	60062	2755	13W-20N	E2
Deer Trail Dr					
10	DYR	46311	3598		C4
Deertrail Ln					
-	DYR	46311	3598		D4
Deer Trail Rd					
400	CHHT	60411	3507	2W-24S	D5
Deer Valley Dr					
100	DRPK	60010	2752	22W-20N	B2
100	PltT	60074	2752	22W-20N	B2
W Deervalley Dr					
13600	HMGN	60441	3343	17W-17S	D6
Deer Valley Ln					
-	HFET	60192	2856	30W-12N	B1
Deerview Dr					
17200	ODPK	60467	3423	13W-20S	B5
Deerview Ln					
7900	BRRG	60527	3208		C2
Deerwood Ct					
9000	PSHL	60465	3209	11W-11S	E7
S Deerwood Dr					
12700	PlsT	60464	3274	9W-15S	D7
12700	PSPK	60464	3274	9W-15S	D7
W Deerwood Dr					
7800	PlsT	60464	3274	9W-15S	C7
Deforest Av					
1300	FDHT	60411	3509	1E-25S	B7
Degener Av					
1200	PvsT	60126	3028		C7
1200	PvsT	60126	3086		C1
Dehne Rd					
2000	NHBK	60062	2757	10W-16N	A7
De Jong Ln					
18200	LNSG	60438	3429	2E-21S	D7
Dekker St					
17800	LNSG	60438	3429	2E-21S	E6
W De Koven St					
500	CHCG	60607	3034	0W-0S	A6
Deland Ct					
8000	TYPK	60477	3424	10W-19S	C1
Delaney Dr					
6000	HFET	60120	2855		E1
6000	HnrT	60120	2855		E1
N Delaplaine Rd					
10	RVSD	60546	3088	9W-3S	D4
S Delaplaine Rd					
10	RVSD	60546	3088	9W-3S	D5

STREET Block	City	ZIP	Map#	CGS	Grid
Delaware Ct					
10	SMBG	60193	2857	27W-10N	D6
300	CPVL	60110	2748		D5
18000	ODPK	60467	3423	13W-21S	A7
S Delaware Dr					
2200	MPPT	60056	2861	16W-10N	E6
Delaware Ln					
600	EGVV	60007	2913		C1
E Delaware Pl					
10	CHCG	60610	3034	0E-1N	C2
10	CHCG	60611	3034	0E-1N	C2
W Delaware Pl					
10	CHCG	60611	3034	0W-1N	B2
500	CHCG	60610	3034	0W-1N	A2
Delaware St					
300	CPVL	60110	2748		D4
Delaware Tr					
1700	WLNG	60090	2754	16W-17N	C5
E Delgado Dr					
500	PLTN	60074	2753	20W-17N	A5
Delicious Ct					
-	PTHT	60070	2808	13W-15N	E1
E Delite Inn Rd					
100	WshT	60401	3864	0E-39S	E7
W Delite Inn Rd					
100	WshT	60401	3864	0W-39S	D7
Dell Av					
-	CHCG	60613	2977	1W-5N	D1
-	ELGN	60120	2855		D6
Dell Ct					
9000	HYHL	60457	3209	11W-9S	E4
Dell Ln					
400	HDPK	60035	2758	7W-20N	C1
Dell Pl					
10	GLNC	60022	2758	5W-17N	E5
3000	GNVW	60025	2810	10W-13N	A6
Dell Rd					
800	NHBK	60062	2757	8W-17N	E4
1000	NHBK	60062	2758	8W-17N	A5
Della Dr					
1400	HFET	60195	2858	25W-12N	B1
Del Lago Dr					
400	SMBG	60173	2859	22W-11N	D4
E Dells Wy					
10	HRVY	60426	3349	1W-17S	E6
100	HRVY	60426	3350	1W-17S	A6
W Dells Wy					
10	HRVY	60426	3349	2W-17S	C6
Del Mar Ct					
700	UYPK	60466	3684	4W-29S	A2
Delmar Ct					
500	EGVV	60007	2913		C1
N Del Mar Dr					
1100	PLTN	60067	2752	20W-17N	E5
Delmonte Dr					
5500	HRPK	60133	2912		A6
Del Ogier Dr					
1600	GNVW	60025	2811	7W-14N	B5
Delphi Ct					
10	TYPK	60477	3505	8W-23S	B4
Delphi Dr					
-	OMFD	60461	3507	3W-24S	A5
Delphia Av					
700	EGVV	60007	2914		D1
700	EGVV	60007	2915		A1
9000	MaiT	60016	2864	10W-11N	A3
9000	NLES	60714	2864	10W-11N	A3
9300	NLES	60016	2864	10W-11N	A3
N Delphia Av					
10	PKRG	60068	2864	10W-9N	A7
10	PKRG	60068	2918	8W-8N	D1
1100	NLES	60714	2864	10W-10N	A5
4700	NRDG	60656	2918	10W-5N	A7
4700	NRDG	60706	2918	10W-5N	A7
5200	CHCG	60656	2918	10W-6N	A5
5500	CHCG	60631	2918	10W-6N	A5
S Delphia Av					
10	PKRG	60068	2918	10W-8N	A3
Delphia Ct					
700	EGVV	60007	2915		A1
Del Prado Dr					
9000	PlsT	60465	3209	11W-11S	E6
9000	PlsT	60480	3209	11W-11S	E6
9000	PSHL	60465	3209	11W-11S	E6
Delrio Rd					
100	CPVL	60110	2748		B4
Delta Ln					
2300	EGVV	60007	2915		E3
Delta Pkwy					
10500	SRPK	60176	2973	13W-5N	A1
Delta Rd					
200	HDPK	60035	2758	7W-20N	C1
18700	HMWD	60430	3508	1W-22S	A2
W Deming Pl					
500	CHCG	60614	2978	0W-3N	A5
4400	CHCG	60639	2976	5W-3N	A5
4800	CHCG	60639	2975	6W-3N	D5
Dempster Av					
700	EGvT	60005	2861	16W-10N	D4
700	EGvT	60056	2861	16W-10N	D4
1500	MPPT	60056	2861	16W-10N	D4
Dempster Ct					
-	PKRG	60068	2863	11W-11N	E4
Dempster St					
100	EVTN	60201	2867	-	C3
100	EVTN	60202	2867	-	C3
300	DSPN	60016	2861	16W-10N	E4
300	DSPN	60056	2861	16W-10N	E4
300	MPPT	60056	2861	16W-10N	E4
500	EGvT	60056	2861	16W-10N	E4
1200	NLES	60714	2863	11W-10N	D4
1200	PKRG	60068	2863	11W-10N	D4
1200	PKRG	60068	2864	10W-10N	A4
1200	PKRG	60714	2863	11W-10N	D4
1800	EVTN	60201	2866	3W-11N	E3
1800	EVTN	60202	2866	3W-11N	E3
2000	MaiT	60016	2863	11W-11N	D4
2600	DSPN	60016	2863	11W-10N	D4
2600	MaiT	60068	2863	11W-10N	D4
2600	PKRG	60016	2863	11W-10N	D4
3300	SKOK	60076	2866	3W-11N	E3
3300	SKOK	60203	2866	3W-11N	E3
4700	SKOK	60076	2865	5W-11N	E4
4700	SKOK	60077	2865	5W-11N	E4
5600	MNGV	60053	2865	6W-11N	E3
6700	MNGV	60053	2864	8W-11N	E3
7000	NLES	60714	2864	8W-11N	E4
Dempster St SR-58					
4800	SKOK	60076	2865	5W-11N	E4
4800	SKOK	60077	2865	6W-11N	E4
5600	MNGV	60053	2865	6W-11N	E3
6700	MNGV	60053	2864	8W-11N	E3
Dempster St US-14					
1200	NLES	60714	2863	11W-10N	D4
1200	PKRG	60068	2863	11W-10N	D4

Chicago & Cook County Street Index

STREET Block	City	ZIP	Map#	CGS	Grid
Dobson St					
3800	SKOK	60076	2866	5W-9N	B6
4600	SKOK	60076	2865	5W-9N	E6
4800	SKOK	60077	2865	6W-9N	D6
W Dobson St					
6800	NLES	60714	2864	8W-9N	D6
Dodd Av					
100	NHLK	60164	3028		D1
Dodge Av					
100	CHCG	60645	2866	3W-9N	E6
100	EVTN	60202	2866	3W-9N	E6
1200	EVTN	60201	2866	3W-10N	E5
9700	FNPK	60131	2973	12W-4N	C3
Doe Ln					
17200	ODPK	60467	3423	13W-20S	A5
N Doe Rd					
1100	PLTN	60067	2751	23W-17N	E5
1300	PLTN	60010	2751	23W-17N	E5
1300	PltT	60010	2751	23W-17N	E5
Doe Tr					
16700	LKPT	60441	3342	20W-17S	A6
Dogleg Ln					
600	BRLT	60103	2910		A1
Dogwood Ct					
10	CTCY	60409	3429	2E-18S	D1
10	SMWD	60107	2857	26W-11N	E4
400	DRPK	60010	2752	22W-20N	B2
500	SMBG	60193	2858	24W-9N	E7
1200	ELGN	60120	2855		D4
1700	HFET	60195	2804	25W-14N	B4
8600	TYPK	60477	3424	10W-22S	B7
Dogwood Dr					
400	DYR	46311	3598		D3
1700	HFET	60195	2804	25W-14N	A3
8800	ODPK	60462	3346	11W-17S	A6
15300	HMGN	60441	3344	15W-18S	C7
21600	MTSN	60443	3594	4W-26S	E2
Dogwood Ln					
1200	BRLT	60103	2910		D7
17700	HLCT	60429	3427	3W-21S	A6
E Dogwood Ln					
1300	MPPT	60056	2808	14W-14N	C4
N Dogwood Ln					
2100	PLTN	60074	2753	19W-18N	C3
S Dogwood Ln					
12200	PSHT	60463	3275	7W-14S	C5
12200	WthT	60463	3275	7W-14S	C5
Dogwood Rd					
10	RGMW	60008	2806	20W-13N	A6
Dogwood St					
10	PKFT	60466	3595	2W-27S	C4
Dogwood Ter					
300	BFGV	60089	2754	16W-20N	D1
300	VrnT	60069	2754	16W-20N	D1
300	VrnT	60089	2754	16W-20N	D1
Dogwood Tr					
500	EGVV	60007	2915		A3
Dolfor Cove					
8300	BRRG	60527	3208		B3
Dolores Dr					
100	BNVL	60106	2972		A4
6200	OKFT	60452	3347	7W-18S	B7
Dolorosa Dr					
17500	ODPK	60467	3423	13W-21S	B6
Dolphin Av					
20100	LYWD	60411	3510	3E-23S	A4
Dolphin Lake Dr					
18100	HMWD	60430	3427	3W-21S	B7
Dolton Av					
-	CTCY	60409	3351	1E-16S	C4
-	CTCY	60419	3351	1E-16S	C4
1300	DLTN	60419	3351	1E-16S	B3
Dolton Rd					
-	CTCY	60419	3351	2E-16S	C4
-	DLTN	60419	3351	2E-16S	C4
1600	CTCY	60409	3351	2E-16S	C4
Domenic Ct					
400	BNVL	60131	2972		C2
N Dominick St					
2000	CHCG	60614	2977	1W-2N	D6
N Donald Av					
10	ANHT	60004	2807	16W-14N	D5
S Donald Av					
10	ANHT	60004	2807	16W-13N	D5
Donald Ct					
2500	MaiT	60025	2864	9W-12N	C1
Donald Ter					
200	MaiT	60025	2864	9W-12N	C1
Donatus Dr					
18000	LNSG	60438	3429	1E-21S	C6
Doncaster Cir					
22600	DRPK	60010	2752	22W-20N	A1
Donegal Ln					
10	RGMW	60008	2806	20W-15N	A3
1000	NHBK	60062	2756	11W-17N	D5
E Donegal Bay					
1200	PLTN	60074	2753	18W-18N	D3
Donlea Rd					
200	BNHL	60010	2749	29W-18N	B4
200	BNHL	60010	2750	28W-18N	A2
Donna Ct					
300	BRLT	60103	2911		A3
600	SMBG	60193	2859	23W-9N	B7
700	WLNG	60090	2755	14W-17N	D6
Donna Ln					
10800	ODPK	60467	3423	13W-21S	A6
Donna Marie Dr					
16000	HMGN	60441	3422	15W-19S	B2
Donnington Dr					
900	MTSN	60443	3505	7W-25S	C7
Donoho Av					
800	BCHR	60401	3864	0E-36S	D1
Donohoe Rd					
15700	LMNT	60439	3270		C5
E Donovan Ct					
10	CRTE	60417	3597	1E-28S	B6
W Donovan Ct					
10	CRTE	60417	3597	1E-28S	B6
Donovan Dr					
1300	CHHT	60411	3507	2W-25S	D7
1400	CHHT	60411	3595	2W-25S	D1
3400	CRTE	60417	3597	1E-28S	B6
3400	STGR	60417	3597	1E-28S	B5
3400	STGR	60475	3597	1E-28S	B5
Donovan Glen Ct					
3100	NfdT	60062	2809	11W-16N	D1
3100	NHBK	60062	2809	11W-16N	D1
Don Powers Al					
-	MNSR	46321	3430		E6
Doogan Av					
11000	WLSP	60480	3208		E4
Doolin St					
10	LMNT	60439	3270		C7
Doolittle Dr					
3100	NHBK	60062	2756	11W-18N	D3
S Doolittle Dr					
24900	MonT	60449	3682	8W-30S	B4
25300	GGnT	60449	3682	8W-30S	A4
S Doonaree Cir					
13500	HMGN	60441	3343	17W-16S	C3
Dooneen Av					
7900	TYPK	60477	3424	9W-20S	C5
Dora St					
2300	FNPK	60164	2973	12W-2N	B6
2300	LydT	60164	2973	12W-2N	B6
3400	FNPK	60131	2973	12W-4N	B3
3700	SRPK	60131	2973	12W-4N	B3
N Dora St					
-	MLPK	60160	2973	12W-2N	B7
2100	LydT	60164	2973	12W-2N	B6
Doral Ct					
10	BRBK	60459	3211	7W-8S	C1
100	DRFD	60015	2757	10W-20N	A2
200	EGVV	60007	2859	22W-9N	D7
1800	PSHT	60463	3347	8W-15S	B2
W Doral Ct					
200	PLTN	60067	2752	21W-17N	D4
Doral Dr					
900	BRLT	60103	2910		C2
S Doral Dr					
25700	MONE	60449	3683	6W-31S	A5
Doral Ln					
8900	ODPK	60462	3346	11W-16S	A2
13800	HMGN	60441	3343	17W-17S	C5
Doral Ter					
400	UYPK	60417	3684	2W-30S	C2
400	UYPK	60466	3684	2W-30S	C2
Dorchester Av					
10400	WSTR	60154	3087	13W-1S	A2
10700	WSTR	60154	3086		D2
14200	DLTN	60419	3351	1E-17S	B5
18000	LNSG	60438	3429	1E-21S	B6
18000	ThtT	60438	3429	1E-21S	B6
S Dorchester Av					
200	GNWD	60425	3509	1E-23S	B3
4700	CHCG	60615	3153	1E-5S	A2
6700	CHCG	60637	3153	1E-8S	A7
7000	CHCG	60619	3153	1E-8S	A7
8700	CHCG	60619	3215	1E-10S	A4
9500	CHCG	60628	3215	1E-11S	A6
Dorchester Ct					
10	SMWD	60107	2856	29W-9N	D7
2200	SMBG	60194	2857	27W-11N	C3
2200	SMBG	60194	2858	26W-11N	A4
Dorchester Ln					
300	EGVV	60007	2914		C3
1000	BRLT	60103	2910		C7
1200	HFET	60194	2858	25W-11N	C3
W Dorchester Rd					
800	PLTN	60067	2805	22W-15N	C2
800	PltT	60067	2805	22W-15N	C2
Dorchester St					
400	ROSL	60172	2912		C6
Doreen Dr					
1200	DSPN	60016	2862	15W-10N	B5
1200	DSPN	60018	2862	15W-10N	B5
Dori Ln					
13900	BmnT	60445	3348	6W-16S	A3
13900	CTWD	60445	3348	6W-16S	A3
Doria Ln					
3500	OMFD	60461	3506	4W-24S	E6
Doriann Dr					
3000	NHBK	60062	2809	11W-15N	D1
E Doric Cir					
10700	PSHL	60465	3274	10W-12S	C2
W Doric Cir					
10700	PSHL	60465	3274	10W-12S	C2
Dorie Ln					
100	TNTN	60476	3428	0E-20S	D5
Dorina Dr					
2300	NHFD	60093	2810	8W-15N	E3
2300	NHFD	60093	2811	8W-15N	A3
Doris Ct					
10400	RSMT	60018	2917	13W-8N	A1
Doris Dr					
500	MLPK	60160	3030	10W-1N	A2
Doris Ln					
100	CHHT	60411	3507	1W-23S	E4
Dorman Dr					
800	SMWD	60107	2857	28W-10N	A7
Dorncliff Ln					
800	BFGV	60089	2754	17W-20N	B1
Dornell Dr					
3200	SCHT	60411	3596	1W-27S	A4
3300	STGR	60475	3596	1W-27S	A4
N Dorothy Av					
-	ANHT	60004	2807	17W-15N	B2
Dorothy Dr					
400	DSPN	60016	2862	15W-10N	A5
E Dorothy Dr					
1200	PLTN	60074	2806	19W-16N	C1
S Dorothy Dr					
24300	CteT	60417	3686	2E-29S	D1
Dorothy Ln					
7300	TYPK	60477	3424	9W-20S	E3
W Dorothy Ln					
-	ElaT	60047	2753	19W-20N	B1
-	LGGV	60047	2753	19W-20N	B1
Dorothy Rd					
-	ANHT	60004	2807	17W-15N	B1
3200	GNVW	60025	2810	10W-15N	A3
W Dorset Av					
400	PltT	60067	2805	21W-15N	D2
800	PLTN	60067	2805	22W-15N	C2
Dorset Cir					
700	WLNG	60090	2755	15W-18N	A3
Dorset Ct					
600	WLNG	60090	2755	15W-18N	A3
Dorset Dr					
900	NHBK	60062	2756	12W-17N	B4
Dorset Ln					
100	SMBG	60193	2859	23W-9N	A6
Dorset St					
400	PTHT	60070	2807	16W-15N	D2
Dorsetshire Dr					
100	CRTE	60475	3596	0W-28S	C7
100	STGR	60475	3596	0W-28S	C6
200	CRTE	60417	3596	0W-28S	C7
Dorshire Ct					
100	SMBG	60193	2857	27W-10N	D6
Dorstep Ln					
8000	ODPK	60462	3346	10W-17S	C4
Dory Ln					
8600	LynT	60480	3208		D4
8600	WLSP	60480	3208		E4
S Doty Av					
-	CHCG	60617	3215	2E-11S	B7
-	CHCG	60633	3351	2E-15S	C2
10300	CHCG	60617	3279	1E-13S	A3
10400	CHCG	60628	3278	1E-13S	E3
S Doty Av					
10400	CHCG	60628	3279	1E-12S	A2
12000	CHCG	60827	3279	1E-14S	A6
12100	CHCG	60633	3278	0E-13S	E5
12100	CHCG	60633	3279	1E-14S	B7
13000	CHCG	60827	3351	2E-15S	C2
E Doty St					
10	CTCY	60409	3352		C7
10	HMND	46320	3352		D7
Douglas Av					
300	CTCY	60409	3352	4E-17S	C6
1300	FSMR	60422	3507	3W-23S	B3
2000	DSPN	60018	2862	14W-9N	D7
2200	DSPN	60018	2916		D1
N Douglas Av					
10	ANHT	60004	2807	17W-14N	B4
10	ANHT	60005	2807	17W-13N	B5
2200	ANHT	60004	2754	17W-16N	B7
S Douglas Av					
300	CHCG	60637	3153	1E-7S	A5
400	ANHT	60005	2861	17W-12N	B1
400	ANHT	60056	2861	17W-12N	B1
400	MPPT	60056	2861	17W-12N	B1
1000	ANHT	60005	2807	17W-12N	B7
1200	MPPT	60005	2861	17W-12N	B1
W Douglas Av					
7200	CHCG	60638	3148	9W-5S	D3
7200	SMMT	60501	3148	9W-5S	D3
7200	SMMT	60638	3148	9W-5S	D3
W Douglas Blvd					
3000	CHCG	60623	3032	4W-1S	D7
Douglas Ct					
10	BlmT	60411	3510	3E-25S	A7
10	HFET	60194	2859	23W-11N	A4
N Douglas Ct					
1600	ANHT	60004	2807	17W-15N	B1
W Douglas Ct					
7700	FftT	60423	3504	9W-24S	D5
Douglas Ln					
1000	CRTE	60417	3596	0W-29S	C7
1400	CRTE	60417	3685	0W-30S	C2
W Douglas Pkwy					
15200	LKPT	60441	3342	20W-18S	A7
Douglas Rd					
1000	HnrT	60107	2856	30W-10N	C7
1000	HnrT	60120	2856	30W-10N	C7
Douglas St					
300	PKFT	60466	3595	3W-25S	A1
400	PKFT	60466	3507	3W-25S	A7
E Douglas St					
10	HMND	46320	3352		D6
Dougshire Ct					
10	BRRG	60527	3146		C4
Dove Av					
1500	MLPK	60160	3029	13W-1N	A2
Dove Ct					
10	SBTN	60010	2803	26W-15N	E3
3100	RGMW	60008	2806	19W-13N	D5
S Dove Ct					
1300	MPPT	60056	2861	16W-11N	D3
W Dove Ln					
7300	FftT	60423	3504	9W-24S	E6
Dove St					
2300	RGMW	60008	2806	19W-13N	D5
Dover Av					
10	LGNG	60525	3087	13W-4S	A6
200	LGPK	60525	3087	13W-3S	A6
N Dover Av					
100	LGPK	60525	3087	13W-4S	A7
Dover Cir					
200	IVNS	60067	2804	23W-15N	E2
800	CPVL	60110	2748		D5
Dover Ct					
10	SMWD	60107	2856	29W-11N	D4
500	ROSL	60172	2912		C6
600	ELGN	60120	2855		D6
1600	HFET	60195	2804	24W-15N	B1
1800	SMBG	60193	2858	25W-9N	A7
11000	ODPK	60467	3345	13W-18S	A7
11000	OrlT	60467	3345	13W-18S	A7
11100	ODPK	60467	3344	13W-18S	E7
11100	OrlT	60467	3344	13W-18S	E7
17600	TYPK	60477	3424	10W-21S	B6
20300	DRPK	60010	2752	22W-20N	B1
N Dover Ct					
1800	ANHT	60004	2807	16W-15N	C1
Dover Dr					
10	DSPN	60018	2862	15W-10N	A6
10	OKBK	60523	3086		B3
400	ROSL	60172	2912		C6
600	ELGN	60120	2855		D6
Dover Ln					
10	GLF	60029	2864	8W-12N	E1
200	DSPN	60018	2862	15W-10N	B6
1200	EGVV	60007	2914		C3
N Dover Ln					
1700	ANHT	60004	2807	16W-15N	C1
Dover Pl					
700	WLNG	60090	2755	15W-18N	A3
W Dover Pl					
100	MPPT	60056	2808	15W-14N	A3
Dover Rd					
5600	OKFT	60452	3347	7W-18S	D7
Dover St					
-	BDVW	60155	3087	12W-1S	B2
-	WSTR	60154	3087	12W-1S	B2
7000	BGVW	60455	3210	8W-10S	E5
N Dover St					
4400	CHCG	60613	2921	1W-5N	D7
4400	CHCG	60640	2921	1W-5N	D7
Dove Valley Ln					
1600	BCHR	60401	3774	0W-35S	D6
N Dovington Ct					
800	HFET	60194	2858	25W-11N	C3
N Dovington Dr					
800	HFET	60194	2858	25W-11N	C3
W Dovington Dr					
1000	HFET	60194	2858	25W-11N	C3
N Dowagiac Av					
6600	CHCG	60646	2919	6W-8N	D2
6600	CHCG	60712	2919	6W-8N	D2
6600	LNWD	60646	2919	6W-8N	D2
6800	SKOK	60646	2919	6W-8N	D2
Downers Dr					
400	DGvT	60439	3270		B1
Downey Ct					
1800	HRPK	60133	2911		D5
Downey Rd					
2000	HMWD	60430	3507	2W-22S	C1
Downey St					
600	HFET	60194	2858	25W-11N	B4
600	SMBG	60194	2858	25W-11N	B4
Downing Av					
1600	WSTR	60154	3087	13W-1S	A2
3000	LGPK	60525	3087	13W-2S	A4
Downing Dr					
800	HFET	60195	2858	24W-12N	D2
800	SMBG	60195	2858	24W-12N	D2
1100	HFET	60195	2804	24W-15N	C1
Downing Rd					
10	ANHT	60004	2754	16W-17N	C5
10	BFGV	60089	2754	16W-17N	C5
200	RVSD	60546	3088	9W-2S	D4
Downing St					
800	NHBK	60062	2756	12W-17N	B4
1200	ROSL	60172	2912		C6
Downs Dr					
1600	BNHM	60633	3351	2E-16S	D4
1600	CTCY	60409	3351	2E-16S	D4
Doyle Ct					
10800	ODPK	60467	3345	13W-16S	A4
10800	OrlT	60467	3345	13W-16S	A4
Doyle Dr					
-	NHLK	60164	3028		D1
S Drackert St					
800	HMND	46320	3352		E7
Dracut Ln					
800	SMBG	60173	2859	22W-11N	C3
Drae Ct					
600	WLNG	60090	2754	16W-18N	E2
Dragonfly Dr					
100	BRRG	60527	3146		C4
Drake Av					
8300	SKOK	60076	2866	4W-10N	C5
9200	SKOK	60203	2866	4W-11N	C2
9400	EVTN	60201	2866	4W-11N	C2
N Drake Av					
500	CHCG	60624	3032	4W-0N	D3
1600	CHCG	60647	3032	5W-1N	A1
1600	CHCG	60651	3032	5W-1N	A1
2400	CHCG	60647	2976	4W-3N	C5
3600	CHCG	60618	2976	4W-4N	C2
4300	CHCG	60625	2976	4W-5N	C1
4400	CHCG	60625	2920	4W-5N	C7
5600	CHCG	60659	2920	4W-7N	C4
6400	CHCG	60712	2920	4W-8N	C3
6400	LNWD	60712	2920	4W-8N	C2
S Drake Av					
1400	CHCG	60623	3032	4W-1S	D7
1600	CHCG	60623	3090	4W-1S	D1
4300	CHCG	60632	3090	4W-4S	D7
4600	CHCG	60632	3150	4W-5S	D1
8500	CHCG	60652	3212	4W-9S	D3
10300	CHCG	60655	3276	4W-12S	D1
10300	ENGN	60655	3276	4W-11S	D1
10300	ENGN	60805	3276	4W-11S	D1
Drake Cir					
400	SMBG	60193	2913		B1
Drake Ln					
100	DSPN	60016	2862	14W-12N	C1
5200	MTSN	60443	3506	6W-25S	A7
5300	MTSN	60443	3505	6W-25S	E7
Drake Rd					
900	GNVW	60025	2810	8W-13N	E6
900	GNVW	60025	2811	8W-13N	A6
Drake Ter					
10	PTHT	60070	2755	15W-16N	A7
1100	WLNG	60070	2755	15W-16N	A7
1100	WLNG	60090	2755	15W-16N	A7
Dralle Rd					
2000	MonT	60449	3683	5W-30S	D3
2000	MonT	60466	3683	5W-30S	D3
2000	UYPK	60449	3683	5W-30S	D3
2000	UYPK	60466	3683	5W-30S	D3
W Dralle Rd					
-	UYPK	60466	3683	5W-30S	C3
4800	MonT	60449	3683	6W-29S	B2
4800	MonT	60466	3683	6W-29S	B2
4800	UYPK	60466	3683	6W-29S	B2
6100	MonT	60449	3682	7W-29S	C2
6100	MonT	60466	3682	7W-29S	C2
6100	UYPK	60449	3682	7W-29S	C2
6100	UYPK	60466	3682	7W-29S	C2
6700	GGnT	60423	3682	9W-29S	A2
6700	GGnT	60449	3682	9W-29S	A2
6700	MonT	60423	3682	9W-29S	A2
W Draper St					
1200	CHCG	60614	2977	1W-3N	D5
Drawbridge Ln					
1200	LMNT	60439	3271		B7
S Dreckslеr Rd					
30900	PtnT	60468	3861	9W-39S	A7
30900	PTON	60468	3861	9W-39S	A7
30900	WilT	60468	3861	9W-39S	A7
W Dresden Av					
200	PLTN	60067	2752	21W-18N	D3
Dresden Ct					
1100	HFET	60195	2804	24W-15N	C2
Dresden Dr					
1000	HFET	60195	2804	24W-15N	C2
W Dresser Dr					
700	MPPT	60056	2807	16W-12N	D7
Drew Av					
100	DGvT	60527	3208		B2
7500	BRRG	60527	3208		C2
N Drew Ct					
-	PLTN	60067	2805	22W-15N	B1
-	PltT	60067	2805	22W-15N	B1
W Drew Ln					
-	PLTN	60067	2805	22W-15N	B1
800	PltT	60067	2805	22W-15N	B1
S Drew St					
10500	CHCG	60643	3277	2W-12S	D1
Drexel Av					
400	GLNC	60022	2758	6W-16N	D7
1000	FDHT	60411	3509	1E-25S	A7
1500	FDHT	60411	3597	1E-25S	A1
14200	DLTN	60419	3351	1E-16S	A4
15400	DLTN	60473	3351	1E-18S	A7
15400	SHLD	60473	3351	1E-18S	A7
15900	SHLD	60473	3429	1E-18S	A1
N Drexel Av					
10	LGNG	60525	3087	13W-4S	A7
100	LGPK	60525	3087	13W-4S	A7
S Drexel Av					
-	CHCG	60615	3152	1E-5S	E2
300	GNWD	60425	3509	1E-23S	A3
7100	CHCG	60619	3152	1E-8S	E7
7100	CHCG	60637	3152	1E-8S	E7
9000	CHCG	60619	3214	1E-10S	E5
9700	CHCG	60628	3214	1E-11S	E6
S Drexel Blvd					
3900	CHCG	60653	3092	1E-4S	E6
4600	CHCG	60615	3092	1E-4S	E7
4700	CHCG	60615	3152	1E-5S	E1
Drexel Ln					
200	GLNC	60022	2758	6W-16N	D7
E Drexel Sq					
800	CHCG	60615	3152	0E-5S	D2
Driftwood Av					
20100	LYWD	60411	3510	3E-23S	B4
N Driftwood Av					
1400	PLTN	60067	2752	21W-17N	D4
Driftwood Ct					
10	SMWD	60107	2857	26W-11N	E4
700	MonT	60466	3684	4W-29S	A2
700	UYPK	60466	3684	4W-29S	A2
1000	WLNG	60090	2754	16W-18N	D3
1100	EGVV	60007	2914		C2
1100	FSMR	60422	3507	3W-23S	A2
1800	HFET	60195	2804	25W-15N	A1
S Driftwood Dr					
20400	FftT	60423	3504	9W-24S	D6
Driftwood Ln					
200	SMBG	60193	2859	21W-10N	E6
300	WLMT	60091	2813	2W-13N	A7
600	NHBK	60062	2757	8W-16N	E7
600	NHBK	60062	2758	8W-17N	A6
1100	BRLT	60103	2910		D7
Dr Korczak Ter					
9100	SKOK	60076	2866	4W-11N	C3
9100	SKOK	60203	2866	4W-11N	C3
S Dr Martin L King Jr Dr					
2200	CHCG	60616	3092	0E-2S	D3
3500	CHCG	60653	3092	0E-4S	D7
4600	CHCG	60615	3092	0E-4S	D7
4700	CHCG	60615	3152	0E-5S	D1
5400	CHCG	60637	3152	0E-5S	D2
7000	CHCG	60619	3152	0E-7S	D6
7500	CHCG	60619	3214	0E-11S	D6
9400	CHCG	60628	3214	0E-11S	D6
10300	CHCG	60628	3278	0E-12S	D2
13000	CHCG	60827	3278	0E-15S	D7
13200	CHCG	60827	3350	0E-15S	D1
Drover Dr					
1200	LMNT	60439	3271		A6
S Drovers Ln					
300	PLTN	60067	2805	22W-15N	B2
Drummer Dr					
1800	SMBG	60173	2805	21W-12N	E7
Drummond Cir					
1400	IVNS	60010	2751	24W-17N	C6
Drummond Ct					
400	ROSL	60172	2912		B5
Drummond Dr					
9200	TYPK	60477	3423	11W-21S	E5
Drummond Pl					
10400	FNPK	60164	2973	13W-3N	A5
10400	LydT	60131	2973	13W-3N	A5
10400	LydT	60164	2973	13W-3N	A5
10600	LydT	60164	2972		E5
W Drummond Pl					
600	CHCG	60614	2978	0W-3N	A5
1100	CHCG	60614	2977	1W-3N	E5
3400	CHCG	60647	2976	4W-3N	D5
4200	CHCG	60639	2976	5W-3N	A5
4800	CHCG	60639	2975	6W-3N	D5
Drury Ln					
2200	NHFD	60093	2811	7W-15N	A2
5400	OKLN	60453	3211	6W-11S	D7
9800	BDVW	60154	3029	12W-1S	C7
9800	BDVW	60155	3029	12W-1S	C7
9800	WSTR	60154	3029	12W-1S	B7
E Drury Ln					
400	BRTN	60010	2751	25W-20N	A1
N Drury Ln					
300	ANHT	60004	2807	16W-14N	C4
1100	PTHT	60004	2807	16W-15N	C3
2600	ANHT	60004	2754	16W-16N	C6
S Drury Ln					
100	ANHT	60004	2807	16W-13N	C5
N Dryden Av					
600	ANHT	60004	2807	17W-14N	B4
N Dryden Ct					
2800	ANHT	60004	2754	17W-17N	B5
N Dryden Ln					
2200	ANHT	60004	2754	17W-16N	B7
N Dryden Pl					
10	ANHT	60004	2807	17W-14N	B4
2700	ANHT	60004	2754	17W-17N	B6
S Dryden Pl					
100	ANHT	60004	2807	17W-13N	B5
300	ANHT	60005	2807	17W-13N	B6
Duane Dr					
-	FftT	60423	3504	10W-25S	C7
Dublin Ct					
100	SMBG	60194	2857	26W-10N	E5
1600	IVNS	60067	2805	22W-15N	A3
14100	HMGN	60441	3343	17W-16S	C2
W Dublin Dr					
13500	HMGN	60441	3343	17W-16S	C3
Dublin Ln					
200	SMBG	60194	2857	26W-10N	E5
Dublin St					
8900	ODPK	60462	3346	11W-17S	A6
Dubois Blvd					
4000	BKFD	60513	3087	11W-4S	D7
4500	BKFD	60513	3147	11W-4S	D1
4600	MCCK	60525	3147	11W-4S	D1
Dubonet Dr					
400	RVWD	60015	2755	13W-20N	E1
Duchess Ct					
-	PTHT	60070	2808	13W-15N	E1
Duchess Ln					
25900	CteT	60417	3685	0W-31S	B5
Duck Ln					
400	WDDL	60191	2914		E7
S Duffy Av					
8700	HMTN	60456	3212	5W-10S	B4
Duffy Ln					
-	BFGV	60089	2754	16W-20N	C2
Duke Dr					
200	BlmT	60411	3598	4E-25S	C1
200	LYWD	60411	3598	4E-25S	C1
5300	MTSN	60443	3505	6W-25S	E7
Dukesberry Ln					
4800	HFET	60010	2804	24W-15N	B1
4900	HFET	60010	2751	24W-16N	B7
Dulles Rd					
10	DSPN	60016	2862	15W-11N	B3
600	DSPN	60016	2861	16W-11N	E3
600	MPPT	60056	2861	16W-11N	E3
Dumfries Ct					
1500	IVNS	60067	2805	22W-15N	A3
Dumke Dr					
5200	OKLN	60453	3211	6W-10S	E6
Dumont Ln					
1700	SMBG	60194	2858	25W-11N	B3
Dunamon Dr					
1200	BRLT	60103	2911		D5
1200	HRPK	60103	2911		D5
S Dunbar Av					
9200	CHCG	60619	3214	0E-10S	D5

STREET Block	City	ZIP	Map#	CGS	Grid
Dunbar Ct					
300	SMWD	60107	2911		A1
800	SMBG	60194	2858	25W-11N	B4
Dunbar Ln					
10	RGMW	60008	2806	20W-14N	A4
100	EDND	60118	2801		C2
Dunbar Rd					
1400	IVNS	60067	2752	23W-16N	A6
Dunbar St					
500	BCHR	60401	3864	1W-36S	B2
700	WshT	60401	3864	1W-36S	B2
1500	FSMR	60422	3506	4W-23S	D3
8600	WLSP	60480	3208		E4
Dunbar Ter					
500	CRTE	60417	3596	0E-28S	E7
500	CRTE	60417	3597	0E-28S	A6
Dunbarton Dr					
600	IVNS	60010	2750	25W-16N	E6
700	IVNS	60010	2751	25W-16N	A6
Duncan Av					
500	DndT	60118	2801		A5
500	ELGN	60120	2801		B7
500	ElgT	60118	2801		B7
800	ELGN	60120	2855		A1
Duncan Rd					
15500	OKFT	60452	3347	7W-18S	D7
Duncan St					
10	PvsT	60126	3028		B7
500	YkTp	60126	3028		B7
Dundee Av					
10	CPVL	60118	2801		C2
10	EDND	60118	2801		C6
100	BRTN	60010	2750	25W-17N	E4
200	ELGN	60120	2855		A2
600	DndT	60118	2801		C4
600	FSMR	60422	3507	3W-22S	C1
600	HMWD	60430	3507	3W-22S	C1
800	BNHL	60010	2750	25W-18N	E4
1500	DndT	60120	2801		B6
1500	ELGN	60118	2801		B7
1500	ELGN	60120	2801		B7
17500	HLCT	60430	3427	3W-21S	C6
17500	HMWD	60430	3427	3W-21S	C6
Dundee Av SR-25					
10	CPVL	60118	2801		C2
10	EDND	60118	2801		C6
600	DndT	60118	2801		C4
1100	ELGN	60120	2855		B1
1300	ELGN	60120	2801		B7
1500	DndT	60120	2801		B6
1500	ELGN	60118	2801		B7
Dundee Ln					
10	BNHL	60010	2750	25W-17N	E5
10	BRTN	60010	2750	25W-17N	E5
Dundee Pkwy					
200	BFGV	60089	2754	17W-18N	C4
Dundee Pl					
9400	TYPK	60477	3423	11W-20S	E4
Dundee Rd					
-	BNHL	60110	2801		E1
-	BNHL	60118	2801		E1
-	BRTN	60010	2750	26W-17N	D5
-	CPVL	60110	2801		D1
-	EDND	60110	2801		E1
-	EDND	60118	2801		E1
-	GLNC	60062	2758	7W-17N	A4
-	IVNS	60010	2750	26W-17N	D5
-	NtrT	60062	2758	7W-17N	A4
-	PLTN	60067	2751	23W-17N	D5
-	PltT	60067	2751	23W-17N	D5
-	WhlT	60062	2755	13W-18N	E4
-	WhlT	60062	2756	12W-17N	A4
-	WLNG	60090	2755	13W-18N	E4
-	WLNG	60090	2756	12W-17N	A4
10	BNHL	60010	2750	26W-17N	D5
100	BNHL	60010	2801		E1
100	BNHL	60010	2802	29W-16N	C1
200	BNHL	60010	2749	28W-16N	E7
300	GLNC	60022	2758	6W-18N	C4
400	NHBK	60062	2758	8W-17N	A4
500	NHBK	60062	2757	8W-18N	D4
2000	IVNS	60010	2751	23W-17N	D5
2000	IVNS	60067	2751	23W-17N	D5
2000	PltT	60010	2751	23W-17N	D5
3800	NHBK	60062	2756	12W-17N	B4
4100	NfdT	60062	2756	12W-17N	A4
Dundee Rd SR-68					
-	BNHL	60110	2801		E1
-	BNHL	60118	2801		E1
-	BRTN	60010	2750	26W-17N	D5
-	CPVL	60110	2801		D1
-	EDND	60110	2801		E1
-	EDND	60118	2801		E1
-	GLNC	60062	2758	7W-17N	A4
-	IVNS	60010	2750	26W-17N	D5
-	NtrT	60062	2758	7W-17N	A4
-	PLTN	60067	2751	23W-17N	D5
-	PltT	60067	2751	23W-17N	D5
-	WhlT	60062	2755	13W-18N	E4
-	WhlT	60062	2756	12W-17N	A4
-	WLNG	60090	2755	13W-18N	E4
-	WLNG	60090	2756	12W-17N	A4
10	BNHL	60010	2750	26W-17N	D5
100	BNHL	60010	2801		E1
100	BNHL	60010	2802	29W-16N	C1
200	BNHL	60010	2749	28W-16N	E7
400	NHBK	60062	2758	8W-17N	A4
500	NHBK	60062	2757	8W-18N	D4
2000	IVNS	60010	2751	23W-17N	D5
2000	IVNS	60067	2751	23W-17N	D5
2000	PltT	60010	2751	23W-17N	D5
2500	NHBK	60062	2756	10W-18N	E4
4100	NfdT	60062	2756	12W-17N	A4
E Dundee Rd					
-	ANHT	60089	2754	17W-18N	B4
-	BFGV	60004	2754	17W-18N	B4
-	PltT	60004	2753	19W-18N	D4
-	WhlT	60062	2755	14W-18N	C4
10	BRTN	60010	2750	25W-17N	E5
10	BRTN	60010	2751	25W-17N	A5
10	IVNS	60010	2750	25W-17N	E5
10	IVNS	60010	2751	24W-17N	B5
10	PLTN	60067	2752	20W-18N	E4
10	PLTN	60067	2753	20W-18N	A4
10	PltT	60067	2753	20W-18N	A4
10	PltT	60074	2752	20W-18N	E4
10	PltT	60074	2753	20W-18N	A4
10	WLNG	60090	2755	14W-18N	C4
100	IVNS	60067	2751	23W-17N	D5
100	PLTN	60074	2753	20W-18N	A4
300	BFGV	60090	2754	16W-18N	D4
600	ANHT	60004	2754	17W-18N	B4
600	BFGV	60089	2754	17W-18N	B4
E Dundee Rd SR-53					
-	PltT	60004	2753	19W-18N	D4
900	PLTN	60074	2753	19W-18N	B4
1500	PltT	60074	2753	19W-18N	C4
E Dundee Rd SR-68					
-	ANHT	60089	2754	17W-18N	B4
-	BFGV	60004	2754	17W-18N	B4
-	PltT	60004	2753	19W-18N	D4
-	WhlT	60062	2755	14W-18N	C4
10	BRTN	60010	2750	25W-17N	E5
10	BRTN	60010	2751	25W-17N	A5
10	IVNS	60010	2750	25W-17N	E5
10	IVNS	60010	2751	24W-17N	B5
10	PLTN	60067	2752	20W-18N	E4
10	PLTN	60067	2753	20W-18N	A4
10	PltT	60067	2753	20W-18N	A4
10	PltT	60074	2752	20W-18N	E4
10	PltT	60074	2753	20W-18N	A4
10	WLNG	60090	2755	14W-18N	C4
100	IVNS	60067	2751	23W-17N	D5
100	PLTN	60074	2753	20W-18N	A4
300	BFGV	60090	2754	16W-18N	D4
600	ANHT	60004	2754	17W-18N	B4
600	BFGV	60089	2754	17W-18N	B4
W Dundee Rd					
-	PltT	60004	2753	19W-18N	D4
-	PltT	60074	2753	19W-18N	D4
10	BFGV	60090	2754	16W-18N	D4
10	WLNG	60089	2754	16W-18N	D4
10	WLNG	60090	2755	15W-18N	A4
100	PLTN	60067	2752	21W-18N	D4
100	PltT	60074	2752	21W-18N	D4
400	ANHT	60004	2754	17W-17N	C4
500	PLTN	60074	2752	21W-17N	C4
700	ANHT	60004	2753	18W-18N	D4
700	BFGV	60089	2753	18W-18N	D4
700	PltT	60067	2752	21W-17N	C4
800	WLNG	60090	2754	15W-17N	E4
1200	ANHT	60089	2754	18W-18N	A4
1200	BFGV	60089	2754	18W-17N	A4
1200	PltT	60010	2752	22W-17N	A4
1500	PLTN	60010	2752	23W-17N	A4
1700	PLTN	60010	2751	23W-17N	E4
1700	PLTN	60067	2751	23W-17N	E5
1700	PltT	60010	2751	23W-17N	E5
1800	PltT	60067	2751	23W-17N	E5
W Dundee Rd SR-53					
-	ANHT	60004	2753	19W-18N	D4
-	PltT	60004	2753	19W-18N	D4
-	PltT	60074	2753	19W-18N	D4
W Dundee Rd SR-68					
-	PltT	60004	2753	19W-18N	D4
-	PltT	60074	2753	19W-18N	D4
10	BFGV	60090	2754	16W-18N	D4
10	WLNG	60089	2754	16W-18N	D4
10	WLNG	60090	2755	15W-18N	A4
100	PLTN	60067	2752	21W-18N	D4
100	PltT	60074	2752	21W-18N	D4
400	ANHT	60004	2754	17W-17N	C4
400	BFGV	60089	2754	17W-17N	C4
500	PLTN	60074	2752	21W-17N	C4
700	ANHT	60004	2753	18W-18N	D4
700	BFGV	60089	2753	18W-18N	D4
700	PltT	60067	2752	21W-17N	C4
800	WLNG	60090	2754	15W-17N	E4
1200	ANHT	60089	2754	18W-18N	A4
1200	PltT	60010	2752	22W-17N	A4
1500	PLTN	60010	2752	23W-17N	A4
1700	PLTN	60010	2751	23W-17N	E5
1700	PLTN	60067	2751	23W-17N	E5
1700	PltT	60010	2751	23W-17N	E5
1800	PltT	60067	2751	23W-17N	E5
E Dundee Quarter Dr					
10	PLTN	60074	2753	19W-18N	C4
Dundee Rd Row					
4200	NfdT	60062	2756	12W-18N	A4
4200	NHBK	60062	2756	12W-18N	A4
Dundonald Rd					
2400	FSMR	60422	3507	3W-23S	B3
Dune Sand Ct					
900	DYR	46311	3598		E3
Dunfries St					
-	FSMR	60422	3506	4W-23S	E3
Dunham Rd					
-	SchT	60177	2909		B5
10	PKFT	60466	3595	2W-27S	C4
10	WYNE	60120	2909		B6
10	WYNE	60174	2909		B5
200	BRLT	60120	2909		B5
200	SchT	60120	2909		B5
400	DGvT	60439	3270		B1
Dunham Rd CO-19					
-	SchT	60177	2909		B5
10	WYNE	60120	2909		B6
10	WYNE	60174	2909		B5
200	BRLT	60120	2909		B5
200	SchT	60120	2909		B5
Dunheath Dr					
1300	IVNS	60010	2751	24W-17N	C4
Dunhill Cir					
1800	GNVW	60025	2810	8W-15N	D2
Dunhill Ct					
1600	NHBK	60062	2757	9W-16N	C6
N Dunhill Ct N					
2000	ANHT	60004	2807	17W-14N	C4
Dunhill Ct N					
1900	ANHT	60004	2807	17W-14N	B4
Dunkirk St					
1500	FSMR	60422	3506	4W-23S	D3
Dunlap Pl					
100	SMBG	60194	2858	25W-10N	A5
Dunlap Rd					
10	PKFT	60466	3595	2W-27S	C4
S Dunlieth Ct					
26700	CteT	60417	3685	0W-32S	C7
Dun Lo Dr					
1500	WhlT	60004	2754	16W-17N	C4
Dunlop Av					
800	FTPK	60130	3030	9W-0S	C7
Dunmore Dr					
-	TYPK	60477	3504	10W-23S	B3
9200	PlsT	60462	3345	11W-15S	E1
Dunmore Ln					
700	BRLT	60103	2911		B4
Dunmore Pl					
1900	HFET	60195	2804	25W-12N	A7
Dunmurry Dr					
9300	PlsT	60462	3345	11W-15S	E2
Dunn Rd					
-	TYPK	60477	3424	10W-21S	B6
Dunning Av					
100	WDND	60118	2801		A4
Dunree Ct					
7800	TYPK	60423	3504	9W-23S	D3
7800	TYPK	60477	3504	9W-23S	D3
Dunree Ln					
11800	ODPK	60467	3422	14W-21S	D6
Dunridge Cir					
200	EDND	60118	2801		B2
Dunridge Ct					
400	EDND	60118	2801		A2
Dunrovin Dr					
100	BNHL	60010	2749	28W-20N	E1
Duns Ct					
900	FKFT	60423	3593	8W-26S	A3
Dunsford Ct					
1800	SMBG	60194	2858	25W-11N	A3
E Dunslow Ln					
1300	LKPT	60441	3342	21W-18S	A7
Dunsten Cir					
500	NHBK	60062	2756	10W-18N	E4
N Dunton Av					
10	ANHT	60004	2807	17W-15N	A3
10	ANHT	60005	2807	17W-14N	A5
2800	ANHT	60004	2754	17W-17N	A5
S Dunton Av					
10	ANHT	60005	2807	17W-14N	A5
1200	ANHT	60005	2861	18W-12N	A1
Duntrune Ln					
100	IVNS	60067	2752	22W-18N	B4
N DuPage Av					
100	EMHT	60126	3028		B1
DuPage St					
300	ELGN	60120	2855		A4
Dupee Pl					
100	EVTN	60091	2813	2W-13N	A7
100	EVTN	60201	2813	2W-13N	A7
100	WLMT	60091	2813	2W-13N	A7
Dupont Av					
4800	PLTN	60067	2805	21W-14N	D4
4800	RGMW	60008	2805	21W-14N	E4
4800	RGMW	60067	2805	21W-14N	D4
Dupont Ct					
600	EGVV	60007	2913		C1
Durham Ct					
10	BRRG	60527	3208		A3
500	HFET	60195	2858	24W-12N	E1
700	HRPK	60133	2858	26W-9N	A7
1100	SMBG	60193	2913		B1
Durham Dr					
100	CRTE	60475	3596	0W-28S	C6
1500	IVNS	60067	2805	23W-15N	A1
1700	IVNS	60067	2804	23W-15N	E1
Durham Ln					
-	SMBG	60195	2858	24W-12N	E2
500	HFET	60195	2858	24W-12N	D1
1200	LMNT	60439	3270		E7
Durkin Rd					
-	TYPK	60477	3424	10W-21S	B6
Dursey Ln					
600	DSPN	60016	2808	13W-13N	D5
600	MPPT	60056	2808	13W-13N	D5
Dusty Tr					
11900	OrlT	60467	3344	14W-16S	C3
Dutch American Wy					
1300	BCHR	60401	3774	0W-35S	C7
Dutch Mill Ct					
5700	HRPK	60133	2911		E5
Dutra Av					
20500	BlmT	60411	3507	2W-24S	C6
20500	CHHT	60411	3507	2W-24S	C6
Dutton Rd					
27000	CteT	60401	3774	0E-33S	E2
Duvan Dr					
7200	TYPK	60477	3424	9W-21S	E5
Duxbury Ct					
-	SMWD	60107	2910		E1
900	SMBG	60193	2858	24W-9N	D7
Duxbury Ln					
600	SMBG	60193	2858	24W-9N	D7
700	BRLT	60103	2910		D5
Duxbury St					
10	RGMW	60008	2805	20W-14N	E4
10	RGMW	60067	2805	20W-14N	E4
Dwight Ct					
8900	ODHL	60477	3424	11W-19S	A3
Dwight St					
300	ELGN	60120	2855		A6
N Dwyer Av					
10	ANHT	60005	2806	18W-14N	E4
S Dwyer Av					
10	ANHT	60005	2806	18W-13N	E5
Dwyer Ct					
-	WNKA	60093	2812	5W-15N	A2
E Dyer Blvd					
200	HMND	46320	3430		D1
Dyer Dr					
-	BRLT	60120	2909		D3
Dystrup Rd					
600	DGvT	60439	3270		C3
E					
W E St					
-	MYWD	60153	3088	10W-1S	A1
-	PvsT	60141	3088	10W-1S	A1
Eagle Av					
100	BmdT	60157	2913		E5
1500	MLPK	60160	3028		E2
Eagle Ct					
10	SMWD	60107	2856	29W-10N	C5
100	DYR	46311	3510		D5
500	RVWD	60015	2756	12W-20N	B1
500	SMBG	60194	2857	26W-11N	E4
1200	BRLT	60103	2910		E7
6700	TYPK	60477	3425	8W-21S	B7
Eagle Dr					
-	BlmT	60411	3509	2E-25S	E7
-	FDHT	60411	3509	2E-25S	E7
400	EGvT	60007	2861	18W-9N	A7
400	EGvT	60007	2915		B1
400	EGVV	60007	2861	18W-9N	A7
400	EGVV	60007	2915		B1
600	BNVL	60106	2915		D7
6700	TYPK	60477	3425	8W-21S	A7
Eagle Ln					
3800	RGMW	60008	2806	19W-13N	C7
N Eagle Ln					
600	PLTN	60067	2752	20W-16N	E6
Eagle St					
8700	HGKN	60525	3147	11W-7S	E5
Eagle Ter					
10	BmdT	60157	2913		E5
N Eagle Wy					
2500	HFET	60195	2803	25W-13N	E6
Eagle Crest Dr					
1200	LMNT	60439	3342	19W-15S	C1
Eagle Grove Ct					
1600	WLNG	60090	2754	16W-18N	D3
E Eagle Lake Rd					
10	WshT	60401	3774	0E-34S	E5
W Eagle Lake Rd					
10	WshT	60401	3774	1W-34S	A5
Eagle Nest Dr					
3400	CRTE	60417	3597	1E-28S	C7
3400	STGR	60417	3597	1E-27S	C5
3400	STGR	60475	3597	1E-27S	C5
Eagle Point Dr					
900	MTSN	60443	3505	7W-25S	C7
Eagle Pointe Dr					
10	BNHL	60010	2801		E1
10	BNHL	60010	2802	30W-16N	A1
Eagle Ridge Dr					
10400	ODPK	60467	3423	13W-21S	B7
10400	OrlT	60477	3423	13W-21S	B7
14700	HMGN	60441	3343	17W-17S	C6
16000	TYPK	60477	3424	10W-19S	C2
Eaker Pl					
300	DSPN	60016	2862	15W-10N	B5
Ealing on Duxbury					
10	RGMW	60008	2805	22W-13N	B6
Earl Av					
1200	DSPN	60016	2862	13W-10N	D5
1200	DSPN	60018	2862	13W-10N	D5
Earl Ct					
10	WDRG	60517	3270		A2
Earl Dr					
500	NHFD	60093	2811	7W-15N	B2
Earls Ct					
300	DRFD	60015	2756	11W-20N	D1
9200	OrlT	60477	3423	11W-21S	E6
N Earls Ct					
1000	PLTN	60067	2752	23W-17N	A5
Earlston Rd					
500	KLWH	60043	2812	4W-14N	C4
W Early Av					
1200	CHCG	60660	2921	1W-7N	D4
Early St					
200	PKFT	60466	3595	3W-25S	B1
East Av					
-	BKFD	60513	3147	12W-4S	D1
-	MCCK	60513	3147	12W-4S	D1
-	SMBG	60173	2860	21W-12N	A2
10	PKRG	60068	2864	9W-9N	C7
10	RVSD	60546	3088	9W-3S	C5
300	CHCG	60631	2864	9W-9N	C7
700	LGNG	60525	3147	12W-5S	D2
700	MCCK	60525	3147	12W-5S	D2
800	CTSD	60525	3147	12W-5S	D2
1000	HRPK	60133	2911		C2
1000	SMWD	60107	2857	27W-9N	C7
1000	SMWD	60107	2911		C1
1000	SMWD	60133	2911		C1
1200	BRWN	60402	3031	8W-1S	A7
1200	OKPK	60304	3031	8W-1S	A7
1500	BRWN	60402	3089	8W-3S	A5
1500	CRTE	60417	3685	0W-30S	C3
1500	CteT	60417	3685	0W-30S	C3
3800	SKNY	60402	3089	8W-3S	A6
5800	HGKN	60525	3147	11W-6S	D5
N East Av					
100	OKPK	60302	3031	8W-0N	A4
S East Av					
100	OKPK	60302	3031	8W-0S	A5
400	OKPK	60304	3031	8W-0S	A6
1100	BRWN	60402	3031	8W-0S	A7
East Av N					
500	OKPK	60302	3031	8W-1N	A2
1200	CHCG	60302	3031	8W-2N	A1
1200	CHCG	60707	3031	8W-2N	A1
East Ct					
600	SHLD	60473	3429	0E-18S	A1
E East Ct					
400	EMHT	60126	3028		B2
East Dr					
-	SMBG	60173	2860	21W-11N	A2
-	TYPK	60477	3504	9W-23S	E3
-	WLNG	60090	2808	14W-16N	D1
10	NHLK	60164	2972		D7
10	NHLK	60164	3028		D1
4800	RNPK	60471	3594	6W-27S	B5
19500	FftT	60423	3504	9W-23S	E3
19500	TYPK	60423	3504	9W-23S	E3
East Rd					
11100	PSHL	60465	3273	11W-13S	E3
East St					
700	LMNT	60439	3270		E6
1100	CRTE	60417	3685	0W-29S	C2
Eastbrook Ct					
1700	SLVL	60411	3597	2E-27S	C5
Eastbrook Dr					
22900	CteT	60417	3597	2E-27S	C5
22900	SLVL	60411	3597	2E-27S	C5
N East Brook Rd					
2400	EDPK	60707	2974	9W-3N	B6
Eastchester Rd					
600	WLNG	60090	2755	15W-17N	A6
N East Cir Av					
5700	CHCG	60631	2918	8W-7N	E4
East End Av					
400	CTCY	60409	3351	2E-17S	C6
700	BKLY	60162	3028		C4
700	BKLY	60163	3028		C4
700	HLSD	60162	3028		C4
700	HLSD	60163	3028		C4
1400	CHHT	60411	3508	0W-25S	B7
1500	CHHT	60411	3596	0W-26S	B2
2500	BlmT	60411	3596	0W-26S	B3
2700	SCHT	60411	3596	0W-26S	B3
3200	SCHT	60475	3596	0W-27S	B4
3200	STGR	60475	3596	0W-27S	B4
15400	DLTN	60473	3351	2E-18S	C6
15600	DLTN	60419	3351	2E-18S	C7
S East End Av					
-	CHCG	60617	3215	2E-9S	B2
4900	CHCG	60615	3153	2E-5S	B1
6700	CHCG	60649	3153	2E-7S	B6
7900	CHCG	60649	3215	2E-9S	B2
Eastern Av					
100	BLWD	60104	3029	12W-0S	B5
100	BNVL	60007	2915		D3
100	BNVL	60106	2915		D3
100	EGVV	60007	2915		D3
100	EGVV	60106	2915		D3
200	BRTN	60010	2751	25W-18N	B2
500	DYR	46311	3510		E5
7000	IHPK	60525	3146		D7
N Eastern Av					
100	BRLT	60103	2910		E2
S Eastern Av					
100	BRLT	60103	2910		E3
Eastgate Av					
200	CHHT	60411	3508	0W-24S	B5
S Eastgate Av					
25900	MONE	60449	3683	6W-31S	A5
Eastgate Dr					
17400	CCHL	60478	3426	5W-20S	D5
Eastgrove Rd					
300	RVSD	60546	3088	9W-3S	D4
Eastham Ct					
10	SMBG	60193	2858	25W-10N	C6
Eastham Ln					
1300	SMBG	60193	2858	25W-10N	B6
Eastings Wy					
-	BrnT	60010	2803	27W-15N	B1
10	SBTN	60010	2803	27W-15N	B1
N Eastlake Ter					
7500	CHCG	60626	2867	1W-9N	D7
N Eastland St					
700	AddT	60126	2972		B6
700	EMHT	60126	2972		B6
East Leamington Dr					
-	BmnT	60445	3347	6W-16S	E3
-	CTWD	60445	3347	6W-16S	E3
Eastman Ct					
500	MPPT	60056	2808	15W-13N	B6
E Eastman Ct					
2000	ANHT	60004	2807	16W-14N	D4
N Eastman Dr					
600	MPPT	60056	2808	15W-13N	B5
E Eastman St					
1300	ANHT	60004	2807	17W-14N	C4
W Eastman St					
-	CHCG	60622	3033	1W-1N	E1
10	ANHT	60004	2807	17W-14N	A4
400	ANHT	60005	2806	18W-14N	E4
700	CHCG	60610	3034	0W-1N	A1
800	CHCG	60610	3033	1W-1N	E1
2100	RGMW	60008	2806	19W-14N	C4
Easton Ct					
1600	BFGV	60089	2754	16W-18N	D4
1600	WLNG	60089	2754	16W-18N	D4
1600	WLNG	60090	2754	16W-18N	D4
5800	HRPK	60133	2911		D5
W Easton Ct					
700	PLTN	60067	2805	21W-15N	C2
Easton Ln					
-	EGVV	60007	2913		E1
Easton Pl					
100	BRRG	60527	3208		D2
N East River Rd					
10	DSPN	60016	2863	12W-12N	C1
10	MaiT	60016	2863	12W-12N	C1
400	MaiT	60016	2809	12W-12N	C7
500	NfdT	60016	2809	12W-12N	C7
4400	CHCG	60656	2917	11W-6N	E7
4700	CHCG	60706	2917	10W-6N	E7
4700	NRDG	60706	2917	10W-6N	E7
5000	NRDG	60656	2917	10W-6N	E6
5500	CHCG	60631	2917	11W-6N	E7
5700	CHCG	60018	2917	10W-7N	E4
5700	PKRG	60068	2917	10W-7N	E4
Eastry Ln					
-	BlmT	60411	3509	2E-23S	D4
-	LYWD	60411	3509	2E-23S	D4
Eastview					
-	ALSP	60803	3276	5W-13S	A4
-	CHCG	60655	3276	5W-13S	A4
Eastview Av					
-	BNVL	60106	2915		D7
Eastview Ct					
600	SMBG	60194	2859	22W-10N	C5
Eastview Dr					
2000	DSPN	60018	2862	13W-9N	E7
2200	DSPN	60018	2916		E1
S East View Pk					
5400	CHCG	60615	3153	2E-5S	B2
Eastview St					
600	ELGN	60120	2855		B4
Eastwick Ln					
500	BRLT	60103	2910		E7
Eastwind Ct					
3800	NHBK	60062	2756	12W-17N	B5
Eastwind Dr					
-	RNPK	60471	3594	6W-27S	A4
Eastwood Av					
2400	EVTN	60201	2867	3W-12N	A1
2500	EVTN	60201	2813	3W-12N	A7
2700	WLMT	60091	2813	3W-13N	A7
2700	WLMT	60201	2813	3W-13N	A7
9300	SRPK	60176	2917	11W-5N	C7
N Eastwood Av					
100	MPPT	60056	2807	15W-13N	E6
W Eastwood Av					
2000	CHCG	60640	2921	2W-5N	B7
2300	CHCG	60625	2921	3W-5N	A7
2900	CHCG	60625	2920	4W-5N	D7
4000	CHCG	60630	2920	5W-5N	B7
5600	CHCG	60630	2919	7W-5N	B7
6300	HDHT	60630	2919	7W-5N	A7
6300	HDHT	60706	2919	7W-5N	A7
8000	NRDG	60706	2918	10W-5N	B7
Eastwood Ct					
1700	SMBG	60195	2859	23W-12N	A1
9900	SRPK	60176	2917	12W-5N	B7
Eastwood Dr					
-	LYWD	60411	3509	2E-23S	D4
10	DRFD	60015	2757	10W-20N	B2
N Eastwood Dr					
1900	ANHT	60004	2807	17W-16N	B1
S Eastwood Dr					
10900	PSHL	60465	3274	9W-12S	D3
Eastwood Ln					
700	BFGV	60089	2754	15W-20N	E1
800	GNVW	60025	2811	7W-13N	B6
1100	NHBK	60062	2757	9W-17N	D5
Eastwood Rd					
900	GLNC	60022	2758	6W-18N	C4
Easy St					
400	DSPN	60016	2862	15W-11N	B3
N Easy St					
400	PLTN	60067	2752	21W-16N	D7
Eaton Ct					
800	SMBG	60193	2859	23W-9N	B7
11000	WSTR	60154	3086		E4
W Eaton Ct					
1100	PLTN	60067	2805	22W-15N	B2
Eaton St					
200	NHFD	60093	2811	7W-15N	B3
E Eaton St					
600	HMND	46320	3352		E7
Ebbtide Pt					
700	SMBG	60194	2859	22W-10N	C4
S Eberhardt St					
19100	BlmT	60425	3508	0E-23S	E3
19100	GNWD	60425	3508	0E-23S	E3
S Eberhart Av					
3100	CHCG	60616	3092	0E-3S	D4

Chicago & Cook County Street Index

STREET Block	City	ZIP	Map#	CGS	Grid
S Eberhart Av					
6000	CHCG	60637	3152	0E-6S	D4
7000	CHCG	60619	3152	0E-8S	D7
7500	CHCG	60619	3214	0E-9S	D2
10000	CHCG	60628	3214	0E-11S	D7
10300	CHCG	60628	3278	0E-12S	D2
13000	CHCG	60827	3278	0E-15S	D7
13100	CHCG	60827	3350	0E-15S	D1
Eberly Av					
4000	BKFD	60513	3087	11W-4S	D7
4000	LGNG	60525	3087	11W-4S	D7
4100	BKFD	60525	3087	12W-4S	D7
4100	LGNG	60513	3087	11W-4S	D7
4500	BKFD	60513	3147	12W-4S	D1
4500	LGNG	60525	3147	12W-4S	D1
4600	MCCK	60513	3147	12W-4S	D1
4600	MCCK	60525	3147	12W-4S	D1
W Ebert Pl					
8500	NLES	60714	2864	10W-10N	A4
W Ebinger Dr					
6500	NLES	60714	2918	8W-8N	E1
6500	NLES	60714	2919	8W-8N	A1
Echo Ln					
500	GNVW	60025	2811	6W-13N	C7
3200	NHBK	60062	2756	11W-16N	D6
S Echo Ln					
500	PLTN	60067	2805	21W-15N	C2
W Echo Ln					
600	PLTN	60074	2752	21W-17N	C5
600	PltT	60067	2752	21W-17N	C5
Ed Bossert Dr					
10	LMNT	60439	3270		D5
Edbrooke Av					
14600	DLTN	60419	3350	0W-17S	D5
14600	DLTN	60827	3350	0W-17S	D5
14600	RVDL	60827	3350	0W-17S	D5
14900	SHLD	60473	3350	0W-17S	D5
S Edbrooke Av					
10500	CHCG	60628	3278	0E-12S	C2
13300	CHCG	60827	3350	0W-15S	D1
13800	RVDL	60827	3350	0W-16S	D3
14500	DLTN	60419	3350	0W-17S	D4
14500	DLTN	60827	3350	0W-17S	D4
Eddy Ln					
100	NHFD	60093	2811	7W-15N	B3
Eddy St					
200	CHHT	60411	3507	1W-23S	E3
W Eddy St					
1100	CHCG	60657	2977	1W-4N	D3
1900	CHCG	60618	2977	2W-4N	B3
3100	CHCG	60618	2976	3W-4N	E3
4000	CHCG	60641	2976	5W-4N	B3
4800	CHCG	60641	2975	7W-4N	C3
5500	CHCG	60634	2975	7W-4N	B3
Edelweiss Dr					
8400	PSPK	60464	3274	10W-13S	C4
Eden Av					
9800	SRPK	60176	2973	12W-4N	B2
Eden Dr					
800	SMBG	60195	2858	24W-12N	D1
W Eden Ln					
400	CteT	60417	3774	0W-33S	C1
Eden Rd					
10	EGVV	60007	2914		D2
Eden Oaks Ln					
10	BlmT	60422	3507	2W-23S	D3
10	FSMR	60422	3507	2W-23S	D3
Edens Av					
-	CHCG	60630	2919	5W-6N	E6
Edens Expwy					
-	CHCG	-	2919	6W-7N	E4
-	CHCG	-	2920	5W-5N	A7
-	GLNC	-	2758	7W-16N	B7
-	GNVW	-	2811	6W-13N	D6
-	HDPK	-	2757	8W-18N	E2
-	LNWD	-	2919	6W-8N	E2
-	MNGV	-	2865	6W-10N	D4
-	NfdT	-	2757	8W-18N	E2
-	NfdT	-	2811	7W-16N	C1
-	NHBK	-	2757	8W-18N	E2
-	NHBK	-	2758	7W-17N	A5
-	NHFD	-	2758	7W-16N	B7
-	NHFD	-	2811	6W-14N	D4
-	NtrT	-	2758	7W-18N	A4
-	NtrT	-	2811	6W-14N	D4
-	SKOK	-	2811	6W-13N	E7
-	SKOK	-	2865	6W-9N	D7
-	SKOK	-	2919	6W-9N	E1
-	WLMT	-	2811	6W-14N	D4
Edens Expwy I-94					
-	CHCG	-	2919	6W-7N	E4
-	CHCG	-	2920	5W-5N	A7
-	GLNC	-	2758	7W-16N	B7
-	GNVW	-	2811	6W-13N	D6
-	LNWD	-	2919	6W-8N	E2
-	MNGV	-	2865	6W-10N	D4
-	NfdT	-	2811	7W-16N	C1
-	NHBK	-	2758	7W-17N	A5
-	NHFD	-	2758	7W-16N	B7
-	NHFD	-	2811	7W-16N	C1
-	NtrT	-	2758	7W-18N	A4
-	NtrT	-	2811	6W-14N	D4
-	SKOK	-	2811	6W-13N	E7
-	SKOK	-	2865	6W-10N	D4
-	SKOK	-	2919	6W-8N	E1
-	WLMT	-	2811	6W-13N	E7
Edens Expwy US-41					
-	GLNC	-	2758	7W-16N	B7
-	HDPK	-	2757	8W-18N	E2
-	NfdT	-	2757	8W-18N	E2
-	NfdT	-	2811	7W-16N	C1
-	NHBK	-	2757	8W-18N	E2
-	NHBK	-	2758	7W-17N	A5
-	NHFD	-	2758	7W-16N	B7
-	NHFD	-	2811	6W-14N	D4
-	NtrT	-	2758	7W-18N	A4
-	NtrT	-	2811	6W-14N	D4
Edens Ln					
400	NHFD	60093	2811	7W-15N	B1
N Edens Pkwy					
5400	CHCG	60630	2919	6W-6N	E5
Edens Expressway Spur					
-	DRFD	-	2756	11W-18N	D2
-	DRFD	-	2757	10W-18N	A3
-	NfdT	-	2756	12W-18N	B2
-	NfdT	-	2757	9W-18N	D3
-	NfdT	-	2758	8W-18N	A3
-	NHBK	-	2756	12W-18N	C2
-	NHBK	-	2757	10W-18N	A3
-	NHBK	-	2758	8W-18N	A3
-	WdfT	-	2756	12W-18N	B2
Edens Expressway Spur I-94					
-	DRFD	-	2756	11W-18N	D2
-	DRFD	-	2757	10W-18N	A3
-	NfdT	-	2756	12W-18N	B2
-	NfdT	-	2757	10W-18N	A3
-	NfdT	-	2758	8W-18N	A3
-	NHBK	-	2756	12W-18N	C2
-	NHBK	-	2757	10W-18N	A3
-	NHBK	-	2758	8W-18N	A3
-	WdfT	-	2756	12W-18N	B2
Edens Expressway Spur E					
-	NfdT	-	2756	12W-20N	B2
-	NfdT	-	2757	10W-18N	A3
-	NHBK	-	2757	8W-18N	E3
-	WdfT	-	2756	12W-20N	B2
Edens Expressway Spur E I-94					
-	NfdT	-	2756	12W-20N	B2
-	NfdT	-	2757	10W-18N	A3
-	NHBK	-	2757	8W-18N	E3
-	WdfT	-	2756	12W-20N	B2
Edens Expressway Spur W					
-	DRFD	-	2756	12W-20N	B1
-	NfdT	-	2757	10W-18N	A3
-	WdfT	-	2756	12W-20N	B1
Edens Expressway Spur W I-94					
-	DRFD	-	2756	12W-20N	B1
-	NfdT	-	2757	10W-18N	A3
-	WdfT	-	2756	12W-20N	B1
Edenwood Dr					
500	BmdT	60172	2912		D6
500	ROSL	60172	2912		D6
Edgar Ln					
18100	OrlT	60477	3423	11W-21S	E7
Edgar St					
3000	PltT	60067	2805	20W-13N	E5
3000	RGMW	60008	2805	20W-13N	E5
3000	RGMW	60067	2805	20W-13N	E5
S Edgar St					
1700	PltT	60067	2805	20W-13N	E5
1700	RGMW	60067	2805	20W-13N	E5
Edgebrook Ct					
100	IHPK	60525	3146		E5
Edgebrook Ln					
800	GLNC	60022	2758	7W-17N	B4
900	NHBK	60062	2757	8W-16N	E7
7000	HRPK	60133	2911		E2
8000	TYPK	60477	3504	10W-23S	C3
11000	IHPK	60525	3146		E5
Edgebrook Rd					
200	WDDL	60191	2915		A7
Edgebrook Ter					
600	ELGN	60120	2855		C6
N Edgebrook Ter					
6700	CHCG	60646	2919	7W-8N	B2
Edgefield Ln					
1400	HFET	60195	2858	25W-12N	B2
Edge Lake Dr					
5600	OKLN	60453	3275	7W-12S	D1
Edgelake Pt					
300	SMBG	60194	2859	23W-10N	A4
Edgemere Ct					
900	EVTN	60202	2867	2W-10N	C4
Edgemont Ln					
500	HFET	60195	2858	24W-12N	D1
500	PKRG	60068	2864	10W-9N	A6
700	SMBG	60195	2858	24W-12N	D1
3000	PKRG	60068	2863	11W-9N	C6
E Edgemont Ln					
10	PKRG	60068	2864	9W-9N	C6
Edgeview Ct					
23500	DRPK	60010	2751	23W-20N	E1
Edgeware Rd					
100	EGVV	60007	2860	18W-9N	E7
Edgewater Av					
4200	HLSD	60162	3029	13W-0S	A7
4300	HLSD	60162	3028		E7
W Edgewater Av					
1400	CHCG	60660	2921	1W-7N	C4
N Edgewater Ct					
1100	PLTN	60067	2752	23W-17N	A4
Edgewater Dr					
-	CCHL	60478	3506	4W-22S	D1
200	BRLT	60103	2909		D4
3600	HLCT	60429	3506	4W-22S	D1
Edgewater Ln					
-	PLTN	60067	2752	22W-17N	A5
S Edgewater Ln					
12700	PlsT	60464	3273	12W-15S	D7
12700	PSPK	60464	3273	12W-15S	D7
W Edgewater Ln					
1400	PLTN	60067	2752	23W-17N	A5
Edgewater Rd					
8000	NRIV	60546	3088	10W-2S	B4
8000	RVSD	60546	3088	10W-2S	B4
Edgewood Av					
-	BNVL	60007	2915		C4
-	EGVV	60007	2915		C4
1200	BNVL	60106	2915		C3
1200	CHHT	60411	3508	1W-25S	A6
1400	CHHT	60411	3596	1W-25S	A1
1600	CHHT	60411	3595	1W-25S	E1
5500	CTSD	60525	3147	13W-6S	A4
5500	LGNG	60525	3147	13W-6S	A4
5500	LynT	60525	3147	13W-6S	A4
N Edgewood Av					
-	EGVV	60007	2915		C4
10	LGNG	60525	3087	13W-4S	A7
200	WDDL	60191	2915		C7
300	LGPK	60525	3087	13W-3S	A6
300	WDDL	60106	2915		C7
S Edgewood Av					
100	LGNG	60525	3087	13W-4S	A7
200	LGNG	60525	3147	13W-5S	A1
500	EMHT	60126	3028		B5
Edgewood Ct					
100	RGMW	60008	2805	21W-13N	D5
1000	LMNT	60439	3270		C7
6300	OKFT	60452	3347	8W-17S	B6
8900	TYPK	60477	3424	11W-21S	A5
Edgewood Dr					
-	LGPK	60525	3087	13W-3S	A4
-	WSTR	60525	3087	13W-3S	A4
10	SMWD	60107	2857	28W-9N	A7
200	WLNG	60090	2755	14W-18N	D3
1200	CTCY	60409	3430	4E-19S	B1
2700	DYR	46311	3598		E4
2800	SjnT	46311	3598		E4
15300	ODPK	60462	3346	10W-18S	B7
W Edgewood Dr					
12000	HMGN	60441	3344	15W-17S	C6
12000	ODPK	60441	3344	15W-17S	C6
12000	ODPK	60467	3344	15W-17S	C6
15300	LKPT	60441	3342	20W-18S	B7
Edgewood Ln					
200	PltT	60067	2805	20W-13N	E6
200	PltT	60067	2806	19W-14N	C3
400	NHFD	60093	2811	8W-15N	A2
500	EGVV	60007	2861	18W-9N	A6
Edgewood Ln					
800	GNVW	60025	2811	7W-13N	B7
1300	NHBK	60062	2757	8W-17N	D5
1300	WNKA	60093	2758	6W-16N	D7
1700	LGGV	60047	2753	18W-20N	D1
S Edgewood Ln					
500	LGNG	60525	3147	13W-5S	A2
500	LynT	60525	3147	13W-5S	A2
600	MPPT	60056	2861	16W-12N	D2
Edgewood Pl					
400	RVFT	60305	3030	10W-0N	B4
W Edgewood Rd					
6700	PSHT	60463	3275	8W-15S	A7
7000	PSHT	60463	3274	8W-15S	E7
W Edgewood St					
6000	CCRO	60804	3089	7W-3S	B4
Edgington St					
2400	FNPK	60131	2973	11W-3N	C5
Edinburgh Ct					
700	IVNS	60010	2751	24W-16N	C7
14600	HMGN	60441	3343	18W-17S	A6
Edinburgh Dr					
1600	BRLT	60103	2855		E7
1600	BRLT	60103	2856	31W-9N	A7
13300	PSHT	60464	3346	10W-15S	C2
Edinburgh Ln					
500	PTHT	60070	2808	14W-14N	B3
S Edinburgh Ln					
19700	FftT	60423	3504	9W-23S	E4
Edison Av					
2800	BLID	60406	3277	3W-15S	A7
3300	BLID	60406	3276	4W-15S	E7
3300	WthT	60406	3276	4W-15S	E7
5300	OKLN	60453	3211	7W-11S	D7
Edison Cir					
1600	HRPK	60133	2911		D5
Edison Pl					
3600	RGMW	60008	2806	20W-15N	B2
W Edmaire St					
1700	CHCG	60643	3277	2W-13S	C3
Edmer Av					
1100	OKPK	60302	3031	7W-1N	A1
Edmond Dr					
400	DYR	46311	3598		D1
Edmund M Burke Rd					
3000	OMFD	60461	3507	4W-24S	A5
3300	OMFD	60461	3506	4W-24S	E5
W Edmunds St					
5400	CHCG	60630	2919	6W-6N	C6
Edna Av					
2300	PKRG	60068	2863	11W-10N	D6
Edward Ct					
400	DSPN	60016	2863	11W-11N	C3
Edward Dr					
3400	CRTE	60417	3597	1E-28S	B6
5700	OKFT	60452	3347	7W-18S	C7
22500	RNPK	60471	3594	4W-27S	D4
E Edward Dr					
800	GNVW	60025	2810	10W-14N	A3
Edward Rd					
900	PTHT	60070	2808	14W-14N	C3
Edward St					
800	WLNG	60090	2755	15W-17N	A5
1000	WLNG	60090	2754	15W-17N	E5
2700	BLID	60406	3349	3W-15S	A1
N Edward St					
10	MPPT	60056	2808	14W-13N	B7
S Edward St					
10	MPPT	60056	2808	15W-12N	B7
400	MPPT	60056	2862	15W-12N	B2
Edward Cul de Sac St					
10	PTHT	60070	2808	14W-14N	D3
Edwards Av					
-	CPVL	60118	2801		A1
10	NHLK	60164	2972		E7
10	NHLK	60164	3028		E1
10	NHLK	60164	3029	12W-2N	A1
10	WDND	60118	2801		A3
900	EDND	60118	2801		A1
17000	CCHL	60478	3426	5W-21S	C7
E Edwards Av					
400	CPVL	60118	2801		A1
Edwards Dr					
-	LMNT	60439	3342	20W-15S	B1
Effingham Ct					
2800	SMBG	60193	2857	27W-10N	D6
Egan Ct					
100	SMWD	60107	2857	27W-11N	C4
Egan Dr					
10	SMWD	60107	2857	27W-11N	C4
Egandale Av					
4900	MCCK	60525	3148	10W-5S	B2
Eggert Ln					
9100	SJHN	46373	3687		E1
Egg Harbour Ct					
10	SMBG	60173	2859	21W-10N	E5
Eggleston Av					
-	BlmT	60411	3508	0W-24S	C5
-	CHHT	60411	3508	0W-24S	C5
S Eggleston Av					
5900	CHCG	60621	3152	0W-6S	B4
7500	CHCG	60621	3214	0W-8S	B1
9500	CHCG	60620	3214	0W-11S	B6
9500	CHCG	60628	3214	0W-11S	B6
10400	CHCG	60628	3278	0W-12S	B2
13700	RVDL	60827	3350	0W-15S	B2
14500	HRVY	60426	3350	0W-16S	B4
Egidi Dr					
200	WLNG	60090	2755	14W-18N	B4
S Egyptian Tr					
25200	MONE	60449	3682	6W-31S	E5
26500	MonT	60449	3682	6W-32S	E7
29700	WIIT	60468	3861	7W-36S	E1
Eicklemann Dr					
-	ITSC	60143	2914		B6
Eileen Ct					
9200	ODPK	60462	3345	11W-16S	E2
E Eisenhower Av					
600	PLTN	60074	2753	20W-16N	B7
Eisenhower Cir					
4200	HFET	60195	2804	24W-15N	D2
E Eisenhower Ct					
200	PLTN	60074	2753	20W-16N	B7
Eisenhower Dr					
2600	DSPN	60018	2917	12W-8N	B1
Eisenhower Expwy					
-	ADSN	-	2914		B7
-	BDVW	-	3029	11W-0S	E6
-	BKLY	-	3028		B5
-	BLWD	-	3029	12W-0S	A6
-	CHCG	-	3031	6W-0S	D6
-	CHCG	-	3032	4W-0S	D5
-	CHCG	-	3033	3W-0S	A5
-	CHCG	-	3034	0W-0S	A5
-	EMHT	-	2972		A7
Eisenhower Expwy					
-	EMHT	-	3028		B3
-	FTPK	-	3030	10W-0S	B6
-	HLSD	-	3028		C5
-	HLSD	-	3029	13W-0S	A6
-	ITSC	-	2914		A7
-	MYWD	-	3029	11W-0S	D6
-	MYWD	-	3030	10W-0S	B6
-	NHLK	-	3028		B2
-	OKPK	-	3030	9W-0S	D5
-	OKPK	-	3031	8W-0S	A6
-	PvsT	-	3028		C6
-	WSTR	-	3029	13W-0S	A6
Eisenhower Expwy I-290					
-	ADSN	-	2914		B7
-	BDVW	-	3029	12W-0S	C6
-	BKLY	-	3028		B3
-	BLWD	-	3029	12W-0S	C6
-	CHCG	-	3031	6W-0S	D6
-	CHCG	-	3032	5W-0S	A6
-	CHCG	-	3033	1W-0S	E5
-	CHCG	-	3034	0W-0S	A5
-	EMHT	-	2972		A7
-	EMHT	-	3028		B4
-	FTPK	-	3030	9W-0S	D5
-	HLSD	-	3028		C5
-	HLSD	-	3029	13W-0S	A6
-	ITSC	-	2914		A7
-	MYWD	-	3029	11W-0S	D6
-	MYWD	-	3030	10W-0S	B6
-	NHLK	-	3028		B2
-	OKPK	-	3030	9W-0S	D5
-	OKPK	-	3031	8W-0S	A6
-	PvsT	-	3028		C6
-	WSTR	-	3029	12W-0S	B6
Eisenhower Expwy US-20					
-	EMHT	-	2972		A7
-	EMHT	-	3028		A1
Eisenhower St					
10	EGvT	60018	2862	15W-9N	A7
Ela Rd					
10	IVNS	60067	2804	23W-16N	E1
100	IVNS	60010	2751	23W-17N	D6
100	IVNS	60067	2751	23W-17N	D5
1700	HFET	60067	2804	23W-13N	E6
1700	HFET	60195	2804	23W-13N	E6
1700	PltT	60195	2804	23W-13N	E6
N Ela Rd					
10	BRTN	60010	2751	23W-20N	D1
10	DRPK	60010	2751	23W-20N	D1
10	ElaT	60010	2751	24W-20N	D1
10	PltT	60010	2751	23W-20N	D1
N Ela Rd CO-V57					
10	BRTN	60010	2751	23W-20N	D1
10	DRPK	60010	2751	23W-20N	D1
10	ElaT	60010	2751	24W-20N	D1
10	PltT	60010	2751	23W-20N	D1
S Ela Rd					
-	DRPK	60010	2751	24W-18N	D3
10	IVNS	60067	2804	23W-14N	E3
100	BRTN	60010	2751	24W-18N	D3
100	PltT	60010	2751	24W-18N	D3
800	HFET	60067	2804	23W-14N	E4
800	HFET	60195	2804	23W-14N	E4
Ela St					
10	BRTN	60010	2751	25W-20N	A2
E Elaine Cir					
10	PTHT	60070	2808	14W-15N	C3
W Elaine Cir					
10	PTHT	60070	2808	14W-15N	B3
Elaine Ct					
1100	FSMR	60422	3507	3W-23S	A2
N Elaine Pl					
3400	CHCG	60657	2978	0W-4N	A3
Elayne Ct					
2700	MPPT	60005	2861	17W-10N	C4
Elbridge Av					
-	PSPK	60464	3274	10W-13S	B5
N Elbridge Av					
3000	CHCG	60618	2976	4W-3N	C4
El Cameno Real Dr					
9900	ODPK	60462	3345	12W-18S	C6
El Camino Ct					
9800	ODPK	60462	3345	12W-18S	D6
El Camino Ln					
9800	ODPK	60462	3345	12W-18S	D6
El Camino Ter					
15200	ODPK	60462	3345	12W-18S	D7
El Cid Ln					
2300	NHBK	60062	2810	10W-15N	A1
Elder Av					
100	CHHT	60411	3507	1W-25S	E7
100	CHHT	60411	3508	1W-25S	A7
Elder Ct					
400	MaiT	60025	2809	10W-12N	E7
700	GLNC	60022	2758	7W-17N	B5
1200	WLNG	60090	2754	16W-18N	E2
3100	NHBK	60062	2756	11W-16N	D6
6900	BGVW	60455	3210	8W-10S	E5
6900	BGVW	60455	3211	8W-10S	A5
15500	HMGN	60441	3343	16W-18S	E7
Elder Ln					
100	HDPK	60035	2758	6W-20N	C1
400	MaiT	60025	2809	11W-12N	E7
500	NfdT	60025	2809	11W-12N	E7
600	WNKA	60093	2812	4W-15N	B3
1600	NHFD	60093	2811	6W-15N	C3
3300	FNPK	60131	2973	12W-4N	B3
3600	SRPK	60131	2973	12W-4N	B3
3600	SRPK	60176	2973	12W-4N	B3
N Elder Ln					
10	LGNG	60525	3087	13W-4S	A7
S Elder Ln					
25800	MONE	60449	3682	6W-31S	E5
Elder Rd					
800	GNWD	60425	3428	1W-21S	B7
800	GNWD	60430	3428	1W-21S	B7
800	HMWD	60430	3428	1W-21S	B7
1300	HMWD	60430	3427	1W-21S	E7
Elderberry Ln					
-	OrlT	60467	3423	12W-20S	B3
400	HnrT	60120	2910		D1
10400	ODPK	60467	3423	13W-20S	B3
E Elderberry Ln					
600	MPPT	60056	2808	14W-14N	B5
Elderwood Ct					
6300	OKFT	60452	3347	7W-17S	B5
Eldorado Dr					
6400	MNGV	60053	2865	8W-11N	A2
Eldorado St					
800	WNKA	60093	2759	5W-16N	A7
800	WNKA	60093	2812		B1
S Eleanor Av					
10000	PSHL	60465	3210	10W-11S	B7
10000	PSHL	60465	3274	10W-11S	B1
Eleanor Dr					
100	PTHT	60070	2755	15W-16N	A6
100	WLNG	60070	2755	15W-16N	A6
100	WLNG	60090	2755	15W-16N	A6
E Eleanor St					
-	ThtT	60476	3428	0E-21S	E5
100	TNTN	60476	3428	0E-21S	D5
S Eleanor St					
2500	CHCG	60608	3091	1W-2S	D3
W Eleanor St					
100	TNTN	60476	3428	0E-21S	D5
Eleanore Ct					
3700	RGMW	60008	2806	20W-13N	A5
Electric Av					
5100	BKLY	60163	3028		C4
5100	HLSD	60162	3028		D4
6000	EMHT	60126	3028		C4
Elgin Av					
10	DndT	60118	2801		A4
300	EDND	60118	2801		A4
700	ELGN	60120	2855		A7
800	FTPK	60130	3030	9W-1S	D7
1400	FTPK	60130	3088	9W-1S	D1
1500	NRIV	60130	3088	9W-1S	D1
Elgin Ln					
1300	SMBG	60194	2858	25W-10N	C5
3300	SKOK	60203	2866	4W-11N	D2
Elgin Rd					
700	EVTN	60201	2867	2W-11N	B2
1600	BNHL	60110	2748		C3
1600	CPVL	60110	2748		C3
1900	DndT	60110	2748		C2
2100	ALGN	60102	2748		C2
2100	ALGN	60110	2748		C2
2100	BNHL	60010	2748		C2
2100	BNHL	60102	2748		C2
2800	EVTN	60201	2866	4W-11N	D2
2800	SKOK	60201	2866	4W-11N	D2
2800	SKOK	60203	2866	4W-11N	D2
Elgin Rd SR-25					
1600	BNHL	60110	2748		C3
1600	CPVL	60110	2748		C3
1900	DndT	60110	2748		C2
2100	ALGN	60102	2748		C2
2100	ALGN	60110	2748		C2
2100	BNHL	60010	2748		C2
2100	BNHL	60102	2748		C2
Elgin O'Hare Expwy					
-	AddT	60143	2914		A4
-	BmdT	-	2913		C3
-	EGVV	-	2913		D3
-	HRPK	-	2912		A4
-	ITSC	-	2913		E3
-	ITSC	60143	2914		A4
-	ROSL	-	2912		E2
-	ROSL	-	2913		B3
-	SMBG	-	2912		A3
-	SmbT	-	2912		E2
Elgin O'Hare Expwy E					
-	HRPK	-	2911		E4
-	HRPK	-	2912		A4
El Greco St					
14900	LMNT	60439	3343	18W-15S	A2
S Elias Ct					
2900	CHCG	60608	3091	1W-2S	E3
Eliasek Ct					
100	SMWD	60107	2857	27W-11N	C4
Elinor Pl					
1400	EVTN	60201	2867	3W-11N	A3
Eliot Tr					
1300	ELGN	60120	2855		E3
Elizabeth Av					
8100	ODPK	60462	3346	10W-16S	C3
N Elizabeth Av					
20500	BFGV	60089	2754	15W-20N	E1
20500	VrnT	60069	2754	15W-20N	E1
S Elizabeth Av					
10	PLTN	60074	2806	19W-15N	C1
Elizabeth Ct					
10	OKPK	60302	3030	8W-0N	E3
100	BRLT	60103	2911		A3
200	BMDL	60157	2913		C7
900	WLNG	60090	2754	16W-16N	D6
1400	HFET	60195	2858	24W-12N	E2
4900	BmnT	60452	3426	6W-20S	A4
4900	BmnT	60477	3426	6W-20S	A4
4900	OKFT	60452	3426	6W-20S	A4
S Elizabeth Ct					
100	PLTN	60074	2806	19W-15N	C1
Elizabeth Dr					
-	BRLT	60103	2856	30W-9N	B7
-	BRLT	60107	2856	30W-9N	B7
-	BRLT	60120	2856	30W-9N	B7
-	HnrT	60120	2856	30W-9N	B7
10	EGvT	60005	2861	16W-9N	E6
900	HnrT	60107	2856	30W-9N	B7
2200	BDVW	60155	3087	11W-2S	D2
N Elizabeth Dr					
2000	ANHT	60004	2753	18W-16N	E7
2000	ANHT	60004	2806	20W-15N	A2
Elizabeth Ln					
-	PSPK	60464	3273	13W-14S	A7
400	DSPN	60018	2862	15W-10N	A5
1300	GNVW	60025	2811	8W-13N	A6
1400	GNVW	60025	2810	8W-13N	E6
20700	FftT	60423	3504	9W-25S	E7
20700	FKFT	60423	3504	9W-25S	E7
S Elizabeth Ln					
14300	HMGN	60441	3343	17W-17S	C5
Elizabeth Pl					
5300	RGMW	60008	2860	19W-12N	C1
Elizabeth St					
10	CTCY	46320	3430	4E-18S	C1
10	CTCY	60409	3430	4E-18S	C1
10	HMND	46320	3430	4E-18S	C1
800	BlmT	60411	3510	4E-25S	C7
800	ELGN	60120	2855		B7
1200	CRTE	60417	3685	0W-29S	B1
10200	PvsT	60154	3087	12W-1S	A1
10200	PvsT	60162	3087	12W-1S	A1
10200	WSTR	60154	3087	12W-1S	A1
E Elizabeth St					
10	CTCY	46320	3430		C1
10	CTCY	60409	3430		C1
10	HMND	46320	3430		C1
N Elizabeth St					
10	CHCG	60607	3033	1W-0N	D4
800	CHCG	60622	3033	1W-1N	D2
S Elizabeth St					
4700	CHCG	60609	3151	1W-5S	E1
5500	CHCG	60636	3151	1W-6S	E4
9200	CHCG	60620	3213	1W-10S	E5
10000	CHCG	60643	3213	1W-11S	E7
11300	CHCG	60643	3277	1W-13S	E4
12200	CTPK	60643	3277	1W-14S	E6

Chicago & Cook County Street Index

STREET Block	City	ZIP	Map#	CGS	Grid
S Elizabeth St					
12200	CTPK	60827	3277	1W-15S	E7
W Elizabeth St					
8200	NLES	60714	2864	10W-11N	A3
Elizabeth Tr					
300	OKPK	60302	3030	8W-0N	E3
Elk Blvd					
300	DSPN	60016	2863	13W-11N	A3
Elk Dr					
17300	ODPK	60467	3423	13W-20S	A5
N Elk Grove Av					
1400	CHCG	60622	3033	2W-1N	C1
E Elk Grove Blvd					
200	EGVV	60007	2914		E1
300	EGVV	60007	2915		A1
W Elk Grove Blvd					
500	EGvT	60007	2860	18W-9N	D7
500	EGVV	60007	2860	18W-9N	D7
500	EGVV	60007	2914		E1
S Elk Grove Rd					
1900	ANHT	60005	2860	18W-11N	E2
1900	ANHT	60007	2860	18W-11N	E3
1900	RGMW	60005	2860	18W-11N	E3
1900	RGMW	60008	2860	18W-11N	E3
Elle Ct					
-	SBTN	60010	2803	27W-15N	A1
Ellen Ct					
5500	BmnT	60477	3425	6W-19S	D2
5500	OKFT	60452	3425	6W-19S	D2
Ellen Dr					
10	BlmT	60411	3510	3E-25S	A7
900	BFGV	60089	2754	16W-17N	C4
900	WhlT	60004	2754	16W-17N	C4
N Ellen Dr					
3100	ANHT	60004	2754	16W-17N	C5
3100	WhlT	60004	2754	16W-17N	C4
3200	BFGV	60089	2754	16W-17N	C4
Ellen Ln					
20700	FftT	60423	3504	9W-25S	E7
20700	FKFT	60423	3504	9W-25S	E7
W Ellen St					
1700	CHCG	60622	3033	2W-1N	C1
Ellendale Dr					
1700	NHBK	60062	2756	10W-16N	E7
Ellendale Rd					
10	DRFD	60015	2757	10W-20N	B2
10	NfdT	60062	2757	10W-20N	B2
Ellington Av					
3800	PvsT	60558	3086		E7
3800	WNSP	60558	3086		E7
5100	WNSP	60558	3146		E2
Ellington Dr					
10	SMBG	60193	2858	25W-10N	B5
10	SMBG	60194	2858	25W-10N	C5
Ellinwood Av					
1400	DSPN	60016	2863	13W-11N	A4
Elliot Ct					
1000	OMFD	60461	3506	4W-25S	D7
Elliot Dr					
1000	MNSR	46321	3510		E1
Elliot Ln					
3000	HMWD	60430	3507	3W-22S	A1
Elliott Av					
1200	PKRG	60068	2863	11W-10N	C5
S Elliott Av					
8100	CHCG	60617	3215	2E-9S	C2
Elliott Ct					
1700	PKRG	60068	2863	11W-10N	C4
Elliott Dr					
5200	HFET	60192	2856	30W-12N	C1
Elliott St					
500	BCHR	60401	3864	1W-36S	B2
1700	PKRG	60068	2863	11W-10N	C4
Ellis Av					
700	FDHT	60411	3509	1E-25S	A6
1400	FDHT	60411	3597	1E-25S	A1
14200	DLTN	60419	3351	1E-17S	A5
15400	SHLD	60473	3351	1E-18S	A7
16100	SHLD	60473	3429	1E-18S	A1
S Ellis Av					
200	GNWD	60425	3509	1E-23S	A3
2700	CHCG	60616	3092	0E-2S	D3
3500	CHCG	60653	3092	1E-3S	E5
4600	CHCG	60615	3092	1E-4S	E7
4700	CHCG	60615	3152	1E-5S	E1
5400	CHCG	60637	3152	1E-6S	E4
7100	CHCG	60619	3152	1E-8S	E7
7800	CHCG	60619	3214	1E-9S	E3
9700	CHCG	60628	3215	1E-11S	A6
11100	CHCG	60628	3278	0E-13S	E3
13000	CHCG	60628	3279	1E-14S	A7
13000	CHCG	60827	3279	1E-15S	A7
13100	CHCG	60827	3351	1E-15S	A1
Ellis Ct					
900	SHLD	60473	3429	1E-19S	A2
N Ellis St					
1000	BNVL	60106	2915		D3
1200	EGVV	60007	2915		D4
W Ellis St					
800	PLTN	60067	2805	22W-15N	C2
800	PltT	60067	2805	22W-15N	C2
Ellisville Ln					
1400	SMBG	60193	2858	25W-10N	B6
Ellridge Cir					
400	HDPK	60035	2757	9W-20N	C1
Elm Av					
-	ELGN	60120	2855		D6
200	NHLK	60164	3028		D2
1700	NHBK	60062	2757	9W-17N	B6
2000	HRPK	60133	2911		C3
2400	EVTN	60201	2812	3W-12N	E7
2400	EVTN	60201	2866	3W-12N	D1
3100	BKFD	60513	3087	11W-3S	E4
4300	LYNS	60534	3088	9W-4S	C7
4500	BKFD	60513	3147	11W-4S	E1
4600	MCCK	60525	3147	11W-4S	E1
8700	LynT	60480	3208		D5
8700	WLSP	60480	3208		D5
9200	MKNA	60448	3504	11W-23S	A3
E Elm Av					
10	LGNG	60525	3087	12W-4S	C7
10	ROSL	60172	2913		A5
700	BKFD	60513	3087	12W-4S	C7
W Elm Av					
10	LGNG	60525	3087	12W-4S	B7
10	ROSL	60172	2913		A5
1400	WNSP	60558	3087	13W-4S	A7
5800	BKLY	60163	3028		C5
5800	HLSD	60162	3028		C5
Elm Cir					
-	GLF	60029	2865	8W-12N	A1
9000	HYHL	60457	3209	11W-10S	E4
E Elm Cir					
700	ITSC	60143	2914		C5
Elm Ct					
-	BmnT	60426	3426	5W-19S	B1
10	CTCY	60409	3429	2E-18S	D1
100	ROSL	60172	2913		A5
200	NfdT	60062	2757	9W-18N	B3
1200	GNVW	60025	2810	9W-13N	D6
1900	HRPK	60133	2911		C3
3600	FSMR	60422	3506	4W-22S	D2
13600	LMNT	60439	3343	17W-15S	B2
16500	SHLD	60473	3428	0E-19S	E2
E Elm Ct					
300	GLNC	60022	2758	6W-18N	C3
S Elm Ct					
10	PSHT	60463	3346	9W-15S	D1
W Elm Ct					
300	GLNC	60022	2758	6W-18N	C3
700	ITSC	60143	2914		C5
900	PLTN	60067	2805	21W-14N	C3
Elm Dr					
-	BmnT	60426	3426	5W-19S	B1
-	CCHL	60478	3506	5W-23S	C2
300	WLNG	60090	2755	13W-17N	D5
1200	SMBG	60194	2858	25W-10N	C4
8600	MaiT	60016	2863	10W-11N	E2
8600	MaiT	60016	2864	10W-11N	A2
12000	BLID	60406	3277	3W-14S	A5
16900	HLCT	60429	3426	4W-20S	E5
W Elm Dr					
7900	NRDG	60706	2918	10W-5N	B7
Elm Ln					
10	HGKN	60525	3147	12W-7S	C5
10	LynT	60458	3209	11W-8S	E1
100	SMWD	60107	2857	28W-10N	A6
6000	MTSN	60443	3505	7W-24S	C6
N Elm Ln					
10	GNWD	60425	3508	0E-22S	E2
2700	ANHT	60004	2754	17W-17N	B6
S Elm Ln					
10	GNWD	60425	3508	0E-22S	E2
Elm Pl					
-	ODHL	60477	3424	11W-19S	A2
800	GLNC	60022	2758	7W-17N	C4
Elm Rd					
100	BRTN	60010	2750	25W-20N	E2
100	BRTN	60010	2751	25W-20N	A1
2000	HMWD	60430	3427	2W-21S	D6
3600	PKFT	60466	3594	4W-26S	E3
3600	RNPK	60471	3594	4W-26S	E3
Elm St					
-	FNPK	60131	2973	11W-4N	E4
-	RVGV	60171	2973	11W-4N	E4
10	CTSD	60525	3147	12W-6S	C4
10	GNVW	60025	2864	9W-12N	D1
10	MNGV	60053	2864	9W-12N	D2
10	MPPT	60056	2807	15W-15N	E3
10	PKFT	60466	3595	3W-26S	C3
10	PKRG	60068	2864	10W-9N	A7
10	PTHT	60056	2807	15W-15N	E3
10	PTHT	60070	2807	15W-15N	E2
10	ROSL	60172	2913		A5
200	WLSP	60480	3209	12W-9S	D3
400	DRFD	60015	2756	11W-20N	E1
400	DYR	46311	3598		D2
500	WNKA	60093	2812	4W-15N	B2
600	BCHR	60401	3864	0W-36S	C2
700	FSMR	60422	3506	4W-22S	E2
700	FSMR	60429	3506	4W-22S	E2
700	HLCT	60429	3506	4W-22S	E2
800	GNVW	60025	2810	9W-13N	D6
800	WNSP	60558	3146		E1
1100	WNKA	60093	2811	5W-15N	E2
1300	PKRG	60068	2863	11W-9N	D7
4800	SKOK	60076	2865	6W-10N	E4
4900	SKOK	60077	2865	6W-10N	D4
6000	MNGV	60053	2865	7W-10N	B4
6400	OKFT	60452	3347	8W-18S	B6
12500	BLID	60406	3277	3W-15S	B7
13500	ODPK	60462	3345	11W-16S	E3
13500	OrlT	60462	3345	11W-15S	E2
13500	PlsT	60462	3345	11W-15S	E2
15400	DLTN	60419	3350	0E-18S	E7
15400	SHLD	60473	3350	0E-18S	E7
16600	SHLD	60473	3428	0E-19S	E3
E Elm St					
10	CHCG	60610	3034	0E-1N	C1
10	CHCG	60611	3034	0E-1N	C1
N Elm St					
10	HNDL	60521	3146		B1
10	PvsT	60162	3028		D6
200	HLSD	60162	3028		D5
200	MPPT	60056	2808	15W-13N	A6
300	HNDL	60521	3086		B7
700	ITSC	60143	2914		C5
1300	PLTN	60067	2753	20W-17N	A4
1500	PLTN	60074	2753	20W-17N	A4
1500	PltT	60067	2753	20W-17N	A4
1500	PltT	60074	2753	20W-17N	A4
2400	RVGV	60171	2973	11W-3N	E5
2600	FNPK	60131	2973	11W-3N	E5
2600	FNPK	60171	2973	11W-3N	E5
S Elm St					
10	MPPT	60056	2808	15W-12N	A7
10	PLTN	60067	2805	21W-14N	C3
100	NHLK	60164	3028		D1
100	PltT	60067	2805	21W-15N	C2
300	ITSC	60143	2914		C7
500	ADSN	60143	2914		C7
600	MPPT	60056	2862	15W-12N	A2
900	DSPN	60016	2862	15W-11N	A3
900	DSPN	60056	2862	15W-11N	A3
1600	DSPN	60018	2863	13W-9N	A6
5500	HNDL	60521	3146		B4
5800	BRRG	60521	3146		B4
6300	WLBK	60527	3146		B6
7200	BRRG	60527	3146		B7
7200	BRRG	60527	3208		B1
12300	PSPK	60464	3273	11W-14S	E6
13900	HMGN	60441	3342	19W-16S	E4
14100	HmrT	60441	3342	19W-16S	E4
W Elm St					
10	CHCG	60611	3034	0W-1N	B2
100	ANHT	60004	2807	18W-14N	A3
100	CHCG	60610	3034	0W-1N	B2
500	ANHT	60004	2806	18W-14N	E3
1000	PLTN	60067	2752	22W-17N	B5
Elm Ter					
4600	SKOK	60076	2866	5W-10N	A4
9600	MaiT	60016	2863	11W-12N	D2
Elma Av					
600	ELGN	60120	2801		B7
900	ELGN	60120	2855		C1
N Elma Av					
1000	ELGN	60120	2801		D7
Elm Cir Dr					
5000	OKLN	60453	3211	6W-11S	E7
Elm Cir Dr					
9900	OKLN	60453	3212	6W-11S	A7
Elmcrest Av					
-	EMHT	60126	2972		A7
-	EMHT	60126	3028		A1
Elmdale Av					
1600	GNVW	60025	2810	10W-14N	A4
1600	NfdT	60025	2810	10W-14N	A4
2400	BmnT	60426	3427	3W-19S	B2
W Elmdale Av					
1200	CHCG	60660	2921	1W-7N	C3
Elmdale Rd					
600	MaiT	60025	2810	10W-13N	A7
600	NfdT	60025	2810	10W-13N	A7
1000	GNVW	60025	2810	10W-13N	A6
Elm Gate Dr					
300	GNVW	60025	2810	9W-13N	C7
W Elmgrove Dr					
7700	EDPK	60707	2974	9W-3N	C4
7900	RVGV	60171	2974	9W-3N	B4
E Elmhurst Av					
200	EMHT	60126	3028		A1
N Elmhurst Av					
10	MPPT	60056	2807	15W-14N	E5
S Elmhurst Av					
100	MPPT	60056	2807	15W-12N	E7
200	MPPT	60056	2861	16W-12N	E1
Elmhurst Ln					
1300	SMBG	60194	2858	25W-11N	C4
Elmhurst Rd					
600	MPPT	60056	2861	16W-11N	E3
700	DSPN	60018	2861	16W-9N	E7
700	EGvT	60007	2861	15W-9N	E7
700	EGvT	60018	2861	16W-9N	E7
700	EGVV	60007	2861	15W-9N	E7
700	EGVV	60018	2861	15W-9N	E7
900	DSPN	60016	2861	16W-10N	E5
900	DSPN	60056	2861	16W-10N	E5
900	EGvT	60007	2915		E1
900	EGvT	60018	2915		E1
900	EGVV	60007	2915		E2
900	EGVV	60018	2915		E2
1700	CHCG	60007	2915		E2
1700	MPPT	60018	2861	16W-9N	E6
Elmhurst Rd CO-8					
2300	EGvT	60007	2915		E3
2300	EGVV	60007	2915		E3
Elmhurst Rd SR-83					
600	MPPT	60056	2861	16W-11N	E3
900	DSPN	60016	2861	16W-10N	E5
900	DSPN	60056	2861	16W-10N	E5
N Elmhurst Rd					
10	MPPT	60070	2808	15W-14N	A3
900	MPPT	60056	2808	15W-14N	A4
900	PTHT	60070	2755	15W-16N	A7
900	WLNG	60090	2755	15W-16N	A7
1000	PTHT	60090	2755	15W-16N	A7
1100	PTHT	60056	2808	15W-14N	A4
1100	PTHT	60070	2808	15W-14N	A4
N Elmhurst Rd SR-83					
10	MPPT	60070	2808	15W-14N	A3
10	PTHT	60070	2808	15W-15N	A1
10	WLNG	60090	2755	15W-18N	A4
900	MPPT	60056	2808	15W-14N	A4
900	PTHT	60056	2755	15W-16N	A7
1000	PTHT	60090	2755	15W-16N	A7
1100	PTHT	60056	2808	15W-14N	A4
S Elmhurst Rd					
10	MPPT	60056	2808	15W-14N	A4
10	MPPT	60070	2808	15W-14N	A4
10	PTHT	60056	2808	15W-14N	A4
10	PTHT	60070	2808	15W-14N	A4
10	WLNG	60090	2755	15W-17N	A5
400	MPPT	60056	2861	15W-12N	E2
800	DSPN	60016	2861	16W-10N	E4
800	DSPN	60056	2861	16W-10N	E4
900	PTHT	60090	2755	15W-17N	A6
1400	DSPN	60018	2861	16W-9N	E6
1400	MPPT	60018	2861	16W-9N	E6
S Elmhurst Rd SR-83					
10	MPPT	60056	2808	15W-14N	A4
10	MPPT	60070	2808	15W-14N	A4
10	PTHT	60056	2808	15W-14N	A4
10	PTHT	60070	2808	15W-14N	A4
10	WLNG	60090	2755	15W-17N	A5
400	MPPT	60056	2861	15W-12N	E2
800	DSPN	60016	2861	16W-10N	E4
900	DSPN	60016	2861	16W-11N	E3
900	PTHT	60090	2755	15W-17N	A6
1400	DSPN	60018	2861	16W-9N	E6
1400	MPPT	60018	2861	16W-9N	E6
Elmhurst St					
100	AddT	60191	2915		B6
100	WDDL	60191	2915		B6
1100	BNVL	60106	2915		D6
Elmira Av					
2100	DSPN	60018	2862	14W-9N	D7
2200	DSPN	60018	2916		D1
Elm Ln Dr					
16800	TYPK	60477	3425	8W-20S	A4
Elmont Ct					
300	SMBG	60193	2859	22W-10N	C6
Elmore Av					
-	MNSR	46321	3430		E7
Elmore Ct					
18100	TYPK	60477	3424	10W-21S	B7
Elmore St					
10	PKRG	60068	2864	9W-9N	B7
10	PKRG	60068	2918	9W-8N	B1
N Elmore St					
8000	NLES	60068	2864	9W-10N	B6
8000	PKRG	60068	2864	9W-10N	B6
8200	MaiT	60714	2864	9W-10N	B5
8200	NLES	60714	2864	9W-10N	B4
El Morro Ct					
5900	OKFT	60452	3347	7W-18S	C6
El Morro Ln					
5900	OKFT	60452	3347	7W-18S	C6
Elm Ridge Dr					
2200	NHBK	60062	2809	10W-15N	E1
2200	NHBK	60062	2810	10W-16N	A1
Elmridge Dr					
900	GLNC	60022	2758	7W-18N	C4
Elm Ridge Rd					
400	CPVL	60110	2748		A7
W Elmscourt Ln					
10	CteT	60417	3685	1W-32S	B7
1200	CteT	60417	3684	2W-32S	D7
S Elm Tree Ln					
100	EMHT	60126	3028		B3
Elmwood Av					
10	LGPK	60525	3087	12W-3S	B6
100	CHCG	60645	2867	2W-9N	B6
400	EVTN	60202	2867	2W-10N	B5
500	WLMT	60091	2813	3W-14N	A5
1000	GNVW	60025	2811	7W-14N	A5
Elmwood Av					
1200	BRWN	60402	3031	8W-1S	A7
1200	EVTN	60201	2867	2W-10N	B4
1200	OKPK	60304	3031	8W-1S	A7
1500	BRWN	60402	3089	8W-2S	A3
2300	WLMT	60091	2812	5W-14N	B5
3500	WLMT	60091	2811	6W-14N	D5
3900	SKNY	60402	3089	8W-4S	A7
8000	SKOK	60077	2865	6W-10N	E5
N Elmwood Av					
10	PLTN	60074	2806	20W-16N	B1
100	OKPK	60302	3031	8W-0N	A3
300	WDDL	60191	2915		B7
400	AddT	60191	2915		B7
1200	PLTN	60074	2753	20W-17N	B5
S Elmwood Av					
10	PLTN	60074	2806	20W-15N	B1
500	OKPK	60302	3031	8W-0S	A5
500	OKPK	60304	3031	8W-0S	A5
1100	BRWN	60402	3031	8W-0S	A7
Elmwood Av N					
1000	OKPK	60302	3031	8W-1N	A1
1200	CHCG	60302	3031	8W-2N	A1
1200	CHCG	60707	3031	8W-2N	A1
E Elmwood Cir					
1900	ANHT	60004	2807	16W-16N	C1
Elmwood Ct					
10	IHPK	60525	3146		E5
300	PltT	60067	2806	20W-13N	A7
Elmwood Dr					
-	DndT	60118	2801		B5
10	IHPK	60525	3146		D4
500	BFGV	60089	2754	17W-18N	B3
700	CPVL	60110	2748		A7
17800	TYPK	60477	3424	11W-21S	A6
E Elmwood Dr					
10	CHHT	60411	3508	1W-23S	A4
W Elmwood Dr					
100	CHHT	60411	3507	1W-23S	E4
100	CHHT	60411	3508	0W-23S	B4
9100	MaiT	60016	2863	11W-12N	D1
9100	NLES	60714	2863	11W-12N	D1
Elmwood Ln					
-	MONE	60449	3683	6W-31S	A5
-	MTSN	60443	3506	5W-25S	B7
200	SMBG	60193	2859	21W-10N	E6
700	WLNG	60090	2754	15W-18N	E2
900	EGVV	60007	2915		A2
N Elmwood Ln					
200	PltT	60067	2806	20W-13N	A7
200	SMBG	60067	2806	21W-12N	A7
S Elmwood Ln					
200	BRLT	60103	2910		C3
300	PltT	60067	2806	20W-13N	A7
300	SMBG	60067	2806	20W-13N	A7
W Elmwood Ln					
1000	BRLT	60103	2910		C3
Elmwood Pl					
200	HNDL	60521	3146		B3
Elmwood Rd					
5000	OKFT	60452	3426	6W-20S	A4
5100	OKFT	60452	3425	6W-20S	E4
Elmwood Sq					
10	IHPK	60525	3146		D5
N Elroy Av					
100	BRLT	60103	2911		A2
S Elroy Av					
100	BRLT	60103	2911		A3
S Elsdon Av					
5400	CHCG	60632	3150	4W-5S	D2
Elsie Dr					
500	MLPK	60160	3029	10W-1N	E1
500	MLPK	60160	3030	10W-1N	A1
N Elston Av					
800	CHCG	60622	3033	1W-1N	D1
1600	CHCG	60622	2977	1W-2N	D7
1900	CHCG	60614	2977	1W-2N	C6
2400	CHCG	60647	2977	2W-3N	B5
2700	CHCG	60618	2977	1W-2N	D7
3100	CHCG	60618	2976	3W-4N	E3
4300	CHCG	60630	2976	5W-5N	B3
4300	CHCG	60641	2976	5W-5N	B1
4400	CHCG	60630	2920	5W-5N	A7
4900	CHCG	60630	2919	5W-6N	E6
5600	CHCG	60646	2919	7W-7N	B4
Elsworth Dr					
-	CHCG	60615	3152	0E-5S	D2
-	CHCG	60637	3152	0E-6S	D2
El Vista Av					
14700	OKFT	60452	3347	6W-17S	D6
Elwood St					
-	LYWD	60411	3510	4E-24S	C6
Ely Ct					
1300	WLNG	60090	2754	16W-18N	E2
Elysees Ct					
3400	HLCT	60429	3426	4W-21S	E7
Elysian Dr					
10	TYPK	60477	3505	8W-23S	B3
Embassy Ln					
1400	FDHT	60411	3509	1E-25S	B6
9000	MaiT	60016	2863	11W-11N	D3
9000	PKRG	60016	2863	11W-11N	D3
9000	PKRG	60068	2863	11W-11N	D3
Embassy Row					
2900	FSMR	60422	3507	3W-22S	A2
S Embers Ln					
2300	ANHT	60005	2861	17W-11N	B3
Emelia Ct					
2600	FSMR	60422	3507	3W-23S	B3
Emelia St					
100	CHHT	60411	3507	1W-24S	E4
100	CHHT	60411	3508	1W-24S	A4
Emerald Av					
400	CHHT	60411	3508	0W-24S	B5
3300	STGR	60475	3596	1W-27S	B5
3700	CteT	60417	3596	1W-28S	B7
3700	CteT	60475	3596	1W-28S	B7
3700	STGR	60417	3596	1W-28S	B7
10400	ODPK	60467	3423	13W-20S	B4
10400	OrlT	60467	3423	13W-20S	B4
15600	HRVY	60426	3428	0W-18S	B1
S Emerald Av					
2600	CHCG	60616	3092	0W-3S	A5
3400	CHCG	60609	3092	0W-4S	A7
5100	CHCG	60609	3152	0W-5S	A2
5500	CHCG	60621	3152	0W-6S	A3
8600	CHCG	60620	3214	0W-10S	A4
9400	CHCG	60628	3214	0W-11S	A6
10300	CHCG	60628	3278	0W-13S	A3
13600	RVDL	60827	3350	1W-15S	A2
14500	HRVY	60426	3350	1W-16S	A4
Emerald Ct					
-	PSHL	60465	3210	10W-11S	C7
8900	HYHL	60457	3210	10W-10S	A5
W Emerald Ct					
7700	FftT	60423	3504	9W-24S	E5
Emerald Dr					
10	SMWD	60107	2856	29W-10N	D5
1000	SMBG	60173	2859	22W-11N	D4
1200	LMNT	60439	3342	19W-15S	D1
S Emerald Dr					
6400	CHCG	60621	3152	1W-7S	A5
Emerald Ln					
300	ALGN	60102	2748		B2
Emerald Wy					
-	MTSN	60443	3506	5W-24S	C5
N Emerald Bay					
1700	PLTN	60074	2753	18W-18N	D4
W Emerald Wy St N					
4300	ALSP	60803	3276	5W-14S	B7
W Emerald Wy St S					
4300	ALSP	60803	3276	5W-14S	B7
Emerson Av					
-	SRPK	60176	2973	12W-4N	B2
2000	LydT	60164	2973	12W-2N	C7
2000	MLPK	60160	2973	12W-2N	C7
2300	FNPK	60131	2973	12W-2N	C7
3100	HLCT	60429	3427	3W-20S	A5
3700	RGMW	60008	2806	20W-14N	A4
4800	PltT	60008	2805	21W-14N	E4
4800	RGMW	60008	2805	21W-14N	D4
4900	RGMW	60067	2805	21W-14N	D4
5100	PLTN	60008	2805	21W-14N	D4
5100	PLTN	60067	2805	21W-14N	D4
W Emerson Av					
10	PLTN	60008	2805	21W-14N	D4
10	PLTN	60067	2805	21W-14N	D4
10	RGMW	60008	2805	21W-14N	D4
10	RGMW	60067	2805	21W-14N	D4
Emerson Ct					
4400	SRPK	60176	2973	12W-5N	B1
S Emerson Ct					
900	MPPT	60056	2862	15W-11N	A2
Emerson Dr					
-	ODPK	60467	3423	11W-19S	E2
10	SMBG	60193	2858	25W-10N	B5
10	SMBG	60194	2858	25W-10N	A5
3800	SRPK	60176	2973	12W-4N	B2
Emerson St					
-	ANHT	60005	2861	18W-12N	A1
-	EVTN	60203	2866	3W-11N	E2
-	SKOK	60076	2865	6W-11N	E2
-	SKOK	60201	2866	3W-11N	E2
-	SKOK	60203	2866	3W-11N	E2
600	EVTN	60201	2867	3W-11N	A2
1800	EVTN	60201	2866	3W-11N	E2
3300	FNPK	60131	2973	12W-4N	B3
3600	SRPK	60176	2973	12W-4N	B3
3900	SKOK	60076	2866	5W-11N	B2
5000	SKOK	60077	2865	6W-11N	E2
5600	MNGV	60053	2865	7W-11N	C2
7200	MNGV	60053	2864	9W-11N	D2
E Emerson St					
100	ANHT	60005	2861	18W-12N	A1
2500	DSPN	60016	2863	11W-11N	C2
2500	MaiT	60016	2863	11W-11N	C2
N Emerson St					
10	MPPT	60056	2808	15W-13N	A6
6000	RSMT	60018	2917	12W-7N	B4
S Emerson St					
10	MPPT	60056	2808	15W-12N	A7
200	MPPT	60056	2862	15W-12N	A1
W Emerson St					
10	ANHT	60005	2861	18W-12N	A1
8600	MaiT	60016	2864	10W-11N	A2
8600	NLES	60016	2864	10W-11N	A2
8600	NLES	60714	2864	10W-11N	A2
8700	NLES	60714	2863	10W-11N	E2
8900	MaiT	60016	2863	11W-11N	D2
9300	DSPN	60016	2863	11W-11N	D2
Emery Ln					
3100	RBBN	60472	3348	4W-16S	D4
Emil Ct					
100	BRLT	60103	2911		A3
Emil St					
700	LMNT	60439	3270		E5
Emile Ln					
10400	FftT	60448	3423	13W-22S	B7
10400	ODPK	60448	3423	13W-22S	B7
10400	ODPK	60467	3423	13W-22S	B7
10400	ODPK	60477	3423	13W-22S	B7
10400	OrlT	60477	3423	13W-22S	B7
Emily Ct					
10	LMNT	60439	3342	19W-15S	C2
17900	TYPK	60477	3424	10W-21S	C6
18600	HLCT	60429	3506	4W-22S	E1
Emily Ln					
10	HmrT	60439	3342	19W-15S	C2
10	HmrT	60441	3342	19W-15S	C2
10	LMNT	60439	3342	19W-15S	C2
E Emma Ct					
10	PLTN	60067	2805	20W-14N	E3
Emmerson Av					
200	ITSC	60143	2914		D7
400	ITSC	60191	2914		D7
400	WDDL	60191	2914		D7
E Emmerson Ln					
1400	MPPT	60056	2808	14W-13N	C7
1500	DSPN	60016	2808	14W-13N	C7
1500	MPPT	60016	2808	14W-13N	C7
N Emmett St					
2600	CHCG	60647	2976	4W-3N	D5
Emory Rd					
-	HFET	60195	2804	24W-12N	E7
Empire Av					
14600	DLTN	60419	3351	0E-17S	A5
Empress Dr					
-	HMND	46320	3280		D2
N Emroy Av					
200	AddT	60126	2972		A5
200	EMHT	60126	3028		A1
600	EMHT	60126	2972		A6
Enclave Ct					
10	BRRG	60527	3208		B5
Enclave Dr					
9000	BRRG	60527	3208		B5
Enclave Ln					
8000	TYPK	60477	3504	10W-23S	C3
W End Av					
-	BlmT	60411	3508	0W-24S	C6
700	CHHT	60411	3508	0W-24S	C6
W End Ln					
13100	CTWD	60445	3347	6W-15S	D1
W End Rd					
600	ROSL	60172	2912		E6
Endicott Cir					
1800	CPVL	60110	2801		D1
Endicott Ct					
11200	ODPK	60467	3344	14W-16S	E4

STREET Block	City	ZIP	Map#	CGS	Grid
Enfield Av					
3600	SKOK	60076	2866	5W-11N	B3
4700	SKOK	60076	2865	5W-11N	E3
5200	SKOK	60077	2865	6W-11N	D3
7100	MNGV	60053	2864	8W-11N	D3
Enfield Dr					
800	NHBK	60062	2810	8W-16N	D1
Engel Blvd					
400	PKRG	60068	2917	11W-8N	E2
W Enger Ln					
8100	RVGV	60171	2974	10W-3N	B4
Engle Ct					
800	DLTN	60419	3351	1E-17S	A5
W Engle Rd					
4800	ALSP	60803	3276	6W-15S	A7
Engle St					
400	DLTN	60419	3350	0E-16S	E4
Englewood Av					
10	BLWD	60104	3029	13W-0N	A4
400	HLSD	60162	3029	13W-0N	A5
W Englewood Av					
400	CHCG	60621	3152	0W-6S	A4
N Englewood Ct					
10	PltT	60067	2805	22W-15N	B2
Englewood Rd					
1000	HFET	60195	2858	24W-12N	C1
English Oak Ln					
100	HnrT	60120	2856	30W-10N	B5
100	SMWD	60120	2856	30W-10N	B5
Enid Ln					
100	NHFD	60093	2811	7W-15N	A3
N Enlund Dr					
2200	PLTN	60074	2753	19W-18N	C2
Ensenada Ct					
100	CPVL	60110	2748		B4
Ensenada Dr					
100	CPVL	60110	2748		B4
Enslen Dr					
2700	DYR	46311	3598		E4
Enterprise Ct					
700	CHHT	60411	3507	2W-24S	D6
Enterprise Dr					
-	GNVW	60025	2810	9W-14N	C4
-	PvsT	60154	3086		D3
600	OKBK	60523	3086		A2
2200	PvsT	60523	3086		D2
2200	WSTR	60154	3086		D2
2200	WSTR	60523	3086		D2
W Enterprise Dr					
300	DSPN	60018	2861	16W-10N	E6
300	MPPT	60018	2861	16W-10N	E6
300	MPPT	60056	2861	16W-10N	E6
Enterprise Rd					
600	CHHT	60411	3507	2W-24S	D6
Enterprise St					
400	ELGN	60120	2855		A2
Enterprise Park Av					
3000	SCHT	60411	3596	1W-27S	A4
3300	STGR	60475	3596	1W-27S	A4
Entertainment Dr					
-	HGKN	60525	3147	12W-6S	C5
Entrance Dr					
800	ANHT	60005	2807	17W-12N	B7
Entrance Rd					
-	ELGN	60123	2801		B6
S Entre Av					
13800	BNHM	60633	3352	3E-16S	B2
Epping Pl					
1700	SMBG	60194	2858	25W-10N	B5
Equestrian Dr					
500	WLNG	60090	2755	15W-16N	A7
700	PTHT	60070	2755	15W-16N	A7
Equestrian Tr					
15600	ODPK	60467	3345	13W-18S	A7
15600	ODPK	60467	3422	14W-19S	E1
15600	OrlT	60467	3345	13W-18S	A7
15600	OrlT	60467	3422	14W-19S	E1
Equestrian Wy					
10	LMNT	60439	3272	15W-14S	A6
Era Dr					
300	NHBK	60062	2756	12W-18N	C3
Eric Av					
200	MPPT	60056	2808	14W-13N	B6
Eric Cir					
-	ELGN	60120	2856	31W-10N	A6
Eric Ct					
300	MPPT	60056	2808	14W-13N	B6
N Eric Dr					
200	PLTN	60067	2752	21W-16N	D7
Ericka Dr					
2200	BDVW	60155	3087	11W-2S	D2
Erickson Ct					
-	ODPK	60467	3423	13W-21S	A7
S Erie Av					
5700	HMND	46320	3352		E7
6000	HMND	46320	3430		E1
Erie Ln					
1900	HFET	60195	2804	25W-12N	A7
1900	HFET	60195	2858	25W-12N	A1
Erie St					
-	BLWD	60104	3029	12W-0N	B3
10	CHCG	60644	3031	7W-0N	B3
10	MYWD	60153	3030	10W-0N	A3
10	OKPK	60302	3031	7W-0N	B3
1000	OKPK	60302	3030	8W-0N	D3
1100	RVFT	60305	3030	8W-0N	D3
4600	BLWD	60104	3028		E3
E Erie St					
10	CHCG	60610	3034	0E-0N	C3
10	CHCG	60611	3034	0E-0N	C3
N Erie St					
2400	RVGV	60171	2974	10W-3N	B5
W Erie St					
10	CHCG	60610	3034	0W-0N	A3
10	CHCG	60611	3034	0W-0N	B3
700	CHCG	60622	3034	0W-0N	A3
1200	CHCG	60622	3033	2W-0N	C3
1900	CHCG	60612	3033	3W-0N	A3
3900	CHCG	60624	3032	4W-0N	C3
4600	CHCG	60644	3032	5W-0N	A3
4700	CHCG	60644	3031	6W-0N	E3
5900	OKPK	60302	3031	7W-0N	B3
Erika Ct					
-	LYWD	60411	3510	3E-23S	A4
Erin Ct					
100	LMNT	60439	3270		C7
S Erin Ct					
14400	HMGN	60441	3343	16W-17S	E5
S Erin Dr					
13500	HMGN	60441	3343	17W-16S	C3
W Erin Dr					
8100	PSHL	60465	3210	10W-11S	C7
Erin Ln					
10	BRRG	60527	3146		C5
200	NHBK	60062	2758	7W-16N	A6

STREET Block	City	ZIP	Map#	CGS	Grid
Erin Ln					
9200	ODPK	60462	3423	11W-18S	D1
15600	ODPK	60462	3345	11W-18S	E7
Ernst Ct					
5200	WNSP	60558	3146		E3
5200	WNSP	60558	3147	13W-5S	A2
N Ernst Ct					
900	CHCG	60611	3034	0E-1N	C2
Ernst St					
2400	LydT	60164	2973	12W-3N	A6
3500	FNPK	60131	2973	12W-4N	A3
Eros Dr					
-	OMFD	60461	3507	3W-24S	A5
Escanaba Av					
200	BNHM	60633	3351	3E-17S	E4
200	CTCY	60409	3351	3E-17S	E4
18500	BlmT	60411	3429	3E-21S	E7
18500	LNSG	60411	3429	3E-21S	E7
18500	LNSG	60438	3429	3E-21S	E7
S Escanaba Av					
7800	CHCG	60617	3215	3E-9S	E2
7800	CHCG	60649	3215	3E-9S	E2
12600	CHCG	60633	3279	3E-14S	E7
13100	CHCG	60633	3351	3E-15S	E1
Eskin Dr					
1300	NfdT	60062	2756	12W-17N	B5
1300	NHBK	60062	2756	12W-17N	B6
S Esmond St					
10900	CHCG	60643	3277	2W-13S	C3
S Essex Av					
7500	CHCG	60649	3153	3E-8S	D7
7500	CHCG	60649	3215	3E-9S	D3
8900	CHCG	60617	3215	3E-10S	D5
Essex Ct					
-	GNVW	60025	2809	11W-13N	D6
-	NfdT	60025	2809	11W-13N	D6
-	SMBG	60193	2858	25W-10N	A5
10	SMBG	60194	2858	25W-10N	A5
700	HRPK	60133	2858	26W-9N	A7
2000	SMWD	60107	2910		E1
5700	HRPK	60133	2911		D5
Essex Dr					
-	HFET	60120	2802	31W-12N	A7
-	HFET	60120	2856	31W-12N	A1
2500	NHBK	60062	2810	10W-15N	A2
Essex Pl					
200	WLMT	60091	2811	5W-13N	E7
W Essex Pl					
900	ANHT	60004	2753	18W-16N	E6
Essex Rd					
10	EGVV	60007	2914		D2
10	KLWH	60043	2812	4W-14N	D4
10	WNKA	60093	2812	4W-14N	D4
5800	OKFT	60452	3347	7W-18S	C7
Essex St					
800	PTHT	60070	2808	15W-16N	A1
10500	WSTR	60154	3087	13W-2S	A3
Essex Wy					
4800	RGMW	60008	2860	19W-12N	C1
Essington Ct					
4900	HFET	60010	2751	24W-16N	B7
Essington Ln					
4900	HFET	60010	2751	24W-16N	B7
Estate Ct					
200	NHBK	60062	2756	12W-18N	A3
Estate Dr					
10	DRFD	60015	2756	10W-20N	E2
10	GLNC	60022	2758	6W-18N	D3
300	BFGV	60089	2754	17W-18N	B3
Estate Ln					
1400	GNVW	60025	2809	10W-14N	E5
W Estates Dr					
1700	MPPT	60056	2861	17W-12N	C1
Estelle Dr					
10000	RSMT	60018	2917	12W-7N	B3
Estes Av					
400	SMBG	60193	2912		D2
700	EGVV	60007	2915		D1
2000	DSPN	60018	2917	12W-8N	B1
4900	LNWD	60712	2919	6W-8N	E1
4900	SKOK	60077	2919	6W-8N	D1
W Estes Av					
1900	CHCG	60626	2921	2W-8N	B1
1900	CHCG	60645	2921	2W-8N	A1
2600	CHCG	60645	2920	3W-8N	E1
4400	LNWD	60712	2920	5W-8N	A1
4700	LNWD	60712	2919	5W-8N	E1
6200	CHCG	60646	2919	7W-8N	A1
6300	NLES	60714	2919	8W-8N	A1
7300	CHCG	60631	2918	9W-8N	C1
Estes Ct					
900	SMBG	60193	2912		D2
Esther Dr					
18000	ODPK	60467	3423	13W-21S	B7
Eternity					
-	MTSN	60443	3505	7W-25S	D7
Ethan Ln					
7200	GGnT	60449	3682	9W-32S	A7
7200	MonT	60449	3682	9W-32S	A7
W Ethans Glen Dr					
1500	PLTN	60067	2752	22W-17N	A5
1700	PLTN	60067	2751	23W-17N	E4
Ethel Ct					
10400	RSMT	60018	2917	13W-8N	A1
W Ethel St					
700	PTON	60468	3860	10W-37S	D4
Ethyl Ln					
9200	TYPK	60477	3423	11W-22S	E7
Eton Ct					
10	SBTN	60010	2804	24W-14N	C3
1200	BFGV	60089	2754	16W-17N	D5
Eton Dr					
1700	HFET	60120	2855		E1
1700	HnrT	60120	2855		E1
E Eton Dr					
1300	ANHT	60004	2754	17W-17N	C6
Eton on Oxford					
10	RGMW	60008	2805	22W-13N	B6
Etowah Av					
400	PTHT	60070	2807	16W-15N	E2
Euclid Av					
100	GLNC	60022	2758	5W-16N	E6
100	PKRG	60068	2918	10W-8N	B1
100	WNKA	60022	2758	5W-16N	E6
100	WNKA	60093	2758	5W-16N	E6
200	WNKA	60093	2811	5W-15N	E2
1200	BRWN	60402	3031	8W-1S	A7
1200	OKPK	60304	3031	8W-1S	A7
1200	OKPK	60402	3031	8W-1S	A7
1400	CHHT	60411	3508	1W-25S	A7
1500	CHHT	60411	3596	1W-26S	A2
2100	ANHT	60005	2806	19W-14N	B4
2100	RGMW	60005	2806	19W-14N	B4
2100	RGMW	60008	2806	19W-14N	B4
2200	BRWN	60402	3089	8W-2S	A3

STREET Block	City	ZIP	Map#	CGS	Grid
Euclid Av					
2500	SCHT	60411	3596	1W-26S	A2
3100	ANHT	60008	2806	19W-14N	B4
3200	BlmT	60411	3596	1W-27S	A4
3200	BlmT	60475	3596	1W-27S	A4
3200	STGR	60411	3596	1W-27S	A4
3200	STGR	60475	3596	1W-27S	A4
3800	SKNY	60402	3089	8W-3S	A6
6300	HMND	46324	3430		E2
7900	MNSR	46321	3430		E6
E Euclid Av					
-	MPPT	60056	2807	15W-14N	E4
-	MPPT	60070	2808	14W-14N	C4
10	ANHT	60004	2807	16W-14N	D4
10	MPPT	60056	2808	14W-14N	C4
10	PTHT	60056	2808	15W-14N	A4
10	PTHT	60070	2808	15W-14N	A4
2000	WhlT	60025	2808	13W-14N	E4
2400	ANHT	60056	2807	16W-14N	D4
N Euclid Av					
100	OKPK	60301	3031	8W-0N	A4
100	OKPK	60302	3031	8W-0N	A3
S Euclid Av					
100	OKPK	60302	3031	8W-0N	A5
500	OKPK	60304	3031	8W-0S	A5
600	EMHT	60126	3028		A7
600	YkTp	60126	3028		A7
1100	BRWN	60402	3031	8W-0S	A7
1100	OKPK	60402	3031	8W-0S	A7
6700	CHCG	60649	3153	2E-7S	C6
7600	CHCG	60649	3215	2E-9S	C2
9500	CHCG	60617	3215	2E-11S	C6
W Euclid Av					
-	ANHT	60056	2807	15W-14N	E4
-	MPPT	60056	2807	15W-14N	E4
-	MPPT	60070	2808	15W-14N	A4
-	PTHT	60056	2808	15W-14N	A4
-	PTHT	60070	2808	15W-14N	A4
-	RGMW	60005	2806	20W-14N	B4
10	ANHT	60004	2807	18W-14N	A4
10	PLTN	60008	2805	21W-14N	E4
10	PLTN	60067	2805	21W-14N	E4
10	RGMW	60008	2805	21W-14N	E4
10	RGMW	60067	2805	21W-14N	E4
500	ANHT	60004	2806	18W-14N	E4
700	ANHT	60005	2806	18W-14N	E4
1100	IVNS	60067	2805	22W-14N	A4
1600	RGMW	60008	2806	18W-14N	D4
Euclid Av N					
500	OKPK	60302	3031	8W-1N	A3
800	OKPK	60302	3030	8W-1N	E2
1200	CHCG	60302	3030	8W-2N	E1
1200	CHCG	60707	3030	8W-2N	E1
1200	OKPK	60707	3030	8W-2N	E1
Euclid Ct					
1100	RNPK	60471	3594	4W-26S	D2
Euclid Dr					
3000	SCHT	60411	3596	1W-27S	A4
Euclid Ln					
1000	RNPK	60471	3594	4W-26S	D2
S Euclid Pkwy					
7400	CHCG	60649	3153	2E-8S	C7
Euclid St					
800	CTCY	60409	3352	3E-17S	A6
Euclid Park Pl					
2700	EVTN	60201	2813	2W-13N	B7
N Eugene Av					
20500	BFGV	60069	2754	16W-20N	E1
20500	BFGV	60089	2754	16W-20N	E1
20500	VrnT	60069	2754	16W-20N	E1
W Eugenie St					
100	CHCG	60614	2978	0W-2N	A7
W Eugenie St SR-64					
100	CHCG	60614	2978	0W-2N	B7
E Eureka Av					
10	LMNT	60439	3270		D6
W Eureka Av					
10	LMNT	60439	3270		C6
Eustace St					
1500	ThtT	60438	3429	1E-21S	C7
W Eva Ln					
1000	MPPT	60056	2861	16W-11N	D3
W Evan Ter					
7800	FftT	60423	3504	9W-23S	D4
Evans Av					
14800	DLTN	60419	3351	0E-17S	A5
15900	SHLD	60473	3351	0E-18S	A7
16300	SHLD	60473	3428	0E-19S	E2
16600	SHLD	60473	3429	0E-19S	A2
S Evans Av					
-	CHCG	60628	3278	0E-15S	E7
4300	CHCG	60653	3092	0E-4S	E7
4600	CHCG	60615	3092	0E-4S	E7
5000	CHCG	60615	3152	0E-5S	E1
6100	CHCG	60637	3152	0E-7S	E5
7200	CHCG	60619	3152	0E-8S	E7
7500	CHCG	60619	3214	0E-9S	E2
13000	CHCG	60827	3278	0E-15S	E7
13400	CHCG	60827	3350	0E-15S	E1
Evans Ct					
300	SMWD	60107	2911		A1
700	DLTN	60419	3351	0E-17S	A5
1400	EGVV	60007	2914		A3
16500	SHLD	60473	3428	0E-19S	E2
17100	SHLD	60473	3429	0E-20S	A3
Evans Dr					
17000	SHLD	60473	3429	0E-20S	A3
Evans Rd					
1000	FSMR	60422	3507	2W-22S	C2
N Evanston Av					
10	ANHT	60004	2807	16W-14N	D5
200	MPPT	60056	2807	16W-13N	D6
S Evanston Av					
10	ANHT	60004	2807	16W-13N	D5
Evanston St					
800	HFET	60194	2859	23W-11N	A3
900	SMBG	60194	2859	23W-11N	A3
900	SMBG	60195	2859	23W-11N	A3
W Evelyn Ln					
8700	CHCG	60656	2917	10W-6N	E5
8700	CHCG	60656	2918	10W-6N	A5
Evelyn Rd					
300	RVSD	60546	3088	9W-2S	D4
Evenhouse Av					
-	RSMT	60018	2917	11W-7N	D4
Evening Song Ct					
1900	SMBG	60194	2858	26W-11N	A3
Everdon Dr					
16100	TYPK	60477	3424	9W-19S	D2
W Everell Av					
7200	CHCG	60631	2918	9W-7N	D3
Everett Av					
1000	DSPN	60018	2862	13W-9N	E6
1400	DSPN	60018	2863	12W-9N	A6
17000	SHLD	60473	3429	1E-20S	B4

STREET Block	City	ZIP	Map#	CGS	Grid
S Everett Av					
5400	CHCG	60615	3153	2E-6S	B2
5400	CHCG	60637	3153	2E-6S	B3
N Everett Dr					
300	PLTN	60074	2753	19W-16N	C7
Everett St					
2800	BLID	60406	3277	3W-15S	A7
Evergreen Av					
-	CHCG	60613	2921	1W-5N	D7
-	CHCG	60613	2977	1W-5N	D1
100	CteT	60475	3596	1W-28S	A7
200	MNSR	46321	3430		C7
1300	DSPN	60016	2862	13W-11N	E3
1300	DSPN	60016	2863	13W-11N	A3
1600	HRPK	60133	2911		D2
E Evergreen Av					
100	DSPN	60016	2862	14W-11N	C3
200	MPPT	60056	2808	15W-12N	B7
900	DSPN	60016	2808	15W-12N	B7
N Evergreen Av					
100	ANHT	60005	2807	17W-14N	A5
1900	ANHT	60004	2807	17W-16N	A1
2300	ANHT	60004	2754	17W-16N	A7
S Evergreen Av					
10	ANHT	60005	2807	17W-13N	A5
1300	ANHT	60005	2861	18W-12N	A1
W Evergreen Av					
-	MPPT	60056	2808	14W-13N	B5
200	MPPT	60056	2807	16W-12N	E7
400	CHCG	60610	3034	0W-1N	A1
800	CHCG	60610	3033	1W-1N	E1
1300	CHCG	60622	3033	1W-1N	D1
2700	CHCG	60622	3032	5W-1N	A1
3200	CHCG	60651	3032	4W-1N	D1
6800	PSHT	60463	3275	8W-15S	A7
Evergreen Cir					
-	BmnT	60426	3426	5W-19S	E5
10	EGVV	60007	2861	18W-10N	A5
1000	MTSN	60443	3506	4W-25S	E7
1000	OMFD	60443	3506	4W-25S	E7
1000	OMFD	60461	3506	4W-25S	E7
Evergreen Ct					
10	DRFD	60015	2757	10W-18N	A3
300	SMBG	60193	2858	23W-10N	E5
1300	GNVW	60025	2811	8W-13N	A5
W Evergreen Ct					
700	PLTN	60067	2805	21W-15N	C3
Evergreen Dr					
-	BmnT	60426	3426	5W-19S	B1
10	LMNT	60439	3270		C6
10	SMWD	60107	2856	29W-9N	D7
1400	PLTN	60074	2753	19W-17N	C5
7300	ODPK	60462	3346	9W-18S	E6
16300	TYPK	60477	3424	10W-19S	C2
E Evergreen Dr					
1200	PLTN	60074	2753	19W-17N	C5
W Evergreen Dr					
8100	FftT	60423	3504	10W-24S	C4
Evergreen Ln					
10	CPVL	60110	2748		C5
100	NtrT	60093	2812	5W-15N	A3
100	WNKA	60093	2812	5W-15N	A3
500	MNSR	46321	3430		D7
600	HFET	60195	2858	24W-12N	D1
700	BRLT	60103	2910		D6
700	SMBG	60195	2858	24W-12N	D1
1700	PKRG	60068	2863	11W-10N	D4
4000	NfdT	60062	2756	12W-16N	B7
Evergreen Pl					
10	LMNT	60439	3270		C6
600	BFGV	60089	2754	17W-18N	B3
Evergreen Rd					
1200	HMWD	60430	3428	1W-22S	A7
1300	HMWD	60430	3427	1W-22S	E7
Evergreen St					
10	EGVV	60007	2861	18W-10N	A6
200	BNVL	60106	2972		B2
Evergreen Ter					
1400	GNVW	60025	2811	8W-14N	A5
16800	HMGN	60441	3422	15W-20S	C4
N Evergreen Ter					
1900	ANHT	60004	2807	16W-16N	C1
Evers Av					
1200	HLSD	60154	3028		E7
1200	HLSD	60162	3028		E7
1200	WSTR	60154	3028		E7
1200	WSTR	60154	3086		E1
Evers St					
14500	DLTN	60419	3350	0E-16S	E4
15300	SHLD	60473	3350	0E-17S	E6
Evert Ct					
2100	NHBK	60062	2757	10W-16N	A7
Ewell Av					
-	BNHM	60633	3352	3E-16S	A3
Ewell Ct					
200	BRLT	60103	2911		A6
Ewing Av					
2000	EVTN	60201	2866	4W-12N	D1
2000	SKOK	60201	2866	4W-11N	D2
2600	EVTN	60201	2812	4W-13N	D7
2700	EVTN	60091	2812	4W-13N	D7
2700	WLMT	60091	2812	4W-13N	D7
8800	SKOK	60076	2866	4W-11N	D3
9400	SKOK	60203	2866	4W-11N	D2
S Ewing Av					
9200	CHCG	60617	3216	4E-10S	B5
10300	CHCG	60617	3280	4E-11S	B1
11800	CHCG	60633	3280	4E-13S	B5
S Ewing Av US-12					
9500	CHCG	60617	3216	4E-10S	B5
S Ewing Av US-20					
9500	CHCG	60617	3216	4E-10S	B5
S Ewing Av US-41					
9200	CHCG	60617	3216	4E-10S	B5
Excalibur Ct					
2000	LYWD	60411	3509	2E-24S	D5
Exchance Av					
-	BNHM	60633	3352	3E-16S	A3
Exchange Av					
200	BNHM	60633	3351	3E-17S	E5
200	CTCY	60409	3351	3E-17S	E5
9000	FNPK	60131	2973	11W-3N	D4
9000	RVGV	60171	2973	11W-3N	D4
16800	LNSG	60438	3429	3E-19S	E3
S Exchange Av					
7100	CHCG	60649	3153	3E-8S	D7
7900	CHCG	60617	3215	3E-9S	E2
7900	CHCG	60649	3215	3E-9S	E2
12700	CHCG	60633	3279	3E-14S	E7
13100	CHCG	60633	3351	3E-15S	E1
W Exchange Av					
800	CHCG	60609	3092	0W-4S	A6
900	CHCG	60609	3091	1W-4S	E6
Exchange Ct					
500	WLNG	60090	2755	14W-17N	B5

STREET Block	City	ZIP	Map#	CGS	Grid
E Exchange St					
10	CRTE	60417	3685	0E-29S	E2
10	CteT	60417	3685	0E-29S	E2
300	CRTE	60417	3686	1E-29S	B2
300	CteT	60417	3686	1E-29S	A2
2900	CteT	60417	3687	3E-30S	B3
3200	CteT	46311	3687	4E-30S	C3
3200	HnrT	46311	3687	4E-30S	C3
3200	SjnT	46311	3687	4E-30S	C3
W Exchange St					
10	CRTE	60417	3685	0W-29S	C2
10	CteT	60417	3685	0W-29S	C2
400	CteT	60417	3684	2W-29S	D2
800	CRTE	60417	3684	2W-29S	D2
2000	UYPK	60417	3684	2W-29S	D2
2300	UYPK	60466	3684	2W-29S	D2
Executive Cir					
1500	GNVW	60025	2809	10W-14N	E5
Executive Ct					
-	HFET	60195	2803	26W-13N	E5
-	SBTN	60195	2803	26W-13N	E5
10	SBTN	60010	2803	26W-13N	E5
W Executive Ct					
7900	CHCG	60634	2974	10W-5N	B1
7900	CHCG	60706	2974	10W-5N	B1
7900	NRDG	60706	2974	10W-5N	B1
Executive Dr					
10	PSHL	60465	3274	9W-13S	D3
500	DGvT	60527	3208		A2
500	WLBK	60527	3208		A2
Executive Ln					
1400	GNVW	60025	2809	10W-14N	E4
Executive Wy					
1000	DSPN	60018	2862	13W-10N	E6
Exeter Ct					
100	ROSL	60172	2912		C5
900	SMBG	60193	2912		E1
1300	WLNG	60090	2754	16W-18N	D2
1400	HFET	60010	2751	24W-16N	B7
13900	ODPK	60467	3344	14W-16S	E3
Exeter Dr					
11200	ODPK	60467	3344	14W-16S	E4
Exeter Ln					
-	NfdT	60062	2756	12W-18N	A2
4300	NHBK	60062	2756	12W-18N	A2
Exeter Rd					
-	MNSR	46321	3510		C4
Exeter on Oxford					
10	RGMW	60008	2805	22W-13N	B6
Exit Rd					
-	ELGN	60123	2801		A7
N Exmoor Av					
500	BRTN	60010	2750	26W-20N	E1
Exmoor Ct					
100	DRFD	60015	2757	10W-20N	A2
Exmoor Dr					
300	SMWD	60107	2857	28W-11N	A4
Exmoor Rd					
500	EGVV	60007	2914		C2
500	KLWH	60043	2812	4W-14N	C4
600	WNKA	60093	2812	4W-14N	C4
700	OMFD	60461	3506	4W-25S	D6
N Exmoore Av					
-	BRTN	60010	2750	26W-20N	E1
Exmore Dr					
1400	SMBG	60194	2858	25W-10N	B5
W Exner Ct					
800	PLTN	60067	2805	22W-15N	C3
Express Center Dr					
-	CHCG	60666	2917	12W-5N	A7
-	CHCG	60666	2973	13W-5N	A1
-	SRPK	60176	2973	13W-5N	A1
Expressway Dr					
700	ITSC	60143	2914		B5
Eynsford Dr					
8200	ODPK	60462	3346	10W-17S	B4

F

STREET Block	City	ZIP	Map#	CGS	Grid
W F St					
-	MYWD	60141	3088	10W-1S	A1
-	MYWD	60153	3088	10W-1S	A1
-	PvsT	60141	3088	10W-1S	A1
Fabish Ct					
2400	SMBG	60193	2857	26W-10N	E6
Fagan St					
100	DYR	46311	3598		D2
S Fair Av					
200	EMHT	60126	3028		B3
Fair Ln					
800	NHBK	60062	2757	10W-17N	A4
Fairbank Rd					
100	RVSD	60546	3088	10W-4S	B6
Fairbanks Ct					
600	SMBG	60194	2859	22W-10N	C4
N Fairbanks Ct					
500	CHCG	60611	3034	0E-0N	C3
Fairbanks Pl					
200	MNSR	46321	3430		D5
Faircroft Rd					
100	BRLT	60103	2909		C3
Fair Elms Av					
4700	WNSP	60558	3146		D2
7100	BRRG	60527	3146		D7
7100	BRRG	60527	3208		D1
7100	IHPK	60525	3146		D7
Fairfax Av					
3800	RGMW	60008	2806	20W-14N	A5
E Fairfax Av					
10	PltT	60008	2805	20W-14N	E5
10	PltT	60067	2805	20W-14N	E5
10	RGMW	60008	2805	20W-14N	E5
10	RGMW	60067	2805	20W-14N	E5
Fairfax Ct					
900	ELGN	60120	2855		C1
16500	TYPK	60477	3425	8W-19S	B3
Fairfax Rd					
5600	OKFT	60452	3347	7W-18S	D7
Fairfax St					
4200	OKLN	60453	3276	5W-12S	B2
Fairfield Av					
6400	BRWN	60402	3089	8W-3S	A4
14800	HRVY	60426	3349	3W-17S	B6
14800	POSN	60426	3349	3W-17S	B6
15000	MKHM	60426	3349	3W-17S	B6
20300	OMFD	60461	3506	4W-24S	E5
N Fairfield Av					
-	MLPK	60160	2973	12W-2N	A7
200	CHCG	60612	3033	3W-0N	A4
1400	CHCG	60622	3033	3W-1N	A1
1500	CHCG	60647	3033	3W-1N	A1
2200	LydT	60164	2973	12W-2N	A6
2300	FNPK	60131	2973	12W-2N	A6
2400	CHCG	60647	2977	3W-3N	A5
2900	CHCG	60618	2976	3W-3N	E4

STREET Block	City	ZIP	Map#	CGS	Grid
N Fairfield Av					
2900	CHCG	60618	2977	3W-3N	A4
5600	CHCG	60625	2920	3W-6N	E5
5600	CHCG	60659	2920	3W-6N	E5
6300	CHCG	60645	2920	3W-7N	E3
7400	CHCG	60645	2866	3W-9N	E7
S Fairfield Av					
900	CHCG	60612	3033	3W-1S	A7
1000	CHCG	60608	3033	3W-1S	A7
1600	CHCG	60608	3091	3W-1S	A1
4100	CHCG	60632	3091	3W-4S	A7
5000	CHCG	60632	3151	3W-6S	A3
6900	CHCG	60629	3151	3W-8S	A7
7900	CHCG	60652	3213	3W-9S	A2
8700	ENGN	60805	3213	3W-10S	A4
9900	CHCG	60655	3213	3W-11S	A7
9900	CHCG	60805	3213	3W-11S	A7
10600	CHCG	60655	3277	3W-12S	A2
Fairfield Cir					
600	EGVV	60007	2860	19W-9N	C7
Fairfield Ct					
400	SMBG	60193	2859	23W-9N	B6
1300	WLNG	60090	2754	16W-18N	D3
W Fairfield Ct					
200	PLTN	60067	2752	21W-17N	D4
Fairfield Dr					
600	BRTN	60010	2751	24W-18N	C3
600	PltT	60010	2751	24W-18N	C3
Fairfield Ln					
1500	HFET	60195	2858	25W-12N	C2
8400	FftT	60423	3504	10W-23S	B4
8400	FftT	60477	3504	10W-23S	B4
8700	FftT	60448	3504	10W-23S	B4
8700	TYPK	60448	3504	11W-23S	A4
8900	MKNA	60448	3504	11W-23S	A4
Fairfield Rd					
1100	GLNC	60022	2758	7W-18N	B4
Fairfield St					
10600	WSTR	60154	3087	13W-2S	A3
Fairford Ln					
2500	NHBK	60062	2756	10W-18N	E4
2500	NHBK	60062	2757	10W-18N	B4
Fairgrounds Ct					
5100	MONE	60449	3683	6W-31S	A6
Fairhaven Ct					
1900	SMBG	60194	2858	26W-11N	A4
Fairhaven Dr					
600	HRPK	60133	2912		A1
Fairhaven Ln					
1800	SMBG	60194	2858	25W-11N	A4
Fairhope Av					
700	GNVW	60025	2811	7W-14N	B3
700	NHFD	60025	2811	7W-14N	B3
700	NHFD	60093	2811	7W-14N	B3
S Fairlane Av					
100	EMHT	60126	3028		B2
Fairlane Ct					
1200	SMBG	60193	2912		B2
Fairlane Dr					
900	SMBG	60193	2912		B1
8800	BGVW	60455	3210	8W-10S	E5
8800	BGVW	60455	3211	8W-10S	A5
Fairlawn Av					
-	ELGN	60120	2855		C6
Fairlawn Dr					
3300	MaiT	60025	2863	11W-12N	E1
3300	MaiT	60025	2864	10W-11N	A2
Fairmont Ct					
800	DSPN	60018	2862	14W-10N	D6
9100	ODPK	60462	3345	11W-17S	E6
9100	ODPK	60462	3346	11W-17S	A6
Fairmont Rd					
-	HFET	60194	2858	25W-12N	C2
-	HFET	60195	2858	25W-12N	C2
W Fairmont St					
100	MPPT	60056	2807	15W-14N	E3
Fair Oaks Av N					
500	OKPK	60302	3031	8W-1N	A3
1200	CHCG	60302	3031	8W-2N	A1
1200	CHCG	60707	3031	8W-2N	A1
Fairoaks Ct					
-	CCHL	60478	3426	6W-21S	A6
W Fairoaks Ct					
10	PLTN	60067	2805	21W-15N	E2
Fairoaks Dr					
4900	CCHL	60478	3426	6W-21S	A6
Fairview					
-	ELGN	60120	2855		C7
Fairview Av					
10	DRFD	60015	2756	11W-20N	D2
200	WNKA	60093	2812	4W-15N	C3
1300	CHHT	60411	3507	2W-25S	D7
1400	CHHT	60411	3595	2W-25S	D1
3000	SCHT	60411	3596	1W-27S	A4
3300	STGR	60475	3596	1W-27S	A4
8900	BKFD	60513	3087	11W-3S	D6
9500	LGPK	60525	3087	11W-3S	D6
12400	BLID	60406	3277	3W-14S	A7
N Fairview Av					
100	MPPT	60056	2807	15W-13N	E6
800	PKRG	60068	2864	10W-9N	A6
900	NLES	60714	2864	10W-9N	A6
5500	CHCG	60631	2918	10W-7N	A5
5500	CHCG	60656	2918	10W-6N	A5
5500	LydT	60631	2918	10W-6N	A5
5500	MaiT	60631	2918	10W-7N	A5
S Fairview Av					
1200	PKRG	60068	2918	10W-7N	A3
1800	CHCG	60068	2918	10W-7N	A4
1800	CHCG	60631	2918	10W-7N	A4
1800	PKRG	60631	2918	10W-7N	A4
Fairview Cir					
500	SMBG	60193	2858	24W-9N	D7
Fairview Ln					
100	NHBK	60062	2756	12W-18N	A3
100	SMWD	60107	2857	28W-9N	A7
500	SMBG	60193	2858	24W-9N	D7
700	BRLT	60103	2910		D4
2000	SHLD	60473	3429	2E-20S	D4
4900	LNWD	60712	2919	6W-8N	E1
4900	SKOK	60712	2919	6W-8N	E1
5300	SKOK	60077	2919	6W-8N	D1
Fairview Rd					
100	GLNC	60022	2758	5W-17N	E5
E Fairview St					
10	ANHT	60005	2807	17W-13N	A6
W Fairview St					
10	ANHT	60005	2807	18W-13N	A6
500	ANHT	60005	2806	18W-13N	E6
Fairway Cir					
12300	BLID	60406	3277	3W-14S	A6
Fairway Ct					
200	PTHT	60070	2808	14W-14N	C4
1900	HFET	60195	2804	24W-13N	B7
1900	HFET	60195	2858	25W-12N	B1
Fairway Ct					
2900	GNVW	60025	2810	10W-13N	B7
3500	CRTE	60417	3596	0W-28S	D6
N Fairway Ct					
900	PLTN	60067	2753	20W-17N	A6
Fairway Dr					
-	GNVW	60025	2811	7W-14N	C5
-	LynT	60525	3208		E2
100	WLSP	60525	3208		E2
200	BCHR	60401	3864	0W-36S	D2
200	MPPT	60056	2808	14W-14N	C4
200	PTHT	60056	2808	14W-14N	C4
200	PTHT	60070	2808	14W-14N	C4
300	BRLT	60103	2910		D1
600	BNVL	60106	2915		D6
600	GNVW	60025	2810	10W-13N	B7
1200	LMNT	60439	3342	20W-15S	B1
3400	CRTE	60417	3596	0W-28S	D6
3900	WLMT	60091	2811	7W-14N	C5
5400	CTWD	60445	3347	6W-15S	D1
5400	WthT	60445	3347	6W-15S	D1
5400	WthT	60463	3347	6W-15S	D1
8800	ODPK	60462	3346	11W-17S	A5
9100	ODPK	60462	3345	11W-17S	E5
9200	MaiT	60016	2863	11W-12N	D1
9200	NLES	60714	2863	11W-12N	D1
N Fairway Dr					
800	PLTN	60067	2753	20W-17N	A6
Fairway Ln					
-	CRTE	60417	3596	0E-29S	E7
-	CRTE	60417	3685	0E-29S	E1
-	CteT	60417	3685	0E-29S	E1
200	BmdT	60143	2913		E6
200	BmdT	60157	2913		E6
200	CPVL	60110	2748		C7
500	IVNS	60067	2751	23W-16N	E6
500	IVNS	60067	2752	23W-16N	A7
1100	NHBK	60062	2757	8W-18N	D3
Fairway Rd					
10	CPVL	60110	2748		C7
Fairway Ter					
4000	BmnT	60430	3426	4W-21S	D7
4000	CCHL	60478	3426	5W-21S	C7
Fairway View Dr					
500	WLNG	60090	2754	16W-18N	E3
S Fairwood Ct					
20100	FftT	60423	3504	9W-24S	E5
Faith Ct					
1900	LYWD	60411	3509	2E-24S	D5
Faith Ln					
800	BRLT	60103	2911		A5
Faith Pl					
5200	MTSN	60443	3505	6W-24S	E5
5200	MTSN	60443	3506	6W-24S	A5
Faithorn Av					
1500	CRTE	60417	3685	0W-30S	C3
1500	CteT	60417	3685	0W-30S	C3
Falcon Ct					
10	SBTN	60010	2803	26W-15N	D3
12800	LMNT	60439	3343	18W-15S	A1
N Falcon Ct					
3600	RGMW	60008	2806	20W-13N	B5
S Falcon Ct					
3500	RGMW	60008	2806	20W-13N	B5
W Falcon Ct					
3000	RGMW	60008	2806	20W-13N	B5
Falcon Dr					
100	BlmT	60411	3509	3E-25S	E7
E Falcon Dr					
600	ANHT	60005	2861	17W-11N	B3
600	ANHT	60056	2861	17W-11N	B3
600	MPPT	60056	2861	17W-11N	B3
S Falcon Dr					
1200	PLTN	60067	2805	22W-14N	B4
1200	RGMW	60067	2805	22W-14N	B4
Falcon Ln					
1400	HFET	60192	2856	30W-12N	B2
Falcon St					
8700	HGKN	60525	3147	11W-7S	E5
Falcon Lakes Dr					
10	SBTN	60010	2803	26W-14N	E3
Falcon Ridge Dr					
9100	BGVW	60455	3210	9W-10S	D5
Falkirk Ln					
10	RGMW	60008	2805	20W-14N	E4
W Falkirk Pl					
400	PLTN	60074	2752	21W-18N	D3
Fall Cir					
400	ROSL	60172	2912		E7
Fall Ct					
1300	WLNG	60090	2754	16W-18N	D2
Fallbrook Ct					
200	EDND	60118	2801		B3
300	SMBG	60194	2857	27W-10N	D5
W Fallbrook Ct					
7600	FftT	60423	3504	9W-24S	E5
Fallbrook Dr					
400	EDND	60118	2801		B3
Falling Leaf Ln					
1700	NHBK	60062	2757	9W-16N	C6
Falling Waters Dr E					
9100	BRRG	60527	3208		C3
9400	DGvT	60527	3208		C3
Falling Waters Dr W					
-	DGvT	60527	3208		A5
9300	BRRG	60527	3208		A6
Fallstone Dr					
10	SMWD	60107	2857	28W-11N	B4
Falmore Dr					
700	BRLT	60103	2911		B4
S Falmore Dr					
1000	PLTN	60067	2805	22W-14N	B4
Falmouth Ct					
2000	SMWD	60107	2910		C1
Falmouth Ln					
500	SMBG	60193	2858	25W-9N	C7
Falmouth Wy					
500	ROSL	60172	2912		C6
Falmouth on Oxford					
10	RGMW	60008	2805	22W-13N	B6
Fane Ct					
11900	ODPK	60467	3422	14W-20S	D5
Fargo Av					
600	EGVV	60007	2861	17W-9N	B7
600	EGVV	60007	2915		B1
1200	DSPN	60018	2862	13W-9N	E7
1800	DSPN	60018	2863	12W-9N	B7
3800	SKOK	60076	2866	4W-9N	B7
5200	SKOK	60077	2865	6W-9N	D7
W Fargo Av					
1900	CHCG	60626	2867	2W-9N	B7
2000	CHCG	60645	2867	2W-9N	B7
2600	CHCG	60645	2866	3W-9N	E7
3100	SKOK	60076	2866	3W-9N	D7
3100	SKOK	60645	2866	3W-9N	D7
W Fargo Av					
6800	NLES	60714	2864	8W-9N	E7
7700	CHCG	60631	2864	9W-9N	C7
Fargo Ct					
4600	SKOK	60076	2866	5W-9N	A7
Far Hills Rd					
10	BNHL	60010	2748		E3
W Farm St					
100	CRTE	60417	3685	1W-30S	B3
Farm Crest Ter					
19000	CCHL	60478	3506	5W-22S	D2
Farmgate Dr					
100	SMBG	60193	2859	23W-9N	A6
200	SMBG	60193	2858	23W-9N	E6
E Farmgate Ln					
10	PLTN	60067	2752	20W-17N	E5
100	PLTN	60067	2753	20W-17N	A5
100	PLTN	60074	2753	20W-17N	A5
Farmhill Av					
8000	PlsT	60464	3274	10W-15S	C7
Farm Hill Dr					
15800	ODPK	60462	3424	10W-18S	A1
S Farmhill Ln					
12700	PlsT	60464	3274	10W-15S	C7
12700	PSPK	60464	3274	10W-15S	C7
Farmhouse Rd					
7800	FftT	60423	3504	9W-24S	D6
Farmington Av					
4400	RNPK	60471	3594	5W-27S	B4
Farmington Ct					
100	RGMW	60008	2805	21W-14N	D5
5800	HRPK	60133	2911		D5
Farmington Dr					
10	BrnT	60010	2803	25W-15N	E2
10	SBTN	60010	2803	25W-15N	E2
S Farmington Ln					
19700	FftT	60423	3504	9W-23S	E4
Farmington Rd					
10	SBTN	60010	2803	25W-15N	E2
2800	NHBK	60062	2809	11W-15N	E1
Farmsley Ct					
5100	OKFT	60452	3426	6W-20S	A4
Farmstead Ln					
7200	HRPK	60133	2912		A1
7200	SMBG	60133	2912		A2
7200	SMBG	60193	2912		A2
Farm Trace Dr					
22900	RNPK	60471	3594	4W-27S	D5
23000	MonT	60466	3594	4W-27S	D5
Farmview Ct					
-	UYPK	60466	3684	3W-30S	B4
16700	TYPK	60477	3424	10W-20S	B3
Farmview Rd					
500	UYPK	60466	3684	3W-30S	B4
600	UYPK	60449	3684	3W-30S	B4
W Farm View St					
13200	HMGN	60441	3343	16W-18S	E7
Farnham Ct					
1900	SMBG	60194	2858	26W-11N	A3
5800	HRPK	60133	2911		D5
N Farnsworth Dr					
8100	NLES	60714	2864	10W-10N	B5
Farnsworth Ln					
2000	NHBK	60062	2757	10W-16N	A6
2500	NHBK	60062	2756	10W-16N	E6
Farquhar Av					
-	BLID	60406	3276	4W-14S	D7
W Farragut Av					
1800	CHCG	60640	2921	2W-6N	B5
2500	CHCG	60625	2921	3W-6N	A5
2700	CHCG	60625	2920	3W-6N	E5
5500	CHCG	60630	2919	6W-6N	C5
7600	CHCG	60656	2918	9W-6N	C6
8300	CHCG	60706	2918	10W-6N	A6
8300	NRDG	60656	2918	10W-6N	A6
8300	NRDG	60706	2918	10W-6N	A6
Farragut St					
200	OMFD	60461	3507	3W-25S	B7
200	PKFT	60466	3507	3W-25S	B7
9700	CHCG	60018	2917	12W-6N	B6
S Farrar Dr					
1200	CHCG	60623	3032	3W-1S	E7
1500	CHCG	60623	3033	2W-1S	B7
1500	CHCG	60623	3091	3W-1S	A1
1800	CHCG	60623	3090	3W-1S	E1
Farrell Av					
1900	PKRG	60068	2863	11W-10N	D4
N Farrell Rd					
700	LKPT	60441	3342	21W-18S	A7
800	HmrT	60441	3342	21W-18S	A7
800	LktT	60441	3342	21W-18S	A7
S Farrell Rd					
-	HmrT	60441	3342	20W-17S	A7
14800	LKPT	60441	3342	21W-17S	A6
14800	LktT	60441	3342	21W-17S	A6
S Farrell St					
2600	CHCG	60608	3091	1W-2S	E2
Farrington Dr					
700	BFGV	60089	2754	17W-20N	B1
Fars Cove					
8300	BRRG	60527	3208		C3
8300	DGvT	60527	3208		C3
Farthing Ln					
400	DSPN	60016	2862	15W-11N	B3
Farwell Av					
1600	DSPN	60018	2917	12W-8N	A2
4900	LNWD	60712	2919	6W-8N	E1
4900	SKOK	60077	2919	6W-8N	D1
W Farwell Av					
1100	CHCG	60626	2921	2W-8N	B1
1900	CHCG	60645	2921	2W-8N	A1
2600	CHCG	60645	2920	3W-8N	E1
4700	LNWD	60712	2919	5W-8N	E1
7200	CHCG	60631	2918	9W-8N	D1
7200	NLES	60631	2918	9W-8N	D1
7200	NLES	60714	2918	9W-8N	D1
Father Burns Dr					
10200	OKLN	60453	3275	6W-11S	E6
Faun Ln					
-	HnrT	60120	2856	31W-11N	A4
Fawn Ct					
-	RchT	60443	3593	8W-25S	B1
10	BRRG	60527	3208		C4
5300	OKFT	60452	3347	6W-18S	E6
13400	ODPK	60462	3346	10W-15S	A2
E Fawn Ln					
400	PLTN	60074	2753	20W-18N	A2
Fawn Pth					
16700	LKPT	60441	3342	20W-17S	A6
16700	LktT	60441	3342	20W-17S	A6
Fawn Tr					
8000	JSTC	60458	3209	11W-9S	E3
Fawn Creek Ln					
11000	ODPK	60467	3344	13W-18S	E7
11000	ODPK	60467	3345	13W-18S	A7
Fawn Creek Ln					
11100	OrlT	60467	3344	13W-18S	E7
15500	OrlT	60467	3345	13W-18S	A7
Fawn Trail Dr					
10800	ODPK	60467	3423	13W-20S	A5
Fay Av					
10	WDND	60118	2801		A3
Fayette St					
500	HMND	46320	3352		D6
E Fayette St					
400	HMND	46320	3352		D6
Fayette Wk					
1700	HFET	60195	2858	25W-12N	B1
Fears Dr					
-	MYWD	60141	3030	10W-1S	A7
-	MYWD	60153	3030	10W-1S	A7
-	PvsT	60141	3029	10W-1S	E7
-	PvsT	60141	3030	10W-1S	A7
Feather Ct					
13400	ODPK	60462	3346	11W-15S	A2
Feathercreek Rd					
5500	MTSN	60443	3505	6W-24S	E6
Featherstone Ct					
2300	SMBG	60194	2857	26W-10N	E5
Federal Ct					
2400	LGGV	60047	2753	19W-20N	C1
9000	MaiT	60016	2863	11W-11N	E3
9000	PKRG	60016	2863	11W-11N	E3
9000	PKRG	60068	2863	11W-11N	E3
Federal Dr					
2300	NRIV	60546	3088	9W-2S	D2
S Federal St					
300	CHCG	60604	3034	0W-0S	B5
500	CHCG	60605	3034	0W-0S	B6
1600	CHCG	60616	3092	0W-1S	B1
4300	CHCG	60609	3092	0W-4S	C7
4700	CHCG	60609	3152	0W-5S	C2
Federal Signal Dr					
2500	MonT	60449	3682	7W-29S	E1
2500	MonT	60466	3682	7W-29S	E1
2500	UYPK	60449	3682	7W-29S	E1
2500	UYPK	60466	3682	7W-29S	E1
Feehanville Rd					
800	MPPT	60056	2808	14W-13N	C6
1600	DSPN	60016	2808	14W-13N	D5
1600	MPPT	60016	2808	14W-13N	D5
Feldner Ct					
100	PSHT	60463	3275	8W-15S	B7
Fencl Ln					
-	WSTR	60154	3028		E7
100	HLSD	60162	3028		E6
Fennel Ct					
700	SMBG	60193	2859	22W-9N	B7
Fennel Ln					
400	SMBG	60193	2859	22W-9N	B7
Fenton Ln					
1800	PKRG	60068	2863	11W-10N	E4
Fenview Ct					
11400	OrlT	60467	3344	14W-17S	E4
Fenwick Ct					
1800	SMBG	60194	2858	25W-11N	B3
Fenwood Ct					
11500	OrlT	60467	3344	14W-17S	D5
Fenwood Ln					
200	HLSD	60162	3028		E5
Fenz Rd					
-	SMBG	60193	2912		B3
Ferdinand Av					
-	BGVW	60455	3210	9W-9S	D3
800	FTPK	60130	3030	9W-0S	C7
S Ferdinand Av					
7100	BGVW	60455	3148	9W-8S	D7
8100	BGVW	60455	3210	9W-9S	D3
W Ferdinand St					
1600	CHCG	60622	3033	2W-0N	B3
1900	CHCG	60612	3033	2W-0N	B3
4200	CHCG	60624	3032	5W-0N	B3
4700	CHCG	60644	3032	5W-0N	A3
4800	CHCG	60644	3031	6W-0N	E3
Fermi Ct					
300	SMBG	60193	2858	24W-10N	D6
Fern					
-	JSTC	60458	3210	10W-9S	C2
Fern Av					
2800	NHBK	60062	2756	11W-16N	E7
4000	LYNS	60534	3088	10W-4S	A7
5400	OKFT	60452	3347	6W-17S	E5
S Fern Av					
500	EMHT	60126	3028		B4
900	YkTp	60126	3028		B6
Fern Ct					
600	SMBG	60193	2859	23W-9N	B7
N Fern Ct					
1700	CHCG	60614	2978	0W-2N	A7
S Fern Ct					
600	EMHT	60126	3028		B5
W Fern Ct					
10	PLTN	60067	2805	21W-14N	E3
Fern Dr					
200	EGVV	60007	2914		E2
S Fern Dr					
1100	MPPT	60056	2861	16W-11N	D3
Fern Ln					
9300	MaiT	60016	2863	11W-11N	D2
Fern St					
-	LNSG	60438	3429	2E-21S	D6
-	ThtT	60438	3429	2E-21S	D6
Fernald Av					
8500	MNGV	60053	2865	7W-10N	B4
N Fernandez Av					
1600	ANHT	60004	2806	18W-15N	E1
1900	ANHT	60004	2753	18W-16N	E7
S Fernandez Av					
1000	ANHT	60005	2806	18W-12N	E7
1100	ANHT	60005	2860	18W-12N	E2
S Fernandez Ct					
1300	ANHT	60005	2860	18W-12N	E1
N Fernandez Pl					
1500	ANHT	60004	2806	18W-15N	E2
Ferndale Av					
1600	NHBK	60062	2757	9W-17N	B4
Ferndale Ct					
200	PTHT	60070	2808	14W-14N	B3
300	SMBG	60193	2859	21W-9N	D6
400	BFGV	60089	2754	16W-20N	D1
1000	WLNG	60090	2754	15W-18N	E2
Ferndale Ln					
400	PTHT	60070	2808	14W-14N	B4
Ferndale Rd					
10	DRFD	60015	2757	9W-20N	B2
10	DRPK	60010	2752	23W-20N	A2
10	PltT	60010	2752	23W-20N	A2
300	GNVW	60025	2811	6W-13N	C6
Ferne Dr					
300	WLNG	60090	2755	13W-17N	D5
Fernwood Ct					
10	SMWD	60107	2857	26W-11N	E4
5600	MTSN	60443	3505	7W-24S	D4
8900	ODPK	60462	3346	11W-17S	A6
Fernwood Dr					
10	BNHL	60010	2748		E7
10	BNHL	60010	2801		E1
10	BNHL	60010	2802	30W-16N	A1
10	MaiT	60025	2864	9W-12N	C1
100	GNVW	60025	2864	9W-12N	C1
Fernwood Ln					
200	GNVW	60025	2864	9W-12N	C1
Fernwood St					
200	HMND	46324	3430		D3
Ferrari Ct					
300	BMDL	60157	2913		B6
Ferris Av					
8500	MNGV	60053	2865	7W-10N	A4
W Fey Ln					
4400	ALSP	60803	3276	5W-13S	B5
Field Av					
3100	BDVW	60155	3087	11W-2S	C2
N Field Blvd					
-	CHCG	60601	3034	0E-0N	D4
Field Dr					
-	SMBG	60173	2860	21W-11N	A3
N Field Dr					
-	CHCG	60601	3034	0E-0N	D4
8100	NLES	60714	2864	10W-10N	B5
Field Ln					
300	SMWD	60107	2857	28W-10N	B5
W Field Pkwy					
21500	DRPK	60010	2752	21W-20N	C1
21500	DRPK	60074	2752	21W-20N	C1
E Field St					
800	HMND	46320	3430		E1
800	HMND	46324	3430		E1
Field Crest Av					
8300	WLSP	60480	3208		E3
Fieldcrest Dr					
-	BRLT	60103	2909		B3
-	MKHM	60426	3426	5W-19S	C1
4500	OKFT	60452	3426	5W-19S	B3
16200	BmnT	60426	3426	5W-19S	C1
16200	OKFT	60426	3426	5W-19S	C2
S Fielding Av					
7700	CHCG	60620	3214	0W-8S	B1
Fielding Dr					
1500	GNVW	60025	2810	9W-14N	C4
Fielding Place Ct					
-	DRPK	60010	2751	23W-18N	D2
-	PltT	60010	2751	23W-18N	D2
Fieldside Dr					
-	MTSN	60443	3505	7W-25S	C7
Fieldstone Ct					
-	IVNS	60010	2750	25W-17N	E6
900	SMBG	60194	2858	24W-11N	D3
1000	ELGN	60120	2855		D1
Fieldstone Dr					
-	WLBK	60527	3146		B6
6700	BRRG	60527	3146		B6
Fieldstone Rd					
10	RGMW	60008	2806	19W-14N	C4
Fieldview Ct					
-	LKPT	60441	3342	20W-18S	B7
Fieldwood Dr					
1700	NHBK	60062	2757	10W-16N	A7
1800	NHBK	60062	2756	10W-16N	E7
Fiesta Dr					
900	UYPK	60466	3684	3W-30S	A2
Fife Ct					
700	IVNS	60010	2751	24W-16N	B6
Figard Ln					
500	DSPN	60016	2862	15W-11N	B3
Figura Dr					
7400	JSTC	60458	3209	11W-8S	E1
Filbert Dr					
100	SMWD	60107	2857	27W-10N	C6
Fillmore Av					
500	DYR	46311	3510		E5
500	MNSR	46321	3510		E5
Fillmore Ln					
10	SMWD	60107	2856	29W-10N	E6
Fillmore St					
-	MYWD	60153	3029	11W-0S	D7
-	MYWD	60153	3030	10W-0S	A7
10	CHCG	60644	3031	7W-0S	B6
10	OKPK	60304	3031	8W-0S	A6
100	YkTp	60126	3028		B7
600	EMHT	60126	3028		A7
800	OKPK	60304	3030	8W-0S	E7
1700	BDVW	60155	3029	11W-0S	D7
7300	FTPK	60130	3030	9W-0S	D7
W Fillmore St					
1300	CHCG	60607	3033	1W-0S	D6
1800	CHCG	60612	3033	2W-0S	D6
2800	CHCG	60612	3032	4W-0S	D6
3100	CHCG	60624	3032	5W-0S	B6
5600	CHCG	60644	3031	7W-0S	C6
5900	OKPK	60304	3031	7W-0S	B6
Filly Dr					
13500	HMGN	60441	3343	16W-18S	D7
Filmore Av					
7400	HRPK	60133	2912		A2
S Financial Pl					
300	CHCG	60604	3034	0W-0S	B5
600	CHCG	60605	3034	0W-0S	B6
800	CHCG	-	3034	0W-0S	B6
800	CHCG	60607	3034	0W-0S	B6
Finbar Pl					
9300	OrlT	60477	3423	11W-21S	E6
Finch Av					
16600	HRVY	60426	3428	1W-19S	A3
Finch Ct					
10	SMWD	60107	2856	30W-10N	C6
3600	RGMW	60008	2806	20W-13N	B5
13000	HMGN	60441	3344	16W-18S	A7
Fincharn Ln					
100	IVNS	60067	2752	22W-16N	A7
Finchley Ct					
1900	SMBG	60194	2858	26W-11N	A3
N Finley Av					
2200	RVGV	60171	2973	11W-2N	D6
2300	FNPK	60131	2973	11W-2N	D6
2300	FNPK	60171	2973	11W-2N	D6
S Finley Av					
13900	RBBN	60472	3348	4W-16S	E3
Finley Dr					
8900	HYHL	60457	3209	11W-9S	E4
8900	HYHL	60457	3210	11W-9S	A4
Finsbury Ln					
200	LGPK	60525	3087	12W-2S	C3
Fir Ct					
200	SMWD	60107	2857	27W-10N	C5
4000	HFET	60195	2804	24W-15N	B3

STREET Block	City	ZIP	Map#	CGS	Grid
Fir Ln					
10	LynT	60458	3209	12W-8S	D1
Fir St					
10	CPVL	60110	2748		C5
10	PKFT	60466	3595	3W-26S	B3
2200	GNVW	60025	2810	9W-13N	C6
8500	ODPK	60462	3346	10W-16S	B2
Fireside Dr					
6400	CHRG	60415	3275	8W-11S	B1
N Firestone Ct					
4100	HFET	60195	2804	24W-15N	D2
Firestone Dr					
13300	ODPK	60462	3346	11W-15S	A2
25500	MONE	60449	3683	6W-31S	B5
N Firestone Dr					
4000	HFET	60195	2804	24W-15N	C3
W Firestone Dr					
800	HFET	60195	2804	24W-15N	D2
N Firestone Ln					
3900	HFET	60195	2804	24W-14N	C3
Firethorn Ct					
10	LMNT	60439	3271		D7
10	LMNT	60439	3343	17W-15S	D1
Firth Rd					
10	IVNS	60067	2804	23W-15N	E2
1600	IVNS	60067	2805	23W-15N	A2
Fisher Ln					
900	WNKA	60093	2759	5W-16N	A7
1000	GLNC	60093	2759	5W-16N	A7
Fisher Pl					
400	MNSR	46321	3510		D1
Fisher St					
400	MNSR	46321	3510		D1
Fishermans Ter					
4100	LYNS	60534	3088	9W-4S	D7
4500	LYNS	60534	3148	9W-4S	D1
Fisk St					
16700	HRVY	60426	3428	1W-19S	A3
17100	EHZC	60429	3428	1W-20S	A5
17400	EHZC	60430	3428	1W-20S	A5
17400	HMWD	60430	3428	1W-20S	A5
Fiskeville Ln					
1100	SMBG	60193	2912		C1
Fitch Av					
4900	SKOK	60077	2919	6W-8N	D1
W Fitch Av					
2400	CHCG	60645	2921	3W-8N	A1
2600	CHCG	60645	2920	3W-8N	E1
3800	LNWD	60712	2920	4W-8N	B1
6300	CHCG	60646	2919	7W-8N	A1
7200	CHCG	60631	2918	9W-8N	D1
7200	NLES	60714	2918	9W-8N	D1
Fitch Rd					
400	CHHT	60411	3507	2W-24S	D5
W Fitzhenry Ct					
700	GNWD	60425	3428	0W-21S	B7
Fitzsimmons Dr					
10400	PlsT	60464	3345	13W-15S	B1
Flagg Ct					
300	HNDL	60521	3146		B1
Flagstaff Ln					
10	HFET	60194	2859	23W-11N	A3
200	HFET	60194	2858	24W-11N	E3
Flagstone Dr					
2200	CPVL	60110	2748		C3
Flagstone Pl					
-	SMBG	60193	2912		B2
E Flake Dr					
1000	PLTN	60074	2753	19W-16N	B7
N Flake Dr					
100	PLTN	60074	2753	19W-16N	C7
S Flambeau Dr					
12000	PSHT	60463	3275	8W-14S	A6
Flamingo Cir					
8400	ODPK	60462	3346	10W-18S	B7
Flamingo Dr					
-	HGKN	60525	3147	11W-7S	E5
10	ROSL	60172	2912		C4
8800	TYPK	60477	3424	11W-21S	A7
W Flamingo Dr					
1200	ROSL	60172	2912		C4
Flamingo Ter					
8400	HYHL	60457	3210	10W-11S	B6
Flanigan Dr					
2900	LNSG	60438	3430	3E-20S	A4
Flannagan Ct					
17700	TYPK	60477	3424	10W-21S	A6
Flat Rock Rd					
2400	DYR	46311	3598		E3
Flavin Rd					
-	PlsT	60480	3209	13W-10S	B6
-	PlsT	60480	3273	13W-12S	B2
-	WLSP	60480	3209	13W-10S	B6
Fleet St					
10600	WSTR	60154	3086		E3
10600	WSTR	60154	3087	13W-2S	A3
Fleetwood Dr					
4000	FNPK	60131	2972		E2
Fleetwood Ln					
200	EGVV	60007	2861	17W-9N	B7
E Fleming Dr N					
1400	ANHT	60004	2754	16W-17N	C5
E Fleming Dr S					
1400	ANHT	60004	2754	16W-17N	C5
Fleming Ln					
200	SMBG	60193	2858	23W-9N	E7
E Flentie Ln					
1400	ANHT	60004	2754	16W-17N	C5
1700	BFGV	60089	2754	16W-17N	C5
Fletcher Av					
10800	FNPK	60131	2972		E4
10800	FNPK	60164	2972		E4
10800	LydT	60164	2972		E4
Fletcher Dr					
10	DSPN	60016	2862	14W-11N	B2
100	WLNG	60090	2754	15W-17N	E5
100	WLNG	60090	2755	15W-17N	A4
S Fletcher Dr					
800	WLNG	60090	2755	15W-17N	A5
900	WLNG	60090	2754	15W-17N	E5
W Fletcher St					
800	CHCG	60657	2977	1W-3N	E4
2100	CHCG	60618	2977	2W-3N	B4
2800	CHCG	60618	2976	3W-3N	E4
4100	CHCG	60641	2976	5W-3N	B4
4800	CHCG	60641	2975	6W-3N	D4
6000	CHCG	60634	2975	7W-3N	B4
6900	CHCG	60634	2974	8W-3N	E4
7900	EDPK	60707	2974	9W-3N	B4
Flicker Ln					
2100	RGMW	60008	2806	20W-14N	B5
Flint Ct					
2300	DYR	46311	3598		E3
Flint Dr					
12000	HMGN	60441	3344	15W-17S	C5

STREET Block	City	ZIP	Map#	CGS	Grid
Flint Dr					
12000	OrlT	60467	3344	15W-17S	C5
Flint Ln					
8600	ODPK	60462	3346	10W-15S	A2
Flintshire Dr					
1800	SMBG	60194	2858	25W-11N	A3
Flora Av					
-	GNVW	60025	2810	9W-12N	C7
100	MaiT	60025	2864	9W-12N	C1
200	GNVW	60025	2864	9W-12N	C1
Flora Pl					
300	HDPK	60035	2758	7W-20N	B1
Floral Av					
8000	SKOK	60077	2865	6W-10N	D5
W Floral Ct					
7700	FftT	60423	3504	9W-24S	E5
Floral Dr					
2800	NHBK	60062	2809	11W-16N	D1
3100	NfdT	60062	2809	11W-16N	D1
Florence Av					
100	CHCG	60645	2867	3W-9N	A6
100	IVNS	60010	2751	23W-16N	D6
200	IVNS	60067	2751	23W-16N	D6
300	EVTN	60202	2867	3W-9N	A6
1200	EVTN	60201	2867	3W-10N	A4
3000	SCHT	60411	3596	0W-27S	B5
3000	STGR	60475	3596	0W-28S	B6
9700	SRPK	60176	2917	12W-6N	C6
N Florence Av					
20500	BFGV	60089	2754	15W-20N	E1
20500	VrnT	60069	2754	15W-20N	E1
Florence Dr					
600	PKRG	60068	2863	11W-9N	D6
6000	HFET	60120	2855		D1
Florence St					
200	HMND	46324	3430		D2
1000	LMNT	60439	3270		D7
2200	BLID	60406	3277	2W-14S	B6
Florence Wy					
4100	NfdT	60025	2809	11W-13N	D7
Florian Dr					
300	DSPN	60016	2862	15W-10N	A4
Florida Ct					
18000	ODPK	60467	3423	13W-21S	A7
Florida Ln					
1000	EGVV	60007	2913		D3
Florina Ct					
100	WDDL	60191	2915		A6
Flossmoor Rd					
2000	BlmT	60430	3507	2W-22S	D2
2000	FSMR	60422	3507	3W-22S	A2
3200	RchT	60422	3507	4W-23S	A2
3200	RchT	60430	3507	4W-23S	A2
3300	RchT	60422	3506	4W-23S	E2
3300	RchT	60430	3506	4W-23S	E2
3400	FSMR	60422	3506	4W-23S	E2
3800	RchT	60478	3506	4W-22S	D2
3900	CCHL	60422	3506	4W-22S	D2
3900	CCHL	60478	3506	6W-23S	A2
3900	FSMR	60478	3506	4W-22S	D2
4200	RchT	60477	3506	6W-23S	A2
4500	CCHL	60477	3506	6W-23S	A2
5400	RchT	60477	3505	7W-22S	D2
5600	TYPK	60477	3505	7W-22S	D2
Flournoy St					
200	OKPK	60304	3031	7W-0S	B6
W Flournoy St					
1200	CHCG	60607	3033	1W-0S	D6
1600	CHCG	60612	3033	2W-0S	C6
2800	CHCG	60612	3032	4W-0S	C6
3100	CHCG	60624	3032	4W-0S	C6
4600	CHCG	60644	3032	5W-0S	A6
4800	CHCG	60644	3031	6W-0S	E6
N Flower Cir					
2000	ANHT	60004	2807	16W-16N	C1
Flower Ct					
2200	SMBG	60194	2857	26W-11N	E4
7400	HRPK	60133	2911		C1
Flowers Av					
800	SMWD	60107	2911		C2
N Floyd Ln					
100	CHHT	60411	3508	1W-23S	A4
S Floyd Ln					
100	CHHT	60411	3508	1W-23S	A4
Flying Dutchman Ter					
500	SMBG	60193	2912		D1
Foliage Ln					
2200	DYR	46311	3598		E2
Foltz Dr					
1600	HFET	60195	2858	25W-12N	B1
Fonda Ln					
5300	HRPK	60133	2911		C6
Fontana Dr					
2400	GNVW	60025	2810	9W-12N	C7
Forbes Av					
-	HFET	60192	2802	28W-13N	D6
Forbes Rd					
-	NRIV	60546	3088	10W-3S	B5
-	RVSD	60546	3088	10W-3S	B5
Forbes Rd SR-171					
-	NRIV	60546	3088	10W-3S	B5
-	RVSD	60546	3088	10W-3S	B5
Ford Av					
600	ELGN	60120	2855		B1
S Ford Av					
2200	CHCG	60616	3092	0W-2S	A2
Ford Ct					
700	ELGN	60120	2855		B1
W Ford Ct					
6000	MONE	60449	3682	7W-31S	D5
Ford Ln					
300	BRLT	60103	2910		D2
S Ford Rd					
11200	PlsT	60464	3272	14W-13S	D5
11800	LMNT	60439	3272	14W-13S	D5
11800	PlsT	60439	3272	14W-13S	D5
W Ford City Dr					
4000	CHCG	60652	3212	5W-8S	B1
Fordham Pl					
400	ROSL	60172	2912		D6
Fore Ct					
1200	WLNG	60090	2754	16W-18N	E2
E Foreman Dr					
-	CHCG	60617	3216	4E-10S	C5
Forest Av					
10	FTPK	60130	3030	9W-0N	C5
10	ROSL	60172	2913		A6
10	RVSD	60546	3088	10W-3S	B5
100	OKPK	60301	3030	8W-0N	E3
100	OKPK	60302	3030	8W-0N	E3
100	WLSP	60480	3209	12W-9S	D3
200	ROSL	60172	2912		E6
400	WLMT	60091	2813	3W-14N	A5
600	ELGN	60120	2855		B4
600	PlsT	60480	3209	12W-9S	D4

STREET Block	City	ZIP	Map#	CGS	Grid
Forest Av					
700	WLMT	60091	2812	3W-14N	E5
900	EVTN	60202	2867	2W-10N	C4
900	GLNC	60022	2758	6W-18N	D3
1000	GNVW	60025	2811	7W-14N	A5
1200	EVTN	60201	2867	2W-11N	C3
1300	CTCY	60409	3430	4E-19S	B2
1300	EDPK	60707	3030	9W-1N	C1
1300	RVFT	60305	3030	9W-1N	C1
2200	FTPK	60130	3088	9W-2S	C2
2200	FTPK	60546	3088	9W-2S	C2
2200	NRIV	60546	3088	9W-2S	C2
2200	RGMW	60008	2806	20W-14N	A4
2900	BKFD	60513	3087	11W-2S	E4
3500	WLMT	60091	2811	6W-14N	D5
3800	PvsT	60558	3086		D6
3800	WNSP	60558	3086		D6
4500	BKFD	60513	3147	11W-4S	E1
4500	MCCK	60525	3147	11W-4S	E1
6900	HMND	46324	3430		C4
8400	MNSR	46321	3430		C7
13800	CHCG	60827	3350	0E-16S	D2
13800	DLTN	60419	3350	0E-16S	D2
15900	OKFT	60452	3426	6W-19S	A2
16800	BmnT	60452	3426	6W-20S	A3
16900	BmnT	60477	3426	6W-20S	A4
16900	OKFT	60477	3426	6W-20S	A4
E Forest Av					
200	EMHT	60126	3028		A3
500	DSPN	60018	2862	14W-10N	C5
1300	DSPN	60018	2863	13W-10N	A5
N Forest Av					
10	PLTN	60074	2806	20W-16N	A1
100	MPPT	60056	2807	16W-13N	E7
100	PLTN	60074	2753	20W-16N	A7
200	HLSD	60162	3028		E5
600	ANHT	60004	2807	16W-13N	E6
600	ANHT	60056	2807	16W-13N	E6
600	MPPT	60004	2807	16W-13N	E5
1200	PltT	60067	2752	22W-17N	B5
2700	RVGV	60171	2974	10W-3N	A5
S Forest Av					
10	PLTN	60074	2806	20W-15N	A1
100	HLSD	60162	3028		E7
300	ITSC	60143	2914		B7
9100	CHCG	60619	3214	0E-11S	D6
9400	CHCG	60628	3214	0E-11S	D6
10300	CHCG	60628	3278	0E-12S	D2
13400	CHCG	60827	3350	0E-15S	D1
19400	BlmT	60425	3508	0W-23S	C3
19400	GNWD	60425	3508	0W-23S	C3
Forest Av N					
500	OKPK	60302	3030	8W-1N	E2
1200	CHCG	60707	3030	8W-1N	E1
Forest Blvd					
10	PKFT	60466	3595	3W-26S	B3
Forest Ct					
400	SMBG	60193	2858	24W-10N	E5
800	BRLT	60103	2910		D6
2300	LNSG	60438	3429	2E-21S	E7
3600	OMFD	60461	3506	4W-24S	D4
4900	OKFT	60452	3426	6W-20S	A3
N Forest Ct					
200	PLTN	60074	2753	20W-16N	A7
Forest Dr					
-	BmnT	60426	3426	5W-19S	B1
-	OKFT	60452	3426	5W-18S	B1
-	TYPK	60477	3424	9W-21S	E6
500	BMDL	60108	2912		E7
500	BMDL	60108	2913		A7
500	BMDL	60172	2913		A7
500	BmdT	60172	2912		E7
500	BmdT	60172	2913		A7
800	SMWD	60107	2857	28W-9N	A7
1400	GNVW	60025	2809	12W-14N	B5
6000	MNGV	60053	2865	7W-11N	B3
8400	HYHL	60457	3209	11W-9S	E3
S Forest Dr					
700	BRTN	60010	2750	26W-18N	D3
800	BNHL	60010	2750	26W-18N	D3
Forest Ln					
10	EGVV	60007	2861	18W-10N	A6
10	HFET	60195	2804	25W-14N	A3
10	SBTN	60010	2804	25W-15N	A3
10	YkTp	60126	3028		B7
300	SMBG	60193	2858	23W-10N	E6
500	CTCY	60409	3430	4E-18S	B1
500	ThtT	60476	3428	0E-21S	E6
500	TNTN	60476	3428	0E-21S	E6
1000	LMNT	60439	3270		E7
2800	LNSG	60438	3510	3E-22S	A1
8900	HYHL	60457	3209	11W-10S	E5
8900	HYHL	60457	3210	11W-10S	A5
10400	CHRG	60415	3275	8W-12S	B2
10600	CHRG	60482	3275	8W-12S	B2
10600	WRTH	60482	3275	8W-12S	B2
13300	DPgT	60441	3342	21W-15S	A2
14500	LKPT	60441	3342	21W-17S	A5
14500	LktT	60441	3342	21W-17S	A5
E Forest Ln					
10	PltT	60067	2805	20W-13N	E5
10	RGMW	60067	2805	21W-13N	E5
200	PltT	60067	2806	20W-13N	A5
W Forest Ln					
1600	CteT	60417	3595	2W-29S	E7
Forest Ln E					
9000	HYHL	60457	3209	11W-10S	E5
Forest Ln W					
9000	HYHL	60457	3209	11W-10S	E5
Forest Pl					
10	BFGV	60089	2754	16W-18N	C3
1300	CTCY	60409	3430	4E-19S	B2
1600	EVTN	60201	2867	2W-11N	C3
9500	MaiT	60016	2809	12W-12N	C7
Forest Rd					
300	HNDL	60521	3086		B7
300	HNDL	60521	3146		B1
600	GNVW	60025	2811	6W-13N	D7
700	LGPK	60525	3087	12W-3S	C5
1600	LGPK	60154	3087	12W-2S	C3
Forest St					
10	CHHT	60411	3596	1W-26S	A2
100	WNKA	60093	2812	4W-15N	B3
9700	SjnT	46311	3687		C3
Forest Tr					
5200	OKFT	60452	3425	6W-20S	E4
Forest Cove Ct					
10	HnrT	60120	2856	29W-9N	E7
10	SMWD	60120	2856	29W-9N	E7
Forest Cove Dr					
1700	EGvT	60056	2861	17W-10N	C5
1700	MPPT	60056	2861	17W-10N	C5
Forestdale Ct					
1300	SMBG	60193	2858	25W-10N	C6

STREET Block	City	ZIP	Map#	CGS	Grid
Forestdale Pk					
10	CTCY	60409	3430	4E-18S	C1
10	HMND	46320	3430	4E-18S	C1
Forest Edge Ln					
600	DSPN	60016	2863	12W-11N	C3
14800	OKFT	60452	3347	6W-17S	E5
Forest Glen Av					
1600	HRPK	60133	2911		D2
N Forest Glen Av					
5200	CHCG	60630	2919	6W-6N	E5
5500	CHCG	60646	2919	6W-6N	E5
5800	CHCG	60646	2920	5W-7N	A4
S Forest Glen Blvd					
12300	PSPK	60464	3274	11W-14S	A6
W Forest Glen Blvd					
9000	PSPK	60464	3273	11W-14S	E6
9000	PSPK	60464	3274	11W-13S	A5
Forest Glen Ct					
800	BRLT	60103	2910		C3
Forest Glen Dr					
-	WNKA	60093	2758	6W-16N	E7
4200	HFET	60195	2804	25W-15N	A2
Forest Glen Dr E					
800	WNKA	60093	2758	5W-16N	E7
Forest Glen Dr N					
1200	WNKA	60093	2758	6W-16N	E7
Forest Glen Dr S					
1200	WNKA	60093	2758	6W-16N	E7
Forest Glen Dr W					
900	WNKA	60093	2758	6W-16N	E7
Forest Glen Ln					
700	OKBK	60523	3086		B1
Forest Glen Rd					
100	AddT	60191	2915		A6
100	WDDL	60191	2915		A6
W Foresthill Ct					
7800	PSHT	60463	3346	9W-15S	D1
W Foresthill Ln					
7700	PSHT	60463	3346	9W-15S	D1
Forest Hill Rd					
7300	BRRG	60527	3208		D2
Forest Hill St					
1000	CTCY	60409	3430	4E-18S	B1
E Forest Knoll Dr					
-	PLTN	60074	2752	20W-18N	E3
200	PLTN	60074	2753	20W-18N	A3
Forest Park Dr					
2300	DYR	46311	3598		C3
Forest Park Ln					
10	HFET	60194	2859	23W-11N	A3
Forest Preserve					
-	PKRG	60068	2917	11W-8N	D2
W Forest Preserve Av					
6700	CHCG	60634	2974	10W-4N	A3
6700	HDHT	60706	2974	8W-5N	E1
6900	NRDG	60706	2974	10W-4N	B3
7000	NRDG	60634	2974	10W-4N	B3
8400	CHCG	60634	2973	10W-4N	E4
8600	RVGV	60171	2973	10W-4N	E4
Forest Preserve Dr					
-	PvsT	60154	3087	12W-2S	B2
-	WSTR	60154	3087	12W-2S	B2
200	LGPK	60154	3087	12W-2S	C3
200	LGPK	60525	3087	12W-2S	C3
2600	CHHT	60411	3596	1W-26S	A3
2600	SCHT	60411	3596	1W-26S	A3
2900	SCHT	60411	3595	1W-27S	E3
3000	BlmT	60466	3595	1W-27S	E4
3000	SCHT	60466	3595	2W-27S	E4
W Forest Preserve Dr					
6400	HDHT	60706	2919	8W-5N	A7
6600	CHCG	60634	2974	8W-5N	E2
6600	HDHT	60706	2974	8W-5N	E2
6600	HDHT	60706	2975	7W-3N	B5
Forest Ridge Dr					
13100	PSHT	60463	3347	7W-15S	B2
13400	BmnT	60463	3347	7W-15S	B2
Forest View Av					
100	WDDL	60191	2915		A7
300	EGvT	60007	2861	18W-9N	A7
300	EGVV	60007	2861	18W-9N	A7
400	EGvT	60007	2915		B1
400	EGVV	60007	2915		B1
Forestview Av					
-	RVDL	60827	3350	0W-15S	B1
500	PKRG	60068	2863	11W-9N	D7
2600	BKFD	60513	3087	11W-2S	E3
N Forestview Av					
2400	RVGV	60171	2974	10W-3N	A5
4400	CHCG	60656	2917	10W-5N	E7
4400	CHCG	60656	2973	10W-5N	E1
W Forestview Av					
-	BKFD	60513	3087	10W-2S	E3
2400	NRIV	60546	3087	11W-2S	E3
2400	PvsT	60546	3087	11W-2S	E3
N Forest View Cir					
1200	PLTN	60067	2752	22W-17N	B4
Forestview Ct					
13200	CTWD	60445	3347	6W-15S	E1
S Forestview Ct					
24300	CteT	60417	3687	3E-29S	B1
Forest View Dr					
4200	NfdT	60062	2756	13W-18N	A3
4200	NHBK	60062	2756	13W-18N	A3
4400	WhlT	60062	2756	13W-18N	A3
4700	NHBK	60062	2755	13W-18N	E3
4700	WhlT	60062	2755	13W-18N	E3
7800	OrlT	60462	3346	10W-17S	C6
8100	ODPK	60462	3346	10W-17S	C6
16700	TYPK	60477	3425	8W-20S	B4
Forestview Dr					
10	HnrT	60120	2856	30W-11N	A4
6000	OKFT	60452	3347	8W-18S	B6
W Forest View Dr					
12000	HMGN	60467	3344	15W-16S	C2
12000	OrlT	60467	3344	15W-16S	C3
Forest View Ln					
18600	LNSG	60438	3429	1E-22S	B7
18600	LNSG	60438	3509	1E-22S	B1
Forestview Ln					
1000	GNVW	60025	2811	7W-13N	A7
11900	PSPK	60464	3274	10W-14S	B5
13100	CTWD	60445	3347	6W-15S	E1
S Forestview Ln					
27500	CteT	60401	3774	0W-33S	C2
W Forest View Ln					
6700	NLES	60714	2918	8W-8N	E1
6700	NLES	60714	2919	8W-8N	A1
Forestview Rd					
2100	EVTN	60201	2866	4W-12N	D1
8800	SKOK	60076	2866	4W-11N	D3
9200	SKOK	60203	2866	4W-11N	D3
10700	CTSD	60525	3147	13W-7S	A6
S Forestview Rd					
12800	PSHT	60463	3275	8W-15S	A7

STREET Block	City	ZIP	Map#	CGS	Grid
S Forestview Rd					
12900	PSHT	60463	3347	8W-15S	A1
13000	WthT	60463	3347	8W-15S	A1
E Forestview Tr					
3000	CteT	60417	3687	3E-29S	B1
Forestway Ct					
10	BFGV	60089	2754	17W-18N	A3
Forestway Dr					
-	GLNC	60093	2758	6W-16N	C7
-	NHFD	60093	2811	6W-16N	C1
-	NtrT	60093	2811	6W-16N	C1
-	WNKA	60093	2758	7W-17N	B5
-	WNKA	60093	2811	6W-16N	C1
10	DRFD	60015	2756	11W-20N	D2
200	NHBK	60062	2758	7W-17N	A6
400	BFGV	60089	2754	17W-18N	A3
800	GLNC	60022	2758	7W-17N	B5
17100	EHZC	60429	3427	2W-20S	D5
Forestway Ln					
300	WLNG	60090	2755	14W-18N	C4
Forest Wood Ln					
10	PKFT	60466	3595	2W-28S	D6
Forest Woods Dr					
11000	LynT	60480	3208		E4
11000	WLSP	60480	3208		E4
N Forrest Av					
10	ANHT	60004	2807	16W-14N	C5
600	PKFT	60004	2807	16W-14N	D3
S Forrest Av					
10	ANHT	60004	2807	16W-13N	C6
500	ANHT	60005	2807	16W-13N	C6
N Forrest Ln					
1800	ANHT	60004	2807	16W-15N	D1
2400	ANHT	60004	2754	16W-16N	C6
S Forrestville Av					
4700	CHCG	60615	3092	0E-4S	D7
4700	CHCG	60615	3152	0E-5S	D1
4700	CHCG	60653	3092	0E-4S	D7
11200	CHCG	60628	3278	0E-13S	D3
13100	CHCG	60827	3278	0E-15S	E7
13100	CHCG	60827	3350	0E-15S	E1
Forster Av					
4800	SRPK	60176	2917	12W-6N	C7
5100	CHCG	60018	2917	12W-6N	C6
5100	SRPK	60018	2917	12W-6N	C7
Forsythe Av					
500	CTCY	60409	3352	4E-18S	C7
S Forsythe Sq					
1900	HMND	46394	3280		D5
Forsythia Dr					
300	DRFD	60015	2756	12W-20N	B1
300	WdfT	60015	2756	12W-20N	B1
Fort Dearborn Dr					
-	CHCG	60616	3092	0E-2S	D2
Fortuna Av					
1100	PKRG	60068	2863	11W-10N	D5
S Fortuna Av					
1100	PKRG	60068	2863	11W-10N	D5
Fortune Bay Ct					
1300	HFET	60195	2804	24W-15N	C2
N Fortwood Ct					
10	PltT	60067	2805	22W-15N	B2
Forum Dr					
500	ROSL	60172	2913		B3
Forum Sq					
700	NfdT	60025	2809	11W-13N	D7
S Forums Ct					
1100	PTHT	60070	2755	15W-16N	A7
1100	PTHT	60090	2755	15W-16N	A7
1100	WLNG	60070	2755	15W-16N	A7
1100	WLNG	60090	2755	15W-16N	A7
E Fosket Dr					
1000	PLTN	60074	2806	20W-15N	A2
N Fosket Dr					
10	PLTN	60074	2806	19W-16N	C1
W Foss Rd					
6800	MonT	60449	3682	8W-30S	B3
7100	GGnT	60449	3682	8W-30S	A3
Fossil Stone Rd					
2500	DYR	46311	3598		E2
Foster Av					
10	AddT	60106	2915		B6
10	BmdT	60157	2913		C6
10	BNVL	60106	2915		B6
10	BNVL	60191	2915		C6
10	WDDL	60106	2915		C6
10	WDDL	60191	2915		C6
100	AddT	60191	2915		B6
100	CHCG	60106	2915		E6
100	ROSL	60157	2913		C6
200	BmdT	60172	2912		B6
500	BRLT	60103	2910		D7
2000	PTHT	60070	2808	14W-15N	C2
2000	PTHT	60090	2808	14W-15N	C2
2000	WLNG	60090	2808	14W-15N	C2
E Foster Av					
100	BMDL	60108	2913		A6
100	ROSL	60172	2913		A7
700	BmdT	60157	2913		B6
700	BmdT	60172	2913		C6
700	ROSL	60157	2913		B6
W Foster Av					
900	CHCG	60640	2921	2W-6N	B5
1900	CHCG	60625	2921	2W-6N	B5
2700	CHCG	60625	2920	3W-6N	D5
3900	CHCG	60630	2920	5W-6N	B6
5600	CHCG	60630	2919	8W-6N	A6
6300	CHCG	60656	2919	8W-6N	A6
6600	CHCG	60656	2918	8W-6N	E5
7200	CHCG	60706	2918	10W-6N	B6
7200	HDHT	60706	2918	10W-6N	B6
7600	NRDG	60706	2918	9W-6N	B6
7900	NRDG	60656	2918	9W-6N	B6
8600	CHCG	60656	2917	11W-6N	E6
9400	SRPK	60018	2917	11W-6N	C6
9400	SRPK	60656	2917	11W-6N	C6
9700	CHCG	60018	2917	12W-6N	B6
9700	CHCG	60176	2917	12W-6N	B6
9700	SRPK	60176	2917	12W-6N	B6
W Foster Av US-41					
900	CHCG	60640	2921	2W-6N	B5
1900	CHCG	60625	2921	2W-6N	B5
W Foster Dr					
-	CHCG	60640	2922	0W-6N	A5
W Foster Ln					
8000	MNGV	60053	2864	9W-11N	B2
8000	NLES	60714	2864	10W-11N	B2
W Foster Pl					
7100	CHCG	60656	2918	8W-6N	D6
7100	CHCG	60706	2918	8W-6N	D6
7100	HDHT	60706	2918	8W-6N	D6
Foster St					
10	BMDL	60108	2913		A6
10	ROSL	60172	2913		A6
600	EVTN	60201	2867	2W-11N	B2

Chicago & Cook County Street Index

STREET Block	City	ZIP	Map#	CGS	Grid
Foster St					
1700	EVTN	60201	2866	3W-11N	E2
3600	SKOK	60203	2866	4W-11N	C2
4200	SKOK	60076	2866	5W-11N	A2
4800	SKOK	60076	2865	6W-11N	E2
5100	SKOK	60077	2865	6W-11N	D2
5400	MNGV	60077	2865	6W-11N	D2
6600	MNGV	60053	2865	8W-11N	A2
7200	MNGV	60053	2864	9W-11N	D2
7900	NLES	60714	2864	9W-11N	B2
E Foster St					
200	ANHT	60005	2861	17W-12N	A2
Founders Dr					
-	NHBK	60062	2757	8W-16N	D7
-	NHBK	60062	2810	8W-16N	D1
Founder's Wy					
-	OMFD	60461	3506	4W-24S	D5
Fountainbleau Dr					
3200	HLCT	60429	3426	4W-21S	E7
3200	HLCT	60429	3427	3W-21S	B6
18200	BmnT	60430	3426	4W-21S	E7
Fountain Grass Cir					
-	BRLT	60103	2909		D3
Fountain Grass Ct					
-	BRLT	60103	2909		C3
Fountain Hill Dr					
-	ODPK	60467	3422	14W-21S	D7
-	ODPK	60467	3423	13W-21S	A7
Fountain Valley Dr					
600	DndT	60118	2801		A5
Fountain View Dr					
800	DRFD	60015	2756	11W-20N	E1
S Fountainview Dr					
27100	CteT	60417	3774	0W-33S	C1
Four Winds Ln					
4400	NHBK	60062	2756	13W-18N	A2
Four Winds Wy					
3800	SKOK	60076	2866	4W-11N	B3
9100	SKOK	60203	2866	4W-11N	B3
Fowler Av					
900	EVTN	60202	2866	3W-10N	D4
1200	EVTN	60201	2866	3W-10N	D4
Fowler Dr					
-	GNVW	60025	2810	9W-13N	C5
Fox Av					
10	WDND	60118	2801		A4
Fox Ct					
9200	ODHL	60477	3423	11W-19S	E2
Fox Ct E					
10	BFGV	60089	2754	16W-20N	D1
Fox Ct W					
10	BFGV	60089	2754	16W-20N	D1
Fox Dr					
-	BmnT	60426	3426	5W-19S	B2
Fox Hllw					
14600	LMNT	60439	3343	18W-15S	A2
Fox Ln					
-	PlsT	60464	3273	13W-14S	A6
-	PSPK	60464	3273	13W-14S	A6
-	RGMW	60008	2805	21W-13N	C5
-	RGMW	60173	2805	21W-13N	C5
-	SMBG	60173	2805	21W-13N	C5
10	WLNG	60090	2755	14W-16N	D7
10	WNKA	60093	2812	5W-14N	A3
1400	HNDL	60521	3086		B5
2000	DSPN	60018	2917	12W-8N	B2
6400	PSHT	60463	3275	8W-15S	B7
6400	WthT	60463	3275	8W-15S	B7
11300	BRRG	60527	3208		E2
13100	LMNT	60439	3343	18W-15S	A2
Fox Ln N					
10	PSPK	60464	3273	13W-14S	A6
Fox Ln S					
10	PSPK	60464	3273	13W-14S	A6
Fox Tr					
1400	IVNS	60067	2805	22W-14N	A3
Foxbend Ct					
15700	ODPK	60462	3424	10W-18S	C1
Foxboro Ct					
10	SMWD	60107	2856	29W-9N	D7
1000	SMBG	60193	2912		D1
1100	BRLT	60103	2910		C5
Foxboro Dr					
400	WLNG	60090	2755	14W-17N	D5
Foxboro Ln					
1100	BRLT	60103	2910		B5
1100	SMBG	60193	2912		C2
Foxborough Pl					
100	BRRG	60527	3208		D2
Foxburrow Ln					
10	LMNT	60439	3343	17W-15S	D2
Fox Chase Rd					
22800	DRPK	60010	2752	22W-20N	A1
Foxcroft on Auburn					
10	RGMW	60008	2806	19W-14N	B3
Foxdale Av					
600	WNKA	60093	2812	5W-16N	A1
800	WNKA	60093	2759	5W-16N	A7
Foxdale Ct					
600	ROSL	60172	2912		C6
W Foxdale Ln					
400	ANHT	60004	2753	18W-18N	E2
400	ANHT	60004	2754	18W-18N	A2
Foxfire Dr					
10	BRBK	60459	3211	7W-8S	C1
Foxford Ln					
1300	LKPT	60441	3342	21W-18S	A7
19500	MKNA	60448	3504	11W-23S	A4
Foxford Rd					
500	BRLT	60103	2911		C5
Foxgate Ln					
5700	HNDL	60521	3146		A4
N Fox Glen Dr					
9700	NLES	60714	2863	11W-12N	D1
Foxglove Ct					
10	SMWD	60107	2856	30W-10N	C6
Foxglove Dr					
2100	NHBK	60062	2756	10W-16N	E7
Fox Glove Ln					
500	BRTN	60010	2751	24W-20N	D1
500	DRPK	60010	2751	24W-20N	D1
Foxglove Ln					
1100	PLTN	60074	2753	19W-18N	C3
Foxgrove Ln					
17100	TYPK	60477	3424	10W-20S	B4
W Fox Hill Ct					
13100	LMNT	60439	3344	16W-15S	A2
Fox Hill Dr					
13100	LMNT	60439	3343	16W-15S	E1
13300	LMNT	60439	3344	16W-15S	A2
13400	HMGN	60441	3344	16W-15S	A2
E Fox Hill Dr					
10	BFGV	60089	2754	16W-20N	D1
S Foxhound Ln					
17900	HMGN	60448	3422	16W-21S	A7
Fox Hound Tr					
1300	BCHR	60401	3774	0W-35S	D7
Fox Hunt Rd					
10	BNHL	60010	2749	29W-20N	B1
Fox Hunt Tr					
100	BRTN	60010	2751	24W-20N	B1
Fox Meadow Cir					
2400	NHFD	60093	2810	8W-15N	E2
Fox Meadow Ct					
2400	NHFD	60093	2810	8W-15N	D2
2400	NHFD	60093	2811	8W-15N	A2
Fox Meadow Dr					
400	NHFD	60093	2810	8W-15N	E2
Fox Meadow Ln					
2400	NHFD	60093	2810	8W-15N	E2
2400	NHFD	60093	2811	8W-15N	A2
Fox Path Ct					
1400	HFET	60192	2856	30W-12N	B2
Fox Path Ln					
-	HFET	60120	2856	30W-12N	B2
5300	HFET	60192	2856	30W-12N	B2
Fox River Dr					
10	DndT	60118	2801		A4
Fox Run Dr					
200	NHBK	60062	2757	9W-18N	D3
1600	ANHT	60004	2754	16W-17N	C6
1800	EGVV	60007	2859	22W-9N	C6
Fox Run Ln					
6200	MTSN	60443	3505	7W-24S	C6
Foxshire Ct					
10	SBTN	60010	2803	26W-14N	D3
Foxtail Ln					
13100	LMNT	60439	3344	16W-15S	A1
Foxwood Ct					
900	SMBG	60194	2858	24W-11N	D3
Foxwood Dr					
26500	MonT	60449	3683	6W-32S	A7
Foxwood Ln					
100	PltT	60010	2752	23W-18N	A2
Foxwoods Ct					
11400	OKLN	60803	3275	6W-13S	D4
Foxwoods Dr					
5400	OKLN	60803	3275	6W-13S	D4
5500	ALSP	60803	3275	6W-13S	D4
Frances Av					
1000	HRPK	60133	2911		D1
1000	SMWD	60107	2857	27W-9N	D7
1000	SMWD	60107	2911		D1
Frances Ct					
10	BFGV	60089	2754	16W-18N	C3
Frances Ln					
10	CHHT	60411	3508	1W-23S	A3
10	PlsT	60467	3344	13W-15S	E1
10	PlsT	60467	3345	13W-15S	A1
200	BRTN	60010	2751	23W-18N	D2
200	PltT	60010	2751	23W-18N	D2
8900	ODPK	60462	3423	11W-18S	D1
8900	ODPK	60462	3424	11W-18S	A1
15500	ODPK	60462	3346	11W-18S	A7
Frances Pkwy					
900	PKRG	60068	2918	10W-7N	A3
1200	PKRG	60068	2917	10W-7N	E3
Frances St					
500	PHNX	60426	3350	0W-18S	B7
Franchesca Ct					
9900	ODPK	60462	3345	12W-18S	C6
Francine Dr					
800	BRLT	60103	2911		A5
Francis Av					
5800	CTSD	60525	3147	12W-6S	C4
Francis Ct					
16400	ODPK	60467	3422	13W-19S	E3
W Francis Dr					
1100	ANHT	60005	2806	18W-13N	D6
Francis Ln					
-	FKFT	60423	3504	11W-24S	A5
Francis Pl					
900	DYR	46311	3598		E4
W Francis Pl					
2600	CHCG	60647	2977	3W-2N	A6
2700	CHCG	60647	2976	3W-2N	E6
E Francis St					
100	TNTN	60476	3428	0E-21S	D6
Franciscan Dr					
1200	LmnT	60439	3271		B4
Francisco Av					
12600	BLID	60406	3277	3W-14S	A7
13100	BLID	60406	3349	3W-15S	A1
13100	WthT	60406	3349	3W-15S	A1
13300	RBBN	60406	3349	3W-16S	A2
14300	BmnT	60469	3349	3W-17S	A4
18300	HMWD	60430	3427	3W-22S	A7
18400	HMWD	60430	3507	3W-22S	A1
N Francisco Av					
10	CHCG	60612	3032	3W-0N	E4
800	CHCG	60622	3032	3W-1N	E2
2400	CHCG	60647	2976	3W-3N	E5
3600	CHCG	60618	2976	3W-4N	E2
4400	CHCG	60618	2920	3W-5N	E7
4400	CHCG	60625	2920	3W-5N	E7
5500	CHCG	60659	2920	3W-6N	E5
6300	CHCG	60645	2920	3W-7N	E3
7300	CHCG	60645	2866	3W-9N	E7
7500	EVTN	60202	2866	3W-9N	E7
S Francisco Av					
10	CHCG	60612	3032	3W-0S	E5
1100	CHCG	60623	3032	3W-0S	E7
2400	CHCG	60623	3090	3W-2S	E2
3500	CHCG	60632	3090	3W-3S	E5
4600	CHCG	60632	3150	3W-5S	E1
5200	CHCG	60632	3151	3W-6S	A3
5400	CHCG	60629	3151	3W-7S	A5
8300	CHCG	60652	3213	3W-9S	A3
8600	ENGN	60652	3213	3W-9S	A4
8700	ENGN	60805	3213	3W-11S	A6
10100	ENGN	60655	3213	3W-11S	A7
10200	CHCG	60655	3277	3W-12S	A1
10200	ENGN	60655	3277	3W-12S	A1
10200	ENGN	60805	3277	3W-12S	A1
14500	POSN	60469	3349	3W-17S	A5
14800	BmnT	60426	3349	3W-17S	A5
14800	BmnT	60469	3349	3W-17S	A5
Francisco Ter					
100	OKPK	60302	3031	7W-0S	C6
Francis Ouimet Cir					
14000	MDLN	60445	3348	6W-16S	A3
Frank Dr					
-	LMNT	60439	3272	15W-14S	B6
6000	HFET	60120	2855		E1
Frank Ln					
1000	CteT	60401	3774	1W-33S	A2
N Frank Pkwy					
4800	NRDG	60706	2918	9W-6N	B6
S Frankfort Square Rd					
-	FKFT	60423	3504	9W-25S	D7
S Frankfort Square Rd					
19900	FftT	60423	3504	9W-25S	D7
W Frankfort Square Rd					
7600	FftT	60423	3504	9W-23S	D4
7900	FftT	60477	3504	9W-23S	D4
7900	TYPK	60423	3504	9W-23S	D4
7900	TYPK	60477	3504	9W-23S	D4
Frankie Ct					
500	PTHT	60070	2807	16W-15N	D2
Franklin Av					
10	FTPK	60130	3030	9W-0N	C5
800	RVFT	60305	3030	9W-1N	C3
1000	CHHT	60411	3507	1W-25S	E7
1500	EDPK	60707	3030	9W-1N	C1
3800	PvsT	60558	3086		E7
3800	WNSP	60558	3086		E7
5300	OKLN	60453	3211	6W-11S	D6
5300	WNSP	60558	3146		E3
9300	FNPK	60131	2973	11W-3N	C4
10600	FNPK	60131	2972		E3
10600	LydT	60131	2972		E3
11500	BNVL	60131	2972		C2
E Franklin Av					
300	LGNG	60525	3087	12W-4S	C7
N Franklin Av					
600	PLTN	60067	2752	22W-16N	C6
S Franklin Av					
5600	LynT	60525	3146		E4
Franklin Blvd					
-	ELGN	60120	2855		B3
W Franklin Blvd					
3000	CHCG	60612	3032	3W-0N	E3
3600	CHCG	60624	3032	4W-0N	C3
Franklin Ct					
10	SMWD	60107	2857	28W-11N	A4
5800	HRPK	60133	2911		D5
9000	ODPK	60462	3346	11W-17S	A5
Franklin Dr					
900	BRLT	60103	2910		C6
1900	GNVW	60062	2809	11W-14N	C3
22400	RNPK	60471	3594	5W-27S	B4
W Franklin Dr					
10	NHLK	60164	3028		D1
500	MPPT	60056	2861	16W-10N	E5
Franklin Ln					
400	EGVV	60007	2859	21W-9N	D7
400	EGVV	60007	2913		D1
Franklin Pl					
1900	HFET	60195	2858	25W-12N	A1
Franklin Rd					
100	GLNC	60022	2758	6W-18N	D3
Franklin St					
-	FNPK	60131	2973	11W-3N	E4
-	RVGV	60171	2973	11W-3N	D4
10	EGvT	60018	2862	15W-9N	A7
100	BRTN	60010	2750	27W-20N	C1
100	BRTN	60010	2751	25W-20N	A1
500	HNDL	60521	3086		B7
7200	FTPK	60130	3030	9W-0N	D4
7200	OKPK	60302	3030	9W-0N	D4
7500	RVFT	60305	3030	9W-0N	C4
E Franklin St					
200	BRTN	60010	2751	25W-20N	A2
N Franklin St					
10	CHCG	60606	3034	0W-0N	B4
400	CHCG	60610	3034	0W-0N	B3
S Franklin St					
10	CHCG	60606	3034	0W-0S	B5
300	CHCG	60607	3034	0W-0S	B5
Frank Mraz Dr					
-	RVDL	60827	3350	1W-16S	A3
N Franks Av					
7000	NLES	60714	2918	8W-8N	E1
7100	NLES	60714	2864	8W-9N	E7
Frank Wagner Av					
2300	BlmT	60411	3509	2E-25S	D7
2300	SLVL	60411	3509	2E-25S	D7
Fran Lin Pkwy					
800	MNSR	46321	3510		E2
Fransean					
-	HGKN	60525	3147	11W-7S	D5
N Franzen St					
300	BNVL	60106	2915		D7
Fred St					
18200	LNSG	60438	3429	3E-21S	E6
Frederick Av					
10	BLWD	60104	3029	12W-0N	A3
500	SMWD	60107	2911		B1
7800	MNSR	46321	3430		D6
Frederick Ct					
200	HFET	60195	2858	23W-12N	E1
1200	ELGN	60120	2855		D1
Frederick Dr					
100	CHHT	60411	3507	1W-23S	E3
3600	OKBK	60523	3086		A6
Frederick Ln					
200	HFET	60195	2858	24W-12N	E1
200	HFET	60195	2859	23W-12N	B1
Frederick Pl					
200	WDDL	60191	2914		E7
Frederick Rd					
22300	CHHT	60411	3596	0E-27S	E4
22300	SCHT	60411	3596	0E-27S	E4
22300	SCHT	60475	3596	0E-27S	E4
22300	STGR	60475	3596	0E-27S	E4
E Frederick St					
1300	ANHT	60004	2807	17W-14N	C3
Frediani Ct					
1700	MPPT	60056	2807	17W-12N	C7
Fredric Ct					
2800	GNVW	60062	2809	11W-15N	D2
Fredrick Ct					
10	BlmT	60411	3510	3E-25S	A7
Freedom Ct					
1700	MPPT	60056	2808	13W-14N	D5
Freehauf St					
200	LMNT	60439	3270		D6
Freeland Av					
300	CTCY	60409	3352	4E-17S	B6
1200	CTCY	60409	3430	4E-19S	B3
Freeman Av					
400	SMWD	60107	2911		A1
Freeman Ct					
700	HFET	60195	2804	23W-15N	D2
700	IVNS	60067	2804	23W-15N	D2
700	IVNS	60195	2804	23W-15N	D2
Freeman Rd					
100	HFET	60195	2804	23W-15N	D2
100	IVNS	60067	2804	24W-15N	C2
100	IVNS	60195	2804	23W-15N	D2
N Freeman Rd					
10	HFET	60195	2804	25W-14N	B5
10	SBTN	60010	2804	25W-14N	B5
E Fremont Av					
10	DSPN	60016	2862	14W-11N	C3
E Fremont Av					
100	EMHT	60126	3028		A1
Fremont Ct					
10	DSPN	60016	2862	15W-11N	B3
1700	HFET	60195	2858	24W-12N	E1
2800	SMBG	60193	2857	27W-10N	D6
E Fremont Ct					
2000	ANHT	60004	2807	16W-14N	C4
Fremont Dr					
1300	HRPK	60133	2911		D4
Fremont Rd					
1700	HFET	60195	2858	24W-12N	E1
Fremont St					
200	LMNT	60439	3270		D5
400	ELGN	60120	2855		A3
900	BRLT	60103	2910		C6
E Fremont St					
10	ANHT	60004	2807	17W-14N	A4
N Fremont St					
100	PLTN	60067	2752	20W-16N	E7
1400	CHCG	60622	3033	1W-1N	E1
1700	CHCG	60614	2977	1W-2N	E7
3500	CHCG	60613	2977	1W-4N	E2
3500	CHCG	60657	2977	1W-4N	E3
S Fremont St					
100	PLTN	60067	2805	20W-15N	E1
W Fremont St					
100	ANHT	60004	2807	18W-14N	A4
1400	ANHT	60005	2806	18W-14N	D4
1700	RGMW	60008	2806	18W-14N	D4
Fresno Ct					
5800	HRPK	60133	2911		E5
Fresno Ln					
3000	HMWD	60430	3507	3W-22S	A1
Friendship Dr					
-	BRLT	60103	2911		B3
S Friendship Dr					
25600	MONE	60449	3682	7W-31S	D4
Friendship Vil					
-	SMBG	60193	2858	23W-10N	E5
-	SMBG	60194	2858	23W-10N	E5
Friendship Village					
-	SMBG	60194	2858	23W-10N	E5
-	SMBG	60194	2859	23W-10N	A5
Fries Av					
-	DndT	60118	2801		A5
Frisco Ct					
200	BMDL	60108	2912		A7
Frisco St					
200	BMDL	60108	2912		A7
200	BMDL	60172	2912		A7
200	BmdT	60172	2912		A7
Fritz					
-	RVDL	60827	3349	1W-16S	E2
Fritz Dr					
17500	LNSG	60438	3430	3E-20S	A5
Front Av					
10300	FNPK	60131	2973	12W-4N	A3
S Front Av					
12100	CHCG	60628	3278	0E-14S	D5
Front St					
-	WLMT	60091	2811	6W-13N	D5
3400	MTSN	60443	3594	4W-25S	E1
3400	PKFT	60443	3594	4W-25S	E1
3400	PKFT	60466	3594	4W-25S	E1
E Front St					
100	WDDL	60191	2915		B7
Frontage					
-	HFET	60194	2858	24W-11N	E2
-	SMBG	60195	2858	24W-11N	E2
Frontage Rd					
-	BlmT	60438	3429	1E-21S	B7
-	BLWD	60104	3029	12W-0S	A6
-	EMHT	60126	3028		A7
-	HLSD	60162	3028		E6
-	MDLN	60445	3348	4W-17S	D4
-	NfdT	60062	2757	8W-18N	E3
-	NHBK	60062	2757	8W-18N	E3
-	NtrT	60093	2811	6W-14N	D4
-	OKBK	60523	3086		A1
-	OKFT	60426	3426	5W-19S	C2
-	SMBG	60193	2912		C2
-	SmbT	60193	2912		C2
-	SRPK	60176	2973	13W-5N	A1
-	ThtT	60438	3429	2E-20S	C5
-	ThtT	60476	3429	1E-21S	B7
-	WNSP	60558	3146		D3
-	YkTp	60523	3028		B7
-	YkTp	60523	3086		A1
1000	SMBG	60194	2858	24W-10N	C5
1200	NHFD	60091	2811	6W-14N	D4
1200	NHFD	60093	2811	6W-14N	D4
2000	DSPN	60018	2863	13W-9N	A7
2200	DSPN	60018	2917	13W-9N	A1
4100	HLSD	60162	3029	13W-0S	A6
4300	OKFT	60452	3426	5W-19S	C2
4700	BmnT	60452	3426	5W-20S	A4
4700	BmnT	60477	3426	5W-20S	A4
4700	BmnT	60478	3426	5W-20S	B4
7300	BGVW	60455	3210	9W-11S	D6
7600	SKOK	60077	2865	6W-9N	C6
7700	MNGV	60053	2865	6W-9N	C6
8600	SKOK	60053	2865	6W-10N	C4
9200	BGVW	60453	3210	8W-10S	E5
9200	OKLN	60453	3210	8W-10S	E5
10000	SKOK	60077	2811	6W-12N	E7
10000	SKOK	60091	2811	6W-13N	E7
10000	WLMT	60091	2811	6W-13N	E7
16100	BmnT	60426	3426	5W-19S	C2
16100	MKHM	60426	3426	5W-19S	C2
18200	LNSG	60438	3429	1E-21S	B7
E Frontage Rd					
-	EGvT	60007	2860	20W-11N	A3
-	RGMW	60007	2860	20W-11N	A3
-	RGMW	60008	2860	20W-11N	A3
-	SMBG	60193	2912		B3
-	SmbT	60193	2912		B3
10	NHFD	60093	2811	6W-14N	D3
2900	RGMW	60008	2806	20W-13N	B6
3400	PltT	60067	2806	20W-13N	B6
3800	PltT	60008	2806	20W-13N	B6
N Frontage Rd					
-	IHPK	60525	3146		D5
-	LynT	60525	3146		D5
200	BRRG	60527	3208		B1
300	DGvT	60527	3208		B1
1200	PLTN	60074	2753	19W-17N	D5
1200	PltT	60074	2753	19W-17N	D5
6900	BRRG	60527	3146		D7
S Frontage Rd					
-	BRRG	60527	3146		D7
-	BRRG	60527	3208		A2
-	DGvT	60439	3270		B1
-	HLSD	60162	3028		D6
-	IHPK	60525	3146		D7
S Frontage Rd					
-	WDRG	60439	3270		B1
10	BlmT	60425	3509	1E-23S	B3
10	GNWD	60425	3509	1E-23S	B3
W Frontage Rd					
-	ANHT	60004	2806	19W-15N	C2
-	PLTN	60004	2806	19W-15N	C2
-	PLTN	60074	2806	19W-15N	C2
-	SMBG	60173	2860	21W-11N	A3
-	WLMT	60091	2811	6W-14N	D4
10	NtrT	60093	2811	6W-14N	D3
400	NHFD	60093	2811	7W-16N	B1
500	NHFD	60093	2758	7W-16N	B7
800	GLNC	60062	2758	7W-16N	B7
1800	RGMW	60008	2806	20W-13N	A6
1800	SMBG	60008	2806	21W-12N	A7
1800	SMBG	60067	2806	21W-12N	A7
1800	SMBG	60173	2806	21W-12N	A7
1900	PltT	60067	2806	20W-13N	A7
5400	MNGV	60053	2865	6W-11N	C2
5400	SKOK	60077	2865	6W-11N	C2
Frontage Rd E					
-	SKOK	60077	2865	6W-9N	D7
Frontage Rd W					
7300	SKOK	60077	2865	6W-9N	D7
W Frontage Ter					
8700	JSTC	60458	3210	11W-9S	A4
S Frontenac Av					
5900	CHCG	60621	3152	0W-6S	A4
W Frontenac Dr					
900	ANHT	60004	2753	18W-16N	E7
Frontier Dr					
200	ROSL	60172	2913		B5
Frontier Wy					
100	BNVL	60106	2915		D4
Frost Dr					
-	MPPT	60056	2861	16W-11N	D3
Frost Rd					
2000	HFET	60195	2804	23W-13N	D6
2000	PltT	60195	2804	23W-13N	D6
W Fry St					
900	CHCG	60622	3033	1W-1N	E2
Fulbright Ln					
10	SMBG	60193	2859	23W-10N	A5
10	SMBG	60194	2859	23W-10N	A5
Fulle St					
2100	RGMW	60008	2806	19W-13N	C7
Fuller Ln					
100	KLWH	60043	2812	4W-15N	D3
100	WNKA	60093	2812	4W-15N	D3
Fuller Rd					
400	HNDL	60521	3086		B7
Fuller St					
-	HNDL	60521	3086		B7
W Fuller St					
1300	CHCG	60608	3091	1W-2S	D3
Fullerton Av					
800	MNSR	46321	3430		E6
1600	FNPK	60131	2973	11W-3N	C6
9100	FNPK	60171	2973	11W-3N	C6
9100	RVGV	60171	2973	11W-3N	C6
9400	FNPK	60164	2973	11W-2N	C6
9400	LydT	60164	2973	11W-2N	C6
E Fullerton Av					
10	NHLK	60164	2972		E6
100	EMHT	60126	2972		A6
300	AddT	60126	2972		A6
300	LydT	60164	2972		E6
W Fullerton Av					
-	NHLK	60164	2972		D6
800	CHCG	60614	2977	2W-3N	C5
1900	CHCG	60647	2977	2W-3N	B5
2700	CHCG	60647	2976	4W-2N	D6
3900	CHCG	60639	2976	5W-2N	B6
4700	CHCG	60639	2975	7W-3N	C6
6300	CHCG	60707	2975	7W-2N	A6
7200	CHCG	60707	2974	9W-2N	D6
7200	EDPK	60707	2974	9W-2N	B6
8000	RVGV	60707	2974	10W-3N	B6
8600	RVGV	60171	2973	11W-3N	E6
8600	RVGV	60171	2974	10W-3N	A6
9000	FNPK	60171	2973	11W-3N	D6
9600	FNPK	60131	2973	12W-2N	A6
9600	FNPK	60164	2973	12W-2N	A6
9600	LydT	60164	2973	12W-2N	A6
10300	LydT	60131	2973	12W-3N	A6
10400	NHLK	60164	2973	13W-3N	A6
W Fullerton Pkwy					
300	CHCG	60614	2978	0W-2N	B5
W Fulton Blvd					
3200	CHCG	60612	3032	4W-0N	D4
3200	CHCG	60624	3032	4W-0N	D4
Fulton Dr					
1000	HnrT	60107	2856	29W-9N	E7
1000	HnrT	60107	2910		E1
1000	SMWD	60107	2856	29W-9N	E7
1000	SMWD	60107	2910		E1
W Fulton Dr					
3600	CHCG	60624	3032	5W-0N	B4
Fulton St					
200	ELGN	60120	2855		A4
2100	BLID	60406	3349	2W-15S	C1
W Fulton St					
500	CHCG	60606	3034	0W-0N	A4
500	CHCG	60661	3034	0W-0N	A4
1200	CHCG	60607	3033	1W-0N	D4
1600	CHCG	60612	3033	3W-0N	A4
2800	CHCG	60612	3032	3W-0N	E4
4400	CHCG	60624	3032	5W-0N	A4
4500	CHCG	60644	3032	5W-0N	A4
5300	CHCG	60644	3031	6W-0N	D4
5900	OKPK	60302	3031	7W-0N	B4
Fulton Ter					
16400	BmnT	60477	3425	7W-19S	C3
16600	TYPK	60477	3425	7W-19S	C3
W Fulton Market					
700	CHCG	60607	3034	0W-0N	A4
700	CHCG	60661	3034		E4
800	CHCG	60607	3033	1W-0N	E4
Fun Dr					
-	ODPK	60462	3345	12W-18S	C7
-	ODPK	60467	3345	12W-18S	C7
-	OrlT	60467	3345	12W-18S	C7
G					
W G St					
-	MYWD	60141	3088	10W-1S	A1
-	MYWD	60153	3088	10W-1S	A1
-	PvsT	60141	3088	10W-1S	A1
-	PvsT	60153	3088	10W-1S	A1
Gable Ct					
1600	HRPK	60133	2911		D6
W Gabreski Ln					
6900	MonT	60449	3682	8W-30S	A3

STREET Block	City	ZIP	Map#	CGS	Grid
Gadwall Ct					
14400	HMGN	60441	3344	15W-17S	B5
Gaelic Ct					
10	IVNS	60010	2750	25W-16N	E7
Gaffield Pl					
800	EVTN	60201	2867	2W-12N	B1
Gage Av					
3900	LYNS	60534	3088	9W-4S	C7
5600	RSMT	60018	2917	11W-7N	C5
9000	FNPK	60131	2973	11W-4N	D4
11000	FNPK	60131	2972		D4
Gage Rd					
100	RVSD	60546	3088	9W-3S	D5
Gage St					
1000	WNKA	60093	2758	5W-16N	E7
1000	WNKA	60093	2759	5W-16N	A7
6100	RSMT	60018	2917	11W-7N	C3
Gail Av					
10	NHLK	60164	3028		D1
5600	MONE	60449	3682	7W-30S	E4
5600	MonT	60449	3682	7W-30S	E4
5600	UYPK	60449	3682	7W-30S	E4
5600	UYPK	60466	3682	7W-30S	E4
Gail Ct					
10	BlmT	60411	3510	3E-25S	A7
N Gail Ct					
300	ANHT	60004	2807	16W-15N	D2
300	PTHT	60070	2807	16W-15N	D2
Gail Ct S					
200	ANHT	60004	2807	16W-15N	D2
200	PTHT	60004	2807	16W-15N	D2
200	PTHT	60070	2807	16W-15N	D2
Gail Ln					
400	CHHT	60411	3507	2W-24S	D4
14000	CTWD	60445	3347	6W-16S	E3
Gailine Av					
21500	SLVL	60411	3597	2E-26S	D2
Gainsborough Pl					
5700	OKFT	60452	3347	7W-18S	D6
E Gaisor Ct					
2100	CteT	60417	3686	2E-29S	E1
E Gaisor Dr					
2000	CteT	60417	3686	2E-29S	D2
Gale Av					
10	FTPK	60130	3030	9W-0N	B5
10	RVFT	60305	3030	9W-0N	B4
W Gale St					
5300	CHCG	60630	2919	6W-6N	D6
N Galena Av					
3900	ANHT	60004	2753	19W-18N	D3
3900	PltT	60004	2753	19W-18N	D3
N Galena Ct					
3800	ANHT	60004	2753	19W-18N	D3
N Galesburg Av					
3900	ANHT	60004	2753	19W-18N	D3
3900	PltT	60004	2753	19W-18N	D3
N Galesburg Ct					
3800	ANHT	60004	2753	19W-18N	D3
3800	PltT	60004	2753	19W-18N	D3
W Galeview Ln					
7600	FftT	60423	3504	9W-24S	D5
Galitz St					
5100	SKOK	60077	2865	6W-9N	D6
5300	MNGV	60053	2865	6W-9N	D6
Galleon Ln					
700	EGVV	60007	2913		D2
Galleon Wy					
400	DSPN	60016	2862	15W-11N	B3
Galloway Cir					
1700	IVNS	60010	2751	24W-16N	C6
Galloway Dr					
1500	IVNS	60010	2751	24W-17N	C5
5200	HFET	60192	2802	30W-12N	C7
Galvin Center Access					
-	SMBG	60173	2805	22W-12N	C7
Galway Ct					
10	LMNT	60439	3272	16W-14S	A7
1100	NHBK	60062	2756	11W-17N	E5
Galway Dr					
700	PTHT	60070	2808	14W-15N	C2
Galway Ln					
10	LMNT	60439	3272	16W-14S	A6
Galway Rd					
10	LMNT	60439	3272	16W-14S	A6
Gannon Ct					
1000	HFET	60194	2858	24W-11N	C3
Gannon Dr					
-	HFET	60195	2858	24W-12N	C2
800	HFET	60194	2858	24W-11N	C3
Gant Cir					
10	SMWD	60107	2857	28W-11N	B4
S Garavogue Av					
14000	HMGN	60467	3344	15W-16S	C4
Garbo Ln					
5300	HRPK	60133	2911		C6
Garden Av					
10	BmdT	60172	2912		D7
10	BNVL	60106	2972		A1
200	BNVL	60106	2916		A7
500	ROSL	60172	2912		D7
1300	CHHT	60411	3507	1W-25S	E7
3800	WNSP	60558	3086		C7
E Garden Av					
10	PLTN	60067	2752	20W-17N	E4
300	PLTN	60067	2753	20W-17N	A4
300	PLTN	60074	2753	20W-17N	A4
N Garden Av					
10	ROSL	60172	2912		D4
S Garden Av					
10	ROSL	60172	2912		D5
500	BmdT	60172	2912		D6
W Garden Av					
10	PLTN	60067	2752	21W-17N	E4
Garden Cir					
200	HFET	60010	2857	27W-11N	C4
200	SMWD	60107	2857	27W-11N	B4
900	SMWD	60010	2857	27W-11N	C4
Garden Ct					
600	GNVW	60025	2810	9W-13N	D7
1200	PTHT	60070	2754	15W-16N	E6
7200	OKPK	60301	3030	9W-0N	D4
7200	RVFT	60305	3030	9W-0N	D4
7900	BGVW	60455	3148	9W-7S	C6
9800	SRPK	60176	2973	12W-4N	B2
W Garden Ct					
100	PLTN	60067	2752	21W-17N	E4
Garden Ln					
-	FftT	60423	3505	8W-23S	A3
-	FftT	60477	3505	8W-23S	A3
-	RchT	60423	3505	8W-23S	A3
-	RchT	60477	3505	8W-23S	A3
100	PTHT	60070	2754	15W-16N	E6
800	WLNG	60090	2754	15W-16N	E6
800	WLNG	60090	2755	15W-16N	A6
6800	BGVW	60455	3148	9W-7S	C6
6800	BGVW	60458	3148	9W-7S	C6
7400	JSTC	60458	3209	11W-8S	E2
Garden St					
700	PKRG	60068	2918	10W-8N	A1
1300	PKRG	60068	2917	10W-8N	E1
3400	NfdT	60062	2756	11W-16N	C7
S Garden St					
1500	PltT	60067	2806	20W-13N	A5
1600	PltT	60008	2806	20W-13N	A5
1600	RGMW	60008	2806	20W-13N	A5
Garden Ter					
2000	HFET	60195	2858	25W-12N	C1
E Garden Wk					
2600	ANHT	60004	2807	16W-14N	D5
Garden Wy					
-	BMDL	60108	2912		D7
-	SMBG	60194	2859	23W-10N	A5
Gardenia Dr					
10	DYR	46311	3598		C1
Gardenia Ln					
300	BFGV	60089	2754	17W-20N	C1
600	BRLT	60103	2910		D7
E Gardenia Ln					
800	PLTN	60074	2753	19W-18N	B3
Garden View Ct					
15600	ODPK	60462	3346	9W-18S	E7
Garden View Ln					
6200	MTSN	60443	3505	7W-25S	C6
Gardner Av					
20500	BlmT	60411	3507	2W-24S	C6
20700	CHHT	60411	3507	2W-25S	C7
Gardner Ct					
5700	HRPK	60133	2911		E5
Gardner Rd					
600	BDVW	60154	3029	12W-1S	C7
600	BDVW	60155	3029	12W-1S	C7
600	WSTR	60154	3029	12W-1S	C7
700	FSMR	60422	3507	2W-22S	C2
1000	WSTR	60155	3029	12W-0S	C7
1400	BDVW	60155	3087	12W-1S	C1
1400	WSTR	60154	3087	12W-1S	C1
2100	BDVW	60154	3087	12W-1S	C2
Gareth Ln					
200	SMBG	60193	2859	22W-10N	C6
Garfield Av					
10	LGPK	60525	3087	12W-3S	C4
400	CTCY	60409	3352	4E-17S	C5
1100	BKFD	60513	3087	12W-3S	C4
6100	HMND	46324	3430		D2
8500	MNSR	46321	3430		D7
E Garfield Av					
10	PltT	60067	2805	20W-13N	E5
10	RGMW	60067	2805	20W-13N	E5
N Garfield Av					
10	HNDL	60521	3146		B1
300	HNDL	60521	3086		B7
S Garfield Av					
10	HNDL	60521	3146		B5
5800	BRRG	60521	3146		B4
6200	WLBK	60527	3146		B5
7200	BRRG	60527	3146		B7
7600	HMND	46324	3430		D5
7900	BRRG	60527	3208		B3
8100	DGvT	60527	3208		B3
W Garfield Av					
300	PTON	60468	3860	9W-37S	E4
E Garfield Blvd					
10	CHCG	60609	3152	0E-5S	C2
10	CHCG	60615	3152	0E-5S	C2
10	CHCG	60621	3152	0E-6S	C3
10	CHCG	60637	3152	0E-5S	C2
W Garfield Blvd					
-	CHCG	60629	3151	2W-5S	B3
-	CHCG	60632	3151	2W-5S	B3
10	CHCG	60609	3152	0W-5S	A2
10	CHCG	60615	3152	0W-5S	C2
10	CHCG	60621	3152	0W-5S	A2
10	CHCG	60637	3152	0W-5S	A2
900	CHCG	60609	3151	1W-5S	D3
900	CHCG	60621	3151	1W-6S	E3
1100	CHCG	60636	3151	1W-6S	E3
Garfield Ct					
900	CPVL	60110	2748		D7
8400	MNSR	46321	3430		D7
Garfield Dr					
900	CPVL	60110	2748		D7
Garfield Ln					
10	SMWD	60107	2856	29W-10N	E6
Garfield St					
10	CHCG	60644	3031	7W-0S	B6
10	OKPK	60304	3031	7W-0S	B6
100	BRTN	60010	2750	27W-20N	C1
800	OKPK	60304	3030	8W-0S	D6
1100	FTPK	60130	3030	8W-0S	D6
Garfield Ridge Ct					
10	WLBK	60527	3146		B6
Garland Av					
600	WNKA	60093	2812	4W-15N	B3
N Garland Ct					
10	CHCG	60603	3034	0E-0N	C4
100	CHCG	60601	3034	0E-0N	C4
100	CHCG	60602	3034	0E-0N	C4
W Garland Ct					
7700	FftT	60423	3504	9W-24S	D5
Garland Ln					
1600	HRPK	60133	2911		D6
Garland Pl					
600	DSPN	60016	2863	12W-11N	B4
Garlands Ln					
1000	BRTN	60010	2751	25W-20N	A1
Garlisch Dr					
10	EGVV	60007	2861	17W-10N	C5
Garman Rd					
10	PKFT	60466	3595	2W-27S	C4
Garnet Cir					
800	SMBG	60193	2913		B1
1400	HFET	60195	2804	24W-15N	B1
Garnet Dr					
1200	NHLK	60164	2972		C5
Garnett Pl					
1000	EVTN	60201	2867	2W-11N	A2
W Garrett Ct					
7600	FftT	60423	3504	9W-23S	E4
Garrett Dr					
10900	ODPK	60467	3423	13W-21S	A5
Garrett Pl					
600	EVTN	60201	2867	2W-12N	C1
Garrison Av					
100	EVTN	60091	2813	2W-13N	B7
100	EVTN	60201	2813	2W-13N	B7
100	WDND	60118	2801		A3
100	WLMT	60091	2813	2W-13N	B7
Garth Rd					
600	WLNG	60090	2755	15W-17N	A6
N Garvey Ct					
200	CHCG	60601	3034		E4
E Garwood Av					
500	MPPT	60056	2808	15W-13N	A5
Gary Av					
-	HRPK	60133	2912		B5
-	ROSL	60172	2912		B5
10	BMDL	60108	2912		B7
10	BMDL	60172	2912		B7
10	BmdT	60172	2912		B7
200	BmdT	60108	2912		B7
Gary Av CO-23					
-	HRPK	60133	2912		B5
10	BMDL	60108	2912		B7
10	BMDL	60172	2912		B7
10	BmdT	60172	2912		B7
200	BmdT	60108	2912		B7
500	ROSL	60172	2912		B7
N Gary Av					
-	HRPK	60133	2912		B4
200	ROSL	60172	2912		B4
200	SMBG	60193	2912		B4
N Gary Av CO-23					
-	HRPK	60133	2912		B4
200	ROSL	60172	2912		B4
200	SMBG	60193	2912		B4
Gary Ct					
1900	SMBG	60193	2912		A3
Gary Dr					
2800	FNPK	60131	2973	13W-3N	A5
2800	LydT	60131	2973	13W-3N	A5
2800	LydT	60164	2973	13W-3N	A5
Garywood Dr					
1400	BRRG	60527	3146		C5
Gasket Dr					
1300	BRLT	60103	2909		D2
1300	ELGN	60120	2909		D2
W Gaslight Square Dr					
3600	ALSP	60803	3276	4W-14S	D6
Gasoline Al					
700	BNVL	60106	2915		E5
Gastes Ln					
14300	HMGN	60441	3343	18W-17S	B5
Gates Av					
700	BmdT	60143	2913		E5
Gatesby Rd					
200	RVSD	60546	3088	9W-2S	C4
Gateshead Av S					
-	EGVV	60007	2914		B2
Gateshead Ln N					
500	EGVV	60007	2914		C2
Gateshead Ln S					
500	EGVV	60007	2914		C2
N Gateway Dr					
-	MTSN	60443	3594	6W-26S	A2
Gateway Ln					
10	OKBK	60523	3086		B6
Gateway Rd					
10	BNVL	60106	2915		E7
N Gatewood Av					
1400	PLTN	60067	2752	21W-17N	D4
Gauger Av					
15900	HRVY	60426	3427	1W-19S	E2
16000	MKHM	60426	3427	1W-19S	E2
N Gay Ct					
200	GNWD	60425	3508	0W-22S	B1
Gayle Ct					
100	SMWD	60107	2857	27W-11N	D4
600	WLNG	60090	2755	14W-17N	D5
2500	MaiT	60025	2864	9W-12N	C1
2500	NHBK	60062	2809	11W-15N	C1
Gaylord St					
10	EGVV	60007	2861	18W-10N	A5
Gaynelle Rd					
6200	TYPK	60477	3425	7W-19S	B3
Gayton Ln					
400	SMBG	60193	2859	22W-9N	B7
Gee Ct					
700	WLNG	60090	2754	16W-18N	D2
Gemini Ln					
2600	RVWD	60015	2755	13W-20N	E1
Genauldi Av					
1700	SMWD	60107	2911		B2
Geneva Av					
10	BLWD	60104	3029	13W-0N	A4
300	MLPK	60160	2973	13W-2N	A7
300	NHLK	60164	2973	13W-2N	A7
400	HLSD	60162	3029	13W-0N	A5
400	LydT	60164	2973	13W-2N	A7
N Geneva Av					
100	EMHT	60126	3028		B2
700	AddT	60126	2972		B6
700	EMHT	60126	2972		B6
Geneva Cir					
700	EGVV	60007	2913		D2
Geneva Ct					
-	IVNS	60010	2750	25W-16N	E7
10	CRTE	60417	3596	0E-28S	E6
300	SMBG	60193	2858	23W-9N	E7
N Geneva Ct					
800	EMHT	60126	2972		B6
Geneva Dr					
200	BlmT	60411	3598	4E-25S	C1
200	HRVY	60426	3428	1W-19S	A3
200	LYWD	60411	3598	4E-25S	C1
1600	WLNG	60090	2808	14W-15N	B1
6800	TYPK	60477	3505	8W-22S	A1
N Geneva Dr					
1300	PLTN	60074	2753	19W-17N	C5
1300	PltT	60074	2753	19W-17N	C5
Geneva Pl					
-	SKOK	60203	2866	4W-12N	C2
10	EVTN	60201	2866	4W-12N	C1
Geneva St					
300	WDND	60118	2801		B3
N Geneva St					
10	ELGN	60120	2855		A4
S Geneva St					
10	ELGN	60120	2855		A4
N Geneva Ter					
2200	CHCG	60614	2978	0W-3N	A5
Genevieve Dr					
9400	SjnT	46311	3687		E2
S Genoa Av					
8700	CHCG	60620	3214	1W-10S	A4
9300	CHCG	60620	3213	1W-11S	E6
9300	CHCG	60643	3213	1W-11S	E6
Gentry Ln					
16700	BmnT	60477	3425	7W-20S	D3
16700	TYPK	60477	3425	7W-20S	D3
Gentry Rd					
1200	HFET	60195	2858	24W-12N	E2
Gentry St					
200	OMFD	60461	3507	3W-25S	B7
200	PKFT	60466	3507	3W-25S	B7
Geo Brown Dr					
14200	ODPK	60462	3345	12W-16S	D4
Geoffrey Rd					
15100	OKFT	60452	3347	7W-18S	D6
George Ct					
1700	GNVW	60025	2810	8W-12N	D7
2700	RGMW	60008	2806	19W-14N	C5
George Dr					
16400	OKFT	60452	3426	5W-19S	B3
George Pl					
4100	SRPK	60176	2973	12W-5N	A2
George Rd					
10	WLNG	60090	2755	15W-17N	A4
George St					
-	RVGV	60171	2973	11W-2N	E7
10	BNVL	60106	2972		A3
200	STGR	60475	3596	0E-27S	E5
400	ELGN	60120	2855		B5
400	WDDL	60143	2914		D7
400	WDDL	60191	2914		E7
800	FNPK	60131	2972		A3
1000	CTCY	60409	3351	3E-17S	E5
1000	CTCY	60409	3352	3E-17S	A5
1200	BrnT	60010	2751	25W-17N	A4
1200	BRTN	60010	2751	25W-17N	A4
1900	MLPK	60160	2973	11W-2N	E7
1900	MLPK	60160	3029	11W-2N	E1
2400	LydT	60164	2973	12W-3N	B6
3500	FNPK	60131	2973	12W-4N	A3
5200	SKOK	60077	2865	6W-9N	D6
5300	MNGV	60053	2865	6W-9N	D6
5300	MNGV	60077	2865	6W-9N	D6
E George St					
100	ITSC	60143	2914		C7
200	ANHT	60005	2807	17W-13N	B5
800	ITSC	60191	2914		D7
800	WDDL	60191	2914		C7
1100	WDDL	60143	2914		C7
N George St					
1600	CHCG	60657	2977	2W-3N	C4
S George St					
10	MPPT	60056	2808	15W-12N	B7
500	MPPT	60056	2862	15W-12N	B2
W George St					
100	ITSC	60143	2914		C7
200	ANHT	60005	2807	18W-13N	A5
500	ANHT	60005	2806	18W-13N	E5
1800	CHCG	60657	2977	2W-3N	B4
2100	RGMW	60008	2806	19W-13N	C5
2400	CHCG	60618	2977	3W-3N	A4
3600	CHCG	60618	2976	4W-3N	C4
3900	CHCG	60639	2976	5W-3N	B4
4600	CHCG	60641	2976	5W-3N	A4
4700	CHCG	60641	2975	7W-3N	C4
5500	CHCG	60634	2975	8W-3N	A4
6700	CHCG	60634	2974	8W-3N	E4
7200	EDPK	60707	2974	9W-3N	C4
Georgean Ln					
800	SMBG	60193	2858	24W-10N	D6
George Brennan Hwy					
17000	BmnT	60452	3426	6W-20S	A5
17000	BmnT	60477	3426	6W-20S	A5
17000	OKFT	60452	3426	6W-20S	A5
17000	OKFT	60477	3426	6W-20S	A5
17200	CCHL	60478	3426	6W-20S	A5
17200	OKFT	60478	3426	6W-20S	A5
17300	BmnT	60452	3425	6W-21S	E5
17300	BmnT	60478	3425	6W-21S	E5
17300	BmnT	60478	3426	6W-20S	A5
17400	BmnT	60477	3425	6W-20S	E5
Georgetown Coms					
7200	FKFT	60423	3593	8W-25S	A1
7200	RchT	60443	3593	9W-25S	A1
Georgetown Dr					
-	SMBG	60133	2912		A2
-	SMBG	60193	2912		B2
5400	MTSN	60443	3505	6W-25S	E7
13100	PlsT	60462	3345	13W-15S	A2
13100	PlsT	60467	3345	13W-15S	A2
Georgetown Ln					
1900	HFET	60195	2804	26W-12N	A7
1900	HFET	60195	2858	26W-12N	A1
Georgetown Rd					
21200	FKFT	60423	3593	9W-25S	A1
Georgetown Sq					
300	ITSC	60143	2914		E7
300	ITSC	60191	2914		E7
300	WDDL	60143	2914		E7
300	WDDL	60191	2914		E7
9400	ODHL	60477	3423	11W-19S	D2
9400	ODPK	60467	3423	11W-19S	D2
Georgia Ct					
1800	SMBG	60193	2912		A2
18000	ODPK	60467	3423	13W-21S	A7
Georgia Dr					
1000	EGVV	60007	2913		D2
W Georgia Dr					
6900	MNGV	60053	2864	8W-10N	E4
6900	NLES	60714	2864	8W-10N	E4
Georgia Ln					
10300	OKLN	60453	3275	6W-12S	D1
Georgian Pl					
900	BRLT	60103	2910		E6
Georgiana Av					
8500	MNGV	60053	2865	7W-10N	B4
Georgina Ln					
3300	BLWD	60104	3029	12W-0N	A5
Georgio Ln					
-	ODPK	60467	3423	13W-21S	B6
Geri Av					
700	PLTN	60067	2752	21W-16N	C6
N Geri Ct					
400	PLTN	60067	2752	21W-16N	C6
Geriln Ln					
-	DSPN	60016	2863	12W-11N	C3
Germaine Ln					
500	EGVV	60007	2861	18W-9N	A7
Germaine Pl					
10	SMBG	60173	2859	22W-10N	D5
500	EGVV	60007	2861	18W-9N	A7
German Church Rd					
10	DGvT	60527	3208		C3
10	LynT	60527	3208		C3
10800	WLSP	60480	3209	13W-9S	A3
10800	WLSP	60525	3209	13W-9S	A3
10900	WLSP	60480	3208		C3
10900	WLSP	60525	3208		C3
11400	BRRG	60480	3208		D3
11500	BRRG	60527	3208		D3
W Germania Pl					
100	CHCG	60610	3034	0W-1N	B1
Geronimo St					
500	HFET	60194	2859	23W-11N	A4
Gerritsen Av					
8800	BKFD	60513	3088	10W-4S	B7
8800	LYNS	60534	3088	10W-4S	B7
8900	BKFD	60513	3087	11W-4S	D7
9500	LGNG	60525	3087	12W-4S	D7
Gerry Dr					
100	WDDL	60191	2915		A5
Gerstung St					
10	PKFT	60466	3595	3W-26S	C2
Gettler St					
2100	DYR	46311	3598		C2
9700	SjnT	46311	3687		C3
10000	HnrT	46311	3687		C3
Getty Av					
900	ELGN	60120	2855		C6
Gettysburg Dr					
4400	RGMW	60008	2805	20W-14N	E3
W Gettysburg Dr					
700	ANHT	60004	2753	18W-16N	E7
Gettysburg St					
300	PKFT	60466	3595	4W-25S	A1
W Gettysburg St					
5400	CHCG	60630	2919	6W-6N	C6
Gianna Dr					
10	BlmT	60422	3507	2W-23S	D3
10	FSMR	60422	3507	2W-23S	D3
N Gibbons Av					
10	ANHT	60004	2807	16W-14N	C5
1000	PTHT	60004	2807	16W-14N	C4
S Gibbons Av					
10	ANHT	60004	2807	16W-13N	C5
400	ANHT	60005	2807	16W-13N	C6
Gibbs Dr					
10	SBTN	60010	2803	26W-13N	C6
Gibson Dr					
1500	EGVV	60007	2859	21W-9N	D7
1700	EGVV	60007	2913		D1
Gibson Ln					
17100	SHLD	60473	3429	1E-20S	B3
Gibson Rd					
10	PKFT	60466	3595	3W-26S	B2
Gibson St					
-	MTSN	60443	3506	6W-24S	A5
Giddings Av					
5700	HNDL	60521	3146		B4
5800	HNDL	60527	3146		B4
7200	BRRG	60527	3146		B7
7200	BRRG	60527	3208		B1
W Giddings St					
2000	CHCG	60625	2921	2W-5N	B7
2000	CHCG	60640	2921	2W-5N	B7
2700	CHCG	60625	2920	3W-5N	E7
5600	CHCG	60630	2919	7W-5N	B7
6200	HDHT	60706	2919	7W-5N	A7
7700	HDHT	60706	2918	9W-5N	C7
7700	NRDG	60706	2918	9W-5N	C7
Gifford Ct					
1300	HRPK	60133	2911		E5
Gifford Pl					
200	ELGN	60120	2855		A5
Gifford Rd					
800	ELGN	60120	2855		D7
900	BRLT	60103	2909		D2
900	ELGN	60120	2909		D2
N Gifford St					
10	ELGN	60120	2855		A3
S Gifford St					
10	ELGN	60120	2855		A4
Gilbert Av					
5200	LynT	60525	3147	13W-5S	A2
5200	WNSP	60558	3147	13W-5S	A2
N Gilbert Av					
10	LGNG	60525	3087	13W-4S	A7
10	WNSP	60558	3087	13W-4S	A7
100	LGPK	60525	3087	13W-4S	A7
Gilbert Ct					
3400	CRTE	60417	3597	1E-28S	B5
S Gilbert Ct					
8400	CHCG	60620	3214	0W-9S	A3
E Gilbert Rd					
10	PLTN	60067	2805	20W-15N	E2
W Gilbert Rd					
500	PLTN	60067	2805	22W-15N	C2
S Gilbert St					
700	SchT	60120	2909		A5
700	SchT	60177	2909		A5
Gilcrest Ct					
2800	SMBG	60193	2857	27W-10N	D6
S Giles Av					
3100	CHCG	60616	3092	0E-3S	C4
3300	CHCG	60653	3092	0E-3S	C4
Giles Ct					
400	BRLT	60103	2910		D3
Gillian St					
1100	LMNT	60439	3270		E7
Gillick St					
-	PKRG	60068	2917	10W-8N	E2
10	CHCG	60631	2918	10W-8N	B2
10	PKRG	60068	2918	10W-8N	A2
Gilman Av					
200	WLNG	60090	2755	14W-16N	B7
N Ginger Cir					
2000	PLTN	60074	2753	19W-18N	C3
Ginger Ct					
-	SjnT	46311	3598		D6
100	RGMW	60008	2805	21W-14N	D5
Ginger Ln					
400	ELGN	60120	2855		E3
Gingerbrook Ln					
200	BRLT	60103	2911		A5
N Ginger Creek Dr					
1900	PLTN	60074	2753	19W-18N	C3
Ginger Creek Ln					
15100	ODPK	60467	3344	14W-18S	E7
Girard Av					
100	EVTN	60091	2813	2W-13N	B7
100	WLMT	60091	2813	2W-13N	B7
2600	EVTN	60201	2813	2W-12N	B7
S Givins Ct					
8500	CHCG	60620	3214	0W-9S	A3
Glacier Ct					
600	ROSL	60172	2913		C3
2100	ALGN	60102	2748		B1
Glacier Dr					
400	HnrT	60107	2856	29W-11N	E4
400	SMWD	60107	2856	29W-11N	E4
Glacier Pkwy					
1100	ALGN	60102	2748		C1
Glacier Tr					
500	ROSL	60172	2913		B3
1500	CPVL	60110	2748		B3
Glad Ln					
-	HFET	60194	2858	24W-11N	E4
Glade Rd					
10	GLNC	60022	2758	6W-18N	D3

STREET Block	City	ZIP	Map#	CGS	Grid
E Glade Rd					
10	PLTN	60067	2805	20W-15N	E2
W Glade Rd					
200	PLTN	60067	2805	21W-15N	D2
Gladiola Av					
7200	HRPK	60133	2911		C1
Gladish Ln					
1200	GNVW	60025	2810	9W-13N	B6
Gladstone Av					
3700	RvsT	60546	3088	9W-3S	C6
3800	LYNS	60534	3088	9W-3S	C6
3800	RvsT	60534	3088	9W-3S	C6
Gladstone Ln					
400	ELGN	60120	2855		E5
400	ELGN	60120	2856	31W-10N	A5
Gladstone St					
-	BDVW	60155	3029	12W-0S	B6
10100	WSTR	60154	3029	12W-0S	B6
10300	HLSD	60162	3029	12W-0S	A6
Gladville Av					
17700	HMWD	60430	3427	2W-21S	D6
18500	HMWD	60430	3507	2W-22S	E1
Gladys Av					
3800	BLWD	60104	3029	12W-0S	A6
3800	BLWD	60162	3029	12W-0S	A6
3800	HLSD	60162	3029	12W-0S	A6
E Gladys Av					
100	EMHT	60126	2972		A7
W Gladys Av					
600	CHCG	60661	3034	0W-0S	A5
700	CHCG	60607	3034	0W-0S	A5
1300	CHCG	60607	3033	1W-0S	D5
2100	CHCG	60612	3033	2W-0S	B5
3300	CHCG	60624	3033	4W-0S	D5
4600	CHCG	60644	3032	5W-0S	A5
4700	CHCG	60644	3031	6W-0S	D5
Gladys Ct					
10	DRFD	60015	2757	9W-20N	B2
Gladys Ln					
8100	HYHL	60465	3210	10W-11S	C7
8100	PSHL	60465	3210	10W-11S	B7
Glamis Ln					
100	IVNS	60067	2752	22W-16N	A7
Glarus Ln					
10	LYWD	60411	3510	4E-25S	C7
10	LYWD	60411	3598	4E-25S	C1
Glasgow Ct					
2700	SMBG	60194	2857	26W-10N	D5
S Glasgow Dr					
19700	FftT	60423	3504	9W-23S	E4
Glasgow Ln					
100	SMBG	60194	2857	26W-10N	E5
600	PTHT	60070	2808	14W-14N	B3
Glastonbury Ln					
900	SMBG	60193	2912		C1
Glastonbury St					
10	MNSR	46321	3510		D3
E Glavin Ct					
1000	PLTN	60074	2753	19W-18N	B2
Gleaston Dr					
-	LYWD	60411	3509	2E-23S	D4
Glen Ct					
500	BMDL	60157	2913		B6
600	BmdT	60157	2913		D5
700	GNVW	60025	2811	7W-13N	A7
Glen Dr					
18000	OrlT	60477	3423	11W-21S	E7
S Glen Dr E					
14300	HMGN	60441	3344	15W-17S	C4
S Glen Dr W					
14300	HMGN	60441	3344	15W-17S	C4
W Glen Dr					
3700	ALSP	60803	3276	4W-14S	D6
Glen Ln					
1100	HFET	60195	2858	25W-12N	C1
Glen Rd					
10	BmdT	60157	2913		D5
S Glen Rd					
11400	PlsT	60464	3272	14W-13S	C5
Glen Ter					
18100	LNSG	60438	3429	3E-21S	E6
Glenayre Dr					
800	GNVW	60025	2811	7W-13N	A6
Glenberry Ln					
8600	TYPK	60477	3504	10W-23S	B3
Glenbrook Ct					
100	IHPK	60525	3146		E5
Glenbrook Dr					
10	PTHT	60070	2754	15W-16N	E7
10	PTHT	60070	2755	15W-16N	A7
10	WLNG	60090	2755	15W-16N	A7
3200	NHBK	60062	2756	11W-17N	D5
Glenbrook Ln					
11000	IHPK	60525	3146		E5
19400	TYPK	60477	3504	10W-23S	C3
Glenbrook Ln E					
6100	IHPK	60525	3146		E5
Glenbrook Ln W					
6100	IHPK	60525	3146		E5
Glenbrook Pl					
8100	TYPK	60477	3504	10W-23S	C3
Glen Byrn Ct					
300	SMBG	60194	2857	27W-10N	D5
Glencoe Av					
5000	MCCK	60525	3148	10W-5S	A2
Glencoe Dr					
800	GLNC	60022	2758	6W-18N	D4
Glencoe Rd					
-	PltT	60067	2752	21W-17N	C5
W Glencoe Rd					
400	PLTN	60067	2805	21W-15N	C1
700	PltT	60067	2805	21W-15N	C1
E Glencoe St					
300	PLTN	60067	2806	20W-15N	A1
300	PLTN	60074	2806	20W-15N	A1
Glencrest Dr					
1000	IVNS	60010	2751	25W-17N	B5
1100	BRTN	60010	2751	25W-17N	B5
Glendale Av					
-	CHCG	60613	2977	1W-5N	D1
-	CteT	60417	3774	1W-32S	B1
10	HNDL	60521	3086		A6
10	HNDL	60523	3086		A6
10	OKBK	60521	3086		A6
10	OKBK	60523	3086		A6
300	WNKA	60093	2811	5W-15N	E2
300	WNKA	60093	2812	5W-15N	A2
1800	NHBK	60062	2757	10W-16N	A7
E Glendale Av					
10	HNDL	60521	3086		A6
10	OKBK	60523	3086		A6
N Glendale Av					
100	BRTN	60010	2751	25W-20N	B2
S Glendale Av					
100	BRTN	60010	2751	25W-18N	B2
Glendale Blvd					
10	HMND	46320	3430		C1
Glendale Ct					
10	SMWD	60107	2857	27W-11N	C4
Glendale Dr					
600	GNVW	60025	2811	7W-13N	A7
600	PTHT	60070	2808	15W-15N	A1
600	WLNG	60090	2808	15W-15N	A1
Glendale Ln					
200	GNVW	60714	2864	10W-12N	A1
400	HFET	60194	2858	24W-11N	E4
N Glendale Ln					
9800	GNVW	60714	2864	10W-12N	A1
9800	NLES	60714	2864	10W-12N	A1
S Glendale Ln					
600	MPPT	60056	2861	16W-12N	D2
Glendale Rd					
-	GNVW	60025	2810	10W-13N	A6
10	BFGV	60089	2754	16W-18N	C3
200	GNVW	60025	2864	10W-12N	A1
200	GNVW	60714	2864	10W-12N	A1
200	NLES	60714	2864	10W-12N	A1
400	MaiT	60025	2810	10W-12N	A7
400	ROSL	60172	2913		C5
500	BmdT	60157	2913		C6
500	ROSL	60157	2913		C6
600	NfdT	60025	2810	10W-13N	A7
Glendale St					
10	WLNG	60090	2755	14W-18N	C4
900	BNVL	60106	2915		D7
Glendale Ter					
100	BMDL	60172	2913		A7
100	BMDL	60108	2913		B7
100	BmdT	60172	2913		A7
300	BmdT	60157	2913		C7
500	BMDL	60172	2912		E7
500	BmdT	60172	2912		E7
2300	HRPK	60133	2911		B3
Glendale Tr					
19400	TYPK	60477	3504	10W-23S	B3
Glendenning Rd					
300	KLWH	60043	2812	4W-14N	C5
300	WLMT	60043	2812	4W-14N	C5
300	WLMT	60091	2812	4W-14N	C5
Glen Eagle Ct					
13500	ODPK	60462	3346	11W-16S	A2
Gleneagle Ln					
800	NHBK	60062	2757	8W-16N	E7
Glen Eagles Ct					
500	IVNS	60067	2752	22W-16N	B6
Glen Eagles Dr					
2400	OMFD	60461	3507	3W-24S	B5
Glen Eagles Ln					
2200	RVWD	60015	2756	12W-20N	A1
Glen Echo Rd					
10	ELGN	60120	2855		E5
10	HnrT	60120	2855		E5
Glen Ellyn Ln					
-	PLTN	60067	2752	21W-17N	D6
Glengary Ct					
1300	WLNG	60090	2754	16W-18N	D3
2300	SMBG	60194	2857	26W-10N	E5
Glengary Ln					
1300	WLNG	60090	2754	16W-18N	D3
Glengate Av					
300	CHHT	60411	3508	0W-24S	B5
E Glengate Av					
10	CHHT	60411	3508	1W-24S	A5
W Glengate Av					
100	CHHT	60411	3508	1W-24S	A5
200	CHHT	60411	3507	2W-24S	E5
Glenhurst Rd					
22800	DRPK	60010	2752	22W-20N	A1
Glen Ivy Dr					
600	ELGN	60120	2855		D6
Glenlake Av					
10	CHCG	60631	2918	9W-7N	B3
10	PKRG	60068	2918	9W-7N	B3
1200	PKRG	60068	2917	10W-7N	E4
9500	RSMT	60018	2917	11W-7N	C3
E Glenlake Av					
10	ROSL	60172	2913		A4
W Glenlake Av					
10	ROSL	60172	2913		A4
100	ROSL	60172	2912		D4
1300	ITSC	60143	2913		E4
1600	CHCG	60660	2921	2W-7N	C3
2300	CHCG	60659	2921	3W-7N	A3
3900	CHCG	60659	2920	4W-7N	B3
4000	CHCG	60646	2920	5W-7N	B3
4700	CHCG	60646	2919	6W-7N	E3
7700	CHCG	60631	2918	9W-7N	C3
7800	PKRG	60068	2918	9W-7N	C3
7800	PKRG	60631	2918	9W-7N	C3
Glenlake Dr					
-	NfdT	60025	2809	11W-14N	D4
-	NfdT	60062	2809	11W-14N	D4
2000	GNVW	60025	2809	11W-14N	D4
3300	GNVW	60025	2810	10W-14N	A3
10800	ODPK	60467	3423	13W-18S	A1
15500	ODPK	60467	3345	13W-18S	A7
Glen Lake Rd					
1400	HFET	60194	2858	25W-12N	C2
1600	HFET	60195	2858	25W-12N	C1
Glenlake St					
9400	RSMT	60018	2917	11W-7N	C3
Glen Leven Ct					
200	SMBG	60194	2857	27W-10N	D5
Glenmora Dr					
100	BRRG	60527	3208		C5
Glenmora Ln					
8900	BRRG	60527	3208		C5
Glenmore Ct					
1000	LKPT	60441	3342	21W-18S	A7
1300	IVNS	60010	2751	24W-17N	C5
Glenmore Pl					
400	ROSL	60172	2912		C6
N Glenmore St					
700	LKPT	60441	3342	21W-18S	A7
Glenn Av					
500	WLNG	60090	2755	14W-17N	C6
W Glenn Av					
3400	RBBN	60472	3348	4W-16S	E3
Glenn Ct					
600	SMBG	60193	2859	23W-9N	B7
Glenn Dr					
400	BRRG	60527	3208		A6
400	DGvT	60527	3208		A6
N Glenn Dr					
400	PLTN	60074	2753	19W-16N	B6
W Glenn Ln					
1200	MPPT	60056	2861	16W-11N	D2
S Glenn Tr					
1100	EGVV	60007	2913		E2
W Glenn Tr					
900	EGVV	60007	2913		E2
Glen Oak Av					
18300	LNSG	60438	3429	3E-21S	E7
Glen Oak Dr					
800	WNKA	60093	2759	5W-16N	A7
1900	GNVW	60025	2811	7W-14N	A4
1900	NHFD	60025	2811	7W-14N	A4
2100	NHFD	60093	2811	7W-14N	A4
Glen Oak Ln					
1200	NHBK	60062	2757	9W-17N	D5
Glen Oak Rd					
8400	ODPK	60462	3346	10W-18S	B7
Glen Oaks Ct					
2300	ALGN	60102	2748		C1
16900	CCHL	60478	3426	4W-20S	D4
Glen Oaks Dr					
16800	CCHL	60478	3426	4W-20S	D4
Glenoble Ct					
10	OKBK	60523	3028		B7
Glenridge Dr					
600	GNVW	60025	2811	7W-13N	A7
Glenridge Ln					
100	SMBG	60193	2857	26W-10N	E6
S Glenroy Av					
10700	CHCG	60643	3277	1W-12S	E2
W Glenshire Dr					
7500	FftT	60423	3504	9W-25S	E7
7500	FKFT	60423	3504	9W-25S	E7
Glenshire Rd					
400	MaiT	60025	2810	10W-12N	A7
400	NfdT	60025	2810	10W-12N	A7
800	GNVW	60025	2810	10W-13N	A7
Glenshire St					
8600	TYPK	60477	3504	11W-23S	A4
8700	MKNA	60448	3504	11W-23S	A4
8700	TYPK	60448	3504	11W-23S	A4
8900	FftT	60448	3504	11W-23S	A4
Glenside Ct					
900	HRPK	60133	2858	26W-9N	A7
Glen Swilly Cir					
18200	TYPK	60477	3425	8W-21S	A7
Glenview Av					
1500	PKRG	60068	2863	11W-10N	D5
Glenview Ct					
2200	SMBG	60194	2857	26W-11N	E4
N Glenview Ct					
900	PLTN	60067	2752	22W-17N	C5
Glenview Dr					
6500	TYPK	60477	3425	8W-20S	B4
11500	OrlT	60467	3344	14W-17S	D4
Glenview Ln					
10	LMNT	60439	3270		E6
N Glenview Ln					
300	PTON	60468	3860	9W-37S	E3
Glenview Rd					
-	WLMT	60091	2812	5W-13N	A7
10	GNVW	60025	2811	7W-13N	B7
10	GNVW	60091	2811	6W-13N	D7
10	WLMT	60091	2811	6W-13N	D7
1400	GNVW	60025	2810	9W-13N	B6
2800	NfdT	60025	2810	9W-13N	B6
3500	NfdT	60025	2809	10W-13N	E6
3800	GNVW	60025	2809	11W-13N	E6
Glenway Dr					
3000	GNVW	60062	2809	11W-15N	D2
3100	GNVW	60025	2809	11W-15N	D2
Glen Wood Av					
10	GLNC	60093	2758	5W-16N	E6
10	GLNC	60093	2759	5W-16N	A6
Glenwood Av					
100	WLSP	60480	3209	12W-9S	B4
300	PlsT	60480	3209	12W-9S	C4
500	ELGN	60120	2801		B7
1300	GNVW	60025	2811	8W-14N	A4
1400	GNVW	60025	2810	8W-14N	E4
N Glenwood Av					
10	GNWD	60425	3508	0W-22S	D1
4900	CHCG	60640	2921	1W-6N	D6
5500	CHCG	60660	2921	1W-7N	D3
6800	CHCG	60626	2921	1W-8N	D1
7100	CHCG	60626	2867	1W-9N	D7
Glen Wood Ln					
14800	HMGN	60441	3343	18W-18S	A7
14800	HmrT	60441	3343	18W-18S	A7
Glenwood Ln					
600	GNVW	60025	2810	10W-13N	A7
600	NfdT	60025	2810	10W-13N	A7
1100	HFET	60010	2804	24W-16N	C1
6800	HRPK	60133	2912		A2
S Glenwood Ln					
600	LGNG	60525	3147	13W-5S	A1
Glenwood Rd					
100	GNWD	60425	3508	0W-23S	C2
200	BlmT	60411	3508	0W-23S	B4
200	CHHT	60411	3508	0W-23S	B4
19200	CHHT	60425	3508	0W-23S	B3
19200	GNWD	60411	3508	0W-23S	B3
19400	BlmT	60425	3508	0W-23S	B3
E Glenwood Rd					
800	GNVW	60025	2811	6W-13N	D7
S Glenwood St					
10	PLTN	60067	2806	20W-15N	A1
Glenwood Tr					
400	ELGN	60120	2801		A7
Glenwood Dyer Rd					
600	BlmT	60411	3509	2E-23S	C4
600	LYWD	60411	3509	2E-23S	C4
2400	BlmT	60411	3510	3E-24S	A5
2400	LYWD	60411	3510	3E-24S	A5
Glenwood Dyer Rd SR-83					
2400	BlmT	60411	3510	3E-24S	A5
2400	LYWD	60411	3509	3E-24S	E5
2400	LYWD	60411	3510	3E-24S	A5
E Glenwood Dyer Rd					
100	BlmT	60425	3508	0E-23S	E2
100	GNWD	60425	3508	0E-23S	E2
400	BlmT	60425	3509	1E-23S	A3
400	GNWD	60425	3509	1E-23S	A3
800	BlmT	60425	3509	1E-23S	B3
Glenwood Lansing Rd					
800	BlmT	60411	3509	2E-22S	C2
800	BlmT	60425	3509	1E-22S	B2
800	GNWD	60425	3509	1E-22S	B2
1800	LYWD	60411	3509	2E-22S	C2
2600	BlmT	60411	3510	3E-22S	A2
2600	LNSG	60438	3510	4E-22S	B2
2600	LYWD	60411	3510	3E-22S	A2
3500	MNSR	46321	3510	4E-22S	B2
E Glenwood Lansing Rd					
200	BlmT	60425	3508	0E-22S	E2
200	GNWD	60425	3508	0E-22S	E2
600	BlmT	60425	3509	1E-22S	A2
600	GNWD	60425	3509	1E-22S	A2
E Glenwood Thornton Rd					
18600	BlmT	60425	3508	0W-22S	C1
18600	GNWD	60425	3508	0W-22S	C1
Glenwoody Ct					
8400	ODPK	60462	3346	11W-16S	A2
Glenys Dr					
400	LMNT	60439	3270		E7
Gloria Ct					
3900	GNVW	60025	2809	11W-13N	D6
Gloria Dr					
1000	EGVV	60007	2913		E3
E Gloria Dr					
1200	PLTN	60074	2753	19W-16N	D7
1200	PLTN	60074	2806	19W-16N	C1
Gloria Jean Dr					
300	BNVL	60106	2972		A3
Glos Av					
2600	BLWD	60104	3029	12W-0N	C4
Gloucester Ct					
-	IVNS	60010	2804	25W-15N	A1
-	SBTN	60010	2804	25W-15N	A1
Gloucester Dr					
-	CRTE	60417	3596	0E-29S	E7
-	CRTE	60417	3685	0E-29S	E1
700	EGVV	60007	2914		C1
Glouchester Cir					
900	SMBG	60193	2913		D4
Glouchester Ct					
1300	HFET	60195	2804	25W-15N	A2
Glouchester Hbr					
1000	SMBG	60193	2913		B1
Glynwood Ln					
3600	HLCT	60429	3426	4W-20S	D5
Godair Cir					
700	DGvT	60527	3146		A5
Godair Dr					
-	BRRG	60527	3146		A5
10	DGvT	60527	3146		A5
S Goebbert Rd					
1900	ANHT	60005	2861	17W-11N	B3
Goesel Dr					
-	TYPK	60477	3424	10W-21S	B7
E Goethe St					
10	CHCG	60610	3034	0E-1N	C1
W Goethe St					
10	CHCG	60610	3034	0W-1N	B1
Gold Cir					
6100	HRPK	60133	2911		E4
Gold St					
200	PKFT	60466	3595	3W-27S	A3
Gold Coast Ln					
200	CTCY	60409	3430	4E-19S	B2
Goldcrest Ct					
10	BRLT	60107	2856	29W-9N	D7
Golden Spur					
10	LMNT	60439	3272	15W-13S	B5
Golden Eagle Dr					
-	FftT	60448	3422	14W-22S	E7
-	MKNA	60448	3422	14W-22S	E7
-	ODPK	60448	3422	14W-22S	E7
-	ODPK	60467	3422	14W-22S	E7
Golden Oak Ct					
8900	HYHL	60457	3209	11W-10S	E5
S Golden Oak Dr					
13700	HMGN	60441	3343	16W-17S	E5
Golden Pheasant Dr					
8800	TYPK	60477	3424	11W-21S	A6
Goldenrod Cir					
600	MTSN	60443	3506	5W-24S	B6
Goldenrod Ln					
1200	HFET	60195	2804	24W-15N	C1
2200	GNVW	60025	2810	9W-15N	B3
Golden Rose Dr					
8700	ODPK	60462	3424	10W-19S	A1
Golden Valley Ct					
10	ALGN	60102	2748		A2
Golden Valley Ln					
500	ALGN	60102	2748		A2
Golf Blvd					
-	ELGN	60120	2856	31W-10N	A6
Golf Ct					
900	CTCY	60409	3352	4E-18S	C7
2100	GNVW	60025	2864	9W-12N	D1
5000	MDLN	60445	3348	6W-17S	A5
Golf Ctr					
10	HFET	60195	2859	23W-11N	A2
Golf Dr					
-	OKBK	60523	3086		A3
W Golf Dr					
7600	PSHT	60463	3346	9W-15S	D1
Golf Ln					
10	NtrT	60093	2812	4W-14N	B3
10	WNKA	60093	2812	4W-15N	B3
300	ALGN	60102	2748		A1
700	BNVL	60106	2915		D6
Golf Pl					
-	RGMW	60008	2860	19W-12N	D2
Golf Rd					
-	ELGN	60120	2855		E2
-	HFET	60010	2856	29W-11N	E3
-	HFET	60010	2857	28W-12N	A3
-	HFET	60107	2856	29W-11N	D3
-	HnrT	60120	2855		E2
-	MNGV	60077	2865	8W-12N	A1
-	RGMW	60173	2860	20W-12N	A2
-	RVSD	60513	3088	10W-3S	B5
-	SMBG	60173	2860	20W-12N	A2
500	HFET	60120	2856	31W-12N	A2
500	HFET	60192	2856	30W-11N	B3
500	HnrT	60120	2856	31W-12N	A2
500	HnrT	60192	2856	30W-11N	B3
900	ANHT	60005	2860	19W-11N	D2
900	RGMW	60005	2860	19W-11N	D2
900	RGMW	60008	2860	19W-11N	D2
1700	GNVW	60025	2864	9W-12N	C2
1700	GNVW	60053	2864	9W-12N	C2
1700	MNGV	60053	2864	9W-12N	C2
2400	MaiT	60025	2864	9W-12N	C2
2500	MaiT	60714	2864	9W-12N	B2
2800	EGvT	60007	2860	19W-12N	B2
3100	EGvT	60008	2860	20W-12N	B2
3100	RGMW	60007	2860	20W-12N	B2
3100	RGMW	60008	2860	20W-12N	B2
3300	EVTN	60201	2866	4W-11N	C2
3300	EVTN	60203	2866	4W-11N	D2
3300	SKOK	60201	2866	4W-11N	D2
3300	SKOK	60203	2866	4W-11N	D2
3400	BKFD	60513	3088	10W-3S	B5
3400	BKFD	60546	3088	10W-3S	A4
3400	RVSD	60546	3088	10W-3S	B5
4000	SKOK	60076	2866	5W-11N	B2
4700	SKOK	60076	2865	5W-12N	E2
4700	SKOK	60077	2865	8W-12N	A1
6100	GLF	60029	2865	7W-12N	B2
6100	GLF	60053	2865	7W-12N	B2
6100	GLF	60077	2865	8W-12N	A1
Golf Rd					
6100	MNGV	60053	2865	7W-12N	B2
6400	MNGV	60029	2865	8W-12N	A2
6700	GLF	60029	2864	8W-12N	E2
9200	MaiT	60016	2863	11W-12N	C2
9200	NLES	60714	2863	11W-12N	C2
9500	DSPN	60016	2863	11W-12N	C2
10500	ODPK	60462	3345	13W-17S	A5
Golf Rd SR-58					
-	ELGN	60120	2855		E2
-	HFET	60010	2856	29W-11N	E3
-	HFET	60010	2857	28W-12N	A3
-	HFET	60107	2856	29W-11N	D3
-	HnrT	60120	2855		E2
-	RGMW	60173	2860	20W-12N	A2
-	SMBG	60173	2860	20W-11N	A2
500	HFET	60120	2856	31W-12N	A2
500	HFET	60192	2856	30W-11N	B3
500	HnrT	60120	2856	31W-12N	A2
500	HnrT	60192	2856	30W-11N	B3
900	ANHT	60005	2860	19W-11N	D2
900	RGMW	60005	2860	19W-11N	D2
900	RGMW	60008	2860	19W-11N	D2
1700	GNVW	60025	2864	9W-12N	C2
1700	GNVW	60053	2864	9W-12N	C2
1700	MNGV	60053	2864	9W-12N	C2
2400	MaiT	60025	2864	9W-12N	C2
2500	MaiT	60714	2864	9W-12N	B2
2800	EGvT	60007	2860	19W-12N	B2
3100	EGvT	60008	2860	20W-12N	B2
3100	RGMW	60007	2860	20W-12N	B2
9200	MaiT	60016	2863	11W-12N	C2
9200	NLES	60714	2863	11W-12N	C2
9500	DSPN	60016	2863	11W-12N	C2
E Golf Rd					
10	ANHT	60005	2861	17W-11N	A2
10	HFET	60195	2859	22W-12N	C2
10	SMBG	60173	2859	22W-12N	C2
10	SMBG	60195	2859	23W-12N	A2
100	HFET	60173	2859	22W-12N	C2
500	DSPN	60016	2862	13W-12N	D2
600	MPPT	60056	2861	17W-11N	B2
800	ANHT	60056	2861	17W-11N	B2
900	MPPT	60005	2861	17W-11N	B2
1300	DSPN	60016	2863	12W-12N	A2
1700	MaiT	60016	2863	12W-12N	A2
1800	SMBG	60173	2860	21W-12N	A2
2000	EGvT	60007	2860	21W-12N	A2
2000	RGMW	60008	2860	21W-12N	A2
2000	RGMW	60173	2860	20W-12N	A2
E Golf Rd SR-58					
10	ANHT	60005	2861	18W-11N	A2
10	HFET	60195	2859	22W-12N	C2
10	SMBG	60173	2859	22W-12N	C2
10	SMBG	60195	2859	23W-12N	A2
100	HFET	60173	2859	22W-12N	C2
500	DSPN	60016	2862	13W-12N	D2
600	MPPT	60056	2861	17W-11N	B2
800	ANHT	60056	2861	17W-11N	B2
900	MPPT	60005	2861	17W-11N	B2
1300	DSPN	60016	2863	12W-12N	A2
1700	MaiT	60016	2863	12W-12N	A2
1800	SMBG	60173	2860	21W-12N	A2
2000	EGvT	60007	2860	21W-12N	A2
2000	RGMW	60008	2860	21W-12N	A2
2000	RGMW	60173	2860	20W-12N	A2
W Golf Rd					
-	HFET	60010	2857	27W-12N	C3
10	ANHT	60005	2861	18W-12N	A2
10	DSPN	60016	2862	15W-11N	B3
10	DSPN	60056	2862	15W-11N	B3
10	HFET	60195	2859	23W-12N	A2
10	MPPT	60016	2862	15W-11N	B2
10	MPPT	60056	2862	15W-11N	B3
10	SMBG	60173	2859	23W-12N	A2
10	SMBG	60195	2859	23W-12N	A2
100	SMBG	60195	2858	25W-12N	C2
300	DSPN	60016	2861	16W-11N	E3
300	HFET	60195	2858	23W-12N	E2
500	ANHT	60005	2860	18W-11N	E2
600	SMBG	60194	2858	24W-12N	D2
700	RGMW	60005	2860	18W-11N	E2
700	RGMW	60008	2860	18W-11N	E2
1200	HFET	60194	2858	25W-11N	C2
1900	MPPT	60056	2861	17W-11N	C2
2000	ANHT	60056	2861	16W-11N	E3
2000	MPPT	60005	2861	16W-11N	E3
2100	HFET	60194	2857	26W-12N	E3
2100	SMBG	60194	2857	26W-12N	E3
8000	MaiT	60025	2864	10W-12N	A2
8000	MaiT	60714	2864	10W-12N	A2
8000	MNGV	60053	2864	10W-12N	A2
8000	NLES	60025	2864	10W-12N	A2
8000	NLES	60714	2864	10W-12N	A2
8500	MaiT	60016	2864	10W-12N	A2
8600	MaiT	60016	2863	11W-12N	E2
8700	MaiT	60714	2863	11W-12N	E2
8700	NLES	60714	2863	11W-12N	E2
8800	NLES	60016	2863	11W-12N	E2
W Golf Rd SR-58					
-	HFET	60010	2857	27W-12N	C3
10	ANHT	60005	2861	18W-12N	A2
10	DSPN	60016	2862	15W-11N	B3
10	DSPN	60056	2862	15W-11N	B3
10	HFET	60195	2859	23W-12N	A2
10	MPPT	60016	2862	15W-11N	B2
10	MPPT	60056	2862	15W-11N	B3
10	SMBG	60173	2859	23W-12N	A2
10	SMBG	60195	2859	23W-12N	A2
100	SMBG	60195	2858	25W-12N	B2
300	DSPN	60016	2861	16W-11N	E3
300	HFET	60195	2858	23W-12N	E2
300	MPPT	60056	2861	16W-11N	E3
500	ANHT	60005	2860	18W-11N	E2
600	SMBG	60194	2858	24W-12N	D2
700	RGMW	60005	2860	18W-11N	E2
700	RGMW	60008	2860	18W-11N	E2
2000	ANHT	60056	2861	16W-11N	E3
2000	MPPT	60005	2861	16W-11N	E3
2100	HFET	60194	2857	26W-12N	E3
2100	SMBG	60194	2857	26W-12N	E3
8000	MaiT	60025	2864	10W-12N	A2
8000	MaiT	60714	2864	10W-12N	A2
8000	MNGV	60053	2864	10W-12N	A2
8000	NLES	60025	2864	10W-12N	A2
8000	NLES	60714	2864	10W-12N	A2
8500	MaiT	60016	2864	10W-12N	A2
8600	MaiT	60016	2863	11W-12N	E2
8700	MaiT	60714	2863	11W-12N	E2
8700	NLES	60714	2863	11W-12N	E2
8800	NLES	60016	2863	11W-12N	E2
Golf Ter					
100	WLMT	60091	2813	2W-13N	A6
9600	MaiT	60016	2863	11W-12N	E2

STREET Block	City	ZIP	Map#	CGS	Grid
Golf Ter					
9600	NLES	60714	2863	11W-12N	E2
E Golf Ter					
10	ANHT	60005	2861	18W-12N	A2
N Golf Cul de Sac St					
800	DSPN	60016	2862	14W-12N	D2
S Golf Cul de Sac St					
800	DSPN	60016	2862	13W-12N	D2
Golfers Ln					
500	BRLT	60103	2910		A1
E Golfhurst Av					
800	MPPT	60056	2862	15W-11N	B2
Golf Mill Ctr					
100	MaiT	60016	2864	10W-11N	A2
100	NLES	60016	2864	10W-11N	A2
100	NLES	60714	2864	10W-11N	A2
Golfview Av					
17500	HLCT	60430	3427	2W-21S	C5
17500	HMWD	60430	3427	2W-21S	C5
18600	HMWD	60430	3507	2W-22S	C1
Golf View Cir					
100	PTHT	60070	2808	14W-14N	C4
Golfview Ct					
10	CPVL	60110	2748		D7
Golf View Dr					
1400	BRLT	60103	2910		A1
Golfview Dr					
-	HMWD	60430	3506	4W-22S	E1
10	NHLK	60164	2972		C7
700	BmdT	60157	2913		C4
700	ROSL	60172	2913		C4
6800	CTSD	60525	3146		E7
8400	ODPK	60462	3346	10W-17S	B5
8400	OrlT	60462	3346	10W-17S	B5
18600	HLCT	60429	3506	4W-22S	E1
E Golfview Dr					
800	MPPT	60056	2862	15W-11N	B2
Golf View Ln					
10	FKFT	60423	3593	9W-26S	A2
10	RchT	60443	3593	9W-26S	A2
Golfview Ln					
10	CPVL	60110	2748		C7
10	CPVL	60110	2801		D1
100	EDND	60118	2801		D1
1100	FSMR	60422	3507	2W-23S	C3
1100	GNVW	60025	2811	7W-13N	A6
S Golfview Ln					
12800	PSHT	60463	3275	8W-15S	B7
12800	PSHT	60463	3347	8W-15S	B1
W Golfview Ln					
6700	PSHT	60463	3347	8W-15S	A1
S Golfview Pl					
800	MPPT	60056	2862	15W-11N	B2
900	DSPN	60016	2862	15W-11N	B2
Golf View Rd					
-	BKFD	60513	3088	10W-2S	A4
-	BKFD	60546	3088	10W-2S	A4
Golfview Rd					
900	GNVW	60025	2811	7W-13N	A6
Golfview Ter					
-	WhlT	60089	2754	16W-17N	C4
10	WLNG	60089	2754	16W-18N	C3
10	WLNG	60090	2754	16W-18N	C3
100	BFGV	60089	2754	16W-17N	C4
800	WhlT	60004	2754	17W-17N	C4
W Golfview Ter					
200	PLTN	60067	2752	21W-17N	D6
Good Av					
200	DSPN	60016	2863	11W-11N	C3
200	MaiT	60016	2863	11W-11N	C3
1700	PKRG	60068	2863	11W-10N	C4
Good Ct					
200	DSPN	60016	2863	11W-11N	C2
Goodenow Av					
-	CteT	60417	3774	1W-32S	B1
E Goodenow Rd					
100	CteT	60401	3774	0E-33S	E2
W Goodenow Rd					
10	CteT	60401	3774	1W-33S	A2
E Goodman Av					
10	LGNG	60525	3147	12W-4S	C1
W Goodman Av					
10	LGNG	60525	3147	13W-4S	A1
1400	WNSP	60558	3147	13W-4S	A1
Goodman Ct					
700	BNHL	60118	2802	30W-15N	A2
W Goodman St					
5600	CHCG	60630	2919	7W-6N	C6
E Goodrich Av					
2600	BNHM	60633	3351	3E-16S	E4
2700	BNHM	60633	3352	3E-16S	A4
W Goodrich Pl					
800	PLTN	60067	2752	22W-17N	B6
Goodridge Ter					
200	BmdT	60172	2912		E7
Good Speed Ln					
2300	SMBG	60194	2857	26W-11N	E3
Goodwin Dr					
600	PKRG	60068	2863	11W-9N	C6
N Goodwin Dr					
1800	PLTN	60074	2753	19W-18N	C3
Goose Lake Dr					
10	BNHL	60010	2750	27W-17N	A5
Gordon Av					
400	CTCY	60409	3352	4E-17S	B6
1300	CTCY	60409	3430	4E-19S	B2
Gordon Dr					
500	CRTE	60417	3685	1W-30S	B3
2400	FSMR	60422	3507	3W-22S	B1
Gordon Ln					
1200	LMNT	60439	3342	20W-15S	C2
1300	HmrT	60439	3342	20W-15S	C2
1300	HmrT	60441	3342	20W-15S	C2
Gordon St					
10	EGVV	60007	2861	18W-10N	A5
Gordon Ter					
600	UYPK	60466	3684	3W-29S	B2
800	WNKA	60093	2758	5W-16N	E7
1000	DRFD	60015	2756	11W-20N	C2
W Gordon Ter					
600	CHCG	60613	2977	1W-5N	E1
600	CHCG	60613	2978	0W-5N	A1
W Gorman Ct					
6600	MONE	60449	3682	8W-32S	B7
S Gorman Tr					
26300	MONE	60449	3682	8W-32S	B7
26300	MonT	60449	3682	8W-32S	B7
Goshawk Ln					
300	VrnT	60015	2755	14W-20N	B1
Goss Av					
4000	SRPK	60176	2973	12W-5N	B2
Gostlin St					
10	BNHM	60633	3352		C4
10	HMND	46327	3352		C4
Gostlin St SR-312					
10	BNHM	60633	3352		C4
10	HMND	46327	3352		C4
E Gostlin St					
300	HMND	46327	3352		E4
Gottschalk Av					
17800	HMWD	60430	3427	2W-21S	D7
18500	HMWD	60430	3507	2W-22S	D1
S Gougar Rd					
15100	HmrT	60441	3342	20W-18S	C7
Gould Ctr					
10	EGvT	60007	2860	19W-12N	C2
10	RGMW	60008	2860	19W-12N	C2
Gould St					
500	BCHR	60401	3864	1W-36S	B2
Gouwens Ln					
15500	DLTN	60419	3351	0E-18S	A7
15500	SHLD	60419	3351	0E-18S	A7
15500	SHLD	60473	3350	0E-18S	E7
15500	SHLD	60473	3351	0E-18S	A7
Governors Dr					
400	SMBG	60193	2858	23W-9N	E7
19900	FSMR	60422	3506	4W-24S	E5
19900	OMFD	60461	3506	4W-24S	E5
Governors Hwy					
800	FSMR	60422	3507	3W-22S	A2
17500	HLCT	60429	3427	3W-21S	B7
17500	HLCT	60430	3427	3W-21S	B7
17500	HMWD	60429	3427	3W-21S	B7
17500	HMWD	60430	3427	3W-21S	B7
18300	HMWD	60430	3507	3W-22S	A2
18400	FSMR	60430	3507	3W-22S	A2
19400	RchT	60422	3507	4W-23S	A3
19600	FSMR	60422	3506	4W-25S	D7
19600	RchT	60422	3506	4W-25S	D7
21100	MTSN	60443	3506	5W-25S	D7
21100	OMFD	60461	3506	5W-25S	D7
21400	MTSN	60443	3594	5W-25S	D1
21800	RNPK	60443	3594	5W-26S	D2
21800	RNPK	60471	3594	5W-27S	D4
22500	RchT	60471	3594	5W-27S	D4
23100	UYPK	60466	3594	5W-27S	C5
23300	MonT	60449	3594	5W-28S	B7
23300	MonT	60466	3594	5W-28S	B7
S Governors Hwy					
400	PTON	60468	3861	9W-37S	A4
24000	MonT	60449	3594	5W-29S	B7
24000	MonT	60449	3683	6W-29S	B1
24000	MonT	60466	3594	5W-29S	B7
24000	UYPK	60466	3594	5W-29S	B7
24000	UYPK	60466	3683	6W-29S	B1
24700	MonT	60466	3683	6W-29S	B1
25100	UYPK	60449	3683	6W-30S	A3
25500	MONE	60449	3682	7W-32S	E7
25500	MONE	60449	3683	6W-31S	A4
26100	MonT	60449	3682	7W-32S	E7
29800	PtnT	60468	3861	9W-36S	A2
29800	WllT	60468	3861	8W-36S	A2
S Governors Hwy SR-50					
-	MonT	60466	3683	6W-29S	B2
-	UYPK	60466	3683	6W-29S	B2
400	PTON	60468	3861	9W-37S	A4
25100	MonT	60449	3683	6W-30S	A3
25100	UYPK	60449	3683	6W-30S	A3
25500	MONE	60449	3682	7W-32S	E7
25500	MONE	60449	3683	6W-31S	A4
26100	MonT	60449	3682	7W-32S	E7
29800	PtnT	60468	3861	9W-36S	A2
29800	WllT	60468	3861	8W-36S	A2
Governors Ln					
-	HFET	60194	2858	25W-12N	A1
1800	HFET	60195	2858	26W-12N	A1
1900	HFET	60195	2857	26W-12N	E1
W Governors Pkwy					
-	CHCG	60624	3032	4W-0N	D4
W Go Wando Av					
600	MPPT	60056	2861	16W-12N	D1
N Grace Av					
10	PKRG	60068	2918	8W-8N	D1
900	PKRG	60068	2864	10W-9N	A6
9800	NLES	60714	2864	10W-12N	A1
S Grace Av					
1600	PKRG	60068	2918	10W-7N	A4
13900	RBBN	60472	3348	4W-16S	D4
Grace Ct					
700	SMBG	60193	2858	24W-9N	D7
S Grace Dr					
1000	MPPT	60056	2861	16W-11N	D3
Grace Ln					
-	MTSN	60443	3505	7W-24S	D6
100	BRTN	60010	2751	24W-18N	C3
100	CHHT	60411	3507	1W-23S	E4
100	PltT	60010	2751	24W-18N	C3
500	SMBG	60193	2858	24W-9N	D7
3800	GNVW	60025	2809	11W-14N	D5
Grace Rd					
2700	NHBK	60062	2756	10W-17N	E5
8600	ODPK	60462	3346	10W-18S	A6
Grace St					
100	BNVL	60106	2972		A2
100	CteT	60475	3596	1W-28S	A7
100	STGR	60475	3596	1W-28S	A7
800	ELGN	60120	2855		A7
1000	DSPN	60016	2862	13W-10N	E5
4000	SRPK	60176	2973	11W-5N	C2
4500	SRPK	60176	2917	11W-5N	C7
W Grace St					
600	CHCG	60613	2978	0W-4N	A2
1400	CHCG	60613	2977	2W-4N	B2
1900	CHCG	60618	2977	3W-4N	A2
2800	CHCG	60618	2976	4W-4N	C2
4000	CHCG	60641	2976	5W-4N	A2
4700	CHCG	60641	2975	6W-4N	E2
5500	CHCG	60634	2975	7W-4N	B2
6800	CHCG	60634	2974	9W-4N	D2
Graceland Av					
-	CHCG	60613	2977	1W-5N	D1
200	DSPN	60016	2863	13W-11N	A2
700	DSPN	60016	2862	13W-10N	E4
Graceland Av US-12					
1000	DSPN	60016	2862	13W-10N	E4
Graceland Av US-45					
800	DSPN	60016	2862	13W-10N	E4
Graceland Ct					
12000	HMGN	60441	3344	15W-18S	C7
Graceland Dr					
15300	HMGN	60441	3344	15W-18S	C7
S Graceland Ln					
19900	FftT	60423	3504	9W-24S	D6
S Grady Ct					
2800	CHCG	60608	3091	1W-2S	D3
Graegin Pl					
800	DYR	46311	3598		E3
Graemere St					
200	NHFD	60093	2811	7W-15N	B3
Graff Av					
10000	RSMT	60018	2917	12W-7N	B3
Grafton Pl					
200	MTSN	60443	3506	5W-24S	B5
Granada Ct					
10600	PSHL	60465	3274	10W-12S	A2
Granada Rd					
100	CPVL	60110	2748		B5
Grand Av					
600	ELGN	60120	2855		B3
3800	PvsT	60558	3086		D7
3800	WNSP	60558	3086		D7
4400	WNSP	60558	3146		D1
4900	MCCK	60525	3148	10W-5S	B1
9100	FNPK	60131	2973	11W-3N	C5
9100	FNPK	60171	2973	11W-3N	D5
9100	RVGV	60171	2973	11W-3N	D5
E Grand Av					
10	BNVL	60106	2972		A5
10	CHCG	60610	3034	0E-0N	C3
10	CHCG	60611	3034	0E-0N	C3
10	EMHT	60106	2972		A5
10	EMHT	60126	2972		A5
100	AddT	60106	2972		B5
100	AddT	60126	2972		A5
100	BNVL	60126	2972		A5
100	FNPK	60131	2972		B5
100	LydT	60131	2972		B5
600	CokC	60611	3034	0E-0N	E3
E Grand Av CO-20					
10	BNVL	60106	2972		A5
10	EMHT	60106	2972		A5
10	EMHT	60126	2972		A5
100	AddT	60106	2972		A5
100	AddT	60126	2972		A5
100	BNVL	60126	2972		A5
100	FNPK	60131	2972		B5
100	LydT	60131	2972		B5
W Grand Av					
-	AddT	60126	2972		B5
-	EMHT	60126	2972		B5
-	LydT	60131	2972		E5
10	CHCG	60610	3034	0W-0N	A3
10	CHCG	60611	3034	0W-0N	A3
700	CHCG	60622	3034	0W-0N	A3
800	CHCG	60622	3033	1W-0N	E3
1900	CHCG	60612	3033	2W-0N	C3
2800	CHCG	60612	3032	3W-0N	E3
2800	CHCG	60622	3032	3W-1N	E2
3100	CHCG	60651	3032	3W-1N	E2
4300	CHCG	60639	3032	5W-1N	B1
4400	CHCG	60639	2976	5W-2N	A7
4700	CHCG	60639	2975	6W-2N	C6
6600	CHCG	60707	2975	8W-3N	A6
6700	CHCG	60707	2974	8W-3N	E6
7100	EDPK	60707	2974	8W-3N	E6
8000	RVGV	60171	2974	9W-3N	B5
8600	RVGV	60171	2973	11W-3N	E5
8900	FNPK	60171	2973	11W-3N	E5
10400	FNPK	60131	2973	13W-3N	A5
10400	FNPK	60164	2973	13W-3N	A5
10400	LydT	60164	2973	13W-3N	A5
10600	LydT	60131	2973	13W-3N	A5
10700	FNPK	60131	2972		E5
10700	LydT	60164	2972		E5
11200	NHLK	60164	2972		C5
Grand Blvd					
300	ELGN	60120	2855		C3
300	PKRG	60068	2864	10W-9N	B7
3100	BKFD	60513	3087	11W-3S	D4
3100	LGPK	60525	3087	11W-3S	D4
N Grand Ct					
8100	NLES	60714	2864	10W-10N	B5
Grand Dr					
2200	NHBK	60062	2809	11W-16N	D1
Grand Pl					
400	AddT	60126	2972		A5
N Grand St					
8800	NLES	60714	2864	10W-11N	B3
Grand Canyon Pkwy					
800	HFET	60194	2858	23W-11N	E3
900	HFET	60194	2859	23W-11N	A2
900	SMBG	60194	2859	23W-11N	A2
900	SMBG	60195	2859	23W-11N	A2
Grand Canyon St					
600	HFET	60194	2858	23W-11N	E4
Grand Central Ln					
10	SMBG	60193	2858	24W-10N	D6
10	SMBG	60194	2858	24W-10N	D5
Grand Oak Ct					
1100	BRLT	60103	2910		C7
S Grand Prairie Ln					
20300	FftT	60423	3504	9W-24S	E6
Grand Traverse Dr					
20300	FftT	60423	3504	11W-24S	A5
20300	FKFT	60423	3504	11W-24S	A6
Grandview Dr					
10500	PlsT	60464	3273	13W-14S	A7
15100	ODPK	60467	3344	14W-18S	D6
17600	HLCT	60429	3427	3W-21S	B6
Grandview Pl					
2200	GNVW	60025	2810	9W-12N	C7
Grange Av					
5400	OKFT	60452	3347	6W-17S	E5
Grange Ct					
10	EGVV	60007	2914		D2
Grange Dr					
10	EGVV	60007	2914		D2
17200	ODPK	60467	3422	14W-20S	C5
Grant Av					
600	CHHT	60411	3508	1W-24S	B5
1300	MLPK	60160	3029	10W-1N	E2
2300	BLWD	60104	3029	12W-0N	C3
3600	PKFT	60466	3594	4W-27S	E4
3600	RNPK	60471	3594	4W-27S	D4
8800	BKFD	60513	3087	11W-3S	D5
9500	LGPK	60525	3087	11W-3S	D5
16400	ODPK	60467	3423	13W-19S	A3
Grant Blvd					
-	CRTE	60417	3685	0E-29S	D1
Grant Cir					
600	HRPK	60133	2912		A1
Grant Ct					
600	BRRG	60527	3146		A4
1500	HRPK	60133	2911		E6
Grant Dr					
1200	CPVL	60110	2748		D7
E Grant Dr					
800	DSPN	60016	2862	13W-10N	D4
W Grant Dr					
800	DSPN	60016	2862	14W-10N	D4
Grant Pl					
300	PKRG	60068	2864	10W-9N	B7
W Grant Pl					
400	CHCG	60614	2978	0W-2N	A6
Grant Rd					
900	LMNT	60439	3271		E2
900	LmnT	60439	3272	16W-12S	A2
1200	NHBK	60062	2757	8W-17N	D6
Grant St					
-	EVTN	60201	2867	3W-12N	A1
100	EGvT	60018	2862	15W-9N	A7
200	PKFT	60466	3595	3W-25S	A1
300	LMNT	60439	3270		E5
500	ROSL	60172	2912		E3
800	BRLT	60103	2911		B5
1200	WLMT	60091	2812	5W-14N	A4
1300	NtrT	60093	2812	5W-14N	A4
1400	SMBG	60193	2912		E2
1400	SmbT	60193	2912		E2
1800	EVTN	60201	2866	3W-12N	E1
3000	OKBK	60523	3086		A4
3300	SKOK	60076	2866	5W-12N	B1
4000	OKLN	60453	3276	5W-12S	C2
14100	DLTN	60419	3350	0E-16S	E4
15600	SHLD	60473	3350	0E-18S	E7
17000	LNSG	60438	3430	4E-20S	B4
19100	LNSG	60438	3510	4E-22S	B2
N Grant St					
10	HNDL	60521	3146		A1
100	BRTN	60010	2750	26W-20N	E2
400	HNDL	60521	3086		A7
S Grant St					
-	DGvT	60527	3208		A5
10	HNDL	60521	3146		A5
5800	BRRG	60521	3146		A4
6200	BRRG	60527	3146		A5
6200	WLBK	60527	3146		A5
7400	BRRG	60527	3208		B2
W Grant Vil					
200	HNDL	60521	3146		A4
Grantham Ln					
-	SMBG	60193	2859	21W-9N	D6
Grantham Pl					
1800	HFET	60195	2858	26W-12N	A1
E Grantley Av					
100	EMHT	60126	3028		A1
Grants Tr					
16500	ODPK	60467	3423	13W-19S	A3
16500	OrlT	60467	3423	13W-19S	A3
Granville Av					
10	AddT	60143	2914		D5
10	BLWD	60104	3029	13W-0N	A5
10	CHCG	60068	2918	9W-7N	C3
10	CHCG	60631	2918	9W-7N	C3
10	ITSC	60143	2914		D5
300	PKRG	60068	2918	10W-7N	A3
500	BLWD	60162	3029	13W-0N	A4
500	HLSD	60162	3029	13W-0N	A5
1200	PKRG	60068	2917	10W-7N	E3
2700	LydT	60164	2973	13W-3N	A5
9800	RSMT	60018	2917	12W-7N	B3
E Granville Av					
10	ROSL	60172	2913		B4
700	BmdT	60157	2913		C4
W Granville Av					
10	ROSL	60172	2913		A4
100	ROSL	60172	2912		E4
900	CHCG	60660	2921	2W-7N	B3
1900	CHCG	60659	2921	3W-7N	A3
3400	CHCG	60659	2920	4W-7N	C3
4000	CHCG	60646	2920	5W-7N	B3
Graphics Ct					
-	TYPK	60477	3504	9W-22S	D1
Graphics Dr					
-	TYPK	60477	3504	9W-22S	D1
Grassmere Rd					
10	EGVV	60007	2914		D1
S Gratten Av					
3000	CHCG	60608	3091	1W-2S	E3
Gray Ct					
600	WLNG	60090	2754	16W-18N	E2
Gray Ln					
13400	LMNT	60439	3343	16W-15S	E1
19400	FftT	60423	3504	9W-23S	E3
19400	TYPK	60423	3504	9W-23S	E3
19400	TYPK	60477	3504	9W-23S	E3
Graycor Dr					
10	HLCT	60430	3427	3W-20S	B5
Grayfriars Ln					
300	IVNS	60067	2805	22W-15N	A2
Gray Hawk Dr					
-	MTSN	60443	3505	8W-25S	B7
-	RchT	60443	3505	8W-25S	B7
-	RchT	60443	3593	8W-25S	C1
N Graylynn Dr					
200	WhlT	60056	2808	13W-13N	E6
Graymoor Ln					
10	BlmT	60422	3507	2W-24S	C4
10	FSMR	60422	3507	2W-24S	C4
10	OMFD	60422	3507	2W-24S	C4
100	OMFD	60461	3507	2W-24S	C5
Grayshire Ct					
1300	ELGN	60120	2801		D7
Graystone Dr					
-	HMGN	60441	3344	15W-16S	B4
-	HmrT	60441	3344	15W-16S	B4
Great Egret Dr					
10400	ODPK	60467	3423	13W-20S	B4
10400	OrlT	60467	3423	13W-20S	B4
Great Glen Ct					
700	IVNS	60010	2751	24W-16N	B6
Great Plains Av					
900	MTSN	60443	3505	7W-25S	C7
Greco Av					
2400	DSPN	60018	2917	12W-8N	A1
Greco Lane Ln					
-	SMBG	60193	2859	21W-9N	D6
Greeley Av					
2500	EVTN	60201	2812	5W-12N	B7
2500	SKOK	60076	2812	5W-12N	B7
2500	SKOK	60201	2812	5W-12N	B7
2500	WLMT	60091	2812	5W-12N	B7
2500	WLMT	60201	2812	5W-12N	B7
N Greeley St					
10	PLTN	60067	2805	21W-16N	E1
S Greeley St					
10	PLTN	60067	2805	21W-15N	D1
Green Ct					
100	SMWD	60107	2857	27W-11N	D4
N Green Dr					
600	WLNG	60090	2755	15W-17N	A5
W Green Dr					
400	WLNG	60090	2755	15W-17N	A5
Green Ln					
100	CPVL	60110	2748		C6
E Green Ln					
1400	MPPT	60056	2808	14W-13N	C7
Green Ln N					
1800	PLTN	60074	2753	19W-18N	C3
Green Ln S					
1800	PLTN	60074	2753	19W-18N	C3
Green Rdg					
10	ELGN	60120	2855		C1
Green St					
-	MTSN	60443	3506	6W-24S	A6
200	MYWD	60153	3030	10W-0S	A5
200	PKFT	60466	3595	3W-27S	A3
700	MYWD	60153	3029	10W-0S	E5
1400	CHHT	60411	3508	0W-25S	C7
1400	CHHT	60411	3596	0W-25S	C1
3000	SCHT	60411	3596	1W-28S	A6
3000	STGR	60475	3596	1W-28S	A6
3700	CteT	60475	3596	1W-28S	A6
14400	HRVY	60426	3350	1W-17S	A5
14600	ODPK	60462	3345	11W-17S	E5
16500	HRVY	60426	3428	1W-19S	B3
E Green St					
10	BNVL	60106	2972		B2
600	BNVL	60131	2972		B2
N Green St					
10	CHCG	60607	3033	1W-0N	E4
600	CHCG	60622	3033	1W-0N	E3
S Green St					
10	CHCG	60607	3033	1W-0S	E5
2600	CHCG	60608	3092	1W-2S	A3
5200	CHCG	60609	3152	1W-5S	A2
5500	CHCG	60621	3152	1W-6S	A4
9000	CHCG	60620	3214	1W-11S	A6
9400	CHCG	60643	3214	1W-11S	A6
10300	CHCG	60643	3278	1W-13S	A3
12200	CTPK	60827	3278	1W-14S	A6
12700	CHCG	60827	3278	1W-14S	A7
Greenacre Dr					
3700	NHBK	60062	2756	12W-17N	B5
Greenacres Ln					
700	GNVW	60025	2811	7W-13N	B6
W Green Acres Ln					
1200	MPPT	60056	2861	16W-11N	D2
Greenbay Av					
700	CTCY	60409	3352	3E-18S	B7
1200	CTCY	60409	3430	3E-19S	B2
17000	LNSG	60438	3430	3E-20S	B4
19500	LNSG	60411	3510	3E-23S	B2
19500	LNSG	60438	3510	3E-23S	B2
S Green Bay Av					
10300	CHCG	60617	3216	3E-11S	B7
10300	CHCG	60617	3280	3E-11S	B1
13000	CHCG	60633	3280	3E-15S	B7
13000	CHCG	60633	3352	3E-15S	B1
13800	BNHM	60633	3352	3E-16S	B4
Green Bay Rd					
10	GLNC	60022	2758	6W-17N	D5
10	GLNC	60093	2758	5W-16N	E7
10	HDPK	60022	2758	7W-20N	B2
10	HDPK	60035	2758	7W-20N	A1
10	KLWH	60043	2812	4W-14N	C4
10	WNKA	60022	2758	5W-16N	E7
10	WNKA	60093	2758	5W-16N	E7
100	EVTN	60201	2812	3W-13N	E7
100	WLMT	60091	2812	3W-13N	E6
100	WLMT	60201	2812	3W-13N	E7
500	WNKA	60093	2812	5W-16N	A1
800	WNKA	60093	2759	5W-16N	A7
1800	EVTN	60201	2867	3W-12N	A1
E Greenbriar Av					
10	CHHT	60411	3508	1W-24S	A5
W Greenbriar Av					
100	CHHT	60411	3508	1W-24S	A5
Greenbriar Ct					
7900	BRRG	60527	3208		D2
Greenbriar Dr					
-	MaiT	60016	2863	11W-12N	E1
-	MaiT	60025	2863	11W-12N	E1
10	DRFD	60015	2757	10W-20N	A2
300	CRTE	60417	3596	0E-28S	E6
1600	SMBG	60173	2859	21W-10N	E5
1600	SMBG	60173	2860	21W-10N	A5
3100	GNVW	60025	2810	10W-12N	A7
3200	MaiT	60025	2810	10W-12N	A7
3300	MaiT	60025	2809	10W-12N	E7
9400	HYHL	60457	3210	10W-10S	A6
S Greenbriar Dr					
26700	MonT	60449	3683	6W-32S	A7
W Greenbriar Dr					
1400	MPPT	60056	2861	16W-12N	D2
Greenbriar Ln					
200	SMWD	60107	2856	29W-10N	E5
400	RVWD	60015	2755	13W-20N	D1
600	EGVV	60007	2913		C2
600	SmbT	60193	2913		C2
800	UYPK	60466	3684	3W-30S	A2
1000	NHBK	60062	2757	10W-17N	A6
1400	ROSL	60172	2913		C2
1400	ROSL	60193	2913		C2
4100	RNPK	60471	3594	5W-26S	C3
E Greenbriar Ln					
1100	PLTN	60074	2753	19W-18N	C3
Greenbriar St					
200	EGVV	60007	2860	18W-9N	E6
200	EGVV	60007	2861	18W-9N	A6
Greenbriar East Dr					
10	DRFD	60015	2757	9W-20N	B2
Green Bridge Ct					
2700	SMBG	60194	2857	26W-10N	E5
Green Bridge Ln					
400	PTHT	60070	2808	14W-14N	B4
W Greenbrier Ct					
1100	ANHT	60004	2806	18W-16N	E1
Greenbrier Ln					
14700	HMGN	60441	3343	17W-17S	D6
Greenbrook Blvd					
10	BRLT	60133	2911		D6
1300	BmdT	60133	2911		D6
1300	HRPK	60133	2911		D6
1600	BRLT	60103	2911		D6
Greenbrook Blvd CO-29					
10	BRLT	60133	2911		D6
1300	BmdT	60133	2911		D6
1300	HRPK	60133	2911		D6
1600	BRLT	60103	2911		D6
Greenbrook Ct					
1300	HRPK	60133	2911		E5
Greencastle Ln					
9100	ODPK	60462	3345	11W-17S	E5
9100	ODPK	60462	3346	10W-17S	A6
Greendale Av					
900	NLES	60714	2864	10W-10N	A5
1200	PKRG	60068	2864	10W-10N	A5
1200	PKRG	60714	2864	10W-10N	A5
1300	PKRG	60068	2863	11W-10N	E5
W Greendale Av					
8100	NLES	60068	2864	10W-10N	B6
8100	NLES	60714	2864	10W-10N	B5
8100	PKRG	60068	2864	10W-10N	B6

STREET Block	City	ZIP	Map#	CGS	Grid
Hackberry Ct					
1200	ELGN	60120	2855		D4
Hackberry Dr					
200	SMWD	60107	2857	27W-10N	C6
E Hackberry Dr					
200	ANHT	60004	2754	17W-17N	B5
W Hackberry Dr					
300	ANHT	60004	2754	18W-17N	A5
500	ANHT	60004	2753	18W-17N	E5
Hackberry Ln					
10	GNVW	60025	2811	6W-13N	D7
1200	WNKA	60093	2811	6W-16N	E1
E Hackberry Ln					
600	MPPT	60056	2808	14W-14N	B5
Hackberry Rd					
1100	DRFD	60015	2756	11W-20N	C1
Hacke Ln					
9500	FNPK	60131	2973	11W-4N	C3
Hackney Cir					
10	SBTN	60010	2803	27W-13N	A5
Hackney Dr					
16100	ODPK	60467	3423	12W-19S	D2
Haddam Pl					
1900	HFET	60195	2858	25W-12N	B1
Haddam Wy					
700	HRPK	60133	2912		A1
Haddington Cir					
500	IVNS	60010	2803	25W-15N	E1
W Haddington Ct					
1200	PLTN	60067	2805	22W-15N	B2
E Haddock Pl					
-	CHCG	60601	3034	0E-0N	C4
W Haddock Pl					
200	CHCG	60601	3034		E4
200	CHCG	60606	3034	0W-0N	B4
W Haddon Av					
2000	CHCG	60622	3033	2W-1N	B2
2700	CHCG	60622	3032	3W-0N	E3
3200	CHCG	60651	3032	4W-1N	D2
4800	CHCG	60651	3031	6W-1N	E2
Haddon St					
1200	MLPK	60160	3029	11W-1N	D2
N Haddow Av					
1500	ANHT	60004	2807	17W-15N	B2
2500	ANHT	60004	2754	17W-16N	B6
S Haddow Av					
1000	ANHT	60005	2807	17W-12N	B7
1200	ANHT	60005	2861	17W-12N	B1
N Haddow Ct					
1100	ANHT	60004	2807	17W-15N	B3
Hadley Ct					
1600	WLNG	60090	2754	16W-18N	D4
W Hadley Rd					
12200	HMGN	60441	3422	16W-20S	A5
13000	HMGN	60448	3422	16W-20S	A5
Hadley Run Ln					
800	SMBG	60173	2859	22W-10N	C5
800	SMBG	60193	2859	22W-10N	C5
Haegers Bend Rd					
11600	ALGN	60010	2748		C2
11800	ALGN	60102	2748		C2
11800	BNHL	60010	2748		C2
11900	ALGN	60110	2748		C2
11900	BNHL	60102	2748		C2
11900	BNHL	60110	2748		C2
W Haft St					
6300	CHCG	60631	2919	7W-7N	A3
6300	CHCG	60646	2919	7W-7N	A3
Hagburg Dr					
-	MNSR	46321	3510		E4
Hagen Ln					
2000	FSMR	60422	3507	2W-22S	C2
N Hager Av					
100	BRTN	60010	2750	26W-20N	D2
S Hager Av					
100	BRTN	60010	2750	26W-18N	D2
Hager Ln					
300	GNVW	60025	2811	6W-13N	C6
Haggard St					
13400	HMGN	60441	3343	16W-18S	D6
N Haig Ct					
2100	PLTN	60074	2753	19W-18N	B3
W Haines St					
800	CHCG	60610	3033	1W-1N	E2
800	CHCG	60622	3033	1W-1N	E2
Hainsworth Av					
2200	FTPK	60130	3088	9W-2S	C3
2200	FTPK	60546	3088	9W-2S	C3
2200	NRIV	60546	3088	9W-2S	C3
2500	RVSD	60546	3088	9W-2S	C3
Haise Ct					
1400	EGVV	60007	2913		E3
Haise Ln					
1400	EGVV	60007	2913		E3
Halbert Ln					
700	IVNS	60010	2751	25W-16N	A7
Hale Av					
-	BRLT	60103	2911		A2
N Hale Av					
100	BRLT	60103	2911		A2
S Hale Av					
100	BRLT	60103	2911		A3
10300	CHCG	60643	3277	2W-12S	C1
11800	BLID	60406	3277	2W-13S	C5
11800	CHCG	60406	3277	2W-13S	C5
Hale Ct					
600	WLNG	60090	2754	16W-18N	E2
Hale Dr					
14900	ODPK	60462	3345	12W-17S	C6
E Hale St					
100	EMHT	60126	3028		A6
N Hale St					
10	PLTN	60067	2805	20W-16N	E1
100	PLTN	60067	2752	20W-16N	E7
S Hale St					
10	PLTN	60067	2805	20W-15N	E2
Halesia Ct					
7500	ODPK	60462	3346	9W-18S	D7
Haley Ct					
-	ODPK	60467	3423	13W-21S	A7
W Haleys Hill Ct					
400	PLTN	60074	2752	21W-18N	D3
Half Ln					
100	SmbT	60172	2913		A3
Halien Ter					
500	PKRG	60068	2863	11W-9N	C7
Halifax Av					
2900	WSTR	60154	3086		E4
3000	PvsT	60558	3086		E4
Halifax Ct					
800	SMBG	60193	2912		D1
Halina Dr E					
2400	GNVW	60025	2809	10W-15N	E3
Halkirk Cir					
100	IVNS	60067	2805	22W-15N	A1

STREET Block	City	ZIP	Map#	CGS	Grid
Hallberg Ln					
1300	PKRG	60068	2863	10W-10N	E4
1300	PKRG	60068	2864	10W-10N	A4
Hallick Dr					
500	HFET	60107	2856	29W-11N	E3
500	HFET	60120	2856	29W-11N	E3
500	HnrT	60120	2856	29W-11N	E3
Halloran Ln					
6000	HFET	60120	2855		D1
Halloway St					
-	MTSN	60443	3506	6W-24S	A5
Halpin Dr					
100	DSPN	60016	2808	13W-13N	E6
Halsey Dr					
2000	DSPN	60018	2917	12W-8N	B2
Halsted Blvd					
3400	STGR	60475	3596	1W-28S	B6
S Halsted Pkwy					
6100	CHCG	60621	3152	0W-7S	A5
Halsted St					
-	EHZC	60426	3428	0W-20S	B4
-	EHZC	60473	3428	0W-20S	B4
-	HRVY	60426	3350	1W-18S	B7
-	PHNX	60426	3350	1W-18S	B7
3000	SCHT	60411	3596	1W-27S	A5
3000	STGR	60475	3596	1W-27S	A5
14300	RVDL	60827	3350	1W-17S	A5
15600	HRVY	60426	3428	1W-18S	B1
16900	SHLD	60473	3428	0W-20S	B4
17200	EHZC	60429	3428	0W-20S	B5
17300	HMWD	60430	3428	0W-20S	B5
18000	GNWD	60425	3428	0W-21S	B7
18000	GNWD	60430	3428	0W-21S	B7
Halsted St SR-1					
-	EHZC	60426	3428	0W-20S	B4
-	EHZC	60473	3428	0W-20S	B4
-	PHNX	60426	3350	1W-18S	B7
14300	HRVY	60426	3350	1W-17S	A5
14300	RVDL	60827	3350	1W-17S	A5
15600	HRVY	60426	3428	1W-18S	B1
16900	SHLD	60473	3428	0W-20S	B4
17200	EHZC	60429	3428	0W-20S	B5
17300	HMWD	60430	3428	0W-20S	B5
18000	GNWD	60425	3428	0W-21S	B7
18000	GNWD	60430	3428	0W-21S	B7
N Halsted St					
10	CHCG	60607	3034	1W-0N	A4
10	CHCG	60661	3034	1W-0N	A4
300	CHCG	60610	3034	0W-0N	A3
300	CHCG	60622	3034	0W-0N	A3
900	CHCG	60610	3033	1W-1N	E1
900	CHCG	60622	3033	1W-1N	E1
1600	CHCG	60610	2977	1W-2N	E7
1600	CHCG	60614	2977	1W-2N	E7
1600	CHCG	60622	2977	1W-2N	E7
2700	CHCG	60657	2977	1W-3N	E4
3500	CHCG	60613	2977	1W-2N	E7
S Halsted St					
-	RVDL	60628	3278	0W-15S	A7
-	RVDL	60643	3278	0W-15S	A7
-	RVDL	60827	3278	0W-15S	A7
10	CHCG	60661	3034	1W-0S	A5
100	CHHT	60411	3508	1W-25S	B7
1100	CHCG	60607	3034	1W-1S	A7
1100	CHCG	60608	3034	1W-1S	A7
1500	CHCG	60616	3034	1W-1S	A7
1500	CHHT	60411	3596	1W-26S	B1
1700	CHCG	60608	3092	0W-3S	A5
1700	CHCG	60616	3092	0W-3S	A5
2500	SCHT	60411	3596	1W-26S	B2
3400	CHCG	60609	3092	1W-3S	A4
4700	CHCG	60609	3152	1W-5S	A1
5500	CHCG	60621	3152	0W-7S	A6
7500	CHCG	60620	3214	0W-8S	A1
9400	CHCG	60628	3214	1W-11S	A7
9400	CHCG	60643	3214	1W-11S	A7
10300	CHCG	60628	3278	1W-12S	A1
10300	CHCG	60643	3278	1W-12S	A1
12200	CTPK	60827	3278	1W-14S	A6
12500	CTPK	60628	3278	1W-14S	A6
12600	CHCG	60827	3278	1W-14S	A7
13100	RVDL	60827	3350	1W-16S	A4
14500	HRVY	60426	3350	1W-16S	A4
18300	GNWD	60425	3428	0W-22S	B7
18300	GNWD	60425	3508	1W-23S	B3
18300	GNWD	60430	3428	0W-22S	B7
18300	HMWD	60430	3428	0W-22S	B7
18500	HMWD	60430	3508	1W-23S	B3
19000	HMWD	60425	3508	0W-23S	B2
19100	BlmT	60411	3508	0W-23S	B3
19300	GNWD	60411	3508	0W-23S	B3
S Halsted St SR-1					
-	RVDL	60628	3278	0W-15S	A7
-	RVDL	60643	3278	0W-15S	A7
-	RVDL	60827	3278	0W-15S	A7
100	CHHT	60411	3508	1W-23S	B4
9900	CHCG	60628	3214	1W-11S	A7
9900	CHCG	60643	3214	1W-11S	A7
10300	CHCG	60628	3278	1W-12S	A1
10300	CHCG	60643	3278	1W-12S	A1
12200	CTPK	60827	3278	1W-14S	A6
12500	CTPK	60628	3278	1W-14S	A6
12600	CHCG	60827	3278	1W-14S	A7
13100	RVDL	60827	3350	1W-16S	A4
14500	HRVY	60426	3350	1W-16S	A4
18300	GNWD	60425	3428	0W-22S	B7
18300	GNWD	60425	3508	1W-23S	B3
18300	GNWD	60430	3428	0W-22S	B7
18300	HMWD	60430	3428	0W-22S	B7
18500	HMWD	60430	3508	1W-23S	B3
19000	HMWD	60425	3508	0W-23S	B2
19100	BlmT	60411	3508	0W-23S	B3
19300	GNWD	60411	3508	0W-23S	B3
Halts Pl					
6100	CHCG	60631	2918	9W-7N	C3
Haman Av					
4200	HFET	60195	2804	24W-15N	C2
4300	IVNS	60067	2804	24W-15N	C2
4300	IVNS	60195	2804	24W-15N	C2
Haman Ct					
4300	HFET	60195	2804	24W-15N	C2
Haman Rd					
10	HFET	60010	2804	24W-15N	D1
10	HFET	60067	2804	24W-15N	D1
10	HFET	60195	2804	24W-15N	D1
10	IVNS	60067	2804	24W-15N	D1
10	IVNS	60195	2804	24W-15N	D1
N Haman Rd					
100	IVNS	60010	2751	24W-16N	D6
S Haman Rd					
10	IVNS	60010	2751	24W-16N	D7
200	HFET	60010	2751	24W-16N	D7
Hamann Ct					
2000	HMND	46394	3280		E5

STREET Block	City	ZIP	Map#	CGS	Grid
Hamann Ct E					
1900	HMND	46394	3280		D5
Hamann Ct W					
1900	HMND	46394	3280		D5
Hamilton Av					
1200	HLSD	60162	3028		C7
1200	PvsT	60126	3028		C7
1200	PvsT	60126	3086		C1
1200	PvsT	60162	3028		C7
1300	PvsT	60162	3086		C1
7200	BRRG	60527	3146		B7
7500	BRRG	60527	3208		B2
15900	MKHM	60426	3427	2W-19S	C2
15900	ThtT	60426	3427	2W-19S	C2
16200	TYPK	60477	3424	9W-19S	D2
N Hamilton Av					
2200	CHCG	60647	2977	2W-2N	B6
3800	CHCG	60618	2977	2W-4N	B2
4400	CHCG	60618	2921	2W-5N	B7
4800	CHCG	60625	2921	2W-6N	B6
6100	CHCG	60659	2921	2W-7N	B3
6800	CHCG	60645	2921	2W-8N	B1
7200	CHCG	60645	2867	2W-9N	B7
S Hamilton Av					
200	CHCG	60612	3033	2W-0S	B5
1000	CHCG	60608	3033	2W-0S	B7
3200	CHCG	60608	3091	2W-3S	B4
3500	CHCG	60609	3091	2W-3S	B5
5300	CHCG	60609	3151	2W-5S	B2
5500	CHCG	60636	3151	2W-6S	B3
7500	CHCG	60620	3213	2W-8S	C1
9500	CHCG	60643	3213	2W-11S	C6
10300	CHCG	60643	3277	2W-12S	C1
Hamilton Ct					
600	BRLT	60103	2910		B5
700	SMBG	60194	2857	26W-11N	E4
1800	IVNS	60010	2751	25W-17N	A6
9200	MaiT	60016	2863	11W-12N	D1
9200	NLES	60714	2863	11W-12N	D1
N Hamilton Ct					
800	PLTN	60067	2752	21W-17N	D6
Hamilton Dr					
8500	MNGV	60053	2865	6W-10N	C4
8500	SKOK	60053	2865	6W-10N	C4
8500	SKOK	60077	2865	6W-10N	C4
22400	RNPK	60471	3594	5W-27S	C4
S Hamilton Dr					
-	CHCG	60620	3213	2W-9S	C2
W Hamilton Dr					
10	PLTN	60067	2752	21W-17N	D6
6900	NLES	60714	2864	8W-10N	E4
W Hamilton Ln					
300	PLTN	60067	2752	21W-17N	D6
Hamilton Pkwy					
1200	ITSC	60007	2914		A3
1200	ITSC	60143	2913		E3
1200	ITSC	60143	2914		A3
Hamilton Pl					
2300	SMBG	60194	2857	26W-11N	E4
Hamilton Rd					
-	UYPK	60466	3684	3W-30S	A3
100	EGvT	60005	2861	16W-9N	D6
900	UYPK	60466	3682	7W-30S	D3
1200	MONE	60449	3682	7W-30S	D4
1200	MONE	60466	3682	7W-30S	D4
1200	MonT	60449	3682	7W-30S	D4
1200	UYPK	60449	3682	7W-30S	D4
W Hamilton Rd					
3400	MonT	60449	3683	4W-30S	E3
3400	MonT	60449	3684	4W-30S	A3
3400	MonT	60466	3683	4W-30S	E3
3400	MonT	60466	3684	4W-30S	A3
3400	UYPK	60449	3684	4W-30S	A3
3400	UYPK	60466	3684	4W-30S	A3
Hamilton St					
10	BNVL	60106	2972		A1
100	CHCG	60106	2972		A1
100	EVTN	60202	2867	2W-10N	B4
Hamilton Wood					
400	BlmT	60422	3507	1W-23S	E3
400	BlmT	60430	3507	1W-23S	E3
400	CHHT	60411	3507	1W-23S	E3
400	CHHT	60430	3507	1W-23S	E3
500	FSMR	60422	3507	1W-23S	E3
500	FSMR	60430	3507	1W-23S	E3
S Hamlet Av					
11100	CHCG	60643	3277	1W-13S	D3
Hamlin Av					
800	FSMR	60422	3506	4W-23S	D3
1000	RchT	60430	3506	4W-23S	D3
7200	LNWD	60712	2866	4W-9N	C7
7300	SKOK	60712	2866	4W-9N	C7
8500	SKOK	60076	2866	4W-10N	C4
9200	MaiT	60016	2863	11W-11N	E3
9200	PKRG	60016	2863	11W-11N	E3
9200	SKOK	60203	2866	4W-11N	C3
9400	NLES	60714	2863	11W-11N	E3
9500	EVTN	60201	2866	4W-11N	C2
14500	MDLN	60445	3348	4W-17S	D4
15400	MDLN	60426	3348	4W-18S	D7
15400	MKHM	60426	3348	4W-18S	D7
15900	MKHM	60426	3426	4W-19S	D2
16600	CCHL	60478	3426	4W-19S	D3
N Hamlin Av					
10	CHCG	60624	3032	4W-0N	C5
10	PKRG	60068	2917	11W-9N	E1
800	PKRG	60068	2863	11W-9N	E6
1600	CHCG	60647	2976	4W-2N	C7
1600	CHCG	60647	3032	4W-1N	C1
1600	CHCG	60651	3032	4W-1N	C1
2700	CHCG	60618	2976	4W-3N	C5
4300	CHCG	60625	2976	4W-5N	C1
4400	CHCG	60625	2920	4W-5N	C7
6100	CHCG	60659	2920	4W-7N	C3
6300	LNWD	60712	2920	4W-7N	C3
7100	SKOK	60076	2920	4W-9N	C1
9400	MaiT	60016	2863	11W-11N	E2
9400	MaiT	60714	2863	11W-11N	E2
9400	NLES	60714	2863	11W-11N	E2
S Hamlin Av					
-	RBBN	60445	3348	4W-16S	D3
600	PKRG	60068	2917	11W-8N	E2
1400	CHCG	60623	3032	4W-1S	C7
1500	CHCG	60623	3090	4W-2S	C3
4500	CHCG	60632	3090	4W-4S	C7
5100	CHCG	60632	3150	4W-6S	C3
5400	CHCG	60629	3150	4W-8S	C7
7300	CHCG	60629	3212	4W-8S	C1
7500	CHCG	60652	3212	4W-8S	C1
9100	CHCG	60805	3212	4W-10S	C5
9100	ENGN	60805	3212	4W-10S	C5
9800	CHCG	60655	3212	4W-11S	C7
10300	CHCG	60655	3276	4W-12S	C2
11400	WthT	60803	3276	4W-14S	D5
11700	ALSP	60803	3276	4W-14S	D5

STREET Block	City	ZIP	Map#	CGS	Grid
S Hamlin Av					
13300	CTWD	60472	3348	4W-16S	D2
13300	RBBN	60472	3348	4W-15S	D2
13300	WthT	60472	3348	4W-15S	D2
14000	CTWD	60445	3348	4W-16S	D3
S Hamlin Blvd					
10	CHCG	60624	3032	4W-0S	C5
Hamlin Ct					
500	PKRG	60068	2917	11W-8N	E2
S Hamlin Ct					
4900	HMND	46320	3352		D5
12600	ALSP	60803	3276	4W-14S	D7
13000	ALSP	60803	3348	4W-15S	D1
Hamlin St					
400	PKFT	60466	3507	3W-25S	A7
400	PKFT	60466	3595	3W-25S	A1
800	EVTN	60201	2867	2W-11N	B2
Hammersmith Ln					
4300	GNVW	60062	2809	11W-14N	C3
Hammond Av					
300	ELGN	60120	2855		A7
2400	BNHM	60633	3351	3E-16S	E4
E Hammond Av					
2600	BNHM	60633	3351	3E-16S	E4
2700	BNHM	60633	3352	3E-17S	A4
Hammond Dr					
2000	SMBG	60173	2805	21W-13N	C6
Hammond Ln					
1400	FDHT	60411	3509	1E-24S	B6
N Hampden Ct					
2600	CHCG	60614	2978	0W-3N	A5
2700	CHCG	60657	2978	0W-3N	A5
N Hampshire Av					
100	EMHT	60126	3028		B2
S Hampshire Av					
400	EMHT	60126	3028		B4
Hampshire Ct					
1100	SMBG	60193	2913		B1
1300	ROSL	60172	2912		A4
Hampshire Dr					
1600	EGVV	60007	2859	21W-9N	D7
1600	EGVV	60007	2913		D1
1800	HFET	60120	2855		E1
Hampshire Ln					
-	LYWD	60411	3509	2E-23S	D4
900	ELGN	60120	2855		C1
Hampshire Pkwy					
800	CRTE	60417	3596	0W-28S	D6
Hampton Av					
3800	PvsT	60558	3086		D7
3800	WNSP	60558	3086		D7
4300	WNSP	60558	3146		D1
Hampton Cir					
500	BRLT	60103	2911		A4
600	ELGN	60120	2855		D5
Hampton Ct					
10	BRRG	60527	3146		C6
10	FSMR	60422	3507	4W-23S	A3
10	RchT	60430	3507	4W-23S	A3
2100	SMWD	60107	2910		C2
4100	GNVW	60025	2809	11W-15N	D3
4100	GNVW	60062	2809	11W-15N	D3
4100	NfdT	60062	2809	11W-15N	D3
13200	PlsT	60462	3345	13W-15S	A2
13600	HMGN	60441	3342	19W-16S	E3
S Hampton Ct					
10	CRTE	60417	3685	0W-29S	C1
200	PLTN	60067	2805	22W-15N	B1
20100	FftT	60423	3504	9W-24S	E5
W Hampton Ct					
10	CRTE	60417	3685	0W-29S	C1
Hampton Dr					
6000	CPVL	60110	2748		D7
S Hampton Hbr					
1000	SMBG	60193	2913		B1
Hampton Ln					
400	ROSL	60172	2912		C6
1300	SMBG	60193	2858	25W-9N	B7
2300	NHBK	60062	2809	11W-16N	D1
Hampton Pkwy					
2700	EVTN	60201	2813	2W-13N	A7
2700	WLMT	60091	2813	2W-13N	A7
Hampton Pl					
300	HNDL	60521	3086		B7
W Hampton Pl					
1200	PLTN	60067	2805	22W-15N	B1
Hampton Rd					
1800	HFET	60195	2858	24W-12N	E1
1900	HFET	60195	2804	24W-12N	E7
10600	PlsT	60462	3345	13W-15S	A2
10700	PlsT	60467	3345	13W-15S	A2
Hamptondale Rd					
1100	WNKA	60093	2758	5W-16N	E7
1100	WNKA	60093	2811	5W-16N	E1
Hampton on Auburn					
10	RGMW	60008	2806	19W-14N	C3
Hamstead Ct					
200	ROSL	60172	2912		C5
W Hamstead Ct					
1300	PLTN	60067	2805	22W-15N	B2
Hanbury Ct					
-	BGVW	60455	3274	9W-11S	D1
Hancock Dr					
1900	HFET	60195	2858	25W-12N	A1
N Hancock Dr					
2000	PLTN	60074	2753	20W-20N	B1
Hancock St					
10900	ODPK	60467	3423	13W-19S	A3
11100	ODPK	60467	3422	14W-19S	E3
Haney Rd					
15200	SHLD	60473	3350	0E-18S	D6
W Hank Ct E					
12600	HMGN	60441	3344	15W-17S	B5
W Hank Ct W					
12700	HMGN	60441	3344	15W-17S	A5
Hanley Ct					
1800	SMBG	60194	2858	25W-11N	B3
Hannah Av					
700	FTPK	60130	3030	9W-1S	D7
1500	FTPK	60130	3088	9W-1S	D1
Hannah Ln					
-	HNDL	60521	3146		C3
Hanover Ct					
-	RGMW	60008	2860	19W-11N	B2
10	BRRG	60527	3208		B4
600	SMBG	60194	2859	23W-10N	A5
Hanover Dr					
7400	TYPK	60477	3424	9W-20S	D4
Hanover Ln					
900	DYR	46311	3510		E6
1800	FSMR	60422	3507	2W-23S	D3
W Hanover Pl					
200	MPPT	60056	2807	15W-14N	E3
Hanover St					
300	HMND	46327	3352		D4

STREET Block	City	ZIP	Map#	CGS	Grid
Hanover St					
1500	CHHT	60411	3596	0W-25S	C1
6900	HRPK	60133	2911		D2
7100	BGVW	60455	3210	8W-10S	E5
E Hanover St					
100	HMND	46327	3352		D4
W Hanover St					
7200	CHCG	60638	3148	9W-5S	D3
7200	SMMT	60501	3148	9W-5S	D3
Hans Brinker Ct					
600	PTON	60468	3860	9W-37S	D4
Hans Brinker Dr					
300	PTON	60468	3860	9W-37S	D4
Hanscom Ct					
2300	SMBG	60193	2857	26W-10N	E6
Hansen Ct					
100	WDDL	60191	2915		A5
Hansen Pl					
700	PKRG	60068	2864	10W-9N	A7
Hansom Ct					
200	WLNG	60090	2755	15W-18N	A2
Hansom Dr					
100	WLNG	60090	2755	15W-18N	A2
S Hanson Ct					
25100	MonT	60449	3682	8W-30S	A3
Happ Rd					
500	NHFD	60093	2811	7W-16N	B1
800	NHFD	60093	2758	7W-16N	B7
900	NHBK	60062	2758	7W-16N	B7
900	NHFD	60062	2758	7W-16N	B7
1000	NHBK	60093	2758	7W-16N	B7
S Happ Rd					
10	NHFD	60093	2811	6W-15N	C3
10	NtrT	60093	2811	6W-14N	C4
10	WLMT	60091	2811	6W-14N	C4
W Happfield Dr					
-	ANHT	60089	2754	18W-18N	A3
-	BFGV	60089	2753	18W-18N	E3
200	BFGV	60004	2754	18W-18N	A4
300	ANHT	60004	2754	18W-18N	A3
300	BFGV	60089	2754	18W-18N	A3
500	ANHT	60004	2753	18W-18N	E3
Happy Hollow Rd					
2400	GNVW	60025	2809	10W-15N	E3
2400	GNVW	60025	2810	10W-15N	A2
Hapsfield Ln					
500	BFGV	60089	2754	17W-18N	B4
Harasek St					
600	LMNT	60439	3270		E6
Harbor Av					
1600	BNHM	60633	3351	2E-16S	D4
1600	CTCY	60409	3351	2E-16S	D4
S Harbor Av					
9200	CHCG	60617	3216	4E-10S	A5
Harbor Cir					
4400	HFET	60195	2804	25W-15N	B2
W Harbor Ct					
7700	FftT	60423	3504	9W-24S	E5
Harbor Dr					
10	WLMT	60091	2813	2W-13N	B6
7900	PSHT	60463	3274	9W-13S	C4
14800	OKFT	60452	3347	7W-17S	C5
N Harbor Dr					
100	CHCG	60601	3034	0E-0N	D4
Harbor Ln					
2800	NHBK	60062	2756	11W-18N	E4
5000	RNPK	60471	3594	6W-26S	A3
Harbor St					
10	GLNC	60022	2759	5W-17N	A6
100	GLNC	60022	2758	5W-17N	E6
Harbor Ter					
400	BRLT	60103	2911		B4
E Harbor Ter					
500	BRLT	60103	2911		C4
Harborside Dr					
10	NHBK	60062	2756	11W-17N	D5
Harbor Town Dr					
15500	ODPK	60462	3346	9W-18S	D7
15600	ODPK	60462	3424	9W-18S	D1
Harbour Ct					
1000	WLNG	60090	2754	16W-16N	D6
1500	SMBG	60193	2912		B2
Harbour Dr					
1000	PTHT	60070	2754	16W-16N	D6
1000	WLNG	60090	2754	16W-16N	D6
1500	ANHT	60004	2754	16W-16N	D7
1500	ANHT	60090	2754	16W-16N	D7
Harcourt St					
5200	BmnT	60452	3425	6W-20S	E4
5200	OKFT	60452	3425	6W-20S	E4
5200	OKFT	60477	3425	6W-20S	E4
Harding Av					
1000	CTCY	60409	3352	3E-17S	A5
1200	DSPN	60016	2862	13W-11N	E3
1300	DSPN	60016	2863	13W-11N	A3
1400	BKLY	60163	3028		C4
1400	CTCY	60409	3351	2E-17S	C5
8000	SKOK	60076	2866	4W-10N	B5
9200	SKOK	60203	2866	4W-11N	B2
9500	EVTN	60201	2866	4W-11N	B2
15300	MDLN	60445	3348	4W-18S	C7
18700	FSMR	60422	3506	4W-22S	D2
18700	FSMR	60429	3506	4W-22S	D2
18700	HLCT	60429	3506	4W-22S	D2
19000	FSMR	60478	3506	4W-22S	D2
20300	OMFD	60461	3507	3W-24S	A5
E Harding Av					
10	LGPK	60525	3087	12W-3S	C5
10	BKFD	60513	3087	12W-3S	C5
N Harding Av					
400	CHCG	60624	3032	4W-0N	C3
700	CHCG	60651	3032	4W-0N	C3
1500	CHCG	60647	3032	4W-2N	C1
1800	CHCG	60647	2976	4W-2N	C7
3300	CHCG	60618	2976	4W-4N	B3
4300	CHCG	60625	2976	4W-5N	B1
4400	CHCG	60625	2920	4W-6N	B6
6000	CHCG	60659	2920	4W-7N	B3
6700	LNWD	60712	2920	4W-8N	B2
S Harding Av					
1200	CHCG	60623	3032	4W-1S	C7
1200	CHCG	60624	3032	4W-1S	C7
2300	CHCG	60623	3090	4W-2S	C4
4500	CHCG	60632	3090	4W-4S	C7
5100	CHCG	60632	3150	4W-5S	C2
7100	CHCG	60629	3150	4W-8S	C7
9100	CHCG	60805	3212	4W-10S	C5
9100	ENGN	60805	3212	4W-11S	C6
10100	CHCG	60655	3212	4W-11S	C7
10200	CHCG	60655	3276	4W-11S	C1
11700	ALSP	60803	3276	4W-13S	C5
11700	WthT	60803	3276	4W-13S	C5
13300	CTWD	60472	3348	4W-15S	C2
13300	RBBN	60472	3348	4W-15S	C2

STREET Block	City	ZIP	Map#	CGS	Grid
W Harding Av					
10	LGPK	60525	3087	12W-3S	B5
Harding Rd					
700	HNDL	60521	3146		D3
1500	NHFD	60093	2811	6W-15N	D3
Harding St					
-	OMFD	60461	3507	3W-25S	B7
10	ELGN	60123	2855		A6
100	EGvT	60018	2862	15W-9N	A7
300	CPVL	60110	2801		D1
Hardt Cir					
-	BRLT	60120	2910		B5
Hardy Dr					
-	HRPK	60133	2911		D6
Harger Rd					
600	OKBK	60523	3086		A1
Harlem Av					
-	CHCG	60638	3148	8W-5S	E2
-	FftT	60477	3504	9W-22S	E1
-	FftT	60477	3505	8W-23S	A2
-	LYNS	60402	3148	8W-5S	E1
-	SMMT	60501	3148	9W-5S	E2
-	SMMT	60534	3148	8W-5S	E2
-	TYPK	60423	3505	8W-23S	A3
-	TYPK	60477	3504	9W-22S	E1
10	GNVW	60025	2864	9W-12N	D1
10	GNVW	60053	2864	9W-11N	D3
10	MNGV	60053	2864	9W-11N	D3
400	GNVW	60025	2810	8W-13N	D7
1100	BRWN	60402	3030	8W-1S	D7
1100	FTPK	60130	3030	8W-1S	D7
1100	OKPK	60304	3030	8W-1S	D7
1500	BRWN	60402	3088	8W-3S	E6
1500	FTPK	60130	3088	8W-1S	D1
1500	NRIV	60130	3088	8W-3S	E6
1700	NRIV	60402	3088	8W-1S	D1
2100	NRIV	60546	3088	8W-1S	D2
2500	RVSD	60546	3088	8W-2S	D3
3200	RVSD	60402	3088	9W-3S	E4
3600	LYNS	60402	3088	8W-3S	E5
3600	LYNS	60534	3088	8W-3S	E5
3800	SKNY	60402	3088	8W-3S	E6
4400	FTVW	60402	3088	8W-4S	E7
4500	FTVW	60402	3148	8W-5S	E1
4500	LYNS	60534	3148	8W-5S	E1
8800	NLES	60714	2864	8W-11N	D3
15900	ODPK	60462	3424	9W-18S	E1
15900	ODPK	60477	3424	9W-18S	E1
15900	TYPK	60477	3424	9W-19S	E3
16300	OrlT	60477	3424	9W-19S	E2
18200	TYPK	60477	3425	8W-22S	A7
19300	TYPK	60477	3505	8W-22S	A2
Harlem Av SR-43					
-	CHCG	60638	3148	8W-5S	E2
-	FftT	60477	3505	9W-22S	A2
-	LYNS	60402	3148	8W-5S	E1
-	SMMT	60501	3148	8W-5S	E2
-	SMMT	60534	3148	8W-5S	E2
1100	BRWN	60402	3030	8W-1S	D7
1100	FTPK	60130	3030	8W-1S	D7
1100	OKPK	60304	3030	8W-1S	D7
1500	BRWN	60402	3088	8W-3S	E6
1500	FTPK	60130	3088	8W-1S	D1
1500	NRIV	60130	3088	8W-3S	E6
1700	NRIV	60402	3088	8W-1S	D1
2100	NRIV	60546	3088	8W-1S	D2
2500	RVSD	60546	3088	8W-2S	D3
3200	RVSD	60402	3088	9W-3S	E4
3600	LYNS	60402	3088	8W-3S	E5
3600	LYNS	60534	3088	8W-3S	E5
3800	SKNY	60402	3088	8W-3S	E6
4400	FTVW	60402	3088	8W-4S	E7
4500	FTVW	60402	3148	8W-5S	E1
4500	LYNS	60534	3148	8W-5S	E1
15900	ODPK	60462	3424	9W-18S	E1
15900	ODPK	60477	3424	9W-18S	E1
15900	TYPK	60477	3424	9W-19S	E3
16300	OrlT	60477	3424	8W-19S	E2
18200	TYPK	60477	3425	8W-22S	A7
19300	TYPK	60423	3505	8W-23S	A3
19300	TYPK	60477	3505	8W-22S	A2
N Harlem Av					
-	FTPK	60305	3030	8W-0N	D4
10	FTPK	60130	3030	8W-0N	D4
10	OKPK	60302	3030	9W-1N	D3
10	OKPK	60304	3030	9W-0N	D5
100	PTON	60468	3861	9W-37S	A3
200	WIIT	60468	3861	9W-37S	A3
300	PtnT	60468	3861	9W-37S	A2
400	OKPK	60301	3030	8W-0N	D4
400	OKPK	60305	3030	9W-1N	D3
400	RVFT	60301	3030	8W-0N	D4
400	RVFT	60305	3030	9W-1N	D3
1500	CHCG	60707	3030	8W-2N	D1
1500	EDPK	60707	3030	8W-2N	D1
1700	CHCG	60707	2974	8W-2N	D7
1700	EDPK	60707	2974	8W-2N	D7
2700	CHCG	60634	2974	9W-4N	D3
3900	NRDG	60634	2974	9W-3N	D4
3900	NRDG	60706	2974	9W-3N	D4
4400	HDHT	60706	2918	8W-5N	D7
4400	NRDG	60706	2918	8W-5N	D7
4700	CHCG	60656	2918	8W-5N	D7
5100	CHCG	60706	2918	8W-6N	D6
5600	CHCG	60631	2918	9W-5N	D7
6500	CHCG	60714	2918	8W-8N	D2
6500	NLES	60631	2918	8W-8N	D2
6500	NLES	60714	2918	9W-5N	D7
7200	CHCG	60631	2864	8W-9N	D7
7200	NLES	60714	2864	9W-9N	D7
7500	CHCG	60714	2864	8W-9N	D7
7500	NLES	60631	2864	8W-9N	D7
8700	MNGV	60053	2864	8W-10N	D4
N Harlem Av SR-43					
-	FTPK	60305	3030	8W-0N	D4
10	FTPK	60130	3030	8W-0N	D4
10	OKPK	60302	3030	9W-1N	D3
10	OKPK	60304	3030	9W-0N	D5
400	OKPK	60301	3030	8W-0N	D4
400	OKPK	60305	3030	9W-1N	D3
400	RVFT	60301	3030	8W-0N	D4
400	RVFT	60305	3030	9W-1N	D3
1500	CHCG	60707	3030	8W-2N	D1
1500	EDPK	60707	3030	8W-2N	D1
1700	CHCG	60707	2974	8W-2N	D7
1700	EDPK	60707	2974	8W-2N	D7
2700	CHCG	60634	2974	9W-4N	D3
3900	NRDG	60634	2974	9W-3N	D4
3900	NRDG	60706	2974	9W-3N	D4
4400	HDHT	60706	2918	8W-5N	D7
4400	NRDG	60706	2918	8W-5N	D7
4700	CHCG	60656	2918	8W-5N	D7
5100	CHCG	60706	2918	8W-6N	D6
5600	CHCG	60631	2918	9W-5N	D7
6500	CHCG	60714	2918	8W-8N	D2
N Harlem Av SR-43					
6500	NLES	60631	2918	8W-8N	D2
6500	NLES	60714	2918	9W-5N	D7
7200	CHCG	60631	2864	8W-9N	D7
7200	NLES	60714	2864	9W-9N	D7
7500	CHCG	60714	2864	8W-9N	D7
7500	NLES	60631	2864	8W-9N	D7
N Harlem Av SR-50					
100	PTON	60468	3861	9W-37S	A3
200	WIIT	60468	3861	9W-37S	A3
300	PtnT	60468	3861	9W-37S	A2
S Harlem Av					
-	BGVW	60453	3210	9W-10S	E5
-	FKFT	60423	3505	9W-25S	A7
-	OKLN	60453	3210	9W-10S	E5
-	OKLN	60455	3210	9W-10S	E5
-	OrlT	60452	3346	9W-17S	E5
-	PlsT	60462	3346	9W-16S	E3
-	PSHT	60462	3346	9W-15S	E2
-	PSHT	60463	3346	9W-15S	E2
-	RchT	60423	3505	9W-25S	A7
-	RchT	60443	3505	9W-25S	A7
-	SMMT	60534	3148	9W-5S	E2
-	TYPK	60423	3505	8W-23S	A3
10	FTPK	60130	3030	9W-0S	D6
10	FTPK	60304	3030	9W-0S	D5
10	OKPK	60302	3030	9W-0S	D5
10	OKPK	60304	3030	9W-0S	D5
100	PTON	60468	3861	8W-37S	A4
300	OKPK	60130	3030	9W-0S	D6
5100	CHCG	60501	3148	8W-5S	E2
5100	FTVW	60402	3148	8W-5S	E2
5400	SMMT	60501	3148	9W-7S	D6
5400	SMMT	60638	3148	8W-5S	E3
6400	BDPK	60638	3148	8W-7S	E5
6400	CHCG	60638	3148	8W-7S	E5
6500	BDPK	60501	3148	9W-7S	D5
6700	BGVW	60455	3148	9W-7S	E6
7100	BGVW	60638	3148	8W-8S	E7
7300	BDPK	60638	3210	8W-8S	E1
7400	BGVW	60638	3210	9W-8S	E1
7700	BGVW	60459	3210	9W-8S	E2
7700	BRBK	60455	3210	9W-8S	E2
7700	BRBK	60459	3210	9W-8S	E2
9200	BGVW	60455	3210	9W-10S	E6
9500	CHRG	60415	3210	8W-11S	E7
9500	CHRG	60455	3210	8W-11S	E7
9500	OKLN	60415	3210	8W-11S	E6
10100	BGVW	60455	3274	9W-11S	E1
10100	CHRG	60415	3274	9W-11S	E1
10100	PSHL	60455	3274	9W-11S	E1
10100	PSHL	60465	3274	9W-11S	E1
10400	CHRG	60482	3274	9W-14S	E7
10400	WRTH	60465	3274	9W-14S	E7
10500	WRTH	60482	3274	9W-14S	E7
11600	PSHT	60463	3274	8W-13S	E5
11600	WRTH	60463	3274	8W-13S	E5
13500	BmnT	60445	3346	9W-17S	E5
13500	BmnT	60462	3346	9W-17S	E5
13500	OrlT	60462	3346	9W-17S	E5
13500	WthT	60445	3346	9W-15S	E2
13500	WthT	60462	3346	9W-15S	E2
13500	WthT	60463	3346	9W-15S	E2
14100	BmnT	60452	3346	9W-17S	E5
15100	ODPK	60462	3346	9W-18S	E6
15200	OKFT	60462	3346	9W-18S	E6
15700	ODPK	60462	3424	9W-18S	E1
15800	ODPK	60477	3424	9W-18S	E1
15800	TYPK	60477	3424	9W-18S	E1
19300	FftT	60423	3505	9W-25S	A7
19300	FftT	60477	3505	8W-23S	A3
19300	RchT	60477	3505	8W-23S	A3
19300	TYPK	60477	3505	8W-23S	A3
19700	MTSN	60443	3505	8W-23S	A4
19800	MTSN	60423	3505	8W-24S	A5
21500	FKFT	60423	3593	8W-26S	A2
22400	FKFT	60443	3593	9W-27S	A3
22400	RchT	60423	3593	9W-27S	A3
23100	FKFT	60449	3593	8W-28S	A7
23100	GGnT	60423	3593	8W-28S	A7
23100	GGnT	60449	3593	8W-28S	A7
23100	MonT	60449	3593	8W-28S	A7
23100	RchT	60449	3593	8W-28S	A7
23900	GGnT	60423	3682	8W-29S	A1
23900	GGnT	60449	3682	9W-30S	A4
23900	MonT	60423	3593	8W-29S	A7
23900	MonT	60423	3682	8W-29S	A1
23900	MonT	60449	3682	9W-30S	A4
29700	PtnT	60468	3861	9W-36S	A1
29700	WIIT	60468	3861	9W-36S	A1
S Harlem Av SR-43					
-	BGVW	60453	3210	9W-10S	E5
-	FKFT	60423	3505	9W-25S	A7
-	OKLN	60453	3210	9W-10S	E5
-	OKLN	60455	3210	9W-10S	E5
-	OrlT	60452	3346	9W-17S	E5
-	PlsT	60462	3346	9W-16S	E3
-	PSHT	60462	3346	9W-15S	E2
-	PSHT	60463	3346	9W-15S	E2
-	RchT	60423	3505	9W-25S	A7
-	RchT	60443	3505	9W-25S	A7
-	SMMT	60534	3148	9W-5S	E2
10	FTPK	60130	3030	9W-0S	D6
10	FTPK	60304	3030	9W-0S	D5
10	OKPK	60302	3030	9W-0S	D5
10	OKPK	60304	3030	9W-0S	D5
300	OKPK	60130	3030	9W-0S	D6
5100	CHCG	60501	3148	8W-5S	E2
5100	FTVW	60402	3148	8W-5S	E2
5400	CHCG	60638	3148	9W-7S	D6
5400	SMMT	60501	3148	9W-7S	D6
5400	SMMT	60638	3148	8W-5S	E3
6300	BDPK	60638	3148	8W-7S	E5
6500	BDPK	60501	3148	9W-7S	D5
6700	BGVW	60455	3148	9W-7S	E6
7100	BGVW	60638	3148	8W-8S	E7
7300	BDPK	60638	3210	8W-8S	E1
7300	BGVW	60455	3210	9W-9S	E3
7400	BGVW	60638	3210	9W-8S	E1
7700	BGVW	60459	3210	9W-8S	E2
7700	BRBK	60455	3210	9W-8S	E2
7700	BRBK	60459	3210	9W-8S	E2
9800	CHRG	60415	3210	9W-11S	E7
9800	CHRG	60455	3210	9W-11S	E7
10100	BGVW	60455	3274	9W-11S	E1
10100	CHRG	60415	3274	9W-11S	E1
10100	PSHL	60455	3274	9W-11S	E1
10100	PSHL	60465	3274	9W-11S	E1
10400	CHRG	60482	3274	9W-14S	E7
10400	WRTH	60465	3274	9W-14S	E7
10500	WRTH	60482	3274	9W-14S	E7
11600	PSHT	60463	3274	8W-13S	E5
11600	WRTH	60463	3274	8W-13S	E5
13500	BmnT	60445	3346	9W-17S	E5
13500	BmnT	60462	3346	9W-17S	E5
S Harlem Av SR-43					
13500	OrlT	60462	3346	9W-17S	E5
13500	WthT	60445	3346	9W-15S	E2
13500	WthT	60462	3346	9W-15S	E2
13500	WthT	60463	3346	9W-15S	E2
14100	BmnT	60452	3346	9W-17S	E5
15100	ODPK	60462	3346	9W-18S	E6
15200	OKFT	60462	3346	9W-18S	E6
15700	ODPK	60462	3424	9W-18S	E1
15800	ODPK	60477	3424	9W-18S	E1
15800	TYPK	60477	3424	9W-18S	E1
19300	FftT	60423	3505	9W-25S	A7
19300	FftT	60477	3505	8W-23S	A3
19300	RchT	60477	3505	8W-23S	A3
19300	TYPK	60423	3505	8W-23S	A3
19700	MTSN	60443	3505	8W-23S	A4
19800	MTSN	60423	3505	8W-24S	A5
21500	FKFT	60423	3593	8W-26S	A2
21500	RchT	60423	3593	8W-26S	A2
22400	FKFT	60443	3593	9W-27S	A3
22400	RchT	60423	3593	9W-27S	A3
S Harlem Av SR-50					
100	PTON	60468	3861	8W-37S	A4
100	WIIT	60468	3861	8W-37S	A4
Harlem Ct					
-	OKPK	60301	3030	8W-0N	D3
-	OKPK	60302	3030	8W-0N	D3
Harlem Dr					
5200	SMMT	60501	3148	9W-5S	E2
Harmess St					
800	CTCY	60409	3352	3E-17S	A6
Harmon Blvd					
700	HFET	60194	2858	25W-11N	B3
700	SMBG	60194	2858	25W-11N	B3
Harmony Ct					
1400	ITSC	60143	2914		E6
Harmony Dr					
400	WLNG	60090	2755	14W-17N	D5
Harmony Ln					
200	EGVV	60007	2914		E2
600	GNVW	60025	2810	8W-13N	E7
Harms Ct					
700	WLNG	60090	2754	16W-18N	E2
Harms Rd					
10	GLF	60025	2865	7W-12N	C1
10	GLF	60077	2865	7W-12N	C1
10	MNGV	60053	2865	7W-12N	C1
10	MNGV	60077	2865	7W-12N	C1
500	GLF	60025	2811	7W-12N	C7
500	GNVW	60025	2811	7W-13N	C7
500	GNVW	60077	2811	7W-12N	C7
500	SKOK	60025	2865	7W-12N	C7
500	SKOK	60077	2811	7W-12N	C7
1300	WLMT	60091	2811	7W-13N	C7
8400	SKOK	60077	2865	6W-10N	D4
Harmswood Ter					
5200	SKOK	60077	2865	6W-11N	D2
Harnew Rd E					
9900	OKLN	60453	3212	6W-11S	A7
Harnew Rd S					
4800	OKLN	60453	3212	6W-11S	A7
4800	OKLN	60453	3276	6W-11S	A1
4900	OKLN	60453	3275	6W-11S	E1
Harnew Rd W					
9900	OKLN	60453	3211	6W-11S	E7
Harold Av					
4800	SRPK	60176	2917	12W-6N	C6
N Harold Av					
100	NHLK	60164	2972		E7
800	LydT	60164	2972		E5
1500	MLPK	60160	3028		E2
1500	MLPK	60164	3028		E2
1500	NHLK	60164	3028		E2
S Harold Av					
100	NHLK	60164	3028		E1
200	MLPK	60160	3028		E1
200	MLPK	60164	3028		E1
11900	PSHT	60463	3274	9W-14S	D6
Harold St					
-	ANHT	60004	2806	18W-16N	E1
16400	OKFT	60452	3426	5W-19S	B2
Harolds Cres					
2800	FSMR	60422	3507	3W-23S	A4
Harper Av					
14400	DLTN	60419	3351	1E-16S	C4
18200	LNSG	60438	3429	1E-21S	C7
18200	ThtT	60438	3429	1E-21S	C7
22200	SLVL	60411	3597	1E-26S	C3
S Harper Av					
-	CHCG	60628	3215	1E-11S	B6
200	GNWD	60425	3509	1E-23S	B3
5500	CHCG	60615	3153	1E-6S	B3
5500	CHCG	60637	3153	1E-6S	B3
7000	CHCG	60619	3153	1E-7S	B6
7700	CHCG	60619	3215	1E-8S	B1
Harper Ct					
5600	CHCG	60637	3153	1E-6S	B3
Harper Ln					
100	LMNT	60439	3342	19W-15S	D1
Harper Rd					
-	TYPK	60477	3424	10W-21S	B6
Harper College Dr					
-	PLTN	60067	2805	22W-13N	B5
E Harriet Ln					
800	BRTN	60010	2751	25W-18N	B2
E Harriet St					
100	TNTN	60476	3428	0E-21S	D6
W Harriet St					
100	TNTN	60476	3428	0E-21S	D6
W Harrington Ln					
4200	CHCG	60646	2920	5W-7N	A4
E Harris Av					
10	LGNG	60525	3087	12W-4S	C7
W Harris Av					
10	LGNG	60525	3087	12W-4S	B7
Harris Ct					
500	BFGV	60089	2754	17W-20N	C1
Harris Dr					
500	BFGV	60089	2754	17W-20N	C1
3400	NHBK	60062	2756	11W-18N	C3
Harrison					
12300	BRTN	60010	2750	26W-20N	E2
Harrison Av					
400	CTCY	60409	3352	4E-17S	B6
800	DYR	46311	3510		D7
1100	BKFD	60513	3087	11W-3S	D5
1100	LGPK	60525	3087	11W-3S	D5
1500	DYR	46311	3598		D1
1500	PvsT	60525	3087	11W-2S	D4
6000	HMND	46320	3430		D1
6000	HMND	46324	3430		D3
7800	MNSR	46321	3430		D6
8700	MNSR	46321	3510		D1
N Harrison Av					
10	PLTN	60067	2805	22W-16N	B1
10	PltT	60067	2805	22W-16N	B1
100	IVNS	60067	2752	22W-16N	B7
100	PLTN	60067	2752	22W-16N	B7
100	PltT	60067	2752	22W-16N	B7
S Harrison Av					
-	PltT	60067	2805	22W-15N	B1
10	PLTN	60067	2805	22W-15N	B1
5900	HMND	46320	3352		D7
5900	HMND	46320	3430		D1
13900	BLID	60406	3349	3W-16S	A3
14700	BmnT	60469	3349	3W-17S	A5
14900	BmnT	60426	3349	3W-17S	A5
14900	POSN	60469	3349	3W-17S	A5
Harrison Ct					
700	CRTE	60417	3685	1W-30S	A3
S Harrison Ct					
300	PLTN	60067	2805	22W-15N	B2
300	PltT	60067	2805	22W-15N	B2
Harrison Ln					
10	SMWD	60107	2856	29W-10N	E6
800	HFET	60195	2804	24W-15N	D3
Harrison Pl					
10	HNDL	60521	3146		A2
700	DYR	46311	3510		E6
Harrison St					
-	BLWD	60153	3029	11W-0S	D6
-	MYWD	60104	3029	11W-0S	D6
-	PvsT	60126	3028		C7
10	CHCG	60644	3031	7W-0S	B6
10	EMHT	60126	3028		B6
10	FTPK	60153	3030	10W-0S	A6
10	MYWD	60130	3030	10W-0S	A6
10	MYWD	60153	3030	10W-0S	A6
10	OKPK	60304	3031	8W-0S	A6
10	YkTp	60126	3028		B6
100	BRTN	60010	2750	25W-20N	E2
200	CPVL	60110	2801		D1
400	CTCY	60409	3352	4E-17S	B5
400	ELGN	60120	2855		B5
700	MYWD	60153	3029	11W-0S	E6
900	PKRG	60068	2918	9W-8N	B2
1000	BDVW	60153	3029	11W-0S	E6
1000	BDVW	60155	3029	11W-0S	E6
1400	MYWD	60155	3029	11W-0S	E6
1700	EVTN	60201	2813	3W-12N	A7
1700	GNVW	60025	2864	9W-12N	B1
1900	EVTN	60201	2812	3W-12N	E7
2600	BLWD	60104	3029	12W-0S	B6
2800	MaiT	60025	2864	10W-12N	A1
2900	EVTN	60201	2866	4W-12N	B1
2900	NLES	60714	2864	10W-12N	B1
3100	GNVW	60714	2864	10W-12N	A1
3300	SKOK	60076	2866	4W-12N	B1
3300	SKOK	60201	2866	4W-12N	B1
4100	HLSD	60162	3028		C7
4100	HLSD	60162	3029	13W-0S	A6
4100	PvsT	60162	3028		C7
4100	WSTR	60154	3029	13W-0S	A6
7200	FTPK	60130	3030	9W-0S	D6
7200	OKPK	60304	3030	9W-0S	D6
7400	HRPK	60133	2912		A1
9300	MaiT	60016	2863	11W-12N	C1
13800	BLID	60406	3349	3W-16S	A3
13800	POSN	60469	3349	3W-16S	A3
E Harrison St					
10	CHCG	60605	3034	0E-0S	C5
500	EMHT	60126	3028		B6
500	YkTp	60126	3028		B6
W Harrison St					
10	CHCG	60605	3034	0W-0S	B6
100	CHCG	60607	3034	0W-0S	B5
800	CHCG	60607	3033	1W-0S	D5
1400	CHCG	60607	3033	3W-0S	A6
2800	CHCG	60612	3032	3W-0S	E6
3100	CHCG	60624	3032	4W-0S	C6
4500	CHCG	60644	3032	5W-0S	A6
4800	CHCG	60644	3031	6W-0S	D6
Harrogate on Oxford					
10	RGMW	60008	2805	22W-13N	B7
Harrow Gate Dr					
2100	IVNS	60010	2751	25W-16N	B7
2300	IVNS	60010	2804	25W-16N	B1
Harry Caray Dr					
-	NHLK	60164	3028		D1
S Harry J Rogowski Dr					
11400	MTPK	60803	3276	3W-13S	E4
Hart Dr					
2900	FNPK	60131	2972		E4
2900	FNPK	60131	2973	13W-3N	A4
18200	HMWD	60430	3428	1W-21S	A7
Hart Rd					
600	BNHL	60010	2750	26W-20N	D1
600	BRTN	60010	2750	26W-20N	D1
Hart St					
1800	DYR	46311	3598		D3
8000	SjnT	46311	3598		D5
N Hart St					
400	CHCG	60612	3033	2W-0N	C3
400	CHCG	60622	3033	2W-0N	C3
S Hart St					
200	PLTN	60067	2805	21W-15N	D1
Hartford Ct					
900	SMBG	60193	2913		A1
1600	HFET	60195	2858	24W-12N	D1
10100	SRPK	60176	2973	12W-4N	B2
E Hartford Ct					
2500	ANHT	60004	2807	16W-15N	D2
E Hartford Dr					
10	SMBG	60193	2913		B1
W Hartford Dr					
10	SMBG	60193	2913		A1
200	SMBG	60193	2858	23W-9N	E7
Hartford Ln					
900	EGVV	60007	2915		A2
Hartford St					
7100	BGVW	60455	3210	8W-10S	E4
Hart Hills Rd					
10	BNHL	60010	2750	26W-18N	C2
N Hartland Ct					
500	CHCG	60622	3033	2W-0N	C3
Hartley Dr					
-	SMBG	60173	2859	21W-12N	E2
Hartmann Dr					
1200	SMBG	60193	2912		B1
1800	HRPK	60133	2912		A1
25400	CRTE	60417	3685	0W-30S	D4
25400	CteT	60417	3685	0W-30S	D4
Hartmann Ln					
500	WLMT	60091	2812	4W-13N	B6
Hartrey Av					
100	CHCG	60645	2866	3W-9N	E6
500	EVTN	60202	2866	3W-10N	E5
2100	EVTN	60201	2866	3W-12N	E1
Hartrey Av					
2500	EVTN	60201	2812	3W-12N	E7
W Harts Rd					
6600	NLES	60714	2865	8W-9N	A7
6600	NLES	60714	2918	8W-8N	E1
6600	NLES	60714	2919	8W-8N	A1
Hartung Rd					
-	RGMW	60008	2805	21W-13N	C5
-	RGMW	60067	2805	21W-13N	D5
-	RGMW	60173	2805	21W-13N	C5
-	SMBG	60067	2805	21W-13N	D5
-	SMBG	60173	2805	21W-13N	C5
Hartwell Av					
600	ELGN	60120	2855		B1
S Hartwell Av					
6600	CHCG	60637	3152	0E-7S	C5
Hartwood Ct					
9200	ODPK	60462	3345	11W-16S	E3
Hartwood Dr					
900	SMWD	60107	2857	27W-9N	C7
900	SMWD	60107	2911		C1
Hartzell St					
2200	EVTN	60201	2812	3W-13N	D7
2900	WLMT	60091	2811	6W-13N	E7
Harvard Av					
10	DSPN	60016	2862	14W-12N	B1
10	MPPT	60016	2862	14W-12N	B1
10	MPPT	60056	2862	14W-12N	B1
100	BNHL	60010	2750	25W-18N	E4
100	BrnT	60010	2750	25W-18N	E4
100	NHLK	60164	3028		C1
200	BrnT	60010	2751	25W-18N	A4
600	BRTN	60010	2751	25W-18N	A4
N Harvard Av					
-	NHLK	60164	3028		C1
100	ANHT	60005	2806	18W-14N	E4
1500	ANHT	60004	2806	18W-15N	E2
4000	ANHT	60004	2753	18W-18N	E2
S Harvard Av					
100	ANHT	60005	2806	18W-13N	D5
1300	ANHT	60005	2860	18W-12N	E1
7100	CHCG	60621	3152	0W-8S	B7
7500	CHCG	60621	3214	0W-8S	B1
7900	CHCG	60620	3214	0W-9S	B2
9500	CHCG	60628	3214	0W-11S	B6
11300	CHCG	60628	3278	0W-14S	B5
Harvard Cir					
1000	SMBG	60193	2912		B1
Harvard Ct					
-	GNVW	60062	2810	10W-15N	B2
100	GNVW	60025	2810	10W-15N	B2
S Harvard Ct					
700	PLTN	60067	2805	22W-15N	B3
S Harvard Dr					
800	PLTN	60067	2805	22W-14N	B3
Harvard Ln					
500	HFET	60195	2858	24W-12N	E1
700	MTSN	60443	3505	6W-25S	E7
900	BFGV	60089	2754	16W-17N	D5
1400	SMBG	60193	2912		B1
17700	CCHL	60478	3426	4W-21S	E6
17700	HLCT	60429	3426	4W-21S	E6
Harvard Rd					
-	FSMR	60422	3507	2W-23S	D4
N Harvard Rd					
1200	ANHT	60004	2806	18W-15N	D2
Harvard St					
-	MYWD	60153	3030	10W-0S	A6
10	CHCG	60644	3031	7W-0S	B6
10	OKPK	60304	3031	8W-0S	A6
600	WLMT	60091	2812	4W-13N	B6
800	OKPK	60304	3030	8W-0S	E6
2500	BDVW	60155	3029	12W-0S	C6
2500	MYWD	60153	3029	12W-0S	C6
7200	FTPK	60130	3030	9W-0S	C6
7200	OKPK	60130	3030	9W-0S	C6
E Harvard St					
10	PvsT	60126	3028		B7
500	EMHT	60126	3028		A7
500	YkTp	60126	3028		A7
W Harvard St					
7100	NLES	60714	2864	8W-9N	D6
Harvard Ter					
900	EVTN	60202	2867	2W-9N	A6
3800	SKOK	60076	2866	5W-9N	B6
5000	SKOK	60077	2865	6W-9N	D6
Harvest Cross					
100	ODPK	60467	3344	14W-17S	D5
Harvest Ct					
3900	GNVW	60025	2809	11W-15N	D3
3900	GNVW	60062	2809	11W-15N	D3
Harvest Dr					
10	SMWD	60107	2856	29W-9N	E7
100	DYR	46311	3598		D4
7800	FftT	60423	3504	10W-24S	C6
16400	LMNT	60439	3342	20W-15S	B1
Harvest Ln					
-	DYR	46311	3598		D5
-	RchT	60443	3593	8W-25S	B1
-	SKOK	60076	2812	5W-12N	A7
400	ROSL	60172	2912		E7
700	MPPT	60056	2808	14W-13N	B6
1200	UYPK	60466	3684	3W-30S	C4
3800	GNVW	60025	2809	11W-15N	E3
3800	GNVW	60062	2809	11W-15N	E3
S Harvest Ln					
26100	CteT	60417	3684	2W-32S	E7
Harvest Pl					
800	ROSL	60172	2912		E7
Harvester Ct					
400	WLNG	60090	2755	15W-17N	B5
Harvester Dr					
-	BRRG	60527	3146		B7
-	BRRG	60527	3208		C1
Harvest Hill Ct					
11700	ODPK	60467	3422	14W-21S	D5
Harvest Hill Dr					
17400	ODPK	60467	3422	14W-20S	D5
Harvest View Ln					
8600	TYPK	60477	3504	10W-23S	B3
Harvey Av					
100	WDDL	60191	2915		A7
1200	BRWN	60402	3031	7W-1S	B7
1200	OKPK	60304	3031	7W-1S	B7
1200	OKPK	60402	3031	7W-1S	B7
1500	BRWN	60402	3089	7W-2S	B3
3800	PvsT	60558	3086		E7
3800	SKNY	60402	3089	7W-3S	B6
3800	WNSP	60558	3086		E7
4400	WNSP	60558	3146		E1
5000	WNSP	60558	3147	13W-5S	A3
5400	LynT	60525	3147	13W-5S	A3
5700	LynT	60525	3146		E4
14500	HRVY	60426	3349	1W-17S	E5

STREET Block City ZIP Map# CGS Grid

S Harvey Av
100 OKPK 60302 3031 7W-0N B4
1000 OKPK 60304 3031 7W-0S B7
1100 BRWN 60402 3031 7W-0S B7
1100 OKPK 60402 3031 7W-0S B7
Harvey Av N
100 OKPK 60302 3031 7W-0N B3
1200 CHCG 60302 3031 7W-2N B1
1200 CHCG 60639 3031 7W-2N B1
Harvey Rd
10 BmdT 60157 2913 C5
300 ROSL 60157 2913 C7
Harvey St
400 DSPN 60016 2862 14W-11N C2
Harwich Ln
800 SMBG 60194 2858 24W-10N D4
Harwinton Pl
2100 HFET 60195 2857 26W-12N E1
2100 HFET 60195 2858 25W-12N B1
Harwood Av
17700 HMWD 60430 3427 2W-22S C7
18400 HMWD 60430 3507 2W-22S C1
18600 FSMR 60422 3507 2W-22S C1
18600 FSMR 60430 3507 2W-22S C1
18600 HMWD 60422 3507 2W-22S C1
Harwood St
- CHCG 60656 2918 8W-6N E6
- CHCG 60706 2918 8W-6N E6
- HDHT 60706 2918 8W-6N E6
N Haskins Av
7700 CHCG 60626 2867 2W-9N C6
Hassell Cir
1200 HFET 60195 2804 25W-12N C7
Hassell Ct
1200 HFET 60195 2804 25W-12N C7
Hassell Dr
1300 HFET 60195 2804 25W-12N C7
1300 HFET 60195 2858 25W-12N C1
Hassell Pl
1400 HFET 60195 2804 24W-13N B7
Hassell Rd
- HFET 60195 2804 26W-12N A7
2300 HFET 60195 2803 26W-12N E7
2300 HFET 60195 2857 26W-12N E1
Hastings Av
10 EGVV 60007 2914 D1
10 NfdT 60062 2758 7W-20N A2
10 NtrT 60035 2758 7W-20N A2
10 NtrT 60062 2758 7W-20N A2
100 HDPK 60035 2758 7W-20N A1
2300 EVTN 60201 2866 4W-12N C1
2500 EVTN 60201 2812 4W-12N C7
Hastings Ct
100 ROSL 60172 2912 B4
700 WLNG 60090 2755 15W-17N A6
1900 SMBG 60194 2858 25W-11N B3
Hastings Dr
1900 HFET 60195 2858 25W-12N C1
7900 ODPK 60462 3346 9W-16S D4
15100 DLTN 60419 3351 1E-17S B6
Hastings Ln
- BFGV 60089 2754 15W-20N E2
- WLNG 60089 2755 15W-18N A2
- WLNG 60090 2754 15W-20N E2
- WLNG 60090 2755 15W-18N A2
100 VrnT 60015 2755 15W-20N A2
100 VrnT 60089 2755 15W-20N A2
700 BFGV 60089 2755 15W-20N A1
700 HRPK 60133 2858 26W-9N A7
800 HRPK 60133 2857 26W-9N E7
Hastings Rd
600 WLNG 60090 2755 15W-17N A6
Hastings St
700 ELGN 60120 2855 B6
700 PKRG 60068 2864 10W-9N A7
10800 WSTR 60154 3086 E2
W Hastings St
1200 CHCG 60608 3033 1W-1S D7
Hastings Mill Rd
100 SMWD 60107 2857 27W-11N C4
Hastings on Oxford
10 RGMW 60008 2805 22W-13N B7
Hathaway Cir
1200 ELGN 60120 2855 D1
Hatherleigh Ct
- MPPT 60005 2861 17W-10N C4
- MPPT 60056 2861 17W-10N C4
W Hatherleigh Ct
1800 MPPT 60056 2861 17W-11N C4
S Hatlen Av
10 ANHT 60005 2807 17W-12N C7
10 MPPT 60056 2807 17W-12N C7
400 MPPT 60056 2861 17W-12N C1
Hatlen Ct
300 MPPT 60056 2861 17W-12N C1
E Hattendorf Av
10 ROSL 60172 2913 A4
W Hattendorf Av
10 ROSL 60172 2913 A4
100 ROSL 60172 2912 D4
E Hauert St
500 PTON 60468 3861 8W-37S A3
N Haussen Ct
3000 CHCG 60618 2976 4W-3N C4
Havana Av
6200 HMND 46320 3430 D1
6200 HMND 46324 3430 D1
Haven Av
15900 ODHL 60477 3424 11W-19S A2
15900 ODPK 60462 3424 11W-19S A2
16200 ODHL 60477 3423 11W-19S E2
Haven Ct
9200 ODHL 60477 3423 11W-19S E3
Haven Dr
600 BRTN 60010 2751 24W-18N C3
600 PltT 60010 2751 24W-18N C3
N Haven Dr
1500 PltT 60067 2752 21W-17N C4
1500 PltT 60074 2752 21W-17N C4
W Haven Dr
300 ANHT 60005 2861 18W-12N A1
900 ANHT 60005 2860 18W-12N E1
N Haven Rd
100 EMHT 60126 3028 A2
Haven St
600 EVTN 60201 2867 2W-12N B1
E Haven St
300 ANHT 60005 2861 17W-12N B1
400 MPPT 60056 2861 17W-12N B1
W Haven St
2100 MPPT 60056 2861 17W-12N B1
Havenwood Av
400 HDPK 60035 2758 7W-20N C2
Havenwood Ct
3200 RGMW 60067 2805 21W-13N D6

Haverford Ct
200 SMBG 60173 2859 21W-10N E4
Haverford Wy
- HFET 60120 2855 E1
- HFET 60120 2856 31W-12N A1
E Haver Hill Ct
300 ITSC 60143 2914 C5
E Haverhill Ct
2500 ANHT 60004 2807 16W-15N D2
Haverhill Ln
100 SMBG 60193 2858 26W-10N A6
14000 ODPK 60467 3344 14W-16S E4
Haverhill on Auburn
10 RGMW 60008 2806 19W-14N B3
Haverman Ct
10 ELGN 60120 2855 C5
Haverton Ct
10 SMWD 60107 2857 28W-11N A5
Hawaii Ct
18000 ODPK 60467 3423 13W-21S A7
Haweswood Ct
3400 CRTE 60417 3596 0E-28S D6
Haweswood Dr
3400 CRTE 60417 3596 0E-28S E6
3400 STGR 60475 3596 0E-28S E6
Hawk Av
1500 MLPK 60160 3029 13W-1N A2
Hawk Ct
200 SMBG 60193 2857 27W-10N D6
2000 RGMW 60008 2806 19W-13N D6
Hawk Dr
100 PltT 60010 2751 24W-18N D2
Hawk Ln
1800 EGVV 60007 2913 C2
2100 RGMW 60008 2806 19W-13N C6
N Hawk St
600 PLTN 60067 2752 20W-16N E6
W Hawkes St
1400 ANHT 60004 2753 18W-18N D2
Hawk Haven Rd
15500 HMGN 60441 3342 19W-16S D3
Hawkins Ct
1200 BRLT 60103 2910 E7
Hawley Av
10 WDND 60118 2801 A3
Hawley Woods Rd
400 BNHL 60010 2750 27W-17N C4
Hawthorn Av
10 GLNC 60022 2758 6W-17N E5
Hawthorn Ct
1400 HNDL 60521 3086 B5
Hawthorn Dr
9000 HYHL 60457 3209 11W-10S E5
14100 LMNT 60439 3343 17W-15S B2
W Hawthorn Dr
900 ITSC 60143 2914 A7
Hawthorn Ln
- PSPK 60464 3273 11W-14S E5
100 HFET 60195 2859 23W-11N B3
300 WNKA 60093 2812 4W-15N C3
Hawthorne Av
- FTPK 60130 3030 9W-0N C4
- RVFT 60305 3030 9W-0N C4
10 AddT 60106 2915 C6
10 BNVL 60106 2915 C6
10 MonT 60466 3594 4W-28S E6
10 PKFT 60466 3594 4W-28S E6
100 WDDL 60191 2915 B6
200 AddT 60191 2915 B6
500 BmdT 60157 2913 C3
1600 WSTR 60154 3087 13W-1S A2
2000 HMWD 60430 3427 2W-21S C6
4500 LYNS 60534 3148 10W-4S B1
4600 MCCK 60525 3148 10W-4S B1
4600 MCCK 60534 3148 10W-4S B1
N Hawthorne Av
- MLPK 60165 3029 12W-2N B1
1900 LydT 60164 2973 12W-2N B7
1900 MLPK 60160 2973 12W-2N B7
1900 MLPK 60160 3029 12W-2N B1
1900 SNPK 60160 3029 12W-2N B1
1900 SNPK 60165 3029 12W-2N B1
2300 FNPK 60131 2973 12W-2N B7
W Hawthorne Av
4800 BKLY 60163 3028 D4
4800 HLSD 60162 3028 D4
5000 BKLY 60162 3028 D4
5000 HLSD 60163 3028 D4
5100 BKLY 60104 3028 E4
5100 BLWD 60104 3028 E4
W Hawthorne Cir
300 MPPT 60056 2861 16W-10N E4
Hawthorne Ct
10 BFGV 60089 2754 16W-18N C3
10 CTCY 60409 3429 2E-18S C1
200 SMBG 60193 2859 22W-9N D6
600 CPVL 60110 2748 A7
1100 WLNG 60090 2754 16W-18N D3
S Hawthorne Ct N
14500 HMGN 60441 3342 19W-17S E5
S Hawthorne Ct S
14700 HMGN 60441 3342 19W-17S E6
Hawthorne Dr
- EHZC 60430 3427 2W-20S D5
- HLCT 60429 3427 2W-20S D5
- HLCT 60430 3427 2W-20S D5
10 CTSD 60525 3147 13W-7S B6
100 PltT 60010 2751 24W-18N C2
10100 ODPK 60462 3345 12W-17S C6
17100 EHZC 60429 3427 2W-20S D5
17500 CCHL 60478 3426 5W-21S B6
Hawthorne Ln
- BNHL 60010 2750 27W-17N B4
10 SMWD 60107 2857 28W-10N B5
100 CHHT 60411 3507 1W-24S E6
100 CHHT 60411 3508 1W-24S A6
100 CPVL 60110 2748 B7
100 EDND 60110 2748 B7
100 EDND 60118 2748 B7
200 DSPN 60016 2863 12W-11N B3
500 BRLT 60103 2910 D4
500 CPVL 60110 2801 A1
800 NHBK 60062 2756 10W-17N E4
1100 EGVV 60007 2914 A2
1200 HNDL 60521 3086 B5
1400 GNVW 60025 2811 7W-14N A5
1900 DRFD 60015 2756 12W-20N B1
1900 RVWD 60015 2756 12W-20N B1
1900 WdfT 60015 2756 12W-20N B1
2000 EVTN 60201 2866 3W-11N D2
2400 FSMR 60422 3507 3W-23S B3
2700 WLMT 60091 2812 5W-13N A5
2900 DYR 46311 3598 C4
2900 WLMT 60091 2811 5W-13N E5
3000 HLCT 60429 3427 3W-21S A5

Hawthorne Ln
4300 RGMW 60008 2806 20W-12N B7
6800 HRPK 60133 2912 A2
9300 ODHL 60477 3423 11W-19S E2
9300 ODPK 60467 3423 11W-19S E2
N Hawthorne Ln
500 PTON 60468 3861 8W-37S B3
500 WIIT 60468 3861 8W-37S B3
W Hawthorne Ln
7400 FftT 60423 3504 9W-25S E6
Hawthorne Pl
10 MPPT 60056 2808 15W-14N A4
10 PTHT 60070 2808 15W-14N A4
W Hawthorne Pl
500 CHCG 60657 2978 0W-4N A3
Hawthorne Rd
10 BNHL 60010 2750 26W-17N D4
10 BRTN 60010 2750 25W-18N E3
300 BFGV 60089 2754 17W-18N B3
5000 OKFT 60452 3425 6W-20S E4
5000 OKFT 60452 3426 6W-20S A4
5200 BmnT 60452 3425 6W-20S E4
Hawthorne Rd SR-59
10 BNHL 60010 2750 26W-17N D4
10 BRTN 60010 2750 25W-18N E3
Hawthorne Sq
10 IHPK 60525 3146 E5
Hawthorne St
- PvsT 60126 3086 C1
- PvsT 60162 3086 C1
3300 FNPK 60131 2973 12W-4N B3
3600 SRPK 60131 2973 12W-4N B3
3600 SRPK 60176 2973 12W-4N B3
E Hawthorne St
10 ANHT 60004 2807 17W-14N B4
N Hawthorne St
6000 RSMT 60018 2917 12W-7N B3
W Hawthorne St
10 ANHT 60004 2807 18W-14N A4
1100 ANHT 60005 2806 18W-14N D4
Hawthorne Ter
1700 DSPN 60016 2863 12W-11N B3
S Hawthorne Tr
26600 MonT 60449 3683 6W-32S A7
Hawthorne Wy
22100 RNPK 60471 3594 5W-26S B3
Hay St
100 PKFT 60466 3595 3W-25S B1
Hayes Av
10 LGNG 60525 3087 12W-4S C7
10 NHLK 60164 2972 D6
W Hayes Av
6600 CHCG 60631 2918 8W-8N E2
6800 CHCG 60714 2918 8W-8N E2
6800 NLES 60714 2918 8W-8N E2
Hayes Av N
1100 OKPK 60302 3031 7W-1N B1
1200 CHCG 60302 3031 7W-2N B1
1200 CHCG 60639 3031 7W-2N B1
Hayes Dr
- CHCG 60637 3153 2E-6S B4
Hayes St
3300 EVTN 60201 2866 4W-12N B1
3300 SKOK 60076 2866 4W-12N B1
W Hayford St
3700 CHCG 60652 3212 4W-8S C1
N Haymond St
2400 RVGV 60171 2974 10W-3N B5
S Haynes Ct
2900 CHCG 60608 3091 1W-2S E3
Haynes Dr
200 AddT 60191 2915 B6
200 WDDL 60191 2915 B6
W Haystack Dr
7400 FftT 60423 3504 9W-24S E6
Hayward Av
600 SMWD 60107 2911 B2
Hazard Rd
10 CPVL 60110 2748 C6
Hazel Av
- LGNG 60525 3087 12W-4S C6
400 GLNC 60022 2758 6W-17N D5
Hazel Ct
600 ROSL 60172 2913 C6
1300 DSPN 60018 2862 13W-9N E6
1300 DSPN 60018 2863 12W-9N A7
10100 ODPK 60462 3345 12W-17S C6
Hazel Dr
300 SMBG 60193 2859 23W-9N A7
Hazel Ln
1500 WNKA 60093 2811 6W-16N D1
3300 HLCT 60429 3426 4W-20S E5
Hazel St
6600 MNGV 60053 2865 8W-11N A3
6700 MNGV 60053 2864 8W-11N E3
N Hazel St
4200 CHCG 60613 2977 1W-5N E1
4400 CHCG 60613 2921 1W-5N E7
4400 CHCG 60640 2921 1W-5N E7
N Hazelcrest Rd
20000 ElaT 60074 2752 20W-20N E1
20600 ElaT 60074 2753 20W-20N A2
20600 PltT 60074 2753 20W-20N A2
S Hazel Hill Dr
1800 MPPT 60056 2861 17W-10N C5
Hazel Nut Ct
600 BRLT 60103 2910 D1
Hazelnut Dr
10 SMWD 60107 2857 27W-10N D7
Hazelnut Ln
2500 RVWD 60015 2755 13W-20N E1
Hazelwood Dr
700 NHBK 60062 2756 11W-18N E4
Hazelwood Ln
300 MaiT 60025 2864 10W-12N A1
400 MaiT 60025 2810 10W-12N A7
Hazelwood Ter
300 BFGV 60089 2754 16W-20N E1
300 VrnT 60069 2754 16W-20N E1
Head Av
16700 HLCT 60429 3427 2W-20S C4
16700 MKHM 60426 3427 2W-20S C4
Headwater Cove
10 SBTN 60010 2803 27W-14N B4
Healy Av
200 ELGN 60120 2855 B5
Healy Rd
- EDND 60118 2801 E4
- EDND 60118 2802 30W-14N A3
- HFET 60118 2801 E4
- HFET 60118 2802 30W-14N A3
10 BNHL 60010 2802 29W-15N B1
10 BNHL 60118 2802 30W-14N A3
Hearth Cir
2000 LNSG 60438 3429 2E-21S D7

Hearth Dr
7500 HRPK 60133 2912 A1
Hearthside Dr
10 RchT 60443 3593 8W-25S A1
Hearthstone Dr
- BRLT 60103 2909 B3
Heartland Dr
4500 RNPK 60471 3594 5W-27S B5
S Heath Av
1300 CHCG 60608 3033 2W-1S B7
Heath Ct
200 BRTN 60010 2751 24W-18N C2
500 SMWD 60107 2911 B1
Heath Wy
10 SBTN 60010 2803 26W-15N D2
Heather Ct
10 SMWD 60107 2857 27W-11N B4
100 RGMW 60008 2805 21W-14N D5
300 SMBG 60193 2859 21W-9N E6
1500 WLNG 60090 2754 16W-17N D6
1800 NHBK 60062 2756 11W-16N E7
8300 TYPK 60477 3424 10W-21S E5
8400 BRRG 60527 3208 B4
15200 ODPK 60462 3346 9W-18S D7
18600 HMWD 60430 3507 1W-22S E1
S Heather Ct
14300 HMGN 60441 3344 15W-17S C4
Heather Dr
3300 MKHM 60426 3348 4W-18S E6
8500 BRRG 60527 3208 B4
Heather Ln
10 SMWD 60107 2857 27W-11N C4
100 WLMT 60091 2811 6W-13N E7
200 WDDL 60191 2915 D6
400 DRPK 60010 2752 22W-20N B1
400 DYR 46311 3598 D4
600 BRLT 60103 2910 D7
700 WNKA 60093 2811 6W-16N D1
800 HFET 60195 2858 24W-12N D1
800 WNKA 60093 2758 6W-16N D7
1000 MNSR 46321 3510 E2
1100 IVNS 60067 2751 23W-17N E5
1200 GNVW 60025 2865 8W-12N A1
1400 DSPN 60018 2862 13W-10N D6
1800 NHBK 60062 2756 11W-16N E7
8200 TYPK 60477 3424 10W-21S C5
8300 OrlT 60477 3424 10W-21S B5
N Heather Ln
2100 PLTN 60074 2753 19W-18N C2
S Heather Ln
14300 HMGN 60441 3344 15W-17S C5
14300 OrlT 60467 3344 15W-17S C5
W Heather Ln
1200 ANHT 60005 2806 18W-14N D4
Heather Rd
1200 HMWD 60430 3508 1W-22S A1
2400 FSMR 60422 3507 3W-22S B1
2400 FSMR 60430 3507 3W-22S B1
2400 HMWD 60430 3507 3W-22S B1
Heather Ter
2000 NHFD 60093 2811 7W-15N B2
Heather Tr
7200 JSTC 60458 3148 10W-8S B7
W Heatherbrook Tr
5300 MonT 60449 3683 6W-32S A7
Heatherfield Ct
- GNVW 60025 2811 6W-13N C6
Heatherfield Ln
1000 GNVW 60025 2811 6W-13N C6
Heather Glen Dr
- ODPK 60467 3423 13W-18S A1
Heather Hill Cres
1100 FSMR 60422 3507 3W-23S A3
Heather Hill Ct
3100 FSMR 60422 3507 3W-23S A4
E Heatherlea Dr
100 PLTN 60067 2752 20W-17N E5
W Heatherlea Dr
10 PLTN 60067 2752 20W-17N E5
Heathermead St
400 RchT 60443 3593 8W-26S B2
Heatherstone Dr
700 SMBG 60173 2859 22W-11N C4
Heatherton Dr
- CteT 60417 3686 3E-31S E6
Heatherwood Ct
10 IHPK 60525 3146 D4
2900 SMBG 60194 2857 27W-10N C5
14300 HMGN 60441 3343 16W-17S D5
Heatherwood Dr
2800 SMBG 60194 2857 27W-10N D5
S Heatherwood Dr
14300 HMGN 60441 3343 17W-17S D4
Heathrow Cir
11400 ODPK 60467 3422 14W-20S E4
Heathrow Ct
400 BRRG 60527 3208 B2
W Heathwood Dr
9000 NLES 60714 2863 11W-12N D1
9100 MaiT 60016 2863 11W-12N D1
Hecht Dr
- BRLT 60120 2909 E4
- BRLT 60120 2910 A4
Hecker Ct
1100 ELGN 60120 2855 D3
Hecker Dr
600 DndT 60118 2801 C5
1000 ELGN 60120 2855 D3
Hedge Row
2300 NHFD 60093 2810 8W-15N E2
2300 NHFD 60093 2811 8W-15N A2
Hedge Run
200 HDPK 60035 2758 7W-20N C1
W Hedge Apple Dr
13000 HMGN 60441 3343 16W-16S E2
13000 HMGN 60441 3344 16W-16S A2
Hedgerow Ln
3000 HMWD 60430 3507 3W-22S A1
Hedgewick Ct
200 RchT 60443 3593 8W-26S B2
N Hedgewood Dr
900 PLTN 60074 2753 20W-17N B5
Heidorn Av
1200 HLSD 60162 3028 D7
1200 WSTR 60154 3028 D7
1400 WSTR 60154 3086 D1
1600 HLSD 60162 3086 D1
Heine Ct
100 SMWD 60107 2857 27W-11N D4
Heine Dr
100 SMWD 60107 2857 27W-11N D4
Heinz Dr
1100 EDND 60118 2801 D4
Helen
- JSTC 60458 3210 10W-9S B2

Helen Ct
10 SMWD 60107 2856 29W-9N E7
Helen Dr
400 NHBK 60062 2756 11W-18N E4
500 BRLT 60103 2909 E2
900 MLPK 60160 3029 11W-1N E2
1000 ALGN 60102 2748 A1
1100 AlqT 60102 2748 A1
2700 MaiT 60025 2864 10W-12N B1
22300 SLVL 60411 3597 1E-27S B4
Helen Ln
1200 EGvT 60007 2914 A1
1200 EGVV 60007 2914 A1
9000 ODPK 60462 3346 11W-18S A7
9100 ODPK 60462 3345 11W-18S E7
14600 HMGN 60441 3343 18W-17S B6
Helen St
1100 PKRG 60068 2863 11W-10N D5
S Helena Av
300 MPPT 60005 2861 17W-12N B1
300 MPPT 60056 2861 17W-12N B1
S Helena Dr
11100 PSHL 60465 3273 11W-13S E3
Helene Ln
1000 SMBG 60193 2858 24W-10N C6
Helen Sandidge Ct
16700 TYPK 60477 3425 7W-20S C3
Helfred Av
3000 SCHT 60411 3595 1W-27S E4
N Helgesen St
700 PltT 60074 2752 21W-18N C2
E Hellen Rd
10 PLTN 60067 2805 20W-15N E2
100 PLTN 60067 2806 20W-15N A2
100 PLTN 60074 2806 20W-15N A2
W Hellen Rd
400 PLTN 60067 2805 21W-15N D2
400 PltT 60067 2805 21W-15N D2
Hellenic Dr
20300 OMFD 60461 3507 4W-24S A6
20400 OMFD 60461 3506 4W-24S E6
Helm Rd
10 CPVL 60110 2748 D5
100 BNHL 60010 2748 D5
100 BNHL 60010 2749 30W-17N A5
100 BNHL 60110 2748 D5
Helsted Av
- CteT 60401 3774 1W-33S B1
- CteT 60417 3774 1W-33S B1
Hemingway Ln
600 OKPK 60302 3031 7W-0S C6
N Hemlock Av
200 WDDL 60191 2915 C7
400 AddT 60191 2915 C7
Hemlock Ct
10 ELGN 60120 2855 D4
9400 MaiT 60016 2863 11W-12N D1
Hemlock Dr
1200 EGVV 60007 2915 A3
7500 ODPK 60462 3346 9W-18S D7
Hemlock Ln
10 HDPK 60035 2757 9W-20N D2
400 ROSL 60172 2912 E6
1200 ELGN 60120 2855 D4
3100 NHBK 60062 2756 11W-16N D6
N Hemlock Ln
1200 MPPT 60056 2808 14W-14N B4
1200 PTHT 60070 2808 14W-14N B4
Hemlock Pl
1800 SMBG 60173 2860 21W-12N A1
Hemlock St
10 PKFT 60466 3595 3W-27S B4
6800 HRPK 60133 2911 C2
7000 SMWD 60107 2911 C2
7000 SMWD 60133 2911 C2
8500 ODPK 60462 3346 10W-16S B3
Hemlock Knoll Ter
1400 NHBK 60062 2756 11W-17N D6
Hempstead Dr
14100 ODPK 60462 3346 9W-16S C4
Hendee St
300 ELGN 60123 2855 A6
Henderson Ln
- ODPK 60467 3344 14W-16S D4
W Henderson St
1200 CHCG 60657 2977 1W-4N D3
1900 CHCG 60618 2977 2W-4N B3
3400 CHCG 60618 2976 4W-4N C3
4100 CHCG 60641 2976 5W-4N B3
4800 CHCG 60641 2975 7W-4N C3
5500 CHCG 60634 2975 7W-4N C3
7000 CHCG 60634 2974 8W-4N E3
Hendricks Rd
3100 RBBN 60472 3348 4W-16S D3
S Hendricks Rd
14100 RBBN 60472 3348 4W-16S D3
Henke Dr
- TYPK 60477 3424 10W-21S B6
Henke Pl
2600 CHCG 60007 2916 A2
Henley Ct
1600 WLNG 60090 2754 16W-18N D4
Henley St
1800 GNVW 60025 2810 9W-13N D6
3300 NfdT 60025 2809 10W-13N E6
3300 NfdT 60025 2810 10W-13N A6
Henneberry Ln
10 GLF 60025 2865 8W-12N A1
10 GLF 60029 2865 8W-12N A1
10 GNVW 60025 2865 8W-12N A1
Henning Ct
6300 MNGV 60053 2865 8W-10N A4
Henrici Dr
- NHBK 60062 2757 8W-18N E2
- NHBK 60062 2758 8W-18N A4
Henrietta Av
9400 BKFD 60513 3087 11W-3S C5
9500 BKFD 60525 3087 11W-3S C5
9500 LGPK 60525 3087 11W-3S C5
Henry Av
800 CTCY 60409 3351 3E-18S E7
1200 DSPN 60016 2862 13W-10N E5
1200 DSPN 60016 2863 13W-10N A5
S Henry Av
4400 HMND 46327 3352 E4
Henry Ct
18800 LNSG 60438 3510 4E-22S B1
W Henry Ct
2700 CHCG 60647 2976 3W-2N E6
Henry Ln
16600 TYPK 60477 3424 10W-19S C3
Henry St
100 ELGN 60120 2855 A4
200 DYR 46311 3598 D2
4300 OKFT 60452 3426 5W-19S B2

Chicago & Cook County Street Index

STREET Block	City	ZIP	Map#	CGS	Grid
Henry St					
8400	SjnT	46311	3598		E7
8700	ODPK	60462	3346	10W-18S	A6
9200	SjnT	46311	3687		E1
17200	LNSG	60438	3430	4E-20S	B4
18700	LNSG	60438	3510	4E-22S	B1
E Henry St					
-	MPPT	60056	2808	14W-13N	C7
10	ANHT	60004	2754	17W-17N	A5
W Henry St					
-	MPPT	60056	2807	16W-13N	D7
-	MPPT	60056	2808	15W-13N	A7
10	ANHT	60004	2754	17W-17N	A5
Henson Ct					
-	MTSN	60443	3506	6W-24S	A5
Herbert Av					
1500	BKLY	60163	3028		C4
Herbert Ct					
8900	ODHL	60477	3424	11W-19S	A3
W Herbert Ct					
4900	MONE	60449	3683	6W-31S	B5
N Herbert Rd					
10	RVSD	60546	3088	9W-3S	D4
S Herbert Rd					
10	RVSD	60546	3088	9W-3S	D5
W Herbert St					
5200	MONE	60449	3683	6W-31S	A5
Hercules Ct					
600	GNVW	60025	2810	10W-14N	A3
Hereford Av					
100	CRTE	60475	3596	0W-28S	C5
Hereford Dr					
10	CRTE	60417	3596	0W-28S	D5
Heren Dr					
-	BNHL	60010	2749	28W-17N	E4
Heritage Blvd					
3100	MTSN	60443	3595	4W-26S	A1
N Heritage Cir					
1900	PLTN	60074	2753	20W-20N	B1
Heritage Ct					
5400	HRPK	60133	2911		E6
5500	WNSP	60558	3146		E3
Heritage Dr					
-	CTCY	60409	3430	3E-19S	B3
-	DYR	46311	3510		D7
10	LYWD	46311	3510		C6
10	LYWD	60411	3510	4E-25S	C6
100	BmdT	60172	2913		A6
200	ROSL	60172	2912		E6
500	HFET	60194	2858	24W-11N	D3
700	SMBG	60194	2858	24W-11N	D3
800	MPPT	60056	2808	13W-14N	D5
800	WhlT	60056	2808	13W-13N	D5
3600	NHBK	60062	2756	12W-17N	C5
11100	PSHL	60465	3274	11W-13S	A3
11900	LynT	60480	3208		C4
11900	LynT	60527	3208		C4
17200	SHLD	60473	3429	2E-20S	D4
19400	TYPK	60477	3504	10W-23S	C4
N Heritage Dr					
1900	PLTN	60074	2753	19W-18N	C3
Heritage Ln					
100	SMWD	60107	2856	29W-9N	E7
Herman Ct					
10	CRTE	60417	3685	0W-30S	C2
Herman St					
200	CRTE	60417	3685	0W-30S	C2
Hermes Av					
1000	LMNT	60439	3270		C7
Hermes Dr					
-	OMFD	60461	3507	3W-24S	A5
W Hermione St					
6300	CHCG	60631	2919	8W-7N	A3
6300	CHCG	60646	2919	8W-7N	A3
Hermitage Av					
16100	MKHM	60426	3427	2W-19S	D3
16500	HLCT	60429	3427	2W-19S	D3
N Hermitage Av					
10	CHCG	60612	3033	2W-0N	C4
400	CHCG	60622	3033	2W-0N	C3
1600	CHCG	60622	2977	2W-2N	C7
2700	CHCG	60614	2977	2W-3N	C5
2700	CHCG	60657	2977	2W-3N	C5
4000	CHCG	60613	2977	2W-5N	C1
4400	CHCG	60613	2921	2W-5N	C7
4400	CHCG	60640	2921	2W-5N	C7
5600	CHCG	60660	2921	2W-7N	C4
6700	CHCG	60626	2921	2W-8N	C2
7500	EVTN	60202	2867	2W-9N	C7
7700	CHCG	60626	2867	2W-9N	C6
S Hermitage Av					
600	CHCG	60612	3033	2W-0S	C6
1000	CHCG	60608	3033	2W-0S	C6
3400	CHCG	60608	3091	2W-3S	C5
3400	CHCG	60609	3091	2W-3S	C5
4700	CHCG	60609	3151	2W-5S	C2
5500	CHCG	60636	3151	2W-6S	C3
7500	CHCG	60620	3213	2W-10S	C5
Hermitage Cir					
1100	HFET	60195	2858	24W-12N	C1
Hermitage Ln					
1000	HFET	60195	2858	24W-12N	C1
S Hermosa Av					
10800	CHCG	60643	3277	2W-12S	D2
Herndon St					
300	PKFT	60466	3595	3W-25S	B1
Heron Av					
1000	PTON	60468	3860	10W-38S	C5
1700	SMBG	60193	2912		A3
Heron Ct					
2200	RGMW	60008	2806	19W-14N	B4
Heron Dr					
6100	OKFT	60452	3425	7W-18S	C1
E Heron Dr					
10	PLTN	60067	2752	20W-16N	E6
Heron Ln					
10	BNHL	60010	2750	27W-17N	A4
Herrick Av					
-	RVGV	60171	2973	11W-3N	D6
9900	FNPK	60131	2973	12W-3N	B6
W Herrick Av					
-	RVGV	60171	2974	10W-3N	A6
8700	RVGV	60171	2973	11W-3N	E6
9000	FNPK	60131	2973	11W-3N	D6
Herrick Rd					
10	RVSD	60546	3088	9W-3S	D5
300	BRWN	60402	3088	9W-3S	D4
300	RVSD	60402	3088	9W-3S	D5
Hess St					
8100	WLSP	60480	3208		E3
8100	WLSP	60525	3208		E3
N Hessing St					
2400	RVGV	60171	2974	10W-3N	B5
Hewes St					
1500	CRTE	60417	3685	0W-30S	C3

STREET Block	City	ZIP	Map#	CGS	Grid
Hewes St					
1500	CteT	60417	3685	0W-30S	C3
Hewitt Dr					
1000	DSPN	60016	2862	15W-10N	B5
1000	DSPN	60018	2862	15W-10N	B5
Hialeah Ct					
14000	HMGN	60467	3344	15W-16S	C4
Hialeah Ln					
1100	HRPK	60133	2911		E6
1100	HRPK	60133	2912		A6
N Hiawatha Av					
6000	CHCG	60646	2920	5W-7N	A3
6700	CHCG	60646	2919	7W-8N	B1
Hiawatha Ct					
700	ELGN	60120	2855		B2
1300	HDPK	60035	2757	8W-20N	E2
S Hiawatha Ct					
700	MPPT	60056	2862	15W-11N	A2
13800	HMGN	60441	3343	16W-16S	E3
Hiawatha Dr					
200	BFGV	60089	2754	17W-18N	C3
500	ELGN	60120	2855		B1
W Hiawatha Dr					
13000	HMGN	60441	3343	16W-16S	E3
13000	HMGN	60441	3344	16W-16S	A3
Hiawatha Ln					
11200	IHPK	60525	3146		D5
Hiawatha Tr					
10	HDPK	60035	2757	8W-20N	E2
10100	ODPK	60462	3345	12W-18S	C6
E Hiawatha Tr					
100	MPPT	60056	2862	15W-12N	A2
W Hiawatha Tr					
10	MPPT	60056	2861	16W-12N	E2
10	MPPT	60056	2862	15W-12N	A2
Hibbard Rd					
10	NHFD	60093	2811	6W-14N	E4
10	NtrT	60093	2811	6W-14N	E4
10	WLMT	60091	2811	6W-13N	E6
10	WLMT	60093	2811	6W-14N	E4
10	WNKA	60093	2811	6W-15N	E2
800	WNKA	60093	2758	6W-16N	E7
Hibiscus Cir					
100	MTSN	60443	3593	7W-26S	C2
Hibiscus Dr					
10100	ODPK	60462	3345	12W-17S	B6
Hickok Av					
500	UYPK	60466	3684	3W-30S	B3
Hickory Av					
-	ANHT	60004	2754	17W-17N	B5
-	ANHT	60089	2754	17W-17N	B5
-	BFGV	60089	2754	17W-17N	B5
100	SMWD	60107	2857	28W-10N	A6
N Hickory Av					
100	BRLT	60103	2910		E2
1000	CHCG	60622	3033	1W-1N	E2
1100	ANHT	60004	2807	17W-15N	B2
S Hickory Av					
10	ANHT	60004	2807	17W-14N	B5
100	BRLT	60103	2910		E3
1200	MPPT	60005	2861	17W-12N	B1
W Hickory Av					
13500	HMGN	60441	3343	18W-16S	B3
13500	LMNT	60439	3343	18W-15S	A2
13500	LMNT	60441	3343	18W-16S	A2
Hickory Ct					
10	BmdT	60157	2913		D7
10	CPVL	60110	2748		C5
10	CTCY	60409	3429	2E-18S	D1
10	PKFT	60466	3595	4W-25S	A1
200	NfdT	60062	2757	9W-18N	C3
300	SMBG	60193	2859	23W-10N	A6
2100	GNVW	60025	2864	9W-12N	D1
17000	ODHL	60477	3424	11W-20S	A4
18500	BlmT	60438	3429	2E-22S	E7
18500	LNSG	60438	3429	2E-22S	E7
S Hickory Ct					
8400	WLSP	60480	3208		D4
24700	CteT	60417	3687	3E-30S	B2
Hickory Dr					
10	CPVL	60110	2748		C5
10	OKBK	60523	3086		B1
400	WLNG	60090	2755	13W-17N	D5
500	BFGV	60089	2754	17W-18N	B2
2300	DYR	46311	3598		E3
8800	ODHL	60477	3424	11W-20S	A4
10200	ODPK	60462	3345	12W-18S	C7
10200	ODPK	60467	3345	12W-18S	C7
19100	CCHL	60478	3506	5W-23S	C3
N Hickory Dr					
300	ITSC	60143	2914		B6
S Hickory Dr					
1400	MPPT	60056	2861	16W-11N	D3
Hickory Gln					
500	RchT	60443	3593	8W-26S	B2
Hickory Ln					
10	ALGN	60102	2748		A1
10	AlqT	60102	2748		A1
10	NHBK	60062	2757	8W-17N	D5
10	PvsT	60523	3086		D4
10	PvsT	60558	3086		D4
10	WSTR	60523	3086		D4
100	SMBG	60193	2859	23W-10N	A6
200	SMBG	60193	2858	24W-10N	E6
300	LynT	60458	3209	11W-8S	E2
400	MNSR	46321	3430		D7
1000	EGVV	60007	2915		A2
1500	WNKA	60093	2758	6W-16N	D7
3300	HLCT	60429	3426	4W-20S	E5
9000	HYHL	60457	3209	11W-10S	E5
15300	OKFT	60452	3347	8W-18S	B7
27300	CteT	60401	3774	1W-33S	A2
E Hickory Ln					
2900	CteT	60417	3687	3E-30S	B2
N Hickory Ln					
10	GNWD	60425	3508	0E-22S	E2
400	PTON	60468	3861	8W-37S	B3
400	WlIT	60468	3861	8W-37S	B3
2500	ANHT	60004	2754	17W-16N	B6
W Hickory Ln					
2000	HFET	60195	2804	23W-13N	E6
2000	PltT	60195	2804	23W-13N	D6
Hickory Pl					
300	ELGN	60120	2855		A3
Hickory Rd					
1100	HMWD	60430	3428	1W-21S	A7
2500	HMWD	60430	3427	3W-21S	B7
3000	HLCT	60429	3427	3W-21S	A7
14500	HMGN	60441	3343	18W-15S	A2
14500	LMNT	60439	3343	18W-15S	A2
14500	LMNT	60441	3343	18W-15S	A2
E Hickory Rdg					
400	GNWD	60425	3509	0E-23S	A3
Hickory St					
-	TYPK	60477	3424	8W-21S	E5

STREET Block	City	ZIP	Map#	CGS	Grid
Hickory St					
10	CHHT	60411	3596	1W-25S	A1
200	CHHT	60411	3595	2W-25S	D1
200	MTSN	60443	3594	4W-25S	E1
200	PKFT	60411	3594	4W-25S	E1
200	PKFT	60466	3594	4W-25S	E1
200	PKFT	60466	3595	4W-25S	A1
700	LMNT	60439	3270		D6
2300	DSPN	60018	2917	12W-9N	B1
6700	HRPK	60133	2911		C3
6800	TYPK	60477	3425	8W-21S	A5
7000	SMWD	60107	2911		C2
7000	SMWD	60133	2911		C3
18200	LNSG	60438	3429	2E-21S	D7
18500	BlmT	60411	3429	2E-22S	E7
18500	BlmT	60438	3429	2E-22S	E7
E Hickory St					
400	HNDL	60521	3146		B1
2000	CteT	60417	3686	2E-30S	D2
S Hickory St					
10	PLTN	60067	2805	21W-15N	D1
100	PltT	60067	2805	21W-15N	D1
200	GNWD	60425	3509	0E-23S	A2
W Hickory St					
10	HNDL	60521	3146		A1
S Hickory Creek Ct					
20700	FftT	60423	3505	8W-24S	A6
W Hickory Creek Dr					
-	MTSN	60443	3505	8W-25S	A6
-	RchT	60423	3505	9W-25S	A6
7200	FftT	60423	3505	9W-25S	A6
7300	FftT	60423	3504	9W-25S	E7
S Hickory Creek Pl					
20700	FftT	60423	3505	9W-25S	A7
S Hickory Crest Ct					
9700	PSHL	60465	3209	11W-11S	E7
Hickory Trace Dr					
10	HYHL	60457	3210	10W-9S	A3
10	JSTC	60457	3210	10W-9S	A3
10	JSTC	60458	3210	10W-9S	A3
N Hicks Pl					
200	PLTN	60067	2753	20W-16N	A7
200	PLTN	60074	2753	20W-16N	A7
Hicks Rd					
1400	PLTN	60067	2806	20W-14N	A4
1400	RGMW	60008	2806	20W-14N	A4
2700	LGGV	60047	2753	20W-20N	B1
2700	PLTN	60047	2753	20W-20N	A2
2700	PLTN	60074	2753	20W-20N	A2
20700	ElaT	60047	2753	20W-20N	B1
Hicks Rd SR-53					
2700	LGGV	60047	2753	20W-20N	B1
2700	PLTN	60047	2753	20W-20N	A2
2700	PLTN	60074	2753	20W-20N	A2
20700	ElaT	60047	2753	20W-20N	B1
N Hicks Rd					
500	PLTN	60067	2753	20W-17N	A5
500	PLTN	60074	2753	20W-17N	A5
1500	PltT	60074	2753	20W-18N	A4
2300	ElaT	60047	2753	20W-20N	A2
2300	LGGV	60047	2753	20W-20N	A2
2300	PLTN	60047	2753	20W-20N	A2
N Hicks Rd SR-53					
2100	PLTN	60074	2753	20W-18N	A2
2300	ElaT	60047	2753	20W-20N	A2
2300	LGGV	60047	2753	20W-20N	A2
2300	PLTN	60047	2753	20W-20N	A2
S Hicks Rd					
200	PLTN	60067	2806	20W-15N	A3
200	PLTN	60074	2806	20W-15N	A3
300	PLTN	60008	2806	20W-15N	A2
300	RGMW	60008	2806	20W-15N	A2
Hidden Brook Ct					
11700	ODPK	60467	3422	14W-20S	D5
Hiddenbrook Ln					
300	WLBK	60527	3146		A5
S Hidden Brook Tr					
1000	PLTN	60067	2805	22W-14N	A4
Hidden Creek Cir					
1700	PLTN	60074	2753	19W-18N	C3
W Hidden Hill Ln					
900	PLTN	60067	2752	22W-16N	B7
900	PltT	60067	2752	22W-16N	B7
Hidden Lake Dr					
10	BRRG	60527	3208		C4
10	LynT	60527	3208		C4
S Hidden Lake Tr					
23100	BlmT	60411	3598	3E-28S	A6
23100	CteT	60411	3598	3E-28S	A6
23100	CteT	60417	3598	3E-28S	A6
Hidden Oaks Dr					
100	PltT	60010	2751	23W-18N	E3
Hidden Pines Dr					
10	DRPK	60010	2752	22W-20N	A2
N Hidden Prairie Ct					
500	PLTN	60067	2752	21W-16N	D6
Hidden Valley Dr					
13100	HMGN	60441	3422	16W-19S	A2
Hidden Valley Cove					
11500	ODPK	60467	3422	14W-21S	D7
W Higgins Av					
5400	CHCG	60630	2919	6W-6N	D6
6300	CHCG	60656	2919	6W-6N	C6
6600	CHCG	60656	2918	8W-6N	E5
7200	CHCG	60631	2918	8W-6N	E5
W Higgins Av SR-72					
7200	CHCG	60631	2918	8W-6N	E5
7200	CHCG	60656	2918	8W-6N	E5
Higgins Rd					
-	CHCG	60007	2916		A1
-	CHCG	60018	2916		B1
-	DndT	60118	2801		D4
-	DSPN	60007	2916		A1
-	DSPN	60018	2916		E1
-	EDND	60118	2801		D4
-	EGvT	60007	2860	20W-11N	A4
-	EGvT	60007	2861	18W-10N	A5
-	EGVV	60007	2861	18W-10N	A5
-	HFET	60118	2801		E4
-	SMBG	60173	2860	20W-11N	A4
700	CHCG	60068	2918	10W-7N	A4
700	CHCG	60631	2918	10W-7N	A4
700	PKRG	60068	2918	10W-7N	A4
1500	CHCG	60018	2917	11W-7N	D4
1500	CHCG	60068	2917	11W-7N	D4
1500	CHCG	60631	2917	11W-7N	E4
1500	PKRG	60068	2917	11W-7N	D4
Higgins Rd SR-72					
-	DndT	60118	2801		D4
-	EDND	60118	2801		D4
-	EGvT	60007	2860	20W-11N	A4
-	EGvT	60007	2861	18W-10N	A5
-	EGVV	60007	2861	18W-10N	A5
-	HFET	60118	2801		E4
-	SMBG	60173	2860	20W-11N	A4

STREET Block	City	ZIP	Map#	CGS	Grid
Higgins Rd SR-72					
700	CHCG	60068	2918	10W-7N	A4
700	CHCG	60631	2918	10W-7N	A4
700	PKRG	60068	2918	10W-7N	A4
1500	CHCG	60018	2917	11W-7N	D4
1500	CHCG	60068	2917	11W-7N	D4
1500	CHCG	60631	2917	11W-7N	E4
1500	PKRG	60068	2917	11W-7N	D4
E Higgins Rd					
-	EGvT	60007	2860	18W-10N	E5
10	HFET	60194	2859	23W-11N	A3
10	HFET	60195	2859	23W-11N	B3
600	SMBG	60194	2859	22W-11N	C3
700	SMBG	60173	2859	21W-11N	D4
1700	SMBG	60173	2860	20W-10N	B4
1900	EGvT	60007	2861	16W-9N	D6
1900	EGVV	60007	2861	16W-9N	D6
2400	EGVV	60007	2915		E1
2600	EGvT	60007	2915		E1
E Higgins Rd SR-72					
-	EGvT	60007	2860	18W-10N	E5
10	EGvT	60007	2861	17W-10N	B5
10	HFET	60194	2859	23W-11N	A3
10	HFET	60195	2859	23W-11N	B3
600	SMBG	60194	2859	22W-11N	C3
700	SMBG	60173	2859	21W-11N	D4
1700	SMBG	60173	2860	20W-10N	B4
1900	EGVV	60007	2861	16W-9N	D6
2400	EGVV	60007	2915		E1
2600	EGVV	60007	2915		E1
W Higgins Rd					
-	CHCG	60018	2916		E2
-	DSPN	60018	2916		E2
-	EDND	60118	2801		E4
-	HFET	60118	2801		E4
-	HFET	60118	2802	28W-13N	D5
-	PKRG	60068	2917	11W-7N	D4
10	BmT	60010	2803	27W-13N	A6
10	HFET	60194	2859	23W-11N	A3
10	HFET	60195	2859	23W-11N	A3
10	SBTN	60010	2803	27W-13N	B6
100	SMBG	60194	2859	23W-11N	A3
100	SMBG	60195	2859	23W-11N	A3
200	BmT	60010	2802	28W-13N	E6
200	HFET	60010	2802	28W-13N	D6
200	HFET	60192	2802	28W-13N	D5
200	HFET	60194	2858	25W-12N	B2
200	SBTN	60010	2802	28W-13N	E6
200	SMBG	60194	2858	24W-12N	D2
200	SMBG	60195	2858	24W-12N	D2
400	SBTN	60118	2802	28W-13N	E6
600	HFET	60195	2858	24W-12N	D2
1900	HFET	60194	2857	26W-12N	E1
1900	HFET	60195	2857	26W-12N	E1
2600	HFET	60010	2857	26W-12N	E1
2900	HFET	60010	2803	27W-12N	D7
3100	HFET	60195	2803	27W-12N	D7
7600	CHCG	60631	2918	10W-7N	B4
7700	PKRG	60631	2918	10W-7N	B4
7800	PKRG	60068	2918	10W-7N	B4
8200	CHCG	60068	2918	10W-7N	B4
8400	CHCG	60631	2917	10W-7N	E4
9300	CHCG	60018	2917	11W-7N	D4
9300	CHCG	60068	2917	11W-7N	D4
9300	RSMT	60018	2917	12W-7N	C3
10000	DSPN	60018	2917	12W-7N	C3
10200	CHCG	60666	2917	13W-8N	A2
10200	RSMT	60666	2917	13W-8N	A2
10700	CHCG	60666	2916		E2
10700	RSMT	60018	2916		E2
W Higgins Rd SR-72					
-	CHCG	60018	2916		E2
-	DSPN	60018	2916		E2
-	EDND	60118	2801		E4
-	HFET	60118	2801		E4
-	PKRG	60068	2917	11W-7N	D4
-	SBTN	60118	2802	28W-13N	E6
10	BmT	60010	2803	27W-13N	A6
10	HFET	60194	2859	23W-11N	A3
10	HFET	60195	2859	23W-11N	A3
10	SBTN	60010	2803	27W-13N	B6
100	SMBG	60194	2859	23W-11N	A3
100	SMBG	60195	2859	23W-11N	A3
200	BmT	60010	2802	28W-13N	E6
200	HFET	60010	2802	28W-13N	D6
200	HFET	60118	2802	30W-14N	A5
200	HFET	60192	2802	28W-13N	D5
200	HFET	60194	2858	25W-12N	B2
200	SBTN	60010	2802	28W-13N	E6
200	SMBG	60194	2858	24W-12N	D2
200	SMBG	60195	2858	24W-12N	D2
500	HFET	60195	2858	25W-12N	B2
1900	HFET	60194	2857	26W-12N	E1
1900	HFET	60195	2857	26W-12N	E1
2600	HFET	60010	2857	26W-12N	E1
2600	HFET	60195	2803	27W-12N	D7
2900	HFET	60010	2803	27W-12N	D7
7600	CHCG	60631	2918	10W-7N	B4
7700	PKRG	60631	2918	10W-7N	B4
7800	PKRG	60068	2918	10W-7N	B4
8200	CHCG	60068	2918	10W-7N	B4
8400	CHCG	60631	2917	10W-7N	E4
9300	CHCG	60018	2917	11W-7N	D4
9300	CHCG	60068	2917	11W-7N	D4
9300	RSMT	60018	2917	12W-7N	C3
10000	DSPN	60018	2917	12W-7N	C3
10200	CHCG	60666	2917	13W-8N	A2
10200	RSMT	60666	2917	13W-8N	A2
10700	CHCG	60666	2916		E2
10700	RSMT	60018	2916		E2
Higginson Ln					
800	WNKA	60093	2812	5W-15N	A3
Higgins Quarters Dr					
1000	HFET	60194	2858	24W-11N	D3
1000	SMBG	60194	2858	24W-11N	D3
High St					
-	CTPK	60827	3277	1W-15S	D7
10	WNKA	60093	2812	4W-14N	C3
800	WLSP	60480	3209	12W-9S	C4
1800	BLID	60406	3277	2W-15S	C7
2000	BKLY	60163	3028		B5
2000	EMHT	60126	3028		B5
2100	BKLY	60162	3028		B6
2100	EMHT	60162	3028		B6
High Bridge Ln					
4200	CHCG	60646	2920	5W-7N	A4
Highbury Ct					
1000	ELGN	60120	2855		D4
Highbury Dr					
10	ELGN	60120	2855		C4
Highbush Rd					
16800	ODPK	60467	3423	13W-20S	B4
Highcrest Dr					
400	WLMT	60091	2812	4W-13N	B6

STREET Block	City	ZIP	Map#	CGS	Grid
Highfield Ct					
8000	TYPK	60477	3504	10W-23S	C3
High Gate Ct					
8200	ODPK	60462	3346	10W-17S	B4
S Highgoal Dr					
1200	WLNG	60090	2755	15W-16N	A7
W Highgoal Dr					
600	WLNG	60090	2755	15W-16N	A7
High Grove Blvd					
-	WLBK	60527	3146		A7
6800	BRRG	60527	3146		A7
N High Grove Ln					
1900	PLTN	60074	2753	19W-18N	C3
Highland					
-	ELGN	60120	2855		C6
Highland Av					
-	CHCG	60613	2977	1W-5N	D1
100	WLNG	60090	2755	14W-17N	C4
700	TNTN	60476	3428	0E-20S	D4
1200	BRWN	60402	3031	7W-1S	B7
1500	BRWN	60402	3089	7W-2S	B3
1600	NfdT	60062	2756	11W-16N	C7
1800	NHBK	60062	2756	11W-16N	C7
2600	EVTN	60201	2812	4W-13N	C7
2700	EVTN	60091	2812	4W-13N	C7
2700	WLMT	60091	2812	4W-13N	C7
3000	WLMT	60091	2811	5W-13N	E6
3800	SKNY	60402	3089	7W-3S	B6
12100	BLID	60406	3277	3W-15S	A7
14300	ODPK	60462	3345	12W-17S	C5
17100	HLCT	60429	3427	3W-20S	B5
17500	BmnT	60477	3425	7W-21S	C6
17500	TYPK	60477	3425	7W-21S	C6
17700	HMWD	60430	3427	2W-21S	D6
18500	HMWD	60430	3507	2W-22S	D1
18800	BlmT	60430	3507	2W-22S	D2
E Highland Av					
200	ELGN	60120	2855		A4
400	MPPT	60056	2808	15W-13N	B5
N Highland Av					
-	ANHT	60005	2807	16W-13N	C6
-	VrnT	60004	2754	18W-18N	A2
-	VrnT	60089	2754	18W-18N	A2
1500	ANHT	60004	2807	18W-15N	A2
3900	BFGV	60089	2754	18W-18N	A2
4200	ANHT	60004	2754	18W-18N	A2
S Highland Av					
-	ANHT	60005	2807	17W-14N	A5
500	OKPK	60302	3031	7W-0S	B5
500	OKPK	60304	3031	7W-0S	B5
600	BRTN	60010	2751	25W-18N	A3
1100	BRWN	60304	3031	7W-0S	B7
1100	BRWN	60402	3031	7W-0S	B7
1200	ANHT	60005	2861	18W-12N	A1
1500	ANHT	60005	2860	18W-12N	E2
25700	MonT	60449	3684	3W-32S	B6
25700	UYPK	60449	3684	3W-31S	B5
25700	UYPK	60466	3684	3W-31S	B5
W Highland Av					
1600	CHCG	60660	2921	2W-7N	C3
2100	CHCG	60659	2921	2W-7N	B3
4300	CHCG	60646	2920	5W-7N	A3
6300	CHCG	60646	2919	7W-7N	A3
6500	CHCG	60646	2919	8W-7N	A3
7100	CHCG	60631	2918	8W-8N	D3
Highland Blvd					
1200	HFET	60195	2858	24W-12N	D1
1200	SMBG	60195	2858	24W-12N	E2
Highland Ct					
2300	SMBG	60194	2857	26W-10N	E5
3400	NfdT	60025	2809	10W-13N	E6
5300	CTWD	60445	3347	6W-15S	E1
17300	HLCT	60429	3427	3W-20S	B5
Highland Dr					
-	PLTN	60067	2805	21W-14N	C4
-	WLNG	60090	2754	15W-16N	E6
1200	DSPN	60018	2862	13W-9N	E7
1200	PTHT	60070	2754	15W-16N	E6
1200	WLNG	60070	2754	15W-16N	E6
1300	DSPN	60018	2863	13W-9N	A7
2400	RGMW	60067	2805	22W-14N	C4
2800	GNVW	60062	2809	11W-15N	E1
2800	NHBK	60062	2809	11W-15N	D1
N Highland Dr					
800	CHHT	60411	3507	1W-24S	E6
W Highland Dr					
200	CHHT	60411	3507	1W-24S	E6
5500	PLTN	60067	2805	21W-14N	C4
5600	RGMW	60067	2805	21W-14N	C4
6600	PSHT	60463	3275	8W-15S	A7
Highland Ln					
900	NfdT	60025	2810	10W-13N	A6
1100	GNVW	60025	2809	10W-13N	E6
1200	GNVW	60025	2810	10W-13N	A5
Highland Pl					
10	GLF	60029	2865	8W-12N	A1
600	HDPK	60035	2758	7W-20N	A1
3700	CCHL	60478	3426	4W-21S	D6
8100	MNSR	46321	3430		D6
Highland Rd					
10	IVNS	60067	2804	23W-16N	E1
100	IVNS	60067	2751	23W-16N	E7
200	MTSN	60443	3505	7W-24S	C6
500	HNDL	60521	3146		C1
3200	NHBK	60062	2809	11W-15N	C1
S Highland Rd					
10500	CHRG	60415	3275	8W-12S	A2
10500	CHRG	60482	3275	8W-12S	A2
10500	WRTH	60482	3275	8W-12S	A2
Highland St					
10	CTCY	60409	3430	4E-18S	C1
10	HMND	46320	3430	4E-18S	C1
100	BMDL	60108	2913		C7
100	BmdT	60108	2913		C7
200	BmdT	60157	2913		C7
6600	HRPK	60133	2911		E3
E Highland St					
10	CTCY	60409	3430		C1
10	HMND	46320	3430		D1
W Highland St					
-	MPPT	60056	2807	15W-13N	E5
-	MPPT	60056	2808	15W-13N	A5
Highland Ter					
1700	GNVW	60025	2811	8W-14N	A4
Highland Grove Ct S					
10	BFGV	60089	2754	17W-20N	B1
Highland Grove Dr					
400	BFGV	60089	2754	16W-20N	C1
Highlands Av					
-	ITSC	60143	2914		E6
S Highlawn Av					
14100	RVDL	60827	3350	0W-16S	B3
Highlington Ct					
500	BCHR	60401	3864	0W-36S	D2

Chicago & Cook County Street Index

STREET Block	City	ZIP	Map#	CGS	Grid
High Point Ct					
300	ROSL	60172	2913		B4
Highpoint Ct					
700	SMBG	60193	2859	22W-9N	B7
High Point Dr					
1500	ELGN	60123	2801		A6
High Point Ln					
900	BRLT	60107	2856	29W-9N	D7
900	SMWD	60107	2856	29W-9N	D7
1200	NHBK	60062	2756	11W-17N	E5
High Point Tr					
100	DYR	46311	3598		D5
High Pointe Rdg					
200	ALGN	60102	2748		B1
Highpoint Park Ln					
19700	HFET	60195	2858	25W-12N	C1
Highridge Av					
1400	WSTR	60154	3086		E1
High Ridge Pkwy					
2200	HLSD	60154	3086		E2
2200	WSTR	60154	3086		E2
Highridge Pkwy					
1200	HLSD	60162	3028		E7
1200	WSTR	60154	3028		E7
High Ridge Rd					
200	HLSD	60162	3028		D5
600	ROSL	60172	2913		C4
700	BmdT	60157	2913		C4
700	ROSL	60157	2913		C4
Highview Av					
800	OMFD	60461	3506	4W-25S	D7
16700	ODHL	60477	3423	11W-20S	E4
S Highview Ln					
19500	FftT	60423	3504	9W-23S	D3
Highwood Ct					
17100	ODPK	60467	3422	14W-20S	D4
Highwood Dr					
17100	ODPK	60467	3422	14W-20S	D5
S Highwood Dr					
11500	PSPK	60464	3274	10W-13S	B5
Hilbrich Ct					
600	DYR	46311	3598		E4
600	SjnT	46311	3598		E4
Hill Av					
200	BRLT	60103	2911		A5
300	EMHT	60126	3028		A4
800	ELGN	60120	2855		A1
Hill Cir					
600	GNVW	60025	2811	7W-13N	A7
Hill Ct					
400	PTHT	60070	2808	15W-15N	A2
Hill Dr					
-	ALSP	60803	3275	7W-15S	D7
-	CTWD	60445	3275	7W-15S	D7
-	WthT	60445	3275	7W-15S	D7
-	WthT	60463	3275	7W-15S	D7
500	HFET	60194	2858	24W-11N	D3
700	SMBG	60194	2858	24W-11N	D3
Hill Ln					
3100	WLMT	60091	2811	6W-13N	D6
Hill Rd					
100	WLBK	60527	3146		A6
400	DGvT	60439	3270		C1
600	WNKA	60093	2812	5W-15N	A3
900	NtrT	60093	2812	5W-15N	A3
1100	NtrT	60093	2811	5W-14N	E3
1100	WNKA	60093	2811	5W-14N	E3
1200	NHFD	60093	2811	5W-14N	E3
8000	FftT	60423	3504	10W-25S	C7
8300	FKFT	60423	3504	10W-25S	C7
W Hill Rd					
600	PLTN	60067	2752	21W-17N	C4
600	PLTN	60074	2752	21W-17N	C4
600	PltT	60067	2752	21W-17N	C4
Hill St					
-	CRTE	60417	3685	1W-30S	B3
10	BmdT	60172	2913		A5
10	EDND	60118	2801		A2
10	ROSL	60172	2913		A5
100	WLSP	60480	3209	12W-9S	C3
3000	WLMT	60091	2811	5W-13N	E6
E Hill St					
100	WhlT	60056	2808	13W-13N	E6
400	MPPT	60056	2808	15W-13N	B6
500	BRTN	60010	2751	25W-18N	A3
W Hill St					
100	CHCG	60610	3034	0W-1N	A2
1300	PltT	60067	2752	22W-17N	B4
Hill Ter					
500	WNKA	60093	2812	4W-15N	B3
S Hill Ter					
9900	PSHL	60465	3210	10W-11S	B7
Hillandale Dr					
400	BRLT	60103	2911		A4
Hillary Ln					
15000	HMGN	60441	3342	19W-17S	D6
15000	HmrT	60441	3342	19W-17S	D6
W Hillberry Ct					
800	LGNG	60525	3147	13W-5S	A2
Hill Creek Ct					
17100	ODPK	60467	3422	14W-20S	E4
S Hillcreek Dr					
12600	PSPK	60464	3274	11W-14S	A7
Hillcrest Av					
10	CHHT	60411	3508	0W-24S	B6
100	HNDL	60521	3146		C2
400	BRTN	60010	2751	25W-18N	A3
1400	HRPK	60133	2911		E2
E Hillcrest Av					
100	AddT	60191	2915		B6
100	WDDL	60191	2915		B6
S Hillcrest Av					
500	EMHT	60126	3028		B5
900	YkTp	60126	3028		B6
Hillcrest Blvd					
10	HFET	60195	2859	23W-12N	A1
10	SMBG	60173	2859	23W-12N	A1
10	SMBG	60195	2859	23W-12N	A1
300	HFET	60195	2858	24W-12N	D1
Hillcrest Cir					
9700	ODPK	60467	3423	12W-19S	D2
Hillcrest Ct					
100	BRTN	60010	2751	24W-18N	C3
100	PltT	60010	2751	24W-18N	C3
500	HFET	60195	2858	24W-12N	E1
Hillcrest Dr					
-	WLNG	60090	2808	15W-15N	B2
10	BRRG	60527	3146		C6
100	BRTN	60010	2751	24W-18N	C3
100	PltT	60010	2751	24W-18N	C3
400	PTHT	60070	2808	15W-15N	A2
500	SMBG	60193	2913		B2
500	SmbT	60193	2913		B2
500	WLNG	60070	2808	15W-15N	B2
600	BmdT	60143	2913		E6
Hillcrest Dr					
600	ITSC	60143	2913		E6
2500	DYR	46311	3598		D3
8200	PlsT	60462	3346	10W-15S	B2
8200	PSHT	60464	3346	10W-15S	B2
8500	ODPK	60462	3346	10W-15S	B2
11800	LMNT	60439	3271		B6
16300	TYPK	60477	3424	10W-19S	C3
16400	MKHM	60426	3426	4W-19S	E3
16600	HLCT	60429	3426	4W-19S	E3
17600	CCHL	60478	3426	4W-21S	E6
W Hillcrest Dr					
10500	PlsT	60464	3345	13W-15S	B2
Hillcrest Ln					
100	BRLT	60103	2910		E3
100	BRLT	60103	2911		A3
200	CRTE	60475	3596	0W-28S	C6
600	DGvT	60439	3270		C3
2800	NHBK	60062	2756	11W-17N	E6
8000	TYPK	60477	3424	10W-19S	C3
W Hillcrest Ln					
9000	PSPK	60464	3273	11W-14S	E6
9000	PSPK	60464	3274	11W-14S	A6
Hillcrest Rd					
1000	GLNC	60022	2758	6W-18N	D3
14200	LMNT	60439	3271		B4
S Hillcrest Rd					
14300	HMGN	60441	3343	18W-17S	A5
30300	BCHR	60401	3864	0W-37S	D2
30300	WshT	60401	3864	0W-37S	D2
W Hillcrest Rd					
600	PltT	60074	2752	21W-18N	C2
Hillcrest Ter					
10	BmdT	60157	2913		C7
100	BMDL	60108	2913		B7
Hillgrove Av					
10	LGNG	60525	3087	13W-3S	A6
10	WNSP	60558	3086		D7
10	WNSP	60558	3087	13W-3S	A6
400	HNDL	60521	3146		B1
1100	WNSP	60558	3146		C1
E Hillgrove Av					
10	LGNG	60525	3087	12W-4S	C6
W Hillgrove Av					
10	LGNG	60525	3087	12W-4S	B7
1400	WNSP	60558	3087	13W-4S	A7
Hilliard Dr					
-	ELGN	60120	2856	31W-9N	A7
S Hillock Av					
2500	CHCG	60608	3091	1W-2S	D3
Hills Av					
1500	DSPN	60016	2863	13W-11N	A3
Hills & Dales Rd					
10	BNHL	60010	2750	27W-17N	B5
Hillsdale Rd					
10700	CTSD	60525	3147	13W-7S	A7
Hillshire Ct					
100	IVNS	60010	2751	25W-17N	A5
Hillshire Dr					
10	BRTN	60010	2751	25W-17N	A5
10	IVNS	60010	2751	25W-17N	A5
Hillside Av					
10	PTHT	60070	2808	15W-15N	A2
15100	OKFT	60452	3347	7W-18S	C6
17100	HLCT	60429	3427	3W-20S	B5
17500	HMWD	60430	3427	2W-21S	C5
E Hillside Av					
100	BRTN	60010	2750	26W-18N	D2
100	BRTN	60010	2751	25W-18N	A3
N Hillside Av					
10	NHLK	60164	3028		D1
10	PvsT	60162	3028		D6
100	NHLK	60164	2972		D7
700	HLSD	60162	3028		D4
800	BKLY	60163	3028		D4
1500	BKLY	60162	3028		D4
S Hillside Av					
100	NHLK	60164	3028		D1
W Hillside Av					
100	BRTN	60010	2750	25W-18N	E3
S Hillside Cir					
10	PSPK	60464	3274	10W-14S	B6
Hillside Ct					
300	SMBG	60193	2859	23W-9N	B7
400	SMWD	60107	2857	28W-10N	B5
500	BRTN	60010	2751	24W-18N	B3
600	BmdT	60157	2913		D5
600	ROSL	60157	2913		D6
900	BRLT	60103	2911		C5
3500	HFET	60195	2804	24W-14N	D4
Hillside Dr					
-	DndT	60118	2801		B5
-	HYHL	60457	3210	10W-10S	A4
-	HYHL	60458	3210	10W-10S	A4
-	JSTC	60458	3210	10W-10S	A4
-	TYPK	60477	3504	9W-23S	E3
300	ROSL	60172	2913		B4
300	SMWD	60107	2857	28W-10N	B5
400	DYR	46311	3598		D4
400	HDPK	60035	2758	7W-20N	A1
22100	RNPK	60471	3594	6W-26S	A3
E Hillside Dr					
300	BNVL	60106	2916		A7
300	CHCG	60106	2916		A7
S Hillside Dr					
8400	PSPK	60464	3274	10W-14S	B7
12600	PlsT	60464	3274	10W-14S	B7
W Hillside Dr					
-	WDDL	60191	2915		C7
300	BNVL	60106	2915		D7
Hillside Ln					
300	EDND	60118	2801		A3
2600	EVTN	60201	2812	4W-13N	B7
Hillside Pl					
5700	TYPK	60477	3425	7W-20S	C3
Hillside Rd					
600	MaiT	60025	2809	10W-13N	E7
600	NfdT	60025	2809	10W-13N	E7
900	NHBK	60062	2757	9W-17N	C5
3500	EVTN	60201	2812	4W-13N	B7
E Hillside Rd					
100	BRTN	60010	2751	23W-18N	E3
100	PltT	60010	2751	23W-18N	E3
200	PltT	60010	2752	23W-18N	A3
S Hillside Rd					
21100	FftT	60423	3504	10W-25S	C7
W Hillside St					
800	PLTN	60067	2805	22W-15N	C1
800	PltT	60067	2805	22W-15N	B1
Hilltop Av					
100	BRTN	60010	2751	24W-20N	B2
1200	BlmT	60411	3507	2W-25S	C7
1200	CHHT	60411	3507	2W-25S	C7
1600	CHHT	60411	3595	2W-25S	C1
16700	ODHL	60477	3424	11W-20S	A4
Hilltop Ct					
10	LMNT	60439	3270		E5
400	SMBG	60193	2858	24W-10N	E5
15100	ODPK	60462	3345	12W-18S	B6
18300	TYPK	60477	3424	11W-22S	A7
Hilltop Dr					
10	SMBG	60193	2858	24W-10N	E6
10	SMBG	60194	2858	24W-10N	E6
600	ITSC	60143	2913		E5
1000	LMNT	60439	3270		E5
1000	LMNT	60439	3271		A5
10200	ODPK	60462	3345	12W-18S	B6
N Hilltop Dr					
900	BmdT	60143	2913		E5
900	BmdT	60157	2913		E5
900	ITSC	60143	2913		E4
1000	ITSC	60157	2913		E4
Hilltop Rd					
1700	HnrT	60120	2856	31W-11N	A3
2000	HFET	60195	2804	24W-12N	C7
S Hilltop Rd					
25700	CteT	60417	3687	3E-31S	A5
Hilltop St					
200	WLSP	60480	3209	12W-9S	B4
Hillview Ct					
400	LMNT	60439	3270		E6
Hillview Dr					
800	LMNT	60439	3270		E7
2000	CHHT	60411	3595	2W-26S	C2
Hillview Rd					
1200	HMWD	60430	3508	1W-22S	A1
1300	HMWD	60430	3507	1W-22S	E1
Hillwick Ln					
200	SMBG	60193	2859	22W-10N	C6
Hilton Dr					
9400	OKLN	60453	3212	5W-10S	A6
Hilton Ln					
200	EDND	60118	2801		B2
Hilton Pl					
100	ELGN	60120	2855		A4
Hilton St					
100	WLSP	60480	3209	12W-9S	D3
S Hi Lusi Av					
10	MPPT	60056	2807	16W-12N	E7
200	MPPT	60056	2861	16W-12N	E1
Hindsell Pl					
100	ELGN	60120	2855		A4
Hines Blvd					
-	MYWD	60153	3030	10W-1S	A7
-	PvsT	60141	3030	10W-1S	A7
-	PvsT	60141	3088	10W-1S	A1
-	PvsT	60153	3030	10W-1S	A7
Hingham Ct					
600	SMBG	60193	2858	24W-9N	D7
Hingham Ln					
500	SMBG	60193	2858	24W-9N	D7
Hinkle Ct					
700	SMBG	60193	2858	24W-10N	D6
Hinkle Ln					
10	SMBG	60193	2858	24W-10N	D6
Hinman Av					
1000	EVTN	60202	2867	2W-10N	B4
1200	EVTN	60201	2867	2W-10N	B4
Hinricher Dr					
100	WLSP	60480	3209	12W-9S	B4
Hinsdale Av					
4900	MCCK	60525	3148	10W-5S	A1
E Hinsdale Av					
10	HNDL	60521	3146		B2
W Hinsdale Av					
10	HNDL	60521	3146		A2
Hinsdale Oasis Rd					
-	BRRG	60521	3146		D4
-	HNDL	60521	3146		D4
Hintz Ln					
1500	WLNG	60090	2754	16W-17N	D6
E Hintz Rd					
10	WhlT	60090	2755	13W-16N	E6
10	WLNG	60090	2755	13W-17N	D6
200	ANHT	60004	2754	16W-17N	C6
1700	WLNG	60004	2754	16W-17N	D6
1700	WLNG	60090	2754	16W-17N	C6
2100	ANHT	60090	2754	16W-17N	D6
2300	PTHT	60070	2754	16W-17N	D6
2500	WLNG	60070	2754	16W-17N	E6
W Hintz Rd					
10	ANHT	60004	2754	18W-17N	A6
10	WLNG	60090	2755	14W-17N	B6
100	WLNG	60070	2754	15W-17N	E6
100	WLNG	60090	2754	15W-17N	E6
300	PTHT	60070	2754	15W-17N	E6
300	WLNG	60004	2754	15W-17N	E6
500	ANHT	60004	2753	18W-17N	E6
800	PTHT	60090	2755	14W-17N	B6
Hipple Ter					
-	SKOK	60076	2866	5W-11N	B2
Hirsch Av					
300	CTCY	60409	3352	4E-17S	B6
E Hirsch Av					
100	NHLK	60164	3028		E1
200	MLPK	60164	3028		E1
300	MLPK	60164	3029	13W-1N	A1
300	NHLK	60164	3029	13W-1N	A1
400	NHLK	60165	3029	13W-1N	A1
400	SNPK	60165	3029	13W-1N	A1
W Hirsch Av					
3000	MLPK	60160	3029	12W-1N	B1
Hirsch Blvd					
900	CTCY	60409	3352	4E-18S	B7
900	CTCY	60409	3430	4E-18S	B1
W Hirsch Dr					
3100	CHCG	60622	3032	3W-1N	E1
3100	CHCG	60651	3032	3W-1N	E1
Hirsch St					
1200	CTCY	60409	3430	4E-19S	B3
4200	NHLK	60164	3029	13W-1N	A1
4200	SNPK	60165	3029	13W-1N	A1
W Hirsch St					
2200	CHCG	60622	3033	3W-1N	A1
2700	CHCG	60622	3032	3W-1N	E1
3200	CHCG	60651	3032	4W-1N	C1
4800	CHCG	60651	3031	7W-1N	C1
5900	OKPK	60302	3031	7W-1N	B1
Hirsch Ter					
-	MLPK	60160	3028		E2
-	MLPK	60160	3029	13W-1N	A2
4600	NHLK	60160	3029	13W-1N	A2
4600	NHLK	60164	3029	13W-1N	A2
Hirschberg Av					
4200	SRPK	60176	2973	12W-5N	B1
4500	SRPK	60176	2917	12W-5N	B7
Hirschberg Ct					
4500	SRPK	60176	2973	11W-5N	D1
Hise Ct					
300	SMWD	60107	2857	27W-11N	C4
Hitching Post Ln					
2000	SMBG	60194	2858	26W-10N	A5
2200	SMBG	60194	2857	26W-10N	E5
Hobart Av					
16700	ODHL	60477	3423	11W-20S	E4
S Hobart Av					
11900	PlsT	60464	3273	11W-14S	E5
12300	PSPK	60464	3273	11W-14S	E6
W Hobart Av					
-	CHCG	60631	2919	8W-7N	A4
6800	CHCG	60631	2918	8W-7N	E4
W Hobbie St					
600	CHCG	60610	3034	0W-1N	A2
Hobble Bush Ln					
1000	ELGN	60120	2855		C1
N Hobson Av					
2000	CHCG	60614	2977	2W-3N	B5
Hodges St					
500	BCHR	60401	3864	0W-36S	C2
900	WshT	60401	3864	1W-36S	B2
Hodlmair Ct					
1400	EGVV	60007	2913		E3
Hodlmair Ln					
1300	EGVV	60007	2913		E2
S Hoey St					
2700	CHCG	60608	3091	1W-2S	E3
Hoffman Av					
1400	PKRG	60068	2863	11W-10N	D5
Hoffman Ct					
3000	DYR	46311	3598		D5
Hoffman Pkwy					
600	DSPN	60016	2862	14W-10N	D4
Hoffman St					
5200	SKOK	60077	2865	6W-10N	D5
E Hoffman St					
300	HMND	46327	3352		E5
Hoffman Ter					
6400	MNGV	60053	2865	8W-11N	A2
Hogarth Ln					
10	GLNC	60022	2758	6W-18N	E4
Hoger Dr					
-	MTSN	60443	3505	7W-25S	D7
Hohlfelder Rd					
1000	GLNC	60022	2758	7W-18N	B4
Hohman Av					
6300	HMND	46324	3430		D2
7400	HMND	46321	3430		D4
7400	MNSR	46321	3430		D7
8600	MNSR	46321	3510		D1
S Hohman Av					
3700	HMND	46327	3352		D4
4800	HMND	46320	3352		D5
5900	HMND	46320	3430		D1
6100	HMND	46324	3430		D1
Hohman St					
9600	SjnT	46311	3687		D2
Holbrook Cir					
10	CHHT	60411	3507	1W-23S	E3
10	CHHT	60411	3508	1W-23S	A3
300	HMWD	60411	3508	1W-23S	A3
Holbrook Dr					
200	WLNG	60090	2808	14W-16N	B1
Holbrook Ln					
-	HFET	60195	2804	26W-12N	A7
1900	HFET	60195	2858	25W-12N	B1
Holbrook Rd					
-	GNWD	60425	3508	1W-23S	A3
10	BlmT	60430	3507	1W-23S	E3
10	CHHT	60411	3507	1W-23S	E3
10	CHHT	60411	3508	1W-23S	A3
10	HMWD	60411	3508	1W-23S	A3
10	HMWD	60430	3507	1W-23S	E3
10	HMWD	60430	3508	1W-23S	A3
200	CHHT	60430	3507	1W-23S	E3
200	FSMR	60422	3507	2W-23S	D3
200	FSMR	60430	3507	1W-23S	E3
800	BlmT	60411	3508	1W-23S	A3
800	HMWD	60425	3508	1W-23S	A3
900	CHHT	60425	3508	1W-23S	A3
1600	BlmT	60422	3507	2W-23S	D3
W Holbrook Rd					
600	BlmT	60411	3508	0W-23S	B3
600	GNWD	60425	3508	0W-23S	B3
600	HMWD	60425	3508	0W-23S	B3
W Holbrook St					
6200	CHCG	60646	2919	7W-7N	A3
Holden Cir					
-	PKFT	60443	3594	4W-26S	E1
-	PKFT	60466	3594	4W-26S	E1
3000	MTSN	60443	3595	4W-26S	A2
3000	PKFT	60443	3595	4W-26S	A2
3000	PKFT	60466	3595	4W-26S	A2
3300	MTSN	60443	3594	4W-26S	E1
N Holden Ct					
10	CHCG	60602	3034		D5
S Holden Ct					
500	CHCG	60605	3034	0E-0S	C6
Holder Ln					
1700	NHFD	60093	2811	6W-15N	C3
Holeman Av					
3200	CHHT	60411	3596	0W-27S	C4
3200	SCHT	60411	3596	0W-27S	C4
3200	STGR	60475	3596	0W-27S	C4
3300	CRTE	60475	3596	0W-28S	C6
Holiday Ct					
15000	ODPK	60462	3345	12W-17S	C6
S Holiday Dr					
12500	ALSP	60803	3275	6W-14S	E7
Holiday Ln					
700	DSPN	60016	2861	16W-10N	E4
700	DSPN	60016	2862	15W-10N	A5
700	MPPT	60056	2861	16W-10N	E4
Holiday Ter					
2300	LNSG	60438	3429	2E-20S	D5
Holiday Plaza Dr					
500	MTSN	60443	3506	6W-25S	A7
500	MTSN	60443	3594	6W-25S	A1
Holland Av					
16600	SHLD	60473	3428	0E-19S	D2
Holland Rd					
18300	LNSG	60438	3429	2E-21S	C7
S Holland Rd					
8600	CHCG	60620	3214	0W-10S	B4
Hollendale Villa					
1700	NHFD	60093	2811	6W-15N	C2
Hollett Dr					
-	CHCG	60629	3150	4W-7S	D6
Holli Ct					
1000	SMBG	60194	2858	24W-11N	C4
Holliston Ct					
900	SMBG	60193	2912		D1
Holliston on Asbury					
10	RGMW	60008	2806	19W-15N	B3
Hollow Tree Rd					
10600	ODPK	60462	3345	13W-17S	A5
Holly Av					
1600	NfdT	60062	2756	11W-16N	C7
1600	NHBK	60062	2756	11W-16N	C7
E Holly Av					
500	MPPT	60056	2808	15W-13N	B5
N Holly Av					
2000	CHCG	60614	2977	2W-2N	C6
2000	CHCG	60622	2977	2W-2N	C6
S Holly Av					
300	EMHT	60126	3028		B4
Holly Ct					
10	WLNG	60090	2754	16W-18N	E4
500	SMWD	60107	2857	28W-10N	B6
900	NHBK	60062	2757	8W-17N	E5
1000	NfdT	60025	2810	10W-13N	B6
1100	OKPK	60301	3030	8W-0N	D3
2200	NfdT	60062	2809	11W-16N	D1
2200	NHBK	60062	2809	11W-16N	D1
3800	CCHL	60478	3426	4W-20S	D5
7300	RVFT	60305	3030	9W-0N	D3
8200	PSHL	60465	3274	10W-13S	B3
10000	ODPK	60462	3345	12W-17S	C5
11900	LMNT	60439	3271		D5
15300	OKFT	60452	3347	6W-18S	E7
17700	TYPK	60477	3423	11W-21S	E6
E Holly Ct					
700	MPPT	60056	2808	15W-13N	B5
W Holly Ct					
300	GNWD	60425	3508	0W-22S	B1
Holly Dr					
300	SMWD	60107	2857	28W-10N	B6
700	BRLT	60103	2910		D4
Holly Ln					
-	HFET	60195	2859	22W-11N	B3
200	EGVV	60007	2860	18W-9N	E7
200	EGVV	60007	2861	18W-9N	A6
1000	MNSR	46321	3510		E2
1300	WNKA	60093	2758	6W-16N	E7
1800	BlmT	60422	3507	2W-23S	C4
1800	FSMR	60422	3507	2W-23S	C4
1800	OMFD	60461	3507	2W-23S	C4
3600	RGMW	60008	2806	20W-13N	A5
10000	MaiT	60016	2809	12W-12N	C7
10000	MaiT	60016	2863	12W-12N	C1
S Holly Ln					
20100	FftT	60423	3504	9W-24S	D5
Holly St					
10	PKFT	60466	3595	3W-26S	B1
E Holly Wy					
800	PLTN	60074	2753	19W-18N	B3
N Holly Wy					
1900	PLTN	60074	2753	19W-18N	B3
Hollyberry Av					
9000	MaiT	60016	2863	11W-11N	D2
Hollybrook Ln					
8400	TYPK	60477	3504	10W-23S	B3
Hollydale Dr					
2700	HMWD	60430	3427	3W-21S	B6
Hollyhock Ct					
15100	ODPK	60462	3346	9W-18S	D6
Hollywood Av					
200	MNSR	46321	3430		C5
800	DSPN	60016	2862	13W-11N	D3
800	ITSC	60143	2914		A5
1300	GNVW	60025	2810	8W-14N	E5
1300	GNVW	60025	2811	8W-14N	A5
1700	HRPK	60133	2911		C1
3300	BKFD	60513	3088	10W-3S	A5
3800	LYNS	60534	3088	10W-3S	A6
W Hollywood Av					
900	CHCG	60640	2921	1W-7N	E4
1500	CHCG	60660	2921	2W-7N	C4
2400	CHCG	60659	2921	3W-7N	A4
3200	CHCG	60659	2920	4W-7N	C4
4300	CHCG	60646	2920	5W-7N	A4
Hollywood Blvd					
100	SBTN	60010	2803	26W-13N	D6
Hollywood Ct					
100	WLMT	60091	2812	4W-13N	B6
700	HMND	46394	3280		D5
Hollywood Dr					
4800	CCHL	60478	3426	6W-21S	A6
8400	ODPK	60462	3346	10W-18S	B6
S Holm Ct					
14500	HMGN	60441	3344	15W-17S	B5
W Holm Dr					
12500	HMGN	60441	3344	15W-17S	B5
S Holmberg Ct					
12000	ALSP	60803	3276	5W-14S	C5
Holmes Av					
-	PSPK	60464	3274	10W-13S	B4
16900	HLCT	60429	3427	3W-20S	A5
S Holmes Av					
11600	PlsT	60464	3274	10W-13S	B5
11600	PSPK	60464	3274	10W-13S	B5
Holmes Dr					
13000	PlsT	60462	3345	13W-15S	A1
13000	PlsT	60464	3345	13W-15S	A1
Holmes St					
100	LMNT	60439	3270		E5
Holmes Wy					
10	SMBG	60193	2857	27W-10N	D5
10	SMBG	60194	2857	27W-10N	D6
Holste Rd					
1800	NHBK	60062	2810	9W-15N	B2
Holyoke Ct					
800	SMBG	60193	2858	24W-10N	C6
800	SMBG	60193	2859	23W-10N	A6
Holyoke on Auburn					
10	RGMW	60008	2806	19W-14N	C3
Homan Av					
-	ALSP	60406	3276	4W-14S	E7
-	RchT	60422	3506	4W-23S	E2
-	RchT	60430	3506	4W-23S	E2
400	PKFT	60466	3507	4W-25S	A7
500	MTSN	60443	3594	4W-25S	E1
500	MTSN	60466	3594	4W-25S	E1
500	PKFT	60443	3594	4W-25S	E1
500	PKFT	60466	3506	4W-25S	E7
500	PKFT	60466	3594	4W-25S	E1
12600	BLID	60406	3276	4W-15S	E7
12800	ALSP	60406	3348	4W-15S	E1
12800	ALSP	60803	3276	4W-15S	E7
12800	ALSP	60803	3348	4W-15S	E1
12800	WthT	60406	3276	4W-15S	E7
12800	WthT	60406	3348	4W-15S	E1
12800	WthT	60803	3276	4W-15S	E7
14300	MDLN	60445	3348	4W-17S	E5
14800	MKHM	60426	3348	4W-18S	E6
15500	MKHM	60426	3426	4W-18S	E1
N Homan Av					
10	CHCG	60624	3032	4W-0N	D4
1100	CHCG	60651	3032	4W-1N	D2
1500	CHCG	60647	3032	4W-2N	D1

STREET Block	City	ZIP	Map#	CGS	Grid
S Homan Av					
10	CHCG	60624	3032	4W-1S	D7
1100	CHCG	60623	3032	4W-1S	D7
1500	CHCG	60623	3090	4W-1S	D1
4500	CHCG	60632	3090	4W-4S	D7
4600	CHCG	60632	3150	4W-5S	D1
5400	CHCG	60629	3150	4W-7S	D5
7500	CHCG	60652	3212	4W-9S	D2
9100	ENGN	60805	3212	4W-11S	D6
10200	CHCG	60655	3276	4W-11S	D1
10200	ENGN	60805	3276	4W-11S	D1
11400	MTPK	60803	3276	4W-13S	E4
11500	CHCG	60803	3276	4W-13S	E4
11600	MTPK	60655	3276	4W-13S	E4
12300	ALSP	60803	3276	4W-14S	E6
12300	WthT	60803	3276	4W-14S	E6
12400	ALSP	60406	3276	4W-14S	E6
12400	WthT	60406	3276	4W-14S	E6
12500	BLID	60406	3276	4W-14S	E6
13300	RBBN	60472	3348	4W-15S	E2
13300	WthT	60472	3348	4W-15S	E2
Homan Cir					
10	PKFT	60466	3594	4W-25S	E1
Home Av					
-	WRTH	60482	3275	7W-13S	B5
-	WthT	60482	3275	7W-13S	B5
100	OKPK	60302	3030	8W-0S	E5
200	ITSC	60143	2914		D7
200	OKPK	60304	3030	8W-0S	E6
500	ADSN	60143	2914		D7
700	EGVV	60007	2913		E1
1100	BRWN	60402	3030	8W-1S	E7
1100	OKPK	60402	3030	8W-0S	E7
3100	BRWN	60402	3088	8W-3S	E6
3900	SKNY	60402	3088	8W-4S	E7
4400	FTVW	60402	3088	8W-4S	E7
4500	FTVW	60402	3148	8W-4S	E1
9200	MaiT	60016	2863	11W-11N	E2
E Home Av					
10	PLTN	60067	2752	20W-17N	E4
100	PLTN	60067	2753	20W-17N	A4
200	PLTN	60074	2753	20W-17N	A4
N Home Av					
10	PKRG	60068	2917	11W-9N	E1
2100	PKRG	60068	2863	11W-11N	E3
2200	MaiT	60016	2863	11W-11N	E3
2200	PKRG	60016	2863	11W-11N	E3
S Home Av					
10	PKRG	60068	2917	11W-8N	E1
23400	MonT	60449	3594	6W-29S	B7
23400	MonT	60449	3683	6W-29S	B1
23400	UYPK	60466	3594	6W-29S	B7
23400	UYPK	60466	3683	6W-29S	B1
W Home Av					
6400	WRTH	60482	3275	8W-13S	A4
6400	WthT	60482	3275	8W-13S	B5
Home Cir					
1500	EGVV	60007	2913		E1
9300	MaiT	60016	2863	11W-11N	E2
Home Ct					
9300	MaiT	60016	2863	11W-11N	E2
N Home Ct					
1300	PLTN	60074	2753	20W-17N	A4
Home Ter					
9200	MaiT	60016	2863	11W-11N	E2
Homeland Rd					
200	MTSN	60443	3506	5W-25S	B7
600	RchT	60443	3506	5W-25S	B7
W Homer St					
1500	CHCG	60622	2977	1W-2N	D7
2000	CHCG	60647	2977	2W-2N	B7
3100	CHCG	60647	2976	3W-2N	D7
4500	CHCG	60639	2976	5W-2N	A7
5100	CHCG	60639	2975	6W-2N	D7
Homestead Dr					
5400	CTWD	60445	3347	6W-15S	D2
5500	WthT	60445	3347	6W-15S	D2
5500	WthT	60463	3347	6W-15S	D2
Homestead Ln					
9100	BGVW	60455	3210	8W-10S	E5
Homestead Rd					
1000	LGPK	60525	3087	12W-3S	C4
Hometown Ln					
8700	HMTN	60456	3212	5W-10S	A4
Homewood Av					
17800	HMWD	60430	3427	2W-21S	D7
18400	HMWD	60430	3507	2W-22S	D1
S Homewood Av					
10900	CHCG	60643	3277	2W-13S	C3
Homewood Ct					
200	CHHT	60411	3508	1W-24S	A4
Honey Ln					
800	CRTE	60417	3597	1E-28S	A6
6300	TYPK	60477	3425	7W-20S	B3
Honey Locust Ct					
800	BRLT	60103	2856	29W-9N	D7
Honey Locust Dr					
300	WLNG	60090	2755	13W-17N	E5
7200	JSTC	60458	3148	10W-7S	B7
Honeysuckle Ct					
100	RGMW	60008	2805	21W-14N	D5
Honeysuckle Dr					
200	NHBK	60062	2755	13W-18N	E3
900	WLNG	60090	2755	15W-16N	A7
Honeysuckle Ln					
1100	BRLT	60103	2910		E6
2400	RGMW	60008	2805	21W-14N	D4
Honor Dr					
-	MTSN	60443	3505	7W-24S	D6
Honore Av					
14100	DXMR	60426	3349	2W-16S	D4
14600	HRVY	60426	3349	2W-17S	D6
15600	HRVY	60426	3427	2W-18S	D1
16100	MKHM	60426	3427	2W-19S	D3
16500	HLCT	60429	3427	2W-19S	D3
Honore St					
-	CHCG	60406	3277	2W-13S	C5
-	CHCG	60643	3277	2W-13S	C5
-	ClmT	60406	3277	2W-13S	C5
-	ClmT	60643	3277	2W-13S	C5
12700	BLID	60406	3277	2W-15S	D7
12700	BLID	60827	3277	2W-15S	D7
12700	CTPK	60827	3277	2W-15S	D7
13000	BLID	60406	3349	2W-15S	D1
N Honore St					
1200	CHCG	60622	3033	2W-1N	C1
1600	CHCG	60622	2977	2W-2N	C7
1900	CHCG	60614	2977	2W-2N	C7
2900	CHCG	60657	2977	2W-3N	C4
4200	CHCG	60613	2977	2W-5N	C1
5200	CHCG	60640	2921	2W-6N	C5
6800	CHCG	60626	2921	2W-8N	C1
7300	CHCG	60626	2867	2W-9N	C7
S Honore St					
100	CHCG	60612	3033	2W-0S	C5

STREET Block	City	ZIP	Map#	CGS	Grid
S Honore St					
3500	CHCG	60608	3091	2W-3S	C5
3500	CHCG	60609	3091	2W-3S	C5
5500	CHCG	60609	3151	2W-6S	C4
5500	CHCG	60636	3151	2W-7S	C6
8400	CHCG	60620	3213	2W-9S	C4
12300	CTPK	60827	3277	2W-14S	D6
12600	BLID	60406	3277	2W-14S	D7
12600	BLID	60827	3277	2W-14S	D7
Hood Av					
18200	HMWD	60430	3427	1W-21S	E7
18800	HMWD	60430	3507	1W-22S	E2
W Hood Av					
1800	CHCG	60660	2921	2W-7N	B3
2000	CHCG	60659	2921	2W-7N	B3
3000	CHCG	60659	2920	3W-7N	D3
7100	CHCG	60631	2918	8W-7N	D3
Hood Ct					
200	BRLT	60103	2911		A5
Hook Rd					
100	CPVL	60110	2748		C6
N Hooker St					
1000	CHCG	60622	3033	1W-1N	E2
Hooks Ct					
-	SHLD	60473	3428	0E-19S	E3
Hoover Ct					
10	SMWD	60107	2856	29W-10N	D6
1800	RGMW	60008	2805	20W-14N	E4
S Hoover Ct					
25800	MONE	60449	3682	7W-31S	D5
Hoover Dr					
200	WDDL	60191	2914		E7
400	CPVL	60110	2748		C7
Hoover St					
-	EGvT	60018	2861	16W-9N	E7
-	EGVV	60007	2861	15W-9N	E7
400	EGvT	60018	2862	15W-9N	A7
4300	RGMW	60008	2805	20W-14N	E4
4300	RGMW	60008	2806	20W-14N	A4
S Hoover St					
25700	MONE	60449	3682	7W-31S	D5
Hope Ct					
1900	LYWD	60411	3509	2E-24S	D5
Hope Pl					
5200	MTSN	60443	3505	6W-24S	E5
5200	MTSN	60443	3506	6W-24S	A5
Hope St					
10000	RSMT	60018	2917	12W-7N	B3
Hopi Ln					
2700	CPVL	60110	2748		C5
E Hopi Ln					
1800	MPPT	60056	2808	13W-14N	E5
2000	WhlT	60025	2808	13W-14N	E5
Hopi Tr					
1600	WLNG	60090	2754	16W-17N	D5
Hopkins Av					
3000	SCHT	60411	3596	0W-27S	C5
3000	STGR	60475	3596	0W-28S	C6
3300	CRTE	60475	3596	0W-28S	C6
Hopkins Ct					
14900	ODPK	60462	3345	12W-17S	C6
W Hopkins Pl					
2000	CHCG	60620	3213	2W-10S	B4
Hopman Dr					
18200	TYPK	60477	3424	10W-21S	B7
Horace Dr					
500	ELGN	60120	2855		E5
Horatio Blvd					
100	BFGV	60089	2754	16W-20N	E1
400	VrnT	60069	2754	16W-20N	E1
Horizon Ct					
8400	FftT	60477	3504	10W-23S	B4
8400	TYPK	60477	3504	10W-23S	B4
Horizon Dr					
400	BRLT	60103	2910		C1
1000	BRLT	60120	2910		C1
Horizon Ln					
1300	NfdT	60062	2756	12W-17N	C5
1300	NHBK	60062	2756	12W-17N	C6
Horizon Tr					
-	WLNG	60004	2754	16W-17N	D5
-	WLNG	60090	2754	16W-17N	D5
Horn Rd					
15100	ODPK	60462	3346	10W-18S	B6
Horne Ter					
1000	DSPN	60016	2862	15W-10N	B5
W Horner Av					
2300	MonT	60449	3682	6W-30S	E4
2300	MonT	60449	3683	6W-30S	A4
2300	UYPK	60449	3682	6W-30S	E4
2300	UYPK	60449	3683	6W-30S	A4
2300	UYPK	60466	3682	6W-30S	E4
N Horner Ln					
-	DSPN	60016	2808	14W-13N	C7
-	MPPT	60016	2808	14W-13N	C7
100	MPPT	60056	2808	14W-13N	C7
Horseshoe Ct					
10	SMWD	60107	2856	30W-10N	C5
Horseshoe Dr					
8400	TYPK	60477	3424	10W-19S	B3
Horseshoe Ln					
-	MonT	60449	3684	3W-31S	C4
-	UYPK	60466	3684	3W-31S	C4
10	LMNT	60439	3272	15W-13S	A4
1200	BRLT	60103	2910		A7
W Hortense Av					
7400	CHCG	60631	2918	9W-7N	C3
7700	PKRG	60068	2918	9W-7N	C3
Hotchkiss Dr					
-	FKFT	60423	3504	10W-24S	B6
N Hough St					
100	BRTN	60010	2750	25W-20N	E1
N Hough St SR-59					
100	BRTN	60010	2750	25W-20N	E1
S Hough St					
100	BRTN	60010	2750	25W-18N	E3
800	BrnT	60010	2750	25W-18N	E3
S Hough St SR-59					
100	BRTN	60010	2750	25W-18N	E3
Houlton Ct					
800	SMBG	60193	2912		E1
Houston Av					
300	CTCY	60409	3352	3E-17S	A5
900	ELGN	60120	2855		C6
S Houston Av					
8700	CHCG	60617	3216	3E-10S	A4
12900	CHCG	60633	3280	3E-15S	A7
13100	CHCG	60633	3352	3E-15S	A1
Houston Dr					
-	FNPK	60131	2973	13W-3N	A5
700	CPVL	60110	2748		B5
Houston St					
500	LMNT	60439	3270		E6
3000	FNPK	60131	2973	13W-3N	A4

STREET Block	City	ZIP	Map#	CGS	Grid
Hovland Ct					
1700	EVTN	60201	2866	3W-11N	E2
Howard Av					
10	DSPN	60018	2862	14W-9N	C7
10	EGvT	60018	2862	14W-9N	B7
10	PvsT	60162	3028		C6
100	EDND	60118	2801		B3
200	HLSD	60162	3028		D5
1200	BKLY	60163	3028		C3
1600	DSPN	60018	2863	12W-9N	A7
3800	PvsT	60558	3086		E7
3800	WNSP	60558	3086		E7
4400	WNSP	60558	3146		E1
5900	LynT	60525	3146		E4
6500	IHPK	60525	3146		E6
7900	LynT	60525	3208		E2
7900	WLSP	60525	3208		E3
N Howard Av					
200	AddT	60126	2972		A5
300	EMHT	60126	3028		A1
600	EMHT	60126	2972		A6
S Howard Av					
10	ROSL	60172	2913		B5
5500	HMND	46320	3352		E7
Howard Ct					
-	MaiT	60016	2863	11W-11N	D4
-	PKRG	60068	2863	11W-11N	D4
10	BlmT	60411	3510	3E-25S	A7
600	EDND	60118	2801		B2
Howard Dr					
1000	SMBG	60193	2913		A1
Howard St					
300	EGvT	60007	2860	18W-9N	E7
300	EGVV	60007	2860	18W-9N	E7
400	EGvT	60018	2861	18W-9N	A7
1000	EGVV	60007	2861	17W-9N	C7
5400	SKOK	60077	2865	6W-9N	C7
5500	NLES	60714	2865	6W-9N	C6
W Howard St					
1300	CHCG	60626	2867	1W-9N	D6
1600	EVTN	60202	2867	2W-9N	B6
1900	CHCG	60645	2867	2W-9N	B6
2200	CHCG	60202	2867	2W-9N	A6
2600	CHCG	60645	2866	3W-9N	E6
2600	EVTN	60202	2866	3W-9N	E6
3100	SKOK	60076	2866	3W-9N	D7
3100	SKOK	60645	2866	3W-9N	D7
4600	SKOK	60076	2865	5W-9N	E7
5600	NLES	60714	2865	7W-9N	C6
5600	SKOK	60077	2865	7W-9N	C6
5900	SKOK	60714	2865	7W-9N	B6
6700	NLES	60714	2864	8W-9N	E7
7100	CHCG	60631	2864	8W-9N	D7
7100	CHCG	60714	2864	8W-9N	D7
7100	NLES	60631	2864	8W-9N	D7
7500	PKRG	60068	2864	9W-9N	C7
W Howdy Ln					
4500	ALSP	60803	3276	5W-13S	B4
Howe Av					
17500	HLCT	60430	3427	2W-21S	C5
17500	HMWD	60430	3427	2W-21S	C5
Howe Ct					
100	PltT	60010	2751	24W-18N	C2
Howe Dr					
13500	OrlT	60462	3345	11W-16S	D2
13500	PlsT	60462	3345	11W-16S	D2
N Howe St					
1100	CHCG	60610	3034	0W-1N	A2
1800	CHCG	60614	2978	0W-2N	A7
Howe Ter					
-	BRTN	60010	2751	24W-18N	C2
100	PltT	60010	2751	24W-18N	C2
W Howland Av					
2100	CHCG	60620	3213	2W-10S	C4
Hoxie Av					
200	BNHM	60633	3351	2E-17S	E6
200	CTCY	60409	3351	2E-17S	E6
S Hoxie Av					
9600	CHCG	60617	3215	2E-11S	D7
10300	CHCG	60617	3279	2E-12S	D1
13400	CHCG	60633	3351	2E-15S	E2
14300	BNHM	60633	3351	2E-16S	E4
14500	CTCY	60409	3351	2E-16S	E4
Hoyne Av					
-	MKHM	60426	3427	2W-19S	C2
13300	BLID	60406	3349	2W-15S	C2
14200	DXMR	60426	3349	2W-16S	C4
14600	HRVY	60426	3349	2W-17S	C6
15600	HRVY	60426	3427	2W-18S	C1
N Hoyne Av					
200	CHCG	60612	3033	2W-0N	B4
700	CHCG	60622	3033	2W-0N	B3
1500	CHCG	60647	3033	2W-1N	B1
2500	CHCG	60647	2977	2W-3N	B5
2900	CHCG	60618	2977	2W-3N	B4
4800	CHCG	60625	2921	2W-6N	B6
6000	CHCG	60659	2921	2W-7N	B3
6200	CHCG	60645	2921	2W-7N	B3
7300	CHCG	60645	2867	2W-9N	B7
7500	EVTN	60202	2867	2W-9N	B7
S Hoyne Av					
1200	CHCG	60608	3033	2W-1S	B7
1200	CHCG	60612	3033	2W-1S	B7
1700	CHCG	60608	3091	2W-2S	B2
3400	CHCG	60609	3091	2W-3S	B5
4700	CHCG	60609	3151	2W-5S	B1
5500	CHCG	60636	3151	2W-6S	B4
7600	CHCG	60620	3213	2W-9S	C2
9500	CHCG	60643	3213	2W-11S	C7
10300	CHCG	60643	3277	2W-12S	C1
Hoyne St					
12700	BLID	60406	3277	2W-15S	C7
13000	BLID	60406	3349	2W-15S	C1
Hoyt Ln					
500	WNKA	60093	2812	4W-15N	C2
Hub Rd					
200	WYNE	60174	2909		A7
500	WYNE	60120	2909		A7
Hubbard Ln					
200	CRTE	60417	3685	0W-30S	C2
6500	TYPK	60477	3425	8W-20S	B3
Hubbard Pl					
1000	WNKA	60093	2759	5W-16N	A7
Hubbard St					
100	TNTN	60476	3428	0E-21S	D6
900	WNKA	60093	2759	5W-16N	A7
E Hubbard St					
10	CHCG	60610	3034	0E-0N	C3
10	CHCG	60611	3034	0E-0N	C3
W Hubbard St					
10	CHCG	60611	3034	0E-0N	C3
600	CHCG	60610	3034	0W-0N	A3
700	CHCG	60622	3034	0W-0N	A3
800	CHCG	60622	3033	2W-0N	B3
1900	CHCG	60612	3033	2W-0N	B3

STREET Block	City	ZIP	Map#	CGS	Grid
W Hubbard St					
4700	CHCG	60644	3032	5W-0N	A3
4800	CHCG	60644	3031	6W-0N	E3
Hubbell Ct					
10	BNHL	60010	2750	25W-17N	E4
Huber Ct					
9400	ODPK	60467	3423	12W-19S	D2
Huber Ln					
400	GNVW	60025	2864	10W-11N	A2
400	NLES	60714	2864	10W-11N	A2
700	GNVW	60025	2810	10W-13N	A7
900	NfdT	60025	2810	10W-13N	A6
N Huber Ln					
9700	NLES	60714	2864	10W-12N	A1
9900	GNVW	60025	2864	10W-12N	A1
N Huber Ovl					
9700	NLES	60714	2864	10W-12N	B1
Huckins Dr					
8500	FKFT	60423	3504	10W-24S	B6
Huckleberry Ln					
400	NHBK	60062	2756	10W-17N	E4
900	GNVW	60025	2811	7W-14N	A4
N Hudson Av					
1300	CHCG	60610	3034	0W-1N	A1
1600	CHCG	60610	2978	0W-2N	A7
2100	CHCG	60614	2978	0W-2N	A6
3100	CHCG	60657	2978	0W-3N	A4
Hudson Ct					
100	ROSL	60172	2912		E5
600	EGVV	60007	2913		D1
1000	BRLT	60103	2910		C5
Hudson Dr					
3900	HFET	60195	2804	24W-14N	D3
Hudson Rd					
700	GNVW	60025	2810	8W-13N	E7
700	GNVW	60025	2811	7W-13N	B7
Hudson St					
500	HMND	46327	3352		D4
E Hudson St					
800	HMND	46327	3352		E4
Hudson Tr					
3200	OMFD	60461	3507	4W-24S	A5
N Hudson Bay					
1700	PLTN	60074	2753	18W-18N	D4
Huehl Rd					
-	DRFD	60015	2756	11W-18N	C2
200	NHBK	60062	2756	11W-18N	C4
E Huehn St					
200	HMND	46327	3352		D4
Huggins Dr					
-	MKHM	60426	3426	4W-19S	D2
Huguelet Pl					
8900	ODPK	60462	3346	11W-18S	A6
Hull Av					
600	WSTR	60154	3029	12W-0S	B7
1400	WSTR	60154	3087	12W-1S	B1
2100	PvsT	60154	3087	12W-1S	B2
2100	PvsT	60525	3087	12W-1S	B2
Hull St					
-	SKOK	60077	2865	7W-9N	B6
3800	SKOK	60076	2866	4W-9N	B6
Hull Ter					
600	EVTN	60202	2867	2W-9N	B6
Humber Ln					
17300	TYPK	60477	3424	10W-21S	B5
Humboldt Av					
700	WNKA	60093	2812	5W-16N	B1
N Humboldt Blvd					
1600	CHCG	60647	2976	3W-2N	E6
N Humboldt Dr					
1000	CHCG	60622	3032	3W-1N	E1
1500	CHCG	60647	3032	3W-2N	E1
S Humboldt Dr					
20700	FftT	60423	3504	9W-25S	E7
Humbracht Cir					
-	BRLT	60103	2910		B4
-	BRLT	60120	2910		B4
Hummingbird Ct					
10	SMWD	60107	2856	30W-10N	C6
400	VrnT	60015	2755	14W-20N	B1
Hummingbird Dr					
-	BlmT	60411	3509	3E-25S	E7
18000	TYPK	60477	3424	11W-21S	A7
Hummingbird Ln					
-	MTSN	60443	3593	8W-25S	B1
-	RchT	60443	3593	8W-25S	B1
10	SMWD	60107	2856	30W-10N	C6
500	VrnT	60015	2755	15W-20N	B2
Hummingbird Wy					
-	BRLT	60103	2910		E6
Hummingbird Hill Dr					
9700	ODPK	60467	3423	12W-19S	D2
Humpfer St					
200	HMND	46324	3430		D3
S Humphrey Av					
500	OKPK	60302	3031	7W-0S	B5
1000	OKPK	60304	3031	7W-0S	B7
1100	CCRO	60804	3031	7W-0S	B7
1100	OKPK	60804	3031	7W-0S	B7
Humphrey Av N					
700	OKPK	60302	3031	7W-1N	B2
1200	CHCG	60302	3031	7W-2N	B1
1200	CHCG	60639	3031	7W-2N	B1
N Hundley St					
600	HFET	60194	2858	25W-11N	B4
W Hundley St					
1400	HFET	60194	2858	25W-11N	B4
Hundley Wy					
1600	HFET	60194	2858	25W-11N	B4
1600	SMBG	60194	2858	25W-11N	B4
S Hunt Av					
5300	SMMT	60501	3148	9W-5S	D3
W Hunt Av					
2000	CHCG	60620	3213	2W-10S	C4
Huntcliff Rd					
1400	BRLT	60103	2910		B7
W Hunt Club Ct					
12900	HMGN	60448	3422	16W-21S	A6
Hunt Club Dr					
10	OKBK	60523	3086		B4
S Hunt Club Dr					
1000	MPPT	60056	2861	16W-11N	E3
W Hunt Club Dr					
17900	HMGN	60448	3422	16W-21S	A7
Hunt Club Ln					
10	OKBK	60523	3086		B4
Hunter Ct					
10	BRRG	60527	3208		A4
500	WLMT	60091	2812	4W-13N	B6
9300	ODHL	60477	3423	11W-19S	E2
Hunter Dr					
-	WLNG	60090	2754	16W-17N	D6
10	ROSL	60172	2912		D5
600	OKBK	60523	3086		A2
1000	ELGN	60120	2855		D3

STREET Block	City	ZIP	Map#	CGS	Grid
Hunter Dr					
9200	ODHL	60477	3423	11W-19S	E2
9200	ODPK	60467	3423	11W-19S	E2
E Hunter Dr					
2200	ANHT	60004	2807	16W-16N	D1
S Hunter Dr					
20300	FftT	60423	3504	9W-24S	E6
Hunter Rd					
500	WLMT	60091	2812	5W-13N	B6
1000	GNVW	60025	2811	6W-13N	C6
N Hunter St					
100	TNTN	60476	3428	0E-20S	D5
S Hunter St					
100	TNTN	60476	3428	0E-21S	D6
Hunter Tr					
16600	TYPK	60477	3425	8W-19S	A3
Hunterdon Ct					
200	SMBG	60194	2857	27W-10N	D5
Hunters Cir					
100	SMBG	60193	2859	23W-9N	A7
Hunter's Dr					
-	BCHR	60401	3774	0W-35S	D6
Hunters Rdg E					
1100	HFET	60192	2856	30W-12N	B2
Hunters Rdg W					
1100	HFET	60192	2856	30W-12N	B2
Hunters Ridge Ct					
5500	HFET	60192	2856	30W-12N	B2
Hunter Woods Dr					
21100	FftT	60423	3504	9W-25S	D7
21100	FKFT	60423	3504	9W-25S	D7
W Hunting Ct					
1100	PLTN	60067	2805	22W-15N	B2
W Hunting Dr					
1000	PLTN	60067	2805	22W-15N	B3
Huntington Blvd					
-	HFET	60194	2858	25W-12N	B2
1800	HFET	60195	2858	25W-12N	B1
2500	SBTN	60010	2804	25W-13N	B6
3600	HFET	60195	2804	25W-14N	B4
4700	HFET	60010	2804	24W-15N	B1
4700	IVNS	60010	2804	24W-15N	B1
Huntington Cir					
7700	HRPK	60133	2857	26W-9N	E7
Huntington Ct					
10	BRRG	60527	3208		D2
200	LGPK	60525	3087	12W-2S	B3
1000	EGVV	60007	2914		A2
1600	FSMR	60422	3507	2W-23S	E4
1700	WLNG	60090	2754	16W-18N	D3
8600	JSTC	60458	3210	10W-8S	A1
10000	ODPK	60462	3345	12W-17S	B6
15200	ODPK	60467	3345	12W-18S	C7
Huntington Dr					
-	HFET	60107	2857	28W-11N	A4
200	SMWD	60107	2857	28W-11N	A4
900	EGVV	60007	2914		A2
1400	CTCY	60409	3429	2E-19S	D3
1400	GNVW	60025	2810	8W-14N	E5
1500	SHLD	60473	3429	2E-19S	D3
N Huntington Dr					
2900	ANHT	60004	2754	17W-17N	C5
Huntington Ln					
10	BFGV	60089	2754	16W-18N	D4
10	BFGV	60090	2754	16W-18N	D4
10	WLNG	60090	2754	16W-18N	D4
600	SMBG	60193	2859	23W-9N	A7
3100	NHBK	60062	2756	11W-16N	D6
E Huntington Ln					
300	EMHT	60126	3028		B3
Huntington Pl					
10200	ODPK	60462	3345	12W-17S	B6
W Huntington St					
6100	CHCG	60646	2919	7W-7N	A3
6300	CHCG	60631	2919	8W-7N	A3
Huntington Ter					
3400	CRTE	60417	3596	0W-28S	D6
3400	CRTE	60475	3596	0W-28S	D6
3400	STGR	60475	3596	0W-28S	D6
W Huntington Commons Rd					
500	DSPN	60016	2861	16W-11N	E3
500	MPPT	60056	2861	16W-11N	E4
Huntingwood Rd					
10	MTSN	60443	3505	7W-24S	D5
Huntleigh Ct					
17900	CCHL	60478	3426	5W-21S	C6
Huntleigh Rd					
10	PSPK	60464	3272	13W-14S	E7
Huntley Ct					
10	CRTE	60417	3597	1E-28S	A6
Huntley Ter					
500	CRTE	60417	3596	0E-28S	E6
700	CRTE	60417	3597	0E-28S	A6
3400	STGR	60417	3597	0E-28S	A6
3400	STGR	60475	3597	0E-28S	A6
Huntley Woods Ct					
800	CRTE	60417	3597	0E-28S	A6
Huntley Woods Dr					
800	CRTE	60417	3597	1E-28S	A5
Huntly					
2100	IVNS	60067	2804	23W-14N	D4
Huntly Ct					
700	SMBG	60194	2857	26W-11N	E4
W Huntmaster Ln					
13100	LMNT	60439	3343	16W-15S	E2
13100	LMNT	60439	3344	16W-15S	A2
Huntsbridge Rd					
10	RchT	60443	3593	8W-26S	B2
Huntsman					
10	LMNT	60439	3272	15W-13S	B5
Hunt Wyck Ct					
1000	ELGN	60120	2855		D2
Huntwyck Ct					
200	SMBG	60173	2859	21W-11N	E3
Hurd Av					
2600	EVTN	60201	2812	4W-13N	D7
2700	WLMT	60091	2812	4W-13N	D7
2700	WLMT	60201	2812	4W-13N	D7
W Hurlbut St					
6500	CHCG	60631	2919	8W-7N	A4
6600	CHCG	60631	2918	8W-7N	E4
Huron Ct					
1000	ELGN	60120	2801		D7
Huron Dr					
800	ELGN	60120	2801		C7
Huron St					
-	BKLY	60163	3028		C3
-	MLPK	60153	3029	10W-0N	E3
-	MLPK	60160	3029	10W-0N	E3
-	MYWD	60153	3029	10W-0N	E3
10	MYWD	60153	3030	10W-0N	A3
400	PKFT	60466	3595	4W-27S	A5
E Huron St					
10	CHCG	60610	3034	0E-0N	C3
10	CHCG	60611	3034	0E-0N	C3

Chicago & Cook County Street Index

Block	City	ZIP	Map#	CGS	Grid
N Huron St					
2200	ANHT	60004	2753	18W-16N	E7
W Huron St					
10	CHCG	60610	3034	0W-0N	A3
10	CHCG	60611	3034	0W-0N	B3
800	CHCG	60622	3033	1W-0N	E3
1900	CHCG	60612	3033	3W-0N	A3
3100	CHCG	60612	3032	4W-0N	D3
3100	CHCG	60624	3032	4W-0N	C3
4600	CHCG	60644	3032	5W-0N	A3
4700	CHCG	60644	3031	7W-0N	C3
5900	OKPK	60302	3031	7W-0N	B3
Hutchings Av					
1100	GNVW	60025	2810	8W-13N	E6
Hutchinson Av					
20500	BlmT	60411	3507	2W-24S	C6
W Hutchinson St					
600	CHCG	60613	2977	1W-5N	E1
600	CHCG	60613	2978		A1
2000	CHCG	60618	2977	2W-5N	B1
3300	CHCG	60618	2976	4W-5N	D1
4400	CHCG	60641	2976	5W-5N	A1
4700	CHCG	60641	2975	6W-5N	E1
5500	CHCG	60634	2975	7W-5N	C1
Hutchison Rd					
-	BlmT	60430	3507	2W-22S	D2
700	FSMR	60422	3507	2W-22S	D2
Huttner Ct					
2000	HFET	60194	2858	26W-12N	A1
Hyacinth Dr					
10100	ODPK	60462	3345	12W-17S	C6
Hyacinth Ln					
100	DRFD	60015	2757	10W-20N	B2
300	MTSN	60443	3593	7W-26S	C2
W Hyacinth St					
6200	CHCG	60646	2919	7W-7N	A3
6300	CHCG	60631	2919	8W-7N	A3
Hyacynth Ln					
900	BRLT	60103	2910		C7
Hyannis Ct					
800	SMBG	60194	2858	24W-10N	D5
Hyde Ct					
2200	SMBG	60194	2857	27W-11N	C3
Hyde Park Av					
10	BLWD	60104	3029	13W-0N	A3
400	HLSD	60162	3029	13W-0N	A5
500	BLWD	60162	3029	13W-0N	A4
N Hyde Park Av					
2600	LydT	60164	2973	13W-3N	A6
E Hyde Park Blvd					
800	CHCG	60615	3152	1E-5S	E1
1000	CHCG	60615	3153	1E-5S	A1
S Hyde Park Blvd					
5100	CHCG	60615	3153	2E-5S	B2
5400	CHCG	60637	3153	2E-6S	B3
Hygate Dr					
1100	ROSL	60172	2912		C5
Hyland Pl					
10200	CHRG	60415	3275	8W-11S	B1
Hyles Blvd					
-	HMND	46320	3352		D6
Hyles Ct					
500	HMND	46320	3352		D7
S Hyslop Pl					
5900	HMND	46320	3430		D1

I

Block	City	ZIP	Map#	CGS	Grid
I-55					
-	BGBK	-	3270		A1
-	BRRG	-	3146		D7
-	DGvT	-	3270		A1
-	DPgT	-	3270		A1
-	IHPK	-	3146		D7
I-55 Joliet Rd					
-	BGBK	-	3270		A1
-	BRRG	-	3146		D7
-	BRRG	-	3208		B1
-	DGvT	-	3270		A1
-	DPgT	-	3270		A1
-	IHPK	-	3146		D7
-	WDRG	-	3270		A1
-	WLBK	-	3208		B1
I-55 Stevenson Expwy					
-	BDPK	-	3147	11W-7S	E6
-	BDPK	-	3148	10W-6S	B4
-	CHCG	-	3089	6W-4S	E6
-	CHCG	-	3090	5W-4S	A6
-	CHCG	-	3091	1W-2S	D3
-	CHCG	-	3092	0E-2S	C2
-	CTSD	-	3146		D7
-	CTSD	-	3147	13W-7S	A7
-	FTVW	-	3089	6W-4S	E7
-	FTVW	-	3148	10W-6S	B4
-	FTVW	-	3149	7W-5S	B1
-	HGKN	-	3147	11W-7S	E6
-	IHPK	-	3146		D7
-	SKNY	-	3089	6W-4S	E6
-	SMMT	-	3148	9W-5S	C2
-	StkT	-	3089	6W-4S	E7
I-57					
-	BLID	-	3277	2W-15S	D7
-	BLID	-	3349	2W-15S	D1
-	BmnT	-	3349	3W-17S	A6
-	BmnT	-	3425	6W-21S	E6
-	BmnT	-	3426	6W-21S	A7
-	CCHL	-	3426	6W-20S	B4
-	CCHL	-	3506	6W-22S	A1
-	CHCG	-	3213	1W-11S	E7
-	CHCG	-	3214	1W-11S	A7
-	CHCG	-	3277	1W-12S	D2
-	ClmT	-	3349	2W-15S	D1
-	CTPK	-	3277	2W-14S	D6
-	DXMR	-	3349	2W-15S	D1
-	MKHM	-	3348	4W-18S	E7
-	MKHM	-	3349	3W-18S	A6
-	MKHM	-	3426	4W-19S	D2
-	MONE	-	3682	7W-32S	D6
-	MonT	-	3593	7W-28S	D7
-	MonT	-	3682	7W-30S	D2
-	MTSN	-	3506	6W-23S	A4
-	MTSN	-	3594	6W-25S	A1
-	OKFT	-	3426	5W-19S	C2
-	POSN	-	3349	3W-17S	C5
-	PtnT	-	3860	11W-39S	B7
-	RchT	-	3426	6W-22S	A7
-	RchT	-	3506	6W-22S	A1
-	RchT	-	3593	7W-28S	D7
-	RNPK	-	3593	6W-26S	E3
-	RNPK	-	3594	6W-26S	A2
-	RVDL	-	3349	3W-17S	B5
-	UYPK	-	3593	7W-28S	D7
-	UYPK	-	3682	7W-29S	D2
I-57 Dan Ryan Expwy					
-	CHCG	-	3214	1W-11S	A7

Block	City	ZIP	Map#	CGS	Grid
I-80					
-	BmnT	-	3426	6W-21S	A6
I-80 Kingery Expwy					
-	LNSG	-	3429	2E-20S	C4
-	LNSG	-	3430		D5
-	MNSR	-	3430	4E-20S	C4
-	ThtT	-	3429	2E-20S	C4
I-80 Moline Expwy					
-	BmnT	-	3425	7W-21S	D7
-	BmnT	-	3426	6W-21S	A6
-	CCHL	-	3426	4W-20S	E4
-	FftT	-	3504	10W-22S	A1
-	HLCT	-	3426	4W-20S	E4
-	HLCT	-	3427	3W-20S	A4
-	MKHM	-	3427	3W-20S	A4
-	MKNA	-	3504	10W-22S	A1
-	RchT	-	3425	7W-21S	D7
-	RchT	-	3505	7W-22S	C1
-	TYPK	-	3504	9W-22S	E1
-	TYPK	-	3505	7W-22S	C1
I-80 Tri State Expwy					
-	HMND	-	3430		D5
-	LNSG	-	3430	4E-20S	C4
-	MNSR	-	3430		D5
I-80 Tri-State Tollway					
-	EHZC	-	3427	2W-20S	D4
-	EHZC	-	3428	1W-20S	A4
-	HLCT	-	3427	2W-20S	C4
-	LNSG	-	3429	1E-20S	C4
-	SHLD	-	3428	0E-20S	E4
-	SHLD	-	3429	1E-20S	A4
-	ThtT	-	3429	1E-20S	A4
-	TNTN	-	3428	0W-20S	C4
I-88 Ronald Reagan Mem Tollway					
-	EMHT	-	3028		C6
-	HLSD	-	3028		C6
-	OKBK	-	3028		B7
-	OKBK	-	3086		A1
-	PvsT	-	3028		C6
-	YkTp	-	3028		B7
-	YkTp	-	3086		B1
I-90 Chicago Skwy					
-	CHCG	-	3152	0E-7S	E6
-	CHCG	-	3153	1E-8S	A7
-	CHCG	-	3215	3E-10S	D4
-	CHCG	-	3216	3E-10S	A6
-	CHCG	-	3280	4E-11S	C1
-	HMND	-	3280	4E-11S	C1
I-90 Chicago Skwy W					
-	CHCG	-	3152	0E-7S	D6
-	CHCG	-	3215	3E-10S	D4
I-90 Dan Ryan Expwy					
-	CHCG	-	3034	0W-1S	A7
-	CHCG	-	3092	0W-3S	B5
-	CHCG	-	3152	0W-6S	B3
I-90 Indiana East-West Toll Rd					
-	CHCG	-	3280		C1
-	HMND	-	3280		C3
-	HMND	-	3352		E4
I-90 Indiana East-W Toll Road					
-	HMND	-	3280		C4
I-90 Kennedy Expwy					
-	CHCG	-	2917	11W-7N	E4
-	CHCG	-	2918	8W-6N	E5
-	CHCG	-	2919	6W-6N	D6
-	CHCG	-	2920	5W-5N	A7
-	CHCG	-	2976	3W-3N	E4
-	CHCG	-	2977	2W-2N	C7
-	CHCG	-	3033	1W-1N	D1
-	CHCG	-	3034	0W-0S	A5
I-90 Kennedy Expwy E					
-	CHCG	-	2919	7W-6N	C6
-	CHCG	-	3034	0W-0S	A5
I-90 Kennedy Expwy W					
-	CHCG	-	3034	0W-0N	A4
I-90 Northwest Tollway					
-	ANHT	-	2860	18W-11N	D3
-	ANHT	-	2861	17W-11N	B4
-	CHCG	-	2916		E1
-	CHCG	-	2917	11W-7N	E4
-	DSPN	-	2861	16W-9N	E6
-	DSPN	-	2862	14W-9N	C7
-	DSPN	-	2916		E1
-	DSPN	-	2917	12W-8N	B2
-	EGvT	-	2860	18W-11N	D3
-	EGvT	-	2861	16W-9N	E6
-	EGvT	-	2862	15W-9N	A7
-	EGVV	-	2861	17W-11N	B4
-	ELGN	-	2801		A7
-	ElgT	-	2801		A7
-	HFET	-	2802	31W-12N	A7
-	HFET	-	2803	27W-12N	C7
-	HFET	-	2804	24W-12N	E7
-	HnrT	-	2801		C7
-	HnrT	-	2802	30W-12N	B7
-	MPPT	-	2861	16W-10N	C6
-	RGMW	-	2859	21W-12N	E1
-	RGMW	-	2860	20W-12N	B1
-	RSMT	-	2916		E1
-	RSMT	-	2917	11W-7N	D4
-	SMBG	-	2804	24W-12N	E7
-	SMBG	-	2805	23W-12N	A7
-	SMBG	-	2859	21W-12N	D1
-	SmbT	-	2805	23W-12N	B7
-	SmbT	-	2859	21W-12N	D1
I-94 Bishop Ford Mem Expwy					
-	CHCG	-	3214	0W-11S	C6
-	CHCG	-	3215	1E-11S	A7
-	CHCG	-	3278	0E-13S	E4
-	CHCG	-	3279	1E-15S	B7
-	CHCG	-	3351	1E-15S	B1
-	CTCY	-	3351	2E-16S	C2
-	DLTN	-	3351	1E-17S	C5
-	SHLD	-	3351	1E-18S	B7
-	SHLD	-	3429	1E-20S	B3
I-94 Dan Ryan Expwy					
-	CHCG	-	3034	0W-1S	A7
-	CHCG	-	3092	0W-3S	B5
-	CHCG	-	3152	0W-7S	C6
-	CHCG	-	3214	0W-10S	C6
I-94 Edens Expwy					
-	CHCG	-	2919	6W-7N	E4
-	CHCG	-	2920	5W-5N	A7
-	GLNC	-	2758	7W-16N	B7
-	GNVW	-	2811	6W-13N	D6
-	LNWD	-	2919	6W-8N	E2
-	MNGV	-	2865	6W-10N	D4
-	NfdT	-	2811	7W-16N	C1
-	NHBK	-	2758	8W-18N	A4
-	NHFD	-	2758	7W-16N	B7
-	NHFD	-	2811	7W-16N	B1
-	NtrT	-	2758	7W-18N	A4

Block	City	ZIP	Map#	CGS	Grid
I-94 Edens Expwy					
-	NtrT	-	2811	6W-14N	D4
-	SKOK	-	2811	6W-13N	E7
-	SKOK	-	2865	6W-9N	D7
-	SKOK	-	2919	6W-8N	E1
-	WLMT	-	2811	6W-13N	D6
I-94 Edens Expressway Spur					
-	DRFD	-	2756	11W-18N	E3
-	DRFD	-	2757	10W-18N	A3
-	NfdT	-	2756	12W-18N	B2
-	NfdT	-	2757	10W-18N	A3
-	NfdT	-	2758	7W-17N	B6
-	NHBK	-	2756	11W-18N	E3
-	NHBK	-	2757	8W-18N	E3
-	NHBK	-	2758	7W-17N	B6
-	WdfT	-	2756	12W-20N	B2
I-94 Edens Expressway Spur E					
-	NfdT	-	2756	12W-20N	B2
-	NfdT	-	2757	10W-18N	A3
-	NHBK	-	2757	8W-18N	E3
-	WdfT	-	2756	12W-20N	B2
I-94 Edens Expressway Spur W					
-	DRFD	-	2756	12W-20N	B1
-	NfdT	-	2757	10W-18N	A3
-	WdfT	-	2756	12W-20N	B1
I-94 Kennedy Expwy					
-	CHCG	-	2920	5W-5N	A7
-	CHCG	-	2976	5W-5N	A1
-	CHCG	-	2977	3W-3N	A5
-	CHCG	-	3033	1W-1N	D1
-	CHCG	-	3034	0W-0N	A4
I-94 Kennedy Expwy E					
-	CHCG	-	3034	0W-0S	A5
I-94 Kennedy Expwy W					
-	CHCG	-	3034	0W-0N	A4
I-94 Kingery Expwy					
-	LNSG	-	3429	3E-20S	E4
-	LNSG	-	3430	3E-20S	A4
-	MNSR	-	3430	4E-20S	C4
-	SHLD	-	3429	1E-18S	B1
-	ThtT	-	3429	1E-20S	C4
I-94 Tri State Expwy					
-	HMND	-	3430		D5
-	LNSG	-	3430	4E-20S	C5
-	MNSR	-	3430		C5
I-94 Tri-State Tollway					
-	DRFD	-	2756	12W-20N	B1
-	WdfT	-	2756	12W-20N	B2
I-190					
-	CHCG	-	2916		E5
-	CHCG	-	2917	12W-7N	B5
-	RSMT	-	2917	11W-7N	E4
I-290					
-	ADSN	-	2914		B7
-	EGvT	-	2860	21W-11N	A3
-	EGvT	-	2914		A1
-	EGVV	-	2914		B3
-	ITSC	-	2914		B5
-	RGMW	-	2860	20W-12N	A1
-	SMBG	-	2860	20W-11N	A3
I-290 Eisenhower Expwy					
-	ADSN	-	2914		B7
-	BDVW	-	3029	11W-0S	E6
-	BKLY	-	3028		C5
-	BLWD	-	3029	11W-0S	C6
-	CHCG	-	3031	7W-0S	C6
-	CHCG	-	3032	4W-0S	E5
-	CHCG	-	3033	1W-0S	D5
-	CHCG	-	3034	0W-0S	A5
-	EMHT	-	2972		A7
-	EMHT	-	3028		B2
-	FTPK	-	3030	10W-0S	A6
-	HLSD	-	3028		E6
-	HLSD	-	3029	13W-0S	A6
-	ITSC	-	2914		B7
-	MYWD	-	3029	12W-0S	B6
-	MYWD	-	3030	10W-0S	A6
-	NHLK	-	3028		B2
-	OKPK	-	3030	8W-0S	E6
-	OKPK	-	3031	8W-0S	A6
-	PvsT	-	3028		C6
-	WSTR	-	3029	12W-0S	B6
I-294 Tri-State Tollway					
-	ALSP	-	3275	7W-13S	B4
-	ALSP	-	3276	5W-15S	A7
-	ALSP	-	3348	5W-15S	B1
-	BGVW	-	3210	9W-10S	C4
-	BKLY	-	3028		C6
-	BmnT	-	3348	3W-17S	E4
-	BmnT	-	3349	3W-17S	B6
-	BRRG	-	3146		D6
-	CHCG	-	2863	12W-9N	C7
-	CHCG	-	2917	12W-6N	B6
-	CHRG	-	3210	9W-11S	E7
-	CHRG	-	3274	8W-11S	E1
-	CHRG	-	3275	8W-12S	A2
-	CTSD	-	3146		E7
-	CTSD	-	3147	13W-8S	A7
-	CTSD	-	3209	12W-8S	B1
-	CTWD	-	3348	5W-15S	C1
-	DRFD	-	2756	12W-20N	B2
-	DSPN	-	2863	12W-10N	C4
-	DSPN	-	2917	12W-8N	C2
-	EHZC	-	3427	2W-20S	D4
-	EHZC	-	3428	0W-20S	C4
-	EMHT	-	3028		C6
-	FNPK	-	2972		C4
-	FNPK	-	2973	12W-4N	A3
-	GNVW	-	2809	11W-13N	C6
-	HGKN	-	3209	12W-8S	C1
-	HLCT	-	3427	2W-20S	C4
-	HLSD	-	3028		C6
-	HNDL	-	3086		C6
-	HNDL	-	3146		D6
-	HYHL	-	3210	10W-9S	B3
-	IHPK	-	3146		D5
-	JSTC	-	3209	11W-9S	E2
-	JSTC	-	3210	10W-9S	B3
-	LNSG	-	3429	1E-20S	C4
-	LydT	-	2972		B5
-	LydT	-	2973	13W-4N	A3
-	LynT	-	3086		C6
-	LynT	-	3146		D4
-	LynT	-	3147	13W-8S	A7
-	LynT	-	3209	12W-8S	B1
-	MaiT	-	2809	11W-13N	C7
-	MaiT	-	2863	12W-12N	C1
-	MDLN	-	3348	4W-16S	D4
-	MKHM	-	3349	3W-18S	B7
-	MKHM	-	3427	3W-19S	B2
-	NfdT	-	2756	12W-17N	A5
-	NfdT	-	2809	11W-14N	C4
-	NHBK	-	2756	12W-18N	B3
-	NHBK	-	2809	12W-16N	C1
-	NHLK	-	2972		C4

Block	City	ZIP	Map#	CGS	Grid
I-294 Tri-State Tollway					
-	NHLK	-	3028		B1
-	OKBK	-	3086		B2
-	PKRG	-	2863	12W-10N	C5
-	POSN	-	3349	3W-18S	B7
-	PvsT	-	3028		C7
-	PvsT	-	3086		C5
-	RBBN	-	3348	4W-16S	D4
-	RSMT	-	2917	12W-8N	C3
-	SHLD	-	3428	0E-20S	E4
-	SHLD	-	3429	1E-20S	A4
-	SRPK	-	2917	12W-6N	C6
-	SRPK	-	2973	12W-4N	A3
-	ThtT	-	3429	1E-20S	B4
-	TNTN	-	3428	0W-20S	C4
-	WdfT	-	2756	13W-17N	A5
-	WhlT	-	2756	12W-18N	A4
-	WLNG	-	2756	12W-18N	A4
-	WLSP	-	3209	12W-8S	C1
-	WNSP	-	3086		C6
-	WNSP	-	3146		C1
-	WRTH	-	3275	8W-12S	A2
-	WthT	-	3275	7W-13S	B5
I-355					
-	ADSN	-	2914		B7
-	ITSC	-	2914		B6
W Ibsen St					
7200	CHCG	60631	2918	9W-8N	D1
7200	NLES	60631	2918	9W-8N	D1
7200	NLES	60714	2918	9W-8N	D1
S Ida Ct					
500	EGvT	60056	2861	16W-10N	E4
500	MPPT	60056	2861	16W-11N	E4
Ida Ln					
9200	MNGV	60053	2865	8W-11N	A2
Ida Pl					
400	GLNC	60022	2758	6W-17N	E5
Ida Rd					
1700	HFET	60195	2858	24W-12N	E1
Ida St					
500	DSPN	60016	2863	13W-11N	A3
Idaho Ct					
18000	ODPK	60467	3423	13W-21S	A7
Idaho Pl					
1500	EGVV	60007	2913		E1
Ideal					
-	MTSN	60443	3505	7W-25S	D7
Idlestone Ln					
10	SMBG	60194	2858	25W-10N	B5
Idle Wild Ct					
100	SMBG	60195	2859	23W-12N	A1
Idlewild Dr					
13500	ODPK	60462	3345	11W-16S	E2
18000	CCHL	60478	3426	5W-21S	C7
Idlewild Ln					
1300	HMWD	60430	3507	2W-22S	D2
1500	BlmT	60430	3507	2W-22S	D2
1800	FSMR	60422	3507	2W-22S	D2
4400	HLSD	60162	3028		E5
Ignace Ct					
12100	HMGN	60441	3422	15W-19S	C2
Iliad Dr					
10	RchT	60423	3505	8W-23S	B4
10	TYPK	60477	3505	8W-23S	B4
Illi Indi Dr					
18400	LNSG	60438	3430	4E-21S	C7
Illinois Av					
10	SMBG	60193	2859	23W-10N	A6
800	ELGN	60120	2855		B7
E Illinois Av					
10	PLTN	60067	2805	20W-15N	E3
200	PLTN	60067	2806	20W-15N	A3
200	RGMW	60008	2805	20W-14N	E3
200	RGMW	60008	2806	20W-15N	A3
300	PLTN	60008	2806	20W-14N	A3
N Illinois Av					
-	GNWD	60430	3428	1W-22S	A7
200	GNWD	60425	3508	1W-22S	A1
200	HMWD	60425	3508	1W-22S	A1
500	GNWD	60425	3428	1W-22S	A7
500	HMWD	60425	3428	1W-22S	A7
500	HMWD	60430	3428	1W-22S	A7
900	ANHT	60005	2806	18W-14N	D3
1200	ANHT	60004	2806	18W-15N	D2
2100	ANHT	60004	2753	18W-16N	D7
W Illinois Av					
10	PLTN	60067	2805	21W-15N	C3
1300	IVNS	60067	2805	22W-14N	A3
Illinois Blvd					
10	HFET	60193	2858	24W-10N	E5
200	HFET	60194	2858	24W-10N	E4
600	HFET	60194	2859	23W-11N	A4
Illinois Ct					
10	PKFT	60466	3595	3W-25S	B1
200	ELGN	60120	2855		B4
10500	ODPK	60467	3423	13W-21S	A7
S Illinois Dr					
200	ANHT	60005	2806	18W-13N	D5
Illinois Rd					
400	WLMT	60091	2812	5W-13N	A5
1800	NfdT	60062	2757	9W-17N	B6
1800	NHBK	60062	2757	9W-17N	B6
2500	NHBK	60062	2756	10W-17N	E6
2600	NtrT	60091	2812	5W-14N	A5
2600	NtrT	60093	2812	5W-14N	A4
2600	WLMT	60093	2812	5W-14N	A4
2800	NtrT	60093	2811	5W-14N	E4
2800	WLMT	60093	2811	5W-14N	E4
3100	NHFD	60091	2811	6W-14N	D4
3400	NHFD	60093	2811	6W-14N	D4
3400	WLMT	60091	2811	6W-14N	D4
Illinois St					
-	BmT	60010	2751	25W-18N	A3
-	BRTN	60010	2751	25W-18N	A3
10	BlmT	60411	3598	4E-26S	C2
10	CHHT	60411	3596	1W-25S	B1
10	DYR	46311	3598		C2
10	DYR	60411	3598	4E-26S	C2
10	ROSL	60172	2913		A3
100	BrnT	60010	2750	25W-18N	E3
100	BRTN	60010	2750	25W-18N	E3
100	CHHT	60411	3595	2W-25S	C1
100	PKFT	60466	3595	4W-25S	A1
400	CPVL	60118	2801		A1
400	EDND	60118	2801		A1
500	PKFT	60466	3594	4W-25S	E1
1400	SMBG	60193	2913		A2
1400	SmbT	60193	2913		A2
1500	ROSL	60193	2913		A2
1600	DSPN	60018	2863	13W-9N	A6
3100	LNSG	60438	3430	3E-21S	B7
E Illinois St					
10	CHCG	60610	3034	0E-0N	C3
10	CHCG	60611	3034	0E-0N	C3
100	LMNT	60439	3270		E5

Block	City	ZIP	Map#	CGS	Grid
N Illinois St					
200	EMHT	60126	3028		A1
S Illinois St					
13700	RVDL	60827	3350	0W-15S	C2
14500	DLTN	60419	3350	0W-16S	B4
W Illinois St					
10	CHCG	60610	3034	0W-0N	A3
10	CHCG	60611	3034	0W-0N	B3
Ill Prairie Pth					
-	BRLT	60103	2909		E3
-	BRLT	60103	2910		A2
-	ELGN	60103	2909		E3
W Imlay St					
6500	CHCG	60631	2919	8W-8N	A2
6600	CHCG	60631	2918	8W-7N	D3
Imperial Av					
1300	CTCY	60409	3430	3E-19S	A2
Imperial Ct					
2900	FSMR	60422	3507	3W-22S	A2
22600	RNPK	60471	3593	6W-27S	E4
W Imperial Ct					
10	PLTN	60067	2805	21W-15N	D2
1600	EGvT	60056	2861	16W-10N	D4
1600	MPPT	60056	2861	16W-10N	C4
Imperial Dr					
1500	GNVW	60025	2809	10W-14N	E4
5200	RNPK	60471	3594	6W-27S	A3
5300	RNPK	60471	3593	6W-27S	E3
Imperial Ln					
11700	ODPK	60467	3422	14W-21S	D7
18200	FftT	60448	3422	14W-21S	D7
Imperial St					
10	CHCG	60631	2918	9W-8N	B2
10	PKRG	60068	2918	9W-8N	B2
Independence Av					
1500	GNVW	60025	2810	9W-14N	C5
5600	OKFT	60452	3347	7W-18S	D7
Independence Blvd					
24400	CRTE	60417	3685	1W-29S	A2
S Independence Blvd					
500	CHCG	60624	3032	4W-0S	C6
1300	CHCG	60623	3032	4W-0S	D6
Independence Ct					
1700	MPPT	60056	2808	13W-14N	D4
15700	OKFT	60452	3347	7W-18S	D7
E Independence Ct					
600	ANHT	60005	2861	17W-11N	B2
Independence Dr					
10	CHHT	60411	3596	1W-25S	A1
1000	BRLT	60103	2910		D7
8100	WLSP	60480	3208		D3
E Independence Dr					
600	PLTN	60074	2753	20W-18N	B2
S Indian Ct					
20200	FftT	60423	3504	10W-24S	C5
Indian Dr					
1100	ELGN	60120	2855		C1
Indian Ln					
100	DndT	60110	2748		A6
1400	CPVL	60110	2748		C4
7300	JSTC	60458	3209	11W-8S	E1
Indian Rd					
1000	GNVW	60025	2811	6W-13N	C6
N Indian Rd					
6000	CHCG	60646	2919	7W-7N	B3
Indian Wy					
600	BRTN	60010	2751	24W-20N	C1
Indiana Av					
-	BNHM	60633	3352	3E-16S	A3
1300	BlmT	60411	3508	0E-25S	D7
1300	CHHT	60411	3508	0E-25S	D7
1900	LNSG	60438	3429	2E-21S	D6
1900	ThtT	60438	3429	2E-21S	D6
2600	LNSG	60438	3430	3E-21S	A6
14600	DLTN	60419	3350	0E-17S	D5
14600	DLTN	60827	3350	0E-17S	D4
14600	RVDL	60827	3350	0E-17S	D4
14900	SHLD	60419	3350	0W-17S	D5
14900	SHLD	60473	3350	0W-17S	D5
E Indiana Av					
10	BCHR	60401	3864	0E-36S	E2
10	WshT	60401	3864	0E-36S	E2
S Indiana Av					
1200	CHCG	60605	3034	0E-1S	C7
1500	CHCG	60616	3034	0E-1S	C7
1600	CHCG	60616	3092	0E-2S	C2
3400	CHCG	60653	3092	0E-3S	C4
4600	CHCG	60615	3092	0E-4S	C7
4700	CHCG	60615	3152	0E-5S	C1
5400	CHCG	60637	3152	0E-6S	C4
7000	CHCG	60619	3152	0E-8S	C7
7500	CHCG	60619	3214	0E-11S	C6
9400	CHCG	60628	3214	0E-11S	C6
10300	CHCG	60628	3278	0E-13S	D3
12900	RVDL	60827	3278	0W-15S	D7
13000	CHCG	60827	3278	0W-15S	D7
13100	CHCG	60827	3350	0W-15S	D2
13400	RVDL	60827	3350	0W-16S	D4
13700	DLTN	60419	3350	0W-16S	D4
13700	RVDL	60419	3350	0W-16S	D4
14500	DLTN	60827	3350	0E-17S	D4
W Indiana Av					
10	BCHR	60401	3864	0W-36S	D2
10	WshT	60401	3864	0W-36S	D2
Indiana Cir					
20900	OMFD	60461	3507	3W-25S	A7
Indiana Ct					
17900	ODPK	60467	3423	12W-21S	C7
Indiana Ln					
700	EGVV	60007	2913		E2
Indiana Pkwy					
9700	MNSR	46321	3510		D3
Indiana St					
100	DYR	46311	3598		D2
100	OMFD	60461	3507	4W-25S	A7
100	PKFT	60461	3507	4W-25S	A7
100	PKFT	60466	3507	4W-25S	A7
100	PKFT	60466	3595	4W-25S	A1
E Indiana St					
800	HMND	46320	3352		E6
N Indiana St					
200	AddT	60126	2972		A7
200	EMHT	60126	2972		A7
200	EMHT	60126	3028		A1
W Indiana St					
1000	GNWD	60425	3428	1W-22S	A7
Indiana East-West Toll Rd					
-	CHCG	-	3280		C1
-	HMND	-	3280		D4
-	HMND	-	3352		D1
Indiana East-West Toll Rd I-90					
-	CHCG	-	3280		C1
-	HMND	-	3280		D4
-	HMND	-	3352		D1

STREET Block	City	ZIP	Map#	CGS	Grid
Indiana East-West Toll Road					
-	HMND	-	3280		C4
Indiana East-W Toll Road					
I-90					
-	HMND	-	3280		C4
S Indianapolis Av					
-	CHCG	60617	3280	4E-11S	C1
10000	CHCG	60617	3216	4E-11S	B7
10600	CHCG	46320	3280	4E-11S	C1
10600	HMND	46320	3280	4E-12S	C1
S Indianapolis Av US-12					
-	CHCG	60617	3280	4E-11S	C1
-	HMND	46320	3280	4E-11S	C1
10000	CHCG	60617	3216	4E-11S	B7
10600	CHCG	46320	3280	4E-11S	C1
S Indianapolis Av US-20					
-	CHCG	46320	3280	4E-11S	C1
-	CHCG	60617	3280	4E-11S	C1
-	HMND	46320	3280	4E-11S	C1
10000	CHCG	60617	3216	4E-11S	B7
S Indianapolis Av US-41					
-	CHCG	46320	3280	4E-11S	C1
-	CHCG	60617	3280	4E-11S	C1
-	HMND	46320	3280	4E-11S	C1
10000	CHCG	60617	3216	4E-11S	B7
S Indianapolis Blvd					
1000	HMND	46320	3280		D3
1000	HMND	46394	3280		D3
10500	CHCG	46320	3280	4E-12S	C1
10500	CHCG	60617	3280		C1
S Indianapolis Blvd US-12					
1000	HMND	46320	3280		D3
1000	HMND	46394	3280		D3
10500	CHCG	46320	3280	4E-12S	C1
10500	CHCG	60617	3280		C1
S Indianapolis Blvd US-20					
1000	HMND	46320	3280		D3
1000	HMND	46394	3280		D3
10500	CHCG	46320	3280	4E-12S	C1
10500	CHCG	60617	3280		C1
S Indianapolis Blvd US-41					
1000	HMND	46320	3280		D3
1000	HMND	46394	3280		D3
10500	CHCG	46320	3280	4E-12S	C1
10500	CHCG	60617	3280		C1
Indian Boundary Dr					
-	MLPK	60165	3029	12W-2N	C1
-	SNPK	60165	3029	12W-2N	C1
1900	MLPK	60160	2973	12W-2N	C7
1900	MLPK	60160	3029	12W-2N	C1
N Indian Boundary Rd					
2700	RVGV	60171	2973	10W-3N	E5
2800	RVGV	60171	2974	10W-3N	B5
Indianhead Ct					
6300	IHPK	60525	3146		E5
Indianhead Tr					
6300	IHPK	60525	3146		E5
Indian Hill Av					
1400	HRPK	60133	2911		D3
Indian Hill Ct					
1400	HRPK	60133	2911		E3
Indian Hill Dr					
200	BFGV	60089	2754	17W-18N	A3
1200	BNVL	60106	2915		C4
1200	EGVV	60106	2915		C3
1200	SMBG	60193	2913		A2
1400	SmbT	60172	2913		A2
1400	SmbT	60193	2913		A2
1500	EGVV	60007	2915		C4
4000	CCHL	60478	3426	5W-20S	C5
S Indian Hill Dr					
1600	SmbT	60172	2913		A3
1600	SmbT	60193	2913		A3
1700	ROSL	60172	2913		A3
Indian Hill Rd					
10	KLWH	60043	2812	4W-14N	B4
10	NtrT	60043	2812	4W-14N	B4
10	NtrT	60093	2812	4W-15N	B3
10	WLMT	60091	2812	5W-14N	A4
10	WNKA	60093	2812	4W-15N	B3
400	DRFD	60015	2756	11W-20N	C1
N Indian Hill Rd					
10	NtrT	60093	2812	5W-14N	B3
10	WNKA	60093	2812	5W-14N	B3
Indian Joe Dr					
2800	BDVW	60154	3029	12W-0S	C6
2800	BDVW	60155	3029	12W-0S	C6
2800	WSTR	60154	3029	12W-0S	C6
Indian Ridge Ct					
2500	GNVW	60025	2809	11W-15N	D2
Indian Ridge Dr					
2300	GNVW	60025	2809	11W-15N	C3
2500	GNVW	60062	2809	11W-15N	C2
Indian Spring Ln					
500	BFGV	60089	2754	17W-20N	B1
Indian Trail Dr					
500	PlsT	60464	3273	12W-14S	C7
Indian Trail Rd					
1100	HNDL	60521	3086		B6
Indian Tree Dr					
10	GLNC	60022	2758	7W-20N	B2
10	HDPK	60022	2758	7W-20N	B2
10	HDPK	60035	2758	7W-20N	B2
Indian Wells Ln					
3600	NHBK	60062	2756	12W-17N	B4
Indianwood Blvd					
10	PKFT	60466	3595	3W-27S	B4
400	MonT	60466	3595	4W-28S	A6
Indianwood Dr					
10	TNTN	60476	3428	0E-20S	E5
Indianwood Ln					
100	IHPK	60525	3146		D5
100	LynT	60525	3146		D5
Indianwood Rd					
2900	WLMT	60091	2811	5W-14N	E5
Indian Woods Dr					
11100	BRRG	60527	3208		E1
11100	IHPK	60527	3208		E1
Indie Ct					
18500	HLCT	60429	3506	4W-22S	D1
Indie Ln					
22300	SLVL	60411	3597	1E-27S	A4
22300	STGR	60411	3597	1E-27S	A4
Indigo Ct					
-	BmdT	60172	2912		A6
-	HRPK	60133	2912		A6
N Indigo Ct					
1700	MPPT	60056	2808	13W-14N	D3
Indigo Dr					
10	SjnT	46311	3598		C6
N Indigo Dr					
1300	MPPT	60056	2808	13W-14N	D4
Indigo Ln					
2300	GNVW	60025	2810	9W-14N	C5

STREET Block	City	ZIP	Map#	CGS	Grid
Indi Illi Pkwy					
6700	CTCY	46324	3430	4E-19S	C3
6700	CTCY	60409	3430	4E-19S	C3
6700	HMND	46324	3430	4E-19S	C3
Industrial Av					
3600	ANHT	60005	2806	20W-15N	B3
3600	RGMW	60005	2806	20W-14N	A3
3600	RGMW	60008	2806	20W-15N	B3
3700	PLTN	60008	2806	20W-15N	C1
3700	PLTN	60067	2806	20W-14N	A3
Industrial Dr					
-	RVDL	60827	3350	1W-15S	A2
-	UYPK	60466	3682	7W-29S	D2
400	BNVL	60106	2915		D5
1300	ITSC	60143	2914		E6
7400	FTPK	60130	3088	9W-1S	C1
8500	JSTC	60458	3210	10W-9S	A3
9600	BGVW	60455	3210	9W-11S	D6
9600	HYHL	60457	3210	9W-11S	D6
W Industrial Dr					
5800	MONE	60449	3682	7W-31S	D6
5900	MonT	60449	3682	7W-31S	D6
Industrial Ln					
200	WhlT	60090	2755	13W-16N	E6
200	WLNG	60090	2755	13W-16N	D6
Industrial Rd					
10	CTCY	46320	3352		C5
10	CTCY	60409	3352		C5
10	HMND	46320	3352		C5
Industrial Park Dr					
16400	LmnT	60439	3270		C5
Ingalls Dr					
10	HRVY	60426	3349	2W-18S	D7
Ingleside Av					
14200	DLTN	60419	3351	1E-16S	A4
15400	DLTN	60473	3351	1E-18S	A7
15400	SHLD	60473	3351	1E-18S	A7
16300	SHLD	60473	3429	1E-19S	A2
S Ingleside Av					
200	GNWD	60425	3509	1E-23S	A3
5100	CHCG	60615	3152	1E-5S	E2
5500	CHCG	60637	3152	1E-6S	E3
7300	CHCG	60619	3152	1E-8S	E7
7500	CHCG	60619	3214	1E-8S	E1
9700	CHCG	60628	3214	1E-11S	E6
13100	CHCG	60827	3351	0E-15S	A1
Ingleside Ct					
16900	SHLD	60473	3429	1E-20S	A3
Ingleside Pk					
500	EVTN	60201	2813	2W-13N	B7
Ingleside Pl					
500	EVTN	60201	2813	2W-13N	B7
Inglewood Ln					
1000	ELGN	60120	2855		C2
Ingraham Av					
300	CTCY	60409	3352	4E-17S	C6
Ingram Pl					
800	DSPN	60016	2862	15W-10N	B4
Ingram St					
200	NHFD	60093	2811	7W-15N	A3
Ingrid Ln					
1600	CHHT	60411	3595	2W-25S	C1
Inland Dr					
300	WLNG	60090	2755	13W-17N	D5
W Inland Dr					
-	ALSP	60803	3276	5W-15S	B7
-	ALSP	60803	3348	5W-15S	B1
Inner Cir Dr					
10	DSPN	60016	2862	15W-12N	B2
100	MPPT	60016	2862	15W-12N	B2
100	MPPT	60056	2862	15W-12N	B2
S Inner Cir Dr					
500	DSPN	60016	2862	13W-11N	D2
500	MPPT	60016	2862	13W-11N	D2
500	MPPT	60056	2862	13W-11N	D2
Innisbrook Ln					
14700	HMGN	60441	3343	17W-17S	C5
Innishmor Ct					
11700	ODPK	60467	3422	14W-21S	D6
Innsbrook Dr					
100	HnrT	60107	2910		E1
100	SMWD	60107	2910		E1
15500	ODPK	60462	3346	9W-18S	C7
15600	ODPK	60462	3424	9W-18S	C1
Innsbruck Ln					
3400	CRTE	60417	3596	0E-28S	E5
3400	STGR	60417	3596	0E-28S	E5
3400	STGR	60475	3596	0E-28S	E5
S Insignia Ct					
10	PLTN	60067	2805	20W-14N	E3
W Institute Pl					
200	CHCG	60610	3034	0W-1N	A2
W Interlochen Ct					
8500	PSHL	60465	3274	10W-12S	B1
S Interlochen Dr					
10300	PSHL	60465	3274	10W-12S	A1
International St					
-	BRRG	60527	3146		A7
Internationale Pkwy					
1000	DGvT	60439	3270		C2
1000	WDRG	60439	3270		C2
1600	WDRG	60517	3270		A2
Interocean Av					
10	SCHT	60411	3596	1W-26S	A2
Interurban Av					
19300	BlmT	60411	3508	1W-23S	B3
19300	HMWD	60411	3508	1W-23S	B3
19300	HMWD	60425	3508	1W-23S	B3
19400	CHHT	60411	3508	1W-23S	B3
Inverary Dr					
7600	FftT	60423	3504	9W-25S	E7
Inverdale Dr					
400	IVNS	60010	2751	23W-16N	D6
Inverness Ct					
100	EGVV	60007	2859	22W-9N	D7
20000	OMFD	60461	3507	3W-24S	B5
Inverness Dr					
1200	ELGN	60120	2855		D5
13500	ODPK	60462	3346	11W-16S	A2
17100	ODHL	60477	3424	11W-20S	A4
17100	TYPK	60477	3424	11W-20S	A5
Inverness Ln					
-	CRTE	60417	3686	0E-29S	A1
-	CteT	60417	3686	0E-29S	A1
1000	ITSC	60143	2914		D5
1200	AddT	60143	2914		D5
2100	GNVW	60025	2810	10W-14N	A3
3500	CRTE	60417	3596	0E-28S	E6
3500	CRTE	60417	3597	0E-28S	A6
W Inverness Ln					
7400	FftT	60423	3504	9W-23S	E4
Inverrary Ln					
100	VrnT	60015	2755	15W-20N	B1
1200	PLTN	60074	2753	19W-18N	C4

STREET Block	City	ZIP	Map#	CGS	Grid
Inverray Rd					
2100	IVNS	60067	2804	23W-15N	D1
Inverway					
10	IVNS	60067	2805	22W-16N	A1
200	IVNS	60067	2751	23W-16N	E7
600	IVNS	60067	2752	23W-16N	A6
Inwood Dr					
200	PTHT	60070	2808	14W-15N	B2
200	PTHT	60090	2808	14W-15N	B2
200	WLNG	60070	2808	14W-15N	B2
200	WLNG	60090	2808	14W-15N	B2
S I-Oka Av					
10	MPPT	60056	2807	16W-12N	E7
200	MPPT	60056	2861	16W-12N	E1
Iona Av					
9700	FNPK	60131	2973	12W-4N	C3
Ionia Av					
3400	OMFD	60461	3506	4W-24S	E6
N Ionia Av					
6000	CHCG	60646	2920	5W-7N	A3
6400	LNWD	60712	2919	6W-8N	D2
6500	CHCG	60712	2919	6W-8N	D2
6700	NLES	60646	2919	6W-8N	C2
6700	SKOK	60646	2919	6W-8N	C2
6800	CHCG	60646	2919	7W-8N	B1
Iota Ct					
1200	WLNG	60090	2754	16W-18N	E2
Iowa Ct					
17900	ODPK	60467	3423	12W-21S	C7
Iowa Dr					
1600	EGVV	60007	2913		D2
Iowa St					
-	MYWD	60153	3029	10W-1N	E3
-	MYWD	60153	3030	10W-1N	A3
10	CHCG	60302	3031	8W-1N	A2
10	CHCG	60651	3031	8W-1N	A2
10	OKPK	60302	3031	8W-1N	A2
700	OKPK	60302	3030	8W-1N	E3
1000	MLPK	60160	3029	11W-1N	D3
7200	RVFT	60305	3030	9W-1N	C2
W Iowa St					
-	HMWD	60425	3508	1W-22S	A1
500	CHCG	60610	3034	0W-1N	A2
1000	GNWD	60425	3508	1W-22S	A1
1800	CHCG	60622	3033	3W-1N	A2
3300	CHCG	60651	3032	5W-1N	B2
4700	CHCG	60651	3031	7W-1N	C2
5900	CHCG	60302	3031	7W-1N	B2
5900	OKPK	60302	3031	7W-1N	B2
Ipswich Ct					
600	EGVV	60007	2860	19W-9N	D7
600	EGVV	60007	2914		D1
N Irene Av					
3200	CHCG	60618	2976	3W-4N	D3
Irene Dr					
6000	HFET	60120	2855		E1
N Irene Dr					
2300	DRPK	60074	2752	21W-18N	E2
2300	PltT	60074	2752	21W-18N	E2
Irenes Courtyard					
7000	TYPK	60477	3425	8W-19S	A2
Iris Av					
7200	HRPK	60133	2911		D1
Iris Ct					
3100	NHBK	60062	2756	11W-16N	D7
Iris Dr					
200	SMWD	60107	2857	27W-10N	C6
N Iris Dr					
1800	PLTN	60074	2753	19W-18N	B3
Iris Ln					
300	CHHT	60411	3507	1W-23S	E3
300	HDPK	60035	2758	7W-20N	C1
2400	DSPN	60018	2917	12W-8N	B1
S Iron St					
3200	CHCG	60608	3091	1W-3S	D5
3200	CHCG	60609	3091	1W-3S	D5
W Ironwood Cir					
13700	HMGN	60441	3343	17W-17S	D5
Ironwood Ct					
10	SMWD	60107	2857	27W-11N	C3
100	RGMW	60008	2805	21W-14N	D5
600	WLNG	60090	2754	16W-18N	D3
1100	ELGN	60120	2855		D1
1200	SMBG	60193	2859	22W-10N	D6
Ironwood Dr					
400	DSPN	60016	2863	11W-11N	D3
600	EGVV	60007	2861	17W-9N	A6
1000	ELGN	60120	2855		D1
16300	TYPK	60477	3424	10W-19S	B3
E Ironwood Dr					
1300	MPPT	60056	2808	14W-14N	C5
N Ironwood Dr					
600	ANHT	60004	2807	16W-14N	D4
Ironwood Ln					
9400	DSPN	60016	2863	11W-11N	D2
9400	MaiT	60016	2863	11W-11N	D2
N Ironwood Pl					
900	MPPT	60056	2808	14W-14N	C5
Iroquois Ct					
1200	BNVL	60106	2915		C3
Iroquois Dr					
900	ELGN	60120	2855		B1
2300	GNVW	60025	2809	11W-15N	C3
Iroquois Ln					
1300	BNVL	60106	2915		C3
Iroquois Rd					
200	HLSD	60162	3028		D5
2600	WLMT	60091	2812	5W-14N	A5
2900	WLMT	60091	2811	5W-14N	E5
S Iroquois Rd					
12400	PSPK	60464	3274	10W-14S	B7
W Iroquois Rd					
8400	PSPK	60464	3274	10W-14S	B6
Iroquois St					
100	PKFT	60466	3595	3W-27S	A5
W Iroquois Tr					
13400	HMGN	60441	3343	16W-16S	D3
Iroquois Trc					
8000	TYPK	60477	3424	10W-21S	C6
Irvine Ct					
400	WLNG	60090	2754	16W-17N	D5
Irving Av					
11900	CHCG	60406	3277	2W-14S	C6
11900	CHCG	60643	3277	2W-14S	C6
12500	BLID	60406	3277	2W-15S	C7
13100	BLID	60406	3349	2W-15S	C1
14100	DLTN	60419	3350	0E-16S	E3
14400	ODPK	60462	3345	12W-17S	C5
15300	SHLD	60473	3350	0E-17S	E6
15900	MKHM	60426	3427	2W-19S	C2
15900	ThtT	60426	3427	2W-19S	C2
N Irving Av					
10	PvsT	60162	3028		D6
700	HLSD	60162	3028		D4
800	BKLY	60162	3028		D4

STREET Block	City	ZIP	Map#	CGS	Grid
N Irving Av					
1200	BKLY	60163	3028		D3
S Irving Av					
100	NHLK	60164	3028		D1
Irving Blvd					
200	CHHT	60411	3507	1W-25S	E7
Irving Pl					
500	UYPK	60466	3684	3W-30S	B3
Irving Park Rd					
-	CHCG	60176	2973	11W-5N	D2
-	CHCG	60634	2973	11W-5N	D2
-	CHCG	60666	2973	13W-5N	A1
-	ELGN	60120	2855		E5
-	FNPK	60666	2973	13W-5N	A1
-	HnrT	60120	2855		E5
-	ROSL	60172	2913		C5
-	SRPK	60666	2973	12W-5N	A1
10	BmdT	60143	2913		C5
10	BmdT	60143	2914		A6
10	BmdT	60157	2913		D5
10	HnrT	60120	2856	31W-10N	A5
10	ITSC	60143	2914		A6
100	HnrT	60107	2856	30W-10N	C6
100	SMWD	60107	2856	30W-10N	C6
100	SMWD	60120	2856	30W-10N	C6
300	BmdT	60172	2913		C5
400	ITSC	60143	2913		E6
800	HRPK	60133	2912		A2
800	SMBG	60133	2912		A2
1200	HRPK	60133	2911		D1
1600	ELGN	60120	2856	31W-10N	A5
1700	SMWD	60107	2911		D1
1700	SMWD	60133	2911		D1
9200	SRPK	60176	2973	11W-5N	D2
Irving Park Rd SR-19					
-	CHCG	60176	2973	11W-5N	D2
-	CHCG	60634	2973	11W-5N	D2
-	CHCG	60666	2973	12W-5N	A1
-	ELGN	60120	2855		E5
-	FNPK	60666	2973	13W-5N	A1
-	HnrT	60120	2855		E5
-	ROSL	60172	2913		C5
-	SRPK	60666	2973	12W-5N	A1
10	BmdT	60143	2913		C5
10	BmdT	60143	2914		A6
10	BmdT	60157	2913		D5
10	HnrT	60120	2856	31W-10N	A5
10	ITSC	60143	2914		A6
100	HnrT	60107	2856	30W-10N	C6
100	SMWD	60107	2856	30W-10N	C6
100	SMWD	60120	2856	30W-10N	C6
300	BmdT	60172	2913		C5
400	ITSC	60143	2913		E6
800	HRPK	60133	2912		A2
800	SMBG	60133	2912		A2
1200	HRPK	60133	2911		D1
1600	ELGN	60120	2856	31W-10N	A5
1700	SMWD	60107	2911		D1
1700	SMWD	60133	2911		D1
9200	SRPK	60176	2973	11W-5N	D2
E Irving Park Rd					
10	BNVL	60106	2972		A1
10	ROSL	60172	2913		B4
10	SMWD	60107	2857	28W-9N	A7
100	ITSC	60143	2914		D6
100	WDDL	60191	2915		B7
300	SMWD	60107	2911		C1
400	BmdT	60172	2913		C5
400	BNVL	60106	2915		C7
900	CHCG	60131	2972		B1
900	HRPK	60107	2911		C1
1000	HRPK	60133	2911		C1
1000	SMWD	60133	2911		C1
1100	BNVL	60131	2972		C1
1100	CHCG	60106	2972		C1
1100	WDDL	60143	2914		D7
1200	WDDL	60191	2914		D7
1300	ITSC	60191	2914		E7
11500	CHCG	60666	2972		C1
E Irving Park Rd SR-19					
10	BNVL	60106	2972		A1
10	ROSL	60172	2913		B4
10	SMWD	60107	2857	28W-9N	A7
100	ITSC	60143	2914		D6
100	WDDL	60191	2915		B7
300	SMWD	60107	2911		C1
400	BmdT	60172	2913		C5
400	BNVL	60106	2915		C7
900	CHCG	60131	2972		B1
900	HRPK	60107	2911		C1
1000	HRPK	60133	2911		C1
1000	SMWD	60133	2911		C1
1100	BNVL	60131	2972		C1
1100	CHCG	60106	2972		C1
1100	WDDL	60143	2914		D7
1200	WDDL	60191	2914		D7
1300	ITSC	60191	2914		E7
11500	CHCG	60666	2972		C1
W Irving Park Rd					
-	BmdT	60143	2914		A6
-	BNVL	60131	2972		C1
-	CHCG	60176	2973	10W-5N	E2
-	CHCG	60634	2973	10W-5N	E2
-	FNPK	60131	2972		E1
-	FNPK	60666	2972		D2
-	HnrT	60107	2856	29W-10N	D6
-	HnrT	60120	2856	29W-10N	D6
-	SMWD	60120	2856	29W-10N	D6
10	BNVL	60106	2915		C7
10	ROSL	60172	2913		A4
10	SMWD	60107	2856	29W-9N	E7
100	ROSL	60172	2912		E4
100	WDDL	60191	2915		A7
200	ITSC	60143	2914		A6
200	WDDL	60191	2914		E7
400	ITSC	60191	2914		E7
400	SMBG	60172	2912		D3
400	SMBG	60193	2912		D3
600	CHCG	60613	2978	0W-5N	A1
700	CHCG	60613	2977	2W-5N	C1
700	SmbT	60193	2912		D3
1400	BmdT	60143	2913		E6
1400	ITSC	60143	2913		E6
1800	SMBG	60133	2912		B2
1900	CHCG	60618	2977	2W-5N	B1
1900	HRPK	60133	2912		B2
2700	CHCG	60618	2976	3W-5N	E1
3900	CHCG	60641	2976	5W-4N	A2
4600	CHCG	60641	2975	7W-5N	B2
5500	CHCG	60634	2975	6W-5N	C2
6600	CHCG	60634	2974	8W-4N	E2
7100	NRDG	60634	2974	8W-5N	D2
7100	NRDG	60706	2974	8W-5N	D2
7500	CHCG	60706	2974	9W-5N	C2
11000	CHCG	60131	2972		C2

STREET Block	City	ZIP	Map#	CGS	Grid
W Irving Park Rd					
11000	CHCG	60666	2972		C2
11000	LydT	60131	2972		C2
W Irving Park Rd SR-19					
-	BmdT	60143	2914		A6
-	BNVL	60131	2972		C1
-	CHCG	60131	2972		C1
-	CHCG	60176	2973	10W-5N	E2
-	CHCG	60634	2973	10W-5N	E2
-	CHCG	60666	2972		D2
-	FNPK	60131	2972		E1
-	FNPK	60666	2972		D2
-	HnrT	60107	2856	29W-10N	D6
-	HnrT	60120	2856	29W-10N	D6
-	SMWD	60120	2856	29W-10N	D6
10	BNVL	60106	2915		C7
10	ROSL	60172	2913		A4
10	SMWD	60107	2856	29W-9N	E7
100	ROSL	60172	2912		E4
100	WDDL	60191	2915		A7
200	ITSC	60143	2914		A6
200	WDDL	60191	2914		E7
400	ITSC	60191	2914		E7
400	SMBG	60172	2912		D3
400	SMBG	60193	2912		D3
600	CHCG	60613	2978	0W-5N	A1
700	CHCG	60613	2977	2W-5N	C1
700	SmbT	60193	2912		D3
1400	BmdT	60143	2913		E6
1400	ITSC	60143	2913		E6
1800	SMBG	60133	2912		B2
1900	CHCG	60618	2977	2W-5N	B1
1900	HRPK	60133	2912		B2
2700	CHCG	60618	2976	3W-5N	D1
3900	CHCG	60641	2976	5W-4N	A2
4600	CHCG	60641	2975	7W-5N	B2
5500	CHCG	60634	2975	6W-5N	C2
6600	CHCG	60634	2974	8W-4N	E2
7100	NRDG	60634	2974	8W-5N	D2
7100	NRDG	60706	2974	8W-5N	D2
7500	CHCG	60706	2974	9W-5N	C2
Irvington Ct					
500	BRLT	60103	2911		A4
500	WynT	60103	2911		A4
Irwin Av					
1000	DSPN	60018	2862	13W-9N	E7
2300	PKRG	60068	2863	11W-9N	C7
Isa Av					
10	CHHT	60411	3508	1W-25S	B7
Isa Dr					
400	WLNG	60090	2755	15W-17N	A5
Isabell St					
3800	SKOK	60076	2866	4W-10N	B5
Isabella St					
200	EVTN	60201	2813	3W-13N	A7
200	WLMT	60091	2813	3W-13N	A7
300	EVTN	60091	2813	2W-13N	A7
400	WLMT	60201	2813	3W-13N	A7
600	EVTN	60091	2812	3W-13N	E7
600	EVTN	60201	2812	3W-13N	E7
800	WLMT	60201	2812	3W-13N	E7
3400	WLMT	60091	2812	4W-13N	B7
E Isabella St					
-	MPPT	60056	2808	15W-13N	A6
W Isabella St					
-	MPPT	60056	2808	15W-13N	A6
800	MPPT	60056	2807	15W-13N	E6
W Isham Av					
7400	CHCG	60631	2918	9W-8N	C2
Ishnala Dr					
13500	ODPK	60462	3346	9W-16S	D2
W Ishnala Dr					
7200	PSHT	60463	3274	9W-15S	E7
7200	PSHT	60463	3346	9W-15S	D1
Island Ct					
-	SMBG	60193	2857	27W-10N	D6
800	DRFD	60015	2756	11W-20N	E1
900	BRLT	60103	2911		B4
Islandview Ct					
1600	HFET	60195	2858	26W-12N	A1
Islay Ln					
-	CRTE	60417	3685	0E-29S	E1
-	CteT	60417	3685	0E-29S	E1
3400	CRTE	60417	3596	0E-28S	E6
E Isle Royal Cir					
1200	PLTN	60074	2753	19W-18N	C3
Isle Royal Bay					
500	ROSL	60172	2913		B3
Islington Ln					
200	SMBG	60193	2857	26W-10N	E6
Itasca St					
300	WDDL	60191	2915		C6
400	WDDL	60106	2915		C6
1100	BNVL	60106	2915		D6
Ithaca Rd					
3500	OMFD	60461	3506	4W-24S	E6
Ithica Ct					
10	TYPK	60477	3505	8W-23S	B4
Ithica Dr					
3400	OMFD	60461	3506	4W-24S	E5
Ivanhoe Av					
9200	FNPK	60176	2973	11W-4N	D3
9200	SRPK	60176	2973	11W-4N	D3
9200	SRPK	60634	2973	11W-4N	D3
Ivanhoe Cir					
3700	SRPK	60176	2973	12W-4N	C3
Ivanhoe Ct					
3800	SRPK	60176	2973	12W-4N	B2
S Ivanhoe Dr					
14300	RVDL	60827	3350	0W-16S	C4
Ivanhoe Ln					
900	DYR	46311	3510		E5
W Ivanhoe Ln					
700	MPPT	60056	2861	16W-11N	E3
Ivarene Ct					
600	CPVL	60110	2748		B7
Iverson Ln					
400	SMBG	60194	2858	25W-11N	B4
Ivory Ln					
500	BRLT	60103	2909		E2
500	BRLT	60103	2910		A2
Ivy Ct					
200	SMWD	60107	2857	27W-10N	C6
300	KLWH	60043	2812	4W-14N	C4
600	WLNG	60090	2754	16W-17N	D5
1100	BRLT	60103	2910		E7
2000	SMBG	60194	2858	26W-10N	A5
15000	HMGN	60441	3344	15W-17S	B6
W Ivy Ct					
7700	FftT	60423	3504	9W-24S	E4
Ivy Dr					
4300	GNVW	60062	2809	11W-14N	C4
Ivy Ln					
10	DYR	46311	3510		C7
100	HDPK	60035	2758	6W-20N	C2

STREET Block	City	ZIP	Map#	CGS	Grid
Ivy Ln					
600	GLNC	60022	2758	6W-16N	C7
600	WNKA	60022	2758	6W-16N	D7
600	WNKA	60093	2758	6W-16N	C7
700	GLNC	60093	2758	6W-16N	C7
1200	ALGN	60010	2748		C1
1200	ALGN	60102	2748		C1
1200	BNHL	60010	2748		C1
1700	NHBK	60062	2756	11W-16N	D7
1900	GNVW	60062	2809	11W-14N	C4
E Ivy Ln					
200	ANHT	60004	2754	17W-16N	B7
1900	MPPT	60056	2808	13W-14N	E4
2000	WhlT	60025	2808	13W-14N	E4
W Ivy Ln					
300	ANHT	60004	2754	18W-16N	A7
N Ivy Pl					
1900	PLTN	60074	2753	19W-18N	B3
S Ivy Pth					
20500	FftT	60423	3504	9W-24S	E6
Ivy Wy					
1900	GNVW	60062	2809	11W-14N	C4
Ivy Log Ter					
600	RchT	60443	3593	8W-26S	B2
Ivy Ridge Dr					
-	HnrT	60120	2802	30W-12N	B7
2000	HFET	60120	2802	30W-12N	B7
J					
Jackpine Ct					
10	BRRG	60527	3208		C2
10	DGvT	60527	3208		C2
N Jackpine Ct					
1200	PLTN	60067	2752	22W-17N	A5
1200	PltT	60067	2752	22W-17N	A5
Jackson Av					
300	GLNC	60022	2758	6W-17N	D6
500	DYR	46311	3510		D6
500	RVFT	60305	3030	9W-0N	D3
700	CPVL	60110	2748		D7
1500	EDPK	60707	3030	9W-1N	C1
1500	RVFT	60707	3030	9W-1N	C1
1900	EVTN	60201	2867	3W-11N	A2
2500	EVTN	60201	2813	3W-12N	A7
2600	CHHT	60411	3596	1W-26S	B3
2600	SCHT	60411	3596	1W-27S	B4
3600	PKFT	60466	3594	4W-27S	E4
3600	RNPK	60471	3594	4W-27S	D4
6200	HMND	46324	3430		D3
7800	MNSR	46321	3430		D6
8800	BKFD	60513	3087	11W-3S	C4
8800	MNSR	46321	3510		D1
9500	BKFD	60525	3087	11W-3S	C4
9500	LGPK	60525	3087	11W-3S	C4
E Jackson Av					
900	LGPK	60525	3087	12W-3S	C5
1100	BKFD	60513	3087	12W-3S	C5
1100	BKFD	60525	3087	12W-3S	C5
S Jackson Av					
5900	HMND	46320	3430		D1
W Jackson Av					
10	LGPK	60525	3087	12W-3S	B4
Jackson Blvd					
10	CHCG	60644	3031	7W-0S	B5
10	OKPK	60304	3031	8W-0S	A5
400	FTPK	60130	3030	9W-0S	D5
400	RVFT	60305	3030	9W-0S	D5
800	OKPK	60304	3030	8W-0S	E5
E Jackson Blvd					
10	CHCG	60604	3034	0E-0S	C5
10	CHCG	60605	3034	0E-0S	C5
100	CHCG	60603	3034	0E-0S	C5
N Jackson Blvd					
300	HLSD	60162	3028		D5
W Jackson Blvd					
10	CHCG	60604	3034	0W-0S	A5
100	CHCG	60606	3034	0W-0S	B5
400	CHCG	60661	3034	0W-0S	A5
700	CHCG	60607	3034	0W-0S	A5
800	CHCG	60607	3033	1W-0S	E5
1500	CHCG	60612	3033	3W-0S	A5
2800	CHCG	60612	3032	3W-0S	E5
3100	CHCG	60624	3032	4W-0S	E5
4500	CHCG	60644	3032	5W-0S	A5
4800	CHCG	60644	3031	6W-0S	E5
5800	OKPK	60304	3031	7W-0S	B5
Jackson Cir					
900	EGVV	60007	2913		D2
Jackson Ct					
200	BRLT	60103	2911		A6
800	DYR	46311	3510		E6
8400	MNSR	46321	3430		D7
22500	RNPK	60471	3594	4W-27S	D4
Jackson Dr					
2700	PTHT	60070	2754	16W-17N	E6
2700	WLNG	60004	2754	16W-17N	E6
2700	WLNG	60090	2754	16W-17N	E6
Jackson Ln					
10	SMWD	60107	2856	29W-10N	E6
Jackson Pl					
900	DYR	46311	3510		E6
Jackson St					
-	ClmT	60406	3349	1W-15S	E1
-	ClmT	60827	3349	1W-15S	E1
-	ClmT	60827	3350	1W-15S	A1
-	RVDL	60827	3349	1W-15S	E1
-	RVDL	60827	3350	1W-15S	A1
10	EDND	60118	2801		A2
100	EGvT	60018	2862	15W-9N	A7
200	BRLT	60103	2911		B6
300	PKFT	60466	3594	4W-25S	E1
600	HRPK	60133	2912		A3
2900	BLWD	60104	3029	12W-0S	A5
3500	LNSG	60438	3430	4E-21S	C5
3800	BLWD	60162	3029	12W-0S	A5
3800	HLSD	60162	3029	12W-0S	A5
14200	DLTN	60419	3350	0E-16S	D4
E Jackson St					
200	EMHT	60126	3028		A6
Jacob Ct					
10	BlmT	60411	3510	3E-25S	A7
Jacobs Ct					
800	DYR	46311	3598		E3
S Jacobs Ln					
26700	CteT	60417	3686	1E-32S	B7
Jacqueline Ct					
10	LMNT	60439	3270		C7
Jacqueline Dr					
1100	CRTE	60417	3597	1E-28S	B6
9000	MaiT	60016	2863	11W-11N	E3
9000	NLES	60714	2863	10W-11N	E3
Jacquelyn Ct					
6000	TYPK	60477	3425	7W-20S	C3
Jacquelyn Dr					
10	BNVL	60106	2972		A4
N Jade Av					
2500	ANHT	60004	2753	18W-16N	D6
Jade Ln					
4500	HFET	60195	2804	24W-15N	C1
James Av					
-	FNPK	60131	2973	13W-3N	A4
James Ct					
10	MaiT	60025	2864	9W-12N	C1
200	BMDL	60157	2913		B7
1400	EGVV	60007	2913		E2
1900	SMBG	60194	2858	25W-11N	A4
N James Ct					
2300	ANHT	60004	2753	18W-16N	E7
James Dr					
-	SKOK	60076	2866	5W-10N	A5
100	BRLT	60103	2909		E2
2500	DYR	46311	3598		E3
5600	OKFT	60452	3347	7W-18S	D7
13900	CTWD	60445	3347	6W-16S	E3
S James Dr					
12100	ALSP	60803	3276	6W-14S	A5
W James Dr					
1500	EGvT	60056	2861	16W-10N	D5
1500	MPPT	60056	2861	16W-10N	D5
James Ln					
5200	CTWD	60445	3347	6W-16S	E3
W James Ln					
7200	GGnT	60449	3682	9W-30S	A3
7200	MonT	60449	3682	9W-30S	A3
James Pl					
4400	MLPK	60160	2973	13W-2N	A7
4500	MLPK	60164	2973	13W-2N	A7
4500	NHLK	60164	2973	13W-2N	A7
5200	OKLN	60453	3211	7W-10S	C6
James St					
100	BRTN	60010	2750	25W-20N	E1
200	BRTN	60010	2751	25W-20N	A1
2400	BLID	60406	3349	3W-15S	B1
6000	BmnT	60477	3425	7W-19S	C2
6100	TYPK	60477	3425	7W-19S	C2
7300	FftT	60423	3504	9W-23S	E3
W James St					
2000	CHCG	60609	3151	2W-5S	C2
James Wy					
1400	EGVV	60007	2913		E3
Jamestown Cir					
1700	HFET	60195	2858	25W-12N	A1
Jamestown Ct					
1100	SMBG	60193	2913		B2
3000	SMWD	60107	2911		A1
N Jamestown Dr					
1900	PLTN	60074	2753	19W-18N	B3
Jamie Ct					
15900	OKFT	60452	3425	6W-19S	E1
18800	HMWD	60430	3508	1W-22S	A2
22700	RNPK	60471	3594	5W-27S	B5
Jamie Ln					
1100	HMWD	60430	3508	1W-22S	A2
1200	HMWD	60430	3507	1W-22S	E2
5400	OKFT	60452	3425	6W-19S	E1
Jamison Dr					
7600	FftT	60423	3504	9W-24S	D5
Jamison Ln					
500	HFET	60195	2804	24W-12N	D7
Janas Dr					
13500	HMGN	60441	3342	19W-16S	D3
Janas Ln					
1200	LMNT	60439	3271		A6
Jane Av					
400	LMNT	60439	3271		B7
400	LMNT	60439	3343	18W-15S	B1
E Jane Av					
1400	ANHT	60004	2807	16W-15N	A1
Jane Ct					
400	LMNT	60439	3271		B7
400	LMNT	60439	3343	18W-15S	B1
W Jane St					
10	GNWD	60425	3508	0E-22S	D2
Jane Wy					
8700	MNSR	46321	3510		D1
Jane Addams Dr					
-	PLTN	60074	2753	19W-16N	B6
Janet Av					
100	SMWD	60107	2856	29W-10N	E6
Janet Ct					
5400	OKFT	60452	3425	6W-19S	E2
Janet Dr					
2200	GNVW	60025	2810	10W-15N	A3
Janet Ln					
6500	CHRG	60415	3211	8W-11S	A7
Janet Pl					
900	DYR	46311	3598		E4
Janice Av					
-	CteT	60417	3774	0W-33S	B1
1900	MLPK	60160	3029	13W-2N	A1
1900	MLPK	60164	3029	13W-2N	A1
2000	MLPK	60160	2973	13W-2N	A7
2000	NHLK	60164	2973	13W-2N	A7
Janice Ct					
400	WLNG	60090	2808	15W-16N	B1
Janice Dr					
1100	SLVL	60411	3597	1E-27S	B3
Janine Ct					
17000	ODPK	60467	3423	13W-20S	B4
Janine Ln					
400	SMBG	60193	2858	24W-9N	E7
Janis Dr					
3800	RNPK	60471	3594	4W-27S	D5
Janke Dr					
1800	NHBK	60062	2757	9W-16N	B7
Jan Marie Ln					
800	ELGN	60120	2855		C5
Jann Ct					
10900	LynT	60525	3146		E5
10900	LynT	60525	3147	13W-6S	A5
Janny Rd					
-	GNVW	60025	2809	10W-15N	E3
N Janssen Av					
2700	CHCG	60614	2977	1W-3N	D5
2700	CHCG	60657	2977	1W-3N	D5
3800	CHCG	60613	2977	1W-4N	D2
4900	CHCG	60640	2921	1W-6N	D6
Jarlath Av					
600	DSPN	60018	2916		D1
5000	SKOK	60077	2865	6W-9N	D7
W Jarlath Av					
4800	LNWD	60712	2865	6W-9N	E7
W Jarlath St					
2600	CHCG	60645	2867	3W-9N	A7
2700	CHCG	60645	2866	3W-9N	E7
3800	LNWD	60712	2866	4W-9N	C7
3800	SKOK	60076	2866	4W-9N	C7
7700	CHCG	60068	2864	9W-9N	C7
7700	CHCG	60631	2864	9W-9N	C7
7700	PKRG	60068	2864	9W-9N	C7
Jarvis Av					
400	DSPN	60018	2862	14W-9N	C7
1200	EGVV	60007	2861	17W-9N	C7
1900	DSPN	60018	2863	12W-9N	B7
3500	SKOK	60076	2866	4W-9N	C7
3700	LNWD	60712	2866	4W-9N	C7
3700	SKOK	60712	2866	4W-9N	C7
4900	LNWD	60712	2865	6W-9N	E7
4900	SKOK	60077	2865	6W-9N	E7
W Jarvis Av					
1200	CHCG	60626	2867	2W-9N	C7
2400	CHCG	60645	2867	3W-9N	A7
2600	CHCG	60645	2866	3W-9N	E7
3100	SKOK	60645	2866	3W-9N	D7
4000	LNWD	60712	2866	5W-9N	A7
4000	SKOK	60076	2866	5W-9N	A7
4600	LNWD	60712	2865	6W-9N	E7
4600	SKOK	60076	2865	6W-9N	E7
4600	SKOK	60077	2865	6W-9N	E7
5600	NLES	60077	2865	7W-9N	C7
5600	NLES	60714	2865	7W-9N	C7
6900	NLES	60714	2864	8W-9N	E7
7100	CHCG	60631	2864	9W-9N	D7
E Jarvis Ct					
400	PLTN	60074	2753	20W-18N	A3
Jasmine Ct					
-	SMWD	60120	2856	30W-10N	B5
1100	BRLT	60103	2910		D7
Jasmine Dr					
7200	HRPK	60133	2911		D1
Jasmine Ln					
2600	RGMW	60008	2805	21W-14N	D5
S Jasmine Ln					
25600	MONE	60449	3683	5W-31S	B5
Jason Ct					
400	SMBG	60173	2859	22W-11N	D4
Jason Ln					
400	SMBG	60173	2859	22W-10N	D4
18000	LNSG	60438	3429	2E-21S	C6
Jaspen Ct					
1200	WLNG	60090	2754	16W-18N	E2
Jasper Ct					
2500	GNVW	60062	2809	11W-15N	D1
2500	NHBK	60062	2809	11W-15N	D2
S Jasper Pl					
3600	CHCG	60609	3091	1W-3S	D5
Jay Av					
1500	MLPK	60160	3028		E2
Jay Ln					
2100	RGMW	60008	2806	19W-14N	C4
Jay St					
700	ELGN	60120	2855		A6
14000	SjnT	46311	3598		E4
Jaymia Ct					
10	LMNT	60439	3271		A5
W Jayne St					
10	LMNT	60439	3270		C7
N Jean Av					
6700	CHCG	60646	2919	7W-8N	B2
S Jean Av					
21400	MTSN	60443	3594	4W-25S	D1
Jean Ct					
14800	OKFT	60452	3348	6W-17S	A5
22400	RNPK	60471	3594	4W-27S	D4
Jean Ln					
16600	TYPK	60477	3425	8W-19S	A3
S Jean St					
400	PTON	60468	3860	10W-37S	D4
W Jean St					
4400	ALSP	60803	3276	5W-13S	B5
Jean Creek Dr					
13200	ODPK	60462	3346	11W-15S	A1
Jeanette Ct					
6400	BmnT	60477	3425	8W-21S	B6
6400	TYPK	60477	3425	8W-21S	B6
Jeanie Ln					
8900	FKFT	60423	3504	11W-25S	A7
Jeanne Ter					
300	WLNG	60090	2755	14W-17N	C5
Jeannette St					
800	DSPN	60016	2862	13W-10N	E4
1200	DSPN	60018	2862	13W-10N	E5
Jeans Rd					
10	DGvT	60439	3271		E1
10	DGvT	60527	3208		A7
10	DGvT	60527	3271		E1
Jefferson Av					
300	GLNC	60022	2758	6W-17N	D6
600	CPVL	60110	2748		D7
600	ELGN	60120	2855		B2
1700	GNVW	60025	2810	8W-14N	E4
6200	HMND	46324	3430		E2
7800	MNSR	46321	3430		E6
8700	MNSR	46321	3510		E1
9300	BKFD	60513	3087	11W-3S	D5
9500	LGPK	60525	3087	11W-3S	C5
14300	ODPK	60462	3345	12W-17S	D4
Jefferson Ct					
10	SMWD	60107	2856	29W-10N	E5
400	WLNG	60090	2808	15W-16N	B1
8800	MNSR	46321	3510		E1
W Jefferson Ct					
7700	FftT	60423	3504	9W-24S	D4
Jefferson Dr					
4400	RNPK	60471	3594	5W-27S	B4
Jefferson Ln					
10	SMWD	60107	2856	29W-10N	E6
10	SMWD	60107	2857	28W-10N	A6
Jefferson Rd					
1300	HFET	60195	2858	24W-12N	E2
Jefferson Sq					
900	EGVV	60007	2914		E2
Jefferson St					
400	DLTN	60419	3350	0E-16S	D4
500	HNDL	60521	3086		B7
600	CRTE	60417	3685	1W-29S	A2
1300	DSPN	60016	2863	12W-11N	B3
14500	HRVY	60426	3350	1W-17S	B5
16200	HRVY	60426	3428	0W-19S	B2
16200	SHLD	60473	3428	0W-19S	B2
E Jefferson St					
-	BNVL	60131	2972		B3
100	BNVL	60106	2972		A3
N Jefferson St					
10	CHCG	60661	3034	0W-0N	A4
400	CHCG	60610	3034	0W-0N	A4
S Jefferson St					
10	CHCG	60661	3034	0W-0S	A5
300	CHCG	60607	3034	0W-1S	A7
1600	CHCG	60616	3092	0W-1S	A1
Jeffery Av					
-	ThtT	60473	3351	2E-17S	C6
400	CTCY	60409	3351	2E-17S	C6
400	DLTN	60419	3351	2E-17S	C6
600	DLTN	60409	3351	2E-17S	C6
600	ThtT	60409	3351	2E-17S	C6
600	ThtT	60419	3351	2E-17S	C6
21500	SLVL	60411	3597	2E-26S	C2
S Jeffery Av					
-	CHCG	60633	3351	2E-15S	C1
-	CTCY	60409	3351	2E-16S	C2
9400	CHCG	60617	3215	2E-11S	C6
S Jeffery Blvd					
6700	CHCG	60649	3153	2E-8S	C7
7500	CHCG	60649	3215	2E-8S	C1
7800	CHCG	60617	3215	2E-8S	C1
Jeffery Ct					
900	SMBG	60193	2858	24W-10N	D6
1400	HMWD	60430	3507	1W-22S	E1
Jeffery Ct N					
1100	NHBK	60062	2757	9W-17N	C5
Jeffery Ct S					
1200	NHBK	60062	2757	9W-17N	D5
Jeffery Ct W					
1100	NHBK	60062	2757	9W-17N	C5
Jeffery Dr					
1200	HMWD	60430	3507	1W-22S	E1
1200	HMWD	60430	3508	1W-22S	A1
S Jeffery Dr					
-	CHCG	60637	3153	2E-7S	C5
-	CHCG	60649	3153	2E-7S	C5
Jeffery Ln					
10	DSPN	60018	2862	15W-10N	B6
100	SMBG	60193	2858	24W-10N	D6
1400	NHBK	60062	2757	9W-17N	C5
Jeffery St					
200	NHFD	60093	2811	7W-15N	A2
Jeffrey Av					
17000	SHLD	60473	3429	2E-20S	C3
E Jeffrey Av					
200	WLNG	60090	2755	13W-17N	D5
W Jeffrey Av					
10	WLNG	60090	2755	14W-17N	C5
E Jeffrey Dr					
1500	MPPT	60056	2808	14W-13N	D6
S Jeffrey Dr					
21200	MTSN	60443	3594	4W-25S	D1
Jeffrey Ln					
300	WLNG	60090	2755	14W-17N	B5
Jenkins Ct					
800	WLNG	60090	2755	15W-17N	A4
Jenks St					
1300	EVTN	60201	2813	2W-13N	A7
1700	EVTN	60201	2812	3W-13N	E7
Jenna Dr					
4500	GNVW	60025	2809	12W-14N	C5
4500	NfdT	60025	2809	12W-14N	C5
Jennifer Av					
6100	TYPK	60477	3425	7W-20S	C4
Jennifer Ct					
-	BNHL	60010	2750	27W-17N	B6
800	ALGN	60102	2748		A1
3400	STGR	60475	3596	1W-28S	A5
N Jennifer Ct					
800	ANHT	60004	2807	17W-15N	B2
Jennifer Dr					
500	BlmT	60411	3510	4E-25S	B7
17500	ODPK	60467	3423	13W-21S	A6
Jennifer Ln					
10	CTCY	60409	3351	2E-16S	C4
300	ROSL	60172	2913		B2
300	SmbT	60172	2913		B3
1800	HFET	60194	2858	25W-12N	A2
3400	CRTE	60417	3597	1E-28S	B6
4000	PltT	60004	2753	19W-18N	C2
W Jennifer Ln					
200	PLTN	60067	2752	21W-16N	D6
Jenny Ln					
15500	ODPK	60467	3345	13W-18S	A7
Jensen Blvd					
7400	HRPK	60133	2911		D1
Jensen Dr					
1600	CHCG	60644	3031	7W-0S	C5
Jerele Av					
1400	BKLY	60163	3028		E4
1400	BLWD	60104	3028		E4
1400	BLWD	60163	3028		E4
Jeremy Ln					
17100	ODPK	60462	3424	10W-20S	B4
17100	ODPK	60477	3424	10W-20S	B4
17100	TYPK	60477	3424	10W-20S	B4
Jerome Av					
3800	SKOK	60076	2866	4W-9N	B7
Jerome Dr					
500	NHLK	60164	2972		D6
Jerome Pl					
300	WLNG	60090	2755	13W-17N	D5
Jerome St					
4800	SKOK	60077	2865	6W-9N	E7
W Jerome St					
2500	CHCG	60645	2867	3W-9N	A7
2600	CHCG	60645	2866	3W-9N	E7
3100	SKOK	60076	2866	3W-9N	D7
3100	SKOK	60645	2866	3W-9N	D7
7700	CHCG	60631	2864	9W-9N	C7
Jerrie Ln					
2900	GNVW	60025	2810	10W-12N	B7
E Jerry Dr					
10	MPPT	60056	2808	14W-13N	D7
N Jersey Av					
5600	CHCG	60625	2920	4W-7N	D4
5600	CHCG	60659	2920	4W-7N	D4
Jersey Ln					
500	EGVV	60007	2913		D1
Jervey Ln					
100	BRLT	60103	2910		E4
Jessen St					
100	PTON	60468	3861	9W-37S	A4
Jessica Ct					
5700	RGMW	60008	2805	21W-14N	C5
Jessica Dr					
200	WDDL	60191	2915		D6
5300	BmnT	60452	3425	6W-20S	E4
5300	OKFT	60452	3425	6W-20S	E4
5500	BmnT	60477	3425	7W-20S	D4
Jessica Ln					
300	BRLT	60103	2910		E2
1900	NHBK	60062	2756	11W-16N	D7
2500	RGMW	60067	2805	21W-13N	D6
2500	SMBG	60173	2805	21W-13N	D6
8200	TYPK	60477	3424	10W-19S	C3
S Jessica Ln					
19900	FftT	60423	3504	9W-24S	D4
Jessie Av					
5100	HMND	46320	3352		E6
Jewel Ct					
1500	PLTN	60074	2806	19W-15N	D2
S Jewel Ct					
300	PLTN	60074	2806	19W-15N	C2
Jewel Dr					
-	MLPK	60160	2973	11W-2N	D7
-	MLPK	60160	3029	11W-2N	D1
Jewel Ln					
-	HGKN	60525	3147	11W-7S	D5
JFK Blvd					
10	EGVV	60007	2914		D2
JFK Memorial Dr					
-	CPVL	60118	2801		C1
-	EDND	60118	2801		C1
10	CPVL	60110	2748		C7
200	EDND	60110	2748		C7
800	CPVL	60110	2801		C1
800	EDND	60110	2801		C1
JFK Memorial Dr SR-25					
-	CPVL	60118	2801		C1
-	EDND	60118	2801		C1
10	CPVL	60110	2748		C7
200	EDND	60110	2748		C7
800	CPVL	60110	2801		C1
800	EDND	60110	2801		C1
Jill Ct					
400	AddT	60126	2972		A5
400	EMHT	60126	2972		A5
500	DSPN	60018	2862	15W-10N	A5
1400	HMWD	60430	3507	1W-22S	E2
1400	RGMW	60008	2805	20W-14N	E3
Jill Ln					
100	SMWD	60107	2857	27W-11N	D4
9200	SRPK	60176	2973	11W-5N	D2
Jill St					
-	FNPK	60131	2973	13W-3N	A5
Jill Ter					
1200	HMWD	60430	3507	1W-22S	E2
1200	HMWD	60430	3508	1W-22S	A2
Jillann Dr					
6200	OKFT	60452	3425	7W-18S	C1
Jillian Rd					
10800	ODPK	60467	3345	13W-18S	A7
10900	OrlT	60467	3345	13W-18S	A7
Jimmick Ln					
-	ODPK	60467	3423	13W-20S	B4
W JI Smith Ln					
7000	MonT	60449	3682	8W-30S	A3
W Jo Ln					
1300	ANHT	60004	2806	18W-15N	D2
S Joalyce Ct					
11800	ALSP	60803	3276	5W-13S	B5
S Joalyce Dr					
11500	ALSP	60803	3276	5W-13S	A4
11500	CHCG	60655	3276	5W-13S	A4
Joan Ct					
300	BRLT	60103	2911		A3
700	ELGN	60120	2855		B6
Joan Dr					
100	PltT	60010	2751	23W-18N	D3
E Joan Dr					
1200	PLTN	60074	2753	19W-16N	C7
Joan Marie Dr					
12000	HMGN	60441	3344	15W-18S	C7
Joann Ln					
15800	OKFT	60452	3425	7W-18S	C1
Joanne Dr					
3800	GNVW	60025	2809	11W-15N	D2
3900	GNVW	60062	2809	11W-15N	D2
W Jobev Ln					
4200	ALSP	60803	3276	5W-13S	C5
Jocare Dr					
9200	JSTC	60458	3209	11W-8S	E1
Jodan Dr					
-	ALSP	60803	3275	6W-12S	E3
10900	OKLN	60453	3275	6W-12S	E3
Jodave Av					
16800	HLCT	60429	3427	2W-20S	D4
17000	EHZC	60429	3427	2W-20S	D4
Jodi Ct					
10	DYR	46311	3510		C7
1200	BRLT	60103	2910		B3
Jodi Ln					
100	BRLT	60103	2910		B3
Jodi Ter					
18900	HMWD	60430	3508	1W-22S	A2
Jody Ct					
4100	RGMW	60008	2806	20W-13N	A5
W Jody Ct					
2100	MPPT	60056	2861	17W-12N	B1
Jody Ln					
600	HFET	60194	2858	24W-11N	C4
6000	BmnT	60477	3425	7W-19S	C2
6100	TYPK	60477	3425	7W-19S	C2
8800	MaiT	60016	2863	11W-12N	E1
Joe Ct					
800	LynT	60458	3209	11W-8S	E1
Joe Fullan Ct					
-	OKBK	60523	3086		A4
Joe Orr Ct					
10	CRTE	60417	3685	0W-29S	C2
Joe Orr Rd					
300	CRTE	60417	3685	0W-29S	C1
E Joe Orr Rd					
-	CHHT	60411	3507	2W-24S	C5
-	CHHT	60461	3507	2W-24S	C5
-	OMFD	60461	3507	2W-24S	C5
10	CHHT	60411	3508	0W-24S	B5
300	BlmT	60411	3508	0E-24S	D5
900	BlmT	60411	3509	0E-24S	A5
1100	FDHT	60411	3509	1E-24S	B5
1700	LYWD	60411	3509	2E-24S	C5
W Joe Orr Rd					
10	CHHT	60411	3507	2W-24S	D5
10	CHHT	60411	3508	1W-24S	A5
500	CHHT	60461	3507	2W-24S	D5
500	OMFD	60411	3507	2W-24S	D5
500	OMFD	60461	3507	2W-24S	D5
Joey Dr					
10	EGvT	60007	2861	17W-10N	B5
10	EGVV	60007	2861	17W-10N	B5
N Joey Dr					
-	NLES	60714	2864	10W-11N	B3
Johanna Av					
9600	FNPK	60131	2973	12W-3N	C5
W Johanna Dr					
8400	MaiT	60714	2864	10W-10N	A4
8400	NLES	60714	2864	10W-10N	A4
W Johanna Ter					
1600	ANHT	60005	2806	18W-14N	D5
John Av					
17700	CCHL	60478	3426	5W-21S	B6
18400	CCHL	60478	3506	5W-22S	B1
18900	RchT	60477	3506	5W-22S	B2

STREET Block	City	ZIP	Map#	CGS	Grid
John Ct					
400	BMDL	60157	2913		C6
500	SMBG	60193	2859	23W-9N	B7
600	LynT	60458	3209	11W-8S	D2
John Dr					
200	BRLT	60103	2911		A4
300	ELGN	60120	2855		C5
1000	HFET	60194	2858	24W-11N	C3
John St					
-	AddT	60126	2972		B4
500	BNVL	60106	2972		B3
800	LMNT	60439	3270		D6
900	AddT	60106	2972		B4
2700	BLID	60406	3349	3W-15S	A1
3500	STGR	60475	3595	1W-28S	E6
John Charles Dr					
18000	ODPK	60467	3423	13W-21S	B7
18200	ODPK	60448	3423	13W-21S	B7
John David					
-	LMNT	60439	3342	20W-15S	B1
John Humphrey Dr					
14200	ODPK	60462	3345	11W-17S	D5
14200	OrlT	60462	3345	11W-17S	D5
John Rolfe Dr					
2300	SMBG	60194	2857	26W-11N	E3
Johns Ct					
2000	GNVW	60025	2810	9W-14N	D3
Johns Dr					
1800	GNVW	60025	2810	9W-14N	D4
John Smith Dr					
2300	HFET	60194	2857	26W-11N	E3
2300	SMBG	60194	2857	26W-11N	E3
John Snow Av					
-	BRTN	60010	2751	25W-18N	B2
Johnson Av					
300	CTCY	60409	3352	3E-17S	A4
3800	PvsT	60558	3086		E7
3800	WNSP	60558	3086		E7
4400	WNSP	60558	3146		E1
S Johnson Av					
3800	HMND	46327	3352		D5
W Johnson Ct					
6800	MonT	60449	3682	8W-30S	B3
Johnson Dr					
-	VrnT	60062	2755	15W-20N	B1
-	VrnT	60089	2755	15W-20N	B1
1000	BFGV	60089	2755	15W-20N	B1
1000	BFGV	60090	2755	15W-20N	B1
W Johnson Rd					
10300	CHCG	60666	2917	13W-8N	A2
10500	CHCG	60666	2916		E2
Johnson St					
10	EDND	60118	2801		A3
W Johnson St					
100	PLTN	60067	2805	21W-15N	D1
Johnston Ln					
12400	HMGN	60441	3422	15W-19S	B2
Johnston Rd					
8500	BRRG	60527	3208		C4
8500	LynT	60527	3208		C4
8700	LynT	60480	3208		C4
Joliet Rd					
7600	LYNS	60534	3088	9W-4S	D7
Joliet Av					
3900	LYNS	60534	3088	9W-4S	C7
3900	RvsT	60534	3088	9W-4S	C6
3900	RvsT	60546	3088	9W-4S	C6
4500	LYNS	60534	3148	10W-5S	C1
4600	MCCK	60534	3148	10W-4S	C1
4700	MCCK	60525	3148	10W-5S	C1
Joliet Dr N					
7800	TYPK	60477	3424	9W-21S	D5
Joliet Dr S					
7700	TYPK	60477	3424	9W-21S	D6
Joliet Rd					
-	BGBK	-	3270		A1
-	DGvT	-	3270		A1
-	DPgT	-	3270		A1
-	IHPK	-	3146		C7
-	WDRG	-	3270		A1
-	WLBK	-	3208		A2
400	BRRG	60527	3208		A2
400	DGvT	60527	3208		A2
800	CTSD	60525	3147	13W-7S	A6
800	LynT	60525	3147	13W-7S	B5
4300	LYNS	60534	3088	9W-4S	C7
6100	HGKN	60525	3147	11W-6S	D4
6500	IHPK	60525	3147	13W-7S	A6
6600	CTSD	60525	3146		E6
6900	BRRG	60525	3146		D7
6900	BRRG	60527	3146		C7
7200	LYNS	60402	3088	9W-4S	E6
7200	SKNY	60402	3088	9W-4S	E6
7900	LYNS	60534	3148	10W-5S	B2
7900	MCCK	60525	3148	10W-5S	B2
7900	MCCK	60534	3148	10W-5S	B2
9000	MCCK	60525	3147	11W-6S	D4
Joliet Rd I-55					
-	BGBK	-	3270		A1
-	BRRG	-	3146		D7
-	BRRG	-	3208		A2
-	DGvT	-	3270		A1
-	DPgT	-	3270		A1
-	IHPK	-	3146		C7
-	WDRG	-	3270		A1
-	WLBK	-	3208		A2
S Joliet Rd					
400	PtnT	60468	3860	10W-36S	D1
400	PTON	60468	3860	9W-36S	E2
Joliet St					
10	BlmT	60411	3598		C2
10	DYR	46311	3598		C2
10	DYR	60411	3598		C2
200	DXMR	60426	3349	2W-17S	C5
300	LMNT	60439	3270		D5
2200	POSN	60469	3349	2W-17S	C5
Joliet St US-30					
10	BlmT	60411	3598		C2
10	DYR	46311	3598		C2
10	DYR	60411	3598		C2
Jon Ct					
300	DSPN	60016	2862	15W-11N	A3
Jon Ln					
500	DSPN	60016	2808	14W-12N	C7
500	DSPN	60016	2862	14W-12N	C1
500	MPPT	60016	2808	14W-12N	C7
500	MPPT	60056	2808	14W-12N	C7
Jon Rd					
15700	OKFT	60452	3425	7W-18S	B1
Jonathan Dr					
1100	IVNS	60010	2803	25W-15N	E1
1100	SBTN	60010	2803	25W-15N	E2
8100	HYHL	60457	3210	10W-10S	B5
N Jonathan Dr					
400	PLTN	60074	2753	19W-16N	C7
Jonathan Ln					
18900	HMWD	60430	3508	1W-22S	A2
E Jonathan Ln					
23700	CteT	60417	3597	3E-29S	E7
23700	CteT	60417	3598	3E-28S	A7
Jonathon Ct					
800	PTHT	60070	2809	13W-15N	A2
Jones Ct					
15000	OKFT	60452	3348	6W-17S	A6
Jones Dr					
100	BRLT	60103	2909		E2
Jones Rd					
-	HFET	60195	2804	24W-12N	D7
1200	HFET	60195	2858	24W-12N	D1
1200	SMBG	60194	2858	24W-12N	D2
1200	SMBG	60195	2858	24W-12N	D1
N Jones St					
2500	CHCG	60647	2977	2W-3N	B5
E Jonquil Cir					
1400	ANHT	60004	2754	16W-16N	C7
Jonquil Ct					
100	RGMW	60008	2805	22W-13N	B5
W Jonquil Ct					
10	SMWD	60107	2856	30W-10N	C5
S Jonquil Ln					
4500	MONE	60449	3683	5W-31S	C5
20100	FftT	60423	3504	9W-24S	D5
Jonquil Ter					
400	DRFD	60015	2756	11W-20N	D1
7100	HRPK	60133	2911		D2
E Jonquil Ter					
1600	ANHT	60004	2754	16W-16N	C7
1600	ANHT	60004	2807	16W-16N	C1
W Jonquil Ter					
1400	CHCG	60626	2867	1W-9N	C6
6800	NLES	60714	2864	8W-9N	E6
7500	PKRG	60068	2864	9W-9N	C6
Joplin Cir					
1600	EGVV	60007	2913		D2
Josef Dr					
16000	HMGN	60441	3422	15W-19S	B2
Joseph Av					
2600	DSPN	60018	2917	12W-8N	B2
Joseph Ct					
100	BRLT	60103	2909		E3
400	BMDL	60157	2913		C6
Josephine Ct					
2300	RGMW	60008	2805	21W-14N	D4
2300	RGMW	60067	2805	21W-14N	D4
S Josephine Ct					
10	DSPN	60016	2862	15W-11N	B2
Josephine St					
8600	MaiT	60016	2863	10W-12N	E1
Joseph J Schwab Rd					
-	DSPN	60016	2863	12W-10N	B5
Joshua Dr					
22300	SLVL	60411	3597	1E-27S	C4
Joshua Ln					
2500	NHBK	60062	2809	11W-15N	D1
Joslyn Dr					
100	ELGN	60120	2855		C3
S Jourdan Ct					
1900	CHCG	60608	3092	1W-1S	A1
Jovanna Dr					
17400	HLCT	60430	3427	3W-20S	C5
17400	HMWD	60430	3427	3W-20S	C5
Joy Ct					
-	BRRG	60527	3208		C5
Joy Ln					
-	LYWD	60411	3509	2E-24S	D5
1600	GNVW	60025	2809	11W-14N	E4
Joyce Av					
800	LydT	60164	2972		E5
E Joyce Av					
1200	PLTN	60074	2806	19W-15N	C1
Joyce Cir					
16200	SHLD	60473	3428	0E-19S	E1
Joyce Ct					
10	CRTE	60417	3685	1W-30S	A2
400	SHLD	60473	3428	0E-19S	E1
Joyce Dr					
1400	DSPN	60018	2862	15W-10N	A5
1400	FSMR	60422	3506	4W-23S	E3
1400	RchT	60430	3506	4W-23S	E3
Joyce Ln					
10	SMWD	60107	2856	29W-10N	E6
100	CHHT	60411	3508	1W-23S	A4
800	ELGN	60120	2855		C4
11200	WLSP	60480	3208		E3
W Joyce Ln					
6200	CHCG	60634	2975	7W-5N	B1
E Joyce Pl					
100	PKRG	60068	2864	9W-9N	C6
Joyce St					
14100	SjnT	46311	3598		E4
Juanita Dr					
11700	ODPK	60467	3422	14W-19S	D2
11700	OrlT	60467	3422	14W-19S	D2
Judd Av					
4000	SRPK	60176	2973	12W-5N	B2
Judith Ct					
10	BlmT	60411	3510	3E-25S	A7
100	BRLT	60103	2911		A3
Judith Ln					
10	CHHT	60411	3508	1W-23S	A3
100	BlmT	60411	3508	1W-23S	A3
E Judith Ann Dr					
10	MPPT	60056	2808	15W-13N	A5
Judson Av					
600	HDPK	60035	2758	8W-20N	A1
1000	EVTN	60202	2867	2W-10N	C4
1200	EVTN	60201	2867	2W-10N	C4
Judy Ct					
5300	OKFT	60452	3425	6W-20S	E4
Judy Dr					
1000	EGVV	60007	2913		E3
Judy Ln					
200	SMWD	60107	2857	27W-11N	D4
Juhlin Dr					
18700	HMWD	60430	3507	1W-22S	E2
Jules Rd					
200	IVNS	60067	2751	23W-16N	E7
E Jules St					
700	ANHT	60004	2807	17W-15N	B2
1000	PTHT	60004	2807	17W-15N	B2
Juli Ct					
600	SMBG	60193	2859	23W-9N	A7
Juli Dr					
400	SMBG	60193	2859	23W-9N	A7
Julia Ct					
1000	GLNC	60022	2758	7W-18N	B4
W Julia Ct					
2700	CHCG	60647	2977	3W-2N	A6
Julia Dr					
9300	SjnT	46311	3687		E2
Julia St					
200	LMNT	60439	3270		E5
N Julian St					
200	TNTN	60476	3428	0E-20S	D5
S Julian St					
100	TNTN	60476	3428	0W-21S	D6
W Julian St					
1600	CHCG	60622	3033	2W-1N	C1
N Julian Ter					
2600	RVGV	60171	2973	10W-3N	E5
Julias Courtyard					
16000	TYPK	60477	3425	8W-19S	A2
Julie Dr					
200	IVNS	60010	2751	24W-17N	D4
1900	EGVV	60007	2913		C1
1900	SMBG	60193	2913		C1
Julie Ln					
10	MaiT	60025	2864	9W-12N	C1
10	MNGV	60053	2864	9W-12N	C2
1000	CRTE	60417	3597	1E-28S	B7
Julie Ann Ln					
800	ELGN	60120	2855		C5
Julie's Wy					
-	ODPK	60467	3345	13W-18S	B7
-	ODPK	60467	3423	13W-18S	B1
E Juliette St					
100	TNTN	60476	3428	0E-21S	D6
W Juliette St					
100	TNTN	60476	3428	0E-21S	D6
Juli Lyn Ct					
1400	NHBK	60062	2756	12W-17N	A6
Juli Lyn Ln					
1400	NHBK	60062	2756	12W-17N	A6
June Ter					
400	BRTN	60010	2751	25W-20N	A2
Juneberry Rd					
300	RVWD	60015	2755	13W-20N	D1
Juneway Av					
700	VrnT	60015	2755	15W-20N	A1
Juneway Ct					
18000	CCHL	60478	3426	5W-21S	C7
W Juneway Ter					
1600	CHCG	60626	2867	2W-9N	C6
1800	EVTN	60202	2867	2W-9N	C6
Junior Ter					
1700	DSPN	60016	2863	12W-11N	B3
W Junior Ter					
600	CHCG	60613	2977	0W-5N	E1
600	CHCG	60613	2978		A1
Juniper Av					
-	ELGN	60120	2855		C7
20100	LYWD	60411	3510	3E-23S	A4
Juniper Cir					
200	SMWD	60107	2857	27W-10N	C5
Juniper Ct					
-	LYWD	60411	3510	3E-23S	B3
10	BFGV	60089	2754	17W-18N	B2
10	SMWD	60107	2857	27W-10N	C5
8200	PSHL	60465	3274	10W-13S	B3
8800	ODPK	60462	3346	11W-17S	A6
8800	TYPK	60477	3424	11W-20S	A5
W Juniper Ct					
200	FftT	60423	3504	9W-24S	E6
Juniper Dr					
10	BmdT	60157	2913		C4
10	ROSL	60157	2913		C4
E Juniper Dr					
400	PLTN	60067	2753	20W-17N	A5
400	PLTN	60074	2753	20W-17N	A5
1100	MPPT	60056	2808	14W-14N	C4
Juniper Ln					
400	SMBG	60193	2858	24W-9N	E6
600	BRLT	60103	2910		E6
800	NHBK	60062	2757	10W-17N	B4
12000	HMGN	60441	3422	15W-20S	C4
E Juniper Ln					
1100	MPPT	60056	2808	14W-14N	C5
N Juniper Ln					
2000	ANHT	60004	2754	18W-16N	A7
2000	ANHT	60004	2807	17W-14N	C4
Juniper Rd					
10	RGMW	60008	2806	19W-15N	C3
1000	GNVW	60025	2811	6W-13N	D6
Juniper St					
200	PKFT	60466	3595	3W-26S	B3
6800	HRPK	60133	2911		D3
Juniper Tree Ct					
300	HFET	60194	2858	24W-11N	E3
Justice					
-	MTSN	60443	3505	7W-25S	D7
Justin Ct					
8000	TYPK	60477	3424	10W-19S	C2
Justina St					
200	HNDL	60521	3146		C1
300	HNDL	60521	3086		C7
Justine St					
14500	HRVY	60426	3349	1W-17S	E5
16100	MKHM	60426	3427	1W-19S	E2
N Justine St					
200	CHCG	60607	3033	1W-0N	D4
S Justine St					
3300	CHCG	60608	3091	1W-3S	D4
4500	CHCG	60609	3091	1W-4S	D7
4700	CHCG	60609	3151	1W-5S	D1
5500	CHCG	60636	3151	1W-6S	D3
8300	CHCG	60620	3213	1W-9S	D3
9400	CHCG	60643	3213	1W-10S	D6
11500	CHCG	60643	3277	1W-13S	D4
12200	CTPK	60827	3277	1W-15S	D7
K					
Kahler Jr Dr					
2100	DYR	46311	3598		D3
Kaindl Dr					
-	HLCT	60429	3427	3W-20S	A4
S Kainer Av					
100	BRTN	60010	2751	25W-18N	B2
Kaitlin Ct					
21200	MTSN	60443	3593	7W-25S	C1
Kaleigh Ct					
-	SBTN	60010	2803	27W-15N	A1
Kalvelage Dr					
2700	BlmT	60411	3597	3E-26S	E2
2700	SLVL	60411	3597	3E-26S	E2
W Kamerling Av					
4000	CHCG	60651	3032	5W-1N	B1
4800	CHCG	60651	3031	6W-1N	E1
Kamp Ct					
17100	TYPK	60477	3424	10W-20S	B4
Kamp Dr					
-	NHBK	60062	2810	8W-16N	D1
Kanawha Av					
13800	CHCG	60827	3350	0E-16S	E3
13800	DLTN	60419	3350	0E-16S	E3
Kane Av					
10	HGKN	60525	3147	11W-7S	D6
E Kane St					
600	HMND	46320	3352		E7
Kankakee Av					
-	BNHM	60633	3352	3E-16S	A3
Kansas Ct					
17900	ODPK	60467	3423	12W-21S	C7
Kanst Dr					
-	CHCG	60629	3151	3W-7S	A6
Kara Ct					
16700	OKFT	60452	3426	6W-20S	A3
Kara Ln					
-	RNPK	60471	3593	6W-27S	E4
Kara St					
-	RNPK	60471	3593	7W-27S	E4
-	RNPK	60471	3594	6W-27S	A4
Karen Ct					
600	CRTE	60417	3685	1W-30S	A3
Karen Dr					
11000	ODPK	60467	3422	13W-19S	E2
11000	ODPK	60467	3423	13W-19S	A2
Karen Ln					
2700	GNVW	60025	2810	10W-12N	B7
W Karen Ln					
700	PLTN	60067	2752	21W-16N	C6
Karey Ct					
500	WLMT	60091	2812	5W-13N	A6
Karli Ln					
17500	ODPK	60467	3422	14W-21S	E5
Karlov Av					
7400	LNWD	60712	2866	5W-9N	B7
9600	SKOK	60076	2866	5W-12N	B1
9900	EVTN	60076	2866	5W-12N	B1
9900	EVTN	60201	2866	5W-12N	B1
14100	CTWD	60445	3348	5W-17S	C5
14200	MDLN	60445	3348	5W-16S	C4
22100	RNPK	60471	3594	5W-27S	D4
N Karlov Av					
10	CHCG	60624	3032	5W-0N	B4
800	CHCG	60651	3032	5W-1N	B1
1500	CHCG	60639	3032	5W-1N	B1
2700	CHCG	60639	2976	5W-3N	B5
2900	CHCG	60641	2976	5W-3N	B4
4500	CHCG	60630	2920	5W-6N	B6
5600	CHCG	60646	2920	5W-7N	B4
6800	LNWD	60712	2920	5W-8N	B1
7200	LNWD	60712	2866	5W-9N	B7
7300	SKOK	60076	2866	5W-9N	B7
S Karlov Av					
10	CHCG	60624	3032	5W-0S	B5
1100	CHCG	60623	3032	5W-1S	B7
2000	CHCG	60623	3090	5W-1S	B1
3900	CHCG	60632	3090	5W-4S	B6
5300	CHCG	60632	3150	5W-6S	B3
5400	CHCG	60629	3150	5W-7S	C5
7700	CHCG	60652	3212	5W-8S	C1
8600	CHCG	60456	3212	5W-9S	C4
8600	HMTN	60456	3212	5W-9S	C4
9100	OKLN	60453	3212	5W-10S	C5
10200	OKLN	60453	3276	5W-12S	C1
11500	ALSP	60803	3276	5W-13S	C4
11500	CHCG	60655	3276	5W-13S	C4
13300	RBBN	60472	3348	5W-15S	C2
N Kaspar Av					
10	ANHT	60005	2806	18W-14N	E4
1500	ANHT	60004	2806	18W-15N	E1
S Kaspar Av					
10	ANHT	60005	2806	18W-14N	E5
1200	ANHT	60005	2860	18W-12N	E1
Kasser Ct					
200	DndT	60110	2748		A5
N Kasson Av					
4400	CHCG	60630	2920	5W-5N	B7
Kasten Dr					
1400	DLTN	60419	3351	1E-16S	B4
Kates Rd					
-	DRFD	60015	2756	10W-20N	E1
300	DRFD	60015	2757	10W-20N	A1
Katherine Ct					
10	BFGV	60089	2754	17W-18N	A3
Katherine Wy					
2700	EGVV	60007	2915		C4
Kathleen Ct					
3000	HMWD	60430	3507	3W-22S	A1
5200	OKFT	60452	3425	6W-20S	E4
10800	PSHL	60465	3274	10W-12S	C2
S Kathleen Ct					
12000	ALSP	60803	3276	4W-14S	C5
E Kathleen Dr					
10	DSPN	60016	2862	14W-11N	C4
100	PKRG	60068	2864	9W-9N	C6
W Kathleen Dr					
10	DSPN	60016	2862	15W-11N	A4
100	PKRG	60068	2864	9W-9N	B6
700	DSPN	60016	2861	16W-11N	E4
700	DSPN	60056	2861	16W-11N	E4
700	MPPT	60056	2861	16W-11N	E4
800	PLTN	60067	2805	22W-15N	C2
Kathleen Ln					
-	FSMR	60422	3507	3W-23S	A4
100	CHHT	60411	3508	1W-23S	A4
4200	OKLN	60453	3276	5W-12S	B2
8600	TYPK	60477	3424	10W-20S	B4
Kathleen Wy					
1400	EGVV	60007	2913		E3
1400	EGVV	60007	2914		A3
Kathryn Ct					
8100	BRRG	60527	3208		B3
Kathryn Ln					
-	MTSN	60443	3505	7W-24S	D5
Kathy Ct					
8900	ODPK	60462	3346	11W-16S	A4
10100	MaiT	60016	2809	11W-12N	D7
10100	NfdT	60016	2809	11W-12N	D7
10100	NfdT	60025	2809	11W-12N	D7
S Kathy Ct					
10300	BGVW	60465	3274	9W-12S	D1
10300	PSHL	60465	3274	9W-12S	D1
Kathy Ln					
500	BRLT	60103	2910		D2
600	SMBG	60173	2859	22W-11N	D3
W Kathy Ln					
8800	MaiT	60016	2863	11W-11N	E2
8800	MaiT	60714	2863	11W-11N	E2
8800	NLES	60016	2863	11W-11N	E2
8800	NLES	60714	2863	11W-11N	E2
Katie Ln					
-	PLTN	60074	2806	19W-15N	C3
Katie Rd					
10	LMNT	60439	3342	19W-15S	D2
Katy Ln					
8100	ODPK	60462	3346	10W-17S	C4
Kaup Ln					
11600	OrlT	60467	3344	14W-16S	D3
Kavalier Ct					
400	SMBG	60194	2857	26W-11N	E5
400	SMWD	60107	2857	26W-11N	E4
W Kay St					
8300	NLES	60714	2864	10W-12N	A1
Kayjay Dr					
3000	NHBK	60062	2809	11W-15N	D1
Kaywood Ln					
1400	GNVW	60025	2811	7W-14N	B5
Kazwell St					
100	WLSP	60480	3209	12W-9S	C3
S Kean Av					
8000	JSTC	60458	3209	11W-9S	E3
8000	JSTC	60480	3209	11W-9S	E3
8000	WLSP	60458	3209	11W-9S	E3
8000	WLSP	60480	3209	11W-9S	E3
8200	HYHL	60457	3209	11W-11S	E7
8200	HYHL	60458	3209	11W-9S	E3
8200	LynT	60458	3209	11W-10S	E6
8500	PlsT	60480	3209	11W-11S	E7
8900	HYHL	60480	3209	11W-10S	E5
9200	PlsT	60457	3209	11W-10S	E5
9400	HYHL	60465	3209	11W-11S	E7
9400	PlsT	60465	3209	11W-11S	E7
9400	PSHL	60465	3209	11W-11S	E7
10000	PlsT	60480	3273	11W-12S	E1
10000	PSHL	60465	3273	11W-12S	E1
10600	PlsT	60465	3273	11W-12S	E2
S Kean Rd					
-	PSPK	60464	3273	11W-13S	E5
11200	PlsT	60464	3273	11W-13S	E5
Kearney Rd					
400	DGvT	60439	3270		E1
S Kearsage Av					
500	EMHT	60126	3028		A4
N Kearsarge Av					
2900	CHCG	60641	2976	5W-3N	B4
Keating Av					
8000	SKOK	60076	2865	5W-10N	E5
14300	CTWD	60445	3348	5W-17S	A5
14800	MDLN	60445	3348	5W-17S	A5
N Keating Av					
1400	CHCG	60651	3032	5W-1N	A1
1500	CHCG	60639	3032	5W-1N	A1
2200	CHCG	60639	2975	5W-2N	E6
2200	CHCG	60639	2976	5W-2N	A6
2800	CHCG	60641	2975	5W-3N	E4
5000	CHCG	60630	2919	5W-6N	E6
6200	CHCG	60646	2919	5W-7N	E3
7000	LNWD	60712	2919	5W-8N	E1
7200	LNWD	60712	2865	5W-9N	E7
S Keating Av					
-	OKLN	60453	3212	5W-10S	A5
4200	CHCG	60632	3090	5W-4S	A7
4600	CHCG	60632	3150	5W-5S	A2
6000	CHCG	60629	3150	5W-7S	A5
7700	CHCG	60652	3212	5W-8S	A1
8600	CHCG	60456	3212	5W-9S	A4
8700	HMTN	60456	3212	5W-10S	A4
10300	OKLN	60453	3276	5W-12S	A1
11000	CHCG	60655	3276	5W-12S	A3
W Keating Dr					
1100	ANHT	60005	2806	18W-13N	D6
Keats Ct					
700	SMBG	60193	2858	24W-9N	E7
Kedvale Av					
7400	LNWD	60712	2866	5W-9N	B7
9600	SKOK	60076	2866	5W-12N	B1
10000	OKLN	60453	3212	5W-11S	C7
10200	OKLN	60453	3276	5W-12S	C1
14300	CTWD	60445	3348	5W-17S	C5
14300	MDLN	60445	3348	5W-17S	C5
16300	BmnT	60426	3426	5W-19S	C3
16300	BmnT	60452	3426	5W-19S	C3
16300	OKFT	60452	3426	5W-19S	C3
16400	MKHM	60452	3426	5W-19S	C3
N Kedvale Av					
800	CHCG	60624	3032	5W-0N	B3
1400	CHCG	60651	3032	5W-1N	B1
1500	CHCG	60639	3032	5W-1N	B1
1600	CHCG	60639	2976	5W-2N	B7
4000	CHCG	60641	2976	5W-5N	B1
4300	CHCG	60630	2976	5W-5N	B1
4700	CHCG	60630	2920	5W-6N	B6
5600	CHCG	60646	2920	5W-6N	B5
6300	LNWD	60646	2920	5W-7N	B3
7200	LNWD	60712	2866	5W-9N	B7
7300	SKOK	60076	2866	5W-9N	B7
S Kedvale Av					
600	CHCG	60624	3032	5W-0S	B6
1200	CHCG	60623	3032	5W-1S	B7
2200	CHCG	60623	3090	5W-2S	B2
4300	CHCG	60632	3090	5W-4S	B7
5400	CHCG	60629	3150	5W-6S	B3
5400	CHCG	60632	3150	5W-6S	B3
7800	CHCG	60652	3212	5W-8S	C1
8600	HMTN	60456	3212	5W-9S	C4
11500	ALSP	60803	3276	5W-13S	C4
11500	CHCG	60655	3276	5W-13S	C4
13600	RBBN	60472	3348	5W-16S	C3
13800	CTWD	60445	3348	5W-16S	C3
Kedzie Av					
-	RBBN	60472	3348	3W-16S	E3
10	EVTN	60202	2867	2W-10N	C5
700	FSMR	60422	3507	3W-23S	A3
700	HMWD	60430	3507	3W-23S	A3
700	MonT	60466	3684	3W-29S	A2
700	RchT	60422	3507	3W-23S	A3
700	UYPK	60466	3684	3W-29S	A2
12700	ALSP	60406	3276	3W-15S	E7
12700	BLID	60406	3276	3W-15S	E7
12700	WthT	60406	3276	3W-15S	E7
12900	WthT	60406	3348	3W-15S	E1
13200	WthT	60472	3348	3W-15S	E1
14100	BLID	60406	3348	3W-16S	E4
14100	RBBN	60406	3348	4W-16S	E4
14300	BmnT	60406	3348	3W-17S	E4
14300	BmnT	60469	3348	3W-17S	E4
14300	MDLN	60406	3348	3W-16S	E4
14900	MDLN	60445	3348	3W-18S	E6
14900	MKHM	60426	3348	3W-18S	E6
14900	POSN	60469	3348	3W-18S	E6
15300	MKHM	60426	3349	4W-18S	A7
16000	MKHM	60426	3427	3W-19S	A2
16600	HLCT	60429	3427	3W-19S	A3
18000	HMWD	60430	3427	3W-21S	A7
18600	HMWD	60422	3507	3W-22S	A1
19800	OMFD	60422	3507	3W-23S	A4
19800	OMFD	60461	3507	3W-23S	A4
N Kedzie Av					
10	CHCG	60612	3032	4W-0N	E5
10	CHCG	60624	3032	4W-0N	E5
700	CHCG	60622	3032	4W-0N	D3
700	CHCG	60651	3032	4W-0N	D3
1500	CHCG	60647	3032	4W-2N	D1

Chicago & Cook County Street Index

STREET Block	City	ZIP	Map#	CGS	Grid
N Kedzie Av					
2200	CHCG	60647	2976	3W-3N	D5
2700	CHCG	60618	2976	3W-4N	D2
4300	CHCG	60625	2976	4W-5N	D1
4400	CHCG	60625	2920	3W-6N	D6
5500	CHCG	60659	2920	3W-6N	D6
6200	CHCG	60645	2920	4W-8N	D1
6200	CHCG	60712	2920	4W-7N	D3
6200	LNWD	60712	2920	4W-8N	D2
6400	LNWD	60645	2920	4W-8N	D2
6900	SKOK	60645	2920	4W-8N	D2
7200	CHCG	60645	2866	3W-9N	D7
7200	SKOK	60076	2866	3W-9N	D7
7200	SKOK	60645	2866	3W-9N	D7
7500	EVTN	60202	2866	3W-9N	D7
S Kedzie Av					
10	CHCG	60612	3032	4W-1S	E7
10	CHCG	60624	3032	4W-1S	E7
1100	CHCG	60623	3032	4W-0S	E7
1600	CHCG	60623	3090	4W-4S	E7
3500	CHCG	60632	3090	4W-4S	E7
4600	CHCG	60632	3150	4W-8S	E7
7300	CHCG	60629	3150	3W-8S	E7
7300	CHCG	60629	3212	4W-8S	D1
7300	CHCG	60652	3212	4W-8S	D1
8500	ENGN	60652	3212	3W-9S	E4
8500	ENGN	60805	3212	4W-11S	E7
10200	CHCG	60655	3276	4W-12S	E2
10200	ENGN	60805	3276	3W-11S	E1
11300	CHCG	60803	3276	3W-13S	E3
11400	MTPK	60655	3276	3W-13S	E3
11400	MTPK	60803	3276	3W-13S	E3
11800	WthT	60655	3276	3W-13S	E5
11800	WthT	60803	3276	3W-13S	E5
12200	ALSP	60803	3276	3W-14S	E6
12300	ALSP	60406	3276	3W-14S	E6
12300	WthT	60406	3276	3W-14S	E6
12500	BLID	60406	3276	3W-14S	E7
13500	RBBN	60472	3348	3W-16S	E3
13900	RBBN	60406	3348	3W-16S	E3
14500	MDLN	60445	3348	4W-17S	E5
14500	POSN	60469	3348	4W-17S	E5
14800	MKHM	60426	3348	3W-17S	E5
W Kedzie St					
7000	NLES	60714	2864	8W-10N	D5
S Keefe Av					
6800	CHCG	60637	3152	0E-7S	D6
Keele Cir					
1500	CPVL	60110	2748		C5
Keele Dr					
1400	CPVL	60110	2748		D5
Keeler Av					
7400	LNWD	60712	2866	5W-9N	B7
7800	SKOK	60076	2866	5W-9N	B6
13500	CTWD	60445	3348	5W-16S	C3
13500	CTWD	60472	3348	5W-16S	C3
13500	RBBN	60472	3348	5W-16S	C3
14200	MDLN	60445	3348	5W-17S	C6
18800	CCHL	60478	3506	5W-22S	C2
20300	MTSN	60443	3506	5W-24S	C5
21200	MTSN	60443	3594	5W-25S	C1
N Keeler Av					
100	CHCG	60624	3032	5W-0N	B4
800	CHCG	60651	3032	5W-1N	B1
1500	CHCG	60639	3032	5W-1N	B1
1600	CHCG	60639	2976	5W-2N	B7
3200	CHCG	60641	2976	5W-4N	B2
4300	CHCG	60630	2976	5W-5N	B1
4700	CHCG	60630	2920	5W-6N	B6
6000	CHCG	60646	2920	5W-7N	B3
6300	LNWD	60712	2920	5W-7N	B3
7200	LNWD	60712	2866	5W-9N	B7
7300	SKOK	60076	2866	5W-9N	B7
S Keeler Av					
-	CHCG	60456	3212	5W-10S	B4
-	CHCG	60652	3212	5W-10S	B4
10	CHCG	60624	3032	5W-1S	B7
1100	CHCG	60623	3032	5W-1S	B7
1500	CHCG	60623	3090	5W-2S	B4
3900	CHCG	60632	3090	5W-4S	B6
4600	CHCG	60632	3150	5W-5S	B3
5400	CHCG	60629	3150	5W-7S	B6
8700	HMTN	60456	3212	5W-10S	B4
9100	OKLN	60453	3212	5W-11S	B7
10700	OKLN	60453	3276	5W-12S	C2
11500	CHCG	60655	3276	5W-13S	C4
12400	ALSP	60803	3276	5W-14S	C6
S Keeley St					
2800	CHCG	60608	3091	1W-2S	E3
Keenan Ln					
3400	GNVW	60025	2809	10W-15N	E3
3400	GNVW	60025	2810	10W-15N	A3
3700	GNVW	60062	2809	10W-15N	E3
N Keene Av					
6200	CHCG	60646	2919	5W-7N	E3
6200	CHCG	60646	2920	5W-7N	A3
Keene Ln					
5200	HRPK	60133	2911		E6
Keenehand Ct					
4400	RNPK	60471	3594	5W-26S	B3
Keeney Ct					
5900	MNGV	60053	2865	7W-10N	B5
Keeney Rd					
10	BMDL	60108	2912		B7
10	BmdT	60108	2912		B7
10	BmdT	60172	2912		B7
400	ROSL	60172	2912		B7
Keeney St					
1600	EVTN	60202	2867	3W-10N	A5
1900	EVTN	60202	2866	3W-10N	E5
3800	SKOK	60076	2866	5W-10N	A5
4700	SKOK	60076	2865	5W-10N	E5
4700	SKOK	60077	2865	5W-10N	E5
5700	MNGV	60053	2865	7W-10N	C5
W Keeney St					
6800	MNGV	60053	2864	8W-10N	E5
7000	NLES	60714	2864	8W-10N	D5
Keep Av					
600	ELGN	60120	2855		B1
Keepataw Ct					
10	LMNT	60439	3270		E6
Keepataw Dr					
400	LMNT	60439	3270		E6
Keepataw Ln					
10	LMNT	60439	3270		E7
Keilman St					
100	DYR	46311	3598		D2
Keim Tr					
1100	BRLT	60103	2910		E7
Keith Ct					
2300	RGMW	60008	2805	20W-14N	E4
Keith Dr					
5000	RNPK	60471	3594	6W-27S	A4
Kelberg Av					
1700	HFET	60120	2855		E1
Kelburn Rd					
300	DRFD	60015	2756	10W-20N	E1
300	DRFD	60015	2757	10W-20N	A1
Keller Dr					
6000	BRRG	60527	3146		A5
Kelley Dr					
1700	HFET	60192	2856	30W-12N	C1
Kelling Ln					
300	GLNC	60022	2758	7W-18N	C3
Kells Dr					
8700	HYHL	60457	3210	10W-10S	A6
Kelly Ct					
9200	ODHL	60477	3423	11W-19S	E2
Kelly St					
10	EGVV	60007	2861	18W-10N	A5
W Kelly St					
1200	ANHT	60004	2753	18W-16N	D6
W Kelly Ann Dr					
800	PLTN	60067	2805	22W-15N	C2
Kelsey Ln					
17500	ODPK	60467	3422	14W-21S	D6
17500	OrlT	60467	3422	14W-21S	D6
N Kelso Av					
4600	CHCG	60630	2920	5W-5N	B7
Kelso Glen Ct					
700	IVNS	60010	2751	23W-16N	D6
700	IVNS	60067	2751	23W-16N	D6
Kelvin Ln					
9400	SRPK	60176	2917	11W-6N	C7
Kemah Ct					
700	SMBG	60193	2858	24W-10N	D6
Kemah Ln					
200	SMBG	60193	2858	24W-10N	D6
Kemman Av					
-	BDVW	60155	3087	11W-2S	D3
-	BDVW	60525	3087	11W-2S	D3
100	BKFD	60513	3087	12W-3S	C4
100	LGNG	60513	3087	12W-3S	C4
100	LGNG	60525	3087	12W-3S	C4
100	LGPK	60525	3087	12W-3S	C4
700	BKFD	60525	3087	11W-3S	C5
1500	PvsT	60525	3087	11W-2S	D3
Kemper Dr					
15500	ODPK	60462	3346	11W-18S	A7
W Kemper Pl					
600	CHCG	60614	2978	0W-2N	A6
N Kendal Ct					
1500	ANHT	60004	2807	16W-15N	C2
Kendal Rd					
10	EGVV	60007	2914		D2
Kendale Ln					
1700	GNVW	60025	2810	8W-14N	E4
Kendall Av					
500	EMHT	60126	3028		A6
500	YkTp	60126	3028		A6
Kendall Ct					
-	LYWD	60411	3509	2E-23S	D3
600	SMBG	60194	2857	27W-11N	C3
Kendall Ln					
8600	ODPK	60462	3346	10W-18S	B7
Kendall on Oxford					
10	RGMW	60008	2805	22W-13N	B6
Kendrick Ct					
200	SMBG	60194	2858	24W-10N	C5
Kenilworth Av					
-	KLWH	60091	2812	4W-14N	C5
-	WLMT	60043	2812	4W-14N	C5
10	EGVV	60007	2914		D3
10	KLWH	60043	2812	4W-14N	C5
500	EDND	60118	2801		A1
1200	BRWN	60402	3030	8W-1S	E7
1200	OKPK	60304	3030	8W-1S	E7
1500	BRWN	60402	3088	8W-1S	E1
1900	WLMT	60091	2812	4W-14N	B4
2600	NtrT	60091	2812	5W-14N	A4
2600	NtrT	60093	2812	5W-14N	A4
4300	SKNY	60402	3088	8W-4S	E7
4400	FTVW	60402	3088	8W-4S	E7
4500	FTVW	60402	3148	8W-4S	E1
E Kenilworth Av					
300	PTHT	60070	2808	15W-15N	B1
300	WLNG	60070	2808	15W-15N	B1
300	WLNG	60090	2808	15W-15N	B1
1200	PLTN	60074	2806	19W-15N	C1
N Kenilworth Av					
10	MPPT	60056	2807	16W-13N	D7
100	OKPK	60301	3030	8W-0N	E3
100	OKPK	60302	3030	8W-0N	E3
300	EMHT	60126	3028		A1
500	EMHT	60126	2972		A6
1200	CHCG	60302	3030	8W-2N	E1
1200	CHCG	60707	3030	8W-2N	E1
1200	OKPK	60707	3030	8W-2N	E1
S Kenilworth Av					
100	EMHT	60126	3028		A4
100	MPPT	60056	2807	16W-12N	D7
100	MPPT	60056	2861	16W-12N	D1
100	OKPK	60302	3030	8W-0N	E5
500	OKPK	60304	3030	8W-0S	E5
1100	BRWN	60402	3030	8W-0S	E7
W Kenilworth Av					
10	PTHT	60070	2807	15W-15N	E2
10	PTHT	60070	2808	15W-15N	A1
200	PLTN	60067	2805	21W-15N	D1
400	PltT	60067	2805	21W-15N	C1
1300	IVNS	60067	2805	22W-15N	A1
Kenilworth Av N					
500	OKPK	60302	3030	8W-1N	E3
Kenilworth Cir					
1900	HFET	60195	2804	25W-12N	B7
1900	HFET	60195	2858	25W-12N	B1
Kenilworth Ct					
400	DSPN	60016	2862	14W-11N	C4
Kenilworth Dr					
400	SMBG	60193	2859	22W-10N	B6
1000	WLNG	60090	2754	16W-18N	E3
1300	CTCY	60409	3430	4E-19S	C3
4600	RGMW	60008	2806	19W-12N	C7
4600	RGMW	60008	2860	19W-11N	B2
Kenilworth Ln					
900	GNVW	60025	2811	7W-14N	A4
1400	GNVW	60025	2810	8W-14N	E4
E Kenilworth Rd					
500	PLTN	60067	2806	20W-15N	A1
500	PLTN	60074	2806	20W-15N	A1
Kenilworth Ter					
600	KLWH	60043	2812	4W-14N	C4
600	WLMT	60091	2812	4W-14N	C4
Kenmare Ct					
600	DSPN	60016	2808	13W-13N	D6
Kenmare Dr					
600	DSPN	60016	2808	13W-13N	D6
900	BRRG	60527	3146		B6
Kenmore Av					
10	DRFD	60015	2756	11W-20N	C2
N Kenmore Av					
2000	CHCG	60614	2977	1W-2N	E6
3000	CHCG	60657	2977	1W-3N	E4
4000	CHCG	60613	2977	1W-5N	E1
4200	CHCG	60613	2921	1W-5N	E7
4200	CHCG	60640	2921	1W-5N	E7
5500	CHCG	60660	2921	1W-6N	E5
6300	CHCG	60626	2921	1W-7N	E4
S Kenmore Av					
100	EMHT	60126	3028		A3
Kenmore Ct					
2400	SMBG	60193	2857	26W-10N	E6
Kennedy Ct					
9000	ODPK	60462	3346	11W-17S	A6
9300	MNSR	46321	3510		D2
W Kennedy Ct					
6000	MONE	60449	3682	7W-31S	D5
Kennedy Dr					
-	PLTN	60074	2753	19W-18N	C4
8900	MaiT	60016	2863	11W-11N	D3
E Kennedy Dr					
1300	SMWD	60107	2857	27W-11N	D4
N Kennedy Dr					
10	CPVL	60110	2748		C5
100	BNHL	60110	2748		C5
1200	SMWD	60107	2857	27W-11N	D4
N Kennedy Dr SR-25					
10	CPVL	60110	2748		C5
100	BNHL	60110	2748		C5
W Kennedy Dr					
100	SMWD	60107	2857	27W-11N	D4
Kennedy Expwy					
-	CHCG	-	2917	11W-7N	E4
-	CHCG	-	2918	10W-7N	A4
-	CHCG	-	2919	7W-6N	A5
-	CHCG	-	2920	5W-5N	A7
-	CHCG	-	2976	4W-4N	C2
-	CHCG	-	2977	2W-2N	C7
-	CHCG	-	3033	1W-1N	D1
-	CHCG	-	3034	0W-0N	A4
Kennedy Expwy I-90					
-	CHCG	-	2917	11W-7N	E4
-	CHCG	-	2918	8W-6N	E5
-	CHCG	-	2919	7W-6N	A5
-	CHCG	-	2920	5W-5N	A7
-	CHCG	-	2976	5W-4N	B2
-	CHCG	-	2977	1W-2N	C7
-	CHCG	-	3033	1W-1N	D1
-	CHCG	-	3034	0W-0N	A4
Kennedy Expwy I-94					
-	CHCG	-	2976	4W-4N	C2
-	CHCG	-	2977	2W-2N	B6
-	CHCG	-	3033	1W-1N	D1
-	CHCG	-	3034	0W-0N	A4
Kennedy Expwy E					
-	CHCG	-	2919	6W-6N	D6
-	CHCG	-	3034	0W-0S	A5
Kennedy Expwy E I-90					
-	CHCG	-	2919	6W-6N	D6
-	CHCG	-	3034	0W-0S	A5
Kennedy Expwy E I-94					
-	CHCG	-	3034	0W-0S	A5
Kennedy Expwy W					
-	CHCG	-	3034	0W-0N	A4
Kennedy Expwy W I-90					
-	CHCG	-	3034	0W-0N	A4
Kennedy Expwy W I-94					
-	CHCG	-	3034	0W-0N	A4
Kennedy Ln					
1000	FDHT	60411	3509	1E-25S	B7
W Kennedy Rd					
4800	WlIT	60468	3861	7W-38S	E6
6400	PtnT	60468	3861	9W-38S	A6
7200	PtnT	60468	3860	9W-38S	E6
Kennedy St					
-	FNPK	60131	2973	11W-3N	E4
-	RVGV	60171	2973	11W-3N	D4
100	EGvT	60018	2862	15W-9N	A7
Kenneth Av					
10	PTHT	60070	2808	15W-16N	A1
7400	LNWD	60712	2866	5W-9N	A7
9000	SKOK	60076	2866	5W-11N	A3
14300	CTWD	60445	3348	5W-17S	B4
14300	MDLN	60445	3348	5W-17S	B4
N Kenneth Av					
200	CHCG	60624	3032	5W-0N	A4
1900	CHCG	60639	2976	5W-2N	A7
2800	CHCG	60641	2976	5W-3N	A4
4300	CHCG	60630	2976	5W-5N	A1
4800	CHCG	60630	2920	5W-6N	A6
5600	CHCG	60646	2920	5W-7N	A4
6800	LNWD	60712	2920	5W-8N	A1
7200	LNWD	60712	2866	5W-9N	A7
7300	SKOK	60076	2866	5W-9N	A7
S Kenneth Av					
700	CHCG	60624	3032	5W-0S	A6
1400	CHCG	60623	3032	5W-1S	A7
1500	CHCG	60623	3090	5W-1S	A1
4700	CHCG	60632	3150	5W-5S	B1
5400	CHCG	60629	3150	5W-7S	B6
8300	CHCG	60652	3212	5W-9S	B3
8700	HMTN	60456	3212	5W-10S	B4
9500	OKLN	60453	3212	5W-11S	B6
10200	OKLN	60453	3276	5W-12S	B1
10800	CHCG	60655	3276	5W-12S	B3
11500	ALSP	60803	3276	5W-13S	B4
Kenneth Cir					
10	ELGN	60120	2855		D2
Kenneth Ct					
14100	CTWD	60445	3348	5W-16S	B3
N Kenneth Ct					
300	GNWD	60425	3428	0W-22S	B7
300	GNWD	60425	3508	0W-22S	B1
S Kenneth Ct					
-	CHCG	60652	3212	5W-9S	B2
Kenneth Dr					
8800	MaiT	60016	2863	11W-12N	E1
W Kenneth Dr					
1600	EGvT	60056	2861	16W-10N	D5
1600	MPPT	60056	2861	16W-10N	D5
Kenneth Ter					
8800	SKOK	60076	2866	5W-11N	A3
N Kennicott Av					
-	BFGV	60089	2753	18W-18N	E3
400	ANHT	60005	2806	18W-14N	E4
600	ANHT	60004	2806	18W-14N	E3
3900	ANHT	60004	2753	18W-18N	E3
4500	CHCG	60630	2920	5W-5N	B7
S Kennicott Av					
100	ANHT	60005	2806	18W-13N	E6
Kennicott Ct					
1700	ANHT	60004	2806	18W-15N	E1
1900	DSPN	60018	2863	12W-9N	B6
N Kennicott Dr					
1900	ANHT	60004	2806	18W-16N	E1
2000	ANHT	60004	2753	18W-16N	E7
S Kennicott Dr					
1500	ANHT	60005	2860	18W-12N	E2
1600	RGMW	60005	2860	18W-12N	E2
1600	RGMW	60008	2860	18W-12N	E2
Kennicott Ln					
4100	GNVW	60025	2809	11W-14N	C5
Kennicott Pl					
800	MPPT	60056	2861	17W-11N	C2
N Kennison Av					
5000	CHCG	60630	2920	5W-6N	A6
Kennsington E					
900	DYR	46311	3510		E6
N Kenosha Av					
3100	CHCG	60641	2976	5W-3N	B4
Kensington Av					
1600	WSTR	60154	3086		E1
2500	WSTR	60154	3087	13W-2S	A4
3000	LGPK	60525	3087	13W-2S	A4
16100	TYPK	60477	3424	9W-19S	D2
E Kensington Av					
100	CHCG	60628	3278	0E-13S	D4
N Kensington Av					
10	LGNG	60525	3087	12W-4S	B7
200	LGPK	60525	3087	12W-3S	B5
S Kensington Av					
10	LGNG	60525	3087	12W-4S	B7
1100	LGNG	60525	3147	12W-5S	B3
5500	CTSD	60525	3147	12W-6S	B4
Kensington Ct					
10	SMWD	60107	2856	29W-11N	E4
500	ROSL	60172	2912		C6
S Kensington Ct					
300	PLTN	60067	2805	22W-15N	B2
Kensington Dr					
300	SMWD	60107	2856	29W-11N	D4
900	NHBK	60062	2810	8W-16N	D1
2100	SMBG	60194	2858	26W-11N	A3
2200	SMBG	60194	2857	26W-11N	E3
Kensington Ln					
1900	HFET	60195	2804	24W-13N	B7
1900	HFET	60195	2858	25W-12N	A1
7600	HRPK	60133	2911		E1
8100	HRPK	60133	2857	26W-9N	E7
8100	SMBG	60193	2857	26W-9N	E7
S Kensington Ln					
-	MonT	60449	3682	9W-31S	A5
25600	GGnT	60449	3682	9W-31S	A5
E Kensington Rd					
100	MPPT	60056	2808	13W-13N	D5
600	ANHT	60004	2807	16W-14N	C5
600	ANHT	60005	2807	16W-14N	C5
1400	WhlT	60056	2808	13W-13N	D5
1900	WhlT	60025	2808	13W-13N	E5
2400	MPPT	60056	2807	16W-14N	D5
W Kensington Rd					
200	MPPT	60056	2808	15W-13N	A5
300	MPPT	60056	2807	15W-13N	E5
600	ANHT	60004	2807	15W-13N	E5
600	ANHT	60056	2807	15W-13N	E5
600	MPPT	60004	2807	15W-14N	E5
Kensington Wy					
9000	ODPK	60462	3345	11W-18S	E6
9000	ODPK	60462	3346	11W-18S	A6
Kensington on Oxford					
10	RGMW	60008	2805	22W-13N	B6
Kent Av					
300	EGvT	60007	2861	17W-9N	B6
300	EGVV	60007	2861	17W-9N	B6
1000	PKRG	60068	2918	10W-7N	A3
S Kent Av					
700	EMHT	60126	3028		A6
W Kent Av					
700	CteT	60417	3685	1W-31S	B5
Kent Cir					
800	BRLT	60103	2910		D5
Kent Ct					
400	SMBG	60193	2858	24W-9N	E7
700	HRPK	60133	2858	26W-9N	A7
Kent Ln					
1400	ELGN	60120	2855		E3
Kent Pl					
3600	CRTE	60417	3596	0E-28S	E6
Kent Rd					
10	WNKA	60093	2758	5W-16N	E7
300	RVSD	60546	3088	9W-2S	D4
700	KLWH	60043	2812	4W-14N	C4
700	NtrT	60043	2812	4W-14N	C4
700	NtrT	60093	2812	4W-14N	C4
1700	HFET	60195	2858	24W-12N	E1
Kent St					
9800	BDVW	60155	3087	12W-1S	C1
9800	WSTR	60154	3087	12W-1S	B1
Kenton Av					
7400	LNWD	60712	2866	5W-9N	A7
8800	SKOK	60076	2866	5W-11N	A3
13500	CTWD	60445	3348	5W-16S	B2
14100	MDLN	60445	3348	5W-17S	B6
15000	MDLN	60452	3348	5W-17S	B6
15000	OKFT	60452	3348	5W-17S	B6
15200	OKFT	60445	3348	5W-18S	B6
15300	BmnT	60445	3348	5W-18S	B7
15300	BmnT	60452	3348	5W-18S	B7
N Kenton Av					
100	CHCG	60624	3032	5W-0N	A4
100	CHCG	60644	3032	5W-0N	A4
700	CHCG	60651	3032	5W-0N	A3
1600	CHCG	60639	3032	5W-1N	A1
2400	CHCG	60639	2976	5W-3N	A5
2700	CHCG	60641	2976	5W-3N	A5
5100	CHCG	60630	2920	5W-6N	A6
5800	CHCG	60646	2920	5W-7N	A4
6400	CHCG	60712	2920	5W-8N	A3
7000	LNWD	60712	2920	5W-8N	A1
S Kenton Av					
10	CHCG	60624	3032	5W-0S	A5
10	CHCG	60644	3032	5W-0S	A5
5800	CHCG	60629	3150	5W-6S	A4
8400	CHCG	60652	3212	5W-9S	A4
8700	HMTN	60456	3212	5W-10S	A4
9300	OKLN	60453	3212	5W-11S	A6
10200	OKLN	60453	3276	5W-12S	A2
11000	CHCG	60655	3276	5W-12S	B3
11500	ALSP	60803	3276	5W-13S	B4
W Kenton Ct					
7700	FftT	60423	3504	9W-24S	E4
Kentucky Av					
14500	HRVY	60426	3350	1W-17S	A5
N Kentucky Av					
4800	CHCG	60630	2920	5W-6N	A6
Kentucky Ct					
10	PKFT	60466	3595	3W-25S	B1
10600	ODPK	60467	3423	13W-21S	B7
Kentucky Ln					
900	EGVV	60007	2913		D2
E Kentucky Rd					
100	WshT	60401	3864	0E-38S	E6
W Kentucky Rd					
100	WshT	60401	3864	1W-38S	A6
Kentucky St					
200	PKFT	60466	3595	3W-25S	B1
Kentwood Ct					
1000	DYR	46311	3510		C6
Kentwood Dr					
1000	DYR	46311	3510	4E-25S	C6
Kenwood Av					
14200	DLTN	60419	3351	1E-16S	B4
15600	SHLD	60473	3351	1E-18S	B7
17000	SHLD	60473	3429	1E-20S	B4
S Kenwood Av					
4800	CHCG	60615	3153	1E-5S	A1
6800	CHCG	60637	3153	1E-7S	A6
7300	CHCG	60619	3153	1E-8S	A7
7800	CHCG	60619	3215	1E-9S	A3
Kenwood Ct					
1200	SHLD	60473	3429	1E-19S	B2
Kenwood Dr					
16200	SHLD	60473	3429	1E-19S	B1
Kenwood Rd					
1500	HFET	60194	2858	25W-12N	B2
1500	HFET	60195	2858	25W-12N	B2
Kenwood St					
10	CTCY	60409	3430		D1
10	HMND	46324	3430		E1
800	HMND	46320	3430		E1
E Kenwood St					
900	HMND	46320	3430		E1
900	HMND	46324	3430		E1
Kenyon Rd					
300	BRLT	60120	2909		A2
300	ElgT	60177	2909		A2
800	SEGN	60177	2909		A2
N Keokuk Av					
4400	CHCG	60630	2920	5W-5N	B7
Keokuk Rd					
6300	IHPK	60525	3146		D5
N Keota Av					
6600	CHCG	60646	2919	7W-8N	C2
Keough St					
1200	LMNT	60439	3271		A7
N Kerbs Av					
5600	CHCG	60646	2919	5W-7N	E4
5700	CHCG	60646	2920	5W-7N	A4
N Kercheval Av					
5700	CHCG	60646	2919	5W-7N	E4
5700	CHCG	60646	2920	5W-7N	A4
S Kerfoot Av					
8300	CHCG	60620	3214	0W-9S	A3
Keri Ln					
10	BRRG	60527	3208		A6
Kerri Ct					
400	SMBG	60173	2859	21W-11N	E4
Kerry Av					
17000	ODPK	60467	3423	13W-20S	B4
Kerry Ct					
400	PTHT	60070	2754	16W-16N	D6
S Kerry Ct					
800	PLTN	60067	2805	21W-14N	D3
W Kerry Ct					
400	PLTN	60067	2805	21W-14N	D3
Kerry Ln					
10	WLNG	60090	2755	14W-16N	C6
300	DRFD	60015	2757	10W-20N	B1
S Kerry Ln					
13500	HMGN	60441	3343	17W-16S	D3
E Kerry Brook Ln					
200	ANHT	60004	2754	17W-17N	A6
S Kerwood St					
10	PLTN	60067	2806	20W-15N	A1
Keswick Rd					
10	EGVV	60007	2914		D1
Kettering Ln					
10	LMNT	60439	3270		D6
Kettering Rd					
2000	HFET	60195	2858	25W-12N	B1
Kettering on Oxford					
10	RGMW	60008	2805	22W-13N	B6
Kettle Ct					
2000	LNSG	60438	3429	2E-21S	D7
E Kevin Cir					
1000	PLTN	60074	2753	19W-18N	B2
Kevin Ln					
-	UYPK	60466	3684	3W-29S	B1
2600	RGMW	60008	2805	21W-13N	C5
Kevin Wy					
-	MTSN	60443	3505	7W-24S	D5
Kevin Morris Ct					
1300	SMWD	60107	2857	27W-11N	D4
Kevyn Ln					
300	BNVL	60106	2915		D7
N Kewanee Av					
4700	CHCG	60630	2920	5W-5N	B7
Kewaunee Ct					
400	PTHT	60070	2807	16W-15N	E2
Keystone Av					
10	FTPK	60130	3030	9W-0N	B5
10	RVFT	60305	3030	9W-0N	B5
800	NHBK	60062	2757	9W-17N	B5
2200	FTPK	60130	3088	9W-2S	C2
2200	FTPK	60546	3088	9W-2S	C2
2200	NRIV	60546	3088	9W-2S	C2
2500	RVSD	60546	3088	9W-2S	C3
7400	LNWD	60712	2866	5W-9N	B7
9700	SKOK	60076	2866	5W-12N	B1
9900	EVTN	60076	2866	5W-12N	B1
9900	EVTN	60201	2866	5W-12N	B1
14300	CTWD	60445	3348	5W-17S	C4
14300	MDLN	60445	3348	5W-17S	C4
19900	MTSN	60443	3506	5W-24S	C5
19900	RchT	60443	3506	5W-24S	C5
N Keystone Av					
200	CHCG	60624	3032	5W-0N	B4
800	CHCG	60651	3032	5W-1N	B2
1500	CHCG	60639	3032	5W-1N	B1
1600	CHCG	60639	2976	5W-2N	B7
4000	CHCG	60641	2976	5W-5N	B1
4400	CHCG	60630	2920	5W-5N	B7
5600	CHCG	60646	2920	5W-7N	B4
6300	LNWD	60712	2920	5W-7N	B3
7200	LNWD	60712	2866	5W-9N	B7
7300	SKOK	60076	2866	5W-9N	B7
S Keystone Av					
13500	RBBN	60472	3348	5W-16S	C2
13700	CTWD	60445	3348	5W-16S	C3
Keystone Ct					
300	GLNC	60022	2759		A5
1400	ELGN	60120	2855		E5
5100	RGMW	60008	2860	19W-12N	C1

STREET Block	City	ZIP	Map#	CGS	Grid
Keystone Pl					
-	HRPK	60133	2912		A2
-	SMBG	60133	2912		A2
-	SMBG	60193	2912		A2
Keystone Rd					
2800	NHBK	60062	2756	11W-17N	D6
7800	ODPK	60462	3346	9W-18S	D7
Keywest Dr					
1200	LKPT	60441	3342	21W-18S	A7
Kickapoo Dr					
19300	TYPK	60477	3504	9W-23S	E3
19400	FftT	60423	3504	9W-23S	E3
19400	TYPK	60423	3504	9W-23S	E3
S Kickapoo Tr					
13500	HMGN	60441	3343	16W-16S	E3
Kiess Dr					
3800	GNVW	60025	2809	11W-15N	D3
Kiest Av					
1800	NHBK	60062	2757	9W-17N	B5
Kilbourn Av					
7400	LNWD	60712	2866	5W-9N	A7
7400	SKOK	60076	2866	5W-9N	A7
14300	CTWD	60445	3348	5W-17S	B5
14300	MDLN	60445	3348	5W-17S	B6
15200	BmnT	60445	3348	5W-18S	B6
15200	OKFT	60445	3348	5W-18S	B6
N Kilbourn Av					
10	CHCG	60624	3032	5W-0N	A4
600	CHCG	60644	3032	5W-0N	A3
600	CHCG	60651	3032	5W-0N	A3
1600	CHCG	60639	2976	5W-2N	A7
1600	CHCG	60639	3032	5W-1N	A1
2700	CHCG	60641	2976	5W-3N	A5
4400	CHCG	60630	2920	5W-5N	A7
5600	CHCG	60646	2920	5W-7N	A4
6800	LNWD	60712	2920	5W-8N	A1
7300	LNWD	60712	2866	5W-9N	A7
7300	SKOK	60076	2866	5W-9N	A7
S Kilbourn Av					
10	CHCG	60624	3032	5W-0S	A5
1100	CHCG	60623	3032	5W-1S	A7
2700	CHCG	60623	3090	5W-3S	A4
4700	CHCG	60632	3150	5W-5S	A2
5400	CHCG	60629	3150	5W-7S	B6
7700	CHCG	60652	3212	5W-9S	B2
8600	HMTN	60652	3212	5W-9S	B4
8700	HMTN	60456	3212	5W-10S	A4
9100	OKLN	60453	3212	5W-11S	B6
10400	OKLN	60453	3276	5W-12S	B2
10800	CHCG	60655	3276	5W-12S	B3
11500	ALSP	60803	3276	5W-13S	B4
Kilchurn Ln					
100	IVNS	60067	2752	22W-16N	B7
Kildare Av					
7400	LNWD	60712	2866	5W-9N	A7
9000	SKOK	60076	2866	5W-11N	B2
13500	CTWD	60445	3348	5W-16S	B2
13500	RBBN	60472	3348	5W-16S	B2
14600	MDLN	60445	3348	5W-17S	C6
21100	MTSN	60443	3506	5W-25S	C7
21100	MTSN	60443	3594	5W-25S	C1
N Kildare Av					
10	CHCG	60624	3032	5W-0N	B4
800	CHCG	60651	3032	5W-1N	B2
1500	CHCG	60639	3032	5W-1N	B1
1600	CHCG	60639	2976	5W-2N	B7
4100	CHCG	60641	2976	5W-5N	A1
4300	CHCG	60630	2976	5W-5N	A1
4700	CHCG	60630	2920	5W-6N	A6
5500	CHCG	60646	2920	5W-6N	B5
6800	LNWD	60712	2920	5W-8N	A1
7200	LNWD	60712	2866	5W-9N	B7
7300	SKOK	60076	2866	5W-9N	B7
S Kildare Av					
10	CHCG	60624	3032	5W-0S	B5
1500	CHCG	60623	3032	5W-1S	B7
1800	CHCG	60623	3090	5W-1S	B1
4000	CHCG	60632	3090	5W-4S	B7
4700	CHCG	60632	3150	5W-5S	B1
5400	CHCG	60629	3150	5W-7S	B6
7900	CHCG	60652	3212	5W-9S	B2
8700	HMTN	60456	3212	5W-10S	B4
10000	OKLN	60453	3212	5W-11S	B7
10200	OKLN	60453	3276	5W-12S	B1
11500	ALSP	60803	3276	5W-13S	B4
13300	RBBN	60472	3348	5W-15S	B2
13400	CTWD	60445	3348	5W-15S	B2
Kildare Ct					
10	DRFD	60015	2757	10W-20N	B1
4300	MTSN	60443	3594	5W-25S	C1
16600	TYPK	60477	3424	9W-19S	E3
Kildare Ln					
10	DRFD	60015	2757	9W-20N	B1
Kildeer Ln					
300	VrnT	60015	2755	14W-20N	B1
Kiley Ln					
11500	ODPK	60467	3422	14W-21S	D5
Kilkenny Av					
19700	TYPK	60448	3504	11W-23S	A4
19800	FftT	60448	3504	11W-23S	A4
Killarney Ct					
-	TYPK	60477	3424	10W-21S	C7
700	SMBG	60193	2859	23W-10N	A6
3600	RGMW	60008	2806	18W-13N	D6
S Killarney Ct					
700	EMHT	60126	3028		B5
Killarney Ln					
1700	NHBK	60062	2758	7W-16N	A7
Killian Ct					
-	WNKA	60093	2812	5W-15N	B1
Kilpatrick Av					
-	OKLN	60456	3212	5W-10S	A5
-	SKOK	60076	2865	5W-9N	E6
200	WLMT	60091	2811	5W-13N	E7
9100	HMTN	60453	3212	5W-10S	A5
9100	HMTN	60456	3212	5W-10S	A5
9100	OKLN	60453	3212	5W-10S	A5
9100	SKOK	60076	2866	5W-11N	A3
10300	OKLN	60453	3276	5W-12S	A2
11000	CHCG	60655	3276	5W-12S	A3
13900	CTWD	60445	3348	5W-17S	A5
15100	MDLN	60445	3348	5W-18S	B7
15100	OKFT	60445	3348	5W-18S	B7
15100	OKFT	60452	3348	5W-18S	B7
16700	BmnT	60477	3426	5W-20S	B3
16700	OKFT	60452	3426	5W-20S	B3
N Kilpatrick Av					
600	CHCG	60644	3032	5W-0N	A3
1400	CHCG	60651	3032	5W-1N	A1
1500	CHCG	60639	3032	5W-1N	A1
1900	CHCG	60639	2976	5W-2N	A7
3600	CHCG	60641	2976	5W-4N	A2
4000	CHCG	60641	2975	5W-5N	E1
4800	CHCG	60630	2919	6W-7N	D4
4900	CHCG	60630	2920	5W-6N	A6
N Kilpatrick Av					
5800	CHCG	60646	2919	5W-7N	E4
6100	CHCG	60646	2920	5W-7N	A3
6300	LNWD	60712	2919	5W-8N	E2
7200	LNWD	60712	2865	5W-9N	E7
S Kilpatrick Av					
10	CHCG	60644	3032	5W-0S	A5
4200	CHCG	60632	3090	5W-4S	A7
5400	CHCG	60629	3150	5W-6S	A3
5400	CHCG	60632	3150	5W-6S	A3
5400	CHCG	60638	3150	5W-6S	A3
7700	CHCG	60652	3212	5W-8S	A1
8600	CHCG	60456	3212	5W-9S	A4
8600	HMTN	60456	3212	5W-9S	A4
Kilpatrick Ln					
8700	HMTN	60456	3212	5W-10S	A4
Kilrea Dr					
9300	PlsT	60462	3345	11W-15S	E2
Kilrenny					
800	IVNS	60067	2804	23W-14N	D3
W Kim Av					
1700	MPPT	60056	2861	17W-12N	C1
Kim Pl					
1000	LMNT	60439	3270		D7
Kimball Av					
6500	HGKN	60525	3147	11W-7S	D6
8200	SKOK	60076	2866	4W-10N	D5
8700	SKOK	60203	2866	4W-10N	D4
18400	HMWD	60430	3506	4W-22S	E1
N Kimball Av					
1600	CHCG	60647	2976	4W-2N	D7
2700	CHCG	60618	2976	4W-3N	D5
4300	CHCG	60625	2976	4W-5N	D1
4400	CHCG	60625	2920	4W-5N	D7
5500	CHCG	60659	2920	4W-7N	D3
7100	LNWD	60076	2920	4W-8N	D1
7100	LNWD	60712	2920	4W-8N	C1
7100	SKOK	60076	2920	4W-8N	C1
W Kimball Av					
600	PLTN	60067	2805	21W-15N	C2
Kimball Pl					
5200	OKLN	60453	3211	6W-10S	D4
Kimball St					
300	ELGN	60120	2855		A3
Kimball Hill Dr					
4800	RGMW	60008	2860	19W-11N	B3
Kimbark Av					
14200	DLTN	60419	3351	1E-17S	B5
15600	SHLD	60473	3351	1E-18S	B7
16700	SHLD	60473	3429	1E-19S	B2
S Kimbark Av					
5300	CHCG	60615	3153	1E-5S	A2
5400	CHCG	60637	3153	1E-5S	A2
7100	CHCG	60619	3153	1E-8S	A7
7700	CHCG	60619	3215	1E-9S	A2
Kimbark Ct					
16700	SHLD	60473	3429	1E-19S	B2
Kimbark Rd					
10	RVSD	60546	3088	10W-3S	B5
E Kimber Ln					
800	ANHT	60005	2861	17W-11N	B4
W Kimber Ln					
8200	PSPK	60464	3274	10W-13S	B4
Kimberley Ln					
600	SMWD	60107	2856	29W-10N	D5
Kimberly Av					
-	PltT	60067	2805	22W-14N	A5
-	PltT	60195	2805	22W-14N	A5
E Kimberly Av					
10	PltT	60067	2805	20W-13N	E5
10	RGMW	60008	2805	20W-13N	E5
10	RGMW	60067	2805	20W-13N	E5
N Kimberly Av					
5000	CHCG	60630	2919	6W-7N	D4
5000	CHCG	60630	2920	5W-6N	A6
Kimberly Ct					
10	DRFD	60015	2756	11W-20N	C2
4800	OKFT	60452	3426	6W-20S	A3
8400	BRRG	60527	3208		A4
S Kimberly Ct					
25100	GGnT	60449	3682	9W-30S	A3
Kimberly Dr					
100	EDND	60118	2801		C2
1600	SMBG	60173	2859	21W-11N	E4
1600	SMBG	60173	2860	21W-11N	A3
6000	BmnT	60477	3425	7W-19S	B2
6100	TYPK	60477	3425	7W-19S	C3
Kimberly Ln					
10800	ODPK	60467	3423	13W-21S	A5
Kimberry Ct					
100	RGMW	60008	2805	21W-14N	D4
Kimmel Ct					
9300	OrlT	60477	3423	11W-21S	E6
9300	TYPK	60477	3423	11W-21S	E6
Kimmey Ln					
9500	FNPK	60131	2973	11W-4N	C3
Kin Ct					
500	WLMT	60091	2811	5W-13N	E6
Kincaid Ct					
10	DSPN	60016	2862	15W-10N	B4
Kincaid St					
500	HDPK	60035	2758	7W-20N	B1
Kindling Ct					
10500	PlsT	60464	3345	13W-15S	B1
Kindrat Ln					
-	HMGN	60441	3342	19W-16S	D4
King Av					
100	DndT	60118	2801		B2
100	EDND	60118	2801		B3
9000	FNPK	60131	2973	11W-4N	D3
11200	FNPK	60131	2972		D4
King Cir					
1200	SHLD	60473	3351	1E-18S	B7
King Ct					
100	WLNG	60090	2755	15W-17N	A4
600	EDND	60118	2801		B3
King Dr					
10	SMWD	60107	2857	27W-9N	C7
10	SMWD	60107	2911		C1
1200	SHLD	60419	3351	1E-18S	B6
1200	SHLD	60473	3351	1E-18S	B6
1500	BKLY	60163	3028		C4
King Ln					
500	DSPN	60016	2862	15W-10N	A4
King Rd					
-	BNHL	60010	2802	30W-15N	A2
-	BNHL	60118	2802	30W-15N	A2
13400	HMGN	60441	3343	18W-15S	A2
13400	LMNT	60439	3343	18W-15S	A2
13400	LMNT	60441	3343	18W-15S	A2
S King Rd					
13700	HMGN	60441	3343	18W-16S	A4
King St					
10	EGvT	60007	2861	17W-10N	B5
10	EGVV	60007	2861	17W-10N	B5
King St					
11000	FNPK	60131	2972		D3
King Arthur Ct					
10	HnrT	60120	2856	31W-10N	A6
10	NHLK	60164	2972		C6
20500	LYWD	60411	3509	2E-24S	E5
N King Arthur Ct					
1100	PLTN	60067	2752	21W-17N	E4
W King Arthur Ct					
10	PLTN	60067	2752	21W-17N	D5
King Arthur Dr					
-	NHLK	60164	2972		C6
20500	LYWD	60411	3509	2E-24S	E5
Kingbird Ct					
10	SBTN	60010	2803	26W-14N	D3
N King Charles Ct					
1000	PLTN	60067	2752	21W-17N	E4
N King Edward Ct					
1300	PLTN	60067	2752	21W-17N	E4
1500	PltT	60074	2752	21W-17N	E4
Kingery Expwy					
-	LNSG	-	3429	2E-20S	C4
-	LNSG	-	3430	3E-20S	A4
-	MNSR	-	3430	4E-20S	C4
-	SHLD	-	3429	1E-20S	B4
-	ThtT	-	3429	1E-20S	C4
Kingery Expwy I-80					
-	LNSG	-	3429	2E-20S	C4
-	LNSG	-	3430	3E-20S	A4
-	MNSR	-	3430	4E-20S	C4
-	ThtT	-	3429	2E-20S	C4
Kingery Expwy I-94					
-	LNSG	-	3429	2E-20S	C4
-	LNSG	-	3430	3E-20S	A4
-	MNSR	-	3430	4E-20S	C4
-	SHLD	-	3429	1E-20S	B4
-	ThtT	-	3429	2E-20S	C4
Kingery Expwy SR-394					
-	SHLD	-	3429	1E-20S	B3
Kingery Expwy US-6					
-	LNSG	-	3430	3E-20S	A4
-	MNSR	-	3430	4E-20S	C4
Kingery Hwy					
-	DGvT	60439	3271		E1
-	DGvT	60527	3271		E1
-	EGVV	60106	2915		D7
-	LmnT	60439	3271		E1
-	LmnT	60439	3272	16W-12S	A2
400	BNVL	60106	2915		D7
Kingery Hwy SR-83					
-	DGvT	60439	3271		E1
-	DGvT	60527	3271		E1
-	EGVV	60106	2915		D7
-	LmnT	60439	3271		E1
-	LmnT	60439	3272	16W-12S	A1
400	BNVL	60106	2915		D7
Kingfisher Ct					
3200	RGMW	60008	2806	19W-13N	C6
Kingfisher Ln					
2100	RGMW	60008	2806	19W-13N	C6
Kingfisher Ln E					
3200	RGMW	60008	2806	19W-13N	C6
N King George Ct					
1300	PLTN	60067	2752	21W-17N	E4
W King George Ct					
10	PLTN	60067	2752	21W-17N	E4
W King Henry Ct					
10	PLTN	60067	2752	21W-17N	D5
Kingman Ln					
10	HFET	60194	2859	23W-11N	A4
10	SMBG	60194	2859	23W-11N	A4
200	HFET	60194	2858	24W-11N	E4
Kings Ct					
-	WSTR	60154	3086		D3
200	LGPK	60525	3087	12W-2S	B3
4800	RNPK	60471	3594	6W-27S	A4
Kings Ln					
900	GNVW	60025	2811	7W-14N	A3
Kings Rd					
100	CPVL	60110	2748		A5
100	DndT	60110	2748		A5
18700	HMWD	60430	3508	1W-22S	B1
S Kings Rd					
3300	BlmT	60466	3595	2W-28S	E7
3300	BlmT	60475	3595	2W-28S	E7
3300	CteT	60466	3595	2W-28S	E7
3300	CteT	60475	3595	2W-28S	E7
3300	STGR	60475	3595	2W-28S	E7
3500	CteT	60417	3595	2W-28S	E6
3500	STGR	60417	3595	2W-28S	E6
24000	CRTE	60417	3684	2W-29S	E1
24000	CteT	60417	3684	2W-29S	E1
24500	UYPK	60417	3684	2W-29S	D2
Kings Row					
100	BRTN	60010	2751	24W-18N	D2
E Kings Row					
800	PLTN	60074	2753	19W-18N	B2
Kingsborough Cove					
10	IVNS	60010	2750	25W-16N	E7
Kingsbridge Rd					
200	EGVV	60007	2914		C2
S Kingsbury Ct					
9700	PSHL	60465	3210	10W-11S	A7
W Kingsbury Ct					
700	ANHT	60004	2753	18W-16N	E6
Kingsbury Dr					
300	SMBG	60193	2857	26W-9N	E7
1300	HRPK	60133	2911		E1
7700	HRPK	60133	2857	26W-9N	E7
8200	HRPK	60193	2857	26W-10N	E7
8200	SMBG	60133	2857	26W-10N	E7
W Kingsbury Dr					
300	ANHT	60004	2754	18W-16N	A6
500	ANHT	60004	2753	18W-16N	E6
N Kingsbury St					
-	CHCG	60610	3033	1W-1N	E1
400	CHCG	60606	3034	0W-0N	B3
900	CHCG	60610	3034	0W-1N	A2
1200	CHCG	60622	3033	1W-1N	E1
1600	CHCG	60614	2977	1W-2N	D7
1600	CHCG	60622	2977	1W-2N	E7
Kings Canyon Dr					
900	HnrT	60107	2856	30W-9N	B7
N Kingsdale Av					
5700	CHCG	60646	2919	5W-7N	E4
5800	CHCG	60646	2920	5W-7N	A4
Kingsdale Rd					
1000	HFET	60194	2858	25W-11N	B3
1500	HFET	60195	2858	25W-12N	C1
Kingsley Ct					
-	ELGN	60120	2855		C4
Kingsley Dr					
1800	SMBG	60194	2858	25W-11N	A4
W Kingsley Dr					
500	ANHT	60004	2754	18W-18N	A3
W Kingsley Dr					
700	ANHT	60004	2753	18W-18N	E3
Kings Mill Ct					
200	SMBG	60193	2859	23W-10N	B5
Kingsmill Ln					
500	PTHT	60070	2808	14W-14N	C4
Kingsport Ct					
1400	NHBK	60062	2756	11W-17N	D6
Kingsport Dr					
100	SMBG	60193	2913		B1
200	SMBG	60193	2859	23W-9N	B7
1000	WLNG	60090	2754	15W-17N	E5
1100	WLNG	60004	2754	15W-17N	E5
Kingsport Rd					
16100	ODPK	60467	3423	13W-19S	A2
S Kingston Av					
7300	CHCG	60649	3153	3E-8S	D7
7500	CHCG	60649	3215	3E-9S	D2
7800	CHCG	60617	3215	3E-10S	D4
Kingston Cir					
1700	CPVL	60110	2748		D7
1700	CPVL	60110	2801		D1
Kingston Ct					
-	SMWD	60107	2911		A2
400	MPPT	60056	2808	14W-13N	C6
500	ROSL	60172	2912		C6
1400	DSPN	60018	2862	13W-10N	D5
1400	SMBG	60193	2858	25W-9N	B7
3000	SMWD	60107	2910		C2
6900	TYPK	60477	3425	8W-19S	A2
S Kingston Ct					
20100	FftT	60423	3504	9W-24S	D5
Kingston Dr					
5000	HFET	60010	2751	24W-16N	B7
5100	IVNS	60010	2751	24W-16N	B7
W Kingston Dr					
7700	FftT	60423	3504	9W-24S	D5
Kingston Ln					
800	BRLT	60103	2910		D5
1600	SMBG	60193	2858	25W-9N	B7
9000	ODPK	60462	3346	11W-18S	A6
Kingston Pl					
100	CHHT	60411	3507	1W-24S	E5
100	CHHT	60411	3508	1W-24S	A5
Kingston Rd					
2500	NHBK	60062	2809	10W-16N	E1
2500	NHBK	60062	2810	10W-16N	A1
6800	TYPK	60477	3425	8W-19S	A2
Kingston St					
10800	WSTR	60154	3086		E3
Kings Walk Dr					
4500	PLTN	60008	2805	20W-14N	E4
4500	PLTN	60067	2805	20W-14N	E4
4500	RGMW	60008	2805	20W-14N	E4
Kingswood Ct					
300	WLBK	60527	3146		A6
Kingswood Dr					
6700	BRRG	60527	3146		A6
6700	WLBK	60527	3146		A6
11400	ODPK	60467	3344	14W-16S	D3
Kingswood Ln					
200	WLNG	60090	2755	14W-18N	D3
King William St					
10	EDND	60118	2801		A2
Kinkaid Ct					
400	DSPN	60016	2862	15W-10N	A4
Kinne Rd					
3200	RBBN	60472	3348	4W-16S	D4
Kinnear Cove					
-	IVNS	60010	2803	25W-15N	E2
-	SBTN	60010	2803	25W-15N	E2
Kinross St					
1400	FSMR	60422	3506	4W-23S	D3
Kinsale Dr					
9000	MKNA	60448	3504	11W-23S	A4
9000	TYPK	60448	3504	11W-23S	A4
Kinsley Pl					
7600	MNSR	46321	3430		D5
Kinvara Av					
8900	MKNA	60448	3504	11W-23S	A3
S Kinvarra Dr					
12500	PlsT	60464	3273	12W-14S	C7
12500	PSPK	60464	3273	12W-14S	C7
N Kinzie Pl					
500	TNTN	60476	3428	0E-20S	D5
E Kinzie St					
10	CHCG	60610	3034	0E-0N	C3
10	CHCG	60611	3034		E4
N Kinzie St					
100	TNTN	60476	3428	0E-21S	D5
S Kinzie St					
100	TNTN	60476	3428	0E-21S	D6
W Kinzie St					
10	CHCG	60610	3034	0W-0N	A4
10	CHCG	60611	3034	0E-0N	C3
100	CHCG	60606	3034	0W-0N	A4
400	CHCG	60661	3034	0W-0N	A3
700	CHCG	60622	3034	0W-0N	A3
800	CHCG	60607	3033	1W-0N	D3
800	CHCG	60622	3033	1W-0N	D3
1400	CHCG	60612	3033	2W-0N	B3
4000	CHCG	60624	3032	5W-0N	B4
4600	CHCG	60644	3032	5W-0N	A4
4800	CHCG	60644	3031	6W-0N	D4
N Kinzua Av					
6700	CHCG	60646	2919	6W-8N	C2
N Kiona Av					
4700	CHCG	60630	2920	5W-5N	B7
S Kiowa Ct					
13700	HMGN	60441	3343	16W-16S	D3
E Kiowa Ln					
1900	MPPT	60056	2808	13W-14N	E4
W Kiowa Ln					
7200	PSHT	60463	3274	9W-14S	D6
7200	PSHT	60463	3346	9W-15S	E1
Kiowa Tr					
400	WLNG	60090	2754	16W-17N	D5
Kip Pl					
1000	LMNT	60439	3270		E7
Kipling Ct					
700	ROSL	60172	2913		B6
Kipling St					
10200	PvsT	60162	3029	12W-1S	A7
10200	WSTR	60154	3029	12W-1S	A7
N Kirby Av					
5800	CHCG	60646	2920	5W-7N	A4
Kirby Dr					
8400	TYPK	60477	3424	10W-21S	B7
W Kirchhoff Rd					
100	ANHT	60005	2807	18W-13N	A7
500	ANHT	60005	2806	18W-13N	E6
1700	RGMW	60008	2806	18W-13N	E6
Kirchoff Rd					
2000	ANHT	60005	2806	19W-13N	D6
2000	RGMW	60008	2806	19W-13N	B5
Kirchoff Rd					
4300	RGMW	60008	2805	20W-14N	E4
4500	RGMW	60067	2805	20W-14N	E4
Kirk Av					
400	EMHT	60126	3028		A7
400	YkTp	60126	3028		A7
500	ELGN	60120	2855		C6
S Kirk Av					
800	EMHT	60126	3028		A6
Kirk Ct					
3700	CCHL	60478	3426	4W-21S	D6
W Kirk Dr					
7500	NLES	60714	2864	9W-9N	C6
7500	PKRG	60068	2864	9W-9N	C6
Kirk St					
1100	EGVV	60007	2915		C4
1300	EVTN	60202	2867	3W-9N	A6
1700	EVTN	60202	2866	3W-9N	E6
3800	SKOK	60076	2866	4W-9N	B6
4800	SKOK	60077	2865	6W-9N	E6
5400	MNGV	60077	2865	6W-9N	D6
6100	MNGV	60053	2865	8W-9N	A6
W Kirk St					
7000	NLES	60714	2864	9W-9N	D6
Kirkcaldy Ct					
8000	PSHT	60464	3346	10W-15S	C2
S Kirkland Av					
2200	CHCG	60623	3090	5W-2S	B2
7900	CHCG	60652	3212	5W-9S	B2
Kirkwall Ct					
1400	IVNS	60010	2751	24W-17N	C5
Kirkwall Ln					
500	SMBG	60193	2859	22W-10N	B6
N Kirkwood Av					
6000	CHCG	60646	2920	5W-7N	A3
6300	LNWD	60712	2920	5W-7N	A3
Kirkwood Dr					
900	IVNS	60067	2751	24W-17N	D5
Kirkwood Cove					
300	BRRG	60527	3208		B3
Kirschoff St					
6200	RSMT	60018	2917	12W-7N	B3
N Kirschoff St					
2000	LydT	60164	2973	12W-2N	B7
2000	MLPK	60160	2973	12W-2N	B7
Kirson Dr					
10	SBTN	60010	2803	26W-13N	C5
Kit Ln					
13700	LMNT	60439	3343	17W-15S	C1
Kit Carson Dr					
6000	HRPK	60133	2911		E4
Kitchner St					
-	BDVW	60155	3029	12W-0S	B6
-	WSTR	60154	3029	12W-0S	B6
Kitson Cir					
1700	IVNS	60067	2751	23W-16N	E7
1700	IVNS	60067	2804	23W-16N	E1
E Kitson Dr					
1000	PLTN	60074	2806	19W-16N	B1
N Kitson Dr					
10	PLTN	60074	2753	19W-17N	B5
10	PLTN	60074	2806	19W-16N	C1
Kittery on Auburn					
10	RGMW	60008	2806	19W-14N	B4
Kitty Av					
6600	CHRG	60415	3211	8W-11S	A7
10100	CHRG	60415	3275	8W-11S	A1
Kitty Ln					
8700	HYHL	60457	3210	10W-10S	A6
Kittyhawk Ln					
1400	GNVW	60025	2810	10W-14N	A5
Klafter Ct					
1200	SMWD	60107	2857	27W-11N	C4
Klehm Ct					
5100	SKOK	60077	2865	6W-10N	D5
Klein Dr					
1200	SMWD	60107	2857	27W-11N	C4
S Klemme Rd					
1500	CteT	60417	3687	3E-31S	A5
Klimm Av					
18300	HMWD	60430	3427	2W-22S	C7
18500	HMWD	60430	3507	2W-22S	C1
Klingenberg Ln					
-	BRTN	60010	2751	25W-18N	A2
Knight Av					
9000	MaiT	60016	2863	10W-11N	E3
9300	NLES	60016	2863	10W-11N	E3
N Knight Av					
10	PKRG	60068	2917	10W-9N	E1
900	PKRG	60068	2863	10W-10N	E6
1100	NLES	60068	2863	10W-10N	E5
4800	CHCG	60656	2917	10W-6N	E7
5000	NRDG	60706	2917	10W-6N	E6
8200	NLES	60714	2863	10W-10N	E5
9300	NLES	60016	2863	11W-11N	E2
S Knight Av					
300	PKRG	60068	2917	10W-8N	E3
Knight St					
3800	GNVW	60025	2809	11W-14N	E5
Knight Bridge Ct					
-	MTSN	60443	3594	6W-25S	A1
Knightbridge Ct					
-	MNSR	46321	3510		D5
Knightbridge Pl					
-	MNSR	46321	3510		D5
Knight Hill Ct					
10	BFGV	60089	2754	17W-20N	A1
Knighton Pl					
-	EMHT	60126	3028		A6
Knightsbridge Ct					
900	SMBG	60195	2858	24W-12N	C1
Knights Bridge Dr					
1800	MPPT	60056	2861	17W-11N	C4
Knightsbridge Ln					
800	HFET	60195	2858	24W-12N	D1
800	SMBG	60195	2858	24W-12N	D1
8900	ODPK	60462	3346	11W-18S	A6
E Knob Hill Dr					
200	ANHT	60004	2754	17W-16N	B7
Knockderry Ln					
100	IVNS	60067	2752	22W-17N	B4
Knoebel Dr					
10	DGvT	60439	3270		C3
Knoll Ct					
10	SBTN	60010	2804	25W-15N	A2
Knoll Ln					
700	HFET	60194	2858	24W-11N	D3
1000	WLMT	60091	2812	4W-14N	B5
Knoll Crest Dr					
400	BRLT	60103	2910		A1
Knoll Ridge Rd					
10	RGMW	60008	2806	20W-13N	A6
Knollwood Av					
-	DndT	60118	2801		C4
-	EDND	60118	2801		B4

STREET Block	City	ZIP	Map#	CGS	Grid
Knollwood Cir					
100	RchT	60443	3593	8W-26S	B1
2200	SMBG	60194	2857	27W-11N	C3
Knollwood Ct					
100	OKBK	60523	3028		B7
300	PltT	60067	2806	20W-13N	A6
2300	SMBG	60194	2857	26W-10N	E5
Knollwood Dr					
-	SMBG	60194	2857	26W-11N	E3
10	FSMR	60422	3507	2W-23S	D3
100	CteT	60475	3596	1W-28S	A7
100	STGR	60475	3596	1W-28S	A7
6300	OKFT	60452	3347	7W-17S	B5
N Knollwood Dr					
10	SMBG	60193	2857	26W-10N	E6
10	SMBG	60194	2857	26W-11N	E3
1000	HFET	60194	2857	26W-11N	E3
1000	PLTN	60067	2752	22W-17N	B5
1400	PltT	60067	2752	22W-17N	B5
1400	PltT	60074	2752	22W-17N	B5
S Knollwood Dr					
10	SMBG	60193	2857	26W-10N	E6
10	SMBG	60194	2857	26W-10N	E6
W Knollwood Dr					
8200	PSPK	60464	3274	10W-14S	B6
Knollwood Ln					
-	NfdT	60025	2809	10W-13N	E6
100	GLNC	60022	2758	6W-18N	D3
1000	BRLT	60103	2910		C3
2800	GNVW	60025	2810	9W-13N	B6
2800	NfdT	60025	2810	10W-13N	A6
3200	HMWD	60430	3506	4W-22S	E1
3200	HMWD	60430	3507	4W-22S	A1
3700	GNVW	60025	2809	11W-13N	E6
8400	ODPK	60462	3346	10W-18S	B7
Knollwood Pl					
2600	HLCT	60429	3427	3W-21S	B6
2600	HLCT	60430	3427	3W-21S	B6
Knottingham Ct					
1200	SMBG	60193	2913		C1
Knottingham Dr					
-	EGVV	60007	2913		C1
-	EGVV	60193	2913		C1
800	SMBG	60193	2913		C1
Knox Av					
600	WLMT	60091	2811	5W-13N	E6
8000	SKOK	60076	2866	5W-10N	A5
14300	CTWD	60445	3348	5W-17S	B5
14300	MDLN	60445	3348	5W-17S	B5
15300	OKFT	60452	3348	5W-18S	B6
N Knox Av					
2200	CHCG	60639	2976	5W-2N	A6
3400	CHCG	60641	2976	5W-4N	A3
4400	CHCG	60630	2920	5W-5N	A7
5600	CHCG	60646	2920	5W-7N	A5
5900	CHCG	60646	2919	5W-7N	E4
6300	LNWD	60712	2920	5W-7N	A3
6400	CHCG	60712	2920	5W-8N	A3
S Knox Av					
4200	CHCG	60632	3090	5W-4S	A7
4600	CHCG	60632	3150	5W-5S	A2
5900	CHCG	60629	3150	5W-6S	A5
7700	CHCG	60652	3212	5W-8S	A2
9000	HMTN	60456	3212	5W-10S	A5
9500	OKLN	60453	3212	5W-11S	A6
10300	OKLN	60453	3276	5W-12S	A1
11500	ALSP	60803	3276	5W-13S	B4
Knox Cir					
10	EVTN	60201	2866	4W-12N	C1
Knox Ct					
200	IVNS	60010	2750	25W-16N	E7
200	IVNS	60010	2751	25W-16N	A7
S Knox Ct					
10100	OKLN	60453	3212	5W-11S	A7
E Knox St					
500	PLTN	60074	2753	20W-17N	A5
Knoxboro Ln					
200	PltT	60010	2751	23W-18N	E2
Koch Ct					
9700	ODPK	60467	3423	12W-19S	D2
Koclanis Av					
200	HLSD	60162	3028		D5
Koehler Dr					
1900	DSPN	60018	2862	13W-9N	E7
8500	TYPK	60477	3424	10W-21S	B7
Koehling Rd					
1700	NfdT	60062	2757	9W-18N	B3
Koepke Rd					
2700	NHBK	60062	2756	11W-16N	E6
Koerper Ct					
500	WLMT	60091	2812	5W-13N	A6
Kolin Av					
-	ALSP	60803	3276	5W-15S	B7
14300	CTWD	60445	3348	5W-17S	B4
14300	MDLN	60445	3348	5W-17S	B4
N Kolin Av					
800	CHCG	60624	3032	5W-1N	B2
800	CHCG	60651	3032	5W-1N	B2
1500	CHCG	60639	3032	5W-1N	B1
S Kolin Av					
1200	CHCG	60623	3032	5W-1S	B7
1200	CHCG	60624	3032	5W-1S	B7
1500	CHCG	60623	3090	5W-1S	B1
4500	CHCG	60632	3090	5W-4S	B7
4700	CHCG	60632	3150	5W-5S	B2
5900	CHCG	60629	3150	5W-7S	B6
8300	CHCG	60652	3212	5W-9S	B3
8700	HMTN	60456	3212	5W-10S	B4
10000	OKLN	60453	3212	5W-11S	B7
10200	OKLN	60453	3276	5W-11S	B1
11500	ALSP	60803	3276	5W-13S	B4
11500	CHCG	60655	3276	5W-13S	B4
13300	RBBN	60472	3348	5W-15S	B2
13400	CTWD	60445	3348	5W-15S	B2
13400	RBBN	60445	3348	5W-15S	B2
Kolmar Av					
7400	LNWD	60712	2866	5W-9N	A7
8200	SKOK	60076	2866	5W-10N	A5
14300	CTWD	60445	3348	5W-17S	B5
14300	MDLN	60445	3348	5W-17S	B5
N Kolmar Av					
200	CHCG	60624	3032	5W-0N	A4
1000	CHCG	60651	3032	5W-1N	A2
1600	CHCG	60639	3032	5W-1N	A1
2000	CHCG	60639	2976	5W-2N	A6
4000	CHCG	60641	2976	5W-5N	A1
4900	CHCG	60630	2920	5W-6N	A6
5800	CHCG	60646	2920	5W-7N	A4
6300	CHCG	60712	2920	5W-7N	A3
6800	LNWD	60712	2920	5W-8N	A1
7300	LNWD	60712	2866	5W-9N	A7
7300	SKOK	60076	2866	5W-9N	A7
S Kolmar Av					
-	CHCG	60623	3032	5W-1S	A7
-	CHCG	60623	3090	5W-1S	A1
600	CHCG	60644	3032	5W-0S	A6
1000	CHCG	60624	3032	5W-0S	A7
4400	CHCG	60632	3090	5W-4S	A7
5500	CHCG	60629	3150	5W-6S	A4
5500	CHCG	60632	3150	5W-6S	A3
7700	CHCG	60652	3212	5W-8S	A2
8600	HMTN	60652	3212	5W-9S	B4
8700	HMTN	60456	3212	5W-10S	A4
9100	HMTN	60453	3212	5W-10S	A5
9200	OKLN	60453	3212	5W-11S	B6
10300	OKLN	60453	3276	5W-12S	B2
11500	ALSP	60803	3276	5W-13S	B4
Kolmar Ln					
-	CTWD	60445	3348	5W-16S	B3
Kolpin Dr					
1200	DSPN	60016	2862	15W-10N	A5
1200	DSPN	60018	2862	15W-10N	A5
Kolze Av					
4000	SRPK	60176	2973	11W-5N	C2
4700	SRPK	60176	2917	11W-5N	C7
S Komensky Av					
1200	CHCG	60623	3032	5W-1S	B7
1200	CHCG	60624	3032	5W-1S	B7
1500	CHCG	60623	3090	5W-1S	B1
4300	CHCG	60632	3090	5W-4S	C7
5400	CHCG	60629	3150	5W-6S	C3
5400	CHCG	60632	3150	5W-6S	C3
7700	CHCG	60652	3212	5W-8S	C1
8600	CHCG	60456	3212	5W-9S	C4
8800	HMTN	60456	3212	5W-10S	C4
9100	OKLN	60453	3212	5W-10S	C5
10700	OKLN	60453	3276	5W-12S	C2
11500	ALSP	60803	3276	5W-13S	C5
11500	CHCG	60655	3276	5W-13S	C5
13300	RBBN	60472	3348	5W-15S	C2
Konrad Av					
4000	LYNS	60534	3088	10W-4S	A7
Kopping Ln					
9100	HYHL	60457	3209	11W-10S	E5
9100	PlsT	60457	3209	11W-10S	E5
9100	PlsT	60480	3209	11W-10S	E5
Korrel Av					
2800	BLWD	60104	3029	12W-0N	C4
Kosan Cir					
200	SMWD	60107	2857	27W-11N	C4
Kostner Av					
-	ALSP	60803	3276	5W-15S	B7
700	MTSN	60443	3506	5W-25S	C6
7400	LNWD	60712	2866	5W-9N	A7
9000	SKOK	60076	2866	5W-11N	A3
13500	CTWD	60445	3348	5W-17S	B4
13500	RBBN	60445	3348	5W-16S	B3
13500	RBBN	60472	3348	5W-16S	B3
14200	MDLN	60445	3348	5W-17S	B6
15200	BmnT	60445	3348	5W-18S	B6
15200	OKFT	60445	3348	5W-18S	B6
17900	CCHL	60478	3426	5W-21S	C7
22100	RNPK	60471	3594	5W-26S	C3
N Kostner Av					
10	CHCG	60624	3032	5W-0N	A4
800	CHCG	60651	3032	5W-1N	A2
1500	CHCG	60639	3032	5W-2N	A1
1600	CHCG	60639	2976	5W-2N	A7
3700	CHCG	60641	2976	5W-5N	A1
4300	CHCG	60630	2976	5W-5N	A1
4700	CHCG	60630	2920	5W-6N	A6
6300	CHCG	60646	2920	5W-7N	A3
6800	LNWD	60712	2920	5W-8N	A1
7200	LNWD	60712	2866	5W-9N	A7
7300	SKOK	60076	2866	5W-9N	A7
S Kostner Av					
-	CHCG	60652	3212	5W-10S	B4
10	CHCG	60624	3032	5W-1S	B7
1100	CHCG	60623	3032	5W-1S	B7
1500	CHCG	60623	3090	5W-2S	B4
3500	CHCG	60632	3090	5W-3S	A5
4700	CHCG	60632	3150	5W-6S	B3
5400	CHCG	60629	3150	5W-7S	B6
7300	CHCG	60629	3212	5W-8S	B1
8700	HMTN	60456	3212	5W-10S	B4
9000	HMTN	60453	3212	5W-10S	B5
9300	OKLN	60453	3212	5W-11S	B7
10200	OKLN	60453	3276	5W-12S	B1
11000	CHCG	60655	3276	5W-12S	B3
11900	ALSP	60803	3276	5W-15S	B7
13300	CTWD	60445	3348	5W-15S	B2
13300	CTWD	60472	3348	5W-15S	B2
13300	RBBN	60472	3348	5W-15S	B2
Kostner Ter					
8800	SKOK	60076	2866	5W-11N	A3
Kotlin Rd					
14700	LMNT	60439	3271		A4
Kott St					
2600	BLID	60406	3349	3W-15S	B1
Kouba Dr					
5800	BKLY	60163	3028		C4
5800	HLSD	60162	3028		C4
Kraft Ct					
10	GNVW	60025	2864	8W-12N	E1
Kramer Av					
900	ELGN	60120	2855		C6
Kraml Dr					
-	DGvT	60527	3208		A4
100	BRRG	60527	3208		A4
Krause Av					
400	SMWD	60107	2911		B1
Krause Ln					
200	WLNG	60090	2755	14W-18N	D3
S Kreiter Av					
9300	CHCG	60617	3216	4E-10S	B5
Kreitzburg St					
9800	SjnT	46311	3687		D3
9900	HnrT	46311	3687		D3
Kris Tr					
9600	PlsT	60462	3345	12W-15S	D2
Kris Howard Dr					
-	PLTN	60067	2805	22W-14N	A5
Kris Howard Drwy					
-	PLTN	60067	2805	22W-14N	B5
E Krista Ct					
900	PLTN	60074	2806	19W-15N	B1
S Krista Ln					
100	PLTN	60074	2806	19W-15N	B1
Kristin Cir					
10	SMBG	60173	2859	23W-12N	A1
10	SMBG	60195	2859	23W-12N	A1
Kristin Dr					
10	SMBG	60173	2859	23W-12N	A1
10	SMBG	60195	2859	23W-12N	A1
Kristine Ln					
22900	RNPK	60471	3594	4W-27S	D5
Kristo Ln					
8000	ODPK	60462	3346	10W-17S	C4
Kristoffer Ct					
11700	OrlT	60467	3344	14W-16S	D2
Kristoffer Ln					
11700	OrlT	60467	3344	14W-16S	D2
Kristy Ln					
600	WLNG	60090	2755	15W-17N	A6
S Kroll Dr					
12600	ALSP	60803	3276	6W-14S	A7
Kromray Rd					
300	LMNT	60439	3271		A5
Kroner Ln					
2000	HMWD	60430	3427	2W-21S	C7
Kropp Ct					
17100	ODPK	60467	3422	14W-20S	E4
Krotiak Rd					
10	PKFT	60466	3595	3W-26S	B2
Krowka Dr					
1800	DSPN	60018	2917	12W-8N	B1
Krueger St					
2300	BLID	60406	3277	2W-14S	B6
N Kruger Av					
4800	CHCG	60630	2919	5W-6N	E6
4800	CHCG	60630	2920	5W-6N	A5
Kruk St					
600	LMNT	60439	3270		E6
S Kuersten Rd					
-	MONE	60449	3683	5W-31S	C6
-	UYPK	60449	3683	5W-31S	C6
26300	MonT	60449	3683	5W-31S	C6
S Kurt Ln					
23700	CteT	60417	3597	3E-28S	E7
Kylemore Ct					
1000	LKPT	60441	3342	21W-18S	A7
1100	DSPN	60016	2808	13W-13N	D6
9200	OrlT	60477	3423	11W-21S	E6
Kylemore Dr					
600	DSPN	60016	2808	13W-13N	D6
600	MPPT	60056	2808	13W-13N	D6
Kylemore Ln					
19300	MKNA	60448	3504	11W-23S	A3
L					
Laburnum Ct					
3500	NHBK	60062	2756	11W-18N	C4
Laburnum Dr					
400	NHBK	60062	2756	12W-18N	C4
Laburnum Rd					
1400	HFET	60195	2804	24W-14N	B3
Lace					
-	CHCG	60646	2919	5W-7N	E4
N Lacey Av					
5700	CHCG	60646	2919	6W-7N	E4
Laconia Ln					
400	SMBG	60193	2912		E1
La Costa Av					
900	BRLT	60103	2910		C2
La Crosse Av					
7800	BRBK	60459	3212	6W-8S	A2
8800	SKOK	60077	2865	6W-11N	E3
10000	SKOK	60077	2811	6W-12N	E7
10000	WLMT	60077	2811	6W-12N	E7
10000	WLMT	60091	2811	6W-12N	E7
15100	OKFT	60452	3348	6W-18S	A6
Lacrosse Av					
600	WLMT	60091	2811	6W-13N	D5
9500	OKLN	60453	3212	6W-11S	A6
10700	OKLN	60453	3276	6W-12S	A2
N La Crosse Av					
100	CHCG	60644	3031	6W-0N	E4
1800	CHCG	60639	2975	6W-2N	E7
4400	CHCG	60630	2975	6W-5N	E1
4400	CHCG	60641	2975	6W-5N	E1
5400	CHCG	60630	2919	6W-6N	E5
6200	CHCG	60646	2919	6W-7N	E3
6300	LNWD	60712	2919	6W-7N	E3
S La Crosse Av					
4500	CHCG	60638	3090	6W-4S	A7
4600	CHCG	60638	3150	6W-5S	A1
6400	BDPK	60638	3150	6W-7S	A5
11700	ALSP	60803	3276	6W-13S	A5
Lacrosse Ct					
-	WLMT	60091	2811	6W-13N	D5
Lacy Av					
400	SMWD	60107	2911		B1
Ladd Ln					
5200	HRPK	60133	2911		C6
W Ladd St					
300	ANHT	60004	2754	18W-16N	A7
600	ANHT	60004	2753	18W-16N	E7
Lady Bar Av					
13700	HMGN	60467	3344	15W-16S	B3
W Lady Bar Av					
13800	HMGN	60467	3344	15W-16S	B3
W Lady Bar Ln					
12100	HMGN	60467	3344	15W-16S	B3
Lady Bird Ln					
9300	DSPN	60016	2863	11W-11N	D2
9300	MaiT	60016	2863	11W-11N	D2
Lady Marion Dr					
200	HnrT	60120	2856	31W-10N	A6
Ladysmith Rd					
500	BRLT	60103	2911		C5
S Lafayette Av					
5500	CHCG	60609	3152	0W-6S	C3
5500	CHCG	60621	3152	0W-6S	C3
7500	CHCG	60620	3214	0W-11S	C6
7500	CHCG	60621	3214	0W-8S	C1
9400	CHCG	60628	3214	0W-11S	C6
10500	CHCG	60628	3278	0W-12S	C1
Lafayette Ln					
200	HFET	60195	2804	24W-12N	E7
200	HFET	60195	2805	23W-12N	A7
200	SMBG	60195	2805	23W-12N	A7
Lafayette Rd					
10	RVSD	60546	3088	9W-3S	D5
Lafayette St					
200	WDDL	60191	2914		C7
N Lafayette St					
2300	ANHT	60004	2753	18W-16N	E7
Lafleur Ln					
3900	HFET	60195	2804	24W-14N	B3
Laflin Av					
16100	MKHM	60426	3427	1W-19S	E2
17100	EHZC	60429	3427	1W-20S	E4
17100	HRVY	60429	3427	1W-20S	E4
17400	HMWD	60430	3427	1W-20S	E5
Laflin Ct					
600	CHCG	60607	3033	1W-0S	D6
S Laflin Pl					
3600	CHCG	60609	3091	1W-3S	D5
Laflin St					
-	CTPK	60827	3277	1W-15S	D7
N Laflin St					
200	CHCG	60607	3033	1W-0N	D4
S Laflin St					
600	CHCG	60607	3033	1W-0S	D6
1200	CHCG	60608	3033	1W-1S	D7
1500	CHCG	60608	3091	1W-1S	D1
4500	CHCG	60609	3091	1W-4S	D7
4700	CHCG	60609	3151	1W-6S	D4
5500	CHCG	60636	3151	1W-7S	D6
7500	CHCG	60620	3213	1W-8S	D1
9400	CHCG	60643	3213	1W-10S	D6
12200	CHCG	60643	3277	1W-14S	D6
12200	CTPK	60827	3277	1W-15S	D7
La Fontaine Ln					
3800	GNVW	60025	2809	11W-14N	D4
Lageschulte St					
100	BRTN	60010	2750	26W-18N	E2
Lago Ln					
13700	ODPK	60462	3346	9W-16S	C2
Lagoon Dr					
100	NHFD	60093	2811	6W-15N	D3
300	NtrT	60093	2811	6W-15N	D3
Lagoon Ln					
-	NtrT	60093	2811	6W-15N	D2
-	WNKA	60093	2811	6W-15N	D2
10	NHFD	60093	2811	6W-14N	D3
La Grande Av					
6000	OKFT	60452	3347	7W-18S	C7
La Grande Ct					
6100	OKFT	60452	3347	7W-18S	C7
La Grange Rd					
-	LynT	60458	3209	11W-8S	D2
-	LynT	60480	3209	11W-10S	D5
-	MKNA	60448	3423	12W-22S	D7
-	PlsT	60480	3209	11W-10S	D5
-	PlsT	60480	3273	12W-12S	D2
-	WLSP	60458	3209	11W-8S	D2
-	WLSP	60480	3209	11W-8S	D2
-	WLSP	60525	3209	12W-8S	D2
16700	ODHL	60477	3423	12W-20S	D4
16700	ODPK	60467	3423	12W-20S	D4
16700	ODPK	60477	3423	12W-20S	D4
16700	OrlT	60467	3423	12W-20S	D4
16700	OrlT	60477	3423	12W-20S	D4
17500	TYPK	60477	3423	11W-20S	D5
18200	FftT	60448	3423	12W-21S	D7
18200	ODPK	60448	3423	12W-21S	D7
La Grange Rd US-12					
-	LynT	60458	3209	11W-8S	D2
-	LynT	60480	3209	11W-10S	D5
-	PlsT	60480	3209	11W-10S	D5
-	WLSP	60458	3209	11W-8S	D2
-	WLSP	60480	3209	11W-8S	D2
-	WLSP	60525	3209	12W-8S	D2
La Grange Rd US-20					
-	LynT	60458	3209	11W-8S	D2
-	LynT	60480	3209	11W-10S	D5
-	PlsT	60480	3209	11W-10S	D5
-	WLSP	60458	3209	11W-8S	D2
-	WLSP	60480	3209	11W-8S	D2
-	WLSP	60525	3209	12W-8S	D2
La Grange Rd US-45					
-	LynT	60458	3209	11W-8S	D2
-	LynT	60480	3209	11W-10S	D5
-	MKNA	60448	3423	12W-22S	D7
-	PlsT	60480	3209	11W-10S	D5
-	PlsT	60480	3273	12W-12S	D2
-	WLSP	60458	3209	11W-8S	D2
-	WLSP	60480	3209	11W-8S	D2
-	WLSP	60525	3209	12W-8S	D2
16700	ODHL	60477	3423	12W-20S	D4
16700	ODPK	60467	3423	12W-20S	D4
16700	ODPK	60477	3423	12W-20S	D4
16700	OrlT	60467	3423	12W-20S	D4
16700	OrlT	60477	3423	12W-20S	D4
17500	TYPK	60477	3423	11W-20S	D5
18200	FftT	60448	3423	12W-21S	D7
18200	ODPK	60448	3423	12W-21S	D7
N La Grange Rd					
-	WSTR	60154	3087	12W-3S	B5
10	LGNG	60525	3087	12W-4S	C6
100	LGPK	60525	3087	12W-3S	C6
1000	PvsT	60525	3087	12W-2S	B4
2500	PvsT	60154	3087	12W-3S	B5
N La Grange Rd US-12					
-	WSTR	60154	3087	12W-3S	B5
10	LGNG	60525	3087	12W-4S	C6
100	LGPK	60525	3087	12W-3S	C6
1000	PvsT	60525	3087	12W-2S	B4
2500	PvsT	60154	3087	12W-3S	B5
N La Grange Rd US-20					
-	WSTR	60154	3087	12W-3S	B5
10	LGNG	60525	3087	12W-4S	C6
100	LGPK	60525	3087	12W-3S	C6
1000	PvsT	60525	3087	12W-2S	B4
2500	PvsT	60154	3087	12W-3S	B5
N La Grange Rd US-45					
-	WSTR	60154	3087	12W-3S	B5
10	LGNG	60525	3087	12W-4S	C6
100	LGPK	60525	3087	12W-3S	C6
1000	PvsT	60525	3087	12W-2S	B4
2500	PvsT	60154	3087	12W-3S	B5
S La Grange Rd					
-	HGKN	60525	3147	12W-8S	C7
-	HGKN	60525	3209	12W-8S	C1
-	PlsT	60480	3273	12W-13S	D4
10	LGNG	60525	3087	12W-4S	C7
300	LGNG	60525	3147	12W-6S	C3
5200	CTSD	60525	3147	12W-5S	C3
7600	WLSP	60525	3209	12W-8S	C1
11800	PlsT	60464	3273	12W-14S	D7
11800	PSPK	60464	3273	12W-14S	D7
12700	PSPK	60464	3345	12W-16S	D3
13000	PlsT	60462	3345	11W-15S	D1
13000	PSPK	60462	3345	11W-15S	D1
13400	OrlT	60462	3345	11W-15S	D2
13500	ODPK	60462	3345	12W-16S	D2
15700	ODPK	60462	3423	11W-18S	D1
15800	ODPK	60467	3423	12W-19S	D2
16600	ODHL	60477	3423	11W-19S	D3
16600	OrlT	60467	3423	11W-19S	D3
S La Grange Rd US-12					
-	CTSD	60525	3147	12W-8S	C7
-	HGKN	60525	3209	12W-8S	C1
-	WLSP	60525	3209	12W-8S	C1
10	LGNG	60525	3087	12W-4S	C7
300	LGNG	60525	3147	12W-6S	C3
6000	HGKN	60525	3147	12W-6S	C5
S La Grange Rd US-20					
-	CTSD	60525	3147	12W-8S	C7
-	HGKN	60525	3147	12W-8S	C7
-	HGKN	60525	3209	12W-8S	C1
-	WLSP	60525	3209	12W-8S	C1
10	LGNG	60525	3087	12W-4S	C7
300	LGNG	60525	3147	12W-6S	C3
S La Grange Rd US-45					
-	HGKN	60525	3147	12W-8S	C7
-	HGKN	60525	3209	12W-8S	C1
-	PlsT	60480	3273	11W-13S	D4
-	WLSP	60525	3209	12W-8S	C1
10	LGNG	60525	3087	12W-4S	C7
300	LGNG	60525	3147	12W-6S	C3
5200	CTSD	60525	3147	12W-5S	C3
11800	PlsT	60464	3273	12W-14S	D7
11800	PSPK	60464	3273	12W-14S	D7
12700	PSPK	60464	3345	12W-16S	D3
13000	PlsT	60462	3345	11W-15S	D1
13000	PSPK	60462	3345	11W-15S	D1
13400	OrlT	60462	3345	11W-15S	D2
13500	ODPK	60462	3345	12W-16S	D2
15700	ODPK	60462	3423	11W-18S	D1
15800	ODPK	60467	3423	12W-19S	D2
16600	ODHL	60477	3423	11W-19S	D3
16600	OrlT	60467	3423	11W-19S	D3
Laguna Ct					
1300	HRPK	60133	2911		E5
1500	WLNG	60090	2754	16W-17N	D5
N Laguna Ct					
1200	PLTN	60067	2752	22W-17N	C4
Laguna Ln					
7800	ODPK	60462	3346	10W-16S	C3
7800	OrlT	60462	3346	10W-16S	C3
La Haigh Rd					
17900	HMWD	60430	3427	1W-21S	E6
Lahinch Ct					
1100	DYR	46311	3510		E7
Lahinch Dr					
10	LMNT	60439	3343	17W-15S	B1
13200	PlsT	60462	3345	11W-15S	E2
Lahon Av					
22300	CHHT	60411	3596	0E-27S	E4
22300	CHHT	60475	3596	0E-27S	E4
22300	SCHT	60475	3596	0E-27S	E4
22300	STGR	60411	3596	0E-27S	E4
22300	STGR	60475	3596	0E-27S	E4
Lahon Rd					
22700	STGR	60475	3596	0E-27S	D5
22800	CRTE	60417	3596	0E-27S	D5
Lahon St					
-	PKRG	60068	2864	9W-9N	B6
1400	PKRG	60068	2863	10W-9N	E6
E Lahon St					
10	PKRG	60068	2864	9W-9N	C6
200	NLES	60714	2864	9W-9N	C6
La Jolla Ter					
900	BRLT	60103	2911		B5
Lake					
-	ELGN	60120	2855		C6
Lake Av					
-	CHCG	60613	2977	1W-5N	D1
-	ELGN	60120	2855		C7
200	PKRG	60068	2918	10W-8N	B1
200	WLMT	60091	2813	3W-14N	A5
700	WLMT	60091	2812	5W-14N	A5
2800	WLMT	60091	2811	6W-13N	D5
3500	GNVW	60025	2811	6W-13N	D5
E Lake Av					
-	NfdT	60025	2810	10W-13N	B5
200	GNVW	60025	2811	7W-14N	B5
200	WLMT	60091	2811	6W-13N	C5
500	WLMT	60025	2811	7W-14N	B5
700	GNVW	60091	2811	7W-14N	B5
1500	GNVW	60025	2810	9W-13N	C5
3800	GNVW	60025	2809	10W-14N	E5
S Lake Av					
1300	HMND	46320	3280		E3
1300	HMND	46394	3280		E5
W Lake Av					
-	WhlT	60025	2809	12W-14N	A4
2400	GNVW	60025	2810	10W-14N	B4
3000	NfdT	60025	2810	10W-14N	A4
3400	GNVW	60025	2809	10W-14N	E4
4100	NfdT	60025	2809	12W-14N	A4
4100	NfdT	60062	2809	11W-14N	D4
4500	GNVW	60062	2809	11W-14N	C4
Lake Av E					
41700	NfdT	60025	2809	12W-14N	A4
Lake Blvd					
-	BFGV	60090	2754	16W-17N	D4
-	WLNG	60090	2754	16W-17N	D4
10	BFGV	60089	2754	16W-17N	D4
Lake Ct					
4900	CCHL	60478	3506	6W-22S	A2
Lake Dr					
-	PLTN	60067	2805	22W-14N	B5
100	OMFD	60461	3507	3W-24S	A5
1700	FSMR	60422	3507	3W-23S	B4
15700	OKFT	60452	3347	7W-18S	D7
15700	OKFT	60452	3425	7W-18S	D1
Lake St					
-	BRLT	60103	2856	31W-9N	A7
-	BRTN	60010	2751	25W-18N	A2
-	ELGN	60103	2856	31W-9N	A7
-	ELGN	60120	2856	31W-9N	A7
-	HnrT	60120	2856	31W-9N	A7
10	BmdT	60172	2912		B6
10	CHCG	60644	3031	7W-0N	B4
10	MYWD	60153	3030	10W-0N	B4
10	OKPK	60302	3031	8W-0N	A4
10	ROSL	60172	2912		C6
10	RVFT	60305	3030	10W-0N	A4
100	WNKA	60093	2758	6W-16N	E7
200	BmdT	60133	2911		E5
200	ELGN	60120	2855		A4
200	EVTN	60201	2867	2W-11N	C3
300	BMDL	60108	2912		D7
300	BMDL	60172	2912		D7
300	BmdT	60108	2912		D7
300	GLNC	60022	2758	6W-17N	E6
300	HRPK	60133	2912		B6
400	HRPK	60172	2912		B6
600	BmdT	60133	2912		B6
600	OKPK	60301	3031	8W-0N	A4
700	MYWD	60153	3029	11W-0N	E3
800	MLPK	60160	3029	10W-0N	E3
800	OKPK	60301	3030	8W-0N	E3
1100	RVFT	60301	3030	8W-0N	D4
1200	DYR	46311	3510		C7
1500	DYR	46311	3598		C1
1500	HRPK	60133	2911		E4
1700	EVTN	60201	2866	3W-11N	E3
3300	SKOK	60203	2866	4W-11N	D3
3400	LNSG	60438	3430	4E-21S	C6
3700	MNSR	46321	3430	4E-21S	C6
5500	MNGV	60053	2865	7W-11N	C3
5500	SKOK	60077	2865	6W-11N	D3
7200	MNGV	60053	2864	9W-11N	D3
7800	NLES	60053	2864	9W-11N	B3
7800	NLES	60714	2864	9W-11N	B3
8000	WLSP	60480	3209	12W-9S	C2

STREET Block	City	ZIP	Map#	CGS	Grid
Lake St US-20					
-	BRLT	60103	2856	31W-9N	A7
-	ELGN	-	2855		D6
-	ELGN	60103	2856	31W-9N	A7
-	ELGN	60120	2856	31W-9N	A7
-	HnrT	60120	2856	31W-9N	A7
10	BmdT	60172	2912		B6
10	ROSL	60172	2912		C6
200	BmdT	60133	2911		E5
200	HRPK	60133	2911		E4
300	BMDL	60108	2912		D7
300	BMDL	60172	2912		D7
300	BmdT	60108	2912		D7
300	HRPK	60133	2912		B6
400	HRPK	60172	2912		B6
600	BmdT	60133	2912		B6
E Lake St					
10	CHCG	60601	3034	0E-0N	C4
10	MLPK	60160	3028		E2
10	NHLK	60164	3028		D2
100	BRLT	60103	2910		E2
100	BRLT	60103	2911		A2
100	BRLT	60107	2910		E2
100	BRLT	60107	2911		A2
100	BRTN	60010	2750	26W-18N	D2
100	BRTN	60010	2751	25W-18N	A2
100	EMHT	60126	2972		A7
100	SMWD	60103	2910		E1
100	SMWD	60107	2910		E2
100	SMWD	60107	2911		A2
200	EMHT	60126	3028		B1
500	HRPK	60133	2911		B2
500	SMWD	60103	2911		A2
1000	BmdT	60133	2911		E5
1000	BmdT	60133	2912		A5
1000	HRPK	60133	2912		A5
E Lake St US-20					
10	MLPK	60160	3028		E2
10	NHLK	60164	3028		D2
100	BRLT	60103	2910		E2
100	BRLT	60103	2911		A2
100	BRLT	60107	2910		E2
100	BRLT	60107	2911		A2
100	SMWD	60103	2910		E1
100	SMWD	60107	2910		E2
100	SMWD	60107	2911		A2
500	HRPK	60133	2911		B2
500	SMWD	60103	2911		A2
1000	BmdT	60133	2911		E5
1000	BmdT	60133	2912		A5
1000	HRPK	60133	2912		A5
W Lake St					
-	EMHT	60126	3028		C1
-	HnrT	60103	2910		C1
-	NHLK	60164	3028		C1
-	SMWD	60120	2910		C1
10	CHCG	60601	3034	0W-0N	A4
100	BRTN	60010	2750	25W-18N	E2
100	CHCG	60606	3034	0W-0N	B4
200	BMDL	60108	2912		D7
200	BMDL	60172	2912		D7
200	BmdT	60108	2912		E7
200	BmdT	60172	2912		D7
200	ROSL	60108	2912		D7
200	ROSL	60172	2912		D7
400	CHCG	60661	3034	0W-0N	A4
500	BRLT	60103	2910		E1
500	BRLT	60107	2910		E1
500	BRLT	60120	2910		E1
500	HnrT	60120	2910		D1
500	SMWD	60103	2910		E1
500	SMWD	60107	2910		E1
600	BRLT	60103	2911		B3
600	HRPK	60103	2911		B3
600	HRPK	60133	2911		B3
600	SMWD	60107	2911		B3
700	CHCG	60607	3034	0W-0N	A4
800	CHCG	60607	3033	1W-0N	E4
900	MLPK	60160	3029	11W-1N	C3
900	MYWD	60153	3029	10W-0N	E3
1100	BRLT	60103	2856	30W-9N	B7
1100	BRLT	60107	2856	30W-9N	B7
1100	BRLT	60120	2856	30W-9N	B7
1100	HnrT	60103	2856	30W-9N	B7
1100	HnrT	60107	2856	30W-9N	B7
1100	HnrT	60120	2856	30W-9N	B7
1100	SMWD	60107	2856	30W-9N	C7
1500	CHCG	60612	3033	2W-0N	D4
2200	BRLT	60133	2911		C3
2800	CHCG	60612	3032	3W-0N	E4
3100	CHCG	60624	3032	3W-0N	E4
3600	SNPK	60160	3029	12W-1N	B2
3700	SNPK	60165	3029	12W-1N	A2
3900	MLPK	60165	3029	12W-1N	A2
4500	CHCG	60644	3032	5W-0N	B4
4600	MLPK	60160	3028		E2
5500	CHCG	60644	3031	6W-0N	C4
5900	OKPK	60302	3031	7W-0N	B4
8000	MNGV	60053	2864	10W-11N	B3
8000	NLES	60053	2864	10W-11N	B3
8000	NLES	60714	2864	10W-11N	B3
W Lake St US-20					
-	HnrT	60103	2910		C1
-	SMWD	60120	2910		C1
10	NHLK	60164	3028		C1
200	BMDL	60108	2912		D7
200	BMDL	60172	2912		D7
200	BmdT	60108	2912		E7
200	BmdT	60172	2912		E7
200	ROSL	60108	2912		D7
200	ROSL	60172	2912		D7
500	BRLT	60103	2910		E1
500	BRLT	60107	2910		E1
500	BRLT	60120	2910		E1
500	HnrT	60120	2910		D1
500	SMWD	60103	2910		E1
500	SMWD	60107	2910		E1
600	BRLT	60103	2911		B3
600	HRPK	60103	2911		B3
600	HRPK	60133	2911		B3
600	SMWD	60107	2911		B3
1100	BRLT	60103	2856	30W-9N	B7
1100	BRLT	60107	2856	30W-9N	B7
1100	BRLT	60120	2856	30W-9N	B7
1100	HnrT	60103	2856	30W-9N	B7
1100	HnrT	60107	2856	30W-9N	B7
1100	HnrT	60120	2856	30W-9N	B7
1100	SMWD	60107	2856	30W-9N	C7
2200	BRLT	60133	2911		C3
4100	MLPK	60160	3029	13W-1N	A2
4100	MLPK	60165	3029	12W-1N	A2
4100	SNPK	60165	3029	13W-1N	A2
4600	MLPK	60160	3028		E2
N Lake Ter					
1900	NfdT	60025	2810	10W-14N	A4
3000	GNVW	60025	2810	10W-14N	A4
Lake Adalyn Dr					
10	SBTN	60010	2803	26W-13N	C6
N Lake Arlington Dr					
-	PTHT	60070	2754	16W-16N	E7
1900	ANHT	60004	2807	16W-16N	D1
2100	ANHT	60004	2754	16W-16N	E7
Lake Bluff Dr					
5800	BmnT	60477	3425	7W-20S	C3
5800	TYPK	60477	3425	7W-20S	C4
Lakebrook Ct					
11300	ODPK	60467	3422	14W-20S	E5
Lakebrook Dr					
17200	ODPK	60467	3422	14W-20S	E5
Lake Cook Rd					
-	AlqT	60010	2749	28W-20N	D2
-	ANHT	60004	2753	19W-20N	C2
-	ANHT	60047	2753	18W-20N	D2
-	BNHL	60010	2749	28W-20N	D2
-	BNHL	60010	2750	26W-20N	D2
-	BRTN	60010	2750	26W-20N	C2
-	ElaT	60004	2753	19W-20N	C2
-	ElaT	60047	2753	19W-20N	C2
-	NfdT	60035	2757	8W-20N	E2
-	PltT	60004	2753	19W-20N	C2
-	PltT	60047	2753	19W-20N	C2
-	PltT	60074	2753	19W-20N	C2
-	VrnT	60047	2753	19W-20N	D2
-	VrnT	60089	2753	18W-20N	D2
-	WhlT	60090	2755	14W-20N	D2
10	NfdT	60062	2757	8W-20N	E2
400	DRFD	60062	2757	10W-18N	A2
500	DRFD	60015	2757	10W-18N	A3
600	DRFD	60062	2756	10W-18N	E2
700	NHBK	60062	2756	10W-18N	E2
900	DRFD	60015	2756	11W-20N	D2
1000	HDPK	60035	2758	8W-18N	A2
1000	NfdT	60062	2758	8W-18N	A2
1000	NtrT	60035	2758	7W-18N	A2
1000	NtrT	60062	2758	7W-18N	A2
1200	HDPK	60035	2757	8W-20N	E2
1300	NHBK	60062	2757	9W-20N	B2
1400	NHBK	60035	2757	9W-18N	C2
1500	HDPK	60062	2757	9W-20N	B2
1900	NfdT	60062	2756	12W-20N	A2
1900	WdfT	60015	2756	12W-20N	A2
1900	WdfT	60062	2756	12W-20N	A2
2200	RVWD	60015	2756	12W-20N	A2
2200	RVWD	60062	2756	12W-20N	A2
2300	NHBK	60015	2756	13W-20N	A2
2700	RVWD	60015	2755	13W-20N	D2
2700	VrnT	60015	2755	13W-20N	E2
2700	VrnT	60062	2755	13W-20N	E2
2700	WhlT	60062	2755	13W-20N	D2
4400	NHBK	60062	2755	13W-20N	D2
22000	DRPK	60010	2752	22W-20N	A2
22000	PltT	60074	2752	22W-20N	C2
22500	PltT	60010	2752	22W-20N	A2
23200	DRPK	60010	2751	23W-20N	E2
23200	ElaT	60010	2751	23W-20N	E2
23200	PltT	60010	2751	23W-20N	E2
23900	BRTN	60010	2751	23W-20N	D2
E Lake Cook Rd					
-	ElaT	60047	2753	20W-20N	B2
-	ElaT	60074	2753	20W-20N	A2
-	LGGV	60047	2753	20W-20N	A2
-	PLTN	60047	2753	19W-20N	B2
-	PLTN	60074	2753	20W-20N	A2
-	PltT	60004	2753	19W-20N	C2
-	PltT	60047	2753	19W-20N	C2
-	PltT	60074	2753	20W-20N	A2
-	VrnT	60062	2755	14W-20N	C2
-	VrnT	60090	2755	14W-20N	C2
-	WhlT	60062	2755	14W-20N	D2
-	WhlT	60090	2755	14W-20N	C2
10	BFGV	60089	2754	16W-18N	C2
100	DRPK	60074	2752	20W-20N	E2
100	ElaT	60074	2752	20W-20N	E2
100	PltT	60074	2752	20W-20N	E2
200	BFGV	60089	2755	15W-18N	A2
200	WLNG	60090	2755	15W-18N	A2
700	WLNG	60089	2755	15W-18N	A2
1100	BFGV	60090	2754	16W-18N	D2
1100	WLNG	60089	2754	16W-18N	D2
1100	WLNG	60090	2754	16W-18N	D2
1400	BFGV	60090	2755	14W-18N	B2
E Lake Cook Rd CO-A50					
100	BFGV	60089	2754	16W-20N	D2
100	WLNG	60089	2754	16W-20N	D2
1300	WLNG	60090	2754	16W-18N	D2
W Lake Cook Rd					
-	ANHT	60004	2753	18W-20N	E2
-	ANHT	60047	2753	18W-20N	E2
-	ANHT	60089	2753	18W-20N	E2
-	VrnT	60004	2753	18W-20N	E2
-	VrnT	60047	2753	18W-20N	E2
-	VrnT	60089	2753	18W-20N	E2
10	BFGV	60089	2754	17W-18N	B2
100	DRPK	60074	2752	21W-20N	D2
100	PltT	60074	2752	21W-20N	D2
500	DRPK	60010	2752	21W-20N	C2
1100	ANHT	60004	2754	17W-20N	A2
1100	VrnT	60004	2754	17W-20N	A2
1100	VrnT	60089	2754	17W-20N	A2
Lake Cornish Ct					
10	ALGN	60102	2748		A3
Lake Cornish Wy					
500	ALGN	60102	2748		A2
Lake Edge Ct					
1300	HFET	60195	2804	24W-15N	C2
Lakefield Dr					
11200	ODPK	60467	3422	14W-20S	E4
Lake Gillian Ct					
10	ALGN	60102	2748		B2
Lake Gillian Wy					
200	ALGN	60102	2748		B2
Lake Hill Ln					
100	CRTE	60417	3596	0W-28S	C6
100	CRTE	60475	3596	0W-28S	C7
Lake Hills Ct					
15700	ODPK	60462	3424	10W-18S	B1
Lake Katherine Dr					
10	PSHT	60463	3274	9W-13S	D5
Lake Knoll Dr					
3300	NHBK	60062	2756	11W-16N	C7
3400	NfdT	60062	2756	11W-16N	C7
Lakeland Ct					
200	SMBG	60173	2859	22W-10N	C5
1000	WLNG	60090	2754	16W-16N	D7
Lakeland Dr					
100	PlsT	60464	3273	12W-14S	B7
600	SMBG	60194	2859	22W-10N	C5
700	SMBG	60173	2859	22W-10N	C5
Lake Lawn Ln					
15100	ODPK	60467	3344	14W-18S	E7
E Lake Louise Dr					
1400	PLTN	60074	2753	19W-16N	C7
Lake Lynwood Dr					
19400	BlmT	60411	3509	3E-23S	E3
19400	LYWD	60411	3509	3E-23S	E3
19700	LYWD	60411	3510	3E-23S	A3
Lake Marian Rd					
10	CPVL	60110	2748		A6
10	DndT	60110	2748		A6
S Lake Park Av					
2900	CHCG	60616	3092	0E-2S	D3
3500	CHCG	60653	3092	1E-4S	E6
4200	CHCG	60653	3093	1E-4S	A7
4600	CHCG	60615	3093	1E-4S	A7
4700	CHCG	60615	3153	1E-5S	A1
5400	CHCG	60637	3153	1E-5S	B2
Lake Park Ct					
2800	LYWD	60411	3510	3E-23S	A2
Lake Park Dr					
2700	LYWD	60411	3510	3E-23S	A2
Lake Placid Ln					
2900	NHBK	60062	2756	11W-17N	D5
Lake Plumleigh Ct					
10	ALGN	60102	2748		B2
Lake Plumleigh Wy					
300	ALGN	60102	2748		B2
Lake Point Dr					
10	ROSL	60172	2913		C4
Lake Ridge Ct					
10	BRRG	60527	3208		B3
Lake Ridge Dr					
8100	BRRG	60527	3208		A3
Lake Ridge Rd					
14300	ODPK	60462	3345	13W-17S	B5
Lake Ridge Club Ct					
10	BRRG	60527	3208		A3
Lake Ridge Club Dr					
10	BRRG	60527	3208		A2
Lakeshore					
10	ROSL	60172	2913		C4
Lake Shore Blvd					
1000	EVTN	60202	2867	2W-10N	C4
1200	EVTN	60201	2867	2W-11N	C3
N Lake Shore Cir					
2100	ANHT	60004	2754	16W-16N	D7
Lake Shore Ct					
1400	BRTN	60010	2751	24W-20N	C1
Lake Shore Dr					
-	CRTE	60417	3596	0E-28S	D7
-	CRTE	60417	3685	0E-29S	D1
10	CPVL	60110	2748		A5
10	DndT	60110	2748		A5
400	EDND	60118	2801		B1
2500	LYWD	60411	3509	3E-23S	E3
11500	ODPK	60467	3422	14W-21S	D7
19400	BlmT	60411	3509	3E-23S	E3
Lakeshore Dr					
-	UYPK	60466	3594	6W-27S	B5
-	UYPK	60471	3594	6W-27S	B5
4900	RNPK	60471	3594	6W-27S	A4
E Lake Shore Dr					
-	CHCG	60616	3092	1E-3S	E4
100	CHCG	60611	3034	0E-1N	C2
N Lake Shore Dr					
-	CHCG	-	2922	0W-5N	A7
-	CHCG	-	2978	0W-3N	B4
-	CHCG	-	3034	0E-1N	C1
-	CHCG	60640	2921	1W-6N	E6
-	CHCG	60660	2921	1W-7N	E4
-	CokC	-	3034	0E-0N	D4
400	PLTN	60067	2752	22W-16N	B6
1100	CHCG	60610	3034	0E-1N	C1
1500	CHCG	60610	2978	0E-1N	C7
3200	CHCG	60657	2978	0W-4N	A2
3500	CHCG	60613	2978	0W-4N	A2
N Lake Shore Dr US-41					
-	CHCG	-	2921	1W-6N	E6
-	CHCG	-	2922	0W-5N	A7
-	CHCG	-	2978	0W-3N	B4
-	CHCG	-	3034	0E-1N	C1
-	CokC	-	3034	0E-0N	D4
N Lake Shore Dr W					
-	CHCG	60614	2978	0W-3N	A4
2800	CHCG	60657	2978	0W-3N	A4
S Lake Shore Dr					
-	CHCG	-	3092	1E-3S	E5
-	CHCG	-	3093	1E-4S	A6
-	CokC	60637	3153	2E-6S	C3
10	CHCG	60601	3034	0E-0S	D5
10	CHCG	60603	3034	0E-0S	D5
100	CHCG	60605	3034	0E-0S	D5
1400	CHCG	60616	3034	0E-1S	D7
5300	CHCG	60615	3153	2E-6S	C3
5300	CHCG	60637	3153	2E-6S	C3
S Lake Shore Dr US-41					
-	CHCG	-	3092	0E-2S	D3
-	CHCG	-	3093	1E-4S	A6
-	CHCG	-	3153	2E-5S	B1
-	CokC	60637	3153	2E-6S	C3
10	CHCG	60601	3034	0E-0S	D5
10	CHCG	60603	3034	0E-0S	D5
100	CHCG	60605	3034	0E-0S	D5
1500	CHCG	60616	3034	0E-1S	D7
5300	CHCG	60637	3153	2E-6S	C3
Lake Shore Dr N					
300	BRTN	60010	2751	24W-20N	C1
Lake Shore Dr S					
1300	BRTN	60010	2751	24W-20N	C1
Lake Shore Dr Ct					
19600	LYWD	60411	3509	3E-23S	E3
Lakeside Av					
3200	NfdT	60062	2756	11W-16N	D7
3200	NHBK	60062	2756	11W-16N	C7
14600	DLTN	60419	3350	0E-17S	D5
Lakeside Ct					
10	SBTN	60010	2803	27W-15N	B2
2800	EVTN	60201	2813	2W-13N	B6
S Lakeside Ct					
24000	CteT	60417	3598	4E-29S	B7
24000	CteT	60417	3687	4E-29S	B1
W Lakeside Ct					
7200	FftT	60423	3504	9W-23S	E3
Lakeside Dr					
10	SBTN	60010	2803	27W-15N	A2
300	ROSL	60172	2913		A4
800	BRLT	60103	2911		C4
7800	FftT	60423	3504	9W-23S	D3
7800	TYPK	60423	3504	9W-23S	D3
7800	TYPK	60477	3504	9W-23S	D3
10900	ODPK	60467	3423	13W-18S	A1
15500	ODPK	60467	3345	13W-18S	A7
N Lakeside Dr					
1000	PltT	60067	2752	21W-17N	C5
W Lakeside Dr					
600	PltT	60067	2752	21W-17N	C5
700	PLTN	60067	2752	22W-17N	C6
7300	FftT	60423	3504	9W-23S	D3
Lakeside Pl					
10	GLNC	60022	2758	6W-20N	C2
400	HDPK	60035	2758	7W-20N	C1
5900	TYPK	60477	3425	7W-20S	C3
W Lakeside Pl					
700	CHCG	60640	2921	1W-5N	E7
N Lakeside Plz					
1900	HFET	60195	2804	24W-12N	D7
1900	HFET	60195	2858	24W-12N	C2
W Lakeside Plz					
800	HFET	60195	2804	24W-12N	D7
Lakeside Ter					
300	GLNC	60022	2758	5W-17N	E5
300	GLNC	60022	2759	5W-17N	A5
S Lakeside Tr					
24000	CteT	60417	3598	4E-29S	B7
24000	CteT	60417	3687	4E-29S	B1
Lakeside Cir Dr					
600	WLNG	60090	2754	16W-17N	D6
Lakeside Manor Rd					
400	HDPK	60035	2758	6W-20N	C1
Lake Superior Dr					
900	MTSN	60443	3506	6W-25S	A7
Lake Trail Dr					
500	PlsT	60464	3273	12W-14S	B7
Lake View					
-	LMNT	60439	3272	15W-13S	B5
N Lakeview Av					
2400	CHCG	60614	2978	0W-3N	A5
2700	CHCG	60657	2978	0W-3N	A4
Lakeview Cir					
400	EGVV	60007	2860	19W-9N	C7
Lakeview Cir E					
18400	TYPK	60477	3425	8W-22S	B7
Lakeview Cir W					
18400	TYPK	60477	3425	8W-22S	B7
Lake View Ct					
300	DRFD	60015	2756	11W-20N	E1
500	BRLT	60103	2910		E4
Lakeview Ct					
200	CRTE	60475	3596	0W-28S	C6
300	BFGV	60089	2754	17W-20N	B1
400	MPPT	60056	2808	14W-13N	C6
500	ROSL	60172	2913		B4
12300	OrlT	60467	3344	14W-16S	C3
21200	FKFT	60423	3504	11W-25S	A7
N Lakeview Ct					
1200	PLTN	60067	2752	22W-17N	C5
W Lake View Ct					
12300	HMGN	60467	3344	15W-16S	B2
W Lakeview Ct					
7900	PSHT	60463	3346	9W-15S	C1
10000	PlsT	60464	3345	12W-15S	C1
Lakeview Dr					
-	ANHT	60090	2754	16W-17N	D6
200	BFGV	60089	2754	17W-20N	C1
600	WLNG	60090	2754	16W-17N	C5
1700	ANHT	60004	2754	16W-17N	C5
3500	HLCT	60429	3426	4W-22S	E7
3500	HLCT	60429	3506	4W-22S	E1
3500	HMWD	60430	3426	4W-22S	E7
4100	CCHL	60478	3426	5W-21S	C6
9200	ODPK	60462	3345	11W-17S	E5
14700	ODPK	60462	3346	11W-17S	A5
N Lakeview Dr					
1200	PLTN	60067	2752	22W-17N	B5
1200	PltT	60067	2752	22W-17N	C5
W Lake View Dr					
12000	HMGN	60467	3344	15W-16S	B2
12000	OrlT	60467	3344	15W-16S	B2
12400	HmrT	60467	3344	15W-16S	B2
Lakeview Ln					
10	BNHL	60010	2750	26W-17N	D5
500	HFET	60194	2858	24W-11N	D4
6500	MONE	60449	3682	8W-31S	B6
21100	FKFT	60423	3504	11W-25S	A7
W Lake View Pl					
12300	HMGN	60467	3344	15W-15S	B2
Lakeview Pt					
700	SMBG	60194	2859	22W-10N	C4
Lakeview Ter					
10	HDPK	60035	2758	6W-20N	C1
7800	FftT	60423	3504	9W-23S	D3
7800	TYPK	60423	3504	9W-23S	D3
7800	TYPK	60477	3504	9W-23S	D3
W Lakeview Ter					
7600	FftT	60423	3504	9W-23S	D3
Lakeview Tr					
12000	HMGN	60441	3344	15W-18S	B7
12000	OrlT	60441	3344	15W-18S	C7
12000	OrlT	60467	3344	15W-18S	C7
12300	HMGN	60441	3422	15W-18S	C1
Lake Villa Av					
16100	TYPK	60477	3424	9W-19S	E2
Lakeway Dr					
6400	MONE	60449	3682	8W-31S	C5
Lakewood Av					
19800	LYWD	60411	3509	3E-23S	E4
N Lakewood Av					
2100	CHCG	60614	2977	1W-2N	D6
2700	CHCG	60657	2977	1W-3N	D5
3900	CHCG	60613	2977	1W-4N	D2
5200	CHCG	60640	2921	1W-6N	D5
6100	CHCG	60660	2921	1W-7N	D3
6600	CHCG	60626	2921	1W-8N	D1
S Lakewood Av					
200	NHLK	60164	3028		D2
11900	PlsT	60464	3273	11W-14S	E5
11900	PSPK	60464	3273	11W-14S	E5
Lakewood Blvd					
-	SBTN	60010	2803	25W-13N	E6
200	PKFT	60466	3595	3W-26S	A3
500	PKFT	60466	3594	4W-26S	E3
1700	HFET	60195	2804	25W-13N	A6
2000	HFET	60195	2803	25W-13N	E6
Lakewood Cir					
100	BRRG	60527	3208		B4
Lakewood Ct					
10	PKFT	60466	3595	4W-27S	A3
600	OKBK	60523	3086		B1
900	BRTN	60010	2751	24W-18N	B2
3300	GNVW	60025	2810	10W-13N	A5
Lakewood Dr					
10	GLNC	60022	2758	6W-18N	E4
900	BRLT	60103	2910		D6
900	BRTN	60010	2751	24W-18N	B2
2300	DYR	46311	3598		C3
16700	BmnT	60477	3425	7W-20S	D3
16700	TYPK	60477	3425	7W-20S	D3
Lakewood Ln					
14300	OrlT	60467	3344	14W-17S	D5
Lakewood Pl					
10	HDPK	60035	2758	7W-20N	C1
Lakewood Plz					
10	CPVL	60110	2748		C7
Lakewood Rd					
1000	ELGN	60123	2801		A7
1000	ELGN	60123	2855		A1
Lake Zurich Rd					
400	BRTN	60010	2751	25W-20N	A1
N Lama Ln					
1300	MPPT	60056	2808	13W-14N	E3
Lamb Dr					
4800	OKLN	60453	3276	6W-11S	A1
4900	OKLN	60453	3275	6W-11S	E1
Lambert Dr					
10	SMBG	60193	2859	23W-10N	B5
10	SMBG	60194	2859	23W-10N	B6
Lambert Ln					
500	BRLT	60103	2909		E1
500	BRLT	60120	2909		E1
700	BRLT	60103	2856	31W-9N	A7
700	ELGN	60120	2856	31W-9N	A7
Lambert Tree Av					
300	HDPK	60035	2758	7W-20N	B1
Lamburt Ln					
-	BRLT	60103	2909		E1
600	BRLT	60103	2856	31W-9N	A7
Lamon Av					
7800	BRBK	60459	3212	6W-9S	A3
8600	BRBK	60453	3212	6W-9S	A4
8600	OKLN	60453	3212	6W-9S	A4
8800	SKOK	60077	2865	6W-11N	E3
10000	SKOK	60077	2811	6W-12N	E7
10000	WLMT	60091	2811	6W-12N	E7
10300	OKLN	60453	3276	6W-12S	A2
13500	CTWD	60445	3348	6W-16S	A3
13800	BmnT	60445	3348	6W-16S	A3
14300	MDLN	60445	3348	6W-17S	A5
14900	OKFT	60452	3348	6W-17S	A6
15700	OKFT	60452	3426	6W-18S	A1
N Lamon Av					
10	CHCG	60644	3031	6W-0N	E4
1400	CHCG	60651	3031	6W-1N	E1
1600	CHCG	60639	3031	6W-1N	E1
1900	CHCG	60639	2975	6W-2N	E7
4200	CHCG	60641	2975	6W-5N	E1
4300	CHCG	60630	2975	6W-5N	E1
4800	CHCG	60630	2919	6W-6N	E6
6800	LNWD	60712	2919	6W-8N	E1
6800	SKOK	60077	2919	6W-8N	E1
6900	SKOK	60712	2919	6W-8N	E1
7200	LNWD	60712	2865	6W-9N	E7
7200	SKOK	60077	2865	6W-9N	E7
S Lamon Av					
-	CHCG	60644	3031	6W-0S	E6
4300	CHCG	60638	3089	6W-4S	E7
4300	CHCG	60638	3090	6W-4S	A7
4600	CHCG	60638	3149	6W-5S	E1
6300	CHCG	60638	3150	6W-7S	A5
6400	BDPK	60638	3150	6W-7S	A5
11200	ALSP	60803	3276	6W-13S	A4
Lamon Ct					
14400	MDLN	60445	3348	6W-17S	A4
Lamont Pkwy					
100	BRLT	60103	2910		E4
Lamorak Ct					
300	SMBG	60193	2859	22W-9N	C6
Lamorak Dr					
600	SMBG	60193	2859	22W-10N	C6
S Lams Ct					
700	MPPT	60056	2807	16W-12N	E7
Lamson Dr					
800	WNKA	60093	2759	5W-16N	A7
Lanark Ln					
1000	IVNS	60067	2751	24W-17N	D5
W Lanark Ln					
800	PLTN	60067	2805	22W-15N	C2
Lanark St					
1400	FSMR	60422	3506	4W-23S	D3
Lancashire Ct					
1800	SMBG	60194	2858	25W-11N	A3
Lancaster Av					
200	ANHT	60004	2807	16W-15N	D2
200	PTHT	60004	2807	16W-15N	D2
200	PTHT	60070	2807	16W-15N	D2
1000	EGVV	60007	2914		D2
S Lancaster Av					
100	MPPT	60056	2807	16W-12N	D7
200	MPPT	60056	2861	16W-12N	D1
Lancaster Ct					
10	BRRG	60527	3208		B3
400	IVNS	60010	2751	24W-17N	C5
1000	HFET	60195	2804	24W-12N	C7
1100	HFET	60195	2858	25W-12N	C1
W Lancaster Ct					
12000	HMGN	60467	3344	15W-16S	C4
Lancaster Dr					
2700	MKHM	60426	3427	3W-19S	B2
5600	OKFT	60452	3347	7W-18S	D7
Lancaster Ln					
10	DSPN	60018	2862	15W-10N	B6
900	DYR	46311	3510		E5
15400	ODPK	60462	3346	11W-18S	A7
Lancaster St					
10900	WSTR	60154	3086		E3
N Lancaster St					
10	MPPT	60056	2807	16W-13N	D7
Lancaster Wy					
-	NHBK	60062	2757	9W-16N	B7
Lancastor Ct					
10	SMWD	60107	2856	29W-9N	E7
Lance Dr					
200	DSPN	60016	2862	15W-11N	A4
S Lancelot Ln					
200	ANHT	60004	2806	19W-15N	D2
200	PLTN	60074	2806	19W-15N	D2
Landau Ln					
200	WLNG	60090	2755	15W-18N	A2
Landau Rd					
500	UYPK	60466	3684	3W-30S	C3
N Landcaster Ct					
1700	ANHT	60004	2807	16W-15N	C1
N Landen Dr					
2400	LydT	60164	2972		E5
2400	NHLK	60164	2972		E6
2600	FNPK	60131	2972		E5
N Landers Av					
6000	CHCG	60646	2919	6W-7N	E3
Landers Dr					
5100	HFET	60192	2856	30W-12N	C1
Landings Dr					
10700	ODPK	60467	3423	13W-20S	A4
10700	OrlT	60467	3423	13W-20S	A4
Landings Ln					
-	DSPN	60016	2863	11W-11N	D3

STREET Block	City	ZIP	Map#	CGS	Grid
Landings Ln					
-	MaiT	60016	2863	11W-11N	D3
14800	OKFT	60452	3347	7W-17S	B6
Landmark					
10	NHFD	60093	2811	6W-15N	C3
Landmark Ln					
20500	DRPK	60010	2752	22W-20N	B1
Landmark Vil					
-	CHCG	60657	2977	2W-3N	C4
Landmeier Rd					
100	EGVV	60007	2860	18W-9N	E7
300	EGvT	60007	2860	18W-9N	E7
300	EGvT	60007	2861	18W-9N	A7
300	EGVV	60007	2861	18W-9N	A7
1100	EGVV	60007	2915		C1
1800	EGvT	60007	2915		D1
2500	EGvT	60018	2861	16W-9N	E7
Landreth Ln					
400	NHFD	60093	2758	8W-16N	A7
Lands End					
9900	MNSR	46321	3510		D4
Landwehr Rd					
600	NHBK	60062	2756	11W-16N	D6
1800	GNVW	60025	2809	11W-14N	D4
1800	NfdT	60025	2809	11W-14N	D4
1800	NfdT	60062	2809	11W-14N	D4
2100	NfdT	60062	2756	11W-16N	D7
2100	NHBK	60062	2809	11W-15N	D1
2600	GNVW	60062	2809	11W-15N	D1
2600	NHBK	60025	2809	11W-15N	D2
Lanford Ln					
200	PTHT	60070	2808	15W-14N	A3
Langdon Pl					
2200	HFET	60195	2857	26W-12N	E1
2200	HFET	60195	2858	25W-12N	C1
Lange Av					
-	BCHR	60401	3864	0W-36S	D1
Lange St					
18000	LNSG	60438	3430	4E-21S	C6
19200	LNSG	60438	3510	4E-22S	C2
Langley Av					
14700	DLTN	60419	3350	0E-17S	E4
15500	SHLD	60473	3350	0E-18S	E7
16600	SHLD	60473	3429	0E-19S	A2
16800	SHLD	60473	3428	0E-19S	E3
S Langley Av					
4600	CHCG	60615	3092	0E-4S	E7
4600	CHCG	60653	3092	0E-4S	E7
4700	CHCG	60615	3152	0E-5S	E1
6000	CHCG	60637	3152	0E-7S	E6
7100	CHCG	60619	3152	0E-8S	E7
7500	CHCG	60619	3214	0E-9S	E3
9400	CHCG	60628	3214	0E-10S	E5
10500	CHCG	60628	3278	0E-12S	E2
13100	CHCG	60827	3278	0E-15S	E7
13100	CHCG	60827	3350	0E-15S	E1
Langley Cir					
2700	GNVW	60025	2810	9W-13N	B5
Langley Ct					
400	SMBG	60193	2859	23W-9N	B6
5000	OKFT	60452	3426	6W-20S	A4
Langley Dr					
300	SMBG	60193	2859	23W-9N	B6
Langston St					
-	FDHT	60411	3509	1E-24S	B6
Langtry Ct					
900	ELGN	60120	2855		C5
N Lansing Av					
5700	CHCG	60646	2919	6W-7N	D4
Lansing St					
10	HNDL	60521	3086		A7
Lanyon Dr					
-	BRLT	60120	2909		D3
Lapalm Ct					
5300	OKFT	60452	3347	6W-17S	E6
Lapalm Dr					
5400	OKFT	60452	3347	7W-17S	D6
La Paz Ct					
15700	OKFT	60452	3347	7W-18S	C7
15700	OKFT	60452	3425	7W-18S	C1
La Paz Dr					
6000	OKFT	60452	3347	7W-18S	C7
Lapier St					
100	GLNC	60022	2758	5W-17N	E6
La Porte Av					
400	NHLK	60164	2972		D7
800	LydT	60164	2972		D5
3100	FNPK	60131	2972		D5
Laporte Av					
600	WLMT	60091	2811	6W-13N	D6
7800	BRBK	60459	3211	6W-8S	E2
8300	BRBK	60459	3212	6W-9S	A3
8600	OKLN	60453	3212	6W-9S	A4
10300	OKLN	60453	3276	6W-12S	A1
14500	MDLN	60445	3348	6W-17S	A5
15100	OKFT	60452	3348	6W-18S	A6
N Laporte Av					
100	CHCG	60644	3031	6W-0N	E4
2000	CHCG	60639	2975	6W-2N	E6
2000	CHCG	60641	2975	6W-4N	E2
4400	CHCG	60630	2975	6W-5N	E1
5200	CHCG	60630	2919	6W-6N	E5
6600	LNWD	60712	2919	6W-8N	E2
6700	SKOK	60077	2919	6W-8N	E2
S Laporte Av					
4500	CHCG	60638	3089	6W-4S	E7
4700	CHCG	60638	3149	6W-5S	E2
6400	BDPK	60638	3149	6W-7S	E5
11600	ALSP	60803	3276	6W-13S	A4
La Porte Ct					
6700	BGVW	60455	3148	9W-7S	C6
Laporte Rd					
-	FftT	60448	3504	11W-23S	A4
-	FftT	60477	3504	10W-23S	B4
-	FKFT	60448	3504	11W-23S	A4
-	FKFT	60477	3504	10W-23S	B4
W La Porte Rd					
-	FftT	60448	3504	11W-24S	A4
-	FKFT	60448	3504	11W-24S	A4
Laporte Meadows Ct					
20000	FKFT	60423	3504	11W-24S	A5
Laporte Meadows Dr					
19900	FKFT	60423	3504	11W-24S	A4
19900	FKFT	60448	3504	11W-24S	A4
La Quienta Dr					
4900	MONE	60449	3683	6W-31S	B5
Laramie Av					
-	CCRO	60804	3089	6W-3S	E6
-	SKNY	60804	3089	6W-4S	E6
500	WLMT	60091	2811	6W-13N	D6
600	GNVW	60025	2811	6W-13N	D7
6800	SKOK	60077	2919	6W-8N	D1
7500	BDPK	60459	3211	6W-8S	E1
7500	BDPK	60638	3211	6W-8S	E1
7500	BRBK	60459	3211	6W-8S	E1
Laramie Av					
7500	BRBK	60638	3211	6W-8S	E1
7500	SKOK	60077	2865	6W-9N	D6
8600	BRBK	60453	3211	6W-9S	E4
8600	OKLN	60453	3211	6W-9S	E4
10300	OKLN	60453	3275	6W-12S	E1
14700	MDLN	60445	3347	6W-17S	E6
14700	MDLN	60452	3347	6W-17S	E6
14700	OKFT	60452	3347	6W-18S	E7
16700	BmnT	60452	3425	6W-20S	E4
16700	OKFT	60452	3425	6W-20S	E4
N Laramie Av					
10	CHCG	60644	3031	6W-0N	D5
700	CHCG	60651	3031	6W-0N	D4
1500	CHCG	60639	3031	6W-2N	D1
1600	CHCG	60639	2975	6W-2N	D7
2700	CHCG	60641	2975	6W-5N	D1
4300	CHCG	60630	2975	6W-5N	D1
4800	CHCG	60630	2919	6W-6N	D6
S Laramie Av					
-	FTVW	60402	3089	6W-4S	E7
-	StkT	60402	3089	6W-4S	E7
10	CHCG	60644	3031	6W-0S	D7
700	CCRO	60804	3031	6W-0S	E7
1500	CCRO	60804	3089	6W-1S	E1
3400	SKNY	60804	3089	6W-3S	E5
4500	CHCG	60638	3089	6W-4S	E7
4500	FTVW	60638	3089	6W-4S	E7
4600	FTVW	60638	3149	6W-4S	E1
4700	StkT	60638	3149	6W-5S	E1
6500	BDPK	60638	3149	6W-7S	E5
6500	CHCG	60638	3149	6W-7S	E5
11100	OKLN	60453	3275	6W-13S	E3
11500	ALSP	60803	3275	6W-13S	E5
Laramie Blvd					
13500	CTWD	60445	3347	6W-16S	E3
13800	BmnT	60445	3347	6W-16S	E3
14000	MDLN	60445	3347	6W-16S	E3
Laramie Ct					
5200	OKFT	60452	3347	6W-18S	E6
Laramie Ln					
19000	CCHL	60478	3506	6W-22S	A2
Laramie Rd					
18600	CCHL	60478	3506	6W-22S	A1
W Laraway Rd					
7200	FKFT	60423	3593	9W-26S	A3
7200	FKFT	60443	3593	9W-27S	A3
7200	RchT	60423	3593	9W-27S	A3
7200	RchT	60443	3593	9W-27S	A3
Larch Av					
4600	GNVW	60025	2809	12W-14N	B4
E Larch Av					
4500	GNVW	60025	2809	12W-14N	C4
Larch Ct					
10	SMBG	60193	2857	27W-10N	D5
Larch Dr					
9300	MNSR	46321	3510		E2
N Larch Dr					
1500	MPPT	60056	2808	13W-15N	D3
Larch Ln					
2300	HRPK	60133	2911		B3
W Larchmont Av					
1800	CHCG	60613	2977	2W-4N	B2
Larchmont Dr					
1200	EGVV	60007	2915		A3
Larchmont Rd					
1900	HFET	60195	2804	23W-12N	E7
1900	SMBG	60195	2804	23W-12N	E7
La Reina Ct					
9900	ODPK	60462	3345	12W-17S	C6
La Reina Real St					
9900	ODPK	60462	3345	12W-17S	C6
Largo Ct					
1800	SMBG	60194	2858	25W-11N	A3
Lariat Ct					
10	LMNT	60439	3272	15W-13S	A4
Lark Av					
1500	MLPK	60160	3028		E2
Lark Ct					
2900	RGMW	60008	2806	19W-14N	C4
W Lark St					
900	PTON	60468	3860	10W-37S	D4
Larkdale Dr					
1700	NHBK	60062	2756	10W-16N	E7
2100	GNVW	60025	2810	9W-13N	D7
W Larkdale Ln					
400	MPPT	60056	2807	15W-14N	E5
600	ANHT	60004	2807	15W-14N	E5
600	MPPT	60004	2807	15W-14N	E5
Larkdale Rd					
10	DRFD	60015	2757	10W-20N	B2
Larkdale East Rd					
10	DRFD	60015	2757	9W-20N	B2
Larkin Dr					
200	WLNG	60090	2755	14W-16N	C7
Larkin Ln					
17600	CCHL	60478	3426	5W-21S	B6
Larkspur Dr					
200	HDPK	60035	2757	8W-20N	E1
Larkspur Ln					
600	MTSN	60443	3506	5W-24S	B6
2700	HLCT	60429	3427	3W-21S	B5
15100	OrlT	60462	3346	9W-18S	D6
15500	ODPK	60462	3346	9W-18S	D7
17700	HMWD	60430	3427	3W-21S	B6
N Larkspur Ln					
1300	PLTN	60074	2753	20W-17N	B5
W Larkspur Ln					
10	SMWD	60107	2856	30W-10N	C5
N Larned Av					
5200	CHCG	60630	2919	6W-6N	D5
Larrabee Ln					
1200	NHBK	60062	2757	9W-17N	D5
N Larrabee St					
600	CHCG	60610	3034	0W-1N	A1
1600	CHCG	60610	2978	0W-2N	A7
1600	CHCG	60614	2978	0W-2N	A7
Larry St					
7800	SjnT	46311	3598		E4
Larsen Av					
700	SMWD	60107	2911		B1
Larson Ln					
500	ROSL	60172	2913		B3
500	SmbT	60172	2913		B3
700	BNVL	60106	2915		E5
700	SmbT	60193	2913		B3
Larue St					
100	PKFT	60466	3595	3W-25S	B1
Lasalle Av					
-	TYPK	60477	3424	9W-21S	D6
N Lasalle Blvd					
300	CHCG	60610	3034	0W-1N	B2
La Salle Ct					
3400	FNPK	60131	2973	12W-4N	C3
Lasalle Ct					
10	SMWD	60107	2856	29W-9N	E7
N Lasalle Dr					
1600	CHCG	60610	2978	0W-2N	B7
1600	CHCG	60614	2978	0W-2N	B7
N Lasalle Dr SR-64					
1600	CHCG	60610	2978	0W-2N	B7
1600	CHCG	60614	2978	0W-2N	B7
W La Salle Dr					
-	CHCG	60614	2978	0W-2N	B7
W La Salle Dr SR-64					
-	CHCG	60614	2978	0W-2N	B7
Lasalle Rd					
100	HnrT	60107	2856	29W-9N	E7
100	SMWD	60107	2856	29W-9N	E7
La Salle St					
-	DSPN	60016	2861	16W-10N	E4
-	MPPT	60056	2861	16W-10N	E4
-	SHLD	60473	3428	0W-20S	C4
-	TNTN	60473	3428	0W-20S	C4
-	TNTN	60476	3428	0W-20S	C4
500	DSPN	60016	2862	14W-11N	C3
14600	DLTN	60419	3350	0W-17S	C5
14600	RVDL	60827	3350	0W-17S	C5
14900	HRVY	60426	3350	0W-17S	C5
15500	SHLD	60473	3350	0W-18S	C7
N Lasalle St					
-	CHCG	60610	3034	0W-0N	B4
10	CHCG	60602	3034	0W-0N	B4
10	CHCG	60603	3034	0W-0N	B4
100	CHCG	60601	3034	0W-0N	B4
S La Salle St					
13800	RVDL	60827	3350	0W-16S	C2
14500	DLTN	60419	3350	0W-16S	C4
S Lasalle St					
10	CHCG	60602	3034	0W-0S	B5
10	CHCG	60603	3034	0W-0S	B5
100	CHCG	60604	3034	0W-0S	B5
300	CHCG	60605	3034	0W-0S	B6
2600	CHCG	60616	3092	0W-2S	B3
3400	CHCG	60609	3092	0W-3S	B4
5300	CHCG	60609	3152	0W-5S	B2
5500	CHCG	60621	3152	0W-6S	B4
7900	CHCG	60620	3214	0W-9S	C2
9800	CHCG	60628	3214	0W-11S	C7
10500	CHCG	60628	3278	0W-12S	C1
W Lasalle St					
10	ANHT	60004	2807	18W-16N	A1
N Las Casas Av					
5600	CHCG	60646	2919	6W-7N	E4
Las Flores Ln					
15100	OKFT	60452	3347	7W-18S	C7
Las Robles Ct					
15200	OKFT	60452	3347	7W-18S	B6
Las Robles St					
15200	OKFT	60452	3347	7W-18S	B6
N Latham Av					
5400	CHCG	60630	2919	6W-6N	E5
Lathrop Av					
10	FTPK	60130	3030	9W-0N	C5
10	RVFT	60305	3030	9W-0N	C5
1500	EDPK	60707	3030	9W-1N	C1
1500	RVFT	60707	3030	9W-1N	C1
2200	FTPK	60130	3088	9W-2S	C2
2200	FTPK	60546	3088	9W-2S	C2
2200	NRIV	60546	3088	9W-2S	C2
15500	HRVY	60426	3350	1W-18S	A7
15500	HRVY	60426	3428	1W-18S	A1
16200	HRVY	60426	3427	1W-19S	E2
16200	MKHM	60426	3427	1W-19S	E2
16700	EHZC	60426	3428	1W-20S	A4
16700	HRVY	60429	3428	1W-20S	A4
17100	EHZC	60429	3428	1W-20S	A5
17300	HMWD	60430	3428	1W-20S	A5
17400	EHZC	60430	3428	1W-20S	A5
Latimer Ln					
700	FSMR	60422	3507	2W-22S	D2
Latonia Ct					
22500	RNPK	60471	3594	5W-27S	B4
Latonia Ln					
22200	RNPK	60471	3594	5W-27S	B5
22800	UYPK	60471	3594	5W-27S	B5
Latoria Ln					
2900	FNPK	60131	2973	13W-3N	A5
2900	LydT	60131	2973	13W-3N	A5
2900	LydT	60164	2973	13W-3N	A5
Latour Ct					
3900	HFET	60195	2804	24W-14N	C3
Latrobe Av					
-	CTWD	60445	3347	6W-16S	E2
100	NHFD	60093	2811	6W-15N	D2
300	NtrT	60093	2811	6W-15N	D2
6800	SKOK	60077	2919	6W-8N	D1
7500	BDPK	60638	3211	6W-8S	E1
7500	BRBK	60459	3211	6W-8S	E1
7500	BRBK	60638	3211	6W-8S	E1
8600	OKLN	60453	3211	6W-9S	E4
9200	SKOK	60077	2865	6W-11N	D2
15600	OKFT	60452	3347	6W-18S	E7
15900	OKFT	60452	3425	6W-19S	E1
N Latrobe Av					
600	CHCG	60644	3031	6W-0N	D3
700	CHCG	60651	3031	6W-0N	D3
1500	CHCG	60639	3031	6W-2N	D1
1900	CHCG	60639	2975	6W-2N	D7
5300	CHCG	60630	2919	6W-6N	D5
S Latrobe Av					
4700	FTVW	60638	3149	6W-5S	E1
4700	StkT	60638	3149	6W-5S	E1
6300	CHCG	60638	3149	6W-7S	E5
6400	BDPK	60638	3149	6W-7S	E5
12300	ALSP	60803	3275	6W-14S	E6
Lauder Ln					
400	IVNS	60067	2804	23W-15N	E2
W Lauffer Rd					
12500	HMGN	60441	3422	16W-20S	A5
12500	HMGN	60448	3422	16W-20S	A5
Laura Ln					
100	CHHT	60411	3507	1W-23S	E4
100	TNTN	60476	3428	0E-20S	D5
900	SLVL	60411	3597	1E-27S	B3
900	STGR	60411	3597	1E-27S	B3
1200	DGvT	60439	3270		C2
1900	DSPN	60018	2917	12W-8N	B1
6100	TYPK	60477	3425	7W-20S	C3
16400	OKFT	60452	3426	5W-19S	C2
S Laura Ln					
24300	CteT	60417	3686	2E-29S	D1
Laurel Av					
200	DSPN	60016	2862	13W-11N	E3
200	WLMT	60091	2813	2W-13N	A6
700	WLMT	60091	2812	3W-13N	E6
1000	DRFD	60015	2756	11W-20N	D2
1000	WNKA	60093	2759	5W-16N	A7
1100	WNKA	60093	2758	6W-16N	D7
Laurel Av					
1100	WNKA	60093	2811	5W-16N	E1
1500	WdfT	60015	2756	11W-20N	C2
1600	HRPK	60133	2911		D2
1800	EVTN	60201	2866	3W-11N	E2
2100	HRPK	60107	2911		C2
2100	SMWD	60107	2911		C2
3600	CCHL	60429	3426	4W-20S	D4
3600	CCHL	60478	3426	4W-20S	D4
3600	HLCT	60429	3426	4W-20S	D4
4600	GNVW	60025	2809	12W-14N	B5
5400	LynT	60525	3146		E4
6200	IHPK	60525	3147	13W-7S	A5
6200	LynT	60525	3147	13W-7S	A5
E Laurel Av					
300	EMHT	60126	3028		B3
Laurel Ct					
10	CRTE	60417	3685	0W-30S	C2
100	ELGN	60120	2855		A4
100	WLNG	60090	2755	15W-17N	A4
300	SMWD	60107	2857	28W-10N	A6
2500	DYR	46311	3598		E3
Laurel Dr					
10	BmdT	60157	2913		D7
600	DYR	46311	3598		E3
4700	RNPK	60471	3594	5W-26S	B3
16100	ODPK	60462	3424	10W-19S	B1
20500	DRPK	60010	2752	23W-20N	A1
N Laurel Dr					
1700	MPPT	60056	2808	13W-15N	D2
1700	PLTN	60074	2753	19W-18N	B3
W Laurel Dr					
7700	FftT	60423	3504	9W-24S	D5
Laurel Ln					
300	SMWD	60107	2857	28W-10N	A6
1300	SMBG	60193	2913		A2
1300	SmbT	60193	2913		A2
2500	WLMT	60091	2812	5W-13N	A6
3200	HLCT	60429	3426	4W-20S	E4
3200	HLCT	60429	3427	4W-20S	A4
3600	CCHL	60429	3426	4W-20S	D5
3600	CCHL	60478	3426	4W-20S	D5
Laurel Rd					
800	NHBK	60062	2757	9W-17N	B4
Laurel St					
200	EGvT	60007	2914		E1
200	EGVV	60007	2914		D1
300	EGvT	60007	2915		A1
300	EGVV	60007	2915		A1
400	ELGN	60120	2855		A4
Laurel Tr					
10	WLNG	60090	2754	16W-17N	E4
Laurel Hill Dr					
11000	ODPK	60467	3423	13W-20S	E3
11100	ODPK	60467	3422	13W-20S	E4
11100	OrlT	60467	3422	13W-20S	E4
Laurel Oak Ct					
10	BRRG	60527	3208		B5
Laurel Oaks Dr					
1300	BRLT	60107	2856	30W-9N	C7
1300	SMWD	60107	2856	30W-9N	C7
1300	SMWD	60120	2856	30W-9N	C7
Lauren Ln					
300	BFGV	60089	2754	16W-18N	C3
N Lauren Ln					
9800	NLES	60714	2864	10W-12N	B1
Laurette Ct					
500	SMBG	60193	2859	22W-9N	B7
S Laurie Av					
11900	PlsT	60464	3274	10W-14S	A5
11900	PSPK	60464	3274	10W-14S	A5
Laurie Ct					
1100	BRRG	60521	3146		C4
Laurie Ln					
500	NHFD	60093	2811	7W-15N	B1
600	BRLT	60103	2909		E2
1000	BRRG	60521	3146		C4
1000	HNDL	60521	3146		C4
1000	HRPK	60133	2857	26W-9N	E7
1500	HRPK	60107	2857	26W-9N	D7
1500	SMWD	60107	2857	26W-9N	D7
Lavender Ct					
5500	RGMW	60008	2860	19W-12N	D2
Lavergne Av					
-	BmnT	60477	3426	6W-21S	A7
-	CCHL	60478	3426	6W-21S	A7
400	WLMT	60091	2811	6W-13N	D6
6800	LNWD	60712	2919	6W-8N	E2
6800	SKOK	60077	2919	6W-8N	E1
7900	BRBK	60459	3211	6W-9S	E2
8600	OKLN	60453	3211	6W-9S	E4
9200	SKOK	60077	2865	6W-11N	E2
10000	SKOK	60077	2811	6W-12N	E7
10300	OKLN	60453	3275	6W-12S	E1
11000	ALSP	60803	3276	6W-12S	A1
11000	OKLN	60453	3276	6W-12S	A1
13500	CTWD	60445	3348	6W-16S	A3
13800	BmnT	60445	3348	6W-16S	A3
14500	MDLN	60445	3348	6W-17S	A5
14900	OKFT	60452	3348	6W-18S	A7
16100	OKFT	60452	3426	6W-19S	A1
18100	BmnT	60478	3426	6W-21S	A7
18100	RchT	60478	3426	6W-21S	A7
N Lavergne Av					
10	CHCG	60644	3031	6W-0N	E4
10	NHLK	60164	3028		D1
500	NHLK	60164	2972		D6
700	CHCG	60651	3031	6W-0N	E3
1500	CHCG	60639	3031	6W-2N	E1
2000	CHCG	60639	2975	6W-2N	E6
2700	CHCG	60641	2975	6W-3N	E5
4300	CHCG	60630	2975	6W-5N	E1
4700	CHCG	60630	2919	6W-6N	E6
S Lavergne Av					
10	CHCG	60644	3031	6W-0S	E4
200	NHLK	60164	3028		D2
4400	CHCG	60638	3089	6W-4S	E7
6500	BDPK	60638	3149	6W-7S	E6
6500	CHCG	60638	3149	6W-7S	E6
11500	ALSP	60803	3276	6W-13S	A5
S Lavergne Dr					
1100	MPPT	60056	2861	17W-11N	C3
Laverne Av					
1200	PKRG	60068	2864	10W-9N	A6
1200	PKRG	60068	2863	11W-9N	E6
N Laverne Av					
200	HLSD	60162	3028		D5
Laverne Ln					
400	BRTN	60010	2750	26W-20N	D1
7100	TYPK	60477	3425	8W-19S	A3
Lavigne Ln					
2000	NHBK	60062	2756	11W-16N	D7
Lavoie Av					
800	ELGN	60120	2855		B7
Lawler Av					
400	WLMT	60091	2811	6W-13N	D6
7600	BRBK	60459	3211	6W-8S	E1
8500	OKLN	60453	3211	6W-9S	E4
9200	SKOK	60077	2865	6W-12N	E1
10300	OKLN	60453	3275	6W-12S	E2
13500	CTWD	60445	3348	6W-16S	A2
13700	BmnT	60445	3348	6W-16S	A3
N Lawler Av					
400	CHCG	60644	3031	6W-0N	E3
800	CHCG	60651	3031	6W-1N	E2
1500	CHCG	60639	3031	6W-1N	E1
2000	CHCG	60639	2975	6W-2N	E6
4000	CHCG	60641	2975	6W-5N	E1
4600	CHCG	60630	2919	6W-5N	E7
S Lawler Av					
4400	CHCG	60638	3089	6W-4S	E7
5000	CHCG	60638	3149	6W-5S	E2
11100	ALSP	60803	3276	6W-13S	A3
11100	OKLN	60453	3276	6W-13S	A3
11500	ALSP	60803	3275	6W-13S	E4
W Lawler Av					
7400	NLES	60714	2864	9W-9N	C6
Lawn Av					
3800	PvsT	60558	3086		D7
3800	WNSP	60558	3086		D7
4400	WNSP	60558	3146		D1
6200	HGKN	60525	3147	12W-7S	D5
Lawn Cir					
900	WNSP	60558	3146		D4
Lawn Ct					
900	WNSP	60558	3146		E4
2500	SMBG	60193	2857	26W-10N	E7
Lawn Dr					
5600	WNSP	60558	3146		D4
Lawn Ln					
300	DSPN	60016	2862	15W-11N	A3
Lawndale					
-	ELGN	60120	2855		C6
Lawndale Av					
-	SKOK	60203	2866	4W-11N	C3
2300	EVTN	60201	2866	4W-12N	C1
2600	EVTN	60201	2812	4W-13N	C7
2700	WLMT	60091	2812	4W-13N	C7
4100	LYNS	60534	3088	10W-4S	B7
4500	LYNS	60534	3148	10W-5S	B1
4600	MCCK	60525	3148	10W-5S	B1
4600	MCCK	60534	3148	10W-4S	B1
5100	SMMT	60501	3148	10W-5S	B2
5100	SMMT	60525	3148	10W-5S	B1
8000	SKOK	60076	2866	4W-10N	C5
14300	MDLN	60445	3348	4W-17S	D4
15400	MKHM	60426	3348	4W-18S	D7
16000	MKHM	60426	3426	4W-19S	D3
16600	CCHL	60478	3426	4W-19S	D3
16600	HLCT	60429	3426	4W-19S	D3
17900	BmnT	60429	3426	4W-21S	D7
17900	BmnT	60430	3426	4W-21S	D7
17900	HLCT	60429	3426	4W-21S	D7
22400	RNPK	60471	3594	4W-27S	E5
N Lawndale Av					
400	CHCG	60624	3032	4W-0N	C3
1500	CHCG	60647	3032	4W-1N	C1
1500	CHCG	60651	3032	4W-1N	C1
1600	CHCG	60647	2976	4W-2N	C7
4100	CHCG	60618	2976	4W-5N	C1
4300	CHCG	60625	2976	4W-5N	C1
4400	CHCG	60625	2920	4W-5N	C7
6000	CHCG	60659	2920	4W-7N	C3
6300	CHCG	60712	2920	4W-7N	C3
6500	LNWD	60712	2920	4W-8N	C2
7000	SKOK	60076	2920	4W-8N	C1
S Lawndale Av					
100	EMHT	60126	3028		A3
1200	CHCG	60623	3032	4W-1S	C7
1200	CHCG	60624	3032	4W-1S	C7
1500	CHCG	60623	3090	4W-3S	C4
4700	CHCG	60632	3150	4W-5S	D1
5400	CHCG	60629	3150	4W-8S	D7
7500	CHCG	60652	3212	4W-8S	D1
8600	CHCG	60805	3212	4W-9S	D4
9200	ENGN	60805	3212	4W-11S	D6
9800	CHCG	60655	3212	4W-11S	D7
11500	CHCG	60655	3276	4W-13S	D4
11500	CHCG	60803	3276	4W-13S	D4
11500	WthT	60803	3276	4W-13S	D4
12000	ALSP	60803	3276	4W-14S	D5
13300	RBBN	60472	3348	4W-15S	D2
W Lawndale Av					
7600	SMMT	60501	3148	9W-5S	C3
Lawndale Dr					
10	MNSR	46321	3430		C7
Lawndale St					
10	CTCY	60409	3430	4E-19S	C3
10	HMND	46324	3430	4E-19S	C3
100	EVTN	60201	2812	4W-13N	C7
100	WLMT	60091	2812	4W-13N	C7
Lawnware Dr					
6100	MNGV	60053	2865	7W-10N	B5
Lawrence Av					
-	CHCG	60656	2917	11W-6N	D7
10	BmdT	60108	2912		A7
100	BMDL	60108	2912		E7
100	BMDL	60108	2913		A7
200	BMDL	60172	2912		A7
200	BmdT	60157	2913		C7
400	BmdT	60172	2912		D7
400	CHHT	60411	3595	2W-26S	D2
400	ROSL	60172	2913		B4
700	ROSL	60157	2913		B4
3200	SCHT	60411	3596	1W-27S	A4
9400	SRPK	60176	2917	11W-6N	D7
W Lawrence Av					
-	CHCG	60640	2922	0W-6N	A6
-	SRPK	60176	2917	11W-6N	D7
700	CHCG	60640	2921	1W-6N	E6
1900	CHCG	60625	2921	2W-5N	B6
2700	CHCG	60625	2920	3W-6N	E6
3900	CHCG	60630	2920	5W-6N	B7
4600	CHCG	60630	2919	7W-5N	E7
6200	HDHT	60706	2919	7W-5N	A7
7200	HDHT	60706	2918	9W-6N	C7
7500	NRDG	60706	2918	9W-6N	C7
8400	CHCG	60656	2918	10W-6N	A7
8500	NRDG	60656	2918	10W-6N	A7
8600	CHCG	60656	2917	11W-5N	E7
8600	NRDG	60706	2917	11W-5N	E7
8700	CHCG	60706	2917	10W-6N	E7
Lawrence Cres					
1300	FSMR	60422	3507	3W-23S	B3
Lawrence Ct					
300	BmdT	60157	2913		D4
9400	SRPK	60176	2917	11W-5N	C7
10100	OKLN	60453	3211	6W-11S	D7
10100	OKLN	60453	3275	6W-11S	D1

STREET Block	City	ZIP	Map#	CGS	Grid
Lawrence Ct					
15200	ODPK	60462	3346	10W-18S	B6
Lawrence Ln					
-	MTSN	60443	3506	6W-24S	A5
1400	NHBK	60062	2757	8W-17N	E6
1700	HDPK	60035	2757	9W-20N	D2
2500	HMWD	60430	3427	3W-21S	B6
3400	GNVW	60062	2809	12W-14N	B4
W Lawrence Ln					
2100	ANHT	60056	2861	17W-12N	B1
2100	MPPT	60056	2861	17W-12N	B1
2200	ANHT	60005	2861	17W-12N	B1
E Lawrence St					
1900	CHHT	60411	3595	2W-26S	D2
W Lawrence St					
1900	CHHT	60411	3595	2W-26S	D2
Lawrence-Wilson Dr					
-	CHCG	60640	2922	0W-6N	A6
Lawson Ln					
10	DXMR	60426	3349	2W-16S	D4
Lawson Rd					
1900	SMBG	60194	2858	25W-11N	A4
3600	GNVW	60025	2809	10W-15N	E2
3600	GNVW	60062	2809	10W-15N	E2
Lawton Av					
9500	OKLN	60453	3211	6W-11S	D6
Lawton Rd					
10	RVSD	60546	3088	9W-3S	D5
300	BRWN	60402	3088	9W-3S	D5
Lazy Ln					
6500	MONE	60449	3682	8W-31S	C5
Lea Rd					
10	DRPK	60010	2752	23W-20N	A1
N Leader Av					
5900	CHCG	60646	2919	6W-7N	D4
Leaf Ct					
700	BRLT	60103	2910		D6
Leahy Cir					
400	DSPN	60016	2862	15W-11N	B3
Leahy Cir E					
500	DSPN	60016	2862	15W-11N	B4
Leamington Av					
500	GNVW	60025	2811	6W-13N	D6
500	WLMT	60091	2811	6W-13N	D6
7600	BRBK	60459	3211	6W-8S	E2
8500	OKLN	60453	3211	6W-9S	E4
N Leamington Av					
100	CHCG	60644	3031	6W-0N	E4
700	CHCG	60651	3031	6W-0N	E3
1500	CHCG	60639	3031	6W-2N	D1
2000	CHCG	60639	2975	6W-2N	D6
4000	CHCG	60641	2975	6W-5N	D1
5200	CHCG	60630	2919	6W-6N	D5
S Leamington Av					
10	CHCG	60644	3031	6W-0S	E5
4400	CHCG	60638	3089	6W-4S	E7
4600	CHCG	60638	3149	6W-5S	E1
7100	BDPK	60638	3149	6W-8S	E7
11100	ALSP	60803	3275	6W-13S	E3
11100	OKLN	60453	3275	6W-13S	E3
W Leamington Dr					
-	BmnT	60445	3347	6W-16S	E3
-	CTWD	60445	3347	6W-16S	E3
Leamington St					
9400	SKOK	60077	2865	6W-11N	E2
Leanne Ct					
2700	GNVW	60025	2809	11W-15N	D2
2700	GNVW	60062	2809	11W-15N	D2
Lear Ct					
400	SMBG	60194	2857	26W-11N	E4
400	SMWD	60107	2857	26W-11N	E4
Leather Leaf Ct					
3600	HFET	60195	2804	25W-14N	A4
Leather Leaf Ln					
3600	HFET	60195	2804	25W-14N	A4
N Leavenworth Av					
5500	CHCG	60630	2919	6W-6N	D5
Leavitt Av					
1000	FSMR	60422	3507	3W-23S	B2
14100	DXMR	60406	3349	2W-17S	C4
14100	DXMR	60426	3349	2W-17S	C4
14600	HRVY	60426	3349	2W-17S	C6
15900	MKHM	60426	3427	2W-19S	C1
15900	ThtT	60426	3427	2W-19S	C1
N Leavitt Av					
3000	CHCG	60618	2977	2W-3N	B4
N Leavitt St					
10	CHCG	60612	3033	2W-0N	B4
700	CHCG	60622	3033	2W-0N	B3
1500	CHCG	60647	3033	2W-1N	B1
1600	CHCG	60647	2977	2W-2N	B7
3100	CHCG	60618	2977	2W-4N	B3
4400	CHCG	60625	2921	2W-5N	B7
6100	CHCG	60659	2921	2W-7N	B3
6300	CHCG	60645	2921	2W-7N	B3
S Leavitt St					
-	CHCG	60609	3151	2W-5S	B1
800	CHCG	60612	3033	2W-0S	B6
1200	CHCG	60608	3033	2W-1S	B7
1700	CHCG	60608	3091	2W-2S	B3
3400	CHCG	60609	3091	2W-3S	B5
8800	CHCG	60620	3213	2W-11S	B6
9400	CHCG	60643	3213	2W-11S	B6
10200	CHCG	60643	3277	2W-12S	C1
Leawood Ct					
1200	ELGN	60120	2855		D3
Leawood Dr					
10	ROSL	60172	2912		D5
1000	ELGN	60120	2855		D3
Lechner Ln					
2300	DSPN	60016	2863	12W-11N	C3
2300	MaiT	60016	2863	12W-11N	C3
Le Claire Av					
6800	LNWD	60712	2919	6W-8N	D2
6800	SKOK	60077	2919	6W-8N	D1
9400	SKOK	60077	2865	6W-11N	E2
13300	CTWD	60445	3347	6W-15S	E2
13700	BmnT	60445	3347	6W-16S	E3
14700	MDLN	60452	3348	6W-17S	A5
14800	OKFT	60452	3348	6W-18S	A7
16700	OKFT	60452	3426	6W-20S	A4
16900	OKFT	60477	3426	6W-20S	A4
18300	BmnT	60477	3426	6W-22S	A7
18300	BmnT	60478	3426	6W-22S	A7
18300	CCHL	60478	3506	6W-22S	A1
18300	RchT	60477	3426	6W-22S	A7
18300	RchT	60478	3426	6W-22S	A7
18300	RchT	60478	3506	6W-22S	A1
Leclaire Av					
-	WLMT	60025	2811	6W-13N	D6
300	GNVW	60025	2811	6W-13N	D6
300	GNVW	60091	2811	6W-13N	D7
300	WLMT	60091	2811	6W-13N	D6
7600	BRBK	60459	3211	6W-9S	E3
8500	OKLN	60453	3211	6W-9S	E4
Leclaire Av					
10700	OKLN	60453	3275	6W-12S	E2
13900	BmnT	60445	3348	6W-16S	A3
13900	CTWD	60445	3348	6W-16S	A3
N Leclaire Av					
400	CHCG	60644	3031	6W-0N	E3
700	CHCG	60651	3031	6W-0N	E3
1500	CHCG	60639	3031	6W-2N	E1
1600	CHCG	60639	2975	6W-2N	E7
2700	CHCG	60641	2975	6W-3N	E5
4800	CHCG	60630	2919	6W-6N	E6
S Leclaire Av					
4400	CHCG	60638	3089	6W-4S	E7
6300	CHCG	60638	3149	6W-7S	E5
6700	BDPK	60638	3149	6W-7S	E6
11100	ALSP	60803	3275	6W-13S	E3
11100	OKLN	60453	3275	6W-13S	E3
Ledochowski St					
500	LMNT	60439	3270		E6
Lee Av					
1200	MLPK	60160	3029	10W-1N	E2
3600	RNPK	60471	3594	4W-27S	E4
16400	ODPK	60467	3423	13W-19S	A3
N Lee Blvd					
600	HLSD	60162	3028		D4
1400	BKLY	60163	3028		D4
1500	HLSD	60163	3028		D4
Lee Ct					
10	GNWD	60425	3508	1W-22S	A1
10	HMWD	60430	3508	1W-22S	A1
800	SMWD	60107	2911		C1
4700	RNPK	60471	3594	5W-26S	B3
N Lee Ct					
1700	PLTN	60074	2753	20W-18N	A4
Lee Ln					
-	EGvT	60007	2861	16W-9N	D7
-	EGVV	60007	2861	16W-9N	D7
S Lee Pkwy					
1800	CHCG	60616	3092	0W-1S	B1
W Lee Pl					
2000	CHCG	60612	3033	2W-0N	B3
2000	CHCG	60622	3033	2W-0N	B3
Lee Rd					
400	NHBK	60062	2757	9W-17N	D6
S Lee Rd					
11500	ALSP	60803	3276	5W-13S	A4
Lee St					
-	BRLT	60103	2911		A6
-	WynT	60103	2911		A6
200	PKFT	60466	3595	3W-25S	A1
700	EGVV	60007	2861	17W-10N	B5
800	EVTN	60202	2867	2W-10N	B4
1100	WLNG	60090	2754	15W-17N	E5
1700	DSPN	60018	2862	13W-9N	E7
1700	EVTN	60202	2866	3W-10N	E4
2200	DSPN	60018	2916		E1
2900	FNPK	60131	2972		E5
2900	LydT	60164	2972		E5
3000	LydT	60131	2972		E4
3100	FNPK	60164	2972		E5
3300	SKOK	60076	2866	5W-10N	B4
4800	SKOK	60076	2865	6W-10N	E4
4900	SKOK	60077	2865	6W-10N	D4
5600	MNGV	60053	2865	7W-10N	C4
16700	ODPK	60467	3423	13W-20S	A3
18700	CCHL	60478	3506	5W-22S	B1
N Lee St					
200	MPPT	60056	2808	13W-13N	E6
200	WhlT	60056	2808	13W-13N	E6
W Lee St					
7600	NLES	60714	2864	9W-10N	C4
7800	MaiT	60714	2864	9W-10N	C4
Leeds Dr					
200	BNHL	60010	2749	28W-18N	E3
Leeds Ln					
1200	EGVV	60007	2914		C3
Leeds Rd					
5800	HFET	60120	2855		E1
5800	HFET	60120	2856	31W-12N	A1
Leeds Pass					
400	SMBG	60194	2858	25W-11N	C4
Leesley Rd					
700	RVSD	60546	3088	9W-2S	D4
Le Fevre Ln					
-	PLTN	60067	2752	21W-16N	D6
Legend Ln					
-	HFET	60194	2858	25W-12N	A4
8200	ODPK	60462	3346	10W-16S	B2
Legends Ct					
2300	RVWD	60015	2756	13W-20N	A1
Legends Ln					
-	BNVL	60106	2972		B4
Legend Trail Ln					
-	ODPK	60462	3346	11W-16S	A3
N Legett Av					
5900	CHCG	60646	2919	6W-7N	E3
Legion Dr					
900	CTCY	60409	3352	4E-18S	C7
900	CTCY	60409	3430	4E-18S	C1
Legion St					
10	MYWD	60153	3030	10W-0S	A5
700	MYWD	60153	3029	10W-0S	E5
Lehigh Av					
-	NLES	60053	2865	7W-9N	B6
-	SKOK	60077	2865	7W-9N	B6
800	GNVW	60025	2810	8W-13N	D6
2600	GNVW	60062	2810	9W-15N	B2
2700	NHBK	60062	2810	9W-15N	B2
8800	MNGV	60053	2865	8W-11N	A3
N Lehigh Av					
6100	CHCG	60646	2919	7W-8N	C1
7000	NLES	60714	2919	7W-8N	C1
7200	CHCG	60646	2865	7W-9N	C7
7200	NLES	60714	2865	7W-9N	C7
7600	SKOK	60077	2865	7W-9N	B7
7600	SKOK	60714	2865	7W-9N	B6
7900	MNGV	60053	2865	7W-9N	B7
7900	NLES	60053	2865	7W-9N	B7
Lehigh Ln					
700	BFGV	60089	2754	17W-17N	B5
Lehman Dr					
-	ELGN	60120	2855		E5
N Lehmann Ct					
2600	CHCG	60614	2978	0W-3N	A5
2700	CHCG	60657	2978	0W-3N	A4
Lehmer St					
7200	FTPK	60130	3030	9W-0S	D5
Leicester Rd					
10	MNSR	46321	3510		C3
200	KLWH	60043	2812	3W-14N	D4
900	EGVV	60007	2914		C2
Leims Rd					
10	PKFT	60466	3595	3W-27S	B4
Leinster Dr					
1200	LMNT	60439	3342	19W-15S	C1
Leitch Av					
200	LGNG	60525	3087	13W-4S	A7
200	LGNG	60525	3147	13W-4S	A1
5500	CTSD	60525	3147	13W-6S	A4
5500	LynT	60525	3147	13W-6S	A4
S Leitch Av					
-	LGNG	60525	3087	13W-4S	A7
Le Jardin Ct					
10	BFGV	60089	2754	16W-20N	E2
Lela Ct					
1000	SMBG	60193	2858	24W-10N	C6
Lela Ln					
10	SMBG	60193	2858	24W-10N	C6
300	BRLT	60103	2910		D2
Leland Av					
1700	EVTN	60201	2866	3W-11N	D2
4000	LYNS	60534	3088	10W-4S	B6
9800	SRPK	60176	2917	12W-5N	B7
W Leland Av					
700	CHCG	60640	2921	1W-5N	E7
1900	CHCG	60625	2921	2W-5N	B7
3400	CHCG	60625	2920	4W-5N	C7
4100	CHCG	60630	2920	5W-5N	B7
4900	CHCG	60630	2919	6W-5N	E7
6800	HDHT	60706	2918	8W-5N	E7
8400	CHCG	60656	2918	10W-5N	A7
8400	NRDG	60706	2918	10W-5N	A7
8600	CHCG	60656	2917	10W-5N	E7
Leland Ct					
100	BNVL	60106	2915		E7
N Le Mai Av					
6200	CHCG	60646	2919	6W-7N	D3
6500	LNWD	60712	2919	6W-8N	E2
6700	SKOK	60077	2919	6W-8N	E2
Lemans Dr					
10	WLNG	60090	2808	14W-15N	B2
Lemar Av					
1800	EVTN	60201	2866	3W-11N	E2
Lemon Ln					
5200	HRPK	60133	2911		C7
N Lemont Av					
6100	CHCG	60646	2919	5W-7N	E3
6200	CHCG	60646	2920	5W-7N	A3
6300	CHCG	60712	2920	5W-7N	A3
6300	LNWD	60712	2920	5W-7N	A3
Lemont Rd					
-	HmrT	60441	3342	19W-17S	D5
-	LMNT	60439	3342	19W-16S	D3
10	DGvT	60439	3270		C1
10	WDRG	60439	3270		C1
10	WDRG	60516	3270		C1
200	DGvT	60517	3270		D3
200	WDRG	60517	3270		D3
300	LMNT	60439	3270		D5
600	DGvT	60516	3270		C1
13500	HMGN	60441	3342	19W-16S	D3
Lemont Rd CO-9					
10	DGvT	60439	3270		C1
10	WDRG	60439	3270		D3
10	WDRG	60516	3270		C1
200	DGvT	60517	3270		D3
200	WDRG	60517	3270		D3
500	LMNT	60439	3270		C3
600	DGvT	60516	3270		C1
Lemont St					
100	LMNT	60439	3270		D5
W Le Moyne Av					
-	NHLK	60164	3029	13W-1N	A1
3200	SNPK	60165	3029	12W-1N	E1
Le Moyne Ct					
-	MLPK	60160	3029	11W-1N	D1
W Le Moyne Dr					
2800	CHCG	60622	3032	3W-1N	E1
Le Moyne Pkwy					
-	OKPK	60302	3030	8W-1N	E1
-	OKPK	60305	3030	8W-1N	D1
-	RVFT	60305	3030	8W-1N	D1
10	CHCG	60651	3031	7W-1N	B1
10	OKPK	60302	3031	8W-1N	A1
Le Moyne St					
7200	OKPK	60302	3030	9W-1N	C1
7200	OKPK	60305	3030	9W-1N	C1
7200	RVFT	60305	3030	9W-1N	C1
E Le Moyne St					
200	NHLK	60164	3028		E1
300	NHLK	60164	3029	13W-1N	A1
400	SNPK	60165	3029	13W-1N	A1
W Le Moyne St					
1400	MLPK	60160	3029	11W-1N	D1
1600	CHCG	60622	3033	2W-1N	C1
2700	CHCG	60622	3032	5W-1N	A1
3200	CHCG	60651	3032	5W-1N	B1
4800	CHCG	60651	3031	6W-1N	E1
5900	OKPK	60302	3031	7W-1N	B1
Lengl Dr					
10	SMBG	60193	2859	23W-10N	A6
Lennan Brook Ln					
17900	ODPK	60467	3422	14W-21S	C6
Lennon Ct					
20500	FKFT	60423	3504	10W-24S	B6
Lennon Dr					
20500	FKFT	60423	3504	10W-24S	B6
Lenore Ln					
18300	OrlT	60477	3423	11W-21S	E7
18300	TYPK	60477	3423	11W-22S	E7
N Lenox Av					
6100	CHCG	60646	2919	6W-7N	E3
6300	LNWD	60646	2919	6W-7N	D3
6300	LNWD	60712	2919	6W-7N	D3
Lenox Ct					
10	LMNT	60439	3270		E5
10	LMNT	60439	3271		B5
100	SMBG	60193	2857	26W-10N	E6
1400	WLNG	60090	2754	16W-18N	D4
Lenox Ln					
-	LMNT	60439	3271		A5
E Lenox Ln					
600	PLTN	60074	2753	20W-17N	B5
Lenox Rd					
700	GNVW	60025	2811	7W-13N	A7
Lenox St					
1000	LMNT	60439	3271		B5
Lenox St W					
400	OKPK	60302	3031	8W-1N	A1
Lentfer Ct					
10800	ODPK	60467	3423	13W-19S	A2
N Lenwood Dr					
2300	DRPK	60074	2752	21W-18N	D2
2300	PltT	60074	2752	21W-18N	D2
Lenzi Av					
6000	HGKN	60525	3147	11W-6S	D4
6000	MCCK	60525	3147	11W-6S	D4
S Leo Ct					
1200	PLTN	60067	2805	22W-14N	C4
E Leon Ln					
10	PTHT	60070	2808	14W-15N	B3
W Leon Ln					
10	PTHT	60070	2808	14W-15N	B3
Leon Pl					
1200	EVTN	60201	2867	2W-11N	A2
Leona					
-	JSTC	60458	3210	10W-9S	B2
N Leona Av					
6200	CHCG	60646	2919	6W-7N	D3
Leona St					
2600	FNPK	60131	2973	12W-3N	C5
W Leona Ter					
1300	ANHT	60005	2806	18W-13N	D5
N Leonard Av					
5500	CHCG	60630	2919	6W-7N	D5
5700	CHCG	60646	2919	7W-7N	C4
Leonard Dr					
-	SMBG	60193	2912		E1
-	SmbT	60193	2912		E2
13900	CTWD	60445	3348	5W-16S	A3
N Leonard Dr					
4800	CHCG	60656	2917	10W-6N	E6
4800	NRDG	60706	2917	10W-6N	E6
5100	NRDG	60656	2917	10W-6N	E6
Leonard Ln					
400	BRRG	60527	3208		B4
S Leonard Ln					
200	ANHT	60005	2807	16W-13N	C7
200	MPPT	60005	2807	16W-13N	C7
200	MPPT	60005	2861	17W-12N	B1
300	MPPT	60056	2861	17W-12N	B1
Leonard Pl					
1100	EVTN	60201	2867	2W-12N	A1
S Leonard Rd					
10	PLTN	60074	2806	19W-15N	B1
W Leonard Rd					
800	PLTN	60067	2805	22W-15N	C1
800	PltT	60067	2805	22W-15N	C1
Leonard St					
200	CHHT	60411	3507	1W-23S	E3
400	PKRG	60068	2864	10W-9N	A7
Leon Cook Dr					
6100	HGKN	60525	3147	11W-8S	D7
W Leonora Ln					
7900	EDPK	60707	2974	9W-2N	B7
7900	EDPK	60707	3030	9W-2N	B1
N Leoti Av					
6500	CHCG	60646	2919	7W-8N	B2
Le Parc Cir					
200	BFGV	60089	2754	15W-20N	E2
Lerose Dr					
300	CHHT	60411	3508	1W-23S	A3
N Leroy Av					
6200	CHCG	60646	2919	6W-7N	D3
6400	LNWD	60712	2919	6W-8N	E2
6700	SKOK	60077	2919	6W-8N	E2
Leslee Ln					
200	HDPK	60035	2758	7W-20N	B1
Leslie Ct					
400	MaiT	60016	2809	12W-12N	C7
Leslie Dr					
8800	ODHL	60462	3424	11W-19S	A3
8800	ODHL	60477	3424	11W-19S	A3
8800	ODPK	60462	3424	11W-19S	A3
Leslie Ln					
300	WLNG	60090	2755	14W-17N	C5
600	SMBG	60194	2858	26W-11N	A4
2400	HRPK	60133	2911		B3
5400	OKFT	60452	3425	6W-19S	D1
5500	BmnT	60477	3425	6W-19S	D1
5500	OKFT	60477	3425	6W-19S	D1
10300	CHRG	60415	3275	8W-12S	A1
N Leslie Ln					
10	PLTN	60067	2805	21W-16N	D1
8800	MaiT	60016	2863	11W-12N	E1
8800	NLES	60016	2863	11W-12N	E1
8800	NLES	60714	2863	11W-12N	E1
S Leslie Ln					
1200	DSPN	60016	2862	15W-10N	A5
1200	DSPN	60018	2862	15W-10N	A5
Leslie Ann Dr					
16300	BmnT	60477	3425	7W-19S	C3
16300	TYPK	60477	3425	7W-19S	C3
Lessenden Pl					
200	ELGN	60120	2855		A5
Lesser Av					
9800	FNPK	60131	2973	12W-4N	B3
N Lessing St					
800	CHCG	60622	3033	1W-1N	E2
N Lester Av					
4900	CHCG	60630	2919	6W-6N	C6
Lester Rd					
10	PKFT	60466	3595	3W-27S	B4
Letterkenny Dr					
8900	TYPK	60448	3504	11W-23S	A4
Leverett St					
300	TNTN	60476	3428	0E-21S	E6
Levine Ct					
500	ELGN	60120	2855		B4
Lewe Ct					
2500	NRIV	60546	3088	10W-2S	B3
Lewis Av					
3400	CRTE	60475	3596	0W-28S	C6
3400	STGR	60475	3596	0W-28S	C6
Lewis Ct					
100	SMBG	60193	2859	23W-10N	A6
Lewis Dr					
-	LYWD	60411	3509	2E-23S	D3
200	WDDL	60191	2914		E3
200	WDDL	60191	2915		A3
Lewis Ln					
1900	HDPK	60035	2757	9W-20N	C2
Lewis St					
2400	BLID	60406	3277	3W-14S	B6
3200	STGR	60475	3596	0W-27S	C5
E Lewis St					
400	HMND	46320	3430		D1
Lewis Ter					
4400	SKOK	60076	2866	5W-11N	A2
Lewis Isle Ln					
500	PTHT	60070	2808	14W-14N	B3
Lexington Av					
600	ROSL	60172	2913		B6
700	YkTp	60126	3028		A6
1000	FDHT	60411	3509	1E-25S	B7
1400	FDHT	60411	3597	1E-25S	B1
9500	BKFD	60513	3087	11W-3S	D4
9500	LGPK	60525	3087	11W-3S	C4
14500	HRVY	60426	3349	1W-17S	E5
15900	HRVY	60426	3427	1W-19S	E2
18500	HMWD	60430	3507	2W-22S	C1
Lexington Cir					
800	HRPK	60133	2912		A1
1500	SMBG	60173	2859	21W-10N	E4
Lexington Cir					
8600	ODPK	60462	3346	10W-18S	B6
Lexington Ct					
10	SMWD	60107	2857	26W-11N	E4
200	SMBG	60173	2859	21W-10N	E4
700	NHBK	60062	2757	8W-17N	E4
6900	TYPK	60477	3425	8W-19S	A2
Lexington Dr					
10	DYR	46311	3510		C7
100	BFGV	60089	2754	15W-18N	E2
200	SMBG	60173	2859	21W-11N	E4
400	VmT	60069	2754	15W-20N	E1
500	WLNG	60090	2754	15W-18N	E2
600	CHHT	60411	3507	2W-24S	C6
1000	BRLT	60103	2910		C7
2400	LGGV	60047	2753	19W-20N	C1
2700	HLCT	60429	3427	3W-20S	A5
3500	HFET	60195	2804	24W-14N	D4
N Lexington Dr					
1900	PLTN	60074	2753	20W-20N	B2
S Lexington Dr					
2200	EGvT	60005	2861	16W-10N	E6
2200	EGvT	60056	2861	16W-10N	E6
2200	MPPT	60056	2861	16W-10N	E6
W Lexington Dr					
1300	ANHT	60004	2753	18W-16N	D7
Lexington Ln					
3000	GNVW	60025	2810	10W-15N	B1
3000	GNVW	60062	2810	10W-15N	B1
N Lexington Ln					
6700	CHCG	60646	2919	7W-8N	A1
6700	NLES	60646	2919	7W-8N	A1
6700	NLES	60714	2919	7W-8N	A1
Lexington Rd					
10	SBTN	60010	2803	27W-14N	B4
Lexington St					
-	FTPK	60130	3030	10W-0S	A6
300	EMHT	60126	3028		A6
300	YkTp	60126	3028		A6
400	MYWD	60153	3030	10W-0S	A6
500	PvsT	60126	3028		B6
600	OKPK	60304	3031	8W-0S	A6
700	MYWD	60153	3029	12W-0S	C6
1200	BDVW	60155	3029	12W-0S	C6
1600	MYWD	60155	3029	11W-0S	D6
7200	OKPK	60304	3030	9W-0S	C6
W Lexington St					
500	CHCG	60607	3034	0W-0S	A6
1200	CHCG	60607	3033	1W-0S	D6
2100	CHCG	60612	3033	2W-0S	B6
2800	CHCG	60612	3032	4W-0S	D6
3100	CHCG	60624	3032	4W-0S	C6
4500	CHCG	60644	3032	5W-0S	A6
4800	CHCG	60644	3031	6W-0S	D6
N Leyden Av					
2200	RVGV	60171	2973	11W-3N	E6
S Leyden Av					
13700	CHCG	60827	3350	0E-15S	D2
13700	DLTN	60419	3350	0E-16S	D2
13700	RVDL	60827	3350	0E-15S	D2
Leyden Ct					
3500	FNPK	60131	2973	11W-4N	C3
Leyden Ln					
700	WLMT	60091	2811	5W-13N	E5
N Liano Av					
5200	CHCG	60630	2919	6W-6N	D5
Liatris Dr					
8800	FKFT	60423	3504	11W-24S	A4
8900	FKFT	60448	3504	11W-24S	A4
Liberty Ct					
400	SMBG	60194	2857	26W-11N	E4
400	SMWD	60107	2857	26W-11N	E4
1700	MPPT	60056	2808	13W-14N	D5
1800	EGVV	60007	2859	22W-9N	D7
15700	ODPK	60462	3423	12W-18S	C1
Liberty Dr					
10	LMNT	60439	3272	16W-13S	A5
200	PKFT	60466	3595	3W-27S	B3
N Liberty Dr					
10	BrnT	60010	2803	27W-14N	A4
10	BrnT	60118	2803	27W-14N	A4
10	SBTN	60010	2803	27W-14N	A4
S Liberty Dr					
10	BrnT	60010	2803	27W-14N	A4
10	BrnT	60118	2803	27W-14N	A4
10	SBTN	60010	2803	27W-14N	A4
Liberty Ln					
-	MTSN	60443	3505	7W-25S	D7
3600	GNVW	60025	2809	10W-13N	E6
Liberty Pl					
1900	HFET	60195	2858	25W-12N	A1
Liberty Sq					
5800	OKFT	60452	3347	7W-18S	C7
Liberty St					
10	WDND	60118	2801		A3
1200	CRTE	60417	3685	1W-29S	A1
1600	HRPK	60133	2911		D4
E Liberty St					
100	BRTN	60010	2750	27W-20N	C1
100	BRTN	60010	2751	25W-20N	A1
N Liberty St					
10	ELGN	60120	2855		B2
N Liberty St SR-25					
10	ELGN	60120	2855		B2
S Liberty St					
10	ELGN	60120	2855		B7
S Liberty St SR-25					
10	ELGN	60120	2855		B6
W Liberty St					
-	CHCG	60607	3034	0W-1S	A7
-	CHCG	60608	3034	1W-1S	A7
100	BRTN	60010	2750	25W-20N	E1
Liberty Grove Dr					
8600	WLSP	60480	3208		E4
10800	WLSP	60480	3209	13W-9S	A4
Library Ln					
-	SRPK	60176	2973	11W-5N	C1
300	SMWD	60107	2911		A1
Library Pl					
600	EVTN	60201	2867	2W-11N	B2
Library Rd					
-	RGMW	60008	2806	19W-13N	B5
Lichfield Dr					
4900	HFET	60010	2751	24W-16N	C7
Lido Ter E					
600	BRLT	60103	2911		B4
Lido Ter W					
600	BRLT	60103	2911		A4
Lido Tr					
200	BRLT	60103	2911		A4
N Lieb Av					
5200	CHCG	60630	2919	6W-6N	D5
N Lightfoot Av					
6600	CHCG	60646	2919	7W-8N	B2

STREET Block	City	ZIP	Map#	CGS	Grid
Lighthouse Ct					
2700	LYWD	60411	3510	3E-23S	A3
Lighthouse Dr					
1000	SMBG	60193	2912		D1
Lighthouse Ln					
11700	PSHT	60463	3274	9W-13S	C5
Lilac Av					
4400	GNVW	60025	2809	12W-14N	C4
W Lilac Av					
4600	MONE	60449	3683	5W-31S	B4
Lilac Ct					
100	RGMW	60008	2805	21W-14N	D5
1900	SMBG	60193	2912		A3
15100	ODPK	60462	3346	9W-18S	D6
Lilac Dr					
10	DYR	46311	3510		C7
300	BCHR	60401	3864	0W-36S	D1
E Lilac Dr					
900	PLTN	60074	2753	19W-18N	B4
Lilac Ln					
-	WLMT	60091	2811	6W-13N	D7
10	GLF	60029	2864	8W-12N	E1
100	BFGV	60089	2754	16W-20N	E2
100	WLNG	60090	2755	14W-17N	C4
300	MTSN	60443	3593	7W-26S	C2
400	EGVV	60007	2915		A1
2900	NHBK	60062	2756	11W-16N	D7
8300	TYPK	60477	3424	10W-21S	B5
Lilac Pl					
1000	PLTN	60074	2753	19W-18N	C4
E Lilac Ter					
1600	ANHT	60004	2807	16W-16N	C1
W Lill Av					
1200	CHCG	60614	2977	1W-3N	D5
W Lill Ct					
7800	NLES	60714	2864	9W-10N	C4
S Lill St					
400	BRTN	60010	2750	25W-18N	E3
Lillian Av					
-	ANHT	60004	2807	17W-15N	B1
E Lillian Av					
10	ANHT	60004	2807	17W-15N	A1
W Lillian Av					
10	ANHT	60004	2807	17W-15N	A1
1500	ANHT	60004	2806	18W-15N	D1
Lillian Ln					
300	DSPN	60016	2861	15W-11N	E3
E Lillian Ln					
2300	ANHT	60004	2807	16W-15N	D1
Lillian Pl					
-	BRLT	60120	2909		E4
Lillibet Ter					
8600	MNGV	60053	2865	7W-10N	C4
Lillie St					
600	ELGN	60120	2855		B3
E Lilly Ct					
900	PLTN	60074	2753	19W-18N	B3
E Lilly Ln					
800	PLTN	60074	2753	19W-18N	B3
Lily Ct					
600	SMBG	60193	2858	23W-9N	E7
19900	FKFT	60423	3504	11W-24S	A4
Lily Ln					
2300	GNVW	60025	2810	9W-15N	C3
3400	SjnT	46311	3598		D6
Limar Ln					
1400	GNVW	60025	2809	10W-14N	E5
Limerick Ln					
600	SMBG	60193	2859	23W-9N	A7
Limestone Ln					
2000	CPVL	60110	2748		C3
Lincoln Av					
10	BNVL	60106	2972		A1
10	CTCY	60409	3352	4E-17S	B6
10	EDND	60118	2801		A2
10	RVSD	60546	3088	10W-3S	B5
200	WDND	60118	2801		A2
300	GLNC	60022	2758	6W-17N	C5
500	WNKA	60093	2812	5W-16N	B1
600	ELGN	60120	2855		B3
800	WNKA	60093	2759	5W-16N	A7
1100	SMWD	60107	2911		C1
1200	CHHT	60411	3508	0W-25S	C7
1400	CTCY	60409	3430	4E-19S	B2
1700	HMND	46394	3280		E4
1800	NHBK	60062	2757	9W-17N	B5
2400	LGGV	60047	2753	19W-20N	C1
2500	ElaT	60047	2753	19W-20N	C1
2500	NRIV	60546	3088	10W-2S	B3
4300	RGMW	60008	2806	20W-14N	A3
4400	RGMW	60008	2805	20W-14N	E4
5200	SKOK	60077	2865	6W-10N	D5
5400	MNGV	60053	2865	7W-10N	B4
5400	MNGV	60077	2865	6W-10N	D4
5400	SKOK	60053	2865	6W-10N	D4
7400	LNWD	60712	2866	5W-9N	A7
7400	SKOK	60076	2866	5W-9N	A7
7500	SKOK	60076	2865	5W-9N	E7
8800	BKFD	60513	3087	11W-3S	D5
9500	LGPK	60525	3087	11W-3S	D5
13800	CHCG	60827	3350	0E-16S	D2
13800	DLTN	60419	3350	0E-16S	D2
14100	DXMR	60426	3349	2W-17S	D4
14300	DLTN	60419	3351	1E-17S	A4
14400	HRVY	60426	3349	2W-17S	D6
15000	CTCY	60409	3351	1E-17S	C5
15000	DLTN	60409	3351	1E-17S	C5
15600	HRVY	60426	3427	2W-18S	D1
16000	MKHM	60426	3427	2W-19S	D2
17500	HLCT	60430	3427	3W-21S	B6
17500	HMWD	60430	3427	3W-21S	B6
Lincoln Av US-41					
7400	LNWD	60712	2866	5W-9N	A7
7400	SKOK	60076	2866	5W-9N	A7
7500	SKOK	60076	2865	5W-9N	E7
7500	SKOK	60077	2865	5W-9N	E7
E Lincoln Av					
-	DSPN	60018	2862	13W-10N	D6
100	BRTN	60010	2750	26W-18N	D2
100	BRTN	60010	2751	25W-18N	A2
300	LGNG	60525	3087	12W-4S	C7
700	BKFD	60513	3087	12W-4S	C7
700	BKFD	60525	3087	12W-4S	C7
1300	DSPN	60018	2863	13W-10N	A6
N Lincoln Av					
10	PKRG	60068	2917	11W-8N	D2
1100	NLES	60068	2863	10W-10N	E5
1100	NLES	60714	2863	10W-10N	E5
1600	PKRG	60068	2863	10W-10N	E4
1800	CHCG	60614	2978	0W-2N	A6
2300	CHCG	60614	2977	0W-2N	E5
2600	CHCG	60657	2977	1W-3N	D4
3500	CHCG	60613	2977	2W-4N	C2
3900	CHCG	60618	2977	2W-4N	B2
4400	CHCG	60618	2921	2W-5N	B7
N Lincoln Av					
4300	CHCG	60625	2921	2W-5N	A7
5500	CHCG	60659	2921	3W-6N	A5
5600	CHCG	60659	2920	3W-7N	E4
6300	CHCG	60712	2920	4W-7N	C3
6300	LNWD	60712	2920	4W-7N	D3
7200	LNWD	60712	2866	5W-9N	A7
7200	SKOK	60076	2866	5W-9N	A7
9000	MaiT	60016	2863	10W-11N	E3
9300	NLES	60016	2863	10W-11N	E3
N Lincoln Av US-41					
5200	CHCG	60625	2921	3W-6N	A5
5500	CHCG	60659	2921	3W-6N	A5
5600	CHCG	60659	2920	3W-7N	E4
6300	CHCG	60712	2920	4W-7N	C3
6300	LNWD	60712	2920	4W-7N	D3
7200	LNWD	60712	2866	5W-9N	A7
7200	SKOK	60076	2866	5W-9N	A7
S Lincoln Av					
10	PKRG	60068	2917	10W-8N	E2
W Lincoln Av					
100	BRTN	60010	2750	25W-18N	E2
7600	SMMT	60501	3148	9W-5S	D3
Lincoln Blvd					
4500	RNPK	60471	3594	5W-27S	B4
Lincoln Ct					
200	WDDL	60191	2914		D7
1200	SMWD	60107	2911		B1
4300	RGMW	60008	2805	20W-14N	E3
7400	FTPK	60130	3030	9W-0N	D4
9000	ODPK	60462	3346	11W-17S	A6
N Lincoln Ct					
1500	ANHT	60004	2807	17W-15N	B2
S Lincoln Ct					
25800	MONE	60449	3682	7W-31S	E5
Lincoln Dr					
-	CRTE	60417	3685	0E-29S	D1
200	BRLT	60103	2911		A5
200	GLNC	60022	2758	6W-18N	D4
400	HFET	60194	2859	23W-11N	A4
400	SMBG	60194	2859	23W-11N	A4
8600	LYNS	60534	3088	10W-4S	A7
15200	MKHM	60426	3349	3W-18S	A7
N Lincoln Dr					
9100	MaiT	60016	2863	11W-11N	D3
Lincoln Hwy					
-	CHHT	60411	3507	2W-25S	C7
2400	OMFD	60461	3507	3W-25S	B7
2500	PKFT	60466	3507	3W-25S	B7
2600	PKFT	60461	3507	3W-25S	B7
3200	MTSN	60443	3506	4W-25S	E7
3200	OMFD	60461	3506	4W-25S	E7
3200	OMFD	60466	3506	4W-25S	E7
3200	PKFT	60466	3506	4W-25S	E7
3600	OMFD	60443	3506	4W-25S	E7
5300	MTSN	60443	3505	6W-25S	E7
6200	RchT	60443	3505	6W-25S	E7
6500	FftT	60423	3505	9W-25S	A7
6500	FKFT	60423	3505	9W-25S	A7
6500	RchT	60423	3505	9W-25S	A7
Lincoln Hwy US-30					
-	CHHT	60411	3507	2W-25S	C7
2400	OMFD	60461	3507	3W-25S	B7
2500	PKFT	60466	3507	3W-25S	B7
2600	PKFT	60461	3507	3W-25S	B7
3200	MTSN	60443	3506	4W-25S	E7
3200	OMFD	60461	3506	4W-25S	E7
3200	OMFD	60466	3506	4W-25S	E7
3200	PKFT	60466	3506	4W-25S	E7
3600	OMFD	60443	3506	4W-25S	E7
5300	MTSN	60443	3505	6W-25S	E7
6200	RchT	60443	3505	6W-25S	E7
6500	FftT	60423	3505	9W-25S	A7
6500	FKFT	60423	3505	9W-25S	A7
6500	RchT	60423	3505	9W-25S	A7
E Lincoln Hwy					
400	BlmT	60411	3508	0E-25S	D7
400	CHHT	60411	3508	0E-25S	D7
800	CHHT	60411	3509	1E-25S	A7
800	FDHT	60411	3509	1E-25S	A7
1400	BlmT	60411	3509	2E-25S	D7
1600	SLVL	60411	3509	2E-25S	D7
2400	BlmT	60411	3510	3E-25S	A7
2800	LYWD	60411	3510	3E-25S	A7
21400	BlmT	60411	3598	4E-25S	C1
21400	LYWD	60411	3598	4E-25S	C1
E Lincoln Hwy US-30					
400	BlmT	60411	3508	0E-25S	D7
400	CHHT	60411	3508	0E-25S	D7
800	CHHT	60411	3509	1E-25S	A7
800	FDHT	60411	3509	1E-25S	A7
1400	BlmT	60411	3509	2E-25S	D7
1600	SLVL	60411	3509	2E-25S	D7
2400	BlmT	60411	3510	3E-25S	A7
2800	LYWD	60411	3510	3E-25S	A7
21400	BlmT	60411	3598	4E-25S	C1
21400	LYWD	60411	3598	4E-25S	C1
W Lincoln Hwy					
7200	FftT	60423	3504	9W-25S	D7
7200	FftT	60423	3505	9W-25S	A7
7200	FKFT	60423	3504	9W-25S	E7
7200	FKFT	60423	3505	9W-25S	A7
7200	RchT	60423	3505	9W-25S	A7
7200	RchT	60443	3505	9W-25S	A7
W Lincoln Hwy US-30					
7200	FftT	60423	3504	9W-25S	D7
7200	FftT	60423	3505	9W-25S	A7
7200	FKFT	60423	3504	9W-25S	E7
7200	FKFT	60423	3505	9W-25S	A7
7200	RchT	60423	3505	9W-25S	A7
7200	RchT	60443	3505	9W-25S	A7
Lincoln Ln					
200	WLNG	60090	2755	13W-17N	D5
800	CTSD	60525	3147	13W-6S	A4
800	LynT	60525	3147	13W-6S	A4
2700	WLMT	60091	2812	5W-13N	A6
N Lincoln Ln					
100	ANHT	60004	2807	17W-14N	B4
S Lincoln Ln					
300	ANHT	60005	2807	17W-13N	B6
W Lincoln Ln					
500	DSPN	60018	2862	15W-10N	A6
700	DSPN	60018	2861	16W-10N	E6
700	MPPT	60018	2861	16W-10N	E6
700	MPPT	60056	2861	16W-10N	E6
Lincoln Ln E					
3800	RBBN	60472	3348	4W-15S	C1
Lincoln Ln W					
4300	CTWD	60472	3348	5W-15S	B1
4300	RBBN	60472	3348	5W-15S	B1
N Lincoln Pk W					
2000	CHCG	60614	2978	0W-2N	B6
Lincoln Pl					
600	CTCY	60409	3352	4E-17S	B6
1400	CTCY	60409	3430	4E-19S	B3
Lincoln Rd					
3000	OKBK	60523	3086		A4
E Lincoln Rd					
200	ANHT	60005	2861	17W-12N	B1
400	ANHT	60056	2861	17W-12N	B1
400	MPPT	60005	2861	17W-12N	B1
400	MPPT	60056	2861	17W-12N	B1
W Lincoln Rd					
2100	MPPT	60005	2861	17W-12N	B1
2100	MPPT	60056	2861	17W-12N	B1
2300	ANHT	60005	2861	17W-12N	B1
2300	ANHT	60056	2861	17W-12N	B1
Lincoln Sq					
900	EGVV	60007	2914		E1
Lincoln St					
10	GNVW	60025	2864	9W-12N	D1
10	GNVW	60053	2864	9W-12N	D2
10	MNGV	60053	2864	9W-12N	D2
200	EGvT	60018	2862	15W-9N	A7
200	HFET	60194	2859	23W-10N	A5
200	LMNT	60439	3270		D5
200	SMBG	60194	2859	23W-10N	A5
300	ROSL	60172	2912		E4
500	EVTN	60201	2867	2W-12N	C1
500	ROSL	60172	2913		A3
900	GNVW	60025	2810	8W-13N	D6
1000	EGVV	60007	2914		B2
1200	CRTE	60417	3685	1W-29S	B2
1400	SMBG	60193	2913		A2
1400	SmbT	60193	2913		A2
1500	SmbT	60172	2913		A2
1800	EVTN	60201	2866	3W-12N	E1
2400	LydT	60164	2973	12W-3N	A6
3500	FNPK	60131	2973	12W-4N	A3
12800	BLID	60406	3277	2W-15S	C7
16700	HLCT	60429	3427	2W-20S	D4
16700	MKHM	60426	3427	2W-20S	D4
17000	EHZC	60429	3427	2W-20S	D4
E Lincoln St					
100	MPPT	60056	2862	15W-12N	A1
100	PLTN	60067	2752	20W-16N	E7
100	PTON	60468	3861	9W-37S	A3
400	PLTN	60067	2753	20W-16N	A7
400	PLTN	60074	2753	20W-16N	A7
1000	DSPN	60016	2862	15W-12N	B1
1000	MPPT	60016	2862	15W-12N	B1
N Lincoln St					
10	HNDL	60521	3146		A1
400	HNDL	60521	3086		A7
S Lincoln St					
10	HNDL	60521	3146		A2
12300	BLID	60406	3277	2W-14S	C6
12300	BLID	60827	3277	2W-14S	C6
12300	CTPK	60406	3277	2W-14S	C6
12300	CTPK	60827	3277	2W-14S	C6
W Lincoln St					
-	MPPT	60056	2862	15W-12N	A1
100	PTON	60468	3860	10W-37S	D3
100	PTON	60468	3861	9W-37S	A3
500	MPPT	60056	2861	17W-12N	C1
2000	MPPT	60005	2861	17W-12N	B1
W Lincoln St SR-83					
-	MPPT	60056	2861	16W-12N	E1
-	MPPT	60056	2862	15W-12N	A1
Lincoln Ter					
200	BFGV	60089	2754	17W-18N	B3
Lincoln Mall Dr					
100	MTSN	60443	3594	5W-25S	B1
4700	MTSN	60443	3506	5W-25S	B7
Lincoln Meadows Cir					
1600	SMBG	60173	2859	21W-10N	E5
Lincoln Meadows Dr					
1600	SMBG	60173	2859	22W-10N	C6
N Lincoln Meadows Dr					
10	SMBG	60173	2859	22W-10N	C6
S Lincoln Meadows Dr					
10	SMBG	60173	2859	21W-10N	E5
Lincolnshire Ct					
200	SMBG	60193	2859	23W-10N	B6
1000	ELGN	60120	2855		C5
Lincolnshire Dr					
7600	BRRG	60527	3208		C1
13500	ODPK	60462	3346	11W-16S	A2
13500	PlsT	60462	3346	11W-16S	A2
Lincolnshire Ln					
600	HFET	60194	2858	25W-10N	B5
Lincolnshire Ter					
-	CRTE	60417	3596	0E-28S	E7
Lincolnwood Dr					
600	SMWD	60107	2857	28W-10N	A6
2100	EVTN	60201	2866	4W-12N	D1
2600	EVTN	60201	2812	4W-13N	D7
2700	WLMT	60091	2812	4W-13N	D7
2700	WLMT	60201	2812	4W-13N	D7
8800	SKOK	60076	2866	4W-11N	D3
9200	SKOK	60203	2866	4W-11N	D2
N Lincolnwood Dr					
6800	LNWD	60712	2919	6W-8N	E2
Lincolnwood Rd					
10	HDPK	60035	2758	7W-20N	C2
N Lind Av					
10	PvsT	60162	3028		D6
200	HLSD	60162	3028		D5
1200	BKLY	60163	3028		D3
5200	CHCG	60630	2919	6W-6N	D5
S Lind Av					
100	NHLK	60164	3028		D1
Linda Ct					
2500	MaiT	60025	2864	9W-12N	C1
Linda Dr					
800	ALGN	60102	2748		A1
Linda Ln					
10	SMWD	60107	2856	29W-10N	E6
200	LYWD	60411	3510	4E-25S	B7
1100	GLNC	60022	2758	6W-18N	C3
9900	MaiT	60016	2863	12W-12N	C1
10000	MaiT	60016	2809	12W-12N	C7
Linda Ter					
600	WLNG	60090	2755	15W-17N	A4
Lindale St					
600	EGvT	60007	2861	18W-10N	A6
600	EGVV	60007	2861	18W-10N	A6
Lindberg Ln					
400	NHBK	60062	2756	11W-18N	D4
Lindberg Rd					
400	BRWN	60402	3088	9W-2S	D4
400	RVSD	60546	3088	9W-2S	D4
Linden Av					
-	KLWH	60043	2812	4W-14N	B4
-	WLMT	60043	2812	4W-14N	B4
-	WLMT	60091	2812	4W-14N	B4
10	BFGV	60090	2755	14W-20N	C2
10	BLWD	60104	3029	12W-0N	B5
10	GLNC	60022	2758	5W-17N	E6
10	GLNC	60093	2758	5W-16N	E7
Linden Av					
100	DndT	60118	2801		B2
100	EDND	60118	2801		B2
100	OKPK	60302	3031	8W-0N	A3
100	WLMT	60091	2813	2W-13N	A6
200	BmdT	60157	2913		C5
600	ELGN	60120	2855		A5
1200	GNVW	60025	2811	7W-14N	A4
1600	HRPK	60133	2911		D2
1600	PKRG	60068	2918	9W-7N	B4
1900	CHCG	60631	2918	9W-7N	B4
1900	LynT	60525	3146		E3
1900	PKRG	60631	2918	9W-7N	B4
3900	WNSP	60558	3086		E7
4600	GNVW	60025	2809	12W-14N	B5
N Linden Av					
10	PLTN	60074	2806	20W-16N	A1
200	PLTN	60074	2753	20W-16N	A7
5400	NpkT	60656	2918	9W-6N	B5
S Linden Av					
10	PLTN	60074	2806	20W-15N	A1
100	EMHT	60126	3028		B2
100	PLTN	60067	2806	20W-15N	A1
25500	MONE	60449	3683	6W-31S	A5
Linden Av N					
700	OKPK	60302	3031	8W-1N	A2
1200	CHCG	60302	3031	8W-2N	A1
1200	CHCG	60707	3031	8W-2N	A1
Linden Cir					
700	ITSC	60143	2914		C5
1000	WNSP	60558	3146		D4
1100	BCHR	60401	3774	0W-36S	C7
1100	BCHR	60401	3864	0W-36S	D1
E Linden Cir					
-	HFET	60194	2859	23W-11N	A3
W Linden Cir					
-	HFET	60194	2859	23W-11N	A3
Linden Ct					
900	WNSP	60558	3146		D4
W Linden Ct					
700	ITSC	60143	2914		D5
Linden Dr					
-	BCHR	60401	3864	0W-36S	C1
-	DndT	60118	2801		A5
100	SMWD	60107	2911		B2
7400	JSTC	60458	3148	10W-8S	B7
8900	TYPK	60477	3424	11W-21S	A6
15500	OKFT	60452	3347	8W-18S	A5
17100	HLCT	60429	3427	4W-20S	A4
S Linden Dr					
800	EMHT	60126	3028		B6
W Linden Dr					
6800	PSHT	60463	3275	8W-15S	A7
Linden Ln					
100	CHHT	60411	3507	1W-24S	E6
200	WLNG	60090	2755	14W-18N	C4
500	PTON	60468	3861	8W-37S	B3
700	YkTp	60126	3028		B7
900	GNVW	60025	2811	7W-14N	A4
1000	WNSP	60558	3146		D4
2000	PltT	60067	2805	20W-13N	E6
2400	PltT	60173	2805	20W-13N	E7
2400	SMBG	60173	2805	20W-13N	E7
4200	RGMW	60008	2806	19W-12N	C7
6100	LynT	60525	3147	13W-6S	A5
E Linden Ln					
1600	MPPT	60056	2808	14W-14N	C5
S Linden Ln					
26700	CteT	60417	3685	0W-32S	C7
Linden Pl					
600	EVTN	60202	2867	2W-10N	B5
N Linden Pl					
2400	CHCG	60647	2976	3W-3N	E5
Linden Rd					
200	NfdT	60062	2757	9W-18N	C3
1400	NHBK	60062	2757	9W-17N	C5
1600	HMWD	60430	3427	2W-21S	D6
3600	PKFT	60466	3594	4W-26S	E2
3600	PKFT	60471	3594	4W-26S	E2
3600	RNPK	60471	3594	4W-26S	E2
Linden Rd N					
300	ANHT	60004	2807	16W-15N	D2
300	PTHT	60004	2807	16W-15N	D2
300	PTHT	60070	2807	16W-15N	D2
Linden Rd S					
200	PTHT	60070	2807	16W-15N	D2
Linden St					
-	FTPK	60130	3030	9W-0N	C4
-	RVFT	60305	3030	9W-0N	C4
100	WNKA	60093	2812	5W-15N	B3
500	CRTE	60417	3685	1W-29S	B2
1600	DSPN	60018	2863	12W-9N	A6
N Linden St					
300	ITSC	60143	2914		C6
Linden Leaf Dr					
1000	GNVW	60025	2810	9W-13N	C6
Lindenwood Ct					
4600	MTSN	60443	3506	5W-25S	B7
Lindenwood Dr					
1100	NtrT	60093	2811	5W-15N	E3
1100	WNKA	60093	2811	5W-15N	E3
4000	MTSN	60443	3506	5W-25S	C7
4000	OMFD	60461	3506	5W-25S	D7
Lindenwood Ln					
3000	GNVW	60025	2810	10W-13N	A5
3700	GNVW	60025	2809	11W-13N	E5
4500	NHBK	60062	2756	13W-18N	A2
Linder Av					
-	MNGV	60077	2865	6W-10N	D5
-	SKOK	60053	2865	6W-10N	D5
-	SKOK	60077	2865	6W-10N	D5
300	NHFD	60093	2811	6W-15N	D2
300	NtrT	60093	2811	6W-15N	D2
7900	BRBK	60459	3211	6W-9S	D4
8200	MNGV	60053	2865	6W-10N	D5
8600	OKLN	60453	3211	6W-9S	D4
8600	OKLN	60459	3211	6W-9S	D4
10700	OKLN	60453	3275	6W-12S	D2
13900	BmnT	60445	3347	6W-16S	D3
13900	CTWD	60445	3347	6W-16S	D3
14100	MDLN	60445	3347	6W-17S	E4
14500	OKFT	60445	3347	6W-17S	E5
14500	OKFT	60452	3347	6W-17S	E4
N Linder Av					
1400	CHCG	60651	3031	6W-1N	D1
1500	CHCG	60639	3031	6W-2N	D1
2400	CHCG	60639	2975	6W-3N	D5
2700	CHCG	60641	2975	6W-3N	D5
4300	CHCG	60630	2975	6W-5N	C1
4400	CHCG	60630	2919	6W-5N	C7
5500	CHCG	60646	2919	6W-6N	C5
S Linder Av					
4700	FTVW	60638	3149	6W-5S	D1
4700	StkT	60638	3149	6W-5S	D1
6300	CHCG	60638	3149	6W-7S	D5
S Linder Av					
7300	BDPK	60638	3149	6W-8S	D7
7300	BDPK	60638	3211	6W-8S	D1
Linder Ct					
5500	CTWD	60445	3347	6W-15S	D1
8400	MNGV	60053	2865	6W-10N	D4
8400	MNGV	60077	2865	6W-10N	D4
8400	SKOK	60053	2865	6W-10N	D4
8400	SKOK	60077	2865	6W-10N	D4
14500	OKFT	60452	3347	6W-17S	E5
Linder Ln					
-	PltT	60010	2751	24W-18N	C2
Lindsay Ct					
10	LMNT	60439	3270		E5
Lindsay Dr					
13700	ODPK	60462	3346	10W-16S	B3
Lindsay St					
9400	ODHL	60477	3423	11W-20S	E3
Line St					
-	ITSC	60143	2914		C6
W Line St					
100	ITSC	60143	2914		C6
W Linecrest Dr					
4300	ALSP	60803	3276	5W-13S	B4
Link Ct					
2700	FSMR	60422	3507	3W-23S	B3
W Linklater Ct					
900	LGNG	60525	3147	13W-5S	A1
900	LynT	60525	3147	13W-5S	A1
Linn Av					
9700	SRPK	60176	2917	12W-6N	C7
Linn Ct					
10900	LynT	60525	3146		E5
10900	LynT	60525	3147	13W-6S	A5
Linnea Ln					
9400	MaiT	60016	2863	11W-12N	C1
S Linneman Rd					
-	EGvT	60005	2861	16W-10N	D5
1000	MPPT	60056	2861	16W-11N	D4
1500	EGvT	60056	2861	16W-11N	D4
Linneman St					
1800	GNVW	60025	2810	9W-13N	C7
2900	NfdT	60025	2810	10W-13N	B7
3300	NfdT	60025	2809	10W-13N	E7
S Linn White Dr					
1300	CHCG	60605	3034	0E-1S	D7
Linsey Av					
400	SMBG	60194	2858	26W-11N	A4
Linton Ct					
1800	SMBG	60193	2912		A2
Lintz St					
300	LMNT	60439	3270		D6
Linus Ln					
10300	OKLN	60453	3275	6W-12S	E1
Linwood Ct					
400	SMBG	60193	2858	24W-10N	E6
Lioncrest Ct					
2000	RNPK	60471	3594	4W-26S	D2
Lioncrest Dr					
1000	RNPK	60471	3594	4W-26S	D3
Lionel Rd					
200	RVSD	60546	3088	9W-3S	D6
300	LYNS	60534	3088	9W-3S	D6
Lions Dr					
100	BRTN	60010	2750	25W-20N	E1
100	EGVV	60007	2914		E1
Lion's Club Dr					
-	MNSR	46321	3430		E7
-	MNSR	46321	3510		E1
Lippitt Ct					
1100	SMBG	60193	2912		C1
N Lipps Av					
4800	CHCG	60630	2919	6W-6N	D6
Lisa Ct					
2300	RGMW	60008	2805	21W-14N	D4
2300	RGMW	60067	2805	21W-14N	D4
2600	NHBK	60062	2810	10W-15N	A2
15300	ODPK	60462	3346	10W-18S	B7
Lisa Ln					
300	LYWD	60411	3510	4E-25S	C7
400	SMWD	60107	2856	29W-10N	E6
800	ELGN	60120	2855		C5
4400	OKFT	60452	3426	5W-19S	B3
8500	HYHL	60457	3210	10W-10S	B4
21100	STGR	60475	3597	0E-27S	A4
Lisadell Dr					
19400	TYPK	60477	3504	10W-23S	B3
Liscanor Av					
-	FftT	60448	3504	11W-23S	A3
9000	MKNA	60448	3504	11W-23S	A3
Lisdowney Dr					
700	LKPT	60441	3342	21W-18S	A7
E Lismore Cir					
20200	FftT	60423	3504	10W-24S	C5
W Lismore Cir					
20200	FftT	60423	3504	10W-24S	C5
Lismore Ct					
16600	TYPK	60477	3424	9W-19S	E3
Lismore Dr					
1000	DSPN	60016	2808	13W-13N	D6
Lismore St					
3700	FSMR	60422	3506	4W-23S	D3
Lissfannon Ct					
11900	ODPK	60467	3422	14W-20S	C5
N Lister Av					
2200	CHCG	60614	2977	2W-2N	C6
2300	CHCG	60647	2977	2W-2N	B6
Litchfield Ln					
400	BRLT	60103	2910		B4
400	WynT	60103	2910		B4
W Lithuanian Plaza Ct					
2400	CHCG	60629	3151	3W-7S	A6
2400	CHCG	60636	3151	3W-7S	A6
Litt Dr					
-	BLWD	60104	3028		E5
-	HLSD	60162	3028		E5
4100	HLSD	60162	3029	13W-0N	A5
Little Bend Rd					
10	BNHL	60010	2748		D1
Little City Dr					
1600	PltT	60067	2805	23W-14N	A4
1700	PltT	60195	2805	23W-14N	A5
Little Creek Ct					
10	SMWD	60107	2856	30W-10N	C5
Little Creek Dr					
100	HnrT	60107	2856	30W-10N	C5
100	SMWD	60107	2856	30W-10N	C5
W Little Creek Dr					
13400	HMGN	60441	3343	16W-16S	E4
Little Elm Bnd					
8900	SKOK	60076	2866	4W-11N	B3
Little Falls Ct					
900	EGVV	60007	2914		B3
Little Falls Dr					
1000	ELGN	60120	2855		D1

Chicago & Cook County Street Index

STREET Block	City	ZIP	Map#	CGS	Grid
Little John Ct					
200	BRLT	60103	2910		D2
1300	HnrT	60120	2856	31W-10N	A6
Little Moose Ln					
1400	NHBK	60062	2756	11W-17N	D6
Little Oak Pth					
-	SKOK	60076	2866	4W-11N	C3
Little Path Rd					
400	DSPN	60016	2862	14W-10N	C5
Little Peninsula Rd					
200	ELGN	60123	2801		B6
Littleton Dr					
300	ELGN	60120	2855		E5
300	HnrT	60120	2855		E5
400	ELGN	60120	2856	31W-10N	A5
700	HnrT	60120	2856	31W-10N	A5
S Lituanica Av					
3100	CHCG	60608	3091	1W-3S	E4
3400	CHCG	60609	3091	1W-3S	E4
3500	CHCG	60608	3092	1W-3S	A5
3500	CHCG	60609	3092	1W-3S	A5
Lively Blvd					
10	EGVV	60007	2861	17W-9N	B7
800	WDDL	60191	2915		B5
900	EGVV	60007	2915		B5
N Lively Blvd					
10	EGVV	60007	2861	17W-10N	B5
Live Oak Ct					
18000	TYPK	60477	3425	8W-21S	B6
N Livermore Av					
6200	CHCG	60646	2919	6W-7N	C3
Livingston Ct					
900	IVNS	60010	2751	25W-16N	A7
Livingston Ln					
800	IVNS	60010	2751	25W-16N	A7
Livingston St					
1700	EVTN	60201	2812	3W-13N	E7
1700	EVTN	60201	2813	3W-13N	A7
Liz Dr					
10900	ODPK	60467	3423	13W-20S	A4
Lizette Ln					
4000	GNVW	60025	2809	11W-14N	D3
4000	GNVW	60062	2809	11W-14N	D3
Lloyd Av					
200	BmdT	60143	2914		A6
200	ITSC	60143	2914		A6
S Lloyd Av					
2900	CHCG	60608	3091	1W-2S	D3
S Lloyd Dr					
10700	WRTH	60482	3275	8W-12S	A2
W Lloyd Dr					
6600	WRTH	60482	3275	8W-12S	A3
Lloyd Pl					
800	WNKA	60093	2759	5W-16N	B7
800	WNKA	60093	2812		B1
Loblolly Ct					
10	LMNT	60439	3271		D7
Loch Ln					
10	SBTN	60010	2803	26W-15N	C2
Lochbrook Ln					
10	IVNS	60010	2750	25W-16N	E7
Lochleven Ln					
10	IVNS	60067	2752	22W-16N	B7
Loch Lomond Dr					
10	IVNS	60067	2752	22W-16N	A7
Loch Lomond Ln					
500	PTHT	60070	2808	14W-14N	B3
Lochwood Pl					
9300	OrlT	60477	3423	11W-21S	E6
S Lock St					
2800	CHCG	60608	3091	1W-2S	D3
Lockerbie Ln					
100	WLMT	60091	2811	6W-13N	D7
Lockport St					
100	LMNT	60439	3270		D5
Lockridge Av					
16400	OKFT	60452	3426	5W-19S	B3
Locksley Dr					
100	SMWD	60107	2910		E1
100	SMWD	60107	2911		A1
Lockwood Av					
-	BmnT	60445	3347	6W-16S	E2
-	CTWD	60445	3347	6W-16S	E2
200	NHFD	60093	2811	6W-15N	D2
300	NtrT	60093	2811	6W-15N	D2
6800	SKOK	60077	2919	6W-8N	D1
7500	BDPK	60638	3211	6W-8S	E1
7500	BRBK	60459	3211	6W-8S	E1
7500	BRBK	60638	3211	6W-8S	E1
8600	OKLN	60453	3211	6W-9S	E4
9300	SKOK	60077	2865	6W-11N	D2
10000	GNVW	60025	2811	6W-12N	D7
10000	SKOK	60077	2811	6W-12N	D7
10500	OKLN	60453	3275	6W-12S	E1
15500	OKFT	60452	3347	6W-18S	E7
16700	BmnT	60452	3425	6W-20S	E4
16700	BmnT	60477	3425	6W-20S	E4
16700	OKFT	60452	3425	6W-20S	E4
N Lockwood Av					
-	CHCG	60646	2919	6W-7N	D4
10	CHCG	60644	3031	6W-0N	D4
700	CHCG	60651	3031	6W-0N	D3
1500	CHCG	60639	3031	6W-2N	D1
2000	CHCG	60639	2975	6W-2N	D6
2700	CHCG	60641	2975	6W-3N	D5
4300	CHCG	60630	2975	6W-5N	D1
4400	CHCG	60630	2919	6W-5N	D7
6700	LNWD	60712	2919	6W-8N	D2
6700	SKOK	60077	2919	6W-8N	D2
S Lockwood Av					
10	CHCG	60644	3031	6W-0S	D6
4700	FTVW	60638	3149	6W-5S	D1
4700	StkT	60638	3149	6W-5S	D2
6300	CHCG	60638	3149	6W-7S	D5
7100	BDPK	60638	3149	6W-8S	E7
7300	BDPK	60638	3211	6W-8S	E1
11900	ALSP	60803	3275	6W-14S	E5
Lockwood Ct					
10600	OKLN	60453	3275	6W-12S	E2
Locust Av					
10	LGNG	60525	3087	12W-4S	C6
4600	GNVW	60025	2809	12W-14N	B5
5100	BKLY	60163	3028		C5
5100	HLSD	60162	3028		C5
17200	TYPK	60477	3424	11W-20S	A4
Locust Cir					
-	BmnT	60426	3426	5W-19S	B1
Locust Ct					
-	BmnT	60426	3426	5W-19S	B2
10	CTCY	60409	3429	2E-18S	C1
1100	BRLT	60103	2910		C4
Locust Dr					
500	WLNG	60090	2754	16W-18N	E2
17000	HLCT	60429	3426	4W-20S	E4
Locust Ln					
400	ROSL	60172	2913		B5
1300	GNVW	60025	2865	8W-12N	A1
1400	GNVW	60025	2864	8W-12N	E1
6100	LynT	60525	3146		E5
S Locust Ln					
400	PTON	60468	3860	10W-37S	D4
W Locust Ln					
1800	MPPT	60056	2861	17W-11N	C3
Locust Pl					
400	DRFD	60015	2756	11W-20N	E1
1700	RGMW	60008	2860	21W-12N	A1
1700	RGMW	60173	2860	21W-12N	A1
1700	SMBG	60173	2860	21W-12N	A1
S Locust Pl					
25900	MONE	60449	3683	6W-31S	A6
Locust Rd					
10	NtrT	60091	2812	5W-14N	A4
10	NtrT	60093	2812	5W-14N	A4
10	WLMT	60091	2812	5W-13N	A7
10	WLMT	60093	2812	5W-14N	A4
300	WNKA	60093	2812	5W-15N	A2
2500	HLCT	60430	3427	3W-21S	B5
2500	HMWD	60430	3427	3W-21S	B5
Locust St					
10	CTCY	46324	3430		C2
10	CTCY	60409	3430		C2
10	HMND	46324	3430		C2
700	WNKA	60093	2812	5W-16N	A1
800	WNKA	60093	2759	5W-16N	A7
2000	DSPN	60018	2863	12W-9N	B7
18200	LNSG	60438	3429	2E-21S	D7
18200	ThtT	60438	3429	2E-21S	D7
21100	MTSN	60443	3506	4W-25S	E7
21500	MTSN	60443	3594	4W-26S	E2
W Locust St					
400	CHCG	60610	3034	0W-1N	A2
S Lode Dr					
6800	WRTH	60482	3275	8W-12S	A2
W Lodge Tr					
400	WLNG	60090	2754	16W-17N	C5
S Loeffel Steel Dr					
14100	RVDL	60827	3350	1W-16S	A3
Logan Av					
600	ELGN	60120	2855		A1
W Logan Blvd					
2200	CHCG	60618	2977	2W-3N	A5
2200	CHCG	60647	2977	3W-3N	A5
2700	CHCG	60647	2976	3W-3N	E5
Logan Ct					
11600	OrlT	60467	3344	14W-16S	D3
Logan Dr					
13600	OrlT	60467	3344	14W-16S	D3
13800	ODPK	60467	3344	14W-16S	D3
Logan St					
400	HMND	46320	3352		D5
400	ROSL	60172	2912		E3
1400	SMBG	60193	2912		E2
1400	SmbT	60193	2912		E2
1500	SmbT	60172	2912		E2
E Logan St					
10	LMNT	60439	3270		D6
800	HMND	46320	3352		E6
W Logan St					
10	LMNT	60439	3270		C6
Logan Ter					
10	GLF	60029	2864	8W-11N	E2
100	GLF	60029	2865	8W-12N	A1
Loganbury Ct					
1100	ELGN	60120	2801		D7
Lois Av					
1000	PKRG	60068	2918	10W-7N	A4
1200	PKRG	60068	2917	10W-7N	E4
Lois Ct					
500	ANHT	60056	2861	17W-12N	B1
500	MPPT	60056	2861	17W-12N	B1
1100	PKRG	60068	2917	10W-7N	E4
Lois Dr					
2200	RGMW	60008	2860	19W-12N	C2
9600	MaiT	60016	2863	10W-12N	E1
Lois Ln					
100	DRPK	60010	2751	23W-20N	D1
900	GNVW	60025	2811	7W-14N	B3
900	NHFD	60025	2811	7W-14N	B3
900	NHFD	60093	2811	7W-14N	B3
N Loleta Av					
6600	CHCG	60646	2919	7W-8N	C2
Lombard Av					
10400	CHRG	60415	3275	7W-12S	C1
11000	ALSP	60482	3275	7W-12S	B3
11000	WRTH	60482	3275	7W-12S	B3
S Lombard Av					
100	OKPK	60302	3031	7W-0S	B5
400	OKPK	60304	3031	7W-1S	B7
1200	BRWN	60402	3031	7W-1S	B7
1200	CCRO	60402	3031	7W-1S	B7
1200	CCRO	60804	3031	7W-1S	B7
1200	OKPK	60402	3031	7W-0S	B7
1200	OKPK	60804	3031	7W-0S	B7
1500	CCRO	60804	3089	7W-1S	B1
2400	CCRO	60402	3089	7W-2S	B2
3100	BRWN	60402	3089	7W-3S	B5
3100	BRWN	60804	3089	7W-3S	B5
3800	SKNY	60402	3089	7W-3S	B6
Lombard Av N					
1100	OKPK	60302	3031	7W-1N	B1
1200	CHCG	60302	3031	7W-2N	B1
1200	CHCG	60639	3031	7W-2N	B1
S Lombard Ln					
12300	ALSP	60803	3276	5W-14S	C6
S Lombard Rd					
300	ITSC	60143	2914		B7
500	ADSN	60143	2914		B7
Lombard St					
3400	FNPK	60131	2973	11W-4N	D3
N Lombard St					
700	AddT	60126	2972		B6
700	EMHT	60126	2972		B6
Lombardy Ct					
4300	HFET	60195	2804	24W-15N	B2
Lombardy Ln					
600	DRFD	60015	2756	11W-20N	D1
4200	HFET	60195	2804	24W-15N	B2
Lomond Dr					
-	IVNS	60067	2751	23W-16N	E7
10	IVNS	60067	2804	23W-16N	E1
N London Av					
4700	CHCG	60630	2919	6W-5N	D7
London Dr					
3000	OMFD	60461	3507	3W-25S	A7
London Ln					
1300	GNVW	60025	2810	8W-14N	D4
1300	GNVW	60025	2811	8W-14N	A5
S London Ln					
12600	PSHT	60463	3274	9W-14S	D7
S London Ln					
12600	PSHT	60464	3274	9W-14S	D7
London Pl					
200	WLNG	60090	2755	15W-18N	A4
London Sq					
600	HFET	60194	2858	24W-11N	D4
Londonderry Ct					
3500	HFET	60067	2804	23W-14N	E4
Loneflower Dr					
10	SjnT	46311	3598		C6
Long Av					
10	SmbT	60193	2912		B3
2100	BlmT	60411	3597	2E-27S	D5
7400	SKOK	60077	2865	6W-9N	D7
7500	BDPK	60638	3211	6W-8S	D1
7500	BRBK	60459	3211	6W-8S	D1
7500	BRBK	60638	3211	6W-8S	D1
7700	MNGV	60053	2865	6W-10N	D5
7800	MNGV	60077	2865	6W-9N	D6
8600	OKLN	60453	3211	6W-9S	D4
10300	OKLN	60453	3275	6W-12S	D1
13500	BmnT	60445	3347	6W-16S	E2
13500	CTWD	60445	3347	6W-16S	E2
13500	WthT	60445	3347	6W-16S	E4
14300	MDLN	60445	3347	6W-17S	E5
14300	OKFT	60452	3347	6W-17S	E5
15900	OKFT	60452	3425	6W-19S	E2
16200	BmnT	60477	3425	6W-19S	E2
N Long Av					
10	CHCG	60644	3031	6W-0N	D5
1400	CHCG	60651	3031	6W-1N	D1
1500	CHCG	60639	3031	6W-2N	D1
1900	CHCG	60639	2975	6W-2N	D6
2700	CHCG	60641	2975	6W-3N	D5
4300	CHCG	60630	2975	6W-5N	D1
4400	CHCG	60630	2919	6W-5N	D7
S Long Av					
4700	FTVW	60638	3149	6W-5S	D1
4700	StkT	60638	3149	6W-5S	D2
6300	CHCG	60638	3149	6W-7S	D5
6400	BDPK	60638	3149	6W-7S	D5
Long Rd					
-	GNVW	60091	2811	6W-13N	D7
800	GNVW	60025	2811	6W-13N	D7
900	WLMT	60091	2811	6W-13N	D7
Longacre Ln					
1200	WLNG	60090	2755	15W-16N	B7
Longacres Ln					
300	PltT	60067	2806	20W-13N	A6
300	SMBG	60008	2806	20W-13N	A7
300	SMBG	60067	2806	20W-13N	A7
Longaker Rd					
900	NHBK	60062	2757	8W-17N	E4
900	NHBK	60062	2758	8W-17N	A5
Longboat Ct					
1000	SMBG	60194	2858	24W-11N	D3
Longboat Dr					
1700	EGVV	60007	2913		C2
Longboat Ln					
800	SMBG	60194	2858	24W-11N	D3
Long Boat Key Ln					
1300	SMWD	60120	2856	30W-9N	C7
Longbow Ct					
1600	WLNG	60090	2754	16W-18N	D4
Longcommon Rd					
200	RVSD	60546	3088	9W-2S	D4
500	BRWN	60402	3088	9W-2S	D3
Long Cove Dr					
10	LMNT	60439	3271		B7
10	LMNT	60439	3343	17W-15S	B1
Longfellow Av					
3000	HLCT	60429	3427	3W-20S	A5
Longfield Av					
10	NHLK	60164	2972		D6
Longford Cir					
1200	ELGN	60120	2855		D4
Longford Ct					
100	ROSL	60172	2912		D5
200	ELGN	60120	2855		D3
Longford Dr					
10	ELGN	60120	2855		D3
600	DSPN	60016	2808	13W-13N	D6
600	MPPT	60056	2808	13W-13N	D6
700	ROSL	60172	2912		D5
Longford Rd					
-	HRPK	60133	2911		C6
900	BRLT	60103	2911		C6
Long Grove Rd					
10	DRPK	60010	2752	22W-20N	A1
100	BRTN	60010	2751	23W-20N	D1
100	DRPK	60010	2751	23W-20N	D1
100	ElaT	60010	2751	23W-20N	E1
100	ElaT	60010	2752	23W-20N	A1
500	DRPK	60074	2752	22W-20N	C1
Long Grove Rd CO-A49					
10	DRPK	60010	2752	22W-20N	A1
100	BRTN	60010	2751	23W-20N	D1
100	DRPK	60010	2751	23W-20N	D1
100	ElaT	60010	2751	23W-20N	E1
100	ElaT	60010	2752	23W-20N	A1
500	DRPK	60074	2752	22W-20N	C1
W Long Grove Rd					
21500	DRPK	60074	2752	21W-20N	C1
21500	ElaT	60074	2752	21W-20N	C1
21700	DRPK	60074	2752	21W-20N	C1
W Long Grove Rd CO-A49					
21500	DRPK	60074	2752	21W-20N	C1
21500	ElaT	60074	2752	21W-20N	C1
21700	DRPK	60074	2752	21W-20N	C1
N Longmeadow Av					
6400	CHCG	60646	2919	6W-8N	E3
6400	LNWD	60646	2919	6W-8N	E3
6500	LNWD	60712	2919	6W-8N	E2
6700	SKOK	60077	2919	6W-8N	E2
Longmeadow Ct					
10	BNHL	60010	2748		E6
10	BNHL	60010	2749	30W-16N	A6
N Long Meadow Ct					
20600	KLDR	60047	2752	21W-20N	C1
Long Meadow Dr					
800	SMBG	60193	2859	23W-9N	A7
900	SMBG	60193	2913		A1
Longmeadow Dr					
10	BNHL	60010	2748		E6
10	BNHL	60010	2749	30W-16N	A6
900	GNVW	60025	2809	10W-13N	E6
900	NfdT	60025	2809	10W-13N	E6
2500	NHBK	60062	2809	10W-16N	E1
2500	NHBK	60062	2810	10W-16N	A1
Longmeadow Ln					
1000	WNSP	60558	3146		D3
1100	GLNC	60022	2758	7W-18N	B4
7100	HRPK	60133	2911		E2
12000	HMGN	60441	3422	15W-20S	C4
Longmeadow Rd					
10	NHFD	60091	2811	6W-14N	D4
10	NHFD	60093	2811	6W-14N	D4
10	NtrT	60093	2811	6W-14N	E4
10	WLMT	60091	2811	6W-14N	D4
1100	NHBK	60062	2757	8W-18N	D3
W Long Run Ct					
13200	HMGN	60441	3343	16W-16S	E3
Long Run Dr					
-	OrlT	60467	3344	14W-16S	D4
11600	ODPK	60467	3344	14W-16S	D4
13700	HMGN	60441	3343	18W-16S	A3
Longstreet Dr					
900	BRLT	60103	2911		B6
Longtree Ct					
-	SMBG	60173	2859	21W-12N	E1
1700	RGMW	60008	2860	21W-12N	A1
1700	RGMW	60173	2860	21W-12N	A1
1700	SMBG	60173	2860	21W-12N	A1
Longtree Dr					
-	WLNG	60070	2754	15W-17N	E6
400	WLNG	60090	2754	15W-17N	E6
Longtree Ln					
1100	WLNG	60004	2754	16W-17N	E6
1100	WLNG	60090	2754	16W-17N	E6
Longvalley Ct					
1600	NHBK	60062	2756	11W-17N	C6
Longvalley Dr					
1600	NHBK	60062	2756	11W-16N	C7
E Long Valley Dr					
1200	PLTN	60074	2753	19W-17N	D5
1200	PltT	60074	2753	19W-17N	D5
Longvalley Rd					
1200	GNVW	60025	2811	8W-12N	A7
1700	GNVW	60025	2810	8W-12N	D7
Longview Dr					
700	CTSD	60525	3147	12W-6S	B4
700	LynT	60525	3147	12W-6S	B4
13500	HMGN	60441	3342	19W-16S	E3
W Longview Ln					
600	PLTN	60067	2805	21W-15N	C2
Longview Rd					
2000	NfdT	60062	2756	11W-16N	C7
Longwood Av					
500	GLNC	60022	2758	5W-17N	E4
Longwood Cir					
11300	ODPK	60467	3422	14W-20S	E5
Longwood Ct					
10	BFGV	60089	2754	17W-18N	A3
400	CHHT	60411	3507	2W-24S	D5
N Longwood Ct					
600	GNWD	60425	3428	0W-21S	B7
S Longwood Ct					
13100	PlsT	60462	3346	10W-15S	C1
13100	PlsT	60464	3346	10W-15S	C1
Longwood Dr					
10	BRRG	60527	3146		C5
400	BFGV	60089	2754	17W-18N	A3
400	CHHT	60411	3507	2W-24S	D5
11900	BLID	60406	3277	2W-14S	C5
11900	CHCG	60406	3277	2W-14S	C5
11900	CHCG	60643	3277	2W-14S	C5
14100	SjnT	46311	3598		E5
17400	ODPK	60467	3422	14W-20S	D4
E Longwood Dr					
3200	CteT	60417	3598	3E-29S	B7
N Longwood Dr					
300	GNWD	60425	3508	0W-22S	B1
500	GNWD	60425	3428	0W-21S	C7
S Longwood Dr					
-	BlmT	46311	3598	4E-28S	C6
-	CteT	46311	3598	4E-28S	C6
-	CteT	60417	3598	4E-28S	C6
-	SjnT	46311	3598	4E-28S	C6
8700	CHCG	60620	3213	2W-10S	C4
9500	CHCG	60643	3213	2W-11S	C7
11100	CHCG	60643	3277	2W-13S	C4
11800	BLID	60406	3277	2W-13S	C5
11800	CHCG	60406	3277	2W-13S	C5
Longwood Ln					
10400	OKLN	60453	3276	5W-12S	C1
Longwood Wy					
10	DPgT	60441	3342	20W-15S	A2
10	LMNT	60439	3342	20W-15S	A2
10	LMNT	60441	3342	20W-15S	A2
E Lonnquist Blvd					
10	MPPT	60056	2862	15W-11N	A2
W Lonnquist Blvd					
10	MPPT	60056	2862	15W-12N	A2
200	MPPT	60056	2861	17W-12N	B2
Lonnquist Dr					
3400	FNPK	60131	2973	12W-4N	C3
Lonsdale Rd					
10	EGVV	60007	2914		D2
200	PTHT	60070	2808	15W-14N	A4
Loomis Av					
-	HRVY	60429	3427	1W-20S	E5
-	ThtT	60426	3349	1W-16S	E4
14400	HRVY	60426	3349	1W-17S	E5
15600	HRVY	60426	3427	1W-18S	E1
16000	MKHM	60426	3427	1W-19S	E2
17100	EHZC	60429	3427	1W-20S	E5
17900	HMWD	60430	3427	1W-21S	E7
18700	HMWD	60430	3507	1W-22S	E1
19100	HMWD	60430	3508	1W-23S	A3
S Loomis Blvd					
4700	CHCG	60609	3151	1W-5S	D2
5500	CHCG	60636	3151	1W-7S	D6
7500	CHCG	60620	3213	1W-9S	D3
Loomis Ct					
13400	CTWD	60445	3347	6W-15S	E2
Loomis Ln					
13500	CTWD	60445	3347	6W-16S	E2
S Loomis Pl					
3600	CHCG	60609	3091	1W-3S	D5
N Loomis St					
100	CHCG	60607	3033	1W-0N	D4
S Loomis St					
10	CHCG	60607	3033	1W-1S	D7
1100	CHCG	60608	3033	1W-1S	D7
1500	CHCG	60608	3091	1W-1S	D1
3900	CHCG	60609	3091	1W-4S	D6
8700	CHCG	60620	3213	1W-11S	D6
9400	CHCG	60643	3213	1W-11S	D6
10800	CHCG	60643	3277	1W-13S	E4
12500	CTPK	60827	3277	1W-14S	E6
23600	CteT	60417	3596	1W-28S	A7
23600	CteT	60475	3596	1W-28S	A7
23600	STGR	60475	3596	1W-28S	A7
23900	CteT	60417	3685	1W-29S	A1
Loop Dr					
-	CHCG	60637	3152	0E-6S	D3
Loras Ct					
-	CCHL	60478	3506	5W-22S	B1
Loras Ln					
18600	CCHL	60478	3506	5W-22S	B2
N Loras Ln					
9200	NLES	60714	2864	10W-11N	B2
Lord St					
10	ELGN	60123	2855		A6
Lorel Av					
6800	SKOK	60077	2919	6W-8N	D1
7500	BDPK	60638	3211	6W-8S	E1
7500	BRBK	60459	3211	6W-8S	E1
7500	BRBK	60638	3211	6W-8S	E1
7900	SKOK	60077	2865	6W-9N	D6
8600	BRBK	60453	3211	6W-9S	E4
8600	OKLN	60453	3211	6W-9S	E4
10500	OKLN	60453	3275	6W-12S	E2
14700	MDLN	60445	3347	6W-17S	E5
14700	MDLN	60452	3347	6W-17S	E5
14800	OKFT	60452	3347	6W-17S	E5
15800	OKFT	60452	3425	6W-18S	E1
N Lorel Av					
10	CHCG	60644	3031	6W-0N	D5
1400	CHCG	60651	3031	6W-1N	D1
1500	CHCG	60639	3031	6W-2N	D1
2000	CHCG	60639	2975	6W-2N	D6
S Lorel Av					
4700	FTVW	60638	3149	6W-5S	D1
4700	StkT	60638	3149	6W-5S	D1
5000	CHCG	60638	3149	6W-5S	D1
6400	BDPK	60638	3149	6W-7S	D5
Lorelei Dr					
500	SMBG	60193	2912		E1
Lorenz Av					
17000	LNSG	60438	3430	3E-20S	A4
18800	LNSG	60438	3510	3E-22S	B1
Lorete Ln					
1400	NHBK	60062	2756	11W-17N	D6
Loretto Ln					
18700	CCHL	60478	3506	5W-22S	B2
18900	CCHL	60477	3506	5W-22S	B2
18900	RchT	60477	3506	5W-22S	B2
Lori Ct					
-	BMDL	60108	2913		B7
22700	RNPK	60471	3594	5W-27S	C5
Lori Dr					
-	GNVW	60025	2810	10W-15N	A3
Lori Ln					
8800	ODPK	60462	3346	11W-16S	A4
S Lori Ln					
10500	PSHL	60465	3274	9W-12S	D2
Loriann Dr					
-	ODPK	60467	3423	13W-21S	A7
Lorien Ct					
200	EDND	60118	2801		B2
Lori Lyn Ln					
1400	NHBK	60062	2756	12W-17N	A6
1500	NfdT	60062	2756	12W-17N	A6
Lorin Ln					
4900	OKFT	60452	3348	6W-17S	A6
N Loring Av					
5200	CHCG	60630	2919	6W-6N	C5
Loriss Pl					
2600	CHCG	60007	2916		A2
N Loron Av					
6800	CHCG	60646	2919	7W-8N	C1
Lorraine Ct					
22600	RNPK	60471	3594	6W-27S	A4
Lorraine Dr					
9700	CTSD	60525	3147	12W-6S	C4
Lorraine Pl					
1200	SMBG	60173	2859	22W-10N	D5
Lorraine Ter					
7000	SKNY	60402	3088	8W-4S	E6
Los Angeles Av					
17900	HMWD	60430	3427	3W-21S	B7
Los Angeles Ct N					
17900	HMWD	60430	3427	3W-21S	B6
Los Angeles Ct S					
18100	HMWD	60430	3427	3W-21S	B7
Losey Ct					
10	LMNT	60439	3270		D6
Los Palos Ln					
9000	PSHL	60465	3209	11W-11S	E7
9100	PlsT	60465	3209	11W-11S	E7
9100	PlsT	60480	3209	11W-11S	E7
S Lothair Av					
11100	CHCG	60643	3277	2W-13S	C3
W Lotta St					
100	GNWD	60425	3508	0W-22S	D2
Lotus Av					
7700	BRBK	60459	3211	6W-8S	D2
7800	MNGV	60053	2865	6W-9N	D6
8600	OKLN	60453	3211	6W-9S	D4
8900	SKOK	60077	2865	6W-11N	D2
N Lotus Av					
600	CHCG	60644	3031	6W-0N	D3
700	CHCG	60651	3031	6W-0N	D3
1600	CHCG	60639	3031	6W-2N	D1
2400	CHCG	60639	2975	6W-3N	D5
2800	CHCG	60641	2975	6W-3N	D4
5300	CHCG	60630	2919	6W-6N	C5
5500	CHCG	60646	2919	6W-6N	C5
S Lotus Av					
10	CHCG	60644	3031	6W-0S	D5
4700	FTVW	60638	3149	6W-5S	D1
4700	StkT	60638	3149	6W-5S	D2
5000	CHCG	60638	3149	6W-5S	D2
Lotus Ct					
500	WLNG	60090	2754	16W-18N	D3
Lotus Dr					
8800	HYHL	60457	3210	11W-10S	A4
Lotus Ln					
400	GNVW	60025	2810	10W-12N	A7
400	GNVW	60025	2864	10W-11N	A2
400	MaiT	60025	2864	10W-11N	A2
500	NfdT	60025	2810	10W-12N	A7
Lotz Dr					
-	RVDL	60827	3350	1W-16S	A2
Loudon Rd					
400	RVSD	60546	3088	9W-2S	C3
Louetta Dr					
-	OrlT	60467	3423	13W-21S	B6
10400	ODPK	60467	3423	13W-21S	B6
Louetta Ln					
10800	ODPK	60467	3423	13W-21S	A6
10800	OrlT	60467	3423	13W-21S	A6
Louis Av					
1000	ALGN	60102	2748		A2
1200	EGVV	60007	2861	17W-9N	C7
16200	SHLD	60473	3428	0E-19S	E2
Louis Ct					
16800	SHLD	60473	3428	0E-19S	E3
Louis Dr					
200	WLSP	60480	3209	11W-9S	D2
Louis St					
2000	LydT	60164	2973	12W-2N	B7

STREET Block	City	ZIP	Map#	CGS	Grid
Louis St					
2000	MLPK	60160	2973	12W-2N	B7
3400	FNPK	60131	2973	12W-4N	B3
N Louis St					
10	MPPT	60056	2808	15W-13N	B7
S Louis St					
10	MPPT	60056	2808	15W-12N	B7
500	MPPT	60056	2862	15W-12N	B2
900	DSPN	60016	2862	15W-11N	B2
900	DSPN	60056	2862	15W-11N	B2
N Louise Av					
5800	CHCG	60646	2919	6W-7N	E4
Louise Ct					
100	WDDL	60191	2915		B7
3200	LNSG	60438	3510	4E-22S	B1
6700	HMND	46324	3430		E3
Louise Dr					
3200	LNSG	60438	3510	4E-22S	B1
E Louise Dr					
18900	LNSG	60438	3510	4E-22S	B1
W Louise Dr					
18800	LNSG	60438	3510	4E-22S	B1
Louise Ln					
-	PTON	60468	3860	10W-37S	D4
N Louise Ln					
1400	PLTN	60074	2752	21W-17N	C4
1400	PltT	60074	2752	21W-17N	C4
W Louise Ln					
700	PTON	60468	3860	10W-37S	D4
Louise St					
3800	SKOK	60076	2866	4W-9N	B6
4800	SKOK	60077	2865	6W-9N	E6
Louisiana Ct					
10700	ODPK	60467	3423	13W-21S	A7
Louisiana Dr					
1800	EGVV	60007	2913		D3
Louis Sherman Dr					
3000	SCHT	60411	3596	0W-27S	C5
3000	STGR	60475	3596	0W-27S	C5
3300	CRTE	60475	3596	0W-27S	C5
Loulla St					
600	CteT	60417	3686	0E-31S	A5
Lourdes Dr					
-	HMGN	60441	3343	17W-18S	D7
Love Dr					
500	PTHT	60070	2808	13W-15N	E1
20400	LYWD	60411	3509	2E-24S	D5
20500	BlmT	60411	3509	2E-24S	D5
Love St					
600	EGvT	60007	2915		A1
600	EGVV	60007	2915		A1
N Lovejoy Av					
5300	CHCG	60630	2919	7W-6N	C5
Loveland Ln					
8400	PSHL	60465	3274	10W-12S	B2
S Loveland St					
12200	ALSP	60803	3276	5W-14S	B6
12800	ALSP	60803	3348	5W-15S	B1
Lovell Ct					
1100	EGVV	60007	2913		E2
Lovell St					
300	ELGN	60120	2855		A2
Loverock Av					
3300	STGR	60475	3596	0W-27S	C5
3400	CRTE	60475	3596	0W-28S	C6
W Loves Ln					
2000	CteT	60417	3684	2W-29S	D2
2000	UYPK	60417	3684	2W-29S	D2
2000	UYPK	60466	3684	2W-29S	D2
E Lowden Ln					
1400	MPPT	60056	2808	14W-13N	C6
1500	DSPN	60016	2808	14W-13N	D6
Lowe Av					
-	BlmT	60411	3508	0W-24S	B4
500	CHHT	60411	3508	0W-24S	B5
1400	CHHT	60411	3596	0W-25S	B1
15900	HRVY	60426	3428	0W-19S	B1
15900	SHLD	60426	3428	0W-19S	B2
16600	HRVY	60473	3428	0W-19S	B3
16600	SHLD	60473	3428	0W-19S	B3
S Lowe Av					
2600	CHCG	60616	3092	0W-3S	A4
3900	CHCG	60609	3092	0W-4S	A6
5100	CHCG	60609	3152	0W-5S	A2
5500	CHCG	60621	3152	0W-6S	A3
7500	CHCG	60620	3214	0W-9S	A2
9400	CHCG	60628	3214	0W-11S	A6
11800	CHCG	60628	3278	0W-14S	B5
14200	RVDL	60827	3350	1W-16S	B4
14500	HRVY	60426	3350	1W-16S	B4
Lowell Av					
7400	LNWD	60712	2866	5W-9N	A7
9000	SKOK	60076	2866	5W-11N	A2
16200	SHLD	60473	3428	0E-19S	E1
17300	HLCT	60429	3427	3W-20S	A5
N Lowell Av					
1600	CHCG	60639	3032	5W-1N	A1
1600	CHCG	60651	3032	5W-1N	A1
2800	CHCG	60639	2976	5W-3N	A4
2800	CHCG	60641	2976	5W-3N	A4
4300	CHCG	60630	2976	5W-5N	A1
4400	CHCG	60630	2920	5W-5N	A7
6100	CHCG	60646	2920	5W-7N	A3
6800	LNWD	60712	2920	5W-8N	A1
7200	LNWD	60712	2866	5W-9N	A7
7300	SKOK	60076	2866	5W-9N	A7
Lowell Cir					
1100	SMBG	60193	2858	24W-9N	C7
Lowell Dr					
7000	CPVL	60110	2748		D7
Lowell Ln					
1000	SMBG	60193	2858	24W-9N	C7
Lowell Ter					
8800	SKOK	60076	2866	5W-11N	A3
N Lower Michigan Av					
300	CHCG	60601	3034	0E-0N	C4
Lowestoft Ln					
500	EGVV	60007	2914		C2
Lowrie Ct					
400	ELGN	60120	2855		A4
Loyalty Ln					
-	MTSN	60443	3505	7W-24S	D6
W Loyola Av					
1000	CHCG	60626	2921	1W-8N	D2
1900	CHCG	60645	2921	2W-8N	B2
3800	LNWD	60712	2920	4W-8N	B2
Luau Dr					
700	DSPN	60016	2862	14W-12N	D1
E Lucas Dr					
10	PSHL	60465	3274	10W-13S	A3
S Lucas Dr					
10	PSHL	60465	3274	11W-13S	A3
W Lucas Dr					
10	PSHL	60465	3274	11W-13S	A3

STREET Block	City	ZIP	Map#	CGS	Grid
Lucas St					
1000	CTCY	60409	3351	3E-17S	E5
1400	CTCY	60409	3352	3E-17S	A5
N Lucerne Av					
6000	CHCG	60646	2919	6W-7N	D3
Lucerne Ct					
100	WLNG	60090	2808	14W-15N	B1
Lucile Av					
500	ELGN	60120	2855		C5
Lucille Av					
300	ELGN	60120	2855		C5
Lucille Ct					
100	BRLT	60103	2911		A3
Lucille Dr					
-	MONE	60449	3683	6W-31S	A5
Lucille Ln					
-	SMBG	60193	2912		E2
1800	HRPK	60133	2911		D6
12500	PlsT	60464	3273	12W-14S	B7
Lucre Ct					
100	SMBG	60173	2859	22W-10N	C5
Lucy Ln					
2900	FNPK	60131	2972		E5
2900	LydT	60164	2972		E5
Luda St					
600	ELGN	60120	2855		B1
Ludington Ct					
4100	HFET	60195	2804	24W-15N	C2
N Ludlam Av					
5200	CHCG	60630	2919	6W-6N	D5
Ludlow Av					
600	ELGN	60120	2855		B1
Luella Av					
10	CTCY	60409	3351	2E-16S	D4
16500	SHLD	60473	3429	2E-19S	D3
S Luella Av					
-	CHCG	60617	3279	2E-11S	D1
-	CHCG	60633	3351	2E-15S	D2
-	CTCY	60409	3351	2E-15S	D2
7100	CHCG	60649	3153	2E-8S	D7
7500	CHCG	60649	3215	2E-9S	D2
7800	CHCG	60617	3215	2E-9S	D3
Luella Ct					
22100	SLVL	60411	3597	2E-26S	D3
Luis Munoz Marin Dr					
1000	CHCG	60622	3032	3W-1N	E2
W Lukas Av					
800	PLTN	60067	2805	22W-14N	C4
Lumber St					
1200	CRTE	60417	3685	1W-29S	B2
S Lumber St					
1400	CHCG	60607	3034	0W-1S	B7
1400	CHCG	60616	3034	0W-1S	B7
2300	CHCG	60608	3091	1W-2S	E2
2300	CHCG	60608	3092		E2
2300	CHCG	60616	3092		E2
Luna Av					
7700	BRBK	60459	3211	6W-8S	D2
7800	SKOK	60077	2865	6W-9N	C6
8800	MNGV	60053	2865	6W-11N	C3
14100	BmnT	60445	3347	6W-16S	D4
14100	MDLN	60445	3347	6W-16S	D4
N Luna Av					
1400	CHCG	60651	3031	6W-1N	C1
1600	CHCG	60639	3031	6W-2N	D1
2400	CHCG	60639	2975	6W-3N	C5
3600	CHCG	60641	2975	6W-4N	C2
5200	CHCG	60630	2919	6W-6N	C5
5500	CHCG	60646	2919	6W-6N	C5
S Luna Av					
4700	FTVW	60638	3149	6W-5S	D1
4700	StkT	60638	3149	6W-5S	D2
5000	CHCG	60638	3149	6W-5S	D2
Lunar Av					
8900	ODPK	60462	3346	11W-17S	A5
Lundergan Av					
1500	PKRG	60068	2863	12W-10N	C4
N Lundy Av					
6200	CHCG	60646	2919	6W-7N	C3
Lundy Ln					
200	SMBG	60193	2859	23W-10N	B6
Lunt Av					
10	SMBG	60193	2913		A2
10	SmbT	60193	2913		A2
200	SmbT	60193	2912		E2
400	SMBG	60193	2912		D2
600	EGVV	60007	2915		B2
1600	DSPN	60018	2917	12W-8N	A1
4900	LNWD	60712	2919	6W-8N	E1
4900	SKOK	60712	2919	6W-8N	E1
5300	SKOK	60077	2919	6W-8N	D1
10400	RSMT	60018	2917	13W-8N	A1
10500	DSPN	60018	2916		E1
10500	RSMT	60018	2916		E1
W Lunt Av					
1100	CHCG	60626	2921	2W-8N	B1
2000	CHCG	60645	2921	2W-8N	B1
2600	CHCG	60645	2920	3W-8N	E1
4500	LNWD	60712	2920	5W-8N	A1
4600	LNWD	60712	2919	5W-8N	E1
4800	SKOK	60077	2919	6W-8N	E1
4800	SKOK	60712	2919	6W-8N	E1
5400	CHCG	60646	2919	6W-8N	C1
7200	CHCG	60631	2918	9W-8N	D1
7200	NLES	60714	2918	9W-8N	D1
7700	PKRG	60068	2918	9W-8N	C1
Lunt Ct					
-	SMBG	60193	2912		E2
-	SmbT	60193	2912		E2
Lurilane Dr					
-	GNVW	60062	2809	12W-14N	B4
Luther Ln					
800	CHHT	60411	3507	2W-24S	E6
1200	ANHT	60004	2806	18W-15N	E2
1600	PKRG	60068	2863	11W-10N	E4
W Luther St					
2600	CHCG	60608	3091	3W-2S	A2
Luthin Rd					
300	OKBK	60523	3086		A5
LW Besinger Dr					
10	CPVL	60110	2748		B7
10	EDND	60110	2748		C7
S Lydia Av					
13900	RBBN	60472	3348	4W-16S	E3
W Lydia Av					
3200	RBBN	60472	3348	4W-16S	D3
Lyle Ln					
3400	CRTE	60417	3597	1E-28S	B6
Lyman Av					
-	GNVW	60016	2809	11W-12N	C7
-	GNVW	60025	2809	11W-12N	C7
-	MaiT	60016	2809	11W-12N	C7
-	MaiT	60016	2863	11W-12N	C1
6500	HMND	46324	3430		D3
10300	CHRG	60415	3275	7W-12S	C1

STREET Block	City	ZIP	Map#	CGS	Grid
Lyman Av					
11000	ALSP	60482	3275	7W-12S	C3
11000	CHRG	60482	3275	7W-12S	C3
S Lyman Av					
300	DSPN	60016	2863	12W-11N	C3
300	MaiT	60016	2863	12W-11N	C3
500	OKPK	60302	3031	7W-0S	B5
700	PKRG	60068	2863	12W-11N	C4
1000	OKPK	60304	3031	7W-0S	B7
1100	CCRO	60804	3031	7W-0S	B7
1100	OKPK	60804	3031	7W-0S	B7
5300	HMND	46320	3352		D6
5900	HMND	46320	3430		D1
6100	HMND	46324	3430		D1
Lyman Ct					
500	HDPK	60035	2758	7W-20N	C1
S Lyman St					
2900	CHCG	60608	3091	1W-2S	E3
Lyn Ct					
18500	HMWD	60430	3507	1W-22S	E1
N Lynch Av					
5300	CHCG	60630	2919	6W-6N	D5
Lynch Dr					
11800	HMGN	60441	3422	14W-18S	C1
11800	OrlT	60467	3422	14W-18S	C1
E Lynda Dr					
400	PLTN	60074	2753	20W-18N	B3
N Lynda Dr					
1600	PLTN	60074	2753	20W-18N	B4
E Lyndale Av					
10	NHLK	60164	2972		E6
300	LydT	60164	2973	13W-2N	A6
300	NHLK	60164	2973	13W-2N	A6
W Lyndale Av					
10400	LydT	60164	2973	13W-2N	A6
10400	NHLK	60164	2973	13W-2N	A6
Lyndale Ln					
2600	RVWD	60015	2755	13W-20N	E1
W Lyndale St					
2100	CHCG	60647	2977	2W-2N	B6
2800	CHCG	60647	2976	3W-2N	E6
4500	CHCG	60639	2976	5W-2N	A6
8600	RVGV	60171	2973	10W-2N	E6
8600	RVGV	60171	2974	10W-2N	A6
E Lynden Ln					
600	ANHT	60005	2807	17W-13N	B5
Lyndon St					
7000	RSMT	60018	2917	13W-8N	A1
7100	DSPN	60018	2917	13W-8N	A1
Lynn Ct					
200	DSPN	60016	2862	15W-11N	B3
3000	EGVV	60005	2861	17W-10N	C5
3000	EGVV	60007	2861	17W-10N	C5
3000	MPPT	60005	2861	17W-10N	C5
E Lynn Ct					
1300	HMWD	60430	3507	1W-22S	E1
Lynn Dr					
10400	ODPK	60467	3423	13W-21S	B7
W Lynn Dr					
200	PLTN	60067	2752	21W-16N	D6
Lynn Ln					
100	WLNG	60090	2755	14W-16N	C7
200	CHHT	60411	3507	1W-23S	E3
S Lynn Ln					
-	MONE	60449	3682	6W-31S	E6
25900	MONE	60449	3683	6W-31S	A5
Lynnbrook Dr					
10	PTHT	60070	2754	15W-16N	E7
10	PTHT	60070	2755	15W-16N	A7
Lynne Ct					
14900	OKFT	60452	3347	6W-17S	E6
Lynne Dr					
-	EGVV	60007	2914		C2
Lynnfield Ln					
100	SMBG	60193	2858	26W-10N	A6
1100	BRLT	60103	2910		B5
E Lynnwood Av					
200	ANHT	60004	2807	17W-15N	A2
W Lynnwood Av					
1400	ANHT	60004	2806	18W-15N	D2
Lynnwood Ct					
-	PlsT	60464	3345	13W-15S	A1
3000	SMWD	60107	2911		A2
Lynwood Ct					
1600	FSMR	60422	3507	2W-23S	D3
Lynwood Dr					
3200	SCHT	60411	3596	1W-27S	A4
5800	OKLN	60453	3211	7W-10S	C5
8600	HYHL	60457	3210	10W-10S	A4
Lynze Ln					
8800	FKFT	60423	3504	11W-24S	A5
S Lyon Av					
9300	CHCG	60619	3214	0E-10S	E5
Lyons St					
-	SKOK	60076	2865	5W-11N	E2
-	SKOK	60076	2866	5W-11N	A2
1300	EVTN	60201	2867	3W-11N	A2
1700	EVTN	60201	2866	3W-11N	E2
3300	SKOK	60203	2866	4W-11N	D2
5400	SKOK	60077	2865	6W-11N	C2
6400	MNGV	60053	2865	8W-11N	A2
7200	MNGV	60053	2864	9W-11N	C2
7900	MNGV	60714	2864	9W-11N	B2
7900	NLES	60053	2864	9W-11N	B2
8600	MaiT	60016	2863	10W-11N	E2
8600	MaiT	60016	2864	10W-11N	A2
8600	NLES	60016	2864	10W-11N	A2
8600	NLES	60714	2864	10W-11N	A2
8700	HGKN	60525	3147	11W-7S	D6
E Lyons St					
800	HMND	46320	3430		E1
W Lyons St					
8000	MNGV	60053	2864	9W-11N	B2
8000	MNGV	60714	2864	9W-11N	B2
8000	NLES	60714	2864	10W-11N	B2
N Lytle Dr					
100	PLTN	60074	2753	19W-16N	C7
S Lytle St					
1000	CHCG	60607	3033	1W-0S	D6
1000	CHCG	60608	3033	1W-0S	D6

M

STREET Block	City	ZIP	Map#	CGS	Grid
Mable Ln					
600	BRLT	60103	2909		E2
N Macalpin Av					
6900	CHCG	60646	2919	7W-8N	B1
6900	NLES	60714	2919	7W-8N	A1
Macalpin Cir					
1400	IVNS	60010	2751	25W-16N	A6
Macalpin Ct					
300	IVNS	60010	2751	25W-16N	A6
Macalpin Dr					
1100	IVNS	60010	2751	25W-16N	A6

STREET Block	City	ZIP	Map#	CGS	Grid
MacArthur					
9100	MaiT	60016	2863	11W-11N	D3
MacArthur Blvd					
800	MNSR	46321	3510		E1
2900	NHBK	60062	2756	11W-18N	D3
MacArthur Ct					
10	BFGV	60089	2754	17W-18N	C3
700	DLTN	60419	3350	0E-16S	E3
700	DLTN	60419	3351	1E-16S	A3
MacArthur Dr					
10	NHLK	60164	2972		D5
200	LydT	60164	2972		D5
500	BFGV	60089	2754	17W-18N	C4
800	BlmT	60411	3507	2W-24S	D6
800	CHHT	60411	3507	2W-24S	D6
2100	GNVW	60025	2864	9W-12N	D1
E MacArthur Dr					
600	PLTN	60074	2753	20W-16N	A7
N MacArthur Dr					
100	MPPT	60056	2807	16W-13N	D6
200	PLTN	60074	2753	20W-16N	A7
Macbain Wy					
400	HFET	60010	2751	24W-16N	C7
400	IVNS	60010	2751	24W-16N	C7
N Macchesney Ct					
-	CHCG	60601	3034		E4
MacDonald Ln					
2200	FSMR	60422	3507	2W-22S	C2
Macfarlane Cres					
2800	FSMR	60422	3507	3W-23S	A3
Mach Dr					
22900	CRTE	60417	3597	0E-27S	A5
22900	STGR	60417	3597	0E-27S	A5
22900	STGR	60475	3597	0E-27S	A5
Macheath Cres					
2800	FSMR	60422	3507	3W-23S	A3
Mackenzie Ln					
1400	ELGN	60120	2855		E3
1400	HnrT	60120	2855		E3
Mackey Ln					
800	ELGN	60120	2855		C4
Mackinac Ct					
16400	HMGN	60441	3422	15W-19S	C3
Mackinac Rd					
12000	HMGN	60441	3422	15W-19S	C3
12000	OrlT	60467	3422	14W-19S	C2
Mackinaw Av					
300	CTCY	60409	3352	3E-17S	A6
1200	CTCY	60409	3430	3E-19S	A2
S Mackinaw Av					
-	CHCG	60617	3280	3E-12S	A3
8700	CHCG	60617	3216	4E-10S	A4
13000	CHCG	60633	3280	3E-14S	A7
13000	CHCG	60633	3352	3E-15S	A1
13900	BNHM	60633	3352	3E-16S	A3
S Mackinaw Av US-41					
8700	CHCG	60617	3216	4E-10S	A4
Mackler Dr					
800	CHHT	60411	3507	2W-24S	E6
Macks Dr					
100	WLSP	60480	3209	12W-9S	B4
Maclaine Ln					
5400	HRPK	60133	2911		C6
Maclean Av					
-	NtrT	60043	2812	4W-14N	C4
-	NtrT	60093	2812	4W-14N	C4
700	KLWH	60043	2812	4W-14N	C4
700	KLWH	60093	2812	4W-14N	C4
700	WNKA	60043	2812	4W-14N	C4
700	WNKA	60093	2812	4W-14N	C4
S Madden Dr					
4900	HMND	46320	3352		D5
Madeline Cir					
10	SMBG	60173	2859	21W-10N	E5
Madelyn Dr					
600	DSPN	60016	2808	13W-13N	D7
Madera Cir					
100	CPVL	60110	2748		C4
Madera St					
-	HRPK	60133	2911		E5
Madisen Ln					
-	UYPK	60466	3684	3W-29S	B1
Madison Av					
200	CTCY	60409	3351	2E-17S	C5
300	GLNC	60022	2758	6W-17N	D6
1000	DYR	46311	3510		E7
1500	DYR	46311	3598		D1
3100	BKFD	60513	3087	11W-3S	D6
3100	LGPK	60525	3087	11W-3S	D6
4500	BKFD	60513	3147	11W-4S	D1
5800	HMND	46320	3352		E7
6200	HMND	46324	3430		E3
7800	MNSR	46321	3430		E6
8700	MNSR	46321	3510		E1
14700	HRVY	60426	3350	1W-17S	B5
15100	DLTN	60419	3351	2E-17S	C6
15500	ThtT	60473	3351	2E-18S	C7
15600	DLTN	60473	3351	2E-18S	C7
N Madison Av					
10	LGNG	60525	3087	12W-4S	B6
100	LGPK	60525	3087	12W-4S	B6
S Madison Av					
10	LGNG	60525	3087	12W-4S	C7
300	LGNG	60525	3147	12W-4S	C1
5500	CTSD	60525	3147	12W-6S	C3
Madison Ct					
800	EGVV	60007	2913		D2
1100	CPVL	60110	2748		D7
6100	MNGV	60053	2865	7W-10N	B5
8800	MNSR	46321	3510		E1
E Madison Ct					
400	EMHT	60126	3028		B5
W Madison Ct					
8300	NLES	60714	2864	10W-10N	A5
Madison Dr					
-	HnrT	60107	2856	29W-10N	D6
500	SMWD	60107	2856	29W-10N	D6
W Madison Dr					
8400	NLES	60714	2864	10W-10N	A5
8600	NLES	60714	2863	10W-10N	E5
E Madison Pk					
1200	CHCG	60615	3153	1E-5S	A1
Madison Pl					
2100	EVTN	60202	2866	3W-10N	E5
Madison St					
-	HNDL	60523	3086		A6
10	CHCG	60644	3031	7W-0N	B5
10	FTPK	60130	3030	10W-0N	B5
10	FTPK	60153	3030	10W-0N	B5
10	FTPK	60305	3030	10W-0N	B5
10	MYWD	60153	3030	10W-0N	B5
10	OKPK	60302	3031	7W-0N	B5
10	OKPK	60304	3031	7W-0N	B5
10	RVFT	60305	3030	10W-0N	B5
400	EGvT	60018	2861	16W-9N	E7

STREET Block	City	ZIP	Map#	CGS	Grid
Madison St					
400	EGvT	60018	2862	15W-9N	A7
600	EDND	60118	2801		B2
600	EVTN	60202	2867	3W-10N	A5
700	OKPK	60302	3030	8W-0N	E5
700	OKPK	60304	3030	8W-0N	E5
800	MYWD	60153	3029	11W-0N	D5
1600	EVTN	60202	2866	3W-10N	E5
2100	BLWD	60104	3029	11W-0N	D5
3300	LNSG	60438	3430	4E-21S	C6
3300	SKOK	60076	2866	4W-10N	D5
3500	OKBK	60523	3086		A6
3900	HLSD	60162	3029	13W-0S	A5
4200	HLSD	60162	3028		E5
4700	SKOK	60076	2865	5W-10N	E5
5100	SKOK	60077	2865	6W-10N	D5
5700	MNGV	60053	2865	7W-10N	B5
5800	BKLY	60163	3028		C5
5800	HLSD	60163	3028		C5
7400	HRPK	60133	2912		A1
8000	RVFT	60130	3030	10W-0N	B5
E Madison St					
10	CHCG	60602	3034	0E-0N	C4
10	CHCG	60603	3034	0E-0N	C4
100	EMHT	60126	3028		A5
N Madison St					
10	HNDL	60521	3146		A1
400	HNDL	60521	3086		A7
900	HNDL	60523	3086		A7
900	OKBK	60521	3086		A7
900	OKBK	60523	3086		A7
S Madison St					
10	BRRG	60527	3208		A6
10	DGvT	60527	3208		A1
10	HNDL	60521	3146		A1
800	DGvT	60521	3146		A7
5800	DGvT	60527	3146		A4
5900	BRRG	60527	3146		A5
6300	WLBK	60527	3146		A5
7200	WLBK	60527	3208		A1
S Madison St CO-8					
5400	DGvT	60521	3146		A7
5400	HNDL	60521	3146		A7
5800	DGvT	60527	3146		A4
5900	BRRG	60527	3146		A5
6300	WLBK	60527	3146		A5
7200	DGvT	60527	3208		A1
7200	WLBK	60527	3208		A1
7600	BRRG	60527	3208		A2
W Madison St					
10	CHCG	60602	3034	0W-0N	A4
10	CHCG	60603	3034	0W-0N	A4
100	CHCG	60606	3034	0W-0N	B4
400	CHCG	60661	3034	0W-0N	A4
700	CHCG	60607	3034	0W-0N	A4
800	CHCG	60607	3033	3W-0S	A5
1500	CHCG	60612	3033	2W-0S	D5
2800	CHCG	60612	3032	4W-0N	C5
3100	CHCG	60624	3032	3W-0S	E5
4500	CHCG	60644	3032	5W-0S	A5
4700	CHCG	60644	3031	6W-0N	E5
5900	OKPK	60302	3031	7W-0N	B5
5900	OKPK	60304	3031	7W-0N	B5
6800	NLES	60714	2864	8W-10N	E5
Madrid Ct					
5700	HRPK	60133	2911		E5
Mae Ct					
1200	WLNG	60090	2754	16W-18N	D3
Maeburn Ter					
-	CRTE	60417	3685	0E-29S	E1
-	CRTE	60417	3686	0E-29S	A1
Mager Dr					
18000	TYPK	60477	3424	10W-21S	B7
N Magnet Av					
5300	CHCG	60630	2919	7W-6N	C5
Magnolia Av					
9200	FftT	60448	3504	11W-23S	A3
9200	MKNA	60448	3504	11W-23S	A3
N Magnolia Av					
1400	CHCG	60622	3033	1W-1N	D1
1900	CHCG	60614	2977	1W-2N	D6
2700	CHCG	60657	2977	1W-3N	D5
3600	CHCG	60613	2977	1W-4N	D2
4400	CHCG	60613	2921	1W-5N	D7
5200	CHCG	60640	2921	1W-6N	D5
5500	CHCG	60660	2921	1W-6N	D5
6300	CHCG	60626	2921	1W-7N	D3
Magnolia Ct					
10	SMWD	60107	2856	30W-10N	C5
300	SMBG	60193	2858	23W-10N	E6
600	HnrT	60120	2856	29W-12N	E2
8800	ODPK	60462	3346	11W-17S	A5
Magnolia Dr					
-	BlmT	60425	3508	0E-22S	E1
-	GNWD	60425	3508	0E-22S	E1
3200	MKHM	60426	3348	4W-18S	E7
4400	RGMW	60008	2806	20W-12N	B7
16900	HLCT	60429	3426	4W-20S	E4
W Magnolia Dr					
10	SMWD	60107	2856	30W-10N	C5
7900	FftT	60423	3504	10W-24S	C5
Magnolia Ln					
500	EGVV	60007	2915		A2
2000	HDPK	60035	2757	9W-20N	C2
2200	HnrT	60120	2856	29W-12N	D2
8900	TYPK	60477	3424	11W-21S	A5
12000	HMGN	60441	3344	15W-18S	C7
S Magnolia Ln					
11400	ALSP	60803	3275	6W-13S	E4
W Magnolia Ln					
1700	MPPT	60056	2861	17W-11N	C3
Magnolia Pl					
200	SCHT	60411	3595	2W-27S	D3
200	SCHT	60411	3596	1W-27S	A3
Magnolia Plz					
3000	SCHT	60411	3595	1W-27S	E3
Magnolia Rd					
2000	HMWD	60430	3427	2W-21S	C6
Magnolia St					
-	GNVW	60062	2809	12W-14N	B4
1400	GNVW	60025	2809	12W-14N	B5
2100	DSPN	60018	2863	12W-9N	B7
2300	DSPN	60018	2917	12W-9N	B1
6800	HRPK	60133	2911		D3
E Magnolia St					
10	ANHT	60005	2807	17W-12N	A7
W Magnolia St					
-	ANHT	60005	2806	18W-12N	E7
-	ANHT	60005	2807	18W-12N	A7
Magnuson Ct					
800	BNHL	60118	2802	30W-15N	A2
Mahoney Dr					
-	BRRG	60527	3208		C6
-	DGvT	60527	3208		C6

STREET Block	City	ZIP	Map#	CGS	Grid
Mahoney Pkwy					
17200	HLCT	60429	3427	3W-20S	B5
Maiden Ln					
10	EDND	60118	2801		A3
10	WDND	60118	2801		A3
S Maiden Ln					
1800	HMND	46394	3280		D4
Maidstone Ct					
300	SMBG	60194	2857	27W-11N	D3
Main Av					
-	CHCG	60613	2977	1W-5N	D1
Main Dr					
-	HGKN	60525	3147	12W-6S	C4
-	WynT	60184	2909		D6
10	CTSD	60525	3147	12W-6S	C4
Main St					
-	CHHT	60411	3595	2W-26S	C2
-	PKFT	60411	3595	2W-26S	C2
-	PKFT	60466	3595	2W-26S	C2
10	GNVW	60093	2810	8W-15N	E3
10	LMNT	60439	3270		E5
10	NHFD	60093	2810	8W-15N	E3
10	PKRG	60068	2918	10W-8N	A1
100	EVTN	60202	2867	2W-10N	C4
100	MYWD	60153	3030	10W-0N	A4
100	ROSL	60172	2913		A4
500	DYR	46311	3510		E5
500	MNSR	46321	3510		E5
800	CRTE	60417	3596	1W-28S	B7
800	CRTE	60417	3685	0W-30S	B2
900	MLPK	60153	3029	11W-0N	E3
900	MYWD	60153	3029	10W-0N	E3
900	MYWD	60160	3029	10W-0N	E3
1100	LmnT	60439	3271		A4
1100	MLPK	60160	3029	11W-0N	D3
1500	CteT	60417	3685	0W-30S	B3
1700	EVTN	60202	2866	3W-10N	E4
2400	BLWD	60104	3029	11W-0N	D3
3300	SKOK	60076	2866	5W-10N	B4
4700	SKOK	60076	2865	6W-10N	E4
4700	SKOK	60077	2865	6W-10N	E4
5300	MNGV	60077	2865	6W-10N	D4
5400	SKOK	60053	2865	6W-10N	D4
6400	MNGV	60053	2865	8W-10N	A5
12700	LmnT	60439	3272	16W-12S	A3
14700	HRVY	60426	3350	1W-18S	A6
21100	MTSN	60443	3506	4W-25S	E7
21100	OMFD	60461	3506	4W-25S	E7
21600	MTSN	60443	3594	4W-26S	E2
21800	PKFT	60443	3594	4W-26S	E2
21800	PKFT	60466	3594	4W-27S	E3
21800	PKFT	60471	3594	4W-26S	E3
21800	RNPK	60471	3594	4W-27S	E4
Main St SR-1					
800	CRTE	60417	3596	1W-28S	B7
800	CRTE	60417	3685	0W-30S	B2
1500	CteT	60417	3685	0W-30S	B3
E Main St					
10	BlmT	60425	3508	0E-22S	E2
10	CHHT	60411	3596	1W-26S	B2
10	EDND	60118	2801		C3
10	GNWD	60425	3508	0E-22S	E2
100	PTON	60468	3861	9W-37S	A3
200	DLTN	60419	3350	0E-16S	D3
200	RVDL	60419	3350	0E-16S	D3
200	RVDL	60827	3350	0E-16S	D3
400	DndT	60118	2801		C3
700	DLTN	60419	3351	1E-16S	A3
E Main St SR-72					
10	EDND	60118	2801		C3
400	DndT	60118	2801		C3
N Main St					
-	BlmT	60425	3508	0W-22S	C1
10	MPPT	60056	2808	15W-13N	A6
100	GNWD	60425	3508	0W-22S	C1
N Main St SR-83					
10	MPPT	60056	2808	15W-13N	A6
S Main St					
-	CHCG	60456	3212	5W-10S	B4
-	CHCG	60805	3212	5W-10S	B4
10	GNVW	60093	2810	8W-15N	E3
10	MPPT	60056	2808	15W-12N	A7
200	LMNT	60439	3270		D6
200	MPPT	60056	2862	15W-12N	A1
400	BRLT	60103	2910		E4
8800	HMTN	60456	3212	5W-10S	B4
9000	HMTN	60453	3212	5W-10S	B5
9000	OKLN	60453	3212	5W-10S	B5
S Main St SR-83					
10	MPPT	60056	2808	15W-12N	A7
200	MPPT	60056	2862	15W-12N	A1
W Main St					
10	CHHT	60411	3596	1W-26S	A2
10	EDND	60118	2801		A2
10	GNWD	60425	3508	0W-22S	D2
10	WDND	60118	2801		A2
100	PTON	60468	3861	9W-37S	A3
200	PTON	60468	3860	9W-37S	E3
4800	MONE	60449	3683	6W-31S	A5
4800	MonT	60449	3683	5W-31S	B5
5500	MONE	60449	3682	6W-31S	E5
6800	NLES	60714	2864	8W-10N	E4
7000	MNGV	60053	2864	8W-10N	D4
7000	MNGV	60714	2864	8W-10N	D4
7700	MaiT	60714	2864	9W-10N	C5
W Main St SR-72					
10	EDND	60118	2801		A2
10	WDND	60118	2801		A2
Maine Ct					
17800	ODPK	60467	3423	13W-21S	A6
Maine Dr					
1800	EGVV	60007	2913		C1
N Maison Ct					
200	EMHT	60126	3028		B2
Major Av					
8400	MNGV	60053	2865	7W-10N	C4
8700	BRBK	60459	3211	7W-10S	D5
8700	OKLN	60453	3211	7W-10S	D6
10400	CHRG	60415	3275	7W-12S	D1
10400	OKLN	60453	3275	7W-12S	D1
11000	ALSP	60482	3275	7W-12S	D3
11000	CHRG	60482	3275	7W-12S	D3
14200	BmnT	60445	3347	7W-16S	D4
14700	OKFT	60452	3347	7W-17S	D5
N Major Av					
1600	CHCG	60639	3031	6W-0S	E7
1600	CHCG	60651	3031	6W-0S	E7
2000	CHCG	60639	2975	7W-2N	C6
2700	CHCG	60634	2975	7W-3N	C5
4300	CHCG	60630	2975	7W-5N	C1
5500	CHCG	60630	2919	7W-7N	C4
5500	CHCG	60646	2919	7W-7N	C4
S Major Av					
5100	StkT	60638	3149	7W-5S	C2
6500	BDPK	60638	3149	7W-7S	D5
6500	CHCG	60638	3149	7W-7S	D6
12500	WthT	60463	3275	7W-14S	D7
12500	WthT	60803	3275	7W-14S	D7
12600	WthT	60445	3275	7W-14S	D7
Major Dr					
200	NHLK	60164	2972		E7
300	NHLK	60164	2973	13W-2N	A7
400	LydT	60164	2973	13W-2N	A7
Malden Av					
10	LGNG	60525	3087	13W-4S	A6
200	LGPK	60525	3087	13W-3S	A6
Malden Ct					
800	SMBG	60193	2858	24W-10N	C6
N Malden St					
4400	CHCG	60613	2921	1W-5N	D7
4400	CHCG	60640	2921	1W-5N	D7
Maley Rd					
-	LMNT	60439	3271		D3
E Malibou Ln					
600	PLTN	60074	2753	20W-16N	A6
Malibu Ct					
10	BRRG	60527	3208		B6
Malik Ct					
2300	GNVW	60025	2864	9W-12N	C1
Mall Dr					
500	SMBG	60173	2859	21W-11N	E3
Mallard Cir					
900	SMBG	60193	2913		B1
15200	ODPK	60462	3346	10W-18S	B7
Mallard Ct					
500	SMBG	60193	2913		B1
600	BRLT	60103	2911		A3
700	VrnT	60015	2755	15W-20N	A1
3500	RGMW	60008	2806	20W-13N	B6
S Mallard Ct					
900	PLTN	60067	2805	22W-14N	B3
Mallard Dr					
400	VrnT	60015	2755	15W-20N	A1
2000	NHBK	60062	2757	10W-16N	A7
3100	FSMR	60422	3507	4W-22S	A1
3100	HMWD	60430	3506	4W-22S	E1
3100	HMWD	60430	3507	4W-22S	A1
5500	MTSN	60443	3505	6W-24S	A5
14000	HMGN	60441	3344	15W-17S	B5
14000	HMGN	60467	3344	15W-16S	C4
N Mallard Dr					
4100	ANHT	60004	2753	18W-20N	D2
S Mallard Dr					
600	PLTN	60067	2805	22W-14N	B3
W Mallard Dr					
1000	PLTN	60067	2805	22W-15N	B2
Mallard Ln					
400	DRFD	60015	2756	11W-20N	D1
600	VrnT	60015	2755	15W-20N	A1
700	ANHT	60004	2754	16W-17N	D6
700	WLNG	60004	2754	16W-17N	D6
700	WLNG	60090	2754	16W-17N	D6
1000	PTON	60468	3860	10W-38S	C4
1100	HFET	60192	2856	30W-12N	B2
1100	HnrT	60192	2856	30W-12N	B2
S Mallard Ln					
1300	MPPT	60056	2861	16W-11N	E3
14400	HMGN	60441	3342	19W-18S	D7
W Mallard Ln					
14400	HMGN	60441	3344	15W-17S	C5
Mallard Rd					
8800	TYPK	60477	3424	11W-21S	A7
S Mallard Lake Dr					
15100	HMGN	60441	3342	19W-18S	D7
15100	HmrT	60441	3342	19W-18S	D7
Mallards Cove					
200	BCHR	60401	3774	0W-35S	D7
Mallette Av					
100	ThtT	60476	3428	0E-21S	E6
100	TNTN	60476	3428	0E-21S	E6
Mallory Ct					
-	BRRG	60527	3146		B6
2300	RGMW	60008	2805	21W-14N	D4
2300	RGMW	60067	2805	21W-14N	D4
S Mallory Dr					
19900	FftT	60423	3504	9W-24S	D4
Mallow Ct					
2400	SMBG	60194	2857	26W-10N	E5
Mallow Dr					
8000	TYPK	60477	3424	10W-21S	C6
Mallow Ridge Dr					
16700	ODPK	60467	3423	13W-20S	A4
Malmo Rd					
2800	EGvT	60005	2861	16W-10N	E5
2800	EGvT	60056	2861	16W-10N	E5
2800	MPPT	60005	2861	16W-10N	E5
2800	MPPT	60056	2861	16W-10N	E5
S Malta St					
9900	CHCG	60643	3213	1W-11S	D7
10000	CHCG	60643	3277	2W-12S	D1
Malthusian Wy					
-	RVFT	60305	3030	9W-1N	B2
W Manawa Tr					
500	MPPT	60056	2861	16W-12N	E2
Mance St					
-	HGKN	60525	3147	12W-7S	C5
Manchester Av					
600	WSTR	60154	3029	12W-0S	C7
1400	WSTR	60154	3087	12W-1S	C1
Manchester Blvd					
1500	HFET	60195	2858	25W-12N	A1
Manchester Cir					
900	SMBG	60193	2913		B1
Manchester Ct					
10	BFGV	60089	2754	17W-20N	C2
10	SMWD	60107	2856	29W-11N	D4
100	SMBG	60193	2913		D4
Manchester Dr					
-	HFET	60195	2858	25W-12N	A1
10	BFGV	60089	2754	17W-20N	C2
100	BRTN	60010	2750	25W-17N	E5
E Manchester Dr					
10	CHHT	60411	3508	1W-24S	A5
200	WLNG	60090	2755	14W-17N	D5
N Manchester Dr					
400	CHHT	60411	3508	1W-24S	A5
W Manchester Dr					
10	WLNG	60090	2755	14W-17N	C5
Manchester Mnr					
7600	HRPK	60133	2912		A1
Manchester Rd					
1000	SMBG	60193	2913		B1
Manchester St					
16400	TYPK	60477	3425	8W-19S	A2
Manda Ln					
400	WLNG	60090	2754	16W-18N	E3
Mandel Av					
1200	HLSD	60154	3028		E7
1200	HLSD	60162	3028		E7
1200	WSTR	60154	3028		E7
1400	WSTR	60154	3086		E2
2100	HLSD	60154	3086		E2
Mandel Ct					
11000	WSTR	60154	3086		E1
Mandel Ln					
10	MPPT	60056	2808	13W-15N	D3
10	MPPT	60070	2808	13W-15N	D3
10	PTHT	60070	2808	13W-15N	D3
N Mandel Ln					
1400	MPPT	60056	2808	13W-14N	D3
1400	MPPT	60070	2808	13W-14N	D3
1400	PTHT	60070	2808	13W-14N	D3
N Mandell Av					
6200	CHCG	60646	2919	7W-7N	C3
Mango Av					
8800	MNGV	60053	2865	7W-11N	C3
N Mango Av					
1600	CHCG	60639	3031	6W-0S	E6
1600	CHCG	60651	3031	6W-0S	E6
2000	CHCG	60639	2975	7W-2N	C6
4400	CHCG	60630	2975	7W-5N	C1
4400	CHCG	60634	2975	7W-5N	C1
4900	CHCG	60630	2919	7W-6N	C6
5500	CHCG	60646	2919	7W-6N	C5
N Manila Av					
5300	CHCG	60630	2919	7W-6N	C5
Manistee Av					
200	BNHM	60633	3351	3E-17S	E5
200	CTCY	60409	3351	3E-17S	E6
S Manistee Av					
7900	CHCG	60617	3215	3E-9S	E3
7900	CHCG	60649	3215	3E-9S	E2
10300	CHCG	60617	3279	3E-11S	E1
12600	CHCG	60633	3279	3E-14S	E7
13100	CHCG	60633	3351	2E-15S	D1
14500	BNHM	60633	3351	3E-16S	E4
14500	CTCY	60409	3351	3E-16S	E4
W Manitoba Dr					
7400	PSHT	60463	3274	9W-15S	D7
Manitou Ct					
16400	HMGN	60441	3422	15W-19S	B2
Manitou Rd					
12200	HMGN	60441	3422	15W-19S	B3
Manitowac St					
300	PKFT	60466	3595	3W-27S	A5
N Mankato Av					
7000	CHCG	60646	2919	7W-8N	B1
Mann Dr					
-	CHCG	60629	3150	3W-7S	E6
-	CHCG	60629	3151	3W-7S	A6
Mann Pl					
500	ELGN	60120	2855		A2
Mann St					
4300	OKFT	60452	3426	5W-19S	B2
Mannheim Rd					
-	CHCG	60176	2917	12W-6N	B6
-	CHCG	60666	2973	12W-5N	B1
-	SRPK	60176	2917	12W-6N	B6
10	BLWD	60104	3029	13W-0N	A3
10	BLWD	60160	3029	13W-0N	A4
10	MLPK	60160	3029	13W-0N	A4
300	DSPN	60016	2863	13W-10N	A4
500	BLWD	60162	3029	12W-0N	A4
500	HLSD	60162	3029	12W-0N	A4
900	DSPN	60016	2862	13W-10N	E5
1000	DSPN	60018	2862	13W-10N	E6
1700	DSPN	60018	2863	13W-9N	A6
2000	DSPN	60018	2917	13W-8N	A1
2000	RSMT	60018	2917	13W-8N	A1
2400	FNPK	60131	2973	12W-3N	A4
2400	FNPK	60164	2973	13W-3N	A6
2400	LydT	60131	2973	13W-3N	A6
2400	LydT	60164	2973	13W-3N	A6
2900	CHCG	60666	2917	12W-7N	A3
2900	RSMT	60666	2917	12W-8N	A2
3700	SRPK	60176	2973	13W-4N	A2
4000	FNPK	60176	2973	13W-4N	A2
Mannheim Rd US-12					
-	CHCG	60176	2917	12W-6N	B6
-	CHCG	60666	2973	12W-5N	B1
-	SRPK	60176	2917	12W-6N	B6
10	BLWD	60104	3029	13W-0N	A4
10	BLWD	60160	3029	13W-0N	A4
10	MLPK	60160	3029	13W-0N	A4
300	DSPN	60016	2863	13W-10N	A4
500	BLWD	60162	3029	12W-0N	A4
500	HLSD	60162	3029	12W-0N	A4
1000	DSPN	60016	2862	13W-10N	E6
1000	DSPN	60018	2862	13W-10N	E6
1700	DSPN	60018	2863	13W-9N	A6
2000	DSPN	60018	2917	13W-8N	A1
2000	RSMT	60018	2917	13W-8N	A1
2400	FNPK	60131	2973	12W-3N	A4
2400	FNPK	60164	2973	13W-3N	A6
2400	LydT	60131	2973	13W-3N	A6
2400	LydT	60164	2973	13W-3N	A6
2900	CHCG	60666	2917	12W-7N	A3
2900	RSMT	60666	2917	12W-8N	A2
3700	SRPK	60176	2973	13W-4N	A2
4000	FNPK	60176	2973	13W-4N	A2
Mannheim Rd US-20					
10	BLWD	60104	3029	13W-0N	A4
10	BLWD	60160	3029	13W-0N	A4
10	MLPK	60160	3029	13W-0N	A4
500	BLWD	60162	3029	12W-0N	A4
500	HLSD	60162	3029	12W-0N	A4
Mannheim Rd US-45					
-	CHCG	60176	2917	12W-6N	B6
-	CHCG	60666	2973	12W-5N	B1
-	SRPK	60176	2917	12W-6N	B6
10	BLWD	60104	3029	13W-0N	A4
10	BLWD	60160	3029	13W-0N	A4
10	MLPK	60160	3029	13W-0N	A4
300	DSPN	60016	2863	13W-10N	A4
500	BLWD	60162	3029	12W-0N	A4
500	HLSD	60162	3029	12W-0N	A4
1000	DSPN	60016	2862	13W-10N	E6
1000	DSPN	60018	2862	13W-10N	E6
1700	DSPN	60018	2863	13W-9N	A6
2000	DSPN	60018	2917	13W-8N	A1
2000	RSMT	60018	2917	13W-8N	A1
2400	FNPK	60131	2973	12W-3N	A4
2400	FNPK	60164	2973	13W-3N	A6
2400	LydT	60131	2973	13W-3N	A6
2400	LydT	60164	2973	13W-3N	A6
2900	CHCG	60666	2917	12W-7N	A3
2900	RSMT	60666	2917	12W-8N	A2
3700	SRPK	60176	2973	13W-4N	A2
4000	FNPK	60176	2973	13W-4N	A2
N Mannheim Rd					
-	BLWD	60160	3029	12W-1N	A3
-	HLSD	60104	3029	12W-0S	A6
-	HLSD	60154	3029	12W-0S	A6
-	WSTR	60154	3029	12W-0S	A6
10	BLWD	60104	3029	12W-0S	A5
10	BLWD	60162	3029	12W-0S	A5
10	HLSD	60162	3029	12W-0S	A5
1500	MLPK	60160	3029	12W-1N	A2
1500	MLPK	60165	3029	12W-1N	A2
1500	SNPK	60165	3029	13W-1N	A2
2000	LydT	60164	2973	13W-2N	A7
2000	MLPK	60160	2973	12W-2N	A7
2000	NHLK	60164	2973	12W-2N	A7
2300	LydT	60131	2973	13W-2N	A7
N Mannheim Rd US-12					
-	BLWD	60160	3029	12W-1N	A3
-	HLSD	60104	3029	12W-0S	A6
-	HLSD	60154	3029	12W-0S	A6
-	WSTR	60154	3029	12W-0S	A6
10	BLWD	60104	3029	12W-0S	A5
10	BLWD	60162	3029	12W-0S	A5
10	HLSD	60162	3029	12W-0S	A5
1500	MLPK	60160	3029	12W-1N	A2
1500	MLPK	60165	3029	12W-1N	A2
1500	SNPK	60165	3029	13W-1N	A2
2000	LydT	60164	2973	13W-2N	A7
2000	MLPK	60160	2973	12W-2N	A7
2000	NHLK	60164	2973	12W-2N	A7
2300	LydT	60131	2973	13W-2N	A7
N Mannheim Rd US-20					
-	BLWD	60160	3029	12W-1N	A3
-	HLSD	60104	3029	12W-0S	A6
-	MLPK	60160	3029	12W-1N	A2
-	MLPK	60165	3029	12W-1N	A2
-	SNPK	60165	3029	12W-1N	A2
-	WSTR	60154	3029	12W-0S	A6
10	BLWD	60104	3029	12W-0S	A5
10	BLWD	60162	3029	12W-0S	A5
10	HLSD	60162	3029	12W-0S	A5
N Mannheim Rd US-45					
-	BLWD	60160	3029	12W-1N	A3
-	HLSD	60104	3029	12W-0S	A6
-	HLSD	60154	3029	12W-0S	A6
-	WSTR	60154	3029	12W-0S	A6
10	BLWD	60104	3029	12W-0S	A5
10	BLWD	60162	3029	12W-0S	A5
10	HLSD	60162	3029	12W-0S	A5
1500	MLPK	60160	3029	12W-1N	A2
1500	MLPK	60165	3029	12W-1N	A2
1500	SNPK	60165	3029	13W-1N	A2
2000	LydT	60164	2973	13W-2N	A7
2000	MLPK	60160	2973	12W-2N	A7
2000	NHLK	60164	2973	12W-2N	A7
2300	LydT	60131	2973	13W-2N	A7
S Mannheim Rd					
-	BLWD	60104	3029	12W-0S	A6
-	HLSD	60154	3029	12W-0S	A6
10	HLSD	60162	3029	12W-0S	A6
10	WSTR	60154	3029	13W-1S	A7
300	PvsT	60162	3029	13W-1S	A7
1300	PvsT	60154	3029	13W-1S	A7
1400	PvsT	60154	3087	12W-1S	A1
1400	PvsT	60162	3087	12W-1S	A1
1400	WSTR	60154	3087	12W-1S	A1
S Mannheim Rd US-12					
-	BLWD	60104	3029	12W-0S	A6
-	HLSD	60154	3029	12W-0S	A6
10	HLSD	60162	3029	12W-0S	A6
10	WSTR	60154	3029	13W-1S	A7
300	PvsT	60162	3029	13W-1S	A7
1300	PvsT	60154	3029	13W-1S	A7
1400	PvsT	60154	3087	12W-1S	A1
1400	PvsT	60162	3087	12W-1S	A1
1400	WSTR	60154	3087	12W-1S	A1
S Mannheim Rd US-20					
-	BLWD	60104	3029	12W-0S	A6
-	HLSD	60154	3029	12W-0S	A6
10	HLSD	60162	3029	12W-0S	A6
10	WSTR	60154	3029	13W-1S	A7
300	PvsT	60162	3029	13W-1S	A7
1300	PvsT	60154	3029	13W-1S	A7
1400	PvsT	60154	3087	12W-1S	A1
1400	PvsT	60162	3087	12W-1S	A1
1400	WSTR	60154	3087	12W-1S	A1
S Mannheim Rd US-45					
-	BLWD	60104	3029	12W-0S	A6
-	HLSD	60154	3029	12W-0S	A6
10	HLSD	60162	3029	12W-0S	A6
10	WSTR	60154	3029	13W-1S	A7
300	PvsT	60162	3029	13W-1S	A7
1300	PvsT	60154	3029	13W-1S	A7
1400	PvsT	60154	3087	12W-1S	A1
1400	PvsT	60162	3087	12W-1S	A1
1400	WSTR	60154	3087	12W-1S	A1
Manomet Ct					
600	SMBG	60173	2859	22W-11N	C3
Manomet Ln					
800	SMBG	60173	2859	22W-11N	C3
Manomet on Auburn					
10	RGMW	60008	2806	19W-14N	C3
Manor Av					
-	PTHT	60070	2807	15W-15N	E2
7600	MNSR	46321	3430		D6
8700	MNSR	46321	3510		D1
14100	DLTN	60419	3350	0E-16S	D3
N Manor Av					
4400	CHCG	60618	2920	3W-5N	E7
4400	CHCG	60625	2920	3W-5N	E7
W Manor Av					
10000	FNPK	60131	2973	12W-3N	B5
Manor Cir					
500	SMBG	60194	2857	26W-11N	E4
Manor Ct					
200	DLTN	60419	3350	0E-16S	D3
600	DSPN	60016	2862	14W-11N	C4
3300	SKOK	60203	2866	4W-11N	D2
W Manor Ct					
800	GNWD	60425	3428	0W-22S	B7
Manor Dr					
10	MTSN	60443	3505	6W-24S	E5
200	BFGV	60089	2754	17W-20N	C1
1000	SMWD	60107	2857	28W-9N	A7
1200	WLMT	60091	2811	6W-14N	D4
2800	NHBK	60062	2809	11W-16N	D1
6300	BRRG	60527	3146		D6
N Manor Dr					
3200	LNSG	60438	3510	4E-22S	B1
S Manor Dr					
400	PTON	60468	3860	9W-37S	D4
3200	LNSG	60438	3510	4E-22S	B1
Manor Ln					
700	BmdT	60143	2913		D6
1500	NLES	60714	2863	11W-10N	D5
1500	PKRG	60714	2863	11W-10N	D5
2700	PKRG	60068	2863	11W-10N	D5
15200	HMGN	60441	3343	18W-18S	B7
N Manor Ln					
5600	CHCG	60631	2918	10W-7N	B5
5600	LydT	60631	2918	10W-7N	B5
5600	MaiT	60631	2918	10W-7N	B5
W Mansard Ln					
1700	EGvT	60056	2861	17W-10N	C5
1700	MPPT	60056	2861	17W-10N	C5
Mansfield Av					
7900	BRBK	60459	3211	7W-9S	C2
8500	BRBK	60453	3211	7W-9S	C4
9300	MNGV	60053	2865	7W-11N	C2
10100	OKLN	60453	3211	7W-11S	C7
10100	OKLN	60453	3275	7W-11S	C1
10400	CHRG	60415	3275	7W-12S	C1
11000	ALSP	60482	3275	7W-12S	C3
11000	CHRG	60482	3275	7W-12S	C3
Mansfield Ct					
300	BRLT	60103	2911		B5
800	SMBG	60194	2858	25W-11N	A3
1600	ROSL	60172	2912		B4
Mansfield Dr					
9000	TYPK	60477	3424	11W-21S	A7
18000	TYPK	60477	3423	11W-21S	E7
S Mansfield St					
12300	ALSP	60803	3275	7W-14S	C7
Mansfield Wy					
200	ROSL	60172	2912		B4
W Manshire Pl					
100	MPPT	60056	2807	16W-14N	D4
Manteca Ct					
700	UYPK	60466	3684	3W-29S	A2
N Manton Av					
5700	CHCG	60646	2919	7W-7N	C4
Mantua Ct					
10	PKFT	60466	3595	4W-27S	A4
Mantua St					
200	PKFT	60466	3594	4W-27S	E4
200	PKFT	60466	3595	4W-27S	A4
Manu Ct					
2700	GNVW	60025	2809	11W-15N	E2
Manzella Ln					
1200	GNVW	60025	2810	10W-13N	A6
Maple					
-	ELGN	60120	2855		C7
Maple Av					
-	CHCG	60613	2977	1W-5N	D1
-	DndT	60118	2801		C4
-	EDND	60118	2801		C4
100	EVTN	60201	2813	2W-13N	B6
100	WLMT	60091	2813	3W-13N	A6
200	SCHT	60411	3595	1W-27S	E4
200	SCHT	60411	3596	1W-27S	A4
400	AddT	60191	2915		B6
400	CPVL	60110	2748		A7
500	WLSP	60480	3209	12W-9S	C4
600	BmdT	60157	2913		D5
600	DLTN	60419	3350	0W-17S	B4
600	PlsT	60480	3209	12W-9S	C4
600	RVDL	60827	3350	0W-17S	B4
800	HMWD	60430	3428	1W-21S	A6
900	EVTN	60202	2867	2W-10N	B4
1200	BRWN	60402	3030	8W-1S	E7
1200	OKPK	60304	3030	8W-1S	E7
1200	WLMT	60091	2812	4W-13N	D6
1400	BRWN	60402	3088	8W-1S	E1
1600	HRPK	60133	2911		C3
1700	EVTN	60201	2867	2W-11N	B2
2000	NHBK	60062	2757	10W-17N	A6
3100	BKFD	60513	3087	11W-3S	D5
3100	LGPK	60513	3087	11W-3S	D5
3100	LGPK	60525	3087	11W-3S	D5
3600	NfdT	60062	2756	12W-17N	B6
3600	NHBK	60062	2756	12W-17N	B6
4000	RNPK	60471	3594	5W-26S	C3
4100	LYNS	60534	3088	9W-4S	D7
4100	SKNY	60402	3088	8W-4S	E7
4400	FTVW	60402	3088	8W-4S	E7
4500	BKFD	60513	3147	11W-4S	D1
4500	FTVW	60402	3148	8W-4S	E1
8900	LynT	60480	3208		D5
8900	WLSP	60480	3208		D5
9900	OKLN	60453	3211	6W-11S	D7
10100	OKLN	60453	3275	6W-11S	D1
11900	BLID	60406	3277	3W-15S	B7
11900	CHCG	60655	3277	3W-14S	B6
13000	BLID	60406	3349	3W-15S	B1
13100	LMNT	60439	3343	18W-15S	B2
13300	HMGN	60441	3343	18W-15S	B2
13800	ODPK	60462	3346	10W-16S	B3
17500	CCHL	60478	3426	5W-21S	C5
18500	CCHL	60478	3506	5W-22S	C1
E Maple Av					
10	ROSL	60172	2913		B5
600	BKFD	60513	3087	12W-4S	D7
600	LGNG	60525	3087	12W-4S	C7
N Maple Av					
-	AddT	60191	2915		B6
-	NRIV	60546	3087	11W-2S	D2
100	BMDL	60108	2913		A7
100	PTHT	60070	2808	15W-15N	A3
200	WDDL	60191	2915		B7
300	OKPK	60302	3030	8W-0N	D3
600	PLTN	60067	2752	22W-16N	C6
700	ITSC	60143	2914		C5
1100	BKFD	60513	3087	11W-2S	D3
1100	LGPK	60513	3087	11W-2S	D4
1100	LGPK	60525	3087	11W-2S	D3
1500	PvsT	60513	3087	11W-2S	D3
1500	PvsT	60525	3087	11W-2S	D3
S Maple Av					
100	HLSD	60162	3028		E7
100	OKPK	60302	3030	8W-0S	D5
900	OKPK	60304	3030	8W-0S	D6
1100	BRWN	60402	3030	8W-0S	D7
W Maple Av					
10	LGNG	60525	3087	12W-4S	B7
10	ROSL	60172	2913		A5
100	BmdT	60172	2912		E5
100	ROSL	60172	2912		E5
800	LGNG	60525	3147	13W-4S	A1
1400	WNSP	60558	3147	13W-4S	A1
5700	BKLY	60163	3028		C4
5700	BLID	60162	3028		C4
5700	HLSD	60163	3028		C4
8100	NRDG	60706	2918	10W-5N	B7
8200	NRDG	60706	2974	10W-5N	A1
8300	CHCG	60656	2974	10W-5N	A1
Maple Av E					
-	ELGN	60120	2855		D7
Maple Ct					
10	CTCY	60409	3351	2E-16S	C4
500	BmdT	60157	2913		D7
600	EGVV	60007	2915		A1
600	MPPT	60056	2808	15W-13N	A5
800	UYPK	60466	3684	3W-30S	A2

STREET Block	City	ZIP	Map#	CGS	Grid
Maple Ct					
900	BRLT	60103	2910		D6
4400	RGMW	60008	2806	19W-12N	C7
6700	BGVW	60455	3148	9W-7S	C6
9100	SJHN	46373	3687		E1
9200	MNGV	60053	2864	9W-11N	C2
15400	OKFT	60452	3347	8W-18S	B7
15500	HMGN	60441	3344	16W-18S	A7
15500	HMGN	60441	3422	16W-18S	A1
16500	SHLD	60473	3428	0E-19S	E2
E Maple Ct					
400	GNWD	60425	3508	0E-22S	E1
S Maple Ct					
100	PLTN	60067	2805	21W-15N	D1
Maple Dr					
400	WLNG	60090	2755	13W-17N	D5
500	BFGV	60089	2754	17W-18N	B2
500	SMWD	60107	2911		B2
7200	JSTC	60458	3148	10W-7S	B7
8800	ODPK	60462	3346	11W-17S	A5
9100	SJHN	46373	3687		E1
9500	RSMT	60018	2917	11W-7N	C3
15300	OKFT	60452	3347	8W-18S	A7
17500	LNSG	60438	3430	4E-20S	C5
E Maple Dr					
100	GNWD	60425	3508	0E-22S	E1
500	GNWD	60425	3509	0E-22S	A1
N Maple Dr					
800	CHHT	60411	3507	1W-24S	E6
800	CHHT	60411	3508	1W-24S	A6
W Maple Dr					
100	CHHT	60411	3507	1W-24S	E6
Maple Ln					
-	BmnT	60426	3426	5W-19S	B2
200	HLSD	60162	3028		E5
200	MNSR	46321	3430		D7
200	ThtT	60476	3428	0E-21S	E6
200	TNTN	60476	3428	0E-21S	E6
300	EGVV	60007	2915		A2
700	BNVL	60106	2915		D7
700	HFET	60194	2858	24W-11N	D4
700	LynT	60458	3209	11W-8S	E1
800	PTHT	60070	2755	15W-16N	A6
800	WLNG	60090	2755	15W-16N	A6
900	BRLT	60103	2910		D6
1100	PTHT	60090	2755	15W-16N	A6
1100	WNSP	60558	3146		D4
1200	GNVW	60025	2811	7W-14N	A4
2300	RGMW	60008	2806	19W-12N	C7
3200	HLCT	60429	3426	4W-20S	E4
3200	HLCT	60429	3427	4W-20S	A4
5500	BmnT	60445	3347	6W-17S	D4
5500	MDLN	60445	3347	6W-17S	D4
9300	MaiT	60016	2863	11W-11N	D2
15300	MKHM	60426	3348	4W-18S	E7
N Maple Ln					
1900	ANHT	60004	2807	16W-16N	C1
S Maple Ln					
10	PTHT	60070	2808	15W-14N	A4
200	MPPT	60056	2808	15W-14N	A4
200	PTHT	60056	2808	15W-14N	A4
8900	HYHL	60457	3210	11W-10S	A5
W Maple Ln					
10	PSHT	60463	3275	8W-14S	B7
800	PTON	60468	3860	10W-37S	D4
1600	CteT	60417	3595	2W-28S	E6
1600	STGR	60417	3595	2W-28S	E6
1700	CteT	60475	3595	2W-28S	E6
8900	HYHL	60457	3209	11W-10S	E5
8900	HYHL	60457	3210	11W-10S	A5
Maple Pl					
1700	SMBG	60173	2859	21W-12N	E1
Maple Rd					
100	BRTN	60010	2751	25W-20N	A1
800	FSMR	60422	3506	4W-22S	D2
2400	HMWD	60430	3427	3W-21S	B6
Maple Row					
200	NHFD	60093	2758	7W-16N	A7
Maple St					
10	CTSD	60525	3147	12W-6S	C4
100	MYWD	60153	3030	10W-0N	A4
100	RVFT	60305	3030	10W-0N	A4
200	BCHR	60401	3864	0W-36S	D1
400	WNKA	60093	2812	4W-15N	B1
700	MYWD	60153	3029	11W-0N	E4
800	WNSP	60558	3086		D7
1400	DSPN	60018	2863	12W-9N	B7
1400	GNVW	60025	2809	12W-14N	B5
1600	GNVW	60062	2809	12W-14N	B5
1700	NHFD	60093	2811	7W-15N	C2
2200	DSPN	60018	2917	12W-8N	B1
2400	FNPK	60171	2973	11W-3N	D6
2400	RVGV	60171	2973	11W-3N	D6
3000	FNPK	60131	2973	11W-3N	D4
6500	MNGV	60053	2865	8W-11N	A2
6600	MNGV	60053	2864	8W-11N	E2
7800	NLES	60053	2864	9W-11N	B2
7800	NLES	60714	2864	9W-11N	B2
15400	DLTN	60419	3350	0E-18S	E7
15400	SHLD	60473	3350	0E-18S	E7
16600	SHLD	60473	3428	0E-19S	E2
18200	LNSG	60438	3430	4E-21S	C7
19200	LNSG	60438	3510	4E-22S	C2
21100	MTSN	60443	3506	4W-25S	D7
21100	OMFD	60461	3506	4W-25S	D7
21200	MTSN	60443	3594	4W-25S	D1
E Maple St					
10	ANHT	60005	2807	17W-13N	A6
10	HNDL	60521	3146		B1
2000	CteT	60417	3686	2E-30S	D2
N Maple St					
10	MPPT	60056	2808	15W-13N	A7
10	PLTN	60067	2805	21W-16N	D1
100	PLTN	60067	2752	21W-16N	D7
200	ITSC	60143	2914		C6
300	PTHT	60070	2808	15W-15N	A2
2400	RVGV	60171	2974	10W-3N	A5
S Maple St					
10	MPPT	60056	2808	15W-12N	A7
100	ITSC	60143	2914		C7
100	PLTN	60067	2805	21W-15N	D1
200	MPPT	60056	2862	15W-12N	A1
900	DSPN	60016	2862	15W-11N	A3
900	DSPN	60056	2862	15W-11N	A3
27400	CteT	60401	3774	1W-33S	A2
W Maple St					
10	ANHT	60005	2807	18W-13N	A6
10	CHCG	60610	3034	0W-1N	B2
10	CHCG	60611	3034	0W-1N	B2
10	HNDL	60521	3146		A1
500	ANHT	60005	2806	18W-13N	E6
3200	ENGN	60805	3212	4W-11S	E6
Maple Ter					
4300	CCHL	60478	3506	5W-22S	C1
Maple Wy					
-	ELGN	60120	2855		C7
Maplebrook Ct					
200	SMBG	60194	2859	22W-10N	C5
Maplebrook Dr					
-	RchT	60443	3593	8W-26S	C2
6200	MTSN	60443	3593	7W-26S	C2
Maple Creek Dr					
-	TYPK	60477	3424	9W-22S	E7
-	TYPK	60477	3504	9W-22S	E1
Maplecreek Dr					
14600	ODPK	60467	3344	14W-17S	D5
14600	OrlT	60467	3344	14W-17S	D5
Maple Crest Ct					
9700	PSHL	60465	3209	11W-11S	E7
Maple Hill Rd					
10	GLNC	60022	2758	6W-18N	D3
Maple Leaf Dr					
3000	GNVW	60025	2810	10W-15N	A3
3600	GNVW	60025	2809	10W-15N	E3
Maple Ln Dr					
6500	TYPK	60477	3425	8W-20S	B3
Maples Ct					
600	NfdT	60025	2809	11W-13N	D7
Mapleton Av					
800	OKPK	60302	3031	7W-1N	B2
Mapletree Ln					
100	DndT	60110	2748		A6
Maplewood Av					
-	MKHM	60426	3427	3W-19S	B3
1400	HRPK	60133	2911		E3
7000	HMND	46324	3430		E4
14700	HRVY	60426	3349	3W-17S	B6
N Maplewood Av					
800	CHCG	60612	3033	3W-1N	A2
1200	CHCG	60622	3033	3W-1N	A1
1500	CHCG	60647	3033	3W-2N	A1
2100	CHCG	60647	2977	3W-2N	A6
4000	CHCG	60618	2977	3W-5N	A1
4400	CHCG	60618	2921	3W-5N	A7
4700	CHCG	60625	2921	3W-5N	A7
5500	CHCG	60659	2921	3W-7N	A4
6300	CHCG	60645	2921	3W-7N	A3
7500	CHCG	60645	2867	3W-9N	A6
7500	EVTN	60202	2867	3W-9N	A6
S Maplewood Av					
200	NHLK	60164	3028		E2
600	CHCG	60612	3033	3W-0S	A6
3500	CHCG	60608	3091	3W-3S	A5
3500	CHCG	60632	3091	3W-3S	A5
4700	CHCG	60632	3151	3W-5S	A1
5500	CHCG	60629	3151	3W-7S	A6
7900	CHCG	60652	3213	3W-9S	B2
9600	ENGN	60805	3213	3W-11S	B7
9800	ENGN	60655	3213	3W-11S	B7
10000	CHCG	60655	3213	3W-11S	B7
10200	CHCG	60655	3277	3W-12S	B2
11800	BLID	60406	3277	3W-13S	B5
Maplewood Ct					
9200	ODHL	60477	3423	11W-19S	E2
16400	TYPK	60477	3425	8W-19S	A3
Maplewood Dr					
800	ITSC	60143	2914		A6
7200	JSTC	60458	3148	10W-8S	A7
7200	JSTC	60458	3210	10W-8S	A1
Maplewood Ln					
-	RchT	60443	3506	5W-25S	B7
200	SMBG	60193	2859	22W-9N	D6
1700	GNVW	60025	2810	8W-13N	E5
S Maplewood Ln					
200	BRLT	60103	2910		C3
W Maplewood Ln					
1000	BRLT	60103	2910		C3
Maplewood Rd					
100	RVSD	60546	3088	10W-3S	B4
1900	NfdT	60062	2757	10W-18N	B2
10700	CTSD	60525	3147	13W-7S	A7
10800	CTSD	60525	3146		E6
Maplewood St					
9000	SJHN	46373	3598		E7
9000	SJHN	46373	3687		E1
Marathon Ct					
20500	OMFD	60461	3506	4W-24S	E6
Marberry Dr					
-	MPPT	60056	2808	15W-14N	A3
-	MPPT	60070	2808	15W-14N	A3
10	PTHT	60070	2808	15W-14N	A3
Marberry Ln					
10	PTHT	60070	2808	15W-14N	A3
Marbilynn Dr					
900	ELGN	60120	2855		C1
Marble Ln					
-	CPVL	60110	2748		B3
W Marble Pl					
10	CHCG	60603	3034	0W-0S	B5
100	CHCG	60606	3034	0W-0S	B5
600	CHCG	60661	3034	0W-0S	A5
E Marble St					
10	CTCY	46327	3352		D4
10	HMND	46327	3352		C4
Marble Hill Ct					
10	SMBG	60193	2859	23W-10N	B5
Marbury Ln					
10	BNHL	60010	2750	25W-17N	E4
Marcee Ln					
1700	NHBK	60062	2757	9W-17N	C5
Marcella Rd					
600	DSPN	60016	2808	14W-12N	C7
600	MPPT	60016	2808	14W-12N	C7
600	MPPT	60056	2808	14W-12N	C7
N Marcella Rd					
10	DSPN	60016	2808	14W-13N	C7
10	MPPT	60056	2808	14W-13N	C6
N Marcey St					
1600	CHCG	60614	2977	1W-2N	E7
Marcia Ct					
300	BRLT	60103	2911		A3
E Marcus Ct					
1400	PKRG	60068	2863	11W-10N	E4
W Marcus Ct					
1400	PKRG	60068	2863	11W-10N	D4
Marcy Av					
2300	EVTN	60201	2866	4W-12N	C1
2700	EVTN	60201	2812	4W-13N	C7
2700	WLMT	60091	2812	4W-13N	C7
Marcy Ln					
1300	WLNG	60090	2754	16W-17N	D4
Marden Ct					
2700	NHBK	60062	2756	10W-17N	E5
Mardjetko Dr					
5200	HFET	60192	2802	30W-12N	C7
Marengo Av					
10	FTPK	60130	3030	9W-0N	D5
1400	FTPK	60130	3088	9W-1S	D1
1500	NRIV	60130	3088	9W-1S	D1
Margail Av					
9300	MaiT	60016	2863	11W-11N	D2
N Margaret Av					
20500	BFGV	60089	2754	16W-20N	E1
20500	VrnT	60069	2754	16W-20N	E1
Margaret Ct					
-	LYWD	60411	3510	3E-23S	A3
Margaret Ln					
8700	TYPK	60477	3424	10W-20S	A4
Margaret Pl					
600	ELGN	60120	2855		B5
Margaret St					
600	DLTN	60419	3350	0E-16S	E4
800	DSPN	60016	2862	13W-10N	E4
1200	DSPN	60018	2862	13W-10N	E5
E Margaret St					
100	TNTN	60476	3428	0E-21S	E6
500	ThtT	60476	3428	0E-21S	E6
W Margaret St					
100	TNTN	60476	3428	0W-21S	B6
300	TNTN	60430	3428	0W-21S	B6
4800	MONE	60449	3683	6W-31S	A6
4800	MonT	60449	3683	6W-31S	B6
5500	MONE	60449	3682	7W-31S	E6
Margaret Curtis Ln					
5100	CTWD	60445	3347	6W-16S	E3
5100	MDLN	60445	3347	6W-16S	E3
5100	MDLN	60445	3348	6W-16S	A3
Margarets Courtyard					
6900	TYPK	60477	3425	8W-19S	A2
Margate Ct					
10	SMBG	60193	2859	23W-10N	B5
Margate Ln					
700	PTHT	60070	2808	14W-14N	C3
W Margate Ter					
800	CHCG	60640	2921	1W-6N	E6
Margate on Oxford					
10	RGMW	60008	2805	20W-14N	E4
Margerita Av					
8300	ODPK	60462	3346	10W-16S	B4
Margie Ln					
5400	OKFT	60452	3425	6W-19S	D1
5500	BmnT	60477	3425	6W-19S	D1
5500	OKFT	60477	3425	6W-19S	D1
Margo Ln					
3000	NHBK	60062	2809	11W-16N	D1
9700	MNSR	46321	3510		D3
Margraf Ct					
200	DYR	46311	3598		D3
Marguerite St					
1500	PKRG	60068	2863	11W-10N	E6
Margust Ln					
14700	HMGN	60441	3343	18W-17S	B6
Maria Av					
2800	NHBK	60062	2756	11W-18N	E3
N Maria Ct					
4600	CHCG	60656	2918	10W-5N	A7
4700	NRDG	60656	2918	10W-5N	A7
4700	NRDG	60706	2918	10W-5N	A7
Maria St					
400	TNTN	60476	3428	0E-21S	E6
Marian Dr					
12700	LMNT	60439	3271		A7
12700	LMNT	60439	3343	18W-15S	A1
Marian Ln					
2500	WLMT	60091	2812	5W-13N	A5
Maricopa Ln					
10	HFET	60194	2859	23W-11N	A4
10	SMBG	60194	2859	23W-11N	A4
100	HFET	60194	2858	23W-11N	E4
Maridon Rd					
7300	CTSD	60525	3209	12W-8S	B1
Marie Dr					
100	IVNS	60010	2751	23W-17N	D5
100	IVNS	60067	2751	23W-17N	D5
500	SHLD	60473	3428	0E-19S	E2
Marie Ln					
300	SMBG	60193	2858	24W-10N	D6
1600	GNVW	60025	2809	11W-14N	E4
9200	SRPK	60176	2973	11W-5N	C2
Mariel Cir					
22400	DRPK	60010	2752	22W-20N	B1
Marigold Cir					
300	MTSN	60443	3593	7W-26S	C2
Marigold Dr					
2600	SLVL	60411	3597	3E-26S	E3
Marigold Ln					
1800	HRPK	60133	2911		C2
W Marigold Ln					
4700	MONE	60449	3683	5W-31S	B4
Marigold Pl					
16100	ODHL	60477	3424	11W-19S	A2
Marik Rd					
900	BLWD	60104	3029	12W-0S	B5
N Marilyn Av					
100	NHLK	60164	2972		E7
100	NHLK	60164	3028		E1
S Marilyn Av					
100	NHLK	60164	3028		E1
Marilyn Ct					
1400	RGMW	60008	2806	20W-14N	A3
11100	ODPK	60467	3344	13W-16S	E4
16500	ODHL	60477	3424	11W-19S	A3
Marilyn Dr					
3800	RNPK	60471	3594	4W-27S	D5
16900	TYPK	60477	3424	10W-20S	C4
17000	OrlT	60477	3424	10W-20S	C4
Marilyn Ter					
14000	ODPK	60467	3344	13W-16S	E3
Marilynn Ln					
14700	HMGN	60441	3343	18W-17S	A6
Marina Ct					
700	UYPK	60466	3684	3W-29S	A2
Marina Dr					
-	ALSP	60803	3275	6W-14S	D6
10	DSPN	60016	2862	15W-12N	B2
100	MPPT	60016	2862	15W-12N	B2
100	MPPT	60056	2862	15W-12N	B2
S Marina Dr					
-	DSPN	60016	2862	15W-12N	B1
-	MPPT	60016	2862	15W-12N	B1
500	MPPT	60056	2862	15W-12N	B1
Marina Ter E					
800	BRLT	60103	2911		B4
Marina Ter W					
800	BRLT	60103	2911		A4
N Marine Dr					
-	CHCG	60613	2922	0W-5N	A7
4000	CHCG	60613	2978	0W-5N	A1
4400	CHCG	60640	2921	0W-5N	E6
4400	CHCG	60640	2922	0W-5N	A7
Mariner Ct					
700	ELGN	60120	2855		D6
2700	LYWD	60411	3510	3E-23S	A3
Mariner Dr					
600	ELGN	60120	2855		D5
Mariner Pt					
700	SMBG	60194	2859	22W-10N	C5
Marino Ct					
10	AddT	60143	2914		D4
10	ITSC	60143	2914		D4
Marion Av					
600	HDPK	60035	2758	7W-20N	A2
2800	LydT	60164	2972		D5
2800	NHLK	60164	2972		D5
3100	FNPK	60131	2972		D5
9100	MNGV	60053	2864	8W-11N	D2
9500	OKLN	60453	3211	7W-11S	B6
10000	CHRG	60415	3211	7W-11S	B7
E Marion Av					
10	PTHT	60070	2808	15W-15N	A2
N Marion Av					
100	BRLT	60103	2911		A2
Marion Ct					
10	BlmT	60411	3510	3E-25S	A7
200	BNVL	60106	2972		A2
300	WLNG	60090	2755	15W-17N	A5
16000	SHLD	60473	3429	1E-18S	A1
N Marion Ct					
200	OKPK	60301	3030	8W-0N	E3
200	OKPK	60302	3030	8W-0N	E3
1200	CHCG	60622	3033	2W-1N	C1
Marion Dr					
8000	BGVW	60455	3210	10W-9S	B3
8000	BGVW	60458	3210	10W-9S	B3
8000	JSTC	60458	3210	10W-9S	B3
15900	SHLD	60473	3429	1E-18S	A1
Marion Ln					
10	SMWD	60107	2857	28W-11N	A4
W Marion Rd					
1000	ANHT	60004	2806	18W-15N	E2
Marion St					
200	BNVL	60106	2972		A2
400	ROSL	60172	2913		A4
1200	DSPN	60016	2862	13W-11N	E4
1400	SMBG	60193	2913		A2
1400	SmbT	60193	2913		A2
1500	ROSL	60193	2913		A2
E Marion St					
-	ThtT	60476	3428	0E-21S	E5
100	EMHT	60126	3028		A2
100	TNTN	60476	3428	0E-21S	D5
600	ANHT	60004	2807	17W-15N	B2
1000	PTHT	60004	2807	17W-15N	B2
N Marion St					
100	OKPK	60301	3030	8W-0N	E4
100	OKPK	60302	3030	8W-0N	E3
200	PLTN	60074	2753	20W-16N	A7
S Marion St					
-	OKPK	60301	3030	8W-0N	E4
100	OKPK	60302	3030	8W-0N	E4
W Marion St					
100	PTHT	60070	2808	15W-15N	A2
200	ANHT	60004	2807	18W-15N	A2
200	TNTN	60476	3428	0E-21S	D5
500	PTHT	60070	2807	16W-15N	D2
Marion St N					
700	OKPK	60302	3030	8W-1N	D2
1200	CHCG	60707	3030	8W-2N	D1
Marion Wy					
800	CHHT	60411	3507	2W-24S	D6
Marissa Ct					
10	BRRG	60527	3208		A6
13500	HMGN	60441	3343	16W-17S	D5
Mark Av					
600	DSPN	60016	2808	13W-13N	D7
600	MPPT	60016	2808	14W-13N	D7
600	MPPT	60056	2808	14W-13N	D7
Mark Dr					
100	GNVW	60025	2811	6W-13N	C5
E Mark Dr					
1500	MPPT	60056	2808	14W-13N	D7
Mark Ln					
300	HFET	60010	2857	27W-11N	D4
300	SMWD	60010	2857	27W-11N	D4
300	SMWD	60107	2857	27W-11N	D4
800	WLNG	60090	2754	16W-16N	D6
900	PTHT	60070	2754	16W-16N	D6
11600	OrlT	60467	3344	14W-16S	D3
16300	BmnT	60477	3425	7W-19S	C2
16300	TYPK	60477	3425	7W-19S	C2
Mark St					
100	WDDL	60191	2915		A4
700	EGVV	60007	2915		B4
700	WDDL	60007	2915		B4
1200	BNVL	60106	2915		C4
1200	EGVV	60106	2915		C4
W Mark Ter					
2000	MPPT	60056	2861	17W-12N	B1
Mark Collins Dr					
-	FDHT	60411	3597	1E-26S	B3
-	SLVL	60411	3597	1E-26S	B3
-	STGR	60411	3597	1E-26S	B3
Market St					
2000	BLID	60406	3349	2W-15S	C1
2100	WLSP	60480	3209	12W-10S	B4
Markey Ln					
1600	FSMR	60422	3507	2W-23S	D4
N Markham Av					
5900	CHCG	60646	2919	7W-7N	C4
Markham Dr					
14700	DLTN	60419	3350	0W-17S	C6
14700	HRVY	60426	3350	0W-17S	C6
Mark Thomas Ln					
-	BRLT	60103	2911		B3
2500	HRPK	60133	2911		B3
Marlboro Cir					
1600	CPVL	60110	2748		D7
Marley Brook Ct					
11200	ODPK	60467	3422	14W-21S	E6
Marley Creek Blvd					
17700	ODPK	60448	3422	14W-21S	E7
17700	ODPK	60467	3422	14W-21S	E7
Marley Creek Ln					
11300	ODPK	60467	3422	14W-21S	E6
Marlin Av					
20100	LYWD	60411	3510	3E-23S	A4
Marlin Ct					
2700	HMWD	60430	3427	3W-21S	B7
20000	LYWD	60411	3510	3E-23S	A4
Marlin Ln					
18000	HMWD	60430	3427	3W-21S	B7
Marlowe Av					
1700	PKRG	60068	2917	11W-8N	E1
E Marmion Pl					
1800	CteT	60417	3686	2E-29S	D1
Marmon Ln					
10	BNHL	60010	2750	26W-18N	C2
Marmora Av					
7600	SKOK	60077	2865	7W-9N	B6
8100	MNGV	60053	2865	7W-10N	C5
N Marmora Av					
2100	CHCG	60639	2975	7W-2N	C6
3200	CHCG	60634	2975	7W-4N	C3
4300	CHCG	60630	2975	7W-5N	B1
4800	CHCG	60630	2919	7W-6N	B6
6000	CHCG	60646	2919	7W-7N	B3
Maroon Dr					
1200	ELGN	60120	2855		D5
Maros Ln					
10	OMFD	60461	3507	3W-25S	A7
E Marquardt Dr					
10	WLNG	60090	2755	14W-16N	C7
Marquette Av					
200	BNHM	60633	3351	3E-17S	E5
200	CTCY	60409	3351	3E-17S	E6
S Marquette Av					
7900	CHCG	60649	3215	3E-9S	E2
9100	CHCG	60617	3215	3E-10S	E5
12600	CHCG	60633	3279	3E-14S	E7
14400	BNHM	60633	3351	3E-16S	E4
14500	CTCY	60409	3351	3E-17S	E4
E Marquette Dr					
2000	CHCG	60637	3153	2E-7S	B5
2000	CHCG	60649	3153	2E-7S	C5
E Marquette Dr US-41					
2000	CHCG	60637	3153	2E-7S	C5
2000	CHCG	60649	3153	2E-7S	C5
Marquette Dr N					
7800	TYPK	60477	3424	9W-21S	D5
Marquette Dr S					
7700	TYPK	60477	3424	9W-21S	D6
Marquette Ln					
1700	HFET	60195	2858	25W-12N	A1
Marquette Pl					
10	BFGV	60090	2755	14W-20N	C2
10	PKFT	60466	3595	3W-27S	A4
Marquette Rd					
10	HDPK	60035	2758	8W-20N	A2
10	NfdT	60062	2758	8W-20N	A2
E Marquette Rd					
10	CHCG	60621	3152	0E-7S	C6
10	CHCG	60637	3152	0E-7S	C6
1100	CHCG	60637	3153	1E-7S	A5
W Marquette Rd					
10	CHCG	60621	3152	0W-7S	B5
10	CHCG	60637	3152	0E-7S	C6
900	CHCG	60621	3151	2W-7S	C6
1100	CHCG	60636	3151	1W-7S	E6
2300	CHCG	60629	3151	2W-7S	B6
2900	CHCG	60629	3150	4W-7S	C6
4700	BDPK	60638	3150	5W-7S	A6
4700	CHCG	60638	3150	5W-7S	A6
Marquette St					
100	PKFT	60466	3595	3W-27S	A4
300	PKFT	60466	3594	4W-27S	E4
Marryat Pl					
100	SMWD	60107	2856	29W-10N	D5
Mars Pl					
10	MPPT	60056	2808	15W-14N	A3
10	PTHT	60070	2808	15W-14N	A3
Marseilles Cir					
500	BFGV	60089	2754	16W-20N	C1
Marseilles Ln					
3500	HLCT	60429	3426	4W-21S	E7
Marsh Ln					
6000	MTSN	60443	3505	7W-24S	C6
N Marsha Dr					
800	PLTN	60067	2753	20W-17N	A6
Marshall Av					
10	BLWD	60104	3029	12W-0N	B3
6000	CHRG	60415	3275	7W-12S	C1
6000	OKLN	60453	3275	7W-12S	C1
S Marshall Blvd					
1900	CHCG	60623	3090	3W-2S	E2
Marshall Ct					
3800	BLWD	60104	3029	12W-0N	A4
E Marshall Ct					
800	PLTN	60074	2753	19W-18N	B3
Marshall Dr					
200	DSPN	60016	2862	15W-10N	A5
200	DSPN	60056	2862	15W-11N	A3
200	MPPT	60016	2862	15W-11N	A3
200	MPPT	60056	2862	15W-11N	A3
1400	DSPN	60018	2862	15W-10N	A6
1600	EGvT	60018	2862	15W-9N	A6
Marshall Rd					
200	BNVL	60106	2915		D7
400	NHBK	60062	2758	8W-17N	A5
500	NHBK	60062	2757	8W-17N	E5
E Marshall St					
1300	ANHT	60004	2807	17W-14N	C3
Marshfield Av					
14100	DXMR	60426	3349	2W-16S	E4
14800	HRVY	60426	3349	2W-18S	E7
15600	HRVY	60426	3427	2W-18S	E1
16100	MKHM	60426	3427	2W-19S	E3
16500	HLCT	60426	3427	2W-19S	E3
16500	HLCT	60429	3427	2W-19S	E3
18300	HMWD	60430	3427	2W-22S	E7
18300	HMWD	60430	3507	2W-22S	E1
N Marshfield Av					
400	CHCG	60612	3033	2W-0N	C3
400	CHCG	60622	3033	2W-0N	C3
1600	CHCG	60622	2977	2W-2N	C7
2400	CHCG	60614	2977	2W-3N	C5
3300	CHCG	60657	2977	2W-4N	C3
3500	CHCG	60613	2977	2W-4N	C3
7400	CHCG	60626	2867	2W-9N	C6
S Marshfield Av					
-	BLID	60406	3277	2W-15S	D7
-	CTPK	60406	3277	2W-15S	D7
700	CHCG	60612	3033	2W-0S	D6
3400	CHCG	60608	3091	2W-3S	D5
3400	CHCG	60609	3091	2W-3S	D5
4700	CHCG	60609	3151	2W-5S	D2
5500	CHCG	60636	3151	2W-6S	D3
7500	CHCG	60620	3213	2W-9S	D3
11100	CHCG	60643	3277	2W-13S	D4
11700	CTPK	60643	3277	2W-13S	D4
12100	BLID	60827	3277	2W-14S	D6
12400	CTPK	60827	3277	2W-15S	D7
Marshfield Ln					
8800	ODHL	60477	3424	11W-19S	A2
N Marshfield St					
500	CHCG	60622	3033	2W-0N	C3
Marske Av					
-	RNPK	60471	3594	4W-27S	E5
Marston Ln					
2000	FSMR	60422	3507	2W-22S	C2
N Mart Ct					
600	PLTN	60067	2752	21W-16N	C6

STREET Block	City	ZIP	Map#	CGS	Grid
W Mart Center Dr					
300	CHCG	60606	3034	0W-0N	A4
Martens St					
3400	FNPK	60131	2973	11W-4N	D3
S Martha Av					
14500	BNHM	60633	3351	3E-16S	E4
14500	CTCY	60409	3351	3E-17S	E4
Martha Ln					
10	EVTN	60201	2866	4W-11N	D2
5300	BmnT	60452	3425	6W-20S	E4
5300	OKFT	60452	3425	6W-20S	E4
W Martha Ln					
1700	MPPT	60056	2861	17W-12N	C2
E Martha Pl					
2600	BNHM	60633	3351	3E-16S	E4
Martha St					
900	EGVV	60007	2914		B2
Marti Rd					
17500	HMGN	60448	3422	15W-21S	B6
Martin Av					
2800	LydT	60164	2972		C5
2800	NHLK	60164	2972		C5
3000	FNPK	60131	2972		C5
3000	FNPK	60164	2972		C5
3000	LydT	60131	2972		C5
18000	HMWD	60430	3427	2W-22S	D7
18400	HMWD	60430	3507	2W-22S	D1
Martin Ct					
10	BlmT	60411	3510	3E-25S	A7
10	LMNT	60439	3272	15W-13S	B3
300	BRTN	60010	2751	25W-20N	B1
3300	RGMW	60008	2806	19W-13N	D6
18900	CCHL	60478	3506	5W-22S	B2
Martin Dr					
700	ELGN	60120	2855		C2
4900	HMND	46320	3352		D5
8700	HGKN	60525	3147	11W-7S	D6
N Martin Dr					
800	PLTN	60067	2752	21W-17N	C6
800	PltT	60067	2752	21W-17N	C6
Martin Ln					
10	EGvT	60007	2861	17W-10N	B5
10	EGVV	60007	2861	17W-10N	B5
10	NHFD	60093	2811	7W-15N	A1
100	CHHT	60411	3508	0W-24S	B6
600	VrnT	60015	2755	15W-20N	B1
2600	RGMW	60008	2806	19W-13N	B6
5400	HRPK	60133	2911		C6
9000	BGVW	60455	3210	8W-10S	E5
18900	CCHL	60478	3506	5W-22S	B2
19000	CCHL	60477	3506	5W-22S	B2
19000	RchT	60477	3506	5W-22S	B2
S Martin Ln					
2200	ANHT	60005	2861	18W-11N	A3
W Martin Ln					
1700	MPPT	60056	2861	17W-12N	C2
Martindale Dr					
10800	WSTR	60154	3086		E3
Martindale Dr E					
2400	WSTR	60154	3086		E3
Martindale Dr W					
2400	WSTR	60154	3086		D3
Martin France Cir					
6600	TYPK	60477	3425	8W-21S	B7
Martingale Dr					
900	BRLT	60103	2910		D6
W Martingale Ln					
12500	HMGN	60441	3344	15W-17S	B5
Martingale Rd					
-	EGvT	60007	2914		A1
-	EGvT	60193	2860	20W-9N	A7
-	EGvT	60193	2914		A1
-	EGVV	60007	2914		A1
-	SMBG	60193	2860	21W-9N	A6
-	SmbT	60193	2860	21W-9N	A7
-	SmbT	60193	2914		A1
N Martingale Rd					
-	SMBG	60193	2860	21W-10N	A6
-	SmbT	60193	2860	21W-10N	A6
10	SMBG	60173	2860	21W-10N	A5
Marvin Pkwy					
800	PKRG	60068	2863	11W-9N	E6
Marvin Pl					
300	WLNG	60090	2755	13W-17N	D5
W Marwood Av					
7400	EDPK	60707	2974	9W-3N	C6
N Marwood St					
2500	RVGV	60171	2974	10W-3N	A5
Mary Ct					
10	SLVL	60411	3597	1E-27S	B4
100	BRLT	60103	2911		A3
4900	CCHL	60478	3506	6W-22S	A1
Mary Dr					
13700	ODPK	60462	3345	11W-16S	E3
13700	OrlT	60462	3345	11W-16S	E3
S Mary Ln					
25600	CteT	60417	3687	3E-31S	A4
Mary Pl					
400	ELGN	60120	2855		A4
Mary St					
10	DSPN	60016	2863	13W-12N	A2
10	GLNC	60022	2759	5W-17N	A6
10	GLNC	60093	2759	5W-17N	A6
200	DYR	46311	3598		D3
200	GLNC	60022	2758	5W-17N	E6
200	GLNC	60093	2758	5W-17N	E6
S Mary St					
2700	CHCG	60608	3091	1W-2S	E3
Mary Ann Ct					
5500	BmnT	60477	3425	6W-19S	D2
5500	OKFT	60452	3425	6W-19S	D2
5500	OKFT	60477	3425	6W-19S	D2
Mary Ann Ln					
18100	CCHL	60478	3426	5W-21S	B7
Maryann Ln					
3100	DYR	46311	3598		C5
Mary Belle Cir					
-	BFGV	60089	2754	16W-20N	D1
Mary Byrne Dr					
800	SLVL	60411	3597	1E-27S	A4
800	STGR	60411	3597	1E-27S	A4
800	STGR	60475	3597	1E-27S	A4
Marycrest Dr					
-	CCHL	60477	3506	6W-22S	A2
-	RchT	60477	3506	6W-22S	A2
18300	CCHL	60478	3426	6W-22S	A7
18300	CCHL	60478	3506	6W-22S	A1
Mary Jane Ln					
2000	PKRG	60068	2863	11W-9N	D6
Mary Kay Ln					
-	GNVW	60025	2810	10W-15N	A2
Marylake Ln					
19000	CCHL	60478	3506	6W-22S	A2
19000	RchT	60477	3506	6W-22S	A2
Maryland Av					
2700	FSMR	60422	3507	3W-23S	B3
15000	SHLD	60473	3351	1E-17S	A5
15500	DLTN	60419	3351	1E-18S	A7
16300	SHLD	60473	3429	1E-19S	A2
S Maryland Av					
-	CHCG	60615	3152	1E-5S	E1
300	GNWD	60425	3509	1E-23S	A3
5600	CHCG	60637	3152	1E-6S	E3
7200	CHCG	60619	3152	1E-8S	E7
7500	CHCG	60619	3214	1E-8S	E1
9700	CHCG	60628	3214	1E-11S	E6
10400	CHCG	60628	3278	1E-12S	E1
13400	CHCG	60827	3350	0E-15S	E1
Maryland Ct					
17800	ODPK	60467	3423	12W-21S	C5
Maryland Dr					
1800	EGVV	60007	2913		D1
N Maryland St					
9000	NLES	60714	2864	10W-11N	A3
Mary Lu Ln					
100	BFGV	60089	2754	17W-18N	B2
S Mary Therese Ln					
20100	FftT	60423	3504	10W-24S	D5
Mary Tree Ln					
-	PTON	60468	3860	10W-37S	D4
Maryview Ct					
300	MTSN	60443	3505	6W-24S	E5
Maryview Pkwy					
100	MTSN	60443	3505	6W-24S	E5
Maryville Dr					
-	DSPN	60016	2808	13W-13N	E7
Mashpee Ln					
300	SMBG	60194	2858	24W-10N	D5
Mason Av					
7500	BRBK	60459	3211	7W-8S	C2
8400	MNGV	60053	2865	7W-10N	B4
9700	OKLN	60453	3211	7W-11S	C7
10300	CHRG	60453	3275	7W-12S	C1
10300	OKLN	60453	3275	7W-12S	C1
10400	CHRG	60415	3275	7W-12S	C1
10400	OKLN	60415	3275	7W-12S	C1
11000	ALSP	60482	3275	7W-12S	C3
11000	CHRG	60482	3275	7W-12S	C3
N Mason Av					
10	CHCG	60644	3031	7W-0N	C5
1000	CHCG	60651	3031	7W-1N	B2
1500	CHCG	60639	3031	7W-2N	B1
2100	CHCG	60639	2975	7W-2N	B6
2700	CHCG	60634	2975	7W-3N	B5
4300	CHCG	60630	2975	7W-5N	B1
5400	CHCG	60630	2919	7W-6N	B5
7000	CHCG	60646	2919	7W-8N	C1
S Mason Av					
10	CHCG	60644	3031	7W-0S	C5
1100	CCRO	60804	3031	7W-0S	C7
1100	CHCG	60804	3031	7W-0S	C7
5100	StkT	60638	3149	7W-5S	C2
5500	CHCG	60638	3149	7W-6S	C3
7200	BDPK	60638	3149	7W-8S	C7
7300	BDPK	60638	3211	7W-8S	C1
12400	ALSP	60803	3275	7W-14S	C7
12700	WthT	60463	3275	7W-15S	C7
12900	WthT	60463	3347	7W-15S	C1
Mason Ct					
1200	CHHT	60411	3508	0W-25S	C7
Mason Dr					
600	LGNG	60525	3147	13W-5S	A1
1300	WNSP	60558	3147	13W-5S	A1
4000	HFET	60195	2804	23W-15N	D3
S Mason Dr					
-	CHCG	60644	3031	7W-0S	C5
-	OKPK	60304	3031	7W-0S	C5
700	LGNG	60525	3147	13W-5S	A2
Mason Ln					
-	TYPK	60477	3424	10W-21S	B6
800	DSPN	60016	2863	12W-10N	B4
14300	ODPK	60462	3345	11W-17S	E4
Mason St					
10	CTCY	60409	3352	4E-18S	B7
10	HMND	46320	3352	4E-18S	C7
E Mason St					
10	CTCY	60409	3352		C7
10	HMND	46320	3352		C7
Massachusetts Ct					
17800	ODPK	60467	3423	12W-21S	C5
Massasoit Av					
7700	BRBK	60459	3211	7W-9S	C2
8600	BRBK	60453	3211	7W-9S	D4
9100	OKLN	60453	3211	7W-11S	D6
10400	CHRG	60415	3275	7W-12S	D1
10400	OKLN	60453	3275	7W-12S	D1
11000	ALSP	60482	3275	7W-12S	D3
11000	CHRG	60482	3275	7W-12S	D3
14700	OKFT	60452	3347	7W-17S	D5
N Massasoit Av					
800	CHCG	60644	3031	7W-1N	C3
800	CHCG	60651	3031	7W-1N	C2
1500	CHCG	60639	3031	7W-2N	C1
S Massasoit Av					
5100	CHCG	60638	3149	7W-5S	C2
5100	StkT	60638	3149	7W-5S	C2
7300	BDPK	60638	3149	7W-8S	C7
7300	BDPK	60638	3211	7W-8S	D1
12500	WthT	60463	3275	7W-14S	D7
12500	WthT	60803	3275	7W-14S	D7
Massasoit Ct					
14800	OKFT	60452	3347	7W-17S	D5
Massey Rd					
2400	DndT	60118	2801		C5
Mast Ct					
1200	FSMR	60422	3507	2W-23S	C2
Matfield Ct					
1000	SMBG	60193	2912		C1
Mather Av					
7000	CHRG	60415	3210	8W-11S	E7
S Mather Av					
11200	ALSP	60803	3275	6W-13S	E3
W Mathews Dr					
7200	FftT	60423	3504	9W-25S	E7
7200	FftT	60423	3505	9W-25S	A7
W Matson Av					
5900	CHCG	60646	2919	7W-7N	B3
Matsushita Ln					
-	FNPK	60131	2973	11W-3N	D5
S Matterhorn Cir					
11600	PSPK	60464	3274	10W-13S	C5
Matteson Av					
-	MTSN	60443	3506	6W-24S	A5
Matteson St					
100	DYR	46311	3598		C1
Matthew Ln					
3000	HMWD	60430	3427	3W-22S	A7
3000	HMWD	60430	3507	3W-22S	A1
N Maud Av					
1900	CHCG	60614	2977	1W-2N	E7
E Maude Av					
10	ANHT	60004	2807	17W-15N	A2
W Maude Av					
10	ANHT	60004	2807	18W-15N	A2
400	ANHT	60004	2806	18W-15N	E1
Maue Dr					
10500	ODPK	60467	3423	13W-21S	A6
Maumell St					
100	HNDL	60521	3086		B7
Maureen Ct					
500	LYWD	60411	3510	4E-25S	C7
Maureen Dr					
200	WLNG	60090	2755	15W-17N	A5
300	WLNG	60090	2754	15W-17N	E5
1500	HFET	60120	2855		D1
W Maverick Tr					
13200	HMGN	60441	3343	16W-18S	E7
Maxey Ct					
3600	RBBN	60472	3348	4W-16S	D4
Maxine Cohen Cir					
-	NHBK	60062	2756	11W-18N	D4
Maxine Cohen Dr					
-	NHBK	60062	2757	9W-18N	D3
E Maxon Ln					
200	SMWD	60107	2857	28W-10N	A5
S Maxon Ln					
100	SMWD	60107	2857	28W-10N	A5
Maxwell St					
300	BCHR	60401	3864	0W-37S	C2
W Maxwell St					
500	CHCG	60607	3034	0W-1S	A7
700	CHCG	60608	3034		E7
900	CHCG	60608	3033	1W-1S	E7
Maxwelton Rd					
400	EDND	60118	2801		B1
May Ct					
200	CHHT	60411	3507	1W-23S	E4
May St					
100	BNVL	60106	2972		A2
300	ELGN	60120	2855		A6
500	ROSL	60172	2913		A3
700	CTCY	60409	3352	3E-18S	B7
4000	HLSD	60162	3029	13W-0S	A7
4000	WSTR	60154	3029	13W-0S	A7
18300	HMWD	60430	3428	1W-22S	A7
18400	HMWD	60430	3508	1W-22S	A1
E May St					
100	EMHT	60126	3028		A4
800	HMND	46320	3352		E7
N May St					
10	CHCG	60607	3033	1W-0N	E4
800	CHCG	60622	3033	1W-1N	E2
S May St					
700	CHCG	60607	3033	1W-0S	E6
1100	CHCG	60608	3033	1W-0S	E6
1800	CHCG	60608	3091	1W-1S	E1
3600	CHCG	60609	3091	1W-3S	E5
5000	CHCG	60609	3151	1W-5S	E2
5500	CHCG	60621	3151	1W-8S	E7
7500	CHCG	60620	3213	1W-10S	E4
9900	CHCG	60643	3213	1W-11S	E7
10500	CHCG	60643	3277	1W-12S	E1
12200	CTPK	60827	3277	1W-14S	E6
E Maya Ln					
-	PTHT	60070	2808	13W-15N	D3
1700	MPPT	60056	2808	13W-15N	D3
Mayapple Ct					
2500	NHBK	60062	2756	10W-16N	E7
2500	NHBK	60062	2757	9W-16N	B7
Mayapple Ln					
2100	NHBK	60062	2756	10W-16N	E7
2100	NHBK	60062	2757	10W-16N	A7
Mayberry Ct					
100	RGMW	60008	2805	21W-14N	D4
Maybrook Dr					
1300	MYWD	60153	3030	10W-0S	A5
Maybrook Sq					
1300	MYWD	60153	3030	10W-0S	B5
Maycliff Dr					
14300	ODPK	60462	3346	10W-17S	A5
Maydell Ct					
-	TYPK	60477	3424	10W-21S	B5
19800	FftT	60448	3504	11W-23S	A4
19800	TYPK	60448	3504	11W-23S	A4
Mayer Av					
10	WLNG	60090	2755	14W-18N	C3
Mayer Ct					
200	DRFD	60015	2756	11W-20N	E2
Mayfair Av					
1600	WSTR	60154	3086		E3
3000	LGPK	60525	3086		E4
3000	PvsT	60558	3086		E4
Mayfair Ct					
-	MNSR	46321	3510		D4
10	LMNT	60439	3270		E5
4300	CCHL	60478	3426	5W-21S	C7
Mayfair Ct N					
500	BFGV	60089	2754	17W-18N	B3
Mayfair Ct S					
600	BFGV	60089	2754	17W-18N	B4
Mayfair Dr					
-	LMNT	60439	3342	20W-15S	B1
1200	CPVL	60110	2748		D5
Mayfair Ln					
-	MTSN	60443	3594	6W-25S	A1
200	SMBG	60193	2859	21W-10N	E6
300	BFGV	60089	2754	17W-18N	B4
1100	GLNC	60022	2758	7W-18N	B4
9200	ODPK	60462	3345	11W-18S	E7
N Mayfair Pl					
100	CHHT	60411	3508	1W-23S	A3
S Mayfair Pl					
10	CHHT	60411	3508	1W-23S	A4
E Mayfair Rd					
600	ANHT	60005	2807	17W-13N	B6
1000	ANHT	60004	2807	17W-13N	B5
2500	ANHT	60056	2807	16W-13N	D5
2500	MPPT	60004	2807	16W-13N	D5
2500	MPPT	60056	2807	16W-13N	D5
Mayfair Wy					
-	MNSR	46321	3510		D4
Mayfield Av					
-	BmnT	60445	3347	7W-17S	C4
8500	OKLN	60459	3211	7W-9S	C4
8700	BRBK	60459	3211	7W-10S	C5
8700	OKLN	60453	3211	7W-10S	C5
9900	CHRG	60453	3211	7W-11S	C7
10100	CHRG	60453	3275	7W-11S	C1
10300	OKLN	60453	3275	7W-12S	C1
10400	CHRG	60415	3275	7W-12S	C1
11000	ALSP	60482	3275	7W-12S	C3
11000	CHRG	60482	3275	7W-12S	C3
N Mayfield Av					
10	CHCG	60644	3031	7W-0N	C4
1000	CHCG	60651	3031	7W-1N	C2
1500	CHCG	60639	3031	7W-2N	C1
1700	CHCG	60639	2975	7W-2N	C7
S Mayfield Av					
10	CHCG	60644	3031	7W-0S	C5
1100	CCRO	60804	3031	7W-0S	C7
5100	CHCG	60638	3149	7W-5S	C2
5100	StkT	60638	3149	7W-5S	C2
6400	BDPK	60638	3149	7W-7S	C5
11500	ALSP	60482	3275	7W-13S	C4
11500	ALSP	60803	3275	7W-13S	C4
Mayfield Ct					
12500	ALSP	60803	3275	7W-14S	C6
Mayfield Dr					
100	SMWD	60107	2857	27W-10N	B5
2600	PKRG	60068	2863	11W-10N	C4
Mayfield Ln					
1000	HFET	60195	2804	24W-12N	C7
Mayfield Pl					
19400	FftT	60423	3504	9W-23S	D3
19400	TYPK	60423	3504	9W-23S	D3
19400	TYPK	60477	3504	9W-23S	D3
Mayflower Ct					
5400	RGMW	60008	2860	19W-12N	D1
Mayflower Ln					
11000	ODPK	60467	3344	13W-16S	E3
11000	ODPK	60467	3345	13W-16S	A3
Mayher Dr					
17500	ODPK	60467	3422	14W-21S	D6
Maynard Dr					
-	NLES	60714	2864	10W-12N	B1
2700	MaiT	60025	2864	10W-12N	B1
W Maynard Dr					
8200	MaiT	60025	2864	10W-12N	B1
8200	NLES	60714	2864	10W-12N	B1
W Maynard Ovl					
8300	NLES	60714	2864	10W-12N	A1
W Maynard Rd					
8300	NLES	60714	2864	10W-12N	A1
8500	GNVW	60025	2864	10W-12N	A1
N Maynard Ter					
9800	NLES	60714	2864	10W-11N	A2
Mayo Dr					
15000	ODPK	60462	3346	11W-17S	A6
Mayors Row					
-	ODHL	60477	3424	11W-19S	A2
W Maypole Av					
1600	CHCG	60607	3033	2W-0N	C4
1600	CHCG	60612	3033	2W-0N	C4
3100	CHCG	60612	3032	3W-0N	E4
3100	CHCG	60624	3032	4W-0N	D4
4500	CHCG	60644	3032	5W-0N	A4
4800	CHCG	60644	3031	6W-0N	E4
Maytree Ln					
400	PTON	60468	3860	10W-37S	C4
S Maywood Av					
5200	HMND	46320	3352		E6
Maywood Dr					
2200	BLWD	60104	3029	11W-0S	C5
2200	MYWD	60153	3029	11W-0S	C5
N Maywood Dr					
1400	MYWD	60153	3029	11W-0S	E5
S Maywood Dr					
1700	MYWD	60153	3029	11W-0S	D5
1900	BLWD	60104	3029	11W-0S	D5
Maywood Ln					
600	HFET	60194	2858	24W-11N	D4
800	SMBG	60194	2858	26W-11N	A3
Mc 8th Dr					
-	CHCG	60616	3092		E2
McBreen Av					
3200	RBBN	60472	3348	4W-16S	E3
McCabe Av					
1100	EGvT	60007	2915		D1
1100	EGVV	60007	2915		D1
McCabe Dr					
10	SMWD	60107	2857	28W-10N	A5
13500	OrlT	60467	3344	14W-16S	D3
13500	PlsT	60467	3344	14W-16S	D3
13800	ODPK	60467	3344	14W-16S	D3
McCain Ct					
200	DSPN	60016	2862	15W-10N	B5
W McCampbell Dr					
6800	MonT	60449	3682	8W-30S	B4
McCarthy Dr					
-	CHCG	60616	3092		E2
McCarthy Rd					
10	PKFT	60466	3595	3W-27S	C4
400	LMNT	60439	3270		E5
1000	LMNT	60439	3271		D6
12200	LMNT	60439	3272	15W-14S	A6
12200	LmnT	60464	3272	15W-14S	A6
12200	PlsT	60464	3272	15W-14S	A6
S McCarthy Rd					
12400	PSHT	60463	3274	9W-14S	D7
12400	PSHT	60464	3274	9W-14S	D7
12400	PSPK	60464	3274	9W-14S	D7
W McCarthy Rd					
7700	PSHT	60463	3274	9W-14S	C6
7700	PSHT	60464	3274	9W-14S	D6
7700	PSPK	60464	3274	9W-14S	C6
9600	PlsT	60464	3273	13W-14S	B6
9600	PSPK	60464	3273	13W-14S	B6
11000	PlsT	60464	3272	14W-14S	D6
11000	PSPK	60464	3272	14W-14S	D6
11600	LMNT	60439	3272	14W-14S	C6
11600	LmnT	60464	3272	14W-14S	C6
McCarthy St					
400	LMNT	60439	3270		E6
McClean Av					
-	NHLK	60164	2972		E7
N McClellan Av					
6100	CHCG	60646	2919	7W-7N	C3
McClellan Ct					
100	BRLT	60103	2911		A5
McClellan St					
100	BRLT	60103	2910		E5
100	BRLT	60103	2911		A5
McClintock Dr					
600	BRRG	60527	3208		C1
N McClurg Ct					
300	CHCG	60611	3034	0E-0N	D3
McConnor Pkwy					
1400	SMBG	60173	2859	21W-12N	E1
1400	SMBG	60173	2860	21W-12N	A1
1800	RGMW	60173	2860	20W-12N	A2
N McCook Av					
5900	CHCG	60646	2919	7W-7N	B4
McCook Ct					
200	BRLT	60103	2911		A5
S McCorkle Av					
25500	MONE	60449	3683	6W-31S	A5
McCormack Dr					
1500	HFET	60195	2858	25W-12N	B1
McCormick Av					
2900	BKFD	60513	3088	10W-2S	A4
3800	LYNS	60534	3088	10W-3S	A6
McCormick Blvd					
1800	EVTN	60201	2866	4W-9N	D6
1800	EVTN	60201	2867	3W-12N	A1
2000	EVTN	60203	2866	4W-11N	D2
2000	SKOK	60201	2866	4W-11N	D2
2000	SKOK	60203	2866	4W-11N	D2
7500	SKOK	60076	2866	4W-9N	D7
N McCormick Blvd					
6400	CHCG	60659	2920	4W-8N	D3
6400	LNWD	60712	2920	4W-8N	D2
7000	SKOK	60076	2920	4W-9N	D1
7000	SKOK	60645	2920	4W-9N	D1
7200	SKOK	60076	2866	4W-9N	D7
7200	SKOK	60645	2866	4W-9N	D7
N McCormick Rd					
6200	CHCG	60659	2920	4W-7N	D3
6200	LNWD	60712	2920	4W-7N	D3
E McCormick Sq					
-	CHCG	60616	3092	0E-2S	D2
McCoy Dr					
-	PvsT	60141	3088	10W-1S	A1
N McCrea Dr					
100	CHCG	60624	3032	4W-0N	C4
McDaniel Av					
900	SKOK	60076	2866	3W-10N	D4
1300	EVTN	60202	2866	3W-11N	D3
1900	EVTN	60201	2866	4W-12N	D1
1900	EVTN	60203	2866	4W-11N	D2
1900	SKOK	60203	2866	4W-11N	D2
2600	EVTN	60201	2812	3W-13N	D7
2700	WLMT	60091	2812	3W-13N	D7
S McDaniel Ct					
13000	ALSP	60803	3348	5W-15S	A1
S McDaniel St					
12200	ALSP	60803	3276	5W-14S	A6
McDaniels St					
12700	ALSP	60803	3276	5W-15S	A7
McDermott Dr					
5200	BKLY	60163	3028		C3
S McDermott St					
2800	CHCG	60608	3091	1W-2S	D3
McDevitt Cir					
1500	EGVV	60007	2913		E1
1500	EGVV	60007	2914		A1
McDonough Dr					
-	HFET	60120	2802	30W-12N	B7
-	HFET	60192	2802	30W-12N	B7
McDonough Rd					
-	HFET	60120	2856	30W-12N	B1
1800	HFET	60120	2802	30W-12N	B7
1800	HFET	60192	2856	30W-12N	B1
1800	HnrT	60192	2856	30W-12N	B1
1900	HFET	60192	2802	30W-12N	B7
5400	HnrT	60192	2802	30W-12N	B7
S McDowell Av					
4500	CHCG	60609	3091	1W-4S	D7
E McEldowney St					
10	CHHT	60411	3596	1W-25S	A1
W McEldowney St					
10	CHHT	60411	3596	1W-25S	A1
McGarity Rd					
10	PKFT	60466	3595	3W-27S	B4
McGlashen Dr					
10	SBTN	60010	2803	26W-13N	D5
McGraw Ln					
10	DndT	60118	2801		C4
10	EDND	60118	2801		C4
McGuire Pkwy					
11200	LmnT	60439	3271		B4
McHenry Rd					
10	BFGV	60089	2754	16W-20N	C1
10	WLNG	60090	2755	15W-18N	A4
500	WLNG	60090	2754	16W-18N	D2
900	WLNG	60089	2754	16W-18N	D2
McHenry Rd SR-83					
10	BFGV	60089	2754	16W-20N	C1
400	WLNG	60090	2755	15W-18N	A3
500	WLNG	60090	2754	16W-18N	D2
900	WLNG	60089	2754	16W-18N	D2
McIntosh Ct					
800	PTHT	60070	2808	13W-15N	E2
McIntosh Dr					
7600	PlsT	60462	3346	9W-15S	D2
7600	PSHT	60462	3346	9W-15S	D2
7600	PSHT	60463	3346	9W-15S	D2
13400	ODPK	60462	3346	9W-15S	D2
McKay St					
11000	LydT	60164	2972		D5
McKenna Ct					
10400	ODPK	60467	3423	13W-20S	B4
E McKenna Ct					
300	YkTp	60126	3028		B7
McKinley Av					
10	STGR	60475	3596	1W-28S	A6
1100	CHHT	60411	3508	0W-25S	B7
S McKinley Av					
500	ANHT	60005	2807	17W-13N	C6
11900	PlsT	60464	3273	11W-14S	E5
11900	PSPK	60464	3273	11W-14S	E5
14700	POSN	60469	3349	3W-17S	B5
McKinley Ln					
10	SMWD	60107	2856	29W-10N	E6
700	HNDL	60521	3146		C3
McKinley St					
400	EGvT	60018	2861	16W-9N	E7
400	EGvT	60018	2862	15W-9N	A7
S McKinley St					
25700	MONE	60449	3682	7W-31S	E5
McKone Ct					
4600	RGMW	60008	2805	20W-13N	E5
E McKone Ct					
400	ANHT	60005	2861	17W-12N	B1
McKool Av					
1500	HRPK	60107	2911		C1
1500	HRPK	60133	2911		C1
1500	SMWD	60107	2911		C2
McLean Av					
9600	FNPK	60131	2973	12W-2N	C7
9600	LydT	60164	2973	12W-2N	C7
9600	MLPK	60131	2973	12W-2N	C7
9600	MLPK	60164	2973	12W-2N	C7
W McLean Av					
2000	CHCG	60614	2977	2W-2N	B6
2000	CHCG	60647	2977	2W-2N	B6
3900	CHCG	60639	2976	4W-2N	B6
3900	CHCG	60647	2976	5W-2N	B6
4700	CHCG	60639	2975	6W-2N	E7
6400	CHCG	60707	2975	8W-2N	A7
10100	LydT	60164	2973	12W-2N	A7
10300	NHLK	60164	2973	12W-2N	A7

STREET Block	City	ZIP	Map#	CGS	Grid
McLean Ct					
1700	GNVW	60025	2810	8W-13N	E6
N McLeod Av					
6000	CHCG	60646	2919	7W-7N	A3
McNerney Dr					
10200	FNPK	60131	2973	12W-4N	A3
McVicker Av					
8700	BRBK	60459	3211	7W-10S	C5
8700	OKLN	60459	3211	7W-10S	C5
9200	OKLN	60453	3211	7W-11S	C7
10700	CHRG	60415	3275	7W-12S	C3
N McVicker Av					
1600	CHCG	60302	3031	6W-0S	E7
1600	CHCG	60639	3031	6W-0S	E7
1600	OKPK	60302	3031	6W-0S	E7
2100	CHCG	60639	2975	7W-2N	B6
4000	CHCG	60634	2975	7W-5N	B1
4300	CHCG	60630	2975	7W-5N	B1
4800	CHCG	60630	2919	7W-6N	B6
5500	CHCG	60646	2919	7W-7N	B4
7200	CHCG	60646	2865	7W-9N	B7
S McVicker Av					
5100	CHCG	60638	3149	7W-6S	C3
5100	StkT	60638	3149	7W-5S	C2
McVickers Av					
8800	MNGV	60053	2865	7W-11N	B3
S McVickers Av					
12400	WthT	60463	3275	7W-15S	C7
12900	WthT	60463	3347	7W-15S	C1
McWalter Dr					
-	SmbT	60172	2913		B3
Meacham Av					
10	PKRG	60068	2918	8W-8N	D1
900	NLES	60714	2864	10W-9N	B6
900	PKRG	60068	2864	10W-9N	B6
N Meacham Ct					
8100	NLES	60714	2864	10W-10N	B5
Meacham Rd					
-	ITSC	60143	2913		D4
200	EGVV	60007	2859	21W-9N	E7
200	EGVV	60193	2859	21W-9N	E7
200	SmbT	60193	2859	21W-9N	E7
300	EGVV	60007	2913		E2
Meacham Rd CO-24					
-	ITSC	60143	2913		D4
N Meacham Rd					
-	SMBG	60193	2859	21W-10N	E5
1200	SMBG	60173	2859	21W-12N	E1
1300	ITSC	60143	2913		E4
1700	SMBG	60173	2805	21W-12N	E7
2500	PltT	60067	2805	20W-13N	E7
S Meacham Rd					
10	SMBG	60173	2859	21W-9N	E7
10	SMBG	60193	2859	21W-9N	E7
500	EGVV	60007	2859	21W-9N	E7
500	SMBG	60007	2859	21W-9N	E7
900	SmbT	60193	2859	21W-9N	E7
1000	EGVV	60193	2859	21W-9N	E7
1500	PltT	60067	2805	21W-13N	E6
1500	RGMW	60008	2805	21W-14N	E5
1500	RGMW	60067	2805	21W-14N	E5
2000	SMBG	60067	2805	21W-13N	E6
2000	SMBG	60173	2805	21W-13N	E6
2100	PltT	60173	2805	21W-13N	E6
Meade Av					
8500	BRBK	60459	3211	7W-9S	C4
8700	OKLN	60459	3211	7W-10S	C5
8800	MNGV	60053	2865	7W-11N	B3
10000	CHRG	60415	3211	7W-11S	B7
10000	OKLN	60453	3211	7W-11S	B7
N Meade Av					
1600	CHCG	60302	3031	6W-0S	E7
1600	CHCG	60639	3031	6W-0S	E7
1600	OKPK	60302	3031	6W-0S	E7
2100	CHCG	60639	2975	7W-2N	B6
2700	CHCG	60634	2975	7W-3N	B5
4300	CHCG	60630	2975	7W-5N	B1
5200	CHCG	60630	2919	7W-6N	B6
5500	CHCG	60646	2919	7W-7N	B4
7200	CHCG	60646	2865	7W-9N	B7
S Meade Av					
5100	StkT	60638	3149	7W-5S	B2
6000	CHCG	60638	3149	7W-7S	B5
7300	BDPK	60638	3149	7W-8S	C7
7300	BDPK	60638	3211	7W-8S	C1
12300	WthT	60463	3275	7W-14S	C6
12900	WthT	60463	3347	7W-15S	C1
Meade Ct					
200	BRLT	60103	2911		A6
Meade Ln					
700	ROSL	60172	2912		C6
W Meade Ln					
1200	ANHT	60004	2753	18W-18N	E2
Meade St					
10900	ODPK	60467	3423	13W-19S	A2
Meadow Ct					
10	SBTN	60010	2803	27W-13N	B5
10	SMBG	60193	2857	27W-10N	D5
600	DSPN	60016	2862	14W-12N	D1
600	EGvT	60007	2860	19W-9N	D7
600	EGVV	60007	2860	19W-9N	D7
600	EGVV	60007	2914		D1
1000	SMWD	60107	2857	28W-9N	B7
3600	OMFD	60461	3506	4W-24S	E5
8100	TYPK	60477	3424	10W-19S	C3
15300	OKFT	60452	3347	6W-18S	E7
S Meadow Ct					
10	SBTN	60010	2803	27W-13N	B5
Meadow Dr					
100	CTSD	60525	3147	12W-7S	B5
600	MaiT	60025	2809	10W-13N	E7
600	NfdT	60025	2809	10W-13N	E7
700	DSPN	60016	2862	14W-12N	D1
2300	RGMW	60008	2806	19W-13N	C6
E Meadow Dr					
500	WLMT	60091	2812	5W-13N	B6
N Meadow Dr					
2300	WLMT	60091	2812	5W-13N	B6
S Meadow Dr					
2300	WLMT	60091	2812	5W-13N	A6
W Meadow Dr					
500	WLMT	60091	2812	5W-13N	A6
Meadow Ln					
10	DGvT	60439	3270		B1
10	WLNG	60090	2755	14W-18N	B3
100	CTSD	60525	3147	13W-7S	B6
100	LynT	60525	3147	13W-7S	B6
100	WNKA	60093	2812	5W-15N	A3
200	CHHT	60411	3507	1W-25S	E6
300	PltT	60067	2806	20W-13N	A6
400	SmbT	60193	2912		B2
500	BCHR	60401	3864	0W-36S	C1
700	BRTN	60010	2750	25W-18N	E3
900	SMWD	60107	2857	28W-9N	B7
1100	HFET	60194	2858	24W-11N	E3

STREET Block	City	ZIP	Map#	CGS	Grid
Meadow Ln					
1400	GNVW	60025	2811	7W-14N	A5
2800	SMBG	60193	2857	27W-10N	D5
2800	SMBG	60194	2857	27W-10N	C5
3200	NfdT	60025	2810	10W-13N	A7
3400	NfdT	60025	2809	10W-13N	E7
6300	WLBK	60527	3146		A6
7400	HMND	46324	3430		D4
8000	TYPK	60477	3424	10W-19S	C3
8700	MNSR	46321	3510		D1
9400	DSPN	60016	2863	11W-11N	C2
9400	MaiT	60016	2863	11W-11N	C2
10000	MaiT	60016	2809	11W-12N	D7
10100	NfdT	60016	2809	11W-12N	D7
14900	OrlT	60462	3346	9W-17S	C6
15000	DLTN	60419	3351	1E-17S	B6
15000	ODPK	60462	3346	9W-17S	C6
18500	HLCT	60429	3506	4W-22S	E1
18500	HMWD	60429	3506	4W-22S	E1
18500	HMWD	60430	3506	4W-22S	E1
20200	DRPK	60010	2751	23W-20N	E1
E Meadow Ln					
600	PLTN	60074	2753	20W-16N	B6
N Meadow Ln					
1000	MPPT	60056	2808	15W-14N	A4
1100	MPPT	60056	2807	15W-14N	E4
S Meadow Ln					
500	PTON	60468	3860	10W-37S	D4
6500	HMND	46324	3430		D2
10700	PSHL	60465	3274	10W-12S	B2
Meadow Ln W					
-	DndT	60118	2801		B5
Meadow Pl					
8100	MNSR	46321	3430		D6
Meadow Rd					
-	NtrT	60093	2812	4W-14N	B3
-	PSPK	60464	3272	14W-14S	D7
500	WNKA	60093	2812	4W-14N	C3
800	NHBK	60062	2757	9W-17N	B5
1000	GLNC	60022	2758	6W-18N	D3
Meadow St					
3400	NfdT	60062	2756	11W-16N	C6
3400	NHBK	60062	2756	11W-16N	C6
Meadow Ter					
4600	MLPK	60160	3029	13W-1N	A2
4600	NHLK	60160	3029	13W-1N	A2
4600	NHLK	60164	3029	13W-1N	A2
Meadow Tr					
300	BRLT	60103	2911		B5
Meadow Bridge Dr					
-	PLTN	60008	2805	21W-14N	D5
-	RGMW	60008	2805	21W-14N	D5
-	RGMW	60067	2805	21W-13N	D5
Meadowbrook Ct					
5500	RGMW	60008	2860	19W-12N	C1
Meadowbrook Dr					
200	NHFD	60093	2758	7W-16N	A7
Meadowbrook Ln					
10	WLNG	60090	2755	14W-17N	C5
200	HNDL	60521	3146		B4
2400	WSTR	60154	3086		C3
6800	HRPK	60133	2912		A2
8000	ODPK	60462	3346	10W-18S	C7
Meadowbrook Industrial Ct					
5400	RGMW	60008	2860	19W-12N	C2
Meadowcrest Dr					
16700	HMGN	60441	3422	15W-20S	C4
Meadowcrest Rd					
900	LGPK	60525	3087	12W-3S	B4
Meadowdale Ct					
100	CPVL	60110	2748		B7
Meadowdale Dr					
16700	OKFT	60452	3426	6W-20S	A3
S Meadow Hill Ln					
13100	LMNT	60439	3344	16W-15S	A2
13200	LMNT	60439	3343	16W-15S	E2
W Meadow Hill Ln					
13100	LMNT	60439	3343	16W-15S	E1
Meadow Hill Rd					
10	BNHL	60010	2749	29W-20N	B2
Meadow Lake Ct					
4800	RNPK	60471	3594	6W-26S	A3
Meadow Lake Dr					
4800	RNPK	60471	3594	6W-26S	A3
E Meadow Lake Dr					
1000	PLTN	60074	2753	19W-17N	C5
Meadowland Dr					
12000	HMGN	60441	3344	15W-17S	C5
12000	OrlT	60467	3344	15W-17S	C5
Meadow Lark					
-	LYWD	60411	3510		C6
10	DYR	46311	3510		C6
Meadowlark Ct					
10	ROSL	60172	2912		C4
13000	HMGN	60441	3344	16W-18S	A7
Meadowlark Dr					
8800	TYPK	60477	3424	11W-21S	A6
13100	PlsT	60462	3346	10W-15S	B1
13100	PlsT	60464	3346	10W-15S	B1
Meadowlark Ln					
10	CPVL	60110	2748		C6
100	CTSD	60525	3147	12W-6S	B5
400	NHFD	60093	2811	7W-15N	B2
1000	GNVW	60025	2810	9W-13N	B6
2700	EVTN	60201	2812	4W-13N	B7
S Meadow Ln Dr					
11500	MTPK	60803	3276	3W-13S	E4
W Meadow Ln Dr					
3100	MTPK	60803	3276	3W-13S	E4
Meadowood Dr					
10	OKBK	60523	3086		B1
Meadowood Ln					
10	NHFD	60093	2811	7W-14N	B3
S Meadowood Rd					
24200	CteT	60417	3684	2W-29S	D1
24200	UYPK	60417	3684	2W-29S	D1
Meadow Ridge Ln					
400	PTHT	60070	2754	16W-16N	D6
Meadows Edge Tr					
8400	TYPK	60477	3504	10W-23S	B3
Meadow View Ct					
14200	ODPK	60462	3346	10W-16S	B4
Meadowview Ct					
2000	NHBK	60062	2757	8W-16N	D7
2800	NHBK	60062	2809	11W-15N	D1
Meadowview Dr					
-	NHBK	60062	2809	11W-15N	C2
4200	NHBK	60025	2809	11W-15N	C2
4400	GNVW	60025	2809	11W-15N	C2
4400	GNVW	60062	2809	11W-15N	C2
8800	ODHL	60477	3424	11W-19S	A2
8800	ODPK	60462	3424	11W-19S	A2
8800	ODPK	60477	3424	11W-19S	A2
9000	HYHL	60457	3209	11W-9S	E4
9000	LynT	60480	3209	11W-9S	E4

STREET Block	City	ZIP	Map#	CGS	Grid
Meadowview Dr					
9200	ODHL	60477	3423	11W-19S	E2
9200	ODPK	60467	3423	11W-19S	E2
9200	ODPK	60477	3423	11W-19S	E2
Meadowview Ln					
12800	HMGN	60441	3422	16W-18S	A1
Meadowview Rd					
10	NHFD	60093	2811	6W-14N	D3
10	NtrT	60093	2811	6W-14N	E3
Meagan Ln					
10	LMNT	60439	3270		C7
Meath Cir					
13600	HMGN	60441	3343	17W-16S	D3
W Meath Dr					
13600	HMGN	60441	3343	17W-16S	D3
N Medford Av					
6900	CHCG	60646	2919	7W-8N	A1
Medford Cir					
800	SMBG	60193	2859	23W-9N	B7
800	SMBG	60193	2913		D3
3800	NHBK	60062	2756	12W-17N	B5
Medford Ct					
3100	BRLT	60103	2910		E1
3100	SMWD	60103	2910		E1
3100	SMWD	60107	2910		E1
W Medford Dr					
600	PLTN	60067	2805	21W-14N	C3
Medill Av					
9100	FNPK	60131	2973	11W-2N	D6
9100	FNPK	60171	2973	11W-2N	D6
9100	RVGV	60171	2973	11W-2N	D6
E Medill Av					
10	NHLK	60164	2972		E6
300	LydT	60164	2973	13W-2N	A6
300	NHLK	60164	2973	13W-2N	A6
W Medill Av					
1600	CHCG	60614	2977	2W-2N	C6
2600	CHCG	60647	2977	3W-2N	A6
3400	CHCG	60647	2976	4W-2N	D6
4800	CHCG	60639	2975	6W-2N	E6
6700	CHCG	60707	2974	8W-2N	E6
6700	CHCG	60707	2975	8W-2N	A6
7100	EDPK	60707	2974	8W-2N	D6
10000	LydT	60164	2973	12W-2N	B6
10400	NHLK	60164	2973	13W-2N	A6
W Medill St					
-	CHCG	60614	2977	1W-2N	D6
N Medina Av					
5800	CHCG	60646	2919	7W-7N	B4
Medina Dr					
13300	ODPK	60462	3346	11W-15S	A2
Medinah					
-	MONE	60449	3683	6W-31S	A5
Medinah Ct					
2100	PSHT	60463	3347	8W-15S	B2
Medinah Dr					
1200	BmdT	60143	2913		E7
1200	BmdT	60143	2914		A7
1200	ITSC	60143	2913		E7
1200	ITSC	60143	2914		A7
25500	MONE	60449	3683	6W-31S	B5
Medinah Rd					
10	BMDL	60157	2913		D7
10	BmdT	60143	2913		D7
10	BmdT	60157	2913		D7
300	ITSC	60143	2913		D4
300	ITSC	60157	2913		D4
300	ROSL	60143	2913		D4
400	ROSL	60143	2913		D6
700	BMDL	60101	2913		D7
Medinah Rd CO-24					
10	BMDL	60157	2913		D7
10	BmdT	60143	2913		D7
10	BmdT	60157	2913		D7
300	ITSC	60143	2913		D4
300	ITSC	60157	2913		D4
300	ROSL	60157	2913		D4
400	ROSL	60143	2913		D6
700	BMDL	60101	2913		D7
Medinah St					
900	BNVL	60106	2915		D7
Meed Ct					
-	PlsT	60464	3345	13W-15S	B1
Meegan Wy					
1400	EGVV	60007	2913		E3
Megan Ct					
21300	MTSN	60443	3593	7W-25S	C1
Meghan Av					
1000	ALGN	60102	2748		A2
Meghan Ct N					
26700	MonT	60449	3683	6W-32S	A7
S Meier Rd					
200	MPPT	60005	2861	17W-12N	B1
200	MPPT	60056	2861	17W-12N	B1
800	ANHT	60005	2861	17W-11N	B2
800	ANHT	60056	2861	17W-11N	B2
Meier St					
300	EDND	60118	2801		A2
Meigs Ct					
10	BNVL	60106	2972		A1
Meijer Dr					
-	ANHT	60005	2860	18W-11N	E2
-	RGMW	60005	2860	18W-11N	E2
-	RGMW	60008	2860	18W-11N	E2
N Melanie Ct					
10	CRTE	60417	3597	1E-28S	B7
200	PltT	60067	2752	22W-16N	B7
S Melanie Ct					
10	CRTE	60417	3597	1E-28S	B7
Melanie Ln					
2500	NHBK	60062	2809	11W-15N	D1
3600	CRTE	60417	3597	1E-28S	B7
Melbrook Dr					
1000	MNSR	46321	3510		E1
Melbrooke Rd					
10	ELGN	60123	2801		A7
Melinda Ln					
200	BFGV	60089	2754	17W-18N	C3
Melise Dr					
1700	GNVW	60025	2810	8W-14N	E4
S Melissa Ct					
26500	MonT	60449	3683	6W-32S	B7
Melissa Dr					
10	LMNT	60439	3342	19W-15S	D2
10600	ODPK	60467	3423	13W-21S	B7
Melody Ct					
500	SMBG	60194	2858	26W-11N	A4
Melody Ln					
-	WthT	60482	3275	7W-13S	B5
200	CPVL	60110	2748		A5
200	DndT	60110	2748		A5
500	HDPK	60035	2758	7W-20N	B1
Melrose Av					
100	KLWH	60043	2812	4W-14N	D4
200	EMHT	60126	3028		A1

STREET Block	City	ZIP	Map#	CGS	Grid
Melrose Av					
400	HLSD	60162	3028		E5
2400	LydT	60164	2972		E5
2400	NHLK	60164	2972		E6
11200	FNPK	60131	2972		C4
Melrose Ct					
3100	WLMT	60091	2811	6W-14N	E5
11200	ODPK	60467	3344	14W-16S	E4
Melrose Ln					
500	BCHR	60401	3864	0W-37S	C2
S Melrose Ln					
26700	CteT	60417	3685	0W-32S	C7
W Melrose St					
400	CHCG	60657	2978	0W-4N	A3
1600	CHCG	60657	2977	2W-4N	B3
2600	CHCG	60618	2977	3W-4N	A3
2700	CHCG	60618	2976	3W-4N	E3
4000	CHCG	60641	2976	5W-4N	B3
5100	CHCG	60641	2975	7W-4N	C3
5500	CHCG	60634	2975	7W-4N	C3
6900	CHCG	60634	2974	8W-4N	E4
Melshane Ct					
10	LMNT	60439	3271		A5
Melvin Dr					
200	NHBK	60062	2756	11W-18N	E3
1000	HDPK	60035	2758	8W-20N	A2
Melvin Pl					
300	WLNG	60090	2755	14W-17N	C5
Melvina Av					
8700	BRBK	60459	3211	7W-10S	B5
8700	OKLN	60453	3211	7W-11S	B7
10000	CHRG	60415	3211	7W-11S	B7
N Melvina Av					
1600	CHCG	60302	3031	6W-0S	E6
1600	CHCG	60639	3031	6W-0S	E6
1600	OKPK	60302	3031	6W-0S	E6
2600	CHCG	60639	2975	7W-3N	B5
2700	CHCG	60634	2975	7W-3N	B5
4200	CHCG	60630	2975	7W-5N	B1
4800	CHCG	60630	2919	7W-6N	B6
5600	CHCG	60646	2919	7W-7N	B4
7200	CHCG	60646	2865	7W-9N	B7
7200	NLES	60714	2865	7W-9N	B7
S Melvina Av					
5100	CHCG	60638	3149	7W-5S	B2
5100	StkT	60638	3149	7W-5S	B2
6400	BDPK	60638	3149	7W-7S	B5
12400	PSHT	60463	3275	7W-14S	C6
12700	WthT	60463	3275	7W-15S	C7
Memorial Dr					
-	PSPK	60464	3274	11W-14S	A6
10	CTCY	60409	3352	4E-17S	B6
10	HMND	46320	3352	4E-17S	C6
1100	CTCY	60409	3351	3E-17S	E6
1900	DLTN	60419	3351	2E-17S	E6
14600	DLTN	60419	3350	0E-17S	E4
N Memorial Dr					
800	CHHT	60411	3507	1W-24S	E6
W Memorial Dr					
100	CHHT	60411	3507	1W-24S	E6
E Memorial Rd					
10	BNVL	60106	2972		A2
Memory Ln					
100	DndT	60110	2748		A6
E Memory Ln					
-	MPPT	60056	2808	15W-13N	A6
W Memory Ln					
-	ANHT	60004	2807	15W-13N	E6
10	MPPT	60056	2808	15W-13N	A6
200	MPPT	60056	2807	16W-13N	E6
8000	CHCG	60656	2918	10W-6N	B6
8000	NRDG	60706	2918	10W-6N	B6
Memphis Cir					
1000	EGVV	60007	2913		D3
Menard Av					
8000	MNGV	60053	2865	7W-10N	C5
8000	SKOK	60077	2865	7W-10N	C5
8700	BRBK	60453	3211	7W-10S	C5
8700	BRBK	60459	3211	7W-10S	C5
8700	OKLN	60453	3211	7W-11S	C6
10100	OKLN	60453	3275	7W-11S	C1
10300	CHRG	60415	3275	7W-12S	C1
11000	ALSP	60482	3275	7W-12S	C3
11000	CHRG	60482	3275	7W-12S	C3
14200	BmnT	60445	3347	7W-16S	D4
14700	BmnT	60452	3347	7W-17S	D6
14700	OKFT	60452	3347	7W-17S	D6
N Menard Av					
10	CHCG	60644	3031	7W-0N	C5
700	CHCG	60651	3031	7W-0N	C3
1500	CHCG	60639	3031	7W-2N	C1
2100	CHCG	60639	2975	7W-2N	C6
2700	CHCG	60634	2975	7W-3N	C5
4300	CHCG	60630	2975	7W-5N	C1
4800	CHCG	60630	2919	7W-5N	C7
6000	CHCG	60646	2919	7W-7N	C3
7500	NLES	60714	2865	7W-9N	C7
7500	SKOK	60077	2865	7W-9N	C7
S Menard Av					
10	CHCG	60644	3031	7W-0S	C5
1100	CCRO	60804	3031	7W-0S	C7
4900	StkT	60638	3149	7W-5S	C2
5900	CHCG	60638	3149	7W-7S	C5
6500	BDPK	60638	3149	7W-7S	C6
12400	ALSP	60803	3275	7W-14S	D7
12400	WthT	60463	3275	7W-14S	D7
12400	WthT	60803	3275	7W-14S	D7
12500	WthT	60445	3275	7W-14S	D7
S Menard Pl					
11700	ALSP	60803	3275	7W-13S	D5
N Mendell St					
1900	CHCG	60614	2977	1W-2N	C6
1900	CHCG	60622	2977	1W-2N	C6
Mendocino Ct					
700	UYPK	60466	3684	3W-29S	A2
Mendon Ln					
10	SMBG	60193	2858	26W-10N	A6
N Mendota Av					
6800	CHCG	60646	2919	7W-8N	B1
6800	CHCG	60714	2919	7W-8N	B1
6800	NLES	60646	2919	7W-8N	B1
6800	NLES	60714	2919	7W-8N	B1
W Menominee Pkwy					
6600	PSHT	60463	3275	8W-14S	A6
W Menomonee St					
100	CHCG	60614	2978	0W-2N	A7
Mensching Rd					
300	BmdT	60172	2912		E6
300	ROSL	60172	2912		E6
Meota St					
300	PKFT	60466	3595	3W-27S	A4
Merc Ln					
-	LKPT	60441	3342	20W-18S	B7
Mercantile Ct					
400	WLNG	60090	2755	15W-17N	B5

STREET Block	City	ZIP	Map#	CGS	Grid
Mercury Ct					
900	SMBG	60193	2912		B1
Mercury Dr					
1000	SMBG	60193	2912		A2
N Meredith Av					
6200	CHCG	60646	2919	7W-7N	C3
Meredith Dr					
10	RVWD	60015	2755	13W-20N	E1
Meredith Ln					
100	SMWD	60107	2857	28W-9N	A7
100	SMWD	60107	2911		A1
Merganser Ln					
600	PTON	60468	3860	10W-38S	D5
Meribel Ct					
200	SMBG	60194	2857	27W-10N	D5
Meridian Rd					
-	DGvT	60439	3271		A1
Merimac Ct					
400	ROSL	60172	2912		E5
Merion Dr					
8800	ODPK	60462	3346	11W-18S	A7
9000	ODPK	60462	3345	11W-18S	E7
25700	MONE	60449	3683	6W-31S	B5
Merioneth Dr					
-	CRTE	60417	3596	0E-29S	E7
-	CRTE	60417	3685	0E-29S	E1
-	CteT	60417	3685	0E-29S	E1
Merle Ln					
500	WLNG	60090	2755	15W-17N	A5
3400	GNVW	60062	2809	12W-14N	B4
3500	GNVW	60025	2809	12W-14N	B4
E Merle Ln					
400	WLNG	60090	2755	15W-17N	A5
S Merle Ln					
600	WLNG	60090	2755	15W-17N	A5
Merlin Ct					
10	DRFD	60015	2756	11W-20N	D2
5700	OKFT	60452	3347	7W-18S	D6
Merlin Dr					
500	SMBG	60193	2859	22W-9N	C7
700	EGVV	60007	2859	22W-9N	C7
700	SMBG	60007	2859	22W-9N	C7
Merlot Ct					
1900	WLNG	60090	2808	14W-15N	B2
Mermaid Ct					
800	SMBG	60193	2912		D1
Merriford Ln					
100	ROSL	60172	2912		B4
Merrill Av					
-	NLES	60714	2864	9W-11N	C3
200	CTCY	60409	3351	2E-17S	D6
9400	MNGV	60053	2864	9W-11N	C2
16600	SHLD	60473	3429	2E-19S	D3
21500	BlmT	60411	3597	2E-26S	D1
21500	SLVL	60411	3597	2E-26S	D2
S Merrill Av					
-	CHCG	60633	3351	2E-15S	C2
-	CTCY	60409	3351	2E-15S	C2
6700	CHCG	60649	3153	2E-7S	C6
7500	CHCG	60649	3215	2E-9S	C2
7800	CHCG	60617	3215	2E-9S	C2
Merrill Ct					
21600	SLVL	60411	3597	2E-26S	D2
Merrill St					
1000	WNKA	60093	2758	5W-16N	E7
1000	WNKA	60093	2759		B7
15400	CTCY	60409	3351	2E-18S	C7
15400	ThtT	60473	3351	2E-18S	C7
E Merrill St					
800	HMND	46320	3430		E1
N Merrill St					
10	PKRG	60068	2864	9W-9N	C7
10	PKRG	60068	2918	9W-8N	C1
8000	NLES	60068	2864	9W-10N	C6
8200	MaiT	60714	2864	9W-10N	C5
8600	NLES	60714	2864	9W-10N	C4
S Merrill St					
300	CHCG	60631	2918	9W-8N	C1
300	PKRG	60068	2918	9W-8N	C1
W Merrill St					
200	BlmT	60425	3508	0W-22S	D1
200	GNWD	60425	3508	0W-22S	D1
Merrillwood Rd					
800	HNDL	60521	3086		A7
Merrimac Av					
7700	BRBK	60459	3211	7W-9S	B2
7800	MNGV	60053	2865	7W-9N	B6
7800	NLES	60714	2865	7W-9N	B6
9900	OKLN	60453	3211	7W-11S	B7
10000	CHRG	60415	3211	7W-11S	B7
N Merrimac Av					
1600	CHCG	60302	3031	6W-0S	E6
1600	CHCG	60639	3031	6W-0S	E6
1600	OKPK	60302	3031	6W-0S	E6
2600	CHCG	60639	2975	7W-3N	B5
3900	CHCG	60634	2975	7W-4N	B2
4400	CHCG	60630	2975	7W-5N	B1
4800	CHCG	60630	2919	7W-6N	A6
7000	CHCG	60646	2919	7W-8N	B1
7600	NLES	60714	2865	7W-9N	B6
7800	MNGV	60053	2865	7W-9N	B6
S Merrimac Av					
4700	StkT	60638	3149	7W-5S	B2
5900	CHCG	60638	3149	7W-6S	B4
Merrimac St					
300	PKFT	60466	3595	3W-27S	A5
S Merrion Av					
9500	CHCG	60617	3215	2E-11S	D6
S Merrion Ln					
8700	CHCG	60456	3212	5W-10S	B4
8700	CHCG	60652	3212	5W-10S	B4
8700	HMTN	60456	3212	5W-10S	B4
11600	MTPK	60803	3276	4W-13S	E4
W Merrion Ln					
3300	CHCG	60655	3276	4W-13S	E4
3300	CHCG	60803	3276	4W-13S	E4
3300	MTPK	60803	3276	4W-13S	E4
Merry Ct					
10	CTSD	60525	3147	12W-6S	B4
Merry Oaks Rd					
10	SMWD	60107	2856	29W-9N	E7
10	SMWD	60120	2856	29W-9N	E7
300	SMWD	60120	2910		E1
400	HnrT	60120	2910		E1
Merton Av					
9900	OKLN	60453	3211	7W-11S	B7
10000	CHRG	60415	3211	7W-11S	B7
Mery Ln					
-	WthT	60482	3275	7W-13S	B5
N Meryls Tr					
1900	PLTN	60074	2752	21W-18N	C3
S Meryton Ct					
9700	PSHL	60465	3210	10W-11S	A7
Mesa Dr					
500	HFET	60194	2858	24W-11N	E3

STREET Block	City	ZIP	Map#	CGS	Grid
Mesquite Dr					
14500	OrlT	60467	3344	14W-17S	E5
Messina Ct					
10	TYPK	60477	3505	8W-23S	B4
Messina Dr					
-	OMFD	60461	3507	3W-24S	A5
Messner Dr					
10	WLNG	60090	2755	14W-16N	C7
S Metron Dr					
12900	CHCG	60633	3279	1E-14S	B7
W Metropole St					
7900	EDPK	60707	2974	9W-3N	B4
7900	RVGV	60171	2974	9W-3N	B4
N Meyer Av					
1600	CHCG	60614	2978	0W-2N	A7
Meyer Ct					
300	SMWD	60107	2857	27W-11N	D4
N Meyer Ct					
10	DSPN	60016	2862	14W-12N	C2
S Meyer Ct					
10	DSPN	60016	2862	14W-11N	C2
Meyer Rd					
300	BNVL	60106	2915		E7
1300	HFET	60194	2858	25W-12N	B2
Meyerson Wy					
10	WLNG	60090	2755	14W-18N	C3
MGM Dr					
11700	ODPK	60467	3422	14W-21S	D7
Mgsr Cardiff Dr					
5100	OKLN	60453	3275	6W-12S	E1
Mgsr McNichols Dr					
5300	OKLN	60453	3211	7W-10S	C6
Mgsr Mulcahey St					
6900	CHCG	60626	2921	2W-8N	C1
W Miami Av					
5900	CHCG	60646	2919	7W-7N	B3
Miami Ln					
1300	DSPN	60018	2862	15W-10N	B6
Miami Rd					
1000	WLMT	60091	2812	5W-14N	A5
3800	BLWD	60104	3029	12W-0N	A4
Miami St					
100	PKFT	60466	3595	4W-27S	A5
200	PKFT	60466	3594	4W-27S	E4
400	RNPK	60471	3594	4W-27S	E3
Michael Av					
17700	CCHL	60478	3426	5W-21S	B6
Michael Ct					
400	DSPN	60016	2862	15W-11N	A3
1300	HFET	60195	2804	24W-15N	C3
5700	RGMW	60008	2805	21W-14N	C5
9300	MNGV	60053	2864	9W-11N	B2
18500	HLCT	60429	3506	4W-22S	D1
Michael Dr					
14000	ODPK	60462	3346	11W-16S	A4
18600	HLCT	60429	3506	4W-22S	D1
N Michael Dr					
1200	WDDL	60191	2915		A3
1500	EGvT	60007	2915		A3
S Michael Dr					
10300	BGVW	60465	3274	9W-12S	D1
10300	PSHL	60465	3274	9W-12S	D1
Michael Ln					
3800	GNVW	60025	2809	11W-15N	D2
3800	GNVW	60062	2809	11W-15N	D2
6200	MTSN	60443	3505	7W-24S	C5
Michael Mnr					
10	MaiT	60025	2864	10W-12N	B1
10	MaiT	60714	2864	10W-12N	B2
10	NLES	60714	2864	10W-12N	B2
300	GNVW	60025	2864	10W-12N	B1
400	GNVW	60025	2810	10W-12N	B7
Michael Rd					
10	DSPN	60016	2862	15W-11N	B3
10	PKFT	60466	3595	2W-27S	C4
Michael St					
500	CRTE	60417	3685	1W-30S	B3
S Michael St					
200	MPPT	60056	2861	17W-12N	C1
Michaele Dr					
15300	OKFT	60452	3347	6W-18S	E7
Michael John Ct					
4400	RNPK	60471	3594	5W-27S	C4
Michael John Dr					
10	NLES	60714	2864	10W-9N	B6
10	PKRG	60068	2864	10W-9N	B6
Michael John Ln					
4400	RNPK	60471	3594	5W-27S	B4
E Michael Manor Ln					
2200	ANHT	60004	2807	16W-15N	D1
Michael McFarlane Dr					
1400	CHCG	60640	2921	1W-6N	C5
S Michaels St					
24700	CteT	60417	3686	2E-30S	C2
Michael Todd Ter					
10300	GNVW	60025	2809	11W-13N	D6
10300	NfdT	60025	2809	11W-13N	D6
Michaux Rd					
10	RVSD	60546	3088	9W-3S	C4
Michele Dr					
1300	PLTN	60074	2753	19W-16N	C7
Michelle Cir					
1300	SMBG	60173	2859	21W-10N	D4
Michelle Ct					
7900	ODPK	60462	3346	9W-17S	C4
S Michelle Ct					
26600	MonT	60449	3683	6W-32S	B7
Michelle Dr					
600	BlmT	60411	3510	4E-25S	C7
700	LYWD	60411	3510	4E-25S	B7
Michelle Ln					
8200	TYPK	60477	3424	10W-19S	B3
Michelle Pl					
100	SMBG	60173	2859	21W-11N	D4
Michelline Ct					
1400	HFET	60195	2804	24W-14N	C3
Michelline Ln					
600	NHBK	60062	2756	12W-18N	B4
Michigan Av					
10	EDND	60118	2801		A2
900	WLMT	60091	2813	3W-14N	A5
1100	WLMT	60091	2812		E4
1200	EVTN	60202	2867	2W-10N	C4
4800	SRPK	60176	2917	12W-6N	C7
5100	CHCG	60018	2917	12W-6N	C7
5100	SRPK	60018	2917	12W-6N	C7
14600	DLTN	60419	3350	0W-17S	C5
14600	DLTN	60827	3350	0W-17S	C5
14600	RVDL	60827	3350	0W-17S	C5
15700	SHLD	60473	3350	0E-18S	D7
16400	SHLD	60473	3428	0E-19S	D2
E Michigan Av					
10	PLTN	60067	2805	20W-15N	E3
N Michigan Av					
10	CHCG	60602	3034	0E-0N	C4
10	CHCG	60603	3034	0E-0N	C4
100	EMHT	60126	3028		A1
200	CHCG	60601	3034	0E-0N	C4
400	CHCG	60611	3034	0E-0N	C3
5200	CHCG	60018	2917	12W-6N	C6
5200	RSMT	60018	2917	12W-6N	C6
S Michigan Av					
10	CHCG	60602	3034	0E-0N	C4
10	CHCG	60603	3034	0E-0S	C4
100	CHCG	60604	3034	0E-0S	C5
200	CHCG	60605	3034	0E-1S	C7
1500	CHCG	60616	3034	0E-1S	C7
1600	CHCG	60616	3092	0E-2S	C2
3400	CHCG	60653	3092	0E-3S	C4
4600	CHCG	60615	3092	0E-4S	C7
4700	CHCG	60615	3152	0E-6S	C3
6600	CHCG	60637	3152	0E-7S	C5
7000	CHCG	60619	3152	0E-8S	C7
9100	CHCG	60619	3214	0E-11S	C6
9400	CHCG	60628	3214	0E-11S	C6
10300	CHCG	60628	3278	0W-14S	C6
13300	CHCG	60827	3350	0W-15S	D1
13500	RVDL	60827	3350	0W-15S	C2
14500	DLTN	60419	3350	0W-17S	C4
14500	DLTN	60827	3350	0W-17S	C4
W Michigan Av					
10	PLTN	60067	2805	21W-15N	D3
Michigan Blvd					
-	NHFD	60093	2811	6W-15N	D3
-	NtrT	60093	2811	6W-15N	D2
-	WNKA	60093	2811	6W-15N	D2
Michigan Ct					
18200	ODPK	60467	3423	13W-21S	B7
Michigan Ln					
600	EGVV	60007	2913		D2
Michigan St					
200	ELGN	60120	2855		A4
E Michigan St					
400	HMND	46320	3352		D5
N Michigan St					
500	EMHT	60126	2972		A7
5200	CHCG	60018	2917	12W-6N	C6
5200	SRPK	60018	2917	12W-6N	C6
5200	SRPK	60176	2917	12W-6N	C6
Michigan City Rd					
-	HMND	46324	3430	4E-19S	C1
10	CTCY	60409	3430	3E-18S	A1
600	CTCY	60409	3352	3E-18S	A7
1000	CTCY	60409	3351	2E-17S	C6
1400	CTCY	60473	3351	2E-18S	D6
1900	DLTN	60419	3351	2E-17S	C6
Mickey Ln					
2000	GNVW	60025	2810	8W-14N	E3
2000	NHFD	60093	2810	8W-14N	E3
Middaugh Dr					
400	DGvT	60439	3270		C1
Middle Dr					
-	SMBG	60173	2805	22W-12N	D7
-	SMBG	60173	2859	21W-11N	E2
-	WLMT	60091	2813	2W-13N	B5
E Middle St					
500	BRLT	60103	2909		B3
500	BRLT	60120	2909		B3
500	ElgT	60120	2909		A3
500	ElgT	60177	2909		A3
500	SEGN	60103	2909		B3
500	SEGN	60120	2909		A3
500	SEGN	60177	2909		A3
Middlebury Ct					
10	SMWD	60107	2857	27W-11N	C3
200	SMBG	60193	2859	21W-10N	E6
Middlebury Ln					
500	EGVV	60007	2860	18W-9N	E7
500	EGVV	60007	2914		D1
1100	WLNG	60090	2754	16W-18N	D3
1200	WLMT	60091	2812	5W-14N	A4
1300	NtrT	60093	2812	5W-14N	A4
Middlebury Rd					
10	BNHL	60010	2748		E2
600	EGVV	60007	2914		E1
Middlefork Rd					
2000	NHFD	60093	2811	7W-16N	B1
Middle Pinecreek Dr					
14600	OrlT	60467	3344	14W-17S	C5
S Middlepoint Av					
25600	MONE	60449	3683	6W-31S	A5
Middlesex Ct					
400	BFGV	60089	2754	16W-17N	D4
Middlesex Dr					
10	CPVL	60110	2748		A4
N Middleton Av					
10	PLTN	60067	2805	22W-16N	B1
10	PltT	60067	2805	22W-16N	B1
100	PLTN	60067	2752	22W-16N	B7
100	PltT	60067	2752	22W-16N	B7
S Middleton Av					
10	PltT	60067	2805	22W-15N	B1
400	PLTN	60067	2805	22W-15N	B2
Middleton Ct					
700	PLTN	60067	2805	22W-15N	B3
1300	DSPN	60016	2808	13W-13N	D6
Middleton Dr					
500	ROSL	60172	2912		C6
Middleton Ln					
600	DSPN	60016	2808	13W-13N	D6
800	BRLT	60103	2910		B5
900	IVNS	60010	2804	25W-15N	A1
Midfield Ln					
600	NHBK	60062	2757	8W-16N	E6
600	NHBK	60062	2758	8W-17N	A6
Midlothian Tpk					
4200	CTWD	60445	3348	5W-16S	A3
4200	RBBN	60472	3348	5W-16S	A3
4800	BmnT	60445	3348	5W-16S	A3
5000	BmnT	60445	3347	7W-16S	D4
5000	MDLN	60445	3347	7W-16S	D4
5000	MDLN	60445	3348	5W-16S	A3
5100	CTWD	60445	3347	6W-16S	E3
5800	BmnT	60452	3347	7W-16S	C4
W Midlothian Tpk					
3600	RBBN	60472	3348	4W-16S	C3
3800	CTWD	60472	3348	4W-16S	C2
3900	CTWD	60445	3348	4W-16S	C3
Midmar Ln					
100	IVNS	60067	2752	22W-16N	B7
Mid Oaks Ln					
10	BNHL	60010	2750	27W-20N	C1
Midway Ct					
10	BNVL	60106	2972		A1
10	CTCY	46324	3430		C3
10	CTCY	60409	3430	4E-19S	C3
10	HMND	46324	3430	4E-19S	C3
1500	EGVV	60007	2861	17W-10N	C6
Midway Dr					
500	DSPN	60018	2861	16W-10N	E6
500	MPPT	60018	2861	16W-10N	E6
500	MPPT	60056	2861	16W-10N	E6
Midway Ln					
1400	GNVW	60025	2810	10W-14N	A5
W Midway Pk					
5700	CHCG	60644	3031	7W-0N	C3
5900	OKPK	60302	3031	7W-0N	B3
Midway Rd					
800	NHBK	60062	2757	8W-17N	E4
1000	NHBK	60062	2758	8W-17N	A5
Midway Plaisance Dr					
-	CHCG	60637	3152	1E-6S	E3
-	CHCG	60637	3153	1E-6S	A4
N Mies Van Der Rohe Wy					
800	CHCG	60611	3034		D2
Milan Ct					
300	SMBG	60193	2858	23W-9N	E7
Milan Ln					
500	HFET	60194	2858	24W-11N	E4
Milbeck Av					
700	EGVV	60007	2914		D1
Milbeck Ct					
700	EGVV	60007	2914		D1
S Milbrook Ln					
1700	ANHT	60005	2861	18W-12N	A2
Milburn Av					
100	CRTE	60417	3685	0W-29S	C1
E Milburn Av					
-	DSPN	60016	2862	15W-12N	B1
-	MPPT	60016	2862	15W-12N	B1
10	MPPT	60056	2862	15W-12N	A1
W Milburn Av					
10	MPPT	60056	2862	15W-12N	A1
700	MPPT	60056	2861	16W-12N	E1
Milburn Pk					
10	EVTN	60201	2813	2W-12N	C7
Milburn St					
500	EVTN	60201	2813	2W-12N	C7
N Mildred Av					
2600	CHCG	60614	2977	1W-3N	E5
2700	CHCG	60657	2977	1W-3N	E5
Mildred Ct					
11400	WLSP	60480	3208		D4
Mildred Ln					
10	CHHT	60411	3508	1W-23S	A4
1000	UYPK	60466	3684	3W-30S	C3
Milford Av					
4600	OKFT	60452	3426	5W-19S	B3
17000	TYPK	60477	3424	9W-20S	D4
Milford Ct					
300	SMBG	60193	2858	24W-9N	E7
Milford Rd					
300	DRFD	60015	2757	10W-20N	A1
400	DRFD	60015	2756	10W-20N	E1
Milford St					
10200	PvsT	60162	3087	12W-1S	A1
10200	WSTR	60154	3087	12W-1S	A1
Milford Haven Wy					
200	MNSR	46321	3510		D3
E Milida Ct					
1200	ANHT	60004	2807	17W-16N	C1
Mill Cir					
600	WLNG	60090	2755	13W-17N	D6
W Mill Ct					
1300	PLTN	60074	2753	20W-17N	B4
Mill Ct E					
9700	PlsT	60464	3345	12W-15S	D1
Mill Dr					
-	RNPK	60471	3594	4W-26S	D3
Mill Dr E					
9700	PlsT	60464	3345	12W-15S	D1
12900	PSPK	60464	3345	12W-15S	D1
Mill Dr W					
9800	PlsT	60464	3345	12W-15S	C1
N Mill Rd					
200	ADSN	60143	2914		D7
200	ITSC	60143	2914		D7
200	ITSC	60191	2914		D7
200	WDDL	60191	2914		D7
S Mill Rd					
12800	PlsT	60464	3273	12W-15S	D7
12800	PlsT	60464	3345	12W-15S	D1
13000	PSPK	60464	3345	12W-15S	D1
Mill St					
1300	CRTE	60417	3685	1W-29S	B2
1600	DSPN	60016	2863	12W-11N	A3
N Mill St					
400	PTON	60468	3860	9W-37S	E3
500	PtnT	60468	3860	9W-37S	E3
S Mill St					
200	PTON	60468	3860	9W-37S	E4
W Mill St					
5300	MONE	60449	3683	6W-31S	A6
5400	MONE	60449	3682	6W-31S	E6
Millard Av					
14300	MDLN	60445	3348	4W-17S	D4
15400	MKHM	60426	3348	4W-18S	D7
15500	MKHM	60426	3426	4W-18S	D1
22700	RNPK	60471	3594	4W-27S	E5
S Millard Av					
1200	CHCG	60623	3032	4W-1S	C7
1200	CHCG	60624	3032	4W-1S	C7
1500	CHCG	60623	3090	4W-2S	D3
5100	CHCG	60632	3150	4W-5S	D2
6600	CHCG	60629	3150	4W-7S	D6
9100	ENGN	60805	3212	4W-10S	D5
9800	CHCG	60655	3212	4W-11S	D7
9800	ENGN	60655	3212	4W-11S	D7
11700	CHCG	60655	3276	4W-13S	D5
11700	WthT	60803	3276	4W-13S	D5
12100	ALSP	60803	3276	4W-14S	D6
S Millard St					
11900	ALSP	60803	3276	4W-14S	D5
11900	WthT	60803	3276	4W-14S	D5
Millbank Dr					
13900	ODPK	60462	3346	10W-16S	C3
Millbridge Rd					
-	LYNS	60534	3088	9W-3S	C6
-	RVSD	60546	3088	10W-3S	C6
-	RvsT	60534	3088	10W-3S	C6
-	RvsT	60546	3088	10W-3S	C6
Millbrook Ct					
1400	SMBG	60193	2858	25W-10N	B6
Millbrook Ln					
100	SMBG	60193	2858	25W-10N	B6
100	WLMT	60091	2811	6W-13N	E7
Mill Creek Dr					
1000	BFGV	60089	2754	17W-17N	B4
1400	ANHT	60004	2754	17W-17N	A5
Millcreek Ln					
2500	RGMW	60008	2805	21W-13N	D5
Millennium Dr					
18300	TYPK	60477	3425	8W-22S	A7
18300	TYPK	60477	3505	8W-22S	A1
Miller Av					
800	SMWD	60107	2911		C1
1100	OKPK	60302	3030	8W-1N	D2
1100	RVFT	60305	3030	8W-1N	D2
2700	SCHT	60411	3596	1W-26S	A3
3300	STGR	60475	3596	1W-27S	A4
Miller Ct					
1900	HMWD	60430	3427	2W-21S	D7
Miller Dr					
3700	GNVW	60025	2809	10W-15N	E2
3800	GNVW	60062	2809	11W-15N	D2
18400	LNSG	60438	3430	4E-21S	C7
Miller Ln					
-	ANHT	60004	2754	17W-17N	A4
300	WDDL	60191	2914		E7
800	BFGV	60089	2754	17W-17N	A4
Miller Pl					
900	PHNX	60426	3350	0W-18S	C7
900	SHLD	60473	3350	0W-18S	C7
Miller Rd					
-	LYNS	60534	3088	9W-3S	D6
-	LYNS	60546	3088	9W-3S	D6
-	RVSD	60546	3088	9W-3S	D6
1600	NHBK	60062	2756	11W-16N	D6
22400	SCHT	60411	3596	0E-27S	D4
22400	SCHT	60475	3596	0E-27S	D4
22400	STGR	60475	3596	0E-27S	D4
22900	CRTE	60417	3596	0E-27S	D5
Miller St					
-	WshT	60401	3864	1W-36S	B1
400	STGR	60475	3596	0E-27S	D4
500	BCHR	60401	3864	0W-36S	B1
S Miller St					
700	CHCG	60607	3033	1W-0S	E6
1900	CHCG	60608	3091	1W-1S	E1
Miller Cir Dr					
5300	MTSN	60443	3505	6W-25S	E7
5300	MTSN	60443	3593	6W-25S	E1
5300	MTSN	60443	3594	6W-25S	A1
Millers Cross					
100	ITSC	60143	2914		C5
Millers Ln					
10	MPPT	60056	2807	16W-13N	D7
E Millers Rd					
10	DSPN	60016	2862	14W-11N	C3
W Millers Rd					
10	DSPN	60016	2862	15W-11N	B3
700	DSPN	60016	2861	16W-11N	E3
700	MPPT	60056	2861	16W-11N	E3
Millis Ln					
100	SMBG	60193	2857	26W-10N	E6
Mill Run Ct					
17100	ODHL	60477	3424	11W-20S	A4
17100	TYPK	60477	3424	11W-20S	A4
Mills St					
200	HNDL	60521	3146		C1
600	HNDL	60521	3086		C7
W Millstone Ct					
10	PSHL	60465	3274	10W-12S	B3
Millstone Ln					
2700	RGMW	60008	2805	21W-13N	C5
Millstone Rd					
17900	HLCT	60429	3427	3W-21S	A6
E Mill Valley Rd					
400	PLTN	60074	2753	20W-17N	A5
E Millwood Dr					
300	BRLT	60103	2911		B5
S Millwood Dr					
900	BRLT	60103	2911		C5
N Miltimore Av					
5600	CHCG	60646	2919	7W-7N	C4
Milton Av					
400	GLNC	60022	2758	6W-17N	C4
1800	NHBK	60062	2757	10W-17N	B5
2000	PKRG	60068	2863	11W-9N	D6
Milton Ct					
5500	RSMT	60018	2917	12W-6N	C5
Milton Ln					
400	HFET	60194	2858	24W-11N	E4
700	SMBG	60194	2858	24W-11N	D4
1200	SMBG	60193	2912		C1
Milton Pkwy					
5400	RSMT	60018	2917	12W-6N	C5
Milton Rd					
600	IVNS	60067	2751	23W-16N	E6
Milton Bridge Ter					
900	FKFT	60423	3593	8W-26S	A2
Milwaukee Av					
500	MaiT	60016	2809	10W-13N	E7
500	MaiT	60025	2809	10W-13N	E7
500	NfdT	60016	2809	10W-13N	E7
500	NfdT	60025	2809	11W-14N	C5
700	GNVW	60025	2809	11W-13N	C5
900	BFGV	60089	2755	14W-20N	C1
900	VrnT	60015	2755	14W-20N	C1
900	VrnT	60062	2755	14W-20N	C1
900	VrnT	60089	2755	14W-20N	C1
1000	RVWD	60015	2755	14W-20N	C1
1600	GNVW	60062	2809	12W-14N	C4
1800	NfdT	60062	2809	12W-15N	B3
2800	PTHT	60062	2809	12W-15N	B3
2800	PTHT	60070	2809	12W-15N	B3
9700	GNVW	60025	2863	10W-12N	E1
9700	GNVW	60025	2864	10W-12N	A1
9700	MaiT	60016	2864	10W-12N	A1
9700	MaiT	60025	2863	11W-12N	E1
9700	MaiT	60714	2864	10W-12N	A1
9700	NLES	60714	2864	10W-12N	A1
9800	MaiT	60016	2863	11W-12N	E1
20400	BFGV	60090	2755	14W-20N	C1
Milwaukee Av SR-21					
500	MaiT	60016	2809	10W-13N	E7
500	MaiT	60025	2809	10W-13N	E7
500	NfdT	60016	2809	10W-13N	E7
500	NfdT	60025	2809	11W-14N	C5
700	GNVW	60025	2809	11W-14N	C5
900	BFGV	60089	2755	14W-20N	C1
900	VrnT	60015	2755	14W-20N	C1
900	VrnT	60062	2755	14W-20N	C1
900	VrnT	60089	2755	14W-20N	C1
1000	RVWD	60015	2755	14W-20N	C1
1600	GNVW	60062	2809	12W-14N	C4
1800	NfdT	60062	2809	12W-15N	B3
2800	PTHT	60062	2809	12W-15N	B3
2800	PTHT	60070	2809	12W-15N	B3
9700	GNVW	60025	2863	10W-12N	E1
9700	GNVW	60025	2864	10W-12N	A1
9700	MaiT	60016	2864	10W-12N	A1
9700	MaiT	60025	2863	11W-12N	E1
9700	MaiT	60714	2864	10W-12N	A1
9700	NLES	60714	2864	10W-12N	A1
9800	MaiT	60016	2863	11W-12N	E1
20400	BFGV	60090	2755	14W-20N	C1
Milwaukee Av US-45					
900	BFGV	60089	2755	14W-20N	C1
900	VrnT	60015	2755	14W-20N	C1
900	VrnT	60062	2755	14W-20N	C1
900	VrnT	60089	2755	14W-20N	C1
1000	RVWD	60015	2755	14W-20N	C1
20400	BFGV	60090	2755	14W-20N	C1
N Milwaukee Av					
-	NfdT	60062	2809	12W-15N	A2
200	CHCG	60606	3034	0W-0N	A4
400	CHCG	60610	3034	0W-0N	A3
400	CHCG	60622	3034	0W-0N	A3
400	CHCG	60661	3034	0W-0N	A3
500	CHCG	60622	3033	1W-1N	D2
500	PTHT	60062	2809	13W-15N	A1
500	PTHT	60070	2809	12W-15N	A2
500	PTHT	60090	2809	13W-15N	A1
500	WhlT	60062	2809	13W-15N	A1
500	WhlT	60090	2809	13W-15N	A1
500	WLNG	60090	2755	14W-18N	C2
800	BFGV	60090	2755	14W-20N	C2
900	BFGV	60089	2755	14W-20N	C1
900	VrnT	60062	2755	14W-20N	C1
900	VrnT	60089	2755	14W-20N	C1
1500	CHCG	60647	3033	2W-2N	B1
1600	CHCG	60647	2977	2W-2N	A7
2200	CHCG	60647	2976	3W-2N	E6
2700	CHCG	60618	2976	4W-3N	D5
3200	CHCG	60641	2976	4W-3N	D5
3900	CHCG	60641	2975	6W-5N	E1
4300	CHCG	60630	2975	6W-5N	E1
4400	CHCG	60630	2919	6W-5N	D7
5500	CHCG	60646	2919	7W-6N	B5
6300	CHCG	60631	2919	8W-7N	A3
6500	NLES	60714	2919	6W-5N	D7
6600	NLES	60714	2918	8W-8N	E1
7200	NLES	60714	2864	9W-9N	D6
7500	CHCG	60631	2864	8W-9N	D7
7500	CHCG	60714	2864	8W-9N	D7
7500	NLES	60631	2864	9W-9N	D7
8300	MaiT	60714	2864	9W-9N	D6
9600	GNVW	60025	2864	9W-9N	D6
9600	MaiT	60016	2864	9W-9N	D6
N Milwaukee Av SR-21					
-	NfdT	60062	2809	12W-15N	A2
500	PTHT	60062	2809	13W-15N	A1
500	PTHT	60070	2809	13W-15N	A1
500	PTHT	60090	2809	13W-15N	A1
500	WhlT	60062	2809	13W-15N	A1
500	WhlT	60090	2809	13W-15N	A1
500	WLNG	60090	2755	14W-18N	C2
800	BFGV	60090	2755	14W-20N	C2
900	BFGV	60089	2755	14W-20N	C1
900	VrnT	60062	2755	14W-20N	C1
900	VrnT	60089	2755	14W-20N	C1
7500	CHCG	60631	2864	9W-9N	D7
7500	CHCG	60714	2864	9W-9N	D7
7500	NLES	60631	2864	9W-9N	D7
7500	NLES	60714	2864	9W-9N	D6
8300	MaiT	60714	2864	9W-9N	D6
9600	GNVW	60025	2864	9W-9N	D6
9600	MaiT	60016	2864	9W-9N	D6
N Milwaukee Av US-45					
500	PTHT	60062	2809	13W-15N	A1
500	PTHT	60070	2809	13W-15N	A1
500	PTHT	60090	2809	13W-15N	A1
500	WhlT	60062	2809	13W-15N	A1
500	WhlT	60090	2809	13W-15N	A1
500	WLNG	60090	2755	14W-18N	C2
800	BFGV	60090	2755	14W-20N	C2
900	BFGV	60089	2755	14W-20N	C1
900	VrnT	60062	2755	14W-20N	C1
900	VrnT	60089	2755	14W-20N	C1
S Milwaukee Av					
10	WLNG	60090	2755	13W-17N	E5
600	WhlT	60090	2755	13W-17N	E5
1100	PTHT	60070	2755	13W-16N	E7
1100	PTHT	60070	2808	13W-16N	E1
1100	PTHT	60070	2809	13W-16N	A1
1100	PTHT	60090	2809	13W-16N	A1
1100	WhlT	60090	2808	13W-16N	E1
1100	WhlT	60090	2809	13W-16N	A1
S Milwaukee Av SR-21					
10	WLNG	60090	2755	13W-17N	E5
600	WhlT	60090	2755	13W-17N	E5
1100	PTHT	60070	2755	13W-16N	E7
1100	PTHT	60070	2808	13W-16N	E1
1100	PTHT	60070	2809	13W-16N	A1
1100	PTHT	60090	2809	13W-16N	A1
1100	WhlT	60090	2808	13W-16N	E1
1100	WhlT	60090	2809	13W-16N	A1
S Milwaukee Av US-45					
10	WLNG	60090	2755	13W-17N	E5
600	WhlT	60090	2755	13W-17N	E5
1100	PTHT	60070	2755	13W-16N	E7
1100	PTHT	60070	2808	13W-16N	E1
1100	PTHT	60070	2809	13W-16N	A1
1100	PTHT	60090	2809	13W-16N	A1
1100	WhlT	60090	2808	13W-16N	E1
1100	WhlT	60090	2809	13W-16N	A1
Milwaukee Ct					
3800	CHCG	60641	2976	5W-4N	A2
Milwaukee Pl					
10	WLNG	60090	2755	14W-18N	D4
Mimosa Dr					
7300	ODPK	60462	3346	9W-18S	E7
Mimosa Ln					
200	EGVV	60007	2914		E2
Miner St					
1200	DSPN	60016	2862	13W-11N	E3
1300	DSPN	60016	2863	13W-11N	A3
Miner St US-14					
1200	DSPN	60016	2862	13W-11N	E3
1300	DSPN	60016	2863	13W-11N	A3
E Miner St					
2400	ANHT	60004	2807	16W-14N	D4
W Miner St					
10	ANHT	60004	2807	17W-14N	A4
200	ANHT	60005	2807	18W-14N	A4
1400	ANHT	60005	2806	18W-14N	D4
1700	RGMW	60008	2806	18W-14N	D4
Minerva Av					
14200	DLTN	60419	3351	1E-17S	A5
15400	SHLD	60473	3351	1E-18S	A7
15900	SHLD	60473	3429	1E-18S	A1
S Minerva Av					
200	BlmT	60425	3509	1E-23S	A3
200	GNWD	60425	3509	1E-23S	A3
6300	CHCG	60637	3153	1E-7S	A5
Mines Dr					
-	CHCG	60616	3092	0E-1S	D1
Minette Ln					
500	CHHT	60411	3595	2W-25S	D1
Minetz Ct					
11600	OrlT	60467	3344	14W-16S	D2

STREET Block	City	ZIP	Map#	CGS	Grid
Minnaqua Dr					
400	PTHT	60070	2807	16W-15N	D2
Minneapolis Av					
9600	FNPK	60131	2973	12W-3N	B4
N Minnehaha Av					
6300	CHCG	60646	2919	6W-8N	D2
6600	LNWD	60712	2919	6W-8N	D2
6600	SKOK	60077	2919	6W-8N	D2
Minneola St					
400	HNDL	60521	3086		C7
Minnesota Av					
-	ALSP	60406	3276	4W-14S	E7
-	ALSP	60406	3277	3W-14S	A7
-	ALSP	60803	3276	4W-14S	E7
-	ALSP	60803	3277	3W-14S	A7
-	BLID	60406	3276	4W-14S	E7
-	BLID	60803	3276	4W-14S	E7
-	BLID	60803	3277	3W-14S	A7
2800	BLID	60406	3277	3W-14S	A7
W Minnesota Av					
200	PLTN	60067	2752	21W-16N	D7
Minnesota Ct					
10800	ODPK	60467	3423	12W-21S	C5
Minnesota Dr					
1600	EGVV	60007	2913		D2
S Minnesota Dr					
6700	BDPK	60638	3148	8W-7S	E7
N Minnetonka Av					
6800	CHCG	60646	2919	6W-8N	D1
Minnick Av					
9500	OKLN	60453	3211	6W-10S	E6
10100	OKLN	60453	3275	6W-11S	E1
Minocqua Ct					
10	PKFT	60466	3595	3W-27S	A4
Minocqua St					
200	PKFT	60466	3595	4W-27S	A4
300	PKFT	60466	3594	4W-27S	E4
Minot Ct					
700	EGVV	60007	2913		D2
Mint Ln					
2100	GNVW	60025	2810	9W-14N	B3
W Mint Julip Dr					
5200	ALSP	60803	3275	6W-13S	E4
Miroballi Dr					
8600	HYHL	60457	3210	11W-9S	A4
Mirta Cir					
10	LMNT	60439	3271		B7
Misko Ct					
10	LMNT	60439	3271		A5
Mission Av					
14700	OKFT	60452	3347	6W-17S	E5
Mission Ct					
300	BMDL	60108	2912		A7
300	BmdT	60108	2912		A7
Mission Dr					
-	PSPK	60464	3273	12W-14S	C7
700	UYPK	60466	3684	3W-30S	B3
4900	RNPK	60471	3594	6W-27S	B4
9900	PlsT	60464	3273	12W-15S	C7
N Mission Dr					
5100	CHCG	60656	2918	9W-6N	B6
5100	NRDG	60706	2918	9W-6N	B6
Mission Hills Ct					
13500	ODPK	60462	3346	10W-16S	A2
Mission Hills Ln					
1800	NfdT	60062	2756	12W-16N	B7
Mission Hills Rd					
1600	NfdT	60062	2756	12W-16N	B6
Mississippi Ct					
10800	ODPK	60467	3423	12W-21S	C5
Mississippi Ln					
900	EGVV	60007	2913		D3
Missouri Ct					
17700	ODPK	60467	3423	13W-21S	A6
Missouri Dr					
1600	EGVV	60007	2913		D2
Mistic Harbour Ln					
500	SMBG	60193	2858	24W-9N	E7
W Misty Dr					
700	PltT	60074	2752	21W-17N	C4
Misty Ln					
16800	TYPK	60477	3424	8W-20S	E3
S Misty Harbour Ln					
12700	PSPK	60464	3272	13W-14S	E7
12700	PSPK	60464	3273	13W-15S	A7
12700	PSPK	60464	3344	13W-15S	E1
12700	PSPK	60467	3344	13W-15S	E1
Misty Hill Rd					
10400	ODPK	60462	3345	13W-17S	B6
Misty Meadow Dr					
-	OrlT	60462	3346	10W-15S	C2
-	PSHT	60462	3346	10W-15S	C2
13200	PlsT	60462	3346	10W-15S	C2
13200	PlsT	60464	3346	10W-15S	C2
13200	PSHT	60464	3346	10W-15S	C1
Misty Pine Ct					
6200	RchT	60477	3425	7W-22S	C7
6200	TYPK	60477	3425	7W-22S	C7
Misty Pines Dr					
-	TYPK	60477	3425	7W-21S	C7
6200	RchT	60477	3425	7W-22S	C7
N Mitchell Av					
1600	ANHT	60004	2807	18W-15N	A1
1700	ANHT	60004	2806	18W-15N	E1
2800	ANHT	60004	2754	18W-17N	A5
S Mitchell Av					
10	ANHT	60005	2807	18W-13N	A7
1200	ANHT	60005	2861	18W-12N	A1
Mitchell Blvd					
1200	SMBG	60193	2912		E3
1500	SMBG	60172	2912		E3
W Mitchell Ct					
400	ANHT	60004	2807	18W-15N	A1
N Mitchell Dr					
3900	ANHT	60004	2754	18W-18N	A3
E Mitchell Ln					
1500	MPPT	60056	2808	14W-13N	D6
Mitchell Tr					
1300	EGVV	60007	2914		A3
N Mittel Blvd					
1200	WDDL	60191	2915		A4
1300	WDDL	60191	2914		E3
1500	EGvT	60007	2914		E3
Mittel Dr					
1000	WDDL	60191	2915		A4
Mobile Av					
8500	BRBK	60459	3211	7W-9S	B4
8700	OKLN	60453	3211	7W-10S	B4
N Mobile Av					
1600	CHCG	60302	3031	7W-2N	B1
1600	CHCG	60639	2975	7W-2N	B7
1600	CHCG	60639	3031	6W-0S	E6
1600	OKPK	60302	3031	7W-2N	B1
4200	CHCG	60630	2975	7W-5N	B1
4200	CHCG	60634	2975	7W-5N	B1
N Mobile Av					
4400	CHCG	60630	2919	7W-5N	A7
7000	CHCG	60646	2919	7W-8N	B1
S Mobile Av					
5100	CHCG	60638	3149	7W-5S	B2
5100	StkT	60638	3149	7W-5S	B2
6400	BDPK	60638	3149	7W-7S	B5
12700	PSHT	60463	3275	7W-15S	B7
12700	WthT	60463	3275	7W-15S	B7
Mobile Cir					
1000	EGVV	60007	2913		D3
Mocassin Ln					
2500	CPVL	60110	2748		C4
Mockingbird Ln					
100	WLNG	60090	2754	16W-18N	E4
18100	TYPK	60477	3424	11W-21S	A7
Moczygemba St					
600	LMNT	60439	3270		E6
Model Ct					
12800	CTWD	60445	3275	6W-15S	E7
Model Airfield Rd					
23500	WynT	60184	2909		E7
Moe Dr					
-	CHCG	60616	3092	0E-2S	D2
E Moehling Dr					
200	MPPT	60056	2862	15W-12N	A1
Moeller St					
2100	DYR	46311	3598		D2
W Moffat St					
2000	CHCG	60622	2977	2W-2N	B7
2000	CHCG	60647	2977	2W-2N	B7
3100	CHCG	60647	2976	3W-2N	E7
Mohave St					
200	HFET	60194	2858	23W-11N	E4
200	HFET	60194	2859	23W-10N	A4
200	SMBG	60194	2859	23W-10N	A4
Mohawk Ct					
10	BFGV	60089	2754	17W-18N	C3
10	SBTN	60010	2804	25W-13N	A5
800	ELGN	60120	2855		C2
1200	SMBG	60193	2913		B1
1300	SmbT	60193	2913		B2
6400	IHPK	60525	3146		D6
Mohawk Dr					
10	SBTN	60010	2804	25W-13N	A5
10	TNTN	60476	3428	0E-20S	E5
200	BNVL	60106	2915		D7
800	ELGN	60120	2855		C1
1300	SmbT	60193	2913		B2
1500	SmbT	60172	2913		B2
Mohawk Ln					
2300	GNVW	60025	2809	11W-15N	C2
13500	ODPK	60462	3346	9W-16S	C2
E Mohawk Ln					
1700	MPPT	60056	2808	13W-15N	D2
1700	PTHT	60070	2808	13W-15N	D2
Mohawk Rd					
1000	WLMT	60091	2812	5W-14N	A5
S Mohawk Rd					
12300	PSPK	60464	3274	10W-14S	B6
Mohawk St					
200	PKFT	60466	3595	4W-27S	A4
300	PKFT	60466	3594	4W-27S	E4
N Mohawk St					
800	CHCG	60610	3034	0W-1N	A2
1600	CHCG	60610	2978	0W-2N	A7
1600	CHCG	60614	2978	0W-2N	A7
Mohawk Tr					
10	BFGV	60089	2754	16W-18N	C3
1500	WLNG	60090	2754	16W-17N	D5
20000	OMFD	60461	3507	4W-24S	A5
20100	OMFD	60461	3506	4W-24S	E5
Mohegan Ln					
900	SMBG	60193	2912		D1
Moher Ct					
19400	MKNA	60448	3504	11W-23S	A3
N Moki Ln					
900	MPPT	60056	2808	13W-14N	E5
Moline Expwy					
-	BmnT	-	3425	7W-21S	D7
-	BmnT	-	3426	6W-21S	A6
-	CCHL	-	3426	5W-20S	B5
-	FftT	-	3504	11W-22S	A1
-	HLCT	-	3426	4W-20S	D4
-	HLCT	-	3427	3W-20S	B4
-	MKHM	-	3427	3W-20S	A4
-	MKNA	-	3504	10W-22S	C1
-	RchT	-	3425	7W-21S	D7
-	RchT	-	3505	8W-22S	A1
-	TYPK	-	3504	10W-22S	C1
-	TYPK	-	3505	8W-22S	A1
Moline Expwy I-80					
-	BmnT	-	3425	7W-21S	D7
-	BmnT	-	3426	6W-21S	A6
-	CCHL	-	3426	5W-20S	B5
-	FftT	-	3504	11W-22S	A1
-	HLCT	-	3426	4W-20S	D4
-	HLCT	-	3427	3W-20S	B4
-	MKHM	-	3427	3W-20S	A4
-	MKNA	-	3504	10W-22S	C1
-	RchT	-	3425	7W-21S	D7
-	RchT	-	3505	8W-22S	A1
-	TYPK	-	3504	10W-22S	C1
-	TYPK	-	3505	8W-22S	A1
Molobay Ter					
900	BRLT	60103	2911		B5
Monaco Dr					
300	ROSL	60172	2912		E4
Monaghan Dr					
8400	FftT	60477	3504	10W-23S	B4
8400	TYPK	60477	3504	10W-23S	B4
8500	FftT	60423	3504	10W-23S	B4
S Monaghan Rd					
13500	HMGN	60441	3343	17W-16S	D2
13500	LMNT	60439	3343	17W-16S	D2
Monaldi Dr					
7900	MNSR	46321	3430		E6
Monaldi Pkwy					
2600	DYR	46311	3598		C3
Monarch Dr					
10	SMWD	60107	2856	30W-9N	C7
10	SMWD	60107	2910		C1
Monarch Ln					
1100	HFET	60195	2804	24W-15N	C1
Monarch Birch Ct					
300	BRLT	60103	2910		A2
Monarch Birch Ln					
400	BRLT	60103	2910		A2
Mondelli Ln					
-	HMGN	60441	3342	19W-17S	E5
Monee Ct					
10	PKFT	60466	3595	3W-28S	B5
Monee Rd					
-	CteT	60417	3686	0E-31S	A5
10	BlmT	60466	3595	3W-27S	B5
Monee Rd					
10	MonT	60466	3595	3W-27S	B5
10	PKFT	60466	3595	3W-28S	B5
200	MonT	60417	3594	4W-28S	E7
200	MonT	60466	3594	4W-28S	E7
200	PKFT	60466	3594	4W-28S	E7
700	CteT	60417	3685	1W-31S	A5
1100	CteT	60417	3684	2W-31S	D5
2100	MonT	60417	3684	2W-31S	D5
2100	MonT	60449	3684	2W-31S	D5
W Monee Rd					
10	CRTE	60417	3685	0W-31S	C5
10	CteT	60417	3685	0W-31S	C5
W Monee Manhattan Rd					
5500	MONE	60449	3682	8W-30S	B4
5500	MONE	60449	3683	6W-30S	A4
5500	MonT	60449	3682	8W-30S	B4
5500	MonT	60449	3683	6W-30S	A4
5500	UYPK	60449	3683	6W-31S	A4
5600	MONE	60466	3682	7W-31S	D4
5600	UYPK	60449	3682	7W-31S	E4
5600	UYPK	60466	3682	7W-31S	E4
6800	GGnT	60449	3682	8W-30S	A4
Monet Ct					
700	SMBG	60193	2858	24W-9N	E7
Monitor Av					
7500	BRBK	60459	3211	7W-8S	C2
9100	OKLN	60453	3211	7W-10S	C5
10700	CHRG	60415	3275	7W-12S	C2
N Monitor Av					
1000	CHCG	60651	3031	7W-1N	C2
1600	CHCG	60639	3031	7W-2N	C1
2100	CHCG	60639	2975	7W-2N	C6
4000	CHCG	60634	2975	7W-5N	C1
4300	CHCG	60630	2975	7W-5N	C1
4900	CHCG	60630	2919	7W-6N	B6
6000	CHCG	60646	2919	7W-7N	B3
S Monitor Av					
900	CHCG	60644	3031	7W-0S	C6
1100	CCRO	60804	3031	7W-0S	C7
5100	CHCG	60638	3149	7W-5S	C2
5100	StkT	60638	3149	7W-5S	C2
12700	ALSP	60803	3275	7W-15S	C7
12700	WthT	60445	3275	7W-15S	C7
12700	WthT	60463	3275	7W-15S	C7
12900	WthT	60463	3347	7W-15S	C1
Monitor St					
400	PKFT	60466	3507	3W-25S	B7
400	PKFT	60466	3595	3W-25S	B1
Monmouth Dr					
1200	LMNT	60439	3271		A6
Monmouth Pl					
-	CRTE	60417	3685	0E-29S	D1
N Monon Av					
7000	CHCG	60646	2919	7W-8N	B1
Monroe Av					
400	GLNC	60022	2758	6W-17N	D6
500	RVFT	60305	3030	9W-0N	D3
800	CPVL	60110	2748		D7
800	OKPK	60304	3030	8W-0S	E5
1500	EDPK	60707	3030	9W-2N	D1
1800	GNVW	60025	2810	8W-14N	E4
6200	HMND	46324	3430		E2
7800	MNSR	46321	3430		E6
8700	MNSR	46321	3510		D1
8800	BKFD	60513	3087	11W-3S	D5
9500	BKFD	60525	3087	11W-3S	C5
9500	LGPK	60525	3087	11W-3S	C5
E Monroe Av					
900	LGPK	60525	3087	12W-3S	C5
1100	BKFD	60513	3087	12W-3S	C5
1100	BKFD	60525	3087	12W-3S	C5
W Monroe Av					
200	LGPK	60525	3087	12W-3S	B5
Monroe Ct					
10	SMWD	60107	2857	28W-10N	A6
1800	GNVW	60025	2810	8W-14N	E4
6000	MNGV	60053	2865	7W-10N	B5
W Monroe Ct					
6900	NLES	60714	2864	8W-10N	E5
Monroe Dr					
1100	BRLT	60103	2910		C7
E Monroe Dr					
100	CHCG	60603	3034	0E-0S	C5
Monroe Ln					
1600	HRPK	60133	2911		E6
Monroe Pl					
500	WDDL	60191	2914		D7
Monroe St					
200	EGvT	60018	2862	15W-9N	A7
400	DLTN	60419	3350	0E-16S	D4
700	EVTN	60202	2867	3W-10N	A5
1100	FTPK	60304	3030	8W-0S	D5
1100	OKPK	60304	3030	8W-0S	D5
1600	EVTN	60202	2866	3W-10N	E5
2900	BLWD	60104	3029	12W-0S	B5
3400	LNSG	60438	3430	4E-21S	C6
3900	HLSD	60162	3029	12W-0S	A5
5200	SKOK	60077	2865	6W-10N	C5
5800	MNGV	60053	2865	7W-10N	B5
7000	WLBK	60527	3146		A7
7600	FTPK	60130	3030	9W-0S	C5
E Monroe St					
10	CHCG	60603	3034	0E-0S	C5
100	EMHT	60126	3028		A5
W Monroe St					
10	CHCG	60603	3034	0W-0S	A5
100	CHCG	60606	3034	0W-0S	B5
400	CHCG	60661	3034	0W-0S	A5
700	CHCG	60607	3034	0W-0S	A5
800	CHCG	60607	3033	1W-0S	D5
2400	CHCG	60612	3033	3W-0S	A5
2800	CHCG	60612	3032	3W-0S	E5
3100	CHCG	60624	3032	4W-0S	D5
4600	CHCG	60644	3032	5W-0S	A5
4800	CHCG	60644	3031	6W-0S	E5
7200	NLES	60714	2864	10W-10N	B5
7900	MaiT	60714	2864	9W-10N	B5
Monson Ct					
200	SMBG	60173	2859	21W-10N	E5
Montabello					
-	BMDL	60172	2912		C7
-	BmdT	60172	2912		C7
Montana Av					
9900	FNPK	60131	2973	12W-3N	B6
Montana Ct					
18200	ODPK	60467	3423	13W-21S	A7
Montana St					
10400	LydT	60131	2973	13W-3N	A6
10400	LydT	60164	2973	13W-3N	A6
10600	LydT	60164	2972		E6
10600	NHLK	60164	2972		E6
W Montana St					
900	CHCG	60614	2977	1W-3N	D5
2300	CHCG	60647	2977	2W-3N	A5
W Montana St					
4400	CHCG	60639	2976	5W-3N	A5
4700	CHCG	60639	2975	6W-3N	D5
Montana Wy					
1500	EGVV	60007	2859	21W-9N	E7
Montclaire Cir					
1300	SMBG	60173	2859	21W-10N	D5
Montclaire Pl					
1200	SMBG	60173	2859	22W-10N	D5
N Mont Clare Av					
2500	CHCG	60707	2974	8W-3N	D5
2700	CHCG	60634	2974	8W-3N	D5
4800	CHCG	60656	2918	8W-6N	D6
4800	HDHT	60656	2918	8W-6N	D7
4800	HDHT	60706	2918	8W-6N	D7
Montego Ct					
200	BMDL	60108	2912		B7
200	BmdT	60108	2912		B7
1200	EGVV	60007	2914		C3
Montego Dr					
500	EGVV	60007	2914		C3
Monterey Av					
19800	LYWD	60411	3510	3E-23S	A4
E Monterey Av					
10	SMBG	60193	2913		A2
400	SmbT	60193	2913		B2
N Monterey Av					
5000	CHCG	60656	2918	9W-6N	B6
5000	NRDG	60656	2918	9W-6N	B6
5000	NRDG	60706	2918	9W-6N	B6
S Monterey Av					
1400	ROSL	60172	2913		C2
1400	ROSL	60193	2913		C2
1400	SmbT	60193	2913		C2
W Monterey Av					
10	SMBG	60193	2913		A2
1600	CHCG	60643	3277	2W-13S	D3
Monterey Ct					
1700	HFET	60194	2858	25W-12N	A2
Monterey Dr					
1400	GNVW	60025	2810	10W-14N	A4
2900	FSMR	60422	3507	3W-22S	A1
3100	HMWD	60430	3507	3W-22S	A1
4800	RNPK	60471	3594	6W-27S	A4
E Monterey Rd					
400	PLTN	60074	2753	20W-17N	A6
Montery Ct					
1000	UYPK	60466	3684	3W-30S	B3
S Montgomery Av					
4000	CHCG	60632	3091	3W-4S	A6
W Montgomery Av					
2600	CHCG	60632	3091	3W-4S	A6
Montgomery Dr					
-	CRTE	60417	3596	0E-29S	E7
-	CRTE	60417	3685	0E-29S	E1
9100	ODPK	60462	3346	10W-17S	A6
9200	ODPK	60462	3345	11W-17S	E5
Montgomery Ln					
100	GNVW	60025	2864	9W-12N	D1
200	WDDL	60191	2914		C7
Montgomery St					
100	GLNC	60022	2758	5W-17N	E5
W Montgomery St					
-	DSPN	60016	2861	16W-10N	E4
-	DSPN	60056	2861	16W-10N	E4
-	MPPT	60056	2861	16W-10N	E4
Montibello Dr					
5500	HRPK	60133	2911		D6
Monticello Av					
7300	SKOK	60076	2866	4W-9N	C7
9400	SKOK	60203	2866	4W-11N	C2
9500	EVTN	60201	2866	4W-11N	C2
N Monticello Av					
400	CHCG	60624	3032	4W-0N	C3
700	CHCG	60651	3032	4W-0N	C3
1500	CHCG	60647	3032	4W-1N	C1
2200	CHCG	60647	2976	4W-2N	C6
3500	CHCG	60618	2976	4W-4N	C2
4300	CHCG	60625	2976	4W-5N	C1
4400	CHCG	60625	2920	4W-5N	C7
6000	CHCG	60659	2920	4W-7N	C3
6300	CHCG	60712	2920	4W-7N	C3
6300	LNWD	60712	2920	4W-7N	C3
S Monticello Av					
13300	RBBN	60472	3348	4W-15S	D2
Monticello Dr					
10	DYR	46311	3510		C7
10	LYWD	60411	3510	4E-25S	C7
S Monticello Pl					
-	PvsT	60558	3086		D4
-	WSTR	60154	3086		D4
-	WSTR	60523	3086		D4
W Monticello Pl					
11300	WSTR	60154	3086		D3
Monticello Rd					
1600	HFET	60195	2858	23W-12N	E1
Monticello St					
700	EVTN	60201	2813	2W-13N	B7
Montmarte Av					
3300	HLCT	60429	3426	4W-21S	E7
Montrose Av					
-	SRPK	60176	2917	12W-5N	B7
-	SRPK	60176	2973	11W-5N	C1
500	CHCG	60666	2917	12W-5N	A7
W Montrose Av					
-	CHCG	60613	2922	0W-5N	A7
-	CHCG	60640	2922	0W-5N	A7
600	CHCG	60613	2921	2W-5N	C7
600	CHCG	60640	2921	2W-5N	C7
1900	CHCG	60618	2921	2W-5N	B7
1900	CHCG	60625	2921	2W-5N	B7
2700	CHCG	60618	2920	3W-5N	E7
2700	CHCG	60625	2920	3W-5N	E7
3200	CHCG	60618	2976	4W-5N	D1
3200	CHCG	60625	2976	4W-5N	D1
3900	CHCG	60630	2976	5W-5N	B1
3900	CHCG	60641	2976	5W-5N	B1
4600	CHCG	60630	2975	7W-5N	B1
4600	CHCG	60641	2975	7W-5N	B1
5500	CHCG	60634	2975	7W-5N	C1
6300	HDHT	60706	2975	7W-5N	A1
6600	HDHT	60706	2974	8W-5N	E1
7200	NRDG	60706	2974	10W-5N	A1
7700	CHCG	60634	2974	9W-5N	C1
7700	NRDG	60634	2974	9W-5N	C1
7800	CHCG	60706	2974	9W-5N	B1
8300	CHCG	60656	2974	10W-5N	A1
8500	CHCG	60634	2973	10W-5N	E1
8500	CHCG	60656	2973	10W-5N	E1
Montrose Blvd					
9900	SRPK	60176	2973	12W-5N	B1
W Montrose Harbor Dr					
-	CHCG	60613	2922	0W-5N	B7
-	CHCG	60613	2978	0W-5N	B1
-	CHCG	60640	2922	0W-5N	B7
W Montvale Av					
1600	CHCG	60643	3277	2W-13S	C3
Monument Av					
100	BRTN	60010	2750	25W-18N	E3
Moody Av					
7700	BRBK	60459	3211	7W-8S	C2
8500	OKLN	60459	3211	7W-9S	C4
8800	MNGV	60053	2865	7W-11N	B3
9800	OKLN	60453	3211	7W-11S	C7
10400	CHRG	60415	3275	7W-12S	C1
N Moody Av					
1600	CHCG	60302	3031	6W-0S	E7
1600	CHCG	60639	3031	6W-0S	E7
1600	OKPK	60302	3031	6W-0S	E7
2600	CHCG	60639	2975	7W-3N	B5
4000	CHCG	60634	2975	7W-5N	B1
4200	CHCG	60630	2975	7W-5N	B1
5200	CHCG	60630	2919	7W-6N	B5
5600	CHCG	60646	2919	7W-7N	B4
S Moody Av					
5100	CHCG	60638	3149	7W-5S	B2
5100	StkT	60638	3149	7W-5S	B2
12400	WthT	60463	3275	7W-14S	C7
12900	WthT	60463	3347	7W-15S	C1
Moody Ct					
300	SEGN	60177	2909		A1
Moon Hill Dr					
2900	NHBK	60062	2756	11W-17N	D5
Moon Lake Blvd					
-	SMBG	60194	2858	25W-12N	A2
1300	HFET	60194	2858	26W-12N	A2
1600	HFET	60194	2857	26W-12N	E2
1600	HFET	60195	2857	26W-12N	E1
Moonlight Ct					
10	MTSN	60443	3506	5W-24S	C5
Moonlight Rd					
10	MTSN	60443	3506	5W-24S	C5
Moore Av					
1600	SMWD	60107	2911		B1
Moore Dr					
700	EGVV	60007	2914		C1
8900	BGVW	60455	3210	9W-10S	D5
Moore Ln					
-	SRPK	60176	2973	11W-5N	C1
Moorefield Ct					
13100	LMNT	60439	3343	16W-15S	E1
W Moorefield Dr					
7600	FftT	60423	3504	9W-24S	E5
Moorehead Dr					
100	BRLT	60103	2909		C3
Moorfield Rd					
400	RchT	60443	3593	8W-26S	B2
Moorings Dr					
10	PSHT	60463	3274	9W-13S	D5
S Moorings Dr					
1000	ANHT	60005	2807	17W-12N	B7
Moorings Ln					
14800	OKFT	60452	3347	7W-17S	C5
N Moorman St					
1300	CHCG	60622	3033	1W-1N	E1
Moose Ln					
10800	ODPK	60467	3423	13W-20S	A4
Mora Ct					
1900	HRPK	60133	2912		A2
1900	SMBG	60193	2912		A2
Mora Rd					
100	CPVL	60110	2748		B4
Moraine Av					
6200	HMND	46324	3430		C2
8400	MNSR	46321	3430		C7
Moraine Ct					
-	HnrT	60107	2856	29W-11N	E5
Moraine Dr					
10	HnrT	60107	2856	29W-11N	E4
10	SMWD	60107	2856	29W-11N	E4
8400	PSHL	60465	3274	10W-13S	B3
Moraine St					
8900	SjnT	46311	3598		C7
9100	SjnT	46311	3687		D1
Moray Ct					
200	CRTE	60417	3596	0E-28S	E6
Moray Dr					
-	IVNS	60010	2803	25W-15N	E1
Moray Ter					
400	CRTE	60417	3596	0E-28S	E6
N Moreland Dr					
5000	CHCG	60656	2918	9W-6N	B6
5000	NRDG	60706	2918	9W-6N	B6
Morey Dr					
100	WDRG	60439	3270		B2
100	WDRG	60517	3270		B2
Morgan Av					
1100	BKFD	60513	3087	11W-2S	D4
1100	LGPK	60525	3087	11W-2S	D4
1500	PvsT	60525	3087	11W-2S	D4
9300	SKOK	60203	2866	4W-11N	D2
Morgan Ct					
10	BRRG	60527	3208		B5
3700	STGR	60475	3596	1W-28S	A6
W Morgan Ct					
12500	HMGN	60441	3344	15W-17S	B5
Morgan Dr					
-	CHCG	60637	3152	0E-6S	D3
1400	EGVV	60007	2913		E3
Morgan Ln					
10	BrnT	60010	2803	27W-14N	A5
10	SBTN	60010	2803	27W-14N	A5
400	HFET	60194	2858	24W-10N	E4
1200	BRLT	60103	2910		C7
16300	ODHL	60477	3423	11W-19S	E2
Morgan St					
200	CHHT	60411	3596	0W-25S	C1
3000	SCHT	60411	3596	1W-27S	A5
3000	STGR	60475	3596	1W-28S	A6
3800	CteT	60475	3596	1W-28S	A7
14900	HRVY	60426	3350	1W-18S	A6
18200	HMWD	60430	3428	1W-21S	A7
18700	HMWD	60430	3508	1W-22S	A2
N Morgan St					
10	CHCG	60607	3033	1W-0N	E4
700	CHCG	60622	3033	1W-0N	E3
S Morgan St					
10	CHCG	60607	3033	1W-0S	E5
1000	CHCG	60608	3033	1W-1S	E7
1600	CHCG	60608	3091	1W-1S	E1
3400	CHCG	60609	3091	1W-4S	E6
4700	CHCG	60609	3151	1W-6S	E3
5500	CHCG	60621	3151	1W-7S	E6
7500	CHCG	60620	3213	1W-8S	E1
9400	CHCG	60643	3213	1W-10S	E6
9900	CHCG	60643	3214	1W-11S	A7
12200	CTPK	60643	3278	1W-14S	A6
12200	CTPK	60827	3278	1W-14S	A6
12700	CHCG	60643	3278	1W-15S	A7

STREET
Block City ZIP Map# CGS Grid

Morgan O'Brien
- DSPN 60016 2862 15W-12N B2
S Mormann Ln
13900 HMGN 60441 3343 18W-16S A4
Morning Glory Ct
13000 HMGN 60441 3344 16W-18S A7
Morning Glory Dr
4500 MTSN 60443 3506 5W-24S B6
Morning Glory Ln
600 BRLT 60103 2910 D7
Morningside Cir
2200 CPVL 60110 2801 D1
Morningside Ct
600 ROSL 60172 2913 C4
600 SMBG 60173 2859 22W-11N C4
Morning Side Dr
900 UYPK 60466 3684 3W-30S A3
Morningside Dr
10 ROSL 60172 2913 C5
800 SMBG 60173 2859 22W-11N C4
Morningside Ln
2100 CPVL 60110 2801 D1
2100 EDND 60118 2801 D1
Morningside Rd
14400 ODPK 60462 3345 13W-17S B5
Morning Song Ct
1900 SMBG 60194 2858 26W-11N A3
Morningview Ct
5300 HFET 60192 2802 30W-12N B7
Morningview Dr
1900 HFET 60192 2802 30W-12N C7
Morray Ct
500 DSPN 60018 2862 15W-10N A5
Morris Av
10 BLWD 60104 3029 12W-0N A3
600 HLSD 60162 3028 D4
700 HLSD 60163 3028 D4
1200 BKLY 60163 3028 D3
18100 HMWD 60430 3427 2W-22S C7
18600 HMWD 60430 3507 2W-22S D1
E Morris Dr
600 PLTN 60074 2753 20W-16N B7
N Morris Dr
200 PLTN 60074 2753 19W-16N C7
Morris Ln
500 HNDL 60521 3086 A7
Morris St
100 PKRG 60068 2864 10W-9N A7
E Morris St
800 HMND 46320 3430 E1
S Morris Hill Dr
1800 MPPT 60056 2861 16W-10N D5
E Morrison Av
100 WhlT 60056 2808 13W-13N E6
N Morrison Av
600 PLTN 60067 2752 22W-16N B6
Morrison Rd
900 NHBK 60062 2757 8W-18N D3
Mors Av
200 WLNG 60090 2755 14W-17N D5
Morse Av
10 SmbT 60193 2913 A2
300 NHLK 60164 3028 E2
300 NHLK 60164 3029 13W-1N A1
400 SNPK 60165 3029 13W-1N A1
500 SMBG 60193 2912 D2
600 EGVV 60007 2915 B2
900 SmbT 60193 2912 D2
1600 DSPN 60018 2917 12W-8N A2
4900 LNWD 60712 2919 6W-8N E1
4900 SKOK 60077 2919 6W-8N E1
E Morse Av
100 BRLT 60103 2910 E2
200 BRLT 60103 2911 A2
W Morse Av
100 BRLT 60103 2910 E2
1100 CHCG 60626 2921 2W-8N B1
2000 CHCG 60645 2921 2W-8N A1
2600 CHCG 60645 2920 3W-8N E1
4500 LNWD 60712 2920 5W-8N A1
4600 LNWD 60712 2919 5W-8N E1
4800 SKOK 60077 2919 6W-8N E1
5400 CHCG 60646 2919 6W-8N E1
5400 SKOK 60646 2919 6W-8N D1
Morse Dr
300 NHLK 60164 3028 E1
Mortimer Rd
200 GLNC 60022 2758 6W-17N E5
Morton Av
1000 ELGN 60120 2855 B1
3100 BKFD 60513 3087 11W-3S D4
3100 LGPK 60525 3087 11W-3S D4
8500 MNGV 60053 2865 7W-10N B4
Morton Ct
5100 HMND 46320 3352 C6
Morton St
800 HFET 60194 2858 24W-11N E3
N Moselle Av
6800 CHCG 60646 2919 7W-8N B1
6800 NLES 60646 2919 7W-8N B1
6800 NLES 60714 2919 7W-8N B1
Moss Ct
8700 TYPK 60477 3424 10W-21S B6
E Moss St
1000 HMND 46320 3430 E2
Motorola
- SMBG 60173 2805 21W-13N D7
Moulin Ln
3800 HFET 60195 2804 24W-14N B3
Mound St
100 WLSP 60480 3209 12W-9S C3
Mt Pleasant Rd
1000 WNKA 60093 2811 5W-15N E2
1000 WNKA 60093 2812 5W-15N A2
Mt Pleasant St
- NtrT 60093 2811 6W-15N D2
- WNKA 60093 2811 6W-15N D2
700 WNKA 60093 2812 5W-15N A2
1700 NHFD 60093 2811 6W-15N C2
Mt Prospect Plz
900 MPPT 60016 2808 14W-13N B7
900 MPPT 60056 2808 14W-13N B7
Mt Prospect Rd
3300 AddT 60126 2972 B4
3300 BNVL 60106 2972 B4
3300 EMHT 60126 2972 B5
3300 FNPK 60131 2972 B4
3300 LydT 60131 2972 B5
3500 BNVL 60131 2972 B4
N Mt Prospect Rd
10 DSPN 60016 2862 15W-12N B2
10 MPPT 60016 2862 15W-12N B1
100 MPPT 60056 2862 15W-12N B2
S Mt Prospect Rd
10 DSPN 60016 2808 14W-12N B7
10 MPPT 60056 2808 14W-12N B7
200 DSPN 60016 2862 15W-12N B1
200 MPPT 60016 2862 15W-12N B1
200 MPPT 60056 2862 15W-12N B1
900 DSPN 60018 2862 14W-10N B5
1800 EGvT 60018 2862 14W-9N B7
2200 DSPN 60018 2916 B1
2200 EGvT 60018 2916 B1
2200 MaiT 60018 2916 B1
2500 CHCG 60018 2916 C2
Mt Vernon Ter
1200 NHBK 60062 2756 10W-17N E5
Mozart Av
16700 MKHM 60426 3427 3W-20S B3
S Mozart Av
14400 POSN 60469 3349 3W-17S A5
14700 BmnT 60469 3349 3W-17S A5
N Mozart Dr
1200 CHCG 60622 3032 3W-1N E1
Mozart St
12700 BLID 60406 3277 3W-15S A7
13400 BLID 60406 3349 3W-16S A2
N Mozart St
100 PLTN 60067 2753 20W-16N A7
200 CHCG 60612 3032 3W-0N E4
800 CHCG 60622 3032 3W-1N E2
2400 CHCG 60647 2976 3W-3N E5
3600 CHCG 60618 2976 3W-4N E2
4400 CHCG 60618 2920 3W-5N E7
4900 CHCG 60625 2920 3W-6N E6
6000 CHCG 60659 2920 3W-7N E3
6300 CHCG 60645 2920 3W-7N E3
S Mozart St
- CHCG 60612 3032 3W-0S E5
1100 CHCG 60623 3032 3W-0S E7
3500 CHCG 60623 3091 3W-3S A5
3500 CHCG 60632 3091 3W-3S A5
4600 CHCG 60632 3151 3W-5S A1
5400 CHCG 60629 3151 3W-7S A5
7900 CHCG 60652 3213 3W-9S A2
8700 ENGN 60805 3213 3W-10S A4
Mueller Dr
300 HLSD 60162 3029 13W-0S A5
W Mueller St
300 ANHT 60004 2807 18W-14N A4
Muenich Ct
10 HMND 46320 3352 C6
Muirfield Dr
800 HRPK 60133 2912 A5
16700 ODPK 60467 3423 13W-20S B3
16700 OrlT 60467 3423 13W-20S B3
Muirfield Ln
400 RVWD 60015 2756 12W-20N A1
Muirfield Rd
800 IVNS 60067 2751 24W-17N D5
Mulberry Av
9900 OKLN 60453 3211 6W-11S D7
10100 OKLN 60453 3275 6W-11S D1
17400 TYPK 60477 3424 11W-20S A5
17500 CCHL 60478 3426 5W-21S B6
Mulberry Ct
- BGVW 60455 3274 9W-11S D1
300 BRLT 60103 2911 B3
500 BFGV 60089 2754 17W-18N B3
8200 PSHL 60465 3274 10W-13S B3
15400 HMGN 60441 3344 16W-18S A7
E Mulberry Ct
400 GNWD 60425 3508 0E-22S E1
400 GNWD 60425 3509 0E-22S A2
2900 CteT 60417 3687 3E-29S A2
Mulberry Dr
- MPPT 60056 2808 14W-14N C4
- MPPT 60070 2808 14W-14N C4
600 PTHT 60070 2808 14W-14N B4
E Mulberry Dr
10 GNWD 60425 3508 0E-22S E2
Mulberry Ln
- BGVW 60455 3274 9W-11S D1
10 GNVW 60025 2811 6W-13N D7
200 EGVV 60007 2914 E3
900 SMWD 60107 2857 28W-9N B7
2500 NHBK 60062 2756 10W-16N E7
E Mulberry Ln
1900 ANHT 60004 2807 16W-16N D1
N Mulberry Ln
1300 MPPT 60056 2808 14W-14N C5
S Mulberry Ln
24500 CteT 60417 3687 3E-29S B2
W Mulberry Ln
1300 ANHT 60005 2806 18W-14N D4
5200 MONE 60449 3683 6W-31S A6
Mulberry Rd
10 DRFD 60015 2757 10W-20N B2
Mulberry St
400 HMND 46324 3430 D3
6900 HRPK 60133 2911 D2
Mulberry Ter
18300 CCHL 60478 3426 5W-22S B7
Mulberry East Rd
10 DRFD 60015 2757 10W-20N B2
Mulcahey Dr
100 DSPN 60016 2808 13W-13N E7
Mulford Ct
200 ELGN 60120 2855 C3
Mulford Dr
10 ELGN 60120 2855 C3
Mulford Ln
200 ROSL 60172 2912 C5
Mulford St
900 EVTN 60202 2867 2W-9N A6
1700 EVTN 60202 2866 3W-9N E6
3900 SKOK 60076 2866 5W-9N B6
5000 SKOK 60077 2865 6W-9N D6
5300 MNGV 60053 2865 6W-9N D6
5500 SKOK 60053 2865 6W-9N D6
W Mulford St
6100 NLES 60714 2865 7W-9N B6
6100 SKOK 60077 2865 7W-9N B6
7200 NLES 60714 2864 9W-9N D6
Mulguy Ct
2100 IVNS 60010 2751 25W-16N A7
Mulguy Dr
2100 IVNS 60010 2751 25W-16N A7
Mulligan Av
7700 BRBK 60459 3211 7W-9S B3
9100 OKLN 60453 3211 7W-10S B5
N Mulligan Av
2600 CHCG 60639 2975 7W-3N A5
4200 CHCG 60630 2975 7W-5N A1
4200 CHCG 60634 2975 7W-5N A1
4400 CHCG 60630 2919 7W-5N A7
4800 HDHT 60706 2919 7W-6N A6
5700 CHCG 60646 2919 7W-7N A4
S Mulligan Av
5100 StkT 60638 3149 7W-5S B2
5800 CHCG 60638 3149 7W-6S B4
N Mulligan Ct
800 PLTN 60067 2752 21W-17N C6
800 PltT 60067 2752 21W-17N C6
Mullingar Ct
100 SMBG 60193 2859 23W-9N A7
Mulranny Dr
13100 HMGN 60441 3343 16W-17S E5
Mumford Ct
4400 HFET 60195 2804 24W-15N C2
Mumford Dr
4100 HFET 60195 2804 24W-15N C1
E Mundhank Rd
10 HFET 60195 2804 25W-14N A5
10 SBTN 60010 2803 26W-14N D5
10 SBTN 60010 2804 25W-14N A5
W Mundhank Rd
10 SBTN 60010 2803 27W-13N B6
Mundhawk Rd
- HFET 60010 2803 28W-12N B7
- HFET 60010 2857 28W-12N B1
Munger Rd
10 BRLT 60103 2910 A7
10 BRLT 60120 2910 A5
10 WynT 60184 2910 A7
400 BRLT 60184 2910 A7
Municipal Dr
- WSTR 60154 3029 12W-1S B7
Munroe Cir
200 DSPN 60016 2862 15W-10N B4
Munroe Cir S
400 DSPN 60016 2862 15W-10N A4
Munster Rd
10 LMNT 60439 3342 19W-15S D1
Munz Rd
- CRTE 60417 3685 0W-30S C4
E Munz Rd
200 CRTE 60417 3685 0E-30S E4
200 CteT 60417 3685 0E-30S E4
200 CteT 60417 3686 0E-30S A4
N Mura Ln
1500 MPPT 60056 2808 13W-15N E2
1800 PTHT 60056 2808 13W-15N E2
1800 PTHT 60070 2808 13W-15N E2
Muret Ct
100 WLNG 60090 2808 14W-15N C1
Muriel Ct
400 WLNG 60090 2808 15W-16N B1
Murphy Av
16900 HLCT 60429 3427 3W-20S B4
22300 BlmT 60411 3598 3E-27S A3
22300 SLVL 60411 3598 3E-27S A3
Murphy Cir
- TYPK 60477 3423 11W-21S E7
18200 OrlT 60477 3423 11W-21S E7
Murphy Ln
9000 SKOK 60076 2866 4W-11N C3
S Murphy Ln
24700 MonT 60449 3682 8W-30S B3
Murphy Rd
- WDRG 60517 3270 C2
700 DGvT 60439 3270 C3
Murphy Lake Ln
100 PKRG 60068 2863 11W-9N D7
Murphy Lake Rd
100 PKRG 60068 2917 11W-9N D1
Murray Av
14300 DLTN 60419 3350 0E-16S E4
Murray Ct
7500 JSTC 60458 3209 11W-8S E1
9300 MNGV 60053 2864 9W-11N B2
Murray Dr
5600 BKLY 60163 3028 C4
S Murray Dr
26500 CteT 60417 3686 2E-32S D7
Murray Ln
600 DSPN 60016 2861 16W-10N E4
600 DSPN 60016 2862 15W-10N A4
600 MPPT 60056 2861 16W-10N E4
E Murray St
900 HMND 46320 3352 E6
S Murvey Ct
13600 HMGN 60467 3344 15W-16S C2
W Murvey Dr
12000 HMGN 60467 3344 15W-16S C2
E Museum Dr
1700 CHCG 60637 3153 2E-6S B3
S Museum Campus Dr
- CHCG 60616 3034 0E-1S D7
- CHCG 60616 3092 0E-1S D1
1400 CHCG 60605 3034 0E-1S D7
W Music Ct Dr
3600 CHCG 60624 3032 4W-0S C5
Muskegon Av
200 BNHM 60633 3351 3E-17S E5
200 CTCY 60409 3351 3E-17S E6
S Muskegon Av
7900 CHCG 60649 3215 3E-9S E2
8300 CHCG 60617 3215 3E-9S E3
10300 CHCG 60617 3279 3E-11S E1
12600 CHCG 60633 3279 3E-14S E7
13100 CHCG 60633 3351 2E-15S D1
14500 BNHM 60633 3351 3E-16S E4
14500 CTCY 60409 3351 3E-17S E4
Mustang Ct
10 SMWD 60107 2856 30W-10N C6
S Mustang Dr
14300 HMGN 60441 3344 15W-17S A5
14300 HmrT 60441 3344 15W-17S A5
Mutual Ter
15600 SHLD 60473 3350 0E-18S E7
W Myrick St
3700 CHCG 60652 3212 4W-8S C2
Myrtle Av
- ELGN 60120 2855 C6
14700 HRVY 60426 3349 1W-17S E6
15900 HRVY 60426 3427 1W-19S E2
16000 MKHM 60426 3427 1W-19S E2
W Myrtle Av
7600 CHCG 60631 2918 9W-7N C3
Myrtle Ct
18200 LNSG 60438 3430 4E-21S C6
W Myrtle Dr
1700 MPPT 60056 2861 17W-12N C2
Myrtle Ln
10 SMWD 60107 2856 29W-10N E6
3100 GNVW 60025 2809 11W-15N D2
3100 GNVW 60062 2809 11W-15N D2
3100 NHBK 60025 2809 11W-15N D2
3100 NHBK 60062 2809 11W-15N D2
Myrtle St
100 WNKA 60093 2812 4W-15N C3
E Myrtle St
900 HMND 46394 3280 E4
W Myrtle St
1000 PLTN 60067 2752 22W-17N B6
Myrtle Park St
1400 SMBG 60193 2913 A2
1400 SmbT 60193 2913 A2
1500 ROSL 60172 2913 A2
1500 ROSL 60193 2913 A2

N

S Nacke Rd
- CRTE 60417 3684 2W-31S D4
24700 CteT 60417 3684 2W-32S D6
24700 UYPK 60417 3684 2W-30S D2
Nacona Ln
10 IHPK 60525 3146 E5
Nagle Av
7700 BDPK 60459 3211 8W-8S B1
7700 BRBK 60459 3211 8W-9S B2
8600 OKLN 60453 3211 8W-9S B4
9200 MNGV 60053 2865 8W-11N A2
N Nagle Av
1600 CHCG 60302 3031 8W-2N A1
1600 CHCG 60707 3031 8W-2N A1
1600 OKPK 60302 3031 8W-2N A1
2000 CHCG 60707 2975 8W-2N A6
3200 CHCG 60634 2975 8W-4N A3
4400 HDHT 60706 2919 8W-5N A7
4400 HDHT 60706 2975 8W-5N A1
4500 CHCG 60630 2919 7W-6N A6
4800 CHCG 60656 2919 7W-6N A6
5600 CHCG 60631 2919 8W-7N A3
5600 CHCG 60646 2919 8W-7N A3
S Nagle Av
5000 StkT 60638 3149 8W-5S B2
5100 CHCG 60638 3149 8W-5S B2
5100 FTVW 60638 3149 8W-5S B2
10700 CHRG 60415 3275 8W-12S B2
10700 CHRG 60482 3275 8W-12S B2
11200 WRTH 60482 3275 8W-13S B4
12100 PSHT 60463 3275 8W-14S B6
Nancy Ln
300 WLNG 60090 2755 14W-17N C5
8600 ODPK 60462 3346 10W-18S B7
S Nancy St
25700 CteT 60417 3686 0E-31S A5
Nancy Ann Ln
800 ELGN 60120 2855 C5
Nanti St
100 PKFT 60466 3595 4W-28S A6
Nantucket Ct
300 BRLT 60103 2911 B6
1300 HFET 60195 2804 24W-15N C2
Nantucket Hbr
200 SMBG 60193 2913 B1
Nantucket Ln
100 PltT 60010 2751 23W-18N E3
Nantucket Cove
7400 HRPK 60133 2912 A1
Naoma Dr
600 CRTE 60417 3685 1W-30S A2
N Naper Av
5900 CHCG 60631 2919 8W-7N A3
Naperville Rd
- BRLT 60103 2856 30W-9N B7
- BRLT 60107 2856 30W-9N B7
- BRLT 60120 2856 30W-9N B7
- HnrT 60107 2856 30W-9N B7
- HnrT 60120 2856 30W-9N B7
- WynT 60103 2910 C4
100 BRLT 60103 2910 B3
100 HnrT 60103 2910 B2
N Naples Av
6000 CHCG 60631 2919 8W-7N A3
6000 CHCG 60646 2919 8W-7N A3
Naples Ln
900 DGvT 60439 3270 C2
900 WDRG 60439 3270 D2
N Napoleon Av
5800 CHCG 60631 2919 8W-7N A4
5800 CHCG 60646 2919 8W-7N A4
Narcissus Av
2000 HRPK 60133 2911 C1
2100 HRPK 60107 2911 C1
2100 SMWD 60107 2911 C1
Narcissus Ct
15100 ODPK 60462 3346 9W-18S D6
Narcissus Ln
7000 ODPK 60462 3346 9W-18S D7
Narragansett Av
7700 BDPK 60459 3211 7W-8S B1
7700 BRBK 60459 3211 8W-9S B2
8700 MNGV 60053 2865 8W-10N A4
N Narragansett Av
10 HDHT 60706 2975 8W-5N A1
1600 CHCG 60302 3031 8W-1N A1
1600 CHCG 60639 2975 7W-2N A7
1600 CHCG 60639 3031 8W-1N A1
1600 CHCG 60707 2975 7W-2N A7
1600 CHCG 60707 3031 8W-1N A1
1600 OKPK 60302 3031 8W-1N A1
2700 CHCG 60634 2975 8W-2N A6
4200 CHCG 60630 2975 8W-5N A1
4400 CHCG 60630 2919 7W-5N A7
4400 HDHT 60706 2919 7W-5N A7
4500 HDHT 60706 2919 7W-5N A7
S Narragansett Av
5100 CHCG 60638 3149 8W-6S B4
5100 StkT 60638 3149 7W-5S B2
7200 BDPK 60638 3149 7W-8S B7
7300 BDPK 60638 3211 8W-8S B1
Nash Ct
- LYWD 60411 3509 2E-23S D3
N Nashotah Av
5800 CHCG 60631 2919 8W-7N A4
Nashua Ln
1200 HRPK 60133 2911 D7
1200 HRPK 60133 2912 A6
Nashua St
100 PKFT 60466 3595 3W-27S A5
Nashville Av
7700 BDPK 60459 3211 8W-8S A1
7700 BRBK 60459 3211 8W-9S A3
8900 MNGV 60053 2865 8W-11N A3
9400 CHRG 60453 3211 8W-10S A6
9400 OKLN 60453 3211 8W-10S A6
9500 GLF 60029 2865 8W-11N A2
9500 MNGV 60029 2865 8W-11N A2
9700 CHRG 60415 3211 8W-11S A7
10300 CHRG 60415 3275 8W-12S A1
N Nashville Av
1600 CHCG 60302 3031 6W-0S D6
1600 CHCG 60707 3031 6W-0S D6
1600 OKPK 60302 3031 6W-0S D6
1700 CHCG 60707 2975 8W-2N A7
4000 CHCG 60634 2975 8W-5N A1
4400 HDHT 60706 2975 8W-5N A1
4800 CHCG 60656 2919 8W-6N A6
4800 HDHT 60706 2919 8W-6N A6
6400 CHCG 60631 2919 8W-8N A2
S Nashville Av
5100 FTVW 60638 3149 8W-5S A2
5900 CHCG 60638 3149 8W-7S A5
6400 BDPK 60638 3149 8W-7S A5
10700 CHRG 60415 3275 8W-12S A2
10700 CHRG 60482 3275 8W-12S A2
10700 WRTH 60482 3275 8W-12S A2
12300 PSHT 60463 3275 8W-14S B6
N Nassau Av
6000 CHCG 60631 2919 8W-7N A3
6000 CHCG 60646 2919 8W-7N A3
6100 CHCG 60631 2918 8W-7N E3
Nassau Ct
10 PKFT 60466 3595 3W-27S B5
Nassau Dr
600 ROSL 60172 2912 D6
Nassau St
300 PKFT 60466 3595 3W-27S B5
Natalie Dr
5400 OKFT 60452 3347 6W-18S D6
Natchez Av
7700 BDPK 60459 3211 8W-8S B1
7700 BRBK 60459 3211 8W-9S B2
8900 MNGV 60053 2865 8W-11N A2
9300 OKLN 60453 3211 8W-10S B5
10200 CHRG 60415 3275 8W-11S B1
N Natchez Av
1600 CHCG 60302 3031 6W-0S D6
1600 CHCG 60707 3031 6W-0S D6
1600 OKPK 60302 3031 6W-0S D6
2000 CHCG 60707 2975 8W-2N A6
4100 CHCG 60634 2975 8W-5N A1
4400 HDHT 60706 2919 8W-5N A7
4400 HDHT 60706 2975 8W-5N A1
4800 CHCG 60656 2919 8W-6N A6
7900 MNGV 60053 2865 8W-9N A6
7900 MNGV 60714 2865 8W-9N A6
7900 NLES 60714 2865 8W-9N A6
S Natchez Av
5100 FTVW 60638 3149 8W-5S A2
6500 BDPK 60638 3149 8W-7S A5
6500 CHCG 60638 3149 8W-7S A6
10700 CHRG 60415 3275 8W-12S B2
10700 CHRG 60482 3275 8W-12S B2
10700 WRTH 60482 3275 8W-12S B2
12100 PSHT 60463 3275 8W-14S B6
Natchez Tr
13500 OrlT 60467 3344 14W-16S D3
13500 PlsT 60467 3344 14W-16S D3
Nathan Rd
500 UYPK 60466 3684 3W-30S C3
Nathaniel Pl
2300 EVTN 60202 2866 3W-10N D4
National Av
8800 MNGV 60053 2864 8W-11N E3
8800 NLES 60714 2864 8W-11N E3
National Pkwy
- SMBG 60193 2859 21W-10N D5
800 SMBG 60173 2859 22W-10N D4
National St
- ELGN 60120 2855 A5
10 ELGN 60123 2855 A5
N National St
8500 NLES 60714 2864 8W-10N E4
Natoma Av
7700 BDPK 60459 3211 8W-8S A1
7700 BRBK 60459 3211 8W-9S A3
8700 OKLN 60453 3211 8W-10S A5
8900 MNGV 60053 2865 8W-11N A3
9700 CHRG 60415 3211 8W-11S A7
9700 CHRG 60453 3211 8W-11S A7
10400 CHRG 60415 3275 8W-12S A1
12600 PSHT 60463 3275 8W-14S B7
N Natoma Av
1600 CHCG 60302 3031 6W-0S D6
1600 CHCG 60707 3031 6W-0S D6
1600 OKPK 60302 3031 6W-0S D6
1700 CHCG 60707 2975 8W-2N A7
2800 CHCG 60634 2975 8W-3N A4
4800 CHCG 60656 2919 8W-6N A6
4800 CHCG 60656 2919 8W-6N A6
4800 HDHT 60706 2919 8W-6N A6
5700 CHCG 60631 2918 8W-7N E4
6200 CHCG 60631 2919 8W-7N A3
6500 CHCG 60631 2919 8W-8N A2
6500 NLES 60714 2919 8W-8N A2
S Natoma Av
5100 CHCG 60638 3149 8W-6S A3
5100 FTVW 60638 3149 8W-5S A2
11100 WRTH 60482 3275 8W-13S A4
Natoma Ct
600 ELGN 60120 2855 D6
Natoma Dr
600 ELGN 60120 2855 D6
Natoma St
400 PKFT 60466 3595 4W-28S A5
Nature Ct
1700 SMBG 60193 2912 A3
Nature Dr
4400 OKFT 60452 3347 8W-18S B7
Nature Center Dr
21500 OKBK 60523 3086 A5
Natwick Ln
200 SMBG 60193 2858 26W-10N A6
Naughton Dr
15000 SHLD 60473 3351 1E-17S A6
Nauset Ln
100 SMBG 60194 2858 24W-10N D5
Nauvoo St
100 PKFT 60466 3595 4W-28S A5
200 PKFT 60466 3594 4W-28S E5
Navaho Av
22100 SLVL 60411 3597 2E-26S E3
W Navaho Tr
13400 HMGN 60441 3343 16W-16S D3
N Navajo Av
6200 CHCG 60646 2919 6W-7N D3
6400 LNWD 60712 2919 6W-8N D2
7000 SKOK 60077 2919 6W-8N D2
Navajo Ct
10 BRRG 60527 3208 D4
E Navajo Ct
12600 PSHT 60463 3275 8W-13S A5
S Navajo Ct W
12600 PSHT 60463 3275 8W-13S A5
Navajo Dr
700 CPVL 60110 2748 C4

STREET Block	City	ZIP	Map#	CGS	Grid
E Navajo Dr					
6600	PSHT	60463	3275	8W-14S	A7
S Navajo Dr					
12600	PSHT	60463	3275	8W-14S	A7
W Navajo Dr					
6700	PSHT	60463	3275	8W-14S	A7
Navajo Ln					
200	HFET	60194	2858	23W-10N	E5
Navajo St					
400	PKFT	60466	3595	4W-28S	A5
Navajo Tr					
100	BFGV	60089	2754	16W-18N	C3
S Navajo Tr					
400	WLNG	60090	2754	16W-17N	D5
Navajo Trc					
17500	TYPK	60477	3424	10W-21S	C6
N Navarre Av					
5800	CHCG	60631	2919	8W-7N	A4
6000	CHCG	60631	2918	8W-7N	E3
Navy Blvd					
2600	GNVW	60025	2810	9W-14N	B4
S Na Wa Ta Av					
400	MPPT	60056	2861	16W-12N	E1
Nawata Pl					
400	PTHT	60070	2807	16W-15N	D2
Neal Cir					
18600	CCHL	60478	3506	6W-22S	A1
Neal Ct					
400	SMBG	60193	2859	22W-9N	B6
Nebel Ln					
700	DSPN	60018	2862	13W-9N	D7
Nebraska Ct					
18100	ODPK	60467	3423	13W-21S	A7
Nebraska Dr					
1600	EGVV	60007	2913		D2
Needles Ct					
-	HMGN	60467	3344	15W-16S	B3
Neenah Av					
7700	BDPK	60459	3211	8W-8S	A1
7700	BRBK	60459	3211	8W-9S	A2
9300	MNGV	60053	2865	8W-11N	A2
N Neenah Av					
2800	CHCG	60707	2975	8W-3N	A5
4100	CHCG	60634	2975	8W-5N	A1
4400	HDHT	60706	2919	8W-5N	A7
4400	HDHT	60706	2975	8W-5N	A1
4900	CHCG	60656	2919	8W-6N	A6
6200	CHCG	60631	2919	8W-7N	A3
S Neenah Av					
5100	CHCG	60638	3149	8W-6S	A3
5100	FTVW	60638	3149	8W-5S	A2
10700	CHRG	60415	3275	8W-12S	B2
10700	CHRG	60482	3275	8W-12S	B2
10700	WRTH	60482	3275	8W-12S	B2
Neil Av					
200	MPPT	60056	2808	14W-13N	B6
Neil Ln					
900	GNVW	60025	2809	11W-13N	E6
900	NfdT	60025	2809	11W-13N	E6
Nellie Ct					
300	MaiT	60025	2864	9W-12N	B1
Nelson Av					
3200	RBBN	60472	3348	4W-16S	D4
Nelson Ln					
500	DSPN	60016	2808	14W-12N	D7
500	MPPT	60016	2808	14W-12N	D7
500	MPPT	60056	2808	14W-12N	D7
Nelson Sq					
2400	WSTR	60154	3086		E3
Nelson St					
10800	WSTR	60154	3086		E3
W Nelson St					
1800	CHCG	60657	2977	2W-3N	B4
2300	CHCG	60618	2977	2W-3N	A4
2700	CHCG	60618	2976	3W-3N	E4
4000	CHCG	60641	2976	5W-3N	B4
4800	CHCG	60641	2975	6W-3N	E4
6000	CHCG	60634	2975	7W-3N	B4
6900	CHCG	60634	2974	8W-3N	E4
N Neola Av					
6000	CHCG	60631	2918	8W-7N	E3
6000	CHCG	60631	2919	8W-7N	A3
Neola St					
300	PKFT	60466	3595	3W-27S	A5
Neosho St					
400	PKFT	60466	3595	4W-28S	A6
Neptune Ct					
500	GNVW	60025	2810	10W-14N	A3
Neptune Ln					
22000	RNPK	60471	3594	6W-26S	B3
Nerbonne Av					
9400	FNPK	60131	2973	11W-4N	C3
Nerge Rd					
1000	EGVV	60007	2914		A2
1100	ITSC	60007	2914		A3
1100	ITSC	60143	2914		A3
1500	EGVV	60007	2913		D2
1900	ROSL	60172	2913		D2
E Nerge Rd					
10	ROSL	60172	2913		B2
10	SmbT	60172	2913		B2
10	SmbT	60193	2913		A2
500	ROSL	60193	2913		B2
800	EGVV	60007	2913		B2
800	ROSL	60007	2913		B2
Nettle Ln					
-	HnrT	60120	2856	30W-10N	B5
-	SMWD	60120	2856	30W-10N	B5
N Nettleton Av					
6000	CHCG	60631	2918	8W-7N	E3
Neutrenton Av					
100	ELGN	60120	2855		E4
100	HnrT	60120	2855		E4
Neva Av					
200	GNVW	60025	2864	8W-12N	E1
7900	BRBK	60459	3210	8W-9S	E2
9300	BGVW	60453	3210	8W-10S	E6
9300	OKLN	60453	3210	8W-10S	E6
N Neva Av					
1600	CHCG	60707	3030	8W-2N	D1
1600	OKPK	60302	3030	8W-2N	D1
1700	CHCG	60707	2974	8W-2N	D7
3200	CHCG	60634	2974	8W-4N	D3
4200	NRDG	60706	2974	8W-5N	D1
4800	CHCG	60656	2918	8W-6N	D6
4800	HDHT	60706	2918	8W-6N	D7
6500	CHCG	60631	2918	8W-8N	D2
6500	CHCG	60714	2918	8W-8N	D2
6500	NLES	60714	2918	8W-8N	D2
8200	NLES	60714	2864	8W-10N	D5
S Neva Av					
5100	CHCG	60638	3148	8W-5S	E2
Neva Ter					
300	BmdT	60143	2913		E6
300	BmdT	60157	2913		E6
Nevada Av					
10000	FNPK	60131	2973	12W-3N	B5
10400	FNPK	60164	2973	13W-3N	A6
10400	LydT	60131	2973	13W-3N	A6
10400	LydT	60164	2973	13W-3N	A6
10600	LydT	60164	2972		E6
Nevada Ct					
1700	ODPK	60467	3423	13W-21S	A7
Nevada Ln					
1500	EGVV	60007	2859	21W-9N	E7
W Nevada St					
1000	GNWD	60425	3428	1W-22S	A7
1100	GNWD	60430	3428	1W-22S	A7
1100	HMWD	60430	3428	1W-22S	A7
New Av					
-	DPgT	60441	3270		A7
-	LmnT	60439	3270		A7
E New Av					
10	LMNT	60439	3270		C5
W New Av					
10	LMNT	60439	3270		B6
200	DPgT	60441	3270		A6
New St					
2700	BLID	60406	3349	3W-15S	A1
N New St					
400	CHCG	60611	3034	0E-0N	D3
New Abby Dr					
10	IVNS	60010	2803	25W-16N	E1
10	IVNS	60010	2804	25W-16N	A1
N Newark Av					
5600	CHCG	60631	2918	8W-7N	E4
5600	CHCG	60656	2918	8W-7N	E4
6400	CHCG	60714	2918	8W-8N	E2
6400	NLES	60714	2918	8W-8N	E1
Newark Ln					
200	HFET	60194	2858	24W-10N	E5
Newberry Av					
-	FftT	60423	3504	10W-25S	D7
10	LGNG	60525	3087	12W-4S	C6
300	LGPK	60525	3087	12W-3S	C5
1500	PvsT	60525	3087	12W-2S	C4
4600	OKFT	60452	3426	5W-19S	B3
S Newberry Av					
1600	CHCG	60608	3092		E2
Newberry Dr					
300	EGVV	60007	2859	22W-9N	C7
300	EGVV	60007	2913		C1
500	SMWD	60107	2857	27W-10N	C6
N Newberry Ln					
1000	MPPT	60056	2808	14W-14N	C5
New Bridge Ct					
200	RGMW	60067	2805	21W-13N	D5
Newbridge Dr					
1200	LKPT	60441	3342	21W-18S	A7
N New Britton Dr					
4000	HFET	60195	2804	24W-15N	C3
W New Britton Dr					
1200	HFET	60195	2804	24W-15N	C3
N Newburg Av					
5900	CHCG	60631	2919	8W-7N	A3
5900	CHCG	60646	2919	8W-7N	A4
6100	CHCG	60631	2918	8W-7N	E3
Newburn Ct					
1600	WLNG	60090	2754	16W-18N	D3
Newbury Ct					
800	SMBG	60173	2859	22W-11N	C3
Newbury Dr					
7900	ODPK	60462	3346	9W-16S	D3
Newbury Ln					
600	SMBG	60173	2859	22W-11N	C3
6000	MTSN	60443	3505	7W-25S	C7
S Newbury Pl					
300	ANHT	60005	2807	17W-13N	B5
Newbury St					
10600	WSTR	60154	3087	13W-2S	A3
New Castle Av					
7700	BDPK	60459	3211	8W-8S	A1
7700	BRBK	60459	3211	8W-9S	A2
8100	BGVW	60459	3211	8W-9S	A3
8600	OKLN	60453	3211	8W-9S	A4
Newcastle Av					
1200	WSTR	60154	3029	12W-1S	B7
1400	WSTR	60154	3087	12W-1S	B1
2100	PvsT	60154	3087	12W-1S	B2
9100	MNGV	60053	2864	8W-11N	E3
N Newcastle Av					
1600	CHCG	60707	3030	8W-1N	E1
1600	OKPK	60302	3030	8W-1N	E1
1600	OKPK	60707	3030	8W-1N	E1
2400	CHCG	60707	2974	8W-3N	E5
2700	CHCG	60634	2974	8W-3N	E5
4200	HDHT	60706	2974	8W-5N	E1
4700	HDHT	60706	2918	8W-5N	E7
4800	CHCG	60706	2918	8W-6N	E6
5400	CHCG	60656	2918	8W-6N	E5
6200	CHCG	60631	2918	8W-7N	E3
6400	CHCG	60714	2918	8W-8N	E2
6400	NLES	60714	2918	8W-8N	E2
8200	NLES	60714	2864	8W-10N	E5
S Newcastle Av					
5100	CHCG	60638	3149	8W-6S	A3
5100	FTVW	60638	3149	8W-5S	A2
5100	StkT	60638	3149	8W-5S	A2
New Castle Ct					
100	RGMW	60008	2805	22W-13N	B5
Newcastle Ct					
400	ROSL	60172	2912		E4
1400	IVNS	60010	2751	25W-17N	A5
9000	TYPK	60477	3423	11W-21S	E7
9000	TYPK	60477	3424	11W-21S	A7
22600	DRPK	60010	2752	22W-20N	A1
New Castle Dr					
7500	FftT	60423	3504	9W-23S	E4
Newcastle Dr					
400	ROSL	60172	2912		D4
Newcastle Ln					
700	PTHT	60070	2808	14W-15N	C2
700	WLNG	60070	2808	14W-15N	C2
1200	HFET	60194	2858	25W-12N	B2
New Devon St					
9800	MNSR	46321	3510		C4
Newell Av					
700	CTCY	60409	3352	3E-18S	A7
New England Av					
-	BDPK	60638	3149	8W-7S	A6
-	NHBK	60062	2757	8W-18N	E2
7700	BDPK	60459	3211	8W-9S	A2
7700	BRBK	60459	3211	8W-9S	A2
8300	BGVW	60459	3211	8W-9S	A4
8700	BGVW	60455	3211	8W-10S	A4
8700	OKLN	60453	3211	8W-10S	A4
8700	OKLN	60455	3211	8W-10S	A4
9100	MNGV	60053	2864	8W-11N	E3
9600	CHRG	60415	3211	8W-11S	A6
15500	OKFT	60452	3347	8W-18S	A7
New England Av					
15600	BmnT	60477	3347	8W-18S	A7
15600	OKFT	60477	3347	8W-18S	A7
15700	BmnT	60477	3425	8W-18S	A1
16700	TYPK	60477	3425	8W-20S	A4
N New England Av					
1600	CHCG	60302	3030	8W-1N	E1
1600	CHCG	60707	3030	8W-1N	E1
1600	OKPK	60302	3030	8W-1N	E1
2400	CHCG	60707	2974	8W-3N	E5
2700	CHCG	60634	2974	8W-3N	E5
4200	HDHT	60706	2974	8W-5N	E1
4400	HDHT	60706	2918	8W-5N	E7
5400	CHCG	60656	2918	8W-6N	E5
6400	CHCG	60631	2918	8W-8N	E2
6400	CHCG	60714	2918	8W-8N	E2
6400	NLES	60714	2918	8W-8N	E2
8000	NLES	60714	2864	8W-10N	E5
8300	MNGV	60053	2864	8W-10N	E5
S New England Av					
5100	CHCG	60638	3148	8W-5S	E2
5100	StkT	60638	3148	8W-5S	E2
6400	BDPK	60638	3148	8W-7S	E5
10700	WRTH	60482	3275	8W-12S	A2
Newfield Ln					
7600	TYPK	60477	3504	9W-23S	D3
N Newgard Av					
6400	CHCG	60626	2921	1W-8N	D2
6400	CHCG	60660	2921	1W-8N	D2
Newgate Ct					
300	SMBG	60193	2859	23W-10N	B5
14000	ODPK	60462	3346	10W-16S	B3
Newgate Ln					
700	PTHT	60070	2808	14W-14N	C3
New Gross Point Rd					
-	NLES	60714	2865	7W-9N	C6
-	SKOK	60077	2865	7W-9N	C6
N New Hampshire Av					
5600	CHCG	60631	2918	8W-7N	E4
New Hampshire Ct					
17700	ODPK	60467	3423	12W-20S	C5
New Haven Av					
3900	ANHT	60004	2753	19W-18N	D3
3900	PltT	60004	2753	19W-18N	D3
New Jersey Ct					
17700	ODPK	60467	3423	13W-21S	A6
N Newkirk Ln					
700	PLTN	60074	2753	19W-16N	D6
Newland Av					
7700	BDPK	60459	3210	8W-9S	E3
7700	BRBK	60459	3210	8W-9S	E3
8200	BGVW	60459	3210	8W-9S	E3
8500	BRBK	60459	3211	8W-9S	A4
8700	BGVW	60455	3211	8W-10S	A4
8700	OKLN	60453	3211	8W-10S	A4
8700	OKLN	60455	3211	8W-10S	A4
N Newland Av					
1600	CHCG	60707	3030	8W-2N	E1
1600	OKPK	60302	3030	8W-2N	E1
1600	OKPK	60707	3030	8W-2N	E1
2300	CHCG	60707	2974	8W-3N	E5
3600	CHCG	60634	2974	8W-4N	E2
4200	HDHT	60706	2974	8W-5N	E1
4200	NRDG	60706	2974	8W-5N	E1
4700	HDHT	60706	2918	8W-5N	E7
5200	CHCG	60656	2918	8W-6N	E5
6400	CHCG	60631	2918	8W-8N	E2
8200	NLES	60714	2864	8W-10N	E5
S Newland Av					
5100	CHCG	60638	3148	8W-5S	E2
5100	StkT	60638	3148	8W-5S	E3
Newland Pl					
600	BmdT	60143	2913		E6
Newman Pl					
4300	HFET	60195	2804	23W-15N	D2
4300	IVNS	60067	2804	23W-15N	D2
4300	IVNS	60195	2804	23W-15N	D2
New Mexico Ct					
700	EGVV	60007	2913		E1
10900	ODPK	60467	3423	13W-21S	A6
New Mexico Tr					
600	EGVV	60007	2859	21W-9N	E7
600	EGVV	60007	2913		E1
New Mills Ct					
300	SMBG	60193	2859	23W-10N	B6
Newport Av					
10	EGVV	60007	2914		D3
W Newport Av					
800	CHCG	60657	2977	1W-4N	D3
1900	CHCG	60618	2977	2W-4N	B3
4000	CHCG	60618	2976	5W-4N	B3
4000	CHCG	60641	2976	5W-4N	B3
5500	CHCG	60641	2975	7W-4N	C3
6000	CHCG	60634	2975	7W-4N	B3
7000	CHCG	60634	2974	8W-4N	E3
Newport Blvd					
-	BRLT	60103	2911		B4
-	BRLT	60133	2911		D6
-	HRPK	60133	2911		D6
-	WynT	60103	2911		B5
Newport Cir					
2000	HRPK	60133	2911		C6
N Newport Ct					
4000	ANHT	60004	2753	18W-18N	D3
Newport Dr					
-	CRTE	60417	3685	1W-29S	A2
5000	RGMW	60008	2860	19W-12N	B1
5100	OKFT	60452	3425	6W-20S	E3
5100	OKFT	60452	3426	6W-20S	A3
19300	MKNA	60448	3504	11W-23S	A3
S Newport Dr					
12700	PlsT	60464	3273	12W-15S	C7
12700	PlsT	60464	3345	12W-15S	C1
Newport Hbr					
1000	SMBG	60193	2913		B1
Newport Ln					
300	BRLT	60103	2911		B4
1400	IVNS	60010	2751	25W-17N	A6
N Newport Ln					
4000	ANHT	60004	2753	19W-18N	D2
4000	PltT	60004	2753	18W-18N	D2
Newport Rd					
2400	NHBK	60062	2809	10W-16N	E1
2400	NHBK	60062	2810	10W-15N	A1
N Newport Rd					
1600	HFET	60195	2858	23W-12N	E1
W Newport Rd					
300	HFET	60195	2804	24W-12N	E7
W Newport St					
700	ROSL	60172	2912		D6
Newport Wy					
3900	PltT	60004	2753	19W-18N	C3
Newport North St					
600	ROSL	60172	2912		D6
Newport S St					
600	ROSL	60172	2912		D6
New Salem St					
300	PKFT	60466	3595	3W-25S	B1
400	PKFT	60466	3507	3W-25S	B7
New Sutton Rd					
-	BNHL	60010	2803	28W-15N	A1
-	BrnT	60010	2802	28W-14N	E4
-	BrnT	60010	2803	28W-15N	A1
-	BrnT	60192	2802	28W-13N	E6
-	HFET	60010	2802	29W-12N	D7
-	HFET	60192	2802	28W-13N	E6
-	HnrT	60192	2802	29W-12N	D7
-	SBTN	60010	2802	28W-13N	E6
-	SBTN	60118	2802	28W-13N	E5
100	BNHL	60010	2750	27W-16N	B6
100	BrnT	60010	2750	27W-16N	B6
700	BNHL	60118	2802	28W-14N	E4
700	BrnT	60118	2802	28W-14N	E4
New Sutton Rd SR-59					
-	BNHL	60010	2803	28W-15N	A1
-	BrnT	60010	2802	28W-14N	E4
-	BrnT	60010	2803	28W-15N	A1
-	BrnT	60192	2802	28W-13N	E6
-	HFET	60010	2802	29W-12N	D7
-	HFET	60192	2802	28W-13N	E6
-	HnrT	60010	2802	29W-12N	D7
-	SBTN	60010	2802	28W-13N	E6
-	SBTN	60118	2802	28W-13N	E6
100	BNHL	60010	2750	27W-16N	B6
100	BrnT	60010	2750	27W-16N	B6
700	BNHL	60118	2802	28W-14N	E4
700	BrnT	60118	2802	28W-14N	E4
New Sutton Rd SR-68					
100	BNHL	60010	2750	27W-16N	B6
100	BrnT	60010	2750	27W-16N	B6
Newton Av					
1600	PKRG	60068	2918	9W-7N	B4
1900	PKRG	60631	2918	9W-7N	B4
2000	CHCG	60631	2918	9W-7N	B4
Newton Ct					
600	SMBG	60194	2857	26W-11N	E4
Newton St					
200	HFET	60194	2858	23W-10N	E5
200	SMBG	60194	2858	23W-10N	E5
New Trier Ct					
1000	WLMT	60091	2811	6W-14N	C5
S New Wilke Rd					
-	ANHT	60008	2806	18W-13N	D6
1100	ANHT	60005	2806	19W-12N	D7
1100	RGMW	60008	2806	19W-12N	D7
1200	ANHT	60005	2860	19W-12N	D2
1400	RGMW	60008	2860	19W-12N	D1
New York Ct					
11000	ODPK	60467	3423	13W-21S	A6
New York Ln					
400	EGVV	60007	2859	22W-9N	C7
400	EGVV	60007	2913		C1
E Niagara Av					
200	EMHT	60126	3028		A4
300	SmbT	60193	2913		B2
400	SMBG	60193	2913		B2
N Niagara Av					
6200	CHCG	60631	2918	8W-7N	E3
W Niagara Av					
10	SMBG	60193	2913		A2
Niagara St					
-	LmnT	60439	3271		B5
300	PKFT	60466	3595	3W-28S	A5
Nicholas Blvd					
700	EGvT	60007	2861	16W-9N	D7
700	EGVV	60007	2861	16W-9N	D7
1100	EGVV	60007	2915		D2
2000	BNVL	60106	2915		D3
2000	EGVV	60106	2915		D3
Nicholas Ct					
5200	OKFT	60452	3425	6W-20S	E5
Nichols Av					
3500	FNPK	60131	2973	11W-4N	C3
Nichols Dr					
-	LYWD	60411	3509	2E-23S	D3
2800	SLVL	60411	3597	3E-26S	E3
2800	SLVL	60411	3598	3E-27S	A4
Nichols Ln					
1100	MYWD	60153	3030	10W-1N	A2
E Nichols Rd					
1000	PLTN	60074	2753	19W-18N	C2
W Nichols Rd					
-	ANHT	60004	2754	18W-18N	A3
-	BFGV	60004	2754	18W-18N	A3
-	BFGV	60089	2754	18W-18N	A3
-	ElaT	60004	2753	19W-20N	C2
-	ElaT	60047	2753	19W-20N	C2
500	BFGV	60004	2753	18W-18N	E3
500	BFGV	60089	2753	18W-18N	E3
2200	ANHT	60004	2753	19W-18N	C2
2200	PltT	60004	2753	19W-18N	C2
Nicholson Dr					
1600	HFET	60192	2856	30W-12N	C1
1600	HnrT	60192	2856	30W-12N	C1
N Nickerson Av					
5800	CHCG	60631	2918	8W-7N	E4
Nicola Dr					
-	ELGN	60120	2855		D2
Nicole Ct					
15200	ODPK	60462	3346	10W-18S	B7
Nicole Dr					
400	BRLT	60103	2911		C6
Nicole Finney Ct					
-	DLTN	60419	3351	1E-17S	A5
-	DLTN	60473	3351	1E-17S	A5
-	SHLD	60473	3351	1E-17S	A5
N Nicolet Av					
5800	CHCG	60631	2918	8W-7N	D4
Nicolette Av					
10	SMBG	60173	2859	21W-10N	D5
Nicolette Dr					
3400	CRTE	60417	3597	1E-28S	B5
3400	STGR	60417	3597	1E-28S	B5
3400	STGR	60475	3597	1E-28S	B5
Nida Ct					
8800	HYHL	60457	3210	11W-10S	A5
Nielsen Dr					
8400	TYPK	60477	3424	10W-21S	B7
Nielsen Plz					
-	GNVW	60062	2809	12W-15N	B1
-	NfdT	60062	2809	12W-15N	B2
10	PTHT	60062	2809	12W-15N	B2
Nielson Ln					
8000	TYPK	60477	3424	10W-21S	C7
S Nightengale Dr					
10	PLTN	60067	2805	22W-14N	B4
Nightengale Ter					
18600	CCHL	60478	3506	6W-22S	A1
Nightingale Ln					
19000	CCHL	60478	3506	6W-22S	A2
Night Song Ct					
1900	SMBG	60194	2857	26W-11N	E3
Niles Av					
7800	SKOK	60077	2865	6W-9N	E6
W Niles Av					
7100	NLES	60714	2864	8W-10N	D4
W Niles Ter					
6900	NLES	60714	2864	8W-9N	E7
Niles Center Rd					
7200	SKOK	60077	2865	6W-9N	D7
8800	SKOK	60076	2865	6W-11N	E3
9000	SKOK	60076	2866	5W-11N	A3
Nimitz Dr					
-	GNVW	60025	2810	9W-14N	C4
2000	DSPN	60018	2917	12W-8N	B2
Nina					
10	BRLT	60103	2910		A3
10	HnrT	60103	2910		A3
Nina Av					
3100	WLMT	60091	2811	6W-13N	E7
N Nina Av					
5700	CHCG	60631	2918	8W-7N	D4
Nippert Dr					
1200	SMWD	60107	2911		B1
Niven Ln					
5300	HRPK	60133	2911		C6
N Nixon Av					
6500	CHCG	60631	2918	8W-8N	D2
6500	CHCG	60714	2918	8W-8N	D2
6500	NLES	60631	2918	8W-8N	D2
6500	NLES	60714	2918	8W-8N	D2
S Noah Ter					
500	MPPT	60056	2861	17W-12N	B2
N Noble St					
1100	CHCG	60622	3033	1W-1N	D1
Noel Av					
1000	WLNG	60090	2755	14W-16N	B6
9200	MaiT	60016	2863	11W-11N	D2
Nogales St					
200	HFET	60194	2858	23W-10N	E5
200	SMBG	60194	2858	23W-10N	E5
N Nokomis Av					
6200	CHCG	60646	2919	6W-7N	D3
6600	LNWD	60712	2919	6W-8N	D2
6700	SKOK	60077	2919	6W-8N	D2
Nokomis St					
300	PKFT	60466	3595	3W-27S	B5
N Nolton Av					
100	WLSP	60480	3209	12W-9S	C3
S Nolton Av					
100	WLSP	60480	3209	12W-9S	C4
600	PlsT	60480	3209	12W-9S	C4
Nona St					
2500	FNPK	60131	2973	12W-3N	C5
Nondorf St					
2100	DYR	46311	3598		D2
Nora Av					
200	GNVW	60025	2864	8W-12N	D1
9400	OKLN	60453	3210	8W-10S	E6
N Nora Av					
3500	CHCG	60634	2974	8W-4N	E2
8000	NLES	60714	2864	8W-10N	D5
Nordic Ln					
12900	LMNT	60439	3343	17W-15S	D1
S Nordic Rd					
1800	EGvT	60005	2861	16W-10N	E5
1800	MPPT	60056	2861	16W-10N	E5
Nordic St					
1100	BNVL	60106	2915		D6
Nordica Av					
200	GNVW	60025	2864	8W-12N	E1
7900	BGVW	60459	3210	8W-9S	E2
7900	BRBK	60459	3210	8W-9S	E2
9300	BGVW	60453	3210	8W-10S	E6
9300	OKLN	60453	3210	8W-10S	E6
N Nordica Av					
1600	CHCG	60707	3030	8W-2N	E1
1600	OKPK	60302	3030	8W-2N	E1
1700	CHCG	60707	2974	8W-2N	E7
3200	CHCG	60634	2974	8W-4N	E3
4300	NRDG	60706	2974	8W-5N	D1
4800	CHCG	60656	2918	8W-6N	E5
4800	HDHT	60706	2918	8W-6N	E6
6200	CHCG	60631	2918	8W-7N	E3
6500	CHCG	60714	2918	8W-8N	E2
6500	NLES	60714	2918	8W-8N	E2
7500	NLES	60714	2864	8W-9N	E6
S Nordica Av					
5100	CHCG	60638	3148	8W-5S	E2
10700	WRTH	60482	3274	8W-12S	E2
Norfolk Av					
-	BRLT	60103	2910		C4
600	WSTR	60154	3029	12W-0S	B7
1200	CteT	60417	3596	1W-28S	A7
1400	CteT	60417	3595	2W-28S	D7
1400	WSTR	60154	3087	12W-1S	B1
1800	MonT	60417	3595	3W-28S	C7
1800	MonT	60466	3595	3W-28S	C7
Norfolk Ct					
100	ROSL	60172	2912		C4
Norfork Rd					
2000	NHFD	60093	2811	7W-16N	B1
Norma Ct					
2700	MaiT	60025	2864	10W-12N	B1
W Norma Ct					
8200	MaiT	60025	2864	10W-12N	B1
8200	NLES	60714	2864	10W-12N	B1
Norma Ln					
2200	DYR	46311	3598		E2
Normal Av					
-	BlmT	60411	3508	0W-24S	C5
400	CHHT	60411	3508	0W-24S	C5
14300	HRVY	60426	3350	0W-17S	B4
14300	RVDL	60827	3350	0W-17S	B4
S Normal Av					
2900	CHCG	60616	3092	0W-3S	A5
3300	CHCG	60609	3092	0W-4S	A6
5200	CHCG	60609	3152	0W-5S	B2
5500	CHCG	60621	3152	0W-6S	B3
7500	CHCG	60620	3214	0W-8S	B1
7500	CHCG	60621	3214	0W-8S	B1
9400	CHCG	60628	3214	0W-11S	B6
10300	CHCG	60628	3278	0W-13S	B4
14200	RVDL	60827	3350	0W-16S	B4
14500	HRVY	60426	3350	0W-16S	B4
W Normal Av					
8400	NLES	60714	2864	10W-10N	A5
8600	NLES	60714	2863	10W-10N	E5
8700	PKRG	60068	2863	10W-10N	E5
S Normal Blvd					
7400	CHCG	60621	3152	0W-8S	B7
W Normal Ct					
8300	NLES	60714	2864	10W-10N	A5

STREET Block	City	ZIP	Map#	CGS	Grid
W Normal Pkwy					
300	CHCG	60621	3152	0W-7S	B6
Norman Blvd					
1700	PKRG	60068	2917	11W-8N	E1
Norman Ct					
10	BRRG	60527	3208		B5
10	DSPN	60016	2862	15W-11N	A3
100	SMBG	60193	2913		A1
Norman Dr					
800	HFET	60195	2804	23W-14N	D4
E Norman Dr					
1200	PLTN	60074	2806	19W-16N	C1
N Norman Dr					
10	PLTN	60074	2753	19W-16N	D7
10	PLTN	60074	2806	19W-16N	D1
Norman Ln					
300	ROSL	60172	2912		C6
E Norman Ln					
100	WLNG	60090	2755	15W-17N	A5
N Norman Ln					
800	WLNG	60090	2755	15W-17N	A4
900	WLNG	60090	2754	15W-17N	E4
W Norman Ln					
100	WLNG	60090	2754	15W-17N	E4
Normandy Av					
7700	BDPK	60459	3211	8W-8S	A1
7700	BRBK	60459	3211	8W-9S	A3
8500	BRBK	60453	3211	8W-9S	A4
8700	OKLN	60453	3211	8W-10S	A4
9300	MNGV	60053	2865	8W-11N	A2
9500	GLF	60029	2865	8W-11N	A2
9800	CHRG	60415	3211	8W-11S	A7
9800	CHRG	60453	3211	8W-11S	A7
10300	CHRG	60415	3275	8W-12S	A1
N Normandy Av					
1600	CHCG	60302	3031	6W-0S	D6
1600	CHCG	60707	3031	6W-0S	D6
1600	OKPK	60302	3031	6W-0S	D6
2400	CHCG	60707	2975	8W-3N	A5
3800	CHCG	60634	2974	8W-4N	E2
4200	CHCG	60634	2975	8W-5N	A1
4200	HDHT	60706	2974	8W-5N	E1
4800	CHCG	60656	2918	8W-6N	E6
4800	HDHT	60706	2918	8W-6N	E6
6200	CHCG	60631	2919	8W-7N	A3
6300	CHCG	60631	2918	8W-8N	E2
6500	CHCG	60714	2918	8W-8N	E2
6500	NLES	60714	2918	8W-8N	E2
S Normandy Av					
5100	CHCG	60638	3149	8W-6S	A4
5100	FTVW	60638	3149	8W-5S	A2
6400	BDPK	60638	3149	8W-7S	A5
10900	WRTH	60482	3275	8W-12S	A3
Normandy Cir					
10	SMBG	60173	2859	21W-10N	E5
Normandy Ct					
-	EGVV	60007	2913		E1
N Normandy Ct					
1800	ANHT	60004	2807	16W-15N	C2
Normandy Dr					
16700	TYPK	60477	3425	8W-20S	B3
E Normandy Dr					
10	CHHT	60411	3508	1W-23S	A4
N Normandy Dr					
100	CHHT	60411	3508	1W-23S	A3
S Normandy Dr					
100	CHHT	60411	3508	1W-23S	A4
W Normandy Dr					
10	CHHT	60411	3508	0W-23S	B4
100	CHHT	60411	3507	1W-23S	E4
Normandy Ln					
700	GNVW	60025	2811	7W-13N	B6
3800	NHBK	60062	2756	12W-18N	B4
17900	HLCT	60429	3426	4W-21S	E6
Normandy Pl					
3000	EVTN	60201	2866	4W-12N	C1
Norridge Ln					
400	HFET	60194	2858	24W-10N	E4
W Norridge St					
7600	HDHT	60706	2918	9W-6N	C6
7600	NRDG	60706	2918	9W-6N	C6
Norris Dr					
10	BRRG	60527	3146		A5
10	DGvT	60527	3146		A5
Norris St					
2300	DXMR	60406	3349	2W-17S	C4
2300	POSN	60469	3349	2W-17S	C4
North Av					
100	BRTN	60010	2751	25W-20N	A1
800	DSPN	60016	2862	13W-11N	D3
E North Av					
-	MLPK	60160	3029	13W-1N	A1
10	NHLK	60164	3028		E1
100	BRLT	60103	2910		E3
100	EMHT	60126	3028		A1
200	BRLT	60103	2911		A3
300	NHLK	60164	3029	13W-1N	A1
400	HRPK	60133	2911		B3
400	MLPK	60164	3029	13W-2N	A1
400	MLPK	60165	3029	13W-1N	A1
400	SNPK	60164	3029	13W-1N	A1
400	SNPK	60165	3029	13W-1N	A1
E North Av SR-64					
-	MLPK	60160	3029	13W-1N	A1
-	MLPK	60164	3029	13W-1N	A1
-	MLPK	60165	3029	13W-1N	A1
-	NHLK	60164	3029	13W-1N	A1
-	SNPK	60164	3029	13W-1N	A1
-	SNPK	60165	3029	13W-1N	A1
10	NHLK	60164	3028		E1
100	EMHT	60126	3028		A1
W North Av					
-	EMHT	60126	3028		B1
-	FftT	60423	3505	9W-25S	A6
-	FKFT	60423	3504	9W-24S	E6
-	MLPK	60164	3029	13W-2N	A1
-	NHLK	60164	3029	13W-2N	A1
10	NHLK	60164	3028		C1
100	CHCG	60610	2978	0W-2N	A7
100	CHCG	60614	2978	0W-2N	A7
200	BRLT	60103	2910		E3
500	MLPK	60160	3030	10W-2N	A1
500	PvsT	60160	3030	10W-1N	A1
700	CHCG	60610	2977	2W-2N	C7
700	CHCG	60614	2977	2W-2N	C7
700	CHCG	60622	2977	2W-2N	C7
1900	CHCG	60622	3033	2W-1N	B1
1900	CHCG	60647	3033	2W-1N	B1
2500	MLPK	60165	3029	12W-2N	B1
2500	SNPK	60165	3029	12W-2N	B1
2800	CHCG	60622	3032	3W-1N	E1
2800	CHCG	60647	3032	3W-1N	E1
3000	MLPK	60160	3029	12W-2N	B1
3100	CHCG	60651	3032	4W-2N	D1
3900	CHCG	60639	3032	5W-2N	B1
4700	CHCG	60639	3031	7W-2N	C1
4700	CHCG	60651	3031	7W-2N	C1
5900	CHCG	60302	3031	7W-2N	B1
5900	OKPK	60302	3031	7W-2N	B1
6300	CHCG	60707	3031	7W-2N	A1
6700	CHCG	60302	3030	8W-1N	E1
6700	CHCG	60707	3030	8W-1N	E1
6700	OKPK	60302	3030	8W-1N	E1
6700	OKPK	60707	3030	8W-2N	E1
7100	EDPK	60707	3030	8W-2N	D1
7100	RVFT	60305	3030	8W-2N	D1
7200	RVFT	60707	3030	9W-2N	D1
7300	EDPK	60305	3030	9W-2N	D1
7600	FftT	60423	3504	9W-24S	E6
8300	RVFT	60160	3030	10W-1N	B1
8300	RVGV	60305	3030	10W-1N	B1
8300	RVGV	60707	3030	10W-1N	B1
8400	MLPK	60171	3030	10W-2N	A1
8400	RVGV	60171	3030	10W-2N	A1
10400	SNPK	60160	3029	12W-2N	B1
W North Av SR-64					
-	EMHT	60126	3028		B1
10	NHLK	60164	3028		C1
100	CHCG	60610	2978	0W-2N	A7
100	CHCG	60614	2978	0W-2N	A7
500	MLPK	60160	3030	10W-2N	A1
500	PvsT	60160	3030	10W-1N	A1
600	MLPK	60160	3029	12W-2N	B1
700	CHCG	60610	2977	2W-2N	C7
700	CHCG	60614	2977	2W-2N	C7
700	CHCG	60622	2977	2W-2N	C7
1900	CHCG	60622	3033	2W-1N	B1
1900	CHCG	60647	3033	2W-1N	B1
2500	MLPK	60165	3029	12W-2N	B1
2500	SNPK	60165	3029	12W-2N	B1
2800	CHCG	60622	3032	3W-1N	E1
2800	CHCG	60647	3032	3W-1N	E1
3100	CHCG	60651	3032	4W-2N	D1
3900	CHCG	60639	3032	5W-2N	B1
4700	CHCG	60639	3031	7W-2N	C1
4700	CHCG	60651	3031	7W-2N	C1
5900	CHCG	60302	3031	7W-2N	B1
5900	OKPK	60302	3031	7W-2N	B1
6300	CHCG	60707	3031	7W-2N	A1
6700	CHCG	60302	3030	8W-1N	E1
6700	CHCG	60707	3030	8W-1N	E1
6700	OKPK	60302	3030	8W-1N	E1
6700	OKPK	60707	3030	8W-2N	E1
7100	EDPK	60707	3030	8W-2N	D1
7100	RVFT	60305	3030	8W-2N	D1
7200	RVFT	60707	3030	9W-2N	D1
7300	EDPK	60305	3030	9W-2N	D1
8300	RVFT	60160	3030	10W-1N	B1
8300	RVGV	60305	3030	10W-1N	B1
8300	RVGV	60707	3030	10W-1N	B1
8400	MLPK	60171	3030	10W-2N	A1
8400	RVGV	60171	3030	10W-2N	A1
10400	SNPK	60160	3029	12W-2N	B1
North Blvd					
10	CHCG	60644	3031	7W-0N	B4
10	OKPK	60302	3031	7W-0N	B4
600	OKPK	60301	3031	8W-0N	A4
700	OKPK	60301	3030	8W-0N	E4
700	OKPK	60302	3030	8W-0N	E4
1100	RVFT	60305	3030	8W-0N	D4
E North Blvd					
10	CHCG	60610	2978	0E-2N	C7
W North Blvd					
10	CHCG	60610	2978	0W-1N	B7
10	CHCG	60614	2978	0W-1N	B7
North Brch					
10	GNVW	60093	2810	8W-15N	D2
N North Cir					
500	ITSC	60143	2914		B5
N North Ct					
500	PLTN	60067	2752	20W-16N	E6
600	PLTN	60067	2753	20W-16N	A6
S North Ct					
20700	FftT	60423	3504	9W-25S	D6
North Dr					
-	PLTN	60067	2805	22W-14N	B4
1900	GNVW	60025	2811	7W-14N	A4
North Ln					
-	MPPT	60056	2861	17W-11N	C3
1600	NHBK	60062	2757	8W-16N	E6
North Pkwy					
10	PTHT	60070	2807	15W-15N	E2
10	PTHT	60070	2808	15W-15N	A2
North Rd					
9100	PlsT	60465	3273	11W-13S	E3
9100	PSHL	60465	3273	11W-13S	E3
North St					
-	MTSN	60443	3594	4W-26S	E1
-	PKFT	60443	3594	4W-26S	E1
-	PKFT	60466	3594	4W-26S	E1
10	AddT	60106	2915		C5
10	CHHT	60411	3595	3W-26S	C1
10	MTSN	60443	3595	3W-25S	A1
10	PKFT	60411	3595	3W-26S	C1
10	PKFT	60443	3595	3W-25S	A1
10	PKFT	60466	3595	3W-26S	B1
100	EDND	60118	2801		A2
200	ELGN	60120	2855		A3
400	CRTE	60417	3685	1W-29S	B2
6700	TYPK	60477	3425	8W-20S	A5
E North St					
10	HNDL	60521	3086		B7
100	ITSC	60143	2914		C5
300	PTON	60468	3861	9W-37S	A3
1200	LKPT	60441	3342	21W-18S	A7
W North St					
-	PtnT	60468	3860	9W-37S	D3
10	HNDL	60521	3086		A7
100	ITSC	60143	2914		B6
100	PTON	60468	3860	9W-37S	E3
100	PTON	60468	3861	9W-37S	A3
1300	PltT	60067	2752	22W-17N	A5
1500	PLTN	60067	2752	22W-17N	A5
W North Ter					
8400	NLES	60714	2864	10W-10N	A5
8500	PKRG	60714	2864	10W-10N	A5
8600	NLES	60068	2863	10W-10N	E5
8600	NLES	60714	2863	10W-10N	E5
8600	PKRG	60068	2863	10W-10N	E5
8600	PKRG	60068	2864	10W-10N	A5
North Tr					
10	LMNT	60439	3272	15W-13S	B4
Northampton Cir					
500	EGvT	60007	2860	19W-9N	D7
500	EGVV	60007	2860	19W-9N	D7
Northampton Dr					
2600	RGMW	60008	2806	19W-12N	B7
Northampton Ln					
400	ROSL	60172	2912		B5
W North Bank Dr					
200	CHCG	60606	3034	0W-0N	B4
200	CHCG	60610	3034	0W-0N	B4
North Branch Rd					
200	GNVW	60025	2810	8W-12N	E7
200	GNVW	60025	2864	8W-12N	E1
N North Branch St					
900	CHCG	60622	3033	1W-1N	E2
Northbridge Ct					
10600	PlsT	60462	3345	13W-15S	A2
Northbridge Dr					
10600	PlsT	60462	3345	13W-15S	A2
Northbrook Av					
800	NHBK	60062	2757	8W-17N	E5
Northbrook Ct					
1000	HDPK	60035	2757	9W-18N	C2
1000	NHBK	60062	2757	9W-18N	C2
Northbrook Ct Dr					
-	DRFD	60015	2757	9W-18N	C2
-	DRFD	60062	2757	9W-18N	C2
-	HDPK	60035	2757	9W-18N	C2
-	HDPK	60062	2757	9W-18N	C2
-	NHBK	60062	2757	9W-18N	D2
Northbury Ct					
200	SMBG	60193	2859	22W-10N	C6
Northbury Ln					
1100	WLNG	60090	2754	15W-18N	E2
N Northcott Av					
5600	CHCG	60631	2919	8W-7N	A4
6000	CHCG	60631	2918	8W-7N	D3
Northeast Ct					
-	CTSD	60525	3147	13W-5S	A3
-	LynT	60525	3147	13W-5S	A3
Northeast Pkwy					
-	LNWD	60712	2920	4W-8N	C1
Northeast Pl					
800	DSPN	60016	2862	13W-10N	D4
North End Av					
100	EMHT	60126	2972		A6
300	AddT	60126	2972		A6
Northern Av					
-	CHCG	60613	2977	1W-5N	D1
Northfield Ln					
7700	TYPK	60477	3504	9W-23S	D2
Northfield Plz					
-	NHFD	60093	2811	7W-16N	B1
Northfield Rd					
100	NHFD	60093	2811	7W-15N	C2
100	NtrT	60093	2811	7W-15N	C2
Northfield Sq					
1700	NHFD	60093	2811	6W-15N	C2
Northgate Av					
2100	NHBK	60093	2758	7W-16N	A7
2100	NHFD	60062	2758	7W-16N	A7
2100	NHFD	60093	2758	7W-16N	A7
Northgate Ct					
400	RVSD	60546	3088	9W-2S	C3
1300	BRLT	60103	2910		B7
Northgate Dr					
400	DYR	46311	3510		D5
1300	BRLT	60103	2910		B7
Northgate Pkwy					
-	BFGV	60090	2755	15W-18N	B2
200	WLNG	60090	2755	15W-18N	B2
600	BFGV	60089	2755	15W-20N	B2
Northgate Pl					
100	BRRG	60527	3208		D2
Northgate Rd					
10	RVSD	60546	3088	9W-2S	C3
2200	FTPK	60130	3088	9W-2S	C2
2200	FTPK	60546	3088	9W-2S	C2
2200	NRIV	60546	3088	9W-2S	C2
Northlake Pkwy					
1400	CPVL	60110	2801		B1
1400	EDND	60110	2801		B1
1500	EDND	60118	2801		B1
Northmoor Ct					
1300	NHBK	60062	2757	10W-17N	A6
N North Park Av					
1300	CHCG	60610	3034	0W-1N	B1
1600	CHCG	60610	2978	0W-2N	B7
1600	CHCG	60614	2978	0W-2N	B7
Northport Dr					
500	EGVV	60007	2914		C3
Northshore Av					
1800	DSPN	60018	2917	12W-8N	B2
W North Shore Av					
1000	CHCG	60626	2921	1W-8N	D2
2400	CHCG	60645	2921	3W-8N	A2
2600	CHCG	60645	2920	3W-8N	E2
3100	LNWD	60645	2920	3W-8N	D2
3700	LNWD	60712	2920	4W-8N	C2
5000	LNWD	60712	2919	6W-8N	D2
7200	CHCG	60631	2918	9W-8N	D2
7200	NLES	60714	2918	9W-8N	D2
7700	PKRG	60068	2918	9W-8N	C2
Northshore Ct					
1100	BRTN	60010	2751	24W-20N	C1
Northshore Dr					
8800	GNVW	60025	2863	11W-12N	E1
8900	MaiT	60016	2863	11W-12N	E1
Northshore Rd					
10	ELGN	60123	2801		A7
Northside Av					
-	ROSL	60172	2913		A2
-	SmbT	60172	2913		A2
Northstar Ct					
18500	TYPK	60477	3504	10W-22S	C1
N Northumberland Pass					
1900	PLTN	60074	2752	21W-18N	D3
Northview Ln					
400	HFET	60195	2804	24W-12N	D7
E North Water St					
100	CHCG	60611	3034	0E-0N	C3
Northway Ct					
300	GLNC	60022	2758	6W-17N	D5
900	HRPK	60133	2912		A1
Northway Dr					
7200	HRPK	60133	2912		A1
7800	HRPK	60133	2858	26W-9N	A7
8200	SMBG	60133	2858	26W-9N	A7
8200	SMBG	60193	2858	26W-9N	A7
Northwest Av					
100	LydT	60164	2972		C6
100	NHLK	60164	2972		C6
100	NHLK	60164	3028		C1
Northwest Ct					
-	LynT	60525	3147	13W-5S	A3
E Northwest Hwy					
-	DSPN	60068	2863	12W-10N	C4
-	PKRG	60016	2863	12W-10N	C4
-	PKRG	60068	2863	12W-10N	C4
-	PLTN	60074	2753	20W-16N	A7
10	ANHT	60004	2807	16W-13N	C6
10	ANHT	60005	2807	16W-13N	C6
10	DSPN	60016	2862	14W-12N	C1
10	MPPT	60056	2808	15W-12N	A7
10	MPPT	60056	2862	13W-11N	D2
10	PLTN	60067	2752	20W-16N	E6
100	BRTN	60010	2751	25W-20N	A1
200	PLTN	60067	2753	20W-16N	A6
400	PLTN	60067	2806	19W-15N	C3
400	PLTN	60074	2806	19W-15N	C2
1700	DSPN	60016	2863	12W-11N	B4
2100	MPPT	60056	2807	16W-13N	D6
E Northwest Hwy US-14					
10	ANHT	60004	2807	16W-13N	C6
10	ANHT	60005	2807	16W-13N	C6
10	DSPN	60016	2862	14W-12N	C1
10	MPPT	60056	2808	15W-12N	A7
10	MPPT	60056	2862	13W-11N	D2
10	PLTN	60067	2752	20W-16N	E6
100	BRTN	60010	2751	25W-20N	A1
200	PLTN	60067	2753	20W-16N	A6
200	PLTN	60074	2753	20W-16N	A7
400	PLTN	60067	2806	19W-15N	C2
400	PLTN	60074	2806	19W-15N	C2
1700	DSPN	60016	2863	12W-11N	B4
2100	MPPT	60056	2807	16W-13N	D6
N Northwest Hwy					
10	PKRG	60068	2864	10W-9N	A7
10	PLTN	60067	2806	20W-15N	A1
10	PLTN	60074	2806	20W-15N	A1
100	BRTN	60010	2751	25W-20N	A1
100	PLTN	60067	2753	20W-16N	A7
100	PLTN	60074	2753	20W-16N	A7
600	PKRG	60068	2863	11W-10N	C5
1500	DSPN	60016	2863	11W-10N	C5
1500	DSPN	60068	2863	11W-10N	C5
1500	PKRG	60016	2863	11W-10N	C5
5000	CHCG	60630	2919	6W-6N	C6
5500	CHCG	60646	2919	7W-7N	B5
5700	CHCG	60631	2919	7W-6N	B5
5900	CHCG	60631	2918	9W-8N	C2
6800	PKRG	60068	2918	9W-8N	C2
N Northwest Hwy US-14					
10	PLTN	60067	2806	20W-15N	A1
10	PLTN	60074	2806	20W-15N	A1
100	BRTN	60010	2751	25W-20N	A1
100	PLTN	60067	2753	20W-16N	A7
100	PLTN	60074	2753	20W-16N	A7
S Northwest Hwy					
-	PLTN	60067	2751	23W-17N	E5
-	PltT	60067	2751	23W-17N	E5
10	PKRG	60068	2918	9W-8N	B1
10	PLTN	60067	2806	20W-15N	A1
10	PLTN	60074	2806	20W-15N	A1
100	BRTN	60010	2751	23W-17N	D4
400	CHCG	60631	2918	9W-8N	C1
1100	PltT	60010	2751	23W-17N	D4
S Northwest Hwy US-14					
-	PLTN	60067	2751	23W-17N	E5
-	PltT	60067	2751	23W-17N	E5
10	PLTN	60067	2806	20W-15N	A1
10	PLTN	60074	2806	20W-15N	A1
100	BRTN	60010	2751	23W-17N	D4
1100	PltT	60010	2751	23W-17N	D4
W Northwest Hwy					
-	PltT	60010	2751	23W-17N	E5
-	PltT	60067	2751	23W-17N	E5
10	ANHT	60005	2807	18W-14N	A4
10	MPPT	60056	2808	15W-12N	A7
10	PLTN	60067	2752	21W-16N	D6
100	BRTN	60010	2750	26W-20N	E1
200	MPPT	60056	2807	16W-13N	D6
300	ANHT	60004	2806	18W-14N	D3
300	ANHT	60005	2806	18W-14N	D3
500	PltT	60067	2752	21W-17N	C6
1300	ANHT	60004	2807	16W-13N	D6
1500	PLTN	60067	2751	23W-17N	E5
1800	ANHT	60074	2806	18W-14N	D3
1800	PLTN	60074	2806	18W-14N	D3
W Northwest Hwy US-14					
-	PltT	60010	2751	23W-17N	E5
-	PltT	60067	2751	23W-17N	E5
10	ANHT	60005	2807	18W-14N	A4
10	MPPT	60056	2808	15W-12N	A7
10	PLTN	60067	2752	21W-16N	D6
100	BRTN	60010	2750	26W-20N	E1
200	MPPT	60056	2807	16W-13N	D6
300	ANHT	60004	2806	18W-14N	D3
300	ANHT	60005	2806	18W-14N	D3
500	PltT	60067	2752	21W-17N	C6
1300	ANHT	60004	2807	16W-13N	D6
1500	PLTN	60067	2751	23W-17N	E5
1800	ANHT	60074	2806	18W-14N	D3
1800	PLTN	60074	2806	18W-14N	D3
Northwest Pl					
800	DSPN	60016	2862	14W-10N	D4
Northwest Rd					
11100	PSHL	60465	3273	11W-13S	E3
Northwest Tollway					
-	ANHT	-	2860	18W-11N	E3
-	ANHT	-	2861	18W-11N	A3
-	CHCG	-	2916		D1
-	CHCG	-	2917	11W-7N	D4
-	DSPN	-	2861	16W-9N	E6
-	DSPN	-	2862	15W-9N	A7
-	DSPN	-	2916		D1
-	DSPN	-	2917	12W-8N	A2
-	EGvT	-	2860	19W-11N	D2
-	EGvT	-	2861	16W-10N	D6
-	EGvT	-	2862	15W-9N	A7
-	EGVV	-	2861	17W-10N	C5
-	ELGN	-	2801		A7
-	ElgT	-	2801		A7
-	HFET	-	2802	29W-12N	D7
-	HFET	-	2803	28W-12N	A7
-	HFET	-	2804	24W-12N	D7
-	HnrT	-	2801		D7
-	HnrT	-	2802	30W-12N	C7
-	MPPT	-	2861	17W-10N	B5
-	RGMW	-	2859	21W-12N	E1
-	RGMW	-	2860	21W-12N	A1
-	RSMT	-	2916		E1
-	RSMT	-	2917	12W-7N	B3
-	SMBG	-	2804	24W-12N	D7
-	SMBG	-	2805	23W-12N	B7
-	SMBG	-	2859	22W-12N	C1
-	SmbT	-	2805	23W-12N	B7
-	SmbT	-	2859	22W-12N	C1
Northwest Tollway I-90					
-	ANHT	-	2860	18W-11N	E3
-	ANHT	-	2861	17W-11N	A4
-	CHCG	-	2916		D1
-	CHCG	-	2917	11W-7N	E4
-	DSPN	-	2861	16W-9N	E6
-	DSPN	-	2862	15W-9N	A7
-	DSPN	-	2916		D1
-	DSPN	-	2917	12W-8N	A2
-	EGvT	-	2860	19W-11N	D2
-	EGvT	-	2861	16W-9N	E7
-	EGvT	-	2862	15W-9N	A7
-	EGVV	-	2861	17W-10N	B5
-	ELGN	-	2801		B7
-	ElgT	-	2801		B7
-	HFET	-	2802	29W-12N	D7
-	HFET	-	2803	27W-12N	C7
-	HFET	-	2804	24W-12N	D7
-	HnrT	-	2801		D7
-	HnrT	-	2802	31W-12N	A7
-	MPPT	-	2861	17W-10N	B5
-	RGMW	-	2859	21W-12N	E1
-	RGMW	-	2860	19W-12N	C2
-	RSMT	-	2916		E1
-	RSMT	-	2917	12W-7N	B3
-	SMBG	-	2804	24W-12N	D7
-	SMBG	-	2805	23W-12N	B7
-	SMBG	-	2859	22W-12N	C1
-	SmbT	-	2805	23W-12N	B7
-	SmbT	-	2859	22W-12N	C1
Northwind Cir					
2100	SMBG	60194	2858	26W-11N	A3
Northwind Dr					
-	LYWD	60411	3509	2E-23S	E3
-	RNPK	60471	3593	6W-27S	E4
-	RNPK	60471	3594	6W-27S	A5
E Northwood Ct					
2400	ANHT	60004	2807	16W-15N	D1
Northwood Dr					
400	GLNC	60022	2758	7W-18N	C3
Northwood Rd					
100	RVSD	60546	3088	9W-2S	C3
Norton Av					
10	LMNT	60439	3270		D6
Norton Dr					
10	LMNT	60439	3270		D6
Norwalk Rd					
1000	LMNT	60439	3270		E7
1000	LMNT	60439	3271		A7
Norway Ln					
1500	PltT	60074	2753	19W-17N	C4
E Norway Tr					
3300	CteT	60417	3687	4E-29S	C1
Norway Pine Ln					
2800	NHBK	60062	2756	11W-16N	E7
2800	NHBK	60062	2809	11W-16N	E1
Norwell Ct					
1300	SMBG	60193	2858	25W-9N	C7
Norwell Ln					
1600	SMBG	60193	2858	25W-9N	B7
Norwich Ct					
-	MNSR	46321	3510		D4
2000	GNVW	60025	2809	10W-14N	E3
Norwich Dr					
-	MNSR	46321	3510		D4
100	BRLT	60103	2909		C3
Norwich Ln					
11200	ODPK	60467	3344	14W-16S	E3
Norwood Av					
1700	MLPK	60160	3029	11W-1N	D2
W Norwood Av					
1200	ITSC	60143	2914		A4
1400	ITSC	60143	2913		E4
Norwood Blvd					
10	PKFT	60466	3595	3W-26S	B2
Norwood Ct					
100	RGMW	60008	2805	21W-14N	D4
3100	SMWD	60107	2911		A2
W Norwood Ct					
6600	HDHT	60706	2974	8W-5N	E1
6600	HDHT	60706	2975	8W-5N	A1
W Norwood Dr					
8000	FftT	60423	3504	10W-24S	C5
Norwood Ln					
500	SMBG	60193	2858	24W-9N	C7
900	BRLT	60103	2910		C5
900	WynT	60103	2910		C5
Norwood St					
9800	RSMT	60018	2917	12W-7N	B4
W Norwood St					
1800	CHCG	60660	2921	2W-7N	B3
1900	CHCG	60659	2921	2W-7N	B3
4300	CHCG	60646	2920	5W-7N	A3
6200	CHCG	60646	2919	7W-7N	A3
7700	CHCG	60631	2918	9W-7N	C4
Norwood Ter					
2700	GNVW	60025	2864	10W-12N	B1
2700	MaiT	60025	2864	10W-12N	B1
Norwood Square Dr					
100	PKFT	60466	3595	3W-26S	C2
Notis Ct					
900	SMBG	60193	2912		D1
E Notre Dame Av					
1800	CteT	60417	3686	2E-29S	D1
Notre Dame Dr					
700	MTSN	60443	3505	6W-25S	E6
1100	LMNT	60439	3271		A7
Nottingham Av					
200	GNVW	60025	2864	8W-12N	E1
2900	MKHM	60426	3427	3W-19S	A2
7900	BRBK	60459	3210	8W-9S	E3
8200	BGVW	60455	3210	8W-9S	E3
8200	BGVW	60459	3210	8W-9S	E3
9500	OKLN	60453	3210	8W-11S	E6
9600	OKLN	60415	3210	8W-11S	E6
9700	CHRG	60415	3210	8W-11S	E7
N Nottingham Av					
3200	CHCG	60634	2974	8W-4N	D3
4300	NRDG	60706	2974	8W-5N	D1
4500	NRDG	60706	2918	8W-5N	D7
4800	HDHT	60656	2918	8W-6N	D6
4800	HDHT	60706	2918	8W-6N	D6
5300	CHCG	60656	2918	8W-6N	D5
5700	CHCG	60631	2918	8W-7N	D4
7500	NLES	60714	2864	8W-9N	E6
S Nottingham Av					
6300	CHCG	60638	3148	8W-7S	E5
7100	BDPK	60638	3148	8W-8S	E7
7300	BDPK	60638	3210	8W-8S	E1
7400	BGVW	60455	3210	8W-8S	E1
7400	BGVW	60638	3210	8W-8S	E1
Nottingham Ct					
1400	WLNG	60090	2754	15W-18N	E3
7700	TYPK	60477	3424	9W-19S	D2
16400	ODPK	60467	3423	13W-19S	A3
Nottingham Dr					
7400	TYPK	60477	3424	9W-19S	D2
Nottingham Ln					
1000	HFET	60195	2804	24W-12N	C7
1100	HnrT	60120	2856	31W-10N	A5
Nottingham Rd					
8000	TYPK	60477	3424	10W-19S	C2

STREET Block	City	ZIP	Map#	CGS	Grid
Nottingwood Av					
16400	OKFT	60452	3426	5W-19S	A2
Nottoway Ct					
-	RGMW	60008	2860	19W-11N	B2
Nottoway Sq					
-	RGMW	60008	2860	19W-12N	C1
Nova Ct					
1200	WLNG	60090	2754	16W-18N	D3
Novak Dr					
17000	HLCT	60429	3427	3W-20S	A4
Noyes Ct					
2300	EVTN	60201	2867	2W-12N	B1
Noyes St					
600	EVTN	60201	2867	3W-12N	A1
1900	EVTN	60201	2866	3W-12N	D1
3300	SKOK	60076	2866	4W-12N	B1
E Noyes St					
400	ANHT	60005	2861	17W-12N	B1
400	ANHT	60056	2861	17W-12N	B1
400	MPPT	60056	2861	17W-12N	B1
W Noyes St					
200	ANHT	60005	2861	18W-12N	A1
1300	ANHT	60005	2860	19W-12N	D1
Nueport Ct S					
8200	WLSP	60480	3208		D3
Nueport Dr S					
8100	WLSP	60480	3208		D3
Nueport Dr W					
11400	WLSP	60480	3208		D3
Nugent St					
-	GNWD	60425	3508	0E-23S	D3
Nugget Cir					
6200	HRPK	60133	2911		E4
Nutmeg Ct					
1300	MPPT	60056	2807	16W-14N	E3
Nuttall Rd					
200	RVSD	60546	3088	9W-2S	C3
W Nutwood Ct					
7600	FftT	60423	3504	9W-24S	D5
Ny-O-Da Pl					
1300	HDPK	60035	2757	8W-20N	E2
O					
Oak					
-	MNGV	60053	2865	8W-10N	A5
Oak Av					
100	HLSD	60162	3029	13W-0S	A6
200	WDDL	60191	2915		B7
400	AddT	60191	2915		B7
1000	WLNG	60070	2755	15W-16N	A7
1000	WLNG	60090	2755	15W-16N	A7
1100	PTHT	60070	2755	15W-16N	A6
1200	EVTN	60202	2867	2W-10N	B3
1300	LMNT	60439	3271		B6
1800	EVTN	60201	2867	2W-11N	B2
2000	HRPK	60133	2911		C3
2100	NHBK	60062	2757	10W-17N	A6
3100	BKFD	60513	3087	11W-3S	E5
3600	NfdT	60062	2756	12W-17N	B6
3600	NHBK	60062	2756	12W-17N	B6
4300	LYNS	60534	3088	9W-4S	D7
4500	BKFD	60513	3147	11W-4S	E1
7200	OKPK	60302	3030	9W-0N	D3
7200	RVFT	60305	3030	10W-0N	B3
10400	CHRG	60415	3275	7W-12S	B2
11000	CHRG	60482	3275	7W-12S	B3
11000	WRTH	60482	3275	7W-12S	B3
15900	OKFT	60452	3426	6W-19S	A2
18400	LNSG	60438	3429	3E-21S	E7
18600	BlmT	60411	3429	3E-22S	E7
18600	BlmT	60438	3429	3E-22S	E7
18700	BlmT	60411	3509	3E-22S	E1
18700	BlmT	60438	3509	3E-22S	E1
18700	LNSG	60411	3509	3E-22S	E1
18700	LNSG	60438	3509	3E-22S	E1
19100	CCHL	60478	3506	5W-23S	D3
19400	LNSG	60411	3510	3E-23S	B2
19400	LNSG	60438	3510	3E-23S	B2
E Oak Av					
1000	LGPK	60525	3087	12W-3S	C5
1100	BKFD	60513	3087	12W-3S	C5
N Oak Av					
100	BRLT	60103	2910		E2
300	BRLT	60107	2910		E1
300	SMWD	60103	2910		E1
300	SMWD	60107	2910		E1
9400	MaiT	60016	2863	11W-11N	D2
S Oak Av					
100	BRLT	60103	2910		E3
4300	HMND	46327	3352		E4
W Oak Av					
10	LGPK	60525	3087	12W-3S	B5
8100	NLES	60714	2864	10W-11N	B3
14300	HMGN	60441	3343	17W-16S	B4
Oak Cir					
300	WLMT	60091	2812	3W-13N	D6
Oak Ct					
10	CTCY	60409	3351	2E-16S	C4
10	LMNT	60439	3270		C6
10	OKBK	60523	3086		B5
100	PltT	60010	2751	24W-18N	C3
1000	FSMR	60422	3506	4W-22S	E2
2900	SMBG	60193	2857	27W-10N	C6
3200	HLCT	60429	3426	4W-20S	E4
13500	LMNT	60439	3343	17W-15S	B2
S Oak Ct					
13000	PSHT	60463	3346	9W-15S	D1
23500	CteT	60417	3595	2W-28S	E6
W Oak Ct					
12800	HMGN	60441	3422	16W-19S	A2
13300	HMGN	60441	3343	16W-17S	E5
Oak Dr					
-	BmnT	60426	3426	5W-19S	A1
400	WLNG	60090	2755	14W-17N	C5
500	EDND	60118	2801		B2
700	GLNC	60022	2758	7W-17N	C4
1000	BCHR	60401	3864	0W-36S	C1
Oak Ln					
-	CRTE	60417	3597	0E-29S	A7
-	CRTE	60417	3686	0E-29S	A1
-	CteT	60417	3686	0E-29S	A1
10	LMNT	60439	3270		C6
10	PKFT	60466	3595	3W-27S	B5
300	LynT	60458	3209	11W-8S	E2
1100	WNSP	60558	3146		D4
2200	ANHT	60005	2806	19W-12N	D7
2200	ANHT	60008	2806	19W-12N	D7
2200	RGMW	60008	2806	19W-12N	C7
12500	PSPK	60464	3272	14W-14S	E7
13200	LMNT	60439	3342	19W-15S	E2
13400	OrlT	60462	3346	9W-15S	D2
13400	PSHT	60462	3346	9W-15S	D2
13400	PSHT	60463	3346	9W-15S	D2
20100	LYWD	60411	3509	3E-23S	E4
N Oak Ln					
10	GNWD	60425	3508	0E-22S	E1
9600	MaiT	60016	2863	11W-12N	D1
S Oak Ln					
10	GNWD	60425	3508	0E-22S	E2
20700	FftT	60423	3504	9W-25S	E6
24700	CteT	60417	3687	4E-30S	B2
W Oak Ln					
8100	NLES	60714	2864	10W-10N	B5
Oak Pl					
14200	ODPK	60462	3345	12W-17S	D4
W Oak Pl					
9500	MaiT	60016	2863	11W-12N	C1
Oak Rd					
600	BRTN	60010	2751	25W-20N	A1
2100	HMWD	60430	3427	2W-21S	C7
15200	OKFT	60452	3347	8W-18S	B6
S Oak Rd					
-	MonT	60449	3682	6W-32S	E6
25600	MONE	60449	3683	6W-31S	A5
25900	MONE	60449	3682	6W-31S	E6
Oak St					
-	MONE	60449	3683	6W-31S	A4
-	WNKA	60093	2811	6W-15N	D2
10	HGKN	60525	3147	12W-7S	C5
100	ELGN	60123	2855		A6
100	MYWD	60153	3030	10W-0N	A4
100	RVFT	60305	3030	10W-0N	A4
300	DSPN	60016	2863	13W-11N	A3
300	PKRG	60068	2918	10W-8N	B1
400	DYR	46311	3598		D2
500	EGVV	60007	2860	18W-9N	E7
500	EGVV	60007	2914		E1
600	ROSL	60172	2912		E6
700	BMDL	60172	2912		E6
700	BmdT	60172	2912		E6
700	MYWD	60153	3029	11W-0N	C4
700	WNKA	60093	2812	5W-15N	B2
800	WNSP	60558	3086		D6
1600	CHHT	60411	3596	1W-25S	A1
1600	HRPK	60133	2911		D4
1800	BLID	60827	3277	2W-15S	C7
1800	CTPK	60406	3277	2W-15S	C7
1800	CTPK	60827	3277	2W-15S	C7
1800	NHFD	60093	2811	7W-15N	C2
2200	BLWD	60104	3029	12W-0N	C4
2200	BLWD	60153	3029	11W-0N	D4
2400	BLID	60406	3277	3W-15S	B7
2400	FNPK	60131	2973	11W-3N	D5
2400	RVGV	60171	2973	11W-3N	D6
3200	HLCT	60429	3426	4W-20S	E4
3500	FSMR	60422	3506	4W-22S	E2
4600	BLWD	60104	3028		E4
5100	BKLY	60104	3028		E4
5100	BKLY	60163	3028		E4
5100	HLSD	60162	3028		E4
5200	OKLN	60453	3211	6W-10S	E5
9200	ODPK	60462	3345	11W-17S	E5
13900	HMGN	60441	3342	19W-16S	E4
14100	HmrT	60441	3342	19W-16S	E4
14200	DLTN	60419	3350	0E-16S	E4
15300	SHLD	60473	3350	0E-17S	E6
18200	LNSG	60438	3430	3E-21S	A6
21100	MTSN	60443	3506	4W-25S	E7
21100	MTSN	60443	3594	4W-25S	E1
21100	OMFD	60461	3506	4W-25S	E7
E Oak St					
10	CHCG	60610	3034	0E-1N	C2
10	CHCG	60611	3034	0E-1N	C2
2000	CteT	60417	3686	2E-29S	D2
N Oak St					
10	PLTN	60067	2805	20W-16N	E1
100	GNWD	60425	3508	0W-22S	D1
200	ITSC	60143	2914		C6
300	HNDL	60521	3086		B7
300	HNDL	60521	3146		C1
300	MPPT	60056	2807	16W-13N	E6
1200	PLTN	60067	2752	20W-17N	E4
1400	PltT	60074	2752	20W-17N	E4
2400	RVGV	60171	2974	10W-3N	A5
4500	NRDG	60706	2918	10W-5N	B7
S Oak St					
10	HNDL	60521	3146		B1
100	PLTN	60067	2805	20W-15N	E1
200	ITSC	60143	2914		C6
400	ADSN	60143	2914		C7
W Oak St					
10	CHCG	60610	3034	0W-1N	B2
10	CHCG	60611	3034	0W-1N	B2
500	PTON	60468	3860	9W-37S	E2
600	PtnT	60468	3860	10W-37S	D2
Oak Ter					
900	GLNC	60022	2758	6W-18N	D4
W Oak Tr					
14300	HMGN	60441	3343	16W-17S	E5
N Oakbrook Cir					
2100	PLTN	60074	2753	19W-20N	C2
Oakbrook Ct					
300	BRLT	60103	2910		D4
Oak Brook Rd					
100	OKBK	60523	3086		A4
100	PvsT	60523	3086		A4
11300	PvsT	60154	3086		D4
11300	PvsT	60558	3086		D4
11300	WSTR	60154	3086		D4
11300	WSTR	60523	3086		D4
Oak Brook Rd CO-34					
100	OKBK	60523	3086		B4
100	PvsT	60523	3086		C4
Oak Center Dr					
4800	OKLN	60453	3276	6W-11S	A1
4900	OKLN	60453	3211	6W-11S	E7
4900	OKLN	60453	3212	6W-11S	A7
Oak Creek Ct					
10	BRRG	60527	3208		B6
Oakcreek Ct					
14800	ODPK	60467	3344	14W-17S	D5
Oak Creek Dr					
-	PTHT	60070	2808	15W-15N	B1
-	WLNG	60070	2808	15W-15N	B1
10	BFGV	60089	2754	16W-18N	C4
10	BRRG	60527	3208		B6
200	WLNG	60090	2808	14W-15N	B1
Oak Creek Rd					
10	RGMW	60008	2806	20W-13N	A6
W Oak Crest Ct					
9000	PSHL	60465	3209	11W-11S	D6
Oak Crest Dr					
10	CPVL	60110	2748		A4
Oakdale Av					
400	GLNC	60022	2758	6W-16N	D6
7100	HMND	46324	3430		E5
14900	HRVY	60426	3350	0W-17S	C6
W Oakdale Av					
300	CHCG	60657	2978	0W-3N	A4
1700	CHCG	60657	2977	2W-3N	B4
2200	CHCG	60618	2977	2W-3N	B4
3600	CHCG	60618	2976	4W-3N	C4
4000	CHCG	60641	2976	5W-3N	B4
4800	CHCG	60641	2975	6W-3N	D4
6900	CHCG	60634	2974	8W-3N	E4
Oakdale Cir					
2100	HRPK	60133	2911		C6
Oakdale Ct					
8900	ODPK	60462	3346	11W-17S	A5
Oakdale Dr					
5200	OKLN	60453	3275	6W-11S	D1
Oakdale Rd					
1900	HFET	60195	2804	25W-12N	C7
1900	HFET	60195	2858	25W-12N	C1
Oakdene Dr					
10	BNHL	60010	2750	26W-18N	C3
10	BRTN	60010	2750	26W-20N	C2
Oakdene Dr E					
10	BNHL	60010	2750	26W-18N	C2
Oakdene Dr W					
200	BNHL	60010	2750	26W-18N	C3
S Oakenwald Av					
4000	CHCG	60653	3092	1E-4S	E6
4200	CHCG	60653	3093	1E-4S	A7
Oak Forest Av					
6000	BmnT	60477	3425	8W-20S	B4
6000	TYPK	60477	3425	8W-20S	B4
E Oak Glen Dr					
100	BRLT	60103	2910		D4
200	BRLT	60103	2911		A4
S Oak Glen Dr					
400	BRLT	60103	2911		A4
W Oak Glen Dr					
100	BRLT	60103	2910		E4
Oak Grove Av					
7100	JSTC	60458	3148	11W-8S	A7
7300	JSTC	60458	3210	11W-8S	A2
9000	LynT	60480	3208		E5
Oakhill Ct					
8600	HYHL	60457	3210	10W-10S	A4
Oak Hill Dr					
100	WDDL	60191	2915		A7
3400	MonT	60417	3594	4W-29S	E7
3400	MonT	60417	3595	4W-29S	A7
11800	HMGN	60441	3344	14W-18S	C7
11800	OrlT	60441	3344	14W-18S	C7
11800	OrlT	60467	3344	14W-18S	C7
Oakhill Rd					
400	ELGN	60120	2855		B1
500	ELGN	60120	2801		B7
W Oak Hills Ct					
7800	PSHT	60463	3346	9W-15S	D1
Oak Hills Pkwy					
-	PSHT	60463	3346	9W-15S	C1
S Oak Hills Pkwy					
7900	PSHT	60463	3346	9W-15S	C2
Oakhurst Ct					
10	MTSN	60443	3505	7W-24S	D5
Oakhurst Rd					
10	MTSN	60443	3505	7W-24S	D5
Oak Knoll Ct					
10	SMWD	60107	2857	26W-11N	E4
200	SMBG	60193	2859	22W-9N	D6
4300	NHBK	60062	2756	12W-18N	A3
Oak Knoll Ln					
4200	HFET	60195	2804	25W-15N	B2
7900	PSHT	60463	3346	9W-15S	C1
Oak Knoll Rd					
10	BNHL	60010	2750	27W-20N	B1
Oak Knoll Ter					
100	HDPK	60035	2758	6W-20N	C2
200	NHBK	60062	2756	12W-18N	A3
300	NfdT	60062	2756	12W-18N	A3
Oakland Av					
600	ELGN	60120	2855		B3
6000	OKFT	60452	3347	7W-18S	C6
Oakland Ct					
1000	BRTN	60010	2751	24W-18N	B2
Oakland Dr					
200	HDPK	60035	2758	7W-20N	B1
1000	BRTN	60010	2751	24W-18N	B3
1000	SMWD	60107	2857	28W-9N	B7
10800	ODPK	60462	3345	13W-17S	A5
10800	ODPK	60467	3345	13W-17S	A5
22800	STGR	60475	3596	0E-27S	E5
22800	STGR	60475	3597	0E-27S	A4
23000	CRTE	60417	3597	0E-27S	A5
S Oakland Crescent St					
4000	CHCG	60653	3092	1E-4S	E6
Oak Lawn Ct					
100	SMBG	60195	2859	23W-12N	A2
W Oakleaf Av					
7800	EDPK	60707	2974	9W-3N	B5
7900	RVGV	60171	2974	9W-3N	B5
Oak Leaf Ct					
1200	CRTE	60417	3685	0W-29S	D1
Oak Leaf Ter					
800	NHBK	60062	2757	9W-17N	C4
Oakley Av					
1100	WNKA	60093	2758	5W-16N	E7
5100	HMND	46320	3352		D6
14300	DXMR	60406	3349	2W-17S	C5
14300	DXMR	60426	3349	2W-17S	C5
14300	ODPK	60462	3345	12W-17S	B5
14600	HRVY	60426	3349	2W-17S	C5
15600	HRVY	60426	3427	2W-18S	C1
15900	ThtT	60426	3427	2W-19S	C2
16100	MKHM	60426	3427	2W-19S	C2
18400	LNSG	60438	3429	3E-21S	E7
18500	BlmT	60411	3429	3E-22S	E7
18500	LNSG	60411	3429	3E-21S	E7
N Oakley Av					
2200	CHCG	60647	2977	2W-2N	B6
2800	CHCG	60618	2977	2W-3N	B5
4700	CHCG	60625	2921	2W-6N	B6
6000	CHCG	60659	2921	2W-7N	A3
6800	CHCG	60645	2921	2W-8N	A1
7500	CHCG	60202	2867	2W-9N	A7
7500	CHCG	60645	2867	2W-9N	A7
7500	EVTN	60202	2867	2W-9N	A7
S Oakley Av					
1200	CHCG	60608	3033	2W-1S	B7
1200	CHCG	60612	3033	2W-1S	B7
1800	CHCG	60608	3091	2W-2S	B2
3400	CHCG	60609	3091	2W-3S	B5
4900	CHCG	60609	3151	2W-5S	B2
5200	HMND	46320	3352		D6
5500	CHCG	60636	3151	2W-6S	B3
7400	CHCG	60620	3213	2W-8S	B1
7400	CHCG	60636	3213	2W-8S	B1
9500	CHCG	60643	3213	2W-11S	B7
10300	CHCG	60643	3277	2W-12S	B1
11800	BLID	60406	3277	2W-13S	B5
11800	CHCG	60406	3277	2W-13S	B5
N Oakley Blvd					
10	CHCG	60612	3033	2W-0N	B4
700	CHCG	60622	3033	2W-0N	B3
1500	CHCG	60647	3033	2W-1N	B1
S Oakley Blvd					
10	CHCG	60612	3033	2W-0S	B6
Oakley Ct					
15400	HRVY	60426	3349	2W-18S	C7
Oak Ln Dr					
20700	OMFD	60461	3506	4W-25S	E7
Oak Ln Rd					
1700	FSMR	60422	3507	3W-23S	B4
1800	FSMR	60461	3507	3W-23S	B4
1800	RchT	60461	3507	3W-23S	B4
Oak Meadow Ct					
10	SMWD	60107	2857	27W-11N	C3
300	SMBG	60193	2859	22W-10N	C6
Oakmeadow Ct					
1300	WLNG	60090	2754	16W-18N	D4
17200	HMGN	60441	3422	16W-20S	A4
Oakmont Av					
1100	FSMR	60422	3507	3W-23S	B3
Oakmont Ct					
10	LMNT	60439	3342	20W-15S	B2
10	SMWD	60107	2857	26W-11N	E4
Oakmont Dr					
10	DRFD	60015	2757	10W-20N	A2
300	BRLT	60103	2910		D4
1200	LMNT	60439	3342	20W-15S	B2
Oakmont Ln					
400	SMBG	60173	2859	22W-11N	C4
600	WLNG	60090	2754	15W-18N	E2
N Oakmont Rd					
-	HFET	60195	2858	25W-12N	B2
1300	HFET	60194	2858	25W-12N	B2
W Oakmont Rd					
1200	HFET	60194	2858	25W-12N	C2
Oak Park Av					
-	BmnT	60445	3347	8W-17S	A5
-	BRBK	60459	3211	8W-10S	A6
-	OKFT	60445	3347	8W-17S	A5
500	BCHR	60401	3864	1W-36S	B2
600	WshT	60401	3864	1W-36S	B2
1200	BRWN	60402	3030	8W-1S	E7
1200	OKPK	60304	3030	8W-1S	E7
1500	BRWN	60402	3088	8W-1S	E1
2000	BRWN	60402	3089	8W-4S	A7
3800	SKNY	60402	3089	8W-4S	A7
4400	FTVW	60402	3089	8W-4S	A7
4500	FTVW	60402	3149	8W-4S	A1
7700	BDPK	60459	3211	8W-8S	A2
8600	OKLN	60459	3211	8W-9S	A4
8700	BGVW	60453	3211	8W-10S	A4
8700	BGVW	60455	3211	8W-10S	A4
8700	OKLN	60453	3211	8W-11S	A6
8700	OKLN	60455	3211	8W-10S	A4
8800	MNGV	60053	2864	8W-11N	E3
9600	CHRG	60415	3211	8W-11S	A6
9800	CHRG	60453	3211	8W-11S	A7
9800	OKLN	60415	3211	8W-11S	A7
10300	CHRG	60415	3275	8W-12S	A2
10300	CHRG	60482	3275	8W-12S	A2
10300	WRTH	60415	3275	8W-12S	A2
10300	WRTH	60482	3275	8W-12S	A2
14500	BmnT	60452	3347	8W-18S	A7
14500	OKFT	60452	3347	8W-18S	A7
15600	BmnT	60477	3347	8W-18S	A7
15600	OKFT	60477	3347	8W-18S	A7
15700	BmnT	60452	3425	8W-18S	A1
15700	BmnT	60477	3425	8W-18S	A1
15700	OKFT	60452	3425	8W-18S	A1
15800	TYPK	60452	3425	8W-18S	A1
15800	TYPK	60477	3425	8W-19S	A3
18200	RchT	60477	3425	8W-21S	A7
18500	RchT	60477	3505	8W-22S	A1
18500	TYPK	60477	3505	8W-23S	A3
N Oak Park Av					
100	OKPK	60301	3030	8W-0N	E4
800	OKPK	60302	3030	8W-1N	E1
1200	CHCG	60707	3030	8W-2N	E1
1600	OKPK	60707	3030	8W-2N	E1
1700	CHCG	60707	2974	8W-2N	E7
2700	CHCG	60634	2974	8W-3N	E6
4100	HDHT	60706	2974	8W-5N	E1
4400	HDHT	60706	2918	8W-5N	E7
4800	CHCG	60706	2918	8W-6N	E6
5400	CHCG	60656	2918	8W-6N	E6
6200	CHCG	60631	2918	8W-7N	E3
6500	CHCG	60714	2918	8W-8N	E2
6500	NLES	60714	2918	8W-8N	E2
7200	NLES	60714	2865	8W-9N	A7
7400	NLES	60714	2864	8W-9N	E7
S Oak Park Av					
100	OKPK	60302	3030	8W-0S	E5
400	OKPK	60304	3030	8W-0N	E5
1100	BRWN	60402	3030	8W-0S	E7
5900	CHCG	60638	3149	8W-7S	A5
7300	BDPK	60638	3149	8W-8S	A7
7300	BDPK	60638	3211	8W-8S	A1
10700	CHRG	60482	3275	8W-12S	A3
10700	WRTH	60482	3275	8W-13S	A4
11900	PSHT	60463	3275	8W-14S	A6
12900	PSHT	60463	3347	8W-15S	A1
13000	WthT	60463	3347	8W-15S	A1
Oak Park Av N					
1000	OKPK	60302	3030	8W-1N	E1
Oak Ridge Av					
10	HLSD	60162	3029	13W-0S	A7
300	PvsT	60162	3029	13W-0S	A7
Oakridge Av					
4600	OKFT	60452	3426	5W-19S	B3
Oak Ridge Cir					
1000	BRTN	60010	2751	24W-18N	B2
Oak Ridge Ct					
1300	WLSP	60480	3209	12W-10S	B4
N Oakridge Ct					
1200	PLTN	60067	2752	22W-17N	C5
S Oak Ridge Ct					
14100	HMGN	60441	3343	16W-16S	E4
W Oak Ridge Ct					
7700	PSHT	60463	3346	9W-15S	D1
Oak Ridge Dr					
900	HnrT	60107	2856	29W-9N	D7
900	SMWD	60107	2856	29W-9N	D7
9000	JSTC	60458	3209	11W-9S	E2
Oakridge Dr					
1000	GLNC	60022	2758	7W-18N	C4
S Oak Ridge Dr					
13800	HMGN	60441	3343	16W-16S	E3
W Oak Ridge Dr					
7800	PSHT	60463	3274	9W-14S	C6
7800	PSPK	60464	3274	9W-14S	C6
Oak Ridge Dr E					
100	BRRG	60527	3208		A6
Oak Ridge Dr W					
100	BRRG	60527	3208		A6
Oak Ridge Ln					
10	DRPK	60010	2751	23W-20N	E2
10	PltT	60010	2751	23W-20N	E2
W Oak Ridge Ln					
13200	HMGN	60441	3343	16W-16S	E4
Oak Ridge Rd					
-	DndT	60110	2748		B7
600	CPVL	60110	2801		B1
600	EDND	60110	2801		B1
600	EDND	60118	2801		B1
1000	CPVL	60110	2748		B7
1000	CPVL	60118	2748		B7
1000	EDND	60110	2748		B7
1000	EDND	60118	2748		B7
1200	BRTN	60010	2751	24W-18N	C2
S Oak Ridge Tr					
13100	PSHT	60463	3346	9W-15S	D1
W Oaks Av					
9000	MaiT	60016	2863	11W-11N	D2
Oaksbury Ct					
2900	RGMW	60008	2806	20W-13N	A5
Oaksbury Ln					
4100	RGMW	60008	2806	20W-13N	A5
4300	PltT	60008	2806	20W-13N	A5
4300	PltT	60067	2806	20W-13N	A5
E Oaksbury Ln					
100	PltT	60008	2806	20W-13N	A5
100	PltT	60067	2806	20W-13N	A5
100	RGMW	60008	2806	20W-13N	A5
300	PltT	60067	2805	20W-13N	E5
Oakside Ln					
800	UYPK	60466	3684	3W-29S	A2
W Oakton Ct					
6900	NLES	60714	2864	8W-10N	E5
Oakton Pl					
1600	DSPN	60018	2862	13W-9N	E6
Oakton St					
-	CHCG	60068	2863	12W-10N	B6
-	DSPN	60018	2863	12W-10N	B6
-	MNGV	60714	2865	8W-10N	A5
-	NLES	60714	2865	8W-10N	A5
100	EGVV	60007	2861	17W-9N	B6
600	EGvT	60007	2861	17W-9N	B6
600	EVTN	60202	2867	3W-9N	A6
900	NLES	60714	2864	10W-9N	A6
900	PKRG	60068	2864	10W-9N	A6
1300	PKRG	60068	2863	11W-10N	D6
1700	EVTN	60202	2866	5W-10N	A6
1900	EGvT	60005	2861	16W-9N	D6
1900	EGVV	60005	2861	16W-9N	D6
2300	SKOK	60076	2866	3W-10N	D6
4700	SKOK	60076	2865	6W-10N	E5
4700	SKOK	60077	2865	7W-9N	A5
5300	MNGV	60053	2865	7W-9N	A5
5500	SKOK	60053	2865	6W-10N	C5
Oakton St SR-72					
1500	EGVV	60007	2861	17W-9N	C6
1800	EGvT	60007	2861	16W-9N	D6
Oakton St SR-83					
1800	EGvT	60007	2861	16W-9N	D6
1800	EGVV	60007	2861	16W-9N	C6
1900	EGvT	60005	2861	16W-9N	D6
1900	EGVV	60005	2861	16W-9N	D6
E Oakton St					
10	ANHT	60004	2807	17W-14N	B3
10	DSPN	60018	2862	14W-9N	C6
1300	DSPN	60018	2863	12W-10N	A6
1600	PTHT	60004	2807	16W-14N	C3
1900	CHCG	60068	2863	12W-10N	A6
2200	EGvT	60005	2861	16W-9N	D6
2200	EGvT	60007	2861	16W-9N	D6
2200	EGVV	60005	2861	16W-9N	D6
2200	EGVV	60007	2861	16W-9N	D6
2300	MPPT	60005	2861	16W-9N	D6
2400	EGvT	60056	2861	16W-9N	D6
2500	MPPT	60056	2861	16W-9N	D6
2600	DSPN	60018	2861	16W-9N	D6
2600	DSPN	60056	2861	16W-9N	D6
E Oakton St SR-83					
2200	EGvT	60005	2861	16W-9N	D6
2200	EGvT	60007	2861	16W-9N	D6
2200	EGVV	60005	2861	16W-9N	D6
2200	EGVV	60007	2861	16W-9N	D6
2300	MPPT	60005	2861	16W-9N	D6
2400	EGvT	60056	2861	16W-9N	D6
2500	MPPT	60056	2861	16W-9N	D6
2600	DSPN	60018	2861	16W-9N	D6
2600	DSPN	60056	2861	16W-9N	D6
W Oakton St					
-	MNGV	60053	2864	8W-10N	E5
10	ANHT	60004	2807	18W-14N	A3
10	DSPN	60018	2862	15W-9N	A6
500	ANHT	60004	2806	18W-15N	D3
900	DSPN	60018	2861	16W-9N	E6
900	DSPN	60056	2861	16W-9N	E6
900	EGvT	60005	2861	16W-9N	E6
900	EGvT	60056	2861	16W-9N	E6
900	MPPT	60018	2861	16W-9N	E6
900	MPPT	60056	2861	16W-9N	E6
1700	ANHT	60074	2806	19W-14N	D3
1700	PLTN	60074	2806	19W-14N	D3
6700	MNGV	60714	2864	8W-10N	E5
6700	NLES	60714	2864	8W-10N	E5
7500	PKRG	60068	2864	8W-10N	E5
7600	NLES	60068	2864	9W-10N	C6
7900	PKRG	60714	2864	9W-10N	B6
W Oakton St SR-43					
7000	NLES	60714	2864	8W-10N	E5
W Oakton St SR-83					
900	DSPN	60018	2861	16W-9N	E6
900	DSPN	60056	2861	16W-9N	E6
900	EGvT	60005	2861	16W-9N	E6
900	EGvT	60056	2861	16W-9N	E6
900	MPPT	60018	2861	16W-9N	E6
900	MPPT	60056	2861	16W-9N	E6
Oak Trail Ct					
10	PSHT	60463	3274	9W-14S	C5
Oak Trails Rd					
300	MaiT	60016	2863	12W-12N	C1
Oaktree Ct					
300	HFET	60194	2858	24W-11N	E3
S Oak Tree Dr					
10600	WRTH	60482	3274	9W-12S	E2
Oak Tree Ln					
500	NHFD	60093	2811	7W-15N	B1
2200	PKRG	60068	2863	11W-10N	D4
Oaktree Ln					
11900	LMNT	60439	3271		D6
Oak Valley Ct					
15900	HMGN	60441	3422	16W-19S	A1

Chicago & Cook County Street Index

STREET Block	City	ZIP	Map#	CGS	Grid
Oak Valley Tr					
12600	HMGN	60441	3422	16W-19S	A2
N Oakview Av					
5500	CHCG	60631	2917	10W-6N	E5
5500	CHCG	60656	2917	10W-6N	E5
Oakview Ct					
400	SMBG	60193	2858	24W-10N	E6
S Oakview Ct					
13300	PSHT	60463	3346	9W-15S	D2
W Oak View Ct					
12900	HMGN	60441	3422	16W-19S	A2
Oakview Rd					
10	MTSN	60443	3505	7W-24S	D4
N Oakview St					
4700	NRDG	60706	2917	10W-5N	E7
5200	CHCG	60656	2917	10W-6N	E6
Oakwerth Ln					
8000	BRRG	60527	3208		C3
Oakwood Av					
400	DGvT	60439	3270		B1
900	DSPN	60016	2862	13W-10N	E4
1100	WLMT	60091	2812	3W-13N	D6
1200	DSPN	60016	2863	13W-10N	A4
1400	HRPK	60133	2911		E3
7300	LYNS	60534	3088	9W-4S	D6
17000	LNSG	60438	3430	3E-20S	A4
17500	CCHL	60478	3426	5W-21S	D6
18600	LNSG	60411	3430	3E-22S	A7
18600	LNSG	60411	3510	3E-22S	A1
18600	LNSG	60438	3510	3E-22S	A1
18800	CCHL	60478	3506	5W-22S	D2
19300	LYWD	60411	3510	3E-23S	A3
N Oakwood Av					
100	WLSP	60480	3209	12W-9S	B3
S Oakwood Av					
100	WLSP	60480	3209	12W-9S	C4
600	PlsT	60480	3209	12W-9S	C4
Oakwood Blvd					
10	ELGN	60120	2855		C3
E Oakwood Blvd					
400	CHCG	60653	3092	0E-4S	D6
Oakwood Ct					
-	LYWD	60411	3510	3E-23S	A4
300	PltT	60067	2806	20W-13N	A6
800	DSPN	60016	2862	13W-10N	D4
1000	SMBG	60193	2912		C1
5100	OKFT	60452	3426	6W-19S	A3
18900	CCHL	60478	3506	5W-22S	D2
Oakwood Dr					
10	EGvT	60007	2861	18W-10N	A6
10	EGVV	60007	2861	18W-10N	A6
10	PlsT	60464	3273	13W-14S	B7
10	PTHT	60070	2754	15W-16N	E7
10	PTHT	60070	2755	14W-16N	B7
200	CRTE	60417	3685	0W-29S	C1
2500	OMFD	60461	3507	3W-24S	B6
8700	HYHL	60457	3209	11W-10S	E5
17500	HLCT	60429	3427	3W-21S	A6
17500	TYPK	60477	3423	11W-21S	E5
17500	TYPK	60477	3424	11W-21S	A5
N Oakwood Dr					
1900	ANHT	60004	2754	16W-16N	D7
1900	ANHT	60004	2807	16W-16N	D1
S Oakwood Dr					
200	WDDL	60191	2915		A7
1100	MPPT	60056	2861	17W-11N	C3
W Oakwood Dr					
13400	HMGN	60441	3343	16W-17S	E5
Oakwood Ln					
100	BRLT	60103	2910		E5
100	BRLT	60103	2911		A5
100	WynT	60103	2910		E5
200	WLNG	60090	2755	14W-18N	D3
1200	GNVW	60025	2811	7W-14N	A3
4100	MTSN	60443	3506	5W-25S	C7
Oakwood Rd					
1600	NfdT	60062	2757	9W-18N	B3
Oakwood St					
200	HMND	46324	3430		D3
300	PKFT	60466	3595	3W-27S	B5
Oakwood Ter					
900	HNDL	60521	3086		B6
2500	OMFD	60461	3507	3W-24S	B6
Oboe Ct					
1200	WLNG	60090	2754	16W-18N	D3
O'Brien Dr					
8800	ODHL	60462	3424	11W-19S	A3
8800	ODHL	60477	3424	11W-19S	A3
8800	ODPK	60462	3424	11W-19S	A3
8800	ODPK	60477	3424	11W-19S	A3
W O'Brien St					
-	CHCG	60607	3034	0W-1S	A7
-	CHCG	60608	3034	1W-1S	A7
Oceanside Ter					
900	BRLT	60103	2911		B4
O'Connell Dr					
7000	CHRG	60415	3210	8W-11S	E7
O'Connor Dr					
100	DSPN	60016	2808	13W-13N	E7
W O'Connor Dr					
8000	EDPK	60707	2974	10W-3N	B4
8000	RVGV	60171	2974	10W-3N	A4
Oconto Av					
9500	MNGV	60053	2864	9W-11N	D2
16700	TYPK	60477	3424	9W-20S	E3
N Oconto Av					
3000	CHCG	60707	2974	9W-3N	D4
3000	EDPK	60707	2974	9W-3N	D4
3100	CHCG	60634	2974	9W-3N	D4
3900	NRDG	60634	2974	9W-4N	D3
3900	NRDG	60706	2974	9W-4N	D3
4900	HDHT	60706	2918	9W-6N	D6
5100	CHCG	60706	2918	9W-6N	D6
5400	CHCG	60656	2918	9W-6N	D5
6500	CHCG	60631	2918	9W-8N	D2
7200	CHCG	60631	2864	9W-9N	D7
7500	NLES	60631	2864	9W-9N	D7
7600	NLES	60714	2864	9W-9N	D6
S Oconto Av					
7500	BGVW	60455	3210	9W-8S	E1
W Oconto Ct					
7200	WRTH	60482	3274	9W-12S	E2
Octavia Av					
8900	MNGV	60053	2864	9W-11N	D3
N Octavia Av					
3000	CHCG	60707	2974	9W-3N	D4
3000	EDPK	60707	2974	9W-3N	D4
3100	CHCG	60634	2974	9W-3N	D4
3900	NRDG	60634	2974	9W-4N	D2
3900	NRDG	60706	2974	9W-4N	D2
4900	HDHT	60706	2918	9W-6N	D6
5400	CHCG	60656	2918	9W-6N	D5
7100	CHCG	60631	2918	9W-8N	D1
7200	CHCG	60631	2864	9W-9N	D7
7700	NLES	60714	2864	9W-10N	D5

STREET Block	City	ZIP	Map#	CGS	Grid
S Octavia Av					
7100	BGVW	60455	3148	9W-8S	E7
9200	BGVW	60455	3210	9W-10S	E6
11200	WRTH	60482	3274	9W-13S	E4
O'Dell Av					
8900	BGVW	60455	3210	9W-10S	E5
9200	MNGV	60053	2864	9W-11N	D2
17300	TYPK	60477	3424	9W-20S	E5
N O'Dell Av					
3000	CHCG	60707	2974	9W-3N	D4
3000	EDPK	60707	2974	9W-3N	D4
3100	CHCG	60634	2974	9W-3N	D4
4000	NRDG	60634	2974	9W-5N	D2
4000	NRDG	60706	2974	9W-5N	D1
4900	HDHT	60706	2918	9W-6N	D6
5400	CHCG	60656	2918	9W-6N	D5
6900	CHCG	60631	2918	9W-8N	D1
7200	CHCG	60631	2864	9W-9N	D7
7800	NLES	60714	2864	9W-9N	D6
O'Dell Ct					
-	HDHT	60706	2918	9W-6N	D7
W O'Dell Ct					
7300	WRTH	60482	3274	9W-12S	E2
Odessa Dr					
-	MTSN	60443	3506	5W-24S	B6
Odlum Ct					
200	SMBG	60194	2857	27W-10N	D5
Odlum Dr					
2700	SMBG	60194	2857	27W-10N	D5
2800	SMBG	60193	2857	27W-10N	D5
Odyssey Blvd					
-	MTSN	60443	3505	8W-23S	B4
-	MTSN	60477	3505	8W-23S	B4
-	TYPK	60477	3505	8W-23S	B4
Odyssey Dr					
10	TYPK	60477	3505	8W-23S	B4
N Ogallah Av					
6600	CHCG	60631	2918	9W-8N	D2
Ogden Av					
-	CHCG	60610	3034	0W-1N	A1
-	HNDL	60521	3086		B6
-	LynT	60521	3086		B6
-	LynT	60558	3086		B6
-	PvsT	60521	3086		B6
100	PvsT	60558	3086		B6
100	WNSP	60558	3086		D6
6200	BRWN	60402	3089	8W-3S	A5
6200	BRWN	60804	3089	8W-3S	A5
6200	CCRO	60804	3089	8W-3S	A5
6800	BRWN	60402	3088	10W-4S	B6
7100	LYNS	60402	3088	10W-4S	B7
7100	LYNS	60534	3088	10W-4S	B7
7100	RVSD	60402	3088	10W-4S	B7
7100	RVSD	60546	3088	10W-4S	B7
7300	LYNS	60546	3088	9W-3S	D6
8700	BKFD	60513	3088	10W-4S	A6
8800	BKFD	60513	3087	11W-4S	D6
9500	LGNG	60525	3087	11W-4S	D6
Ogden Av US-34					
-	HNDL	60521	3086		B6
-	LynT	60521	3086		B6
-	LynT	60558	3086		B6
-	PvsT	60521	3086		B6
100	PvsT	60558	3086		B6
100	WNSP	60558	3086		D6
7200	BRWN	60402	3088	10W-4S	B7
7200	LYNS	60402	3088	10W-4S	B7
7200	LYNS	60534	3088	10W-4S	B7
7200	RVSD	60402	3088	10W-4S	B7
7200	RVSD	60546	3088	10W-4S	B7
7300	LYNS	60546	3088	9W-3S	D6
8700	BKFD	60513	3088	10W-4S	A6
8800	BKFD	60513	3087	11W-4S	D6
9500	LGNG	60525	3087	11W-4S	D6
E Ogden Av					
10	LGNG	60525	3087	12W-4S	C6
400	HNDL	60521	3086		C6
400	LynT	60521	3086		C6
500	LynT	60558	3086		C6
9600	BKFD	60513	3087	12W-4S	D6
E Ogden Av US-34					
10	LGNG	60525	3087	12W-4S	C6
400	HNDL	60521	3086		C6
400	LynT	60521	3086		C6
500	LynT	60558	3086		C6
9600	BKFD	60513	3087	12W-4S	D6
N Ogden Av					
10	CHCG	60607	3033	1W-0N	D4
300	CHCG	60622	3033	1W-0N	D4
1400	CHCG	60610	3034		C1
W Ogden Av					
10	HNDL	60521	3086		A7
10	LGNG	60525	3087	12W-4S	C6
1200	LGPK	60525	3087	13W-4S	A6
1500	CHCG	60607	3033	2W-0S	C5
1500	CHCG	60612	3033	2W-0S	C5
1500	WNSP	60558	3087	13W-3S	A6
1600	PvsT	60558	3087	13W-3S	A6
2300	CHCG	60608	3033	3W-1S	A7
2700	CHCG	60623	3033	3W-1S	A7
2800	CHCG	60623	3032	3W-1S	E7
2800	CHCG	60623	3090	3W-1S	E1
4400	CCRO	60804	3090	5W-2S	A2
4800	CCRO	60804	3089	7W-3S	C4
6100	BRWN	60402	3089	7W-3S	B4
6100	BRWN	60804	3089	7W-3S	B4
W Ogden Av US-34					
10	HNDL	60521	3086		A7
10	LGNG	60525	3087	12W-4S	C6
1200	LGPK	60525	3087	13W-3S	A6
1500	WNSP	60558	3087	13W-3S	A6
1600	PvsT	60558	3087	13W-3S	A6
E Ogden St					
10	CTCY	60409	3352	4E-18S	C6
10	HMND	46320	3352		D6
Oglesby Av					
10	CTCY	60409	3351	2E-16S	D4
S Oglesby Av					
-	CHCG	60633	3351	2E-15S	D2
-	CTCY	60409	3351	2E-15S	D2
6700	CHCG	60649	3153	2E-7S	D6
7500	CHCG	60649	3215	2E-9S	D2
9300	CHCG	60617	3215	2E-10S	D5
10300	CHCG	60617	3279	2E-11S	D1
Ogorman Dr					
11100	PSHL	60465	3274	10W-12S	A3
O'Hare Ct					
10	BNVL	60106	2972		A1
S O'Hare Ct					
25200	MonT	60449	3682	8W-30S	B4
O'Hare Dr					
4100	HFET	60195	2804	24W-15N	D3
O'Hare Cargo Area Rd					
-	CHCG	60666	2916		C7
-	CHCG	60666	2972		C1

STREET Block	City	ZIP	Map#	CGS	Grid
Ohio Ct					
18100	ODPK	60467	3423	13W-21S	B7
Ohio St					
10	MYWD	60153	3030	10W-0N	A3
E Ohio St					
10	CHCG	60610	3034	0E-0N	C3
10	CHCG	60611	3034	0E-0N	C3
W Ohio St					
10	CHCG	60611	3034	0W-0N	B3
300	CHCG	60610	3034	0W-0N	A3
700	CHCG	60622	3034	0W-0N	A3
1000	GNWD	60425	3508	1W-22S	A1
1000	HMWD	60425	3508	1W-22S	A1
1200	CHCG	60622	3033	2W-0N	B3
1900	CHCG	60612	3033	3W-0N	A3
3000	CHCG	60612	3032	4W-0N	D3
3100	CHCG	60624	3032	4W-0N	C3
4600	CHCG	60644	3032	5W-0N	A3
5200	CHCG	60644	3031	6W-0N	D3
5900	OKPK	60302	3031	7W-0N	B3
Ohlendorf Rd					
3000	MonT	60449	3683	4W-31S	D6
3000	MonT	60449	3684	3W-31S	A6
Ojibwa Tr					
-	MPPT	60056	2861	16W-12N	D2
S Ojibwa Tr					
400	MPPT	60056	2861	16W-12N	D1
Oketo Av					
8800	NLES	60053	2864	9W-11N	D4
8800	NLES	60714	2864	9W-11N	D4
9300	MNGV	60053	2864	9W-11N	D2
16700	TYPK	60477	3424	9W-20S	E3
N Oketo Av					
3000	CHCG	60707	2974	9W-3N	D4
3000	EDPK	60707	2974	9W-3N	D4
3100	CHCG	60634	2974	9W-3N	D4
3900	NRDG	60706	2974	9W-5N	D1
4400	HDHT	60706	2918	9W-5N	D7
4400	NRDG	60706	2918	9W-5N	D7
5100	CHCG	60656	2918	9W-5N	D7
6600	CHCG	60631	2918	9W-8N	D2
7200	CHCG	60631	2864	9W-9N	D7
8000	NLES	60714	2864	9W-10N	D5
8700	MNGV	60053	2864	9W-10N	D5
8700	NLES	60053	2864	9W-10N	D5
S Oketo Av					
7100	BGVW	60455	3148	9W-8S	D7
7500	BGVW	60455	3210	9W-10S	D4
11200	WRTH	60482	3274	9W-13S	E4
Oklahoma Cir					
600	EGVV	60007	2859	21W-9N	E7
Oklahoma Ct					
-	OrlT	60477	3423	12W-21S	B7
18200	ODPK	60467	3423	13W-21S	B7
Oklahoma Wy					
600	EGVV	60007	2859	21W-9N	E7
600	EGVV	60007	2913		E1
Olcott Av					
8800	NLES	60714	2864	9W-11N	D4
9200	MNGV	60053	2864	9W-11N	C2
15900	ODPK	60462	3424	9W-18S	E1
15900	TYPK	60477	3424	9W-19S	E2
16700	OrlT	60477	3424	9W-20S	E4
N Olcott Av					
3000	CHCG	60707	2974	9W-3N	C4
3000	EDPK	60707	2974	9W-3N	C4
3900	CHCG	60634	2974	9W-4N	C2
3900	NRDG	60706	2974	9W-4N	C2
4600	HDHT	60706	2918	9W-5N	C7
4600	NRDG	60706	2918	9W-5N	C7
5100	CHCG	60656	2918	9W-6N	C6
6800	CHCG	60631	2918	9W-8N	C1
7200	CHCG	60631	2864	9W-9N	C7
8100	NLES	60714	2864	9W-10N	C4
8600	MNGV	60053	2864	9W-10N	C4
Olcott Ct					
17300	TYPK	60477	3424	9W-20S	E5
Old Arlington Ct					
900	ANHT	60004	2754	17W-17N	A4
900	ANHT	60089	2754	17W-17N	A4
900	BFGV	60089	2754	17W-17N	A4
N Old Arlington Heights Rd					
-	BFGV	60004	2754	17W-17N	A5
3200	ANHT	60004	2754	17W-17N	A5
3200	ANHT	60089	2754	17W-17N	A5
3200	BFGV	60089	2754	17W-17N	A5
Old Barn Ct					
16700	TYPK	60477	3424	10W-20S	C3
E Old Barn Ln					
700	ANHT	60005	2807	17W-12N	B7
Old Barrington Rd					
-	HFET	60195	2803	25W-13N	E6
-	SBTN	60010	2803	25W-13N	E6
Old Bartlett Rd					
-	BNHL	60010	2750	27W-16N	A7
-	BNHL	60010	2803	27W-16N	A1
-	BrnT	60010	2803	27W-16N	A1
-	SBTN	60010	2803	27W-16N	A1
Old Beach Rd					
800	DYR	46311	3598		E2
Old Bender Rd					
10	DSPN	60016	2863	12W-11N	B3
Old Bluff Rd					
-	DGvT	60439	3271		B1
Old Brennan Hwy					
-	BmnT	60478	3426	6W-20S	A5
-	CCHL	60478	3426	6W-20S	A5
Old Briar Rd					
1600	HDPK	60035	2757	9W-20N	C2
E Old Bridge Rd					
100	PLTN	60067	2752	20W-17N	E5
100	PLTN	60067	2753	20W-17N	A5
100	PLTN	60074	2753	20W-17N	A5
N Old Bridge Rd					
1000	PLTN	60067	2752	20W-17N	E4
Old Buffalo Grove Rd					
-	BFGV	60089	2754	16W-18N	C4
-	WhlT	60004	2754	16W-18N	C4
-	WhlT	60089	2754	16W-18N	C4
N Old Buffalo Grove Rd					
-	ANHT	60004	2754	16W-17N	C6
-	ANHT	60090	2754	16W-17N	C6
-	WLNG	60090	2754	16W-17N	C6
3500	BFGV	60089	2754	16W-17N	C4
3500	WhlT	60004	2754	16W-17N	C4
3500	WhlT	60089	2754	16W-17N	C4
Old Cargo Rd					
500	CHCG	60666	2917	12W-6N	A6
Old Checker Ct					
700	BFGV	60089	2754	17W-20N	B1
Old Checker Rd					
300	BFGV	60089	2754	17W-20N	B1
Old Church Rd					
1000	SMBG	60107	2857	27W-11N	D5
1000	SMBG	60194	2857	27W-11N	D5

STREET Block	City	ZIP	Map#	CGS	Grid
Old Church Rd					
1000	SMWD	60107	2857	27W-11N	D5
1000	SMWD	60194	2857	27W-11N	D5
Old Coach Dr					
10	SBTN	60010	2803	26W-14N	D4
S Old Coach Tr					
19500	FftT	60423	3504	9W-23S	D3
Old Creek Ct					
700	EGVV	60007	2914		B3
1000	ELGN	60120	2801		D7
Old Creek Ln					
6000	MTSN	60443	3505	7W-24S	D6
Old Creek Rd N					
10	PSPK	60464	3272	14W-14S	D7
Old Creek Rd S					
10	PSPK	60464	3272	14W-15S	D7
10	PSPK	60464	3344	14W-15S	E1
Old Dundee Rd					
100	BNHL	60010	2750	27W-16N	B6
100	BrnT	60010	2750	27W-16N	B6
Olde Farm Rd					
1200	SMBG	60173	2805	21W-13N	D6
18200	ThtT	60438	3429	2E-21S	D6
18300	LNSG	60438	3429	2E-21S	D7
18500	BlmT	60411	3429	2E-21S	D7
Olde Gatehouse Rd					
6800	TYPK	60477	3425	8W-19S	A3
Old Elm Dr					
16900	CCHL	60478	3426	4W-20S	D4
Old Elm Ln					
1000	GLNC	60022	2758	6W-18N	C3
Old Elm Pl					
900	GLNC	60022	2758	6W-18N	C4
Olde Oaks Rd					
1100	SMBG	60173	2805	21W-13N	D6
Olde Salem Cir					
7200	HRPK	60133	2912		A1
7200	SMBG	60133	2912		A2
Olde Salem Rd					
7300	HRPK	60133	2912		A1
E Olde Virginia Ct					
1000	PLTN	60074	2753	19W-17N	B5
E Olde Virginia Rd					
1000	PLTN	60074	2753	19W-17N	C5
Olde Western Av					
13200	BLID	60406	3349	3W-15S	B1
Old Farm Dr					
600	ROSL	60172	2912		D7
Old Farm Ln					
10	DndT	60110	2748		A5
Old Farm Rd					
-	LYWD	46311	3510		C6
-	LYWD	60411	3510		C6
100	NHFD	60093	2811	7W-16N	A1
200	NfdT	60093	2811	7W-16N	A1
200	NHFD	60093	2758	7W-16N	A7
700	MTSN	60443	3505	7W-24S	D6
900	DYR	46311	3510		C6
Old Forge Ct					
600	UYPK	60466	3684	3W-30S	B4
S Old Forge Ct					
1200	PLTN	60067	2805	21W-14N	D4
Old Forge Ln					
600	UYPK	60466	3684	3W-30S	B4
Old George's Wy					
-	OMFD	60461	3506	4W-24S	D4
Old Georges Wy					
7900	PSHT	60463	3346	9W-15S	C2
Old Glenview Rd					
2000	WLMT	60091	2812	4W-13N	B6
2100	EVTN	60201	2812	4W-13N	B7
2200	WLMT	60201	2812	4W-13N	B7
3200	SKOK	60077	2811	6W-13N	D7
3200	WLMT	60091	2811	6W-13N	D7
3300	GNVW	60025	2811	6W-13N	D7
3300	GNVW	60091	2811	6W-13N	D7
Old Green Bay Rd					
10	GLNC	60093	2759	5W-16N	A7
10	WNKA	60093	2759	5W-17N	A6
100	GLNC	60022	2759	5W-17N	A6
700	GLNC	60022	2758	6W-18N	D4
Oldham Rd					
14100	ODPK	60467	3344	14W-16S	D4
S Old Harlem Av					
6500	BDPK	60638	3148	9W-7S	E6
6500	CHCG	60638	3148	9W-7S	E6
Old Hart Rd					
10	BNHL	60010	2750	26W-20N	C1
Old Hickory Rd					
10	RGMW	60008	2806	19W-14N	C3
Old Hicks Rd					
2300	ElaT	60047	2753	19W-20N	B1
2300	LGGV	60047	2753	19W-20N	B1
E Old Hicks Rd					
2000	PLTN	60074	2753	19W-18N	B2
2300	LGGV	60047	2753	19W-20N	B2
N Old Hicks Rd					
1800	PLTN	60074	2753	19W-18N	B3
Old Higgins Rd					
-	EDND	60118	2801		E4
-	HFET	60010	2803	27W-12N	C7
-	HFET	60010	2857	27W-12N	D1
-	HFET	60118	2801		E4
-	HFET	60118	2802	30W-14N	A4
-	HFET	60194	2857	27W-12N	D1
2700	EGvT	60007	2915		E1
2700	EGVV	60007	2915		E1
2800	EGVV	60007	2916		A1
2900	CHCG	60007	2916		A1
2900	CHCG	60018	2916		A1
3000	DSPN	60007	2916		A1
3000	DSPN	60018	2916		A1
Old Hunt Rd					
-	NfdT	60062	2757	8W-16N	E7
-	NfdI	60062	2758	8W-16N	A7
-	NfdT	60093	2757	8W-16N	E7
-	NfdT	60093	2758	8W-16N	A7
-	NHBK	60062	2758	8W-16N	A7
-	NHBK	60093	2758	8W-16N	A7
-	NHFD	60093	2758	8W-16N	A7
10	NHBK	60062	2757	8W-16N	E7
10	NHBK	60093	2757	8W-16N	E7
10	NHFD	60093	2757	8W-16N	E7
Old Irving Park Rd					
11500	CHCG	60666	2972		C1
Old Kings Ct					
2300	SMBG	60194	2857	27W-11N	C3
2300	SMWD	60107	2857	27W-11N	C3
Old Lake St					
200	HnrT	60120	2910		E1
200	SMWD	60120	2910		E1
300	BRLT	60103	2910		D1
300	BRLT	60120	2910		D1
Old Lemont Rd					
-	LmnT	60439	3270		D4

STREET Block	City	ZIP	Map#	CGS	Grid
Old Meadow Rd					
500	MTSN	60443	3505	7W-24S	D6
Old Mill Ct					
10	BRRG	60527	3146		C7
10	BRTN	60010	2751	24W-18N	B2
Old Mill Dr					
100	SMBG	60193	2859	23W-9N	A6
N Old Mill Dr					
1000	PLTN	60067	2752	20W-17N	E5
Old Mill Ln					
-	BRRG	60527	3146		C7
1000	HRPK	60133	2911		E1
1200	EGVV	60007	2914		B3
2600	RGMW	60008	2805	21W-13N	C5
E Old Mill Ln					
10	BRRG	60527	3146		D7
N Old Mill Ln					
10	BRRG	60527	3146		C7
S Old Mill Ln					
10	BRRG	60527	3146		D7
W Old Mill Ln					
10	BRRG	60527	3146		C7
Old Mill Rd					
10	MTSN	60443	3505	7W-24S	C5
100	BRTN	60010	2751	24W-18N	C2
1100	HNDL	60521	3086		B6
1100	OKBK	60523	3086		B6
3200	NHBK	60062	2756	11W-16N	D7
3300	NHBK	60062	2809	11W-16N	C1
7900	FftT	60423	3504	10W-24S	C5
Old Monee Rd					
23900	MonT	60417	3594	4W-29S	E7
23900	MonT	60466	3594	4W-28S	E7
24000	MonT	60417	3683	4W-29S	E1
24000	UYPK	60466	3683	4W-29S	E2
24700	MonT	60449	3683	4W-30S	D3
24700	MonT	60466	3683	4W-30S	D2
25500	UYPK	60449	3683	5W-31S	D5
W Old Monee Rd					
500	CRTE	60417	3685	1W-30S	B4
500	CteT	60417	3685	1W-30S	B4
1300	CRTE	60417	3684	2W-30S	D4
1300	CteT	60417	3684	2W-30S	D4
2000	MonT	60417	3684	2W-30S	D4
2000	MonT	60449	3684	2W-30S	D4
2000	UYPK	60417	3684	2W-30S	D4
2000	UYPK	60466	3684	2W-30S	D4
Old Mud Rd					
500	CteT	60417	3685	0E-31S	E6
500	CteT	60417	3686	0E-31S	A6
W Old Northwest Hwy					
400	BRTN	60010	2750	26W-20N	D1
Old Oak Ct					
-	BmnT	60426	3426	5W-19S	A1
Old Oak Ct E					
100	BFGV	60089	2754	16W-18N	C4
Old Oak Ct W					
100	BFGV	60089	2754	16W-18N	C4
Old Oak Dr					
-	BRLT	60103	2910		E1
-	SMWD	60103	2910		E1
-	SMWD	60107	2910		E1
-	SMWD	60107	2911		A2
10	BFGV	60089	2754	16W-18N	C3
10	WLNG	60089	2754	16W-18N	D3
Old Oak Tr					
10	PSHT	60463	3274	9W-14S	C5
Old Orchard Ct					
10100	SKOK	60076	2812	5W-12N	A7
15700	ODPK	60462	3424	10W-18S	C1
Old Orchard Ln E					
13300	DPgT	60441	3342	21W-15S	A2
13300	LktT	60441	3342	21W-15S	A2
Old Orchard Ln N					
16900	DPgT	60441	3342	21W-15S	A2
Old Orchard Rd					
4000	EVTN	60076	2866	5W-12N	B1
4000	EVTN	60201	2866	5W-12N	A1
4000	SKOK	60076	2866	5W-12N	A1
4000	SKOK	60201	2866	5W-12N	B1
4700	SKOK	60076	2865	5W-12N	E1
4800	SKOK	60077	2865	6W-12N	E1
5200	GNVW	60025	2811	6W-13N	D7
5200	SKOK	60077	2811	6W-13N	D7
5200	SKOK	60091	2811	6W-13N	D7
5200	WLMT	60091	2811	6W-13N	D7
5700	GLF	60025	2811	7W-12N	C7
5700	SKOK	60025	2811	7W-12N	C7
Old Orchard Shopping Ctr					
-	SKOK	60076	2865	6W-12N	E1
10	SKOK	60077	2865	6W-12N	E1
Old Plank Blvd					
6000	MTSN	60443	3593	8W-25S	B1
6300	RchT	60443	3593	8W-25S	B1
Old Plank Road Tr					
-	MTSN	60443	3594	6W-25S	A1
Old Plum Grove Rd					
5200	RGMW	60067	2805	21W-13N	D5
5200	SMBG	60067	2805	21W-13N	D5
5200	SMBG	60173	2805	21W-13N	D5
W Old Plum Grove Rd					
10	PltT	60067	2805	21W-13N	D5
10	RGMW	60008	2805	21W-13N	D5
10	RGMW	60067	2805	21W-13N	D5
Old Post Rd					
200	NHBK	60062	2757	8W-18N	D3
700	ANHT	60004	2754	17W-17N	B5
700	BFGV	60089	2754	17W-17N	B5
13600	OrlT	60467	3344	14W-16S	C3
E Old Post Rd					
2300	CteT	60417	3686	3E-29S	E1
2300	CteT	60417	3687	3E-29S	A1
S Old Post Rd					
23900	CteT	60417	3597	2E-29S	E7
23900	CteT	60417	3686	2E-29S	E1
S Old Prague Pth					
11500	PSPK	60464	3274	10W-13S	C4
Old Quarry Rd					
-	LMNT	60439	3270		C6
Old River Rd					
4100	SRPK	60176	2973	11W-5N	D1
Old Saybrook on Auburn					
10	RGMW	60008	2806	19W-14N	B4
Old Schaumburg Rd					
-	SMBG	60173	2859	21W-10N	E6
-	SMBG	60193	2859	21W-10N	E6
Old Spanish Tr					
11800	OrlT	60467	3344	14W-16S	C3
Old Stone Ct					
400	MNSR	46321	3510		D1
Old Surrey Rd					
400	DGvT	60521	3146		A4
400	DGvT	60527	3146		A4
400	HNDL	60521	3146		A4

STREET Block	City	ZIP	Map#	CGS	Grid
Old Sutton Rd					
-	CokC	60010	2802	28W-13N	D5
-	CokC	60118	2802	28W-13N	D5
-	HFET	60010	2802	28W-13N	D5
-	HFET	60118	2802	28W-13N	D5
-	HFET	60192	2802	28W-13N	D6
10	BNHL	60010	2802	28W-14N	D4
10	BNHL	60118	2802	28W-15N	D3
10	BrnT	60010	2802	28W-15N	D3
10	BrnT	60118	2802	28W-15N	D3
200	BNHL	60010	2749	28W-16N	D6
300	AlqT	60010	2749	28W-16N	D6
Old Tamerack Ln					
10	ODPK	60462	3345	13W-16S	B4
10	OrlT	60462	3345	13W-16S	B4
Old Timber Ct					
1100	HFET	60195	2804	24W-15N	C1
Old Timber Ln					
10	PSPK	60464	3272	13W-14S	E7
10	PSPK	60464	3273	13W-14S	A7
1200	HFET	60195	2804	24W-15N	C1
W Old Town Ct					
300	CHCG	60610	3034	0W-1N	A1
Old Trail Rd					
17800	HLCT	60429	3427	3W-21S	A6
Old Valley Rd					
10	RGMW	60008	2806	20W-13N	A6
Old Western Av					
2400	PKFT	60466	3595	3W-28S	C5
13300	BLID	60406	3349	3W-15S	B1
Old Wick Ln					
100	IVNS	60067	2752	22W-18N	B3
S Old Wilke Rd					
1200	ANHT	60005	2860	19W-12N	D1
1200	RGMW	60008	2860	19W-12N	D1
Old Williams Rd					
10	DndT	60102	2748		A4
800	CPVL	60110	2748		A4
800	DndT	60110	2748		A4
Old Willow Rd					
1800	GNVW	60025	2810	9W-15N	B3
1800	NHBK	60062	2810	9W-15N	B3
1800	NHFD	60093	2811	7W-15N	B2
2600	GNVW	60062	2810	9W-15N	C3
2600	NHBK	60025	2810	9W-15N	C3
E Old Willow Rd					
-	MPPT	60056	2808	13W-15N	D2
-	PTHT	60070	2808	13W-15N	D2
-	WLNG	60090	2808	13W-15N	D2
W Old Willow Rd					
100	PTHT	60070	2808	14W-15N	D2
100	WLNG	60090	2808	14W-15N	C2
Old York Rd					
400	EMHT	60126	3028		A6
400	YkTp	60126	3028		A6
Oleander Av					
8800	NLES	60714	2864	9W-11N	C4
9200	MNGV	60053	2864	9W-11N	C2
9500	GNVW	60025	2864	9W-11N	C2
16700	OrlT	60477	3424	9W-20S	E3
16700	TYPK	60477	3424	9W-20S	E3
N Oleander Av					
3000	CHCG	60707	2974	9W-3N	C4
3000	EDPK	60707	2974	9W-3N	C4
3100	CHCG	60634	2974	9W-3N	C4
3900	CHCG	60706	2974	9W-4N	C2
3900	NRDG	60706	2974	9W-4N	C2
5200	CHCG	60656	2918	9W-6N	C6
5200	HDHT	60706	2918	9W-6N	C6
6800	CHCG	60631	2918	9W-8N	C1
7200	CHCG	60631	2864	9W-9N	C7
8200	NLES	60714	2864	9W-10N	C4
8600	MNGV	60053	2864	9W-10N	C4
Oleander Dr					
300	SMBG	60173	2859	21W-11N	E4
O'Leary Dr					
10	BNVL	60106	2972		B1
10	CHCG	60106	2972		B1
Oliphant Av					
9300	MNGV	60053	2864	9W-11N	C2
N Oliphant Av					
6400	CHCG	60631	2918	9W-8N	C2
6400	PKRG	60068	2918	9W-8N	C2
E Olive Av					
100	PTHT	60070	2808	15W-15N	A2
W Olive Av					
100	PTHT	60070	2808	15W-15N	A2
400	ANHT	60004	2807	16W-15N	D2
400	PTHT	60004	2807	16W-15N	D2
400	PTHT	60070	2807	16W-15N	D2
1400	CHCG	60660	2921	2W-7N	C4
3200	CHCG	60659	2920	4W-7N	D4
7200	CHCG	60631	2918	9W-7N	D4
7800	NpkT	60631	2918	9W-7N	B5
Olive Ct					
10	ELGN	60120	2855		C5
Olive Pkwy					
600	BRLT	60103	2910		D1
Olive Rd					
900	HMWD	60430	3428	1W-21S	A7
1200	HMWD	60430	3427	2W-21S	E7
3000	HLCT	60429	3427	3W-21S	A7
Olive St					
800	ELGN	60120	2855		C5
800	HFET	60194	2858	24W-11N	E3
2200	BLID	60406	3277	2W-14S	B7
E Olive St					
10	ANHT	60004	2807	17W-15N	C2
1000	PTHT	60004	2807	17W-15N	C2
1400	PLTN	60074	2806	19W-15N	D2
1500	ANHT	60004	2806	19W-15N	D2
1500	ANHT	60074	2806	19W-15N	D2
W Olive St					
10	ANHT	60004	2807	18W-15N	A2
1600	ANHT	60004	2806	18W-15N	D2
1700	PLTN	60074	2806	18W-15N	D2
Oliver Ct					
100	SMBG	60193	2913		A1
Oliver St					
100	BRLT	60103	2910		D3
Olivia Av					
21500	SLVL	60411	3597	2E-26S	C2
Olivia Ct					
6000	MTSN	60443	3593	7W-25S	D1
S Olivia Ct					
26500	MonT	60449	3683	6W-32S	B7
Olivia Ln					
1500	HRPK	60133	2857	26W-9N	D7
17500	ODPK	60467	3423	13W-21S	A6
Olivia St					
1000	DSPN	60018	2862	13W-10N	E5
Ollie Ct					
800	CPVL	60110	2748		B7
Olmstead Dr					
-	HFET	60010	2804	24W-15N	C1

STREET Block	City	ZIP	Map#	CGS	Grid
Olmstead Dr					
-	MonT	60417	3684	3W-31S	B4
-	MonT	60449	3684	3W-31S	B4
-	UYPK	60417	3684	3W-31S	B4
-	UYPK	60449	3684	3W-30S	C4
-	UYPK	60466	3684	3W-31S	B4
4400	HFET	60195	2804	24W-15N	B2
N Olmsted Av					
6600	CHCG	60631	2918	9W-8N	C2
6800	PKRG	60068	2918	9W-8N	C2
Olmsted Rd					
100	RVSD	60546	3088	9W-3S	D5
300	BRWN	60402	3088	9W-3S	E5
E Oltendorf Ct					
10	SMWD	60107	2857	28W-10N	A7
E Oltendorf Rd					
10	SMWD	60107	2857	28W-9N	A7
N Oltendorf Rd					
10	SMWD	60107	2857	28W-11N	A4
300	HFET	60107	2857	28W-11N	A4
S Oltendorf Rd					
10	SMWD	60107	2857	28W-10N	A6
N Olympia Av					
5000	CHCG	60656	2918	9W-6N	C6
6600	CHCG	60631	2918	9W-8N	C2
E Olympia Cir					
10700	PSHL	60465	3274	10W-12S	B2
W Olympia Cir					
10700	PSHL	60465	3274	10W-12S	B2
Olympia Ct					
300	ELGN	60120	2855		E3
Olympia Dr					
18000	CCHL	60478	3426	5W-21S	D7
Olympia Ln					
1000	ROSL	60172	2912		C5
Olympian Wy					
20500	OMFD	60461	3507	4W-25S	A6
20800	MTSN	60443	3506	4W-24S	D6
20800	OMFD	60461	3506	4W-24S	D6
21100	MTSN	60443	3594	5W-25S	C1
Olympic Dr					
6800	BGVW	60453	3211	8W-10S	A5
6800	BGVW	60455	3211	8W-10S	A5
6800	OKLN	60453	3211	8W-10S	A5
6900	BGVW	60455	3210	8W-10S	E4
8700	BGVW	60459	3210	8W-10S	E4
25700	MONE	60449	3683	6W-31S	B5
Olympic Ln					
-	HmrT	60441	3342	20W-18S	B7
-	LKPT	60441	3342	20W-18S	B7
Olympic Vil					
10	CHHT	60411	3507	2W-25S	D7
Olympus Dr					
10	TYPK	60477	3505	8W-23S	B4
Omaha Cir					
1600	EGVV	60007	2913		D2
Omaha Dr					
8400	BRRG	60527	3208		D3
8400	LynT	60527	3208		D4
Omni Dr					
10	SMBG	60193	2859	23W-9N	A7
N Onarga Av					
6500	CHCG	60631	2918	9W-8N	D2
Onarga St					
300	PKFT	60466	3595	3W-27S	B5
E Oneida Av					
-	BRLT	60103	2910		E3
100	EMHT	60126	3028		A5
200	BRLT	60103	2911		A3
N Oneida Av					
5000	NRDG	60706	2918	9W-6N	C6
6400	CHCG	60631	2918	9W-8N	C2
W Oneida Av					
100	BRLT	60103	2910		E3
Oneida Ct					
1600	MPPT	60056	2808	13W-15N	E3
Oneida Dr					
500	SmbT	60193	2913		B2
N Oneida Ln					
1800	MPPT	60056	2808	13W-15N	E2
W Onekema Dr					
6700	PSHT	60463	3275	8W-14S	A6
One Renaissance Pl					
10	PLTN	60067	2752	20W-16N	E6
Onie Ct					
10	CPVL	60110	2801		B2
10	EDND	60110	2801		B2
10	EDND	60118	2801		B2
W Onondaga Tr					
13200	HMGN	60441	3343	16W-16S	E3
Ontario Ct					
10	OKPK	60302	3030	8W-0N	D3
Ontario St					
10	CHCG	60644	3031	7W-0N	B3
600	OKPK	60301	3031	8W-0N	A3
600	OKPK	60302	3031	8W-0N	A3
800	OKPK	60302	3030	8W-0N	E3
1000	OKPK	60301	3030	8W-0N	D3
1100	OKPK	60305	3030	8W-0N	D3
1100	RVFT	60305	3030	8W-0N	D3
E Ontario St					
10	CHCG	60610	3034	0E-0N	C3
10	CHCG	60611	3034	0E-0N	C3
W Ontario St					
10	CHCG	60610	3034	0W-0N	A3
10	CHCG	60611	3034	0W-0N	B3
1600	CHCG	60622	3033	2W-0N	C3
3900	CHCG	60624	3032	4W-0N	C3
Ontarioville Rd					
1900	HRPK	60133	2911		D4
Onyx Ct					
400	SMBG	60194	2857	26W-11N	E4
N Opal Av					
3200	EDPK	60707	2974	9W-4N	C4
4400	CHCG	60634	2974	9W-5N	B1
4400	CHCG	60706	2974	9W-5N	B1
4400	NRDG	60706	2974	9W-5N	B1
4800	NRDG	60706	2918	9W-6N	B7
Opal Dr					
4400	HFET	60195	2804	24W-15N	C1
Orange Av					
16200	ODPK	60467	3422	13W-19S	E3
16600	OrlT	60467	3422	13W-19S	E3
N Orange Av					
3200	EDPK	60707	2974	9W-4N	B4
4400	CHCG	60634	2974	9W-5N	B1
4400	CHCG	60706	2974	9W-5N	B1
4400	NRDG	60706	2974	9W-5N	B1
4800	NRDG	60706	2918	9W-6N	B7
5700	CHCG	60631	2918	9W-7N	B5
5700	NpkT	60631	2918	9W-7N	B5
Orange Ct					
1400	MPPT	60056	2807	16W-14N	E3
Orange Ln					
600	HFET	60194	2858	24W-10N	D5

STREET Block	City	ZIP	Map#	CGS	Grid
Orange Ln					
5800	OKFT	60452	3347	7W-18S	D7
Orange Blossom Dr					
15600	ODPK	60462	3346	9W-18S	D7
Orange Brace Rd					
2800	RVWD	60015	2755	13W-20N	D1
Orchard Av					
10	BNVL	60106	2972		A1
100	HLSD	60162	3028		E7
200	BNVL	60106	2916		A7
200	CHCG	60106	2916		A7
200	PvsT	60162	3028		E7
1000	MYWD	60153	3030	10W-0S	A5
1200	CHHT	60411	3507	2W-25S	D7
1600	SMBG	60193	2912		A3
12700	ALSP	60803	3276	5W-15S	C7
19800	LYWD	60411	3509	3E-23S	E4
Orchard Ct					
100	PTON	60468	3860	9W-38S	E5
100	PTON	60468	3861	9W-37S	A4
500	DSPN	60016	2862	14W-11N	D3
600	ROSL	60172	2913		C6
8400	TYPK	60477	3424	10W-19S	B3
19700	LYWD	60411	3509	3E-23S	E3
Orchard Dr					
-	TYPK	60477	3424	9W-21S	E7
200	WDDL	60191	2915		A6
500	CRTE	60417	3685	1W-30S	B3
8600	HYHL	60457	3210	10W-10S	A4
21000	OMFD	60461	3507	3W-25S	A7
N Orchard Dr					
10	PKFT	60466	3595	3W-26S	B3
400	OMFD	60461	3507	3W-25S	A7
400	PKFT	60466	3507	3W-25S	A7
S Orchard Dr					
10	PKFT	60466	3595	3W-27S	B5
700	BRTN	60010	2750	26W-18N	E3
W Orchard Dr					
6300	PSHT	60463	3275	7W-14S	B6
8100	FftT	60423	3504	10W-24S	C5
Orchard Ln					
10	GLF	60029	2865	8W-12N	A1
200	BCHR	60401	3864	0W-36S	C1
400	WNKA	60093	2812	4W-15N	B2
500	GLNC	60022	2758	7W-18N	B4
1400	NHBK	60062	2757	9W-17N	C6
1700	NHFD	60093	2811	6W-15N	C2
2700	WLMT	60091	2812	5W-13N	A5
2900	WLMT	60091	2811	5W-13N	E5
4100	MTSN	60443	3506	5W-24S	C5
7000	HRPK	60133	2912		A2
9100	BGVW	60455	3211	8W-10S	A5
10500	CHRG	60415	3275	8W-12S	B2
12800	ALSP	60803	3276	5W-15S	B7
12800	ALSP	60803	3348	5W-15S	B1
15000	HMGN	60441	3342	18W-16S	E3
15000	HMGN	60441	3343	18W-16S	A3
15300	OKFT	60452	3347	8W-18S	B7
17100	CCHL	60478	3426	4W-20S	D4
E Orchard Ln					
10	PLTN	60067	2805	20W-15N	E3
Orchard Pl					
10	HNDL	60521	3146		B1
2800	DSPN	60018	2917	12W-8N	A2
3000	RSMT	60018	2917	12W-8N	A2
W Orchard Pl					
10	MPPT	60056	2861	16W-11N	E2
10	MPPT	60056	2862	15W-11N	A2
1400	ANHT	60005	2806	18W-13N	D7
1400	RGMW	60008	2806	18W-13N	D7
Orchard St					
1400	DSPN	60018	2863	12W-9N	A6
2400	BLID	60406	3277	3W-14S	A6
8800	WLSP	60480	3208		D5
E Orchard St					
100	EMHT	60126	3028		A4
100	ITSC	60143	2914		C6
1000	ANHT	60005	2807	17W-13N	B7
N Orchard St					
1600	CHCG	60610	2978	0W-2N	A7
2100	CHCG	60614	2978	0W-2N	A6
3100	CHCG	60657	2978	0W-3N	A4
S Orchard St					
12200	ALSP	60803	3276	5W-14S	B6
W Orchard St					
10	ANHT	60005	2807	17W-13N	A7
100	ITSC	60143	2914		C6
Orchard Ter					
300	ROSL	60172	2913		B6
3400	CRTE	60417	3596	0E-28S	E6
3400	STGR	60417	3596	0E-28S	E6
3400	STGR	60475	3596	0E-28S	E6
Orchard Tr					
5200	MONE	60449	3683	6W-31S	A6
5400	MONE	60449	3682	6W-31S	E6
15100	LMNT	60439	3342	18W-15S	E1
Orchard Ridge Av					
16700	HLCT	60426	3427	2W-20S	C4
16700	HLCT	60429	3427	2W-20S	C4
16700	MKHM	60426	3427	2W-20S	C4
Orchards Pass					
500	BRLT	60103	2910		E6
Orchid Ct					
-	SMWD	60120	2856	30W-10N	B5
15300	ODPK	60462	3346	9W-18S	D7
Orchid Dr					
600	SHLD	60473	3350	0E-18S	E7
3400	SjnT	46311	3598		C6
Orchid Ln					
700	BRLT	60103	2910		D7
15100	ODPK	60462	3346	9W-18S	D6
N Orchid Ln					
2100	ANHT	60004	2754	16W-16N	C7
Ord Ct					
200	BRLT	60103	2911		A5
Oregon Av					
10	WDND	60118	2801		A3
Oregon Ln					
18100	ODPK	60467	3423	13W-21S	B7
Oregon Tr					
700	ROSL	60172	2913		C3
1500	EGVV	60007	2913		E1
3200	OMFD	60461	3506	4W-24S	E5
3200	OMFD	60461	3507	4W-24S	A4
11800	OrlT	60467	3344	14W-16S	C2
Orenia Ct					
8400	ODPK	60462	3346	10W-16S	B3
Oriole Av					
8800	MNGV	60053	2864	9W-11N	C3
8800	NLES	60714	2864	9W-11N	C4
17100	TYPK	60477	3424	9W-20S	D5
E Oriole Av					
400	EMHT	60126	3028		B4
N Oriole Av					
3200	CHCG	60634	2974	9W-4N	C3

STREET Block	City	ZIP	Map#	CGS	Grid
N Oriole Av					
3200	CHCG	60707	2974	9W-4N	C4
3200	EDPK	60707	2974	9W-4N	C4
3800	CHCG	60706	2974	9W-4N	C2
3800	NRDG	60706	2974	9W-4N	C2
4500	NRDG	60706	2918	9W-5N	C7
4600	HDHT	60706	2918	9W-5N	C7
4900	CHCG	60706	2918	9W-6N	C6
5000	CHCG	60656	2918	9W-6N	C6
5000	HDHT	60656	2918	9W-6N	C6
6800	CHCG	60631	2918	9W-8N	C1
7200	CHCG	60631	2864	9W-9N	C7
7500	PKRG	60068	2864	9W-9N	C6
8200	NLES	60714	2864	9W-10N	C4
8600	MNGV	60053	2864	9W-10N	C4
N Oriole Av SR-72					
-	CHCG	60631	2918	9W-7N	C4
Oriole Ct					
200	DYR	46311	3510		D6
8500	ODPK	60462	3346	10W-18S	B7
Oriole Dr					
-	BlmT	60411	3509	3E-25S	E7
-	SmbT	60193	2913		C2
600	SMWD	60107	2857	27W-9N	C7
700	PtnT	60468	3860	10W-38S	C5
700	PTON	60468	3860	10W-38S	C5
1800	EGVV	60007	2913		C2
9300	MNSR	46321	3510		E2
Oriole Ln					
2600	RGMW	60008	2806	19W-13N	C6
W Oriole Ln					
400	MPPT	60056	2807	15W-14N	E5
600	ANHT	60004	2807	15W-14N	E5
600	MPPT	60004	2807	15W-14N	E5
Oriole Rd					
10	MTSN	60443	3505	7W-24S	D5
Orion Av					
2400	BlmT	60411	3597	2E-26S	D3
2400	SLVL	60411	3597	2E-26S	D3
Orlan Brook Dr					
15100	ODPK	60462	3346	10W-18S	B7
15700	ODPK	60462	3424	10W-19S	B1
Orland Ct					
9000	ODPK	60462	3346	11W-17S	A6
Orland Pkwy					
-	FftT	60467	3423	13W-21S	B7
-	ODPK	60467	3423	13W-21S	B7
-	OrlT	60448	3423	12W-21S	D7
-	OrlT	60477	3423	12W-21S	D7
-	TYPK	60477	3423	12W-21S	D7
10300	FftT	60448	3423	12W-21S	D7
10300	ODPK	60448	3423	13W-22S	B7
10300	ODPK	60477	3423	12W-22S	D7
Orland Park Pl					
200	ODPK	60462	3345	11W-18S	E6
Orland Square Dr					
10	ODPK	60462	3345	11W-17S	E5
Orland Woods Ln					
17500	ODPK	60448	3422	14W-20S	E5
17500	ODPK	60467	3422	14W-20S	E5
Orleans Cir					
1800	EGVV	60007	2913		D3
Orleans Dr					
18100	HLCT	60429	3426	4W-21S	E7
Orleans Ln					
400	SMBG	60193	2858	25W-10N	B6
N Orleans St					
300	CHCG	60610	3034	0W-0N	B3
400	CHCG	60606	3034	0W-0N	B3
2000	CHCG	60614	2978	0W-2N	B6
Orogrande Ct					
15300	OKFT	60452	3347	7W-18S	B7
Orogrande St					
15300	OKFT	60452	3347	7W-18S	B7
Orrington Av					
1800	EVTN	60201	2867	2W-11N	B2
2500	EVTN	60201	2813	2W-12N	B7
Orrington Ct					
10	SMBG	60173	2859	22W-10N	C5
1300	WLNG	60090	2754	16W-18N	D4
N Osage Av					
3200	EDPK	60707	2974	9W-4N	B4
3600	CHCG	60634	2974	9W-4N	B3
4400	NRDG	60634	2974	9W-5N	B1
4400	NRDG	60706	2918	9W-5N	B7
4400	NRDG	60706	2974	9W-5N	B1
5700	CHCG	60631	2918	9W-7N	B5
Osage Ct					
600	DYR	46311	3598		E3
2500	CPVL	60110	2748		C4
Osage Dr					
400	DYR	46311	3598		D3
2500	GNVW	60025	2809	11W-15N	C2
Osage Ln					
700	HFET	60194	2858	24W-10N	D5
700	SMBG	60194	2858	24W-10N	D5
900	WLMT	60091	2812	5W-14N	A5
2000	HRPK	60133	2911		C1
E Osage Ln					
400	PLTN	60074	2753	20W-18N	A3
Osage St					
300	PKFT	60466	3595	3W-27S	B5
Osage Ter					
-	WLNG	60089	2754	16W-20N	D2
200	BFGV	60089	2754	16W-20N	D2
Osceola Av					
8800	NLES	60053	2864	9W-11N	D4
8800	NLES	60714	2864	9W-11N	D4
9100	MNGV	60053	2864	9W-11N	D2
17300	TYPK	60477	3424	9W-20S	E5
N Osceola Av					
3000	CHCG	60707	2974	9W-3N	D4
3000	EDPK	60707	2974	9W-3N	D4
3100	CHCG	60634	2974	9W-3N	D4
3900	NRDG	60706	2974	9W-5N	C1
5200	HDHT	60706	2918	9W-6N	C6
5500	CHCG	60656	2918	9W-6N	D5
6800	CHCG	60631	2918	9W-8N	D1
7200	CHCG	60631	2864	9W-9N	D7
8000	NLES	60714	2864	9W-10N	D4
8600	MNGV	60053	2864	9W-10N	D4
Osceola Tr					
6600	IHPK	60525	3146		D6
N Oshkosh Av					
6500	CHCG	60068	2918	9W-8N	C2
6500	CHCG	60631	2918	9W-8N	C2
6500	PKRG	60068	2918	9W-8N	C2
Osprey Ct					
-	BRLT	60103	2909		D3
-	SMWD	60107	2856	29W-9N	D7
Ostrander Av					
1100	BKFD	60513	3087	11W-2S	D4
1100	LGPK	60525	3087	11W-2S	D4
1500	PvsT	60525	3087	11W-2S	D4

STREET Block	City	ZIP	Map#	CGS	Grid
Oswego Av					
8800	MNGV	60053	2864	9W-11N	C3
8800	NLES	60714	2864	9W-11N	C4
Oswego St					
300	PKFT	60466	3595	3W-27S	B5
N Oswego St					
400	CHCG	60612	3033	2W-0N	C3
400	CHCG	60622	3033	2W-0N	C3
Otis Pl					
1100	NHBK	60062	2757	8W-17N	E5
1100	NHBK	60062	2758	8W-17N	A5
Otis Rd					
10	BNHL	60010	2750	27W-18N	C4
10	BRTN	60010	2750	27W-18N	C4
200	BNHL	60010	2749	28W-18N	E4
N Otsego Av					
6500	CHCG	60631	2918	9W-8N	C2
6600	CHCG	60068	2918	9W-8N	C2
6600	PKRG	60068	2918	9W-8N	C2
Ottawa Av					
600	CHCG	60631	2864	9W-9N	C7
600	PKRG	60068	2864	9W-9N	C6
8800	MNGV	60053	2864	9W-11N	C3
8800	NLES	60714	2864	9W-11N	C4
17300	TYPK	60477	3424	9W-20S	D5
N Ottawa Av					
3200	CHCG	60634	2974	9W-4N	C3
3200	EDPK	60707	2974	9W-4N	C4
3800	CHCG	60706	2974	9W-4N	C2
3800	NRDG	60706	2974	9W-5N	C1
4500	HDHT	60706	2918	9W-5N	C7
4500	NRDG	60706	2918	9W-5N	C7
5600	CHCG	60631	2918	9W-7N	C4
5600	CHCG	60656	2918	9W-6N	C5
6600	CHCG	60068	2918	9W-8N	C2
6600	PKRG	60068	2918	9W-8N	C2
7200	CHCG	60631	2864	9W-9N	C7
8000	NLES	60068	2864	9W-10N	C5
8000	PKRG	60068	2864	9W-10N	C5
8300	NLES	60714	2864	9W-10N	C4
Ottawa Ct					
10	JSTC	60458	3209	11W-8S	E1
1600	WLNG	60090	2754	16W-17N	D5
Ottawa Ln					
900	WLMT	60091	2812	5W-14N	A5
Ottawa St					
-	DSPN	60016	2863	12W-11N	C3
300	PKFT	60466	3595	3W-27S	B5
Otto Av					
5200	CHCG	60018	2917	12W-6N	C6
5200	SRPK	60018	2917	12W-6N	C6
5200	SRPK	60176	2917	12W-6N	C6
Otto Blvd					
1200	CHHT	60411	3508	1W-25S	A7
1400	CHHT	60411	3596	1W-25S	B1
Otto Ln					
3200	EVTN	60201	2812	4W-13N	C7
Otto Pl					
5100	OKLN	60453	3211	6W-10S	E5
Otto St					
3200	LNSG	60438	3430	4E-22S	B7
5200	CHCG	60018	2917	12W-6N	C6
5200	RSMT	60018	2917	11W-6N	C5
Ouilmette Ln					
600	WLMT	60091	2812	4W-13N	B6
Overbrook Rd					
10	SBTN	60010	2803	26W-14N	D3
Overhill Av					
600	CHCG	60631	2864	9W-9N	C7
600	PKRG	60068	2864	9W-9N	C6
9300	MNGV	60053	2864	9W-11N	C2
17100	TYPK	60477	3424	9W-20S	D4
N Overhill Av					
3200	EDPK	60707	2974	9W-4N	C4
3600	CHCG	60634	2974	9W-4N	C2
4000	NRDG	60706	2974	9W-5N	C1
4500	HDHT	60706	2918	9W-5N	C7
4600	NRDG	60706	2918	9W-5N	C7
5000	CHCG	60656	2918	9W-6N	C6
5100	CHCG	60706	2918	9W-6N	C6
5900	CHCG	60631	2918	9W-7N	C3
7200	CHCG	60631	2864	9W-9N	C7
8000	NLES	60068	2864	9W-10N	C5
8000	PKRG	60068	2864	9W-10N	C5
8500	NLES	60714	2864	9W-10N	C4
Overhill Ct					
9300	MNGV	60053	2864	9W-11N	C2
Overland Ct					
700	ROSL	60172	2913		C3
Overland Tr					
600	ROSL	60172	2913		C2
11900	HMGN	60467	3344	14W-16S	C3
11900	OrlT	60467	3344	14W-16S	C3
20000	OMFD	60461	3506	4W-24S	E5
Overland Pass					
3200	GNVW	60025	2809	11W-14N	C3
3200	NfdT	60062	2809	11W-14N	C3
Overlook Ct					
300	BNHL	60010	2748		E3
Overlook Dr					
-	WLMT	60091	2813	2W-14N	B5
10	GLF	60025	2865	8W-12N	A1
10	GLF	60029	2865	8W-12N	A1
10	GLF	60053	2865	8W-12N	A2
10	GNVW	60025	2865	8W-12N	A1
10	MNGV	60053	2865	7W-11N	A2
1300	GLF	60029	2864	8W-12N	E1
1300	GNVW	60025	2864	8W-12N	E1
1300	GNVW	60029	2864	8W-12N	E1
1300	GNVW	60029	2865	8W-12N	A1
1500	GLF	60029	2864	8W-12N	E1
Overton Ct					
10	LMNT	60439	3270		E7
Overton Dr					
1300	LMNT	60439	3270		E7
1300	LMNT	60439	3271		A7
N Owen Av					
6900	CHCG	60631	2918	9W-8N	C1
6900	PKRG	60068	2918	9W-8N	C1
Owen Ct					
300	PTHT	60070	2808	15W-15N	B2
Owen Dr					
10400	ODPK	60467	3423	13W-21S	B6
Owen Pl					
10	PTHT	60070	2808	15W-14N	B3
Owen St					
-	PTHT	60070	2808	15W-15N	B3
N Owen St					
10	MPPT	60056	2808	15W-13N	B6
S Owen St					
10	MPPT	60056	2808	15W-12N	B7
800	MPPT	60056	2862	15W-11N	B2
900	DSPN	60016	2862	15W-11N	B2
900	DSPN	60056	2862	15W-11N	B2
900	MPPT	60016	2862	15W-11N	B2

Chicago & Cook County Street Index

Block	City	ZIP	Map#	CGS	Grid
Owl Dr					
2900	RGMW	60008	2806	19W-13N	B6
Owl Ln					
2700	RGMW	60008	2806	19W-14N	B5
Oxbow Ln					
600	BRTN	60010	2751	24W-20N	C1
Oxford Av					
600	MTSN	60443	3506	6W-25S	A7
10300	CHRG	60415	3275	7W-12S	B2
11000	WRTH	60482	3275	7W-12S	B3
N Oxford Av					
6700	CHCG	60631	2918	9W-8N	D2
Oxford Cir					
400	ROSL	60172	2912		B6
500	EGVV	60007	2913		D1
Oxford Ct					
1900	SMBG	60194	2858	26W-11N	A3
2000	FSMR	60422	3507	2W-23S	D3
4000	SMWD	60107	2911		A1
12100	LMNT	60439	3271		D6
W Oxford Ct					
900	PLTN	60067	2805	22W-14N	C3
Oxford Dr					
15000	OKFT	60452	3347	7W-18S	D6
15200	ODPK	60462	3345	11W-18S	E7
16100	MKHM	60426	3427	3W-19S	B3
16300	TYPK	60477	3425	8W-19S	A3
N Oxford Dr					
2700	MKHM	60426	3427	3W-19S	B2
S Oxford Dr					
2600	MKHM	60426	3427	3W-19S	B3
Oxford Ln					
900	WLMT	60091	2812	4W-14N	B5
1200	GNVW	60025	2811	7W-13N	A5
1200	HRPK	60133	2911		E1
1900	HFET	60195	2804	26W-12N	A7
1900	HFET	60195	2858	25W-12N	B1
3000	NHBK	60062	2756	11W-16N	D7
E Oxford Ln					
1100	ANHT	60004	2807	17W-16N	C1
Oxford Pl					
400	ROSL	60172	2912		C6
800	WLNG	60090	2755	15W-18N	A3
10200	MNSR	46321	3510		E4
W Oxford Pl					
10	MPPT	60056	2808	15W-14N	A4
Oxford Rd					
10	CPVL	60102	2748		A4
10	CPVL	60110	2748		A4
10	DndT	60102	2748		A4
10	DndT	60110	2748		A4
100	KLWH	60043	2812	3W-14N	D4
200	DSPN	60016	2862	14W-11N	C3
1400	DSPN	60018	2862	14W-10N	C6
6400	WLBK	60527	3146		B6
Oxford St					
10	RGMW	60008	2805	20W-14N	E4
7000	BGVW	60455	3210	8W-10S	E5
10200	WSTR	60154	3087	13W-1S	A2
10700	WSTR	60154	3086		E1
Oxhill Ct					
2300	SMBG	60194	2857	26W-11N	E4
Oxley Ct					
1500	WLNG	60090	2754	16W-18N	D4
Ozanam Av					
800	CHCG	60068	2918	9W-8N	C2
800	CHCG	60631	2918	9W-8N	C2
800	PKRG	60068	2918	9W-8N	C2
9500	MaiT	60025	2864	9W-11N	C2
9500	MNGV	60053	2864	9W-12N	C2
N Ozanam Av					
3200	EDPK	60707	2974	9W-4N	C4
4000	CHCG	60634	2974	9W-5N	C1
4000	CHCG	60706	2974	9W-5N	C2
4000	NRDG	60634	2974	9W-5N	C2
4000	NRDG	60706	2974	9W-5N	C1
4900	NRDG	60706	2918	9W-6N	C6
5100	CHCG	60656	2918	9W-6N	C6
5100	CHCG	60706	2918	9W-6N	C6
6400	CHCG	60068	2918	9W-8N	C2
6900	CHCG	60631	2918	9W-8N	C1
6900	PKRG	60068	2918	9W-8N	C1
8000	NLES	60068	2864	9W-10N	C6
8000	PKRG	60068	2864	9W-10N	C6
8200	MaiT	60714	2864	9W-10N	C5
8400	NLES	60714	2864	9W-10N	C4
Ozark Av					
15900	TYPK	60477	3424	9W-19S	D2
N Ozark Av					
-	PKRG	60068	2918	9W-8N	C2
3200	CHCG	60634	2974	9W-4N	C3
3200	EDPK	60707	2974	9W-4N	C4
4000	CHCG	60706	2974	9W-5N	C2
4000	NRDG	60706	2974	9W-5N	C1
4600	NRDG	60706	2918	9W-5N	C7
5600	CHCG	60656	2918	9W-7N	C5
6900	CHCG	60631	2918	9W-8N	C1
7000	PKRG	60631	2918	9W-8N	C1
7400	CHCG	60631	2864	9W-9N	C7
7400	PKRG	60068	2864	9W-9N	C7
8400	NLES	60714	2864	9W-10N	C4
8700	MNGV	60053	2864	9W-10N	C4
Ozark Pkwy					
1900	ALGN	60102	2748		B1
Ozark St					
8800	NLES	60053	2864	9W-11N	C4
8800	NLES	60714	2864	9W-11N	C4
8900	MNGV	60053	2864	9W-11N	C3
P					
Pacer Tr					
10	SBTN	60010	2803	27W-14N	A5
W Pacesetter Pkwy					
400	RVDL	60827	3350	0W-15S	B2
Pacific Av					
800	HFET	60194	2857	26W-11N	E3
800	SMWD	60107	2857	26W-11N	E4
9600	FNPK	60131	2973	12W-4N	B3
N Pacific Av					
3200	EDPK	60707	2974	9W-4N	B4
3200	RVGV	60171	2974	9W-4N	B4
3200	RVGV	60707	2974	9W-4N	B4
3600	CHCG	60634	2974	10W-4N	B2
5200	CHCG	60656	2918	10W-6N	B6
5200	LydT	60656	2918	10W-6N	B6
5200	NpkT	60656	2918	10W-6N	B6
Pacific Ct					
400	WLNG	60090	2754	16W-17N	D5
9500	BRRG	60527	3208		A6
S Pacific Dr					
11200	WRTH	60482	3274	9W-13S	E3
Packard Dr					
-	BLID	60406	3349	2W-15S	B2
600	ELGN	60120	2855		D6
S Packers Av					
4000	CHCG	60609	3091	1W-4S	D7
Paddington Cres					
-	MNSR	46321	3510		C5
Paddock					
10	LMNT	60439	3272	15W-13S	B5
Paddock Ct					
11000	ODPK	60467	3423	13W-18S	A1
Paddock Dr					
1400	GNVW	60025	2810	9W-15N	C2
E Paddock Dr					
1000	PLTN	60074	2753	19W-16N	C7
S Paddock Dr					
1200	WLNG	60090	2755	15W-16N	A7
W Paddock Dr					
500	WLNG	60090	2755	15W-16N	A7
Paddock Ln					
15300	HMGN	60441	3343	16W-18S	E7
Paddock Pl					
1300	BRLT	60103	2910		B7
Padre Ln					
-	ODPK	60467	3423	13W-21S	B6
Paganica Dr					
10	BNHL	60010	2750	27W-20N	C1
Page Av					
600	ELGN	60120	2855		B1
14100	DXMR	60426	3349	2W-16S	D4
14700	HRVY	60426	3349	2W-18S	D7
15600	HRVY	60426	3427	2W-18S	D1
16000	MKHM	60426	3427	2W-19S	D2
16700	HLCT	60429	3427	2W-20S	D4
18500	HMWD	60430	3507	2W-22S	D1
N Page Av					
3200	CHCG	60171	2974	10W-4N	B4
3200	RVGV	60171	2974	10W-4N	B4
3600	CHCG	60634	2974	10W-4N	B2
Page Ct					
12900	BLID	60406	3277	2W-15S	D7
18300	HMWD	60430	3427	2W-22S	D7
Page St					
-	BLID	60406	3277	2W-14S	D5
-	BLID	60827	3277	2W-14S	D5
-	CTPK	60827	3277	2W-14S	D5
-	CTPK	60406	3277	2W-15S	D5
12900	CTPK	60406	3277	2W-15S	D7
N Page St					
3300	ANHT	60004	2754	17W-17N	B4
S Page St					
11900	CHCG	60643	3277	2W-14S	D5
11900	CTPK	60643	3277	2W-14S	D5
11900	CTPK	60827	3277	2W-14S	D5
12700	CTPK	60406	3277	2W-15S	D7
12800	BLID	60406	3277	2W-15S	D7
Pagni Dr					
1100	EGVV	60007	2861	17W-10N	C5
Pahl Rd					
700	EGVV	60007	2914		B1
Paisley Ct					
1400	HFET	60010	2751	24W-16N	B7
Palace Ct					
500	SMBG	60194	2857	26W-11N	E4
Palamino Ct					
1200	BRLT	60103	2910		E7
W Palatine Av					
6400	CHCG	60631	2919	8W-7N	A3
6400	CHCG	60646	2919	8W-7N	A3
6600	CHCG	60631	2918	8W-7N	E3
7700	PKRG	60068	2918	9W-7N	C3
Palatine Rd					
-	IVNS	60010	2804	24W-15N	B1
-	SBTN	60010	2804	24W-15N	B1
1300	HFET	60010	2804	24W-15N	B1
1300	HFET	60195	2804	24W-15N	B1
E Palatine Rd					
-	ANHT	60004	2806	19W-16N	D1
-	NfdT	60090	2809	13W-15N	A1
-	PLTN	60004	2806	19W-16N	D1
-	PTHT	60070	2809	13W-15N	A1
-	WhlT	60090	2809	13W-15N	A1
10	ANHT	60004	2807	16W-15N	C1
10	BNHL	60010	2803	27W-15N	B1
10	BrnT	60010	2803	27W-15N	B1
10	IVNS	60010	2803	26W-16N	E1
10	PLTN	60067	2805	20W-15N	E1
10	PTHT	60090	2809	13W-15N	A1
10	WLNG	60090	2808	14W-15N	D1
100	PTHT	60070	2808	15W-16N	A1
300	PLTN	60067	2806	20W-16N	A1
300	SBTN	60010	2803	27W-16N	B1
300	WLNG	60070	2808	15W-16N	B1
1000	PLTN	60074	2806	19W-15N	C1
2500	PTHT	60070	2807	16W-15N	D1
2600	PTHT	60004	2807	16W-16N	E1
W Palatine Rd					
-	HFET	60010	2804	25W-15N	A1
-	HFET	60195	2804	25W-15N	A1
-	PLTN	60074	2806	19W-16N	D1
-	WLNG	60090	2808	14W-16N	C1
10	ANHT	60004	2807	17W-16N	A1
10	IVNS	60010	2804	25W-15N	A1
10	PLTN	60067	2805	21W-16N	E1
10	PTHT	60070	2807	15W-15N	A1
10	PTHT	60070	2808	15W-15N	A1
10	SBTN	60010	2804	25W-15N	A1
200	PTHT	60004	2807	16W-16N	E1
300	ANHT	60004	2806	18W-16N	E1
300	BNHL	60010	2803	25W-15N	E1
300	BrnT	60010	2803	25W-15N	E1
300	IVNS	60010	2803	25W-15N	E1
300	WLNG	60070	2808	15W-15N	B1
700	PlT	60067	2805	21W-15N	C1
1200	IVNS	60067	2805	22W-16N	A1
1800	IVNS	60067	2804	23W-15N	E1
2400	IVNS	60010	2804	24W-15N	D1
Palatine Frontage Rd					
300	WLNG	60090	2808	14W-16N	B1
E Palatine Frontage Rd					
10	WLNG	60090	2808	14W-15N	C1
Palisades Dr					
10	OKBK	60523	3086		B1
W Palisades Dr					
3100	MTPK	60803	3276	3W-13S	E4
Palisades Ln					
100	CTSD	60525	3147	12W-7S	B5
100	LynT	60525	3147	13W-7S	B5
Palisades St					
300	SMBG	60194	2859	22W-10N	C4
Palm Ct					
7500	ODPK	60462	3346	9W-18S	D7
Palm Dr					
100	DRPK	60010	2752	23W-18N	A2
100	PlT	60010	2752	23W-18N	A2
1100	WLNG	60090	2754	16W-17N	E4
7600	ODPK	60462	3346	9W-18S	D7
W Palm Dr					
600	GNWD	60425	3428	0W-21S	B7
1200	MPPT	60056	2861	16W-11N	D3
Palm Ln					
3000	NHBK	60062	2756	11W-16N	D7
Palma Ln					
6400	MNGV	60053	2865	8W-11N	A2
7200	MNGV	60053	2864	9W-11N	D2
Palma Pl					
4400	SKOK	60076	2866	5W-11N	A2
5200	SKOK	60077	2865	6W-11N	D2
Palm Canyon Dr					
3600	NHBK	60062	2756	12W-17N	B4
Palmer Av					
2400	MonT	60449	3682	7W-30S	E3
2400	UYPK	60466	3682	7W-30S	E3
9600	FNPK	60131	2973	12W-2N	C6
9600	LydT	60164	2973	12W-2N	C6
18400	HMWD	60430	3507	2W-22S	C1
E Palmer Av					
10	NHLK	60164	2972		E6
300	LydT	60164	2973	13W-2N	A6
300	NHLK	60164	2973	13W-2N	A6
S Palmer Av					
14200	POSN	60469	3349	3W-17S	B4
14800	POSN	60426	3349	3W-17S	B5
W Palmer Av					
10	NHLK	60164	2972		D6
10000	LydT	60164	2973	12W-2N	B6
10400	NHLK	60164	2973	13W-2N	A6
Palmer Blvd					
17200	HLCT	60429	3427	3W-20S	B5
17200	HLCT	60430	3427	3W-20S	B5
17300	HMWD	60430	3427	3W-20S	B5
Palmer Cir					
18600	HMWD	60430	3507	2W-22S	C1
Palmer Ct					
300	RVWD	60015	2755	13W-20N	E1
300	RVWD	60015	2756	13W-20N	A1
1100	FSMR	60422	3507	3W-22S	A1
Palmer Dr					
2000	SMBG	60173	2805	21W-13N	C6
N Palmer Dr					
100	EMHT	60126	3028		A2
S Palmer Dr					
100	EMHT	60126	3028		A2
E Palmer Ln					
1500	PLTN	60074	2753	19W-16N	C4
W Palmer Sq					
3000	CHCG	60647	2976	4W-2N	D6
W Palmer St					
2200	CHCG	60647	2977	2W-2N	B6
2800	CHCG	60647	2976	3W-2N	E6
3900	CHCG	60639	2976	5W-2N	A6
4700	CHCG	60639	2975	6W-2N	D6
6300	CHCG	60707	2975	8W-2N	A6
6800	CHCG	60707	2974	9W-2N	D6
7100	EDPK	60707	2974	9W-2N	D6
8600	RVGV	60171	2973	11W-2N	E6
8600	RVGV	60171	2974	10W-2N	A6
9000	FNPK	60131	2973	11W-2N	D6
9000	FNPK	60160	2973	11W-2N	D6
9000	MLPK	60160	2973	11W-2N	D6
9000	RVGV	60131	2973	11W-2N	D6
9000	RVGV	60160	2973	11W-2N	D6
Palmer C Singleton Jr Dr					
-	MNSR	46321	3510		E4
Palmgren Ct					
200	BFGV	60089	2754	16W-17N	D5
Palmgren Dr					
1900	GNVW	60025	2810	8W-13N	D7
Palomino Ct					
14500	HMGN	60441	3344	15W-17S	B5
N Palos Av					
900	PLTN	60067	2752	22W-17N	A5
1200	PltT	60067	2752	22W-17N	A5
1300	PltT	60010	2752	22W-17N	A5
1300	PltT	60074	2752	22W-17N	A5
S Palos Av					
12700	PSHT	60463	3274	9W-15S	E7
W Palos Av					
7200	PSHT	60463	3274	9W-15S	E7
7900	PSPK	60464	3274	9W-14S	C5
S Palos Dr					
10700	PSHL	60465	3274	10W-12S	B2
Palos Pl					
10500	PSHL	60465	3274	9W-12S	C2
Palos Rd					
300	GLNC	60022	2758	5W-17N	E5
Palos Springs Dr					
8800	ODPK	60462	3346	11W-15S	A1
Palos West Dr					
10400	PlsT	60464	3273	13W-14S	A7
Palwaukee Dr					
400	WLNG	60090	2755	14W-17N	C5
Pam Ct					
500	WLNG	60090	2754	16W-18N	E3
Pam Rd					
-	ELGN	60123	2801		A7
Pam Anne Dr					
1300	GNVW	60025	2809	10W-13N	E5
Pamela Cir					
400	HNDL	60521	3146		C3
Pamela Ct					
16100	OKFT	60452	3425	6W-19S	E2
Pamela Dr					
10	BNVL	60106	2972		A4
200	AddT	60126	2972		A4
Pamela Dr N					
100	CHHT	60411	3508	1W-23S	A4
200	BlmT	60411	3508	1W-23S	A4
Pamela Dr S					
10	CHHT	60411	3508	1W-24S	A4
Pamela Ln					
6400	CHRG	60415	3275	8W-12S	B1
10800	ODPK	60467	3423	13W-21S	B5
Pamela Pl					
-	DLTN	60419	3350	0E-16S	D2
Pamella Ln					
4000	NfdT	60062	2756	12W-18N	B2
4000	NHBK	60062	2756	12W-18N	B2
Pan Am Blvd					
2400	EGVV	60007	2915		E4
N Panama Av					
3200	CHCG	60171	2974	10W-4N	B4
3200	CHCG	60634	2974	10W-4N	B3
3200	RVGV	60171	2974	10W-4N	B4
5400	CHCG	60656	2918	10W-6N	B5
5400	LydT	60656	2918	10W-6N	B5
Panasonic Ct					
-	FNPK	60131	2973	11W-3N	D5
W Panorama Dr					
-	PltT	60067	2752	22W-17N	B5
800	PLTN	60067	2752	22W-17N	B5
Panoramic Dr					
10200	FNPK	60131	2973	12W-4N	A3
Pansey Ln					
100	MTSN	60443	3593	7W-26S	C2
Papoose Rd					
1700	CPVL	60110	2748		C4
Papworth St					
10	BmdT	60108	2912		C7
10	BmdT	60172	2912		C7
200	ROSL	60172	2912		C7
Paradise Av					
1500	MLPK	60160	3029	13W-1N	A2
Paradise Ln					
7300	ODPK	60462	3346	9W-18S	E6
7300	OrlT	60462	3346	9W-18S	E6
E Parallel St					
300	PLTN	60067	2806	20W-15N	A1
300	PLTN	60074	2806	20W-15N	A1
N Paris Av					
3000	RVGV	60171	2974	10W-3N	B4
3100	CHCG	60171	2974	10W-3N	B4
3100	CHCG	60634	2974	10W-4N	B3
4400	CHCG	60706	2974	10W-5N	B1
4400	NRDG	60706	2974	10W-5N	B1
5400	CHCG	60656	2918	10W-6N	B5
Paris Ln					
500	HFET	60194	2858	24W-10N	E5
500	SMBG	60194	2858	24W-10N	E5
Paris Rd					
2800	OMFD	60461	3507	3W-25S	A7
Park					
-	HGKN	60525	3147	12W-7S	C5
N Park					
-	DSPN	60018	2917	12W-8N	C2
S Park					
-	DSPN	60018	2917	12W-8N	C2
Park Av					
-	DndT	60118	2801		A5
-	PvsT	60513	3087	11W-2S	E4
10	CTCY	60409	3429	2E-19S	C2
10	FTPK	60130	3030	9W-0N	C5
10	FTPK	60305	3030	9W-0N	C5
10	GLNC	60022	2758	6W-17N	D5
10	LynT	60458	3209	11W-8S	E1
10	RVFT	60305	3030	9W-0N	C5
100	BRTN	60010	2750	25W-18N	E2
100	BRTN	60010	2751	25W-18N	A2
100	CPVL	60110	2748		A6
100	DndT	60110	2748		A6
100	EVTN	60201	2812	3W-13N	D7
100	WLMT	60091	2812	3W-13N	D6
200	WLNG	60090	2755	13W-17N	D4
700	TNTN	60476	3428	0E-20S	E5
700	WNKA	60093	2812	4W-16N	B1
1000	FDHT	60411	3509	1E-25S	A7
1200	CHHT	60411	3508	1W-25S	B7
1400	CHHT	60411	3596	1W-25S	B1
1500	EDPK	60707	3030	9W-1N	C1
1600	HRPK	60133	2911		D2
2200	FTPK	60130	3088	9W-2S	C2
2200	FTPK	60546	3088	9W-2S	C2
2200	NRIV	60546	3088	9W-2S	C2
2500	RVSD	60546	3088	9W-2S	C3
2600	BKFD	60513	3087	11W-3S	E5
3700	CteT	60475	3596	1W-28S	A7
3700	STGR	60475	3596	1W-28S	A7
3800	CteT	60417	3596	1W-28S	A7
4500	BKFD	60513	3147	11W-4S	E1
5800	BKLY	60163	3028		C2
6200	BRWN	60402	3089	7W-3S	B4
6200	CCRO	60804	3089	7W-3S	B4
6200	MNGV	60053	2865	7W-10N	A5
7200	SMMT	60501	3148	9W-5S	D2
7600	SKOK	60077	2865	6W-9N	D6
13800	CHCG	60827	3350	0E-16S	D2
13800	DLTN	60419	3350	0E-16S	D3
14300	RVDL	60827	3350	0W-17S	B5
14500	HRVY	60426	3350	0W-17S	B5
14700	OKFT	60452	3347	6W-17S	D5
15600	HRVY	60426	3428	1W-18S	A1
15900	HRVY	60426	3427	1W-19S	E2
16000	MKHM	60426	3427	1W-19S	E2
16500	HLCT	60426	3427	1W-19S	E3
16700	HLCT	60429	3427	2W-21S	D5
17000	EHZC	60429	3427	2W-21S	D5
17000	LNSG	60438	3430	3E-20S	A4
17500	EHZC	60430	3427	2W-20S	D5
17900	HMWD	60430	3427	2W-21S	C7
19400	LNSG	60411	3510	3E-23S	A2
19400	LNSG	60438	3510	3E-23S	A2
19500	LYWD	60411	3510	3E-23S	A2
19800	LYWD	60411	3509	3E-23S	E4
E Park Av					
100	EMHT	60126	3028		B3
N Park Av					
10	HNDL	60521	3146		B1
1000	PLTN	60067	2752	22W-17N	A5
1200	PltT	60067	2752	22W-17N	A5
S Park Av					
400	HNDL	60521	3146		B3
1100	SMWD	60107	2857	28W-9N	A7
1200	SMWD	60107	2911		A2
2000	BRLT	60103	2911		A2
5800	MNGV	60053	2865	7W-10N	B4
6000	BRRG	60527	3146		B5
8100	BRRG	60527	3208		B3
8100	DGvT	60527	3208		B3
27500	CteT	60401	3774	0E-33S	E3
27500	WshT	60401	3774	0E-35S	E6
28700	BCHR	60401	3774	0E-35S	E6
W Park Av					
5600	CCRO	60804	3089	7W-3S	C4
7800	NLES	60714	2864	9W-11N	B3
Park Blvd					
100	EGVV	60007	2914		B4
100	EGVV	60143	2914		B4
100	ITSC	60143	2914		B4
17700	LNSG	60438	3430	3E-20S	A5
N Park Blvd					
10	SMWD	60107	2857	28W-11N	B4
300	HFET	60010	2857	28W-11N	B4
300	SMWD	60010	2857	28W-11N	B4
S Park Blvd					
10	SMWD	60107	2857	28W-10N	B7
Park Ct					
10	ROSL	60172	2913		A4
200	BLWD	60104	3029	12W-0N	A4
3000	RGMW	60008	2806	19W-13N	C5
13000	CTWD	60445	3347	6W-15S	E1
Park Dr					
-	CHCG	60611	3034	0E-0N	E3
-	DndT	60118	2801		A5
-	RVFT	60305	3030	9W-0N	C4
10	GNVW	60025	2810	9W-13N	B6
200	PltT	60067	2805	20W-13N	E7
300	NHBK	60062	2758	7W-17N	A6
400	PltT	60067	2806	20W-13N	A6
500	KLWH	60043	2812	4W-14N	C4
600	FSMR	60422	3507	3W-22S	B2
600	FSMR	60430	3507	3W-22S	B2
600	HMWD	60430	3507	3W-22S	B2
700	WLMT	60091	2812	4W-14N	C4
900	MLPK	60160	3029	11W-1N	E1
1600	SMBG	60194	2858	25W-10N	B5
3600	OMFD	60461	3506	4W-24S	E4
3700	FSMR	60422	3506	4W-24S	E4
N Park Dr					
-	CHCG	60601	3034	0E-0N	C4
-	CHCG	60611	3034	0E-0N	C3
200	GNWD	60425	3508	0W-22S	C1
200	GNWD	60425	3428	0W-22S	C7
1500	MPPT	60056	2808	13W-15N	E3
1600	MPPT	60056	2809	13W-15N	A2
1800	PTHT	60070	2809	13W-15N	A2
Park Ln					
10	GLF	60029	2864	8W-12N	E1
10	GLF	60029	2865	8W-12N	A1
10	PKRG	60068	2863	11W-9N	D7
100	DRFD	60015	2756	11W-20N	C2
200	ROSL	60172	2913		B4
200	SLVL	60411	3597	2E-25S	D1
400	BRTN	60010	2751	25W-20N	A1
400	WDDL	60191	2914		E7
700	HFET	60195	2804	23W-15N	D2
700	WNKA	60093	2812	4W-16N	B1
1100	GNVW	60025	2810	9W-13N	B6
1100	WNSP	60558	3146		D3
1400	FDHT	60411	3509	1E-25S	B7
4100	CCHL	60478	3426	5W-20S	C5
5200	CTWD	60445	3347	6W-15S	E1
5400	MONE	60449	3682	6W-31S	E6
5400	MONE	60449	3683	6W-31S	A6
9400	MaiT	60016	2863	11W-11N	D2
9400	NLES	60016	2863	11W-11N	D2
9400	NLES	60714	2863	11W-11N	D2
14700	ODPK	60462	3345	12W-17S	C5
14900	OrlT	60462	3346	9W-17S	D6
15400	DLTN	60419	3350	0E-18S	E7
15400	SHLD	60473	3350	0E-18S	E7
S Park Ln					
200	PLTN	60074	2806	19W-15N	B2
W Park Ln					
8600	NLES	60714	2863	10W-10N	E4
8600	NLES	60714	2864	10W-10N	A4
8600	PKRG	60714	2863	10W-10N	E4
Park Pl					
10	RVSD	60546	3088	10W-3S	B4
300	GLNC	60022	2758	6W-18N	C3
500	LMNT	60439	3270		C6
900	LynT	60525	3146		E3
900	WNSP	60558	3146		E4
1400	DSPN	60016	2863	13W-11N	A3
2300	EVTN	60201	2812	3W-13N	D7
3500	FSMR	60422	3506	4W-23S	E4
5700	CTWD	60445	3275	7W-15S	D7
5700	WthT	60445	3275	7W-15S	D7
7400	HMND	46324	3430		D4
9200	ODHL	60477	3423	11W-19S	E3
12700	WthT	60463	3275	7W-14S	D7
E Park Pl					
1300	CHCG	60637	3153	1E-6S	A2
1800	WhlT	60004	2754	16W-17N	D4
S Park Pl					
5900	HMND	46320	3430		D1
W Park Pl					
300	ANHT	60004	2807	18W-14N	A4
Park Plz					
16000	SHLD	60473	3428	0E-18S	E1
Park Rd					
1200	CRTE	60417	3685	1W-29S	B1
N Park Rd					
10	LGNG	60525	3087	13W-4S	A7
300	LGPK	60525	3087	13W-3S	A6
S Park Rd					
100	LGNG	60525	3087	13W-4S	B7
200	LGNG	60525	3147	13W-4S	A1
5500	CTSD	60525	3147	13W-6S	B3
5500	LynT	60525	3147	13W-6S	B3
Park Row					
10	ELGN	60120	2855		A4
Park St					
10	PKFT	60466	3595	3W-26S	B2
100	WLSP	60480	3209	12W-9S	C3
200	BNVL	60106	2972		A2
200	HNDL	60521	3146		B4
300	ELGN	60120	2855		A3
500	BCHR	60401	3864	0W-36S	C2
500	DndT	60118	2801		B2
500	EDND	60118	2801		B2
1300	CRTE	60417	3685	0W-30S	C2
2100	RGMW	60008	2806	19W-13N	C5
2600	FNPK	60131	2973	12W-3N	B5
E Park St					
10	ANHT	60005	2807	17W-13N	B6
1800	ANHT	60004	2807	16W-13N	D6
N Park St					
10	ROSL	60172	2913		A4
S Park St					
10	ROSL	60172	2913		A5
W Park St					
10	ANHT	60005	2807	18W-13N	A6
1300	ANHT	60005	2806	18W-13N	D6
Park Ter					
200	SCHT	60411	3595	1W-27S	E4
200	SCHT	60411	3596	1W-27S	A4
S Park Ter					
800	CHCG	60605	3034	0W-0S	B6
Park Barrington Dr					
-	BrnT	60010	2751	25W-17N	A4
400	BRTN	60010	2751	25W-17N	A5
Park Barrington Wy					
500	BRTN	60010	2751	25W-17N	A5
Park Center Dr					
-	ODPK	60462	3424	9W-19S	E1
-	ODPK	60477	3424	9W-19S	E1
-	TYPK	60477	3424	9W-19S	E1
Park Central Dr N					
7800	TYPK	60477	3424	9W-21S	D5
Park Central Dr S					
7800	TYPK	60477	3424	9W-21S	D6
Parkchester Rd					
100	EGVV	60007	2914		C3
Parkcrest Ln					
8800	HYHL	60457	3210	11W-10S	A5
Parke Av					
9900	OKLN	60453	3212	5W-11S	A7
Parker Av					
-	FNPK	60131	2973	12W-3N	B5
W Parker Av					
4000	CHCG	60647	2976	5W-3N	B5
4600	CHCG	60639	2976	5W-3N	A5

Chicago & Cook County Street Index

STREET Block	City	ZIP	Map#	CGS	Grid
S Pinecreek Dr					
11900	OrlT	60467	3344	14W-17S	C6
Pinecrest Cir					
11300	ODPK	60467	3422	14W-20S	E3
Pinecrest Ct					
-	BRRG	60527	3146		C5
700	DGvT	60527	3146		A4
Pinecrest Dr					
600	PTHT	60070	2808	13W-15N	D1
Pinecrest Ln					
400	WLMT	60091	2812	4W-13N	B6
2400	WSTR	60154	3086		D3
Pinecroft Dr					
200	ROSL	60172	2913		B5
Pine Forest Ln					
800	PTHT	60070	2808	14W-14N	C3
N Pine Grove Av					
2700	CHCG	60614	2978	0W-3N	A5
2900	CHCG	60657	2978	0W-3N	A4
3500	CHCG	60613	2978	0W-4N	A2
Pine Grove Ct					
11900	ODPK	60467	3344	14W-18S	C6
W Pine Grove Ct					
13200	HMGN	60441	3343	16W-17S	E5
S Pine Grove Dr					
14400	HMGN	60441	3343	16W-17S	E5
N Pinehill Ct					
300	PLTN	60067	2752	22W-16N	B7
300	PlT	60067	2752	22W-16N	B7
S Pine Hill Rd					
19900	FftT	60423	3504	10W-24S	C5
W Pine Hill Rd					
7800	FftT	60423	3504	9W-24S	D4
Pinehurst Av					
200	DSPN	60016	2862	14W-12N	C1
500	DSPN	60016	2808	14W-12N	C7
Pinehurst Ct					
10	BRBK	60459	3211	7W-8S	C1
300	PSHT	60463	3347	8W-15S	B1
Pinehurst Dr					
300	PSHT	60463	3347	8W-15S	B1
1300	GNVW	60025	2810	9W-13N	C5
25700	MONE	60449	3683	6W-31S	B5
Pinehurst Ln					
800	SMBG	60193	2858	24W-9N	C7
800	SMBG	60193	2912		C1
1600	FSMR	60422	3507	2W-23S	D3
Pine Lake Ct					
18300	TYPK	60477	3425	8W-22S	B7
Pine Lake Dr					
6500	TYPK	60477	3505	8W-22S	B1
18300	TYPK	60477	3425	8W-22S	B7
Pine Manor Dr					
400	WLMT	60091	2812	4W-13N	C6
Pine Needles Dr					
10	LMNT	60439	3343	17W-15S	C1
Pine Point Dr					
10	HDPK	60035	2758	6W-20N	C2
6500	TYPK	60477	3425	8W-20S	B4
Pine Ridge Ct					
6300	TYPK	60477	3425	7W-22S	C7
Pine Ridge Dr					
-	RchT	60477	3425	7W-22S	C7
6300	TYPK	60477	3425	7W-22S	C7
Pine Trace Ct					
1500	MonT	60466	3594	4W-29S	D7
1500	UYPK	60466	3594	4W-29S	D7
N Pinetree Dr					
1900	ANHT	60004	2807	17W-16N	B1
2000	ANHT	60004	2754	17W-16N	B7
Pine Tree Ln					
10	BRRG	60527	3208		B3
200	LGPK	60525	3087	12W-2S	B3
900	WNKA	60093	2758	6W-16N	C7
Pinetree Ln					
300	SMBG	60193	2859	21W-9N	E6
1100	BRLT	60103	2910		E7
Pine Tree Rd					
10	DRFD	60015	2757	9W-18N	B2
10	NfdT	60062	2757	9W-18N	B2
14700	ODPK	60462	3345	13W-17S	A6
Pinetree St					
6600	HRPK	60133	2911		D3
Pine Valley Dr					
1100	SMBG	60173	2805	21W-13N	D6
Pine Valley Rd					
10	RGMW	60008	2806	19W-14N	C4
Pineview Ct					
14400	OrlT	60467	3344	14W-17S	D5
Pineview Dr					
11600	OrlT	60467	3344	14W-17S	D5
16700	HMGN	60441	3422	15W-20S	C4
Pine Wood Ct					
18300	TYPK	60477	3425	7W-21S	C7
Pinewood Ct					
14500	OrlT	60467	3344	14W-17S	C5
Pinewood Dr					
500	EGVV	60007	2915		A2
500	GLNC	60022	2758	7W-18N	B3
14300	ODPK	60467	3344	14W-17S	C5
14300	OrlT	60467	3344	14W-17S	C5
14500	HMGN	60441	3344	14W-17S	C5
W Pinewood Dr					
3600	MonT	60449	3683	4W-31S	E5
Pinewood Ln					
-	MONE	60449	3683	6W-31S	A5
4100	MTSN	60443	3506	5W-25S	C6
6500	TYPK	60477	3425	8W-22S	B7
S Pinewood Ln					
25500	MonT	60449	3683	4W-31S	E5
Pine Woods Ct					
1400	MonT	60466	3683	4W-29S	D1
1400	UYPK	60466	3683	4W-29S	D1
Pin Oak Ct					
18000	TYPK	60477	3425	8W-21S	B6
S Pin Oak Ct					
16100	HMGN	60441	3422	16W-19S	A2
W Pin Oak Ct					
13200	HMGN	60441	3343	16W-16S	E4
Pin Oak Dr					
-	PTHT	60070	2754	16W-16N	E6
-	WLNG	60004	2754	16W-16N	E6
-	WLNG	60070	2754	16W-16N	E6
200	WLMT	60091	2812	4W-13N	C6
E Pinoak Dr					
2000	MPPT	60056	2808	13W-14N	E4
2000	WhlT	60025	2808	13W-14N	E4
S Pinoak Dr					
300	BRLT	60103	2910		E4
W Pin Oak Dr					
12800	HMGN	60441	3344	16W-16S	A4
13000	HMGN	60441	3343	16W-16S	E4
W Pinoak Dr					
400	BRLT	60103	2910		E3
Pin Oak Ln					
800	UYPK	60466	3684	3W-30S	B2
1000	PTHT	60070	2754	16W-16N	E7
Pintail Ct					
700	VrnT	60015	2755	15W-20N	B1
E Pintail Ct					
1100	PLTN	60067	2805	22W-14N	B3
Pintail Ln					
400	VrnT	60015	2755	15W-20N	B1
Pintail St					
500	VrnT	60015	2755	15W-20N	B1
Pinto Ct					
10	SMWD	60107	2856	30W-10N	C5
Pinto Ln					
800	NHBK	60062	2756	12W-17N	A4
Pinto St					
15300	HMGN	60441	3343	16W-18S	E7
N Pioneer Av					
3200	CHCG	60171	2974	10W-4N	B4
3200	CHCG	60634	2974	10W-4N	B3
3200	RVGV	60171	2974	10W-4N	B4
5400	CHCG	60656	2918	10W-6N	B5
Pioneer Ct					
900	ROSL	60172	2912		C5
Pioneer Ln					
2000	WLMT	60091	2812	4W-13N	B7
Pioneer Rd					
2100	EVTN	60201	2866	3W-12N	E1
2500	EVTN	60201	2812	3W-12N	E7
Piper Ct					
3500	RGMW	60008	2806	20W-13N	B6
Piper Ln					
10	PTHT	60070	2808	13W-15N	D1
10	WLNG	60090	2808	13W-15N	D1
Pipers Dr					
100	BRLT	60103	2910		E5
100	BRLT	60103	2911		A5
W Pippin St					
3700	CHCG	60652	3212	4W-8S	C1
Pirates Cove					
-	RGMW	60067	2805	21W-13N	D6
-	SMBG	60173	2805	21W-13N	D6
Pitner Av					
900	EVTN	60202	2866	3W-10N	E4
1200	EVTN	60201	2866	3W-10N	E4
S Pitney Ct					
3000	CHCG	60608	3091	1W-2S	D3
N Pittsburgh Av					
3200	CHCG	60634	2974	10W-4N	A4
3200	RVGV	60171	2974	10W-4N	A4
5200	CHCG	60706	2918	10W-6N	B6
5200	NRDG	60706	2918	10W-6N	B6
5300	CHCG	60656	2918	10W-6N	A5
Piute Tr					
8000	TYPK	60477	3424	10W-21S	C6
Placid Ct					
200	EGVV	60007	2914		E2
Placid Wy					
200	EGVV	60007	2914		E2
S Plahm Ct					
10700	WRTH	60482	3275	8W-12S	A2
N Plainfield Av					
3200	CHCG	60634	2974	10W-4N	A4
3200	RVGV	60171	2974	10W-4N	A4
4500	NRDG	60706	2918	10W-5N	A7
5300	CHCG	60656	2918	10W-6N	A6
Plainfield Dr					
1700	DSPN	60018	2862	13W-9N	D7
Plainfield Rd					
100	BRRG	60527	3146		A7
100	WLBK	60527	3146		A7
8400	LYNS	60534	3088	10W-4S	A7
8700	BKFD	60513	3088	10W-4S	A7
8800	BKFD	60513	3087	11W-4S	E7
8800	BKFD	60513	3147	11W-4S	E1
9100	MCCK	60525	3147	11W-4S	E1
12000	IHPK	60527	3146		A7
12000	IHPK	60558	3146		A7
12000	LynT	60527	3146		A7
12000	LynT	60558	3146		A7
Plainfield Rd CO-31					
100	BRRG	60527	3146		C6
100	WLBK	60527	3146		B6
E Plainfield Rd					
10	CTSD	60525	3147	12W-5S	C2
10	LGNG	60525	3147	12W-5S	C2
500	MCCK	60525	3147	12W-5S	C2
W Plainfield Rd					
-	BRRG	60527	3146		D5
-	IHPK	60527	3146		D5
-	LynT	60527	3146		D5
10	CTSD	60525	3147	13W-6S	A4
10	LGNG	60525	3147	13W-6S	A4
800	LynT	60525	3147	13W-6S	B3
1500	LynT	60525	3146		D5
2000	IHPK	60525	3146		E5
11400	IHPK	60558	3146		D5
11400	LynT	60558	3146		D5
Plainview Dr					
16500	MKHM	60426	3426	4W-19S	E3
16600	HLCT	60429	3426	4W-19S	E3
Plainview Rd					
1400	CPVL	60110	2801		C1
1400	CPVL	60118	2801		B1
1400	EDND	60110	2801		B1
1400	EDND	60118	2801		B1
Plank Trail Ct					
21100	FKFT	60423	3504	9W-25S	E7
Plank Trail Dr					
-	FftT	60423	3504	9W-25S	E7
-	FKFT	60423	3504	9W-25S	E7
Plant Rd					
1000	WLNG	60090	2755	13W-16N	D6
Plate Dr					
500	DndT	60118	2801		D4
500	EDND	60118	2801		D4
E Plate Dr					
800	PLTN	60074	2753	19W-16N	B6
Platte Tr					
3200	OMFD	60461	3506	4W-24S	E5
W Plattner Dr					
5200	ALSP	60803	3275	6W-14S	E6
E Playfield Dr					
12700	CTWD	60445	3275	6W-15S	E7
12900	CTWD	60445	3347	6W-15S	E1
W Playfield Dr					
12700	CTWD	60445	3275	6W-15S	E7
12900	CTWD	60445	3347	6W-15S	E1
Plaza Ct					
-	CHHT	60411	3507	1W-24S	E5
-	CHHT	60411	3508	1W-24S	A5
7500	WLBK	60527	3208		A1
Plaza Dr					
-	PTHT	60070	2808	13W-15N	E1
-	RGMW	60008	2806	19W-13N	B5
N Plaza Dr					
800	SMBG	60173	2859	21W-11N	E2
Plaza 33 Service Rd					
-	SRPK	60176	2917	12W-5N	B7
Plaza Service Rd					
-	HLCT	60426	3427	2W-19S	C3
-	HLCT	60429	3427	3W-19S	C3
-	MKHM	60426	3427	3W-19S	B3
Pleasant Av					
400	HDPK	60035	2758	7W-20N	A1
8700	HYHL	60457	3210	10W-10S	A4
9200	TYPK	60477	3423	11W-22S	E7
9300	FftT	60477	3423	11W-22S	E7
N Pleasant Av					
100	BMDL	60108	2913		B7
S Pleasant Av					
-	CHCG	60643	3213	2W-10S	C6
9000	CHCG	60620	3213	2W-10S	C4
Pleasant Blvd					
5600	CHRG	60415	3275	7W-12S	D2
5600	OKLN	60453	3275	7W-12S	D2
Pleasant Ct					
12800	CTWD	60445	3275	6W-15S	E7
15200	HMGN	60441	3342	19W-16S	E3
Pleasant Dr					
10	SMBG	60193	2859	23W-10N	A5
10	SMBG	60194	2859	23W-10N	A5
100	CHHT	60411	3507	1W-23S	E4
100	CHHT	60411	3508	0W-23S	B4
200	EGVV	60007	2914		E2
200	HFET	60194	2859	23W-10N	A5
400	SMBG	60193	2912		B2
400	SmbT	60193	2912		B2
22400	RNPK	60471	3594	6W-27S	B4
N Pleasant Dr					
200	GNWD	60425	3508	0W-22S	B1
400	GNWD	60425	3428	0W-22S	C7
Pleasant Ln					
400	DSPN	60018	2862	15W-10N	A6
700	GNVW	60025	2811	7W-14N	A4
700	GNVW	60093	2811	7W-14N	B4
700	NHFD	60093	2811	7W-14N	B4
1400	GNVW	60025	2810	8W-14N	E4
5200	CTWD	60445	3275	6W-15S	E7
Pleasant Pl					
600	SMWD	60107	2857	28W-9N	B7
1000	OKPK	60302	3030	8W-0N	E4
1100	LMNT	60439	3271		A7
Pleasant Run					
3200	GNVW	60025	2809	11W-14N	D3
3200	GNVW	60062	2809	11W-14N	D3
3200	NfdT	60062	2809	11W-14N	D3
Pleasant St					
10	BNVL	60106	2915		E7
10	HFET	60194	2858	24W-10N	D5
10	OKPK	60302	3031	8W-0N	A4
1000	OKPK	60302	3030	8W-0N	E4
1100	FTPK	60130	3030	8W-0N	D4
3400	NfdT	60062	2756	11W-16N	C6
3400	NHBK	60062	2756	11W-16N	C6
Pleasant Ter					
200	RchT	60443	3593	8W-26S	B2
Pleasantdale Ct					
7100	CTSD	60525	3147	13W-8S	A7
Pleasantdale Dr					
10	DGvT	60439	3270		B1
7100	CTSD	60525	3147	13W-8S	A7
W Pleasant Hill Blvd					
10	PLTN	60067	2805	21W-15N	D2
S Pleasant Hill Ct					
23700	CteT	60417	3598	3E-28S	A7
S Pleasant Hill Dr					
23600	CteT	60417	3598	3E-28S	A7
Pleasant Park Wy					
-	CHCG	60620	3213	2W-10S	C5
Pleasant Run Dr					
-	PTHT	60070	2755	15W-16N	A7
-	WLNG	60070	2755	15W-16N	A7
1100	WLNG	60090	2755	15W-16N	A7
1200	PTHT	60090	2755	15W-16N	A7
Pleasant View Av					
8300	WLSP	60480	3208		D3
Pleasantview Ln					
10	NHFD	60093	2811	7W-15N	B2
Plum Ct					
300	ELGN	60120	2855		A2
1400	MPPT	60056	2807	16W-14N	D3
8400	TYPK	60477	3424	10W-20S	B4
Plum St					
200	ELGN	60120	2855		A2
Plum Blossom Tr					
3300	RGMW	60067	2805	21W-13N	D6
Plum Creek Dr					
100	DYR	46311	3598		D2
300	WLNG	60090	2755	13W-17N	D6
Plum Grove Cir					
-	BFGV	60004	2754	18W-18N	A3
800	BFGV	60089	2754	17W-18N	A2
W Plum Grove Cir					
200	ANHT	60004	2754	18W-18N	A2
200	BFGV	60004	2754	18W-18N	A2
200	BFGV	60089	2754	18W-18N	A2
Plum Grove Dr					
3200	RGMW	60008	2860	20W-12N	B1
3300	RGMW	60008	2806	20W-12N	B7
Plum Grove Rd					
-	RGMW	60067	2805	21W-13N	D6
-	SMBG	60067	2805	21W-13N	D6
-	SMBG	60173	2805	21W-13N	D6
1800	PLTN	60008	2805	21W-14N	E4
1800	PLTN	60067	2805	21W-14N	E4
1800	RGMW	60008	2805	21W-14N	E4
2400	PlT	60008	2805	21W-14N	E4
2400	PlT	60067	2805	21W-14N	E5
N Plum Grove Rd					
-	HFET	60194	2859	22W-11N	C4
-	SMBG	60193	2859	22W-10N	C5
-	SMBG	60194	2859	22W-11N	C4
10	PLTN	60067	2805	21W-16N	E1
100	BmdT	60157	2913		C4
100	ROSL	60157	2913		C4
200	BmdT	60172	2913		C3
500	ROSL	60172	2913		C4
700	ROSL	60193	2913		C4
700	SmbT	60172	2913		C4
700	SmbT	60193	2913		C4
900	PLTN	60067	2752	20W-17N	E5
1000	SMBG	60173	2859	22W-11N	C2
20100	DRPK	60074	2752	21W-20N	E2
20100	ElaT	60074	2752	21W-20N	E2
20100	PlT	60074	2752	21W-20N	E2
20400	KLDR	60047	2752	21W-20N	E1
S Plum Grove Rd					
-	EGVV	60193	2913		C1
10	PLTN	60067	2805	20W-15N	E2
10	SMBG	60173	2859	22W-10N	C5
10	SMBG	60193	2859	22W-10N	C6
10	SMBG	60194	2859	22W-10N	C5
300	EGVV	60007	2859	22W-10N	C6
300	EGVV	60193	2859	22W-10N	C6
600	SMBG	60007	2859	22W-9N	C7
800	PLTN	60008	2805	21W-14N	E3
800	RGMW	60008	2805	21W-14N	E3
900	EGVV	60007	2913		C2
900	SMBG	60193	2913		C2
1400	SmbT	60007	2913		C2
1400	SmbT	60172	2913		C2
1400	SmbT	60193	2913		C2
1500	ROSL	60172	2913		C2
1500	ROSL	60193	2913		C2
Plum Island Dr					
3000	NHBK	60062	2756	11W-17N	D5
Plummer Av					
10	CTCY	60409	3352	4E-17S	C5
10	HMND	46320	3352	4E-17S	C5
Plumrose Ct					
10	SMBG	60194	2859	23W-10N	B5
Plumrose Ln					
-	SMBG	60193	2859	23W-10N	A5
10	SMBG	60194	2859	23W-10N	A5
Plum Tree Ct					
10	SMWD	60107	2857	26W-11N	D5
700	WLNG	60090	2754	16W-18N	D3
1200	SMBG	60193	2859	21W-10N	D6
S Plum Tree Ct					
1000	PLTN	60067	2805	21W-14N	C3
Plum Tree Dr					
15500	ODPK	60462	3346	10W-18S	B7
15600	ODPK	60462	3424	10W-18S	B1
Plum Tree Ln					
100	WLMT	60091	2811	5W-13N	E7
1300	WNKA	60093	2758	6W-16N	E7
2400	PLTN	60008	2805	22W-14N	B5
2400	PLTN	60067	2805	22W-14N	B5
2400	RGMW	60008	2805	22W-14N	B5
2400	RGMW	60067	2805	22W-14N	B5
6800	HRPK	60133	2911		C3
7000	SMWD	60107	2911		C3
7000	SMWD	60133	2911		C3
S Plum Tree Ln					
1000	PLTN	60067	2805	21W-14N	C4
26100	MONE	60449	3683	6W-31S	A6
Plum Tree Rd					
100	DRFD	60015	2756	11W-20N	D2
S Plum Valley Dr					
23600	CteT	60417	3598	3E-29S	A7
23900	CteT	60417	3687	3E-29S	A1
Plumwood Ct					
400	SMBG	60173	2859	22W-11N	C4
Plumwood Dr					
-	HFET	60194	2859	22W-11N	C4
800	SMBG	60173	2859	22W-11N	C4
N Plumwood Dr					
20500	KLDR	60047	2753	20W-20N	A1
Pluskota Dr					
8000	ODPK	60462	3346	10W-16S	C3
Plymouth Av					
2600	WSTR	60154	3086		D3
Plymouth Cir					
1500	CPVL	60110	2748		D7
Plymouth Ct					
100	BRLT	60103	2911		A4
100	IVNS	60067	2805	23W-15N	A1
7000	TYPK	60477	3425	8W-19S	A2
S Plymouth Ct					
300	CHCG	60604	3034	0W-0S	B5
800	CHCG	60605	3034	0W-0S	B6
W Plymouth Ct					
1300	ANHT	60004	2753	18W-16N	D7
Plymouth Dr					
100	IVNS	60067	2805	23W-15N	A1
200	CHHT	60411	3595	1W-26S	E1
200	SMWD	60107	2857	28W-11N	B4
16100	MKHM	60426	3427	3W-19S	B2
W Plymouth Dr					
1400	ANHT	60004	2753	18W-16N	D7
Plymouth Ln					
400	SMBG	60193	2858	25W-9N	B7
1300	GNVW	60025	2810	8W-14N	E5
1300	GNVW	60025	2811	8W-14N	A5
2000	NHBK	60062	2757	10W-16N	B7
Plymouth Pl					
10	LGPK	60525	3087	12W-3S	C6
1400	GNVW	60025	2810	8W-14N	E5
Plymouth Rd					
700	HFET	60195	2804	23W-14N	D3
Pocasset Ct					
100	SMBG	60193	2858	25W-10N	C6
Pocasset on Asbury					
10	RGMW	60008	2806	19W-14N	B3
Pochet Ct					
300	SMBG	60193	2858	24W-10N	D6
Pochet Ln					
200	SMBG	60193	2858	24W-10N	D6
Podlin Dr					
400	BNVL	60131	2972		C2
Poe Av					
17300	HLCT	60429	3427	3W-20S	A5
N Poe St					
1800	CHCG	60614	2977	1W-2N	E7
Pohlers Ct					
14400	DLTN	60419	3350	0E-16S	E4
Poinsetta Ln					
1100	BRLT	60103	2910		E7
NW Point Blvd					
10	EGvT	60007	2861	18W-10N	A4
10	EGVV	60007	2861	18W-10N	A4
S Point Ct					
1200	SMBG	60193	2913		C1
E Point Dr					
900	SMBG	60193	2913		C1
N Point Dr					
600	SMBG	60193	2913		C1
S Point Dr					
600	SMBG	60193	2913		C2
W Point Dr					
900	SMBG	60193	2913		C1
18500	TYPK	60477	3505	8W-22S	B1
W Point Pl					
-	TYPK	60477	3505	8W-22S	B1
N Point St					
2000	CHCG	60647	2977	3W-2N	A6
2100	CHCG	60647	2976	4W-2N	D7
Pointe Dr					
5500	HMND	46320	3352		D6
17100	ODPK	60467	3423	13W-20S	A5
S Pointe Dr					
6700	RchT	60477	3425	8W-22S	A7
6700	TYPK	60477	3425	8W-22S	A7
Polk Av					
300	CPVL	60110	2748		D7
700	DYR	46311	3510		D6
3600	RNPK	60471	3594	4W-27S	D5
3800	RchT	60471	3594	4W-27S	D5
Polk Ct					
10	SMWD	60107	2856	29W-10N	D6
200	BRLT	60103	2911		A5
1800	RGMW	60008	2805	20W-14N	E4
Polk St					
200	EGvT	60018	2862	15W-9N	A7
4000	RchT	60471	3594	5W-27S	C5
7400	HRPK	60133	2912		A1
7600	FTPK	60130	3030	9W-0S	C6
S Polk St					
25700	MONE	60449	3682	7W-31S	E5
W Polk St					
10	CHCG	60605	3034	0W-0S	B6
200	CHCG	60607	3034	0W-0S	B6
1000	CHCG	60607	3033	1W-0S	E6
1600	CHCG	60612	3033	2W-0S	E6
2800	CHCG	60612	3032	4W-0S	D6
3100	CHCG	60624	3032	4W-0S	C6
4500	CHCG	60644	3032	5W-0S	A6
4800	CHCG	60644	3031	6W-0S	E6
Polly Ct					
1000	ELGN	60120	2855		B1
Polly Ln					
2900	FSMR	60422	3507	3W-23S	A3
Polo Dr					
-	OKBK	60523	3086		A4
10	SBTN	60010	2803	26W-14N	D4
1400	BRLT	60103	2910		B7
Polo Ln					
800	GNVW	60025	2811	7W-13N	B7
Poloma Dr					
8200	PlsT	60462	3346	10W-15S	B2
8200	PSHT	60464	3346	10W-15S	C2
8500	ODPK	60462	3346	10W-15S	B2
Polynesian Dr					
500	DSPN	60016	2808	13W-12N	E7
Pomo Ct					
2500	SLVL	60411	3597	2E-26S	E3
Pomona Ln					
2300	WLMT	60091	2812	5W-13N	A6
E Pompano Ln					
600	PLTN	60074	2753	20W-16N	B6
N Ponchartrain Blvd					
6500	CHCG	60646	2919	7W-8N	C2
Pond Dr					
500	WDDL	60191	2915		A6
Ponderosa Ct					
100	BRTN	60010	2751	24W-20N	D1
7800	ODPK	60462	3346	9W-18S	D6
W Ponderosa Ct					
7900	ODPK	60462	3346	9W-18S	C6
S Ponderosa Dr					
12700	PSHT	60463	3274	9W-15S	D7
W Ponderosa Dr					
7600	PSHT	60463	3274	9W-15S	D7
Ponderosa Ln					
900	HFET	60010	2751	24W-16N	C7
Pond Gate Dr					
500	BNHL	60010	2802	30W-14N	A3
500	BNHL	60118	2801		E3
500	BNHL	60118	2802	30W-14N	A3
Pondside Dr					
1700	NHBK	60062	2756	10W-16N	E7
Pond View Ct					
18300	TYPK	60477	3425	8W-22S	B7
Pondview Ct					
800	SMBG	60194	2858	24W-10N	D5
Pond View Dr					
-	MTSN	60443	3505	7W-25S	C7
6600	RchT	60477	3425	8W-22S	B7
6600	TYPK	60477	3425	8W-22S	B7
N Pondview Dr					
300	PLTN	60067	2752	22W-16N	C7
Pond View Ln					
400	BRLT	60103	2910		D3
N Pontiac Av					
3200	CHCG	60634	2974	10W-4N	A3
3200	RVGV	60171	2974	10W-4N	A4
3200	RVGV	60634	2974	10W-4N	A4
4800	NRDG	60706	2918	10W-6N	A6
Pontiac Dr					
6300	IHPK	60525	3146		D6
Pontiac Rd					
1000	WLMT	60091	2812	5W-14N	A5
Ponto Dr					
7200	MNGV	60053	2864	9W-11N	D2
Pony Ln					
800	NHBK	60062	2756	12W-17N	A4
W Pope Blvd					
15700	VrnT	60069	2754	16W-20N	E1
15700	VrnT	60089	2754	15W-20N	E1
16200	BFGV	60069	2754	16W-20N	D1
16200	BFGV	60089	2754	16W-20N	D1
W Pope John Paul II Dr					
2400	CHCG	60609	3091	3W-4S	A7
2400	CHCG	60632	3091	3W-4S	A7
2800	CHCG	60632	3090	3W-4S	E7
Poplar Av					
-	EVTN	60201	2812	3W-13N	E7
-	WLMT	60091	2812	3W-13N	E7
-	WLMT	60201	2812	3W-13N	E7
200	BmdT	60157	2913		C3
200	ROSL	60157	2913		C3
400	YkTp	60126	3028		B7
1600	HRPK	60133	2911		D2
2100	HRPK	60107	2911		C2
2100	SMWD	60107	2911		C2
2100	SMWD	60133	2911		C2
2300	EVTN	60201	2867	3W-12N	A1
2400	EVTN	60201	2866	3W-12N	E1
4100	RNPK	60471	3594	5W-26S	C3
16100	BmnT	60426	3427	3W-19S	B2
18300	HMWD	60430	3427	1W-22S	E7
18400	HMWD	60430	3507	1W-22S	E1
N Poplar Av					
300	BNVL	60106	2915		C7
300	WDDL	60106	2915		C7
400	WDDL	60191	2915		C7
S Poplar Av					
100	EMHT	60126	3028		A4
600	YkTp	60126	3028		B7
2700	CHCG	60608	3091	1W-2S	E3
3000	CHCG	60608	3092	1W-2S	A3
Poplar Ct					
10	BFGV	60089	2754	17W-18N	B3
100	NHBK	60062	2755	13W-18N	E2
100	NHBK	60062	2756	13W-18N	A2
400	ELGN	60120	2855		B3
1300	HMWD	60430	3507	1W-22S	E1
14600	ODPK	60462	3346	11W-17S	A5

Block	City	ZIP	Map#	CGS	Grid
E Poplar Ct					
2700	CteT	60417	3687	3E-29S	A2
Poplar Dr					
100	EVTN	60201	2812	3W-13N	E7
100	WLMT	60091	2812	3W-13N	E6
100	WLMT	60201	2812	3W-13N	E7
300	WLNG	60090	2755	13W-17N	E5
Poplar Ln					
100	LynT	60458	3209	11W-8S	E2
400	MaiT	60025	2809	10W-12N	E7
800	DRFD	60015	2756	11W-20N	E1
900	BRLT	60103	2910		D6
2000	SLVL	60411	3509	2E-25S	D7
2000	SLVL	60411	3597	2E-25S	D1
8200	PSHL	60465	3274	10W-13S	B3
17900	CCHL	60478	3426	6W-21S	A7
E Poplar Ln					
2800	CteT	60417	3687	3E-29S	A2
Poplar Pl					
-	FSMR	60422	3506	4W-23S	D2
-	RchT	60430	3506	4W-23S	D2
1700	SMBG	60173	2859	21W-12N	E1
N Poplar Pl					
10	LGNG	60525	3087	13W-4S	A7
Poplar Rd					
200	HDPK	60035	2757	9W-20N	D1
3600	FSMR	60422	3506	4W-22S	D2
4600	RNPK	60471	3594	5W-26S	B3
9000	ODPK	60462	3346	11W-17S	A5
9100	ODPK	60462	3345	11W-17S	E5
Poplar St					
200	WNKA	60093	2812	4W-15N	C2
1500	NLES	60714	2863	11W-10N	E5
1500	PKRG	60068	2863	11W-10N	E5
8900	TYPK	60477	3424	11W-21S	A6
N Poplar St					
100	PLTN	60067	2752	22W-17N	A5
W Poplar St					
800	PltT	60067	2752	22W-17N	C5
1300	PLTN	60067	2752	22W-17N	A5
Poplar Creek Ct					
700	SMWD	60107	2857	28W-10N	A6
15200	ODPK	60467	3344	14W-18S	E7
Poplar Creek Dr					
10	ELGN	60120	2855		D4
1400	HFET	60194	2857	26W-12N	E2
Poplar Creek Ln					
11200	ODPK	60467	3344	14W-18S	E6
Poplar Ct Ct					
-	SBTN	60010	2803	25W-15N	E2
-	SBTN	60010	2804	25W-15N	A2
Poplar View Bnd					
2600	HnrT	60120	2856	31W-11N	A4
Popp Ln					
1700	LGGV	60047	2753	19W-20N	D1
Poppy Ln					
200	BNVL	60106	2915		E7
200	MTSN	60443	3593	7W-26S	C2
700	BRLT	60103	2910		D7
2300	GNVW	60025	2810	9W-15N	C3
N Portage Av					
1200	PLTN	60067	2752	22W-17N	A4
1200	PltT	60067	2752	22W-17N	A4
1300	PltT	60010	2752	22W-17N	A4
W Portage Ct					
1500	PLTN	60067	2752	22W-17N	A5
1500	PltT	60067	2752	22W-17N	A5
Portage Ln					
4100	HFET	60195	2804	24W-15N	B2
Portage Run					
1500	GNVW	60025	2809	11W-14N	D5
Portage Tr					
7200	FTVW	60402	3148	9W-5S	D1
7200	LYNS	60534	3148	9W-5S	D1
Port Arthur Ct					
1400	HFET	60195	2804	24W-15N	B2
Port Center Dr					
1500	IVNS	60067	2805	23W-14N	A5
1500	PltT	60067	2805	23W-14N	A5
1700	PltT	60195	2805	23W-14N	A5
Porter Ct					
200	BRLT	60103	2911		B5
400	ELGN	60120	2855		B3
2700	GNVW	60025	2809	11W-15N	D2
2700	NHBK	60062	2809	11W-15N	D2
Porter St					
400	LMNT	60439	3270		E5
N Porter St					
10	ELGN	60120	2855		B4
S Porter St					
10	ELGN	60120	2855		B4
Portland Av					
1200	CHHT	60411	3508	0W-25S	C7
1400	CHHT	60411	3596	0W-25S	C1
2500	BlmT	60411	3596	0W-26S	C2
S Portland Av					
4500	CHCG	60609	3092	0W-4S	B7
Portland Dr					
800	SMBG	60194	2858	25W-11N	B3
Port O Call Dr					
1300	PLTN	60074	2753	19W-17N	C4
Portshire Ct					
3300	HFET	60067	2804	23W-14N	E4
W Portsmith Ln					
1600	ANHT	60004	2753	18W-18N	D3
Portsmouth Av					
600	WSTR	60154	3029	12W-0S	B7
1400	WSTR	60154	3087	12W-1S	B1
2100	PvsT	60154	3087	12W-1S	B2
Portsmouth Ct					
10	SMBG	60194	2858	25W-10N	B5
1400	NHBK	60062	2757	9W-17N	C5
Portsmouth Ln					
1600	SMBG	60194	2858	25W-10N	A5
Portsmouth Pl					
600	WLNG	60090	2755	15W-18N	A3
Port Washington Ct					
20300	FKFT	60423	3504	11W-24S	A5
Port Washington Dr					
8800	FKFT	60423	3504	11W-24S	A6
Portwine Rd					
-	WLNG	60090	2755	13W-18N	E4
10	ROSL	60172	2913		B4
200	RVWD	60015	2755	13W-20N	E2
200	VrnT	60015	2755	13W-20N	E2
200	VrnT	60062	2755	13W-20N	E2
200	WhlT	60062	2755	13W-20N	E2
S Possum Dr					
11100	PSHL	60465	3274	11W-13S	A3
Possum Hllw					
1600	LGPK	60525	3087	13W-2S	A3
1600	PvsT	60525	3087	13W-2S	A3
1600	WSTR	60154	3087	13W-2S	A3
1600	WSTR	60525	3087	13W-2S	A3

Block	City	ZIP	Map#	CGS	Grid
Post Cir					
100	HNDL	60521	3146		B1
Post Ct					
800	SMWD	60107	2857	27W-10N	C5
Post Ln					
800	SMWD	60107	2857	27W-10N	C5
N Post Pl					
200	CHCG	60606	3034		E4
Post Rd					
100	BRRG	60527	3146		C6
2000	NfdT	60062	2756	12W-16N	B7
2000	NfdT	60062	2809	12W-16N	C1
2000	NHBK	60062	2809	12W-16N	C1
S Post Rd					
12300	PlsT	60464	3273	13W-14S	A6
12300	PSPK	60464	3273	13W-14S	A6
Post Oak Pl					
2000	SMBG	60173	2805	22W-13N	B7
Postoffice Dr					
-	WNSP	60558	3146		D1
Post Office Rd					
-	CHCG	60666	2916		D7
-	CHCG	60666	2972		D1
Poston Rd					
10	WLSP	60480	3209	12W-9S	C2
Potawatami Tr					
10	IHPK	60525	3146		E6
Potawatomi Dr					
7200	PSHT	60463	3274	9W-15S	D7
S Potawatomi Tr					
13500	HMGN	60441	3343	16W-16S	D3
N Potawatomie St					
4400	CHCG	60656	2973	11W-5N	E1
4700	NRDG	60706	2917	10W-5N	E7
5200	CHCG	60656	2917	10W-6N	E6
Poteet Av					
10	IVNS	60067	2804	23W-15N	D2
100	IVNS	60010	2751	23W-16N	D7
300	HFET	60195	2804	23W-15N	D1
300	IVNS	60195	2804	23W-15N	D2
Poteet Rd					
10	IVNS	60010	2751	23W-16N	D7
W Potomac Av					
1300	CHCG	60622	3033	1W-1N	D1
2700	CHCG	60622	3032	3W-1N	E1
3200	CHCG	60651	3032	4W-1N	D1
4800	CHCG	60651	3031	7W-1N	C1
5900	OKPK	60302	3031	7W-1N	B1
Potomac Ct					
-	CRTE	60417	3685	1W-29S	A1
Potomac Dr					
10	DYR	46311	3510		C7
Potomac Ln					
400	EGVV	60007	2859	22W-9N	D7
400	EGVV	60007	2913		D1
E Potomac Ln					
1100	PLTN	60074	2753	19W-17N	C5
Potowatomie Pnd					
5400	WhlT	60062	2755	13W-18N	D3
5400	WLNG	60090	2755	13W-18N	D3
S Pottawatomi Ct					
12800	PSHT	60463	3274	9W-14S	D6
W Pottawatomi Dr					
-	PSHT	60463	3274	9W-15S	E7
Pottawattami Dr					
8900	SKOK	60076	2866	4W-11N	B3
Pottawattomi Tr					
8000	TYPK	60477	3424	10W-21S	C6
Potter Ln					
10	BNHL	60010	2802	30W-15N	A1
Potter Rd					
1100	PKRG	60068	2863	11W-10N	D5
1800	DSPN	60016	2863	11W-10N	D4
1800	MaiT	60068	2863	11W-10N	D4
1800	PKRG	60016	2863	11W-10N	D4
3200	GNVW	60062	2809	11W-14N	C4
3500	NfdT	60062	2809	11W-14N	C4
10000	MaiT	60016	2809	11W-12N	D7
10000	MaiT	60016	2863	11W-11N	D1
10000	NfdT	60016	2809	11W-12N	D7
10000	NfdT	60025	2809	11W-12N	D7
Povalish Ct					
10	LMNT	60439	3270		C5
Powder Horn Dr					
200	NHBK	60062	2757	9W-18N	D3
Powell Av					
3800	LYNS	60534	3088	9W-3S	D6
3800	RVSD	60546	3088	9W-3S	D6
W Powell Rd					
9600	PlsT	60464	3273	12W-14S	C7
9600	PSPK	60464	3273	12W-14S	C7
Powell St					
3400	FNPK	60131	2972		C4
Powers Ct					
8700	ODPK	60462	3424	10W-19S	B1
Powers Dr					
-	MNSR	46321	3510		E4
Powis Rd					
-	WynT	60120	2909		E5
10	BRLT	60184	2909		D7
10	WynT	60184	2909		D7
Prague Av					
800	BFGV	60090	2755	14W-20N	C2
Prairie Av					
10	PKRG	60068	2918	10W-8N	A1
100	WLMT	60091	2812	4W-13N	D6
100	WLMT	60201	2812	3W-13N	E7
200	CTCY	60409	3351	2E-17S	C5
400	BCHR	60401	3864	0W-37S	C2
800	BRLT	60103	2911		A5
1000	BrnT	60010	2751	25W-17N	A4
1200	BRTN	60010	2751	25W-17N	A4
1300	CHHT	60411	3507	1W-25S	E7
1600	NfdT	60062	2756	11W-16N	C7
1600	NHBK	60062	2756	11W-17N	C6
1800	PKRG	60068	2917	11W-8N	D1
2300	EVTN	60201	2866	3W-12N	E1
2400	DSPN	60016	2863	11W-11N	C3
2400	MaiT	60016	2863	11W-11N	C3
2500	EVTN	60201	2812	3W-12N	E7
2900	BKFD	60513	3087	11W-4S	E6
4000	SRPK	60176	2973	12W-5N	C2
4400	BKFD	60513	3147	11W-4S	E1
4500	MCCK	60525	3147	11W-4S	E1
16200	SHLD	60473	3428	0E-19S	D2
22100	SLVL	60411	3597	2E-26S	C3
E Prairie Av					
400	DSPN	60016	2862	13W-11N	D4
1300	DSPN	60016	2863	13W-11N	A4
N Prairie Av					
100	BMDL	60108	2913		B7
S Prairie Av					
200	ANHT	60005	2807	16W-13N	C7
200	ANHT	60005	2861	17W-12N	B1
200	MPPT	60005	2861	17W-12N	B1

Block	City	ZIP	Map#	CGS	Grid
S Prairie Av					
200	MPPT	60056	2807	16W-13N	C7
200	MPPT	60056	2861	17W-12N	B1
300	EMHT	60126	3028		A4
500	BRTN	60010	2751	25W-18N	A3
1400	CHCG	60605	3034	0E-1S	C7
1900	CHCG	60616	3092	0E-1S	C1
3800	CHCG	60653	3092	0E-3S	C5
4600	CHCG	60615	3092	0E-4S	C7
4700	CHCG	60615	3152	0E-5S	C1
5400	CHCG	60637	3152	0E-6S	C4
7000	CHCG	60619	3152	0E-8S	D7
7500	CHCG	60619	3214	0E-9S	D2
9400	CHCG	60628	3214	0E-11S	D6
10300	CHCG	60628	3278	0E-12S	D2
13200	CHCG	60827	3350	0E-15S	D1
Prairie Cir					
1100	PTHT	60070	2754	16W-16N	E6
W Prairie Cir					
300	ITSC	60143	2914		B5
Prairie Ct					
8000	TYPK	60477	3424	10W-19S	C3
11900	LmnT	60439	3271		B6
W Prairie Ct					
12300	HMGN	60441	3344	15W-17S	B5
Prairie Dr					
1000	ALGN	60102	2748		B1
3400	SjnT	46311	3598		D6
16300	TYPK	60477	3424	10W-19S	C3
S Prairie Dr					
12000	ALSP	60803	3276	5W-14S	C5
W Prairie Dr					
4100	ALSP	60803	3276	5W-14S	B5
12300	HMGN	60441	3344	15W-17S	B5
Prairie Ln					
5800	RGMW	60067	2805	22W-14N	C4
Prairie Rd					
400	RchT	60443	3593	8W-26S	C2
700	GLNC	60022	2758	6W-17N	C5
E Prairie Rd					
7400	LNWD	60712	2866	4W-9N	B7
8400	SKOK	60076	2866	4W-10N	C4
8800	SKOK	60203	2866	4W-11N	C3
9400	EVTN	60201	2866	4W-11N	D2
9400	EVTN	60203	2866	4W-11N	D2
NE Prairie Rd					
6600	LNWD	60712	2920	4W-8N	B2
7200	LNWD	60712	2866	4W-9N	B7
7300	SKOK	60076	2866	4W-9N	B7
Prairie Sq					
1900	SMBG	60173	2805	21W-12N	E7
Prairie St					
300	ELGN	60120	2855		A4
1900	GNVW	60025	2810	9W-13N	D6
2000	BLID	60406	3277	2W-15S	C7
3000	FNPK	60131	2973	13W-3N	A4
3300	MTSN	60443	3594	4W-26S	E2
3300	MTSN	60443	3595	4W-26S	A2
E Prairie Brook Dr					
1200	PLTN	60074	2753	19W-17N	C5
Prairie Center Dr					
-	SMBG	60193	2859	22W-10N	C5
-	SMBG	60194	2859	22W-10N	C5
Prairie Hill Dr					
13700	HMGN	60441	3342	19W-16S	D3
13700	HmrT	60441	3342	19W-16S	D3
Prairie Lake Rd					
100	EDND	60110	2748		E7
100	EDND	60110	2801		E1
Prairie Lawn Rd					
800	GNVW	60025	2810	10W-13N	B7
800	NfdT	60025	2810	10W-13N	B7
Prairie Park Dr					
-	WLNG	60090	2755	14W-18N	C2
Prairie Pointe Ln					
10	SMWD	60107	2856	29W-10N	D6
Prairie Stone Pkwy					
-	HFET	60118	2802	29W-13N	C5
5000	HFET	60192	2802	30W-13N	B6
S Prairie View Av					
25700	CteT	60417	3686	3E-31S	E5
Prairie View Dr					
100	PlsT	60464	3273	12W-14S	C7
Prairie View Ln					
200	WLNG	60090	2755	14W-18N	D3
Prairie Wind Ln					
1900	SMBG	60173	2805	21W-12N	E7
Prarie Av					
-	BNHM	60633	3352	3E-16S	A3
N Prater Av					
10	NHLK	60164	3028		E1
100	NHLK	60164	2972		E7
800	LydT	60164	2972		D5
3100	FNPK	60131	2972		D5
S Prater Av					
100	NHLK	60164	3028		E1
Pratt Av					
1600	DSPN	60018	2917	12W-8N	B2
1600	RSMT	60018	2917	12W-8N	A2
W Pratt Av					
3300	LNWD	60712	2920	5W-8N	A2
4700	LNWD	60712	2919	5W-8N	E2
4800	SKOK	60077	2919	6W-8N	D1
5300	CHCG	60646	2919	6W-8N	D1
7200	CHCG	60631	2918	9W-8N	D2
7200	NLES	60631	2918	9W-8N	D2
7200	NLES	60714	2918	9W-8N	D2
Pratt Av N					
400	SMBG	60193	2912		D2
Pratt Blvd					
10	ROSL	60172	2913		A2
10	ROSL	60193	2913		A2
10	SmbT	60172	2913		A2
10	SmbT	60193	2913		A2
100	ROSL	60172	2912		E2
100	SmbT	60172	2912		E2
100	SmbT	60193	2912		E2
600	EGVV	60007	2915		B2
2100	CHCG	60007	2915		D2
W Pratt Blvd					
1000	CHCG	60626	2921	2W-8N	C1
1900	CHCG	60645	2921	2W-8N	B1
2600	CHCG	60645	2920	3W-8N	E1
3100	LNWD	60645	2920	3W-8N	D2
3100	LNWD	60712	2920	3W-8N	D2
Pratt Ct					
2000	EVTN	60201	2867	2W-11N	B2
E Pratt Dr					
800	PLTN	60074	2753	19W-16N	B6
Pratum Av					
-	HnrT	60192	2802	29W-13N	C7
2300	HFET	60192	2802	29W-13N	C6
S Preller Av					
11100	WRTH	60482	3274	8W-13S	E3

Block	City	ZIP	Map#	CGS	Grid
W Prendergast Ln					
2100	MPPT	60056	2861	17W-12N	B2
Prescott Av					
3900	LYNS	60534	3088	9W-4S	C7
4500	LYNS	60534	3148	9W-4S	C1
4600	MCCK	60534	3148	9W-4S	C1
N Prescott Av					
6100	CHCG	60646	2919	6W-7N	C3
Prescott Dr					
-	BRLT	60103	2909		C3
700	ROSL	60172	2912		C6
Prescott Ln					
2400	WSTR	60154	3086		D3
7300	CTSD	60525	3209	13W-8S	A1
Preserve Tr					
1100	BRLT	60103	2910		C4
Presidential Dr					
10	ROSL	60172	2912		E4
Presidents Dr					
17700	HMWD	60430	3428	1W-21S	A6
Presidio Ct					
100	SMBG	60195	2859	23W-12N	A2
Prestbury Ct					
700	NHBK	60062	2756	11W-18N	D4
Prestbury Dr					
1000	ELGN	60120	2855		D1
Preston Av					
10	ELGN	60120	2855		B4
N Preston Av					
400	ELGN	60120	2855		B1
Preston Ln					
-	BlmT	60411	3509	2E-23S	E4
-	LYWD	60411	3509	2E-23S	E4
600	SMBG	60193	2859	22W-9N	C7
Preston St					
10400	WSTR	60154	3087	13W-2S	A3
Prestwick Dr					
-	FKFT	60423	3593	9W-26S	A1
-	RchT	60443	3593	9W-26S	A1
1700	IVNS	60067	2804	23W-15N	E2
7500	TYPK	60477	3424	9W-20S	D4
Prestwick Ln					
10	RGMW	60008	2805	23W-12N	B7
400	WLNG	60090	2755	13W-17N	D5
1200	ITSC	60143	2913		E7
1200	ITSC	60143	2914		A7
3200	NHBK	60062	2756	11W-17N	C6
3300	NfdT	60062	2756	11W-17N	C6
8800	ODPK	60462	3346	11W-15S	A2
Prestwick Pl					
4800	HFET	60010	2751	25W-16N	A7
4800	HFET	60010	2804	24W-16N	B1
Price Av					
300	CTCY	60409	3352	4E-17S	B6
1200	CTCY	60409	3430	4E-19S	B2
Price Dr					
1000	ELGN	60120	2855		D3
Price St					
600	CTCY	60409	3352	4E-17S	B6
Pride Ct					
4500	RGMW	60008	2805	20W-14N	E3
Primrose Cir					
500	ROSL	60172	2912		D6
600	MTSN	60443	3506	5W-24S	B6
Primrose Ct					
-	BRLT	60103	2909		D2
15300	ODPK	60462	3346	9W-18S	D7
20500	DRPK	60010	2751	23W-20N	E1
Primrose Dr					
10	SjnT	46311	3598		C6
Primrose Ln					
-	BRLT	60103	2909		C2
600	MTSN	60443	3506	5W-24S	B6
600	SMBG	60194	2858	26W-11N	A4
1500	GNVW	60025	2810	9W-14N	C5
9000	HYHL	60457	3209	11W-9S	E3
15100	ODPK	60462	3346	9W-18S	D6
15100	OrlT	60462	3346	9W-18S	D6
S Primrose Ln					
16400	LKPT	60441	3342	20W-18S	B7
Prince Dr					
1200	SHLD	60419	3351	1E-18S	B6
1200	SHLD	60473	3351	1E-18S	B6
16200	SHLD	60473	3429	1E-19S	B3
Prince St					
2500	NHBK	60062	2809	10W-15N	E1
Prince Charles Ct					
800	SMBG	60195	2858	24W-12N	D1
Prince Charles Ln					
800	HFET	60195	2858	24W-12N	D1
800	SMBG	60195	2858	24W-12N	D1
Prince Edward Cir					
600	SMBG	60193	2913		C1
Prince Edward Dr					
600	EGVV	60007	2913		C1
600	SMBG	60193	2913		C1
Princess Av					
10400	CHRG	60415	3275	7W-12S	B2
11000	CHRG	60482	3275	7W-12S	B3
11000	WRTH	60482	3275	7W-12S	B3
Princess Ct					
10	WSTR	60154	3086		E3
S Princess Ln					
25900	CteT	60417	3685	1W-31S	B5
Princess Elizabeth Ct					
17600	TYPK	60477	3424	11W-21S	A6
Princeton Av					
100	BNHL	60010	2750	25W-17N	E4
100	BrnT	60010	2750	25W-17N	E4
200	BrnT	60010	2751	25W-17N	A4
600	BRTN	60010	2751	25W-17N	A4
800	MTSN	60443	3505	7W-25S	E7
2600	EVTN	60201	2812	4W-13N	B7
14600	DLTN	60419	3350	0W-17S	B5
14600	RVDL	60827	3350	0W-17S	B5
16100	TYPK	60477	3424	9W-19S	C2
N Princeton Av					
800	ANHT	60004	2806	18W-14N	D3
800	ANHT	60005	2806	18W-14N	D3
S Princeton Av					
100	ITSC	60143	2914		D7
200	ANHT	60005	2806	18W-13N	D6
500	ADSN	60143	2914		D7
1300	ANHT	60005	2860	18W-12N	D1
2100	CHCG	60616	3092	0W-1S	B1
3500	CHCG	60609	3092	0W-3S	B5
4700	CHCG	60609	3152	0W-6S	B3
5500	CHCG	60621	3152	0W-6S	B4
9100	CHCG	60620	3214	0W-10S	B5
9500	CHCG	60628	3214	0W-11S	B6
10300	CHCG	60628	3278	0W-12S	B1
Princeton Cir					
900	HRPK	60133	2911		E1
900	HRPK	60133	2912		A1

Block	City	ZIP	Map#	CGS	Grid
Princeton Ct					
800	EMHT	60126	3028		B5
1500	SMBG	60193	2912		B1
4000	SMWD	60107	2911		A1
S Princeton Ct					
10	ANHT	60005	2806	18W-13N	D5
Princeton Dr					
1100	BRLT	60103	2910		C7
Princeton Ln					
100	GNVW	60025	2810	10W-15N	B2
400	DRFD	60015	2756	11W-20N	D1
1300	SMBG	60193	2912		B1
17700	CCHL	60429	3426	4W-21S	E6
17700	CCHL	60478	3426	4W-21S	E6
17700	HLCT	60429	3426	4W-21S	E6
Princeton Pl					
1200	WLMT	60091	2812	5W-14N	A4
Princeton Rd					
10	HNDL	60521	3146		C1
1600	FSMR	60422	3507	2W-23S	D4
1700	BlmT	60422	3507	2W-23S	D4
1700	CHHT	60422	3507	2W-23S	D4
Princeton St					
10	DSPN	60016	2862	14W-12N	C1
100	HFET	60194	2858	24W-10N	D5
E Princeton St					
500	PLTN	60074	2753	20W-17N	A5
Princeton Cir Dr					
-	HRPK	60133	2912		A3
Principle Ln					
-	MTSN	60443	3505	7W-24S	D6
W Prindiville St					
2700	CHCG	60647	2977	2W-3N	C5
N Prindle Av					
10	ANHT	60004	2807	16W-14N	D5
2200	ANHT	60004	2754	16W-16N	C7
2600	WLNG	60004	2754	16W-16N	D6
2600	WLNG	60090	2754	16W-16N	D6
S Prindle Av					
10	ANHT	60004	2807	16W-13N	D6
E Priscilla Ln					
2400	CteT	60417	3597	3E-28S	E7
2500	CteT	60417	3598	3E-28S	A7
Pristine Pl					
16100	ODHL	60477	3424	11W-19S	A2
Private Dr					
-	MaiT	60016	2863	12W-12N	C1
8700	ODPK	60462	3346	10W-16S	A4
Private Rd					
800	WNKA	60093	2759	5W-16N	A7
W Proctor Cir					
3900	ANHT	60004	2754	18W-18N	A3
W Proesel Av					
6400	CHCG	60659	2920	4W-8N	B3
6400	LNWD	60712	2920	4W-8N	C2
Progress Av					
600	MNSR	46321	3510		D3
Promethian Wy					
20600	OMFD	60461	3507	3W-24S	B6
S Promontory Dr					
6400	CHCG	60649	3153	2E-7S	C5
Prospect Av					
200	WDDL	60191	2914		D7
300	WDDL	60143	2914		D7
600	BRTN	60010	2750	25W-20N	E1
700	WNKA	60093	2812	5W-16N	B1
800	WLSP	60480	3209	12W-9S	C4
800	WNKA	60093	2759	5W-16N	A7
1200	DSPN	60018	2862	13W-9N	E7
1600	DSPN	60018	2863	12W-9N	A7
2100	EVTN	60201	2866	4W-12N	C1
2500	EVTN	60201	2812	4W-12N	C7
4300	WNSP	60558	3086		D7
4300	WNSP	60558	3146		D1
5800	BKLY	60163	3028		C5
5800	HLSD	60162	3028		C5
11300	ITSC	60143	2914		E6
E Prospect Av					
-	DSPN	60016	2862	15W-12N	B1
10	MPPT	60056	2808	14W-13N	B5
100	MPPT	60056	2862	15W-12N	A1
N Prospect Av					
10	ITSC	60143	2914		D5
100	BRLT	60103	2911		A2
100	PKRG	60068	2864	10W-9N	B7
300	AddT	60143	2914		D5
900	NLES	60068	2864	10W-9N	B7
900	NLES	60714	2864	10W-9N	B7
900	PKRG	60714	2864	10W-9N	B7
4800	NRDG	60706	2918	10W-6N	B7
5500	CHCG	60631	2918	10W-7N	A5
5500	CHCG	60656	2918	10W-6N	A5
5500	LydT	60631	2918	10W-6N	A5
5500	MaiT	60631	2918	10W-7N	A5
N Prospect Av CO-10					
10	ITSC	60143	2914		D5
300	AddT	60143	2914		D5
S Prospect Av					
10	PKRG	60068	2918	10W-8N	A1
100	BRLT	60103	2911		A5
100	ITSC	60143	2914		D7
200	WDDL	60143	2914		D7
200	WDDL	60191	2914		D7
700	WynT	60103	2911		A4
1800	CHCG	60631	2918	10W-7N	A4
1800	PKRG	60631	2918	10W-7N	A4
9500	CHCG	60620	3213	2W-11S	D6
9500	CHCG	60643	3213	2W-11S	D6
10200	CHCG	60643	3277	2W-12S	D2
S Prospect Av CO-10					
100	ITSC	60143	2914		D7
200	WDDL	60143	2914		D7
200	WDDL	60191	2914		D7
W Prospect Av					
10	MPPT	60056	2808	15W-12N	A7
1000	MPPT	60056	2807	16W-13N	D6
Prospect Blvd					
800	ELGN	60120	2855		A2
Prospect Ct					
10	PTHT	60070	2807	15W-15N	E3
W Prospect Ct					
8000	NLES	60714	2864	10W-10N	B6
Prospect Dr					
-	BRTN	60010	2751	24W-18N	C2
10	PTHT	60070	2755	15W-16N	A6
10	WLNG	60090	2755	15W-16N	A6
100	PltT	60010	2751	24W-18N	C2
Prospect Ln					
1000	DSPN	60018	2862	13W-9N	E6
Prospect Pl					
11100	ODPK	60467	3423	13W-21S	A6
S Prospect Sq					
9100	CHCG	60620	3213	2W-10S	C5
Prospect St					
400	ELGN	60120	2855		A2

STREET Block	City	ZIP	Map#	CGS	Grid
W Randolph St					
100	CHCG	60606	3034	0W-0N	B4
400	CHCG	60661	3034	0W-0N	A4
800	CHCG	60607	3033	1W-0N	E4
2000	CHCG	60612	3033	2W-0N	B4
3100	CHCG	60612	3032	3W-0N	E3
E Randville Dr					
1100	PLTN	60074	2753	19W-17N	B5
Raneys Ln					
14300	ODPK	60462	3345	12W-17S	C4
Ranger Dr					
500	CHHT	60411	3507	2W-24S	C6
Raoul Wallenberg Dr					
-	SKOK	60077	2811	6W-12N	C7
Raphael Av					
400	BFGV	60089	2754	15W-20N	E1
400	VrnT	60069	2754	15W-20N	E1
400	VrnT	60089	2754	15W-20N	E1
N Raphael Av					
20500	BFGV	60089	2754	15W-20N	E1
20500	VrnT	60069	2754	15W-20N	E1
20500	VrnT	60089	2754	15W-20N	E1
Raphael St					
13100	LMNT	60439	3343	18W-15S	A2
W Rascher Av					
2000	CHCG	60640	2921	2W-6N	B5
2500	CHCG	60625	2921	3W-6N	A5
2600	CHCG	60625	2920	3W-6N	E5
6200	CHCG	60630	2919	7W-6N	A5
6600	CHCG	60656	2919	8W-6N	A5
7200	CHCG	60656	2918	9W-6N	D5
7900	NpkT	60656	2918	9W-6N	B5
8000	LydT	60656	2918	10W-6N	B5
W Rathfarn Dr					
14400	HMGN	60441	3343	18W-17S	B6
S Rathje Rd					
200	PTON	60468	3860	10W-37S	D3
32300	PtnT	60468	3860	10W-39S	D7
Raupp Blvd					
10	BFGV	60089	2754	17W-18N	C3
Raven Ct					
-	LYWD	60411	3509	2E-23S	D3
Raven Dr					
5500	MTSN	60443	3505	6W-24S	E5
Raven Ln					
-	LYWD	60411	3509	2E-23S	D3
3800	RGMW	60008	2806	19W-13N	C7
W Raven Ln					
1000	PLTN	60067	2805	22W-15N	B2
W Raven St					
6200	CHCG	60646	2919	7W-7N	A3
6300	CHCG	60631	2919	7W-7N	A3
6600	CHCG	60631	2918	8W-7N	E3
Ravengate Ct					
11100	ODPK	60467	3422	14W-19S	E2
Ravenscraig Ln					
10	IVNS	60067	2752	22W-17N	B4
10	IVNS	60067	2805	22W-15N	A1
N Ravenswood Av					
3400	CHCG	60657	2977	2W-4N	C3
3600	CHCG	60613	2977	2W-5N	C1
4400	CHCG	60613	2921	2W-5N	C7
4400	CHCG	60640	2921	2W-5N	C7
5500	CHCG	60660	2921	2W-6N	C4
6300	CHCG	60626	2921	2W-7N	C3
E Ravine Av					
200	WLSP	60480	3209	12W-9S	C3
W Ravine Av					
200	WLSP	60480	3209	12W-9S	C3
Ravine Dr					
13000	LMNT	60439	3342	19W-15S	E1
Ravine Ln					
1600	CPVL	60110	2748		C7
1600	CPVL	60110	2801		C1
Ravine Rd					
100	HNDL	60521	3086		B7
600	CPVL	60110	2748		B7
600	EDND	60118	2748		B7
600	EDND	60118	2801		B1
900	WNKA	60093	2759	5W-16N	A7
Ravine Wy					
2300	GNVW	60025	2810	9W-15N	D2
2500	NHBK	60062	2810	9W-15N	D2
Ravine Glade St					
100	GLNC	60022	2758	5W-17N	E5
W Ravine Hills Ct					
1200	PLTN	60067	2805	22W-14N	B4
S Ravinia Av					
-	ODPK	60467	3423	12W-18S	D1
14200	ODPK	60462	3345	12W-18S	D7
15400	ODPK	60462	3423	12W-18S	D1
Ravinia Ct					
9700	ODPK	60462	3345	12W-17S	D4
Ravinia Dr					
6500	TYPK	60477	3425	8W-20S	B4
Ravinia Ln					
9700	ODPK	60462	3345	12W-17S	D4
Ravinia Pl					
100	ODPK	60462	3345	12W-18S	D6
Ravinia Glen Pl					
700	HDPK	60035	2758	7W-20N	B2
Ravinia Park Rd					
200	HDPK	60035	2758	7W-20N	B2
Ravisloe Ln					
-	HMWD	60430	3427	3W-21S	B7
Ravisloe Ter					
17800	CCHL	60478	3426	5W-21S	C7
Rawls Rd					
10	DSPN	60018	2862	14W-10N	C6
N Raye Dr					
200	CHHT	60411	3507	1W-23S	E3
200	CHHT	60411	3508	1W-23S	A4
W Raye Dr					
100	CHHT	60411	3507	1W-23S	E3
Raymond Av					
100	BRTN	60010	2750	26W-20N	E2
1100	BKFD	60513	3087	11W-3S	D4
1100	LGPK	60525	3087	11W-3S	D4
1500	PvsT	60525	3087	11W-2S	D4
4500	BKFD	60513	3147	11W-4S	D1
4600	MCCK	60513	3147	11W-4S	D1
4600	MCCK	60525	3147	11W-4S	D1
9200	OKLN	60453	3211	6W-10S	E6
Raymond Ct					
500	SMBG	60193	2859	22W-9N	B7
Raymond Dr					
1800	NHBK	60062	2810	9W-16N	B1
4200	HLSD	60162	3028		E5
4200	HLSD	60162	3029	13W-0S	A5
23700	CteT	60417	3597	2E-28S	E7
Raymond Rd					
-	BFGV	60069	2754	16W-20N	D1
-	BFGV	60089	2754	16W-20N	D1
-	VrnT	60069	2754	16W-20N	D1

STREET Block	City	ZIP	Map#	CGS	Grid
Raymond St					
200	ELGN	60120	2855		A5
900	ElgT	60120	2855		A7
900	ElgT	60177	2855		A7
1100	SEGN	60177	2855		A7
1200	SEGN	60120	2855		A7
1200	SEGN	60120	2909		A1
1200	SEGN	60177	2909		A1
Rayson Ln					
8800	TYPK	60477	3424	11W-21S	A6
Reading Cir					
1600	CPVL	60110	2748		C5
W Reading Ct					
100	PLTN	60067	2805	21W-14N	D3
Reading Dr					
-	BRLT	60103	2910		C4
-	WynT	60103	2910		C4
Reba Ct					
10	MNGV	60053	2865	7W-10N	B5
Reba Pl					
700	EVTN	60202	2867	2W-10N	B5
Reba St					
5400	SKOK	60077	2865	6W-10N	B5
5700	MNGV	60053	2865	7W-10N	C5
Reba Ln Rd					
1100	ELGN	60123	2801		A7
Rebecca Av					
-	ELGN	60120	2855		D7
Rebecca Ct					
900	SMBG	60193	2912		D1
Rebecca Dr					
10	BNHL	60010	2802	28W-15N	D2
1300	HFET	60194	2858	25W-12N	A2
Rebecca Ln					
2400	GNVW	60025	2810	10W-15N	A2
N Rebecca St					
10	GNWD	60425	3508	0E-22S	D2
S Rebecca St					
10	GNWD	60425	3508	0E-22S	D2
N Recreation Dr					
3400	CHCG	60613	2978	0W-4N	A2
N Recreation Dr SR-19					
-	CHCG	60613	2978	0W-5N	A1
Recreation Rd					
-	ELGN	60123	2801		A7
Red Dr					
13100	LMNT	60439	3343	17W-15S	C1
S Red Ln					
26700	CteT	60417	3687	4E-32S	C7
Red Barn Ln					
100	BRTN	60010	2751	24W-18N	B2
100	NHFD	60093	2811	7W-15N	A3
Red Barn Rd					
10	MTSN	60443	3505	7W-24S	C4
10	MTSN	60477	3505	7W-23S	C4
Redbud Av					
1000	BCHR	60401	3864	0W-36S	D1
Red Bud Ct					
700	BRLT	60103	2910		D1
Redbud Ln					
800	WLMT	60091	2811	5W-13N	E5
800	WLMT	60091	2812	5W-13N	A5
1400	GNVW	60025	2810	8W-14N	D5
Red Bud Pl					
200	BFGV	60089	2754	16W-20N	D1
Redbud Rd					
10	RGMW	60008	2806	19W-14N	C3
Redcastle Dr					
9000	FftT	60448	3504	11W-23S	A4
9000	TYPK	60448	3504	11W-23S	A4
Red Cedar Dr					
100	SMWD	60107	2857	27W-10N	C6
Red Cedar Tr					
15500	HMGN	60441	3344	15W-18S	C7
Red Coach Ln					
200	NHBK	60062	2757	9W-18N	C3
E Redcoat Dr					
13100	LMNT	60439	3343	16W-15S	E2
N Redcoat Dr					
13300	LMNT	60439	3343	16W-15S	D2
S Redcoat Dr					
13500	LMNT	60439	3343	16W-15S	E2
W Redcoat Dr					
13300	LMNT	60439	3343	16W-15S	D2
Redeker Rd					
1200	DSPN	60016	2862	13W-12N	E2
1300	DSPN	60016	2863	13W-11N	A2
N Redfield Ct					
200	PKRG	60068	2863	11W-9N	D7
S Redfield Ct					
300	PKRG	60068	2917	11W-8N	D1
Redfield Dr					
-	CHCG	60629	3150	4W-7S	D6
-	CHCG	60629	3151	3W-7S	A7
Redford Ln					
5400	HRPK	60133	2911		C6
5500	BRLT	60103	2911		C6
Red Fox Ct					
13200	LMNT	60439	3343	16W-15S	E2
Red Fox Ln					
100	EGVV	60007	2859	22W-9N	C6
Red Haw Rd					
10	NHBK	60062	2757	9W-17N	D4
10	RGMW	60008	2806	19W-14N	C4
Red Hill Ln					
10	SBTN	60010	2804	25W-13N	A5
Reding Cir					
-	DSPN	60016	2863	12W-12N	C2
9600	MaiT	60016	2863	12W-12N	C2
Red Maple Ln					
600	ROSL	60172	2912		D6
Redmond Ct					
600	BNVL	60106	2972		B3
Red Oak Ct					
10	BFGV	60089	2754	17W-18N	B3
700	BRLT	60103	2910		D1
1200	ELGN	60120	2855		D4
W Red Oak Ct					
12800	HMGN	60441	3422	16W-19S	A2
Red Oak Dr					
700	BRLT	60103	2910		D1
800	BRLT	60103	2856	29W-9N	D7
900	SMWD	60107	2856	29W-9N	D7
2400	DYR	46311	3598		D3
5700	HFET	60120	2856	31W-12N	A2
Red Oak Ln					
10	HDPK	60035	2757	9W-20N	C1
10	NHBK	60062	2757	9W-18N	C2
700	UYPK	60466	3684	3W-29S	B2
8200	ODPK	60462	3346	10W-16S	B2
E Red Oak Ln					
3200	CteT	60417	3687	4E-32S	B7
Red Oak Rd					
200	NfdT	60062	2757	9W-18N	B3
200	NHBK	60062	2757	9W-18N	B3

STREET Block	City	ZIP	Map#	CGS	Grid
Red Oak St					
100	BNVL	60106	2972		A3
Redondo Ln					
7800	ODPK	60462	3346	9W-16S	C3
7800	OrlT	60462	3346	9W-16S	D3
Red Ridge Cir					
10	SBTN	60010	2803	27W-15N	A2
Redwing Ct					
3900	RGMW	60008	2806	20W-13N	B6
Redwing Dr					
300	VrnT	60015	2755	14W-20N	B1
Redwing Ln					
300	VrnT	60015	2755	14W-20N	B1
W Redwing Pl					
23300	ElaT	60010	2751	23W-20N	E1
Redwing St					
-	LYWD	60411	3509	2E-23S	D3
Redwood Av					
200	EGVV	60007	2861	17W-9N	B7
1600	HRPK	60133	2911		D2
20100	LYWD	60411	3510	3E-23S	A4
S Redwood Av					
1500	EGvT	60005	2861	16W-11N	D4
1500	MPPT	60056	2861	16W-11N	D4
Redwood Ct					
10	SMWD	60107	2857	27W-10N	C6
3100	FSMR	60422	3507	3W-22S	A1
9300	MaiT	60016	2863	11W-12N	D1
17000	ODHL	60477	3424	11W-20S	A4
W Redwood Ct					
15300	LKPT	60441	3342	20W-18S	B7
Redwood Dr					
1000	ALGN	60102	2748		C1
1100	ALGN	60010	2748		C1
1100	BNHL	60010	2748		C1
13800	ODPK	60462	3346	10W-16S	B3
22700	RNPK	60471	3594	6W-27S	B5
N Redwood Dr					
4400	CHCG	60634	2974	10W-5N	B1
4400	CHCG	60706	2974	10W-5N	B1
4400	NRDG	60706	2974	10W-5N	B1
4800	NRDG	60706	2918	10W-6N	B7
5400	CHCG	60656	2918	10W-6N	B5
5400	LydT	60656	2918	10W-6N	B5
5600	CHCG	60631	2918	10W-7N	B5
5600	MaiT	60631	2918	10W-7N	B5
5600	MaiT	60656	2918	10W-7N	B5
S Redwood Dr					
1400	MPPT	60056	2861	16W-11N	D3
Redwood Ln					
100	BRTN	60010	2751	24W-20N	D2
400	SMBG	60193	2858	24W-9N	E7
600	FSMR	60422	3507	3W-22S	A1
600	GLNC	60022	2758	6W-16N	C6
600	HMWD	60422	3507	3W-22S	A1
600	HMWD	60430	3507	3W-22S	A1
700	GNVW	60025	2811	7W-13N	B7
800	BRLT	60103	2911		A5
1700	CPVL	60110	2748		C5
1900	NHBK	60062	2757	10W-17N	B4
17500	TYPK	60477	3424	11W-21S	A5
E Redwood Ln					
600	ANHT	60004	2807	17W-16N	B1
Redwood St					
10	CPVL	60110	2748		C5
Redwood Tr					
10	WLNG	60090	2754	15W-17N	E4
Reed St					
600	BCHR	60401	3864	0W-36S	B2
Reedham Pass					
100	SMBG	60194	2858	25W-10N	B5
Reef Ct					
800	WLNG	60090	2755	15W-16N	A6
Reef Rd					
700	LKPT	60441	3342	21W-18S	A7
N Reef Rd					
600	LKPT	60441	3342	21W-18S	A7
Rees Rd					
100	BRLT	60120	2910		A4
Reese Av					
500	EDND	60118	2801		B2
2600	EVTN	60201	2812	4W-13N	D7
2700	EVTN	60091	2812	4W-13N	D7
2700	WLMT	60091	2812	4W-13N	D7
2700	WLMT	60201	2812	4W-13N	D7
E Reese St					
900	HMND	46394	3280		E4
E Reeves Ct					
9600	FNPK	60131	2973	12W-4N	C3
W Reeves Ct					
9700	FNPK	60131	2973	12W-4N	C3
S Reeves Rd					
13900	RBBN	60472	3348	4W-16S	E3
Regal Ct					
200	ROSL	60172	2912		C4
1900	SMBG	60194	2858	25W-11N	A4
4900	CTWD	60445	3348	6W-16S	A2
Regalia Ct					
500	IVNS	60010	2751	24W-16N	C6
Regalia Dr					
400	HFET	60010	2751	24W-16N	C7
400	IVNS	60010	2751	24W-16N	C7
Regan Blvd					
300	BNHL	60010	2748		D4
Regan Ct					
1500	HFET	60195	2804	24W-15N	B2
Regan Dr					
500	EDND	60118	2801		B3
Regatta Pt					
300	SMBG	60194	2859	22W-11N	C4
Regency Ct					
10	SMWD	60107	2856	29W-9N	E7
200	BRLT	60103	2910		D3
1100	SMBG	60193	2912		C2
1300	ROSL	60172	2912		B5
1400	CTCY	60409	3429	2E-19S	D3
1700	MPPT	60056	2808	13W-14N	D4
8300	WLSP	60480	3208		E3
S Regency Ct E					
10	ANHT	60004	2807	16W-14N	E5
S Regency Ct W					
10	ANHT	60004	2807	16W-14N	D5
Regency Dr					
100	BRLT	60103	2910		D3
600	DSPN	60016	2808	14W-12N	D7
1100	SMBG	60193	2912		C2
4300	GNVW	60025	2809	11W-13N	C7
4300	NfdT	60025	2809	11W-13N	C7
11000	WSTR	60154	3086		E4
22400	RNPK	60471	3594	4W-27S	D4
N Regency Dr E					
10	ANHT	60004	2807	16W-14N	E5
N Regency Dr W					
10	ANHT	60004	2807	16W-14N	D5

STREET Block	City	ZIP	Map#	CGS	Grid
S Regency Dr E					
10	ANHT	60004	2807	16W-13N	D5
10	ANHT	60056	2807	16W-14N	E5
10	MPPT	60056	2807	16W-14N	E5
S Regency Dr W					
10	ANHT	60004	2807	16W-13N	D5
10	MPPT	60056	2807	16W-14N	D5
Regent Cir					
10	SMBG	60193	2859	23W-10N	B5
Regent Ct					
10	BRRG	60527	3208		B5
Regent Ct E					
10	BFGV	60089	2754	17W-18N	A3
Regent Ct W					
10	BFGV	60089	2754	17W-18N	A3
Regent Dr					
200	BFGV	60089	2754	17W-18N	A3
300	WLNG	60090	2755	14W-18N	C3
1300	NfdT	60062	2756	12W-17N	C5
1300	NHBK	60062	2756	12W-17N	C6
3400	HFET	60067	2804	23W-14N	E4
15100	ODPK	60462	3345	11W-18S	E7
Regent Ln					
600	PTHT	60070	2808	14W-14N	B3
1400	FDHT	60411	3509	1E-25S	B6
Regent Rd					
500	UYPK	60466	3684	3W-30S	C3
Regent St					
400	ELGN	60120	2855		A5
Regent Wood Rd					
-	GNVW	60025	2810	8W-15N	E3
10	NHFD	60093	2810	8W-15N	E3
10	NHFD	60093	2811	7W-15N	A3
S Regina Ln					
12600	PlsT	60464	3274	9W-14S	D7
12600	PSPK	60464	3274	9W-14S	D7
N Regis Ct					
700	PLTN	60067	2752	21W-16N	C6
700	PltT	60067	2752	21W-16N	C6
Reichert Av					
1700	SLVL	60411	3597	2E-27S	C4
E Reichert Dr					
3200	CteT	60417	3687	4E-31S	B6
3200	HnrT	46311	3687	4E-31S	B5
Reid St					
1300	WNSP	60558	3086		D7
S Reilly Ter					
7700	CHCG	60652	3212	4W-8S	D2
Rembrandt Ct					
5800	HRPK	60133	2911		E4
W Remington Cir					
-	SMBG	60173	2859	23W-12N	A2
10	SMBG	60195	2859	23W-12N	A2
Remington Dr					
-	BNHL	60010	2749	30W-17N	A6
-	BrnT	60010	2749	30W-17N	A6
200	BRLT	60103	2909		C4
W Remington Ln					
10	SMBG	60195	2859	23W-12N	A2
Remington Rd					
10	SMBG	60173	2859	22W-12N	C2
10	SMBG	60195	2859	23W-12N	A2
Renaissance Dr					
1400	PKRG	60068	2863	12W-10N	C5
Rene Ct					
1000	PKRG	60068	2864	10W-10N	A6
Renee Ter					
200	WLNG	60090	2755	15W-17N	A5
Renmore Rd					
14400	HMGN	60441	3343	18W-17S	B6
Rennes Ct					
3000	NHBK	60062	2756	11W-17N	D6
Rennie Smith Dr					
3200	SCHT	60411	3596	0W-27S	C4
3200	SCHT	60475	3596	0W-27S	C4
Repton Rd					
10	RVSD	60546	3088	9W-2S	C3
Republic Ct					
600	SMBG	60193	2859	23W-9N	A7
E Reseda Pkwy					
100	PLTN	60067	2752	20W-17N	E5
200	PLTN	60067	2753	20W-17N	A5
300	PLTN	60074	2753	20W-17N	A5
N Reserve Av					
4400	CHCG	60656	2917	10W-5N	E7
4400	CHCG	60656	2973	11W-5N	E1
Reserve Dr					
8900	LynT	60480	3208		C5
8900	WLSP	60480	3208		C5
Reston Ct					
100	ROSL	60172	2912		E5
N Reta Av					
3500	CHCG	60613	2977	1W-4N	E3
3500	CHCG	60657	2977	1W-4N	E3
N Reuter Dr					
10	ANHT	60005	2806	18W-14N	D4
S Reuter Dr					
10	ANHT	60005	2806	18W-13N	D6
Reuter St					
2600	FNPK	60131	2973	12W-3N	C5
Revell Ct					
8000	ODPK	60462	3346	10W-17S	C4
Revere Cir					
1500	SMBG	60193	2858	25W-10N	B6
Revere Ct					
1200	CRTE	60417	3685	1W-29S	A1
15700	OKFT	60452	3347	7W-18S	D7
15700	OKFT	60452	3425	7W-18S	D1
Revere Dr					
10	HDPK	60035	2757	8W-18N	D2
10	NHBK	60062	2757	8W-18N	D2
10	SBTN	60010	2803	27W-14N	B4
Revere Ln					
1800	EGVV	60007	2859	22W-9N	C7
W Revere Ln					
500	PLTN	60067	2805	21W-14N	C3
Revere Rd					
600	MaiT	60025	2809	10W-13N	E7
800	NfdT	60025	2809	10W-13N	E6
900	GNVW	60025	2809	10W-13N	E6
Revere St					
1900	CHHT	60411	3595	2W-26S	D2
Reverend Edw H Baseheart Dr					
1600	CHCG	60640	2921	2W-6N	C5
Reverend Morrison Blvd					
100	EGVV	60007	2914		E1
Reverend Rogers Dr					
5500	BRBK	60459	3211	6W-9S	D2
Rexford Rd					
3800	CTWD	60445	3348	4W-17S	C4
3800	MDLN	60445	3348	4W-17S	C4
3800	RBBN	60445	3348	4W-17S	C4
3800	RBBN	60472	3348	4W-17S	C4
Rexford St					
13300	BLID	60406	3349	2W-15S	B2

STREET Block	City	ZIP	Map#	CGS	Grid
S Rexford St					
12200	ALSP	60803	3276	5W-14S	A6
E Reynolds Dr					
1300	PLTN	60074	2753	19W-16N	C7
N Reynolds Dr					
300	PLTN	60074	2753	19W-16N	D7
Reynolds Ln					
15500	OKFT	60452	3347	7W-18S	D7
15700	OKFT	60452	3425	7W-18S	D1
Rhema Dr					
10	BlmT	60430	3507	1W-23S	E3
10	CHHT	60411	3507	1W-23S	E3
Rhiannon Ct					
4800	PLTN	60067	2805	21W-14N	E4
4800	RGMW	60067	2805	21W-14N	E4
Rhode Av					
5700	HMND	46320	3352		E7
6000	HMND	46320	3430		E1
6800	HMND	46324	3430		E3
Rhode Ct					
7900	SjnT	46311	3598		E5
Rhode Island Ct					
17600	ODPK	60467	3423	13W-21S	A6
Rhodes Av					
2700	LydT	60164	2972		C5
2700	NHLK	60164	2972		C5
3000	FNPK	60131	2972		C4
3000	LydT	60131	2972		C5
N Rhodes Av					
2400	RVGV	60171	2973	11W-3N	E6
S Rhodes Av					
3500	CHCG	60616	3092	0E-3S	D5
3500	CHCG	60653	3092	0E-3S	D5
6000	CHCG	60637	3152	0E-7S	D6
7000	CHCG	60619	3152	0E-7S	D6
7500	CHCG	60619	3214	0E-9S	D2
10000	CHCG	60628	3214	0E-11S	D7
10300	CHCG	60628	3278	0E-12S	D2
13100	CHCG	60827	3278	0E-15S	E7
13100	CHCG	60827	3350	0E-15S	D1
19100	BlmT	60425	3508	0E-23S	E2
19100	GNWD	60425	3508	0E-23S	E3
Ribbon Ct					
5100	MONE	60449	3683	6W-31S	A6
Rice Av					
-	MLPK	60160	3029	10W-1N	E3
-	MYWD	60153	3029	10W-1N	E3
-	MYWD	60153	3030	10W-1N	A3
1000	BLWD	60104	3029	12W-0S	B6
Rice St					
600	HDPK	60035	2758	7W-20N	B1
900	MLPK	60160	3029	11W-1N	D3
W Rice St					
-	CHCG	60622	3032	3W-1N	E2
1800	CHCG	60622	3033	2W-1N	C2
3300	CHCG	60651	3032	4W-1N	D2
5800	CHCG	60651	3031	7W-1N	C3
5900	OKPK	60302	3031	7W-1N	B3
Rich Ct					
10	PKFT	60466	3595	4W-27S	A3
Rich Ln					
600	BRLT	60103	2909		E2
Rich Rd					
200	PKFT	60466	3595	3W-27S	A3
Richard Av					
-	RVGV	60171	2973	11W-3N	D5
1000	BKLY	60163	3028		C3
4300	OKFT	60452	3426	5W-19S	B2
9200	FNPK	60131	2973	11W-3N	D5
N Richard Av					
100	EMHT	60126	3028		B2
S Richard Av					
11900	PSHT	60463	3274	9W-14S	D6
Richard Ln					
700	EGvT	60007	2861	16W-9N	D7
700	EGvT	60007	2915		D1
700	EGVV	60007	2915		D1
Richard Rd					
800	DYR	46311	3598		E2
W Richard St					
-	FNPK	60131	2973	11W-3N	D5
8700	RVGV	60171	2973	11W-3N	E5
Richards Ct					
1700	FSMR	60422	3507	2W-23S	D4
8300	TYPK	60477	3424	10W-20S	C3
Richards Dr					
16500	TYPK	60477	3424	10W-20S	C4
N Richards Dr					
100	PLTN	60074	2753	19W-16N	D7
100	PLTN	60074	2806	19W-16N	D1
S Richards Dr					
-	CHCG	60649	3153	2E-7S	C5
6400	CHCG	60637	3153	2E-7S	C5
Richards Rd					
7200	BGVW	60455	3210	9W-11S	E6
Richard S McClaughry Dr					
-	MNSR	46321	3510		D4
S Richardson Av					
13900	RBBN	60472	3348	4W-16S	E3
Richardson Dr					
300	DndT	60118	2801		A4
Richardson Ln					
7600	TYPK	60477	3504	9W-23S	D3
Richardson Rd					
-	EDND	60118	2801		B4
10	DndT	60118	2801		B4
Richert Ct					
300	ELGN	60120	2855		A5
Richert Rd					
200	WDDL	60191	2915		B5
Richmond Av					
10	LGPK	60525	3087	12W-3S	A6
15900	MKHM	60426	3427	3W-18S	A1
E Richmond Av					
1000	LGPK	60525	3087	12W-3S	C6
1100	BKFD	60513	3087	12W-3S	C6
S Richmond Av					
-	CHCG	60652	3213	3W-10S	A4
-	ENGN	60805	3213	3W-10S	A4
14500	POSN	60469	3349	3W-17S	A5
14900	BmnT	60426	3349	3W-17S	A5
Richmond Ct					
100	ROSL	60172	2912		E5
900	EGVV	60007	2913		D2
1000	DYR	46311	3510		C6
1900	SMBG	60194	2858	25W-11N	B3
4000	MTSN	60443	3594	5W-26S	D2
10600	PlsT	60462	3345	13W-15S	A2
Richmond Dr					
400	ROSL	60172	2912		E5
Richmond Ln					
1200	WLMT	60091	2812	4W-14N	D4
1300	KLWH	60043	2812	4W-14N	D4
1800	LGGV	60047	2753	18W-20N	D1
1800	VrnT	60047	2753	18W-20N	D1

Chicago & Cook County Street Index

STREET Block	City	ZIP	Map#	CGS	Grid
Richmond Rd					
-	KLWH	60043	2812	4W-14N	B4
21600	MTSN	60443	3594	5W-26S	D2
Richmond St					
10	PLTN	60067	2752	21W-16N	E7
200	EVTN	60202	2866	3W-9N	E6
13300	RBBN	60406	3349	3W-16S	A2
13300	WthT	60406	3349	3W-15S	A1
13400	BLID	60406	3349	3W-16S	A2
16700	HLCT	60426	3427	3W-20S	A3
16700	HLCT	60429	3427	3W-20S	A3
16700	MKHM	60426	3427	3W-20S	A3
16700	MKHM	60429	3427	3W-20S	A3
N Richmond St					
800	CHCG	60622	3032	3W-1N	E2
2000	CHCG	60647	2976	3W-2N	E6
3600	CHCG	60618	2976	3W-4N	E2
4400	CHCG	60618	2920	3W-5N	E7
4400	CHCG	60625	2920	3W-5N	E7
5900	CHCG	60659	2920	3W-7N	E3
6300	CHCG	60645	2920	3W-7N	E3
S Richmond St					
1100	CHCG	60612	3032	3W-0S	E7
1100	CHCG	60623	3032	3W-0S	E7
3500	CHCG	60623	3090	3W-3S	E5
4000	CHCG	60632	3090	3W-4S	E6
4700	CHCG	60632	3150	3W-5S	E1
7100	CHCG	60629	3150	3W-8S	E7
7700	CHCG	60652	3212	3W-8S	E1
7900	CHCG	60652	3213	3W-9S	A2
W Richmond St					
1300	ANHT	60004	2806	18W-16N	D1
1500	ANHT	60004	2753	18W-16N	D7
Richnee Ln					
3400	RGMW	60008	2805	20W-13N	E6
Richton Pl					
1000	RNPK	60471	3594	4W-26S	D3
Richton Rd					
10	CRTE	60417	3596	0W-28S	C7
100	CRTE	60475	3596	0W-28S	C7
300	STGR	60475	3596	0W-28S	C7
1700	CteT	60417	3595	2W-28S	E6
1700	CteT	60475	3595	2W-28S	D5
1700	STGR	60417	3595	2W-28S	E6
1700	STGR	60475	3595	2W-28S	E6
1900	BlmT	60466	3595	2W-28S	D6
1900	CteT	60466	3595	2W-28S	D5
21600	MTSN	60443	3594	4W-26S	D2
21800	RNPK	60471	3594	4W-26S	D3
E Richton Rd					
10	CRTE	60417	3596	0E-28S	D7
400	CRTE	60417	3597	1E-28S	A7
800	CteT	60417	3597	3E-28S	E7
2500	CteT	60417	3598	3E-29S	A7
W Richton Rd					
10	CRTE	60417	3596	1W-28S	B7
10	CteT	60417	3596	1W-28S	A6
10	CteT	60475	3596	1W-28S	A6
10	STGR	60417	3596	1W-28S	B7
10	STGR	60475	3596	1W-28S	A6
200	CteT	60417	3595	1W-28S	E6
200	CteT	60475	3595	1W-28S	E6
200	STGR	60475	3595	1W-28S	E6
300	STGR	60417	3595	1W-28S	E6
Richton Square Rd					
22300	RNPK	60471	3594	4W-27S	D5
22700	RchT	60471	3594	4W-27S	D4
22900	MonT	60466	3594	4W-27S	D5
Richwood Ter					
10	BlmT	60422	3507	2W-23S	E3
10	FSMR	60422	3507	2W-23S	D3
Rickerman Rd					
14400	HmrT	60441	3342	20W-17S	B5
Ridge Av					
-	WDDL	60191	2914		E3
100	CHCG	60645	2867	2W-9N	B6
100	EVTN	60202	2867	2W-9N	B6
100	WNKA	60093	2812	5W-15N	B3
500	EGvT	60007	2860	18W-9N	E7
500	EGvT	60007	2914		E1
500	EGVV	60007	2860	18W-9N	E7
500	EGVV	60007	2914		E1
1700	EVTN	60201	2867	2W-10N	B5
2400	EVTN	60201	2813	2W-13N	B7
5100	HLSD	60162	3028		C5
5800	BKLY	60163	3028		C5
12300	PSPK	60464	3274	11W-14S	A6
14300	ODPK	60462	3345	12W-17S	B5
E Ridge Av					
300	EMHT	60126	3028		B4
N Ridge Av					
10	ANHT	60005	2806	18W-14N	E5
10	MPPT	60056	2807	15W-13N	E7
600	ANHT	60004	2806	18W-14N	E3
2500	ANHT	60004	2754	18W-16N	A6
3200	ANHT	60004	2753	18W-17N	E4
4200	ANHT	60089	2753	18W-18N	E2
4200	VmT	60004	2753	18W-18N	E2
4200	VmT	60089	2753	18W-18N	E2
5600	CHCG	60640	2921	1W-7N	D4
5600	CHCG	60660	2921	1W-7N	D4
6300	CHCG	60626	2921	2W-7N	C2
N Ridge Av US-14					
5600	CHCG	60640	2921	1W-7N	D4
5600	CHCG	60660	2921	1W-7N	D4
S Ridge Av					
1000	ANHT	60005	2806	18W-12N	E7
1100	ANHT	60005	2860	18W-12N	E1
W Ridge Av					
10	PTHT	60070	2807	15W-15N	E1
10	PTHT	60070	2808	15W-15N	A1
N Ridge Blvd					
6400	CHCG	60626	2921	2W-8N	B2
6400	CHCG	60660	2921	2W-8N	C2
6500	CHCG	60645	2921	2W-8N	B2
7200	CHCG	60645	2867	2W-9N	B7
7500	EVTN	60202	2867	2W-9N	B6
Ridge Cir					
10	SMWD	60107	2857	28W-10N	B7
Ridge Cross					
5400	HRPK	60133	2911		D6
5500	BRLT	60133	2911		D6
Ridge Ct					
-	BRRG	60527	3208		A2
400	ROSL	60172	2913		B5
600	SMBG	60193	2859	22W-9N	B7
900	EGVV	60007	2914		E1
900	EVTN	60202	2867	2W-10N	A4
9000	WLSP	60527	3208		C5
N Ridge Ct					
10	SMWD	60107	2857	27W-11N	C4
W Ridge Ct					
500	ANHT	60004	2806	18W-15N	E2
Ridge Dr					
2100	GNVW	60025	2810	9W-15N	C3

STREET Block	City	ZIP	Map#	CGS	Grid
Ridge Dr					
2300	NfdT	60062	2809	11W-16N	D1
2300	NHBK	60062	2809	11W-15N	C1
6500	CHRG	60415	3275	8W-12S	A2
10000	CHCG	60614	2978	0W-2N	B6
10600	CHRG	60482	3275	8W-12S	A2
10600	WRTH	60482	3275	8W-12S	A2
N Ridge Dr					
1900	CHCG	60614	2978	0W-2N	B6
S Ridge Dr					
1600	ANHT	60005	2860	18W-12N	E2
Ridge Ln					
1100	WNSP	60558	3146		D4
1500	DSPN	60018	2862	15W-10N	A6
8800	ODHL	60477	3424	11W-19S	A2
Ridge Pl					
500	SMWD	60107	2857	27W-10N	B6
Ridge Rd					
-	TNTN	60476	3428	0W-21S	C6
10	AlqT	60010	2749	28W-20N	D2
10	BNHL	60010	2749	28W-20N	D2
10	HDPK	60035	2757	9W-20N	D1
10	LMNT	60439	3270		C6
10	LNSG	60438	3430	3E-21S	A6
10	MNSR	46321	3430		C6
10	NHBK	60062	2757	9W-20N	D1
100	EVTN	60201	2812	4W-13N	C7
100	WLMT	60091	2812	4W-13N	C7
300	EGVV	60007	2860	18W-9N	E7
300	KLWH	60043	2812	4W-13N	C6
300	KLWH	60091	2812	4W-14N	C5
300	WLMT	60043	2812	4W-14N	C5
400	EGvT	60007	2860	18W-9N	E7
400	ROSL	60172	2913		B5
400	TNTN	60430	3428	0W-21S	B6
500	HMWD	60430	3428	1W-21S	A7
500	NtrT	60043	2812	4W-13N	C6
500	NtrT	60091	2812	4W-14N	C4
500	NtrT	60093	2812	4W-13N	C6
1800	LNSG	60438	3429	3E-21S	E6
1800	ThtT	60438	3429	2E-21S	E6
2100	HMWD	60430	3427	2W-21S	C6
7900	OrlT	60462	3346	9W-16S	D3
E Ridge Rd					
300	ANHT	60004	2754	17W-16N	B7
Ridge Sq					
900	EGVV	60007	2914		E1
Ridge St					
800	HMND	46324	3430		E2
W Ridge St					
8700	RVGV	60171	2973	10W-3N	E6
Ridge Ter					
200	PKRG	60068	2918	10W-8N	B1
800	EVTN	60201	2813	2W-12N	B7
W Ridge Tr					
200	PLTN	60067	2752	21W-17N	D5
Ridge Connector Dr					
10000	CHCG	60614	2978	0W-2N	B6
Ridge Cove Dr					
-	CHRG	60482	3274	8W-12S	E2
Ridge Farm Rd					
10	BRRG	60527	3146		B5
Ridgefield Dr					
400	ROSL	60172	2912		D5
E Ridgefield Dr					
2400	CteT	60417	3687	3E-31S	A5
Ridgefield Ln					
-	TYPK	60477	3504	9W-23S	E3
10	WLBK	60527	3146		B6
900	WLNG	60090	2755	15W-16N	B6
Ridgeland Av					
-	CHCG	60613	2977	1W-5N	D1
-	CteT	60417	3774	1W-32S	B1
-	PSHT	60463	3347	7W-16S	B3
1200	BRWN	60402	3031	7W-1S	B7
1200	OKPK	60304	3031	7W-1S	B7
1500	BRWN	60402	3089	8W-4S	B7
3800	SKNY	60402	3089	8W-4S	B7
4200	StkT	60402	3089	7W-4S	B7
8700	BRBK	60459	3211	8W-11S	B7
8700	OKLN	60453	3211	8W-11S	B7
9400	CHRG	60453	3211	8W-10S	B6
9800	CHRG	60415	3211	8W-11S	B7
10200	CHRG	60415	3275	8W-12S	B2
10600	CHRG	60482	3275	8W-12S	B2
10600	WRTH	60415	3275	8W-12S	B2
10600	WRTH	60482	3275	8W-12S	B2
14500	BmnT	60445	3347	7W-16S	B3
14500	BmnT	60463	3347	7W-16S	B3
15000	BmnT	60452	3347	8W-18S	B7
15000	OKFT	60452	3347	8W-18S	B7
15700	BmnT	60477	3425	7W-18S	B1
15700	OKFT	60452	3425	7W-18S	B1
17200	TYPK	60477	3425	8W-21S	B5
18000	LNSG	60438	3429	2E-21S	C6
18000	ThtT	60438	3429	2E-21S	C6
18200	RchT	60477	3425	7W-21S	C7
18400	RchT	60477	3505	7W-22S	C1
18400	TYPK	60477	3505	7W-22S	C1
19300	MTSN	60477	3505	8W-23S	C4
21000	MTSN	60443	3505	8W-25S	C7
21000	MTSN	60443	3593	8W-25S	C1
21000	RchT	60443	3505	8W-25S	C7
21000	RchT	60443	3593	8W-26S	C1
22600	MonT	60449	3593	8W-26S	C3
N Ridgeland Av					
900	OKPK	60302	3031	7W-1N	A1
1200	CHCG	60302	3031	7W-2N	B1
1200	CHCG	60639	3031	7W-2N	B1
S Ridgeland Av					
100	OKPK	60302	3031	8W-0N	A4
400	OKPK	60304	3031	7W-0N	A5
1100	BRWN	60402	3031	7W-0S	A7
6700	CHCG	60649	3153	2E-7S	B6
7900	CHCG	60649	3215	2E-9S	B2
8200	CHCG	60617	3215	2E-9S	B2
10700	CHRG	60415	3275	7W-13S	B3
10700	CHRG	60482	3275	7W-13S	B3
10700	WRTH	60415	3275	7W-13S	B3
10700	WRTH	60482	3275	8W-14S	B7
11500	ALSP	60482	3275	8W-13S	B5
11600	WthT	60482	3275	8W-13S	B5
11700	ALSP	60803	3275	7W-13S	B5
11800	ALSP	60463	3275	7W-14S	B5
11800	PSHT	60463	3275	7W-14S	B5
11800	PSHT	60482	3275	7W-14S	B5
11800	WthT	60463	3275	7W-14S	B5
13000	PSHT	60463	3347	8W-15S	B1
13000	WthT	60463	3347	7W-15S	B1
13300	BmnT	60445	3347	8W-15S	B1
13300	BmnT	60463	3347	8W-15S	B1
20000	MTSN	60443	3505	8W-24S	C6
20800	RchT	60443	3505	8W-25S	C7
23100	MonT	60449	3593	8W-28S	C7
23100	MonT	60471	3593	8W-28S	C7

STREET Block	City	ZIP	Map#	CGS	Grid
S Ridgeland Av					
23100	RchT	60443	3593	8W-28S	C7
23100	RchT	60471	3593	8W-28S	C7
23900	MonT	60449	3682	8W-29S	C2
25700	MONE	60449	3682	8W-32S	C7
Ridgeland Ln					
10	CTSD	60525	3147	12W-7S	B6
4000	NfdT	60062	2756	12W-17N	A6
4000	NHBK	60062	2756	12W-17N	A6
S Ridgeland Rd					
29500	WIIT	60468	3861	8W-36S	C1
Ridgeland Manor Dr					
-	MTSN	60443	3505	7W-25S	D7
21100	MTSN	60443	3593	7W-25S	C1
Ridgelee Rd					
1600	HDPK	60035	2757	9W-20N	D2
Ridgemont Dr					
19500	TYPK	60477	3504	10W-23S	B4
Ridgemont Ln					
5700	CHRG	60415	3275	7W-12S	D2
Ridgemoor Ct					
300	WLBK	60527	3146		A6
Ridgemoor Dr					
300	WLBK	60527	3146		A6
Ridgemore Dr					
1900	BRLT	60103	2909		C3
Ridge Point Dr					
6800	BmnT	60452	3347	8W-18S	A6
6800	OKFT	60452	3347	8W-18S	A6
Ridgepoint Dr					
8100	BRRG	60527	3208		B3
Ridgeview Dr					
-	IVNS	60010	2804	25W-15N	A1
1000	IVNS	60010	2803	25W-15N	E1
1000	SBTN	60010	2803	25W-15N	E2
Ridgeway Av					
800	MNSR	46321	3430		E6
8700	SKOK	60076	2866	4W-10N	C4
9100	SKOK	60203	2866	4W-11N	C3
9500	EVTN	60201	2866	4W-11N	C2
14300	MDLN	60445	3348	4W-17S	D4
15400	MKHM	60426	3348	4W-18S	D7
15500	MKHM	60426	3426	4W-18S	D1
22000	RNPK	60471	3594	4W-26S	D3
23000	MonT	60466	3594	4W-27S	D5
N Ridgeway Av					
400	CHCG	60624	3032	4W-0N	C3
1300	CHCG	60651	3032	4W-1N	C1
1500	CHCG	60647	3032	4W-2N	C1
2300	CHCG	60647	2976	4W-3N	C5
3700	CHCG	60618	2976	4W-4N	C2
4300	CHCG	60625	2976	4W-5N	C1
4800	CHCG	60625	2920	4W-6N	C6
6200	CHCG	60659	2920	4W-7N	C3
6300	CHCG	60712	2920	4W-7N	C3
6300	LNWD	60712	2920	4W-7N	C3
7000	SKOK	60076	2920	4W-8N	C1
S Ridgeway Av					
1400	CHCG	60623	3032	4W-1S	C7
1500	CHCG	60623	3090	4W-2S	C3
4800	CHCG	60632	3150	4W-5S	C1
7100	CHCG	60629	3150	4W-8S	C7
7500	CHCG	60652	3212	4W-8S	D1
9100	CHCG	60805	3212	4W-10S	D5
9100	ENGN	60805	3212	4W-11S	D6
9800	CHCG	60655	3212	4W-11S	D7
10500	CHCG	60655	3276	4W-12S	D2
11700	WthT	60803	3276	4W-13S	D4
11900	ALSP	60803	3276	4W-14S	D5
13300	RBBN	60472	3348	4W-15S	D2
Ridgeway Ct					
900	SMBG	60194	2858	24W-11N	D4
Ridgeway St					
2300	EVTN	60201	2866	4W-12N	C1
2500	EVTN	60201	2812	4W-12N	C7
Ridgewood Av					
17000	LNSG	60438	3430	3E-20S	A4
18800	LNSG	60438	3510	3E-22S	A1
N Ridgewood Av					
4800	CHCG	60656	2917	10W-6N	E7
5000	NRDG	60706	2917	10W-6N	E6
Ridgewood Ct					
2700	DYR	46311	3598		D4
S Ridgewood Ct					
5400	CHCG	60615	3153	1E-5S	A2
Ridgewood Dr					
500	SMWD	60107	2856	29W-10N	D5
1200	NHBK	60062	2757	9W-17N	D5
5500	WNSP	60558	3146		D4
5800	LynT	60525	3146		D4
10400	PlsT	60464	3345	13W-15S	A1
13000	PlsT	60462	3345	13W-15S	B1
14800	OKFT	60452	3347	7W-17S	B5
16000	HMGN	60441	3422	16W-19S	A2
17700	HLCT	60429	3427	3W-21S	A6
Ridgewood Ln					
10	DYR	46311	3598		C4
400	BFGV	60069	2754	16W-20N	E1
400	BFGV	60089	2754	16W-20N	E1
400	VmT	60069	2754	16W-20N	E1
1700	HFET	60195	2804	25W-15N	A3
7500	BRRG	60527	3208		D1
E Ridgewood Ln					
1700	GNVW	60025	2811	7W-14N	A4
N Ridgewood Ln					
1000	PLTN	60067	2753	20W-17N	A5
W Ridgewood Ln					
1800	GNVW	60025	2811	7W-14N	A4
Ridgewood Rd					
10	EGVV	60007	2861	18W-9N	A6
100	RVSD	60546	3088	10W-3S	B5
200	BKFD	60513	3088	10W-3S	B5
200	RVSD	60513	3088	10W-3S	B5
Riedle Ct					
17900	HMWD	60430	3427	2W-21S	C6
Riegel Rd					
18100	HMWD	60430	3427	1W-21S	E7
18400	HMWD	60430	3507	1W-22S	E2
18900	BlmT	60430	3507	1W-22S	E2
19100	CHHT	60411	3507	1W-23S	E3
S Riegel Farm Rd					
1300	MonT	60449	3684	3W-30S	C4
1300	UYPK	60449	3684	3W-30S	C4
1300	UYPK	60466	3684	3W-30S	C4
Riegel Oaks Ln					
10	BlmT	60430	3507	1W-22S	E2
10	HMWD	60430	3507	1W-22S	E2
Rieger St					
-	OMFD	60461	3507	3W-25S	C7
E Rietveld Dr					
1300	CteT	60417	3686	2E-29S	C2
Riley Av					
-	PTHT	60070	2808	14W-15N	B3
Riley St					
10	ELGN	60123	2855		A6

STREET Block	City	ZIP	Map#	CGS	Grid
E Rimbach St					
10	CTCY	60409	3352		C6
10	HMND	46320	3352		C6
E Rimini Ct					
300	PLTN	60067	2753	20W-16N	A6
300	PLTN	60074	2753	20W-16N	A6
S Rincker Rd					
26000	CteT	60417	3686	1E-31S	C6
Ring Ct					
5700	HRPK	60133	2911		D5
Ring Rd					
-	EGvT	60007	2860	20W-12N	B2
-	RGMW	60008	2860	20W-12N	B2
1300	CTCY	60409	3429	2E-19S	D2
Rio Verde Av					
6200	OKFT	60452	3347	7W-18S	B6
Rio Vista Rd					
400	GNVW	60025	2811	8W-12N	A7
Ripple Brook Ct					
700	ELGN	60120	2855		C2
Ripplebrook Ct					
200	SMBG	60173	2859	21W-11N	E3
Ripple Brook Ln					
700	ELGN	60120	2855		C2
Rising Ct					
10300	WDRG	60517	3270		B2
Rita Ct					
100	BRLT	60103	2911		A3
Rita Dr					
3800	RNPK	60471	3594	4W-27S	D5
Rita Rd					
2400	DSPN	60016	2863	11W-11N	C3
18100	TYPK	60477	3425	8W-21S	B7
N Ritchie Ct					
1300	CHCG	60610	3034		C1
Riva Rdg					
10	LMNT	60439	3272	15W-13S	B5
River Av					
-	ITSC	60191	2914		E6
-	WDDL	60191	2914		E6
River Dr					
10	LNSG	60438	3430		C4
400	MNSR	46321	3430		D5
700	HMND	46324	3430		E5
900	GNVW	60025	2810	8W-13N	E6
1200	CTCY	60409	3430	3E-19S	A2
8000	MNGV	60053	2865	7W-10N	A5
E River Dr					
300	CHCG	60611	3034	0E-0N	C3
1200	DSPN	60018	2863	12W-10N	B5
River Rd					
10	LMNT	60439	3270		D5
100	DRFD	60015	2757	9W-20N	B2
3000	NRIV	60546	3088	10W-2S	B4
3600	HLCT	60429	3506	4W-22S	D1
4000	SRPK	60176	2973	11W-5N	D1
4500	SRPK	60176	2917	11W-6N	D6
5100	SRPK	60656	2917	11W-6N	C6
6100	HGKN	60525	3148	11W-6S	A5
6500	HGKN	60525	3147	11W-8S	D7
6500	HGKN	60525	3209	12W-8S	C1
6500	WLSP	60525	3209	12W-8S	C1
N River Rd					
400	WhIT	60056	2808	13W-13N	E6
600	MPPT	60056	2808	13W-13N	E5
600	WhIT	60025	2808	13W-13N	E5
700	DSPN	60016	2808	13W-12N	E7
700	DSPN	60016	2809	13W-12N	A7
700	DSPN	60016	2863	13W-12N	A1
700	MaiT	60016	2808	13W-12N	E7
700	MaiT	60016	2809	13W-12N	A7
700	MaiT	60016	2863	13W-12N	A1
1300	MPPT	60056	2809	13W-15N	A3
1300	WhIT	60025	2809	13W-14N	A3
1300	WhIT	60062	2809	13W-15N	A3
1500	PTHT	60070	2809	13W-15N	A3
5200	CHCG	60018	2917	11W-6N	C6
5200	CHCG	60656	2917	11W-6N	C6
5200	SRPK	60176	2917	11W-6N	C6
5200	SRPK	60656	2917	11W-6N	C6
5300	RSMT	60018	2917	11W-6N	C5
6200	DSPN	60018	2917	11W-8N	C3
N River Rd US-45					
400	WhIT	60056	2808	13W-13N	E6
600	MPPT	60056	2808	13W-13N	E5
600	WhIT	60025	2808	13W-13N	E5
700	DSPN	60016	2808	13W-12N	E7
700	DSPN	60016	2809	13W-12N	A7
700	DSPN	60016	2863	13W-12N	A1
700	MaiT	60016	2808	13W-12N	E7
700	MaiT	60016	2809	13W-12N	A7
700	MaiT	60016	2863	13W-12N	A1
1300	MPPT	60056	2809	13W-15N	A3
1300	WhIT	60025	2809	13W-14N	A3
1300	WhIT	60062	2809	13W-15N	A3
1500	PTHT	60070	2809	13W-15N	A3
S River Rd					
10	DSPN	60016	2863	13W-11N	A2
1200	MPPT	60056	2809	12W-15N	A2
1200	PTHT	60070	2809	13W-15N	A2
1200	WhIT	60062	2809	13W-15N	A2
1800	DSPN	60018	2863	12W-9N	B7
2300	CHCG	60018	2917	12W-8N	C1
2300	DSPN	60018	2917	12W-8N	C1
21100	FftT	60423	3504	10W-25S	C7
S River Rd US-12					
-	DSPN	60016	2863	13W-11N	A3
S River Rd US-45					
10	DSPN	60016	2863	13W-11N	A2
1200	MPPT	60056	2809	13W-15N	A2
1200	PTHT	60070	2809	13W-15N	A2
1200	WhIT	60062	2809	13W-15N	A2
W River Rd					
10	ELGN	60123	2801		A7
River St					
1600	DSPN	60016	2863	12W-11N	A3
9400	SRPK	60176	2917	11W-6N	D6
N River St					
10	EDND	60118	2801		A2
S River St					
10	EDND	60118	2801		A3
River Ash Ct					
1200	BRLT	60103	2910		B1
River Bend Dr					
-	MNSR	46321	3430		D5
River Bend Rd					
11300	ODPK	60467	3422	14W-21S	E6
River Birch Dr					
5700	HFET	60120	2856	31W-12N	A2
River Bluff Rd					
400	ELGN	60120	2855		A1
Rivercrest Ct					
5100	CTWD	60445	3347	6W-15S	E2
Rivercrest Dr					
13100	CTWD	60445	3347	6W-15S	E1

STREET Block	City	ZIP	Map#	CGS	Grid
Rivercrest Dr					
13100	CTWD	60445	3348	6W-15S	A1
S Riverdale Av					
13200	CHCG	60827	3350	0E-15S	D1
Riverdale Dr					
300	NHBK	60062	2758	7W-16N	A7
300	NHFD	60062	2758	7W-16N	A7
300	NHFD	60093	2758	7W-16N	A7
River Falls Dr					
3100	NHBK	60062	2756	11W-17N	D6
3400	NfdT	60062	2756	12W-17N	C6
River Forest Ct					
800	BNVL	60106	2972		B4
River Forest Dr					
800	BNVL	60106	2972		B4
W River Grove Av					
8400	RVGV	60171	2974	10W-3N	A5
W River Loft Ct					
2300	CHCG	60618	2977	2W-3N	A4
River Mill Pkwy					
600	WhIT	60090	2755	13W-17N	E6
600	WLNG	60090	2755	13W-17N	D6
River Oaks W					
400	CTCY	60409	3429	2E-19S	E1
River Oaks Ctr					
10	CTCY	60409	3429	3E-19S	E1
River Oaks Dr					
10	CTCY	60409	3430	4E-19S	B1
10	HMND	46324	3430	4E-19S	C2
10	HMND	60409	3430	4E-19S	C2
500	RVFT	60305	3030	10W-0N	B3
1000	CTCY	60409	3429	3E-19S	E1
River Oaks Center Dr					
10	CTCY	60409	3429	3E-19S	E2
River Ridge St					
1900	NHBK	60062	2758	7W-16N	A7
1900	NHBK	60093	2758	7W-16N	A7
1900	NHFD	60093	2758	7W-16N	A7
N Riversedge Ter					
5200	CHCG	60630	2920	5W-6N	B5
Riverside Av					
10	WDND	60118	2801		A3
4300	LYNS	60534	3088	10W-4S	B7
4500	LYNS	60534	3148	10W-4S	B1
4600	LYNS	60525	3148	10W-4S	B1
4600	MCCK	60525	3148	10W-4S	B1
8400	BKFD	60513	3088	10W-3S	A6
8400	RVSD	60513	3088	10W-3S	B5
8400	RVSD	60546	3088	10W-3S	B5
14900	HRVY	60426	3350	0W-17S	C6
14900	SHLD	60426	3350	0W-17S	D6
14900	SHLD	60473	3350	0W-17S	C6
N Riverside Av					
6500	NLES	60714	2918	8W-8N	E1
6500	NLES	60714	2919	8W-8N	A1
Riverside Ct					
1600	GNVW	60025	2810	8W-14N	E4
Riverside Dr					
10	DRFD	60015	2756	11W-20N	E2
100	NfdT	60093	2811	7W-15N	C3
100	NHFD	60093	2811	7W-15N	C3
200	DLTN	60419	3350	0W-17S	B5
600	PKRG	60068	2863	11W-9N	C7
3400	WLMT	60091	2811	6W-14N	D4
4800	LYNS	60525	3148	10W-5S	B1
4800	LYNS	60534	3148	10W-5S	B1
4800	MCCK	60525	3148	10W-5S	B1
5100	RNPK	60471	3594	6W-27S	A4
6500	TYPK	60477	3425	8W-20S	B3
6700	BRWN	60402	3089	8W-2S	A2
6800	BRWN	60402	3088	8W-2S	E3
7100	RVSD	60546	3088	8W-2S	D3
14700	SHLD	60426	3350	0W-17S	C6
14900	PHNX	60426	3350	0W-17S	C6
E Riverside Dr					
14700	DLTN	60419	3350	0W-17S	C5
14700	HRVY	60426	3350	0W-17S	C5
14700	SHLD	60426	3350	0W-17S	C5
14700	SHLD	60473	3350	0W-17S	C5
N Riverside Dr					
10	SHLD	60473	3350	0E-17S	D6
7100	NLES	60714	2864	8W-9N	E7
7100	NLES	60714	2918	8W-8N	E1
N Riverside Plz					
10	CHCG	60606	3034		D5
S Riverside Plz					
10	CHCG	60606	3034		D5
Riverside Rd					
8100	RVSD	60546	3088	9W-3S	C5
Riverside St					
2600	FNPK	60131	2973	12W-3N	B5
W Riverton Ct					
7600	FftT	60423	3504	9W-23S	D4
Riverview Av					
1400	DSPN	60018	2863	13W-9N	A6
Riverview Dr					
-	DndT	60118	2801		A5
300	SEGN	60177	2855		A7
300	SEGN	60177	2909		A1
500	SHLD	60473	3350	0E-18S	E7
800	SHLD	60473	3351	1E-18S	A7
W Riverview Pkwy					
2700	CHCG	60618	2977	3W-4N	A3
Riverwald Dr					
3900	LYNS	60534	3088	10W-4S	B6
3900	RvsT	60534	3088	10W-4S	B6
3900	RvsT	60546	3088	10W-4S	B6
River Walk Dr					
700	WLNG	60090	2755	13W-17N	D6
Riverwalk Dr					
-	BFGV	60090	2755	14W-20N	C2
N River Walk Dr					
2900	CHCG	60618	2977	2W-3N	A4
N Riverwalk Dr					
-	BFGV	60090	2755	14W-20N	C1
-	VmT	60062	2755	14W-20N	C1
N River West Ct					
1500	MPPT	60056	2808	13W-15N	E3
1500	MPPT	60056	2809	13W-15N	A3
1500	WhIT	60062	2809	13W-15N	A3
Riverwood Dr					
-	ALGN	60102	2748		A2
Riverwoods Dr					
1700	MLPK	60160	3030	10W-1N	B1
1700	MLPK	60171	3030	10W-1N	B1
1700	RVGV	60171	3030	10W-1N	B1
Riviera Ct					
3700	NHBK	60062	2756	12W-17N	B4
Riviera Dr					
4800	MONE	60449	3683	6W-31S	B5
Riviera Pkwy					
8900	ODPK	60462	3346	11W-17S	A4
Roach Av					
9000	BKFD	60513	3087	11W-2S	E4
9100	LGPK	60513	3087	11W-2S	D4

STREET Block	City	ZIP	Map#	CGS	Grid
Rose Ln					
-	ELGN	60120	2856	31W-9N	A7
400	BRLT	60103	2910		A1
700	MTSN	60443	3506	5W-25S	C6
800	PTHT	60070	2755	15W-16N	A6
800	PTHT	60090	2755	15W-16N	A6
800	WLNG	60090	2754	15W-16N	E6
800	WLNG	60090	2755	15W-16N	A6
S Rose Ln					
25600	MONE	60449	3683	5W-31S	C5
Rose St					
100	BNVL	60106	2972		A2
2000	FNPK	60131	2973	12W-2N	C6
2000	LydT	60164	2973	11W-2N	C7
2000	MLPK	60131	2973	12W-2N	C7
2300	FNPK	60164	2973	11W-2N	C6
2400	LydT	60131	2973	11W-3N	C6
3600	SRPK	60176	2973	12W-2N	C6
5000	SRPK	60176	2917	11W-6N	C6
17800	LNSG	60438	3429	2E-21S	D6
19700	LYWD	60411	3509	2E-23S	D4
E Rose St					
10	GNWD	60425	3508	0E-22S	E2
N Rose St					
10	PLTN	60067	2805	21W-16N	D1
100	PLTN	60067	2752	21W-16N	D7
5200	CHCG	60018	2917	11W-6N	C6
5200	RSMT	60018	2917	11W-6N	C6
5200	SRPK	60018	2917	11W-6N	C6
5200	SRPK	60176	2917	11W-6N	C6
S Rose St					
100	PLTN	60067	2805	21W-15N	D2
W Rose St					
10	GNWD	60425	3508	0E-22S	D2
Rosebrook Cir					
-	PvsT	60154	3086		E4
-	PvsT	60558	3086		E4
3000	WSTR	60154	3086		E4
Rosebud Pl					
16100	ODHL	60477	3424	11W-19S	A2
Rosebury Dr					
-	FftT	60423	3504	10W-25S	C6
Rose Bush Ln					
500	DYR	46311	3510		C6
500	DYR	46321	3510		C6
500	LYWD	60411	3510		C6
500	MNSR	46321	3510		C6
800	LYWD	46311	3510	4E-24S	C6
Rosecrans Ct					
300	BRLT	60103	2911		B5
Rosedale Av					
10	BMDL	60108	2912		E7
10	BmdT	60172	2912		E6
200	ROSL	60172	2912		E6
500	BmdT	60108	2912		E7
W Rosedale Av					
1200	CHCG	60660	2921	1W-7N	D4
6100	CHCG	60646	2919	7W-7N	A4
6300	CHCG	60631	2919	8W-7N	A4
7400	CHCG	60631	2918	9W-7N	C4
7800	CHCG	60068	2918	9W-7N	C4
7800	PKRG	60068	2918	9W-7N	C4
Rosedale Ln					
800	HFET	60195	2804	25W-12N	C7
Rosedale Rd					
600	NfdT	60025	2809	10W-13N	E7
Rosedale Ter					
600	CRTE	60417	3596	0E-28S	E7
600	CRTE	60417	3597	0E-28S	A7
Rosefield Tr					
-	TYPK	60477	3504	9W-23S	D2
Rosehill Dr					
300	LMNT	60439	3270		D6
E Rosehill Dr					
1400	ANHT	60004	2807	16W-16N	C1
1900	ANHT	60004	2754	16W-16N	D7
W Rosehill Dr					
1600	CHCG	60660	2921	2W-7N	C4
Roselawn St					
10	CTCY	60409	3430	4E-20S	C3
10	HMND	46324	3430		C3
Roselle Rd					
10	IVNS	60067	2805	22W-16N	A1
10	PLTN	60067	2805	22W-16N	A1
100	IVNS	60067	2752	22W-16N	A7
300	BMDL	60108	2913		A6
300	BMDL	60172	2913		A6
300	ROSL	60172	2913		A6
Roselle Rd CO-4					
300	BMDL	60108	2913		A6
300	BMDL	60172	2913		A6
300	ROSL	60172	2913		A6
N Roselle Rd					
-	SMBG	60173	2805	23W-12N	A7
10	ROSL	60172	2913		A4
10	SMBG	60193	2859	23W-10N	A5
10	SMBG	60194	2859	23W-10N	A5
200	HFET	60194	2859	23W-10N	A4
800	HFET	60195	2859	23W-12N	A2
1000	SMBG	60173	2859	23W-12N	A2
1000	SMBG	60195	2859	23W-12N	A2
2000	PltT	60195	2805	22W-13N	A6
2000	SMBG	60195	2805	23W-12N	A7
2100	PLTN	60067	2805	22W-13N	A6
2100	PltT	60067	2805	22W-13N	A6
N Roselle Rd CO-4					
300	ROSL	60172	2913		A3
S Roselle Rd					
10	IVNS	60067	2805	22W-15N	A2
10	PLTN	60067	2805	22W-15N	A2
10	ROSL	60172	2913		A5
10	SMBG	60193	2859	23W-10N	A6
10	SMBG	60194	2859	23W-9N	A6
700	BMDL	60108	2913		A6
800	SMBG	60193	2913		A1
1300	SmbT	60193	2913		A2
1400	SmbT	60172	2913		A2
1700	PltT	60067	2805	22W-14N	A5
1700	PltT	60195	2805	22W-13N	A5
S Roselle Rd CO-4					
10	ROSL	60172	2913		A5
700	BMDL	60108	2913		A6
Rose Manor Ter					
3600	MKHM	60426	3426	4W-19S	D2
Rosemary Av					
100	IVNS	60010	2751	24W-16N	C6
Rosemary Ct					
1400	DYR	46311	3510		C7
1500	DYR	46311	3598		C1
5800	CTSD	60525	3147	12W-6S	C4
Rosemary Ln					
1200	NHBK	60062	2757	9W-18N	D3
N Rosemary Ln					
6800	NLES	60714	2918	8W-8N	E1
S Rosemary Ln					
11700	ALSP	60803	3276	5W-13S	B5
Rosemary Rd					
1600	HDPK	60035	2757	9W-20N	C1
Rosemear Av					
3500	BKFD	60513	3088	10W-3S	A5
3800	LYNS	60534	3088	10W-4S	A6
Rosemere Ct					
8100	WLSP	60480	3208		D3
Rosemont Av					
10	ROSL	60172	2913		A3
100	ROSL	60172	2912		E3
600	PKRG	60068	2918	10W-7N	A3
10000	RSMT	60018	2917	12W-7N	B3
W Rosemont Av					
900	CHCG	60660	2921	1W-7N	D3
2100	CHCG	60659	2921	3W-7N	A3
3500	CHCG	60659	2920	4W-7N	B3
4000	CHCG	60646	2920	5W-7N	B3
4700	CHCG	60646	2919	6W-7N	E3
Rosemont St					
9900	RSMT	60018	2917	12W-7N	B3
N Rosetree Ln					
1600	MPPT	60056	2808	13W-15N	D3
W Roseview Dr					
8400	MaiT	60714	2864	10W-10N	A4
8400	NLES	60714	2864	10W-10N	A4
8500	PKRG	60068	2864	10W-10N	A4
Rosewood Av					
-	CteT	60417	3774	1W-33S	B1
200	BFGV	60089	2754	17W-18N	C3
300	WNKA	60093	2812	5W-15N	A2
700	WNKA	60093	2759		B7
1200	DRFD	60015	2756	11W-20N	C1
6700	HMND	46324	3430		C3
12900	PSPK	60464	3274	11W-14S	A6
Rosewood Ct					
300	NHBK	60062	2758	7W-17N	A5
900	BRLT	60103	2910		E6
1200	ELGN	60120	2855		D4
1200	SMBG	60193	2859	21W-10N	D5
9300	MaiT	60016	2863	11W-12N	C1
N Rosewood Ct					
1200	PLTN	60067	2752	22W-17N	B5
S Rosewood Ct					
20100	FftT	60423	3504	10W-24S	C5
Rosewood Dr					
-	HnrT	60120	2856	30W-10N	B5
-	SMWD	60120	2856	30W-10N	B5
10	ROSL	60172	2912		D5
400	CPVL	60110	2748		B6
12400	HMGN	60441	3344	15W-17S	B6
17600	LNSG	60438	3429	2E-20S	D5
17700	ThtT	60438	3429	2E-21S	D5
S Rosewood Dr					
19900	FftT	60423	3504	10W-24S	C5
Rosewood Ln					
10	CHHT	60411	3508	1W-23S	A3
100	BlmT	60411	3508	1W-23S	A3
17500	TYPK	60477	3424	11W-21S	A5
Rosewood Rd					
10	RGMW	60008	2806	19W-14N	B4
Rosewood St					
7200	HRPK	60133	2911		D2
Rosewood Ter					
17700	CCHL	60478	3426	5W-21S	B6
Rosiclaire Ct					
3000	SCHT	60411	3595	1W-27S	E4
W Rosiland Rd					
400	PLTN	60074	2752	21W-18N	C3
E Rosita Dr					
1300	PLTN	60074	2753	19W-16N	C7
Roslara Ct					
200	BRLT	60103	2910		E2
Roslyn Ct					
1000	SMBG	60194	2858	24W-11N	C4
Roslyn Ln					
1100	SMBG	60194	2858	24W-11N	C4
W Roslyn Pl					
400	CHCG	60614	2978	0W-3N	A5
Roslyn Rd					
400	EDND	60118	2801		A1
500	KLWH	60043	2812	4W-14N	D3
900	MTSN	60443	3506	4W-25S	D7
900	OMFD	60461	3506	4W-25S	D7
1400	SmbT	60172	2913		B2
1600	SmbT	60193	2913		A3
1700	ROSL	60172	2913		A3
Roslyn Ter					
700	EVTN	60201	2813	2W-13N	B6
800	WLMT	60091	2813	2W-13N	B6
Rosner Dr					
600	ROSL	60172	2913		C5
S Ross Av					
6500	CHCG	60621	3152	0W-7S	B5
Ross Cres					
1700	SLVL	60411	3597	2E-27S	C4
Rossell Av					
1100	OKPK	60302	3031	8W-1N	A1
1200	CHCG	60302	3031	8W-2N	A1
1200	CHCG	60707	3031	8W-2N	A1
Rosslyn Ln					
100	IVNS	60067	2752	22W-16N	B7
Rotary Dr					
-	BrnT	60010	2751	25W-17N	B4
10	BRTN	60010	2751	25W-17N	B4
Roth Av					
100	PltT	60010	2751	24W-18N	C2
Roth Ct					
1200	WLNG	60090	2754	16W-18N	E2
Roth Ter					
3700	SKOK	60076	2866	4W-10N	C4
Rothbury Ct					
1100	SMBG	60193	2913		B1
Rothenburg Rd					
10500	DGvT	60439	3270		D2
10500	WDRG	60439	3270		D2
Round Barn Rd					
10	BNHL	60010	2750	27W-17N	C4
Round House Rd					
-	CRTE	60417	3685	0E-31S	E5
-	CteT	60417	3685	0E-31S	E5
Roundstone Ln					
10	BNHL	60010	2748		E5
Route 1 Cto					
-	CHHT	60411	3508	1W-25S	A6
Route 1 Cto SR-1					
-	CHHT	60411	3508	1W-25S	A6
Routh Ct					
200	SMBG	60195	2859	23W-12N	A2
Rowe Av					
800	PKRG	60068	2863	11W-9N	D6
Rowlett Av					
800	LydT	60164	2972		E5
Rowley Ct					
4100	SMWD	60107	2911		A1
Roxanne Av					
300	BNVL	60106	2972		A2
Roxborough Pl					
100	IVNS	60010	2751	24W-17N	C6
Roxbury Ct					
10	DSPN	60018	2862	15W-10N	B5
900	HRPK	60133	2857	26W-9N	E7
900	HRPK	60133	2858	26W-9N	A7
Roxbury Ln					
-	DSPN	60018	2862	14W-10N	C5
800	SMBG	60194	2858	24W-11N	D4
N Roy Av					
100	NHLK	60164	2972		E6
800	LydT	60164	2972		E5
1500	MLPK	60160	3028		E2
1500	NHLK	60164	3028		E2
S Roy Av					
100	NHLK	60164	3028		E1
200	MLPK	60160	3028		E2
Roy St					
700	DYR	46311	3598		E4
16400	OKFT	60452	3426	5W-19S	B2
17100	LNSG	60438	3430	4E-20S	B4
19100	LNSG	60438	3510	4E-22S	B2
Royal Ct					
-	CTWD	60445	3348	6W-16S	A2
200	ANHT	60004	2807	16W-15N	D2
200	PTHT	60004	2807	16W-15N	D2
200	PTHT	60070	2807	16W-15N	D2
900	SMBG	60193	2858	24W-9N	D7
17300	SHLD	60473	3429	2E-20S	D4
S Royal Ct					
300	PLTN	60067	2805	21W-15N	E2
Royal Dr					
2700	NHBK	60062	2756	10W-17N	E6
8800	BRRG	60527	3208		B5
9000	DGvT	60527	3208		B5
W Royal Ln					
600	PTON	60468	3860	9W-37S	D4
Royal Rd					
18700	GNWD	60425	3508	1W-22S	A2
18700	HMWD	60430	3508	1W-22S	A2
Royal Wy					
10	BNHL	60010	2748		E4
Royal Creek Ln					
15200	ODPK	60467	3344	14W-18S	E7
S Royal Crest Dr					
26100	CteT	60417	3687	3E-31S	A6
Royal Dublin Ln					
700	DYR	46311	3510		E7
Royale Ln					
17900	HLCT	60429	3426	4W-21S	E6
Royal Foxhunt Rd					
15100	ODPK	60462	3346	11W-18S	A7
Royal Georgian Rd					
15100	ODPK	60462	3346	11W-18S	A7
Royal Glen Ct					
400	OKBK	60523	3028		B7
15500	ODPK	60467	3345	13W-18S	A7
Royal Glen Dr					
10800	ODPK	60467	3345	13W-18S	A7
Royal Oak Ct					
17900	TYPK	60477	3425	8W-21S	B6
Royal Oak Ln					
1300	GNVW	60025	2810	8W-13N	E5
1300	GNVW	60025	2811	8W-13N	A5
Royal Oaks Ln					
10900	ODPK	60467	3344	13W-17S	E5
10900	ODPK	60467	3345	13W-17S	A5
Royal Ridge Dr					
2000	NHBK	60062	2757	8W-16N	E7
2200	NHBK	60062	2810	8W-16N	E1
E Royal Ridge Dr					
2400	CteT	60417	3686	3E-31S	E6
2500	CteT	60417	3687	3E-31S	A6
Royal Troon Ct					
2400	RVWD	60015	2756	13W-20N	A1
W Royce Ct					
7600	FftT	60423	3504	9W-24S	E6
Royce Ln					
200	ROSL	60172	2912		D5
S Ruble St					
-	CHCG	60607	3034		E7
1600	CHCG	60616	3092	0W-1S	A1
Ruby St					
2000	MLPK	60160	2973	12W-2N	C7
2200	LydT	60164	2973	12W-2N	C6
2800	FNPK	60131	2973	12W-3N	C5
3600	SRPK	60131	2973	12W-4N	C3
4500	SRPK	60176	2973	12W-5N	C1
4800	SRPK	60176	2917	12W-6N	C7
5200	OKLN	60453	3211	6W-10S	E5
5900	RSMT	60018	2917	12W-7N	B3
N Ruby St					
1900	LydT	60164	2973	12W-2N	C7
1900	MLPK	60160	2973	12W-2N	C7
1900	MLPK	60160	3029	12W-2N	C1
S Ruby St					
25900	MONE	60449	3683	6W-31S	A6
Rucci Ct					
10	BRRG	60527	3146		C6
Rudolph Dr					
1200	NHBK	60062	2757	9W-18N	D2
Rudolph St					
1200	CTCY	60409	3430	3E-19S	A1
Rue Chamonix					
500	DRPK	60010	2752	22W-20N	C1
Rue Jardin					
100	DRPK	60010	2752	22W-20N	B2
100	PltT	60074	2752	22W-20N	B2
Rue Orleanais					
500	DRPK	60010	2752	22W-20N	C1
Rue Royale					
500	DRPK	60010	2752	22W-20N	C1
500	DRPK	60074	2752	22W-20N	C1
Rue St. James Pl					
-	PltT	60067	2805	22W-14N	A5
Rue Touraine					
100	DRPK	60010	2752	22W-20N	C2
100	DRPK	60074	2752	22W-20N	C2
Ruffled Feathers Dr					
10	LMNT	60439	3271		D7
10	LMNT	60439	3343	17W-15S	C1
Rugby Pl					
10	ELGN	60120	2855		A4
300	SMBG	60194	2858	24W-11N	C4
Rugeley Rd					
100	WNSP	60558	3146		E2
100	WNSP	60558	3147	13W-5S	A2
Rugen Rd					
2100	GNVW	60025	2810	9W-14N	D5
3700	GNVW	60025	2809	11W-13N	D5
Ruggles Ct					
10	HMGN	60467	3344	14W-16S	C4
10	ODPK	60467	3344	14W-16S	C4
10	OrlT	60467	3344	14W-16S	C4
W Ruhl Rd					
-	PltT	60074	2752	21W-18N	C3
500	PLTN	60074	2752	21W-18N	C3
Rumford on Asbury					
10	RGMW	60008	2806	19W-14N	B3
Rumsey Av					
4500	OKLN	60453	3212	5W-10S	A5
W Rundell Pl					
1000	CHCG	60607	3033	1W-0S	E5
Runge St					
3400	FNPK	60131	2972		C4
3600	LydT	60131	2972		C3
Rush St					
400	ROSL	60172	2913		B6
2000	SLVL	60411	3509	2E-25S	D7
N Rush St					
300	ITSC	60143	2914		C6
400	CHCG	60611	3034	0E-0N	C3
1000	CHCG	60610	3034	0E-1N	C2
S Rush St					
200	ITSC	60143	2914		C6
200	ROSL	60172	2913		B5
Rushmore Dr					
100	BRLT	60103	2909		D3
100	ELGN	60120	2909		D3
Ruskin Cir					
400	EGVV	60007	2860	19W-9N	C7
Ruskin Ct					
800	SMBG	60193	2858	25W-9N	C7
800	SMBG	60193	2912		D1
Ruskin Dr					
500	EGVV	60007	2860	19W-9N	C7
500	EGVV	60007	2914		B1
Russel					
1200	WLNG	60090	2754	15W-17N	E5
N Russel St					
100	MPPT	60056	2807	15W-13N	E6
W Russell Ct					
1400	ANHT	60005	2860	19W-12N	D1
Russell Dr					
-	CHCG	60637	3152	0E-6S	D3
1400	HFET	60120	2855		E2
6100	ELGN	60120	2855		D2
Russell St					
10	CTCY	60409	3352		C6
10	HMND	46320	3352		D6
500	WLNG	60090	2754	15W-17N	E5
600	ELGN	60120	2855		B6
E Russell St					
100	BRTN	60010	2750	26W-18N	D2
100	BRTN	60010	2751	25W-18N	A2
300	HMND	46320	3352		D6
W Russell St					
100	BRTN	60010	2750	25W-18N	E2
Russellwood Ct					
300	SMBG	60193	2857	26W-9N	E7
Russet Ln					
700	SMWD	60107	2857	28W-10N	B7
Russet Wy					
4000	CCHL	60478	3426	5W-20S	C5
4000	GNVW	60062	2809	11W-15N	D3
E Russet Wy					
10	PLTN	60067	2752	20W-17N	E5
200	PLTN	60067	2753	20W-17N	A5
200	PLTN	60074	2753	20W-17N	A5
Russett Ct					
600	SMBG	60193	2858	23W-9N	E7
3800	NHBK	60062	2756	12W-17N	B5
Russett Ln					
300	HDPK	60035	2757	9W-20N	C1
3700	NHBK	60062	2756	12W-17N	B5
4700	SKOK	60076	2811	7W-13N	B7
4700	SKOK	60076	2812	5W-12N	A7
Russetwood Ct					
1100	WLNG	60004	2754	15W-17N	E6
1100	WLNG	60090	2754	15W-17N	E6
Russetwood Dr					
-	ANHT	60004	2807	16W-15N	D2
-	PTHT	60070	2807	16W-15N	D2
Rust St					
200	WLSP	60480	3209	12W-9S	B4
E Rust Tr					
200	WLSP	60480	3209	11W-9S	D2
Rust Tr N					
400	WLSP	60480	3209	12W-9S	D2
Rust Tr W					
200	WLSP	60480	3209	12W-9S	D2
Rustic Dr					
300	WLNG	60090	2755	13W-17N	D5
Rusty Dr					
2600	DSPN	60018	2917	12W-8N	C1
W Rusty Dr					
1700	MPPT	60056	2861	17W-12N	C1
Rusty Rd					
10	LMNT	60439	3272	15W-13S	A4
Rutgers Ct					
100	GNVW	60025	2810	10W-15N	A2
Rutgers Ln					
500	EGVV	60007	2913		D1
4000	NHBK	60062	2756	12W-17N	B5
Ruth Av					
2200	PKRG	60068	2863	11W-10N	D5
Ruth St					
10	HMND	46320	3352	4E-18S	C7
500	CTCY	60409	3352	4E-18S	B7
3000	FNPK	60131	2973	13W-3N	A4
7700	DYR	46311	3598		E4
7700	SjnT	46311	3598		E4
E Ruth St					
10	CTCY	60409	3352		C7
10	HMND	46320	3352		C7
Rutherford Av					
7700	BDPK	60459	3211	8W-8S	A1
7700	BRBK	60459	3211	8W-9S	A3
9500	OKLN	60453	3211	8W-11S	A7
9800	CHRG	60415	3211	8W-11S	A7
9800	OKLN	60415	3211	8W-11S	A7
N Rutherford Av					
1600	CHCG	60302	3030	8W-2N	E1
1600	CHCG	60707	3030	8W-2N	E1
1600	OKPK	60302	3030	8W-2N	E1
2400	CHCG	60707	2974	8W-3N	E5
3700	CHCG	60634	2974	8W-4N	E2
4300	HDHT	60706	2974	8W-5N	E1
4800	CHCG	60656	2918	8W-6N	E5
4800	CHCG	60706	2918	8W-6N	E6
4800	HDHT	60706	2918	8W-6N	E6
S Rutherford Av					
5100	CHCG	60638	3149	8W-6S	A4
5100	FTVW	60638	3149	8W-5S	A2
10700	WRTH	60482	3275	8W-12S	A3
Rutherford Ln					
9000	ODPK	60462	3346	11W-18S	A6
Ruth Lake Ct					
700	DGvT	60527	3146		A5
Rutland Ct					
1500	SMBG	60173	2859	21W-10N	E5
Rutland Ln					
1500	SMBG	60173	2859	21W-10N	E5
Rutledge St					
400	OMFD	60461	3595	3W-25S	C1
400	PKFT	60466	3595	3W-25S	C1
Ruzich Dr					
-	BRLT	60120	2909		E3
-	ELGN	60120	2909		E3
Ryan Cir					
-	MTSN	60443	3505	7W-24S	D5
E Ryan Ct					
200	ANHT	60005	2861	17W-12N	B1
Ryan Ln					
17500	ODPK	60467	3423	13W-21S	A6
Ryan Pkwy					
1300	ALGN	60102	2748		A1
1300	AlqT	60102	2748		A1
Ryan Rd					
-	ROSL	60172	2912		B4
S Ryan Rd					
8800	HMTN	60456	3212	5W-10S	C4
9000	OKLN	60453	3212	5W-10S	B5
Ryan Wy					
-	ROSL	60172	2912		B4
Rycon Dr					
13000	HMGN	60441	3422	16W-21S	A5
Ryehill Cir					
16200	ODPK	60467	3423	13W-19S	A2
Ryeland Dr					
8000	FftT	60423	3504	10W-24S	C5
Rynberk Ct					
14200	HmrT	60441	3342	20W-16S	B4
Rywick Ct					
3700	RGMW	60008	2806	20W-13N	A5
S					
Sable Dr					
2700	GNVW	60025	2810	9W-14N	B4
Sable Ln					
1700	EGvT	60056	2861	17W-10N	C5
1700	MPPT	60056	2861	17W-10N	C5
Sacramento Av					
-	BmnT	60469	3349	3W-17S	A4
-	POSN	60469	3349	3W-17S	A4
12600	ALSP	60406	3277	3W-14S	A6
12600	ALSP	60803	3277	3W-14S	A6
12600	BLID	60406	3277	3W-15S	A7
12600	BLID	60803	3277	3W-14S	A6
13300	RBBN	60406	3349	3W-16S	A2
13300	WthT	60406	3349	3W-16S	A2
13300	WthT	60472	3349	3W-16S	A2
13700	BLID	60406	3349	3W-16S	A2
13700	RBBN	60472	3349	3W-16S	A2
15100	BmnT	60426	3349	3W-18S	A6
15100	MKHM	60426	3349	3W-18S	A6
17900	HLCT	60429	3427	3W-21S	A7
17900	HMWD	60430	3427	3W-21S	A7
18500	HMWD	60430	3507	3W-22S	A1
N Sacramento Av					
1000	CHCG	60622	3032	3W-1N	E2
2200	CHCG	60647	2976	3W-2N	E6
3500	CHCG	60618	2976	3W-4N	E2
4400	CHCG	60618	2920	3W-5N	E7
4400	CHCG	60625	2920	3W-5N	E7
5600	CHCG	60659	2920	3W-7N	E4
6300	CHCG	60645	2920	3W-7N	E3
7200	CHCG	60645	2866	3W-9N	E7
7500	EVTN	60202	2866	3W-9N	E7
S Sacramento Av					
-	CHCG	60652	3212	3W-10S	E4
-	ENGN	60652	3212	3W-10S	E4
-	ENGN	60805	3212	3W-10S	E4
-	POSN	60469	3349	3W-17S	A4
2200	CHCG	60623	3090	3W-2S	E2
3500	CHCG	60632	3090	3W-3S	E5
4600	CHCG	60632	3150	3W-5S	E1
5400	CHCG	60629	3150	3W-6S	E4
10300	CHCG	60655	3276	3W-12S	E1
11100	CHCG	60655	3277	3W-13S	A3
11200	MTPK	60803	3277	3W-13S	A3
13800	BLID	60406	3349	3W-16S	A2
13800	BLID	60472	3349	3W-16S	A2
13800	RBBN	60406	3349	3W-16S	A2
13800	RBBN	60472	3349	3W-16S	A2
14800	MKHM	60426	3349	3W-17S	A5
14800	MKHM	60469	3349	3W-17S	A5
14900	BmnT	60426	3349	3W-17S	A5
14900	POSN	60426	3349	3W-17S	A5
N Sacramento Blvd					
700	CHCG	60612	3032	3W-0N	E3
700	CHCG	60622	3032	3W-0N	E3
S Sacramento Blvd					
10	CHCG	60612	3032	3W-0S	E6
1100	CHCG	60623	3032	3W-0S	E7
Sacramento Ct					
1600	CPVL	60110	2748		B6
Sacramento Dr					
-	MTPK	60803	3276	4W-13S	E5
1200	CPVL	60110	2748		C5
1300	HRPK	60133	2911		E4
S Sacramento Dr					
-	CHCG	60612	3032	3W-0S	E7
1200	CHCG	60623	3032	3W-1S	E7
1500	CHCG	60623	3090	3W-1S	E1
11500	MTPK	60803	3276	3W-13S	E4
Sacramento Dr N					
-	CHCG	60629	3150	3W-7S	E6
Sacramento Dr S					
-	CHCG	60629	3150	3W-7S	E7
W Sacramento Sq					
3000	CHCG	60612	3032	3W-0N	E3
Saddle Ct					
10	BRRG	60527	3208		B4
Saddle Ln					
1000	LMNT	60439	3271		A5
Saddlebred Ct					
8600	FKFT	60423	3504	10W-25S	B7
Saddlebrook Ln					
12200	LMNT	60439	3272	16W-14S	A6
S Saddle Brook Ln					
14300	HMGN	60441	3343	17W-17S	C5
S Saddle Ridge Ct					
1000	PLTN	60067	2805	22W-14N	B3
W Saddlewood Dr					
16500	LKPT	60441	3342	20W-18S	A7
Sadler Av					
300	ELGN	60120	2855		C5

STREET Block	City	ZIP	Map#	CGS	Grid
Saffron Ct					
10900	ODPK	60467	3423	13W-20S	A3
Sagamore Ct					
200	SMBG	60194	2858	24W-10N	D5
Sagamore Dr					
900	SMBG	60194	2858	24W-10N	C5
Sage Ct					
13100	HMGN	60441	3343	16W-18S	E7
Sage Brush Ct					
-	SMWD	60120	2856	30W-10N	C5
Saginaw Av					
200	BNHM	60633	3351	3E-17S	E5
200	CTCY	60409	3351	3E-17S	E6
S Saginaw Av					
7500	CHCG	60649	3153		E7
7800	CHCG	60617	3215	3E-8S	E1
7900	CHCG	60649	3215	3E-9S	E2
12600	CHCG	60633	3279	3E-14S	E7
13800	BNHM	60633	3351	3E-16S	E3
14500	CTCY	60409	3351	3E-17S	E4
Saginaw Pl					
10	PKFT	60466	3594	4W-27S	E4
Sahler Av					
8800	BKFD	60513	3147	11W-4S	E1
9500	LGNG	60525	3147	11W-4S	D1
Sailfish Dr					
2800	HMWD	60430	3427	3W-21S	B6
Sailor Ln					
18300	LNSG	60438	3429	3E-21S	E7
St. Albans on Oxford					
10	RGMW	60008	2805	22W-13N	B6
St. Andrew Cir					
1200	ITSC	60143	2914		A7
St. Andrew's Ct					
12700	LMNT	60439	3270		D7
12700	LMNT	60439	3342	19W-15S	E1
15100	ODPK	60462	3346	10W-18S	C6
20100	OMFD	60461	3507	3W-24S	C5
St. Andrew's Dr					
500	CRTE	60417	3596	0E-28S	E6
600	CRTE	60417	3597	0E-28S	A7
2400	OMFD	60461	3507	3W-24S	B5
8200	ODPK	60462	3346	10W-18S	C7
St. Andrew's Ln					
500	IVNS	60067	2752	22W-16N	A7
E St. Andrew's Ln					
10	DRFD	60015	2757	9W-20N	B1
W St. Andrew's Ln					
10	DRFD	60015	2757	10W-20N	B1
St. Andrew's St					
-	LNSG	60438	3429	1E-21S	B7
-	ThtT	60438	3429	1E-21S	B7
St. Ann Dr					
1600	HRPK	60133	2911		D6
St. Anne Ct					
1200	LMNT	60439	3271		B4
St. Anthony Ct					
1200	LMNT	60439	3271		B4
St. Armand Ct					
10	WLNG	60090	2754	15W-18N	E4
St. Armand Ln					
10	WLNG	60090	2754	15W-18N	E4
St. Bonaventure Ct					
1200	LMNT	60439	3271		C4
St. Boniface Ln					
-	MONE	60449	3683	6W-31S	A6
St. Brendans Ct					
1200	LMNT	60439	3271		A7
S St. Cecilia Dr					
500	MPPT	60056	2861	17W-12N	B2
St. Charles Pl					
10	GLNC	60022	2758	7W-20N	B2
10	HDPK	60035	2758	7W-20N	B2
3700	BLWD	60104	3029	12W-0N	B3
St. Charles Rd					
400	MYWD	60153	3030	10W-0N	A4
800	MYWD	60153	3029	10W-0N	E4
2100	BLWD	60104	3029	11W-0N	D4
4700	BLWD	60104	3028		E3
5000	BKLY	60163	3028		D3
5000	BLWD	60163	3028		E3
E St. Charles Rd					
-	BKLY	60163	3028		B3
100	EMHT	60126	3028		A3
St. Charles St					
300	ELGN	60120	2855		B7
900	ElgT	60120	2855		B7
1100	ElgT	60120	2909		B1
St. Charles St SR-25					
800	ELGN	60120	2855		B7
900	ElgT	60120	2855		B7
1100	ElgT	60120	2909		B1
N St. Clair St					
500	CHCG	60611	3034	0E-0N	C3
St. Claire Cir					
10	SMBG	60173	2859	21W-10N	D5
St. Claire Ct					
1200	LMNT	60439	3271		C4
St. Claire Pl					
1200	SMBG	60173	2859	22W-10N	D5
St. Colette Ct					
1200	LMNT	60439	3271		B4
St. Francis Ct					
100	BMDL	60108	2913		C7
100	BmdT	60157	2913		C7
W St. Francis Rd					
-	MTSN	60423	3505	8W-24S	A5
-	MTSN	60443	3505	8W-24S	A5
-	RchT	60423	3505	8W-24S	A5
-	RchT	60443	3505	8W-24S	A5
7200	FftT	60423	3504	9W-24S	E5
7200	FftT	60423	3505	9W-24S	A5
8400	FKFT	60423	3504	9W-24S	E5
W St. George Ct					
2700	CHCG	60647	2976	4W-2N	D7
2700	CHCG	60647	2977	2W-3N	C5
St. George Dr					
10	RGMW	60008	2805	23W-12N	B7
10	RGMW	60008	2806	20W-15N	A3
W St. Helen St					
2700	CHCG	60647	2977	2W-3N	C5
St. Ives Ct					
300	MNSR	46321	3510		D3
3000	RNPK	60471	3594	4W-26S	D2
St. Ives Ln					
3000	RNPK	60471	3594	4W-26S	D3
St. James Ct					
5600	OKLN	60453	3275	7W-12S	D1
6300	BRRG	60527	3146		D5
8100	ODPK	60462	3346	10W-18S	C6
10400	CHRG	60415	3275	7W-12S	D1
W St. James Ct					
1300	IVNS	60067	2805	22W-15N	A2
1300	PLTN	60067	2805	22W-15N	A2
St. James Dr					
8000	ODPK	60462	3346	10W-18S	C7
St. James Pl					
900	PKRG	60068	2918	10W-8N	A2
W St. James Pl					
400	CHCG	60614	2978	0W-3N	A5
1500	ANHT	60005	2806	18W-14N	D4
St. James St					
2000	ANHT	60005	2806	19W-14N	C4
3100	RGMW	60008	2806	19W-14N	B4
E St. James St					
200	ANHT	60004	2807	17W-14N	A4
W St. James St					
10	ANHT	60004	2807	17W-14N	A4
800	ANHT	60005	2806	18W-14N	E4
St. James Wy					
12200	LMNT	60439	3271		D6
St. John Ln					
8600	MaiT	60016	2863	10W-11N	E3
8600	MaiT	60016	2864	10W-11N	A3
St. John St					
1000	ELGN	60120	2855		A1
St. John's Av					
-	GLNC	60022	2758	7W-20N	C2
300	HDPK	60035	2758	7W-20N	B1
N St. John's Ct					
5800	CHCG	60646	2920	5W-7N	A4
W St. John's Pl					
800	PLTN	60067	2752	22W-16N	C7
W St. Joseph Av					
8500	CHCG	60656	2918	10W-6N	A6
St. Joseph Ct					
1200	LMNT	60439	3271		C4
St. Lawrence Av					
4000	MTSN	60443	3594	5W-25S	C1
S St. Lawrence Av					
-	CHCG	60827	3278	0E-15S	E7
4100	CHCG	60653	3092	0E-4S	D7
4600	CHCG	60615	3092	0E-4S	D7
4700	CHCG	60615	3152	0E-5S	D1
6000	CHCG	60637	3152	0E-7S	D6
7000	CHCG	60619	3152	0E-8S	D7
7500	CHCG	60619	3214	0E-9S	D3
10000	CHCG	60628	3214	0E-11S	E7
11100	CHCG	60628	3278	0E-13S	E3
13100	CHCG	60827	3350	0E-15S	E1
19100	BlmT	60425	3508	0E-23S	E3
19100	GNWD	60425	3508	0E-23S	E3
St. Louis Av					
8000	SKOK	60076	2866	4W-10N	D5
8700	SKOK	60203	2866	4W-10N	D4
14400	MDLN	60445	3348	4W-17S	E6
14800	MKHM	60426	3348	4W-17S	E5
14800	MKHM	60445	3348	4W-17S	E5
15700	MKHM	60426	3426	4W-19S	E2
N St. Louis Av					
200	CHCG	60624	3032	4W-0N	D4
1600	CHCG	60647	3032	4W-1N	D1
1600	CHCG	60651	3032	4W-2N	D1
2400	CHCG	60647	2976	4W-3N	D5
2700	CHCG	60618	2976	4W-3N	D5
4300	CHCG	60625	2976	4W-5N	D1
5000	CHCG	60625	2920	4W-6N	C6
5500	CHCG	60659	2920	4W-6N	C5
6400	CHCG	60712	2920	4W-8N	C3
6400	LNWD	60712	2920	4W-8N	C2
S St. Louis Av					
10	CHCG	60624	3032	4W-0S	D5
1100	CHCG	60623	3032	4W-1S	D7
1500	CHCG	60623	3090	4W-1S	D1
3700	CHCG	60632	3090	4W-3S	D5
4700	CHCG	60632	3150	4W-5S	D1
5900	CHCG	60629	3150	4W-7S	D5
8200	CHCG	60652	3212	4W-9S	D3
9100	ENGN	60805	3212	4W-11S	D6
10200	ENGN	60655	3276	4W-11S	D1
10300	CHCG	60655	3276	4W-13S	D4
10300	ENGN	60805	3276	4W-11S	D1
11600	MTPK	60803	3276	4W-13S	D4
13300	WthT	60472	3348	4W-15S	D1
13500	RBBN	60472	3348	4W-16S	D2
St. Mark's Ct					
1500	EVTN	60201	2867	2W-11N	A3
N St. Mark's Pl					
1500	PLTN	60067	2752	21W-17N	D4
N St. Marks Pl					
1500	PLTN	60067	2752	21W-17N	D4
N St. Mark's Pl					
1500	PltT	60074	2752	21W-18N	D4
St. Mary Cir					
13500	ODPK	60462	3346	10W-16S	A2
St. Mary's Pkwy					
10	BFGV	60089	2754	16W-18N	C2
10	WLNG	60089	2754	16W-18N	C2
W St. Mary's St					
2700	CHCG	60647	2976	4W-2N	D7
2700	CHCG	60647	2977	2W-3N	C5
N St. Michael's Ct					
1600	CHCG	60614	2978		C7
St. Moritz Dr					
10	PSPK	60464	3274	10W-13S	C5
St. Patrick Rd					
-	DGvT	60439	3270		E1
-	DGvT	60439	3271		A1
St. Paul Av					
3300	BLWD	60104	3029	12W-0N	B5
4000	BLWD	60162	3029	12W-0N	A5
4000	HLSD	60162	3029	12W-0N	A5
St. Paul Ct					
4800	HLSD	60162	3028		D4
W St. Paul's Av					
200	CHCG	60614	2978	0W-2N	B7
2000	CHCG	60622	2977	2W-2N	B7
2000	CHCG	60647	2977	2W-2N	B7
4800	CHCG	60639	2975	6W-2N	E7
St. Stephen's Grn					
2400	NHBK	60062	2757	10W-17N	A5
St. Vincents Dr					
1200	LMNT	60439	3271		B7
Sakas Dr					
200	DSPN	60016	2863	13W-11N	A2
Salado Ct					
100	SMBG	60195	2859	23W-12N	A2
Salceda Dr					
2500	NHBK	60062	2810	10W-15N	A2
N Salem Av					
10	ANHT	60005	2806	18W-14N	E4
800	ANHT	60004	2806	18W-14N	E3
S Salem Av					
10	ANHT	60005	2806	18W-14N	E5
N Salem Blvd					
1300	ANHT	60004	2806	18W-15N	E2
Salem Cir					
10	EVTN	60201	2866	4W-11N	D2
10	SKOK	60203	2866	4W-11N	D2
Salem Ct					
1600	EGVV	60007	2859	21W-9N	D7
4700	RNPK	60471	3594	5W-26S	B3
17000	TYPK	60477	3424	9W-20S	D4
E Salem Ct					
18700	LNSG	60438	3510	4E-22S	B1
N Salem Ct					
600	PLTN	60074	2753	20W-16N	A6
S Salem Ct					
700	SMBG	60193	2858	24W-9N	D6
W Salem Ct					
18700	LNSG	60438	3510	4E-22S	B1
N Salem Dr					
10	HFET	60194	2858	24W-10N	D5
10	SMBG	60193	2858	24W-10N	D5
10	SMBG	60194	2858	24W-11N	D4
4100	ANHT	60004	2753	18W-18N	E2
S Salem Dr					
10	HFET	60194	2858	24W-10N	D6
10	SMBG	60193	2858	24W-10N	D6
10	SMBG	60194	2858	24W-10N	D6
800	SMBG	60193	2912		D1
Salem Ln					
10	SKOK	60203	2866	4W-11N	D2
800	CPVL	60110	2748		B5
S Salem Ln					
1100	ANHT	60005	2806	18W-12N	E7
1100	ANHT	60005	2860	18W-12N	E1
Salem Wk					
-	GNVW	60062	2809	12W-14N	B4
3400	NfdT	60062	2809	12W-14N	B4
Salford Dr					
1200	SMBG	60193	2913		C2
Salim Pl					
1000	LMNT	60439	3270		C7
Salinas Dr					
-	MKNA	60448	3504	11W-22S	A1
Salisbury Av					
8000	LYNS	60534	3088	10W-4S	B6
Salisbury Dr					
100	MNSR	46321	3510		C4
N Salk Rd					
3200	BFGV	60089	2754	16W-17N	D5
3200	WhlT	60004	2754	16W-17N	D5
3200	WhlT	60089	2754	16W-17N	D5
3300	BFGV	60004	2754	16W-17N	D4
Sally Ct					
600	ROSL	60172	2912		E6
3800	GNVW	60025	2809	11W-13N	D6
Sally Dr					
3400	BlmT	60475	3596	1W-28S	A6
3400	STGR	60475	3596	1W-28S	A6
Sally Ln					
9200	SRPK	60176	2973	11W-5N	D6
Salt Creek Cir					
-	OKBK	60523	3086		A6
Salt Creek Ln					
10	HNDL	60521	3086		B6
W Salt Creek Ln					
3000	ANHT	60005	2806	20W-14N	B3
3000	ANHT	60008	2806	20W-14N	B3
3000	RGMW	60008	2806	20W-14N	B3
Salt Creek Rd					
10	ROSL	60172	2913		C4
Salvatori Ct					
8000	ODPK	60462	3346	10W-16S	C3
Salvington Pl					
1400	BFGV	60089	2754	16W-17N	E4
1400	WLNG	60090	2754	16W-17N	D4
Samantha Dr					
-	PltT	60067	2805	22W-16N	B1
Samoset Ct					
500	SMBG	60193	2858	24W-10N	E6
Samoset Ln					
10	SMBG	60193	2858	24W-10N	D6
Samoset Tr					
8900	SKOK	60076	2866	4W-11N	C3
9100	SKOK	60203	2866	4W-11N	C3
Samson Ct					
1000	UYPK	60466	3684	3W-30S	C3
Samson Dr					
900	UYPK	60466	3684	3W-30S	C3
Samuel Ct					
100	SMWD	60107	2911		A1
Samuel Dr					
10	SMWD	60107	2856	30W-10N	B6
10	SMWD	60107	2857	28W-9N	A7
10	SMWD	60107	2911		A1
San Bernardino Dr					
17500	ODPK	60467	3423	13W-21S	B6
E Sanborn Dr					
1200	PLTN	60074	2753	19W-16N	C6
N Sanborn Dr					
800	PLTN	60074	2753	19W-17N	C6
Sancastle Dr					
9600	PlsT	60465	3209	11W-11S	D7
9600	PlsT	60480	3209	11W-11S	D7
9600	PSHL	60465	3209	11W-11S	D7
Sandalwood Ct					
10	SMWD	60107	2857	26W-11N	E4
900	BRLT	60103	2911		C5
Sandalwood Dr					
7300	TYPK	60477	3424	9W-21S	E5
13500	ODPK	60462	3346	10W-16S	B2
Sandalwood Ln					
10	BNHL	60010	2750	26W-18N	C3
300	SMBG	60193	2859	21W-10N	E6
Sanday Ln					
700	IVNS	60010	2751	25W-16N	A7
Sandbloom Rd					
10	ALGN	60102	2748		A3
10	DndT	60102	2748		A4
100	AlqT	60102	2748		A1
Sandburg Ct					
9900	PlsT	60464	3345	12W-15S	C1
Sandburg Dr					
1400	SMBG	60173	2859	21W-10N	E5
Sandburg St					
400	OMFD	60461	3595	3W-25S	B1
400	PKFT	60466	3595	3W-25S	B1
N Sandburg Ter					
1200	CHCG	60610	3034	0W-1N	B1
1500	CHCG	60610	2978		D7
1500	CHCG	60614	2978		D7
Sandcastle Dr					
2200	DYR	46311	3598		E2
Sander Ct					
1500	PTHT	60070	2808	15W-16N	A1
1500	WLNG	60070	2808	15W-16N	A1
1500	WLNG	60090	2808	15W-16N	A1
Sanders Dr					
8800	MaiT	60016	2863	11W-11N	E2
Sanders Ln					
5700	CTSD	60525	3147	13W-6S	A4
5700	LynT	60525	3147	13W-6S	A4
Sanders Rd					
-	RVWD	60015	2756	12W-18N	A2
-	RVWD	60062	2756	12W-18N	A2
-	WdfT	60015	2756	12W-18N	A2
-	WdfT	60062	2756	12W-18N	A2
10	NfdT	60062	2756	12W-18N	A2
10	NHBK	60062	2756	12W-16N	B6
2300	GNVW	60062	2809	12W-16N	B1
2300	NfdT	60062	2809	12W-15N	B2
2400	PTHT	60062	2809	12W-15N	B2
Sanderson Av					
14300	DLTN	60419	3350	0E-16S	E4
Sandhurst Ct					
10	SMWD	60107	2857	26W-11N	E4
1200	SMBG	60193	2859	22W-10N	D6
San Diego Av					
18000	HMWD	60430	3427	3W-21S	A7
San Diego Pl					
600	BRLT	60103	2911		B4
Sandlewood Ln					
4200	HFET	60195	2804	24W-15N	B2
Sandpebble Dr					
500	SMBG	60193	2912		D1
1500	PTHT	60070	2808	15W-16N	B1
1500	WLNG	60070	2808	15W-16N	B1
1500	WLNG	60090	2808	15W-16N	B1
Sandpiper Ct					
700	MonT	60466	3684	3W-29S	A2
900	BRLT	60103	2911		C4
9100	ODPK	60462	3346	11W-17S	A6
W Sandpiper Ct					
800	PLTN	60067	2805	22W-14N	C4
Sandpiper Ln					
500	VrnT	60015	2755	15W-20N	B2
Sandra Av					
1100	LydT	60164	2972		D5
1100	NHLK	60164	2972		D5
3000	FNPK	60131	2972		D4
Sandra Dr					
600	UYPK	60466	3684	3W-29S	B2
Sandra Ln					
300	CHHT	60411	3507	2W-24S	D5
400	ELGN	60120	2855		C5
600	WLNG	60090	2755	15W-17N	A4
8900	HYHL	60457	3209	11W-10S	E5
8900	HYHL	60457	3210	11W-10S	A5
13700	CTWD	60445	3347	6W-16S	D3
13800	BmnT	60445	3347	6W-16S	D3
Sandra St					
3700	FNPK	60131	2972		D3
3700	LydT	60131	2972		D3
Sandridge Ct					
2300	LYWD	60411	3509	2E-24S	E5
Sandridge Dr					
20600	LYWD	60411	3509	2E-24S	E5
Sandridge Ln					
2200	DYR	46311	3598		E2
Sandstone Dr					
1400	PTHT	60070	2808	15W-16N	A1
1400	WLNG	60090	2808	15W-16N	A1
W Sandstone Dr					
13700	HMGN	60441	3343	17W-17S	C5
Sandy Ct					
-	MonT	60449	3683	5W-31S	D5
-	UYPK	60449	3683	5W-31S	D5
Sandy Ln					
400	DSPN	60016	2862	15W-11N	A3
400	WLMT	60091	2812	4W-13N	B6
3100	GNVW	60025	2810	10W-15N	A2
7200	TYPK	60477	3424	9W-20S	E3
Sandy Beach Rd					
1100	ELGN	60123	2801		A7
Sandy Ridge Dr					
3000	SCHT	60475	3596	0W-27S	C5
3000	STGR	60475	3596	0W-27S	C5
Sanford Ct					
1300	GNVW	60025	2810	8W-13N	E5
Sanford Ln					
1300	GNVW	60025	2810	8W-13N	E5
San Francisco Ter					
800	BRLT	60103	2911		B4
Sangamon Ct					
10	PKFT	60466	3594	4W-27S	E5
Sangamon St					
200	PKFT	60466	3594	4W-27S	E5
200	PKFT	60466	3595	4W-27S	A5
300	RNPK	60471	3594	4W-27S	E4
600	CHHT	60411	3508	1W-24S	A6
3000	SCHT	60411	3596	1W-27S	A5
3000	STGR	60475	3596	1W-28S	A6
3800	CteT	60417	3596	1W-28S	A7
14400	HRVY	60426	3350	1W-17S	A5
N Sangamon St					
10	CHCG	60607	3033	1W-0N	E4
600	CHCG	60622	3033	1W-0N	E3
S Sangamon St					
-	CRTE	60417	3596	1W-29S	A7
-	CteT	60417	3685	1W-29S	A1
10	CHCG	60607	3033	1W-0S	E5
1300	CHCG	60608	3033	1W-1S	E7
1300	CRTE	60417	3685	1W-30S	A3
1800	CHCG	60608	3091	1W-1S	E1
3500	CHCG	60609	3091	1W-3S	E5
5200	CHCG	60609	3151	1W-5S	E2
5500	CHCG	60621	3151	1W-6S	E4
7300	CHCG	60621	3152	1W-8S	A7
7500	CHCG	60620	3214	1W-9S	A3
9500	CHCG	60643	3214	1W-11S	A6
12200	CTPK	60643	3278	1W-14S	A6
12200	CTPK	60827	3278	1W-14S	A6
12700	CHCG	60643	3278	1W-15S	A7
12700	CHCG	60827	3278	1W-14S	A7
23900	CteT	60417	3596	1W-29S	A7
San Juan Rd					
100	CPVL	60110	2748		B4
San Luis Ln					
10400	ODPK	60467	3423	13W-20S	B5
10400	OrlT	60467	3423	13W-20S	B5
San Simeon Dr					
1100	HRPK	60133	2912		A6
1200	HRPK	60133	2911		D6
Santa Anita Dr					
1100	HRPK	60133	2912		A6
1300	HRPK	60133	2911		E6
Santa Barbara Dr					
5600	HRPK	60133	2911		D6
Santa Cruz Dr					
5500	HRPK	60133	2911		E6
Santa Cruz Ln					
10400	ODPK	60467	3423	13W-21S	B5
10400	OrlT	60467	3423	13W-21S	B5
Santa Fe Av					
600	CPVL	60110	2748		D4
Santa Fe Ct					
10	WLSP	60480	3208		D5
Santa Fe Dr					
6700	HGKN	60525	3147	12W-7S	D7
7000	HGKN	60525	3209	12W-8S	C1
7600	HGKN	60480	3209	12W-8S	C1
Santa Fe Ln					
100	LynT	60480	3208		D5
100	WLSP	60480	3208		D6
Santa Fe St					
-	BRLT	60103	2910		C4
Santa Fe Tr					
700	BmdT	60108	2912		B7
700	BmdT	60172	2912		B7
3300	OMFD	60461	3506	4W-24S	E5
13600	OrlT	60467	3344	14W-16S	C2
Santa Rosa Dr					
500	DSPN	60018	2916		C1
N Santee Ln					
1300	MPPT	60056	2808	13W-14N	E4
Santuit Ct					
800	SMBG	60194	2858	24W-10N	D5
Sapling Ln					
600	DRFD	60015	2756	12W-20N	C1
Sapphire Dr N					
4500	HFET	60195	2804	24W-15N	B1
Sapphire Dr W					
1400	HFET	60195	2804	24W-15N	B1
Sara Av					
400	LMNT	60439	3270		E7
Sara Ct					
23700	CteT	60417	3597	2E-28S	E7
Sara Ln					
10	BNHL	60010	2750	25W-17N	E4
Sara Ann Ln					
6300	OKFT	60452	3425	8W-18S	B1
Sarah Av					
3700	FNPK	60131	2973	12W-4N	B2
3700	SRPK	60131	2973	12W-4N	B2
3700	SRPK	60176	2973	12W-4N	B2
Sarah Ct					
200	WLNG	60090	2755	15W-17N	A4
17800	CCHL	60478	3426	4W-21S	D6
Sarah Ln					
3600	CCHL	60478	3426	4W-21S	D6
Sarah St					
2400	FNPK	60164	2973	12W-3N	B6
2400	LydT	60164	2973	12W-3N	B6
2800	FNPK	60131	2973	12W-3N	B5
3600	SRPK	60176	2973	12W-4N	B3
Sarah Constant Ln					
900	SMBG	60194	2857	27W-11N	D3
Sarahs Grove Ln					
10	SMBG	60193	2858	24W-10N	E5
10	SMBG	60193	2859	23W-10N	A6
Saranac Ct					
2400	GNVW	60025	2809	11W-15N	C2
Saranac Ln					
1100	NHBK	60062	2756	10W-17N	E5
2400	GNVW	60025	2809	11W-15N	D3
Sarasota Dr					
300	SMWD	60107	2857	28W-11N	A4
1100	WLNG	60090	2754	16W-18N	E3
Saratoga Dr					
-	CPVL	60110	2801		A1
500	CHHT	60411	3507	2W-24S	C5
6800	BGVW	60455	3211	8W-10S	A4
6900	BGVW	60455	3210	8W-10S	E4
11000	ODPK	60467	3422	14W-19S	E2
11000	ODPK	60467	3423	13W-19S	A2
N Saratoga Dr					
900	PLTN	60074	2753	20W-17N	B5
Saratoga Ln					
700	BFGV	60089	2754	17W-17N	B5
1500	GNVW	60025	2810	10W-14N	A5
Saratoga Rd					
4500	RNPK	60471	3594	5W-26S	B3
Saratoga St					
400	DGvT	60439	3270		C1
Sarson Wy					
700	HRPK	60133	2912		A1
Sassabee St					
10	PKFT	60466	3594	4W-27S	E4
Saucer Ct					
10	SBTN	60010	2803	27W-13N	B6
N Sauganash Av					
6000	CHCG	60646	2920	5W-7N	A3
6400	LNWD	60712	2919	6W-8N	D2
6700	CHCG	60646	2919	6W-8N	D2
6800	SKOK	60646	2919	6W-8N	C1
N Sauganash Ln					
5900	CHCG	60646	2920	5W-7N	B4
Sauganash St					
300	PKFT	60466	3594	4W-27S	E5
300	RNPK	60471	3594	4W-27S	E5
Saugatuck St					
400	PKFT	60466	3594	4W-27S	E5
Saugus Ln					
200	SMBG	60173	2859	21W-10N	E5
Sauk Ct					
10	PKFT	60466	3595	3W-27S	B4
N Sauk Ln					
1400	MPPT	60056	2808	13W-14N	E3
Sauk Tr					
-	BlmT	60411	3595	2W-27S	E4
-	SCHT	60411	3595	2W-27S	E4
10	BlmT	60466	3595	2W-27S	C4
10	IHPK	60525	3146		E6
10	PKFT	60466	3595	2W-27S	C4
300	PKFT	60466	3594	4W-26S	E3
400	RNPK	60471	3594	6W-26S	A3
5300	RchT	60471	3593	6W-27S	E3
5300	RNPK	60471	3593	7W-27S	C3
5400	RNPK	60443	3593	7W-27S	C3
5600	RchT	60443	3593	8W-26S	A3
6500	FKFT	60443	3593	8W-27S	A3
7100	FKFT	60423	3593	9W-27S	A3
7100	RchT	60423	3593	9W-27S	A3
E Sauk Tr					
10	CHHT	60411	3596	0W-27S	B4
10	SCHT	60411	3596	0W-27S	B4
400	CHHT	60475	3596	0E-26S	E3
400	SCHT	60475	3596	0E-27S	D3
400	STGR	60411	3596	0W-27S	C4
400	STGR	60475	3596	0W-27S	C4
600	BlmT	60411	3596	0W-27S	C4
600	BlmT	60475	3597	0E-26S	A3
600	BlmT	60475	3597	0E-26S	A3
600	SLVL	60411	3597	2E-26S	D3
600	STGR	60411	3597	0E-26S	A3
600	STGR	60475	3597	0E-26S	A3
2700	BlmT	60411	3598	3E-26S	A2
3600	DYR	46311	3598	4E-26S	C2
3600	DYR	60411	3598	4E-26S	C2
E Sauk Tr US-30					
3600	BlmT	60411	3598	4E-26S	C2
3600	DYR	46311	3598	4E-26S	C2

STREET Block	City	ZIP	Map#	CGS	Grid
E Sauk Tr US-30					
3600	DYR	60411	3598	4E-26S	C2
W Sauk Tr					
-	FKFT	60423	3593	9W-26S	A3
-	RchT	60423	3593	9W-26S	A3
-	RchT	60443	3593	9W-26S	A3
10	SCHT	60411	3596	1W-27S	A4
200	SCHT	60411	3595	1W-27S	E4
300	BlmT	60411	3595	2W-27S	E4
300	BlmT	60466	3595	2W-27S	E4
Sauk Pointe Dr					
22400	SLVL	60411	3597	1E-27S	B3
Saunders Rd					
10	NHBK	60062	2756	12W-20N	A2
10	RVWD	60015	2756	12W-20N	A1
10	RVWD	60062	2756	12W-20N	A2
10	WdfT	60015	2756	12W-20N	A1
10	WdfT	60062	2756	12W-20N	A2
400	DRFD	60015	2756	12W-20N	A1
Saunders Rd CO-W24					
10	NHBK	60062	2756	12W-20N	A2
10	RVWD	60015	2756	12W-20N	A1
10	RVWD	60062	2756	12W-20N	A2
10	WdfT	60015	2756	12W-20N	A1
10	WdfT	60062	2756	12W-20N	A2
400	DRFD	60015	2756	12W-20N	A1
Sausalito Ct					
1100	BRLT	60103	2911		C5
Savanna Ln					
3300	MTSN	60443	3594	4W-26S	E1
Savannah Ln					
-	HRPK	60133	2912		A3
1400	SMBG	60193	2912		A2
Savoy Ct					
400	SMBG	60193	2858	24W-9N	D6
1000	EGVV	60007	2914		B3
Savoy Ln					
-	BGVW	60455	3274	9W-11S	D1
-	BlmT	60411	3509	2E-23S	D3
-	LYWD	60411	3509	2E-23S	D3
Sawgrass Av					
-	RNPK	60471	3593	6W-27S	E5
-	RNPK	60471	3594	6W-27S	A5
Sawgrass Ct					
2300	RVWD	60015	2756	12W-20N	A1
8000	ODPK	60462	3346	10W-18S	C7
Sawgrass Dr					
-	MONE	60449	3683	6W-31S	A4
10	BRBK	60459	3211	7W-8S	C1
10	LMNT	60439	3343	17W-15S	B1
200	PSHT	60463	3275	7W-14S	B5
200	PSHT	60463	3347	8W-15S	B1
Sawgrass Ln					
200	PSHT	60463	3347	8W-15S	B1
14900	HMGN	60441	3343	17W-17S	C6
Saw Horse Dr					
5200	HFET	60192	2802	30W-12N	C7
Sawyer Av					
-	MKHM	60426	3348	4W-17S	E6
10	LGNG	60525	3087	12W-4S	C7
13700	RBBN	60472	3348	4W-16S	E3
14500	MDLN	60445	3348	4W-17S	E5
15600	MKHM	60426	3349	4W-18S	A7
15600	MKHM	60426	3427	4W-18S	A1
16600	HLCT	60429	3427	4W-19S	A3
N Sawyer Av					
500	CHCG	60624	3032	4W-0N	D3
700	CHCG	60651	3032	4W-0N	D3
1600	CHCG	60647	2976	4W-2N	D7
3600	CHCG	60618	2976	4W-4N	D2
4300	CHCG	60625	2976	4W-5N	D1
4700	CHCG	60625	2920	4W-6N	D6
5500	CHCG	60659	2920	4W-6N	D5
S Sawyer Av					
1200	CHCG	60624	3032	4W-1S	D7
1400	CHCG	60623	3032	4W-1S	D7
1500	CHCG	60623	3090	4W-1S	D1
4300	CHCG	60632	3090	4W-4S	E7
4600	CHCG	60632	3150	4W-5S	E1
5400	CHCG	60629	3150	4W-6S	E4
7900	CHCG	60652	3212	4W-9S	E2
9900	ENGN	60805	3212	4W-11S	E7
10200	CHCG	60655	3276	4W-12S	E1
10200	ENGN	60805	3276	4W-11S	E1
Saxon Ct					
1000	ELGN	60120	2855		C5
Saxon Pl					
800	BFGV	60089	2754	16W-17N	D4
800	BFGV	60090	2754	16W-17N	D4
800	WLNG	60090	2754	16W-17N	D4
Sayer Rd					
200	BRLT	60103	2910		C5
200	WynT	60103	2910		C5
E Sayles Dr					
800	PLTN	60074	2753	19W-16N	B6
Saylesville Ln					
1100	SMBG	60193	2912		C1
Sayre Av					
7600	BDPK	60459	3210	8W-9S	E4
7600	BDPK	60638	3210	8W-8S	E1
7600	BGVW	60459	3210	8W-8S	E1
7800	BRBK	60459	3210	8W-9S	E4
8700	BGVW	60455	3210	8W-10S	E4
8700	OKLN	60455	3210	8W-10S	E6
9100	MNGV	60053	2864	8W-11N	E2
9300	BGVW	60453	3210	8W-10S	E6
9500	OKLN	60453	3210	8W-11S	E6
9600	OKLN	60415	3210	8W-11S	E6
9700	CHRG	60415	3210	8W-11S	E7
15500	OKFT	60452	3347	8W-18S	A7
15600	BmnT	60462	3347	8W-18S	A7
15600	BmnT	60462	3425	8W-18S	A1
15600	BmnT	60477	3347	8W-18S	A7
15600	BmnT	60477	3425	8W-18S	A1
15600	ODPK	60462	3347	8W-18S	A7
15600	ODPK	60462	3425	8W-18S	A1
15700	ODPK	60477	3425	8W-18S	A1
16700	TYPK	60477	3425	8W-20S	A4
N Sayre Av					
1600	CHCG	60707	3030	8W-2N	E1
1600	OKPK	60302	3030	8W-2N	E1
1600	OKPK	60707	3030	8W-2N	E1
1700	CHCG	60707	2974	8W-2N	E7
3600	CHCG	60634	2974	8W-4N	E2
4200	HDHT	60706	2974	8W-5N	E1
4200	NRDG	60706	2974	8W-5N	E1
4400	HDHT	60706	2918	8W-5N	E7
4400	NRDG	60706	2918	8W-5N	E7
5400	CHCG	60656	2918	8W-6N	E5
6500	CHCG	60631	2918	8W-8N	E2
6500	CHCG	60714	2918	8W-8N	E2
6500	NLES	60714	2918	8W-8N	E2
S Sayre Av					
-	BDPK	60638	3148	8W-8S	E7
5100	CHCG	60638	3148	8W-5S	E3
5100	StkT	60638	3148	8W-5S	E2
7300	BDPK	60638	3210	8W-8S	E1
7500	BDPK	60459	3210	8W-8S	E1
7500	BGVW	60455	3210	8W-8S	E1
7500	BGVW	60459	3210	8W-8S	E1
W SBC Center Dr					
-	HFET	60195	2804	25W-13N	A6
Scanlon Dr					
600	WLNG	60090	2754	15W-18N	E2
Scarboro Ln					
-	SMBG	60193	2859	21W-9N	D6
Scarborough Ct					
14600	OKFT	60452	3347	7W-17S	D5
Scarborough Ln					
-	BmnT	60445	3347	6W-17S	D5
-	BmnT	60452	3347	6W-17S	D5
5500	OKFT	60452	3347	6W-17S	D5
Scarborough on Oxford					
10	RGMW	60008	2805	22W-13N	B6
Scarbrough Cir					
600	HFET	60194	2858	25W-10N	B5
Scarlet Ct					
1600	BRLT	60103	2910		A2
Scarsdale Ct					
200	SMBG	60193	2859	22W-10N	C6
S Scarsdale Ct					
900	ANHT	60005	2807	17W-13N	B7
Scenic Dr					
8100	BRRG	60527	3208		E3
8100	WLSP	60480	3208		E3
Schaaf Ct					
22100	RNPK	60471	3594	6W-26S	A3
N Schaefer Rd					
4000	ANHT	60004	2753	18W-18N	D2
4200	ANHT	60047	2753	18W-20N	D2
4200	VrnT	60047	2753	18W-20N	D2
4200	VrnT	60089	2753	18W-20N	D2
Schaeffer Ct					
14200	HmrT	60441	3342	20W-16S	B4
Schaeffer Rd					
-	ANHT	60004	2753	18W-20N	D2
-	ANHT	60047	2753	18W-20N	D2
1400	LGGV	60047	2753	18W-20N	D1
1800	VrnT	60047	2753	18W-20N	D2
1800	VrnT	60089	2753	18W-20N	D2
Schaller Dr					
-	MYWD	60141	3088	10W-1S	A1
-	MYWD	60153	3088	10W-1S	A1
-	PvsT	60141	3088	10W-1S	A1
Schaumburg Ct					
100	SMBG	60193	2859	22W-10N	B6
Schaumburg Rd					
1000	HnrT	60120	2856	30W-10N	B5
1000	SMWD	60120	2856	30W-10N	B5
1300	HnrT	60107	2856	30W-10N	C5
1300	SMWD	60107	2856	30W-10N	C5
E Schaumburg Rd					
-	SMBG	60173	2860	21W-10N	A6
-	SMBG	60193	2857	27W-10N	D5
10	SMBG	60193	2859	22W-10N	C5
10	SMBG	60194	2859	23W-10N	A5
10	SMWD	60107	2857	27W-10N	C5
700	SMBG	60173	2859	22W-10N	D5
1000	SMBG	60107	2857	27W-10N	C5
1000	SMBG	60194	2857	27W-10N	C5
W Schaumburg Rd					
10	SMBG	60193	2859	23W-10N	A5
10	SMBG	60194	2859	23W-10N	A5
10	SMWD	60107	2856	29W-11N	D5
10	SMWD	60107	2857	28W-11N	A5
100	HnrT	60107	2856	28W-11N	E5
100	SMBG	60193	2858	26W-10N	A5
100	SMBG	60194	2858	26W-10N	A5
400	HFET	60193	2858	24W-10N	E5
400	HFET	60194	2858	24W-10N	E5
1500	HnrT	60120	2856	30W-10N	C5
1500	SMWD	60120	2856	30W-10N	C5
2000	SMBG	60193	2857	26W-10N	D6
2000	SMBG	60194	2857	26W-10N	D6
Scheer Dr					
8500	TYPK	60477	3424	10W-21S	B7
N Schick Pl					
-	CHCG	60610	3034	0W-1N	A1
Schierhorn Ln					
3300	FNPK	60131	2973	11W-4N	D4
Schiller Av					
1900	WLMT	60091	2812	4W-13N	B5
Schiller Blvd					
9300	FNPK	60131	2973	13W-3N	A4
Schiller St					
600	ITSC	60143	2914		D6
E Schiller St					
10	CHCG	60610	3034	0E-1N	C1
100	EMHT	60126	3028		A2
N Schiller St					
200	PLTN	60067	2752	20W-16N	E7
W Schiller St					
10	CHCG	60610	3034	0W-1N	B1
1900	CHCG	60622	3033	2W-1N	B1
Schilling Av					
1000	CHHT	60411	3507	1W-25S	E6
1200	CHHT	60411	3508	1W-25S	A6
1400	CHHT	60411	3596	0W-25S	B1
1500	CHHT	60411	3595	1W-25S	E1
Schilling Dr					
700	DYR	46311	3598		E3
N Schilling Rd					
6400	CHCG	60666	2917	13W-8N	A3
Schirra Ct					
1500	EGVV	60007	2913		E1
E Schirra Dr					
800	PLTN	60074	2753	19W-16N	B7
N Schirra Dr					
500	PLTN	60074	2753	19W-16N	B7
Schlick Av					
-	BmdT	60157	2913		D5
Schmidt Dr					
10	DYR	46311	3598		C4
Schneider Av					
1100	OKPK	60302	3030	8W-1N	D2
1100	RVFT	60305	3030	8W-1N	D2
Schoenbeck Rd					
10	WLNG	60090	2754	16W-17N	E6
300	WLNG	60004	2754	16W-17N	E6
700	PTHT	60070	2754	16W-17N	E6
N Schoenbeck Rd					
-	ANHT	60056	2807	16W-14N	E4
-	MPPT	60004	2807	16W-14N	E4
10	MPPT	60056	2807	16W-15N	E3
10	PTHT	60070	2807	15W-15N	E1
700	ANHT	60004	2807	15W-15N	E1
800	PTHT	60004	2807	15W-15N	E1
1000	PTHT	60070	2754	15W-16N	E7
1200	WLNG	60004	2754	15W-16N	E7
1200	WLNG	60090	2754	15W-16N	E7
2100	ANHT	60004	2754	16W-16N	E7
2200	PTHT	60004	2754	16W-16N	E7
Scholtz Ln					
23100	BlmT	60466	3595	2W-28S	C5
23100	CteT	60475	3595	2W-28S	C5
School Av					
700	MTSN	60443	3506	5W-25S	B7
School Dr					
-	NHBK	60062	2810	10W-16N	A1
2100	RGMW	60008	2806	19W-14N	C5
3500	CCHL	60429	3426	4W-21S	D6
3500	CCHL	60478	3426	4W-21S	D6
3500	HLCT	60429	3426	4W-21S	D6
3600	BmnT	60430	3426	4W-21S	D6
E School Ln					
200	PTHT	60070	2808	15W-14N	B3
S School Ln					
100	PTHT	60070	2808	15W-14N	A4
200	MPPT	60056	2808	15W-14N	A4
200	PTHT	60056	2808	15W-14N	A4
School St					
-	MYWD	60153	3029	11W-0N	E5
100	MYWD	60153	3030	10W-0N	A5
100	WDDL	60191	2915		A6
200	WDDL	60191	2914		E6
500	MNSR	46321	3430		D6
1600	CHHT	60411	3596	1W-25S	A1
2800	FSMR	60422	3507	3W-22S	A2
5900	BKLY	60163	3028		C5
5900	OKFT	60452	3347	7W-18S	C6
8100	WLSP	60525	3208		E3
8200	WLSP	60480	3208		E3
8500	MNGV	60053	2865	7W-10N	B4
16200	SHLD	60473	3428	0E-19S	E2
17700	LNSG	60438	3430	3E-21S	A6
N School St					
200	MPPT	60056	2808	15W-13N	A6
800	PTHT	60070	2808	15W-16N	A1
7300	NLES	60714	2864	8W-9N	E7
S School St					
10	MPPT	60056	2808	15W-12N	A7
500	MPPT	60056	2862	15W-12N	A2
900	DSPN	60016	2862	15W-11N	A3
900	DSPN	60056	2862	15W-11N	A3
900	MPPT	60016	2862	15W-11N	A3
13600	RVDL	60827	3350	0W-16S	B3
14500	DLTN	60419	3350	0W-16S	B4
W School St					
10	GNWD	60425	3508	0E-22S	D1
900	CHCG	60657	2977	1W-4N	D3
1900	CHCG	60618	2977	2W-4N	B3
2900	CHCG	60618	2976	3W-4N	E3
4000	CHCG	60641	2976	5W-4N	B3
4700	CHCG	60641	2975	7W-4N	C3
5500	CHCG	60634	2975	7W-4N	B3
6700	CHCG	60634	2974	10W-4N	B3
School House Ct					
10	PKFT	60466	3595	3W-26S	B3
Schooner Ln					
600	EGVV	60007	2913		D2
600	EGVV	60193	2913		D2
Schooner Pt					
600	SMBG	60194	2859	23W-10N	A5
W Schorsch St					
6500	CHCG	60634	2975	8W-4N	A3
W Schrader Dr					
3400	CHCG	60624	3032	4W-0N	D4
Schreiber Av					
10	ROSL	60172	2913		A3
100	ROSL	60172	2912		E3
W Schreiber Av					
1600	CHCG	60626	2921	2W-8N	C2
3900	LNWD	60712	2920	4W-8N	B2
6600	CHCG	60631	2919	8W-8N	A2
7100	CHCG	60631	2918	8W-8N	D2
S Schroeder Av					
500	PtnT	60468	3860	9W-37S	E4
500	PTON	60468	3860	9W-37S	E4
Schrum Rd					
10	CTCY	60409	3430	4E-19S	C2
Schubert Av					
10400	FNPK	60131	2973	13W-3N	A5
10400	FNPK	60164	2973	13W-3N	A5
10400	LydT	60131	2973	13W-3N	A5
10400	LydT	60164	2973	13W-3N	A5
10600	LydT	60164	2972		E5
W Schubert Av					
600	CHCG	60614	2978	0W-3N	A5
700	CHCG	60614	2977	1W-3N	E5
2300	CHCG	60647	2977	3W-3N	A5
2700	CHCG	60647	2976	3W-3N	E5
3900	CHCG	60639	2976	5W-3N	B5
4800	CHCG	60639	2975	7W-3N	B5
6700	CHCG	60707	2975	8W-3N	A5
7200	CHCG	60707	2974	9W-3N	D5
7200	EDPK	60707	2974	9W-3N	D5
N Schubert Ct					
100	PLTN	60067	2753	20W-16N	A7
Schulte St					
200	DYR	46311	3598		D2
Schultz Dr					
-	LNSG	60438	3430	4E-21S	C7
N Schultz Dr					
3200	LNSG	60438	3430	4E-21S	B7
S Schultz Dr					
3200	LNSG	60438	3430	4E-21S	B7
Schultz St					
400	LMNT	60439	3270		E6
900	LMNT	60439	3271		A6
Schwab St					
100	TNTN	60476	3428	0E-21S	E6
Science Dr					
-	CHCG	60637	3153	2E-6S	B3
Science Rd					
10	GNWD	60425	3508	0W-22S	C2
Scioto Dr					
25700	MONE	60449	3683	6W-31S	B5
Scotch Ln					
3000	RVWD	60015	2755	13W-20N	D1
Scotch Pine Dr					
6400	TYPK	60477	3425	8W-22S	B7
Scotch Pine Ln					
2100	NHBK	60062	2756	11W-16N	D7
Scotdale Rd					
10	LGPK	60525	3087	12W-2S	B3
10	PvsT	60525	3087	12W-2S	B3
Scots Ct					
500	IVNS	60067	2752	22W-16N	B6
Scotsglen Rd					
-	ODPK	60467	3345	13W-18S	A7
-	ODPK	60467	3423	13W-18S	A1
Scott Av					
-	BNHM	60633	3352	3E-16S	A3
100	GLNC	60093	2759	5W-16N	A6
200	WNKA	60093	2759	5W-16N	A7
1000	CHHT	60411	3507	2W-25S	E7
1100	WNKA	60093	2758	6W-16N	D7
1400	CHHT	60411	3595	2W-25S	E1
Scott Cir					
1900	CPVL	60110	2748		D5
Scott Cres					
3000	FSMR	60422	3507	3W-23S	A3
Scott Ct					
200	BRLT	60103	2911		A6
400	ROSL	60172	2913		B5
6300	TYPK	60477	3425	7W-20S	B4
Scott Dr					
-	BDVW	60141	3087	10W-1S	E1
-	BDVW	60155	3087	10W-1S	E1
-	OMFD	60461	3506	4W-25S	E6
-	OMFD	60461	3507	3W-24S	A6
-	PvsT	60141	3087	10W-1S	E1
-	PvsT	60141	3088	10W-1S	A1
-	PvsT	60155	3087	10W-1S	E1
100	EDND	60118	2801		C2
200	PvsT	60141	3029	10W-1S	E7
200	PvsT	60141	3030	10W-1S	A7
600	SMBG	60193	2913		C1
22000	RNPK	60471	3594	6W-26S	A3
W Scott Dr					
3600	ALSP	60803	3276	4W-14S	D6
Scott Ln					
5200	OKLN	60453	3211	6W-11S	E7
6600	BRLT	60103	2911		C3
6600	HRPK	60133	2911		C3
14000	ODPK	60462	3346	9W-16S	D4
Scott Rd					
2100	NHBK	60062	2757	10W-16N	A7
Scott St					
10	EGvT	60007	2861	17W-10N	B5
10	EGVV	60007	2861	17W-10N	B5
200	WLNG	60090	2754	16W-17N	D5
2000	LydT	60164	2973	12W-2N	B7
2000	MLPK	60160	2973	12W-2N	B7
2300	FNPK	60131	2973	12W-3N	B6
2300	FNPK	60164	2973	12W-2N	B6
3600	SRPK	60131	2973	12W-4N	B3
3600	SRPK	60176	2973	12W-5N	B2
4300	OKFT	60452	3426	5W-19S	B2
4800	SRPK	60176	2917	12W-6N	B7
E Scott St					
10	CHCG	60610	3034	0E-1N	C1
N Scott St					
-	DSPN	60018	2917	12W-7N	B3
6000	RSMT	60018	2917	12W-7N	B3
S Scott St					
2200	DSPN	60018	2863	12W-9N	B7
2300	DSPN	60018	2917	12W-8N	B1
W Scott St					
600	CHCG	60610	3034	0W-1N	A1
W Scott Ter					
2000	MPPT	60056	2861	17W-12N	B1
Scott Foresman Rd					
-	GNVW	60025	2810	8W-14N	D5
Scottlynne Dr					
2800	PKRG	60068	2863	11W-9N	C7
S Scottsdale Av					
8100	CHCG	60652	3212	5W-9S	A2
Scottsvale Av					
600	ANHT	60004	2807	16W-14N	D4
Scottswood Rd					
10	RVSD	60546	3088	10W-3S	B6
Scotty Ln					
400	DYR	46311	3598		D4
Scoville Av					
1200	BRWN	60402	3031	8W-1S	A7
1200	OKPK	60304	3031	8W-1S	A7
1500	BRWN	60402	3089	8W-2S	A2
3900	SKNY	60402	3089	8W-4S	A7
N Scoville Av					
100	OKPK	60302	3031	8W-0N	A3
S Scoville Av					
500	OKPK	60302	3031	8W-0S	A5
500	OKPK	60304	3031	8W-0S	A5
1100	BRWN	60402	3031	8W-0S	A7
Scully Ct					
200	SMBG	60193	2859	23W-10N	A6
Scully Dr					
10	SMBG	60193	2859	23W-10N	A6
S Sea Biscuit Ct					
13900	HMGN	60467	3344	15W-16S	C3
Sea Biscuit Ln					
1300	HRPK	60133	2911		E6
Seacrest Ln					
800	BRLT	60103	2911		B5
Seafarer Dr					
600	SMBG	60193	2912		D1
Seagull Ln					
11700	PSHT	60463	3274	9W-13S	C5
Sean Dr					
17500	ODPK	60467	3423	13W-21S	A6
Seapines Dr					
7800	ODPK	60462	3346	9W-18S	C7
Searle Pkwy					
4800	SKOK	60076	2865	6W-10N	E5
4800	SKOK	60077	2865	6W-10N	E5
Sears Pkwy					
-	HFET	60118	2802	30W-13N	B5
-	HFET	60192	2802	30W-13N	B5
Seaside Ct					
800	SMBG	60193	2912		D1
Seaton Ln					
1600	SMBG	60194	2858	25W-10N	B5
Seaver Ln					
2100	HFET	60194	2857	26W-12N	E2
2100	HFET	60194	2858	26W-12N	A2
Seaview Ct					
1000	SMBG	60193	2912		E1
Seberger Dr					
500	MNSR	46321	3430		D7
Sebring Cir					
1200	ELGN	60120	2855		D3
Sebring Dr					
1000	ELGN	60120	2855		D3
S Secretariat Ln					
13700	HMGN	60467	3344	15W-16S	B3
Sedge Blvd					
5000	HFET	60192	2802	29W-13N	C5
Sedgfield Ct					
2300	SMBG	60194	2857	26W-10N	E5
Sedgley Ct					
6000	BRRG	60527	3146		B4
Sedgley Rd					
300	BRRG	60527	3146		B4
Sedgwick Dr					
10600	PlsT	60464	3273	13W-14S	A7
N Sedgwick St					
600	CHCG	60610	3034	0W-0N	B3
1600	CHCG	60610	2978	0W-2N	A7
1600	CHCG	60614	2978	0W-2N	B7
Seegers Av					
10	EGVV	60007	2861	17W-10N	C6
Seegers Rd					
600	DSPN	60016	2862	14W-11N	D2
E Seegers Rd					
10	ANHT	60005	2861	17W-11N	A2
W Seegers Rd					
10	ANHT	60005	2861	18W-11N	A2
S See Gwun Av					
200	MPPT	60056	2807	16W-12N	E7
400	MPPT	60056	2861	16W-11N	E2
Seeley Av					
900	PKRG	60068	2863	11W-9N	E6
1000	FDHT	60411	3509	1E-25S	A7
1600	FDHT	60411	3597	1E-25S	A1
13000	BLID	60406	3277	2W-15S	C7
13300	BLID	60406	3349	2W-15S	C1
14000	DXMR	60406	3349	2W-16S	C3
14100	DXMR	60426	3349	2W-16S	D4
15300	HRVY	60426	3349	2W-18S	D7
N Seeley Av					
100	CHCG	60612	3033	2W-0N	B4
2300	CHCG	60647	2977	2W-2N	B6
3800	CHCG	60618	2977	2W-4N	B2
4400	CHCG	60618	2921	2W-5N	B7
4800	CHCG	60625	2921	2W-6N	B6
6000	CHCG	60659	2921	2W-7N	B3
6900	CHCG	60645	2921	2W-8N	B1
7300	CHCG	60645	2867	2W-9N	B7
7500	EVTN	60202	2867	2W-9N	B7
S Seeley Av					
10	CHCG	60612	3033	2W-0S	B5
2300	CHCG	60608	3091	2W-2S	B2
3500	CHCG	60609	3091	2W-3S	C5
5200	CHCG	60609	3151	2W-5S	C2
5500	CHCG	60636	3151	2W-6S	C3
7500	CHCG	60620	3213	2W-8S	C1
9500	CHCG	60643	3213	2W-11S	C7
10300	CHCG	60643	3277	2W-12S	C1
Seers Ct					
200	SMBG	60173	2859	22W-10N	D4
Seers Dr					
800	SMBG	60173	2859	22W-10N	C4
Seger St					
-	WLMT	60091	2811	5W-13N	E6
Seine Ct					
3400	HLCT	60429	3426	4W-21S	E7
W Seipp St					
2600	CHCG	60652	3213	3W-9S	A3
Selborne Rd					
300	RVSD	60546	3088	9W-2S	D3
Selkirk Ct					
1900	IVNS	60010	2751	25W-16N	B6
Selkirk Dr					
400	SMBG	60194	2858	25W-11N	C4
Selkirk St					
-	FSMR	60422	3506	4W-23S	D3
Sell Rd					
100	CHCG	60007	2916		A1
Sell St					
10	CHCG	60007	2916		A2
10	DSPN	60007	2916		A2
10	DSPN	60018	2916		A2
Selleck St					
1300	CRTE	60417	3685	0W-30S	C2
Sellstrom Dr					
10	PLTN	60067	2806	20W-15N	A1
10	PLTN	60074	2806	20W-15N	A1
W Selma Av					
7300	SMMT	60501	3148	9W-5S	D2
Selva Ln					
13800	ODPK	60462	3346	9W-16S	D4
13800	OrlT	60462	3346	9W-16S	D4
Selwyn Ln					
100	BFGV	60089	2754	16W-17N	D5
Seminary Av					
2400	DSPN	60016	2863	11W-11N	C3
2400	MaiT	60016	2863	11W-11N	C3
N Seminary Av					
10	PKRG	60068	2917	11W-8N	D2
700	PKRG	60068	2863	11W-9N	E6
1900	CHCG	60614	2977	1W-2N	E7
2700	CHCG	60657	2977	1W-3N	E5
3800	CHCG	60613	2977	1W-4N	E2
S Seminary Av					
700	PKRG	60068	2917	11W-8N	E2
Seminary Dr					
100	DYR	46311	3510		D5
500	DYR	46321	3510		D5
500	MNSR	46321	3510		D5
Seminole Ct					
2400	RVWD	60015	2756	13W-20N	A1
8100	ODPK	60462	3346	10W-18S	C7
Seminole Dr					
800	ELGN	60120	2855		C1
N Seminole Dr					
4400	GNVW	60025	2809	11W-15N	C2
4400	GNVW	60062	2809	11W-15N	C2
S Seminole Dr					
4400	GNVW	60025	2809	11W-15N	C2
Seminole Ln					
1600	CPVL	60110	2748		D4
E Seminole Ln					
1700	MPPT	60056	2808	13W-15N	E2
1700	PTHT	60070	2808	13W-15N	E2
1800	PTHT	60056	2808	13W-15N	E2
2000	MPPT	60056	2809	13W-15N	A2
2000	PTHT	60070	2809	13W-15N	A2
2100	WhlT	60062	2809	13W-15N	A2
Seminole Rd					
900	WLMT	60091	2812	5W-14N	A5
1000	WLMT	60091	2811	5W-14N	E5
S Seminole Rd					
12200	PSPK	60464	3274	10W-14S	B6
Seminole St					
300	PKFT	60466	3594	4W-27S	E5
300	RNPK	60471	3594	4W-27S	E5
W Seminole St					
5600	CHCG	60646	2919	7W-7N	C4
7200	CHCG	60631	2918	9W-7N	D4
7800	NpkT	60631	2918	9W-7N	B5
8000	MaiT	60631	2918	10W-7N	B4
W Seminole Tr					
13500	HMGN	60441	3343	16W-16S	D3
Semmler Ct					
-	TYPK	60477	3424	10W-21S	B6
Semmler Dr					
-	TYPK	60477	3424	10W-21S	B7
Senate Dr					
9000	MaiT	60016	2863	11W-11N	D3
9300	DSPN	60016	2863	11W-11N	D3

Chicago & Cook County Street Index

STREET Block	City	ZIP	Map#	CGS	Grid
W Shirley Rd					
21000	KLDR	60074	2752	21W-20N	E1
W Shirra Ct					
1600	ANHT	60004	2753	18W-16N	D6
Shoal Creek Ct					
2400	RVWD	60015	2756	13W-20N	A1
Shoal Creek Dr					
25500	MONE	60449	3683	6W-31S	B5
Shoals Dr					
1200	LKPT	60441	3342	21W-18S	A7
Shoe Factory Rd					
-	ELGN	60120	2855		D1
-	HFET	60010	2803	27W-12N	D7
-	HFET	60010	2856	29W-12N	D1
-	HFET	60010	2857	27W-12N	C1
-	HFET	60120	2855		D1
-	HFET	60194	2857	27W-12N	C1
-	HFET	60195	2803	27W-12N	D7
-	HnrT	60120	2855		E1
10	HFET	60120	2856	31W-12N	A1
10	HnrT	60120	2856	31W-12N	A1
500	HFET	60192	2856	30W-12N	B1
500	HnrT	60192	2856	30W-12N	B1
600	HFET	60120	2802	30W-12N	B7
600	HnrT	60120	2802	30W-12N	A7
S Sholer Av					
7100	BGVW	60455	3148	9W-8S	C7
7300	BGVW	60455	3210	9W-8S	C1
Shore Ct					
100	BRRG	60527	3208		A3
900	SMBG	60193	2913		A1
1400	WLNG	60090	2754	16W-18N	D4
S Shore Ct					
1400	BRTN	60010	2751	24W-20N	C1
Shore Dr					
10	BRRG	60527	3208		A3
10	SMBG	60193	2913		A1
200	HRVY	60426	3350	1W-16S	A4
200	RVDL	60827	3350	1W-16S	A4
E Shore Dr					
9600	OKLN	60453	3211	6W-11S	D6
W Shore Dr					
9500	OKLN	60453	3211	6W-11S	D6
Shoreham Cir					
22500	DRPK	60010	2752	22W-20N	B1
Shoreline Cir					
100	SMBG	60173	2859	22W-10N	C5
100	SMBG	60194	2859	22W-10N	C5
Shoreline Ct					
300	GLNC	60022	2759	5W-17N	A5
Shoreline Dr					
200	PKRG	60068	2863	11W-9N	D7
Shorely Dr					
500	BRTN	60010	2751	25W-20N	B1
N Shoreside Ct					
1200	PLTN	60067	2752	22W-17N	C5
Shoreside Dr					
10	SBTN	60010	2803	27W-15N	B2
Shorewood Ct					
800	BRLT	60103	2911		B4
4400	HFET	60195	2804	25W-15N	B2
Shorewood Dr					
800	BRLT	60103	2911		B4
1700	HFET	60195	2804	25W-15N	B1
Short Av					
1700	HRPK	60107	2911		C2
1700	HRPK	60133	2911		C2
1700	SMWD	60107	2911		C2
Short Dr					
13500	CTWD	60445	3347	6W-16S	D2
Short Ln					
500	GNVW	60025	2810	9W-12N	C7
Short St					
100	WDND	60118	2801		A4
200	LMNT	60439	3270		D6
S Short St					
2700	CHCG	60608	3091	1W-2S	D3
14500	POSN	60469	3349	2W-17S	B4
Short Ter					
1500	DSPN	60018	2862	15W-10N	A6
S Shoshone Rd					
12700	PSHT	60463	3274	9W-15S	D7
Shoshone Tr					
8000	TYPK	60477	3424	10W-21S	C6
Shoshonee Tr					
1700	WLNG	60090	2754	16W-17N	D5
S Shoshoni Dr					
14000	HMGN	60441	3343	16W-16S	D4
Shotkoski Dr					
5100	HFET	60192	2802	30W-12N	C7
W Shure Dr					
1100	ANHT	60004	2753	18W-17N	D4
W Sibley Av					
10	CHCG	60631	2864	9W-9N	B7
10	PKRG	60068	2864	9W-9N	B7
10	PKRG	60631	2864	9W-9N	B7
Sibley Blvd					
-	DLTN	60409	3351	1E-17S	C5
-	DLTN	60419	3351	1E-17S	C5
10	CTCY	60409	3352	3E-17S	B5
10	HMND	46320	3352	4E-17S	C5
1100	CTCY	60409	3351	2E-17S	C5
Sibley Blvd SR-83					
-	DLTN	60409	3351	1E-17S	C5
-	DLTN	60419	3351	1E-17S	C5
1400	CTCY	60409	3351	2E-17S	C5
E Sibley Blvd					
-	DLTN	60409	3351	1E-17S	C5
10	DLTN	60419	3350	0E-17S	D5
10	HRVY	60426	3349	1W-17S	E5
10	SHLD	60419	3350	0E-17S	D5
10	SHLD	60473	3350	0E-17S	D5
100	DLTN	60473	3350	0E-17S	D5
100	HRVY	60426	3350	1W-17S	A5
400	HRVY	60419	3350	0W-17S	B5
500	DLTN	60426	3350	0W-17S	B5
700	DLTN	60419	3351	1E-17S	A5
700	DLTN	60473	3351	1E-17S	A5
800	SHLD	60473	3351	1E-17S	A5
E Sibley Blvd SR-83					
-	DLTN	60409	3351	1E-17S	C5
10	DLTN	60419	3350	0E-17S	D5
10	HRVY	60426	3349	1W-17S	E5
10	SHLD	60419	3350	0E-17S	D5
100	DLTN	60473	3350	0E-17S	D5
100	HRVY	60426	3350	1W-17S	A5
400	HRVY	60419	3350	0W-17S	B5
500	DLTN	60426	3350	0W-17S	B5
500	SHLD	60473	3350	1W-17S	A5
700	DLTN	60419	3351	1E-17S	A5
700	DLTN	60473	3351	1E-17S	A5
800	SHLD	60473	3351	1E-17S	A5
W Sibley Blvd					
10	DLTN	60419	3350	0W-17S	C5
10	HRVY	60426	3349	2W-17S	D5
10	SHLD	60419	3350	0W-17S	D5
10	SHLD	60473	3350	0W-17S	C5
100	DXMR	60426	3349	2W-17S	D5
200	HRVY	60426	3350	0W-17S	C5
2200	POSN	60469	3349	2W-17S	C5
W Sibley Blvd SR-83					
10	DLTN	60419	3350	0W-17S	C5
10	HRVY	60426	3349	2W-17S	D5
10	SHLD	60419	3350	0W-17S	D5
10	SHLD	60473	3350	0W-17S	C5
100	DXMR	60426	3349	2W-17S	D5
200	HRVY	60426	3350	0W-17S	C5
2200	POSN	60469	3349	2W-17S	C5
E Sibley St					
10	CHCG	60631	2864	9W-9N	C7
10	CTCY	60409	3352		D6
10	HMND	46320	3352		D6
10	PKRG	60068	2864	9W-9N	C7
10	PKRG	60631	2864	9W-9N	C7
200	NLES	60714	2864	9W-9N	C7
W Sibley St					
1600	PKRG	60068	2863	11W-9N	D7
Sicilia					
-	BMDL	60172	2912		C7
Siems Cir					
10	ROSL	60172	2913		A6
Sienna Ct					
200	SMBG	60193	2858	23W-9N	E7
200	SMBG	60193	2859	23W-9N	A7
1600	WLNG	60090	2808	14W-15N	B1
Sienna Dr					
600	SMBG	60193	2859	23W-9N	A7
700	SMBG	60193	2858	23W-9N	E7
800	SMBG	60193	2912		E1
Sierra Ct					
1000	UYPK	60466	3684	3W-30S	B3
Sierra Dr					
15500	OKFT	60452	3347	7W-18S	C7
W Sierra Ln					
9000	PSHL	60465	3209	11W-11S	E7
W Sierra St					
7000	CHCG	60620	3214	0W-9S	B3
Sierra Pass					
-	SMBG	60194	2857	27W-11N	D3
Sierra Pass Dr					
100	SMBG	60194	2857	27W-10N	D5
Siesta Ct					
100	CPVL	60110	2748		B5
Siesta Rd					
100	CPVL	60110	2748		B5
Siesta Key Ln					
1100	SMWD	60120	2856	30W-10N	C7
Sievert Ct					
100	BNVL	60106	2915		E5
100	CHCG	60106	2915		E5
Sieverwood Ct					
10	SMWD	60107	2857	26W-11N	E4
Sigwalt Ct					
2700	RGMW	60008	2806	19W-14N	C5
Sigwalt St					
3400	RGMW	60008	2806	20W-14N	B5
E Sigwalt St					
10	ANHT	60005	2807	17W-13N	A5
W Sigwalt St					
100	ANHT	60005	2807	18W-13N	A5
400	ANHT	60005	2806	18W-14N	E5
Silbury Dr					
-	BRLT	60120	2909		E3
Silentbrook Ln					
5400	RGMW	60008	2805	21W-14N	C5
5600	RGMW	60067	2805	21W-14N	C5
Silk Oak Ln					
1200	BRLT	60103	2910		B2
S Silo Ct					
15100	HMGN	60441	3343	16W-18S	E6
S Silo Dr					
15100	HMGN	60441	3343	16W-18S	E7
W Silo Dr					
7400	FftT	60423	3504	9W-24S	E6
Silo Ridge Dr					
10	ODPK	60467	3344	14W-17S	D6
Silo Ridge Rd E					
10	ODPK	60467	3344	14W-17S	E6
Silo Ridge Rd N					
10	ODPK	60467	3344	14W-17S	D5
Silo Ridge Rd S					
10	ODPK	60467	3344	14W-17S	D6
Silo Ridge Rd W					
10	ODPK	60467	3344	14W-17S	D6
Silvana Ct					
1000	SMBG	60173	2859	22W-11N	D4
Silver Ct					
7800	OrlT	60462	3346	9W-17S	D6
Silver Ln					
100	MLPK	60160	3030	10W-1N	A2
N Silver Ln					
1500	PLTN	60074	2753	19W-17N	C4
1500	PltT	60074	2753	19W-17N	C4
Silver Creek Dr					
2400	LydT	60164	2973	12W-3N	B6
2600	FNPK	60131	2973	12W-3N	B5
Silver Creek Ln					
-	MLPK	60160	3029	11W-1N	D1
Silverdale Dr					
8900	ODPK	60462	3346	11W-17S	A6
S Silver Fox Dr					
12900	LMNT	60439	3343	16W-15S	D1
Silver Lake Dr					
8000	ODPK	60462	3346	10W-17S	C5
8000	OrlT	60462	3346	10W-17S	C5
N Silver Lake Rd					
1900	ANHT	60004	2807	16W-16N	E1
Silver Pine Dr					
-	HFET	60010	2751	24W-16N	C7
1100	HFET	60010	2804	24W-16N	C1
1600	NHBK	60062	2756	11W-16N	D6
Silverpine Dr					
2200	GNVW	60025	2810	9W-13N	C5
Silverside Dr					
-	FKFT	60423	3504	10W-23S	B4
19500	TYPK	60477	3504	10W-23S	B4
19700	FftT	60477	3504	10W-23S	B4
19800	FftT	60423	3504	10W-23S	B4
Silver Spur Dr					
10	LMNT	60439	3272	15W-13S	B4
Silverstone Dr					
-	BNHL	60110	2748		C3
-	CPVL	60110	2748		B3
-	DndT	60110	2748		B3
E Silver Strand Cir					
1500	PLTN	60074	2753	19W-18N	C3
N Silverton Ct					
10	PltT	60067	2805	22W-15N	B2
Silverwillow Dr					
1800	GNVW	60025	2810	8W-14N	D4
Silverwood Ct					
300	SMBG	60193	2859	22W-9N	D6
1100	WLNG	60090	2754	16W-18N	E2
N Simonds Dr					
-	CHCG	60640	2921	0W-6N	E5
-	CHCG	60640	2922	0W-6N	A5
Simone Dr					
300	DSPN	60016	2808	14W-12N	C7
300	DSPN	60016	2862	14W-12N	C1
Simonsen Ln					
2800	GNVW	60025	2810	10W-13N	B6
Simplon Cir					
300	LYWD	60411	3598	4E-25S	C1
Simpson St					
-	SKOK	60076	2866	4W-12N	B2
800	EVTN	60201	2867	2W-12N	B1
1700	EVTN	60201	2866	3W-11N	E2
2900	SKOK	60203	2866	4W-12N	C1
7000	MNGV	60053	2864	8W-11N	D2
Sinatra Ln					
5400	HRPK	60133	2911		C6
Sinclair Av					
6400	BRWN	60402	3089	8W-3S	A4
Singer Av					
400	LMNT	60439	3270		D6
Singleton Dr					
1100	ROSL	60172	2912		C5
Singletree Rd					
100	ODPK	60467	3344	14W-17S	D6
Sioux Av					
100	BNHL	60010	2748		D5
100	BNHL	60110	2748		D5
100	CPVL	60110	2748		D4
N Sioux Av					
6600	CHCG	60646	2919	6W-8N	C2
Sioux Dr					
800	ELGN	60120	2855		C1
N Sioux Ln					
1900	MPPT	60056	2808	13W-14N	E5
S Sioux Ln					
13000	PSHT	60463	3346	9W-15S	E1
Sioux Rd					
7800	ODPK	60462	3346	9W-16S	C2
Sioux St					
300	PKFT	60466	3594	4W-27S	E5
300	RNPK	60466	3594	4W-27S	E5
300	RNPK	60471	3594	4W-27S	E5
Sioux Tr					
2700	GNVW	60025	2809	11W-15N	D2
2700	GNVW	60062	2809	11W-15N	D2
6400	IHPK	60525	3146		D6
Sippel Dr					
17000	TYPK	60477	3424	10W-21S	B6
S Sir Galahad Ln					
1300	MPPT	60056	2861	16W-11N	E3
S Sir Lancelot Ln					
1300	MPPT	60056	2861	16W-11N	E3
E Sitka Ln					
1800	MPPT	60056	2808	13W-14N	D3
Sivert Dr					
800	WDDL	60191	2915		B5
900	EGVV	60007	2915		B5
S Sivic St					
-	ANHT	60005	2807	17W-12N	C7
-	MPPT	60056	2807	17W-12N	C7
Skender Ct					
13800	HMGN	60441	3343	18W-16S	A3
S Skidmore Ct					
19600	FftT	60423	3504	9W-23S	D4
Skipping Stone Ln					
400	DGvT	60521	3146		A4
400	HNDL	60521	3146		A4
Skokiana Ter					
4100	SKOK	60076	2866	5W-11N	B2
Skokie					
-	WNKA	60093	2811	6W-16N	D1
Skokie Blvd					
10	HDPK	60035	2757	8W-18N	E2
10	HDPK	60062	2757	8W-18N	E2
10	NfdT	60062	2757	8W-18N	E3
10	NHBK	60062	2757	8W-18N	E2
400	NHBK	60062	2758	8W-18N	A4
1200	GLNC	60062	2758	8W-18N	A4
1800	NHFD	60093	2758	7W-16N	B7
7400	LNWD	60712	2865	5W-9N	E7
7400	SKOK	60077	2865	6W-12N	E1
7500	SKOK	60076	2865	6W-12N	E1
10000	SKOK	60076	2811	5W-13N	E7
10000	SKOK	60077	2811	5W-13N	E7
10000	WLMT	60076	2811	5W-12N	E7
10000	WLMT	60077	2811	5W-12N	E7
10000	WLMT	60091	2811	5W-12N	E7
Skokie Blvd SR-50					
7400	LNWD	60712	2865	5W-9N	E7
7400	SKOK	60077	2865	5W-9N	E7
7500	SKOK	60076	2865	5W-9N	E7
Skokie Blvd US-41					
7500	SKOK	60076	2865	6W-12N	E1
7500	SKOK	60077	2865	6W-12N	E1
10000	SKOK	60076	2811	5W-13N	E7
10000	SKOK	60077	2811	5W-13N	E7
10000	WLMT	60076	2811	5W-12N	E7
10000	WLMT	60077	2811	5W-12N	E7
10000	WLMT	60091	2811	5W-12N	E7
Skokie Ct					
300	WLMT	60091	2811	5W-13N	E6
Skokie Hwy					
-	HDPK	-	2757	8W-20N	E1
-	NfdT	-	2757	8W-20N	E1
-	NHBK	-	2757	8W-20N	E1
Skokie Hwy US-41					
-	HDPK	-	2757	8W-20N	E1
-	NfdT	-	2757	8W-20N	E1
-	NHBK	-	2757	8W-20N	E1
N Skokie Ln					
300	GLNC	60022	2758	6W-16N	D6
S Skokie Ln					
600	GLNC	60022	2758	6W-16N	D6
Skokie Rd					
-	NHFD	60093	2811	6W-14N	D5
-	SKOK	60077	2811	5W-13N	E7
-	WLMT	60077	2811	5W-13N	E7
-	WLMT	60091	2811	6W-14N	D5
-	WLMT	60093	2811	6W-14N	D5
Skokie Rd US-41					
-	NHFD	60093	2811	6W-14N	D5
-	SKOK	60077	2811	5W-13N	E7
-	WLMT	60077	2811	5W-13N	E7
-	WLMT	60091	2811	6W-14N	D5
-	WLMT	60093	2811	6W-14N	D5
Skokie Ditch					
-	KLWH	60043	2812	3W-15N	D3
Skokie Ridge Dr					
900	GLNC	60022	2758	7W-17N	C4
Skokie Valley Rd					
-	HDPK	-	2757	9W-20N	D1
10	HDPK	60062	2757	8W-20N	E2
10	NHBK	60062	2757	8W-20N	E2
Skokie Valley Rd US-41					
-	HDPK		2757	9W-20N	D1
Skye Ct					
1500	FSMR	60422	3506	4W-23S	D3
S Skye Dr					
19500	FftT	60423	3504	9W-23S	E4
Skye Ln					
600	IVNS	60010	2751	24W-16N	B6
W Skylark Ct					
1000	PLTN	60067	2805	22W-14N	B4
W Skylark Dr					
1000	PLTN	60067	2805	22W-14N	B4
Skylark Ln					
400	VrnT	60015	2755	14W-20N	B1
Skyline Dr					
100	DndT	60110	2748		B6
200	BRTN	60010	2750	25W-18N	E3
200	CPVL	60110	2748		B6
7200	JSTC	60458	3148	10W-8S	A7
16400	TYPK	60477	3425	8W-19S	B3
Skytrain Ln					
400	GNVW	60025	2810	10W-14N	A3
400	GNVW	60062	2810	10W-14N	A3
Skyvue Ln					
300	SMBG	60194	2857	26W-10N	E5
Skywater Dr					
1700	SMBG	60008	2806	21W-12N	A7
1700	SMBG	60173	2805	21W-12N	E7
1700	SMBG	60173	2806	21W-12N	A7
Slade Av					
600	ELGN	60120	2855		B2
E Slade St					
10	PLTN	60067	2805	20W-16N	E1
W Slade St					
-	PLTN	60067	2805	21W-16N	E1
Slate Dr					
-	CPVL	60110	2748		B3
Slawin Ct					
500	MPPT	60056	2808	14W-13N	C5
E Slayton Dr					
800	PLTN	60074	2753	19W-16N	B6
Sleeping Bear Rd					
8900	SKOK	60076	2866	4W-11N	B3
Sleepy Hllw					
2000	NHBK	60062	2756	11W-16N	C7
Sleepy Hollow Ct					
1700	HFET	60195	2859	23W-12N	A1
1700	SMBG	60195	2859	23W-12N	A1
Sleepy Hollow Rd					
1300	GNVW	60025	2810	8W-13N	E5
S Sligo Wy					
18100	BmnT	60477	3426	6W-21S	B7
18100	CCHL	60477	3426	6W-21S	B7
18100	CCHL	60478	3426	6W-21S	B7
W Sligo Wy					
4800	CCHL	60478	3426	6W-21S	A7
Slingerland Dr					
300	SMBG	60193	2858	25W-9N	A7
W Slippery Rock Dr					
500	PLTN	60067	2805	21W-14N	C4
Small Dr					
-	SMBG	60193	2857	27W-10N	D6
E Small Ln					
1400	MPPT	60056	2808	14W-13N	C6
Smethwick Ln					
10	EGVV	60007	2914		D1
W Smethwick Ln					
2100	HFET	60195	2858	25W-12N	B1
Smith Ct					
1600	SMWD	60107	2857	27W-11N	D4
W Smith Ln					
8100	RVGV	60171	2974	10W-3N	B4
Smith Rd					
-	DPgT	60441	3270		A7
-	LMNT	60439	3270		A7
-	NHBK	60062	2756	11W-16N	D6
1200	DPgT	60441	3342	20W-15S	A1
1200	LMNT	60439	3342	20W-15S	A1
1200	LMNT	60441	3342	20W-15S	A1
1300	HmrT	60441	3342	20W-17S	A5
1300	LktT	60441	3342	20W-17S	A5
14700	LKPT	60441	3342	20W-17S	A6
Smith St					
-	NtrT	60093	2811	6W-15N	E3
-	WNKA	60093	2811	6W-15N	E3
2400	RGMW	60008	2805	21W-14N	D5
2400	RGMW	60067	2805	21W-14N	D5
N Smith St					
10	PLTN	60067	2805	21W-16N	D1
100	PLTN	60067	2752	21W-17N	D5
1500	PltT	60074	2752	21W-17N	D5
S Smith St					
900	PLTN	60067	2805	21W-14N	D4
1200	RGMW	60067	2805	21W-14N	D4
Smithwood Dr					
10	MNGV	60053	2865	7W-10N	B4
Smoketree Cir					
1300	BRLT	60103	2910		B1
Smoke Tree Ct					
3100	HLCT	60429	3427	3W-21S	A6
Smoketree Ln					
400	BRLT	60103	2910		B2
Snowbird Ln					
3900	NHBK	60062	2756	12W-17N	B5
Snow Drift Cir					
400	BRLT	60103	2910		B2
Snow Drift Ct					
300	BRLT	60103	2910		A2
Sobieski St					
600	LMNT	60439	3270		E6
Sodaro Av					
500	BMDL	60157	2913		B7
Sodaro Rd					
500	BMDL	60157	2913		B7
E Soffel Av					
100	MLPK	60160	3028		E2
100	MLPK	60164	3028		E2
100	NHLK	60164	3028		E2
300	MLPK	60160	3029	13W-1N	A2
300	NHLK	60160	3029	13W-1N	A2
300	NHLK	60164	3029	13W-1N	A2
400	NHLK	60165	3029	13W-1N	A2
400	SNPK	60165	3029	13W-1N	A2
W Soffel Av					
-	SNPK	60160	3029	12W-1N	B1
10	NHLK	60164	3028		D1
2900	MLPK	60160	3029	12W-1N	B1
3200	SNPK	60165	3029	12W-1N	B1
4600	NHLK	60160	3029	13W-1N	A2
W Soffel Av					
4600	NHLK	60164	3029	13W-1N	A2
Soffel Ter					
-	MLPK	60160	3028		E2
4600	MLPK	60160	3029	13W-1N	A2
S Sohl Av					
4900	HMND	46320	3352		D7
4900	HMND	46327	3352		D5
5900	HMND	46320	3430		E1
Solar Ln					
800	GNVW	60025	2811	7W-13N	B7
Soleri Dr					
4000	BmnT	60430	3426	5W-21S	C7
4000	CCHL	60478	3426	5W-21S	C7
E Solidarity Dr					
600	CHCG	60605	3034	0E-1S	D7
Somer Ln					
10800	ODPK	60467	3423	13W-18S	A1
Somerglen Ct					
15600	ODPK	60467	3423	13W-18S	A1
Somerglen Ln					
10800	ODPK	60467	3345	13W-18S	A7
10800	ODPK	60467	3423	13W-18S	B1
W Somerset Av					
6400	CHCG	60631	2919	8W-7N	A4
6400	CHCG	60646	2919	8W-7N	A4
Somerset Cir					
800	HRPK	60133	2912		A3
Somerset Ct					
-	ANHT	60004	2807	17W-15N	C2
-	PTHT	60004	2807	17W-15N	C2
10	SBTN	60010	2804	24W-14N	C4
100	WLBK	60527	3146		A6
1500	SMBG	60193	2858	25W-10N	B6
9000	ODPK	60462	3346	11W-17S	A6
14100	HMGN	60467	3344	15W-16S	C4
Somerset Dr					
100	SMWD	60107	2857	28W-11N	A4
300	HFET	60107	2857	28W-11N	B4
1100	GNVW	60025	2811	7W-13N	A6
Somerset Ln					
500	NHFD	60093	2811	7W-15N	A2
1100	EGVV	60007	2914		C2
1200	SMBG	60193	2858	25W-10N	B6
1300	ITSC	60143	2914		D3
1800	NHBK	60062	2757	10W-16N	B7
3400	CRTE	60417	3596	0W-28S	D6
N Somerset Ln					
200	ANHT	60005	2807	16W-13N	C6
W Somerset Ln					
9800	PSPK	60464	3273	12W-14S	C7
Somerset Rd					
100	WLBK	60527	3146		A6
11800	ODPK	60467	3344	14W-16S	C4
11900	HMGN	60467	3344	14W-16S	C4
12100	HMGN	60441	3344	15W-16S	C4
Somerset Hills Ct					
400	RVWD	60015	2756	13W-20N	A1
Somersworth Pl					
2100	HFET	60195	2858	26W-12N	A1
Somerton Dr					
4900	HFET	60010	2751	24W-16N	C7
Sommerset Av					
2600	WSTR	60154	3087	13W-2S	A3
Sommerset Ct					
1000	ELGN	60120	2855		D5
Sommersville Ct					
600	MTSN	60443	3506	5W-24S	B6
Somme Woods					
10	NHBK	60062	2757	9W-18N	C4
Somonauk Ct					
10	PKFT	60466	3594	4W-27S	E5
Somonauk St					
200	PKFT	60466	3594	4W-27S	E5
200	PKFT	60466	3595	4W-27S	A5
300	RNPK	60466	3594	4W-27S	E5
300	RNPK	60471	3594	4W-27S	E5
Songbird Cir					
10400	ODPK	60467	3423	13W-20S	B4
Song Sparrow Ct					
1900	SMBG	60173	2805	21W-12N	E7
Sonia Ln					
2500	FNPK	60131	2973	12W-3N	C5
Soo Line Ln					
4400	SRPK	60176	2973	11W-5N	C1
Soper Av					
300	BRRG	60527	3208		A1
300	DGvT	60527	3208		A1
300	WLBK	60527	3208		A1
Sophia Dr					
6100	MTSN	60443	3505	7W-25S	D7
6100	MTSN	60443	3593	7W-25S	C1
S Sophies Ln					
1800	HMND	46394	3280		E4
Soreng Av					
9500	SRPK	60176	2973	12W-4N	C2
Sorrel					
10	LMNT	60439	3272	15W-13S	A5
Sorrel Dr					
3400	NHBK	60062	2756	11W-18N	C3
Sorrento Dr					
10	PSHT	60463	3275	8W-14S	B5
Souster Av					
10	ELGN	60123	2855		A6
South Av					
10	GLNC	60022	2759	5W-17N	A5
100	GLNC	60022	2758	6W-17N	D5
9800	SRPK	60176	2917	12W-6N	B7
South Blvd					
10	CHCG	60644	3031	8W-0N	A4
10	OKPK	60302	3031	8W-0N	A4
600	EVTN	60202	2867	3W-10N	A5
800	OKPK	60302	3030	8W-0N	E4
1100	FTPK	60130	3030	8W-0N	D4
1600	EVTN	60202	2866	3W-10N	E5
South Brch					
10	GNVW	60093	2810	8W-15N	D3
South Ct					
2900	RGMW	60008	2806	19W-13N	C5
South Dr					
-	WLNG	60090	2808	14W-16N	D1
700	BRRG	60521	3146		C4
South Ln					
-	MPPT	60056	2861	17W-11N	C3
200	GLNC	60022	2758	6W-17N	E5
1700	NHBK	60062	2757	8W-16N	E7
1700	NHBK	60062	2758	8W-16N	A7
3000	DSPN	60018	2917	12W-8N	B3
South Pkwy					
10	PTHT	60070	2807	15W-15N	E2
10	PTHT	60070	2808	15W-15N	A2
South Rd					
600	PLTN	60074	2752	21W-18N	C2
600	PltT	60074	2752	21W-18N	C2
1500	RchT	60477	3505	8W-23S	B2

STREET Block	City	ZIP	Map#	CGS	Grid
SR-1 S Halsted St					
100	CHHT	60411	3508	0W-23S	B4
9900	CHCG	60628	3214	1W-11S	A7
9900	CHCG	60643	3214	1W-11S	A7
10300	CHCG	60628	3278	1W-13S	A3
10300	CHCG	60643	3278	1W-13S	A3
12200	CTPK	60827	3278	1W-14S	A6
12500	CTPK	60628	3278	1W-14S	A6
12600	CHCG	60827	3278	1W-14S	A7
13100	RVDL	60827	3350	1W-17S	A6
14500	HRVY	60426	3350	1W-16S	A4
18300	GNWD	60425	3428	0W-22S	B7
18300	GNWD	60425	3508	1W-24S	B5
18300	GNWD	60430	3428	0W-21S	B7
18300	HMWD	60430	3428	0W-21S	B7
18500	HMWD	60430	3508	1W-24S	B5
19000	HMWD	60425	3508	0W-23S	B2
19100	BlmT	60411	3508	0W-23S	B3
19300	GNWD	60411	3508	0W-23S	B3
SR-1 Main St					
800	CRTE	60417	3596	1W-29S	B7
800	CRTE	60417	3685	0W-32S	B6
1500	CteT	60417	3685	0W-30S	B3
SR-1 Route 1 Cto					
-	CHHT	60411	3508	1W-24S	B6
SR-1 Vincennes Rd					
-	PHNX	60426	3350	1W-18S	B7
14900	HRVY	60426	3350	1W-18S	B7
SR-7 W 143rd St					
9800	ODPK	60462	3345	12W-16S	C4
10600	OrlT	60462	3345	13W-16S	B4
10700	ODPK	60467	3345	13W-16S	A4
10700	OrlT	60467	3345	13W-16S	A4
10900	ODPK	60467	3344	13W-17S	E6
10900	OrlT	60467	3344	13W-17S	E6
SR-7 W 159th St					
11200	ODPK	60467	3422	14W-18S	E1
11200	OrlT	60467	3422	13W-18S	E1
11800	HMGN	60441	3422	14W-18S	C1
SR-7 Southwest Hwy					
10600	CHRG	60482	3274	9W-12S	E2
10600	WRTH	60482	3274	9W-12S	E2
10800	PSHL	60465	3274	9W-13S	D4
11100	WRTH	60465	3274	9W-13S	D3
11200	PSHT	60465	3274	9W-13S	D4
11400	PSHT	60463	3274	9W-13S	D4
11800	PSPK	60464	3274	11W-14S	A7
12600	PlsT	60464	3346	11W-15S	A1
12600	PSPK	60464	3346	11W-15S	A1
13000	ODPK	60462	3346	11W-15S	A1
13000	PlsT	60462	3346	11W-15S	A1
13100	ODPK	60462	3345	11W-16S	E3
13100	OrlT	60462	3345	11W-16S	E3
13100	PlsT	60462	3345	11W-16S	E3
SR-7 Wolf Rd					
14300	ODPK	60467	3344	13W-17S	E4
14300	OrlT	60467	3344	13W-17S	E4
15600	ODPK	60467	3422	15W-19S	B1
15600	OrlT	60467	3422	15W-19S	B1
SR-19 E Chicago St					
300	ELGN	60120	2855		B4
1400	HnrT	60120	2855		E5
SR-19 Irving Park Rd					
-	CHCG	60176	2973	11W-5N	E2
-	CHCG	60634	2973	11W-5N	E2
-	CHCG	60666	2973	13W-5N	A1
-	ELGN	60120	2855		E5
-	FNPK	60666	2973	13W-5N	A1
-	HnrT	60120	2855		E5
-	ROSL	60172	2913		C5
-	SRPK	60666	2973	13W-5N	A1
10	BmdT	60143	2913		D5
10	BmdT	60143	2914		E7
10	BmdT	60157	2913		D5
10	HnrT	60120	2856	30W-10N	B5
10	ITSC	60143	2914		E7
100	HnrT	60107	2856	30W-10N	C6
100	SMWD	60107	2856	30W-10N	C6
100	SMWD	60120	2856	30W-10N	B5
300	BmdT	60172	2913		C5
400	ITSC	60143	2913		E6
800	HRPK	60133	2912		C3
800	SMBG	60133	2912		A2
1200	HRPK	60133	2911		C1
1600	ELGN	60120	2856	31W-10N	A5
1700	SMWD	60107	2911		D1
1700	SMWD	60133	2911		D1
9200	SRPK	60176	2973	13W-5N	A1
SR-19 E Irving Park Rd					
10	BNVL	60106	2972		A1
10	ROSL	60172	2913		A4
10	SMWD	60107	2857	28W-9N	A7
100	ITSC	60143	2914		C6
100	WDDL	60191	2915		B7
400	BmdT	60172	2913		C5
400	BNVL	60106	2915		C7
800	SMWD	60107	2911		C1
900	CHCG	60131	2972		B1
900	HRPK	60107	2911		C1
1000	HRPK	60133	2911		C1
1000	SMWD	60133	2911		C1
1100	BNVL	60131	2972		C1
1100	CHCG	60106	2972		C1
1100	WDDL	60143	2914		D7
1200	WDDL	60191	2914		D7
1300	ITSC	60191	2914		E7
11500	CHCG	60666	2972		C1
SR-19 W Irving Park Rd					
-	BmdT	60143	2914		A6
-	BNVL	60131	2972		C1
-	CHCG	60131	2972		C1
-	CHCG	60176	2973	11W-5N	E2
-	CHCG	60634	2973	10W-5N	E2
-	CHCG	60666	2972		D2
-	FNPK	60131	2972		E1
-	FNPK	60666	2972		D2
-	HnrT	60107	2856	29W-10N	D6
-	HnrT	60120	2856	29W-10N	C6
-	SMWD	60120	2856	29W-10N	C6
10	BNVL	60106	2915		E7
10	ROSL	60172	2913		D5
10	SMWD	60107	2856	29W-10N	D6
100	ROSL	60172	2912		E4
100	WDDL	60191	2915		C7
200	ITSC	60143	2914		C6
200	WDDL	60191	2914		E7
400	ITSC	60191	2914		E7
400	SMBG	60172	2912		D3
400	SMBG	60193	2912		D3
600	CHCG	60613	2978	0W-5N	A1
700	CHCG	60613	2977	3W-4N	A2
700	SmbT	60193	2912		B2
1400	BmdT	60143	2913		E6
1400	ITSC	60143	2913		E6
1800	SMBG	60133	2912		A2
1900	CHCG	60618	2977	2W-5N	B1
1900	HRPK	60133	2912		A2
2700	CHCG	60618	2976	3W-4N	E2
3900	CHCG	60641	2976	5W-4N	A2
4600	CHCG	60641	2975	7W-4N	B2
5500	CHCG	60634	2975	6W-5N	C2
6600	CHCG	60634	2974	8W-4N	D2
7100	NRDG	60634	2974	8W-5N	D2
7100	NRDG	60706	2974	8W-5N	D2
7500	CHCG	60706	2974	9W-5N	C2
SR-19 N Recreation Dr					
-	CHCG	60613	2978	0W-4N	A1
SR-21 Milwaukee Av					
500	MaiT	60016	2809	10W-13N	E7
500	MaiT	60025	2809	10W-13N	E7
500	NfdT	60016	2809	10W-13N	E7
500	NfdT	60025	2809	11W-13N	E7
700	GNVW	60025	2809	11W-13N	D6
900	BFGV	60089	2755	14W-20N	C1
900	VrnT	60015	2755	14W-20N	C1
900	VrnT	60062	2755	14W-20N	C1
900	VrnT	60089	2755	14W-20N	C1
1000	RVWD	60015	2755	14W-20N	C1
1600	GNVW	60062	2809	12W-14N	C4
1800	NfdT	60062	2809	12W-14N	C4
2800	PTHT	60062	2809	12W-15N	A2
2800	PTHT	60070	2809	12W-15N	A2
9700	GNVW	60025	2863	10W-12N	E1
9700	GNVW	60025	2864	10W-12N	A1
9700	MaiT	60016	2864	10W-12N	A1
9700	MaiT	60025	2863	10W-12N	E1
9700	MaiT	60714	2864	10W-12N	A1
9700	NLES	60714	2864	10W-12N	A1
9800	MaiT	60016	2863	10W-12N	E1
20400	BFGV	60090	2755	14W-20N	C1
SR-21 N Milwaukee Av					
-	NfdT	60062	2809	12W-15N	A2
500	PTHT	60062	2809	13W-15N	A1
500	PTHT	60070	2809	13W-15N	A1
500	PTHT	60090	2809	13W-15N	A1
500	WhlT	60062	2809	13W-15N	A1
500	WhlT	60090	2809	13W-15N	A1
500	WLNG	60090	2755	14W-18N	C3
800	BFGV	60090	2755	14W-20N	C2
900	BFGV	60089	2755	14W-20N	C1
900	VrnT	60062	2755	14W-20N	C1
900	VrnT	60089	2755	14W-20N	C1
7500	CHCG	60631	2864	9W-9N	D7
7500	CHCG	60714	2864	9W-9N	D7
7500	NLES	60631	2864	9W-9N	D7
7500	NLES	60714	2864	9W-9N	D6
8300	MaiT	60714	2864	9W-10N	C5
9600	GNVW	60025	2864	10W-12N	A1
9600	MaiT	60016	2864	10W-12N	A1
SR-21 S Milwaukee Av					
10	WLNG	60090	2755	14W-18N	D4
600	WhlT	60090	2755	13W-17N	E5
1100	PTHT	60070	2755	13W-16N	E7
1100	PTHT	60070	2808	13W-16N	E1
1100	PTHT	60070	2809	13W-16N	A1
1100	PTHT	60090	2809	13W-16N	A1
1100	WhlT	60090	2808	13W-16N	E1
1100	WhlT	60090	2809	13W-16N	A1
SR-25					
-	BRLT	60103	2909		B3
-	BRLT	60120	2909		B4
-	BRLT	60177	2909		B4
-	ELGN	60120	2855		B1
-	ElgT	60120	2909		B2
-	ElgT	60177	2909		B2
-	SchT	60120	2909		A5
-	SchT	60177	2909		A5
-	SEGN	60103	2909		B3
-	SEGN	60120	2909		B3
-	SEGN	60177	2909		B3
SR-25 Bluff City Blvd					
500	ELGN	60120	2855		B6
SR-25 Dundee Av					
10	CPVL	60118	2801		C2
10	EDND	60118	2801		C2
600	DndT	60118	2801		C4
1100	ELGN	60120	2855		B1
1300	ELGN	60120	2801		B7
1500	DndT	60120	2801		B6
1500	ELGN	60118	2801		B7
SR-25 Elgin Rd					
1600	BNHL	60110	2748		C2
1600	CPVL	60110	2748		C2
1900	DndT	60110	2748		C2
2100	ALGN	60102	2748		C2
2100	ALGN	60110	2748		C2
2100	BNHL	60010	2748		C2
2100	BNHL	60102	2748		C2
SR-25 JFK Memorial Dr					
-	CPVL	60118	2801		C1
-	EDND	60118	2801		C1
10	CPVL	60110	2748		C6
200	EDND	60110	2748		C7
800	CPVL	60110	2801		C1
800	EDND	60110	2801		C1
SR-25 N Kennedy Dr					
10	CPVL	60110	2748		C6
100	BNHL	60110	2748		C4
SR-25 N Liberty St					
10	ELGN	60120	2855		B2
SR-25 S Liberty St					
10	ELGN	60120	2855		B4
SR-25 St. Charles St					
800	ELGN	60120	2855		B6
900	ElgT	60120	2855		B7
1100	ElgT	60120	2909		B1
SR-38 Roosevelt Rd					
-	EMHT	60126	3028		B7
-	EMHT	60523	3028		B7
-	OKBK	60126	3028		B7
-	OKBK	60523	3028		A7
-	PvsT	60523	3028		B7
-	WSTR	60154	3028		D7
-	YkTp	60126	3028		B7
-	YkTp	60523	3028		B7
4000	HLSD	60162	3029	13W-1S	A7
4000	PvsT	60162	3029	13W-1S	A7
4000	WSTR	60154	3029	13W-0S	A7
4300	HLSD	60162	3028		D7
4300	PvsT	60162	3028		D7
4400	HLSD	60154	3028		E7
11900	PvsT	60126	3028		B7
SR-38 W Roosevelt Rd					
10900	HLSD	60154	3028		E7
10900	HLSD	60162	3028		E7
10900	WSTR	60154	3028		E7
SR-43 Harlem Av					
-	CHCG	60638	3148	8W-5S	E2
-	FftT	60477	3505	8W-23S	A2
-	LYNS	60402	3148	9W-5S	E1
-	SMMT	60501	3148	9W-5S	E2
-	SMMT	60534	3148	8W-5S	E2
-	TYPK	60477	3505	8W-23S	A3
1100	BRWN	60402	3030	8W-0S	D7
1100	FTPK	60130	3030	8W-0S	D7
1100	OKPK	60304	3030	8W-0S	D7
1500	BRWN	60402	3088	9W-1S	D1
1500	FTPK	60130	3088	8W-1S	D1
1500	NRIV	60130	3088	9W-1S	D1
1700	NRIV	60402	3088	8W-1S	D1
2100	NRIV	60546	3088	8W-1S	D2
2500	RVSD	60546	3088	8W-2S	D3
3200	RVSD	60402	3088	9W-3S	E4
3600	LYNS	60402	3088	8W-3S	E5
3600	LYNS	60534	3088	8W-3S	E5
3800	SKNY	60402	3088	8W-3S	E6
4400	FTVW	60402	3088	8W-4S	E7
4600	FTVW	60402	3148	8W-4S	E1
4600	LYNS	60534	3148	8W-4S	E1
15900	ODPK	60462	3424	9W-18S	E1
15900	ODPK	60477	3424	9W-18S	E1
15900	TYPK	60477	3424	9W-21S	E6
16300	OrlT	60477	3424	9W-19S	E2
18200	TYPK	60477	3425	8W-21S	A7
19300	TYPK	60423	3505	8W-23S	A3
SR-43 N Harlem Av					
-	FTPK	60305	3030	8W-0N	D4
10	FTPK	60130	3030	8W-0N	D4
10	OKPK	60302	3030	9W-0S	D6
10	OKPK	60304	3030	9W-0N	D5
400	OKPK	60301	3030	8W-0N	D4
400	OKPK	60305	3030	9W-0S	D6
400	RVFT	60301	3030	8W-0N	D4
400	RVFT	60305	3030	9W-0S	D6
1500	CHCG	60707	3030	8W-2N	D1
1500	EDPK	60707	3030	8W-2N	D1
1700	CHCG	60707	2974	8W-2N	D7
1700	EDPK	60707	2974	8W-2N	D7
2700	CHCG	60634	2974	9W-3N	D5
3900	NRDG	60634	2974	9W-3N	D5
3900	NRDG	60706	2974	9W-3N	D5
4400	HDHT	60706	2918	8W-5N	D7
4400	NRDG	60706	2918	8W-5N	D7
4700	CHCG	60656	2918	8W-5N	D7
5100	CHCG	60706	2918	8W-6N	D6
5600	CHCG	60631	2918	9W-6N	D6
6500	CHCG	60714	2918	8W-8N	D2
6500	NLES	60631	2918	8W-8N	D2
6500	NLES	60714	2918	9W-6N	D6
7200	CHCG	60631	2864	8W-9N	D7
7200	NLES	60714	2864	8W-9N	D7
7500	CHCG	60714	2864	8W-9N	D7
7500	NLES	60631	2864	8W-9N	D7
SR-43 S Harlem Av					
-	BGVW	60453	3210	9W-10S	E5
-	FKFT	60423	3505	9W-25S	A7
-	OKLN	60453	3210	9W-10S	E5
-	OKLN	60455	3210	9W-10S	E5
-	OrlT	60452	3346	9W-17S	E5
-	PlsT	60462	3346	9W-16S	E2
-	PSHT	60462	3346	9W-17S	E6
-	PSHT	60463	3346	9W-17S	E6
-	SMMT	60534	3148	9W-5S	E2
-	TYPK	60423	3505	8W-23S	A3
10	FTPK	60130	3030	9W-0S	D5
10	FTPK	60304	3030	9W-0S	D5
10	OKPK	60302	3030	9W-0S	D5
10	OKPK	60304	3030	9W-0S	D5
300	OKPK	60130	3030	9W-0S	D5
5100	CHCG	60501	3148	9W-5S	E1
5100	CHCG	60638	3148	9W-5S	E1
5100	FTVW	60402	3148	9W-5S	E1
5300	SMMT	60501	3148	9W-6S	E4
5400	SMMT	60638	3148	8W-5S	E3
6300	BDPK	60638	3148	8W-7S	E5
6500	BDPK	60501	3148	9W-7S	D5
6700	BGVW	60455	3148	9W-7S	E6
7100	BGVW	60638	3148	8W-8S	E7
7300	BDPK	60638	3210	8W-8S	E1
7300	BGVW	60455	3210	9W-8S	E1
7400	BGVW	60638	3210	9W-8S	E1
7700	BGVW	60459	3210	9W-8S	E2
7700	BRBK	60455	3210	9W-8S	E2
7700	BRBK	60459	3210	9W-8S	E2
9800	CHRG	60415	3210	9W-11S	E7
9800	CHRG	60455	3210	9W-11S	E7
10100	BGVW	60455	3274	9W-11S	E1
10100	CHRG	60415	3274	9W-11S	E1
10100	PSHL	60455	3274	9W-11S	E1
10100	PSHL	60465	3274	9W-11S	E1
10400	CHRG	60482	3274	9W-15S	E7
10400	WRTH	60465	3274	9W-15S	E7
10500	WRTH	60482	3274	9W-15S	E7
11600	PSHT	60463	3274	8W-13S	E5
11600	WRTH	60463	3274	8W-13S	E5
13500	BmnT	60445	3346	9W-17S	E6
13500	BmnT	60462	3346	9W-17S	E6
13500	OrlT	60462	3346	8W-16S	E2
13500	WthT	60445	3346	9W-17S	E6
13500	WthT	60462	3346	9W-17S	E6
13500	WthT	60463	3346	9W-17S	E6
14100	BmnT	60452	3346	8W-16S	E4
15100	ODPK	60462	3346	9W-18S	E6
15200	OKFT	60462	3346	9W-18S	E6
15700	ODPK	60462	3424	9W-18S	E1
15800	ODPK	60477	3424	9W-18S	E1
15800	TYPK	60477	3424	9W-18S	E1
19300	FftT	60423	3505	8W-23S	A3
19300	FftT	60477	3505	8W-23S	A3
19300	RchT	60423	3505	9W-24S	A6
19300	RchT	60477	3505	8W-23S	A3
19300	TYPK	60477	3505	8W-23S	A3
19700	MTSN	60443	3505	9W-24S	A6
19700	RchT	60443	3505	9W-24S	A6
19800	MTSN	60423	3505	9W-24S	A6
21500	FKFT	60423	3593	9W-25S	A1
21500	RchT	60443	3593	9W-25S	A1
22400	FKFT	60443	3593	9W-27S	A5
22400	RchT	60423	3593	9W-27S	A3
SR-43 W Oakton St					
7000	NLES	60714	2864	8W-10N	E5
SR-43 Waukegan Rd					
10	DRFD	60015	2757	10W-20N	A2
10	DRFD	60062	2757	10W-20N	A2
10	GNVW	60025	2864	8W-12N	E1
10	MNGV	60053	2864	8W-10N	E4
100	GNVW	60025	2810	8W-13N	E6
100	GNVW	60093	2810	8W-15N	E3
100	NHFD	60025	2810	8W-15N	E3
100	NHFD	60093	2810	8W-15N	E2
300	NHBK	60062	2810	8W-15N	E2
400	NfdT	60062	2757	10W-18N	B3
600	DRFD	60015	2756	10W-20N	E1
600	NHBK	60062	2757	9W-18N	B4
2100	NHFD	60062	2810	8W-16N	E1
8400	MNGV	60714	2864	8W-10N	E4
8400	NLES	60714	2864	8W-10N	E4
SR-43 N Waukegan Rd					
8000	NLES	60714	2864	8W-10N	E5
8300	MNGV	60053	2864	8W-10N	E5
8300	MNGV	60714	2864	8W-10N	E5
SR-43 S Waukegan Rd					
10	DRFD	60015	2757	10W-18N	A2
10	DRFD	60062	2757	10W-18N	A2
10	NfdT	60062	2757	10W-18N	A2
SR-50					
-	PtnT	60468	3860	9W-38S	E6
-	PtnT	60468	3861	9W-38S	A4
-	PTON	60468	3860	9W-38S	E6
-	PTON	60468	3861	9W-37S	A4
SR-50 Cicero Av					
-	ALSP	60803	3348	5W-15S	A1
-	CTWD	60803	3348	5W-15S	A1
13100	CTWD	60445	3348	6W-15S	A1
13900	BmnT	60445	3348	5W-16S	A3
14300	MDLN	60445	3348	5W-18S	A7
14700	MDLN	60452	3348	5W-18S	A7
14800	OKFT	60452	3348	5W-17S	A5
14900	OKFT	60445	3348	5W-17S	A6
15700	BmnT	60426	3426	6W-21S	B7
15700	OKFT	60452	3426	6W-21S	B7
16200	OKFT	60426	3426	6W-21S	B7
16700	BmnT	60477	3426	5W-20S	A3
16700	OKFT	60477	3426	5W-20S	A3
16800	BmnT	60452	3426	5W-20S	A4
17000	BmnT	60478	3426	6W-20S	B4
17000	CCHL	60477	3426	6W-20S	B4
17000	CCHL	60478	3426	6W-20S	B4
18400	CCHL	60478	3506	6W-25S	B7
18800	CCHL	60477	3506	5W-22S	B2
18800	RchT	60477	3506	5W-22S	B2
19900	MTSN	60443	3506	5W-24S	B5
19900	MTSN	60477	3506	5W-24S	B4
19900	RchT	60443	3506	5W-24S	B4
21100	MTSN	60443	3594	6W-26S	B2
21900	RNPK	60471	3594	6W-26S	B2
22700	UYPK	60471	3594	6W-27S	B5
22900	UYPK	60466	3594	6W-27S	B5
SR-50 N Cicero Av					
10	CHCG	60644	3031	6W-0N	E5
700	CHCG	60651	3031	6W-1N	E2
1500	CHCG	60639	3031	6W-2N	E1
1600	CHCG	60639	2975	6W-2N	E7
2700	CHCG	60641	2975	6W-5N	E1
4300	CHCG	60630	2975	6W-5N	E1
4400	CHCG	60630	2919	6W-5N	E7
5600	CHCG	60646	2919	6W-7N	E4
6300	LNWD	60712	2919	6W-6N	E5
7200	LNWD	60712	2865	5W-9N	E7
7300	SKOK	60077	2865	5W-9N	E7
SR-50 S Cicero Av					
-	CTWD	60445	3348	5W-15S	A1
-	CTWD	60803	3348	5W-15S	A1
-	MonT	60466	3683	6W-29S	B2
-	UYPK	60466	3683	6W-29S	B2
10	CHCG	60644	3031	6W-0S	E5
800	CHCG	60644	3032	6W-0S	A6
1000	CCRO	60804	3032	6W-0S	A7
1500	CCRO	60804	3090	6W-1S	A1
3400	SKNY	60804	3090	6W-3S	A5
3700	CHCG	60804	3090	6W-3S	A6
4200	CHCG	60632	3090	6W-4S	A7
4200	CHCG	60638	3090	6W-4S	A7
4600	CHCG	60632	3150	5W-6S	A3
4600	CHCG	60638	3150	5W-6S	A3
6100	CHCG	60629	3150	6W-7S	A6
6400	BDPK	60638	3150	6W-7S	A6
6700	BDPK	60629	3150	5W-7S	A7
7300	BDPK	60638	3212	5W-8S	A1
7300	CHCG	60629	3212	5W-8S	A1
7300	CHCG	60638	3212	5W-8S	A1
7400	BRBK	60459	3212	6W-8S	A1
7400	CHCG	60652	3212	6W-8S	A1
8500	CHCG	60459	3212	5W-9S	A4
8600	BRBK	60453	3212	6W-9S	A4
8600	CHCG	60456	3212	6W-9S	A4
8600	HMTN	60456	3212	6W-9S	A4
8600	OKLN	60453	3212	6W-9S	A4
8700	OKLN	60456	3212	6W-10S	A4
10200	OKLN	60453	3276	6W-13S	A3
11000	CHCG	60655	3276	5W-12S	A3
12800	ALSP	60803	3276	5W-15S	A7
13100	ALSP	60803	3348	5W-15S	A1
23100	MonT	60449	3594	6W-28S	B7
23100	MonT	60466	3594	6W-28S	B7
23100	RNPK	60471	3594	6W-27S	B5
23100	UYPK	60466	3594	6W-28S	B6
23100	UYPK	60471	3594	6W-27S	B5
24000	MonT	60449	3683	6W-31S	A5
SR-50 S Governors Hwy					
-	MonT	60466	3683	6W-29S	B2
-	UYPK	60466	3683	6W-29S	B2
400	PTON	60468	3861	9W-37S	A4
25100	MonT	60449	3683	6W-30S	A3
25100	UYPK	60449	3683	6W-30S	A3
25500	MONE	60449	3682	7W-31S	E6
25500	MONE	60449	3683	6W-31S	A4
26100	MonT	60449	3682	7W-32S	E7
29800	PtnT	60468	3861	9W-36S	A2
29800	WllT	60468	3861	9W-37S	A2
SR-50 N Harlem Av					
100	PTON	60468	3861	9W-37S	A3
200	WllT	60468	3861	9W-37S	A3
300	PtnT	60468	3861	9W-37S	A2
SR-50 S Harlem Av					
100	PTON	60468	3861	9W-37S	A3
100	WllT	60468	3861	9W-37S	A3
SR-50 Skokie Blvd					
7400	LNWD	60712	2865	5W-9N	E7
7400	SKOK	60077	2865	6W-9N	E7
7500	SKOK	60076	2865	6W-9N	E7
SR-53					
-	ANHT	-	2753	18W-16N	D7
-	ANHT	-	2806	19W-15N	B2
-	EGvT	-	2860	20W-12N	A1
-	EGvT	-	2914		A1
-	EGVV	-	2914		A1
-	PLTN	-	2753	18W-16N	D7
-	PLTN	-	2806	20W-14N	A3
-	PltT	-	2753	18W-16N	D7
-	PltT	-	2806	20W-13N	A6
-	RGMW	-	2806	19W-15N	B2
-	RGMW	-	2860	20W-12N	A1
-	SMBG	-	2806	20W-13N	A6
-	SMBG	-	2860	20W-12N	A1
SR-53 EXT					
-	PLTN	-	2753	19W-18N	D3
SR-53 Biesterfield Rd					
1000	EGVV	60007	2914		A7
SR-53 E Dundee Rd					
-	PltT	60004	2753	19W-18N	D4
900	PLTN	60074	2753	19W-18N	C4
1500	PltT	60074	2753	19W-18N	C4
SR-53 W Dundee Rd					
-	ANHT	60004	2753	19W-18N	D4
-	PltT	60004	2753	19W-18N	D4
-	PltT	60074	2753	19W-18N	D4
SR-53 Hicks Rd					
2700	LGGV	60047	2753	20W-20N	B1
2700	PLTN	60047	2753	20W-20N	A2
2700	PLTN	60074	2753	20W-20N	A2
20700	ElaT	60047	2753	20W-20N	B1
SR-53 N Hicks Rd					
2100	PLTN	60074	2753	20W-20N	B2
2300	ElaT	60047	2753	20W-20N	A2
2300	LGGV	60047	2753	20W-20N	A2
2300	PLTN	60047	2753	20W-20N	A2
SR-53 Rand Rd					
2000	PLTN	60074	2753	20W-18N	A3
SR-53 N Rand Rd					
1600	PLTN	60074	2753	19W-18N	B4
SR-53 Rohlwing Rd					
10	BmdT	60143	2914		A7
800	EGVV	60007	2914		A2
1000	ITSC	60007	2914		A3
1000	ITSC	60143	2914		A3
1100	AddT	60143	2914		A4
SR-53 N Rohlwing Rd					
200	BmdT	60143	2914		A6
200	ITSC	60143	2914		A6
SR-56 Butterfield Rd					
4000	BLWD	60104	3029	13W-0N	A5
4000	BLWD	60162	3029	13W-0N	A4
4000	HLSD	60162	3029	13W-0N	A5
4300	BLWD	60104	3028		E5
4300	HLSD	60162	3028		E5
5200	BKLY	60162	3028		C5
5200	BKLY	60163	3028		C5
5200	HLSD	60163	3028		C5
5900	EMHT	60162	3028		C6
6000	EMHT	60126	3028		B6
SR-56 E Butterfield Rd					
500	BKLY	60162	3028		B6
500	BKLY	60163	3028		B6
500	EMHT	60126	3028		B6
500	EMHT	60162	3028		B6
SR-56 Washington Blvd					
4000	BLWD	60104	3029	12W-0N	A4
4000	BLWD	60162	3029	12W-0N	A4
4000	HLSD	60162	3029	13W-0N	A4
SR-58 Dempster St					
4800	SKOK	60076	2865	5W-11N	E4
4800	SKOK	60077	2865	6W-11N	E4
5600	MNGV	60053	2865	7W-10N	B4
6700	MNGV	60053	2864	8W-10N	E4
SR-58 Golf Rd					
-	ELGN	60120	2855		E3
-	HFET	60010	2856	29W-11N	E3
-	HFET	60010	2857	28W-12N	A3
-	HFET	60107	2856	29W-11N	D3
-	HnrT	60120	2855		E3
-	RGMW	60007	2860	20W-12N	A2
-	RGMW	60173	2860	20W-12N	A2
-	SMBG	60173	2860	20W-12N	A2
500	HFET	60120	2856	30W-11N	B3
500	HFET	60192	2856	30W-11N	B3
500	HnrT	60120	2856	30W-11N	B3
500	HnrT	60192	2856	30W-11N	B3
900	ANHT	60005	2860	18W-11N	E2
900	RGMW	60005	2860	18W-11N	E2
900	RGMW	60008	2860	21W-11N	A2
1700	GNVW	60025	2864	10W-11N	B2
1700	GNVW	60053	2864	10W-11N	B2
1700	MNGV	60053	2864	10W-11N	B2
2100	EGvT	60007	2860	21W-11N	A2
2400	MaiT	60025	2864	9W-12N	C2
2500	MaiT	60714	2864	9W-12N	B2
3100	EGvT	60008	2860	20W-12N	B2
9200	MaiT	60016	2863	11W-12N	D2
9200	NLES	60714	2863	11W-12N	D2
9500	DSPN	60016	2863	11W-12N	C2
SR-58 E Golf Rd					
10	ANHT	60005	2861	17W-11N	B2
10	HFET	60195	2859	23W-12N	A2
10	SMBG	60195	2859	23W-12N	A2
100	HFET	60173	2859	23W-12N	B2
500	DSPN	60016	2862	13W-12N	E2
600	MPPT	60056	2861	17W-11N	B2
800	ANHT	60056	2861	17W-11N	B2
900	MPPT	60005	2861	17W-11N	B2
1300	DSPN	60016	2863	11W-11N	D2
1400	SMBG	60173	2859	23W-11N	A2
1700	MaiT	60016	2863	11W-11N	D2
2000	EGvT	60007	2860	20W-11N	A2
2000	RGMW	60008	2860	20W-12N	A2
2000	RGMW	60173	2860	20W-12N	A2
2000	SMBG	60173	2860	20W-12N	A2
SR-58 W Golf Rd					
-	HFET	60010	2857	27W-12N	C3
10	ANHT	60005	2861	18W-11N	A2
10	DSPN	60016	2862	15W-11N	A3
10	DSPN	60056	2862	15W-11N	A3
10	HFET	60195	2859	23W-12N	A2
10	MPPT	60016	2862	15W-11N	A3
10	MPPT	60056	2862	15W-11N	A3
10	SMBG	60173	2859	23W-12N	A2
10	SMBG	60195	2859	23W-12N	A2
100	SMBG	60195	2858	25W-11N	B2
300	DSPN	60016	2861	16W-11N	E3
300	HFET	60195	2858	23W-12N	E2
300	MPPT	60056	2861	16W-11N	D3
500	ANHT	60005	2860	18W-11N	E2
600	HFET	60194	2858	24W-12N	D2
700	RGMW	60005	2860	18W-11N	E2
700	RGMW	60008	2860	18W-11N	E2
1600	SMBG	60194	2858	25W-12N	B2
2000	ANHT	60056	2861	17W-11N	B2
2000	MPPT	60005	2861	17W-11N	B2
2100	HFET	60194	2857	27W-11N	C3
2100	SMBG	60194	2857	27W-11N	C3
8000	MaiT	60025	2864	10W-12N	B2
8000	MaiT	60714	2864	10W-12N	B2
8000	MNGV	60053	2864	9W-12N	B2
8000	NLES	60025	2864	10W-12N	B2
8000	NLES	60714	2864	10W-12N	B2
8500	MaiT	60016	2864	10W-12N	A2
8700	MaiT	60016	2863	10W-12N	E2
8700	MaiT	60714	2863	11W-12N	E2
8700	NLES	60714	2863	11W-12N	E2
8800	NLES	60016	2863	11W-12N	E2
SR-58 Summit St					
600	ELGN	60120	2855		C3

STREET	Block	City	ZIP	Map#	CGS	Grid
Stagecoach Rd						
	11800	ODPK	60467	3344	14W-16S	C3
	11800	OrlT	60467	3344	14W-16S	C3
Stairway Dr						
	2000	HRPK	60133	2911		C6
	2000	WynT	60133	2911		C6
Stalford Rd						
	6500	CTSD	60525	3147	13W-7S	A6
	6500	LynT	60525	3147	13W-7S	A6
Stamford Ct						
	800	SMBG	60193	2858	23W-9N	E7
Standish Dr						
	10	DRFD	60015	2757	10W-20N	B1
Standish Ln						
	10	SMBG	60193	2858	25W-10N	C6
	10	SMBG	60194	2858	25W-10N	C6
Standish St						
	300	CHHT	60411	3595	2W-26S	D2
Stanford Cir						
	600	EGVV	60007	2860	19W-9N	C7
	1400	CPVL	60110	2748		D5
Stanford Dr						
	6800	BGVW	60455	3211	8W-10S	A5
	6900	BGVW	60455	3210	8W-10S	E5
N Stanford Dr						
	2800	ANHT	60004	2754	16W-17N	C5
Stanford Ln						
	600	BFGV	60089	2754	17W-17N	B5
Stanley Av						
	10	PKRG	60068	2918	9W-8N	B2
	3700	RvsT	60546	3088	9W-3S	C6
	3800	LYNS	60534	3088	9W-3S	C6
	3800	RvsT	60534	3088	9W-3S	C6
	6400	BRWN	60402	3089	8W-3S	A4
	6800	BRWN	60402	3088	8W-3S	E4
	7100	RVSD	60546	3088	8W-3S	E4
Stanley Blvd						
	1200	CTCY	60409	3430	4E-19S	B3
Stanley Ct						
	2100	SMBG	60194	2858	26W-11N	A3
Stanley St						
	10	EGvT	60007	2861	17W-10N	B6
	100	EGVV	60007	2861	17W-10N	B6
	1800	NHBK	60062	2757	9W-16N	B7
S Stanley Av						
	1200	HMND	46320	3280		E3
	1200	HMND	46394	3280		E3
Stanton Ct						
	10	SMBG	60193	2859	23W-10N	B5
Stanton Ct N						
	1900	ANHT	60004	2807	18W-16N	A1
Stanton Dr						
	-	BRLT	60120	2909		D3
W Stanton Ln						
	400	CteT	60417	3774	0W-32S	C1
Stanton St						
	400	PKFT	60466	3595	3W-25S	A1
Star Dr						
	5600	HRPK	60133	2911		E6
Star Ln						
	10	SBTN	60010	2803	27W-13N	B6
	13500	HmrT	60439	3342	20W-16S	A3
	13500	HmrT	60441	3342	20W-16S	A3
	13500	LMNT	60439	3342	20W-16S	A3
Starboard Pt						
	700	SMBG	60194	2859	23W-10N	A5
Stargrass Ln						
	200	SjnT	46311	3598		D5
Stark Dr						
	8700	LynT	60527	3208		D4
E Stark Dr						
	600	PLTN	60074	2753	20W-16N	B7
N Stark Dr						
	400	PLTN	60074	2753	20W-17N	A6
Stark Pl						
	1100	DSPN	60016	2862	15W-10N	B5
	1100	DSPN	60018	2862	15W-10N	B5
S Stark St						
	2500	CHCG	60608	3091	1W-2S	E2
Starling Ln						
	2800	RGMW	60008	2806	19W-13N	B6
Starr Rd						
	1000	WNKA	60093	2812	5W-16N	A1
E State Pkwy						
	10	SMBG	60173	2859	23W-12N	B1
	10	SMBG	60195	2859	23W-12N	A1
N State Pkwy						
	1200	CHCG	60610	3034	0W-1N	B1
	1200	CHCG	60611	3034	0E-1N	B1
State Rd						
	-	OKLN	60453	3211	8W-9S	B4
	5100	BDPK	60459	3211	6W-8S	E1
	5100	BDPK	60638	3211	6W-8S	E1
	5100	BRBK	60459	3211	7W-9S	B4
	5100	BRBK	60638	3211	6W-8S	E1
S State Rd						
	7300	BDPK	60638	3150	6W-8S	A7
	7300	BDPK	60638	3211	6W-8S	E1
	7300	BDPK	60638	3212	6W-8S	A1
	7300	BRBK	60459	3211	6W-8S	E1
	7300	CHCG	60629	3150	5W-8S	A7
	7300	CHCG	60638	3150	6W-8S	A7
State St						
	-	CHHT	60425	3508	0W-25S	D7
	-	HMGN	60441	3342	19W-17S	D6
	-	HmrT	60441	3342	19W-17S	D6
	10	CTCY	60409	3352	3E-17S	A4
	10	HMND	46320	3352	4E-17S	C5
	10	LMNT	60439	3270		D6
	200	BlmT	60411	3508	0W-24S	D5
	200	BlmT	60425	3508	0W-24S	D5
	200	CHHT	60411	3508	0W-24S	D5
	400	DSPN	60016	2862	14W-12N	C2
	700	BNHM	60633	3352	3E-17S	A4
	700	CTCY	60633	3352	3E-17S	A4
	1200	LMNT	60439	3342	19W-15S	D2
	1400	BlmT	60411	3596	0W-25S	D1
	1400	CHHT	60411	3596	0W-25S	D1
	1600	BNHM	60633	3351	2E-17S	D4
	1600	CTCY	60409	3351	2E-17S	C4
	2700	SCHT	60411	3596	0E-26S	D3
	3100	SCHT	60475	3596	0E-27S	D4
	3100	STGR	60475	3596	0E-27S	D4
	14600	DLTN	60419	3350	0W-17S	C5
	14600	RVDL	60827	3350	0W-17S	C4
	14900	SHLD	60473	3350	0W-17S	C5
	15000	SHLD	60419	3350	0W-18S	D7
	15900	SHLD	60473	3428	0W-19S	D2
	16800	SHLD	60476	3428	0W-19S	D3
	16800	TNTN	60476	3428	0W-19S	D3
	23000	CRTE	60417	3596	0E-27S	D5
	23000	CRTE	60475	3596	0E-27S	D5
E State St						
	10	CTCY	60409	3352		C6
	800	HMND	46320	3352		E6
	2200	BNHM	60409	3351	3E-17S	E4
	2200	BNHM	60633	3351	3E-17S	E4
	2200	CTCY	60409	3351	3E-17S	E4
	2700	BNHM	60633	3352	3E-17S	A4
	2900	CTCY	60633	3352	3E-17S	A4
N State St						
	10	CHCG	60602	3034	0E-0N	C4
	10	CHCG	60603	3034	0E-0N	C4
	10	GNWD	60425	3508	0W-22S	D1
	100	BlmT	60425	3508	0W-22S	D1
	100	CHCG	60601	3034	0E-0N	C4
	300	CHCG	60610	3034	0E-0N	C3
	300	CHCG	60611	3034	0E-0N	C3
S State St						
	-	CHHT	60411	3508	0E-23S	D4
	-	CHHT	60425	3508	0E-23S	D4
	10	CHCG	60602	3034	0E-0N	C4
	10	CHCG	60603	3034	0E-0S	C5
	100	BlmT	60425	3508	0E-23S	D3
	100	CHCG	60604	3034	0E-0S	C5
	100	GNWD	60425	3508	0E-23S	D3
	600	CHCG	60605	3034	0E-1S	C7
	1500	CHCG	60616	3034	0W-1S	C7
	1700	CHCG	60616	3092	0E-2S	C3
	3400	CRTE	60417	3596	0W-28S	D6
	3400	CRTE	60475	3596	0W-28S	D6
	3400	STGR	60475	3596	0W-28S	D6
	3600	CHCG	60609	3092	0W-4S	C7
	3600	CHCG	60653	3092	0W-4S	C7
	4600	CHCG	60615	3092	0W-4S	C7
	4700	CHCG	60609	3152	0W-5S	C1
	4700	CHCG	60615	3152	0W-5S	C1
	5400	CHCG	60637	3152	0E-8S	C7
	5500	CHCG	60621	3152	0E-8S	C7
	7000	CHCG	60619	3152	0E-8S	C7
	7400	CHCG	60619	3214	0E-8S	C1
	7400	CHCG	60620	3214	0E-8S	C1
	7400	CHCG	60621	3214	0E-8S	C1
	9400	CHCG	60628	3214	0W-11S	C7
	10300	CHCG	60628	3278	0W-13S	C3
	13600	RVDL	60827	3350	0W-15S	C2
	14500	DLTN	60419	3350	0W-16S	C4
	25200	CRTE	60417	3685	0E-30S	E4
	25200	CteT	60417	3685	0E-30S	E4
State Line Av						
	1100	CTCY	60409	3430		C3
	1100	HMND	46324	3430		C3
	6400	HMND	60409	3430		C3
	6600	CTCY	46324	3430	4E-19S	C2
	7500	LNSG	60438	3430	4E-21S	C6
	7500	MNSR	46321	3430	4E-21S	C6
	7500	MNSR	60438	3430	4E-21S	C6
S State Line Av						
	-	CTCY	46320	3352	4E-17S	C5
	5400	CTCY	60409	3352	4E-18S	C7
	5400	HMND	46320	3352	4E-18S	C7
	5900	CTCY	46320	3430	4E-18S	C1
	5900	CTCY	60409	3430	4E-18S	C1
	5900	HMND	46320	3430	4E-18S	C1
	6100	HMND	46324	3430	4E-18S	C1
State Line Rd						
	600	CTCY	60409	3352	4E-17S	C6
	600	HMND	46320	3352	4E-17S	C6
	1300	CTCY	60409	3430	4E-20S	C4
	1300	HMND	46320	3430	4E-20S	C4
	1300	HMND	60409	3430	4E-20S	C4
	1400	CTCY	46324	3430	4E-19S	C2
	11600	CteT	46311	3687		C7
	11600	CteT	60417	3687		C7
	11600	HnrT	46311	3687		C7
S State Line Rd						
	13900	BNHM	60633	3352	4E-15S	C2
	13900	HMND	46327	3352	4E-15S	C2
	23700	CteT	60417	3598	4E-29S	C7
	23700	SjnT	46311	3598	4E-29S	C7
	24000	CteT	60417	3687		C2
	24000	SjnT	46311	3687		C2
	24300	CteT	46311	3687	4E-32S	C7
	25000	HnrT	46311	3687	4E-32S	C7
Stately Oaks Cir						
	14300	HMGN	60441	3342	19W-17S	D5
	14300	HmrT	60441	3342	19W-17S	D5
Stately Oaks Dr						
	15600	HMGN	60441	3342	19W-17S	D5
	15700	HmrT	60441	3342	19W-17S	D5
Station Dr						
	-	ITSC	60191	2914		E7
	200	WDDL	60191	2914		E7
	3400	MTSN	60443	3594	4W-25S	E1
E Station St						
	-	BRTN	60010	2751	25W-18N	A2
	100	BRTN	60010	2750	26W-18N	D2
W Station St						
	100	BRTN	60010	2750	25W-18N	E2
N Stave St						
	2000	CHCG	60647	2977	3W-2N	A6
	2100	CHCG	60647	2976	4W-2N	D7
Stavros Ln						
	1000	WLNG	60090	2755	13W-16N	E7
Staycoff Ln						
	-	CHCG	60456	3212	5W-10S	A4
	-	CHCG	60652	3212	5W-10S	A4
	8700	HMTN	60456	3212	5W-10S	A4
Stearns Rd						
	10	BRLT	60103	2910		A5
	10	BRLT	60120	2909		C5
	10	BRLT	60120	2910		A5
	10	BRLT	60184	2909		C5
	10	SchT	60120	2909		C5
	10	WynT	60120	2909		C5
	10	WynT	60184	2909		E5
	100	BRLT	60103	2911		A6
	500	WynT	60103	2911		A6
Stearns Rd CO-29						
	10	BRLT	60103	2910		A5
	10	BRLT	60120	2909		C5
	10	BRLT	60120	2910		A5
	10	BRLT	60184	2909		E5
	10	SchT	60120	2909		C5
	10	WynT	60120	2909		C5
	10	WynT	60184	2909		E5
	100	BRLT	60103	2911		A6
	500	WynT	60103	2911		A6
E Stearns Rd						
	-	BRLT	60133	2911		D6
	-	HRPK	60133	2911		C6
	200	BRLT	60103	2911		C6
	200	WynT	60103	2911		B6
E Stearns Rd CO-29						
	-	BRLT	60133	2911		D6
	-	HRPK	60133	2911		C6
	200	BRLT	60103	2911		C6
	200	WynT	60103	2911		B6
W Stearns Rd						
	100	BRLT	60103	2910		E6
	500	BRLT	60120	2910		A5
W Stearns Rd CO-29						
	100	BRLT	60103	2910		D6
	500	BRLT	60120	2910		A5
Stech St						
	100	DYR	46311	3598		C2
Stedhall Rd						
	18400	HMWD	60430	3507	3W-22S	B1
	18500	FSMR	60422	3507	3W-22S	B1
	18500	FSMR	60430	3507	3W-22S	B1
Steeple Dr						
	100	BFGV	60089	2754	16W-20N	D2
	8500	TYPK	60477	3424	10W-20S	B5
Steeplechase Ct						
	200	SMBG	60173	2859	21W-11N	E3
	200	SMBG	60173	2860	21W-10N	A5
Steeplechase Ln						
	10	NfdT	60093	2811	8W-16N	A1
	10	NHFD	60093	2811	8W-16N	A1
W Steeplechase Ln						
	1200	PLTN	60067	2805	22W-14N	A3
Steeplechase Pkwy						
	11300	ODPK	60467	3422	14W-20S	E4
Steeplechase Rd						
	10	BNHL	60010	2750	28W-20N	A1
	100	BNHL	60010	2749	28W-20N	E2
Steeples Rd						
	13700	LMNT	60439	3271		D6
Steepleside Dr						
	8100	BRRG	60480	3208		D3
	8100	BRRG	60527	3208		D3
	8100	WLSP	60480	3208		D3
Steepleview Ln						
	13800	LMNT	60439	3271		C6
Steffen Dr						
	1800	HFET	60120	2855		E1
Steger Rd						
	3600	MonT	60466	3594	4W-27S	D5
	3600	PKFT	60466	3594	4W-27S	D5
	3600	RNPK	60466	3594	4W-27S	D5
	3800	MonT	60471	3594	4W-27S	D5
	5100	RchT	60471	3594	6W-27S	A5
	5100	RNPK	60471	3594	6W-27S	A5
	5100	UYPK	60449	3594	6W-27S	A5
	5100	UYPK	60466	3594	6W-27S	A5
	5100	UYPK	60471	3594	6W-27S	A5
E Steger Rd						
	10	CRTE	60417	3596	0E-27S	D5
	10	CRTE	60475	3596	0E-27S	D5
	10	STGR	60475	3596	0E-27S	D5
	400	STGR	60417	3596	0E-27S	D5
	600	CRTE	60417	3597	1E-27S	B5
	600	STGR	60417	3597	1E-27S	B5
	600	STGR	60475	3597	1E-27S	B5
	700	CRTE	60475	3597	1E-27S	A5
	1400	STGR	60411	3597	1E-27S	B5
	1600	CteT	60417	3597	2E-27S	D5
	1600	SLVL	60411	3597	2E-27S	C5
	1700	BlmT	60411	3597	2E-27S	E5
	1700	BlmT	60417	3597	2E-27S	D5
	2300	CteT	60411	3597	2E-27S	D5
	2500	BlmT	60411	3598	3E-27S	A5
	2500	CteT	60411	3598	3E-27S	A5
	2500	CteT	60417	3598	3E-27S	A5
	3400	BlmT	46311	3598	3E-27S	B5
	3400	CteT	46311	3598	3E-27S	A5
	3500	SjnT	46311	3598	3E-27S	A5
W Steger Rd						
	-	MonT	60471	3593	7W-27S	C5
	-	UYPK	60471	3593	7W-27S	E5
	10	STGR	60475	3596	1W-27S	A5
	100	BlmT	60475	3596	1W-27S	A5
	300	BlmT	60466	3595	1W-27S	E5
	300	BlmT	60475	3595	1W-27S	E5
	300	CteT	60466	3595	1W-27S	E5
	300	CteT	60475	3595	1W-27S	E5
	300	STGR	60475	3595	1W-27S	E5
	2200	MonT	60466	3595	2W-27S	C5
	2200	PKFT	60466	3595	3W-27S	C5
	4800	RchT	60449	3593	6W-27S	E5
	4800	RchT	60449	3594	6W-27S	A5
	4800	RchT	60471	3593	6W-27S	E5
	4800	RchT	60471	3594	6W-27S	A5
	4800	RNPK	60449	3593	6W-27S	E5
	4800	RNPK	60449	3594	6W-27S	A5
	4800	RNPK	60471	3593	6W-27S	E5
	4800	RNPK	60471	3594	6W-27S	A5
	4800	UYPK	60449	3593	6W-27S	E5
	4800	UYPK	60449	3594	6W-27S	A5
	4800	UYPK	60466	3594	6W-27S	A5
	4800	UYPK	60471	3594	6W-27S	A5
	5800	FKFT	60423	3593	8W-27S	B5
	5800	FKFT	60443	3593	8W-27S	A5
	5800	FKFT	60449	3593	8W-27S	A5
	5800	MonT	60443	3593	8W-27S	B5
	5800	MonT	60449	3593	8W-27S	B5
	5800	RchT	60443	3593	8W-27S	A5
Stella Blvd						
	3700	CteT	60417	3596	1W-28S	A7
	3700	CteT	60475	3596	1W-28S	A7
	3700	STGR	60417	3596	1W-28S	A7
	3700	STGR	60475	3596	1W-28S	B6
Stella Ct						
	500	ELGN	60120	2855		B4
Stella St						
	400	ELGN	60120	2855		A4
Stepeeple Hl						
	8600	HYHL	60457	3209	11W-10S	E4
N Stephan Dr						
	400	PLTN	60067	2752	21W-16N	C6
	600	PltT	60067	2752	21W-16N	C6
Stephanie Ct						
	100	BRLT	60103	2911		A3
S Stephanie Ct						
	26500	MonT	60449	3683	6W-32S	A7
Stephen Dr						
	10300	CHRG	60415	3275	8W-12S	A1
S Stephen Dr						
	13300	PlsT	60464	3345	13W-15S	B2
Stephen St						
	400	LMNT	60439	3270		D5
Stephens St						
	-	MTSN	60443	3506	6W-24S	A5
Stepp Dr						
	5400	SMMT	60501	3148	9W-5S	C3
Sterling Av						
	600	FSMR	60422	3507	3W-22S	B2
	600	FSMR	60430	3507	2W-22S	C1
	600	HMWD	60430	3507	2W-22S	C1
	17400	CCHL	60429	3426	4W-20S	D5
	17400	CCHL	60478	3426	4W-20S	D5
	17400	HLCT	60429	3426	4W-20S	D5
	17400	HLCT	60478	3426	4W-20S	D5
N Sterling Av						
	800	PLTN	60067	2752	22W-16N	B6
	900	PltT	60067	2752	22W-17N	B5
	900	PltT	60074	2752	22W-17N	B5
Sterling Ct						
	700	BRLT	60103	2911		B3
	17300	SHLD	60473	3429	2E-20S	D4
Sterling Dr						
	10	HmrT	60441	3342	20W-16S	B3
	1000	HmrT	60439	3342	20W-15S	B3
	1000	LMNT	60439	3342	20W-15S	B3
	11800	ODPK	60467	3344	14W-16S	C4
	16600	LMNT	60439	3270		B7
W Sterling Dr						
	7600	FftT	60423	3504	9W-24S	D6
Sterling Ln						
	100	EVTN	60091	2812	4W-13N	C7
	100	EVTN	60201	2812	4W-13N	C7
	100	NHFD	60093	2811	7W-15N	B2
	100	WLMT	60091	2812	4W-13N	C7
	9800	SRPK	60176	2973	12W-4N	B2
Sterling Rd						
	-	KLWH	60043	2812	4W-14N	C5
	600	IVNS	60067	2751	23W-16N	E6
Sterling St						
	-	LynT	60458	3209	12W-8S	D1
	-	WLSP	60480	3209	12W-8S	D1
Sterling St E						
	400	LynT	60458	3209	11W-8S	E2
Sterling St W						
	600	LynT	60458	3209	11W-8S	E2
N Stetson Av						
	100	CHCG	60601	3034	0E-0N	C4
W Steuben St						
	1700	CHCG	60643	3277	2W-13S	D3
Steven Ct						
	14800	LMNT	60439	3271		A7
	14800	LMNT	60439	3343	18W-15S	A1
Steven Dr						
	8800	MaiT	60016	2863	11W-12N	E2
	8800	NLES	60714	2863	11W-12N	E2
Steven Ln						
	2500	NHBK	60062	2809	11W-15N	C1
Steven Pl						
	8400	TYPK	60477	3424	10W-19S	B2
N Stevens Av						
	6000	CHCG	60646	2920	4W-7N	B3
	6000	CHCG	60659	2920	5W-7N	B3
Stevens Dr						
	10	SMBG	60173	2859	21W-10N	E5
	1700	GNVW	60025	2810	8W-13N	E5
	8700	BRBK	60453	3211	6W-10S	E4
	8700	BRBK	60459	3211	6W-10S	E4
	8700	OKLN	60453	3211	6W-10S	E4
Stevenson Ct						
	1000	BmdT	60157	2913		D4
	1000	ROSL	60157	2913		D4
Stevenson Dr						
	9100	MaiT	60016	2863	11W-11N	D3
Stevenson Expwy						
	-	BDPK	-	3147	11W-7S	E6
	-	BDPK	-	3148	10W-6S	B4
	-	CHCG	-	3089	6W-4S	E6
	-	CHCG	-	3090	4W-3S	D5
	-	CHCG	-	3091	3W-3S	A4
	-	CHCG	-	3092	1W-2S	A2
	-	CTSD	-	3146		D7
	-	CTSD	-	3147	13W-7S	A7
	-	FTVW	-	3089	6W-4S	D7
	-	FTVW	-	3148	8W-5S	E2
	-	FTVW	-	3149	8W-5S	A1
	-	HGKN	-	3147	11W-7S	E7
	-	IHPK	-	3146		D7
	-	SKNY	-	3089	6W-4S	E7
	-	SMMT	-	3148	9W-5S	C2
	-	StkT	-	3089	6W-4S	D7
Stevenson Expwy I-55						
	-	BDPK	-	3147	11W-7S	E7
	-	BDPK	-	3148	10W-6S	B4
	-	CHCG	-	3089	6W-4S	E6
	-	CHCG	-	3090	4W-3S	C5
	-	CHCG	-	3091	3W-3S	A4
	-	CHCG	-	3092	0W-2S	C2
	-	CTSD	-	3146		D7
	-	CTSD	-	3147	13W-7S	A7
	-	FTVW	-	3089	6W-4S	D7
	-	FTVW	-	3148	8W-5S	E2
	-	FTVW	-	3149	8W-5S	A1
	-	HGKN	-	3147	11W-7S	E7
	-	IHPK	-	3146		D7
	-	SKNY	-	3089	6W-4S	E7
	-	SMMT	-	3148	9W-5S	C2
	-	StkT	-	3089	6W-4S	D7
N Stevenson Ln						
	10	DSPN	60016	2808	14W-13N	C7
	10	MPPT	60016	2808	14W-13N	C7
	10	MPPT	60056	2808	14W-13N	C7
Stewart Av						
	400	PKRG	60068	2918	10W-8N	A1
	600	DLTN	60419	3350	0E-17S	E5
	600	ELGN	60120	2801		B7
	1000	CTCY	60409	3351	3E-17S	E5
	1000	CTCY	60409	3352	3E-17S	A5
	1400	PKRG	60068	2917	11W-8N	E1
	1700	DSPN	60018	2863	12W-10N	B5
	2100	CHHT	60411	3596	0W-26S	C2
	2500	BlmT	60411	3596	0W-26S	C2
	2600	EVTN	60201	2812	3W-13N	E7
	3300	CRTE	60475	3596	0W-27S	C5
	3300	STGR	60475	3596	0W-27S	C5
	18000	HMWD	60430	3427	3W-22S	B7
	18200	LNSG	60438	3430	4E-21S	B6
	18400	HMWD	60430	3507	3W-22S	B1
S Stewart Av						
	2200	CHCG	60616	3092	0W-2S	B3
	3800	CHCG	60609	3092	0W-3S	B5
	5500	CHCG	60609	3152	0W-6S	B3
	5500	CHCG	60621	3152	0W-6S	B3
	7500	CHCG	60621	3214	0W-8S	B1
	7900	CHCG	60620	3214	0W-9S	B3
	11100	CHCG	60628	3278	0W-14S	B5
	14000	RVDL	60827	3350	0W-16S	B4
E Stewart Ct						
	600	HMND	46394	3280		D4
Stewart Ter						
	-	CRTE	60417	3596	0E-29S	E7
	-	CRTE	60417	3597	0E-29S	A7
Stewart Wy						
	-	BlmT	60411	3508	0W-24S	C5
	-	CHHT	60411	3508	0W-24S	C5
Stickney Av						
	7200	BGVW	60455	3148	9W-8S	C7
	7500	BGVW	60455	3210	9W-8S	C2
Still Water Ct						
	200	RGMW	60067	2805	22W-13N	B5
Stillwater Rd						
	1000	ELGN	60120	2855		C2
N Stillwater Rd						
	1900	ANHT	60004	2807	16W-16N	D1
Stillwell Dr						
	300	BFGV	60089	2754	17W-18N	C3
	3000	DSPN	60018	2917	12W-8N	B2
	3100	RSMT	60018	2917	12W-8N	B3
Stillwell Pl						
	4000	OKLN	60453	3276	5W-12S	C2
Stirling Av						
	1000	BlmT	60411	3507	2W-25S	D7
	1000	CHHT	60411	3507	2W-25S	D7
Stirling Ln						
	10	RGMW	60008	2806	20W-15N	A3
	100	SMBG	60194	2857	26W-10N	E5
	600	PTHT	60070	2808	14W-14N	C4
Stirrup Ct						
	10	LMNT	60439	3271		A5
S Stirrup Ct						
	14500	HMGN	60441	3344	15W-17S	B5
Stirrup Ln						
	100	BRRG	60527	3146		C6
	1000	LMNT	60439	3271		A5
Stirrup Pl						
	100	BRRG	60527	3146		C6
Stockbridge Ct						
	700	SMBG	60194	2858	25W-11N	B4
	1000	ELGN	60120	2855		D1
Stockbridge Pl						
	800	ELGN	60120	2855		D2
	800	HFET	60120	2855		D2
Stockport Ct						
	200	ROSL	60172	2912		C5
Stock Port Ln						
	200	SMBG	60193	2859	23W-10N	B6
Stockton Av						
	1000	DSPN	60018	2862	13W-9N	E7
	1600	DSPN	60018	2863	12W-9N	A7
	18500	HMWD	60430	3507	3W-22S	A1
Stockton Dr						
	1800	HFET	60195	2858	25W-12N	C1
	1800	NHFD	60093	2811	7W-15N	C3
N Stockton Dr						
	1600	CHCG	60614	2978	0W-2N	B7
Stockton Ln						
	13900	ODPK	60467	3344	14W-16S	E3
Stockton St						
	-	WNKA	60093	2811	6W-15N	D2
N Stokes Av						
	-	CHCG	60018	2917	12W-6N	B6
	-	SRPK	60018	2917	12W-6N	B6
	-	SRPK	60176	2917	12W-6N	B6
W Stolting Rd						
	8600	NLES	60714	2863	10W-10N	E4
	8600	NLES	60714	2864	10W-10N	A4
	8600	PKRG	60714	2863	10W-10N	E4
N Stone Av						
	100	LGNG	60525	3087	12W-4S	B6
	200	LGPK	60525	3087	12W-3S	B5
S Stone Av						
	10	LGNG	60525	3087	12W-4S	B7
	300	LGNG	60525	3147	12W-4S	B1
	1200	CTSD	60525	3147	12W-5S	B3
Stone Ln						
	-	BlmT	60411	3509	2E-25S	D7
	-	FDHT	60411	3509	2E-25S	D7
	1100	SLVL	60411	3509	2E-25S	D7
Stone Pl						
	300	WLNG	60090	2755	14W-17N	D5
Stone St						
	500	DSPN	60016	2862	14W-12N	C1
N Stone St						
	1200	CHCG	60610	3034	0E-1N	C1
	1200	CHCG	60611	3034	0E-1N	C1
Stonebridge Ct						
	1100	ELGN	60120	2855		D2
E Stonebridge Ct						
	800	PLTN	60074	2806	19W-15N	B1
W Stonebridge Ct						
	10	PSHL	60465	3274	10W-12S	B3
Stonebridge Dr						
	-	ANHT	60004	2753	18W-16N	E6
	-	ANHT	60004	2754	18W-16N	A7
	17500	HLCT	60429	3427	3W-21S	A6
N Stonebridge Dr						
	-	ANHT	60004	2753	18W-16N	E6
Stonebridge Ln						
	700	BFGV	60089	2754	17W-17N	B5
	2500	NHBK	60062	2757	10W-18N	A4
Stonebridge Sq						
	-	HLCT	60429	3427	3W-21S	A5
Stonebridge Wy						
	900	DGvT	60439	3270		D2
	900	WDRG	60439	3270		D2
Stone Brook Ct						
	600	EGVV	60007	2914		B3
Stonebrook Ct						
	10	SBTN	60010	2803	27W-13N	B6
Stonebrook Rd						
	100	MTSN	60443	3506	5W-24S	C5
Stonebrooke Ct						
	9400	TYPK	60477	3423	11W-20S	D5
W Stone Canyon Cir						
	500	IVNS	60010	2750	25W-17N	E5
	700	IVNS	60010	2751	25W-17N	A6
	800	BRTN	60010	2751	25W-17N	A5
Stone Canyon Wy						
	-	IVNS	60010	2750	25W-17N	E6
Stone Cir Ct						
	600	SMBG	60194	2859	22W-10N	C5
Stone Cir Dr						
	4900	OKLN	60453	3212	6W-11S	A7
Stone Creek Dr						
	10	LMNT	60439	3272	15W-13S	B4
Stonecreek Dr						
	18400	HLCT	60429	3426	4W-22S	D7
	18400	HLCT	60429	3506	4W-22S	E1
Stonefield Cir						
	900	IVNS	60067	2751	23W-17N	D6
Stonefield Ct						
	200	SMBG	60173	2860	20W-10N	A5
Stonefield Pl						
	800	ROSL	60172	2912		D6
Stone Gate Cir						
	400	SMBG	60193	2859	23W-9N	A7
Stonegate Ct						
	10	BFGV	60089	2754	17W-18N	A2
	300	WLBK	60527	3146		A6
	3100	FSMR	60422	3507	3W-22S	A2
Stone Gate Dr						
	700	HDPK	60035	2758	7W-20N	A2
Stonegate Dr						
	8000	TYPK	60477	3504	10W-23S	C4

Chicago & Cook County Street Index

STREET Block	City	ZIP	Map#	CGS	Grid
E Sunset Rd					
10	MPPT	60056	2862	15W-11N	A2
N Sunset Rd					
2200	PLTN	60074	2752	21W-18N	C2
W Sunset Rd					
10	MPPT	60056	2862	15W-11N	A2
300	BRTN	60010	2750	26W-18N	E3
400	BNHL	60010	2750	26W-18N	D3
500	MPPT	60056	2861	16W-11N	E2
8600	NLES	60714	2863	10W-10N	E5
8600	NLES	60714	2864	10W-10N	A5
8600	PKRG	60714	2863	10W-10N	E5
Sunset Ter					
100	BmdT	60157	2913		C7
600	BMDL	60108	2913		B7
600	BMDL	60157	2913		B7
600	BmdT	60108	2913		B7
1400	WNSP	60558	3086		C7
E Sunset Ter					
1400	ANHT	60004	2807	16W-14N	C5
W Sunset Ter					
1200	ANHT	60005	2806	18W-14N	D5
Sunset Tr					
3200	NfdT	60062	2809	11W-16N	C1
3200	NHBK	60062	2809	11W-16N	C1
Sunset Park Dr					
10	DndT	60118	2801		C5
Sunset Ridge Ct					
8300	ODPK	60462	3346	10W-18S	B6
S Sunset Ridge Ct					
15700	ODPK	60462	3424	10W-18S	C1
Sunset Ridge Dr					
15100	ODPK	60462	3346	10W-18S	B6
15600	ODPK	60462	3424	10W-18S	C1
16700	CCHL	60478	3426	4W-20S	D3
Sunset Ridge Rd					
100	GNVW	60025	2811	8W-15N	A2
100	NHFD	60093	2811	8W-15N	A2
100	WLBK	60527	3146		A5
600	NfdT	60093	2811	8W-15N	A2
800	NHBK	60062	2758	8W-17N	A4
1800	NHBK	60093	2758	8W-16N	A7
1800	NHFD	60093	2758	8W-16N	A7
2000	NfdT	60093	2758	8W-16N	A7
Sunset View Rd					
10	DRPK	60010	2751	23W-20N	E1
Sunshine Ln					
8600	ODPK	60462	3346	11W-15S	A2
20000	DRPK	60010	2752	22W-20N	B1
Suntone Dr					
15800	SHLD	60473	3350	0W-18S	C7
15800	SHLD	60473	3428	0W-18S	C1
S Sun Valley Ct					
10500	PSHL	60465	3274	10W-12S	A2
W Sun Valley Dr					
8400	PSHL	60465	3274	10W-12S	B2
Sunview Ln					
1200	WNKA	60093	2811	6W-16N	E1
Superior Av					
300	CTCY	60409	3352	3E-17S	A6
400	MNSR	46321	3510		D3
1200	CTCY	60409	3430	3E-19S	A2
Superior Ct					
10	SMBG	60193	2859	23W-10N	A6
Superior St					
10	CHCG	60644	3031	7W-0N	B3
10	MYWD	60153	3030	10W-0N	A3
10	OKPK	60302	3031	8W-0N	A3
1000	MLPK	60153	3029	10W-0N	E3
1000	MLPK	60160	3029	11W-0N	E3
1000	MYWD	60153	3029	11W-0N	E3
1000	OKPK	60302	3030	8W-0N	D3
1100	RVFT	60305	3030	8W-0N	D3
5800	BKLY	60163	3028		C3
E Superior St					
10	CHCG	60610	3034	0E-0N	C3
10	CHCG	60611	3034	0E-0N	C3
W Superior St					
10	CHCG	60610	3034	0W-0N	A3
10	CHCG	60611	3034	0W-0N	C3
1400	CHCG	60622	3033	2W-0N	C3
2100	CHCG	60612	3033	3W-0N	A3
4600	CHCG	60644	3032	5W-0N	A3
4700	CHCG	60644	3031	6W-0N	E3
5900	OKPK	60302	3031	7W-0N	B3
Supreme Dr					
400	BNVL	60106	2915		D5
400	CHCG	60106	2915		E4
Surf Ct					
500	WLNG	60090	2754	16W-17N	D5
900	BRLT	60103	2911		C4
2600	LYWD	60411	3509	3E-23S	E2
W Surf St					
600	CHCG	60657	2978	0W-3N	A4
1700	CHCG	60657	2977	2W-3N	C4
Surfside Pl					
300	GLNC	60022	2759	5W-17N	A5
Surfside Pt					
600	SMBG	60194	2859	23W-10N	A4
Surrey					
10	LMNT	60439	3272	15W-14S	A6
Surrey Ct					
200	BRLT	60103	2910		E4
700	SMWD	60107	2857	28W-9N	B7
N Surrey Ct					
2400	CHCG	60614	2977	1W-3N	D5
S Surrey Ct					
12800	PlsT	60464	3273	12W-15S	C7
12800	PlsT	60464	3345	12W-15S	C1
Surrey Dr					
700	SMWD	60107	2857	28W-9N	B7
8400	TYPK	60477	3424	10W-19S	B2
Surrey Ln					
100	BRRG	60527	3146		C7
100	BRTN	60010	2751	24W-20N	C2
300	CRTE	60417	3596	0E-28S	E6
600	GNVW	60025	2811	7W-13N	B7
900	EGVV	60007	2913		C1
900	EGVV	60193	2913		C1
900	NHBK	60062	2757	9W-17N	D5
900	SMBG	60193	2913		C1
1000	ITSC	60143	2914		D5
3000	HLCT	60429	3427	3W-21S	A6
12300	HMGN	60441	3344	15W-17S	B4
S Surrey Ln					
1500	ANHT	60005	2860	18W-12N	E1
W Surrey Pk					
8700	PSHL	60465	3210	10W-11S	A7
Surrey Rd					
100	WYNE	60174	2909		B7
200	WLNG	60090	2755	15W-18N	A2
S Surrey Hill Ct					
10	PSHT	60463	3274	9W-14S	D6
Surrey Hill Rd					
10	PSHT	60463	3274	9W-14S	D6
W Surrey Park Ln					
-	RGMW	60008	2860	19W-12N	D1
1800	ANHT	60005	2860	19W-12N	D1
S Surrey Ridge Dr					
1500	ANHT	60005	2861	18W-12N	A2
Surry Ln					
-	UYPK	60466	3684	3W-30S	B4
Susan Ct					
500	SMBG	60193	2859	22W-9N	C7
900	ALGN	60102	2748		A2
1000	EGVV	60007	2913		E3
N Susan Ct					
8100	NLES	60714	2864	10W-10N	A5
Susan Dr					
10	MPPT	60056	2861	16W-12N	C1
1300	DSPN	60018	2862	15W-10N	A5
Susan Ln					
100	STGR	60475	3596	1W-28S	A5
400	DRFD	60015	2756	12W-20N	C1
16800	ODPK	60448	3423	13W-20S	A4
16800	ODPK	60467	3423	13W-20S	A4
16800	OrlT	60448	3423	13W-20S	A4
S Susan Ln					
25500	CteT	60417	3687	3E-31S	B4
Sussex Av					
2900	MKHM	60426	3427	3W-19S	A2
Sussex Cir					
100	SMBG	60193	2859	23W-10N	B6
Sussex Ct					
-	RGMW	60008	2806	19W-12N	B7
100	ROSL	60172	2912		B4
400	BFGV	60089	2754	16W-17N	D4
500	EGVV	60007	2860	18W-9N	E7
500	EGVV	60007	2914		E1
14500	OKFT	60452	3347	6W-17S	D5
16100	MKHM	60426	3427	3W-19S	A2
Sussex Dr					
900	NHBK	60062	2756	11W-17N	D4
16400	ODPK	60462	3424	10W-19S	B3
Sussex Ln					
2300	GNVW	60025	2809	11W-15N	D3
2300	GNVW	60062	2809	11W-15N	D3
Sussex Rd					
6800	TYPK	60477	3425	8W-19S	A2
Sussex Ter					
700	CRTE	60417	3597	0E-28S	A7
Sussex Wk					
1700	HFET	60195	2858	25W-12N	B1
Sussex Corner Ln					
700	PTHT	60070	2808	14W-14N	C4
Susy Ln					
9200	SRPK	60176	2973	11W-5N	D2
Sutherland Ct					
600	SBTN	60010	2803	25W-15N	E2
N Sutherland Ct					
800	PLTN	60074	2753	19W-17N	B6
Sutherland Ln					
400	PTHT	60070	2808	14W-14N	C4
Sutherland Pl					
2000	HFET	60195	2858	25W-12N	B1
N Suthers Ln					
2300	PltT	60074	2752	21W-18N	C2
Sutter Dr					
1300	HRPK	60133	2911		E4
Sutton Cir					
700	WLNG	60090	2755	15W-18N	A3
Sutton Ct					
600	WLNG	60090	2755	15W-18N	A3
9100	ODPK	60462	3345	11W-17S	E6
9100	ODPK	60462	3346	11W-17S	A6
W Sutton Ct					
1000	PLTN	60067	2752	22W-17N	B6
Sutton Dr					
800	NHBK	60062	2756	12W-17N	B4
Sutton Ln					
1700	SMBG	60194	2858	25W-10N	A5
Sutton Pl					
-	HNDL	60521	3146		B4
9200	TYPK	60477	3423	11W-21S	E6
10200	MNSR	46321	3510		E4
N Sutton Pl					
1300	CHCG	60610	3034	0W-1N	B1
Sutton Rd					
-	BRLT	60103	2856	29W-9N	C7
-	BRLT	60107	2856	29W-9N	C7
-	BRLT	60120	2910		C6
-	HFET	60010	2856	29W-12N	D1
-	HFET	60120	2856	29W-11N	D3
-	SMWD	60107	2910		C1
-	SMWD	60120	2910		C1
10	BRLT	60103	2910		C6
10	WynT	60103	2910		C4
100	HnrT	60120	2856	30W-9N	C7
100	SMWD	60120	2856	30W-9N	C7
200	HFET	60107	2856	29W-11N	D3
200	HnrT	60107	2856	29W-11N	D3
200	SMWD	60107	2856	29W-11N	D3
Sutton Rd SR-59					
-	BRLT	60103	2856	29W-9N	C7
-	BRLT	60107	2856	29W-9N	C7
-	BRLT	60120	2910		C6
-	HFET	60010	2856	29W-12N	D1
-	HFET	60120	2856	29W-11N	D3
-	SMWD	60107	2910		C1
-	SMWD	60120	2910		C1
10	BRLT	60103	2910		C6
10	WynT	60103	2910		C4
100	HnrT	60120	2856	30W-9N	C7
100	SMWD	60120	2856	30W-9N	C7
200	HFET	60107	2856	29W-11N	D3
200	HnrT	60107	2856	29W-11N	D3
200	SMWD	60107	2856	29W-11N	D3
S Sutton Rd					
10	HnrT	60107	2856	29W-10N	C6
10	SMWD	60107	2856	29W-10N	C6
S Sutton Rd SR-59					
10	HnrT	60107	2856	29W-10N	C6
10	SMWD	60107	2856	29W-10N	C6
Suwanee St					
300	PKFT	60466	3594	4W-27S	E4
Suzann Ter					
1500	NHBK	60062	2757	9W-16N	C6
Suzanne Ln					
800	ELGN	60120	2855		C5
Swainwood Dr					
2000	GNVW	60025	2810	9W-13N	C6
Swallow Ct					
800	VrnT	60015	2755	15W-20N	A1
Swallow Ln					
400	VrnT	60015	2755	15W-20N	A1
2900	RGMW	60008	2806	19W-13N	B6
10600	ODPK	60467	3423	13W-20S	B4
Swallow St					
800	VrnT	60015	2755	15W-20N	A1
Swan Blvd					
400	VrnT	60015	2755	15W-20N	A1
Swan Ct					
400	VrnT	60015	2755	15W-20N	A1
Swan Dr					
600	DYR	46311	3510		D6
Swan Ln					
800	VrnT	60015	2755	15W-20N	A1
2100	RGMW	60008	2806	19W-14N	B4
W Swann St					
200	CHCG	60609	3092	0W-4S	B7
Swansea Ct					
1100	SMBG	60193	2912		C1
Swansway					
20500	DRPK	60010	2752	22W-20N	B1
W Swaps Ct					
12300	HMGN	60467	3344	15W-16S	B3
Swartmore Ct					
900	SMBG	60193	2912		A1
Sweetbriar Ln					
2400	PvsT	60523	3086		D3
2400	WSTR	60154	3086		D3
Sweetflower Dr					
900	HFET	60194	2858	25W-11N	B3
W Sweetwater Dr					
13600	HMGN	60441	3343	16W-17S	D5
Sweetwood Ct					
10	IHPK	60525	3146		E5
Swift Dr					
1800	OKBK	60523	3086		B1
Swilly Ct					
11800	ODPK	60467	3422	14W-21S	D5
Swindon Pl					
1900	HFET	60195	2858	26W-12N	A1
Swinford Rd					
600	BRLT	60103	2911		D5
600	HRPK	60133	2911		D5
Swinton St					
-	WNKA	60093	2811	6W-15N	D2
Sycamore Av					
10	CPVL	60110	2748		C6
100	SMWD	60107	2911		B2
200	BmdT	60157	2913		C5
400	ROSL	60157	2913		C6
500	ROSL	60172	2913		C6
1600	HRPK	60133	2911		C2
2400	HRPK	60107	2911		B2
17500	CCHL	60478	3426	5W-21S	C6
Sycamore Ct					
10	CTCY	60409	3429	2E-18S	C1
900	HFET	60195	2804	24W-14N	D4
7400	ODPK	60462	3346	9W-18S	E6
8700	HYHL	60457	3209	11W-10S	E4
8800	TYPK	60477	3424	11W-20S	A4
S Sycamore Ct					
15400	LKPT	60441	3342	20W-18S	B7
W Sycamore Ct					
100	PLTN	60067	2805	21W-15N	E2
Sycamore Dr					
-	HLCT	60429	3426	4W-20S	E5
10	MonT	60466	3595	3W-28S	C6
10	PKFT	60466	3595	2W-28S	C6
400	DYR	46311	3598		D3
500	EGVV	60007	2915		A3
7500	ODPK	60462	3346	9W-18S	D6
8900	HYHL	60457	3209	11W-10S	E4
8900	HYHL	60457	3210	11W-10S	A4
9100	PlsT	60480	3209	11W-10S	E4
10500	CHRG	60415	3275	8W-12S	B2
17500	HMWD	60430	3427	2W-21S	D5
S Sycamore Dr					
19900	FftT	60423	3504	10W-24S	C4
Sycamore Ln					
200	MNSR	46321	3430		D7
500	WLNG	60090	2754	15W-17N	E6
600	GLNC	60022	2758	7W-17N	B5
900	BRLT	60103	2910		D6
1400	NHBK	60062	2757	9W-17N	C6
4400	RGMW	60008	2806	20W-12N	B7
4900	OKFT	60452	3426	6W-20S	A4
4900	OKFT	60477	3426	6W-20S	A4
11200	PSHL	60465	3274	10W-13S	C4
N Sycamore Ln					
10	GNWD	60425	3508	0E-22S	E2
1000	MPPT	60056	2808	14W-14N	C5
S Sycamore Ln					
10	GNWD	60425	3508	0E-22S	E2
12700	PSHT	60463	3274	9W-15S	D7
12900	PSHT	60463	3346	9W-15S	E1
Sycamore Pl					
1500	SMBG	60173	2805	21W-12N	E7
Sycamore Rd					
500	BFGV	60089	2754	17W-18N	B3
600	BRTN	60010	2750	25W-20N	E1
1800	HMWD	60430	3427	2W-21S	D7
Sycamore St					
1000	BCHR	60401	3864	0W-36S	D1
1600	DSPN	60018	2863	12W-9N	B6
2800	DSPN	60018	2917	12W-8N	A2
Sylvan Ct					
10	EGVV	60007	2914		D1
1600	CHHT	60411	3507	2W-23S	D3
1600	FSMR	60422	3507	2W-23S	D3
Sylvan Rd					
200	GLNC	60022	2758	6W-18N	C3
Sylvan Glen Ct					
10	BRRG	60527	3208		A6
Sylviawood Av					
500	PKRG	60068	2863	11W-9N	D7
Symonds Dr					
100	HNDL	60521	3146		B1
Syracuse Ln					
-	HRPK	60133	2858	25W-9N	A7
-	HRPK	60133	2912		A1
-	HRPK	60193	2858	25W-9N	A7
1600	SMBG	60193	2912		A1
1900	SMBG	60193	2858	25W-9N	A7

T

STREET Block	City	ZIP	Map#	CGS	Grid
Tacoma St					
1000	CPVL	60110	2748		C6
Tadmore Ct					
500	SMBG	60194	2858	25W-11N	A4
Taelevale Ct					
12800	HMGN	60441	3422	15W-20S	A4
Taft Av					
1700	PLTN	60008	2805	20W-14N	E4
1700	PLTN	60067	2805	20W-14N	E4
1700	RGMW	60008	2805	20W-14N	E4
N Taft Av					
10	HLSD	60162	3028		C6
10	PvsT	60162	3028		C6
300	BKLY	60162	3028		C5
300	BKLY	60163	3028		C4
N Taft Av					
300	HLSD	60163	3028		C5
Taft Cir					
700	HRPK	60133	2912		A1
Taft Ct					
10	SMWD	60107	2856	29W-10N	D6
300	GNVW	60025	2811	6W-13N	C6
E Taft Dr					
10	SHLD	60473	3428	0E-19S	D2
W Taft Dr					
10	SHLD	60473	3428	0W-19S	C2
400	HRVY	60426	3428	0W-19S	B2
Taft Rd					
-	BRRG	60521	3146		C3
700	HNDL	60521	3146		C3
Taft St					
-	DSPN	60018	2862	15W-9N	A7
100	EGVT	60018	2862	15W-9N	A7
S Taft St					
25700	MONE	60449	3682	7W-31S	E5
Tahoe Dr					
200	CHHT	60411	3507	1W-23S	E4
Tahoe Pkwy					
1900	ALGN	60102	2748		B1
Tahoe St					
-	LKPT	60441	3342	21W-17S	A6
10	TNTN	60476	3428	0E-20S	E5
400	PKFT	60466	3594	4W-28S	E6
E Tahoe Tr					
500	PLTN	60074	2753	20W-16N	B6
Tahoe Cir Dr					
1600	WLNG	60090	2754	16W-17N	C5
1700	ANHT	60004	2754	16W-17N	C5
N Tahoma Av					
6400	CHCG	60646	2919	6W-8N	C2
Talala St					
400	PKFT	60466	3594	4W-28S	E6
400	PKFT	60466	3595	4W-28S	A6
Talandis Dr					
2400	SLVL	60411	3597	2E-26S	E3
E Talbot St					
700	ANHT	60004	2807	17W-15N	B2
Talbots Ln					
1000	EGVV	60007	2914		B2
Talcot St					
400	LMNT	60439	3270		D5
W Talcott Av					
6700	CHCG	60656	2918	8W-7N	D4
6900	CHCG	60631	2918	9W-7N	C4
7700	CHCG	60068	2918	9W-7N	C4
7700	PKRG	60068	2918	9W-7N	C4
Talcott Pl					
200	PKRG	60068	2918	10W-7N	B3
N Talcott Rd					
10	PKRG	60068	2917	11W-9N	D1
100	PKRG	60068	2863	11W-9N	C7
W Talcott Rd					
10	CHCG	60068	2918	9W-7N	C3
10	CHCG	60631	2918	9W-7N	C3
10	PKRG	60068	2918	10W-8N	A2
1400	PKRG	60068	2917	11W-8N	E2
Talia Ln					
2500	NHBK	60062	2809	11W-15N	C1
Tall Grass Ct					
-	HnrT	60107	2856	29W-11N	D3
Tallgrass Dr					
300	BRLT	60103	2911		B5
Tall Grass Tr					
800	MTSN	60443	3505	7W-25S	C6
Tallgrass Tr					
13500	ODPK	60462	3346	11W-16S	A3
E Tall Oaks Dr					
300	ITSC	60143	2914		C4
Tall Oaks Ln					
4500	RGMW	60008	2805	20W-13N	E6
4600	RGMW	60067	2805	20W-13N	E6
Tall Timbers Rd					
1100	SMBG	60173	2805	21W-13N	D6
Tall Tree Ln					
1200	SMWD	60107	2910		E1
Tall Tree Rd					
-	GNVW	60025	2810	8W-14N	D5
Tall Trees Cir					
100	BRTN	60010	2751	24W-20N	C2
Tall Trees Ct					
4500	PltT	60067	2805	20W-14N	E5
Tall Trees Dr					
100	BRTN	60010	2751	24W-20N	D1
E Tall Trees Ln					
200	PltT	60067	2805	20W-14N	E5
200	PltT	60067	2806	20W-14N	A5
Tally Ho Ln					
8900	ODPK	60462	3346	11W-18S	A7
Talman Av					
14900	HRVY	60426	3349	3W-17S	B6
14900	POSN	60426	3349	3W-17S	B6
15000	MKHM	60426	3349	3W-17S	B6
N Talman Av					
200	CHCG	60612	3033	3W-0N	A4
1400	CHCG	60622	3033	3W-1N	A1
1500	CHCG	60647	3033	3W-1N	A1
1600	CHCG	60647	2977	3W-2N	A7
3200	CHCG	60618	2977	3W-4N	A3
4700	CHCG	60625	2921	3W-6N	A6
5600	CHCG	60659	2921	3W-7N	A4
6300	CHCG	60645	2921	3W-7N	A3
7400	CHCG	60645	2867	3W-9N	A7
S Talman Av					
1200	CHCG	60608	3033	3W-1S	A7
1200	CHCG	60612	3033	3W-1S	A7
4200	CHCG	60632	3091	3W-4S	A7
4600	CHCG	60632	3151	3W-5S	A1
5400	CHCG	60629	3151	3W-6S	A3
7900	CHCG	60652	3213	3W-9S	A2
8700	ENGN	60805	3213	3W-10S	A4
9900	CHCG	60655	3213	3W-11S	A7
9900	ENGN	60655	3213	3W-11S	A7
10300	CHCG	60655	3277	3W-12S	A1
Tamar Ln					
17300	TYPK	60477	3424	10W-20S	B5
Tamarac Dr					
1000	CPVL	60110	2748		A7
1000	CPVL	60110	2801		A1
Tamarack Ct					
5100	HFET	60010	2751	24W-16N	C7
Tamarack Dr					
-	BRLT	60103	2910		B1
S Tamarack Dr					
1100	ANHT	60005	2861	17W-11N	B3
1100	ANHT	60056	2861	17W-11N	B3
1300	MPPT	60056	2861	17W-11N	C3
Tamarack Dr N					
4900	HFET	60010	2751	24W-16N	C7
Tamarack Dr W					
1100	HFET	60010	2751	24W-16N	C7
Tamarack Ln					
-	BNHL	60010	2802	28W-15N	D1
-	HMGN	60467	3422	15W-20S	C4
-	ODPK	60467	3422	15W-20S	C4
12000	HMGN	60441	3422	15W-20S	C4
13700	ODPK	60462	3346	10W-16S	A3
Tamarack St					
400	MonT	60466	3594	4W-28S	E6
400	MonT	60466	3595	4W-28S	A6
400	PKFT	60466	3594	4W-28S	D6
400	PKFT	60466	3595	4W-28S	A6
Tamarind Dr					
3400	NHBK	60062	2756	11W-18N	C3
Tamarind Ln					
3600	HLCT	60429	3426	4W-20S	D5
Tamarisk Ln					
10	DRFD	60015	2757	9W-20N	B2
Tamaroa Ter					
8900	SKOK	60076	2866	4W-11N	C3
Tameling					
7900	PSHL	60465	3274	9W-12S	C2
Tameling Ct					
400	ELGN	60103	2910		A3
400	HnrT	60103	2910		A3
Tameling Dr					
16400	HmrT	60441	3342	20W-16S	A4
16700	LktT	60441	3342	20W-16S	A4
Tamer Ln					
900	GNVW	60025	2809	11W-13N	E6
Tamerton Pkwy					
300	BRRG	60527	3208		B3
Tam O Shanter Ct					
20000	OMFD	60461	3507	3W-24S	B5
S Tam O Shanter Ct					
26800	CteT	60417	3685	0W-32S	D7
26800	CteT	60417	3774	0W-33S	D2
W Tam O Shanter Dr					
10	CteT	60417	3774	0W-32S	C1
Tampa St					
200	MonT	60466	3595	4W-28S	A6
200	PKFT	60466	3594	4W-28S	E6
200	PKFT	60466	3595	4W-28S	A6
Tamworth Pl					
10	SMBG	60194	2858	25W-10N	A5
S Tan Ct					
1900	CHCG	60616	3092	0W-1S	B1
Tanager Ct					
200	VrnT	60015	2755	14W-20N	B1
Tanbark Dr					
8200	TYPK	60477	3424	10W-19S	C3
Tandragee Dr					
9200	PlsT	60462	3345	11W-15S	E1
Tanglewood Av					
1600	HRPK	60133	2911		D1
N Tanglewood Av					
1400	PLTN	60067	2752	21W-18N	D4
W Tanglewood Av					
300	PLTN	60067	2752	21W-17N	D4
E Tanglewood Cir					
10100	PlsT	60464	3345	12W-15S	C1
12700	PlsT	60464	3273	12W-15S	C7
W Tanglewood Cir					
12700	PlsT	60464	3273	12W-15S	C7
12700	PlsT	60464	3345	12W-15S	C1
Tanglewood Ct					
10	IHPK	60525	3146		E5
200	EGVV	60007	2861	18W-9N	A7
2000	HDPK	60035	2757	9W-20N	C2
17800	HLCT	60429	3427	3W-21S	A6
W Tanglewood Ct					
10000	PlsT	60464	3345	12W-15S	C1
Tanglewood Dr					
100	EGVV	60007	2861	18W-9N	A6
200	SMWD	60107	2856	29W-10N	D5
800	WLNG	60090	2755	15W-16N	A6
1800	GNVW	60025	2810	8W-14N	D4
W Tanglewood Dr					
200	ANHT	60004	2754	18W-17N	A5
500	ANHT	60004	2753	18W-17N	E5
Tanglewood Rd					
500	RchT	60443	3593	8W-26S	B2
Tanglewood St					
1400	FSMR	60422	3507	3W-22S	A2
1400	RchT	60422	3507	3W-22S	A2
Tannery Ridge Rd					
1100	ELGN	60120	2855		C1
E Tano Ln					
1800	MPPT	60056	2808	13W-14N	E3
2000	WhlT	60025	2808	13W-14N	E3
Tanoak Ct					
300	BRLT	60103	2910		E4
Tantallon Ln					
100	IVNS	60067	2752	22W-18N	B4
W Taos Dr					
8700	PSHL	60465	3274	10W-12S	A1
Tapper Av					
5700	HMND	46320	3352		E7
5900	HMND	46320	3430		E1
6700	HMND	46324	3430		E4
7900	MNSR	46321	3430		E6
S Tara Dr					
13500	HMGN	60441	3343	17W-16S	C3
Tarbat Ct					
700	IVNS	60010	2751	24W-16N	C6
Tarpey Ln					
2700	RVGV	60171	2974	10W-3N	A5
Tarpon Ct					
500	SMBG	60193	2912		E1
2700	HMWD	60430	3427	3W-21S	A6
17900	HLCT	60429	3427	3W-21S	A7
Tarrington Dr					
4800	HFET	60010	2804	24W-16N	B1
4900	HFET	60010	2751	24W-16N	B7
W Tartan Rd					
7400	FftT	60423	3504	9W-23S	E4
Tartan Ridge Rd					
-	HNDL	60521	3146		C3
10	BRRG	60521	3146		C3
N Tatge Av					
-	BRLT	60103	2911		A3
100	BRLT	60103	2910		E2
Taub Dr					
200	DRFD	60015	2757	10W-20N	B2
Taunton Ct					
1000	SMBG	60193	2912		C1
Taupo Ln					
400	DRFD	60015	2756	10W-20N	E1
Taylor Av					
3600	RNPK	60471	3594	4W-27S	D4
E Taylor Av					
100	BRLT	60103	2911		A2
S Taylor Av					
100	OKPK	60302	3031	7W-0N	B4
500	OKPK	60304	3031	7W-0S	B5
1100	CCRO	60804	3031	7W-0S	B7

STREET Block City ZIP Map# CGS Grid

Chicago & Cook County Street Index

STREET Block	City	ZIP	Map#	CGS	Grid
Thornwood Av					
4000	OMFD	60461	3506	5W-24S	C5
Thornwood Cir					
20800	OMFD	60461	3506	4W-25S	E7
Thornwood Ct					
17200	SHLD	60473	3429	0E-20S	A4
Thornwood Dr					
10	FSMR	60422	3507	2W-23S	D3
500	BFGV	60089	2754	17W-18N	B3
500	SHLD	60473	3428	0E-20S	E3
600	SHLD	60473	3429	0E-20S	A4
1200	SMBG	60193	2913		A2
9200	TYPK	60477	3423	11W-20S	E4
20700	OMFD	60461	3506	4W-25S	E6
Thornwood Ln					
500	NHFD	60093	2811	7W-15N	A1
800	GNVW	60025	2811	8W-13N	A7
1800	NHBK	60062	2757	10W-17N	B4
3400	GNVW	60025	2809	10W-14N	E5
3400	GNVW	60025	2810	10W-14N	A5
3400	NfdT	60025	2810	10W-14N	A5
W Thornwood Ln					
1800	MPPT	60056	2861	17W-11N	C3
15300	HMGN	60441	3342	19W-17S	D6
15500	HmrT	60441	3342	19W-17S	D5
Thornwood St					
7200	HRPK	60133	2911		D1
Thoroughbred Ln					
300	ROSL	60172	2912		E4
300	SMBG	60172	2912		E3
Thousand Oaks Dr					
1100	BRLT	60103	2910		C7
Three Lakes Dr					
-	NHBK	60062	2810	8W-16N	E1
-	NHFD	60093	2810	8W-15N	E1
Three Lakes Rd					
10	BNHL	60010	2750	27W-18N	B2
S Three Willow Ct					
800	PLTN	60067	2805	22W-14N	B3
Throop St					
-	HRVY	60426	3427	1W-20S	E5
500	CHCG	60607	3033	1W-0S	D6
17100	EHZC	60429	3427	1W-20S	E5
17400	HMWD	60430	3427	1W-20S	E5
N Throop St					
10	CHCG	60607	3033	1W-0N	D4
1000	CHCG	60622	3033	1W-1N	E2
1700	CHCG	60622	2977	1W-2N	D7
S Throop St					
200	CHCG	60607	3033	1W-0S	D5
1300	CHCG	60608	3033	1W-1S	D7
1600	CHCG	60608	3091	1W-1S	D1
4700	CHCG	60609	3151	1W-5S	E2
5500	CHCG	60636	3151	1W-6S	E3
7600	CHCG	60620	3213	1W-8S	E1
9400	CHCG	60643	3213	1W-11S	E7
10300	CHCG	60643	3277	1W-12S	E1
12200	CTPK	60643	3277	1W-14S	E6
12200	CTPK	60827	3277	1W-15S	E7
Thrush Ct					
3100	RGMW	60008	2806	19W-13N	B6
Thrush Ln					
2900	RGMW	60008	2806	19W-13N	B6
Thrush St					
10	CPVL	60110	2748		D6
Thunderbird Dr					
6400	IHPK	60525	3146		D6
Thurlow St					
10	DGvT	60527	3208		A5
200	HNDL	60521	3146		A3
5600	DGvT	60521	3146		A4
6400	DGvT	60527	3146		A6
E Thurston Dr					
1200	PLTN	60074	2753	19W-16N	C6
W Thurston Pl					
1000	ANHT	60004	2753	18W-18N	E2
Thyne Ct					
1200	WLNG	60090	2754	16W-18N	D3
Thyra Ln					
1000	IVNS	60067	2804	23W-14N	E4
1500	IVNS	60067	2805	23W-14N	A3
Tiburon Ct					
1300	HRPK	60133	2911		E6
W Ticknor Ct					
1300	SMBG	60193	2912		B2
Tide Ct					
800	WLNG	60090	2755	15W-16N	A6
Tieri Ln					
23200	CteT	60475	3595	2W-28S	D6
23200	PKFT	60466	3595	2W-28S	D6
23200	PKFT	60475	3595	2W-28S	D6
Tiffany Cir					
10	SBTN	60010	2803	27W-13N	B5
W Tiffany Ct					
7900	PSHL	60465	3274	9W-12S	C2
Tiffany Dr					
2000	SMBG	60194	2858	26W-10N	A5
2100	SMBG	60194	2857	26W-10N	E5
2200	CteT	60417	3597	2E-28S	E7
7300	ODPK	60462	3424	9W-18S	E1
Tiffany Ln					
200	ROSL	60172	2912		E6
Tiger Ln					
-	TYPK	60477	3424	9W-21S	D7
Tiger Trails					
-	WSTR	60154	3086		E2
Tilbury Ln					
200	WLNG	60090	2755	15W-18N	A3
N Tilden Av					
10	LGNG	60525	3087	12W-3S	C6
S Tilden Av					
10	LGNG	60525	3087	12W-4S	C7
W Tilden St					
-	CHCG	60607	3033	1W-0S	E6
-	CHCG	60607	3034		D6
Tilia Ct					
10	SMWD	60120	2856	30W-10N	B5
Tilipi Ct					
10	SMBG	60193	2858	24W-10N	D5
Tilipi Ln					
600	SMBG	60193	2858	24W-10N	D5
600	SMBG	60194	2858	24W-10N	E6
Timber Ct					
-	PSHT	60463	3347	7W-15S	C2
100	SMWD	60107	2857	28W-10N	A5
4900	OKFT	60452	3426	6W-20S	A3
8800	TYPK	60477	3424	11W-20S	A4
Timber Dr					
1200	EGVV	60007	2914		A2
7000	TYPK	60477	3424	9W-21S	D6
Timber Ln					
10	NHBK	60062	2757	9W-17N	C5
100	GLNC	60022	2758	6W-18N	D3
100	LGPK	60525	3087	12W-2S	B3
1000	WLMT	60091	2812	4W-14N	B5
11900	PSPK	60464	3274	10W-14S	C5
W Timber Ln					
12800	HMGN	60448	3422	16W-21S	A6
Timber Tr					
-	PSHT	60463	3347	7W-15S	B1
10	SMWD	60107	2856	28W-10N	E5
10	SMWD	60107	2857	28W-10N	A5
Timbercrest Ct					
300	SMBG	60193	2858	23W-10N	E6
Timbercrest Dr					
100	SMBG	60193	2858	23W-10N	E6
E Timberedge Ct					
3000	CteT	60417	3687	3E-29S	B1
Timber Edge Dr					
-	EMHT	60523	3028		A7
-	EMHT	60523	3086		A1
-	OKBK	60523	3028		A7
-	OKBK	60523	3086		A1
11900	ODPK	60467	3344	14W-18S	C7
Timber Edge Ln					
100	PlsT	60464	3273	12W-14S	C7
Timber Hill Rd					
10	BFGV	60089	2754	17W-18N	A3
600	DRFD	60015	2756	11W-20N	D1
700	HDPK	60035	2758	7W-20N	A2
W Timberlane Ct					
13900	HMGN	60441	3343	17W-17S	C5
Timberlane Dr					
4000	NfdT	60062	2756	12W-16N	A7
N Timberlane Dr					
1100	PLTN	60067	2753	20W-17N	A5
S Timberlane Dr					
12500	PlsT	60464	3274	9W-14S	C7
12500	PSPK	60464	3274	9W-14S	C7
Timberlane Rd					
10	MTSN	60443	3505	7W-24S	D5
Timberlea Ct					
3900	CCHL	60478	3426	4W-20S	D5
N Timberlea Dr					
900	PLTN	60067	2752	20W-17N	E5
Timberline Ct					
10	LMNT	60439	3270		C6
10400	ODPK	60462	3345	13W-17S	B6
E Timberline Ct					
2900	CteT	60417	3687	3E-29S	B1
Timberline Dr					
-	BRLT	60103	2910		B1
10	LMNT	60439	3270		B6
700	GNVW	60025	2811	7W-13N	B6
Timberline Pl					
10	LMNT	60439	3270		B6
S Timberline Tr					
24200	CteT	60417	3687	3E-29S	A1
Timber Ln Dr					
100	PLTN	60067	2752	20W-17N	E4
100	PLTN	60067	2753	20W-17N	A4
Timber Mill Dr					
20500	FftT	60423	3504	10W-24S	C6
Timber Ridge Ct					
6100	IHPK	60525	3146		E5
6100	LynT	60525	3146		E5
15200	ODPK	60467	3344	14W-18S	D7
Timber Ridge Dr					
300	BRLT	60103	2910		D2
Timber Ridge Rd					
-	MTSN	60443	3593	8W-26S	C2
2000	HFET	60195	2804	23W-13N	D5
2000	PltT	60195	2804	23W-13N	D5
21700	RchT	60443	3593	8W-26S	B2
Timbers Bluff Tr					
200	BCHR	60401	3774	0W-35S	D7
Timbers Edge Ln					
3700	GNVW	60025	2809	12W-14N	B4
3700	GNVW	60062	2809	12W-14N	B4
Timbers Pointe Dr E					
8600	TYPK	60477	3424	11W-22S	A7
Timber Trails Rd					
9000	ODPK	60462	3345	11W-16S	E3
9000	ODPK	60462	3346	11W-16S	A3
Timberview					
10	LMNT	60439	3272	15W-13S	B4
Timberview Ln					
11200	LynT	60525	3146		E4
Timberwood Ln					
8900	TYPK	60477	3424	11W-22S	A7
Times Dr					
1500	DSPN	60018	2862	13W-10N	E6
Times Square Rd					
10	ELGN	60120	2855		A5
Timothy Ct					
400	SMBG	60193	2859	22W-9N	B6
700	EDND	60118	2801		B3
8900	ODPK	60462	3346	11W-16S	A3
Timothy Dr					
2200	GNVW	60025	2810	9W-14N	C5
14000	ODPK	60462	3346	11W-16S	A4
Timothy Ln					
10	CTCY	60409	3351	2E-16S	C4
600	DSPN	60016	2808	13W-13N	D7
Timrick Dr					
10	MNSR	46321	3430		C7
10	MNSR	46321	3510		D1
W Tim Tam Ct					
12300	HMGN	60467	3344	15W-16S	B3
Tina Ln					
1500	FSMR	60422	3507	2W-23S	E4
Tinbury Pl					
200	CRTE	60475	3596	0W-28S	C6
Tinder					
5500	RGMW	60008	2860	19W-12N	D2
Tinker Wy					
1200	GNVW	60025	2810	8W-13N	D5
Tinley Park Dr					
6700	TYPK	60477	3425	8W-20S	A3
Tinnerella Av					
1300	SMWD	60107	2911		C1
Tioga Av					
200	BNVL	60106	2915		D7
Tioga St					
300	PKFT	60466	3594	4W-28S	E6
Tipperary Ct					
700	SMBG	60193	2859	23W-9N	A7
Tipton Av					
17800	HMWD	60430	3427	2W-21S	C6
Tiree Ct					
-	FSMR	60422	3506	4W-23S	D3
Tisbury Ln					
1000	SMBG	60193	2912		D1
Titonka St					
400	PKFT	60466	3594	4W-28S	E6
Tiverton Ct					
900	SMBG	60193	2912		C1
Tiverton Ln					
200	CRTE	60475	3596	0W-28S	C6
300	CRTE	60417	3596	0W-28S	C6
Toastmaster Dr					
1400	ELGN	60120	2801		D7
1400	ELGN	60120	2855		D1
Tobey Ct					
1000	SMBG	60194	2858	24W-10N	C5
S Tod Dr					
10400	PSHL	60465	3274	9W-12S	C2
Todd Ct					
10	CRTE	60417	3685	1W-30S	A2
Todd St					
200	PKFT	60466	3595	3W-25S	C1
400	OMFD	60461	3595	3W-25S	C1
Todd Ter					
200	LYWD	60411	3598	4E-25S	C1
Todor Ct					
10	BRRG	60527	3208		B4
Tod William Dr					
8700	ODPK	60462	3346	11W-16S	A3
Tolios Dr					
-	DGvT	60439	3270		C2
Tollview Dr					
600	EHZC	60429	3428	0W-20S	B4
600	EHZC	60473	3428	0W-20S	B4
600	SHLD	60429	3428	0W-20S	B4
600	SHLD	60473	3428	0W-20S	B4
3000	RGMW	60008	2860	20W-12N	B1
Tollview Rd					
10	ELGN	60123	2801		A7
S Tom Pkwy					
1800	CHCG	60616	3092	0W-1S	B1
Tomah Av					
400	PTHT	60070	2807	16W-15N	D2
Tomahawk Ct					
2400	CPVL	60110	2748		C4
Tomahawk Rd					
900	DYR	46311	3598		E3
Tomahawk St					
400	PKFT	60466	3594	4W-28S	E6
Tomaszewski St					
600	LMNT	60439	3270		E6
Tomawadee Dr					
800	PKRG	60068	2863	11W-9N	E6
Tomcin Tr					
5100	OKLN	60453	3275	6W-12S	E2
Tomlin Cir					
10	BRRG	60527	3146		C5
Tomlin Dr					
700	BRRG	60521	3146		C4
700	BRRG	60527	3146		C4
Ton Av					
17400	LNSG	60438	3430	3E-20S	A4
S Tonne Dr					
-	ANHT	60005	2861	18W-12N	A2
Tonne Rd					
300	EGVV	60007	2861	18W-9N	A7
600	EGVV	60007	2915		A2
2000	EGvT	60007	2915		A3
2100	WDDL	60007	2915		A3
2100	WDDL	60191	2915		A3
Tonset Ct					
100	SMBG	60193	2858	25W-10N	B6
Tonset Ln					
1400	SMBG	60193	2858	25W-10N	B6
N Tonty Av					
6800	CHCG	60646	2919	7W-8N	B1
W Tooker Pl					
10	CHCG	60610	3034	0W-1N	B2
N Topanga Dr					
900	PLTN	60074	2753	20W-17N	A6
Topaz Dr					
4500	HFET	60195	2804	24W-15N	C1
Topaz Ln					
400	BRLT	60103	2910		A1
Topeka Dr					
600	CPVL	60110	2748		B6
Topeka St					
400	PKFT	60466	3594	4W-28S	E6
Topp Ln					
1500	GNVW	60025	2810	8W-14N	E5
Tori Ct					
10	BRRG	60527	3208		B5
Toro Cir					
100	CPVL	60110	2748		B4
Torrence Av					
200	BNHM	60633	3351	3E-17S	E4
200	CTCY	60409	3351	2E-18S	E7
900	CTCY	60409	3429	2E-21S	E6
1400	LNSG	60438	3429	2E-19S	E3
18500	BlmT	60438	3429	2E-22S	E7
19000	BlmT	60411	3509	2E-22S	E2
19000	BlmT	60438	3509	2E-22S	E1
19000	LNSG	60411	3509	2E-22S	E1
19000	LNSG	60438	3509	2E-22S	E1
19300	LYWD	60411	3509	2E-22S	E2
20900	FDHT	60411	3509	2E-24S	E6
21100	SLVL	60411	3509	2E-25S	E7
21300	BlmT	60411	3597	2E-26S	E2
21300	SLVL	60411	3597	2E-26S	E2
22900	CteT	60417	3597	2E-27S	E5
Torrence Av SR-83					
400	CTCY	60409	3351	2E-18S	E7
900	CTCY	60409	3429	2E-21S	E7
1400	LNSG	60438	3429	2E-19S	E3
18500	BlmT	60438	3429	2E-22S	E7
19000	BlmT	60411	3509	2E-22S	E2
19000	BlmT	60438	3509	2E-22S	E1
19000	LNSG	60411	3509	2E-22S	E1
19000	LNSG	60438	3509	2E-22S	E1
19300	LYWD	60411	3509	2E-22S	E2
Torrence Av US-6					
1100	CTCY	60409	3429	2E-21S	E7
1400	LNSG	60438	3429	2E-19S	E3
S Torrence Av					
3700	HMND	46327	3352		E3
9500	CHCG	60617	3215	3E-11S	E7
10300	CHCG	60617	3279	3E-12S	E3
11700	CHCG	60633	3279	3E-14S	E7
13000	CHCG	60633	3351	2E-15S	E1
13800	BNHM	60633	3351	2E-17S	E5
14500	CTCY	60409	3351	3E-17S	E4
23100	BlmT	60411	3597	2E-28S	E6
23100	CteT	60411	3597	2E-28S	E6
23100	CteT	60417	3597	2E-28S	E6
Torrence Pl					
9400	SjnT	46311	3687		E1
Torrence St					
8400	SjnT	46311	3598		E6
Torrey Ct					
20500	FKFT	60423	3504	10W-24S	B6
Torrey Pines Dr					
15600	ODPK	60462	3346	11W-18S	A7
15600	ODPK	60462	3424	11W-18S	A1
Torrey Pines Pkwy					
3600	NHBK	60062	2756	12W-17N	B4
Torri Ln					
800	ELGN	60120	2855		C5
Torrin Rocks Cove					
10	IVNS	60010	2750	26W-16N	D7
Tory Ct					
800	SMBG	60173	2859	22W-10N	C5
Tory Ln					
10	RGMW	60008	2805	20W-14N	E4
10	RGMW	60008	2806	20W-14N	A4
Tosca Dr					
200	WDDL	60191	2915		B7
Tosoana					
-	BMDL	60172	2912		C7
-	BmdT	60172	2912		C7
Tottenham Ln					
100	EGVV	60007	2914		C3
Touhy Av					
-	LNWD	60712	2919	6W-9N	E1
600	EGVV	60007	2915		B1
2500	EGvT	60007	2915		E1
2500	EGvT	60018	2915		E1
5000	SKOK	60077	2919	6W-8N	D1
5300	SKOK	60077	2865	6W-9N	C7
5400	NLES	60077	2865	6W-9N	C7
5400	NLES	60714	2865	6W-9N	C7
Touhy Av SR-72					
2500	EGvT	60007	2915		E1
2500	EGvT	60018	2915		E1
2500	EGVV	60007	2915		E1
E Touhy Av					
10	CHCG	60631	2918	9W-9N	C1
10	PKRG	60068	2918	9W-9N	C1
10	PKRG	60631	2918	9W-9N	C1
200	CHCG	60018	2916		C1
200	DSPN	60018	2916		C1
200	MaiT	60018	2916		C1
1200	RSMT	60018	2916		E1
1300	DSPN	60018	2917	13W-8N	A1
1300	RSMT	60018	2917	13W-8N	A1
2100	CHCG	60018	2917	12W-8N	B1
E Touhy Av SR-72					
200	CHCG	60018	2916		C1
200	DSPN	60018	2916		C1
200	MaiT	60018	2916		C1
W Touhy Av					
-	CHCG	60018	2917	11W-9N	D1
-	PKRG	60018	2917	11W-9N	D1
-	SKOK	60077	2919	5W-8N	E1
10	DSPN	60018	2916		A1
10	EGvT	60018	2916		A1
10	MaiT	60018	2916		A1
10	PKRG	60068	2918	10W-8N	A1
300	CHCG	60007	2916		A1
300	CHCG	60018	2916		A1
1200	CHCG	60626	2867	1W-9N	D7
1300	PKRG	60068	2917	11W-8N	D1
1900	CHCG	60645	2867	3W-9N	A7
2700	CHCG	60645	2866	3W-9N	E7
2800	EGvT	60007	2915		E1
2800	EGvT	60018	2915		E1
2800	EGVV	60007	2915		E1
2800	EGVV	60007	2916		A1
2800	EGVV	60018	2916		A1
3000	CHCG	60645	2920	4W-8N	D1
3100	LNWD	60645	2920	3W-9N	D1
3100	LNWD	60712	2920	3W-9N	D1
3100	SKOK	60645	2920	3W-9N	D1
3200	SKOK	60076	2920	4W-9N	D1
3300	LNWD	60076	2920	4W-9N	D1
4700	LNWD	60712	2919	5W-8N	E1
5600	NLES	60077	2865	7W-9N	C7
5600	NLES	60714	2865	8W-9N	A7
5600	SKOK	60077	2865	7W-9N	C7
5700	CHCG	60646	2865	8W-9N	A7
5900	NLES	60646	2865	7W-9N	B7
6600	NLES	60714	2864	8W-9N	E7
7100	CHCG	60631	2918	8W-8N	D1
7100	NLES	60714	2918	8W-8N	D1
7700	PKRG	60631	2918	9W-9N	C1
W Touhy Av SR-72					
10	DSPN	60018	2916		A1
10	EGvT	60018	2916		A1
10	MaiT	60018	2916		A1
300	CHCG	60007	2916		A1
300	CHCG	60018	2916		A1
2800	EGvT	60007	2915		E1
2800	EGvT	60018	2915		E1
2800	EGVV	60007	2915		E1
2800	EGVV	60007	2916		A1
2800	EGVV	60018	2916		A1
Touhy Ct					
100	EGvT	60018	2916		C1
100	MaiT	60018	2916		C1
Toulon Ct					
1400	HDPK	60035	2757	8W-20N	D1
Toulon Dr					
100	BFGV	60089	2754	16W-20N	C1
3100	NHBK	60062	2756	11W-17N	D6
Touraine Ter					
600	NHBK	60062	2756	12W-18N	B4
Towanda Ct					
10	PKFT	60466	3595	4W-28S	A6
Towanda St					
200	PKFT	60466	3594	4W-28S	E6
200	PKFT	60466	3595	4W-28S	A6
Tower Av					
21100	MTSN	60443	3594	4W-25S	D1
Tower Cir					
-	BmnT	60426	3426	5W-19S	B1
4000	SKOK	60076	2866	5W-11N	B2
20800	OMFD	60461	3507	4W-25S	A7
Tower Ct					
16600	TYPK	60477	3424	10W-19S	C3
E Tower Ct					
900	PLTN	60074	2753	19W-18N	B2
N Tower Ct					
6400	LNWD	60712	2919	6W-8N	E2
Tower Dr					
100	BRRG	60527	3146		C7
1800	GNVW	60025	2810	9W-14N	B4
3900	RNPK	60471	3594	4W-26S	D3
10600	ODPK	60467	3423	13W-20S	A3
S Tower Dr					
900	MPPT	60056	2862	15W-11N	A2
Tower Ln					
100	EGVV	60007	2860	18W-9N	E7
200	EGvT	60007	2860	18W-9N	E7
1000	BNVL	60106	2915		C4
S Tower Ln					
900	MPPT	60056	2862	15W-11N	A2
W Tower Pl					
100	PLTN	60067	2752	21W-16N	D7
Tower Rd					
-	GLNC	60062	2758	7W-16N	B7
-	GLNC	60093	2758	7W-16N	B7
-	NfdT	60093	2758	6W-16N	C7
-	NHFD	60093	2758	7W-16N	B7
700	WNKA	60093	2759	5W-16N	A7
1000	WNKA	60093	2758	6W-16N	C7
1100	SMBG	60173	2859	22W-12N	D1
1700	HRPK	60133	2911		D1
8300	WLSP	60480	3208		E3
W Tower Rd					
300	BRTN	60010	2750	26W-18N	E3
Tower Cir Dr					
-	SMBG	60173	2805	22W-12N	D7
Towering Oaks Ct					
1100	BRLT	60103	2910		C7
Tower Manor Dr					
900	WNKA	60093	2759	5W-16N	A7
N Towers Cir Dr					
6500	LNWD	60712	2919	6W-8N	E2
S Towle Av					
3700	HMND	46327	3352		D3
Towle St					
8500	SjnT	46311	3598		D6
Town St					
400	WLNG	60090	2755	15W-17N	B4
Town Acres Ln					
100	ROSL	60172	2913		A4
Towncenter Dr					
10	MonT	60466	3684	3W-29S	A1
10	UYPK	60466	3684	3W-29S	A1
Town Center Rd					
100	MTSN	60443	3594	6W-25S	B1
200	MTSN	60443	3506	6W-25S	B7
E Towne Blvd					
2400	ANHT	60004	2754	16W-16N	D7
2400	ANHT	60004	2807	16W-16N	E1
2400	PTHT	60004	2807	16W-16N	E1
2400	PTHT	60070	2807	16W-16N	E1
Town Place Cir					
300	BFGV	60089	2754	16W-20N	C1
Town Place Pkwy					
-	BFGV	60089	2754	16W-20N	C1
Town Square Dr					
-	RGMW	60008	2806	19W-13N	B5
Trace Dr					
-	BFGV	60089	2754	18W-18N	A4
800	BFGV	60089	2753	18W-18N	E4
Tracey Ct					
4000	GNVW	60025	2809	11W-13N	D6
S Tracy Av					
13800	RVDL	60827	3350	0W-16S	B2
Tracy Ct					
900	SMBG	60193	2913		A1
2000	HRPK	60133	2911		D6
Tracy Ter					
400	DSPN	60016	2808	14W-12N	C7
Traditions Dr					
-	FSMR	60422	3506	4W-24S	D4
-	MTSN	60443	3506	4W-24S	D4
-	OMFD	60461	3506	4W-24S	D4
Trafalgar Ct					
8000	ODPK	60462	3346	10W-16S	C3
13600	OrlT	60462	3346	10W-16S	C2
Trail Ridge Ct					
10	HnrT	60107	2856	30W-10N	C5
10	SMWD	60107	2856	30W-10N	C5
Trail Ridge St					
1800	ANHT	60004	2753	19W-18N	D2
1800	PltT	60004	2753	19W-18N	D2
Trails Dr					
-	OMFD	60461	3506	4W-24S	E5
10	SMBG	60193	2859	22W-10N	C5
10	SMBG	60194	2859	22W-10N	C5
Trails Edge Dr					
1800	NHBK	60062	2757	9W-16N	C7
W Trails End Ct					
13100	HMGN	60441	3343	16W-16S	E4
S Trails End Dr					
13900	HMGN	60441	3343	16W-16S	E3
Trailside Ct					
4400	HFET	60195	2804	24W-15N	C2
N Trailside Ct					
1400	PLTN	60067	2752	21W-17N	C4
1400	PLTN	60074	2752	21W-17N	C4
1400	PltT	60074	2752	21W-17N	C4
Trailside Dr					
1300	BCHR	60401	3774	0W-35S	D7
15300	HMGN	60441	3344	16W-18S	A7
15500	HMGN	60441	3422	16W-18S	A1
Trailside Ln					
400	DSPN	60016	2863	12W-11N	C3
900	BRLT	60103	2911		C5
Trailwood Ct					
200	NHBK	60062	2756	12W-18N	A3
Trailwood Ln					
100	NHBK	60062	2756	12W-18N	A2
Tralee Ct					
600	SMBG	60193	2859	23W-9N	A7
Tralee Ln					
1200	LKPT	60441	3342	21W-18S	A7
Tralee Tr					
-	TYPK	60477	3424	10W-21S	C7
Tramore Ct					
9500	PlsT	60462	3345	11W-15S	D1
Tramore Ln					
19200	MKNA	60448	3504	11W-23S	A3
19300	FftT	60448	3504	11W-23S	A3
S Trankle Ct					
5000	HMND	46327	3352		E5
Transportation Dr					
-	BlmT	60411	3509	2E-25S	D7
-	FDHT	60411	3509	2E-25S	D7
-	SLVL	60411	3509	2E-25S	D7
-	SLVL	60411	3597	2E-25S	D1
Transworld Rd					
4200	SRPK	60176	2973	13W-5N	A1
Trapet Av					
16700	HLCT	60429	3427	2W-20S	C4
16700	MKHM	60426	3427	2W-20S	C4
Trapp Ln					
1200	WNKA	60093	2811	6W-16N	E1
Traube St					
7600	NRIV	60546	3088	9W-2S	C2
Travers Av					
600	CHHT	60411	3507	2W-24S	C6
600	CHHT	60461	3507	2W-24S	C6
600	OMFD	60461	3507	2W-24S	C6
700	BlmT	60411	3507	2W-24S	C6
Travers Ct					
600	CHHT	60411	3507	2W-24S	C5
Travers Ln					
700	FSMR	60422	3507	2W-22S	C2
Travis Ct					
200	SMBG	60195	2859	23W-12N	A2

Chicago & Cook County Street Index

STREET Block	City	ZIP	Map#	CGS	Grid
Travis Pkwy					
-	ROSL	60172	2912		B4
Treadway Rd					
900	MNSR	46321	3510		E4
Treasure Ln					
10	RVWD	60015	2755	13W-20N	E1
Treaty Ln					
3400	HFET	60195	2804	23W-14N	D4
Tree Ln					
800	PTHT	60070	2808	13W-15N	E2
Treebark Ct					
10	SMBG	60193	2858	24W-10N	E5
Treebark Dr					
10	HFET	60193	2858	24W-10N	E5
10	HFET	60194	2858	24W-10N	E5
10	SMBG	60193	2858	24W-10N	E5
10	SMBG	60194	2858	24W-10N	E5
Treehouse Ct					
10	MTSN	60443	3506	5W-24S	C4
Treehouse Rd					
-	RchT	60443	3506	5W-24S	C5
10	MTSN	60443	3506	5W-24S	C5
Treetop Dr					
9800	ODPK	60462	3345	12W-18S	C7
Tremont St					
6300	WLBK	60527	3146		A5
W Tremont St					
400	CHCG	60621	3152	0W-6S	B3
Trent Ct					
10	BRRG	60527	3208		D1
2000	GNVW	60025	2809	10W-14N	E4
8700	TYPK	60477	3424	10W-20S	B5
Trent Ln					
600	SMBG	60193	2859	22W-9N	C7
Trenton Av					
14100	ODPK	60462	3345	11W-16S	E4
Trenton Ct					
10	SBTN	60010	2803	27W-14N	B4
200	SMBG	60193	2859	22W-10N	C6
Tricia Ln					
10	BNHL	60010	2802	28W-15N	D2
Trillium Blvd					
-	HFET	60118	2802	29W-13N	C5
5200	HFET	60192	2802	29W-13N	B6
Trillium Dr					
10	SjnT	46311	3598		C6
Trillium Ln					
1000	BRLT	60103	2911		B6
1100	WynT	60103	2911		B6
Trinity Cir					
7900	TYPK	60477	3504	9W-23S	D3
Trinity Ct					
100	EVTN	60201	2866	4W-12N	C1
400	BFGV	60089	2754	16W-17N	D4
Trinity Dr					
8700	ODPK	60462	3424	10W-19S	A1
Trinity Pl					
5200	MTSN	60443	3505	6W-24S	E5
5200	MTSN	60443	3506	6W-24S	A5
Triple Crown Ct					
1200	BRLT	60103	2910		E7
Tripp Av					
-	PvsT	60141	3030	10W-1S	A7
-	PvsT	60141	3088	10W-1S	A1
7400	LNWD	60712	2866	5W-9N	B7
9000	SKOK	60076	2866	5W-11N	B2
14300	CTWD	60445	3348	5W-17S	C4
14300	MDLN	60445	3348	5W-17S	C4
N Tripp Av					
500	CHCG	60624	3032	5W-0N	B3
800	CHCG	60651	3032	5W-1N	B2
1500	CHCG	60639	3032	5W-1N	B1
2800	CHCG	60639	2976	5W-3N	B4
3400	CHCG	60641	2976	5W-4N	B3
4300	CHCG	60630	2976	5W-5N	B1
4700	CHCG	60630	2920	5W-6N	B6
5600	CHCG	60646	2920	5W-7N	B4
6300	LNWD	60712	2920	5W-7N	B3
7200	LNWD	60712	2866	5W-9N	B7
7300	SKOK	60076	2866	5W-9N	B7
S Tripp Av					
600	CHCG	60624	3032	5W-0S	B6
1200	CHCG	60623	3032	5W-1S	B7
2600	CHCG	60623	3090	5W-2S	B3
4300	CHCG	60632	3090	5W-4S	B7
4700	CHCG	60632	3150	5W-5S	B2
5400	CHCG	60629	3150	5W-7S	B5
7900	CHCG	60652	3212	5W-9S	B2
8600	HMTN	60456	3212	5W-9S	B4
9100	OKLN	60453	3212	5W-10S	B5
10200	OKLN	60453	3276	5W-12S	B1
11000	CHCG	60655	3276	5W-12S	B3
11600	ALSP	60803	3276	5W-13S	B4
Tripp Ct					
10700	OKLN	60453	3276	5W-12S	B2
S Tripp St					
13300	RBBN	60472	3348	5W-15S	C2
13400	CTWD	60445	3348	5W-15S	C2
Tri State Expwy					
-	HMND	-	3430		C5
-	LNSG	-	3430		C5
-	MNSR	-	3430		C5
Tri State Expwy I-80					
-	HMND	-	3430		C5
-	LNSG	-	3430		C5
-	MNSR	-	3430		C5
Tri State Expwy I-94					
-	HMND	-	3430		C5
-	LNSG	-	3430		C5
-	MNSR	-	3430		C5
Tri State Expwy US-6					
-	HMND	-	3430		C5
-	LNSG	-	3430		C5
-	MNSR	-	3430		C5
Tri State Expwy US-41					
-	HMND	-	3430		E5
Tri-State Tollway					
-	ALSP	-	3275	7W-13S	C5
-	ALSP	-	3276	6W-14S	A6
-	ALSP	-	3348	5W-15S	B1
-	BGVW	-	3210	9W-10S	D5
-	BKLY	-	3028		C3
-	BmnT	-	3348	3W-17S	E4
-	BmnT	-	3349	3W-17S	A6
-	BRRG	-	3146		D4
-	CHCG	-	2863	12W-9N	C7
-	CHCG	-	2917	12W-8N	C1
-	CHRG	-	3210	9W-11S	E7
-	CHRG	-	3274	8W-11S	E1
-	CHRG	-	3275	7W-13S	C5
-	CTSD	-	3146		E7
-	CTSD	-	3147	13W-8S	A7
-	CTSD	-	3209	13W-8S	A1
-	CTWD	-	3348	5W-15S	C1
-	DRFD	-	2756	12W-18N	B2
-	DSPN	-	2863	12W-10N	C4
-	DSPN	-	2917	12W-8N	C1
-	EHZC	-	3427	1W-20S	E4
-	EHZC	-	3428	0W-20S	C4
-	EMHT	-	3028		C6
-	FNPK	-	2972		E3
-	FNPK	-	2973	12W-4N	A3
-	GNVW	-	2809	11W-13N	C7
-	HGKN	-	3209	12W-8S	C1
-	HLCT	-	3427	3W-19S	B3
-	HLSD	-	3028		C5
-	HNDL	-	3086		C6
-	HNDL	-	3146		D5
-	HYHL	-	3210	10W-9S	B3
-	IHPK	-	3146		D5
-	JSTC	-	3209	12W-8S	C2
-	JSTC	-	3210	10W-9S	B3
-	LNSG	-	3429	1E-20S	C4
-	LydT	-	2972		E3
-	LydT	-	2973	13W-4N	A3
-	LynT	-	3086		C6
-	LynT	-	3146		D5
-	LynT	-	3147	13W-8S	A7
-	LynT	-	3209	12W-8S	D2
-	MaiT	-	2809	11W-13N	C7
-	MaiT	-	2863	12W-11N	C3
-	MDLN	-	3348	4W-16S	D4
-	MKHM	-	3349	3W-17S	B6
-	MKHM	-	3427	3W-19S	B2
-	NfdT	-	2756	12W-16N	A6
-	NfdT	-	2809	11W-13N	C7
-	NHBK	-	2756	12W-18N	A3
-	NHBK	-	2809	12W-16N	C1
-	NHLK	-	2972		C7
-	NHLK	-	3028		B1
-	OKBK	-	3086		C2
-	PKRG	-	2863	12W-11N	C4
-	POSN	-	3349	3W-17S	B6
-	PvsT	-	3028		C7
-	PvsT	-	3086		C5
-	RBBN	-	3348	4W-16S	D4
-	RSMT	-	2917	12W-7N	C4
-	SHLD	-	3428	0W-20S	C4
-	SHLD	-	3429	1E-20S	A4
-	SRPK	-	2917	12W-6N	C6
-	SRPK	-	2973	12W-4N	A2
-	ThtT	-	3429	1E-20S	B4
-	TNTN	-	3428	0W-20S	C4
-	WdfT	-	2756	12W-20N	B1
-	WhlT	-	2756	12W-18N	A4
-	WLNG	-	2756	12W-16N	A6
-	WLSP	-	3209	12W-8S	C2
-	WNSP	-	3086		C7
-	WNSP	-	3146		D5
-	WRTH	-	3275	7W-13S	C5
-	WthT	-	3275	7W-13S	B4
Tri-State Tollway I-80					
-	EHZC	-	3427	1W-20S	E4
-	EHZC	-	3428	0W-20S	C4
-	HLCT	-	3427	2W-20S	C4
-	LNSG	-	3429	1E-20S	C4
-	SHLD	-	3428	0W-20S	C4
-	SHLD	-	3429	1E-20S	A4
-	ThtT	-	3429	1E-20S	A4
-	TNTN	-	3428	0W-20S	C4
Tri-State Tollway I-94					
-	DRFD	-	2756	12W-20N	B1
-	WdfT	-	2756	12W-20N	B1
Tri-State Tollway I-294					
-	ALSP	-	3275	7W-13S	C5
-	ALSP	-	3276	6W-14S	A6
-	ALSP	-	3348	5W-15S	B1
-	BGVW	-	3210	9W-10S	C4
-	BKLY	-	3028		C3
-	BmnT	-	3348	3W-17S	E4
-	BmnT	-	3349	3W-17S	B6
-	BRRG	-	3146		D4
-	CHCG	-	2863	12W-9N	C7
-	CHCG	-	2917	12W-8N	C1
-	CHRG	-	3210	9W-11S	E7
-	CHRG	-	3274	8W-11S	E1
-	CHRG	-	3275	7W-13S	C5
-	CTSD	-	3146		E7
-	CTSD	-	3147	13W-8S	A7
-	CTSD	-	3209	12W-8S	B1
-	CTWD	-	3348	5W-15S	C1
-	DRFD	-	2756	12W-20N	B2
-	DSPN	-	2863	12W-11N	C3
-	DSPN	-	2917	12W-8N	C1
-	EHZC	-	3427	1W-20S	E4
-	EHZC	-	3428	0W-20S	C4
-	EMHT	-	3028		C6
-	FNPK	-	2972		E3
-	FNPK	-	2973	12W-4N	A3
-	GNVW	-	2809	11W-13N	C7
-	HGKN	-	3209	12W-8S	C1
-	HLCT	-	3427	3W-19S	B3
-	HLSD	-	3028		C5
-	HNDL	-	3086		C6
-	HNDL	-	3146		D5
-	HYHL	-	3210	9W-9S	C4
-	IHPK	-	3146		D7
-	JSTC	-	3209	12W-8S	C2
-	JSTC	-	3210	10W-9S	B3
-	LNSG	-	3429	1E-20S	C4
-	LydT	-	2972		E3
-	LydT	-	2973	13W-4N	A3
-	LynT	-	3086		C6
-	LynT	-	3146		D4
-	LynT	-	3147	13W-8S	A7
-	LynT	-	3209	11W-8S	D2
-	MaiT	-	2809	11W-13N	C7
-	MaiT	-	2863	12W-11N	C3
-	MDLN	-	3348	4W-16S	D4
-	MKHM	-	3349	3W-17S	B6
-	MKHM	-	3427	3W-19S	B2
-	NfdT	-	2756	12W-18N	A3
-	NfdT	-	2809	11W-13N	C7
-	NHBK	-	2756	12W-18N	A3
-	NHBK	-	2809	12W-16N	C1
-	NHLK	-	2972		C7
-	NHLK	-	3028		C1
-	OKBK	-	3086		C2
-	PKRG	-	2863	12W-10N	C4
-	POSN	-	3349	3W-17S	B6
-	PvsT	-	3028		C7
-	PvsT	-	3086		C5
-	RBBN	-	3348	5W-16S	C2
-	RSMT	-	2917	12W-7N	C4
-	SHLD	-	3428	0W-20S	C4
-	SHLD	-	3429	1E-20S	A4
-	SRPK	-	2917	12W-6N	C6
-	SRPK	-	2973	12W-4N	A3
-	ThtT	-	3429	1E-20S	B4
-	TNTN	-	3428	0W-20S	C4
-	WdfT	-	2756	12W-20N	B2
-	WhlT	-	2756	12W-18N	A4
-	WLNG	-	2756	12W-16N	A6
-	WLSP	-	3209	12W-8S	C2
-	WNSP	-	3086		C7
-	WNSP	-	3146		D5
-	WRTH	-	3275	7W-13S	C5
-	WthT	-	3275	7W-13S	B4
W Triton Wy					
5700	MONE	60449	3682	7W-31S	D5
Triumvera Dr					
-	MaiT	60016	2809	11W-13N	D7
-	NfdT	60016	2809	11W-13N	D7
3900	NfdT	60025	2809	11W-13N	D7
Troon Cir					
900	FKFT	60423	3593	9W-26S	A2
Troon Ln					
-	CRTE	60417	3596	0E-29S	E7
-	CRTE	60417	3685	0E-29S	E1
Troon St					
3800	FSMR	60422	3506	4W-23S	D3
Troon Ter					
900	FKFT	60423	3593	9W-26S	A3
N Troons Cross					
1900	PLTN	60074	2752	21W-18N	D3
Troost Av					
900	FTPK	60130	3030	9W-0S	C7
Trout Av					
1200	ELGN	60120	2801		B7
Troutman Dr					
100	BRLT	60103	2909		C3
Trout Park Blvd					
400	ELGN	60120	2801		B7
Trout View Ct					
16700	BmnT	60477	3425	7W-20S	D3
Trowbridge Ct					
2100	GNVW	60025	2809	10W-14N	E3
Trowbridge Rd					
200	EGVV	60007	2914		C3
Troy Av					
13600	RBBN	60472	3348	3W-16S	E3
15100	MKHM	60426	3349	3W-18S	A7
15700	MKHM	60426	3427	3W-18S	A1
S Troy Av					
14500	POSN	60469	3348	3W-17S	E5
14700	MKHM	60426	3348	3W-17S	E5
Troy Cir					
2400	OMFD	60461	3507	3W-25S	B7
S Troy Dr					
11500	MTPK	60803	3276	3W-13S	E4
N Troy St					
500	CHCG	60612	3032	3W-0N	E3
700	CHCG	60622	3032	3W-0N	E3
1600	CHCG	60647	2976	3W-2N	E7
3500	CHCG	60618	2976	3W-4N	D2
4300	CHCG	60625	2976	3W-5N	D1
5100	CHCG	60625	2920	3W-6N	D6
6000	CHCG	60659	2920	3W-7N	D3
6300	CHCG	60645	2920	3W-7N	D3
S Troy St					
-	ENGN	60652	3212	3W-10S	E4
100	CHCG	60612	3032	3W-0S	E5
1100	CHCG	60623	3032	3W-1S	E7
1600	CHCG	60623	3090	3W-1S	E1
4300	CHCG	60632	3090	3W-4S	E7
4600	CHCG	60632	3150	3W-4S	E1
5500	CHCG	60629	3150	3W-7S	E5
7500	CHCG	60652	3212	3W-8S	E1
9500	ENGN	60805	3212	3W-11S	E6
10300	CHCG	60655	3276	3W-12S	E2
11300	CHCG	60803	3276	3W-13S	E3
11400	MTPK	60803	3276	3W-13S	E4
Truman Ct					
10	SMWD	60107	2856	29W-10N	D6
S Truman Ct					
25800	MONE	60449	3682	7W-31S	D5
Truman Ln					
10	SMWD	60107	2856	29W-10N	E6
Truman St					
300	DSPN	60018	2862	15W-9N	A7
300	EGvT	60018	2862	15W-9N	A7
7400	HRPK	60133	2912		A1
E Truman St					
700	HMND	46320	3352		E6
S Truman St					
25700	MONE	60449	3682	7W-31S	D5
Trumbull Av					
-	MKHM	60426	3348	4W-17S	E6
-	MKHM	60445	3348	4W-17S	E5
8300	SKOK	60076	2866	4W-10N	D5
8700	SKOK	60203	2866	4W-11N	D4
14400	MDLN	60445	3348	4W-17S	E5
15700	MKHM	60426	3426	4W-18S	E1
N Trumbull Av					
500	CHCG	60624	3032	4W-0N	D3
700	CHCG	60651	3032	4W-0N	D3
2300	RVGV	60171	2973	10W-2N	E6
6400	CHCG	60659	2920	4W-8N	D3
6400	CHCG	60712	2920	4W-8N	D3
6400	LNWD	60712	2920	4W-8N	D2
S Trumbull Av					
300	CHCG	60624	3032	4W-0S	D5
1400	CHCG	60623	3032	4W-1S	D7
1500	CHCG	60623	3090	4W-1S	D1
4300	CHCG	60632	3090	4W-4S	D7
5100	CHCG	60632	3150	4W-5S	D2
5500	CHCG	60629	3150	4W-6S	D3
7500	CHCG	60652	3212	4W-8S	D1
9500	ENGN	60805	3212	4W-11S	D6
10200	CHCG	60655	3276	4W-12S	D1
10200	CHCG	60655	3276	4W-11S	D1
10200	ENGN	60805	3276	4W-11S	D1
12300	ALSP	60803	3276	4W-14S	D6
12300	WthT	60803	3276	4W-14S	D6
12500	BLID	60406	3276	4W-14S	E6
13500	RBBN	60472	3348	4W-16S	E2
Truro Ct					
300	SMBG	60194	2858	24W-10N	C4
Trustee Dr					
-	MTSN	60443	3505	7W-24S	D6
Tryall Dr					
1000	DYR	46311	3510		E6
Tucker Rd					
500	PtnT	60468	3861	9W-37S	A4
500	PTON	60468	3861	9W-37S	A4
500	WIIT	60468	3861	9W-37S	A4
Tucker Rd CO-25					
500	PtnT	60468	3861	9W-37S	A4
500	PTON	60468	3861	9W-37S	A4
500	WIIT	60468	3861	9W-37S	A4
Tudor Cir					
8300	WLSP	60480	3208		E3
Tudor Ct					
300	GLNC	60022	2758	6W-17N	D5
10200	MNSR	46321	3510		E4
Tudor Dr					
100	BRTN	60010	2751	24W-18N	D2
Tudor Ln					
-	NHBK	60062	2757	9W-16N	B6
200	SMBG	60193	2859	23W-10N	B6
8000	TYPK	60477	3424	10W-20S	C3
Tudor Pl					
10	KLWH	60043	2812	3W-14N	E4
10	WLMT	60043	2812	3W-14N	E4
10	WLMT	60091	2812	3W-14N	E4
Tudor Rd					
15400	OKFT	60452	3347	7W-18S	C7
Tugwell St					
4000	FNPK	60131	2972		E2
W Tulip Av					
4500	MONE	60449	3683	5W-31S	B5
Tulip Cir					
200	MTSN	60443	3593	7W-26S	D2
Tulip Ct					
200	SMBG	60193	2857	26W-10N	E6
1400	WLNG	60090	2754	16W-18N	D3
15300	ODPK	60462	3346	9W-18S	C7
Tulip Dr					
3300	HLCT	60429	3426	4W-20S	E4
E Tulip Dr					
300	GNWD	60425	3508	0E-22S	E1
400	GNWD	60425	3509	0E-22S	A1
Tulip Ln					
-	BmnT	60426	3426	5W-19S	A1
1200	BRLT	60103	2910		C7
17700	TYPK	60477	3424	10W-21S	C6
E Tulip Wy					
900	PLTN	60074	2753	19W-18N	B4
Tuliptree Ct					
1500	GNVW	60025	2810	8W-14N	E5
Tulip Tree Ln					
2400	DYR	46311	3598		D3
Tullamore Ct					
700	SMBG	60193	2859	23W-9N	A7
Tullamore Dr					
8500	TYPK	60477	3504	10W-23S	B3
Tullamore Ter					
200	RchT	60443	3593	8W-26S	B1
Tulley Av					
8700	BRBK	60453	3211	6W-10S	E4
8700	BRBK	60459	3211	6W-10S	E4
8700	OKLN	60453	3211	6W-10S	E4
Tully Pl					
200	PTHT	60070	2808	15W-14N	A4
Tulsa Av					
300	CPVL	60110	2748		B6
Tulsa Ct					
300	CPVL	60110	2748		B6
Tuppeny Ct					
1500	ROSL	60172	2912		A4
S Tures Ln					
700	DSPN	60018	2862	13W-9N	D7
Turf Ln					
14400	HMGN	60441	3344	15W-17S	B5
Turkey Ct					
1400	IVNS	60067	2805	23W-14N	A3
Turkey Tr					
1400	IVNS	60067	2805	23W-14N	A3
Turlington Av					
14700	HRVY	60426	3350	1W-17S	A6
15600	HRVY	60426	3428	1W-18S	A1
Turnberry Ct					
10	BRRG	60527	3208		A5
800	HRPK	60133	2912		B5
Turnberry Dr					
4400	BmdT	60172	2912		A6
4400	HRPK	60133	2912		B5
4400	HRPK	60172	2912		A6
4800	HFET	60010	2804	24W-16N	C1
4900	ROSL	60172	2912		A5
9000	BRRG	60527	3208		A5
Turnberry Ln					
800	NHBK	60062	2757	8W-16N	D7
8900	TYPK	60477	3424	11W-20S	A4
13500	HmrT	60467	3344	15W-16S	B3
Turnberry Tr					
15100	LMNT	60439	3342	19W-15S	E1
Turnbull Wood					
-	GLNC	60022	2758	7W-18N	B2
Turnbull Woods Ct					
10	HDPK	60035	2758	7W-20N	A2
10	NtrT	60035	2758	7W-20N	A2
10	NtrT	60062	2758	7W-20N	A2
Turner Av					
10	EGVV	60007	2914		D3
10	ITSC	60143	2914		D3
300	BmdT	60157	2913		C6
300	ROSL	60157	2913		C6
400	ROSL	60172	2913		C6
600	BmdT	60172	2912		E5
600	ROSL	60172	2912		E5
13300	RBBN	60472	3348	4W-16S	E2
14000	RBBN	60406	3348	4W-16S	E4
14700	MDLN	60445	3348	4W-17S	E6
14700	MKHM	60426	3348	4W-17S	E5
15700	MKHM	60426	3426	4W-18S	E1
16600	HLCT	60429	3426	4W-19S	E3
E Turner Av					
300	ROSL	60172	2913		B6
600	BmdT	60157	2913		C6
S Turner Av					
9200	ENGN	60805	3212	4W-10S	E5
10200	CHCG	60655	3276	4W-11S	E1
10200	ENGN	60805	3276	4W-11S	E1
W Turner Av					
10	BmdT	60172	2913		A6
10	ROSL	60172	2913		A6
100	BmdT	60172	2912		E6
Turner Ct					
-	CCHL	60478	3506	6W-22S	A2
Turner Ln					
1500	HRPK	60133	2911		E6
Turning Shore Dr					
10	SBTN	60010	2803	27W-14N	C3
Turtle Run					
11200	ODPK	60467	3422	14W-21S	E7
E Turtle Creek Cir					
1300	PLTN	60074	2753	19W-17N	C5
Turtlecreek Dr					
2600	HLCT	60429	3427	3W-21S	B5
17700	HMWD	60430	3427	3W-21S	B6
Turtle Pond Ln					
-	ODPK	60462	3346	9W-15S	D2
-	ODPK	60463	3346	9W-15S	D2
13400	PSHT	60463	3346	9W-15S	C2
Turtle Run Ct					
18100	ODPK	60467	3422	14W-21S	E7
Tuscany Ct					
1400	GNVW	60025	2811	8W-14N	A3
2100	NHFD	60093	2811	8W-14N	A3
Tuttle Dr					
8600	PSHL	60465	3274	10W-13S	A3
Tweed Rd					
1800	IVNS	60067	2751	23W-17N	E5
Twilight Ln					
10	CTCY	60409	3351	2E-16S	C4
800	WLNG	60090	2755	15W-16N	A6
900	PTHT	60070	2754	15W-16N	E6
900	WLNG	60090	2754	15W-16N	E6
Twilight Tr					
300	SMWD	60107	2857	28W-10N	A6
S Twin Creek Ln					
14300	HMGN	60441	3343	18W-17S	A5
Twining Av					
4200	BLWD	60104	3029	13W-0N	A4
4600	BLWD	60104	3028		E4
5000	BKLY	60163	3028		E4
Twin Lakes Dr					
11200	ODPK	60467	3422	14W-21S	D7
15500	HMGN	60441	3344	15W-18S	C7
15500	HMGN	60441	3422	15W-18S	C1
E Twin Lakes Dr					
1200	PLTN	60074	2806	19W-15N	C2
S Twin Oak Ct					
16100	HMGN	60441	3422	16W-19S	A2
S Twin Oaks Ct					
13800	HMGN	60441	3342	18W-16S	E3
Twin Oaks Ln					
9200	MaiT	60016	2863	11W-11N	D3
Twin Oaks St					
1100	BNVL	60106	2915		D7
Twisted Oak Ln					
700	BFGV	60089	2754	17W-20N	A1
Tyburn Dr					
1200	SMBG	60194	2858	25W-10N	C5
Tyler Av					
700	DYR	46311	3510		D6
Tyler Ct					
10	SMWD	60107	2856	29W-10N	D6
Tyler Dr					
500	CPVL	60110	2748		C7
1100	SMBG	60193	2913		A1
2000	LYWD	60411	3509	2E-24S	D5
20500	BlmT	60411	3509	2E-24S	D5
22400	RNPK	60471	3594	5W-27S	C4
Tyler St					
-	EGVV	60007	2861	15W-9N	E7
500	EGvT	60018	2861	16W-9N	E7
500	EGvT	60018	2862	15W-9N	A7
W Tymore Ct					
1100	PLTN	60067	2805	22W-14N	C4
Tyne Ct					
600	IVNS	60010	2751	24W-16N	B6
Tyrell Av					
1400	PKRG	60068	2863	11W-10N	D5
Tyson Rd					
2200	BDVW	60155	3087	11W-1S	D1

U

STREET Block	City	ZIP	Map#	CGS	Grid
Ulm Pl					
10	HNDL	60521	3146		B2
Una Av					
300	LMNT	60439	3270		E7
Union Av					
-	BRLT	60103	2910		C4
-	WynT	60103	2910		C4
500	CHHT	60411	3508	0W-24S	B5
1500	CHHT	60411	3596	0W-25S	B1
2500	BlmT	60411	3596	0W-26S	B2
3000	SCHT	60411	3596	0W-27S	B4
3000	SCHT	60475	3596	0W-27S	B4
3000	STGR	60475	3596	1W-28S	B6
3600	CRTE	60475	3596	1W-28S	B6
3700	CRTE	60417	3596	1W-28S	B7
13700	RVDL	60827	3350	1W-15S	A2
14400	HRVY	60426	3350	1W-17S	A5
16400	HRVY	60426	3428	0W-19S	B3
N Union Av					
200	CHCG	60661	3034	0W-0N	A4
400	CHCG	60610	3034	0W-0N	A3
S Union Av					
1200	CHCG	60607	3034	0W-1S	A7
1500	CHCG	60616	3034	0W-1S	A7
2000	CHCG	60616	3092		E3
3400	CHCG	60609	3092	0W-4S	A7
4700	CHCG	60609	3152	0W-6S	A3
6700	CHCG	60621	3152	0W-7S	A6
7500	CHCG	60620	3214	0W-8S	A1
9400	CHCG	60628	3214	0W-11S	A6
10300	CHCG	60628	3278	0W-13S	A3
14200	ODPK	60462	3345	12W-16S	C4
14200	RVDL	60827	3350	1W-16S	A4
14500	HRVY	60426	3350	1W-16S	A4
Union Cir					
400	EGVV	60007	2913		D1
Union Ct					
-	BRLT	60103	2910		C4
1200	WLNG	60090	2754	16W-18N	D2
Union Dr					
700	UYPK	60466	3684	3W-30S	C3
Union St					
-	CTPK	60827	3277	2W-15S	C7
1800	BLID	60406	3277	2W-15S	C7
1800	CTPK	60406	3277	2W-15S	C7
Unit Ct					
5700	HRPK	60133	2911		E5
United Ln					
2300	EGVV	60007	2915		E4
United Pkwy					
4100	SRPK	60176	2973	13W-5N	A1
University Av					
800	MTSN	60443	3506	5W-25S	C7
14200	DLTN	60419	3351	1E-16S	B4
15400	SHLD	60419	3351	1E-18S	B7
15900	SHLD	60473	3351	1E-18S	B7
16200	SHLD	60473	3429	1E-19S	A1
S University Av					
200	GNWD	60425	3509	1E-23S	A3
4400	CHCG	60653	3093	1E-4S	A7
5100	CHCG	60615	3153	1E-6S	A3
5500	CHCG	60637	3153	1E-6S	A3
7100	CHCG	60619	3153	1E-8S	A7
8000	CHCG	60619	3215	1E-9S	A2
9500	CHCG	60628	3215	1E-11S	A6
University Cross					
-	MonT	60466	3594	6W-29S	A7
-	MonT	60466	3683	6W-29S	A1
University Ct					
-	FSMR	60422	3507	2W-23S	D4
10	BFGV	60089	2754	16W-17N	D5
16400	SHLD	60473	3429	1E-19S	A2

STREET Block	City	ZIP	Map#	CGS	Grid
University Dr					
10	ANHT	60004	2754	16W-17N	C5
10	BFGV	60089	2754	16W-17N	C5
200	MPPT	60056	2808	14W-13N	B5
200	MPPT	60056	2862	15W-12N	A1
9000	MNSR	46321	3510		E1
16300	OKFT	60452	3426	5W-19S	C3
16600	CCHL	60478	3426	5W-19S	C3
16600	OKFT	60478	3426	5W-19S	C3
E University Dr					
10	ANHT	60004	2754	17W-17N	A5
900	BFGV	60004	2754	17W-17N	B5
900	BFGV	60089	2754	17W-17N	B5
W University Dr					
10	ANHT	60004	2754	18W-17N	A5
300	ANHT	60004	2753	18W-17N	E5
University Ln					
200	EGVV	60007	2859	22W-9N	C7
200	SMBG	60193	2859	22W-9N	C7
W University Ln					
800	CHCG	60607	3034		E7
800	CHCG	60608	3034		E7
University Pkwy					
-	PKFT	60466	3594	5W-29S	C7
400	CteT	60417	3684	3W-29S	C2
400	MonT	60466	3684	3W-29S	B1
400	UYPK	60417	3684	3W-29S	C2
400	UYPK	60466	3684	3W-29S	B1
1100	MonT	60417	3684	3W-29S	B1
4400	MonT	60466	3594	5W-28S	C7
4400	UYPK	60466	3594	5W-28S	C7
4600	MonT	60449	3594	5W-28S	B7
4800	MonT	60449	3593	6W-28S	E7
4800	MonT	60466	3593	6W-28S	E7
4800	UYPK	60449	3593	6W-28S	E7
24000	MonT	60466	3683	5W-29S	D1
24000	UYPK	60466	3683	5W-29S	D1
W University Pkwy					
3300	MonT	60417	3683	4W-29S	E1
3300	MonT	60417	3684	4W-29S	A1
3300	MonT	60466	3683	4W-29S	E1
3300	MonT	60466	3684	4W-29S	A1
3300	UYPK	60417	3683	4W-29S	E1
3300	UYPK	60466	3683	4W-29S	E1
University Pl					
600	EVTN	60201	2867	2W-11N	B2
University St					
2200	DSPN	60016	2863	12W-11N	C3
2200	MaiT	60016	2863	12W-11N	C2
Upland Dr					
-	TYPK	60477	3423	11W-21S	E6
17900	OrlT	60477	3423	11W-21S	E6
Upper Dr					
-	WLMT	60091	2813	2W-13N	B5
N Upper Columbus Dr					
100	CHCG	60601	3034	0E-0N	C4
Upper Express Dr					
-	CHCG	60018	2916		D1
Upper Pond Rd					
10	SBTN	60010	2803	27W-14N	B3
Ups Wy					
-	HGKN	60525	3209	13W-8S	B1
10	WLSP	60525	3209	13W-8S	A1
Upton on Asbury					
10	RGMW	60008	2806	19W-15N	B3
S Urban Av					
9100	CHCG	60619	3214	0E-10S	C5
Ursula Dr					
10800	WLSP	60480	3208		E4
10800	WLSP	60480	3209	13W-9S	A4
US-6 159th St					
-	SHLD	60473	3429	1E-19S	C1
1400	CTCY	60409	3429	2E-19S	E1
4700	BmnT	60426	3426	5W-18S	B1
4700	OKFT	60452	3426	5W-18S	B1
5100	OKFT	60452	3425	7W-19S	C1
5400	BmnT	60477	3425	6W-18S	D1
5400	OKFT	60477	3425	6W-18S	D1
6400	TYPK	60452	3425	8W-18S	B1
6500	BmnT	60452	3425	8W-18S	B1
6700	TYPK	60477	3425	8W-18S	A1
6900	ODPK	60477	3425	8W-18S	A1
US-6 E 159th St					
10	HRVY	60426	3427	1W-18S	E1
100	HRVY	60426	3428	1W-18S	A1
300	HRVY	60473	3428	0W-18S	B1
300	SHLD	60426	3428	0W-18S	B1
300	SHLD	60473	3428	0W-18S	B1
US-6 W 159th St					
-	OKFT	60452	3426	5W-18S	B1
10	HRVY	60426	3427	2W-18S	E1
200	MKHM	60426	3427	2W-19S	C1
200	ThtT	60426	3427	2W-18S	C1
2300	BmnT	60426	3427	2W-19S	C1
3300	MKHM	60426	3426	4W-19S	E1
3800	BmnT	60426	3426	4W-19S	E1
7000	ODPK	60462	3425	8W-18S	A1
7000	ODPK	60477	3425	8W-18S	A1
7000	TYPK	60477	3425	8W-18S	A1
7100	ODPK	60462	3424	11W-18S	A1
7100	TYPK	60477	3424	11W-18S	A1
7200	ODPK	60477	3424	9W-18S	E1
7400	TYPK	60462	3424	9W-18S	E1
8700	ODHL	60462	3424	10W-18S	A1
8700	ODHL	60477	3424	10W-18S	A1
9100	ODHL	60477	3423	11W-18S	E1
9100	ODPK	60462	3423	11W-18S	E1
9100	ODPK	60477	3423	11W-18S	E1
9300	ODPK	60467	3423	11W-18S	E1
9900	OrlT	60467	3423	12W-18S	C1
10800	ODPK	60467	3422	13W-18S	E1
10800	OrlT	60467	3422	13W-18S	E1
US-6 E 162nd St					
10	SHLD	60473	3428	0E-19S	D1
700	SHLD	60473	3429	0E-19S	A1
US-6 W 162nd St					
10	SHLD	60473	3428	0E-19S	D1
500	HRVY	60426	3428	0W-18S	B1
500	HRVY	60473	3428	0W-18S	B1
500	SHLD	60426	3428	0W-18S	B1
US-6 Kingery Expwy					
-	LNSG	-	3429	3E-20S	E4
-	LNSG	-	3430	3E-20S	A4
-	MNSR	-	3430	3E-20S	A4
US-6 Southwest Hwy					
-	NlxT	60448	3422	15W-21S	C7
-	OrlT	60467	3422	14W-21S	D6
11300	ODPK	60467	3422	14W-21S	E5
17700	ODPK	60448	3422	14W-21S	D6
17700	OrlT	60448	3422	14W-21S	D6
17900	HMGN	60448	3422	14W-21S	C7
US-6 Torrence Av					
1100	CTCY	60409	3429	2E-19S	D1
1400	LNSG	60438	3429	2E-19S	E3

STREET Block	City	ZIP	Map#	CGS	Grid
US-6 Tri State Expwy					
-	HMND	-	3430		D5
-	LNSG	-	3430	4E-20S	D5
-	MNSR	-	3430		D5
US-6 Wolf Rd					
15900	ODPK	60467	3422	13W-19S	E1
15900	OrlT	60467	3422	13W-19S	E1
16800	OrlT	60448	3422	13W-20S	E4
17200	ODPK	60448	3422	13W-20S	E5
US-12 95th St					
-	HYHL	60457	3209	11W-10S	E6
-	HYHL	60465	3209	11W-10S	E6
-	PlsT	60465	3209	11W-10S	E6
-	PlsT	60480	3209	11W-10S	E6
-	PSHL	60465	3209	11W-10S	E6
US-12 E 95th St					
10	CHCG	60619	3214	0E-10S	D5
10	CHCG	60620	3214	0E-10S	C6
10	CHCG	60628	3214	0E-10S	D5
900	CHCG	60619	3215	1E-10S	A5
900	CHCG	60628	3215	1E-10S	A5
1500	CHCG	60617	3215	3E-10S	E5
3000	CHCG	60617	3216	3E-10S	A5
US-12 W 95th St					
-	BGVW	60455	3210	8W-10S	E6
-	BGVW	60457	3210	9W-11S	D6
-	CHCG	60619	3214	0E-10S	C6
-	HYHL	60455	3210	9W-11S	D6
-	OKLN	60453	3210	9W-11S	D6
10	CHCG	60620	3214	0W-10S	B6
10	CHCG	60628	3214	0W-10S	B6
700	CHCG	60643	3214	0W-10S	A6
900	CHCG	60620	3213	1W-10S	D6
2400	CHCG	60643	3213	3W-10S	A6
2400	ENGN	60805	3213	3W-10S	A6
2900	ENGN	60805	3212	3W-10S	E6
3900	OKLN	60453	3212	4W-10S	C6
4900	OKLN	60453	3211	7W-10S	C6
6300	CHRG	60453	3211	7W-10S	B6
7600	HYHL	60457	3210	9W-11S	D6
8700	HYHL	60465	3210	10W-10S	A6
8700	PSHL	60465	3210	10W-10S	A6
8900	HYHL	60457	3209	11W-10S	E6
8900	PSHL	60465	3209	11W-10S	E6
9000	HYHL	60465	3209	11W-10S	E6
9000	PlsT	60465	3209	11W-10S	E6
9000	PlsT	60480	3209	11W-10S	E6
US-12 S Ewing Av					
9500	CHCG	60617	3216	4E-11S	B6
US-12 Graceland Av					
800	DSPN	60016	2862	13W-10N	E4
US-12 S Indianapolis Av					
-	CHCG	46320	3280	4E-11S	C1
10000	CHCG	60617	3216	4E-11S	B7
10300	CHCG	60617	3280	4E-11S	C1
10600	HMND	46320	3280	4E-12S	C1
US-12 S Indianapolis Blvd					
1000	HMND	46320	3280		D2
1000	HMND	46394	3280		E4
10500	CHCG	46320	3280		C1
10500	CHCG	60617	3280		C1
US-12 La Grange Rd					
-	LynT	60458	3209	12W-8S	D1
-	LynT	60480	3209	12W-8S	D1
-	PlsT	60480	3209	11W-9S	D4
-	WLSP	60458	3209	12W-8S	D1
-	WLSP	60480	3209	11W-10S	D5
-	WLSP	60525	3209	12W-8S	D1
US-12 N La Grange Rd					
-	WSTR	60154	3087	12W-2S	A2
10	LGNG	60525	3087	12W-4S	C6
100	LGPK	60525	3087	12W-3S	C6
1000	PvsT	60525	3087	12W-2S	B4
2500	PvsT	60154	3087	12W-2S	B2
US-12 S La Grange Rd					
-	HGKN	60525	3209	12W-8S	C1
-	WLSP	60525	3209	12W-8S	C1
10	LGNG	60525	3087	12W-4S	C7
300	LGNG	60525	3147	12W-7S	C5
5200	CTSD	60525	3147	12W-5S	C3
6000	HGKN	60525	3147	12W-6S	C5
US-12 Mannheim Rd					
-	CHCG	60176	2917	12W-6N	B6
-	CHCG	60666	2973	12W-5N	A1
-	SRPK	60176	2917	12W-6N	B6
-	SRPK	60176	2973	12W-5N	A1
10	BLWD	60104	3029	12W-0N	A3
10	BLWD	60160	3029	12W-1N	A3
10	MLPK	60160	3029	12W-1N	A3
500	BLWD	60162	3029	12W-0N	A4
500	HLSD	60162	3029	12W-0N	A4
600	DSPN	60016	2863	13W-11N	A3
900	DSPN	60016	2862	13W-10N	E4
1000	DSPN	60018	2862	13W-10N	E5
1700	DSPN	60018	2863	13W-9N	A7
2000	DSPN	60018	2917	13W-8N	A2
2000	RSMT	60018	2917	13W-8N	A2
2400	FNPK	60131	2973	13W-3N	A6
2400	FNPK	60164	2973	13W-3N	A6
2400	LydT	60131	2973	13W-3N	A6
2400	LydT	60164	2973	13W-3N	A6
2900	CHCG	60666	2917	12W-7N	B4
2900	RSMT	60666	2917	12W-8N	A2
4000	FNPK	60176	2973	13W-2N	A7
US-12 N Mannheim Rd					
-	BLWD	60104	3029	12W-1N	A3
-	BLWD	60160	3029	12W-1N	A3
-	HLSD	60104	3029	12W-0S	A6
-	HLSD	60154	3029	12W-0S	A6
-	WSTR	60154	3029	12W-0S	A6
10	BLWD	60162	3029	12W-0S	A6
10	HLSD	60162	3029	12W-0S	A6
1500	MLPK	60160	3029	13W-1N	A2
1500	MLPK	60165	3029	13W-1N	A2
1500	SNPK	60165	3029	13W-1N	A2
2000	LydT	60164	2973	12W-2N	A7
2000	MLPK	60160	2973	12W-2N	A7
2000	NHLK	60164	2973	12W-2N	A7
2300	LydT	60131	2973	13W-2N	A6
US-12 S Mannheim Rd					
-	BLWD	60104	3029	12W-0S	A6
-	HLSD	60154	3029	12W-0S	A6
10	HLSD	60162	3029	13W-0S	A7
10	WSTR	60154	3029	13W-0S	A7
300	PvsT	60162	3029	12W-0S	A7
1300	PvsT	60154	3029	12W-1S	A7
1400	PvsT	60154	3087	12W-1S	A1
1400	PvsT	60162	3087	12W-1S	A1
1400	WSTR	60154	3087	12W-3S	B5
US-12 Rand Rd					
10	DSPN	60016	2808	14W-12N	C7
10	MPPT	60016	2808	14W-12N	C7
10	MPPT	60056	2808	14W-12N	B7
300	DSPN	60016	2862	13W-11N	E2
600	DRPK	60074	2752	21W-20N	D1

STREET Block	City	ZIP	Map#	CGS	Grid
US-12 Rand Rd					
600	ElaT	60074	2752	21W-20N	D1
1200	DSPN	60016	2863	13W-11N	A2
2000	PLTN	60074	2753	20W-18N	A3
US-12 E Rand Rd					
10	ANHT	60004	2754	17W-16N	A7
10	MPPT	60056	2808	15W-13N	A5
200	ANHT	60004	2807	15W-14N	E4
900	DSPN	60016	2808	14W-13N	B7
900	MPPT	60016	2808	14W-13N	B7
1200	PTHT	60004	2807	17W-15N	C2
2400	MPPT	60004	2807	16W-14N	D3
2400	MPPT	60056	2807	16W-14N	D3
2400	WhlT	60004	2807	16W-14N	D3
2500	ANHT	60056	2807	16W-14N	E4
US-12 N Rand Rd					
-	ANHT	60004	2753	19W-17N	D5
-	ANHT	60074	2753	19W-17N	D5
-	PltT	60004	2753	19W-17N	D5
1200	PLTN	60074	2753	20W-18N	B3
2100	PltT	60074	2753	20W-18N	A2
2200	DRPK	60074	2752	20W-20N	E2
2200	ElaT	60074	2752	20W-20N	E2
2200	PltT	60074	2752	20W-18N	E2
20200	KLDR	60074	2752	21W-20N	E1
20400	KLDR	60047	2752	21W-20N	D1
US-12 W Rand Rd					
-	ANHT	60074	2753	19W-17N	D5
10	ANHT	60004	2754	17W-16N	A7
10	MPPT	60056	2808	15W-13N	B6
300	MPPT	60056	2807	15W-14N	E4
400	ANHT	60004	2753	18W-17N	D6
600	ANHT	60056	2807	15W-14N	E4
700	ANHT	60004	2807	16W-14N	E4
700	MPPT	60004	2807	16W-14N	E4
1200	PltT	60004	2753	18W-17N	D6
US-12 S River Rd					
-	DSPN	60016	2863	13W-11N	A3
US-14 N Broadway St					
5200	CHCG	60640	2921	1W-6N	D5
5500	CHCG	60660	2921	1W-6N	D4
US-14 Caldwell Av					
7900	MNGV	60053	2864	8W-10N	E4
7900	NLES	60714	2864	8W-10N	E4
US-14 N Caldwell Av					
-	NLES	60053	2865	8W-9N	A6
6000	CHCG	60646	2919	6W-7N	D3
6800	CHCG	60714	2919	7W-8N	B1
6800	NLES	60646	2919	7W-8N	B1
6800	NLES	60714	2919	7W-8N	B1
7200	CHCG	60646	2865	8W-9N	A7
7200	NLES	60714	2865	8W-9N	A6
7900	MNGV	60053	2865	8W-9N	A6
7900	MNGV	60714	2865	8W-9N	A6
8000	MNGV	60053	2864	8W-10N	E5
8000	MNGV	60714	2864	8W-10N	E5
8000	NLES	60714	2864	8W-10N	E5
US-14 Dempster St					
1200	NLES	60714	2863	10W-10N	E4
1200	PKRG	60068	2863	10W-10N	E4
1200	PKRG	60068	2864	10W-10N	A4
1200	PKRG	60714	2863	10W-10N	E4
2000	MaiT	60016	2863	11W-11N	D4
2600	DSPN	60016	2863	11W-10N	D4
2600	MaiT	60068	2863	11W-10N	D4
2600	PKRG	60016	2863	11W-10N	D4
6900	MNGV	60053	2864	8W-10N	E4
7000	NLES	60714	2864	8W-10N	E4
US-14 E Dempster St					
2300	DSPN	60016	2863	12W-10N	C4
2300	PKRG	60068	2863	12W-10N	C4
2400	PKRG	60016	2863	11W-10N	D4
2500	MaiT	60016	2863	11W-10N	D4
2500	MaiT	60068	2863	11W-10N	D4
US-14 W Dempster St					
7000	MNGV	60053	2864	8W-11N	E4
7000	NLES	60053	2864	8W-11N	E4
7000	NLES	60714	2864	8W-11N	E4
7100	MNGV	60714	2864	8W-11N	D4
8500	PKRG	60068	2864	10W-10N	A4
US-14 Miner St					
1200	DSPN	60016	2862	13W-11N	E3
1600	DSPN	60016	2863	11W-10N	E4
US-14 E Northwest Hwy					
10	ANHT	60004	2807	17W-14N	A4
10	ANHT	60005	2807	17W-14N	A4
10	DSPN	60016	2862	14W-12N	C1
10	MPPT	60056	2808	15W-12N	A7
10	MPPT	60056	2862	13W-11N	E3
10	PLTN	60067	2752	20W-16N	E6
100	BRTN	60010	2751	25W-20N	A1
200	PLTN	60067	2753	20W-16N	A7
200	PLTN	60074	2753	20W-16N	A7
400	PLTN	60067	2806	20W-15N	A1
400	PLTN	60074	2806	20W-15N	A1
1700	DSPN	60016	2863	12W-11N	A4
2100	MPPT	60056	2807	16W-13N	D6
US-14 N Northwest Hwy					
10	PLTN	60067	2806	20W-16N	A1
10	PLTN	60074	2806	20W-16N	A1
100	BRTN	60010	2751	25W-20N	A2
300	PLTN	60067	2753	20W-16N	A7
300	PLTN	60074	2753	20W-16N	A7
US-14 S Northwest Hwy					
-	PLTN	60067	2751	23W-17N	E5
-	PltT	60067	2751	23W-17N	E5
10	PLTN	60067	2806	18W-14N	D3
10	PLTN	60074	2806	18W-14N	D3
100	BRTN	60010	2751	24W-17N	D4
1100	PltT	60010	2751	23W-17N	D4
US-14 W Northwest Hwy					
-	PltT	60010	2751	23W-17N	E5
-	PltT	60067	2751	23W-17N	E5
10	ANHT	60004	2807	17W-14N	A4
10	ANHT	60005	2807	17W-14N	A4
10	MPPT	60056	2808	15W-12N	A7
10	PLTN	60067	2752	22W-17N	A5
200	MPPT	60056	2807	15W-12N	E7
500	ANHT	60004	2806	18W-14N	E4
500	ANHT	60005	2806	18W-14N	E4
500	BRTN	60010	2750	26W-20N	D1
500	PltT	60067	2752	21W-17N	C6
1500	PLTN	60067	2751	23W-17N	E5
1800	ANHT	60074	2806	19W-14N	D3
1800	PLTN	60074	2806	19W-14N	D3
US-14 W Peterson Av					
1700	CHCG	60660	2921	2W-7N	B3
1900	CHCG	60659	2921	2W-7N	B3
2700	CHCG	60659	2920	3W-7N	E3
3800	CHCG	60646	2920	4W-7N	B4
4700	CHCG	60646	2919	5W-7N	E4
US-14 N Ridge Av					
5600	CHCG	60640	2921	1W-7N	D4
5600	CHCG	60660	2921	1W-7N	D4

STREET Block	City	ZIP	Map#	CGS	Grid
US-14 Waukegan Rd					
8500	MNGV	60053	2864	8W-10N	E4
US-20 95th St					
-	HYHL	60457	3209	11W-10S	E6
-	HYHL	60465	3209	11W-10S	E6
-	PlsT	60465	3209	11W-10S	E6
-	PlsT	60480	3209	11W-10S	E6
-	PSHL	60465	3209	11W-10S	E6
US-20 E 95th St					
10	CHCG	60619	3214	0E-11S	D6
10	CHCG	60620	3214	0E-10S	C6
10	CHCG	60628	3214	0E-11S	D6
900	CHCG	60619	3215	1E-10S	A5
900	CHCG	60628	3215	1E-10S	A5
1500	CHCG	60617	3215	3E-11S	E5
3000	CHCG	60617	3216	3E-10S	A5
US-20 W 95th St					
-	BGVW	60455	3210	8W-10S	E6
-	BGVW	60457	3210	9W-11S	D6
-	CHCG	60619	3214	0E-10S	C6
-	HYHL	60455	3210	9W-11S	D6
-	OKLN	60453	3210	9W-11S	D6
10	CHCG	60620	3214	0W-11S	B6
10	CHCG	60628	3214	0W-11S	B6
700	CHCG	60643	3214	0W-10S	A6
2400	CHCG	60620	3213	3W-11S	A6
2400	CHCG	60643	3213	3W-11S	A6
2400	ENGN	60805	3213	3W-11S	A6
2900	ENGN	60805	3212	3W-11S	E6
3900	OKLN	60453	3212	4W-10S	C6
4900	OKLN	60453	3211	7W-11S	C6
6300	CHRG	60453	3211	7W-10S	B6
7600	HYHL	60457	3210	9W-11S	D6
8700	HYHL	60465	3210	10W-10S	A6
8700	PSHL	60465	3210	10W-10S	A6
8900	HYHL	60457	3209	11W-11S	E6
8900	PSHL	60465	3209	11W-11S	E6
9000	HYHL	60465	3209	11W-10S	E6
9000	PlsT	60465	3209	11W-10S	E6
9000	PlsT	60480	3209	11W-10S	E6
US-20 Eisenhower Expwy					
-	EMHT	-	2972		A7
-	EMHT	-	3028		B1
US-20 S Ewing Av					
9500	CHCG	60617	3216	4E-11S	B6
US-20 S Indianapolis Av					
-	CHCG	46320	3280	4E-11S	C1
-	HMND	46320	3280	4E-11S	C1
10000	CHCG	60617	3216	4E-11S	B7
10300	CHCG	60617	3280	4E-11S	C1
US-20 S Indianapolis Blvd					
1000	HMND	46320	3280		D2
1000	HMND	46394	3280		E4
10500	CHCG	46320	3280		C1
10500	CHCG	60617	3280		C1
US-20 La Grange Rd					
-	LynT	60458	3209	12W-8S	D1
-	LynT	60480	3209	12W-8S	D1
-	PlsT	60480	3209	11W-9S	D4
-	WLSP	60458	3209	12W-8S	D1
-	WLSP	60480	3209	11W-10S	D5
-	WLSP	60525	3209	12W-8S	D1
US-20 N La Grange Rd					
-	WSTR	60154	3087	12W-2S	A2
10	LGNG	60525	3087	12W-4S	C6
100	LGPK	60525	3087	12W-3S	C6
1000	PvsT	60525	3087	12W-2S	B4
2500	PvsT	60154	3087	12W-2S	B2
US-20 S La Grange Rd					
-	CTSD	60525	3147	12W-8S	C7
-	HGKN	60525	3209	12W-8S	C1
-	WLSP	60525	3209	12W-8S	C1
10	LGNG	60525	3087	12W-4S	C7
300	LGNG	60525	3147	12W-7S	C5
6000	HGKN	60525	3147	12W-6S	C5
US-20 Lake St					
-	BRLT	60103	2856	31W-9N	A7
-	ELGN	-	2855		D6
-	ELGN	60103	2856	31W-9N	A7
-	ELGN	60120	2856	31W-10N	A7
-	HnrT	60120	2856	31W-9N	A7
10	BmdT	60172	2912		C6
10	ROSL	60172	2912		C6
200	BmdT	60133	2911		E5
200	HRPK	60133	2911		E5
300	BMDL	60108	2912		D7
300	BMDL	60172	2912		D7
300	BmdT	60108	2912		D7
300	HRPK	60133	2912		B6
400	HRPK	60172	2912		B6
500	BmdT	60133	2912		A5
US-20 E Lake St					
10	MLPK	60160	3028		E2
10	NHLK	60164	3028		D2
100	BRLT	60103	2910		E2
100	BRLT	60103	2911		B2
100	BRLT	60107	2910		E2
100	BRLT	60107	2911		B2
100	SMWD	60103	2910		E1
100	SMWD	60107	2910		E2
100	SMWD	60107	2911		B2
500	SMWD	60103	2911		A2
1000	BmdT	60133	2911		E5
1000	BmdT	60133	2912		A5
1000	HRPK	60133	2911		E5
1000	HRPK	60133	2912		A5
US-20 W Lake St					
-	HnrT	60103	2910		C1
-	SMWD	60120	2910		C1
10	NHLK	60164	3028		E2
200	BMDL	60108	2912		E7
200	BMDL	60172	2912		E7
200	BmdT	60108	2912		E7
200	BmdT	60172	2912		E7
200	ROSL	60108	2912		E7
200	ROSL	60172	2912		E7
500	BRLT	60103	2910		D1
500	BRLT	60107	2910		D1
500	BRLT	60120	2910		D1
500	HnrT	60120	2910		D1
500	SMWD	60103	2910		D1
500	SMWD	60107	2910		D1
600	BRLT	60103	2911		B2
600	HRPK	60103	2911		B2
600	HRPK	60133	2911		B2
600	SMWD	60107	2911		B2
1100	BRLT	60103	2856	30W-9N	B7
1100	BRLT	60107	2856	30W-9N	B7
1100	BRLT	60120	2856	30W-9N	B7
1100	HnrT	60103	2856	30W-9N	B7
1100	HnrT	60107	2856	30W-9N	B7
1100	HnrT	60120	2856	30W-9N	B7
1100	SMWD	60107	2856	30W-9N	C7
2200	BRLT	60133	2911		C3
4100	MLPK	60160	3029	13W-1N	A2

STREET Block	City	ZIP	Map#	CGS	Grid
US-20 W Lake St					
4100	MLPK	60165	3029	12W-1N	A2
4100	SNPK	60165	3029	13W-1N	A2
4700	MLPK	60160	3028		E2
US-20 Mannheim Rd					
10	BLWD	60104	3029	12W-0N	A3
10	BLWD	60160	3029	12W-1N	A3
10	MLPK	60160	3029	12W-1N	A3
500	BLWD	60162	3029	12W-0N	A4
500	HLSD	60162	3029	12W-0N	A4
US-20 N Mannheim Rd					
-	BLWD	60104	3029	12W-1N	A3
-	BLWD	60160	3029	12W-1N	A3
-	HLSD	60104	3029	12W-0S	A6
-	HLSD	60154	3029	12W-0S	A6
-	MLPK	60160	3029	13W-1N	A3
-	MLPK	60165	3029	13W-1N	A3
-	SNPK	60165	3029	13W-1N	A3
-	WSTR	60154	3029	12W-0S	A6
10	BLWD	60162	3029	12W-0S	A6
10	HLSD	60162	3029	12W-0S	A6
US-20 S Mannheim Rd					
-	BLWD	60104	3029	12W-0S	A6
-	HLSD	60154	3029	12W-0S	A6
10	HLSD	60162	3029	13W-0S	A7
10	WSTR	60154	3029	13W-0S	A7
300	PvsT	60162	3029	12W-0S	A7
1300	PvsT	60154	3029	12W-1S	A7
1400	PvsT	60154	3087	12W-1S	A1
1400	PvsT	60162	3087	12W-1S	A1
1400	WSTR	60154	3087	12W-3S	B5
US-20 Villa St					
-	ELGN	-	2855		E6
US-20 BUS Villa St					
-	ELGN	60120	2855		D6
US-20 E Villa St					
1500	ELGN	60120	2855		E7
1500	ELGN	60120	2856	30W-9N	B7
US-30 E 14th St					
10	CHHT	60411	3508	1W-25S	A7
300	BlmT	60411	3508	0W-25S	D7
US-30 W 14th St					
10	CHHT	60411	3508	1W-25S	A7
100	CHHT	60411	3507	1W-25S	E7
700	OMFD	60461	3507	2W-25S	C7
US-30 Joliet St					
10	BlmT	60411	3598	4E-26S	C2
10	DYR	46311	3598		C2
10	DYR	60411	3598	4E-26S	C2
US-30 Lincoln Hwy					
-	CHHT	60411	3507	2W-25S	C7
2400	OMFD	60461	3507	3W-25S	A7
2500	PKFT	60466	3507	3W-25S	A7
2600	PKFT	60461	3507	3W-25S	A7
3200	MTSN	60443	3506	4W-25S	E7
3200	OMFD	60461	3506	4W-25S	E7
3200	OMFD	60466	3506	4W-25S	E7
3200	PKFT	60466	3506	4W-25S	E7
3600	OMFD	60443	3506	4W-25S	E7
5300	MTSN	60443	3505	7W-25S	C7
6200	RchT	60443	3505	7W-25S	C7
6500	FftT	60423	3505	9W-25S	A7
6500	FKFT	60423	3505	9W-25S	A7
6500	RchT	60423	3505	9W-25S	A7
US-30 E Lincoln Hwy					
400	BlmT	60411	3508	0E-25S	E7
400	CHHT	60411	3508	0E-25S	E7
800	CHHT	60411	3509	1E-25S	A7
800	FDHT	60411	3509	1E-25S	A7
1400	BlmT	60411	3509	3E-25S	E7
1600	SLVL	60411	3509	3E-25S	E7
2400	BlmT	60411	3510	3E-25S	A7
2800	LYWD	60411	3510	3E-25S	A7
21400	BlmT	60411	3598		D2
21400	LYWD	60411	3598		D2
US-30 W Lincoln Hwy					
7200	FftT	60423	3504	9W-25S	E7
7200	FftT	60423	3505	8W-25S	A7
7200	FKFT	60423	3504	9W-25S	E7
7200	FKFT	60423	3505	8W-25S	A7
7200	RchT	60423	3505	8W-25S	A7
7200	RchT	60443	3505	8W-25S	A7
US-30 E Sauk Tr					
3600	BlmT	60411	3598	4E-26S	C2
3600	DYR	46311	3598	4E-26S	C2
3600	DYR	60411	3598	4E-26S	C2
US-34 Ogden Av					
-	HNDL	60521	3086		C6
-	LynT	60521	3086		C6
-	LynT	60558	3086		C6
-	PvsT	60521	3086		C6
10	LGPK	60525	3087	13W-4S	B6
10	PvsT	60558	3087	13W-4S	B6
10	WNSP	60558	3087	13W-4S	B6
100	PvsT	60558	3086		A7
100	WNSP	60558	3086		A7
7200	BRWN	60402	3088	9W-3S	D6
7200	LYNS	60402	3088	9W-3S	D6
7200	LYNS	60534	3088	9W-3S	D6
7200	RVSD	60402	3088	9W-3S	D6
7200	RVSD	60546	3088	9W-3S	D6
7300	LYNS	60546	3088	9W-3S	D6
8700	BKFD	60513	3088	10W-4S	A6
8800	BKFD	60525	3087	11W-4S	E6
9500	LGNG	60525	3087	12W-4S	D6
US-34 E Ogden Av					
10	LGNG	60525	3087	12W-4S	C6
400	HNDL	60521	3086		C6
400	LynT	60521	3086		C6
500	LynT	60558	3086		C6
9600	BKFD	60513	3087	12W-4S	D6
US-34 W Ogden Av					
10	HNDL	60521	3086		A7
10	LGNG	60525	3087	12W-4S	C6
1200	LGPK	60525	3087	13W-3S	A6
1500	WNSP	60558	3087	13W-3S	A6
1600	PvsT	60558	3087	13W-3S	A6
US-41 E 85th St					
3200	CHCG	60617	3216	4E-9S	A3
US-41 E 87th St					
3200	CHCG	60617	3216	4E-9S	A3
US-41 S Baker Av					
8400	CHCG	60617	3216	3E-9S	A3
US-41 S Burley Av					
8500	CHCG	60617	3216	4E-9S	A3
US-41 Calumet Av					
-	HMND	46320	3430		E1
6200	HMND	46324	3430		E1
US-41 S Calumet Av					
1400	HMND	46394	3280		E7
2100	HMND	46320	3280		E5
3000	HMND	46320	3352		E5
3000	HMND	46327	3280		E7
3000	HMND	46327	3352		E5
5900	HMND	46320	3430		E2

Chicago & Cook County Street Index

STREET Block	City	ZIP	Map#	CGS	Grid
US-41 S Calumet Av					
6100	HMND	46324	3430		E2
US-41 S Coast Guard Dr					
6400	CHCG	60637	3153	2E-7S	C5
6400	CHCG	60649	3153	2E-7S	C5
US-41 Edens Expwy					
-	GLNC	-	2758	7W-16N	B7
-	HDPK	-	2757	8W-20N	E2
-	NfdT	-	2757	8W-18N	E2
-	NfdT	-	2811	7W-16N	C1
-	NHBK	-	2757	8W-18N	E2
-	NHBK	-	2758	7W-17N	A4
-	NHFD	-	2758	7W-16N	B7
-	NHFD	-	2811	6W-14N	D4
-	NtrT	-	2758	7W-18N	A4
-	NtrT	-	2811	6W-14N	D4
US-41 S Ewing Av					
9200	CHCG	60617	3216	4E-10S	A5
US-41 W Foster Av					
900	CHCG	60640	2921	1W-6N	E5
1900	CHCG	60625	2921	2W-6N	B5
US-41 S Indianapolis Av					
-	CHCG	60617	3280	4E-11S	C1
10000	CHCG	60617	3216	4E-11S	B7
10600	CHCG	46320	3280	4E-11S	C1
10600	HMND	46320	3280	4E-12S	C1
US-41 S Indianapolis Blvd					
1000	HMND	46320	3280		D2
1000	HMND	46394	3280		D3
10500	CHCG	46320	3280	4E-12S	C1
10500	CHCG	60617	3280		C1
US-41 N Lake Shore Dr					
-	CHCG	-	2921	0W-6N	E6
-	CHCG	-	2922	0W-5N	A7
-	CHCG	-	2978	0W-4N	A3
-	CHCG	-	3034	0E-0N	D4
-	CokC	-	3034	0E-0N	D4
US-41 S Lake Shore Dr					
-	CHCG	-	3092	0E-1S	D1
-	CHCG	-	3093	1E-4S	A6
-	CHCG	-	3153	2E-5S	B1
-	CokC	60637	3153	2E-6S	C3
10	CHCG	60601	3034	0E-1S	D7
10	CHCG	60603	3034	0E-1S	D7
100	CHCG	60605	3034	0E-0S	D5
1400	CHCG	60616	3034	0E-1S	D7
5300	CHCG	60637	3153	2E-7S	D5
US-41 Lincoln Av					
7400	LNWD	60712	2866	5W-9N	A7
7400	SKOK	60076	2866	5W-9N	A7
7500	SKOK	60076	2865	5W-9N	E7
7500	SKOK	60077	2865	5W-9N	E7
US-41 N Lincoln Av					
5200	CHCG	60625	2921	3W-6N	A5
5500	CHCG	60659	2921	1W-6N	D5
5600	CHCG	60659	2920	3W-7N	E4
6300	CHCG	60712	2920	4W-7N	C3
6300	LNWD	60712	2920	3W-7N	E4
7200	LNWD	60712	2866	5W-9N	A7
7200	SKOK	60076	2866	5W-9N	A7
US-41 S Mackinaw Av					
8700	CHCG	60617	3216	4E-10S	B6
US-41 E Marquette Dr					
2000	CHCG	60637	3153	2E-7S	C5
2000	CHCG	60649	3153	2E-7S	C5
US-41 Skokie Blvd					
7500	SKOK	60076	2865	6W-12N	E1
7500	SKOK	60077	2865	6W-12N	E1
10000	SKOK	60076	2811	5W-12N	E7
10000	SKOK	60077	2811	5W-12N	E7
10000	WLMT	60076	2811	5W-12N	E7
10000	WLMT	60077	2811	5W-12N	E7
10000	WLMT	60091	2811	5W-12N	E7
US-41 Skokie Hwy					
-	HDPK	-	2757	8W-18N	E3
-	NfdT	-	2757	8W-18N	E3
-	NHBK	-	2757	8W-18N	E3
US-41 Skokie Rd					
-	NHFD	60093	2811	5W-13N	E6
-	SKOK	60077	2811	5W-13N	E7
-	WLMT	60077	2811	5W-13N	E7
-	WLMT	60091	2811	5W-13N	E6
-	WLMT	60093	2811	5W-13N	E6
US-41 Skokie Valley Rd					
-	HDPK	60035	2757	9W-20N	D1
US-41 E South Shore Dr					
2400	CHCG	60649	3153	3E-7S	D6
US-41 S South Shore Dr					
6700	CHCG	60649	3153	2E-7S	D5
7700	CHCG	60649	3215	3E-8S	E1
7800	CHCG	60617	3216	3E-8S	A1
7800	CHCG	60649	3216	3E-8S	A1
US-41 Tri State Expwy					
-	HMND	-	3430		E5
US-45 96th Av					
-	PlsT	60464	3273	11W-13S	D4
-	PlsT	60465	3273	12W-13S	D4
-	PlsT	60480	3273	12W-13S	D4
US-45 N Des Plaines River Rd					
10	DSPN	60016	2863	13W-12N	A2
100	MaiT	60016	2863	13W-12N	A1
900	DSPN	60016	2808	13W-13N	E7
900	MaiT	60016	2808	13W-13N	E7
900	WhlT	60016	2808	13W-13N	E7
1000	WhlT	60056	2808	13W-13N	E6
US-45 Graceland Av					
800	DSPN	60016	2862	13W-10N	E4
US-45 La Grange Rd					
-	LynT	60458	3209	12W-8S	C1
-	LynT	60480	3209	12W-8S	C1
-	MKNA	60448	3423	12W-22S	D7
-	PlsT	60480	3209	11W-11S	D7
-	PlsT	60480	3273	11W-12S	D1
-	WLSP	60458	3209	12W-8S	C1
-	WLSP	60480	3209	11W-9S	D4
-	WLSP	60525	3209	12W-8S	C1
16700	ODHL	60477	3423	11W-20S	D3
16700	ODPK	60467	3423	11W-19S	D3
16700	OrlT	60467	3423	11W-20S	D3
16700	OrlT	60477	3423	11W-20S	D3
16900	TYPK	60477	3423	11W-20S	D4
18200	FftT	60448	3423	12W-21S	D7
18200	ODPK	60448	3423	12W-21S	D7
18200	ODPK	60477	3423	12W-21S	D7
US-45 N La Grange Rd					
-	WSTR	60154	3087	12W-2S	A2
10	LGNG	60525	3087	12W-4S	C6
100	LGPK	60525	3087	12W-3S	C6
1000	PvsT	60525	3087	12W-2S	B4
2500	PvsT	60154	3087	12W-2S	B2
US-45 S La Grange Rd					
-	HGKN	60525	3147	12W-8S	C7
-	HGKN	60525	3209	12W-8S	C1
-	PlsT	60480	3273	12W-13S	D4
-	WLSP	60525	3209	12W-8S	C1
US-45 S La Grange Rd					
10	LGNG	60525	3087	12W-4S	C7
300	LGNG	60525	3147	12W-7S	C5
5200	CTSD	60525	3147	12W-5S	C3
11800	PlsT	60464	3273	12W-15S	D7
11800	PSPK	60464	3273	12W-15S	D7
12700	PSPK	60464	3345	12W-15S	D1
13000	PlsT	60462	3345	11W-15S	D1
13000	PSPK	60462	3345	11W-15S	D1
13400	OrlT	60462	3345	11W-15S	D2
13500	ODPK	60462	3345	12W-16S	D2
15700	ODPK	60462	3423	11W-18S	D1
15800	ODPK	60467	3423	12W-20S	D5
16600	ODHL	60477	3423	11W-19S	D3
16600	OrlT	60467	3423	11W-19S	D3
US-45 Mannheim Rd					
-	CHCG	60176	2917	12W-6N	B6
-	CHCG	60666	2973	12W-5N	A1
-	SRPK	60176	2917	12W-6N	B6
-	SRPK	60176	2973	12W-5N	A1
10	BLWD	60104	3029	12W-0N	A3
10	BLWD	60160	3029	12W-1N	A3
10	MLPK	60160	3029	12W-1N	A3
500	BLWD	60162	3029	12W-0N	A4
500	HLSD	60162	3029	12W-0N	A4
600	DSPN	60016	2863	13W-11N	A4
900	DSPN	60016	2862	13W-10N	E4
1000	DSPN	60018	2862	13W-10N	E5
1700	DSPN	60018	2863	13W-9N	A7
2000	DSPN	60018	2917	13W-8N	A2
2000	RSMT	60018	2917	13W-8N	A2
2400	FNPK	60131	2973	13W-3N	A6
2400	FNPK	60164	2973	13W-3N	A6
2400	LydT	60131	2973	13W-3N	A6
2400	LydT	60164	2973	13W-3N	A6
2900	CHCG	60666	2917	12W-6N	B7
2900	RSMT	60666	2917	12W-8N	A2
4000	FNPK	60176	2973	13W-4N	A4
US-45 N Mannheim Rd					
-	BLWD	60104	3029	13W-1N	A3
-	BLWD	60160	3029	13W-1N	A3
-	HLSD	60104	3029	12W-0S	A6
-	HLSD	60154	3029	12W-0S	A6
-	WSTR	60154	3029	12W-0S	A6
10	BLWD	60162	3029	12W-0S	A6
10	HLSD	60162	3029	12W-0S	A6
1500	MLPK	60160	3029	13W-1N	A3
1500	MLPK	60165	3029	12W-1N	A3
1500	SNPK	60165	3029	13W-1N	A1
2000	LydT	60164	2973	12W-2N	A7
2000	MLPK	60160	2973	12W-2N	A7
2000	NHLK	60164	2973	12W-2N	A7
2300	LydT	60131	2973	13W-2N	A6
US-45 S Mannheim Rd					
-	BLWD	60104	3029	12W-0S	A6
-	HLSD	60154	3029	12W-0S	A6
10	HLSD	60162	3029	13W-0S	A7
10	WSTR	60154	3029	13W-0S	A7
300	PvsT	60162	3029	12W-0S	A7
1300	PvsT	60154	3029	12W-1S	A7
1400	PvsT	60154	3087	12W-1S	A1
1400	PvsT	60162	3087	12W-1S	A1
1400	WSTR	60154	3087	12W-4S	C6
US-45 Milwaukee Av					
900	BFGV	60089	2755	14W-20N	C1
900	VrnT	60015	2755	14W-20N	C1
900	VrnT	60062	2755	14W-20N	C1
900	VrnT	60089	2755	14W-20N	C1
1000	RVWD	60015	2755	14W-20N	C1
20400	BFGV	60089	2755	14W-20N	C1
US-45 N Milwaukee Av					
500	PTHT	60062	2809	13W-15N	A1
500	PTHT	60070	2809	13W-15N	A1
500	PTHT	60090	2809	13W-15N	A1
500	WhlT	60062	2809	13W-15N	A1
500	WhlT	60090	2809	13W-15N	A1
500	WLNG	60090	2755	13W-17N	D5
800	BFGV	60090	2755	14W-20N	C2
900	BFGV	60089	2755	14W-20N	C1
900	VrnT	60062	2755	14W-20N	C1
900	VrnT	60089	2755	14W-20N	C1
US-45 S Milwaukee Av					
10	WLNG	60090	2755	14W-18N	D4
600	WhlT	60090	2755	13W-17N	E5
1100	PTHT	60070	2755	13W-16N	E7
1100	PTHT	60070	2808	13W-16N	E1
1100	PTHT	60070	2809	13W-16N	A1
1100	PTHT	60090	2809	13W-16N	A1
1100	WhlT	60090	2808	13W-16N	E1
1100	WhlT	60090	2809	13W-16N	A1
US-45 N River Rd					
400	WhlT	60056	2808	13W-13N	E6
600	MPPT	60056	2808	13W-13N	E6
600	WhlT	60025	2808	13W-13N	E6
700	DSPN	60016	2808	13W-12N	E7
700	DSPN	60016	2809	13W-12N	A7
700	MaiT	60016	2808	13W-12N	E7
700	MaiT	60016	2809	13W-12N	A7
1300	MPPT	60056	2809	13W-14N	A3
1300	WhlT	60025	2809	13W-14N	A3
1300	WhlT	60062	2809	13W-14N	A3
1500	PTHT	60070	2809	13W-15N	A2
US-45 S River Rd					
10	DSPN	60016	2863	13W-11N	A3
1200	MPPT	60056	2809	13W-15N	A2
1200	PTHT	60070	2809	12W-15N	A2
1200	WhlT	60062	2809	13W-15N	A2
Usufruct Av					
10	CHCG	60616	3092	0W-3S	B4
Utah Cir					
700	EGVV	60007	2913		E1
Utah Ct					
10500	ODPK	60467	3423	13W-21S	A7
Utah St					
700	EGVV	60007	2859	21W-9N	E7
700	EGVV	60007	2913		E1
W Ute Ln					
7200	PSHT	60463	3346	9W-15S	E1
Utica Av					
13600	RBBN	60472	3349	3W-16S	A3
S Utica Av					
-	CHCG	60652	3212	3W-10S	E4
-	ENGN	60652	3212	3W-10S	E4
9600	ENGN	60805	3212	3W-11S	E6
Uvedale Ct					
400	RVSD	60546	3088	9W-2S	C3
Uvedale Rd					
200	RVSD	60546	3088	9W-2S	C4
Uxbridge Dr					
8100	ODPK	60462	3346	10W-16S	C4
V					
Vada Ct					
1800	SMBG	60193	2912		A2
Vail Av					
14300	DXMR	60426	3349	2W-17S	C5
14700	HRVY	60426	3349	2W-17S	C6
N Vail Av					
10	ANHT	60005	2807	17W-14N	A5
1800	ANHT	60004	2807	17W-15N	A1
S Vail Av					
1000	ANHT	60005	2807	18W-12N	A7
1200	ANHT	60005	2861	18W-12N	A1
Vail Ct					
500	WLNG	60090	2754	16W-18N	E3
15100	ODPK	60467	3344	14W-18S	D6
W Vail Dr					
8700	PSHL	60465	3274	10W-12S	A2
Valencia Av					
-	BRTN	60010	2751	25W-20N	A1
E Valencia Av					
400	BRTN	60010	2751	25W-20N	A1
Valencia Ct					
1400	CTCY	60409	3429	2E-19S	D3
Valencia Dr					
2000	NHBK	60062	2810	10W-15N	A1
Valentina Dr					
15100	ODPK	60462	3346	10W-18S	A6
Valerie Ct					
200	MaiT	60025	2864	9W-12N	B1
10800	ODPK	60467	3423	13W-21S	A6
Valerie Dr					
500	BlmT	60411	3510	4E-25S	C7
500	LYWD	60411	3510	4E-25S	C7
Valewood Ct					
10	SMWD	60107	2856	29W-9N	D7
Valewood Dr					
1100	BRLT	60107	2856	29W-9N	D7
1100	HnrT	60107	2856	29W-9N	D7
1100	SMWD	60107	2856	29W-9N	D7
Valewood Rd					
900	BRLT	60103	2910		C6
E Vallette St					
400	BKLY	60163	3028		B4
400	EMHT	60126	3028		B4
Valley					
-	ELGN	60120	2855		C6
S Valley Cir					
600	PLTN	60067	2805	21W-14N	C3
Valley Ct					
8100	PSHL	60465	3274	10W-12S	C3
10600	ODPK	60462	3345	13W-17S	A6
N Valley Ct					
300	BRTN	60010	2751	24W-20N	C1
Valley Dr					
10	BNHL	60010	2749	28W-18N	D4
600	LMNT	60439	3270		C6
8000	PSHL	60465	3274	10W-12S	C3
17100	ODPK	60462	3424	10W-20S	B4
17100	ODPK	60477	3424	10W-20S	B4
17100	TYPK	60477	3424	10W-20S	B4
22700	RNPK	60471	3594	6W-27S	A5
Valley Ln					
-	HFET	60195	2858	24W-11N	E2
-	SMBG	60195	2858	24W-11N	E3
700	BmdT	60143	2913		D5
1000	HFET	60194	2858	24W-11N	E3
5000	SMWD	60107	2911		A2
E Valley Ln					
-	SMWD	60107	2911		A1
200	ANHT	60004	2754	17W-16N	B7
S Valley Ln					
800	PLTN	60067	2805	21W-14N	C3
W Valley Ln					
600	PLTN	60067	2805	21W-14N	C3
Valley Rd					
10	BmdT	60172	2912		E5
10	HDPK	60035	2758	7W-20N	B2
10	NtrT	60062	2758	7W-20N	B2
100	ROSL	60172	2912		E5
800	GLNC	60022	2758	7W-17N	C4
2100	NHBK	60062	2756	11W-16N	C7
N Valley Rd					
100	BRTN	60010	2751	24W-20N	C1
S Valley Rd					
100	BRTN	60010	2751	24W-18N	C2
W Valley Rd					
400	ITSC	60143	2914		B7
Valley St					
100	BRLT	60103	2910		E3
Valley Brook Dr					
11500	ODPK	60467	3422	14W-20S	D5
Valley Forge Dr					
17300	TYPK	60477	3424	10W-20S	C5
Valley Lake Dr					
1000	IVNS	60067	2805	22W-14N	A4
1200	SMBG	60173	2859	23W-12N	A1
1200	SMBG	60195	2858	23W-12N	E2
1200	SMBG	60195	2859	23W-12N	A1
1400	PLTN	60067	2805	22W-14N	A4
Valley Lo Ln					
2100	GNVW	60025	2810	8W-14N	E3
Valley Stream Dr					
800	WLNG	60090	2755	15W-18N	A3
900	WLNG	60090	2754	16W-18N	E3
Valley View Ct					
10	LMNT	60439	3342	20W-15S	A2
200	WLMT	60091	2811	5W-13N	E7
8100	TYPK	60477	3424	10W-20S	C5
14500	OrlT	60467	3344	14W-17S	D5
Valley View Dr					
10	DPgT	60441	3342	20W-15S	A2
10	LMNT	60439	3342	20W-15S	A2
200	WLMT	60091	2811	5W-13N	E7
700	SMBG	60193	2912		B2
1600	SmbT	60193	2912		B2
8000	TYPK	60477	3424	10W-20S	C5
Valleyview Dr					
14400	OrlT	60467	3344	14W-17S	D5
E Valleyview Dr					
400	BRLT	60103	2911		C5
Valley View Ln					
2300	CteT	60417	3684	2W-29S	C1
2300	MonT	60466	3684	2W-29S	C1
Valleyview Ln					
100	DYR	46311	3598		C5
100	SjnT	46311	3598		D5
Valley View Rd					
1900	NHFD	60093	2758	7W-16N	A7
6600	HRPK	60133	2911		D3
Valleywood Dr					
100	CteT	60417	3596	1W-28S	A7
100	STGR	60417	3596	1W-28S	A7
Valley Wy Dr					
400	NHBK	60062	2758	8W-16N	A7
400	NHBK	60093	2758	8W-16N	A7
400	NHFD	60093	2758	8W-16N	A7
500	NHFD	60093	2757	8W-16N	E7
Valor Ct					
2000	GNVW	60025	2810	9W-14N	B3
S Valor Ct					
300	PLTN	60074	2806	19W-15N	D2
Valor Dr					
2600	GNVW	60025	2810	9W-14N	B4
Valparaiso Dr					
9600	MNSR	46321	3510		E3
Vals Ct					
10	LYWD	60411	3598	4E-25S	C1
Vana Dr					
100	WLSP	60480	3209	12W-9S	D3
N Van Auken St					
400	EMHT	60126	2972		A6
800	AddT	60126	2972		A6
S Van Beverin Dr					
12000	ALSP	60803	3276	5W-14S	C5
Van Buren Av					
900	DYR	46311	3510		D6
1200	DSPN	60018	2862	13W-10N	E5
1200	DSPN	60018	2863	13W-10N	A5
6100	HMND	46324	3430		D2
8100	MNSR	46321	3430		D6
Van Buren Ct					
8400	MNSR	46321	3430		D7
Van Buren St					
-	HLSD	60162	3028		C6
-	MYWD	60104	3029	11W-0S	D6
-	MYWD	60153	3030	10W-0S	A6
10	CHCG	60644	3031	7W-0S	B5
10	OKPK	60304	3031	8W-0S	A5
300	EGvT	60018	2862	15W-9N	A7
800	OKPK	60304	3030	8W-0S	E5
1000	DSPN	60018	2862	13W-10N	E5
1000	MYWD	60153	3029	11W-0S	C6
2500	BLWD	60104	3029	12W-0S	C6
3800	HLSD	60162	3029	12W-0S	A6
7600	FTPK	60130	3030	9W-0S	C5
7700	RVFT	60305	3030	9W-0S	C5
14400	DLTN	60419	3351	0E-16S	A4
E Van Buren St					
10	CHCG	60604	3034	0E-0S	C5
10	CHCG	60605	3034	0E-0S	C5
100	EMHT	60126	3028		A6
N Van Buren St					
10	EDND	60118	2801		A2
500	CPVL	60118	2801		A1
S Van Buren St					
10	EDND	60118	2801		A2
W Van Buren St					
10	CHCG	60604	3034	0W-0S	B5
10	CHCG	60605	3034	0W-0S	B5
100	CHCG	60606	3034	0W-0S	B5
100	CHCG	60607	3034	0W-0S	A5
400	CHCG	60661	3034	0W-0S	A5
800	CHCG	60607	3033	1W-0S	E5
1500	CHCG	60612	3033	2W-0S	B5
2800	CHCG	60612	3032	3W-0S	E5
3500	CHCG	60624	3032	4W-0S	D5
4600	CHCG	60644	3032	5W-0S	A5
4700	CHCG	60644	3031	6W-0S	E5
Van Dam Rd					
-	CTCY	60409	3429	1E-19S	C1
15900	SHLD	60473	3429	1E-19S	B1
Vandenburgh Dr					
-	SBTN	60010	2803	26W-13N	C6
S Vanderpoel Av					
9200	CHCG	60620	3213	2W-10S	D5
9500	CHCG	60643	3213	2W-11S	D6
Vanderwalker Ln					
400	BlmT	60430	3507	1W-23S	E3
400	CHHT	60411	3507	1W-23S	E3
E Vandrunen Dr					
2500	CteT	60417	3686	3E-31S	E5
2500	CteT	60417	3687	3E-31S	A5
Van Drunen Rd					
15600	PHNX	60426	3350	0W-18S	C7
15600	PHNX	60473	3350	0W-18S	C7
15600	SHLD	60426	3350	0W-18S	C7
15600	SHLD	60473	3350	0W-18S	C7
15600	SHLD	60473	3428	0W-18S	C1
Vandustrial Ln					
16000	HRVY	60426	3428	0W-18S	B1
16000	SHLD	60473	3428	0W-18S	B1
Van Gough Dr					
300	PTON	60468	3860	9W-37S	E3
Vankalker Dr					
2000	CteT	60417	3686	2E-31S	D6
Vanna Ct					
300	HLSD	60162	3028		E5
Van Nostrand Pl					
600	ELGN	60120	2855		B5
Van Selow Dr					
-	DSPN	60018	2917	11W-7N	D3
Vantage Ln					
-	GNVW	60025	2810	10W-15N	A3
3600	GNVW	60025	2809	10W-15N	E3
S Van Vlissingen Rd					
9600	CHCG	60617	3215	2E-11S	C7
N Vapor Ln					
6400	MNGV	60053	2865	8W-9N	A6
6400	MNGV	60714	2865	8W-9N	A6
6400	NLES	60714	2865	8W-9N	A6
Vardon					
-	CRTE	60417	3596	0E-29S	E7
-	CRTE	60417	3685	0E-29S	E1
-	CteT	60417	3685	0E-29S	E1
Vardon Ln					
2000	FSMR	60422	3507	2W-22S	C2
2000	FSMR	60430	3507	2W-22S	C2
2000	HMWD	60430	3507	2W-22S	C2
Vardon Pl					
2400	FSMR	60422	3507	3W-22S	C2
E Vargo Ln					
1000	ANHT	60004	2754	17W-16N	C7
Varsity Dr					
600	ELGN	60120	2855		C6
Vassar Ct					
1700	SMBG	60193	2912		B1
Vassar Ln					
400	DSPN	60016	2862	14W-12N	C1
500	DSPN	60016	2808	14W-12N	C7
800	SMBG	60193	2912		B1
Vaysee Ct					
15200	HMGN	60441	3342	19W-16S	E3
S Venetian Ct					
13700	HMGN	60467	3344	15W-16S	C3
W Venetian Wy					
10	HMGN	60467	3344	15W-16S	C3
10	OrlT	60467	3344	15W-16S	C3
Veneto					
-	BMDL	60172	2912		C7
-	BmdT	60172	2912		C7
Venice Ct					
-	NfdT	60025	2809	11W-13N	D6
Venice Ct					
600	SMBG	60193	2858	24W-9N	E7
Venice Ln					
10400	ODPK	60467	3423	13W-21S	B6
10400	OrlT	60467	3423	13W-21S	B6
N Ventura Dr					
900	PLTN	60074	2753	20W-17N	A5
3700	ANHT	60004	2753	18W-18N	D3
Ventura St					
15200	OKFT	60452	3347	7W-18S	C6
Ventura Club Dr					
300	ROSL	60172	2913		B4
Vera Ct					
15900	OKFT	60452	3425	6W-19S	D1
Vera Ln					
-	EGvT	60007	2861	16W-9N	D7
-	EGVV	60007	2861	16W-9N	D7
800	WLNG	60090	2754	15W-17N	E5
800	WLNG	60090	2755	15W-17N	A5
1100	WLNG	60004	2754	15W-17N	E5
E Vera Ln					
2600	CteT	60417	3687	3E-29S	A2
Verbena Dr					
9100	MNSR	46321	3510		E2
N Verde Av					
1700	ANHT	60004	2806	18W-15N	E1
S Verde Ct					
1700	MPPT	60056	2861	17W-12N	C1
Verde Dr					
200	SMBG	60173	2859	22W-10N	D4
N Verde Dr					
1900	ANHT	60004	2806	18W-16N	D1
2000	ANHT	60004	2753	18W-16N	E7
S Verde Dr					
1700	MPPT	60056	2861	17W-12N	C1
W Verde Dr					
1700	MPPT	60056	2861	17W-12N	C1
Verde Ln					
400	EGVV	60007	2915		A1
E Vermillion Ln					
1600	PLTN	60074	2753	19W-18N	C3
Vermont Av					
-	NHBK	60062	2757	8W-18N	E2
W Vermont Av					
600	CHCG	60628	3278	0W-15S	A7
700	CHCG	60643	3278	0W-15S	A7
1000	CTPK	60643	3278	1W-15S	A7
1000	CTPK	60827	3277	1W-15S	E7
1000	CTPK	60827	3278	1W-15S	A7
1500	BLID	60406	3277	1W-15S	D7
1500	CTPK	60406	3277	1W-15S	D7
Vermont Ct					
1700	RGMW	60008	2806	20W-14N	A3
18100	ODPK	60467	3423	13W-21S	B7
Vermont Dr					
300	EGVV	60007	2859	22W-9N	D7
1600	SmbT	60193	2859	22W-9N	D7
Vermont Pl					
1800	BLID	60406	3349	2W-15S	C1
Vermont St					
1400	PLTN	60067	2806	20W-14N	A3
1400	RGMW	60008	2806	20W-14N	A3
1700	BLID	60406	3277	2W-15S	D7
1700	CTPK	60406	3277	2W-15S	D7
1700	CTPK	60827	3277	2W-15S	D7
1800	BLID	60406	3349	3W-15S	A1
2000	RGMW	60008	2805	20W-14N	E4
2600	WthT	60406	3349	3W-15S	A1
S Vermont St					
400	PLTN	60067	2805	20W-15N	E2
1100	RGMW	60067	2805	21W-14N	D4
1300	PLTN	60008	2805	21W-14N	D4
1300	RGMW	60008	2805	21W-14N	D4
Verne Cir					
10	BRTN	60010	2751	25W-20N	B2
Verne Ln					
800	FSMR	60422	3507	3W-22S	B2
Vernon Av					
200	GLNC	60022	2758	6W-17N	D4
200	WNKA	60022	2758	6W-16N	D7
200	WNKA	60093	2758	6W-16N	D7
1400	PKRG	60068	2863	11W-10N	E4
2900	BKFD	60513	3087	11W-3S	E5
4600	BKFD	60513	3147	11W-4S	E1
4600	MCCK	60525	3147	11W-4S	E1
S Vernon Av					
2800	CHCG	60616	3092	0E-2S	D3
3500	CHCG	60653	3092	0E-3S	D5
6000	CHCG	60637	3152	0E-7S	D5
7000	CHCG	60619	3152	0E-8S	D7
7500	CHCG	60619	3214	0E-8S	D1
10000	CHCG	60628	3214	0E-11S	D7
10300	CHCG	60628	3278	0E-13S	D3
13100	CHCG	60827	3278	0E-15S	D7
13100	CHCG	60827	3350	0E-15S	D1
Vernon Cir					
1900	EGVV	60007	2913		C1
Vernon Ct N					
600	BFGV	60089	2754	17W-18N	B3
Vernon Ct S					
700	BFGV	60089	2754	17W-18N	B4
Vernon Dr					
1000	GNVW	60025	2810	8W-13N	E6
Vernon Ln					
-	ANHT	60004	2754	17W-18N	B4
500	BFGV	60089	2754	17W-18N	B3
Vernon St					
-	BKFD	60513	3147	11W-5S	E2
-	MCCK	60525	3147	11W-5S	E2
2200	BLID	60406	3277	2W-14S	B6
S Vernon St					
3300	CHCG	60616	3092	0E-3S	D4
W Vernon Park Pl					
-	CHCG	60607	3034		D6
1000	CHCG	60607	3033	1W-0S	E6
Verona Ct					
600	SMBG	60193	2858	24W-9N	E7
Veronica Cir					
-	BRLT	60103	2909		D2
Versailles Cir					
600	EGVV	60007	2914		C1
Versailles Ct					
10	WLNG	60090	2808	14W-15N	C2
600	IVNS	60010	2751	24W-17N	B5
Versailles Dr					
300	NHBK	60062	2756	12W-18N	C3
Versailles Ln					
500	BRLT	60103	2909		E1
500	BRLT	60103	2910		A1
500	BRLT	60120	2909		E1
18000	HLCT	60429	3426	4W-21S	E6
18000	HLCT	60429	3427	4W-21S	A7
Versailles Rd					
3700	HFET	60195	2804	24W-14N	B3

STREET Block	City	ZIP	Map#	CGS	Grid
Veterans Dr					
-	NRIV	60546	3088	9W-2S	D3
-	RVSD	60546	3088	9W-2S	D3
W Veterans Dr					
2400	POSN	60469	3349	3W-17S	B5
Vial Pkwy					
5700	LynT	60525	3146		E4
E Viator Ct					
1000	ANHT	60004	2807	17W-15N	B3
Vicki Ln					
2400	NHBK	60062	2809	11W-15N	D1
Vicky Ln					
16700	ODHL	60477	3424	11W-20S	A3
S Vicky Ln					
10400	PSHL	60465	3274	9W-12S	C2
Victor Av					
1200	ELGN	60120	2801		C7
2300	MaiT	60025	2864	9W-12N	B1
Victor Ln					
8600	MaiT	60016	2863	10W-11N	E3
8600	MaiT	60016	2864	10W-11N	A3
Victoria Av					
1000	BKLY	60163	3028		C3
S Victoria Av					
3700	HMND	46327	3352		C2
Victoria Cir					
900	BlmT	60411	3510	4E-25S	C7
900	BlmT	60411	3598	4E-25S	C1
900	LYWD	60411	3510	4E-25S	C7
900	LYWD	60411	3598	4E-25S	C1
Victoria Ct					
6100	MTSN	60443	3593	7W-25S	C1
6100	OKFT	60452	3347	7W-18S	C7
12000	HMGN	60441	3344	15W-17S	C5
Victoria Dr					
3800	RNPK	60471	3594	4W-27S	D4
4000	HFET	60195	2804	24W-15N	C3
5600	OKFT	60452	3347	7W-18S	C7
6600	BmnT	60452	3347	8W-18S	A7
E Victoria Dr					
300	NHLK	60164	3028		E1
300	NHLK	60164	3029	13W-1N	A1
N Victoria Dr					
700	PLTN	60074	2753	19W-16N	D6
4000	HFET	60195	2804	24W-15N	C2
W Victoria Dr					
-	EGvT	60056	2861	17W-10N	C5
1700	MPPT	60056	2861	17W-10N	C5
Victoria Ln					
200	EGVV	60007	2914		E1
600	SMBG	60193	2858	24W-10N	D6
800	EGVV	60007	2915		A2
N Victoria Ln					
10	SMWD	60107	2857	28W-11N	B5
S Victoria Ln					
10	SMWD	60107	2857	28W-10N	B5
26100	CteT	60417	3687	3E-31S	A6
W Victoria Ln					
200	ANHT	60005	2861	18W-12N	A2
500	ANHT	60005	2860	18W-12N	E2
Victoria Pl					
10700	ODPK	60467	3423	13W-20S	A3
Victoria Rd					
600	DSPN	60016	2862	15W-11N	B4
Victoria St					
200	BRTN	60010	2751	25W-20N	A1
W Victoria St					
1400	CHCG	60660	2921	1W-7N	C4
4000	CHCG	60646	2920	5W-7N	B4
4000	CHCG	60659	2920	5W-7N	B4
7700	CHCG	60068	2918	9W-7N	B4
7700	CHCG	60631	2918	9W-7N	B4
7700	PKRG	60068	2918	9W-7N	B4
7700	PKRG	60631	2918	9W-7N	B4
Victory Dr					
300	PKFT	60466	3595	3W-27S	B4
Victory Ln					
800	LynT	60458	3209	11W-8S	E1
Victory Pkwy					
400	AddT	60126	2972		A5
600	EMHT	60126	2972		A5
E Victory Pkwy					
100	AddT	60126	2972		A5
100	EMHT	60126	2972		A5
S Vienna Av					
11500	PSPK	60464	3274	10W-13S	C4
View St					
500	WDND	60118	2801		A3
Villa Ct					
11500	ALSP	60803	3276	5W-13S	B4
14000	ODPK	60462	3346	10W-16S	B3
E Villa Dr					
900	DSPN	60016	2862	13W-10N	D4
W Villa Dr					
900	DSPN	60016	2862	14W-10N	D4
Villa Pl					
200	ELGN	60120	2855		A4
Villa Rd					
100	SMWD	60107	2857	28W-10N	B5
Villa St					
700	ELGN	60120	2855		B5
Villa St US-20					
-	ELGN	-	2855		E6
Villa St US-20 BUS					
700	ELGN	60120	2855		B5
E Villa St					
1500	ELGN	60120	2855		E7
1500	ELGN	60120	2856	31W-10N	A7
E Villa St US-20					
1500	ELGN	60120	2855		E7
1500	ELGN	60120	2856	31W-10N	A7
Villa Cir Dr					
100	RGMW	60173	2805	21W-13N	C5
100	SMBG	60173	2805	21W-13N	C5
Village Coms					
4900	MTSN	60443	3506	6W-24S	A6
5000	MTSN	60443	3505	6W-24S	E6
Village Ct					
10	ELGN	60120	2855		C3
100	DSPN	60016	2862	14W-12N	C1
600	GLNC	60022	2758	6W-17N	C5
13200	CTWD	60445	3347	6W-15S	E1
N Village Ct					
200	PLTN	60067	2752	21W-16N	E7
W Village Ct					
800	CHCG	60608	3034		E7
900	CHCG	60608	3033	1W-1S	E7
Village Dr					
10	NHLK	60164	2972		E7
200	MPPT	60056	2862	15W-12N	A1
300	NHLK	60164	2973	13W-2N	A7
1200	LMNT	60439	3271		B4
1400	ANHT	60004	2806	18W-15N	E2
3700	HLCT	60429	3506	4W-22S	D1
E Village Dr					
-	NHLK	60164	2972		D7
Village Ln					
13100	CTWD	60445	3347	6W-15S	E1
Village Pl					
10	HNDL	60521	3146		B2
Village Cir Dr					
-	PlsT	60464	3345	12W-15S	B1
Village Grove Dr					
1000	EGVV	60007	2914		D2
Village In the Lk					
-	EGVV	60007	2914		C1
Village Square Ln					
4500	BKFD	60513	3147	11W-5S	E1
Village West Dr					
3500	HLCT	60429	3506	4W-22S	E1
18300	HLCT	60429	3426	4W-22S	E7
Village Woods Dr					
10	CteT	60417	3774	0W-32S	C1
Villa Verde Rd					
10	ANHT	60004	2753	18W-17N	E4
10	ANHT	60004	2754	18W-17N	A4
10	ANHT	60089	2753	18W-17N	E4
10	BFGV	60089	2753	18W-17N	E4
10	BFGV	60089	2754	18W-17N	A4
Vinan Dr					
2900	LydT	60164	2972		E5
Vincennes Av					
1200	CHHT	60411	3508	1W-25S	A7
1500	CHHT	60411	3596	1W-25S	B1
S Vincennes Av					
3500	CHCG	60653	3092	0E-4S	D7
4600	CHCG	60615	3092	0E-4S	D7
4700	CHCG	60615	3152	0E-5S	D1
7000	CHCG	60621	3152	0W-8S	B7
7500	CHCG	60620	3214	0W-9S	A3
7500	CHCG	60621	3214	0W-8S	B1
9100	CHCG	60620	3213	1W-11S	E6
9400	CHCG	60643	3213	1W-11S	E7
10300	CHCG	60643	3277	2W-13S	D3
11800	BLID	60406	3277	2W-13S	C5
Vincennes Rd					
-	PHNX	60426	3350	0W-17S	B6
-	PHNX	60426	3428	0W-18S	B1
-	PHNX	60473	3428	0W-18S	B1
300	SHLD	60476	3428	0E-20S	D4
300	TNTN	60473	3428	0E-20S	D4
300	TNTN	60476	3428	0E-20S	D4
11900	BLID	60406	3277	2W-14S	C6
11900	CHCG	60643	3277	2W-14S	C6
14400	HRVY	60426	3349	1W-17S	E4
14400	HRVY	60426	3350	1W-17S	A5
14400	ThtT	60426	3349	1W-17S	E4
15500	SHLD	60473	3350	0W-18S	B7
15700	HRVY	60426	3428	0W-18S	B1
15700	HRVY	60473	3428	0W-18S	B1
15700	SHLD	60426	3428	0W-18S	B1
15700	SHLD	60473	3428	0W-19S	C1
18300	BlmT	60425	3428	0W-22S	D7
18300	BlmT	60476	3428	0W-22S	D7
18300	TNTN	60425	3428	0W-22S	D7
18400	BlmT	60425	3508	0W-22S	C1
Vincennes Rd SR-1					
-	PHNX	60426	3350	1W-18S	B7
14900	HRVY	60426	3350	1W-17S	A6
Vincennes St					
1300	CRTE	60417	3685	1W-30S	B3
Vine Av					
1600	PKRG	60068	2918	10W-7N	B4
1900	CHCG	60631	2918	10W-7N	B4
1900	PKRG	60631	2918	10W-7N	B4
14400	HRVY	60426	3349	1W-17S	E5
15600	HRVY	60426	3427	1W-18S	E1
16000	MKHM	60426	3427	1W-19S	E2
N Vine Av					
-	MaiT	60631	2918	10W-6N	B5
4800	NRDG	60706	2918	10W-6N	B7
5400	CHCG	60631	2918	10W-6N	B5
5400	CHCG	60656	2918	10W-6N	B5
5400	LydT	60631	2918	10W-6N	B5
5600	LydT	60656	2918	10W-7N	B5
5600	MaiT	60656	2918	10W-7N	B5
Vine Ct					
300	WLMT	60091	2812	5W-13N	B6
400	HMND	46324	3430		D2
Vine Ln					
-	EGVV	60193	2913		D1
600	EGVV	60007	2913		D1
Vine St					
10	CTCY	60409	3430		C2
300	BRRG	60527	3208		A1
300	DGvT	60527	3208		A1
300	WLMT	60091	2812	5W-13N	A7
400	HMND	46324	3430		D2
900	SMWD	60107	2857	28W-9N	B7
900	WNKA	60093	2759	5W-16N	A7
5200	OKFT	60452	3347	6W-17S	D6
6900	IHPK	60525	3146		E7
7600	FTPK	60130	3030	9W-0N	C5
7600	RVFT	60305	3030	9W-0N	C5
13400	BLID	60406	3349	3W-15S	A2
N Vine St					
10	HNDL	60521	3146		A1
400	HNDL	60521	3086		A7
1600	CHCG	60610	2978	0W-2N	A7
1600	CHCG	60614	2978	0W-2N	A7
S Vine St					
200	BRRG	60527	3208		A5
200	DGvT	60527	3208		A5
700	HNDL	60521	3146		A3
7100	BRRG	60527	3146		A7
7100	DGvT	60527	3146		A7
W Vine St					
10	ANHT	60004	2807	18W-14N	A3
600	ANHT	60004	2806	18W-14N	E4
1200	ANHT	60005	2806	18W-14N	D4
Vinewood Av					
700	WLSP	60480	3209	12W-9S	D3
Vintage Ct					
14300	ODPK	60462	3346	11W-17S	A4
Vintage Ln					
200	BFGV	60089	2754	17W-20N	C1
Viola Ct					
100	RGMW	60008	2805	21W-14N	D4
700	SMBG	60194	2858	26W-11N	A4
Viola Ln					
200	PTHT	60070	2807	15W-15N	E1
Violet Ct					
15600	ODPK	60462	3346	9W-18S	E7
Violet Dr					
-	BmdT	60172	2912		A6
-	HRPK	60133	2912		A6
Violet Ln					
3100	NHBK	60062	2756	11W-16N	D7
3400	SjnT	46311	3598		D5
Violet Ln					
4000	MTSN	60443	3506	5W-25S	C6
S Violet Ln					
25600	MONE	60449	3683	5W-31S	B4
Violet Rd					
18300	LNSG	60438	3429	2E-21S	E7
Violet St					
2400	GNVW	60025	2810	9W-15N	C3
Virgil Av					
600	ELGN	60120	2855		C6
Virgina Ln					
6200	MTSN	60443	3505	7W-24S	C5
Virginia Av					
10	BMDL	60108	2912		B7
10	BMDL	60172	2912		B7
10	BmdT	60172	2912		B7
500	BlmT	60411	3510	4E-25S	B7
500	LYWD	60411	3510	4E-25S	B7
6800	CHRG	60415	3210	8W-11S	E7
6800	CHRG	60415	3211	8W-11S	A7
9900	CHRG	60415	3275	8W-11S	A1
N Virginia Av					
200	GNWD	60425	3508	1W-22S	B1
500	GNWD	60425	3428	1W-22S	B7
4500	CHCG	60625	2921	3W-5N	A7
5200	CHCG	60625	2920	3W-6N	E5
5500	CHCG	60659	2920	3W-6N	E5
Virginia Ct					
100	SMWD	60107	2856	30W-10N	B6
100	SMWD	60107	2910		E1
1100	BRLT	60103	2910		E7
7200	FKFT	60423	3593	9W-25S	A1
9200	ODPK	60462	3345	11W-16S	E3
Virginia Dr					
1600	EGVV	60007	2913		D3
E Virginia Dr					
1300	PLTN	60074	2753	19W-16N	C7
Virginia Ln					
-	GNVW	60025	2810	10W-12N	B7
500	AddT	60126	2972		A5
500	EMHT	60126	2972		A5
1100	NtrT	60093	2811	5W-14N	E5
1100	WLMT	60091	2811	5W-14N	E5
1100	WLMT	60093	2811	5W-14N	E5
2500	NHBK	60062	2810	10W-15N	A2
18000	HMGN	60448	3422	16W-21S	A7
18300	NlxT	60448	3422	16W-22S	A7
N Virginia Ln					
900	AddT	60126	2972		A5
900	EMHT	60126	2972		A5
Virginia Pkwy					
-	SMBG	60193	2859	23W-10N	A6
Virginia Pl					
300	WLNG	60090	2755	13W-17N	D5
2700	HMWD	60430	3427	3W-21S	B6
Virginia Rd					
400	BmdT	60172	2912		B6
400	ROSL	60172	2912		B6
Virginia St					
300	BNVL	60106	2972		A2
1000	CTCY	60409	3351	3E-18S	E7
1000	CTCY	60409	3352	3E-18S	A7
2300	PKRG	60068	2863	11W-9N	D6
N Virginia Lake Ct					
800	PLTN	60074	2753	19W-17N	C6
N Virn Allen Ct					
700	PLTN	60067	2752	21W-16N	C6
Vista Ct					
200	WLMT	60091	2812	5W-13N	A7
1800	SMBG	60193	2912		A2
2200	NHBK	60062	2810	10W-15N	A1
Vista Dr					
-	BRRG	60527	3208		E2
-	WLSP	60527	3208		E2
200	WLMT	60091	2812	5W-13N	A7
8200	ODPK	60462	3346	10W-16S	C3
15500	OKFT	60452	3347	7W-18S	C7
17800	CCHL	60478	3426	6W-21S	A6
N Vista Dr					
900	ALGN	60102	2748		A1
S Vista Dr					
900	ALGN	60102	2748		A2
Vista Ln					
400	EDND	60118	2801		C2
500	EDND	60110	2801		C2
1400	CRTE	60417	3685	0W-30S	C2
1700	HFET	60194	2858	25W-12N	B2
N Vista Rd					
2700	ANHT	60004	2754	17W-17N	B6
Vista Wk					
1400	HFET	60194	2858	25W-12N	B2
Vita Dr					
400	WLNG	60090	2755	14W-17N	D5
Vivian Ct					
18000	ODPK	60467	3423	13W-21S	A6
Vivian Tr					
-	ELGN	60120	2855		C5
Vivienne Dr					
-	MTSN	60443	3505	7W-25S	C7
21200	MTSN	60443	3593	7W-25S	C1
Viviparous Wy					
7500	HDHT	60706	2918	9W-5N	C7
7500	NRDG	60706	2918	9W-5N	C7
Vogay Ln					
2800	NfdT	60062	2809	12W-15N	B2
2800	PTHT	60062	2809	12W-15N	B2
Vogt St					
6500	TYPK	60477	3425	8W-20S	B4
Volbrecht Ct					
1600	SHLD	60473	3429	2E-20S	C4
Volbrecht Rd					
17500	LNSG	60438	3429	1E-20S	C5
17500	ThtT	60438	3429	1E-20S	C5
S Volbrecht Rd					
23100	CteT	60417	3597	1E-28S	C6
23100	SLVL	60411	3597	2E-27S	C5
24000	CteT	60417	3686	1E-29S	C1
Volid Dr					
1400	HFET	60194	2858	25W-12N	B2
1400	HFET	60195	2858	25W-12N	B2
Volkamer Tr					
1300	EGVV	60007	2913		E3
Vollbrecht Dr					
1600	SHLD	60473	3429	2E-20S	C4
Vollbrecht Rd					
17000	SHLD	60473	3429	1E-20S	C4
17200	ThtT	60473	3429	1E-20S	C4
Vollmer Rd					
-	BlmT	60411	3508	0W-24S	B4
-	BlmT	60411	3509	1E-23S	B4
-	CHHT	60411	3508	1W-23S	A4
-	LYWD	60411	3509	1E-23S	B4
1400	CHHT	60411	3507	1W-24S	E4
1500	CHHT	60422	3507	1W-23S	E4
1500	FSMR	60422	3507	2W-23S	C4
Vollmer Rd					
1800	BlmT	60411	3507	2W-23S	D4
1800	BlmT	60422	3507	2W-23S	D4
2000	OMFD	60422	3507	2W-23S	D4
2000	OMFD	60461	3507	2W-23S	D4
2400	FSMR	60461	3507	2W-23S	C4
2400	RchT	60461	3507	2W-23S	C4
3200	FSMR	60422	3506	4W-23S	E4
3200	OMFD	60461	3506	4W-23S	E4
3400	FSMR	60461	3506	4W-23S	E4
3800	MTSN	60443	3506	6W-23S	A4
3800	RchT	60443	3506	4W-23S	D4
4700	MTSN	60477	3506	6W-23S	A4
4700	RchT	60477	3506	6W-23S	A4
5000	MTSN	60443	3505	6W-23S	E4
5000	RchT	60443	3505	6W-23S	E4
5000	RchT	60477	3505	6W-23S	E4
6100	MTSN	60477	3505	6W-23S	E4
6300	TYPK	60477	3505	6W-23S	E4
W Vollmer Rd					
6400	MTSN	60443	3505	8W-23S	B4
6400	MTSN	60477	3505	8W-23S	B4
6400	RchT	60477	3505	8W-23S	B4
6400	TYPK	60477	3505	8W-23S	B4
6700	MTSN	60423	3505	8W-23S	B4
6700	RchT	60423	3505	8W-23S	B4
6800	FftT	60423	3505	8W-23S	A4
6800	RchT	60443	3505	8W-23S	A4
Voltz Ct					
1600	NHBK	60062	2757	9W-16N	D6
Voltz Rd					
200	NHBK	60062	2758	7W-17N	A6
500	NHBK	60062	2757	9W-16N	C6
1100	NfdT	60062	2757	9W-17N	D6
N Volz Dr E					
3200	ANHT	60004	2754	17W-17N	C4
N Volz Dr W					
3100	ANHT	60004	2754	17W-17N	B5
Von Av					
5600	MONE	60449	3682	7W-31S	E4
Von Braun Tr					
1500	EGVV	60007	2914		A3
1600	EGVV	60007	2913		E3
Voss Dr					
10700	ODPK	60467	3423	13W-21S	A6
Voyager Dr					
700	BRLT	60103	2911		B4
Vrin Ct					
10	LYWD	60411	3598	4E-25S	B1
Vulcan Blvd					
-	BRLT	60103	2909		D1
-	ELGN	60120	2909		D1
W					
Waban Ct					
10	SMBG	60193	2858	25W-10N	A6
Waban Ln					
1800	SMBG	60193	2858	25W-10N	A6
W Wabansia Av					
1300	CHCG	60622	2977	1W-2N	D7
2400	CHCG	60647	2977	3W-2N	A7
2800	CHCG	60647	2976	5W-2N	B7
4700	CHCG	60639	2976	5W-2N	A7
4800	CHCG	60639	2975	8W-2N	A7
6300	CHCG	60707	2975	8W-2N	A7
6700	CHCG	60707	2974	8W-2N	E7
7100	EDPK	60707	2974	9W-2N	C7
Wabash Av					
5100	OKLN	60453	3211	6W-11S	E6
14600	DLTN	60419	3350	0W-17S	C5
14600	RVDL	60827	3350	0W-17S	C5
15000	SHLD	60419	3350	0E-17S	D6
15000	SHLD	60473	3350	0E-17S	D6
15900	SHLD	60473	3428	0E-18S	D1
N Wabash Av					
10	CHCG	60602	3034		D5
10	CHCG	60603	3034		D5
10	GNWD	60425	3508	0E-22S	D1
100	CHCG	60601	3034	0E-0N	C4
300	CHCG	60611	3034	0E-0N	C3
S Wabash Av					
-	CHCG	60628	3214	0E-11S	C6
10	CHCG	60602	3034	0E-0N	C4
10	CHCG	60603	3034	0E-0S	C4
10	GNWD	60425	3508	0E-22S	D2
100	CHCG	60604	3034	0E-0S	C5
300	CHCG	60605	3034	0E-1S	C7
1400	CHCG	60616	3034	0E-1S	C7
1600	CHCG	60616	3092	0E-2S	C2
3600	CHCG	60653	3092	0E-4S	C7
3900	HMND	46327	3352		D3
4600	CHCG	60615	3092	0E-4S	C7
4700	CHCG	60615	3152	0E-5S	C2
5400	CHCG	60637	3152	0E-6S	C4
7000	CHCG	60619	3152	0E-7S	C6
7500	CHCG	60619	3214	0E-9S	C2
10300	CHCG	60628	3278	0E-12S	C1
13700	RVDL	60827	3350	0W-15S	C2
14500	DLTN	60419	3350	0W-16S	C4
Wabash Ct					
15600	SHLD	60473	3350	0E-18S	D7
Wabash St					
9800	SjnT	46311	3687		D2
Wachter Ln					
9000	HYHL	60457	3209	11W-10S	E5
E Wacker Dr					
200	CHCG	60601	3034	0E-0N	C4
N Wacker Dr					
10	CHCG	60606	3034	0W-0N	B4
S Wacker Dr					
-	CHCG	60607	3034	0W-0S	B5
10	CHCG	60606	3034	0W-0S	B5
W Wacker Dr					
100	CHCG	60601	3034	0W-0N	B4
100	CHCG	60606	3034	0W-0N	B4
E Wacker Pl					
10	CHCG	60601	3034	0E-0N	C4
E Wacker Dr Dr					
-	CHCG	60601	3034	0E-0N	C4
Waco Ln					
500	CPVL	60110	2748		B6
Wade St					
2400	EVTN	60201	2866	3W-11N	D2
Wadsworth Rd					
8400	WLSP	60480	3208		E4
Wagman St					
4100	OKFT	60452	3426	5W-19S	B2
Wagner Av					
4000	SRPK	60176	2973	12W-5N	C2
Wagner Dr					
10	NHLK	60164	2972		D6
W Wagner Dr					
6800	MonT	60449	3682	8W-30S	B3
Wagner Rd					
10	NHFD	60093	2811	7W-14N	B5
600	GNVW	60025	2811	7W-13N	B7
2000	NHFD	60025	2811	7W-14N	B3
Wahl St					
12600	ALSP	60406	3277	3W-14S	A6
12600	ALSP	60803	3277	3W-14S	A6
12600	BLID	60406	3277	3W-15S	A7
Waikiki Dr					
400	DSPN	60016	2862	14W-12N	D1
Wainsford Dr					
600	HFET	60194	2858	25W-11N	C4
N Wainwright Ct					
2000	PLTN	60074	2753	19W-18N	B3
Wainwright Dr					
300	NHBK	60062	2756	11W-18N	D3
Wainwright Pl					
4000	OKLN	60453	3276	5W-12S	C3
N Waiola Av					
10	LGNG	60525	3087	12W-4S	B6
200	LGPK	60525	3087	12W-3S	B5
S Waiola Av					
10	LGNG	60525	3087	12W-4S	B7
300	LGNG	60525	3147	12W-4S	B1
Waitkus Dr					
10	LMNT	60439	3272	15W-13S	B4
10	LmnT	60464	3272	15W-13S	B4
Wakeby Ln					
1300	SMBG	60193	2858	25W-10N	C6
Wakefield Dr					
1000	ELGN	60120	2855		D2
3000	CPVL	60110	2748		D7
3000	CPVL	60110	2801		D1
3000	EDND	60118	2801		D1
Wakefield Ln					
10	BFGV	60089	2754	17W-20N	B1
200	SMBG	60193	2858	24W-10N	C6
1100	BRLT	60103	2910		B5
Wakefield St					
10500	WSTR	60154	3087	13W-2S	A3
10700	WSTR	60154	3086		E3
Wald St					
3200	GNVW	60025	2864	10W-12N	A1
3200	MaiT	60025	2864	10W-12N	A1
Walden Ct					
10	SMWD	60107	2857	28W-11N	A5
800	SMBG	60193	2912		A1
14500	OKFT	60452	3347	6W-17S	D5
Walden Dr					
200	GLNC	60022	2758	6W-18N	D4
1300	ELGN	60120	2855		E6
N Walden Dr					
700	PLTN	60067	2752	21W-16N	C6
700	PltT	60067	2752	21W-17N	C6
Walden Ln					
400	PTHT	60070	2754	16W-16N	D7
3100	WLMT	60091	2811	6W-14N	E5
E Walden Ln					
2200	ANHT	60004	2754	16W-16N	D7
2200	ANHT	60004	2807	16W-16N	D1
S Walden Ln					
24000	CteT	60417	3598	3E-29S	A7
24000	CteT	60417	3687	3E-29S	A1
S Walden Pkwy					
9700	CHCG	60643	3213	2W-11S	C7
10100	CHCG	60643	3277	2W-12S	C1
Walden Rd					
600	WNKA	60093	2812	5W-16N	A1
Walden Tr					
10	SMWD	60107	2857	28W-11N	A4
Walden Office Sq					
-	RGMW	60008	2806	21W-12N	A7
-	SMBG	60008	2806	21W-12N	A7
1800	SMBG	60173	2806	21W-12N	A7
Waldman Dr					
300	PKFT	60466	3594	4W-26S	E2
300	PKFT	60466	3595	4W-26S	A2
Waldo Erickson Dr					
-	WNSP	60558	3146		D1
E Waldron Dr					
500	CHCG	60605	3034	0E-1S	D7
500	CHCG	60616	3034	0E-1S	D7
Walker Av					
1600	SMWD	60107	2911		B1
Walker Ct					
20600	FKFT	60423	3504	10W-24S	B6
N Walker Ln E					
3100	ANHT	60004	2754	17W-17N	C5
N Walker Ln W					
3100	ANHT	60004	2754	17W-17N	C5
Walker Pl					
10	ELGN	60120	2855		A4
Walker Rd					
11200	LMNT	60439	3271		B7
Walker St					
500	HNDL	60521	3086		B7
1300	WNSP	60558	3086		D7
1400	WNSP	60558	3146		C1
Wall St					
1600	MPPT	60056	2861	16W-10N	E5
Wallace Av					
3000	SCHT	60411	3596	0W-27S	B5
3000	STGR	60475	3596	0W-28S	B6
Wallace Ct					
1100	CHHT	60411	3507	1W-25S	E7
E Wallace Ct					
100	BRLT	60103	2911		A6
Wallace Dr					
2500	FSMR	60422	3507	3W-22S	B2
Wallace St					
-	BlmT	60411	3508	0W-24S	B4
400	CHHT	60411	3508	0W-24S	B5
1400	CHHT	60411	3596	0W-25S	B1
2500	BlmT	60411	3596	0W-26S	B2
14300	RVDL	60827	3350	1W-17S	B6
14700	DLTN	60419	3350	0W-17S	B6
14700	HRVY	60419	3350	0W-17S	B6
14700	HRVY	60426	3350	0W-17S	B6
14700	SHLD	60426	3350	0W-17S	B6
14800	PHNX	60426	3350	0W-17S	B6
15700	HRVY	60426	3428	0W-18S	B1
16100	SHLD	60426	3428	0W-19S	B2
16200	SHLD	60473	3428	0W-19S	B1
17000	HRVY	60473	3428	0W-20S	B4
E Wallace St					
100	BRLT	60103	2910		E5
100	BRLT	60103	2911		A6
S Wallace St					
2400	CHCG	60616	3092	0W-2S	A2
3300	CHCG	60609	3092	0W-4S	A6
5300	CHCG	60609	3152	0W-5S	A2
7600	CHCG	60620	3214	0W-8S	A1
9400	CHCG	60628	3214	0W-11S	A6
10300	CHCG	60628	3278	0W-14S	B5
14200	RVDL	60827	3350	1W-16S	B4

STREET Block	City	ZIP	Map#	CGS	Grid
S Wallace St					
14500	HRVY	60426	3350	0W-16S	B4
W Wallen Av					
1600	CHCG	60626	2921	2W-8N	C2
3700	LNWD	60712	2920	4W-8N	C2
N Waller Av					
400	CHCG	60644	3031	7W-0N	C3
700	CHCG	60651	3031	7W-0N	C3
1500	CHCG	60639	3031	7W-2N	C1
S Waller Av					
10	CHCG	60644	3031	7W-0S	C5
1100	CCRO	60804	3031	7W-0S	C7
Wallingford Ln					
20000	DRPK	60010	2752	22W-20N	B1
20000	PltT	60010	2752	22W-20N	B2
20000	PltT	60074	2752	22W-20N	B2
Walnut					
-	HGKN	60525	3147	12W-7S	C5
Walnut Av					
200	WLNG	60090	2755	14W-17N	D4
300	NHFD	60093	2811	6W-15N	C1
900	HRPK	60133	2912		A3
900	SMBG	60193	2912		A3
1200	HRPK	60133	2911		C3
1500	WLMT	60091	2812	4W-14N	C5
2300	BRLT	60103	2911		C3
2300	BRLT	60133	2911		C3
2300	HRPK	60103	2911		C3
2600	EVTN	60201	2812	3W-13N	E7
2700	WLMT	60201	2812	3W-13N	E7
3500	WLMT	60091	2811	6W-14N	D5
9000	FNPK	60131	2973	11W-3N	D4
9000	RVGV	60171	2973	11W-3N	D4
18600	CCHL	60478	3506	5W-22S	C1
E Walnut Av					
900	DSPN	60016	2862	13W-10N	E5
1200	DSPN	60016	2863	13W-10N	A4
N Walnut Av					
100	ITSC	60143	2914		C6
300	WDDL	60191	2915		B7
400	AddT	60191	2915		B7
500	ANHT	60005	2806	18W-14N	E4
1600	ANHT	60004	2806	18W-15N	E1
2500	ANHT	60004	2754	18W-16N	A6
4000	ANHT	60004	2753	18W-18N	E2
S Walnut Av					
100	ANHT	60005	2806	18W-13N	E5
100	ITSC	60143	2914		C7
1200	ANHT	60005	2860	18W-12N	E1
W Walnut Av					
10	DSPN	60016	2862	15W-10N	B4
14400	HMGN	60441	3343	18W-16S	B4
Walnut Cir					
1700	NfdT	60062	2757	10W-18N	B3
2100	DRFD	60062	2757	10W-18N	B3
Walnut Ct					
800	DSPN	60016	2862	13W-10N	D5
2100	GNVW	60025	2864	9W-12N	C1
2200	HRPK	60133	2911		C3
3900	RGMW	60008	2806	20W-13N	A6
9300	MaiT	60016	2863	11W-12N	D1
11600	BRRG	60527	3208		D3
15600	HMGN	60441	3422	16W-18S	A1
N Walnut Ct					
10	SMWD	60107	2856	29W-11N	D4
2500	ANHT	60004	2754	18W-16N	A6
W Walnut Ct					
10	ROSL	60172	2913		A6
Walnut Dr					
100	SMWD	60107	2856	29W-10N	E5
Walnut Ln					
10	SBTN	60010	2803	27W-15N	B3
200	EGVV	60007	2914		E3
200	LynT	60458	3209	11W-8S	E2
300	EGVV	60007	2915		A3
1100	NHBK	60062	2757	10W-17N	B5
9000	TYPK	60477	3423	11W-20S	E5
9000	TYPK	60477	3424	11W-20S	A5
N Walnut Ln					
10	GNWD	60425	3509	0E-22S	A1
10	SMBG	60193	2858	25W-10N	A5
100	SMBG	60194	2857	26W-10N	E5
500	SMBG	60194	2858	26W-11N	A4
1100	HFET	60194	2858	25W-11N	A3
S Walnut Ln					
10	GNWD	60425	3509	0E-22S	A2
10	SMBG	60193	2858	25W-9N	A7
10	SMBG	60194	2858	26W-10N	A6
500	SMBG	60133	2858	25W-9N	A7
Walnut Rd					
2900	HMWD	60430	3427	3W-21S	A6
15200	OKFT	60452	3347	8W-18S	B7
S Walnut Rdg					
11500	PSPK	60464	3274	10W-13S	B5
Walnut St					
-	FNPK	60131	2973	11W-3N	E4
-	MYWD	60153	3029	11W-0N	E4
-	RVGV	60171	2973	11W-3N	D4
10	ALGN	60102	2748		A1
10	CPVL	60110	2748		C5
100	PKFT	60466	3594	4W-26S	E3
200	MYWD	60153	3030	10W-0N	A4
200	WNKA	60093	2812	4W-15N	B2
300	BmdT	60157	2913		C6
300	ROSL	60157	2913		C6
500	BmdT	60172	2912		E6
500	BmdT	60172	2913		A6
500	LMNT	60439	3270		D6
500	ROSL	60172	2912		E6
700	WLSP	60480	3209	12W-9S	D3
1400	WNSP	60558	3086		C7
1500	HNDL	60521	3086		C7
1900	PKRG	60068	2863	11W-10N	D5
2000	BLID	60406	3277	2W-15S	C7
8500	ODPK	60462	3346	10W-16S	B2
E Walnut St					
10	ROSL	60172	2913		B6
400	HNDL	60521	3146		B1
500	PTON	60468	3861	8W-37S	A3
N Walnut St					
200	BNVL	60106	2915		E7
700	ITSC	60143	2914		C5
S Walnut St					
10	PLTN	60067	2805	21W-15N	C1
100	PltT	60067	2805	21W-15N	C1
200	BlmT	60425	3509	0E-23S	A2
200	GNWD	60425	3509	0E-23S	A2
800	BmdT	60108	2913		B6
800	BmdT	60157	2913		B6
800	ROSL	60108	2913		B6
800	ROSL	60157	2913		B6
800	ROSL	60172	2913		B6
24600	CteT	60417	3686	2E-29S	D2
W Walnut St					
10	HNDL	60521	3146		A1

STREET Block	City	ZIP	Map#	CGS	Grid
W Walnut St					
400	MPPT	60056	2807	15W-13N	E7
600	CHCG	60661	3034	0W-0N	A4
700	CHCG	60607	3034	0W-0N	A4
1600	CHCG	60607	3033	2W-0N	C4
1600	CHCG	60612	3033	2W-0N	C4
2800	CHCG	60612	3032	4W-0N	D4
3100	CHCG	60624	3032	4W-0N	D4
4600	CHCG	60644	3032	5W-0N	A4
S Walnut Ter					
-	HYHL	60465	3210	10W-11S	B7
9900	PSHL	60465	3210	10W-11S	B7
Walnut Creek Dr					
-	FftT	60423	3504	10W-24S	B6
-	FKFT	60423	3504	10W-24S	B6
Walnut Oaks Dr					
600	ROSL	60172	2913		A6
Walpole Ln					
900	SMBG	60193	2912		D1
Walpole Rd					
10	EGVV	60007	2914		D2
Walredon Av					
8300	BRRG	60527	3208		B4
W Walsh Ln					
8100	RVGV	60171	2974	10W-3N	B4
Walter Av					
200	EGvT	60007	2860	19W-9N	C7
200	EGVV	60007	2860	19W-9N	C7
800	DSPN	60016	2862	13W-11N	D3
S Walter Av					
5500	HMND	46320	3352		D7
Walter Dr					
200	ROSL	60172	2913		A4
13900	CTWD	60445	3348	6W-16S	A3
W Walter Dr					
10500	PlsT	60464	3345	13W-15S	B2
W Walter Ln					
3800	ALSP	60803	3276	4W-15S	C7
Walter St					
900	LMNT	60439	3270		D7
17100	LNSG	60438	3430	4E-20S	B4
19100	LNSG	60438	3510	4E-22S	B2
Walter Hagen Ln					
14100	BmnT	60445	3347	6W-16S	E4
14100	MDLN	60445	3347	6W-16S	E4
14100	MDLN	60445	3348	6W-16S	A4
Walter Payton Dr					
-	SMBG	60173	2859	21W-12N	D2
-	SMBG	60173	2860	21W-12N	A2
Walters Av					
2000	NHBK	60062	2757	10W-17N	A6
2500	NHBK	60062	2756	11W-17N	E6
3500	NfdT	60062	2756	11W-17N	E6
E Walters Ln					
100	ITSC	60143	2914		C5
W Walters Ln					
-	ITSC	60143	2914		C5
W Walter Zimny Dr					
2300	DXMR	60406	3349	3W-17S	B5
2300	POSN	60469	3349	3W-17S	B5
Waltham Ln					
1100	BRLT	60103	2910		B5
Waltham St					
10	CTCY	46320	3352	4E-18S	C7
10	CTCY	60409	3352	4E-18S	B7
10	HMND	46320	3352	4E-18S	C7
E Waltham St					
10	CTCY	46320	3352		D7
10	CTCY	60409	3352		D7
10	HMND	46320	3352		D7
300	HMND	46320	3430		D1
Walton Av					
15200	PHNX	60426	3350	0W-18S	B7
S Walton Dr					
-	CHCG	60617	3216	4E-10S	C6
Walton Ln					
17900	HMWD	60430	3428	1W-21S	A6
E Walton Pl					
10	CHCG	60610	3034	0E-1N	C2
10	CHCG	60611	3034	0E-1N	C2
Walton St					
-	DSPN	60016	2862	13W-12N	E1
-	DSPN	60016	2863	13W-12N	A1
100	BRTN	60010	2751	25W-18N	A2
500	MYWD	60153	3030	10W-1N	A2
700	MYWD	60153	3029	11W-1N	D3
800	MLPK	60160	3029	10W-1N	E2
W Walton St					
10	CHCG	60610	3034	0W-1N	B2
10	CHCG	60611	3034	0W-1N	B2
1300	CHCG	60622	3033	1W-1N	D2
3000	CHCG	60622	3032	3W-1N	E2
4200	CHCG	60651	3032	5W-1N	B2
4700	CHCG	60651	3031	6W-1N	E2
5900	CHCG	60302	3031	7W-1N	B2
5900	OKPK	60302	3031	7W-1N	B2
Waltz Ct					
800	PTHT	60070	2808	15W-16N	A1
W Waltz Dr					
10	WLNG	60090	2755	14W-17N	C6
N Wanda Ln					
400	PLTN	60067	2752	21W-16N	D7
Wandsworth Cir					
400	ROSL	60172	2912		B5
S Wa Pella Av					
10	MPPT	60056	2807	16W-12N	E7
200	MPPT	60056	2861	16W-12N	E1
Wapoos Ct					
200	SMBG	60194	2858	24W-10N	D5
Warbler Ln					
17000	ODPK	60467	3423	13W-20S	A4
Wareham Ln					
10	SMBG	60193	2858	25W-10N	A6
10	SMBG	60194	2858	25W-10N	A6
Warington Ln					
1000	HFET	60194	2858	24W-11N	C3
Warkworth Ln					
100	IVNS	60067	2752	22W-16N	B7
Warner Av					
400	LMNT	60439	3270		D6
W Warner Av					
1800	CHCG	60613	2977	2W-5N	B1
1900	CHCG	60618	2977	2W-5N	B1
3200	CHCG	60618	2976	4W-5N	D1
4800	CHCG	60641	2975	6W-5N	E1
6400	CHCG	60634	2975	8W-5N	A1
Warner Cir					
10	LMNT	60439	3270		D7
Warren Av					
400	PKRG	60068	2917	11W-8N	E2
2100	BLWD	60104	3029	11W-0N	C5
2100	MYWD	60153	3029	11W-0N	C5
2200	IVNS	60067	2804	23W-15N	D1
3700	HLSD	60162	3029	12W-0N	A5
5000	HLSD	60162	3028		C5

STREET Block	City	ZIP	Map#	CGS	Grid
Warren Av					
5100	BKLY	60163	3028		C5
9700	OKLN	60453	3211	6W-11S	D7
S Warren Av					
400	PLTN	60074	2806	19W-15N	D3
W Warren Blvd					
600	CHCG	60661	3034		D5
1500	CHCG	60607	3033	3W-0N	A4
1500	CHCG	60612	3033	3W-0N	A4
2800	CHCG	60612	3032	3W-0N	E5
3100	CHCG	60624	3032	3W-0N	E4
Warren Cir					
3100	OMFD	60461	3507	3W-25S	A7
Warren Ct					
500	HNDL	60521	3086		A7
500	WDDL	60191	2914		D7
5900	MNGV	60053	2865	7W-10N	B5
N Warren Ovl					
300	GNVW	60025	2864	10W-12N	A1
300	GNVW	60714	2864	10W-12N	A1
300	NLES	60714	2864	10W-12N	A1
Warren Rd					
400	GNVW	60025	2864	10W-11N	A2
400	GNVW	60714	2864	10W-11N	A2
400	NLES	60714	2864	10W-11N	A2
500	GNVW	60025	2810	10W-12N	A7
N Warren Rd					
9900	GNVW	60025	2864	10W-12N	A1
9900	GNVW	60714	2864	10W-12N	A1
9900	NLES	60714	2864	10W-12N	A1
Warren St					
-	BLWD	60104	3029	11W-0N	D5
10	CTCY	60409	3352	4E-18S	B7
10	HMND	46320	3352	4E-18S	C7
100	MYWD	60153	3030	10W-0N	A5
1700	MYWD	60153	3029	11W-0N	D5
1900	EVTN	60202	2866	3W-10N	E5
3800	SKOK	60076	2866	4W-10N	C5
4900	SKOK	60077	2865	6W-10N	E5
5700	MNGV	60053	2865	7W-10N	C5
7400	FTPK	60130	3030	9W-0N	D5
E Warren St					
10	CTCY	60409	3352		C7
10	HMND	46320	3352		C7
Warren Ter					
400	HNDL	60521	3086		A7
Warren-Allen Dr					
100	WDDL	60191	2915		B5
Warrington Ct					
2100	GNVW	60025	2809	10W-14N	E3
N Warrington Rd					
10	DSPN	60016	2862	14W-12N	C2
100	MPPT	60016	2862	14W-12N	C1
100	MPPT	60056	2862	14W-12N	C1
S Warrington Rd					
10	DSPN	60016	2862	14W-12N	C2
Warsaw Av					
4500	LYNS	60525	3148	10W-4S	A1
4500	LYNS	60534	3148	10W-4S	A1
4500	MCCK	60525	3148	10W-4S	A1
S Warwick Av					
1400	HMND	46394	3280		E4
W Warwick Av					
4000	CHCG	60618	2976	5W-4N	B2
4000	CHCG	60641	2976	5W-4N	B2
4700	CHCG	60641	2975	6W-4N	D2
5500	CHCG	60634	2975	7W-4N	B2
Warwick Cir N					
1000	HFET	60194	2858	24W-11N	C3
Warwick Cir S					
1100	HFET	60194	2858	24W-11N	C3
Warwick Ct					
10	PKFT	60466	3595	3W-26S	A3
10	SMWD	60107	2857	26W-11N	E4
100	SMBG	60193	2858	25W-10N	A6
1600	WLNG	60090	2754	16W-18N	D3
5800	OKFT	60452	3347	7W-18S	D6
E Warwick Ct					
2600	ANHT	60004	2807	16W-15N	C2
Warwick Dr					
9700	MTSN	60443	3505	7W-25S	D7
3600	CRTE	60417	3596	0W-28S	C7
3600	CRTE	60475	3596	0W-28S	C7
15400	OKFT	60452	3347	7W-18S	D7
Warwick Ln					
100	KLWH	60043	2812	3W-14N	D4
1000	EGVV	60007	2915		A2
1600	SMBG	60193	2858	26W-10N	A6
2100	GNVW	60025	2809	10W-14N	E3
2200	SMBG	60193	2857	26W-10N	E6
Warwick Pl					
10	ELGN	60120	2855		A4
Warwick Rd					
200	KLWH	60043	2812	4W-14N	C3
600	WNKA	60093	2812	4W-14N	C3
E Warwick Rd					
400	PLTN	60074	2753	20W-16N	A6
Warwick St					
100	PKFT	60466	3595	3W-26S	A3
E Warwick St					
600	BRTN	60010	2751	25W-18N	B2
Wasdale Av					
1300	EGVV	60007	2914		D3
1300	ITSC	60143	2914		D3
W Waseca Pl					
1600	CHCG	60643	3277	2W-13S	D3
W Washburne Av					
1200	CHCG	60608	3033	1W-1S	D7
Washington Av					
10	LGNG	60525	3087	12W-4S	D7
10	SMWD	60107	2856	29W-10N	E6
300	GLNC	60022	2758	6W-17N	D5
300	WLMT	60091	2813	3W-13N	A5
700	WLMT	60091	2812	3W-13N	E5
1200	CRTE	60417	3685	1W-29S	A2
2900	WLMT	60091	2811	5W-13N	D6
3800	LYNS	60534	3088	9W-3S	C6
3800	RvsT	60534	3088	9W-3S	C6
3800	RvsT	60546	3088	9W-3S	C6
4200	MTSN	60443	3594	5W-25S	C1
8400	BKFD	60513	3088	10W-3S	A5
8400	RVSD	60513	3088	10W-3S	A5
8400	RVSD	60546	3088	10W-3S	A5
8700	BKFD	60513	3087	11W-3S	E5
9500	LGPK	60525	3087	11W-3S	E5
9800	OKLN	60453	3211	6W-11S	D7
10200	OKLN	60453	3275	6W-12S	D1
11900	BLID	60406	3277	2W-14S	C5
11900	CHCG	60406	3277	2W-14S	C5
11900	CHCG	60643	3277	2W-14S	C5
14700	HRVY	60426	3350	1W-17S	A6
17500	HMWD	60430	3427	2W-21S	A6
N Washington Av					
10	PKRG	60068	2864	9W-9N	B7
10	PKRG	60068	2918	8W-8N	D2

STREET Block	City	ZIP	Map#	CGS	Grid
N Washington Av					
900	NLES	60714	2864	10W-9N	B6
900	PKRG	60714	2864	10W-9N	B6
S Washington Av					
1600	PKRG	60068	2918	10W-7N	B4
1900	CHCG	60631	2918	9W-7N	B4
1900	PKRG	60631	2918	9W-7N	B4
10700	OKLN	60453	3275	6W-12S	D2
Washington Blvd					
10	CHCG	60644	3031	7W-0N	B4
10	HFET	60193	2858	24W-10N	D5
10	MYWD	60153	3030	10W-0N	A4
10	OKPK	60302	3031	8W-0N	A4
10	RVFT	60305	3030	10W-0N	B4
10	SMBG	60193	2858	24W-10N	D5
600	HFET	60194	2858	24W-11N	E4
700	MYWD	60153	3029	11W-0N	D4
800	OKPK	60302	3030	8W-0N	E4
1100	FTPK	60130	3030	8W-0N	D4
2100	BLWD	60104	3029	12W-0N	B4
3900	BLWD	60162	3029	12W-0N	A4
3900	HLSD	60162	3029	12W-0N	B4
Washington Blvd SR-56					
4000	BLWD	60104	3029	12W-0N	B4
4000	BLWD	60162	3029	12W-0N	A4
4000	HLSD	60162	3029	12W-0N	B4
W Washington Blvd					
500	CHCG	60606	3034	0W-0N	A4
500	CHCG	60661	3034	0W-0N	A4
700	CHCG	60607	3034	0W-0N	A4
800	CHCG	60607	3033	1W-0N	D4
1500	CHCG	60612	3033	2W-0N	D4
2800	CHCG	60612	3032	4W-0N	D4
3400	CHCG	60624	3032	5W-0N	A4
4500	CHCG	60644	3032	5W-0N	A4
5100	CHCG	60644	3031	6W-0N	D5
5900	OKPK	60302	3031	7W-0N	B4
S Washington Cir					
10	HNDL	60521	3146		A3
Washington Ct					
-	PKRG	60068	2918	10W-7N	B3
10	PKFT	60466	3594	4W-26S	E3
10	SMWD	60107	2856	29W-10N	E6
200	PLTN	60067	2805	21W-15N	D1
700	HDPK	60035	2758	7W-20N	A1
1000	BRLT	60103	2910		C6
1200	WLMT	60091	2812	3W-13N	D5
17700	ODPK	60467	3423	13W-21S	A6
Washington Dr					
-	OMFD	60461	3507	3W-25S	C7
4300	RNPK	60471	3594	5W-27S	B4
N Washington Dr					
9000	MaiT	60016	2863	11W-11N	D3
Washington Ln					
-	PKRG	60068	2918	9W-7N	B3
Washington Pl					
400	HDPK	60035	2758	7W-20N	A1
600	GLNC	60022	2758	6W-17N	C5
1200	PKRG	60068	2918	9W-7N	C3
Washington Rd					
10	MaiT	60025	2864	10W-12N	B1
10	MaiT	60714	2864	9W-12N	B2
10	MNGV	60053	2864	9W-12N	B2
300	GNVW	60025	2864	10W-12N	B1
400	GNVW	60025	2810	10W-12N	B7
Washington Sq					
200	EGVV	60007	2914		E1
200	WDDL	60191	2914		D7
Washington St					
-	EGvT	60018	2861	16W-9N	E7
-	EGVV	60007	2861	15W-9N	E7
-	EGVV	60018	2861	15W-9N	E7
-	PTON	60468	3861	9W-37S	A2
10	AddT	60106	2915		C5
10	GNVW	60025	2864	9W-12N	D1
10	MNGV	60053	2864	9W-12N	D2
100	BRTN	60010	2750	27W-20N	C1
100	BRTN	60010	2751	25W-20N	A1
100	EGvT	60018	2862	15W-9N	A7
100	PKFT	60466	3594	4W-26S	E3
100	WDND	60118	2801		A2
400	AddT	60191	2915		B6
400	HMND	46320	3430		D1
400	HMND	46324	3430		D1
400	WDDL	60191	2915		B6
500	DLTN	60419	3350	0E-16S	D3
700	EVTN	60202	2867	2W-10N	B5
800	GNVW	60025	2810	8W-13N	D7
1000	BRLT	60103	2910		C7
1000	CHHT	60411	3508	0W-25S	C7
1600	EVTN	60202	2866	3W-10N	E5
3200	FNPK	60131	2973	11W-4N	D4
3300	LNSG	60438	3430	4E-21S	B2
3700	MNSR	46321	3430	4E-21S	C6
3700	OKBK	60523	3086		A6
3800	HNDL	60521	3086		A6
3800	OKBK	60521	3086		A6
4600	HLSD	60162	3028		D5
4600	SKOK	60076	2866	5W-10N	A5
4700	SKOK	60076	2865	6W-10N	E5
5100	BKLY	60163	3028		C5
5200	SKOK	60077	2865	6W-10N	D5
5800	MNGV	60053	2865	7W-10N	B5
6000	CHRG	60415	3275	7W-12S	B1
7200	FTPK	60130	3030	9W-0N	C4
7200	OKPK	60302	3030	9W-0N	D4
7400	HRPK	60133	2912		A3
E Washington St					
10	CHCG	60602	3034	0E-0N	C4
10	PLTN	60067	2805	20W-15N	E1
100	BNVL	60106	2972		A2
100	ITSC	60143	2914		C7
1100	WDDL	60143	2914		D7
1200	DSPN	60016	2862	13W-11N	D6
1200	WDDL	60191	2914		D7
1300	DSPN	60016	2863	13W-11N	A3
N Washington St					
-	MaiT	60631	2918	10W-6N	B5
-	MaiT	60656	2918	10W-6N	B5
-	NpkT	60631	2918	10W-6N	B5
10	HNDL	60521	3146		A1
500	HNDL	60521	3086		A7
900	OKBK	60521	3086		A7
900	OKBK	60523	3086		A7
5300	CHCG	60656	2918	9W-6N	B5
5300	LydT	60656	2918	10W-6N	B5
5300	NpkT	60656	2918	10W-6N	B5
8000	NLES	60714	2864	10W-10N	B5
8000	PKRG	60068	2864	9W-10N	B6
8000	PKRG	60714	2864	9W-10N	B6
9000	MNGV	60053	2864	10W-11N	B3
9000	MNGV	60714	2864	9W-11N	B3
9000	NLES	60053	2864	9W-11N	B3
9500	MaiT	60025	2864	10W-11N	B3
9500	MaiT	60714	2864	10W-11N	B3

STREET Block	City	ZIP	Map#	CGS	Grid
S Washington St					
5700	BRRG	60521	3146		A4
5700	BRRG	60527	3146		A4
5700	HNDL	60521	3146		A4
W Washington St					
10	CHCG	60602	3034	0W-0N	B4
10	PLTN	60067	2805	21W-15N	E1
100	CHCG	60606	3034	0W-0N	B4
100	ITSC	60143	2914		C7
400	CHCG	60661	3034	0W-0N	A4
S Washington Park Ct					
4000	CHCG	60615	3152	0E-5S	D1
Washtenaw Av					
14800	HRVY	60426	3349	3W-17S	B6
14800	POSN	60426	3349	3W-17S	B6
15000	MKHM	60426	3349	3W-17S	B6
15600	MKHM	60426	3427	3W-18S	A1
N Washtenaw Av					
200	CHCG	60612	3033	3W-0N	A4
700	CHCG	60622	3033	3W-1N	A2
1500	CHCG	60647	3033	3W-2N	A1
2400	CHCG	60647	2977	3W-3N	A5
3000	CHCG	60618	2977	3W-4N	A3
4700	CHCG	60625	2921	3W-6N	A6
5300	CHCG	60625	2920	3W-6N	E5
5600	CHCG	60659	2920	3W-7N	E4
6300	CHCG	60645	2920	3W-7N	E3
7200	CHCG	60645	2866	3W-9N	E7
7500	EVTN	60202	2866	3W-9N	E7
S Washtenaw Av					
500	CHCG	60612	3033	3W-1S	A7
1000	CHCG	60608	3033	3W-1S	A7
1600	CHCG	60608	3091	3W-2S	A2
4100	CHCG	60632	3091	3W-4S	A7
5000	CHCG	60632	3151	3W-6S	A4
5400	CHCG	60629	3151	3W-8S	A7
7500	CHCG	60652	3213	3W-9S	A2
9600	ENGN	60805	3213	3W-11S	A7
9800	CHCG	60655	3213	3W-11S	A7
9800	ENGN	60655	3213	3W-11S	A7
10700	CHCG	60655	3277	3W-13S	A3
Washtenaw St					
10	ALGN	60102	2748		A1
10	AlqT	60102	2748		A1
Watch Ct					
300	ELGN	60120	2855		A5
Watch St					
200	ELGN	60120	2855		A5
Water St					
10	EDND	60118	2801		A2
10	PKFT	60466	3595	3W-26S	B2
200	TNTN	60476	3428	0E-21S	E5
Waterbury Cir					
1800	GNVW	60025	2810	8W-15N	D2
N Waterbury Cir					
1400	PLTN	60074	2753	20W-17N	A4
Waterbury Ct					
5300	CTWD	60445	3347	6W-16S	E3
Waterbury Dr					
5300	BmnT	60445	3347	6W-16S	E3
5300	CTWD	60445	3347	6W-16S	E3
Waterbury Ln					
10	SMBG	60193	2859	23W-10N	A6
10	SMBG	60194	2859	23W-10N	A6
400	ROSL	60172	2912		C5
5300	CTWD	60445	3347	6W-16S	E3
Waterbury Wy					
5300	CTWD	60445	3347	6W-16S	E3
Watercrest Ct					
10	SBTN	60010	2803	27W-13N	A6
Waterford Av					
-	MKNA	60448	3504	11W-23S	A4
Waterford Ct					
400	WLBK	60527	3146		A5
500	ROSL	60172	2912		D5
1000	DSPN	60016	2808	13W-13N	D6
Waterford Dr					
-	CTCY	60409	3429	2E-20S	D3
-	LNSG	60409	3429	2E-20S	D3
-	LNSG	60438	3429	2E-20S	D3
-	SHLD	60473	3429	2E-20S	D3
100	WLBK	60527	3146		A6
200	PTHT	60070	2808	14W-15N	C2
400	DGvT	60527	3146		A6
600	DSPN	60016	2808	13W-13N	D6
600	HRPK	60133	2912		A1
8300	TYPK	60477	3424	10W-20S	B4
10400	PvsT	60154	3087	13W-1S	A1
10400	PvsT	60162	3087	13W-1S	A1
10400	WSTR	60154	3087	13W-1S	A1
N Waterford Dr					
10	SMBG	60194	2859	22W-10N	C5
Waterford Ln					
400	IVNS	60010	2751	24W-17N	C5
900	EGVV	60007	2914		A2
900	NHBK	60062	2757	8W-16N	D7
9300	ODPK	60462	3423	11W-18S	E1
19200	FftT	60448	3504	11W-23S	A3
19200	MKNA	60448	3504	11W-23S	A3
E Waterford Ln					
1600	PLTN	60074	2753	18W-18N	D3
Waterford Rd					
1000	BRLT	60103	2911		D5
S Waterford Rd					
600	SMBG	60193	2859	23W-9N	A7
Waterfront Dr					
8700	PSHL	60465	3274	11W-13S	A3
Watergate Dr					
10	SBTN	60010	2803	26W-14N	C4
N Waterloo Ct					
3000	CHCG	60657	2978	0W-3N	A4
Waterman Av					
200	ANHT	60004	2807	16W-15N	D2
200	PTHT	60004	2807	16W-15N	D2
200	PTHT	60070	2807	16W-15N	D2
N Waterman Av					
1100	PTHT	60004	2807	16W-15N	D3
1500	ANHT	60004	2807	16W-15N	D2
1500	PTHT	60070	2807	16W-15N	D2
2500	ANHT	60004	2754	16W-16N	D6
2500	WLNG	60090	2754	16W-16N	D6
2600	ANHT	60090	2754	16W-16N	D6
S Waterman Av					
10	ANHT	60004	2807	16W-13N	D6
600	MPPT	60056	2807	16W-13N	D6
Waterman Ct					
15200	SHLD	60473	3351	1E-17S	A6
Waterman Dr					
15000	DLTN	60419	3351	1E-17S	A5
15000	SHLD	60473	3351	1E-17S	A5
Waters Edge Ct					
500	NHBK	60062	2757	9W-18N	D4
Water's Edge Dr					
-	ODPK	60467	3422	14W-21S	D7
-	ODPK	60467	3423	13W-21S	A7

Chicago & Cook County Street Index

STREET Block	City	ZIP	Map#	CGS	Grid
Waters Edge Ln					
1200	NHBK	60062	2757	9W-18N	C3
Waterside Cir					
11500	ODPK	60467	3422	14W-21S	D7
Waterside Pl					
10	BRRG	60527	3208		D1
Waterton Dr					
10	HnrT	60107	2856	29W-11N	E5
10	SMWD	60107	2856	29W-11N	E5
S Water Tower Dr					
2900	CteT	60417	3687	3E-31S	B5
Waterville Ln					
1600	SMBG	60194	2858	25W-11N	B4
Waterway Ct					
11600	ODPK	60467	3422	14W-21S	D7
S Watkins Av					
11400	CHCG	60643	3277	2W-13S	D4
11800	BLID	60406	3277	2W-13S	C5
W Watling Rd					
1000	ANHT	60004	2806	18W-15N	D3
Watres Pl					
300	ELGN	60120	2855		B5
Watseka St					
400	PKFT	60466	3594	4W-26S	E3
Watson Ct					
13000	PlsT	60464	3345	13W-15S	A1
W Watson Rd					
5800	MONE	60449	3682	6W-32S	E7
5800	MonT	60449	3682	7W-32S	E7
Waubansee Dr					
6400	IHPK	60525	3146		D6
Waubansee Ln					
-	IHPK	60525	3146		D6
Waubansee Rd					
100	BKFD	60513	3088	10W-3S	B6
100	RVSD	60513	3088	10W-3S	B6
100	RVSD	60546	3088	10W-3S	B5
Waukegan Rd					
10	DRFD	60015	2757	10W-20N	A1
10	GNVW	60025	2864	8W-11N	E3
10	MNGV	60053	2864	8W-11N	E3
100	GNVW	60025	2810	8W-13N	E6
100	GNVW	60093	2810	8W-15N	E3
100	NHFD	60025	2810	8W-15N	E3
100	NHFD	60093	2810	8W-15N	E1
300	NHBK	60062	2810	8W-15N	E2
400	DRFD	60062	2757	9W-18N	B4
400	NfdT	60062	2757	9W-18N	B4
600	NHBK	60062	2757	9W-16N	D6
2100	NHFD	60062	2810	8W-16N	E1
8400	MNGV	60714	2864	8W-10N	E4
8400	NLES	60714	2864	8W-10N	E4
Waukegan Rd SR-43					
10	DRFD	60015	2757	10W-20N	A1
10	GNVW	60025	2864	8W-11N	E3
10	MNGV	60053	2864	8W-11N	E3
100	GNVW	60025	2810	8W-13N	E6
100	GNVW	60093	2810	8W-15N	E3
100	NHFD	60025	2810	8W-15N	E3
100	NHFD	60093	2810	8W-15N	E1
300	NHBK	60062	2810	8W-15N	E2
400	DRFD	60062	2757	9W-18N	B4
400	NfdT	60062	2757	9W-18N	B4
600	NHBK	60062	2757	9W-16N	D6
2100	NHFD	60062	2810	8W-16N	E1
8400	MNGV	60714	2864	8W-10N	E4
8400	NLES	60714	2864	8W-10N	E4
Waukegan Rd SR-58					
8800	MNGV	60053	2864	8W-11N	E3
9500	GNVW	60025	2864	8W-11N	E2
Waukegan Rd US-14					
8500	MNGV	60053	2864	8W-10N	E4
N Waukegan Rd					
7200	NLES	60714	2864	8W-9N	E6
8300	MNGV	60053	2864	8W-10N	E5
8300	MNGV	60714	2864	8W-10N	E5
N Waukegan Rd SR-43					
8000	NLES	60714	2864	8W-10N	E5
8300	MNGV	60053	2864	8W-10N	E5
8300	MNGV	60714	2864	8W-10N	E5
S Waukegan Rd					
10	DRFD	60015	2757	10W-18N	A2
10	DRFD	60062	2757	10W-18N	A2
10	NfdT	60062	2757	10W-18N	A2
S Waukegan Rd SR-43					
10	DRFD	60015	2757	10W-18N	A2
10	DRFD	60062	2757	10W-18N	A2
10	NfdT	60062	2757	10W-18N	A2
N Waukesha Av					
6700	SKOK	60646	2919	6W-8N	C2
6800	CHCG	60646	2919	6W-8N	C1
Wausau Av					
16200	SHLD	60473	3428	0E-19S	D1
Wausau Ct					
16400	SHLD	60473	3428	0E-19S	D2
Waveland Av					
1000	BNVL	60106	2972		C3
1000	BNVL	60131	2972		C3
9600	FNPK	60176	2973	12W-4N	B3
9600	SRPK	60131	2973	12W-4N	B3
9600	SRPK	60176	2973	12W-4N	B3
10400	FNPK	60131	2973	13W-4N	A2
10500	FNPK	60131	2972		E3
W Waveland Av					
600	CHCG	60613	2978	0W-4N	A2
700	CHCG	60613	2977	2W-4N	C2
1900	CHCG	60618	2977	2W-4N	B2
2800	CHCG	60618	2976	3W-4N	E2
3900	CHCG	60641	2976	5W-4N	A2
4700	CHCG	60641	2975	7W-4N	C2
5500	CHCG	60634	2975	7W-4N	B2
6800	CHCG	60634	2974	8W-4N	E2
Waverley Ln					
200	SMBG	60193	2858	25W-10N	A6
Waverly Av					
400	SMWD	60107	2857	28W-10N	B6
1400	WSTR	60154	3087	13W-1S	A1
14700	MDLN	60445	3348	4W-17S	C5
15100	BmnT	60445	3348	5W-18S	B6
15200	OKFT	60445	3348	5W-18S	B6
15300	OKFT	60452	3348	5W-18S	B7
S Waverly Av					
800	MPPT	60056	2861	16W-11N	D2
Waverly Ct					
10	PKFT	60466	3594	4W-27S	E3
200	CPVL	60110	2748		B7
E Waverly Ct					
1500	ANHT	60004	2754	16W-16N	C7
N Waverly Ct					
300	ELGN	60120	2855		C3
S Waverly Ct					
300	ELGN	60120	2855		C3
W Waverly Ct					
300	ANHT	60004	2754	18W-16N	A6
1600	ANHT	60004	2753	18W-16N	D6

STREET Block	City	ZIP	Map#	CGS	Grid
Waverly Dr					
200	ELGN	60120	2855		C3
E Waverly Dr					
600	ANHT	60004	2754	17W-16N	B6
Waverly Ln					
700	WLNG	60090	2755	15W-18N	A3
E Waverly Ln					
1900	ANHT	60004	2754	16W-16N	D7
1900	WLNG	60090	2754	16W-16N	D7
E Waverly Pl					
1200	ANHT	60004	2754	17W-16N	C6
N Waverly Pl					
100	MPPT	60056	2807	16W-13N	D7
S Waverly Pl					
100	MPPT	60056	2807	16W-12N	D7
300	MPPT	60056	2861	16W-12N	D1
E Waverly Rd					
10	ANHT	60004	2754	17W-16N	A6
W Waverly Rd					
10	ANHT	60004	2754	17W-16N	A6
Waverly St					
300	PKFT	60466	3594	4W-26S	E3
300	PKFT	60466	3595	4W-27S	A3
N Waverly St					
10	MPPT	60056	2807	16W-13N	D7
Waxwing Ct					
1600	SMBG	60173	2805	21W-12N	E7
Wayland Av					
500	KLWH	60043	2812	4W-14N	C4
Wayland Ct					
1900	SMBG	60193	2858	25W-10N	A6
Wayland Ln					
1900	SMBG	60193	2858	26W-10N	A6
S Wayman Ln					
14000	RBBN	60472	3348	4W-16S	E3
W Wayman St					
600	CHCG	60661	3034	0W-0N	A4
700	CHCG	60607	3034	0W-0N	A4
800	CHCG	60607	3033	1W-0N	E4
4600	CHCG	60644	3032	5W-0N	A4
N Wayne Av					
2500	CHCG	60614	2977	1W-3N	D5
2700	CHCG	60657	2977	1W-3N	D5
3900	CHCG	60613	2977	1W-4N	D2
5200	CHCG	60640	2921	1W-6N	D5
5600	CHCG	60660	2921	1W-7N	D4
6800	CHCG	60626	2921	1W-8N	D1
Wayne Ct					
10	PKFT	60466	3595	4W-26S	A2
200	BRLT	60103	2911		A2
Wayne Dr					
700	CRTE	60417	3685	1W-30S	A3
1200	DSPN	60018	2862	13W-10N	D5
E Wayne Pl					
200	WLNG	60090	2755	15W-17N	B5
N Wayne Pl					
600	WLNG	60090	2755	15W-17N	A4
S Wayne Pl					
500	WLNG	60090	2755	15W-17N	A5
W Wayne Pl					
10	WLNG	60090	2755	15W-17N	A4
Wayne St					
300	PKFT	60466	3595	4W-26S	A2
E Weathersfield Wy					
10	SMBG	60193	2859	23W-9N	B7
700	EGVV	60007	2859	22W-9N	C7
W Weathersfield Wy					
-	SMWD	60107	2857	26W-10N	E6
10	SMBG	60193	2859	23W-9N	A7
200	SMBG	60193	2858	24W-9N	E7
2200	SMBG	60193	2857	26W-10N	E6
W Weathersfield Wy Ct					
500	SMBG	60193	2858	24W-9N	D7
Weatherstone Rd					
100	PlIT	60010	2751	23W-18N	D2
N Weatherstone Rd					
20400	KLDR	60047	2752	20W-20N	E1
Weather Vane Ln					
15300	HMGN	60441	3343	16W-18S	E7
Webb St					
10	CTCY	60409	3352	4E-18S	B7
10	HMND	46320	3352	4E-18S	C7
E Webb St					
10	CTCY	60409	3352		C7
10	HMND	46320	3352		D7
Weber Dr					
4200	ANHT	60008	2806	19W-12N	D7
4200	RGMW	60008	2806	19W-12N	D7
4300	ANHT	60005	2806	19W-12N	D7
4900	ANHT	60005	2860	19W-12N	D1
4900	RGMW	60008	2860	19W-12N	D1
5000	RGMW	60005	2860	19W-12N	D1
Weber Ln					
5100	SKOK	60077	2865	6W-12N	D1
Weber Park Pl					
9300	SKOK	60077	2865	6W-11N	E2
Webford Av					
500	DSPN	60016	2862	13W-11N	E3
1300	DSPN	60016	2863	12W-11N	B3
Webley Ct					
700	SMBG	60193	2859	22W-9N	C7
Webley Ln					
600	SMBG	60193	2859	22W-9N	C7
Webster Av					
200	BmdT	60157	2913		C6
200	ROSL	60157	2913		C6
400	BmdT	60172	2912		A6
400	ROSL	60172	2913		C6
500	HRPK	60133	2912		A6
700	BRLT	60103	2910		D6
E Webster Av					
300	EMHT	60126	3028		B3
W Webster Av					
300	CHCG	60614	2978	0W-2N	A6
700	CHCG	60614	2977	2W-2N	B6
1900	CHCG	60647	2977	2W-2N	B6
Webster Ct					
-	TYPK	60477	3424	10W-21S	B5
300	SMBG	60193	2858	25W-10N	B6
Webster Ln					
10	SMBG	60193	2858	25W-10N	B6
10	SMBG	60194	2858	25W-10N	B5
800	DSPN	60016	2862	13W-10N	E4
1000	SMBG	60193	2912		B1
1200	DSPN	60018	2862	13W-10N	E5
2200	DSPN	60018	2916		D1
N Webster St					
2400	EDPK	60707	2974	10W-3N	B6
2400	RVGV	60171	2974	10W-3N	B6
2400	RVGV	60707	2974	9W-3N	B6
Wedel Ln					
800	GNVW	60025	2810	10W-13N	B6
800	NfdT	60025	2810	10W-13N	B6
Wedgewood Av					
1400	DSPN	60018	2862	14W-10N	C6

STREET Block	City	ZIP	Map#	CGS	Grid
Wedgewood Av					
16600	HLCT	60426	3426	4W-19S	E3
16600	HLCT	60429	3426	4W-19S	E3
16600	MKHM	60426	3426	4W-19S	E3
Wedgewood Ct					
300	WLBK	60527	3146		A7
500	HNDL	60521	3086		A7
6100	MTSN	60443	3505	7W-24S	C4
Wedgewood Dr					
100	DRPK	60010	2752	23W-18N	A3
100	PlIT	60010	2752	23W-18N	A3
600	HRPK	60133	2912		A1
900	GNVW	60025	2810	9W-13N	B6
8500	BRRG	60527	3208		B4
8500	DGvT	60527	3208		B4
12200	HMGN	60441	3422	15W-20S	B4
Wedgewood Ln					
1800	SMBG	60193	2858	25W-10N	A6
6600	WLBK	60527	3146		A6
N Wedgewood Ln					
-	MPPT	60056	2807	16W-13N	D5
1100	MPPT	60056	2808	15W-14N	A4
Wedgewood Rd					
10	MTSN	60443	3505	7W-24S	C4
Wedgewood Glens Dr					
14200	ODPK	60462	3346	10W-16S	C4
Wedgwood Dr					
-	BDVW	60154	3029	12W-0S	C6
-	BDVW	60155	3029	12W-0S	C6
-	WSTR	60154	3029	12W-0S	B6
W Weed St					
-	CHCG	60611	3034	0E-0N	D3
800	CHCG	60610	3033	1W-1N	E1
900	CHCG	60622	3033	1W-1N	E1
Weeg Wy					
1500	PKRG	60068	2863	11W-10N	E4
Weeping Willow Dr					
800	WLNG	60090	2755	15W-16N	A6
Weeping Willow Rd					
-	CTSD	60525	3147	12W-7S	C6
-	HGKN	60525	3147	12W-7S	C6
We Go Ct					
300	DRFD	60015	2756	12W-20N	B1
We Go Tr					
1600	DRFD	60015	2756	12W-20N	C1
S We Go Tr					
10	MPPT	60056	2807	16W-12N	D7
100	MPPT	60056	2861	16W-12N	D1
Wehrheim Rd					
10	DRPK	60010	2752	23W-20N	A2
10	PlIT	60010	2752	23W-20N	A2
Wehrman Av					
3700	FNPK	60131	2973	12W-4N	B2
3700	SRPK	60176	2973	12W-4N	B2
Wehrman Pl					
10100	SRPK	60176	2973	12W-4N	B2
Weidner Ct					
10	BFGV	60089	2754	17W-18N	B3
Weidner Ct S					
800	BFGV	60089	2754	17W-18N	B4
Weidner Rd					
-	BFGV	60089	2754	17W-20N	A2
-	VrnT	60089	2754	17W-20N	A2
Weiland Rd					
100	BFGV	60089	2754	16W-18N	D2
100	LkeC	60089	2754	16W-18N	D2
100	WLNG	60089	2754	16W-18N	D2
100	WLNG	60090	2754	16W-18N	D2
300	BFGV	60069	2754	16W-20N	D1
300	VrnT	60069	2754	16W-20N	D1
Weiland Rd CO-W17					
100	BFGV	60089	2754	16W-20N	D2
100	WLNG	60089	2754	16W-20N	D2
300	BFGV	60069	2754	16W-20N	D1
300	VrnT	60069	2754	16W-20N	D1
S Weiler Rd					
100	EGvT	60005	2861	16W-9N	E6
Weimer Av					
10	LMNT	60439	3270		D7
W Welch Ct					
7000	MonT	60449	3682	8W-30S	B4
Welch Wy					
-	CCHL	60478	3506	6W-22S	A2
Well Ct					
10	PKFT	60466	3595	3W-26S	A2
Well St					
100	PKFT	60466	3595	3W-26S	B2
Welland Ct					
1400	ROSL	60172	2912		C4
Weller Ln					
2800	NHBK	60062	2756	11W-17N	E6
S Weller Ln					
100	MPPT	60056	2807	16W-12N	D7
100	MPPT	60056	2861	16W-12N	D1
Wellesley Cir					
10	NHBK	60062	2756	12W-18N	A2
Wellesley Ct					
100	GNVW	60025	2810	10W-15N	A2
200	SMBG	60193	2858	25W-10N	A6
Wellesley Ln					
200	SMBG	60193	2858	25W-10N	A6
Wellingborough Ct					
10	SBTN	60010	2804	25W-15N	A2
Wellington Av					
-	FNPK	60131	2972		E4
-	FNPK	60131	2973	13W-3N	A4
100	ELGN	60120	2855		A4
200	EGVV	60007	2914		C2
2400	WSTR	60154	3086		D3
W Wellington Av					
300	CHCG	60657	2978	0W-3N	A4
700	CHCG	60657	2977	2W-3N	B4
1900	CHCG	60618	2977	2W-3N	B4
2700	CHCG	60618	2976	3W-3N	E4
3900	CHCG	60641	2976	5W-3N	B4
4700	CHCG	60641	2975	7W-3N	C4
5500	CHCG	60634	2975	8W-3N	A4
6700	CHCG	60634	2974	8W-3N	E4
7200	CHCG	60707	2974	9W-3N	C4
7200	EDPK	60707	2974	9W-3N	C4
Wellington Ct					
-	RGMW	60008	2806	19W-13N	B5
-	SMBG	60173	2859	23W-12N	B1
2500	EVTN	60201	2812	5W-12N	A7
3600	HLCT	60429	3426	4W-20S	D5
N Wellington Ct					
1300	PLTN	60067	2752	21W-18N	D4
Wellington Dr					
300	SMWD	60107	2857	28W-11N	B4
500	DYR	46311	3510		E6
500	MNSR	46321	3510		E6
17400	HLCT	60429	3426	4W-20S	D5
N Wellington Dr					
1200	PLTN	60067	2752	21W-17N	D5

STREET Block	City	ZIP	Map#	CGS	Grid
W Wellington Dr					
200	PLTN	60067	2752	21W-17N	D5
Wellington Pl					
1800	HFET	60195	2858	26W-12N	A1
Wellington Rd					
10	NHBK	60062	2757	9W-18N	C2
Wellington St					
500	ELGN	60120	2855		A6
10800	FNPK	60131	2972		E4
10800	LydT	60164	2972		E4
Wells Av					
10	DXMR	60426	3349	1W-17S	E5
10	HRVY	60426	3349	2W-17S	E5
Wells Ct					
800	DYR	46311	3598		E3
N Wells St					
10	CHCG	60602	3034	0W-0N	B4
10	CHCG	60603	3034	0W-0N	B4
10	CHCG	60606	3034	0W-0N	B4
100	CHCG	60601	3034	0W-0N	B4
300	CHCG	60610	3034	0W-1N	B1
1600	CHCG	60610	2978	0W-2N	B7
1600	CHCG	60614	2978	0W-2N	B7
S Wells St					
10	CHCG	60602	3034	0W-0S	B5
10	CHCG	60603	3034	0W-0S	B5
10	CHCG	60606	3034	0W-0S	B5
100	CHCG	60604	3034	0W-0S	B5
300	CHCG	60605	3034	0W-0S	B6
300	CHCG	60607	3034	0W-0S	B6
1800	CHCG	60616	3092	0W-1S	B1
4100	CHCG	60609	3092	0W-4S	B7
4700	CHCG	60609	3152	0W-5S	B1
5500	CHCG	60621	3152	0W-5S	B1
Welter Ct					
14300	HMGN	60441	3344	16W-17S	A4
14300	HmrT	60441	3344	16W-17S	A4
Welter Dr					
200	WDDL	60191	2914		D7
Welwyn Av					
1800	DSPN	60018	2863	12W-9N	B7
Wembley Ct					
800	ELGN	60120	2855		D2
E Wend St					
10	LMNT	60439	3270		D7
W Wend St					
10	LMNT	60439	3270		C7
W Wendell St					
300	CHCG	60610	3034	0W-1N	A2
Wendt Av					
500	EDND	60118	2801		B2
Wendy Dr					
1100	NHBK	60062	2757	9W-17N	D5
Wenholz Av					
10	EDND	60118	2801		A2
Wennes Ct					
500	HNDL	60521	3086		A6
500	OKBK	60523	3086		A6
Wenonah Av					
-	OKPK	60402	3030	8W-1S	E7
500	OKPK	60302	3030	8W-0S	E5
500	OKPK	60304	3030	8W-0S	E5
1200	BRWN	60402	3030	8W-1S	E7
1600	BRWN	60402	3088	8W-1S	E1
3800	SKNY	60402	3088	8W-4S	E6
4400	FTVW	60402	3088	8W-4S	E7
4500	FTVW	60402	3148	8W-4S	E1
N Wente Ct					
800	PLTN	60074	2753	19W-17N	B6
Wentworth Av					
-	SHLD	60473	3428	0W-20S	C4
-	TNTN	60473	3428	0W-20S	C4
-	TNTN	60476	3428	0W-20S	C4
10	CTCY	60409	3352	4E-18S	C7
10	GLNC	60022	2759	5W-17N	A6
100	GLNC	60022	2758	5W-17N	E6
900	CTCY	60409	3430	4E-18S	C1
1100	CHHT	60411	3508	0W-25S	C7
1500	CHHT	60411	3596	0W-26S	C2
1600	LNSG	60438	3430	4E-20S	C5
2500	BlmT	60411	3596	0W-26S	C2
14800	DLTN	60419	3350	0W-17S	C5
14900	HRVY	60419	3350	0W-17S	C5
14900	HRVY	60426	3350	0W-17S	C5
15500	SHLD	60473	3350	0W-18S	C7
18700	LNSG	60438	3510	4E-22S	C1
19400	LNSG	60411	3510	4E-22S	C2
22700	SCHT	60475	3596	0W-27S	D5
22700	STGR	60475	3596	0W-27S	D5
22800	CRTE	60417	3596	0W-27S	C5
22800	CRTE	60475	3596	0W-27S	C5
S Wentworth Av					
2200	CHCG	60616	3092	0W-4S	B7
3400	CHCG	60609	3092	0W-3S	B4
4700	CHCG	60609	3152	0W-5S	B1
5500	CHCG	60621	3152	0W-8S	B7
7400	CHCG	60621	3214	0W-8S	B1
9100	CHCG	60620	3214	0W-11S	B7
9400	CHCG	60628	3214	0W-11S	B7
10300	CHCG	60628	3278	0W-14S	C6
13600	RVDL	60827	3350	0W-16S	C2
14500	DLTN	60419	3350	0W-16S	C4
Wenz Av					
6500	HGKN	60525	3147	11W-7S	D6
Werch Dr					
10000	WDRG	60517	3270		B2
Werline Av					
1000	FDHT	60411	3509	1E-25S	A7
Wescott Ln					
10	SBTN	60010	2803	26W-13N	D6
Wescott Rd					
1400	NHBK	60062	2757	10W-17N	A6
Wesley Av					
-	OKPK	60402	3031	8W-1S	A7
100	OKPK	60302	3031	8W-0N	A5
400	OKPK	60304	3031	8W-0N	A5
500	EVTN	60202	2867	3W-10N	A5
1200	BRWN	60402	3031	8W-1S	A7
1200	EVTN	60201	2867	3W-11N	A3
3200	BRWN	60402	3089	8W-3S	A5
3900	SKNY	60402	3089	8W-4S	A6
S Wesley Av					
500	OKPK	60302	3031	8W-0S	A5
500	OKPK	60304	3031	8W-0S	A5
1100	BRWN	60402	3031	8W-0S	A7
1100	OKPK	60402	3031	8W-0S	A7
N Wesley Ct					
5200	CHCG	60018	2917	11W-6N	C6
5200	CHCG	60656	2917	11W-6N	C6
5200	RSMT	60018	2917	11W-6N	C6
Wesley Dr					
900	PKRG	60068	2863	11W-9N	C6
Wesley Ln					
900	ALGN	60102	2748		A1

STREET Block	City	ZIP	Map#	CGS	Grid
Wesley Rd					
6300	WLBK	60527	3146		A5
Wesley St					
100	BRTN	60010	2751	24W-20N	B2
Wesley Ter					
3800	SRPK	60176	2973	11W-5N	C2
4500	SRPK	60176	2917	11W-5N	C7
N Wesley Ter					
5200	CHCG	60018	2917	11W-6N	C6
5200	CHCG	60656	2917	11W-6N	C6
5200	SRPK	60018	2917	11W-6N	C6
5200	SRPK	60176	2917	11W-6N	C6
5200	SRPK	60656	2917	11W-6N	C6
S Wespark Av					
1900	HMND	46394	3280		E5
Wessling Dr					
1300	NfdT	60062	2756	12W-17N	B5
1300	NHBK	60062	2756	12W-17N	B5
West Av					
-	HRVY	60426	3428	1W-19S	A3
-	ODPK	60462	3423	12W-18S	C1
-	SMBG	60173	2860	21W-12N	A2
10	RVSD	60546	3088	10W-3S	B5
6800	HRPK	60133	2911		C2
7000	HRPK	60107	2911		C2
7000	SMWD	60107	2911		C2
7000	SMWD	60133	2911		C2
14300	ODPK	60462	3345	12W-17S	C4
West Brch					
1300	GNVW	60093	2810	8W-15N	D3
West Ct					
600	SHLD	60473	3428	0E-18S	E1
West Dr					
-	SMBG	60173	2805	22W-12N	D7
-	SMBG	60173	2859	21W-11N	E2
10	NHLK	60164	3028		D1
1700	CTCY	60409	3429	2E-19S	D1
West Ln					
-	BNHL	60010	2750	27W-17N	C5
West St					
18200	LNSG	60438	3430	4E-21S	C6
N West St					
100	PTON	60468	3860	9W-37S	E3
500	PtnT	60468	3860	9W-37S	E3
2000	MLPK	60160	2973	11W-2N	E6
2000	RVGV	60171	2973	11W-3N	E6
S West St					
100	PTON	60468	3860	9W-37S	E4
500	PtnT	60468	3860	9W-37S	E4
Westberry Ln					
8400	TYPK	60477	3424	10W-19S	B1
Westbourne Ln					
800	BFGV	60089	2754	17W-20N	B1
Westbridge Ct					
1700	SMBG	60194	2858	25W-11N	A3
4400	HFET	60195	2804	24W-15N	B2
17500	TYPK	60477	3424	10W-21S	B5
Westbridge Ln					
1600	HFET	60194	2858	25W-11N	B3
1600	SMBG	60194	2858	25W-11N	B3
Westbridge Rd					
8700	TYPK	60477	3424	11W-21S	A5
Westbrook Dr					
-	HMGN	60448	3422	14W-21S	C6
2400	FNPK	60131	2973	12W-3N	B6
2400	LydT	60164	2973	12W-3N	C6
17400	ODPK	60467	3422	14W-21S	C6
N West Brook Rd					
2400	EDPK	60707	2974	9W-3N	B6
Westbrook Corporate Ctr					
10	HLSD	60154	3086		D2
10	WSTR	60154	3086		D2
Westbury Dr					
1000	HFET	60195	2804	24W-15N	B2
1000	IVNS	60067	2804	24W-15N	D2
1000	IVNS	60195	2804	24W-15N	D2
Westchester Blvd					
-	PvsT	60525	3087	12W-1S	B2
600	WSTR	60104	3029	12W-0S	B7
600	WSTR	60154	3029	12W-1S	B7
1400	WSTR	60154	3087	12W-1S	B1
2100	PvsT	60154	3087	12W-1S	B2
Westchester Cir					
900	SMBG	60193	2913		B1
Westchester Dr					
900	HRPK	60133	2912		A2
900	SMBG	60193	2912		A2
1200	HRPK	60133	2911		E2
Westchester Rd					
400	SMBG	60193	2913		B1
N West Cir Av					
5700	CHCG	60631	2918	8W-7N	D4
W West End Av					
4000	CHCG	60624	3032	5W-0N	B4
4500	CHCG	60644	3032	5W-0N	A4
5400	CHCG	60644	3031	7W-0N	C4
5900	OKPK	60302	3031	7W-0N	B4
W West End Dr					
3700	CHCG	60624	3032	4W-0N	C4
West End Rd					
10	ROSL	60172	2912		E5
200	BmdT	60172	2912		E5
Westerfield Dr					
800	WLMT	60091	2812	3W-14N	E4
900	KLWH	60043	2812	3W-14N	E4
900	WLMT	60043	2812	3W-14N	E4
Western					
-	BRTN	60010	2750	26W-20N	D1
Western Av					
-	CHCG	60613	2977	1W-5N	D1
-	HMWD	60422	3507	3W-25S	C7
700	FSMR	60422	3507	3W-24S	C5
800	NHBK	60062	2757	10W-16N	A7
1300	CHHT	60411	3507	2W-25S	C7
1300	OMFD	60461	3507	2W-25S	C7
1500	CHHT	60411	3595	3W-28S	C5
1500	OMFD	60461	3595	2W-25S	C1
1500	PKFT	60466	3595	3W-28S	C5
1600	NfdT	60062	2756	12W-16N	C6
1600	NHBK	60062	2756	12W-16N	C6
1800	OMFD	60422	3507	2W-23S	C4
1800	PKFT	60411	3595	2W-26S	C1
3700	BlmT	60466	3595	3W-27S	C5
4300	WNSP	60558	3086		C7
11900	BLID	60406	3277	3W-15S	B7
11900	CHCG	60406	3277	3W-14S	B6
11900	CHCG	60643	3277	3W-14S	B6
13100	BLID	60406	3349	3W-15S	B1
13800	DXMR	60406	3349	2W-16S	B3
13800	POSN	60406	3349	2W-16S	B3
13900	DXMR	60469	3349	2W-16S	B3
13900	POSN	60469	3349	2W-16S	B3
14900	HRVY	60426	3349	2W-18S	C7
15600	HRVY	60426	3427	3W-18S	C1
15600	MKHM	60426	3427	3W-18S	C1

Block	City	ZIP	Map#	CGS	Grid
Western Av					
15900	BmnT	60426	3427	2W-19S	C2
15900	ThtT	60426	3427	2W-19S	C2
16700	HLCT	60426	3427	2W-20S	C4
16700	HLCT	60429	3427	2W-20S	C4
17500	HLCT	60430	3427	2W-21S	C6
17500	HMWD	60430	3427	2W-21S	C6
18400	HMWD	60430	3507	2W-22S	C1
18500	FSMR	60430	3507	2W-22S	C1
20300	BlmT	60411	3507	2W-24S	C6
20500	OMFD	60411	3507	2W-24S	C6
23400	MonT	60466	3595	3W-28S	C6
23500	CteT	60417	3595	3W-28S	C7
23500	CteT	60466	3595	3W-28S	C6
23500	MonT	60417	3595	3W-28S	C7
24100	CteT	60417	3684	2W-29S	C2
24100	CteT	60466	3684	2W-29S	C2
24100	MonT	60466	3684	2W-29S	C2
24100	UYPK	60466	3684	2W-29S	C2
24300	UYPK	60417	3684	2W-29S	C2
N Western Av					
10	CHCG	60612	3033	2W-0N	B4
10	PKRG	60068	2917	11W-8N	D2
100	BRLT	60103	2910		E3
700	CHCG	60622	3033	2W-0N	B3
700	PKRG	60068	2863	11W-9N	E6
1300	PKRG	60714	2863	10W-10N	E5
1500	CHCG	60647	3033	3W-1N	A1
1600	CHCG	60647	2977	3W-2N	A7
1800	MaiT	60016	2863	11W-11N	E3
1800	MaiT	60068	2863	11W-11N	E3
2000	PKRG	60016	2863	10W-11N	E3
2700	CHCG	60618	2977	3W-2N	A6
4400	CHCG	60618	2921	3W-5N	A7
4400	CHCG	60625	2921	3W-5N	A7
5500	CHCG	60659	2921	2W-6N	A5
6300	CHCG	60645	2921	3W-8N	A1
7200	CHCG	60645	2867	2W-9N	A7
7500	EVTN	60202	2867	2W-9N	A7
8800	GNVW	60025	2863	11W-12N	E1
8800	MaiT	60714	2863	11W-11N	E2
8800	NLES	60714	2863	11W-11N	E2
9300	NLES	60016	2863	11W-11N	E2
S Western Av					
-	CHCG	60608	3091	3W-3S	B4
10	CHCG	60612	3033	3W-0S	B6
10	PKRG	60068	2917	10W-7N	E3
100	BRLT	60103	2910		E4
300	DSPN	60016	2862	13W-11N	E3
1100	CHCG	60608	3033	3W-0S	B7
3400	CHCG	60632	3091	3W-3S	B5
4300	CHCG	60609	3091	2W-4S	B7
4700	CHCG	60609	3151	2W-5S	B2
4700	CHCG	60632	3151	3W-7S	B6
5400	CHCG	60629	3151	3W-5S	B3
5500	CHCG	60636	3151	3W-6S	B3
7400	CHCG	60620	3151	2W-8S	B7
7500	CHCG	60620	3213	3W-11S	B7
7500	CHCG	60629	3213	2W-8S	B1
7500	CHCG	60652	3213	3W-11S	B7
8300	CHCG	60805	3213	3W-9S	B4
9400	CHCG	60643	3213	2W-10S	B6
9400	ENGN	60805	3213	2W-10S	B5
9700	ENGN	60643	3213	2W-11S	B6
9800	CHCG	60655	3213	2W-11S	B7
9800	ENGN	60655	3213	2W-11S	B7
10200	CHCG	60643	3277	3W-13S	B4
10200	CHCG	60655	3277	3W-13S	B4
11800	BLID	60406	3277	2W-13S	B5
11800	CHCG	60406	3277	2W-13S	B5
14000	DXMR	60406	3349	2W-16S	B3
14000	DXMR	60469	3349	2W-16S	B3
14000	POSN	60406	3349	2W-16S	B3
14000	POSN	60469	3349	2W-17S	C5
14100	DXMR	60426	3349	2W-17S	C5
14600	HRVY	60426	3349	2W-17S	C5
24700	UYPK	60417	3684	3W-31S	C5
24700	UYPK	60466	3684	3W-31S	C5
25400	CteT	60417	3684	2W-29S	C2
26000	MonT	60417	3684	3W-31S	C5
26000	MonT	60449	3684	3W-31S	C5
S Western Blvd					
3300	CHCG	60608	3091	2W-3S	B4
3400	CHCG	60609	3091	2W-3S	B5
Western St					
300	HFET	60194	2858	24W-11N	D4
Westfield Av					
-	FftT	60477	3504	9W-23S	E3
-	TYPK	60477	3504	9W-23S	E3
Westfield Ct					
-	TYPK	60477	3504	9W-23S	D3
Westfield Ln					
10	DSPN	60018	2862	15W-10N	B5
800	SMBG	60193	2912		D1
3600	GNVW	60025	2809	10W-15N	E2
Westfield Wy					
200	BrnT	60010	2749	30W-17N	A5
Westgate Av					
100	EGVV	60007	2860	18W-9N	E6
100	EGVV	60007	2861	18W-9N	A6
200	CHHT	60411	3507	1W-24S	E5
Westgate Ct					
500	SMWD	60107	2857	27W-10N	C6
13300	ODPK	60462	3346	11W-15S	A2
Westgate Dr					
300	PKFT	60466	3594	4W-26S	E3
300	PKFT	60466	3595	4W-26S	A3
400	RNPK	60471	3594	4W-26S	E3
S Westgate Dr					
12700	PSHT	60463	3275	8W-15S	A7
12800	PSHT	60463	3347	8W-15S	A1
N Westgate Rd					
10	DSPN	60016	2808	14W-13N	C7
10	DSPN	60016	2862	14W-12N	C2
10	MPPT	60016	2808	14W-13N	C7
800	MPPT	60056	2808	14W-14N	C5
1200	PTHT	60070	2808	14W-14N	C5
S Westgate Rd					
200	DSPN	60016	2862	14W-11N	C3
Westgate St					
1100	OKPK	60301	3030	8W-0N	D4
1100	RVFT	60305	3030	8W-0N	D4
Westgate Ter					
300	SMWD	60107	2857	27W-10N	C6
W Westgate Ter					
1200	CHCG	60607	3033	1W-0S	D6
Westgate Valley Dr					
-	PSHT	60463	3347	8W-15S	B1
-	WthT	60463	3347	8W-15S	B1
Westhaven Ct					
4800	HFET	60010	2804	24W-16N	B1
Westlake Dr					
10	BNHL	60010	2803	27W-15N	A1
10	BrnT	60010	2803	27W-15N	A1
10	SBTN	60010	2803	27W-15N	A1

Block	City	ZIP	Map#	CGS	Grid
West Lake Rd					
17200	LNSG	60438	3430	3E-20S	A4
Westlake Ter					
4200	MLPK	60165	3029	13W-1N	A2
4200	SNPK	60165	3029	13W-1N	A2
4300	MLPK	60160	3029	13W-1N	A2
4300	SNPK	60160	3029	13W-1N	A2
Westleigh Dr					
-	NHBK	60062	2810	8W-15N	D2
-	NHFD	60093	2810	8W-15N	E2
1800	GNVW	60025	2810	8W-15N	D2
Westley Rd					
400	GLNC	60022	2758	7W-18N	B3
Westmere Rd					
300	DSPN	60016	2862	15W-11N	A3
Westmere St					
10	DSPN	60016	2862	15W-11N	B3
Westminster Av					
3700	CCHL	60478	3426	4W-20S	D5
3700	HLCT	60429	3426	4W-20S	D5
Westminster Cir					
500	ROSL	60172	2912		B6
Westminster Ct					
200	SMBG	60193	2857	27W-10N	D6
Westminster Dr					
-	PvsT	60154	3086		E4
-	PvsT	60558	3086		E4
200	BMDL	60108	2912		D7
300	BRRG	60527	3208		B5
4000	CCHL	60430	3426	4W-21S	D6
4000	CCHL	60478	3426	5W-21S	C6
4100	RNPK	60471	3594	5W-27S	C4
11000	WSTR	60154	3086		E4
15500	ODPK	60462	3345	11W-18S	E7
15600	ODPK	60462	3423	11W-18S	E1
N Westminster Dr					
300	PLTN	60067	2752	22W-16N	B7
Westminster Ln					
900	MNSR	46321	3510		E5
1100	EGVV	60007	2914		A2
Westminster Pl					
-	MNSR	46321	3510		D4
Westmoor Rd					
900	WNKA	60093	2812	5W-16N	A1
1100	WNKA	60093	2811	5W-16N	E1
Westmoor Tr					
1200	WNKA	60093	2811	6W-16N	E1
Westmoreland Dr					
200	WLMT	60091	2812	5W-13N	A7
N Westmoreland Dr					
2100	PLTN	60074	2753	19W-18N	B3
Weston Ct					
-	BRLT	60103	2909		B3
10	SMWD	60107	2856	29W-11N	E4
W Weston Dr					
1200	ANHT	60004	2753	18W-18N	D3
Weston Ln					
1900	SMBG	60193	2858	25W-10N	A6
Westover Av					
2200	FTPK	60130	3088	9W-2S	C2
2200	FTPK	60546	3088	9W-2S	C2
2200	NRIV	60546	3088	9W-2S	C2
2500	RVSD	60546	3088	9W-2S	C3
Westover Ct					
100	SMBG	60193	2858	25W-10N	B6
Westover Ln					
10	SMBG	60193	2858	25W-10N	B6
1000	SMBG	60193	2912		B1
Westpark Pl					
-	DRPK	60074	2752	21W-20N	C1
Westport Dr					
8100	WLSP	60480	3208		D3
S Westport Dr					
10100	PlsT	60464	3345	12W-15S	C1
12700	PlsT	60464	3273	12W-15S	C7
W Westport Dr					
7900	FftT	60423	3504	10W-24S	C5
Westridge Blvd					
100	BRLT	60103	2909		C3
100	HnrT	60103	2909		C3
1800	ELGN	60120	2909		D3
N Westshore Dr					
200	CHCG	60601	3034	0E-0N	D4
Westview Av					
16700	SHLD	60473	3428	0W-20S	C4
17000	TNTN	60473	3428	0W-20S	B4
17000	TNTN	60476	3428	0W-20S	B4
17100	SHLD	60476	3428	0W-20S	C4
17200	EHZC	60429	3428	0W-20S	C4
Westview Dr					
1000	EGVV	60007	2914		E2
2000	DSPN	60018	2862	13W-9N	D7
2200	DSPN	60018	2916		D1
3200	GNVW	60025	2809	11W-14N	D4
3200	NfdT	60025	2809	11W-14N	D4
3200	NfdT	60062	2809	11W-14N	C4
3300	GNVW	60062	2809	11W-14N	C4
6800	OKFT	60452	3347	8W-18S	A7
S Westview Dr					
13100	PSHT	60463	3346	9W-15S	C2
Westview Rd					
100	NtrT	60093	2811	5W-15N	E3
100	WNKA	60093	2811	5W-15N	E3
1100	GNVW	60025	2811	7W-13N	A7
Westview St					
10	HFET	60194	2858	24W-10N	D5
Westward Ho Dr					
10	NHLK	60164	3028		C1
200	NHLK	60164	2972		C7
Westway Wk					
15900	TYPK	60477	3424	9W-19S	E1
Westwind Ct					
7100	TYPK	60477	3425	8W-20S	A3
Westwind Dr					
-	RNPK	60471	3593	6W-27S	E5
16700	TYPK	60477	3425	8W-20S	A3
West Winds Ln					
18200	ODPK	60467	3422	14W-21S	E7
Westwood Ct					
10	IHPK	60525	3146		E6
10	PKFT	60466	3595	3W-26S	A2
600	WLNG	60090	2754	16W-17N	D6
1300	NHBK	60062	2757	10W-17N	A6
17000	ODHL	60477	3424	11W-20S	A4
Westwood Dr					
10	IHPK	60525	3146		E6
10	PKFT	60466	3595	3W-26S	A2
300	BRTN	60010	2750	26W-18N	D3
900	SMBG	60173	2805	21W-13N	C6
2200	HLSD	60154	3086		E3
2200	WSTR	60154	3086		E3
7700	EDPK	60707	2974	9W-3N	B5
7900	RVGV	60171	2974	9W-3N	B5
8800	ODHL	60477	3424	11W-20S	A4
14500	ODPK	60462	3345	12W-17S	C5

Block	City	ZIP	Map#	CGS	Grid
S Westwood Dr					
10900	PSHL	60465	3274	9W-12S	C3
W Westwood Dr					
800	GNWD	60425	3508	0W-22S	B1
Westwood Ln					
-	BlmT	60411	3510	4E-24S	B6
-	LYWD	60411	3510	4E-24S	B6
500	GLNC	60022	2758	7W-18N	B3
700	WLMT	60091	2811	5W-13N	E5
N Westwood Ln					
2300	PltT	60074	2752	21W-18N	D2
S Westwood Ln					
2200	PltT	60067	2805	20W-13N	E7
2300	SMBG	60067	2805	21W-12N	E7
2300	SMBG	60173	2805	21W-12N	E7
Westwood Sq					
10	IHPK	60525	3146		D5
Wetumka Ct					
500	WLNG	60090	2754	16W-17N	D5
Wexford Ct					
10	LMNT	60439	3271		A5
1100	DSPN	60016	2808	13W-13N	D6
16600	TYPK	60477	3424	9W-19S	E3
Wexford Dr					
300	LMNT	60439	3270		E5
500	LMNT	60439	3271		A5
Wexford Ln					
15300	ODPK	60462	3346	11W-18S	A7
Weyers Ct					
1400	SMBG	60193	2912		B2
Weymouth Cir					
600	HRPK	60133	2912		A1
Weymouth Ct					
100	SMBG	60193	2858	26W-10N	A6
Weymouth Ln					
100	SMBG	60193	2858	25W-10N	A6
Whalom Ln					
600	SMBG	60173	2859	22W-11N	C3
Wheat Ln					
600	WDDL	60191	2915		A5
Wheatfield Dr					
7800	FftT	60423	3504	9W-24S	D6
Wheatfield Rd					
300	MTSN	60443	3505	7W-24S	C5
Wheaton Rd					
10	BMDL	60108	2912		C7
10	BmdT	60108	2912		C7
10	BmdT	60172	2912		C7
200	ROSL	60172	2912		C7
Wheeler Ct					
10	LMNT	60439	3270		E5
10	LMNT	60439	3271		B5
Wheeler Dr					
200	LMNT	60439	3270		E5
300	LMNT	60439	3271		A5
7000	ODPK	60462	3346	9W-18S	E7
7000	ODPK	60462	3347	8W-18S	A7
9000	ODPK	60462	3345	11W-18S	E7
W Wheeler St					
-	ANHT	60004	2807	17W-16N	A1
Wheeling Av					
10	WLNG	60090	2755	14W-17N	C5
Wheeling Rd					
10	WLNG	60090	2755	14W-16N	B7
1400	WLNG	60090	2808	14W-16N	B1
N Wheeling Rd					
400	PTHT	60090	2808	15W-15N	B2
400	WLNG	60070	2808	15W-15N	B2
400	WLNG	60090	2808	15W-15N	B2
500	MPPT	60056	2808	14W-13N	B5
1200	PTHT	60070	2808	15W-14N	B5
S Wheeling Rd					
10	PTHT	60070	2808	15W-14N	B4
100	MPPT	60056	2808	15W-14N	B4
Wheelwood Ct					
3600	HLCT	60429	3426	4W-20S	D5
Wherry Ln					
9200	ODPK	60462	3345	11W-18S	E7
Whidah Ct					
200	SMBG	60194	2858	24W-10N	C5
Whipple Av					
15700	MKHM	60426	3427	3W-18S	A1
W Whipple Dr					
3100	MTPK	60803	3276	3W-13S	E4
Whipple St					
14000	BLID	60406	3349	3W-16S	A3
N Whipple St					
400	CHCG	60612	3032	3W-0N	E3
2000	CHCG	60647	2976	3W-2N	E6
3400	CHCG	60618	2976	3W-4N	E3
4400	CHCG	60618	2920	3W-5N	E7
4400	CHCG	60625	2920	3W-5N	E7
6200	CHCG	60659	2920	3W-7N	E3
6800	CHCG	60645	2920	3W-8N	E1
S Whipple St					
10	CHCG	60612	3032	3W-0S	E5
1100	CHCG	60623	3032	3W-0S	E6
2200	CHCG	60623	3090	3W-2S	E3
4200	CHCG	60632	3090	3W-4S	E7
5500	CHCG	60632	3150	3W-6S	E3
7100	CHCG	60629	3150	3W-8S	E7
7900	CHCG	60652	3212	3W-9S	E2
10200	CHCG	60805	3276	3W-11S	E1
10200	ENGN	60805	3212	3W-11S	E7
10200	ENGN	60805	3276	3W-11S	E1
10300	CHCG	60655	3276	3W-12S	E1
11200	CHCG	60803	3276	3W-13S	E3
11300	MTPK	60803	3276	3W-13S	E4
14600	POSN	60469	3349	3W-17S	A5
14700	MKHM	60426	3349	3W-17S	A5
14700	MKHM	60469	3349	3W-17S	A5
Whipple Tree Rd					
10	WLNG	60090	2755	15W-18N	A3
Whippoorwill Ct					
10	ROSL	60172	2912		C4
S Whippoorwill Ln					
1000	PLTN	60067	2805	22W-14N	C4
Whirlaway Ct					
14000	HMGN	60467	3344	15W-16S	C4
Whirlaway Dr					
3300	NHBK	60062	2809	11W-16N	C1
3400	NfdT	60062	2809	11W-16N	C1
3500	NfdT	60062	2756	12W-16N	B7
Whirlaway Ln					
1300	HRPK	60133	2911		E6
Whispering Ct					
10	SMWD	60107	2856	29W-10N	D6
Whispering Dr					
10	SMWD	60107	2856	29W-10N	D7
Whispering Hill Dr					
11600	ODPK	60467	3422	14W-21S	D6
11600	OrlT	60467	3422	14W-21S	D6
W Whispering Hill Ln					
6900	GGnT	60449	3682	8W-31S	A4
6900	MonT	60449	3682	8W-31S	A4

Block	City	ZIP	Map#	CGS	Grid
Whispering Lake Dr					
100	PlsT	60464	3273	12W-14S	C7
Whispering Oaks Ct					
700	PLTN	60074	2753	20W-18N	B3
E Whispering Oaks Ct					
600	PLTN	60074	2753	20W-18N	A2
N Whispering Oaks Dr					
700	PLTN	60074	2753	20W-18N	A3
Whispering Oaks Ln					
100	PltT	60010	2751	23W-18N	E3
S Whispering Oaks Ln					
25000	CteT	60417	3687	3E-30S	B3
Whispering Pines Ct					
300	IVNS	60010	2751	25W-16N	A7
E Whispering Springs Cir					
1300	PLTN	60074	2753	18W-18N	D4
Whispering Trails Ct					
3900	HFET	60195	2804	25W-15N	B3
Whispering Trails Dr					
3900	HFET	60195	2804	25W-14N	A3
Whisperwoods Ct					
3100	NfdT	60062	2756	11W-16N	D7
3100	NHBK	60062	2756	11W-16N	D7
Whitcomb Av					
1200	DSPN	60018	2862	13W-9N	D6
1200	DSPN	60018	2863	13W-10N	A5
N Whitcomb Dr					
600	PLTN	60074	2753	19W-16N	C6
White Av					
7900	LYNS	60534	3088	10W-4S	B7
White St					
1000	DSPN	60016	2863	12W-10N	A5
1200	DSPN	60018	2863	12W-9N	A6
White Tr					
1500	EGvT	60007	2914		A1
1500	EGVV	60007	2913		E1
1500	EGVV	60007	2914		A1
White Ash Dr					
7200	JSTC	60458	3148	10W-8S	A7
White Birch Ln					
6000	MTSN	60443	3505	7W-24S	C6
White Branch Ct N					
100	SMBG	60194	2857	27W-11N	D3
White Branch Ct S					
100	SMBG	60194	2857	27W-11N	D3
White Bridge Ct					
7500	HRPK	60133	2911		E1
White Bridge Ln					
900	HRPK	60133	2912		A1
1000	HRPK	60133	2911		E2
Whitebridge Ln					
100	WNKA	60093	2759		A6
Whitebridge Hill Dr					
100	GLNC	60093	2759	5W-17N	A6
100	WNKA	60093	2759	5W-17N	A6
Whitebridge Hill Rd					
1100	GLNC	60093	2759	5W-17N	A6
1100	WNKA	60093	2759	5W-17N	A6
White Chappel Dr					
1800	MPPT	60056	2861	17W-11N	C4
White Cloud Dr					
-	RchT	60443	3505	8W-25S	B7
-	RchT	60443	3593	8W-25S	B1
3800	SKOK	60076	2866	4W-11N	C3
White Deer Cir					
10800	ODPK	60467	3423	13W-20S	A4
S White Fence Ct					
20300	FftT	60423	3504	9W-24S	E6
White Fence Tr					
10	SMWD	60107	2856	30W-10N	C5
White Gate Ct					
500	PltT	60010	2751	23W-18N	D2
Whitegate Ct					
700	MPPT	60056	2807	16W-12N	E7
Whitegate Dr					
900	MPPT	60056	2807	16W-12N	D7
Whitehall Av					
10	NHLK	60164	2972		D7
300	MLPK	60160	2973	13W-2N	A7
300	NHLK	60164	2973	13W-2N	A7
Whitehall Ct					
10	BFGV	60089	2754	17W-18N	A2
10	SMWD	60107	2857	26W-11N	E4
700	SMBG	60194	2858	25W-11N	A4
1600	WLNG	60090	2754	16W-18N	D3
S Whitehall Ct					
100	PLTN	60067	2805	22W-15N	B1
Whitehall Dr					
-	LYWD	60411	3509	2E-23S	D4
900	BFGV	60089	2754	17W-18N	A2
1000	ANHT	60004	2754	17W-18N	A2
1000	BFGV	60004	2754	17W-18N	A2
1000	NHBK	60062	2757	9W-17N	C5
S Whitehall Dr					
200	PLTN	60067	2805	22W-15N	A2
W Whitehall Dr					
-	BFGV	60089	2754	18W-18N	A2
200	ANHT	60004	2754	18W-18N	A2
200	BFGV	60004	2754	18W-18N	A2
300	ANHT	60004	2753	18W-20N	D2
Whitehall Gdn					
9700	MNSR	46321	3510		D4
Whitehall Ln					
4200	RNPK	60471	3594	5W-26S	C3
9200	ODPK	60462	3345	11W-18S	E7
Whitehorse Ln					
1400	BRLT	60103	2910		B7
White Mountain Dr					
1000	NHBK	60062	2756	11W-17N	D5
White Oak Cir					
2100	NHBK	60062	2756	11W-16N	C7
White Oak Ct					
100	SMBG	60195	2859	23W-12N	A1
200	BRTN	60010	2751	24W-20N	D1
11600	BRRG	60527	3208		D2
18300	TYPK	60477	3424	11W-21S	A7
S White Oak Ct					
10	PSHT	60463	3274	9W-14S	C5
W White Oak Ct					
12800	HMGN	60441	3422	16W-19S	A2
White Oak Dr					
400	ROSL	60172	2913		B6
2100	NfdT	60062	2756	11W-16N	C7
2100	NHBK	60062	2756	11W-16N	C7
2200	NfdT	60062	2809	11W-15N	C1
2200	NHBK	60062	2809	11W-15N	C1
White Oak Ln					
-	HnrT	60120	2856	31W-12N	A1
200	WNKA	60093	2812	5W-15N	A2
400	RVWD	60015	2755	13W-20N	D1
600	BRLT	60103	2856	29W-9N	D7
600	BRLT	60103	2910		C1
800	UYPK	60466	3684	3W-30S	B2
1600	HFET	60120	2856	31W-12N	A1
1600	SMBG	60195	2859	23W-12N	A1

Block	City	ZIP	Map#	CGS	Grid
White Oak Ln					
18300	TYPK	60477	3424	11W-22S	A7
S White Oak Ln					
24900	CteT	60417	3686	2E-30S	D3
E White Oak St					
10	ANHT	60005	2861	18W-12N	A1
W White Oak St					
10	ANHT	60005	2861	18W-12N	A1
500	ANHT	60005	2860	19W-12N	D1
1700	RGMW	60008	2860	19W-12N	D1
2100	MPPT	60005	2861	17W-12N	B1
2100	MPPT	60056	2861	17W-12N	B1
White Oaks Rd					
10	MTSN	60443	3505	7W-24S	C5
White Pine Ct					
15600	HMGN	60441	3422	15W-18S	C1
White Pine Dr					
10	SMBG	60193	2858	23W-10N	E5
10	SMBG	60193	2859	23W-10N	A5
2800	NHBK	60062	2756	11W-16N	D7
W White Pine Pl					
7600	PSHT	60463	3274	9W-15S	D7
White Pine Rd					
400	BFGV	60089	2754	17W-18N	B4
White Pine Tr					
12100	HMGN	60441	3422	15W-18S	C1
12200	HMGN	60441	3344	15W-18S	C7
Whitesail Dr					
700	SMBG	60194	2859	22W-10N	C5
White Sands Bay					
500	ROSL	60172	2913		B3
N White Sands Bay					
1700	PLTN	60074	2753	18W-18N	D4
Whitetail Ln					
10	PltT	60010	2751	23W-18N	D3
White Tail Run					
10600	ODPK	60467	3423	13W-20S	A5
White Tail Wy					
14900	LKPT	60441	3342	21W-17S	A6
14900	LktT	60441	3342	21W-17S	A6
White Tailed Ln					
6700	TYPK	60477	3425	8W-21S	B7
E White Water Ln					
1200	PLTN	60074	2753	19W-18N	C4
S White Willow Bay					
700	PLTN	60067	2805	22W-15N	B3
Whitewood Dr					
200	SMWD	60107	2857	27W-10N	C5
Whitfield Rd					
900	NHBK	60062	2757	8W-17N	E5
1100	NHBK	60062	2758	8W-17N	A5
W Whiting Ln					
600	ANHT	60004	2753	18W-18N	E3
Whiting Wy					
26000	MONE	60449	3682	7W-31S	D6
Whitingham Ln					
1800	HFET	60195	2858	26W-12N	A1
Whitman Av					
17100	HLCT	60429	3427	3W-20S	A4
Whitman Ct					
1400	SMBG	60173	2859	21W-10N	E5
Whitman Dr					
10	SMBG	60173	2859	21W-10N	E5
100	SMBG	60193	2859	21W-10N	E6
Whitman Ln					
18000	LNSG	60438	3429	2E-21S	C6
Whitney Av					
21200	MTSN	60443	3593	7W-25S	C1
Whitney Dr					
100	BRTN	60010	2751	25W-20N	B2
Whitney Ln					
10	DGvT	60439	3270		C3
Whittier Av					
17100	HLCT	60429	3427	3W-20S	B4
Whittier Ct					
200	SMBG	60193	2858	25W-10N	A6
Whittier Ln					
400	NHFD	60093	2811	7W-15N	A2
1800	SMBG	60193	2858	25W-10N	A6
Whittington Dr					
7800	TYPK	60477	3424	9W-19S	C2
W Whytecliff Rd					
1000	PLTN	60067	2805	22W-15N	A2
1300	IVNS	60067	2805	22W-15N	B2
Wianno Ln					
200	SMBG	60194	2858	24W-10N	C5
Wichman Rd					
-	BNHL	60118	2802	29W-14N	C5
-	HFET	60118	2802	29W-14N	C5
-	HFET	60192	2802	29W-13N	C5
Wick Dr					
4800	OKLN	60453	3276	6W-11S	A1
4900	OKLN	60453	3211	6W-11S	E7
5000	OKLN	60453	3275	6W-11S	E1
Wicke Av					
900	DSPN	60018	2862	13W-10N	E6
1300	DSPN	60018	2863	12W-10N	A5
Wicker Av					
600	SMWD	60107	2857	28W-9N	B7
600	SMWD	60107	2911		B1
Wicker Dr					
200	DRPK	60010	2752	22W-20N	B1
N Wicker Park Av					
1400	CHCG	60622	3033	2W-1N	C1
Wickham Dr					
200	SMBG	60194	2858	25W-10N	C5
Wicklow Rd					
500	DRFD	60015	2757	9W-20N	B1
Widgeon Dr					
600	WLNG	60090	2754	16W-17N	C6
700	ANHT	60004	2754	16W-17N	D5
700	WLNG	60004	2754	16W-17N	D5
Wieboldt Dr					
200	DSPN	60016	2862	14W-11N	D3
N Wieland St					
1400	CHCG	60610	2978		D7
1400	CHCG	60610	3034	0W-1N	B1
1400	CHCG	60614	2978		D7
Wight St					
10200	WSTR	60154	3087	12W-1S	A1
W Wigwam Tr					
1400	MPPT	60056	2861	16W-12N	C1
Wilco Dr					
14900	ODPK	60467	3344	14W-17S	C6
15000	HMGN	60441	3344	15W-17S	C6
Wilcox Av					
2900	BLWD	60104	3029	12W-0S	B5
3900	HLSD	60162	3029	12W-0S	A5
Wilcox Ct					
200	BRLT	60103	2911		A5
Wilcox Dr					
100	BRLT	60103	2910		E5
100	BRLT	60103	2911		A5
Wilcox St					
10	MYWD	60153	3030	10W-0S	A5

Chicago & Cook County Street Index

STREET Block	City	ZIP	Map#	CGS	Grid
Wilcox St					
700	MYWD	60153	3029	10W-0S	E5
7600	FTPK	60130	3030	9W-0S	C5
E Wilcox St					
-	HMND	46320	3352		D5
W Wilcox St					
2300	CHCG	60612	3033	2W-0S	B5
2800	CHCG	60612	3032	3W-0S	E5
3800	CHCG	60624	3032	5W-0S	B5
4500	CHCG	60644	3032	5W-0S	A5
Wildberry Ct					
300	SMBG	60193	2859	22W-9N	D7
1100	WLNG	60090	2754	16W-18N	D3
Wildberry Dr					
1700	GNVW	60025	2810	8W-15N	D3
1700	NHFD	60025	2810	8W-15N	E3
1700	NHFD	60093	2810	8W-15N	E3
Wild Cherry Ln					
10	PSPK	60464	3273	12W-14S	C7
9600	PlsT	60464	3273	12W-14S	C7
Wilder St					
1300	EVTN	60202	2867	3W-10N	A4
3300	SKOK	60076	2866	4W-10N	D4
Wilderness Tr					
20200	OMFD	60461	3507	4W-24S	A5
Wildewoode Wy					
17000	CCHL	60478	3426	4W-20S	D4
Wildflower Ct					
1700	SMBG	60173	2860	21W-10N	A5
2800	NHBK	60025	2809	11W-15N	D1
Wildflower Dr					
-	FftT	60448	3504	11W-23S	A4
-	FKFT	60448	3504	11W-24S	A4
19900	FKFT	60423	3504	11W-24S	A5
Wildflower Ln					
-	SMBG	60173	2859	21W-10N	E6
-	SMBG	60193	2859	21W-10N	E6
10	SMBG	60173	2860	20W-10N	A6
200	WLSP	60525	3208		E2
1000	DYR	46311	3510		D7
Wildflower Rd					
10500	ODPK	60462	3345	13W-17S	B5
21600	MTSN	60443	3594	4W-26S	E2
Wildflower Wy					
10	HnrT	60120	2856	30W-10N	C6
10	SMWD	60107	2856	30W-10N	C6
400	SMWD	60120	2856	30W-10N	B5
Wild Oak Ct					
10	LMNT	60439	3271		B6
Wild Oak Dr					
1000	LMNT	60439	3271		A6
Wildplum Ct					
10	LMNT	60439	3271		A6
Wildridge St					
11200	WSTR	60154	3086		D3
Wild Rock Ter					
300	RchT	60443	3593	8W-26S	B1
Wildrose Ct					
-	CPVL	60110	2748		A6
10	HnrT	60107	2856	29W-9N	E7
10	SMWD	60107	2856	29W-9N	E7
Wild Rose Ln					
15600	ODPK	60462	3346	9W-18S	E7
Wildspring Ct					
200	ITSC	60143	2914		C5
Wildwood Av					
-	CHCG	60613	2977	1W-5N	D1
18200	LNSG	60438	3430	3E-21S	A7
18500	LNSG	60411	3430	3E-21S	A7
19000	LNSG	60438	3510	3E-22S	A2
19300	LNSG	60411	3510	3E-22S	A2
19300	LYWD	60411	3510	3E-22S	A2
N Wildwood Av					
6700	CHCG	60646	2919	7W-8N	B1
Wildwood Ct					
800	OKBK	60523	3086		B1
800	SMWD	60107	2857	27W-9N	B7
900	BRLT	60103	2911		B5
1700	GNVW	60025	2810	8W-14N	E4
4400	HFET	60195	2804	24W-15N	C2
S Wildwood Ct					
24500	CteT	60417	3687	3E-29S	B2
Wildwood Dr					
10	ROSL	60172	2912		E5
300	PKFT	60466	3594	4W-26S	E3
300	PKFT	60466	3595	4W-26S	A2
10500	PlsT	60464	3273	13W-14S	A7
S Wildwood Dr					
10	PTHT	60070	2754	15W-16N	E7
10	PTHT	60070	2755	14W-16N	B7
Wildwood Dr E					
900	PTHT	60070	2755	15W-16N	A7
Wildwood Dr N					
10	PTHT	60070	2754	15W-16N	E7
10	PTHT	60070	2755	14W-16N	B7
Wildwood Dr W					
900	PTHT	60070	2754	15W-16N	E7
Wildwood Ln					
700	SMWD	60107	2857	28W-9N	B7
900	NHBK	60062	2757	8W-17N	D6
1100	GNVW	60025	2811	7W-14N	A4
6100	BRRG	60527	3146		A5
16100	HMGN	60441	3422	16W-19S	A2
E Wildwood Ln					
1200	MPPT	60056	2808	14W-13N	C6
Wildwood Pl					
10	EGVV	60007	2861	18W-9N	A6
Wildwood Rd					
10	CTCY	60409	3430		C1
10	EGVV	60007	2861	18W-9N	A6
10	HMND	46320	3430		D1
10	RGMW	60008	2806	19W-14N	B4
200	HMND	46324	3430		D1
Wildwood Ter					
-	GNVW	60025	2810	8W-14N	E5
Wild Wood Tr					
10	PSPK	60464	3272	13W-14S	E7
10	PSPK	60464	3273	13W-15S	A7
S Wildwood Tr					
24500	CteT	60417	3687	3E-29S	B2
Wiley Rd					
1000	SMBG	60173	2859	22W-12N	C1
N Wiley Rd					
1100	SMBG	60173	2859	22W-12N	D1
Wiley Farm Ct					
700	SMBG	60173	2859	22W-12N	C1
Wilke Rd					
200	ANHT	60005	2806	19W-13N	D6
2300	RGMW	60005	2806	19W-13N	D6
3400	RGMW	60008	2806	19W-13N	D7
3800	ANHT	60008	2806	19W-13N	D7
N Wilke Rd					
-	PltT	60074	2753	19W-16N	D7
-	VrnT	60047	2753	19W-20N	D2
10	ANHT	60074	2806	19W-16N	D1
10	PLTN	60074	2753	19W-16N	D7
10	PLTN	60074	2806	19W-16N	D1
600	ANHT	60005	2806	19W-14N	D4
600	RGMW	60008	2806	19W-14N	D4
1600	PLTN	60004	2806	18W-15N	D2
1900	ANHT	60004	2753	18W-17N	D6
1900	ANHT	60004	2806	18W-16N	D1
3100	PltT	60004	2753	18W-18N	D3
Wilkening Ct					
1500	SMBG	60173	2859	23W-12N	A1
Wilkening Rd					
1200	HFET	60173	2859	23W-12N	B2
1200	HFET	60195	2859	23W-12N	B2
1200	SMBG	60173	2859	23W-12N	B1
Wilkens Dr					
200	DSPN	60016	2862	15W-11N	B3
200	MPPT	60056	2862	15W-11N	B3
Wilkinson Pkwy					
700	PKRG	60068	2863	11W-9N	E6
Willams Ln					
-	CRTE	60417	3597	0E-29S	A7
-	CRTE	60417	3686	0E-29S	A1
Willard Av					
-	HRVY	60426	3428	1W-19S	A3
10	ELGN	60120	2855		C5
N Willard Ct					
100	CHCG	60607	3033	1W-0N	E4
900	CHCG	60622	3033	1W-1N	D2
S Will Center Rd					
25100	MonT	60449	3683	5W-30S	B3
25100	UYPK	60449	3683	5W-30S	B3
25100	UYPK	60466	3683	5W-30S	B2
25500	MONE	60449	3683	5W-32S	B7
Will Cook Rd					
-	HMGN	60441	3344	14W-17S	C6
-	HMGN	60448	3422	14W-20S	C5
-	HMGN	60467	3422	14W-20S	C5
-	ODPK	60441	3344	14W-17S	C6
-	ODPK	60448	3422	14W-21S	C7
-	ODPK	60467	3344	14W-17S	C6
10	LmnT	60439	3272	15W-13S	C4
10	LMNT	60464	3272	15W-13S	C4
10	PlsT	60439	3272	15W-13S	C4
10	PlsT	60464	3272	15W-13S	C4
1200	HMGN	60441	3422	14W-19S	C1
1200	ODPK	60467	3422	14W-20S	D4
1200	OrlT	60467	3422	14W-20S	D4
S Will Cook Rd					
-	LmnT	60439	3344	14W-15S	C1
-	LmnT	60464	3344	14W-15S	C1
-	LmnT	60467	3344	14W-15S	C1
-	PlsT	60464	3344	14W-15S	C1
-	PlsT	60467	3344	14W-15S	C1
11700	LMNT	60439	3272	14W-14S	C6
11700	PlsT	60439	3272	14W-14S	C6
11700	PlsT	60464	3272	14W-14S	C6
12100	LmnT	60464	3272	14W-14S	C7
13500	HMGN	60467	3344	15W-15S	C2
13500	OrlT	60467	3344	15W-15S	C2
14900	HMGN	60441	3344	14W-18S	C7
14900	ODPK	60441	3344	14W-17S	C6
14900	ODPK	60467	3344	14W-17S	C6
15400	OrlT	60441	3344	14W-18S	C7
15600	HMGN	60441	3422	14W-18S	C1
15600	ODPK	60467	3422	14W-18S	C1
15600	OrlT	60467	3422	14W-18S	C1
Wille Av					
10	WLNG	60090	2755	14W-17N	D5
Wille Rd					
-	DSPN	60018	2861	16W-9N	E6
10	DSPN	60018	2862	15W-9N	B6
10	EGvT	60018	2862	15W-9N	B6
N Wille St					
10	MPPT	60056	2808	15W-13N	A6
S Wille St					
10	MPPT	60056	2808	15W-12N	A7
200	MPPT	60056	2862	15W-12N	A1
N Willetts Ct					
2500	CHCG	60647	2976	3W-3N	E5
Willgate Ter					
500	GLNC	60022	2758	6W-17N	E5
N William					
100	NHLK	60164	2972		E7
100	NHLK	60164	3028		E1
William Av					
800	DndT	60118	2801		A3
800	EDND	60118	2801		A3
2500	MaiT	60025	2864	9W-12N	B1
N William Av					
20500	BFGV	60089	2754	15W-20N	E1
20500	VrnT	60069	2754	15W-20N	E1
William Ct					
-	ODPK	60462	3345	11W-16S	E3
William Dr					
14000	ODPK	60462	3345	11W-16S	E3
William St					
-	FSMR	60422	3506	4W-23S	E3
-	RchT	60430	3506	4W-23S	E3
400	FTPK	60130	3030	9W-0N	D4
400	FTPK	60305	3030	9W-0N	D4
1200	RVFT	60305	3030	9W-1N	D1
1500	EDPK	60305	3030	9W-2N	D1
1500	EDPK	60707	3030	9W-2N	D1
17000	LNSG	60438	3430	4E-20S	B4
18700	LNSG	60438	3510	4E-22S	C1
N William St					
200	MPPT	60056	2808	15W-13N	B6
S William St					
10	MPPT	60056	2808	15W-12N	B7
400	MPPT	60056	2862	15W-12N	B2
900	DSPN	60016	2862	15W-11N	B2
900	DSPN	60056	2862	15W-11N	B2
W William St					
-	MONE	60449	3682	7W-31S	E6
William Wy					
-	BMDL	60108	2912		D7
William Clifford Ln					
1400	EGVV	60007	2914		A3
E William L McFetridge Dr					
400	CHCG	60605	3034	0E-1S	D7
S Williams Av					
400	PLTN	60074	2806	19W-15N	C2
9100	CHCG	60619	3214	0E-10S	D5
Williams Ct					
800	SMBG	60193	2858	24W-10N	D6
1500	CRTE	60417	3685	1W-30S	A3
4100	HFET	60195	2804	23W-15N	D3
Williams Dr					
100	SMBG	60193	2858	24W-10N	D6
3200	FNPK	60131	2973	13W-4N	A4
E Williams Dr					
1000	PLTN	60074	2806	19W-16N	B1
1100	PLTN	60074	2753	19W-16N	C7
N Williams Dr					
10	PLTN	60074	2806	19W-16N	B1
100	PLTN	60074	2753	19W-16N	C7
Williams Ln					
3500	CRTE	60417	3597	0E-28S	A6
Williams Pl					
200	EDND	60118	2801		A3
4400	OKLN	60453	3212	5W-11S	B7
Williams Rd					
-	HFET	60010	2751	24W-16N	C7
200	HFET	60195	2804	24W-15N	C1
200	IVNS	60010	2751	24W-16N	C7
200	IVNS	60067	2804	24W-15N	C1
700	CPVL	60110	2748		A6
700	DndT	60110	2748		A6
800	DndT	60102	2748		A6
Williams St					
-	RSMT	60018	2917	11W-6N	C5
300	ROSL	60172	2912		E4
800	CTCY	60409	3430	3E-19S	A1
1300	FDHT	60411	3509	1E-25S	B7
3500	CteT	60417	3595	1W-28S	E6
3500	STGR	60417	3595	1W-28S	E6
3500	STGR	60475	3595	1W-28S	E6
E Williams St					
10	CTCY	60409	3352		C7
10	HMND	46320	3352		D7
N Williams St					
100	TNTN	60476	3428	0E-20S	D5
S Williams St					
100	TNTN	60476	3428	0E-21S	D7
17500	BlmT	60425	3428	0W-21S	D7
17500	BlmT	60476	3428	0W-21S	D7
17500	TNTN	60425	3428	0W-21S	D7
Williamsburg Cir					
10	SKOK	60203	2866	4W-11N	C3
Williamsburg Ct					
-	GNVW	60025	2809	11W-13N	D7
10	SKOK	60203	2866	4W-11N	C3
500	WLNG	60090	2754	15W-18N	E3
4100	NfdT	60025	2809	11W-13N	D7
4400	RGMW	60008	2805	21W-14N	D4
4400	RGMW	60008	2806	20W-15N	A3
Williamsburg Dr					
100	BRLT	60103	2910		E3
1000	NHBK	60062	2757	9W-18N	D3
1200	SMBG	60193	2859	21W-10N	D6
1700	HFET	60195	2858	26W-12N	A1
1800	SMWD	60107	2857	26W-11N	E4
2000	HFET	60194	2857	26W-11N	E4
N Williamsburg Dr					
1900	PLTN	60074	2753	20W-20N	B1
Williamsburg Ln					
10	SKOK	60203	2866	4W-11N	C3
400	PTHT	60070	2808	14W-14N	B3
Williamsburg Rd					
10	SKOK	60203	2866	4W-11N	C3
1100	CCHL	60429	3506	5W-22S	C1
1100	CCHL	60478	3506	5W-22S	C1
1100	HLCT	60429	3506	5W-22S	C1
N Williamsburg St					
2200	ANHT	60004	2753	18W-16N	D7
Williamsburg Ter					
10	SKOK	60203	2866	4W-11N	C3
Willigan Rd					
-	ThtT	60476	3429	1E-21S	A6
Willington Dr					
400	SMBG	60194	2858	25W-11N	A4
Willis Av					
1100	WLNG	60090	2755	14W-16N	B7
Willis St					
500	ELGN	60123	2855		A6
Willoby Ct					
200	SMBG	60173	2859	21W-11N	E3
Willoby Ln					
1000	ELGN	60120	2855		D1
Willow					
-	ITSC	60143	2914		B6
Willow Av					
-	LMNT	60439	3343	18W-15S	B2
10	DRFD	60015	2756	11W-20N	D2
1300	DSPN	60016	2862	13W-11N	E2
1300	DSPN	60016	2863	13W-11N	A2
2000	HRPK	60133	2911		C3
17500	CCHL	60478	3426	5W-21S	C6
18900	CCHL	60478	3506	5W-22S	C2
Willow Blvd					
2100	WLSP	60480	3209	13W-9S	B4
Willow Ct					
10	CTCY	60409	3429	2E-18S	D1
10	CTSD	60525	3147	12W-6S	C4
100	MTSN	60443	3505	7W-24S	C5
100	SMWD	60107	2857	27W-10N	C5
400	DRPK	60010	2752	22W-20N	B1
700	BRLT	60103	2910		D6
700	ITSC	60143	2914		B5
9400	MaiT	60016	2863	11W-12N	D1
15500	HMGN	60441	3344	16W-18S	A7
15500	HMGN	60441	3422	16W-18S	A1
18800	CCHL	60478	3506	5W-22S	C2
E Willow Ct					
10	CTCY	60409	3352		D6
10	HMND	46320	3352		D6
500	PLTN	60074	2753	20W-16N	A7
Willow Dr					
-	LMNT	60439	3342	20W-15S	B1
600	CHHT	60411	3507	1W-24S	E6
800	CHHT	60411	3508	1W-24S	A6
8100	PSHL	60465	3274	10W-13S	B4
8700	JSTC	60458	3210	10W-8S	A1
20100	LYWD	60411	3509	3E-24S	E4
Willow Ln					
-	TYPK	60477	3504	10W-23S	B3
100	EGVV	60007	2861	18W-9N	A6
100	WLSP	60480	3209	11W-9S	D3
400	DYR	46311	3598		D3
500	BCHR	60401	3864	0W-36S	C1
1100	LynT	60458	3209	11W-8S	D2
1100	NHBK	60062	2757	8W-17N	D6
1500	CRTE	60417	3685	1W-30S	B3
2200	RGMW	60008	2806	19W-12N	C7
3300	MKHM	60426	3348	4W-18S	E7
3600	GNVW	60025	2809	11W-15N	E2
8900	FftT	60448	3504	11W-23S	A3
8900	MKNA	60448	3504	11W-23S	A3
9100	BGVW	60455	3210	8W-10S	E5
14000	CTWD	60445	3348	5W-16S	A3
15100	BmnT	60452	3347	8W-18S	B6
15100	OKFT	60452	3347	8W-18S	B6
18300	LNSG	60438	3430	4E-21S	C7
N Willow Ln					
10	GNWD	60425	3508	0E-22S	E2
9200	NLES	60714	2864	10W-11N	B3
S Willow Ln					
10	GNWD	60425	3508	0E-22S	E2
W Willow Ln					
900	MPPT	60056	2861	16W-11N	D3
1800	ANHT	60005	2861	17W-11N	B3
1800	ANHT	60056	2861	17W-11N	B3
Willow Rd					
-	NfdT	60062	2809	11W-15N	E2
-	NfdT	60062	2810	9W-15N	B2
-	NfdT	60090	2809	11W-15N	E2
-	NHFD	60093	2810	8W-15N	E2
10	MTSN	60443	3505	7W-24S	C6
10	RchT	60443	3505	7W-23S	D4
10	WLNG	60090	2808	14W-15N	B2
100	BRTN	60010	2751	25W-20N	B1
100	SMWD	60107	2857	27W-10N	C5
600	WNKA	60093	2812	5W-15N	A2
1100	WNKA	60093	2811	5W-15N	E2
1300	GNVW	60025	2810	8W-15N	E2
1300	GNVW	60062	2810	9W-15N	C2
1300	NHBK	60025	2810	10W-15N	A2
1300	NHBK	60062	2810	8W-15N	E2
1300	NHFD	60093	2811	8W-15N	A2
1300	NtrT	60093	2811	6W-15N	D2
1400	SMBG	60173	2859	21W-10N	E4
1500	HMWD	60430	3507	2W-22S	D1
2600	GNVW	60025	2809	10W-15N	E2
2600	NHBK	60025	2809	10W-15N	E2
2600	NHBK	60062	2809	10W-15N	E2
2700	GNVW	60062	2809	10W-15N	E2
3100	SCHT	60411	3595	1W-27S	E4
3700	FNPK	60176	2973	11W-4N	D2
3700	SRPK	60176	2973	11W-4N	D2
8700	HYHL	60457	3209	11W-10S	E4
8700	HYHL	60457	3210	11W-10S	A4
E Willow Rd					
10	PTHT	60070	2808	15W-15N	A2
N Willow Rd					
100	EMHT	60126	3028		A1
400	EMHT	60126	2972		A7
W Willow Rd					
10	PTHT	60070	2808	15W-15N	A2
100	PTHT	60070	2807	16W-15N	D2
500	ANHT	60004	2807	16W-15N	D2
700	PTHT	60004	2807	16W-15N	D2
Willow St					
10	BmdT	60172	2913		A5
100	IVNS	60010	2751	23W-16N	D7
100	PKFT	60466	3595	3W-26S	A3
100	ROSL	60172	2913		A5
300	AddT	60126	2972		A5
300	IVNS	60067	2751	23W-16N	E7
800	ITSC	60143	2914		B5
1400	WNSP	60558	3086		C7
2800	FNPK	60131	2973	11W-3N	D5
3500	FSMR	60422	3506	4W-22S	E2
14500	ODPK	60462	3345	11W-17S	E5
14500	OrlT	60462	3345	11W-17S	E5
E Willow St					
10	ANHT	60004	2807	17W-14N	A3
N Willow St					
200	ITSC	60143	2914		B6
S Willow St					
200	GNWD	60425	3508	0E-23S	E3
W Willow St					
200	CHCG	60614	2978		C7
400	ANHT	60004	2807	18W-14N	A3
800	CHCG	60614	2977	1W-2N	E7
800	PLTN	60067	2752	22W-16N	B7
900	PltT	60067	2752	22W-16N	B7
1400	CHCG	60622	2977	1W-2N	D7
2000	CHCG	60647	2977	2W-2N	B7
Willow Tr					
10	WLNG	60090	2754	15W-17N	E4
Willow Bay Dr					
10	SBTN	60010	2803	27W-13N	B5
Willow Brook Ct					
100	SMBG	60195	2859	23W-12N	B1
E Willow Brook Ct					
2800	CteT	60417	3687	3E-30S	A3
Willowbrook Dr					
800	WLNG	60090	2755	15W-16N	A6
S Willow Brook Tr					
24500	CteT	60417	3687	3E-29S	A2
Willowbrook Centre Pkwy					
500	DGvT	60527	3208		A1
500	WLBK	60527	3208		A1
Willow Creek Dr					
6100	RSMT	60018	2917	11W-7N	C3
Willow Creek Ln					
100	WLSP	60480	3209	13W-10S	A5
11200	ODPK	60467	3344	14W-18S	E7
S Willow Creek Ln					
25500	MonT	60449	3682	8W-31S	B5
Willow Creek Church Dr					
-	BrnT	60010	2803	25W-14N	E3
-	BrnT	60010	2804	25W-14N	A3
-	SBTN	60010	2803	25W-14N	E3
-	SBTN	60010	2804	25W-14N	A3
Willow Crest Ct					
14900	MDLN	60445	3348	5W-17S	C6
Willow Crest Dr					
-	MDLN	60445	3348	5W-17S	C6
Willow Hill Ct					
1800	NHFD	60093	2811	7W-15N	B2
Willow Hills Ln					
800	PTHT	60070	2808	14W-14N	C3
Willowick Dr					
16000	OKFT	60452	3426	5W-19S	B3
Willow Lake Rd					
1100	ELGN	60123	2801		B6
Willow Ln Dr					
6300	TYPK	60477	3425	8W-20S	B3
Willowmere Dr					
10	SBTN	60010	2803	25W-15N	E3
10	SBTN	60010	2804	25W-15N	A2
Willowood Ct					
7400	ODPK	60462	3346	9W-18S	E6
W Willowood Ct					
7500	ODPK	60462	3346	9W-18S	D6
Willow Ridge Dr					
9000	WLSP	60480	3208		C5
9000	WLSP	60527	3208		C5
11900	BRRG	60527	3208		C5
11900	DGvT	60527	3208		C5
Willows Edge Ct					
100	PlsT	60480	3209	13W-10S	A5
100	WLSP	60480	3209	13W-10S	A5
Willow Springs Rd					
10	LGNG	60525	3087	13W-4S	A7
10	WNSP	60558	3087	13W-4S	A7
4400	LGNG	60525	3147	13W-5S	A2
4600	LGNG	60558	3147	13W-5S	A2
5300	LynT	60525	3147	13W-7S	A5
5300	WNSP	60558	3147	13W-7S	A5
5400	CTSD	60525	3147	13W-5S	A3
6400	IHPK	60525	3147	13W-7S	A6
7200	CTSD	60525	3209	13W-8S	A1
7200	LynT	60525	3209	13W-9S	A2
7400	HGKN	60525	3209	13W-9S	A2
7500	WLSP	60525	3209	13W-9S	A2
8100	WLSP	60480	3209	13W-9S	A3
Willow Terrace Dr					
8800	ODHL	60477	3424	11W-19S	A1
Willow Tree Av					
22200	SLVL	60411	3598	3E-26S	A3
Willow Tree Ct					
300	HFET	60194	2858	23W-11N	E3
Willow Tree Ln					
600	GLNC	60022	2758	7W-17N	B4
Willowview Ter					
1800	NHFD	60093	2811	7W-15N	B2
S Willow Walk Dr					
800	PLTN	60067	2805	22W-14N	A3
Willow West Dr					
8300	WLSP	60480	3208		E4
8300	WLSP	60480	3209	13W-9S	A3
8300	WLSP	60525	3209	13W-9S	A3
N Willow Wood Dr					
300	PLTN	60074	2753	20W-16N	A7
W Willow Wood Dr					
6300	PSHT	60463	3275	7W-14S	B6
6300	WthT	60463	3275	7W-14S	B6
Will Scarlet Ln					
100	HnrT	60120	2856	31W-10N	A7
Willson Dr					
800	DSPN	60016	2862	15W-10N	A5
Wilma Ln					
900	EGVV	60007	2914		A2
Wilma Pl					
100	PKRG	60068	2864	9W-9N	C6
Wilmette Av					
10	WLMT	60091	2811	6W-13N	D6
100	GNVW	60025	2811	6W-13N	C6
500	CPVL	60110	2748		A7
500	CPVL	60110	2801		A1
500	CPVL	60118	2801		A1
500	EDND	60118	2801		A1
1000	WLMT	60091	2812	4W-13N	D6
4300	RGMW	60008	2806	20W-14N	A3
4400	RGMW	60008	2805	20W-14N	E3
E Wilmette Av					
10	PLTN	60067	2805	20W-14N	E3
100	PLTN	60008	2805	20W-14N	E3
100	RGMW	60008	2805	20W-14N	E3
Wilmette Ct					
200	SMBG	60193	2859	21W-10N	D6
E Wilmette Rd					
600	PLTN	60074	2806	20W-15N	B2
Wilmington Dr					
300	BRLT	60103	2911		A3
Wilmington Ln					
1000	HFET	60194	2858	24W-11N	C3
W Wilmington Rd					
500	PtnT	60468	3860	9W-37S	E4
500	PTON	60468	3860	10W-37S	C4
N Wilmot Av					
1800	CHCG	60647	2977	2W-2N	B7
Wilmot Rd					
10	DRFD	60015	2756	12W-20N	C1
100	WdfT	60015	2756	11W-20N	C2
Wilmslow Ln					
100	SMBG	60194	2858	25W-10N	A5
Wilrose Ct					
13700	ODPK	60467	3344	13W-16S	E3
Wilshire Av					
900	EGVV	60007	2915		A1
2900	MKHM	60426	3427	3W-19S	A2
N Wilshire Av					
1700	ANHT	60004	2807	16W-15N	C1
Wilshire Blvd					
4800	CCHL	60478	3426	6W-21S	A5
Wilshire Ct					
-	LMNT	60439	3270		A7
100	SMWD	60107	2856	29W-10N	E5
2900	MKHM	60426	3427	3W-19S	A2
5800	HRPK	60133	2911		E4
N Wilshire Ct					
300	PLTN	60074	2753	20W-16N	B7
Wilshire Dr					
-	WLMT	60091	2812	5W-13N	A6
100	WLNG	60090	2755	15W-18N	A4
900	WLNG	60090	2754	15W-18N	E4
3400	HFET	60067	2804	23W-14N	E4
3500	HFET	60195	2804	23W-14N	E4
15300	ODPK	60462	3345	12W-18S	D7
N Wilshire Dr					
600	MPPT	60056	2808	15W-13N	B5
W Wilshire Dr					
400	HFET	60067	2804	23W-14N	E4
400	HFET	60195	2804	23W-14N	E4
Wilshire Dr E					
300	WLMT	60091	2812	5W-13N	A7
Wilshire Dr W					
300	WLMT	60091	2812	5W-13N	A7
Wilshire Ln					
800	CRTE	60417	3596	0W-28S	C6
800	CRTE	60475	3596	0W-28S	C6
2700	NHBK	60062	2756	10W-18N	E4
N Wilshire Ln					
600	ANHT	60004	2807	16W-14N	C4
3000	ANHT	60004	2754	16W-17N	C5
S Wilshire Ln					
-	ANHT	60005	2807	16W-13N	C6
100	ANHT	60004	2807	16W-13N	C5
Wilshire St					
300	PKFT	60466	3594	4W-26S	E3
400	RNPK	60471	3594	4W-26S	E3
Wilson Av					
400	CTCY	60409	3352	4E-17S	C5
1200	CHHT	60411	3507	2W-25S	D7
1300	CPVL	60110	2748		D7
1400	CHHT	60411	3595	2W-25S	D1
1400	CTCY	60409	3351	2E-17S	C5
1900	DLTN	60419	3351	2E-17S	C5
4100	RGMW	60008	2805	20W-14N	E4
4100	RGMW	60008	2806	20W-14N	A4
9900	SRPK	60176	2917	12W-5N	B7
9900	SRPK	60176	2973	12W-5N	B1
W Wilson Av					
-	CHCG	60640	2922	0W-5N	A7
700	CHCG	60640	2921	2W-5N	B7
1900	CHCG	60625	2921	3W-5N	A7
2700	CHCG	60625	2920	3W-5N	E7
4000	CHCG	60630	2920	5W-5N	B7
5300	CHCG	60630	2919	6W-5N	D7
7200	HDHT	60706	2918	9W-5N	C7
7200	NRDG	60706	2918	9W-5N	C7
8400	CHCG	60656	2918	10W-5N	A7
8400	CHCG	60706	2918	10W-5N	A7
8600	CHCG	60656	2917	10W-5N	E7

STREET Block	City	ZIP	Map#	CGS	Grid
Wilson Ct					
10	PKFT	60466	3594	4W-26S	E3
10	PKFT	60466	3595	3W-26S	A2
100	BNVL	60106	2915		E7
N Wilson Ct					
100	PLTN	60067	2752	22W-16N	C7
100	PLTN	60067	2805	22W-15N	B1
100	PltT	60067	2805	22W-15N	B1
Wilson Ln					
500	DSPN	60016	2863	12W-11N	B3
700	HNDL	60521	3146		C3
N Wilson Pl					
1800	ANHT	60004	2807	18W-15N	A1
Wilson St					
-	MONE	60449	3683	6W-31S	A5
10	WNKA	60093	2812	4W-15N	B2
100	PKFT	60466	3594	4W-26S	E3
100	PKFT	60466	3595	4W-26S	A3
200	AddT	60126	2972		A5
200	EMHT	60126	2972		A5
600	HRPK	60133	2912		A1
E Wilson St					
10	PLTN	60067	2805	20W-16N	E1
100	EMHT	60126	3028		A5
200	PTON	60468	3861	9W-37S	A3
400	PLTN	60067	2806	20W-16N	A1
400	PLTN	60074	2806	20W-16N	A1
W Wilson St					
-	MONE	60449	3683	5W-31S	B5
200	PTON	60468	3860	9W-37S	E3
200	PTON	60468	3861	8W-37S	B3
800	PLTN	60067	2805	22W-16N	B1
800	PltT	60067	2805	22W-16N	B1
5600	MONE	60449	3682	7W-31S	E5
Wilson Ter					
4400	SKOK	60076	2866	5W-11N	A2
7200	MNGV	60053	2864	9W-11N	D2
7900	MNGV	60714	2864	9W-11N	B2
7900	NLES	60714	2864	9W-11N	B2
N Wilton Av					
2600	CHCG	60614	2977	1W-3N	E5
3500	CHCG	60613	2977	1W-4N	E3
3500	CHCG	60657	2977	1W-4N	E3
E Wilton Ct					
600	PLTN	60074	2753	20W-16N	B7
Wilton Ln					
300	SMBG	60193	2858	25W-10N	B6
Wiltse Dr					
10	NHLK	60164	3028		D1
Wiltshire Ct					
10	SMBG	60193	2859	23W-9N	A7
Wimbledon Cir					
500	PTHT	60070	2808	13W-15N	E2
Wimbledon Pl					
-	BMDL	60172	2912		D7
-	ROSL	60108	2912		D7
-	ROSL	60172	2912		D7
200	BMDL	60108	2912		D7
W Wimbolton Dr					
10	MPPT	60056	2807	15W-14N	E4
10	MPPT	60056	2808	15W-14N	A4
Winchester Av					
4500	LYNS	60534	3148	10W-4S	B1
4600	MCCK	60525	3148	10W-4S	B1
12700	BLID	60406	3277	2W-15S	C7
12700	BLID	60827	3277	2W-15S	C7
12700	CTPK	60827	3277	2W-15S	C7
13100	BLID	60406	3349	2W-15S	C1
14100	DXMR	60426	3349	2W-16S	D4
14600	HRVY	60426	3349	2W-18S	D7
16100	MKHM	60426	3427	2W-20S	D3
16500	HLCT	60429	3427	2W-20S	D3
17000	EHZC	60429	3427	2W-20S	D4
N Winchester Av					
400	CHCG	60612	3033	2W-0N	C3
800	CHCG	60622	3033	2W-1N	C2
1600	CHCG	60622	2977	2W-2N	C7
2300	CHCG	60614	2977	2W-3N	B5
4200	CHCG	60613	2977	2W-5N	C1
4400	CHCG	60613	2921	2W-5N	B7
4400	CHCG	60640	2921	2W-5N	B7
6000	CHCG	60660	2921	2W-7N	B3
6400	CHCG	60626	2921	2W-8N	B2
7300	CHCG	60626	2867	2W-9N	B7
7500	EVTN	60202	2867	2W-9N	B7
S Winchester Av					
200	CHCG	60612	3033	2W-0S	C5
2300	CHCG	60608	3091	2W-2S	C2
3500	CHCG	60609	3091	2W-3S	C5
4700	CHCG	60609	3151	2W-5S	C2
5500	CHCG	60636	3151	2W-7S	C5
7500	CHCG	60620	3213	2W-9S	C3
9500	CHCG	60643	3213	2W-11S	C6
12400	BLID	60406	3277	2W-14S	C6
12400	BLID	60827	3277	2W-14S	C6
12400	CTPK	60827	3277	2W-14S	C6
Winchester Ct					
600	BRLT	60103	2910		E7
1600	SMBG	60193	2858	25W-10N	B6
14200	HMGN	60467	3344	15W-16S	C4
Winchester Dr					
100	SMWD	60107	2856	29W-9N	E7
Winchester Ln					
800	NHBK	60062	2756	11W-17N	D4
1600	SMBG	60193	2858	25W-10N	B6
2100	GNVW	60025	2810	10W-14N	A3
3400	GNVW	60025	2809	10W-14N	E3
Winchester Rd					
12000	HMGN	60467	3344	15W-16S	C4
W Winchester Rd					
400	CHHT	60411	3507	2W-24S	D5
Windemera Ct					
-	ODPK	60467	3344	14W-16S	C4
Windemere Av					
8800	BKFD	60513	3087	11W-4S	D6
8800	BKFD	60513	3088	11W-4S	A6
8800	LYNS	60534	3088	11W-4S	A6
Windemere Cir					
2000	SMBG	60194	2858	26W-12N	A2
Windemere Ct					
1100	BRLT	60103	2910		E7
Windemere Ln					
10	HFET	60010	2804	24W-14N	C3
10	HFET	60195	2804	24W-14N	C3
10	SBTN	60010	2804	24W-14N	C3
Windermere on Duxbury					
10	RGMW	60008	2805	22W-13N	B6
Windfield Ct					
1200	ROSL	60172	2912		A4
Windfield Wy					
1300	ROSL	60172	2912		B4
Windgate Ct					
10	SMWD	60107	2857	27W-11N	B4
E Windgate Ct					
500	ANHT	60005	2861	17W-12N	B2
N Windham Ct N					
2000	ANHT	60004	2807	17W-14N	C4
Windham Ct N					
1900	ANHT	60004	2807	17W-14N	B4
Windham Ln					
1100	EGVV	60007	2914		A2
Windham Tr					
400	CPVL	60110	2748		A7
S Windhill Dr					
1000	PLTN	60067	2805	22W-14N	B3
W Windhill Dr					
1200	PLTN	60067	2805	22W-14N	A4
1300	IVNS	60067	2805	22W-14N	A4
Windhill Ln					
2900	DYR	46311	3598		D4
Winding Canyon Ct					
10	ALGN	60102	2748		A2
Winding Canyon Wy					
100	ALGN	60102	2748		A2
Winding Creek Ct					
11400	ODPK	60467	3422	14W-20S	E4
Winding Creek Dr					
11300	ODPK	60467	3422	14W-20S	E4
Winding Run Ln					
10	SMWD	60107	2857	27W-11N	C3
Winding Trail Ln					
3600	HFET	60195	2804	25W-14N	A3
Winding Trails Ct					
9100	WLSP	60480	3208		D5
Winding Trails Dr					
11700	WLSP	60480	3208		C6
N Windmere Cir					
100	RchT	60443	3593	8W-26S	B1
S Windmere Cir					
300	RchT	60443	3593	8W-26S	B2
W Windmill Dr					
7400	FftT	60423	3504	9W-24S	E5
Windmill Rd					
10	ODPK	60467	3344	14W-17S	D6
Windmill Turn					
10	ODPK	60467	3344	14W-17S	D6
Windosr Ct					
16600	LMNT	60439	3270		B7
Windover Cir					
500	BFGV	60089	2754	17W-20N	C1
Wind Point Ct					
2700	LYWD	60411	3510	3E-23S	A3
Wind Ridge Rd					
10	SBTN	60010	2803	27W-15N	B1
E Wind River Ter					
1200	PLTN	60074	2753	19W-18N	C3
Windrush Ln					
10	BNHL	60010	2750	26W-18N	C4
2500	NHBK	60062	2757	10W-18N	A4
Windsong Ct					
2300	SMBG	60194	2857	26W-11N	E3
Windsong Dr					
-	HFET	60194	2858	26W-12N	A3
1800	SMBG	60194	2857	26W-11N	E3
1900	SMBG	60194	2858	26W-11N	A3
Windsor Av					
6400	BRWN	60402	3089	8W-3S	A4
6800	BRWN	60402	3088	8W-3S	E4
7100	RVSD	60546	3088	8W-3S	E4
W Windsor Av					
700	CteT	60417	3685	1W-31S	B5
800	CHCG	60640	2921	1W-5N	E7
2100	CHCG	60625	2921	2W-5N	B7
2700	CHCG	60625	2920	3W-5N	E7
5100	CHCG	60630	2919	7W-5N	C7
7000	HDHT	60706	2918	8W-5N	D7
7000	NRDG	60706	2918	8W-5N	D7
8400	CHCG	60656	2918	10W-5N	A7
Windsor Cir					
500	IVNS	60067	2804	23W-15N	E3
1400	CPVL	60110	2748		D7
Windsor Ct					
10	SBTN	60010	2803	26W-14N	D3
10	SMWD	60107	2857	27W-11N	C4
100	DRFD	60015	2756	11W-20N	E2
1300	ELGN	60120	2855		E3
4400	RNPK	60471	3594	5W-26S	B3
8200	BRRG	60527	3208		B3
17300	SHLD	60473	3429	2E-20S	D4
Windsor Dr					
10	DSPN	60018	2862	15W-10N	B5
100	EDND	60110	2801		E1
100	OKBK	60523	3086		B2
200	BFGV	60089	2754	17W-18N	B3
200	BRLT	60103	2911		A6
200	EGVV	60007	2914		C4
200	ITSC	60143	2914		C4
200	ROSL	60172	2912		D5
600	SMBG	60193	2859	23W-9N	A7
9000	ODPK	60462	3346	11W-18S	A7
9000	PSHL	60465	3209	11W-11S	E7
9100	ODPK	60462	3345	11W-18S	E7
9100	PlsT	60465	3209	11W-11S	E7
9100	PlsT	60480	3209	11W-11S	E7
10400	WSTR	60154	3087	13W-2S	A3
10700	WSTR	60154	3086		E3
N Windsor Dr					
600	MPPT	60056	2808	15W-13N	A5
1200	PTHT	60004	2807	16W-15N	C3
1500	ANHT	60004	2807	17W-15N	C1
2000	ANHT	60004	2754	16W-16N	C7
3200	BFGV	60089	2754	17W-17N	C5
3200	WhlT	60004	2754	17W-17N	C5
3200	WhlT	60089	2754	17W-17N	C5
S Windsor Dr					
10	ANHT	60004	2807	16W-13N	C5
500	ANHT	60005	2807	16W-13N	C6
12500	PlsT	60464	3273	12W-14S	D7
12500	PSPK	60464	3273	12W-14S	D7
Windsor Ln					
-	LYWD	60411	3509	2E-23S	D4
300	IVNS	60010	2751	23W-16N	D6
900	DYR	46311	3510		E6
1100	HRPK	60133	2911		E1
2200	CCHL	60478	3506	5W-22S	C1
2500	NHBK	60062	2810	10W-15N	A1
8800	BGVW	60455	3211	8W-10S	A5
Windsor Pkwy					
-	OrlT	60477	3423	11W-21S	E5
9200	TYPK	60477	3423	11W-21S	E5
Windsor Pl					
10200	MNSR	46321	3510		E4
Windsor Rd					
500	IVNS	60067	2804	23W-15N	E2
500	IVNS	60067	2805	23W-15N	A2
600	GNVW	60025	2811	7W-13N	B7
Windsor St					
300	PKFT	60466	3595	4W-27S	A4
Windsor Mall					
2300	PKRG	60068	2917	11W-8N	D2
Windward Dr					
100	SMBG	60194	2859	22W-10N	C5
Windward Tr					
13100	PlsT	60462	3346	10W-15S	B1
13100	PlsT	60464	3346	10W-15S	B1
N Windy Wy					
9900	NLES	60714	2864	10W-12N	A1
Windy Hill Dr					
1500	NHBK	60062	2757	9W-16N	C6
21300	FKFT	60423	3504	10W-25S	B7
Windy Hill Ln					
2000	HDPK	60035	2757	9W-20N	C1
Winesap Ct					
800	PTHT	60070	2808	13W-15N	E2
Winfal Dr					
800	SMBG	60173	2859	22W-10N	C5
Winfield Av					
-	MONE	60449	3682	8W-31S	C6
-	MonT	60449	3682	8W-31S	C6
Winfield Cir					
10	NHFD	60093	2811	6W-14N	E4
Winfield Ct					
300	SMBG	60194	2857	27W-10N	D5
Winfield Dr					
10	NHFD	60093	2811	6W-14N	D4
10	NtrT	60093	2811	6W-14N	E4
Winfield Ln					
400	IVNS	60010	2751	25W-16N	A7
S Winfield Rd					
26300	MONE	60449	3682	8W-32S	C7
26300	MonT	60449	3682	8W-32S	C7
Wing St					
2100	RGMW	60008	2806	19W-14N	C4
E Wing St					
1400	ANHT	60004	2807	16W-14N	C5
W Wing St					
100	ANHT	60005	2807	18W-14N	A5
1000	ANHT	60005	2806	18W-14N	E5
Wingate Cir					
10	CRTE	60417	3685	0W-29S	C1
Wingate Dr					
200	SMBG	60193	2859	22W-9N	C7
300	CRTE	60417	3685	0W-29S	B1
14900	HMGN	60441	3344	15W-17S	B6
Wingate Rd					
900	OMFD	60461	3506	4W-25S	D7
1000	MTSN	60443	3506	4W-25S	D7
6400	WLBK	60527	3146		A6
Wingfoot Dr					
5000	MONE	60449	3683	6W-31S	A5
Winkleman Rd					
-	PTHT	60062	2809	12W-15N	B2
3800	NfdT	60062	2809	12W-15N	B2
N Winnebago Av					
1700	CHCG	60647	2977	2W-2N	A7
S Winnebago Rd					
12700	PSHT	60463	3274	9W-15S	D7
12800	PSHT	60463	3346	9W-15S	D1
Winnebago St					
300	PKFT	60466	3594	4W-26S	E2
300	PKFT	60466	3595	4W-26S	A2
400	PKFT	60471	3594	4W-26S	E2
400	RNPK	60471	3594	4W-26S	E2
W Winneconna Pkwy					
400	CHCG	60620	3214	0W-8S	B1
W Winnemac Av					
1400	CHCG	60640	2921	1W-6N	C6
1900	CHCG	60625	2921	3W-6N	A6
2700	CHCG	60625	2920	3W-6N	E6
4800	CHCG	60630	2919	6W-6N	E6
6700	CHCG	60656	2918	8W-6N	E6
7400	HDHT	60706	2918	9W-6N	C6
7500	HDHT	60656	2918	9W-6N	C6
8000	NRDG	60706	2918	10W-6N	B6
Winnemac St					
400	PKFT	60466	3594	4W-26S	E3
Winners Cup Ct					
1200	BRLT	60103	2910		E7
Winnetka Av					
100	KLWH	60043	2812	4W-15N	D3
100	WNKA	60093	2812	4W-14N	C3
500	NtrT	60093	2812	4W-14N	C3
3900	RGMW	60008	2806	20W-14N	A3
Winnetka Cir					
1600	RGMW	60008	2806	20W-14N	A3
Winnetka Ct					
-	GNVW	60025	2811	8W-15N	A3
-	NHFD	60093	2811	8W-15N	A3
Winnetka Mw					
600	WNKA	60093	2812	5W-16N	A1
Winnetka Rd					
1300	NHFD	60093	2811	6W-15N	D3
1300	NtrT	60093	2811	6W-14N	E3
1300	WNKA	60093	2811	6W-14N	E3
1500	NHFD	60093	2810	8W-15N	E3
1800	NfdT	60093	2811	7W-15N	C3
2200	GNVW	60025	2811	6W-15N	D3
2200	NHFD	60025	2811	7W-15N	A3
3300	GNVW	60025	2809	10W-15N	E3
3300	GNVW	60025	2810	10W-15N	A3
W Winnetka St					
1200	PLTN	60067	2752	22W-17N	A5
Winnsboro Ct					
200	SMBG	60193	2857	27W-10N	D6
Winona Av					
9400	SRPK	60176	2917	11W-6N	C6
Winona Rd					
10	HDPK	60035	2757	8W-20N	E2
10	NfdT	60062	2757	8W-20N	E2
Winona St					
300	PKFT	60466	3594	4W-26S	E3
W Winona St					
1800	CHCG	60640	2921	2W-6N	B6
2200	CHCG	60625	2921	3W-6N	A6
2700	CHCG	60625	2920	3W-6N	E6
4900	CHCG	60630	2919	6W-6N	E6
7600	CHCG	60656	2918	9W-6N	C6
7600	HDHT	60706	2918	9W-6N	C6
7800	NRDG	60706	2918	9W-6N	C6
S Winslow Rd					
11900	PSPK	60464	3274	10W-14S	B5
W Winslow Rd					
8400	PSPK	60464	3274	10W-14S	B5
Winslow St					
10	PKFT	60466	3595	3W-26S	B2
Winslowe Dr					
1400	PLTN	60074	2753	19W-17N	B4
E Winslowe Dr					
1500	PLTN	60074	2753	19W-17N	B4
Winsor Ln					
15000	HMGN	60441	3344	15W-17S	B6
S Winston Av					
9500	CHCG	60620	3213	1W-11S	D6
9500	CHCG	60643	3213	1W-11S	D6
Winston Cir					
3500	HFET	60195	2804	23W-14N	D4
Winston Ct					
400	MLPK	60160	3030	10W-1N	A2
17500	CCHL	60478	3426	4W-21S	D5
Winston Dr					
400	VrnT	60015	2755	14W-20N	B1
500	MLPK	60160	3030	10W-1N	A2
600	EGvT	60007	2860	19W-9N	C7
600	EGVV	60007	2860	19W-9N	C7
700	EGvT	60007	2914		B1
700	EGVV	60007	2914		B1
700	MLPK	60160	3029	10W-1N	E2
3500	HFET	60195	2804	23W-15N	D3
6800	TYPK	60477	3425	8W-19S	A3
17500	CCHL	60478	3426	4W-21S	D6
N Winston Dr					
10	PLTN	60074	2806	19W-16N	C1
100	PLTN	60074	2753	19W-16N	C7
S Winston Dr					
10	PLTN	60074	2806	19W-15N	C1
Winston Ln					
400	CHHT	60411	3507	2W-24S	D5
1900	SMBG	60193	2858	25W-10N	A6
3800	HFET	60195	2804	23W-14N	D3
S Winston Ln					
26000	CteT	60417	3685	1W-31S	B5
Winston Pl					
3600	HFET	60195	2804	23W-14N	D3
Winterberry Ct					
10	SMWD	60120	2856	29W-9N	E7
Winterberry Ln					
16700	ODPK	60467	3423	13W-20S	B4
Wintercress Cir					
2500	NHBK	60062	2756	11W-16N	D6
E Wintergreen Av					
2000	MPPT	60056	2808	13W-15N	E2
2000	MPPT	60056	2809	12W-15N	A2
W Wintergreen Dr					
8200	FftT	60423	3504	10W-24S	C5
S Winterhaven Ct					
400	PLTN	60067	2805	22W-15N	C2
Winter Park Dr					
10300	PSHL	60465	3274	10W-12S	A1
Winterport on Auburn					
10	RGMW	60008	2806	19W-15N	B3
W Winters Dr					
10	LydT	60164	2972		E5
10	NHLK	60164	2972		D5
Winterset Dr					
10700	ODPK	60467	3423	13W-19S	B3
Winterwood Ct					
800	ROSL	60172	2912		E7
Winterwood Dr					
400	ROSL	60172	2912		D6
N Winthrop Av					
5200	CHCG	60640	2921	1W-6N	E5
5500	CHCG	60660	2921	1W-6N	E5
6500	CHCG	60626	2921	1W-8N	D2
Winthrop Ct					
1700	SMBG	60193	2858	25W-10N	B6
Winthrop Dr					
1600	DSPN	60018	2862	14W-9N	C6
Winthrop Ln					
1600	SMBG	60193	2858	25W-10N	B6
Wireton Rd					
2800	BLID	60406	3276	4W-15S	E7
2800	BLID	60406	3277	3W-15S	A7
2800	BLID	60406	3349	3W-15S	A1
2800	WthT	60406	3349	3W-15S	A1
Wiscasset on Auburn					
10	RGMW	60008	2806	19W-14N	B3
Wisconsin Av					
300	OKPK	60302	3030	8W-0N	E5
1200	BRWN	60402	3030	8W-1S	E7
1200	OKPK	60304	3030	8W-1S	E7
3900	BRWN	60402	3088	8W-4S	E6
3900	SKNY	60402	3088	8W-4S	E6
4400	FTVW	60402	3088	8W-4S	E7
4500	FTVW	60402	3148	8W-4S	E1
E Wisconsin Av					
100	BRTN	60010	2750	25W-18N	E3
200	BRTN	60010	2751	25W-18N	A3
Wisconsin Ct					
11100	ODPK	60467	3423	12W-20S	C5
Wisconsin Dr					
10	DSPN	60016	2808	14W-12N	C7
10	MPPT	60056	2808	14W-12N	B7
Wisconsin Ln					
800	EGVV	60007	2913		D2
W Wisconsin St					
200	CHCG	60614	2978	0W-2N	A7
800	CHCG	60614	2977	1W-2N	E7
1000	GNWD	60425	3508	1W-22S	A1
1000	HMWD	60425	3508	1W-22S	A1
Wise Rd					
600	HRPK	60133	2912		A2
600	SMBG	60133	2912		A2
600	SMBG	60193	2912		A2
E Wise Rd					
-	EGVV	60007	2913		D1
-	EGVV	60193	2913		D1
10	SMBG	60193	2913		A1
W Wise Rd					
10	SMBG	60193	2913		A1
200	SMBG	60193	2912		E1
1200	SmbT	60193	2912		C1
1800	HRPK	60133	2912		A2
W Wishing Well Dr					
7400	FftT	60423	3504	9W-24S	E6
N Wisner Av					
2900	CHCG	60618	2976	4W-3N	D4
Wisner St					
10	PKRG	60068	2864	9W-9N	B7
10	PKRG	60068	2918	9W-8N	B1
N Wisner St					
8000	NLES	60714	2864	9W-10N	B5
8000	PKRG	60068	2864	9W-10N	B6
8000	PKRG	60714	2864	9W-10N	B6
8200	MaiT	60714	2864	9W-10N	B5
Wissing Ln					
600	GNVW	60025	2810	9W-13N	C7
Wisteria Ct					
12600	PlsT	60464	3273	13W-14S	B7
Wisteria Dr					
300	SMWD	60107	2857	27W-10N	D7
Wisteria Ln					
10	SMBG	60173	2859	21W-10N	E5
10	SMBG	60173	2860	20W-10N	A6
E Wistoria Ct					
1800	MPPT	60056	2808	13W-14N	D4
Witham Ct					
8600	TYPK	60477	3424	10W-20S	B5
Withorn Ln					
1500	IVNS	60067	2752	23W-16N	A6
W Withorn Ln					
200	MPPT	60056	2807	16W-13N	E6
Witt Rd					
10	SBTN	60010	2803	26W-14N	C4
Wittington Ct					
14200	ODPK	60462	3346	9W-16S	C4
Woburn Ct					
10300	ODPK	60462	3345	12W-17S	B5
Woburn Dr					
1200	LMNT	60439	3271		A6
Woburn Ln					
200	SMBG	60173	2859	21W-10N	E5
Woburn Rd					
17500	TYPK	60477	3424	11W-21S	A6
Wolcott Av					
-	BLID	60406	3277	2W-13S	C5
-	CHCG	60406	3277	2W-13S	C5
-	CHCG	60643	3277	2W-13S	C5
-	ClmT	60406	3277	2W-13S	C5
16100	MKHM	60426	3427	2W-19S	D2
16500	HLCT	60429	3427	2W-19S	D3
N Wolcott Av					
-	CHCG	60657	2977	2W-3N	C5
10	CHCG	60612	3033	2W-0N	C4
300	CHCG	60622	3033	2W-0N	C4
1600	CHCG	60622	2977	2W-2N	C7
1900	CHCG	60614	2977	2W-2N	C7
4200	CHCG	60613	2977	2W-5N	C1
4400	CHCG	60613	2921	2W-5N	C7
4400	CHCG	60640	2921	2W-5N	C7
6000	CHCG	60660	2921	2W-7N	C3
6700	CHCG	60626	2921	2W-8N	B1
7200	CHCG	60626	2867	2W-9N	B7
7500	EVTN	60202	2867	2W-9N	C7
S Wolcott Av					
1200	CHCG	60608	3033	2W-1S	C7
1200	CHCG	60612	3033	2W-1S	C7
1900	CHCG	60608	3091	2W-2S	C2
3400	CHCG	60609	3091	2W-3S	C5
4700	CHCG	60609	3151	2W-5S	C2
5500	CHCG	60636	3151	2W-7S	C5
7500	CHCG	60620	3213	2W-9S	C3
Wolcott Ct					
100	SMBG	60193	2859	23W-10N	A5
N Wolcott St					
100	TNTN	60476	3428	0E-20S	D5
S Wolcott St					
100	TNTN	60476	3428	0E-21S	D6
Wolf Rd					
-	HLSD	60154	3086		D4
-	PlsT	60480	3208		E7
-	PlsT	60480	3272	14W-11S	E1
-	WLSP	60480	3208		E4
600	MTSN	60443	3505	7W-24S	C6
2500	WSTR	60154	3086		D4
2900	PvsT	60154	3086		D4
2900	PvsT	60558	3086		E7
3200	FNPK	60131	2972		D3
3200	LydT	60164	2972		D4
3600	LydT	60131	2972		D3
3800	WNSP	60558	3086		E7
4500	WNSP	60558	3146		E2
5400	LynT	60525	3146		E3
5500	LynT	60558	3146		E4
5500	WNSP	60525	3146		E4
6000	IHPK	60525	3146		E5
6800	CTSD	60525	3146		E7
7000	BRRG	60525	3146		E7
7100	BRRG	60527	3146		E7
7100	IHPK	60527	3146		E7
7200	BRRG	60527	3208		E1
7200	IHPK	60527	3208		E1
7300	IHPK	60525	3208		E1
7300	LynT	60525	3208		E1
7400	BRRG	60525	3208		E1
7400	LynT	60527	3208		E1
7500	WLSP	60527	3208		E1
8000	BRRG	60480	3208		E3
8000	WLSP	60525	3208		E3
8500	LynT	60480	3208		E4
13100	PlsT	60467	3344	13W-15S	E2
13200	OrlT	60467	3344	13W-15S	E2
13500	ODPK	60467	3344	14W-17S	E6
15600	ODPK	60467	3422	14W-20S	E4
15600	OrlT	60467	3422	14W-19S	E2
16800	OrlT	60448	3422	13W-20S	E4
17200	ODPK	60448	3422	13W-20S	E5
17900	FftT	60448	3422	14W-21S	E7
18300	MKNA	60448	3422	13W-22S	E7
Wolf Rd SR-7					
14300	ODPK	60467	3344	14W-17S	E6
14300	OrlT	60467	3344	14W-17S	E6
15600	ODPK	60467	3422	14W-19S	E2
15600	OrlT	60467	3422	14W-19S	E2
Wolf Rd US-6					
15900	ODPK	60467	3422	14W-20S	E4
15900	OrlT	60467	3422	14W-20S	E4
16800	OrlT	60448	3422	13W-20S	E4
17200	ODPK	60448	3422	13W-20S	E5
N Wolf Rd					
-	MLPK	60160	3028		D3
-	MLPK	60163	3028		D3
10	HLSD	60162	3028		D4
10	NHLK	60164	3028		D1
10	PvsT	60162	3028		D6
10	WLNG	60090	2755	14W-18N	C3
100	DSPN	60016	2862	14W-12N	D1
100	NHLK	60164	2972		D7
300	DSPN	60016	2808	14W-13N	D6
300	MPPT	60056	2808	14W-13N	D6
600	MPPT	60016	2808	14W-13N	D7
800	DSPN	60056	2808	14W-13N	D5
800	LydT	60164	2972		D5
800	WhlT	60056	2808	14W-13N	D5
1200	BKLY	60163	3028		D3
1300	PTHT	60070	2808	14W-14N	D3
3100	FNPK	60131	2972		D5
S Wolf Rd					
10	HLSD	60162	3028		D7
10	NHLK	60164	3028		D1
10	PTHT	60070	2808	14W-15N	D2
10	PvsT	60162	3028		D7
10	WLNG	60090	2755	14W-17N	C5
100	DSPN	60016	2862	14W-11N	C3
100	MPPT	60056	2808	14W-14N	D3
1100	DSPN	60018	2862	14W-10N	D5
1100	WLNG	60070	2808	14W-15N	D1
1200	WLNG	60090	2808	14W-15N	D2
1400	HLSD	60154	3086		D2
1400	HLSD	60162	3086		D2
1400	PvsT	60162	3086		D2
1700	PTHT	60090	2808	14W-15N	D3
2100	DSPN	60018	2916		D2
2100	WSTR	60154	3086		D2
2400	CHCG	60018	2916		D1

Chicago & Cook County Street Index

STREET Block	City	ZIP	Map#	CGS	Grid
Yale Av					
100	BmT	60010	2751	25W-18N	A4
900	WLMT	60091	2812	4W-14N	B5
1900	CHHT	60411	3595	2W-26S	D2
N Yale Av					
10	ANHT	60005	2806	18W-14N	D4
800	ANHT	60004	2806	18W-14N	D3
2000	ANHT	60004	2753	18W-16N	D7
S Yale Av					
10	ANHT	60005	2806	18W-13N	D5
1300	ANHT	60005	2860	19W-12N	D1
5900	CHCG	60621	3152	0W-7S	B5
7900	CHCG	60620	3214	0W-9S	B2
9900	CHCG	60628	3214	0W-11S	B7
11300	CHCG	60628	3278	0W-13S	B3
Yale Cir					
2100	HFET	60120	2802	30W-12N	B7
2100	HFET	60192	2802	30W-12N	B7
2100	HnrT	60192	2802	30W-12N	B7
Yale Ct					
100	GNVW	60025	2810	10W-15N	B2
600	DSPN	60016	2862	14W-12N	D2
1500	EGVV	60007	2859	21W-9N	D7
N Yale Ct					
1600	ANHT	60004	2806	18W-15N	D1
W Yale Ct					
1000	PLTN	60067	2805	22W-14N	B3
Yale Ln					
600	MTSN	60443	3505	6W-24S	E6
1400	SMBG	60193	2912		B1
5200	MTSN	60443	3506	6W-24S	A6
17700	CCHL	60478	3426	4W-21S	E6
17700	HLCT	60429	3426	4W-21S	E6
Yale Rd					
1700	FSMR	60422	3507	2W-23S	D4
Yardley Ln					
10	SMBG	60194	2858	26W-10N	A5
600	HFET	60194	2858	25W-11N	C4
Yarmouth Ct					
1300	SMBG	60193	2858	25W-10N	C6
E Yarmouth Ct					
2600	ANHT	60004	2807	16W-15N	D2
Yarmouth Ln					
100	SMBG	60193	2858	25W-10N	C6
N Yarmouth Pl					
1400	MPPT	60056	2807	16W-14N	D4
Yarmouth Rd					
200	EGVV	60007	2914		C2
Yarrow Ct					
100	RGMW	60008	2805	21W-13N	E5
Yarrow Ln					
2400	RGMW	60008	2805	21W-14N	D5
Yarwood St					
300	ELGN	60120	2855		A5
Yates Av					
200	BNHM	60633	3351	2E-17S	D6
200	CTCY	60409	3351	2E-17S	D6
22100	SLVL	60411	3597	2E-27S	D4
S Yates Av					
-	CHCG	60633	3351	2E-15S	D2
7900	CHCG	60617	3215	2E-9S	D2
7900	CHCG	60649	3215	2E-9S	D2
10500	CHCG	60617	3279	2E-12S	D1
14300	BNHM	60633	3351	2E-16S	D4
14300	CTCY	60409	3351	2E-16S	D4
S Yates Blvd					
7100	CHCG	60649	3153	2E-8S	D7
7500	CHCG	60649	3215	2E-8S	D1
7800	CHCG	60617	3215	3E-8S	D1
N Yates Ln					
100	MPPT	60056	2808	14W-13N	D6
Yates St					
17100	SHLD	60473	3429	2E-20S	D4
Yearling Crossing Dr					
10600	ODPK	60467	3423	13W-20S	A4
Yellowstone Dr					
1400	HnrT	60107	2856	30W-9N	B7
Yellowstone Pkwy					
1200	ALGN	60102	2748		B1
Yew Ct					
1100	ELGN	60120	2855		D4
York Cir					
1000	CPVL	60110	2748		D5
York Ct					
700	NHBK	60062	2757	8W-17N	E4
700	ROSL	60172	2913		B6
22400	RNPK	60471	3594	4W-27S	D4
York Dr					
-	LYWD	60411	3509	2E-23S	D4
1300	CPVL	60110	2748		D5
York Rd					
-	EMHT	60523	3028		A7
-	EMHT	60523	3086		A1
-	OKBK	60523	3086		A1
-	YkTp	60523	3028		A7
-	YkTp	60523	3086		A1
400	BRWN	60402	3088	9W-3S	D4
400	RVSD	60546	3088	9W-3S	D4
600	GNVW	60025	2811	8W-13N	A7
3600	HNDL	60521	3086		B6
3700	OKBK	60521	3086		B6
York Rd CO-8					
2700	OKBK	60523	3086		B3
3600	HNDL	60521	3086		B6
3700	OKBK	60521	3086		B6
N York Rd					
100	BNVL	60106	2915		E7
300	CHCG	60106	2915		E7
500	HNDL	60521	3086		B7
800	EGVV	60007	2915		E7
800	EGVV	60106	2915		E7
N York Rd CO-8					
200	BNVL	60106	2915		E7
300	CHCG	60106	2915		E7
800	EGVV	60007	2915		E7
800	EGVV	60106	2915		E7
S York Rd					
-	EMHT	60523	3028		A7
1000	EMHT	60126	3028		A7
1000	YkTp	60126	3028		A6
York St					
-	BDVW	60155	3029	12W-0S	C6
-	CTPK	60827	3277	1W-15S	D7
-	WSTR	60154	3029	12W-0S	C6
2200	BLID	60406	3277	3W-15S	B7
7600	FTPK	60130	3030	9W-0S	C6
S York St					
600	EMHT	60126	3028		A5
E Yorkfield Av					
200	EMHT	60126	3028		A6
300	YkTp	60126	3028		B6
York Lake Ct					
10	OKBK	60523	3086		B5
Yorkshire Ct					
1100	ELGN	60120	2855		D5

STREET Block	City	ZIP	Map#	CGS	Grid
Yorkshire Ct					
3300	HFET	60067	2804	23W-14N	E4
8000	HRPK	60133	2858	26W-9N	A7
12600	HMGN	60441	3344	15W-17S	A6
Yorkshire Dr					
700	HRPK	60133	2858	26W-9N	A7
700	SMBG	60133	2858	25W-9N	A7
700	SMBG	60193	2858	25W-9N	A7
900	HRPK	60133	2857	26W-9N	E7
1300	SMWD	60107	2857	27W-9N	D7
12400	HMGN	60441	3344	15W-17S	B6
Yorkshire Ln					
600	DSPN	60016	2808	14W-12N	D7
1400	SMBG	60194	2858	25W-10N	B5
4000	NHBK	60062	2756	12W-17N	B5
15300	ODPK	60462	3345	11W-18S	E7
Yorkshire Pl					
200	WLNG	60090	2755	15W-18N	B3
Yorkshire Ter					
800	CRTE	60417	3596	0W-28S	C6
Yorkshire Woods					
10	OKBK	60523	3086		A1
Yorktown Ct					
10	SBTN	60010	2803	27W-14N	B4
9100	ODPK	60462	3345	11W-16S	E3
Yorktown Dr					
9100	ODPK	60462	3345	11W-16S	E4
Yorktown Rd					
500	CHHT	60411	3507	2W-24S	C6
7300	FKFT	60423	3593	8W-25S	A1
Yosemite Ct					
500	ROSL	60172	2913		C3
Yosemite Pkwy					
1200	ALGN	60102	2748		C1
Yosemite Tr					
400	ROSL	60172	2913		C3
Yost Av					
10	CHCG	60068	2918	9W-7N	C3
10	CHCG	60631	2918	9W-7N	C3
10	PKRG	60068	2918	9W-7N	B3
Young Cir					
1500	EGVV	60007	2914		A1
Young St					
800	LMNT	60439	3271		A6
S Young St					
10	GNWD	60425	3508	0E-22S	D2
Yuba St					
7600	FTPK	60130	3030	9W-0S	C7
E Yuma Ln					
1900	MPPT	60056	2808	13W-15N	E3
Yy Rd					
-	CteT	60417	3685	0E-29S	E2

Z

STREET Block	City	ZIP	Map#	CGS	Grid
Zee Ct					
1300	WLNG	60090	2754	16W-18N	D2
Zemke Blvd					
-	CHCG	60666	2917	13W-7N	A3
Zenith Dr					
-	GNVW	60025	2809	11W-13N	D6
W Zermatt Dr					
8400	PSHL	60465	3274	10W-12S	B2
E Zinnia Ln					
800	PLTN	60074	2753	19W-18N	B3
Zuelke Dr					
200	BLWD	60104	3029	12W-0N	B4
Zurich Ct					
10	CRTE	60417	3596	0E-28S	E6
6800	TYPK	60477	3425	8W-22S	A7
Zurich Dr					
100	LYWD	60411	3510	4E-25S	C7
100	LYWD	60411	3598	4E-25S	C1
Zurich Ln					
6800	TYPK	60477	3425	8W-22S	A7
18400	TYPK	60477	3505	8W-22S	A1

#

STREET Block	City	ZIP	Map#	CGS	Grid
1st Av					
-	FTPK	60130	3030	10W-1S	A7
-	LYNS	60525	3148	10W-4S	A1
-	MYWD	60153	3088	10W-1S	A1
-	NRIV	60546	3088	10W-1S	A2
-	PvsT	60130	3088	10W-1S	A1
-	PvsT	60141	3088	10W-1S	A1
10	BRLT	60103	2909		E3
10	EGvT	60005	2861	16W-10N	D6
10	MPPT	60005	2861	16W-10N	D6
400	DSPN	60016	2862	13W-11N	E3
1900	MLPK	60160	3030	10W-1N	A1
1900	MLPK	60171	3030	10W-1N	A1
1900	PvsT	60160	3030	10W-1N	A1
1900	RVGV	60171	3030	10W-1N	A1
2100	MYWD	60153	3030	10W-1S	A7
2100	PvsT	60130	3030	10W-1S	A7
3900	BKFD	60513	3088	10W-4S	A7
3900	LYNS	60534	3088	10W-4S	A7
3900	RVSD	60513	3088	10W-4S	A7
3900	RVSD	60546	3088	10W-4S	A7
4500	LYNS	60534	3148	10W-4S	A1
4600	MCCK	60525	3148	10W-4S	A1
14400	ODPK	60462	3345	12W-17S	C4
15100	PHNX	60426	3350	0W-18S	B6
1st Av SR-171					
-	FTPK	60130	3030	10W-1S	A7
-	MYWD	60153	3088	10W-1S	A1
-	NRIV	60546	3088	10W-1S	A2
-	PvsT	60130	3088	10W-1S	A1
-	PvsT	60141	3088	10W-1S	A1
1900	MLPK	60160	3030	10W-1N	A1
1900	MLPK	60171	3030	10W-1N	A1
1900	PvsT	60160	3030	10W-1N	A1
1900	RVGV	60171	3030	10W-1N	A1
2100	MYWD	60153	3030	10W-1S	A7
2100	PvsT	60130	3030	10W-1S	A7
3900	BKFD	60513	3088	10W-4S	A7
3900	LYNS	60534	3088	10W-4S	A7
3900	RVSD	60513	3088	10W-4S	A7
3900	RVSD	60546	3088	10W-4S	A7
N 1st Av					
10	MYWD	60153	3030	10W-0N	A4
700	MLPK	60153	3030	10W-1N	A2
700	MLPK	60160	3030	10W-0N	A3
700	RVFT	60305	3030	10W-1N	A3
1600	MLPK	60160	2974	10W-2N	A7
1600	MLPK	60171	3030	10W-2N	A1
1600	PvsT	60160	3030	10W-2N	A1
1600	RVGV	60171	2974	10W-2N	A6
1600	RVGV	60171	3030	10W-2N	A1
N 1st Av SR-171					
10	MYWD	60153	3030	10W-0N	A4
700	MLPK	60153	3030	10W-1N	A2
700	RVFT	60305	3030	10W-1N	A3
1600	MLPK	60160	2974	10W-2N	A7

STREET Block	City	ZIP	Map#	CGS	Grid
N 1st Av SR-171					
1600	MLPK	60160	3030	10W-2N	A1
1600	MLPK	60171	3030	10W-2N	A1
1600	PvsT	60160	3030	10W-0N	A3
1600	RVGV	60171	2974	10W-2N	A6
1600	RVGV	60171	3030	10W-2N	A1
S 1st Av					
-	BKFD	60513	3088	10W-2S	A3
-	LYNS	60534	3088	10W-3S	B6
-	PvsT	60130	3030	10W-0S	A7
-	RVSD	60513	3088	10W-3S	B6
100	MYWD	60153	3030	10W-0S	A5
100	RVFT	60305	3030	10W-0S	A5
1700	FTPK	60130	3030	10W-0S	A6
1700	FTPK	60153	3030	10W-0S	A6
2200	NRIV	60546	3088	10W-2S	A3
2200	PvsT	60141	3088	10W-2S	A3
2500	BKFD	60546	3088	10W-2S	A3
3500	RVSD	60546	3088	10W-3S	B6
S 1st Av SR-171					
-	BKFD	60513	3088	10W-2S	A3
-	LYNS	60534	3088	10W-3S	B6
-	PvsT	60130	3030	10W-0S	A7
-	RVSD	60513	3088	10W-3S	B6
100	MYWD	60153	3030	10W-0S	A5
100	RVFT	60305	3030	10W-0S	A5
1700	FTPK	60130	3030	10W-0S	A6
1700	FTPK	60153	3030	10W-0S	A6
2200	NRIV	60546	3088	10W-2S	A3
2200	PvsT	60141	3088	10W-2S	A3
2500	BKFD	60546	3088	10W-2S	A3
3500	RVSD	60546	3088	10W-3S	B6
1st St					
100	ITSC	60143	2914		C6
200	WLNG	60090	2755	14W-18N	C3
400	CRTE	60417	3685	1W-29S	A2
400	LMNT	60439	3271		A6
1100	ELGN	60120	2855		B1
1200	NHBK	60062	2757	10W-17N	B5
1900	GNVW	60025	2810	10W-14N	A4
E 1st St					
100	EDND	60118	2801		A2
100	EMHT	60126	3028		A2
300	CPVL	60118	2801		A1
400	HNDL	60521	3146		B1
N 1st St					
100	PTON	60468	3860	9W-37S	E3
100	WDND	60118	2801		A2
100	WLNG	60090	2755	14W-18N	C3
S 1st St					
100	PTON	60468	3860	9W-37S	E3
100	WDND	60118	2801		A3
W 1st St					
10	HNDL	60521	3146		A2
N 1st Bank Dr					
500	PLTN	60067	2753	20W-16N	A6
500	PLTN	60074	2753	20W-16N	A6
1st Park Av					
-	DSPN	60018	2917	11W-7N	D3
1st Private Rd					
2600	FSMR	60422	3507	3W-23S	B3
2nd Av					
10	EGvT	60005	2861	16W-10N	D6
10	MPPT	60005	2861	16W-10N	D6
100	BRLT	60103	2909		E3
14400	ODPK	60462	3345	12W-17S	C4
15100	PHNX	60426	3350	0W-18S	B6
N 2nd Av					
10	DSPN	60016	2862	13W-12N	D2
10	MYWD	60153	3030	10W-0N	A3
S 2nd Av					
400	DSPN	60016	2862	13W-10N	E4
1200	DSPN	60018	2862	13W-10N	E5
1800	MYWD	60153	3030	10W-0S	A6
2200	NRIV	60546	3088	10W-2S	A2
2200	PvsT	60141	3088	10W-2S	A3
2500	BKFD	60546	3088	10W-2S	A3
2nd St					
200	WLNG	60090	2755	14W-18N	C3
500	CRTE	60417	3685	1W-29S	A1
500	LMNT	60439	3271		A6
2000	NHBK	60062	2757	10W-16N	B7
2000	NHBK	60062	2810	10W-16N	B1
E 2nd St					
10	EDND	60118	2801		A2
200	EMHT	60126	3028		A2
300	CPVL	60118	2801		A2
N 2nd St					
100	PTON	60468	3861	9W-37S	A3
100	WDND	60118	2801		A2
S 2nd St					
100	PTON	60468	3861	9W-37S	A4
100	WDND	60118	2801		A3
W 2nd St					
10	HNDL	60521	3146		A2
2nd Park Av					
-	DSPN	60018	2917	11W-7N	D3
2nd Private Rd					
2600	FSMR	60422	3507	3W-23S	B3
3rd Av					
-	MYWD	60153	3088	10W-1S	A1
-	PvsT	60141	3088	10W-1S	A1
-	PvsT	60153	3088	10W-1S	A1
10	EGvT	60005	2861	16W-10N	D6
10	MPPT	60005	2861	16W-10N	D6
100	BRLT	60103	2909		E3
14400	ODPK	60462	3345	12W-17S	D4
15200	PHNX	60426	3350	0W-18S	B7
N 3rd Av					
10	MYWD	60153	3030	10W-0N	A3
200	DSPN	60016	2862	13W-12N	D1
500	DSPN	60016	2808	13W-12N	D7
S 3rd Av					
400	DSPN	60016	2862	13W-10N	D5
1200	DSPN	60018	2862	13W-10N	D5
1800	MYWD	60153	3030	10W-0S	A6
2200	NRIV	60546	3088	10W-2S	A2
2200	PvsT	60141	3088	10W-2S	A2
2500	BKFD	60546	3088	10W-2S	A3
3rd Ct					
10	BRLT	60103	2909		E3
3rd St					
10	PKRG	60068	2918	10W-8N	A1
100	EVTN	60201	2813	2W-13N	A7
100	WLMT	60091	2813	2W-13N	A6
200	WLNG	60090	2755	14W-18N	C3
300	GNVW	60093	2810	8W-15N	E3
500	CRTE	60417	3685	1W-29S	B1
500	LMNT	60439	3271		A6
E 3rd St					
10	EDND	60118	2801		A2
100	EMHT	60126	3028		A1
300	CPVL	60118	2801		A1
500	HNDL	60521	3146		C2

STREET Block	City	ZIP	Map#	CGS	Grid
N 3rd St					
100	WDND	60118	2801		A2
S 3rd St					
100	PTON	60468	3861	9W-37S	A4
100	WDND	60118	2801		A3
500	PtnT	60468	3861	9W-37S	A4
W 3rd St					
10	HNDL	60521	3146		A2
3rd Park Av					
-	DSPN	60018	2917	11W-7N	D3
4th Av					
10	EGvT	60005	2861	16W-10N	D6
10	MPPT	60005	2861	16W-10N	D6
100	BRLT	60103	2909		E2
15100	PHNX	60426	3350	0W-18S	B7
15100	SHLD	60426	3350	0W-18S	B7
N 4th Av					
10	DSPN	60016	2862	14W-12N	D2
10	MYWD	60153	3030	10W-0N	A3
500	DSPN	60016	2808	14W-12N	D7
S 4th Av					
400	DSPN	60016	2862	14W-11N	D3
1200	DSPN	60018	2862	13W-10N	D6
1800	MYWD	60153	3030	10W-0S	A6
2100	PvsT	60141	3030	10W-0S	A7
2100	PvsT	60153	3030	10W-0S	A7
2200	NRIV	60546	3088	10W-2S	A3
2200	PvsT	60141	3088	10W-2S	A3
2500	BKFD	60513	3088	10W-2S	A3
2500	BKFD	60546	3088	10W-2S	A3
4th St					
100	EVTN	60091	2813	2W-13N	A7
100	EVTN	60201	2813	2W-13N	A7
100	WLMT	60091	2813	2W-13N	A7
300	LMNT	60439	3271		A6
400	GNVW	60093	2810	8W-15N	E3
E 4th St					
10	HNDL	60521	3146		B2
200	EDND	60118	2801		A2
N 4th St					
100	PTON	60468	3861	9W-37S	A3
S 4th St					
100	PTON	60468	3861	9W-37S	A4
W 4th St					
10	HNDL	60521	3146		A2
4th Park Av					
-	DSPN	60018	2917	11W-7N	D3
5th Av					
-	MYWD	60141	3088	10W-1S	A1
-	MYWD	60153	3030	10W-1S	A7
-	MYWD	60153	3088	10W-1S	A1
-	PvsT	60141	3030	10W-1S	A7
-	PvsT	60141	3088	10W-1S	A1
-	PvsT	60153	3088	10W-1S	A1
10	EGvT	60005	2861	16W-10N	D6
10	MPPT	60005	2861	16W-9N	D6
100	BRLT	60103	2909		E2
1100	CHHT	60411	3508	0W-25S	C7
1400	CHHT	60411	3596	0W-25S	C1
15100	PHNX	60426	3350	0W-18S	B7
15100	SHLD	60426	3350	0W-18S	B7
N 5th Av					
-	RVGV	60171	3030	10W-2N	A1
10	DSPN	60016	2862	14W-12N	D2
10	MYWD	60153	3030	10W-0N	A3
500	DSPN	60016	2808	14W-12N	D7
1100	MLPK	60160	3030	10W-1N	A2
1100	MYWD	60160	3030	10W-1N	A2
1700	MLPK	60160	2974	10W-2N	A7
1700	PvsT	60160	3030	10W-1N	A1
1700	RVGV	60160	2974	10W-2N	A7
1700	RVGV	60171	2974	10W-2N	A7
S 5th Av					
10	MYWD	60153	3030	10W-0S	A6
1000	HMND	46320	3280		D3
1200	DSPN	60016	2862	14W-10N	D5
1200	DSPN	60018	2862	14W-10N	D5
2100	PvsT	60141	3030	10W-0S	A7
2100	PvsT	60153	3030	10W-0S	A7
2200	NRIV	60546	3088	10W-2S	A2
2200	PvsT	60141	3088	10W-2S	A3
2500	BKFD	60513	3088	10W-2S	A3
W 5th Av					
2800	CHCG	60612	3032	4W-0S	D5
3400	CHCG	60624	3032	4W-0S	D5
4500	CHCG	60644	3032	5W-0S	A6
E 5th Ct					
400	DSPN	60016	2862	14W-11N	D3
5th St					
100	EVTN	60201	2813	3W-13N	A7
100	WLMT	60091	2813	3W-13N	A6
100	WLMT	60201	2813	3W-13N	A7
200	WLNG	60090	2755	14W-18N	C3
400	LMNT	60439	3271		A6
500	CRTE	60417	3685	1W-29S	B1
500	GNVW	60093	2810	8W-15N	E3
E 5th St					
10	HNDL	60521	3146		B2
W 5th St					
10	HNDL	60521	3146		A2
5th Av Cto					
10000	CTSD	60525	3147	12W-8S	C7
10200	CTSD	60525	3209	13W-8S	B1
10700	LynT	60525	3209	13W-8S	A1
5th Park Av					
-	DSPN	60018	2917	11W-7N	D3
6th Av					
10	EGvT	60005	2861	16W-10N	D6
10	LGNG	60525	3087	12W-4S	C7
10	MPPT	60005	2861	16W-10N	D6
100	BRLT	60103	2909		E2
300	LGNG	60525	3147	12W-4S	C1
5600	CTSD	60525	3147	12W-6S	C3
15100	PHNX	60426	3350	0W-18S	B7
15100	SHLD	60426	3350	0W-18S	B7
N 6th Av					
10	DSPN	60016	2862	14W-12N	D2
10	MYWD	60153	3030	10W-0N	A3
400	DSPN	60016	2808	14W-12N	D7
1100	MLPK	60160	3030	10W-1N	A2
1100	MYWD	60160	3030	10W-1N	A3
S 6th Av					
100	MYWD	60153	3030	10W-0S	A5
600	DSPN	60016	2862	14W-11N	D4
1200	DSPN	60018	2862	14W-10N	D5
2100	MYWD	60141	3030	10W-0S	A7
2100	PvsT	60141	3030	10W-0S	A7
2200	NRIV	60141	3088	10W-2S	A2
2200	NRIV	60546	3088	10W-2S	A3
2200	PvsT	60141	3088	10W-2S	A3
2500	BKFD	60513	3088	10W-2S	A3
6th Ct					
10	BRLT	60103	2909		E2
6th St					
100	EVTN	60201	2813	3W-13N	A7

STREET Block	City	ZIP	Map#	CGS	Grid
6th St					
100	WLMT	60091	2813	3W-13N	A6
100	WLMT	60201	2813	3W-13N	A7
100	WLNG	60090	2755	14W-18N	C3
500	LMNT	60439	3271		A6
600	GNVW	60093	2810	8W-15N	E3
E 6th St					
500	HNDL	60521	3146		C2
N 6th St					
300	PTON	60468	3861	8W-37S	B3
W 6th St					
10	HNDL	60521	3146		A2
7th Av					
10	EGvT	60005	2861	16W-10N	D6
10	LGNG	60525	3087	12W-4S	C7
10	MPPT	60005	2861	16W-9N	D6
100	BRLT	60103	2909		E2
500	LGNG	60525	3147	12W-5S	C2
5500	CTSD	60525	3147	12W-6S	C3
15100	PHNX	60426	3350	0W-18S	C7
15100	SHLD	60426	3350	0W-18S	C7
N 7th Av					
10	DSPN	60016	2862	14W-12N	D2
10	MYWD	60153	3030	10W-0N	A3
400	DSPN	60016	2808	14W-12N	D7
900	MYWD	60153	3029	10W-1N	E2
1100	MLPK	60160	3029	10W-1N	E2
S 7th Av					
1800	MYWD	60153	3030	10W-0S	A6
2100	MYWD	60141	3030	10W-0S	A7
2100	PvsT	60141	3030	10W-0S	A7
2200	NRIV	60546	3088	10W-2S	A2
2200	PvsT	60141	3088	10W-2S	A3
2200	PvsT	60546	3088	10W-2S	A3
2500	BKFD	60513	3088	10W-2S	A3
7th Ct					
10	BRLT	60103	2909		E2
7th Pl					
100	CHHT	60411	3508	0W-24S	B6
7th St					
-	CteT	60417	3685	1W-30S	A4
200	WLNG	60090	2755	14W-18N	C3
300	WLMT	60091	2812	3W-13N	E6
700	GNVW	60093	2810	8W-15N	E3
E 7th St					
700	HNDL	60521	3146		C2
W 7th St					
10	HNDL	60521	3146		A2
8th Av					
10	EGvT	60005	2861	16W-10N	D6
10	MPPT	60005	2861	16W-10N	D6
100	BRLT	60103	2909		E2
100	LGNG	60525	3087	12W-4S	C7
300	LGNG	60525	3147	12W-4S	C1
1000	CTSD	60525	3147	12W-5S	C2
15100	PHNX	60426	3350	0W-18S	C7
15100	SHLD	60426	3350	0W-18S	C7
N 8th Av					
10	MYWD	60153	3029	10W-0N	E3
100	DSPN	60016	2862	14W-12N	D1
S 8th Av					
1800	MYWD	60153	3029	10W-0S	E6
2100	PvsT	60141	3029	10W-0S	E7
2100	PvsT	60153	3029	10W-0S	E7
2200	NRIV	60546	3088	10W-2S	A2
2200	PvsT	60141	3088	10W-2S	A3
2200	PvsT	60546	3088	10W-2S	A3
2500	BKFD	60513	3088	10W-2S	A3
8th Pl					
400	HNDL	60521	3146		A3
800	FDHT	60411	3509	1E-24S	B6
8th St					
-	OMFD	60461	3507	2W-24S	C6
200	WLNG	60090	2755	14W-18N	B3
300	CHHT	60411	3507	2W-24S	C6
400	WLMT	60091	2812	3W-14N	E5
500	BlmT	60411	3507	2W-24S	C6
800	GNVW	60093	2810	8W-15N	E3
1000	BlmT	60411	3509	1E-24S	A6
1000	FDHT	60411	3509	1E-24S	A6
E 8th St					
10	CHCG	60605	3034	0E-0S	C6
400	HNDL	60521	3146		B3
W 8th St					
10	HNDL	60521	3146		A3
9th Av					
10	BRLT	60103	2909		E2
10	EGvT	60005	2861	16W-10N	D6
10	MPPT	60005	2861	16W-10N	D6
200	LGNG	60525	3087	12W-4S	C7
500	LGNG	60525	3147	12W-5S	C2
5600	CTSD	60525	3147	12W-6S	C4
15100	SHLD	60426	3350	0W-18S	C7
15100	SHLD	60473	3350	0W-18S	C7
15300	PHNX	60426	3350	0W-18S	C7
N 9th Av					
-	MLPK	60160	2973	10W-2N	E7
10	MLPK	60153	3029	10W-0N	E3
10	MLPK	60160	3029	10W-2N	E1
10	MYWD	60153	3029	10W-0N	E3
10	MYWD	60160	3029	10W-0N	E3
S 9th Av					
10	MLPK	60153	3029	10W-0N	E3
10	MYWD	60153	3029	11W-1S	E7
2100	BDVW	60141	3029	11W-1S	E7
2100	BDVW	60155	3029	11W-1S	E7
2100	PvsT	60141	3029	11W-1S	E7
2100	PvsT	60153	3029	11W-1S	E7
2200	BDVW	60155	3087	11W-2S	E2
2200	NRIV	60546	3087	11W-2S	E2
2200	PvsT	60155	3029	10W-1S	E7
2200	PvsT	60546	3087	11W-2S	E2
2400	PvsT	60141	3087	11W-1S	E1
2500	PvsT	60155	3087	11W-1S	E1
2700	BDVW	60141	3087	11W-1S	E1
9th Ct					
200	HNDL	60521	3146		B3
9th St					
100	EVTN	60091	2812	3W-13N	E7
100	EVTN	60201	2812	3W-13N	E7
100	WLMT	60201	2812	3W-13N	E7
200	WLNG	60090	2755	14W-18N	B3
400	WLMT	60091	2812	3W-13N	E5
900	GNVW	60093	2810	8W-15N	E3
1100	FDHT	60411	3509	1E-24S	B6
E 9th St					
10	CHCG	60605	3034	0E-0S	C6
400	HNDL	60521	3146		B3
W 9th St					
10	CHCG	60605	3034	0W-0S	B6
100	HNDL	60521	3146		A3
300	DGvT	60521	3146		A3
10th Av					
10	BRLT	60103	2909		E2
10	EGvT	60005	2861	16W-10N	D6

Chicago & Cook County Street Index

STREET Block	City	ZIP	Map#	CGS	Grid
N 10th Av					
900	MLPK	60160	3029	11W-1N	E2
S 10th Av					
100	MYWD	60153	3029	11W-0S	E5
500	LGNG	60525	3147	12W-5S	C1
2100	BDVW	60155	3029	11W-0S	E7
2200	BDVW	60155	3087	11W-2S	E2
2200	NRIV	60546	3087	11W-2S	E2
10th Pl					
800	FDHT	60411	3509	1E-25S	A6
10th St					
10	CHHT	60411	3508	1W-25S	A6
100	CHHT	60411	3507	1W-24S	E6
200	WLNG	60090	2755	14W-18N	B3
500	BlmT	60411	3507	2W-24S	D6
1000	FDHT	60411	3509	1E-24S	A6
1000	GNVW	60093	2810	8W-15N	E3
1400	KLWH	60043	2812	3W-14N	E5
1400	WLMT	60043	2812	3W-14N	E5
1400	WLMT	60091	2812	3W-14N	E5
1600	KLWH	60091	2812	3W-14N	E5
E 10th St					
100	CHHT	60411	3508	0W-24S	B6
11th Av					
10	BRLT	60103	2909		E2
10	EGvT	60005	2861	16W-10N	D6
700	LGNG	60525	3147	12W-5S	C2
800	CTSD	60525	3147	12W-5S	C2
N 11th Av					
100	MLPK	60160	3029	11W-0N	E3
S 11th Av					
1800	MYWD	60153	3029	11W-1S	E7
2100	BDVW	60155	3029	11W-1S	E7
2200	BDVW	60155	3087	11W-2S	E2
2200	NRIV	60546	3087	11W-2S	E2
2400	PvsT	60546	3087	11W-2S	E3
11th Pl					
800	FDHT	60411	3509	1E-25S	A7
W 11th Pl					
300	CHHT	60411	3507	2W-25S	E7
11th St					
200	WLNG	60090	2755	14W-18N	B3
800	CHHT	60411	3509	1E-25S	A6
800	FDHT	60411	3509	1E-25S	A6
800	WLMT	60091	2812	3W-14N	E5
1100	GNVW	60093	2810	8W-15N	E3
E 11th St					
10	CHCG	60605	3034	0E-0S	C6
200	CHHT	60411	3508	0W-25S	C7
900	FDHT	60411	3509	1E-25S	A6
12th Av					
10	BRLT	60103	2909		E2
10	EGvT	60005	2861	16W-10N	D6
700	LGNG	60525	3147	12W-5S	D2
800	CTSD	60525	3147	12W-5S	D2
N 12th Av					
700	MLPK	60160	3029	11W-1N	E2
S 12th Av					
100	MYWD	60153	3029	11W-0N	E5
2100	BDVW	60155	3029	11W-0S	E7
2200	BDVW	60155	3087	11W-2S	E2
2200	NRIV	60155	3087	11W-2S	E2
2200	NRIV	60546	3087	11W-2S	E2
W 12th Pl					
600	CHCG	60607	3034	0W-1S	A7
2600	CHCG	60608	3033	3W-1S	A7
2700	CHCG	60623	3033	3W-1S	A7
3400	CHCG	60623	3032	4W-1S	D7
4600	CCRO	60804	3032	5W-1S	A7
12th St					
10	WLNG	60090	2755	14W-18N	B3
700	WLMT	60091	2812	3W-14N	D5
1000	FDHT	60411	3509	1E-25S	A7
1200	GNVW	60093	2810	8W-15N	D3
E 12th St					
10	CHHT	60411	3508	0W-25S	B7
W 12th St					
300	CHHT	60411	3507	2W-25S	D7
W 12th Place Dr					
2800	CHCG	60608	3033	2W-1S	B7
2800	CHCG	60623	3032	3W-1S	E7
2800	CHCG	60623	3033	2W-1S	B7
N 13th Av					
100	MLPK	60160	3029	11W-0N	E3
S 13th Av					
1500	BDVW	60153	3029	11W-0S	E6
1800	BDVW	60155	3029	11W-1S	E7
1800	MYWD	60153	3029	11W-1S	E7
2200	NRIV	60155	3087	11W-2S	E2
2200	NRIV	60546	3087	11W-2S	E2
2400	BDVW	60155	3087	11W-1S	E1
2400	PvsT	60546	3087	11W-2S	E3
13th Pl					
1400	FDHT	60411	3509	1E-25S	B7
W 13th Pl					
2600	CHCG	60608	3033	3W-1S	A7
3400	CHCG	60623	3032	4W-1S	D7
13th St					
-	BDVW	60155	3029	11W-1S	D7
-	MYWD	60153	3030	10W-1S	A7
-	PvsT	60130	3030	10W-1S	A7
-	PvsT	60141	3029	11W-1S	E7
-	PvsT	60141	3030	10W-1S	A7
-	PvsT	60155	3029	11W-1S	E7
100	EVTN	60091	2812	3W-13N	D7
100	EVTN	60201	2812	3W-13N	D7
400	BlmT	60411	3508	0E-25S	D7
800	CHHT	60411	3509	1E-25S	A7
800	FDHT	60411	3509	1E-25S	A7
900	WLMT	60091	2812	3W-14N	D5
6200	BRWN	60402	3031	8W-1S	A7
6200	CCRO	60402	3031	7W-1S	B7
6200	CCRO	60804	3031	7W-1S	A7
6800	BRWN	60402	3030	9W-1S	D7
7100	FTPK	60130	3030	9W-1S	D7
E 13th St					
10	CHCG	60605	3034	0E-1S	C7
200	CHHT	60411	3508	0W-25S	C7
W 13th St					
10	CHCG	60605	3034	0W-1S	B7
100	CHHT	60411	3507	1W-25S	E7
100	CHHT	60411	3508	1W-25S	A7
1000	CHCG	60608	3033	1W-1S	D7
3100	CHCG	60623	3032	4W-1S	D7
4600	CCRO	60804	3032	5W-1S	A7
5600	CCRO	60804	3031	7W-1S	B7
6100	BRWN	60402	3031	7W-1S	B7
6100	CCRO	60402	3031	7W-1S	B7
N 14th Av					
1500	MLPK	60160	3029	11W-1N	E1
S 14th Av					
1200	MYWD	60153	3029	11W-0S	E6
1500	BDVW	60153	3029	11W-0S	E6
1800	BDVW	60155	3029	11W-0S	E7
2200	BDVW	60155	3087	11W-2S	E2
2200	NRIV	60155	3087	11W-2S	E2
2200	NRIV	60546	3087	11W-2S	E2
14th Ct					
-	MLPK	60160	3029	11W-1N	D1
14th Pl					
1400	FDHT	60411	3509	1E-25S	B7
1400	SLVL	60411	3509	1E-25S	B7
E 14th Pl					
10	CHCG	60605	3034	0E-1S	C7
W 14th Pl					
100	CHHT	60411	3507	1W-25S	E7
100	CHHT	60411	3508	1W-25S	A7
400	CHCG	60607	3034	0W-1S	A7
700	CHCG	60608	3034	1W-1S	A7
1200	CHCG	60608	3033	1W-1S	E7
14th St					
100	EVTN	60091	2812	4W-13N	D7
100	EVTN	60201	2812	4W-13N	D7
100	WLMT	60091	2812	3W-13N	D7
6200	BRWN	60402	3031	8W-1S	A7
6200	CCRO	60804	3031	7W-1S	B7
6800	BRWN	60402	3030	9W-1S	D7
7100	FTPK	60130	3030	9W-1S	D7
E 14th St					
10	CHCG	60605	3034	0E-1S	C7
10	CHHT	60411	3508	0W-25S	C7
300	BlmT	60411	3508	0W-25S	C7
E 14th St US-30					
10	CHHT	60411	3508	0W-25S	C7
300	BlmT	60411	3508	0W-25S	C7
W 14th St					
-	PvsT	60141	3029	11W-1S	E7
10	CHCG	60605	3034	0W-1S	C7
10	CHHT	60411	3508	1W-25S	A7
100	CHHT	60411	3507	2W-25S	E7
700	CHCG	60607	3034	0W-1S	A7
700	CHCG	60608	3034	1W-1S	A7
700	OMFD	60461	3507	2W-25S	C7
2200	BDVW	60155	3029	11W-1S	D7
2400	CHCG	60608	3033	3W-1S	A7
2700	CHCG	60623	3033	3W-1S	A7
3800	CHCG	60623	3032	5W-1S	B7
4600	CCRO	60804	3032	5W-1S	A7
5500	CCRO	60804	3031	7W-1S	B7
6100	BRWN	60402	3031	7W-1S	B7
W 14th St US-30					
10	CHHT	60411	3508	1W-25S	A7
100	CHHT	60411	3507	2W-25S	E7
700	OMFD	60461	3507	2W-25S	C7
N 15th Av					
-	MYWD	60153	3029	11W-0N	E3
10	MLPK	60160	3029	11W-0N	D3
1900	MLPK	60160	2973	11W-2N	D7
S 15th Av					
-	MLPK	60160	3029	11W-0N	D3
10	MYWD	60153	3029	11W-0N	E5
1500	BDVW	60153	3029	11W-0S	E6
1500	MYWD	60155	3029	11W-0S	E6
1800	BDVW	60155	3029	11W-1S	E7
2200	BDVW	60155	3087	11W-2S	E2
2200	NRIV	60546	3087	11W-2S	E2
15th Pl					
1400	FDHT	60411	3597	1E-25S	B1
1400	SLVL	60411	3597	1E-25S	B1
E 15th Pl					
200	CHCG	60605	3034	0E-1S	C7
W 15th Pl					
-	CHCG	60608	3033	1W-1S	D7
-	CHCG	60623	3090	5W-1S	A1
100	CHHT	60411	3595	1W-25S	E1
800	CHCG	60607	3034		E7
800	CHCG	60608	3034		E7
2700	CHCG	60623	3033	3W-1S	A7
3100	CHCG	60623	3032	3W-1S	E7
4600	CCRO	60804	3090	5W-1S	A1
5500	CCRO	60804	3089	6W-1S	D1
15th St					
-	BDVW	60155	3087	11W-1S	D1
-	PvsT	60141	3087	11W-1S	E1
100	EVTN	60201	2812	4W-13N	D7
100	WLMT	60091	2812	4W-13N	D6
100	WLMT	60201	2812	4W-13N	D7
900	FDHT	60411	3509	1E-25S	A7
1000	FDHT	60411	3597	1E-25S	A1
1400	SLVL	60411	3597	1E-25S	B1
6200	BRWN	60402	3031	8W-1S	A7
6200	CCRO	60804	3031	7W-1S	B7
6800	BRWN	60402	3030	8W-1S	E7
6900	BRWN	60402	3088	9W-1S	D1
7100	FTPK	60130	3088	9W-1S	D1
E 15th St					
100	CHHT	60411	3596	0W-25S	B1
200	CHCG	60605	3034	0E-1S	C7
W 15th St					
10	CHCG	60605	3034	0W-1S	B7
10	CHHT	60411	3596	1W-25S	A1
100	CHHT	60411	3595	1W-25S	E1
700	CHCG	60607	3034	0W-1S	A7
700	CHCG	60608	3034	0W-1S	A7
700	OMFD	60461	3595	2W-25S	C1
700	PKFT	60466	3595	2W-25S	C1
1300	CHCG	60608	3033	1W-1S	D7
3200	CHCG	60623	3032	5W-1S	B7
5600	CCRO	60804	3031	7W-1S	B7
6100	BRWN	60402	3031	7W-1S	B7
W 15th Place Dr					
2800	CHCG	60608	3033	2W-1S	B7
2800	CHCG	60623	3033	2W-1S	B7
N 16th Av					
10	MLPK	60160	3029	11W-0N	D3
S 16th Av					
10	MYWD	60153	3029	11W-0N	D5
1500	MYWD	60155	3029	11W-0S	D6
1800	BDVW	60155	3029	11W-1S	D7
2400	BDVW	60155	3087	11W-1S	D1
E 16th Pl					
100	CHHT	60411	3596	0W-25S	B1
W 16th Pl					
10	CHHT	60411	3596	1W-25S	A1
500	CHHT	60411	3595	2W-25S	C1
16th St					
100	EVTN	60201	2812	4W-13N	C7
100	WLMT	60201	2812	4W-13N	C7
400	WLMT	60091	2812	4W-13N	C6
900	FDHT	60411	3597	1E-25S	A1
1200	KLWH	60043	2812	4W-13N	C5
1300	SLVL	60411	3597	1E-25S	B1
6200	BRWN	60402	3089	8W-1S	A1
6200	CCRO	60804	3089	7W-1S	B1
6800	BRWN	60402	3088	8W-1S	E1
7100	FTPK	60130	3088	8W-1S	D1
7100	NRIV	60130	3088	8W-1S	D1
7300	PvsT	60130	3088	9W-1S	D1
E 16th St					
10	CHCG	60605	3034	0E-1S	C7
10	CHCG	60616	3034	0E-1S	C7
10	CHHT	60411	3596	0W-25S	B1
300	BlmT	60411	3596	0W-25S	B1
W 16th St					
-	BDVW	60155	3087	11W-1S	E1
-	PvsT	60141	3087	11W-1S	E1
-	PvsT	60155	3087	11W-1S	E1
10	CHCG	60605	3034	0W-1S	C7
10	CHCG	60616	3034	0W-1S	B7
10	CHHT	60411	3596	1W-25S	A1
100	CHHT	60411	3595	2W-25S	D1
400	CHCG	60607	3034	0W-1S	A7
700	CHCG	60608	3034	1W-1S	A7
800	CHCG	60608	3033	1W-1S	E7
1300	CHCG	60608	3091	2W-1S	C1
2700	CHCG	60623	3091	3W-1S	A1
3100	CHCG	60623	3090	5W-1S	A1
4500	CCRO	60804	3090	5W-1S	A1
4800	CCRO	60804	3089	7W-1S	C1
6100	BRWN	60402	3089	7W-1S	B1
N 17th Av					
10	MLPK	60160	3029	11W-2N	D1
1900	MLPK	60160	2973	11W-2N	D7
2000	FNPK	60131	2973	11W-2N	D7
2000	FNPK	60160	2973	11W-2N	D7
S 17th Av					
-	PvsT	60513	3087	11W-2S	D2
-	PvsT	60525	3087	11W-2S	D2
900	MYWD	60153	3029	11W-0S	D7
1600	BDVW	60155	3029	11W-0S	D7
1600	MYWD	60155	3029	11W-0S	D5
2200	BDVW	60155	3087	11W-1S	D2
2200	NRIV	60546	3087	11W-1S	D2
W 17th Pl					
700	CHCG	60608	3092	0W-1S	A1
700	CHCG	60616	3092	1W-1S	A1
17th St					
-	FNPK	60160	2973	11W-2N	D7
-	KLWH	60043	2812	4W-14N	C5
-	KLWH	60091	2812	4W-14N	C5
-	MLPK	60160	2973	11W-2N	D7
-	MYWD	60153	3088	10W-1S	A1
-	PvsT	60130	3088	10W-1S	A1
-	PvsT	60141	3088	10W-1S	A1
-	PvsT	60153	3088	10W-1S	A1
100	EVTN	60201	2812	4W-13N	C7
400	WLMT	60091	2812	4W-14N	C5
800	CHHT	60411	3597	1E-25S	A1
900	FDHT	60411	3597	1E-25S	A1
1300	SLVL	60411	3597	1E-25S	B1
2300	FNPK	60131	2973	11W-2N	D7
E 17th St					
10	CHHT	60411	3596	0W-25S	B1
W 17th St					
200	CHHT	60411	3595	2W-25S	D1
700	CHCG	60608	3092	0W-1S	A1
700	CHCG	60616	3092	1W-1S	A1
1100	CHCG	60608	3091	1W-1S	E1
4200	CHCG	60623	3090	5W-1S	B1
N 18th Av					
-	MYWD	60153	3029	11W-0N	D3
1900	MLPK	60160	2973	11W-2N	D7
1900	MLPK	60160	3029	11W-2N	D1
2000	FNPK	60131	2973	11W-2N	D7
S 18th Av					
10	MYWD	60153	3029	11W-0N	D5
1900	BDVW	60155	3029	11W-1S	D7
2200	BDVW	60546	3087	11W-2S	D2
2200	NRIV	60546	3087	11W-2S	D2
2400	BDVW	60155	3087	11W-1S	D1
E 18th Dr					
400	CHCG	60616	3092	0E-1S	D1
W 18th Dr					
2800	CHCG	60608	3091	3W-1S	A1
2800	CHCG	60623	3091	3W-1S	A1
W 18th Pl					
900	CHCG	60608	3091	1W-1S	E1
4300	CHCG	60623	3090	5W-1S	B1
18th St					
-	KLWH	60043	2812	4W-14N	C5
-	WLMT	60091	2812	4W-14N	C5
6200	BRWN	60402	3089	8W-1S	A1
6200	CCRO	60804	3089	7W-1S	B1
6800	BRWN	60402	3088	8W-1S	E1
7100	NRIV	60130	3088	8W-1S	D1
7100	NRIV	60402	3088	8W-1S	D1
E 18th St					
10	CHCG	60616	3092	0E-1S	C1
W 18th St					
10	CHCG	60616	3092	0W-1S	B1
700	CHCG	60608	3092	1W-1S	A1
800	CHCG	60608	3091	2W-1S	B1
900	BDVW	60155	3087	11W-1S	E1
900	PvsT	60141	3087	11W-1S	E1
900	PvsT	60155	3087	11W-1S	E1
2700	CHCG	60623	3091	3W-1S	A1
3600	CHCG	60623	3090	5W-1S	B1
4700	CCRO	60804	3090	5W-1S	A1
4800	CCRO	60804	3089	6W-1S	E1
6100	BRWN	60402	3089	7W-1S	B1
S 19th Av					
-	MLPK	60160	3029	11W-0N	D3
10	MYWD	60153	3029	11W-0N	D4
1900	BDVW	60155	3029	11W-1S	D7
2200	NRIV	60155	3087	11W-2S	D2
2200	NRIV	60546	3087	11W-2S	D2
2800	BDVW	60155	3087	11W-1S	D2
2900	BDVW	60546	3087	11W-1S	D2
E 19th Pl					
10	CHHT	60411	3596	1W-26S	A1
W 19th Pl					
700	CHCG	60608	3092	0W-1S	A1
700	CHCG	60616	3092	0W-1S	A1
900	CHCG	60608	3091	1W-1S	E1
19th St					
6200	BRWN	60402	3089	8W-1S	A1
6200	CCRO	60804	3089	7W-1S	B1
6800	BRWN	60402	3088	8W-1S	E1
7100	NRIV	60130	3088	8W-1S	D1
W 19th St					
10	CHHT	60411	3596	1W-26S	A1
700	CHCG	60608	3092	0W-1S	A1
700	CHCG	60616	3092	1W-1S	A1
900	BDVW	60155	3087	11W-1S	E1
2600	CHCG	60608	3091	3W-1S	A1
2700	CHCG	60623	3091	3W-1S	A1
3600	CHCG	60623	3090	5W-1S	B1
4600	CCRO	60804	3090	5W-1S	A1
5500	CCRO	60804	3089	6W-1S	D1
6100	BRWN	60402	3089	7W-1S	B1
N 20th Av					
10	MLPK	60160	3029	11W-1N	D2
S 20th Av					
10	MYWD	60153	3029	11W-0N	D5
1900	BDVW	60155	3029	11W-1S	D7
2400	BDVW	60155	3087	11W-1S	D1
W 20th Pl					
500	CHCG	60616	3092	0W-1S	A1
1100	CHCG	60608	3091	1W-1S	E1
20th St					
700	WLMT	60091	2812	4W-13N	C6
W 20th St					
4600	CCRO	60804	3090	5W-1S	A1
N 21st Av					
10	MLPK	60160	3029	11W-0N	D3
S 21st Av					
1800	MYWD	60153	3029	11W-0S	D6
1900	BDVW	60155	3029	11W-1S	D7
2500	BDVW	60155	3087	11W-1S	D1
21st Pl					
2700	BDVW	60155	3087	12W-1S	C2
2700	WSTR	60154	3087	12W-1S	C2
W 21st Pl					
700	CHCG	60608	3092		E2
700	CHCG	60616	3092		E2
2800	CHCG	60608	3091	3W-1S	A2
2800	CHCG	60623	3090	3W-1S	E1
2800	CHCG	60623	3091	3W-1S	A2
4600	CCRO	60804	3090	5W-1S	A2
5500	CCRO	60804	3089	6W-1S	D2
21st St					
1200	WLMT	60091	2812	4W-14N	B5
6200	BRWN	60402	3089	8W-1S	A1
6200	CCRO	60804	3089	7W-1S	B1
6800	BRWN	60402	3088	8W-1S	E2
7100	NRIV	60130	3088	8W-1S	D2
E 21st St					
10	CHCG	60616	3092	0E-1S	C1
10	CHHT	60411	3596	1W-26S	A2
W 21st St					
-	BDVW	60155	3087	11W-1S	E2
10	CHHT	60411	3596	1W-26S	A2
600	CHCG	60616	3092	0W-1S	A1
700	CHCG	60608	3092	1W-1S	A1
1200	CHCG	60608	3091	3W-1S	A1
2700	CHCG	60623	3091	3W-1S	A1
2800	CHCG	60623	3090	3W-1S	E1
4600	CCRO	60804	3090	5W-1S	A1
4800	CCRO	60804	3089	6W-1S	E1
6100	BRWN	60402	3089	7W-1S	B1
22nd Av					
100	BLWD	60104	3029	11W-0N	D5
1100	BLWD	60153	3029	11W-0S	D6
N 22nd Av					
10	MLPK	60160	3029	11W-0N	D3
S 22nd Av					
1800	MYWD	60153	3029	11W-0S	D7
2400	BDVW	60155	3029	11W-1S	D7
2400	BDVW	60155	3087	11W-1S	D1
W 22nd Pl					
200	CHCG	60616	3092	0W-2S	B2
800	CHCG	60608	3091	1W-2S	E2
800	CHCG	60608	3092	1W-2S	A2
2700	CHCG	60623	3091	3W-2S	A2
2800	CHCG	60623	3090	3W-2S	E2
4800	CCRO	60804	3089	6W-2S	E2
4800	CCRO	60804	3090	5W-2S	A2
9000	NRIV	60546	3087	11W-2S	E2
E 22nd St					
10	CHHT	60411	3596	0W-26S	C2
W 22nd St					
100	OKBK	60523	3086		B2
23rd Av					
100	BLWD	60104	3029	11W-0N	D5
1100	BLWD	60153	3029	11W-0S	D6
N 23rd Av					
10	MLPK	60160	3029	11W-0N	C3
S 23rd Av					
1800	MYWD	60153	3029	11W-0S	D6
2400	BDVW	60155	3029	11W-1S	D7
23rd Pl					
2500	BDVW	60155	3087	12W-2S	C2
2500	PvsT	60155	3087	12W-2S	C2
W 23rd Pl					
200	CHCG	60616	3092	0W-2S	B2
2100	CHCG	60608	3091	2W-2S	B2
2700	CHCG	60623	3091	3W-2S	A2
2800	CHCG	60623	3090	3W-2S	E2
4800	CCRO	60804	3089	7W-2S	C2
4800	CCRO	60804	3090	5W-2S	A2
9000	NRIV	60546	3087	11W-2S	E2
23rd St					
2500	BDVW	60155	3087	12W-2S	C2
6200	BRWN	60402	3089	8W-2S	A2
6200	CCRO	60804	3089	7W-2S	B2
6800	BRWN	60402	3088	8W-2S	E2
E 23rd St					
10	CHCG	60616	3092	0E-2S	C2
200	CHHT	60411	3596	0W-26S	C2
W 23rd St					
-	BRWN	60402	3088	9W-2S	D2
-	CHCG	60616	3092	0W-2S	C2
-	NRIV	60546	3088	9W-2S	D2
10	CHHT	60411	3596	1W-26S	A2
800	CHCG	60608	3092	1W-2S	A2
1800	CHCG	60608	3091	2W-2S	C2
2700	CHCG	60623	3091	3W-2S	A2
2800	CHCG	60623	3090	4W-2S	D2
4800	CCRO	60804	3089	7W-2S	B2
4800	CCRO	60804	3090	5W-2S	A2
6100	BRWN	60402	3089	7W-2S	B2
9000	NRIV	60546	3087	11W-2S	D2
9200	BDVW	60155	3087	11W-2S	D2
24th Av					
200	BLWD	60104	3029	11W-0N	C5
1100	BLWD	60153	3029	11W-0S	C6
N 24th Av					
100	MLPK	60160	3029	11W-0N	C3
S 24th Av					
1800	MYWD	60153	3029	11W-0S	C7
1900	BDVW	60155	3029	11W-0S	C6
3000	BDVW	60155	3087	11W-2S	D2
W 24th Blvd					
2800	CHCG	60623	3090	3W-2S	E2
E 24th Pl					
10	CHCG	60616	3092	0E-2S	C2
W 24th Pl					
-	CCRO	60804	3090	5W-2S	A2
200	CHCG	60616	3092	0W-2S	B2
2300	CHCG	60608	3091	3W-2S	A2
4000	CHCG	60623	3090	5W-2S	B2
4800	CCRO	60804	3089	6W-2S	E2
24th St					
6200	BRWN	60402	3089	8W-2S	A2
6200	CCRO	60804	3089	7W-2S	B2
6900	BRWN	60402	3088	8W-2S	E2
E 24th St					
10	CHCG	60616	3092	0E-2S	C2
300	CHHT	60411	3596	0W-26S	C2
W 24th St					
10	CHCG	60616	3092	0W-2S	C2
10	CHHT	60411	3596	1W-26S	A2
2100	CHCG	60608	3091	3W-2S	A2
2700	CHCG	60623	3091	3W-2S	A2
2800	CHCG	60623	3090	5W-2S	B2
4800	CCRO	60804	3089	7W-2S	B2
4800	CCRO	60804	3090	5W-2S	A2
6100	BRWN	60402	3089	7W-2S	B2
7200	BRWN	60402	3088	9W-2S	D2
7200	NRIV	60546	3088	9W-2S	D2
8700	NRIV	60546	3087	11W-2S	E2
25th Av					
-	BDVW	60153	3029	11W-0S	C6
-	BDVW	60155	3029	11W-0S	C6
-	BLWD	60153	3029	11W-0S	C6
-	MYWD	60153	3029	11W-0S	C6
100	BLWD	60104	3029	11W-0N	C5
100	MLPK	60160	3029	11W-0N	C3
3800	SRPK	60176	2973	12W-5N	C2
4500	SRPK	60176	2917	12W-5N	B7
N 25th Av					
100	BLWD	60104	3029	12W-1N	C3
100	MLPK	60160	3029	12W-1N	C3
1900	FNPK	60131	2973	12W-2N	C7
1900	MLPK	60160	2973	12W-2N	C7
2000	LydT	60164	2973	12W-2N	C7
2000	MLPK	60131	2973	12W-2N	C7
S 25th Av					
-	BDVW	60525	3087	11W-2S	C2
-	PvsT	60525	3087	11W-2S	C2
1800	BDVW	60153	3029	12W-0S	C7
1800	BDVW	60155	3029	12W-0S	C7
1800	MYWD	60153	3029	12W-0S	C7
2400	BDVW	60155	3087	12W-1S	C2
3100	PvsT	60155	3087	11W-2S	C2
W 25th Pl					
-	CHCG	60616	3092	0W-2S	C2
2600	CHCG	60608	3091	3W-2S	A2
2800	CHCG	60623	3090	3W-2S	E3
2800	CHCG	60623	3091	3W-2S	A3
5200	CCRO	60804	3089	6W-2S	D3
25th St					
6200	BRWN	60402	3089	8W-2S	A2
6200	CCRO	60402	3089	7W-2S	B2
6200	CCRO	60804	3089	7W-2S	B2
6800	BRWN	60402	3088	8W-2S	E3
E 25th St					
10	CHCG	60616	3092	0E-2S	C2
300	CHHT	60411	3596	0W-26S	C2
W 25th St					
10	CHCG	60616	3092	0W-2S	C2
10	CHHT	60411	3596	1W-26S	A2
2300	CHCG	60608	3091	3W-2S	A2
2800	CHCG	60623	3090	5W-2S	B2
2800	CHCG	60623	3091	3W-2S	A2
4800	CCRO	60804	3089	7W-2S	B3
4800	CCRO	60804	3090	5W-2S	A2
6100	BRWN	60402	3089	7W-2S	B2
6100	CCRO	60402	3089	7W-2S	B2
7200	BRWN	60402	3088	9W-2S	D2
7200	NRIV	60546	3088	9W-2S	D2
8700	NRIV	60546	3087	11W-2S	E3
8800	PvsT	60546	3087	11W-2S	E3
26th Av					
200	BLWD	60104	3029	12W-0N	C4
S 26th Av					
3000	BDVW	60155	3087	12W-2S	C2
3100	PvsT	60155	3087	12W-2S	C2
26th Pkwy					
7000	BRWN	60402	3088	8W-2S	E3
26th Pl					
6400	BRWN	60402	3089	8W-2S	A3
7000	BRWN	60402	3088	8W-2S	E3
9000	BKFD	60513	3087	11W-2S	E3
9100	LGPK	60525	3087	11W-2S	D3
W 26th Pl					
-	CHCG	60608	3091	3W-2S	A3
10	CHCG	60616	3092	0W-2S	B3
26th St					
-	SCHT	60411	3595	2W-26S	E2
-	SCHT	60466	3595	2W-26S	E2
100	BlmT	60466	3595	2W-26S	C2
100	PKFT	60466	3595	2W-26S	C2
300	CHHT	60411	3595	2W-26S	E2
400	LGPK	60525	3087	12W-2S	C3
1000	PvsT	60525	3087	12W-2S	C3
1900	PvsT	60513	3087	12W-2S	C3
6200	BRWN	60402	3089	7W-2S	B3
6200	CCRO	60402	3089	7W-2S	B3
6200	CCRO	60804	3089	7W-2S	B3
6800	BRWN	60402	3088	8W-2S	E3
7100	NRIV	60546	3088	8W-2S	D3
7100	RVSD	60546	3088	8W-2S	D3
9000	BKFD	60513	3087	11W-2S	E3
E 26th St					
10	BlmT	60411	3596	0W-26S	C2
10	CHCG	60616	3092	0E-2S	C3
10	CHHT	60411	3596	0W-26S	C2
10	SCHT	60411	3596	1W-26S	B2
W 26th St					
-	CHCG	60608	3091	1W-2S	E3
10	CHCG	60616	3092	0W-2S	A3
10	CHHT	60411	3596	1W-26S	A2
10	SCHT	60411	3596	1W-26S	A2
200	BlmT	60466	3595	2W-26S	E2
200	CHHT	60411	3595	1W-26S	E2
200	SCHT	60411	3595	1W-26S	E2
200	SCHT	60466	3595	2W-26S	E2
700	CHCG	60608	3092	1W-2S	A2
2800	CHCG	60623	3090	4W-2S	C3
2800	CHCG	60623	3091	3W-2S	A3
4800	CCRO	60804	3089	7W-2S	B3
4800	CCRO	60804	3090	5W-2S	A3
6100	BRWN	60402	3089	7W-2S	B3
6100	CCRO	60402	3089	7W-2S	B3
7200	BRWN	60402	3088	9W-2S	D3
7200	NRIV	60546	3088	9W-2S	C3
7200	RVSD	60546	3088	9W-2S	B3
8100	BKFD	60546	3088	10W-2S	A3
8500	BKFD	60513	3088	10W-2S	A3
8700	BKFD	60513	3087	11W-2S	E3
8700	NRIV	60546	3087	11W-2S	E3
8700	PvsT	60546	3087	11W-2S	E3
27th Av					
300	BLWD	60104	3029	12W-0N	C4
N 27th Av					
1100	MLPK	60160	3029	12W-1N	C2
S 27th Av					
2300	BDVW	60155	3087	12W-1S	C1
27th Pl					
6400	BRWN	60402	3089	8W-2S	A3

STREET Block	City	ZIP	Map#	CGS	Grid
W 27th Pl					
100	SCHT	60411	3596	1W-26S	A3
27th St					
6200	BRWN	60402	3089	8W-2S	A3
6200	CCRO	60804	3089	7W-2S	B3
6800	BRWN	60402	3088	8W-2S	E3
9000	BKFD	60513	3087	11W-2S	E3
9100	LGPK	60525	3087	11W-2S	D3
E 27th St					
10	SCHT	60411	3596	1W-26S	B3
500	CHCG	60616	3092	0E-2S	D3
W 27th St					
10	SCHT	60411	3596	1W-26S	A3
400	CHCG	60616	3092	0W-2S	A3
800	CHCG	60608	3091	1W-2S	E3
800	CHCG	60608	3092	0W-2S	A3
2700	CHCG	60623	3091	3W-2S	A3
3000	CHCG	60623	3090	5W-2S	B3
5800	CCRO	60804	3089	7W-2S	B3
6100	BRWN	60402	3089	7W-2S	B3
8000	NRIV	60546	3088	10W-2S	B3
8000	RVSD	60546	3088	10W-2S	B3
28th Av					
200	BLWD	60104	3029	12W-0N	C4
28th Pl					
6400	BRWN	60402	3089	8W-2S	A3
E 28th Pl					
100	CHCG	60616	3092	0E-2S	C3
W 28th Pl					
10	SCHT	60411	3596	1W-26S	A3
400	CHCG	60616	3092	0W-2S	A3
4900	CCRO	60804	3089	6W-2S	E3
28th St					
1000	LGPK	60525	3087	12W-2S	C3
6200	BRWN	60402	3089	7W-2S	B3
6200	CCRO	60804	3089	7W-2S	B3
7100	BRWN	60402	3088	8W-2S	E3
9000	BKFD	60513	3087	11W-2S	E3
E 28th St					
10	CHCG	60616	3092	0E-2S	C3
10	SCHT	60411	3596	1W-26S	B3
W 28th St					
-	CHCG	60608	3091	3W-2S	A3
100	SCHT	60411	3596	1W-26S	A3
300	CHCG	60616	3092	0W-2S	A3
700	CHCG	60608	3092	1W-2S	A3
3000	CHCG	60623	3090	3W-2S	E3
4800	CCRO	60804	3090	5W-2S	A3
5800	CCRO	60804	3089	7W-2S	B3
6100	BRWN	60402	3089	7W-2S	B3
8000	NRIV	60546	3088	10W-2S	B3
8000	RVSD	60546	3088	10W-2S	B3
29th Av					
200	BLWD	60104	3029	12W-0N	C4
W 29th Ct					
8000	NRIV	60546	3088	10W-2S	B3
8000	RVSD	60546	3088	10W-2S	B3
29th Pl					
6800	BRWN	60402	3088	8W-2S	E3
6800	BRWN	60402	3089	8W-2S	A3
E 29th Pl					
400	CHCG	60616	3092	0E-2S	D3
W 29th Pl					
10	SCHT	60411	3596	1W-26S	A3
300	CHCG	60616	3092	0W-2S	A3
4900	CCRO	60804	3089	6W-2S	D3
29th St					
-	BlmT	60475	3597	1E-27S	B4
-	STGR	60475	3597	1E-27S	B4
10	PvsT	60525	3087	12W-2S	B3
900	LGPK	60525	3087	12W-2S	C3
1900	BKFD	60513	3087	11W-2S	D3
6200	BRWN	60402	3089	7W-2S	B4
6200	CCRO	60804	3089	7W-2S	B4
6900	BRWN	60402	3088	8W-2S	E3
7100	RVSD	60546	3088	8W-2S	D3
8600	BKFD	60513	3088	10W-2S	A3
E 29th St					
200	CHCG	60616	3092	0E-2S	C3
W 29th St					
10	SCHT	60411	3596	1W-26S	A3
100	CHCG	60616	3092	0W-2S	B3
700	CHCG	60608	3092	1W-2S	A3
800	CHCG	60608	3091	1W-2S	B3
4800	CCRO	60804	3089	6W-2S	E3
4800	CCRO	60804	3090	5W-2S	A3
8000	NRIV	60546	3088	10W-2S	B3
8000	RVSD	60546	3088	10W-2S	B3
30th Av					
200	BLWD	60104	3029	12W-0N	C4
N 30th Av					
-	MLPK	60165	3029	12W-2N	C1
1300	MLPK	60160	3029	12W-1N	C2
1700	SNPK	60165	3029	12W-1N	C1
30th Pl					
500	MNSR	46321	3430		D6
6800	BRWN	60402	3088	8W-2S	E4
6800	BRWN	60402	3089	8W-2S	A4
E 30th Pl					
10	STGR	60475	3596	0W-27S	B4
W 30th Pl					
10	SCHT	60411	3596	1W-27S	A3
10	STGR	60475	3596	1W-27S	B4
300	CHCG	60616	3092	0W-2S	B3
4900	CCRO	60804	3089	6W-2S	E4
30th St					
-	PvsT	60525	3087	12W-2S	B4
-	STGR	60475	3597	1E-27S	B4
100	LGPK	60525	3087	12W-2S	B4
500	MNSR	46321	3430		D6
1900	BKFD	60513	3087	11W-2S	D4
7100	BRWN	60402	3088	8W-2S	E4
7100	RVSD	60546	3088	8W-2S	D4
E 30th St					
10	CHCG	60616	3092	0E-2S	C3
W 30th St					
-	SCHT	60411	3595	1W-27S	E3
10	SCHT	60411	3596	1W-26S	A3
10	STGR	60475	3596	1W-27S	A4
400	CHCG	60616	3092	0W-2S	A3
700	CHCG	60608	3092	1W-2S	A3
2700	CHCG	60608	3091	3W-2S	A3
2700	CHCG	60623	3091	3W-2S	A3
3100	CHCG	60623	3090	5W-2S	B3
4800	CCRO	60804	3089	6W-2S	D4
4800	CCRO	60804	3090	5W-2S	A3
8000	NRIV	60546	3088	10W-2S	B4
8000	RVSD	60546	3088	10W-2S	B4
31st Av					
300	BLWD	60104	3029	12W-0N	C4
N 31st Av					
1100	MLPK	60160	3029	12W-1N	B2
W 31st Blvd					
2700	CHCG	60608	3091	3W-2S	A3

STREET Block	City	ZIP	Map#	CGS	Grid
E 31st Pl					
10	STGR	60475	3596	1W-27S	B5
400	CHCG	60616	3092	0E-3S	D4
W 31st Pl					
10	STGR	60475	3596	1W-27S	B5
900	CHCG	60608	3091	1W-3S	E4
4900	CCRO	60804	3089	6W-3S	E4
31st St					
6400	BRWN	60402	3089	8W-2S	A4
6800	BRWN	60402	3088	8W-2S	E4
8400	BKFD	60513	3088	10W-2S	A4
8400	BKFD	60546	3088	10W-2S	A4
8400	NRIV	60546	3088	10W-2S	A4
8400	RVSD	60546	3088	10W-2S	A4
8800	BKFD	60513	3087	11W-2S	E4
9100	LGPK	60513	3087	11W-2S	D4
10600	LGPK	60525	3087	13W-3S	A4
10600	WSTR	60154	3087	13W-3S	A4
10600	WSTR	60525	3087	13W-3S	A4
10700	LGPK	60525	3086		E4
10700	PvsT	60558	3086		E4
10700	WSTR	60154	3086		E4
10900	PvsT	60154	3086		E4
E 31st St					
10	CHCG	60616	3092	0E-2S	C3
10	LGPK	60525	3087	11W-3S	D4
10	PvsT	60525	3087	12W-2S	B4
10	STGR	60475	3596	1W-27S	B5
1100	BKFD	60513	3087	11W-3S	D4
1900	LGPK	60513	3087	11W-3S	D4
W 31st St					
10	BlmT	60475	3596	1W-27S	A5
10	CHCG	60616	3092	0W-2S	B3
10	SCHT	60411	3596	1W-27S	A4
10	STGR	60475	3596	1W-27S	A5
300	LGPK	60525	3087	12W-2S	B4
300	PvsT	60525	3087	12W-2S	B4
400	WSTR	60525	3087	12W-2S	A4
700	CHCG	60608	3092	1W-2S	A3
1000	WSTR	60154	3087	12W-2S	A4
2400	CHCG	60608	3091	3W-3S	A4
2700	CHCG	60623	3091	3W-3S	A4
2800	CHCG	60623	3090	5W-3S	B4
4600	CCRO	60804	3090	5W-3S	A4
4800	CCRO	60804	3089	7W-2S	B4
6100	BRWN	60804	3089	7W-2S	B4
8000	NRIV	60546	3088	10W-3S	B4
8000	RVSD	60546	3088	10W-3S	B4
32nd Av					
200	BLWD	60104	3029	12W-0N	B4
1700	MLPK	60160	3029	12W-1N	B1
1700	SNPK	60160	3029	12W-1N	B1
1700	SNPK	60165	3029	12W-1N	B1
N 32nd Av					
1100	MLPK	60160	3029	12W-1N	B2
1700	SNPK	60160	3029	12W-1N	B1
1700	SNPK	60165	3029	12W-1N	B1
E 32nd Pl					
10	STGR	60475	3596	0W-27S	B5
500	CHCG	60616	3092	0E-3S	D4
W 32nd Pl					
10	STGR	60475	3596	1W-27S	B5
1000	CHCG	60608	3091	1W-3S	E4
4900	CCRO	60804	3089	6W-3S	E4
32nd St					
-	SCHT	60411	3596	0W-27S	C4
-	SCHT	60475	3596	0W-27S	C4
-	STGR	60475	3596	0E-27S	D4
6200	CCRO	60804	3089	7W-3S	B4
6800	BRWN	60402	3088	8W-3S	E4
6800	BRWN	60402	3089	8W-3S	A4
7100	RVSD	60546	3088	8W-3S	E4
E 32nd St					
100	STGR	60475	3596	0W-27S	C5
400	SCHT	60411	3596	0E-27S	D4
400	SCHT	60475	3596	0E-27S	D4
600	CHCG	60616	3092	0E-3S	D4
1000	STGR	60475	3597	1E-27S	A5
W 32nd St					
10	STGR	60475	3596	1W-27S	A5
100	BlmT	60475	3596	1W-27S	A5
800	CHCG	60608	3092	0W-3S	A4
800	CHCG	60616	3092	1W-3S	A4
2000	CHCG	60608	3091	2W-3S	B4
4300	CHCG	60623	3090	5W-3S	B4
4800	CCRO	60804	3090	5W-3S	A4
6100	BRWN	60402	3089	7W-3S	B4
6100	CCRO	60804	3089	7W-3S	B4
N 33rd Av					
1100	MLPK	60160	3029	12W-1N	B1
1400	SNPK	60165	3029	12W-1N	B1
1700	SNPK	60160	3029	12W-1N	B1
E 33rd Blvd					
10	CHCG	60616	3092	0E-3S	C4
E 33rd Pl					
10	STGR	60475	3596	0W-27S	B5
600	CHCG	60616	3092	0E-3S	D4
W 33rd Pl					
10	STGR	60475	3596	1W-27S	B5
800	CHCG	60608	3092	1W-3S	A4
800	CHCG	60616	3092	1W-3S	A4
1600	CHCG	60608	3091	2W-3S	C4
33rd St					
3200	STGR	60475	3596	0W-27S	C5
6200	BRWN	60402	3089	7W-3S	B5
6200	CCRO	60804	3089	7W-3S	B4
E 33rd St					
10	STGR	60475	3596	0W-27S	B5
400	CHCG	60616	3092	0E-3S	D4
W 33rd St					
10	SCHT	60411	3596	1W-27S	B4
10	STGR	60475	3596	1W-27S	A5
100	BlmT	60475	3596	1W-27S	A5
800	CHCG	60608	3092	1W-3S	A4
800	CHCG	60616	3092	1W-3S	A4
1200	CHCG	60608	3091	1W-3S	E4
3700	CHCG	60623	3090	4W-3S	C4
6000	CCRO	60804	3089	7W-3S	B4
N 34th Av					
1200	MLPK	60160	3029	12W-1N	B2
1500	SNPK	60165	3029	12W-1N	B2
E 34th Pl					
10	STGR	60475	3596	0E-27S	D4
W 34th Pl					
10	STGR	60475	3596	1W-28S	B5
800	CHCG	60608	3092	1W-3S	A4
800	CHCG	60616	3092	1W-3S	A4
1800	CHCG	60608	3091	2W-3S	C4
34th St					
-	MNSR	46321	3430		E7
10	SCHT	60475	3596	0E-27S	D4
10	STGR	60475	3596	0E-27S	D4
6200	BRWN	60804	3089	7W-3S	B5
6200	CCRO	60804	3089	7W-3S	B5
6400	BRWN	60402	3089	8W-3S	A5

STREET Block	City	ZIP	Map#	CGS	Grid
34th St					
6800	BRWN	60402	3088	8W-3S	E5
7100	RVSD	60546	3088	8W-3S	E5
E 34th St					
10	SCHT	60411	3596	0W-27S	C4
10	SCHT	60475	3596	0W-27S	B4
10	STGR	60475	3596	1W-27S	B4
100	CRTE	60475	3596	0W-27S	C5
300	CRTE	60417	3596	0W-27S	C5
400	CHCG	60616	3092	0E-3S	D4
W 34th St					
200	CHCG	60616	3092	0W-3S	B4
800	CHCG	60608	3092	1W-3S	A4
2400	CHCG	60608	3091	3W-3S	A4
3700	CHCG	60623	3090	4W-3S	C4
4600	CCRO	60804	3090	5W-3S	A4
5200	CCRO	60804	3089	7W-3S	B4
6100	BRWN	60402	3089	7W-3S	B4
6100	BRWN	60804	3089	7W-3S	B4
N 35th Av					
1200	MLPK	60160	3029	12W-1N	B2
1500	SNPK	60160	3029	12W-1N	B2
1500	SNPK	60165	3029	12W-1N	B2
35th Pl					
-	CCRO	60804	3090	5W-2S	A3
E 35th Pl					
10	STGR	60475	3596	1W-28S	B6
W 35th Pl					
10	STGR	60475	3596	1W-28S	B6
800	CHCG	60609	3092	1W-3S	A5
900	CHCG	60609	3091	1W-3S	E5
2600	CHCG	60632	3091	3W-3S	A5
4100	CHCG	60623	3090	5W-3S	B4
4100	CHCG	60632	3090	5W-3S	B4
35th St					
6200	BRWN	60402	3089	8W-3S	A5
6200	CCRO	60804	3089	7W-3S	B5
6800	BRWN	60402	3088	8W-3S	E5
7100	RVSD	60546	3088	8W-3S	E5
E 35th St					
10	CHCG	60609	3092	0E-3S	C4
10	CHCG	60616	3092	0E-3S	C4
10	CHCG	60653	3092	0E-3S	D4
10	STGR	60475	3596	1W-28S	B6
100	CRTE	60475	3596	0W-28S	C6
W 35th St					
10	CHCG	60609	3092	0W-3S	A4
10	CHCG	60616	3092	0W-3S	A4
10	CHCG	60653	3092	0W-3S	A4
10	STGR	60475	3596	1W-28S	A6
200	STGR	60475	3595	2W-28S	E6
500	CteT	60475	3595	2W-28S	E6
700	CHCG	60608	3092	1W-3S	A4
800	CHCG	60608	3091	3W-3S	A5
800	CHCG	60609	3091	1W-3S	E5
2400	CHCG	60632	3091	3W-3S	A5
2700	CHCG	60623	3091	3W-3S	A5
2800	CHCG	60623	3090	3W-3S	E5
2800	CHCG	60632	3090	3W-3S	E5
5200	CCRO	60804	3089	7W-3S	B5
5200	SKNY	60804	3089	6W-3S	D5
6100	BRWN	60402	3089	7W-3S	B5
N 36th Av					
1200	MLPK	60160	3029	12W-1N	B2
1400	SNPK	60160	3029	12W-1N	B2
1400	SNPK	60165	3029	12W-1N	B2
E 36th Pl					
10	CHCG	60609	3092	0W-3S	C5
10	STGR	60475	3596	1W-28S	B6
500	CHCG	60653	3092	0E-3S	D5
W 36th Pl					
10	STGR	60475	3596	1W-28S	B6
1200	CHCG	60609	3091	1W-3S	E5
2600	CHCG	60632	3091	3W-3S	A5
2800	CHCG	60632	3090	3W-3S	E5
36th St					
6200	BRWN	60402	3089	8W-3S	A5
6200	CCRO	60804	3089	7W-3S	B5
7000	BRWN	60402	3088	8W-3S	E5
7100	RVSD	60546	3088	8W-3S	E5
E 36th St					
10	CHCG	60609	3092	0W-3S	C5
10	CHCG	60653	3092	0W-3S	C5
10	STGR	60475	3596	0W-28S	B6
100	CRTE	60475	3596	0W-28S	B6
W 36th St					
10	STGR	60475	3596	1W-28S	A6
500	CHCG	60609	3092	0W-3S	A5
1600	CHCG	60609	3091	2W-3S	B5
2400	CHCG	60632	3091	3W-3S	A5
2800	CHCG	60632	3090	3W-3S	E5
4000	CHCG	60623	3090	5W-3S	B5
5200	CCRO	60804	3089	7W-3S	C5
5200	SKNY	60804	3089	6W-3S	D5
6100	BRWN	60402	3089	7W-3S	B5
N 37th Av					
1200	MLPK	60160	3029	12W-1N	B2
1200	SNPK	60160	3029	12W-1N	B2
1500	MLPK	60165	3029	12W-1N	B2
1500	SNPK	60165	3029	12W-1N	B2
E 37th Pl					
10	CHCG	60609	3092	0W-3S	C5
500	CHCG	60653	3092	0E-3S	D5
W 37th Pl					
100	STGR	60475	3596	1W-28S	A6
800	CHCG	60609	3092	1W-3S	A5
900	CHCG	60609	3091	1W-3S	E5
2600	CHCG	60632	3091	3W-3S	A5
3000	CHCG	60632	3090	4W-3S	D5
37th St					
6200	BRWN	60402	3089	8W-3S	A5
6200	CCRO	60804	3089	7W-3S	B5
6800	BRWN	60402	3088	8W-3S	E5
E 37th St					
10	CHCG	60609	3092	0W-3S	C5
10	CHCG	60653	3092	0E-3S	C5
10	CRTE	60475	3596	0W-28S	B6
10	STGR	60475	3596	0W-28S	B6
W 37th St					
10	STGR	60475	3596	1W-28S	A6
800	CHCG	60609	3092	0W-3S	A5
1200	CHCG	60609	3091	1W-3S	D5
5200	CCRO	60804	3089	7W-3S	B5
5200	SKNY	60804	3089	6W-3S	D5
6100	BRWN	60402	3089	7W-3S	B5
N 38th Av					
-	MLPK	60160	3029	12W-1N	B1
1700	SNPK	60165	3029	12W-1N	B1
38th Pl					
7200	BRWN	60402	3088	9W-3S	D6
7200	LYNS	60402	3088	9W-3S	D6
7300	LYNS	60534	3088	9W-3S	D6
E 38th Pl					
800	CHCG	60653	3092	1E-3S	E5

STREET Block	City	ZIP	Map#	CGS	Grid
W 38th Pl					
800	CHCG	60609	3091	1W-3S	E5
800	CHCG	60609	3092	1W-3S	A5
2700	CHCG	60632	3091	3W-3S	A5
2800	CHCG	60632	3090	4W-3S	E5
38th St					
6200	BRWN	60402	3089	8W-3S	A6
6200	CCRO	60804	3089	7W-3S	B5
6800	BRWN	60402	3088	8W-3S	E6
7100	LYNS	60402	3088	8W-3S	E6
7100	LYNS	60534	3088	8W-3S	E6
E 38th St					
10	CHCG	60609	3092	0E-3S	C5
900	CHCG	60653	3092	1E-3S	E5
W 38th St					
300	CHCG	60609	3092	0W-3S	A5
900	CHCG	60609	3091	1W-3S	E5
2400	CHCG	60632	3091	3W-3S	A5
2900	CHCG	60632	3090	4W-3S	C5
5200	SKNY	60804	3089	6W-3S	D6
5600	CCRO	60804	3089	7W-3S	C5
6100	BRWN	60402	3089	7W-3S	B6
N 39th Av					
1500	MLPK	60160	3029	12W-1N	A2
1500	SNPK	60160	3029	12W-1N	A2
1500	SNPK	60165	3029	12W-1N	A2
W 39th Pl					
2500	CHCG	60632	3091	3W-4S	A6
2800	CHCG	60632	3090	3W-4S	E6
39th St					
10	LGNG	60525	3087	13W-3S	A5
10	LGPK	60525	3087	13W-3S	A5
10	WNSP	60558	3086		E6
10	WNSP	60558	3087	13W-3S	A5
7300	LYNS	60534	3088	9W-4S	D6
7300	LYNS	60546	3088	9W-4S	D6
7300	RVSD	60546	3088	9W-4S	D6
N 40th Av					
1500	MLPK	60160	3029	12W-1N	A2
1500	MLPK	60165	3029	12W-1N	A2
1500	SNPK	60165	3029	12W-1N	A1
40th Ct					
18300	CCHL	60478	3426	5W-22S	D7
18300	HLCT	60429	3426	5W-22S	D7
40th Pl					
7000	SKNY	60402	3088	8W-4S	E6
7100	LYNS	60402	3088	8W-4S	E6
7100	LYNS	60534	3088	8W-4S	E6
W 40th Pl					
300	CHCG	60609	3092	0W-4S	A6
2800	CHCG	60632	3090	3W-4S	E6
2800	CHCG	60632	3091	3W-4S	A6
40th St					
10	LGNG	60525	3087	13W-3S	A6
10	WNSP	60558	3086		E6
10	WNSP	60558	3087	13W-3S	A6
6400	SKNY	60402	3089	8W-4S	A6
6800	SKNY	60402	3088	8W-4S	E6
7200	LYNS	60402	3088	9W-4S	D6
7200	LYNS	60534	3088	9W-4S	D6
8700	BKFD	60513	3088	11W-4S	A6
E 40th St					
10	CHCG	60609	3092	0W-4S	C6
400	CHCG	60653	3092	0E-4S	D6
W 40th St					
10	CHCG	60609	3092	0W-4S	C6
10	CHCG	60653	3092	0W-4S	C6
900	CHCG	60609	3091	1W-4S	E6
2400	CHCG	60632	3091	3W-4S	A6
2800	CHCG	60632	3090	3W-4S	E6
41st Ct					
7800	LYNS	60534	3088	9W-4S	C7
41st Pl					
7600	LYNS	60534	3088	9W-4S	C6
E 41st Pl					
1000	CHCG	60653	3092	1E-4S	E6
W 41st Pl					
3000	CHCG	60632	3090	3W-4S	E6
41st St					
10	LGNG	60525	3087	13W-4S	A7
10	WNSP	60558	3086		E7
10	WNSP	60558	3087	13W-4S	A7
6300	SKNY	60402	3089	8W-4S	A6
6800	SKNY	60402	3088	8W-4S	E6
7100	LYNS	60402	3088	8W-4S	E6
7100	LYNS	60534	3088	8W-4S	E6
E 41st St					
10	CHCG	60609	3092	0W-4S	C6
800	CHCG	60653	3092	1E-4S	E6
W 41st St					
600	CHCG	60609	3092	0W-4S	A6
1300	CHCG	60609	3091	1W-4S	D6
2700	CHCG	60632	3091	3W-4S	A6
3000	CHCG	60632	3090	3W-4S	E6
4800	CHCG	60632	3089	6W-4S	E7
4800	CHCG	60804	3089	6W-4S	E7
4800	CHCG	60804	3090	5W-4S	A6
4800	SKNY	60804	3089	6W-4S	E7
4900	FTVW	60402	3089	6W-4S	E7
42nd Ct					
1400	SNPK	60165	3029	13W-1N	A2
8000	LYNS	60534	3088	10W-4S	B7
42nd Pl					
7800	LYNS	60534	3088	9W-4S	C7
E 42nd Pl					
800	CHCG	60653	3092	1E-4S	E6
1100	CHCG	60653	3093	1E-4S	A6
W 42nd Pl					
300	CHCG	60609	3092	0W-4S	B6
2300	CHCG	60609	3091	2W-4S	B6
3100	CHCG	60632	3090	3W-4S	E6
42nd St					
10	LGNG	60525	3087	13W-3S	A6
10	WNSP	60558	3086		E7
10	WNSP	60558	3087	13W-3S	A6
6400	SKNY	60402	3089	8W-4S	A7
6800	SKNY	60402	3088	8W-4S	E7
7100	LYNS	60402	3088	8W-4S	E7
8600	LYNS	60534	3088	10W-4S	A7
8700	BKFD	60513	3088	10W-4S	A7
8700	LYNS	60513	3088	10W-4S	A7
E 42nd St					
10	CHCG	60609	3092	0W-4S	C6
10	CHCG	60653	3092	0E-4S	C6
W 42nd St					
300	CHCG	60609	3092	0W-4S	B6
2200	CHCG	60609	3091	2W-4S	B6
2400	CHCG	60632	3091	3W-4S	A6
2800	CHCG	60632	3090	3W-4S	E6
43rd Av					
-	MLPK	60160	3029	13W-1N	A2
200	NHLK	60164	3029	13W-1N	A2
200	SNPK	60165	3029	13W-1N	A2
1400	MLPK	60165	3029	13W-1N	A2

STREET Block	City	ZIP	Map#	CGS	Grid
43rd Ct					
1400	MLPK	60165	3029	13W-1N	A2
1400	SNPK	60165	3029	13W-1N	A2
43rd Pl					
8200	LYNS	60534	3088	10W-4S	B7
W 43rd Pl					
700	CHCG	60609	3092	0W-4S	A7
43rd St					
400	WNSP	60558	3086		E7
6400	SKNY	60402	3089	8W-4S	A7
6400	StkT	60402	3089	8W-4S	A7
6800	SKNY	60402	3088	8W-4S	E7
8500	LYNS	60534	3088	10W-4S	A7
8700	BKFD	60513	3088	10W-4S	A7
8700	LYNS	60513	3088	10W-4S	A7
E 43rd St					
10	CHCG	60609	3092	0W-4S	C6
10	CHCG	60653	3092	0E-4S	D6
1100	CHCG	60653	3093	1E-4S	A6
W 43rd St					
-	CHCG	60632	3091	3W-4S	B7
10	CHCG	60609	3092	0W-4S	B6
10	CHCG	60653	3092	0W-4S	B6
1000	CHCG	60609	3091	2W-4S	C7
3200	CHCG	60632	3090	4W-4S	D7
4700	CHCG	60638	3090	6W-4S	A7
4800	CHCG	60638	3089	6W-4S	E7
44th Av					
200	NHLK	60165	3029	13W-1N	A1
200	SNPK	60165	3029	13W-1N	A1
1400	MLPK	60160	3029	13W-1N	A2
1400	MLPK	60165	3029	13W-1N	A2
1400	SNPK	60160	3029	13W-1N	A2
1500	NHLK	60164	3029	13W-1N	A1
1500	SNPK	60164	3029	13W-1N	A2
S 44th Av					
300	NHLK	60164	3029	13W-1N	A2
300	NHLK	60165	3029	13W-1N	A2
300	SNPK	60165	3029	13W-1N	A2
400	SNPK	60164	3029	13W-1N	A2
44th Ct					
1400	MLPK	60160	3029	13W-1N	A2
1400	SNPK	60160	3029	13W-1N	A2
1400	SNPK	60165	3029	13W-1N	A2
5000	LYNS	60534	3088	10W-4S	B7
S 44th Ct					
12300	ALSP	60803	3276	5W-14S	B6
44th Pl					
8500	LYNS	60534	3088	10W-4S	A7
8800	BKFD	60513	3087	11W-4S	E7
8800	BKFD	60513	3088	11W-4S	A7
E 44th Pl					
500	CHCG	60653	3092	0E-4S	D7
1200	CHCG	60653	3093	1E-4S	A7
S 44th Pl					
-	ALSP	60803	3276	5W-13S	B4
-	CHCG	60655	3276	5W-13S	B4
W 44th Pl					
200	CHCG	60609	3092	0W-4S	B7
4100	CHCG	60632	3090	5W-4S	B7
4800	CHCG	60638	3089	6W-4S	E7
44th St					
6800	SKNY	60402	3088	8W-4S	E7
6800	SKNY	60402	3089	8W-4S	A7
8000	LYNS	60534	3088	10W-4S	B7
8700	BKFD	60513	3088	10W-4S	A7
8700	LYNS	60513	3088	10W-4S	A7
E 44th St					
10	CHCG	60609	3092	0W-4S	C7
900	CHCG	60653	3092	1E-4S	E7
1100	CHCG	60653	3093	1E-4S	A7
W 44th St					
400	CHCG	60609	3092	0W-4S	A7
2400	CHCG	60609	3091	3W-4S	A7
2400	CHCG	60632	3091	3W-4S	A7
4300	CHCG	60632	3090	5W-4S	B7
4700	CHCG	60638	3090	5W-4S	A7
4800	CHCG	60638	3089	6W-4S	E7
5100	FTVW	60638	3089	6W-4S	E7
45th Av					
10	LNSG	60438	3510	4E-22S	C2
10	MNSR	46321	3510		D2
200	NHLK	60164	3029	13W-1N	A2
1400	MLPK	60160	3029	13W-1N	A2
S 45th Av					
12200	ALSP	60803	3276	5W-14S	B6
45th Ct					
8000	LYNS	60534	3088	10W-4S	B7
45th Pl					
8500	LYNS	60534	3088	10W-4S	A7
8600	LYNS	60534	3148	10W-4S	A1
8700	BKFD	60513	3148	10W-4S	A1
8800	BKFD	60513	3147	11W-5S	E1
E 45th Pl					
400	CHCG	60653	3092	0E-4S	D7
N 45th Pl					
1400	MLPK	60160	3029	13W-1N	A2
W 45th Pl					
200	CHCG	60609	3092	0W-4S	B7
2400	CHCG	60609	3091	3W-4S	A7
2400	CHCG	60632	3091	3W-4S	A7
3800	CHCG	60632	3090	4W-4S	C7
45th St					
10	LGNG	60525	3147	13W-4S	A1
10	WNSP	60558	3146		E1
10	WNSP	60558	3147	13W-4S	A1
800	MNSR	46321	3510		E2
6800	FTVW	60402	3088	8W-4S	E7
6800	FTVW	60402	3089	8W-4S	A7
6800	SKNY	60402	3088	8W-4S	E7
6800	SKNY	60402	3089	8W-4S	A7
8000	LYNS	60534	3088	10W-4S	B7
8700	BKFD	60513	3088	10W-4S	A7
E 45th St					
10	CHCG	60609	3092	0W-4S	C7
10	CHCG	60653	3092	0E-4S	C7
1100	CHCG	60653	3093	1E-4S	A7
W 45th St					
200	CHCG	60609	3092	0W-4S	B7
2300	CHCG	60609	3091	3W-4S	A7
2400	CHCG	60632	3091	3W-4S	A7
2800	CHCG	60632	3090	3W-4S	E7
4700	CHCG	60638	3090	5W-4S	A7
4800	CHCG	60638	3089	6W-4S	E7
5100	FTVW	60638	3089	6W-4S	E7
46th Av					
10	BLWD	60104	3029	13W-0N	A4
200	MLPK	60164	3029	13W-1N	A1
200	NHLK	60164	3029	13W-1N	A1
300	MLPK	60160	3029	13W-1N	A1
300	NHLK	60160	3029	13W-1N	A1
500	HLSD	60162	3029	13W-0N	A5
N 46th Av					
1400	MLPK	60160	3029	13W-1N	A2

STREET Block	City	ZIP	Map#	CGS	Grid
S 46th Ct					
1600	CCRO	60804	3090	5W-1S	A1
E 46th Pl					
400	CHCG	60653	3092	0E-4S	D7
W 46th Pl					
100	CHCG	60609	3092	0W-4S	C7
2400	CHCG	60609	3091	3W-4S	A7
2400	CHCG	60632	3091	3W-4S	A7
3800	CHCG	60632	3150	4W-5S	D1
46th St					
10	LGNG	60525	3147	13W-4S	A1
10	WNSP	60558	3146		E1
10	WNSP	60558	3147	13W-4S	A1
400	MLPK	60160	3029	13W-1N	A2
400	MLPK	60164	3029	13W-1N	A2
400	NHLK	60160	3029	13W-1N	A2
400	NHLK	60164	3029	13W-1N	A2
6800	FTVW	60402	3148	8W-4S	E1
6800	FTVW	60402	3149	8W-4S	A1
7600	LYNS	60534	3148	10W-4S	B1
E 46th St					
10	CHCG	60609	3092	0E-4S	C7
900	CHCG	60653	3092	1E-4S	E7
1100	CHCG	60653	3093	1E-4S	A7
W 46th St					
200	CHCG	60609	3092	0W-4S	B7
1200	CHCG	60609	3091	1W-4S	E7
2400	CHCG	60632	3091	3W-4S	A7
2800	CHCG	60632	3090	4W-4S	D7
4700	CHCG	60638	3090	5W-4S	A7
4800	CHCG	60638	3089	6W-4S	E7
5100	FTVW	60638	3089	6W-4S	E7
47th Av					
-	BKLY	60163	3028		C2
-	BKLY	60164	3028		C2
-	NHLK	60164	3028		C2
10	BLWD	60104	3028		E4
N 47th Av					
1400	MLPK	60160	3028		E2
S 47th Av					
1200	CCRO	60804	3032	5W-1S	A7
1200	CHCG	60644	3032	5W-1S	A7
1900	CCRO	60804	3090	5W-1S	A1
S 47th Ct					
1600	CCRO	60804	3090	5W-1S	A1
E 47th Pl					
800	CHCG	60615	3152	1E-5S	E1
1300	CHCG	60615	3153	1E-5S	A1
W 47th Pl					
600	CHCG	60609	3152	1W-5S	A1
1000	CHCG	60609	3151	1W-5S	E1
2400	CHCG	60632	3151	3W-5S	B1
3200	CHCG	60632	3150	4W-5S	D1
47th St					
10	LGNG	60525	3147	13W-4S	A1
10	LGNG	60558	3147	13W-4S	A1
10	WNSP	60558	3146		D1
10	WNSP	60558	3147	13W-4S	A1
7200	FTVW	60402	3148	8W-4S	E1
7200	LYNS	60534	3148	10W-4S	A1
7400	MCCK	60534	3148	10W-4S	A1
8000	MCCK	60525	3148	10W-4S	B1
8300	LYNS	60525	3148	10W-4S	B1
8700	BKFD	60513	3148	10W-4S	A1
8700	MCCK	60513	3148	10W-4S	A1
8800	BKFD	60513	3147	11W-5S	D1
8800	MCCK	60525	3147	11W-5S	D1
9100	MCCK	60513	3147	11W-4S	D1
E 47th St					
10	CHCG	60609	3092	0E-4S	C7
10	CHCG	60615	3092	0E-4S	C7
10	CHCG	60653	3092	0E-4S	C7
10	LGNG	60525	3147	12W-4S	C1
700	BKFD	60513	3147	12W-4S	C1
700	MCCK	60513	3147	12W-4S	C1
700	MCCK	60525	3147	12W-4S	C1
1100	CHCG	60615	3093	1E-5S	A7
1100	CHCG	60653	3093	1E-5S	A7
W 47th St					
10	CHCG	60609	3092	0W-4S	B7
10	CHCG	60615	3092	0W-4S	C7
10	CHCG	60653	3092	0W-4S	C7
10	LGNG	60525	3147	13W-4S	A1
500	CHCG	60609	3152	0W-5S	A1
800	CHCG	60609	3151	1W-5S	D1
1400	LGNG	60558	3147	13W-4S	A1
1400	WNSP	60558	3147	13W-4S	A1
2400	CHCG	60632	3151	3W-4S	A1
2900	CHCG	60632	3150	5W-4S	B1
4700	CHCG	60638	3150	5W-4S	A1
4800	CHCG	60638	3149	6W-4S	D1
5100	FTVW	60638	3149	6W-4S	E1
5300	StkT	60638	3149	6W-4S	D1
48th Av					
10	BLWD	60104	3028		E4
S 48th Ct					
1200	CCRO	60804	3031	6W-1S	E7
1200	CHCG	60644	3031	6W-1S	E7
1500	CCRO	60804	3089	6W-1S	E1
8900	OKLN	60453	3212	6W-10S	A4
E 48th Pl					
400	CHCG	60615	3152	0E-5S	D1
W 48th Pl					
600	CHCG	60609	3152	0W-5S	A1
2200	CHCG	60609	3151	2W-5S	B1
2800	CHCG	60632	3151	3W-5S	A1
3200	CHCG	60632	3150	4W-5S	D1
48th St					
-	LGNG	60525	3147	13W-5S	A1
-	LGNG	60558	3147	13W-5S	A1
-	WNSP	60558	3147	13W-5S	A1
500	WNSP	60558	3146		D1
E 48th St					
10	CHCG	60609	3152	0E-5S	C1
10	LGNG	60525	3147	12W-5S	C1
900	CHCG	60615	3152	1E-5S	E1
1100	CHCG	60615	3153	1E-5S	A1
W 48th St					
10	LGNG	60525	3147	12W-5S	B1
600	CHCG	60609	3152	0W-5S	A1
700	LynT	60525	3147	12W-5S	B1
1000	CHCG	60609	3151	2W-5S	C1
1300	WNSP	60558	3146		D1
2700	CHCG	60632	3151	3W-5S	A1
3800	CHCG	60632	3150	5W-5S	B1
4700	CHCG	60638	3150	5W-5S	A1
4800	CHCG	60638	3149	6W-5S	E1
5100	StkT	60638	3149	6W-5S	E1
49th Av					
10	BLWD	60104	3028		E4
S 49th Av					
1200	CCRO	60804	3031	6W-1S	E7
1200	CHCG	60644	3031	6W-1S	E7
1500	CCRO	60804	3089	6W-2S	E2
8900	OKLN	60453	3212	6W-10S	A5
S 49th Ct					
1200	CCRO	60804	3031	6W-1S	E7
1200	CHCG	60644	3031	6W-1S	E7
1500	CCRO	60804	3089	6W-1S	E1
8700	BRBK	60459	3211	6W-10S	E4
8700	OKLN	60453	3211	6W-10S	E4
9000	OKLN	60453	3212	6W-10S	A5
49th Ct N					
1400	WNSP	60558	3146		D2
49th Ct S					
1400	WNSP	60558	3146		D2
W 49th Pl					
-	CHCG	60632	3151	3W-5S	B1
700	CHCG	60609	3152	1W-5S	A1
1200	CHCG	60609	3151	1W-5S	D1
3000	CHCG	60632	3150	3W-5S	E1
49th St					
800	WNSP	60558	3146		D2
E 49th St					
10	CHCG	60615	3152	0E-5S	C1
10	LGNG	60525	3147	12W-5S	C1
700	MCCK	60525	3147	12W-5S	C1
1100	CHCG	60615	3153	1E-5S	A1
8600	MCCK	60525	3148	10W-5S	B1
W 49th St					
10	LGNG	60525	3147	12W-5S	B2
600	CHCG	60609	3152	0W-5S	A1
700	LynT	60525	3147	12W-5S	B2
1100	CHCG	60609	3151	2W-5S	B1
4600	CHCG	60632	3150	5W-5S	A1
4700	CHCG	60638	3150	5W-5S	A1
4800	CHCG	60638	3149	6W-5S	D1
5100	StkT	60638	3149	6W-5S	E1
50th Av					
10	BLWD	60104	3028		E3
500	HLSD	60104	3028		E5
500	HLSD	60162	3028		E5
S 50th Av					
1200	CCRO	60804	3031	6W-1S	E7
1200	CHCG	60644	3031	6W-1S	E7
1500	CCRO	60804	3089	6W-2S	E2
8700	BRBK	60459	3211	6W-10S	E5
8700	OKLN	60453	3211	6W-10S	E5
S 50th Ct					
1200	CCRO	60804	3031	6W-1S	E7
1200	CHCG	60644	3031	6W-1S	E7
2800	CCRO	60804	3089	6W-2S	E3
9500	OKLN	60453	3211	6W-11S	E6
50th Pl					
200	WNSP	60558	3146		E2
E 50th Pl					
400	CHCG	60615	3152	0E-5S	D1
1600	CHCG	60615	3153	2E-5S	B1
W 50th Pl					
700	CHCG	60609	3152	0W-5S	A1
900	CHCG	60609	3151	1W-5S	E1
1400	LGNG	60525	3147	13W-5S	A2
1400	WNSP	60558	3147	13W-5S	A2
3700	CHCG	60632	3150	4W-5S	C2
50th St					
-	MCCK	60525	3147	11W-5S	E2
-	MCCK	60525	3148	10W-5S	A2
800	WNSP	60558	3146		D2
E 50th St					
10	LGNG	60525	3147	12W-5S	C2
900	CHCG	60615	3152	1E-5S	E1
1000	MCCK	60525	3147	12W-5S	C2
1100	CHCG	60615	3153	1E-5S	A1
8400	MCCK	60525	3148	10W-5S	B2
W 50th St					
10	LGNG	60525	3147	12W-5S	B2
200	CHCG	60609	3152	0W-5S	B1
700	LynT	60525	3147	12W-5S	B2
900	CHCG	60609	3151	2W-5S	B1
2400	CHCG	60632	3151	3W-5S	A1
4000	CHCG	60632	3150	5W-5S	B1
4700	CHCG	60638	3150	5W-5S	A1
4800	CHCG	60638	3149	6W-5S	E1
5100	StkT	60638	3149	6W-5S	E1
51st Av					
400	HLSD	60162	3028		E5
S 51st Av					
1200	CCRO	60804	3031	6W-1S	E7
1200	CHCG	60644	3031	6W-1S	E7
1500	CCRO	60804	3089	6W-2S	E2
8700	BRBK	60459	3211	6W-10S	E5
8700	OKLN	60453	3211	6W-10S	E5
51st Av S					
10	BKLY	60163	3028		E3
10	BLWD	60163	3028		E3
300	BLWD	60104	3028		E4
S 51st Ct					
1200	CCRO	60804	3031	6W-1S	E7
1200	CHCG	60644	3031	6W-1S	E7
1500	CCRO	60804	3089	6W-1S	E1
10300	OKLN	60453	3275	6W-12S	E1
51st Pl					
100	WNSP	60558	3146		E2
100	WNSP	60558	3147	13W-5S	A2
W 51st Pl					
300	CHCG	60609	3152	0W-5S	B2
900	CHCG	60609	3151	1W-5S	B2
7000	CHCG	60638	3148	8W-5S	E2
51st St					
10	LGNG	60525	3147	13W-5S	A2
10	WNSP	60558	3147	13W-5S	A2
100	WNSP	60558	3146		E2
E 51st St					
10	CHCG	60609	3152	0E-5S	C1
10	CHCG	60615	3152	0E-5S	D1
10	LGNG	60525	3147	12W-5S	C2
400	CTSD	60525	3147	12W-5S	C2
W 51st St					
10	CHCG	60609	3152	0W-5S	A1
10	CHCG	60615	3152	0W-5S	A1
10	LGNG	60525	3147	12W-5S	B2
700	LynT	60525	3147	12W-5S	B2
900	CHCG	60609	3151	2W-5S	B2
1400	WNSP	60558	3147	13W-5S	A2
2400	CHCG	60632	3151	3W-5S	B2
2900	CHCG	60632	3150	4W-5S	D2
4700	CHCG	60638	3150	5W-5S	A2
4800	CHCG	60638	3149	6W-5S	E2
5100	StkT	60638	3149	6W-5S	E2
6400	FTVW	60638	3149	8W-5S	A2
6800	CHCG	60638	3148	8W-5S	E2
6800	StkT	60638	3148	8W-5S	E2
52nd Av					
10	BKLY	60163	3028		E3
10	BLWD	60104	3028		E3
10	BLWD	60163	3028		E3
500	HLSD	60104	3028		E5
500	HLSD	60162	3028		E5
S 52nd Av					
8700	BRBK	60459	3211	6W-10S	E4
8700	OKLN	60453	3211	6W-10S	E4
10100	OKLN	60453	3275	6W-11S	E1
S 52nd Ct					
3100	CCRO	60804	3089	6W-3S	D4
9100	OKLN	60453	3211	6W-10S	E5
52nd Pl					
-	LynT	60525	3147	13W-5S	A3
-	WNSP	60558	3147	13W-5S	A3
300	WNSP	60558	3146		E3
E 52nd Pl					
1500	CHCG	60615	3153	1E-5S	B2
W 52nd Pl					
300	CHCG	60609	3152	0W-5S	B2
1300	LynT	60525	3147	13W-5S	A3
1300	WNSP	60558	3147	13W-5S	A3
2000	CHCG	60609	3151	2W-5S	C2
4000	CHCG	60632	3150	5W-5S	B2
52nd St					
800	WNSP	60558	3146		E2
E 52nd St					
10	LGNG	60525	3147	12W-5S	C2
800	CHCG	60615	3152	1E-5S	E2
1100	CHCG	60615	3153	1E-5S	A2
W 52nd St					
10	LGNG	60525	3147	12W-5S	B2
200	CHCG	60609	3152	0W-5S	B2
700	LynT	60525	3147	12W-5S	B2
2000	CHCG	60609	3151	2W-5S	C2
2400	CHCG	60632	3151	3W-5S	A2
2800	CHCG	60632	3150	4W-5S	D2
5000	CHCG	60638	3149	8W-5S	B2
6800	CHCG	60638	3148	8W-5S	E2
53rd Av					
400	BLWD	60104	3028		E4
500	HLSD	60162	3028		E5
S 53rd Av					
2200	CCRO	60804	3089	6W-2S	D2
9100	OKLN	60453	3211	6W-10S	E5
10100	OKLN	60453	3275	6W-11S	E1
S 53rd Ct					
2900	CCRO	60804	3089	6W-2S	D3
8700	BRBK	60459	3211	6W-10S	E4
8700	OKLN	60453	3211	6W-10S	E4
W 53rd Pl					
800	CHCG	60609	3152	1W-5S	A2
900	CHCG	60609	3151	1W-5S	E2
1200	LynT	60525	3147	13W-5S	A3
1200	WNSP	60558	3147	13W-5S	A3
3400	CHCG	60632	3150	4W-5S	D2
5200	CHCG	60638	3149	6W-5S	D2
53rd St					
10	WNSP	60558	3147	13W-5S	A3
600	WNSP	60558	3146		D3
E 53rd St					
10	CHCG	60609	3152	0E-5S	C2
900	CHCG	60615	3152	1E-5S	E2
1100	CHCG	60615	3153	1E-5S	A2
W 53rd St					
10	CHCG	60609	3152	0W-5S	B2
10	CTSD	60525	3147	12W-5S	B3
10	LGNG	60525	3147	12W-5S	B3
700	LynT	60525	3147	12W-5S	B3
1000	CHCG	60609	3151	1W-5S	E2
2400	CHCG	60632	3151	3W-5S	A2
3600	CHCG	60632	3150	4W-5S	C2
4700	CHCG	60638	3150	5W-5S	A2
5600	CHCG	60638	3149	8W-5S	A2
6800	CHCG	60638	3148	8W-5S	E2
7200	SMMT	60501	3148	9W-5S	D2
8400	MCCK	60525	3148	10W-5S	A2
S 54th Av					
1200	CCRO	60804	3031	6W-1S	D7
1200	CHCG	60644	3031	6W-1S	D7
3400	CCRO	60804	3089	6W-3S	D5
9100	OKLN	60453	3211	6W-11S	D7
S 54th Ct					
3100	CCRO	60804	3089	6W-3S	D4
9100	OKLN	60453	3211	6W-10S	D5
54th Pl					
-	LynT	60525	3146		E3
-	LynT	60558	3146		E3
-	WNSP	60525	3146		E3
-	WNSP	60558	3146		E3
E 54th Pl					
900	CHCG	60615	3152	1E-5S	E2
1400	CHCG	60615	3153	1E-5S	A2
W 54th Pl					
300	CHCG	60609	3152	0W-5S	B2
900	CHCG	60609	3151	1W-5S	E2
1200	LynT	60525	3147	13W-5S	A3
1600	LynT	60525	3146		E3
1700	LynT	60558	3146		E3
1700	WNSP	60525	3146		E3
1700	WNSP	60558	3146		E3
3000	CHCG	60632	3150	3W-5S	E2
5800	CHCG	60638	3149	7W-5S	C3
54th St					
800	WNSP	60558	3146		D3
E 54th St					
10	CHCG	60609	3152	0E-5S	C2
900	CHCG	60615	3152	1E-5S	E2
1600	CHCG	60615	3153	2E-5S	B2
W 54th St					
10	CHCG	60609	3152	0W-5S	C2
300	CTSD	60525	3147	12W-5S	B3
300	LGNG	60525	3147	12W-5S	B3
1000	CHCG	60609	3151	1W-5S	E2
1300	LynT	60525	3147	13W-5S	A3
1600	LynT	60525	3146		E3
1600	LynT	60558	3146		E3
1600	WNSP	60558	3146		E3
2400	CHCG	60632	3151	3W-5S	A2
3600	CHCG	60632	3150	5W-5S	B2
4600	CHCG	60638	3150	5W-5S	A2
5200	CHCG	60638	3149	6W-5S	D2
6800	CHCG	60638	3148	8W-5S	E3
7100	SMMT	60501	3148	8W-5S	E3
S 55th Av					
1600	CCRO	60804	3089	6W-1S	D1
8700	BRBK	60459	3211	6W-10S	D4
8700	OKLN	60453	3211	6W-10S	D4
8700	OKLN	60459	3211	6W-10S	D4
S 55th Ct					
1200	CCRO	60804	3031	6W-1S	D7
3100	CCRO	60804	3089	6W-3S	D4
8700	BRBK	60459	3211	6W-10S	D4
8700	OKLN	60453	3211	6W-10S	D4
8700	OKLN	60459	3211	6W-10S	D4
E 55th Pl					
-	CHCG	60615	3153	1E-6S	A2
200	CHCG	60637	3152	0E-6S	D3
1300	CHCG	60637	3153	1E-6S	A2
W 55th Pl					
1000	CTSD	60525	3147	13W-6S	A3
1600	LynT	60525	3146		E3
1600	LynT	60525	3147	13W-6S	A3
2000	WNSP	60558	3146		E3
3600	CHCG	60629	3150	4W-6S	C3
7300	SMMT	60501	3148	9W-6S	D3
55th St					
800	LynT	60525	3146		D3
800	WNSP	60558	3146		D3
1100	HNDL	60558	3146		D3
E 55th St					
-	HNDL	60558	3146		B3
-	WNSP	60558	3146		B3
400	HNDL	60521	3146		B3
500	BRRG	60521	3146		C3
800	CHCG	60615	3152	1E-6S	E2
800	CHCG	60637	3152	1E-6S	E2
1100	CHCG	60615	3153	1E-5S	A2
1100	CHCG	60637	3153	1E-5S	A2
9000	MCCK	60525	3147	11W-5S	D3
9500	CTSD	60525	3147	11W-5S	E3
E 55th St CO-35					
400	HNDL	60521	3146		C3
W 55th St					
10	CTSD	60525	3147	13W-5S	A3
10	HNDL	60521	3146		A3
300	DGvT	60521	3146		A3
400	LGNG	60525	3147	12W-5S	B3
800	LynT	60525	3147	13W-5S	A3
1500	LynT	60525	3146		E3
1700	WNSP	60525	3146		E3
1900	WNSP	60558	3146		E3
2400	CHCG	60609	3151	3W-5S	B3
2400	CHCG	60629	3151	3W-5S	A3
2400	CHCG	60632	3151	3W-5S	A3
2900	CHCG	60629	3150	4W-5S	C3
2900	CHCG	60632	3150	5W-5S	B3
4500	CHCG	60638	3150	5W-5S	B3
4800	CHCG	60638	3149	6W-5S	D3
W 55th St CO-35					
10	HNDL	60521	3146		A3
300	DGvT	60521	3146		A3
S 56th Ct					
1200	CCRO	60804	3031	7W-1S	C7
1200	CHCG	60644	3031	7W-1S	C7
1500	CCRO	60804	3089	7W-1S	C1
3800	SKNY	60402	3089	7W-3S	C6
3800	SKNY	60804	3089	7W-3S	C6
E 56th Pl					
700	CHCG	60637	3152	0E-6S	E3
W 56th Pl					
300	CHCG	60621	3152	0W-6S	B3
3600	CHCG	60629	3150	4W-6S	C3
7300	SMMT	60501	3148	9W-6S	D3
E 56th St					
10	CHCG	60621	3152	0E-6S	C3
100	HNDL	60521	3146		B3
800	CHCG	60637	3152	1E-6S	E3
1100	CHCG	60637	3153	1E-6S	A3
9500	CTSD	60525	3147	12W-6S	C3
9500	MCCK	60525	3147	12W-6S	C3
W 56th St					
-	CTSD	60525	3147	12W-6S	C3
400	CHCG	60621	3152	0W-6S	A3
500	DGvT	60521	3146		A3
500	HNDL	60521	3146		A3
900	CHCG	60621	3151	1W-6S	D3
1900	LynT	60525	3146		E4
2300	CHCG	60636	3151	2W-6S	B3
2400	CHCG	60629	3151	3W-6S	A3
2900	CHCG	60629	3150	4W-6S	D3
5600	CHCG	60638	3149	7W-6S	D3
6800	CHCG	60638	3148	8W-6S	E3
7100	SMMT	60638	3148	8W-6S	E3
7200	SMMT	60501	3148	9W-6S	D3
S 57th Av					
1200	CCRO	60804	3031	7W-1S	C7
1200	CHCG	60644	3031	7W-1S	C7
1500	CCRO	60804	3089	7W-2S	C2
3800	SKNY	60402	3089	7W-3S	C6
3800	SKNY	60804	3089	7W-3S	C6
S 57th Ct					
1200	CCRO	60804	3031	7W-1S	C7
1200	CHCG	60644	3031	7W-1S	C7
1500	CCRO	60804	3089	7W-1S	C1
3800	SKNY	60402	3089	7W-3S	C6
3800	SKNY	60804	3089	7W-3S	C6
W 57th Pl					
10	CHCG	60621	3152	0W-6S	C3
10	CHCG	60637	3152	0W-6S	C3
3500	CHCG	60629	3150	4W-6S	D3
5700	CHCG	60638	3149	7W-6S	C3
7200	CHCG	60638	3148	9W-6S	D3
7200	SMMT	60501	3148	9W-6S	D3
E 57th St					
10	CHCG	60621	3152	0E-6S	C3
400	HNDL	60521	3146		B4
700	CHCG	60637	3152	1E-6S	E3
1100	CHCG	60637	3153	1E-6S	A3
9600	CTSD	60525	3147	12W-6S	C4
9600	MCCK	60525	3147	12W-6S	C4
W 57th St					
-	CTSD	60525	3147	13W-6S	A4
-	LynT	60525	3146		E4
-	LynT	60525	3147	13W-6S	A4
10	CHCG	60621	3152	0W-6S	C3
10	CHCG	60637	3152	0W-6S	C3
10	HNDL	60521	3146		A4
300	DGvT	60521	3146		A4
900	CHCG	60621	3151	1W-6S	D3
1100	CHCG	60636	3151	2W-6S	C3
2300	CHCG	60629	3151	3W-6S	A3
3600	CHCG	60629	3150	5W-6S	B3
5600	CHCG	60638	3149	7W-6S	D3
6800	CHCG	60638	3148	8W-6S	E3
7200	SMMT	60501	3148	9W-6S	D3
S 58th Av					
1200	CCRO	60804	3031	7W-1S	C7
1200	CHCG	60644	3031	7W-1S	C7
3200	CCRO	60804	3089	7W-3S	C5
3800	SKNY	60402	3089	7W-3S	C6
S 58th Ct					
1200	CCRO	60804	3031	7W-1S	C7
1200	CHCG	60644	3031	7W-1S	C7
1500	CCRO	60804	3089	7W-2S	C3
3800	SKNY	60402	3089	7W-3S	C6
58th Pl					
400	DGvT	60521	3146		A4
400	HNDL	60521	3146		A4
W 58th Pl					
500	DGvT	60521	3146		A4
1800	LynT	60525	3146		E4
3500	CHCG	60629	3150	4W-6S	D4
7200	CHCG	60638	3148	9W-6S	D4
7200	SMMT	60501	3148	9W-6S	D4
7200	SMMT	60638	3148	9W-6S	D4
E 58th St					
10	CHCG	60621	3152	0E-6S	C3
100	HNDL	60521	3146		B4
800	CHCG	60637	3152	1E-6S	E3
1000	CHCG	60637	3153	1E-6S	A3
W 58th St					
400	CHCG	60621	3152	0W-6S	A3
500	DGvT	60521	3146		A4
500	HNDL	60521	3146		A4
800	LynT	60525	3147	13W-6S	B4
900	CHCG	60621	3151	1W-6S	D3
1100	CHCG	60636	3151	2W-6S	C3
2300	CHCG	60629	3151	3W-6S	A3
2900	CHCG	60629	3150	5W-6S	B3
5600	CHCG	60638	3149	7W-6S	D4
6800	CHCG	60638	3148	8W-6S	E4
7200	SMMT	60501	3148	9W-6S	D4
9600	CTSD	60525	3147	12W-6S	C4
9600	MCCK	60525	3147	12W-6S	C4
S 59th Av					
1200	CCRO	60804	3031	7W-1S	C7
1200	CHCG	60644	3031	7W-1S	C7
1500	CCRO	60804	3089	7W-2S	C2
3800	SKNY	60402	3089	7W-3S	C6
S 59th Ct					
1200	CCRO	60804	3031	7W-1S	C7
1200	CHCG	60644	3031	7W-1S	C7
1200	CHCG	60804	3031	7W-1S	C7
3200	CCRO	60804	3089	7W-3S	C5
3800	CCRO	60402	3089	7W-3S	C6
3800	SKNY	60402	3089	7W-3S	C6
59th Pl					
1500	LynT	60525	3146		E4
1500	LynT	60525	3147	13W-6S	A4
W 59th Pl					
200	CHCG	60621	3152	0W-6S	B4
3600	CHCG	60629	3150	4W-6S	C4
7400	SMMT	60501	3148	9W-6S	D4
E 59th St					
10	BRRG	60527	3146		B4
10	CHCG	60621	3152	0E-6S	C3
300	BRRG	60521	3146		B4
300	HNDL	60521	3146		B4
800	CHCG	60637	3152	1E-6S	E3
1000	CHCG	60637	3153	1E-6S	A3
W 59th St					
10	BRRG	60521	3146		A4
10	BRRG	60527	3146		A4
10	CHCG	60621	3152	0W-6S	A4
10	CHCG	60637	3152	0W-6S	C3
10	HNDL	60521	3146		A4
400	CTSD	60525	3147	13W-6S	B4
700	DGvT	60521	3146		A4
700	DGvT	60527	3146		A4
700	LynT	60525	3147	12W-6S	B4
900	CHCG	60621	3151	1W-6S	D4
1100	CHCG	60636	3151	2W-6S	B4
1900	LynT	60525	3146		E4
2000	LynT	60558	3146		E4
2000	WNSP	60525	3146		E4
2000	WNSP	60558	3146		E4
2300	CHCG	60629	3151	3W-6S	A4
2900	CHCG	60629	3150	4W-6S	E4
4600	CHCG	60638	3150	5W-6S	A4
5700	CHCG	60638	3149	8W-6S	A4
7200	CHCG	60638	3148	9W-6S	C4
7200	SMMT	60501	3148	9W-6S	C4
7200	SMMT	60638	3148	9W-6S	C4
S 60th Ct					
1200	CCRO	60804	3031	7W-1S	B7
1200	OKPK	60304	3031	7W-1S	B7
1200	OKPK	60804	3031	7W-1S	B7
1500	CCRO	60804	3089	7W-2S	B3
3800	SKNY	60402	3089	7W-3S	B6
60th Pl					
10	CTSD	60525	3147	12W-6S	C4
400	BRRG	60527	3146		A5
W 60th Pl					
200	CHCG	60621	3152	0W-6S	B4
3300	CHCG	60629	3150	4W-6S	D4
6800	CHCG	60638	3149	8W-6S	A4
7100	CHCG	60638	3148	9W-6S	D4
7100	SMMT	60501	3148	9W-6S	D4
60th St					
10	BRRG	60527	3146		B4
10	HNDL	60521	3146		B4
10	HNDL	60527	3146		B4
1200	LynT	60525	3147	13W-6S	A4
1500	LynT	60525	3146		E5
E 60th St					
10	CHCG	60621	3152	0E-6S	C4
10	CHCG	60637	3152	0E-6S	C4
1000	CHCG	60637	3153	1E-6S	A4
W 60th St					
10	CHCG	60621	3152	0W-6S	C4
10	CHCG	60637	3152	0W-6S	C4
900	CHCG	60621	3151	1W-6S	D4
1100	CHCG	60636	3151	2W-6S	C4
2400	CHCG	60629	3151	3W-6S	A4
2900	CHCG	60629	3150	5W-6S	B4
5600	CHCG	60638	3149	8W-6S	A4
6900	CHCG	60638	3148	8W-6S	E4
7100	SMMT	60638	3148	8W-6S	E4
7600	SMMT	60501	3148	9W-6S	C4
S 61st Av					
1200	CCRO	60804	3031	7W-1S	B7
1200	OKPK	60304	3031	7W-1S	B7
1200	OKPK	60804	3031	7W-1S	B7
1500	CCRO	60804	3089	7W-2S	B2
3800	SKNY	60402	3089	7W-3S	B6
S 61st Ct					
1200	CCRO	60804	3031	7W-1S	B7
1200	OKPK	60304	3031	7W-1S	B7
1200	OKPK	60804	3031	7W-1S	B7
1500	CCRO	60804	3089	7W-2S	B3
3800	SKNY	60402	3089	7W-3S	B6
61st Pl					
300	BRRG	60527	3146		B5
600	CTSD	60525	3147	12W-6S	B5
600	LynT	60525	3147	12W-6S	B5
E 61st Pl					
1400	CHCG	60637	3153	1E-6S	A4
W 61st Pl					
200	CHCG	60621	3152	0W-6S	B4
3200	CHCG	60629	3150	4W-6S	D4
7200	CHCG	60638	3148	9W-6S	D4
7200	SMMT	60501	3148	9W-6S	D4
61st St					
-	BRRG	60527	3146		B5
400	CTSD	60525	3147	13W-6S	B5
1200	LynT	60525	3147	13W-6S	A5
E 61st St					
10	CHCG	60621	3152	0E-6S	C4

STREET Block	City	ZIP	Map#	CGS	Grid
E 61st St					
10	CHCG	60637	3152	0E-6S	C4
1000	CHCG	60637	3153	1E-6S	A4
W 61st St					
10	CHCG	60637	3152	0W-6S	C4
200	CHCG	60621	3152	0W-6S	A4
900	CHCG	60621	3151	1W-6S	D4
1100	CHCG	60636	3151	2W-6S	C4
2400	CHCG	60629	3151	3W-6S	A4
2900	CHCG	60629	3150	5W-6S	B4
4700	CHCG	60638	3150	5W-6S	A4
5600	CHCG	60638	3149	8W-6S	A4
7100	CHCG	60638	3148	9W-6S	D4
7100	SMMT	60501	3148	9W-6S	D4
62nd Av					
17600	BmnT	60477	3425	7W-21S	C6
17600	TYPK	60477	3425	7W-21S	C6
62nd Pl					
1200	LynT	60525	3147	13W-6S	A5
E 62nd Pl					
1400	CHCG	60637	3153	1E-6S	A4
W 62nd Pl					
-	CHCG	60638	3148	8W-6S	E5
3200	CHCG	60629	3150	4W-6S	D5
7200	SMMT	60501	3148	9W-6S	C5
62nd St					
200	BRRG	60527	3146		B5
800	CTSD	60525	3147	13W-6S	A5
800	LynT	60525	3147	13W-6S	A5
10900	LynT	60525	3146		E5
E 62nd St					
900	CHCG	60637	3152	1E-6S	E4
1100	CHCG	60637	3153	1E-6S	A4
W 62nd St					
400	CHCG	60621	3152	0W-6S	A4
900	CHCG	60621	3151	1W-6S	E4
1100	CHCG	60636	3151	1W-6S	E4
2300	CHCG	60629	3151	3W-6S	A4
2900	CHCG	60629	3150	4W-6S	D4
5600	CHCG	60638	3149	7W-6S	C5
7100	CHCG	60638	3148	9W-6S	D5
7100	SMMT	60501	3148	9W-6S	D5
E 63rd Dr					
-	CHCG	60637	3153	2E-6S	B4
W 63rd Pkwy					
800	CHCG	60621	3151	1W-6S	E4
800	CHCG	60621	3152	1W-6S	A4
63rd Pl					
900	LynT	60525	3147	13W-7S	A5
E 63rd Pl					
800	CHCG	60637	3152	1E-7S	E5
1400	CHCG	60637	3153	1E-7S	A5
W 63rd Pl					
-	BDPK	60501	3148	9W-7S	C5
-	BDPK	60638	3148	9W-7S	E5
600	CHCG	60621	3152	0W-7S	A5
3200	CHCG	60629	3150	4W-7S	D5
5000	CHCG	60638	3149	6W-7S	E5
6800	CHCG	60638	3148	8W-7S	E5
7400	SMMT	60501	3148	9W-7S	D5
63rd St					
-	HGKN	60525	3147	12W-6S	C5
10	DGvT	60527	3146		A5
400	BRRG	60527	3146		A5
400	WLBK	60527	3146		A5
800	CTSD	60525	3147	13W-6S	A5
800	LynT	60525	3147	13W-6S	A5
10800	IHPK	60525	3147	13W-6S	A5
63rd St CO-38					
10	DGvT	60527	3146		A5
E 63rd St					
10	CHCG	60621	3152	0E-6S	C4
10	CHCG	60637	3152	1E-6S	E4
1100	CHCG	60637	3153	1E-6S	A4
W 63rd St					
10	CHCG	60621	3152	0W-6S	B5
10	CHCG	60637	3152	0E-6S	C4
900	CHCG	60621	3151	2W-6S	D5
1100	CHCG	60636	3151	3W-6S	A5
2300	CHCG	60629	3151	3W-6S	A5
2900	CHCG	60629	3150	4W-6S	C5
4700	CHCG	60638	3150	5W-6S	A5
4900	CHCG	60638	3149	8W-6S	A5
6900	CHCG	60638	3148	8W-6S	E5
7200	SMMT	60501	3148	9W-6S	C5
64th Ct					
18200	TYPK	60477	3425	8W-21S	B7
E 64th Pl					
800	CHCG	60637	3152	1E-7S	E5
W 64th Pl					
3200	CHCG	60629	3150	4W-7S	D5
5400	CHCG	60638	3149	8W-7S	A5
7200	BDPK	60638	3148	9W-7S	E5
7200	CHCG	60638	3148	9W-7S	E5
7400	BDPK	60501	3148	9W-7S	D5
7400	SMMT	60501	3148	9W-7S	D5
64th St					
10	DGvT	60527	3146		A5
10	WLBK	60527	3146		A5
900	CTSD	60525	3147	13W-7S	A5
900	LynT	60525	3147	13W-7S	A5
E 64th St					
400	CHCG	60637	3152	0E-7S	D5
1100	CHCG	60637	3153	1E-7S	A5
W 64th St					
10	CHCG	60637	3152	0W-7S	C5
200	CHCG	60621	3152	0W-7S	B5
900	CHCG	60621	3151	1W-7S	D5
2200	CHCG	60636	3151	2W-7S	B5
2400	CHCG	60629	3151	3W-7S	B5
2900	CHCG	60629	3150	4W-7S	D5
4700	CHCG	60638	3150	5W-7S	A5
4900	CHCG	60638	3149	6W-7S	E5
6800	CHCG	60638	3148	8W-7S	E5
7100	BDPK	60638	3148	8W-7S	E5
7400	SMMT	60501	3148	9W-7S	D5
65th Av					
18200	TYPK	60477	3425	8W-22S	B7
65th Ct					
16300	TYPK	60477	3425	8W-19S	B2
65th Pl					
1500	CTSD	60525	3147	13W-7S	A6
1500	IHPK	60525	3147	13W-7S	A6
1700	IHPK	60525	3146		E6
E 65th Pl					
1400	CHCG	60637	3153	1E-7S	B5
W 65th Pl					
400	CHCG	60621	3152	0W-7S	B5
4500	CHCG	60629	3150	5W-7S	A5
7600	BDPK	60501	3148	9W-7S	C6
65th St					
1500	CTSD	60525	3147	13W-7S	A6
1500	IHPK	60525	3147	13W-7S	A6
1500	LynT	60525	3147	13W-7S	A6

STREET Block	City	ZIP	Map#	CGS	Grid
E 65th St					
400	CHCG	60637	3152	0E-7S	D5
1300	CHCG	60637	3153	1E-7S	B5
W 65th St					
10	CHCG	60637	3152	0W-7S	C5
200	CHCG	60621	3152	0W-7S	B5
900	CHCG	60621	3151	1W-7S	E5
1400	CHCG	60636	3151	2W-7S	B5
2600	CHCG	60629	3151	3W-7S	A5
4600	CHCG	60629	3150	5W-7S	A5
4700	BDPK	60638	3150	5W-7S	A5
4700	CHCG	60638	3150	5W-7S	A5
4900	BDPK	60638	3149	7W-7S	B5
4900	CHCG	60638	3149	7W-7S	B5
6800	BDPK	60638	3148	8W-7S	E5
6800	CHCG	60638	3148	8W-7S	E5
7200	SMMT	60501	3148	9W-7S	B5
7600	BDPK	60501	3148	9W-7S	C5
66th Av					
18100	TYPK	60477	3425	8W-21S	B7
18300	RchT	60477	3425	8W-22S	B7
66th Ct					
14500	BmnT	60452	3347	8W-17S	B5
14500	OKFT	60452	3347	8W-17S	B5
18100	TYPK	60477	3425	8W-21S	B7
18200	RchT	60477	3425	8W-21S	B7
E 66th Pl					
10	CHCG	60621	3152	0E-7S	C5
10	CHCG	60637	3152	0E-7S	C5
1400	CHCG	60637	3153	1E-7S	B5
W 66th Pl					
400	CHCG	60621	3152	0W-7S	B5
3200	CHCG	60629	3150	4W-7S	D6
5200	BDPK	60638	3149	6W-7S	E6
7000	BDPK	60638	3148	8W-7S	E6
7600	BDPK	60501	3148	9W-7S	C6
7800	BDPK	60455	3148	9W-7S	C6
E 66th St					
10	CHCG	60621	3152	0E-7S	C5
400	CHCG	60637	3152	0E-7S	D5
W 66th St					
100	CHCG	60621	3152	0W-7S	B5
900	CHCG	60621	3151	1W-7S	E5
2200	CHCG	60636	3151	3W-7S	A5
2300	CHCG	60629	3151	3W-7S	A5
2900	CHCG	60629	3150	5W-7S	B5
4700	BDPK	60638	3150	5W-7S	A5
4700	CHCG	60638	3150	5W-7S	A5
4800	BDPK	60638	3149	6W-7S	E6
7200	BDPK	60638	3148	9W-7S	E6
7600	BDPK	60501	3148	9W-7S	C6
67th Av					
17200	TYPK	60477	3425	8W-20S	B4
67th Ct					
16300	TYPK	60477	3425	8W-19S	A3
67th Pl					
500	WLBK	60527	3146		A6
E 67th Pl					
1400	CHCG	60637	3153	1E-7S	B6
1500	CHCG	60649	3153	1E-7S	B6
W 67th Pl					
2000	CHCG	60636	3151	2W-7S	C6
3600	CHCG	60629	3150	4W-7S	C6
67th St					
6900	HGKN	60525	3147	11W-7S	E6
9200	CTSD	60525	3147	12W-7S	E6
E 67th St					
500	CHCG	60637	3152	1E-7S	E5
1100	CHCG	60637	3153	1E-7S	A5
1500	CHCG	60649	3153	2E-7S	C5
W 67th St					
4800	BDPK	60638	3150	6W-7S	A6
4800	CHCG	60629	3150	6W-7S	A6
4800	CHCG	60638	3150	6W-7S	A6
4900	BDPK	60638	3149	6W-7S	E6
68th Ct					
17400	TYPK	60477	3425	8W-21S	A5
S 68th Ct					
9400	OKLN	60453	3211	8W-10S	A6
11900	PSHT	60463	3275	8W-14S	A6
W 68th Pl					
2000	CHCG	60636	3151	2W-7S	C6
3600	CHCG	60629	3150	4W-7S	C6
68th St					
500	WLBK	60527	3146		A6
E 68th St					
500	CHCG	60637	3152	0E-7S	E6
1300	CHCG	60637	3153	1E-7S	A6
2000	CHCG	60649	3153	2E-7S	C6
W 68th St					
10	CHCG	60621	3152	0W-7S	C6
900	CHCG	60621	3151	1W-7S	D6
1100	CHCG	60636	3151	2W-7S	C6
2300	CHCG	60629	3151	3W-7S	A6
3600	CHCG	60629	3150	4W-7S	C6
6600	BDPK	60638	3148	8W-7S	E6
6600	BDPK	60638	3149	8W-7S	A6
69th Av					
17100	TYPK	60477	3425	8W-20S	A5
S 69th Av					
9300	BGVW	60453	3211	8W-10S	A6
9300	OKLN	60453	3211	8W-10S	A6
11900	PSHT	60463	3275	8W-14S	A7
S 69th Ct					
9300	BGVW	60453	3211	8W-10S	A6
9300	BGVW	60455	3211	8W-10S	A6
9300	OKLN	60453	3211	8W-10S	A6
11900	PSHT	60463	3275	8W-14S	A6
E 69th Pl					
200	CHCG	60637	3152	0E-7S	C6
1400	CHCG	60637	3153	1E-7S	B6
1500	CHCG	60649	3153	1E-7S	B6
W 69th Pl					
2000	CHCG	60636	3151	2W-7S	C6
3600	CHCG	60629	3150	4W-7S	C6
E 69th St					
10	CHCG	60637	3152	0E-7S	C6
1400	CHCG	60637	3153	1E-7S	B6
1500	CHCG	60649	3153	1E-7S	B6
W 69th St					
10	CHCG	60621	3152	0W-7S	B6
10	CHCG	60637	3152	0W-7S	C6
900	CHCG	60621	3151	1W-7S	D6
1100	CHCG	60636	3151	2W-7S	B6
2300	CHCG	60629	3151	2W-7S	B6
3600	CHCG	60629	3150	4W-7S	C6
5800	BDPK	60638	3149	7W-7S	C6
70th Av					
17500	TYPK	60477	3425	8W-21S	A5
S 70th Av					
11900	PSHT	60463	3275	8W-15S	A7
70th Ct					
17500	TYPK	60477	3425	8W-21S	A5
S 70th Ct					
11900	PSHT	60463	3274	8W-14S	E6

STREET Block	City	ZIP	Map#	CGS	Grid
S 70th Ct					
12900	PSHT	60463	3275	8W-15S	A7
12900	PSHT	60463	3347	8W-15S	A1
13000	WthT	60463	3347	8W-15S	A1
15200	ODPK	60462	3347	8W-18S	A7
15200	OKFT	60462	3347	8W-18S	A7
70th Pl					
11200	IHPK	60525	3146		D7
E 70th Pl					
300	CHCG	60637	3152	0E-7S	D6
2200	CHCG	60649	3153	2E-7S	D6
W 70th Pl					
300	CHCG	60621	3152	0W-7S	B6
2000	CHCG	60636	3151	2W-7S	C7
3600	CHCG	60629	3150	4W-7S	C7
5100	BDPK	60638	3149	6W-7S	D7
E 70th St					
10	CHCG	60637	3152	0E-7S	C6
1200	CHCG	60637	3153	1E-7S	A6
2000	CHCG	60649	3153	2E-7S	B6
W 70th St					
100	CHCG	60621	3152	1W-7S	A6
900	CHCG	60621	3151	1W-7S	D6
2200	CHCG	60636	3151	3W-7S	A6
2300	CHCG	60629	3151	3W-7S	A6
4100	CHCG	60629	3150	5W-7S	C6
7900	BGVW	60455	3148	9W-7S	C7
7900	BGVW	60458	3148	9W-7S	C7
71st Av					
17100	TYPK	60477	3425	8W-20S	A5
S 71st Av					
11900	PSHT	60463	3274	8W-14S	E6
12800	PSHT	60463	3346	8W-15S	E1
12900	WthT	60463	3346	8W-15S	E1
71st Ct					
17600	TYPK	60477	3425	8W-21S	A6
S 71st Ct					
10800	WRTH	60482	3274	8W-12S	E2
11900	PSHT	60463	3274	8W-14S	E6
13000	PSHT	60463	3346	8W-15S	E1
13000	WthT	60463	3346	8W-15S	E1
15500	ODPK	60462	3346	8W-18S	E7
15700	ODPK	60462	3424	8W-18S	E1
15800	ODPK	60462	3425	8W-18S	A1
15800	ODPK	60477	3425	8W-18S	A1
15800	TYPK	60477	3425	8W-18S	A1
71st Pl					
10200	CTSD	60525	3147	12W-8S	B7
E 71st Pl					
1300	CHCG	60619	3153	1E-8S	A7
1500	CHCG	60649	3153	1E-8S	A7
W 71st Pl					
1200	CHCG	60621	3151	1W-8S	E7
1200	CHCG	60636	3151	1W-8S	E7
3400	CHCG	60629	3150	4W-8S	D7
7000	BDPK	60638	3148	8W-8S	E7
7100	BGVW	60455	3148	8W-8S	E7
7100	BGVW	60638	3148	8W-8S	E7
71st St					
700	BRRG	60527	3146		A7
700	DGvT	60527	3146		A7
700	WLBK	60527	3146		A7
10600	CTSD	60525	3147	13W-7S	A7
11200	BRRG	60525	3146		D7
11200	IHPK	60525	3146		D7
11200	IHPK	60527	3146		D7
E 71st St					
10	CHCG	60619	3152	0E-7S	C6
10	CHCG	60621	3152	0E-7S	C6
10	CHCG	60637	3152	0E-7S	C6
1000	CHCG	60619	3153	1E-7S	A6
1000	CHCG	60637	3153	1E-7S	A6
2500	CHCG	60649	3153	3E-7S	D6
W 71st St					
10	CHCG	60619	3152	0W-7S	C7
10	CHCG	60621	3152	0W-7S	B7
10	CHCG	60637	3152	0W-7S	C6
900	CHCG	60621	3151	2W-7S	C7
1100	CHCG	60636	3151	1W-7S	E7
2300	CHCG	60629	3151	2W-7S	B7
2900	CHCG	60629	3150	4W-7S	E7
7100	BDPK	60638	3148	8W-7S	E7
7100	BGVW	60455	3148	9W-7S	D7
8600	BDPK	60458	3148	10W-7S	B7
8600	BDPK	60501	3148	10W-7S	A7
8600	BGVW	60458	3148	10W-7S	A7
8600	BGVW	60501	3148	10W-7S	A7
8600	JSTC	60458	3148	10W-7S	A7
8600	JSTC	60501	3148	10W-7S	A7
N 72nd Ct					
1600	EDPK	60707	3030	9W-2N	D1
1600	RVFT	60305	3030	9W-2N	D1
2400	EDPK	60707	2974	9W-3N	D5
2900	CHCG	60707	2974	9W-3N	D5
S 72nd Ct					
5300	SMMT	60501	3148	9W-6S	E3
12000	PSHT	60463	3274	9W-14S	E6
15200	ODPK	60462	3346	9W-18S	E6
E 72nd Pl					
1300	CHCG	60619	3153	1E-8S	A7
2500	CHCG	60649	3153	3E-8S	D7
W 72nd Pl					
1200	CHCG	60621	3151	1W-8S	D7
1200	CHCG	60636	3151	1W-8S	D7
3400	CHCG	60629	3150	4W-8S	D7
7000	BDPK	60638	3148	8W-8S	E7
7100	BGVW	60455	3148	8W-8S	E7
7100	BGVW	60638	3148	8W-8S	E7
72nd St					
700	DGvT	60527	3146		A7
700	WLBK	60527	3146		A7
11200	BRRG	60525	3146		D7
11200	BRRG	60527	3146		D7
11200	IHPK	60525	3146		D7
11200	IHPK	60527	3146		E7
E 72nd St					
10	CHCG	60621	3152	0E-8S	C7
900	CHCG	60619	3152	1E-8S	E7
1000	CHCG	60619	3153	1E-8S	A7
1500	CHCG	60649	3153	1E-8S	A7
W 72nd St					
10	CHCG	60621	3152	0W-8S	B7
900	CHCG	60621	3151	1W-8S	E7
2200	CHCG	60636	3151	3W-8S	A7
2300	CHCG	60629	3151	3W-8S	A7
2900	CHCG	60629	3150	4W-8S	D7
4400	BDPK	60629	3150	5W-8S	A7
4400	BDPK	60638	3150	5W-8S	A7
7100	BGVW	60455	3148	9W-8S	E7
7100	BGVW	60638	3148	9W-8S	E7
7900	BGVW	60458	3148	9W-8S	C7
8600	JSTC	60458	3148	10W-8S	A7
N 73rd Av					
1600	EDPK	60707	3030	9W-2N	D1

STREET Block	City	ZIP	Map#	CGS	Grid
N 73rd Av					
1600	RVFT	60305	3030	9W-2N	D1
1600	RVFT	60707	3030	9W-2N	D1
1700	EDPK	60707	2974	9W-2N	D7
2900	CHCG	60707	2974	9W-3N	D5
S 73rd Av					
5300	SMMT	60501	3148	9W-5S	D3
10300	BGVW	60455	3274	9W-12S	E1
10300	PSHL	60455	3274	9W-12S	E1
10300	PSHL	60465	3274	9W-12S	E1
12000	PSHT	60463	3274	9W-14S	E6
15100	ODPK	60462	3346	9W-18S	E6
15100	OrlT	60462	3346	9W-18S	E6
N 73rd Ct					
1600	EDPK	60707	3030	9W-2N	D1
1600	RVFT	60305	3030	9W-2N	D1
2400	EDPK	60707	2974	9W-3N	D5
2900	CHCG	60707	2974	9W-3N	D5
S 73rd Ct					
5200	SMMT	60501	3148	9W-5S	D2
10300	BGVW	60455	3274	9W-12S	E1
10300	PSHL	60465	3274	9W-12S	E1
12000	PSHT	60463	3274	9W-14S	E6
73rd Pl					
11200	BRRG	60527	3208		D1
11200	IHPK	60525	3208		E1
11200	IHPK	60527	3208		E1
11200	LynT	60525	3208		E1
E 73rd Pl					
1500	CHCG	60619	3153	1E-8S	B7
2500	CHCG	60649	3153	3E-8S	D7
W 73rd Pl					
1200	CHCG	60621	3151	1W-8S	D7
1200	CHCG	60636	3151	1W-8S	D7
3400	CHCG	60629	3150	4W-8S	D7
7000	BDPK	60638	3148	8W-8S	E7
7100	BGVW	60455	3148	8W-8S	E7
7800	BGVW	60455	3210	9W-8S	C1
7900	JSTC	60455	3210	9W-8S	C1
8500	JSTC	60458	3210	10W-8S	A1
8900	JSTC	60458	3209	11W-8S	E1
73rd St					
100	BRRG	60527	3208		B1
700	DGvT	60527	3208		A1
700	WLBK	60527	3208		A1
E 73rd St					
10	CHCG	60619	3152	0E-8S	C7
10	CHCG	60621	3152	0E-8S	C7
1000	CHCG	60619	3153	1E-8S	A7
1500	CHCG	60649	3153	1E-8S	A7
W 73rd St					
10	CHCG	60621	3152	0W-8S	B7
900	CHCG	60621	3151	1W-8S	E7
1100	CHCG	60636	3151	2W-8S	C7
2300	CHCG	60629	3151	3W-8S	A7
4800	BDPK	60638	3149	8W-8S	A7
4800	BDPK	60638	3150	6W-8S	A7
4800	CHCG	60629	3150	6W-8S	A7
7000	BDPK	60638	3148	9W-8S	D7
7100	BGVW	60455	3148	9W-8S	D7
7900	JSTC	60455	3148	9W-8S	C7
8600	JSTC	60458	3148	10W-8S	A7
N 74th Av					
1600	EDPK	60305	3030	9W-2N	D1
1600	EDPK	60707	3030	9W-2N	D1
1600	RVFT	60305	3030	9W-2N	D1
2400	EDPK	60707	2974	9W-3N	D5
2900	CHCG	60707	2974	9W-3N	D5
S 74th Av					
5300	SMMT	60501	3148	9W-5S	D3
6400	BDPK	60501	3148	9W-7S	D5
10300	BGVW	60455	3274	9W-12S	D1
10300	BGVW	60465	3274	9W-12S	D1
10300	PSHL	60465	3274	9W-12S	D1
11900	PSHT	60463	3274	9W-14S	E6
15200	ODPK	60462	3346	9W-18S	E6
N 74th Ct					
1600	EDPK	60305	3030	9W-2N	D1
1600	EDPK	60707	3030	9W-2N	D1
1600	RVFT	60305	3030	9W-2N	D1
2500	EDPK	60707	2974	9W-3N	D5
2900	CHCG	60707	2974	9W-3N	D5
S 74th Ct					
6000	SMMT	60501	3148	9W-6S	D4
15100	OrlT	60462	3346	9W-18S	E6
E 74th Pl					
1500	CHCG	60619	3153	1E-8S	B7
2600	CHCG	60649	3153	3E-8S	E7
W 74th Pl					
1200	CHCG	60621	3151	1W-8S	E7
1700	CHCG	60636	3151	2W-8S	D7
5300	BDPK	60638	3211	6W-8S	D1
7000	BDPK	60638	3210	8W-8S	E1
7800	BGVW	60455	3210	9W-8S	C1
7900	JSTC	60455	3210	9W-8S	C1
7900	JSTC	60458	3210	9W-8S	C1
74th St					
600	BRRG	60527	3208		A1
600	DGvT	60527	3208		A1
600	WLBK	60527	3208		A1
10500	CTSD	60525	3209	13W-8S	A1
11200	LynT	60525	3208		D1
E 74th St					
10	CHCG	60619	3152	0E-8S	C7
10	CHCG	60621	3152	0E-8S	C7
1200	CHCG	60619	3153	1E-8S	A7
1500	CHCG	60649	3153	1E-8S	A7
W 74th St					
10	CHCG	60621	3152	0W-8S	C7
900	CHCG	60621	3151	1W-8S	E7
2200	CHCG	60636	3151	3W-8S	B7
2300	CHCG	60629	3151	3W-8S	B7
3400	CHCG	60629	3150	4W-8S	D7
3700	CHCG	60629	3212	4W-8S	C1
6100	BDPK	60638	3211	8W-8S	B1
7000	BDPK	60638	3210	9W-8S	E1
7100	BGVW	60455	3210	9W-8S	E1
7900	JSTC	60455	3210	9W-8S	C1
7900	JSTC	60458	3210	9W-8S	C1
N 75th Av					
1600	EDPK	60707	3030	9W-2N	C1
1600	RVFT	60305	3030	9W-2N	C1
1600	RVFT	60707	3030	9W-2N	C1
1700	EDPK	60707	2974	9W-2N	C7
2900	CHCG	60707	2974	9W-3N	C5
S 75th Av					
5600	SMMT	60501	3148	9W-6S	D4
6400	BDPK	60501	3148	9W-7S	D5
10300	BGVW	60455	3274	9W-12S	D1
10300	BGVW	60465	3274	9W-12S	D1
10300	PSHL	60465	3274	9W-12S	D1
11900	PSHT	60463	3274	9W-14S	D6
75th Ct					
15900	ODPK	60462	3424	9W-19S	D1
15900	TYPK	60462	3424	9W-19S	D1

STREET Block	City	ZIP	Map#	CGS	Grid
75th Ct					
15900	TYPK	60477	3424	9W-19S	D1
N 75th Ct					
1600	EDPK	60707	3030	9W-2N	C1
1600	RVFT	60305	3030	9W-2N	C1
1600	RVFT	60707	3030	9W-2N	C1
1700	EDPK	60707	2974	9W-2N	C6
2900	CHCG	60707	2974	9W-3N	C5
S 75th Ct					
6000	SMMT	60501	3148	9W-6S	D4
10300	BGVW	60455	3274	9W-12S	D1
10300	BGVW	60465	3274	9W-12S	D1
10300	PSHL	60465	3274	9W-12S	D1
15100	ODPK	60462	3346	9W-18S	D6
E 75th Pl					
1500	CHCG	60619	3215	1E-8S	B1
1500	CHCG	60649	3215	1E-8S	B1
2700	CHCG	60649	3153	3E-8S	E7
S 75th Pl					
15100	ODPK	60462	3346	9W-17S	D6
15100	OrlT	60462	3346	9W-17S	D6
W 75th Pl					
1600	CHCG	60620	3213	2W-8S	D1
3500	CHCG	60652	3212	4W-8S	D1
5200	BDPK	60459	3211	6W-8S	E1
5200	BDPK	60638	3211	6W-8S	E1
5800	BRBK	60459	3211	7W-8S	C1
75th St					
-	LynT	60525	3209	13W-8S	A1
600	DGvT	60527	3208		A1
9800	HGKN	60480	3209	12W-8S	B1
9800	HGKN	60525	3209	13W-8S	A1
11200	BRRG	60525	3208		D1
11200	BRRG	60527	3208		D1
11200	LynT	60525	3208		D1
11200	LynT	60527	3208		D1
E 75th St					
10	CHCG	60619	3152	0E-8S	C7
1000	CHCG	60619	3153	1E-8S	A7
1500	CHCG	60649	3153	3E-8S	E7
W 75th St					
-	CHCG	60629	3212	5W-8S	C1
10	CHCG	60619	3214	0E-8S	C1
10	CHCG	60621	3214	0W-8S	B1
800	CHCG	60620	3214	1W-8S	A1
800	CHCG	60621	3152	1W-8S	A7
900	CHCG	60621	3151	1W-8S	E7
2700	CHCG	60620	3213	2W-8S	B1
2700	CHCG	60629	3213	2W-8S	B1
2700	CHCG	60636	3213	2W-8S	B1
3400	CHCG	60652	3212	4W-8S	D1
5200	BDPK	60459	3211	6W-8S	D1
5200	BDPK	60638	3211	6W-8S	D1
5200	BRBK	60459	3211	6W-8S	D1
5200	BRBK	60638	3211	6W-8S	D1
6400	BDPK	60638	3210	8W-8S	E1
7100	BGVW	60638	3210	8W-8S	E1
7800	BGVW	60455	3210	9W-8S	C1
8600	JSTC	60458	3210	11W-8S	A1
8900	JSTC	60458	3209	11W-8S	E1
76th Av					
15900	ODPK	60462	3424	9W-19S	D1
16000	TYPK	60477	3424	9W-19S	D2
18700	FftT	60477	3504	9W-22S	E2
18700	TYPK	60477	3504	9W-22S	E2
N 76th Av					
1600	EDPK	60707	3030	9W-2N	C1
1600	RVFT	60305	3030	9W-2N	C1
1600	RVFT	60707	3030	9W-2N	C1
1700	EDPK	60707	2974	9W-2N	C7
2900	CHCG	60707	2974	9W-3N	C4
3100	CHCG	60634	2974	9W-3N	C4
S 76th Av					
-	HYHL	60455	3210	9W-11S	D7
-	OrlT	60462	3346	9W-15S	D2
6000	SMMT	60501	3148	9W-7S	D5
6400	BDPK	60501	3148	9W-7S	D5
7300	BGVW	60455	3148	9W-8S	D7
9600	BGVW	60455	3210	9W-11S	D7
9600	HYHL	60457	3210	9W-11S	D7
10000	BGVW	60455	3274	9W-11S	D1
10000	BGVW	60465	3274	9W-11S	D1
10000	PSHL	60465	3274	9W-11S	D1
10800	WRTH	60465	3274	9W-12S	D2
10800	WRTH	60482	3274	9W-12S	D3
10900	PSHL	60482	3274	9W-12S	D3
11900	PSHT	60463	3274	9W-15S	D7
12800	PSHT	60463	3346	9W-15S	D1
12900	PlsT	60462	3346	9W-15S	D2
13300	PSHT	60462	3346	9W-15S	D2
15700	ODPK	60462	3424	9W-18S	D1
15800	TYPK	60477	3424	9W-18S	D1
N 76th Ct					
1600	EDPK	60707	3030	9W-2N	C1
1600	RVFT	60305	3030	9W-2N	C1
1600	RVFT	60707	3030	9W-2N	C1
2600	EDPK	60707	2974	9W-3N	C4
3100	CHCG	60634	2974	9W-3N	C4
S 76th Ct					
9300	BGVW	60457	3210	9W-10S	D6
9300	HYHL	60457	3210	9W-10S	D6
E 76th Pl					
1500	CHCG	60619	3215	1E-8S	B1
1500	CHCG	60649	3215	1E-8S	B1
W 76th Pl					
2100	CHCG	60620	3213	2W-8S	B1
3400	CHCG	60652	3212	4W-8S	D1
5200	BRBK	60459	3211	6W-8S	D1
8800	JSTC	60458	3209	11W-8S	E1
8800	JSTC	60458	3210	11W-8S	A1
E 76th St					
10	CHCG	60619	3214	0E-8S	C1
10	CHCG	60620	3214	0E-8S	C1
1000	CHCG	60619	3215	1E-8S	A1
1500	CHCG	60649	3215	1E-8S	A1
2800	CHCG	60649	3153	3E-8S	E7
W 76th St					
-	CHCG	60619	3214	0E-8S	C1
10	CHCG	60620	3214	1W-8S	A1
1000	CHCG	60620	3213	2W-8S	C1
2400	CHCG	60652	3213	3W-8S	B1
3500	CHCG	60652	3212	4W-8S	D1
5000	BRBK	60459	3211	6W-8S	E1
5100	BDPK	60459	3211	6W-8S	E1
5100	BDPK	60638	3211	6W-8S	E1
5100	BRBK	60638	3211	6W-8S	E1
7900	BGVW	60455	3210	9W-8S	C1
7900	BGVW	60458	3210	9W-8S	C1
7900	JSTC	60458	3210	9W-8S	C1
77th Av					
400	DYR	46311	3598		E4
400	SjnT	46311	3598		E4
N 77th Av					
1600	EDPK	60707	3030	9W-2N	C1
1600	RVFT	60305	3030	9W-2N	C1

STREET Block	City	ZIP	Map#	CGS	Grid
N 77th Av					
2100	EDPK	60707	2974	9W-2N	C6
3100	CHCG	60634	2974	9W-3N	C4
S 77th Av					
6500	BDPK	60501	3148	9W-7S	C6
6700	BGVW	60455	3148	9W-7S	D6
8700	BGVW	60455	3210	9W-10S	D4
9000	BGVW	60457	3210	9W-10S	D6
9000	HYHL	60457	3210	9W-10S	D6
15600	ODPK	60462	3346	9W-18S	D7
15600	ODPK	60462	3424	9W-18S	D1
15800	TYPK	60477	3424	9W-18S	D1
N 77th Ct					
1600	EDPK	60707	3030	9W-2N	C1
1600	RVFT	60305	3030	9W-2N	C1
2800	EDPK	60707	2974	9W-3N	C4
3100	CHCG	60634	2974	9W-3N	C4
S 77th Ct					
6500	BDPK	60501	3148	9W-7S	C5
8300	BGVW	60455	3210	9W-9S	C3
9300	HYHL	60457	3210	9W-10S	D6
77th Pl					
-	PSHT	60462	3346	9W-15S	D2
-	PSHT	60463	3346	9W-15S	D2
E 77th Pl					
2800	CHCG	60649	3215	3E-8S	E1
W 77th Pl					
10	CHCG	60620	3214	0W-8S	C1
2100	CHCG	60620	3213	2W-8S	B1
4200	CHCG	60652	3212	5W-8S	B1
5200	BRBK	60459	3211	6W-8S	E1
77th St					
11200	BRRG	60527	3208		D2
11200	LynT	60527	3208		D2
11200	WLSP	60527	3208		D2
E 77th St					
10	CHCG	60619	3214	0E-8S	D1
10	CHCG	60620	3214	0E-8S	C1
1200	CHCG	60619	3215	1E-8S	A1
1600	CHCG	60649	3215	2E-8S	B1
W 77th St					
10	CHCG	60620	3214	0W-8S	B1
900	CHCG	60620	3213	2W-8S	C1
2300	CHCG	60652	3213	3W-8S	B1
3700	CHCG	60652	3212	4W-8S	C1
5000	BRBK	60459	3211	6W-8S	E1
6300	BDPK	60459	3211	7W-8S	B1
6900	BDPK	60459	3210	8W-8S	E1
6900	BRBK	60459	3210	8W-8S	E1
7200	BGVW	60455	3210	9W-8S	D1
7900	BGVW	60458	3210	9W-8S	C1
8800	JSTC	60458	3209	11W-8S	D1
8800	JSTC	60458	3210	11W-8S	A2
78th Av					
15900	ODPK	60462	3424	9W-19S	D1
15900	TYPK	60462	3424	9W-19S	D1
15900	TYPK	60477	3424	9W-19S	D1
N 78th Av					
1600	EDPK	60707	3030	9W-2N	C1
1600	RVFT	60305	3030	9W-2N	C1
1700	EDPK	60707	2974	9W-2N	C6
3100	CHCG	60634	2974	9W-3N	C4
S 78th Av					
6500	BDPK	60501	3148	9W-7S	C6
6700	BGVW	60455	3148	9W-7S	C6
7300	BGVW	60455	3210	9W-10S	C4
8200	JSTC	60458	3210	9W-10S	C4
8600	JSTC	60455	3210	9W-10S	C4
9900	HYHL	60457	3210	9W-11S	D7
9900	HYHL	60465	3210	9W-11S	D7
9900	PSHL	60465	3210	9W-11S	D7
10100	PSHL	60465	3274	9W-11S	D1
15700	ODPK	60462	3424	9W-18S	D1
15800	TYPK	60477	3424	9W-18S	D1
20700	FftT	60423	3504	9W-25S	D7
20700	FKFT	60423	3504	9W-25S	D7
N 78th Ct					
1600	EDPK	60707	2974	9W-2N	C7
1600	EDPK	60707	3030	9W-2N	C1
1600	RVFT	60305	3030	9W-2N	C1
3100	CHCG	60634	2974	9W-3N	C4
S 78th Ct					
7500	BGVW	60455	3210	9W-8S	C1
8300	JSTC	60458	3210	9W-9S	C3
9300	HYHL	60457	3210	9W-10S	C6
12900	PSHT	60463	3346	9W-15S	D1
E 78th Pl					
2900	CHCG	60649	3215	3E-8S	E1
W 78th Pl					
10	CHCG	60620	3214	0W-8S	C1
1200	CHCG	60620	3213	1W-8S	E1
3700	CHCG	60652	3212	4W-8S	C2
5200	BRBK	60459	3211	6W-8S	E2
E 78th St					
10	CHCG	60619	3214	1E-8S	E1
10	CHCG	60620	3214	0E-8S	C1
1200	CHCG	60619	3215	1E-8S	A1
2200	CHCG	60649	3215	3E-8S	E1
3000	CHCG	60649	3216	3E-8S	A1
W 78th St					
-	CHCG	60620	3214	0W-8S	B1
2100	CHCG	60620	3213	2W-8S	B1
2300	CHCG	60652	3213	2W-8S	B1
4600	CHCG	60652	3212	6W-8S	A1
4700	BRBK	60459	3212	6W-8S	A1
5400	BRBK	60459	3211	8W-8S	A2
6900	BDPK	60459	3210	8W-8S	E2
6900	BRBK	60459	3210	8W-8S	E2
7200	BGVW	60455	3210	9W-8S	D2
7200	BRBK	60455	3210	9W-8S	D2
7900	BGVW	60458	3210	9W-8S	C2
7900	JSTC	60458	3210	9W-8S	C2
79th Av					
-	TYPK	60477	3424	9W-20S	D5
N 79th Av					
1600	EDPK	60707	3030	9W-2N	B1
1600	RVFT	60305	3030	9W-2N	B1
1600	RVFT	60707	3030	9W-2N	B1
2800	EDPK	60707	2974	9W-3N	B5
3100	CHCG	60634	2974	9W-3N	B4
S 79th Av					
6700	BGVW	60455	3148	9W-7S	C6
8300	BGVW	60455	3210	9W-9S	C3
8300	JSTC	60458	3210	9W-10S	C4
8600	BGVW	60458	3210	9W-10S	C4
9200	HYHL	60457	3210	9W-10S	C5
12300	PSPK	60464	3274	9W-14S	C6
12900	PSHT	60463	3346	9W-15S	C1
21100	FftT	60423	3504	9W-25S	D7
N 79th Ct					
1700	EDPK	60707	2974	9W-2N	B7
S 79th Ct					
8300	BGVW	60455	3210	9W-9S	C3
8300	JSTC	60458	3210	9W-9S	C3
8600	BGVW	60458	3210	9W-9S	C4
9400	HYHL	60457	3210	9W-10S	C6
E 79th Pl					
1100	CHCG	60619	3215	1E-9S	A2
3000	CHCG	60617	3215	3E-9S	E2
3000	CHCG	60617	3216	3E-9S	A1
W 79th Pl					
400	CHCG	60620	3214	0W-9S	B2
2000	CHCG	60620	3213	2W-9S	C2
2500	CHCG	60652	3213	3W-9S	A2
4200	CHCG	60652	3212	5W-9S	B2
5000	BRBK	60459	3211	6W-9S	E2
7700	BGVW	60455	3210	9W-9S	C2
7800	BGVW	60458	3210	9W-9S	C2
8800	JSTC	60458	3210	11W-9S	A2
79th St					
100	BRRG	60527	3208		C2
200	DGvT	60527	3208		B2
10900	LynT	60525	3208		B2
10900	LynT	60525	3209	13W-8S	A2
10900	WLSP	60525	3209	13W-8S	A2
11100	LynT	60527	3208		E2
11100	WLSP	60525	3208		E2
E 79th St					
10	CHCG	60619	3214	0E-8S	E1
10	CHCG	60620	3214	0E-8S	C2
1000	CHCG	60619	3215	1E-8S	A1
1500	CHCG	60617	3215	1E-8S	A1
1500	CHCG	60649	3215	1E-8S	A1
3000	CHCG	60617	3216	3E-8S	A1
3000	CHCG	60649	3216	3E-8S	A1
W 79th St					
-	CHCG	60619	3214	0E-8S	C2
10	CHCG	60620	3214	0W-8S	B2
1000	CHCG	60620	3213	1W-8S	E2
2400	CHCG	60652	3213	3W-8S	A2
2900	CHCG	60652	3212	5W-8S	B2
4700	BRBK	60459	3212	5W-8S	A2
4900	BRBK	60459	3211	8W-8S	A2
6900	BDPK	60459	3210	8W-8S	E2
6900	BGVW	60459	3210	8W-8S	E2
6900	BRBK	60459	3210	10W-8S	B2
7400	BGVW	60455	3210	9W-8S	D2
7900	BGVW	60458	3210	9W-8S	C2
7900	JSTC	60455	3210	9W-8S	C2
8800	JSTC	60458	3209	11W-8S	E2
8800	JSTC	60458	3210	11W-8S	A2
9100	LynT	60458	3209	11W-8S	E2
9200	WLSP	60458	3209	11W-8S	E2
9200	WLSP	60480	3209	11W-8S	E2
9300	LynT	60480	3209	11W-8S	E2
80th Av					
-	FftT	60448	3504	9W-22S	D2
15900	ODPK	60462	3424	10W-18S	C1
15900	TYPK	60477	3424	10W-20S	C3
17300	OrlT	60477	3424	9W-20S	C5
18000	FftT	60477	3424	9W-21S	C7
18600	FftT	60477	3504	9W-22S	C1
18600	TYPK	60477	3504	9W-22S	D2
18700	MKNA	60448	3504	9W-22S	D1
18700	MKNA	60477	3504	9W-22S	D2
N 80th Av					
2600	EDPK	60707	2974	9W-3N	B5
2600	RVGV	60171	2974	9W-3N	B5
3100	CHCG	60634	2974	9W-3N	B5
3100	RVGV	60707	2974	9W-3N	B5
S 80th Av					
-	FftT	60448	3504	9W-22S	D2
11900	PSPK	60464	3274	9W-14S	C6
12100	PSHT	60463	3274	9W-14S	C6
12600	PlsT	60464	3274	9W-14S	C7
12800	PlsT	60463	3274	9W-15S	C7
12900	PlsT	60464	3346	9W-15S	C1
13000	PlsT	60463	3346	10W-15S	C1
13500	ODPK	60463	3346	10W-16S	C4
13500	OrlT	60462	3346	10W-16S	C4
13500	OrlT	60463	3346	10W-16S	C4
13500	OrlT	60464	3346	10W-16S	C4
13500	PSHT	60463	3346	10W-16S	C4
13500	PSHT	60464	3346	10W-16S	C4
14800	ODPK	60462	3346	10W-18S	C7
15600	ODPK	60462	3424	10W-18S	C1
15800	TYPK	60477	3424	10W-18S	C1
19700	FftT	60423	3504	9W-25S	D7
19700	FftT	60477	3504	9W-23S	D4
19700	TYPK	60423	3504	9W-23S	D4
19700	TYPK	60477	3504	10W-23S	D3
S 80th Ct					
8700	HYHL	60457	3210	10W-10S	C4
10000	PSHL	60465	3210	10W-11S	C7
10400	PSHL	60465	3274	10W-12S	C2
13100	PlsT	60464	3346	10W-15S	C1
80th Pl					
11000	LynT	60525	3208		E3
11100	BRRG	60527	3208		E3
E 80th Pl					
2900	CHCG	60617	3215	3E-9S	E2
3000	CHCG	60617	3216	3E-9S	A2
W 80th Pl					
-	CHCG	60620	3214	0W-9S	A2
2000	CHCG	60620	3213	2W-9S	C2
2500	CHCG	60652	3213	3W-9S	A2
4000	CHCG	60652	3212	5W-9S	C2
5100	BRBK	60459	3211	6W-9S	C2
7600	BGVW	60455	3210	9W-9S	C2
7800	BGVW	60458	3210	9W-9S	C2
80th St					
10	BRRG	60527	3208		C3
10	DGvT	60527	3208		C3
E 80th St					
10	CHCG	60619	3214	0E-9S	C2
10	CHCG	60620	3214	0E-9S	C2
1100	CHCG	60619	3215	1E-9S	A2
2600	CHCG	60617	3215	3E-9S	E2
3000	CHCG	60617	3216	3E-9S	A2
W 80th St					
10	CHCG	60620	3214	1W-9S	A2
900	CHCG	60620	3213	2W-9S	C2
2300	CHCG	60652	3213	3W-9S	A2
2900	CHCG	60652	3212	4W-9S	E2
5600	BRBK	60459	3211	7W-9S	B2
6900	BRBK	60459	3210	8W-9S	E2
7200	BGVW	60455	3210	9W-9S	D2
7800	BGVW	60458	3210	9W-9S	C2
8000	JSTC	60458	3210	10W-9S	B2
81st Av					
13900	SjnT	46311	3598		C5
14400	DYR	46311	3598		C5
15700	BlmT	46311	3598	4E-27S	C5
15700	CteT	46311	3598	4E-27S	C5
15700	CteT	60417	3598	4E-27S	C5
16800	TYPK	60477	3424	10W-20S	C3
18500	TYPK	60477	3504	10W-22S	C1
S 81st Av					
7900	BGVW	60458	3210	10W-9S	C2
8300	JSTC	60455	3210	10W-9S	C3
8300	JSTC	60458	3210	10W-9S	C3
9200	HYHL	60457	3210	10W-10S	C6
9800	PSHL	60465	3210	10W-11S	C6
10000	PSHL	60465	3274	10W-12S	C1
12300	PSPK	60464	3274	10W-14S	C6
14300	ODPK	60462	3346	10W-17S	C4
14900	OrlT	60462	3346	10W-17S	C6
81st Ct					
16800	TYPK	60477	3424	10W-20S	C3
S 81st Ct					
9700	HYHL	60457	3210	10W-11S	C7
9700	PSHL	60465	3210	10W-11S	C7
10100	PSHL	60465	3274	10W-12S	C1
12700	PlsT	60464	3274	10W-15S	C7
12700	PSPK	60464	3274	10W-15S	C7
14900	ODPK	60462	3346	10W-17S	C6
14900	OrlT	60462	3346	10W-17S	C6
E 81st Pl					
1100	CHCG	60619	3215	1E-9S	A2
2900	CHCG	60617	3215	3E-9S	E2
W 81st Pl					
500	CHCG	60620	3214	0W-9S	B2
2200	CHCG	60620	3213	2W-9S	B2
2500	CHCG	60652	3213	3W-9S	A2
3500	CHCG	60652	3212	4W-9S	D2
6400	BRBK	60459	3211	8W-9S	B2
7000	BRBK	60459	3210	8W-9S	E2
7100	BGVW	60459	3210	8W-9S	E3
7700	BGVW	60455	3210	9W-9S	C3
7900	JSTC	60458	3210	9W-9S	C3
81st St					
-	BGVW	60455	3210	9W-9S	D2
100	DGvT	60527	3208		C3
200	BRRG	60527	3208		B3
E 81st St					
10	CHCG	60619	3214	0E-9S	C2
10	CHCG	60620	3214	0E-9S	C2
1100	CHCG	60619	3215	1E-9S	A2
1800	CHCG	60617	3215	2E-9S	C2
3000	CHCG	60617	3216	3E-9S	A2
W 81st St					
10	CHCG	60620	3214	0W-9S	A2
900	CHCG	60620	3213	2W-9S	C2
2300	CHCG	60652	3213	3W-9S	A2
4400	CHCG	60652	3212	5W-9S	B2
4700	BRBK	60459	3212	5W-9S	A2
5200	BRBK	60459	3211	7W-9S	D2
6900	BRBK	60459	3210	8W-9S	E2
7100	BGVW	60459	3210	8W-9S	E2
7300	BGVW	60455	3210	9W-9S	D2
7900	BGVW	60458	3210	9W-9S	C2
8200	JSTC	60458	3210	10W-9S	B3
8800	JSTC	60458	3209	11W-9S	E3
9100	JSTC	60480	3209	11W-9S	E3
9100	WLSP	60458	3209	11W-9S	E3
9100	WLSP	60480	3209	11W-9S	E3
82nd Av					
-	FftT	60423	3504	10W-25S	C7
14800	SjnT	46311	3598		D5
16700	TYPK	60477	3424	10W-20S	C4
18800	MKNA	60448	3504	10W-22S	C2
S 82nd Av					
7900	JSTC	60458	3210	10W-9S	B3
8600	HYHL	60457	3210	10W-9S	B4
9800	PSHL	60465	3210	10W-11S	B7
9900	HYHL	60465	3210	10W-11S	B7
10200	PSHL	60465	3274	10W-12S	B1
11600	PSPK	60464	3274	10W-13S	C4
12600	PlsT	60464	3274	10W-14S	C7
12900	PlsT	60462	3346	10W-15S	C1
13300	PlsT	60462	3346	10W-15S	C2
13500	ODPK	60462	3346	10W-18S	C7
13500	OrlT	60462	3346	10W-16S	C3
13500	PSHT	60464	3346	10W-16S	C3
15600	ODPK	60462	3424	10W-18S	C1
20800	FftT	60423	3504	10W-25S	C7
S 82nd Ct					
7900	JSTC	60458	3210	10W-9S	B3
8400	HYHL	60457	3210	10W-9S	B4
9900	HYHL	60465	3210	10W-11S	B7
9900	PSHL	60465	3210	10W-11S	B7
10200	PSHL	60465	3274	10W-12S	B1
11600	PSPK	60464	3274	10W-13S	C5
12700	PlsT	60464	3274	10W-15S	B7
12900	PlsT	60462	3346	10W-15S	C1
12900	PlsT	60464	3346	10W-15S	C1
12900	PSPK	60464	3346	10W-15S	C1
82nd Pl					
13600	ODPK	60462	3346	10W-16S	C3
E 82nd Pl					
1100	CHCG	60619	3215	1E-9S	A2
2900	CHCG	60617	3215	3E-9S	E2
W 82nd Pl					
2000	CHCG	60620	3213	2W-9S	C2
2500	CHCG	60652	3213	3W-9S	A3
3400	CHCG	60652	3212	4W-9S	D3
5100	BRBK	60459	3211	6W-9S	E3
7100	BGVW	60459	3210	8W-9S	E3
7100	BRBK	60459	3210	8W-9S	E3
7700	BGVW	60455	3210	9W-9S	C3
8700	JSTC	60458	3210	10W-9S	A3
82nd St					
600	BRRG	60527	3208		A3
E 82nd St					
10	CHCG	60619	3214	0E-9S	C2
10	CHCG	60620	3214	0E-9S	C2
1000	CHCG	60619	3215	1E-9S	A2
1900	CHCG	60617	3215	2E-9S	C2
3000	CHCG	60617	3216	3E-9S	A2
W 82nd St					
10	CHCG	60620	3214	0W-9S	C2
900	CHCG	60620	3213	2W-9S	C2
2400	CHCG	60652	3213	3W-9S	A2
3600	CHCG	60652	3212	4W-9S	C2
4900	BRBK	60459	3211	6W-9S	E2
4900	BRBK	60459	3212	6W-9S	A2
6900	BRBK	60459	3210	8W-9S	E3
7100	BGVW	60459	3210	8W-9S	E3
8000	BGVW	60455	3210	10W-9S	C3
8200	JSTC	60458	3210	10W-9S	B3
83rd Av					
13300	PlsT	60462	3346	10W-15S	C2
13700	ODPK	60462	3346	10W-16S	B3
S 83rd Av					
7900	JSTC	60458	3210	10W-9S	B3
8700	HYHL	60457	3210	10W-10S	B4
10000	PSHL	60465	3210	10W-11S	B7
10000	PSHL	60465	3274	10W-11S	B1
12400	PSPK	60464	3274	10W-14S	B7
83rd Ct					
8300	ODPK	60462	3346	10W-16S	B3
S 83rd Ct					
7900	JSTC	60458	3210	10W-9S	B2
8300	HYHL	60457	3210	10W-9S	B3
10000	PSHL	60465	3210	10W-11S	B7
10500	PSHL	60465	3274	10W-12S	B2
12700	PlsT	60464	3274	10W-15S	B7
12700	PSPK	60464	3274	10W-15S	B7
12900	PlsT	60464	3346	10W-15S	B1
12900	PSPK	60464	3346	10W-15S	B1
E 83rd Pl					
600	CHCG	60619	3214	0E-9S	E3
1500	CHCG	60617	3215	1E-9S	B3
1500	CHCG	60619	3215	1E-9S	B3
3100	CHCG	60617	3216	3E-9S	A3
W 83rd Pl					
2600	CHCG	60652	3213	3W-9S	A3
3000	CHCG	60652	3212	4W-9S	C3
6400	BRBK	60459	3211	8W-9S	B3
7300	BGVW	60455	3210	9W-9S	D3
8000	JSTC	60458	3210	10W-9S	C3
8800	HYHL	60457	3209	11W-9S	E3
8800	JSTC	60457	3209	11W-9S	E3
8800	JSTC	60458	3209	11W-9S	E3
83rd St					
10	BRRG	60527	3208		A3
E 83rd St					
10	CHCG	60619	3214	0E-9S	E2
10	CHCG	60620	3214	0E-9S	C3
1000	CHCG	60619	3215	1E-9S	A2
1900	CHCG	60617	3215	3E-9S	E2
3000	CHCG	60617	3216	3E-9S	A2
W 83rd St					
-	CHCG	60619	3214	0E-9S	C3
10	CHCG	60620	3214	1W-9S	A3
900	CHCG	60620	3213	2W-9S	B3
2100	CHCG	60652	3213	2W-9S	B3
2900	CHCG	60652	3212	4W-9S	D3
4700	BRBK	60459	3212	6W-9S	A3
4900	BRBK	60459	3211	8W-9S	A3
6800	BGVW	60459	3211	8W-9S	A3
6900	BGVW	60459	3210	9W-9S	D3
6900	BRBK	60459	3210	8W-9S	E3
7600	BGVW	60455	3210	10W-9S	B3
7700	JSTC	60458	3210	10W-9S	B3
7900	JSTC	60455	3210	10W-9S	B3
8400	HYHL	60457	3210	10W-9S	B3
8400	JSTC	60457	3210	10W-9S	A3
8800	HYHL	60457	3209	11W-9S	E3
8800	HYHL	60458	3209	11W-9S	E3
8800	JSTC	60457	3209	11W-9S	E3
8800	JSTC	60458	3209	11W-9S	E3
84th Av					
-	PSPK	60464	3274	10W-14S	B5
15900	ODPK	60462	3424	10W-18S	B1
15900	TYPK	60477	3424	10W-20S	B5
16800	OrlT	60477	3424	10W-20S	B4
S 84th Av					
-	FftT	60423	3504	10W-25S	C7
-	HYHL	60465	3210	10W-11S	B7
-	PSHL	60465	3210	10W-11S	B7
7900	JSTC	60458	3210	10W-9S	B2
8300	HYHL	60457	3210	10W-9S	B3
8300	JSTC	60457	3210	10W-9S	B3
10200	PSHL	60465	3274	10W-12S	B1
11800	PSPK	60464	3274	10W-13S	B5
12600	PlsT	60464	3274	10W-14S	B7
13300	PlsT	60462	3346	10W-15S	B2
13300	PlsT	60464	3346	10W-15S	B2
13500	ODPK	60462	3346	10W-16S	B3
20500	FKFT	60423	3504	10W-24S	C6
84th Ct					
16500	TYPK	60477	3424	10W-19S	B3
S 84th Ct					
8300	HYHL	60457	3210	10W-9S	B4
8300	HYHL	60458	3210	10W-9S	B4
8300	JSTC	60457	3210	10W-9S	B4
8300	JSTC	60458	3210	10W-9S	B4
13200	PlsT	60464	3346	10W-15S	B1
W 84th Ct					
14700	SjnT	46311	3598		E6
84th Pl					
11000	WLSP	60480	3208		E3
16000	TYPK	60477	3424	10W-19S	B2
E 84th Pl					
700	CHCG	60619	3214	0E-9S	E3
1500	CHCG	60617	3215	1E-9S	B3
1500	CHCG	60619	3215	1E-9S	B3
W 84th Pl					
2600	CHCG	60652	3213	3W-9S	A3
4500	CHCG	60652	3212	5W-9S	A3
4800	BRBK	60459	3212	6W-9S	A3
4900	BRBK	60459	3211	6W-9S	E3
7100	BRBK	60459	3210	8W-9S	E3
7200	BGVW	60455	3210	9W-9S	D3
8000	JSTC	60458	3210	10W-9S	C3
8800	HYHL	60457	3209	11W-9S	E3
8800	HYHL	60458	3209	11W-9S	E3
8800	JSTC	60458	3209	11W-9S	E3
E 84th St					
10	CHCG	60619	3214	0E-9S	D3
1400	CHCG	60619	3215	1E-9S	B3
2100	CHCG	60617	3215	2E-9S	D3
3200	CHCG	60617	3216	4E-9S	B3
W 84th St					
10	CHCG	60620	3214	0W-9S	C3
900	CHCG	60620	3213	1W-9S	E3
2600	CHCG	60652	3213	3W-9S	A3
3000	CHCG	60652	3212	4W-9S	E3
4800	BRBK	60459	3212	6W-9S	A3
4900	BRBK	60459	3211	6W-9S	E3
6900	BRBK	60459	3210	9W-9S	E3
7000	BGVW	60459	3210	8W-9S	E3
7100	BGVW	60455	3210	9W-9S	E3
7700	JSTC	60458	3210	10W-9S	C3
8800	HYHL	60457	3209	11W-9S	E3
8800	HYHL	60458	3209	11W-9S	E3
8800	JSTC	60458	3209	11W-9S	E3
S 84th Ter					
9900	PSHL	60465	3210	10W-11S	B7
10100	PSHL	60465	3274	10W-11S	B1
85th Av					
-	PSPK	60464	3274	10W-13S	B4
16100	TYPK	60477	3424	10W-19S	B2
S 85th Av					
8200	JSTC	60458	3210	10W-9S	B3
8700	HYHL	60457	3210	10W-10S	B5
11100	PSHL	60465	3274	10W-13S	B3
11700	PSPK	60464	3274	10W-13S	B5
13000	PlsT	60464	3346	10W-15S	B1
13500	ODPK	60462	3346	10W-16S	B2
13500	PlsT	60462	3346	10W-16S	B2
85th Ct					
16100	TYPK	60477	3424	10W-19S	B2
19100	FftT	60448	3504	10W-23S	B2
19100	MKNA	60448	3504	10W-23S	B2
S 85th Ct					
8300	JSTC	60458	3210	10W-9S	A4
9100	HYHL	60457	3210	10W-10S	B6
11500	PSPK	60464	3274	10W-13S	B4
12900	PlsT	60464	3346	10W-15S	B1
W 85th Ct					
14600	SjnT	46311	3598		E6
85th Pl					
11200	WLSP	60480	3208		E4
14500	SjnT	46311	3598		D6
16000	TYPK	60477	3424	10W-19S	B1
E 85th Pl					
1500	CHCG	60617	3215	1E-9S	B3
1500	CHCG	60619	3215	1E-9S	B3
S 85th Pl					
19100	MKNA	60448	3504	10W-23S	B2
W 85th Pl					
2600	CHCG	60652	3213	3W-9S	A3
3200	CHCG	60652	3212	4W-9S	D3
4800	BRBK	60459	3212	6W-9S	A3
4900	BRBK	60459	3211	6W-9S	E3
7100	BRBK	60459	3210	8W-9S	E4
7300	BGVW	60455	3210	9W-9S	D4
8000	JSTC	60458	3210	10W-9S	C4
8800	HYHL	60457	3209	11W-9S	E4
8800	HYHL	60458	3209	11W-9S	E4
8800	JSTC	60458	3209	11W-9S	E4
13900	SJHN	46373	3598		E6
85th St					
10900	WLSP	60480	3208		E4
10900	WLSP	60480	3209	13W-9S	A4
E 85th St					
800	CHCG	60619	3214	1E-9S	E3
1300	CHCG	60619	3215	1E-9S	B3
2200	CHCG	60617	3215	3E-9S	E3
3200	CHCG	60617	3216	4E-9S	A3
E 85th St US-41					
3200	CHCG	60617	3216	4E-9S	A3
W 85th St					
10	CHCG	60620	3214	0W-9S	C3
1000	CHCG	60620	3213	2W-9S	C3
2600	CHCG	60652	3213	3W-9S	A3
2900	CHCG	60652	3212	4W-9S	E3
4700	BRBK	60459	3212	6W-9S	A3
4900	BRBK	60459	3211	8W-9S	A3
6900	BRBK	60459	3210	9W-9S	E3
7100	BGVW	60455	3210	9W-9S	E3
7100	BGVW	60459	3210	8W-9S	E3
8200	HYHL	60457	3210	10W-9S	B3
8600	JSTC	60458	3210	10W-9S	A3
8800	HYHL	60457	3209	11W-9S	E3
8800	HYHL	60458	3209	11W-9S	E3
8800	JSTC	60458	3209	11W-9S	E3
86th Av					
13300	ODPK	60462	3346	10W-15S	B2
13300	PlsT	60462	3346	10W-15S	B2
15700	ODPK	60462	3424	10W-18S	B1
15800	TYPK	60477	3424	10W-18S	B1
S 86th Av					
-	HYHL	60458	3210	10W-9S	A4
7100	JSTC	60458	3148	10W-8S	A7
7900	JSTC	60458	3210	10W-9S	A2
8300	JSTC	60457	3210	10W-9S	A3
9500	HYHL	60457	3210	10W-11S	A6
9900	HYHL	60465	3210	10W-11S	A7
9900	PSHL	60465	3210	10W-11S	A7
10100	PSHL	60465	3274	10W-11S	A1
11500	PlsT	60464	3274	10W-14S	B7
11500	PSPK	60464	3274	10W-14S	B7
12900	PlsT	60464	3346	10W-15S	B1
12900	PSPK	60464	3346	10W-15S	B1
13000	PlsT	60462	3346	10W-15S	B1
13100	ODPK	60462	3346	10W-15S	B1
13100	ODPK	60464	3346	10W-15S	B1
86th Ct					
8600	SjnT	46311	3598		D6
14000	ODPK	60462	3346	10W-16S	B4
S 86th Ct					
7100	JSTC	60458	3148	10W-8S	A7
7900	JSTC	60458	3210	10W-9S	A3
9100	HYHL	60457	3210	10W-10S	A6
9900	PSHL	60465	3210	10W-11S	A7
10100	PSHL	60465	3274	10W-11S	A1
86th Pl					
14500	SjnT	46311	3598		E6
E 86th Pl					
500	CHCG	60619	3214	0E-9S	D3
1500	CHCG	60617	3215	1E-9S	B3
1500	CHCG	60619	3215	1E-9S	B3
W 86th Pl					
800	CHCG	60620	3214	1W-9S	A3
2600	CHCG	60652	3213	3W-9S	A4
3600	CHCG	60652	3212	4W-9S	C4
4800	BRBK	60459	3212	6W-9S	A4
6200	BRBK	60459	3211	7W-9S	B4
7000	BRBK	60459	3210	8W-9S	E4
8700	JSTC	60458	3210	10W-9S	A4
86th St					
11300	WLSP	60480	3208		E4
E 86th St					
10	CHCG	60619	3214	0E-9S	D3
10	CHCG	60620	3214	0E-9S	C3
1400	CHCG	60619	3215	1E-9S	B3
1500	CHCG	60617	3215	1E-9S	B3
3200	CHCG	60617	3216	4E-9S	A3
W 86th St					
-	BGVW	60455	3210	9W-9S	D4
800	CHCG	60620	3214	1W-9S	A3
900	CHCG	60620	3213	2W-9S	C3
2900	CHCG	60652	3213	3W-9S	A3
2900	WLSP	60480	3208		E4
3900	CHCG	60652	3212	6W-9S	A4
4700	BRBK	60459	3212	6W-9S	A4
4700	CHCG	60459	3212	6W-9S	A4
4900	BRBK	60459	3211	6W-9S	E4
6900	BRBK	60459	3210	9W-9S	E4
7100	BGVW	60459	3210	8W-9S	E4
8600	LynT	60480	3208		E4
8800	HYHL	60457	3209	11W-9S	E4
8800	HYHL	60457	3210	11W-9S	A4
8800	HYHL	60458	3209	11W-9S	E4
8800	JSTC	60457	3209	11W-9S	E4
8800	JSTC	60458	3209	11W-9S	E4
8800	JSTC	60458	3210	11W-9S	A4
S 86th Ter					
9900	PSHL	60465	3210	10W-11S	B7
10100	PSHL	60465	3274	10W-11S	B1
87th Av					
-	HYHL	60457	3210	10W-9S	A4
-	HYHL	60458	3210	10W-9S	A4
-	JSTC	60458	3210	10W-9S	A4
14800	SjnT	46311	3598		C6
15500	CteT	60417	3598		C6
S 87th Av					
7100	JSTC	60458	3148	10W-8S	A7

STREET Block	City	ZIP	Map#	CGS	Grid
S 87th Av					
8600	HYHL	60458	**3210**	**10W-9S**	**A4**
8600	JSTC	60458	**3210**	**10W-9S**	**A4**
9600	HYHL	60457	**3210**	**10W-11S**	**A6**
9600	HYHL	60465	**3210**	**10W-11S**	**A6**
9600	PSHL	60465	**3210**	**10W-11S**	**A6**
9900	PSHL	60465	**3274**	**10W-11S**	**A1**
12100	PSPK	60464	**3274**	**10W-14S**	**A6**
12700	PlsT	60464	**3274**	**10W-15S**	**A7**
14000	ODPK	60462	**3346**	**10W-17S**	**A4**
87th Ct					
14100	ODPK	60462	**3346**	**10W-16S**	**A4**
17100	TYPK	60477	**3424**	**10W-20S**	**A4**
S 87th Ct					
7100	JSTC	60458	**3148**	**10W-8S**	**A7**
7900	JSTC	60458	**3210**	**10W-9S**	**A2**
9100	HYHL	60457	**3210**	**10W-10S**	**A5**
9900	PSHL	60465	**3210**	**10W-11S**	**A7**
10100	PSHL	60465	**3274**	**10W-11S**	**A1**
E 87th Pl					
400	CHCG	60619	**3214**	**0E-10S**	**E4**
1200	CHCG	60619	**3215**	**1E-10S**	**A4**
1600	CHCG	60617	**3215**	**2E-10S**	**B4**
W 87th Pl					
4100	HMTN	60456	**3212**	**5W-10S**	**A4**
5600	OKLN	60453	**3211**	**7W-10S**	**C4**
7300	BGVW	60455	**3210**	**9W-10S**	**D4**
8500	HYHL	60457	**3210**	**10W-10S**	**B4**
87th St					
10	BRRG	60527	**3208**		**A4**
10	DGvT	60527	**3208**		**A4**
10	LynT	60527	**3208**		**A4**
E 87th St					
10	CHCG	60619	**3214**	**0E-9S**	**E3**
10	CHCG	60620	**3214**	**0E-9S**	**C4**
1000	CHCG	60619	**3215**	**1E-9S**	**A3**
1500	CHCG	60617	**3215**	**2E-9S**	**C3**
3000	CHCG	60617	**3216**	**3E-10S**	**A3**
E 87th St US-41					
3200	CHCG	60617	**3216**	**4E-9S**	**A3**
W 87th St					
-	CHCG	60619	**3214**	**0E-9S**	**C4**
10	CHCG	60620	**3214**	**0W-10S**	**A4**
900	CHCG	60620	**3213**	**2W-9S**	**B4**
1000	PlsT	60480	**3209**	**12W-9S**	**C4**
1000	WLSP	60480	**3209**	**12W-9S**	**C4**
2300	CHCG	60652	**3213**	**3W-9S**	**B4**
2300	CHCG	60805	**3213**	**3W-9S**	**B4**
2400	ENGN	60805	**3213**	**3W-9S**	**A4**
2800	ENGN	60652	**3213**	**3W-9S**	**A4**
2900	CHCG	60652	**3212**	**5W-9S**	**B4**
2900	ENGN	60805	**3212**	**5W-9S**	**B4**
3000	ENGN	60652	**3212**	**3W-9S**	**E4**
3300	CHCG	60805	**3212**	**4W-9S**	**D4**
4000	CHCG	60456	**3212**	**5W-9S**	**C4**
4200	HMTN	60456	**3212**	**5W-10S**	**B4**
4400	HMTN	60652	**3212**	**5W-9S**	**B4**
4700	BRBK	60453	**3212**	**6W-9S**	**A4**
4700	BRBK	60459	**3212**	**6W-9S**	**A4**
4700	OKLN	60453	**3212**	**6W-9S**	**A4**
4900	BRBK	60459	**3211**	**6W-9S**	**E4**
4900	OKLN	60453	**3211**	**6W-9S**	**E4**
5100	BRBK	60453	**3211**	**6W-9S**	**E4**
5400	OKLN	60459	**3211**	**6W-9S**	**D4**
7000	BGVW	60455	**3210**	**9W-9S**	**D4**
7000	BGVW	60459	**3210**	**9W-9S**	**D4**
7000	BRBK	60459	**3210**	**8W-9S**	**E4**
7000	OKLN	60453	**3210**	**8W-9S**	**E4**
7000	OKLN	60455	**3210**	**8W-9S**	**E4**
7700	JSTC	60455	**3210**	**9W-9S**	**C4**
7700	JSTC	60458	**3210**	**9W-9S**	**C4**
7800	BGVW	60458	**3210**	**9W-10S**	**C4**
8000	HYHL	60457	**3210**	**10W-10S**	**C4**
8500	HYHL	60458	**3210**	**10W-10S**	**A4**
8900	HYHL	60457	**3209**	**11W-9S**	**E4**
9100	LynT	60480	**3209**	**12W-9S**	**C4**
11200	LynT	60480	**3208**		**E4**
11300	WLSP	60480	**3208**		**E4**
S 87th Ter					
-	HYHL	60457	**3210**	**10W-9S**	**A4**
-	HYHL	60458	**3210**	**10W-9S**	**A4**
8700	JSTC	60458	**3210**	**10W-9S**	**A4**
88th Av					
13900	ODPK	60462	**3346**	**10W-16S**	**A3**
17100	ODHL	60477	**3424**	**11W-21S**	**A5**
17100	ODPK	60462	**3424**	**11W-21S**	**A5**
17100	ODPK	60477	**3424**	**11W-21S**	**A5**
17100	TYPK	60477	**3424**	**11W-21S**	**A5**
S 88th Av					
8300	JSTC	60458	**3210**	**10W-9S**	**A3**
9500	HYHL	60457	**3210**	**11W-11S**	**A7**
9500	HYHL	60465	**3210**	**11W-11S**	**A7**
9500	PSHL	60465	**3210**	**11W-11S**	**A7**
10100	PSHL	60465	**3274**	**10W-12S**	**A2**
11900	PlsT	60464	**3274**	**10W-14S**	**A6**
11900	PSPK	60464	**3274**	**10W-14S**	**A6**
13100	ODPK	60462	**3346**	**10W-16S**	**A2**
13100	PlsT	60462	**3346**	**11W-15S**	**A1**
13100	PlsT	60464	**3346**	**11W-15S**	**A1**
15900	ODHL	60462	**3424**	**10W-19S**	**A2**
15900	ODHL	60477	**3424**	**10W-20S**	**A4**
15900	ODPK	60462	**3424**	**10W-20S**	**A4**
15900	ODPK	60477	**3424**	**10W-19S**	**A2**
17000	TYPK	60477	**3424**	**10W-20S**	**A4**
19000	FftT	60448	**3504**	**10W-23S**	**B3**
19000	MKNA	60448	**3504**	**10W-23S**	**B3**
19200	TYPK	60477	**3504**	**10W-23S**	**B3**
19500	FftT	60477	**3504**	**10W-23S**	**B4**
19500	TYPK	60448	**3504**	**10W-23S**	**B3**
19700	FKFT	60448	**3504**	**10W-23S**	**B4**
19700	FKFT	60477	**3504**	**10W-23S**	**B4**
20000	FftT	60423	**3504**	**10W-24S**	**B5**
20000	FKFT	60423	**3504**	**10W-24S**	**B4**
29700	PtnT	60468	**3860**	**11W-38S**	**B5**
W 88th Av					
15200	SjnT	46311	**3598**		**D7**
88th Ct					
14000	ODPK	60462	**3346**	**10W-16S**	**A3**
16700	ODHL	60477	**3424**	**11W-20S**	**A3**
S 88th Ct					
9100	HYHL	60457	**3210**	**11W-10S**	**A5**
E 88th Pl					
300	CHCG	60619	**3214**	**0E-10S**	**D4**
1200	CHCG	60619	**3215**	**1E-10S**	**A4**
W 88th Pl					
4500	HMTN	60456	**3212**	**5W-10S**	**A4**
6600	BGVW	60453	**3211**	**8W-10S**	**A4**
6600	BGVW	60455	**3211**	**8W-10S**	**A4**
6600	OKLN	60453	**3211**	**8W-10S**	**A4**
6800	OKLN	60455	**3211**	**8W-10S**	**A4**
6900	BGVW	60455	**3210**	**8W-10S**	**E4**
6900	OKLN	60453	**3210**	**8W-10S**	**E4**
6900	OKLN	60455	**3210**	**8W-10S**	**E4**
E 88th St					
10	CHCG	60620	**3214**	**0E-10S**	**C4**
300	CHCG	60619	**3214**	**0E-10S**	**D4**
1200	CHCG	60619	**3215**	**1E-10S**	**A4**
2500	CHCG	60617	**3215**	**3E-10S**	**E4**
3200	CHCG	60617	**3216**	**4E-10S**	**A4**
W 88th St					
200	CHCG	60620	**3214**	**1W-10S**	**A4**
900	CHCG	60620	**3213**	**2W-10S**	**D4**
2600	ENGN	60805	**3213**	**3W-10S**	**A4**
2900	ENGN	60805	**3212**	**3W-10S**	**E4**
4500	HMTN	60456	**3212**	**5W-10S**	**A4**
4700	OKLN	60453	**3212**	**6W-10S**	**A4**
4700	OKLN	60456	**3212**	**6W-10S**	**A4**
4900	OKLN	60453	**3211**	**6W-10S**	**E4**
7700	BGVW	60455	**3210**	**9W-10S**	**C4**
8000	HYHL	60457	**3210**	**10W-10S**	**C4**
S 88th Ter					
8500	JSTC	60458	**3210**	**10W-9S**	**A4**
89th Av					
16700	ODHL	60477	**3424**	**11W-20S**	**A3**
S 89th Av					
9100	HYHL	60457	**3210**	**11W-10S**	**A5**
9500	HYHL	60465	**3210**	**11W-11S**	**A6**
9500	PSHL	60465	**3210**	**11W-11S**	**A6**
10200	PSHL	60465	**3274**	**11W-11S**	**A1**
12400	PSPK	60464	**3274**	**11W-14S**	**A7**
16400	ODPK	60462	**3424**	**11W-19S**	**A2**
89th Ct					
16600	ODHL	60477	**3424**	**11W-19S**	**A3**
S 89th Ct					
9200	HYHL	60457	**3210**	**11W-10S**	**A6**
11900	PlsT	60464	**3274**	**11W-14S**	**A5**
11900	PSPK	60464	**3274**	**11W-14S**	**A5**
16400	ODPK	60462	**3424**	**11W-19S**	**A2**
E 89th Pl					
10	CHCG	60619	**3214**	**0E-10S**	**C4**
10	CHCG	60620	**3214**	**0E-10S**	**C4**
1300	CHCG	60619	**3215**	**1E-10S**	**A4**
W 89th Pl					
-	CHCG	60620	**3213**	**2W-10S**	**C4**
2600	ENGN	60805	**3213**	**3W-10S**	**A4**
4000	HMTN	60456	**3212**	**5W-10S**	**C4**
4700	OKLN	60453	**3212**	**6W-10S**	**A4**
4700	OKLN	60456	**3212**	**6W-10S**	**A4**
5700	OKLN	60453	**3211**	**7W-10S**	**C4**
6600	BGVW	60453	**3211**	**8W-10S**	**A4**
6600	BGVW	60455	**3211**	**8W-10S**	**A4**
7800	HYHL	60457	**3210**	**10W-10S**	**C5**
14100	SJHN	46373	**3598**		**E7**
89th St					
10	DGvT	60527	**3208**		**A5**
400	BRRG	60527	**3208**		**A5**
E 89th St					
10	CHCG	60619	**3214**	**0E-10S**	**C4**
10	CHCG	60620	**3214**	**0E-10S**	**C4**
1300	CHCG	60619	**3215**	**1E-10S**	**B4**
1500	CHCG	60617	**3215**	**1E-10S**	**B4**
3100	CHCG	60617	**3216**	**4E-10S**	**A4**
W 89th St					
400	CHCG	60620	**3214**	**1W-10S**	**A4**
2100	CHCG	60620	**3213**	**2W-10S**	**B4**
2600	CHCG	60805	**3213**	**3W-10S**	**A4**
2600	ENGN	60805	**3213**	**3W-10S**	**A4**
2900	ENGN	60805	**3212**	**3W-10S**	**E4**
4500	HMTN	60456	**3212**	**5W-10S**	**A4**
4800	OKLN	60453	**3212**	**6W-10S**	**A4**
4800	OKLN	60456	**3212**	**6W-10S**	**A4**
4900	OKLN	60453	**3211**	**6W-10S**	**E4**
7800	HYHL	60457	**3210**	**10W-10S**	**B4**
8900	HYHL	60457	**3209**	**11W-10S**	**E5**
8900	PlsT	60480	**3209**	**11W-10S**	**E5**
90th Av					
14500	SjnT	46311	**3598**		**E7**
15900	ODHL	60477	**3424**	**11W-19S**	**A1**
S 90th Av					
8300	HYHL	60457	**3209**	**11W-9S**	**E3**
8300	HYHL	60458	**3209**	**11W-9S**	**E3**
8300	JSTC	60457	**3209**	**11W-9S**	**E3**
8300	JSTC	60458	**3209**	**11W-9S**	**E3**
9500	PSHL	60465	**3209**	**11W-11S**	**E7**
10000	PSHL	60465	**3273**	**11W-11S**	**E1**
10300	PSHL	60465	**3274**	**11W-12S**	**A1**
11900	PSPK	60464	**3274**	**11W-14S**	**A5**
16400	ODHL	60462	**3424**	**11W-19S**	**A2**
16400	ODHL	60477	**3424**	**11W-19S**	**A2**
16400	ODPK	60462	**3424**	**11W-19S**	**A2**
16400	ODPK	60477	**3424**	**11W-19S**	**A2**
W 90th Av					
14000	SJHN	46373	**3598**		**E7**
90th Ct					
14700	SjnT	46311	**3598**		**D7**
S 90th Ct					
12000	PSPK	60464	**3273**	**11W-14S**	**E5**
14400	ODPK	60462	**3345**	**11W-17S**	**E4**
W 90th Ct					
14100	SJHN	46373	**3598**		**E7**
90th Pl					
14700	SjnT	46311	**3598**		**D7**
E 90th Pl					
500	CHCG	60619	**3214**	**0E-10S**	**D4**
1400	CHCG	60619	**3215**	**1E-10S**	**A4**
W 90th Pl					
200	CHCG	60620	**3214**	**0W-10S**	**B4**
1700	CHCG	60620	**3213**	**2W-10S**	**D5**
2600	ENGN	60805	**3213**	**3W-10S**	**A5**
4000	CHCG	60805	**3212**	**5W-10S**	**C5**
4000	HMTN	60456	**3212**	**5W-10S**	**B5**
5700	OKLN	60453	**3211**	**7W-10S**	**C5**
7200	BGVW	60455	**3210**	**9W-10S**	**E5**
7900	HYHL	60457	**3210**	**9W-10S**	**C5**
90th St					
600	BRRG	60527	**3208**		**A5**
600	DGvT	60527	**3208**		**A5**
E 90th St					
900	CHCG	60619	**3214**	**1E-10S**	**E4**
1300	CHCG	60619	**3215**	**1E-10S**	**B4**
2800	CHCG	60617	**3215**	**3E-10S**	**E4**
3000	CHCG	60617	**3216**	**3E-10S**	**A4**
W 90th St					
400	CHCG	60620	**3214**	**1W-10S**	**A4**
900	CHCG	60620	**3213**	**1W-10S**	**E4**
2600	ENGN	60805	**3213**	**3W-10S**	**A4**
2900	ENGN	60805	**3212**	**3W-10S**	**E4**
4700	HMTN	60456	**3212**	**5W-10S**	**A5**
4700	OKLN	60456	**3212**	**5W-10S**	**A5**
4800	OKLN	60453	**3212**	**6W-10S**	**A5**
5000	OKLN	60453	**3211**	**7W-10S**	**C5**
6700	BGVW	60453	**3211**	**8W-10S**	**A5**
6700	BGVW	60455	**3211**	**8W-10S**	**A5**
7200	BGVW	60455	**3210**	**9W-10S**	**D5**
7900	HYHL	60457	**3210**	**9W-10S**	**C5**
91st Av					
15900	ODHL	60477	**3424**	**11W-19S**	**A1**
15900	ODPK	60462	**3424**	**11W-19S**	**A1**
S 91st Av					
12300	PSPK	60464	**3273**	**11W-14S**	**E6**
13900	ODPK	60462	**3345**	**11W-16S**	**E3**
13900	OrlT	60462	**3345**	**11W-16S**	**E3**
W 91st Av					
14200	SJHN	46373	**3687**		**E1**
15200	SjnT	46311	**3598**		**D7**
15700	CteT	60417	**3598**	**4E-29S**	**C7**
E 91st Pl					
-	CHCG	60619	**3214**	**1E-10S**	**E5**
1600	CHCG	60617	**3215**	**2E-10S**	**B5**
W 91st Pl					
300	CHCG	60620	**3214**	**0W-10S**	**B5**
1700	CHCG	60620	**3213**	**2W-10S**	**D5**
4000	ENGN	60805	**3212**	**5W-10S**	**C5**
4000	OKLN	60453	**3212**	**5W-10S**	**B5**
4900	OKLN	60453	**3211**	**6W-10S**	**E5**
6600	BGVW	60453	**3211**	**8W-10S**	**A5**
6600	BGVW	60455	**3211**	**8W-10S**	**A5**
8800	HYHL	60457	**3210**	**11W-10S**	**A5**
8900	HYHL	60457	**3209**	**11W-10S**	**E5**
9100	HYHL	60480	**3209**	**11W-10S**	**E5**
9100	PlsT	60480	**3209**	**11W-10S**	**E5**
91st St					
-	TYPK	60477	**3424**	**11W-22S**	**A7**
10	BRRG	60527	**3208**		**A5**
10	DGvT	60527	**3208**		**A5**
10	WLSP	60527	**3208**		**A5**
11300	LynT	60480	**3208**		**C5**
11400	WLSP	60480	**3208**		**D5**
E 91st St					
10	CHCG	60620	**3214**	**0E-10S**	**C5**
300	CHCG	60619	**3214**	**0E-10S**	**D4**
1400	CHCG	60619	**3215**	**1E-10S**	**B4**
2800	CHCG	60617	**3215**	**3E-10S**	**E4**
3000	CHCG	60617	**3216**	**4E-10S**	**A4**
W 91st St					
-	CHCG	60619	**3214**	**0E-10S**	**C5**
10	CHCG	60620	**3214**	**0W-10S**	**B5**
900	CHCG	60620	**3213**	**2W-10S**	**D5**
2300	CHCG	60805	**3213**	**3W-10S**	**A5**
2300	ENGN	60805	**3213**	**3W-10S**	**A5**
2900	ENGN	60805	**3212**	**4W-10S**	**D5**
3500	CHCG	60805	**3212**	**4W-10S**	**D5**
3900	OKLN	60456	**3212**	**5W-10S**	**C5**
4500	HMTN	60453	**3212**	**5W-10S**	**A5**
4500	HMTN	60456	**3212**	**5W-10S**	**A5**
4500	OKLN	60453	**3212**	**6W-10S**	**A5**
4900	OKLN	60453	**3211**	**6W-10S**	**E5**
6700	BGVW	60453	**3211**	**8W-10S**	**A5**
6700	BGVW	60455	**3211**	**8W-10S**	**A5**
6900	BGVW	60455	**3210**	**8W-10S**	**E5**
7700	HYHL	60457	**3210**	**10W-10S**	**B5**
92nd Av					
16100	ODHL	60477	**3423**	**11W-19S**	**E2**
18300	OrlT	60477	**3423**	**11W-22S**	**E7**
18300	TYPK	60477	**3423**	**11W-22S**	**E7**
S 92nd Av					
11900	PlsT	60464	**3273**	**11W-14S**	**E5**
11900	PSPK	60464	**3273**	**11W-14S**	**E5**
13600	ODPK	60462	**3345**	**11W-16S**	**E3**
S 92nd Ct					
14300	ODPK	60462	**3345**	**11W-17S**	**E4**
14300	OrlT	60462	**3345**	**11W-17S**	**E4**
W 92nd Ln					
14000	SJHN	46373	**3687**		**E1**
92nd Pl					
15600	CteT	60417	**3687**		**C1**
15600	SjnT	46311	**3687**		**C1**
E 92nd Pl					
900	CHCG	60619	**3214**	**1E-10S**	**E5**
1300	CHCG	60619	**3215**	**1E-10S**	**A5**
1600	CHCG	60617	**3215**	**2E-10S**	**B5**
W 92nd Pl					
-	ENGN	60805	**3213**	**2W-10S**	**B5**
1000	CHCG	60620	**3213**	**1W-10S**	**E5**
6200	OKLN	60453	**3211**	**7W-10S**	**B5**
7200	BGVW	60455	**3210**	**9W-10S**	**E5**
7600	BGVW	60457	**3210**	**9W-10S**	**D5**
8000	HYHL	60457	**3210**	**10W-10S**	**C5**
9000	HYHL	60457	**3209**	**11W-10S**	**E5**
9000	PlsT	60457	**3209**	**11W-10S**	**E5**
9000	PlsT	60480	**3209**	**11W-10S**	**E5**
E 92nd St					
10	CHCG	60619	**3214**	**0E-10S**	**C5**
1400	CHCG	60619	**3215**	**1E-10S**	**B5**
1500	CHCG	60617	**3215**	**1E-10S**	**B5**
3000	CHCG	60617	**3216**	**3E-10S**	**A5**
W 92nd St					
10	CHCG	60620	**3214**	**0W-10S**	**C5**
1000	CHCG	60620	**3213**	**2W-10S**	**D5**
2800	ENGN	60805	**3213**	**3W-10S**	**A5**
2900	ENGN	60805	**3212**	**4W-10S**	**E5**
4600	OKLN	60453	**3212**	**5W-10S**	**A5**
4900	OKLN	60453	**3211**	**6W-10S**	**E5**
6600	BGVW	60453	**3211**	**8W-10S**	**A5**
6600	BGVW	60455	**3211**	**8W-10S**	**A5**
7700	BGVW	60455	**3210**	**9W-10S**	**C5**
7700	BGVW	60457	**3210**	**9W-10S**	**C5**
7700	HYHL	60457	**3210**	**9W-10S**	**C5**
8900	HYHL	60457	**3209**	**11W-10S**	**E5**
9100	PlsT	60480	**3209**	**11W-10S**	**E5**
93rd Av					
17000	ODHL	60477	**3423**	**11W-20S**	**E4**
S 93rd Av					
11900	PlsT	60464	**3273**	**11W-14S**	**E6**
11900	PSPK	60464	**3273**	**11W-14S**	**E6**
W 93rd Av					
14000	SJHN	46373	**3687**		**E1**
14000	SjnT	46311	**3687**		**E1**
14000	SjnT	46373	**3687**		**E1**
93rd Ln					
14500	SjnT	46311	**3687**		**E1**
W 93rd Ln					
14300	SJHN	46373	**3687**		**E1**
93rd Pl					
-	ODPK	60462	**3345**	**11W-16S**	**E4**
14400	SjnT	46311	**3687**		**E1**
W 93rd Pl					
200	CHCG	60620	**3214**	**0W-10S**	**B5**
1600	CHCG	60620	**3213**	**2W-10S**	**D5**
2600	ENGN	60805	**3213**	**3W-10S**	**A5**
4000	OKLN	60453	**3212**	**5W-10S**	**C5**
6200	OKLN	60453	**3211**	**7W-10S**	**B5**
7100	OKLN	60453	**3210**	**8W-10S**	**E5**
8500	HYHL	60457	**3210**	**10W-10S**	**A6**
8800	HYHL	60457	**3209**	**11W-10S**	**E5**
14000	SjnT	46311	**3687**		**E1**
E 93rd St					
600	CHCG	60619	**3214**	**0E-10S**	**E5**
1500	CHCG	60617	**3215**	**1E-10S**	**B5**
1500	CHCG	60619	**3215**	**1E-10S**	**B5**
3000	CHCG	60617	**3216**	**3E-10S**	**A5**
W 93rd St					
300	CHCG	60620	**3214**	**0W-10S**	**B5**
1700	CHCG	60620	**3213**	**2W-10S**	**C5**
2800	ENGN	60805	**3213**	**3W-10S**	**A5**
2900	ENGN	60805	**3212**	**4W-10S**	**E5**
3900	OKLN	60453	**3212**	**5W-10S**	**B5**
5800	OKLN	60453	**3211**	**8W-10S**	**A5**
6600	BGVW	60453	**3211**	**8W-10S**	**A5**
6800	BGVW	60455	**3211**	**8W-10S**	**A5**
6900	BGVW	60453	**3210**	**8W-10S**	**E5**
6900	BGVW	60455	**3210**	**8W-10S**	**E5**
6900	OKLN	60453	**3210**	**8W-10S**	**E5**
7600	BGVW	60457	**3210**	**9W-10S**	**D5**
7600	HYHL	60455	**3210**	**9W-10S**	**D5**
8800	HYHL	60457	**3210**	**11W-10S**	**A6**
8900	HYHL	60457	**3209**	**11W-10S**	**E5**
9000	PlsT	60480	**3209**	**11W-10S**	**E6**
94th Av					
16700	ODHL	60477	**3423**	**11W-20S**	**E4**
16700	ODPK	60477	**3423**	**11W-21S**	**E6**
17000	TYPK	60477	**3423**	**11W-21S**	**E7**
17300	OrlT	60477	**3423**	**11W-21S**	**E7**
18200	FftT	60477	**3423**	**11W-21S**	**E7**
S 94th Av					
12800	PlsT	60462	**3345**	**11W-15S**	**E1**
12800	PlsT	60464	**3273**	**11W-15S**	**E7**
12800	PlsT	60464	**3345**	**11W-15S**	**E1**
14400	ODPK	60462	**3345**	**11W-17S**	**E5**
14400	OrlT	60462	**3345**	**11W-17S**	**E4**
15500	ODPK	60462	**3423**	**11W-18S**	**E1**
15800	ODPK	60467	**3423**	**11W-19S**	**E2**
15900	ODHL	60477	**3423**	**11W-19S**	**E2**
16200	ODPK	60477	**3423**	**11W-19S**	**E2**
W 94th Av					
14000	SjnT	46311	**3687**		**E1**
94th Ct					
17200	TYPK	60477	**3423**	**11W-20S**	**E5**
W 94th Ct					
13900	SjnT	46311	**3687**		**E1**
94th Pl					
14600	SjnT	46311	**3687**		**E1**
W 94th Pl					
300	CHCG	60620	**3214**	**0W-10S**	**B5**
2400	CHCG	60620	**3213**	**3W-10S**	**B6**
2400	ENGN	60805	**3213**	**3W-10S**	**B6**
6400	CHRG	60453	**3211**	**8W-10S**	**B6**
6400	OKLN	60453	**3211**	**8W-10S**	**B6**
7000	OKLN	60453	**3210**	**8W-10S**	**E6**
8600	HYHL	60457	**3210**	**10W-11S**	**A6**
14100	SjnT	46311	**3687**		**E1**
94th St					
700	BRRG	60527	**3208**		**A6**
E 94th St					
10	CHCG	60619	**3214**	**0E-10S**	**C5**
1100	CHCG	60619	**3215**	**1E-10S**	**A5**
2000	CHCG	60617	**3215**	**3E-10S**	**D5**
3500	CHCG	60617	**3216**	**4E-10S**	**B5**
W 94th St					
10	CHCG	60620	**3214**	**0W-10S**	**B5**
1600	CHCG	60620	**3213**	**2W-10S**	**C5**
2600	ENGN	60805	**3213**	**3W-10S**	**A5**
2900	ENGN	60805	**3212**	**4W-10S**	**D5**
4500	OKLN	60453	**3212**	**5W-10S**	**B5**
5000	OKLN	60453	**3211**	**6W-10S**	**E6**
6900	OKLN	60453	**3210**	**8W-10S**	**E6**
7600	BGVW	60455	**3210**	**9W-10S**	**D6**
7600	HYHL	60457	**3210**	**9W-10S**	**D6**
E 95th Pl					
1200	CHCG	60628	**3215**	**1E-11S**	**A6**
2000	CHCG	60617	**3215**	**2E-11S**	**C6**
W 95th Pl					
-	ENGN	60805	**3212**	**4W-11S**	**D6**
400	CHCG	60628	**3214**	**0W-11S**	**B6**
1100	CHCG	60643	**3213**	**1W-11S**	**E6**
2700	ENGN	60805	**3213**	**3W-11S**	**A6**
6800	OKLN	60453	**3211**	**8W-11S**	**A6**
6900	OKLN	60453	**3210**	**8W-11S**	**E6**
95th St					
-	HYHL	60457	**3209**	**11W-10S**	**E6**
-	HYHL	60465	**3209**	**11W-10S**	**E6**
-	PlsT	60465	**3209**	**11W-10S**	**E6**
-	PlsT	60480	**3208**		**E6**
-	PlsT	60480	**3209**	**12W-10S**	**B6**
-	PSHL	60465	**3209**	**11W-10S**	**E6**
95th St US-12					
-	HYHL	60457	**3209**	**11W-10S**	**E6**
-	HYHL	60465	**3209**	**11W-10S**	**E6**
-	PlsT	60465	**3209**	**11W-10S**	**E6**
-	PlsT	60480	**3209**	**11W-10S**	**E6**
-	PSHL	60465	**3209**	**11W-10S**	**E6**
95th St US-20					
-	HYHL	60457	**3209**	**11W-10S**	**E6**
-	HYHL	60465	**3209**	**11W-10S**	**E6**
-	PlsT	60465	**3209**	**11W-10S**	**E6**
-	PlsT	60480	**3209**	**11W-10S**	**E6**
-	PSHL	60465	**3209**	**11W-10S**	**E6**
E 95th St					
10	CHCG	60619	**3214**	**1E-10S**	**E5**
10	CHCG	60620	**3214**	**0E-10S**	**C6**
10	CHCG	60628	**3214**	**1E-10S**	**E5**
900	CHCG	60619	**3215**	**1E-10S**	**A5**
900	CHCG	60628	**3215**	**1E-10S**	**A5**
1500	CHCG	60617	**3215**	**1E-10S**	**A5**
3000	CHCG	60617	**3216**	**3E-10S**	**A5**
E 95th St US-12					
10	CHCG	60619	**3214**	**1E-10S**	**E5**
10	CHCG	60620	**3214**	**0E-10S**	**C6**
10	CHCG	60628	**3214**	**1E-10S**	**E5**
900	CHCG	60619	**3215**	**1E-10S**	**A5**
900	CHCG	60628	**3215**	**1E-10S**	**A5**
1500	CHCG	60617	**3215**	**1E-10S**	**A5**
3000	CHCG	60617	**3216**	**3E-10S**	**A5**
E 95th St US-20					
10	CHCG	60619	**3214**	**1E-10S**	**E5**
10	CHCG	60620	**3214**	**0E-10S**	**C6**
10	CHCG	60628	**3214**	**1E-10S**	**E5**
900	CHCG	60619	**3215**	**1E-10S**	**A5**
900	CHCG	60628	**3215**	**1E-10S**	**A5**
1500	CHCG	60617	**3215**	**1E-10S**	**A5**
3000	CHCG	60617	**3216**	**3E-10S**	**A5**
W 95th St					
-	BGVW	60455	**3210**	**10W-10S**	**A6**
-	BGVW	60457	**3210**	**9W-11S**	**D6**
-	CHCG	60619	**3214**	**0E-10S**	**C6**
-	HYHL	60455	**3210**	**10W-10S**	**A6**
10	CHCG	60620	**3214**	**0W-10S**	**B6**
10	CHCG	60628	**3214**	**0W-10S**	**B6**
700	CHCG	60643	**3214**	**0W-10S**	**A6**
2400	CHCG	60620	**3213**	**3W-10S**	**B6**
2400	CHCG	60643	**3213**	**3W-10S**	**B6**
2400	ENGN	60805	**3213**	**3W-10S**	**B6**
2900	ENGN	60805	**3212**	**5W-10S**	**A6**
3900	OKLN	60453	**3212**	**4W-10S**	**C6**
4900	OKLN	60453	**3211**	**8W-10S**	**A6**
6300	CHRG	60453	**3211**	**7W-10S**	**B6**
7000	OKLN	60453	**3210**	**8W-10S**	**E6**
7600	HYHL	60457	**3210**	**9W-11S**	**D6**
8700	HYHL	60465	**3210**	**10W-10S**	**A6**
8700	PSHL	60465	**3210**	**10W-10S**	**A6**
8900	HYHL	60457	**3209**	**11W-10S**	**E6**
8900	PSHL	60465	**3209**	**11W-10S**	**E6**
9000	HYHL	60465	**3209**	**11W-10S**	**E6**
9000	PlsT	60465	**3209**	**11W-10S**	**E6**
9000	PlsT	60480	**3209**	**11W-10S**	**E6**
W 95th St US-12					
-	BGVW	60455	**3210**	**10W-10S**	**A6**
-	BGVW	60457	**3210**	**9W-11S**	**D6**
-	CHCG	60619	**3214**	**0E-10S**	**C6**
-	HYHL	60455	**3210**	**10W-10S**	**A6**
-	OKLN	60453	**3210**	**8W-10S**	**E6**
10	CHCG	60620	**3214**	**0W-10S**	**B6**
10	CHCG	60628	**3214**	**0W-10S**	**B6**
700	CHCG	60643	**3214**	**0W-10S**	**A6**
900	CHCG	60620	**3213**	**1W-10S**	**D6**
900	CHCG	60643	**3213**	**1W-10S**	**D6**
2400	ENGN	60805	**3213**	**3W-10S**	**B6**
2900	ENGN	60805	**3212**	**5W-10S**	**A6**
3900	OKLN	60453	**3212**	**4W-10S**	**C6**
4900	OKLN	60453	**3211**	**8W-10S**	**A6**
6300	CHRG	60453	**3211**	**7W-10S**	**B6**
7600	HYHL	60457	**3210**	**9W-11S**	**D6**
8700	HYHL	60465	**3210**	**10W-10S**	**A6**
8700	PSHL	60465	**3210**	**10W-10S**	**A6**
8900	HYHL	60457	**3209**	**11W-10S**	**E6**
8900	PSHL	60465	**3209**	**11W-10S**	**E6**
9000	HYHL	60465	**3209**	**11W-10S**	**E6**
9000	PlsT	60465	**3209**	**11W-10S**	**E6**
9000	PlsT	60480	**3209**	**11W-10S**	**E6**
W 95th St US-20					
-	BGVW	60455	**3210**	**10W-10S**	**A6**
-	BGVW	60457	**3210**	**9W-11S**	**D6**
-	CHCG	60619	**3214**	**0E-10S**	**C6**
-	HYHL	60455	**3210**	**10W-10S**	**A6**
-	OKLN	60453	**3210**	**8W-10S**	**E6**
10	CHCG	60620	**3214**	**0W-10S**	**B6**
10	CHCG	60628	**3214**	**0W-10S**	**B6**
700	CHCG	60643	**3214**	**0W-10S**	**A6**
2400	CHCG	60620	**3213**	**3W-10S**	**B6**
2400	CHCG	60643	**3213**	**3W-10S**	**B6**
2400	ENGN	60805	**3213**	**3W-10S**	**B6**
2900	ENGN	60805	**3212**	**5W-10S**	**A6**
3900	OKLN	60453	**3212**	**4W-10S**	**C6**
4900	OKLN	60453	**3211**	**8W-10S**	**A6**
6300	CHRG	60453	**3211**	**7W-10S**	**B6**
7600	HYHL	60457	**3210**	**9W-11S**	**D6**
8700	HYHL	60465	**3210**	**10W-10S**	**A6**
8700	PSHL	60465	**3210**	**10W-10S**	**A6**
8900	HYHL	60457	**3209**	**11W-10S**	**E6**
8900	PSHL	60465	**3209**	**11W-10S**	**E6**
9000	HYHL	60465	**3209**	**11W-10S**	**E6**
9000	PlsT	60465	**3209**	**11W-10S**	**E6**
9000	PlsT	60480	**3209**	**11W-10S**	**E6**
96th Av					
-	PlsT	60464	**3273**	**11W-13S**	**D4**
-	PlsT	60465	**3273**	**12W-13S**	**D3**
-	PlsT	60480	**3273**	**12W-13S**	**D3**
-	SjnT	46311	**3687**		**E2**
96th Av US-45					
-	PlsT	60464	**3273**	**12W-13S**	**D3**
-	PlsT	60465	**3273**	**12W-13S**	**D3**
-	PlsT	60480	**3273**	**12W-13S**	**D3**
W 96th Av					
14100	SjnT	46311	**3687**		**E2**
E 96th Pl					
1200	CHCG	60628	**3215**	**1E-11S**	**A6**
2700	CHCG	60617	**3215**	**3E-11S**	**E6**
W 96th Pl					
400	CHCG	60628	**3214**	**0W-11S**	**B6**
2600	ENGN	60805	**3213**	**3W-11S**	**A6**
3000	ENGN	60805	**3212**	**3W-11S**	**E6**
4800	OKLN	60453	**3212**	**6W-11S**	**A6**
6800	OKLN	60453	**3211**	**8W-11S**	**A6**
6900	OKLN	60415	**3210**	**8W-11S**	**E6**
6900	OKLN	60453	**3210**	**8W-11S**	**E6**
7700	HYHL	60457	**3210**	**9W-11S**	**D6**
8600	PSHL	60465	**3210**	**10W-11S**	**A6**
E 96th St					
100	CHCG	60628	**3214**	**0E-11S**	**D6**
1400	CHCG	60628	**3215**	**1E-11S**	**B6**
2200	CHCG	60617	**3215**	**2E-11S**	**D6**
3400	CHCG	60617	**3216**	**4E-10S**	**B6**
W 96th St					
10	CHCG	60628	**3214**	**0W-11S**	**B6**
800	CHCG	60643	**3214**	**1W-11S**	**A6**
1700	CHCG	60643	**3213**	**2W-11S**	**C6**
2500	ENGN	60805	**3213**	**3W-11S**	**B6**
2900	ENGN	60805	**3212**	**3W-11S**	**E6**
4000	OKLN	60453	**3212**	**5W-11S**	**B6**
6600	CHRG	60453	**3211**	**8W-11S**	**A6**
6600	OKLN	60453	**3211**	**8W-11S**	**A6**
6900	OKLN	60453	**3210**	**8W-11S**	**E6**
7100	OKLN	60415	**3210**	**8W-11S**	**E6**
8600	HYHL	60457	**3210**	**10W-11S**	**A6**
8600	HYHL	60465	**3210**	**10W-11S**	**A6**
8600	PSHL	60465	**3210**	**10W-11S**	**A6**
S 97th Av					
16400	ODPK	60467	**3423**	**12W-19S**	**D2**
97th Ct					
15800	SjnT	46311	**3687**		**C2**
97th Ln					
15400	SjnT	46311	**3687**		**D2**
97th Pl					
6800	CHRG	60415	**3211**	**8W-11S**	**A6**
6800	OKLN	60453	**3211**	**8W-11S**	**A6**
15400	SjnT	46311	**3687**		**D2**
E 97th Pl					
1400	CHCG	60628	**3215**	**1E-11S**	**B6**
2500	CHCG	60617	**3215**	**3E-11S**	**D6**
W 97th Pl					
400	CHCG	60628	**3214**	**0W-11S**	**B6**
1200	CHCG	60643	**3213**	**1W-11S**	**E6**
2800	ENGN	60805	**3213**	**3W-11S**	**A6**
2900	ENGN	60805	**3212**	**3W-11S**	**E6**
4800	OKLN	60453	**3212**	**6W-11S**	**A6**
6900	CHRG	60415	**3210**	**8W-11S**	**E6**
7700	HYHL	60457	**3210**	**9W-11S**	**C7**
7700	PSHL	60465	**3210**	**9W-11S**	**C7**
97th St					
-	BRRG	60527	**3208**		**A7**
-	DGvT	60527	**3208**		**A7**
E 97th St					
100	CHCG	60628	**3214**	**0E-11S**	**D6**
1000	CHCG	60628	**3215**	**1E-11S**	**A6**
2700	CHCG	60617	**3215**	**3E-11S**	**E6**
3400	CHCG	60617	**3216**	**4E-10S**	**B6**
W 97th St					
-	ENGN	60805	**3212**	**3W-11S**	**E6**
100	CHCG	60628	**3214**	**0W-11S**	**A6**
800	CHCG	60643	**3214**	**1W-11S**	**A6**
1100	CHCG	60643	**3213**	**1W-11S**	**E6**

STREET Block City ZIP Map# CGS Grid

W 97th St
2500 ENGN 60805 3213 3W-11S B6
4900 OKLN 60453 3212 6W-11S A6
6100 OKLN 60453 3211 7W-11S B6
6600 CHRG 60453 3211 8W-11S A6
6700 CHRG 60415 3211 8W-11S A6
6900 CHRG 60415 3210 8W-11S E6
6900 OKLN 60415 3210 8W-11S E6
6900 OKLN 60453 3210 8W-11S E6
7700 HYHL 60457 3210 10W-11S C6
7800 PSHL 60465 3210 10W-11S C6
8100 HYHL 60465 3210 10W-11S C6
8900 PSHL 60465 3209 11W-11S D7
98th Av
14500 SjnT 46311 3687 D2
98th Pl
15300 SjnT 46311 3687 D2
E 98th Pl
800 CHCG 60628 3214 1E-11S E6
1400 CHCG 60628 3215 1E-11S B6
2000 CHCG 60617 3215 2E-11S C6
W 98th Pl
200 CHCG 60628 3214 0W-11S B6
700 CHCG 60643 3214 1W-11S A6
1300 CHCG 60643 3213 1W-11S E6
2600 ENGN 60805 3213 3W-11S A7
3300 ENGN 60805 3212 4W-11S E6
4600 OKLN 60453 3212 6W-11S A7
5600 OKLN 60453 3211 7W-11S D7
7500 BGVW 60455 3210 9W-11S D7
7500 HYHL 60457 3210 9W-11S D7
8600 PSHL 60465 3210 11W-11S A7
8800 PSHL 60465 3209 11W-11S E7
98th St
6800 CHRG 60415 3211 8W-11S A7
6800 OKLN 60453 3211 8W-11S A7
7000 CHRG 60415 3210 8W-11S E7
E 98th St
800 CHCG 60628 3214 1E-11S E6
1400 CHCG 60628 3215 1E-11S B6
2600 CHCG 60617 3215 3E-11S E6
3000 CHCG 60617 3216 3E-10S A6
W 98th St
200 CHCG 60628 3214 0W-11S B6
700 CHCG 60643 3214 1W-11S A6
1800 CHCG 60643 3213 2W-11S C6
2400 ENGN 60643 3213 3W-11S B6
2400 ENGN 60805 3213 3W-11S B6
3500 ENGN 60805 3212 4W-11S E6
4600 OKLN 60453 3212 5W-11S A6
6600 CHRG 60415 3211 8W-11S A7
6600 CHRG 60453 3211 8W-11S A7
6600 OKLN 60453 3211 8W-11S A7
7600 HYHL 60457 3210 9W-11S D7
8000 PSHL 60465 3210 10W-11S C7
8600 HYHL 60465 3210 11W-11S A7
8900 PSHL 60465 3209 11W-11S E7
99th Pl
- CHRG 60453 3211 8W-11S A7
- CteT 46311 3687 C3
- CteT 60417 3687 C3
6500 CHRG 60415 3211 8W-11S A7
6500 OKLN 60415 3211 8W-11S A7
6500 OKLN 60453 3211 8W-11S A7
7000 CHRG 60415 3210 8W-11S E7
15900 SjnT 46311 3687 C3
W 99th Pl
400 CHCG 60628 3214 0W-11S B7
2600 CHCG 60655 3213 3W-11S A7
2800 CHCG 60805 3213 3W-11S A7
2800 ENGN 60805 3213 3W-11S A7
4000 CHCG 60655 3212 5W-11S B7
4000 OKLN 60453 3212 5W-11S B7
5400 OKLN 60453 3211 6W-11S D7
6300 CHRG 60415 3211 7W-11S B7
7800 HYHL 60457 3210 9W-11S C7
7800 HYHL 60465 3210 9W-11S C7
7800 PSHL 60465 3210 9W-11S C7
8800 PSHL 60465 3209 11W-11S D7
99th St
6400 CHRG 60415 3211 8W-11S A7
6400 CHRG 60453 3211 8W-11S A7
6400 OKLN 60453 3211 8W-11S A7
6700 OKLN 60415 3211 8W-11S A7
7000 CHRG 60415 3210 8W-11S E7
7100 BGVW 60455 3210 8W-11S E7
7100 CHRG 60455 3210 8W-11S E7
E 99th St
10 CHCG 60628 3214 0E-11S C7
1000 CHCG 60628 3215 1E-11S A7
1900 CHCG 60617 3215 2E-11S C6
3600 CHCG 60617 3216 4E-11S B6
W 99th St
10 CHCG 60628 3214 0W-11S B7
700 CHCG 60643 3214 1W-11S A7
1100 CHCG 60643 3213 2W-11S C7
2300 CHCG 60655 3213 3W-11S A7
2300 ENGN 60643 3213 2W-11S B7
2300 ENGN 60655 3213 3W-11S A7
2300 ENGN 60805 3213 3W-11S A7
2700 CHCG 60805 3213 3W-11S A7
2900 ENGN 60805 3212 5W-11S B7
3600 CHCG 60655 3212 5W-11S B7
3600 ENGN 60655 3212 4W-11S D7
3900 OKLN 60453 3212 6W-11S A7
4900 OKLN 60453 3211 7W-11S D7
6300 CHRG 60415 3211 7W-11S B7
6300 CHRG 60453 3211 7W-11S B7
7500 BGVW 60455 3210 9W-11S D7
7600 HYHL 60457 3210 10W-11S B7
7600 PSHL 60465 3210 11W-11S A7
8100 HYHL 60465 3210 10W-11S B7
8800 PSHL 60465 3209 11W-11S E7
W 99th Ter
8400 PSHL 60465 3210 10W-11S B7
S 100th Av
12500 PlsT 60464 3273 12W-14S C7
12500 PSPK 60464 3273 12W-14S C7
E 100th Dr
3800 CHCG 60617 3216 4E-11S C6
100th Pl
15900 SjnT 46311 3687 C3
E 100th Pl
700 CHCG 60628 3214 0E-11S E7
1100 CHCG 60628 3215 1E-11S A7
W 100th Pl
300 CHCG 60628 3214 0W-11S B7
1200 CHCG 60643 3213 2W-11S D7
2600 CHCG 60655 3213 3W-11S A7
2800 CHCG 60805 3213 3W-11S A7
2800 ENGN 60805 3213 3W-11S A7
3000 ENGN 60805 3212 3W-11S E7
4400 OKLN 60453 3212 5W-11S B7
5600 OKLN 60453 3211 7W-11S D7
5800 CHRG 60453 3211 7W-11S C7

W 100th Pl
7200 CHRG 60415 3210 9W-11S D7
7600 BGVW 60455 3210 9W-11S D7
7800 PSHL 60465 3210 9W-11S C7
100th St
7000 CHRG 60415 3210 8W-11S E7
E 100th St
- CHCG 60628 3215 1E-11S B7
10 CHCG 60628 3214 0E-11S C7
2000 CHCG 60617 3215 3E-11S E7
3600 CHCG 60617 3216 4E-11S B7
W 100th St
10 CHCG 60628 3214 0W-11S B7
700 CHCG 60643 3214 1W-11S A7
1000 CHCG 60643 3213 1W-11S E7
2300 CHCG 60655 3213 3W-11S B7
2700 CHCG 60805 3213 3W-11S A7
2700 ENGN 60805 3213 3W-11S A7
3000 ENGN 60805 3212 3W-11S E7
3600 ENGN 60805 3212 4W-11S D7
4000 CHCG 60655 3212 5W-11S C7
4400 OKLN 60453 3212 5W-11S B7
5600 OKLN 60453 3211 7W-11S C7
5800 CHRG 60453 3211 7W-11S C7
7800 HYHL 60465 3210 9W-11S C7
8800 PSHL 60465 3209 11W-11S E7
8800 PSHL 60465 3210 11W-11S A7
W 100th Ter
- PSHL 60465 3210 10W-11S B7
W 101st Av
13800 HnrT 46311 3687 D3
13800 SjnT 46311 3687 D3
15800 CteT 46311 3687 D3
15800 CteT 60417 3687 D3
E 101st Pl
600 CHCG 60628 3214 0E-11S E7
W 101st Pl
300 CHCG 60628 3214 0W-11S B7
1200 CHCG 60643 3213 1W-11S D7
2800 CHCG 60655 3213 3W-11S A7
2800 ENGN 60805 3213 3W-11S A7
3000 ENGN 60805 3212 3W-11S E7
3900 CHCG 60655 3212 4W-11S C7
4500 OKLN 60453 3212 5W-11S B7
5700 OKLN 60453 3211 7W-11S D7
7800 PSHL 60465 3274 9W-11S C1
101st St
300 DGvT 60439 3270 C1
300 WDRG 60439 3270 B1
300 WDRG 60517 3270 B1
E 101st St
10 CHCG 60628 3214 0E-11S C7
900 CHCG 60628 3215 1E-11S A7
2800 CHCG 60617 3215 3E-11S E7
3500 CHCG 60617 3216 4E-11S B7
W 101st St
10 CHCG 60628 3214 1W-11S A7
700 CHCG 60643 3214 1W-11S A7
1600 CHCG 60643 3213 2W-11S D7
2600 CHCG 60655 3213 3W-11S A7
2700 ENGN 60805 3213 3W-11S A7
3100 ENGN 60805 3212 3W-11S E7
3500 CHCG 60805 3212 4W-11S D7
4000 CHCG 60655 3212 5W-11S B7
4700 OKLN 60453 3212 5W-11S A7
5600 OKLN 60453 3211 7W-11S D7
5800 CHRG 60453 3211 7W-11S C7
6100 CHRG 60415 3211 7W-11S B7
7800 PSHL 60465 3210 9W-11S C7
8700 PSHL 60465 3274 11W-11S A1
W 101st Ter
8400 PSHL 60465 3210 10W-11S B7
8500 PSHL 60465 3274 10W-11S B1
102nd Ct
- PlsT 60464 3273 12W-14S C7
102nd Pl
6400 CHRG 60415 3275 8W-11S A1
E 102nd Pl
600 CHCG 60628 3214 0E-11S E7
W 102nd Pl
300 CHCG 60628 3214 0W-11S B7
1200 CHCG 60643 3213 1W-11S D7
1500 CHCG 60643 3277 1W-11S D1
2600 CHCG 60655 3277 3W-11S A1
2800 ENGN 60655 3277 3W-11S A1
2800 ENGN 60805 3277 3W-11S A1
3900 CHCG 60655 3276 4W-11S C1
4500 OKLN 60453 3276 5W-11S A1
8300 PSHL 60465 3274 10W-11S B1
E 102nd St
10 CHCG 60628 3214 0E-11S C7
2800 CHCG 60617 3215 3E-11S E7
3400 CHCG 60617 3216 4E-11S B7
W 102nd St
10 CHCG 60628 3214 0W-11S B7
700 CHCG 60643 3214 1W-11S A7
1900 CHCG 60643 3213 2W-11S C7
2600 CHCG 60655 3213 3W-11S A7
2700 ENGN 60655 3213 3W-11S A7
2700 ENGN 60805 3213 3W-11S A7
3200 ENGN 60805 3212 4W-11S E7
3900 CHCG 60655 3212 4W-11S C7
4000 OKLN 60453 3212 5W-11S B7
4500 OKLN 60453 3276 5W-11S B1
5200 OKLN 60453 3275 7W-11S D1
5800 CHRG 60453 3275 7W-11S C1
8800 PSHL 60465 3274 11W-11S A1
W 102nd Ter
8500 PSHL 60465 3274 10W-11S B1
E 103rd Pl
700 CHCG 60628 3278 0E-12S E1
W 103rd Pl
400 CHCG 60628 3278 0W-12S B1
1000 CHCG 60643 3278 1W-12S A1
1400 CHCG 60643 3277 1W-12S D1
2600 CHCG 60655 3277 3W-12S A1
5500 OKLN 60453 3275 6W-12S D1
8800 PSHL 60465 3274 11W-12S A1
103rd St
- WDRG 60517 3270 B2
6000 CHRG 60453 3275 7W-12S C1
6000 OKLN 60453 3275 7W-12S C1
6300 CHRG 60415 3275 8W-11S A1
7000 BGVW 60455 3274 8W-11S E1
7000 CHRG 60415 3274 8W-11S E1
7000 PSHL 60455 3274 8W-11S E1
7000 PSHL 60465 3274 8W-11S E1
15700 WDRG 60516 3270 C1
16100 DGvT 60439 3270 C1
E 103rd St
10 CHCG 60628 3278 0E-12S C1
800 CHCG 60628 3214 1E-11S E7
1000 CHCG 60628 3215 1E-11S A7
1600 CHCG 60617 3215 1E-11S A7
3200 CHCG 60617 3216 4E-11S B7

W 103rd St
10 CHCG 60628 3278 0W-12S B1
700 CHCG 60643 3278 0W-11S A1
1000 CHCG 60643 3277 3W-11S A1
2300 CHCG 60655 3277 3W-11S A1
2900 CHCG 60655 3276 5W-11S B1
3100 ENGN 60805 3276 3W-11S E1
3400 ENGN 60655 3276 4W-11S D1
3500 CHCG 60805 3276 4W-11S D1
3900 OKLN 60453 3276 4W-11S C1
4900 OKLN 60453 3275 6W-11S E1
5800 CHRG 60453 3275 7W-11S C1
5900 CHRG 60415 3275 7W-12S C1
7200 BGVW 60455 3274 9W-11S C1
7200 CHRG 60415 3274 9W-11S C1
7200 PSHL 60455 3274 9W-11S C1
7200 PSHL 60465 3274 9W-11S C1
7300 BGVW 60465 3274 9W-12S D1
8800 PSHL 60465 3273 11W-11S E1
9000 PlsT 60480 3273 11W-12S E1
W 103rd Ter
8400 PSHL 60465 3274 10W-11S B1
104th Av
- PlsT 60464 3273 12W-13S B3
- PlsT 60480 3273 12W-12S B3
15900 ODPK 60467 3423 13W-20S B4
15900 OrlT 60467 3423 13W-20S B4
17700 OrlT 60477 3423 12W-21S B6
18200 ODPK 60448 3423 12W-21S B7
18200 ODPK 60477 3423 12W-21S B7
S 104th Av
- PlsT 60480 3273 12W-13S B3
12500 PlsT 60464 3273 12W-13S B4
12800 PlsT 60464 3345 13W-15S B2
104th Pl
6600 CHRG 60415 3275 8W-12S A1
6700 CHRG 60482 3275 8W-12S A1
6700 WRTH 60482 3275 8W-12S A1
E 104th Pl
100 CHCG 60628 3278 0E-12S C1
W 104th Pl
10 CHCG 60628 3278 0W-12S C1
1000 CHCG 60643 3278 1W-12S A1
1600 CHCG 60643 3277 2W-12S D1
2500 CHCG 60655 3277 3W-12S B1
3900 CHCG 60655 3276 4W-12S C1
3900 OKLN 60453 3276 4W-12S C1
7900 PSHL 60465 3274 9W-12S C1
104th St
6600 CHRG 60415 3275 8W-12S A1
E 104th St
700 CHCG 60628 3278 1E-12S E1
800 CHCG 60628 3279 1E-12S A1
2500 CHCG 60617 3279 3E-11S E1
3300 CHCG 60617 3280 4E-11S B1
W 104th St
10 CHCG 60628 3278 0W-12S C1
700 CHCG 60643 3278 1W-12S A1
1000 CHCG 60643 3277 1W-12S E1
2300 CHCG 60655 3277 2W-12S B1
3000 CHCG 60655 3276 4W-12S D1
3900 OKLN 60453 3276 5W-12S C1
5600 OKLN 60453 3275 7W-12S D1
5900 CHRG 60415 3275 7W-12S C1
8000 PSHL 60465 3274 10W-12S C1
105th Ct
16300 ODPK 60467 3423 13W-19S B2
E 105th Pl
600 CHCG 60628 3278 0E-12S E1
W 105th Pl
200 CHCG 60628 3278 0W-12S B1
1400 CHCG 60643 3277 1W-12S D1
3200 CHCG 60655 3276 4W-12S D1
4000 CHCG 60453 3276 5W-12S C1
4900 OKLN 60453 3275 6W-12S E1
6900 WRTH 60482 3275 8W-12S A2
105th St
6300 CHRG 60415 3275 7W-12S B1
6700 CHRG 60482 3275 8W-12S A1
6700 WRTH 60482 3275 8W-12S A1
E 105th St
10 CHCG 60628 3278 0E-12S D1
2400 CHCG 60617 3279 3E-11S E1
3300 CHCG 60617 3280 4E-11S B1
W 105th St
10 CHCG 60628 3278 0W-12S C1
800 CHCG 60643 3278 1W-12S A1
1000 CHCG 60643 3277 1W-12S E1
2300 CHCG 60655 3277 3W-12S B1
3000 CHCG 60655 3276 4W-12S D1
3900 OKLN 60453 3276 6W-12S A1
5000 OKLN 60453 3275 6W-12S E1
5600 CHCG 60415 3275 7W-12S C1
5900 OKLN 60415 3275 7W-12S C1
7200 CHRG 60482 3274 9W-12S D1
7200 PSHL 60465 3274 9W-12S D1
106th Ct
- ODPK 60467 3423 13W-19S B3
106th Pl
6500 CHRG 60415 3275 8W-12S A2
6700 CHRG 60482 3275 8W-12S A2
6700 WRTH 60482 3275 8W-12S A2
W 106th Pl
10 CHCG 60628 3278 0W-12S B1
1700 CHCG 60643 3277 2W-12S D2
2600 CHCG 60655 3277 3W-12S A2
4000 CHCG 60655 3276 5W-12S C2
4000 OKLN 60453 3276 5W-12S C2
4900 OKLN 60453 3275 6W-12S E2
6900 WRTH 60482 3275 8W-12S A2
106th St
5600 OKLN 60453 3275 7W-12S D2
6100 CHRG 60415 3275 7W-12S B2
6700 CHRG 60482 3275 8W-12S A2
6700 WRTH 60482 3275 8W-12S A2
E 106th St
600 CHCG 60628 3278 0E-12S E1
2400 CHCG 60617 3279 3E-11S E1
2800 CHCG 60617 3280 3E-11S A1
4000 CHCG 46320 3280 4E-12S C1
4000 HMND 46320 3280 4E-12S C1
W 106th St
- CHCG 60643 3277 1W-12S E1
400 CHCG 60628 3278 0W-12S B1
700 CHCG 60643 3278 1W-12S A1
2300 CHCG 60655 3277 3W-12S B1
3000 CHCG 60655 3276 3W-12S E1
3900 OKLN 60453 3276 5W-12S C1
4900 OKLN 60453 3275 6W-12S E2
8000 PSHL 60465 3274 10W-12S B2
107th Av
16500 ODPK 60467 3423 13W-19S B3
107th Pl
5800 CHRG 60415 3275 7W-12S C2

W 107th Pl
200 CHCG 60628 3278 0W-12S B2
1000 CHCG 60643 3278 1W-12S A2
1800 CHCG 60643 3277 2W-12S C2
2200 CHCG 60655 3277 2W-12S B2
3800 CHCG 60655 3276 4W-12S C2
4300 OKLN 60453 3276 5W-12S B2
6900 WRTH 60482 3275 8W-12S A2
107th St
- LmnT 60439 3272 15W-12S B2
- LmnT 60480 3272 15W-12S B2
- PlsT 60465 3273 11W-12S E2
- PlsT 60480 3272 14W-12S C2
- PlsT 60480 3273 13W-12S A2
5600 CHRG 60415 3275 7W-12S D2
5600 OKLN 60453 3275 7W-12S D2
6300 CHRG 60482 3275 7W-12S B2
6300 WRTH 60415 3275 7W-12S B2
6300 WRTH 60482 3275 7W-12S B2
E 107th St
700 CHCG 60628 3278 0E-12S E2
2500 CHCG 60617 3279 2E-12S D1
3200 CHCG 60617 3280 4E-12S B1
4000 CHCG 46320 3280 4E-12S C1
4000 HMND 46320 3280 4E-12S C1
W 107th St
- CHCG 60643 3277 1W-12S E2
10 CHCG 60628 3278 0W-12S B2
700 CHCG 60643 3278 0W-12S A2
2300 CHCG 60655 3277 2W-12S B2
3000 CHCG 60655 3276 5W-12S B2
3900 OKLN 60453 3276 6W-12S A2
4900 OKLN 60453 3275 6W-12S E2
6400 CHRG 60415 3275 8W-12S A2
6400 CHRG 60482 3275 8W-12S A2
6400 WRTH 60415 3275 8W-12S B2
6400 WRTH 60482 3275 8W-12S A2
6900 WRTH 60482 3274 9W-12S E2
7500 PSHL 60465 3274 9W-12S D2
8800 PlsT 60465 3273 11W-12S E2
8800 PlsT 60480 3273 11W-12S E2
8800 PSHL 60465 3273 11W-12S E2
108th Av
13000 PlsT 60462 3345 13W-15S A2
13000 PlsT 60464 3345 13W-15S A2
13000 PlsT 60467 3345 13W-15S A2
13900 ODPK 60467 3345 13W-18S A7
13900 OrlT 60467 3345 13W-16S A4
14100 ODPK 60462 3345 13W-18S A7
14200 OrlT 60462 3345 13W-18S A7
15600 ODPK 60467 3423 13W-20S A4
15700 OrlT 60467 3423 13W-20S A4
108th Pl
5800 CHRG 60415 3275 7W-12S C2
W 108th Pl
10 CHCG 60628 3278 0W-12S B2
1000 CHCG 60643 3278 1W-12S A2
2000 CHCG 60643 3277 2W-12S C2
2300 CHCG 60655 3277 2W-12S B2
3200 CHCG 60655 3276 4W-12S E2
4200 OKLN 60453 3276 5W-12S D2
5200 OKLN 60453 3275 6W-12S D2
7200 WRTH 60482 3274 9W-12S E2
108th St
4200 OKLN 60453 3276 5W-12S B2
5700 CHRG 60415 3275 7W-12S D2
6300 WRTH 60482 3275 7W-12S B2
E 108th St
10 CHCG 60617 3280 4E-12S B2
10 HMND 46320 3280 C2
600 CHCG 60628 3278 0E-12S E2
2500 CHCG 60617 3279 2E-12S D2
W 108th St
10 CHCG 60628 3278 0W-12S C2
900 CHCG 60643 3278 1W-12S A2
1200 CHCG 60643 3277 1W-12S E2
2600 CHCG 60655 3277 3W-12S A2
3000 CHCG 60655 3276 4W-12S E2
4700 OKLN 60453 3276 6W-12S A2
5400 OKLN 60453 3275 6W-12S D2
6400 CHRG 60415 3275 8W-12S B2
6400 WRTH 60482 3275 8W-12S B2
7000 WRTH 60482 3274 8W-12S E2
7900 PSHL 60465 3274 9W-12S C2
109th Av
12800 HnrT 46311 3687 D5
15100 ODPK 60467 3345 13W-18S A6
15100 OrlT 60467 3345 13W-18S A7
109th Pl
5800 CHRG 60415 3275 7W-12S C2
W 109th Pl
10 CHCG 60628 3278 0W-12S C2
900 CHCG 60643 3278 1W-12S A2
1600 CHCG 60643 3277 2W-12S D2
2500 CHCG 60655 3277 3W-12S B2
3800 CHCG 60655 3276 4W-12S C2
6800 WRTH 60482 3275 8W-12S A2
7400 WRTH 60482 3274 9W-12S D3
7500 PSHL 60465 3274 9W-12S D3
7500 PSHL 60482 3274 9W-12S D3
109th St
600 DGvT 60439 3270 C3
600 LMNT 60439 3270 C3
5600 CHRG 60415 3275 7W-12S C2
5600 OKLN 60453 3275 7W-12S C2
6300 WRTH 60482 3275 7W-12S B2
E 109th St
10 CHCG 60628 3278 0E-12S D2
2500 CHCG 60617 3279 2E-12S D2
3900 CHCG 60617 3280 4E-12S C2
4000 HMND 46320 3280 4E-12S C2
W 109th St
10 CHCG 60628 3278 1W-12S A2
700 CHCG 60643 3278 1W-12S A2
1200 CHCG 60643 3277 1W-12S E2
2300 CHCG 60655 3277 2W-12S B2
4000 CHCG 60655 3276 5W-12S B2
4600 OKLN 60453 3276 6W-12S A2
4900 OKLN 60453 3275 6W-12S E2
6400 CHRG 60415 3275 8W-12S B2
6400 WRTH 60482 3275 8W-12S B2
7200 WRTH 60482 3274 9W-12S E2
7500 PSHL 60482 3274 9W-12S D2
8500 PSHL 60465 3274 10W-12S B2
110th Av
13500 ODPK 60467 3345 13W-16S A3
13500 OrlT 60467 3345 13W-16S A3
13500 PlsT 60467 3345 13W-16S A3
110th Ct
17200 ODPK 60467 3423 13W-20S A5
17200 OrlT 60448 3423 13W-20S A5
E 110th Pl
10 CHCG 60628 3278 0E-12S C2
W 110th Pl
10 CHCG 60628 3278 0W-12S C2

W 110th Pl
1000 CHCG 60643 3278 1W-12S A2
2000 CHCG 60643 3277 2W-12S C2
2500 CHCG 60655 3277 3W-12S B3
3800 CHCG 60655 3276 4W-12S C3
4500 OKLN 60453 3276 5W-12S B3
7200 WRTH 60482 3274 9W-12S E3
110th St
5600 CHRG 60415 3275 7W-12S C3
5600 OKLN 60453 3275 7W-12S C3
6300 WRTH 60482 3275 7W-12S B3
E 110th St
- CHCG 60617 3279 2E-12S D2
300 HMND 46320 3280 D2
700 CHCG 60628 3278 0E-12S E2
3200 CHCG 60617 3280 4E-12S C2
W 110th St
10 CHCG 60628 3278 0W-12S C2
1000 CHCG 60643 3278 1W-12S A2
2400 CHCG 60643 3277 3W-12S B2
2400 CHCG 60655 3277 3W-12S B2
3200 CHCG 60655 3276 4W-12S C2
3900 CHCG 60453 3276 4W-12S C2
3900 OKLN 60453 3276 4W-12S C2
5200 OKLN 60453 3275 6W-12S E3
5400 CHRG 60415 3275 6W-12S D3
5400 CHRG 60453 3275 6W-12S D3
6800 WRTH 60482 3275 8W-12S A3
7100 WRTH 60482 3274 9W-12S E3
111th Pl
- PSHL 60465 3274 9W-13S C3
E 111th Pl
400 CHCG 60628 3278 0E-13S D3
W 111th Pl
10 CHCG 60628 3278 0W-13S B3
1000 CHCG 60643 3277 1W-13S E3
2200 CHCG 60655 3277 2W-13S B3
6700 WRTH 60482 3275 8W-13S A3
7200 WRTH 60482 3274 8W-13S E3
7900 PSHL 60465 3274 9W-13S C3
111th St
- PlsT 60464 3272 14W-12S E3
- PlsT 60464 3273 13W-13S A3
- PlsT 60480 3273 13W-13S A3
12200 LMNT 60439 3272 15W-12S E3
12200 LmnT 60464 3272 14W-12S E3
111th St SR-83
- PlsT 60464 3272 14W-12S E3
- PlsT 60464 3273 13W-13S A3
- PlsT 60480 3273 13W-13S A3
12200 LMNT 60439 3272 15W-12S E3
12200 LmnT 60464 3272 14W-12S E3
E 111th St
- CHCG 60628 3279 1E-13S A3
10 CHCG 60628 3278 1E-12S E3
3300 CHCG 60617 3280 4E-12S B2
4000 HMND 46320 3280 4E-12S C2
W 111th St
10 CHCG 60628 3278 0W-12S B3
700 CHCG 60643 3278 0W-12S A3
1900 CHCG 60643 3277 2W-12S B3
2300 CHCG 60655 3277 2W-12S B3
3000 CHCG 60655 3276 5W-12S B3
3900 CHCG 60453 3276 4W-12S C3
4300 OKLN 60453 3276 5W-12S B3
4800 ALSP 60803 3276 6W-12S A3
5000 ALSP 60803 3275 6W-12S E3
5000 OKLN 60453 3275 6W-12S E3
5200 ALSP 60453 3275 6W-12S E3
5200 ALSP 60482 3275 6W-12S E3
5200 OKLN 60482 3275 6W-12S E3
5400 CHRG 60415 3275 6W-13S D3
5400 CHRG 60453 3275 6W-13S D3
5400 OKLN 60803 3275 6W-13S D3
5600 CHRG 60482 3275 7W-12S D3
6100 WRTH 60482 3275 8W-12S A3
7000 WRTH 60482 3274 9W-12S D3
7400 PSHL 60465 3274 10W-12S A3
7400 WRTH 60465 3274 9W-12S D3
9000 PlsT 60465 3273 11W-12S E3
9000 PSHL 60465 3273 11W-12S E3
9200 PlsT 60480 3273 11W-12S D3
112th Ct
15500 ODPK 60467 3344 14W-18S E7
15500 OrlT 60467 3344 14W-18S E7
15600 OrlT 60467 3422 14W-18S E1
15700 ODPK 60467 3422 14W-18S E1
112th Pl
- PSHL 60465 3274 10W-13S C3
E 112th Pl
10 CHCG 60628 3278 0E-13S C3
W 112th Pl
10 CHCG 60628 3278 0W-13S C3
1000 CHCG 60643 3277 1W-13S E3
1000 CHCG 60643 3278 1W-13S A3
2300 CHCG 60655 3277 2W-13S B3
3200 CHCG 60655 3276 4W-13S A3
4900 ALSP 60803 3276 6W-13S D3
6500 WRTH 60482 3275 8W-13S A3
7700 WRTH 60482 3274 9W-13S D3
7900 PSHL 60465 3274 9W-13S C3
E 112th St
- CHCG 60617 3279 3E-12S E3
100 CHCG 60617 3280 C3
100 HMND 46320 3280 C3
800 CHCG 60628 3278 1E-13S E3
W 112th St
10 CHCG 60628 3278 0W-13S B3
700 CHCG 60643 3278 1W-13S A3
2100 CHCG 60643 3277 2W-13S C3
2600 CHCG 60655 3277 3W-13S A3
3000 CHCG 60655 3276 3W-13S E3
6500 WRTH 60482 3275 8W-13S A3
7100 WRTH 60482 3274 8W-13S E3
7900 PSHL 60465 3274 9W-13S C3
113th
- CHCG 60655 3276 5W-13S C3
113th Av
15500 OrlT 60467 3344 14W-18S E7
15700 OrlT 60467 3422 14W-18S E1
15800 ODPK 60467 3422 14W-18S E1
S 113th Av
12300 PlsT 60464 3272 14W-14S E6
12300 PSPK 60464 3272 14W-14S E6
W 113th Av
14300 CteT 60417 3687 D6
14300 HnrT 46311 3687 D6
113th Ct
15700 OrlT 60467 3422 14W-18S E1
15800 ODPK 60467 3422 14W-18S E1
W 113th Ct
5100 ALSP 60803 3276 6W-13S A3
E 113th Pl
10 CHCG 60628 3278 0E-13S C3

Chicago & Cook County Street Index

STREET Block	City	ZIP	Map#	CGS	Grid
W 113th Pl					
10	CHCG	60628	3278	0W-13S	C3
1000	CHCG	60643	3277	1W-13S	E3
1000	CHCG	60643	3278	1W-13S	A3
2300	CHCG	60655	3277	2W-13S	B3
3000	CHCG	60655	3276	3W-13S	E3
3000	MTPK	60803	3276	3W-13S	E3
5100	ALSP	60803	3276	6W-13S	A3
6700	WRTH	60482	3275	8W-13S	A4
6900	WRTH	60482	3274	9W-13S	E4
7900	PSHL	60465	3274	9W-13S	C4
E 113th St					
-	CHCG	60617	3279	3E-12S	E3
800	CHCG	60628	3278	1E-13S	E3
3300	CHCG	60617	3280	4E-12S	B3
W 113th St					
10	CHCG	60628	3278	0W-13S	C3
700	CHCG	60643	3278	0W-13S	A3
2200	CHCG	60643	3277	2W-13S	B3
2400	CHCG	60655	3277	3W-13S	B3
3000	CHCG	60655	3276	3W-13S	E3
3000	CHCG	60803	3276	3W-13S	E3
3000	MTPK	60803	3276	3W-13S	E3
5000	ALSP	60803	3276	6W-13S	A3
5100	ALSP	60803	3275	6W-13S	E3
6400	WRTH	60482	3275	8W-13S	B3
6900	WRTH	60482	3274	9W-13S	E3
7900	PSHL	60465	3274	9W-13S	C3
114th					
-	CHCG	60655	3276	5W-13S	C4
114th Av					
15600	OrlT	60467	3422	14W-18S	E1
15800	ODPK	60467	3422	14W-18S	E1
S 114th Av					
12300	PlsT	60464	3272	14W-14S	E6
12300	PSPK	60464	3272	14W-14S	E6
114th Ct					
15700	ODPK	60467	3422	14W-18S	E1
15700	OrlT	60467	3422	14W-18S	E1
114th Pl					
-	PSHL	60465	3274	9W-13S	D4
-	PSHT	60465	3274	9W-13S	D4
E 114th Pl					
500	CHCG	60628	3278	0E-13S	D3
W 114th Pl					
10	CHCG	60628	3278	0W-13S	C3
900	CHCG	60643	3277	1W-13S	E3
900	CHCG	60643	3278	1W-13S	A3
3000	MTPK	60803	3276	3W-13S	E4
3100	CHCG	60803	3276	3W-13S	E4
3100	MTPK	60655	3276	3W-13S	E4
3600	CHCG	60655	3276	4W-13S	D4
5100	ALSP	60803	3276	6W-13S	A4
6800	WRTH	60482	3275	8W-13S	A4
6900	WRTH	60482	3274	9W-13S	E4
114th St					
-	PSHL	60465	3274	9W-13S	C4
600	HMND	46394	3280		E3
E 114th St					
500	CHCG	60628	3278	0E-13S	E3
800	HMND	46394	3280		E3
2600	CHCG	60617	3279	3E-12S	E3
3400	CHCG	60617	3280	4E-13S	B3
W 114th St					
10	CHCG	60628	3278	0W-13S	C3
700	CHCG	60643	3278	0W-13S	A3
2300	CHCG	60643	3277	2W-13S	B3
2300	CHCG	60655	3277	2W-13S	B3
3000	CHCG	60803	3276	3W-13S	E3
3000	MTPK	60803	3276	3W-13S	E3
3100	MTPK	60655	3276	3W-13S	E3
3200	CHCG	60655	3276	4W-13S	E3
5100	ALSP	60803	3276	6W-13S	A4
6400	WRTH	60482	3275	7W-13S	B4
6900	WRTH	60482	3274	9W-13S	E4
115th Av					
11400	FftT	60448	3422	14W-22S	E7
11400	ODPK	60448	3422	14W-22S	E7
11400	ODPK	60467	3422	14W-22S	E7
15800	OrlT	60467	3422	14W-18S	E1
S 115th Av					
12300	PlsT	60464	3272	14W-14S	D6
12300	PSPK	60464	3272	14W-14S	D6
115th Ct					
15700	ODPK	60467	3422	14W-18S	D1
15700	OrlT	60467	3422	14W-18S	D1
W 115th Pl					
900	CHCG	60643	3278	1W-13S	A4
2500	CHCG	60655	3277	3W-13S	B4
3400	CHCG	60655	3276	4W-13S	C4
3400	MTPK	60803	3276	4W-13S	C4
3600	WthT	60655	3276	4W-13S	D4
3600	WthT	60803	3276	4W-13S	D4
4300	ALSP	60803	3276	5W-13S	B4
6800	WRTH	60482	3275	8W-13S	A4
7000	WRTH	60482	3274	8W-13S	E4
115th St					
-	PSPK	60464	3274	10W-13S	B4
10	LMNT	60439	3272	15W-13S	A4
12300	LmnT	60464	3272	15W-13S	B4
E 115th St					
10	CHCG	60628	3278	0E-13S	D4
600	HMND	46394	3280		E3
3600	CHCG	60617	3280	4E-13S	B3
W 115th St					
-	CHCG	60655	3276	5W-13S	B4
10	CHCG	60628	3278	0W-13S	B4
700	CHCG	60643	3278	0W-13S	A4
2100	CHCG	60643	3277	2W-13S	C4
2300	CHCG	60655	3277	3W-13S	A4
2900	MTPK	60803	3277	3W-13S	A4
3000	MTPK	60803	3276	4W-13S	C4
3100	CHCG	60803	3276	3W-13S	E4
3600	WthT	60803	3276	4W-13S	D4
4200	ALSP	60803	3276	5W-13S	B4
5000	ALSP	60803	3275	6W-13S	E4
5300	OKLN	60803	3275	6W-13S	E4
5600	ALSP	60482	3275	7W-13S	D4
6000	WRTH	60482	3275	7W-13S	C4
6900	WRTH	60482	3274	9W-13S	E4
116th Av					
15500	OrlT	60467	3344	14W-18S	D7
15600	OrlT	60467	3422	14W-18S	D1
S 116th Av					
12300	PlsT	60464	3272	14W-14S	D6
12300	PSPK	60464	3272	14W-14S	D6
15500	OrlT	60467	3344	14W-18S	D7
116th Ct					
15500	OrlT	60467	3344	14W-18S	D7
15600	OrlT	60467	3422	14W-18S	D1
W 116th Pl					
600	CHCG	60628	3278	0W-13S	A4
900	CHCG	60643	3278	1W-13S	A4
2200	CHCG	60643	3277	2W-13S	B4
2500	CHCG	60655	3277	3W-13S	B4
3400	CHCG	60655	3276	4W-13S	D4
3400	CHCG	60803	3276	4W-13S	D4
3400	MTPK	60655	3276	4W-13S	D4
3400	MTPK	60803	3276	4W-13S	D4
3600	WthT	60803	3276	4W-13S	D4
4400	ALSP	60803	3276	5W-13S	B4
116th St					
-	CHCG	60617	3279	2E-13S	D4
8400	PSPK	60464	3274	10W-13S	B4
8500	PlsT	60464	3274	10W-13S	B4
E 116th St					
-	CHCG	60617	3280	3E-13S	A4
10	CHCG	60628	3278	0E-13S	C4
600	HMND	46394	3280		E4
W 116th St					
600	CHCG	60628	3278	0W-13S	A4
800	CHCG	60643	3278	1W-13S	A4
2000	CHCG	60643	3277	2W-13S	C4
2400	CHCG	60655	3277	3W-13S	B4
3100	CHCG	60655	3276	4W-13S	C4
3100	CHCG	60803	3276	4W-13S	C4
3100	MTPK	60803	3276	4W-13S	C4
3600	WthT	60655	3276	4W-13S	D4
3600	WthT	60803	3276	4W-13S	D4
4800	ALSP	60803	3276	6W-13S	A4
5000	ALSP	60803	3275	6W-13S	E4
6800	WRTH	60482	3275	8W-13S	A4
7000	WRTH	60482	3274	8W-13S	E4
117th Av					
15500	OrlT	60467	3344	14W-18S	D7
15600	OrlT	60467	3422	14W-18S	D1
W 117th Av					
13400	HnrT	46311	3687		E7
117th Ct					
15500	OrlT	60467	3344	14W-18S	D7
15600	OrlT	60467	3422	14W-18S	D1
117th Pl					
600	HMND	46394	3280		D4
E 117th Pl					
10	CHCG	60628	3278	0E-13S	C4
W 117th Pl					
600	CHCG	60628	3278	0W-13S	A4
700	CHCG	60643	3278	0W-13S	A4
2100	CHCG	60643	3277	2W-13S	C4
2500	CHCG	60655	3277	3W-13S	B4
5800	ALSP	60803	3275	7W-13S	C5
117th St					
-	LMNT	60439	3271		B5
-	PSHT	60463	3274	9W-13S	C4
-	PSHT	60465	3274	9W-13S	C4
-	PSPK	60464	3274	10W-13S	B5
600	HMND	46394	3280		E4
E 117th St					
200	CHCG	60628	3278	0E-13S	D4
2600	CHCG	60617	3279	3E-13S	E4
3600	CHCG	60617	3280	4E-13S	B4
W 117th St					
100	CHCG	60628	3278	0W-13S	B4
800	CHCG	60643	3278	1W-13S	A4
1900	CHCG	60643	3277	2W-13S	C4
2400	CHCG	60655	3277	3W-13S	B4
3400	CHCG	60803	3276	4W-13S	D4
3400	MTPK	60655	3276	4W-13S	D4
3500	CHCG	60655	3276	4W-13S	C4
3500	MTPK	60803	3276	4W-13S	C4
3500	WthT	60803	3276	4W-13S	C4
4900	ALSP	60803	3276	6W-13S	A4
5000	ALSP	60803	3275	6W-13S	E4
118th Av					
15500	OrlT	60467	3344	14W-18S	D7
15900	OrlT	60467	3422	14W-19S	D1
16000	ODPK	60467	3422	14W-19S	D2
118th Pl					
-	OrlT	60467	3422	14W-19S	D3
E 118th Pl					
10	CHCG	60628	3278	0E-13S	C4
W 118th Pl					
700	CHCG	60628	3278	0W-13S	A4
700	CHCG	60643	3278	0W-13S	A4
2500	CHCG	60655	3277	3W-13S	B5
4100	ALSP	60803	3276	5W-13S	B5
118th St					
-	PlsT	60464	3274	10W-13S	B5
-	PSPK	60464	3274	10W-13S	B5
1100	LMNT	60439	3271		B5
E 118th St					
10	CHCG	60628	3278	0E-13S	C4
600	HMND	46394	3280		E4
3400	CHCG	60617	3280	4E-13S	B4
W 118th St					
10	CHCG	60628	3278	0W-13S	A4
700	CHCG	60643	3278	0W-13S	A4
1000	CHCG	60643	3277	1W-13S	E4
2400	CHCG	60655	3277	3W-13S	B4
3600	MTPK	60803	3276	4W-13S	C4
3600	WthT	60803	3276	4W-13S	C4
4700	ALSP	60803	3276	6W-13S	A5
5700	ALSP	60803	3275	7W-13S	C5
8200	PSPK	60464	3274	10W-13S	B5
11800	PlsT	60464	3272	14W-13S	D5
11900	LMNT	60439	3272	14W-13S	C5
11900	PlsT	60439	3272	14W-13S	C5
119th Pl					
2000	BLID	60406	3277	2W-14S	B5
E 119th Pl					
300	CHCG	60628	3278	0E-14S	D5
W 119th Pl					
4700	ALSP	60803	3276	5W-14S	B5
7200	PSHT	60463	3274	9W-14S	E5
8400	PSPK	60464	3274	10W-14S	B5
119th St					
1000	LMNT	60439	3271		A5
7500	PSHT	60463	3274	9W-14S	C5
7900	PSHT	60464	3274	9W-13S	C5
7900	PSPK	60463	3274	9W-13S	C5
7900	PSPK	60464	3274	9W-13S	C5
119th St SR-83					
7500	PSHT	60463	3274	9W-14S	C5
7900	PSHT	60464	3274	9W-13S	C5
7900	PSPK	60463	3274	9W-13S	C5
7900	PSPK	60464	3274	9W-13S	C5
E 119th St					
10	CHCG	60628	3278	0E-13S	C5
600	HMND	46394	3280		E4
W 119th St					
10	CHCG	60628	3278	0W-13S	B5
700	CHCG	60643	3278	0W-13S	A5
1000	CHCG	60643	3277	1W-13S	E5
1500	CHCG	60827	3277	1W-13S	D5
1500	CTPK	60643	3277	1W-13S	D5
1500	CTPK	60827	3277	1W-13S	D5
1800	BLID	60406	3277	3W-13S	A5
1800	BLID	60643	3277	2W-13S	D5
1800	CHCG	60406	3277	3W-13S	A5
1800	ClmT	60406	3277	2W-13S	C5
1800	ClmT	60643	3277	2W-13S	C5
1800	CTPK	60406	3277	2W-13S	D5
2400	CHCG	60655	3277	3W-13S	A5
2600	BLID	60655	3277	3W-13S	A5
2600	MTPK	60803	3277	3W-13S	A5
2600	WthT	60655	3277	3W-13S	A5
2600	WthT	60803	3277	3W-13S	A5
3000	MTPK	60655	3276	3W-13S	E5
3000	MTPK	60803	3276	4W-13S	D5
3000	WthT	60655	3276	4W-14S	D5
3000	WthT	60803	3276	4W-14S	D5
4700	ALSP	60803	3276	6W-14S	A5
5000	ALSP	60803	3275	6W-14S	E5
8000	PSPK	60464	3274	10W-14S	C5
8500	PlsT	60464	3274	10W-13S	B5
8900	PlsT	60464	3273	11W-13S	E5
8900	PSPK	60464	3273	11W-13S	E5
120th Pl					
2600	BLID	60406	3277	3W-14S	B5
E 120th Pl					
10	CHCG	60628	3278	0E-14S	C5
W 120th Pl					
3600	ALSP	60803	3276	4W-14S	D5
3600	WthT	60803	3276	4W-14S	D5
5000	ALSP	60803	3275	6W-14S	E5
8800	PSPK	60464	3274	11W-14S	A5
120th St					
2000	BLID	60406	3277	2W-14S	B5
E 120th St					
700	CHCG	60628	3278	0E-13S	E5
700	HMND	46394	3280		E5
W 120th St					
10	CHCG	60628	3278	1W-14S	A5
700	CHCG	60643	3278	1W-14S	A5
1000	CHCG	60643	3277	1W-14S	E5
1500	CHCG	60827	3277	1W-14S	D5
1600	CTPK	60827	3277	2W-14S	D5
1800	BLID	60406	3277	2W-14S	D5
1800	BLID	60827	3277	2W-14S	D5
3600	ALSP	60803	3276	4W-14S	D5
3600	WthT	60803	3276	4W-14S	D5
5600	ALSP	60803	3275	7W-14S	D5
6800	PSHT	60463	3275	8W-14S	A5
7000	PSHT	60463	3274	9W-14S	E5
7900	PSPK	60464	3274	9W-14S	C5
9100	PSPK	60464	3273	11W-14S	E5
121st Pl					
2100	BLID	60406	3277	2W-14S	B5
E 121st Pl					
10	CHCG	60628	3278	0E-14S	D5
W 121st Pl					
3800	ALSP	60803	3276	4W-14S	C5
5200	ALSP	60803	3275	6W-14S	E5
121st St					
-	BLID	60827	3277	2W-14S	D5
-	CTPK	60827	3277	2W-14S	D5
1100	LMNT	60439	3271		B6
2100	BLID	60406	3277	2W-14S	B5
E 121st St					
200	CHCG	60628	3278	0E-14S	D5
700	HMND	46394	3280		E5
W 121st St					
10	CHCG	60628	3278	0W-14S	C5
1400	CHCG	60643	3277	1W-14S	D5
1500	CHCG	60827	3277	1W-14S	D5
1600	CTPK	60827	3277	2W-14S	D5
3600	ALSP	60803	3276	4W-14S	D5
3600	WthT	60803	3276	4W-14S	D5
5000	ALSP	60803	3275	6W-14S	E5
6800	PSHT	60463	3275	8W-14S	A5
7200	PSHT	60463	3274	9W-14S	E5
7800	PSPK	60464	3274	10W-14S	C5
9000	PSPK	60464	3273	11W-14S	E6
9300	PlsT	60464	3273	11W-14S	E6
122nd Pl					
2600	BLID	60406	3277	3W-14S	A6
E 122nd Pl					
10	CHCG	60628	3278	0E-14S	C5
W 122nd Pl					
3600	ALSP	60803	3276	4W-14S	D6
8400	PSPK	60464	3274	10W-14S	B6
122nd St					
-	LMNT	60439	3272	16W-14S	A6
2400	BLID	60406	3277	3W-14S	A5
E 122nd St					
10	CHCG	60628	3278	0E-14S	C5
800	HMND	46320	3280		E5
900	HMND	46394	3280		E5
1600	CHCG	60633	3279	2E-14S	C5
1900	CHCG	60617	3279	2E-13S	D5
W 122nd St					
-	CTPK	60406	3277	2W-14S	D5
10	CHCG	60628	3278	1W-14S	A5
700	CHCG	60643	3278	1W-14S	A5
1000	CHCG	60643	3277	1W-14S	E5
1500	CHCG	60827	3277	1W-14S	D5
1600	BLID	60406	3277	2W-14S	D5
1600	BLID	60827	3277	2W-14S	D5
1600	CTPK	60827	3277	2W-14S	D5
4400	ALSP	60803	3276	5W-14S	A5
5000	ALSP	60803	3275	6W-14S	E6
6400	PSHT	60463	3275	8W-14S	B6
7800	PSHT	60463	3274	9W-14S	C6
7900	PSPK	60464	3274	9W-14S	C6
9300	PSPK	60464	3273	11W-14S	E6
123rd Pl					
2200	BLID	60406	3277	2W-14S	B6
W 123rd Pl					
3400	ALSP	60803	3276	4W-14S	D6
3400	WthT	60803	3276	4W-14S	D6
5200	ALSP	60803	3275	6W-14S	E6
7600	PSHT	60463	3274	9W-14S	D6
7700	PSPK	60464	3274	9W-14S	D6
11400	PSPK	60464	3272	14W-14S	D6
11500	PlsT	60464	3272	14W-14S	D6
123rd St					
2000	BLID	60406	3277	3W-14S	A6
2800	ALSP	60803	3277	3W-14S	A6
2800	WthT	60406	3277	3W-14S	A6
2800	WthT	60655	3277	3W-14S	A6
3000	ALSP	60803	3276	3W-14S	E6
3000	WthT	60655	3276	3W-14S	E6
3000	WthT	60803	3276	3W-14S	E6
E 123rd St					
10	CHCG	60628	3278	0E-14S	C6
W 123rd St					
10	CHCG	60628	3278	1W-14S	A6
700	CHCG	60643	3278	1W-14S	A6
700	CTPK	60827	3278	1W-14S	A6
900	CTPK	60643	3277	1W-14S	D6
1000	CHCG	60643	3277	1W-14S	A6
1000	CTPK	60827	3277	1W-14S	D6
1200	CTPK	60643	3277	1W-14S	E6
1600	BLID	60406	3277	2W-14S	D6
1600	BLID	60827	3277	2W-14S	D6
1600	CHCG	60827	3277	1W-14S	D6
3200	ALSP	60803	3276	6W-14S	A6
3200	WthT	60655	3276	4W-14S	D6
3200	WthT	60803	3276	4W-14S	D6
5000	ALSP	60803	3275	6W-14S	E6
6000	WthT	60463	3275	7W-14S	C6
6000	WthT	60803	3275	7W-14S	C6
6400	PSHT	60463	3275	8W-14S	B6
7000	PSHT	60463	3274	9W-14S	E6
8100	PSPK	60464	3274	10W-14S	A6
9000	PSPK	60464	3273	11W-14S	E6
9300	PlsT	60464	3273	11W-14S	E6
E 124th Pl					
10	CHCG	60628	3278	0W-14S	C6
W 124th Pl					
3400	ALSP	60406	3276	4W-14S	E6
3400	WthT	60406	3276	4W-14S	E6
3400	WthT	60803	3276	4W-14S	E6
3800	ALSP	60803	3276	4W-14S	C6
5800	ALSP	60803	3275	7W-14S	C6
6200	PSHT	60463	3275	7W-14S	B6
7600	PSHT	60463	3274	9W-14S	D6
E 124th St					
-	CHCG	60628	3278	0E-14S	E6
W 124th St					
10	CHCG	60628	3278	0W-14S	B6
700	CTPK	60827	3278	1W-14S	A6
1000	CTPK	60827	3277	1W-14S	E6
1800	BLID	60827	3277	2W-14S	C6
1900	BLID	60406	3277	2W-14S	C6
3400	ALSP	60803	3276	4W-14S	E6
3400	WthT	60803	3276	4W-14S	D6
5800	ALSP	60803	3275	7W-14S	C6
5800	WthT	60463	3275	7W-14S	C6
5800	WthT	60803	3275	7W-14S	C6
6400	PSHT	60463	3275	8W-14S	B6
7000	PSHT	60463	3274	9W-14S	E6
8000	PSPK	60464	3274	10W-14S	C6
9100	PSPK	60464	3273	11W-14S	E6
E 125th Pl					
10	CHCG	60628	3278	0W-14S	C6
W 125th Pl					
10	CHCG	60628	3278	0W-14S	C6
5800	ALSP	60803	3275	7W-14S	C7
5800	WthT	60463	3275	7W-14S	C7
6100	PSHT	60463	3275	7W-14S	B7
W 125th St					
500	CHCG	60628	3278	0W-14S	A6
1000	CTPK	60827	3277	2W-14S	D6
1000	CTPK	60827	3278	1W-14S	A6
1900	BLID	60406	3277	2W-14S	C6
1900	BLID	60827	3277	2W-14S	C6
3400	ALSP	60406	3276	4W-14S	E6
3600	ALSP	60803	3276	4W-14S	D6
3600	BLID	60406	3276	4W-14S	D6
6000	ALSP	60803	3275	7W-14S	C6
6000	WthT	60463	3275	7W-14S	C6
6200	PSHT	60463	3275	8W-14S	B6
7000	PSHT	60463	3274	8W-14S	E6
8000	PSPK	60464	3274	10W-14S	C6
9100	PSPK	60464	3273	11W-14S	E7
E 126th Pl					
100	CHCG	60628	3278	0W-14S	D7
2600	CHCG	60633	3279	3E-14S	E6
2600	CHCG	60633	3280	3E-14S	A6
W 126th Pl					
10	CHCG	60628	3278	0W-14S	C6
5800	ALSP	60803	3275	7W-14S	C7
6400	PSHT	60463	3275	8W-14S	B7
126th St					
-	ALSP	60406	3276	3W-14S	E6
-	ALSP	60406	3276	3W-14S	E6
-	ALSP	60803	3277	3W-14S	A6
E 126th St					
10	CHCG	60628	3278	0W-14S	C6
W 126th St					
-	PlsT	60464	3273	12W-14S	C7
200	CHCG	60628	3278	0W-14S	B6
700	CTPK	60628	3278	0W-14S	A6
700	CTPK	60827	3278	0W-14S	A6
1200	CTPK	60827	3277	1W-14S	D6
1900	BLID	60406	3277	2W-14S	C6
1900	BLID	60827	3277	2W-14S	C6
4000	ALSP	60803	3276	5W-14S	C7
5600	WthT	60463	3275	7W-14S	D6
5800	ALSP	60803	3275	7W-14S	C7
6300	PSHT	60463	3275	7W-14S	B7
7200	PSHT	60463	3274	9W-14S	E7
8000	PSPK	60464	3274	10W-14S	C7
9000	PSPK	60464	3273	11W-14S	E7
W 127th Pl					
500	CHCG	60628	3278	0W-15S	B7
4900	ALSP	60803	3276	6W-15S	A7
6000	WthT	60463	3275	7W-15S	C7
6300	PSHT	60463	3275	7W-15S	B7
E 127th St					
10	CHCG	60628	3278	0W-14S	C7
2600	CHCG	60633	3279	3E-14S	E6
2900	CHCG	60633	3280	3E-14S	A6
W 127th St					
10	CHCG	60628	3278	0W-14S	B7
10	LMNT	60439	3270		E7
700	CHCG	60643	3278	0W-14S	A7
700	CHCG	60827	3278	0W-14S	A7
700	CTPK	60827	3278	0W-14S	A7
900	CTPK	60643	3278	1W-14S	A7
1000	CTPK	60827	3277	1W-14S	E7
3600	ALSP	60803	3276	6W-14S	A7
3600	WthT	60406	3276	4W-14S	C7
3600	WthT	60803	3276	4W-14S	C7
5100	ALSP	60803	3275	7W-14S	C7
5200	CTWD	60445	3275	6W-14S	E7
5200	CTWD	60803	3275	6W-14S	E7
5400	CTWD	60445	3275	6W-14S	D7
5500	ALSP	60463	3275	6W-14S	E7
5500	CTWD	60463	3275	6W-14S	D7
5600	WthT	60445	3275	7W-14S	D7
6000	WthT	60463	3275	7W-15S	C7
6200	PSHT	60463	3275	7W-14S	B7
7000	PSHT	60463	3274	9W-14S	C7
7600	PlsT	60463	3274	9W-14S	C7
7600	PSPK	60463	3274	9W-14S	C7
7600	PSPK	60464	3274	9W-14S	C7
10000	PlsT	60464	3273	12W-14S	C7
10000	PSPK	60464	3273	12W-14S	C7
14500	LMNT	60439	3271		A7
16800	DPgT	60441	3342	21W-15S	A1
16800	LMNT	60439	3342	21W-15S	A1
16800	LMNT	60441	3342	21W-15S	A1
W 127th St SR-83					
4800	ALSP	60803	3276	6W-14S	A7
5100	ALSP	60803	3275	7W-14S	C7
5200	CTWD	60445	3275	6W-14S	E7
5200	CTWD	60803	3275	6W-14S	E7
128th Pl					
-	ALSP	60803	3276	5W-15S	B7
5400	CTWD	60445	3275	7W-15S	D7
W 128th Pl					
400	CHCG	60628	3278	0W-15S	A7
700	CHCG	60643	3278	0W-15S	A7
3600	ALSP	60803	3276	4W-15S	D7
6000	WthT	60463	3275	7W-15S	C7
6300	PSHT	60463	3275	7W-15S	B7
8000	PlsT	60464	3274	10W-15S	C7
128th St					
2800	BLID	60406	3277	3W-15S	A7
5700	CTWD	60445	3275	7W-15S	D7
5700	WthT	60445	3275	7W-15S	D7
15100	LMNT	60439	3342	18W-15S	E1
E 128th St					
2600	CHCG	60633	3279	3E-14S	E7
W 128th St					
400	CHCG	60628	3278	0W-15S	B7
1200	CTPK	60827	3277	1W-15S	E7
1700	BLID	60406	3277	2W-15S	D7
1700	BLID	60827	3277	2W-15S	D7
1700	CTPK	60406	3277	2W-15S	D7
4500	ALSP	60803	3276	5W-15S	A7
6000	WthT	60463	3275	7W-15S	C7
7600	PSHT	60463	3274	9W-15S	D7
8300	PlsT	60464	3274	10W-15S	B7
129th Pl					
5400	CTWD	60445	3347	6W-15S	D1
W 129th Pl					
400	CHCG	60628	3278	0W-15S	A7
700	CHCG	60643	3278	0W-15S	A7
900	CTPK	60827	3278	1W-15S	A7
1100	CTPK	60827	3277	1W-15S	E7
6000	WthT	60463	3275	7W-15S	C7
6300	PSHT	60463	3347	7W-15S	B1
6300	WthT	60463	3347	7W-15S	B1
8400	PlsT	60464	3346	10W-15S	B1
129th St					
100	HMND	46320	3280		E7
600	HMND	46394	3280		E7
5700	CTWD	60445	3275	7W-15S	D7
5700	WthT	60445	3275	7W-15S	D7
5700	WthT	60463	3275	7W-15S	D7
15100	LMNT	60439	3342	19W-15S	E1
E 129th St					
800	HMND	46320	3280		E7
800	HMND	46394	3280		E7
2600	CHCG	60633	3279	3E-14S	E7
2900	CHCG	60633	3280	3E-14S	A7
W 129th St					
4000	ALSP	60803	3276	5W-15S	C7
4400	ALSP	60803	3348	5W-15S	B1
5700	CTWD	60445	3275	7W-15S	C7
5700	WthT	60445	3275	7W-15S	C7
6000	WthT	60463	3275	7W-15S	C7
7800	PlsT	60463	3274	9W-15S	C7
8000	PlsT	60464	3274	10W-15S	C7
8000	PSHT	60463	3274	10W-15S	C7
8000	PSPK	60464	3274	10W-15S	C7
8200	PlsT	60464	3346	10W-15S	B1
8200	PSPK	60464	3346	10W-15S	B1
E 130th Av					
-	CHCG	60827	3279	1E-15S	A7
W 130th Ct					
4600	ALSP	60803	3348	5W-15S	A1
130th Pl					
15300	LMNT	60439	3342	19W-15S	D1
E 130th Pl					
-	CHCG	60628	3279	1E-14S	A7
600	CHCG	60827	3278	0E-15S	E7
700	CHCG	60827	3279	0E-15S	A7
W 130th Pl					
6000	WthT	60463	3347	7W-15S	C1
130th St					
-	RVDL	60827	3350	1W-15S	A1
E 130th St					
-	CHCG	60628	3279	1E-14S	A7
-	CHCG	60827	3279	1E-14S	A7
-	RVDL	60827	3278	0E-14S	D7
200	CHCG	60628	3278	0E-14S	D7
200	CHCG	60827	3278	0E-14S	D7
1400	CHCG	60633	3279	3E-15S	E7
2900	CHCG	60633	3280	3E-15S	A7
W 130th St					
4300	ALSP	60803	3348	5W-15S	C1
5400	CTWD	60445	3347	6W-15S	D1
7000	PSHT	60463	3346	8W-15S	E1
7000	PSHT	60463	3347	8W-15S	A1
8000	PlsT	60464	3346	10W-15S	C1
131st Ct					
1200	LMNT	60439	3342	20W-15S	C2
131st Pl					
3100	WthT	60406	3348	3W-15S	E1
3100	WthT	60406	3349	3W-15S	A1
E 131st Pl					
200	CHCG	60827	3350	0E-15S	D1
600	HMND	46320	3352		E1
600	HMND	46327	3352		E1
W 131st Pl					
8800	PlsT	60462	3346	11W-15S	A1
131st St					
2900	BLID	60406	3349	3W-15S	A1
2900	WthT	60406	3349	3W-15S	A1
3000	WthT	60406	3348	4W-15S	E1
3200	ALSP	60406	3348	4W-15S	E1
3200	ALSP	60803	3348	4W-15S	E1
5100	CTWD	60445	3347	6W-15S	D1
5500	WthT	60445	3347	6W-15S	D1
5500	WthT	60463	3347	6W-15S	D1
E 131st St					
500	CHCG	60827	3278	0E-15S	E7
700	CHCG	60827	3279	0E-15S	A7
1100	CHCG	60827	3351	1E-15S	A1
2700	CHCG	60633	3279	3E-15S	E7
3000	CHCG	60633	3280	3E-15S	A7
W 131st St					
3400	ALSP	60406	3348	4W-15S	D1
3400	ALSP	60803	3348	4W-15S	D1
3400	WthT	60406	3348	4W-15S	D1
5700	WthT	60463	3347	7W-15S	C1
6600	PSHT	60463	3347	8W-15S	A1
7000	PSHT	60463	3346	8W-15S	E1
7000	WthT	60463	3346	8W-15S	E1
7100	PSHT	60462	3346	8W-15S	E1
7100	WthT	60462	3346	8W-15S	E1
7200	PSHT	60462	3346	10W-15S	C1
7900	PlsT	60463	3346	9W-15S	C1
7900	PlsT	60464	3346	11W-15S	A1
8800	PSPK	60462	3346	11W-15S	A1
8800	PSPK	60464	3346	11W-15S	A1
9000	ODPK	60462	3346	11W-15S	A1

STREET Block	City	ZIP	Map#	CGS	Grid
W 148th St					
2500	POSN	60469	3349	3W-17S	B5
2800	BmnT	60469	3349	3W-17S	A5
W 149th Pl					
200	HRVY	60426	3349	2W-17S	C6
149th St					
-	ODPK	60462	3345	12W-17S	D6
-	POSN	60469	3348	3W-17S	E5
3200	MDLN	60445	3348	4W-17S	D5
3200	MKHM	60426	3348	4W-17S	D5
3300	MKHM	60445	3348	4W-17S	D5
3500	MDLN	60426	3348	4W-17S	D5
4700	OKFT	60452	3348	6W-17S	A5
5000	MDLN	60452	3348	6W-17S	A5
5100	MDLN	60452	3347	6W-17S	E5
5100	OKFT	60452	3347	6W-17S	E5
E 149th St					
-	SHLD	60473	3350	0W-17S	C6
10	DLTN	60419	3350	0W-17S	C5
10	HRVY	60426	3349	1W-17S	E6
500	HRVY	60426	3350	0W-17S	C6
500	SHLD	60426	3350	0W-17S	B6
800	HMND	46327	3352		E5
900	DLTN	60419	3351	1E-17S	A5
W 149th St					
10	DLTN	60419	3350	0W-17S	C5
200	HRVY	60426	3349	3W-17S	B6
2600	POSN	60426	3349	3W-17S	B5
2600	POSN	60469	3349	3W-17S	B5
2700	BmnT	60469	3349	3W-17S	A5
2800	BmnT	60426	3349	3W-17S	A5
2900	MKHM	60426	3349	3W-17S	A5
2900	MKHM	60469	3349	3W-17S	A5
3100	MDLN	60445	3348	3W-17S	E5
3100	MKHM	60426	3348	3W-17S	E5
3100	POSN	60469	3348	3W-17S	E5
150th Pl					
5700	OKFT	60452	3347	7W-17S	D6
E 150th Pl					
800	SHLD	60473	3351	1E-17S	A5
1000	DLTN	60419	3351	1E-17S	A5
1000	SHLD	60419	3351	1E-17S	A5
W 150th Pl					
200	HRVY	60426	3349	2W-17S	C6
150th St					
3600	MDLN	60426	3348	4W-17S	D6
3600	MKHM	60426	3348	4W-17S	E6
4200	MDLN	60445	3348	5W-17S	B6
5700	OKFT	60452	3347	7W-17S	D6
E 150th St					
800	HMND	46327	3352		E5
W 150th St					
2700	BmnT	60469	3349	3W-17S	B5
2900	BmnT	60426	3349	3W-17S	A6
2900	MKHM	60426	3349	3W-17S	A5
2900	POSN	60426	3349	3W-17S	A5
2900	POSN	60469	3349	3W-17S	A6
151st Pl					
3900	BmnT	60445	3348	4W-18S	C6
3900	MDLN	60445	3348	4W-18S	C6
E 151st Pl					
900	PHNX	60426	3350	0W-18S	C6
900	SHLD	60473	3350	0W-18S	C6
W 151st Pl					
300	HRVY	60426	3349	2W-18S	C6
151st St					
-	CTCY	60409	3351	2E-17S	C5
-	CTCY	60419	3351	2E-17S	C5
-	DLTN	60409	3351	2E-17S	C5
-	DLTN	60419	3351	2E-17S	C5
3600	MDLN	60426	3348	4W-17S	D6
3600	MKHM	60426	3348	4W-17S	D6
3600	MKHM	60445	3348	4W-17S	D6
3900	BmnT	60445	3348	4W-18S	C6
4200	MDLN	60445	3348	6W-17S	A6
4500	MDLN	60452	3348	5W-17S	B6
4500	OKFT	60452	3348	6W-17S	A6
4600	OKFT	60445	3348	6W-17S	A6
5100	OKFT	60452	3347	8W-17S	B6
6000	BmnT	60452	3347	7W-17S	C6
E 151st St					
-	SHLD	60473	3350	0E-17S	D5
10	HRVY	60426	3349	1W-17S	E6
100	HRVY	60426	3350	1W-18S	A6
300	PHNX	60426	3350	0W-17S	B6
500	DLTN	60419	3350	0E-17S	E5
500	SHLD	60419	3350	0E-17S	E5
600	SHLD	60426	3350	0W-17S	B6
800	DLTN	60473	3351	0E-17S	A5
800	SHLD	60473	3351	0E-17S	A5
1000	DLTN	60419	3351	1E-17S	B6
1000	SHLD	60419	3351	1E-17S	A5
W 151st St					
-	BmnT	60452	3346	9W-17S	E6
-	BmnT	60462	3346	9W-17S	E6
10	HRVY	60426	3349	2W-17S	C6
1200	LKPT	60441	3342	21W-17S	A7
1300	HmrT	60441	3342	21W-17S	A7
1300	LktT	60441	3342	21W-17S	A7
3100	MKHM	60426	3348	3W-17S	E6
3100	MKHM	60426	3349	3W-17S	A6
7200	ODPK	60462	3346	10W-17S	C6
7200	OrlT	60462	3346	10W-17S	B6
9000	ODPK	60462	3345	12W-17S	C6
11200	ODPK	60467	3344	15W-17S	B6
11200	OrlT	60467	3344	15W-17S	B6
12000	HMGN	60441	3344	15W-17S	C6
12000	ODPK	60441	3344	14W-17S	C6
12800	HMGN	60441	3343	17W-17S	C6
14600	HMGN	60441	3342	19W-17S	D6
W 151st Ter					
-	HRVY	60426	3349	2W-18S	C6
W 152nd Ct					
7200	ODPK	60462	3346	9W-18S	E6
152nd Pl					
300	CTCY	60409	3352	4E-17S	B6
3600	MDLN	60445	3348	4W-18S	D6
E 152nd Pl					
900	PHNX	60426	3350	0W-18S	C7
900	SHLD	60473	3350	0W-18S	C7
W 152nd Pl					
7200	ODPK	60462	3346	9W-18S	E6
152nd St					
-	MKHM	60426	3348	4W-18S	E6
3600	MDLN	60445	3348	4W-18S	D6
4300	BmnT	60445	3348	5W-18S	B6
4600	MDLN	60452	3348	5W-18S	B6
5000	OKFT	60452	3348	6W-18S	A6
5100	OKFT	60452	3347	6W-18S	E6
E 152nd St					
10	HRVY	60426	3349	1W-18S	E6
10	SHLD	60473	3350	0E-17S	D6
100	HRVY	60426	3350	1W-18S	A6
500	PHNX	60426	3350	0W-18S	B6
600	DLTN	60419	3350	0E-17S	E6

STREET Block	City	ZIP	Map#	CGS	Grid
E 152nd St					
600	SHLD	60419	3350	0E-17S	E6
800	SHLD	60419	3351	1E-17S	A6
800	DLTN	60419	3351	1E-17S	A6
800	DLTN	60473	3351	1E-17S	A6
800	SHLD	60473	3351	1E-17S	A6
1100	SHLD	60419	3351	1E-17S	A6
W 152nd St					
10	HRVY	60426	3349	2W-18S	D6
10	SHLD	60473	3350	0W-17S	D6
7200	ODPK	60462	3346	9W-18S	E6
7300	OrlT	60462	3346	9W-18S	E6
W 153rd Ct					
7200	ODPK	60462	3346	9W-18S	E7
153rd Pl					
200	CTCY	60409	3352	4E-17S	B6
3600	MDLN	60445	3348	4W-18S	D7
E 153rd Pl					
1000	SHLD	60473	3351	1E-17S	A6
W 153rd Pl					
10	SHLD	60473	3350	0W-17S	C6
7200	ODPK	60462	3346	9W-18S	E7
7300	OrlT	60462	3346	9W-18S	E7
153rd St					
-	MKHM	60426	3348	4W-18S	E6
10	HMND	46320	3352	4E-17S	C6
1000	CTCY	60409	3352	3E-17S	A6
1400	CTCY	60409	3351	2E-17S	D6
3600	MDLN	60445	3348	4W-18S	D7
3900	BmnT	60445	3348	4W-18S	C7
5100	OKFT	60452	3347	6W-18S	E6
5100	OKFT	60452	3348	6W-18S	A6
E 153rd St					
-	DLTN	60419	3351	1E-17S	B6
10	HRVY	60426	3349	1W-18S	E7
100	HRVY	60426	3350	1W-18S	A7
500	DLTN	60419	3350	0E-17S	E6
500	PHNX	60426	3350	0W-18S	B7
500	SHLD	60419	3350	0E-17S	E6
700	SHLD	60473	3351	1E-17S	A6
900	SHLD	60426	3350	0W-18S	C7
900	SHLD	60473	3350	0W-18S	C7
W 153rd St					
2500	HRVY	60426	3349	3W-18S	B7
3100	MKHM	60426	3348	3W-18S	E6
3100	MKHM	60426	3349	3W-18S	A6
7000	ODPK	60462	3346	9W-18S	E6
7000	OKFT	60462	3346	9W-18S	E6
7000	OKFT	60462	3347	8W-18S	A6
7300	OrlT	60462	3346	9W-18S	E7
9600	ODPK	60462	3345	13W-18S	A7
10100	ODPK	60467	3345	12W-18S	C7
10600	OrlT	60467	3345	13W-18S	A7
11000	ODPK	60467	3344	13W-18S	E7
11000	OrlT	60467	3344	13W-18S	E7
154th Pl					
10	CTCY	60409	3352	4E-18S	C6
10	HMND	46320	3352	4E-18S	C6
6900	OKFT	60452	3347	8W-18S	A7
E 154th Pl					
500	HRVY	60426	3350	0W-18S	B7
500	PHNX	60426	3350	0W-18S	B7
600	SHLD	60426	3350	0E-18S	E6
600	SHLD	60473	3351	0E-18S	A6
1400	DLTN	60419	3351	1E-18S	B6
1600	DLTN	60473	3351	2E-18S	C6
W 154th Pl					
100	HRVY	60426	3349	2W-18S	C7
3700	BmnT	60426	3348	4W-18S	D7
3700	MKHM	60426	3348	4W-18S	D7
7300	ODPK	60462	3346	9W-18S	E7
7300	OrlT	60462	3346	9W-18S	E7
154th St					
4800	OKFT	60452	3348	6W-18S	A7
5100	OKFT	60452	3347	6W-18S	E7
E 154th St					
10	HRVY	60426	3349	1W-18S	E7
500	HRVY	60426	3350	0W-18S	B7
600	DLTN	60419	3350	0E-17S	E6
600	PHNX	60426	3350	0W-18S	B7
600	SHLD	60473	3350	0E-17S	E6
700	DLTN	60419	3351	1E-17S	A6
700	SHLD	60419	3351	0E-18S	A6
700	SHLD	60473	3351	0E-18S	A6
800	DLTN	60473	3351	1E-18S	A6
1600	ThtT	60419	3351	1E-17S	A6
1600	ThtT	60473	3351	1E-17S	A6
1700	CTCY	60409	3351	2E-17S	A6
1700	ThtT	60409	3351	1E-17S	A6
W 154th St					
-	BmnT	60426	3348	4W-18S	C7
-	BmnT	60445	3348	4W-18S	C7
-	MDLN	60445	3348	4W-18S	D7
-	MKHM	60426	3348	4W-18S	D7
-	MKHM	60445	3348	4W-18S	D7
-	OKFT	60462	3346	9W-18S	E7
10	HRVY	60426	3349	2W-18S	C7
10	SHLD	60473	3350	0W-17S	C6
100	PHNX	60426	3350	0W-17S	C6
100	SHLD	60426	3350	0W-17S	C6
3800	MDLN	60445	3348	4W-18S	C7
7300	ODPK	60462	3346	9W-18S	E7
7300	OrlT	60462	3346	9W-18S	E7
9700	ODPK	60462	3345	12W-18S	D7
E 155th Ct					
700	PHNX	60426	3350	0W-18S	B7
155th Pl					
10	CTCY	46320	3352	4E-18S	C7
10	CTCY	60409	3352	4E-18S	B7
10	HMND	46320	3352	4E-18S	C7
6800	OKFT	60452	3347	8W-18S	A7
E 155th Pl					
10	SHLD	60473	3350	0E-18S	D7
500	PHNX	60426	3350	0W-18S	B7
700	SHLD	60419	3351	0E-18S	A7
700	SHLD	60473	3351	0E-18S	A7
1400	DLTN	60419	3351	1E-18S	B7
W 155th Pl					
10	SHLD	60473	3350	0W-18S	D6
10	HRVY	60426	3349	2W-18S	D7
155th St					
10	CTCY	60409	3352	4E-18S	C6
10	HMND	46320	3352	4E-18S	C6
4500	OKFT	60452	3348	6W-18S	A7
5100	OKFT	60452	3347	6W-18S	E7
E 155th St					
10	HRVY	60426	3349	1W-18S	E7
100	HRVY	60426	3350	1W-18S	A7
500	PHNX	60426	3350	0W-18S	B7
500	SHLD	60473	3350	0E-18S	E6
800	DLTN	60419	3351	1E-18S	A6
800	SHLD	60419	3351	1E-18S	A6
800	SHLD	60473	3351	1E-18S	A6
900	SHLD	60426	3350	0W-18S	C7
W 155th St					
-	ODPK	60467	3344	14W-18S	D7

STREET Block	City	ZIP	Map#	CGS	Grid
W 155th St					
10	SHLD	60473	3350	0W-18S	C6
2400	HRVY	60426	3349	3W-18S	B7
2400	MKHM	60426	3349	3W-18S	B7
3400	MKHM	60426	3348	4W-18S	D7
3800	BmnT	60426	3348	4W-18S	C7
7300	ODPK	60462	3346	9W-18S	E7
7300	OrlT	60462	3346	9W-18S	E7
11200	OrlT	60467	3344	14W-18S	E7
156th Pl					
10	CTCY	60409	3352	4E-18S	C7
10	HMND	46320	3352	4E-18S	C7
1000	CTCY	60409	3351	3E-18S	E7
6800	OKFT	60452	3347	8W-18S	A7
E 156th Pl					
400	SHLD	60473	3350	0E-18S	E7
700	SHLD	60473	3351	0E-18S	A7
1000	DLTN	60419	3351	1E-18S	A7
1100	SHLD	60419	3351	1E-18S	A7
W 156th Pl					
100	HRVY	60426	3427	2W-18S	C1
200	MKHM	60426	3427	2W-18S	C1
156th St					
10	CTCY	60409	3352	4E-18S	B7
10	HMND	46320	3352	4E-18S	C7
1000	CTCY	60409	3351	3E-18S	E7
4700	OKFT	60452	3348	6W-18S	A7
5100	OKFT	60452	3347	6W-18S	E7
6800	BmnT	60452	3347	8W-18S	A7
7100	ODPK	60462	3346	9W-18S	E7
11200	OrlT	60467	3344	14W-18S	E7
E 156th St					
10	HRVY	60426	3349	1W-18S	E7
10	SHLD	60473	3350	0E-18S	D7
100	HRVY	60426	3350	1W-18S	A7
800	SHLD	60419	3351	1E-18S	A7
800	SHLD	60473	3351	1E-18S	A7
1400	DLTN	60419	3351	1E-18S	B7
W 156th St					
10	HRVY	60426	3349	2W-18S	C7
3200	MKHM	60426	3349	3W-18S	A7
3600	MKHM	60426	3426	4W-18S	D1
3700	BmnT	60426	3426	4W-18S	C1
157th Pl					
6200	OKFT	60452	3347	7W-18S	B7
6800	BmnT	60452	3425	8W-18S	A1
6800	BmnT	60477	3425	8W-18S	A1
6800	OKFT	60452	3425	8W-18S	A1
6900	ODPK	60462	3425	8W-18S	A1
6900	ODPK	60477	3425	8W-18S	A1
E 157th Pl					
-	SHLD	60473	3350	0E-18S	D7
600	HRVY	60426	3428	0W-18S	B1
700	DLTN	60419	3351	0E-18S	A7
700	HRVY	60473	3428	0W-18S	B1
700	SHLD	60426	3351	0E-18S	A7
700	SHLD	60473	3428	0W-18S	B1
W 157th Pl					
100	HRVY	60426	3427	2W-18S	C1
100	MKHM	60426	3427	2W-18S	C1
7600	ODPK	60462	3424	9W-18S	D1
157th St					
10	CTCY	60409	3352	4E-18S	C7
10	HMND	46320	3352	4E-18S	C7
4800	OKFT	60452	3348	6W-18S	A7
6000	OKFT	60452	3347	8W-18S	B7
6800	BmnT	60452	3347	8W-18S	A7
6800	BmnT	60477	3347	8W-18S	A7
E 157th St					
-	ThtT	60473	3351	2E-18S	C7
10	HRVY	60426	3427	1W-18S	E1
100	HRVY	60426	3428	0W-18S	B1
100	SHLD	60426	3350	0E-18S	D7
700	SHLD	60473	3351	0E-18S	A7
1600	DLTN	60419	3351	2E-18S	C7
W 157th St					
10	SHLD	60473	3350	0W-18S	C7
100	PHNX	60426	3350	0W-18S	C7
100	SHLD	60426	3350	0W-18S	C7
200	MKHM	60426	3427	2W-18S	C1
300	HRVY	60426	3427	3W-18S	B1
3300	MKHM	60426	3426	4W-18S	E1
7000	ODPK	60462	3347	8W-18S	A7
7100	ODPK	60462	3346	9W-18S	E7
7400	ODPK	60462	3424	10W-18S	B1
11200	ODPK	60467	3422	14W-18S	E1
11200	OrlT	60467	3422	14W-18S	D1
W 158th Ct					
7700	ODPK	60462	3424	9W-18S	D1
158th Pl					
10	CTCY	60409	3429	2E-18S	C1
5800	OKFT	60452	3425	7W-18S	C1
E 158th Pl					
10	SHLD	60473	3350	0E-18S	D7
W 158th Pl					
10	HRVY	60426	3427	2W-18S	D1
158th St					
600	CTCY	60409	3352	3E-18S	A7
4800	OKFT	60452	3426	6W-18S	A1
5100	OKFT	60452	3425	6W-18S	E1
7100	ODPK	60462	3424	9W-18S	E1
11200	ODPK	60467	3422	14W-18S	E1
11200	OrlT	60467	3422	14W-18S	E1
E 158th St					
10	HRVY	60426	3427	1W-18S	E1
100	HRVY	60426	3428	1W-18S	A1
400	SHLD	60473	3350	0E-18S	C7
700	DLTN	60473	3351	0E-18S	A7
700	SHLD	60426	3428	0W-18S	B1
700	SHLD	60473	3428	0W-18S	B1
900	DLTN	60419	3351	1E-18S	A7
1200	SHLD	60473	3351	1E-18S	B7
1600	SHLD	60419	3351	1E-18S	C7
1800	ThtT	60473	3351	2E-18S	C7
1900	CTCY	60473	3351	2E-18S	C7
W 158th St					
2100	HRVY	60426	3427	2W-18S	C1
2100	MKHM	60426	3427	2W-18S	C1
3400	MKHM	60426	3426	4W-18S	E1
159th Ct					
-	BmnT	60426	3427	3W-19S	B1
E 159th Ct					
600	SHLD	60473	3350	0E-18S	E7
159th Pl					
7400	TYPK	60477	3424	9W-19S	D1
9000	ODHL	60477	3424	11W-19S	A1
E 159th Pl					
600	SHLD	60473	3428	0E-18S	E1
900	SHLD	60473	3429	1E-18S	A1
1100	SHLD	60473	3351	1E-18S	A7
W 159th Pl					
3800	MKHM	60426	3426	4W-19S	D1
3900	BmnT	60426	3426	4W-19S	D1
159th St					
-	SHLD	60473	3429	1E-19S	C1

STREET Block	City	ZIP	Map#	CGS	Grid
159th St					
10	CTCY	60409	3430	4E-18S	C1
10	HMND	46320	3430	4E-18S	C1
10	HMND	46324	3430	4E-18S	C1
1400	CTCY	60409	3429	2E-18S	D1
2400	BmnT	60426	3427	3W-19S	B1
2400	ThtT	60426	3427	3W-19S	B1
4700	BmnT	60426	3426	5W-18S	A1
4700	OKFT	60452	3426	5W-18S	A1
5100	OKFT	60452	3425	6W-18S	E1
5400	BmnT	60477	3425	6W-18S	D1
5400	OKFT	60477	3425	6W-18S	D1
6400	TYPK	60452	3425	8W-18S	B1
6500	BmnT	60452	3425	8W-18S	B1
6700	TYPK	60477	3425	8W-18S	A1
6900	ODPK	60477	3425	8W-18S	A1
159th St US-6					
-	SHLD	60473	3429	1E-19S	C1
1400	CTCY	60409	3429	2E-18S	D1
4700	BmnT	60426	3426	5W-18S	A1
4700	OKFT	60452	3426	5W-18S	A1
5100	OKFT	60452	3425	6W-18S	E1
5400	BmnT	60477	3425	6W-18S	D1
5400	OKFT	60477	3425	6W-18S	D1
6400	TYPK	60452	3425	8W-18S	B1
6500	BmnT	60452	3425	8W-18S	B1
6700	TYPK	60477	3425	8W-18S	A1
6900	ODPK	60477	3425	8W-18S	A1
E 159th St					
10	HRVY	60426	3427	1W-19S	E1
10	SHLD	60473	3350	0E-18S	D7
100	HRVY	60426	3428	1W-18S	A1
300	HRVY	60473	3428	1W-18S	A1
300	SHLD	60426	3428	1W-18S	A1
300	SHLD	60473	3428	1W-18S	A1
E 159th St US-6					
10	HRVY	60426	3427	1W-19S	E1
100	HRVY	60426	3428	1W-18S	A1
300	HRVY	60473	3428	1W-18S	A1
300	SHLD	60426	3428	1W-18S	A1
300	SHLD	60473	3428	1W-18S	A1
W 159th St					
-	OKFT	60452	3426	5W-18S	B1
10	HRVY	60426	3427	2W-18S	D1
200	MKHM	60426	3427	2W-18S	C1
200	ThtT	60426	3427	2W-18S	C1
2300	BmnT	60426	3427	2W-18S	C1
3300	MKHM	60426	3426	5W-18S	B1
3800	BmnT	60426	3426	5W-18S	B1
7000	ODPK	60462	3425	8W-18S	A1
7000	ODPK	60477	3425	8W-18S	A1
7000	TYPK	60477	3425	8W-18S	A1
7100	ODPK	60462	3424	10W-18S	A1
7100	TYPK	60477	3424	10W-18S	A1
7200	ODPK	60477	3424	9W-18S	E1
7400	TYPK	60462	3424	9W-18S	E1
8700	ODHL	60462	3424	10W-18S	A1
8700	ODHL	60477	3424	10W-18S	A1
9100	ODHL	60477	3423	12W-18S	B1
9100	ODPK	60462	3423	12W-18S	B1
9100	ODPK	60477	3423	12W-18S	B1
9300	ODPK	60467	3423	11W-18S	E1
9900	OrlT	60467	3423	12W-18S	C1
10800	ODPK	60467	3422	15W-18S	C1
10800	OrlT	60467	3422	15W-18S	C1
11800	HMGN	60441	3422	14W-18S	C1
W 159th St SR-7					
11200	ODPK	60467	3422	14W-18S	E1
11200	OrlT	60467	3422	13W-18S	E1
11800	HMGN	60441	3422	14W-18S	C1
W 159th St US-6					
-	OKFT	60452	3426	5W-18S	B1
10	HRVY	60426	3427	2W-18S	D1
200	MKHM	60426	3427	2W-18S	C1
200	ThtT	60426	3427	2W-18S	C1
2300	BmnT	60426	3427	2W-18S	C1
3300	MKHM	60426	3426	5W-18S	B1
3800	BmnT	60426	3426	5W-18S	B1
7000	ODPK	60462	3425	8W-18S	A1
7000	ODPK	60477	3425	8W-18S	A1
7000	TYPK	60477	3425	8W-18S	A1
7100	ODPK	60462	3424	10W-18S	A1
7100	TYPK	60477	3424	10W-18S	A1
7200	ODPK	60477	3424	9W-18S	E1
7400	TYPK	60462	3424	9W-18S	E1
8700	ODHL	60462	3424	10W-18S	A1
8700	ODHL	60477	3424	10W-18S	A1
9100	ODHL	60477	3423	12W-18S	B1
9100	ODPK	60462	3423	12W-18S	B1
9100	ODPK	60477	3423	12W-18S	B1
9300	ODPK	60467	3423	11W-18S	E1
9900	OrlT	60467	3423	12W-18S	C1
10800	ODPK	60467	3422	15W-18S	C1
10800	OrlT	60467	3422	15W-18S	C1
E 160th Ct					
600	SHLD	60473	3428	0E-18S	E1
160th Pl					
900	CTCY	60409	3430	3E-19S	A2
8200	TYPK	60477	3424	10W-19S	B1
9000	ODHL	60477	3424	11W-19S	A2
E 160th Pl					
300	HRVY	60426	3428	0W-19S	B2
300	SHLD	60426	3428	0W-19S	B2
400	SHLD	60473	3428	0E-18S	E1
1100	SHLD	60473	3429	1E-18S	B1
160th St					
600	CTCY	60409	3430	3E-19S	B1
4800	BmnT	60426	3426	6W-19S	A1
4800	OKFT	60452	3426	6W-19S	A1
5000	OKFT	60452	3425	6W-19S	E1
7900	TYPK	60477	3424	10W-19S	C1
10700	ODPK	60467	3423	13W-19S	A1
E 160th St					
10	HRVY	60426	3427	1W-19S	E1
200	HRVY	60426	3428	0W-19S	B1
200	SHLD	60426	3428	0E-18S	D1
700	SHLD	60473	3429	0E-18S	A1
W 160th St					
10	HRVY	60426	3427	2W-19S	D2
2100	ThtT	60426	3427	2W-19S	C2
2300	BmnT	60426	3427	2W-19S	C1
3200	MKHM	60426	3427	3W-19S	A1
3300	MKHM	60426	3426	4W-19S	E1
161st Pl					
8000	TYPK	60477	3424	10W-19S	C2
9000	ODHL	60477	3424	11W-19S	A2
9100	ODHL	60477	3423	11W-19S	E2
E 161st Pl					
200	SHLD	60473	3428	0E-18S	E1
1100	SHLD	60473	3429	1E-18S	B1
W 161st Pl					
8700	ODHL	60462	3424	10W-19S	A2
8700	ODHL	60477	3424	10W-19S	A2
8700	ODPK	60462	3424	10W-19S	A2

STREET Block	City	ZIP	Map#	CGS	Grid
161st St					
-	TYPK	60477	3424	9W-19S	E1
-	TYPK	60477	3425	8W-19S	A2
200	CTCY	60409	3430	4E-19S	B2
4800	BmnT	60426	3426	6W-19S	A1
4800	OKFT	60452	3426	6W-19S	A1
5200	OKFT	60452	3425	6W-19S	E1
10700	ODPK	60467	3423	13W-19S	A2
E 161st St					
-	HRVY	60426	3428	0W-19S	B2
600	SHLD	60473	3428	0E-18S	E1
600	SHLD	60473	3429	0E-18S	A1
W 161st St					
1700	HRVY	60426	3427	2W-19S	D2
1700	MKHM	60426	3427	2W-19S	D2
2200	ThtT	60426	3427	2W-19S	C2
3300	MKHM	60426	3426	4W-19S	E2
162nd Pl					
10	CTCY	60409	3430	4E-19S	C2
7400	TYPK	60477	3424	9W-19S	D2
E 162nd Pl					
10	SHLD	60473	3428	0E-19S	D1
900	SHLD	60473	3429	1E-19S	A1
W 162nd Pl					
3700	MKHM	60426	3426	4W-19S	D2
162nd St					
100	CTCY	60409	3430	4E-19S	C2
4800	BmnT	60426	3426	6W-19S	A2
4800	OKFT	60452	3426	6W-19S	A2
5200	OKFT	60452	3425	6W-19S	E2
7400	TYPK	60477	3424	9W-19S	D2
9000	ODHL	60477	3423	11W-19S	E2
9000	ODHL	60477	3424	11W-19S	A2
9400	ODPK	60467	3423	11W-19S	E2
E 162nd St					
10	SHLD	60473	3428	0E-18S	D1
200	HRVY	60426	3428	1W-19S	A2
700	SHLD	60473	3429	1E-19S	A1
E 162nd St US-6					
10	SHLD	60473	3428	0E-18S	D1
700	SHLD	60473	3429	1E-19S	A1
W 162nd St					
10	SHLD	60473	3428	0W-19S	C1
500	HRVY	60426	3428	0W-18S	B1
500	HRVY	60473	3428	0W-18S	B1
500	SHLD	60426	3428	0W-18S	B1
1400	HRVY	60426	3427	2W-19S	E2
1400	MKHM	60426	3427	2W-19S	D2
2500	BmnT	60426	3427	3W-19S	B2
3300	MKHM	60426	3426	4W-19S	E2
8700	ODHL	60477	3424	10W-19S	A2
8700	ODHL	60462	3424	10W-19S	A2
8700	ODPK	60477	3424	10W-19S	A2
W 162nd St US-6					
10	SHLD	60473	3428	0W-19S	C1
500	HRVY	60426	3428	0W-18S	B1
500	HRVY	60473	3428	0W-18S	B1
500	SHLD	60426	3428	0W-18S	B1
163rd Ct					
7900	TYPK	60477	3424	9W-19S	C2
E 163rd Ct					
10	SHLD	60473	3428	0E-19S	D2
163rd Pl					
-	MKHM	60426	3427	3W-19S	A2
10	CTCY	60409	3430	4E-19S	C2
6600	TYPK	60477	3425	8W-19S	A2
7900	TYPK	60477	3424	9W-19S	C2
10400	ODPK	60467	3423	13W-19S	B2
10400	OrlT	60467	3423	12W-19S	B2
E 163rd Pl					
700	SHLD	60473	3428	0E-19S	E2
700	SHLD	60473	3429	0E-19S	A2
W 163rd Pl					
2100	MKHM	60426	3427	2W-19S	C2
163rd St					
-	ODHL	60477	3423	11W-19S	E2
-	ODPK	60467	3423	11W-19S	E2
-	ODPK	60477	3423	11W-19S	E2
-	TYPK	60477	3425	8W-19S	A2
700	CTCY	60438	3430	3E-19S	A2
700	LNSG	60438	3430	3E-19S	A2
800	CTCY	60409	3430	3E-19S	A2
4000	BmnT	60426	3426	5W-19S	C2
4000	BmnT	60452	3426	5W-19S	C2
4000	MKHM	60426	3426	5W-19S	C2
4000	MKHM	60452	3426	5W-19S	C2
4800	OKFT	60426	3426	6W-19S	A2
4800	OKFT	60452	3426	6W-19S	A2
5400	BmnT	60477	3425	6W-19S	D2
5400	OKFT	60452	3425	6W-19S	D2
7300	TYPK	60477	3424	9W-19S	D2
8500	ODPK	60462	3424	10W-19S	B2
E 163rd St					
200	HRVY	60426	3428	1W-19S	A2
600	SHLD	60473	3428	0E-19S	E2
1100	SHLD	60473	3429	1E-19S	B1
W 163rd St					
1400	HRVY	60426	3427	2W-19S	E2
1400	MKHM	60426	3427	2W-19S	D2
3300	MKHM	60426	3426	4W-19S	E2
4200	BmnT	60426	3426	5W-19S	C2
4200	OKFT	60452	3426	5W-19S	C2
8600	ODPK	60462	3424	10W-19S	B2
8600	TYPK	60477	3424	10W-19S	B2
8800	ODHL	60462	3424	11W-19S	A2
8800	ODHL	60477	3424	11W-19S	A2
8800	ODPK	60477	3424	11W-19S	A2
164th Ct					
7900	TYPK	60477	3424	9W-19S	C2
E 164th Ct					
800	SHLD	60473	3429	1E-19S	A2
164th Pl					
10	CTCY	60409	3430	4E-19S	C3
6400	TYPK	60477	3425	8W-19S	B2
7900	TYPK	60477	3424	9W-19S	C2
10400	ODPK	60467	3423	13W-19S	B3
10400	OrlT	60467	3423	13W-19S	B3
E 164th Pl					
200	SHLD	60473	3428	0E-19S	D2
1100	SHLD	60473	3429	1E-19S	B2
W 164th Pl					
8600	ODPK	60462	3424	10W-19S	B2
164th St					
400	CTCY	60409	3430	3E-19S	B2
6600	TYPK	60477	3425	8W-19S	A2
8200	TYPK	60477	3424	10W-19S	C2
E 164th St					
300	HRVY	60426	3428	0W-19S	B2
300	SHLD	60473	3428	0E-19S	D2
1200	SHLD	60473	3429	1E-19S	B2
W 164th St					
1400	HRVY	60426	3427	1W-19S	E2
3200	MKHM	60426	3427	3W-19S	A2
3300	MKHM	60426	3426	4W-19S	E2
8700	ODPK	60462	3424	11W-19S	A2

STREET Block	City	ZIP	Map#	CGS	Grid
W 164th St					
8900	ODHL	60477	3424	11W-19S	A2
8900	ODPK	60477	3424	11W-19S	A2
165th Av					
-	ODPK	60467	3423	12W-19S	D3
165th Pl					
10	CTCY	60409	3430	4E-19S	C3
6600	TYPK	60477	3425	8W-19S	A3
8400	TYPK	60477	3424	10W-19S	B3
E 165th Pl					
300	SHLD	60473	3428	0E-19S	D2
800	SHLD	60473	3429	1E-19S	A2
W 165th Pl					
8600	ODPK	60462	3424	10W-19S	B3
8600	TYPK	60477	3424	10W-19S	B3
165th St					
-	CTCY	46324	3430	4E-19S	C3
-	CTCY	60409	3430	3E-19S	B3
10	HMND	46324	3430		D2
10	HMND	60409	3430		D2
4000	MKHM	60426	3426	5W-19S	C3
4000	OKFT	60426	3426	5W-19S	C3
4000	OKFT	60452	3426	5W-19S	C3
6600	TYPK	60477	3425	8W-19S	A2
7400	TYPK	60477	3424	9W-19S	D3
10700	ODPK	60467	3423	13W-19S	A3
E 165th St					
200	HRVY	60426	3428	1W-19S	B3
200	SHLD	60473	3428	0E-19S	D2
800	SHLD	60473	3429	1E-19S	A2
W 165th St					
1500	HRVY	60426	3427	2W-19S	D3
2700	MKHM	60426	3427	3W-19S	B3
3300	MKHM	60426	3426	4W-19S	E3
W 166th Ct					
9400	ODPK	60467	3423	11W-19S	E3
166th Pl					
10	CTCY	60409	3430	4E-19S	C3
7600	TYPK	60477	3424	9W-19S	D3
E 166th Pl					
400	SHLD	60473	3428	0E-19S	E2
1200	SHLD	60473	3429	1E-19S	B2
W 166th Pl					
3800	MKHM	60426	3426	4W-19S	D3
8700	ODHL	60462	3424	10W-19S	A3
8700	ODHL	60477	3424	10W-19S	A3
8700	ODPK	60462	3424	10W-19S	A3
8700	ODPK	60477	3424	10W-19S	A3
9400	ODHL	60477	3423	11W-19S	E3
9400	ODPK	60467	3423	11W-19S	E3
9400	ODPK	60477	3423	11W-19S	E3
166th St					
-	MKHM	60426	3427	3W-19S	B3
10	CTCY	60409	3430	4E-19S	B3
4100	OKFT	60452	3426	5W-19S	C3
6000	BmnT	60477	3425	7W-19S	C3
6000	TYPK	60477	3425	7W-19S	E3
7100	OrlT	60477	3424	8W-19S	E3
7600	TYPK	60477	3424	9W-19S	D3
E 166th St					
200	HRVY	60426	3428	1W-19S	A3
200	SHLD	60473	3428	0E-19S	E2
700	SHLD	60473	3429	1E-19S	A2
W 166th St					
3000	MKHM	60426	3427	3W-19S	A3
3600	MKHM	60426	3426	4W-19S	D3
8700	ODHL	60477	3424	10W-19S	A3
8700	ODPK	60462	3424	10W-19S	A3
8700	ODPK	60477	3424	10W-19S	A3
167th Pl					
-	HMND	46324	3430	4E-20S	C3
10	CTCY	60409	3430	4E-20S	C3
3700	CCHL	60478	3426	4W-20S	D3
7900	TYPK	60477	3424	10W-20S	C3
8800	ODHL	60462	3424	11W-20S	A3
8800	ODHL	60477	3424	11W-20S	A3
8800	ODPK	60462	3424	11W-20S	A3
10900	ODPK	60467	3423	13W-20S	A3
E 167th Pl					
400	SHLD	60473	3428	0E-19S	E3
1300	SHLD	60473	3429	1E-19S	B3
W 167th Pl					
800	HRVY	60426	3428	1W-20S	A3
8600	ODPK	60462	3424	10W-20S	B3
8700	ODHL	60477	3424	10W-20S	A3
167th St					
-	BmnT	60478	3426	5W-19S	C3
-	CCHL	60477	3426	5W-19S	C3
10	CTCY	60409	3430	4E-20S	C3
800	HMND	46324	3430		E2
4000	CCHL	60478	3426	5W-19S	D3
4000	MKHM	60426	3426	5W-19S	D3
4000	OKFT	60478	3426	5W-19S	C3
4100	OKFT	60452	3426	6W-19S	A3
4500	BmnT	60477	3426	5W-19S	B3
4500	OKFT	60477	3426	5W-19S	B3
5000	BmnT	60452	3425	8W-19S	B3
5000	OKFT	60452	3425	8W-19S	B3
5200	BmnT	60477	3425	6W-19S	E3
5600	TYPK	60477	3425	7W-19S	D3
7100	TYPK	60477	3424	9W-19S	D3
7400	OrlT	60477	3424	10W-20S	B3
9000	ODHL	60477	3423	11W-19S	E3
9000	ODHL	60477	3424	11W-19S	A3
9300	ODPK	60477	3423	11W-19S	E3
9400	ODPK	60467	3423	11W-19S	E3
9400	OrlT	60467	3423	11W-19S	E3
E 167th St					
200	HRVY	60426	3428	0W-20S	B3
300	HRVY	60473	3428	0W-19S	B3
400	SHLD	60473	3428	0E-19S	E2
700	SHLD	60473	3429	0E-19S	A2
W 167th St					
400	SHLD	60473	3428	0W-19S	B2
1500	HLCT	60426	3427	3W-19S	A3
1500	HLCT	60429	3427	3W-19S	A3
1500	HRVY	60426	3427	1W-19S	E3
1500	MKHM	60426	3427	3W-19S	A3
2900	MKHM	60426	3427	3W-19S	A3
3300	HLCT	60429	3426	4W-19S	D3
3300	MKHM	60426	3426	4W-19S	D3
3400	HLCT	60426	3426	4W-19S	E3
3600	CCHL	60478	3426	4W-19S	D3
8500	ODPK	60462	3424	10W-19S	A3
8500	ODPK	60477	3424	11W-19S	A3
8500	TYPK	60462	3424	11W-19S	A3
8500	TYPK	60477	3424	11W-19S	A3
8700	ODHL	60462	3424	10W-19S	A3
8700	ODHL	60477	3424	10W-19S	A3
9600	ODHL	60477	3423	12W-19S	C3
9600	ODPK	60467	3423	12W-19S	C3
9600	OrlT	60467	3423	12W-19S	C3
11100	ODPK	60467	3422	14W-19S	D3
11100	OrlT	60467	3422	14W-19S	D3
11800	HMGN	60467	3422	14W-19S	C3
W 167th St					
12800	HMGN	60441	3422	16W-19S	A3
E 168th Ct					
-	SHLD	60473	3428	0E-19S	E3
168th Pl					
3700	CCHL	60478	3426	4W-20S	D4
7200	TYPK	60477	3424	9W-20S	E3
E 168th Pl					
200	SHLD	60473	3428	0E-19S	D3
700	SHLD	60473	3429	0E-19S	A3
W 168th Pl					
300	HRVY	60426	3428	1W-20S	B4
168th St					
1600	HLCT	60429	3427	2W-20S	D3
3700	CCHL	60478	3426	4W-20S	D3
3700	HLCT	60429	3426	4W-20S	D3
6800	TYPK	60477	3425	8W-20S	A3
7100	TYPK	60477	3424	9W-20S	E3
10900	ODPK	60467	3423	13W-20S	A4
E 168th St					
10	SHLD	60473	3428	0E-19S	D3
800	SHLD	60473	3429	1E-19S	A3
W 168th St					
10	SHLD	60473	3428	0W-19S	C3
800	HRVY	60426	3428	1W-20S	A3
8600	ODPK	60462	3424	10W-20S	B3
8600	TYPK	60462	3424	10W-20S	B3
8600	TYPK	60477	3424	10W-20S	B3
8700	ODHL	60462	3424	10W-20S	A3
8700	ODHL	60477	3424	10W-20S	A3
169th Ct					
3400	LNSG	60438	3430	4E-19S	B3
E 169th Ct					
900	SHLD	60473	3429	1E-19S	A3
169th Pl					
800	HMND	46324	3430		E3
8900	ODHL	60477	3424	11W-20S	A4
9200	ODHL	60477	3423	11W-20S	E4
9300	ODPK	60477	3423	11W-20S	E4
E 169th Pl					
200	SHLD	60473	3428	0E-19S	D3
800	SHLD	60473	3429	1E-19S	A3
169th St					
10	CTCY	60409	3430	4E-20S	C4
10	HMND	46324	3430	4E-20S	C4
1600	HLCT	60429	3427	2W-20S	D4
3700	CCHL	60478	3426	4W-20S	D4
5200	BmnT	60452	3425	6W-20S	E3
5200	BmnT	60477	3425	6W-20S	E3
5200	OKFT	60452	3425	6W-20S	E3
6800	TYPK	60477	3425	8W-20S	A3
8000	TYPK	60477	3424	10W-20S	C4
8300	OrlT	60477	3424	10W-20S	B4
8500	TYPK	60462	3424	10W-20S	B4
8800	ODHL	60462	3424	11W-20S	A4
8800	ODHL	60477	3424	11W-20S	A4
8800	ODPK	60462	3424	11W-20S	A4
E 169th St					
600	SHLD	60473	3428	0E-19S	E3
800	SHLD	60473	3429	1E-19S	A3
W 169th St					
10	SHLD	60473	3428	0W-19S	B3
8600	ODPK	60462	3424	10W-20S	B4
8600	TYPK	60462	3424	10W-20S	B4
8600	TYPK	60477	3424	10W-20S	B4
8700	ODHL	60462	3424	10W-20S	A4
8700	ODHL	60477	3424	10W-20S	A4
170th Pl					
1000	HMND	46324	3430		E3
3400	LNSG	60438	3430	4E-20S	B3
5200	OKFT	60452	3425	6W-20S	E4
7200	TYPK	60477	3424	9W-20S	D4
8100	OrlT	60477	3424	10W-20S	C4
8500	ODPK	60462	3424	10W-20S	B4
8500	TYPK	60462	3424	10W-20S	B4
9200	ODHL	60477	3423	11W-20S	E4
E 170th Pl					
200	SHLD	60473	3428	0E-20S	D3
1400	SHLD	60473	3429	1E-20S	B3
W 170th Pl					
8600	ODPK	60462	3424	10W-20S	B4
8600	TYPK	60462	3424	10W-20S	B4
8600	TYPK	60477	3424	10W-20S	B4
8700	ODHL	60477	3424	10W-20S	A4
170th St					
800	HMND	46324	3430		E3
1700	HLCT	60429	3427	2W-20S	D4
5200	BmnT	60477	3425	6W-20S	E4
5200	OKFT	60452	3425	6W-20S	E4
6800	TYPK	60477	3425	8W-20S	A4
8300	OrlT	60477	3424	10W-20S	B4
8500	TYPK	60462	3424	10W-20S	B4
8500	TYPK	60477	3424	10W-20S	B4
8800	ODHL	60477	3424	11W-20S	A4
8800	ODPK	60462	3424	11W-20S	A4
9100	ODHL	60477	3423	11W-20S	E4
E 170th St					
200	SHLD	60473	3428	0E-20S	D3
1300	SHLD	60473	3429	1E-19S	B3
2100	CTCY	60409	3429	2E-20S	D3
2200	LNSG	60409	3429	2E-20S	D3
2200	LNSG	60438	3429	3E-20S	E3
2600	LNSG	60438	3430	3E-19S	A3
W 170th St					
8600	ODPK	60462	3424	10W-20S	B4
8600	TYPK	60462	3424	10W-20S	B4
8600	TYPK	60477	3424	10W-20S	B4
8700	ODHL	60477	3424	10W-20S	A4
11400	ODPK	60467	3422	14W-20S	E4
E 171st Ct					
2000	SHLD	60473	3429	2E-20S	D3
171st Pl					
3700	CCHL	60478	3426	4W-20S	D4
5600	BmnT	60477	3425	7W-20S	D4
5600	OKFT	60452	3425	7W-20S	D4
7700	TYPK	60477	3424	9W-20S	D4
E 171st Pl					
200	SHLD	60473	3428	0E-20S	D4
1800	SHLD	60473	3429	2E-20S	D4
171st St					
-	CCHL	60478	3426	4W-20S	D5
-	HLCT	60429	3426	4W-20S	D5
-	HLCT	60430	3427	3W-20S	C4
-	HLCT	60478	3426	4W-20S	D5
-	OrlT	60477	3423	11W-20S	D4
-	TNTN	60476	3428	0E-20S	D4
500	HMND	46324	3430		D3
800	EHZC	60426	3428	1W-20S	A4
800	EHZC	60429	3428	1W-20S	A4
800	EHZC	60473	3428	0W-20S	B4
800	HRVY	60426	3428	1W-20S	A4
800	HRVY	60429	3428	1W-20S	A4
800	SHLD	60473	3428	0W-20S	B4
1300	EHZC	60429	3427	2W-20S	D4
1300	HRVY	60426	3427	1W-20S	E4
171st St					
1300	HRVY	60429	3427	2W-20S	D4
3000	HLCT	60429	3427	3W-20S	A4
3400	LNSG	60438	3430	4E-20S	B4
4800	BmnT	60477	3426	6W-20S	A4
4800	BmnT	60478	3426	6W-20S	A4
5000	BmnT	60452	3426	6W-20S	A4
5000	OKFT	60452	3426	6W-20S	A4
5000	OKFT	60477	3426	6W-20S	A4
6500	TYPK	60477	3425	8W-20S	A4
7200	TYPK	60477	3424	10W-20S	C4
8100	OrlT	60477	3424	10W-20S	C4
8500	ODPK	60462	3424	10W-20S	B4
8500	TYPK	60462	3424	10W-20S	B4
8600	ODPK	60477	3424	10W-20S	B4
8700	ODHL	60477	3424	10W-20S	A4
9000	ODHL	60477	3423	11W-20S	E4
9000	TYPK	60477	3423	11W-20S	E4
9200	ODPK	60477	3423	11W-20S	E4
E 171st St					
200	SHLD	60473	3428	0E-20S	D4
1900	SHLD	60473	3429	2E-20S	D3
W 171st St					
11400	ODPK	60467	3422	14W-20S	E4
172nd Pl					
-	SHLD	60473	3429	2E-20S	C4
10	CTCY	60409	3430		C4
10	HMND	46324	3430	4E-20S	C4
1700	EHZC	60429	3427	2W-20S	D4
3400	LNSG	60438	3430	4E-20S	B4
4000	CCHL	60478	3426	5W-20S	C5
7900	TYPK	60477	3424	9W-20S	C4
172nd St					
-	TNTN	60476	3428	0E-20S	D4
10	CTCY	60409	3430		C4
10	HMND	46324	3430		C4
1000	EHZC	60429	3428	1W-20S	A4
1800	EHZC	60429	3427	2W-20S	D5
2200	LNSG	60438	3429	3E-20S	E4
2800	HLCT	60429	3427	3W-20S	A4
3600	LNSG	60438	3430	4E-20S	C4
3700	CCHL	60478	3426	4W-20S	D5
3700	HLCT	60429	3426	4W-20S	D5
3700	HLCT	60478	3426	4W-20S	D5
6800	TYPK	60477	3425	8W-20S	A4
7900	TYPK	60477	3424	9W-20S	C4
10900	ODPK	60467	3423	13W-20S	A4
E 172nd St					
1100	SHLD	60473	3429	1E-20S	B4
W 172nd St					
-	EHZC	60426	3428	0W-20S	B4
-	EHZC	60429	3428	0W-20S	B4
-	HRVY	60426	3428	0W-20S	B4
400	TNTN	60476	3428	0W-20S	B4
500	SHLD	60473	3428	0W-20S	B4
500	SHLD	60476	3428	0W-20S	B4
500	TNTN	60473	3428	0W-20S	B4
700	EHZC	60473	3428	0W-20S	B4
173rd Ct					
3700	LNSG	60438	3430	4E-20S	C4
173rd Pl					
800	HMND	46324	3430		E4
2800	LNSG	60438	3430	3E-20S	A4
6500	TYPK	60477	3425	8W-20S	B5
7200	TYPK	60477	3424	9W-20S	E5
9200	TYPK	60477	3423	11W-20S	E5
E 173rd Pl					
-	SHLD	60473	3428	0E-20S	E4
1100	SHLD	60473	3429	1E-20S	B4
173rd St					
1000	EHZC	60429	3428	1W-20S	A5
1900	EHZC	60429	3427	2W-20S	D5
1900	EHZC	60430	3427	2W-20S	D5
1900	HLCT	60430	3427	2W-20S	D5
2200	LNSG	60438	3429	2E-20S	E4
2800	HLCT	60429	3427	4W-20S	A5
3000	LNSG	60438	3430	3E-20S	A4
3200	HLCT	60429	3426	4W-20S	E5
4800	BmnT	60478	3426	6W-20S	A5
4800	CCHL	60478	3426	6W-20S	A5
5600	BmnT	60477	3425	7W-20S	D4
6600	TYPK	60477	3425	8W-20S	B4
7200	TYPK	60477	3424	9W-20S	D5
9400	TYPK	60477	3423	11W-20S	E5
E 173rd St					
10	HMND	46324	3430		D4
10	SHLD	60473	3428	0E-20S	D4
10	SHLD	60476	3428	0E-20S	D4
10	TNTN	60473	3428	0E-20S	D4
10	TNTN	60476	3428	0E-20S	D4
1300	SHLD	60473	3429	1E-20S	B4
174th Ct					
3600	LNSG	60438	3430	4E-20S	C4
174th Pl					
800	HMND	46324	3430		E4
7000	TYPK	60477	3425	8W-20S	A5
7200	TYPK	60477	3424	9W-20S	E5
174th St					
200	HMND	46324	3430		D4
800	EHZC	60429	3428	1W-20S	A5
800	EHZC	60430	3428	1W-20S	A5
800	HMWD	60429	3428	1W-20S	A5
800	HMWD	60430	3428	1W-20S	A5
1900	EHZC	60429	3427	2W-20S	D5
1900	EHZC	60430	3427	2W-20S	D5
1900	HLCT	60430	3427	2W-20S	D5
2700	HLCT	60429	3427	3W-20S	A5
5400	BmnT	60452	3425	6W-20S	E5
5400	BmnT	60477	3425	6W-20S	E5
5400	BmnT	60478	3425	6W-20S	E5
6400	TYPK	60477	3425	8W-20S	B5
7200	TYPK	60477	3424	9W-20S	D5
9400	TYPK	60477	3423	11W-20S	E5
175th Pl					
800	HMND	46324	3430		E5
3600	CCHL	60429	3426	4W-21S	D5
3600	CCHL	60478	3426	4W-21S	D5
3600	HLCT	60429	3426	4W-21S	D5
6800	TYPK	60477	3425	8W-21S	A5
175th St					
-	TNTN	60430	3428	0W-20S	B5
-	TNTN	60476	3428	0W-20S	B5
500	HMND	46324	3430		D4
800	EHZC	60430	3428	1W-21S	A5
800	HMWD	60430	3428	1W-21S	A5
1000	EHZC	60429	3428	1W-20S	A5
1200	EHZC	60429	3427	1W-20S	E5
1200	HMWD	60430	3427	1W-20S	E5
1500	EHZC	60430	3427	1W-20S	E5
2000	HLCT	60430	3427	2W-20S	D5
2000	LNSG	60438	3429	2E-20S	D5
2500	HLCT	60429	3427	4W-20S	A5
3200	CCHL	60429	3426	4W-20S	E5
3200	CCHL	60478	3426	6W-20S	A5
3200	HLCT	60429	3426	4W-20S	E5
175th St					
3600	LNSG	60438	3430	4E-20S	C5
3600	MNSR	60438	3430	4E-20S	C5
3700	HLCT	60478	3426	4W-20S	D5
4800	BmnT	60477	3426	6W-20S	A5
5300	BmnT	60477	3425	7W-20S	C5
5300	BmnT	60477	3426	6W-20S	A5
5300	BmnT	60478	3425	6W-20S	E5
6800	TYPK	60477	3425	8W-21S	A5
7200	TYPK	60477	3424	11W-20S	A5
9100	TYPK	60477	3423	11W-20S	D5
9400	OrlT	60477	3423	11W-20S	D5
11100	ODPK	60448	3422	13W-20S	E5
11100	ODPK	60467	3422	13W-20S	E5
11100	ODPK	60467	3423	13W-20S	A5
11100	OrlT	60448	3422	13W-20S	E5
11100	OrlT	60448	3423	13W-20S	A5
11100	OrlT	60467	3423	13W-20S	A5
176th Ct					
400	HMND	46324	3430		D5
176th Pl					
800	HMND	46324	3430		E5
2100	ThtT	60438	3429	2E-20S	D5
2400	LNSG	60438	3429	3E-20S	E5
3600	CCHL	60429	3426	4W-21S	E6
3600	HLCT	60429	3426	4W-21S	E6
3600	LNSG	60438	3430	4E-20S	C5
3700	CCHL	60478	3426	4W-21S	D6
3700	MNSR	46321	3430	4E-20S	C5
6800	TYPK	60477	3425	8W-21S	A5
176th St					
-	CCHL	60429	3426	4W-21S	E5
-	CCHL	60478	3426	4W-21S	E5
-	HLCT	60429	3426	4W-21S	E5
-	HLCT	60429	3427	4W-21S	A5
-	TYPK	60477	3423	11W-21S	E5
800	HMND	46324	3430		E5
3100	LNSG	60438	3430	3E-20S	B5
6600	TYPK	60477	3425	8W-21S	A5
8700	TYPK	60477	3424	11W-21S	A5
177th Pl					
-	TYPK	60477	3424	8W-21S	E6
800	HMND	46324	3430		E5
2200	LNSG	60438	3429	2E-20S	D5
2200	ThtT	60438	3429	2E-20S	D5
3600	LNSG	60438	3430	4E-20S	C5
4300	CCHL	60478	3426	5W-21S	B6
7000	TYPK	60477	3425	8W-21S	A5
177th St					
-	LNSG	60438	3429	2E-20S	D5
800	HMND	46324	3430		E5
1900	ThtT	60438	3429	2E-20S	D5
2700	LNSG	60438	3430	3E-20S	A5
3200	HLCT	60429	3426	4W-21S	E5
3200	HLCT	60429	3427	4W-21S	A6
3500	CCHL	60429	3426	4W-21S	E6
3700	MNSR	46321	3430	4E-20S	C5
3700	MNSR	60438	3430	4E-20S	C5
4000	CCHL	60478	3426	5W-21S	B6
5400	BmnT	60477	3425	6W-21S	E5
6200	TYPK	60477	3425	8W-21S	B5
178th Pl					
3100	LNSG	60438	3430	3E-21S	B5
3700	CCHL	60478	3426	4W-21S	D6
178th St					
-	TYPK	60477	3425	8W-21S	A6
2200	LNSG	60438	3429	2E-21S	E5
2700	LNSG	60438	3430	3E-21S	A5
4000	CCHL	60478	3426	5W-21S	C6
8800	TYPK	60477	3424	11W-21S	A6
9100	TYPK	60477	3423	11W-21S	E6
179th Pl					
4600	CCHL	60478	3426	5W-21S	B6
6800	TYPK	60477	3425	8W-21S	A6
179th St					
-	CCHL	60478	3426	6W-21S	A6
-	TYPK	60477	3423	13W-21S	A6
-	TYPK	60477	3424	10W-21S	B6
2600	LNSG	60438	3429	3E-21S	E5
2700	LNSG	60438	3430	3E-21S	A5
3500	BmnT	60430	3426	4W-21S	D6
6200	BmnT	60477	3425	8W-21S	A5
6200	TYPK	60477	3425	8W-21S	A5
9900	ODPK	60467	3423	12W-21S	B6
9900	ODPK	60477	3423	12W-21S	D6
9900	OrlT	60467	3423	12W-21S	B6
9900	OrlT	60477	3423	13W-21S	A6
11100	ODPK	60467	3422	14W-21S	E6
11100	OrlT	60467	3422	14W-21S	D6
11400	ODPK	60448	3422	14W-21S	E6
11400	OrlT	60448	3422	14W-21S	D6
W 179th St					
12000	HMGN	60448	3422	15W-21S	C6
12000	ODPK	60467	3422	15W-21S	C6
180th Ct					
6800	TYPK	60477	3425	8W-21S	A6
180th Pl					
1800	LNSG	60438	3429	2E-21S	C6
1800	ThtT	60438	3429	2E-21S	C6
6400	BmnT	60477	3425	8W-21S	B6
6400	TYPK	60477	3425	8W-21S	B6
180th St					
-	ODPK	60467	3422	14W-21S	E6
-	TYPK	60477	3424	11W-21S	A6
1600	ThtT	60438	3429	2E-21S	C6
2500	LNSG	60438	3429	3E-21S	E6
2700	LNSG	60438	3430	3E-21S	A6
4300	CCHL	60478	3426	5W-21S	C6
6500	TYPK	60477	3425	8W-21S	A6
181st Pl					
1500	LNSG	60438	3429	1E-21S	C6
3300	LNSG	60438	3430	4E-21S	B6
4500	CCHL	60478	3426	5W-21S	B7
6400	TYPK	60477	3425	8W-21S	B7
181st St					
-	LNSG	60438	3429	1E-21S	B6
-	ThtT	60438	3429	1E-21S	B6
2700	LNSG	60438	3430	3E-21S	A6
4200	CCHL	60478	3426	5W-21S	C7
4700	BmnT	60478	3426	5W-21S	B7
6200	TYPK	60477	3425	8W-21S	B6
182nd Pl					
1800	HMWD	60430	3427	2W-21S	D7
2200	LNSG	60438	3429	2E-21S	E6
3000	LNSG	60438	3430	3E-21S	A6
4300	CCHL	60478	3426	5W-21S	C7
4700	BmnT	60478	3426	5W-21S	B7
6400	TYPK	60477	3425	8W-21S	B7
182nd St					
1400	ThtT	60438	3429	2E-21S	C6
1500	LNSG	60438	3429	1E-21S	B6
4400	CCHL	60478	3426	5W-21S	B7
6400	TYPK	60477	3425	8W-21S	B7
183rd Pl					
2600	LNSG	60438	3429	3E-21S	E7
183rd Pl					
8200	TYPK	60477	3424	10W-22S	C7
8200	TYPK	60477	3504	10W-22S	B1
11200	FftT	60448	3422	14W-22S	E7
11200	MKNA	60448	3422	14W-22S	E7
11300	ODPK	60448	3422	14W-22S	E7
W 183rd Pl					
1900	LNSG	60438	3429	2E-21S	D7
183rd St					
-	BlmT	60425	3428	0W-21S	C7
-	BlmT	60425	3429	1E-21S	A7
-	BlmT	60438	3429	1E-21S	A7
-	BlmT	60476	3428	0W-21S	C7
-	BlmT	60476	3429	1E-21S	A7
-	ODPK	60448	3422	14W-22S	D7
-	ThtT	60425	3429	1E-21S	A7
-	ThtT	60476	3429	1E-21S	A7
-	TNTN	60425	3428	0W-21S	C7
-	TNTN	60476	3428	0W-21S	C7
800	GNWD	60425	3428	0W-21S	B7
800	GNWD	60430	3428	0W-21S	B7
800	HMWD	60430	3428	1W-21S	A7
1200	HMWD	60430	3427	2W-21S	C7
1800	ThtT	60438	3429	2E-21S	C6
2600	LNSG	60438	3429	3E-21S	E6
3000	HLCT	60429	3427	3W-21S	A7
3000	LNSG	60438	3430	3E-21S	A6
3200	HLCT	60430	3426	4W-21S	D7
3200	HMWD	60430	3426	4W-21S	D7
3500	BmnT	60430	3426	4W-21S	E7
3600	BmnT	60429	3426	4W-21S	D7
3900	CCHL	60429	3426	4W-21S	D7
3900	CCHL	60478	3426	6W-21S	A7
4800	BmnT	60478	3426	6W-21S	A7
4900	RchT	60478	3426	6W-21S	A7
5000	BmnT	60477	3426	6W-21S	A7
5000	RchT	60477	3426	6W-21S	A7
5200	BmnT	60477	3425	6W-21S	E7
5200	RchT	60477	3425	6W-21S	E7
5900	TYPK	60477	3425	6W-21S	E7
7600	FftT	60477	3424	9W-21S	C7
8500	TYPK	60477	3424	11W-21S	A7
9200	TYPK	60477	3423	11W-22S	E7
9300	FftT	60477	3423	11W-21S	E7
9400	OrlT	60448	3423	11W-21S	E7
10700	FftT	60448	3423	13W-21S	B7
10700	FftT	60467	3423	13W-21S	B7
10700	ODPK	60448	3423	13W-21S	A7
10700	ODPK	60467	3423	13W-21S	A7
11100	FftT	60448	3422	14W-21S	E7
11100	ODPK	60448	3422	14W-22S	D7
15500	ODPK	60477	3423	13W-21S	A7
15500	OrlT	60477	3423	13W-21S	A7
184th Ct					
4900	CCHL	60478	3506	6W-22S	A1
184th Pl					
1600	HMWD	60430	3507	2W-22S	D1
2200	LNSG	60438	3429	2E-21S	D7
4700	CCHL	60478	3426	5W-22S	B7
4700	CCHL	60478	3506	5W-22S	B1
13000	NlxT	60448	3422	16W-22S	A7
184th St					
2400	LNSG	60438	3429	3E-21S	E7
2800	LNSG	60438	3430	3E-21S	A7
3200	HMWD	60430	3426	4W-22S	E7
3200	HMWD	60430	3427	4W-22S	A7
3200	HMWD	60430	3506	4W-22S	E2
4700	CCHL	60478	3426	5W-22S	B7
185th Ct					
2300	LNSG	60438	3429	2E-21S	E7
4900	CCHL	60478	3506	6W-22S	A1
185th Pl					
1000	HMWD	60430	3508	1W-22S	A1
2200	LNSG	60438	3429	2E-21S	D7
3200	HMWD	60430	3506	4W-22S	E1
3200	HMWD	60430	3507	4W-22S	A1
4200	CCHL	60478	3506	5W-22S	C1
185th St					
1000	HMWD	60430	3508	1W-22S	A1
1600	LNSG	60438	3429	2E-21S	C7
2800	LNSG	60438	3430	3E-21S	A7
4400	CCHL	60478	3506	5W-22S	B1
7600	TYPK	60477	3504	10W-22S	B1
7700	FftT	60477	3504	10W-22S	C1
186th Pl					
-	CCHL	60478	3506	5W-22S	B1
1000	HMWD	60430	3508	1W-22S	A1
1500	HMWD	60430	3507	2W-22S	D1
2400	BlmT	60438	3429	3E-22S	E7
2400	LNSG	60438	3429	3E-22S	E7
186th St					
1000	HMWD	60430	3508	1W-22S	A1
1400	BlmT	60438	3429	2E-22S	D7
1400	LNSG	60438	3429	3E-21S	E7
1400	ThtT	60438	3429	2E-22S	D7
1500	HMWD	60430	3507	1W-22S	E1
1600	BlmT	60411	3429	3E-21S	E1
2500	LNSG	60438	3429	3E-21S	E7
2700	BlmT	60411	3430	3E-21S	A7
2700	LNSG	60411	3430	3E-21S	A7
2700	LNSG	60438	3430	3E-21S	A7
4300	CCHL	60478	3506	5W-22S	C1
8000	FftT	60477	3504	10W-22S	C1
8000	TYPK	60477	3504	10W-22S	C1
187th Ct					
3200	LNSG	60438	3510	4E-22S	B1
187th Pl					
2400	BlmT	60411	3509	3E-22S	E1
2400	BlmT	60438	3509	3E-22S	E1
2400	LNSG	60438	3509	3E-22S	E1
4000	CCHL	60478	3506	5W-22S	C1
187th St					
-	FftT	60448	3504	11W-22S	A1
-	HMWD	60425	3508	1W-22S	A1
300	MKNA	60448	3504	10W-22S	B1
800	GNWD	60425	3508	1W-22S	B1
800	HMWD	60430	3508	1W-22S	A1
1200	HMWD	60430	3507	2W-22S	D1
1900	FSMR	60422	3507	2W-22S	D1
2400	BlmT	60411	3429	3E-22S	E7
2400	BlmT	60438	3429	3E-22S	E7
2400	LNSG	60438	3429	3E-22S	E7
3400	LNSG	60438	3430	4E-22S	B7
3900	FSMR	60422	3506	5W-22S	D1
3900	FSMR	60429	3506	4W-22S	D1
3900	HLCT	60429	3506	5W-22S	D1
4300	CCHL	60478	3506	6W-22S	A1
W 187th St					
500	GNWD	60425	3508	0W-22S	B1
900	HMWD	60430	3508	0W-22S	B1
188th Pl					
3100	LNSG	60438	3510	3E-22S	B1
4200	CCHL	60478	3506	5W-22S	C2
188th St					
2400	BlmT	60411	3509	3E-22S	E1

Chicago & Cook County Street Index

STREET Block	City	ZIP	Map#	CGS	Grid
188th St					
2400	BlmT	60438	**3509**	**3E-22S**	**E1**
2400	LNSG	60411	**3509**	**3E-22S**	**E1**
2400	LNSG	60438	**3509**	**3E-22S**	**E1**
3000	LNSG	60438	**3510**	**3E-22S**	**A1**
3800	FSMR	60422	**3506**	**4W-22S**	**D2**
3900	CCHL	60478	**3506**	**5W-22S**	**C1**
8100	MKNA	60448	**3504**	**10W-22S**	**C1**
189th Pl					
2800	LNSG	60438	**3510**	**3E-22S**	**A1**
4100	CCHL	60478	**3506**	**5W-22S**	**C2**
189th St					
-	MKNA	60448	**3504**	**11W-22S**	**A2**
2800	LNSG	60438	**3510**	**3E-22S**	**A1**
3800	FSMR	60422	**3506**	**4W-22S**	**D2**
4400	CCHL	60478	**3506**	**5W-22S**	**B2**
8000	MKNA	60477	**3504**	**10W-22S**	**C2**
8000	TYPK	60477	**3504**	**10W-22S**	**C2**
190th Pl					
2800	LNSG	60438	**3510**	**3E-22S**	**A1**
4100	CCHL	60478	**3506**	**5W-22S**	**C2**
190th St					
-	MKNA	60448	**3504**	**10W-22S**	**B2**
1200	HMWD	60430	**3507**	**1W-22S**	**E2**
1200	HMWD	60430	**3508**	**1W-22S**	**A2**
1400	BlmT	60430	**3507**	**1W-22S**	**E2**
2800	LNSG	60438	**3510**	**3E-22S**	**A1**
3900	FSMR	60422	**3506**	**5W-22S**	**D2**
4000	CCHL	60422	**3506**	**4W-22S**	**D2**
4900	CCHL	60478	**3506**	**6W-22S**	**A2**
191st Ct					
4100	CCHL	60478	**3506**	**5W-23S**	**C2**
191st Pl					
2800	LNSG	60438	**3510**	**3E-22S**	**A2**
3600	BlmT	60438	**3510**	**4E-22S**	**C2**
4000	CCHL	60478	**3506**	**5W-23S**	**C2**
8400	MKNA	60448	**3504**	**10W-23S**	**B2**
E 191st Pl					
400	BlmT	60425	**3508**	**0E-23S**	**E2**
400	GNWD	60425	**3508**	**0E-22S**	**E1**
700	GNWD	60425	**3509**	**1E-23S**	**A2**
191st St					
1100	HMWD	60430	**3508**	**1W-22S**	**A2**
1200	HMWD	60430	**3507**	**1W-22S**	**E2**
1300	BlmT	60430	**3507**	**1W-22S**	**E2**
3400	LNSG	60438	**3510**	**4E-22S**	**B1**
W 191st St					
-	FftT	60477	**3505**	**8W-22S**	**A2**
-	TYPK	60477	**3505**	**8W-22S**	**A2**
7500	FftT	60477	**3504**	**9W-22S**	**E2**
7500	TYPK	60477	**3504**	**9W-22S**	**E2**
7800	FftT	60448	**3504**	**9W-22S**	**E2**
8000	MKNA	60448	**3504**	**9W-22S**	**E2**
192nd Ct					
-	CCHL	60478	**3506**	**5W-23S**	**C3**
192nd Pl					
-	CCHL	60478	**3506**	**5W-23S**	**C3**
3500	LNSG	60438	**3510**	**4E-22S**	**C2**
4000	RchT	60478	**3506**	**5W-23S**	**D3**
8500	MKNA	60448	**3504**	**10W-23S**	**B2**
E 192nd Pl					
900	GNWD	60425	**3509**	**1E-23S**	**B3**
192nd St					
3200	FSMR	60422	**3507**	**4W-23S**	**A2**
3200	LNSG	60438	**3510**	**4E-22S**	**B2**
3200	RchT	60422	**3507**	**4W-23S**	**A3**
3200	RchT	60430	**3507**	**4W-23S**	**A3**
3300	RchT	60430	**3506**	**4W-23S**	**E3**
3800	RchT	60478	**3506**	**4W-23S**	**D3**
4100	CCHL	60478	**3506**	**5W-23S**	**C3**
8400	MKNA	60448	**3504**	**10W-23S**	**B2**
E 192nd St					
400	BlmT	60425	**3508**	**0E-23S**	**E3**
400	GNWD	60425	**3508**	**0E-23S**	**E3**
500	GNWD	60425	**3509**	**1E-23S**	**A3**
W 192nd St					
8400	FftT	60448	**3504**	**11W-23S**	**A2**
8400	MKNA	60448	**3504**	**11W-23S**	**A2**
193rd Ct					
3600	LNSG	60438	**3510**	**4E-22S**	**C2**
4100	CCHL	60478	**3506**	**5W-23S**	**C3**
193rd Pl					
800	BlmT	60411	**3508**	**1W-23S**	**A3**
900	CHHT	60411	**3508**	**1W-23S**	**A3**
3600	LNSG	60438	**3510**	**4E-22S**	**C2**
4100	CCHL	60478	**3506**	**5W-23S**	**C3**
E 193rd Pl					
600	GNWD	60425	**3509**	**1E-23S**	**B3**
193rd St					
-	CCHL	60478	**3506**	**5W-23S**	**C3**
3600	LNSG	60438	**3510**	**4E-22S**	**C2**
4000	FSMR	60422	**3506**	**5W-23S**	**D3**
8500	MKNA	60448	**3504**	**10W-23S**	**B2**
E 193rd St					
700	GNWD	60425	**3509**	**1E-23S**	**B3**
194th Ct					
4100	CCHL	60478	**3506**	**5W-23S**	**C3**
194th Pl					
800	BlmT	60411	**3508**	**1W-23S**	**A3**
900	CHHT	60411	**3508**	**1W-23S**	**A3**
3000	LNSG	60411	**3510**	**3E-23S**	**A2**
4100	CCHL	60478	**3506**	**5W-23S**	**C3**
E 194th Pl					
1000	GNWD	60425	**3509**	**1E-23S**	**B3**
194th St					
800	BlmT	60411	**3508**	**1W-23S**	**A3**
900	CHHT	60411	**3508**	**1W-23S**	**A3**
2800	LNSG	60438	**3510**	**3E-22S**	**A2**
3200	FSMR	60422	**3506**	**4W-23S**	**E3**
3200	FSMR	60422	**3507**	**4W-23S**	**A3**
3200	RchT	60422	**3506**	**4W-23S**	**E3**
3200	RchT	60422	**3507**	**4W-23S**	**A3**
3200	RchT	60430	**3506**	**4W-23S**	**E3**
4100	CCHL	60478	**3506**	**5W-23S**	**C3**
7200	FftT	60423	**3505**	**9W-23S**	**A3**
7200	FftT	60477	**3505**	**9W-23S**	**A3**
7200	RchT	60423	**3505**	**9W-23S**	**A3**
7200	TYPK	60477	**3505**	**9W-23S**	**A3**
7300	TYPK	60477	**3504**	**9W-23S**	**E3**
E 194th St					
600	GNWD	60425	**3509**	**1E-23S**	**A3**
W 194th St					
300	CHHT	60411	**3508**	**0W-23S**	**C3**
300	CHHT	60425	**3508**	**0W-23S**	**C3**
300	GNWD	60425	**3508**	**0W-23S**	**C3**
195th Ct					
3000	LNSG	60411	**3510**	**3E-23S**	**A2**
195th Pl					
-	LYWD	60411	**3510**	**3E-23S**	**A3**
195th St					
700	BlmT	60411	**3508**	**0W-23S**	**B3**
700	BlmT	60425	**3508**	**0W-23S**	**B3**
700	CHHT	60411	**3508**	**0W-23S**	**B3**
700	CHHT	60425	**3508**	**0W-23S**	**B3**
700	GNWD	60425	**3508**	**0W-23S**	**B3**
2900	LYWD	60411	**3510**	**3E-23S**	**A2**
3200	FSMR	60422	**3506**	**4W-23S**	**E3**
3200	FSMR	60422	**3507**	**4W-23S**	**A3**
3200	RchT	60422	**3506**	**4W-23S**	**E3**
3200	RchT	60422	**3507**	**4W-23S**	**A3**
4100	CCHL	60478	**3506**	**5W-23S**	**C3**
7200	FftT	60423	**3505**	**9W-23S**	**A3**
7200	RchT	60423	**3505**	**9W-23S**	**A3**
W 195th St					
300	BlmT	60425	**3508**	**0W-23S**	**C3**
300	CHHT	60411	**3508**	**0W-23S**	**C3**
300	CHHT	60425	**3508**	**0W-23S**	**C3**
300	GNWD	60425	**3508**	**0W-23S**	**C3**
196th St					
700	BlmT	60411	**3508**	**0W-23S**	**B4**
700	CHHT	60411	**3508**	**0W-23S**	**B4**
3000	LYWD	60411	**3510**	**3E-23S**	**A3**
3300	FSMR	60422	**3506**	**4W-23S**	**E3**
3300	FSMR	60422	**3507**	**3W-22S**	**A2**
3300	RchT	60422	**3506**	**4W-23S**	**E3**
3300	RchT	60422	**3507**	**3W-22S**	**A2**
3400	RchT	60430	**3506**	**4W-23S**	**E4**
197th Pl					
-	CHHT	60411	**3508**	**0W-23S**	**B4**
-	LYWD	60411	**3510**	**3E-23S**	**A3**
197th St					
700	CHHT	60411	**3508**	**0W-23S**	**B4**
3000	LYWD	60411	**3510**	**3E-23S**	**A3**
198th Pl					
-	LYWD	60411	**3510**	**3E-23S**	**A3**
2000	LYWD	60411	**3509**	**2E-23S**	**D3**
198th St					
2400	BlmT	60411	**3509**	**3E-23S**	**E3**
2400	LYWD	60411	**3509**	**3E-23S**	**E3**
2700	LYWD	60411	**3510**	**3E-23S**	**A3**
3300	RchT	60422	**3506**	**4W-23S**	**E4**
3600	FSMR	60422	**3506**	**4W-23S**	**D4**
3600	RchT	60443	**3506**	**4W-23S**	**D4**
199th St					
2200	LYWD	60411	**3509**	**2E-23S**	**D4**
200th Pl					
2900	LYWD	60411	**3510**	**3E-23S**	**A4**
200th St					
2400	LYWD	60411	**3509**	**3E-23S**	**E4**
2600	LYWD	60411	**3510**	**3E-23S**	**A4**
201st Pl					
2600	LYWD	60411	**3509**	**3E-23S**	**E4**
2600	LYWD	60411	**3510**	**3E-23S**	**A4**
201st St					
2400	LYWD	60411	**3509**	**3E-23S**	**E4**
2700	LYWD	60411	**3510**	**3E-23S**	**A4**
202nd St					
200	CHHT	60411	**3507**	**2W-24S**	**E5**
2900	LYWD	60411	**3510**	**3E-24S**	**A4**
203rd St					
3200	LYWD	60411	**3510**	**4E-24S**	**B4**
3600	OMFD	60461	**3506**	**4W-24S**	**D5**
4600	MTSN	60443	**3506**	**5W-24S**	**B5**
204th St					
3100	OMFD	60461	**3507**	**4W-24S**	**A6**
3200	BlmT	60411	**3510**	**4E-24S**	**B5**
3200	LYWD	60411	**3510**	**4E-24S**	**B5**
4000	MTSN	60443	**3506**	**5W-24S**	**C6**
4000	OMFD	60461	**3506**	**5W-24S**	**C6**
205th Pl					
500	DYR	46311	**3510**		**D5**
205th St					
2200	LYWD	60411	**3509**	**2E-24S**	**E5**
3200	OMFD	60461	**3506**	**4W-24S**	**E6**
3200	OMFD	60461	**3507**	**4W-24S**	**A6**
4000	MTSN	60443	**3506**	**5W-24S**	**C6**
206th Pl					
500	DYR	46311	**3510**		**D5**
4200	MTSN	60443	**3506**	**5W-24S**	**C6**
206th St					
600	DYR	46311	**3510**		**E5**
4000	MTSN	60443	**3506**	**5W-24S**	**C6**
4000	OMFD	60461	**3506**	**5W-24S**	**C6**
207th Pl					
2200	LYWD	60411	**3509**	**2E-24S**	**D6**
207th St					
2400	BlmT	60411	**3507**	**3W-24S**	**B6**
2400	OMFD	60411	**3507**	**3W-25S**	**B6**
2400	OMFD	60461	**3507**	**3W-24S**	**B6**
4000	MTSN	60443	**3506**	**6W-24S**	**A6**
4000	OMFD	60461	**3506**	**5W-24S**	**D6**
4400	RchT	60443	**3506**	**6W-24S**	**A6**
E 207th St					
2300	LYWD	60411	**3509**	**2E-24S**	**E5**
W 207th St					
2200	BlmT	60411	**3507**	**2W-25S**	**C6**
2200	CHHT	60411	**3507**	**2W-24S**	**D6**
2300	OMFD	60461	**3507**	**2W-24S**	**C6**
209th Ct					
700	DYR	46311	**3510**		**E6**
209th St					
500	CHHT	60411	**3507**	**2W-25S**	**C7**
600	DYR	46311	**3510**		**E6**
2200	BlmT	60411	**3507**	**2W-25S**	**C7**
2300	OMFD	60461	**3507**	**2W-25S**	**C7**
210th Pl					
600	DYR	46311	**3510**		**D6**
210th St					
700	DYR	46311	**3510**		**E6**
211th Pkwy					
5600	MTSN	60443	**3505**	**7W-25S**	**D7**
211th Pl					
600	DYR	46311	**3510**		**E7**
3600	MTSN	60443	**3506**	**4W-25S**	**D7**
211th St					
600	DYR	46311	**3510**		**E6**
3200	LYWD	60411	**3510**	**4E-25S**	**B7**
212th Pl					
500	DYR	46311	**3510**		**D7**
3600	MTSN	60443	**3594**	**4W-25S**	**E1**
212th St					
600	DYR	46311	**3510**		**E7**
213th Pl					
500	DYR	46311	**3510**		**D7**
3500	MTSN	60443	**3594**	**4W-25S**	**D1**
213th St					
400	DYR	46311	**3510**		**D7**
3900	MTSN	60443	**3594**	**4W-25S**	**D1**
214th Pl					
3600	MTSN	60443	**3594**	**4W-25S**	**D1**
214th St					
500	DYR	46311	**3510**		**D7**
3900	MTSN	60443	**3594**	**4W-25S**	**D1**
215th Pl					
1600	SLVL	60411	**3597**	**2E-26S**	**C2**
2200	BlmT	60411	**3597**	**2E-26S**	**D2**
215th St					
400	DYR	46311	**3510**		**C7**
3600	MTSN	60443	**3594**	**4W-26S**	**D1**
216th Ct					
2000	SLVL	60411	**3597**	**2E-26S**	**D2**
216th Pl					
1600	SLVL	60411	**3597**	**2E-26S**	**C2**
3600	MTSN	60443	**3594**	**4W-26S**	**D2**
216th St					
1600	SLVL	60411	**3597**	**2E-26S**	**C2**
3600	MTSN	60443	**3594**	**5W-26S**	**C1**
217th Pl					
2000	SLVL	60411	**3597**	**2E-26S**	**D2**
217th St					
500	BlmT	60411	**3596**	**0E-26S**	**E2**
500	BlmT	60411	**3597**	**0E-26S**	**A2**
500	SLVL	60411	**3597**	**0E-26S**	**A2**
3600	MTSN	60443	**3594**	**4W-26S**	**D2**
218th Pl					
1800	SLVL	60411	**3597**	**2E-26S**	**C2**
3400	MTSN	60443	**3594**	**4W-26S**	**E2**
218th St					
1700	SLVL	60411	**3597**	**2E-26S**	**C2**
3400	MTSN	60443	**3594**	**4W-26S**	**E2**
3400	PKFT	60466	**3594**	**4W-26S**	**E2**
219th Pl					
1800	SLVL	60411	**3597**	**2E-26S**	**D3**
219th St					
500	BlmT	60411	**3596**	**0E-26S**	**E2**
500	BlmT	60411	**3597**	**0E-26S**	**A2**
500	SLVL	60411	**3596**	**0E-26S**	**E2**
500	SLVL	60411	**3597**	**0E-26S**	**A2**
3900	MTSN	60443	**3594**	**4W-26S**	**D2**
3900	RNPK	60443	**3594**	**4W-26S**	**D2**
3900	RNPK	60471	**3594**	**4W-26S**	**D2**
220th St					
2200	SLVL	60411	**3597**	**2E-26S**	**D3**
221st St					
1800	SLVL	60411	**3597**	**2E-26S**	**D3**
222nd Pl					
2400	SLVL	60411	**3597**	**2E-26S**	**D3**
222nd St					
2400	SLVL	60411	**3597**	**2E-26S**	**D3**
223rd Pl					
1800	SLVL	60411	**3597**	**2E-27S**	**D3**
2200	BlmT	60411	**3597**	**2E-27S**	**D3**
2800	SLVL	60411	**3598**	**3E-27S**	**A3**
E 223rd St					
1900	SLVL	60411	**3597**	**2E-27S**	**D3**
2400	BlmT	60411	**3597**	**2E-27S**	**D3**
2800	BlmT	60411	**3598**	**3E-26S**	**B3**
2900	SLVL	60411	**3598**	**3E-27S**	**A3**
224th Ct					
1600	SLVL	60411	**3597**	**2E-27S**	**C3**
224th Pl					
2800	SLVL	60411	**3597**	**3E-27S**	**E4**
2800	SLVL	60411	**3598**	**3E-27S**	**A4**
224th St					
1700	SLVL	60411	**3597**	**2E-27S**	**C4**
2800	SLVL	60411	**3598**	**3E-27S**	**A3**
225th Pl					
2800	SLVL	60411	**3597**	**3E-27S**	**E4**
2900	SLVL	60411	**3598**	**3E-27S**	**A4**
225th St					
1700	SLVL	60411	**3597**	**2E-27S**	**C4**
2800	SLVL	60411	**3598**	**3E-27S**	**A4**
226th Pl					
2800	SLVL	60411	**3597**	**3E-27S**	**E4**
2800	SLVL	60411	**3598**	**3E-27S**	**A4**
263rd St					
900	CteT	60417	**3686**	**1E-31S**	**B6**
265th St					
900	CteT	60417	**3686**	**1E-32S**	**B7**

Chicago & Cook County Points of Interest Index

Airports

FEATURE NAME Address City ZIP Code	MAP#	CGS	GRID
Chicago Midway, CHCG	3150	5W-6S	A3
Chicago-O'Hare International, SRPK	2973	13W-5N	A1
FBM Company Landing Strip, MonT	3684	4W-29S	A2
Haedtler Landing Strip, UYPK	3594	5W-28S	B6
Lansing Municipal, LNSG	3510	4E-23S	B2
Palwaukee Municipal, WLNG	2755	13W-16N	D7
Schaumburg Municipal Helistop, SMBG	2859	22W-11N	D2
Schaumburg Regional, SMBG	2912	24W-8N	D3

Beaches, Harbors & Water Rec

FEATURE NAME Address City ZIP Code	MAP#	CGS	GRID
12th Street Beach, CHCG	3034	0E-1S	E7
A1 Millennium Marina, BNHM	3351	2E-16S	D3
Ardmore Hollywood Beach, CHCG	2921	1W-7N	E4
Beach, SBTN	2803	26W-14N	C4
Belmont Harbor, CHCG	2978	0W-3N	B3
Chicago Yacht Club, CHCG	3034	0E-0S	D4
Chicago Yacht Club, CHCG	2978	0W-4N	A3
Clark Street Beach, EVTN	2867	2W-11N	C2
Columbia Yacht Club, CHCG	3034	0E-0N	D4
Croissant Marina, BNHM	3351	2E-16S	D3
Crowleys Yacht Yard, CHCG	3091	1W-2S	E2
Dempster Street Beach, EVTN	2867	2W-11N	C3
Foster Avenue Beach, CHCG	2922	0W-6N	A5
Hammond Marina, HMND	3280		E2
Lee Street Beach, EVTN	2867	1W-10N	C4
Loyola Avenue Beach, CHCG	2921	1W-8N	E2
Loyola Beach, CHCG	2921	1W-8N	D1
Montrose Harbor, CHCG	2922	0W-5N	A7
Montrose-Wilson Beach, CHCG	2922	0W-5N	B7
North Avenue Beach, CHCG	2978	0E-2N	C7
Oak Street Beach, CHCG	3034	0E-1N	C2
Ohio Street Beach, CHCG	3034	0E-0N	D3
Public Beach, GLNC	2758	5W-18N	E4
Public Beach, KLWH	2812	3W-15N	D3
South Boulevard Beach, EVTN	2867	1W-10N	C5
South Branch Marina, CHCG	3092	0W-2S	A2
South Pier, CHCG	3034	0E-0N	D3
Triplex Marina, RVDL	3350	0W-15S	A1
Yacht Harbor, CHCG	3153	2E-7S	C5

Buildings

FEATURE NAME Address City ZIP Code	MAP#	CGS	GRID
80th Avenue Industrial Park MKNA, 60448	3504	10W-22S	C1
Abbott Laboratories 1 E 95th St, CHCG, 60628	3214	0E-11S	C6
Allstate 2775 Sanders Rd, NfdT, 60062	2809	12W-15N	B2
Ameritech 12601 S Pulaski Rd, ALSP, 60803	3276	4W-14S	C7
Amoco Oil 2939 S Calumet Av, HMND, 46320	3352		E1
Annico Business Park HMGN, 60441	3422	16W-18S	A1
Argonne National Laboratory DGvT, 60439	3271	18W-11S	A1
AT&T Corporate Center 227 W Monroe St, CHCG, 60606	3034	0W-0S	B5
Baxter International 1 Baxter Pkwy, WdfT, 60015	2756	12W-20N	B1
Brunswick 520 Lake Cook Rd, DRFD, 60062	2757	10W-18N	A2
Carbide & Carbon Building 230 N Michigan Av, CHCG, 60601	3034	0E-0N	C4
Centex Industrial Park Lunt Av, EGVV, 60007	2915	16W-8N	D2
Chicago Board of Trade Building 141 W Jackson Blvd, CHCG, 60604	3034	0W-0S	B5
Corporate Corridors W 191st St, MKNA, 60448	3504	11W-23S	A2
Donohue Building 711 S Dearborn St, CHCG, 60605	3034	0W-0S	B6
Equitable Building 401 N Michigan Av, CHCG, 60611	3034	0E-0N	C3
Federal Center & Plaza 219 S Dearborn St, CHCG, 60604	3034	0W-0S	B5
Fine Arts Building 410 S Michigan Av, CHCG, 60605	3034	0E-0S	C5
First National Bank Plaza 1 W Monroe St, CHCG, 60603	3034	0W-0S	B5
Fisher Building 343 S Dearborn St, CHCG, 60604	3034	0W-0S	B5
Flat Iron Building 1581 N Milwaukee Av, CHCG, 60622	3033	2W-1N	C1
Ford Motor Company-Assembly Plant CHCG, 60633	3279	2E-14S	D6
Ford Motor Stamping Plant CHHT, 60411	3596	0E-25S	E1
Fox River Business Park ELGN, 60123	2801	34W-14N	A6
Franklin Building 720 S Dearborn St, CHCG, 60605	3034	0W-0S	B6
General Motors Electro-Motive MCCK, 60525	3147	11W-5S	D2
Governors Gateway Industrial Park UYPK, 60466	3682	7W-30S	D3
Higgins Industrial Park Brummel Dr, EGVV, 60007	2861	17W-9N	C6
Hilton Chicago & Towers 720 S Michigan Av, CHCG, 60605	3034	0E-0S	C6
Hoffman Tower 3910 Riverwald Dr, LYNS, 60534	3088	10W-4S	B6
Illinois Center N Michigan Av, CHCG, 60601	3034	0E-0N	C4
Internationale Centre WDRG, 60517	3270	20W-12S	A2
Internationale Centre Business Park WDRG, 60517	3270	20W-12S	B2
Jewel Food Stores 1955 W North Av, MLPK, 60160	3029	11W-1N	D1
John Hancock Center 875 N Michigan Av, CHCG, 60611	3034	0E-1N	C2
Kraft General Foods 555 Three Lakes Dr, NHFD, 60093	2810	8W-16N	E1
Lake Business Center MNSR, 46321	3510		E2
Marquette Building 140 S Dearborn St, CHCG, 60603	3034	0W-0S	B5
Merchandise Mart 222 W North Bank Dr, CHCG, 60606	3034	0W-0N	A4
Mi-Jack Corporation HLCT, 60429	3427	3W-20S	A3
Motorola Corporate Headquarters 1303 E Algonquin Rd, SMBG, 60173	2805	21W-13N	D7
Motorola Corporate Office Tower Tower Cir Dr, SMBG, 60173	2805	22W-12N	D7
NBC Tower 455 N Cityfront Plaza Dr, CHCG, 60611	3034	0E-0N	C3
Northwest Tower Building 1600 N Milwaukee Av, CHCG, 60647	2977	2W-2N	B7
One Financial Place 440 S Lasalle St, CHCG, 60605	3034	0W-0S	B5
One South Dearborn 21 S Clark St, CHCG, 60603	3034	0W-0S	B4
Pontiac Building 542 S Dearborn St, CHCG, 60605	3034	0W-0S	B5
Prudential Building 130 E Randolph St, CHCG, 60601	3034	0E-0N	C4
Rand McNally Corporate Headquarters 8255 Central Park Av, SKOK, 60076	2866	4W-10N	C5
Reliance Building 32 N State St, CHCG, 60602	3034	0W-0N	C4
River East Center E Illinois St, CHCG, 60611	3034	0E-0N	D3
Santa Fe Building 224 S Michigan Av, CHCG, 60604	3034	0E-0S	C5
Sears Merchandise Headquarters Sears Pkwy, HFET, 60192	2802	29W-13N	B5
Sears Tower 233 S Wacker Dr, CHCG, 60606	3034	0W-0S	A5
South Barrington Executive Center Executive Ct, SBTN, 60010	2803	26W-13N	E5
South Barrington Office Center W Higgins Rd, SBTN, 60010	2803	27W-13N	A7
Stone Container Building 150 N Michigan Av, CHCG, 60601	3034	0E-0N	C4
The Chicago Sun-Times 401 N Wabash Av, CHCG, 60611	3034	0E-0N	C4
The Rookery Building 209 S Lasalle St, CHCG, 60604	3034	0W-0S	B5
Time Life Building 303 E Ohio St, CHCG, 60611	3034	0E-0N	C3
Tootsie Roll Industries 7401 S Cicero Av, CHCG, 60629	3150	5W-8S	A7
Tribune Tower 435 N Michigan Av, CHCG, 60611	3034	0E-0N	C3
Trompe L'Oeil Building 1207 W Division St, CHCG, 60622	3033	1W-1N	D2
Underwriters Laboratories NHBK, 60062	2756	10W-18N	E3
United Airlines 1200 E Algonquin Rd, EGvT, 60005	2861	16W-10N	D4
Walgreen Company Corporate-Headquarters 200 Wilmot Rd, WdfT, 60015	2756	12W-20N	C2
Water Filtration Plant Park Dr, CHCG, 60611	3034	0E-0N	E2
Water Filtration Plant CHCG, 60649	3216	4E-8S	A1
Water Tower Place 835 N Michigan Av, CHCG, 60611	3034	0E-1N	C2
William Wrigley Jr Company 3535 S Ashland Av, CHCG, 60609	3091	1W-3S	D5
Wrigley Building 400 N Michigan Av, CHCG, 60611	3034	0E-0N	C3
WW Grainger 5500 Howard St, SKOK, 60077	2865	7W-9N	C6
Zenith Electronics 1000 Milwaukee Av, GNVW, 60025	2809	11W-13N	C6

Buildings - Governmental

FEATURE NAME Address City ZIP Code	MAP#	CGS	GRID
Administration Building S Cicero Av, CHCG, 60638	3150	5W-6S	A4
Administrative Office Ill Court 222 N Lasalle St, CHCG, 60601	3034	0W-0N	B4
Alsip Village Hall 4500 W 123rd St, ALSP, 60803	3276	5W-14S	B6
Appellate Court 1st District 160 N Lasalle St, CHCG, 60601	3034	0W-0N	B4
Arlington Heights Vil Hall & Vil-Board 3436 N Kennicott Av, ANHT, 60004	2753	18W-17N	E4
Barrington Hills Village Hall 112 Algonquin Rd, BNHL, 60010	2750	28W-16N	A7
Barrington Twp Office 620 S Hough St, BRTN, 60010	2750	25W-18N	E3
Barrington Village Hall 200 S Hough St, BRTN, 60010	2750	25W-18N	E2
Bartlett Village Hall 228 S Main St, BRLT, 60103	2910	29W-8N	E3
Bedford Park Village Hall 6701 S Archer Rd, BDPK, 60501	3148	9W-7S	C6
Beecher Village Hall 724 Penfield St, BCHR, 60401	3864	0W-36S	C2
Bellwood Village Hall 3200 Washington Blvd, BLWD, 60104	3029	12W-0N	B4
Bensenville Village Hall 700 W Irving Park Rd, BNVL, 60106	2915	16W-5N	E7
Berkeley Village Hall 5819 Electric Av, BKLY, 60163	3028	14W-0N	C4
Berwyn City Hall 6700 26th St, BRWN, 60402	3089	8W-2S	A3
Bloomingdale Twp Office 123 Rosedale Av, BmdT, 60108	2912	23W-6N	E7
Bloom Twp Municipal Office 21460 E Lincoln Hwy, LYWD, 60411	3510	4E-25S	B7
Blue Island City Hall 2434 Vermont St, BLID, 60406	3349	3W-15S	B1
Bremen Twp Hall Kedzie Av, MKHM, 60426	3427	3W-19S	A3
Bridgeview 5th District Court 10220 S 76th Av, BGVW, 60455	3274	9W-11S	D1
Bridgeview Village Hall 7500 S Oketo Av, BGVW, 60455	3210	9W-8S	D1
Broadview Village Hall 2350 S 25th Av, BDVW, 60155	3029	12W-1S	C7
Brookfield Village Hall 8820 Brookfield Av, BKFD, 60513	3088	10W-3S	A5
Buffalo Grove Village Hall 50 Raupp Blvd, BFGV, 60089	2754	17W-18N	C2
Burbank City Hall 6530 W 79th St, BRBK, 60459	3211	8W-8S	A2
Burr Ridge Village Hall 7660 S County Line Rd, BRRG, 60527	3208	15W-8S	C2
Calumet City Hall 204 Pulaski Rd, CTCY, 60409	3352	4E-17S	C6
Calumet Park Village Hall 12409 S Throop St, CTPK, 60827	3277	1W-14S	E6
Carpentersville Village Hall 1200 LW Besinger Dr, CPVL, 60110	2748	33W-17N	B7
Chicago City Hall 121 N Lasalle St, CHCG, 60602	3034	0W-0N	B4
Chicago Heights City Hall 1601 Chicago Rd, CHHT, 60411	3596	1W-25S	A1
Chicago Public School Administration-HQs W Pershing Rd, CHCG, 60609	3091	2W-4S	C6
Chicago Ridge Village Hall 10455 Ridgeland Av, CHRG, 60415	3275	7W-12S	B1
Chicago Youth Center 100 N Western Av, CHCG, 60612	3033	3W-0N	A4
Cicero Town Hall 4936 W 26th St, CCRO, 60804	3089	6W-2S	E2
Circuit Court Clerk 2245 W Ogden Av, CHCG, 60612	3033	2W-0S	B6
Circuit Court Clerk 9511 Harrison St, MaiT, 60016	2863	11W-12N	C1
Circuit Court Clerk 200 E Wood St, PLTN, 60067	2752	20W-16N	E7
Clerk Office Ridge Rd, LNSG, 60438	3430	3E-21S	A6
Clerk of the Circuit Court 28 N Clark St, CHCG, 60602	3034	0W-0N	B4
Clerk of the Circuit Courts 5555 W Grand Av, CHCG, 60639	2975	6W-2N	D6
Clerk's Office 1500 Maybrook Dr, MYWD, 60153	3030	10W-0S	B5
Comm Unit Sch District 300 Board of-Edu 300 Cleveland Av, CPVL, 60110	2801	33W-16N	A1
Cook County Building 118 N Clark St, CHCG, 60602	3034	0W-0N	B4
Cook County Circuit Court 55 W Randolph St, CHCG, 60602	3034	0W-0N	B4
Cook County Circuit Court 1340 S Michigan Av, CHCG, 60605	3034	0E-1S	C7
Cook County Circuit Court 155 W 51st St, CHCG, 60609	3152	0W-5S	B2
Cook County Circuit Court 321 N Lasalle Blvd, CHCG, 60610	3034	0W-0N	B4
Cook County Circuit Court 3150 W Flournoy St, CHCG, 60612	3032	3W-0S	E6
Cook County Circuit Court 2452 W Belmont Av, CHCG, 60618	2977	3W-4N	A3
Cook County Circuit Court 937 N Wood St, CHCG, 60622	3033	2W-1N	C2
Cook County Circuit Court 2600 S California Av, CHCG, 60623	3091	3W-2S	A3
Cook County Circuit Court 727 E 111th St, CHCG, 60628	3278	0E-13S	E3
Cook County Circuit Court 5555 W Grand Av, CHCG, 60639	2975	6W-2N	D6
Cook County Criminal Court 2600 S California Blvd, CHCG, 60608	3091	3W-2S	A3
Cook County Department of Health 1010 Lake St, OKPK, 60301	3030	8W-0N	E3
Country Club Hills Village Hall 3700 175th Pl, CCHL, 60478	3426	4W-21S	D5
Countryside City Hall 5550 East Av, CTSD, 60525	3147	12W-6S	D3
County Clerk N Meadow Dr, WLMT, 60091	2812	5W-13N	A6
Court of Appeals-Province Chicago 20 N Wacker Dr, CHCG, 60606	3034	0W-0N	B4
Crestwood Village Hall 13840 Cicero Av, CTWD, 60445	3348	5W-16S	A3
Crete Village Hall 524 W Exchange St, CRTE, 60417	3685	1W-29S	B2
Crossroads Adult Transition Center 3210 W Arthington St, CHCG, 60624	3032	4W-0S	D6
Daley Civic Center 50 W Washington St, CHCG, 60602	3034	0W-0N	B4
Department Adm Hearings 400 W Superior St, CHCG, 60610	3034	0W-0N	A3
Department of Justice 230 S Wood St, CHCG, 60612	3033	2W-0S	C5
Des Plaines City Hall 1420 Miner St, DSPN, 60016	2863	13W-11N	A3
Dixmoor Village Hall 170 W 145th St, HRVY, 60426	3349	2W-17S	E5
Dolton Village Hall 14014 Park Av, DLTN, 60419	3350	0E-16S	D3
Dyer Town Hall Hart St, DYR, 46311	3598		D2
East Dundee Village Hall 120 Barrington Av, EDND, 60118	2801	33W-16N	A2
East Hazel Crest City Hall 1904 174th St, EHZC, 60429	3427	2W-20S	D5
Elk Grove Twp Hall 2400 S Arlington Heights Rd, ANHT, 60005	2861	18W-11N	A3
Elk Grove Village Hall 901 Wellington Av, EGVV, 60007	2914	19W-8N	C2
Elmhurst City Hall 209 N York St, EMHT, 60126	3028	15W-1N	A1
Elmwood Park Village Hall 11 W Conti Pkwy, EDPK, 60707	2974	9W-3N	C5
Evanston City Hall 1200 Ridge Av, EVTN, 60201	2867	2W-12N	B1
Evergreen Park Village Hall 9418 S Kedzie Av, ENGN, 60805	3212	4W-10S	E5
Federal Court 194 E Delaware Pl, CHCG, 60611	3034	0E-1N	C2
Flossmoor Village Hall 2800 Flossmoor Rd, FSMR, 60422	3507	3W-23S	B2
Ford Heights Village Hall 1343 Ellis Av, FDHT, 60411	3509	1E-25S	A7
Forest Park City Hall 517 Des Plaines Av, FTPK, 60130	3030	9W-0S	C5
Forest View Village Hall 7000 46th St, FTVW, 60402	3088	8W-4S	E7
Franklin Park Village Hall 9545 W Belmont Av, FNPK, 60131	2973	11W-3N	C4
Glencoe Village Hall 325 Hazel Av, GLNC, 60022	2758	6W-17N	D5
Glenview Village Hall 1225 Waukegan Rd, GNVW, 60025	2810	8W-13N	E5
Glenwood Village Hall 13 S Rebecca St, GNWD, 60425	3508	0E-22S	D2
Golf Village Hall 1 Briar Rd, GLF, 60029	2864	8W-12N	E1
Hammond City Court 5925 S Calumet Av, HMND, 46320	3430		E1
Hammond City Hall 5925 S Calumet Av, HMND, 46320	3430		E1
Hanover Park Village Hall 2121 W Lake St, HRPK, 60133	2911	27W-8N	C3
Harvey City Hall 15320 Broadway Av, HRVY, 60426	3350	1W-18S	A7
Harwood Heights Village Hall 7300 W Wilson Av, HDHT, 60706	2918	9W-5N	D7
Hazel Crest City Hall 3000 Kaindl Dr, HLCT, 60429	3427	3W-20S	A4
Hickory Hills Village Hall 8652 W 95th St, HYHL, 60457	3210	10W-10S	A6
Hillside Village Hall 30 N Wolf Rd, HLSD, 60162	3028	14W-0S	D6
Hinsdale Village Hall 19 W Chicago Av, HNDL, 60521	3146	15W-4S	B1
Hodgkins Village Hall 8990 Lyons St, HGKN, 60525	3147	11W-7S	D6
Hoffman Estates Village Hall 1900 Hassell Rd, HFET, 60195	2804	25W-12N	A7
Homer Glen Village Hall 14331 S Golden Oak Dr, HMGN, 60441	3343	16W-17S	E4
Homer TWP Administration Center W 151st St, HMGN, 60441	3343	18W-17S	B6
Hometown City Hall 4331 Southwest Hwy, HMTN, 60456	3212	5W-10S	B5
Homewood Village Hall 2020 Chestnut Rd, HMWD, 60430	3427	2W-21S	D6
House Of Corrections S California Av, CHCG, 60623	3091	3W-2S	A3
Illinois Forest District Appellate-Court 160 N Lasalle St, CHCG, 60601	3034	0W-0N	B4
Illinois Supreme Court 160 N Lasalle St, CHCG, 60601	3030	0W-0N	B4
Indian Head Park Village Hall 201 Acacia Dr, IHPK, 60525	3146	13W-7S	E6
Inverness Village Hall 1400 Baldwin Rd, IVNS, 60067	2752	22W-17N	A6
Itasca Village Hall 100 W Irving Park Rd, ITSC, 60143	2914	20W-6N	B6

Buildings - Governmental

FEATURE NAME	Address City ZIP Code	MAP#	CGS	GRID
Jessie Houston Adult Transition-Center	14127 Leavitt Av, DXMR, 60426	3349	2W-16S	C4
Judicary Courts of the State Ill	222 N Lasalle St, CHCG, 60601	3034	0W-0N	B4
Justice Village Hall	7800 S Archer Rd, JSTC, 60458	3210	11W-8S	A2
Kenilworth Village Hall	419 Richmond Rd, KLWH, 60043	2812	4W-14N	C4
La Grange Park Village Hall	447 N Catherine Av, LGPK, 60525	3087	12W-3S	B6
La Grange Village Hall	53 S La Grange Rd, LGNG, 60525	3087	12W-4S	C7
Lake County Superior Court	232 Russell St, HMND, 46320	3352		D6
Lansing Village Hall	18200 Chicago Av, LNSG, 60438	3430	3E-21S	A6
Lemont Twp Office	16020 W 127th St, LMNT, 60439	3342	20W-15S	C1
Lemont Village Hall	418 Main St, LMNT, 60439	3270	19W-13S	D5
Lincolnwood Village Hall	6900 N Lincoln Av, LNWD, 60712	2920	5W-8N	B1
Lyons Village Hall	7801 Ogden Av, LYNS, 60534	3088	9W-4S	C6
Maine Twp Hall	1700 W Ballard Rd, MaiT, 60068	2863	11W-11N	E3
Markham 6th District Court	16501 Kedzie Av, MKHM, 60426	3427	3W-19S	A3
Markham City Hall	16313 Kedzie Av, MKHM, 60426	3427	3W-19S	A2
Matteson Village Hall	4900 Village Coms, MTSN, 60443	3506	6W-24S	A6
Maywood 4th District Court	1500 Maybrook Dr, MYWD, 60153	3030	10W-0S	B5
Maywood Village Hall	115 S 5th Av, MYWD, 60153	3030	10W-0N	A4
McCook Village Hall	5000 Glencoe Av, MCCK, 60525	3148	10W-5S	B2
Melrose Park Village Hall	706 N 18th Av, MLPK, 60160	3029	11W-1N	D3
Merrionette Park Village Hall	11720 S Kedzie Av, MTPK, 60803	3276	4W-13S	E4
Midlothian Village Hall	14801 Pulaski Rd, MDLN, 60445	3348	4W-17S	C5
Monee Branch Court	5130 W Court St, MONE, 60449	3683	6W-31S	A5
Monee Village Hall	5130 W Court St, MONE, 60449	3683	6W-31S	A5
Morton Grove Village Hall	6101 Capulina Av, MNGV, 60053	2865	7W-10N	B4
Mt Prospect Village Hall	100 S Emerson St, MPPT, 60056	2808	15W-12N	A7
Munster Town Hall	1005 Ridge Rd, MNSR, 46321	3430		E7
National Safety Council	1121 Spring Lake Dr, ITSC, 60143	2914	20W-6N	A7
Native American Education Service	2838 W Peterson Av, CHCG, 60659	2920	3W-7N	E4
Niles Twp Hall	5255 Main St, SKOK, 60077	2865	6W-10N	D5
Niles Village Hall	1000 Civic Center Dr, NLES, 60714	2864	8W-9N	E6
Norridge Village Hall	4020 N Olcott Av, NRDG, 60706	2974	9W-5N	C2
Northbrook Village Hall	1225 Cedar Ln, NHBK, 60062	2757	10W-17N	B5
Northfield Village Hall	361 S Happ Rd, NHFD, 60093	2811	6W-15N	C2
Northlake City Hall	55 E North Av, NHLK, 60164	3028	13W-1N	D1
North Lawndale Adult Transition-Center	2839 W Fillmore St, CHCG, 60612	3032	3W-0S	E6
North Riverside Village Hall	2400 Des Plaines Av, NRIV, 60546	3088	10W-2S	B2
North Twp Hall	5947 S Hohman Av, HMND, 46320	3430		D1
Oak Forest City Hall	15440 Central Av, OKFT, 60452	3347	7W-18S	D7
Oak Park Village Hall	1 Madison St, OKPK, 60304	3031	7W-0S	B5
Olympia Fields Village Hall	20701 Governors Hwy, OMFD, 60461	3506	4W-25S	D6
Orland Hills Village Hall	16033 S 94th Av, ODHL, 60477	3423	11W-19S	E2
Orland Park Village Hall	14700 S Ravinia Av, ODPK, 60462	3345	12W-17S	D5
Palatine Village Hall	200 E Wood St, PLTN, 60067	2752	20W-16N	E7
Palos Heights City Hall	7607 119th St, PSHT, 60463	3274	9W-14S	D5
Palos Hills City Hall	10335 S Roberts Rd, PSHL, 60465	3274	9W-12S	C1
Palos Park Village Hall	8901 W 123rd St, PSPK, 60464	3274	11W-14S	A6
Park Forest Village Hall	350 Victory Dr, PKFT, 60466	3595	3W-27S	B4
Park Ridge City Hall	505 Butler Pl, PKRG, 60068	2918	10W-8N	B1
Peotone Village Hall	208 E Main St, PTON, 60468	3861	9W-37S	A3
Phoenix Village Hall	15240 Vincennes Rd, PHNX, 60426	3350	0W-18S	B6
Posen Village Hall	2440 W 147th St, POSN, 60469	3349	3W-17S	B5
Prospect Heights City Hall	14 E Camp McDonald Rd, PTHT, 60070	2808	15W-15N	A3
Public Works Facilities	Bittersweet Dr, BRLT, 60103	2911	28W-6N	B6
Richton Park Village Hall	4455 Sauk Tr, RNPK, 60471	3594	5W-27S	C3
Riverdale Village Hall	325 W 144th St, RVDL, 60827	3350	0W-16S	C4
River Forest Twp Hall	8020 Madison St, RVFT, 60305	3030	10W-0N	B5
River Forest Village Hall	400 Park Av, RVFT, 60305	3030	9W-0N	C4
River Grove Village Hall	2601 N Thatcher Av, RVGV, 60171	2974	10W-3N	A5
Riverside Village Hall	27 Riverside Rd, RVSD, 60546	3088	9W-3S	C5
Riverwoods Village Hall	300 Portwine Rd, RVWD, 60015	2755	13W-20N	E1
Robbins Village Hall	3327 W 137th St, RBBN, 60472	3348	4W-16S	E2
Rolling Meadows 3rd District Court	2121 Euclid Av, RGMW, 60008	2806	19W-14N	D4
Rolling Meadows City Hall	3600 Kirchoff Rd, RGMW, 60008	2806	20W-13N	B5
Roselle Village Hall	31 S Prospect St, ROSL, 60172	2913	23W-7N	A4
Rosemont Village Hall	9501 E Devon Av, RSMT, 60018	2917	11W-7N	C3
Safety & Justice Building	S Halsted St, CHHT, 60411	3596	0W-25S	B1
Sauk Village Town Hall	21701 Torrence Av, SLVL, 60411	3597	3E-26S	E2
Schaumburg Village Hall	101 Schaumburg Ct, SMBG, 60193	2859	22W-10N	B5
Schiller Park Village Hall	9526 Irving Park Rd, SRPK, 60176	2973	11W-5N	C1
Skokie 2nd District Court	5600 Old Orchard Rd, SKOK, 60077	2811	7W-12N	C7
Skokie Court House	5600 Old Orchard Rd, SKOK, 60077	2811	7W-12N	C7
Skokie Village Hall	5127 Oakton St, SKOK, 60077	2865	6W-9N	D6
South Barrington Village Hall	30 S Barrington Rd, SBTN, 60010	2803	26W-13N	E6
South Chicago Heights Village Hall	2729 Chicago Rd, SCHT, 60411	3596	1W-27S	B4
South Holland Village Hall	16226 Wausau Av, SHLD, 60473	3428	0E-19S	D1
Steger Village Hall	35 W Steger Rd, STGR, 60475	3596	1W-27S	A5
Stickney Village Hall	6533 Pershing Rd, SKNY, 60402	3089	8W-4S	A6
Stone Park Village Hall	1629 N Mannheim Rd, SNPK, 60165	3029	12W-1N	A2
Streamwood Village Hall	301 E Irving Park Rd, SMWD, 60107	2857	28W-9N	A7
Summit Village Hall	5810 S Archer Rd, SMMT, 60501	3148	9W-6S	D4
Thornton Twp Hall	333 E 162nd St, SHLD, 60473	3428	0E-19S	E1
Thornton Village Hall	115 E Margaret St, TNTN, 60476	3428	0E-21S	D6
Tinley Park Village Hall	16250 Oak Park Av, TYPK, 60477	3425	8W-19S	A2
United States Courthouse	219 S Dearborn St, CHCG, 60604	3034	0W-0S	B5
United States District Court	507 E State St, HMND, 46320	3352		D6
University Park Village Hall	698 Burnham Dr, UYPK, 60466	3684	3W-29S	A1
Westchester Village Hall	10240 W Roosevelt Rd, WSTR, 60154	3029	12W-0S	B7
West Dundee Village Hall	102 S 2nd St, WDND, 60118	2801	34W-16N	A2
Western Springs Village Hall	740 Hillgrove Av, WNSP, 60558	3086	13W-4S	E7
West Side Adult Transition Center	121 N Campbell Av, CHCG, 60612	3033	3W-0N	A4
Wheeling Village Hall	255 W Dundee Rd, WLNG, 60090	2755	14W-18N	B4
Willow Springs Village Hall	8480 Archer Av, WLSP, 60480	3209	12W-9S	C3
Wilmette Village Hall	1200 Wilmette Av, WLMT, 60091	2812	3W-13N	D6
Winnetka Village Hall	510 Green Bay Rd, WNKA, 60093	2812	5W-15N	B2
Wood Dale City Hall	404 N Wood Dale Rd, WDDL, 60191	2915	18W-6N	A7
Worth Twp Hall	11601 S Pulaski Rd, ALSP, 60803	3276	4W-13S	C4
Worth Village Hall	7112 W 111th St, WRTH, 60482	3274	8W-12S	E3

Cemeteries

FEATURE NAME	MAP#	CGS	GRID
Acacia Cem, CHCG	2974	10W-5N	B1
Adams Cem, CRTE	3685	1W-29S	A2
All Saints Cem, CHCG	2917	11W-7N	D4
All Saints Cem, DSPN	2808	13W-12N	E7
Archer Woods Cem, HYHL	3209	11W-9S	E3
Arlington Cem, EMHT	2972	15W-2N	B7
Arlington Heights Cem, ANHT	2807	16W-14N	D4
Assumption Cem, BlmT	3508	0E-23S	E4
Bethania Cem, JSTC	3210	10W-8S	A2
Bethel & Ridgeland Cem, CHCG	2920	5W-7N	B4
Beverly Cem, WthT	3276	3W-14S	E5
Bluff City Cem, ELGN	2855	32W-10N	D7
Bohemian National Cem, CHCG	2920	4W-6N	C5
Bronswood Cem, OKBK	3086	16W-3S	A6
Burr Oak Cem, ALSP	3276	5W-14S	A6
Calvary Cem, BlmT	3595	2W-27S	C5
Calvary Cem, EVTN	2867	2W-9N	C6
Cedar Park Cem, CTPK	3278	1W-14S	A6
Chapel Hill Gardens South Cem, OKLN	3275	6W-13S	D3
Concordia Cem, FTPK	3030	9W-0S	B5
Concordia Cem, HMND	3430		E2
County Cem, BmnT	3426	5W-19S	C1
Crete Cem, CRTE	3685	1W-29S	B2
Danish Cem, LMNT	3342	20W-15S	C1
Deerfield Cem, DRFD	2756	10W-20N	E1
Dundee Twp Cem East, EDND	2801	32W-15N	C3
Eden Memorial Park, SRPK	2973	12W-5N	B1
Elk Grove Cem, EGVV	2861	18W-11N	A4
Elm Lawn Mausoleum & Cem, EMHT	2972	15W-2N	B7
Elmwood Memorial Cem, RVGV	2974	10W-3N	A4
Evergreen Cem, BRTN	2750	26W-18N	E3
Evergreen Cem, ENGN	3212	4W-9S	D4
Evergreen Hills Memorial Gardens, -CteT	3596	1W-28S	A7
Fairmount-Willow Hills Cem, PlsT	3209	13W-10S	A6
Fairview Memorial Park Cem, NHLK	2972	14W-3N	D6
First Evangelical Lutheran Cem, ALSP	3276	5W-15S	C7
Forest Home Cem, FTPK	3030	10W-0S	B6
Fullersburg Cem, HNDL	3086	15W-4S	A7
Glencoe Pioneer Cem, HDPK	2758	7W-20N	C2
Glen Oak Cem, PvsT	3029	13W-1S	A7
Graceland Cem, CHCG	2977	1W-5N	D1
Hebrew Cem, CHCG	2977	1W-4N	D2
Holy Cross Cem, CTCY	3430	3E-18S	A1
Holy Sepulchre Cem, ALSP	3275	7W-13S	C3
Immanuel Cem, HLSD	3086	13W-2S	D2
Irving Park Boulevard Cem, CHCG	2974	9W-4N	B2
Jewish Cemeteries, FTPK	3030	9W-1S	C7
Jewish Waldheim Cem, NRIV	3088	9W-1S	D1
Knopf Cem, BFGV	2754	17W-20N	A1
Lakewood Memorial Park, HnrT	2856	30W-10N	A7
Lincoln Cem, WthT	3276	4W-14S	E6
Lithuanian National Cem, JSTC	3209	11W-9S	E3
Little Woods Cem, WYNE	2909	33W-7N	B5
Lutheran Cem, NLES	2864	8W-10N	D4
Lutheran Cem, TYPK	3425	7W-20S	C3
Maine Cem, PKRG	2917	11W-8N	D1
Mary Hill Cem, MaiT	2864	10W-10N	B4
Memorial Park Cem, SKOK	2866	5W-12N	A1
Memory Gardens Cem, ANHT	2807	16W-14N	D4
Menorah Gardens Cem, BDVW	3087	11W-1S	D1
Montrose Cem, CHCG	2920	5W-6N	B5
Mt Auburn Cem, SKNY	3089	8W-4S	A7
Mt Carmel Cem, HLSD	3028	14W-0S	C7
Mt Emblem Cem, EMHT	2972	15W-3N	B5
Mt Forest Cem, ThtT	3428	0E-20S	E5
Mt Glenwood Cem, BlmT	3428	0E-22S	D7
Mt Greenwood Cem, CHCG	3277	3W-12S	A2
Mt Hope Cem, CHCG	3277	3W-13S	A4
Mt Hope Cem, ELGN	2855	32W-10N	C6
Mt Mayriv Cem, CHCG	2975	8W-4N	A2
Mt Olive Cem, CHCG	2975	8W-4N	A2
Mt Olivet Cem, CHCG	3277	3W-13S	A3
Mt Vernon Memorial Estates, LMNT	3271	16W-14S	D6
Oak Glen Lutheran Cem, LNSG	3429	2E-21S	D6
Oak Hill Cem, HMND	3430		D2
Oak Hill Cem, PSPK	3346	11W-15S	A1
Oak Hill Cem, WthT	3276	4W-14S	D5
Oakland Cem, DLTN	3351	2E-17S	C6
Oak Lawn Cem, TNTN	3428	0W-21S	B6
Oak Ridge Cem, LNSG	3429	2E-21S	C6
Oak Ridge Cem, PvsT	3086	13W-1S	E1
Oakwoods Cem, CHCG	3152	1E-7S	E6
Orland-Tinley Park Cem, TYPK	3424	10W-20S	B4
Parkholm Cem, LGPK	3087	12W-2S	B3
Peotone Cem, WllT	3861	8W-37S	B3
Queen of Heaven Cem, PvsT	3086	14W-1S	C1
Randhill Park Cem, PltT	2753	18W-17N	D5
Resthaven Cem, CHCG	2916	15W-5N	B7
Restvale Cem, ALSP	3275	6W-13S	E4
Resurrection Cem, JSTC	3210	10W-8S	B1
Ridgewood Cem, MaiT	2863	11W-12N	D1
River Valley Memorial Gardens Cem, -WDND	2801	34W-14N	A5
Rosehill Cem, CHCG	2921	2W-7N	A4
Rosemont Cem, CHCG	2975	8W-4N	A2
Sacred Heart Cem, NHBK	2757	8W-18N	D4
Sacred Heart Cem, PlsT	3209	11W-11S	E7
St. Adalbert Cem, NLES	2918	8W-8N	E1
St. Alphonsus Cem, LMNT	3270	19W-14S	D7
St. Anne's Cem, PKFT	3595	4W-27S	A4
St. Benedict Catholic Cem, CTWD	3348	5W-15S	B2
St. Boniface Cem, CHCG	2921	1W-6N	D6
St. Casimir Lithuanian Cem, CHCG	3276	5W-13S	B3
St. Gabriel Cem, BmnT	3426	5W-19S	A2
St. James Cem, LmnT	3272	15W-12S	A2
St. James Cem, SLVL	3597	2E-26S	C3
St. Johannes Cem, CHCG	2916	15W-6N	B7
St. John's Cem, HGKN	3147	12W-7S	C6
St. John's Cem, WshT	3864	0E-37S	E4
St. Joseph's Cem, RVGV	2974	10W-3N	A4
St. Lucas Cem, CHCG	2920	5W-6N	B5
St. Luke's Cem, WshT	3864	0W-37S	D3
St. Mary's Cem, CHCG	3212	4W-10S	C4
St. Mathew Cem, LMNT	3270	20W-14S	C7
St. Michael the Archangel Cem, PLTN	2805	22W-13N	B6
St. Nicholas Cem, CHCG	2917	11W-7N	E4
St. Patrick's Cem, DGvT	3271	18W-11S	A1
St. Paul Cem, BlmT	3507	2W-23S	C4
St. Paul Lutheran Cem, MPPT	2807	15W-13N	E7
St. Paul's Cem, MONE	3683	6W-31S	A6
St. Paul's Cem, SKOK	2865	6W-10N	D4
St. Paul's Cem, WshT	3774	1W-36S	A7
St. Peter's Cem, SKOK	2865	6W-10N	E5
Skyline Memorial Park, MonT	3683	6W-30S	A2
Smyna German Cem, HRPK	2911	27W-7N	D5
SS Cyril & Methodius Cem, LMNT	3270	19W-14S	D7
Sunset Memorial Lawns, GNVW	2810	10W-15N	A3
Trinity Cem, CteT	3685	0W-30S	B3
Union Cem, BNHL	2749	30W-17N	B6
Union Ridge Cem, CHCG	2918	8W-6N	E5
Waldheim Cem, FTPK	3030	10W-0S	B6
Washington Memory Gardens, TNTN	3428	0W-21S	B7
Westlawn Cem, CHCG	2974	10W-5N	B1
Woodlawn Cem, FTPK	3088	9W-1S	C1
Wunders Cem, CHCG	2977	1W-4N	D2
Zion Cem, CteT	3685	0W-30S	B4
Zion Lutheran Cem, OMFD	3506	4W-25S	E7
Zion Luthern Cem, OKBK	3086	15W-3S	A6

Colleges & Universities

FEATURE NAME	Address City ZIP Code	MAP#	CGS	GRID
Catholic Theological Union Chicago	5401 S Cornell Av, CHCG, 60615	3153	2E-5S	B2
Chicago City Wide College	226 W Jackson Blvd, CHCG, 60606	3034	0W-0S	B5
Chicago National College of-Naprapathy	3333 N Milwaukee Av, CHCG, 60641	2976	4W-4N	B3
Chicago State University	9501 S Dr Martin L King Jr Dr, CHCG, 60628	3214	0E-11S	D6
Columbia College	600 S Michigan Av, CHCG, 60605	3034	0E-0S	C6
Concordia University	7400 Augusta St, RVFT, 60305	3030	9W-1N	D2
DePaul University-Lincoln Park-Campus	2250 N Kenmore Av, CHCG, 60614	2977	1W-2N	E6
DePaul University-Loop Campus	1 E Jackson Blvd, CHCG, 60604	3034	0E-0S	C5
DePaul University-Oak Forest Campus	16333 University Dr, OKFT, 60452	3426	5W-19S	C2
DePaul University-O'Hare Campus	3166 Des Plaines River Rd, DSPN, 60018	2917	11W-8N	D2
DePaul University-Rolling Meadows-Campus	2550 Golf Rd, RGMW, 60008	2860	19W-12N	C2
DeVry University	3300 N Campbell Av, CHCG, 60618	2977	3W-4N	A3
Dominican University	7900 Division St, RVFT, 60305	3030	9W-1N	B2
Dominican University-Priory Campus	7300 Division St, RVFT, 60305	3030	9W-1N	D1
East West University	816 S Michigan Av, CHCG, 60605	3034	0E-0S	C6
Erikson University	420 N Wabash Av, CHCG, 60611	3034	0W-0N	C3
Fox College	4201 W 93rd St, OKLN, 60453	3212	5W-10S	B5
Governors State University	1 University Pkwy, UYPK, 60466	3683	5W-29S	C1
Harold Washington College	30 E Lake St, CHCG, 60601	3034	0E-0N	C4
Harper College	1200 W Algonquin Rd, PLTN, 60067	2805	22W-13N	B5
Harry S Truman College	1145 W Wilson Av, CHCG, 60640	2921	1W-5N	D7
IBEW-NECA Technical Institute	W 115th St, ALSP, 60482	3275	7W-13S	B4
Illinois College of Optometry	3241 S Michigan Av, CHCG, 60616	3092	0E-3S	C4
Illinois Institute of Art-Chicago	350 N Orleans St, CHCG, 60606	3034	0W-0N	A4
Illinois Institute of Art-Schaumburg	1000 N Plaza Dr, SMBG, 60173	2859	21W-11N	E3
Illinois Institute of Technology	3300 S Federal St, CHCG, 60616	3092	0W-3S	C4
ITT Technical Institute	7040 High Grove Blvd, BRRG, 60527	3146	15W-7S	A7
ITT Technical Institute	600 Holiday Plaza Dr, MTSN, 60443	3506	6W-25S	A7
John Marshall Law School	315 S Plymouth Ct, CHCG, 60604	3034	0W-0S	C5
Kaes College	5909 N Rogers Av, CHCG, 60646	2920	5W-7N	B4
Kendall College	2408 Orrington Av, EVTN, 60201	2867	2W-12N	B1
Kennedy-King College	6800 S Wentworth Av, CHCG, 60621	3152	0W-7S	B6
Loyola Mundelein College	6435 W Sheridan Rd, CHCG, 60626	2921	1W-8N	E2
Loyola University-Mallinckrodt-Campus	1041 Ridge Rd, WLMT, 60091	2812	4W-14N	C5
Loyola Univ of Chicago-Lakeshore-Campus	6525 N Sheridan Rd, CHCG, 60626	2921	1W-8N	D2

Chicago & Cook County Points of Interest Index

Chicago & Cook County Points of Interest Index

Law Enforcement

FEATURE NAME / Address City ZIP Code	MAP#	CGS	GRID
Chicago Police-District 25 Central 5555 W Grand Av, CHCG, 60639	2975	6W-2N	C6
Chicago Ridge Police Dept 10501 Oxford Av, CHRG, 60415	3275	7W-12S	B1
Cicero Police Dept 4932 W 26th St, CCRO, 60804	3089	6W-2S	E2
Cook County Sheriff's Dept 1401 Maybrook Dr, MYWD, 60153	3030	10W-0S	B5
Country Club Hills Police Dept 3700 175th Pl, CCHL, 60478	3426	4W-21S	D5
Countryside Police Dept 5550 East Av, CTSD, 60525	3147	12W-6S	D3
Crestwood Police Dept 13840 Cicero Av, CTWD, 60445	3348	5W-16S	A3
Crete Police Dept 1370 Benton St, CRTE, 60417	3685	1W-29S	B2
Des Plaines Police Dept 1420 Miner St, DSPN, 60016	2863	13W-11N	A3
Dixmoor Police Dept 170 W 145th St, HRVY, 60426	3349	2W-17S	E5
Dolton Police Dept 14030 Park Av, DLTN, 60419	3350	0E-16S	D3
Dyer Police Dept 230 Schulte St, DYR, 46311	3598		D2
East Dundee Police Dept 120 Barrington Av, EDND, 60118	2801	34W-16N	A2
East Hazel Crest Police Dept 17223 Throop St, EHZC, 60429	3427	1W-20S	E5
Elk Grove Village Police Dept 901 Wellington Av, EGVV, 60007	2914	19W-8N	C2
Elmhurst Police Dept 125 E 1st St, EMHT, 60126	3028	15W-1N	A2
Elmwood Park Police Dept 11 W Conti Pkwy, EDPK, 60707	2974	9W-3N	C5
Evanston Police Dept 1454 Elmwood Av, EVTN, 60201	2867	2W-11N	B3
Evergreen Park Police Dept 9420 S Kedzie Av, ENGN, 60805	3212	4W-10S	E6
Flossmoor Police Dept 2800 Flossmoor Rd, FSMR, 60422	3507	3W-23S	B2
Ford Heights Police Dept 1343 Ellis Av, FDHT, 60411	3509	1E-25S	A7
Forest Park Police Dept 517 Des Plaines Av, FTPK, 60130	3030	9W-0S	C5
Forest View Police Dept 7000 46th St, FTVW, 60402	3088	8W-4S	E7
Franklin Park Police Dept 9545 W Belmont Av, FNPK, 60131	2973	11W-3N	C4
Glencoe Police Dept 325 Hazel Av, GLNC, 60022	2758	6W-17N	D5
Glenview Police Dept 1215 Waukegan Rd, GNVW, 60025	2810	8W-13N	E6
Glenwood Police Dept 1 S Rebecca St, GNWD, 60425	3508	0E-22S	D2
Golf Police Dept 1 Briar Rd, GLF, 60029	2864	8W-12N	E1
Hammond Police Dept 5925 S Calumet Av, HMND, 46320	3430		E1
Hanover Park Police Dept 2121 W Lake St, HRPK, 60133	2911	27W-8N	C3
Harvey Police Dept 15301 Dixie Hwy, HRVY, 60426	3349	2W-18S	C7
Harwood Heights Police Dept 7300 W Wilson Av, HDHT, 60706	2918	9W-5N	D7
Hickory Hills Police Dept 8652 W 95th St, HYHL, 60457	3210	10W-10S	A6
Hillside Police Dept 30 N Wolf Rd, HLSD, 60162	3028	14W-0S	D6
Hinsdale Police Dept 121 Symonds Dr, HNDL, 60521	3146	15W-4S	B1
Hodgkins Police Dept 6015 Lenzi Av, HGKN, 60525	3147	11W-6S	D4
Hoffman Estates Police Dept 1200 Gannon Dr, HFET, 60194	2858	24W-12N	C2
Hometown Police Dept 4331 Southwest Hwy, HMTN, 60456	3212	5W-10S	B5
Homewood Police Dept 17950 Dixie Hwy, HMWD, 60430	3427	2W-21S	D6
Indian Head Park Police Dept 201 Acacia Dr, IHPK, 60525	3146	13W-7S	E6
Itasca Police Dept 411 N Prospect Av, ITSC, 60143	2914	18W-6N	E5
Justice Police Dept 7800 S Archer Rd, JSTC, 60458	3210	11W-8S	A2
Kenilworth Police Dept 419 Richmond Rd, KLWH, 60043	2812	4W-14N	C4
La Grange Park Police Dept 447 N Catherine Av, LGPK, 60525	3087	12W-3S	B6
La Grange Police Dept 304 W Burlington Av, LGNG, 60525	3087	12W-4S	B7
Lansing Police Dept 2710 E 170th St, LNSG, 60438	3430	3E-19S	A3
Lemont Police Dept 416 Main St, LMNT, 60439	3270	19W-13S	D5
Lincolnwood Police Dept 6900 N Lincoln Av, LNWD, 60712	2920	5W-8N	B1
Lynwood Police Dept 21460 E Lincoln Hwy, LYWD, 60411	3510	4E-25S	B7
Lyons Police Dept 7801 Ogden Av, LYNS, 60534	3088	9W-4S	C6
Markham Police Dept 16313 Kedzie Av, MKHM, 60426	3427	3W-19S	A2
Matteson Police Dept 20500 Cicero Av, MTSN, 60443	3506	6W-24S	B6
Maywood Police Dept 125 S 5th Av, MYWD, 60153	3030	10W-0N	A4
Melrose Park Police Dept 101 Broadway St, MLPK, 60160	3029	11W-0N	D3
Merrionette Park Police Dept 11750 S Kedzie Av, MTPK, 60803	3276	4W-13S	E4
Midlothian Police Dept 14801 Pulaski Rd, MDLN, 60445	3348	4W-17S	C5
Morton Grove Police Dept 6101 Capulina Av, MNGV, 60053	2865	7W-10N	B4
Mt Prospect Police Dept 112 E Northwest Hwy, MPPT, 60056	2808	15W-12N	A7
Munster Police Dept 1007 Ridge Rd, MNSR, 46321	3430		E7
Niles Police Dept 7200 N Milwaukee Av, NLES, 60714	2864	8W-9N	E7
Norridge Police Dept 4020 N Olcott Av, NRDG, 60706	2974	9W-5N	C2
Northbrook Police Dept 1401 Landwehr Rd, NHBK, 60062	2756	11W-17N	D6
Northfield Police Dept 350 Walnut Av, NHFD, 60093	2811	6W-15N	C2
Northlake Police Dept 55 E North Av, NHLK, 60164	3028	13W-1N	E1
North Riverside Police Dept 2359 Des Plaines Av, NRIV, 60546	3088	9W-2S	C2
Oak Forest Police Dept 15440 Central Av, OKFT, 60452	3347	7W-18S	D7
Oak Lawn Police Dept 9446 Raymond Av, OKLN, 60453	3211	6W-10S	E6
Oak Park Police Dept 1 Madison St, OKPK, 60304	3031	7W-0S	B5
Olympia Fields Police Dept 20701 Governors Hwy, OMFD, 60461	3506	4W-25S	D6
Orland Hills Police Dept 16039 S 94th Av, ODHL, 60477	3423	11W-19S	E2
Orland Park Police Dept 14600 S Ravinia Av, ODPK, 60462	3345	12W-17S	D5
Palatine Police Dept 200 E Wood St, PLTN, 60067	2752	20W-16N	E7
Palos Heights Police Dept 7607 119th St, PSHT, 60463	3274	9W-14S	D5
Palos Hills Police Dept 8555 W 103rd St, PSHL, 60465	3274	10W-12S	B1
Palos Park Police Dept 12301 S 90th Av, PSPK, 60464	3274	11W-14S	A6
Park Forest Police Dept 200 Lakewood Blvd, PKFT, 60466	3595	3W-26S	B3
Park Ridge Police Dept 200 Vine Av, PKRG, 60068	2918	10W-8N	B1
Peotone Police Dept 208 E Main St, PTON, 60468	3861	9W-37S	A3
Phoenix Police Dept 15240 Vincennes Rd, PHNX, 60426	3350	0W-18S	B7
Posen Police Dept 2440 W Walter Zimny Dr, POSN, 60469	3349	3W-17S	B5
Prospect Heights Police Dept 14 E Camp McDonald Rd, PTHT, 60070	2808	15W-15N	A3
Richton Park Police Dept 4455 Sauk Tr, RNPK, 60471	3594	5W-27S	C3
Riverdale Police Dept 14140 S Emerald Av, RVDL, 60827	3350	1W-16S	A2
River Forest Police Dept 7810 Central Av, RVFT, 60305	3030	9W-0N	C4
River Grove Police Dept 2621 N Thatcher Av, RVGV, 60171	2974	10W-3N	A5
Riverside Police Dept 31 Riverside Rd, RVSD, 60546	3088	9W-3S	C5
Robbins Police Dept 3323 W 137th St, RBBN, 60472	3348	4W-16S	E2
Rolling Meadows Police Dept 3600 Kirchoff Rd, RGMW, 60008	2806	20W-13N	B5
Roselle Police Dept 103 S Prospect St, ROSL, 60172	2913	23W-7N	A5
Rosemont Police Dept 9501 E Devon Av, RSMT, 60018	2917	11W-7N	C3
Sauk Village Police Dept 21701 Torrence Av, SLVL, 60411	3597	3E-26S	E2
Schaumburg Police Dept 1000 W Schaumburg Rd, SMBG, 60194	2858	24W-10N	D5
Schiller Park Police Dept 9526 Irving Park Rd, SRPK, 60176	2973	11W-5N	C1
Skokie Police Dept 8350 Laramie Av, SKOK, 60077	2865	6W-10N	D5
South Chicago Heights Police Dept 2729 Jackson Av, SCHT, 60411	3596	1W-26S	B3
South Holland Police Dept 16220 Wausau Av, SHLD, 60473	3428	0E-19S	D1
Steger Police Dept 35 W Steger Rd, STGR, 60475	3596	1W-27S	B5
Stickney Police Dept 6533 Pershing Rd, SKNY, 60402	3089	8W-4S	A6
Stone Park Police Dept 1629 N Mannheim Rd, SNPK, 60165	3029	12W-1N	A2
Streamwood Police Dept 401 E Irving Park Rd, SMWD, 60107	2857	28W-9N	A7
Summit-Argo Police Dept 5810 S Archer Rd, SMMT, 60501	3148	9W-6S	D4
Thornton Police Dept 700 Park Av, TNTN, 60476	3428	0E-20S	D5
Tinley Park Police Dept 17355 68th Ct, TYPK, 60477	3425	8W-20S	A5
University Park Police Dept 698 Burnham Dr, UYPK, 60466	3684	3W-29S	A1
Westchester Police Dept 10300 W Roosevelt Rd, WSTR, 60154	3029	12W-0S	B7
Western Springs Police Dept 740 Hillgrove Av, WNSP, 60558	3086	13W-4S	E7
Wheeling Police Dept 255 W Dundee Rd, WLNG, 60090	2755	14W-18N	B4
Willow Springs Police Dept 8480 Archer Av, WLSP, 60480	3209	12W-9S	C3
Wilmette Police Dept 710 Ridge Rd, WLMT, 60091	2812	4W-13N	C6
Winnetka Police Dept 410 Green Bay Rd, WNKA, 60093	2812	4W-15N	B2
Wood Dale Police Dept 404 N Wood Dale Rd, WDDL, 60191	2915	18W-6N	A7

Libraries

FEATURE NAME / Address City ZIP Code	MAP#	CGS	GRID
Acorn Public 15624 Central Av, OKFT, 60452	3347	7W-18S	D7
Alsip Merrionette Park 11960 S Pulaski Rd, ALSP, 60803	3276	5W-14S	C5
Arlington Heights Memorial 500 N Dunton Av, ANHT, 60004	2807	17W-14N	A4
Barrington Area 505 N Northwest Hwy, BRTN, 60010	2751	25W-20N	A1
Bartlett Public 800 S Bartlett Rd, BRLT, 60103	2910	29W-7N	E5
Bedford Park Public 7816 W 65th Pl, BDPK, 60501	3148	9W-7S	C5
Bellwood Public 600 Bohland Av, BLWD, 60104	3029	12W-0N	B5
Berkeley Public 1637 N Taft Av, BKLY, 60163	3028	14W-0N	C4
Berwyn Public 2701 Harlem Av, BRWN, 60402	3088	8W-2S	E3
Blue Island 2433 York St, BLID, 60406	3277	3W-15S	B7
Bradford Anderson Oblesby 16640 Kedzie Av, MKHM, 60426	3427	4W-19S	A3
Bridgeview Public 7840 W 79th St, BGVW, 60455	3210	9W-8S	C2
Broadview Public 2226 S 16th Av, BDVW, 60155	3029	11W-1S	D7
Brookfield 3609 Grand Blvd, BKFD, 60513	3087	11W-3S	E5
Calumet City 660 Manistee Av, CTCY, 60409	3351	3E-17S	E6
Calumet Park 1500 W 127th St, CTPK, 60827	3277	1W-14S	D7
Chicago-Albany Park 5150 N Kimball Av, CHCG, 60625	2920	4W-6N	D6
Chicago-Altgeld 950 E 132nd Pl, CHCG, 60827	3351	1E-15S	A1
Chicago-American 50 E Huron St, CHCG, 60611	3034	0E-0N	C3
Chicago-Archer Heights 5148 S Archer Av, CHCG, 60632	3150	5W-5S	B2
Chicago-Austin 5615 W Race Av, CHCG, 60644	3031	7W-0N	C3
Chicago-Austin Irving 6110 W Irving Park Rd, CHCG, 60634	2975	7W-5N	B2
Chicago-Avalon 8828 S Stony Island Av, CHCG, 60619	3215	1E-10S	B4
Chicago-Back of the Yards 4650 S Damen Av, CHCG, 60609	3091	2W-4S	C7
Chicago-Bessie Coleman 731 E 63rd St, CHCG, 60637	3152	0E-7S	E5
Chicago-Beverly 2121 W 95th St, CHCG, 60643	3213	2W-11S	C6
Chicago-Bezazian 1226 W Ainslie St, CHCG, 60640	2921	1W-6N	D6
Chicago-Blackstone 4904 S Lake Park Av, CHCG, 60615	3153	1E-5S	B1
Chicago-Brainerd 8945 S Loomis St, CHCG, 60620	3213	1W-10S	E4
Chicago-Brighton Park 4314 S Archer Av, CHCG, 60632	3090	3W-4S	E7
Chicago-Canaryville 642 W 43rd St, CHCG, 60609	3092	0W-4S	A6
Chicago-Chicago Lawn 6120 S Kedzie Av, CHCG, 60629	3150	4W-6S	E4
Chicago-Chinatown 2353 S Wentworth Av, CHCG, 60616	3092	0W-2S	B2
Chicago-Clearing 6423 W 63rd Pl, CHCG, 60638	3149	8W-7S	B5
Chicago-Damen Avenue 2056 N Damen Av, CHCG, 60647	2977	2W-2N	B6
Chicago-Dirkwales 345 W Fullerton Pkwy, CHCG, 60614	2978	0W-2N	A5
Chicago-Douglas 3353 W 13th St, CHCG, 60623	3032	4W-1S	D7
Chicago-Eckhart Park 1371 W Chicago Av, CHCG, 60622	3033	1W-0N	D3
Chicago-Edgebrook 5426 W Devon Av, CHCG, 60646	2919	6W-8N	D2
Chicago-Edgewater 1210 W Elmdale Av, CHCG, 60660	2921	1W-7N	D3
Chicago-Gage Park 2807 W 55th St, CHCG, 60629	3151	3W-6S	A3
Chicago-Galewood/Mont Clare 6969 W Grand Av, CHCG, 60707	2974	8W-2N	E6
Chicago-Hall 4801 S Michigan Av, CHCG, 60615	3152	0E-5S	C1
Chicago-Hansberry 4314 S Cottage Grove Av, CHCG, 60653	3092	0E-4S	E6
Chicago-Harold Ickes 2420 S State St, CHCG, 60616	3092	0W-2S	C2
Chicago-Harper 1116 E 59th St, CHCG, 60637	3153	1E-6S	A3
Chicago-Hegewisch 3048 E 130th St, CHCG, 60633	3280	3E-14S	A7
Chicago Heights Public 25 W 15th St, CHHT, 60411	3596	1W-25S	A1
Chicago-Humbolt 1605 N Troy St, CHCG, 60647	2976	3W-2N	E7
Chicago-Independence 3548 W Irving Park Rd, CHCG, 60618	2976	4W-5N	C1
Chicago-Jefferson Park 5363 W Lawrence Av, CHCG, 60630	2919	6W-5N	D7
Chicago-Jeffery Manor 2435 E 100th St, CHCG, 60617	3215	3E-11S	D7
Chicago-Kelly 6151 S Normal Av, CHCG, 60621	3152	0W-6S	B4
Chicago-Lincoln Belmont W Belmont Av, CHCG, 60657	2978	0W-4N	A3
Chicago-Lincoln Park 1150 W Fullerton Av, CHCG, 60614	2977	1W-3N	D5
Chicago-Logan Square 3255 W Altgeld St, CHCG, 60647	2976	4W-3N	D5
Chicago-Mabel Manning 6 S Hoyne Av, CHCG, 60612	3033	2W-0S	B5
Chicago-Marshall Square 2724 W Cermak Rd, CHCG, 60608	3091	3W-1S	A2
Chicago-Martin Luther King Jr 3436 S Dr Martin L King Jr Dr, CHCG, 60616	3092	0E-3S	D4
Chicago-Mayfair 4400 W Lawrence Av, CHCG, 60630	2920	5W-6N	A6
Chicago-Mayfield 4200 W Lawrence Av, CHCG, 60630	2920	5W-6N	B6
Chicago-McKinley Park 1915 W 35th St, CHCG, 60609	3091	2W-3S	C5
Chicago-Midwest 2335 W Chicago Av, CHCG, 60612	3033	2W-0N	B3
Chicago-Mt Greenwood 11010 S Kedzie Av, CHCG, 60655	3276	4W-12S	E3
Chicago-Near North Branch 310 W Division St, CHCG, 60610	3034	0W-1N	B1
Chicago-North Austin 5724 W North Av, CHCG, 60639	3031	7W-2N	C1
Chicago-North Lake View 3754 N Southport Av, CHCG, 60613	2977	1W-4N	D2
Chicago-Northtown 6435 N California Av, CHCG, 60645	2920	3W-8N	E2
Chicago-Portage/Cragin 5108 W Belmont Av, CHCG, 60641	2975	6W-4N	D4
Chicago Public-Budlong Woods Branch 5630 N Lincoln Av, CHCG, 60625	2921	3W-6N	A5
Chicago Public-Garfield 6348 S Archer Av, CHCG, 60638	3149	7W-5S	B3
Chicago Public-Roden 6083 N Northwest Hwy, CHCG, 60631	2918	8W-7N	E3
Chicago Public-T. Roosevelt 1101 W Taylor St, CHCG, 60607	3033	1W-0S	E6
Chicago Public-Toman 4005 W 27th St, CHCG, 60623	3090	5W-2S	C3
Chicago-Pullman 11001 S Indiana Av, CHCG, 60628	3278	0E-12S	D2
Chicago-Richard J Daley 3400 S Halsted St, CHCG, 60608	3092	1W-3S	A4
Chicago Ridge 10400 Oxford Av, CHRG, 60415	3275	7W-12S	B1
Chicago-Robert Taylor 5120 S Federal St, CHCG, 60609	3152	0W-5S	B2
Chicago-Rogers Park 6907 N Clark St, CHCG, 60626	2921	2W-8N	C1
Chicago-Rudy Lozano 1805 S Loomis St, CHCG, 60608	3091	1W-1S	D1
Chicago-Scottsdale 4101 W 79th St, CHCG, 60652	3212	5W-9S	C2
Chicago-Sherman Park 5440 S Racine Av, CHCG, 60609	3151	1W-5S	E2
Chicago-South Chicago 9055 S Houston Av, CHCG, 60617	3216	3E-10S	A4
Chicago-Stateway 3647 S State St, CHCG, 60653	3092	0E-3S	C5
Chicago-Sulzer Regional 4455 N Lincoln Av, CHCG, 60625	2921	2W-5N	B7
Chicago-Thurgood Marshall 7506 S Racine Av, CHCG, 60620	3213	1W-8S	E1
Chicago-Tuley Park 501 E 90th Pl, CHCG, 60619	3214	0E-10S	D4
Chicago-Uptown 929 W Buena Av, CHCG, 60613	2977	1W-5N	E1
Chicago-Vodak/East Side 10542 S Ewing Av, CHCG, 60617	3280	4E-11S	B1
Chicago-Walker 11071 S Hoyne Av, CHCG, 60643	3277	2W-12S	C3
Chicago-West Addison 7536 W Addison St, CHCG, 60634	2974	9W-4N	C3
Chicago-West Belmont 3104 N Narragansett Av, CHCG, 60634	2975	8W-3N	A4
Chicago-West Lawn 4020 W 63rd St, CHCG, 60629	3150	5W-6S	C5
Chicago-Whitney M Young Jr 7901 S Dr Martin L King Jr Dr, CHCG, 60619	3214	0E-9S	D2
Chicago-Woodson Regional 9525 S Halsted St, CHCG, 60628	3214	0W-11S	A6
Chicago-Wrightwood 2519 W 79th St, CHCG, 60652	3213	3W-9S	B2
Christian Lending 1025 Pleasant Pl, OKPK, 60302	3030	8W-0N	E4

Chicago & Cook County Points of Interest Index

Libraries

Military Installations

Museums

Open Space

Chicago & Cook County Points of Interest Index

Other

Park & Ride

Chicago & Cook County Points of Interest Index

Parks & Recreation

FEATURE NAME Address City ZIP Code	MAP#	CGS	GRID
Abbott Pk, CHCG	3214	0E-11S	C6
Abrahamsen Pk, SMBG	2859	22W-10N	B6
Adam Perry Pk, EVTN	2866	3W-11N	E2
Adams Pk, CHCG	3215	1E-8S	A1
Ada Pk, CHCG	3277	1W-13S	E3
Addams Pk, CHCG	3033	1W-1S	D7
Ahlstrand Pk, HRPK	2911	27W-8N	C2
Aiello Pk, CHCG	2975	7W-2N	B6
Alcott Center & Pk, BFGV	2754	17W-18N	B3
Alexander Pk, EVTN	2867	3W-11N	A3
Algonquin Lakes Pk, ALGN	2748	33W-19N	A3
Algonquin Pk, PKFT	3595	2W-26S	C2
Allan Weissburg Pk, SKOK	2866	5W-12N	B1
Allemong Pk, MTSN	3505	7W-24S	C5
Almond Pk, CHCG	3277	2W-13S	B4
Altgeld Pk, CHCG	3033	3W-0S	A6
Altman Pk, PSHT	3274	9W-13S	D4
American Lane Pk, SMBG	2859	22W-11N	D2
Amundsen Pk, CHCG	2975	7W-2N	B7
Ancient Oaks Pk, BRLT	2910	30W-6N	B7
Andersen Pk, OKPK	3031	7W-1N	B2
Anderson Pk, CHCG	3092	0E-3S	C5
Anderson Pk, HMTN	3212	5W-10S	B5
Andres Pk, CPVL	2748	33W-18N	B5
Andrews Pk, EGVV	2861	18W-9N	A6
Anniversary Pk, SMWD	2856	29W-9N	E7
Apollo Pk, ALSP	3276	5W-14S	B6
Apollo Pk, BLWD	3029	12W-0S	B5
Apollo Pk, HMWD	3508	1W-22S	A2
Apollo Pk, SMBG	2859	22W-9N	B6
Applegate Pk, SMBG	2859	23W-10N	A6
Apple Orchard Greenway Pk, BRLT	2910	29W-6N	D6
Apple Orchard Pk, BRLT	2910	29W-7N	E5
Appleseed Pk, EGVV	2860	18W-9N	E7
Aquarius Pk, SMWD	2856	29W-10N	E6
Aquatic Pk, ALSP	3276	5W-14S	B5
Arbor Day Pk, PlsT	3345	12W-15S	D2
Arcade Pk, CHCG	3278	0E-13S	E3
Arcadia Pk, OMFD	3506	4W-24S	E6
Archer Pk, CHCG	3150	5W-5S	A1
Argyle-Keeler Pk, CHCG	2920	5W-6N	B6
Armour Square Pk, CHCG	3092	0W-3S	B4
Armstrong Pk, HFET	2858	25W-12N	B2
Arndt Pk, DSPN	2863	13W-9N	A7
Arne & Mary Oldberg Pk, EVTN	2867	2W-11N	B2
Arnie Gunther Sports Fields, TYPK	3424	9W-20S	D4
Arquilla Pk, GNWD	3508	0W-22S	C1
Arrigo Pk, CHCG	3033	1W-0S	D6
Ashburn Pk, CHCG	3212	3W-9S	E3
Ashmore Pk, CHCG	2919	6W-6N	E6
Ashwood Pk, PLTN	2752	20W-16N	E6
Aspen Trail Pk, MPPT	2808	13W-15N	E2
Atcher Pk, SMBG	2858	25W-9N	B7
Athletic Field Pk, CHCG	2976	4W-4N	C2
Atkin Pk, CCHL	3426	5W-21S	C6
Audubon Pk, EGVV	2914	18W-8N	E1
Austin-Foster Pk, CHCG	2919	7W-6N	B5
Austin Gardens Pk, OKPK	3030	8W-0N	E3
Austin Pk, CHCG	3031	7W-0N	B4
Austin Pk, MNGV	2865	7W-10N	B5
Austin Town Hall Pk, CHCG	3031	7W-0N	C4
Austin View Pk, ALSP	3275	7W-14S	C6
Avondale Pk, CHCG	2976	4W-4N	C3
Babe Ruth Pk, BLWD	3029	11W-0S	C5
Baker Pk, EVTN	2867	2W-10N	C5
Ballard Pk, NLES	2864	10W-11N	A3
Bambrick Pk, DPgT	3342	21W-15S	A2
Barnard Pk, CHCG	3277	2W-12S	C1
Barnes Pk, ALSP	3276	5W-13S	B4
Barrie Pk, OKPK	3031	7W-0S	B6
Bartlett Pk, BRLT	2910	29W-8N	E3
Bartlett Pk, SMWD	2857	28W-9N	A7
Bartrum Pk, EGVV	2915	18W-9N	A1
Bataan Pk, MLPK	3029	11W-1N	E2
Bauler Pk, CHCG	2978	0W-2N	A7
Beach Oak Pk, LGPK	3087	12W-3S	C5
Beau Drive Pk, DSPN	2862	15W-11N	A3
Beaver Pond Pk, BRLT	2910	29W-7N	C5
Beck Pk, EVTN	2866	4W-11N	D2
Beilfuss Pk, CHCG	2976	4W-2N	C7
Bel-Aire Pk, MKHM	3349	3W-18S	B7
Bell Pk, CHCG	2974	8W-3N	E4
Bensley Pk, CHCG	3215	3E-11S	D6
Bent Pk, EVTN	2812	4W-12N	C7
Berbecker Pk, ANHT	2807	16W-14N	C4
Berger Beach & Pk, CHCG	2921	1W-7N	E3
Berguin Recreation & Field Pk, BRWN	3089	8W-2S	A4
Berkeley Community Pk, BKLY	3028	14W-0N	C4
Bessemer Pk, CHCG	3215	3E-10S	E4
Bettenhausen Pk, TYPK	3424	9W-19S	D2
Beverly Pk, BDVW	3087	11W-2S	D2
Beverly Pk, CHCG	3213	3W-11S	B7
Bicentennial Pk, OMFD	3506	4W-24S	E5
Bicentennial Pk, TYPK	3425	8W-19S	A2
Bickerdike Square Pk, CHCG	3033	1W-0N	D3
Bill Young Pk, ODPK	3345	12W-18S	C7
Birch Pk, HFET	2859	23W-11N	B3
Birchwood Pk, PLTN	2805	21W-14N	D3
Birchwood South Pk, PLTN	2805	21W-14N	D3
Bison Pk, BFGV	2754	17W-17N	B4
Bixler Pk, CHCG	3153	1E-6S	A3
Black Bear Pk, HFET	2856	31W-12N	A1
Blackhawk Pk, CHCG	2975	6W-2N	E6
Blackhawk Pk, DSPN	2862	14W-11N	B2
Black Hawk Pk, IHPK	3146	13W-7S	E6
Blackstone Pk, DLTN	3351	1E-17S	B4
Blackweider Pk, CHCG	3277	2W-13S	C4
Block Pk, CHCG	3278	0W-12S	B1
Bluedingen Pk, TYPK	3424	10W-19S	B3
Blue Star Memorial Woods, GNVW	2811	7W-13N	C6
Bluett Pk, MPPT	2808	14W-13N	C6
Bock Pk, SMBG	2858	25W-10N	C6
Bogan Pk, CHCG	3212	4W-9S	C2
Bohn Pk, CHCG	3277	2W-12S	C3
Bosley Pk, CHCG	3091	1W-2S	E3
Brainerd Pk, CHCG	3213	1W-10S	E5
Brandenberry Pk, ANHT	2807	16W-15N	D3
Brandenburg Pk, SMBG	2857	26W-11N	E4
Brands Pk, CHCG	2976	3W-4N	E3
Brandt Pk, OKLN	3211	6W-10S	E4
Bremen Heights Pk, MDLN	3348	5W-17S	B4
Brentwood Pk, DSPN	2862	15W-11N	B3
Brentwood Pk, ODPK	3346	11W-16S	A2
Bretman Pk, BNVL	2972	15W-5N	A1
Briar Pointe Pk, SMBG	2912	25W-8N	A3
Briarwood Pk, DRFD	2757	9W-20N	B1
Brickyard Pk, DRFD	2756	11W-20N	E1
Briggs Ellis Pk, ThtT	3349	1W-16S	E4
Bristol Pk, TYPK	3424	9W-21S	D5
Brook Pk, HNDL	3146	14W-5S	C2
Brookrose Pk, ROSL	2912	24W-7N	D5
Brooks Pk, CHCG	2918	9W-8N	D1
Brown Pk, HDPK	2758	7W-20N	B1
Brown Pk, ODPK	3345	13W-17S	B5
Buffalo Pk, CHCG	2920	3W-5N	E7
Bulger Pk, MLPK	3029	11W-1N	D1
Burbank Pk, EGVV	2914	18W-8N	E2
Burlington Pk, HNDL	3146	15W-5S	A1
Burnham Pk, BNHM	3352	3E-16S	A2
Burnham Pk, CHCG	3092	0E-1S	D1
Burnham Shores Pk, EVTN	2867	1W-10N	C4
Burning Bush Trail Pk, MPPT	2808	13W-14N	E4
Burn Pk, HNDL	3146	15W-4S	A1
Burnside Pk, CHCG	3215	1E-10S	A5
Burr Ridge District Pk, DGvT	3208	16W-10S	A5
Bush Hill Pk, HNDL	3146	15W-4S	B1
Busse Pk, MPPT	2808	15W-13N	B7
Busse Pk, SMBG	2859	21W-10N	E5
Butler Pk, EVTN	2866	3W-11N	E2
Butterfield Pk, EMHT	3028	15W-0S	B6
Butterfield Pk, HMWD	3508	1W-23S	A3
Butterfly Pk, SMWD	2857	27W-10N	C7
Buzz 'N Bloom Prairie Pk, PSHT	3274	9W-13S	E5
Cachey Pk, ODPK	3346	10W-18S	B7
California Pk, CHCG	2976	3W-4N	E2
Calumet Pk, CHCG	3216	4E-10S	C6
Calumet Pk, HRVY	3350	1W-17S	A4
Calvary Pk, PSHL	3274	9W-13S	C3
Camberley Pk, PvsT	3086	14W-2S	C3
Cambridge Pk, BFGV	2754	16W-17N	D4
Camelot Pk, ANHT	2754	17W-16N	B6
Cameno Real Pk, ODPK	3345	12W-18S	C6
Campanelli Pk, SMBG	2858	24W-9N	C6
Campbell Pk, RGMW	2806	19W-14N	B4
Campus Pk, ELGN	2855	31W-10N	E5
Candlewood Pk, BFGV	2755	15W-20N	A1
Candy Cane Pk, BKFD	3087	11W-2S	E3
Cannon Crossings Pk, HnrT	2856	30W-12N	B1
Canterbury Fields Pk, HFET	2855	32W-12N	D1
Canterbury Pk Place, HFET	2855	32W-12N	D2
Cardinal Pk, PLTN	2805	21W-14N	D3
Carefree Pk, ANHT	2861	17W-12N	B1
Carmen Garcia Memorial Arboretum Pk, - DndT	2801	33W-16N	B2
Carousel Pk, ANHT	2754	16W-16N	D6
Carriage Walk Pk, ANHT	2807	17W-14N	C3
Carroll Pk, OKPK	3030	8W-0S	E6
Carson Pk, EGVV	2913	21W-8N	E3
Carver Pk, CHCG	3351	0E-15S	A1
Ceaser Pk, CTWD	3348	5W-16S	B3
Cedar Pk, PKFT	3595	2W-27S	C3
Cedar Pk, PLTN	2805	21W-15N	D1
Celtic Pk, PLTN	2753	19W-17N	B4
Centennial Pk, ANHT	2754	17W-17N	C5
Centennial Pk, BLID	3277	2W-15S	C7
Centennial Pk, CHCG	2918	8W-7N	E3
Centennial Pk, EVTN	2867	2W-11N	C3
Centennial Pk, LMNT	3342	20W-15S	C1
Centennial Pk, ODPK	3345	12W-18S	C7
Centennial Pk, OKLN	3211	8W-10S	A5
Centennial Pk, PKRG	2917	11W-8N	E1
Centennial Pk, RVFT	3030	9W-0N	C3
Centennial Pk, TYPK	3424	9W-20S	D3
Centennial Pk, WLMT	2812	5W-13N	B7
Central Pk, AddT	2915	17W-6N	B6
Central Pk, BLID	3277	2W-15S	C7
Central Pk, CHCG	3032	4W-0N	C3
Central Pk, DSPN	2863	13W-10N	A4
Central Pk, GNVW	2810	8W-13N	E7
Central Pk, LNWD	2920	4W-8N	C2
Central Pk, OKFT	3347	6W-18S	D7
Central Pk, OKLN	3212	5W-10S	A5
Central Pk, SKOK	2866	4W-11N	C2
Central Pk Wetlands, PKFT	3595	3W-26S	A3
Chandler Pk, EVTN	2867	2W-12N	A1
Channel Runne Pk, LNWD	2920	4W-8N	D1
Channelside Pk, SKOK	2866	4W-10N	D5
Charlemagne Pk, HFET	2804	24W-14N	B4
Chase Avenue Beach & Pk, CHCG	2867	1W-9N	D7
Chase Pk, CHCG	2921	1W-5N	C7
Chatburg Pk, ROSL	2912	25W-7N	C5
Chatham Lions Pk, BFGV	2754	17W-18N	B3
Cherokee Pk, DSPN	2863	13W-10N	A5
Cherrywood Pk, PLTN	2752	20W-17N	E5
Chestnut Pk, FNPK	2973	12W-3N	B5
Chestnut Pk, HFET	2858	25W-11N	C3
Chestnut Pk, PLTN	2806	19W-16N	C1
Cheyenne Pk, DSPN	2808	14W-12N	C7
Chicago Blaze Rugby, LMNT	3342	20W-15S	A1
Childerly Pk, WLNG	2755	15W-18N	A3
Chino Pk, HFET	2859	23W-11N	A4
Chippewa Pk, CHCG	2920	3W-8N	D2
Chippewa Pk, DSPN	2862	14W-12N	D1
Chopin Pk, CHCG	2975	6W-4N	D3
Churchill Pk, CHCG	2977	2W-2N	C7
Citizen's Pk, BRTN	2751	25W-20N	B1
City Pk, CHCG	3150	5W-6S	B4
City Pk, CTSD	3147	12W-6S	B5
City Pk, ELGN	2855	33W-11N	A4
City Pk, HMND	3430		E1
C Kelly Franson Pk, RVDL	3350	0W-16S	B4
Claire Lane Pk, PTHT	2808	14W-15N	C2
Claremont Pk, CHCG	3033	2W-0S	B6
Clarendon Pk, CHCG	2921	1W-5N	E7
Clark Pk, CHCG	3032	5W-0S	A5
Clark Pk, EGVV	2913	21W-8N	D1
Clarkson Pk, NHFD	2811	7W-15N	B2
Clark Square Pk, EVTN	2867	1W-10N	C5
Clauss Rec Area, ROSL	2912	24W-6N	E6
Clemente Pk, CHCG	3033	2W-1N	B1
Clyde Pk, CCRO	3089	7W-2S	C3
Coast Guard Pk, NHBK	2757	10W-18N	A4
Cole Pk, GNVW	2811	7W-14N	B4
Colonial Pk, ODPK	3345	11W-16S	E3
Colony Lake Pk, SMBG	2858	24W-11N	C3
Colony Pk, EGVV	2913	22W-9N	C1
Colony Pk, HFET	2751	24W-16N	C7
Columbia Avenue Beach & Pk, CHCG	2921	1W-8N	E2
Columbus Manor Pk, OKLN	3211	7W-11S	C6
Columbus Pk, CCRO	3089	6W-3S	D4
Columbus Pk, CHCG	3031	7W-0S	C6
Commissioner's Pk, ALSP	3276	4W-14S	E6
Commissioner's Pk, BGVW	3210	9W-9S	D2
Commissioner's Pk, CHHT	3508	1W-23S	A3
Commissioner's Pk, CHRG	3275	7W-12S	C2
Commissioner's Pk, CTCY	3352	3E-17S	A6
Commissioner's Pk, JSTC	3210	11W-8S	A1
Commissioner's Pk, TYPK	3424	10W-19S	C2
Commons Pk, BFGV	2754	17W-20N	C1
Commons Pk, NRIV	3088	9W-2S	C2
Community Pk, CCHL	3426	5W-20S	C5
Community Pk, FftT	3504	9W-24S	D5
Community Pk, HFET	2858	23W-11N	E3
Community Pk, PLTN	2806	20W-16N	A1
Community Pk, PTON	3860	9W-37S	E4
Community Pk, TYPK	3424	10W-20S	C4
Community Pk, WSTR	3087	12W-1S	A2
Conrad Fischer Pk, AddT	2972	15W-3N	A5
Constitution Pk, RVFT	3030	9W-1N	C1
Container Pk, DLTN	3350	0E-16S	D4
Continental Pk, ELGN	2855	33W-10N	A6
Convent Pk, OKFT	3347	7W-17S	D5
Cooney Meadow, EGVV	2859	22W-9N	D7
Cooper Pk, BFGV	2754	17W-18N	A2
Cooper Pk, CHCG	3277	1W-13S	E4
Cooper Pk, HRVY	3349	2W-17S	C6
Copley Pk, SMBG	2859	23W-12N	B2
Cornell Pk, CHCG	3153	2E-5S	B2
Cornell Pk, DSPN	2862	14W-12N	C1
Cornell Square Pk, CHCG	3151	2W-5S	C1
Cornet Pk, CHHT	3595	2W-25S	D1
Corrine Deinert Pk, TYPK	3424	10W-20S	B5
Cotton Tail Pk, CHCG	3034	0W-1S	B7
Cottonwood Pk, HFET	2804	25W-12N	B7
Cottonwood Pk, RGMW	2805	21W-13N	C5
Country Aire Pk, MKHM	3348	4W-18S	D6
Country Club Estates Pk, ODPK	3346	10W-17S	B5
Country Club Pk, ITSC	2914	19W-7N	D5
Country Gardens Pk, PTHT	2754	15W-16N	E7
Countryside Pk, CTSD	3147	12W-6S	B4
Countryside Pk, GNVW	2809	10W-13N	E6
Countryside Pk, MPPT	2862	15W-11N	A2
Countryside Pk, NfdT	2757	10W-18N	B3
Countryside Pk, RGMW	2805	20W-14N	E4
Countryside Pk, SMWD	2857	28W-10N	A5
Cove Pk, SMBG	2912	24W-9N	E1
Covington Knolls Pk, LMNT	3270	18W-14S	E7
Cragin Pk, CHCG	2975	6W-3N	D5
Craig Manor Pk, DSPN	2808	13W-13N	D7
Creekside Pk, ALSP	3276	6W-13S	A3
Creekside Pk, MTSN	3505	7W-24S	C6
Creekside Pk, RGMW	2806	20W-13N	A6
Creekside Pk, TYPK	3424	9W-19S	D3
Creekside Pk, WLBK	3146	15W-7S	A5
Creekside West Pk, ANHT	2753	18W-18N	D2
Crescent Pk, CHCG	3277	2W-12S	B2
Crestview Pk, EMHT	2972	15W-2N	A6
Crestwood Pk, NHBK	2757	9W-17N	B4
Crete Pk, CRTE	3685	1W-29S	B1
Cronin Pk, ANHT	2807	18W-13N	A5
Crow Island Woods, WNKA	2811	5W-15N	E2
Crowley Pk, GNVW	2810	10W-13N	A7
Crusoe Pk, FNPK	2973	11W-4N	D3
Cubs Care Pk, CHCG	3034	0W-1N	A1
Culver Pk, HMGN	3343	17W-17S	D5
Cumberland Pk, PKRG	2918	10W-8N	A1
Cumberland Terrace Pk, DSPN	2862	14W-11N	C3
Cunliff Pk, GNVW	2811	7W-12N	C7
Curie Pk, CHCG	3150	4W-5S	C1
Cypress Pk, ANHT	2807	18W-12N	A7
Cypress Pk, FSMR	3506	4W-23S	D3
Dalenberg Pk, SHLD	3428	0E-19S	D3
Dauphin Pk, CHCG	3214	1E-10S	E4
Davis Pk, CHCG	3031	6W-1N	D2
Davis Square Pk, CHCG	3091	2W-4S	C7
Dawes Pk, CHCG	3213	2W-9S	C2
Dawes Pk, EVTN	2867	2W-11N	C3
Dearborn Pk, CHCG	3034	0W-0S	B6
Debra Pk, EGVV	2914	21W-8N	A1
Dedra Pk, SMBG	2858	26W-10N	A6
Dee Pk, MaiT	2863	11W-11N	D2
Deering Estate Pk, EVTN	2813	2W-13N	C7
Deer Point Estates Pk, ODPK	3423	13W-20S	A5
Denning Pk, LGNG	3147	13W-5S	A1
Depot Pk, BCHR	3864	0W-36S	B2
Devonshire Pk, DSPN	2862	15W-10N	B5
Devonshire Pk, SKOK	2866	5W-11N	A3
De Youngs Grove Pk, SHLD	3350	0E-18S	D7
Dickinson Pk, CHCG	2975	6W-5N	E1
Diedrich Pk, GLF	2864	8W-12N	E1
Dillion Pk, OKLN	3211	6W-11S	E7
Dimucci Pk, DSPN	2862	14W-12N	B1
Discovery Pk, ODPK	3422	14W-20S	E5
Doherty Pk, SMBG	2913	22W-9N	B1
Dolphin Lake Pk, HMWD	3427	3W-21S	B7
Dolphin Pk, SMWD	2857	28W-10N	B6
Dolton Pk, DLTN	3350	0E-17S	E4
Dominic J Sesto Pk, CHHT	3595	2W-25S	C1
Don Burns Pk, OKFT	3426	6W-20S	A3
Donovan Pk, CHCG	3091	1W-3S	E5
Doogan Pk, ODPK	3345	12W-17S	C5
Dooley Pk, SMBG	2858	24W-9N	C7
Dougherty Pk, CHCG	3215	3E-10S	D5
Douglas Pk, CHCG	3032	3W-1S	E7
Doug Lindberg Pk, PLTN	2753	19W-16N	C6
Dove Pk, PLTN	2753	19W-18N	C3
Dover Pond Pk, DRPK	2752	22W-20N	B1
Downey Pk, CTCY	3351	2E-17S	C4
Drake Field, ELGN	2855	33W-10N	B6
Drake Pk, LNWD	2920	4W-8N	C2
Dr Edwin B Tharp Pk, TYPK	3424	9W-21S	D5
Dresser Pk, MKHM	3349	3W-18S	A7
Drexel Square Pk, CHCG	3152	0E-5S	E1
Drury Lane Pk, WSTR	3029	12W-1S	C7
Dryden Pk, ANHT	2807	17W-13N	B7
Dubkin Pk, CHCG	2867	2W-9N	C7
Duffy Pk, ENGN	3212	4W-10S	D5
Dunbar Pk, CHCG	3092	0E-2S	C3
Dunham Pk, CHCG	2919	7W-5N	A7
Durkin Pk, CHCG	3212	5W-9S	B3
Durso Pk, CHCG	3034	0W-1N	A2
Dusable Pk, CHCG	3034	0E-0N	D3
Duxbury Pk, SMBG	2858	24W-9N	C7
Dvorak Pk, CHCG	3091	1W-1S	E1
Dwyer Pk, WNKA	2812	5W-15N	A2
Eagle Pk, PLTN	2752	20W-17N	E4
Eagle Pk, SMBG	2858	24W-9N	D7
Eagle Ridge II Pk, ODPK	3422	14W-21S	E5
Eagle Ridge Pk, ODPK	3423	13W-21S	A7
East Avenue Pk, SEGN	2909	33W-8N	A3
East End Pk, EMHT	3028	15W-1N	B1
Eastgate Pk, PKFT	3595	2W-26S	C2
East River Pk, CHCG	2920	3W-6N	E6
Eastview Pk, LGNG	3147	12W-5S	C1
Eaton Field Pk, DSPN	2917	12W-8N	C2
Eckersall Pk, CHCG	3215	3E-9S	D2
Eckhart Pk, CHCG	3033	1W-1N	D2
Edgebrook Pk, CHCG	2919	6W-8N	D2
Edge Brook Pk, HRPK	2911	26W-8N	E2
Edison Pk, CHCG	2918	9W-8N	C1
Edison Pk, HMND	3430		D3
Edward Mraz Pk, ROSL	2913	22W-8N	B2
Ehler Pk, CHCG	2977	2W-2N	B7
Ehlert Pk, BKFD	3087	11W-4S	E7
Einstein Pk, DSPN	2862	15W-10N	A4
Eisenhower Pk, HLSD	3028	13W-0N	D4
Elaine Bond Pk, SMBG	2858	25W-10N	B6
Elder Lane Pk, WNKA	2812	4W-15N	D3
Eleanor Pk, HNDL	3146	15W-5S	A1
Elks Pk, EVTN	2867	2W-9N	B6
Elliot Pk, EVTN	2867	1W-10N	C4
Elliot Woods Pk, OMFD	3506	4W-25S	D7
Ellis Pk, CHCG	3092	0E-3S	D5
El Morro Pk, OKFT	3347	7W-18S	C7
Elm Pk, LGNG	3087	12W-4S	B7
Elnora Smith Pk, EVTN	2867	3W-11N	A2
Emerson Pk, MPPT	2808	15W-13N	A6
Emerson Pk, SKOK	2865	6W-11N	E2
Emily Pk, SKOK	2866	5W-9N	A6
Emmerich East Pk, BFGV	2754	16W-18N	C2
Emmerich Pk, BFGV	2754	17W-18N	C2
Emmerson Pk, CHCG	2921	2W-7N	B3
Enneth B Shipley Memorial Field, - STGR	3596	0W-28S	B6
Equestrian Pk, OrlT	3423	13W-18S	A1
Erfert Pk, LNSG	3510	3E-22S	A1
Eric Nasebandt Pk, TYPK	3424	9W-20S	E5

Chicago & Cook County Points of Interest Index

Parks & Recreation

Chicago & Cook County Points of Interest Index

FEATURE NAME Address City ZIP Code	MAP#	CGS	GRID
Rutherford Pk, CHCG	2974	8W-2N	E6
Ruth MacIntyre Pk, SMBG	2858	24W-9N	D7
Ruzicka Memorial Pk, BRLT	2911	28W-7N	B4
Sacajawea Pk, IHPK	3146	14W-7S	D5
Sacramento Pk, CHCG	2976	3W-4N	E3
Safari Springs Family Aquatic Center, - HRPK	2911	27W-7N	D5
Saganashkee Slough, PlsT	3272	15W-12S	B3
St. Boniface Pk, TYPK	3425	8W-19S	A2
St. Claire Pk, SMBG	2859	22W-10N	D4
St. Francis Pk, ELGN	2855	33W-12N	A2
Salceda Pk, NHBK	2756	13W-18N	A2
Salk Pk, SMBG	2858	24W-10N	D5
Salt Creek Pk, EGVV	2914	19W-8N	D2
Sandburg Pk, HRVY	3349	1W-17S	E4
Sanders Pk, EGVV	2861	18W-9N	A7
Sangamon Pk, CHHT	3508	1W-24S	A5
Sarah's Grove Pk, SMBG	2859	23W-10N	A5
Sauganash Pk, CHCG	2920	5W-7N	A4
Sauk School Pk, RNPK	3594	5W-26S	C3
Savannah Pk, SMBG	2912	26W-8N	A2
Sayre Pk, CHCG	2974	8W-2N	E6
Schiller Pk, ITSC	2914	19W-6N	D6
Schiller Pk, SRPK	2973	12W-5N	B2
Schoppe Pk, BRLT	2911	28W-8N	A2
Schreiber Pk, CHCG	2921	2W-8N	C2
Schroeder Pk, BDVW	3087	11W-1S	E1
Schultz Pk, LNSG	3430	4E-21S	B7
Schussler Pk, ODPK	3346	11W-17S	A5
Schuster Pk, BNVL	2972	15W-5N	B1
Scottsdale Pk, CHCG	3212	5W-9S	A3
Scout Pk, MDLN	3348	5W-17S	B5
Scoville Pk, OKPK	3030	8W-0N	E3
Searle Pk, SKOK	2865	6W-10N	E5
Sears Pk, ALSP	3276	4W-14S	D6
Seifer Pk, CHHT	3596	0W-25S	D1
Seminole Pk, DSPN	2917	12W-8N	B2
Seminole Pk, HFET	2804	25W-14N	A3
Seneca Pk, CHCG	3034	0E-1N	C2
Seneca Pk, SKOK	2866	5W-10N	B4
Senior Citizens Memorial Pk, CHCG	2977	2W-2N	A6
Senka Pk, CHCG	3150	4W-6S	D3
Senn Pk, CHCG	2921	1W-7N	C4
Sequoya Pk, SKOK	2865	6W-11N	D2
Sergeant Mean's Pk, OMFD	3507	3W-25S	B6
Sesquintennial Pk, DSPN	2863	12W-11N	A2
Seward Pk, CHCG	3034	0W-1N	A2
Shabbona Pk, CHCG	2974	8W-4N	E3
Shabbona Pk, PKFT	3595	3W-28S	A5
Shabonee Pk, SKOK	2866	5W-12N	B1
Shady Oaks Pk, SMWD	2857	28W-10N	A6
Shana Elman Pk, DRFD	2757	10W-20N	B2
Sharp Pk, MLPK	3029	12W-1N	B2
Shawmut Pk, LGNG	3087	12W-4S	C6
Sheed Pk, CHCG	3090	4W-2S	C2
Sheffield Pk, HFET	2858	25W-12N	A2
Sheffield Ridge Pk, SMBG	2858	26W-11N	A3
Sheil Pk, CHCG	2977	1W-4N	D3
Shelton Pk, GLNC	2758	5W-17N	E6
Shenandoah Pk, EGVV	2913	21W-8N	E3
Shepard Pk, DRFD	2756	11W-20N	D1
Sheridan Pk, CHCG	3033	1W-0S	E6
Sherman Pk, CHCG	3151	1W-5S	D2
Shermer Pk, MNGV	2864	9W-11N	D2
Sherwin Avenue Beach & Pk, CHCG	2867	1W-9N	D7
Sherwood Pk, CHCG	3152	0W-6S	B3
Simmons Pk, CHCG	2976	4W-2N	D7
Sioux Pk, DSPN	2808	14W-12N	C7
Sippel Memorial Field, BCHR	3864	0W-36S	C2
Site 21 Pk, BFGV	2754	17W-20N	A1
Skinner Pk, CHCG	3033	1W-0S	D5
Skokie Sculpture Pk, SKOK	2866	4W-11N	D3
Skokie Sports Pk, SKOK	2866	4W-9N	C6
Skokie Valley Pk, SKOK	2866	5W-9N	A7
Sleepy Hollow Pk, GNVW	2810	8W-13N	E5
Slinglerland Pk, SMBG	2913	23W-9N	A1
Sloan Pk, HFET	2858	24W-11N	D3
Smirz Pk, BRWN	3089	7W-3S	B5
Smith Memorial Pk, CHHT	3507	2W-25S	E7
Smith Pk, CHCG	3033	3W-0N	A3
Smith Pk, LYNS	3088	10W-4S	B7
Snapper Field Pk, ALGN	2748	33W-20N	A1
Soehrman Pk, CTSD	3147	13W-7S	A7
Somonauk Pk, PKFT	3594	4W-27S	E5
Southeast Pk, ENGN	3212	3W-11S	E7
South End Pk, WDND	2801	34W-15N	A4
Southfield Knoll Pk, BCHR	3864	0W-37S	C3
South Pk, DRFD	2756	11W-20N	C1
South Pk, IVNS	2804	23W-14N	E3
South Pk, PKRG	2918	10W-8N	A3
South Ridge Lake Pk, HFET	2804	24W-15N	B3
South Twin Pk, HFET	2804	24W-12N	D7
Southwest Pk, PKRG	2917	10W-7N	E3
Sparrow Pk, PLTN	2805	22W-15N	B2
Spirit Creek Pk, ODPK	3344	14W-18S	E6
Spirit Trail Pk, OMFD	3506	4W-25S	E7
Springdale Pk, WNSP	3146	13W-5S	E3
Springfield Pk, BMDL	2912	24W-5N	D7
Springhill Pk, ROSL	2913	22W-7N	C5
Spring Rock Pk, WNSP	3146	14W-4S	D1
Spruce Pk, CHCG	3153	1E-5S	A2
Stahlak Pk, WRTH	3275	8W-13S	B3
Stanton Schiller Pk, CHCG	3034	0W-1N	A1
Stars & Stripes Pk, CHCG	3148	8W-5S	E2
Stateway Pk, CHCG	3092	0W-3S	B5
Station Pk, FTPK	3030	9W-0S	D6
Stevenson Pk, BLWD	3029	12W-0N	B4
Stevenson Pk, BRBK	3211	7W-9S	C3
Stevenson Pk, OKPK	3031	7W-0N	B4
Stevens Pk, BRRG	3208	15W-9S	B4
Stonegate Pk, NHBK	2809	11W-16N	C1
Stone Hollow Pk, HLCT	3427	3W-21S	A6
Stone Monroe Pk, LGPK	3087	12W-3S	B5
Stoney Island Pk, CHCG	3215	2E-10S	C4
Stout Pk, CHCG	3152	1E-5S	E2
Streamside Pk, HRVY	3350	1W-17S	A4
Strohacker Pk, CHCG	3150	5W-5S	B3
Struckman Basin, BRLT	2910	29W-6N	E7
Sullivan Pk, OKLN	3212	5W-11S	B7
Summit Pk, SMMT	3148	9W-6S	C4
Sundance Pk, HFET	2804	24W-15N	C2
Sunken Gardens Pk, CHCG	2921	3W-5N	A7
Sunnydale Pk, SMWD	2911	27W-9N	B1
Sunny Side Pk, ODPK	3346	10W-16S	A2
Sunrise Pk, BNVL	2972	15W-4N	A2
Sunrise Pk, BRLT	2910	29W-6N	D7
Sunrise Pk, MPPT	2862	15W-11N	B2
Sunset Meadows Pk, ANHT	2806	18W-13N	D6
Sunset Pk, ANHT	2753	18W-18N	E2
Sunset Pk, BRLT	2910	29W-6N	D7
Sunset Pk, MPPT	2861	16W-11N	E2
Sunset Pk, SMBG	2913	22W-8N	B1
Sunset Ridge Pk, CCHL	3426	6W-21S	A6
Sunshine Pk, BRWN	3088	8W-2S	E3
Sunshine Pk, DLTN	3350	0E-16S	E2
Superior Pk, CHCG	3033	2W-0N	B3
Surkey Wood Pk, SMWD	2856	29W-11N	D4
Sweet Briar Pk, WSTR	3086	14W-2S	D3
Swenson Pk, GNVW	2810	9W-13N	C6
Swiss Valley, CRTE	3596	0E-28S	E5

FEATURE NAME Address City ZIP Code	MAP#	CGS	GRID
Sycamore Pk, HFET	2858	23W-12N	E1
Sycamore Pk, PLTN	2753	19W-17N	B6
Sycamore Trails Pk, MPPT	2808	14W-14N	C5
Taft Pk, HRVY	3428	0W-19S	B2
Tall Grass Pk, BRLT	2911	28W-7N	B5
Tallmadge Pk, EVTN	2867	2W-12N	B1
Tall Oaks Pk, HFET	2856	31W-12N	A2
Tall Tree Pk, GNVW	2810	8W-14N	E5
Tamarack Trails Pk, MPPT	2808	13W-14N	E5
Tartan Pk, BFGV	2754	16W-20N	D1
Taylor-Lauridsen Pk, CHCG	3092	0W-4S	A6
Taylor Pk, CHCG	3152	0W-5S	C1
Taylor Pk, OKPK	3031	8W-1N	A2
Terada Pk, SMBG	2858	24W-10N	D6
Terminal Pk, SKOK	2866	5W-11N	A2
Terrace Pk, BNVL	2915	17W-7N	C3
Terrace View Pk, SHLD	3429	1E-19S	B3
Terry Steczo Pk, OKFT	3347	7W-17S	C5
The Bowl, LMNT	3270	19W-13S	D5
The Pk Of River Oaks, CTCY	3429	2E-19S	C2
Thiele Pk, HLSD	3028	13W-0S	E5
Thomas T Hamilton Pk, PLTN	2752	21W-17N	E5
Thornbark Pk, HFET	2804	24W-15N	C2
Thorncreek Pk, SHLD	3429	1E-20S	A4
Thorndale Pk, SHLD	3428	0E-20S	E4
Thornwood Pk, SHLD	3428	0E-20S	D4
Thornwood Pk, WLMT	2812	5W-14N	A4
Throop Pk, CHCG	3151	1W-5S	D1
Tilton Pk, CHCG	3032	5W-0N	B4
Timbercrest Pk, SMBG	2859	23W-10N	A6
Timberline Pk, LMNT	3270	20W-14S	B6
Timber Ridge Pk, SKOK	2866	4W-11N	C3
Tinley Gardens Pk, TYPK	3423	11W-22S	E7
Tolentine Pk, OMFD	3506	4W-24S	D6
Tomahawk Pk, DSPN	2862	14W-11N	B3
Tomahawk Pk, SHLD	3350	0W-18S	C6
Tom Ping Memorial Pk, CHCG	3092	0W-1S	B1
Touhy Herbert Pk, CHCG	3033	2W-0S	B5
Touhy Pk, CHCG	2867	2W-9N	C7
Tower Pk, CCHL	3426	4W-20S	D4
Tower Road Pk, WNKA	2759	5W-16N	B7
Town & Country Pk, DLTN	3350	0W-17S	B5
Town Center Pk, HMGN	3343	17W-17S	B5
Town Pointe Pk, TYPK	3424	10W-21S	B6
Trails End Pk, BRLT	2911	27W-7N	C5
Trail Tree Pk, DRFD	2757	9W-20N	B1
Travelers Pk, BlmT	3507	2W-25S	C6
Trebes Pk, CHCG	2977	1W-2N	D6
Tree Nursery Pk, SMWD	2856	28W-10N	E6
Treetop Pk, ODPK	3345	12W-18S	C7
Triangle Pk, CHCG	3032	5W-0N	B3
Triangle Pk, DLTN	3351	1E-17S	B6
Triangle Pk, HRVY	3428	1W-19S	A3
Tri-County State Pk, BRLT	2909	32W-7N	C4
Trout Pk, ELGN	2801	33W-13N	B7
Trumbull Pk, CHCG	3279	2E-11S	D1
Tuley Pk, CHCG	3214	0E-10S	D4
Turner Pk, HMND	3352		E5
Turner Pk, ROSL	2913	23W-7N	A4
Twiggs Pk, EVTN	2866	3W-12N	E1
Twin Lakes Pk, HMGN	3344	15W-18S	B7
Udall Pk, EGVV	2861	17W-9N	B6
Ulrich Pk, BGVW	3210	9W-8S	D1
Union Creek Community Pk, FftT	3504	10W-23S	C4
Union Pk, CHCG	3033	1W-0N	D4
Unity Pk, CHCG	2976	4W-3N	D5
Valley Forge Pk, CHCG	3148	8W-6S	E4
Valley Pk, BmdT	2912	23W-6N	E5
Valley Pk, HFET	2804	23W-15N	D2
Van Laten Pk, LNSG	3429	2E-21S	C7
Van Oostenbrugge Pk, SHLD	3350	0E-18S	E7
Van Voorst Pk, EMHT	3028	15W-0N	B5
Vattmann Pk, WLMT	2812	4W-13N	C5
Veeck Pk, HNDL	3146	14W-4S	C1
Veteran Pk, SMBG	2857	26W-10N	E5
Veterans Memorial Pk, GLNC	2758	6W-17N	D4
Veterans Memorial Pk, LNSG	3430	4E-19S	B3
Veterans Memorial Pk, PKFT	3595	3W-26S	B3
Veterans Memorial Pk, SHLD	3428	0E-18S	E1
Veterans Memorial Pk, STGR	3596	0W-28S	B6
Veterans Pk, CHCG	3215	3E-11S	E6
Veterans Pk, CTCY	3430	3E-19S	B3
Veterans Pk, NRIV	3088	9W-2S	C3
Veterans Pk, ODPK	3346	9W-18S	D7
Veterans Pk, SKOK	2865	6W-10N	D5
Veterans Pk, SMWD	2857	28W-10N	B5
Veterans Pk, TYPK	3424	9W-19S	D1
VFW Little League Pk, HMWD	3428	1W-21S	A6
Victoria Pk, HFET	2858	25W-11N	B3
Victory Pk, ANHT	2860	18W-12N	D1
Village Green Pk, CTCY	3429	2E-18S	C1
Village Green Pk, NHBK	2757	9W-17N	B5
Village Green Pk, WNKA	2812	4W-15N	B2
Village in the Pk, SMBG	2858	23W-12N	E1
Village Square Pk, ODPK	3344	11W-18S	E7
Vine Pk, SMWD	2857	28W-9N	B7
Virginia Terrace Pk, ANHT	2806	18W-15N	D2
Vittum Pk, CHCG	3149	6W-5S	E1
Vogelei Pk, HFET	2858	24W-12N	D2
Vogt Woods Community Pk, TYPK	3425	8W-20S	B4
Volbrecht Pk, SHLD	3429	1E-20S	B4
Volkening Pk, SMBG	2858	24W-10N	C5
Volunteer Pk, TYPK	3424	10W-21S	C5
Volz Pk, ANHT	2806	18W-14N	E4
Wacker Pk, CHHT	3508	0W-25S	B6
Wagner Pk, CHCG	3151	1W-5S	E1
Waiola Pk, LGNG	3147	12W-5S	B1
Wales S Stamper Pk, OMFD	3507	3W-24S	A5
Walker Pk, CTWD	3347	6W-16S	E3
Walker Pk, LynT	3208	13W-8S	E1
Wallace Pk, CHCG	3214	0W-10S	A5
Wally Degner Pk, PltT	2805	22W-15N	B1
Warren Pk, CCRO	3089	7W-1S	C1
Warren Pk, CHCG	2921	2W-8N	A2
Washington Circle Pk, HNDL	3146	15W-5S	A3
Washington Commons Pk, RVFT	3030	9W-0N	B4
Washington Pk, CHCG	3152	0E-6S	D3
Washington Pk, EMHT	3028	15W-0N	A4
Washington Pk, HMWD	3428	1W-21S	A5
Washington Pk, ITSC	2914	19W-6N	C7
Washington Square Pk, CHCG	3034	0W-1N	B2
Washington Square Pk, RVFT	3030	9W-0N	B4
Washington Triangle Pk, RVFT	3030	9W-0N	C4
Washtenaw Pk, CHCG	2977	3W-3N	A4
Wastenaw Pk, CHCG	3091	3W-2S	A2
Waterford Pk, WLBK	3146	15W-7S	A6
Water Tower Pk, BCHR	3864	1W-36S	B2
Watts Pk, GLNC	2758	6W-17N	D6
Waverly Creekside Pk, OKFT	3348	5W-18S	A7
Waverly Pk, MDLN	3348	4W-17S	D4
Weber Pk, SKOK	2865	6W-11N	E2
Wedgewood Commons Pk, ODPK	3346	10W-16S	C4
Wedgewood Estates Pk, ODPK	3346	10W-17S	B4
Wedgewood Pk, MPPT	2808	15W-14N	A4
We Go Pk, MPPT	2807	16W-12N	D7
Weidner Pk, BFGV	2754	17W-18N	B2
Wellers Creek Pk, MPPT	2861	16W-12N	E2
Welles Pk, CHCG	2921	2W-5N	A7
Wentland Athletic Field, MLPK	3029	11W-1N	E3
Wentworth Gardens Pk, CHCG	3092	0W-3S	B5

FEATURE NAME Address City ZIP Code	MAP#	CGS	GRID
Wentworth Pk, CHCG	3149	7W-6S	B3
Wescott Pk, NHBK	2757	10W-16N	A6
Wesley G Usher Memorial Pk, ITSC	2914	19W-6N	C6
Westbury Lake Pk, HFET	2804	24W-15N	C2
West Chatham Pk, CHCG	3214	0W-9S	B2
Westdale Pk, LydT	2972	14W-3N	D4
West Elm Street Pk, WNKA	2811	5W-15N	E1
Western Pk, CHCG	3033	2W-1N	B2
Westfield Pk, DSPN	2862	14W-10N	C4
West Fork Pk, GNVW	2810	8W-15N	D2
Westgate Valley Pk, PSHT	3347	8W-15S	A1
West Lawn Pk, CHCG	3150	5W-7S	B5
West Morton Pk, CCRO	3089	6W-2S	D2
West Pk, DSPN	2862	14W-11N	D3
West Pk, NHBK	2756	11W-16N	D6
West Pullman Pk, CHCG	3278	0W-14S	B6
West Ridge Pk, HDPK	2757	9W-20N	C1
West River Pk, CHCG	2920	3W-6N	E6
Whealan Pool, CHCG	2919	7W-8N	B2
Whihala Beach County Pk, HMND	3280		E3
Whippoorwill Pk, PLTN	2805	22W-14N	B3
Whispering Willow Pk, HGKN	3147	12W-7S	C6
White Pk, CHCG	3277	1W-14S	E5
Whittaker Pk, BRRG	3208	15W-8S	B2
Wierzba Pk, BGVW	3210	9W-8S	D2
Wigwam Pk, SHLD	3350	0E-18S	D7
Wild Meadow Pk, EMHT	3028	15W-0N	B4
Wildwood Pk, ANHT	2754	16W-16N	D7
Wildwood Pk, CHCG	2919	7W-8N	B1
Wilkins Pk, ALSP	3276	5W-15S	B7
William Aldis Sr Pk, WDND	2801	34W-15N	A3
Williamsburg Pk, NHBK	2757	9W-18N	D3
Williams Pk, CHCG	3092	0W-2S	B3
Williams Pk, OKLN	3212	5W-11S	B7
Willowbrook Pk, SHLD	3428	0E-19S	D2
Willow Pk, ANHT	2807	17W-16N	C1
Willow Pk, CHCG	3152	1E-5S	E2
Willow Pk, DSPN	2863	13W-11N	A2
Willow Pk, GNVW	2810	10W-15N	A2
Willow Pk, HFET	2804	24W-14N	C4
Willow Pk, NHFD	2811	7W-15N	B2
Willow Pk, PLTN	2753	20W-16N	A6
Willow Stream Pk, BFGV	2754	17W-20N	B1
Willow Trails Pk, PTHT	2808	13W-15N	E1
Wilmington Pk, HFET	2858	24W-11N	C2
Wilson Pk, CHCG	3091	1W-3S	E4
Windemere Pk, EGVV	2913	22W-8N	C2
Winding Creek Pk, BRLT	2911	28W-7N	A5
Windsor Pkway Pk, ANHT	2807	17W-13N	C5
Windsor Ridge Pk, BFGV	2754	17W-18N	B4
Windy Oaks Pk, BRLT	2910	30W-9N	B1
Winfield Pk, BFGV	2754	18W-18N	A3
Winnebago Pk, PKFT	3595	4W-26S	A2
Winnebago Pk, SKOK	2866	5W-10N	B5
Winnemac Pk, CHCG	2921	2W-6N	B6
Winston Pk, PLTN	2806	19W-15N	C1
Winterhoff Pk, LNSG	3430	3E-21S	B6
Wlodarski Pk, ODPK	3424	10W-19S	A3
Wolf Lake Pk, HMND	3280		D6
Wolf Pk, CCHL	3506	5W-22S	B1
Wolf Pk, CHCG	3280	3E-12S	A2
Womens Welfare Pk, BCHR	3864	1W-36S	B1
Woodborough Pk, HMWD	3508	1W-22S	A1
Woodbridge Pk, HDPK	2757	8W-20N	D2
Wood Dale Community Pk, WDDL	2915	18W-7N	A5
Woodgate Pk, MTSN	3505	7W-24S	D5
Woodhull Pk, CHCG	3153	2E-8S	B7
Woodland Pk, CHCG	3092	0E-3S	D4
Woodland Pk, HYHL	3209	11W-10S	E5
Woodland Pk, PKRG	2863	11W-10N	E5
Woodland Pk, SMWD	2857	27W-10N	C7
Woodland Trails Pk, MPPT	2808	14W-14N	C4
Woodlawn Pk, FftT	3504	9W-25S	E7
Woodstock Pk, SMBG	2858	24W-9N	E7
Worthbrook Pk, OKLN	3211	7W-10S	B4
Worth Woods Pk, WRTH	3274	9W-12S	D3
Worthy Pk, HRVY	3349	3W-18S	B6
Wright Pk, ELGN	2855	32W-10N	C6
Wright Pk, SKOK	2865	6W-10N	E4
Wrightwood Pk, CHCG	2977	1W-3N	D5
Yangas Pk, HMGN	3344	15W-16S	C3
Yellowstone Pk, ALGN	2748	32W-20N	B1
York Commons, EMHT	3028	15W-0N	A5
Young Pk, CHCG	3033	1W-0S	D5
Youth Pk, BLWD	3029	12W-0N	B4
Ziebell Pk, HRVY	3349	3W-17S	B6
Zocher Pk, SMBG	2858	24W-11N	D3

Post Offices

FEATURE NAME Address City ZIP Code	MAP#	CGS	GRID
AMF O'Hare Finance 11600 W Irving Park Rd, CHCG, 60666	2972	14W-5N	D2
Arlington Heights Main 909 W Euclid Av, ANHT, 60005	2806	18W-14N	E4
Ashburn 3639 W 79th St, CHCG, 60652	3212	4W-9S	D2
Auburn Park 8345 S Ashland Av, CHCG, 60620	3213	1W-9S	D3
Barrington Main 1515 S Grove Av, BRTN, 60010	2751	25W-17N	A5
Bartlett 160 Railroad Av, BRLT, 60103	2910	29W-8N	E3
Bedford Park 6801 W 73rd St, BDPK, 60638	3149	8W-8S	A7
Beecher 712 Penfield St, BCHR, 60401	3864	0W-36S	C2
Bellwood Main 2800 St. Charles Rd, BLWD, 60104	3029	12W-0N	C4
Bensenville Main 303 E Green St, BNVL, 60106	2972	15W-5N	A1
Berwyn 6625 Cermak Rd, BRWN, 60402	3089	8W-2S	A2
Blue Island Main 2441 Vermont St, BLID, 60406	3349	3W-15S	B1
Bridgeview 7401 W 100th Pl, BGVW, 60455	3210	9W-11S	D7
Broadview 2131 S 17th Av, BDVW, 60155	3029	11W-0S	D7
Brookfield Main 3731 Prairie Av, BKFD, 60513	3087	11W-3S	E5
Buffalo Grove 255 N Buffalo Grove Rd, BFGV, 60089	2754	16W-20N	C1
Burbank 7401 W 100th Pl, BGVW, 60455	3210	9W-11S	D7
Calumet City Main 1200 159th St, CTCY, 60409	3429	2E-19S	D1
Cardiss Collins 433 W Harrison St, CHCG, 60607	3034	0W-0S	B6
Carpentersville Main 100 N Kennedy Dr, CPVL, 60110	2748	33W-18N	C5
Chicago Heights 1333 W End Av, CHHT, 60411	3508	0W-25S	B7
Chicago Ridge Main 10525 Ridgeland Av, CHRG, 60415	3275	7W-12S	B1
Cicero 2440 S Laramie Av, CCRO, 60804	3089	6W-2S	D2
Clearing 5645 S Archer Av, CHCG, 60638	3149	6W-5S	E2
Country Club Hills Branch 4053 183rd St, CCHL, 60478	3426	5W-22S	C7

Post Offices

Schools

Chicago & Cook County Points of Interest Index

FEATURE NAME Address City ZIP Code	MAP#	CGS	GRID
Dayspring Christian Academy 5133 W Fullerton Av, CHCG, 60639	2975	6W-3N	D5
DD Eisenhower High School 12700 Sacramento Av, BLID, 60406	3277	3W-14S	A7
Decatur Classical Elementary School 7030 N Sacramento Av, CHCG, 60645	2920	3W-8N	E1
De Diego Community Academy 1313 N Claremont Av, CHCG, 60622	3033	2W-1N	B1
Deer Creek Christian School 425 University Pkwy, UYPK, 60466	3684	3W-29S	B1
Delano Elementary School 3937 W Wilcox St, CHCG, 60624	3032	4W-0S	C5
De La Salle Institute-Main Campus 3455 S Wabash Av, CHCG, 60616	3092	0E-3S	C4
De La Salle Institute-West Campus 1040 W 32nd Pl, CHCG, 60608	3091	1W-3S	D4
Deneen Elementary School 7240 S Wabash Av, CHCG, 60619	3152	0E-8S	C7
Depriest Elementary School 139 S Parkside Av, CHCG, 60644	3031	7W-0S	C5
Dett Elementary School 2306 W Maypole Av, CHCG, 60612	3033	2W-0N	B4
Dever Elementary School 3436 N Osceola Av, CHCG, 60634	2974	9W-4N	C3
Devonshire Elementary School 1401 Pennsylvania Av, DSPN, 60018	2862	15W-10N	B5
Devonshire Elementary School 9040 Kostner Av, SKOK, 60076	2866	5W-11N	A3
Dewey Academy of Fine Arts 5415 S Union Av, CHCG, 60609	3152	0W-5S	A2
Dewey Elementary School 1551 Wesley Av, EVTN, 60201	2867	3W-11N	A3
DeWitt Clinton Elementary School 6110 N Fairfield Av, CHCG, 60659	2920	3W-7N	E3
Diekman Elementary School 15121 Dorchester Av, DLTN, 60419	3351	1E-17S	B6
Dirksen Elementary School 8601 W Foster Av, CHCG, 60656	2918	10W-6N	A6
Dirksen Elementary School 116 W Beech Dr, SMBG, 60193	2859	23W-10N	A6
Dirksen Middle School 1650 Pulaski Rd, CTCY, 60409	3351	2E-17S	D6
Disney Magnet Elementary School 4140 N Marine Dr, CHCG, 60613	2978	0W-5N	A1
Divine Infant Jesus School 1640 Newcastle Av, WSTR, 60154	3087	12W-1S	B1
Divine Providence School 2500 Mayfair Av, WSTR, 60154	3086	13W-2S	E3
Dixon Elementary School 8306 S St. Lawrence Av, CHCG, 60619	3214	0E-9S	D3
Dodge Renaissance Academy 2651 W Washington Blvd, CHCG, 60612	3033	3W-0N	A4
Dooley Elementary School 622 Norwood Ln, SMBG, 60193	2858	24W-9N	D7
Doolittle East School 535 E 35th St, CHCG, 60653	3092	0E-3S	D4
Dorn Primary Center 7840 W 92nd St, HYHL, 60457	3210	9W-10S	C5
Douglass Junior High Academy 543 N Waller Av, CHCG, 60644	3031	7W-0N	C3
Dr Charles E Gavin Elementary-School 280 E 12th St, CHHT, 60411	3508	0W-25S	C7
Drexel Elementary School 5407 W 36th St, CCRO, 60804	3089	6W-3S	D5
Dr Julian Rogus School 20027 S 88th Av, FftT, 60477	3504	10W-23S	B4
Dryden Elementary School 722 S Dryden Pl, ANHT, 60005	2807	17W-13N	B6
Dulles Elementary School 6311 S Calumet Av, CHCG, 60637	3152	0E-7S	D5
Dumas Elementary School 6650 S Ellis Av, CHCG, 60637	3152	1E-7S	E5
Dundee-Crown High School 1 Charger Country Dr, CPVL, 60110	2748	33W-18N	A5
Dunne Elementary School 10845 S Union Av, CHCG, 60628	3278	0W-12S	A2
Durkin Park Elementary School 8445 S Kolin Av, CHCG, 60652	3212	5W-9S	B3
Dusable High School 4934 S Wabash Av, CHCG, 60615	3152	0E-5S	C1
Dvorak Math-Science Tech Academy 3615 W 16th St, CHCG, 60623	3090	4W-1S	D1
Dwight D Eisenhower School 700 N Schoenbeck Rd, PTHT, 60070	2807	16W-15N	E1
Dyett Academic Center 555 E 51st St, CHCG, 60615	3152	0E-5S	D2
Eads Elementary School 8000 Jackson Av, MNSR, 46321	3430		D6
Eagles Wings Urban Academy 2447 W Granville Av, CHCG, 60659	2921	3W-7N	A3
Earhart Elementary School 1710 E 93rd St, CHCG, 60617	3215	2E-10S	B5
East Leyden High School 3400 Rose St, FNPK, 60131	2973	12W-4N	C3
East Prairie Elementary School 3907 Dobson St, SKOK, 60076	2866	4W-9N	B6
Eastview Elementary School 3411 Hopkins St, CRTE, 60475	3596	0W-28S	C5
Eastview Middle School 321 N Oak Av, BRLT, 60103	2910	28W-8N	E2
Echo Early Childhood Program 640 E 168th Pl, SHLD, 60473	3428	0E-19S	E3
Edgar Allen Poe Classical School 10538 S Langley Av, CHCG, 60628	3278	0E-12S	E1
Edgar A Poe Elementary School 2800 N Highland Av, ANHT, 60004	2754	18W-17N	A6
Edgebrook Elementary School 6525 N Hiawatha Av, CHCG, 60646	2919	6W-8N	D2
Edison Elementary School 246 S Fair Av, EMHT, 60126	3028	15W-1N	B3
Edison Elementary School 7025 Madison Av, HMND, 46324	3430		E3
Edison Elementary School 4100 Scoville Av, SKNY, 60402	3089	8W-4S	A6
Edison Regional Gifted Center 6220 N Olcott Av, CHCG, 60631	2918	9W-7N	C3
Edmund Burke Elementary School 5356 S King Dr, CHCG, 60615	3152	0E-5S	D2
Edward Everett Elementary School 3419 S Bell Av, CHCG, 60608	3091	2W-3S	B4
Eggers Middle School 5825 Blaine Av, HMND, 46320	3352		D7
Einstein Elementary School 1100 Laurie Ln, HRPK, 60133	2857	26W-9N	E7
Eisenhower Elementary School 16001 Minerva Av, SHLD, 60473	3429	1E-18S	B1
Eisenhower Junior High School 800 Hassell Rd, HFET, 60195	2804	24W-12N	D7
Elgin Academy 350 Park St, ELGN, 60120	2855	33W-11N	A3
Elgin High School 1200 Maroon Dr, ELGN, 60120	2855	32W-10N	D5
Eli Whitney Elementary School 2815 S Komensky Av, CHCG, 60623	3090	5W-2S	C3
Elizabeth Blackwell School 345 N Walnut Ln, SMBG, 60194	2858	26W-10N	A5
Elk Grove High School 500 W Elk Grove Blvd, EGVV, 60007	2860	18W-9N	D7
Ellington Branch Elementary School 243 N Parkside Av, CHCG, 60644	3031	7W-0N	C4
Ellington Elementary School 224 N Central Av, CHCG, 60644	3031	7W-0N	C4
Ellis Middle School 225 S Liberty St, ELGN, 60120	2855	33W-11N	B4
Elm Elementary School 15w201 60th St, BRRG, 60527	3146	15W-6S	B4
Elmer G Kich Elementary School 191 W 155th Pl, HRVY, 60426	3349	2W-18S	D7
Elm Middle School 7607 W Cortland St, EDPK, 60707	2974	9W-2N	C7
Elmwood Elementary School 2319 N 76th Av, EDPK, 60707	2974	9W-2N	C6
Elmwood Park High School 8201 W Fullerton Av, RVGV, 60171	2974	10W-2N	B6
Emerson Elementary School 3105 Clinton Av, BRWN, 60402	3088	8W-3S	E4
Emerson Elementary School 311 Washington Blvd, MYWD, 60153	3030	10W-0N	A4
Emerson Middle School 8101 N Cumberland Av, NLES, 60714	2864	10W-10N	A5
Emiliano Zapata Academy 2728 S Kostner Av, CHCG, 60623	3090	5W-2S	B3
Emmanuel Christian School 8301 S Damen Av, CHCG, 60620	3213	2W-9S	C3
Enders-Salk Elementary School 345 N Salem Dr, SMBG, 60194	2858	24W-10N	D4
Englewood Academy High School 6201 S Stewart Av, CHCG, 60621	3152	0W-6S	B4
Entrepreneurship School 7627 S Constance Av, CHCG, 60649	3215	2E-8S	C1
Ericson Scholastic Academy 3600 W 5th Av, CHCG, 60624	3032	4W-0S	C5
Esmond Elementary School 1865 W Montvale Av, CHCG, 60643	3277	2W-13S	C3
Euclid Elementary School 1211 N Wheeling Rd, MPPT, 60056	2808	14W-14N	B4
Eugene Field Elementary School 7019 N Ashland Blvd, CHCG, 60626	2921	1W-8N	C1
Eugene Field Elementary School 707 Wisner St, PKRG, 60068	2864	9W-9N	B6
Eugene Field Elementary School 51 Saint Armand Ln, WLNG, 60090	2754	15W-18N	E4
Evangelical Christian School 9130 S Vincennes Av, CHCG, 60620	3213	1W-10S	E5
Evangelic Assembly of God Academy 5100 W Diversey Av, CHCG, 60641	2975	6W-3N	E5
Evanston Twp High School 1600 Dodge Av, EVTN, 60201	2866	3W-11N	E3
Everett F Kerr Middle School 12915 Maple Av, BLID, 60406	3277	3W-15S	B7
Evergreen Middle Academy 3537 S Paulina St, CHCG, 60609	3091	2W-3S	C5
Evergreen Park High School 9901 S Kedzie Av, ENGN, 60805	3212	3W-11S	E7
Evers Elementary School 9811 S Lowe Av, CHCG, 60628	3214	0W-11S	A6
Fairfield Academy 6201 S Fairfield Av, CHCG, 60629	3151	3W-6S	A4
Fairview Elementary School 375 Arizona Blvd, HFET, 60194	2859	23W-11N	B4
Fairview Elementary School 300 N Fairview Av, MPPT, 60056	2807	15W-13N	E6
Fairview South Elementary School 7040 Laramie Av, SKOK, 60077	2919	6W-8N	D1
Falconer Elementary School 3020 N Lamon Av, CHCG, 60641	2975	6W-3N	E4
Faraday Elementary School 3250 W Monroe St, CHCG, 60624	3032	4W-0S	D5
Farnsworth Elementary School 5414 N Linder Av, CHCG, 60630	2919	6W-6N	C5
Farragut Career Academy 2345 S Christiana Av, CHCG, 60623	3090	4W-2S	D2
Farren Fine Arts Elementary School 5055 S State St, CHCG, 60615	3152	0E-5S	C1
Faulkner School 7110 S Coles Av, CHCG, 60649	3153	3E-8S	D6
FB McCord Elementary School 8450 Nashville Av, BRBK, 60459	3211	8W-9S	A3
Fenger Academy High School 11220 S Wallace St, CHCG, 60628	3278	0W-13S	A3
Fenwick High School 505 Washington Blvd, OKPK, 60302	3031	8W-0N	A5
FE Peacock Middle School 301 E North St, ITSC, 60143	2914	19W-6N	C5
Fermi Elementary School 1415 E 70th St, CHCG, 60637	3153	1E-7S	A6
Fernway Park Elementary School 16600 S 88th Av, ODPK, 60462	3424	11W-19S	A3
Fernwood Elementary School 10041 S Union Av, CHCG, 60628	3214	0W-11S	A7
Fieldcrest Elementary School 4100 Wagman St, OKFT, 60452	3426	5W-19S	C2
Field Elementary School 295 N Emroy Av, EMHT, 60126	3028	15W-1N	A1
Field Middle School 2055 Landwehr Rd, NHBK, 60062	2756	11W-16N	D7
Field Park Elementary School 4335 Howard Av, WNSP, 60558	3086	13W-4S	E7
Field-Stevenson Elementary School 925 Beloit Av, FTPK, 60130	3030	9W-0S	D6
Fierke Elementary School 6535 Victoria Dr, OKFT, 60452	3347	8W-18S	B7
Finkl Elementary School 2332 S Western Av, CHCG, 60608	3091	3W-2S	B2
Finley Junior High School 10835 Lombard Av, CHRG, 60415	3275	7W-12S	C2
Fiske Elementary School 6145 S Ingleside Av, CHCG, 60637	3152	1E-6S	E4
Fleming Branch Elementary School 4918 W 64th St, CHCG, 60638	3149	6W-7S	E5
Flossmoor Hills Elementary School 3721 Beech St, FSMR, 60422	3506	4W-22S	D1
Foreman High School 3235 N Leclaire Av, CHCG, 60641	2975	6W-4N	E4
Forest Elementary School 1375 S 5th Av, DSPN, 60018	2862	14W-10N	D5
Forest Hills Elementary School 5020 Central Av, WNSP, 60558	3146	14W-5S	D2
Forest Park Middle School 925 Beloit Av, FTPK, 60130	3030	9W-0S	D6
Forest Road Elementary School 901 Forest Rd, LGPK, 60525	3087	12W-3S	C4
Forest Trail Middle School 215 Wilson St, PKFT, 60466	3594	4W-26S	E3
Forest View Elementary School 1901 W Estates Dr, MPPT, 60056	2861	17W-12N	C2
Fort Dearborn Elementary School 9025 S Throop St, CHCG, 60620	3213	1W-10S	E4
Foster Elementary School 5931 School St, OKFT, 60452	3347	7W-18S	C6
Foster Park Elementary School 8530 S Wood St, CHCG, 60620	3213	2W-9S	C3
Foundations Elementary School 2040 W Adams St, CHCG, 60612	3033	2W-0S	B5
Fox Elementary School 1035 Parkview Dr, HRPK, 60133	2911	26W-9N	E1
Fox River Country Day School 1600 Dundee Av, DndT, 60118	2801	33W-14N	B7
Frances Xavier Warde School 120 S Des Plaines Av, CHCG, 60611	3034	0E-0N	C2
Francis Parker School 2233 N Clark St, CHCG, 60614	2978	0W-2N	B6
Frank C Whitely Elementary School 4335 Haman Av, HFET, 60195	2804	24W-15N	D2
Frankfort Square Elementary School 7710 W Kingston Dr, FftT, 60423	3504	9W-24S	D5
Franklin Elementary School 14701 Chicago Rd, DLTN, 60419	3350	0E-17S	E5
Franklin Elementary School 1000 116th St, HMND, 46394	3280		E4
Franklin Fine Arts Center 225 W Evergreen Av, CHCG, 60610	3034	0W-1N	B1
Franzen Intermediate School 730 Catalpa Av, ITSC, 60143	2914	20W-7N	B5
Frazier Elementary School 4027 W Grenshaw St, CHCG, 60624	3032	5W-0S	B7
Freedom Middle School 3016 Ridgeland Av, BRWN, 60402	3089	8W-2S	B4
Friendship Junior High School 550 Elizabeth Ln, DSPN, 60018	2862	15W-10N	A5
Frost Junior High School 320 W Wise Rd, SMBG, 60193	2912	23W-9N	E1
Fuller Elementary School 4214 S St. Lawrence Av, CHCG, 60653	3092	0E-4S	D6
Fulton Elementary School 5300 S Hermitage Av, CHCG, 60609	3151	2W-5S	C2
Fulton School 6601 171st St, TYPK, 60477	3425	8W-20S	B4
Funston Elementary School 2010 N Central Park Av, CHCG, 60647	2976	4W-2N	C7
Gage Park High School 5630 S Rockwell St, CHCG, 60629	3151	3W-6S	A3
Gale Community Academy 1631 W Jonquil Ter, CHCG, 60626	2867	2W-9N	C6
Galileo Scholastic Academy 820 S Carpenter St, CHCG, 60607	3033	1W-0S	E6
Gallistel Branch School 10200 S Avenue J, CHCG, 60617	3216	4E-11S	B7
Gallistel Language Academy 10347 S Ewing Av, CHCG, 60617	3280	4E-11S	B1
Garfield Elementary School 140 E 23rd St, CHHT, 60411	3596	0W-26S	B2
Garfield Elementary School 420 May St, ELGN, 60120	2855	33W-10N	A5
Garfield Elementary School 543 Hannah Av, FTPK, 60130	3030	9W-0S	D5
Garfield Elementary School 1514 S 9th Av, MYWD, 60153	3029	11W-0S	E6
Garrett A Morgan Elementary School 8407 S Kerfoot Av, CHCG, 60620	3214	0W-9S	A3
Garvy Elementary School 5225 N Oak Park Av, CHCG, 60656	2918	8W-6N	E5
Gemini Junior High School 8955 N Greenwood Av, NLES, 60714	2864	10W-11N	A3
General Patton Elementary School 13700 S Stewart Av, RVDL, 60827	3350	0W-15S	B2
George Armstrong Elementary School 2110 W Greenleaf Av, CHCG, 60645	2921	2W-8N	B1
George Carpenter Elementary School 300 N Hamlin Av, PKRG, 60068	2863	11W-9N	E7
George R Clark Elementary School 1045 S Monitor Av, CHCG, 60644	3031	7W-0S	C6
George Schneider Elementary School 2957 N Hoyne Av, CHCG, 60618	2977	2W-3N	B4
George Washington Elementary School 12545 S Homan Av, ALSP, 60406	3276	4W-14S	E6
George Washington Elementary School 3611 E 114th St, CHCG, 60617	3280	4E-13S	B3
George Washington Elementary School 1500 Stewart Av, PKRG, 60068	2917	11W-8N	E1
George Washington Elementary School 4835 Michigan Av, SRPK, 60176	2917	12W-6N	C7
George Washington High School 3535 E 114th St, CHCG, 60617	3280	4E-13S	B3
George Washington Middle School 4040 Joliet Av, LYNS, 60534	3088	10W-4S	C6
George W Curtis Elementary School 32 E 115th St, CHCG, 60628	3278	0E-13S	C4
Gillespie Elementary School 9301 S State St, CHCG, 60619	3214	0E-10S	C5
G Kerkstra Elementary School 14950 Laramie Av, OKFT, 60452	3347	6W-17S	E6
Gladstone Elementary School 1231 S Damen Av, CHCG, 60608	3033	2W-1S	C7
Glenbrook Elementary School 315 Garden Cir, SMWD, 60107	2857	27W-11N	C4
Glenbrook North High School 2300 Shermer Rd, NHBK, 60062	2810	10W-16N	B1
Glenbrook South High School 4000 W Lake Av, GNVW, 60025	2809	11W-14N	D4
Glen Grove Elementary School 3900 Glenview Rd, GNVW, 60025	2809	11W-13N	E6
Glen Oaks Elementary School 9045 S 88th Av, HYHL, 60457	3210	10W-10S	A5
Glenwood School 18700 S Halsted St, HMWD, 60430	3508	1W-22S	B1
Global Visions Academy 2710 E 89th St, CHCG, 60617	3215	3E-10S	E4
Goethe Elementary School 2236 N Rockwell St, CHCG, 60647	2977	3W-2N	A6
Goldblatt Elementary School 4257 W Adams St, CHCG, 60624	3032	5W-0S	B5
Goldsmith Elementary School 10211 S Crandon Av, CHCG, 60617	3215	2E-11S	D7
Golf Middle School 9401 Waukegan Rd, MNGV, 60053	2864	8W-11N	E2
Golfview Elementary School 124 Golfview Ln, CPVL, 60110	2801	32W-17N	D1
Gompers Fine Arts Optional School 12302 S State St, CHCG, 60628	3278	0W-14S	C6
Goodings Grove Elementary School 12914 W 143rd St, HmrT, 60441	3344	16W-16S	A4
Goodlow Magnet Elementary School 2040 W 62nd St, CHCG, 60636	3151	2W-6S	C4
Goodwin Elementary School 2625 S Austin Blvd, CCRO, 60804	3089	7W-2S	C3
Gordon School 14100 S Harrison Av, POSN, 60469	3349	3W-16S	A3
Gordon Tech High School 3633 N California Av, CHCG, 60618	2976	3W-4N	E2
Goudy Elementary School 5120 N Winthrop Av, CHCG, 60640	2921	1W-6N	D6
Gower Middle School 7941 S Madison St, BRRG, 60527	3208	15W-9S	A2
Grace Lutheran School 4106 W 28th St, CHCG, 60623	3090	5W-2S	B3
Grace Lutheran School 7300 Division St, RVFT, 60305	3030	9W-1N	D2
Graham Elementary School 4436 S Union Av, CHCG, 60609	3092	0W-4S	A7
Grant Elementary School 1300 N 34th Av, MLPK, 60160	3029	12W-1N	B2
Grant Elementary School 2712 Miller Av, SCHT, 60411	3596	1W-26S	A3
Grant-White Elementary School 147 Circle Av, FTPK, 60130	3030	9W-0N	D4
Graves Elementary School 6021 S 74th Av, SMMT, 60501	3148	9W-6S	D4

FEATURE NAME Address City ZIP Code	MAP#	CGS	GRID
Gray Elementary School 3730 N Laramie Av, CHCG, 60641	2975	6W-4N	D2
Gray M Sanborn Elementary School 101 N Oak St, PLTN, 60067	2805	20W-16N	E1
Greeley Elementary School 275 Fairview Av, WNKA, 60093	2812	4W-15N	C3
Greeley Regional Gifted Center 832 W Sheridan Rd, CHCG, 60613	2977	1W-4N	E2
Greenbriar Elementary School 101 W Greenbriar Av, CHHT, 60411	3508	1W-24S	A5
Greenbriar Elementary School 1225 Greenbriar Ln, NHBK, 60062	2757	10W-17N	A5
Greenbrier Elementary School 2330 N Verde Dr, ANHT, 60004	2753	18W-16N	D7
Greenbrook Elementary School 5208 Arlington Cir, HRPK, 60133	2911	26W-6N	E6
Greene Elementary School 3525 S Honore St, CHCG, 60609	3091	2W-3S	C5
Greenwood Elementary School 16801 Greenwood Av, SHLD, 60473	3429	1E-19S	A3
Gregory Elementary School 3715 W Polk St, CHCG, 60624	3032	4W-0S	C6
Gresham Elementary School 8524 S Green St, CHCG, 60620	3214	1W-9S	A3
Grissom Elementary School 12810 S Escanaba Av, CHCG, 60633	3279	3E-14S	E7
Grissom Middle School 17000 80th Av, TYPK, 60477	3424	10W-20S	C4
Gross Middle School 3524 Maple Av, BKFD, 60513	3087	11W-3S	D5
Grove Avenue Elementary School 900 S Grove Av, BRTN, 60010	2751	25W-18N	A3
Grove Elementary School 1000 Pfingsten Rd, NHBK, 60062	2756	11W-17N	E5
Grove Junior High School 777 W Elk Grove Blvd, EGVV, 60007	2914	18W-8N	E1
Guerin Prep High School 8001 Belmont Av, RVGV, 60171	2974	10W-3N	B4
Guggenheim Elementary School 7141 S Morgan St, CHCG, 60621	3151	1W-8S	E7
Gunsaulus Scholastic Academy 4420 S Sacramento Av, CHCG, 60632	3090	3W-4S	E7
Gurrie Middle School 1001 S Spring Av, LGNG, 60525	3147	12W-5S	B2
Gwendolyn Brooks Middle School 14741 Wallace St, HRVY, 60426	3350	0W-17S	B5
Hadley School 15731 S Bell Rd, HMGN, 60441	3422	15W-18S	A1
Haines Elementary School 247 W 23rd Pl, CHCG, 60616	3092	0W-2S	B2
Hale Elementary School 6140 S Melvina Av, CHCG, 60638	3149	7W-6S	B4
Hale Elementary School 1300 W Wise Rd, SMBG, 60193	2912	25W-9N	C1
Hales Franciscan High School 4930 S Cottage Grove Av, CHCG, 60615	3152	0E-5S	E1
Hamilton Elementary School 1650 W Cornelia Av, CHCG, 60657	2977	2W-4N	C3
Hamline Branch Elementary School 1548 W 48th St, CHCG, 60609	3151	1W-5S	D1
Hamline Elementary School 4747 S Bishop St, CHCG, 60609	3151	1W-5S	D1
Hamlin Upper Grade Center 12150 S Hamlin Av, ALSP, 60803	3276	4W-14S	D5
Hammond Elementary School 2819 W 21st Pl, CHCG, 60623	3090	3W-1S	E2
Hammond High School 5926 S Calumet Av, HMND, 46320	3430		E1
Hampton Fine & Performing Arts-School 3434 W 77th St, CHCG, 60652	3212	4W-8S	D1
Hancock College Prep 4034 W 56th St, CHCG, 60629	3150	5W-6S	B3
Hancock High School 4350 W 56th St, CHCG, 60629	3150	5W-6S	B3
Hanna Sacks Bais Yaakov High School 3021 W Devon Av, CHCG, 60659	2920	3W-8N	E2
Hannum Elementary School 9800 S Tripp Av, OKLN, 60453	3212	5W-11S	B7
Hanover Countryside Elementary-School 6 S Bartlett Rd, SMWD, 60107	2857	28W-10N	A5
Hanover Highlands Elementary School 1451 Cypress Av, HRPK, 60133	2911	26W-8N	E2
Hanson Park Elementary School 5411 W Fullerton Av, CHCG, 60639	2975	6W-2N	D6
Harlan Community Academy High-School 9652 S Michigan Av, CHCG, 60628	3214	0E-11S	C6
Harnew Elementary School 9101 Meade Av, OKLN, 60453	3211	7W-10S	C5
Harold Washington Elementary School 9130 S University Av, CHCG, 60619	3215	1E-10S	A5
Harper Elementary School 1101 Dartmouth St, WLMT, 60091	2812	5W-14N	A5
Harper High School 6520 S Wood St, CHCG, 60636	3151	2W-7S	C5
Harriet Tubbman Elementary School 333 E 142nd St, DLTN, 60419	3350	0E-16S	D3
Harte Elementary School 1556 E 56th St, CHCG, 60637	3153	2E-6S	B3
Harvard Elementary School 7525 S Harvard Av, CHCG, 60620	3214	0W-8S	B1
Hatch Elementary School 1000 N Ridgeland Av, OKPK, 60302	3031	7W-1N	B1
Haugan Elementary School 4540 N Hamlin Av, CHCG, 60625	2920	4W-5N	C7
Haven Middle School 2417 Prairie Av, EVTN, 60201	2866	3W-12N	E1
Havlicek Elementary School 6401 15th St, BRWN, 60402	3089	8W-1S	A1
Hawthorne Scholastic Academy 3319 N Clifton Av, CHCG, 60657	2977	1W-4N	E3
Hay Elementary Community Academy 1018 N Laramie Av, CHCG, 60651	3031	6W-1N	D2
Hayt Elementary School 1518 W Granville Av, CHCG, 60660	2921	1W-7N	C3
Hazelgreen Elementary School 11751 S Lawler Av, ALSP, 60803	3275	6W-13S	E4
Healy Elementary School 3010 S Parnell Av, CHCG, 60616	3092	0W-2S	A3
Healy Elementary School Annex 3040 S Parnell Av, CHCG, 60616	3092	0W-2S	A3
Hearst Elementary School 4640 S Lamon Av, CHCG, 60638	3149	6W-4S	E1
Heather Hill Elementary School 1439 Lawrence Cres, FSMR, 60422	3507	3W-23S	B3
Hedges Branch Elementary School 1954 W 48th St, CHCG, 60609	3151	2W-5S	C1
Hedges Elementary School 4747 S Winchester Av, CHCG, 60609	3151	2W-5S	C1
Hefferan Elementary School 4409 W Wilcox St, CHCG, 60624	3032	5W-0S	A5
Helen Keller Elementary School 7846 163rd St, TYPK, 60477	3424	9W-19S	D2
Henderson Elementary School 5650 S Wolcott Av, CHCG, 60636	3151	2W-6S	C3
Hendricks Community Academy 4316 S Princeton Av, CHCG, 60609	3092	0W-4S	B7
Henking Elementary School 2941 Linneman St, GNVW, 60025	2810	10W-13N	B7
Henry D Lloyd Elementary School 2103 N Lamon Av, CHCG, 60639	2975	6W-2N	E6
Henry H Nash Elementary School 4837 W Erie St, CHCG, 60644	3031	6W-0N	E3
Henry R Clissold Elementary School 2350 W 110th Pl, CHCG, 60643	3277	2W-12S	B2
Henson Elementary School 1326 S Avers Av, CHCG, 60623	3032	4W-1S	C7
Herbert Elementary School 2131 W Monroe St, CHCG, 60612	3033	2W-0S	B5
Heritage Elementary School 507 Arnold Av, SMWD, 60107	2911	28W-9N	B1
Heritage Middle School 6850 31st St, BRWN, 60402	3088	8W-3S	E4
Heritage Middle School 19250 Burnham Av, LNSG, 60438	3510	3E-22S	B2
Heritage Middle School 6021 S 74th Av, SMMT, 60501	3148	9W-6S	D4
Herzl Elementary School 3711 W Douglas Blvd, CHCG, 60623	3032	4W-1S	C7
Hester Junior High School 2836 Gustav St, FNPK, 60131	2973	12W-3N	C5
Hiawatha Elementary School 6539 26th St, BRWN, 60402	3089	8W-2S	A3
Hibbard Elementary School 3244 W Ainslie St, CHCG, 60625	2920	4W-6N	D6
Hickory Bend Elementary School 600 E 191st Pl, GNWD, 60425	3509	1E-23S	A2
Hickory Elementary School 1009 Blackhawk Dr, UYPK, 60466	3684	3W-30S	B3
Hickory Point School 500 Laburnum Dr, NHBK, 60062	2756	12W-18N	C3
Higgins Community Academy 11710 S Morgan St, CHCG, 60643	3278	1W-13S	A4
Highcrest Middle School 569 Hunter Rd, WLMT, 60091	2812	5W-13N	B6
Highland Elementary School 9700 Crawford Av, SKOK, 60076	2866	5W-12N	B1
Highlands Elementary School 3420 Laurel Ln, HLCT, 60429	3426	4W-20S	E4
Highlands Elementary School 5850 Laurel Av, LynT, 60525	3146	13W-6S	E4
Highlands Middle School 1850 W Plainfield Rd, LynT, 60525	3146	13W-6S	E4
High Point Elementary School 14825 West Av, ODPK, 60462	3345	12W-17S	C5
Hillcrest High School 17401 Pulaski Rd, CCHL, 60478	3426	4W-20S	D5
Hillel Torah North Day School 7120 Laramie Av, SKOK, 60077	2919	6W-8N	D1
Hille Middle School 5800 151st St, OKFT, 60452	3347	7W-17S	D6
Hillside Academy 431 N Hillside Av, HLSD, 60162	3028	14W-0N	D5
Hillside Elementary School 4804 Harrison St, HLSD, 60162	3028	14W-0S	D6
Hinsdale Adventist Academy 631 E Hickory St, HNDL, 60521	3146	14W-4S	C1
Hinsdale Central High School 200 W 55th St, HNDL, 60521	3146	15W-6S	A3
Hinsdale Middle School 100 S Garfield Av, HNDL, 60521	3146	15W-5S	B2
Hinton Elementary School 644 W 71st St, CHCG, 60621	3152	0W-7S	A6
Hiram H Belding Elementary School 4257 N Tripp Av, CHCG, 60641	2976	5W-5N	B1
Hirsch Metropolitan High School 7740 S Ingleside Av, CHCG, 60619	3214	1E-8S	E1
Hitch Elementary School 5625 N McVicker Av, CHCG, 60646	2919	7W-7N	B4
HL Richards High School 10601 Central Av, OKLN, 60453	3275	6W-12S	D1
H McNelty School 2100 Main St, MLPK, 60160	3029	11W-0N	D3
Hodgkins Elementary School 6516 Kane Av, HGKN, 60525	3147	11W-7S	D6
Hoffman Elementary School 2000 Harrison St, GNVW, 60025	2810	9W-12N	D7
Hoffman Estates High School 1100 W Higgins Rd, HFET, 60195	2858	24W-12N	C2
Holden Elementary School 1104 W 31st St, CHCG, 60608	3091	1W-2S	E3
Hollywood Elementary School 3423 Hollywood Av, BKFD, 60513	3088	10W-3S	A5
Holmes Elementary School 955 W Garfield Blvd, CHCG, 60621	3151	1W-6S	E3
Holmes Elementary School 16000 Carse Av, HRVY, 60426	3428	1W-19S	B2
Holmes Elementary School 508 N Kenilworth Av, OKPK, 60302	3030	8W-1N	E3
Holmes Junior High School 1900 W Lonnquist Blvd, MPPT, 60056	2861	17W-12N	C2
Holmes Middle School 221 S Wolf Rd, WLNG, 60090	2755	14W-17N	C4
Holy Angels School 545 E Oakwood Blvd, CHCG, 60653	3092	0E-4S	D6
Holy Family Catholic Academy 2515 Palatine Rd, HFET, 60195	2804	24W-15N	C1
Holy Family Lutheran School 4256 W Walton St, CHCG, 60651	3032	5W-1N	B2
Holy Ghost School 260 N Wood Dale Rd, WDDL, 60191	2915	18W-5N	A7
Holy Trinity High School 1443 W Division St, CHCG, 60622	3033	1W-1N	D2
Home Elementary School 4400 Home Av, SKNY, 60402	3088	8W-4S	E7
Homer Junior High School 15711 S Bell Rd, HMGN, 60441	3422	15W-18S	A1
Hometown Elementary School 8870 S Duffy Av, HMTN, 60456	3212	5W-10S	B4
Homewood Community Academy 18620 Kedzie Av, HMWD, 60430	3507	4W-22S	A1
Homewood-Flossmoor High School 999 Kedzie Av, FSMR, 60422	3507	3W-22S	A2
Hoover Elementary School 1259 Superior Av, CTCY, 60409	3430	3E-19S	A1
Hoover Elementary School 315 N Springinsguth Rd, SMBG, 60194	2858	25W-10N	B5
Hope College Preparatory High-School 5515 S Lowe Av, CHCG, 60621	3152	0W-6S	A3
Hope Lutheran School 6416 S Washtenaw Av, CHCG, 60629	3151	3W-7S	A5
Horace Mann Elementary School 8050 S Chappel Av, CHCG, 60617	3215	2E-9S	C2
Horace Mann Elementary School 921 N Kenilworth Av, OKPK, 60302	3030	8W-1N	E2
Horizon Elementary School 1701 Greenbrook Blvd, HRPK, 60133	2911	27W-6N	D6
Hough Street Elementary School 310 S Hough St, BRTN, 60010	2750	25W-18N	E2
Hoyne School 8905 S Crandon Av, CHCG, 60617	3215	2E-10S	D4
Hubbard High School 6200 S Hamlin Av, CHCG, 60629	3150	4W-6S	C4
Hubbard Woods Elementary School 1110 Chatfield Rd, WNKA, 60093	2758	5W-16N	E7
Huff Elementary School 801 Hastings St, ELGN, 60120	2855	32W-10N	B6
Humboldt Community Christian School 1847 N Humboldt Blvd, CHCG, 60647	2976	3W-2N	E7
Hunting Ridge Elementary School 1105 W Illinois Av, PLTN, 60067	2805	22W-14N	B3
Hurley Elementary School 3849 W 69th Pl, CHCG, 60629	3150	4W-7S	C6
Hyde Park Academy High School 6220 S Stony Island Av, CHCG, 60637	3153	1E-6S	B4
Hynes Elementary School 9000 Belleforte Av, MNGV, 60053	2864	8W-11N	E3
Ida Crown Jewish Academy 2828 W Pratt Blvd, CHCG, 60645	2920	3W-8N	E1
Ideal Elementary School 9901 W 58th St, CTSD, 60525	3147	12W-6S	C4
Illiana Christian High School 2261 Indiana Av, LNSG, 60438	3429	2E-21S	D6
Illinois Primary Center 210 Illinois St, PKFT, 60466	3595	3W-25S	B1
Immaculate Conception School 1431 N North Park Av, CHCG, 60610	3034	0W-1N	B1
Immaculate Conception School 8739 S Exchange Av, CHCG, 60617	3215	3E-10S	E3
Immaculate Conception School 7263 W Talcott Av, CHCG, 60631	2918	9W-7N	D4
Immaculate Heart of Mary High-School 10900 W Cermak Rd, WSTR, 60154	3086	13W-1S	E2
Immanuel Lutheran School 5 S Van Buren St, EDND, 60118	2801	33W-16N	A2
Immanuel Lutheran School 148 E 3rd St, EMHT, 60126	3028	15W-1N	A1
Immanuel Lutheran School 200 N Plum Grove Rd, PLTN, 60067	2752	21W-16N	E7
Incarnation School 5705 W 127th St, WthT, 60463	3275	7W-15S	D7
Independence Junior High School 6610 W Highland Dr, PSHT, 60463	3275	8W-15S	A7
Indiana Elementary School 165 Indiana St, PKFT, 60466	3595	3W-25S	A1
Indian Grove Elementary School 1340 N Burning Bush Ln, MPPT, 60056	2808	13W-14N	E4
Indian Trail Elementary School 20912 S Frankfort Square Rd, FftT, 60423	3504	9W-25S	D7
Infant Jesus of Prague School 1101 Douglas Av, FSMR, 60422	3507	3W-23S	B2
Infinity High School 3120 S Kostner Av, CHCG, 60623	3090	5W-3S	A4
Inter-American Magnet School 919 W Barry Av, CHCG, 60657	2977	1W-3N	E4
Iroquois Community School 1836 E Touhy Av, DSPN, 60018	2917	12W-9N	B1
Irving Elementary School 3501 Clinton Av, BRWN, 60402	3088	8W-3S	E5
Irving Elementary School 4727 S Pine Av, HMND, 46327	3352		E4
Irving Elementary School 805 S 17th Av, MYWD, 60153	3029	11W-0N	D5
Irving Park Middle School 3815 N Kedvale Av, CHCG, 60641	2976	5W-4N	B2
Ivy Hill Elementary School 2211 N Burke Dr, ANHT, 60004	2754	17W-16N	B7
Jackson Language Academy 1340 W Harrison St, CHCG, 60607	3033	1W-0S	D5
Jacob Beidler Elementary School 3151 W Walnut St, CHCG, 60612	3032	3W-0N	E4
Jacqueline B Kennedy School 7644 Central Av, BRBK, 60459	3211	7W-8S	D1
Jahn Elementary School 3149 N Wolcott Av, CHCG, 60657	2977	2W-3N	C4
James B Conant High School 700 E Cougar Tr, HFET, 60194	2859	22W-11N	C4
James G Blaine Elementary School 1420 W Grace St, CHCG, 60613	2977	1W-4N	D2
James Hart School 18220 Morgan St, HMWD, 60430	3428	1W-21S	A7
James Madison Elementary School 7433 S Dorchester Av, CHCG, 60619	3153	1E-8S	A7
James Monroe Elementary School 3651 W Schubert Av, CHCG, 60647	2976	4W-3N	C5
James R Lowell Elementary School 3320 W Hirsch St, CHCG, 60651	3032	4W-1N	D1
James Shields Elementary School 4250 S Rockwell St, CHCG, 60632	3091	3W-4S	A6
James Thorp Elementary School 8914 S Buffalo Av, CHCG, 60617	3216	4E-10S	A4
Jamieson Elementary School 5650 N Mozart St, CHCG, 60659	2920	3W-7N	E4
Jane Addams Elementary School 910 Division St, MLPK, 60160	3029	11W-1N	E2
Jane Addams Elementary School 1020 E Sayles Dr, PLTN, 60074	2753	19W-16N	C6
Jane A Neil Elementary School 8555 S Michigan Av, CHCG, 60619	3214	0E-9S	C3
Jane Stenson Elementary School 9201 Lockwood Av, SKOK, 60077	2865	6W-11N	D2
J Calhoun North Elementary School 2833 W Adams St, CHCG, 60612	3032	3W-0S	E5
Jefferson Elementary School 225 46th Av, BLWD, 60104	3029	13W-0N	A4
Jefferson Elementary School 7035 16th St, BRWN, 60402	3088	8W-1S	E1
Jefferson Elementary School 176 E 11th St, CHHT, 60411	3508	0W-25S	B7
Jefferson Elementary School 360 E Crescent Av, EMHT, 60126	3028	15W-0N	A5
Jefferson Elementary School 560 W 144th St, RVDL, 60827	3350	0W-16S	B4
Jenner Academy of the Arts 1119 N Cleveland Av, CHCG, 60610	3034	0W-1N	A2
Jensen Scholastic Academy 3030 W Harrison St, CHCG, 60612	3032	3W-0S	E6
Jerling Junior High School 8851 W 151st St, ODPK, 60462	3346	11W-18S	A6
Jesse Sherwood Elementary School 245 W 57th St, CHCG, 60621	3152	0W-6S	B3
JFH Educational Academy 7642 W Irving Park Rd, NRDG, 60706	2974	9W-5N	C2
J Giles Elementary School 4251 N Oriole Av, NRDG, 60706	2974	9W-5N	C1
J Leigh Elementary School 8151 W Lawrence Av, NRDG, 60706	2918	10W-5N	B7
Joan Dachs Bais Yaakov 3200 W Peterson Av, CHCG, 60659	2920	3W-7N	D3
John Barry Elementary School 2828 N Kilbourn Av, CHCG, 60641	2976	5W-3N	A4
John B Drake Elementary School 2722 S King Dr, CHCG, 60616	3092	0E-2S	D3
John C Burroughs Elementary School 3542 S Washtenaw Av, CHCG, 60632	3091	3W-3S	A5
John C Coonley Elementary School 4046 N Leavitt St, CHCG, 60618	2977	2W-5N	B1
John C Dore Elementary School 6108 S Natoma Av, CHCG, 60638	3149	8W-6S	A4
John F Eberhart Elementary School 3400 W 65th Pl, CHCG, 60629	3150	4W-7S	D5
John F Kennedy Elementary School 3945 Wehrman Av, SRPK, 60176	2973	12W-4N	B2

Chicago & Cook County Points of Interest Index

FEATURE NAME Address City ZIP Code	MAP#	CGS	GRID
John F Kennedy High School 6325 W 56th St, CHCG, 60638	3149	8W-6S	A3
John Hersey High School 1900 E Thomas St, ANHT, 60004	2807	16W-15N	D2
John Jay Elementary School 1835 W Pheasant Tr, MPPT, 60056	2861	17W-11N	C3
John Laidlaw Elementary School 4072 Forest Av, WNSP, 60558	3086	14W-4S	D7
John L Marsh Elementary School 9810 S Exchange Av, CHCG, 60617	3215	3E-11S	E6
John Middleton Elementary School 8300 St. Louis Av, SKOK, 60076	2866	4W-10N	C5
John Mills Elementary School 2824 N 76th Av, EDPK, 60707	2974	9W-3N	C5
John Muir Literacy Academy 1973 Kensington Ln, HFET, 60195	2858	25W-12N	A1
Johnnie Coleman Academy 1441 W 119th St, CHCG, 60643	3277	1W-14S	D5
Johnson Elementary School 1420 S Albany Av, CHCG, 60623	3032	3W-1S	E7
John W Cook Elementary School 8150 S Bishop St, CHCG, 60620	3213	1W-9S	D2
Jonathan Burr Elementary School 1621 W Wabansia Av, CHCG, 60622	2977	2W-2N	C7
Jones College Prep High School 606 S State St, CHCG, 60605	3034	0W-0S	B6
Jordan Community Academy 7414 N Wolcott Av, CHCG, 60626	2867	2W-9N	B7
Josephine Perry Elementary School 251 Amarillo Dr, CPVL, 60110	2748	33W-18N	B4
Josephinum Academy 1501 N Oakley Blvd, CHCG, 60622	3033	2W-1N	B1
Joseph Sears Elementary School 542 Abbotsford Rd, KLWH, 60043	2812	4W-14N	C4
JS Morton East High School 2423 S Austin Blvd, CCRO, 60804	3089	7W-2S	C2
JS Morton West High School 2400 Home Av, BRWN, 60402	3088	8W-2S	E2
Juarez Community Academy 2150 S Laflin St, CHCG, 60608	3091	1W-1S	D1
Julian High School 10330 S Elizabeth St, CHCG, 60643	3277	1W-12S	E1
Julia Ward Howe Elementary School 720 N Lorel Av, CHCG, 60644	3031	6W-0N	D3
Juliette Low Elementary School 1530 S Highland Av, ANHT, 60005	2861	18W-12N	A1
Jungman Elementary School 1746 S Miller St, CHCG, 60608	3091	1W-1S	E1
JW James Christian School 911 S 6th Av, MYWD, 60153	3030	10W-0N	A5
Kahler Middle School 600 Joliet St, DYR, 46311	3598		D2
Kanoon Magnet Elementary School 2233 S Kedzie Av, CHCG, 60623	3090	3W-2S	E2
Kellar School 14123 S Lydia Av, RBBN, 60472	3348	4W-16S	E3
Keller Junior High School 820 Bode Rd, SMBG, 60194	2858	24W-11N	D3
Keller Regional Gifted Center 3020 W 108th St, CHCG, 60655	3276	3W-12S	E2
Kellman Corporate Community Elem-School 751 S Sacramento Blvd, CHCG, 60612	3032	3W-0S	E6
Kellogg Elementary School 9241 S Leavitt St, CHCG, 60620	3213	2W-10S	C5
Kelly High School 4136 S California Av, CHCG, 60632	3091	3W-4S	A6
Kelvyn Park High School 4343 W Wrightwood Av, CHCG, 60639	2976	5W-3N	B5
Kennedy Elementary School 1013 Division St, CHHT, 60411	3507	2W-25S	D6
Kenwood Academy High School 5015 S Blackstone Av, CHCG, 60615	3153	1E-5S	A1
Kenwood Elementary School 6416 Hohman Av, HMND, 46324	3430		C2
Kershaw Elementary School 6450 S Lowe Av, CHCG, 60621	3152	0W-7S	A5
Key Elementary School 517 N Parkside Av, CHCG, 60644	3031	7W-0N	C3
Keystone Montessori School 7415 North Av, RVFT, 60305	3030	9W-1N	D1
Kilmer Elementary School 655 Golfview Ter, BFGV, 60089	2754	16W-18N	C4
Kilmer Elementary School 6700 N Greenview Av, CHCG, 60626	2921	1W-8N	C2
Kimball Hill Elementary School 2905 Meadow Dr, RGMW, 60008	2806	19W-13N	C5
King College Prep High School 4445 S Drexel Blvd, CHCG, 60653	3092	1E-4S	E7
King Elementary School 740 S Campbell Av, CHCG, 60612	3033	3W-0S	A6
Kingsley Elementary School 2300 Green Bay Rd, EVTN, 60201	2867	3W-12N	A1
Kinzie Elementary School 5625 S Mobile Av, CHCG, 60638	3149	7W-6S	B3
Kipling Elementary School 9351 S Lowe Av, CHCG, 60620	3214	0W-10S	A5
KIPP Ascend Academy Charter School 715 S Kildare St, CHCG, 60624	3032	5W-0S	B6
Kirby Elementary School 17300 Ozark Av, OrlT, 60477	3424	9W-20S	D5
Kohn Elementary School 10414 S State St, CHCG, 60628	3278	0W-12S	C1
Kolb Elementary School 9620 Normandy Av, OKLN, 60453	3211	8W-11S	A6
Kolmar Avenue Elementary School 10425 S Kolmar Av, OKLN, 60453	3276	5W-12S	B1
Kolmar Elementary School 4500 143rd St, CTWD, 60445	3348	5W-16S	B4
Komarek Elementary School 8940 W 24th St, NRIV, 60546	3087	11W-2S	E2
Komensky Elementary School 2515 Cuyler Av, BRWN, 60402	3089	7W-2S	B3
Koraes Elementary School 11025 S Roberts Rd, PSHL, 60465	3274	9W-12S	C3
Kozminski Community Academy 936 E 54th St, CHCG, 60615	3152	1E-5S	E2
Kruse Education Center 7617 Hemlock Dr, ODPK, 60462	3346	9W-18S	D7
Lafayette Elementary School 2714 W Augusta Blvd, CHCG, 60622	3033	3W-1N	A2
Lafayette Elementary School 856 E Sibley St, HMND, 46320	3352		E6
Lake Louise Elementary School 500 N Jonathan Dr, PLTN, 60074	2753	19W-16N	D7
Lake Park High School East Campus 600 Medinah Rd, ROSL, 60143	2913	22W-6N	C6
Lake Park High School West Campus 500 W Bryn Mawr Av, ROSL, 60172	2912	24W-7N	D5
Lake Shore School 5611 N Clark St, CHCG, 60660	2921	1W-7N	C4
Lakeview Elementary School 615 Lakeview Ln, HFET, 60194	2858	24W-11N	E4
Lake View High School 4015 N Ashland Av, CHCG, 60613	2977	2W-5N	C1
Lakewood School 1651 Ravine Ln, CPVL, 60110	2748	33W-17N	C7
Lane Elementary School 4600 W 123rd St, ALSP, 60803	3276	5W-14S	B6
Langston Hughes Elementary School 226 W 104th St, CHCG, 60628	3278	0W-12S	B1
Lansing Christian School 3660 Randolph St, LNSG, 60438	3430	4E-21S	C6
Lara Academy 4619 S Wolcott Av, CHCG, 60609	3091	2W-4S	C7
Larsen Middle School 665 Dundee Av, ELGN, 60120	2855	33W-12N	A2
Lasalle Language Academy 1734 N Orleans St, CHCG, 60614	2978	0W-2N	B7
Lathrop Elementary Academy 1440 S Christiana Av, CHCG, 60623	3032	4W-1S	D7
Latin School of Chicago 1531 N Dearborn Pkwy, CHCG, 60610	3034	0W-1N	B1
Laura S Ward Elementary School 410 N Monticello Av, CHCG, 60624	3032	4W-0N	C3
Laurel Hill Elementary School 1750 Laurel Av, HRPK, 60133	2911	27W-9N	D2
Lavizzo Elementary School 138 W 109th St, CHCG, 60628	3278	0W-12S	C2
Lawndale Community Academy 3500 W Douglas Blvd, CHCG, 60623	3032	4W-1S	D7
Lawn Manor Primary Center 4300 W 108th Pl, OKLN, 60453	3276	5W-12S	B2
Lawrence Elementary School 9928 S Crandon Av, CHCG, 60617	3215	2E-11S	D7
Lee Elementary School 6448 S Tripp Av, CHCG, 60629	3150	5W-7S	B5
Leland Elementary School 5221 W Congress Pkwy, CHCG, 60644	3031	6W-0S	D6
Lemont High School 800 Porter St, LMNT, 60439	3270	19W-13S	E5
Lemoyne Elementary School 851 W Waveland Av, CHCG, 60613	2977	1W-4N	E2
Lenart Regional Gifted Center 8101 S Lasalle St, CHCG, 60620	3214	0W-9S	B2
Leo High School 7901 S Sangamon St, CHCG, 60620	3214	1W-9S	A2
Lewis Elementary School 1431 N Leamington Av, CHCG, 60651	3031	6W-1N	E1
Lexington Elementary School 415 Lexington St, MYWD, 60153	3030	10W-0S	A6
LH Day School 1720 W 87th St, CHCG, 60620	3213	2W-9S	D4
Libby Elementary School 5300 S Loomis Blvd, CHCG, 60609	3151	1W-5S	D2
Liberty Elementary School 121 Naperville Rd, BRLT, 60103	2910	30W-8N	B3
Liberty Elementary School 4946 W 13th St, CCRO, 60804	3031	6W-1S	E7
Liberty Elementary School 8801 W 151st St, ODPK, 60462	3346	10W-18S	A6
Liberty Junior High School 5900 W 81st St, BRBK, 60459	3211	7W-9S	C2
Liberty Temple Academy 2255 W 79th St, CHCG, 60620	3213	2W-9S	B2
Lieb Elementary School 9101 Pembroke Ln, BGVW, 60455	3211	8W-10S	A5
Lincoln Elementary School 4300 Grove Av, BKFD, 60513	3087	11W-4S	E7
Lincoln Elementary School 3420 Jackson St, BLWD, 60104	3029	12W-0S	B5
Lincoln Elementary School 3545 S 61st Av, CCRO, 60804	3089	7W-3S	B5
Lincoln Elementary School 615 W Kemper Pl, CHCG, 60614	2978	0W-2N	A6
Lincoln Elementary School 1520 Center Av, CHHT, 60411	3596	0W-25S	B1
Lincoln Elementary School 410 157th St, CTCY, 60409	3352	4E-18S	B7
Lincoln Elementary School 14151 Lincoln Av, DLTN, 60419	3350	0E-16S	E3
Lincoln Elementary School 14100 Honore Av, DXMR, 60426	3349	2W-16S	D4
Lincoln Elementary School 910 Forest Av, EVTN, 60202	2867	2W-10N	C4
Lincoln Elementary School 4221 S Towle Av, HMND, 46327	3352		D3
Lincoln Elementary School 811 Chicago Av, MYWD, 60153	3029	10W-1N	E3
Lincoln Elementary School 1111 S Grove Av, OKPK, 60304	3030	8W-0S	E6
Lincoln Elementary School 1021 N Ridgewood Ln, PLTN, 60067	2753	20W-17N	A5
Lincoln Elementary School 511 Park Av, RVFT, 60305	3030	9W-0N	C3
Lincoln Hall Middle School 6855 N Crawford Av, LNWD, 60712	2920	4W-8N	B1
Lincoln Junior High School 14151 Lincoln Av, DLTN, 60419	3350	0E-16S	E3
Lincoln Junior High School 700 W Lincoln St, MPPT, 60056	2861	16W-12N	E1
Lincoln Junior High School 7839 Lincoln Av, SKOK, 60077	2865	6W-9N	E6
Lincoln Middle School 6432 16th St, BRWN, 60402	3089	8W-1S	A1
Lincoln Middle School 200 S Lincoln Av, PKRG, 60068	2917	10W-8N	E1
Lincoln Middle School 4050 Wagner Av, SRPK, 60176	2973	12W-5N	C2
Lincoln Park High School 2001 N Orchard St, CHCG, 60614	2978	0W-2N	A6
Lincoln Prairie Elementary School 500 Hillcrest Blvd, HFET, 60195	2858	24W-12N	E1
Lincoln School 2140 Broadway St, BLID, 60406	3349	2W-15S	C1
Lincolnwood Elementary School 2600 Colfax St, EVTN, 60201	2866	4W-12N	D1
Lindblom College Prep High School 6130 S Wolcott Av, CHCG, 60636	3151	2W-6S	C4
Lindop Elementary School 2400 S 18th Av, BDVW, 60155	3029	11W-1S	D7
Lines Elementary School 217 Eastern Av, BRTN, 60010	2751	24W-18N	B2
Link Elementary School 900 W Glenn Tr, EGVV, 60007	2913	21W-8N	E1
Lions Park Elementary School 300 E Council Tr, MPPT, 60056	2862	15W-12N	A1
Little Village Academy 2620 S Lawndale Av, CHCG, 60623	3090	4W-2S	C3
Living Word Christian Academy 501 Bellwood Av, BLWD, 60104	3029	12W-0N	B4
LJ Hauser Junior High School 65 Woodside Rd, RVSD, 60546	3088	9W-3S	C5
Locke 21st Century School 3141 W Jackson Blvd, CHCG, 60612	3032	3W-0S	E5
Locke Elementary School 2828 N Oak Park Av, CHCG, 60634	2974	8W-3N	E5
Logandale Middle School 3212 W George St, CHCG, 60618	2976	4W-3N	D4
London Middle School 1001 W Dundee Rd, WLNG, 60090	2754	15W-18N	E4
Longfellow Elementary School 501 Arlington Heights Rd, BFGV, 60089	2754	17W-18N	A3
Longfellow Elementary School 715 Highland Av, OKPK, 60304	3031	7W-0S	B5
Longwood Elementary School 441 N Longwood Dr, GNWD, 60425	3508	0W-22S	B1
Loop Lab School 300 N Michigan Av, CHCG, 60601	3034	0E-0N	C4
Lords Park Elementary School 323 Waverly Dr, ELGN, 60120	2855	32W-11N	C3
Lovett Elementary School 6333 W Bloomingdale Av, CHCG, 60639	2975	7W-2N	B7
Lowell-Longfellow Elementary School 15636 Lexington Av, HRVY, 60426	3427	1W-18S	E1
Loyola Academy 1100 Laramie Av, WLMT, 60091	2811	6W-14N	D5
Lutheran School of St. Luke 410 S Rush St, ITSC, 60143	2914	19W-6N	C7
Luther Burbank Elementary School 8235 Linder Av, BRBK, 60459	3211	6W-9S	D3
Luther Burbank Elementary School 2035 N Mobile Av, CHCG, 60639	2975	7W-2N	B7
Luther East High School 2750 Glenwood Lansing Rd, LNSG, 60438	3510	3E-22S	A2
Luther High School North 5700 W Berteau Av, CHCG, 60634	2975	7W-5N	C1
Luther High School South-Junior High-School 3130 W 87th St, CHCG, 60652	3212	3W-9S	E3
Lycee Francais de Chicago 613 W Bittersweet Pl, CHCG, 60613	2978	0W-5N	A1
Lyle Elementary School 7801 W 75th St, BGVW, 60455	3210	9W-8S	C1
Lyman A Budlong Elementary School 2701 W Foster Av, CHCG, 60625	2920	3W-6N	E6
Lyon Elementary School 1335 Waukegan Rd, GNVW, 60025	2810	8W-13N	E5
Lyons Twp High School-North 100 S Brainard Av, LGNG, 60525	3087	13W-4S	A7
Lyons Twp High School-South 4900 Gilbert Av, WNSP, 60558	3147	13W-5S	A2
MacArthur Elementary School 1800 Chippendale Rd, HFET, 60195	2858	24W-12N	C1
MacArthur Middle School 1310 N Wolf Rd, BKLY, 60163	3028	14W-0N	D3
MacArthur Middle School 700 N Schoenbeck Rd, PTHT, 60070	2807	16W-15N	E1
Maddock Elementary School 8258 South Sayre Av, BRBK, 60459	3210	8W-9S	E3
Madero Middle School 3202 W 28th St, CHCG, 60623	3090	4W-2S	E3
Madison Elementary School 611 S Madison St, HNDL, 60521	3146	15W-5S	A2
Madison Elementary School 15700 Orchid Dr, SHLD, 60473	3350	0E-18S	E7
Madison Elementary School 5100 Madison St, SKOK, 60077	2865	6W-10N	D5
Mae Jemison School 3450 W 177th St, HLCT, 60429	3426	4W-21S	E6
Mahalia Jackson Elementary School 917 W 88th St, CHCG, 60620	3214	1W-10S	A4
Maine East High School 2601 Dempster St, PKRG, 60068	2863	11W-10N	D4
Maine South High School 1111 S Dee Rd, PKRG, 60068	2917	11W-8N	D2
Maine West High School 1755 S Wolf Rd, DSPN, 60018	2862	14W-9N	D6
Manierre Elementary School 1420 N Hudson Av, CHCG, 60610	3034	0W-1N	A1
Manley Career Academy High School 2935 W Polk St, CHCG, 60612	3032	3W-0S	E6
Mannheim Middle School 2600 Hyde Park Av, LydT, 60164	2973	13W-3N	A5
Maple Middle School 2370 Shermer Rd, NHBK, 60062	2810	10W-16N	B1
Maranatha Christian Academy 115 W 108th St, CHCG, 60628	3278	0W-12S	C2
Marconi Community Academy 230 N Kolmar Av, CHCG, 60624	3032	5W-0N	A4
Marcus M Garvey Elementary School 10309 S Morgan St, CHCG, 60643	3278	1W-12S	A1
Maria High School 6727 S California Av, CHCG, 60629	3151	3W-7S	A6
Marian Catholic High School 700 Ashland Av, CHHT, 60411	3507	2W-24S	D5
Marie Murphy Middle School 2921 Illinois Rd, WLMT, 60091	2811	5W-14N	E4
Marion Jordan Elementary School 100 N Harrison Av, PLTN, 60067	2805	22W-16N	B1
Marist High School 4200 W 115th St, CHCG, 60655	3276	5W-13S	C4
Markham Park Elementary School 16239 Lawndale Av, MKHM, 60426	3426	4W-19S	D2
Mark Sheridan Academy 533 W 27th St, CHCG, 60616	3092	0W-2S	A3
Mark Twain Elementary School 515 Merle Ln, WLNG, 60090	2755	15W-17N	A5
Marquette Elementary School 6550 S Richmond St, CHCG, 60629	3150	3W-7S	E5
Marshall Elementary School 2501 Oak St, BLWD, 60104	3029	12W-0N	C4
Marshall Metropolitan High School 3250 W Adams St, CHCG, 60624	3032	4W-0S	D5
Marshall Middle School 3900 N Lawndale Av, CHCG, 60618	2976	4W-4N	C2
Marti Bilingual Education Center 5126 N Kenmore Av, CHCG, 60640	2921	1W-6N	E6
Martin Luther King Elementary-School 14600 Seeley Av, DXMR, 60426	3349	2W-17S	C5
Marva Collins Preparatory School 8035 S Honore St, CHCG, 60620	3213	2W-9S	C2
Marya Yates Elementary School 6131 Allemong Dr, MTSN, 60443	3505	7W-24S	C5
Mary Lyon Elementary School 2941 N McVicker Av, CHCG, 60634	2975	7W-3N	B4
Mary Seat of Wisdom School 1352 S Cumberland Av, PKRG, 60068	2918	10W-7N	A3
Mason Elementary School 4217 W 18th St, CHCG, 60623	3090	5W-1S	B1
Maternity BVM School 1537 N Lawndale Av, CHCG, 60651	3032	4W-1N	C1
Mather High School 5835 N Lincoln Av, CHCG, 60659	2920	3W-7N	E4
Matteson Elementary School 21245 Main St, MTSN, 60443	3594	4W-25S	E1
Maya Angelou Elementary School 15748 Page Av, HRVY, 60426	3427	2W-18S	D1
May Community Academy 512 S Lavergne Av, CHCG, 60644	3031	6W-0S	E6
Mayer Elementary School 2250 N Clifton Av, CHCG, 60614	2977	1W-2N	D6
Mayo Elementary School 249 E 37th St, CHCG, 60653	3092	0E-3S	C5
Maywood Elementary School 1001 165th St, HMND, 46324	3430		E2
McAuliffe Elementary School 1841 N Springfield Av, CHCG, 60647	2976	4W-2N	C7
McAuliffe Elementary School 8944 174th St, TYPK, 60477	3424	11W-20S	A5
McClellan Elementary School 3527 S Wallace St, CHCG, 60609	3092	0W-3S	A5
McClure Junior High School 4225 Wolf Road, WNSP, 60558	3086	13W-4S	E7
McCorkle Elementary School 4421 S State St, CHCG, 60653	3092	0E-4S	C7
McCormick Elementary School 2712 S Sawyer Av, CHCG, 60623	3090	4W-2S	D3

Chicago & Cook County Points of Interest Index

FEATURE NAME Address City ZIP Code	MAP#	CGS	GRID
McCosh Elementary School 6543 S Champlain Av, CHCG, 60637	3152	0E-7S	E5
MCC School 8601 Menard Av, MNGV, 60053	2865	7W-10N	C4
McCutcheon Branch Elementary School 4850 N Kenmore Av, CHCG, 60640	2921	1W-6N	E6
McCutcheon Elementary School 4865 N Sheridan Rd, CHCG, 60640	2921	1W-6N	E6
McDade Classical Elementary School 8801 S Indiana Av, CHCG, 60619	3214	0E-10S	C4
McDowell Elementary School 1419 E 89th St, CHCG, 60619	3215	1E-10S	B4
McKay Elementary School 6901 S Fairfield Av, CHCG, 60629	3151	3W-7S	A6
McKenzie Elementary School 649 Prairie Av, WLMT, 60091	2812	3W-13N	D6
McKinley Elementary School 3317 Butterfield Rd, BLWD, 60104	3029	12W-0N	B4
McKinley Elementary School 5900 W 14th St, CCRO, 60804	3031	7W-1S	C7
McKinley Elementary School 25 W 16th Pl, CHHT, 60411	3596	1W-25S	A1
McKinley Elementary School 850 E 170th St, SHLD, 60473	3429	1E-19S	A3
McKinley Junior High School 16949 Cottage Grove Av, SHLD, 60473	3429	1E-19S	A3
McKinley Park Elementary School 2744 W Pershing Rd, CHCG, 60632	3091	3W-3S	A6
McPherson Elementary School 4728 N Wolcott Av, CHCG, 60640	2921	2W-5N	C7
Mead Junior High School 1765 Biesterfield Rd, EGVV, 60007	2913	22W-9N	D1
Meadowbrook Elementary School 1600 Walters Av, NHBK, 60062	2757	9W-17N	C6
Meadowdale Elementary School 14 Ash St, CPVL, 60110	2748	32W-17N	C6
Meadow Lane Intermediate Center 11800 S Meadow Ln Dr, MTPK, 60803	3276	3W-13S	E5
Meadow Ridge School 10959 W 159th St, ODPK, 60467	3423	13W-19S	A1
Meadowview Elementary School 4701 179th Pl, CCHL, 60478	3426	5W-21S	B6
Meca Elementary Christian Academy 425 Bohland Av, BLWD, 60104	3029	12W-0N	B4
Medgar Evers Primary Academy Center 1101 E 10th St, FDHT, 60411	3509	1E-24S	B6
Medill Elementary School 1301 W 14th St, CHCG, 60608	3033	1W-1S	D7
Medinah Christian School 900 Foster Av, ROSL, 60157	2913	22W-6N	C6
Medinah Intermediate School 7n330 Medinah Rd, BmdT, 60157	2913	22W-7N	D5
Medinah Middle School 700 E Granville Av, ROSL, 60172	2913	22W-7N	C4
Medinah Primary School 22W300 Sunnyside Rd, BmdT, 60157	2913	22W-6N	C5
Melody Elementary School 412 S Keeler Av, CHCG, 60624	3032	5W-0S	B5
Melrose Park Elementary School 1715 W Lake St, MLPK, 60160	3029	11W-1N	D3
Melzer School 9400 Oriole Av, MNGV, 60053	2864	9W-11N	C2
Memorial Elementary School 6701 179th St, TYPK, 60477	3425	8W-21S	B6
Memorial Junior High School 2721 Ridge Rd, LNSG, 60438	3430	3E-21S	A6
Metcalfe Community Academy 12339 S Normal Av, CHCG, 60628	3278	0W-14S	B6
Metro Prep School 2525 E Oakton St, EGvT, 60005	2861	16W-9N	E6
Middlefork Primary School 405 Wagner Rd, NHFD, 60093	2811	7W-15N	B2
Midwestern Christian Academy 3465 N Cicero Av, CHCG, 60641	2975	5W-4N	E3
Millennium Elementary School 17830 84th Av, TYPK, 60477	3424	10W-21S	B6
Millennium School 18211 Aberdeen St, HMWD, 60430	3428	1W-21S	A7
Mitchell Branch Elementary School 2315 W Erie St, CHCG, 60612	3033	2W-0N	B3
Mitchell Elementary School 2233 W Ohio St, CHCG, 60612	3033	2W-0N	B3
ML King Junior Lab School 2424 Lake St, EVTN, 60201	2866	3W-11N	D3
M Moody Christian School 3811 W 139th St, RBBN, 60472	3348	4W-16S	D3
Mohawk Elementary School 917 W Hillside Dr, BNVL, 60106	2915	16W-6N	D7
Mohawk Elementary School 301 Mohawk St, PKFT, 60466	3595	4W-27S	A4
Mollison Elementary School 4415 S King Dr, CHCG, 60653	3092	0E-4S	D7
Monee Elementary School 5154 W Main St, MONE, 60449	3683	6W-31S	A5
Monroe Elementary School 210 N Madison St, HNDL, 60521	3146	16W-4S	A1
Montessori School House 5935 S Hohman Av, HMND, 46320	3430		D1
Morgan Park Academy 2153 W 111th St, CHCG, 60643	3277	2W-12S	B2
Morgan Park High School 1744 W Pryor Av, CHCG, 60643	3277	2W-12S	D3
Morrill Elementary Math & Science-School 6011 S Rockwell St, CHCG, 60629	3151	3W-6S	A4
Morse Elementary Tech School 620 N Sawyer Av, CHCG, 60624	3032	4W-0N	D3
Morton Career Academy 431 N Troy St, CHCG, 60612	3032	3W-0N	E3
Morton-Gingerwood Elementary School 16936 Forest Av, OKFT, 60452	3426	6W-20S	A4
Most Holy Redeemer School 9536 S Millard Av, ENGN, 60805	3212	4W-11S	D6
Mother McAuley Liberal Arts High-School 3737 W 99th St, CHCG, 60655	3212	4W-11S	D7
Mt Assisi Academy 13860 Main St, LmnT, 60439	3271	17W-13S	C4
Mt Carmel Academy-East Lakeview 720 W Belmont Av, CHCG, 60657	2978	0W-4N	A3
Mt Carmel High School 6410 S Dante Av, CHCG, 60637	3153	1E-7S	B5
Mt Greenwood Elementary School 10841 S Homan Av, CHCG, 60655	3276	4W-12S	E2
Mount Vernon Elementary School 10540 S Morgan St, CHCG, 60643	3278	1W-12S	A1
Mozart Elementary School 2200 N Hamlin Av, CHCG, 60647	2976	4W-2N	C6
Murphy Elementary School 3539 W Grace St, CHCG, 60618	2976	4W-4N	C2
Murray Language Academy 5335 S Kenwood Av, CHCG, 60615	3153	1E-5S	A2
Namaste Charter School 3540 S Hermitage Av, CHCG, 60609	3091	2W-3S	C5
Nathan Hale Elementary School 19055 Burnham Av, LNSG, 60438	3510	4E-22S	B1
Nathan Hale Intermediate School 5312 135th St, CTWD, 60445	3347	6W-15S	E2
Nathan Hale Middle School 5220 135th St, CTWD, 60445	3347	6W-15S	E2
Nathan Hale Primary School 5324 135th St, CTWD, 60445	3347	6W-15S	E2
Nathan S Davis Elementary School 3014 W 39th Pl, CHCG, 60632	3090	3W-4S	E6
National Teacher's Academy 55 W Cermak Rd, CHCG, 60616	3092	0W-2S	B1
Nativity BVM School 6820 S Washtenaw Av, CHCG, 60629	3151	3W-7S	A6
Nature Ridge Elementary School 1899 Westridge Blvd, BRLT, 60103	2909	32W-8N	D3
Navajo Heights Elementary School 12401 S Oak Park Av, PSHT, 60463	3275	8W-14S	A6
Nazareth Academy 1209 W Ogden Av, LGPK, 60525	3087	13W-3S	A6
Near North Montessori School 1434 W Division St, CHCG, 60622	3033	1W-1N	D1
Neil Armstrong Elementary School 5030 Imperial Dr, RNPK, 60471	3594	6W-27S	A4
Nelson Elementary School 8901 N Ozanam Av, NLES, 60714	2864	9W-11N	C3
Nettelhorst Elementary School 3252 N Broadway St, CHCG, 60657	2978	0W-4N	A3
Newberry Math-Science Academy 700 W Willow St, CHCG, 60614	2978	0W-2N	A7
New Covenant Christian Academy 15213 5th Av, PHNX, 60426	3350	0W-18S	B6
New Field Primary School 1707 W Morse Av, CHCG, 60626	2921	2W-8N	C1
New Sullivan Elementary School 8331 S Mackinaw Av, CHCG, 60617	3216	4E-9S	A2
Newton Bateman Elementary School 4220 N Richmond St, CHCG, 60618	2976	3W-5N	E1
New Trier High School Northfield-Campus 7 Happ Rd, NHFD, 60093	2811	6W-14N	C4
New Trier Twp Winnetka Campus 385 Winnetka Av, WNKA, 60093	2812	4W-15N	C3
Nicholas Senn High School 5900 N Glenwood Av, CHCG, 60660	2921	1W-7N	C4
Nichols Middle School 800 Greenleaf St, EVTN, 60202	2867	2W-10N	B4
Nicholson Specialty School 6006 S Peoria St, CHCG, 60621	3152	1W-6S	A4
Nightingale Elementary School 5250 S Rockwell St, CHCG, 60632	3151	3W-5S	A2
Niles North High School 9800 Lawler Av, SKOK, 60077	2865	6W-12N	E1
Niles West High School 5701 Oakton St, SKOK, 60077	2865	7W-9N	C6
Ninos Heros Academic Center 8344 S Commercial Av, CHCG, 60617	3215	3E-9S	E2
Nixon Elementary School 2121 N Keeler Av, CHCG, 60639	2976	5W-2N	B6
Nobel Elementary School 4127 W Hirsch St, CHCG, 60651	3032	5W-1N	B1
Nob Hill Elementary School 3701 168th St, CCHL, 60478	3426	4W-20S	D4
Noble Street Charter School 1012 N Noble St, CHCG, 60622	3033	1W-1N	D2
Norman Bridge School 3800 N New England Av, CHCG, 60634	2974	8W-4N	E2
Northbrook Junior High School 1475 Maple Av, NHBK, 60062	2757	9W-17N	C6
Northeast Elementary School 9058 S California Av, ENGN, 60805	3213	3W-10S	A5
North Elementary School 1789 Rand Rd, DSPN, 60016	2863	12W-11N	B3
North Elementary School 9500 Gage Av, FNPK, 60131	2973	11W-4N	C4
North Grand High School 4338 W Wabansia Av, CHCG, 60639	2976	5W-2N	A7
North Kenwood Charter School 1119 E 46th St, CHCG, 60653	3093	1E-4S	A7
Northlake Middle School 202 S Lakewood Av, NHLK, 60164	3028	13W-1N	D2
North Lawndale Charter High School 1616 S Spaulding Av, CHCG, 60623	3090	4W-1S	D1
North Park Elementary School 2017 W Montrose Av, CHCG, 60618	2977	2W-5N	B1
Northridge Prep School for Boys 8320 W Ballard Rd, NLES, 60714	2864	10W-11N	A3
North River Elementary School 4416 N Troy St, CHCG, 60625	2920	3W-5N	D7
North Shore Country Day School 310 Green Bay Rd, WNKA, 60093	2812	5W-15N	B2
North Shore Junior Academy 5220 N California Av, CHCG, 60625	2920	3W-6N	E5
Northside Academy-St. Gertrude 6216 N Glenwood Av, CHCG, 60660	2921	1W-7N	D3
Northside Catholic Academy-St. Ita 5525 N Magnolia Av, CHCG, 60640	2921	1W-6N	D5
Northside College Prep High School 5501 N Kedzie Av, CHCG, 60625	2920	3W-6N	D5
Northwest Elementary School 9200 Millard Av, ENGN, 60805	3212	4W-10S	D5
Northwest Institute Learning-Academy 5108 W Division St, CHCG, 60651	3031	6W-1N	E2
Northwest Middle School 5252 W Palmer St, CHCG, 60639	2975	6W-2N	D6
Norwood Park Elementary School 5900 N Nina Av, CHCG, 60631	2918	8W-7N	E4
Notre Dame High School 3000 N Mango Av, CHCG, 60634	2975	7W-3N	C4
Notre Dame High School 7655 W Dempster St, NLES, 60714	2864	9W-10N	C4
Oakdale Christian Academy 9440 S Vincennes Av, CHCG, 60620	3213	1W-10S	E5
Oak Elementary School 950 S Oak St, HNDL, 60521	3146	15W-5S	B3
Oak Forest High School 15201 Central Av, OKFT, 60452	3347	6W-18S	D6
Oak Glen Elementary School 2101 182nd St, LNSG, 60438	3429	2E-21S	D6
Oakhill Elementary School 502 S Oltendorf Rd, SMWD, 60107	2857	28W-10N	A6
Oak Lawn Community High School 9400 Southwest Hwy, OKLN, 60453	3211	7W-10S	C5
Oaklawn Hometown Middle School 5345 W 99th St, OKLN, 60453	3211	6W-11S	D7
Oak Park Christian School 931 Lake St, OKPK, 60301	3030	8W-0N	E4
Oak Park-River Forest High School 201 N Scoville Av, OKPK, 60302	3031	8W-0N	A3
Oak Prairie Junior High School 15161 S Gougar Rd, HmrT, 60441	3342	19W-18S	C7
Oak Ridge Elementary School 8791 W 103rd St, PSHL, 60465	3274	10W-12S	A1
Oakton Elementary School 436 Ridge Av, EVTN, 60202	2867	2W-9N	B6
Oakwood Elementary School 1130 Kim Pl, LMNT, 60439	3270	19W-14S	D7
Octavio Paz Charter School-Congress 2401 W Congress Pkwy, CHCG, 60612	3033	3W-0S	A5
Ogden Avenue Elementary School 501 W Ogden Av, LGNG, 60525	3087	12W-4S	B6
Ogden Elementary School 24 W Walton St, CHCG, 60610	3034	0W-1N	B2
Oglesby Elementary School 7646 S Green St, CHCG, 60620	3214	1W-8S	A1
O'Keeffe Elementary School 6940 S Merrill Av, CHCG, 60649	3153	2E-7S	C6
Old Orchard Junior High School 9310 Kenton Av, SKOK, 60076	2866	5W-11N	A2
Old Quarry Middle School 16100 127th St, LMNT, 60439	3342	20W-15S	C1
Olive-Mary Stitt Elementary School 303 E Olive St, ANHT, 60004	2807	17W-15N	B2
Oliver McCracken Middle School 8000 E Prairie Rd, SKOK, 60076	2866	4W-10N	B5
OL Westside-Presentation School 3900 W Lexington St, CHCG, 60624	3032	4W-0S	C6
Onahan Elementary School 6634 W Raven St, CHCG, 60631	2919	8W-7N	A3
Ontarioville Elementary School 2100 Elm Av, HRPK, 60133	2911	27W-8N	C3
Orchard Hill Farm School 16800 Kilpatrick Av, BmnT, 60477	3426	5W-20S	B3
Orchard Place Elementary School 2727 Maple St, DSPN, 60018	2917	12W-8N	B2
Oriole Park Elementary School 5424 N Oketo Av, CHCG, 60656	2918	9W-6N	D5
Orland Center Elementary School 9407 W 151st St, ODPK, 60462	3345	11W-18S	E6
Orland Junior High School 14855 West Av, ODPK, 60462	3345	12W-17S	C6
Orland Park Elementary School 9960 W 143rd St, ODPK, 60462	3345	12W-16S	C4
Orozco Elementary School 1940 W 18th St, CHCG, 60608	3091	2W-1S	C1
Orr High School 730 N Pulaski Rd, CHCG, 60624	3032	5W-0N	B3
Orrington Elementary School 2636 Orrington Av, EVTN, 60201	2813	2W-13N	B7
Ortiz de Dominguez Elementary-School 3000 S Lawndale Av, CHCG, 60623	3090	4W-2S	C3
Otis Elementary School 525 N Armour St, CHCG, 60622	3033	1W-0N	D3
O'Toole Elementary School 6550 S Seeley Av, CHCG, 60636	3151	2W-7S	C5
Our Lady of Charity School 3620 S 57th Ct, CCRO, 60804	3089	7W-3S	C5
Our Lady of Destiny South Campus 1880 Ash St, DSPN, 60018	2862	13W-9N	E6
Our Lady of Grace School 2446 N Ridgeway Av, CHCG, 60647	2976	4W-3N	C5
Our Lady of Guadalupe School 9050 S Burley Av, CHCG, 60617	3216	4E-10S	A4
Our Lady of Loretto School 9003 S Kostner Av, HMTN, 60456	3212	5W-10S	B5
Our Lady of Tepeyac High School 2228 S Whipple St, CHCG, 60623	3090	3W-2S	E2
Our Lady of Tepeyac School 2235 S Albany Av, CHCG, 60623	3090	3W-2S	E2
Our Lady of the Gardens School 13300 S Langley Av, CHCG, 60827	3350	0E-15S	E1
Our Lady of the Ridge School 10859 Ridgeland Av, CHRG, 60415	3275	7W-12S	B2
Our Lady of the Snows School 4810 S Leamington Av, CHCG, 60638	3149	6W-5S	E1
Our Lady of the Wayside School 432 S Mitchell Av, ANHT, 60005	2807	18W-13N	A5
Our Lady of Perpetual Help School 1123 Church St, GNVW, 60025	2810	8W-13N	E6
Our Lady of Victory School 4434 N Laramie Av, CHCG, 60630	2919	6W-5N	D7
Overton Elementary School 221 E 49th St, CHCG, 60615	3152	0E-5S	C1
Owen Scholastic Academy 8247 S Christiana Av, CHCG, 60652	3212	4W-9S	E3
Owens Community Academy 12450 S State St, CHCG, 60628	3278	0W-14S	C6
OW Huth Middle School 3718 213th Pl, MTSN, 60443	3594	4W-25S	D1
Pablo Casals Elementary School 3501 W Potomac Av, CHCG, 60651	3032	4W-1N	D1
Paderewski Learning Academy 2221 S Lawndale Av, CHCG, 60623	3090	4W-2S	C2
Palatine High School 1111 N Rohlwing Rd, PLTN, 60074	2753	20W-17N	B5
Palmer Elementary School 5051 N Kenneth Av, CHCG, 60630	2920	5W-6N	A6
Palos East Elementary School 7700 W 127th St, PSHT, 60463	3274	9W-14S	D7
Palos South Middle School 13100 S 82nd Av, PlsT, 60464	3346	10W-15S	C1
Palos West Elementary School 12700 S 104th Av, PlsT, 60464	3273	13W-14S	B7
Parker Community Academy 6800 S Stewart Av, CHCG, 60621	3152	0W-7S	B6
Parker Junior High School 2810 School St, FSMR, 60422	3507	3W-22S	B2
Park Junior High School 325 N Park Rd, LGPK, 60525	3087	12W-3S	B6
Parkman Elementary School 245 W 51st St, CHCG, 60609	3152	0W-5S	B2
Park Manor Elementary School 7037 S Rhodes Av, CHCG, 60637	3152	0E-7S	D6
Park School 14200 S Wentworth Av, RVDL, 60827	3350	0W-16S	C3
Parkside Community Academy 6938 S East End Av, CHCG, 60649	3153	2E-7S	B6
Parkview Elementary School 100 Richton Rd, CteT, 60475	3596	1W-28S	A7
Park View School 6200 Lake St, MNGV, 60053	2865	7W-11N	B3
Parkwood Elementary School 2150 Laurel Av, HRPK, 60133	2911	27W-9N	C2
Passages Charter School 1447 W Montrose Av, CHCG, 60613	2921	1W-5N	D7
Passow Elementary School 2838 Calwagner St, FNPK, 60131	2973	12W-3N	C5
Pasteur Elementary School 5825 S Kostner Av, CHCG, 60629	3150	5W-6S	B4
Patrick Henry Elementary School 4250 N Saint Louis Av, CHCG, 60618	2976	4W-5N	C1
Patton Elementary School 1616 N Patton Av, ANHT, 60004	2806	18W-15N	E1
Paul Revere Intermediate School 12331 Gregory St, BLID, 60406	3277	2W-14S	B6
Paul Revere Primary School 2300 123rd Pl, BLID, 60406	3277	2W-14S	B6
Peabody Elementary School 1444 W Augusta Blvd, CHCG, 60622	3033	1W-1N	D2
Peck Elementary School 3826 W 58th St, CHCG, 60629	3150	4W-6S	C3
Peirce International Studies School 1423 W Bryn Mawr Av, CHCG, 60640	2921	1W-6N	D4
Penn Elementary School 1616 S Avers Av, CHCG, 60623	3090	4W-1S	C1
Pennoyer Elementary School 5200 N Cumberland Av, NRDG, 60706	2918	10W-6N	A6
Peotone Elementary School 426 N Conrad St, PTON, 60468	3860	9W-37S	E3
Peotone High School 605 W North St, PTON, 60468	3860	9W-37S	D3
Peotone Junior High School 1 Blue Devil Dr, PTON, 60468	3860	9W-37S	E4

Chicago & Cook County Points of Interest Index

FEATURE NAME Address City ZIP Code	MAP#	CGS	GRID
Percy Julian Middle School 416 S Ridgeland Av, OKPK, 60302	3031	7W-0N	A5
Perez Elementary School 1241 W 19th St, CHCG, 60608	3091	1W-1S	D1
Pershing Magnet Humanities School 3113 S Rhodes Av, CHCG, 60616	3092	0E-3S	D3
Pershing West Middle School 3200 S Calumet Av, CHCG, 60616	3092	0E-3S	D4
Perspectives Charter School 1930 S Archer Av, CHCG, 60616	3092	0W-1S	B1
Peterson Elementary School 5510 N Christiana Av, CHCG, 60625	2920	4W-6N	D5
Philip Rogers Elementary School 7345 N Washtenaw Av, CHCG, 60645	2866	3W-9N	E7
Phillips Academy High School 244 E Pershing Rd, CHCG, 60653	3092	0E-3S	C5
Piccolo Specialty School 1040 N Keeler Av, CHCG, 60651	3032	5W-1N	B2
Pickard Elementary School 2301 W 21st Pl, CHCG, 60608	3091	2W-1S	B1
Pilgrim Lutheran School 4300 N Winchester Av, CHCG, 60613	2977	2W-5N	B1
Pilsen Community Academy 1420 W 17th St, CHCG, 60608	3091	1W-1S	D1
Piper Elementary School 2435 Kenilworth Av, BRWN, 60402	3088	8W-2S	E2
Pirie Magnet Elementary School 650 E 85th St, CHCG, 60619	3214	0E-9S	E3
Plainfield Elementary School 1850 Plainfield Dr, DSPN, 60018	2862	13W-9N	D6
Plamondon Elementary School 2642 W 15th Pl, CHCG, 60608	3033	3W-1S	A7
Plato Academy 8535 Georgiana Av, MNGV, 60053	2865	7W-10N	B4
Player Early Childhood Center 8600 S Roberts Rd, JSTC, 60458	3210	10W-9S	C4
Pleasantdale Elementary School 8100 School St, WLSP, 60525	3208	13W-9S	E3
Pleasantdale Middle School 7450 Wolf Rd, BRRG, 60527	3208	14W-8S	E1
Pleasant Hill Elementary School 434 W Illinois Av, PLTN, 60067	2805	21W-15N	D3
Pleasant Ridge School 1730 Sunset Ridge Rd, GNVW, 60025	2811	8W-14N	A4
Plum Grove Junior High School 2600 Plum Grove Rd, RGMW, 60008	2805	21W-14N	E5
Pope Elementary School 1852 S Albany Av, CHCG, 60623	3090	3W-1S	E1
Pope John Paul II School 4325 S Richmond St, CHCG, 60632	3090	3W-4S	E7
Pope John XXIII School 1120 Washington St, EVTN, 60202	2867	2W-10N	A5
Portage Park Elementary School 5330 W Berteau Av, CHCG, 60641	2975	6W-5N	D1
Posen School 14545 S California Av, POSN, 60469	3349	3W-17S	A4
Powell Academy 7530 S South Shore Dr, CHCG, 60649	3153	3E-8S	E7
Prairie-Hills Junior High School 3035 W 163rd St, MKHM, 60426	3427	3W-19S	A2
Prairie Junior High School 11910 S Kostner Av, ALSP, 60803	3276	5W-14S	B5
Prairie Oak Elementary School 1427 Oak Park Av, BRWN, 60402	3031	8W-1S	A7
Prairie School 14200 S 82nd Av, ODPK, 60462	3346	10W-16S	C4
Prairie View Middle School 8500 175th St, TYPK, 60477	3424	10W-20S	B5
Prescott Elementary School 1632 W Wrightwood Av, CHCG, 60614	2977	2W-3N	C5
Price Elementary School 4351 S Drexel Blvd, CHCG, 60653	3092	1E-4S	E7
Prichett Elementary School 200 Horatio Blvd, BFGV, 60089	2754	16W-20N	E1
Primary Academic Center 3055 W 163rd St, MKHM, 60426	3427	3W-19S	A2
Princeton AC Elementary School 5125 S Princeton Av, CHCG, 60609	3152	0W-5S	B2
Pritzker Elementary School 2009 W Schiller St, CHCG, 60622	3033	2W-1N	B1
Prologue Alt High School 640 W Irving Park Rd, CHCG, 60613	2978	0W-4N	A2
Prospect High School 801 W Kensington Rd, MPPT, 60056	2807	15W-13N	E5
Protestant Reformed School 16511 S Park Av, SHLD, 60473	3428	0E-19S	E2
Protsman Elementary School 1121 Harrison Av, DYR, 46311	3510		D7
Providence St. Mel School 119 S Central Park Blvd, CHCG, 60624	3032	4W-0S	D5
Proviso East High School 807 S 1st Av, MYWD, 60153	3030	10W-0N	A5
Proviso West High School 4701 Harrison St, HLSD, 60162	3028	13W-0S	D6
Prussing Elementary School 4650 N Menard Av, CHCG, 60630	2919	7W-5N	C7
Pulaski Community Academy 2230 W McLean Av, CHCG, 60647	2977	2W-2N	B6
Pullman Elementary School 11311 S Forrestville Av, CHCG, 60628	3278	0E-13S	E3
Queen of All Saints School 6230 N Lemont Av, CHCG, 60646	2920	5W-7N	A3
Queen of Angels School 4520 N Western Av, CHCG, 60625	2921	3W-5N	A7
Queen of Martyrs School 3550 W 103rd St, ENGN, 60805	3276	4W-11S	D1
Queen of the Rosary School 690 W Elk Grove Blvd, EGVV, 60007	2914	18W-9N	E1
Queen of the Universe School 7130 S Hamlin Av, CHCG, 60629	3150	4W-8S	C7
Queen of Peace High School 7659 Linder Av, BRBK, 60459	3211	6W-8S	D1
Quest Academy 500 N Benton St, PLTN, 60067	2752	20W-16N	E7
Ralph J Bunche Elementary School 16500 Park Av, MKHM, 60426	3427	1W-19S	E3
Ramirez Computer Science School 2435 N Western Av, CHCG, 60647	2977	3W-3N	A5
Randolph Magnet Elementary School 7316 S Hoyne Av, CHCG, 60636	3151	2W-8S	C7
Ravenswood Baptist Christian School 4437 N Seeley Av, CHCG, 60625	2921	2W-5N	B7
Ravenswood Elementary School 4332 N Paulina St, CHCG, 60613	2977	2W-5N	C1
Ray Elementary School 5631 S Kimbark Av, CHCG, 60637	3153	1E-6S	A3
Reavis Elementary School 834 E 50th St, CHCG, 60615	3152	1E-5S	E1
Reavis Elementary School 17121 Roy St, LNSG, 60438	3430	4E-20S	B4
Reavis High School 6034 W 77th St, BRBK, 60459	3211	7W-8S	B1
Red Oak Elementary School 530 Red Oak Ln, HDPK, 60035	2757	9W-20N	C1
Reed Elementary School 6350 S Stewart Av, CHCG, 60621	3152	0W-7S	B5
Reed Elementary School 14939 W 143rd St, HmrT, 60441	3343	18W-17S	A4
Regina Dominican High School 701 Locust Rd, WLMT, 60091	2812	5W-13N	A6

FEATURE NAME Address City ZIP Code	MAP#	CGS	GRID
Reilly Elementary School 3650 W School St, CHCG, 60618	2976	4W-4N	C3
Reinberg Elementary School 3425 N Major Av, CHCG, 60634	2975	7W-4N	C3
Resurrection High School 7500 W Talcott Av, CHCG, 60631	2918	9W-7N	C3
Revere Elementary School 1010 E 72nd St, CHCG, 60619	3152	1E-8S	E7
Rhodes Elementary School 8931 Fullerton Av, RVGV, 60171	2973	11W-3N	E6
Richard Byrd Elementary School 8259 Lavergne Av, BRBK, 60459	3211	6W-9S	E3
Richard Edwards Elementary School 4815 S Karlov Av, CHCG, 60632	3150	5W-5S	B1
Richards Career Academy 5009 S Laflin St, CHCG, 60609	3151	1W-5S	D1
Rich Central High School 3600 W 203rd St, OMFD, 60461	3506	4W-24S	D5
Rich East High School 300 Sauk Tr, PKFT, 60466	3595	3W-27S	A4
Rich South High School 5000 Sauk Trl, RNPK, 60471	3594	6W-26S	A3
Rickover Junior High School 22151 Torrence Av, SLVL, 60411	3597	3E-26S	E3
Ridge Central Elementary School 10800 Lyman Av, CHRG, 60415	3275	7W-12S	C2
Ridge Circle Elementary School 420 Ridge Cir, SMWD, 60107	2857	27W-10N	C6
Ridge Lawn Elementary School 5757 105th St, CHRG, 60415	3275	7W-12S	C1
Ridgewood Community High School 7500 W Montrose Av, NRDG, 60706	2974	9W-5N	C1
Riley Elementary School 1209 E Burr Oak Dr, ANHT, 60004	2754	17W-17N	C5
Riley Elementary School 123 S Wolf Road, NHLK, 60164	3028	13W-1N	D1
River Grove Elementary School 2650 Thatcher Av, RVGV, 60171	2974	10W-3N	A5
Riverside-Brookfield Twp High-School 160 Ridgewood Rd, RVSD, 60546	3088	10W-3S	B5
River Trails Middle School 1000 N Wolf Rd, MPPT, 60056	2808	14W-14N	D5
Robert A Black Branch Magnet School 7133 S Coles Av, CHCG, 60649	3153	3E-8S	D6
Robert A Black Magnet School 9101 S Euclid Av, CHCG, 60617	3215	2E-10S	C4
Robert Emmet Elementary School 5500 W Madison St, CHCG, 60644	3031	6W-0N	D5
Robert Frost Elementary School 1308 S Cypress Dr, MPPT, 60056	2861	16W-11N	D3
Robert Frost Middle School 2206 W 167th St, MKHM, 60426	3427	2W-19S	C3
Robert L Grimes Middle School 5450 W 64th Pl, CHCG, 60638	3149	6W-7S	D5
Robeson High School 6835 S Normal Blvd, CHCG, 60621	3152	0W-7S	B6
Robinson Elementary School 4225 S Lake Park Av, CHCG, 60653	3093	1E-4S	A6
Robinson Elementary School 4431 Gage Av, LYNS, 60534	3088	9W-4S	C7
Rodolfo Lozano Bilingual and Int'l Study-Ctr 1424 N Cleaver St, CHCG, 60622	3033	1W-1N	D1
Rolling Meadows High School 2901 Central Rd, RGMW, 60008	2806	19W-12N	C7
Romona Elementary School 600 Romona Rd, WLMT, 60091	2811	5W-13N	E6
Ronald Brown Academy 12607 S Union Av, CHCG, 60628	3278	0W-14S	A6
Ronald E McNair Academic Center 4820 W Walton St, CHCG, 60651	3031	6W-1N	E2
Roosevelt Elementary School 1927 S 15th Av, BDVW, 60155	3029	11W-0S	E6
Roosevelt Elementary School 1500 S 50th Av, CCRO, 60804	3031	6W-1S	E7
Roosevelt Elementary School 1345 Sunnyside Av, CHHT, 60411	3507	1W-25S	E7
Roosevelt Elementary School 111 W 146th St, DLTN, 60419	3350	0W-17S	C4
Roosevelt High School 3436 W Wilson Av, CHCG, 60625	2920	4W-5N	C7
Roosevelt Junior High School 111 W 146th St, DLTN, 60419	3350	0W-17S	C4
Roosevelt Middle School 2500 Oak St, BLWD, 60104	3029	12W-0N	C4
Roosevelt Middle School 7560 Oak Av, RVFT, 60305	3030	9W-0N	C3
Roque de Du Prey Elementary School 1405 N Washtenaw Av, CHCG, 60622	3033	3W-1N	A1
Rosa Parks Middle School 14700 Robey Av, HRVY, 60426	3349	2W-17S	D5
Rosario Castellanos Middle School 2524 S Central Park Av, CHCG, 60623	3090	4W-2S	D2
Roseland Christian School 314 W 108th St, CHCG, 60628	3278	0W-12S	B2
Roselle Middle School 500 S Park St, ROSL, 60172	2913	23W-6N	A6
Rosemont Elementary School 6101 Ruby St, RSMT, 60018	2917	12W-7N	C3
Rosenwald Branch Elementary School 2541 W 80th St, CHCG, 60652	3213	3W-9S	A2
Rosenwald-Carroll School 2601 W 80th St, CHCG, 60652	3213	3W-9S	A2
Roycemore School 640 Lincoln St, EVTN, 60201	2867	2W-12N	B1
Roy Elementary School 533 N Roy Av, NHLK, 60164	2972	13W-2N	E6
Ruben Salazar Bilingual Center 160 W Wendell St, CHCG, 60610	3034	0W-1N	B2
Ruggles Elementary School 7831 S Prairie Av, CHCG, 60619	3214	0E-8S	D1
Ruiz Elementary School 2410 S Leavitt St, CHCG, 60608	3091	2W-2S	B2
Rupley Elementary School 305 Oakton St, EGVV, 60007	2861	18W-9N	A6
Rutledge Hall Elementary School 6850 N East Prairie Rd, LNWD, 60712	2920	4W-8N	B1
Ryder Elementary School 8716 S Wallace St, CHCG, 60620	3214	0W-10S	A4
Ryerson Elementary School 646 N Lawndale Av, CHCG, 60624	3032	4W-0N	C3
Sabin Magnet School 2216 W Hirsch St, CHCG, 60622	3033	2W-1N	B1
Sacred Heart School 2906 E 96th St, CHCG, 60617	3215	3E-11S	E6
Sacred Heart School 6250 N Sheridan Rd, CHCG, 60660	2921	1W-7N	E3
Sacred Heart School 815 N 16th Av, MLPK, 60160	3029	11W-1N	D3
Sacred Heart School 1095 Gage St, WNKA, 60093	2758	5W-16N	E7
St. Agnes of Bohemia School 2643 S Central Park Av, CHCG, 60623	3090	4W-2S	D3
St. Agnes School 1501 Chicago Rd, CHHT, 60411	3596	1W-25S	A1
St. Ailbe School 9037 S Harper Av, CHCG, 60619	3215	1E-10S	B4
St. Albert the Great School 5535 State Rd, BRBK, 60459	3211	6W-9S	D2

FEATURE NAME Address City ZIP Code	MAP#	CGS	GRID
St. Alexander School 126 126th St, PSHT, 60463	3274	8W-14S	E7
St. Alphonsus Liguori School 411 N Wheeling Rd, WLNG, 60090	2808	14W-15N	B2
St. Andrew Lutheran School 3659 S Honore St, CHCG, 60609	3091	2W-3S	C5
St. Andrew School 1710 W Addison St, CHCG, 60613	2977	2W-4N	C2
St. Andrew's Lutheran School 260 N Northwest Hwy, PKRG, 60068	2864	10W-9N	A7
St. Angela School 1332 N Massasoit Av, CHCG, 60651	3031	7W-1N	C1
St. Anne School 319 Franklin St, BRTN, 60010	2751	25W-20N	A2
St. Ann School 2211 W 18th Pl, CHCG, 60608	3091	2W-1S	B1
St. Ann School 3014 Ridge Rd, LNSG, 60438	3430	3E-21S	A6
St. Athanasius School 2510 Ashland Av, EVTN, 60201	2813	3W-12N	A7
St. Barbara School 8900 Windemere Av, BKFD, 60513	3087	11W-4S	E6
St. Barbara School 2867 S Throop St, CHCG, 60608	3091	1W-2S	E3
St. Barnabas School 10121 S Longwood Dr, CHCG, 60643	3213	2W-11S	C7
St. Bartholomew School 4941 W Patterson Av, CHCG, 60641	2975	6W-4N	E2
St. Beatrice School 4141 Atlantic Av, SRPK, 60176	2973	12W-5N	C1
St. Bede the Venerable School 4440 W 83rd St, CHCG, 60652	3212	5W-9S	B3
St. Benedict High School 3900 N Leavitt St, CHCG, 60618	2977	2W-4N	A2
St. Benedict School 2324 New St, BLID, 60406	3349	2W-15S	B1
St. Benedict School 3920 N Leavitt St, CHCG, 60618	2977	2W-4N	B2
St. Bernadette School 9311 S Francisco Av, ENGN, 60805	3213	3W-10S	A5
St. Bernardine School 815 Elgin Av, FTPK, 60130	3030	9W-0S	D6
St. Bruno School 4839 S Harding Av, CHCG, 60632	3150	4W-5S	C1
St. Cajetan School 2447 W 112th St, CHCG, 60655	3277	3W-13S	B3
St. Casimir School 4329 S Cameron Av, HMND, 46327	3352		D3
St. Catherine Laboure School 3425 Thornwood Av, GNVW, 60025	2809	10W-14N	E5
St. Catherine of Alexandria School 10621 Kedvale Av, OKLN, 60453	3276	5W-12S	C2
St. Catherine-St. Lucy School 27 Washington Blvd, OKPK, 60302	3031	7W-0N	B4
St. Celestine School 3017 N 77th Av, EDPK, 60707	2974	9W-3N	C4
St. Charles Borromeo School 145 E Grand Av, BNVL, 60106	2972	15W-3N	A4
St. Christina School 3333 W 110th St, CHCG, 60655	3276	4W-12S	E3
St. Christopher School 14611 Keeler Av, MDLN, 60445	3348	5W-17S	C5
St. Clement School 2524 N Orchard St, CHCG, 60614	2978	0W-3N	A5
St. Cletus School 700 W 55th St, LGNG, 60525	3147	12W-5S	B3
St. Colette School 3900 Pheasant Dr, RGMW, 60008	2806	19W-13N	C6
St. Columbanus School 7120 S Calumet Av, CHCG, 60619	3152	0E-8S	D7
St. Constance School 5841 W Strong St, CHCG, 60630	2919	7W-6N	B6
St. Cornelius School 5252 N Long Av, CHCG, 60630	2919	6W-6N	D5
St. Cyprian School 2561 Clinton St, RVGV, 60171	2974	10W-3N	B5
St. Damian School 5300 155th St, OKFT, 60452	3347	6W-18S	E7
St. Daniel the Prophet School 5337 S Natoma Av, CHCG, 60638	3149	8W-5S	A2
St. Domitilla School 605 N Hillside Av, HLSD, 60162	3028	14W-0N	D5
St. Dorothy School 7740 S Eberhart Av, CHCG, 60619	3214	0E-8S	D1
St. Edmund School 200 S Oak Park Av, OKPK, 60302	3030	8W-0N	E4
St. Edward School 4343 W Sunnyside Av, CHCG, 60630	2920	5W-5N	A7
St. Elizabeth School 4052 S Wabash Av, CHCG, 60653	3092	0E-4S	C6
St. Emily School 1400 E Central Rd, MPPT, 60056	2808	14W-13N	C7
St. Ethelreda School 8734 S Paulina St, CHCG, 60620	3213	2W-10S	D4
St. Eugene School 7930 W Foster Av, CHCG, 60656	2918	9W-6N	B6
St. Ferdinand School 3131 N Mason Av, CHCG, 60634	2975	7W-3N	B4
St. Florian School 13110 S Baltimore Av, CHCG, 60633	3280	3E-15S	A7
St. Frances of Rome School 1401 S Austin Blvd, CCRO, 60804	3031	7W-1S	C7
St. Francis Borgia School 3535 N Panama Av, CHCG, 60634	2974	10W-4N	B3
St. Francis de Sales High School 10155 S Ewing Av, CHCG, 60617	3216	4E-11S	B7
St. Francis Xavier School 145 N Waiola Av, LGNG, 60525	3087	12W-4S	B6
St. Francis Xavier School 808 Linden Av, WLMT, 60091	2812	3W-13N	E6
St. Gabriel School 607 W 45th St, CHCG, 60609	3092	0W-4S	A7
St. Gall School 5515 S Sawyer Av, CHCG, 60629	3150	4W-6S	E3
St. Genevieve School 4854 W Montana St, CHCG, 60639	2975	6W-3N	E5
St. George School 6700 176th St, TYPK, 60477	3425	8W-21S	B5
St. Gerald School 9320 S 55th Ct, OKLN, 60453	3211	6W-10S	D5
St. Germaine School 9735 S Kolin Av, OKLN, 60453	3212	5W-11S	B6
St. Giles School 1034 Linden Av, OKPK, 60302	3031	8W-1N	A1
St. Gregory High School 1677 W Bryn Mawr Av, CHCG, 60640	2921	2W-7N	C4
St. Helena of the Cross School 10115 S Parnell Av, CHCG, 60628	3214	0W-11S	B7
St. Helen School 2347 W Augusta Blvd, CHCG, 60622	3033	2W-1N	B2
St. Hilary School 5614 N Fairfield Av, CHCG, 60659	2920	3W-7N	E4
St. Hubert School 255 Flagstaff Ln, HFET, 60194	2858	23W-11N	E3
St. Hyacinth School 3640 W Wolfram St, CHCG, 60618	2976	4W-3N	C4
St. Ignatius College Prep School 1076 W Roosevelt Rd, CHCG, 60607	3033	1W-0S	E6
St. Isaac Jogues School 421 S Clay St, HNDL, 60521	3146	15W-5S	A2

Chicago & Cook County Points of Interest Index

FEATURE NAME	Address City ZIP Code	MAP#	CGS	GRID
St. James Lutheran School	2101 N Fremont St, CHCG, 60614	2977	1W-2N	E6
St. James School	821 N Arlington Heights Rd, ANHT, 60004	2807	17W-14N	A3
St. Jane de Chantal School	5201 S McVicker Av, CHCG, 60638	3149	7W-5S	C2
St. Jerome School	2801 S Princeton Av, CHCG, 60616	3092	0W-2S	B3
St. Joan of Arc School	9245 Lawndale Av, SKOK, 60203	2866	4W-11N	C2
St. John Berchmans School	2509 W Logan Blvd, CHCG, 60647	2977	3W-3N	A5
St. John Brebeuf School	8301 N Harlem Av, NLES, 60714	2864	8W-10N	D5
St. John de La Salle Elementary-School	10212 S Vernon Av, CHCG, 60628	3214	0E-11S	D7
St. John Fisher School	10200 S Washtenaw Av, CHCG, 60655	3213	3W-11S	A7
St. John Lutheran School	305 Circle Av, FTPK, 60130	3030	9W-0N	D5
St. John of the Cross School	708 51st St, WNSP, 60558	3146	13W-5S	E2
St. John's Lutheran School	4231 183rd St, CCHL, 60478	3426	5W-22S	C7
St. John's Lutheran School	4939 W Montrose Av, CHCG, 60641	2975	6W-5N	E1
St. John's Lutheran School	505 S Park Rd, LGNG, 60525	3147	13W-5S	B1
St. John's Lutheran School	18100 Wentworth Av, LNSG, 60438	3430	4E-21S	C6
St. John the Evangelist School	513 Parkside Cir, SMWD, 60107	2857	28W-10N	B6
St. John Vianney School	27 N Lavergne Av, NHLK, 60164	3028	14W-2N	D1
St. Josaphat School	2245 N Southport Av, CHCG, 60614	2977	1W-2N	D6
St. Joseph High School	1840 Mayfair Av, WSTR, 60154	3086	13W-1S	E2
St. Joseph School	430 Joliet St, DYR, 46311	3598		D2
St. Joseph School	17949 Dixie Hwy, HMWD, 60430	3427	2W-21S	D6
St. Joseph School	5641 S 73rd Av, SMMT, 60501	3148	9W-6S	D3
St. Joseph School	1740 Lake Av, WLMT, 60091	2812	4W-14N	C5
St. Juliana School	7400 W Touhy Av, CHCG, 60631	2918	9W-8N	D1
St. Kieran School	700 195th St, CHHT, 60411	3508	0W-23S	B3
St. Ladislaus Catholic School	3330 N Lockwood Av, CHCG, 60641	2975	6W-4N	D3
St. Laurence High School	5556 W 77th St, BRBK, 60459	3211	6W-8S	D1
St. Lawrence O'Toole School	4101 St. Lawrence Av, MTSN, 60443	3594	5W-25S	C1
St. Leonard School	3322 Clarence Av, BRWN, 60402	3089	8W-3S	A4
St. Liborius School	24201 S Kings Rd, CRTE, 60417	3684	2W-29S	D1
St. Liborius School	3440 Halsted Blvd, STGR, 60475	3596	1W-28S	A5
St. Linus School	10400 Lawler Av, OKLN, 60453	3275	6W-12S	E1
St. Louis de Montfort School	8840 Ridgeland Av, OKLN, 60453	3211	8W-10S	B4
St. Louise de Marillac School	1125 Harrison Av, LGPK, 60525	3087	11W-2S	D4
St. Luke Academy	1500 W Belmont Av, CHCG, 60657	2977	1W-4N	D3
St. Luke School	519 Ashland Av, RVFT, 60305	3030	9W-0N	C3
St. Malachy School	2252 W Washington Blvd, CHCG, 60612	3033	2W-0N	B4
St. Margaret Mary School	7318 N Oakley Av, CHCG, 60645	2867	2W-9N	A7
St. Margaret of Scotland School	9833 S Throop St, CHCG, 60643	3213	1W-11S	E7
St. Maria Goretti School	10050 Ivanhoe Av, SRPK, 60176	2973	12W-4N	B2
St. Mary of Czestochowa School	3001 S 49th Av, CCRO, 60804	3089	6W-2S	E3
St. Mary of the Angels School	1810 N Hermitage Av, CHCG, 60622	2977	2W-2N	C7
St. Mary of the Lake School	1026 W Buena Av, CHCG, 60613	2977	1W-5N	E1
St. Mary of the Woods School	7033 N Moselle Av, CHCG, 60646	2919	7W-8N	B1
St. Mary School	50 N Buffalo Grove Rd, BFGV, 60089	2754	16W-20N	C2
St. Mary School	103 S Gifford St, ELGN, 60120	2855	33W-11N	A4
St. Mary School	227 Monee Rd, MonT, 60466	3594	4W-28S	E6
St. Mary School	97 Herrick Rd, RVSD, 60546	3088	9W-3S	C5
St. Mary Star of the Sea School	6424 S Kenneth Av, CHCG, 60629	3150	5W-7S	B5
St. Matthias School	4910 N Claremont Av, CHCG, 60625	2921	2W-6N	A6
St. Michael School	14355 Highland Av, ODPK, 60462	3345	12W-17S	C4
St. Michael the Archangel School	8231 S South Shore Dr, CHCG, 60617	3216	3E-9S	A2
St. Monica School	5115 N Mont Clare Av, CHCG, 60656	2918	8W-6N	D6
St. Nicholas of Tolentine School	3741 W 62nd St, CHCG, 60629	3150	4W-6S	C4
St. Nicholas Ukrainian Catholic-School	2200 W Rice St, CHCG, 60622	3033	2W-1N	B2
St. Norbert School	1817 Walters Av, NHBK, 60062	2757	9W-17N	B6
St. Odilo Elementary School	6617 23rd St, BRWN, 60402	3089	8W-2S	A2
St. Pascal School	6143 W Irving Park Rd, CHCG, 60634	2975	7W-4N	B2
St. Patricia School	9000 S 86th Av, HYHL, 60457	3210	10W-10S	A5
St. Patrick High School	5900 W Belmont Av, CHCG, 60634	2975	7W-4N	B3
St. Paul Lutheran Academy	5201 Galitz St, SKOK, 60077	2865	6W-9N	D6
St. Paul Lutheran School	846 N Menard Av, CHCG, 60651	3031	7W-1N	C2
St. Paul Lutheran School	1025 W Lake St, MLPK, 60160	3029	11W-0N	E3
St. Paul Lutheran School	8601 Harrison Av, MNSR, 46321	3430		D7
St. Paul Lutheran School	18 S School St, MPPT, 60056	2808	15W-12N	A7
St. Paul Lutheran School	5650 N Canfield Av, NpkT, 60631	2918	9W-7N	B5
St. Paul Lutheran School	4660 W 94th St, OKLN, 60453	3212	5W-10S	A5
St. Paul of the Cross School	140 S Northwest Hwy, PKRG, 60068	2918	10W-8N	B1
St. Paul-Our Lady of Vilna School	2114 W 22nd Pl, CHCG, 60608	3091	2W-2S	B2
St. Paul's Lutheran School	330 W Highland Dr, CHHT, 60411	3507	2W-24S	E6
St. Peter Lutheran School	111 W Olive St, ANHT, 60004	2807	17W-15N	A2
St. Peter Lutheran School	208 E Schaumburg Rd, SMBG, 60194	2859	23W-10N	B5
St. Peter School	8140 Niles Center Rd, SKOK, 60077	2865	6W-10N	E5
St. Peter the Apostle School	500 N Cherry St, ITSC, 60143	2914	19W-6N	C5
St. Philip Lutheran School	2500 W Bryn Mawr Av, CHCG, 60659	2921	3W-7N	A4
St. Philip Neri School	2110 E 72nd St, CHCG, 60649	3153	2E-8S	C7
St. Pius V School	1919 S Ashland Av, CHCG, 60608	3091	1W-1S	D1
St. Priscilla School	7001 W Addison St, CHCG, 60634	2974	8W-4N	E3
St. Procopius School	1625 S Allport St, CHCG, 60608	3091	1W-1S	E1
St. Raymond School	300 S Elmhurst Av, MPPT, 60056	2861	16W-12N	E1
St. Rene Goupil School	6340 S New England Av, CHCG, 60638	3148	8W-7S	E5
St. Richard School	5025 S Kenneth Av, CHCG, 60632	3150	5W-5S	B2
St. Rita of Cascia High School	7740 S Western Av, CHCG, 60652	3213	3W-8S	B1
St. Robert Bellarmine School	6036 W Eastwood Av, CHCG, 60630	2919	7W-5N	B7
St. Sabina Academy	7801 S Throop St, CHCG, 60620	3213	1W-8S	E1
Sts. Alphonsus & Patrick School	20W145 Davey Rd, LMNT, 60439	3270	19W-13S	D5
St. Scholastica Academy	7416 N Ridge Blvd, CHCG, 60645	2867	2W-9N	B7
Sts. Cyril & Methodius School	607 Sobieski St, LMNT, 60439	3270	19W-14S	E5
Sts. Faith Hope & Charity School	180 Ridge Av, WNKA, 60093	2812	5W-15N	B3
St. Stanislaus Bishop-Martyr School	14418 S McKinley Av, POSN, 60469	3349	3W-17S	B4
St. Stanislaus Kostka School	1255 N Noble St, CHCG, 60622	3033	1W-1N	D1
St. Sylvester School	3027 W Palmer Blvd, CHCG, 60647	2976	3W-2N	E6
St. Symphorosa School	6125 S Austin Av, CHCG, 60638	3149	7W-6S	C4
St. Tarcissus School	6040 W Ardmore Av, CHCG, 60646	2919	7W-7N	B4
St. Thecla School	6323 N Newcastle Av, CHCG, 60631	2918	8W-7N	E3
St. Theresa School	445 N Benton St, PLTN, 60067	2752	20W-16N	E7
St. Therese School	247 W 23rd St, CHCG, 60616	3092	0W-2S	B2
St. Thomas More School	8435 Calumet Av, MNSR, 46321	3430		E7
St. Thomas of Canterbury School	4827 N Kenmore Av, CHCG, 60640	2921	1W-6N	E6
St. Thomas of Villanova School	1141 E Anderson Dr, PLTN, 60074	2753	19W-16N	C7
St. Thomas the Apostle School	5467 S Woodlawn Av, CHCG, 60615	3153	1E-5S	A2
St. Turibius School	4120 W 57th St, CHCG, 60629	3150	5W-6S	B3
St. Viator High School	1213 E Oakton St, ANHT, 60004	2807	17W-14N	B3
St. Viator School	4140 W Addison St, CHCG, 60641	2976	5W-4N	B3
St. Vincent Ferrer School	1515 Lathrop Av, RVFT, 60305	3030	9W-1N	C1
St. Walter School	11741 S Western Av, CHCG, 60643	3277	2W-13S	B4
St. Walter School	201 W Maple Av, ROSL, 60172	2912	23W-7N	E5
St. William School	2559 N Sayre Av, CHCG, 60707	2974	8W-3N	E5
St. Zachary School	567 W Algonquin Rd, DSPN, 60018	2862	15W-10N	A5
Salem Christian Academy	11816 S Indiana Av, CHCG, 60628	3278	0E-13S	D4
Salem Christian School	2845 W McLean Av, CHCG, 60647	2976	3W-2N	E6
Salt Creek Elementary School	65 JF Kennedy Blvd, EGVV, 60007	2914	19W-8N	D2
Sandburg Elementary School	14500 Myrtle Av, HRVY, 60426	3349	1W-17S	E5
Sandburg Middle School	345 E St. Charles Rd, EMHT, 60126	3028	15W-0N	B3
Sanders Academy of Excellence	1425 W 112th St, CHCG, 60643	3277	1W-13S	D3
Sandidge Elementary School	16600 66th Av, TYPK, 60477	3425	8W-19S	B3
Sandoval Elementary School	5534 S St. Louis Av, CHCG, 60629	3150	4W-6S	D3
Sandridge Elementary School	2950 Glenwood Dyer Rd, BlmT, 60411	3510	3E-24S	A6
San Miguel-Gary Comer School	819 N Leamington Av, CHCG, 60651	3031	6W-1N	E3
Santa Lucia School	3017 S Wells St, CHCG, 60616	3092	0W-2S	B3
Saucedo Scholastic Academy	2850 W 24th Blvd, CHCG, 60623	3091	3W-2S	A2
Sauganash Elementary School	6040 N Kilpatrick Av, CHCG, 60646	2919	5W-7N	E3
Sauk Elementary School	4435 S Churchill Dr, RNPK, 60471	3594	5W-26S	C3
Saukview Elementary School	3341 Miller Av, SCHT, 60411	3596	1W-27S	A4
Sawyer Elementary School	5247 S Spaulding Av, CHCG, 60632	3150	4W-5S	E2
Sayre Language Academy	1850 N Newland Av, CHCG, 60707	2974	8W-2N	E7
Scammon Elementary School	4201 W Henderson St, CHCG, 60641	2976	5W-4N	B3
Scarlet Oak Elementary School	5731 Albert Dr, OKFT, 60452	3347	7W-18S	D7
Schaumburg Christian School	200 N Roselle Rd, SMBG, 60194	2859	23W-10N	A4
Schaumburg High School	1100 W Schaumburg Rd, SMBG, 60194	2858	24W-10N	C5
Schiller Middle School	640 W Scott St, CHCG, 60610	3034	0W-1N	A1
Schmid Elementary School	9755 S Greenwood Av, CHCG, 60628	3215	1E-11S	A6
School of Technology	7529 S Constance Av, CHCG, 60649	3215	2E-8S	C1
School of the Arts	7529 S Constance Av, CHCG, 60649	3215	2E-8S	C1
Schrum Memorial School	485 165th St, CTCY, 60409	3430	4E-19S	B3
Schubert Elementary School	2727 N Long Av, CHCG, 60639	2975	6W-3N	D5
Schurz High School	3601 N Milwaukee Av, CHCG, 60641	2976	5W-4N	B2
Science & Arts Academy	1825 Miner St, DSPN, 60016	2863	12W-11N	B4
Science Academy of Chicago	2601 N Meade Av, CHCG, 60639	2975	7W-3N	B5
Scott Elementary School	2250 Scott St, LydT, 60164	2973	12W-2N	B6
Scott Joplin Elementary School	7931 S Honore St, CHCG, 60620	3213	2W-9S	C2
Serena Hills Elementary School	255 Pleasant Drive, CHHT, 60411	3507	1W-23S	E4
Seward Arts Academy	4600 S Hermitage Av, CHCG, 60609	3091	2W-4S	C7
Seward Branch Academy	4541 S Wood St, CHCG, 60609	3091	2W-4S	C7
Sexton Elementary School	6020 S Langley Av, CHCG, 60637	3152	0E-6S	E4
Shabonee School	2929 Shabonee Trl, NHBK, 60062	2756	11W-17N	E5
Shedd Branch of Bennett School	200 E 99th St, CHCG, 60628	3214	0E-11S	D6
Shepard High School	13049 S Ridgeland Av, WthT, 60463	3347	7W-15S	B1
Shepard Middle School	440 Grove Av, DRFD, 60015	2756	11W-20N	E1
Sheridan Elementary School	510 Franklin Blvd, ELGN, 60120	2855	33W-11N	B3
Sherlock Elementary School	5347 W 22nd Pl, CCRO, 60804	3089	6W-2S	D2
Shoesmith Elementary School	1330 E 50th St, CHCG, 60615	3153	1E-5S	A1
Shoop Academy of Math Science &-Technology	1460 W 112th St, CHCG, 60643	3277	1W-13S	D3
Sieden Prairie School	725 Notre Dame Dr, MTSN, 60443	3505	6W-25S	E6
Simmons Middle School	6450 W 95th St, CHRG, 60453	3211	8W-10S	B6
Sir Miles Davis Academy	6723 S Wood St, CHCG, 60636	3151	2W-7S	C6
Skinner Classical Elementary School	111 S Throop St, CHCG, 60607	3033	1W-0S	D5
Skokie School	520 Glendale Av, WNKA, 60093	2811	5W-15N	E1
Smyser Elementary School	4310 N Melvina Av, CHCG, 60634	2975	7W-5N	B1
Smyth Elementary School	1059 W 13th St, CHCG, 60608	3033	1W-1S	E7
Socrates School	5701 N Redwood Dr, CHCG, 60631	2918	10W-7N	B5
Solomon Elementary School	6206 N Hamlin Av, CHCG, 60659	2920	4W-7N	C3
Solomon Schechter Day School	3210 Dundee Rd, NHBK, 60062	2756	11W-18N	D4
Solomon Schechter Day School	9301 Gross Point Rd, SKOK, 60076	2865	5W-11N	E2
South Chicago Community Area Elem-School	8255 S Houston Av, CHCG, 60617	3216	3E-9S	A2
Southeast Elementary School	9800 S Francisco Av, ENGN, 60805	3213	3W-11S	A6
South Elementary School	1535 Everett Av, DSPN, 60018	2863	13W-9N	A6
South Elementary School	266 Linden Av, GLNC, 60022	2758	5W-17N	E6
South Loop Elementary School	1212 S Plymouth Ct, CHCG, 60605	3034	0W-1S	B7
South Middle School	400 S Highland Av, ANHT, 60005	2807	18W-13N	A5
South Park Elementary School	1421 Hackberry Rd, DRFD, 60015	2756	11W-20N	C1
South Side Baptist School	5345 W 99th St, OKLN, 60453	3211	6W-11S	E7
Southwest Christian School	17171 84th Av, TYPK, 60477	3424	10W-20S	B4
Southwest Elementary School	9900 S Central Park Av, ENGN, 60805	3212	4W-11S	D7
Southwood Middle School	18635 S Lee St, CCHL, 60478	3426	5W-21S	C7
Spaulding Elementary School	14811 Turner Av, MDLN, 60445	3348	4W-17S	E5
Speed Therapeutic Elementary School	16121 Central Park Av, MKHM, 60426	3426	4W-19S	E2
Spencer Math-Science Academy	214 N Lavergne Av, CHCG, 60644	3031	6W-0N	E4
Spring Avenue Elementary School	1001 S Spring Av, LGNG, 60525	3147	12W-5S	B2
Springfield Elementary School	14620 Springfield Av, MDLN, 60445	3348	4W-17S	C5
Spring Hills Elementary School	560 Pinecroft Dr, ROSL, 60172	2913	22W-6N	B6
Springman Middle School	2701 Central Rd, GNVW, 60025	2810	9W-12N	B7
Spring Wood Middle School	5540 Arlington Dr E, HRPK, 60133	2912	25W-6N	A6
Spry Elementary School	2400 S Marshall Blvd, CHCG, 60623	3090	3W-2S	E2
Stagg Elementary School	7424 S Morgan St, CHCG, 60621	3151	1W-8S	E7
Steinmetz Academic Center High-School	3030 N Mobile Av, CHCG, 60634	2975	7W-3N	A4
Stevenson Elementary School	8010 S Kostner Av, CHCG, 60652	3212	5W-9S	B2
Stevenson Elementary School	1414 Armstrong Ln, EGVV, 60007	2913	21W-8N	E2
Stevenson Elementary School	9000 Capitol Dr, MaiT, 60016	2863	11W-11N	D3
Stevenson Elementary School	1630 N 20th Av, MLPK, 60160	3029	11W-1N	D1
Stevenson Middle School	4350 W 79th St, CHCG, 60652	3212	5W-8S	B2
Stewart Elementary School	4525 N Kenmore Av, CHCG, 60640	2921	1W-5N	E7
Stockton Specialty School	4420 N Beacon St, CHCG, 60640	2921	1W-5N	D7
Stone Church Christian Academy	6330 W 127th St, PSHT, 60463	3275	7W-14S	B7
Stone Scholastic Academy	6239 N Leavitt St, CHCG, 60659	2921	2W-7N	B3
Stony Creek Elementary School	11700 S Kolin Av, ALSP, 60803	3276	5W-13S	B4
Stowe Elementary School	3444 W Wabansia Av, CHCG, 60647	2976	4W-2N	D7
Strassburg Elementary School	2002 223rd St, SLVL, 60411	3597	2E-27S	D3
Streamwood High School	701 W Schaumburg Rd, SMWD, 60107	2856	29W-10N	D5
Stuart R Paddock Elementary School	225 W Washington St, PLTN, 60067	2805	21W-15N	E1
Sullivan High School	6631 N Bosworth Av, CHCG, 60626	2921	1W-8N	C2
Summit Hill Junior High School	20130 S Rosewood Dr, FftT, 60423	3504	10W-24S	C5
Summit School	611 E Main St, EDND, 60118	2801	33W-15N	B3
Sumner Elementary School	4320 W 5th Av, CHCG, 60624	3032	5W-0S	B6
Sunnydale Elementary School	716 Sunnydale Blvd, SMWD, 60107	2857	27W-9N	C7
Sunny Hill Elementary School	2500 Helm Rd, CPVL, 60110	2748	32W-18N	C5
Sunnyside Elementary School	5412 St. Charles Rd, BKLY, 60163	3028	14W-0N	D3

Chicago & Cook County Points of Interest Index

Shopping Centers

Chicago & Cook County Points of Interest Index

FEATURE NAME / Address City ZIP Code	MAP#	CGS	GRID
Canterbury Shopping Center Kedzie Av, MKHM, 60426	3427	3W-19S	A1
Central Maywood Shopping Center Washington Blvd, MYWD, 60153	3030	10W-0N	A4
Century Plaza W Northwest Hwy, PLTN, 60067	2752	21W-16N	D6
Century Shopping Center 2828 N Clark St, CHCG, 60657	2978	0W-3N	A4
Century Tile Plaza Cicero Av, MTSN, 60443	3506	5W-25S	B7
Cermak Plaza Shopping Center Cermak Rd, BRWN, 60402	3088	8W-2S	E2
Chase Plaza N Arlington Heights Rd, BFGV, 60089	2754	17W-20N	A2
Cherry Creek Shopping Center Governors Hwy, HMWD, 60430	3427	3W-21S	B7
Chicago Place Mall 700 N Michigan Av, CHCG, 60611	3034	0E-0N	C3
Church Street Plaza Church St, EVTN, 60201	2867	2W-11N	A3
Cicero Marketplace Shopping Center S Cicero Av, CCRO, 60804	3090	5W-2S	A3
Civic Center Plaza N Waukegan Rd, NLES, 60714	2864	8W-9N	E6
Clock Tower Shopping Center National St, ELGN, 60120	2855	33W-10N	A5
Cobblers Crossing Shopping Center Summit St, ELGN, 60120	2855	32W-12N	C2
Colony Square Shopping Center W Camp McDonald Rd, PTHT, 60070	2808	15W-15N	A3
Country Club Plaza 167th St, CCHL, 60478	3426	5W-20S	C3
Country Court Shopping Center W Dundee Rd, BFGV, 60089	2754	16W-17N	C4
Countryside Court Shopping Center S Elmhurst Rd, MPPT, 60056	2861	16W-11N	E3
Countryside Plaza S La Grange Rd, CTSD, 60525	3147	12W-6S	B4
Countryview Plaza Willow Springs Rd, LynT, 60525	3147	13W-6S	A4
Crossroads Shopping Center Skokie Valley Rd, HDPK, 60035	2757	8W-20N	D2
Crystal Court Shopping Center W Algonquin Rd, MPPT, 60056	2861	17W-10N	C4
Deerbrook Mall S Waukegan Rd, DRFD, 60062	2757	10W-18N	A2
Deer Grove Centre N Rand Rd, PLTN, 60074	2753	20W-18N	A3
Deer Grove Crossing E Dundee Rd, PLTN, 60074	2753	20W-17N	B4
Deer Park Town Center N Rand Rd, DRPK, 60074	2752	21W-20N	D1
Dempster Plaza Dempster St, NLES, 60714	2864	10W-10N	A4
Downtown Oak Park N Harlem Av, OKPK, 60301	3030	8W-0N	D3
Dundee Point Shopping Center W Dundee Rd, BFGV, 60089	2754	16W-18N	C4
Dunhurst Plaza S Elmhurst Rd, WLNG, 60090	2755	15W-17N	A4
Edens Plaza Lake Av, WLMT, 60091	2811	6W-14N	D5
Elk Crossing Biesterfield Rd, EGVV, 60007	2914	19W-8N	D1
Elk Grove Annex S Arlington Heights Rd, EGVV, 60007	2914	19W-8N	D2
Eurofresh Plaza W Northwest Hwy, PLTN, 60067	2752	21W-16N	D6
Evanston Center W Howard St, CHCG, 60645	2867	3W-9N	A7
Evanston Galleria Church St, EVTN, 60201	2867	2W-11N	B2
Evanston Plaza Shop Center Dempster St, EVTN, 60202	2866	3W-10N	E4
Flossmoor Commons Shopping Center Governors Hwy, FSMR, 60422	3506	4W-23S	E4
Ford City Mall 7601 S Cicero Av, CHCG, 60652	3212	5W-8S	A1
Ford City North S Cicero Av, CHCG, 60652	3212	5W-8S	A1
Forest Park Mall 7600 Roosevelt Rd, FTPK, 60130	3030	9W-1S	C7
Fountainbleau Court Shopping Center Kedzie Av, HLCT, 60429	3427	3W-21S	A7
French Village Shopping Center 183rd St, HLCT, 60429	3427	3W-21S	A7
Fresh Farms Plaza E Dundee Rd, WLNG, 60090	2755	14W-18N	C4
Garden Market Shopping Center 47th St, WNSP, 60558	3146	13W-5S	E1
Georgetown Square Shopping Center George St, WDDL, 60191	2914	18W-6N	E7
Glen Oak Plaza 1411 Waukegan Rd, GNVW, 60025	2810	8W-14N	E5
Glenwood Plaza S Halsted St, GNWD, 60425	3428	0W-22S	B7
Golf Center N Roselle Rd, HFET, 60195	2859	23W-11N	A2
Golf Flaggs Shopping Center N Milwaukee Av, NLES, 60714	2864	10W-11N	A2
Golf Glen Mart Shopping Center W Golf Rd, NLES, 60714	2863	11W-12N	D2
Golf Mill Shopping Center 239 Golf Mill Ctr, NLES, 60714	2864	10W-11N	A2
Golf Milwaukee Plaza W Golf Rd, NLES, 60714	2864	10W-12N	A1
Golf Plaza W Golf Rd, MPPT, 60056	2861	17W-11N	C3
Golf Plaza II W Golf Rd, MPPT, 60056	2861	16W-11N	E3
Governors Plaza Sauk Tr, RNPK, 60471	3594	4W-27S	D3
Grand Plaza Grand Av, FNPK, 60131	2973	12W-3N	A5
Grant Square W Chicago Av, HNDL, 60521	3146	15W-4S	A1
Green Oaks Shopping Center S Cicero Av, OKLN, 60453	3212	5W-11S	A6
Grenoble Square Shopping Center 183rd St, HLCT, 60429	3426	4W-21S	E7
Halsted Indoor Mall 11444 S Halsted St, CHCG, 60643	3278	1W-13S	A3
Harlem-Foster Shopping Center N Harlem Av, CHCG, 60656	2918	9W-6N	D5
Harlem-Irving Plaza 4200 N Harlem Av, NRDG, 60706	2974	9W-5N	D1
Harwood Commons N Harlem Av, HDHT, 60706	2918	9W-6N	D7
Hawthorne Works Shopping Center S Cicero Av, CCRO, 60804	3090	5W-2S	A2
Hazel Crest Center 175th St, HLCT, 60429	3427	3W-21S	A5
Heritage Plaza 175th St, CCHL, 60478	3426	5W-21S	C5
Hickory Palos Shopping Center W 95th St, HYHL, 60457	3210	10W-11S	B6
Hill Creek Shopping Center S 88th Av, HYHL, 60457	3210	11W-11S	A6
Hoffman Plaza N Roselle Rd, HFET, 60195	2859	23W-11N	A2
Hoffman Village Shopping Center Barrington Rd, HFET, 60194	2857	26W-11N	E3
Holiday Plaza Shopping Center N Harlem Av, HDHT, 60706	2918	8W-5N	D7
Homewood Square 17715 Halsted St, HMWD, 60430	3428	0W-21S	B6
Huntington Plaza Charlemagne Dr W, HFET, 60195	2804	24W-14N	B3
Indian Trails Shopping Center W 127th St, PSHT, 60463	3275	8W-15S	B7
International Plaza Shopping Center E Golf Rd, ANHT, 60005	2861	17W-12N	B2
Jewel Plaza State St, LMNT, 60439	3342	19W-15S	D1
Kmart Plaza E Sibley Blvd, DLTN, 60419	3351	1E-17S	A5
Lake Cook Plaza Lake Cook Rd, DRFD, 60062	2757	10W-18N	A2
Lake View Plaza W 159th St, ODPK, 60462	3423	12W-18S	D1
Lansing Commons Torrence Av, LNSG, 60438	3429	2E-20S	E4
Lansing Square 176th Pl, LNSG, 60438	3429	3E-20S	E5
Lemont Plaza Weimer Av, LMNT, 60439	3270	19W-14S	D7
Lincoln Crossing Shopping Center W 14th St, CHHT, 60411	3507	2W-25S	C7
Lincoln Mall 208 Lincoln Mall Dr, MTSN, 60443	3594	5W-25S	B1
Lincolnwood Town Center 3333 W Touhy Av, LNWD, 60712	2920	4W-8N	D1
Long Run Marketplace 13460 S Archer Av, LMNT, 60439	3342	19W-15S	D2
Lynwood Center Torrence Av, LYWD, 60411	3509	3E-23S	E3
Main Place Mall W 143rd St, ODPK, 60462	3345	11W-16S	D4
Market Place Golf Rd, RGMW, 60008	2860	18W-12N	E2
Marketplace of Matteson Crawford Av, MTSN, 60443	3506	5W-25S	C7
Market Place of Oak Lawn W 87th St, OKLN, 60453	3212	6W-10S	A4
Market Square 901 Ridge Rd, MNSR, 46321	3430		E7
Matteson Plaza Governors Hwy, MTSN, 60443	3506	4W-25S	D7
Matteson Town Center Cicero Av, MTSN, 60443	3594	6W-25S	A1
Meadowdale Shopping Center Lake Marian Rd, CPVL, 60110	2748	33W-17N	C6
Melrose Crossing Shopping Center N Mannheim Rd, MLPK, 60160	3029	13W-2N	A1
Melrose Park Venture Shopping-Center 1st Av, MLPK, 60160	3030	10W-1N	A1
Merrionette Park Shopping Center W 115th St, MTPK, 60803	3276	4W-13S	E4
Mid Oak Plaza Cicero Av, MDLN, 60445	3348	6W-17S	A5
Midway Square S Pulaski Rd, CHCG, 60632	3150	4W-5S	C2
Mt Prospect Plaza Mt Prospect Plz, MPPT, 60056	2808	14W-13N	B7
Nantucket Square E Wise Rd, SMBG, 60193	2913	23W-9N	A1
Norridge Commons N Harlem Av, NRDG, 60706	2974	8W-5N	D1
North & 9th Shopping Center W North Av, MLPK, 60160	3029	11W-2N	E1
North Bridge E Ohio St, CHCG, 60611	3034	0E-0N	C3
Northbrook Court 2171 Northbrook Ct, NHBK, 60062	2757	9W-18N	C2
Northlake Commons Shopping Center S Hillside Av, NHLK, 60164	3028	14W-1N	D1
North Pier 435 E Illinois St, CHCG, 60611	3034	0E-0N	D3
Northpoint Shopping Center N Arlington Heights Rd, ANHT, 60004	2754	17W-16N	A7
North Quentin Center N Quentin Rd, PLTN, 60067	2752	22W-16N	C6
North Riverside Park Mall 7501 W Cermak Rd, NRIV, 60546	3088	9W-2S	D2
North Riverside Plaza W Cermak Rd, NRIV, 60546	3088	9W-2S	D2
Northwest Shopping Center E Dundee Rd, PLTN, 60074	2753	20W-17N	A4
Norwood Square Shopping Center 500 Norwood Square Dr, PKFT, 60466	3595	3W-26S	B2
Oak Creek Shopping Center 159th St, OKFT, 60452	3425	7W-18S	D1
Oak Forest Commons Shopping Center Central Av, OKFT, 60452	3425	6W-18S	D1
Oak Lawn Shopping Center W 95th St, OKLN, 60453	3212	5W-11S	C6
Oak Mill Mall W Oakton St, NLES, 60714	2864	9W-9N	C6
OK Shopping Center 3715 W 26th St, CHCG, 60623	3090	4W-2S	C3
Old Church Plaza Old Church Rd, SMWD, 60107	2857	27W-11N	D4
Olde Church Centre Old Church Rd, SMWD, 60107	2857	27W-11N	C5
Olympia Corners Lincoln Hwy, OMFD, 60461	3507	2W-25S	C7
Olympia Glen Shopping Center Vollmer Rd, OMFD, 60461	3507	3W-24S	A4
Olympia Plaza Dixie Hwy, CHHT, 60411	3507	1W-24S	E5
Olympia Square Shopping Center Governors Hwy, OMFD, 60461	3506	4W-24S	E4
One Milwaukee Place Shops N Milwaukee Av, WLNG, 60090	2755	14W-18N	D4
Orland Consumer Square Shopping-Center W 159th St, ODPK, 60462	3424	9W-18S	E1
Orland Greens Shopping Center S La Grange Rd, ODPK, 60462	3345	12W-17S	D6
Orland Park Place Shopping Center 1400 Orland Park Pl, ODPK, 60462	3345	11W-18S	D7
Orland Park Shopping Plaza S La Grange Rd, ODPK, 60462	3345	12W-16S	D4
Orland Plaza S 94th Av, ODPK, 60462	3423	11W-18S	E1
Orland Square Shopping Center 288 Orland Square Dr, ODPK, 60462	3345	11W-17S	E6
Orland Towne Center W 159th St, ODHL, 60477	3423	11W-19S	E1
Pacesetter Park Plaza E 162nd St, SHLD, 60473	3429	1E-18S	A1
Palatine Centre E Northwest Hwy, PLTN, 60067	2753	20W-16N	A7
Palatine Mall N Hicks Rd, PLTN, 60074	2753	20W-16N	A6
Palatine Plaza E Northwest Hwy, PLTN, 60067	2752	20W-16N	E7
Palatine Windsor Shopping Center N Windsor Dr, ANHT, 60004	2807	17W-15N	C1
Park Center Harlem Av, TYPK, 60477	3424	9W-19S	E1
Park Place Harlem Av, TYPK, 60477	3424	9W-19S	E2
Park Place Plaza Ridge Rd, HMWD, 60430	3428	1W-21S	B6
Park Place Shopping Center E Dundee Rd, PLTN, 60074	2753	19W-17N	C4
Park St. Claire Plaza N Meacham Rd, SMBG, 60173	2859	21W-11N	D4
Parkside Plaza 80th Av, TYPK, 60477	3424	9W-20S	C3
Plaza Del Lago Sheridan Rd, WLMT, 60091	2812	3W-14N	E4
Plaza Del Prado Pfingsten Rd, GNVW, 60025	2809	10W-15N	E2
Pointe Plaza W Touhy Av, NLES, 60714	2865	7W-9N	C7
Popular Creek Plaza W Golf Rd, SMBG, 60194	2858	25W-11N	A3
Prairie Town Center S Barrington Rd, SMBG, 60194	2857	26W-10N	E5
Prairie View Plaza Waukegan Rd, MNGV, 60053	2864	8W-10N	E4
Prospect Crossing Shopping Center E Rand Rd, ANHT, 60004	2807	17W-15N	C2
Prospect Heights Plaza S Elmhurst Rd, PTHT, 60070	2808	15W-14N	A3
Quentin Corners N Quentin Rd, PLTN, 60067	2752	21W-17N	C6
Randhurst Commons W Rand Rd, MPPT, 60056	2807	15W-14N	E5
Randhurst Shopping Center 999 N Elmhurst Rd, MPPT, 60056	2808	15W-14N	A5
Ravinia Plaza W 153rd St, ODPK, 60462	3345	12W-18S	D7
Regency Plaza W Euclid Av, PLTN, 60067	2805	21W-14N	C4
Ridge Plaza Shopping Center W Dundee Rd, BFGV, 60089	2754	18W-18N	A4
Rivercrest Center Cicero Av, CTWD, 60445	3348	6W-15S	A1
Rivercrest Shopping Center Cicero Av, CTWD, 60445	3348	5W-16S	A2
River Oaks Shopping Center 1201 River Oaks Dr, CTCY, 60409	3429	3E-19S	E1
River Oaks West Shopping Center 1451 159th St, CTCY, 60409	3429	2E-19S	D1
River Place Shop Center Torrence Av, LNSG, 60438	3429	3E-19S	E3
Riverside Plaza S Milwaukee Av, WLNG, 60090	2755	13W-18N	D4
River Valley Square E Main St, EDND, 60118	2801	33W-15N	C3
Rolling Meadows Shopping Center Kirchoff Rd, RGMW, 60008	2806	19W-13N	B5
Salem Square S Brainard Av, CTSD, 60525	3147	12W-6S	B3
Scharrington Square S Barrington Rd, SMBG, 60193	2857	26W-10N	E6
Schaumburg Corners Shopping Center E Golf Rd, SMBG, 60173	2859	23W-12N	A2
Schaumburg Town Center W Wise Rd, SMBG, 60193	2913	23W-9N	A1
Shoppes At Mill Creek W 131st St, PSPK, 60464	3345	12W-15S	D1
Shopping Center West Dr, CTCY, 60409	3429	2E-19S	D1
Shops At Coopers Grove Pulaski Rd, CCHL, 60478	3426	5W-21S	C7
Shops At Schaumburg Court W Schaumburg Rd, SMBG, 60194	2857	27W-10N	D5
Sibley Crossing Shopping Center E Sibley Blvd, DLTN, 60419	3351	1E-17S	B5
Southfield Plaza S Harlem Av, BGVW, 60455	3210	8W-10S	E4
South Holland Plaza E 163rd St, SHLD, 60473	3428	0E-19S	D2
Southpoint Shopping Center E Palatine Rd, ANHT, 60004	2807	17W-15N	A1
South Point Shopping Center E Camp McDonald Rd, WLNG, 60090	2808	14W-15N	D3
Southwest Square Dixie Hwy, HRVY, 60426	3349	2W-17S	C6
State Road Plaza Shopping Center W 87th St, OKLN, 60453	3211	7W-10S	B4
Stearns Crossing W Stearns Rd, BRLT, 60103	2910	30W-7N	C6
Stonebrook Plaza W 115th St, MTPK, 60803	3276	4W-13S	E4
Streamwood Market Square E Irving Park Rd, SMWD, 60107	2911	27W-9N	C1
Streets Of Woodfield Shopping-Center 601 N Martingale Rd, SMBG, 60173	2860	21W-11N	A3
Summit Shopping Center S Cicero Av, BRBK, 60459	3212	6W-9S	A2
Summit Square Shopping Center Summit St, ELGN, 60120	2855	32W-12N	C2
Sunset Plaza 422 S Governors Hwy, PTON, 60468	3861	8W-37S	A4
Surrey Ridge Shopping Center W Algonquin Rd, ANHT, 60005	2860	18W-12N	E2
The Commons Of Chicago Ridge Shopping-Center Ridgeland Av, CHRG, 60415	3211	8W-11S	A7
The Commons Shopping Center W 159th St, ODPK, 60462	3424	9W-18S	E1
The Depot Division St, WDDL, 60191	2915	17W-5N	B7
The Franklin Park Mall Mannheim Rd, FNPK, 60131	2973	12W-3N	A4
The Glen Town Center Patriot Blvd, GNVW, 60025	2810	9W-14N	B4
The Grove RGMW, 60067	2805	21W-14N	E5
The Grove Shopping Center McHenry Rd, BFGV, 60089	2754	16W-20N	C2
The Hall Plaza W Diversey Av, CHCG, 60641	2976	5W-3N	A4
The Landings Torrence Av, LNSG, 60438	3429	3E-19S	E2
The Market Place At Six Corners Shopping-Ctr N Milwaukee Av, CHCG, 60641	2975	6W-5N	D1
The Oaks Of Des Plaines Shopping-Center Mannheim Rd, DSPN, 60018	2862	13W-10N	E5
The Plaza 9730 S Western Av, ENGN, 60805	3213	3W-11S	B6
The Quarry Joliet Rd, HGKN, 60525	3147	12W-6S	C5
The Shops At North Bridge E Illinois St, CHCG, 60611	3034	0E-0N	C3
The Shops of Kildeer N Rand Rd, KLDR, 60047	2752	21W-20N	D1
The Village Centre E 162nd St, SHLD, 60473	3428	0E-18S	E1
The Village Market N La Grange Rd, LGPK, 60525	3087	12W-3S	B6

Chicago & Cook County Points of Interest Index

Subdivisions & Neighborhoods

Transportation

Visitor Information

FEATURE NAME Address City ZIP Code	MAP#	CGS	GRID

CUT ALONG DOTTED LINE

RAND McNALLY

Thank you for purchasing this Rand McNally Street Guide!
We value your comments and suggestions.

Please help us serve you better by completing this postage-paid reply card.
This information is for internal use ONLY and will not be distributed or sold to any external third party.

Missing pages? Maybe not... Please refer to the "Using Your Street Guide" page for further explanation.

Street Guide Title: Chicago & Cook County **ISBN-13# 978-0-5288-5973-1** **MKT: CHG**

Today's Date: ____________ Gender: ☐M ☐F Age Group: ☐18-24 ☐25-31 ☐32-40 ☐41-50 ☐51-64 ☐65+

1. What type of industry do you work in?
☐Real Estate ☐Trucking ☐Delivery ☐Construction ☐Utilities ☐Government
☐Retail ☐Sales ☐Transportation ☐Landscape ☐Service & Repair
☐Courier ☐Automotive ☐Insurance ☐Medical ☐Police/Fire/First Response
☐Other, please specify: ____________
2. What type of job do you have in this industry?____________
3. Where did you purchase this Street Guide? (store name & city) ____________
4. Why did you purchase this Street Guide? ____________
5. How often do you purchase an updated Street Guide? ☐Annually ☐2 yrs. ☐3-5 yrs. ☐Other:____________
6. Where do you use it? ☐Primarily in the car ☐Primarily in the office ☐Primarily at home ☐Other: ____________
7. How do you use it? ☐Exclusively for business ☐Primarily for business but also for personal or leisure use
☐Both work and personal evenly ☐Primarily for personal use ☐Exclusively for personal use
8. What do you use your Street Guide for?
☐Find Addresses ☐In-route navigation ☐Planning routes ☐Other: ____________
Find points of interest: ☐Schools ☐Parks ☐Buildings ☐Shopping Centers ☐Other:____________
9. How often do you use it? ☐Daily ☐Weekly ☐Monthly ☐Other: ____________
10. Do you use the internet for maps and/or directions? ☐Yes ☐No
11. How often do you use the internet for directions? ☐Daily ☐Weekly ☐Monthly ☐Other:____________
12. Do you use any of the following mapping products in addition to your Street Guide?
☐Folded paper maps ☐Folded laminated maps ☐Wall maps ☐GPS ☐PDA ☐In-car navigation ☐Phone maps
13. What features, if any, would you like to see added to your Street Guide? ____________
14. What features or information do you find most useful in your Rand McNally Street Guide? (please specify)
15. Please provide any additional comments or suggestions you have. ____________

We strive to provide you with the most current updated information available if you know of a map correction, please notify us here.

Where is the correction? Map Page #:__________ Grid #:__________ Index Page #:__________

Nature of the correction: ☐Street name missing ☐Street name misspelled ☐Street information incorrect
☐Incorrect location for point of interest ☐Index error ☐Other: ____________

Detail: ____________

I would like to receive information about updated editions and special offers from Rand McNally
☐via e-mail E-mail address: ____________
☐via postal mail
Your Name: ____________ Company (if used for work): ____________
Address: ____________ City/State/ZIP: ____________

Thank you for your time and help. We are working to serve you better.
This information is for internal use ONLY and will not be distributed or sold to any external third party.

CUT ALONG DOTTED LINE

TAPE SHUT

TAPE SHUT

get directions at
randmcnally.com

CUT ALONG DOTTED LINE

2ND FOLD LINE

NO POSTAGE
NECESSARY
IF MAILED
IN THE
UNITED STATES

BUSINESS REPLY MAIL
FIRST-CLASS MAIL PERMIT NO. 388 CHICAGO IL
POSTAGE WILL BE PAID BY ADDRESSEE

RAND MCNALLY
CONSUMER AFFAIRS
PO BOX 7600
CHICAGO IL 60680-9915

1ST FOLD LINE

RAND McNALLY

The most trusted name on the map.

You'll never need to ask for directions again with these Rand McNally products!

- EasyFinder® Laminated Maps
- Folded Maps
- Street Guides
- Wall Maps
- CustomView Wall Maps
- Road Atlases
- Motor Carriers' Road Atlases

CUT ALONG DOTTED LINE

SGTG_07